D0116515
DICTIONARY OF AMERICAN BIOGRAPHY
CSS
FOR REFERENCE

DICTIONARY
OF
AMERICAN BIOGRAPHY

DICTIONARY OF American Biography

Supplement Ten

1976–1980

Kenneth T. Jackson
Editor in Chief

Karen E. Markoe
General Editor

Arnold Markoe
Associate Editor

WITH AN INDEX GUIDE TO THE SUPPLEMENTS

Charles Scribner's Sons
Simon & Schuster Macmillan

Charles Scribner's Sons
An Imprint of Simon & Schuster Macmillan
866 Third Avenue
New York, NY 10022

Library of Congress Cataloging-in-Publication Data
(Revised for suppl. 9)

Dictionary of American biography. Supplement three–

Supplement 9– editor in chief: Kenneth T. Jackson
Includes index.
Supplements 1–2 comprise v. 11 of the edition of the main work published in 10 v., 1946–1958.
Contents: —3. 1941–1945. —4. 1946–1950. —[etc.]—10. 1976–1980.
1. United States—Biography—Dictionaries.
I. Garraty, John Arthur, 1920– II. Jackson, Kenneth T.
E176.D563 Suppl. 920′.073 77–2942

ISBN 0-684-19399-X

3 5 7 9 11 13 15 17 19 V/C 20 18 16 14 12 10 8 6 4 2

Printed in the United States of America

∞ The paper used in this publication meets the minimum requirements of the American National Standard for Information Sciences—Permanence of Paper for Printed Library Materials, ANSI Z39.48-1984.

Acknowledgment is gratefully made for permission to reprint the following:

Except from "Florida" from *The Complete Poems 1927–1979* by Elizabeth Bishop. Copyright © 1979, 1993 by Alice Helen Methfessel. Reprinted by permission of Farrar, Straus & Giroux, Inc.

EDITORIAL STAFF

Project Editor

TIMOTHY J. DEWERFF

Copy Editors, Researchers

ERIC C. BANKS   JEFFREY L. BENEKE   MELISSA A. DOBSON
STEPHEN FLANDERS   PHILIP G. HOLTHAUS   LOUISE B. KETZ
MARK STEVEN LONG   LELAND S. LOWTHER   MARCIA M. MEANS
ANN LESLIE TUTTLE   ELIZABETH I. WILSON

Proofreaders

CAROL HOLMES   ADRIAN SAICH

Senior Editor

SYLVIA K. MILLER

Publisher

KAREN DAY

PREFACE

Since 1928, the *Dictionary of American Biography* has been the preeminent retrospective reference work on persons who have made significant contributions to our national past. During its long and distinguished history, it has always maintained the highest standards of accuracy, balanced judgment in interpretation, and a consistent focus on "just portraiture." With this supplement, which contains the biographies of 519 Americans, written by more than 300 separate authors, the *DAB* extends its coverage through 1980 and reaches a total of 19,173 sketches.

Although this supplement has been produced independently of the American Council of Learned Societies, the editors have followed traditional *DAB* procedure. Supplement 10 covers Americans who died in the five-year period between Jan. 1, 1976, and Dec. 31, 1980. In general, the editors have included individuals who made major professional or artistic contributions while living in the United States, whether or not they were born here or ever actually became citizens. Similarly, we have not included persons, such as Golda Meir, who lived several years in the United States but whose major achievements took place in other countries.

In selecting a few hundred persons from the almost ten million Americans who died in those years, the editors followed the practice established by their predecessors seventy years ago. First, they compiled a list of several thousand candidates from a variety of sources. Second, they classified the names according to profession or occupation. Third, they submitted the lists to specialists or groups of specialists who helped to rank the potential biographees. Fourth, an advisory board consisting of Stuart W. Bruchey, Richard H. Gentile, Joshua Lederberg, and Arthur M. Schlesinger, Jr., reviewed the final list and made recommendations for additions or deletions. Finally, the editors assigned biographies to those best qualified to write them.

The 519 individuals who are profiled in these pages lived extraordinary lives, and in conspicuous ways they set themselves apart from the rest of us. Some won fame on the battlefield or in the halls of government. Others distinguished themselves by their books, their research efforts, or their creative genius. Still others became household names because of their achievements as performing artists or sports heroes. But taken together, these unusual individuals reflected the diversity of the nation they called home. Representing virtually every race, ethnic group, and socioeconomic class, they came from nearly every state and from every region of the United States. Many were born to privilege; others were born to sharecroppers or to penniless immigrants. All took advantage of their natural gifts to leave a permanent mark on a continental nation. As a review of an earlier supplement noted several years ago, "There is much to be said for a source in which anthropologists, jazz musicians, football players, and poets mingle."

Contributors to this volume were asked not only to appraise the circumstances and influences that shaped the careers of the biographees, but also to provide basic biographical data, including the full dates of birth and death, the full names and occupations of parents, the number of siblings, the educational institutions attended and degrees granted, the names of spouses and the dates of marriages and divorces, and the number of children. Wherever appropriate, we have also included information on residences, cause and place of death, and place of burial. The length of articles was determined both by the relative significance of the subject and by the completeness of the biographical information available.

As in the case of any large-scale research effort, Supplement 10 could not have been produced without the cooperation and enthusiasm of hundreds of persons, some who were new to this venture, and others who have contributed to the *DAB* almost since its inception. For example, Irving Dilliard of Collinsville, Ill., who had previously written ninety-nine biographical sketches for the *DAB* over a period of more than six decades, has now contributed exactly one hundred entries. Similarly, Timothy J. DeWerff and Sylvia K. Miller of the reference division of Charles Scribner's Sons were not even alive when the first *DAB* supplements began to appear. But their tireless and distinguished contributions as project directors have been profound in recent years, and they have done everything necessary to maintain the high standards that have characterized this collaborative effort for so many decades. Finally, we wish to record our gratitude to Karen Day, the head of the reference division of Charles Scribner's Sons, who dreamed of keeping the *DAB* alive and who had the energy and the devotion to make her vision come true. Everyone who uses this volume will be in her debt.

Special mention must go to Leland S. Lowther, a former managing editor of the *DAB* who prepared the original master list from which these entries were chosen and whose recent death reminds us that he had long been a wise counselor to everyone associated with the *DAB*. With gratitude and respect, we dedicate this volume to him.

KENNETH T. JACKSON
KAREN E. MARKOE
ARNOLD MARKOE
Aug. 15, 1994

A

ABERNETHY, ROY (Sept. 29, 1906–Feb. 28, 1977), automobile executive, was born in West Monterey, Pa., near Pittsburgh, the seventh and youngest child of Thomas R. Abernethy, a coal miner, and Susanah A. Nichols. He attended a one-room grammar school and graduated from East Brady High School in 1924. Abernethy, whose first jobs were caring for coal mine mules and laying track with a railroad section gang, was a master salesman who had a lifelong fascination with automobiles. He began his career in the automobile industry in 1925, working as an apprentice mechanic (a "grease monkey") for 18 cents per hour at Burke Packard in Pittsburgh. While working as a mechanic, Abernethy took night courses in bridge and highway engineering at Carnegie Institute of Technology. He became a salesman for Packard in 1926. He married Florence Ruth Nunally in October 1932; they had two children.

Abernethy's career at Packard progressed rapidly. At one time or another, he held every sales position in the Packard organization. He moved from retail sales to district manager in 1932. In 1943, Packard transferred Abernethy to Kansas City, Mo., as regional manager. Two years later, he was back in Pittsburgh as zone manager for Packard dealerships. He became a Packard vice-president and eastern regional manager in 1948. Abernethy left Packard management to open his own dealership in Hartford, Conn., later in 1948. He sold more than $1 million worth of automobiles in a single year. His outstanding success as a dealer brought him back into Packard management in 1950, as general manager for Packard New York and, later that year, as assistant general sales manager for Packard Motor Car Company.

In 1953, Abernethy joined Willys Motors in Toledo, Ohio, as vice-president and sales manager. He was recruited by George Romney to join the newly formed American Motors Company (AMC) in October 1954. American Motors had been formed by a merger of the Hudson Motor Company and the Nash-Kelvinator Corporation in May 1954. Abernethy's position as vice-president of Nash-Kelvinator sales was to rebuild the "floundering, apathetic, overlapping dealer organization so that it would contribute to, rather than detract from, AMC's sales strength." After the merger, AMC was beset by sales complacency and poor management, a debt of $65 million, and diminished public confidence reflected in shrinking automobile sales. The Nash Rambler, a compact car that was more economical to run and maintain, was AMC's hope for improving market share, but it stood in competition not only with other Detroit models but also with AMC's full-sized Nash and Hudson models.

In the automobile industry, the manufacturer sells to franchised dealers who in turn sell to the public. Abernethy's task at AMC was twofold. First, he had to streamline an inefficient and costly dealer system while building outlets for service, parts, and accessories. Second, he had to sell the concept of a compact car to AMC dealers, who were in the habit of selling cars that were bigger, heavier, and more powerful with each new model.

Abernethy, who rallied to a challenge, was eager to go to work for AMC. He believed, as did Romney, that AMC could outflank Detroit's "Big Three"—General Motors, Ford, and Chrysler—by taking advantage of middle-class America's move to the suburbs and its abandonment of downtown business centers. AMC proposed to win back market share by providing automobile customers with an efficient alternative to "gas-guzzling dinosaurs." Beginning in 1955, Abernethy set about reorganizing Nash sales. He drew up a checklist to measure dealer effectiveness and traveled at least 50,000 miles each year, visiting dealerships, working out management and sales problems, and redeploying his sales staff. A large, gregarious, hard-driving salesman, Abernethy was known to be fair-minded and to balance private ambition with consideration for dealers, whom he came to know as colleagues. He established a Dealer Advisory Board that sent dealers to regularly scheduled meetings with AMC executives where they could advise and make recommendations that directly affected manufacturing. He kept open communications, taking calls directly and responding personally to dealers' concerns. He believed that in the automobile industry, success depended as much on teamwork and a strong dealer organization as it did on a strong product line.

In 1955, Abernethy was promoted to vice-president of automotive distribution and marketing for the Nash and Hudson divisions of AMC. He expanded the Dealer Advisory Board by creating a Dealer's Council that met regularly with AMC's senior executives, bringing automobile sales, manufacturing, and market know-how to an open forum in order to strengthen the connection between the consumer and the manufacturer. After three years of steady losses at AMC, American consumers embraced the idea of a smaller, fuel-efficient, compact car. Abernethy's planning provided AMC with the sales structure to turn a $26 million profit in 1958 after losing $12 million in 1957.

In December 1960, Abernethy was promoted to executive vice-president in charge of both automotive and Kelvinator appliance distribution and marketing. Less than a year later, he became AMC's executive vice-president and general manager. Abernethy succeeded George Romney as president and chief operations officer, and subsequently as chief executive officer of American Motors in 1962.

By 1963, the compact Rambler had led AMC to an average market share of 6.6 percent, representing 426,346 compact cars sold in that year and bringing the company out of debt; however, Americans' love affair with "muscle cars" eventually made the Rambler seem dowdy and pedestrian. Against Ford's new line of sportier, sexier "pony cars," like the Mustang and Pinto, AMC's compact cars began losing market share. By 1966, despite larger engines and sportier lines and names, AMC's compact cars accounted for 9 percent of the company's sales. AMC's sales accounted for only 3.1 percent of total market share. Although Abernethy continued to build his sales network and promote his product, AMC could not compete with either compact cars or standard-sized models. By midyear, AMC's market share fell to 2.8 percent. In January 1967, AMC's board of directors requested Abernethy's resignation. He complied with the same grace and candor that had marked his earlier successes. He acknowledged that after a lifetime of selling cars, industry changes and pressures from the major automobile manufacturers came faster than AMC could accommodate. His commitment to a smaller, more efficient automobile anticipated later energy and environmental concerns, but at the time they could not compete with American dream cars.

Following his retirement, Abernethy continued to serve on the AMC board of directors and as president of the Automobile Manufacturers Association. A heart attack six months after leaving AMC forced his resignation from both positions later in 1967, and he and his wife moved to Tequesta, Fla., where he died.

[News clippings and news releases are available from the Chrysler Historical Foundation, Detroit, Mich. Alumni offices at Ohio Wesleyan University, Tri-State University, and Baldwin-Wallace College have files of clippings related to Abernethy's career and early life. "How to Get New Sales Power from Your Dealers," *Management Methods*, May 1959, discusses Abernethy's management strategies at AMC. Obituaries are in the *New York Times* and *Detroit Free Press*, both Mar. 1, 1977; and in *Automotive News*, Mar. 7, 1977.]

WENDY HALL MALONEY

ALBERS, JOSEF (Mar. 19, 1888–Mar. 25, 1976), painter, printmaker, designer, and teacher, was born in Bottrop, in the industrial Ruhr district of Germany, the oldest son of Lorenz Albers, a housepainter, and Magdalena Schumacher, a descendant of blacksmiths. Throughout his life Albers remained proud of his artisan background, which taught him that technical mastery is the foundation of all creative undertakings.

Albers attended the Präparanden-Schule in Langenhorst from 1902 to 1905 and graduated in 1908 from the Lehrerseminar (Teachers' College) in Büren, where he earned his teaching certificate. He excelled in drawing and demonstrated a propensity for teaching. Also in 1908 he discovered the paintings of Cézanne, a lifelong influence, and of Matisse. From 1908 to 1913 he taught elementary school in small towns in the Westphalian region and spent the following two years at the Königliche Kunstschule in Berlin, where he studied teaching techniques and produced vivid still lifes and drawings influenced by Albrecht Dürer.

After Albers received his certificate to teach art in 1915, he went on to study at the Kunstgewerbeschule (School for Applied Arts) in Essen, where he explored printmaking, drawing, and stained glass design. During these apprentice years, Albers began to develop his own unique aesthetic style, which he described as creating the "maximum effect from minimum means."

In 1919 he traveled to Munich to attend the Königliche bayerische Akademie der bildenden Kunst, where he studied painting with Max Doerner. The following year he attended the Bauhaus School in Weimar, where he began his experiments with furniture design and glass assemblages, which he constructed from fragments found in the city dump. At the Bauhaus, Albers abandoned figurative art for the purely abstract forms that became the hallmark of his mature style. From 1922 to 1924 he was commissioned to design windows, including two for houses designed by the architect Walter Gropius. All were destroyed in World War II.

In 1925 the Bauhaus moved to Dresden, where Albers was made a Bauhaus Master. On May 9 of that year he married Anneliese Fleischmann, a student, who became known for her woven tapestries and fabric design. The couple enjoyed a long, artistically supportive marriage. They had no children.

While in Dresden, Albers developed a technique for fabricating sandblasted flashed (fused) glass paintings that he arranged in refined, geometric compositions. Albers referred to the works of this period as his "thermometer style" because of the straight black lines he painted on the glass. He also experimented with typography, furniture design (one of his most successful designs was for a laminated bentwood chair that could be quickly assembled), metalwork, and architecture.

Albers held the directorships of the Bauhaus furniture and wallpaper workshops from 1928 to 1933 and in 1930 he became assistant director to Ludwig Mies van der Rohe, head of the Bauhaus. In addition to his administrative responsibilities, Albers continued to make his signature sandblasted glass paintings, some of which were shown in a major Bauhaus exhibit in Zurich that included works by Paul Klee and Wassily Kandinsky.

In 1932 he painted the *Treble Clef* series of gouaches and glass constructions in variations of black, white, and gray. This was his first major use of a repetitive single motif that was varied only by subtle color modulations.

After the Bauhaus was closed by the Nazis in 1933, Albers and his wife received an invitation from the young American architect Philip Johnson to accept teaching positions at the new experimental Black Mountain College located near Asheville, N.C. Even though Albers spoke no English, he and his wife accepted the college's offer. During his sixteen years at Black Mountain, Albers became one of the two most prominent art teachers in the country (the other was Hans Hofmann).

Albers's move to the United States brought him recognition from the American art and academic community. At Walter Gropius's invitation he lectured at Harvard from 1936 to 1940, and during those years he exhibited work from the Bauhaus period in over twenty solo shows in American galleries. In 1939, Albers became an American citizen, and beginning in 1942 he began to assume greater administrative responsibilities at Black Mountain College.

In 1947 Albers began his *Variant* series, in which he further developed his concept of a static form that is altered only by changing variations in color. Through his intensive explorations with color and color theory, Albers exploited the emotional range present in various chromatic schemes.

Albers left Black Mountain College in 1950 to take the position of head of the department of design at Yale University. Also in that year he began painting his *Homages to the Square*, to which he devoted the last twenty-five years of his life. Each painting in the *Homages*, his most renowned series, consists of a nested grouping of three or four squares painted with a palette knife and unmixed pigments taken directly from the tube. In this series Albers explored his fascination with color relationships and the varied emotional responses they could evoke in the viewer.

Albers retired from Yale in 1960 and published *The Interaction of Color* in 1963. The artist spent his retirement working in a basement studio in the modest suburban house he shared with his wife. In 1971 he became the first living artist to be given a retrospective exhibition at the Metropolitan Museum of Art in New York City.

In his later years Albers received numerous prestigious fellowships, honorary degrees, and awards, and continued to work until his death in New Haven, Conn. Shortly after his death, the Yale University Art Gallery opened a permanent exhibition space devoted to Albers's work, and the Josef Albers Museum opened in Bottrop, Germany.

As one of the twentieth century's preeminent teachers, Albers influenced generations of American artists, and his wide-ranging experimentation with design and color have had an important impact on modern art.

[For Albers's color theories see his *Interaction of Color* (1963). For a comprehensive catalog with biographical and critical essays see Nicholas F. Weber et al., *Josef Albers: a Retrospective* (1988). Other catalogs include *Josef Albers: The American Years* (1965); Sam Hunter, ed., *Josef Albers: Paintings and Graphics 1917–1970* (1971); and Jo Miller, *Josef Albers: Prints 1915–1970* (1973). See also Eugen Gomringer, *Josef Albers* (1968); Werner Spies, *Josef Albers* (1970); and Nicholas Fox Weber, *The Drawings of Josef Albers* (1984). For a film on Albers see Hans Namuth, *Homage to the Square* (1969). An obituary is in the *New York Times*, Mar. 26, 1976.]

CHRISTINE STENSTROM

ALLEN, JAMES BROWNING (Dec. 28, 1912–June 1, 1978), lawyer and politician, was born in Gadsden, Ala., the son of George C. Allen and Mary Ethel Browning. Allen attended Gadsden public schools and graduated from the University of Alabama in 1931 and its law school in 1933. He was admitted to the Alabama bar in 1935 and practiced law in Gadsden either full-time or part-time until 1968.

While in his twenties, Allen began a lifelong political career. Serving in the Alabama House of Representatives from Etowah County from 1939 to 1943, he resigned during World War II to become a naval officer. After the war, Allen was elected in 1946 to the Alabama State Senate from Etowah and St. Clair counties. He served from 1947 to 1951 and was next elected lieutenant governor of Alabama (Gordon Persons was elected governor), a post he held from 1951 to 1955. In 1952 he was a state delegate to the Democratic National Convention. He sought the Democratic nomination for the governorship in 1954 but lost to former governor James E. Folsom (1947–1951), who won the general election.

Allen took a nine-year break from elected office to practice law full-time until 1963, when he successfully ran for lieutenant governor again with gubernatorial candidate George C. Wallace. In 1968, when Lister Hill chose to retire after serving thirty years in the United States Senate, Allen ran for the seat in the Democratic primary against Congressman Armistead I. Selden, Jr., who was endorsed by Senator Hill, a distant cousin. Allen, a poor and easily embarrassed public speaker, was hampered by his pedestrian campaign style and personal shyness, but he had the advantage of a close association with Governor Wallace (Allen enthusiastically supported Wallace's third-party 1968 presidential bid). On the strength of that association, as well as Allen's frequent attacks on the so-called "Washington crowd," he won a close runoff primary against Selden and then, much more handily, the general election. Once in office Allen's popularity grew to such a degree that he was elected to a second term in 1974 almost without opposition.

Allen's tenure in the Senate followed the long-lived tradition of conservative southern senators whose allegiances to southern interests and right-wing principles made their loyalty to the national Democratic party a tenuous matter at best. In fact, demographic and political changes in the South had very nearly depleted the Dixiecrat ranks by the time Allen was elected. He was, therefore, somewhat of an anachronism even at the beginning of his career in Washington. Moreover, by entering the Senate at the age of fifty-six, Allen seemingly violated the southern practice of electing young legislators who, through the accumulation of seniority, ended up exercising a disproportionate degree of power for their numbers.

Nevertheless, Allen quickly became an expert on the details of Senate procedure, another route to power for southern senators, who used their parliamentary skills to outmaneuver their northern colleagues. He soon became known among his colleagues as the "wizard of the rule book," and Senator Edward M. Kennedy, a longtime foe of Allen's who served with him on the Senate Judiciary Committee, praised him as "perhaps the greatest parliamentarian ever to sit in the United States Senate." The success Allen enjoyed in the Senate, however, owed as much to hard work as to procedural wiliness.

Despite his modest speaking abilities, Allen became a master of the filibuster and emerged as a speaker who could outtalk nearly all of his fellow senators. The six-foot, 200-pound Allen, his red hair parted in the middle and worn slicked back, would occupy the Senate floor for days, sustained only by generous doses of cherry-flavored glucose. The issues that gave rise to what Allen called "extended floor debate" were typical of those that had concerned southerners for generations. Although Allen carefully eschewed any overtly racist vocabulary, he spoke out often against school desegregation and busing. One of his most noteworthy filibusters sought unsuccessfully over a five-week period to derail passage of the Equal Employment Opportunity Act in 1972. Another filibuster stalled creation of a federal consumer protection agency for several years. Allen also led the unsuccessful fight against the Panama Canal treaties in 1978. Issues dear to the business community also regularly won his allegiance, as did the Constitutional issue of separation of powers. His parliamentary skills and personal tenacity led his longtime ally, Senator Sam Ervin of North Carolina, to rhapsodize, "If I had to stand with one man at Armageddon and battle for the Lord, I hope that man would be Jim Allen."

Allen was notably courteous and spurned most of the perquisites of office. Despite his quiet and reserved manner, Allen kept his McLean, Va., residence telephone number publicly listed so that his constituents could reach him to express their views. Allen flew back home often, always traveling coach and carrying his own bags. Allen died of a heart attack in Foley, Ala., during of one of his visits back to the voters.

On Mar. 16, 1940, Allen married Marjorie Jo Stephens, who died in January 1956; they had three children. On Aug. 7, 1964, Allen married Maryon Pittman Mullins, who was appointed to Allen's seat by Governor Wallace on June 13, 1978, after her husband's death. Maryon Allen had surprising political gifts of her own, and was almost nominated for the special election held later in the year to elect a senator to complete Allen's term.

[Allen's papers and correspondence covering the years 1968–1978 are held in the Alabama Department of Archives and History in Montgomery. See also Sarah Glazer, "James B. Allen: Democratic Senator from Alabama," in *Ralph Nader Congress Project: Citizens Look at Congress* (1972); "Alabama's Allen: Bucking the Anti-Business Tide," *Nation's Business*, Jan. 1976; Victor Gold, "Jim Allen RIP," *National Review*, June 23, 1978; and Michael Barone et al., *Almanac of American Politics* (1978, 1984). An obituary is in the *New York Times*, June 2, 1978.]

DAVID HART NELSON

ALSOP, MARY O'HARA (July 10, 1885–Oct. 14, 1980), author and composer, was born in Cape May Point, N.J., one of four children of the Reverend Reese Fell Alsop, an Episcopal clergyman, and Mary Lee Spring. She was a descendant of Jonathan Edwards and William Penn. Alsop was educated at the Packer Institute near her home in Brooklyn Heights, N.Y., and at the Ingleside School in New Milford, Conn. She also studied music and languages in Europe for several years.

In October 1905, Alsop married a distant cousin, Elisha Kent Kane Parrot, a car salesman who later became a lawyer and political figure; they had two children. In 1908 the Parrots moved from New York to California. After her divorce from Parrot in 1916, Alsop worked for several Hollywood silent film companies as a reader and a script and continuity writer. Her most successful adaptations and script continuities were *Toilers of the Sea* (1923), *Black Oxen* (1924), *Turn to the Right* (1927), and *The Prisoner of Zenda* (1927). During this period, Alsop began restudying music, taking lessons in both piano and composition. In addition, she explored Hindu mysticism and a variety of religious philosophies under the tutelage of George Edwin Burnell.

In August 1922, Alsop married Helge Sture-Vasa, a Swede whom she had met at a film studio. In the 1930's the couple purchased and moved to a Wyoming horse-breeding and dairy ranch, which they operated as a boy's camp in the summer in order to supplement the family income. The Remount Ranch was the inspiration for several of Alsop's novels, which she began publishing after leaving the film industry.

In her autobiography, *Flicka's Friend*, Alsop wrote: "I was destined to be a writer. I might almost say predestined, for I wrote my first short story when I was seven. . . . As soon as it was finished I wrote another, and since then have never stopped writing." Most of Alsop's works were printed under her pen name, Mary O'Hara. Her breakthrough as a writer occurred in the summer of 1940 when, at age fifty-five, she traveled to New York City and took an extension course in writing at Columbia University. Through this class, she made contacts in the literary world that led to the publication of her most successful novel, the best-seller *My Friend Flicka* (1941). The novel, a story of a boy and his horse, was immensely popular and eventually was printed in fourteen foreign-language editions. It was the first of a trilogy that also included *Thunderhead* (1943) and *Green Grass of Wyoming* (1946). The main characters of the first novel are a ten-year-old boy and his beloved wild horse, Flicka, who live on a Wyoming ranch. Alsop explores the dynamics of family relationships as the young boy finds both conflict with his strong-willed, military-trained father and understanding from his artistic, sensitive mother. The difficulties of ranch life and family relationships and a boy's love for spirited horses are continuing themes of the trilogy's second and third novels, as the boy matures into a young man of seventeen. Critics praised the author for her skillful, vivid use of imagery and her sensitive character portrayals. In 1943, *New York Times* book reviewer Orville Prescott wrote, "In Miss O'Hara, I believe, we have one of the most important and most enduring novelists now writing in America. . . . Timeless tales like hers will always find a new public awaiting them as fast as new generations who like children and like horses grow up enough to read them." Twentieth Century–Fox produced film versions of each of the novels (1943, 1945, and 1948), and in 1957, an ABC-TV series was based on *My Friend Flicka*.

In the early 1940's, having failed to achieve economic success in ranching, Alsop and her husband sold their Wyoming property and moved to Santa Barbara, Calif. In 1947 they were divorced and Alsop legally resumed her maiden name. The following year she returned to the East to make her home near Monroe, Conn.

While Alsop was writing film scripts, novels, and short stories, she also was producing musical compositions. Throughout her life she enjoyed playing the piano daily and once wrote that she believed music was "my true vocation and writing merely an avocation . . . but when the inspiration for a story seized me, I would decide it was the other way around, and writing was my vocation." Among the better-known of her many early musical compositions for piano were "Esperan" (1943), "May God Keep You" (1946), "Wyoming Suite for Piano" (1946), and "Windharp."

After reaching what most would consider retirement age, Alsop wrote five more books, each very intimate in the way it reflected different aspects of her life and personality. *The Son of Adam Wyngate* (1952) drew on some of the mysticism and religious philosophies she had explored; *Novel-in-the-Making* (1954), on the art of writing a book, was her first autobiography; *Wyoming Summer* (1963), a fictionalized adaptation of her summer diary written many years earlier, reintroduced Western themes while also revealing her personal insights on life; and *A Musical in the Making* (1966) was an intimate account of nine years of her trials and tribulations in creating a musical. She also wrote a play, *The Catch Colt* (1964), for which she composed the musical score. This folk musical was first produced at Catholic University of America under the title *Oh, Wyoming!* and later at Lincoln Theatre, Cheyenne, Wyo., where it was called *Top O' the Big Hill*. In 1979, *The Catch Colt* was published as a novella.

In the early 1970's Alsop moved to the Washington, D.C., area to be near her son, who was assisting her as agent and public relations adviser for her musical. She died of arteriosclerosis in Chevy Chase, Md., at the age of ninety-five.

[The University of Wyoming's American Heritage Center in Laramie, Wyo., has a collection of some of Alsop's papers and photographs, including the book manuscripts of her best-selling trilogy. Alsop's last and most complete autobiography is *Flicka's Friend* (1982), although her earlier *Novel-in-the-Making* (1954) and *A Musical in the Making* (1966) are also autobiographical. In addition to her novels cited above, Alsop wrote *Let Us Say Grace* (1930). A number of musical compositions, besides those mentioned, were published by Presser of Philadelphia and G. Schirmer of New York. Some reviews of her books are in the *New York Times*, Aug. 27, 1941, Oct. 6, 1943, and Oct. 27, 1946. Obituaries are in the *New York Times*, Oct. 16, 1980, and the *Washington Post*, Oct. 15, 1980.]

MARILYNN WOOD HILL

ANDERSON, EDWARD ("EDDIE") (Sept. 18, 1906–Feb. 28, 1977), radio, film, and television actor and comedian, was born in Oakland, Calif., the son of "Big Ed" Anderson, a minstrel performer, and Ella Mae Anderson, a circus tightrope walker. At age twelve, while selling the *San Francisco Bulletin*, he strained his vocal cords and, so the legend goes, permanently acquired the hoarse, scratchy voice that would be his signature.

At age fourteen, Anderson began performing in all-black musical revues such as *Struttin' Along*, and he sang with a trio, the Three Black Aces. He toured with a band called the California Collegians and as half of a two-person song-and-dance act with his older brother, Cornelius. Eventually he settled in Los Angeles and became a regular entertainer at Sebastian's Cotton Club; he began auditioning for the bit "race" parts in Hollywood films available to an African-American thespian.

After a tiny role as James in *What Price Hollywood?* (1932), Anderson was cast as an unnamed young Negro in *Show Boat* (1936). His important character role as Noah in the all-black biblical musical *Green Pastures* (1936) should have brought better parts to Anderson, but instead he was relegated, in 1938, to three stereotyped roles: as a doorman in *Gold Diggers in Paris*, as a janitor in *Thanks for the Memory*, and as a groom in *Going Places*.

Fortunately for Anderson, a new career was to open up for him. Comedian Jack Benny, who was moving his popular radio program to Los Angeles in 1937, was preparing an episode about his train trip from New York. Benny's writers had included a role for a black porter, and Benny planned to utilize his regular performer, Benny Rubin, who did dialect roles. However, writer Bill Morrow insisted that the part must be played by a black actor. "The one we hired . . . was the least impressive in the reading," Benny said of Anderson's audition, "but he had a deep husky growl in his voice and his words came up through his larynx like there was a pile of gravel down there."

Anderson's several-minutes-long first appearance on Easter, 1937, as a Pullman porter skeptical that there's a place on the train's route—or on earth—called Albuquerque, caused a sensation. By popular demand the porter appeared again, and in a third program he visited Benny in Los Angeles and stayed on as the comedian's valet and chauffeur. Along the way, Anderson's character acquired a name: Rochester.

"Within two years," Benny said of Anderson, "he was making $150,000 a year and lived in a gorgeous mansion with his charming wife, Maymie, and his family. He diverted himself with such hobbies as raising thoroughbred horses." One of his horses, Burnt Cork, ran in the 1943 Kentucky Derby.

As Rochester, Anderson became widely recognized and much beloved. "It has been said that Eddie Anderson talks to more Americans every Sunday night than any colored man in history," wrote a critic in the 1940's. Anderson also was instrumental in advancing Benny's movie career. They made three films together at Paramount—*Man About Town* (1939), *Buck Benny Rides Again* (1940), and *Love Thy Neighbor* (1940)—and much of the box office success was attributed to Anderson's spirited participation. Concerning *Man About Town*, *New York Times* critic Frank S. Nugent declared, "A sly little gentleman's gentleman—or comedian's comedian—called Rochester has restored Jack Benny to the comic map and cleared a sizable place there for himself."

Paramount wanted Anderson for one of its Bob Hope pictures, but Benny refused, saying, "It's bad enough having him steal my pictures. I won't have him helping out another actor." However, Anderson's radio and film popularity qualified him for his best role by far in a movie. He was cast as Little Joe Jackson, the singing and dancing romantic lead, in the film version of the Broadway musical *Cabin in the Sky* (1943), directed by Vincente Minnelli. Anderson headed an all-star black cast that included Lena Horne, Ethel Waters, and Louis Armstrong. The movie was a major MGM hit.

Anderson's starring performance in *Cabin in the Sky* must be contrasted with the minuscule "race" roles he had been squeezed into in other movies—including Uncle Peter in *Gone with the Wind* (1939)—when he wasn't being Rochester. Perhaps his most demeaning part was as an eye-rolling chauffeur in *Topper Returns* (1941), scared of ghosts and of his own shadow. In 1945, Anderson's film *Brewster's Millions* was banned in Memphis, Tenn., because he, a black man, stood too close to Helen Walker, a white actress. Even *Cabin in the Sky* had its racial tensions: actress Lena Horne recalled that during her screen test with Anderson, MGM personnel kept smearing her face with dark makeup to match Anderson's skin tone.

Anderson never got a chance to star in his pet project, a biographical tribute to the African-American vaudevillian Bert Williams. He summed up his outlook on life in a 1943 interview: "A colored man's just . . . gotta laugh. If I don't laugh, I reckon pretty quick I'd die."

Ultimately, the questions critics ask about Anderson concern the character of Rochester, with whom he was associated for forty years. Was Rochester, loyal black manservant to Jack Benny, a degrading racial stereotype? Or did Rochester's sarcastic wit and sparkling intelligence undercut his boss's penny-pinching authority more than it bolstered it? Benny himself supplied perhaps the best answer: "Rochester was never a servile, supplicating Stepin Fetchit. I was . . . the fall guy for Rochester."

When the "Jack Benny Show" moved to television (CBS, 1950–1964; NBC, 1964–1965), Anderson stayed on as Benny's valet. Asked in the 1950's about his television Rochester and about Hattie McDaniel's black television maid, Beulah, Anderson said, "I haven't seen anything objectionable. I don't know why certain characters are called stereotypes. The Negro characters being represented are not labeling the Negro race . . . any more than is Beulah, who is not playing the part of thousands of Negroes."

Anderson made guest appearances on television shows including "Bachelor Father" (1962), the "Dick Powell Theatre" (1963), and "Love American Style" (1969). His last film role was as a cab driver in the 1963 comedy *It's a Mad, Mad, Mad, Mad World*. He lived in semiretirement, devoting time to his race horses. He died at the Motion Picture House and Hospital in Los Angeles. His first wife, Maymie Anderson, died in 1954. He was divorced from his second wife, Eva Anderson. He had three children.

[An interview with Anderson is Florabel Muir, "What's That, Boss?" *Saturday Evening Post*, June 19, 1943. Anderson's career is discussed in Peter Noble, *The Negro in Films* (1948); Donald Bogle, *Toms, Coons, Mulattoes, Mammies, and Bucks* (1973, rev. ed. 1989); and Jack Benny's *Sunday Nights at Seven* (1990), with Joan Benny. An obituary is in the *New York Times*, Mar. 1, 1977.]

GERALD PEARY

ARONSON, BORIS SOLOMON (Oct. 15, 1900–Nov. 16, 1980), painter, sculptor, and scenic designer, was born in Kiev, Russia (now Ukraine), one of ten children of Solomon Aronson, a rabbi, and Deborah Turovsky. He attended State Art School, Kiev (1912–1918), and studied art and design with Ilya Mashkov at the School of Modern Painting, Moscow; Alexandra Exter at the School of the Theatre, Kiev; and Herman Strauch in Berlin. He left for Berlin in 1922 and immigrated to the United States in 1923.

In New York he began designing sets for Yiddish theater productions, first with the experimental Unser Theater and then the Yiddish Art Theater. Toward the end of his career, Aronson admitted that he experienced his greatest artistic gratification during this early period when he was allowed freedom to experiment. He next worked with Eva Le Gallienne's Civic Repertory Theatre. During the Great Depression he joined the artistic collective The Group Theater and designed their productions of *Awake and Sing!* (1935), *Paradise Lost* (1935), and *The Gentle People* (1939).

By the 1930's he was frequently designing for Broadway shows, including *Three Men on a Horse* (1935) and *The Merchant of Yonkers* (1938).

By the 1940's he had expanded his design work to ballet (Ballet Theatre, Ballet Russe de Monte Carlo) and musical theater (*Cabin in the Sky* [1940]; *South Pacific* [1949]). In 1945 he married Lisa Jalowetz, an artistic assistant since 1943, who would continue to work with him professionally. His outstanding designs of the 1950's included the New York productions of *The Country Girl* (1950), *The Rose Tattoo* (1951), *I Am a Camera* (1951), the ballet *Ballade* (1952), *The Crucible* (1953), *Bus Stop* (1955), *The Diary of Anne Frank* (1955), *Orpheus Descending* (1957), and *J. B.* (1958). He also designed *Coriolanus* (1959) at Stratford-upon-Avon, England.

Aronson's greatest recognition and critical success came in the 1960's and 1970's with his work on musicals, considered to be his most innovative designs, especially those done in collaboration with producer Harold Prince. Notable among his musical designs were those for *Fiddler on the Roof* (1964), *Cabaret* (1966), *Zorba* (1968), *Company* (1970), *Follies* (1972), *A Little Night Music* (1973), and *Pacific Overtures* (1976). For the Metropolitan Opera he designed *Mourning Becomes Electra* (1967) and *Fidelio* (1970). In 1976 he designed Mikhail Baryshnikov's staging of *The Nutcracker*, his final project.

During a career that spanned five decades, Aronson, termed by director and critic Harold Clurman the "master visual artist of the stage," won the Antoinette Perry (Tony) Award for best design for *The Rose Tattoo, The Country Girl, Season in the Sun* (1951), *Cabaret*, *Zorba*, *Company*, *Follies*, and *Pacific Overtures*. He received six additional Tony nominations. His work was recognized by fellowships from the Guggenheim (1950) and Ford (1962) foundations.

Aronson's designs, for approximately 125 productions, were noted for their originality, their strong sense of line and form, and a subtle but evocative use of color. In 1940 he demonstrated for the first time a technique he called "projected scenery," a method of projecting colored slides (collages) on neutral or textured scenery in order to create and alter mood and space ("painting with light"). He rarely repeated himself in his design work, using influences not only from his teachers but from the work of Marc Chagall (known for his cubist-fantastic style), Alexander Tairov (the antinaturalistic director of Moscow's Kamerny Theatre), and Nathan Altman (the designer for the Moscow Jewish Theatre), in addition to his childhood experiences in Russia and his travels in prewar Europe. A lifelong interest in Japanese popular arts was most clearly reflected in his designs for *Pacific Overtures*. In defining the stage designer's job, Aronson wrote, "I strongly believe that for each play you first and foremost must create a space which, inherent in its design, already holds the mystique of the entire event."

Many consider Aronson the most respected American scenic designer of the mid-twentieth century. He was a first-rate artist and his paintings and designs have been exhibited on many occasions in New York, Paris, and London, most notably in 1947 at the Museum of Modern Art in New York, in 1981 at the New York Library for the Performing Arts at Lincoln Center, and in 1989 at the Katonah (N.Y.) Gallery. Aronson wrote two books, both in Russian: *Marc Chagall* (1923) and *Modern Graphic Art* (1924). He died near his home in suburban Nyack, N.Y., survived by his wife and one son.

[The definitive study of Aronson is Frank Rich with Lisa Aronson, *The Theatre Art of Boris Aronson* (1987), which includes an extensive bibliography. His designs are in the collections of Lisa Aronson, the New York Public Library, the Museum of the City of New York, and various private collectors. Files of clippings are in the New York Public Library of the Performing Arts at Lincoln Center and the Harvard Theatre Collection. See also John Mason Brown, introduction to *Art in the Theatre* (1927); Shepard Traube, "Boris Aronson," *Theatre Guild Magazine*, Jan. 1931; Eric Weitz, "The Long-Forgotten Magic Lantern," *Interiors*, Dec. 1948; Harold Clurman, "Master of Visual Art," *New York World Journal Telegram*, Apr. 16, 1967; Mel Gussow, "The Stage Worlds of Boris Aronson," *New York Times*, Apr. 3, 1981; Frank Rich with Lisa Aronson, "He Made the Stage," *New York Times*, Oct. 11, 1987; Frank Rich, "Boris Aronson, Stage Design As Visual Metaphor," *Theatre Design and Technology*, Fall 1989; and Eric Weitz, "Boris Aronson: Stages in Design," *New York Times*, Oct. 28, 1989. Obituaries are in the *New York Times*, Nov. 17, 1980, and *Variety*, Nov. 19, 1980.]

DON B. WILMETH

ARVEY, JACOB M. (Nov. 3, 1895–Aug. 25, 1977), politician and lawyer, was born in Chicago, one of seven children of Israel and Bertha Arvey, Russian-Jewish immigrants. His father, a milk dealer and peddler, moved the family soon after Jacob's birth to the growing Jewish neighborhood on the city's West Side. He died when Jacob was only thirteen years old.

Arvey worked many odd jobs while attending Crane High School and later the John Marshall Law School. In 1916 he was admitted to the Illinois bar; that same year he married Edith Freeman. They had three children. It was also at this time that Arvey joined the local Democratic political organization of Mike and Moe Rosenberg, emerging power brokers in West Side Jewish politics.

He became a precinct captain for the Rosenbergs and soon after that was named assistant states attorney for Cook County. In less than two years he left that position to join a law firm headed by a fellow West Sider and noted politician, Joseph Kostner. Kostner, a Czech, lived in the adjoining Bohemian neighborhood; Arvey saw the advantages of forging ethnic alliances.

In 1923, Arvey, under the protective wing of the Rosenbergs, was elected alderman of the predominantly Jewish Twenty-fourth Ward. He served in this post until 1941. In 1934 he succeeded the remaining Rosenberg brother to become Twenty-fourth Ward Democratic committeeman, thereby gaining direct access to the high tribunal of local Democratic politics, the county central committee.

Under Arvey's leadership the Twenty-fourth Ward became the most vote-potent and deliverable Democratic district in the country. Arvey maximized the ward's religious cohesiveness with his own aggressive brand of politics. He combined community and politics into an all-powerful social service machine. Nothing happened in the Twenty-fourth Ward without "Jake's OK." Arvey enforced his will through hard work, compassion, and, when necessary, a little muscle. Though diminutive in size, Arvey became a giant on Chicago's West Side.

An example of Arvey's power can best be seen in the 1936 Democratic gubernatorial primary. The Democratic governor, Henry Horner, had broken with the Democratic organization headed by Chicago's mayor, Ed Kelly, and Democratic county chairman Pat Nash. Horner, a well-known Jewish leader, expected heavy support from the Twenty-fourth Ward. In the name of party loyalty and unity, Arvey supported Horner's non-Jewish opponent, Herman Bundeson, who won an unlikely victory in this overwhelmingly Jewish ward. Years later Arvey called his anti-Horner decision the most difficult of his political career but, according to Arvey, "I had given my word to the party and I had to keep it."

Throughout the 1930's, Arvey moved up the power ladder in Chicago politics. Journalists began referring to the local Democratic organization as the "Kelly-Nash-Arvey" machine. In 1941, following the Pearl Harbor bombing, Arvey, age forty-six, resigned from the council to join the Illinois Thirty-third Infantry Division. He served four years as a judge advocate, including two years in the South Pacific, and when he came home in late 1945 he carried the rank of lieutenant colonel.

Arvey quickly returned full time to Chicago's political wars. His old friend, Mayor Ed Kelly, appointed Arvey to the patronage-heavy Park District Board. The Democratic machine was sputtering, and several party leaders looking for harmony and leadership persuaded Arvey to become county chairman. The 1946 general election proved disastrous for local Democrats and convinced Arvey that the party and its organization had to go in a different direction if it wanted to regain its former stature. In the next two years Arvey transformed the leadership and image of local Democratic politics.

In late 1946 he convinced Ed Kelly not to seek reelection for a fifth term. Arvey then endorsed a local businessman, Martin Kennelly, for mayor. Kennelly ran as a reformer and with begrudging support from many astonished party leaders won the mayor's race as a "liberal Democrat" in the spring of 1947.

One year later Arvey was at it again. Conventional wisdom said the Illinois Democrats would not be competitive in the 1948 United States Senate and gubernatorial races. Arvey thought otherwise. He orchestrated the party nomination of Paul Douglas, University of Chicago economics professor and antimachine Chicago alderman, for the Senate, and the patrician lawyer Adlai Stevenson for governor. Douglas and Stevenson went on to win their respective statewide races with landslide majorities, putting Arvey at the height of his political power. He was called a "genius" and Democratic savior even though in the same year, 1948, he had unsuccessfully tried to dump the incumbent president, Harry Truman, in favor of war hero Dwight Eisenhower.

Arvey's political glow would shine for only a short time. In 1950 another off-year election disaster rocked the local Democratic party. Corruption charges against a local candidate for sheriff helped cost the seat of Senate Democratic leader Scott Lucas. Arvey accepted responsibility for the defeat and resigned as party chairman. The colonel remained national party committeeman, but a new leader was emerging to challenge his power within the local Democratic party. By 1955, Richard J. Daley would consolidate party control and the mayoralty under his sole leadership, forcing old-timers like Arvey to the background.

Though still considered a player in Chicago politics, Arvey spent the next quarter century enjoying himself as party statesman, civic leader, and fund-raiser for the State of Israel. It was his idea in 1951 that Israel start a bond-sale program in the United States. Arvey joined various social clubs, including the German-Jewish Standard Club, which in a previous era would have rejected him for his eastern European background. He also prospered as the lead partner in the LaSalle Street law firm of Arvey, Hodes and Mantynbond, and reveled in being called "colonel" by almost everyone in Chicago.

Arvey never enjoyed a close relationship with Daley. Both men, in old-school tradition, did not speak openly about the coolness between them, but legend has it that Daley never forgave Arvey for not slating him in 1950 for the office of Cook County board president. As fate would have it, Arvey outlived Daley by only eight months; the passing of both men ended an era in Chicago politics. At Arvey's funeral service, held at a fashionable lakefront synagogue (his old West Side community was now part of Chicago's black ghetto), it was said that throughout his life Arvey lived his mother's admonition, "It is never necessary to be rude to anybody."

[Arvey's papers are at the Chicago Historical Society. They contain little information about his political career. Secondary sources are also somewhat sparse on Arvey's political influence. For Arvey's early career, see Alex Gottfried, *Boss Cermak of Chicago* (1962). See also Len O'Connor, *Clout* (1975); and Milton L. Rakove, *We Don't Want Nobody Nobody Sent* (1979). An obituary is in the *New York Times*, Aug. 26, 1977.]

PAUL M. GREEN

ARZNER, DOROTHY EMMA (Jan. 3, 1897–Oct. 1, 1979), film director and editor, was born in San Francisco, Calif., one of two children of Louis Adolph Arzner and Jenette Hay Young, immigrants from Germany and Scotland, respectively. Dorothy's mother presumably died before she was eight, and in 1905 her father married Mabel Gorsuch and moved the family to Los Angeles, where he became proprietor of a café popular with actors and filmmakers. Mabel Arzner, wishing to refine Dorothy's tomboy ways, sent her to board at the Westlake School for Girls. Active, competitive, and popular, Dorothy graduated in 1915.

From 1915 to 1917 she studied at the University of Southern California and contemplated medical school, but when the United States entered World War I, she enlisted in the Los Angeles Emergency Ambulance Corps. In 1919 her corps commander suggested a career in film and arranged an interview with William deMille at Famous Players–Lasky Studio (later Paramount Pictures). DeMille told her to look around the studio for a week. "I remember making the observation," she wrote later, "if one was going to be in this movie business, one should be a director because he was the one who told everyone what to do." She told deMille, however, that she would start at the bottom and began work in the script department as a typist.

After three months she did her first work on a set as the script girl for actress Alla Nazimova, and within a few months she rose to script supervisor. Instructed by film cutter Nan Heron, Arzner learned to edit. She left the studio to obtain a promotion at Universal, but in 1921 Paramount made her sole editor at their Realart Studios, giving her thirty-five pictures to cut in one year. In 1922 she gained her first screen credit, as editor of *Blood and Sand*, intercutting stock footage with shots of Rudolph Valentino to create the film's bullfight sequences.

Her success led director James Cruze to bring her on location to edit *The Covered Wagon* (1923). Now well established—according to British film historian Kevin Brownlow, "the only editor from the entire silent era to be officially remembered"—Arzner turned to writing scenarios. She sold a few Westerns to Film Booking Office but returned to Paramount as editor and scenarist on Cruze's *Old Ironsides* (1926).

In 1927, while negotiating with Harry Cohn to direct at fledgling Columbia Pictures, producer Walter Wanger intervened and persuaded Paramount to give Arzner a film to get into production in two weeks. Daunted but determined, she directed the silent *Fashions for Women* (1927), starring Esther Ralston. The two were also paired for *Ten Modern Commandments* (1927). The pairing, however, proved uncongenial, and Paramount found the director a new star in Clara Bow.

With Bow and Charles Rogers, Arzner made another comedy, *Get Your Man* (1927), and, with Nancy Carroll and Richard Arlen, *Manhattan Cocktail* (1928). By now Arzner's reputation was so considerable that Paramount chose her to make Bow's first sound picture, *The Wild Party* (1929). Arzner picked Fredric March, who had made only one other film, to play the male lead—the first of many apt castings of newcomers who would later become stars. In collaboration with a sound technician she developed the first boom microphone (on a "fish pole"), an innovation typical of the collaborative spirit on her pictures.

In 1930 she made the first of four films with writer Zoë Akins. *Sarah and Son*, about the trials of a German immigrant (played by Ruth

Chatterton), proved so successful that the studio thereafter let Arzner choose her own stories. She picked another Akins screenplay, *Anybody's Woman* (1930), again with Chatterton. In the same year she directed an episode in *Paramount on Parade* and worked on *Behind the Makeup* and *Charming Sinners*, films assigned to other directors. In 1931 she directed *Honor Among Lovers* with Claudette Colbert, Fredric March, and Ginger Rogers.

Arzner's string of successes ended with *Working Girls* (1931), an Akins script with two heroines, one who is victimized by sex and another who exploits it. Now praised for its frankness and innovation, it found no favor with the studio. The total ambiguity of Arzner's work continued with *Merrily We Go to Hell* (1932), a dark Prohibition comedy about alcoholism and marriage starring Sylvia Sidney and March. It is the ambiguity itself—a disturbing, socially subversive presence in much of Arzner's work—that is emphasized by modern critics.

In 1933, Arzner left Paramount to become an independent director, working first for David O. Selznick at RKO on *Christopher Strong*, again picking an "unlikely" star—Katharine Hepburn, whom she found making a jungle movie "up a tree with a leopard skin on." In *Christopher Strong*, Hepburn played a champion aviator.

After making *Nana* (1934) for Samuel Goldwyn, Arzner became an associate producer for Cohn at Columbia. She made *Craig's Wife* (1936) but almost lost control of the picture when Cohn objected to her expensive sets and her choice of another newcomer, Rosalind Russell, to star. The film was admired by Joan Crawford and Louis B. Mayer, who brought Arzner to MGM for *The Bride Wore Red* with Crawford in 1937. She also contributed to *The Last of Mrs. Cheney*, without credit. Arzner then refused three scripts suggested by Mayer, calling them "frivolous," and was put on suspension.

Two years later, she stepped in after a week's shooting to take over the RKO film *Dance, Girl, Dance* (1940). Arzner rewrote the script and made what has become her most widely discussed picture. Especially notable is the scene in which Maureen O'Hara, playing an idealistic ballet dancer, has a fistfight with stripper Lucille Ball and berates the male audience of a burlesque house.

Arzner made training films for the Women's Army Corps early in World War II but returned to Columbia to make her last film, *First Comes Courage* (1943), a drama with Merle Oberon about Norwegian resistance to the Nazis. Near completion of the film, Arzner fell ill with pneumonia, and at her recovery a year later she unexpectedly retired as a film director. She was forty-six. In later years, she spoke of hating the tension of working for tyrants like Mayer and Cohn: "I had no defenses. I would rather walk away."

After leaving the studios, she directed plays and from 1952 to 1954 was the first head of cinema and television at the Pasadena Playhouse. In 1959 she began directing Pepsi-Cola television commercials for her friend Joan Crawford and in 1965 joined the Film Department at the University of California at Los Angeles for four years, where she championed the work of her student Francis Ford Coppola. She never married. For the last fourteen years of her life Arzner retired to a desert home near Palm Springs, Calif., where she undertook a historical novel on the settling of Los Angeles. She died in La Quinta, Calif.

"Try as man may," Arzner said in 1927, "he will never get the woman's viewpoint in telling certain stories." The tonal uneasiness and questioning of social values in her films have come to be identified with the "woman's viewpoint" of which she spoke, an element that deliberately disturbed the "male gaze" of traditional studio films. Her sympathetic but unsentimental portrayals of independent women stand alone among Hollywood films of the 1930's and 1940's, and Arzner has become an icon to students of feminist film theory. Arzner was the first woman to gain membership in the Directors Guild; her professional skill, industry, and independence became models for the work of later women filmmakers. As she said at her 1915 high school commencement, "We enjoy ourselves only in our work, our doing; and our best doing is our best enjoyment."

[The University of California at Los Angeles and the Academy of Motion Picture Arts and Sciences, Beverly Hills, Calif., maintain Arzner collections. See also Francine Parker, "Approaching the Art of Dorothy Arzner," *Action*, July/Aug. 1973; Gerald Peary, "Dorothy Arzner," *Cinema*, Fall 1974; Mary Murphy, "Tribute to an Unsung Pioneer," *Los Angeles Times*, Jan. 24, 1975; C. Johnston, ed., *The Work of Dorothy Arzner: Towards a Feminist Cinema* (1975); John Wakeman, ed., *World Film Di-*

rectors (1987); and Judith Mayne, *Directed by Dorothy Arzner* (1994). Obituaries are in the *Los Angeles Times*, Oct. 8, 1979, and the *New York Times*, Oct. 12, 1979.]

ALAN BUSTER

ASCOLI, MAX (June 25, 1898–Jan. 1, 1978), writer, publisher, and political scientist, was born in Ferrara, Italy, the only child of Adriana Finzi and Enrico Ascoli, a successful coal and lumber merchant. From childhood Ascoli suffered from eye problems. At four he started wearing glasses, and at school he avoided all sports, on doctor's orders. Ascoli later recalled: "For over fifty years, people who cared about me were concerned about my eyes. I was living on borrowed sight." Although he depended on friends to read aloud to him at times, Ascoli graduated from the University of Ferrara in 1920 with an LL.D. degree in jurisprudence and earned a doctorate in philosophy from the University of Rome in 1928.

Ascoli's wide-ranging writing career began in 1921 with the publication in Paris of *Georges Sorel*, a critique of the French socialist and revolutionary syndicalist. In his 1924 book *Le Vie dalla croce*, Ascoli, who was Jewish and regarded himself as deeply religious, framed his own religious philosophy within a discussion of Judaism and Christianity. Between 1922 and 1925, Ascoli spoke out forcefully against Mussolini and the rise of fascism in *Rivoluzione liberale*, *Il quarto stato*, and other antifascist publications. After Mussolini became dictator in 1925, Ascoli started writing for *Non mollare*, an underground paper. Ascoli later said that he "ceased to write for it after a man in Florence whom the Fascists considered the writer of an article of mine was murdered."

From 1926 to 1928, Ascoli taught jurisprudence at the University of Camerino. In the latter year Mussolini's Fascist police arrested him in Milan. He was jailed for several weeks and then sentenced to two years of modified house arrest, later reduced to six months. "All the trouble I had with Fascism," he once said, "was because of what I had written and most of all because I would *refuse* to enter the Fascist Party." Three years of humiliation and police surveillance followed. Ascoli lost his teaching post, his writings were suppressed in Italy, and he was barred from accepting a chair in philosophy at the University of Rome, which he had won in a national competition. Ascoli was an associate professor of jurisprudence and political philosophy at the University of Cagliari in Sardinia from 1929 to 1931, when he was dismissed for refusing to join the Fascist party.

In 1931, with the promise of a Rockefeller Foundation Fellowship in his pocket and a painting by Gauguin and one by Tintoretto under his arm, Ascoli boarded a ship in Naples and sailed to America. He spent his first two years in the United States traveling around the country, stopping to study at Harvard, at the University of Chicago, and at the University of Wisconsin. When his fellowship expired, Ascoli, who faced arrest if he returned to Italy, chose political exile. In late 1933 he became a charter member of the graduate faculty of political and social science at the New School for Social Research in New York City. The Rockefeller Foundation paid half of his salary during the first year. The University in Exile, Ascoli later recalled, began with seventeen refugee German scholars and "one lonely Italian" professor of political philosophy. When he became an American citizen in 1939, Ascoli said, "I am in a large group of friends over here, a community which is growing out of the work of each one of us, and mutual confidence, and common beliefs." He served as dean of the graduate faculty from 1940 to 1941.

Besides teaching at the New School, Ascoli wrote article after article, book after book, mostly dealing with his "pet obsession": "how, in the democratic climate of our times, freedom can perish." Ascoli saw his task as "searching for the point at which democratic institutions fail to work in strengthening freedom." In his 1938 book *Fascism for Whom?* (a collaboration with Arthur Feiler), Ascoli described fascism as "a parasitic growth on the democratic structure."

Ascoli married twice. His first wife, Anna Maria Cochetti, wrote poetry under the name Anna Maria Armi. They divorced in 1940. That same year, on October 5, he married Marion Rosenwald, the wealthy daughter of Julius Rosenwald, the chairman of Sears, Roebuck; they had one child.

Ascoli was named the first president of the Mazzini Society, an Italian-American anti-Fascist organization, in 1940, but stepped down the following year when he became associate director of cultural relations in the office of the coordinator of Inter-American affairs, under Nelson Rockefeller, in Washington, D.C. He spent the next two years traveling in Latin

America, gathering intelligence and extolling the virtues of America to the Italian communities there. At the end of 1944, Ascoli set up his own foundation to revive and promote the production and sale of Italian arts and crafts.

Ascoli left the New School in 1950 to work on the *Reporter*, an award-wining, biweekly magazine based in New York that he founded (1949), edited, and published until it ceased publication in 1968. Known for its aggressive journalism and distinguished staff of editors and correspondents, the magazine included an editorial by Ascoli in nearly every issue. Ascoli described his magazine as "an experiment in adult journalism." Read by liberals, the magazine studied news issues including McCarthyism, illegal wiretapping, the effects of radioactive fallout, and the Vietnam War. Ascoli's greatest impact as a political scientist came from his involvement with the *Reporter*. In *Illustrious Immigrants*, Laura Fermi wrote: "Ascoli has not forced his conclusions on his readers or considered world events in black or white. The partiality he has imparted to his magazine has consisted in his refusal to compromise with principle. And principle may sometimes be very personal."

Ascoli died in New York City.

[Ascoli's files of the *Reporter* are in the Department of Special Collections, Mugar Library, Boston University. Major publications by Ascoli include *Intelligence in Politics* (1936); *Political and Economic Democracy*, edited with Fritz Lehmann (1937); *The Fall of Mussolini*, as editor, translated by Francis Frenaye (1948); *The Power of Freedom* (1949); *The Reporter Reader*, as editor (1956); and *Our Times: The Best from the Reporter* (1960). For a discussion of his political ideas and personality, see Martin K. Doudna, "The Liberalism of Max Ascoli," in his *Concerned About the Planet* (1977). Peter M. Rutkoff and William B. Scott discuss Ascoli in *New School* (1986). An obituary is in the *New York Times*, Jan. 2, 1978.]

JUDITH R. GOODSTEIN

ASHFORD, EMMETT LITTLETON (Nov. 23, 1914–Mar. 1, 1980), baseball umpire, was born in Los Angeles and abandoned in early childhood by his father. Emmett and his older brother were raised by their mother, an ambitious and strong-willed woman who was a secretary at the *California Eagle*, a black-oriented newspaper. His supportive home life served him well in overcoming the problems of being the first black umpire in major league baseball.

Ashford attended public schools in Los Angeles, earning varsity letters in track and baseball at the predominantly white Jefferson High School. He was an excellent student and became the first black to serve as student body president and newspaper editor. He was also the first black to hold a cashier job at the neighborhood grocery store.

Ashford began umpiring in sandlot and recreation-league games in 1937, after a regular umpire failed to show. His officiating initially caused an uproar, the crowd never having seen a black umpire before, but after the game he received a nice collection of money from the crowd. It was only after Jackie Robinson was signed by the Brooklyn Dodgers in 1947, thus breaking the color barrier, however, that Ashford thought of umpiring professionally.

Ashford matriculated at Los Angeles City College, then transferred to Chapman College in Orange, Calif., in 1941. He lettered in track and baseball and served as sports editor of the college newspaper. In 1943, Ashford left Chapman because of a lack of funds and joined the navy.

Decommissioned in 1947, Ashford took a civil service job with the U.S. Post Office in Los Angeles. He devoted his recreational time to umpiring sandlot, high school, junior college, and college games and also began playing semiprofessional baseball with the Mystery Nine. A centerfielder with a somewhat unreliable arm, he spent a lot of time on the bench. When the umpire failed to show up to one of the games, Ashford was asked to take his place. He reportedly did so in two-tone shoes, green slacks, and a sports coat. Pandemonium broke out, but the crowd eventually calmed down, approved of his work, and the team got a large collection. His umpiring was successful on all levels, including the college circuit, with Division I schools such as University of Southern California and UCLA.

Noted for his friendliness, his sense of humor, and his acrobatic style, Ashford attracted the attention of professional baseball scouts. In 1951, at a time of strong racial intolerance in the United States, he was given a tryout in Mexicali, Mexico, about twenty miles south of El Centro, Calif. During a four-game tryout, the white umpires refused to work with him. Ashford recruited someone from the stands to work the bases and spent the entire four games behind the plate. His showy, ebullient style was so exciting to the fans that they cheered rather than jeered—the latter treatment, or worse, was the fate for most umpires. On the recommendation of a major league scout, Rosey Gilhousen, Ashford became the first black umpire in professional baseball in 1951. Offered a contract to finish the 1951 season of the Class C Southwest League, he took a leave of absence from his job at the post office.

In 1951, he was offered a one-year contract. Unable to obtain another leave, Ashford resigned from his job in the finance and payroll division of the post office, giving up fifteen years of seniority and the possibility of being promoted to supervisor. Six months into the season, the Southwest League folded. The five white umpires were quickly placed, and weeks later the league was reorganized as the Class C Arizona-Texas League. Ashford's perennial humor and repartee, for which he became renowned, served him well during this period. He was tested by biased fans, players, managers, and other umpires, but the *El Paso Press* hailed Ashford's "great display of guts and courage plus very good umpiring."

During fifteen years in the minor leagues, he umpired in the Southern International League (Class C) from 1951 to 1953, the Arizona-Texas League (Class C) in 1952, the Western International League (Class A) in 1953, and the Pacific Coast League (Class AAA) from 1954 to 1965. He also umpired three winter seasons in the Dominican Republic (1958–1959 and 1964). It was Clarence Rowland, president of the Pacific Coast League, who hired Ashford as the first black umpire in the league in 1954. In 1963, Ashford was promoted to umpire in chief by Rowland's successor, Dervey Soriano, whose influence was instrumental in getting Ashford into the majors. Soriano recognized Ashford's special gifts and used him to boost attendance at various parks and in difficult assignments. When Ashford was the arbiter, it was a certainty that the ballpark's attendance would increase.

In 1966, Ashford finally reached the major leagues. Joe Cronin, the president of the American League, bought Ashford's contract from the Pacific Coast League. Some twenty years after Jackie Robinson's integration as a player, the first black umpire was hired. Ashford's first regular-season game was the season opener between the Washington Senators and the Cleveland Indians at Washington, D.C., Stadium in 1966. His umpire crew consisted of the crew chief Johnny Stevens, Bob Steward, and Bill Haller, all veterans. Vice-President Hubert Humphrey substituted for President Lyndon Johnson in throwing out the ceremonial first pitch. Ashford had more difficulties getting past incredulous Secret Service men than he had in his duties as officiator. But Cronin had told Ashford to be himself, and the five foot seven, 187 pound extrovert was just that. He made history in that first game and no errors. Ashford went on to umpire the 1967 All-Star Game and the 1970 World Series. He conducted umpiring clinics in Asia, Europe, and Canada.

Ashford's major league career was filled with controversy, replete with racial slurs and hostilities from players and managers. Some umpires resented his popularity with the fans and the press. He was criticized for his flamboyance, as symbolized by his French cuffs, which extended just beyond his jacket, his spit-shined shoes and suit that looked just pressed, and especially for his mannerisms in making calls. He was called a "showboat," a "clown," and a "Hollywood hot dog" who sacrificed accuracy for attention. When calling strikes, he assumed a semi-squat stance, his right arm extended out to the side; when it reached its apex, down it would come like a cleaver or karate chop while Ashford pumped his left leg and let out a resounding "Stirriike!" that could be heard blocks away; or, he reached up and gave two quick jerks like a person pulling on a train whistle; or, from the squat position, he reached out and motioned with his arm as if he were slamming a car door. He even swept home plate with style, finishing with a cross-stroke that left him standing on one foot. He was known to run toward first base with the runner, then do a stiff-legged Chaplin walk on returning to home plate, or race with the runner around the base path. He pirouetted out of the way of hit balls. He took to the outfield to determine if a ball had been cleanly caught or trapped. Others were critical because they felt that he was promoted to the majors only because of pressures from civil rights groups and the federal government. The criticisms were unwarranted: Ashford had spent fifteen years honing his skills in the minor leagues, and umpire schools then were for whites only. Even though his skills had deteriorated slightly by the time he reached the majors, he proved himself highly competent in addition to being popular.

After retiring in 1970, Ashford umpired Pacific-10 Conference college games, served as commissioner and umpire in chief of the pro-amateur American International League, and worked until his death as the West Coast public relations representative for Baseball Commissioner Bowie Kuhn.

Ashford married Margaret Cloud Kirby, who worked for American Airlines. They had three children before her death. He was living with his second wife, Virginia, when he died of a heart attack in Los Angeles. Ashford was elected posthumously to Chapman College Hall of Fame on Feb. 26, 1981.

[A clippings file is in the National Baseball Hall of Fame Library, Cooperstown, N.Y., and Chapman College Hall of Fame, Anaheim, Calif.; Ashford's firsthand account of his umpiring start is in Art Rust, Jr., *"Get That Nigger Off the Field!"* (1976). See also "Delayed Calls," *Newsweek*, Apr. 25, 1966; "Ashford Arrives," *Ebony*, June 1966; "Emmett Ashford: Ultra Ump," *Look*, Oct. 4, 1966; and Arthur R. Ashe, Jr., *A Hard Road to Glory* (1988). An obituary is in the *New York Times*, Mar. 4, 1980.]

SAMUEL VON WINBUSH

AUCHINCLOSS, HUGH DUDLEY, JR. (Aug. 15, 1897–Nov. 20, 1976), stockbroker and lawyer, was born at Hammersmith Farm, Newport, R.I., the son of Hugh Dudley Auchincloss, a merchant and financier, and Emma Brewster Jennings. The first Auchinclosses arrived in the United States in 1803 and established a business in the import and distribution of yarn. They later branched out into dry-goods, merchandising and investments in nitrates, railroads, banking, and real estate. The family name is intertwined through marital and business alliances with such famed American families as the Rockefellers, Tiffanys, and Vanderbilts. Among his relatives were his cousin, Louis S. Auchincloss, the novelist and New York lawyer, and James C. Auchincloss, the longtime representative of New Jersey's Third Congressional District in the United States House of Representatives. Much of his considerable inherited wealth came from his mother, who was the daughter of Oliver B. Jennings, one of the founders of the Standard Oil Company.

After graduating from the Groton School in Massachusetts, Auchincloss entered Yale, from which he received his bachelor's degree in 1920, having interrupted his studies briefly to serve in the navy during World War I. After the war he studied at Kings College, Cambridge; traveled to Russia in 1922 to assist university students in connection with the Student Friendship Fund; and earned his law degree from Columbia University in 1924.

He practiced as a lawyer in New York from 1924 to 1926, when he moved to Washington to serve as a special agent in aeronautics at the Commerce Department. In 1927, Auchincloss was appointed an aviation specialist in the Western European Division of the State Department. In 1931, he requested permission to maintain his position in the State Department while establishing a stock-brokerage firm with his friends Chauncey Parker and Albert G. Redpath. When the request was denied, he resigned his government post to join the newly formed Auchincloss, Parker, and Redpath. Later that year he bought a seat on the New York Stock Exchange. The company came to have fifteen offices in East Coast cities.

Auchincloss married Maya (Maria) de Chrapovitsky, the daughter of a Russian naval officer, on June 4, 1925. They had one child and were divorced in 1932. His second marriage, on Oct. 8, 1935, was to Nina Gore Vidal, daughter of Senator Thomas P. Gore from Oklahoma, former wife of Eugene L. Vidal, and mother of the writer Gore Vidal. Following an extended legal battle, Auchincloss and Nina were divorced in September 1941. That same year he began dating Janet Lee Bouvier, a divorcée with two daughters, Jacqueline and Lee. They were married in June 1942, on the morning of the day he left for Kingston, Jamaica, to serve as a lieutenant in the wartime planning unit of the Office of Naval Intelligence. His overseas service was cut short by his mother's death in September 1942, and he returned to Washington, where he held a desk job in the War Department. He and Janet had two children.

Auchincloss attended exclusive social gatherings and was known to be socially refined, dependable, intensely private, and somewhat staid. He also had a proclivity for long, repetitive stories and absentmindedness. "Uncle Hughdie," as he was known to his stepdaughters, would recite the Auchincloss motto before meals, beginning "obedience to the Unenforceable" and continuing for what seemed like an eternity.

Auchincloss gave Jacqueline Bouvier the start on her journalism career in Washington by placing a call to his friend Arthur Krock at the *New York Times*, who in turn called Frank Waldrop of the *Washington Times-Herald*, which hired her. On Sept. 12, 1953, standing in for the absent Jack Bouvier, he escorted Jacqueline down the aisle at her wedding to Senator John F. Kennedy. The marriage was to cause Auchincloss some trouble in 1960. Usually a substantial Republican campaign contributor, that year he contributed $500 to Kennedy's presidential campaign. As he told Richard Nixon's campaign manager, "You see, I happen to be the step-father-in-law of one of the candidates for President, and his name isn't Nixon. I want to live in harmony with Mrs. Auchincloss and all the other members of the family."

Auchincloss's ancestral homes, Merrywood in McLean, Va., and Hammersmith Farm in Newport, R.I., played an important part in his life. Merrywood, which Gore Vidal used as the setting for his novel *Washington, D.C.* (1967), was described as a secure place, removed from the tensions of the twentieth century. In the early 1960's, Auchincloss's carefully guarded privacy was encroached upon when he made a contract to sell the forty-six-acre Merrywood estate. Developers intended to erect a tall apartment building that would have intruded on the skyline on the Virginia side of the Potomac River. Although the sale eventually went through, local opposition to the project was strong and the construction of the buildings was blocked in 1963 by President Kennedy, who instructed the Interior Department to intervene.

Late in life severe financial difficulties, caused by the stock market's decline and poor real estate investments, struck Hugh Auchincloss, who had always been known as the one Auchincloss who really did have money. Auchincloss intervened in 1970 with his own personal money in an attempt to save his failing brokerage firm. When this maneuver failed, the firm merged with the brokerage house of Thomson and McKinnon, the new firm being known as Thomson and MacKinnon Auchincloss Kohlmeyer. Later that year his finances deteriorated further, and he realized that he would be forced to sell Hammersmith Farm. He retained only a servant's house for the use of his family. Auchincloss died in Washington, D.C.

Auchincloss had an interest in many philanthropic organizations and was director of both the Boys Club of Newport County, R.I., and the Boys Club of America. He was on the board of the Redwood Library in Newport.

[See Joanna Russell Auchincloss and Caroline Auchincloss Fowler, *John and Elizabeth (Buck) Auchincloss: Their Descendants and Their Ancestry* (1957); Benjamin Bradlee, *Conversations with Kennedy* (1975); Peter Collier and David Horowitz, *The Kennedys* (1984); and C. David Heymann, *A Woman Named Jackie* (1989). An obituary is in the *New York Times*, Nov. 22, 1976.]

CAROL R. BERKIN

B

BAILEY, BILL (1912–Dec. 12, 1978), tap dancer, was born in Newport News, Va., one of four children of Ella Mae and Joseph James Bailey, a cement worker by day and a minister by night. The family moved to Washington, D.C., in 1922, where Willie (as he was called at home) attended Garnett-Patterson Public School. One of Bailey's three sisters, singer-entertainer Pearl Bailey, suggested in her memoirs that the Bailey children were drawn to music by their father's highly active and highly musical church in Washington, the House of Prayer. "The House of Prayer is a holy and sanctified church; they really shout. As in the Bible, they declare themselves speaking in tongues," she wrote in 1968. Bill Bailey began his theatrical career dancing for pennies on street corners in Washington.

In the late 1920's, Bailey's parents separated and his mother moved to Philadelphia, leaving the children with her husband. According to family legend, Bill followed her there on his bicycle. Although he did not have her address, he found his mother more or less by accident. He lived with her as he tried to find a place in show business, and he brought his sisters to Philadelphia as well. After a series of peripheral jobs, including one selling candy at the Pearl Theater, Bailey started getting work as a dancer in Philadelphia and on tour.

In the mid-1930's, Bailey established himself in the New York City entertainment world and married dancer Jessie Scott. The date of the dissolution of this marriage is uncertain, as are the dates of his subsequent marriages, of which there were at least two. He had a total of eleven children.

Bailey formed an important professional partnership in the 1930's, becoming a protégé of famed tap dancer Bill ("Bojangles") Robinson, whom he replaced in 1937 at the Cotton Club. Like Robinson, Bailey performed as a "tapologuist," that is, he accompanied his tap-dance routine with patter directed at the audience.

During the 1930's and early 1940's, Bailey performed in vaudeville, nightclubs, and even a few motion pictures. At one time or another his tap percussion accompanied most of the major African-American bands of the day, including those of Count Basie and Duke Ellington. His most important theatrical role was a supporting part in the pioneering all-black Broadway musical *Cabin in the Sky* in 1940; he also appeared in the 1943 motion picture of the same name.

Bailey worked steadily and his performances were generally well received critically, although he never moved beyond comparisons to Robinson to establish a strong independent image in the press. He was widely known for his gift of gab and sense of humor. Despite his show-business success, he suffered from a number of personal problems, many of them drug related. In 1946 he attempted to put his drug addiction behind him by shifting careers and following his father into the ministry. He wrote in the September 1951 issue of *Negro Digest*: "I was a sinner and was therefore well qualified to help others. I had known the ravages of dissipation, drink and the devil. For years I had squandered my life on petty things and foolish pleasures. I displeased God and he let me know it." Bailey spent a year engaged in itinerant preaching in southern states, then returned to his former theatrical home base in New York City.

In 1950, after preaching for several years on New York's streets, he opened a small church above a pool hall on West 126th Street. He was particularly interested in reaching fellow entertainers with his message of salvation and drew performers from the nearby Apollo Theater to his congregation. Bailey noted, "My background had equipped me with the understanding and idiom of show people. I felt I had a special mission to help them spiritually." Stagehands from the Apollo helped him build his altar, and the theater's owner, Frank Schiffman, donated seats for the church.

Despite the goodwill and financial support of many entertainers, including his sister Pearl, Bailey was unable to make a living as a minister. He returned to dancing from time to time beginning in 1951. He stated in print that he was still doing God's work—"I've taken wings off my back and put 'em on my feet"—noting that it seemed ordained from on high that he once more step into the shoes of Bill Robinson, who had died in 1949.

Throughout the 1950's and early 1960's, Bailey obtained sporadic work on the stage. He performed with Duke Ellington, Cab Calloway, Miles Davis, and Pearl Bailey. He also kept his name in the public eye through semi-regular appearances on Ed Sullivan's television variety show. In 1959 he was picked up by the police for illegal possession of narcotics, and *Variety* noted that the arrest was his sixth since 1946. His sister Pearl, who enjoyed working with him throughout most of his career, noted that around this time he began to resent her success. In 1968 she described his bitterness: "Bill had many, many good moments with the show, but he began to do some things to destroy himself in the business that he dearly loved. From the outside came the tidbits and the needling of other people, which always set the harm within. Sometimes he would scream, 'You stole things from me, that's where you got it.' "

Bailey's health deteriorated in the late 1960's, and a series of operations on his legs ended his dancing career. He died in Philadelphia. After his death, his contribution to show business was honored in the 1989 film *Tap*, in which he was credited with inventing the dance step known as the moonwalk.

[The Billy Rose Theatre Collection of the New York Public Library for the Peforming Arts maintains a clipping file on Bailey. See Bill Bailey, "Why I'm Dancing Again," *Negro Digest*, Sept. 1951. He was profiled in "Tap Dancer Turned Preacher," *Ebony*, Aug. 1950. Other sources on his life are brief references in the writings of his sister Pearl Bailey, particularly in *The Raw Pearl* (1968), *Talking to Myself* (1971), and *Between You and Me* (1989). Obituaries are in the *New York Times*, Dec. 18, 1978; and *Jet*, Jan. 4, 1979.]

TINKY ("DAKOTA") WEISBLAT

BALDWIN, FAITH (Oct. 1, 1893–Mar. 19, 1978), author, was born in New Rochelle, N.Y., the daughter of Stephen Charles Baldwin, a well-known trial lawyer, and Edith Hervey Finch. When she was three, the family moved to Manhattan, in the heart of New York City, and later to a brownstone mansion across the East River in Brooklyn Heights.

Baldwin was reared in a mixture of what she later called "wild extravagance" and "protectionism." By age three she was able to read. She attended the Brooklyn Heights Academy and finishing schools in Brooklyn and Briarcliff Manor, N.Y. Her education, along with gatherings of family and social equals at teatime, solo trips to visit relatives in Kansas City and California, and private luncheons with actresses to whom she had written fan letters, helped to create a personal sophistication that was later reflected in her stories.

Between 1914 and 1916, as World War I raged in Europe, Baldwin lived in Germany with a close friend of her mother's. "Life didn't change for us because of the war," she said. "I was sent to cooking school and learned German, but we continued to go to the opera." Back home, she worked for the War Camp Community Service.

On Nov. 6, 1920, she married Hugh Hamlin Cuthrell, an American navy pilot she had met a year earlier; they had four children. He later became president and chairman of the board of the Brooklyn Union Gas Company. In her last years, she lived and wrote outside Norwalk, Conn., in "Fable Farm," a fourteen-room house built in 1800.

Baldwin's first book, *Mavis of Green Hill* (1921), and several others set in the fictional town of Divine Corners were written for teenagers. From 1925 on, almost all of her novels were for women. In 1927 she sold her first serial to *Good Housekeeping*. Later she sold serialization rights to her books for as much as $55,000. She agreed with critics who complained that her novels of romance among the wealthy created fantasies in the minds of lower- and middle-class women, saying that the "fantasy element" in her books allowed readers to identify with her characters. "The girl on the subway reads about the rich heroes and hopes she'll meet a man with $500,000. But she also reads that the two young millionaires come together not through money but through love and personal honesty. So the reader understands that even if she can't marry a millionaire, she may have other rewards if she is true to herself."

In the 1930's, an era of frothy movies and radio soap operas, Baldwin reached the height of her success. In 1936, in the depths of the Great Depression, she earned more than $300,000. Many of the three dozen novels and a handful of novelettes she wrote in that decade were first serialized in major national magazines, including *Collier's*, *Good Housekeeping*, *Woman's Home Companion*, *Cosmopolitan*, and *American*, and then published in book form. She also published two volumes of short stories. Two dozen of her books went into reprint editions. Three volumes were republished in England, and some were translated into German, French, or Spanish editions. Some of her novels were republished in omnibus editions, each volume containing several titles.

Twice she collaborated with another prolific writer, Achmed Abdullah, on novels about the New York theater world. The first, *Broadway Interlude* (1929), was adapted (by the coauthors) as a play with the same title; the reviewers were not impressed. *Girl-on-the-Make* (1932) was their second book.

Several of her novels focused on love triangles involving businessmen, their wives, and attractive secretaries. (A critic of these books said that Baldwin looked at the globe and found it triangular.) Three of these and five other Baldwin novels were filmed with such major actors as Henry Fonda, Clark Gable, and Jean Harlow, including *Wife Versus Secretary* (1936) and *Comet over Broadway* (1938). In spite of all the Hollywood talent involved, one reviewer commented that the former film was, like many others, "inspired by Faith, produced in hope, and not always received with charity." William K. Everson of the New School for Social Research said Baldwin's were the kind of stories "especially prevalent in the Thirties, a natural for housewives and spinsters. They'd all avidly consume the book, argue over the casting choices, see the films, and argue some more."

Baldwin said, "People had to have some escape hatch, some way to get out of themselves, especially during the Depression." The *New York Times* said that she told "lonely working people" that they shared "certain problems and preoccupations about love and friendship . . . with everybody. . . . Women found in her stories solace as well as entertainment." *Time* said she "was an unabashed old pro who could write a chapter a day [combining] the surefire elements of romantic love and great wealth." But *Time* also noted that her stories "always stopped at the bedroom door."

Despite Baldwin's protestations that during World War II, "nothing was more important than the headlines," escapist fare dominated the some two dozen books and two volumes of verse she published in the 1940's and the 1950's. In all, she wrote one hundred volumes of fiction and verse, and numerous short stories, poems, and articles, leading the *New York Times* to call her the "doyenne of American light-fiction writers" and "one of the most successful writers of light fiction on the American scene." Baldwin also was at times a columnist for several New York newspapers and, in the mid-1960's, for *Woman's Day*.

Despite declining health in the months before she died at eighty-four in her Norwalk, Conn., home, she was still writing a book.

[An obituary is in the *New York Times*, Mar. 19, 1978.]

CLARENCE A. ANDREWS

BAROODY, WILLIAM JOSEPH (Jan. 29, 1916–July 28, 1980), public-policy analyst and research institute executive, was born in Manchester, N.H., the son of Joseph Assad Baroody, an immigrant Lebanese stonecutter, and Helen Hasney. After attending local Catholic schools, Baroody entered St. Anselm's College in Manchester. On Oct. 15, 1935, he married Nabeeha Marion Ashooh; they had seven children. Working in grocery stores to support his family, Baroody received a B.A. from St. Anselm's in 1936 and did graduate work at the University of New Hampshire in the 1937–1938 academic year and at American University in 1938.

From 1937 to 1940, Baroody was an assistant statistician at the New Hampshire Unemployment Compensation Agency; he was supervisor of the fiscal research and legislative planning sections of the agency from 1941 to 1944. He also served as research associate of the New Hampshire Legislative Commission on Disability Benefits from 1940 to 1944 and as director of the statistics division, New Hampshire War Finance Committee, in 1943 and 1944.

Baroody enlisted in the Naval Reserve and served as a lieutenant on the escort carrier *Mission Bay* in 1944 and 1945. At the Veterans Administration in Washington, D.C., he was chief of the research and statistics division, readjustment allowance service, from 1946 to 1949. He served next in the United States Chamber of Commerce, from 1950 to 1953, as executive secretary of the committee on economic security and associate editor of *American Economic Security*.

In 1954, Baroody became executive vice-president of the American Enterprise Association. This small public policy research organization had been founded by Lewis Herold Brown in 1943, but when Baroody joined, it was only marginally engaged in debating the issues confronting American society. As a first-generation American, Baroody saw the United States as a land of opportunity; throughout his life he maintained that "competition of ideas is fundamental to a free society." He felt the ideas of the New Deal, such as the growth of governmental regulation and bureaucracy and the centralization of power in Washington, deserved to be challenged and enlisted leading scholars who agreed, including Milton Friedman, Roscoe Pound, Gottfried Haberler, Paul W. McCracken, and Glenn Campbell, who was research director of the organization (1954–1960) before going to the Hoover Institution.

In 1962, Baroody became president of the association and changed its name to the American Enterprise Institute for Public Policy Research (AEI). Patient and low-keyed, he had a talent for mixing people and ideas. As William F. Buckley, Jr., wrote, "he combined a gentleness of manner with a resolution of purpose and a conciliator's good nature." As head of AEI, Baroody helped to bring conservative ideas into the national public policy debate and helped achieve a new level of acceptance for views that had not previously been taken seriously by government and the media. A devout member of the Melkite Greek Catholic Church, Baroody held family values and religion to be particularly important issues and made them the focus of studies at his institute. He believed that the debate on the legitimacy of the free enterprise system was about more than economics, and as a result, AEI paid more attention to religious thought and political theory than did other research centers concerned with preserving a free market economy.

Even those who did not share his viewpoint were often impressed by the high quality of research done at AEI, which grew in size and influence under Baroody's leadership, with a budget of $8 million and some 125 staff members. Barry Goldwater, Richard M. Nixon, and Gerald R. Ford sought Baroody's advice. In 1977 former president Gerald R. Ford became a distinguished fellow at AEI and participated in its seminars and lectures at many universities. Melvin Laird, Bryce Harlow, Arthur Burns, Herbert Stein, Jeane Kirkpatrick, and Ben Wattenberg were among those associated with Baroody's institute. Of diverse political affiliations, most AEI scholars strongly supported free markets and firmly opposed Communism. They also favored market or voluntary approaches to policy issues instead of the use of government power. Journalists sometimes called AEI a conservative counterpart of the liberal Brookings Institution. The functions of the two think tanks were similar (and they both provided places for prominent members of previous presidential administrations), but Baroody's institute had a different and much more difficult role, since it promoted ideas and viewpoints that were unfashionable with most academics before 1980. A comment by Robert H. Bork indicates a special function that AEI performed: "Persons who often, particularly in those years, felt intellectually isolated, even beleaguered, on their own campuses were drawn into a larger intellectual community."

Baroody was a founder of Georgetown University's Center for Strategic and International Studies, a member of the board of overseers at the Hoover Institution from 1960 to 1980, and chairman of the board of the Woodrow Wilson International Center for Scholars from 1972 to 1979. In 1978, Baroody was succeeded as president of AEI by his son William J. Baroody, Jr., and became chairman of AEI's development committee, a post he retained until his death.

A decade before the Berlin Wall came down in 1989, the Cold War appeared far from over and its outcome uncertain. Baroody believed that shifts in the political balance of power should be irrelevant in determining one's conduct. Speaking about his father in 1980, William J. Baroody, Jr., said, "What he taught us to do was to compete . . . not just because we have to win, because he knew we might not."

While many scholars and journalists were

writing in the 1970's about American decline, Baroody held the opposite view. Noting the importance of AEI in 1980, liberal historian James MacGregor Burns observed that victory in the presidential election had gone to conservatives because of their successful effort "to build their intellectual case and to use invigorated and broadened conservative ideas as vehicles to political power." Former president Gerald R. Ford said, in November 1980, "If the way is well prepared to offer a new vision for this country, no one in the postwar history of the United States deserves more credit than does Bill Baroody." Baroody's institute helped create an intellectual climate for political changes that would take place during the 1980's in the United States and in other parts of the world, especially Eastern Europe. AEI scholars who would serve in the Reagan administration included Murray Weidenbaum (chairman of the Council of Economic Advisers), Jeane Kirkpatrick (ambassador to the United Nations), James Miller (chairman of the Federal Trade Commission), and David Gergen (director of communications). A few months after Baroody's death from a heart attack in Alexandria, Va., where he had made his home, President-elect Ronald Reagan said in a speech at AEI, "One of Bill Baroody's greatest accomplishments was in building an institution that said, 'Here is a place where you can develop your ideas,' that said to others, 'Here is a place you can turn to for advice,' that said to all of us who were concerned about our country's future, 'You are not alone.' "

[Baroody's papers are at the Library of Congress. For his role in the conservative political and intellectual movement, see Paul W. McCracken, Robert H. Bork, Irving Kristol, and Michael Novak, with additional remarks by Ronald W. Reagan and Gerald R. Ford, *William J. Baroody, Sr.: The Francis Boyer Lectures on Public Policy* (1981). For a liberal view of Baroody's AEI, see James MacGregor Burns, *The Crosswinds of Freedom* (1989). *William J. Baroody, January 29, 1916–July 28, 1980* (1980), published by AEI, contains a biographical sketch. See also Myra MacPherson, "The Baroody Connection," *Washington Post Potomac*, Aug. 17, 1975; and Nick Thimmesch, "Bill Baroody Deserved More Years," *Washington Post*, Aug. 9, 1980. Obituaries are in the *Washington Post*, July 30, 1980; the *New York Times*, July 30, 1980; the *Washington Star*, editorial tribute, July 31, 1980; and *National Review*, Aug. 22, 1980.]

RALPH KIRSHNER

BARRIE, WENDY (Apr. 18, 1912–Feb. 2, 1978), actress, was born Margaret Wendy Jenkins in Hong Kong, the daughter of F. C. Jenkins, one of the most important barristers in Asia, and Nell MacDonagh, who was descended from the Irish king Brian Boru; her uncle, Sir James Barrie, later ran Scotland Yard. She took her professional name from her godfather, Sir James Matthew Barrie, who wrote *Peter Pan*.

Barrie spent her early years in Hong Kong, where her father had his law practice. Her education was uneven, caused as much by her high spirits as her parents' keen social aspirations. She first attended the Peak School in Hong Kong and, when she was old enough to travel unattended, the Holy Child and Assumption convent in London. She completed her education at a fashionable finishing school in Lausanne, Switzerland. Along the way, Barrie traveled widely across the Continent; by the time she was seventeen, she had traveled around the world at least seven times.

After a gala debut in society sponsored by Winston Churchill, Barrie dabbled in a number of careers: apprenticing in a beauty parlor, working as a secretary, selling clothing in a London department store. Barrie's entry into show business had the ring of a fairy tale: in 1932, when she was nineteen years old, she was "discovered" by the producer Alexander Korda as she was having lunch at London's Savoy Grill. Her fun-loving mother was thrilled, but her father was appalled. However, her father was thousands of miles away, so at Korda's request Barrie took a screen test, leading to a five-year contract with his studio.

Her initial roles in "quota quickies" (films produced to satisfy the law that a certain percentage of films released in Britain be British-made) were as forgettable as the films themselves. Her one memorable role among her seventeen British films was *The Private Life of Henry VIII* (1933). In the film, which won its star, Charles Laughton, an Oscar, Barrie played Henry's third wife, Jane Seymour.

Building on her success at home, Barrie decided to try her luck in Hollywood. Ten days after her arrival, she landed her first American movie role in *It's a Small World* (1935), starring Spencer Tracy. "A looker, but not much of an actress," *Variety* reported. "A good-looking ingenue with plenty of class," the reviewer added. The evaluation would remain with her for much of her cinema career. In part, this was due to the roles she was given. "I always have to be a lady, or a professor's daughter, or something like that," she complained in a rare moment. "I'd like to get hold of a part I could be mean in."

Nonetheless, she did not devote much of her time to her career. Her name was always in the society gossip columns, usually for dating glamorous heirs Howard Hughes and Woolworth Donahue (to whom she was engaged), entertainers Rudy Vallee and Milton Berle, and gangster Benjamin ("Bugsy") Siegel. She devoted much of her time to nightclub hopping, playing golf and tennis, and learning to pilot an airplane. Nonetheless, her agent Herbert ("Zeppo") Marx of Marx Brothers fame signed her to a long-term contract with Paramount. At five feet, five inches tall and 110 pounds, the socialite-actress with the reddish gold hair and blue-green eyes was pleasant to work with and a surefire box office draw because of her offscreen antics.

The high point of Barrie's film career was *Dead End* (1937), starring Joel McCrea and Sylvia Sidney, in which Barrie played a mistress living in an expensive apartment in Manhattan. Her tour de force was a scene in which she recoiled in horror during a visit to a slum apartment. She was also in *The Hound of the Baskervilles* (1939), starring Basil Rathbone.

On Jan. 9, 1941, Barrie became an American citizen. About the same time, her film career started to wind down. In 1942 she made her Broadway debut in *The Morning Star*, which ran for only six weeks. Barrie then returned briefly to film work. On June 5, 1945, Barrie married New York textile manufacturer David L. Meyers. They were divorced on Apr. 24, 1950. It was through her husband, however, that Barrie's television career was launched.

As the wife of a wealthy businessman, Barrie was called on to entertain clients at golf outings. Her golfing prowess attracted golf pro Johnny Farrell, who invited Barrie to appear on his televised sports show. Her relaxed, cheerful personality was an instant hit on the small screen and led to a hostess job on a children's program, "Okey Dokey Ranch." She enjoyed working with children, she said, because they ensured that she would not have to worry about action. "At least they'd spit in your face or do something," she observed.

In television, Barrie made her mark. She turned down a starring role in "Topper" and on Sept. 12, 1949, began her own talk show on ABC. The program ran through the mid-1950's. Her method of interviewing was unique. As one critic commented, "Garnished with bubbling impertinence and unbelievable naivete, she manages to elicit a good deal of enlightening information." When the show went off the air, irate viewers demanded the return of "their Wendy." In 1954, Barrie became the host of a talk show on Channel 5 in New York City and did a brief stint as the cohost of NBC's "$64,000 Question."

Thereafter, Barrie turned to charity work, chairing the women's division of the Committee for Deborah Hospital in 1960. She died in Englewood, N.J.

[See James Robert Parish, *The RKO Gals* (1974). See also a brief article in the *New York Times*, Jan. 10, 1942. An obituary is in the *New York Times*, Feb. 4, 1978.]

LAURIE ROZAKIS

BARTH, ALAN (Oct. 21, 1906–Nov. 20, 1979), journalist and author, was born in New York City, the son of Jacob Lauchheimer, who owned a small department store, and Flora Barth. Named Alan Barth Lauchheimer at birth, he legally changed his name to Alan Barth as an adult. He was educated at Phillips Academy in Andover, Mass. After graduating in 1924, he traveled around the world and then entered Yale University, from which he graduated in 1929 with a Ph.B. Barth then worked as both a free-lance writer and a salesman until he became a reporter and editorial writer for the *Beaumont* (Tex.) *Enterprise and Journal* in 1936 and 1937. From 1938 to 1941 he was the Washington, D.C., correspondent of the McClure Newspaper Syndicate. On July 1, 1939, Barth married Adrienne Mayer; they had two children. He served as a speechwriter for Secretary of the Treasury Henry Morgenthau, and on the staff of the Office of War Information, from 1941 to 1943, when he became an editorial writer for the *Washington Post*.

Although already well known for his editorials in the *Washington Post*, Barth's reputation was secured by the first of his five books, *The Loyalty of Free Men* (1951). In it, Barth attacked what he called the "cult of loyalty," then at its most intense. In separate chapters he exposed the House Committee on Un-American Activities (HUAC), the government's loyalty program, and the Federal Bureau of Investigation, as well as special violations of human rights involving government-sponsored research and academic freedom.

Although some who defended the Bill of Rights did so for partisan reasons, Barth was not in any way sympathetic to Communism or to the Communist party of the United States. He argued, rather, that individual freedom "is the supreme end which the government of the United States was instituted to secure." However, it is also "a source of strength if it is used wisely. It cannot provide a guarantee against ruinous mistakes; but it can provide a means of correcting mistakes, a means denied to those who live in a society where dissent is silenced."

This book was widely praised for the clarity and strength of its reasoning, which did not keep it from being unfairly attacked. Conservative anti-Communists detested it. So also did Irving Kristol, then managing editor of *Commentary*, a monthly journal of opinion on political and cultural matters of special interest to Jews. Kristol had not yet become a conservative, but he believed that American Communism was dangerous. Barth aroused his anger by maintaining that it did not threaten national security, and Kristol attributed Communist sympathies to Barth that he did not have. Time was on Barth's side, and the facts as well.

Unlike academic critics of the "red scare," Barth lacked the protection of tenure. His outspoken editorials exposed the *Washington Post* to many attacks and once nearly cost him his job. To Philip L. Graham, his publisher, a 1950 editorial by Barth on the right of Communist party chairman Earl Browder not to give names to a congressional committee was the last straw. Only the intervention of Supreme Court associate justice Felix Frankfurter saved Barth from being fired and the *Post* from making what would have proved to be a most embarrassing mistake. Fortunately, Barth had no compromising associations in his past and could not be effectively smeared by red-baiters. His only loss occurred after the Republicans came to power, when *The Loyalty of Free Men* was removed from government-sponsored libraries overseas.

Barth elaborated on the threat to freedom in *Government by Investigation* (1955), a long and detailed inquiry into the use of Congress's investigative power to achieve political ends. He discussed what he called "legislative trials," hearings in which committees investigated persons punitively, to ruin their good names and otherwise punish them for opinions and activities that were not illegal. This prerogative of Congress was being so abused at the time that Barth feared that the balance of power between government's branches had become adversely affected. He warned against the danger of a "legislative tyranny" that would subvert the Constitution itself.

With the passing of the McCarthy era, Barth turned his attention to the abuse of individual rights in criminal cases. *The Price of Liberty* (1961) argued that American society as a whole had much at stake in protecting accused persons against summary seizures, unwarranted searches, forced confessions, denial of counsel, and other violations of constitutionally protected rights. Although Barth was not a lawyer, his explication of cases and clarity of analysis was admired by reviewers, including Abe Fortas, later an associate justice of the Supreme Court. Barth anticipated a direction the Supreme Court would soon take in an important series of decisions expanding the rights of criminal defendants. He would subsequently write other books as well as numerous magazine articles.

Barth, who once saw a man shot to death on the streets of Washington, was an ardent supporter of gun control. After the assassination of President John F. Kennedy, he declared war on the National Rifle Association, writing more than one thousand editorials in favor of gun control, seventy-seven of them on consecutive days. This was a losing cause, unlike school desegregation and home rule for the District of Columbia, both of which he supported long before they became law. He was instrumental in changing the editorial position of the *Washington Post* on racial issues. It was in his words that the paper came out in 1945 against a threatened strike by white transit workers to prevent blacks from being hired. "To bar men from serving in these jobs because of their race or color," he wrote, "is at once to hamper the war program and to subvert the principles for which it is being waged."

During his distinguished career as journalist, editorial writer, and explicator of constitutional law to laymen, Barth received many honors: the Sigma Delta Chi Award for distinguished service to American journalism in 1947, the Sidney Hillman Award of the American Newspaper Guild for distinguished editorial writing in 1948, the Oliver Wendell Holmes Bill of Rights Award in 1964, and the Florence Lasker Civil Liberties Award in 1967, among others. He was also a Nieman Fellow of Harvard University (1948–1949) and a research professor at the University of California on a Ford Foundation grant (1958–1959). When he retired from the *Washington Post* in 1973, the columnist Roger Wilkins said Barth was considered "the liberal conscience of Washington by those who knew his work." He died in Washington, D.C.

[Obituaries are in the *New York Times*, Nov. 21, 1979; the *Washington Post*, Nov. 21, 1979; and *Newsweek*, Dec. 3, 1979.]

WILLIAM L. O'NEILL

BARTLETT, DEWEY FOLLETT (Mar. 28, 1919–Mar. 1, 1979), politician, businessman, and rancher, was born in Marietta, Ohio, the son of David A. Bartlett, a banker, and Jessie B. Follett. He was educated in Marietta public schools and graduated from the Lawrenceville (N.J.) School in 1938. Bartlett's father financed oil properties in Oklahoma, which he consolidated into the Keener Oil and Gas Company. Bartlett worked summers on family oil leases while pursuing a B.S. degree in geological engineering at Princeton University, where he was president of both his junior and senior classes, chairman of the honor committee and undergraduate council, and an all-league basketball selection. He graduated in 1942.

Bartlett served as a U.S. Marine Corps bomber pilot in the Pacific Theater during World War II. On Apr. 2, 1945, he married Ann Chilton Smith; they had three children.

After leaving military service as a captain, Bartlett moved to Tulsa, Okla., and entered the family petroleum business with his brother, involved primarily in secondary oil recovery through water flooding methods. Enjoying considerable success, they established the Keener Oil and Gas Company as a leading independent Oklahoma oil producer. In the 1950's, Bartlett founded the Dewey Supply Company, an oil field equipment firm, and served as its president from 1953 to 1956. Starting in 1958, he acquired extensive ranch lands in Wagoner, Tulsa, and Delaware Counties, Okla.

In 1952, Bartlett served as a Tulsa precinct Republican chairman in the presidential campaign of Dwight D. Eisenhower. In 1962, he ran for the state senate representing Tulsa County and was elected with the state's first Republican governor, Henry Bellmon. Bartlett was reelected to the state senate in 1964. He ran for governor in 1966, promising to bring industry to Oklahoma, to veto any tax increases, and to operate state government with existing revenues. Benefiting from an efficient Republican political organization and divisions among state Democrats, Bartlett won the Republican primary and runoff elections, then defeated Democrat Preston J. Moore in the general election.

As governor, Bartlett traveled extensively throughout the country in an effort to attract business and industry to Oklahoma. At the end of his term in 1971, he claimed that more than thirty-five thousand new jobs had been created and that $692 million in new industrial investment had been generated. He utilized the expertise of business executives to streamline the operation of state agencies and to cut expenditures. With corporate financial assistance, he created a private organization to provide loans and other assistance for vocational and technical training for minority groups, while also encouraging minority management and ownership of businesses. In 1967, in conjunction with the sixtieth anniversary of Oklahoma statehood, he launched a flamboyant public relations campaign designed to upgrade the state's image and that of the term "Okie," complete with lapel pins, honorary state-resident certificates, and the phrases "Oklahoma, Key to Industrial Expansion" and "Oklahoma, Key to Intelligence and Enterprise."

An advocate of law and order, Bartlett's reelection bid in 1970 was adversely affected by allegations surrounding the Office of Inter Agency Cooperation, a secret, quasi-official state agency Bartlett had created in June 1968, ostensibly to prevent civil disorder and monitor dissent; the existence of the agency only came to light through the investigative efforts of a Tulsa journalist in the summer of 1970. Bartlett was assailed by the American Civil Liberties Union and the state civil liberties chapter for creating an organization perceived as a threat to free speech and an invasion of privacy. Critics charged that the agency compiled dossiers and blacklisted individuals, all of which he denied. Bartlett further alienated many educators by his reluctance to support pay raises for public school teachers, his veto of a statewide kindergarten system, and his criticism of the president of the University of Oklahoma. He was defeated by Democrat David Hall by a margin of only 2,181 votes, the closest race in the state's history.

After leaving office, Bartlett returned to his oil and ranching interests. In March 1972 he announced for the Republican nomination to the United States Senate. Easily winning the primary, he entered the general election as an underdog to Democratic congressman Ed Edmondson, but riding the coattails of President Richard Nixon's landslide reelection triumph, Bartlett defeated Edmondson by a thirty thousand-vote margin.

In the Senate, Bartlett was a staunchly ideological conservative, a partisan supporter of Republican policies, a vocal defender of oil interests, and, from his position on the Armed Services Committee, an outspoken critic of NATO conventional forces, which he deemed insufficient and ill-prepared to confront potential Soviet military encroachments in Europe. Bartlett traveled widely, visiting South Vietnam and Cambodia for a week early in 1975 with Congressman Pete McCloskey at President Gerald Ford's behest. In July he made a brief trip to Somalia, investigating the plight of drought-stricken refugees and also examining the facilities in the northern port city of Berbera, where he warned about the creation of a Soviet missile storage and refueling operation. On his return to the United States, he recommended a $15 million appropriation for a military base on Diego Garcia Island in the Indian Ocean to counter the Soviet presence in the region. He made a one-day visit to Angola in February 1976 and led the opposition to a Democratic-sponsored bill that cut aid to the pro-Western rebels in the Angolan civil war. After a tour of NATO defenses with Democratic senator Sam Nunn in 1976, he issued a joint report to the Senate Armed Services Committee urging the strengthening of conventional forces and ammunition stocks, the improvement of air defenses, and the positioning of ground forces closer to Warsaw Pact borders.

Bartlett opposed the Panama Canal Treaty in 1977 and in 1978 proposed a resolution cutting off all diplomatic relations with Cuba. He also opposed taxpayer funding of legal aid lawyers involved in busing cases, voted against raising the minimum wage, and opposed abortion except to save the life of the mother.

In January 1977, Bartlett was diagnosed with lung cancer and underwent surgery. He returned to the Senate in February and in June underwent a second cancer operation. In failing health, Bartlett declined to run for reelection in 1978. After his term ended, he returned to his home in Tulsa, where he died.

[Bartlett's administrative files as governor of Oklahoma are located at the Oklahoma Department of Libraries in Oklahoma City. See also "Bartlett Eager to Boost Exploration in Oklahoma," *Oil and Gas Journal*, May 29, 1967; and Neil A. Martin, "The Governor Is a Businessman," *Dun's Review and Modern Industry*, June 1970. Obituaries are in the Oklahoma City *Daily Oklahoman*, Mar. 2, 1979, and in the *New York Times* and the *Washington Post*, both Mar. 3, 1979.]

EDWARD J. TASSINARI

BATESON, GREGORY (May 9, 1904–July 4, 1980), natural and social scientist, was born in Grantchester, England, a small village on the outskirts of Cambridge, one of three children born to Caroline Beatrice Durham and William Bateson, a British geneticist at Cambridge University. After the untimely deaths of his two older brothers in 1918 and 1922, Bateson began his adulthood reading zoology (1922–1925) at St. John's College, Cambridge, as his father had done (and where his grandfather had been headmaster). For his master's degree (1930), however, he switched to anthropology, the first of many shifts throughout his life.

Bateson's first field experience, among the Baining of New Britain (1927–1928), was unhappy, as the Baining people were too reserved for fruitful observation. His second field experience, however, among the Iatmul of nearby New Guinea (1929–1930), provided Bateson with the material for his master's thesis. In 1932 he again visited New Guinea, where he met fellow anthropologist Margaret Mead and gathered the material for *Naven* (1936), his first book. He and Mead were married in Singapore in 1936. From there, they traveled to Bali, where their fieldwork (1936–1938) led to their jointly authored *Balinese Character: A Photographic Analysis* (1942).

Following the birth of their daughter in 1939, Bateson and Mead settled in the United States. The family spent little time together, as both Mead and Bateson sought out opportunities to contribute to the American war effort (though Bateson did not become an American citizen until 1956). During this time he served on the Committee for National Morale, analyzed German propaganda films, and finally, from 1943 to 1945, worked in Southeast Asia for the Office of Strategic Services. Bateson and Mead separated in 1946 and were divorced in 1950, although their intellectual lives continued to intertwine. In particular, they both helped organize conferences on cybernetics, the new science of self-regulating recursive systems. Although cybernetics originally developed from the study of mechanical systems, both Bateson and Mead felt that cybernetic thought could make a valuable contribution to the understanding and even redirection of human societies.

Bateson never returned to anthropological fieldwork. Instead, he turned to psychiatric observation, joining the staff at the Veterans Administration Hospital in Palo Alto, Calif., as an ethnologist in 1949, where he observed and interacted with the psychiatric staff and their patients. He also worked with the psychiatrist Jurgen Ruesch, through a two-year appointment at the University of California Medical School (1948–1949), on a project studying communication in psychiatric treatment, resulting in their book *Communication: The Social Matrix of Psychiatry* (1951). The project's research secretary, Betty Sumner, became Bateson's second wife in 1951. They had three children before divorcing in 1958.

Working with a series of grants in the 1950's, Bateson directed a small team of researchers investigating the problem of paradox in differing levels of human communication and learning. The team focused on schizophrenia and its possible origins in family communicational paradoxes that produced in schizophrenics "double-bind" situations, severely altering the language with which they communicated about themselves and the world. Simultaneously, Bateson also began observing levels of communication and learning in nonhuman species—first otters and then octopuses, which he collected with Lois Cammack, who became his third wife in 1961; they had one child. He kept his octopuses in tanks, first in the morgue of the Palo Alto hospital and then in his living room.

His interest in nonhuman species led Bateson to break off his psychiatric observations and move on, first to the Virgin Islands (1963–1964) and then to Hawaii (1965–1972), in both instances to study communication and learning in dolphins. Bateson's research at this time can be seen as a return to the zoology with which he began, but with a difference: where zoologists of the early twentieth century had been interested in animals only as individual representatives of evolving species, Bateson's interest was in animals as part of living interactive groups, learning and communicating and evolving not in a linear sequence but as parts of a far more complex whole.

Not until he returned to California in 1972 did Bateson begin, as a teacher, writer, and lecturer, to challenge the world with the ideas and concerns—holism, ecology, a new sense of the sacred—that had become associated with his name by the time of his death. But the ideas and concerns of his last phase had been present in his thinking from his earliest days in Cambridge. His training as a zoologist had instilled in him an interest in patterns, in the relationships between things rather than the things themselves. In the naven ceremonies of the Iatmul, which marked the development of boys into men and girls into women, he had found two patterns of "schismogenesis," or mutually reinforcing behavior, in the differentiation of sexual roles. He also was aware that as an anthropologist, he, too, was not separate from the phenomena he observed but was an interactive part, an awareness he later brought to his observation of the dynamics of psychotherapy. Schizophrenics and alcoholics were best understood as part of interactive systems that included not only the individuals themselves but also their families, their culture, and their therapeutic environment, as parts of interactive communication-learning systems gone awry. Bateson labeled such systems "epistemologies" and began to question the stability—the sustainability—of Occidental culture's epistemology, one that separates mind from nature and the observer from the observed and that thinks exclusively in terms of linear cause and effect.

In cybernetics, Bateson found models for both stable and unstable systems. In either case, the systems were holistic rather than linear. Function, purpose, and even mind were not isolable elements but were immanent throughout a system. Bateson in his last years asked Western culture to develop a new epistemology based on the cybernetic model before it brought on its own destruction. In keeping with his turn from the West, he spent his final months at the

Esalen Institute, an alternative community on the cliffs of Big Sur, Calif. After his health failed beyond recovery, he spent his final days with his family at the Zen Center in San Francisco.

[The Bateson Archive is located at the Library of the University of California, Santa Cruz. In addition to the books mentioned above, see also Bateson's *Mind and Nature: A Necessary Unity* (1979) and *Angels Fear: Towards an Epistemology of the Sacred* (1987), completed by his daughter Mary Catherine Bateson, as well as two collections of essays: Vern Carroll, ed., *Steps to an Ecology of Mind* (1972); and Rodney E. Donaldson, ed., *A Sacred Unity* (1991). Bateson also edited *Perceval's Narrative: A Patient's Account of His Psychosis, 1830–1832* (1961). A full bibliography of Bateson's published works, interviews, quotations, and miscellania is in Rodney E. Donaldson, ed., *A Sacred Unity* (1991).

The chief biographical source is David Lipset, *Gregory Bateson: The Legacy of a Scientist* (1980); also valuable are Margaret Mead, *Blackberry Winter* (1972); Stewart Brand, "Both Sides of the Necessary Paradox," *Harper's*, Nov. 1973; and Mary Catherine Bateson, *With a Daughter's Eye* (1984). Evaluations and appreciations can be found in John Brockman, ed., *About Bateson* (1977); and Robert W. Rieber, ed., *The Individual, Communication, and Society: Essays in Memory of Gregory Bateson* (1989). An obituary is in the *New York Times*, July 7, 1980.]

PAUL JOHNSTON

BAYH, MARVELLA BELLE HERN (Feb. 14, 1933–Apr. 24, 1979), civic worker and advocate for cancer education and research, was born in Enid, Okla., the daughter of Delbert Murphy Hern and Bernett Monson, who were farmers. Delbert Hern was also active in local Democratic politics. Faced with straitened circumstances during the Great Depression, the Herns took extra jobs that supplemented their farm income and enabled them to provide their only child with educational and extracurricular opportunities. At a very early age, Bayh took elocution lessons and was soon performing and winning public speaking contests. In 1950, as a result of her student leadership and speaking talents, she was chosen governor of the Oklahoma Girls' State and the president of Girls' Nation in Washington, D.C. Throughout her life, Bayh noted these two events as key experiences in her development. After graduating from Enid High School in 1951, where she was the first female to be elected president of the student body, Bayh studied for one year at Oklahoma A&M (now Oklahoma State University) at Stillwater. In college, she continued to be recognized as both a leader and a public speaker. She won the American Farm Bureau's national public speaking contest in December 1951, the first woman ever selected. At the competition she met Birch Evan Bayh, Jr., whom she married on Aug. 24, 1952; they had one child, Birch Evan Bayh III, who was elected governor of Indiana in 1988 and 1992. The couple moved to the Bayh family farm near Terre Haute, Ind.

Bayh attended Indiana State Teachers College (now Indiana State University) in Terre Haute from 1952 to February 1954, when she had to withdraw because of injuries sustained in an automobile accident. In 1954, Birch Bayh was elected to the Indiana state legislature. Three years later, while continuing to serve as a legislator, Birch Bayh entered Indiana University law school, and Marvella Bayh enrolled in the undergraduate school. In 1960 she earned a B.S. degree in education, with honors.

While a student at Indiana University, Bayh served as vice-president of the Indiana Democratic Women's Club in 1959. From 1962 to 1974 she served as a counselor at the Indiana Girls' State, and on occasion she spoke at Girls' Nation. Viewing herself as a full partner in her husband's political campaigns, Bayh was involved in his successful bid for the United States Senate in 1962. She was recognized by her husband and others as an effective campaigner and a driving force behind his career. Her researching of issues and traveling throughout the state, using her talents as a public speaker, were repeated in his victorious Senate campaigns of 1968 and 1974. Senator Bayh once stated, "My wife has a better political head than anybody who works for me. Marvella is my political confidante and my adviser."

Bayh was described as intelligent, vivacious, attractive, and ambitious, and she and her husband were a popular and well-publicized young couple during the Kennedy and Johnson administrations. After their move to Washington, D.C., her oratorical abilities were noted by the Democratic National Committee, and she was recruited as part of a speakers' bureau of public figures who traveled the country giving speeches on behalf of Democratic candidates and administration programs. Bayh was particularly interested in promoting Head Start and child-care programs and in supporting the passage of the Equal Rights Amendment. Lady Bird Johnson appointed her as a member of the National Beautification Speakers' Committee. In 1964 she was chosen by women journalists as Indiana Woman of the Year, in 1965 she was recognized as one of the Outstanding Young Women of the Nation, and in 1967 she received the Oklahoma Pride of the Plainsmen Award.

In her autobiography, *Marvella: A Personal Journey*, Bayh discussed the difficulties of being a political wife, particularly for a strong and outspoken woman. Most difficult for her were the psychological pressures that resulted from being submerged in a husband's career, a situation that she believed had thwarted her personal development, and the tensions that existed between office staff and family, especially for a woman who assumed an important role in her husband's political life.

Bayh's most significant public contribution was the result of her being diagnosed with breast cancer in 1971, an experience that led her to pursue a more independent and personally fulfilling life. At a time when breast cancer was not talked about openly and mammography was not widely used for screening, she was the first prominent public figure to discuss her cancer and mastectomy in the national media. In addition to her forthright disclosure, Bayh lobbied for early-detection programs and increased funding for research. In magazines and newspapers, and on television, she openly and frankly discussed her breast cancer and treatment as well as her anxieties and fears and, as a result, elicited an enormous national response. She was commended by doctors and cancer patients, who credited her with helping women face the disease; by editors, who said she helped remove the stigma from the public discussion of breast cancer; and by ordinary citizens, who noted that her personal message had educated them on the importance and methods of cancer detection. In 1973, Bayh served as state cochairman of the American Cancer Society's (ACS) annual crusade in Indiana, and in 1974 she was appointed cochairman of the national crusade. In the national campaign she crisscrossed the country with a film, *The Marvella Bayh Story*, disseminating information and advocating research for the prevention, treatment, and cure of cancer. In late 1974 she was hired by ACS as a consultant and special representative, a position she held until 1979. From 1974 until July 1976, she hosted a short NBC Sunday television program, the "Bicentennial Reporter."

In 1978 Bayh's cancer returned in an inoperable, metastasized form. In spite of declining health, she continued working on behalf of cancer education programs. She also established the Washington, D.C., office of ACS's Public Issues Committee, a center for lobbying for cancer-associated legislation and research programs. In her last year of public interviews and speeches, Bayh's message stressed the importance of religious faith as well as medicine in fighting cancer. In all, she gave over 175 speeches and countless interviews to increase the public's awareness of the disease. Because of her personal example and work on behalf of cancer, Bayh received the 1977 American Society of Surgical Oncologists' James Ewing Memorial Award for a layman and the ACS's 1979 Hubert Humphrey Inspirational Award for Courage. After her death, the *Washington Post* noted: "To the rest of the country hers was the most exceptional life . . . for the way she took the most cruel news about her fate . . . and turned that news into a gift of strength for anyone who ever saw or heard her." Bayh died in Bethesda, Md.

[Marvella Bayh's personal papers are in private hands. The best source on her life is her autobiography, *Marvella: A Personal Journey* (1979), written with Mary Lynne Kotz. Bayh contributed to publications, including *Ladies' Home Journal*, Jan. 1975; and *Today's Health*, June 1972. An account of the Bayhs as a political couple is in Myra MacPherson, *Power Lovers* (1975). Information on Bayh can also be found in *Life*, July 26, 1963; *Ladies' Home Journal*, May 1971; the *New York Times*, June 18, 1972, Mar. 26, 1974, and Oct. 14, 1979; *People*, Sept. 30, 1974, and May 14, 1979; and the *Washington Post*, Oct. 12, 1979, and Dec. 12, 1979. Obituaries are in the *Washington Post*, Apr. 25, 1979; the *New York Times*, Apr. 25, 1979; and the *Chicago Tribune*, Apr. 26, 1979.]

MARILYNN WOOD HILL

BELKIN, SAMUEL (Dec. 12, 1911–Apr. 18, 1976), educator and rabbi, was born in Swislocz, Russian Poland, the son of Solomon Belkin, a Talmudic scholar, and Mina Sattir. He received a traditional Jewish education. After attending the yeshivas (Jewish academies) of Mir and Slonim, he was ordained at the yeshiva of Radom by Rabbi Shimon Shkop in 1928.

Belkin immigrated to the United States with a student visa in 1929, educated in Polish, Hebrew, and Yiddish but with no knowledge of

English. He lived in Philadelphia, in the home of Rabbi Bernard L. Levinthal. By 1934, after a year studying at Harvard, his mastery of English was such that he was accepted at Brown University with an honorary fellowship. In 1935 he received his Ph.D. from that institution, with a dissertation titled "Philo and the Oral Law," and was elected to Phi Beta Kappa.

Later in 1935, Belkin was appointed an instructor in Greek at Yeshiva College in New York City. On November 10 of that year he married Selma Ehrlich; they had two children and later divorced. (He married Abby Polesie on Jan. 3, 1963.) In 1936 he became an instructor in Talmud at the Rabbi Isaac Elchanan Theological Seminary, an affiliate of Yeshiva College. In 1937 he was named secretary of the faculty of the newly organized graduate school. In 1939 he was appointed a member of Yeshiva College's Executive Committee, which, because of the absence of a dean, was acting as the policymaking body for that office. Belkin became a full professor in 1940.

With the death in 1940 of Dr. Bernard Revel, founder and first president of Yeshiva College and head of the Rabbi Isaac Elchanan Theological Seminary, Belkin was named dean of the seminary and member of the seven-man Executive Board, which exercised presidential functions pending the election of a new president. He became an American citizen in 1941.

On May 23, 1944, Belkin was inaugurated as president of Yeshiva College and the seminary. He immediately started a broad program of academic and physical expansion. This resulted in the granting of university status to Yeshiva by the New York State Board of Regents in November 1945, making Yeshiva the first university in the United States under Jewish auspices.

As president, Belkin initiated far-reaching and innovative programs that had a great impact on Jewish academic and cultural life in America. In 1954 the first liberal arts college for women under Jewish auspices—Stern College—was established. In 1955 the Albert Einstein College of Medicine, the first American medical school under Jewish sponsorship, was opened. He personally visited a reluctant Albert Einstein to obtain permission to use his name for the new school. Other schools were the Belfer Graduate School of Science, the Ferkauf Graduate School of Humanities and Social Sciences, and the Wurzweiler School of Social Work. In 1976, Yeshiva University opened the Benjamin N. Cardozo School of Law.

Under Belkin's leadership, the university's enrollment rose from 850 to 7,000, full-time faculty grew from 94 to 1,500, and the number of schools and affiliates increased from 4 to 15. The physical facilities expanded from one building in Washington Heights in Manhattan to four major campuses in Manhattan and the Bronx.

Belkin described himself as "a rabbi who doesn't preach, a doctor who doesn't cure, and a professor who doesn't teach." Yet for decades he was a leader in education. By establishing a strong symbiotic relationship between Jewish education and secular ideas, he was able to serve not only Jewish communities around the world but also American society as a whole.

Belkin was also a scholar and authority on Jewish law and Hellenistic literature. His major work, based on his doctoral dissertation, was *Philo and the Oral Law: The Philonic Interpretation of Biblical Law in Relation to the Palestinian Halakah* (1940), in which he wrote that the oral law of the Palestinian Jews was known and practiced by Jews outside Palestine, and that Philo's Jewish law was based on this Palestinian law. Two other books, *Essays in Traditional Jewish Thought* (1956) and *In His Image: The Jewish Philosophy of Man as Expressed in Rabbinic Tradition* (1960), contain Belkin's formulation of a religious philosophy of Judaism as reflected in Jewish law.

Belkin wrote numerous scholarly articles and served as associate editor of Rabbinics for the *Universal Jewish Encyclopedia* (1940). He also won wide acclaim for his monographs, which include *What Makes a Good Jew*, *Parent as Teacher and Teacher as Parent*, *Man and His Creator*, and *The Philosophy of Purpose*. His "The Four Dimensions of Higher Education" is in *Introduction to College Life, a Book of Readings* (1962).

Belkin belonged to numerous scholarly, civic, and communal organizations. He was on the board of directors of the Council of Higher Educational Institutions in New York City, Youth Aid, and the Society of Friends of Touro Synagogue. He was also on the advisory council of the New York State Board of Regents, the advisory committee of the United Negro College Fund, and the National Advisory Board of the United World Federalists.

In June 1959 his alma mater, Brown University, bestowed upon him an honorary D.D. degree. In 1963, Mayor Robert F. Wagner awarded Belkin the bronze medal of the City of New York for his service to higher education. On his thirtieth anniversary as president of Yeshiva, in 1973, he was awarded the New York City 75th Anniversary Medal and the New York City Scroll of Distinguished Service.

In 1975, Belkin resigned as president because of illness and assumed the new post of chancellor. He died in New York City.

[Additional publications by Belkin include "The Problem of Paul's Background," *Journal of Biblical Literature* 54 (1935); *The Alexandrian Halakah in Apologetic Literature of the First Century* C.E. (1936); "Dissolution of Vows and the Problem of Antisocial Oaths in the Gospels and Contemporary Jewish Literature," *Journal of Biblical Literature* 55 (1936); and "The Alexandrian Source for Contra Opionem II," *Jewish Quarterly Review* 27 (1936–1937). See also Gilbert Klaperman, *History of Yeshiva University* (1969). Obituaries are in the *New York Times*, Apr. 19, 1976; and *Jewish Press*, Apr. 23, 1976.]

SARA REGUER

BERGEN, EDGAR (Feb. 16, 1903–Oct. 1, 1978), ventriloquist and actor, was born Edgar John Berggren in Chicago, one of five children of John Berggren, a factory worker, and Nellie Swanson, who had emigrated from Sweden. Edgar attended Lane Tech and Lakeview High School in Chicago.

In the fall of 1919, Bergen paid a carpenter $36 to construct the head of a ventriloquist's dummy. He added a monocle, a top hat, and tails. At the Lakeview High School winter recital he introduced the world to Charlie McCarthy, his wisecracking alter ego. For the next fifty-nine years Bergen acted as the genteel foil for Charlie's one-line insults. Much of his material was developed from a mail-order wizard's manual he bought so he could become a magician.

In his senior year Bergen's English teacher warned him, "I shouldn't count on graduating." However, when she saw him perform at the senior pageant, she agreed that he should graduate, declaring, "The world needs laughter more than another history teacher."

In the fall of 1921, Bergen enrolled as a drama student at Northwestern University. While still a student, between June 1922 and August 1925 he performed professionally every summer on the Chautauqua circuit and at the Lyceum Theater in the Chicago area as a ventriloquist and magician. During this time he perfected his act with Charlie and legally changed his name to Edgar Bergen.

In 1925, Bergen began his full time, professional career in vaudeville. He developed the characters of Mortimer Snerd and Effie Klinker, both the opposites of McCarthy. Snerd was a country hayseed who, despite his ignorant appearance, often got the best of both Bergen and slickster McCarthy. The same held true for spinisterish Klinker, whom Bergen used less in later years.

On Dec. 17, 1936, Bergen and Charlie first appeared on NBC Radio in New York City with W. C. Fields. With this program Bergen began a twenty-year radio career, and Charlie and Fields also began their famous feud. On one occasion Charlie quipped, "Are you eating a tomato or is that your nose?" Fields retorted, "Why, you blockhead! I'm going to feed you into a pencil sharpener!" Another time, when Fields declared that McCarthy's head was full of sawdust, Charlie replied, "Pink Elephants take aspirin to get rid of W. C. Fields."

Less than six months later, Bergen and McCarthy began their own show on NBC Radio for Chase and Sanborn Coffee. One of their standard jokes over the next nineteen years was McCarthy accusing Bergen of moving his lips. Bergen might reply, "I've taken a lot from you." Charlie McCarthy would respond, "Yes, and you have kept every penny."

During the late 1930's and early 1940's, Bergen's program became the number-one show on radio. Ultimately, Bergen earned as much as $10,000 per week. In this golden era of radio, with rival programs like "The Jack Benny Show," "The Fred Allen Show," "Fibber McGee and Molly," "The Green Hornet," "The Mercury Theater," and "The Walter Winchell Show," Bergen and McCarthy remained a prime-time hit until the advent of television in the mid-1950's.

Opposing networks, primarily CBS, tried to unseat Bergen with comedy and dramatic shows in his time slot. Finally, when they could not beat him, they joined him. On Feb. 11, 1949, CBS announced it had hired Bergen and company, beginning Sept. 1, 1949.

In 1952, Charlie had a much publicized radio wedding to Marilyn Monroe. Monroe commented she was "wearing my wedding dress . . .

something borrowed." McCarthy replied, "You didn't borrow enough."

Beginning in the 1930's, Bergen played a variety of character roles in twenty-five full-length movies or shorts. Among these were *Charlie McCarthy, Detective* (1939), with Robert Cummings and Constance Moore; *Stage Door Canteen* (1943), directed by Sol Lesser, with stars such as Ray Bolger, Harpo Marx, Guy Lombardo, and Kay Kyser; *Fun and Fancy Free* (1947), a Disney cartoon with Jiminy Cricket; *I Remember Mama* (1948), in which he played Mr. Thorkelson opposite Irene Dunne, Barbara Bel Geddes, Oscar Homolka, Philip Dern, and Sir Cedric Hardwicke; *Don't Make Waves* (1967), with Tony Curtis, Claudia Cardinale, Sharon Tate, and Jim Backus; and the television movie *The Homecoming* (1970).

In 1937, Bergen won a special Academy Award for lifetime achievement and community service. He subsequently married Frances Westerman, a model; they had two children. Their daughter, Candice, became a film and television actress, notably in the CBS television situation comedy "Murphy Brown."

In 1956, Bergen retired from radio. He continued his career in television, on stage, and in nightclubs. On Sept. 21, 1978, in Hollywood, he announced his final retirement. He declared he was making one last tour with singer Andy Williams. In typical fashion, Charlie McCarthy joked, "How can you retire when you haven't worked since you met me?" When asked what it had been like working with Bergen, Charlie remarked, "It hasn't been easy. The man has no talent." During the same press conference Bergen announced that Charlie McCarthy would also retire and be sent to the Smithsonian Institution in Washington, D.C., to be preserved as a national treasure. Although Charlie was pleased, he regretted leaving Bergen. McCarthy concluded, "Well, at least I won't be the only dummy in Washington."

Ironically, Bergen never got to retire. Following his Sept. 30, 1978, performance at Caesars Palace in Las Vegas, Nev., he returned to his room, where he died in his sleep. Thousands sent their condolences, including President Jimmy Carter. As an *Atlanta Constitution* editorial assured its readers, "For sure . . . with Edgar Bergen's death there will be less laughter in Washington and throughout the land."

[Candice Bergen, *Knock Wood* (1984), includes reminiscences of her father. See also Bob Thomas, "Bergen Announces Retirement," *New York Times*, Sept. 22, 1978. Obituaries and appreciations are in *Newsweek*, Oct. 2, 1978; the *Atlanta Constitution*, Oct. 3, 1978; *Time*, Oct 9, 1978; and the *New York Times*, Nov. 6, 1978.]

WILLIAM HEAD

BERKELEY, BUSBY (Nov. 29, 1895–Mar. 14, 1976), choreographer and motion-picture director, was born William Berkeley Enos in Los Angeles, the son of Wilson Enos and Gertrude Berkeley. Both parents had impressive theatrical résumés: Wilson Enos directed T. Daniel Frawley's stock company in Los Angeles, and Gertrude Enos was an established actress. Indeed, Berkeley got his nickname—and eventually his stage name—from Frawley's company, when family friends named him "Busby" in honor of Frawley's leading lady, Amy Busby. In 1914, after graduating from the Mohegan Lake Military Academy in upstate New York, Berkeley worked at a box shop and a shoe manufacturing plant in Athol, Mass., but spent his spare time directing a dance band.

When the United States declared war on Germany in April 1917, Berkeley immediately enlisted in the army, where he earned the rank of second lieutenant and became General John Pershing's entertainment officer. During his two years in France, Berkeley's duties included designing and rehearsing marching drills for the American and French forces. Following the war, he organized numerous stage shows for enlisted men.

With Berkeley's family connections, his entrance into the world of the theater was assured, although his precise direction was not. He launched his adult show business career as an actor, largely because a part was waiting for him when he returned from the service, in the cross-country touring production of *The Man Who Came Back*. By 1921 he was combining acting with directing, showing particular skill with musical productions. His breakthrough came in 1927, when he directed the dance sequences for Rodgers and Hart's *The Connecticut Yankee*. For the next three years he alternately (and at times simultaneously) produced, directed, and acted in about twenty Broadway productions. With *The Street Singer* in 1929, Berkeley became the first man to serve as both dance and general director for a production.

In 1930, Samuel Goldwyn, hoping that Berkeley's Broadway success could be transferred to the screen, hired him to direct the dance sequences for the United Artists movie *Whoopee*, which starred Eddie Cantor. With his move to Hollywood, Berkeley discovered the medium that would bring him fame, fortune, and eventually the appreciation of film critics and scholars. While it would have been natural to choreograph the dance numbers from the camera perspective of a theater audience, as others had always done, he immediately grasped the revolutionary implications of filmmaking technology. And when the current technology did not suit his needs, he invented something that did, such as a camera mounted on a monorail. With *Whoopee*, he dreamed up the "top shot" of dancers, with the camera suspended above the action. This camera position enabled Berkeley to design sequences that emphasized the dance troupe's collective shape, rather than the moves of individual dancers, a lesson he had learned while organizing military drills.

Berkeley's Goldwyn years (1930–1933) were his apprenticeship for the masterful work he would do at Warner Brothers (1933–1939). Warner Brothers gave Berkeley something that the tight-fisted Goldwyn would not: a very big budget for his routines. The money allowed him to realize the many outrageous ideas that he reportedly thought up every day during his morning bath—ideas that had little to do with the internal logic of the picture, but everything to do with sheer extravaganza. The results were sensual (several film critics have labeled them "orgiastic"), mind-boggling film experiences that will probably never be duplicated.

Berkeley's first musical for Warner Brothers, *42nd Street* (1933), was a box office triumph that redefined the possibilities of the genre. The film viewer spends most of the movie watching the chorus line practice their singing and dancing while dressed in their rehearsal tights and shorts. These scenes are purposefully hardheaded and unmagical, as the director, Lloyd Bacon, strips the veneer off a "typical" Broadway production. Near the end of the movie, however, Berkeley's numbers (which include "Shuffle Off to Buffalo" and "42nd Street") transform the dancers through the use of the top shot and other exotic angle shots. By having the dance troupe manipulate banners, flags, and other material, he made the dancers disappear altogether, so that all that remained was a kaleidoscopic, swirling mass of wonderment.

In the *Gold Diggers of 1933*, Berkeley used sixty women dancers holding neon-lighted violins to create numerous stunning effects. These included a top shot of the small violins forming the shape of a giant violin—the dancers themselves could not be seen in the darkened studio—and a neon "bow" playing in time to the music. The film also contained the powerful "Forgotten Man" sequence, which bemoaned the degradation (and emasculation) of the World War I veterans who had recently marched to Washington, D.C., to demand their bonuses. His juxtaposition of fantasy and social realism reminded the audience of the horrors of the Great Depression even while they were being allowed to escape into the movie theater for a few hours.

With each new film in the 1930's, Berkeley designed ever more elaborate and complicated numbers, including the wild "By a Waterfall" sequence in *Footlight Parade* (1933), which featured geometric shapes formed by women's legs against a cascading fountain. Film critic Jean Comolli later wrote, "One can suspect Busby Berkeley of having given himself the ballet as an alibi for his mad frenzy . . . to show in all possible fashions . . . the largest possible number of uniformly dressed blonde girls, in the splendor of an impeccable alignment of their legs . . . with a shameless camera."

Berkeley began directing his own films with *Gold Diggers of 1935*, which traded much of the narrative charm of *42nd Street* for more lavish production numbers. These included Berkeley's signature sequence, the "Lullaby of Broadway." Berkeley's directorial efforts never matched his dance work—he cared too much for spectacle and too little for the niceties of pacing, plot, and the like. In 1939 he moved to Metro-Goldwyn-Mayer (MGM) when Warner Brothers decided its big-budget musical extravaganzas had run their course. His MGM work tended to be more dancer- and star-oriented, featuring Judy Garland and Mickey Rooney in *Babes in Arms* (1939) and *Strike Up the Band* (1940), and Garland and Gene Kelly in the standout *For Me and My Gal* (1942). He also acted as dance director for a number of MGM musicals, including his last real blowout production, *The Gang's All Here* (1943) starring Carmen Miranda. One film critic later called

The Gang's All Here "awe-inspiring in its total outrageousness."

Throughout his Hollywood period, Berkeley gained an image as a carouser and a womanizer, as well as an extremely hardworking director. The combination helps explain his five stormy and generally short-lived marriages—many annulled after less than a year. In the mid-1940's, Berkeley's life-style may have contributed to his physical and mental collapse, which kept him out of show business for a number of years. It also may have slowed him down enough so that his fifth marriage, with Marge Pemberton, lasted from 1945 to 1954. His last significant contribution to cinema came in the early 1950's, when he directed the water ballets for Esther Williams in *Million Dollar Mermaid* (1952) and *Easy to Love* (1953). When Hollywood no longer had any use for him, Berkeley married for the last time, in 1958; his sixth wife, Etta Dunn, remained with him until his death.

Although Berkeley's pictures had always scored big at the box office, contemporary critics had tended to view his aesthetic as excessive and grotesque. In the mid-1960's, however, a revival of interest in depression-era "camp" brought Berkeley into the spotlight. Critics praised his work for its sensuality, playfulness, and above all its inventiveness with the camera and with the dance troupe. He found himself lecturing at colleges and art houses across the country, extolling the benefits of "old-fashioned" entertainment values. Although he made a successful return to Broadway directing *No, No, Nanette* in 1971 (starring his favorite performer from his Warner Brothers pictures, Ruby Keeler), he was never able to produce the extravaganzas he had envisioned for television.

Berkeley died at his home near Palm Springs, Calif.

[Berkeley's work must be seen to be appreciated. Besides the films listed above, see *Roman Scandals* (1933), *Gold Diggers of 1937*, *Babes on Broadway* (1941), and *Take Me Out to the Ballgame* (1949). Critical commentary may be found in Bob Pike and Dave Martin, *The Genius of Busby Berkeley* (1973); and Barbara Siegel and Scott Siegel, *The Encyclopedia of Hollywood* (1990). Biographical material may be found in John Gruen, *Close Up* (1971). An obituary is in the *New York Times*, Mar. 15, 1976.]

MICHAEL GOLDBERG

BERNSTEIN, THEODORE MENLINE (Nov. 17, 1904–June 27, 1979), journalist, journalism educator, and authority on the English language, was born in New York City, the son of Saul Bernstein, a lawyer, and Sarah Menline, who had taught in the New York public schools.

At DeWitt Clinton High School he was associate editor of the *Magpie*, the school's literary magazine, and he was managing editor of the *Daily Spectator* at Columbia College, from which he graduated with a B.A. in 1924. Rejecting his parents' advice to become a lawyer, he went on to the Columbia School of Journalism, where he graduated with a B.Litt. in 1925.

Bernstein began work at the *New York Times* in May 1925. He started out at the copy desk, where he worked for five years and made his reputation as a copy editor. J. Y. Smith of the *Washington Post* wrote at the time of Bernstein's death that the job of copy editor is an important one because "the copy editors are the last to read stories before they are set in type. They see that the stories make sense. They also write the headlines for them. Unlike reporters, who get bylines on their stories, copy editors are largely anonymous so far as the public is concerned." Bernstein was named suburban editor in 1930, a position he held until 1932, when he transferred to the foreign desk as assistant cable editor. On Sept. 2, 1930, he married Beatrice Alexander; they had one child.

Bernstein taught copy editing at Columbia's School of Journalism after his graduation in 1925 and continued teaching there until 1950. He started out as an instructor, and in 1934 was named an associate in journalism along with Robert E. Garst, who had preceded Bernstein on the staff of the *Times* in 1925. They collaborated on the book *Headlines and Deadlines: A Manual for Copyeditors* (1933). In the preface, they noted that the ideal copy editor not only would have complete mastery over the technical phases of his work, such as editing copy and writing headlines, but also would possess sound and swift judgment, be an expert rhetorician and grammarian, and be thoroughly versed in a variety of subjects. Noting that a book cannot instill judgment, they settled for instructions in the techniques of copy editing. Nevertheless, the book contained germs of Bernstein's future work in chapters entitled "Abused Words" and "How the Headlines Say It," which provided examples of Bernstein's judgments on word usage and clarity of expression. In 1939, Bernstein and Garst were named associate professors.

In 1939, Bernstein was promoted to cable editor at the *Times*, which was the equivalent of foreign editor. At age thirty-five, he was the youngest person to hold that position. He supervised the foreign correspondents covering World War II and the foreign copy desk, as well as the production of as many as six maps in one night, wrote the war headlines and news roundup on page one, and often worked from 3 P.M. to 3 A.M. Near the end of the war, Bernstein noted the difficulty of covering war news because of censorship and because so much territory was controlled by the enemy. He said, "It is as if we are standing outside a walled fortress and reporting on what is going on inside." The day of the Normandy invasion, Bernstein headed home at midnight and was about to have a highball when the newsroom called to say that the Germans were reporting the invasion. He downed the highball and headed back to the newsroom, where the next day's edition was produced using maps, drawings, and information Bernstein had prepared ahead of time.

In 1948, Bernstein became the assistant night managing editor, helping to select and place stories on the front page, and in 1950 he was named news editor. In 1952 he became assistant managing editor, an important assistant to Turner Catledge, who wanted brighter writing and editing in the *Times*. Bernstein held that position until 1969. In one incident during that time, Bernstein favored a more prominent place for and a fuller version of a story on the Cuban exiles that ran in the *Times* several days before the Bay of Pigs invasion on Apr. 17, 1961. As assistant managing editor, he brought about innovations in the presentation of the news such as the daily news summary and index and the "man in the news" profile. He also became famous in the newsroom as a "shirt sleeved vigilante" and "linguistic policeman." He was called a "tyrant of type" by his own newspaper. According to the *Times*, he never knew, because of his benevolence and affability, that he ruled by fear. At the time of Bernstein's death, executive editor A. M. Rosenthal said that Bernstein had been the "guiding spirit" of the *Times* for years, and that "I always felt he was looking over my shoulder. I wrote for Theodore Bernstein. He shaped this newspaper as much as anyone in its history."

Bernstein began publishing an in-house newsletter in the autumn of 1951 that he called *Winners and Sinners*, "a bulletin of second-guessing issued occasionally from the southeast corner of the *Times* newsroom." It started out with a circulation of about 600, intended for the writers and editors of the *Times*, but eventually 5,000 outsiders—"freeloaders," Bernstein called them—were on the mailing list. He wrote 389 issues of *Winners and Sinners* before turning it over to successors in January 1978. In it he cataloged errors (not mentioning names) and examples of good writing (mentioning names) under various headings, and ended with "Helpful Hints for Hatchet Men," a brief lecture on the editing process. He loved puns and often laced his comments on imprecise or ungrammatical language with humor. For example, in response to the sentence "He had become the father of a curly blond-haired boy," he wrote, "This kid needs straightening out." Under the heading "Jet Propelled Dictator," he listed the following sentence: "Overhead new Sabre jets, given to Spain by the United States, whistled low over the trees . . . General Franco himself could be seen on the reviewing stand following the fighters as they swept out of sight."

Using material from *Winners and Sinners*, Bernstein published *Watch Your Language* (1958) and *More Language That Needs Watching* (1962). In *Watch Your Language* he stated his approach to grammar and usage: "On one side are the stiff-necked grammarians, brandishing rigid rules, which they wield whether or not the rules are supported by history, idiom, or certificates of convenience or necessity. On the other side are the soothing champions of the masses, with their battle cry, 'whatever the people say is okay by me; the people speak real good.' This wordmonger refuses to join either camp; he takes up his position a trifle right of center." Bernstein published a more extensive reference in 1965, *The Careful Writer*, which listed more than 2,000 words and examples of usage. In *Miss Thistlebottom's Hobgoblins* (1971) he dealt with outmoded rules and changing usage, and in *Dos, Don'ts and Maybes of English Usage* (1977) he published more examples of usage taken from his column, "Bernstein on Words." Through these books Bernstein became a widely recognized authority on the English language.

In 1960, Bernstein went to Paris to direct the editorial revision and expansion of the international edition of the *Times*. In the fall of 1969 he became editorial director of the *Times* book division, but he returned to the news department when the book division was closed in 1971. He was executive editor of the *New York Times Encyclopedic Almanac* from 1969 to 1971 and was a consultant on usage for the *Random House Dictionary* beginning in 1966 and the *American Heritage Dictionary* beginning in 1969. He retired on July 1, 1972, but stayed on as a consulting editor at the *Times*, writing a column, "Bernstein on Words," three times per week. Bernstein died in New York City.

[Bernstein's papers are in the Columbia University Libraries; they include some 200 items of correspondence, lecture notes, and printed materials concerning his books, courses he taught, and *Winners and Sinners*. In addition to books mentioned in the text, Bernstein wrote a pamphlet, *How to Get the Most out of Your Newspaper* (1956); and *Bernstein's Reverse Dictionary* (1975). Memoirs that have significant recollections of Bernstein include Gay Talese, *The Kingdom and the Power* (1969); Turner Catledge, *My Life and the Times* (1971); and James Reston, *Deadline* (1991). See the following issues of the *New York Times*: Apr. 23, 1939; Mar. 5, 1944; Feb. 17, 1955; Nov. 18, 1962; Oct. 6, 1969; June 24, 1972; June 28, 1979; June 29, 1979. See also *Time*, June 15, 1953; "It's Better in Black and White," *Saturday Review*, Aug. 24, 1968; and the *Washington Post*, June 28 and July 6, 1979.]

ROBERT T. BRUNS

BIBLE, DANA XENOPHON (Oct. 8, 1891–Jan. 19, 1980), college football coach and administrator, was born in Jefferson City, Tenn., the son of Jonathan David Bible, a classics professor, and Cleopatra Willis. He received a B.A. degree in 1912 from Carson-Newman College, where he played quarterback on the football team. Bible pursued graduate studies in physical education at the University of North Carolina, Ohio State University, and Centre College. He next served as athletic director and football coach at Brandon Prep School in Shelbyville, Tenn., and occasionally entered the lineup. His coaching skills were developed by consulting the era's great collegiate mentors: Fielding Yost, Robert Zuppke, Henry Williams, Glenn Warner, and Amos Alonzo Stagg. In 1913, Mississippi College hired Bible as head football coach, Latin professor, and athletic director. Mississippi College compiled eighteen wins, eight losses, and one tie from 1913 through 1915 under Bible and upset Tulane University, 20–8, in 1915.

Texas A&M University appointed Bible its freshman football coach in 1916 and loaned him that October to Louisiana State University, which had lost its head coach. The Bengals finished 2–0–2 under Bible. Bible returned to Texas A&M as head football coach from 1917 through 1928 with a 72–19–7 record. His 1917 Aggies won all eight games, outscoring opponents 270–0. Bible spent 1918 as a flight instructor in the United States Army. His 1919 Aggies shut out all ten opponents, averaging over twenty-seven points per contest; his 1920 team, with a record of 6–1–1, surrendered only one touchdown. Texas A&M garnered five Southwest Conference crowns (1917, 1919, 1921, 1925, 1927) under Bible and often routed opponents, trouncing Dallas by 98–0 in 1917 and Daniel Baker College by 110–0 in 1920. Bible's biggest thrill came in the Dixie Classic on Jan. 1, 1922, when the Aggies upset heavily favored Centre College, 22–14. The Cadet Corps started a tradition of providing the players with a "twelfth man" by standing and cheering throughout the contest. His 1927 Aggies, led by halfback Joel Hunt, finished 8–0–1. During his tenure at Texas A&M, he married Rowena Jones on Dec. 19, 1923; the couple had two children.

The bald, lip-smacking Bible impressed others as confident, astute, poised, sportsmanlike, expressive, and resolute. A perfectionist, he commanded discipline and respect, admonished players who performed without enthusiasm, and organized his teams into loyal, spirited groups. He adeptly used psychology, challenging his team's desire to win and courage to fight adversity. His bullfrog voice mellowed over time, as he frequently quoted Scripture and preached solid, fundamental football. The Minnesota shift, single wingback, and double wingback were his basic formations, with the fake punt and run play on third down his favorite strategy.

From 1929 to 1936, Bible coached the University of Nebraska football squads to a 50–15–7 record. The Cornhuskers won six Big Six Conference titles (1929, 1931–1933, 1935–1936), lost only three conference games altogether, and fared well except against the University of Minnesota and the University of Pittsburgh. Nebraska fullbacks George Sauer (1933) and Sam Francis (1936) were named All-Americans.

Bible restored the University of Texas as a national football power with a 63–31–3 mark as head coach from 1937 through 1946. In 1937 he signed a ten-year contract as head football coach and athletic director at $15,000 annually, one of the best coaching contracts up to that time. The Texas legislature raised the university president's salary by $7,000 to match Bible's. Bible pledged to make the last-place Longhorns a championship team within five years, but Texas finished last in the Southwest Conference in his first two seasons. Texas steadily improved under Bible, winning three Southwest Conference titles (1942, 1943, 1945) and appearing in three Cotton Bowls. The Longhorns defeated Georgia Tech, 14–7, in 1943; tied Randolph Field, 7–7, in 1944; and trounced the University of Missouri, 40–27, in 1946, with the teams' sixty-seven combined points establishing a Cotton Bowl record. Texas quarterback Bobby Layne figured in all Longhorn points, completing eleven of twelve passes for two touchdowns, running for three touchdowns, catching a long pass for a sixth score, and kicking four extra points. Ends Mal Kutner (1941) and Hubert Bechtol (1945–1946), an All-American, also starred for Texas. Altogether, Bible's thirty-three seasons as a head football coach produced 205 wins, 73 losses, and 20 ties with 14 conference championships and three Cotton Bowl appearances.

Bible's book, *Championship Football* (1947), remains a classic text for molding a winning team. He described his intricate system of scouting potential recruits and future opponents. His scouts answered forty-two mimeographed pages of questions on each future game and completed eight more pages with comments and diagrams involving offensive and defensive strategies. Bible advised teams to employ running plays within their own forty-yard line, passes or runs between the two forty-yard lines, passes between their opposition's forty- and twenty-yard lines, special plays (backward and lateral passes, double reverses, and fake run and pass plays) between their opposition's twenty- and five-yard lines, and running plays for the remaining yardage.

Bible, a Baptist, spent twenty-seven years on the NCAA Rules Committee, presided over the American College Football Coaches Association, and helped modernize football after World War II. As Texas athletic director from 1937 to 1957, he built the Longhorns' athletic program into an excellent, very profitable enterprise. His successful Bible Plan utilized alumni to recruit players throughout Texas, stressing the importance of athletes as students. Bible received the Amos Alonzo Stagg Award and the New York Touchdown Club's 1954 award for outstanding service to football. By the time of his death in Austin, Tex., Bible had been elected to the Helms Athletic Foundation and the National Football Foundation College Football halls of fame.

[Dana X. Bible, *Championship Football* (1947), contains his coaching philosophy. Edwin Pope, *Football's Greatest Coaches* (1956), summarizes Bible's career. On Bible as head football coach see Hollis Limprecht, Hollis Silber, and James Denner, *Go Big Red* (1966); Wilbur Evans and H. B. McElroy, *The Twelfth Man* (1974); Denne H. Freeman, *Hook 'Em, Horns* (1974); and John D. McCallum, *Big Eight Football* (1979). An obituary is in the *New York Times*, Jan. 20, 1980.]

DAVID L. PORTER

BIEBER, MARGARETE (July 31, 1879–Feb. 25, 1978), ancient art historian and pioneer in women's education, was born in Schoenau, Kreis Schwetz, West Prussia (now Przechowo, Poland), the daughter of a prosperous Jewish industrialist, Jacob Heinrich Bieber, and Valli Bukofzer. She attended local schools and then boarding schools in Dresden and Berlin. In 1901 she matriculated at the Friedrich-Wilhelms-Universität in Berlin. As a woman, she needed to secure her professors' permission to attend their lectures. She heard the greatest classical scholars of the time: Hermann Diels (Greek philosophy), Eduard Meyer (ancient history), and Ulrich von Wilamowitz-Moellendorff (Greek literature), for whom she wrote a paper in Latin on the Greek sources of Catullus. She began to study Greek sculpture with Reinhard Kekule von Stradonitz, but his lectures bored her. She transferred to Bonn and became the student of Georg Loeschcke, her mentor and dissertation adviser, whose portrait always hung in her study. Her dissertation, on Greek sculpture and acting, anticipated her lifework. She received her Ph.D. in 1907.

Bieber spent the years 1907–1914 in Italy, Greece, and Asia Minor, where she visited ancient sites and museums and met the greatest archaeologists of the day: Wilhelm Dörpfeld, Sir Arthur Evans, Franz Studniczka, and Theodor Wiegand. In 1915 she published her exemplary catalog of the ancient sculptures in the museum at Kassel, Germany. Her interpretation of the Kassel Apollo remains authoritative.

While working intensively with her sister for the Red Cross during World War I, Bieber gave instruction privately from 1915 to 1918 in Berlin. From 1919 to 1933 she taught archaeology at the university of Giessen, progressing from lecturer to positions comparable to associate professor and department chairman. She lectured on a wide variety of subjects but was not paid a salary until 1926 and did not receive a regular budget line until 1931. Although she had always thought of herself as a German, not a Jew, she was forced to retire by the Nazis on July 1, 1933. She wisely decided to emigrate immediately.

After a disappointing year at Oxford University, Bieber arrived in New York City on Sept. 21, 1934, to serve as a visiting lecturer at Barnard College. In 1935 she became a member of the Department of Fine Arts and Archaeology at Columbia University, where she eventually reached the rank of associate professor. During her years at Columbia, on Sept. 26, 1940, Bieber was naturalized as an American citizen. After retiring in 1948, she continued to teach at Columbia's School of General Studies (1948–1956) and at the New School for Social Research (1948–1950). She also had an appointment as a visiting lecturer at Princeton University (1949–1951). She made a last trip to Europe (1951–1952) but did not visit Germany.

Bieber published some 350 books, monographs, articles, and reviews. Her scholarly reputation rests largely on three great books: *The History of the Greek and Roman Theater* (1939, rev. ed. 1961); *the Sculpture of the Hellenistic Age* (1955, rev. ed. 1961); and *Ancient Copies: Contributions to the History of Greek and Roman Art* (1977). They endure because they are sound compilations of central subjects, profusely illustrated, free of obscurantist theory, and contain valuable bibliographies. She was a synthesizer rather than an interpreter. In the tradition of earlier German "monumental philology," she used texts and monuments to elucidate each other. She valued Roman art for what it was rather than as a means to learn about lost Greek masterpieces. She did for American archaeologists, who because of the anti-German feeling generated by World War I, tended not to read German, what Werner Jaeger had done for classicists: she made the German achievement available and exciting. She regularly reviewed and summarized German books in American journals. Her necrologies of German colleagues were widely read. She even wrote an often-reprinted textbook to teach American students how to read German art historians. Her two most influential students were the Greek art historian Evelyn Byrd Harrison and the Etruscologist Larissa Bonfante.

Bieber's life is also important for those concerned with the emergence of academic women. She opened art history and archaeology to women in Germany both in universities and in the foreign institutes. She gained her first teaching posts only because her father's wealth allowed her to serve without salary. As the first woman who had ever taught them, she astonished students at Berlin and Giessen, but her competence and good nature quickly won them over. She was as much a victim of prejudice at Columbia as she had been in Germany: she was overworked, poorly paid, and repeatedly denied promotions. Even the title "emeritus" with its concomitant benefits was withheld from her. She was ninety-five before she was awarded the gold medal of the Archaeological Institute of America in 1974.

Bieber also has historical importance as one of the refugee scholars who changed American higher education both by reviving the German tradition of research in the face of rampant English dilettantism and by opening tenured posts in American universities to American Jews for the first time. She remained loyal both to Germany and her adopted country. She bore no grudge against her fellow Germans. After 1945 she sent numerous food and gift packages to her former colleagues and students in Germany, some of whom had spoken against her earlier, and she wrote letters exonerating them.

Bieber never married, but she did adopt a daughter in 1932. Her students were also her family. Her apartment at 605 West 113th Street became a salon where European and American scholars met, exchanged ideas, and learned from one another. Through public interviews she became an inspiration to older people because the last thirty years of her long life were her most productive and satisfying. She died in her sleep in New Canaan, Conn.

[Bieber's personal library and many of her papers are in the Tulane University Library, New Orleans, La. See Larissa Bonfante Warren and Rolf Winkes, *Bibliography of the Works of Margarete Bieber for Her Ninetieth Birthday, July 31, 1969* (1975), with addenda in the *American Journal of Archaeology*, 1975; and Larissa Bonfante, "Margarete Bieber," *Gnomon*

51 (1979). The best evaluation of her work is Evelyn B. Harrison, "Margarete Bieber (1879–1978)," *American Journal of Archaeology* 82 (1978). The authoritative biography is Larissa Bonfante, "Margarete Bieber (1879–1978)," in Claire Richter Sherman with Adele M. Holcomb, eds., *Women as Interpreters of the Visual Arts, 1820–1979* (1981). An obituary is in the *New York Times*, Feb. 25, 1978.]

WILLIAM M. CALDER III

BIERMAN, BERNARD WILLIAM ("BERNIE") (Mar. 11, 1894–Mar. 8, 1977), football coach, was born near Springfield, Minn., the son of William August Bierman, a farmer, and Lydia Ruessler. Osteomyelitis crippled Bierman as a youngster and kept him from participating in athletics until 1911. He graduated from Litchfield High School in 1912, having captained the football team and competed in basketball and track. Bierman earned a B.A. degree in 1916 from the University of Minnesota, where he lettered three times each in football and track and field and once in basketball, and won the Western Conference medal for academic and athletic achievement. Under football coach Henry L. Williams, the reserved, well-conditioned halfback captained the 1915 Western Conference championship squad and made several Western Conference teams.

Nicknamed "The Silver Fox of the Northland," Bierman began his football coaching career in 1916 at Butte (Mont.) High School. Butte outscored opponents 300–6, trouncing Billings, 54–0, in the state championship game. During World War I, Bierman entered the United States Marine Corps in 1917 as a second lieutenant and was discharged in 1919 as a captain. From 1919 to 1921 he compiled thirteen wins, seven losses, and three ties as head football coach at the University of Montana. Bierman installed Williams's Minnesota-shift system for his Grizzly players, who averaged under 160 pounds. In 1920 his Montana squad routed Mount St. Charles, 133–0.

Bierman married Clara Louise MacKenzie on June 6, 1921; they had two sons, both of whom would play football under Bierman at Minnesota. Bierman in 1922 entered the investment banking business in Minneapolis, Minn. In 1923, Clark Shaughnessy, a former teammate who was the head football coach at Tulane University, persuaded Bierman to relocate his investment banking business to New Orleans and become his assistant coach. Bierman joined Mississippi A&M University as head football, basketball, and track coach in 1925, compiling an 8–8–1 football record in two seasons there. He developed the buck lateral series, in which the fullback ran with the ball, handed it off, or made jump passes.

From 1927 to 1931, Tulane University employed Bierman as head football coach. The Green Wave finished 36–10–1 under Bierman and won twenty-eight of thirty games from 1929 through 1931, outscoring opponents 880 to 110. Bierman's 1931 squad did not experience defeat until the University of Southern California triumphed over them 21–12, in the 1932 Rose Bowl. Tulane boasted four All-Americans, including end Jerry Dalrymple (1930–1931) and halfback Don Zimmerman (1931–1932).

Bierman restored the University of Minnesota as a national football power, guiding the Golden Gophers to a 93–34–6 mark as head coach from 1932 to 1941 and from 1945 to 1950. Minnesota had not won a Western Conference title since 1915, Bierman's last season as a player. The Golden Gophers, using a relentless, single-wing attack behind an unbalanced line, outscored opponents 2,586 to 1,130 during Bierman's tenure. His players, who averaged 200 pounds, blocked well, enabling Minnesota to concentrate on a running game with speed and power. Bierman stressed physical conditioning, discipline, precise execution of fundamentals, crisp blocking, and hard tackling. Under him, Minnesota enjoyed the greatest decade in its gridiron history. The Golden Gophers won five of eight games in 1932, then did not suffer another defeat until the 1936 Northwestern University game. Minnesota won twenty-one consecutive games from 1933 to 1936, recorded five undefeated seasons (1933–1935, 1940–1941), earned five outright Western Conference titles (1934, 1937–1938, 1940–1941), shared a sixth with Ohio State University (1935), and garnered five national championships (1934–1936, 1940–1941) under Bierman. During Bierman's first three seasons, only the University of Wisconsin scored more than one touchdown against Minnesota, and during the entire 1932–1941 span only Notre Dame beat the Golden Gophers by as much as two touchdowns. Bierman's 1934 squad, sparked by All-American back Francis ("Pug") Lund, was his best and favorite team and ranks among the greatest all-time college aggregates. Bierman's masterful backfield juggling when Heisman Trophy and All-American halfback Bruce

Smith was sidelined with knee injuries brought him United Press Coach of the Year honors in 1941. Bierman served as a colonel in the United States Marine Corps from 1942 to 1945 and coached the Navy's Pre-Flight School football team at Iowa State University. Minnesota struggled in football under Bierman from 1945 to 1947 and narrowly missed going to the Rose Bowl following the 1948 and 1949 seasons. Bierman retired after the Golden Gophers plunged to a dismal 1–7–1 mark in 1950 and Minnesota fans hanged him in effigy.

Bierman completed his illustrious twenty-six-year college coaching career with 163 wins, 57 losses, and 11 ties. The shy, reticent, unemotional football genius did not believe in fiery pep talks. He coached fifteen All-Americans at Minnesota, including Lund, Smith, end Frank Larson (1933–1934), center Clayton Tonnemaker (1940), and tackles Ed Widseth (1936), Dick Wildung (1942), and Leo Nomellini (1948–1949). Bierman became a charter member of the National Football Foundation College Football Hall of Fame in 1955 and belonged to the Helms Athletic Foundation Hall of Fame. In addition to presiding over the American College Football Coaches Association, he wrote a popular text, *Winning Football* (1937), with Frank Mayer. Other coaching assignments included the East team in the Shrine All-Star game at San Francisco and the College All-Stars against the National Football League champions at Soldier Field in Chicago.

Bierman, whose Minnesota record remains unmatched, ranks among the greatest college football mentors. His career spanned a major transitional period in college football. Coaches recruited more aggressively by 1950 and, to Bierman's dismay, relied more extensively on the forward pass.

Bierman, an Episcopalian, was a football commentator for WCCO in Minneapolis in the early 1950's and then retired to southern California. In 1969 he moved into a retirement community at Laguna Hills, Calif., where he died.

[Bernard Bierman and Frank Mayer, *Winning Football* (1937), contains his coaching philosophy. Edwin Pope, *Football's Greatest Coaches* (1956), summarizes Bierman's career. For Bierman's role at Minnesota, see Stan W. Carlson, *Dr. Henry L. Williams* (1938); Howard Roberts, *The Big Nine* (1948); George A. Barton, *My Lifetime in Sports* (1957); University of Minnesota, *One Hundred Years of Golden Gopher Football* (1981); and James P. Quirk, *Minnesota Football, the Golden Years* (1984). An article in the *New York Times*, Nov. 22, 1971, recounts Bierman's retirement years. An obituary is in the *New York Times*, Mar. 9, 1977.]

DAVID L. PORTER

BIERWIRTH, JOHN EDWARD (Apr. 21, 1895–Apr. 3, 1978), business executive, was born in Brooklyn, N.Y., the son of Carl Julius Bierwirth, a physician, and Nettie Gheradine Cocks. He attended the Brooklyn Latin School, graduated from the Hotchkiss School in Lakeville, Conn., in 1913, and received a B.A. degree from Yale in 1917. During his youth he developed an enthusiasm for and high proficiency in sports that lasted a lifetime. He excelled on his high school and college baseball and hockey teams and was named by Grantland Rice to the 1917 All-America college hockey team.

At Yale, Bierwirth joined the Battery, a precursor to ROTC. The summer before graduation his unit trained in Texas, partially in response to a perceived threat from Pancho Villa's raiders. The class of 1917 graduated early, sending many of its young men to the American Expeditionary Force in Europe. Bierwirth was a first lieutenant in the 308th Field Artillery and saw combat.

Upon returning to New York City, Bierwirth joined Thompson, Starrett Company, building contractors. He remained with this firm for ten years and became vice-president. He married Alice von Bernuth on May 24, 1922; they had two children. Bierwirth continued to participate in athletics as a player and captain of the St. Nick's amateur hockey team of New York City.

Bierwirth joined the New York Trust Company, the predecessor of Chemical Bank, in 1929 as vice-president. As a banker he became involved, through the extension and supervision of the bank's credit, with the recovery of many industrial firms from the Great Depression. He was president and trustee of the bank from 1941 to 1949. In recognition of the bank's investment role and of its president's financial expertise, many corporations sought Bierwirth's participation as a director. His eventual list of board memberships included Textron, Owens Corning Fiberglass, Milliken, National Petro-Chemicals, and Bell Aerospace.

In 1942, Bierwirth joined the board of directors of the National Distillers Products Corporation, a producer of a highly profitable line of spirits including Old Grand Dad bourbon and Gilbey's gin. He did not, as a matter of personal taste, drink alcohol but he did not disapprove of its use. In 1948 management began to recruit him as the firm's president. Bierwirth did not accept until 1949, when he received assurances from the directors that he could pursue a course of product diversification for National Distillers.

During the next twenty-six years, as president and chief executive officer after 1952, and as chairman of the board after 1958, Bierwirth led the development of National Distillers into a major chemical concern with important involvement in liquor, wine, textiles, and metals. National's expansion into the chemical industry began quickly. A plant in Ashtabula, Ohio, for the production of metallic sodium and chlorine was built in 1950, and U.S. Industrial Chemicals, a firm that produced chemicals, resins, insecticides, and antifreezes, was made a subsidiary of National in 1951. In quick succession Algonquin Chemical Corporation, Intermountain Chemical Corporation, and National Petro-Chemicals Corporation were also acquired. In 1954, 25 percent of National's $500 million business was in chemicals, and the liquor business continued to thrive. Bridgeport Brass was acquired in 1961, at a time when chemicals and plastics were rivaling the liquor sales. In 1966, Beacon Manufacturing and Inwood Knitting added a significant position in textiles. Almaden Vineyards was acquired in 1967. Net sales of all products exceeded $1 billion in 1970.

The growth of National Distillers was also fueled by its entering international markets. Bierwirth's son, John C., joined the corporation in 1957 and became international vice-president in 1958. The European economy was taking off, and National established subsidiaries in Germany, Belgium, Italy, Sweden, and Northern Ireland. Although plastics were well established in the United States, European markets were ready for rapid growth.

Bierwirth served as a director of the Federal Reserve Bank of New York for six years, the last three as chairman (1957–1959). He relinquished the presidency of National Distillers in 1965, retaining his role as chief executive officer and chairman of the board. Bierwirth resigned as CEO in 1970 and as chairman in 1975. He remained on the board as chairman of the executive committee. During the post-Bierwirth years National Distillers became predominantly a liquefied petroleum gas and petrochemicals concern, changing its name to Quantum Chemical Corporation in 1987.

Bierwirth had a strong interest in education. He was a loyal supporter of the Hotchkiss School, serving on the board of trustees from 1942 to 1946 and from 1946 to 1962 as president of the board. He also donated the hockey rink at Hotchkiss that bears his name. National Distillers, under Bierwirth's leadership, established a corporate program of aid to education in 1956. The corporation supported the National Merit Scholarship program and created a major teaching endowment fund at Hotchkiss in Bierwirth's honor. He was also a trustee of Presbyterian and Beekman hospitals in New York City.

The Bierwirths lived in suburban Cedarhust, N.Y. Their family life was characterized by enthusiasm for athletics and outdoor recreation. Family vacations included fishing trips, visits to working ranches, and other vigorous activities. Bierwirth hunted and fished regularly, and remained an active and skillful golfer, with a handicap of six. Bierwirth died in Cedarhurst, N.Y.

[Further information can be found in articles in the *New York Times*, Jan. 31, 1954; and *Business Week*, Oct. 21, 1961. An obituary is in the *New York Times*, Apr. 4, 1978.]

MICHAEL F. HAINES

BIGGS, EDWARD GEORGE POWER (Mar. 29, 1906–Mar. 10, 1977), organist, was born in Westcliff-on-Sea, Essex, England, the son of Clarence Power-Biggs, an auctioneer, and Alice Maud Tredgett. His father died when Biggs was three. At age seven, Biggs entered Hurstpierpoint College in Sussex, a "public" (that is, private) school, where he excelled at mathematics and science, studied piano, and enjoyed tinkering with mechanical things. After graduating at age sixteen, he went to London to apprentice with an engineering firm.

At age eighteen, Biggs began organ studies with J. Stuart Archer, a well-known recitalist. At Archer's suggestion, in 1926 he applied for and won the Thomas Threfall organ scholarship to the Royal Academy of Music. There he studied with George D. Cunningham, then at the height of his career as a concert organist. Cunningham became his role model and seems to have exerted considerable influence over his choice of career. While still a student, Biggs won the Hubert Kiver Organ Prize in 1927 and was chosen to play two concertos for organ and orchestra under the direction of Sir Henry Wood and a solo recital at Queens' Hall, which one reviewer termed "a remarkably brilliant performance." He graduated in 1929, winning highest honors in organ, harmony and counterpoint, and piano. During these years his name appeared on various programs as E. G. Biggs, Edward G. P. Biggs, Edward Power Biggs, and Power Biggs, but by 1929 he had settled on the professional name E. Power Biggs.

Perhaps inspired by Cunningham's concert tour of the United States in the spring of 1929, Biggs embarked on a six-month tour of the United States in September 1929, serving as organist, pianist, and accompanist for the Cambrian Concert Company. A year later he took up permanent residence in the United States as organist at the Emmanuel Episcopal Church in Newport, R.I., and began his concert career in earnest.

Seeking a better base of operations for a concert career, Biggs looked for a church opening in New York City to no avail, but in February 1932 he accepted a job as organist at Christ Church in Cambridge, Mass., and soon thereafter played several organ recitals in the Boston-Cambridge area. In March 1932 he played a recital at the Wanamaker Auditorium in New York City. According to the *Diapason*'s critic, his later performance at the August convention of the National Association of Organists in Rochester, N.Y., "aroused the audience to sustained applause and bravos." And in September he began teaching organ at the Longy School of Music in Cambridge, a post he held until 1951. It was also in 1932 that he met French pianist Colette Lionne, a graduate of the New England Conservatory, whom he married in June 1933. They had no children.

In May 1935, Biggs was appointed organist and music director of Harvard Congregational Church in Brookline, Mass., and continued in that capacity until Dec. 30, 1956, although he spent increasing amounts of time concertizing. Following his appointment, he made the first of many recital tours of the United States and Canada, to critical acclaim, and in 1937 he became a naturalized American citizen.

Biggs's refusal to perform on electronic organs substantially influenced organ building in the United States. After learning of an experimental organ built by G. Donald Harrison, he suggested that it be housed in the Busch-Reisinger Museum of Germanic Culture at Harvard University. In 1937 he gave the opening recitals on the Harrison organ at Harvard, and he was closely associated with this organ for many years. Reviewing Biggs's performance in the *Boston Herald*, Alexander Williams said, "The effect of listening to that organ played with such knowledge and ability was electrifying." His concerts at the Busch-Reisinger Museum received wide acclaim. The *Diapason*'s critic wrote, "His playing was marked by beautifully defined rhythm . . . coupled with a real appreciation of the traditional manner of playing such music."

In a series of twelve recitals (1937–1938), Biggs performed the complete organ works of Johann Sebastian Bach. But his repertoire was not confined to established classics; indeed, he encouraged many contemporary composers to write organ works. For example, Biggs asked American composer Leo Sowerby to write a concerto for organ and orchestra, which he premiered in 1938 with the Boston Symphony, conducted by Serge Koussevitzky. At the Busch-Reisinger Museum he was often assisted by members of the Stradivarius Quartet, Arthur Fiedler's Sinfonietta, and the Boston Symphony. He made his first recording there, a five-record album called *A Bach Organ Recital* (1938).

A performance as organ soloist at the Library of Congress in Washington, D.C., in 1940 led to Biggs's initial contact with arts patron Elizabeth Sprague Coolidge. In 1942 she sponsored a series of ten, half-hour organ recitals by Biggs to be broadcast over CBS radio from the Busch-Reisinger Museum. The response to the concerts was overwhelming, and the series of Sunday morning recitals continued as a regular weekly feature on the CBS radio network until 1958. Constantly seeking new music for his weekly radio program, Biggs invited contemporary composers to write organ works and broadcast world premieres of pieces by Piston, Harris, Hanson, Porter, Templeton, Britten, Sowerby, and Pinkham. He also edited much of the traditional organ repertoire for publication. As a result of radio exposure, Biggs's fame spread beyond sophisticated music circles to the general public. A critic for the *New York Times* wrote that Biggs "in no small way, created a kind of musical renaissance of that great instrument—the organ."

In 1944, Biggs's first marriage ended in divorce. On Mar. 10, 1945, he married Margaret ("Peggy") Allen, who, though not a musician herself, remained closely involved with his work throughout his life. They had no children and resided in Cambridge, Mass.

In the years 1945 and 1946 Biggs played the entire organ works of Bach for the first time on radio, a feat he repeated in 1949–1950 in honor of the bicentenary of Bach's death. In 1948 he played the first radio performance of Charles Ives's *Variations on America*. In 1950, he performed Antonio Soler's Concerto in G for Two Organs by recording one part prior to broadcast and playing along with it for the "live" performance.

From 1939 to 1947, Biggs made twenty-six recordings for Victor Red Seal Records; after 1947 he recorded exclusively for Columbia Records, eventually making 118 recordings for that label. In 1950 he began a series of recordings of performances on the historical organs of Europe. This project continued for the last twenty-five years of his life. A genial man with a dry wit, he once told an interviewer, "We had to record at night, because the crowds and motor scooters made so much noise in the daytime." Informed that Trondheim Cathedral in Norway was haunted, he said, "Wouldn't want to record there at night."

In the last years of his life arthritis forced Biggs to curtail his concertizing, but he continued to record and to edit organ works for publication. His last public appearance was in June 1976 as soloist with the Boston Pops Orchestra under conductor Arthur Fiedler. He died in Boston and was buried at Mt. Auburn Cemetery, Cambridge.

[Biggs's correspondence, notebooks, programs, and other papers are in the Organ Library of the Boston Chapter of the American Guild of Organists at Boston University. Additional material can be found in the archives of United Parish Church of Brookline (formerly Harvard Congregational Church), Brookline, Mass. See also Barbara Owen, *E. Power Biggs, Concert Organist* (1987). An obituary is in the *New York Times*, Mar. 12, 1977.]

SUSAN FLEET

BISHOP, ELIZABETH (Feb. 8, 1911–Oct. 6, 1979), poet, was born in Worcester, Mass., the only child of William Thomas Bishop and Gertrude Bulmer, both of Canadian descent. Her father was a wealthy builder but died before Elizabeth reached her first birthday. Her mother became mentally unstable and returned to her parents' home in Great Village, Nova Scotia, Canada, and was confined to a sanatorium shortly thereafter. After age five, Elizabeth never saw her mother again. At age six she returned to Worcester and was raised by her father's relatives.

Bishop's childhood was marked by loneliness and frequent illnesses (she suffered from asthma), but her solitary pursuits heightened her pleasures in reading and in music. During the summer months she sometimes returned to Nova Scotia or visited Wellfleet, Mass. From the time she was fifteen to her senior year, Bishop attended Walnut Hill School, a boarding school in Natick, Mass. After graduation in 1930 she entered Vassar College in Poughkeepsie, N.Y., where she became close friends with the novelist Mary McCarthy, was a regular contributor to the *Vassar Review*, and helped start the literary magazine *Con Spirito*. After receiving a B.A. in English in 1934, she met the poet Marianne Moore through an introduction arranged by the Vassar College librarian, Fannie Borden. Moore was to have a far-ranging impact on Bishop's life and work. Indeed, Brett C. Millier, in her biography *Elizabeth Bishop: Life and the Memory of It*, states that "Moore was without doubt the most important single influence on Bishop's poetic practice and career." Both women shared a passion for precise, exotic details, and both remained, in their poems, reticent about their personal lives. (A short essay in tribute to Moore, "Efforts of Affection," can be found in Bishop's *Collected Prose*.)

The beneficiary of a small inheritance from her father, Bishop spent the year immediately following college in New York City, taking up residence at 16 Charles Street in Greenwich Village. She had frequent meetings with Moore, and then in July 1935, tiring of the city, set sail for Europe. For two years she explored France, Spain, North Africa, Ireland, and Italy. From 1938 to 1942 she lived in Key West, Fla. In an interview published in the winter 1966 issue of *Shenandoah*, Bishop told Ashley Brown: "I can't say Key West offered any advantages for a writer. But I loved living there. The light and blaze of colors made a good impression on me." Some of that light and blaze of colors found their way into a poem called "Florida," which opens, "The state with the prettiest name, / the state that floats in brackish water, / held together by mangrove roots / that bear while living oysters in clusters."

Although Bishop had been writing poetry from early childhood, it was not until 1946 that her first book, *North and South*, was published. Selected from some 800 poetry manuscripts entered in the Houghton Mifflin poetry competition, *North and South* assured Bishop's poetic reputation. As poet and critic Randall Jarrell later wrote: "The best poems in Elizabeth Bishop's *North and South* are so good that it takes a geological event like *Paterson* to overshadow them. 'The Fish' and 'Roosters' are two of the most calmly beautiful, deeply sympathetic poems of our time."

In the years that immediately followed publication of *North and South*, Bishop started corresponding with fellow poet Robert Lowell. The two became great friends (at one time Lowell considered proposing marriage to Bishop). The friendship endured to the end of Bishop's life and had lasting impact on her career as a poet.

In 1951, Bishop sailed to South America aboard a freighter. Her original destination was Tierra del Fuego, but while visiting a friend in Rio de Janeiro, Brazil, she ate some cashew nuts that brought on a severe allergic reaction. She was hospitalized and remained in Brazil, which became her home for the next twenty years. While she was recovering from her illness, Maria Carlota Costellat de Macedo Soares, or Lota, as she was affectionately known, invited Bishop to recuperate at her house in Petrópolis, a resort town about an hour from Rio. Lota and Elizabeth fell in love and lived together for the next fifteen years.

One of Bishop's great delights was geography; *Questions of Travel* (1965) and *Geography III* (1976) are titles of two of her poetry collections, and the poem "The Map" opens *The Complete Poems* (1969). She later told an interviewer, "I think geography comes first in my work, and then animals. But I like people, too. I've written a few poems about people." The beauties and poverties of Brazil also exerted considerable influence over Bishop's development as a poet, as a translator (*The Diary of "Helena Morley,"* 1957), and as a writer of prose, including the Brazil volume in the Life World Library series (1970). In 1972, she and Emanuel Brasil edited *An Anthology of Twentieth Century Brazilian Poetry*.

In 1965, Bishop returned to the United States to teach poetry at the University of Washington in Seattle and to take up the post of consultant in poetry to the Library of Congress, but before leaving Brazil, she bought a colonial house in Ouro Prêto, Minas Gerais, and returned to it frequently until the suicide of Lota in 1967.

In 1971, after Robert Lowell recommended that Bishop take over his creative writing course for a semester, she began teaching at Harvard University in Cambridge, Mass., and for a time she divided her teaching duties between Harvard and the University of Washington. In 1973 she collected her belongings from the house in Ouro Prêto and for the remaining years of her life she lived in an apartment on the Boston waterfront (Lewis Wharf). And, of course, there was still much travel. Harvard awarded her a four-year teaching contract, commencing in the spring of 1974. She had formed an intimate relationship with a woman named Alice Methfessel, but that relationship was severely tested by Bishop's bouts with alcoholism (a condition Bishop had battled throughout her life) and depression.

Still, the final years of Bishop's life were marked by numerous awards for her poetry. In 1970 the Brazilian government awarded Bishop the Order of Rio Branco. She won the National Book Award in 1970 for *The Complete Poems* and the National Book Critics Circle Award in 1976 for *Geography III*. Also in 1976 she became the first woman to win the Neustadt International Prize for literature. In 1978 she was awarded a Guggenheim Fellowship to work on a new volume of poems to be called *Grandmother's Glass Eye* and a book-length poem entitled *Elegy*.

Bishop died in Boston of a ruptured cerebral aneurysm.

[More than 500 of Bishop's letters are collected in Robert Giroux, ed., *One Art* (1994). See also Bishop's *The Collected Prose* (1984). Biographies are Anne Stevenson, *Elizabeth Bishop* (1966); Lloyd Schwartz and Sybil P. Estes, eds., *Elizabeth Bishop and Her Art* (1983); Lorrie Goldensohn, *Elizabeth Bishop* (1992); and Brett C. Millier, *Elizabeth Bishop* (1993). See also Candace W. MacMahon, *Elizabeth Bishop: A Bibliography, 1927–1979* (1979); Diana E. Wyllie, *Elizabeth Bishop and Howard Nemerov: A Reference Guide* (1983); David Kalstone, *Becoming a Poet* (1989); and Lloyd Schwartz, "Elizabeth Bishop and Brazil," *New Yorker*, Sept. 30, 1991. An obituary is in the *New York Times*, Oct. 8, 1979.]

LOUIS PHILLIPS

BLACK, DOUGLAS MACRAE (July 24, 1895–May 15, 1977), publisher, was born in Brooklyn, N.Y., the son of John William Black, a music critic and the editor of the Saturday edition of the *Brooklyn Times*, and Flora E. Blayney, a schoolteacher. From his parents, Black gained an appreciation for books.

Although remembered primarily as an executive associated with book publisher Doubleday and Company, Black began his career as a lawyer. He received a B.A. degree from Columbia College in 1916 and an LL.B. from the Columbia University Law School in 1918. Soon thereafter, he went to Europe as a field artillery sergeant with the American Expeditionary Force, returning a member of the French Legion of Honor. He passed the New York bar examination in 1919 and then joined the law firm of Kellogg, Emery and Inness-Brown, becoming a member in 1924. Black married Maude Thornell Bergen on Sept. 11, 1920; they had one child.

Black's connection with Doubleday started in 1914, when he worked in Doubleday, Page and Company's Pennsylvania Station bookshop. For three years he gained valuable book-trade experience while completing his undergraduate education. The association deepened during the 1920's and early 1930's, when, as an employee of Kellogg, Emery and Inness-Brown, he performed legal work for Doubleday. Black acquired Doubleday as a client when he opened his own law firm in 1935, and he became a director of the publishing company in 1939.

Black's intelligence, knowledge of the book industry, and ability to produce worthwhile results sufficiently impressed Nelson Doubleday, the president and chairman of Doubleday's board of directors, to ask him to become first vice-president of the publishing firm. Black accepted the post in January 1944 and rose to the presidency after Doubleday relinquished that position in October 1946. When Doubleday died in 1949, Black assumed complete responsibility for the business. He remained president until February 1961, when he became chairman of the board. He retired from the company in June 1964, fifty years after he began working in the Pennsylvania Station bookshop.

While president, Black led Doubleday through a period of substantial expansion and innovation. He sought to produce high-quality products and to organize the firm for long-term success. He increased the number of printing plants, retail bookstores, and book clubs associated with the company. He established editorial offices on the West Coast of the United States, as well as in London and Paris. He expanded the company's export department in order to compete in postwar European markets.

Through Black's efforts, Doubleday became one of the first large publishing houses to recruit writers from, and to promote its products in, the western United States. The firm also pioneered, in 1946, a department with the sole purpose of investigating and processing ideas for new publishing ventures.

Black deserves credit for bringing several major projects to Doubleday. His friendships with Dwight David Eisenhower and Harry S. Truman helped the company win the publishing rights to General Eisenhower's *Crusade in Europe* (1948) and the first volume of President Truman's memoirs, *Year of Decisions* (1955). Black's affiliation with Columbia University undoubtedly helped the company acquire *The Columbia Historical Portrait of New York* (1953), a monumental work by John A. Kouwenhoven of Barnard College and sponsored by the Columbia University Bicentennial Committee.

Black's experience working in the Pennsylvania Station bookshop made him sensitive to the needs of booksellers. As president of the company, he strove to have Doubleday sales personnel work more closely with booksellers, including requiring them to monitor stock levels personally and to perform reordering duties. Those actions lightened booksellers' work loads, kept inventories of Doubleday books in balance, and ensured that a cross section of products appeared before the public.

In 1953, Doubleday and Company instituted Anchor Books, a division that concentrated on publishing and distributing high-quality trade paperback books through bookstores rather than mass-market outlets. The division surprised the publishing industry completely: within two years of its founding, Anchor Books had sold one million copies of its books and won the Carey-Thomas Award for creative publishing.

During Black's presidency, Doubleday became heavily involved in textbook publishing. Other publishers had been involved in the field for years, but Doubleday waited until the late 1950's and early 1960's, when America's renewed emphasis on education increased the market for textbooks.

An ardent and articulate advocate of the freedom to speak, to write, and to exchange ideas, Black was unafraid to publish books that contained ideas different from his own or that held the potential to create public or legal controversy. For example, he published Immanuel Velikovsky's *Worlds in Collision* (1950), a speculative book about ancient astronomical occurrences, after Macmillan chose to halt publication in the wake of a threatened boycott by scientists. In 1946 he produced Edmund Wilson's *Memoirs of Hecate County*, only to see the book declared obscene in New York. He also published *Anne Frank: The Diary of a Young Girl* (1952) when no other company would do so.

Black fought censorship through the efforts of the American Book Publishers Council (predecessor of the Association of American Publishers), which he helped found in December 1942. As president from 1952 to 1954, he was responsible for the June 1953 document "The Freedom to Read," which promoted reading and books. He also became chairman of the American Book Publishers Council Anti-Censorship Committee in 1954. During this period, he involved himself in issues related to international copyright law and U.S. postal rates for books.

Black divided his time between his Park Avenue apartment in Manhattan and his summer home in Shelter Island, N.Y., where he and his family dug clams and sailed on his yacht. Heavily involved in civic affairs, he became a member of numerous organizations and boards, as well as life trustee of Columbia University. A member of the Presbyterian church, Black became director of its national board of Christian education in 1942. He was an adequate golfer.

Black died in New York City.

[*Publishers Weekly*, June 5, 1954, contains an interview with Black. Charles A. Madison, *Book Publishing in America* (1966); and John Tebbel, *A History of Book Publishing in the United States*, vol. 4 (1981), and *Between Covers* (1987) discuss the history of Doubleday and Company, including Black's involvement. Obituaries appear in the *New York Times*, May 17, 1977; and *Publishers Weekly*, May 30, 1977.]

GLEN E. AVERY

BLANSHARD, PAUL (Aug. 27, 1892–Jan. 27, 1980), author, social critic, and reformer, was born in Fredericksburg, Ohio, one of two children of Francis George Blanshard, a Congregational minister, and Emily Coulter. His mother was burned to death in an accident at her parents' farm a year after Paul's birth. His twin brother, Brand, became one of the nation's leading philosophers and had a distinguished teaching career at Yale. Paul Blanshard was Phi Beta Kappa and earned a B.A. at the University of Michigan (1914) and did graduate study at Harvard, Columbia, and Union Theological Seminary. In 1937 he received an LL.B. from Brooklyn Law School. He married three times. His first wife was Julia Anderson, a journalist, whom he wed in 1915. They had two children before her death in 1934. The next year he married Mary W. Hillyer, who died in 1965. His third wife was Beatrice Enselman Mayer, whom he married in 1965.

Ordained a Congregational minister in 1917, Blanshard served for one year as pastor of the First Church in Tampa, Fla., but he soon became disillusioned with his role as a clergyman and with institutional religion in general. From then on, if pressed, he would list his church affiliation as Unitarian, but at a conference late in his life he said, "I have come to the conclusion that Christianity is so full of fraud that any honest man should repudiate the whole shebang and espouse atheism." By then (1972), he had become a highly vocal critic of the Roman Catholic Church, whose politics and hierarchy he believed represented a threat to fundamental freedoms both in the United States and around the world.

At the end of 1918, Blanshard left the ministry for the trade union movement. In the tumultuous strike-torn year that followed World War I, when wartime protections for labor were lifted, he worked initially as a labor organizer. From 1920 to 1924 he was educational director for the Amalgamated Clothing Workers of America in Rochester, N.Y., and in 1925 he became field secretary of the League for Industrial Democracy, a position he held until 1933. In 1923, Blanshard published his first book, *An Outline of the British Labor Movement*. During this period, he began his relationship with Norman Thomas and the Socialist party and took an active role in Thomas's unsuccessful campaign for the presidency of the United States in 1928.

As the 1930's began, Blanshard turned his attention from labor and socialism to urban reform. From 1930 to 1933 he served as executive director of the City Affairs Committee, a good-government group in New York City. His investigations on behalf of the committee led to a second book, *What's the Matter with New York*, which he coauthored with Norman Thomas in 1932. The book attacked Tammany Hall and old-line government as the principal source of the city's corruption. In the mayoral campaign the following year, Blanshard gave his support to Fiorello H. La Guardia, the reform candidate who pledged to implement the recommendations of the Seabury Commission, which in 1931 had revealed widespread corruption in the municipal court system and elsewhere.

La Guardia made Blanshard commissioner of accounts (in reality, the commissioner of investigations) and gave him a broad mandate to clean up city hall, a charge that eventually led to the conviction, dismissal, or resignation of 122 holdovers from the Tammany-driven administration of James ("Jimmy") Walker. By 1937, Blanshard's relationship with La Guardia had cooled. Calling the mayor "a temperamental and ruthless taskmaster," Blanshard resigned his commissioner's office to complete his third book, *Investigating City Government* (1937), and to take up a private law practice after admission to the New York bar in 1938.

Three years later he moved to Washington, D.C., as an economic analyst and consultant to the Caribbean Commission of the Department of State, leaving that post in 1946 to become a full-time writer. His *Democracy and Empire in the Caribbean* appeared the next year to mixed reviews. By then, he was the Vatican correspondent for the *Nation* and, in the spring of 1948, produced a series of twelve articles on the political role of the Roman Catholic Church in the modern world, a series that Blanshard reworked in 1949 into a best-selling and highly controversial book, *American Freedom and Catholic Power*.

Attacked by Catholic critics as the herald of the "New Nativism," applauded by Protestants for striking "valiant blows" for freedom, banned for a time, along with the *Nation*, in the New York public schools, *American Freedom and Catholic Power* was premised on Blanshard's conviction that the Roman Catholic Church was institutionally antithetical to democracy and politically antagonistic to American pluralism and individual liberty. His quarrel, Blanshard wrote, was not with doctrine or belief; it was directed toward the Church's hierarchy, the policies of which, he wrote, were nothing more than the "medieval prejudices of an inflexible, authoritarian ecclesiastical system," which, having entered the American political and social arena, was seeking to control "foreign affairs, social hygiene, public education and modern science." The Church, operating on orders from Rome, had become "more and more aggressive in extending the frontiers of Catholic authority." Citing the Church's historic opposition to birth control and divorce, its demand for public funds to support its schools, its censorship of books and movies, and the pressure-group tactics it applied to its critics in the media or in business, Blanshard argued that the Roman Catholic Church was out of touch with the realities of modern America and with the Constitution and posed a clear danger to American life.

Blanshard repeated variations on that argument in a half-dozen titles over the next fifteen years. *Communism, Democracy and Catholic Power* (1951), *The Right to Read* (1955), *The Irish and Catholic Power* (1953), *God and Man in Washington* (1960), *Freedom and Catholic Power in Spain and Portugal* (1962), and *Religion and the Schools: The Great Controversy* (1963) all carried the message of *American Freedom and Catholic Power*, but without its impact on public discussion. His final assessment came in *Paul Blanshard on Vatican II* in 1966, when he wrote that while the Church was no longer "a monolithic glacier of reactionary thought," the Vatican II conference was only a beginning and that most of the institutional policies that made freedom anathema to the Church continued unchanged. His last book, *Classics of Free Thought*, was published in 1977. He died three years later in St. Petersburg, Fla., where he had been a columnist for the *St. Petersburg Times*, until just before his death.

[Blanshard published two memoirs: *Personal and Controversial: An Autobiography* (1973) and *Some of My Best Friends Are Christians* (1974). See also August Heckscher, *When La Guardia Was Mayor* (1978); and Thomas Kessner, *Fiorello H. La Guardia and the Making of Modern New York* (1989). An obituary is in the *New York Times*, Jan. 30, 1980.]

Allan L. Damon

BLISS, GEORGE WILLIAM (July 21, 1918–Sept. 11, 1978), journalist, was born in Denver, Colo., the son of William Lane Bliss, a newspaper reporter, and Marie Bresnan. His father worked for the *Denver Post*, then moved the family to the western suburbs of Chicago in the 1920's when he joined the *Chicago Herald and Examiner* as labor editor. From childhood, Bliss wanted to become a top reporter for a Chicago newspaper. After graduation from Lyons Township High School in La Grange, Ill., he studied for a year at Northwestern University, then dropped out to become a news clerk for the *Chicago Evening American* in 1937. He was promoted to reporter in 1939. He began his long association with the *Chicago Tribune* in 1942, joining the metropolitan staff as a reporter. During World War II, he served in the United States Navy in the Pacific. He returned to the *Tribune* in 1945 and was a general-assignment and police reporter until 1951.

In 1951, Bliss exposed a scandal in a state-run juvenile home, documenting abuse inflicted on residents of the home so vividly that reforms were implemented. Crime and political corruption were his specialties. Bliss was appointed the *Tribune*'s labor editor in 1953, a position that he held until 1968. In 1953, he reported on the attempt by organized crime figures Joey Glimco and Angelo Inciso to take over the Chicago Conference of Teamsters. Bliss and his colleague Sandy Smith prepared one of the first published charts of the Chicago crime syndicate's hierarchy.

Bliss was a tenacious investigator: tough but fair, objective and thorough in his reporting. In August 1961 the *Tribune* published his series of articles that uncovered widespread corruption at the Metropolitan Sanitary District of Greater Chicago. Bliss detailed waste, fraud, padded payrolls, kickbacks, public land giveaways to special interests, rigged contracts, and the link between organized crime and the commissioners of the sanitary district. In 1962 he won the first of his three Pulitzer Prizes for this series.

In 1966, Bliss reported that trucks engaged in intrastate commerce were using cheaper out-of-state licenses to avoid paying higher fees for Illinois plates. A front-cover advertisement in the July 23, 1966, issue of *Editor and Publisher* promoted his investigation: "Illegal out-of-state truck licenses were costing Illinois millions in lost taxes . . . until the *Chicago Tribune* exposed the racket."

Tribune management was less supportive of Bliss after McCormick Place, the lakefront exhibition hall named for the late *Tribune* editor Robert R. McCormick, burned in January 1967. *Tribune* editor William Donald Maxwell, who had been the driving force in the construction of the hall, sought political support to have it rebuilt. He conferred with Illinois secretary of state Paul Powell, former speaker of the Illinois House of Representatives, who had much influence in the legislature. Powell's office had authority over truck licensing and had been seriously tarnished by the Bliss reports. Bliss had reported that Powell's chief investigator had a criminal background, a story that led to the aide's resignation and Powell's claim that he had been unaware of the situation. Bliss was continuing his investigation of Powell's office, but after the meeting between Maxwell and Powell he was ordered to abandon his truck-licensing probe. Bliss resigned from the *Tribune*.

From 1968 until 1971, Bliss served as chief investigator for the Better Government Association (BGA), a civic organization that had been fighting waste, fraud, and corruption in Chicago since the 1920's. Under his direction, the BGA worked closely with investigative reporters at all four Chicago daily newspapers. Bliss received a tip from the owner of an ambulance firm about payoffs to police. He conducted the BGA's undercover investigation of ambulance firms in cooperation with *Tribune* reporter William Jones, who obtained a license as an ambulance attendant. Bliss staged a heart attack, and a *Tribune* photographer took pictures of an ambulance attendant stealing money from Bliss. The Jones series documented mistreatment of patients, Medicaid fraud, and police payoffs. As a result of the series, three ambulance firms were banned from transporting welfare patients, two firms were decertified by Medicare officials, and a grand jury indicted ten policemen and six ambulance company officials. Jones won a Pulitzer Prize for the ambulance series. Bliss also had himself placed in a nursing home as part of a *Tribune* investigation of nursing homes.

Bliss returned to the *Tribune* in 1971, after Maxwell's retirement. He investigated police brutality after records showed that only 27 of 827 complaints against policemen had been sustained by internal investigations. Bliss had sources in the Federal Bureau of Investigation and the Chicago Police Department who provided him with police records. He and his team studied 500 cases, interviewing victims and witnesses, and arranging for lie detector tests. Bliss also studied medical records. In his series, he focused on thirty-seven cases. *Time* magazine said that the Bliss investigation was "probably the most thorough examination of police brutality ever published in a U.S. newspaper." Several policemen were indicted after the Bliss articles, and the Chicago Police Department was ordered to develop policies to reduce the use of excessive force.

In December 1971, as director of the *Tribune* task force of investigative reporters, Bliss launched a probe of vote fraud. Registered letters were mailed by the *Tribune* to 5,495 voters in 14 precincts where vote fraud was suspected. More than 700 letters were returned because the registered voter had died, had moved, or never existed. Bliss had seventeen *Tribune* staff members and eight BGA investigators named as Republican election judges and poll watchers. Though they challenged persons voting under false names, Democratic precinct captains overruled them in violation of election law. Two days after the March primary, *Tribune* articles documented the vote fraud.

Bliss turned his evidence over to United States Attorney James R. Thompson and a federal grand jury, but no action was taken. He then placed one of his reporters, William Mullen, as a clerk for the Chicago Board of Election Commissioners. Mullen brought Bliss the ballot applications for the March 1972 primary. Bliss copied the applications, and Mullen returned the originals to the elections board. Bliss and Mullen compiled evidence of more than 1,000 ghost voters, forgeries, and other violations. Mullen's articles were published in September 1972. A federal grand jury indicted seventy-nine election judges for fraud. All but a handful pleaded guilty or were convicted. Bliss and Mullen won the 1973 Pulitzer Prize for local reporting.

In 1975, Bliss and *Tribune* colleague Chuck Neubauer spent seven months examining the Federal Housing Administration's program of mortgage insurance to aid poor people in buying homes. They reported $4 billion in waste and showed how mortgage firms were defrauding taxpayers. Their series reported a cover-up by officials at the Department of Housing and Urban Development (HUD) and collusion between mortgage companies and federal officials. The series prompted several congressional investigations and a shakeup of HUD. Bliss, Neubauer, and four others shared the 1976 Pulitzer Prize for local reporting.

"George Bliss was a journalism school for a generation of investigative reporters," said Bernard M. Judge, the *Tribune*'s city editor in the 1970's. "Bliss was the pre-eminent investigative reporter of his time." When the *Tribune* began publishing an afternoon edition in 1974, Bliss was asked to help launch the new edition. His response was three major exclusives on three consecutive days.

Bliss married Helen Jeanne Groble in June 29, 1940; they had six children. She died in childbirth in 1959, and Bliss married Therese O'Keefe on Aug. 11, 1960; they had one child. After the death of his first wife, Bliss began suffering depression. In late 1977 he took a seven-month leave from the *Tribune* and was hospitalized. He returned to work on May 18, 1978. On Sept. 11, 1978, in their Evergreen Park, Ill., home, Bliss shot and killed his wife, then fatally shot himself.

"George Bliss was, in effect, a victim of his own intense devotion to journalism," said Clayton Kirkpatrick, editor of the *Tribune*. "He was a perfectionist who was never satisfied with his stories." Kirkpatrick added that Bliss "undoubtedly was the foremost investigative reporter in the nation."

["Unethical Newspaper Practices," in *The Press*, compiled and edited by Allan Kent MacDougall (1972), is an account of the events leading to Bliss's resignation from the *Tribune*. James H. Dygert, *The Investigative Journalist* (1976), includes a profile of Bliss. Bliss's articles that won the Pulitzer Prize are summarized in Heinz Dietrich Fischer, *The Pulitzer Prize Archive*, vol. 3, *Local Reporting, 1947–1987* (1989). An obituary is in the *Chicago Tribune*, Sept. 12, 1978.]

STEVE NEAL

BLIVEN, BRUCE ORMSBY (July 27, 1889–May 27, 1977), journalist and editor, was born in Emmetsburg, Iowa, the son of Charles F. Bliven and Lilla C. Ormsby. Bliven's early childhood was comfortable; his father, a farmer, also worked for the family mortgage and loan company. Unfortunately, that firm never quite recovered from the panic of 1893. Over the years his father slowly sold off the family farm and his mother took part-time jobs. It was only because a cousin volunteered to finance his education that Bliven was able to enroll at Stanford University in 1907. He graduated in 1911.

Bliven's interest in journalism began in high school, when he started his own paper. The paper lasted for four or five issues, but his enthusiasm remained. At Stanford he was college correspondent for the *San Francisco Bulletin* (1909–1912) and worked summers as a cub reporter. After he left Stanford, he wrote advertising copy in Los Angeles. In May 1913 he married Rose Frances Emery; they had one child. Newspapers remained Bliven's first professional interest, however, and soon he was a theater critic for the *Los Angeles Evening News* and a part-time journalism instructor at the University of Southern California. By 1914 he was director of the journalism department, enabling him to leave advertising. Unsatisfied by teaching alone, Bliven continued to do free-lance writing for trade publications and newspapers in his spare time.

One of those trade publications, *Printers' Ink*, offered him an editorial position in 1916. Bliven accepted, and he and his wife moved to New York City. A 1919 assignment to interview the publisher of the *New York Globe* led to his employment as that publication's chief editorial writer. A year later, he became managing editor. He remained with the publication until it changed ownership and format in 1923.

Bliven is best known for his work on the *New Republic*. He began his association with the weekly magazine while still employed by the *Globe*, by writing free-lance pieces. In 1923, the *New Republic* engaged him as managing editor; in 1930, he was named editor in chief. Bliven is generally credited with shifting the *New Republic*'s editorial line to the left politically. In 1932, for example, the publication endorsed Socialist party candidate Norman Thomas for president. A year later, however, it came out in support of both the domestic and the foreign policies of Franklin Roosevelt. By the end of the 1930's, Bliven and the *New Republic* had moderated somewhat, remaining liberal but becoming anti-Communist.

During Bliven's tenure the *New Republic* published the writings of such well-known authors as Edmund Wilson, John Dewey, Charles Beard, John Dos Passos, Malcolm Cowley, and Felix Frankfurter. In 1946, Bliven hired Roosevelt's third-term vice-president, Henry Wallace, as an editor until his 1948 run for the presidency forced him to resign.

Bliven was not content merely to handle editorial matters at the *New Republic*; he also contributed pieces from time to time. He helped expose the scandals in the Harding administration, interviewed Nicola Sacco and Bartolomeo Vanzetti just before their execution, toured the country to report on conditions during the nadir of the Great Depression, and in 1938 wrote an open letter to Joseph Stalin urging him to conduct the Moscow trials by Western standards.

Besides his work at the *New Republic*, Bliven served as the New York correspondent for the *Guardian* for twenty years (1927 to 1947); wrote free-lance pieces, particularly on propaganda, consumer issues, and science; and gave public lectures. He was a director of the Twentieth Century Club and belonged to the Consumers' League of New York and the Foreign Policy Association of the United States.

Several heart attacks prompted the workaholic Bliven to cut back on his activities. In 1947, after a heart attack, he had to resign from the *Guardian*. In 1953, on his doctor's advice that he move to a milder climate, Bliven also resigned from the *New Republic* and returned to Palo Alto, Calif., taking up residence on the Stanford campus.

In California, Bliven entered a period of semiretirement, writing, speaking, and teaching an occasional journalism class. He followed up his first book on science and technology, *The Men Who Make the Future* (1942), with a second, *Preview for Tomorrow* (1953), and wrote a history of the 1930's and 1940's, *The World Changers* (1965). At the time of his death in Palo Alto, he was working on a manuscript detailing the history of the late nineteenth century.

[Bliven's papers are housed in the Stanford University Library. See also his autobiography, *Five Million Words Later* (1970). An obituary is in the *New York Times*, May 29, 1977.]

JUDY KUTULAS

BLODGETT, KATHARINE BURR (Jan. 10, 1898–Oct. 12, 1979), physicist, was born in Schenectady, N.Y., the daughter of George Reddington Blodgett, a patent attorney, and Katharine Buchanan Burr. Her father died before she was born, having been shot by an intruder in the family home. She was raised in

New York City and attended the Rayson School there. In 1913, Blodgett entered Bryn Mawr College, graduating with a B.S. degree in 1917; she received an M.S. degree from the University of Chicago in 1918. In 1919 she began a forty-four-year association with the scientific staff of the General Electric (GE) Research Laboratory in Schenectady, where her father had worked.

For many years Blodgett worked as an assistant to, and later as a coworker of, Irving Langmuir, a physical chemist who won the Nobel Prize in chemistry in 1932. He later described her as a "gifted experimenter" with a "rare combination of theoretical and practical ability." Other colleagues remarked on her untiring persistence and her habitual and contagious cheerfulness. Langmuir advised Blodgett to seek her doctorate, and she entered Newnham College of Cambridge University in 1924. There she studied under Sir Ernest Rutherford, and in 1926 she received the first Ph.D. in physics awarded to a woman by that institution. She returned to GE in that same year, the first woman scientist with a doctorate to be employed by GE; there she assisted Langmuir in improving tungsten filaments in electric light bulbs.

In 1933, Blodgett turned to the research for which she became best known, on monomolecular films. She invented a step gauge (also called a color gauge), a device that could measure the thickness of films down to one-millionth of an inch. Each layer of film would reflect a particular shade of white light, depending on its thickness. In 1938, GE announced that she had developed a nonreflecting "invisible" glass. This was accomplished by applying forty-four thin soap films one molecule (or about four-millionths of an inch) thick to ordinary glass, eliminating glare and in effect rendering the glass invisible. Blodgett and other scientists continued research on durable nonglare film, which later was used on camera lenses and optical equipment. These nonreflective surface coatings allow the efficient passage of 99 percent of the light striking them, compared with 92 percent passing through ordinary glass. This development also proved invaluable to the American war effort during World War II. Blodgett later developed electrically conducting glass.

Another phase of Blodgett's work involved the placement of thin films on leaded glass. Different numbers of layers produced a variety of colors when their thickness ranged between two-millionths and thirty-millionths of an inch. During World War II, Blodgett worked on methods of deicing airplane wings and developed a denser, more rapidly accumulating smoke screen. A machine she devised needed only two quarts of oil to cover several acres, and the resulting smoke hovered longer before dissipating because the oil droplets were of microscopic size. The chief of the Army Chemical Warfare Service praised the protective qualities of the device, stating that it had been the "greatest lifesaver of our troops and was responsible for the small number of casualties" during the Sicilian campaign. While at work on a project for the United States Army Signal Corps after World War II, Blodgett adapted thin films for use in a device measuring humidity at very high altitudes when carried by weather balloons. Her last published study prior to her retirement from GE, a joint project with T. A. Vanderslice, had to do with the cleansing of gases in ionization gauges. Blodgett retired from GE in 1963.

Blodgett received honorary degrees from Elmira College, Western College, Russell Sage College, and Brown University. She was given the Achievement Award of the American Association of University Women in 1945, the Francis P. Garvan Medal of the American Chemical Society in 1951, and, in 1972, the Progress Medal of the Photographic Society of America, the first woman to be so honored. An energetic woman of less than average height, she was active in the civic affairs of Schenectady. Blodgett was president of both the local Traveler's Aid Society and the Zonta Club, a service organization of executive and professional women. She also enjoyed performing in amateur theatricals, an interest she first cultivated when in college. She spent her summer weekends in a cottage on the shores of Lake George, where she enjoyed swimming and boating. Blodgett died in Schenectady, N.Y.

[The archives of Bryn Mawr College and of GE's Hall of History Foundation have extensive holdings of materials concerning Blodgett's life and professional activities. There is no published biography. The *Schenectady* (N.Y.) *Gazette* provides extensive coverage of her civic work and other accomplishments. Unpublished family sources were also utilized in the writing of this sketch. An obituary is in the *New York Times*, Oct. 13, 1979.]

KEIR B. STERLING

BLONDELL, JOAN (Aug. 30, 1912–Dec. 25, 1979), actress, was born Rose Blondell in New York City, the daughter of Edward Blondell and Kathryn Cain, vaudevillians. She became a member of Blondell and Company while still an infant: she was carried on stage when only four months old for an appearance in *The Great Lover*. As her parents toured the United States, Blondell and her brother and sister made stage appearances and attended schools one week at a time in cities on the national vaudeville circuit, often just a step ahead of the authorities from the Gerry Society, a group concerned with protecting employed children.

Blondell made her Broadway debut in the *Trial of Mary Dugan* (1927); won a role in *Maggie the Magnificent* (1929), a musical; and was featured in *Penny Arcade* (1930). When Al Jolson bought the film rights to *Penny Arcade* and brought Blondell and fellow unknown James Cagney to Hollywood to star in the production (renamed *Sinners' Holiday*), Warner Brothers decided the film needed well-known stars and relegated the young actors to minor roles. However, when early rushes revealed Blondell's and Cagney's talent, the two were signed to long contracts. Blondell became a workhorse in the Warner Brothers acting stable, making as many as five films in one year, often collapsing in exhaustion. Whether cast as a reporter, gun moll, gold digger, chorus girl, or the heroine's wisecracking best friend, Blondell never compromised her standards of professionalism, and never gave a bad performance.

Often costarring with Cagney or Dick Powell (seven times each), Blondell delivered creditable performances in both dramas and musicals. Between 1930 and 1939 she appeared in fifty films, among them *Public Enemy* (1931), *Blonde Crazy* (1931), *Miss Pinkerton* (1932), *The Greeks Had a Word for Them* (1932), *The Crowd Roars* (1932), *Gold Diggers of 1933*, *Footlight Parade* (1933), *Bullets or Ballots* (1936), *Colleen* (1936), *The King and the Chorus Girl* (1937), *Gold Diggers of 1937*, and *Good Girls Go to Paris* (1939). She appeared in a number of Busby Berkeley extravaganzas such as *Dames* (1934), which features her memorable "The Girl at the Ironing Board" number. Often her appearances in these spectaculars drew attention away from the stars. When her Warner Brothers contract expired, Blondell began to free-lance and thereafter had more control over her roles and the number of films she would make.

Blondell's 1933 marriage to cameraman George Barnes ended in divorce in 1935. Her son by that marriage was adopted by singer-actor Dick Powell when he and Blondell married in July 1936; the couple had one additional child. Powell and Blondell divorced in 1945. On July 5, 1947, she married producer Mike Todd. This third marriage also ended in divorce, in 1950.

During World War II, Blondell maintained her film career, appearing in the story of nurses caught in the Battle of Bataan, *Cry Havoc* (1943). She also toured regularly for the United Service Organizations. She was a big hit with the servicemen, for she performed a comic striptease involving a stuck zipper.

As Blondell matured, she began to select character parts, a move that helped her to extend her career. She gave a memorable performance as Aunt Cissy in *A Tree Grows in Brooklyn* (1945), her favorite role. She was nominated for an Academy Award for best supporting actress in *The Blue Veil* (1951). She also appeared in *The Corpse Came C.O.D.* (1947), *Nightmare Alley* (1947), and *For Heaven's Sake* (1950).

Blondell returned to Broadway after a thirteen-year absence for the 1943 Mike Todd production of *The Naked Genius*, a play written by Gypsy Rose Lee. She toured in such plays as *Call Me Madam* (1952), *A Tree Grows in Brooklyn* (1952), *Copper and Brass* (1952), *Crazy October* (1958), *The Dark at the Top of the Stairs* (1959–1960), *Bye Bye Birdie* (1962), and *Watch the Birdie* (1964). She appeared on Broadway in *The Rope Dancers* (1957) and in *The Effect of Gamma Rays on Man-in-the Moon Marigolds* (1971).

Late in her career, Blondell played a number of supporting roles, including performances in *The Desk Set* (1957), *Will Success Spoil Rock Hunter* (1957), *The Cincinnati Kid* (1965), *Support Your Local Gunfighter* (1971), *Grease* (1978)—for which she won a Golden Globe nomination—and the Zeffirelli remake of the 1930 classic, *The Champ* (1979).

Blondell also added television to her list of acting credits, appearing in more than forty shows between 1951 and 1972, including "Studio One," "Playhouse 90." "Twilight Zone," "General Electric Theater," "U.S. Steel Hour," "Wagon Train," "The Lucy

Show," "Petticoat Junction," and "Bob Hope Presents the Chrysler Theater." Particularly noteworthy was her portrayal of the maternal Lottie Hatfield, a bartender in the series "Here Come the Brides" (1968–1970). This series was a "spin-off" from the film *Seven Brides for Seven Brothers*, for which she received an Emmy nomination for best supporting actress. She also played Peggy Revere, the operator of a secretarial agency, in the detective series "Banyon" (1972–1973) on NBC. Moreover, in 1972 she published a novel, *Center Door Fancy*, whose heroine Nora Marten shared life experiences with Blondell.

Her blond, blue-eyed beauty accented by two beauty marks on her cheek, earned Blondell some assignments as the leading lady, but more often she was cast in a secondary role, typically as a breezy (sometimes blowsy), wisecracking, dependable "pal" with a strong, self-reliant inner core. A consummate professional, she was given a National Board of Film Reviewers award as best supporting actress for her performance in *The Cincinnati Kid*, not only for her performance in that film but also as a long-delayed tribute to her entire career.

Starting with her long string of films in the 1930's, Blondell epitomized the new, self-reliant, independent movie heroines. In *Blondie Johnson* (1933) she capably portrayed the head of a gang of criminals. Blondell's presence added another dimension to movie roles: women no longer had to be either vapid ingenues or deadly femme fatales. It was an image that women in the last half of the century could admire and respect.

[For further information on Blondell, see clippings and scrapbooks in the Billy Rose Theatre Collection, New York Public Library for the Performing Arts at Lincoln Center; and Ted Hook, *Joan Blondell* (prepared Sept. 1965), in the above collection. Blondell is also discussed in Clive Hirschorn, *Hollywood Musicals* (1983); and James Vinson, ed., *International Dictionary of Films and Film Makers*, vol. 3, *Actors and Actresses* (1986). See also the interview with Leonard Maltin in *Film Fan Monthly*, Sept. 1969; and the interview with John Kobal in *Focus on Film*, Spring 1976. An obituary is in the *New York Times*, Dec. 26, 1979.]

ELIZABETH R. NELSON

BLOOMGARDEN, KERMIT (Dec. 15, 1904–Sept. 20, 1976), theatrical producer, was born in the Williamsburg section of Brooklyn, N.Y., the son of Russian-born Zemad Bloomgarden and Annie Groden. His father owned a matzoh factory, ran a chicken market, and was a butcher. Bloomgarden attended Commercial High School in Brooklyn before working his way through night school at New York University, from which he graduated with a degree in accounting in 1926.

Following five years of employment as a certified public accountant, Bloomgarden served as accountant to Broadway producer Arthur Beckhard in 1932, worked as general manager for producer-director Herman Shumlin for a decade from 1935, and was employed as the Group Theatre's business manager. He married Hattie Richardson (who sang under the name Linda Lee) in 1939; she died in 1942. In September 1943 he wed actress Virginia Kaye, from whom he was eventually divorced. They had two children.

Bloomgarden made his producing debut with a flop, *Heavenly Express* (1940), starring John Garfield; was manager of the Stage Door Canteen during World War II; and became a full-time producer in 1945, coproducing (an occasional practice) Arnaud d'Usseau's and James Gow's controversial play (477 performances) *Deep Are the Roots*, about a black soldier's racial problems (including intermarriage) on returning home from combat. Bloomgarden's productions often demonstrated a commitment to meaningful drama with socially provocative content, but he always insisted that good playwriting took precedence over any particular message. He honored the playwright over the director, whom he felt was too dominant in modern theater. Other powerful Bloomgarden productions of the 1940's were the 182-performance *Another Part of the Forest* (1946) by Lillian Hellman (whose earlier plays had been produced by Shumlin), about younger versions of the rapacious characters in her *The Little Foxes*; William Wister Haines's *Command Decision* (1947), a riveting war drama (408 performances); and, his greatest contribution, Arthur Miller's modern classic about the failure of the American dream, the award-winning, 742-performance *Death of a Salesman* (1949), starring Lee J. Cobb.

The decade's failures included *Woman Bites Dog* (1946) and Hellman's adaptation of Emmanuel Robles's *Montserrat* (1949). Those in the 1950's included *The Man* (1950), *The Legend of Sarah* (1950), Hellman's *The Autumn*

Garden (1951), *The Wedding Breakfast* (1954), *The Night of the Auk* (1956), *Maiden Voyage* (1957), which closed out of town, *The Gang's All Here* (1959), and Jean Anouilh's *The Fighting Cock* (1959).

Nevertheless, Bloomgarden chalked up a remarkable list of distinguished hits and near-hits; in the 1955–1956 season he contributed four major works. The skein began with a modestly successful revival of Hellman's *The Children's Hour* (1952) and continued with Miller's 197-performance, Tony-winning *The Crucible* (1953), which suggested the House Un-American Activities Committee hearings on Communism via a tale about the Salem witch-hunts; Miller's vibrant drama about Brooklyn longshoremen, *A View from the Bridge*, on a double bill with *A Memory of Two Mondays* (1955); *The Diary of Anne Frank* (1955), Frances Goodrich and Albert Hackett's moving, 717-performance, Pulitzer Prize–winning adaptation of the Holocaust victim's story; Anouilh's Joan of Arc drama, *The Lark* (1955), adapted by Hellman and starring Julie Harris (229 performances); and Bloomgarden's first musical, Frank Loesser's 676-performance *The Most Happy Fella* (1956), adapted from a 1924 Sidney Howard play and winner of the New York Drama Critics Circle Award. Also successful were *Look Homeward, Angel* (1957), Ketti Frings's version of Thomas Wolfe's autobiographical novel (564 performances) and another musical, Meredith Willson's *The Music Man* (1957), which, true to Bloomgarden's instincts for trying new things, introduced heretofore dramatic actor Robert Preston as a musical comedy star (1,375 performances). Of these theatrical landmarks, Bloomgarden considered his finest work to be *The Lark*, because of its elegantly simplified production relying on projections and lights. He often called for less heavy scenery and more imaginative means in production.

The 1960's, when Bloomgarden increasingly shared producer credit, was a decade riddled with failures, with the exceptions of Hellman's *Toys in the Attic* (1960), a 556-performance drama about the twisted relationship between two spinster sisters and their scapegrace brother (Jason Robards, Jr.); John Hersey's depiction of the Warsaw ghetto uprising, *The Wall* (1960), starring George C. Scott; and *Ilya Darling* (1967), the musical version of the film *Never on Sunday* (318 performances).

Among the decade's failures were the musical *The Gay Life* (1961); Bloomgarden's first off-Broadway production, *A Moon on a Rainbow Shawl* (1962); the musical *Nowhere to Go but Up* (1962); Hellman's *My Mother, My Father, and Me* (1963); off Broadway's *Next Time I'll Sing to You* (1963); Stephen Sondheim's musical *Anyone Can Whistle* (1964); *The Playroom* (1965); and Athol Fugard's *Hello and Goodbye* (1960), off Broadway.

During his mostly successful final decade, Bloomgarden again mixed off Broadway—which he found invigorating—with Broadway, beginning with a Japanese off-Broadway rock musical import, *The Golden Bat* (1970). He grappled with illness for several seasons (his right leg was amputated in 1971 as a result of complications from arteriosclerosis), but returned with the long-running (1,166 performances) off-Broadway Lanford Wilson comedy–drama, *The Hot L Baltimore* (1973), about the denizens of a sleazy hotel; Edward Albee's Pulitzer Prize–winning but commercially weak fantasy *Seascape* (1975); *Ionescopade* (1974), an off-Broadway dud; and the Broadway transfer of English dramatist Peter Shaffer's hugely successful (1,209 performances), Tony-winning drama, *Equus* (1974), starring Anthony Hopkins and depicting the psychiatric treatment of a boy who has maimed a group of horses.

Shy, nervous, and soft-spoken, Bloomgarden could become distractingly preoccupied. Owl-faced, and stockily built, he wore conservatively tailored suits and chain-smoked cigars and cigarettes until ordered by a doctor to stop. He liked to wear a battered hat as a good-luck charm to his openings. Bloomgarden was an avid baseball fan and, in his late sixties, enjoyed discotheques. Much honored for his taste and integrity, he received the Sam S. Shubert Foundation's Annual Gold Medal in 1956, served as president of the League of New York Theatres from 1957 to 1958, headed the Council of Living Theater the same year, and ran the American Theatre Wing in the 1940's and 1950's. Many Bloomgarden shows won major awards, and in 1958, when *Look Homeward, Angel* and *The Music Man* won, respectively, the New York Drama Critics Circle Awards for best play and best musical, he became the first producer ever to win both in the same season.

Bloomgarden supported the development of new audiences, and often arranged nominally priced tickets for students. One of his quirks was never to hold opening-night parties, so as to avoid the potential pain of hearing negative reviews. He believed that the quality of a script took precedence over its potential moneymaking possibilities; a play in which he believed personally held a 35–40 percent chance of success, while one selected merely as a gold mine had a 5 percent chance. Still, he admitted, each experience was a new one, and little could be learned from previous ones.

Raising money was always a nasty problem, and many of his biggest hits originally ran into obstacles in finding backers. Bloomgarden liked to involve a large number of backers (eighty-two on *Death of a Salesman*), both to prevent anyone from losing too much and to avoid any backer's having undue power. His producing included participation at rehearsals, where he served as the oil to lubricate the relationship between author and director. He considered producing a creative endeavor not merely a business arrangement. When he died of a brain tumor in New York City, he was in the process of producing Pavel Kohout's *Poor Murderer*.

[A major source of information is the Kermit Bloomgarden clipping file in the Billy Rose Theatre Collection at the New York Public Library for the Performing Arts. A useful article is Ward Morehouse, "Broadway's Bloomgarden: Prize Productions and Profits," *Theatre Arts*, Apr. 1958. An obituary is in the *New York Times*, Sept. 21, 1976.]

SAMUEL L. LEITER

BOLTON, FRANCES PAYNE BINGHAM (Mar. 29, 1885–Mar. 9, 1977), United States representative, was born in Cleveland, Ohio, the daughter of Charles William Bingham, a financier, and of Mary Perry Payne. Her maternal grandfather was a United States senator, and she inherited a fortune from a maternal uncle who was a founder of Standard Oil.

Like other women of her era and class, she was educated by governesses and in finishing schools, including the Hathaway-Brown School in Cleveland and the Dieudonné Burnel in Oise, France (1899–1900). In 1904 she graduated from Miss Spence's School for Girls in New York City and then studied music prior to her marriage to Chester Castle Bolton, an attorney, on Sept. 14, 1907. They had four children, one of whom died at birth.

For three decades, Bolton was a traditional wife, moving between Washington, D.C., and Ohio to support her husband's political interests. When he was appointed to the War Industries Board in 1917, she developed her lifelong interest in nursing through volunteerism during World War I. She was influential in persuading the secretary of war to establish the Army School of Nursing, and nursing education became a priority for the Payne Foundation, which she established in 1917. For the rest of her life, Bolton administered foundation grants ranging from research in parapsychology to children's literature.

Chester Bolton was elected to Congress as a Republican in 1928, during the disastrous Democratic presidential year of Al Smith's candidacy. By 1936, Franklin D. Roosevelt's New Deal had made inroads against incumbent Republicans, even in Bolton's affluent district of Cleveland Heights, and he was defeated. Frances Bolton served on the state Republican committee when they returned to Ohio, and in 1938 her husband was again elected to Congress. He died only a few months after taking office, and she was easily elected to fill his term the following February.

At age fifty-four, Bolton was the first woman in Congress from Ohio. One of her initial acts was to return to the United States Treasury the pension to which she was entitled as the widow of a congressman. The news media frequently referred to Bolton as "perhaps the richest member of Congress." Nonetheless, she devoted her career to the less-fortunate. Bolton was expected to be merely a caretaker finishing up her husband's term, but she surprised pundits by running in and winning the 1940 election by a larger margin than her husband ever had.

Though elected as an isolationist Republican, Bolton quickly developed global views after she was appointed to the House Foreign Affairs Committee in January 1941. She would go on to support the Roosevelt administration's foreign initiatives more often than those of her party. Bolton even voted against the Republicans on such domestic issues as antistrike legislation and was a prime sponsor of a 1949 bill to establish a national network of low-rent housing. In addition, she sponsored equal-pay legislation in 1953 that finally became law in 1963.

Bolton's most important wartime legislation was the 1943 Bolton bill, which provided funds to nursing students and nursing schools; one of the first federal appropriations aimed primarily at women, it was directly responsible for the training of more than 120,000 wartime nurses. Bolton also sponsored legislation to improve conditions for dietitians, therapists, and other War Department employees whose secondary status was gender-based. To check on medical delivery at the front, she paid her own way to Europe in the summer of 1944; she was in London during bombing raids and went to Paris two days after its liberation, where "in grim tents" she saw medical "miracles performed."

Bolton was conflicted by President Roosevelt's proposed draft of nurses late in the war. While her friends in the Army Nurse Corps believed that she shared their quiet opposition, Bolton, recognized by her peers as their best-informed member on nursing issues, did not join the opposition, and the bill passed. Bolton's position was complex, for it was the singling out of nurses that concerned her, not the unprecedented drafting of women. At the war's end, she proposed a genderless draft. Seemingly oblivious to conservative opinion, in 1949 she wrote an article for *American Magazine* with the blunt title "Women Should Be Drafted." At the same time, Bolton was a sponsor of the 1948 Women's Armed Services Integration Act, which regularized rank and benefits for women, and both during and after the war, she pressured officials for racial integration of the military.

In 1943, Bolton became one of six drafters of the Republican party's foreign-policy platform plank, and when the Republicans became the majority party in the House, she chaired the Foreign Affairs Subcommittee on the Near East and Africa. In 1945 she was granted an audience with the pope, and the following year, she was the first woman received by the king of Saudi Arabia. When, in 1946, the Republicans won a majority in the House, Bolton became the first woman to lead a congressional mission abroad. The following year, she chaired the Subcommittee on National and International Movements; the report of this body, *The Strategy and Tactics of World Communism* (1948), became an important diplomatic and military document.

The election of 1952 was of special significance to Bolton, for not only did Republicans retake the White House for the first time in twenty years but she also became the first congresswoman to have a child serving simultaneously in Congress. Oliver Payne Bolton, the youngest of her three sons, was elected from the Eleventh Ohio District that year; his mother represented the adjacent, Twenty-second District. Newspapers throughout the nation noted this electoral milestone. "We do not always see eye to eye," she said, "but I am happy in his independence. . . . He should make a good congressman."

Although Bolton delivered the anti-Communist line that was standard in the 1950's, she held to her moderate views during the worst of the McCarthy years. Indeed, Democratic Representative Mary Norton said that she was "never so proud of being a woman in politics" as when she witnessed Bolton on the House floor: "A member noted for his use of vilification cast a slur on the patriotism of [actor] Melvyn Douglas. Seated a few rows away was his wife, Representative Helen Gahagan Douglas of California. . . . Quietly and with great dignity, Mrs. Bolton got up from her seat on the Republican side, came across the aisle and sat down beside Helen." Nor was this merely a case of identifying with another wealthy white woman, for in the same repressive era when the National Association for the Advancement of Colored People kept its membership lists secret, Bolton was praised by the *Negro History Bulletin* for "changing the pattern" of the "droning" debate over South Africa.

Bolton supported federal aid for education when opposition to it—and the school integration it implied—was a litmus test of conservatism in the late 1950's. Called "the African Queen" by some reporters because of her deep interest in that continent, she financed several trips there, not only for herself but also for expert advisers. Bolton's interest in Africa deepened as a result of her service as the first female congressional delegate to the United Nations. Appointed by President Eisenhower and confirmed by the Senate, she and Democratic Congressman James P. Richards of South Carolina served during the Eighth General Assembly in 1953 and 1954. This was a historic time as the still-new United Nations struggled with decolonialization not only in Africa but all around the globe. A particular problem during Bolton's tenure was the independence movement in Puerto Rico that was critical of the United States.

With the death of Republican Edith Nourse Rogers in 1960, Bolton became "Dean of the Women of Congress," having served longer than any other woman; she also became the senior Republican on the Foreign Affairs Committee and was an alternate delegate to a 1961 North Atlantic Treaty Organization conference. Her longevity in Congress was partially explained by her willingness to spend her own money on a staff large enough to keep in close touch with voters; her moderate views were also key to winning fifteen consecutive elections. Another factor was her personal energy, despite routine days from 6 A.M. to 10 P.M. Bolton practiced yoga, and reporters noted that she did "not remotely appear her age."

In 1968, Bolton faced a new district when reapportionment forced her and an incumbent Democratic man to run against each other. Moreover, the nation faced unprecedented domestic tumult, especially among young people, and not surprisingly, the eighty-three-year-old Bolton finally lost an election.

Bolton had served in Congress for twenty-nine years. She had been awarded the French Legion of Honor (1956), and the United States Air Force had made her an honorary flight nurse (1968). She supported a host of mainstream organizations but also gave time and money to such less-known ones as the National Association of Colored Graduate Nurses. She was a trustee of the Tuskegee Institute and of the Museum of African-American Art, and her membership in the Society of Women Geographers reflected both her feminism and her global interests. Perhaps the most important of Bolton's philanthropies was the establishment of the Frances Payne Bolton School of Nursing at Western Reserve University with an endowment of more than $1 million in 1929. She also bought more than five hundred acres of land opposite Mount Vernon to protect it from commercialization.

Bolton enjoyed less than a decade of retirement before dying in the Cleveland suburb of Lyndhurst shortly before her ninety-second birthday.

[Western Reserve Historical Society in Cleveland holds Frances Bolton's papers. *Report on the Eighth Session of the General Assembly of the United Nations* (1954), Appendix 2, summarizes Bolton's official statements as one of two delegates from Congress. She is frequently cited in the records of the Army Nurse Corps during and immediately after World War II, as well as in the *U.S. State Department Bulletin*, especially in 1953, when she was a subcommittee chair. See also articles in *Time*, Feb. 12, 1940; *Life*, Mar. 11, 1940, and June 12, 1944; *Collier's*, Aug. 28, 1943; *American Magazine*, June 1949; *Saturday Evening Post*, Aug. 15, 1953; and *U.S. News & World Report*, Sept. 9, 1955. Bolton was also regularly featured by *Independent Woman*, the publication of the Business and Professional Women's Clubs, between 1940 and 1955. An obituary is in the *New York Times*, Mar. 10, 1977.]

DORIS WEATHERFORD

BOSWELL, CONNIE (CONNEE) (Dec. 3, 1907–Oct. 11, 1976), jazz singer, was born in Kansas City, Mo., the daughter of Alfred Clyde Boswell and Meldania Foore. During the 1880's her father had appeared in tent shows, danced, and played "stride"-style piano; her mother, although never in show business, was also very fond of music. In 1911, Connie contracted polio, and from then on she could walk only if she held onto something. In spite of her disability, she was not treated differently from her sisters Martha and Helvetia ("Vet"). Boswell was expected to do the same chores, including jobs such as raking leaves.

In 1914, Connie's father took a job as manager for Fleischmann's Yeast Company and moved the family to New Orleans, La. There Meldania Boswell enrolled all three girls in music lessons at a very young age. The sisters were classically trained by a German music teacher, Otto Fink: Martha studied piano, Connie studied cello, and Vet studied violin. The three girls attended McDonogh Elementary School in New Orleans and Francis T. Nicholls School for Girls (a commercial art school); because Connie could not walk to school, her mother bought her a tricycle. Their mother instilled a sense of unity among the three sisters through music; they remained inseparable throughout adulthood.

Boswell and her sisters grew up hearing their parents and their aunt and uncle harmonize in a barbershop quartet style of singing as well as the singing of the family's black servants. Often the young girls would go to the French Market to hear blacks singing, and they even sat outside of black churches during services. In addition, the Boswell home was filled with music played by friends such as trumpet player Louis Prima and cornetist Emmet Hardy. Connie also credited local singer Maimie Smith and recordings of operatic singer Enrico Caruso as important influences.

The sisters played and sang in the blues-jazz style then prevalent in New Orleans. Martha played "stride" piano; Connie, saxophone and piano; and Vet, the banjo. By the time the Boswell sisters were in their teens, they were interspersing jazz with classical music. (Later, during Connie's solo career, she recorded swing versions of classics such as "Amapola," a traditional Spanish song, and "Martha," a classical piece by Frederick Von Flatow.)

The sisters first recorded in 1925, on a Victor mobile unit. In 1928, although their father was reluctant to let them go, the trio left home to perform on the road. The first stop was Chicago, to audition for several vaudeville agents. The Boswells were supposed to play a classical set on violin, cello, and piano; a jazz set on banjo, piano, and sax; Vet would dance; and finally the girls would sing. They became so nervous, however, that they were unable to play their instruments and instead just sang, harmonizing as they had always done at home. From then on they were asked only to sing.

Soon afterward the Boswell Sisters trio embarked on a rigorous vaudeville tour from the Midwest to the West Coast. Connie created many of the vocal arrangements and encouraged the group's musical energy; she had a strong solo alto voice and sang the majority of the solo choruses in the trio's arrangements. The Boswell Sisters were one of the few white singing groups of the time who utilized wordless vocals (in a 1987 interview, Vet Boswell said the sisters called this "gibberish," a kind of made-up family language). The Boswell Sisters' harmonies and vocal arrangements were unlike those of most vocal groups in the early 1930's. The trio utilized cross voicings in harmony, change of musical "rhythmic feel," and changes in tempo and key within one song. Examples of their unique arrangements and vocal sound can be heard on "Crazy People," "Everybody Loves My Baby," "If It Ain't Love," and many more reissued recordings of their work.

During the trio's travel, there was no wheelchair for Connie, so her sisters found the best way to move her was with Connie sitting in their crossed arms. In California, a young hotel clerk, Harry Leedy, heard the Boswell Sisters on a radio show and recognized their unique sound and special talent. When Leedy happened to check the sisters into a San Francisco hotel, the four became friends, and he became the trio's manager. In 1930, Leedy arranged the Boswell Sisters' first coast-to-coast broadcast from Los Angeles on "California Melodies."

After this initial nationwide appearance the sisters appeared on many network radio shows. Their special sound and rhythm made them stars. The trio did fifteen-minute programs; Connie had her own fifteen-minute program on alternating nights. The sisters were regulars with Bing Crosby on "The Woodbury Hour"; they began recording for Okeh Records in 1930 and later appeared on Brunswick Records. These early recordings are still considered inventive vocal arrangements. Musicians who recorded with the Boswell Sisters included the Dorsey Brothers, Joe Venuti, Eddie Lang, Bunny Berigan, and Mannie Klein.

As a trio, the Boswell Sisters' performing career spanned the years 1931 to 1936. By 1935 each of the sisters had married. Connie married the trio's manager, Harry Leedy, on Dec. 14, 1935. The sisters appeared in several movies and film shorts. One of their best movie performances, which demonstrated their special vocal sound, was in *The Big Broadcast of 1932*, in which they sang "Crazy People." Although Martha and Vet retired from show business, Connie continued her career as a vocalist.

Connie Boswell's recordings eventually sold 75 million copies. She won a large audience on the radio shows "Camel Caravan," "Good News," and "The Ken Murray Show," and made frequent guest appearances on "The Bing Crosby Show." Frank Sinatra once said that Connie Boswell was the most widely imitated singer of all time. Among the many vocalists she influenced was jazz singer Ella Fitzgerald. Throughout the 1930's and 1940's, Boswell continued to record for Decca. She had her own television show on ABC, and appeared with Ed Sullivan, Perry Como, Steve Allen, Bob Crosby, Arthur Godfrey, and Frank Sinatra. During her solo career, Boswell changed the spelling of her name to Connee. (Some say she received a fan letter with her name spelled thus and decided to adopt it.)

When Boswell performed as a soloist, she concealed her handicap by wearing floor-length gowns that hid a stool on which she was wheeled onto the stage. She performed in movies, introducing such songs as "Stormy Weather" and "Whispers in the Dark." She appeared in *Artists and Models* (1937), *Syncopation* (1942), *Swing Parade* (1946), and *Senior Prom* (1958). She also appeared in the Broadway show *Star Time* (1944).

Boswell and entertainer Eddie Cantor were among the original founders of the March of

Dimes. From the 1960's on, her public performances were limited to benefits for hospitals and institutions for the handicapped. She also curtailed appearances because of Leedy's ill health.

Boswell's last professional appearance as a vocalist was in New York City on Sept. 19, 1975, with Benny Goodman at Shepheards in the Drake Hotel, during a Jazz at Noon jam session. Following the death of her husband in 1975, Boswell lost her vigor and energy. In early 1976, she was diagnosed with stomach cancer. She died in New York City.

Although some of Boswell's recordings demonstrate her unique jazz phrasing, they do not transmit the energy and charisma of her live performances. Irving Berlin called her "the best ballad singer in the business." Boswell was most proud of the fact that she and her sisters "revolutionized trio and group singing." Besides the trio's influence on group singing, Boswell's solo work influenced many singers, bridging the gap between blues singing and early jazz singing.

[The Boswell Collection, written and compiled by Jan Shapiro, is housed at the libraries at Howard University, Washington, D.C.; Berklee College, Boston, Mass.; and the Rutgers Institute of Jazz Studies, Newark, N.J. See also Jan Shapiro, *Filling in the Gaps in the History of Vocal Jazz, Connee Boswell and the Boswell Sisters* (1990), and "Connee Boswell and the Boswell Sisters: Pioneers in Vocal Jazz," *Jazz Educators Journal*, Spring 1990. Other articles appear in *Down Beat* (1944); *The Second Line* (1971); *Melody Maker* (Oct. 1976); and *Storyville* (1977). An obituary is in the *New York Times*, Oct. 12, 1976.]

JAN SHAPIRO

BOYD, JULIAN PARKS (Nov. 3, 1903–May 28, 1980), historian and librarian, was born in the rural town of Converse, S.C., one of three children of Robert Jay Boyd, a railroad telegrapher, and Melona Parks. After dropping out of high school during his freshman year and working as an assistant bank cashier in a small South Carolina town, Boyd graduated in 1921 from Baird's Preparatory School in Charlotte, N.C. He attended Duke University, graduating summa cum laude in 1925 and earning a master's degree in political science a year later. On Dec. 21, 1927, he married Grace Wiggins Welch of Edenton, N.C., and shortly thereafter left the Methodist church to which generations of his ancestors belonged. They had two sons, one of whom drowned at an early age in an ice-skating accident.

After college, Boyd moved north, working for a year as an instructor in American history at the University of Pennsylvania, the only college teaching position he ever held. In 1928, Boyd became editor of *The Susquehanna Company Papers* for the Wyoming Historical and Geological Society in Wilkes-Barre, Pa. During the next four years, Boyd earned his historical spurs by producing the first four volumes of this series, a meticulously edited collection of documents dealing with the much disputed efforts of an eighteenth-century Connecticut land company to settle the Susquehanna Valley, and by publishing a number of essays on the subject.

In 1932, Boyd was appointed director of the New York State Historical Association at Ticonderoga. During his two-year tenure, Boyd established a quarterly bulletin, in which he called for microfilming critically important privately owned collections of historical manuscripts before they were offered for sale at auction and for surveying college and university archives to facilitate the work of historical researchers. At the same time, his concern about improving the professional standards of the guardians of America's documentary heritage led him to become an early advocate of what later became the Society of American Archivists.

The Historical Society of Pennsylvania appointed Boyd its librarian in 1934. Under his dynamic leadership the society moved beyond its traditional role as a haven for genealogists and became as well a center for historical research. Boyd transformed the *Pennsylvania Magazine of History and Biography* into one of the leading historical journals in the country, began an extensive publications program to which he himself contributed *Indian Treaties Printed by Benjamin Franklin, 1736–1762* (1938), launched what became a useful guide to the society's holdings, and published a monograph, *Anglo-American Union: Joseph Galloway's Plans to Preserve the British Empire, 1774–1788* (1941).

In 1940 he became librarian of Princeton University. In addition to discharging the manifold duties of a university librarian, Boyd continued to produce a steady stream of articles and book reviews dealing with various subjects in early American history, as well as two short books: *The Declaration of Independence* (1943) and *The Scheide Library* (1947). In recognition of Boyd's many scholarly and administrative achievements, President Franklin D. Roosevelt, to whose political party Boyd was undyingly faithful, personally urged him twice in 1944 to become Archibald MacLeish's successor as librarian of Congress. On each occasion Boyd reluctantly declined to serve, devoting himself instead to what remains his greatest contribution to American historical scholarship: launching the definitive edition of Thomas Jefferson's papers.

Conceived of by Boyd during his tenure in 1943 as historian of the Thomas Jefferson Bicentennial Commission, *The Papers of Thomas Jefferson* (1950–) was a scholarly response to the inadequacies of existing editions of Jefferson's papers and an ideological response to the challenge of totalitarianism to liberal democratic values. Boyd persuaded the federally appointed commission that a definitive edition of Jefferson's papers would, in the context of World War II, be the most fitting way to commemorate the historical legacy of the foremost symbol of American democracy. With the approval of the commission, the sponsorship of Princeton University and Princeton University Press, and the financial assistance of Arthur Hays Sulzberger of the New York Times Company, Boyd assumed editorship in 1944 of an ambitious enterprise that was dedicated to the publication in thirteen years of fifty-two volumes that would account in one way or another for the approximately forty-five thousand surviving papers written and received by Jefferson. Boyd continued to serve concurrently as librarian of Princeton until 1952, when he resigned this position to devote himself wholly to editing the Jefferson papers.

Boyd's editorship of the Jefferson papers falls into two clearly defined phases. During the first fifteen years of the project, with the help of an efficient editorial staff and by keeping his historical commentary on the documents at a moderate length, Boyd produced fifteen volumes covering Jefferson's career through the end of his ministry to France in 1789. These volumes revolutionized the art of historical editing in the United States and earned Boyd virtually universal praise for his masterly handling of what one reviewer called "one of the greatest editorial and publishing ventures in the nation's history." It was largely on the basis of this accomplishment that Boyd served as president of the American Historical Association in 1964 and as president of the American Philosophical Society from 1973 to 1976.

During the last twenty-one years of Boyd's tenure as editor, however, production of the Jefferson papers slackened and his approach began to draw criticism. Beginning with the papers relating to Jefferson's term as secretary of state, Boyd radically increased the scale of his historical commentaries on the documents, convinced that the great struggle between Jeffersonian republicanism and Hamiltonian centralism required an unprecedented level of analysis by a historical editor. But even as Boyd broadened his editorial scope, financial constraints forced him to reduce his staff, while a series of prolonged illnesses and advancing age began to sap his once formidable energies. As a result Boyd produced only five more volumes of the Jefferson papers before his death, which led a growing number of critics to call for him to concentrate on editing the texts with a minimum of scholarly commentary. Nevertheless, the twenty volumes of the Jefferson papers Boyd published remain as monuments of historical editing, though he fell far short of his goal of completing the project (now expected to require about seventy-five volumes) in fifty-two volumes in thirteen years.

Boyd collapsed while working at home on an editorial note to the Jefferson papers, and died of a combination of cancer and cardiac failure at Princeton Medical Center.

[Boyd's papers are at Princeton University Library; the personal reminiscences of Grace W. Boyd, Lyman H. Butterfield, and Ruth W. Lester were helpful in preparing this entry. See also Lyman H. Butterfield, *Julian P. Boyd: A Bibliographical Record* (1950); James R. Wiggins, "Julian Parks Boyd," in Massachusetts Historical Society, *Proceedings* (1981); and Whitfield J. Bell, Jr., "Julian Parks Boyd," in American Philosophical Society, *Year Book* (1983). An obituary is in the *New York Times*, May 29, 1980.]

EUGENE R. SHERIDAN

BOYER, CHARLES (Aug. 28, 1899–Aug. 26, 1978), actor, was born in Figeac, Lot, France, the son of Maurice Boyer, a farm-machinery merchant, and Augustine Durand. He acted in school plays from age seven. Audience reaction to entertainments he organized while working as a hospital volunteer during World War I confirmed his desire to be an actor. From the College Champollion in Figeac, he went to Paris in

1918 to study philosophy at the Sorbonne and acting at the Conservatoire Nationale. Awaiting admission to the Conservatoire, he shared an apartment with two young actors, attended Sorbonne classes, met theater people, and auditioned for parts.

In 1920, Boyer, recommended as a quick study, replaced a sick actor in an opening-night emergency. Memorizing his lines and stage directions in twelve hours, he made his unrehearsed professional stage debut as leading man in a Conservatoire-sponsored revival of *Les Jardins de Murcie*. After Paris first-nighters had cheered his feat, the instant celebrity was gratefully admitted to the Conservatoire. Between subsequent acting engagements he worked part time as a nightclub violinist and briefly as a Surété detective until he graduated in 1922. He soon became a "draw" at Paris box offices, his salary escalating as he progressed through a series of starring parts in short-lived mediocre plays. His first leading role in a film, in *L'Esclave* (1923), established his name throughout France.

In 1923, playwright-producer Henry Bernstein offered to take Boyer under his management; Boyer declined but acted in plays Bernstein wrote for him over the next six years, during which time he became one of the highest paid actors on the French stage. Although Boyer regarded himself as a character actor, Bernstein envisioned him as a romantic leading man and created roles to fit that vision; this casting problem annoyed Boyer most of his professional life.

Boyer sought out like-minded, seriously committed professionals. He befriended literally everyone who was or soon would be important in Paris's performing arts world.

Silent films negated Boyer's greatest asset, his voice; after appearing in Alberto Cavalcanti's 1927 film *Le Capitaine Fracassé*, he rejected subsequent film offers and embarked on a stage tour of Belgium, Egypt, Syria, Turkey, and Romania. He then starred in Bernstein's *Melo*, the Paris box-office sensation of 1929, but before the end of its run, he left the play to make his first journey to Hollywood.

"Talkies" had arrived, but dubbing of "lip-synched" dialogue had not yet been conceived, so native-speaking actors were in demand to make duplicate foreign-language versions of many films. Boyer was hired to act in French versions of German, British, and Hollywood films. His friend Maurice Chevalier, starring in American movie musicals, urged him to learn English, which Boyer had resisted adding to his five European languages.

Three successive annual Hollywood trips failed to make any significant impression. In 1934 the frustrated Boyer was back again, when he met Patricia Paterson, a vivacious musical-comedy actress from England, eleven years his junior, who, like himself, was struggling for Hollywood recognition. Twenty-two days later, on Valentine's Day, they married in Yuma, Ariz.

The independent Boyer decided to free-lance rather than take a studio contract: studios dictated parts played by contract players and controlled their private lives, "even into the bedroom." His new Hollywood agent, Charles Feldman, chosen partly for his support of Boyer's decision, negotiated a $40,000 contract for seven weeks' work on the musical *Caravan* (1934), the same rate as a major star. The film was a box-office failure.

When Boyer's love scenes with Claudette Colbert in *Private Worlds* (1935) turned it into a very successful "woman's picture," Henry Bernstein's romantic vision of Boyer became Hollywood's, to Boyer's lasting chagrin. Producer Walter Wanger marketed Boyer as "the greatest screen lover since Valentino" and Boyer exploded across American screens as earlier European films were imported to exploit his Hollywood success. His Paris friends toasted their "French Ambassador in Hollywood." Boyer partnered major female stars of the 1930's and 1940's in such films as the French *Mayerling* (1936) with Danielle Darrieux, *Algiers* (1938) with Hedy Lamarr, *Love Affair* (1939) with Irene Dunne, *All This and Heaven, Too* (1940) with Bette Davis, and *Gaslight* (1944) with Ingrid Bergman. Boyer was not to be recognized as a serious actor until after World War II.

Active political liberals, Charles and Pat Boyer worked for Franklin Roosevelt's 1936 re-election campaign and for antifascist causes before Americans were fully aware of the threat. Even at the peak of his Hollywood popularity Boyer was a devoted French patriot. In France when World War II started, the forty-year-old Boyer joined the French army, serving eleven weeks as a private before Premier Daladier released him in December 1939 to do more appropriate work as a goodwill ambassador in Hollywood. But throughout the war he made acting secondary to war work. In June 1940, when the Nazis entered Paris, Boyer was in France evacuating his mother and helping friends find refuge in England. An ardent supporter of General de Gaulle, he was in London when de Gaulle arrived to lead the Free French, as de Gaulle's government-in-exile, of which Boyer was a member, was called; he recorded de Gaulle's London radio address to France and its English version for broadcast to America.

Boyer played a central role in the Free French Movement in America. He cofounded the French War Relief Committee with war refugee Henry Bernstein, then financed the French Research Foundation in Los Angeles, collecting and providing Hollywood with materials for more authentic films about France and serving as a cover for people escaping Nazi-occupied Europe. In 1942 his foundation work brought him a special Academy Award, and both Boyers became American citizens. But Boyer also kept his French citizenship.

In 1943, after years of trying, pregnancy surprised Pat Boyer; Michael Charles Boyer's early arrival on Dec. 3, 1943, surprised his elated father at the studio, where he was working on his Academy Award–nominated performance in *Gaslight*.

After the war, Boyer fought to reunite faction-torn France, pleading for reconciliation between anti-Nazi resisters and those, like Chevalier, accused of collaboration. His arguments at the first postwar Cannes Film Festival received an ovation.

Charles Boyer worked on both sides of the Atlantic throughout his career, eventually appearing in twenty-nine European and forty-seven American films. He returned to the stage in 1948, making his Broadway debut in *Red Gloves* (Jean-Paul Sartre's *Les Mains Sales*). Sartre disowned the production, claiming that textual alterations had turned his play into "vulgar melodrama with an anti-communist bias" to cash in on American Cold War prejudices. Though he agreed with Sartre's criticism, Boyer stayed in the play, receiving excellent personal reviews. In 1950 he joined Agnes Moorehead, Cedric Hardwicke, and Charles Laughton in innovative platform readings of the *Don Juan in Hell* interlude from G. B. Shaw's *Man and Superman*. The First Drama Quartet's seven hundred performances on two tours in the United States and England surprised collegiate and regional audiences, revealing Boyer's brilliant, classically trained verbal mastery, and creating an audience for "reader's theater" performances. Many considered Boyer's portrayal of Don Juan his greatest acting achievement on stage or screen. Later stage appearances would be in much lighter fare, ending with Terence Rattigan's *Man and Boy* (1964), in which Boyer also made his London stage debut and returned to the Paris stage after a twenty-year absence.

In 1952 the Boyers left Hollywood to escape the ugly aftermath of hearings by the House Un-American Activities Committee. Several suicides among his blacklisted friends caused Boyer to view the committee and Hollywood's studio heads as "murderers." In later years the Boyers returned to Beverly Hills, but only as temporary residents.

Dick Powell convinced Boyer and fellow actors David Niven and Ida Lupino to join him in forming Four Star Productions in 1952 to produce dramatic programs for television. The partners and other Hollywood stars appeared in many television dramas. Four Star eventually produced as many as five hundred programs per year under various series titles, grossing nearly $50 million annually. Boyer and Niven withdrew, considerably richer, when Four Star later went public.

Boyer's son, who had entered television as an associate producer for Four Star, had little success outside the company. On Sept. 25, 1965, Boyer was recalled to Beverly Hills from filming in Paris; his son was dead, an apparent suicide. Divesting themselves of all other residences and possessions, the grieving parents moved to a small apartment in Geneva, from which Boyer continued working for another decade.

In 1977, after medical checkups, Boyer learned he urgently needed prostate surgery and that his wife had inoperable cancer, with only months to live. Conspiring with doctors to conceal Pat's condition from her, Boyer moved her to Paradise Valley, Ariz., celebrating their forty-fifth anniversary there. She died on Aug. 24, 1978, as Boyer held her hand. He did not attend her funeral, but spent the day putting his affairs in order before taking a fatal dose of barbiturates just two days before his seventy-ninth birthday. Those who had cast Charles Boyer as a great lover had been right, after all.

[The only biography of Boyer is Larry Swindell, *Charles Boyer: The Reluctant Lover* (1983). A number of Boyer's films are available on videocassette.

The *New York Times*, Aug. 27, 1978, reported Boyer's death; other stories appeared on August 29. A delayed obituary written by drama critic Walter Kerr is in the *New York Times*, Sept. 4, 1978.]

DANIEL S. KREMPEL

BRADEN, SPRUILLE (Mar. 13, 1894–Jan. 10, 1978), miner, businessman, and diplomat, was born at Elkhorn, Mont., the only child of William Braden and Mary Kimball. His father was a mining engineer who did consulting work out of Helena, Mont., and in 1896 he worked for the Amalgamated Copper in Chile. The result was the opening of El Teniente mine and a partnership with the Guggenheim brothers and Anaconda Copper.

His father's extensive travels and desire to have his family with him delayed Braden's formal education but brought him a wide knowledge of Spanish, which he could speak fluently, with regional or national variations. These trips provided Braden with a large number of private and government contacts in Latin America that he would use throughout his career.

At age nine, Braden entered Ridley College in St. Catharines, Ontario, a High Church of England school noted for its academics and renowned for its stern discipline. After a year he left the school. He returned to the United States in 1910 and entered Betts Academy to prepare for the Yale entrance exams. One year later he passed the entrance exams, enrolled in Yale's Sheffield Scientific School, and graduated in 1914 with a Ph.B. in mining engineering.

After graduation Braden joined his father in a variety of Latin American business enterprises, including mining, export-import, rural electrification, petroleum exploration, and shipping. On Sept. 15, 1915, Braden married Maria Humeres del Solar; they had six children. During the 1920's he organized Cohoe Process (1926) and reorganized Englishtown Carpet and renamed it Monmouth Rug Mills (1925–1929). In 1933, following American recognition of the Soviet Union, Braden formed the Capital Goods Corporation, to sell excess or used railroad equipment in return for Russian manganese ore. Nothing came of this venture.

In 1920, Braden entered the diplomatic world as a delegate to the second Pan-American Financial Conference. After the Democrats returned to power in 1933, Braden was appointed a delegate to the Seventh International Conference of American States in Montevideo, Uruguay. He was appointed to a newly formed Latin the American advisory committee to the State Department and was the de facto chairman of the American delegation to the Pan American Commercial Conference in 1935 and 1936.

In 1935, Braden was chairman of the American delegation to the Chaco Peace Conference, negotiating an end to the long war between Bolivia and Paraguay. Originally this assignment was to last only six months, but it stretched to four years. Braden played a central role in establishing the peace treaty in July 1938. Following his success at the Chaco Peace Conference, Braden spent seven years as the United States ambassador to Colombia (1939–1942), the first full ambassador at that post; to Cuba (1942–1945); and to Argentina (1945). In Bogotá he assisted in resolving the Colombian debt question, negotiating new assistance loans, and removing the German involvement in the Colombian airline, SCADTA, transforming it into a new national airline, AVIANCA. This action ensured the security of the Panama Canal on the eve of World War II. During his tenure in Havana, Braden negotiated new sugar trade accords and assisted in securing American military airfields for the defense of the Caribbean.

In May 1945, Braden went to Buenos Aires to help restore relations with Argentina that had been broken during the war as a result of Argentina's support for the Axis. He clashed with Juan Perón, the emerging leader of Argentina, over fulfillment of treaties and the removal of fascist elements within Argentina. In September 1945, Braden returned to the United States to become assistant secretary of state for American republic affairs.

In his new post, Braden wrote *Consultation Among the American Republics with Respect to the Argentina Situation* (known as the Blue Book, 1946), a State Department study that condemned Perón and Argentina for supporting the Axis. The Blue Book was released on the eve of the Argentine elections, resulting in charges of Yankee intervention. It failed to prevent Perón from winning the presidency.

In 1947, Braden left the State Department over differences in hemispheric policy and moved his family to New York City. He and his wife quickly renewed friendships and carried on an active cultural and social life until she died in 1962. On May 29, 1964, Braden married Verbena Victoria Williams Hebbard. She died in 1977. Braden also returned to business and consulting work, advising companies like Anaconda, United Fruit, American Foreign Power, and Lone Star Cement on business in Latin America.

Braden stayed active in international affairs, becoming a member of the Foreign Affairs Committee of the National Association of Manufacturers, the Avenue of the Americas Association, the Americas Foundation, and the Colombia Association. He was president of a number of these organizations. Fanatically conservative in his old age, he was a member of the John Birch Society.

After leaving the State Department, Braden was honored by a number of countries for his work. Among his honors were Chile's officer of the Order of Merit of O'Higgins; Bolivia's Condor of the Andes, grand cross; as well as grand crosses from Peru, Brazil, Colombia, Paraguay, and Haiti. The American government awarded him the Medal of Freedom.

Braden remained a staunch champion of the free-enterprise system, democracy, and old-fashioned values: "I believe in complete honesty, judgment, energy, and tolerance. In the exercise of these qualities and carrying them through to a conclusion, one inevitably will arrive at the fifth condition—a belief in God."

Braden died in Los Angeles.

[Braden's papers are collected at Columbia University. His memoirs are titled *Diplomats and Demagogues* (1971). An obituary is in the *New York Times*, Jan. 11, 1978.]

JOHN C. KESLER

BRAUN, WERNHER VON (Mar. 23, 1912–June 16, 1977), rocket engineer and scientist, was born in Wirsitz, East Prussia (now part of Poland), the son of Emmy von Quisturp and Magnus Alexander Maximilian Freiherr von Braun, then the chief magistrate (*Landrat*) of the governmental district and later the minister of nutrition and agriculture in the last two governments of the Weimar Republic before the Nazi seizure of power. The second of three sons in an aristocratic and cultured family, von Braun acquired his lifelong interest in astronomy when his mother, an amateur astronomer, gave him a telescope in place of the customary gold watch when he was confirmed in the Lutheran church at age twelve. An interest in the universe soon expanded into curiosity about space travel.

Despite this background, von Braun was not a good student and was especially weak in mathematics and physics while attending the French Gymnasium in Berlin. This prompted his father to send him to a less humanistically oriented *Oberrealschule* founded by the pedagogue Hermann Lietz. At two different Lietz schools, he responded positively to the progressive teaching methods.

A more significant stimulus appears to have been von Braun's purchase in 1925 of the book *Die Rakete zu den Planeträumen* (The Rocket to Interplanetary Space) by the space pioneer Hermann Oberth. It was filled with incomprehensible formulas, which spurred him to study mathematics and physics. Upon completion of secondary school, he enrolled in the Berlin-Charlottenburg Institute of Technology, earning a bachelor of science in mechanical engineering and aircraft construction in 1932. He followed this up with a Ph.D. in physics at the University of Berlin in 1934.

Meanwhile, von Braun began to assist Oberth in testing a small, liquid-propellant rocket engine. In September 1930, after Oberth returned to a teaching position in his native Romania, von Braun continued experimental work under the auspices of the German Society for Space Travel. With the ensuing depression, this organization fell on financial hard times. In the fall of 1932, von Braun accepted a research grant from the Ordnance Department of the German army to investigate larger rocket engines for military application.

Von Braun worked with a small staff at the Kummersdorf Army Proving Grounds near Berlin, obtaining the information needed for his doctoral dissertation. Following receipt of his degree, he continued work as a rocket-development engineer at Kummersdorf. There he and his small group successfully designed two liquid-propellant rockets (designated A-2s), which they launched to an altitude of roughly 6,500 feet from Borkum, an island in the North Sea, in December 1934.

This success brought increased funding, and the experimental station grew to about eighty people by early 1937, making the constricted quarters at Kummersdorf too confining. At a site suggested by von Braun's mother, Peenemünde on the Baltic coast, the German army and air force constructed a large experimental facility. In April 1937, von Braun and most of his group moved there, with him serving as technical director of the army portion of the operation. They continued development of their A series of rockets through the A-3 and A-5 until they arrived at the A-4 long-range ballistic missile employed against London and other Allied cities in the waning days of World War II.

While the A-4 (better known as the V-2) was far from strategically decisive because of its relative lack of accuracy, it was by far the largest and in many ways the most sophisticated rocket yet developed anywhere in the world. In partnership with German industry and institutions of higher learning, the engineers and scientists at Peenemünde had overcome numerous problems in integrating pumps, valves, mixture-control orifices, ignition techniques, the guidance system, and a multitude of other intricate components into a functional system that provided a basis for future rocket development.

In the process, von Braun had apparently felt compelled to join the Nazi party and even its elite SS quasi-military component. This issue needs to be studied further, but available American records, based on those in what was then West Germany, fail to suggest any Nazi sentiments on his part. They indicate that he joined the Nazi party on May 1, 1937, and the SS on May 1, 1940, but support his assertions that he had to join in order to continue his work on rockets, which he pursued primarily in the interest of their utility to science and to future space travel. This does not exonerate him from responsibility for the actual use of the rockets or for the concentration-camp prisoners who produced them, but there appears to be no evidence that von Braun actively wanted to build weapons or exploit slave labor.

Near the end of World War II, von Braun led his employees at Peenemünde to central Germany, where they ultimately surrendered to American forces. Subsequently some 118 of them went to Fort Bliss, Tex., where he became project director of guided missile development for the United States Army and engaged in high-altitude research at nearby White Sands, N.Mex., using captured V-2 rockets. A highlight of this effort was the joint development and launch of the so-called Bumper-WAC with the Jet Propulsion Laboratory (JPL) in California. This combination of a V-2 with a WAC Corporal rocket serving as the second stage reached a record altitude of almost 250 miles on Feb. 24, 1949.

Meanwhile, von Braun had returned briefly to Germany, where he married his second cousin, Maria Louise von Quistorp, on Mar. 1, 1947; they had three children. The family resided in Huntsville, Ala., where the rocket team from Germany had been relocated in 1950. Von Braun became a naturalized American citizen on Apr. 14, 1955.

At Huntsville, von Braun held a succession of positions at the Redstone Arsenal, culminating in February 1956 with his appointment as director of the Development Operations Division of the Army Ballistic Missile Agency. Here, he and his team first developed the Redstone missile, essentially an offspring of the V-2 but featuring an improved inertial guidance system and other modifications. The first large, medium-range, guided ballistic missile in the United States military inventory, it was deployed in 1958.

While von Braun and his team improved the Redstone, they also began work on the Jupiter intermediate-range ballistic missile. They again cooperated with the JPL to produce the Jupiter C, a combination of a modified Redstone as a first stage and two clustered stages of solid-propellant rockets on top of that. On Aug. 8, 1957, a Jupiter C launched a nose cone that became the first man-made object recovered from outer space. On Jan. 31, 1958, Juno I—a four-stage Jupiter C—launched the first United States satellite, Explorer I, into orbit. Unlike the previously launched Russian Sputniks, it made the significant scientific discovery of what came to be called the Van Allen radiation belts around the earth.

On July 1, 1960, von Braun and his rocket team transferred to the recently created National Aeronautics and Space Administration (NASA), forming the nucleus of what soon became the George C. Marshall Space Flight Center in Huntsville, which von Braun directed for the next decade. Among the many achievements of this period, undoubtedly the most important was the complex, highly successful development of the massive Saturn family of launch vehicles: the Saturn I, Saturn IB, and the Saturn V. These three vehicles, each more powerful than its predecessor in the series, featured different combinations of clustered rockets using liquid oxygen and a kerosene-based fuel as propellants for the first stage. The upper stages used liquid-oxygen and liquid-hydrogen propellants.

The principal purpose of the Saturn family was to support the Apollo program. On Oct. 11, 1968, a Saturn IB placed three men in earth orbit, where they remained for almost eleven days. Then on July 16, 1969, a Saturn V launched lunar and command modules into orbit around the moon, whence the lunar module landed two astronauts on the moon and returned, fulfilling a pledge made by President John F. Kennedy on May 25, 1961.

Assigning individual credit for this achievement is impossible, but certainly von Braun deserves a significant share. He frequently stated that the time had passed when one person could make major contributions to technology, and he always gave credit to the many people who contributed to the extraordinarily complex projects involved in rocket development and space exploration. Nevertheless, his own contributions were multifarious. As a manager, von Braun could be curt, but he showed a remarkable ability to develop team spirit. This, plus the experience in rocket development that he and his fellow Germans had brought from Peenemünde, may have constituted their most important contribution to the American rocket and space programs. In addition, von Braun exhibited an extraordinary ability to grasp complex technical matters and express them in terms everyone could understand while encouraging others to participate in decision making. His capability to adapt the organizational structure to the task at hand enabled the rocket team to cope with the increasing size and complexity of the launch vehicles they managed.

Von Braun thus showed himself to possess not only the qualities of the engineer and scientist he had trained to become but also those of the manager and leader. But his role did not stop there. In numerous articles that appeared in *Collier's* magazine and *Popular Science* as well as other forums, in books, in speeches, in testimony before congressional committees, and elsewhere he perhaps did more than any other person to popularize the space effort. He also addressed numerous related issues, such as America's educational needs and the relationship between science and religion, arguing that the latter were complementary rather than in conflict.

Over six feet tall and imposing in appearance, von Braun had an enormously positive popular image, but he was not without his critics. Many of them claimed, for example, that he was excessively conservative in his engineering and that he showed favoritism to Germans. While these criticisms are valid, it should also be noted that his conservatism was rooted in long experience and a desire to ensure safety, and that he was flexible enough to change his mind in the face of persuasive arguments. As to the Germans, he did place many of them in positions of leadership in his organizations in the United States, but he did not do so entirely to the exclusion of Americans.

Besides his space-related activities, Wernher von Braun loved music and played the piano and cello. He could converse knowledgeably about many subjects in French and English as well as German. He flew airplanes, sailed, hunted, and fished all over the world, all with great zest.

In March 1970, von Braun transferred to NASA headquarters in Washington, D.C., where as deputy associate administrator for planning he had significant planning responsibilities. In May 1972 he resigned from the agency to become vice-president for engineering and development of Fairchild Industries, an aerospace company. When he died a little less than five years later in Alexandria, Va., President Jimmy Carter stated that he "was not only a skillful engineer, but also a man of bold vision; his inspirational leadership helped mobilize and maintain the effort we needed to reach the moon and beyond."

[The Manuscript Division of the Library of Congress holds many of von Braun's papers, principally covering the period 1950–1970; the NASA History Division in Washington, D.C., contains other papers plus many of his writings, speeches, interviews, newspaper clippings, and the United States Army documents relevant to his Nazi party and SS memberships; interviews with him and members of his rocket team, plus related materials, are available at the National Air and Space Museum in Washington D.C., and the Alabama Space and Rocket Center in Huntsville. His numerous writings include an article on liquid-propellant rockets in *Die Umschau*, June 4, 1932; "Prelude to Space Travel," in Cornelius Ryan, ed., *Across the Space Frontier* (1952); *Exploration of Mars*, with Willy Ley (1956); and *History of Rocketry and Space Travel*, with Frederick I. Ordway III (1966). There is as yet no scholarly biography, but Bernd Ruland, *Wernher von Braun* (1969); Erik Bergaust, *Wernher von Braun* (1976); and Ernst Stuhlinger and Frederick I. Ordway III, *Wernher von*

Braun (1994) cover his life. Obituaries are in the *Washington Post* and the *New York Times*, both June 18, 1977; a tribute appears in *Spaceflight*, Sept. 9, 1977.]

J. D. HUNLEY

BRENT, GEORGE (Mar. 15, 1904–May 26, 1979), actor, was born George Brendan Nolan in Shannonbridge, Ireland. His father, John Nolan, a newspaperman, died when Brent was seven; his mother, Mary McGuinne, died four years later, whereupon he and his sister relocated to their maternal grandparents' home in Dublin. During World War I, the two children boarded the SS *Philadelphia* and traveled to New York City to live with an aunt. There Brent successively attended the Dwight Preparatory School, the High School of Commerce, and the Rand School of Social Science. He joined a radical group in New York, the Pearson Club, where he met the Irish journalist and writer Frank Harris.

In October 1921, Brent traveled to London and soon returned to Dublin, where he was enrolled for about six months at the National University. It was there that Brent became interested in acting; he was given minor roles at the university and with the Abbey Theatre. Concurrently, he became a dispatch carrier for the Irish Irregulars, a nationalist organization that opposed the signing, on Dec. 6, 1921, of the treaty to establish the Irish Free State. After the assassination of Michael Collins, who supported the Irish Free State, on Aug. 22, 1922, Brent was forced to flee the country and finally escaped to Montreal. (It should be noted that there are many discrepancies in published sources regarding Brent's political activity and early marriages.)

Determined to become an actor, he took the stage name George Brent and engaged in a two-year tour with a Canadian stage company and next with a Bronx stock theater. His first major stage success came in 1925, when he began a twenty-two-month American tour as Abie in *Abie's Irish Rose;* he left the tour when it reached Denver to join Elitch's Gardens Theatre (1926), where he performed in seventeen productions. Next, he established and co-managed several theatrical stock companies in Rhode Island, Florida, and Massachusetts. According to his own later estimates, his performances during the 1920's and 1930's totaled more than 300 plays, which included both minor and leading roles and some Broadway appearances, in *Golden Dawn* (1927) and *Love, Honor, and Betray* (1930), among others. Brent's tall, handsome appearance, along with his memorization skills (he could learn 25 pages of script in an hour), were attractive attributes for the stage.

In 1931, Brent moved to Hollywood in search of a film career and was cast in minor parts in several of that year's films, including *Charlie Chan Carries On* and *Ex-Bad Boy*, as well as a movie serial, *The Lightning Warrior*, featuring the dog Rin-Tin-Tin. Brent also signed a contract to star in Erich von Stroheim's remake of *Blind Husbands* (1919), but the production was canceled. Low on funds and discouraged with his career (especially after a reported thirty-one unsuccessful screen tests), Brent lived for several months with his sister in New York City.

Back in Hollywood, Brent impressed actress Ruth Chatterton during a screen test for Warner Brothers and was signed to a seven-year contract. In his first films for Warner Brothers he played the leads in *The Rich Are Always with Us* (the first of four films with Chatterton) and *So Big* (both 1932); the latter was the first of five films with Barbara Stanwyck and eleven with Bette Davis. With *The Keyhole* (1933), he teamed up with Kay Francis for the first of their six films together; the most popular was *Living on Velvet* (1935). In 1933, Jack Warner included him in the cross-country train promotion of *42nd Street*, in which Brent played Ginger Rogers's romantic interest.

Greta Garbo requested Brent as the lead in *The Painted Veil* (1934). In 1936 he appeared in a popular Technicolor film, *God's Country and the Woman*, shot in Washington state by director William Keighley. During the filming of *Submarine D1* (1937) with Pat O'Brien and Wayne Morris, the three were submerged for twenty-five minutes in the tiny submarine bell, which had broken down. Coming out safely to the fresh air, Brent commented: "Realism frequently becomes synonymous with sadism." (Also in 1937, Brent became a naturalized American citizen.)

With Bette Davis he made *Jezebel* (1938), *Dark Victory* and *The Old Maid* (both 1939), and *The Great Lie* (1941); the role of Dr. Frederick Steele in *Dark Victory* is generally acclaimed as his most outstanding work. In the late 1930's, after refusing to play certain roles, filing an unsuccessful lawsuit against Warner Brothers, and being temporarily suspended, he signed a better contract, attaining a prewar weekly rate of $3,000. Radio also interested him during the 1930's, and he performed three or four times a year for Cecil B. DeMille's "Lux Radio Theatre," including the 1938 productions of *The Girl from Tenth Avenue* with Loretta Young and *The Lady Is Willing* with Kay Francis.

In September 1942, Brent became a civilian flying instructor at an Oxnard, Calif., training school as a means of demonstrating his effort to help win the war. He made only a few films during the war years and afterward signed a two-year contract with RKO, beginning with the 1945 releases *The Spiral Staircase*, Robert Siodmak's thriller in which Brent played the villain, and *Tomorrow Is Forever*. In 1949 he made the comic hit *Bride for Sale*. From 1946 to 1953, Brent starred in some twenty films.

Thereafter, he occasionally appeared on television, in dramatizations on CBS's "Schlitz Playhouse of Stars" (1953), "Mirror Theatre" (1953), and "Rawhide" (Apr. 3, 1959); NBC's "Ford Theatre" (1953), "Fireside Theatre" (1955), and "Mystery Show" (July 24, 1960); and ABC's "Crossroads" (1956). In the mid-1950's, he made one episode for the ABC television series "Wire Service." At actor George Raft's suggestion, he even made an automobile commercial, which he considered a most grueling experience. His last screen appearance was in the role of Judge Gerhard Gesell in the Frank Capra, Jr., production of Charles Colson's autobiography, *Born Again* (1978).

Although he was never nominated for an Academy Award, Brent acquired respect from the studios and from fellow actors for his solid professionalism and hard-working dependability. He was a "really good masculine foil" and an "intelligent, self-contained man thoroughly trained in the mechanics of acting," Ben Maddox wrote in 1932. He worked with some of the greatest male and female stars and the most prominent directors of Hollywood's Golden Age; the variety of his films attests to how ably Brent adapted his early theatrical experience to his cinematic career.

Until his last marriage, Brent's personal life did not reflect his romantic screen image. When he was nineteen he married a young stock actress, to whom he referred in various interviews as Helen ("Molly") Campbell or Lewis, which lasted less than a month and ended in divorce. Ruth Chatterton became Brent's second wife on Aug. 13, 1932; they traveled to Europe in 1933, only to divorce on Oct. 4, 1934. An Australian actress, Constance Worth, became his third wife on May 10, 1937; they separated on June 14 and divorced on Dec. 7, 1937. On Jan. 5, 1942, Brent married actress Ann Sheridan, with whom he had first worked in *Honeymoon for Three* (1941). They were divorced on Jan. 5, 1943. When he married model Janet Michael on Dec. 17, 1947, he at last entered into a stable, happy marriage; they had two children.

During his semiretirement in the 1950's, Brent concentrated on breeding horses at his ranch in Ventura, Calif.; after selling the ranch in 1965, he moved to Rancho Santa Fe, Calif., and engaged in racing his horses. Brent died in Solana Beach, near San Diego.

[James Robert Parish and Don E. Stanke, "George Brent," chap. 1 in T. Allan Taylor, ed., *The Debonairs* (1975), contains a detailed filmography. See also Ben Maddox, "George Brent," *Silver Screen*, May 1932; James Robert Parish, "George Brent and Kay Francis," in T. Allan Taylor, ed., *Hollywood's Great Love Teams* (1974); and James Robert Parish with Gregory W. Mank, *The Hollywood Reliables* (1980). A bibliography is in Mel Schuster, *Motion Picture Performers* (1971 and 1976). Obituaries are in the *New York Times*, May 28, 1979, and the *Times* (London), May 28, 1979.]

MADELINE SAPIENZA

BRITTON, BARBARA (Sept. 26, 1920–Jan. 17, 1980), actress, was born Barbara Brantingham in Long Beach, Calif., the only child of Adna W. Brantingham, a city employee, and Clara Ginn. Following graduation from Polytechnic High School, Britton enrolled in Long Beach Junior College as a drama major. In her second year there Britton won a place on the Long Beach float for the 1941 Rose Bowl Parade. Her photo, which appeared in numerous southern California newspapers, caught the attention of Hollywood agents. On the advice of her drama teacher, Britton invited them to see her performance in the Long Beach Junior College production *The Old Maid*. By the end of January 1941, Britton had signed a contract with Paramount Pictures, taken her grandmother's surname, and started her movie career.

Between 1941 and 1943, Britton graced more than one hundred magazine covers and appeared in ten movies. Those early films tended to minimize both her beauty and her talent. In her first film, *Secret of the Wastelands* (1941), Paramount's press release stated that "Barbara's big blue eyes were framed by large, horn-rimmed goggles, her natural blonde hair was done up under a horror of a crude, old-fashioned hat, [and] her knees were concealed from view by long dresses."

Britton received her first major role in the 1944 film *Till We Meet Again* in which she portrayed a French nun aiding an American aviator's escape from the Nazis. Director Frank Borzage insisted on casting the relatively unknown Britton, whom he had screen tested for *Stage Door Canteen* when the scheduled star, Maureen O'Hara, had to withdraw because of illness. Despite Britton's wardrobe, "consisting of a nun's robes, two decidedly unglamorous dresses, a black head shawl and an old trench coat," Paramount noted, "she managed to look like an angel." After viewing of the film's first rough cuts, Britton's billing was upgraded from a feature role to that of a costar.

While shooting *Till We Meet Again*, Britton suffered a nervous breakdown, and, upon the recommendation of a friend, began seeing Dr. Eugene J. Czukor, a specialist in psychosomatic medicine. Through therapy, Britton, a self-described pleaser who had a compulsion to be liked, learned to take control of her life, make more mature decisions, and, when necessary, say "no" to the studio and publicists. Eventually Czukor went from being Britton's doctor to being her friend, business manager, and husband. They were married on Apr. 2, 1945; they had four children, two of whom lived past infancy.

Britton played starring roles in the 1946 remake of *The Virginian* with Joel McCrea; the 1948 Western *Albuquerque* opposite Randolph Scott; *Champagne for Caesar* in 1950, with Ronald Colman, Celeste Holm, and Vincent Price; and, also in 1950, *Bandit Queen*, in which she played the title role. In 1952 she starred in the first Natural Vision three-dimension feature movie, *Bwana Devil*, with Robert Stack. In 1955 she appeared in her last film, *The Spoilers*.

Britton's first professional stage appearance occurred in the 1950 Los Angeles production of *Strange Bedfellows*. During the next two years she appeared in a number of plays produced in Los Angeles and in numerous summer stock theaters on the East Coast. In 1951 she debuted on Broadway in a revival of George Bernard Shaw's *Getting Married*. Other Broadway plays, including *Wake Up, Darling* (1956), followed. Her last Broadway performance was in the 1967 production of *Spofford*.

While performing on Broadway in 1951, Britton was cast to portray Pam North in the television series "Mr. and Mrs. North," which aired on CBS in October 1952. In January 1954 the show moved to NBC, where it remained until its cancellation in July of that year. Although this was Britton's first television series, her first appearance on television was in December 1950 on "Robert Montgomery Presents" (also called "The Lucky Strike Theatre"). Between 1950 and 1980, Britton was a guest star in thirteen television dramas, starred in two series and one series pilot, became a regular on two soap operas, and filmed three specials, the last one airing after her death. She also spent twelve years as the official commercial spokeswoman for Revlon.

During her forty-year career, Britton appeared in no fewer than thirty-five films, twenty-one television shows, and eleven stage plays. Although she never won any industry awards for her work, in 1949 she received two distinct and divergent public honors. The first came from her hometown, the city of Long Beach, when it named Britton Drive after her. The second came from Peruvian artist Alberto Varga, who proclaimed that Britton possessed "thighs that sigh," a widely reported comment that set off a furor of controversy among her fans, who felt she was above such a demeaning "honor."

Never one to succumb to the Hollywood lifestyle, Britton once described herself as "the dullest person in Hollywood." Press agents, in her opinion, hated her because she never did anything exciting. Rather than attend nightclubs or Hollywood parties, Britton preferred teaching Sunday school or delivering sermons at the North Glendale Methodist Church, recording books for the blind, and working for a variety of local and national charities. At various times she served on the boards of the Salvation Army, the Protestant Council, the National Council of Churches, and the Rare Blood Club. The YMCA and the plight of underprivileged youth also received special attention and support from Britton. In 1975 she was the honorary chairperson of the Connecticut Heart Fund Campaign.

In 1957, following a successful movie career and in the midst of a burgeoning television and stage career, Britton and her husband moved their family to New York City. Except for a few television appearances and one run on Broadway, she spent the next two decades focused on her family and her charities. She returned to television in 1979, a year before her death, when she joined the cast of the ABC soap opera "One Life to Live." Britton died in New York City.

[Newspaper clippings and studio biographies are at the Academy of Motion Picture Arts and Sciences' Margaret Herrick Library in Beverly Hills, Calif., and at the American Film Institute Louis B. Mayer Library in Los Angeles. For listings of Britton's films, see John T. Weaver, *Forty Years of Screen Credits* (1970). For information on her television appearances see James R. Parish, *The Complete Actor's TV Credits* (1989). Obituaries are in the *Los Angeles Times*, Jan. 19, 1980; and the *New York Times*, Jan. 20, 1980.]

DIANE E. COOPER

BROWN, GEORGE SCRATCHLEY (Aug. 17, 1918–Dec. 5, 1978), United States Air Force officer, was born in Montclair, N.J., the son of Thoburn Kaye Brown, a career army officer, and Frances Katherine Scratchley. Brown and a younger brother grew up on various army bases. His early exposure to military life instilled in him a deep sense of order, purpose, loyalty, and commitment, and pride in the service. In his youth he excelled in football, tennis, and horseback riding.

Brown graduated from Immaculata High School, Leavenworth, Kans., in June 1936, spent a year at the University of Missouri (1936–1937), then transferred to West Point (1937–1941). In his senior year he was appointed cadet captain and regimental adjutant, distinctions that placed him among the five top cadet officers in the corps. Brown graduated on June 11, 1941, earning a B.S. degree and a commission as a second lieutenant. He married Alice Calhoun on May 19, 1942; they had three children.

Brown selected the Air Corps as his base branch of the service. On Aug. 20, 1941, he began training, receiving his wings on Mar. 7, 1942, and completing his instruction in August. He departed for the European Theater on Sept. 1, 1942, with the 329th Bomb Squadron, 93d Group. He flew twenty-five missions from England, then transferred to the Italian front. In February 1943 he was promoted to major, and the following September, he became a lieutenant colonel. The latter promotion was due largely to his performance in one of the most celebrated raids of World War II. On Aug. 1, 1943, in his plane, *Queenie*, Brown took part in a low-altitude raid over the oil fields at Ploesti, Romania, part of a series of Allied bombings launched from Italy against the main railway traffic centers in eastern Europe, in the battle to liberate the Russian homeland. When his group commander and ten other planes were shot down, Brown assumed command. For his leadership of the raid and the safe return of the remaining members of his group, he was awarded the Distinguished Service Cross. The Ploesti raid changed the nature of Allied bombing policy. Oil fields became prime military objectives for both the British and the Americans. Also, where up to this point most air raids involved area bombing, the Ploesti raid proved the value of low-altitude, surgical bombing of strategic targets. This new method was adopted by Air Chief Marshal Sir Arthur Tedder in Operation Overlord.

Brown returned to the United States in November 1944. That December, he was promoted to colonel, only three years and two months after his graduation from West Point. After a series of assignments at various posts, on July 1, 1947, he was appointed assistant chief of staff for operations, Air Defense Command Headquarters. This assignment brought Brown to Washington, D.C., for the first time. He spent much time at the Pentagon, getting plans approved and then going to Congress for the funding. In 1949, when the Air Defense Command became the Continental Air Command, Brown was charged with developing a new air strategy, designed to meet the increasing Soviet atomic threat.

From July 1951 to April 1952, Brown served at Selfridge Air Force Base, Mich., and from May 1952 to June 1953 he was with the Fifth Air Force in Korea, where he was director of operations, planning and supervising combat missions and coordinating them with the other services and other national forces. After serving as commander of the 3,525th Pilot Training Wing at Williams Air Force Base, Ariz. (July 1953–July 1956), Brown was sent to the National War College in Washington, D.C. (August 1956–June 1957).

From July 1957 to June 1959, Brown served as executive officer to the air force chief of staff, General Thomas D. White; he next was appointed military assistant to Deputy Secretary of Defense Thomas S. Gates, Jr. (June 1959–August 1961). When Gates became secretary of defense on Aug. 1, 1959, Brown was promoted to brigadier general. Gates established the Integrated Targeting Strategic Plan, which was set up under the Strategic Air Command in Omaha, Nebr., to coordinate the strategic missile systems of the navy and air force. Brown demonstrated his ability to reconcile conflicting interests in the Pentagon when disagreements occurred between the chief of naval operations, Admiral Arleigh Burke, and the air force chief of staff, General Nathan Twining. In 1961, Gates was succeeded as defense secretary by Robert McNamara. Brown became McNamara's air force assistant and was promoted to major general. McNamara was hated by much of the military brass, and Brown became an effective buffer between the Defense Department and the Joint Chiefs of Staff.

After six years in Washington, D.C., Brown was transferred in August 1963 to McGuire Air Force Base in New Jersey, to assume command of the Eastern Transport Air Force, a component of the Military Air Transport Service, which was converting to an all-jet service. It was the largest command Brown had held up to that time. He was responsible for all air operations between the Mississippi River and the western border of India, and all airlifts to Europe, Africa, and the Middle East. From September 1964 to May 1966, Brown was at Sanchez, N.Mex.

On May 1, 1966, Brown was appointed assistant to the chairman of the Joint Chiefs of Staff, Army General Earle G. Wheeler, and promoted to lieutenant general. The Vietnam conflict was ongoing, and Brown was drawn into the tensions between military demands on the one hand and congressional-executive strictures on the other. Two incidents during this period brought the Joint Chiefs of Staff under fire.

The *Liberty* incident occurred in June 1967, when the American reconnaissance ship *Liberty* entered the war zone off the Egyptian coast and was bombed by an Israeli plane. The *Pueblo* incident involved an American intelligence ship that, on Jan. 23, 1968, was seized with its crew of eighty-three by four North Korean patrol boats. President Lyndon Johnson reacted instantly, ordering 14,787 air force and navy reservists to report to active duty. Shortly after, the *Pueblo* was returned to the United States. Questions were raised regarding the joint chiefs' responsibility for the *Pueblo*'s location at the time of its seizure.

In August 1968, Brown was promoted to four-star general and was shipped to Vietnam, to take command of the Seventh Air Force, as deputy commander of all air operations there. He remained in Vietnam until August 1970. In September 1970, Brown came to national attention when he became commander of the Air Force Systems Command Headquarters, at Andrews Air Force Base in Maryland, a position that required him to perform, among other duties, a considerable amount of public relations. He quickly proved himself a superb speaker and an excellent debater whose public addresses were often quoted, excerpted, and reprinted in the national press.

In August 1973, Brown became air force chief of staff. In October 1973, during the Yom Kippur War, Brown assigned Major General George F. Keegan the responsibility of handling the crisis. In July 1974, Brown was promoted to chairman of the joint chiefs of staff. He brought to this job a deep conviction of the need for increased defense expenditures to back up the United States policy of détente. But his tenure as chairman was marred by controversy. On Oct. 10, 1974, a year after the Yom Kippur War, Brown, answering a question from the audience after a speech at Duke University Law School, condemned the influence of Israel on Congress and the American Jewish community, which he said controlled all the banks and newspapers. There was a general uproar. President Gerald Ford personally rebuked him. Nevertheless, in spite of nationwide opposition, Ford renewed Brown's appointment as chairman of the joint chiefs for two years (1976–1978), citing his exemplary military record.

In his second term, Brown, during a congressional hearing, blasted America's four closest allies: Great Britain, the Netherlands, Iran, and Israel. This time President Ford refused to reprimand him, determining that Brown was the Pentagon's problem. The Department of Defense was silent on the subject.

Several crises occurred during Brown's terms

as chairman of the Joint Chiefs of Staff: the Cyprus civil war, which required the evacuation of all American and British civilians from the island; the capture by a Cambodian boat of the American merchant ship *Mayaguez;* and the evacuation of American citizens from Lebanon. In each one of these, Brown delegated responsibility to subordinates. In fact, when the news about the *Mayaguez* had reached the Pentagon, Brown was incommunicado, presumably fishing in the wilds of the Northwest Territory in Canada.

In June 1978, Brown completed his second term as chairman of the Joint Chiefs of Staff. In December of that year he died at Andrews Air Force Base. Besides the Distinguished Service Cross, his decorations included the Silver Star, the Legion of Merit with two oak leaf clusters, the Distinguished Flying Cross with one oak leaf cluster, the Bronze Star, and the Air Medal with three oak leaf clusters.

[Brown's papers are held at the Historical Division, Joint Staff to the JCS, at the Pentagon in Arlington, Va. His most important addresses are reprinted in *Vital Speeches of the Day*, Mar. 15, June 15, and Nov. 1, 1971; July 1 and Oct. 1, 1973; Sept. 15, 1975; and Mar. 15, 1977. Highlights of policy speeches are in *Aviation Week and Space Technology*, Sept. 6, 1971; Sept. 18, 1972; Mar. 26, 1973; Feb. 25, 1974; and Feb. 23, 1976. Interviews with Brown are in *U.S. News and World Report*, Feb. 25, 1974, and Nov. 1, 1976; and in *Aviation Week and Space Technology*, Feb. 13, 1978. Brown participated in a symposium published as *The Role of the JCS in National Policy* (1978). See also "Meaning of Shifts at the Pentagon," *U.S. News and World Report*, May 27, 1974; "What Brown Really Said," *U.S. News and World Report*, Nov. 25, 1974; "The General and the Jews," *Newsweek*, Nov. 25, 1974; "Foreign Policy: Brown's Bomb," *Time*, Nov. 25, 1974; and S. J. Ungar, "Problem at the Pentagon," *Atlantic Monthly*, Feb. 1977. Additional references are in *Howitzer* (1937–1941); *West Point Yearbook* (1941); *History of the Air Force Systems Command* (1970–1971, 1971–1972, 1972–1973); and in the records of the Air Force historian, Washington, D.C. A biography is Edgar F. Puryear, Jr., *George S. Brown, General, U.S. Air Force: "Destined for Stars"* (1983). Obituaries are in the *New York Times* and the *Washington Post*, both Dec. 6, 1978.]

SHOSHANA KLEBANOFF

BRUCE, DAVID KIRKPATRICK ESTE (Feb. 12, 1898–Dec. 5, 1977), statesman and diplomat, was born in Baltimore, Md., to William Cabell Bruce and Louise Este Fisher. His father, a member of a distinguished southern family that owned one of the largest plantations in Southside, Va., was a prominent lawyer who served as a United States senator from 1923 to 1929 and authored a Pulitzer Prize–winning biography of Benjamin Franklin. His mother was a socialite descended from one of Baltimore's most distinguished families. Bruce attended the Gilman Country School, an exclusive private school in Baltimore. He entered Princeton University in 1915, leaving in 1917 to join the United States Army, in which he served until the end of World War I. He was discharged with the rank of lieutenant. His work for the Army Courier Service during the Versailles Peace Conference and his subsequent personal travels during the 1920's enabled him to visit most of the capital cities of Europe.

Upon his return to the United States, Bruce studied law at the University of Virginia from 1919 to 1920 and then at the University of Maryland from 1920 to 1922 but did not earn a degree. Nonetheless he was admitted to the Maryland bar in 1923 and began a law practice in Baltimore. He won election as a Democrat to the Maryland House of Delegates, where he served from 1924 to 1926.

On May 29, 1926, Bruce married Ailsa Mellon, the only daughter of Treasury Secretary Andrew W. Mellon, a multimillionaire financier and philanthropist. President Calvin Coolidge, the vice-president, five Supreme Court justices, the Speaker of the House, General John Pershing, and many other high-ranking officials attended the ceremony presided over by the Episcopal bishop of Washington, D.C. After passing the Foreign Service examination in 1925, Bruce assumed his first overseas assignment as vice-consul at the United States embassy in Rome in 1926. Ailsa soon became ill and required medical attention at spas outside of Italy, however, and Bruce left the Foreign Service in 1927 to return home with his ailing wife.

Bruce then devoted his attention to Staunton Hill, the Bruce family estate at Brookneal in Charlotte County, Va. The estate had become too much for Bruce's father to handle and he had sold it during the 1920's to be used as a hunt club in which his two sons held some financial interest. With an improved financial portfolio, David Bruce purchased it as outright owner. During this period he also operated a

5,000-acre tobacco plantation and ran a parachute manufacturing company. Meanwhile, he engaged in highly remunerative legal work for such prominent firms as Bankers Trust and W. A. Harriman and Company. Bruce also assisted his father-in-law and Ailsa's brother, Paul, with the establishment of the National Gallery of Art in Washington, D.C.; the National Gallery and its contents, Andrew Mellon's renowned personal art collection, were the financier's unique "gift to the nation." Bruce was one of the National Gallery's first five general trustees and served as vice-president and then president of the board during the early years of World War II. In 1939 he won election to the Virginia House of Delegates as a Democrat and served there until 1942.

On June 28, 1940, Bruce traveled to England as chief representative in Great Britain for the American Red Cross. He made another trip to England at the end of the year. Various newspaper publications of his letters from abroad and his subsequent radio broadcasts at home in the United States reported on the fortitude of the English during the Battle of Britain and their need for assistance, and helped to build support for the United States' entry into World War II.

On July 11, 1941, President Franklin D. Roosevelt authorized William J. Donovan to head a new government agency, which became the Office of Strategic Services (the OSS), the predecessor of the Central Intelligence Agency. Donovan recruited Bruce, who began his wartime responsibilities on Oct. 10, 1941. With the rank of United States Army colonel, Bruce served as the London-based director of the OSS European Theater of Operations (ETO) from 1943 to 1945. He witnessed and participated in most of the major Allied military events of the ETO and entered liberated Paris in the company of Ernest Hemingway.

Bruce was divorced from Ailsa in 1945, and on April 23 of that year, he married Evangeline Bell, daughter of an American diplomat and fellow OSS worker. He had one daughter, Audrey, with Ailsa; and two sons and a daughter with Evangeline. Both of his daughters died tragically: Audrey and her husband, Stephen Richard Currier, were on a January 1967 chartered flight that disappeared between Puerto Rico and the Virgin Islands; Bruce's second daughter, Alexandra Bruce Michaelides, died of a gunshot wound on Nov. 9, 1975.

The postwar period launched Bruce into a succession of political appointments and diplomatic activities. As assistant secretary of commerce to W. Averell Harriman from 1947 to 1948, Bruce oversaw the Bureau of Foreign and Domestic Commerce; he then served as chief of the Economic Cooperation Administration mission to France from 1948 to 1949 and promoted the Marshall Plan there; then he was appointed United States ambassador to France, a post he held from 1949 to 1952. He next served as under secretary of state and alternate governor of the International Monetary Fund from 1952 to 1953; as governor of the International Bank for Reconstruction and Development (World Bank) and special United States observer at the Interim Committee of the European Defense Community in 1953; and as special American representative to the European High Authority for Coal and Steel from 1953 to 1954. In 1956, President Dwight Eisenhower appointed Bruce to the newly created President's Board of Consultants on Foreign Intelligence Activities. In 1957, Eisenhower appointed Bruce ambassador to the Federal Republic of Germany, where he served until 1959. In 1961, President Kennedy named Bruce ambassador to Great Britain, a post he held until 1969, thereby serving longer than any previous United States ambassador to the Court of St. James. As a consultant for the Department of State, he signed the Nuclear Non-Proliferation Treaty in London in July 1968. On July 1, 1970, President Richard Nixon used a nationwide television speech to announce Bruce's appointment as chief United States negotiator at the Vietnam peace talks in Paris. Reportedly frustrated by the attitudes of the North Vietnamese, a little more than a year later Bruce offered his resignation. However, some credit Bruce with paving the way for the secret talks between Secretary of State Henry A. Kissinger and North Vietnamese negotiators that ended the Vietnam War. Diplomatically active even in his last years, Bruce became the first chief of the United States mission to the People's Republic of China from 1973 to 1974, and then served in Brussels as ambassador to NATO from 1974 to 1976.

During his lifetime, Bruce received numerous American and foreign awards and military decorations, including the Distinguished Service Medal, the Legion of Merit, the French croix de guerre, and the Legion of Honor. President Gerald R. Ford awarded him the Medal of

Freedom on Feb. 10, 1976. He died of a heart attack in Washington, D.C.

Bruce was the first American diplomat to serve as ambassador to the three most prestigious European posts of the postwar era: France, the Federal Republic of Germany, and Great Britain. Throughout his extensive, impressive career, he won admiration and respect for his gracious personality and refined sensibilities, and particularly for his inherent capability to mitigate negotiation tensions. Such diplomatic agility was a most admirable asset for a major world power during such critical times.

[Bruce's papers are at the Virginia Historical Society in Richmond. His published writings include *Seven Pillars of the Republic* (1936); *Revolution to Reconstruction* (1939); and his World War II diaries, *OSS Against the Reich* (1991), edited by Nelson Douglas Lankford. For Bruce's diplomatic career, see the *Political Profiles* series published by Facts on File: *The Truman Years* (1978), *The Eisenhower Years* (1980), and *The Nixon/Ford Years* (1979), edited by Eleanore W. Schoenebaum; and *The Kennedy Years* (1976) and *The Johnson Years* (1976), edited by Nelson Lichtenstein. Bruce's connection with the Mellons and the establishment and first years of the National Gallery are described in Philip Kopper, *America's National Gallery of Art* (1991). An obituary is in the *New York Times*, Dec. 6, 1977.]

MADELINE SAPIENZA

BRUNO, ANGELO (1911–Mar. 21, 1980), organized crime leader, was born Angelo Annaloro in Villaba, Sicily. Raised in South Philadelphia, where his parents operated a small grocery store, Bruno was arrested in 1935 for operating an illegal still above his father's business, and in 1940 for possession of illegal gambling receipts. Apart from another gambling arrest in 1953, he remained out of jail until 1970, when he was remanded (until 1973) for refusing to answer questions put to him by the New Jersey Commission of Investigation. In 1956, because of his success in the Philadelphia rackets, Bruno was made underboss, second in command, of the crime family. By 1959, he was named boss, a rank he would hold for the next twenty-one years, during which time his criminal influence would extend into New Jersey, Delaware, Maryland, and New York.

Known as the "Docile Don" because of his reputation for seeking nonviolent, negotiated solutions to problems, Bruno survived anticrime campaigns in the 1960's and 1970's relatively unscathed. A combination of cunning and shrewdness enabled him to avoid arrest.

Bruno did not fit the image of the flashy, Capone-style gangster: he lived modestly with his wife Sue and two children and seemed more like a small-time businessman than a powerful mobster. Like other prominent underworld figures, he disapproved of narcotics but could do little to stop drug dealing among his associates. He cleverly disguised his illegitimate businesses by forming partnerships and investing indirectly through friends and relatives. In fact, he reported and paid income taxes on earnings from a vending machine business that he owned legitimately. This business in particular provided him with the expertise and knowledge to penetrate the lucrative casinos in Atlantic City, N.J.

His success in legitimate enterprises and the decision to permit other crime families opportunities in and around Atlantic City produced tensions within his organization. Bruno's talent in legitimate business may have been his undoing. He was increasingly cut off from the street crime upon which many of his subordinates depended, and their discontent mounted: a struggle for control of the family instigated by his top associates would eventually lead to Bruno's assassination.

The Bruno crime family was not an illicit enterprise as such. Rather, it was a power structure, membershp in which provided distinct advantages in carrying on illegal activities. The organization fashioned by Bruno created partnerships in various illicit enterprises, thereby spreading and minimizing risks, and making it possible to exploit capital resources and expertise. In gambling and loan-sharking operations, for example, associates of Mafia members took a percentage of the profits earned from clients they recruited. Since their income was linked to their personal initiative, there was little need for much vigilance—everyone had an incentive to do well. And because these criminal enterprises were decentralized, the threat of criminal conspiracy prosecutions was minimized. The system maximized independence, required low levels of administration, and insulated the family leadership from overt complicity in criminal activities.

Among those who participated in family enterprises, a central principle was that the businesses of members or their associates were protected from raids by other members or by outsiders. This was a distinct advantage of membership or affiliation.

The Bruno crime family was part of a national system of crime organizations. This meant that its members could call upon contacts in other cities in their legal and illegal businesses. Members, their associates, and their customers constituted a complex system of mutual obligations and exchange of favors. Members and associates of the Bruno family carried on their legal and illegal businesses within the informal framework of rules and obligations. The quasi-governmental functions of the family constituted the most important way that associations with the family had an impact on the business activities of those within its influence.

Like many important organized crime figures, Bruno was still active as he approached his seventieth birthday. His chief criminal skills lay in his ability to blur the distinctions between underworld activities and legitimate business interests. The key to his longevity as an underworld leader was his capacity to ensure earnings for his associates and to minimize the violence characteristic of criminal enterprises. Few organized crime figures before him evaded notoriety and imprisonment as he had.

Bruno was killed by a shotgun blast to his head as he sat in his car in front of his South Philadelphia home. After his death, the crime family was torn apart by warfare among its competing factions. By 1988, two family bosses who had conspired to kill Bruno were themselves killed, along with nine other Mafia members and their associates. A third boss, a protégé of Bruno's, was imprisoned for life. The strength and durability of the crime family that Bruno had carefully nurtured was severely and irreversibly damaged.

[See Howard Abadinsky, *Organized Crime*, 2d ed. (1985); Robert J. Kelly, "The Evolution of Criminal Syndicates," *Law Enforcement Intelligence Analysis Digest* (Winter 1988); U.S. Senate, Permanent Subcommittee on Investigations, *Hearings, Overview of the Philadelphia La Cosa Nostra Criminal Activity* (1988); Pennsylvania Crime Commission, *Organized Crime in Pennsylvania* (1990); and Mark Haller, *Life Under Bruno* (1991). The *New York Times* reported Bruno's death on Mar. 22, 1980.]

ROBERT J. KELLY

BUCHANAN, EDGAR (Mar. 20, 1903–Apr. 4, 1979), film and television actor and dentist, was born William Edgar Buchanan, Jr., in Humansville, Mo., the son of William Edgar Buchanan, a teacher, high school principal, and later a dentist, and Rose Kee. He spent the first years of his life in Humansville, a town of six hundred people, and attended its school. When he was seven, he moved west with his parents and four sisters to Eagle Point, Oreg., and later to Ashland. He graduated from Ashland High School in 1921.

Buchanan's father encouraged his son to be a doctor, and Edgar entered the University of Oregon at Portland in the premedical program. His grades were poor, however, and in an attempt to raise his average he took the suggestion of his sister, a fellow student, to enroll in a course in the interpretation of plays. He enjoyed the class and began to devote more time to drama than to premedical studies.

This worried Buchanan's father, who believed his son had ability as an actor but was troubled by the uncertainty of an acting career. He arranged for his son to transfer to North Pacific Dental College, also in Portland. Edgar had not given up on acting, however. He proceeded to join three theater companies and combined acting with the study of dentistry. He was so good at the former that he was awarded a two-year drama scholarship to Yale. Once again, though, he yielded to his father's wishes, declined the scholarship, and completed dental school.

In 1928, Buchanan married a classmate, Mildred Spence; they adopted a son. In 1929 the Buchanans established a practice together in Eugene, Oreg. Edgar became chief of oral surgery at Eugene Hospital in 1930 and served in that capacity until 1937. Acting was by no means forgotten, and during these years he was active in local theater and joined the University of Oregon's drama department as assistant director. He helped to establish Eugene's Very Little Theatre, and acted with the Portland Civic Theatre and Henry Duffy's Stock Company.

In the winters of the late 1930's, Buchanan took time off from dentistry to travel to Pasadena, Calif., where he acted at the noted Pasadena Playhouse. In the summers he returned north to resume his practice. Buchanan took dentistry seriously, but his heart was on stage.

In 1939, Buchanan left Eugene permanently and set up his practice in Altadena, Calif., so as to be near the Pasadena Playhouse. Its proximity to Hollywood had not been overlooked. During his time at the playhouse, Buchanan appeared in eleven plays. His first role was as a ragged soldier in Maxwell Anderson's *Valley Forge*. It was Anderson's play *Both Your Houses*, in which he played a colorful senator, that sealed his future as an actor. During this production he caught the attention of scouts from Columbia Pictures. They invited Buchanan to audition for the director Wesley Ruggles, who was filling roles for his upcoming Western *Arizona* (1940). Buchanan was cast not in the bit part he had anticipated but in the prominent role of Judge Bogardus. This assignment led to a seven-year contract with Columbia. About this time Dr. William Edgar Buchanan, Jr., became simply Edgar Buchanan.

His unique gravelly voice, subtle facial expressions, and portly build made Buchanan particularly well suited to character roles. Over the next thirty-five years he appeared in more than ninety movies and four television series. By and large, he was cast in Westerns. His characters were often on the wrong side of the law but revealed an appealing quality. Buchanan referred to them as "lovable rogues."

As his new career developed, Buchanan's dental practice dwindled. He turned his office over to his wife and in his new life felt mentally and physically healthier. He did continue to practice, however, treating patients once or twice a year, more often when there was a lull (rare though that was) in his acting. He retained his licenses in both Oregon and California.

Buchanan's favorite movie, *Texas* (1941), was one in which he played a dentist. Not surprisingly, this performance drew high praise from the critics and favorable letters from dentists. Buchanan also received complimentary reviews for another of his favorite films, *Penny Serenade* (1941). In this movie he played a linotype operator, known as Applejack, who befriends a troubled couple played by Cary Grant and Irene Dunne.

Buchanan could be relied upon to give a sound performance, although he thought that he occasionally overdramatized (and consequently valued a good director). The movies, though not always memorable, were entertaining, and some of them were extraordinary, such as *The Talk of the Town* (1943) and *Shane* (1953).

In the early 1950's, Buchanan moved into television after receiving an offer to play Red Connors, the sidekick to William Boyd's Hopalong Cassidy. He did forty episodes of this show, which was especially popular with children. A few years later he was hired as the lead in the television series "Judge Roy Bean."

The television comedy "Petticoat Junction" afforded Buchanan his longest-running role, that of Joe Carson. Uncle Joe, as he was more readily known, was the self-proclaimed manager of the Shady Rest Hotel. Too lazy to do any serious managing, he would spend his time lounging on the front porch or cooking up schemes by which to get rich quickly, then get into trouble trying to put them into effect. Off screen, Buchanan entertained other cast members with his amusing jokes and yarns.

Buchanan's last series was "Cade's County" with Glenn Ford, in which he was a deputy to Ford. The show ran for one year in 1971. By this time, Buchanan had made several hundred appearances in local theater, movies, and television. From time to time he heard people say of his acting, "Anybody could do that." Buchanan took this as a compliment because it meant to him that he had appeared natural in his roles–an objective he worked hard to achieve.

Under Buchanan's picture in his high school yearbook was the caption "With grace to win and heart to dare." Buchanan hoped that he had fulfilled this assessment. He continued his acting career into his seventies, making his last appearance in the movie *Benji* (1974). He died in Palm Desert, Calif.

[A collection of clippings, including interviews, reviews, and other articles, is in the New York Public Library for the Performing Arts at Lincoln Center. See also Richard West, *Television Westerns* (1987). Obituaries are in the *New York Times*, Apr. 5, 1979, and *Variety*, Apr. 11, 1979.]

ELIZABETH MCKAY

BURNETT, CHESTER ARTHUR ("HOWLIN' WOLF") (June 19, 1910–Jan. 10, 1976), blues musician, was born on a plantation between West Point and Aberdeen, Miss., one of six children of Gertrude and Dock Burnett, poor farm laborers. He had little formal education, leaving school early to help his family with farm work. The Delta region, characterized by harsh poverty and hard physical labor in the fields, produced a rich music now recognized worldwide as one of America's great twentieth-century cultural artifacts. Young Burnett learned traditional field chants and spirituals in his childhood, and in his teens he learned the blues music endemic to small backwoods bars ("juke joints") where black workmen relaxed on weekends. He also strongly admired the music of white country blues singer Jimmie Rodgers, whose blues yodeling stemmed from African-American blues music.

From the late 1920's into the 1930's and 1940's, Burnett was an itinerant musician; he eventually chose the name "Howlin' Wolf" from a series of nicknames that included "Foot" and "Bull Cow." He also turned from Rodgers's hillbilly yodeling, not suited to his voice, to blues shouting style: "I just stuck to the Wolf. I could do no yodelin' so I turned to Howlin'." His chosen name also alludes to a hit song of the same title sung by John ("Funny Papa") Smith in the early 1930's. Its effect was undoubtedly intensified by the physical presence of the 300-pound, luminous-skinned Burnett.

From the late 1920's, Burnett developed his style largely under the influence of, and often under direct instruction from, more established blues musicians, especially Robert Johnson, Rice Miller (one of two bluesmen called "Sonny Boy Williamson," who taught him to play harmonica), Blind Lemon Jefferson, Texas Alexander, and Charley Patton of Cleveland, Miss. According to Bertha Lee Patton, Charley Patton's wife, Burnett worked all day with Patton to master his technique. His other instrument was the guitar.

After marrying and divorcing fellow bluesman Willie Brown's sister during the 1930's, Burnett married Lillie Handley (also in the 1930's); they had four children. During World War II he served in the United States Army (1941–1945), frequently entertaining troops. After the war he moved to Twist, Ark., and Penton, Miss., where he did farm work. In 1947, however, at Lake Cummins, Miss., he formed his own band to work in juke joints. At various times his band included James Cotton, Herman ("Little Junior") Parker, and teenage pianist and part-time talent scout Ike Turner. From 1948 to 1952 he worked at radio station KWEM in West Memphis, Ark., as disc jockey, performer, and salesman; he also began recording, first with Sam Phillips of the Sun label and then with Leonard Chess of Chess Records, to whom Phillips introduced him. He continued recording with Chess for well over a decade; his first hit, "Moanin' at Midnight," was in 1951.

In 1952, in a decisive transition, Howlin' Wolf moved to Chicago to become part of the impressive blues scene there. Through the 1950's and 1960's he was one of the foremost figures in urban blues, along with singers like Muddy Waters (McKinley Morganfield) and Jimmy Reed, performing on the South Side and the West Side of Chicago and increasingly on tour. From 1961 to 1964 he toured with the American Blues Festival, playing concerts in England and Europe; he also performed at the First International Jazz Festival, in Washington, D.C. (1952). The live performances were interspersed with frequent radio performances; he also made one appearance on network television, on "Shindig" (1965), with the Rolling Stones. By this time he was a blues celebrity; his performance caused a sensation at the 1966 Folk Festival at Newport, R.I.

Burnett's urban status in the second half of his life never obscured or fundamentally changed the rural roots of his country blues style and technique. These roots largely accounted for his influence on younger rock musicians; among the English and American groups who recorded his songs or who were openly indebted to Burnett's rhythm and blues style were some of the most famous names in international rock, including the Butterfield Blues Band, Cream, the Grateful Dead, and especially the Rolling Stones. He also had a profound influence on younger blues musicians, including Johnny Shines ("Little Wolf") and B. B. King. In 1975, his album *The Back Door Wolf* won the Montreaux Festival Award.

Burnett's last public performance was at the Chicago Amphitheater, with B. B. King, in November 1975. He died in the Veterans Administration hospital in Hines, Ill., and was buried at Oakridge Cemetery in Hillside, Ill.

Burnett's songs included "Howlin' Blues," "The Killing Floor," "Smokestack Lightnin'," "Who's Been Talkin'?," "Work for Your Money," and "Worried About My Baby." His deeply traditional repertoire sustained a strong if limited following throughout his career; his return to celebrity status was stimulated by the interest of largely British rock groups, who "rediscovered" him, went to see him, and brought him to Europe. In what was not a direct financial exploitation, but was certainly cross-cultural aggrandizement, his Delta roots helped to revitalize and nourish the post-1960 transatlantic rock phenomenon, as well as to stabilize and to establish blues in American folk music.

[See Peter Guralnick, *Feel Like Going Home* (1971), and *Lost Highway* (1979); and Barry Pearson, *"Sounds So Good to Me"* (1984). An obituary is in the *New York Times*, Jan. 12, 1976.]

MARGIE BURNS

BURNS, RAYMOND JOSEPH (Mar. 25, 1886–July 7, 1977), security industry executive, was born in Columbus, Ohio, one of five children of William J. Burns and Annie Ressler. His father was a detective and Secret Service operative whose efforts to rid San Francisco of graft and political corruption in the early years of the twentieth century won national attention; he later headed the Bureau of Investigation, the predecessor of the FBI.

William Burns left the Secret Service in 1909 and with a partner, William Sheridan, founded the Burns and Sheridan Detective Agency. Within a year Sheridan sold out his interest in the company, which became the William J. Burns National Detective Agency in 1910. William Burns was president and his second son, Raymond, who had graduated from Ohio State University in 1908 with a law degree, served as secretary-treasurer and manager of the Chicago headquarters.

Burns was just twenty-four years old, and barely out of school, when he went into business with his father. There was some skepticism about his appointment to the Chicago office. "Word got around that bank robbers would have a field day," Raymond Burns later recalled. But the younger Burns was no stranger to the detective business. He grew up hearing stories of his father's adventures as a Secret Service agent and had assisted in the San Francisco graft case. The robbery of the First National Bank of Chatsworth, Ill., gave Burns the opportunity to prove his ability as a detective. He solved the case in three weeks.

A few months later, in October 1910, the fledgling agency began an investigation of the bombing of the *Los Angles Times* building. This act of terrorism, which resulted in twenty-one deaths, was widely believed to be a union plot. Father and son hesitated before taking the case; they did not want to plunge the company into the morass of labor disputes. But in the final analysis, they accepted the assignment, and it brought the agency national recognition.

Burns doggedly pursued leads in the Midwest until he apprehended two key figures associated with the *Times* bombing. The confessions of these men tied the bombing to the National Association of Structural Iron and Bridge Workers, confirming that the crime was part of a bitter labor dispute. On Apr. 9, 1907, Burns married Gladys Sykes; they had one child.

Burns effectively took over leadership of the company when his father died in 1932. He served as president of the Burns National Detective Agency from 1949 until 1955, when he became chairman of the board. In 1964 he rose to the position of executive committee chairman, which he held until 1970 when his brother, W. Sherman Burns, succeeded him. Raymond Burns, at age eighty-four, then became director of the agency. In the 1930's, Burns wrote a series of newspaper articles analyzing major crimes such as the Lindbergh kidnapping and the death of Dutch Schultz.

Although prevention of crime was the major business of the Burns Detective Agency, it found itself from time to time accused of a crime. The most serious accusations revolved around labor disputes. Although William J. Burns attempted to keep the company out of conflicts between companies and unions, the agency did get involved in labor disputes under the leadership of Raymond and W. Sherman Burns. In 1936, the company was accused of hiring men to infiltrate the workplace and inform corporate leaders about union activities and membership. The agency was also accused of supplying strikebreakers and hiring guards who were convicted criminals.

Even though Raymond Burns emphatically denied such accusations, the agency gained a reputation for this activity. In 1938, the regular guards who policed the stadium of the New York Giants in Manhattan picketed on opening day. They complained that the National Exhibition Company, owners of the Giants, had contracted the Burns Detective Agency to supply the special police. The regular guards, as union members, refused to join the Burns Agency "because of its strike-breaking activities."

The dispute was quelled, but in 1939 the Workers Defense League protested the Burns Agency request to renew its state license on the grounds that the agency was involved in industrial spying and strikebreaking. The agency's license was renewed, and once again Burns steered his company back to smooth waters.

With an eye toward the future, Burns established an electronics division in 1956, and the agency became a leader in electronic surveillance techniques. By 1959, the Burns Detective Agency was one of the largest organizations furnishing protective services to industrial and commercial clients. In fact, 95 percent of the agency's $29 million revenue in 1960 derived from supplying uniformed guards to industrial and commercial clients.

Raymond Burns was a capable administrator. Before his death in 1977, he saw the agency founded by his father grow to thirty-six thousand employees working out of several regional offices. It guarded everything from golf tournaments to the Nevada Nuclear Test Site. He presided over the company as executive committee chairman when it grew to be an international concern and changed its name to the William J. Burns International Detective Agency, Inc.

[See Gene Caesar, *Incredible Detective* (1968). Relevant articles in the *New York Times* appear Apr. 11 and 17, 1936; Mar. 9 and 10, 1937; Apr. 20, 1938; Apr. 14, 1939; Aug. 23, 1961; Jan. 18, 1966; and Oct. 28, 1972. An obituary is in the *New York Times*, July 8, 1977.]

LYNNE E. OHMAN

BURPEE, DAVID (Apr. 5, 1893–June 24, 1980), developer of seeds, was born in Philadelphia, one of three children of Washington Atlee Burpee, a seed merchant, and Blanche Simons. His father had built a successful mail-order business, W. Atlee Burpee and Company, from a small seed shop opened in Philadelphia in 1876. In 1888, W. Atlee Burpee bought the 500-acre Fordhook Farm near Doylestown in Bucks County, making it the family residence and the experimental growing center for the seed company. Burpee went to Europe annually and brought back seeds from Germany, Italy, France, Belgium, Hungary, and the Netherlands, in order to develop seeds for immigrants who wanted vegetables from the old country. At the age of eight, David Burpee began accompanying his father to Europe to look for new seeds. At the age of ten, David picked sage seeds on his father's farm for five cents per hour. He also worked as a roguer, picking out imperfect plants.

David Burpee loved gardening but also viewed it as a challenge. When he was fourteen years old, his father offered him $1,000 if he could develop a yellow sweet pea. David went to Washington, D.C., and obtained numerous species of the flower from the Bureau of Seed and Plant Introduction. He grew more than forty varieties of sweet peas on the family farm but failed in his effort to develop a yellow sweet pea.

Burpee, who said that he had a "very poor formal education," attended Culver Military Academy in Indiana and Cornell University, but he dropped out after his first term when his father became seriously ill. W. Atlee Burpee died in 1915 and the twenty-two-year-old David succeeded him as chief executive officer of what had become the world's largest mail-order seed business. His brother W. Atlee Burpee, Jr., became vice-president and treasurer of the firm. "Fortunately, I had a great deal of experience in the horticultural end of the business," David Burpee recalled in 1976. "But then business management was entirely new to me."

A crisis struck shortly afterward that threatened the future of the Burpee company. "The sweet pea had been the most popular flower grown from seed for many years. Then just about the time of my father's death, the sweet pea developed a fungus root rot. That disease gradually spread all over the United States where summers were hot. So the demand for sweet peas fell off increasingly year after year."

After months of testing, Burpee concluded in the summer of 1919 that the marigold should be developed as the flower of the future. "It had plenty of faults," Burpee later recalled, noting that the flower was "late blooming, scrawny, [had] limited color range, and it had an odor in the foliage that some people didn't like. But underneath I saw a garden Cinderella." He spent decades developing the marigold and got rid of its turpentine smell when a missionary sent him an ounce of Tibetan marigold seeds that had no odor. Though the plants had no smell, the Tibetan marigolds had puny blossoms and only one good bloom, which was a mutation. Burpee and his employees sniffed more than half a million growing marigolds looking for other mutations. An employee found an entire row of odorless plants. Through hybridization, Burpee created some of the more colorful marigolds in the world. From 1920 until 1954, Burpee sought to develop a white marigold that would grow two and a half inches or more across. In 1954, he offered a $10,000 prize to the first gardener who could develop a pure white marigold, a challenge that met with success: he presented a check to Alice Vonk of

Sully, Iowa, in 1976. Burpee launched a campaign in 1959 to make the marigold the national flower and gained the support of Senator Everett M. Dirksen of Illinois. Calling the marigold "the flower of all the people," Burpee registered as a lobbyist and brought truckloads of marigolds to Capitol Hill, giving bouquets and packets of seeds to legislators. Though Burpee won supporters, he failed to build a political consensus for the marigold.

Tall and angular with a folksy demeanor, David Burpee was a Norman Rockwell character sprung to life. Working in his gardens, he wore three-piece suits. He had prominent, expressive, bushy eyebrows and wore wire-framed glasses. During his fifty-five years as the head of the Burpee Company, he wrote a "dear fellow gardeners" letter to millions of customers. About 4 million catalogs were mailed to gardeners every winter. About 21 million packages of seeds were sold annually from mail-order centers in Warminster, Pa., Clinton, Iowa, and Riverside, Calif. Millions more were sold through stores on Burpee racks. Bulk-seed vegetable sales were made to farmers and commercial growers and bulk flower sales were made to nurseries and florists.

Like his father, David Burpee was an innovator. W. Atlee Burpee had introduced iceberg lettuce in 1894, bush lima beans in 1907, and had also developed Golden Bantam sweet corn and Golden self-blanching celery. David Burpee's own first major success was in 1934 when he developed an all-color double nasturtium. Until the late 1930's, Burpee used selection to improve plant varieties. But he became a pioneer in hybridizing, crossing two strains of the same or different species to create a new flower or vegetable. Burpee demonstrated that hybrids are stronger growing, more disease resistant, and more attractive than their parents.

Among the Burpee hybrids that followed years of crossing were these innovations: Burpee's red and gold hybrid marigold, which in 1939 became the first hybrid flower to be sold commercially; Supreme and Topper hybrid snapdragons; Zenith hybrid zinnias; and Burpee hybrid cucumbers, tomatoes, and cantaloupes. Burpee's geneticists used X rays to alter the genes of seeds and also made extensive use of the drug colchicine, which doubles the chromosome number in plants and changes its characteristics. Colchicine produces stronger stems, darker foliage, and richer colors. Among the flowers developed with the drug were giant marigolds and snapdragons. A common wildflower, the black-eyed Susan, was transformed into spectacular Gloriosa daisies with the help of colchicine. Burpee said that his customers wanted "what is easy to grow and spectacular to look at."

Burpee was a tireless promoter. He hosted annual press luncheons at Fordhook Farm, where garden writers could preview his new flowers and vegetables. Before mailing out his catalogs, Burpee would invite garden club members, horticulturists, and the news media to the Waldorf-Astoria Hotel in New York City for an exhibition of his new seed offerings. He named a new flower every year for a prominent American such as Mrs. Douglas MacArthur, Senator Everett Dirksen, Mrs. Dwight D. Eisenhower, Pearl Buck, Kate Smith, and Helen Hayes. His customers included the Duke of Windsor, Madame Chiang Kai-shek, and General George C. Marshall. Burpee corresponded regularly with mail-order customers and guaranteed refunds if they were less than satisfied with their flowers or vegetables.

Burpee met his wife, Lois Torrance, a horticulturist, in 1936 at a flower show in Baltimore. They were married on July 18, 1938, and had two children. Their son Jonathan later headed Burpee's customer service department. The Burpee family lived in a 300-year-old farmhouse on Fordhook Farm. In 1970, Burpee sold his business to the General Foods Corporation, remaining as a consultant. In 1979, the Burpee Company was purchased by the International Telephone and Telegraph Corporation. Burpee died at Doylestown (Pa.) Hospital in 1980. Six years later, the Burpee Company was sold by ITT to the Recreation Company, a New York investment group. It was acquired in 1991 by George J. Ball, Inc., a Chicago-based seed company.

David Burpee took positive joy in his work. He often said: "If you want to be happy for an hour, get drunk. If you want to be happy for a weekend, get married. If you want to be happy for a whole week, kill your pig and eat it. But if you want to be happy all your life, become a gardener."

Burpee's place in the history of American gardening was summed up in 1976 by Ruth Snyder, who was then editor of *Flower and Garden* magazine: "David Burpee is a direct link with the history of American gardening. He's been there almost from the beginning. Although some universities have turned out giants of horticulture, their work doesn't always boil down to the people. Burpee brought his innovations to the people and made it all available for a quarter a packet."

[Burpee talked about his life and career in "David W. Burpee: Gardener of the People," in *Philadelphia Inquirer* magazine, May 23, 1976; and in "The Gardener's Gardener," *Time*, June 6, 1960. See also Anne Raver, "Where Burpee First Tilled," *New York Times*, Aug. 23, 1992, for a useful history of the Burpee seed company. Obituaries are in the *Philadelphia Inquirer*, June 25, 1980; and the *New York Times*, June 26, 1980.]

STEVE NEAL

BUTTRICK, GEORGE ARTHUR (Mar. 23, 1892–Jan. 23, 1980), Protestant minister, lecturer, and writer, was born in Seaham Harbour, Northumberland, England, the son of Tom Buttrick, an itinerant minister, and Jessie Lambert of Aberdeen, Scotland, a shop clerk at the time of her marriage. Buttrick attended Lancaster Theological College in Manchester and Victoria University, graduating in 1915 with a degree in philosophy. That same year he visited the United States and stayed to be ordained as a minister in the Congregational Church. He became pastor of the First Union Congregational Church of Quincy, Ill. On June 27, 1916, Buttrick married Agnes Gardner; they had three children. Buttrick became a naturalized citizen of the United States in 1923.

Following his pastorage in Quincy, Buttrick served churches in Rutland, Vt., and Buffalo, N.Y. In 1927 he became pastor of the Madison Avenue Presbyterian Church in New York City. In that pulpit from 1927 to 1954, he became known as a spokesman for many causes, which he advocated with conviction regardless of their public popularity. He was outspoken in his opposition to the fundamentalist theology so prevalent in the 1920's by insisting that "literal infallibility of Scripture is a fortress impossible to defend." As president of the Federal Council of Churches from 1939 to 1941, Buttrick visited Franklin Roosevelt at the White House to encourage the president in his attempts to restore peace after the German invasion of Poland. A pacifist, Buttrick strongly opposed American involvement in World War II. His opposition to the war was not political but was that of a consistent pacifist. After the war, Buttrick pointed out that Communist successes in China were largely attributable to the failures of Chiang Kai-shek and also stated that the arms race with the Soviet Union was a formula for mutual disaster.

In 1955, Buttrick became Preacher to the University at Harvard and Plummer Professor of Christian Morals in the Divinity School. After retirement from Harvard in 1960, Buttrick continued his career of teaching, writing, lecturing, and preaching at a number of other universities and seminaries.

Buttrick is perhaps best remembered as a scholar and an author, but he also had a profound influence on the thousands who heard him preach. Although he was associated with major universities and seminaries for much of his life, Buttrick was always a preacher first and foremost. His sermon content never took on the tone of abstract academic research but always dealt with the vital questions of applying the Christian faith to daily life. Listeners were impressed with his warmth and humility. His sermons were described as having "gravity without mordancy, devotion without applied solemnity." Throughout his lengthy public career Buttrick was known as a thoughtful, clear, and edifying preacher.

A prolific writer, Buttrick wrote and published steadily from the beginning of his tenure at the Madison Avenue Church until almost the time of his death. His books are marked by erudition and a canny observation of daily life. His pragmatic application of Christian ideals makes all his books, even those from the 1920's and 1930's, readable today. Buttrick assumed the good sense of his readers without patronizing them and employed a wide-ranging set of illustrations that evidenced sound common sense. One reviewer noted that he was "closer in mood and manner to the Fables of Aesop, the Canterbury tales of Chaucer, or the stories of Abraham Lincoln than to the careful allegories of the *Rabbais* or the elaborations of the Schoolmen."

Buttrick's most lasting contributions to theological scholarship are the twelve-volume commentary *The Interpreter's Bible* (1951) and the four-volume companion *The Interpreter's Dictionary of the Bible* (1962), both of which he edited. Although these works were compiled by nearly three hundred scholars from fifteen nations, the Buttrick stamp on them is clear. The commentary uses two sections to interpret the biblical text: one section is scholarly technical comment, and the other is astute application of biblical principles to everyday life, larded with allusions to and quotes from a wide range of sources in music and literature. Buttrick died in Louisville, Ky., and was buried in Charlevoix, Mich.

[Among the most influential of Buttrick's works are *So We Believe, So We Pray* (1951); *The Beatitudes* (1968); and *The Power of Prayer Today* (1968). A volume of sermons in Buttrick's honor, *To God Be the Glory*, was published in 1972. An obituary is in the *New York Times*, Jan. 24, 1980.]

MICHAEL R. BRADLEY

C

CABOT, CHARLES SEBASTIAN THOMAS (July 6, 1918–Aug. 23, 1977), actor, was born in London, England, the son of Oscar Charles Cabot and Sophie Augustine Nubertine Brimbois. Both his parents were Belgian, his mother a refugee from World War I and his father a banker who was ruined during the Great Depression.

His father's financial failure forced Cabot to leave school at the age of fourteen to work as a garage helper. Cabot subsequently held a series of odd jobs, including that of a cook, an occupation to which he later attributed his famous rotund figure. His weight fluctuated throughout his adult life, but generally remained between 260 and 300 pounds, a considerable bulk for his five foot, nine inch frame.

"Sabby," as his friends called him, also worked as a chauffeur for the British actor Frank Pentingell. While working for Pentingell, with neither training nor experience, Cabot successfully launched his professional acting career by talking a series of repertory theaters into hiring him on the basis of a fake résumé of respectable credits. The managers of the various theaters that hired Cabot eventually discovered his chicanery, but before they did, he managed to obtain valuable acting experience. By the mid-1930's he was landing bit parts in feature films. In the late 1930's, Cabot performed as a wrestler under the moniker of "Pierre Savage." His wrestling career only lasted about three years, however, because of a hernia he suffered while performing.

Cabot worked as a "voice" actor for the British Broadcasting Corporation in the early 1940's, appearing on more than five hundred radio programs, according to his own estimate. One of the best-known programs was "Dick Barton Strikes Back," in which he played several roles as heavies. Cabot also did love scenes on radio, a feat that his physical appearance kept him from duplicating in films and on television. His radio career was briefly interrupted toward the end of World War II when he went abroad to entertain Allied troops.

In 1945, Cabot made his London stage debut in *A Bell for Adano*. During his early stage career he was dubbed "The Great Faffler" by actor Charles Laughton, a reference to Cabot's tendency to employ stalling gestures, such as scratching his behind, while he struggled to remember his lines.

In 1947, Cabot came to the United States and appeared in John Gielgud's production of *Love for Love* on Broadway. A role in 1950 as a drunk had him growing a beard, which he continued to wear from then on and for which he became as well known as for his corpulence. Cabot also appeared in more than fifty movies, including *Romeo and Juliet* (1954), *Kismet* (1955), and *The Time Machine* (1960). Cabot often played the villain, as he did in *Othello* (1946) as Iago. Cabot never had a lead role in a feature film but generally received good notices for his work as a character actor.

By the middle of the 1950's, Cabot was appearing frequently on television. His first major role was in the 1956 British series "The Three Musketeers," in which he played the character Porthos. From 1960 to 1962 he appeared in "Checkmate," a series about a San Francisco detective firm dedicated to preventing crime before it happened. Cabot played the firm's criminologist, Carl Hyatt, an urbane Bostonian, and it was in this series that Cabot began to develop a persona as a cultured gentleman. He is best remembered for his role as Giles French, the genteel butler and male nanny on the CBS series "Family Affair," which aired from 1966 until 1971. Although critics generally praised the show, commending Cabot's performance in particular, on several occasions Cabot expressed ambivalence about the character he played. After the series was canceled, he announced that he was looking forward to playing the heavy again.

During the 1972–1973 television season Cabot appeared as a host for NBC's "Ghost Story," a series of stories about the occult, psychic phenomena, and mystery. Cabot played the role of Winston Essex, the owner of an apartment hotel that was featured as the show's locale. The show, which aired for less than a year, was the last series in which Cabot regularly appeared.

Cabot's career in television extended to doing commercials for such products as wine and refrigerators; he also appeared as a regular panelist on the quiz show "Stump the Stars" during the summers of 1964 and 1965. Toward the end of his life, Cabot appeared in several television movies, including *The Spy Killer* and *Miracle on 34th Street*. In the late 1960's and early 1970's, Cabot did several tours with USO shows in Southeast Asia, entertaining the troops.

Cabot embodied a curious combination of the popular and the elite. Although the genteel persona that Cabot developed on "Checkmate" and "Family Affair" might suggest otherwise, he was far from being a highbrow snob. Cabot welcomed television roles, much preferring them to the stage, which he abandoned completely after he began acquiring regular television work; he claimed that doing the same performance every night was a bore. He also spent much of the spring and fall months of his later years touring college campuses and literary societies where he read his favorite poems, scenes from plays, and passages from books.

Cabot married in 1940. He and his wife Kathleen had three children. Although Cabot moved his family to the United States in 1955, he never became an American citizen, explaining that he never felt the need to because, in his view, the English and Americans were so much alike. His primary residence in the United States was in Los Angeles. He also kept a summer home on Vancouver Island, British Columbia, where he died of a stroke.

[See Bob Johnson, "He Uses His Beard and Bulk Shamelessly," *TV Guide*, Apr. 20, 1960; Carolyn Gaiser, "Sitting Pretty—in a Fragile Chair," *New York Times*, Nov. 27, 1966; and Roberta Brandes Gratz, "Sebastian Cabot: The Butler Did It," *New York Post*, Dec. 10, 1966. An obituary is in the *New York Times*, Aug. 24, 1977.]

JOHN GILLOOLY

CAIN, HARRY PULLIAM (Jan. 10, 1906–Mar. 3, 1979), United States senator, was born in Nashville, Tenn., one of two children of George William Cain, a lumber businessman, and Grace Pulliam. The family moved to Tacoma, Wash., in 1911 where George Cain became publisher of the journal *West Coast Lumberman*. Cain's mother died when he was eleven and the loss affected him deeply. Before attending college he was a reporter for the *Portland Telegram*. He graduated with a B.A. in 1929 from the University of the South in Sewanee, Tenn., with a major in classical literature and languages.

He returned to Tacoma to work for the Bank of California in the trust department and later established the bank's business department. He married Marjorie Dils of Seattle in 1934. The couple had two children. In 1939 he resigned from the bank and entered the Tacoma mayoralty race. After placing third in the Republican primary he decided to drop out. Four days before the election, however, one of the two leading candidates died. Cain reentered the race and won and was reelected in 1942. As mayor, Cain earned praise for his efforts to improve health and moral conditions. Tacoma became the first northwestern city to close its houses of prostitution. Cain also cracked down on gambling. Following the outbreak of World War II, Cain was one of the few public officials to go on record as opposing the internment of Japanese-Americans.

In May 1943, Cain took a leave of absence and accepted a commission as a major in the army's Military Government Corps. In August he went overseas to North Africa and later saw service in Italy. Called from the field in October, Cain headed the civil administration and public relations departments of the Allied Control Commission in Naples. In March 1944 he was transferred to a public relations position in Supreme Headquarters, Allied Expeditionary Forces, under the command of General Dwight D. Eisenhower. Following his promotion to lieutenant colonel in August 1944, Cain returned to combat duty with the Eighteenth Corps. That same year he ran in absentia for the United States Senate but lost to Warren Magnuson. During the Battle of the Bulge in the winter of 1944–1945 he was promoted to full colonel.

Cain returned to Tacoma a highly decorated veteran to finish his term as mayor, which expired in June 1946. Rather than seek reelection, Cain ran as a Republican for the Senate seat occupied by Democrat Hugh B. Mitchell. Using the slogan "Raising Cain," he campaigned against the federal government's food and housing programs and won the election. Mitchell resigned before his term ended and Governor Mon Wallgren appointed Cain to fill Mitchell's term. *U.S. News* predicted that year that the young senator would be part of the liberal pro-labor Republican bloc. The first area Cain worked on was housing. He proposed a 15 percent rent increase for tenants in federal housing and encountered stiff opposition when he proposed a bill to dispose of wartime housing by making it available to veterans at low cost. The idea met with opposition in Seattle and Spokane, where it was feared low-priority families already living in the units would be dispossessed, but was favored by the real estate industry. He later failed to halt the extension of rent controls despite a twelve hour and eight minute filibuster. Although Cain said he never resented being known as the "number one real estate lobbyist in the country," he tempered his support, perhaps out of fear that it would hurt his reelection chances.

In foreign and military affairs, he supported the withdrawal of Allied forces from Germany and an end to the denazification program. Cain was also one of only two senators to vote against expanding the United States Air Force to seventy groups. In 1947 he reluctantly voted for American aid to Greece and Turkey, even though he believed it set a poor precedent. During the Korean War, Cain supported General Douglas MacArthur's plan to cross the Yalu River into China. Cain simultaneously introduced a resolution for Congress to declare war on China and another for the withdrawal of all American forces. Cain explained: "There is not now, nor will there ever be, any middle ground." MacArthur's plan was not put into effect and the resolutions were never passed.

On domestic matters, Cain supported the Taft-Hartley Act of 1947, which imposed various restrictions on labor unions, despite the endorsements he earlier received from labor. In 1949, Cain made national headlines with a filibuster against President Harry S. Truman's nomination of Mon Wallgren as chairman of the National Security Resources Board. Cain did not think his fellow Washingtonian was qualified and said he was "soft on communism." On March 8 he filibustered for six and three-quarter hours against the nomination. The Armed Services Committee later tabled the nomination. Shortly before the filibuster Cain called an unusual press conference to announce his divorce but by summer the papers had been withdrawn.

In 1950, with two more years remaining in his term, Cain proposed resigning to go head-to-head with Senator Magnuson in the 1950 election. If he won, Cain reasoned, Republican Governor Arthur Langlie could appoint another Republican to the vacant seat. Cain decided not to go through with the plan. That same year *Time* magazine described Cain as one of the Senate's "most expendable members." Cain attacked the writer of the story on the floor of the Senate calling him "smug, arrogant, self-centered, vain, and frustrated." The *Chicago Tribune*, however, included Cain on a list of senators "every patriot should vote for." During the presidential campaign of 1952 Cain's name came up as a possible replacement for Richard Nixon as Eisenhower's running mate. That same year Cain ran for reelection with the slogan "Retain Cain." His opponent, Representative Henry M. Jackson, called Cain the "talkingest man in the state." Cain's votes on labor issues and his opposition to public electrical power cooperatives had alienated many Washingtonians and he lost the election.

In 1953, President Eisenhower appointed Cain to a three-year term on the Subversive Activities Control Board because the former senator had earned a reputation as a supporter of Senator Joseph McCarthy. In 1955, however, Cain delivered a speech sharply criticizing the administration's personnel security program, which was designed to rid the federal payroll of Communists. In another speech he called for the liquidation of the attorney general's list of subversive organizations. In both cases Cain said he wanted to "better protect individuals from unintended oppression." His shift in position openly angered administration officials. Cain subsequently broke with McCarthy over the Communist hunter's disrespect for civil rights and the use of smear tactics. Cain's shift in position came about after learning of the detrimental effects Communist-hunting tactics were having on the lives of ordinary people caught in webs of allegations. After leaving the board in 1956, Cain briefly taught at Yale University before moving to Florida, where he hosted a thirty-minute talk show, became associated with a real estate firm, and later joined Miami's First Federal Savings and Loan. In 1958 he divorced Marjorie and married La Vonne Bonnie Strachan Kneisly.

In 1963, Cain indicated he was interested in running for the Senate from Florida but did not do so. In a partisan shift, Cain headed Democrat Lyndon Johnson's presidential campaign in Florida in 1964 and later chaired Dade County's War on Poverty program. In 1972 he was elected to the Dade County Commission after serving a two-year appointment to fill a vacancy on the commission. He sponsored a resolution declaring the county bilingual, and, as a former smoker, led the campaign to ban smoking in public buildings. He served on the commission until 1976, when he was defeated in the primaries. Cain remained active in a variety of civic activities, and in his later years he worked to secure equal rights for homosexuals in Dade County. Cain died at Miami Lakes, Fla.

[Cain's papers are at the Washington State Historical Society in Tacoma. See also James Stevens, "Harry Cain: Freshman U.S. Senator from Tall Timber of Washington," *Sunday Oregonian*, Mar. 16, 1947; James C. Derieux, " 'Hurry' Cain Out of the West," *Collier's*, Aug. 13, 1949; Douglas Cater, "Senator Cain, Washington Hamlet," the *Reporter*, Sept. 2, 1952; L. Edgar Prina, "The Harry Cain 'Mutiny,' " *Collier's*, Sept. 2, 1955; and Melvin B. Voorhees, "Harry Cain Rides Once More Out of Their Past," *Argus* (Seattle), Dec. 6, 1963. An obituary is in the *New York Times*, Mar. 4, 1979.]

DANIEL LIESTMAN

CAIN, JAMES MALLAHAN (July 1, 1892–Oct. 27, 1977), author and journalist, was born in Annapolis, Md., one of five children born to James William Cain, professor of English at St. John's College who later became president of Washington College, and Rose Cecelia Mallahan, an aspiring opera singer who had given up her career for marriage. Cain grew up in an academic household where his parents instilled in him a love of music and books. He read voraciously and was allowed to skip years in elementary school. He entered Washington College in Chestertown, Md., when only fourteen and graduated with a B.A. degree in 1910. Along with his formal education, his college years exposed him to the language of the common man—specifically, a campus bricklayer named Ike Newton. Cain's use of vernacular dialogue was often praised by the critics, and he would later express indebtedness to Newton.

Cain held various jobs, many of which later provided background for his novels, before returning to Washington College to teach and work on a master's degree in drama. He graduated in 1917 and moved to Baltimore. While trying to sell short stories, he joined the *Baltimore American* and later the *Sun*, covering the police and financial beats. In 1918 and 1919 he served in the United States Army's Seventy-ninth Division in France, where he saw little action, but edited the division's newspaper, the *Lorraine Cross*. Back home, Cain returned to work on the *Sun*. He married his college sweetheart, Mary Rebekah Clough, in 1920.

During the early 1920's, Cain published articles in the *Nation* and the *Atlantic Monthly*. He also met and befriended H. L. Mencken, who published his work in the *American Mercury*. In 1924, after a brief stint teaching at St. John's College, he went to work for Walter Lippmann, the editor of the *New York World*. Cain's first play, *Crashing the Gates*, the story of a false messiah, was produced in 1926 but closed after two weeks.

In 1927 he divorced his wife to marry Elina Sjosted Tyszecka of Finland, whom he had met four years earlier. For nine months in 1931 he was managing editor of the *New Yorker*, but he left to write screenplays in Hollywood. Between then and 1948 he wrote for nearly every major studio. Because he was either dropped from various projects, or they were never produced, he received screen credit for only three of the dozens of films on which he worked: *Algiers* (1938), *Stand Up and Fight* (1939), and *Gypsy Wildcat* (1944).

His first novel, *The Postman Always Rings Twice*, was published in 1934 by Alfred A. Knopf. Cain's tale of a drifter who plots with a conniving wife to murder her husband was an immediate best-seller, and Cain won praise for his realistic, "hard-boiled" technique. He was favorably compared with Hemingway and Tolstoy. The story was serialized, a play was made out of it (and ran on Broadway), and in 1946 the first of two film versions appeared, starring John Garfield and Lana Turner. That, too, was an immediate success, and it is today recognized as one of the films that broadened the motion-picture industry's perspectives by forcing Hollywood's censoring arm, the Hays Office, to consider the darker side of human nature as appropriate material for motion pictures.

Knopf later published *Serenade* (1937), *Mildred Pierce* (1941), and *Love's Lovely Counterfeit* (1942). In 1943 the originally serialized "Double Indemnity," "Career in C Major," and "The Embezzler" were reprinted in *Three of a Kind*. In 1942, Cain and Elina Tyszecka were divorced, and he married actress Aileen Pringle in 1944. Also in that year Warner Brothers produced *Double Indemnity*, followed by *Mildred Pierce* in 1945. Both films met with enormous popular and critical success, the former setting the standard for film noir and the latter winning Joan Crawford an Academy Award.

In 1946, Cain's novel set in the Old West, *Past All Dishonor*, the result of endless hours of library research, was published to disappointingly mixed reviews. His other works include *Our Government* (1930), *Sinful Woman* (1947), *The Moth* (1948), *Jealous Woman* (1950), *Galatea* (1953), *Mignon* (1962), *The Magician's Wife* (1965), *Rainbow's End* (1975), and *The Institute* (1976).

In 1946 he also began to campaign for the creation of the American Authors' Authority (AAA), a board that would grant writers more control over the rights to their works. The AAA became the subject of fierce national debate among writers, and Cain was accused of being a Communist, even though his plan would have exploited the capitalist system to the benefit of writers, whom he felt were being cheated by publishers, networks, and studios. After two years, Cain, tired of constant setbacks and a lack of positive interest on the part of those he intended to help, abandoned the project.

Cain and Aileen Pringle were divorced in 1947, and he married Florence Macbeth, a retired opera singer. That same year, *The Butterfly*, a novel of rural incest, was published, and a year later, he and Florence moved to Hyattsville, Md., where they would remain until their deaths.

Cain's remaining years were spent researching his many interests, writing book reviews, articles, and novels, none of which achieved the same popularity as his earlier works. *Cain × 3* (1969), a reprinting of *The Postman Always Rings Twice, Double Indemnity*, and *Mildred Pierce*, introduced his writing to a new generation of readers. Years after his death, the writer who called himself "a newspaper man" is the subject of doctoral dissertations and numerous scholarly examinations of his lean prose style, which shed a unique light on the drama of American life.

[A large collection of Cain's letters and other papers is at the Library of Congress. Roy Hoopes, *Cain* (1982), is a detailed biography written in cooperation with Cain himself. See also David Madden, *James M. Cain* (1970); Thomas Chastain, "Publishers Weekly Interviews: James M. Cain," *Publishers Weekly*, July 24, 1972; Gary Giddins, "James M. Cain Rings Again," *Village Voice*, Apr. 8–14, 1981; and Paul Skenazy, *James M. Cain* (1989). A detailed account of Cain's involvement in the AAA is Richard Fine, *James M. Cain and the American Authors' Authority* (1992). Obituaries appear in the *Los Angeles Times*, Oct. 28, 1977; the *New York Times* and the *Washington Post*, both Oct. 29, 1977; and *Time* and *Newsweek*, both Nov. 7, 1977.]

KEVIN LAUDERDALE

CALDER, ALEXANDER (July 22, 1898–Nov. 11, 1976), sculptor, painter, and printmaker, was born in Philadelphia into a family of accomplished artists. His mother, Nanette Lederer, was a painter; his father, Alexander Stirling Calder, and his grandfather, Alexander Milne Calder, were well-known sculptors.

Calder's childhood home was a virtual studio. He was a model for both parents' work: at the age of four he posed for his father's sculpture *Man Cub* (1902), and later for his mother's oil paintings. He became familiar early on with the materials and processes of painting and sculpture. At the age of five, Calder was making little wire and wood figures; by eight he was making jewelry for his older sister Peggy's dolls. Nevertheless, he did not seem to desire art as a career. Instead, he preferred his workshop and was adept at using tools of all sorts. Consequently, in 1917, after graduating from Lowell High School in Berkeley, Calif., Calder entered the Stevens Institute of Technology in Hoboken, N.J., where he earned a degree in mechanical engineering in 1919. His keen knowledge of materials and construction (his marks in descriptive geometry were the highest ever given), coupled with his innovative artistic spirit, would become one of the hallmarks of his art.

Between 1919 and 1921, Calder held a number of jobs, including draftsman, mapmaker, and letterer for machine designers. These experiences may have awakened earlier artistic interests. In the autumn of 1923, after taking some drawing classes at night school, he enrolled in the Art Students League in New York City. There he studied, at various times, with Kenneth Hayes Miller, Thomas Hart Benton, Guy Pène duBois, George Luks, and John Sloan. A year later, as a free-lance artist, he was doing line drawings of sporting events for the *National Police Gazette*. His lifelong fascination with the circus began during his tenure with the *Gazette*. In the spring of 1925 Calder, armed with a two-week pass to cover the Barnum and Bailey Circus, spent every evening sketching the performances. This experience developed into the miniature circus performances that became his signature work in the late 1920's. Composed of wire figures that he ingeniously animated, Calder's circus performances became the talk of the Paris art world between 1927 and 1930. The circus not only brought Calder his first success as a sculptor but also introduced him to important members of the European avant-garde.

In 1930, Calder became a member of the Abstraction-Création group that included Theo van Doesburg, Jean Arp, Piet Mondrian, Robert Delaunay, Antoine Pevsner, and Jean Hélion. Joan Miró became a lifelong friend. Marcel Duchamp, an important ally both in Paris and the United States, suggested the term "mobile" for Calder's movable sculptures; Arp coined the term "stabile" for Calder's stationary works. Fernand Léger wrote a preface for the catalog of Calder's first exhibition of abstract constructions, held at the Galerie Percier (April–May 1931). He was one of the few Americans represented in the only group exhibition of surrealist artists held in the United States, First Papers of Surrealism (October–November 1942). Moreover, Calder was one of a handful of American artists to gain the respect of the European moderns at this time.

In the fall of 1930, Calder visited Mondrian's studio, an event that would have a profound effect on the future development of his work. It was Mondrian, of all his notable associates, whom Calder would later acknowledge as a direct influence on his career. After a chance visit to one of Calder's circus performances in his Paris studio, Mondrian, impressed with Calder's work, invited him to visit his studio. Mondrian's studio, with its immaculate white walls and removable rectangles of brilliant primary colors, provided "the necessary shock" that led Calder into abstraction. Calder remarked later how enlightening this experience was for him: "Though I had heard the word 'modern' before, I did not consciously know or feel the term 'abstract.' So now, at thirty-two, I wanted to paint and work in the abstract." His enthusiasm for painting was short-lived, however, lasting only three weeks. More important, Calder adopted Mondrian's spartan palette of the primary colors, black, and white, which he would use throughout his career in his sculpture and graphic work.

Shortly after his return to America, Calder married Louisa Cushing James on Jan. 17, 1931; they had two children. After his return to Paris the same year, Calder's newfound interest in abstraction was realized with his exhibition at the Galerie Percier. In the winter he began making works with movable parts that were both hand-cranked and run by an electric motor.

Although Calder's oeuvre is vast, the work for which he is best known is his kinetic sculpture. In fact, his name is synonymous with movement in art. His sculpture is so much his own that it necessitated its own lexicon: mobiles, stabiles, totems, constellations, gongs, and crags. There are several theories on the origin of Calder's interest in movable art. It is suggested that as a young man in San Francisco, he came under the spell of the cable cars with their intricate machinery (especially the wires and cables) and the movement of the brightly colored cars. More directly, in 1929, he saw a collection of eighteenth-century mechanical birds in cages in New York that inspired his first moving sculptures: a series of mechanized works in which fish swim about. Of course Calder was no stranger to making works of art move. His earlier circus performances provided ample precedent. Calder had said that even before he had visited Mondrian's studio, he "felt that art was too static to reflect our world of movement."

Calder was not the first artist to investigate movement. In the early 1910's the Italian Futurists tried to suggest the illusion of movement in their paintings and sculptures, but their works remained physically static. The Russian-born constructivist sculptor Naum Gabo was an early pioneer of kinetic works. However, Gabo's *Kinetic Sculpture* (1920) offered only the rhythmic swing of a single element. Calder's innovation was to allow multiple objects to move simultaneously. In the words of Jean Lipman: "Although not the first to make sculpture move, Calder was the first to create an art of motion." Some of the early constructions were mechanically driven by small electric motors that set up programmed trajectories. The large (thirty-three by fifty-five feet) lobby sculpture installation in the Sears Tower, *Universe* (1974), is a later important example of this last type.

The motorized works had one drawback: they could become monotonous in their prescribed patterns of movement. Calder's solution was to allow for a freer natural movement. The result was his first wind-operated mobile. Although he continued to work on both the mechanized sculpture and the wind mobiles simultaneously between 1930 and 1933, it was the latter that proved more successful, both critically and aesthetically for his future production in this medium. Many of the mobiles feature several shapes of differing sizes and are painted in primary colors. They are delicately balanced on pivoting rods that move with the slightest air current. This allows for an ever-shifting play of forms and relationships in space. *France Forever* (1944, dedicated to the French Resistance) is an early sculpture of this type. The philosopher Jean-Paul Sartre wrote the introductory essay to the catalog for an exhibition of Calder's mobiles at the Galerie Louis Carré in Paris in 1946. He saw a connection between Calder's work and his own existential philosophy. He wrote: "Calder's mobiles signify nothing, they do not send one back to anything but to themselves: they are, that is all: they are absolutes." The level of abstraction that Mondrian had initiated, Calder had successfully achieved in the mobiles.

While Calder did not want to openly imitate nature, he did want to suggest the things of the life world. For the catalog of a Caracas exhibition (1955), he wrote: "From the beginnings of my abstract work, even when it might not have seemed so, I felt there was no better model for me to choose than the Universe." Many of his themes, his symbols, and his images are related to the cosmos: sun, moon, stars, and spirals. These images appear again and again in the numerous gouaches that he began painting in the 1930's. Calder's world of imagery is both macro and micro. He also created shapes that suggest insects and crabs. Calder's particular genius was his ability to work on a grand scale (some works are as large as fifty-nine feet high), using structural steel and bold forms, and at the same time to create intimate worlds through his delicate jewelry or his small sculptures of fish and animals.

The stabiles became Calder's largest endeavors in sculpture, approaching the scale of architecture. His first large-scale stabile, *Whale*, was constructed in 1937. Calder's later work, especially after 1950, began to outgrow his studios and his ability to execute the work himself. As large public commissions came his way in the 1960's and 1970's, Calder needed the assistance of factories skilled in iron and steel fabrication. Many of his public pieces were commissioned by some of the leading architects of the time. I. M. Pei in 1966 commissioned *La Grande Voile*, a monumental stabile forty feet high and weighing twenty-five tons, for the Massachusetts Institute of Technology. Calder's stabiles have been installed in cities throughout the world: from New York to Los Angeles in the United States; from Mexico City to Caracas, Venezuela; from Sydney, Australia, to Rotterdam and Amsterdam in the Netherlands. Well into his seventies, Calder continued to produce stabiles that grew steadily in scale and boldness. He brought to a public who knew little about contemporary art sculpture that was a curious blend of whimsy and formal rigor. Many cities that were recipients of his work used the occasion as a reason to celebrate. Chicago held a Calder festival in 1974 for the dedication of two major pieces: *Universe*, a motorized mural for the Sears Tower, and *Flamingo*, a stabile commissioned by the General Services Administration for the Federal Center Plaza. In addition, the Museum of Contemporary Art in Chicago held a large retrospective exhibition.

After 1930, Calder had numerous international one-man exhibitions. His first retrospective, at age forty, was at the George Walter Vincent Smith Art Gallery, in Springfield, Mass. (November 1938). James Johnson Sweeney, his future biographer, wrote the foreword to the catalog. Sweeney later organized a major exhibition of Calder's work at the Museum of Modern Art in New York City that opened on Sept. 29, 1943. In 1955, Calder was featured as one of the pioneers of motion in art in the first exhibition devoted exclusively to kinetic art, Le Mouvement, organized by the Galerie Denise René in Paris.

Calder exhibited at the Venice Biennale in 1952 and received first prize for sculpture; the following year he was awarded a prize at the São Paulo Bienal. He was honored with the Grand Prix National des Arts et Lettres by the French Ministry of Culture and the United Nations Peace Medal in 1974 and 1975, respectively.

Known primarily for his work in traditional media—painting, sculpture, drawing, and printmaking—Calder explored various other forms of expression. Throughout his career he was involved in several theatrical productions. Most notable are his mobiles for Martha Graham's *Panorama* (1935) and another set of mobiles for a production of Erik Satie's 1920 symphonic drama, *Socrate*, produced at the Wadsworth Atheneum in Hartford, Conn. (1936). *Works in Progress*, a "ballet" conceived by Calder that featured an array of mobiles, stabiles, and large painted backdrops, was produced with electronic music at the Rome Opera House in 1968.

One of Calder's most celebrated ventures in unconventional media involved the painting of a 157-foot McDonnell-Douglas jet aptly called *Flying Colors*, which was commissioned by Braniff International in 1973. Two years later Braniff asked Calder to design a flagship for its American fleet in celebration of the nation's bicentennial. The result was *Flying Colors of the United States*, a 727-200 jet painted with a rippled image of red, white, and blue echoing the waving American flag.

On Oct. 14, 1976, the Whitney Museum of American Art in New York City mounted the largest retrospective of Calder's work to date. Less than one month later, he died of a heart attack in New York City.

Calder's legacy is far-reaching. Not only did he leave an abundant body of work, but many of his most important sculptures are on public view around the world. His pioneering use of industrial materials and fabrication processes has informed much contemporary sculpture. An appropriate epitaph for Calder can be found in the words of the art historian and critic John Russell: "In the man, as in the work, iron is the metal."

[See Alexander Calder, *Calder: An Autobiography with Pictures* (1966). See also James Johnson Sweeney, *Alexander Calder*, 2d ed. (1951); Jean Lipman, *Calder's Universe* (1976); Margaret Calder Hayes, *Three Alexander Calders* (1977); Daniel Marchesseau, *The Intimate World of Alexander Calder* (1989); and Joan M. Marter, *Alexander Calder* (1991). Also see Jean Davidson, "Four Calders," *Art in America*, Winter 1962; and John Russell, "Alexander Calder in Saché," *Vogue*, July 1967. An obituary is in the *New York Times*, Nov. 12, 1976.]

COREY POSTIGLIONE

CALLAS, MARIA (Dec. 2, 1923–Sept. 16, 1977), singer, was born Maria Anna Cecelia Sofia Kalogeropoulos in New York City, one of three children of Evangelia Dimitriadu and George Kalogeropoulos, recent immigrants from Meligala, Greece. The family first lived in Astoria, Queens, where Maria's father, who had owned a pharmacy in his native Greece, worked for a drugstore chain; like many immigrants, Maria's father changed his last name to something more easily pronounced by Americans, choosing Callas, and by 1927 he owned his own drugstore in a Greek neighborhood in Manhattan. However, he did not meet with the economic success he had enjoyed in Greece, was forced to give up his store, and thereafter worked as a pharmacist for various drugstore chains.

Maria's mother was the daughter of a Greek officer. Although she admired music and the arts, she was not a gifted musician. However, from early on, Evangelia did recognize the musical talents of her two daughters, Cynthia ("Jackie") and Maria. Evangelia was determined that the two girls would be trained for musical careers. She bought records of opera singers and was delighted to hear four-year-old Maria sing along with the arias on these recordings. As the girls grew older, Evangelia became even more determined that they continue their music studies, regardless of personal sacrifice. Eleven-year-old Maria, though shy and awkward, participated in children's contests and sang on radio programs. In one such competition, Maria was awarded second prize by comedian Jack Benny. Unfortunately, Evangelia's ambition for her daughters was the source of many family arguments between her and George.

In the 1930's the Great Depression was devastating America. The Callas family suffered financially like many other American families at that time. Evangelia decided that the only way to afford her daughters' musical studies was to send them to Greece. Despite protests from her husband, Evangelia first sent her older daughter Jackie to Greece for piano studies, and then in 1937 she accompanied Maria to Greece. Maria auditioned for voice teacher Maria Trivella, who taught at the National Conservatory in Athens; she helped Maria win a scholarship to study voice. The conservatory thought that Maria was sixteen, but she was only thirteen. (The young Maria was overweight. She would battle this image for a number of years, later dropping eighty pounds and generally maintaining a slim physique.) Two years after her acceptance, she began study with Elvira de Hidalgo, an artist-teacher at the leading conservatory in Athens, the Odeon Athenon. In 1940, Callas made her professional stage debut at the National Lyric Theater, appearing in the operetta *Boccaccio*.

At the end of World War II, in part because she wished to break away from her mother's control, Callas returned to the United States, where she lived with her father and pursued her operatic career. This trip home, however, was professionally disappointing, so she left for Italy in 1947.

On June 29, 1947, Callas met Giovanni Battista Meneghini, a building materials tycoon and multimillionaire who was also an avid opera fan. Meneghini took an active interest in Callas and her musical career. Though he was twenty years older than Callas, they married within the year. Meneghini thereafter served as his wife's manager and agent. Though she remained an American citizen, Callas chose to make Italy her home.

Callas made her Italian opera debut singing the title role of La Gioconda at the Verona Arena in August 1947. She went on to sing the parts of Isolde and Turandot in Venice, and Aïda in Turin. Critics began to recognize her talents—not only her extraordinary voice, but her emotional interpretations of the parts she sang. In November 1948, Callas made her debut in Florence, singing as Norma for the first time: she would be associated with this role throughout her career, performing *Norma* ninety times in eight countries. In 1954, Maria Callas finally made her United States debut, singing in *Norma* with the Chicago Lyric Opera. Two years later she again sang the same role for her Metropolitan Opera debut. Thereafter she performed at all the greatest opera houses of the world: La Scala, Covent Garden, the Paris Opera House, and many more.

As Callas gained fame as a prominent opera singer, the media seemed to follow her every move. Newspapers wrote of her "diva" temperament, reporting that she was difficult to work with and prone to temper tantrums. Meneghini disputed her critics, saying that Callas was warranted in the performance demands she made. Callas herself was a perfectionist; she stated, "To me the art of music is magnificent and I cannot bear to see it treated in a shabby way. When it is respected I will work hard and always give my best. But if music is treated in a shabby or second best way, I do not want to be associated with it."

Though an accomplished vocalist, possessing a two-and-a-half octave range, she was plagued by many mixed reviews concerning her musical performances—some hailed her as the greatest singer of bel canto opera, while others criticized her voice as flawed, undependable, thin, and "metal-like" in the upper register. Callas's own colleagues were also split regarding her talent. Audiences, however, loved Maria Callas and the aura that seemed to surround her. Callas's every performance was said to command an audience; when singing a role, her charisma was astounding.

Callas's personal life was constantly sensationalized in the papers. Her disputes with conductors about repertoire and her illnesses, which some claimed were phony, were front-page news. The more prominent she became as a performer, the more the media became interested in both her professional life and her personal life as well. In later years, her long romantic relationship with the Greek shipbuilding tycoon Aristotle Onassis was an ongoing serial dramatized in newspaper society and gossip columns.

When Maria became famous, her husband and manager Meneghini demanded for her—and received—ever larger sums of money. She became rich but Meneghini invested her money and made it difficult for Callas to have access to it. Meanwhile, Callas's mother expected her daughter to share her fortune. Her mother's demands, coupled with bad memories about her mother's arguments with her father and lingering resentment of her mother's dominance caused Callas to become estranged from her mother and her sister, although she consistently sent money weekly to both of them.

When Callas fell in love with Onassis, she decided to end her first marriage. The divorce proceedings proved lengthy. Meanwhile Maria Callas lived with Onassis but never married him. For the first time in her life her career became secondary to her personal life.

Her life with Onassis shifted back and forth between happiness and sadness. She endured verbal humiliation by Onassis in front of others, as well as his philandering with a variety of women. When Onassis married Jacqueline Kennedy, Callas quietly moved to Paris. Later, when his marriage to Kennedy was deteriorating, Onassis resumed his friendship with Callas, now pleading for her to marry him. Maria refused but maintained a relationship. Onassis died in 1975.

Callas took chances with her voice to mesh voice and drama together, unlike other opera singers of her time. Vocal risks as well as fatigue probably contributed to her vocal demise. Her career lasted barely twenty years. Her most famous roles included Norma, Lucia, Violetta (*La Traviata*), Elvira (*I Puritani*), Tosca, and Lady Macbeth. She was eventually fired from the Metropolitan Opera because Meneghini constantly demanded more money for his wife's performances, while Callas disagreed with Met manager Rudolf Bing on the selection of operas that she would sing.

Callas recorded more than twenty albums for EMI-Angel records and also made recordings for the Seraphim label. Her best recordings date from the early to mid-1950's. In 1965, Callas made her last public opera performance, at New York's Metropolitan Opera House. Thereafter her singing career virtually ended, although Callas and Giuseppe di Stefano joined together to sing in a worldwide tour in 1974; her performances were well received by Callas fans, but panned by the critics.

Two years after the death of Ari Onassis, Maria Callas died in Paris of an apparent heart attack. She was only fifty-three. Her revival of forgotten repertoire and her dramatic vocal presentation influenced all opera singers who followed her.

[Biographies of Callas include George Jellinek, *Portrait of a Prima Donna* (1960); John Ardoin, *The Callas Legacy* (1977; rev. ed. 1982); Arianna Stassinopoulos, *Maria Callas* (1981); and Nadia Stancioff, *Maria Callas Remembered* (1987). See also Walter Legge, "Callas Remembered: La Divina," *Opera News*, Nov. 1977. An obituary is in the *New York Times*, Sept. 17, 1977.]

JAN SHAPIRO

CAMBRIDGE, GODFREY MACARTHUR (Feb. 26, 1933–Nov. 29, 1976), actor and comedian, was born in the Harlem section of New York City, the son of Sarah and Alexander Cambridge, who had emigrated from British Guiana to Sydney, Nova Scotia, before arriving in New York. His father worked at blue-collar jobs, despite his skill as a bookkeeper; his mother worked in the garment district, although she was a skilled stenographer and had been a teacher in Guiana. His parents sent Cambridge to live with his grandparents in Sydney, Nova Scotia, so that he could attend school there. His grandfather was a coal miner and also operated a small grocery store. Cambridge's grandparents were strong disciplinarians who were not averse to corporal punishment.

Cambridge rejoined his parents when he was thirteen years old and entered high school in the Queens neighborhood of Flushing, where he was popular and active in extracurricular activities. A superior student, he graduated in three years and was awarded a scholarship to Hofstra College (now Hofstra University) in Hempstead, N.Y. He entered Hofstra in 1951 intending to pursue premedical studies with a major in psychology. Early on, however, he became interested in acting and switched his major to English. (As a child he entertained his family and friends with his comic talents.) While at Hofstra, he played one of the murderers in *Macbeth* in his first onstage experience. He left Hofstra in 1953 when his grief over his father's death, overwork, and a renewed awareness of his "blackness," when taunted by members of a new fraternity on campus, made studying difficult. Of this incident he later said, "I couldn't concentrate any more. All my life I ignored being colored. I never felt racial prejudice because I was the only Negro. . . . It's terrible for someone to reach the age of 21 and realize he's Negro, to spend all that time leading a sheltered life." In 1954 he enrolled as a drama major at City College (CCNY), but he left before he received his degree. Later in life he admitted that he did not "recommend dropping out to anyone." Cambridge then considered joining the paratroopers but was classified 4F.

While working at various odd jobs, Cambridge acted in his free time in church groups and sought full-time work as an actor. His first professional acting part was as a bartender in the off-Broadway production *Take a Giant Step* (1956), and his first Broadway show was *Nature's Way*. But acting jobs were scarce, and he was continually turned away by casting directors who told him, "We can't use you because there's no Negro part." To which he would reply, "Use me and I'll make it Negro." Later in his career he played "male" rather than "Negro" roles, that is, an Irishman in *The Troublemaker* (1964), a CIA agent in *The President's Analyst*, a concert violinist in *The Biggest Bundle*, and a Jewish cab driver in *Bye Bye Braverman*.

His first major acting role was as a white woman in the off-Broadway production of Genet's *The Blacks* (1961). Cambridge was a critical success and received an Obie Award. After that, he played the role of Uncle Gitlow in the Broadway production of *Purlie Victorious*, a part that playwright Ossie Davis wrote especially for him. For that performance he received an Antoinette Perry ("Tony") Award nomination in 1962. He repeated his role in the film version of this play, *Gone Are the Days!* (1963). Godfrey was part of an improvisational group, The Living Premise, and for six months in 1963 appeared in its satirical review. Before *The Blacks*, he had bit parts on Broadway in *Detective Story* and *Lost in the Stars*. One of his most successful roles was that of Pseudolus the slave in the road production of *A Funny Thing Happened on the Way to the Forum*, a role Zero Mostel had played on Broadway. In his last show he joined Molly Picon in *How to Be a Jewish Mother* (1967).

Among the films in which Cambridge performed were *The Last Angry Man* (1959), *The President's Analyst* (1967), *The Busy Body* (1967), *The Biggest Bundle of Them All* (1968), and *Bye Bye Braverman* (1968). *The Night the Sun Came Out* was the original title for his next film, released as *Watermelon Man* (1970), in which he appeared as a white man who finds himself suddenly with black skin. The title change caused Cambridge to break his friendship with the director Melvin Van Peebles, contending that too many violent things were happening to blacks for them to accept such a title. His last pictures were *Cotton Comes to Harlem* (1970) and its sequel, *Come Back Charleston Blue* (1972).

Cambridge also had considerable television exposure, appearing on such programs as "The U.S. Steel Hour," "Naked City," "Search for Tomorrow," "Ellery Queen," "I've Got a Secret," and "Sergeant Bilko." He attributed his acceptance as a television comedian to his three appearances on "The Tonight Show" with Jack Paar in 1964. The following year he received an Emmy Award for his role in "Beyond the Blues," the premier episode of the experimental CBS series "Stage II." In 1968 he signed a ten-year contract with CBS-TV.

As a stand-up comedian, Cambridge wrote his own material and he performed in some of the best cafés and supper clubs in the country. His routines were funny, but he was no proselytizer; he maintained that "I don't do a racial act. I do a funny act." His comedy routines were recorded on the Epic label: *Them Cotton Pickin' Days Is Over, Godfrey Cambridge Toys with the World, The Godfrey Cambridge Show* and his first, *Ready or Not, Here's Godfrey Cambridge* (1964), which became one of the top five best-selling albums at the time of its release.

His philosophical orientation may be inferred from these quotations: "I've got a responsibility not only to myself but to those 20 million black folks out there," and "I'm interested in black kids having heroes. I've given up being ashamed of Africa, ashamed of who I was, ashamed of that hair pomade because I didn't have any heroes." Shunning violence, Cambridge almost continually found himself fighting the little man's battles, jousting with taxi drivers who refused to pick up blacks; with real estate people who not only overcharged blacks but defrauded them; and with other low-level bureaucrats.

A voracious eater, Cambridge fought the problem of obesity throughout his adult life. He was five feet, ten and a half inches tall, and his weight fluctuated between a high of 370 pounds and a low of 180 pounds. Of one instance of weight loss, he said, "I've lost 12 Twiggies"—the reference is to slim British actress Twiggy.

Cambridge sought peace of mind in reading; he maintained that "You can't be a public person 24 hours a day." He enjoyed the classics, but his serious reading also included speeches of Malcolm X and Black Panther Eldridge Cleaver's *Soul on Ice* (1968), this last considered by him to be "the most definitive book written on the racial question in many a year." Cambridge, a social person at heart, numbered among his friends James Earl Jones, Harry Belafonte, Ossie Davis, Robert Culp, Bill Cosby, and Sidney Poitier. "God" was Poitier's nickname for Cambridge. His friend Sammy Davis, Jr., was responsible for his intense interest in photography.

Louie Robinson, writing in *Ebony* in 1967, estimated that Cambridge was earning a quarter of a million dollars per year. Earnings were augmented by income from his record royalties, his business interests in several singers, his investment in Royal Crown sodas, his writing (he wrote for *Monocle*, a British publication; his book *Put-Downs and Put-Ons* was published in 1967), and his board game, 50 Easy Steps to the White House. Nevertheless, he lived relatively frugally. While married to actress Barbara Ann Teer (1962–1965), he lived in a middle-income housing development in New York City. After a divorce that left him bitter, he moved to a four-and-a half room West End Avenue apartment in Manhattan. In 1974 he moved to an expensive home in Ridgefield, Conn.

Cambridge died of a heart attack on the Warner Brothers set of *Victory at Entebbe* (1976), while playing the role of Uganda's president, Idi Amin. A funeral service was held on Dec. 1, 1976, at the Hollywood Church of the Hills and Cambridge was interred in Forest Lawn Cemetery.

[There is no published biography of Cambridge. Feature articles may be found in *Esquire*, Nov. 1964; the *New York Times*, Dec. 31, 1965, and Nov. 20, 1966; *Negro Handbook* (1966); *Ebony*, Oct. 1967; the *New York Post*, Dec. 28, 1968; and *Look*, Jan. 7, 1969. An obituary is in the *New York Times*, Nov. 30, 1976.]

HAROLD L. WATTEL

CAPEHART, HOMER EARL (June 6, 1897–Sept. 3, 1979), politician and businessman, was born on a farm near Algiers, Ind., one of three children of Alvin Thomas Capehart and Susan Kelso. His father, a farmer, had briefly been a cowboy in Colorado.

Although most of his school years were spent in Indiana, Capehart graduated in 1916 from high school in Polo, Ill., where his family had moved in 1915. After high school he worked at various jobs in Wisconsin and Indiana before enlisting in the United States Army in April 1917. At posts in Missouri, Arizona, California, and Washington, he became aware of the opportunities that the wider world offered. He was discharged with the rank of sergeant in 1919.

Upon returning to civilian life, Capehart worked as a cook in Rockford, Ill., and then as a demonstrator of electric milking machines, but soon entered the world of salesmanship. His first sales job was with the J. I. Case firm of Racine, Wis., selling a new-model tractor. Organizing plowing and tractor-pull contests against other makes of tractors, Capehart became the top Case salesman in his Nebraska territory. After the farm depression of 1921–1922 caused farm-equipment sales to nosedive, Capehart sold commercial popcorn machines for a company called Holcomb and Hoke out of Indianapolis, then had brief stints in advertising and hardware. By the mid-1920's, he had rejoined Holcomb and Hoke, first as regional sales manager working out of Minneapolis and then as general sales manager supervising 325 employees. In 1927 he returned to Indiana to launch the Capehart Automatic Phonograph Corporation, which manufactured and sold what soon were known as jukeboxes.

In 1929 he married Irma Mueller, a schoolteacher of Wrightstown, Wis.; the couple had two children.

In a decade after enlisting in the army, the former Hoosier farm boy, at five feet, eleven inches tall, weighing some two hundred pounds, and sporting an ever-present cigar, was an unquestioned business success and a recognized sales expert. Sales for his firm grew rapidly, but as the 1930's dawned, the corporation lost money, probably because Capehart shifted his market from commercial coin-operated machines to the home phonograph market and did not reduce prices as the depression deepened. In 1932, dismissed by his board of directors, Capehart was nearly bankrupt.

Undaunted, he soon joined forces with the Wurlitzer Company, a musical instrument firm, and moved to the firm's North Tonawanda, N.Y., headquarters. Capehart persuaded Wurlitzer to convert its phonograph to a coin-operated version. The resulting Wurlitzer jukebox quickly became a staple of American life. While the economy in general remained stagnant for several years, Wurlitzer, with Capehart's leadership, saw increasing profits throughout the 1930's.

By 1940, Capehart had returned to Indiana to revive the Packard Manufacturing Corporation, formerly the Packard Piano Company, which he had bought in 1932, and to pursue a political career. Although his focus was still on jukeboxes, he anticipated the coming demand for war production. In 1941 the firm began to produce cartridge slides for army carbines, tank battery boxes, and slip rings for tank and bomber turrets.

Meanwhile, Capehart had begun to buy Indiana farmland, eventually owning more than 2,500 acres. This asset became an important source of income and facilitated his entrance into politics. It also enabled him to host one of the most unusual events in American political history, the 1938 Cornfield Conference.

Although his family had traditionally supported Democrats, by the mid-1930's, Capehart had aligned himself with the Republican party, which was staggering under its 1936 defeat. Following his usual marketing flair, he invited some ten thousand Republican officials, primarily from Indiana but many from across the nation, to a rally on an alfalfa field of his southern Indiana farm. Dozens of open tents, including one that would seat all in attendance, were erected to prepare and serve meals and accommodate the media. The conference, with its county-fair atmosphere, invigorated Republican forces and tabbed Capehart as a rising star in the party.

Capehart became a sought-after speaker for Republican events and the focus of widespread speculation about his future leadership role in politics. He even enjoyed a brief flurry of support for the party's 1940 presidential nomination. After the 1940 election, he was selected Republican party chairman for his congressional district. With his customary energy he traveled throughout the district, drumming up support for Republican candidates.

The Republican party began a comeback in the midterm elections in November 1940, nearly doubling its numbers in the House of Representatives and gaining a 50 percent increase in the Senate. The resurgence was especially marked in Indiana, which voted Republican in the election for president, after having voted Democratic in 1932 and 1936. In 1942, Republicans swept the Indiana congressional delegation and gained control of both chambers of the state legislature.

As 1944 approached, Capehart announced he would seek a Senate seat that year. After a bitter contest for his party's nomination, he defeated Governor Henry Shricker by fewer than 22,000 votes, trailing the other Republican candidates for major office. Capehart established the style he pursued in every campaign, traveling statewide, making several speeches a day. In 1950 he defeated Assistant United States Attorney General Alexander Campbell by more than 100,000 votes, and more than doubled that margin in 1956 in defeating former secretary of agriculture Claude R. Wickard.

In Congress, Capehart was identified with the Republican faction led by Senator Joseph McCarthy of Wisconsin. But Capehart's links to McCarthy's ultraconservative point of view were never as close as those of his fellow Hoosier William E. Jenner. After 1953, Capehart aligned himself with the moderate wing of the party led by President Dwight Eisenhower, but he never denounced McCarthy and was critical of Eisenhower's foreign policy in the late 1950's. He endorsed housing legislation to aid middle-income home buyers and military families, and, after joining the Senate Foreign Relations Committee in 1953, he became an enthusiastic spokesman for trade with Latin America, where he traveled extensively.

Capehart's defeat by less than 11,000 votes in 1962 to the youthful Birch Bayh maintained Indiana's tradition of not letting its senators serve more than eighteen years. Never expressing any bitterness over his loss of office, Capehart moved to Indianapolis, where he headed a family business devoted to real estate and farming, and where he died and was buried.

[See John R. Taylor, "Homer E. Capehart: United States Senator, 1944–1962" (Ph.D. diss., Ball State University, 1977); and William B. Pickett, *Homer E. Capehart* (1990). An account of Capehart's early political career is William B. Pickett, "The Capehart Cornfield Conference and the Election of 1938: Homer E. Capehart's Entry into Politics," *Indiana Magazine of History*, Dec. 1977. Obituaries are in the *Indianapolis Star*, Sept. 4, 1979, and the *New York Times*, Sept. 5, 1979.]

THOMAS P. WOLF

CAPP, AL (Sept. 28, 1909–Nov. 5, 1979), cartoonist, writer, and social critic, was born Alfred Gerald Caplin in New Haven, Conn., the eldest of four children of Latvian natives Matilda Davidson and Otto Philip Caplin. His father studied law but became an unsuccessful salesman with a penchant for drawing cartoons. The young Caplin attended the public schools of Bridgeport, Conn. His main interests were sports, girls, and hitchhiking. At nine years of age, while jumping from the back of a moving ice truck, he was hit by a street car, resulting in amputation of his left leg and the need to use a prosthesis for the rest of his life. By eleven he was drawing cartoons for sale to neighboring children. At Bridgeport High School, he did well in history and English, but he failed geometry nine times, so he never graduated. When he was fifteen, he spent a summer hitchhiking to Memphis, for the first and only time seeing the backwoods South, which he later used as the locale for his comic strip.

Capp attended a variety of art schools in Philadelphia and Boston. Because his family was poor and he was working his way through school, he regularly told school officials that the "check was in the mail" and then attended classes until they caught up with him. At this point he would go to another school and repeat the charade. At a Boston art school, he met Catherine Wingate Cameron, and in 1930 they were married, eventually having three children.

In 1932 the Associated Press Feature Service made him the nation's youngest cartoonist by hiring him to carry on "Mr. Gilfeather," an already established strip. He was a failure. He went back to art school and, to make ends meet, did illustrations, usually of attractive women with windblown skirts, for a Boston newspaper. In 1934, Ham Fisher, the creator of the "Joe Palooka" strip, hired him as an assistant. When Fisher went on vacation, a group of hillbillies, principally one named Big Leviticus, appeared for the first time in the strip. Fisher and Capp both later claimed to have created these characters.

After less than a year, Capp left Fisher's employ when he sold his own strip about hillbillies, "Li'l Abner," to United Feature. The strip, which began on Aug. 13, 1934, in eight newspapers, quickly became one of the nation's most popular comic strips in its forty-three-year run, appearing in one thousand newspapers at its peak in the early 1960's. Its characters became national bywords. The ignorant but innocently appealing Li'l Abner Yokum (the name taken from the words "yokel" and "hokum"), his corncob smoking mother, Mammy Yokum, and curvaceous Daisy Mae Scragg were regulars in the mythical town of Dogpatch, but there was an ever-expanding supporting cast: Senator Jack S. ("Good old Jack S.") Phogbound; Marryin' Sam; Lena the Hyena, the world's ugliest woman; the lovable Schmoo; Skonk Works proprietor, Big Barnsmell; hog tycoon, J. Roaringham Fatback; Appassionata Van Climax; Joe Bftsplk, the man with his own perpetual bad luck cloud; Evil-Eye Fleegle and his triple whammy; Moonbeam McSwine; and Jubilation T. Cornpone. Sadie Hawkins Day, the one day each year in Dogpatch when women could chase men for marriage, became a fixture in many colleges, high schools, and adult social gatherings every November.

Capp used his comic strip to satirize all aspects of American society: sex, politics, law enforcement, outdoor advertising signs, John Steinbeck's *The Grapes of Wrath*, and even other comic strips. One of his characters, Fearless Fosdick, was a satire on the popular Dick Tracy. Early on, some conservatives found his satire un-American, and several times individual newspapers refused to print some segments, usually because the female characters were considered too suggestive. Capp believed his cartooning talent gave him a place among the leading storytellers of his age; he also wrote several books and numerous articles for popular magazines, served as a movie and drama critic, was a newspaper columnist, did regular radio spots, and was a frequent guest on television talk shows. His artwork appeared in leading galleries. Capp also wrote the story line for the cartoon feature "Abbie an' Slats." "Li'l Abner" was made into two movies and a Broadway musical, and Capp helped write an unsuccessful song about it. During World War II, he created a comic book (*"Al Capp," by Li'l Abner*) about his own experience in losing his leg; the military distributed this to injured fighting men. Capp also created a Sunday cartoon feature entitled "Small Change" for the War Bond Division of the Treasury Department.

During the McCarthy era in the early 1950's, the national attitude opposing any criticism of American life upset Capp, and he supported liberal causes and politicians. By the 1960's, however, he became a conservative critic who particularly lambasted student radicals in hundreds of abrasive speeches on college campuses each year. "The lunatics are running the asylum," he thundered, while simultaneously praising Vice-President Spiro Agnew. Whereas once his satire and criticism had been lighthearted, it now became harsh and bitter. In commenting on the student deaths at Kent State

University in 1970, for example, he told shocked audiences: "The real martyrs at Kent State were the kids in National Guard uniforms." When this harshness began to be reflected in "Li'l Abner," Capp's readership plummeted. In 1972 he pleaded guilty to attempted adultery with a Wisconsin coed and became a recluse. He announced his retirement in 1977, and the last "Li'l Abner" appeared on November 13 that year. Capp died from emphysema two years later in Cambridge, Mass.

Capp was a dark, heavy-set man with a thick crop of hair and a booming voice. He laughed loudly and frequently at his own and others' jokes. He seemed never to appear without a cigarette in his mouth and flicked ashes in all directions as he spoke. He was a regular on the New York social scene, though he was a teetotaler who regularly took antacids for a chronically upset stomach.

Critics have placed Capp in the company of Lewis Carroll, Mark Twain, Charles Dickens, and François Rabelais. John Steinbeck thought him the greatest writer of his age and worthy of a Nobel Prize. A contemporary newspaper once said of his comic strip that it was "as much a part of the national life as ice cream cones and taxes."

[Capp's papers ("Li'l Abner" cartoon strips, 1958–1965) are located in the Boston University Library. His own books are *Life and Times of the Schmoo* (1948); *The World of Li'l Abner*, with an introduction by John Steinbeck and a foreword by Charlie Chaplin (1953); *From Dogpatch to Slobbovia* (1964); *The Hardhat's Bedtime Story Book* (1971); *Li'l Abner Dailies*, 3 vols. (1988). See also Arthur Asa Berger, *Li'l Abner: A Study in American Satire* (1970); E. J. Kahn, Jr., "Profiles: OOFF!!! (GULP!!) EEP!!! ZOWIE!!!!," *New Yorker*, Nov. 29–Dec. 6, 1947; "Die Monstersinger," *Time*, Nov. 6, 1950; and Richard Woodley, "Cappital Punishment," *Esquire*, Nov. 1970. Obituaries are in the *Washington Post* and the *New York Times*, both Nov. 6, 1979.]

JOHN F. MARSZALEK

CAREY, MAX GEORGE ("SCOOPS") (Jan. 11, 1890–May 30, 1976), baseball player, was born Maximilian Carnarius in Terre Haute, Ind., one of four children of Frank Carnarius, a contractor, and Catherine Astroth. His parents wanted young Max to become a Lutheran minister, and accordingly Max entered Concordia College in Fort Wayne, Ind., in 1903. There he found time to run track and play on the school baseball team despite his divinity studies. In 1909 he won a tryout with the South Bend baseball team of the Central League, and changed his name to Max Carey in order to protect his amateur status and college eligibility. He had a poor first season but improved markedly the next year. He completed his degree requirements in 1909 but did not proceed with his plans to enter the ministry after his contract was sold to the Pittsburgh Pirates in the National League. He married Aurelia Berens in 1913; the couple had two children.

Originally a shortstop, Carey moved to the outfield when Pittsburgh player-manager Fred Clarke was injured. He spent the next twenty years of his career in center field. It was once thought that Carey earned the nickname "Scoops" because of his ability to handle low line drives, but actually he received the title because of baseball tradition. A nineteenth-century first-base man, George Carey, had been called "Scoops" and Max Carey inherited the nickname label, regardless of his abilities. In 1935, when Tom Carey (no relation) came up with the Cleveland Browns, he too was nicknamed "Scoops."

At five feet, ten inches, and weighing 170 pounds, Max Carey was not a power hitter, preferring instead to "spray" the ball to all fields. A consistent hitter, he had a lifetime batting average of .285. But it was his skills on the base paths that established his claim to fame. Carey led the National League in stolen bases ten times; his career total of 738 was a record that stood for decades. The scourge of catchers, in 1922 Carey was thrown out only twice in 53 attempts. He was also a fine defensive player: his 6,363 putouts set a record that lasted forty years (to be broken by Willie Mays, who had a longer career), and his career total of 339 assists set a National League record.

Carey's best season came in 1925 when he hit a career-high .343 and led the Pirates to victory in the World Series, during which he batted an incredible .458. In the decisive seventh game of the series, Carey smacked four hits off pitching legend Walter Johnson, driving in two runs, scoring three times himself, and stealing a base—all this despite playing with two broken ribs. The next year, after a dispute with Pirates management, he was sold to the Brooklyn Dodgers.

He played for the Dodgers through the 1929 season, despite his advancing age. In his first appearance in Pittsburgh in a Dodger uniform, Carey received a thunderous ovation from the fans when he stepped up to the plate. The umpire called time; after stepping out of the batter's box and nodding to the crowd, Carey asked to resume play. The umpire refused, saying, "Not while you're crying, Max." He coached with the Pirates in 1930. Then in 1932 the Dodgers signed Carey as their manager. The Dodgers finished third in 1932; when they fell to sixth in 1933, Carey was fired. His replacement was a rookie coach named Casey Stengel.

Leaving baseball reluctantly, Carey went into the real estate business in Florida. He was a founder of the All-American Girls Professional Baseball League that played during World War II. In 1955, Carey scouted for the Baltimore Orioles. He ended his baseball career as manager of the Louisville team in the American Association in 1956. Thereafter he worked as a racing official in Miami Beach, Fla. He was elected to the Baseball Hall of Fame in 1961.

Although gifted with extraordinary athletic prowess, Carey was a deliberate and low-key individual off the field. He was the kind of player who would stop in a bar (before and after Prohibition) for a beer after a game, drink it, and go home. Beside road games the only thing that ever separated him from his wife of sixty-three years was his death, which occurred in Miami Beach.

[See Frederick Lieb, *The Pittsburgh Pirates* (1948). An obituary is in the *New York Times*, May 31, 1976.]

WILLIAM E. ESPOSITO

CARLSON, RICHARD DUTOIT (Apr. 29, 1912–Nov. 25, 1977), stage, film, and television actor, was born in Albert Lea, Minn., the youngest of four children born to Henry Clay Carlson, a corporate attorney. When Richard was four his family moved to Minneapolis. Richard was a bookish youngster who became a high school prodigy, a scholar-athlete who edited the school newspaper, led the drama club, wrote a play later adopted by dozens of other high schools, and even attempted a novel about Africa. He maintained his academic success at the University of Minnesota while writing, acting in, and directing over twenty plays, one of which was an adaptation of Joseph Conrad's *Victory*. He graduated summa cum laude, was elected to Phi Beta Kappa, and then earned a master's degree. He taught briefly in Minnesota's English department but quickly left the position and used a $2,500 scholarship grant and a loan from his father to establish the Minnesota Repertory Company in St. Paul. When the group failed six months later, Carlson left for California, where he joined the Pasadena Community Playhouse in 1936. He starred in *Henry IV* and directed *Richard II* there before deciding to move on to Broadway.

In New York City, Carlson visited a college friend, working as the assistant stage manager of *Three Men on a Horse*, and immediately won a role in that show's road company. According to theater lore, legendary producer George Abbott intervened to give Carlson a role because it amused him to employ an actor with a Phi Beta Kappa key, but in fact a bit player had to be quickly replaced. Whatever the case, Carlson's career benefited and in March 1937 he made his Broadway debut in *Now You've Done It*. While acting, he wrote a play called *Western Waters* and found backing to produce it even as he began to appear opposite Ethel Barrymore in *The Ghost of Yankee Doodle*. He quit that role to direct his own play, but it closed after seven performances. Brooks Atkinson remarked that before Carlson "writes and directs another [play], this column fervently prays that he try and pull himself together." The crushed playwright appeared in *White Oaks* early in 1938 but soon decided that the West Coast offered him greater opportunity.

In 1938 the "triply talented" Carlson was hired by David Selznick as a writer, but in typical Hollywood fashion he soon had a movie career. Janet Gaynor insisted he appear (in kilts) with her in *The Young in Heart*; a major role in *The Duke of West Point* quickly followed. Carlson was unhappy playing the juvenile, friend-of-the-hero roles in which he was typecast and left Hollywood to appear on Broadway with Ethel Merman in *Stars in Your Eyes* in February 1939. That decision might inadvertently have cost him true movie stardom, for he was unable to accept the lead in *Golden Boy*, which went to William Holden and launched his long career as a leading man.

After 1939, Carlson returned to Hollywood, where he played lightweight romantic leads for years. He was consistently employed, but rarely moved beyond B picture rank. On June 10, 1939, he married Mona Mayfield; the couple had two sons. His early films included *Winter*

Carnival (1939) and *The Howards of Virginia* (1940), and during 1941 he acted in five more, notably *Back Street* and *The Little Foxes*. Late that year he and Mona moved to a home in the San Fernando Valley that he had designed; there they established the first "victory garden" in Hollywood. Carlson's film interests expanded in 1943 when he began to collect movie memorabilia; in time his holdings included Charlie Chaplin's derby, Harold Lloyd's horn-rimmed glasses, and the leopard skin Elmo Lincoln wore as Hollywood's first Tarzan. With the rank of lieutenant, Carlson served in the United States Army from 1943 to 1946, writing and directing war documentaries. Meanwhile, his articles and stories appeared in such varied publications as the *Minnesota Quarterly*, *Good Housekeeping*, *American Magazine*, *Women's Home Companion*, *McCall's*, and *Reader's Digest*.

The postwar years saw his film career decline; one harsh critic noted that Carlson had "played the juvenile role for so long he had nothing to give to mature roles." Carlson thereafter transformed himself into a character actor worthy of featured roles, and often starring ones in B movies. He remarked that he had no desire to be "either a playboy or a star," but believed film success would allow him to test other areas of creativity. During these years he was extensively involved in the Screen Actor's Guild, serving almost continually on its board or as an officer from 1947 to 1953.

In 1950, Carlson was featured in *King Solomon's Mines* and chronicled the film company's experience in articles on Africa for *Collier's* and the *Saturday Evening Post*. Once again he was "hot" as an actor, and he made use of the opportunity to create well-made science fiction features that he variously wrote, directed, or helped produce. *The Magnetic Monster* and *It Came from Outer Space* appeared in 1953, with *Riders to the Stars* and *Creature from the Black Lagoon* following in 1954.

Carlson was among the first Hollywood personalities to recognize the potential of television. His own production company created shows for the Japanese market and a television pilot, *Poor Richard's Almanac*, that was deemed too intellectual by the networks. He declared that TV was a "gold mine" for actors: he asked and received $2,000 per show. After many guest appearances on such shows as "Studio One," "Schlitz Playhouse of the Stars," and "Climax," he achieved TV stardom and financial success with "I Led Three Lives," which ran from 1953 to 1956. This docudrama was based on the true story of Herbert Philbrick, a Boston advertising executive who for nine years did lead three lives: as an average citizen, a member of the Communist party, and a spy for the Federal Bureau of Investigation. With its pro-FBI, anti-Communist sentiment, the show reflected the right-wing paranoia of the McCarthy era. Carlson lectured widely, discussing the show and the Cold War. He used the profits of stardom to finance and direct several sci-fi thrillers. In 1958 and 1959 he starred in and directed many episodes of "MacKenzie's Raiders," in which he played a cavalry officer pursuing Mexican bandits in the 1870's. He confessed that he enjoyed doing TV because "I love money. The more of it the better. I want prosperity for my family, and television gives it to me."

Carlson belonged to the Actors, the Directors, and the Writers guilds and maintained his activity in all three fields during the 1960's. His last movie role was in 1969, but he continued to appear in, write, and direct TV shows such as "Perry Mason," "The Virginian," and "Owen Marshall." He lived quietly with his wife, wrote poetry, traveled extensively, was active in community affairs and served as president of an animal rights organization, Actors and Others for Animals. His active pace in three creative areas sapped his strength, and he died in Encino, Calif., of a cerebral hemorrhage at age sixty-five.

[Clippings files on Carlson's career are held at the New York Public Library for the Performing Arts at Lincoln Center and at the Academy Foundation, National Film Information Service, in Beverly Hills, Calif. No book-length study of Carlson's career exists, nor has he been the subject of articles. An obituary is in the *New York Times*, Nov. 27, 1977.]

GEORGE J. LANKEVICH

CARPENTER, WALTER SAMUEL, JR. (Jan. 8, 1888–Feb. 2, 1976), industrialist, was born in Wilkes-Barre, Pa., the son of Walter S. Carpenter, an engineering contractor, and Belle Morgan. After attending public schools in his hometown, he enrolled in Wyoming Seminary, a prep school, in Kingston, Pa., in 1902. Following graduation in 1906, he entered Cornell University, where he majored in civil engineering. His older brother, R. R. M. ("Ruly") Carpenter, was working for Du Pont and helped the younger Carpenter to find summer jobs with the firm during each of his first three years at Cornell.

In the fall of 1909 the brothers met at the Cornell-Penn football game in Philadelphia, at which time Ruly told his younger brother about an immediate opening Du Pont had in Chile. Walter Carpenter left Cornell, never to return to complete his degree, to begin full-time work for Du Pont as treasurer of its nitrate company in Chile. The Chilean nitrate market was very competitive, but Carpenter did well obtaining the immense quantities Du Pont needed. After two years in Chile he was rewarded with assignment to the firm's development department in Wilmington, Del. The development department was a good place to be just when Du Pont began its diversification, during which it shifted from being almost exclusively an explosives manufacturer and became a diverse chemical company. Big changes began following the purchase of the firm by the "three cousins," Pierre, Irénée, and Lammot du Pont, and its division in the aftermath of the first Du Pont antitrust case.

Carpenter married Mary Wootten, to whom he had been introduced by Irénée du Pont, on June 3, 1914; the couple had three children.

In 1917, as the United States entered World War I and the market for Du Pont explosives soared, Carpenter was made head of the development division. By 1919 he was a vice-president and the firm's youngest director and executive committee member to that time. Pierre, Irénée, and Lammot du Pont were reshaping the venerable family firm during these years and Carpenter was one of the key people they counted on as they moved forward. His role in making the modern Du Pont Company was significant because the firm's development division, which he headed, was literally creating new chemicals and new products, such as ammonia derivatives, rayon, celluloid, and lacquers, each of which became the departure point for major new families of chemicals and production divisions that spurred the company's growth. Carpenter was at the center of the firm's research effort at the crucial moment.

In 1922, Carpenter was elected treasurer and served as chairman of the finance committee and vice-chairman of the executive committee. As head of the finance committee he continued Du Pont's high level of investment in research and promoted the construction of new plants for new products even during the Great Depression. In 1917 he was one of a group of Du Pont executives elected to the board of General Motors after the firm made a major investment in the automaker and served until 1959, after the second Du Pont antitrust case.

In May 1940, as the United States geared up to enter World War II, Carpenter was elected president of the firm, succeeding Lammot du Pont, who became chairman. He was the first president of the firm since its founding in 1802 who was not a member of the du Pont family. Carpenter's presidency was marked by Du Pont's participation in the American war effort, which required production levels never imagined in peacetime. The company did an excellent job under his leadership of meeting these wartime challenges. Du Pont designed, built, and operated fifty defense plants during the war, and expanded production in its prewar plants. One major accomplishment of Carpenter's presidency was Du Pont's design and operation of the Hanford Engineering Works, which played a key role in the development of the atomic bomb by manufacturing plutonium in quantities never before imagined.

After leading the company through reconversion to a peacetime economy, Carpenter stepped down as president in favor of Crawford Greenwalt in 1948 and then served fourteen years as chairman of the board. In 1962 he accepted the rarely bestowed title of honorary chairman, which he held until 1975, when he chose not to stand for reelection to the board, ending a sixty-five-year career with Du Pont.

Carpenter was a strong proponent of owner management of large industrial firms, seeing it as one of the great strengths Du Pont had drawn on over its long history. He felt that managers should have a stake in the company beyond their salaries by becoming major stockholders, a point he made frequently in speeches and interviews and in a well-known letter to a stockholder who had written suggesting that Carpenter and other top managers take pay cuts to increase stockholder dividends.

During his long career he served on the boards of General Motors, the Wilmington Trust Company, the Diamond State Telephone Company, and the du Pont family holding company, Christiana Securities. He also served for a time on the board of the Sloan Foundation.

He served as a trustee of both Wyoming Seminary and Cornell University and contributed generously to both, especially Cornell, although almost always doing so anonymously. He also served as a trustee of the University of Delaware during its period of greatest growth and was a generous benefactor of that institution as well.

As a young man Carpenter had played football and baseball and been a member of a championship track team at Cornell. He loved tennis and won club championships until well past age sixty, defeating men half his age.

Carpenter was known by his peers as a thoughtful man who was able to grasp key points quickly and to see future needs and opportunities clearly. His personal modesty hid a powerful intellect. When he joined Du Pont in 1909, the firm was almost solely focused on manufacturing explosives, but when he retired as chairman of the board it was manufacturing more than 1,600 products and had plants or offices in thirty-four states and many foreign countries. Carpenter died at his home in Wilmington.

[Biographical material concerning Carpenter is held at the Hagley Museum and Library, Wilmington, Del. See also Larston D. Farrar, "Walter S. Carpenter, Jr.," in B. C. Forbes, ed., *America's Fifty Foremost Business Leaders* (1948). An obituary is in the *New York Times*, Feb. 3, 1976.]

WILLIAM H. MULLIGAN, JR.

CARR, JOHN DICKSON (Nov. 30, 1906–Feb. 27, 1977), author of mystery fiction and drama, was born in Uniontown, Pa., the son of Wood Nicholson Carr, a lawyer and member of Congress from 1913 to 1916, and Amanda Julia Cook. Once while the senior Carr was "thundering in Congress," young John stood on a table in the members' anteroom, reciting Hamlet's famous soliloquy to James Thomas Heflin and other congressmen.

By age eleven, Carr was writing articles on court proceedings and murder cases for his grandfather's Uniontown newspaper. By fifteen he had a column, mostly about boxing. At Hill School in Pottstown, Pa. (1921–1925), he wrote for the school paper, and at Haverford College he was an editor of the *Haverfordian* and wrote verses and historical adventure stories for the magazine. One of his early Henry Bercolin tales, "The Shadow of the Goat," appeared in the November–December 1926 issue. In another issue, he offered a reward of $25 to any student who could solve the mystery in one of his unfinished stories. To his dismay, a fellow student quickly came up with the solution. Carr had to borrow the money to pay him.

In 1928 his parents sent him to the Sorbonne in Paris for further study, but Carr spent all his time writing a short novel, *Grand Guignol*. It was published in the *Haverfordian* in 1929, a year after he took a B.A. degree from Haverford College. The story was expanded into *It Walks by Night* (1930); Harper and Brothers published it, and it sold fifteen thousand copies. The book's success led to Carr's career as a mystery novelist.

From 1930 to 1933, Carr made several voyages—to England, Africa, and Madagascar. In 1931 he married Clarice Cleaves of Bristol, England, whom he had met on one trip. They had three children.

The couple lived in London until 1948. Carr was elected to the Savage and Garrick clubs and, in 1936, to the exclusive Detection Club. During World War II, Carr wrote propaganda broadcasts for the British Broadcasting Corporation and a weekly radio mystery, "Appointment with Fear." In 1948, unhappy with the post-war British labour governments, the politically conservative Carrs returned to the United States.

They made their home in Mamaroneck, N.Y., in suburban Westchester County but continued to travel to England, France, and North Africa. After their return, Carr initiated the "Suspense" series on American radio. Six stories, some of which were based on tales by Edgar Allan Poe and other mystery writers and still others on his own stories, were published, with additional short stories, in *The Door to Doom and Other Detections* (1980); nine others were published in *The Dead Sleep Lightly* (1983).

From 1930 on, under his own name as well as the pseudonyms Carter Dickson, Dickson Carr, and Roger Fairbairn, Carr wrote two nonfiction books, *The Murder of Sir Edmund Godfrey* (1936) and *The Life of Sir Arthur Conan Doyle* (1949, 1975); forty-seven short stories, including fourteen "juvenilia"; three or four novelettes; two stage plays; and seventy-one novels, many of which featured the crime investigators Henry Bercolin, Patrick Rossiter, John Gaunt, Sir Henry Merrivale, and Dr. Gideon Fell, an Oxford don modeled on the writer G. K. Chesterton. Some novels were set in historical periods, others in contemporary times; some dealt with the supernatural. The prolific

Carr kept two American publishers busy with both first editions and subsequent reprints, and a British firm reprinted many of the American books under new titles. Many were published in both hardcover and paperback editions and in translations into all the principal European languages and Turkish. A number of his books were later issued in omnibus editions.

Beginning in 1950, Carr set many of his mysteries in England's Regency and Restoration periods, including his favorite, *The Devil in Velvet* (1951), which sold more copies than any other of his books. He also published five volumes of short stories and wrote several plays for radio. Films were made from several of his novels, including *The Man with a Cloak* (1951), *Dangerous Crossing* (1953), *Colonel March of Scotland Yard* (1954), and *The Burning Court* (1963).

Carr acknowledged Edgar Allan Poe and Arthur Conan Doyle as influences, saying that Poe invented the mystery tale and originated all the devices used by himself and others. A "master of the locked-room mystery," Carr once said that he never misled readers; he just stated the evidence and let the readers mislead themselves. His success was due in part to his intriguing tales, in part to his story-telling ability, in part to his style. Critic S. T. Joshi has commented that "his true virtues . . . are an unrelenting vigor that matches the bizarrerie of his plots"; Dorothy Sayers noted his "ability to change the atmosphere with startling suddenness."

In 1949, after two years of research, Carr published, with Adrian Conan Doyle (son of the mystery writer), *The Life of Sir Arthur Conan Doyle*, a book that demonstrated that Sherlock Holmes's companion, Dr. Watson, was based on a real person, Dr. James Watson. He became a member of the Baker Street Irregulars, an organized group of Holmes admirers.

Inspired by the desire to produce stories of the "old Doyle vintage," Carr also collaborated with Adrian Conan Doyle on *The Exploits of Sherlock Holmes* (1954). Of the twelve stories, based on story ideas originally suggested by Arthur Conan Doyle, Carr wrote two and collaborated with Adrian Conan Doyle on two more; Doyle wrote the others.

Carr served several terms as president of the Mystery Writers of America. In 1949 and 1962 he won the club's Edgar Award (named for Poe) and, in 1962, its Grand Master Award for collections of short stories.

From 1969 to 1976, Carr wrote a witty book column in *Ellery Queen's Mystery Magazine*. Carr's last book was *The Hungry Goblin* (1972). He died in Greenville, S.C., where he had made his home since 1965.

[See *Crime and Mystery Writers* (1985); and S. T. Joshi, *John Dickson Carr: A Critical Study* (1990). An obituary is in the *New York Times*, Mar. 1, 1977.]

CLARENCE A. ANDREWS

CARTER, MAYBELLE ADDINGTON (May 10, 1909–Oct. 23, 1978), guitarist, was born and grew up in southwestern Virginia in a rural area near Nickelsville, the daughter of Margaret and Hugh Jack Addington. Her father ran a general store and mill. Music was a major form of entertainment among the mountain families, and members of the Addington brood quickly learned to pick, play, and sing. By the age of twelve, Carter was accomplished on the guitar, autoharp, and banjo.

Carter married Ezra ("E. J.") Carter, a mail clerk, on Mar. 23, 1926. During their early married life the couple lived in a one-room log cabin with a lean-to kitchen near Maces Springs, Va., her husband's hometown. They had three daughters, Helen, June, and Anita. Even though she was busy with her career, Carter made her children's clothes, washed, ironed, cooked, and gardened.

By the mid-1920's, Carter was performing with Ezra's older brother, Alvin Pleasant ("A. P.") Delaney Carter, and his wife, Sara Dougherty Carter, at local church socials, parties, and community gatherings. The group had a "down-home" style that was popular with audiences. A collector of English and Irish folk tunes, A. P. sang bass and led the group. Sara sang lead and accompanied on guitar and autoharp, but Maybelle Carter's original guitar technique provided the foundation for their musical presentation. The "Carter Family lick," featured her picking the melody on the bass strings and strumming rhythm on the treble strings. Instead of placing instrumentation subordinate to voices, as was common practice in traditional country music, the group created complex vocal and instrumental arrangements to match Carter's syncopated bass lead.

In the summer of 1927, the Carters made a journey to Bristol, Tenn., in hopes of auditioning for a record company. The trek along rutted, washed-out dirt roads seemed even more perilous because of Carter's pregnancy with her first child. The trio made a favorable impression on talent scout Ralph Peer, who signed them to a five-year contract with RCA Victor Records. They were asked to record six songs that day, an event that marked one of the first commercial country music recording sessions ever and launched what was to become a fruitful and productive career for the Original Carter Family.

Among the memorable recordings the Carters made during their sixteen years together were "Keep on the Sunny Side," "Wabash Cannonball," "I'm Thinking Tonight of My Blue Eyes," and Carter's famous rendition of "Wildwood Flower." She also wrote "My Home Among the Hills" and "It's a Long Road to Travel." The Original Carter Family's recordings had a significant influence on the developing country music tradition and contributed to the preservation of traditional folk and mountain music.

Hoping to widen their audience, the Carters appeared on daily broadcasts from the powerful Mexican border radio stations in Del Rio, Tex. For three years beginning in 1938, their programs were produced first by XERA, then XEG and XENT. The group became known to households across the United States, and it was at this point that the Carter children began performing.

A. P. and Sara Carter, who had divorced, returned to private life in 1943. Maybelle Carter continued to perform, this time with her daughters. From 1943 to 1948, Mother Maybelle and the Carter Sisters were featured on WRVA in Richmond, Va., on a program called "Old Dominion Barn Dance." In 1950 the four Carter women began a seventeen-year relationship with WSM's "Grand Ole Opry" in Nashville, Tenn. They also recorded for Victor and Columbia records and toured with Chet Atkins, Elvis Presley, and Johnny Cash. During these years Carter built a repertoire that included family originals and "commercial" country music songs that were popular at the time.

The revival of folk music during the 1960's and 1970's brought a renewed interest in the Original Carter Family, and such musicians as Joan Baez and Bob Dylan were strongly influenced by Carter. The "matriarch of country music" lived up to her reputation by giving moving performances in the United States and Europe. They included appearances at the Newport Folk Festivals of 1963 and 1967, when she was reunited with Sara Carter. Carter was a regular on the "Johnny Cash Show" (Cash married her daughter June) and recorded the albums "An Historic Reunion" (1967) with Sara and "Will the Circle Be Unbroken" (1971) with the Nitty Gritty Dirt Band. Carter was on hand in 1970 when the Original Carter Family was inducted into the Country Music Hall of Fame. Mother Maybelle Carter died in Nashville, Tenn.

[For biographical sketches, discography, and bibliography, see John Atkins, ed., *The Carter Family* (1973); and Robert K. Krishef and Stacy Harris, *The Carter Family* (1978). An obituary is in *Rolling Stone*, Nov. 24, 1978.]

LINDA ELSROAD

CASSIDY, JACK (Mar. 5, 1927–Dec. 12, 1976), stage, television, and film actor, was born John Edward Joseph Cassidy in Richmond Hill, Queens, New York City. Cassidy's childhood was "classically unhappy." He attended parochial school and high school in Richmond Hill, both of which he found "a bore." "I never had time for games and things," he explained in a 1966 interview. "I wanted to make money, to be a man quickly." Cassidy later blamed his unhappy childhood for his initial inhibitions as an actor. At the age of sixteen, Cassidy answered an open audition for actors and singers for Michael Todd's production of *Something for the Boys*, which toured the nation in 1943. Cassidy gained his early entry into show business largely because of a dearth of available young male actors owing to the draft.

After World War II, Cassidy made his way to Broadway, where he appeared in the chorus in numerous musicals, including *Sadie Thompson* (1945), *The Red Mill* (1945), and *Around the World in Eighty Days* (1946). In these and other productions during the late 1940's, Cassidy found himself typecast as a "pretty chorus boy," so he developed "a tough facade for compensation." The result was that his new attitude and his good looks classified him as a "cocky, self-centered smart aleck" in the eyes of directors. In 1948, Cassidy got a break from such roles in the comic revue *Small Wonder*, when director Payton Price encouraged him to develop his feeling for comedy. With this part, he discovered "the best side of me was the light side, not the sorrowful." He established himself further with his work in the dramatic musical *Sandhog*. One critic labeled his rendering of the Irish melody, "Johnny O," with Betty Oakes, "a beguiling piece of work." In 1949, Cassidy appeared in Rodgers and Hammerstein's *South Pacific*.

By the mid-1950's, Cassidy had developed a singing style that critics consistently praised. He had also honed his talents as an actor and dancer. His multiplicity of talents kept him steadily employed in television, film, and theater. "If there was no song-and-dance work one season, I could play comedy," he told an interviewer; "if comedy was hard to find, I could handle a dramatic role."

Cassidy married Evelyn Ward on Oct. 31, 1948. The couple had one son, David, and were divorced in 1956. During this time, Cassidy had been struggling with the legacy of his childhood and his inability to establish a satisfying personal and theatrical identity. In the mid-1950's, Cassidy began exorcizing some of his childhood demons by writing a fictionalized autobiography. "It was a strictly amateur effort," Cassidy later explained, "but putting the things that troubled me on paper had quite a cathartic effect."

Although Cassidy indicated to an interviewer that his first marriage had been unstable, the divorce was probably instigated by his relationship with actress and singer Shirley Jones. The two first met on a State Department–sponsored European tour of *Oklahoma!* (1955), where Cassidy played the lead role of Curley opposite Jones's Laurey. Both received enthusiastic reviews from critics and from each other. According to Cassidy, "When I first met Shirley, everything positive seemed to fall into place." The two married on Aug. 5, 1956, during their joint appearance in *The Beggar's Opera*. The marriage fared better than the play, which was generally panned, but both Jones and Cassidy were praised for their singing. The couple had three children, including Shaun, a singer and actor.

Jones and Cassidy developed a supper-club act, which allowed them to spend more time together. They took the act to British television with *A Date with Shirley and Jack* in 1959. They went on to make a number of records, including *With Love from Hollywood*, and *Speaking of Love*. Cassidy also recorded several albums on his own.

During the early 1960's, Cassidy and Jones followed separate though occasionally intertwined careers, yet managed to maintain their relationship. Cassidy began appearing in numerous low-budget movies, cast in the role of a sophisticated, sinister villain. His television work during this period, including appearances in "Gunsmoke," "Wagon Train," "77 Sunset Strip," and other programs, was of a similar type. Cassidy also appeared in several theatrical productions during this time.

Cassidy's breakthrough role came in 1963, with a small but significant part in the musical *She Loves Me*. "I knew I'd be lost in the show if I didn't do something pretty positive, and decided to make it the broadest kind of caricature. It was a nervy, tricky thing to do, but at that point I'd developed the kind of freedom and ease that happens when you begin to like yourself." Cassidy's hilarious rendition of a preening Don Juan earned him honors in the New York drama critics poll, the *Saturday Review* critics poll, and a Tony Award, as well as notices in *Newsweek*, *Time*, *Life*, and the *New Yorker*. The following year, he starred in *Fade Out, Fade In*, with Carol Burnett. Cassidy earned high praise for his portrayal of film star Byron Perry, "who is never without a hand mirror to admire the dimples on his handsome face." Cassidy perfected his rendition of a leading man parodying leading men with *It's a Bird . . . It's a Plane . . . It's Superman!* (1966), another musical that was lauded by critics. Stanley Kauffmann wrote, "Mr. Cassidy is a skillful pro, to whom a song and dance is a chance to comment on the world of song and dance."

Cassidy appeared ready for a move into true stardom, but failed to get the necessary roles in film, television, or theater to capitalize on his growing reputation. He did land a supporting role in the comedy series "He and She," repeating his leading man parody as television star Oscar North. Unfortunately, the series, which featured Richard Benjamin and Paula Prentiss, was canceled after a year and a half. Cassidy made numerous one-shot appearances on television shows ranging from "The Carol Burnett Show" to "Cannon," as well as several made-for-television movies. His best television performance was as the defense lawyer in the television version of the play *The Andersonville Trial* (1970), which earned Cassidy an Emmy nomination. He also kept busy with supporting parts in movies, including *A Guide for the Married Man* (1967), *Bunny O'Hare* (1971), *The Eiger Sanction* (1975), and W. C. *Fields and*

Me (1976). The last again had him playing a leading man, this time the actor John Barrymore. Cassidy made only irregular appearances on the stage in the late 1960's and 1970's.

Cassidy and Jones continued to appear together occasionally, although they never repeated the critical raves of their earliest collaboration. Of their performance in *Maggie Flynn* (1969), *New York Times* critic Clive Barnes wrote, "I only wish I had seen them in *Oklahoma!*" The pair toured their club act in the early 1970's, appearing at the MGM Grand in Las Vegas and other top nightclub spots. Jones had by this time established herself as a national star with her television role as the singing (and single) mom in "The Partridge Family." Cassidy's son David starred in the show as one of Jones's children and launched a successful career from this role. Jack Cassidy remarked that "ever since the 1950's I've been known as Shirley Jones's husband. But all that's changed; now I'm David Cassidy's father!" The strain of two separate show-business careers finally took its toll on Jones and Cassidy's marriage, and Jones filed for divorce in 1975, claiming "irreconcilable differences."

Cassidy's life ended the following year, when a fire ravaged his penthouse apartment in West Hollywood. The fire was believed to have been caused by a cigarette left burning on a couch. Jones was not mentioned in Cassidy's will, and his son David was specifically cut out of his inheritance.

[A revealing interview with Cassidy is in the *New York Times*, May 15, 1966. For Cassidy's Broadway notices, see the *New York Times Index to Theater Reviews*. An assortment of smaller pieces on Cassidy may be found in the clippings file at the Television Academy Library in Los Angeles. An obituary is in the *New York Times*, Dec. 13, 1976.]

MICHAEL GOLDBERG

CATTON, CHARLES BRUCE (Oct. 9, 1899–Aug. 28, 1978), author and editor, was born in Petoskey, Mich., the son of George R. Catton, a Congregational minister and teacher, and Adella M. Patten. A winner of both the Pulitzer Prize and the National Book Award, Catton was perhaps the most widely read and influential Civil War historian of his time. His books most often centered on the experiences of small-town men and boys who had been drawn into the awful carnage of combat but managed to hold on to some of the innocence and much of the strength of the world they had left behind, a world much like Benzonia, Mich., where Catton had lived as a boy and whose homespun values he carried throughout his life. It was, he said of Benzonia (population 350), "about as small a small town as there ever was, and I think about as pleasant a place, in the last of the preautomobile age, for a child to grow up."

After graduating from Benzonia Academy, a preparatory school presided over by his father, Catton entered Oberlin College in 1916. On America's entrance into World War I, he enlisted in the United States Navy as a gunner's mate, returning to college after the armistice. At the end of his junior year, he left Oberlin for good to become a newspaperman, breaking with the family tradition of entering the ministry or teaching. From 1920 to 1926 he reported variously for the *Cleveland News*, the *Boston American*, and the *Cleveland Plain Dealer*. On Aug. 16, 1925, he married Hazel H. Cherry; they had one child.

From 1926 to 1941, Catton wrote for the Newspaper Enterprise Association, moving through a series of specialized roles as a feature assignment reporter, editorial writer, book reviewer, and syndicated columnist based in Washington, D.C. During World War II he served as director of information for the War Production Board and, after the war, in the same capacity for the Department of the Interior. He was a special assistant to the secretary of commerce in 1948, the year he published *The War Lords of Washington*, a firsthand account of the bickering, backbiting, and intrigue that marked the struggle for power between high-level civilian officials and the military during World War II. The book received mixed reviews and was little read, but its reception was encouraging enough for him to strike out on his own as a free-lance writer.

His subject was the Civil War, which had long been the focus of his recreational reading and a source of fascination since his boyhood in Benzonia, where he had heard countless war stories from the town's aging veterans of the Grand Army of the Republic. Their recollections were so vivid, he wrote, that he felt "the whole affair had taken place in the next county just a few years ago." Over time he had collected and avidly read regimental histories, soldiers' diaries, and little-known memoirs, most of which, he believed, had been overlooked by other Civil War historians. He initially thought to write a novel, a literary form he had earlier tackled with little success (his two efforts in the 1930's, he told an interviewer, were "quite worthless"), but he soon abandoned fiction for straight narrative history.

In 1951 he offered *Mr. Lincoln's Army* to three publishing houses before Doubleday agreed to take it. The first volume in a trilogy about the Army of the Potomac, it was followed by *Glory Road* in 1952 and *A Stillness at Appomattox* in 1953. The last volume won Catton a large and faithful audience and established his reputation as an elegant writer of narrative history, with a unique ability to recreate the life of common soldiers as well as the mood of the era he described. Highly praised by academic historians and daily book reviewers alike, *A Stillness at Appomattox* won both the Pulitzer Prize for history and the National Book Award, the latter's citation praising Catton for combining "historical accuracy with poetic insight."

In 1954, Catton became the first editor of *American Heritage*, a magazine of popular history that quickly became a publishing success. By 1959, the demands on his time as a writer and lecturer became so great that he relinquished editorial control of the magazine to become senior editor, a position he held until his death. Between 1950 and 1978, he published fourteen books relating to the Civil War. In addition to his trilogy on the Army of the Potomac, he wrote *The Coming Fury* (1961), *Terrible Swift Sword* (1963), and *Never Call Retreat* (1965), which collectively formed *The Centennial History of the Civil War*. Less successful with academic critics were three volumes that moved away from Catton's familiar narrative territory to speculations about the causes and consequences of the war. His critics accused him of reductionism, unsubstantiated generalizations, and overblown prose in *U. S. Grant and the American Military Tradition* (1954), a preliminary examination of Grant's place in American history; *This Hallowed Ground* (1956), an assessment of the meaning of the Union's victory; and *America Goes to War* (1958), a series of essays on the war's military legacy derived from the lectures he delivered as Frank B. Weeks Visiting Professor of History at Wesleyan University in Middletown, Conn.

Returning to the narrative form, Catton gained critical favor for *Grant Moves South* (1960) and *Grant Takes Command* (1969), which completed the three-volume biography begun by Lloyd Lewis, who had died shortly after he completed the first volume, *Captain Sam Grant*, in 1950. In addition, Catton wrote the narrative for *The American Heritage Picture History of the Civil War*, which won him and Stephen Sears, the picture editor, a special Pulitzer citation in 1961. In his later years, he published a memoir, *Waiting for the Morning Train* (1972); a battle history, *Gettysburg: The Final Fury* (1974); and a volume in the State and Nation Series, *Michigan: A Bicentennial History* (1976). He twice collaborated with his son, William, a professor of American history at Middlebury College in Vermont: in 1963 on *Two Roads to Sumter* and in 1978 on *The Bold and Magnificent Dream: America's Founding Years, 1492–1815*.

Catton was a highly disciplined and well-organized writer who rose early and worked late. An avid fisherman and baseball fan, he was fond of good food and drink. For many years the Algonquin Hotel in New York City kept a corner table for him at lunch. Although he could be a blunt-spoken critic in editorial sessions, he was, said an associate, "a positive pussycat" in his face-to-face meetings with writers whose work he had to reject. Tall and unassuming, he had, a colleague wrote, "the faintly courtly good manners of the old Midwest."

Catton received the Presidential Medal of Freedom from Gerald Ford in 1977. He died in Frankfort, Mich.

[An interview with Catton is in the *Wilson Library Bulletin*, June 1954; Oliver Jensen provides a memoir entitled "Working with Bruce Catton" in *American Heritage*, Feb. 1979. An obituary is in the *New York Times*, Nov. 6, 1978.]

ALLAN L. DAMON

CAVANAGH, JEROME PATRICK ("JERRY") (June 16, 1928–Nov. 27, 1979), politician, was born in Detroit, Mich., one of six children of Sylvester J. Cavanagh, a boilermaker at the Ford Motor Company, and Mary Irene Timmins. Both his parents had been born in Ireland and had originally emigrated to Canada. They moved to Detroit so that the elder Cavanagh could find work with Ford. Cavanagh graduated from St. Cecilia High School in Detroit in 1946. He received his Ph.B. in political science from the University of Detroit in 1950 and his law degree from its law school in 1954. Cavanagh married Mary Helen Martin on Nov. 22, 1952; the couple had eight children.

After law school he practiced with the firm of Sullivan, Romanoff, Cavanagh and Nelson, but his real passion was Detroit city politics. In 1961 he challenged incumbent mayor Louis C. Miriani and won. He was the second-youngest mayor in the history of Detroit, and his youth and energy attracted wide national attention and many favorable comparisons to the young Irish-American president, John F. Kennedy.

The Kennedy and Lyndon Johnson administrations both saw Detroit as an ideal test site for their many programs designed to address the problems plaguing urban America in the 1960's and viewed its Democratic mayor as a natural political ally. The city received a large infusion of federal money for urban renewal, economic redevelopment, and programs to improve race relations. Detroit was widely hailed by the national press and media as a model city in all three areas owing to Cavanagh's leadership and the federal assistance the city was given.

Cavanagh was regularly featured in the national press as an exemplar of the new breed of urban mayors, reversing the decline of America's older industrial cities. He was also a highly visible figure around Motor City, promoting the arts and its cultural institutions, pushing for greater racial integration of the police force, and overseeing many federal programs to rebuild and renew Detroit.

In 1965, Cavanagh was reelected with 69 percent of the vote and was considered a rising star on the national political scene. In 1966 he served as president of both the United States Conference of Mayors and the National League of Cities. He was one of the first ten fellows selected in 1966 by the Kennedy Institute at Harvard University.

In 1966, Cavanagh sought the Democratic nomination for the United States Senate and in the course of the primary campaign came out publicly against the Vietnam War. This was a bold and dramatic step, but it left him isolated both nationally and in Michigan from the mainstream of the Democratic party, which was still supportive of President Johnson and the war. His stand led to a very bitter, public break with President Johnson and reductions in federal assistance for Detroit. His defeat by former Governor G. Mennen Williams in the Democratic primary marked the end of Cavanagh's political ascent. In later years he referred to himself and his life as a "walking Irish tragedy."

In the summer of 1967 a police raid on an after-hours club quickly escalated into a riot. A series of errors and delays, as well as pent-up frustration and grievances against the police force in the city's black community, expanded the riot into one of the most violent and destructive civil disturbances in American history. Federal assistance was slow to arrive, and as the city burned, its failures as a model city and those of its mayor were laid bare for all to see. Once order was restored, the task of rebuilding the city was slowed and made more difficult by the deep rift between Cavanagh and President Johnson.

In 1968, Cavanagh faced additional personal and political traumas. That year he and his wife divorced, which in 1968 was a major liability for an Irish-Catholic politician. There were also allegations (never substantiated) of widespread corruption in his administration's handling of the federal grant money that had flowed through Detroit. Cavanagh chose not to seek reelection in 1969 and moved to Ann Arbor at the end of his term in 1970.

Cavanagh married Kathleen M. Disser on June 30, 1972, and they adopted one child. For several years he practiced law, taught politics and government at the University of Michigan, and served as president of Urban Synergistics, a New York City–based urban policy think tank exploring solutions to the urban problems that the riots of 1967 and 1968 had brought forward on the national agenda.

In 1974, Cavanagh attempted a political comeback, seeking the Democratic nomination for governor. Illness that took him away from the campaign for a great deal of time and vivid images in the minds of Michigan voters of Detroit in flames and occupied by federal troops combined to defeat him in the primary. He returned to the practice of law following the primary election. His name frequently surfaced as a potential candidate for office, but he was plagued by poor health and never again sought elective office. He died in Lexington, Ky.

[Information on Cavanagh can be found at the Archives of Labor History and Urban Affairs, Wayne State University, Detroit. See also Sidney Fine, *Violence in the Model City: The Cavanagh Adminis-*

tration, Race Relations, and the Detroit Riot of 1967 (1989). An obituary is in the *New York Times*, Nov. 28, 1979.]

WILLIAM H. MULLIGAN, JR.

CAVERT, SAMUEL McCREA (Sept. 9, 1888–Dec. 21, 1976), clergyman, ecumenist, and interdenominational executive, was born in Charlton, N.Y., one of four children of Elizabeth Brann and Walter I. Cavert, a farmer and civic worker. Cavert attended Charlton Academy, a private school, for eleven years before graduating from Schenectady High School in 1906. From 1906 to 1910 he attended Union College (Schenectady), where he served as president of the senior class and the student YMCA. He received a B.A. degree, summa cum laude, and was chosen valedictorian and a member of Phi Beta Kappa. From 1910 to 1912, he was director of Union College's student YMCA, and during his second year of employment at the college, he also was an instructor of Greek. In 1912 he enrolled as a divinity student at Union Theological Seminary in New York City, and he simultaneously studied philosophy at Columbia University, where he received an M.A. degree in 1914. In 1915, he received a B.D. degree, summa cum laude, from Union Seminary, and he was awarded the school's traveling fellowship. On Oct. 29, 1915, he was ordained as a minister of the Presbyterian Church (U.S.A.). From 1915 to 1916, Cavert served as an assistant to William Adams Brown in the Department of Systematic Theology at Union Seminary. Cavert credited Brown with sparking his interest in the ecumenical movement and interdenominational work.

In the fall of 1916, Cavert traveled to India and the Far East for a year of study on his fellowship. After his return to the United States in the fall of 1917, Cavert was employed as assistant secretary of the General War-Time Commission of the Churches, an organization that served as the official agency through which the government dealt with the various Protestant denominations in matters concerning the religious welfare of American soldiers and sailors. In October 1918 he enlisted as a chaplain in the United States Army, serving in the rank of first lieutenant. On Nov. 14, 1918, Cavert married Ruth Miller, and three months later, following his discharge from the army, the couple moved to New York City, where Cavert was employed by the Federal Council of Churches of Christ in America (FCC) as secretary of the Committee on the War and the Religious Outlook. The committee studied issues of American church unity, mission, and education as well as the impact of postwar industrial reconstruction on the American people. Cavert assisted in writing and editing several of the committee's studies, which were published in the 1920's.

In 1920, after fifteen months of marriage, Ruth Cavert died from complications that followed the birth of the Caverts' only child. Later in 1920, Cavert became associate secretary of the Federal Council of Churches, and in 1921, he became one of two general secretaries of the FCC as well as the editor of the *Federal Council Bulletin*. In the post of general secretary (which he held until 1950), Cavert was instrumental in leading the FCC through the period when it had its greatest impact on the development of interchurch cooperation in the United States, and his own philosophical outlook was influential in determining the nature of the FCC's work. During his early career, Cavert espoused a social-centered philosophy that evolved from his Protestant faith, a faith that advocated cooperative social action and outreach as a means to a more perfect world. Though Cavert was an advocate of Christian social action for the rest of his life, in the 1930's he began to believe that social and evangelical action needed a firmer basis in theology, a point of view he and others called theological realism. With the brothers Reinhold and Richard Niebuhr and other American neo-Orthodox theologians, he joined the Theological Discussion Group to explore religious and social issues of the day.

On June 28, 1927, Cavert married Ruth Twila Lytton, an educator and eventual leader in furthering the role of women in the national and international movements for Christian unity.

In 1930, Cavert became the sole general secretary and the chief executive officer of the Federal Council of Churches. Under Cavert's leadership during the decade of the 1930's, the FCC had to confront criticisms of its alleged "liberal" stands on issues ranging from disarmament and pacifism to family planning and parenting, controversial issues that challenged the council's ability to achieve its goal of greater church unity in America. During this period Cavert played a major role in the movement to organize Christian churches from around the world into a cooperative association, or ecumenical federation. He was a participant in a meeting in May 1933 in England where the first steps were taken toward the formal unification of various ecumenical organizations in Europe and the United States. In 1937, he was one of the members of the Committee of Thirty-Five, a group of church leaders who designed the plan for an international organization of churches. It was Cavert who suggested that the body be named the World Council of Churches (WCC). In 1938, following the approval of the global organization's plan by several European conferences and church groups, a WCC constitution was drafted at a meeting in Utrecht, Holland, which was attended by Cavert. He was selected as a member of the World Council's provisional committee, a position he held for ten years until the WCC was officially constituted as the representative body for 150 independent national churches in forty-two countries.

Because of World War II, the formal establishment of the WCC was delayed. During this period Cavert and other church leaders focused their attention on maintaining positive American-European church relationships in order to preserve the progress that had been made toward a cooperative unity. Cavert was also instrumental in creating a plan for postwar church reconstruction and relief that would be under the auspices of the World Council leadership. During the war, Cavert served as a member of the board of directors of the United Service Organizations (USO), and President Roosevelt appointed him a member of the Advisory Committee on Political Refugees. He also served on the governing board of the United States Committee for the Care of European Children.

In September 1945, Cavert took a six-month leave from the Federal Council to go to Geneva and assist the provisional committee with postwar plans for finalizing the formal organization of the WCC. While in Europe, Cavert served as a representative at a Stuttgart meeting that established a reconciliation with the German church, an issue that was key to the future success of the WCC. Because of his effective work with German church leaders during the strained, prewar years as well as the postwar reconciliation period, Cavert was appointed by the Truman administration in 1946 as a temporary Protestant liaison officer for the United States government in Europe. In this capacity, he served as intermediary between the German Protestant churches and the United States Office of Military Government for Germany. His responsibilities also included working with American chaplains in Europe.

By 1950, as a former president of the WCC has noted, Cavert's ecumenical work had solidified his role as "both an architect and builder of the two most widely-known councils for Christian unity in this century": the World Council of Churches and the National Council of Churches of Christ in the U.S.A. Cavert chaired the committee on arrangements for, and attended, the First Assembly of the WCC held in Amsterdam in August 1948, and he also attended succeeding assemblies in Evanston, Ill. (1954), New Delhi (1961), and Uppsala (1968).

In 1950, as the general secretary of the Federal Council of Churches, Cavert led in bringing that organization together with seven other interdenominational agencies in the United States to form the National Council of Churches (NCC), an organization that represented a national membership of nearly 32 million from the Protestant and Eastern Orthodox faiths. Cavert was chosen the first general secretary, or chief executive officer, a post he held from 1951 to 1954.

On his retirement from the NCC, Cavert served as the executive secretary of the New York office of the WCC for four years (1954–1957). Although semiretired, he continued to work in religion-related enterprises. He served as editorial secretary of the Religious Book Club (1958–1969) and as the director of the Interchurch Center in New York City (1963–1964). He was a guest of the Second Vatican Council in Rome in 1964.

In the last decade of his life, Cavert devoted his time to writing. In 1968 he published *The American Churches in the Ecumenical Movement, 1900–1968*, and in 1970 he published *Church Cooperation and Unity in America, 1900–1970*. He also wrote numerous articles for religious journals. Because he was a participant in the great ecumenical events of his time, his writings on the history of ecumenism are considered standard sources on the movements. He died at age eighty-eight of heart failure in suburban Bronxville, N.Y. His ashes are interred in the Christ Church (Episcopal) Columbarium in Bronxville.

[Cavert was the author or editor of over a dozen books and reports. In addition to the two works listed above, his books include *On the Road to Christian Unity* (1961) and *The Adventure of the Church* (1927). With Henry P. Van Dusen, Cavert edited *The Church Through Half a Century* (1936). Representative of his numerous articles are "Separation of Church and State: Why It Matters," *The Christian Century*, May 15, 1940; and "Is the Ecumenical Movement Slowing Down?," *The Christian Century*, May 1, 1974. The best source on his life is a biography by William J. Schmidt, *Architect of Unity* (1978). George Hugh Wilson is the author of "The Role of Samuel McCrea Cavert in the Federal Council of Churches of Christ in America" (Master's thesis, Hartford Seminary Foundation, 1957). An obituary is in the *New York Times*, Dec. 23, 1976.]

MARILYNN WOOD HILL

CHALIAPIN, BORIS FYODOROVICH (Oct. 5, 1904–May 18, 1979), artist, was born in Moscow, Russia, where he spent most of his childhood and youth. His Italian-born mother, Iole Tornaghi, had been a ballerina before her marriage, and his father, Fyodor Chaliapin, was a widely celebrated opera singer. Among the older Chaliapin's most famous roles was Boris Gudonov, for whom his son was named. Chaliapin exhibited a talent for drawing at an early age, and sketching was one of the major preoccupations of his boyhood. Despite his family's ample means, the peasant origins of his father prevented Chaliapin from enrolling in Russia's elite lyceums, which were reserved for the aristocracy. As a result, he received his basic education at one of Moscow's less-exclusive gymnasiums.

In the years immediately following the Russian Revolution, Chaliapin's family was sympathetic to their country's new Communist order, and his father, who was proclaimed a People's Artist, at one point undertook concert tours abroad to raise money for relieving the postrevolutionary famine in Soviet Russia. The younger Chaliapin embarked on the formal study of art. In 1919 he spent several months at Petrograd's academy of art, and on his return to Moscow, he worked in the studios of painters Abram Arkipov and Dimitri Kardovsky.

Shortly after completing his secondary education in 1922, Chaliapin was admitted to the State Higher Arts and Technology Workshops. He wanted to study painting there, but because of crowded enrollments in the school's painting curriculum, he had to settle for courses in sculpture, under the tutelage of Sergei Konenkov. Chaliapin's primary interest remained painting, and so, after several failed efforts to shift into the workshops' painting classes, he immigrated to Paris to pursue an art training more to his liking. He was supported in that decision by his father, whose disillusionment with the Soviet regime had by then led to his own immigration to the French capital.

Arriving in Paris in the summer of 1925, Chaliapin studied with a number of painters, including the fellow Russian émigré Konstantin Korovin and an artist identified only as Gerin. It was through Gerin's timed drawing exercises, Chaliapin later said, that he developed his unusual facility for rapid and sure draftsmanship.

In 1928, while appearing in an opera at London's Covent Garden, Chaliapin's father arranged for the first public exhibition of his son's work there. Consisting mostly of scenes recalling rural Russian life, the show drew complimentary newspaper notices, and over the next seven years, Chaliapin's work was included in several group shows in Paris. Among his pieces from this period is a striking portrait of Russian composer Sergei Rachmaninoff, a family friend at whose French country house he was a frequent visitor. In 1929, Chaliapin married Maria Bobrik; they had one child.

Chaliapin was always a steadfast realist in his painting and in later years dismissed the abstractionist trends in twentieth-century art as a "cultivated approach to insanity" fostered by "incurable delinquents." The lack of sympathy for modernism ultimately made him ill at ease in the Paris art world, where the avant-garde was becoming ever more dominant. Yet another source of dissatisfaction was his failure to make a decent living from his art in Paris.

In 1935 he sailed for the United States in the hope of finding an art community and market more receptive to his work. Settling in New York City, Chaliapin concentrated mostly on painting portraits. Owing largely to his family's connections in the world of the performing arts, many of his early subjects were actors, dancers, and musicians, among them violinist Jascha Heifetz and members of the Ballet Russe de Monte Carlo.

On Apr. 11, 1942, shortly after obtaining a divorce from his first wife, Chaliapin married Helen Davidson, and a year later he became an American citizen. He received his first commission from *Time* magazine in 1942 for a newsmaker cover portrait, a likeness of Indian leader Jawaharlal Nehru. When a few weeks later Chaliapin filled a request for a second cover portrait on a moment's notice, it was clear that his talents meshed unusually well with the magazine's needs. The crisp realism of his portraiture was entirely compatible with *Time*'s style, and his ability to meet short press deadlines substantially increased the magazine's capacity for shifting cover subjects in the face of late-breaking news. Soon Chaliapin numbered among *Time*'s regular cover artists, and between 1942 and 1970 he produced more than four hundred covers for the publication.

Chaliapin's success at *Time* was the turning point of his career, and soon after his first cover was published, several advertising agencies, including J. Walter Thompson, began enlisting his services. Among his advertising work was a series of likenesses done for Magnavox of leading musical figures, such as conductor Arturo Toscanini and singer Lily Pons. His covers for *Time* also enhanced his standing as a studio portraitist, and in the coming years he painted noncommercial likenesses of many notables, among them conductor Fritz Reiner, novelist Theodore Dreiser, and dancer Katherine Dunham.

A major exhibition of Chaliapin's work took place in the Soviet Union in 1975 under the sponsorship of the cultural exchange program between the United States and the Soviet Union. Today the largest collection of his work—consisting mostly of his original *Time* covers—resides at the National Portrait Gallery of the Smithsonian Institution in Washington, D.C. Another important repository of his work is his childhood home in Moscow, now a museum dedicated to his father. Chaliapin died in New York City.

[A small collection of Chaliapin's papers resides at the Archives, American Heritage Center, University of Wyoming in Laramie. The artist's family retains other records of his career, including early childhood drawings. The most complete treatment of Chaliapin's views on art is William Michefelder, "His War Against Phonies!!" *New York World-Telegram*, Apr. 18, 1959. For biographical material, see William F. Woo, "Artist Boris Chaliapin: Fast Man on the Draw," *St. Louis Post-Dispatch*, May 23, 1963, and Semyon Markovich Chertok, *Artist Boris Chaliapin* (1975), a work in Russian containing color reproductions of many of the artist's works. An obituary is in the *New York Times*, May 19, 1979.]

FREDERICK S. VOSS

CHAMPION, GOWER (June 22, 1919–Aug. 25, 1980), dancer, choreographer, and director, was born in Geneva, Ill., to John W. Champion, an advertising executive, and Beatrice Carlisle, a custom dressmaker. After his parents divorced, Champion was raised by his mother in Los Angeles, where he studied dance under Ernest Belcher. He quit Fairfax High School at age seventeen, after winning an amateur dance contest, and began touring fashionable clubs with his partner, Jeanne Tyler. They billed themselves as "Gower and Jeanne, America's Youngest Dancers." They danced together all the way to Hollywood, where they had cameo roles in *Streets of Paris* (1939), *The Lady Comes Across* (1942), and *Count Me In* (1942).

Champion joined the United States Coast Guard during World War II, and the service recognized his talents by allowing him to tour with the patriotic musical *Tars and Spars*. After the war, he appeared in the motion picture *Till the Clouds Roll By* (1946). In 1947 he rediscovered his childhood sweetheart, Marjorie Celeste ("Marge") Belcher, the daughter of his former mentor. She became his dance partner and on Oct. 5, 1947, they were married. They had two children. Working together as the dance team of Gower and Bell, the pair became a dancing sensation, and their stylish and energetic performances were especially suited to the new medium of television. They appeared on the "Admiral Broadway Revue" in 1949 and performed later on virtually every TV variety show of the 1950's. So great was their renown that in 1957 they starred in a situation comedy, the "Marge and Gower Champion Show," in which they played themselves. Their career also included the big screen, with roles in such motion pictures as *Mr. Music* (1950), *Show Boat* (1951), *Everything I Have Is Yours* (1952), *Give a Girl a Break* (1953), *Jupiter's Darling* (1955), and *The Girl Most Likely* (1955).

In 1948, Champion discovered Carol Channing and cast her in *Lend an Ear*, his first effort at directing and choreographing a musical stage production. The play was a Broadway hit and a success with the critics—Champion won the first of his seven Tony Awards. He did not, however, return to Broadway as director-choreographer until 1960, with the smash hit *Bye Bye Birdie*. He received Tonys for the plays's animated choreography and direction. Critical and popular acclaim swelled as one hit musical followed another: *Carnival!* (1961),

Hello, Dolly! (1964), with Tony Awards for his direction and choreography, and *I Do! I Do!* (1966). No one who saw *Dolly* on stage could ever forget the waiters capering and duelling with shish kebabs in the Harmonia Gardens.

For a performer, Champion was unusually shy. After a show, he often disappeared for hours at a time, especially on opening nights. As cast and crew rustled off to await the reviews at some posh restaurant, Champion would hide in the sets, enjoying people's candid observations about the performance. When Gower missed the reviews of *Dolly*, Marge returned to the theater to tell him the play was a hit—and found him in the set for the Harmonia Gardens.

Work on *Carnival!* introduced Champion to producer David Merrick and began a fruitful, though stormy, collaboration. Irked by the choreographer's dictatorial attitude on the set, Merrick once called him the "Presbyterian Hitler." Champion disputed only the first part of that characterization—he was an avowed agnostic. And he was demanding—one stagehand later recalled having to "audition" twenty pushcarts before Champion saw one he liked. Champion and Merrick disagreed loudly, passionately, and often about who should have final control over the finished production, and both asserted more than once that their latest play would be their last together. Nevertheless, they overcame their differences, personal and professional, to stage seven productions over a span of twenty years, most of which were critical and financial successes.

Champion's most complete failures as an artist came in his attempts to direct dramatic productions for stage and screen. A natural as a dancer, choreographer, and musical director, his stage production of Lillian Hellman's *My Mother, My Father and Me* (1963) and the movie *My Six Loves* (1963) both flopped. He was more successful at directing television variety specials and won considerable respect as a "show doctor," called in from the wings to cure ailing Broadway musicals. Oddly, although he saved several productions, including Liza Minnelli's *The Act*, Champion did not direct or choreograph a hit show for the better part of ten years—with the notable exception of *Irene* (1973). Such experimental plays as *The Happy Time* (1968), *Mack and Mabel* (1974), and *Rockabye Hamlet* (1976), the first two for producer David Merrick, were critical failures. His professional crisis was mirrored in his personal life: in 1973 the Champions divorced. Three years later, he married longtime friend interior landscaper Karla Most.

After nearly five years' absence from the director's chair, Champion accepted Merrick's challenge to choreograph and direct a theatrical adaptation of the movie musical *42nd Street* (1933), which had starred Ruby Keeler. He also knew he was not Merrick's first choice (Michael Bennett had already declined the offer). Yet the simple, old-fashioned musical was a perfect vehicle for the dance master's unique talents; both he and the play were charmingly and purposely anachronistic. He was not successful as a cutting-edge innovator like his friends Bob Fosse or Jerome Robbins; his style was sophisticated yet engagingly unpretentious, energetic yet reminiscent of Broadway's more innocent past.

A year earlier, Champion's doctors had informed him that he had a rare blood disease and recommended inactivity. He chose to work, but the grueling pace of rehearsals debilitated him quickly. Unable to hide his growing infirmity, Champion told cast, crew, and producer that he had a virus and fought with Merrick to hasten production. Champion died only hours before *42nd Street* opened on Broadway. Merrick, normally reclusive, came on stage after the show and ten curtain calls were over to tell cast and audience that Champion was dead. Few at the Winter Garden Theater missed the pervasive sense of tragic irony. *42nd Street* was rife with show-business clichés—the ingenue, the fading star, the tough director who falls in love with the ingenue—which could only be topped by the ultimate Broadway cliché: with its directory lying dead in the hospital, the show had gone on.

[For his life and work see David Payne-Carter, "Gower Champion and the American Musical Theater" (Ph.D. diss., New York University, 1989). See also William Goldman, *The Season* (1969). An obituary is in the *New York Times*, Aug. 27, 1980.]

DAVID M. ESPOSITO

CHAPLIN, CHARLES SPENCER ("CHARLIE") (Apr. 16, 1889–Dec. 25, 1977), film actor, director, producer, writer, and composer, was born in London, England, the son of Charles Chaplin and Hannah Harriet Pedlingham Hill. Both of Chaplin's parents sang in

English music halls, his mother under the stage name Lily Harley. Chaplin's childhood was unstable. Charles, Sr., separated from the family in 1890 and provided only minimal and sporadic support for his son after that time. An alcoholic, he died in 1901 at the age of thirty-seven. After ending her singing career, his mother tried to support Chaplin and his half brother Sydney through sewing. From 1895 on, she was in and out of hospitals and asylums with physical and emotional problems. For the next five years, Chaplin and his brother Sydney lived in a variety of homes and institutions, including the Lambeth workhouse. It was during this time that Chaplin received his only four years of (intermittent) formal education.

From the time he was very young, Chaplin was a gifted mime. His first performance before an audience came in 1894, when his mother's singing voice failed on stage, and he was called upon to sing a popular ditty. By late 1898, Chaplin had his first job as a performer, touring with a group called the Eight Lancashire Lads. Between 1903 and 1907, Chaplin played roles in a number of plays, some in London and some touring the British Isles. In 1908 he was hired by Fred Karno, whose comedy troupes were popular in the English music halls. While working for Karno, Chaplin honed his skills at pantomime and twice toured the United States and Canada. On the second tour, he came to the attention of leaders in the burgeoning movie industry, and in 1913 he signed a contract to appear in comic movies made at Mack Sennett's Keystone Studios in Los Angeles.

Chaplin arrived at Keystone in December 1913, a propitious moment in the development of the film industry. The "star system" was just beginning, as studios between 1910 and 1913 began featuring the names of movie actors and actresses and publicizing their lives as a method of marketing their films. Chaplin became a chief beneficiary of that system and one of the most popular and lasting stars in the history of American movies. His first film, *Making a Living*, was released in February 1914. Later that month, Chaplin assembled the costume that became his trademark for more than twenty years. Consisting of a tight-fitting coat, baggy pants, floppy shoes, a derby hat, a narrow moustache, and a cane, the costume looked to be that of a genteel figure fallen on hard times. The character Chaplin created wearing that costume—variously called the Tramp, the Little Fellow, or Charlie—served as his comic screen persona in nearly all his films through *Modern Times* (1936).

Chaplin appeared in thirty-five films at Keystone in 1914, nearly all of them one-reelers and two-reelers. Beginning in April, he was also given the opportunity to direct the films he appeared in; after leaving Keystone, he always directed the films in which he starred. Near the end of his one-year contract with Keystone, his movies were already becoming vastly popular, and companies were bidding for his services.

In 1915, Chaplin left Keystone for Essanay, on a one-year contract. He made fourteen films, mostly two-reelers, at Essanay in 1915 and the first months of 1916 and began to move away from pure slapstick and the sometimes crude humor of the Keystone films by blending romance and pathos with comedy in such films as *The Tramp* and *The Bank*. Chaplin's Essanay films were so successful with movie audiences that, as one contemporary journalist put it, the United States experienced a case of "Chaplinitis." Fan magazines featured stories about Chaplin, companies marketed products using the Charlie image, Chaplin songs enjoyed popularity, Chaplin look-alike contests were held around the country, and movies featuring Chaplin imitators began to appear. The Chaplin craze of 1915 firmly established his status as a major star in the movies.

That status led to greater financial security and creative independence for Chaplin under the terms of his next contract, with the Mutual Film Corporation, where he made twelve two-reel films. He slowed his working pace, completing those twelve films in 1916 and 1917. He later recalled that period as the happiest of his life. A number of his most memorable comic shorts were made at Mutual, including *The Vagabond*, *One A.M.*, *The Pawnshop*, *The Rink*, *Easy Street*, and *The Immigrant*. Film historians and critics differ on which films represent Chaplin's greatest creative achievement, some arguing for the short comic films, some favoring the features from *The Gold Rush* (1925) through *Limelight* (1952). Those who defend the short comedies find much to support their position in the Mutual films.

At the end of his year with Mutual, Chaplin signed a contract with the First National Exhibitors' Circuit to make eight short films with complete creative control. He also began to build his own studio on La Brea Avenue at

Sunset Boulevard in Los Angeles, which ensured him a degree of financial and creative control almost unheard-of in Hollywood before or since.

In 1918, Chaplin began making and releasing his First National films, including *A Dog's Life* and *Shoulder Arms*. The latter film, in which Charlie plays a soldier who dreams of capturing Kaiser Wilhelm II, constitutes part of Chaplin's effort to support American and British involvement in World War I; that same year, Chaplin also helped sell Liberty Bonds by touring the East and South on a fund-raising drive and making a short Liberty Loan film called *The Bond*.

In January 1919, fearing the growing consolidation of the film industry, Chaplin joined with film stars Mary Pickford and Douglas Fairbanks and director D. W. Griffith to found United Artists, a company formed to distribute the films that each of the founders independently produced. All of Chaplin's films from *A Woman of Paris* (1923), his first film after fulfilling the First National contract, to *Limelight* were released through United Artists.

Chaplin had difficulty completing his First National contract. In 1919, only the relatively unsuccessful *Sunnyside* and *A Day's Pleasure* were released. Meanwhile, Chaplin's first marriage, to Mildred Harris on Oct. 23, 1918, began to break up after their only child died three days after its birth in July 1919. A divorce was granted in November 1920. The next year, Chaplin's most acclaimed First National film, an ambitious six-reeler called *The Kid*, was released. After completing *The Idle Class* that same year, Chaplin took a two-month trip to New York and Europe. Upon his return, he fulfilled his First National obligations with *Pay Day* (1922) and *The Pilgrim* (1923).

The United Artists period began with *A Woman of Paris* and included seven more feature films through 1952. A serious melodrama set in France and starring Edna Purviance and Adolphe Menjou, *A Woman of Paris* seemed calculated to establish Chaplin as a serious filmmaker. Although the film did not do particularly well at the box office, it did garner critical acclaim and won favor among the intelligentsia. Throughout the 1920's and much of the 1930's, in fact, Chaplin enjoyed an unusually high public reputation, both among the mass moviegoing audience and among intellectuals, many of whom felt that Chaplin's work represented an artistry far superior to that of the typical commercial products of Hollywood. His personal magnetism and charm also contributed to his broad popularity.

Chaplin's next film was *The Gold Rush*, a comic feature he later said was the film for which he most hoped to be remembered. Made as Chaplin was reaching the height of his powers, it portrays the Charlie character trying to survive hunger, isolation, frigid cold, and human brutality during the Klondike gold rush of 1898 and includes a number of his most famous scenes of comedy and pathos: eating a shoe for Thanksgiving dinner, doing a dance with forks and rolls ("the Oceana Roll"), standing alone outside the dance hall on New Year's Eve while the townspeople celebrate.

During the production of his next feature, *The Circus* (1928), Chaplin's second marriage began to fail. He and Lita Grey had married on Nov. 26, 1924; they had two children. But his all-consuming work habits when he was making a film caused him to neglect his family. His wife filed a much-publicized divorce complaint in January 1927, and the divorce was granted in August. Chaplin, who had suspended production for six months during the divorce proceedings, then resumed work on *The Circus*, in which Charlie has comic misadventures while working with a traveling circus. The film was released to strong critical reviews in January 1928.

While Chaplin was finishing that film, Hollywood was rocked by the introduction of talking motion pictures, a technological advance that eventually contributed to the erosion of Chaplin's stardom. Because his comic persona depended for much of his appeal on pantomime, Chaplin decided to make his next film, *City Lights*, a sound film that included only a recorded musical score and sound effects, with no dialogue. After a long and troubled production schedule he released the successful *City Lights* in early 1931 and then immediately embarked on a world tour, lasting until June 1932, during which he drew huge appreciative crowds and met with famous artists and political figures around the world. The tour probably represented the apogee of Chaplin's stardom and popularity in the United States.

During the trip Chaplin became aware of the distress wrought by the worldwide depression and interested in formulating possible solutions to the crisis. These experiences, as well as the calls by critics in the early 1930's for a socially conscious art, influenced Chaplin as he began his next film, *Modern Times*, which introduced a more specific topicality and social criticism into his comedies, a trend he continued in his next two films. In this comedy set in the Great Depression, workers struck, factories closed, people were homeless and hungry, and police shot to kill while breaking up groups of rioting strikers. Despite this sobering focus, the film contains some of Chaplin's most hilarious routines, from the hysteria induced by an assembly-line speedup and a feeding machine that goes berserk to a gibberish song that Charlie sings near the film's conclusion. The film's sound track, like that of *City Lights*, contains almost no dialogue, relying nearly exclusively on image, music, sound effects, and the comic antics of Charlie—in his last incarnation—to achieve its aims.

In 1938, Chaplin began work on his next film, a satirical attack on Adolf Hitler and the Nazi dictatorship. As his first film with dialogue, *The Great Dictator* required a more finished script than Chaplin customarily prepared for his films. In it he played two roles, a dictator named Adenoid Hynkel (the Phooey of Tomania) and a quiet Jewish barber. The movie concludes with the barber, disguised as Hynkel, making a six-minute speech pleading for human understanding and opposition to the dictators. Although critics were divided about the final speech when the film was released in 1940, it proved to be Chaplin's greatest box office success in its American run.

Chaplin's public reputation in the United States declined seriously during the 1940's, owing in part to publicity surrounding a paternity suit filed against him by the actress Joan Barry. Chaplin had secretly married actress Paulette Goddard (the female lead of both *Modern Times* and *The Great Dictator*) in 1936, and he met Barry in 1941, the same year he and Goddard decided to divorce amicably for professional reasons. In June 1943, Barry charged that Chaplin was the father of the child she expected in October.

Shortly before blood tests proved in February 1944 that Chaplin was not the father of Barry's child, a federal grand jury in Los Angeles indicted Chaplin on four counts, including the Mann Act (which prohibited transporting a woman across state lines for sexual purposes) and violations of Barry's civil rights. Chaplin pleaded not guilty on all counts and was found not guilty on the Mann Act charges. The other federal charges were dropped. After the first paternity suit ended in a hung jury, Chaplin was found guilty in the second trial, despite the blood tests, which were then inadmissible evidence in California state courts. Press coverage of the charges and the trials was extensive, helping to portray Chaplin as a womanizer, an image reinforced when the fifty-four-year-old Chaplin, shortly after the charges were first filed, married eighteen-year-old Oona O'Neill, the daughter of playwright Eugene O'Neill, on June 16, 1943.

Chaplin's public reputation also suffered because of his public political activities. In 1942 he gave six public addresses in support of opening a second front in Europe that would force the Nazis to split their troops between the Soviet Union and a western or southern front. In the speeches Chaplin also praised the fighting spirit of the Russian people, then under attack by the Nazis. Although polls in 1942 indicated that his Second Front position was supported by a majority of Americans, Chaplin's positive comments about the Russians came back to haunt him when the Cold War began. He was branded by conservative groups and veterans' organizations as a radical. The fact that he had retained his British citizenship while living in the United States for more than thirty years also made him a target of attack.

This conservative critique led to protests and boycotts against Chaplin's next two films, *Monsieur Verdoux* (1947), in which he played a bluebeard who marries and then murders rich widows to support his wife and child, and the more personal and autobiographical *Limelight*, in which he played Calvero, an aging music-hall comedian in pre–World War I England who has lost his ability to make audiences laugh. Picketing and threats of boycotts at movie theaters canceled some shows and hurt attendance at others. Both films failed at the box office in the United States, particularly *Monsieur Verdoux*, yet both did quite well in European releases, especially *Limelight*, which also won the Foreign Film Critics' Best Film Award for 1952.

These attacks on Chaplin culminated in 1952 in what might best be called his banishment from the United States. To obtain permission to travel abroad for the London and Paris premieres of *Limelight*, Chaplin, as a resident alien, applied for and received a reentry permit from the Immigration and Naturalization Service (INS). Two days after he and his family set sail for England, United States Attorney General James P. McGranery revoked Chaplin's reentry permit and announced that Chaplin would have to go before an INS board to prove his moral and political worth if he wished to return to the country. Frustrated by this treatment and gratified by the welcome he received in England and France, Chaplin made sure his assets in the United States were secure and in April 1953 turned in his reentry permit to the American embassy in Switzerland.

For the rest of his life, Chaplin lived at Manoir de Ban in Vevey, Switzerland, where he and his wife raised their eight children, one of whom, Geraldine, became an actress. After selling his studio in 1953 and his remaining interest in United Artists in 1955, Chaplin directed two more films. The first was *A King in New York* (1957), a satire on various aspects of American culture, including advertising, wide-screen movies, progressive education, and McCarthyism, with Chaplin playing the role of a deposed king visiting New York. The second, *The Countess from Hong Kong* (1967), starred Marlon Brando and Sophia Loren, with Chaplin in a brief cameo appearance as a ship steward.

As the political climate in the United States shifted in the 1960's, Chaplin and his films began to return to public favor. A limited rerelease of his films in New York in 1963 and 1964 and the publication of *My Autobiography* in 1964 generated renewed interest in Chaplin's life and films. A more general release of his earlier films began in 1971, leading in April 1972 to Chaplin's first and only visit to the United States after his departure twenty years earlier. After being feted by the Lincoln Center Film Society in New York, he was given a special Oscar in Los Angeles for his "incalculable effect in making motion pictures the art form of the century."

Returning to Switzerland, he completed a new book, *My Life in Pictures* (1974), and, despite failing health, collaborated on composing a musical score for *A Woman of Paris*. In 1975 he was knighted by Queen Elizabeth of England. He died in Vevey.

Although Chaplin was never an innovator in film style and although his public reputation suffered in the United States during the late 1940's and 1950's, he was one of the key creative figures in American film history, owing particularly to his creation of the mythic comic persona Charlie. Most agree that Chaplin and Buster Keaton were the most brilliant silent film comedians of the 1920's. Chaplin surpassed Keaton in the longevity of his career and the rich variety of his films, thanks in no small part to the financial and creative control he enjoyed through most of his career. Filmmaker René Clair expressed a widely shared sentiment when he said that through his comic persona Charlie, Chaplin "was a monument of the cinema in all countries and all times."

[Chaplin's papers are presently unavailable to scholars. Clippings are in the Robinson Locke Collection at the New York Public Library for the Performing Arts at Lincoln Center. Relevant studio records are in the United Artists Collection at the Wisconsin State Historical Library. Besides his autobiography, Chaplin published *My Trip Abroad* (1922) and *A Comedian Sees the World* (1933). Bibliographical works referencing the voluminous writings on Chaplin are Timothy Lyons, *Charles Chaplin* (1979); and Wes Gehring, *Charlie Chaplin* (1983). Biographies include Theodore Huff, *Charlie Chaplin* (1951); and David Robinson, *Chaplin* (1985), which draws on Chaplin's personal papers and records. See also Georges Sadoul, *Vie de Charlot* (1952) and *Charles Spencer Chaplin* (1978); Roger Manvell, *Chaplin* (1974); John McCabe, *Charlie Chaplin* (1978); Raoul Sobel and David Francis, *Chaplin* (1978); and Charles J. Maland, *Chaplin and American Culture* (1989). A three-part television series by Kevin Brownlow and David Gill, "The Unknown Chaplin" (1983), contains rare footage from Chaplin's personal film archives. An obituary is in the *New York Times*, Dec. 26, 1977.]

CHARLES J. MALAND

CHAPMAN, OSCAR LITTLETON (Oct. 22, 1896–Feb. 7, 1978), lawyer and government official, was "born under a tobacco plant" near Omega, Halifax County, Va., the son of James Jackson Chapman, a farmer, and Rosa Archer Blount. He was educated in public and private schools, and enlisted in the United States Navy following graduation from Randolph-Macon Academy (Bedford, Va.) in June 1918. Chapman served as a pharmacist's mate on hospital ships, crossing the Atlantic thirty-six times before contracting tuberculosis. He was sent to Fort Lyon Hospital in Denver, Colo., where he recovered.

Believing "there was more independence of thought in the Western states," Chapman remained in Denver, where he married Olga Pauline Edholm, a nurse, on Dec. 21, 1920; they had no children. She died in 1932. Chapman's increasingly progressive thought, stemming from his rural Populist roots, was reinforced in 1921 when he met the liberal Benjamin B. Lindsey, judge of the Juvenile Court of Denver. Chapman served the court as assistant chief probation officer (1922–1924) while taking night classes at the University of Denver, and later as chief probation officer (1924–1927). He also began the study of law at this time.

Chapman's humanitarian concerns led him to study the social sciences at the University of New Mexico (1927–1928) and culminated with his receiving an LL.B. from the Westminster Law School in 1929. He was admitted to the Colorado bar and joined the Denver law firm of Edward P. Costigan, a friend of Lindsey's, that same year. His ability to work behind the scenes as a political strategist first became evident when he nominated, then successfully managed, Costigan's United States Senate bid in 1930, a role he repeated for Alva B. Adams two years later. Chapman also promoted Franklin D. Roosevelt's 1932 presidential campaign in a five-state western area.

Declining the offer of a higher-paying but less desirable federal appointment, Chapman entered public office as an assistant secretary of the interior in May 1933. The youngest member of the "Little Cabinet," he held the position for the next thirteen years, routinely passed over for the post of undersecretary. Yet, having few political ambitions of his own, Chapman quietly carried out his duties under outspoken Interior Secretary Harold Ickes, the "Old Curmudgeon."

Raised amid the social injustices of the post-Reconstruction South, Chapman championed civil rights and humanitarian causes throughout his lifetime. He served as chairman of the American Legion's State Child Welfare Committee in Colorado and as president of the state board of control of the Colorado Boys' Industrial School (1930–1936). Chapman continued the tradition in the District of Columbia by serving on the Public Works Board, the Committee on Race Relations, and the advisory board of the National Training School for Boys. He also assisted numerous governmental humanitarian committees and headed charitable fund drives. When anti-Semitism strengthened in Europe in the late 1930's, Chapman organized the Washington branch of the Emergency Committee to Save the Jewish People. His most noteworthy act during this period was orchestrating the 1939 Easter Sunday concert by Marian Anderson on the steps of the Lincoln Memorial after she was refused permission to sing in Constitution Hall and was denied use of a school auditorium because of her race. Fittingly, he later became a chief sponsor of the mural painted in an Interior Department hallway commemorating the event.

On Feb. 24, 1940, Chapman married Ann Kendrick, his secretary; they had one child. Soon afterward, he became coordinator of Roosevelt's 1940 election activities in the eleven western states. During World War II he served on an interdepartmental committee considering charges of subversive activity by federal employees and chaired the personnel advisory board of the Army's Office of the Provost Marshal General. Chapman was considered a contender to fill the Colorado Senate seat vacated following the death of Alva Adams in 1942. He decided not to run, for his primary concern was the continuation of New Deal politics—party leaders feared that a defeat might directly reflect upon the president during the election.

In 1944, Chapman served as western campaign manager for the Roosevelt-Truman ticket even though he had supported the renomination of Henry A. Wallace for vice-president at the Democratic National Convention.

Chapman served as acting secretary of the interior following the resignation of Ickes in February 1946 and was promoted to undersecretary to Julius Krug a month later. He embraced Truman's Fair Deal politics and became one of the architects, as well as unofficial manager, of the president's upset victory over Republican candidate Thomas E. Dewey in 1948. Initially considered as a possible running mate, Chapman tirelessly campaigned as Truman's advance man, traveling more than twenty-five thousand miles to promote the Democratic platform and bring disparate groups together in support of the president. The dossier he compiled enabled Truman to discuss local concerns at whistle-stops across the country while placing blame for political ineptitude upon Congress. As a result, Dewey's accusations carried less weight with the public in the closing weeks of the campaign.

As a reward for his efforts in the presidential election, Chapman was nominated in November 1949 to succeed Krug, who had predicted Truman's defeat and had become an embarrassment to the administration. Yet the nomination was also made because Chapman knew more about the workings of the Interior Department than anyone else. Finally, it put a westerner in charge of a "western" department. After sixteen years in subordinate posts, Chapman became secretary of the interior in January 1950, with unanimous Senate approval. In September, following the outbreak of the Korean conflict and rising anti-Communist anxieties, Senator Andrew F. Schoeppel charged Chapman with involvement in subversive organizations. The secretary, an unabashed liberal, was quickly cleared of any misconduct.

Steadfast in his New Deal beliefs, Chapman sought both conservation and development during his tenure as secretary. He successfully incorporated the Jackson Hole National Monument into Grand Teton National Park and authorized the opening of a large portion of the Joshua Tree National Monument to mining. As oil became a critical issue in the early 1950's, Chapman pursued the possibilities of exploration in Alaska and along the continental shelf. He also furthered research on synthetic fuel from coal and oil shale. Western irrigation projects, especially the proposal to use Dinosaur National Monument as a reservoir area, proved quite controversial. Chapman came to disagree with Ickes over the Bureau of Indian Affairs' attempts to regulate lawyers' contracts with native Americans.

In 1952, Chapman served as campaign adviser to Adlai Stevenson after once again being considered as a vice-presidential candidate. He resigned his post in 1953 following Stevenson's defeat. After twenty years of public life, "the smilingest man in Washington" established a successful law practice that focused on domestic and international energy and trade. Remaining active in civic and humanitarian affairs, he died in Washington, D.C., and was interred at Arlington National Cemetery.

[Chapman's papers are held at the Harry S. Truman Library in Independence, Mo. For an extensive biography of his years in government, see Clayton R. Koppes, "Oscar L. Chapman: A Liberal at the Interior Department, 1933–1953" (Ph.D. diss., University of Kansas, 1974); a condensed version is "Environmental Policy and American Liberalism: The Department of the Interior, 1933–1953," *Environmental Review* 7, no. 1 (Spring 1983). Obituaries are in the *New York Times* and the *Washington Post*, both Feb. 9, 1978.]

WILLIAM E. FISCHER, JR.

CHASE, ILKA (Apr. 8, 1905–Feb. 15, 1978), actress, novelist, radio and television personality, and playwright, was born in New York City, to Francis Dane Chase, a hotel manager, and Edna Alloway Woolman, editor-in-chief of *Vogue* magazine. Her parents divorced early in her life, and although her ancestry and upbringing had been Quaker, she was sent to convent schools, where she was first introduced to the theater and starred in the school plays. Later, she went to Mrs. Dowe's School in Briarcliff Manor, N.Y., and then, at the age of sixteen, she went to France to study for two years rather than go to college.

In 1923 she returned to the United States and devoted herself to becoming an actress. Her new career began slowly, with bit parts in the acting company of Henry Miller, whom she considered a great actor-manager. In 1926 she married Louis Calhern, an actor. They divorced later that year, after which she moved to Hollywood to pursue a career in films.

While in Hollywood, she appeared in such movies as *Fast and Loose* (1930), *Once a Sinner* (1931), *The Animal Kingdom* (1932), and, her most popular, *Now Voyager* (1942). But her creative talents were not dedicated to just one medium. During this time, she also acted on Broadway in such shows as *Days Without End* (1934), *The Women* (1936), *Forsaking All Others* with Tallulah Bankhead, and *Present Laughter* (1975).

On July 13, 1935, Chase married William B. Murray, a radio advertising executive, whom she had met in Hollywood. They made their home in New York. With Murray's support, Chase started her own radio program called "Luncheon at the Waldorf," designed for the "upper middle class and the slightly educated" even though it aired during the daytime. On the show, which aired from 1938 to 1945, she offered women advice on careers and interviewed a variety of professionals, including a Harvard anthropologist, the head of a New York department store, religious leaders, socialites, and female business owners. Eventually, the program was moved to the evening hours, and the name was changed to "Penthouse Party." Shortly after her appearance with Bette Davis in *Now Voyager*, Chase went on the lecture circuit discussing her philosophy of being a woman.

Chase even tried a few musicals, *Revenge with Music* and *Keep Off the Grass*. She later adapted one of her own novels, *In Bed We Cry*

(1943), for the stage and played the leading role in its first production on Broadway at the Belasco Theatre, opening on Nov. 14, 1944. Along with *In Bed We Cry*, Chase wrote numerous other novels and two autobiographies, *Past Imperfect* (1942) and *Free Admission* (1948), books on travel, and an entertainment guide. She also authored a syndicated weekly newspaper column.

In 1945, Chase's marriage to Murray ended in divorce, and in 1945 she married a doctor, Norton Sager Brown. During the 1950's, Chase appeared on television from time to time. Critics of the new medium, who claimed that television was demoralizing society with its sex and violence, took aim at her when she and Faye Emerson appeared on television in low-cut dresses. Chase came out of the brouhaha with an interview show on CBS called "Glamour-Go-Round" (1950). Another of her shows on television was "Masquerade Party" (1952–1958), a popular show in which she appeared as a panelist trying to identify the guests, who had been disguised by makeup artists for the production. In addition, in 1957 she appeared in the television special "Cinderella," starring Julie Andrews and Jon Cypher.

Chase was concerned about social issues. Among the causes and organizations she supported were the protection of wildlife, United Hospital Funds, and the Council of Actors Equity. Chase and Brown traveled extensively together and published books on their travels. She chronicled their trips and he took the photographs, in such places as the Balkan countries (*Fresh from the Laundry*, 1967), Italy and Greece (*The Varied Airs of Spring*, 1969), and North Africa, India, and Japan (*Around the World and Other Places*, 1970). She died in Mexico City.

[Three autobiographical works by Chase are *Past Imperfect* (1942); *Free Admission* (1948), and, with her mother, *Always in Vogue* (1954). For information about her television shows, see Arthur Shulman and Roger Youman, *How Sweet It Was* (1966); and Harry Castleman and Walter J. Podrazik, *Watching TV* (1982). An obituary is in the *New York Times*, Feb. 16, 1978.]

LISA M. ARMSTRONG

CHILDS, RICHARD SPENCER (May 24, 1882–Sept. 26, 1978), business executive and political reformer, was born in Manchester, Conn., the son of Nellie White Spencer and William Hamlin Childs, who founded the Bon Ami Company and became a wealthy businessman. In 1892 the family moved to Brooklyn, N.Y., where Richard attended Adelphi Academy and then the Polytechnic Preparatory School from 1897 to 1900. He went to Yale University from 1900 to 1904 and graduated with a B.A. degree. His first job was with Erickson Advertising Company (1904–1918), but he also worked for Bon Ami Company (1911–1920); A. E. Chew Company, an exporting business (1921–1928); and American Cyanamid Company (1928–1947). From 1935 to 1944 he was executive vice-president of Lederle Laboratories, a division of American Cyanamid that marketed serums and biological medicines. Childs married Grace Pauline Hatch of Chicago on June 15, 1912. They had four children.

His father, a progressive Republican who was active in the reform movement in New York City, had an important influence on him. In 1897 he took his son to a political rally for Seth Low, the Citizens Union candidate for mayor. There the young Childs witnessed an outburst of righteous anger directed against the local Democratic machine (Tammany Hall). It was then that he began to develop an interest in reform, which his father encouraged. In 1903, Childs, accompanied by his father, cast his first vote in the mayoralty election and was surprised to discover that he knew the top four candidates by name and nothing about the other fifteen. Stymied by the long ballot, he voted a straight Republican ticket. He was shocked to learn that his father, whom he believed to be a "brilliant and politically active man," knew no more than he did and voted similarly. This experience made a deep impression on him.

A foe of entrenched political machines, Childs made reform his avocation by the time he was in his mid-twenties. Drawn to civic organizations, in 1908 he joined the City Club of New York and the National Municipal League and the following year the Citizens Union of New York. It was then also that the young Progressive thought out the short ballot doctrine. Defining the long ballot, typically American, as one in which "there are many offices to be filled simultaneously by popular vote," he reasoned that, in effect, voters delegated their choice of minor candidates to the party's "ticket makers." He came to believe that the inattentive electorate would not cast an informed ballot for obscure offices they deemed trivial and uninteresting—and never would (it became an axiom of political science).

Defining democracy as "government by elected officers," he counseled that each voter should vote "only for officials *important* enough for him to care about, *few* enough for him to know about, and given *power* enough [to appoint lesser officials] to be held to account." The visibility of naturally conspicuous elective offices—the sine qua non of a practical and workable democracy—would engage popular attention and permit concentrated public scrutiny at the election, Childs pointed out.

Childs published a pioneer article, "The Short Ballot," in *The Outlook*, a reform-minded journal, on July 17, 1909, initiating the "short ballot movement." The National Short Ballot Organization, which he founded with Woodrow Wilson as its president, was formally launched on Jan. 21, 1910, in New York City to encourage the adoption of the short ballot principle in municipal, county, and state government. Although it had merged with the National Municipal League by 1921, Childs continued to advance the short ballot principle throughout his long life. Arguing that unifying the powers of government was another essential for democracy, he warned that power divided among many separately elected officials—in effect constituting many little governments—defied popular control and obscured responsibility. He supported, for example, efforts to integrate state government by reorganizing and consolidating administrative agencies.

Childs was a major figure in the reform movement during the Progressive Era. The "father of the council-manager plan" (also known as the city manager plan), as he came to be called, he set about promoting his new "invention." Under his theory, which was first implemented in Sumter, S.C., on June 11, 1912, when the city voted to adopt the council-manager plan, every municipal power was possessed by a council—a single group of elective officers (the short ballot). Childs wanted the council member elected with the largest number of votes to be the "mayor" (rather than to be separately elected) and his power to be little or no greater than that of the other councilmen: the voter's attention would then be focused on the entire council. The council would appoint a chief executive, the city manager, who would be under their continuous control and serve at their pleasure (integrated government).

Childs's council-manager plan combined democracy (a conspicuously responsible and hence accountable council) with efficiency (a manager in charge of the entire city administration). By 1976 the council-manager form of municipal government, which gave rise to the new profession of city management and which had clear advantages over traditional mayor-council government, was in operation in 2,441 cities, including 70 with populations over 100,000.

Childs rose to leadership positions in the civic community: president of the National Municipal League from 1927 to 1931, president of the City Club of New York from 1926 to 1938, and chairman of the Citizens Union of New York from 1941 to 1950. In October 1947 he retired from business to become a full-time volunteer at the National Municipal League, where he worked until the end of his life. In 1949 he embarked on a crusade to abolish the elective lay county-coroner system, prevalent throughout the United States. He believed that coroners, including those few who were physicians, should not be popularly elected. By the mid-1960's, about one-half of the elected coroners in the United States had been replaced with qualified appointive medical examiners, and the National Association of Medical Examiners was organized at Childs's suggestion.

Another reform project he took on, initiated in 1960, was a state-by-state study of legislative malapportionment, or election districts of widely unequal population, in state legislatures. His efforts to secure reapportionment to reflect increasingly more populous urban districts anticipated the "one man, one vote" decision of the United States Supreme Court in *Baker* v. *Carr* (1962).

Childs defined a reformer as "one who sets forth cheerfully toward sure defeat. His serene persistence against stone walls invites derision from those who have never been touched by his religion and do not know what fun it is. . . . Yet, in time, the reformer's little movement becomes respectable and his little minority proves that it can grow." Selecting causes that he felt were worthy and having "the sense of time of a geologist" he knew a reformer needed, Childs devised and in his forthright and vigorous manner urged the adoption of mechanisms to solve the difficulties of democracy in the United States.

Childs died in Ottawa, Canada, on a visit to one of his children.

[Childs's personal papers and correspondence are at the Butler Library, Columbia University. The Oral History Collection of Columbia University contains transcripts of two tape-recorded biographical interviews with Childs by Owen Bombard and Robert Sink, from 1950 and 1975, respectively. His books are *Short-Ballot Principles* (1911), *Civic Victories* (1952), and *The First 50 Years of the Council Manager Plan of Municipal Government* (1965). He edited the *Short Ballot Bulletin* from 1911 to 1920. Childs's articles on wide-ranging reform topics appear in the *National Municipal Review*, *National Civic Review*, the *American City*, the *New Republic*, and the *American Journal of Economics and Sociology*, among many others. See particularly "The Theory of the New Controlled-Executive Plan," *National Municipal Review*, Jan. 1913; "A Democracy That Might Work," *The Century*, Jan. 1930; and "Citizen Organization for Control of Government," *The Annals of the American Academy of Political and Social Science*, Mar. 1954.

For an overview of the council-manager plan see John Porter East, *Council-Manager Government: The Political Thought of Its Founder, Richard S. Childs* (1965). See also William M. Ringle, "The Businessman Who Brought the Pro to City Hall," *Nation's Business*, Dec. 1971; "The Reformer," *National Civic Review*, June 1972; John E. Behout, "Richard S. Childs, Happy Reformer," *National Civic Review*, Jan. 1979; and Bernard Hirschhorn, "Richard S. Childs (1882–1978)," *The American Journal of Forensic Medicine and Pathology*, Sept. 1983, and "Richard S. Childs," *Judicature*, Dec.–Jan. 1990. An obituary is in the *Brooklyn Heights Press*, Oct. 5, 1978, and tributes appear in the *New York Times*, Dec. 16, 1978, and *National Civic Review*, Nov. 1978 and Jan. 1979.]

BERNARD HIRSCHHORN

CHURCH, THOMAS DOLLIVER (Apr. 27, 1902–Aug. 30, 1978), landscape architect, was born in Boston, Mass., the son of Alfred Church and Wilda Wilson. His father, an inventor, is credited with inventing the first popular washing machine; his mother was an elocutionist and drama coach. After his parents separated, Church moved to Ojai Valley, Calif., with his mother and sister, settling near his maternal grandparents. Church showed an early interest in gardening; at age twelve he designed and did all the work for his first garden area on a slope adjoining his home.

After graduating from Berkeley High School in 1918, Church entered the University of California at Berkeley with the intention of following the Church family tradition of studying law. During his second year, however, a course in the history of garden design persuaded him to change his major. He graduated in 1923 with a B.A. in landscape architecture. He then returned to the Boston area to study at the Harvard Graduate School of Landscape Architecture, entering in 1924 and graduating with an M.S. in 1926. Awarded a Sheldon Traveling Fellowship while at Harvard, Church used his grant to visit gardens in France, Spain, and Italy, and then wrote his master's thesis concerning their adaptability to California, which shares many Mediterranean-like conditions. Since the turn of the century, California garden design had reflected traditional ideas imposed by landscape architects arriving from the East, who made the site fit the design, rather than the reverse. Church's recognition at an early age that climate and site conditions were important factors in garden design would be hallmarks of his long career.

With his formal education completed, Church taught as an assistant professor at Ohio State University from 1927 to 1929 and at the University of California at Berkeley from 1929 to 1930. In 1929 he began work with the architect William Wurster, designing the landscaping and siting the houses for the Pasatiempo Estates, a community of homes built around a golf course near Santa Cruz, Calif. Wurster designed a home/studio on the grounds for Church and his wife. Church had married Elizabeth Roberts in 1930; the couple had two children.

Church opened his own office in San Francisco in 1932, and he continued to practice there until his retirement in 1977. Throughout the 1930's, Church's gardens reflected traditional design principles set in areas that were compact and clearly defined, a style appropriate to the austere financial climate of the Great Depression. During this period, however, Church became increasingly aware of, and excited by, current trends in art and architecture. Cubism with its expression of different spatial perspectives and the International Style's emphasis on form following function in architecture began to influence the development of his landscape designs. On a trip to Europe to see firsthand the architecture of Le Corbusier and other avant-garde practitioners, he met Alvar Aalto, the Finnish architect, who was experimenting with sinuous forms in both his buildings and his furnishings. Curvilinear forms and abstract patterns would appear in future Church garden designs as he shifted from the geometric, center-axis designs of the past to accommodate the demands of the site and existing house.

Church was no dogmatist of either the classical or the modern school. While rejecting the notion that a garden must conform to certain rules, he learned from the past and noted that good design played an equally important role in contemporary gardens where simplicity, function, and relatively carefree maintenance would predominate. This approach reflected the California way of life, where people were moving outside again, encouraged by a new kind of architecture that opened onto the outdoors. They wanted spaces that suited their needs in a lifestyle emphasizing recreation and multifaceted use of their yards. Dispensing with broad front lawns, he incorporated barbecue areas, terraces, play areas for children, small gardens, and pools within artistic landscape schemes. By the innovative use of walls, fences, and trellises, Church was able to create oases of calm and privacy in both small and large spaces. He could make small yards seem larger by his ability to interrelate various functional areas within the design as a whole, and he had the ability to site buildings to their environment by relating the use of outdoor space to the architecture of the house, creating an effortless flow between the two.

During the 1930's, Church worked on many private gardens, the first of approximately two thousand that he would eventually design in many states and abroad, but primarily in California. This number is especially impressive given the fact that Church not only designed them, but also played a role in supervising their construction, paying close attention to the selection of materials and plants, always important elements in his artistic vision. He was known to appear in clients' gardens years after his designs had been executed to see how things were progressing, and he was not shy about pruning here and there if he felt it necessary.

While Church was focusing on this private work, his firm was also contracted to do a select number of public projects. One of his best-known commissions in the San Francisco area was the design of the War Memorial Opera House Garden Court, done in 1935. Other large projects followed over the years: the Treasure Island Exposition Garden in 1940, the Valencia Gardens housing project in 1944, the large Parkmerced housing project built through the 1940's—all in San Francisco—and the General Motors Research Center in Warren, Mich., in 1945, designed in collaboration with architect Eero Saarinen. Church also received many major campus contracts. In the 1950's and 1960's he was the landscape consultant for Stanford University; he designed the master plans for the University of California campuses at Berkeley and Santa Cruz in the 1960's; and he also designed the master plans for Harvey Mudd College and Scripps College, both in Claremont, Calif., in the 1960's.

While winning fame for these projects, Church's first love remained residential garden design. During twenty-five years following World War II, he executed some of his most renowned designs. An increased sophistication in the manipulation of garden forms was evident in his work even while the themes of unity between landscape and house, the proper scale of elements within the whole design, and the imaginative selection of natural and manmade materials continued to be his hallmarks. The designs were diverse, reflecting the sites' demands and his own flexibility. In the 1960's he even returned to the classical, center-line garden when either the site or the client called for it.

During these years Church became well known through his own numerous articles on garden design or other author's articles about him and his designs that appeared in such magazines as *Bonanza*—the weekly magazine of the *San Francisco Chronicle*—*Sunset*, *House and Garden*, *California Arts and Architecture* (where he was on the editorial staff), *House Beautiful*, *Landscape Architecture*, and *Architectural Forum*. Furthering the public's awareness of Church's work was the publication of his two popular books on garden design: *Gardens Are for People*, in 1955 (revised by his associates for a second edition in 1983), and *Your Private World: A Study of Intimate Gardens*, in 1969.

Church exercised further influence over the future of modern landscape design by employing and teaching many talented young landscape architects, including Douglas Baylis, Lawrence Halprin, Casey Kawamoto, and Robert Royston. Church himself received numerous awards, including the Fine Arts Medal of the American Institute of Architects in 1951, the Gold Medal of the New York Architectural League in 1953, the Gold Medal of the American Society of Landscape Architects in 1976, and designation as a Fellow in the American Academy of Arts and Sciences in 1978. In 1992 the American Society of Landscape Architects bestowed its prestigious Classic Award, recognizing significant contributions to landscape architecture, on Church's Donnell Garden designed in 1948 in Sonoma, Calif.

Church was described by landscape architect Garrett Eckbo as "the last great traditional designer and the first great modern designer." He died in San Francisco.

[Church's papers, including drawings and plans, were willed to the College of Environmental Design, the University of California at Berkeley. The Regional Oral History Office, Bancroft Library, the University of California at Berkeley, houses *Thomas D. Church: Landscape Architect*, two volumes of interviews with Church's wife, associates, and clients, conducted by Suzanne B. Riess.

Book-length studies of Church remain to be published. Useful articles include Michael Laurie, "Thomas Church and the Evolution of the California Garden," *Landscape Design* 101 (1973), and "The Gift of Thomas Church," *Horticulture* 63 (Spring 1985); and Pam-Anela Messenger, "Thomas D. Church: His Role in American Landscape Architecture," *Landscape Architecture* 67, no. 2 (Mar. 1977). Obituaries are in the *New York Times* and the *San Francisco Chronicle*, both Aug. 31, 1978.]

JUDY CONNORTON

CLARK, TOM CAMPBELL (Sept. 23, 1899–June 13, 1977), Supreme Court justice, was born in Dallas, Tex., the son of Virginia Maxey Falls and William Henry Clark, an attorney. After graduating from Bryan High School in 1917, he enrolled in Virginia Military Institute to prepare for military service. A year later he joined a Texas national guard unit that was federalized late in World War I. Clark, who held the rank of sergeant, never saw combat duty. In January 1919 he enrolled at the University of Texas, from which he received the B.A. degree in 1921 and his law degree in 1922. Admitted to the Texas bar soon thereafter, he joined his father's Dallas law firm. On Nov. 8, 1924, he married Mary Jane Ramsey, daughter of a Texas supreme court justice; they had three children. Three years later he accepted his first public post as civil district attorney for Dallas County, a position in which, reportedly, he never lost a case during his six-year tenure. Active in Democratic politics, Clark became a protégé of Senator Tom Connally and Congressman Sam Rayburn, whose political influence helped him to land an appointment in 1937 as special attorney in the Bureau of War Risk Litigation; the following year he became special assistant to the attorney general in the Antitrust Division.

During the next several years, Clark handled antitrust, war claims, and war fraud cases and coordinated the government's relocation of Japanese-Americans living on the West Coast during World War II. His success in litigating the war fraud cases—his conviction rate exceeded 90 percent—won him a reputation as a vigorous and skillful prosecutor. Clark rose quickly through the Justice Department's ranks. In 1942 he became chief of the War Frauds Unit of the Antitrust Division, where he worked closely with the Special Senate Committee Investigating the War Program, chaired by Senator Harry S. Truman. The prosecutor and senator worked well together and became close friends. In 1943, Clark was appointed assistant attorney general in charge of the Antitrust Division. Later in the same year he was assigned to head the Criminal Division. He supported Truman for vice-president in 1944, and when Truman succeeded to the presidency in 1945, he made Clark his attorney general. Clark thus became the first person to rise through the ranks to head the Justice Department.

During his four years as attorney general, Clark continued his vigorous antitrust litigation. He instituted 160 antitrust actions and personally argued three cases before the Supreme Court. He also actively supported the Truman administration's civil rights initiatives, submitting an amicus curiae brief that helped to persuade the Supreme Court to rule in *Shelley* v. *Kraemer* (1948) that racially restrictive housing deeds and covenants were unconstitutional. In taking this action he broke with the Justice Department's earlier policy and positioned the agency to play a leading role in the civil rights movement.

Clark had an important hand in developing the Truman administration's domestic anti-Communist program. Influenced by the Cold War, he firmly believed that subversive activity represented a serious and growing threat to national security. He obtained broader investigative authority for his department and the

Federal Bureau of Investigation and advocated loyalty standards for federal employees. He compiled the first attorney general's list of subversive political organizations and was responsible for prosecuting the conspiracy cases against American leaders of the Communist party. Alger Hiss, a former State Department official, was among those he prosecuted. In the 1948 presidential election, when Republicans charged that Truman had been "soft on Communism," Clark defended him by pointing to the administration's loyalty program and its successful prosecution of Communist leaders. Truman rewarded Clark in 1949 by appointing him to the United States Supreme Court to fill the seat vacated by the death of Justice Frank Murphy. Although the appointment was protested by many liberals, who considered Clark to be a foe of civil liberties, he was overwhelmingly confirmed by the Senate, 73–8.

During his early years on the Court, Clark showed little judicial independence. Greatly influenced by the strong personality of fellow justice Felix Frankfurter, he voted rather consistently with the conservative bloc, loyally following the lead of another Truman appointee, Chief Justice Fred Vinson. An exception was his 1952 vote against the president in the steel-seizure case (*Youngstown Sheet and Tube Company* v. *Sawyer*), when he held that Truman's taking control of the strike-bound steel mills violated the Taft-Hartley Act. In the same year he wrote two opinions for a unanimous Court that demonstrated a firm attachment to First Amendment principles. The first of these declared unconstitutional an Oklahoma loyalty oath required of state employees and teachers; the other declared unconstitutional New York's censorship of the film *The Miracle*. Even so, Clark was not especially sympathetic to civil liberties issues, nor was he pro-labor in his opinions. On free-speech matters he usually voted with the conservative bloc, disagreeing with liberal justices Hugo Black and William O. Douglas at least three-fourths of the time. He generally upheld governmental regulatory authority and sustained loyalty-security programs at state and federal levels.

After five or six years on the Court, Clark became more independent and original in his thinking. His opinions became more profound and penetrating, reflecting a high level of judicial craftsmanship. After 1953, when Vinson died and was succeeded by Earl Warren, Clark played a much more active role, writing a high percentage of the Court's opinions. In addition, he was the Court's specialist in antitrust matters. During the Warren years Clark maintained his conservative posture on loyalty-security questions but supported the Court's antisegregation rulings. On these and other issues he was often the swing vote between the conservative and liberal blocs. He dissented strongly in 1957 when the Court overturned the convictions of fourteen American Communists whose prosecution he had overseen as attorney general. In the early 1960's he continued to attach importance to loyalty-security issues. In 1961, for example, he voted to sustain the investigative powers of the House Un-American Activities Committee and was part of the five-judge majority that upheld key provisions of the 1950 Internal Security Act (the McCarran Act).

But loyalty-security questions disappeared as the Court focused its attention on civil rights, criminals rights, and reapportionment. In a very important 1961 criminal-rights case, *Mapp* v. *Ohio*, Clark wrote the majority opinion, holding that evidence obtained illegally was inadmissible in state courts. In several other cases expanding the rights of criminal defendants, however, he dissented. In one important 1957 case, *Jencks* v. *United States*, he dissented very strongly. The Court ruled that defendants must be allowed to see certain sensitive government documents held by the prosecution. Clark denounced the majority opinion because he feared it would give criminals a "Roman holiday for rummaging through confidential information as well as vital national secrets." His solitary dissent was, in some respects, an invitation for Congress to change the law in order to protect intelligence and law-enforcement agencies. He again voted with the minority on the landmark 1966 *Miranda* case, which defined constitutional limitations of the power of police to question criminal suspects.

Justice Clark supported the Warren Court's attacks on the unfair and discriminatory legislative apportionment practices of the states. Breaking with Felix Frankfurter, he voted with the majority in *Baker* v. *Carr*, a 1962 case that allowed voters whose franchise was diluted by unfair, unequal, or discriminatory apportionment of legislative seats to seek relief in the federal courts. The following year he wrote the majority opinion in *School District of Abington* v. *Schempp* (1963), the decision ruling that

Bible-reading exercises in the public schools violated the Constitution's establishment-of-religion clause.

Clark unflinchingly supported the Court's efforts to dismantle segregation, beginning with the landmark *Brown* v. *Board of Education of Topeka* decision of 1954. His authorship of three Court opinions in 1964 had a decided impact upon the course of the civil rights movement. The first of these decisions struck down as unconstitutional a Louisiana statute requiring a candidate's race to be printed on the ballot. In December 1964, following the passage of the 1964 Civil Rights Act, he wrote the unanimous opinion in *Heart of Atlanta Motel, Inc.* v. *United States*. The decision upheld the constitutionality of the public accommodations section of the Civil Rights Act, thereby ensuring the rapid desegregation of motels, restaurants, and other public accommodations. In the third opinion, he spoke for the Court on the criminal trespass conviction of sit-in demonstrators who had attempted to integrate lunch counters in South Carolina and Arkansas. Those convictions were overturned by his decision. Thousands of convictions that preceded the passage of the 1964 Civil Rights Act were thereby reversed.

In 1967, when his son Ramsey was appointed attorney general, Clark resigned from the Court to avoid possible conflict of interest. Criticized by some for bringing the Cold War to the Court and for emphasizing the needs of government and society over the rights of the individual, Clark was, nevertheless, the ablest of Truman's four appointees to the Supreme Court. He grew with the job and became one of the Court's ablest judicial craftsmen. In retirement Clark accepted assignments to sit on various circuit courts and became the only retired justice in history to sit on all eleven circuits. He died while visiting his son Ramsey in New York City.

[Clark's papers are in the Harry S. Truman Library, Independence, Mo. There is no biography of Clark. His legal career, his role on the Supreme Court, and the significance of his judicial opinions are assessed in C. B. Dutton, "Mr. Justice Tom C. Clark," *Indiana Law Journal*, Winter 1951; John P. Frank, *The Warren Court* (1964); Richard Kirkendall, "Tom C. Clark," in Leon Friedman and Fred L. Israel, eds., *The Justices of the United States Supreme Court, 1789–1969*, vol. 4 (1969); and Charles A. Buckley, "Tom Campbell Clark," in Nelson Lichtenstein, ed., *Political Profiles: The Johnson Years* (1976).

On his appointment as attorney general and confirmation to the Supreme Court, see the *Washington Post*, July 29, 1949; the *New York Times*, July 29, 1949; the *Wall Street Journal*, Aug. 13, 1949; and Jack Alexander, "The President's New Lawyer," *Saturday Evening Post*, Sept. 29, 1945. Obituaries are in the *New York Times*, June 14, 1977, and the *Washington Post*, June 14, 1977.]

CHARLES D. LOWERY

CLAY, LUCIUS DuBIGNON (Apr. 23, 1897–Apr. 16, 1978), army officer, businessman, and political adviser, was born in Marietta, Ga., the son of Alexander Stephens Clay, a United States senator, and Sarah Francis. He entered West Point in 1915, and graduated in only three years because of the need for officers during World War I. On June 12, 1918, Clay was commissioned second lieutenant, promoted to first lieutenant, and made a temporary captain. On Sept. 21, 1918, he married Marjorie McKeown; they had two children.

From 1918 to 1940, Clay served as a teacher in various army schools and as an army engineer both in the United States and abroad, including service in the Panama Canal Zone and the Philippines. In October 1940 he was appointed to the Airport Approval Board to enhance the nation's defense posture. In just under two years Clay oversaw the improvement of 277 airports and the construction of 197 new ones in the United States, Alaska, and some Pacific islands.

In March 1942 (temporary) Brigadier General Clay was named director of matériel, Army Service Forces, carrying out one of the largest logistical tasks in military history. At the special request of Supreme Allied Commander Dwight D. Eisenhower, Clay was placed in charge of the port of Cherbourg, through which most supplies for the Allies in Europe passed following the Normandy invasion of 1944. Within three weeks Clay had repaired the damage inflicted by the retreating Germans and had organized an efficient system of supply that allowed the Allies to make a rapid dash across France toward the German border.

At the conclusion of World War II, Germany was divided into American, British, French, and Soviet zones of occupation. The former German capital, Berlin, was approximately ninety miles inside the Soviet zone but the city was jointly governed by the four Allies. In 1945, Clay was made deputy military governor of the American zone; two years later he became military governor as well as commander of United States forces in Europe.

On Mar. 5, 1948, Clay sent a message to Washington warning that American-Soviet relations in Germany might deteriorate to the point of war with "dramatic suddenness." Since this message followed close on the heels of a successful Communist coup in Czechoslovakia, it gained the attention of the Pentagon and of the White House. On Mar. 31, 1948, the Soviets notified Clay that they intended to stop the passage of all United States personnel and freight traveling through the Soviet zone, in order to check for proper documentation. Clay proposed to confront the Soviets with an armed convoy whose commander was under orders to use force to get through to Berlin. President Harry S. Truman, however, was not prepared to go this far, and American forces were told to use force only in self-defense. When an American troop train commander refused to allow Soviet inspection, the train was turned back; freight shipments continued uninterrupted.

A major confrontation arose when Britain, France, and the United States jointly issued a new currency for West Germany and West Berlin. The creation of the Deutschmark was the first step toward creating an independent West German state. This was a challenge to the Soviet policy of occupation and frustrated the Soviet tactic of grossly inflating the German currency to inhibit economic development. On June 24, 1948, two days after the new currency's issue, all land access to West Berlin was severed by the Soviets. The obvious Soviet intention was to starve the civilian population of the city, so as to force the Western allies to abandon their occupation. Clay felt abandoning Berlin would be a diplomatic and political disaster, and President Truman agreed. An airlift entailed the least risk in challenging the Soviets and in supplying the two million civilian inhabitants of West Berlin.

Utilizing his World War II experience in constructing airports and organizing supplies, Clay was allowed to collect United States military aircraft from all over the world to supply the more than eleven hundred tons of food Berlin needed each day. The magnitude of this challenge is better understood when it is remembered that the primary American cargo plane at that time was the C-47, with a capacity of three tons. Clay, through the United States Air Force commander at Wiesbaden, West Germany, General Curtis LeMay, asked for forty-five C-54 aircraft, each with a cargo capacity of ten tons. This request met strong opposition from military commanders in other parts of the world, who opposed concentrating so many military resources in so small an area. President Truman, however, staunchly supported Clay. By autumn, over one hundred C-54 aircraft had been placed under Clay, who also coordinated the effort with the Allies. Soon Clay was able to say that the airlift could continue indefinitely. Called to testify before committees of both houses of Congress on short notice, Clay amazed the members with his ability to present facts and figures without the use of notes.

The Western allies approached the Soviets through the United Nations almost as soon as the blockade began, seeking a peaceful resolution to the blockade. These contacts made slow progress in 1948, but when even the adverse weather conditions of the winter of 1948–1949 failed to stop the flow of food and supplies to Berlin, the Soviet attitude changed. When the Soviets tacitly recognized the failure of the blockade by ending it on May 12, 1949, Clay had organized and coordinated over 250,000 flights in what was called "the greatest transportation achievement of all time."

Although a very able military officer, Clay achieved promotion to high rank rather slowly, in part because he served in so specialized a field. His promotion to the permanent rank of brigadier came in March 1946, and in 1948 he received the rank of major general with a temporary rank of full general. The latter rank was made permanent by President Truman on Clay's retirement on May 26, 1949. The following year Clay became chief executive officer and board chairman of Continental Can Company. Under his leadership Continental Can diversified into other types of containers, becoming the leader in its field.

Clay was instrumental in convincing Dwight Eisenhower to be a candidate for the presidency in 1952. Following Eisenhower's election, Clay advised him on matters relating to Berlin. When the East German government again blocked border-crossing points in the city and began construction of the Berlin Wall in August 1961, Clay was once more called into service, this time by President John F. Kennedy. As personal representative of the President in Berlin, Clay became a symbol of American determination to protect and support the city. Because of a tendency of his to force issues, Clay sometimes suggested initiatives that alarmed the State Department, but his views usually reflected those of the West German government in Bonn.

Following his service in Berlin, Clay advised Kennedy on foreign aid. The Agency for International Development (AID) had recently been created and Kennedy thought Clay would be an ideal head for the agency, since his leadership would overcome many conservative objections. Clay agreed to serve on a committee to evaluate AID, and although the committee did not give the agency a ringing endorsement, he added a positive note to its comments and made several useful suggestions. Clay also helped raise almost $2 million to ransom prisoners who had been captured at the Bay of Pigs in a failed attempt to invade Cuba in 1961.

Clay retired as head of Continental Can in 1962 but remained active as a senior partner with Lehman Brothers and served as a director of numerous other companies. He died in Chatham, Mass.

During his military career Clay received the Distinguished Service Medal with two oak leaf clusters, a Bronze Star, and the Legion of Merit. A street in Berlin, Clay Allee, is named for him. Clay was buried at the United States Military Academy at West Point, N.Y.

[Clay's papers are collected in Jean Edward Smith, ed., *The Papers of Lucius D. Clay: Germany, 1945–1949*, 2 vols. (1974). Clay wrote *Decision in Germany* (1950) and *Germany and the Fight for Freedom* (1950). See also John H. Backer, *Winds of History* (1983); and Jean Edward Smith, *Lucius D. Clay* (1990). An obituary is in the *New York Times*, Apr. 17, 1978.]

MICHAEL R. BRADLEY

CLURMAN, HAROLD EDGAR (Sept. 18, 1901–Sept. 9, 1980), director, theater critic, and author, was born in New York City, the son of Samuel M. Clurman, a physician, and Bertha Saphir. He dated his "passionate inclination toward the theater" to his childhood, when his father took him, at the age of six, to see the great Yiddish actor Jacob P. Adler in *Uriel Acosta*. He briefly attended Columbia University and in 1921 went to Paris, where he shared an apartment with the composer Aaron Copland, who became a lifelong friend. He attended lectures and productions at Jacques Copeau's Théâtre du Vieux Colombier, saw the Moscow Art Theater on tour, and met Konstantin Stanislavsky, among other current and future arts notables of the Parisian avant-garde. In 1923 he graduated from the Sorbonne with a degree in letters, having written his thesis on French drama from 1890 to 1914.

Returning to New York in 1924, he began his fifty-six-year theatrical career as an extra in Stark Young's *The Saint*, produced by Kenneth MacGowan, Robert Edmond Jones, James Light, and Eugene O'Neill's new company at the Greenwich Village Playhouse. After playing small parts for the Theatre Guild, he advanced to stage manager of the Guild's *Garrick Gaieties of 1925* and then to a position as play reader. At the Guild, he met Lee Strasberg, Cheryl Crawford, Sanford Meisner, and others who were soon to become his colleagues. While studying directing under Richard Boleslavsky at the Laboratory Theatre, he met actress Stella Adler, the youngest daughter of his childhood idol, Jacob Adler. Their long and stormy love affair began just as Clurman and his friends' shared artistic dreams were beginning to take shape.

Clurman, as the actress Aline MacMahon said later, literally "talked the Group [Theatre] into existence" by fervent, evangelical "torrents" of talk at twenty-five weekly late-night meetings between November 1930 and May 1931, describing his vision of a permanent acting ensemble studying their craft together to produce creative expressions that would convey the life of the times through theater. Although the Group Theatre never achieved its central aim of establishing an institutional theater, its decade of creative achievement on Broadway was of seminal importance. The first plays of members Clifford Odets, Irwin Shaw, and William Saroyan were staged by the Group. The actors Bobby Lewis and Elia Kazan directed for the Group before becoming Broadway directors. Cheryl Crawford, who along with Clurman and Strasberg was one of the Group's three founding directors, became a Broadway producer when the Group dissolved in 1941.

With Lewis and Kazan, Crawford founded the Actors Studio in 1947, carrying forward the Group's most lasting contribution: they had introduced Stanislavsky's approach to acting and directing to Broadway, permanently changing American production methods. Later generations of actors and acting teachers, taught by Strasberg at the Actors Studio and by Stella

Adler, Sanford Meisner, and other Group members at rival studios, passionately debated and reshaped Stanislavsky's system into the "Method" that dominates actors' training throughout the United States.

For the Group Theatre, Clurman directed Clifford Odets's *Awake and Sing!* (1935), *Paradise Lost* (1935), *Golden Boy* (1937), *Rocket to the Moon* (1938), and *Night Music* (1940) and Irwin Shaw's *The Gentle People* (1939) and *Retreat to Pleasure* (1940), the Group's last production. He was the Group's managing director from 1937, when Crawford and Strasberg resigned, until the end. Depressed by the Group's dissolution after ten years of struggle, Clurman went to Hollywood in 1941, working as a producer and directing a film written by Odets, *Deadline at Dawn* (1946). He also wrote *The Fervent Years* (1945), his memoir-history of the Group. During the 1940's he directed four plays on Broadway, none a success, and coproduced Arthur Miller's *All My Sons* (1947).

For Clurman, whom Stella Adler once described as "all mind, which accelerates into passion," women were a lifelong complication. He and Adler finally married in 1943 and were divorced in 1960 (there was vagueness on both their parts about precise dates). He married the actress Juleen Compton that same year. They, in turn, were divorced a couple of years later. Both wives remained good but not always tolerant friends of Clurman's: in 1980, Adler boycotted the Harold Clurman Theatre's dedication party, objecting to the seating arrangement of his former wives and his companion, Joan Ungaro. Clurman wryly remarked, "I can handle Stanislavsky. I can handle criticism. I can handle the Group Theatre. But I can't handle my women."

His directing career revived in 1950 when Robert Whitehead asked him to direct Carson McCullers's *Member of the Wedding*, the tremendous popular success of which surprised Clurman and made a star of Julie Harris. He then directed, among others, Lillian Hellman's *The Autumn Garden* (1951), a revival of Eugene O'Neill's *Desire Under the Elms* (1952), Jean Anouilh's *Mademoiselle Colombe* (1954), William Inge's *Bus Stop* (1955), Jean Giraudoux's *Tiger at the Gates* (1955), Anouilh's *The Waltz of the Toreadors* (1957), and Tennessee Williams's *Orpheus Descending* (1957). In the 1960's he directed two O'Neill plays in Tokyo, Anton Chekhov's *Uncle Vanya* in Los Angeles, and several New York productions, including Arthur Miller's *Incident at Vichy* (1965).

Clurman wrote theater criticism for the *New Republic* (1949–1952), the *Nation* (1953–1980), and the *London Observer* (1955–1963). He lectured widely and was a professor at Hunter College from 1964 until his death, publishing three collections of his essays and two more books. He died in New York.

The *New York Times* writer John Corry called Clurman "a dapper gallant whose profound love of the stage manifested itself in a single-minded and scholarly intensity that both inspired and amused his colleagues and friends." He was one of the creators of the modern American theater, yet gloried in the classics and in his heritage of European culture: of many honors, he most proudly wore the lapel ribbon of a chevalier of the French Legion of Honor. He decried the tendency of younger artists and academics to dismiss the great classics as irrelevant to modern life. As a critic "he did not so much judge a play as put it into context," relating each experience to a larger world of culture and history.

To fellow critic Walter Kerr, he was "Broadway's best invisible director because he permitted the author's work to absorb his powers and his personality so entirely. Lost not in the clouds, but in another man's creation." In this, he epitomized the ideals of the mentors of his youth, Jacques Copeau and Konstantin Stanislavsky, and like them, he created a theater company that profoundly changed his country's theatrical culture.

[Parts of Clurman's voluminous correspondence are housed at the Billy Rose Theatre Collection of the New York Public Library for the Performing Arts at Lincoln Center, the John Gassner Collection at the University of Texas at Austin, and the Wisconsin Center for Theatre Research at Madison. Clurman wrote an autobiography, *All People Are Famous* (1974).

His collected drama criticism and theater essays were published as *Lies Like Truth* (1958), *The Naked Image* (1966), and *The Divine Pastime* (1974). *On Directing* (1972) detailed his artistic approaches. His last published work was *Ibsen* (1977).

"Reunion," edited by Helen Krich Chinoy, with documents, photographs, and statements from Clurman and more than a dozen Group alumni, appears in the *Educational Theatre Journal*, Dec. 1976. An obituary is in the *New York Times*, Sept. 10, 1980.]

DANIEL S. KREMPEL

COBB, LEE J. (Dec. 9, 1911–Feb. 11, 1976), actor, was born Leo Jacob Cobb in New York City to Benjamin Jacob Cobb, a compositor for a foreign-language newspaper, and Kate Neilecht. He was educated in the New York City public school system. As a youth Cobb studied the violin in hopes of becoming a symphony-quality musician; he showed promise but a broken wrist and consequent lack of muscular control in his hand ended this dream. By the time he graduated from high school in 1929, Cobb had a new dream—to become an actor. He went to Los Angeles in the hopes of finding work in the movies but made no progress. He soon returned to New York City, where he worked selling radio tubes during the day and took classes in accounting at City College of New York at night. In 1931 he set out again for Los Angeles and a second try at breaking into the movies. Although he did not have success in Hollywood, he did land a job with the Pasadena Playhouse, where he worked as an actor and director from 1931 to 1933. After this period of apprenticeship, he spent another two years acting with various touring companies and on the New York stage.

His big career break came in 1935, when he was asked to join the Group Theatre, a company that had been founded in 1931 in New York City with the intention of presenting American plays with serious social content—in contrast to the mainstream "entertainments" produced on Broadway. The Group Theatre, with its leftist sympathies, emphasis on the Stanislavsky system of acting (so-called Method acting), and encouragement of such American playwrights as Clifford Odets and William Saroyan, had a profound effect on American theater and eventually American movies before its dissolution in 1941. Besides Odets and Saroyan, Cobb's associates in the Group included Elia Kazan, Lee Strasberg, and Stella Adler. Cobb played a variety of parts in the Group productions of *Waiting for Lefty* (1935), *Till the Day I Die* (1935), *Johnny Johnson* (1936), and *Thunder Rock* (1939). *Golden Boy* (1937), one of the Group's greatest successes, launched Cobb's film career; when the play was made into a movie in 1939, Cobb was asked to join the Hollywood cast. He had earlier appeared on screen in 1937 in *North of the Rio Grande*.

Between 1939 and 1943, Cobb moved back and forth from the stage to the movies. He acted in such plays as *The Fifth Column* (1940), *Clash by Night* (1941), and *Jason* (1942) and had parts in the films *This Thing Called Love* (1941), *Men of Boys Town* (1941), *Paris Calling* (1941), *The Moon Is Down* (1943), *Tonight We Raid Calais* (1943), and *Song of Bernadette* (1943). In 1943, Cobb enlisted in the United States Army Air Forces as a private. Because of his theatrical talents he was assigned to a radio production unit in California. Cobb served until the end of the war and was discharged with the rank of corporal.

Cobb then returned to Hollywood and a film career that eventually included roles in some eighty movies. His facial features—a large nose, heavy jowls, a prominent chin, and a lower lip that he could loosen to express contempt or debauched satisfaction—and his large physique caused him to be typecast as a powerful and often villainous character; he became one of the most reliable heavies in the business. His parts as Johnny Friendly, a corrupt union boss, in Elia Kazan's *On the Waterfront* (1954), a Chinese warlord in Edward Dmytryk's *The Left Hand of God* (1955), a loudmouthed bully in Sidney Lumet's *Twelve Angry Men* (1957), an outlaw leader in Anthony Mann's *Man of the West* (1958), and a mobster in Nicholas Ray's *Party Girl* (1958) demonstrate some of his best work in this mode. He was not, however, always cast as the villain; over the course of his long career he also had the opportunity to play a prime minister, a newspaper editor, a scientist, a judge, a race car driver, a businessman, a cop (on numerous occasions), and even a playwright. As he aged Cobb was given the chance to play benign, patriarchal characters in *Exodus* (1960) and *How the West Was Won* (1962). Cobb occasionally appeared in television shows during the 1950's and had a featured role as Judge Garth in the television series "The Virginian" from 1962 to 1966.

Despite his success in Hollywood, Cobb was probably most proud of his stage work in Arthur Miller's *Death of a Salesman*. He introduced the part of Willy Loman when the play premiered in New York City in 1949 and continued to play the part for two years. The role was a once-in-a-lifetime chance, and Cobb knew it; he later said, "When I read the script, I knew there was no living unless I played Willy Loman." Critics raved about the play and had nothing but praise for Cobb's performance. Indeed, Cobb's Willy Loman has long been elevated to the status of Broadway legend. He reprised the role for the 1961 television adaptation. In 1969 Cobb returned to the stage for one last time, giving a remarkable series of performances as King Lear at New York City's Lincoln Center.

Cobb married actress Helen Beverley on Feb. 6, 1940; the couple had two children. This marriage ended in divorce in 1952. In July 1957, Cobb married schoolteacher Mary Hirsch; they also had two children.

[An obituary is in the *New York Times*, Feb. 12, 1976.]

P. M. W. THODY

COCHRAN, JACQUELINE (May 11, 1910?–Aug. 9, 1980), aviator and businesswoman, was born near Muscogee, Fla. The exact place and date of her birth and her parents' identity are unknown. A family of impoverished sawmill workers adopted Cochran as an infant. When she was about eight years old, the family moved to Columbus, Ga., to work in a cotton mill. There Cochran earned enough money to buy her first shoes, but she chose a pair of high heels too uncomfortable to wear.

Though Cochran was haunted by her mysterious origins, she took advantage of the situation to reinvent herself. She would go to church alone as a child, and, in her early teens, she chose the last name Cochran from a telephone book. Her formal early education did not go beyond the second grade because her beloved teacher, a Miss Bostwick from Cincinnati, did not return to teach. Bostwick had taught the barefoot, wiry Cochran the importance of cleanliness and self-respect.

When the cotton mill closed, nine-year-old Cochran found work as a live-in assistant to a beautician in Columbus. A chance for higher wages drew her to another job as a beautician in Montgomery, Ala. One of her clients convinced Cochran to study nursing. Her grades were poor, but her clinical performance was outstanding. Cochran never took the written certification exam because she was afraid she would fail it. Instead she went back to the sawmills as a doctor's assistant.

But the poverty of the mills depressed her. Cochran soon returned to work as a beautician, which took her from Pensacola, Fla., to Biloxi, Miss., to Philadelphia, and finally to New York City, where she got a job at Antoine's salon at Saks Fifth Avenue. A client introduced Cochran to Floyd Bostwick Odlum, a millionaire investor who was unhappily married. A few years after he and Cochran met, Odlum divorced his wife. He and Cochran were married on May 11, 1936. They had no children.

Odlum helped Cochran realize her childhood fantasies, and he lived vicariously through her adventures. For example, knowing that when she was a child she had planned to run off with a traveling circus and was crushed when it left without her, Odlum arranged for her to ride a circus elephant in Madison Square Garden. Together they bought a 900-acre ranch in Indio, Calif., where they entertained guests ranging from President Dwight Eisenhower to Amelia Earhart. By 1941, Odlum had developed severe arthritis that left him crippled and too fragile to be touched.

When she met Odlum in 1932, Cochran wanted to leave Antoine's to sell cosmetics on the road for a manufacturer. Odlum encouraged her to take up flying so she could cover more territory. He bet her she wouldn't be able to get her pilot's license in six weeks. She got it in less than three weeks and flew solo on her third day of class at Roosevelt Field on Long Island. The first time she flew, she knew it was her passion. "Pity the man or woman who doesn't have the chance to love the way I loved flying," she once said.

In 1933, Cochran got her commercial pilot's license from the Ryan Flying School in San Diego, Calif. Her lack of formal education forced her to take her written exams as orals. She learned how to fly by instruments alone from one of the best aviators at the time, Wesley Smith.

In 1934, Cochran became the first woman to enter the annual Bendix Transcontinental Air Race, but her plane blew up on the factory test block before the race started. That same year, she was the only American woman to enter the MacRobertson London-to-Melbourne Race, but she had to abandon the race in Bucharest, Romania, when her plane's wing flaps failed to function. In 1935 she finished the Bendix. In 1937, Cochran won third place in the Bendix and became the first woman to make a "blind" landing. A year later, she took first place in the Bendix.

By 1939, Cochran was setting world records for both men and women. She held more international speed, altitude, and distance records than anyone else in the history of aviation, but she is best known as the first woman to fly faster than the speed of sound, which she did in 1953 in a F-86 Sabrejet. She was the only woman to receive the Gold Medal from the Fédération Aéronautique Internationale (1954), and in 1958 she was elected that organization's first female president. During her career, she won fifteen Harmon trophies for her excellence as a female pilot.

While Cochran struggled to establish her aviation career in the 1930's, she was also starting her own cosmetics business in New York. Jacqueline Cochran Cosmetics began manufacturing in 1935 and soon became famous for the moisturizer Flowing Velvet, the lip balm Lipsaver, and the compact Perk-Up travel kit. Along with Helena Rubenstein, Dorothy Gray, and Elizabeth Arden, Cochran pioneered the American cosmetics industry. Associated Press editors voted her "Woman of the Year in Business" in 1953 and 1954. She created new hair dyes and the lipstick Marilyn Monroe used in *Gentlemen Prefer Blondes*. With her large, soft brown eyes and creamy skin, Cochran was considered the glamour girl of aviation. At the end of a race, she never left the cockpit until she had applied fresh lipstick and combed her hair. After World War II she devoted herself to her business between air races. She flew 90,000 miles a year selling her products.

Throughout her career, Cochran encountered men who wanted to keep women out of aviation. In June 1941, as the first woman to pilot a bomber across the Atlantic, she proved women could handle heavy aircraft as well as men could. The bigger challenge was on the ground before the flight. Male pilots taunted her during practice flights. And on the day she flew the bomber, she discovered before takeoff that her oxygen supply had been sabotaged, her antifreeze tank emptied, and a cockpit window smashed.

In England Cochran tried to enter combat, but the only pilot who would fly with her was taken prisoner. England had a program that trained women pilots for transport so that men would be free for combat duty. Cochran trained twenty-five American women, then went back to the United States to direct women's flight training for the armed forces. In July 1943, she founded the separate Women's Air Force Service Program, which trained more than 1,000 women. Her efforts brought her a Distinguished Service Medal in 1945. That year, she began traveling as a correspondent for *Liberty* magazine, and was the first American woman to enter Japan after the war.

Cochran once described her career as having gone "from sawdust to stardust." Friends included President Eisenhower, for whom she campaigned in 1952, and President Lyndon Johnson, whose life she helped save during his race for senator in 1948. Johnson was suffering from a kidney stone that had failed to pass, and Cochran's training as a nurse helped her recognize the seriousness of his condition. She flew him to a clinic that had the technology to save him. Cochran herself dabbled in politics in 1956, when she lost a race to represent California's Twenty-sixth Congressional District.

Cochran had few female friends, but one of her closest was Amelia Earhart. The women felt they could communicate by telepathy. When Earhart attempted her trip around the world in 1937—it would be her last—she asked Cochran to "look out" for her. Cochran claimed she saw in her mind where and when Earhart's plane crashed in the Pacific.

A heart attack forced Cochran to use a pacemaker for the last ten years of her life. It was not the first time her body had slowed her down. A poorly done appendectomy as a teenager left her with intestinal scars that on seven occasions required her to undergo further surgery. The pacemaker, however, kept her from flying, and Cochran found being bound to the ground frustrating. She died in Indio, Calif.

[See Cochran's autobiography, *Jackie Cochran* (1987), written with Maryann Bucknum Brinley. An obituary is in the *New York Times*, Aug. 10, 1980.]

ALISON GARDY

COE, VIRGINIUS ("FRANK") (1907–June 2, 1980), economic adviser and alleged spy, was born in Richmond, Va. He was a graduate of the University of Chicago, where he also did postgraduate work. Before joining the Treasury Department in 1934, he was a faculty member of the Johns Hopkins Institute of Law, the University of Chicago, and the Brookings Institution.

In 1939, Coe became economic adviser to the Federal Security Agency. He later served as financial adviser to the National Security Council, special assistant to the United States embassy in London, assistant to the director of the Board of Economic Warfare, assistant administrator of the Foreign Economic Administration, and director of monetary research in the Treasury Department. In 1946 he became the first person to hold the post of secretary of the newly formed International Monetary Fund (IMF), an agency of the United Nations.

Two years later, Coe was accused of being a spy by Elizabeth Bentley, a confessed Soviet agent. At hearings before the House Un-American Activities Committee, he denied the charges and returned to his job at the Washington-based IMF. Similar allegations were made against Coe in 1952, at which time, in hearings before the Subcommittee on Internal Security of the Senate Judiciary Committee, he invoked the Fifth Amendment against self-incrimination sixty-five times. Indignant senators demanded he be removed from his position at IMF. Two days after his testimony, he was forced to resign. As secretary, he had participated in all meetings of the board of governors and directors of the IMF.

Coe was accused of using his position at the IMF to participate in a conspiracy to prevent a devaluation of the Austrian currency. Such a devaluation was viewed as favorable to American interests but unfavorable to the Soviet Union. Although witnesses testified that Coe had instructed them to end currency negotiations with the Austrians, his superior at the IMF, H. Merle Cochran, said that during that time, Coe had actually been traveling in the Middle East.

In 1953, Coe was called to testify before the Senate Investigations Subcommittee chaired by Senator Joseph McCarthy. His appearance was complicated by the fact that he was out of the country when the committee first called him. His wife stated she did not know his whereabouts, saying only that he had left two months earlier. The Senate committee then asked the Justice Department to help track Coe down. Coe returned to the United States soon after, stating that he had been in Mexico seeking employment, since he could no longer find work in the United States. At the hearings, he again invoked his constitutional right against self-incrimination, refusing to answer when asked whether he was or had been a Communist or whether he had engaged in espionage while serving at the IMF. He said he was not currently engaged in espionage and that he was not engaged in espionage on Dec. 2, 1952. He would not answer the question as it applied to Dec. 1, 1952, his last day with the IMF. After his appearance, Senator McCarthy publicly called on the State Department to prevent Coe from leaving the country. Coe accused the senator of persecuting him, charging that the request to the State Department was being made to prevent him from seeking employment. He claimed that, on his trip to Mexico, he had not knowingly met with any members of the Soviet secret police but refused to say whether he had met with members of the Communist party.

In 1956, Coe waived his Fifth Amendment rights and testified that he had not been a Soviet spy, although he continued to refuse to answer questions about Communism. In 1958, he imigrated to China, where he lived for the remainder of his life. At the time of his death, the official Chinese press agency described him as "a close friend of the Chinese people" and said that several senior officials had visited him during his illness.

His first marriage, to Nora Mallinson, ended in divorce. They had two children. He later married Ruth Evans. They also had two children.

[Obituaries are in the *New York Times*, June 6, 1980, and the *Washington Post*, June 8, 1980.]

RICHARD CONIGLIONE

COHEN, MEYER HARRIS ("MICKEY") (1914–July 29, 1976), racketeer, was born in the Brownsville section of Brooklyn, N.Y., the sixth child of Sam and Fanny Cohen, Russian-Jewish immigrants. His father died when Mickey was two months old. His mother left his siblings with relatives and, with Cohen, resettled in the Boyle Heights section of Los Angeles.

Cohen dropped out of school in the sixth grade and worked in Los Angeles as a sparring partner to prepare boxers for upcoming fights. In his teens, Cohen left home to become a boxer in Cleveland, Ohio, where he fell in with bootleggers and gangsters. Cohen embraced the gangster life-style rather than return to the drudgery of the small grocery store his mother operated. Eventually he came to the attention of the Chicago syndicate that was impressed with his nerve and cunning; Cohen's involvements with Al Capone and other mob bosses inflated his reputation as a strong-arm man with brains and opened up opportunities for him in gambling enterprises.

Cohen moved back to the West Coast after a gunplay episode in Chicago and joined Benjamin ("Bugsy") Siegel of the New York syndicate in loan-sharking, gambling, and movie industry rackets. With Siegel's assassination in 1947, Cohen emerged as the undisputed boss representing Chicago underworld interests. He lived sumptuously in a large mansion on Lake Michigan fully equipped with sophisticated security devices.

Cohen identified with the Hollywood mystique, moved in fashionable circles, and lavishly entertained many of the movie industry's biggest stars. Cohen was noted for his expensive clothes and fastidious taste in food and for his obsessive personal hygiene: he showered many times a day and washed his hands constantly. Apart from his chief preoccupations with vice and movie racketeering in which he played a role in manipulating the labor unions, he bought a haberdashery, invested in a supermarket chain, and dabbled in the promotion of prizefighters.

Having achieved notoriety with his open connections with movie stars, law enforcement officials, politicians, and hoodlums in a community that thrived on publicity and flamboyance, in 1947 Cohen agreed to raise money and material support for the Jewish struggle in Palestine. He met with Menachem Begin, at the time one of the leaders of the Irgun, a radical underground group believed to be a terrorist organization. Cohen's contacts with teamsters and stevedores persuaded Begin and other Jewish activists that he could assemble war surplus and ordnance for shipment to the Irgun and the more moderate Haganah statehood movement. Nearly $1 million was collected for the Israeli cause at Hollywood benefits and functions that Cohen arranged. But according to Mafia informants, the entire scheme was nothing more than an elaborate and callous scam. Three months after the funds had been collected, Cohen claimed that the ship he had contracted for the transportation of the weapons and supplies to the Jews fighting in Palestine was mysteriously sunk. Cohen also claimed that the funds donated were used to buy weapons and bribe government officials.

In November 1950, Cohen testified before the Kefauver Committee of the United States Senate investigating racketeering and illegal gambling activities in the United States. Asked to explain his many arrests in Cleveland, Chicago, and Los Angeles, as well as his scale of living, he denied he was a racketeer, said that his principal business was a tailor shop, and that his affluence was attributable to his knowledge of sports and his sheer luck in betting. Even less convincingly, he claimed that he was the beneficiary of gifts in the amount of $300,000 from friends and Hollywood associates. Within two years of his appearance before the Senate committee, he was convicted of tax evasion and served two years at the McNeil Island federal prison in Washington.

Again in 1959, Cohen was subpoenaed to testify before the McClellan Subcommittee investigating labor racketeering. His sardonic remarks in answering questions led to still another tax investigation and conviction.

While serving a fifteen-year sentence in the Atlanta Federal Penitentiary, Cohen was assaulted by an inmate in 1963 and was partially paralyzed from a head injury. He was released in 1972, moved to a modest abode in southern California, and faded from public view until 1974, when he campaigned for prison reform and attracted attention when he met with the Hearsts about the sensational events surrounding the 1974 kidnapping of their daughter, Patricia, by the Symbionese Liberation Army. Cohen intimated that he could locate Patty Hearst and arrange for her safe return. The Hearst family confirmed that they knew Cohen and had met with him about their daughter but denied that they had accepted his offer to help find her.

In a turbulent underworld career spanning more than three decades, Mickey Cohen was indeed lucky. He managed to evade a murder charge that was declared a justifiable homicide; to survive two bombings of his home; a gunshot wound; and a prison assault that partially paralyzed him for the rest of his life. Cohen's only marriage did not survive, however. It collapsed because of his wife's incapacitating emotional problems induced by the mayhem of her husband's stormy life-style. The marriage was childless. A succession of showgirls and Hollywood starlets filled Cohen's life thereafter.

Cohen wrote a book in 1975 about his colorful life and made television appearances in which he described the underworld as full of misfits and freaks. His rejection of his former way of life may have been an effort to change his image as a thug and to vindicate himself. He urged the government to vigorously prosecute organized criminals and to root out corrupt government officials without which, he said, racketeers could not flourish. He died of stomach cancer at the University of California Medical Center.

[See Mickey Cohen as told to John Peer Nugent, *Mickey Cohen, In My Own Words* (1975). An obituary is in the *New York Times*, July 30, 1976.]
ROBERT J. KELLY

COLE, ARTHUR CHARLES (Apr. 22, 1886–Feb. 26, 1976), historian, was born in Ann Arbor, Mich., the son of Harry Loomis Cole, a building contractor, and Pauline Kuster. He was educated at Ann Arbor High School, the University of Michigan (B.A., 1907; M.A., 1908), and the University of Pennsylvania (Ph.D., 1911). At Pennsylvania, he was awarded a Harrison Fellowship in history (1909–1911) and a Harrison Senior Fellowship in research (1911–1912). In 1907 he married Ethel Sleight; they had two children. Between 1908 and 1909 he taught at Short Ridge High School in Indianapolis, and in 1912 he accepted a position at the University of Illinois, where he rose from instructor to associate professor of history.

Accepting a professorship at Ohio State University in 1920, he remained in Columbus until 1930, when he transferred to Western Reserve University in Cleveland. In 1944 he was a member of the Secret Committee of Historians of the Air Force in Washington, D.C., where he performed studies concluding that Germany could not be subdued by bombing alone. Joining the faculty of Brooklyn College that same year, he moved to Brooklyn, N.Y., where he was active until his retirement in 1956 and served as chair of the Department of History after 1950. He was also a visiting professor at the University of Wisconsin, Columbia University, and the Brookings Graduate School, and taught summer school at the Universities of Michigan (1909, 1914, 1926), Pennsylvania (1912), Texas (1920), Wisconsin (1928), Oregon (1930), Washington (1934), and Southern California (1942). After leaving Brooklyn College, he served as Whitney Professor at C.W. Post College (1956–1957). After his retirement, he moved to Naples, Fla.

Specializing in the Civil War period, Cole made valuable contributions to his field in various books and articles. In 1914 he published his innovative study, *The Whig Party in the South*, for which he had received the American Historical Association's Justin Winsor Prize in 1912. The book demonstrated the appeal of the Whigs to the large slaveholders of the section, and in his 1914 review in the *American Historical Review*, William E. Dodd called it an "important book" with "a poise and certainty of touch" marking its author as "a sound and discriminating scholar." Charles Ambler, in the *Mississippi Valley Historical Review*, pronounced it "the best contribution to the political history of the South that has yet been made."

In 1919 Cole's second work appeared. Entitled *The Era of the Civil War, 1848–1870*, it constituted the third volume of the *Centennial History of Illinois*, published by the Illinois State Library. Not only was it praised for its incisive social insights, but its author was also asked to contribute a chapter to the *Centennial History*'s twentieth-century volume, in which he covered World War I and was singled out for special praise by the historian Dixon Ryan Fox. At the same time, he also edited the *Constitutional Debates of 1847* for the Illinois State Library.

Cole's best-known work was his contribution to the History of American Life series, edited by Dixon Ryan Fox and Arthur M. Schlesinger. Entitled *The Irrepressible Conflict, 1850–1865*, it appeared in 1934 and stressed the development of two separate civilizations as the principal cause of the Civil War. Even historian Charles Ramsdell, whose views diverged sharply from Cole's, conceded that it was "a solid and notable contribution to the social history of the American people." Written at a time when the moral issues of the Civil War tended to be minimized, *The Irrepressible Conflict* continued to uphold the antislavery ideal, a stance for which Cole was criticized by such contrary-minded historians as Avery Craven, who thought the author depicted the South "very much as the abolitionists would have had it."

Cole's next book, *A Hundred Years of Mount Holyoke College: The Evolution of an Educational Ideal* (1940), was also praised by eminent scholars. Merle Curti stated that "no student of the history of women, of education, and of social life in the United States should neglect it." An indefatigable searcher for hidden sources, both printed and manuscript, Cole was a splendid social historian whose books have remained as easily read as they were when first written. He also contributed numerous articles on social and political history to various learned publications, including his famous exchange with J. G. de Roulhac Hamilton in the 1931 and 1932 issue of the *American Historical Review*, "Lincoln's Election an Immediate Menace to Slavery in the States?" in which he took the negative point of view, and *The Puritan and Fair Terpsichore*, which appeared in book form in 1942.

Widely recognized by the profession, Cole served as a member of the board of editors of the *American Historical Review* from 1928 to 1934, as one of the editors of the *Mississippi Valley Historical Review* (now the *Journal of American History*) between 1921 and 1924, and as its managing editor from 1930 to 1940. Cole also delivered the prestigious Walter B. Fleming Lectures in Southern History at Louisiana State University in 1944.

Throughout his life, Cole was a firm believer in civil liberties in general and academic freedom in particular. An opponent of America's participation in World War I, he was the subject of an investigation of Illinois University trustees in a loyalty probe in which he was completely exonerated. A prominent member of the American Civil Liberties Union (ACLU)—for which he served as chair of the Academic Freedom Committee during the McCarthy period—and of the American Association of University Professors, he defended many a colleague in difficulties because of politically or personally unpopular views. It was in keeping with his devotion to freedom of expression that when the *American Historical Review* refused to review W. E. B. Du Bois's controversial *Black Reconstruction in America* (1935), Cole not only accepted it for the *Mississippi Valley Historical Review* but critiqued it himself. His willingness to allow his opponents to review his own books in the journal also showed his devotion to academic freedom. During his retirement years, Cole enjoyed swimming, ice skating, bicycling, and horseback riding; he also devoted his time to growing fruit trees. He died in Naples, Fla.

[There is a file on Cole in the Department of History at Brooklyn College. The archives of the ACLU are at the Seeley G. Mudd Manuscript Library, Princeton University. See also the festschrift *Toward a New View of America: Essays in Honor of Arthur C. Cole*, edited by Hans L. Trefousse (1977). Obituaries are in the *New York Times*, and the *Naples News*, both Feb. 28, 1976.]

HANS L. TREFOUSSE

COLE, CHARLES WOOLSEY (Feb. 8, 1906–Feb. 6, 1978), educator, author, and diplomat, was born in Montclair N.J., the son of Charles Buckingham Cole and Bertha Woolsey Dwight. A summa cum laude graduate of Amherst College (1927), he earned an M.A. (1928) at Columbia University and on August 28 of that year married Katharine Bush Salmon; they had two children. The first Mrs. Cole died on Feb. 20, 1972. Cole married Marie Greer Donahoe on May 15, 1974.

Cole began his teaching career in 1929 as an instructor in history at Columbia, where he earned his Ph.D. in 1931. Returning to Amherst in 1935 as an associate professor, he was appointed George C. Olds Professor of Economics in 1937. Three years later, he was named professor of history at Columbia. During World War II he was a New York region executive in the Office of Price Administration (1942–1943), where, as *Time* put it, he pinned "ceiling price tags on laundry tickets and the work of stevedores." In the 1943–1944 academic year he taught at both the United States Navy School of Military Government and Administration and the United States Army School of Military Government.

In 1946, shortly after Amherst celebrated its 125th anniversary, Cole became its twelfth president. Only thirty-nine years old, he had established a national reputation for his scholarship and had recently chaired an alumni committee to consult with the Amherst faculty on the college's postwar plans. Like other college administrators of the period, he was confronted with a student population made substantially different by returning veterans under the G.I. Bill of Rights and by a national desire to make higher education available to all who could benefit from it. As the youngest president in Amherst's history, Cole introduced a series of broad reforms in the school's academic and social policies that reached far beyond its Massachusetts campus.

In 1948, Cole ushered in the "new curriculum," which was to last until 1966 and was widely influential among other small liberal arts colleges in the Northeast and the Midwest. Requiring a common core of science and humanities courses for all freshmen and sophomores, the new curriculum was designed to cross the traditional lines that had long separated the academic disciplines from one another. Freshman physics lectures, for example, were intended to give students not only an introduction to the physical sciences but were also to provide an awareness of how the scientific mind works. Thus, physics lecturers often posed ethical questions that were being simultaneously considered in philosophy and writing classes. Physics problems were keyed to lessons being taught in mathematics sections as well. Every effort was made to provide a similar approach to learning in all areas of the curriculum. The emphasis in each discipline was on the process of knowing, on the uniqueness of knowledge in a given area, and on the interdependency of intellectual inquiry.

The new curriculum was designed to give all students a common base for discussion outside the classroom and to produce a collegiality of learning that Cole and the faculty believed was absent, or at least more difficult to sustain, in the free elective program that historically had served at Amherst and other schools. "It is important for the students to receive a common body of knowledge," Cole told the *New York Times*, adding that "we need a basic education for a democratic people."

Under Cole's direction, the college's fraternities were forced to renounce the policies of their national organizations that barred blacks, Jews, and specific ethnic groups from membership. Any fraternity chapter at Amherst failing to remove such discriminatory clauses from its national charter had to disaffiliate from its national organization or be closed down.

The policy changes bore Cole's imprint and reflected the broad range of his own interests. A liberal, he prized democratic values and sought to break down ethnic and racial barriers that had earlier limited admissions to the nation's select colleges. Before his presidency ended with his resignation in 1960, Cole increased the then all-male college's enrollment from 1,000 to 1,200 students, built up its endowment from $16 million to $42 million, and attracted a number of leading scholars to the faculty. He was known for his easy accessibility to students, aided, one of his relatives said, by his "boyish, blue-eyed appearance, which often caused him to be mistaken for a student himself." He was a passionate and skilled fly-fisherman, working trout streams and rivers from Alaska to Tierra del Fuego. His other nonacademic interest was gardening.

On his retirement from Amherst in 1960, Cole became a vice-president of the Rockefeller Foundation. In the fall of 1961, President John F. Kennedy appointed him ambassador to Chile, where he opened the new embassy building in Santiago. He resigned his post in 1964. He served as a director of the Federal Reserve Bank in Boston from 1966 to 1968.

Cole's area of academic expertise was seventeenth-century France and mercantilism. His major scholarly work was *Colbert and a Century of French Mercantilism*, a two-volume study that appeared first in 1939 and was revised and reprinted in 1964. His other books include *French Mercantilist Doctrines Before Colbert* (1931; rev. ed. 1969) and *French Mercantilism, 1683–1700* (1943; rev. ed. 1965). Cole was coauthor of several textbooks: *History of Europe Since 1500* (1949; rev. ed. 1956) and *History of Western Civilization* (1962), both with Carlton J. H. Hayes and Marshall Baldwin; *Economic History of Europe* (1941), with Shephard B. Clough; a two-volume history, *A Free People* (1970), with H. P. Bragdon and S. P. McCutcheon; and *A History of a Free People* (1973), with H. P. Bragdon. Cole also served as an editor of Macmillan's Career Books series.

Cole had honorary degrees from a dozen schools, including Amherst, Columbia, Wesleyan, Williams, Hamilton, Trinity, and Doshisha University in Japan. He received the grand cross of the Order of Merit from the government of Chile and was honored by the government of Honduras as a grand officer of the Order of Morazan. He was a member of the American Academy of Arts and Sciences and the Council on Foreign Relations. Cole died on board a cruise ship off Los Angeles while returning to his home in Seattle.

[Cole's papers are at Amherst College. An early profile, "Cole to Amherst," appears in *Time*, Feb. 4, 1946. See also *Amherst Alumni News*, Spring 1978. An obituary is in the *New York Times*, Feb. 8, 1978].

ALLAN L. DAMON

COLEMAN, JOHN ALOYSIUS (Dec. 24, 1901–Feb. 24, 1977), chairman of the New York Stock Exchange (NYSE), was born in New York City, the son of Irish-American Catholics; his father was a policeman. He left high school at the age of fourteen to help support the family. He drifted to Wall Street, where he found work in 1916 as a page and then as a clerk at E. H. Stern and Company, a member firm of the New York Curb Market, an outdoor market on Broad Street that traded shares in companies not listed on the NYSE. It was the forerunner of the American Stock Exchange.

This was a period when career options at the NYSE and its member firms were limited for young men of eastern European, southern European, or Irish ancestry. The most they might hope for was a senior clerkship after two decades or so of work. A few Curb Exchange brokers managed to make the jump to the NYSE, usually as representatives for commission houses. Promotion to specialists, the individuals who made markets for shares, standing ready to buy and sell from commission house representatives, was a rare occurrence. It was different at the Curb Exchange, however, which was dominated by eastern European Jews and Irish Catholics.

By 1922 the Curb Exchange had moved indoors to a site on the west side of Trinity Church, and Stern and Company purchased a seat for Coleman. He performed well, and in 1924 became a partner and made the move to the NYSE, where he became its youngest specialist. Stern retired in 1928, and Coleman and Paul Adler, the second in command, reorganized the firm as Adler, Coleman and Company.

Now in his late twenties, Coleman had a reputation as intelligent, honest, and hardworking. Uninterested in the clubby environment at the NYSE, he devoted much time to affairs of the Roman Catholic Church, attending Mass regularly and participating in charitable activities. In 1920, at the age of nineteen, he became a member of the Cardinal's Committee of the Laity, helping raise funds for the New York diocese; in 1934 he became its executive chairman. In 1930, Coleman married Ann Marie Meehan; they had three children.

Prior to the stock market crash of 1929, investment bankers had been the dominant powers in the NYSE. They remained influential during the early 1930's, but as underwritings and related business dried up, their influence waned. This left a vacuum at the NYSE that was filled by the specialists, of whom Coleman was a rising star.

In 1937 the NYSE established the Conway Commission to study possible changes in its organization. The following year it recommended a new management structure including a salaried president, a chairman selected from the membership, and increased responsibilities for the staff. The report was approved on Mar. 17, 1938, the same day former chairman Richard Whitney, who represented banker control, was expelled on charges of embezzlement. The following June, William McChesney Martin was elected president; Coleman and other specialists were named to the board of governors, on which Coleman soon became a dominant force. The tasks before Martin, Coleman, and their supporters was to provide the exchange with a reputation for honesty and integrity, which they did forcefully. Coleman, who was on the floor each day, policed activities there with an iron fist. He became the man to see for specialists hoping to be assigned one of the few new issues coming to the floor. Should a specialist be negligent in his duties, Coleman would see to it that he lost companies for which he made markets. Between 1943 and 1947, Coleman was chairman of the NYSE. Even after stepping down, he was considered the most powerful force there.

Adler, Coleman became one of the most powerful specialist units. By the late 1940's it was making markets for forty-seven stocks, including those of American Tobacco, Armour, Wilson, Liggett & Myers, International Minerals, Curtiss Wright, and General Public Service.

Coleman had an unvarying schedule. He left his Park Avenue apartment at 7:00 A.M., attended church services, and arrived at his office at 9:00 A.M. He was on the Exchange floor fifteen minutes later. After the 3:30 P.M. closing, he would return to the office for a few hours, then go home, have dinner, and attend to charitable and political activities. He played an occasional round of golf, but otherwise he had no hobbies.

Pope Pius XI appointed Coleman a Knight of St. Gregory the Great in 1937, and in 1940 he was named a Knight of Malta. Coleman was appointed a papal chamberlain in 1957, and in 1966 Cardinal Spellman named a parochial high school in Kingston, N.Y., in his honor. Coleman was awarded the Johannes XXIII Peace and Humanitarian Medal by the Wall Street Synagogue.

Coleman never truly retired. He was still on the NYSE floor in the mid-1970's, although by then he had relinquished leadership at Adler, Coleman to his two sons, who had earlier entered the firm. He died in New York City.

[There is no biography of Coleman. His career is covered in Robert Sobel, *N.Y.S.E.* (1975). An obituary is in the *New York Times*, Feb. 25, 1977.]

ROBERT SOBEL

COLOMBO, JOSEPH ANTHONY (June 16, 1923–May 22, 1978), racketeer, was born in Brooklyn, N.Y. His father, Anthony Colombo, was born in Brazil to Italian parents; little information on his mother is available. After the family moved to the United States, Anthony drifted into the organized crime orbit of Mafia boss Joseph Profaci. In 1938, when Joseph was fifteen, his father was found strangled to death in a car, apparently the victim of a gangland execution.

Colombo attended New Utrecht High School in Brooklyn for two years and joined the Coast Guard during World War II. Discharged after three years with a mental disability, he began a career in crime. He was arrested several times for gambling and other minor offenses. His legitimate jobs, of longshoreman and meat salesman, stemmed from Mafia contacts.

Colombo stood five foot six and had a round, pleasant face. His talents were more of the diplomat than the thug, although he was widely believed to have participated in several murders sanctioned by Profaci. He rose steadily in the crime family as a loan shark and truck hijacker until the early 1960's, when he became a *caporegime*, or captain, under Profaci's successor, Joseph Magliocco. Colombo helped negotiate an end to a rebellion by a faction led by "Crazy Joey" Gallo of Brooklyn's Red Hook section.

Meanwhile, a plot was afoot to kill the bosses of two other New York City Mafia families, Carlo Gambino and Thomas Lucchese. The plotters allegedly included Magliocco and Joseph Bonanno, head of another crime family. Colombo apparently warned Gambino, who foiled the plot and helped Colombo become Magliocco's successor when Magliocco died in 1963. Colombo was easily the city's youngest Mafia boss. "What experience has he got?" asked New Jersey mobster Simone DeCavalcante in a conversation secretly recorded by the Federal Bureau of Investigation. "What does he know?"

In 1970, Colombo's twenty-three-year-old son Joseph Junior was arrested by federal agents for allegedly conspiring to melt down old silver coins and sell the silver, profiting from the disparity between the coins' face value and the prevailing price of silver. Claiming his son was being harassed, Colombo led picketing outside the FBI's New York office and founded the Italian-American Civil Rights league.

Joseph Cantalupo, a crime family hanger-on who later became an FBI informer, said the boss was genuinely outraged. The government, he heard Colombo complain shortly after his son's arrest, "ain't satisfied going after me, they gotta go after my kids. . . . This is discrimination, that's what it is. It's because the kid's named Colombo, because his name ends in a vowel. . . . They want to screw Italians. You don't see them do this to Jews or the Irish. . . . I'm not gonna let them get away with it."

The campaign that followed flagrantly violated the spirit of *omerta*, the Mafia's traditional vow of secrecy, and Colombo received commensurate attention from the news media. In speeches and interviews, Colombo repeated three themes: He and his relatives were not criminals, there was no such thing as the Mafia, and the government was discriminating against Italian-Americans.

The league succeeded in having the terms "Mafia" and "La Cosa Nostra" (in Italian, "this thing of ours") deleted from the script of the film *The Godfather* and from the television series *The FBI*. Attorney General John Mitchell directed Justice Department employees to stop using such terms on the ground that they offended "decent Italian-Americans." After the Staten Island *Advance* printed a series of articles about reputed mafiosi who lived on the island, league members picketed the newspaper building and interfered with delivery trucks. The *New York Times* was also picketed.

The league raised large sums of cash through dues and testimonial dinners. A "Unity Day" rally at Columbus Circle in Manhattan on June 29, 1970, drew about fifty thousand people, including many politicians. A concert by Frank Sinatra and others at Madison Square Garden's Felt Forum raised a reported $500,000.

Informers told the police that other mob bosses, notably Gambino, were appalled by the publicity generated by Colombo's crusade. The government, meanwhile, refused to back off. Colombo was arrested in connection with a jewel theft that had occurred in 1967. He allegedly mediated a dispute between participants in the $750,000 heist and collected a commission of $7,500. He also was arrested with several other men and charged with operating a gambling operation. He was released on bail and immediately went to FBI headquarters to picket.

At the Unity Day rally on June 28, 1971, a black man posing as a news photographer approached Colombo shortly before the event was to begin. He pulled out a gun and shot him in the head and neck. The gunman, Jerome A. Johnson, immediately was shot to death, possibly by a Colombo bodyguard. No arrests were ever made in the shootings, and investigators disagreed on whether Johnson had been hired or had attacked Colombo for his own reasons.

Police said Johnson had a criminal record but no known organized crime connections. Suspicion focused on Joey Gallo, who had been released from prison in May. In a characteristic departure from Mafia custom, Gallo had made friends behind bars with several black inmates. Some investigators believed he had hired Johnson through these prison contacts, presumably with Gambino's approval.

Almost totally paralyzed by the shooting, Colombo spent the rest of his life far from Brooklyn, at his estate in Blooming Grove, N.Y. A court-ordered medical report in 1975 described him as able to move only the forefinger and thumb of his right hand. A year later, he was reported to be able to utter a few words and recognize people. He died of a heart attack less than a month shy of his fifty-fifth birthday, survived by his wife, Lucille, and their five children.

In the months that followed, Joey Gallo's men began moving in on Colombo rackets, especially along the Brooklyn waterfront. On Apr. 7, 1972, Gallo was celebrating his birthday at Umberto's Clam House in Manhattan's Little Italy when three gunmen entered the restaurant and opened fire, killing Gallo and wounding his bodyguard.

[See also Gay Talese, *Honor Thy Father* (1971); the Colombo entry in Carl Sifakis, *The Mafia Encyclopedia* (1987); Joseph Cantalupo and Thomas C. Renner, *Body Mike* (1990); and Howard Abadinsky, *Organized Crime* (1990). An obituary is in the *New York Times*, May 24, 1978.]

RICK HAMPSON

COMBS, EARLE BRYAN (May 14, 1899–July 21, 1976), baseball player, was born in Pebworth, Ky., one of six children of James Combs, a hill farmer, and Nannie Brandenburg. Sleek and graceful (he was six feet tall and weighed 185 pounds), Combs did not start out seeking to become a professional baseball player. Instead, he trained to be a teacher. He graduated from Berea College and Eastern Kentucky Normal School, and spent two years at Eastern Teachers' College in Richmond, Ky. He began teaching school in a one-room schoolhouse and played ball for a mining company in order to supplement his income. His athletic skill was quickly recognized, and he landed a minor league contract with the Louisville Colonels of the American Association. Combs married Ruth McCollum on Oct. 16, 1922; they had three children.

In 1923, after Combs batted .380 with the Colonels, the New York Yankees purchased his contract for a reported $50,000, a huge sum in those days. Yet his career nearly ended as quickly as it had begun. After playing in only a handful of games early in the 1924 season, he suffered a badly broken ankle that could have ended his career. His tenacity brought him back to the lineup in 1925, when he established himself as a bona fide star, playing center field in 150 games and hitting an impressive .342.

Handsome and prematurely gray, Combs was nicknamed "the Kentucky Colonel" by the New York Press because of his soft-spoken and modest politeness. He was always considered the gentleman of the Yankee clubs for which he played, spending his entire major-league career of twelve seasons with the "Bronx Bombers." Never a power hitter, Combs was overshadowed by Babe Ruth and Lou Gehrig, but gifted with superb speed, an excellent glove, and a lifetime batting average of .325, he is considered by baseball historians to be among the greatest leadoff hitters of all time.

Legend has it that in spring training in 1925 Combs told Yankee manager Miller Huggins that in Louisville he was known as "the Mail Carrier," a reference to his terrific speed. The wry Huggins was reported to have replied, "Up here we'll call you 'the Waiter.' When you get to first base, you just wait there for Ruth or Gehrig, or one of the other fellows, to send you the rest of the way around." And "wait" is just what Combs did. Although he may have missed out on becoming one of the greatest base stealers in the game (he never had more than 16 steals in one season), he wound up scoring 1,186 runs in his career. His patience rewarded his team with many victories.

Combs's excellent speed served him well in many other ways. Playing between Bob Meusel in left field and Ruth in right, he could reach balls the other two sluggish fielders could not, and so his quickness compensated for a weakness in the defense of the Yankee outfield.

Combs had only an average throwing arm, but his release was quick and his instincts were excellent. He seldom missed a cutoff man and knew where the runners were going. A right-handed thrower, Combs batted left and was able to beat out many ground balls for hits. In eight seasons he hit 30 or more doubles, and three times he led the American League in triples. In 1927 he hit 23 triples, the following season he hit 21, and in 1930 he hit 22 triples, which established Combs as a great triples hitter.

Combs's best season was in 1927 with the legendary "Murderers' Row" team, which many historians of the game consider the greatest club ever to take the field. That season, Combs not only led the league in triples, but also in hits (231) and at-bats (648). In addition, he scored 137 runs and batted .356. Combs had great seasons with the 1929 Yankees when he hit .345, and in 1930 when his average was .344. For eight straight years he scored well over 100 runs, and in 1932 he scored 143 times. Also notable are the statistics for his four World Series, including a 1932 World Series batting average of .375 and a career .350 World Series batting average. When the Yankees started wearing numbers on their uniforms in 1928, Combs, because he was leadoff hitter, was given the number "1".

In 1934, Combs fractured his skull when he crashed into the outfield wall in St. Louis while chasing a fly ball. He was carried off the field unconscious and placed on the hospital's critical list, and doctors feared for his life. Combs declared from his hospital bed, "You'll see, I'm made of tough stuff. They said I was through in 1924 when I broke my ankle. I fooled them once and I believe I will do it again." He spent two months in the hospital and was back in a Yankee uniform for the 1935 season.

His comeback was short-lived, for Combs broke his collarbone before midseason. He remained on the job as a full-time coach; his first assignment was to train his replacement, a rookie from San Francisco named Joe DiMaggio. Ed Barrow, then general manager of the Yankees, wrote Combs, "If this boy does as well as you, I'll be satisfied."

After leaving his coaching job in New York City, Combs coached in St. Louis, Philadelphia, and Boston; served on the Board of Regents at Eastern Kentucky University; and was Kentucky's banking commissioner. Combs was inducted into the Baseball Hall of Fame in 1970. Joe Cronin, the president of the American League, stated at the ceremony, "He was the tablesetter for Ruth and Gehrig. He was always on base, it seemed, when they'd hit a homer." During his induction speech Combs modestly remarked, "When I heard I'd been named, it was like a bullet shot between my eyes. It was the last thing I expected. I thought the Hall of Fame was for superstars, not just average players like I was."

Combs died in Richmond, Ky., after a long illness. Once discussing the famed 1927 team, Hall of Fame catcher Bill Dickey said, "The only one I could guarantee as a full-fledged gentleman was Earle Combs."

[Memorabilia and newspaper clippings are in the National Baseball Hall of Fame, Cooperstown, N.Y. Obituaries are in the *New York Times*, July 22, 1976; and *Time* and *Newsweek*, both Aug. 2, 1976.]

STUART BARTOW

CONANT, JAMES BRYANT (Mar. 26, 1893–Feb. 11, 1978), scientist, university president, and diplomat, was born in Dorchester, Mass., the son of James Scott Conant, owner of a photoengraving company, and Jennett Orr Bryant, both members of old New England families. He attended Roxbury Latin School, where his science teacher, Newton Henry Black, trained him so well in chemistry that he entered Harvard in 1910 with advanced standing and completed the B.A. requirements in three years. Conant then began graduate study in inorganic chemistry with Theodore Richards, the first American Nobel laureate in chemistry, and in organic chemistry with Elmer Kohler, receiving the Ph.D. in 1916 with a double dissertation in the two fields. His later research focused on chlorophyll and the quantitative study of organic reactions.

After a sadly unsuccessful effort at manufacturing chemicals, Conant joined the army as an officer and engaged in developing the poison gas lewisite. In 1919 he returned to Harvard as assistant professor; by 1931 he was Emery professor of organic chemistry and chairman of the department of chemistry. He married Grace Thayer Richards on Apr. 17, 1921; they had two children.

In the 1920's, Conant expanded his professional expertise through visits to England and the Continent. Particularly valuable were the contacts he made with German scholars and laboratories during a long stay in 1925.

When President Abbott Lawrence Lowell announced his retirement from Harvard in 1932, Conant was not mentioned as a possible candidate for the office. Although, as Mrs. Conant later reminded him, he had told her early in their engagement of three great ambitions—to be America's leading organic chemist, then president of Harvard, then finally a cabinet secretary—he was surely surprised to be approached early in 1933 by Robert Homans, a member of the Harvard Corporation (equivalent to the board of trustees) and sounded out regarding possible candidates. Homans, a distinguished Boston lawyer, found Conant's ideas for improving Harvard so convincing that he urged Conant's candidacy on an initially reluctant corporation. On Apr. 24, 1933, Conant's selection as president was announced. An unenthusiastic President Lowell brought Conant the news in his laboratory. Conant later wrote, "My only reply was a rather resigned 'Well.' "

Conant's early actions and pronouncements were more radical than many contemporaries realized. His concept of a university was closer to the German ideal than was Lowell's English collegiate institution; outstanding scholars and facilities were its substance, its aim the advancement of learning. He started on this path in his first year, with a program of national scholarships to attract students from outside Harvard's traditional northeastern recruiting ground, and the establishment of university professorships, without departmental limitations, to lure renowned scholars. Not so visible was his concern with the hard facts of declining income and of a faculty overweighted with younger men for whom there was no chance of permanent appointment. But, while there were doubts about Conant's new style at Harvard, the euphoria of the splendid tercentenary celebration in 1936, when Harvard was for weeks literally the center of the intellectual world, with outstanding scholars presenting memorable addresses, gave him international prestige.

From the start Conant also proclaimed the concept of academic freedom against its ideological foes. A much-noted early example of this was his rejection in 1934 of a scholarship for study in Germany offered by Ernst Hanfstaengl (class of 1909), a devout follower of Hitler. This, like the award of honorary degrees in 1935 to Albert Einstein and Thomas Mann, indicated his and Harvard's attitude toward the Nazi system. Yet Conant was unwilling to reject invitations to the jubilees of two German universities (Heidelberg and Göttingen) in the 1930's, evidently hoping to uphold the banner of a free academic world even in the face of the facts.

The first major clash within the Harvard faculty came in 1937: the Walsh-Sweezy case, named for two instructors in economics, Raymond Walsh and Alan Sweezy, who received two-year "concluding appointments" in April instead of the three-year contracts recommended by the department. Both were leftists, officers of the Harvard Teachers' Union, and popular instructors; their cause was widely taken up as an alleged example of political injustice. Press reports spread the news, and Conant, as he admitted, erred badly in handling the affair. A petition signed by 131 faculty members led to the appointment of an investigating committee of eight professors, whose report found no indication of political bias. The report was approved by the faculty, but the corporation refused to reconsider the Walsh-Sweezy appointments.

After a deceptively quiet year, during which the Committee of Eight presented a second, general report on promotion and tenure (1939), the faculty's repressed wrath broke out as the implications of Conant's policy for young colleagues became clear. The faculty meetings in October and November resembled a palace revolution. Here was a constitutional issue: traditionally the power of appointment and tenure belonged to the corporation and the overseers, not to the faculty. When, after a series of increasingly bitter meetings, Conant admitted serious errors of communication, a professor of government introduced a resolution for a committee to investigate the role of the faculty in governance of the university—a moment of high drama. Then a professor of mathematics moved to table the motion—hence to block action on it—that surprisingly went unopposed. Conant was saved.

The war in Europe was raging while the Harvard faculty debated. Although Conant had long respected German science and education, he was intensely pro-Allies in 1939. In late September he wrote an open letter to Alf Landon, head of the Republican party, urging revision of the neutrality law to permit shipment of implements of war to the Allies. That was of course out of step with the generally isolationist mood, especially among students. When the western front crumbled in May 1940, Conant joined William Allen White's Committee to Defend America by Aiding the Allies, and broadcast its message over CBS on May 29. Overnight, he wrote later, he became "one of the leading interventionists."

Soon Conant moved into high government circles. Vannevar Bush invited him to join the National Defense Research Committee (NDRC). This and successor organizations enabled civilian scientists to carry on unrestricted research without military direction. In 1942, Conant worked with Bernard Baruch to develop the manufacture of synthetic rubber, and by 1944 American production reached a million tons annually. Conant became head of Division B of the NDRC, concerned with bombs, fuels, gases, and chemical warfare. His position led him to "the most extraordinary experience of my life," a mission to England, early in 1941, to set up a London office for the NDRC. He met Winston Churchill, the king, and scores of British leaders, and he brought back information on radar and on the possibility of an atomic bomb.

Pearl Harbor ended the dispute about entering the war. Conant immediately declared Harvard to be at the disposal of the government, a potentially risky policy that on the whole was carried out intelligently. He was an early member of the Top Policy Group, which dealt with research on materials for developing atomic energy. His autobiography describes the American procedures for building the bomb and the complex military-civilian operation at Los Alamos, N.Mex., where he worked closely with General Leslie Groves and J. Robert Oppenheimer. He was appointed to the Interim Committee, which recommended use of the atomic bomb against Japan. In retrospect, Conant argued that this was justified, since it gave Japan the chance to surrender "with honor," yielding not to military force but to a new, almost supernatural technical creation. Recently this view has been sharply contested. The Interim Committee also favored international supervision of atomic energy, with the Soviet Union included.

Conant's role in atomic affairs continued; in 1947 he was made head of the General Advisory Committee of the Atomic Energy Commission. Seven years later he was a witness in the hearings regarding Oppenheimer's loyalty. He firmly defended his former associate, pointing out that he, like Oppenheimer, had opposed developing the hydrogen bomb.

Harvard had kept afloat during the war thanks especially to effective administration by Provost Paul Buck. A passable amount of undergraduate and graduate instruction was offered. Conant inaugurated a study of curriculum reform that led to the general education program for a broader, better-integrated curriculum. Advances were made in other areas: reform and development of the schools of Education and of Public Administration; even the admission of Radcliffe students to Harvard courses —not coeducation but "joint education." Harvard also pioneered fairer methods of faculty appointments, especially the use of ad hoc committees with members from other universities.

Conant may have thought of resuming his scientific career and of establishing a nuclear institute at Harvard. But when he failed to be elected president of the National Academy of Sciences in 1950, he turned to public service elsewhere.

Conant was already known as a "cold warrior" and a sponsor of universal military training when he was appointed high commissioner for Germany in 1953. There he fostered the complex transformation from occupation to alliance in the hectic years of shifting Soviet strategies, French (and German) objections to German rearmament, and strong American support for Chancellor Konrad Adenauer and a separate West Germany. In 1955 the Allies recognized the Federal Republic of Germany as a sovereign state, and Conant became American ambassador. He did not, however, have warm support from Secretary of State John Foster Dulles or from Adenauer. Conant resigned in 1957 and turned to still another career as an advocate of improved public education in America. He had already begun work in this field, and his book *Education and Liberty* (1953), opposing the expansion of private schools, was severely criticized. Now, with Carnegie Foundation support, he proclaimed his support for comprehensive schools, bringing together the potential college student and the nonintellectual youth, and for two-year colleges, as valuable weapons for democracy. And in his book *Slums and Suburbs* (1961) he dealt with the danger of a separated society that was producing "social dynamite" in the poor areas of American cities.

In the early 1960's, Conant developed a "pedagogical center" with the support of Mayor Willy Brandt of West Berlin and the Ford Foundation, with the aim of giving prestige to embattled West Berlin through establishment of an institution for the study of new educational trends and introduction of modern American ideas in the still rigid German schools. The Conants spent the years 1963–1965 in Berlin, then returned to America, where Conant resumed his role of spokesman for reformed public education as an instrument for creating a classless society.

Soon, however, Conant's once inexhaustible vigor declined. He published his autobiography, *My Several Lives*, in 1970. Its subtitle, *Memoirs of a Social Inventor*, shows how he wished to be remembered: not as a militant warrior or leader into an "atomic age" that he deplored but as a prophet of a fluid social order with equal opportunity for every individual and generation.

Conant died in Hanover, N.H.

[The Harvard University Archives contain hundreds of boxes of Conant's official presidential papers; a separate set of personal papers; a valuable typescript of William Bentinck-Smith's interviews with Provost Paul Buck in 1974; the annual President's Reports; and anniversary volumes of the class of 1914. Conant's list of publications (omitting scientific articles) as of 1950 is in Virginia Proctor's bibliography, *Journal of General Education*, Oct. 1950. Conant's autobiography, *My Several Lives: Memoirs of a Social Inventor* (1970), covers rather selectively his various careers.

The most important study of Conant is James Hershberg, *James B. Conant: Harvard to Hiroshima and the Making of the Nuclear Age* (1993). See also William M. Tuttle, Jr., *James B. Conant, Pressure Groups, and the National Defense, 1933–1945* (1970); Charles D. Biebel, *Politics, Pedagogues, and Statesmanship* (1971); *James Bryant Conant, a Remembrance* (1978); Paul Bartlett, in *Biographical Memoirs, National Academy of Sciences* 54 (1983); and Jeanne E. Amster, *Meritocracy Ascendant* (1990). An obituary is in the *New York Times*, Feb. 12, 1978.]

REGINALD H. PHELPS

CONE, FAIRFAX MASTICK (Feb. 21, 1903–June 20, 1977), advertising executive, was born in San Francisco, Calif., the son of William H. Cone, a mining engineer and prospector, and Isabelle Williams, a former teacher. His mother supplemented the family's income by tutoring students and taught her sons at home through the sixth grade. Cone attended University High School in Oakland, Calif.

At sixteen, Cone signed on as a merchant seaman with the SS *Haxtum*, a transatlantic freighter. In later years, he claimed that his eight months aboard the *Haxtum* had provided him with a touchstone for testing the effectiveness of his advertising copy. "Many a time in writing advertising," he wrote, "I have asked myself whether everyone on the *Haxtum* would know what I was trying to say. If I thought the answer might be no, I changed the copy."

Cone enrolled at the University of California at Berkeley in 1921, flunked out twice in his first two years, then settled down and received better grades. He studied literature with the intention of becoming an English teacher. While in college he held a summer job as a copy boy on the *San Francisco Bulletin*. In 1926, a friend from college, William Randolph Hearst, Jr., son of the publisher, helped him get a position as a want-ad clerk, writer, and illustrator for the Hearst-owned *San Francisco Examiner*, a post he held for three years. His first work for an advertising agency was with L. H. Waldron, where he was an artist.

The major break in Cone's career occurred in 1929, when he was hired to work as a copywriter in the San Francisco office of one of the most famous and successful advertising firms of that time, Lord and Thomas, then owned by industry pioneer Albert D. Lasker. Cone rose through the ranks to account executive and then to manager of the San Francisco office in 1939.

In 1941, Lasker moved Cone to New York City, made him vice-president in charge of the agency's creative work there, and gave him the Lucky Strike cigarette account. With the president of American Tobacco, George Washington Hill, Cone developed the famous slogan, "L.S./M.F.T.—Lucky Strike Means Fine Tobacco." Later, Cone was made vice-president in the firm's office in Chicago, where he was to spend the rest of his career.

When Lasker retired and dissolved Lord and Thomas in late 1942, three vice-presidents—Cone in Chicago, Emerson Foote in New York, and Don Belding in Los Angeles—picked up the firm's clients and formed a new agency, Foote Cone and Belding (FCB).

Among the memorable advertising campaign slogans with which Cone and his agency were associated were "You'll wonder where the yellow went" (Pepsodent toothpaste); "When you care enough to send the very best" (Hallmark cards); "Aren't you glad you use Dial? Don't you wish everybody did?" (Dial soap); "Raid kills bugs dead" (Raid insecticide); and "Does she . . . or doesn't she?" (Clairol hair coloring).

Cone was chairman of FCB's executive committee from its founding until 1948 and again after 1958. He was chairman of the board from 1948 to 1951, and president from 1951 to 1957. In 1963, FCB became the second advertising agency to sell stock ownership to the general public. From 1967 until 1975, five years after his retirement from FCB, Cone remained a director of the company.

Cone's reputation for honesty and integrity and his outspoken criticism of advertising practices he abhorred earned him praise. *Time* magazine called him the industry's "most respected scold." David Ogilvy, founder of Ogilvy and Mather, called him advertising's "most admirable statesman." Leo Burnett, another midcentury advertising great, referred to him as "the Abraham Lincoln of Advertising." *Business Week* said he was one of the "authentic heroes of advertising," and *Advertising Age* called him "one of the true giants of the 20th century advertising world."

Cone understood the need for honesty in advertising, the skill of the average consumer in assessing advertised products, and the fundamental selling nature of the advertising process. He wrote, "No one has yet developed better judgment than the average woman standing in the middle of a supermarket thinking about her money . . . she is not going to be led into any foolishness by any . . . advertising. She may be cheated once in a while, but she always gets even."

Cone committed many of his ideas about advertising to his "blue streaks," memos to his staff. Some of those memos written between 1948 and 1969 were the subject of his book *The Blue Streak* (1973).

Of his chosen field he wrote in a 1968 memorandum: "Advertising is a business. It is not a profession and it is not an art . . . its sole purpose is to substitute for personal salesmanship."

Cone served as chairman of the American Association of Advertising Agencies (1950–1951) and of the Advertising Council (1951–1952). He was for many years a director of the Advertising Federation of America (now the American Advertising Federation). Active in civic affairs, he was a member of the Chicago Board of Education (1961–1963) and chairman of the University of Chicago board of trustees (1963–1970).

Cone was named "Ad Man of the Year" by *Printer's Ink* in 1956 and elected to the Advertising Hall of Fame of the American Advertising Federation in 1975. He was also a Berkeley fellow at the University of California.

Cone married Gertrude Kennedy, a teacher, on June 29, 1929. They had one child. Cone died in Carmel, Calif.

[Cone's papers are at the Regenstein Library at the University of Chicago. His books are *With All Its Faults* (1969), an autobiography, and *The Blue Streak* (1973). Among his articles are "Advertising Is Not a Plot," *Atlantic Monthly*, Jan. 1958; "What's Bad for TV Is Worse for Advertising," *Fortune*, July 1965; "Advertising Is No Joke," *Advertising Age*, Dec. 15, 1969; and "When Advertising Talks to Everyone," *Saturday Review*, Oct. 10, 1970. Articles on Cone are in *Voice of St. Jude*, Oct. 1961; *National Observer*, Apr. 15, 1963; the *New York Times*, Jan. 5, 1964; and *Newsweek*, Aug. 16, 1965. An obituary is in the *New York Times*, June 21, 1977.]

RICHARD L. TINO

CONNELLY, MARCUS COOK ("MARC") (Dec. 13, 1890–Dec. 21, 1980), playwright, was born in McKeesport, Pa., one of two children born to Mabel Louise Fowler Cook and Patrick Joseph Connelly. His parents were touring actors until their baby daughter died of pneumonia. They then moved to McKeesport and opened the Hotel White, which became a stopping place for touring theatrical companies and the backdrop for Marc's early interest in the theater.

After his father died in 1902, Connelly was sent to Trinity Hall, a boarding school in Washington, Pa.; he stayed there until 1907, when his mother lost the hotel through bankruptcy. His formal schooling virtually ended, he gave up plans to attend Harvard and sought employment with several newspapers, first the *Pittsburgh Press* and later the *Pittsburgh Gazette Times*, where he was drama critic and writer of a column entitled "Jots and Tittles."

After a brief attempt at writing lyrics, Connelly began work as theater reporter for the *New York Morning Telegraph* in 1917. He collaborated with George S. Kaufman on *Dulcy* (1921), a play based on a popular Franklin P. Adams character. This stage hit made Lynn Fontanne a star and was followed by another successful collaboration, *To the Ladies!* (1922), starring Helen Hayes.

Connelly and Kaufman wrote several other plays, including two reasonably successful ones, *Merton of the Movies* (1922) and a fantasy, *Beggar on Horseback* (1924), still a respected play. None of his later plays enjoyed the same degree of success achieved by the first two, however. By 1924, the collaboration was essentially at an end, although the two men remained friends until Kaufman's death in 1961. After a fairly successful solo play, *The Wisdom Tooth* (1926), which balanced realism and expressionism, Connelly collaborated with Herman J. Mankiewicz on *The Wild Man of Borneo* (1927). Connelly also wrote *How's the King?* (1925, produced 1927) and five plays known as the Kenneth Mercer skits (1925–early 1930's).

Connelly was a member of the Algonquin Round Table, a group of theatrical and literary kindred spirits that included Franklin P. Adams, Deems Taylor, Robert Benchley, Mankiewicz, Dorothy Parker, and Harold Ross. When Ross created the *New Yorker* magazine, he listed the better-known Algonquins as his "Advisory Board." In 1927 the magazine published a number of Connelly's short pieces, including several short stories. One of his short stories, "Coroner's Inquest," appeared in *Collier's* in 1930 and won the O. Henry Award.

Connelly's major contribution to the stage and to literature was *The Green Pastures*, a musical about the creation that took its impetus from Roark Bradford's dialect stories, *Ol' Man Adam an' His Chillun* (1928). Connelly researched black dialect and customs in New Orleans, but when the play was completed, he had considerable difficulty locating a producer willing to risk the potential public response to the portrayal of God as a black man. Two circumstances made the play both possible and successful: the decision of retired stockbroker Rowland Stebbins to back the play and the discovery of Richard B. Harrison, who had never acted, to play the lead.

The play opened on Feb. 26, 1930, in New York City. It ran for 640 performances, followed by five years of touring in various parts of the country before its return to New York for a second run, bringing the total of performances to 1,642. It brought Connelly the Pulitzer Prize in 1930. The second New York run ended after seventy-three performances, when Richard B. Harrison died; Connelly spent the next dozen years searching unsuccessfully for a replacement. In 1935, Warner Brothers purchased the film rights, giving Connelly carte blanche in directing, staging, and casting. A 1951 stage revival of the play by Connelly ran from March 15 to April 21, partly because of Harrison's absence and partly because by the 1950's, blacks were viewed differently by the world and themselves. The play is reputed to have grossed over $3 million during the five-year period of its popularity, leaving Connelly independently wealthy.

Although Connelly never again achieved the success of *The Green Pastures*, he continued to write. In addition to several one-act plays, he and Frank B. Elser wrote a full-length play, *The Farmer Takes a Wife* (1934), based on Walter D. Edmonds's novel, *Rome Haul*. It was made into a motion picture starring Henry Fonda in 1935.

Connelly remained active in the theater during the 1940's, 1950's, and 1960's, producing, staging, and acting in several productions. He also served from 1947 to 1952 as professor of playwriting at Yale University and lectured at several other universities. In addition he published an interesting but not much acclaimed novel, *A Souvenir from Qam* (1965), about the quest for a virtuous society and a virtuous man.

Although Connelly, who married Madeline Hurlock on Oct. 4, 1930, and was divorced from her in 1935, was childless, he is reputed to have had some twenty godchildren who, every Thanksgiving, watched the Macy's parade from Connelly's Central Park West apartment. By the accounts of those who knew him, the balding and portly Connelly was mischievous, funloving, and congenial. In *Voices Offstage: A Book of Memoirs* (1968), Connelly presents a charming and engaging account of his personal and professional life that supports the general view of him held by his acquaintances.

A month before Connelly's death in New York City, Mayor Ed Koch presented him a certificate of appreciation for his many and varied contributions to the theater.

[The bulk of Connelly's manuscripts, papers, letters, and other documents are in the Mugar Memorial Library at Boston University. Other manuscripts, papers, letters, and various documents are scattered among several libraries, including the New York Public Library and the American Academy of Arts and Letters in New York.

Connelly is also discussed in drama surveys, including John Mason Brown, *Dramatis Personae* (1952); and Bernard Hewitt, *Theatre USA* (1959). The only full-length study of Connelly's life and work is Paul T. Nolan, *Marc Connelly* (1960), which provides a thorough study of Connelly's work through 1966 and has the advantage of having been read before publication by Connelly. An obituary is in the *New York Times*, Dec. 22, 1980.]

MARY BOYLES

CONRAD, MAXIMILIAN ARTHUR, JR. (Mar. 6, 1903–Apr. 3, 1979), aviator, was born in Winona, Minn., one of six children of Maximilian Arthur Conrad and Elizabeth Dolores Conrad. His father owned a store that processed and sold fur coats and clothes. All the family members worked in the business as soon as they were old enough. Conrad began when he was six, carrying letters and messages. His father was also the part-time manager of the Winona semiprofessional baseball team. A domineering patriarch, he pushed his oldest surviving son to love baseball, hunting, fishing, and the fur business as he did. His persistence caused Conrad to hate all his father's passions. Instead, he loved gymnastics, running track, and racing cars, boats, and (later) airplanes. He also enjoyed tinkering with engines.

Despite an indifferent school career, Conrad graduated from the local high school in June 1921 and enrolled at Marquette University that fall, majoring in mechanical engineering at his father's "request." Unfortunately, dazzled by college life, he soon overloaded himself with too many classes and an evening job as a musician in a dance band. After a year he dropped out of school.

In September 1922, Conrad entered the University of Colorado at Boulder. He dropped out again because of a lack of money and moved to Detroit, where he worked in a Cadillac, and later a Plymouth, automobile assembly plant. In 1924 he returned to college at the University of California, Berkeley. He excelled at track and field, trying out for the United States Olympic team that year. Failing to make the team, he soon dropped out of school and returned to Minnesota, where he enrolled at the University of Minnesota in September 1926, majoring in aeronautical engineering.

Although he never graduated, his studies and Charles Lindbergh's 1927 transatlantic flight inspired Conrad to become a pilot. On May 18, 1928, he bought his first plane, a Laird Swallow, in Wichita, Kans. He took his first flight exactly one year after Lindbergh's historic flight. Within five months he had made his first solo flight, and by the end of the year he had established Conrad Aviation, a flying school and charter service based in Winona.

In October 1929, after Conrad had given a ride to a cousin and his girlfriend, the young woman was struck and killed by the rotating propeller when she exited the plane on the wrong side. Trying to save her, Conrad was struck on the head and severely injured. Only the heroic efforts of surgeon Robert Krieg, the determination of his mother, and a long difficult convalescence at the Mayo Clinic enabled him to return to flying. He became right-brain dominant and had to relearn common skills such as writing using his left hand. In addition, his motor abilities were impaired, and his speech and hearing were affected.

In late 1930, Conrad resumed flying and running his company at the Winona airfield. He had built a gravel and dirt runway in a pasture owned by one of his father's best friends. On July 23, 1931, he married the pasture owner's daughter, Betty Biesanz; they had ten children. She soon took over the company books and turned what had been a haphazard business into a money-maker.

By the summer of 1931, Conrad had a growing charter service to the upper Midwest, to Canada, and even some runs to California. Both of his younger brothers worked with him and flew many of the routes. But on July 24, 1931, Conrad's brother Arthur and four passengers were killed in a crash near Winona. To make matters worse, the circumstances of the crash led to lawsuits against Conrad's company. Even though they were settled favorably, the resulting pressures caused Conrad to experience periodic bouts of depression for the rest of his life.

From 1932 to 1944, the company purchased seven Ford trimotor passenger planes and tried to run an airline. During World War II, Conrad's airfield was a government-sponsored private flight-training facility. Even so, the business slowly deteriorated, and he was finally forced to sell all his assets and go to work as a test pilot for Honeywell in Minneapolis. In 1950 his growing family and his debts from the business forced him to move the family to Switzerland in an effort to save money and shield his assets.

Conrad soon signed an agreement with the Piper Aircraft Company to ferry small aircraft across the Atlantic. He gained fame and fortune by setting several small single-engine-aircraft records. Ultimately, he flew a record 50,000 solo hours and set six distance and endurance records. In late 1950, Conrad flew a Piper Pacer solo from New York to Geneva. It was the first of 200 such flights (150 across the Atlantic and 50 across the Pacific), and by 1952 he was able to move his family to San Francisco. In 1954 he set a speed record for a single-engine solo flight from New York to Paris. It was the first such flight since Lindbergh's in 1927.

In 1959, Conrad, by then known as "the flying grandfather," flew 7,683 miles, solo, nonstop from Casablanca, Morocco, to Los Angeles. The flight, in a Piper Comanche, took fifty-eight hours and thirty-eight minutes. On July 6, 1960, he set a world record for a light plane marathon flight, traveling 6,920 miles in 60 hours on a closed course in California.

The next year Conrad set a record when he flew alone in a Piper Cherokee around the world in eight days, eighteen hours, and forty-nine minutes. Over the next two decades, he continued to excite the public with his daring flights. Twice, in 1968 and in 1973, he tried and failed to fly around the world by going over the poles. His wife once remarked, "People are always saying to me, 'Well, someday, you know, he'll settle down.' I think to myself, 'That will be the day,' because he won't, of course. It won't ever happen. And I admire him for it."

Conrad died in Summit, N.J. Even in his last days, he was planning flying adventures and flights that would set world records for his age group.

[See Sally Buegeleisen, *Into the Wind* (1973); and Dee Mosteller, "Living Legends: Max Conrad," *Flying*, Nov. 1977. An obituary is in the *New York Times*, Apr. 4, 1979.]

WILLIAM HEAD

CORT, STEWART SHAW (May 9, 1911–May 25, 1980), steel executive and marketing expert, was born in Duquesne, Pa., the son of Stewart Joseph Cort and Carolyn Myrtilla Schreiner. The family moved to Bethlehem, Pa., in 1917, when Cort's father got work as an open hearth superintendent at the Bethlehem Steel Corporation. By the time of his retirement, Cort's father had become a company vice-president. Cort attended public schools until 1928, then Blair Academy in New Jersey for two years. He received a B.A. in economics from Yale in 1934 and an M.B.A. from Harvard in 1936.

Cort began his lifelong career with the Bethlehem Steel Corporation in 1937 as a clerk in the commercial research department. Thirty-three years later, he became the fifth chief executive officer of the nation's number two steel corporation. Bethlehem Steel engineered and constructed some of America's most impressive landmarks: the George Washington Bridge and the Waldorf-Astoria Hotel in New York City, the Golden Gate Bridge in San Francisco, the Merchandise Mart in Chicago, and the National Gallery of Art in Washington, D.C.

In 1939, Cort was transferred to the sales department of the company's Pacific Coast division. During World War II, he became manager of the commercial research department and of the sheet and tinplate sales department. By 1946, Bethlehem had built and repaired more ships than any other private shipbuilder in the world. In later years, the company constructed missile silos for the United States Air Force and other national defense equipment.

After the war, promotions took Cort back and forth between California and Pennsylvania. From 1954 to 1960 he served as vice-president in charge of sales for the Pacific Coast. In 1960 he was transferred back to Bethlehem's head office and named assistant general manager of sales for the entire corporation. A year later, he returned to California as vice-president of the Pacific Coast division. In 1963, he returned to Bethlehem as president of the corporation and a director. He was the first company president to have risen through the ranks of the sales division. In 1970, Cort was appointed chief executive officer by his predecessor, Edmund F. Martin. He served in the top position until his retirement in 1974 and continued as a director until 1977.

Cort held the reins of the corporation during the beginning of its decline in the 1970's. Competition from Japan and Europe crept up on American steel corporations, whose fat years of profit and growth had blinded them to technological and global market changes. Bethlehem Steel was especially known for its rigid corporate structure and conservative attitude toward technological innovation. For example, during the 1960's, when the technological breakthrough of continuous casting was taken up by steel mills around the world, Bethlehem and other American steel corporations failed to incorporate what is now considered an essential cost-saving, energy-efficient part of any modern steel mill.

Bethlehem experimented twice with continuous casting in the 1960's. The first experiment was successful, but Bethlehem's executives felt the technique was not adaptable to high-volume output and therefore abandoned the innovation. The Japanese soon adapted continuous casting for high-volume output. Glowing reports of technological advances convinced Bethlehem to try continuous casting again, but, against the advice of their own research department, company executives decided to build a caster in a plant that was too small. After a loss of $10 million, the project was abandoned. Bethlehem's research department often struggled against the corporation's conservative vision.

In 1973 and 1974, company profits climbed as a result of the country's demand for steel. However, foreign competition, along with Bethlehem's outdated technology and increasingly hostile management-labor relations, soon crippled the steel giant and the entire steel industry.

The epitome of the old-style Bethlehem executive, Cort was a company man who enjoyed the luxurious life-style of its top executives. He was an avid golfer. As president, he encouraged the construction at company expense of Weyhill, one of the most exclusive golf courses in the eastern United States. The impetus for a new golf course came about when Cort was leaving the overcrowded course at the local Saucon Valley Country Club and saw a woman in golf clothes changing her baby's diaper on the hood of his car. The Weyhill course, which was restricted to clients and top executives, barred women.

Cort, a staunch Republican, supported Richard Nixon's presidential race in 1972 and served from 1971 to 1973 as chairman and director of Radio Free Europe, which broadcast behind the Iron Curtain. Like many other Bethlehem executives, Cort expected his employees to share his loyalty to the Republican party. When an executive's wife admitted at a dinner party that she had not voted for Nixon in 1972, Cort angrily confronted her. Like many other business executives of his generation, Cort believed that wives should not speak their mind or pursue careers of their own.

Cort was married twice, but there is little public information about either marriage or either wife. On Apr. 15, 1961 he married Elizabeth Fiske Brumiller. In 1978 he married Alys Faurot.

In 1970, the year Cort became chief executive officer, Bethlehem suffered a crushing blow to its reputation as a construction giant when it lost its bid to build the World Trade Center towers in downtown New York City. Bethlehem had originally beaten out its larger competitor, U.S. Steel, but then was accused by New York's Port Authority of price rigging. The job of building the towers went instead to several small companies that imported foreign steel. Even though Bethlehem's engineers had done a significant part of the towers' design, the company never received credit for its contribution.

In 1973, under Cort's leadership, Bethlehem became the largest industrial plant to face a Labor Department ultimatum that declared that discrimination against minority workers would have to be corrected or the company would lose all of its federal contracts. Discriminatory practices that held back women, blacks, and Latinos had long gone uncontested at Bethlehem and other steel companies. In the wake of the civil rights movement, however, the government forced nine of the country's steel companies, including Bethlehem, to pay compensation to minority workers that amounted to the most costly civil rights settlement in American history.

Known for his fondness for hard liquor and occasionally excessive reveling, Cort was in poor health when he retired in 1974. He died in Bethlehem, Pa. He left the company in the hands of Lewis W. Foy, whom he had praised for his ability to bargain and his abstinence from alcohol.

[John Strohmeyer, *Crisis in Bethlehem* (1986), contains anecdotes about Cort as a Bethlehem executive. For documentation of discrimination, see Maryland Commission on Human Relations, *Systemic Discrimination: A Report on Patterns of Discrimination at the Bethlehem Steel Corporation, Sparrows Point, Maryland* (1968). An obituary is in the *New York Times*, May 27, 1980.]

ALISON GARDY

COUGHLIN, CHARLES EDWARD (Oct. 25, 1891–Oct. 27, 1979), Catholic priest and political figure, was born in Hamilton, Ontario, Canada, the son of Thomas J. Coughlin, a Great Lakes seaman and church sexton, and Amelia Mahoney, a seamstress. Thomas Coughlin was a United States citizen; Amelia Coughlin, a Canadian.

From earliest childhood Coughlin was immersed in Irish-Catholic doctrine and culture. After graduating from St. Mary's elementary school in Hamilton, he entered St. Michael's High School in Toronto, where he excelled in mathematics and athletics. He then attended St. Michael's College, where he played fullback on the rugby team and gained a reputation as a public speaker. In 1911, Coughlin entered the Basilian novitiate of St. Michael's. On June 29, 1916, he was ordained a priest and was assigned to Assumption College in Windsor, Ontario, across the river from Detroit, where he taught English, psychology, and logic for seven years. He was also known for his production of Shakespearean plays.

When the Basilian community in Canada separated from its French parent order, Coughlin became a priest under the jurisdiction of the Archdiocese of Detroit. The popularity of his sermons at St. Leo's Church soon brought him to the attention of Bishop Michael Gallagher, who selected him to establish a new parish in the growing suburb of Royal Oak. The Ku Klux Klan welcomed the new pastor into the community by burning a cross into the parish lawn. This, coupled with the tiny congregation's inability to financially support the operation of the parish, influenced Father Coughlin to try an innovative technique to combat the church's woes.

Coughlin was one of the first priests to utilize radio to spread Catholic tenets to the community. He believed that radio would serve the many immigrants who were unable to read. His first broadcast was on Oct. 17, 1926, on the Detroit station WJR. He was successful from the beginning and more stations began carrying his sermons. Coughlin initially confined his sermons to biblical parables and stories about the life of Christ. In 1930 his format changed, and he began attacking bolshevism and socialism as anti-Christian systems of government. In 1931 he denounced President Herbert Hoover for failing to combat the depression. He received more than a million letters supporting his stance. Thereafter, his radio "sermons" became exclusively political, economic, and social in content. He stressed the concept of social justice as espoused by Pope Leo XIII's 1891 encyclical, *Rerum novarum*, which committed the Catholic church to the improvement of the lot of the working man. Coughlin's favorite scapegoats were international bankers, whom he claimed ran a supranational organization that controlled the world.

Coughlin broadcast on Sunday afternoons from the top of a seven-story granite "Crucifixion Tower" adjoining the Shrine of the Little Flower Church, which he had constructed in 1928 with listener contributions. Newspapers around the country ran stories about Coughlin's Sunday sermons, and national magazines carried feature articles about the "radio priest." By 1934 he was receiving more than ten thousand letters per day, many of them enclosing cash. His clerical staff at times numbered more than a hundred, and he had four personal secretaries. The first edition of Coughlin's complete radio discourses, published in 1933, sold nearly a million copies.

Father Coughlin, who weighed about two hundred pounds and was five feet, ten inches tall, possessed charm, geniality, and good humor. He exuded charisma and convinced people that he actually knew the answers to the nation's problems. His rich, crisp voice with its slight Irish brogue was called "without a doubt one of the great speaking voices of the twentieth century."

As his sermons became more controversial, CBS requested that he tone down his oratory. Instead, on Jan. 4, 1931, he devoted his talk to the attempts of CBS to censor him. Pro-Coughlin letters deluged the network and provided the priest with the notion that he could now safely speak out on any subject. CBS promptly canceled his contract. Undaunted, Coughlin established his own network of more than thirty stations stretching from Maine to California. His sermons were occasionally heard by as many as 40 million persons, the largest radio audience in the world.

In 1932, Coughlin became an ardent supporter of Franklin D. Roosevelt and considered himself at least partially responsible for his election victory. Often referring to FDR as "the boss," Coughlin sprinkled his 1933 sermons with such slogans as "Roosevelt or Ruin" and "The New Deal Is Christ's Deal." Roosevelt never reciprocated this sycophancy and always treated Father Coughlin with diffidence, but considered his adulation useful in attracting the Catholic vote.

Coughlin asserted that the solution to the depression was to place more money in circulation, and he assured his audiences that the president was on the brink of initiating these inflationary policies. When Roosevelt did not push for such legislation, Coughlin became more strident in his insistence upon the nationalization of credit, currency, and the Federal Reserve System.

In 1934, Coughlin established the National Union for Social Justice, which, he explained, was not a political party but a nationwide, nonpartisan people's lobby. Its sixteen principles sought to protect the common working man from the abuses of capitalism. The NUSJ's greatest victory was its eleventh-hour campaign to block the administration's attempt to have the United States join the World Court. In a special nationwide broadcast, Coughlin decried the loss of national sovereignty that this membership would cause. An avalanche of 40,000 anti-Court telegrams helped stop Senate passage of the bill. Although the National Union attracted approximately 5 million members, it failed to influence further legislation. In 1936, Coughlin launched a weekly newspaper called *Social Justice* to promote congressional candidates and reinforce his radio themes.

Disillusioned with FDR, Father Coughlin created the Union party a few months before the election of 1936, and chose as its standard-bearer Representative William Lemke of North Dakota. Other supporters included the remnants of Huey P. Long's "Share the Wealth" movement led by Gerald L. K. Smith, and Dr. Francis E. Townsend's group, which sought government pension payments of $200 per month for all over age sixty-five. Coughlin spoke at rallies around the country, castigating FDR and the New Deal. In Cleveland he referred to FDR as a "great betrayer and liar." Lemke captured only 1 million votes, but Coughlin simply became more extreme in his views and more hysterical in his crusade against Communism.

In 1938, Coughlin accused the Jews of being responsible for all the nation's ills. "The Protocols of the Elders of Zion," an account of a purported Jewish conspiracy to seize control of the world, appeared in *Social Justice*. Henry Ford had published this same forged document more than a decade earlier. In a particularly outrageous speech, Coughlin defended Nazi actions against Communism and accused the Jews of financing the Russian Revolution. His newspaper even reprinted excerpts from the speeches of Nazi propaganda minister Joseph Goebbels.

In August 1938, Coughlin organized the Christian Front as the "last defense" against Communism. Consisting mostly of young Catholic thugs, its principal activity was baiting and violently beating Jewish people. The Royal Oak priest justified this behavior by alluding to Christ's use of physical force in driving the money changers out of the temple. Finally the vitriol became too much. Coughlin was forced off the air in 1940 by a National Association of Broadcasters code that forbade controversial broadcasts.

After Pearl Harbor, Coughlin continued to be involved with isolationist, pro-Nazi groups who claimed the war had been caused by a British-Jewish-Roosevelt conspiracy. On May 1, 1942, Archbishop Mooney ordered Father Coughlin to desist or be defrocked. The priest obeyed. The postmaster general banned his publications from the mails. Coughlin remained pastor of the Shrine of the Little Flower until his retirement in 1966. For the most part he restricted himself to priestly duties, but occasionally he issued a parish bulletin or a sermon warning of the dangers of Communism. After his forced retirement, Coughlin moved to another suburb, living comfortably but privately, saying Mass each morning in his private chapel. He died at his home in nearby Birmingham, Mich.

Father Coughlin was the first American to utilize the radio to advocate political doctrines. He also was a pioneer in pushing American Catholicism into the arena of political activism. Whether or not Father Coughlin ever constituted a threat to democracy, he undoubtedly was one of the most powerful figures outside of the government during the Depression era.

[Major sources include Charles J. Tull, *Father Coughlin and the New Deal* (1965); David H. Bennett, *Demagogues in the Depression* (1969); and Sheldon Marcus, *Father Coughlin: The Tumultuous Life of the Priest of the Little Flower* (1973). An obituary is in the *New York Times*, Oct. 28, 1979.]

FRANCIS R. MCBRIDE

COZZENS, JAMES GOULD (Aug. 19, 1903–Aug. 9, 1978), writer and novelist, was born in

Chicago, the only child of Mary Bertha Wood and Henry William Cozzens. His father sold printing equipment. He grew up in the borough of Staten Island in New York City and in 1922 graduated from the Kent School in Connecticut. At age sixteen, while at Kent, Cozzens had an article accepted by the *Atlantic Monthly*. He attended Harvard University for two years and in the spring of 1924 took a leave of absence, never to return. In 1924 he published *Confusion*, a novel he had completed while a freshman at Harvard. The title was based on a passage from Marcus Aurelius, and the setting was France and North Africa. From 1925 to 1926, Cozzens taught in Cuba, where he accumulated background for some of his later fiction.

In August 1926, Cozzens accompanied his mother to France and for one year worked as a tutor. While there he wrote "The Minor Catholicon" and began "The Careless Livery," both unpublished. Upon returning to the United States, he served for a short period as a librarian at the New York Athletic Club. On Dec. 31, 1927, he married Sylvia Bernice Baumgarten, a literary agent. They had no children.

Cock Pit (1928), the first of Cozzens's novels set in Latin America, was a financial and literary success. It was followed by *The Son of Perdition* (1928). *S.S. San Pedro* (1931), a novelette about ships and the sea, drew some comparisons to the fiction of Joseph Conrad and Stephen Crane. In 1944, William McFee included it in his anthology *World's Great Tales of the Sea*.

In the 1930's, Cozzens published a large number of short stories and essays as well as several complex novels, nearly all of them focusing on professional men. In the *Last Adam* (1933), the protagonist is a physician; *Men and Brethren* (1936) deals with an Episcopal minister. In these novels his heroes are upper class, conservative, and admirable, but susceptible to human frailties. *The Last Adam*, a Book-of-the-Month Club selection, established him as an important writer. The title is drawn from the writings of St. Paul, who describes Christ as the last Adam. There is nothing Christlike, however, about the novel's central figure, Dr. Bull, a cynical, less than competent practitioner who attempts to control a typhoid epidemic in a small New England town. *Men and Brethren* brought Cozzens critical praise for undertaking the difficult task of describing a religious figure who combines Christian spirituality with a realistic view of his environment. In 1940, Cozzens produced *Ask Me Tomorrow*, a short autobiographical novel about his years in Europe.

Through the *Just and the Unjust* (1942), based on a New Jersey murder trial, Cozzens reached a much larger audience; more than 250,000 copies of the work were sold. The *Harvard Law Review* called it a fine fictional account of the daily life of lawyers and recommended that it be made required reading for law students.

During World War II, Cozzens was a writer in the Army Air Corps and was discharged with the rank of major in October 1945. Diaries he kept during this period provided material for *Guard of Honor* (1948), the story of a young general faced with a case of racial discrimination, which was awarded the Pulitzer Prize. Cozzens's most important and popular work was *By Love Possessed* (1957), which sold some 6 million copies and won the William Dean Howells Medal of the American Academy of Arts and Letters. The book covers two traumatic days in the life of Arthur Winner, Jr., a middle-aged lawyer who has an almost Victorian sense of noblesse oblige but at times buckles under the moral testing he is obliged to endure. Critical praise included suggestions that Cozzens deserved the Nobel Prize for literature and that *By Love Possessed* was the most important novel in years. Some critics dissented. The *National Review* cited the work's consistent anti-Catholic bias, and Dwight Macdonald wrote, "Such reviews, such enthusiasm, such unanimity, such nonsense!" He believed that Cozzens had received undue attention because he had not been sufficiently praised for his earlier works. In *Children and Others* (1964), Cozzens brought together seventeen short stories, two of which had not been previously published. It enjoyed a reasonably good popular and critical reception. Cozzens's last novel, *Morning, Noon and Night* (1968), received scattered and generally hostile reviews.

Despite the popular recognition that came with *By Love Possessed*, Cozzens refused to become a public figure. He declined to participate in literary tours or to give radio or television interviews. Living in the rural New Jersey countryside at Lambertville, and later at Williamstown, Mass., he confessed to enjoying the life of a semirecluse. When it was reported that he had not attended a play or concert in over two decades, he was asked how he could write about life and people with so little contact. He replied, "The thing you have to know about yourself, is you are people." He believed his fiction to be a "just representation" of what people endure and that he had no thesis except that "people get a very raw deal from life."

Cozzens died of pneumonia in Stuart, Fla. His literary reputation continues to be debatable. Matthew Bruccoli wrote, "Since 1924 Mr. Cozzens has stayed home and written novels. His works have a distinction that makes some of William Faulkner's work look amateurish." Yet within a decade after his death, Cozzens was little read.

[Cozzens's manuscripts and other papers are at the Princeton University Library. See Dwight Macdonald, "By Cozzens Possessed," in his *Against the American Grain* (1962); Matthew J. Bruccoli, ed., *Just Representations* (1978); and Matthew J. Bruccoli, *James Gould Cozzens* (1983). An obituary is in the *Chicago Tribune*, Aug. 13, 1978.]

ESTELLE M. SHANLEY

CRAIG, CLEO FRANK (Apr. 6, 1893–Apr. 21, 1978), telephone company executive, was born in Rich Hill, Mo., the youngest of seven children of John Stuman Craig, a salesman, and Missouri Ann Davis, who had founded the mining town during the 1880's. His parents had selected the name Cleo before his birth, hoping for a daughter.

Craig attended public schools in Rich Hill, where he was valedictorian of his high school class in 1909, and he graduated from the University of Missouri with a B.S. in electrical engineering in 1913. Immediately after graduation, he went to work in St. Louis for the American Telephone and Telegraph Company (AT&T) as a plant equipment inspector. On Sept. 7, 1914, he married Laura Heck; they had three children.

Craig held a variety of positions at AT&T plants in the Midwest, including division inspector (1913), district plant chief (1919), and district plant superintendent (1920). In 1922 he was transferred to AT&T's Long Lines Division in New York City, where he was a plant accountant. He spent the years 1925–1927 in Atlanta as a division plant superintendent in charge of Long Lines facilities in the southeastern states, then returned to New York City as special representative in AT&T's General Department.

Craig became general manager of Long Lines in 1933 and in 1940 was elected vice-president of Long Lines and made a member of its board of directors. The following year he joined the board of Bell Telephone Laboratories and was appointed AT&T's vice-president in charge of personnel relations. Craig was in charge of AT&T's labor relations during World War II and the immediate postwar period. He negotiated with the National Federation of Telephone Workers and settled the telephone workers' 1947 strike against AT&T.

Craig was considered a possible successor to AT&T president Walter S. Gifford when Gifford resigned from AT&T to become ambassador to Great Britain in 1948. The presidency, however, went to another AT&T vice-president, LeRoy A. Wilson. Craig took over Wilson's vacated post of vice-president for finance and revenue and was elected to the AT&T board of directors in 1949. When Wilson died in June 1951, the board of directors elected Craig as AT&T's president on July 2, 1951.

Craig headed AT&T at a time when it was expanding and upgrading its facilities to satisfy pent-up postwar demand. The number of telephones in the AT&T system increased from 22 million to 35 million between 1945 and 1950, and grew to 46 million by 1955. AT&T's annual revenues increased accordingly: $1.9 billion in 1945, $3.3 billion in 1950, and $5.3 billion in 1955.

AT&T made numerous technological advances during Craig's presidency: the replacement of thousands of central office switches to inaugurate the beginnings of nationwide direct-dial long-distance service; the installation of more than 200,000 miles of coaxial cables and microwave relays to accommodate the rapidly expanding national television networks, NBC, CBS, and ABC; and the laying of the world's first undersea telephone cable.

The new direct-dial technology eliminated the need for large numbers of telephone operators and reduced the cost of long-distance services in comparison with the still-expensive local service. Congressional pressure prompted AT&T to develop new accounting and separations procedures, starting with the Charleston Conference separations plan of 1953, which resulted in long-distance rates subsidizing local telephone service. This cross-subsidization encouraged the growth of competing long-distance telephone companies during the following decades.

Craig was also involved in the negotiations with the United States Department of Justice that ended an antitrust case filed against AT&T in 1949. The 1956 consent decree accepted by Craig allowed AT&T to retain ownership of its Western Electric production facilities, but it had to refrain from any manufacturing activities not related to telephone operations. The consent decree prevented AT&T from entering the computer business, which experienced a period of rapid growth after the invention of the transistor by AT&T's Bell Telephone Laboratories in 1948. AT&T made its transistor technology available to any company willing to pay a licensing fee, thereby feeding the growth of the lucrative new industry from which it had agreed to exclude itself.

Craig oversaw AT&T's laying of the world's first undersea telephone cable, a joint venture of AT&T, the British Post Office, and the Canadian Overseas Telecommunications Corporation. The $42 million line ran from Newfoundland to Scotland and could carry thirty-six simultaneous telephone conversations, which was three times the previous capacity of the existing radio-telephone link. On Sept. 25, 1956, Craig conducted the line's first telephone conversation, with British Postmaster General Dr. Charles Hill.

In late 1956, Craig became AT&T's chairman of the board, and Frederick Kappel succeeded him as AT&T's president. Craig retired as chairman the following year, but he remained a member of AT&T's board of directors until 1960. Craig's wife died in 1962, and he married Esther Abbott Sutton in 1965. Craig, who enjoyed golf, hunting, and fishing, was a trustee of the Metropolitan Museum of Art, Cooper Union, Grand Central Art Galleries, and Presbyterian Hospital in New York City.

Craig was one of a cadre of white Anglo-Saxon Protestant executives who rose to power under the guidance, and during the long tenure, of AT&T president Walter Gifford. He continued Gifford's policy of presenting AT&T to the public as a unique company carrying out a national mission to provide full-service telephone operations under a government-protected monopoly. But the financial accounting and separations procedures initiated in the 1950's led to cross-subsidies, which, combined with the development of the new microwave and computer technologies, later caused the rise of competing telephone equipment manufacturers and providers of long-distance telephone service—and the breakup of AT&T in the 1980's.

Craig died near his home in Ridgewood, N.J.

[Craig's papers at AT&T were destroyed, apparently at his request, at the time of his retirement. There is no book-length biography, but *Fortune*, Nov. 1951, contains "'Craig of AT&T," a biographical profile; and *U.S. News and World Report*, Jan. 22, 1954, contains "Miracles Ahead in Telephone Age," an interview. John Brooks, *Telephone* (1976), describes Craig's role in settling the 1947 strike, as well as the impact of the 1956 consent decree in the antitrust case. Peter Temin, *The Fall of the Bell System* (1987), discusses the separations conferences of the 1950's and other factors leading to the eventual AT&T divestiture. An obituary is in the *New York Times*, Apr. 22, 1978.]

STEPHEN G. MARSHALL

CRANE, BOB EDWARD (July 13, 1928–June 29, 1978), actor, was born in Waterbury, Conn., the son of Alfred T. Crane and Rosemary Senich. Graduation from high school in Waterbury completed his formal education. From an early age Crane aspired to go into show business. Although he was to attain television fame, he set out to be a drummer. He started by playing with the Connecticut Symphony from 1944 to 1946. Afterward, he played on both coasts with traveling dance bands. Meanwhile, he completed a hitch in the Connecticut National Guard from 1948 to 1950. On May 20, 1949, he married Anne Terzian, whom he had known from childhood; they had three children.

Despite a promising start to his drumming career, Crane's interests in his late teens turned toward radio. In 1950 he began realizing his new dream by beating out forty applicants for an announcer position at WLEA in Hornell, N.Y. A year later, Crane sent a recording of his voice to WBIS in Bristol, Conn., which hired him as an announcer. After several weeks on his new job, his manager asked why his on-air voice sounded different from his recording. It turned out that the station had played his recording at the wrong speed, lowering his voice an octave. Crane regarded this accident as one in a long string of lucky breaks that shaped his career.

Crane

Later in 1951, Crane moved to WICC in Bridgeport, Conn., where his ratings and salary began to climb. Other offers came in, including one from Boston, but he stayed in Bridgeport for five years, hoping for an offer from New York City or Los Angeles. His break finally came in 1956 when Ralph Story left a high-rated morning talk show on Los Angeles's KNX. Crane replaced him. His initial ratings were so poor that he went on the "banquet circuit," making 256 public appearances in one year to build his name recognition. New listeners discovered his humor, and his ratings shot up. By the end of the decade his was southern California's highest-rated radio show.

Crane meanwhile began acting at little theaters and making contacts with show-business celebrities through his radio show. These contacts led to his getting small parts on television. His first was on a February 1960 episode of "The Lucy Show." He also provided the off-camera voice of a radio announcer on a "Twilight Zone" episode broadcast in March 1961. Later that year, he appeared on "General Electric Theater." He was on "The Dick Van Dyke Show" in 1962, and on "The Donna Reed Show" twice in 1963. During this period, Crane also had small parts in two feature films, *Return to Peyton Place* and *Mantrap* (both 1963).

As the new season began in September 1964, Crane's role as neighbor Dr. Dave Kelsey on "The Donna Reed Show" became permanent. While working on this series, Crane continued his daily radio program until he got his own television series. In 1965 he became the star of "Hogan's Heroes," playing an Army Air corps colonel, Robert Hogan. Many critics and viewers regarded this sitcom about Allied officers in a German prison camp during World War II as vulgar buffoonery, but it was an immediate hit, ending the year as television's ninth-ranked show. The series ran from Sept. 17, 1965, through July 4, 1971, raising Crane himself to national stardom. In spite of his show's lowbrow reputation, Crane received Emmy Award nominations as best comedy-series actor during its first two seasons.

Success on television allowed Crane to retire from radio permanently, but he kept himself busy throughout the series's six-year run with other work. He made guest appearances on "The Lucy Show" in February 1966, "Love American Style" in October 1969 and February 1971, and other shows, and he occasionally guest-hosted Johnny Carson's and Merv Griffin's talk shows. In 1967 he appeared in the film *The Wicked Dreams of Paula Shultz*; and in 1969 he starred with Lillian Gish and Helen Hayes in a television production of the play *Arsenic and Old Lace*.

In June 1970, Crane divorced his first wife, and on October 16 of that year, he married Patricia Olsen, who played Hilda on "Hogan's Heroes" under her stage name, Sigrid Valdis; they had one child (she already had a child from a previous marriage).

After "Hogan's Heroes" ended in 1971, Crane made more guest appearances on such television shows as "The Doris Day Show," "Night Gallery," "Police Woman," and others. He appeared in the films *Superdad* in 1972 and *Gus* in 1976. In March 1975 his career reached a high-water mark with a new television series bearing his own name, "The Bob Crane Show." In this show, he played Bob Wilcox, a middle-aged insurance salesman returning to school to become a doctor—an ironic twist, since Crane's first regular television role was as a doctor. After running a minimal thirteen weeks, the show was canceled.

Crane did not work in television again until the following year, when he was a guest on both Lloyd Bridges's "Joe Forrester" series and "Ellery Queen" as well as two other short-lived series, "Spencer's Pilots" and "Gibbsville." In 1977 he appeared on television only once, in an April episode of "The Hardy Boys/Nancy Drew Mysteries." His last television work was the Jan. 7, 1978, episode of "The Love Boat."

Through these years, Crane turned more to theater. He appeared in stage productions of *Cactus Flower* and *Send Me No Flowers*, and toured dinner clubs with *Beginner's Luck*. While appearing in this latter production in Scottsdale, Ariz., Crane met his unlucky end. On June 29, 1978, he was found beaten to death in his bed in an apartment rented by the dinner theater. Although there was considerable speculation about possibly unsavory elements of Crane's personal life, no clear motive was established for his murder and no arrests were made. The case remained a mystery until mid-1992, when a man who had been a suspect since the time of Crane's murder was finally arrested.

[No biographical works on Crane are available. Obituaries are in the *Los Angeles Times* and the *New York Times*, both June 30, 1978.]

R. KENT RASMUSSEN

CRAWFORD, JOAN (Mar. 23, 1906–May 10, 1977), actress, was born Lucille Fay LeSueur in San Antonio, Tex., the daughter of Thomas LeSueur, a ne'er-do-well French Canadian drifter, and Anna Bell Johnson, a waitress. Before her birth LeSueur deserted his family. Anna promptly moved to Lawton, Okla., where she divorced LeSueur and, in 1907, wed Henry Cassin. Lucille was renamed Billie Cassin and adored the man she regarded as her true father. Cassin, who operated the local "opera house," encouraged the girl to attend rehearsals and performances, to practice dance steps, and to enjoy the freedom and creativity of theatrical life, despite the objections of Anna, who was determined that her daughter not become an entertainer.

In 1913, Cassin was accused of embezzlement, and although he was cleared of all charges, he was forced to leave town. The Cassins moved to Kansas City, Mo., where he and Anna operated a rundown boardinghouse. In 1916 he left Anna and his two children. Again, Anna filed for divorce and quickly remarried. Her new husband did not want Billie around, and the girl was shunted from one convent school to another, working on the premises in the laundry and waiting on tables to pay her tuition. She became popular with boys, having turned into a pretty though plump teenager and a good dancer.

In 1922, because of superior grades, Billie was awarded a scholarship at Stephens College, but she left before completing her first term to join a touring dance company. The company failed, and she returned to Kansas City to work in a department store until another stage offer came along. This time she was successful, the popular "pony"—the smallest chorus girl—in the Detroit tryout of *Innocent Eyes*, a revue starring the fabled Mistinguette. At this time, she changed her name back to Lucille LeSueur. After the show moved on to triumph in New York City, the impresario J. J. Shubert commented, "She had something. I don't know how to define it, but every man in the audience picked her out. She wasn't particularly sexy, but she seemed to enjoy herself every minute she was onstage, and that made the audience enjoy the show more."

When *Innocent Eyes* left Broadway for a national road tour, Lucille stayed on in New York to dance in another Shubert Brothers musical. It was then that Harry Rapf, a Metro-Goldwyn-Mayer (MGM) talent scout, spotted the vivacious dancer, gave her a screen test, and persuaded her to go to Hollywood. On the way, she stopped in Kansas City for a strained reunion with her mother, who disapproved of her career; her stepfather, who still did not want her around; and her brother, whom she had come to dislike. On Jan. 1, 1925, she entrained for Hollywood.

Crawford was delighted with the opportunity to roam the MGM lot to watch such stars as Greta Garbo and Norma Shearer at work. She soon realized, after reading her contract thoroughly, that she could be dropped (as a majority of film hopefuls were) after six months. Shortly before her first deadline, terrified but determined, she bullied Rapf to find her a part. Back to the chorus she went in a revue titled *Pretty Ladies* (1925). In this film she was "noticed," as was another contract hopeful named Myrna Loy (they became lifelong friends), and she appeared in a succession of such nondescript films as *The Only Thing* (1925) and *Old Clothes* (1925). Audiences became so aware of the girl that Louis B. Mayer decided to promote her with a publicity campaign, the first step involving a contest to change her name. Thus, Lucille LeSueur became Joan Crawford. "I hated the name at first—it sounded like 'crawfish'—but it wasn't long before I felt as though I'd always been Joan Crawford."

Before the year ended, MGM publicist Pete Smith, prodded by Crawford, persuaded studio heads to cast her in a major film, *Sally, Irene, and Mary* (1925), supporting such "real" stars as Constance Bennett and Sally O'Neil. The film was a smash success, and Crawford established herself as an actress as well as a dancer. Film after film followed, as many as five in a year, most of which (in Crawford's words) were "forgettables."

Although her career was secured, her personal life was chaotic, topped by a publicized romance with Michael Cudahy, an alcoholic packing-plant heir. Then her brother arrived in Hollywood and moved in with her, informing the actress that "you can support me, now that you're a big star." Crawford's dislike of her brother, whom her mother had always favored, soon turned to hatred. She sent for her mother (again divorced) and turned her bungalow over to the pair, removing herself to a better house. For the rest of their lives, Crawford supported them.

In 1929, Crawford made her first landmark film, *Our Modern Maidens*, costarring Douglas Fairbanks, Jr. The pairing led to a romance publicized—with MGM's blessing—throughout the world, and on June 3, 1929, they were wed. It was a press agent's dream: the chorus girl from the wrong side of the tracks marrying into the Fairbanks-Pickford aristocracy. Crawford took her role seriously, learned all she could about china and silver services and entertainment etiquette, and even attempted to learn French. The marriage disintegrated when Fairbanks proved more at home with his cronies in Hollywood's British colony than with Joan. On May 13, 1933, they were divorced. Two more marriages also ended in divorce: to actors Franchot Tone (Oct. 11, 1935–Apr. 11, 1939) and Philip Terry (July 21, 1942–Apr. 25, 1946). On May 10, 1955, she married Pepsi-Cola president Alfred Steele, a union that lasted until his death in 1959.

Unable to bear children—she claimed that a bacillus found in raw milk she had drunk in her childhood caused her seven miscarriages—Crawford satisfied her maternal instincts through the adoption of four children. As a strict—and perhaps cruel—disciplinarian, her treatment of her children has been a topic of severe criticism, manifesting itself most notably in her daughter Christina's book *Mommie Dearest* (1978).

Crawford's golden years at MGM extended from 1931 to 1941, during which time she made a number of films that have become regarded as classics: *Possessed* (1931), *Rain* (1932), *Grand Hotel* (1932), *Dancing Lady* (1933), *The Shining Hour* (1939), *The Women* (1939), *Strange Cargo* (1940), *Susan and God* (1940), and *A Woman's Face* (1941). (Many of these films paired her with Clark Gable; they were on-and-off lovers for more than two decades.) Crawford's vast following worshipped her as a star, and she played the part to perfection, usually gowned by Adrian, always totally convincing in her roles, even those requiring extreme bitchiness (*The Women*) or actual physical ugliness (*A Woman's Face*). In 1943, however, as one of many actresses labeled "box office poison," Crawford left MGM.

Despite the loss of studio protection and an increasing addiction to alcohol, Crawford's greatest triumph was yet to come—Warner Brothers' *Mildred Pierce* (1945), for which she won the best actress Academy Award. A few other laudable films followed, including *Humoresque* (1946), *Possessed* (1947), *Harriet Craig* (1950), *Female on the Beach* (1955), and *Autumn Leaves* (1956). The box office magic was gone, however, and studios and audiences preferred younger actresses. In 1962, in what turned out to be a stroke of near genius, Robert Aldrich cast Crawford and Bette Davis in *Whatever Happened to Baby Jane?* The film was a box office smash, helped by the publicized feud between the two stars, who loathed each other.

From her marriage to Alfred Steele in 1955 until his death in 1959, Crawford's career played second fiddle. She accompanied Steele on Pepsi-Cola sales and merchandising excursions throughout the world, took an active role in company affairs, and after his death assumed a role on the executive board. (Two years later she was forced out.) Steele did not leave a large estate: despite his enormous salary, Crawford was left with debts that she paid by the sale of personal property, a move to a less expensive apartment, and sporadic appearances in low-budget films and television soap operas. At her death in New York City as a Christian Scientist she did not admit to having cancer, nor did she consult a physician—she left a relatively small estate to her adopted "twins"; she was estranged from Christina and Christopher, who had borne the brunt of her discipline.

[See Joan Crawford and Jane Kesner Ardmore, *A Portrait of Joan* (1962); Joan Crawford, *My Way of Life* (1971); Christina Crawford, *Mommie Dearest* (1978); Bob Thomas, *Joan Crawford: A Biography* (1978); and Roy Newquist, *Conversations with Joan Crawford* (1980). Obituaries are in the *New York Times* and the *Los Angeles Times*, both May 11, 1977.]

ROY NEWQUIST

CROSBY, HARRY LILLIS ("BING") (May 2, 1903–Oct. 14, 1977), singer and actor, was born in Tacoma, Wash., the fourth of seven children of Harry Lowe Crosby, a bookkeeper, and Kate Harrigan. His nickname was derived from that of a popular comic strip figure he admired as a child.

Crosby graduated from Gonzaga University High School in Spokane, Wash., and then enrolled at Gonzaga University. Before dropping out, Crosby had been singing with a local group. In 1925 he and the band's piano player, Al Rinker, went to Los Angeles, where they developed a singing act. In 1927 they were hired by the immensely successful Paul Whiteman, whose big band helped define the Jazz Age. Later, Crosby and Rinker were joined by Harry Barris, a singer and songwriter. The trio performed as Paul Whiteman's Rhythm Boys. (One of Crosby's first successful recordings was the Harry Barris–Gordon Clifford song "I Surrender, Dear," which also provided the title for a two-reeler featuring Crosby that was produced by Mack Sennett in 1931.) After touring separately and with Whiteman, the Rhythm Boys appeared with Whiteman's big band in an early talking picture, *The King of Jazz*, in 1930.

The next year Crosby became a solo star after William S. Paley, president of the Columbia Broadcasting System, began giving him air time on a sustained basis. Although Crosby had already done some film work, it was his growing radio audiences, and a record run of performances at the Paramount Theater in New York City in 1932, that made him a popular idol and guaranteed more and better parts in movies. He had several radio programs during the 1930's, enjoying his greatest success with "The Kraft Music Hall," of which he became host in 1935. The program featured as guests many of the biggest names in show business and included a resident comedian with whom Crosby exchanged wisecracks. The annual highlight of this series was Crosby's Christmas show, which later became a feature of the holiday season on television.

Crosby's singing style, known as "crooning"—a relaxed, seemingly effortless rendition of sunny songs and ballads—was welcomed by Americans suffering from the Great Depression blues. So, too, was the humor employed on his radio shows and in films. A natural ad-libber, Crosby had the timing of a comedian and could perform equally well as straight man or comic. His growing popularity was of great benefit to the recording industry, which had suffered near catastrophic losses during the Great Depression. Record sales nationwide had fallen from $73 million in 1928 to only $5 million in 1934 when Crosby became the first artist to sign with Decca Records, enabling the firm to survive hard times and become a leader in the industry.

Although Crosby always had an attractive voice, in early recordings his style resembles that of jazz singers of the 1920's, Al Jolson in particular. He often sang near the top of his range and with greater intensity than in later years. As he matured, Crosby stayed with his natural baritone, avoiding the thinner, high end of his range and abandoning jazz mannerisms as a rule, although he continued to slur certain notes ("groaning," it was called, and he was sometimes called "the groaner").

Crosby was one of the first popular singers to take advantage of electronic amplification, thereby pioneering a revolution in pop music. Before the microphone was introduced, lung power and projection were important to pop singers, whose styles were built around these requirements. Crosby, in contrast, developed an intimate, almost conversational way of putting over a song, knowing that the microphone would carry his subtleties of inflection and phrasing to every audience member. Though other singers followed his lead, none equaled his mastery of the idiom he had created.

Crosby was often compared with Fred Astaire, another great popular artist who made what he did look easy, but in some ways he was closer to Franklin D. Roosevelt, the first major politician to adapt his oratorical style to radio—notably in the "fireside chats." Crosby's influence persists to this day, for although the popularity of his kind of ballad faded with the coming of rock and roll in the 1950's, the apparent informality and naturalness of contemporary "soft" rock singers result from Crosby's innovations.

In addition to his long career on radio and television, Crosby appeared in one hundred motion pictures—including two-reelers, travelogues, and cameo performances. Among the most popular feature films were his "road" movies—*The Road to Singapore* (1940), *The Road to Zanzibar* (1941), and seven others, in which he costarred with Bob Hope. Their mock feuding in pictures and over the air was one of the staples of American popular culture for several decades. Another long association, that with Louis Armstrong, dated from 1936, when they both appeared in the hit film *Pennies from Heaven*. They performed together often after that and made outstanding recordings as well, the last being "Bing and Satchmo" in 1960.

Although most of his films exploited his singing voice and easy charm, Crosby had considerable dramatic gifts, winning an Oscar in 1944 as best actor for his role as a priest in *Going My Way*. His performance opposite Grace Kelly as an alcoholic husband in the 1954 film *The Country Girl*, though it did not result in an Oscar, was the most accomplished of his career. Beginning in 1943, Crosby was among the top ten box office attractions for twelve consecutive years. In five of those years he headed the list. Since he was also recording and performing on the air, he was at this time easily the number one star in show business.

Of his many films Crosby's personal favorite was *High Society* (1956), which had a superb score by Cole Porter and featured Grace Kelly again, plus Frank Sinatra and a stellar cast including Louis Armstrong, Louis Calhern, and Celeste Holm. It also resulted in the twentieth and last of his records to sell a million copies, "True Love," a duet sung with Kelly.

During World War II, Crosby entertained the troops at home and abroad. Although "Silent Night" was the most popular song he ever recorded, the most popular song of the war was Irving Berlin's "White Christmas," introduced by Crosby in the film *Holiday Inn* (1942). It was the first song in a decade to sell more than one million copies of sheet music, and led the Hit Parade—music's equivalent of a Nielsen rating—nine times. As sung by Crosby, it embodied the overwhelming nostalgia induced by the war's separation of loved ones better than any other piece of music.

After the war Crosby led the music industry through its next technical revolution, becoming the first performer to record his radio show on audiotape. He did this when he left "The Kraft Music Hall" and started a new program, "Philco Radio Time," on the American Broadcasting Company network in 1946. This step marked the beginning of the end of live radio performances. From taping his shows Crosby progressed to recording vocals in Los Angeles over instrumental tracks recorded earlier in London. In his fifty-one years as a recording artist, he went from recording on wax to using thirty-two-track tapes.

Crosby recorded more than 1,600 songs that sold at least 500 million copies. He seldom rerecorded, unlike many artists, who recorded their most popular songs over and over again. There were some notable exceptions, such as the five-record Decca album, *Bing—A Musical Biography*, which was released in 1954. Near the end of his life a two-record set of his London Palladium concerts, *Big Crosby Live at the London Palladium*, included a selection of his hits from the 1920's through the 1970's. Crosby was always most interested in fresh material; few, if any, popular artists equaled him in the number of new songs introduced. Curiously, he never learned to read music.

By the late 1950's Crosby's long and brilliant career in show business was winding down. Ballads were giving way to rock. The tastes of movie audiences had changed. After 1960 he appeared in only seven films, two of them travelogues. His portrayal of a drunken physician in the remake of *Stagecoach* (1966) was much admired by critics. He appeared on television in his Christmas specials, as a guest on other shows, and as one of the rotating hosts of a series called "Hollywood Palace," which ran from 1964 to 1970. His only series, "The Bing Crosby Show," a situation comedy, lasted just one season (1964).

In 1975, Crosby made his first theater appearance in many years at a tribute honoring the Mills Brothers. The next year he organized and starred in his own concert, which was highly successful at the box office and praised by critics. He gave many such concerts thereafter, including several at the London Palladium—one engagement there lasted for two weeks. These concerts typically lasted two hours, with Crosby being on stage throughout, and ended with a thirty-minute medley of his favorite hits. For a man over seventy, who had had part of a lung removed as a result of a fungus acquired in Africa, these were considerable feats.

Crosby married Wilma Winifred Wyatt, an actress known professionally as Dixie Lee, on Sept. 29, 1930; they had four sons. Her death in 1952 ended a marriage that had survived despite many difficulties, some a result of Crosby's harsh disciplining of his children—a futile regime that produced more rebelliousness than obedience. In October 1957, Crosby married Kathryn Grant, an actress thirty years his junior. They had three children.

Crosby was one of the best-paid entertainers in the country and, despite the high taxes levied on earned income during the 1940's and 1950's, amassed a fortune. He made light of his wealth, telling Barbara Walters in a 1977 interview for one of her television specials that he would leave an estate of about $1.2 million. They were, at the time, on the grounds of his Hillsborough, Calif., mansion, which alone was worth more than that. Crosby had incorporated himself in 1936, shortly after he began earning big money. Over the years his companies, limited partnerships, copartnerships, and corporate affiliations spanned an enormous range of businesses, including investments in real estate; frozen orange juice; mines; oil wells; cattle; race horses; a horse breeding farm; a race track; music publishing; videotape and audiotape recordings and machines; professional baseball, football, and hockey teams; prizefighters; radio and television stations; banks; and television and motion picture production companies. At his death he was probably worth in excess of $150 million.

Apart from show business, sport was Crosby's great passion. He enjoyed hunting, fishing, and going on safaris, but his dedication to golf, which he played expertly, was world famous. The Bing Crosby Pro-Amateur Golf Tournament, held annually at Pebble Beach, Calif., became one of golf's classic events. In 1950, Crosby was awarded the William D. Richardson Memorial Trophy for his contributions to the game. He died as he must have wished to, suddenly, of a massive heart attack, while playing at the Moralejo Golf Club near Madrid, Spain. Crosby was buried at Holy Cross Cemetery, Los Angeles.

As a young man Crosby had pursued wine and women in addition to song. Indeed, it appears that Paul Whiteman let the Rhythm Boys go because of Crosby's drinking—which was interfering with his performances. Crosby was spendthrift as well, and had little to show for his money when it first began to roll in. But during the early 1930's, as his star rose, Crosby changed. He stopped drinking excessively, created an organization to handle his business affairs in which his brothers Laurance and Everett held key positions, and became the complete professional.

As so often in show business, the public image of Crosby as an easygoing, unflappable charmer was part of his act. In private he was more disciplined, more reserved, sterner, and not especially generous. However, his work as a performing artist was close to faultless. From the time he began taking his career seriously until his last performance, at the London Palladium four days before his death, Bing Crosby gave the public its money's worth each and every time. One of the greatest American popular artists, he was important, too, for personifying gentlemanliness and grace. Crosby was loved all over the world, but he also had the world's respect.

[Crosby's autobiography is *Call Me Lucky* (1953), as told to Pete Martin. There are many biographies, among them Charles Thompson, *Bing* (1976); Laurence J. Zwisohn, *Bing* (1978), which includes basic information on all his recordings; and Donald Shepherd and Robert F. Slatzer, *Bing Crosby* (1981), which contains a listing of all his movie appearances. An obituary is in the *New York Times*, Oct. 15, 1977.]

WILLIAM L. O'NEILL

CUNNINGHAM, IMOGEN (Apr. 12, 1883–June 24, 1976), photographer, was born in Portland, Oreg., the daughter of Susan Elizabeth and Isaac Burns Cunningham, whose trades included farming, logging, and road grading. The fifth of ten children, Cunningham grew up with little money. The family moved to Seattle, Wash., in 1889. By the time Cunningham was eighteen, she had settled on photography as her profession, and though her father would have preferred her to be a teacher, he showed his support by building her a darkroom in the woodshed. She would remain active in photography until her death.

Cunningham enrolled at the University of Washington in Seattle in 1903, wanting to be an art major. As there was no art department, she settled on chemistry instead, wrote her thesis ("The Scientific Development of Photography"), and graduated with honors in 1907. That same year, she took a job in the portrait studio of Edward S. Curtis. Among her duties was the printing of some of his now-famous photographs of native Americans. She worked for Curtis until 1909 when she was awarded a $500 scholarship by her sorority to study photochemistry in Dresden, Germany.

On her return to Seattle in 1910, Cunningham set up her own portrait studio. Little remains of her early professional work, as she destroyed the heavy glass negatives she used for portraiture when she moved to the San Francisco Bay area in 1917, but the personal photographs she took at the time show a preference for romantic, soft-focus images reminiscent of English Victorian-era photography. She often put friends in costume, placed them in wooded settings, and had them strike dramatic poses for the camera. In 1915, Cunningham married Roi Partridge, an etcher, and she took nude photos of him on Mt. Rainier that same year. The photos were greeted by the public with shock, and she withdrew them from view for more than fifty years.

Partridge took a position teaching art at Mills College in Oakland, Calif., in 1920. By this time, the couple had three sons, and Cunningham had to balance her photographic career with her need to take care of her children and her home. When time allowed, Cunningham pursued her photography, often in the garden while her children played. During this period she created the plant studies that are often considered her finest work. *Magnolia Blossom*, created in 1925, stands as one of her finest achievements.

In 1932, Cunningham was a founding member of the influential Group f/64 along with six other photographers, including Edward Weston and Ansel Adams. The informal group helped set the standard for the West Coast style of photography by insisting on clear, sharp photography rather than the painterly, soft-focus style then still in vogue. The associations forged between Cunningham and the other seminal photographers lasted throughout their lives. Unlike most others in the group, Cunningham was not a photographic purist. She eagerly experimented with multiple exposures, and she cropped her negatives freely when she felt it was appropriate.

Cunningham began taking photographs for the magazine *Vanity Fair* in 1931, and in 1934 she was invited to complete an assignment for the magazine in New York City. She accepted, feeling this was an important step in her career. Her husband objected strongly, and the incident aggravated the couple's growing marital friction and led to their divorce that same year. The two remained friends, and Cunningham never remarried.

Though Cunningham continued to pick up occasional magazine assignments for *Vanity Fair*, she supported herself predominantly with portrait work well into the 1960's, living frugally and laboring in relative obscurity. She preferred environmental portraiture over studio work and was known for establishing immediate rapport with her sitters, rapidly taking numerous photos while talking constantly about whatever she thought might interest them. Her sitters often commented that being photographed by Cunningham was as much an experience as it was a portrait session. Never a perfectionist and considering technique secondary to the visual and emotional strength of a photo, Cunningham was known to print a somewhat out-of-focus negative over a perfectly sharp one if she felt the less technically perfect shot was more evocative. Much of her personal work during this time was portraiture as well, usually of artists and friends. Her 1950 photograph of the painter Morris Graves among rocks and foliage is often considered to be one of the finest portraits of its kind.

It was not until the 1960's, when Cunningham was in her eighties, that she gained wide recognition, and her work did not begin selling well in galleries until 1974. She continued her portrait work, though she became more selective about her clients, photographing only people who interested her. Two collections of her works were published, adding considerably to her reputation: *Imogen Cunningham: Photographs* (1970) and *Imogen!* (1974). Somewhat bitter about her late fame, she nevertheless took to notoriety in style, adopting a black cape and a close-fitting cap as a kind of uniform, which made her instantly recognizable around San Francisco; newspaper columnist Herb Caen declared her the new sex symbol of the city.

Cunningham kept up an exhausting schedule of photographic work, teaching, and a vigorous social life. She had numerous friends and admirers and was known for her biting, irreverent wit, often at the expense of others. At age ninety-two, Cunningham decided to begin a book that was to be published as *After Ninety* in 1977. The book contains portraits of people who were in their nineties or a little younger; more than half of the photos were taken by Cunningham after her own ninetieth year. She died in San Francisco.

Cunningham's importance as a photographer is subject to debate. While some consider her an interesting but second-rate photographer, others believe that her photographic output spanning seven decades contains both a one-woman history of modern photography and a wealth of first-rate photographs.

[Cunningham's papers are in the Smithsonian Institution's Archives of American Art, Washington, D.C. Her negatives and a collection of prints are in the Imogen Cunningham Trust, Berkeley, Calif. Biographical information and collections of her photos can be found in *Imogen Cunningham: Photographs* (1970); *Imogen!* (1974); *After Ninety* (1977);

and *Imogen Cunningham: A Portrait* (1979). Films featuring Cunningham include *Two Photographers: Imogen Cunningham and Wynn Bullock* (1966); *Imogen Cunningham, Photographer* (1972); and *Never Give Up: Imogen Cunningham* (1974). An obituary is in the *New York Times*, June 26, 1976.]

DAVID SAFIER

CUSHMAN, AUSTIN THOMAS ("JOE") (Dec. 18, 1901–June 12, 1978), retailer and businessman, was born in Albuquerque, N.Mex., the son of Charles Otis Cushman, a men's clothing retailer, and Lena Hughes. As a boy, Cushman attended the Culver Military Institute, then the New Mexico Military Institute. He learned about the retail business by working in his father's store. Cushman studied for three years at the University of California but left in 1926, before graduating, to work as a salesman for Montgomery Ward. He married Paula Hannah Paiver on Nov. 6, 1926; they had one child. At Montgomery Ward, Cushman rose to the rank of department manager in Oakland. In 1930, when Montgomery Ward was laying off and demoting employees, he refused to accept a demotion and left the company.

He joined Montgomery Ward's archrival, Sears, Roebuck, in 1931 as a part-time salesman in its Oakland store. The following year he was named manager in San Francisco, and in 1939, only eight years after he had joined Sears, he was put in charge of all of the company's operations in the San Francisco area. He held a number of other executive positions until 1945, when he became general manager of Sears stores in the Los Angeles area.

Four years later, Cushman was promoted to vice-president in charge of Sears's Pacific Coast territory. In this capacity, he directed all retail stores and mail-order outlets in nine western states. He was noted for his passion for constructing huge, free-standing retail stores surrounded by enormous parking lots. The parking was free, and the stores were one story with high ceilings that created a sense of expansive space.

Known as "a retailer's retailer," Cushman earned a reputation for surrounding himself with enthusiastic and resourceful salesmen. His advice to them was: "A salesman has to be friendly, and he has to be sincere. He has to know his product and believe in what he is selling." Cushman had no tolerance for lackluster personalities. He would say often that there was no place at Sears for a man whose blood got tired.

Cushman convinced Sears's board to spend more money on opening stores in the West rather than other regions of the United States. From 1949 to 1962, Sears's sales grew 200 percent in the West, compared with 98 percent nationwide. By 1962, one out of every three American families was a Sears customer, and Sears had become the largest retail operation in the world. The company's sales had topped $4.5 billion a year, and it offered 140,000 items, from farm supplies to luxury goods.

In 1962, Sears's chief executive officer, Charles Kellstadt, retired. Instead of choosing the president of Sears to replace him, Kellstadt selected Cushman, who was then sixty years old, as his successor. The nomination was approved by the company's board of directors and 160,000 stockholders.

It was speculated that Kellstadt chose Cushman because he felt a common bond with him. Each man had gotten his start in the retail business by working in his father's store. Each had directed one of the company's five regional divisions. And each bought his clothes at Sears. Moreover, Kellstadt had left Cushman with a $210 million mission to expand the company's number of stores over the next three years.

Shortly before he assumed the helm, Cushman said he had no plans for sweeping changes. But once in office, he exceeded Kellstadt's expectations. During his five years at the helm (1962–1967), Cushman opened 164 additional stores and modernized catalog merchandise distribution centers in an $800 million expansion. He transplanted the model of the colossal California-style store to the East Coast and directed the construction of the company's gigantic landmark store in suburban Hicksville, N.Y., as well as other supersize stores in Washington, D.C., and Middleburg Heights, Ohio, outside Cleveland.

Cushman was the third Sears chief executive officer to have come from Montgomery Ward. The first was "General" Robert Wood, who replaced Charles Kittle, and the second was Theodore Houser. Cushman's promotion required him to leave California for Chicago, where Sears's head office was located. An associate said of him that he was "a master of the fireside-chat method of communication." Cushman described himself in more modest terms: as a "clean-desk man" who liked to keep business in order and in motion. His son remembered Cushman as saying, "There are three important things: merchandise, money and men. And the most important are people."

"I'm not a dynamic character," Cushman said, "but I'm a good businessman. I like people, I can sell, and I love to make money." Though people might have come first with Cushman, making money did indeed seem to be his favorite pastime. He once said of a forty-foot fishing boat he had owned, "The two happiest things about my boating experience were the day I bought [the boat] and the day I sold it." The reason was that he didn't lose anything on the boat.

By 1964, Sears had a bigger sales volume than the tobacco or furniture industries. As shopping centers sprouted across the country, they often organized around the focal point of a Sears store. Sears even had its own shopping center development subsidiary, Homart Development, which was created in 1960. The price of Sears's stock soared. Cushman used his annual bonus to buy shares at an average cost of $2 per share. By the time he retired as chief executive officer in 1967, he had 90,000 shares of company stock, worth about $5 million.

When Cushman retired at the age of sixty-six, he had increased Sears's sales by about two-thirds. He moved back to the West Coast and lived in San Marino, Calif. By the time he died in Pasadena, Calif., Sears's sales had increased by a further 40 percent.

[Donald F. Katz, *The Big Store* (1987), and Cecil C. Hoge, *The First Hundred Years Are the Toughest* (1988), provide general background on Sears and details on Cushman's influence. See also James C. Worthy, *Shaping an American Institution* (1984), for background on Sears. "New Boss at Sears," *Time*, Feb. 16, 1962, and "Clean Desk Man," *Newsweek*, Feb. 19, 1962, contain information on Cushman's appointment as chief executive officer of Sears. An obituary is in the *New York Times*, June 13, 1978.]

ALISON GARDY

D

DAILEY, DAN, JR. (Dec. 14, 1915–Oct. 16, 1978), singer, dancer, and actor, was born in New York City, one of four children of Daniel J. Dailey, manager of the Roosevelt Hotel, and Helen Riley, an actress. Dailey attended private schools in Baldwin, Long Island, but gave up further education to foster his dancing career, initiated when he responded to a call for male dancers at his sister's dancing school. Although his father would have preferred Dan to pursue a career in the hotel business, Dan was stage-struck early and began dancing professionally while still a young teenager in minstrel shows, on the vaudeville circuit (especially Publix), in burlesque (Minsky's in 1937), and as part of the chorus line at the Roxy in New York City. He also worked as a social director at various Catskills summer resorts. He won a role in the Broadway success *Babes in Arms* in 1937, played in *I Married an Angel* in 1938, and then was offered the leading role in the musical *Stars in Your Eyes* in 1939. Spotted by a Metro-Goldwyn-Mayer agent during the Los Angeles run of the play, he was signed to a movie contract, making his debut with a minor role in *The Captain Is a Lady* in 1940.

In the first years of his Hollywood career, Dailey was sometimes cast in straight dramatic roles, as in the film *The Mortal Storm* (1940), where he played a Nazi storm trooper. He was also cast as a juvenile lead in such lackluster movies as *Dulcy* (1940), *Hullabaloo* (1940), and *Washington Melodrama* (1941). He had not yet developed a strong screen image, and his versatility as a dancer and actor confused producers in their assignment of roles. Moreover, he photographed looking more mature than his real age, yet he was too young to take character parts. Although undeniably handsome—he was six feet, four inches tall, weighed 210 pounds, and had sandy hair and light blue eyes—he was considered too rugged to earn stardom as a dancer. He never considered himself an elegant dancer like Fred Astaire or an athletic dancer like Gene Kelly: he always regarded himself as a "hoofer." His screen persona was finally beginning to take shape when World War II interrupted his career. He had appeared in the musicals *Ziegfeld Girl* (1941), *Lady Be Good* (1941), and *Panama Hattie* (1942). He was cast to star with Eleanor Powell in *For Me and My Girl*, but he lost the part when he was drafted into the armed forces (Gene Kelly's movie career was launched when he replaced Dailey).

Dailey served in the United States Army Signal Corps from 1942 to 1946, leaving with the rank of second lieutenant. Upon his discharge from the army, he returned to Hollywood and signed a new contract with Twentieth Century–Fox. He immediately became a mainstay of postwar Hollywood musicals. He appeared in *Mother Wore Tights* (1947) with Betty Grable, *You Were Meant for Me* (1948) with Jeanne Crain, *Give My Regards to Broadway* (1948), and *When My Baby Smiles at Me*, in which he outshone costar Grable in the part that won him his Academy Award nomination for best actor (1948), playing a former burlesque clown whose career had faded. Dailey was praised for his charm and vitality and labeled a performer of distinction.

His late 1940's successes were followed by appearances in *My Blue Heaven* (1950); *Call Me Mister* (1951), with Betty Grable; *There's No Business Like Show Business* (1954), with Donald O'Connor, Ethel Merman, and Mitzi Gaynor, in which he played the father of O'Connor and Gaynor, while he was hardly older than they were; *It's Always Fair Weather* (1955), where he played a wonderful scene as a drunken advertising executive at a party; *Meet Me in Las Vegas* (1956); and *The Best Things in Life Are Free* (1956). In 1955 he was one of Hollywood's top moneymakers, but his film career had peaked by 1957 as interest in musicals waned. With the popularity of variety shows on television, few movie patrons were willing to leave home to watch singing and dancing on the big screen.

Although most famous for his roles in musicals and comedies, Dailey also had some memorable dramatic parts. He appeared in three dramas directed by John Ford: *When Willie Comes Marching Home* (1950); *What Price Glory*, a Technicolor remake of the Maxwell Anderson play, with James Cagney (1952); and *The Wings of Eagles* (1957). One of his most famous roles was Dizzy Dean in the Hollywood biography of the baseball pitcher, *The Pride of St. Louis* (1952). After appearing with Jayne Mansfield in *The Wayward Bus* (1957) and with Mexican actor Cantinflas in *Pepe* (1960), Dailey made his last Hollywood film, *Hemingway's Adventures of a Young Man*, in 1962.

In the 1960's and 1970's Dailey worked steadily on the stage and on television. He returned to New York for his first straight acting role on Broadway in *Catch Me if You Can* in 1965. He toured extensively in productions such as *The Odd Couple* (1965–1967) as Oscar Madison, *Plaza Suite* (1969) with Lee Grant, and *Take Me Along* (1975).

On television, he guest-starred on a number of shows, including "G. E. Theater," "The Untouchables," "Alfred Hitchcock Presents," "Here's Lucy," and "The Wonderful World of Disney." He also starred in three television series: "The Four Just Men" (1959), featuring international stars; a half-hour situation comedy, "The Governor and J. J." (Sept. 1969–Aug. 1972), with Julie Sommars, and the mystery series "Faraday and Co." (Sept. 1973–Aug. 1974).

Dailey married four times. His first marriage, to Esther Rodier, lasted barely a year, 1940 to 1941. His second marriage, to Elizabeth Hofert, lasted from 1942 to 1951; the couple had one child, a son who predeceased his father in 1975. For his third wife, Dailey chose Gwendolyn O'Connor, the former wife of fellow hoofer and film star Donald O'Connor; this marriage lasted from 1955 to 1961. A fourth marriage, to Carole Warner, had ended in divorce before Dailey's death.

Whatever the medium, Dailey's performances were always professional; he was able to make the most mundane vehicle a bit more attractive. His niche in entertainment history, however, is definitely because of his work in musicals; he was the consummate hoofer, ready to beguile audiences with his fancy footwork.

[For further information on Dailey's career, consult the clippings file in the Billy Rose Theatre Collection, New York Public Library for the Performing Arts at Lincoln Center. An interview with Dailey conducted by J. E. Albert is in *Film Fan Monthly*, Mar. 1974. Most film encyclopedias contain entries on Dailey, and his name comes up regularly in histories and studies of the Hollywood musical. Obituaries are in *Variety* and in the *New York Times*, both Nov. 6, 1978.]

ELIZABETH R. NELSON

DALEY, RICHARD JOSEPH (May 15, 1902–Dec. 20, 1976), mayor of Chicago, was born in Chicago, the only child of Michael Daley, a sheet-metal worker and union organizer, and Lillian Dunne. The grandson of Irish immigrants, Daley grew up near the Chicago stockyards in the working-class neighborhood of Bridgeport, where he lived throughout his life. In his youth, Daley sold newspapers and worked for a vegetable peddler. He attended public and parochial elementary schools and graduated from De La Salle Institute, a Roman Catholic high school, in 1919. As a teenager he took a job as a stockyards cowboy, riding horseback and penning cattle. His shorthand and typing skills, acquired through high school courses, led to a promotion to an office job at the stockyards. He joined the Eleventh Ward's Democratic organization around 1920 and became active in the Hamburg Athletic Association as a player, coach, and manager. "He was a plugger," Daley's close friend William J. Lynch told the *Chicago Daily News*. "Dick was inherently shy. He had to counteract his shyness with a sense of determination and become aggressive. He kept the Hamburg club alive with that determination and aggressiveness."

For more than ten years Daley worked during the day and attended the De Paul University law school at night. In 1933 he graduated from De Paul and was admitted to the Illinois bar. For Irish Americans of Daley's generation, there were few opportunities in Chicago's law firms and executive suites. Although Daley opened his own law office, he viewed politics as his means of ascent.

At twenty-one, Daley was a precinct captain in the Eleventh Ward Regular Democratic organization. His hard work and organizational skills impressed Joseph P. McDonough, the ward's Democratic committeeman and alderman, who appointed Daley as his ward secretary and aide. When McDonough was elected Cook County treasurer in 1930, Daley served as his administrative assistant, a position he held under four county treasurers, gaining a keen understanding of public finance and taxation that would be invaluable in his political career.

After winning his first election in 1936, Daley held public office for the next forty years. He was first elected to the Illinois House of Representatives as a write-in candidate when a Republican state legislator died. Two years later, in 1938, Daley was elected to the Illinois Senate, where he seldom gave speeches but gained influence by outworking most of his colleagues and by forging alliances. From 1941 until 1946, Daley was the senate's Democratic minority leader. He sponsored legislation for school lunch programs, public housing developments, junior colleges, and equitable tax assessments. He authored legislation in 1939 providing for a state income tax to ease the tax burden on the poor; it was finally adopted in 1969.

Daley married Eleanor Guilfoyle after five years of courtship on June 23, 1936; they had seven children. His wife was Daley's closest friend and confidant. Although Daley maintained a busy political schedule, he usually spent nights at home, reading the Grimms' fairy tales, Hans Christian Andersen, and Dickens to his close-knit Irish Catholic family.

In 1946, Daley gave up his seat in the legislature for an unsuccessful campaign for Cook County sheriff. After his loss he was appointed controller of Cook County. Returning to Springfield, the state capital, in January in 1949, as Governor Adlai E. Stevenson's director of revenue, Daley shaped Stevenson's budget and lined up legislative support for Stevenson's programs. Daley sought but failed to win the Democratic party's endorsement in 1949 for the presidency of the Cook County board of commissioners.

When the Cook County clerk died in 1950, Daley was appointed acting clerk and won election to a full term in the November election. In this office, Daley was in charge of county elections and the maintenance of records. He modernized services by microfilming records, installing Photostat machines, and using voting machines in elections. He easily won reelection in 1954.

Since his election as Democratic ward committeeman in 1947, Daley had become a force in the Cook County Democratic party. Following Republican victories in the 1950 state and county elections, Daley engineered the ouster of Colonel Jacob M. Arvey as Democratic chairman. Three years later, Daley replaced caretaker chairman Joseph Gill and formally took over the leadership of the Cook County Democratic Central Committee. The central committee was made up of committeemen from the city's fifty wards and the county's thirty suburban townships. Under Daley's leadership, the Cook County Democratic organization became the largest, most disciplined, and most successful political machine of the postwar era. As party chairman, Daley ran for mayor of Chicago in 1955, challenging two-term Democratic incumbent Martin H. Kennelly for renomination. The Democratic organization endorsed Daley over Kennelly, setting the stage for a bitter primary and election. Three of the city's four major newspapers opposed Daley's nomination and election. His opponents warned that Daley's election would mean a throwback to the era of vice and corruption.

Daley responded: "When I walk down the street where I live, I see every street in the City of Chicago. . . . My neighbors are all the people of this city. No one who knows me believes that I want anything else for this city than to make it fine and beautiful and strong." He defeated Kennelly in the primary and Republican Robert E. Merriam in the general election.

Chicago was a city in decline when Daley took office. There had been almost no building activity in the central business district, or Loop, since the 1920's, and the skyline looked old and dingy. After nearly a century as the nation's transportation center, Chicago was losing its edge. The airport was small and overcrowded. With fewer people traveling by streamliner, the railroad terminals were empty between rush hours. There were no expressways. Once fashionable neighborhoods on the near South and West sides had deteriorated into slums. Middle-class residents were abandoning the city.

Over the next two decades, Daley transformed Chicago into what became known as the city that worked. In an era of troubles for American cities, Daley presided over a construction boom that changed Chicago's skyline. He worked closely with the business establishment and organized labor in promoting large-scale projects. Mass-transit lines and expressways were built. Daley annexed onion fields and a military base that had previously been beyond the city limits and built O'Hare International Airport with privately financed revenue bonds and federal aid. He was responsible for the construction of McCormick Place, a convention center on the city's lakefront, and the nation's largest water-filtration plant. The accomplishment for which he was most proud was the creation of a Chicago campus for the University of Illinois.

Daley centralized his power by retaining his position as Democratic party chairman. At the peak of his influence, he controlled ten congressmen, the governorship of Illinois, the Democratic caucuses in both houses of the state legislature, and city and county government. In his dual role as party chairman and mayor, Daley obtained state and federal aid for Chicago and promoted revenue-sharing and urban-renewal programs.

For example, under the Model Cities Act, for which Daley helped Lyndon B. Johnson win congressional approval in September 1966 after a stormy debate, block grants of federal funds were made available to cities for the revival of slum neighborhoods.

Daley took firm control over the city's finances. One of his first actions as mayor was to take over the responsibility for drafting the budget from the City Council. He also sought and was granted authority from the state legislature for the city to set real estate tax rates. At the 1970 Illinois Constitutional Convention, Daley obtained broad new taxing authority to impose taxes under the home-rule provision of the new constitution.

His staying power was extraordinary. In a city whose voters turned out Daley's predecessor and three of his four successors, Daley won a record six terms. He won landslide reelections in 1959, 1963, 1967, 1971, and 1975. A decade after his death, Daley was still rated favorably by three out of four Chicago residents, according to a Gallup Poll commissioned for the *Chicago Sun-Times*. Daley considered seeking the Illinois governorship in 1960 but instead supported Judge Otto Kerner, who was elected over Republican governor William G. Stratton.

Daley was among John F. Kennedy's key allies in the 1960 presidential election, providing him with critical support that helped Kennedy win a first-ballot nomination at the Democratic National Convention. Daley also produced a 456,000-vote plurality for Kennedy in the Nov. 8, 1960, election that enabled Kennedy to carry Illinois by 8,858 votes over Richard M. Nixon. Daley's critical role in the 1960 election established his reputation as a political kingmaker. He turned down invitations to serve in the administrations of Kennedy and Lyndon B. Johnson but frequently was consulted by both presidents on domestic policy.

In 1968, Daley hosted the Democratic National Convention at Johnson's request. "As long as I am mayor of this city, there's going to be law and order in Chicago," Daley declared in welcoming convention delegates, even as about ten thousand demonstrators gathered outside to protest Johnson's Vietnam War policies. Daley brought in a security force of twenty-five thousand, including Chicago police officers and members of the Illinois National Guard. A week of confrontations culminated in a riot in Grant Park in which three hundred people were injured. Senator Abraham A. Ribicoff of Connecticut, who denounced the "Gestapo tactics" of Chicago police as he spoke from the convention podium, was jeered by Daley from the convention floor. Though Daley termed the demonstrators a "lawless, violent group of terrorists," a committee of the President's Commission on the Cause and Prevention of Violence blamed a "police riot" for the convention violence. Ironically, Daley had been a private critic of the Vietnam War and had urged Johnson to withdraw American forces. However, Daley's national reputation was seriously tarnished as a result of the excessive use of force by Chicago policemen during the 1968 convention.

Daley was among the leaders of a movement to draft Senator Edward M. Kennedy for the 1968 Democratic presidential nomination following the assassination of Senator Robert F. Kennedy. He supported Hubert H. Humphrey for the presidential nomination only after the last Kennedy brother took himself out of the running. Humphrey, who narrowly lost the presidential election to Nixon, said that the convention riots contributed to his defeat. "I thought we should have had a stronger candidate," said Daley.

In 1972, Daley was dealt a series of blows when a critic of his administration, Dan Walker, won the Democratic nomination for governor and the election. Daley's candidate for state's attorney was defeated in the primary and a Republican won the general election. Daley was embarrassed that summer when the Democratic National Convention refused to seat his Illinois delegation because of noncompliance with new selection rules. A full vote of the convention rejected Daley's delegation. Former Senator George S. McGovern, the 1972 Democratic presidential nominee, said later that the expulsion of the Daley slate was a political mistake. At the 1974 Democratic midterm convention in Kansas City, Daley received a tumultuous welcome. Two years later, Jimmy Carter said that Daley's endorsement a month before the Democratic National Convention clinched his first-ballot nomination for the presidency. That same year, Daley's candidate defeated Walker for renomination in the gubernatorial primary but lost the general election to Republican James R. Thompson by a wide margin. Partly because of the Thompson landslide, Daley failed to deliver Illinois for Carter.

Daley's administration was tainted by scandals linked to political influence in the operation of traffic court and the handling of municipal court bail bonds. In 1960, eight policemen were convicted for running a burglary ring on the city's North Side. Daley reformed the police department and named a University of California criminology professor, Orlando Wilson, as the new superintendent. In the early 1970's a Chicago police spying unit was put under federal injunction to prevent it from violating the rights of private citizens.

During his tenure as United States attorney in the Nixon and Ford administrations, Thompson prosecuted and convicted several of Daley's associates, including aldermen, ward committeemen, the county clerk, former governor Kerner, and two senior Daley aides. But the mayor was never implicated in any wrongdoing.

African Americans were a major component of Daley's political coalition, providing him with winning margins in his two closest mayoral elections. Daley's relationship with blacks became strained, however, after the riots that followed the 1968 murder in Memphis of the Reverend Dr. Martin Luther King, Jr. Eleven persons were killed in the rioting, looting, and firebombing. Even Daley's critics acknowledged that the disorder had been put down with restraint by Chicago policemen. But in a rare display of temper Daley said at a press conference that policemen should shoot to kill arsonists and shoot to maim looters. When his remarks provoked a controversy, Daley backpedaled, saying that the "minimum force necessary" should be used in containing riots.

Daley was angered by news reports in the early 1970's that his administration had shown favoritism to an insurance firm that employed one of his sons. The company was paid $2 million for casualty insurance on city buildings and his son John Patrick received $100,000 in commissions. "What kind of a world is this if a man can't put his arm around his own son?" Daley said.

Daley was short, broad-shouldered, and stocky, with a ruddy face and high forehead. He had a hearty laugh and sparkling eyes that could turn cold. He retained the values of his blue-collar neighborhood and was suspicious of outsiders. A devout Roman Catholic, Daley attended mass every day.

A series of court rulings against political patronage diminished Daley's political influence in his final term, which was interrupted by his death in Chicago of a heart attack; he was buried in suburban Worth, Ill. Daley's political organization declined, but his legacy continued to be felt in Chicago in the person of Richard M. Daley, the mayor's eldest son, who was elected mayor of Chicago in April 1989.

In a political career that spanned more than half a century, Daley rose from a precinct captain to a position of national power and influence. As the six-term mayor of Chicago, he was a dominant force, transforming the city's skyline and building on a monumental scale. In his role as the last of the big-city Democratic political bosses, he was an important ally to three Democratic presidents of the United States. "He's the best political brain in the country," said Lyndon B. Johnson, who frequently sought Daley's advice in shaping urban policy. Former president Gerald R. Ford said that Daley's participation in the making of national legislation and policies reflected "his strong belief in and dedication to the vitality of the American cities." Senator Edward M. Kennedy, whose family had close ties to Daley, said in 1976: "Richard Daley will be remembered as one of America's greatest mayors, a leader who understood the needs and aspirations of his city, who made Chicago livable, who kept his city as a beacon of wise and responsible leadership for every other major city in this nation."

[The municipal reference section of Chicago's Harold Washington Library has an extensive collection of Daley's official papers and a comprehensive Daley bibliography. Biographies include Bill Gleason, *Daley of Chicago* (1970); Mike Royko, *Boss: Richard J. Daley of Chicago* (1971); Len O'Connor, *Clout: Mayor Daley and His City* (1975) and *Requiem: The Decline and Demise of Mayor Daley and His Era* (1977); Eugene Kennedy, *Himself!: The Life and Times of Mayor Richard J. Daley* (1978); and Milton L. Rakove, *We Don't Want Nobody Nobody Sent: An Oral History of the Daley Era* (1980). See also David Halberstam, "Daley of Chicago," *Harper's*, Aug. 1968. Obituaries are in the *Chicago Sun-Times*, the *Chicago Tribune*, and the *New York Times*, all Dec. 21, 1976.]

STEVE NEAL

DAVIS, ABRAHAM LINCOLN, JR. (Nov. 2, 1914–June 24, 1978), civil rights leader and the first black city councilman in New Orleans since Reconstruction, was born in Bayou Goula, La. His father, for whom he was named, founded the Pilgrim Baptist Church in that town and served as its pastor for fifty years. His mother, Jennie Edigeson, cared for the couple's six children. Although Davis periodically interrupted his studies to work and help send his siblings to school, in 1932 he received a diploma from J. W. Hoffman Junior High School in New Orleans and went on to graduate from McDonogh No. 35 Senior High School in 1935. On August 13 of that year, the New Zion Baptist Church in New Orleans elected Davis as pastor, a position he held for the rest of his life. He subsequently attended Leland College in Baker, La., from which he received his B.A. in 1938. A year later he was awarded a D.D. by Union Baptist Theological Seminary in New Orleans.

Over the next decade, Davis became involved in a number of religious and educational organizations. He was named president of the Interdenominational Ministerial Alliance in 1941, and a trustee of Union Baptist Theological Seminary in 1942 and of Leland College in 1947. In 1947 he was appointed to the Advisory Board of the Louisiana Educational Association.

As the struggle against racial segregation gained momentum in the later 1940's, Davis turned his energies to social activism. In 1947 he was elected president of the Louisiana Progressive Voters League, and in 1948 he organized a New Orleans chapter of the League to oppose a purge of black voters from registration lists. In 1950 he was named a member of the Advisory Commission to the Mayor of New Orleans. The following year, Davis organized the First Baptist Church baseball teams in order to provide children in the neighborhood around his church with recreational opportunities. Throughout his life, he continued to organize activities for black youth. He never married or had children of his own.

In December 1955, African Americans in Montgomery, Ala., began a bus boycott to protest the segregation laws that required blacks to ride in the back of the bus and to give up seats to white people. The boycott dragged on for thirteen months, and local protest movements, often led by black clergy, sprang up in cities throughout the South. In New Orleans, Davis used his contacts as head of the Interdenominational Ministerial Alliance to organize peaceful protests. In March 1956 he urged a crowd of 5,000 to "rise up and let white citizens know the time is out for segregation." In the following year, he was a plaintiff in a successful legal challenge that forced the city to integrate its transportation system in the summer of 1958. When integration on the buses created racial tensions, Davis called for harmony and won the praise of Mayor de Lesseps S. Morrison, who said, "New Orleans had been spared turmoil and racial unrest because of the sane leadership of Abraham Lincoln Davis, Jr., and others." A few blacks accused Davis of behaving like an "Uncle Tom." Davis calmly responded, "If sponsoring radical ideas of eliminating racial segregation and saving a city is Uncle Tom-ing, then so be it."

Following the bus boycotts, local civil rights leaders, spurred by Dr. Martin Luther King, began planning ways to coordinate their efforts. Ninety-seven clergy gathered on Feb. 14, 1957, at Davis's church in New Orleans to form the Southern Christian Leadership Conference (SCLC). King was elected president and Davis, second vice-president. Under King's charismatic leadership, the SCLC provided the organizational core of the early civil rights movement. In 1957, Davis was a principal organizer and leader of the first march on Washington, D.C., during which 27,000 people demanded that President Dwight Eisenhower and the federal government take steps to overturn racial discrimination.

Meanwhile, Davis continued to work for educational, employment, and recreational opportunities for blacks in New Orleans. In 1961, Mayor Morrison chose him as the city's first director of race relations. Two years later, police arrested Davis during a sit-in at City Hall, where he was trying to speak against racial discrimination in the hiring of blacks. That same year, 13,000 people joined the first peaceful march for freedom for blacks in New Orleans, which Davis organized. In 1965, Davis began a two-year voter-registration drive and filed suit when he felt electoral officials were dragging their feet. He scored a stunning victory on September 3 when 463 voters registered in one day. Davis continued to work both publicly and behind the scenes, building bridges between black voters and white politicians, to further racial justice. In 1965 he was appointed to the Louisiana Commission on Race Relations, Rights and Responsibilities; in 1971, to the Housing Authority of New Orleans; and in 1972, to the commission that brought the Superdome to New Orleans.

In the mid-1970's the City Council was mired in a legal controversy over demands to reapportion districts to better represent black voters. When a seat on the Council became vacant in 1975, members unanimously appointed Davis, who became the first African American since Reconstruction to hold that office in New Orleans. In the election of 1976, Davis easily won a popular mandate from voters in District B. His career in public service, from his founding of the Progressive Voters League nearly thirty years before, had gained him a citywide reputation as a wise and cautious leader. In 1977 another black politician, James Singleton, ran a well-organized campaign, charging that Davis had not done enough in recent years to win gains for African Americans in New Orleans. Singleton unseated Davis in November.

When Davis died in New Orleans, he was honored throughout the city. Former mayor Morrison paid tribute: "New Orleans has lost a rare citizen, one who made lasting contributions both spiritually and politically." Throughout his career, Davis defied easy categorization; conservative critics regarded him as a radical, and black separatists accused him of compromising too quickly. However, his steady work and many achievements—from his early efforts at educational reform, to his role in the founding of the SCLC, to his being the first black man to serve on the New Orleans City Council in the twentieth century—assure his lasting importance as an example of a generation of civil rights leaders who believed in integration and racial harmony.

[The New Zion Baptist Church in New Orleans has preserved clippings and other material on Davis. Detailed biographical information is in the *Greater Plaquemine Post*, Jan. 23, 1975. On City Council elections, see the *New Orleans Times-Picayune*, especially James H. Gillis's column, "Politics, Power and the People," Jan. 18, 1975, and Nov. 15, 1977. Obituaries are in the *New York Times*, June 26, 1978, and the *New Orleans Times-Picayune*, June 30, 1978.]

CORINNE T. FIELD

DAVIS, JOHN WARREN (Feb. 11, 1888–July 12, 1980), educator, was born in Milledgeville, Ga., the son of Robert Marion Davis, a grocery store clerk in Savannah, Ga., and Katie Mann, a laundress. When he was five and one-half years old, he was sent to Americus, Ga., to live with elderly relatives, the Reverend and Mrs. Sylvannus Carter, as a result of financial exigencies in his large family. Carter, an itinerate Baptist preacher and an important black community leader during the 1890's, exerted a significant impact on Davis's formative years. With segregation still a constitutionally mandated principle and lynching a commonly used control mechanism, Davis learned from Carter the value of a life of noncombativeness without servility and of intellectual achievement without arrogance. This became his ladder to success.

The Carters sent Davis to the McKay Hills Elementary School and to Atlanta Baptist College, a high school for black youths. In 1903 this was exceptional: only a generation earlier it had been illegal to educate blacks. In 1907, Davis was admitted to Morehouse College in Atlanta, a leading institution for educating blacks. He supported himself with summer jobs at the Chicago stockyards and janitorial work at Morehouse. Following graduation from Morehouse in 1911, Davis enrolled as a graduate student in chemistry and physics at the University of Chicago. In 1911 he returned to Morehouse as a teacher; he later became registrar, serving until 1917. Morehouse awarded him an M.A. degree in 1920. Davis's intellectual abilities, social skills, and religious contacts brought him to the attention of the Young Men's Christian Association (YMCA), and beginning in 1917, he was executive secretary of the Twelfth Street branch of the YMCA in Washington, D.C.

By 1919, when West Virginia State College was seeking a new president, Davis was appropriately positioned for such a job. Although only thirty-one years old, he was hailed as a diplomat who could work with both blacks and whites.

As president of West Virginia State College for thirty-four years, Davis developed contacts with important legislators and interest groups. He used their support to expand the college's curriculum, including liberal arts courses, like drama and theater, that served to meet cultural needs of the entire state. His successful leadership was due also to his appointments of both staff and faculty. This in turn attracted students of the highest intellectual caliber. As a result, West Virginia State College won regional accreditation in 1927: it was one of four African-American institutions so recognized at that time. During World War II, Davis established technological training programs at the college and set the stage for integration of black and white students. A Civilian Pilot Training Program for the college was authorized in 1939 by the government, and a Reserve Officers' Training Corps was established in 1942.

Davis was aided in his earliest endeavors by the political contacts of his wife, Bessie Rucker, whom he married on Aug. 24, 1916; they had two children. She died in 1920. Davis's second wife was Ethel McGhee, whom he married on Sept. 2, 1932; they had one child. She was active in promoting the total program of the college. A well-educated teacher and administrator who had a master's degree from Columbia University, Ethel McGhee had been dean of women at Spelman College in Atlanta. Together, the Davises created at West Virginia State College an integrated environment for all the social, cultural, political, and educational functions that the college offered. Contacts with presidents Franklin Roosevelt and Harry Truman resulted in significant opportunities for Davis to develop his favorite theme: that racism was the weakest link in democracy. In 1948, Truman issued an executive order integrating the armed services, as Davis had hoped.

Davis retired from the presidency of West Virginia State College in 1953 and was immediately appointed head of the Technical Cooperative Administration in Liberia. When the United States Supreme Court declared segregation in education unconstitutional in 1954, however, Davis reentered the educational arena. Encouraged by Thurgood Marshall, he agreed to direct the newly established Department for Teacher Information and Security of the NAACP's Legal Defense and Educational Fund. For the next twenty years he used the litigation process to help protect black teachers and principals; he used the economic process to secure funds to educate blacks in colleges and universities nationwide. This latter goal was aided by the establishment in 1964 of the Herbert Lehman Educational Fund. This program's finances expanded as a result of its sponsorship by Mrs. Herbert Lehman, an NAACP board member with tremendous political, educational, and financial power, and of the public relations efforts of Davis.

A supplementary program was begun in 1972. Named the Earl Warren Legal Training Program, and with Davis as director, it made a concerted effort to recruit, educate, and activate a cadre of highly competent black attorneys to defend black students and educators. During Davis's lifetime this program enabled more than eight hundred students to attend law school.

At age eighty-four, Davis moved into advisory and consultant positions within these organizations. He died at his home in Englewood, N.J., eight years later. His leadership had resulted in integration of educational activities even before 1954, and in educating litigators to protect emerging civil rights. Together these accomplishments contributed to Davis's goal of both a diplomatic and a positive end to segregation.

[Davis's papers are at Howard University, West Virginia State College Archives, and the NAACP Legal Defense Fund. For a study of his leadership style, see Angel Patricia Johnson, "A Study of the Life and Works of a Pioneer Black Educator" (Ph.D. Rutgers University, 1987). An obituary is in the *New York Times*, July 15, 1980. The Oral History Collection at Columbia University contains a 1976 tape-recorded autobiographical interview with Davis. There is also a 1979 videotape at West Virginia State

College in which Davis discusses his administrative goals.]

ALICE FLEETWOOD BARTEE

DAVIS, MEYER (Jan. 10, 1885–April 5, 1976), bandleader, was born in Ellicott City, Md., one of four children of Rose Benjamin and Sol Davis. When Meyer was eight, his father, who had been in the shoe business, moved the family to Washington, D.C., where he opened a coal and feed store. Meyer started taking violin lessons and played in a family quartet. When he was rejected by the school orchestra at the age of thirteen, he organized a five-piece band to play high school dances. The band played for $25 an evening; the budding businessman paid $12 to the other players and kept the rest for himself. He also took a part-time job as second violinist in a theater.

After completing a two-year high-school course in bookkeeping and stenography at Business High School in 1910, Davis entered George Washington University as a law student. He also worked briefly part-time as secretary to a clergyman and then became a court reporter on the *Washington Post*. Throughout this period he continued to lead his band and, while still a law student, began building his musical empire by starting a second group.

At a time when the Marine Corps Band played little but Sousa marches and Strauss waltzes at social events in Washington and new dance rhythms were beginning to be heard, Davis headed out West during a law school vacation to explore syncopation. He returned to Washington with a mastery of the dance music of the turkey trot, the bunny hug, and the grizzly bear, and within a year he had challenged the dominance of the Marine Corps musicians. Davis introduced his music to Washington society in 1913 and enjoyed a near monopoly as high society's undisputed favorite for a quarter of a century.

In the summer of 1913, Davis and his pianist brother Uriel traveled to Bar Harbor, Maine. He persuaded the manager of the Malvern Hotel to hire his group to alternate with the Marine Band. As a result of his success, the summer resorts' wealthy residents, previously served only by vacationing members of the Boston Symphony Orchestra, invited him to play at their Philadelphia and New York homes during the winter.

The following year, Davis received his first steady engagement, providing music at lunch and dinner at Washington's New Willard Hotel. The discovery that he could take in $90 per week after salaries and expenses made him leave law school to become a full-time bandleader. By his early twenties, the musical entrepreneur had offices in Washington, Philadelphia, and New York.

Davis hired Hilda Emery as a pianist for his Bar Harbor orchestra and married her on June 17, 1917. They had five children. Hilda, like her husband, often composed songs for special occasions. In 1939, Davis wrote the words and music for *Ev'ry Thought, Ev'ry Breath, Ev'ry Dream* with Kenneth Case and Byron Bradley.

Davis described himself as a businessman with an astute appreciation of music rather than a musician. He became a corporation that could have as many as thirty bands playing somewhere on any given evening, commanding a payroll in excess of $3 million a year. During one season in Newport, R.I., he played at fifty-nine of sixty top-flight parties. His resourceful press agent was Harry Sobol.

Each band consisted of hand-picked musicians, playing a repertoire of some five hundred arrangements approved by Davis and under a Davis-trained conductor. The "millionaire maestro" himself appeared at only the most important and lucrative engagements. In 1965, for example, of the 1,421 private engagements his bands filled, he appeared at 127. Davis sometimes made as many as five personal appearances in a single night, whisking from one party to another by chartered plane or private limousine. The dignified Davis turned into a gyrating evangelist of the dance, losing more than five pounds and going through an average of three dress shirts in an evening. To keep up his energy he catnapped and took an occasional sniff on a tube of inhalant. It was not unusual for him to lead one orchestra for a Long Island wedding until 9 P.M., take a taxi to the airport, and, changing his soaked clothes on the way, ride a shuttle plane to Washington, where he would conduct another of his bands at a coming-out party until 4 A.M.

Society parties were popular during the 1920's and 1930's, dropped off during World War II, picked up again in the 1950's, and increased some 25 percent in the 1960's. Meyer Davis orchestras played annually at such social events as the Maryland Hunt Ball in Baltimore, the April in Paris Ball and the Junior Assembly in New York, the December Ball in Chicago, and the Hospital Ball in Palm Beach. He played for royalty, including King George VI and Queen Elizabeth of England and Princess Grace of Monaco. He was chosen to take his band to France in 1958 to play at the international Versailles debutante ball in the Royal Palace and took his musicians to Rio de Janeiro for an American debutante ball in the Brazilian capital. His first White House engagement, at the age of eighteen, was for President Woodrow Wilson. Davis played at seven inaugural balls—for Calvin Coolidge, twice for Franklin D. Roosevelt, for Harry S. Truman, at both of Dwight D. Eisenhower's inaugurals, and for John F. Kennedy—and led orchestras at the White House many times. He had played for Jacqueline Bouvier's debut and her wedding to John F. Kennedy, as well as at the wedding of Jacqueline's mother and the debut of her sister, Lee.

The list of elite families for whom Davis played includes the Fords, Firestones, Astors, du Ponts, Rockefellers, Vanderbilts, Dukes, and Drexels. His engagements were often booked two or three years in advance or more. Debuts, which represented around one-third of Davis's business and cost about $300,000 each, or $200 per young lady in a mass cotillion, often were booked ten to fifteen years in advance. Proud of the continuity of his appeal from one generation to another, he noted his bookings with reference to the debuts of mothers, aunts, and sometimes grandmothers at which he also played.

In addition to performing for private patrons, Davis's musicians provided music at luxury hotels and aboard the liners *United States* and *America*. He kept location orchestras at resorts, such as the Greenbrier at White Sulphur Springs in West Virginia, and at exclusive clubs in such places as the Bahamas. They also played in the pits of many Broadway shows. Davis began to finance Broadway shows during World War II, beginning with *By Jupiter!* in 1942, and became one of Broadway's leading angels, investing his money in as many as fifteen shows playing at the same time. Among the more than two hundred shows that Davis backed were such successes as *The Music Man*, *J.B.*, and *The Dark at the Top of the Stairs*. He also invested in bowling alleys, restaurants, dance halls, an amusement park, and a film production company, not all of which were successful.

Davis described his "sound," better known as "the society beat," as a "distinctive, well-integrated musical throb." His aim was to provide atmosphere through "continuous music," a type of "orchestrated pulse that works on people in a subliminal way, urging them into dancing and easy conversation." Davis's style of playing always sounded the same, which suited the ritual-bound social set from San Francisco to Newport. About half of his music was old standards, particularly Viennese waltzes, and often 75 percent of the music played was requests. His music seldom appeared on records or radio.

Several notables who began their careers with Davis bands were Benny Goodman, Tommy Dorsey, Jimmy Dorsey, and Jan Peerce. Davis worked out a system whereby one section of the orchestra played while the other rested, so that there were few interruptions between numbers, because hostesses were afraid of losing guests during breaks. Musicians were permitted one drink an hour.

Those who knew him spoke of his urbanity, courtesy, tact, and affability. He was an inveterate poker player, and he relaxed by performing chamber music on the violin with his brother-in-law Pierre Monteux on the viola.

The Davises had an extensive collection of Byroniana, including Byron's last will and testament, his writing desk, and signed first editions of his works. Meyer Davis also framed and displayed copies of some of his larger checks in his office. He was a director of the Composers Laboratory Orchestra and belonged to the Congressional Club in Washington and the Lotos, Friars, and Lambs clubs in New York City.

Davis was active as late as December 1975, when he led the orchestra at Philadelphia's Assembly Ball for the fifty-second consecutive year. He died at his home at 101 Central Park West in New York City.

[References to Davis can be found in George T. Simon, *The Big Bands*, with a foreword by Frank Sinatra (1967). See also Beth Day, "Bands of Gold," *Saturday Evening Post*, Apr. 20, 1963; and George Frazier, "The Next Dance Will Be 'What Is Meyer Davis Doing While Oedipus and the Mothers Drop Trousers?' Foxtrot," *Esquire*, Jan. 1966. Portraits are in *Saturday Review*, Feb. 23, 1957; the *Washington Post*, Jan. 8, 1961; and the *New York Post*, Jan. 18, 1961. An obituary is in the *New York Times*, Apr. 6, 1976.]

PHYLLIS BADER-BOREL

DAY, DOROTHY (Nov. 8, 1897–Nov. 29, 1980), Catholic pacifist and cofounder of the Catholic Worker movement, was born in Brooklyn, N.Y., the third of five children of John I. Day and Grace Satterlee. Her father was a sportswriter who in his later years worked for the New York *Morning Telegraph* and helped found the Hialeah racetrack in Florida, where he was a steward and partner. Day's childhood, spent mainly in Chicago, was not a religious one, although for a brief period she attended a neighborhood Episcopal Church. In high school she declared herself an atheist.

From 1914 to 1916, Day attended the University of Illinois, where, in her words, she was bored and rather "shiftless." There she met and befriended Samson Raphaelson and Rayna Simons, who introduced her to socialist ideas. Day quit the university, moved to New York City, met Mike Gold, and found a job with *The Call*, a socialist newspaper. In the winter of 1917 she interviewed Leon Trotsky, who was in New York at the time. Day next worked for *The Masses*, edited by Max Eastman.

In November 1917, Day, with a group of suffragettes, picketed the White House and was arrested. She was sent to Occoquan Prison, where, to pass the time, she read the Bible "with the sense of coming back to something of my childhood that I had lost."

Upon her return to Greenwich Village in New York City and a circle of friends who included Eugene O'Neill, Agnes Boulton, Allen Tate and Caroline Gordon, and Peggy and Malcolm Cowley, Day started writing for *The Liberator*. Needing a steady income, she took up nursing at Kings County Hospital in Brooklyn, where she met Lionel Moise, a hard-drinking, pugnacious, sometime newspaper reporter. In 1919, Day became pregnant by Moise, who threatened to leave her unless she had an abortion. She had the abortion, which haunted her the rest of her life; Moise deserted her anyway.

On the rebound, in the spring of 1920, Day married Barkeley Tobey, a charlatan. For a year they lived in Europe, mainly in Italy, where Day began writing her novel, *The Eleventh Virgin*, published in 1924. On their return to New York, Day left Tobey.

Around 1925, Day met Forster Batterham, brother-in-law of literary critic Kenneth Burke. She and Batterham began living together in a small cottage that she had bought on Staten Island. Day wrote; Batterham fished and drank. As Day noted in her journal, the closeness to nature reawakened in her a longing—for a child, and for God.

In March 1927, Day bore Batterham's child and in July had her christened Tamar Teresa at the local Catholic church. In December, Day converted to Catholicism. Batterham, an atheist who detested the Catholic Church, left her, and many of her Greenwich Village friends drifted away from her. For Day, however, her course was set: her quest was God, and she would never regret it.

The next few years found her briefly in Hollywood and then in Mexico, where she wrote articles for American Catholic magazines such as *The Sign*, *America*, and *Commonweal*. In 1932 she reported on the Hunger March in Washington, D.C. On a visit to the Shrine of the Immaculate Conception on December 8 (the feast of the Immaculate Conception), Day "prayed fervently" for a way to live her Catholic faith in concert with her concern for the poor.

The next day, a man named Peter Maurin arrived at Day's New York apartment. In her words, "he was the saint . . . the one who showed me the way." Maurin, often mistaken for a tramp, was a French peasant, former Christian Brother, and intellectual who had come to the United States in 1911. He introduced Day to the Christian personalism of Nicholas Berdyaev and Jacques Maritain, to Catholic humanism and the doctrine of the common good of St. Thomas Aquinas, and to the decentralism of the English Distributists: Father Vincent McNabb, G. K. Chesterton, and Eric Gill. Maurin's communitarian vision was rooted in voluntary poverty and the corporal works of mercy by which there is a direct engagement with the poor. At his urging Day started the *Catholic Worker* (CW) newspaper to promote this vision of society. First published on May Day 1933, within a year the CW monthly reached a circulation of 100,000 copies, at a penny per copy. Numerous Catholic Worker communities for the poor and farming communes sprang up throughout the country. Day helped Catherine de Hueck Doherty start Friendship House, an interracial center in Harlem.

Intellectuals took note of the CW, which published articles by Emmanuel Mounier, among others. Jacques Maritain and Hilaire Belloc were among hundreds who over the years lectured at the New York CW house. A young

Thomas Merton visited, as did John F. Kennedy.

In the pages of the CW, Day bucked the Catholic hierarchy, which was pro-Franco, decrying the violence of both sides in the Spanish Civil War in 1936. With the outbreak of World War II, Day's pacifism remained unshakable, dismissing from the CW those who did not embrace absolute pacifism. Ruling the CW autocratically, Day never countenanced criticism or disagreement; she was uncompromising when it came to ideology and morality.

In the 1950's, Day led protests against compulsory air-raid drills in New York, saying that they fostered a "war mentality." She supported the gravediggers on strike at the Catholic cemeteries. In 1962, Day made a controversial visit to Castro's Cuba and was criticized by the American press for her uncritical remarks about the Communist dictator. In the mid-1960's, Father Daniel Berrigan joined the CW in leading protests against the Vietnam War.

In the fall of 1965, Day went to Rome to be present for the Second Vatican Council's discussion on war and peace. Day had sent to every bishop in the world a special issue of the CW on peace. She went on a fast with nineteen other women, led by Lanzo del Vasto of the Community of the Ark. Ultimately Vatican II noted the value of Gospel nonviolence and the right of conscientious objection to war, which was reiterated by the American bishops in 1968.

In 1972, Day visited Mother Teresa in Calcutta, and in the summer of 1973 she joined César Chávez and the United Farm Workers in their strike in California. Her participation in Farm Workers' demonstrations led to her arrest and a brief jail term.

Day's last public appearance was in 1976 in Philadelphia at the International Eucharistic Congress. She spoke on August 6, the thirty-first anniversary of the atomic bombing of Hiroshima. That morning the bishops had celebrated a mass in honor of the American armed forces. Acknowledging her love for the church, Day voiced her sadness at the insensitivity to the memory of those who had died on that date and asked the eight thousand people gathered to beg "God to forgive us."

Day died at Maryhouse, a CW shelter for the homeless, on the Lower East Side of New York City; she was buried in Resurrection Cemetery, Staten Island. In 1972 the University of Notre Dame had awarded her its prestigious Laetare Medal for her long life of "comforting the afflicted and afflicting the comfortable." Three years after her death, the American bishops in their pastoral letter, "God's Promise and Our Response," cited Day as having had a "profound effect upon the life of the Church in the United States."

[Day's papers, as well as those of Peter Maurin and the CW movement, are at Marquette University. Day's major publications include her autobiographical *The Long Loneliness* (1952) and *Loaves and Fishes* (1963), an anecdotal history of the CW. See also Robert Ellsberg, ed., *By Little and by Little, the Selected Writings of Dorothy Day* (1983).

For a biography, unfortunately without notes and with undue emphasis on Day's early life, see William Miller, *Dorothy Day* (1982). See also Dwight MacDonald, "Revisiting Dorothy Day," *New York Review of Books*, Jan. 28, 1971.

For a scholarly analysis of Day, the CW, and Catholic radicalism, see Mel Piehl, *Breaking Bread* (1982); and Patrick G. Coy, ed., *A Revolution of the Heart* (1988). Obituaries are in the *New York Times*, Nov. 30 and Dec. 1, 1980.]

GEOFFREY B. GNEUHS

DENNIS, PATRICK. See TANNER, EDWARD EVERETT, III.

DEVERS, JACOB LOUCKS (Sept. 8, 1887–Oct. 15, 1979), army officer, was born in York, Pa., the eldest of four children of Philip Devers, a watchmaker, and Ella Kate Loucks. At York High School he was class president for three years, debating team president, basketball captain, and football quarterback. Admitted to the United States Military Academy in 1905, Devers played shortstop on the varsity baseball team and twice captained the basketball team under coach Joseph Stilwell. He finished thirty-ninth out of 103 cadets in the class of 1909, ahead of George S. Patton, William H. Simpson, and Robert Eichelberger, all of whom became four-star generals in World War II.

Devers was commissioned in the field artillery and assigned to Fort Russell, Wyo. On Oct. 18, 1911, he married Georgie Hays Lyon, niece of his battalion commander at Fort Russell; they had one child. Devers taught mathematics at West Point from 1912 to 1916 and coached the baseball and basketball teams. Wartime assignments followed in Hawaii and at Fort Sill, Okla., and postwar tours of duty in France and Germany. In 1919 Devers returned to West

Point as an instructor of field artillery tactics and commander of the field artillery detachment. In 1924 and 1925 he attended the Command and General Staff School at Fort Leavenworth, Kans.

After assignments at Fort Sill and in Washington, D.C., Devers completed the Army War College in 1933 and commanded a field artillery unit at Fort Myer, Va. In 1936 he again returned to West Point, as executive officer and graduate manager of athletics. In 1939, General George C. Marshall sent him to the Panama Canal Zone, to put it on a wartime footing after the outbreak of war in Europe.

Marshall, impressed by Devers's performance, recalled him to Washington, D.C., in the spring of 1940 and promoted him over 474 other colonels as the United States Army's youngest brigadier general. Chosen by President Franklin D. Roosevelt to represent the army, Devers served on the committee that selected sea and air bases for lease from Great Britain in exchange for fifty destroyers. Promoted to major general in October 1940, Devers was sent to Fort Bragg, N.C., to command the Ninth Infantry Division and to expand the post's training facilities. Army critic Westbrook Pegler had kind words for Devers, and the *Washington Post* commented that Devers's "energy spawned legends."

In July 1941, Marshall placed Devers in charge of the armored forces at Fort Knox, Ky., with responsibility for creating a tank army of sixteen armored divisions. A main challenge was to create a modern tank that could compete with German models. Devers developed the M-4 medium Sherman tank, of which fifty thousand were manufactured before the war's end. He also developed the 105-mm self-propelled howitzer, which became standard weaponry of the armored divisions. Devers played a major role in developing the DUKW amphibious truck, which proved indispensable in the invasions of Sicily, Italy, and France.

In May 1943 Devers was sent to London to command the European Theater of Operations. He trained a million-man invasion force for the 1944 crossing of the English Channel and directed the Eighth Air Force's strategic bombing campaign against targets in France and Germany. In January 1944 Devers replaced General Dwight D. Eisenhower as United States theater commander in the Mediterranean. He also became deputy allied supreme commander in Algiers, under British general Henry Maitland Wilson. Devers devoted himself to rebuilding Mark Clark's Fifth Army in Italy, where German resistance had halted the Allies at Cassino. Devers's efforts were rewarded on June 4, 1944, when Rome fell.

Devers helped plan and organize the invasion of southern France. After the June 6, 1944, invasion of Normandy, Eisenhower's forces were unable to break out of the beachhead perimeter. Eisenhower urged that the invasion of southern France be launched to relieve the situation and recommended that Devers direct the invasion. Devers's Seventh Army and the First French Army went ashore along the Riviera beaches on Aug. 15, 1944, with Devers overhead in a fighter plane. The invasion was a brilliant success; the surprised enemy began retreating immediately to Toulon, Marseilles, Avignon, Lyons, and Dijon. On Sept. 11, 1944, Devers's forces joined with Patton's Third Army west of Dijon.

In October 1944 the opposing armies regrouped. Eisenhower ordered a broad-front offensive to end the war, but only Devers's armies made important gains. On November 19 the Rhine was reached; Strasbourg was liberated four days later.

On December 16, the Battle of the Bulge began when Hitler launched a surprise attack in the Ardennes. Devers's forces took over Patton's sector so that the Third Army could hurry north to Bastogne. When Hitler saw his Ardennes hopes fading, he ordered a New Year's attack against Devers's spread-out forces in Alsace-Lorraine. Enemy penetrations were made in the Vosges Mountains near Strasbourg, but Devers refused to pull back. Finally, on January 26, Hitler was compelled to halt the failed offensive.

In March 1945, Devers was promoted to full general, ahead of Omar Bradley and Patton. His forces crossed the Rhine and captured Stuttgart, Ulm, Munich, Berchtesgaden, and Salzburg. Before V-E Day, Devers accepted the surrender of German Field Marshal Alfred Kesselring's Army Group G.

In June 1945, Devers succeeded Joseph Stilwell as head of the army ground forces. He retired in September 1949, after forty-four years of service. From 1959 to 1969 he was chairman of the American Battle Monuments Commission. His wife died in 1967, and he married Dorothy C. B. Ham in May 1975. He died in Washington, D.C.

[A rather comprehensive archive of Devers's correspondence and unpublished papers is at the Historical Association of York County, York, Pa., as are extensive oral histories of Devers and two dozen of his professional colleagues. An article about Devers is Martin Blumenson and James L. Stokesbury, "Masters of the Art: Jake Devers," *Army*, Feb. 1973. Obituaries are in the *Washington Post* and the *Washington Star*, both Oct. 16, 1979, and in the *New York Times*, Oct. 17, 1979.]

FRANKLIN L. GURLEY

DEVINE, ANDREW ("ANDY") (Oct. 7, 1905–Feb. 18, 1977), screen, stage, and television personality, was born in Flagstaff, Arizona Territory, the son of Thomas Devine, a hotel keeper, and Amy Ward, the daughter of Admiral James H. Ward, a founder of the United States Naval Academy. When he was a year old, the family moved to Kingman, Ariz. There, when he was four, he fell while holding a curtain rod in his mouth. The healing process left him with a high-pitched yet gravelly voice that, combined with an adult weight exceeding three hundred pounds, made him an ideal comic foil. Devine recognized that "my voice was my fortune."

Devine attended Arizona public schools. Admittedly an indifferent student, he was a natural athlete, and because of his size he was a football lineman at military school, at Arizona Teachers College, and finally as guard center at Santa Clara University in the 1924 and 1925 seasons. He left without earning a degree and in 1925 played professionally for the Los Angeles Angels for $35 per week. The family had moved to Hollywood, Calif., after his father died, and Devine attempted to break into the movies. In Hollywood legend, he was wearing his Santa Clara sweater when a producer, who thought SC meant Southern California, asked if he played football and if he would try out for a part in a serial called *The Collegians* (1926–1928). He earned $150 per month for two years of episodes.

By 1928, Devine had appeared in many movies even though he never took a single acting lesson; he later remembered playing three different roles in a single day. Like many silent screen performers, his career was threatened by "talkies"; his unusual voice made a film future questionable. Parts were no longer offered, and he joined the U.S. Lighthouse Service, delivering supplies to Bering Sea outposts. On completing his term of service, he worked at the odd jobs seemingly required of unemployed actors, including lifeguard duty on Venice Beach in California. His career was again saved by his football background; in 1930 he was offered the role of Truck McCall in *The Spirit of Notre Dame*. His portrayal of a dumb but essentially noble Irishman who played despite broken ribs brought him heavy fan mail and steady employment. Devine joked that all his portrayals were ultimately based on his girth and "a lot of Arizona hayseed," but directors realized that his voice was so distinctive in conjunction with his size that he was invaluable as a character actor. He was never out of work again, appearing in as many as nine films in a year during the 1930's. Most were forgettable roles, but he did play in such classic films as *Destry Rides Again* (1932), *A Star Is Born* (1937), and *Stagecoach* (1939). Critics consider Buck, the stage driver, in *Stagecoach* as his best performance.

During the filming of *Dr. Bull* in 1933, Will Rogers introduced Devine to Dorothy Irene House. Their whirlwind courtship ended with a wedding in Las Vegas on Oct. 28, 1933; they had two children. Dorothy recalled Andy's career as just work; "It doesn't matter a tinker's damn to him which star he plays with," so long as the check was good. After 1935, Devine appeared regularly on Jack Benny's radio program. His "Hi-ya, buck" greeting became copied nationwide and led to a motion picture, *Buck Benny Rides Again* (1940). Devine also appeared with George Jessel, Lum 'n' Abner, and Al Pearce and His Gang, and hosted "Melody Round-up" (1944). During the war, he played in many camp and hospital shows and also owned a flying school called Provo Divine.

From the mid-1930's until 1957, the Devines lived on a five-acre ranch in the San Fernando Valley; Andy served as honorary mayor of Van Nuys, Calif., from 1938 to 1955. He raised jumping horses, rode with Clark Gable and Phil Harris, flew pigeons with Roy Rogers when they were not making movies together, and dabbled in real estate. He later remarked that he could hardly dislike shopping malls, since he had sold the land on which to build them. Like many actors, his career soared with the advent of television; from 1951 to 1956 he played Jingles B. Jones in 113 episodes of "Wild Bill Hickock." Devine agreed to accept a low salary, but his 10 percent of gross revenues made Jingles his most profitable role. When the series ended, Devine, who had already made more than three hundred movies in a twenty-five-year career, was more beloved than ever. His own show, "Andy's Gang," appeared from 1955 to 1960.

In 1957 the Devines moved to Newport Beach, Calif., so that Andy, an ardent sailor, could enjoy the ocean. He made his stage debut, as Captain Andy in *Show Boat*, at the Jones Beach Marine Theater on Long Island. Devine said the show would be a hit because "I'm lucky," and in subsequent years he played the role more than four hundred times. He compounded his luck by investing in a Captain Andy restaurant chain. He appeared on stage in *My Three Angels, Never Too Late, On Borrowed Time,* and *Anything Goes,* and did a host of movie and television productions. His last movie appearance was as a voice-over in *The Mouse and His Child* (1977).

In Devine's later years he became active in conservative politics; he campaigned for George Wallace in 1968 and supported Ronald Reagan in 1976. He also basked in honors. Kingman, Ariz., gave him a day and named a street in his honor (Oct. 3, 1970); the Pacific Pioneers Broadcasters feted his forty years on radio; and John Wayne hosted a Hollywood testimonial on Devine's seventieth birthday. In June 1976, while attending the summer encampment of the Bohemian Club, a males-only society of the political and business elite, Devine suffered kidney failure. A combination of illnesses caused his death in Orange, Calif.

[Clippings files are at the New York Library for the Performing Arts at Lincoln Center and at the Academy Foundation, National Film Information Service, in Beverly Hills, Calif. Personal reminiscences are in David Rothel, *Those Great Cowboy Sidekicks* (1984). Obituaries are in the *Los Angeles Times*, Feb. 19, 1977, and the *New York Times*, Feb. 20, 1977.]

GEORGE J. LANKEVICH

DILL, CLARENCE CLEVELAND (Sept. 21, 1884–Jan. 14, 1978), United States senator, was born in Fredericktown, Ohio, the only child of Theodore Marshall Dill, a farmer, and Amanda Kunkel. As a youth, Dill enjoyed debating and planned to enter politics. He attended public schools and graduated from Ohio Wesleyan University in 1907, after which he worked briefly as a newspaper reporter for the *Cleveland Press*. Later that year he began teaching high school in Dubuque, Iowa, and wrote for the *Dubuque Journal*. He moved to Spokane, Wash., in 1908 after working briefly as a reporter in Butte, Mont. In Spokane, Dill worked as a teacher and during the summers as a police reporter for the Spokane *Spokesman-Review* until 1909. Having pursued the study of law on his own, he was admitted to the Washington bar in 1910 and opened a practice in Spokane. From 1911 to 1913, Dill was a deputy prosecuting attorney for Spokane County. In 1912 he became chairman of the state Democratic convention, and the following year he served briefly as private secretary to Governor Ernest Lister.

In 1914, Dill was elected to Congress from the Fifth Congressional District as the first Washington State Democrat in Congress in eighteen years. Dill worked to open Indian lands to settlement and to secure new mail routes for his district. After winning reelection in 1916, in his second term he voted against the declaration of war on Germany and then chaired a congressional special committee investigating conditions in army camps, which toured the western front in November 1917. Although he easily won the Democratic renomination in 1918, he lost the election to John Stanley Webster; Dill blamed the defeat on his war-declaration vote. Dill returned to Spokane to practice law and campaigned for the United States Senate in 1922. Drawing support from disaffected farmers and postwar isolationists, he won an upset victory over conservative Republican senator Miles Poindexter.

In the Senate, Dill earned a reputation for advocating federal control of the airwaves, in much the way the government oversaw railroads and telephone and telegraph lines. Dill coauthored the Radio Act of 1927, which he proudly called the "Magna Charta of the radio listeners." The law created the Federal Radio Commission to regulate radio station frequencies, allow equal access for political candidates, and prevent network monopolies through the licensing of stations. Dill was also the principal sponsor of the Federal Communications Act of 1934, which created the Federal Communications Commission, and also supported federal control of the fledgling aviation industry.

In 1927, Dill surprised many people by announcing his engagement to Rosilie Gardiner Jones, an outspoken leader in the woman suffrage movement. The couple had no children, and the marriage ended in divorce in 1936.

Dill won reelection in 1928, again as the only

Democrat from his state to win a seat in the Congress. During his second term he sat on the Senate Public Lands Committee, which investigated the Teapot Dome Scandal. During Prohibition, although he was a dry, he criticized the manner in which federal agents disregarded the civil rights of suspects. He also introduced the first Railroad Retirement Act. In 1930 he was among the group of senators who unsuccessfully opposed President Herbert Hoover's nomination of Charles Evans Hughes to be chief justice. Dill also fought private utilities and railroad mergers.

Dill is best known for being the "father of the Grand Coulee Dam." He first discussed the need for a high dam for Washington's Columbia River with President Hoover, outlining the necessity for electricity and irrigation in the West. Hoover balked at the projected cost of the project. In 1931, Dill approached Franklin D. Roosevelt, then governor of New York, with the idea. At the close of their conversation, Roosevelt said, "Well, I don't suppose I'll ever be President; but if I am, I'll build that dam." After Roosevelt's victory in the 1932 election, however, he decided against construction of the dam as "too big." Dill went to the White House and argued with the president, who compromised by issuing an executive order to start construction on a low dam for $60 million as opposed to a high dam for $450 million. Roosevelt and Dill agreed that the project could later be expanded. Congress authorized construction of the high dam after Dill had left the Senate. With the dam approved, Dill was accused of purchasing large tracts of land in the Columbia River basin in anticipation of rising land values. Dill denied the allegations and no charges were brought. In a surprise announcement in 1934, Dill said he was tired of public life and chose not to run for a third term. He planned "never to seek public life again," even though he enjoyed bipartisan support and many pundits predicted he could have won.

After leaving the Senate, Dill returned to his legal practice and maintained offices in both Washington, D.C., and Spokane, where he specialized in communications and public power law. He taught radio law at the Washington College of Law from 1936 to 1938. On Apr. 16, 1939, he married Mabel Dickson, a Spokane socialite and teacher who established the home economics department at the local Whitworth College. They had no children. In 1940, Dill ran for governor and lost narrowly to Arthur B. Langlie, the former mayor of Seattle. Two years later he was defeated in a bid to return to Congress. From 1945 to 1948 he served on the Columbia Basin Commission of the State of Washington. He served as a special assistant to the United States attorney general in charge of the Bonneville Power Administration condemnation work at four Northwest sites from 1946 to 1953, and in 1955 he accepted a position as legislative consultant to the Senate Committee on Interstate and Foreign Commerce chaired by fellow Washingtonian Warren Magnuson. Dill continued to practice law in Spokane until shortly before his death there.

[Dill's papers are housed at the Eastern Washington State Historical Society in Spokane, Wash. His autobiography is *Where Water Falls* (1971). He also authored *How Congress Makes Laws* (1936); *Radio Law: Practice and Procedure* (1937); *Our Government* (1939); and *History of the State of Washington* (1941). See also *A History of the State of Washington*, vol. 4, edited by Lloyd Spencer (1937); and Richard W. Larsen, "How C. C. Dill Interested F.D.R. in Grand Coulee Dam," *Seattle Times Magazine*, Jan. 3, 1971. Obituaries are in the *Spokane Spokesman-Review* and the Seattle *Post-Intelligencer*, both Jan. 15, 1978.]

DANIEL LIESTMAN

DONNELL, FORREST C. (Aug. 20, 1884–Mar. 3, 1980), state governor and United States senator, was born in Quitman, a small town in northwestern Missouri, the son of John Cary Donnell and Barbara Lee Waggoner. His father operated a general store in Quitman, and then in nearby Maryville. Donnell graduated from Maryville High School in 1900, then attended the University of Missouri in Columbia, earning his B.A. in 1904 and his law degree there in 1907. He was high school, college, and law school valedictorian, and was elected to Phi Beta Kappa and to the Order of the Coif, the legal honor society. Growing up in the age of William Jennings Bryan, when oratory and forensics rivaled football as prestigious school activities, Donnell early won recognition as an able orator and debater. He married Hilda Hayes on Jan. 29, 1913; they had two children.

Donnell was admitted to the bar in 1907 and began a long and successful law practice in St. Louis. He earned the reputation of being a hardworking, public-spirited attorney who was scrupulous about the fees he charged and was determined to represent only clients he knew to be innocent or wronged. He held to strict religious and moral ideas learned from his parents and was an active Methodist layman, teaching a men's Sunday School class and holding many church offices over the years. He also served on the boards of various civic and benevolent organizations, and like his fellow Missourian, Harry Truman, served as grand master of the Missouri Masonic Lodge.

Although his father was a Democrat, Donnell early became an active Republican, apparently inspired by Theodore Roosevelt's presidency. By 1916, he was president of the Young Republicans of Missouri. After World War I, he opposed America's entry into the League of Nations but favored a world court and served as president of the St. Louis World Court Committee.

Donnell became well known throughout Missouri, and in 1940 Republican leaders persuaded him to run for governor. The Democrats, the dominant party, were plagued by division and charges of corruption. Donnell proved to be an energetic and persuasive campaigner and was the only Republican on the ballot to win a state office. The victory margin was so narrow—3,613 votes out of 1,819,447—that the Democrat-controlled legislature at first refused to certify the victory, alleging fraud. On Jan. 13, 1941, a writ of mandamus from the state supreme court, backed by irate public opinion, forced Donnell's confirmation as governor, thwarting what the press called the "Missouri governorship steal." Donnell's two major accomplishments as governor were a revised, unified tax structure and inclusion of more than half of all state employees in a merit system. As governor, Donnell alienated many of his own party leaders by avoiding the customary patronage appointment process; thus, they did not support his entry into the senatorial race in 1944. He nevertheless won the primary, and then a general election victory—1,900 votes out of more than 1.5 million—while the national Roosevelt-Truman ticket and the Democrats easily carried the state.

As senator, Donnell allied himself closely with the conservative Robert Taft wing of the party to oppose nearly all of Truman's domestic and foreign policy initiatives. He voted for the Marshall Plan but opposed the NATO treaty as unconstitutional. As a constitutional lawyer and consistent strict constructionist, he vigorously opposed all claims to any "inherent powers" of the president. He especially irked Truman by attacking and often delaying presidential nominations he considered "cronyism." Donnell and Taft cast the two votes against Robert Hannegan to be postmaster general and he voted alone against Washington hostess Perle Mesta's nomination to be minister to Luxembourg. He shared the prevalent fear of Communism but never followed Senator Joseph McCarthy in making undocumented charges.

Politeness and a gentlemanly, mild manner characterized Donnell in his personal relationships; but when he took the floor of the Senate, he was an articulate, aggressive advocate for his cause. He came well armed with data, and his powerful voice needed no microphone. Critics considered his speeches tedious, long-winded, and overlegalistic, and joked he was the only senator who could explain at length the difference between a jot and a tittle. Admirers viewed him as an able constitutional lawyer with high ethical standards. He was never known to drink, smoke, swear, or be touched by any hint of personal or political scandal. A tireless campaigner, he rose to an evangelistic fervor when attacking federal aid to education, "socialized medicine," and other Fair Deal proposals. He never indulged in personal attacks on his opponents; indeed, he often surprised his audiences by praising them. Thus Donnell remained throughout his Senate career an anomaly in Washington politics. After one term he was defeated by Thomas Hennings, Jr., in 1950 and returned to his St. Louis law practice. He died in St. Louis.

Donnell was a representative, however untypical, of growing midwestern reaction to the domestic programs of the late New Deal and the Fair Deal. In foreign affairs he never moved much beyond his youthful isolationism. His achievements as a governor in confrontation with a hostile legislature were modest, his role as a senator essentially negative as he opposed the expanding power of the presidency and national government. His individualistic political style and extraordinarily strict ethical standards mark Donnell as an unusual and unforgettable figure in Missouri and national history.

[A large collection of Donnell's papers is indexed in the library of the State Historical Society of Missouri in Columbia. His speeches are available in the *Congressional Record.* No biography has been published. Articles of interest include Paul Healy, "The

Senate's Big Itch," *Saturday Evening Post*, Dec. 3, 1949; election articles in *The Nation*, Oct. 14, 1950; and *Newsweek*, Oct. 23, 1950, and Nov. 20, 1950. A brief obituary is in the *St. Louis Post Dispatch*, Mar. 4, 1980.]

WAYNE C. BARTEE

DOUGLAS, AARON (May 26, 1899–Feb. 2, 1979), artist, illustrator, and educator, was born in Topeka, Kans., where he grew up. He received a B.A. degree from the University of Kansas in 1923, a B.F.A. degree from the University of Nebraska in 1922, and an M.F.A. degree from Columbia University in 1944. In addition, he studied in Paris on a Barnes Foundation grant in 1928 and 1929, and he received Rosenwald grants in 1931 and 1938.

After working as a high school art teacher in Kansas City, Mo. (1923–1925), Douglas moved to New York City. In 1926 he married Alta Sawyer, who died in 1958. In New York he studied until 1927 with artist Winold Reiss, who encouraged him to use his own culture as subject matter for his art. Douglas became interested in the art of Africa and was one of the first painters to be considered an Africanist. He often painted fellow African Americans. Much of his work is characterized by geometric forms and stylized figures, typically found in African art.

In the 1920's, Douglas became one of the leading artists of the Harlem Renaissance. He felt that the purpose of art is to chronicle history, to reveal thought, and to transform myths. Douglas wrote that few African-American artists could escape becoming part of the Harlem Renaissance: "When unsuspecting Negroes were found with a brush in their hands, they were immediately hauled away and held for interpretation. They were given places of honor and bowed to with much ceremony." Douglas illustrated the works of such well-known literary contemporaries as W. E. B. Du Bois, Countee Cullen, Langston Hughes, and James Weldon Johnson. His illustration of Johnson's *God's Trombones* is one of his masterpieces. His work also appeared in magazines such as *Vanity Fair*, *Theatre Arts*, and *American Mercury*.

During the 1930's, Douglas painted murals for the WPA. In 1934 he completed a four-part mural for the Countee Cullen Branch of the New York Public Library on the history of American blacks. The first mural depicted the African background; the second, the joy over emancipation, followed by the terror of the Ku Klux Klan; the third, the horrors of lynching combined with the African-American will to survive; and the fourth, the migration of African Americans from the South to the North. He also executed a mural on black history for Fisk University. In addition he painted murals for the Ebony Club in New York City and the Hotel Sherman in Chicago, both of which depict African dance.

In addition to his mural painting, most of which is distinctly geometric, Douglas produced a number of portraits that show a clearly representative style using elongation, angularities, and mystical light patterns. Three of his best-known portraits in this style are of Mary McLeod Bethune, Marian Anderson, and Alexander Dumas.

In 1939, Douglas joined the faculty at Fisk University in Nashville, Tenn., where he later founded and chaired the art department; he retired in 1966. He was known as a demanding taskmaster; a campus editor once wrote that he occasionally distributed "praise in weak microscopic pills." He died in Nashville, Tenn.

Art historian David Driskell said of Douglas, "Few people have been so prophetic in their art as Aaron Douglas. . . . His art spoke prophetically of the beauty of the black man and his culture in this hemisphere."

[Aaron Douglas is mentioned briefly in articles and books pertaining to African-American art. The articles below are devoted exclusively to him: "The Art of Aaron Douglas," *Crisis*, May 1931; and Rose Henderson, "Aaron Douglas, Negro Painter," *Southern Workman*, Sept. 1931.]

RENNIE SIMSON

DOUGLAS, HELEN GAHAGAN (Nov. 25, 1900–June 28, 1980), actress and politician, was born in Boonton, N.J., the daughter of Walter Hamer Gahagan II and Lillian Rose Mussen. Her father, an Ohio-born engineer, prospered in construction and shipbuilding; her mother had taught school prior to marriage. Reared in cosmopolitan turn-of-the-century Brooklyn, she once described her house as resembling the set of *Life with Father*, "with large, airy high-ceilinged rooms, marble fireplaces in every room, tall windows looking out over the garden, and fine paneling everywhere." She expressed early a desire to become an actress, causing her father, in an attempt to diminish her interest in what was then still considered a disreputable profession, to demand that she first attend college. Selecting to attend Barnard College at Columbia University because of its proximity to Broadway, Douglas discovered that Barnard suited her ambitions perfectly. She enrolled in every acting course the school offered, joined the college drama society, and—as an indication of her later political interests—championed the cause of Irish independence as a member of the debating team. At the end of her first year, she appeared in an off-Broadway production of *Shoot* by Henry Wagstaff Gribble and then took a summer-stock role in *Manhattan*. Douglas attracted the attention of playwright Owen Davis who, needing an ingenue, offered her a role in his Broadway romance, *Dreams for Sale* (1922). She did not think much of the play's quality, but it proved to be the making of her professional career since she impressed the influential critic Heywood Broun, who praised her performance, declaring her to be one of the twelve most beautiful women in America. Abandoning college, Douglas appeared in plays around the country for several years before going to Europe to study opera.

In October 1930 she returned to America to play the opera singer feminine lead in David Belasco's last production, *Tonight or Never*. Her costar was Melvyn Douglas. After their working relationship blossomed into romance, they married in her parents' home on Apr. 15, 1931. Helen had two children with Melvyn Douglas and also raised a stepson, from her husband's previous marriage. Over the next decade, continuing to perform under the name Helen Gahagan, she took parts in plays, operas, and films (she made her film debut in Rider Haggard's *She* in 1936). These years also saw the emergence of her political consciousness, beginning with her support of Franklin D. Roosevelt's New Deal and her vocal opposition to the Nazi party, whose brutalities she had witnessed firsthand while performing in Germany in the 1930's. Douglas became a champion of progressive causes in California: She called attention to the plight of subsistence farmers and migrant workers, promoted civil rights and the growth of organized labor, and took a particular interest in environmental issues including offshore oil drilling and land reclamation.

Her endorsement of Roosevelt for a third presidential term led to her selection as a Democratic national committeewoman for California in 1940. Her intelligence and commitment combined with her physical attractiveness and effective speaking manner to make her a natural choice for elective office. In 1944 she won the congressional seat in California's Fourteenth District; she was reelected in 1946 and 1948. In Congress, Douglas steadfastly supported President Roosevelt's New Deal and President Harry S. Truman's Fair Deal. Never shy of confrontations, she defended the record of black soldiers in World War II against the scurrilous attacks of John Rankin, a white supremacist congressman from Mississippi. She voted against increased funding for the House Un-American Activities Committee and coauthored with Senator Brien McMahon of Connecticut the Atomic Energy Act designed to control what she described as "this unparalleled instrument of destruction." Meanwhile, Douglas made powerful future enemies for herself in California by endorsing Truman's opposition to attempts by the states of Texas, Louisiana, and California to gain jurisdiction over coastal tidelands where significant deposits of oil had been discovered.

On foreign policy questions, Douglas stood more left of center than most of her Democratic colleagues. On the pivotal issue of American aid to democratic governments in Greece and Turkey that were attempting to stave off Communist challenges, she opposed Truman's decision to provide unilateral American aid, arguing that all such efforts should be coordinated with the United Nations collective-security system. Despite her liberal sympathies, Douglas, who as a delegate to the Democratic National Convention in 1944 had strongly backed Henry Wallace for the vice-presidential nomination, broke with Wallace when he formed the Progressive party to oppose Truman's reelection in 1948.

The defining moment in the career, and indeed the life, of Helen Gahagan Douglas occurred in 1950 when she ran for the United States Senate against Richard M. Nixon. Douglas had decided to oppose the incumbent Democratic senator Sheridan Downey because of the latter's opposition to reclamation and his ties to California oil interests. Her depiction of Downey as a do-nothing senator under the control of big-business lobbyists caused him to abandon the race, bitterly complaining that he was not physically capable of "waging a personal and militant campaign against vicious and unethical propaganda" against him. Conservative Democrats then persuaded Manchester Boddy, publisher of the *Los Angeles Daily News*, to challenge Douglas. Boddy, an inept campaigner, characterized Douglas as one of a "small subversive clique of red-hots" out to take over the Democratic party. Douglas easily won the primary and polled nearly as many votes as Nixon had in winning the Republican nomination. There then ensued what one Nixon supporter called "the most hateful campaign" that California had experienced in many years. An editorial in the conservative *Los Angeles Times* succinctly suggested the tenor of the campaign the Nixon forces waged when it described Douglas as a "glamorous actress who though not a Communist voted the Communist Party line in Congress innumerable times" and referred to her as "the darling" of Hollywood parlor pinks and reds. Nixon's campaign manager Murray Chotiner, perhaps the first of a new breed of political consultants, produced the campaign's most controversial document, "the Pink Sheet." This leaflet attempted to align Douglas with Congressman Vito Marcantonio, described as the "notorious Communist Party Liner" from New York City. The Pink Sheet charged that since 1945 Douglas had voted the same as Marcantonio 354 times and that the issues on which they most "saw eye to eye" were un-American activities and internal security. Nixon, the Pink Sheet declared, had voted "exactly opposite to the Douglas-Marcantonio Axis." Eventually Chotiner printed and distributed more than half a million copies of the leaflet. Nixon over the years denied that he ever said or inferred that Helen Douglas was a Communist. But the Pink Sheet certainly implied that she was. A highly respected reference service, Editorial Research, concluded that on ten major congressional issues on the so-called Communist threat, Douglas voted against Marcantonio in favor of a policy opposing a real or imagined Communist threat.

In light of later events, the 1950 campaign produced some interesting endorsements. Congressman John F. Kennedy contributed $1,000 to Nixon's campaign, while Ronald Reagan, then a leading figure in the Screen Actors Guild, campaigned for Douglas. The circulation of the Pink Sheet produced a response in kind from the Douglas campaign in the form of a yellow-colored broadside that proclaimed: "The Big Lie. Hitler invented it, Stalin perfected it, Nixon uses it." Douglas went so far as to charge Nixon with being allied to Marcantonio on "every key vote against America in its fight to defeat Communism." The *New York Times* found each side accusing the other "of hitting a new low in distortion."

Nixon's anti-Communist strategy benefited greatly from the surprise attack by the North Korean Communist government on South Korea in June 1950, an event Nixon attributed to Secretary of State Dean Acheson's declaration that Korea and Formosa were outside the American defensive perimeter in Asia. By making Nixon appear prescient on the Communist menace, the outbreak of war in Korea guaranteed his election. But although victorious in the senatorial race and positioned firmly for his nomination and election as the 1952 Republican vice-presidential candidate, Nixon suffered lasting political damage in 1950, not the least from the name Democrats used to denounce his tactics against Douglas—"Tricky Dick"—an epithet he could not shake to the end of his career.

Nixon received 2.2 million votes to 1.5 million for Douglas. Afterward, Douglas steadfastly refused to discuss the campaign, although she did express her opinion during the Watergate crisis that Nixon deserved to be impeached. In her posthumous autobiography, Douglas revealed the pain she had suffered in 1950 and observed, "Before Watergate and its revelations of Nixon's character, I was among those who didn't believe it was possible for him to be a great President, contending that his technique for success involved vicious campaigning." She concluded that Nixon had condoned the Watergate break-in because under stress he "reverted to what had served him in the past, which was to wage a dirty campaign." After the 1950 election Douglas retired from politics and lived the rest of her life in comparative obscurity. She died at the Memorial Sloan-Kettering Cancer Center in New York City.

[Douglas wrote an autobiography, *A Full Life/Helen Gahagan Douglas* (1982). For a biography, see Ingrid Winther Scobie, *Center Stage: Helen Gahagan Douglas, A Life* (1992). Detailed accounts of the 1950 California senate campaign can be found in Richard M. Nixon, *RN: The Memoirs of Richard Nixon* (1978); Herbert S. Parmet, *Richard Nixon and His America* (1990); and Tom Wicker, *One of Us: Richard Nixon and the American Dream* (1991). An obituary is in the *New York Times*, June 29, 1980.]

JOHN B. DUFF

DOUGLAS, PAUL HOWARD (Mar. 26, 1892–Sept. 24, 1976), economist and United States senator, was born in Salem, Mass., the son of James Howard Douglas, a traveling salesman, and Annie Smith. His mother died when he was four years old. Douglas spent his childhood on his uncle's farm in northern Maine and attended Newport (Maine) public schools. He received a B.A. degree from Bowdoin College in 1913, with Phi Beta Kappa honors. Douglas earned a master's degree from Columbia University in 1915 and a doctorate in 1921, having studied at Harvard University in 1915 and 1916. His doctoral dissertation was titled "American Apprenticeship and Industrial Relations."

Douglas was an instructor in economics at the University of Illinois (1916–1917) and assistant professor of economics at Reed College in Portland, Oreg. (1917–1918). Although a Quaker pacifist, he volunteered for military service in 1917. He was rejected, however, because of markedly defective eyesight. Douglas arbitrated labor disputes with the Emergency Fleet Corporation in 1918 and 1919 and resumed teaching as an associate professor of economics at the University of Washington in the 1919–1920 academic year.

In 1920, Douglas joined the faculty of the University of Chicago, as assistant professor of industrial relations (1920–1923), associate professor (1923–1925), and professor (1925–1948). Amherst College appointed him visiting professor of economics from 1924 to 1927. Douglas, who spent 1931 in Europe on a Guggenheim Fellowship, wrote influential books on wages, social security, and unemployment. He specialized in production functions, the mathematical analysis relating labor to capital. *Wages and the Family* (1925) analyzed the family allowance system of wage payments. Books written with others include *The Worker in Modern Economic Society* (1923), *Adam Smith (1776–1926)* (1928), *Movement of Real Wages (1926–1928)* (1930), and *The Problem of Unemployment* (1931). *Real Wages in the United States* (1930) and *The Theory of Wages* (1934) were his most distinguished books, the latter bringing him a $5,000 prize in international competition. Douglas also wrote *Standards of Unemployment Insurance* (1933), *Controlling Depressions* (1935), and *Social Security in the United States* (1936).

These publications brought Douglas several state and national government appointments. He chaired the board of arbitration for the newspaper industry from 1925 to 1941, handing down eighty-five decisions. During 1930, Douglas was acting director of the Swarthmore Unemployment Study, secretary to the Pennsylvania Commission on Unemployment, and economic adviser to the New York Committee to Stabilize Employment. As an Illinois Housing Commission member from 1931 to 1933, he drafted the Utilities Act of 1933, which reduced electricity and gas rates. Douglas also framed the Illinois Old Age Pension Act of 1935 and the Illinois State Unemployment Insurance Act of 1937. From 1933 to 1935, he served on the Consumers' Advisory Board of the National Recovery Administration (NRA). NRA administrators, however, persuaded Douglas to resign after he raised the truth-in-lending issue. From 1937 to 1939 Douglas was a member of the advisory committee to the United States Senate and the Social Security Board on revision of the original Social Security Act, which he had helped to draft.

Douglas urged formation of an American labor party in *The Coming of a New Party* (1932). His baptism in elective politics came as an alderman in Chicago, representing the Fifth Ward from 1939 to 1942. Raymond McKeough, backed by the Chicago machine, defeated Douglas in the 1942 Democratic primary for the United States Senate seat held by Republican C. Wayland Brooks. The fifty-year-old Douglas immediately joined the United States Marines as a private and fought with the First Marine Division in the Pacific Theater. He was wounded at Peleliu and Okinawa and spent fourteen months in hospitals before being discharged as a lieutenant colonel. In 1945, Douglas resumed his professorship at the University of Chicago and arranged the National Labor-Management Conference agenda. Although he had been a delegate at large to the 1948 Democratic party convention, Douglas supported Dwight D. Eisenhower over incumbent Harry Truman for president.

In 1948, Douglas unseated Brooks by over four hundred thousand votes. The Democratic State Committee and the Cook County Democratic party machine initially favored lawyer Adlai Stevenson for the senatorial post, but veterans, labor organizations, and independent voters persuaded Democratic officials to run

Stevenson for governor instead. The illustrious group of freshman senators in 1949 included Lyndon Johnson of Texas and Hubert Humphrey of Minnesota.

Douglas, a tall, heavy man with shaggy white hair and a carved-in-granite face, demonstrated an idealism and independence that kept him outside the Senate's inner circle. He disclosed his income and net worth annually, refused to accept political donations over $2.50, and favored financial disclosure by all members of Congress, public financing of elections, and reform of the seniority system. His battles for social and economic justice built a body of far-reaching legislation for the disadvantaged. Service on the Labor and Public Welfare, Banking and Currency, and Finance committees and chairmanship on the Joint Committee on the Economic Report (Eighty-fourth Congress) and the Joint Economic Committee (Eighty-sixth and Eighty-eighth Congresses) afforded Douglas ample opportunity to frame pioneering domestic legislation.

Douglas sought civil rights legislation, urged repeal of the Taft-Hartley Act, and championed low-cost public housing, national health insurance, federal aid to education, expanded Social Security and unemployment insurance protection, a higher minimum wage, and welfare and pension-fund regulation. In 1951, Douglas and Humphrey occupied the Senate floor for several days in an unsuccessful attempt to close tax loopholes in the Revenue Act. Douglas opposed removing federal control over taxes on gasoline in interstate commerce and leasing of offshore oil deposits to private interests. A staunch anti-Communist, he endorsed the Marshall Plan, the North Atlantic Treaty Organization, and American military intervention in the Korean War.

Douglas served as a delegate at large to the 1952, 1956, 1964, and 1968 Democratic party conventions. In 1952 he backed Estes Kefauver of Tennessee over Stevenson for the Democratic presidential nomination. Illinois voters re-elected Douglas to two United States Senate terms: by 237,000 votes over Republican Joseph Meek in 1954 and by 437,000 votes over Republican Samuel Witwer in 1960. During those terms, his proposals for outlawing discrimination in public places, employment, labor unions, and voting registration were incorporated into the Civil Rights Acts of 1964 and the Voting Rights Act of 1965. Douglas adamantly defended American military intervention in South Vietnam, believing that the United States should stop Communism from spreading in Southeast Asia.

In 1966, Republican Charles Percy ousted Douglas from the Senate by 420,000 votes. Advancing age, defense of President Lyndon Johnson's Vietnam War policy, and growing white backlash against civil rights contributed to the setback for Douglas. In 1967 he taught at the New School for Social Research in New York City and chaired the National Commission on Urban Problems. Finding one-third of the American population still ill housed, the Douglas Commission recommended a system of federal revenue sharing with the states and cities, and encouraged the consolidation of local governments with metropolitan areas.

Between 1951 and 1972, Douglas wrote six books: *Federal Budget* (1951), *Ethics in Government* (1952), *Economy in the National Government* (1952), *America in the Market Place* (1966), and *In Our Time* (1968). His memoirs, *In the Fullness of Time* (1972), features his voluminous legislative efforts on economic and social issues. The American Economic Association elected Douglas as its president in 1947. Douglas also was a member of the Econometric Society, the American Academy of Arts and Sciences, the American Statistical Association, the Royal Economic Association, and several veterans' groups. He frequently contributed articles to the *American Economic Review*, *Journal of Political Economy*, and *Political Science Quarterly*.

On Aug. 21, 1915, Douglas married Dorothy Wolff, the daughter of a New York City banker; they had four children. They were divorced in 1930, and in 1931 Douglas married Emily Taft, daughter of renowned sculptor Lorado Taft; they had one child. In 1945 and 1946 she served as a Democratic member at large from Illinois in the House of Representatives. Douglas died in Washington, D.C.

[Douglas's papers are housed at the Chicago Historical Society. The best source remains his memoirs, *In the Fullness of Time* (1972). Jerry M. Anderson, "Paul H. Douglas: Insurgent Senate Spokesman for Human Causes, 1949–1963" (Ph.D. diss., Michigan State University, 1964), recounts Douglas's Senate career. An obituary is in the *New York Times*, Sept. 25, 1976.]

DAVID L. PORTER

DOUGLAS, WILLIAM ORVILLE (Oct. 16, 1898–Jan. 19, 1980), Supreme Court justice, was born in Maine, Minn., one of three children of William Douglas, a Presbyterian minister, and Julia Fisk. When he was three years old, his parents moved to Estrella, Calif., and then to Cleveland, Wash., where the Reverend Douglas died in 1904. The family then moved to Yakima, Wash.

While living in Minnesota, the young William, whom his mother called "Treasure," contracted polio, which caused paralysis in his legs. His mother nursed him constantly, bathing his legs in warm salt water and massaging them every two hours. Gradually he regained limited use of his legs, but he was a sickly child at the time of his father's funeral.

Between the strong will of his mother and his own self-determination, Douglas overcame his physical disabilities. He started to hike in the mountains with his younger brother Arthur, an experience that not only built up his strength but turned into a lifelong devotion to the environment. The drive to build himself physically carried over into other areas of his life. The Yakima High School yearbook of 1916 noted that its valedictorian that year had been "born for success." Douglas enrolled in Whitman College in Walla Walla, Wash., in the fall of 1916 on a full scholarship, although he continued to work hard and, free from his mother's eye, play hard as well.

After graduation from Whitman, he worked in Yakima for a while. In the summer of 1922, with $75 in his pocket, he went east to attend Columbia Law School. He started the journey to New York as guardian of two thousand sheep bound for Minnesota. Douglas embellished the details of the trip over the years, but there is no doubt that few if any of his classmates at Columbia University had ever spent time riding the rails with hoboes or running from the "bulls" who policed the railroad yards.

Douglas entered Columbia at a time when its faculty had just begun to explore new areas of legal research that would eventually lead to the "Legal Realism" movement. The Realists believed that in order to understand the law and the behavior of legal institutions, one had to use the social sciences to understand the causes of particular actions. Douglas became a devoted adherent to this new philosophy. He graduated in 1925. After a miserable two years working in a Wall Street law firm, he returned to Columbia Law School as a teacher in 1927. Within a year, however, he resigned to accept a position at the Yale Law School, which, under the leadership of its brilliant young dean, Robert Maynard Hutchins, quickly became the center of Legal Realism, with Douglas as one of its star exponents.

His tenure at Yale may have been the most peaceful in his life. He had married Mildred Riddle (whom he had met during a brief stint as a teacher in Yakima) in 1924, and they had two children. At Yale, Douglas enjoyed a good salary at a time when the country was plunged into depression; he did important work in the law of bankruptcy and protective committees; and he seemed to have enjoyed the company and intellectual stimulation of his colleagues. But beneath the surface he remained restless, especially when he looked to Washington and saw the dynamic activities going on under the New Deal umbrella.

In 1934, Douglas secured an assignment from the newly created Securities and Exchange Commission (SEC) to study protective committees, the agency stockholders use during bankruptcy reorganization to protect their interests. He began commuting between New Haven, Conn., and Washington, D.C., and soon came to the attention of the SEC chair, Joseph P. Kennedy, who arranged for the then thirty-seven-year-old Douglas to be named to the commission in 1936. Two years later President Roosevelt named Douglas chair of the SEC.

Douglas's two years on Wall Street had left him with little respect for the big financiers who often manipulated stock offerings and bankruptcy proceedings to line their own pockets. He had no illusions that the stock market was anything more than a crap shoot, but he demanded that the players observe the rules. Investors deserved to be fully informed about the companies whose stock they were asked to buy. Once they had that information, they could decide how much risk they wanted to take.

Wall Street, which had had little trouble with Kennedy or his successor, James Landis, now prepared to do battle with Douglas, who directed a small army of lawyers. The opposition collapsed, however, with the disclosure of embezzlement by the scions of one of America's most elite families. Richard Whitney, a former president of the New York Stock Exchange, had diverted funds from a trust account to cover his brokerage's stock losses. With Whitney's arrest, the governors of the stock exchange quickly agreed to abide by the SEC rules.

During these years in Washington, Douglas became part of Franklin D. Roosevelt's inner circle and often joined the weekly poker games at the White House. There was a great deal of speculation that the bright, handsome westerner might have a future in politics. In fact, Douglas had already tired of the game and wanted to return to Yale. When a messenger interrupted a golf game on Mar. 19, 1939, to tell Douglas that the president wanted to see him at the White House, Douglas almost did not go since he fully expected that Roosevelt was going to ask him to take over the troubled Federal Communications Commission. But after teasing him for a few minutes, Roosevelt offered Douglas the seat on the Supreme Court vacated by Louis D. Brandeis a month earlier. Although Douglas always claimed the offer came as a surprise, in fact he had had his friends busily at work promoting his name for the opening. Following the bruising battle surrounding Roosevelt's "court-packing" scheme in 1937, the president wanted to make sure that his appointees would support his programs, and in Douglas he had a confirmed New Deal liberal, someone who could handle confrontations with conservatives, who had a quick mind, and was a westerner and a loyal personal friend.

Douglas, one of the youngest persons ever appointed to the Supreme Court, would establish a record of longevity for service before illness forced him to retire in late 1975. Douglas always claimed that the work of the Court never took more than three or four days a week. He read petitions rapidly, rarely agonized over decisions, could get to the heart of an issue instantly, and wrote his opinions quickly. This left him time for other activities, such as travel, lecturing, writing, climbing mountains, and, some critics claimed, getting into trouble.

Douglas joined the Court during one of its great historical transformations. From the end of the Civil War until the late 1930's, the main items on the Court's agenda had been property rights and the limits on how far government could go in restricting the use of private property. Since then the Court has been concerned primarily with individual rights. The great court fight of 1937 had marked an end to the conservative domination of the bench, and with the arrival of the Roosevelt appointees the Court essentially gave federal and state governments an almost unlimited power to regulate property in the name of the public welfare. Douglas himself wrote one of the major opinions upholding state power, *Williamson* v. *Lee Optical Co.* (1955).

Douglas served on the bench more than thirty-six years and wrote thousands of opinions. His most important contribution to modern jurisprudence may have been his development of a constitutionally protected right to privacy, enunciated in the landmark case of *Griswold* v. *Connecticut* (1965).

Douglas's name was often associated with that of Hugo L. Black, the acknowledged leader of the Court's liberal, activist wing. The two men believed government should interfere as little as possible in people's lives. Douglas wanted to keep the government off the backs of the people, and he could be just as eloquent as his colleague and friend in espousing a preferred position for First Amendment rights. The Constitution said Congress shall make no law abridging freedom of speech, and the two men believed it meant just that. Douglas in particular opposed any and all obscenity laws. The courts, he believed, had no business acting as censors.

Critics complained that Douglas wanted the Court to be too active and that he ignored the inherent conservatism of the judicial role. Douglas believed that, at least in the areas of civil rights and liberties, the judiciary should be active defenders of liberty. And much to his opponents' chagrin, Douglas, like any good law professor, could produce precedents to support whatever side he took, although he often said he would rather create a precedent than cite one.

Douglas's record was far from consistent, however. In the Japanese internment cases during World War II, he voted with the majority to validate one of the worst violations of civil rights in American history. Douglas did have qualms about these cases, but he went along with the majority. And, although in his memoirs Douglas extolled his efforts to prevent the executions of convicted spies Julius and Ethel Rosenberg, he failed to note that on five occasions he had voted against the Court's accepting their case for review. Several scholars have also noted his reflexive tendency to vote against the Internal Revenue Service in tax cases.

Despite his inconsistencies, however, Douglas had a very real commitment to libertarian jurisprudence. He was willing to strike down racial segregation long before *Brown* v. *Board of Education* (1954), and during the heyday of McCarthyism only he and Black stood up for free speech. His dissent in *Dennis* v. *United States* (1951) remains an outstanding testimony to his courage.

Many scholars and sympathetic colleagues believe that Douglas could have been more effective if he had tried to be a team player. He enjoyed his role as a dissenter, but he often made it hard for others to join him because he would insist on taking the most extreme stance. One of his colleagues noted that Douglas would "put two or three sentences in a dissent that were so outrageous, you just couldn't join him."

Some of Douglas's opinions were sloppy in their legal reasoning and proofs. His biographer, James Simon, suggests that after his first decade on the Court Douglas stopped writing for lawyers and law school professors and began aiming his opinions and dissents at the general public. He certainly had the ability to write solid technical opinions, but for the most part chose not to do so. He could write far more clearly than most judges or lawyers, and he hoped the people would understand his pleas for religious and racial tolerance and his explanations of why civil liberties had to be protected in a democracy.

Douglas was a results-oriented jurist who cared more about the final decision than the means by which one arrived at that decision. This has led some critics to call him an "anti-judge" because of his disdain for the accepted modes of judicial discourse. In response, his supporters have suggested that Douglas followed the older common law tradition, in which the purpose of the law is to seek justice even if it requires unusual arguments.

Every court needs a libertarian conscience such as Douglas, but it also needs a craftsman who can forge coherent and persuasive legal and moral arguments. For most of his career Douglas could rely on either Black or William Brennan to take care of the arguments while he went after the results. He never saw his role as having to teach others the law and thus cared little about the legal niceties of opinion writing. He preferred to be the loner on the bench, the dissident voice of conscience. It may have proven personally satisfying, but one can lament that a person so intellectually gifted chose not to exercise his talents in a more effective and lasting manner.

Douglas had a wanderlust, which he started to indulge soon after World War II. Although in his letters he often claimed to have traveled at his own expense, he rarely paid for trips directly. In most instances he would contract with a publisher or magazine—frequently *National Geographic*—for an article or book and use the advance to cover the costs of the adventure or bill the expenses to the publisher. He also took advantage of frequent speaking engagements in faraway places. The results were a series of engagingly written books and articles reflecting his wide-ranging mind and insatiable curiosity.

When he traveled, he sought to leave the beaten path frequented by the diplomats and Foreign Service officers. As a result Douglas learned a great deal about what the common people thought, and this frequently ran against the grain of official American policy. He incurred President Harry Truman's wrath for suggesting that the United States recognize the People's Republic of China, and long before the revolution in Iran he warned the Kennedy and Johnson administrations about opposition to the shah. Often he claimed to be an "expert" after spending a couple of weeks in a country, but on many occasions his analyses of the problems proved far more prescient than those of overly optimistic State Department officers.

Douglas remained a deeply committed environmentalist his entire life, and he feared the encroachment of "progress" in the ever-shrinking wilderness areas. He opposed cutting trails or campsites. If people wanted to get into wilderness areas, he argued, they should park their cars, strap on a backpack, and hike. People who wanted comfort should stay in motels.

Douglas helped lead a publicized effort in opposition to paving over the old C & O Canal next to the Potomac River, running northwest from Washington. Every year he led a hike along the canal, and eventually Congress voted funds to turn it into a national park, with the towpaths devoted to hikers and cyclists and the canal itself reserved for canoeists. Fittingly, the park was dedicated to Douglas.

Douglas believed that as a citizen he had a right to speak out on any issue that might affect him, and he saw his judicial responsibilities as limiting him only in that he should not comment on matters that might come before the Court. He resigned from several environmental groups when they began litigation to protect natural resources, but he rationalized his statements on foreign affairs by claiming that such issues rarely came before the Court. Some of his activities, however, including his involvement in the Albert Parvin Foundation (whose creator then faced potential criminal charges in regard to other activities) did involve potential conflicts of interest.

Efforts to impeach Douglas intensified during the Nixon presidency and grew primarily out of political motivations. His outspoken liberalism, his half-muted criticism of government policy (including the war in Vietnam), and above all the Republicans' desire to take the high court away from the liberal activists led Congressman Gerald Ford in April 1970 to demand an investigation of Douglas on charges that he had abused his judicial office.

The four charges leveled by Ford claimed that Douglas had sold an article, and accepted money for it, from a man involved in litigation that might reach the Supreme Court; that Douglas had received money from the Parvin Foundation; that Douglas had worked for and spoken to "leftist" groups; and that his book *Points of Rebellion* (1970) was un-American and urged resistance to government. Some of the suspicions about Douglas related to his various marriages. His union with Mildred had begun disintegrating in the 1940's, and they were divorced in 1953. In December 1954, Douglas married Mercedes Hester Davidson, whom he had known for a number of years. That marriage fell apart in 1961 when, on a speaking tour, Douglas met and fell in love with twenty-one-year-old Joan Martin, a student at Allegheny College. They were married in 1963, but the pressure on the young bride as the wife of a well-known political figure in Kennedy's Washington proved too much. In 1964, less than a year after their wedding, she ran off to Europe. Douglas finally met his match in another young woman, Cathleen Heffernan, and despite the forty-four-year difference in their ages, their marriage, which lasted from 1966 until his death, proved a happy one, perhaps because, as Douglas's daughter said, Cathleen "was the only one of Dad's wives who categorically refused to wait on him."

The Judiciary Committee hearings completely exonerated Douglas, which he erroneously considered to be a vindication of his conduct. Although the committee concluded that he had not committed an impeachable offense, many people were troubled by the exposure of his off-the-court activities.

At the time of the impeachment hearings, Douglas had been considering retirement so that he could spend more time with his wife. Left alone, it is likely, as his letters indicate, that he would have stepped down. Instead, he decided to stay as long as he could, and although Black was gone, Brennan proved just as fine a champion of liberal causes at his side.

In December 1974, Douglas suffered a stroke, while vacationing in Nassau. He tried to return to the bench in March 1975 but could no longer handle the work and finally retired from the Court in November. He had published the first volume of his memoirs, *Go East, Young Man*, just prior to his illness, and its charm won widespread acclaim. (Actually, an earlier volume, *Of Men and Mountains*, was his first autobiographical work, published in 1950). Following his resignation he worked on another volume, *The Court Years*, which was published after his death, but it is an inferior work, marred by error and petty judgments.

Douglas died in Washington, D.C. Although denounced by his critics as an atheist, he had made arrangements for a funeral service in the National Presbyterian Church, after which he was buried in Arlington National Cemetery, twenty feet away from the grave of another of the Court's great dissenters, Oliver Wendell Holmes.

[The Douglas Papers are in the Library of Congress; a selection of them is in Melvin I. Urofsky and Philip E. Urofsky, eds., *The Douglas Letters* (1987). Three volumes make up the Douglas memoirs: *Of Men and Mountains* (1950); *Go East, Young Man* (1974); and *The Court Years* (1980). An excellent biography is James F. Simon, *Independent Journey* (1980). Legal Realism is examined in Laura Kalman, *Legal Realism at Yale, 1927–1960* (1986); the SEC is detailed in Michael Parrish, *Securities Regulation and the New Deal* (1970). Some of Douglas's more important opinions are collected in Vern Countryman, ed., *The Douglas Opinions* (1977). Various aspects of his career are covered sympathetically in the various essays in Stephen L. Wasby, ed. "*He Shall Not Pass This Way Again*" (1990). An obituary is in the *New York Times*, Jan. 20, 1980.]

MELVIN I. UROFSKY

DRURY, NEWTON BISHOP (Apr. 9, 1889–Dec. 14, 1978), conservationist, was born in San Francisco, Calif., one of four children of

Wells Drury, a newspaper editor and columnist, and Ella Lorraine Bishop. While attending high school in Berkeley, Calif., he was a dance band cornetist. From 1906 to 1911 he was a reporter for San Francisco and Oakland newspapers. Meanwhile, he entered the University of California at Berkeley, studied journalism, and was active in debating clubs and campus politics. In his senior year he was elected student body president. His graduating class of 1912 included two other Californians who would attain national distinction—Governor and Chief Justice Earl Warren and conservationist Horace M. Albright. From 1912 to 1918 he served as administrative assistant to the university president, Benjamin I. Wheeler, and lecturer in English literature.

On June 29, 1918, Drury married Elizabeth Frances Schilling of Berkeley. They had three children. During World War I Drury served overseas as an aerial observer in the United States Army Balloon Corps. He later declared that the destruction he had witnessed strongly influenced him to favor conservation.

In 1919, Newton and his brother, Aubrey, formed the Drury Brothers Company, an advertising and public relations agency, in San Francisco. The company soon acquired several prestigious clients, including the Mark Hopkins Hotel. Organizers of the Save-the-Redwoods League also sought assistance with publicity and fund-raising from Drury Brothers. The league was founded in 1918 under the leadership of Henry Fairfield Osborn, president of the American Museum of Natural History in New York City; Madison Grant, chairman of the New York Zoological Society; and John C. Merriam, president of the Carnegie Institution in Washington, D.C. Drury became the league's first executive secretary and formulated its early objectives: preservation of representative areas of primeval forests, cooperation with the federal and state governments to create a national and a state redwood park, purchase of redwood groves by private subscription, protection of timber along certain highways, and support for reforestation and forest conservation.

From 1919 to 1940, Drury conducted a vigorous campaign to attain the objectives of the league. He led efforts to obtain legislation authorizing a California state park commission, a park site survey, and a park bond issue. He solicited and obtained memorial-grove donations, including a donation of $3 million from the John D. Rockefeller, Jr., family. Under his leadership the league by 1933 had either purchased or assisted the state of California in acquiring 30,000 acres of redwood forest in Mendocino, Humboldt, and Del Norte counties at a cost of $3 million of its own funds. After approval of a park bond referendum, the California State Park Commission employed Drury as its land-acquisition officer, a position that he held from 1929 to 1940, concurrent with his duties as executive secretary of the Save-the-Redwoods League.

Drury's outstanding work for park preservation in California influenced Secretary of the Interior Harold L. Ickes to offer him the position of director of the National Park Service in 1933 and again in 1940, when Drury accepted. As director, Drury became widely known for his opposition to special-interest demands for park uses during World War II and immediately thereafter. Early in the war he opposed demands of western ranchers to open the national parks to cattle grazing. He contended that the parks contained insufficient forage to serve any wartime needs and that their resources should remain "unimpaired." Some preservationists, however, criticized Drury for compromises in 1943 and 1947 that tended to favor loggers who sought to cut spruce timber in Olympic National Park in the state of Washington. Nevertheless, he continued to oppose commercial uses in several national monuments and parks, including Death Valley in California and Glacier Bay in Alaska. His administration was also notable for additions to the national park system, including a large portion of the Everglades National Park in Florida, Independence National Historical Park in Pennsylvania, and the Jackson Hole area in Grand Teton National Park in Wyoming.

Drury's protection of the national parks was put to its greatest test when the Bureau of Reclamation and Army Corps of Engineers discovered potential in the parks for water power, flood control, and irrigation and proposed related projects in Big Bend (Texas), Grand Canyon (Arizona), Mammoth Cave (Kentucky), and other parks. In opposing these proposed projects Drury declared: "If we are going to succeed in preserving the greatness of national parks, they must be held inviolate." He therefore expressed opposition to the Bureau of Reclamation's proposed billion-dollar Colorado River storage project in Utah, which included an Echo Park dam within the Dinosaur National Monument. His position was supported by several prominent conservationists, including Irving N. Brant, Bernard De Voto, David R. Brower, Ira N. Gabrielson, and Howard Zahniser. It was not supported, however, by the new secretary of the interior, Oscar Chapman, who forced Drury to resign as director of the National Park Service in 1951. Actually, Drury was given the choice of becoming governor of distant Samoa or a special assistant to the secretary with few duties. He preferred to resign from the Department of the Interior.

Drury returned to California and in 1951 was appointed by Governor Warren as chief of the State Division of Beaches and Parks. In this position he led efforts in establishing several new parks in desert and redwood forest areas, along beaches, and at historic sites. He retired in 1959 and returned to the position of executive secretary of the Save-the-Redwoods League, replacing Aubrey Drury, who had died after having served in the position since 1940. During the 1960's, Drury conducted the league's campaign for a redwood national park, which was successful in 1968, despite opposition from the lumber industry and differences between the league and the Sierra Club. He was president of the league from 1971 to 1975 and chairman of its board of directors from 1975 until his death in Berkeley.

Drury was known as a person of poise and high principles. He was seen as moderate in dealing with opponents but also as tenacious in defense of his fundamental belief that America's great natural, scenic, and historic areas should be preserved inviolate. Two California redwood groves, Drury Brothers Grove in Prairie Creek State Park and Newton B. Drury Grove in Humboldt Redwoods State Park, have been designated as living memorials.

[Records concerning Drury's service as chief of the California Division of Beaches and Parks and his work as executive secretary of the Save-the-Redwoods League are in the Bancroft Library, University of California at Berkeley. Records concerning his administration of the National Park Service are in the National Archives, Washington, D.C. The transcript of an oral history interview of Drury entitled *Parks and Redwoods, 1917–1971* (1972) by Amelia R. Fry and Susan R. Schrepfer is in the University of California Regional Oral History Office. A critical study of Drury's campaign for preservation of the redwood forests is Schrepfer's doctoral dissertation, "A Conservative Reform: Saving the Redwoods, 1917 to 1940" (University of California at Riverside, 1971). Obituaries are in the *New York Times*, Dec. 16, 1978; and *National Parks and Conservation Magazine*, June 1979.]

HAROLD T. PINKETT

DU BOIS, SHIRLEY LOLA GRAHAM (Nov. 11, 1904–Mar. 27, 1977), author, biographer, and composer, was born in Indianapolis, Ind., one of five children born to David A. Graham, a minister in the African Methodist Episcopal church, teacher, and the organizer of a local NAACP chapter, and Etta Bell. The family moved frequently; she attended schools in Detroit, Chicago, Nashville, and Colorado Springs, before graduating from Lewis and Clark High School in Spokane, Wash.

When Graham was thirteen years old, W. E. B. Du Bois came to Colorado Springs to deliver a speech; his stay with her family made a lasting impression on the young teenager. Influenced by his words, she wrote an article during her first year of high school that criticized the YWCA for refusing to accept her in a swimming class because of her race. Graham married Shadrack T. McCanns in 1923; they had two children before his death in 1926.

From 1927 to 1928, McCanns attended the Howard School of Music in Washington, D.C., and from 1929 to 1932 she taught music at Morgan College (now Morgan State University) in Baltimore. In 1932 she enrolled in Oberlin College, from which she received a bachelor's degree in 1934 and a master's degree in 1935. McCanns studied piano, pipe organ, and voice, as well as music history; her master's thesis was entitled "Survivals of Africanism in Modern Music." While at Oberlin she produced a musical, *Tom-Tom*, depicting the history of African Americans from the days of slavery through the Harlem Renaissance. An abridged version of her play was broadcast by NBC radio on June 26, 1932; and the complete version was performed at the Cleveland Stadium from June 29 to July 6, 1932.

In 1935, McCanns returned to teaching at Tennessee Agricultural and Industrial State college (now Tennessee State University) in Nashville, where she served as chair of the Fine Arts Department. That year she renewed her acquaintance with Du Bois when he invited her to attend a teachers' conference with him in Lexington, Ky.

In 1936, McCanns again gave up her teaching career, this time to work at the Federal Theater in Chicago as the supervisor of the African-American division. There she adapted such well-known works as *The Hairy Ape*, *The Mikado*, and *Little Black Sambo* for a black cast.

From 1938 to 1940, McCanns held a Julius Rosenwald Grant; during that time, she spent a year at the Yale School of Drama where she revised *Tom-Tom*. She also wrote and saw a number of plays produced, including *Dust to Earth*, *I Gotta Home*, *Elijah's Ravens*, *Deep Rivers*, *It's Mornin'*, and *Track Thirteen*. In 1941 she saw her play *Mississippi Rainbow* produced in Indianapolis.

The years during World War II were hectic and varied for McCanns. She worked for the USO in Arizona, then moved to New York City, where she wrote political articles and won another Rosenwald grant. In 1943 she became a field secretary for the NAACP. In 1947 she received the $6,500 Messner Award for her historical novel about Frederick Douglass, *There Once Was a Slave*. With this money she purchased a house in St. Albans, in the New York City borough of Queens.

From 1945 to 1947, McCanns held a Guggenheim Fellowship and attended classes at New York University. At this point she focused on writing biographies for young audiences, including works about Benjamin Banister, Phyllis Wheatley, Jean Baptiste Pointe de Sable, and Booker T. Washington. In 1950 her work was recognized with an award given by the National Institute of Arts and Letters.

After 1950, McCanns became increasingly interested and involved in politics, espousing Communist doctrines. She was alarmed at the conservative trend of American politics and the hysteria of the McCarthy era. This interest in politics brought her once again into close contact with W. E. B. Du Bois, who returned to work for the NAACP after being forced to retire from Atlanta University at the age of seventy-five because of his radical political views. Du Bois's wife of fifty-five years, Nina Du Bois, died early in 1950; he and McCanns were married on Feb. 14, 1951. They bought a house in Brooklyn from playwright Arthur Miller and resided there until they left the United States for Ghana in 1961. Du Bois died in Ghana in 1963, and Shirley remained there until 1967, after which she resided in Cairo, Egypt. In 1971 she published *His Day Is Marching On*, and in 1976 *A Pictorial History of* W. E. B. *Du Bois*, both tributes to her husband.

Du Bois was not allowed to return to the United States until 1971, because the State Department felt her Communist ties to be a security threat. She died in Beijing, China, where she had gone for cancer treatment.

As is often the case with the wives of famous men, Shirley Du Bois was largely identified by the public as the wife of W. E. B. Du Bois, even though by the time she married him, she had produced numerous critically acclaimed musicals, plays, and biographies. Of particular significance are her biographies of famous African Americans meant for young people. Her style is simple and straightforward, letting her readers come in contact with history in a manner sure to intrigue them and whet their appetite for more.

[The Julius Rosenwald Archives at Fisk University, Nashville, Tenn., contain materials dating from Shirley Du Bois's 1938 grant application to the end of 1946. The Black Oral History Collection in the Fisk Library includes an oral history interview with Du Bois. Two articles worth noting are Deborah Mason, "The Du Bois Legend Carries on in Cairo," *Sepia*, Jan. 1975; and Bernard Peterson, "Shirley Graham Du Bois: Composer and Playwright," *Crisis*, May 1977. An obituary is in the *New York Times*, Apr. 5, 1977.]

RENNIE SIMSON

DUFFY, FRANCIS RYAN (June 23, 1888–Aug. 16, 1979), judge, lawyer, and politician, was born in Fond du Lac, Wis., the son of Francis F. Duffy, a lawyer, and Hattie E. Ryan. Educated in the public schools of Fond du Lac, he graduated from Fond du Lac High School in 1906. He graduated from the University of Wisconsin in 1910 with a B.A. and then entered the University of Wisconsin Law School, where he earned an LL.B. in 1912.

Duffy practiced law in Fond du Lac with his father. Between 1917 and 1919 he served in the United States Army, first on the Mexican border and then as a member of the American Expeditionary Force in France. After World War I he was discharged with the rank of major, Motor Transport Corps, and returned to the practice of law in Fond du Lac.

On Jan. 26, 1918, Duffy married Louise Haydon of Springfield, Ky. They had four children, including F. Ryan Duffy, Jr., who later became a county judge in Milwaukee.

Between 1919 and 1933, Duffy became deeply involved in American Legion activities. After his election as commander of the Wisconsin Department in 1922, he served first as national vice-commander and then as a member of the national executive committee until 1925. Through his work on the American veterans' bonus legislation he developed a deep interest in national politics.

A liberal Democrat, Duffy was a strong supporter of Franklin D. Roosevelt during the Wisconsin presidential primary of April 1932. Elected as a Roosevelt delegate to the Democratic national convention in Chicago, he served as chairman of the state delegation. Duffy was elected to the United States Senate in November 1932 by defeating Republican John B. Chapple, who had made the alleged "red menace" the central theme in the campaign.

Duffy's liberal stance placed him in disagreement with the conservatives who dominated the Wisconsin Democratic party in the 1930's. His relationship with the state party became even more complicated in 1934, when the Progressive party assumed power in Wisconsin. During his subsequent senatorial career, he often cooperated in Washington with the congressional Progressives, whose liberal views frequently agreed with his own.

While in the Senate, Duffy served on several important committees, including Foreign Relations, Military Affairs, and Appropriations. He was also a member of the Patents, Interoceanic Canals, and Privileges and Elections committees. Among his primary interests were national defense issues and copyright legislation. At a time when isolationism prevailed in Wisconsin politics, he argued for substantial defense expenditures. Because of his expertise in foreign and military affairs, Duffy sometimes served in a quasi-diplomatic capacity. In 1935 he served as a member of the American economic and diplomatic mission to China, Japan, and the Philippines, and two years later he was selected as one of three senators to participate in the dedication of American battle monuments in Europe.

When Duffy ran for reelection to the Senate in 1938, his liberalism and the influence of third-party farmer-labor politics in Wisconsin combined to ensure his defeat. Although Duffy ran 150,000 votes ahead of the Democratic gubernatorial candidate, he divided the liberal vote with Progressive party candidate Herman Ekern. As a result of disunity on the left, Republican Alexander Wiley succeeded Duffy in an election that also spelled disaster for liberal Congressional and gubernatorial candidates nationwide.

Following his defeat Duffy returned to Fond du Lac, where he resumed his law practice with Russell E. Hanson. In June 1939, President Roosevelt appointed him United States district judge for the eastern district of Wisconsin in Milwaukee. In 1949, President Harry S. Truman elevated him to the United States Court of Appeals for the Seventh Circuit. Duffy's political experience led to his frequent selection to important judicial advisory committees, such as the Bankruptcy Committee of the Judicial Council of the United States and the Committee of the Judicial Conference of the United States on Judicial Retirement and Tenure. Duffy was able to use skills acquired in the Senate to advance the administration of justice and upgrade the standards of the judicial profession.

Characteristic of Duffy's conduct of the courts were the innovations he introduced as district judge. In order to conserve time and save money, he required pretrial conferences in all civil cases. Not long after taking office, he also established a probation department, a step intended to emphasize both rehabilitation and economy in the administration of justice. These measures reflected Duffy's commitment to litigants' interests, defendants' rights, and efficiency of operation.

Throughout his judicial career, Duffy remained active in civic and fraternal affairs, maintaining membership in the University of Wisconsin Alumni Association, the Wisconsin Bar Association, and the Legal Aid Society. The liberalism that had sparked his political career was evident in his commitment to free legal service for the disadvantaged long before it became an accepted practice. In 1946, Duffy became a director of the Milwaukee chapter of the Legal Aid Society of the United States, and in 1960 was elected its president. Duffy also served two terms on the board of directors of the National Legal Aid and Defender Association, starting in 1958.

Duffy retired in 1966 but continued to serve as senior circuit judge until 1978, when he left the court. He died in Milwaukee, Wis.

[F. Ryan Duffy's personal, political, and judicial papers are in the Archives and Manuscripts Division at the State Historical Society of Wisconsin in Madison. Because little has been written on Duffy's career, the papers constitute the primary reference source on his career. However, brief biographical articles appear in *Wisconsin Blue Book* (1937); Fred Holmes, ed., *Wisconsin* (1946); and *Biographical Directory of the American Congress, 1774–1989* (1989). Additional biographical sketches and an oral history by *Milwaukee Journal* reporter Richard L. Kenyon may be found in Box 1 of the Duffy Papers. Obituaries are in the *Milwaukee Journal*, Aug. 17, 1979; *Wisconsin State Journal*, Aug. 17, 1979; and the *New York Times*, Aug. 18, 1979.]

JAMES J. LORENCE

DURANTE, JAMES FRANCIS ("JIMMY") (Feb. 10, 1893–Jan. 29, 1980), comedian, was born in New York City, the son of Bartolomeo Durante, a barber, and Rosa Millino, both Italian immigrants. Raised in an impoverished neighborhood on the Lower East Side of Manhattan, he left public school at age ten to earn money as a newspaper boy, coal-wagon driver, stable hand, and photo engraver's assistant. Never a pretty child, young Jimmy resented his playmates nicknaming him "Naso," Italian for "nose." Bitter over such slights, he turned inward, becoming a sensitive and lonely boy. Later, as an entertainer, although he made his famous nose the hallmark of his humor, he scrupulously avoided poking fun at others with similar features.

Encouraged by his father to study classical piano, Durante soon discovered ragtime music, embracing its exuberant chords as a release from his personal introversion. Calling himself "Ragtime Jimmy," at age sixteen he played in the cabarets, honky tonks, and smoky dives of Coney Island, Harlem, and Chinatown. By 1917, Durante was earning $45 per week at Harlem's infamous Club Alamo. Self-effacing dialogue, mispronounced words and scrambled syntax, a raspy voice, and brilliant timing characterized the unique humor of the mature Durante. But in his early years this shy entertainer hid behind the piano, refusing to banter with his audience for fear that they might laugh at him. On June 19, 1921, Durante married Jeanne Olsen, who was a singer at Club Alamo. They had no children.

Durante first made his mark as a composer of ragtime scores, often collaborating with black musician Chris Smith and journalist Walter Winchell. While working at Club Alamo he formed a friendship with Eddie Jackson, a singing waiter, and together they opened a Manhattan speakeasy called Club Durant in 1923. Within a few weeks they added as a third partner Lou Clayton, a cabaret dancer with vague connections to the New York underworld. Prompted by Jackson and Clayton, a reticent Durante began interspersing his piano playing with humorous monologues and jokes. After Sime Silverman, editor of *Variety*, gave the antics of Durante, Clayton, and Jackson ebullient reviews, Club Durant drew an eclectic audience of businessmen, journalists, show people, politicians, artists, and gangsters who howled at the trio's zany anarchy. Performances often climaxed with Durante demolishing his piano.

Clayton recognized Durante's star potential and charted the course of his friend's career. He endowed Durante with the moniker "Schnozzola," which, together with a battered fedora, became the performer's signature. Shortly after Prohibition agents closed Club Durant, Clayton led his partners onto the Broadway stage, where for three years the Durante entourage grew in popularity. Booked at Loew's State Theatre in March 1927, they played to record audiences and weeks later drew even larger crowds into the Palace, vaudeville's premier venue. Florenz Ziegfeld signed the comedy team to play slapstick "stagehands" in his 1929 review *Show Girl*. Their buffoonery stole the show, with the great "Schnozzola" receiving the highest raves.

Hollywood producers soon recognized Durante's appeal, and in 1931 Metro-Goldwyn-Mayer signed him to a five year contract. Ever loyal to his friends, he retained Clayton as his business manager and Jackson as his personal assistant. His film *The New Adventures of Get-Rich-Quick Wallingford* (1931) brought Durante immediate popularity with millions of Americans who responded to his sidewalk humor. Unfortunately, there followed a series of low-budget pictures that little enhanced his reputation. In 1933 he returned to Broadway, starring in the successful musical comedy *Strike Me Pink*. After a three-month run he was recalled to California because of his movie contract.

Trapped by Hollywood's studio system and forced to act in mediocre films and short features, Durante dutifully fulfilled his obligations. He eventually completed twenty-nine largely forgettable movies, but in one, *Palooka*, he introduced the tune "Inka Dinka Doo," which became his trademark song. Throughout his career Durante wrote melodies that fitted his cheerful public image, including "I Ups Ta Him, and He Ups Ta Me," "I'm Jimmy, That Well-Dressed Man," "I Know Darn Well I Can Do Without Broadway (Can Broadway Do Without Me?)."

Free of his MGM obligations in 1935, Durante went to New York City to appear in Billy Rose's spectacular musical *Jumbo*, playing an unscrupulous press agent for a bankrupt circus. He left his critically acclaimed role the following year for a European tour that included two weeks at London's Palladium. Thereafter his career entered a brief eclipse. Critics complained that his humor was old-fashioned and dated, and Durante endured personal tragedies. Profoundly depressed by his father's death in 1940, he soon learned that his wife was stricken with cancer. She died in February 1943.

In the spring of that year, the Columbia Broadcasting System hired Durante to cohost a weekly radio program, and his popularity revived. Teamed with the fast-talking and popular Garry Moore, Durante found the medium well suited to his talents. No stranger to the airwaves—he first appeared on radio in 1934—he delighted listeners with his working man's responses to the sophisticated Moore. Whenever Moore corrected his diction, Durante retorted, "You teach me to say dem woids right and we're both outa a job." In 1947 the partnership ended amiably as Moore moved on to other stages.

Beginning with his 1943 radio show, Durante closed each of his performances by saying "Goodnight, Mrs. Calabash, wherever you are." Journalists speculated that it might have been a mystic message to his late wife, and he once hinted that it was a secret greeting to a long lost sweetheart of his grammar school days.

One radio performance earned Durante a footnote in legal history. Following his reading of the poem "One-Room House" by Alfred Kreymborg, its author sued the comedian and the network for copyright infringement. A federal judge eventually dismissed the suit, ruling that poems did not possess the same copyright protections as dramatic scripts.

Before Lou Clayton died in 1950 he urged Durante to enter the new medium of television. Complying with his friend's wish, the "Schnozzola" burst into American homes, finding the small screen ideal for his spontaneous clowning, singing, and butchered English. He ended his Saturday evening program at the height of its popularity in 1956, and thereafter he appeared on television once or twice each year as a guest on variety or comedy shows. He received a George Foster Peabody Award in 1951 in recognition of his public service and distinguished television achievement.

Durante married Marjorie Little on Dec. 14, 1960, and they had one daughter by adoption. He began to limit his activities to occasional club performances and charitable benefits. Durante's benefits raised millions of dollars for the Damon Runyon Foundation for Cancer Research, and he gave away much of his wealth to panhandlers and acquaintances down on their luck. In 1962 he starred in the film *Billy Rose's Jumbo*, which was based on the earlier musical. The following year he made a memorable cameo appearance in the comedy hit *Its a Mad, Mad, Mad, Mad World*. Felled by a stroke in 1972, he lingered until his death at his Santa Monica, Calif., home.

Durante's ever-smiling, merry public persona masked an intensely lonely, almost pathetic private man. He craved the company of others, insisting upon the constant attendance of his closest friends, especially Clayton, Jackson, and Jack Roth, his longtime drummer. Possessed by a compelling desire to be loved by everyone, he feared offending anyone and cleansed his material of all indecent references, especially double entendres. Identifying with the working masses, he became famous for his altruism. When teased for his easy touch, he responded: "Maybe we ain't all born equal, but it's a cinch we all die equal."

[Biographies include Gene Fowler, *Schnozzola, the Story of Jimmy Durante* (1951); William Cahn, *Good Night, Mrs. Calabash* (1963); Irene Adler, *I Remember Jimmy* (1980); and Jhan Robbins, *Inka Dinka Doo* (1991). See also Frank Capra, "Unforgettable Jimmy Durante," *Reader's Digest*, Nov. 1981. An obituary is in the *New York Times*, Jan. 30, 1980.]

FRED A. BAILEY

DU VIGNEAUD, VINCENT (May 18, 1901–Dec. 11, 1978), biochemist and Nobel laureate, was born in Chicago, the son of Alfred Joseph Du Vigneaud, an inventor and machine designer, and Mary Theresa O'Leary. He attended public schools in Chicago, graduating from Carl Schurz High School in 1918. Showing an early avid interest in science, he and his young high school friends, working in the laboratory which he set up in his basement, experimented with gunpowder, tried to grow supersized rats using glandular extracts, and investigated techniques of taxidermy with cats, the latter inquiry being frowned upon by his parents as might be expected.

Du Vigneaud entered the University of Illinois at Urbana in 1918, graduating in 1923 with a B.S. in organic chemistry. He studied biochemistry with Professors W. C. Rose and H. B. Lewis, becoming intensely interested in the field. He began his research activities as an undergraduate under the tutelage of Professor C. S. Marvel with whom he continued to study for his M.S., completed in 1924. His thesis research, which involved an attempt to synthesize a drug having the effects both of local anesthesia and pressor activity, set him on his lifelong interest in the relationship between chemical structure and biological function. In 1924 he spent six months at the Jackson Laboratories of E. I. du Pont de Nemours and Company in Wilmington, Del. On June 12 of that year he married Zella Zon Ford; they had two children.

From 1924 to 1925, Du Vigneaud was an assistant biochemist at Philadelphia General Hospital, where he was exposed to the clinical side of biochemistry, and at the Graduate School of Medicine of the University of Pennsylvania, where he worked with W. G. Karr. He was invited by John R. Murlin in 1925 to join his endocrinology and metabolism department at the newly opened University of Rochester School of Medicine, which stressed the importance of the physiological approach to medical research. Du Vigneaud's doctoral research demonstrated that the amino acid cystine was the source for the disulfide in insulin. He received the Ph.D. from the University of Rochester in 1927. From 1927 to 1929 he received a number of postdoctoral fellowships: at the Johns Hopkins School of Medicine (National Research Council Fellowship) with John Jacob Abel of the Department of Pharmacology, focusing on the study of insulin (1927); the Kaiser Wilhelm Institute, Dresden, Germany, with Max Bergmann (the most renowned of Emil Fischer's students), pursuing research on peptides and amino acids, particularly the amino acids cysteine and cystine from which the sulfur of insulin is derived (1928); the University of Edinburgh Medical School with George Barger (1928); and University College, London, with Sir Charles Robert Harington (also in 1928). Du Vigneaud's early research set the course for his subsequent pathbreaking work on sulfur-containing compounds, particularly biotin, penicillin, and the hormones oxytocin and vasopressin.

Upon returning to the United States in 1929, Du Vigneaud joined the physiological chemistry faculty at the University of Illinois where W. C. Rose was serving as departmental chairman. Granted exceptional professional latitude in his assignment, he taught biochemistry, directed graduate studies, and carried on his research. An offer came in 1932 from George Washington University School of Medicine to serve as a full professor in biochemistry and chairman of the department. He eagerly accepted the post, which afforded him the opportunity to organize the teaching program as well as a long-range research program on the chemistry and metabolism of sulfur compounds, on insulin, and on posterior pituitary hormones. In 1938 he was made professor and head of the biochemistry department at Cornell Medical College in New York City. The *New York Times* characterized his oversight of the department during the next three decades as producing "some of the most important discoveries in biochemistry in this century." In collaboration with Donald Melville and Klaus Hofmann at Cornell and a team of researchers at Western Reserve University School of Medicine led by Paul Gyorgy, Du Vigneaud discovered in 1940 that both vitamin H and coenzyme R were identical to the vitamin biotin. Under his direction a new technique was developed for isolating this very scarce substance from liver, which was known to be rich in vitamin H. After continuing the research, on Oct. 9, 1942, his group reported the structure of biotin. On Nov. 8, 1946, Du Vigneaud and his colleagues announced their production of a synthetic penicillin (penicillin G). This monumental achievement rendered unnecessary reliance on the tedious, living-mold process for producing penicillin and made possible the synthesis of other analogues of penicillin. These synthetic drugs offered an alternative to individuals allergic to natural penicillin and provided a means to combat bacteria resistant to the natural product.

In 1950, Du Vigneaud delivered the Messenger lectures at Cornell University, which were subsequently published in book form in 1952 as *A Trail of Research in Sulfur Chemistry and Metabolism and Related Fields.* In October 1953 he reported the successful synthesis of oxytocin. The hormone, produced by the posterior pituitary gland, is responsible for uterine contractions at childbirth and for the stimulation of mother's milk. The landmark accomplishment was the first synthesis of a polypeptide hormone (composed of two or more amino acids). Du Vigneaud's laboratory also achieved the isolation and synthesis of vasopressin, an antidiuretic hormone likewise secreted by the posterior pituitary gland. The test-tube forms of oxytocin and vasopressin were shown to be as effective as their natural counterparts, and various analogues of both hormones were also synthesized. Du Vigneaud received the Nobel Prize for Chemistry in 1955 for his synthesis of oxytocin and work on biochemically important sulfur compounds.

In 1967, Du Vigneaud relinquished his post at Cornell Medical School but remained active as a professor of chemistry at Cornell University in Ithaca, N.Y., until 1975. Du Vigneaud was a distinguished visiting lecturer at many universities throughout the world and served as a trustee of the Rockefeller Institute for Medical Research (now Rockefeller University). Among his many honors, in addition to the Nobel Prize, were the Hildebrand Award of the Washington Chemical Society (1936); the Lasker Award of the American Public Health Association (1948); the Passano Foundation Award (1955); and the Columbia University Chandler Medal for outstanding scientific research (1955). He was a fellow of the American Academy of Arts and Sciences and served at different times as president of the Harvey Society and of the American Society of Biological Chemistry, and as chair of the Federation of the American Societies of Experimental Biology. From 1958 to 1960 he was chair of the biochemistry section of the National Academy of Sciences. He died in White Plains, N.Y.

Beyond his own world-class achievements in biochemistry, Du Vigneaud mentored many students and researchers who went on to make outstanding contributions in their own right. Described as a rather tall man, with sparse gray hair, and a trim moustache, Du Vigneaud championed close cooperation in biochemical research between scientists and clinicians. He believed that the research chemist was best able to contribute to difficult biochemical challenges, such as the synthesis of penicillin, when permitted to engage in fundamental, pioneering research. In essence, Du Vigneaud was characterizing the kind of unfettered research environment that had allowed him to utilize best his own prodigious talents.

[Du Vigneaud's papers are held at the Cornell University Medical School, New York City. See also "The Lasker Awards of 1948," *American Journal of Public Health* 38 (1948); and Tyler Wasson, ed., *Nobel Prize Winners* (1987). An obituary is in the *New York Times*, Dec. 12, 1978.]

LESLIE S. JACOBSON

E

EAMES, CHARLES ORMAND, JR. (June 17, 1907–Aug. 21, 1978), designer, architect, and filmmaker, was born in St. Louis, Mo., the son of Charles Ormand Eames, a Pinkerton security officer and amateur photographer, and Marie Celine Adele Pauline Lambert. The family resided briefly in Buffalo and Brooklyn, N.Y., before returning to St. Louis, where Charles entered elementary school. While in elementary school, he worked part-time for a printing shop, a grocer, and a druggist. His father died in 1919. The following year Eames found his father's photographic materials and experimented with wet-plate printing.

Eames attended Yeatman High School in St. Louis, where he served as senior class president and captain of the football team; he also worked weekends and summers for a steel company. After graduation in 1925 he had a summer job with a lighting fixture company and then entered Washington University, where he studied architecture with the aid of a scholarship. He remained in college until 1928, combining his studies with part-time and summer work for the architectural firm Trueblood and Graf.

Eames married Catherine Dewey Woermann, a fellow architectural student, in 1929. They had one child and were divorced in May 1941. Their honeymoon trip took them to Europe, where they became aware of the work of early modern architects and designers, including Walter Gropius, Ludwig Mies van der Rohe, and Le Corbusier.

Eames helped to form the architectural firm of Gray and Eames (later Gray, Eames, and Pauley) in St. Louis in 1930. In 1933, Eames designed sets for the St. Louis Municipal Opera outdoor theater, and he remained active with the firm until 1934, designing domestic and religious structures. After spending eight months in Mexico, Eames returned to St. Louis in 1935 and opened a new architectural firm, Eames and Walsh. The firm designed residences and churches, among them St. Mary's Church in Helena, Ark., for which it also designed vessels, lighting fixtures, and vestments. The church came to the attention of Eliel Saarinen, the Finnish-born architect and director of the Cranbook Academy of Art in Michigan, who would later advise Eames and Walsh on the design of the Meyer house (1936–1938) at Huntleigh, west of St. Louis. It had furniture and stained glass designed by Eames, as well as draperies and carpets woven by Loja Saarinen and sculpture by Carl Milles. The design of the Meyer house illustrates key elements of the early development, and, later, the professional practice of Eames. His success was in large measure brought about by his ability to benefit from mentoring by seasoned professionals and by his ability to work well in collaboration.

In the autumn of 1938, with the aid of a fellowship, Eames began studies in architecture and design at Cranbrook. In 1940, Eames joined the faculty to teach design, and he began working for Saarinen's architectural firm. While at Cranbrook, Eames assisted Carl Milles in his St. Louis commission for a fountain with symbolic figures, *Meeting of the Waters*, completed in 1940. The chief contribution of Eames was the design for the basin. In 1939, in collaboration with Saarinen's son Eero, Eames designed the installation of the faculty exhibition in Cranbrook Pavilion. On visits to Chicago, Eames conferred with Laszlo Moholy-Nagy, director of the School of Design in Chicago.

Eames next collaborated with Eero Saarinen

Eames

on winning designs for the competition Organic Design in Home Furnishings, announced in 1940 by the Museum of Modern Art in New York, including three plywood chairs molded into complex curves by laminating thin layers of veneers and glue. They were assisted in preparing their entries by three Cranbrook students, Harry Bertoia, Don Albinson, and Ray Kaiser. Although the winning designs were supposed to have been put into production and sold by a network of cooperating department stores, World War II prevented any immediate attempt at mass production. Nevertheless, prototypes of the designs, produced at great expense, were part of an exhibition (organized by the Museum of Modern Art and the Modern Art Society of Cincinnati) that toured American museums in 1941 and 1942.

Eames married Ray Kaiser on June 20, 1941; the couple had met at Cranbrook and soon after their wedding moved to Los Angeles, where they began a working partnership that lasted until the death of Charles. They had no children. While in California, Charles worked on movie sets for Metro-Goldwyn-Mayer until the summer of 1942. Meanwhile, he and his wife continued to experiment with plywood. With the help of John Entenza, Gregory Ain, and Griswald Raetze, they began to develop molded-plywood leg splints and stretchers for the United States Navy.

In July 1943 the Eames workshop, with a staff of more than twenty, became the Molded Plywood Division of Detroit-based Evans Products Company. Later that year Molded Plywood moved into a converted garage in Venice, Calif., and expanded production to include plywood parts for aircraft. At the end of the war the Eameses began to produce molded plywood furniture.

In March 1946 the Museum of Modern Art opened an exhibition of the furniture of Eames. In summer, production began on chairs developed from those shown in March, including a dining chair with back and seat units of plywood, bent into compound curves, attached by shock mounts to a leg-and-spine unit of bent slender metal rods. In 1949 the chairs began to be manufactured by the Herman Miller Furniture Company of Zeeland, Mich. This chair has become a classic; probably more of them are in museum collections worldwide than any other item. The Eameses continued to carry out commissions for Herman Miller, creating graphic designs for advertisements and catalogues, showroom interiors, and a range of furniture, as well as films. Highlights were a 1950 molded fiberglass armchair with metal legs and a 1956 leather-covered plywood lounge chair with a metal swivel base and a related ottoman. Charles Eames and Kenneth Acker designed a Los Angeles showroom building for Herman Miller in 1949; the interior was redesigned periodically, in collaboration with George Nelson or Alexander Girard.

The finest achievement of Eames as an architect is the house and studio in Pacific Palisades, Calif., in which he and Ray lived and worked. Its design began (with Eero Saarinen) in 1945 as a case-study house for *Arts and Architecture* magazine. The design was radically altered with the assistance of Acker, and the house and studio were constructed in 1949, utilizing the prefabricated parts originally ordered for the 1945 design. The result was exposed metal frames, glass walls alternating with solid panels, dramatic touches of color, and open, light-flooded interiors looking out on trees and other plants on the site. The straight lines and right angles of the living areas were softened by furniture and plants and displays of antique toys and artifacts.

The Eames firm continued to use the converted garage in Venice, with a staff at times numbering as many as seventy-five people. The firm designed a number of creative toys for Tigrett Enterprises of Jackson, Tenn., from 1951 to 1961; some were sold through Sears, Roebuck and Company catalogues. The best known of the toys, "House of Cards," was later reissued by other firms. Films and exhibitions increasingly became a major part of the office's work. *Glimpses of USA*, for the American National Exhibition in Moscow in 1959, was a film presentation on seven large screens depicting the everyday lives of a cross section of Americans. A series of exhibitions commissioned by International Business Machines included *Mathematica* (1961) for the California Museum of Science and Industry in Los Angeles and *A Computer Perspective* (1971) for the IBM Exhibit Center in New York City. The most complex exhibition undertaken by the Eames office was *The World of Franklin and Jefferson*, which was shown in Europe, the United States, and Mexico from 1975 to 1977.

Other films included *A Computer Perspective* (related to the exhibition), *Powers of Ten* (1968;

new version 1977), *Toccata for Toy Trains* (1957), with music by Elmer Bernstein, and *Tops* (1969).

Charles and Ray Eames developed a close relationship with India; in 1957 they were invited by the national government to investigate design opportunities presented by the possible interrelationship of Western design and technology and India's traditional culture. This invitation led to *The Eames Report* (1958), which has become a classic of its kind: sensitive and informed advice, practical and without condescension, for a developing country. Their work led to the establishment of the National Institute of Design in Ahmadabad in 1961. In 1965 the Eameses used the NID as a working base to set up a Jawaharlal Nehru memorial exhibition, *Jawaharlal Nehru: His Life and Times,* that opened in New York City and was later seen on four continents.

Significant recognition came with the first Kaufmann International Design Award, given jointly to Charles and Ray Eames in New York City in 1960. Charles Eames delivered a series of six Charles Eliot Norton lectures at Harvard University in 1970 and 1971, an honor he considered a high point of his career. He died in St. Louis while serving as a consultant for a new project at the Missouri Botanical Gardens.

[The Eames Archive in the Library of Congress in Washington, D.C., has about 2,000 design drawings; 750,000 photographic prints, negatives, and transparencies; and numerous manuscripts. It is expected to add about ninety films, ranging in length from one to thirty minutes. The Vitra Design Museum in Weil am Rhein, Germany, has numerous examples of experimental objects and prototypes. The best source of information is John Neuhart, Marilyn Neuhart, and Ray Eames, *Eames Design; the Work of the Office of Charles and Ray Eames* (1989). See also Peter Smithson and Alison Smithson, "An Eames Celebration," *Architectural Design*, Sept. 1966; Luciano Rubino, *Ray & Charles Eames* (1981); Robert Judson Clark et al., *Design in America: the Cranbrook Vision, 1923–1950* (1983); Elizabeth Lidén, *Between Water and Heaven; Carl Milles: Search for American Commissions* (1986); and Rose DeNeve, "Creative Destruction: India's Search for Design Identity," *Print*, Sept./Oct. 1988.

Charles Eames was coauthor of *A Computer Perspective* (1973; new edition, 1990), with Ray Eames and the Eames office; *The World of Franklin & Jefferson* (1976), with Ray Eames, Jehane Burns, Barbara Diamond, and Jeannine Oppewall; and "The Eames Report, April, 1958," *Design Issues; History, Theory, Criticism*, Spring 1991, with Ray Eames. An obituary is in the *Los Angeles Times*, Aug. 23, 1978. For audiovisual materials, see *An Eames Celebration, The Films of Charles and Ray Eames* (1989–1993); and *901; After 45 Years of Working* (1990).]

LLOYD C. ENGELBRECHT

EASTER, LUSCIOUS LUKE (Aug. 4, 1915–Mar. 29, 1979), baseball player, was born in Jonestown, Miss., the son of James Easter, a farmer, and Maude Williams. In 1922, Easter's mother died and in 1924 his father sold his farm and moved the family to St. Louis, Mo., where he remarried and worked as a shoveler in a glass factory.

Of African-American ancestry, Easter dropped out of Vashon High School in St. Louis in the ninth grade to work in a dry-cleaning store. He played semiprofessional baseball in the 1930's for the St. Louis Titanium Giants, a team sponsored by the National Lead Company, while working on the Titanium plant's rigging crew.

In 1941, Easter suffered a broken ankle in an automobile accident, which delayed his induction into the military. He served in the United States Army at Fort Leonard Wood, Mo., between 1942 and 1944 and received a medical discharge because of ankle problems. He then worked for a time in a Portland, Oreg., shipyard before returning to St. Louis in the spring of 1945. Easter tried out unsuccessfully with Negro League baseball teams but was spotted playing in a Chicago industrial league and was offered a contract to play with a barnstorming baseball team. A big, powerful man (at six feet, four inches tall and 235 pounds), Easter rapidly acquired a reputation for long-ball hitting. He was noticed and signed by sporting impresario Abe Saperstein, who ran the Cincinnati Crescents, which was affiliated with the Negro League. With the Crescents, Easter amassed impressive batting statistics capped by a 1946–1947 exhibition series in Hawaii in which he hit twelve home runs in nineteen games.

Easter's hitting gained the attention of the Washington-Homestead Grays, the premier Negro League team. In the spring of 1947 the Grays acquired his contract and paid him $700 per month. Playing first base and in the outfield for the Grays in 1947 and 1948, Easter became one of the league's leading sluggers. He continued his long-ball heroics while playing in Venezuela and Puerto Rico in the winters of 1947–1948 and 1948–1949.

Easter's growing repute prompted the owner of the Cleveland Indians, Bill Veeck, to make a special trip to Puerto Rico to scout him. Veeck purchased Easter's contract for a reported $5,000 in 1949 and sent him to San Diego in the Pacific Coast League, where he became the league's most feared slugger and greatest drawing card, hitting long home runs and displaying surprising speed and defensive ability around first base. At the time, Easter claimed his age was twenty-seven, although in reality he was thirty-three years old.

Easter injured his knee in a spring-training collision and later suffered a broken kneecap after being hit by a pitch, but he continued playing despite increasing pain. In less than half a season with San Diego, before going to Cleveland for knee surgery, he hit .363 with 25 home runs and 92 runs batted in as attendance figures soared. After surgery he was sidelined for six weeks, his weight ballooned to 256 pounds, and he hit poorly in limited appearances with Cleveland late in the season.

In 1950, after a slow start, Easter hit .280 with 28 home runs and 107 runs batted in. That included a 477-foot home run, the longest ever hit in Cleveland's Municipal Stadium. In 1951, Easter suffered a torn elbow muscle and torn knee cartilage, yet he still hit .270 with 27 home runs and 103 runs batted in.

Easter underwent another knee operation in the winter of 1951–1952. An accumulation of injuries and vision and sinus problems plagued him early in 1952. After a terrible start, he was sent to the Indianapolis farm team in late June. Recalled by Cleveland after two weeks, he finished the season with 31 home runs, 97 runs batted in, and a .263 average. He was named the *Sporting News* American League player of the year.

In 1953, Easter signed a $20,000 contract, his highest ever. Early in the season he was hit by a pitch, suffering a broken foot that sidelined him for over two months. The next year he was sent to Ottawa in the International League and was generally considered to be finished as a player. Yet he played in the minor leagues until 1964 with Ottawa, San Diego, Charleston, and, most memorably, with Buffalo (1956–1959) and Rochester (1959–1964), becoming a fan favorite and hitting 113 home runs in a three-year span (1956–1958). After struggling early in the 1959 season, he was released on May 14 and signed a few days later by Rochester as player-coach. As in Buffalo, Easter became one of the most popular players in franchise history. He retired in 1965.

Easter was married three times and had four children. One of his first two wives was Mildred Squires, whom he married on Mar. 19, 1948. He married his third wife, Virgil Love, on Dec. 10, 1950. They had three children. After retiring, Easter returned to Cleveland and worked as a metal polisher at a plant that manufactured aircraft components. Earlier business ventures operating a hotel restaurant and a sausage company had been unsuccessful. Easter became the chief steward with the Aircraft Workers Alliance Union and established a reputation for honesty and sincerity in dealings with fellow workers and management. He returned to baseball briefly in 1969 as a coach with the Cleveland Indians to qualify for a major league baseball pension.

Easter often cashed employee paychecks as personal favors. On the morning of Mar. 29, 1979, he left the Cleveland Trust branch in suburban Euclid with over $40,000 in cash. He was approached by two armed men and shot and killed by a single shotgun blast.

A gregarious, warm-hearted man, Easter was one of the most popular players in baseball and one of its greatest drawing cards. He took the time to assist younger players, to sign autographs and talk to fans long after the game, to appear before adult and youth groups, and to make friends for the franchise. He was a community fixture in Cleveland, actively involved in civic causes and worker-management relations within his union responsibilities. More than one thousand people, including the mayor of Cleveland, attended his funeral.

[A clippings file on Easter is in the National Baseball Hall of Fame, Cooperstown, N.Y. Major league statistics are in *The Baseball Encyclopedia*, 9th ed. (1993). Minor league statistics are in *Minor League Baseball Stars*, vol. 2 (1985). Two articles by Daniel J. Cattau clarify many biographical details about Easter's early life: "So Maybe There Really Is Such a Thing as 'The Natural,' " *Smithsonian*, July 1991; and "Luke Easter—The First Black Major Leaguer From St. Louis," *St. Louis Post-Dispatch Magazine*, Apr. 5, 1992. See also A. S. ("Doc") Young, *Great Negro Baseball Stars* (1953); and Joseph M. Overfield, "Easter Captivated Buffalo Fans," *Baseball Research Journal* 13 (1984).

Obituaries and tributes are in the *New York Times*, Mar. 30, 1979; the *Cleveland Plain Dealer*, Mar. 30, 1979, Apr. 1, 1979, and Apr. 4, 1979; and *Sporting News*, Apr. 14, 1979.]

EDWARD J. TASSINARI

EATON, CYRUS STEPHEN (Dec. 27, 1883–May 9, 1979), industrialist, was born in Pugwash, Nova Scotia, Canada, the son of Joseph H. Eaton and Mary McPherson. His father owned three farms and ran a general store in Pugwash. Eaton was schooled in Canada at Amherst Academy, Woodstock College, and McMaster University. Before enrolling at McMaster in preparation for the Baptist ministry, Eaton visited his uncle, the Reverend Charles A. Eaton, in Cleveland. In the summer of 1901, Charles Eaton introduced young Cyrus to Mr. and Mrs. John D. Rockefeller, Sr., who were members of his congregation. Rockefeller soon hired Cyrus as a messenger in the telegraph room at his mansion.

Eaton came to Cleveland from McMaster every summer to work for Rockefeller's Cleveland Gas Company. After Eaton earned his B.A. in philosophy in 1905, Rockefeller wanted to hire him full time. Instead, Eaton spent two years as a cowboy in western Canada and as a lay minister before he finally returned to work for Rockefeller in 1907. That December, Eaton married Margaret House; they had seven children and were divorced in 1934.

Eaton's initial assignment for Rockefeller was in Manitoba, where he negotiated franchises for a natural-gas and electricity network. When the Rockefellers backed out of this venture during the Panic of 1907, Eaton constructed the power plants in Canada with the financial assistance of Lord Beaverbrook, a Canadian financier. These became the nucleus of the Continental Gas and Electric Company, which by the mid-1920's was the third-largest public utility corporation in North America. He earned his first \$2 million at Continental Gas, which had properties on both sides of the U.S.-Canadian border.

In 1912, Eaton moved his growing family to his 850-acre estate, Acadia Farms, outside Cleveland. He became a naturalized American citizen in 1913. Three years later he joined the Otis and Company investment bank as a partner. It was through Otis that he would multiply his wealth with shrewd investments in rubber, iron, coal, and steel.

An early example of Eaton's entrepreneurial skill was his flamboyant gesture to the directors of the troubled Trumbull Steel Company of Warren, Ohio, in 1925. Eaton presented the astonished businessmen, who at the time were unaware of the scope of his wealth, with a personal check for \$18 million and assumed control of the company. The following year he launched Continental Shares Incorporated, which purchased undervalued steel and rubber companies. In 1930, Eaton consolidated his steel holdings into the Republic Steel Company, the nation's third-largest steel producer.

Although Eaton lost \$100 million in the Wall Street crash of 1929, unlike many of his colleagues, he was not left completely destitute. A maverick financier, he opposed the J. P. Morgan Company's control of investment banking in the railroad industry during this era. In the 1930's, Eaton and the Van Swearingen brothers of Cleveland were successful in opening up railroad investment banking to competitive bidding, thus breaking the Morgan monopoly. Later in the decade, Eaton also helped found the Sherwin-Williams Paint Company.

He made his second fortune early in World War II. At the Steep Rock Iron Mines in Quebec, he drained a lake of 121 billion gallons of water to access a rich iron lode beneath. The wartime demand for this iron helped propel Eaton to the head of a business empire valued in the billions. The industrialist was assisted further by John L. Lewis, the president of the United Mineworkers Union (UMW). Lewis invested union pension funds in Eaton's businesses in 1942 in return for unionization at iron and coal mines Eaton acquired in Kentucky and Ohio. This arrangement eventually led to a congressional investigation when a UMW-funded mine failed and lawmakers learned Eaton had enjoyed interest-free use of union money.

In 1943, with the help of railroad magnate Robert R. Young, Eaton bought a major portion of the Chesapeake and Ohio Railway, the country's largest bituminous coal transporter. In 1954 he became chairman of the board of the Chesapeake and Ohio, which acquired the Baltimore and Ohio in 1963. Eaton chaired the firm until 1973, when it became the Chessie System, and continued as a director until 1978. Throughout his career he served on the boards of dozens of companies and was a trustee of many institutions, including Denison University and the University of Chicago.

Eaton personally knew every American president from Theodore Roosevelt to Jimmy Carter. A staunch Republican until the early 1930's, he became a Democrat and supported Franklin D. Roosevelt in the 1932 presidential campaign. He believed Roosevelt best able to redress the economic crisis of the Great Depression and save America's capitalist system. With the onset of the atomic age, Eaton's interest in international affairs grew. In the mid-1950's, he became an early proponent of improved relations with the Soviet Union. He sponsored a meeting of nuclear scientists from both the Western and Communist blocs at his summer home in Nova Scotia in 1955. The gathering evolved into the annual Pugwash Conference, named for its original site, which brings together scientists, scholars, and intellectuals from all over the world for discussions.

Eaton sometimes found himself embroiled in controversy. When he criticized the Federal Bureau of Investigation during a television interview in 1958, the tycoon was threatened with a subpoena from the House Committee on Un-American Activities. In 1960 he became one of the few Americans to receive the Soviet Union's Lenin Peace Prize. Much of the impetus for Eaton's Soviet interests had come from his second wife, Anne Kinder Jones, whom he married in December 1957. Despite suffering from poliomyelitis, Anne Eaton abounded with energy. She learned Russian in order to assist her husband with his dealings with the Soviets, and she accompanied him on his many trips abroad. Between 1956 and 1965, Cyrus Eaton met Communist leaders including János Kádár of Hungary, and Nikita Khrushchev, Anastas Mikoyan, and Alexei Kosygin of the Soviet Union. The industrialist advocated increased trade with the USSR as the best way to improve relations between America and the Communist bloc. Many of his critics considered Eaton a tool of the Soviets because he promoted increased contacts with Moscow and nuclear disarmament. However, Eaton's main goal was business. Washington's barriers to trade with Moscow limited his efforts, and his chief export to the Soviet Union was cattle-breeding stock.

In 1965, Eaton urged President Lyndon B. Johnson to stop the bombing of North Vietnam, suggesting that otherwise Communist China and the Soviet Union would jointly attack the United States. In 1969, at the height of the Vietnam War, he and his wife traveled to Hanoi to meet North Vietnamese Premier Pham Van Dong. Eaton strongly endorsed United States–Soviet détente in the early 1970's and continued to press for normalized relations with China and Cuba.

Besides his business and political interests, the soft-spoken, nattily attired Eaton was also an avid reader of philosophy, history, and poetry. Until very late in life he skied, played ice hockey and tennis, and took long walks on his estates in Ohio and Nova Scotia. He also raised Scottish shorthorn cattle and quarter horses. He served as a trustee of the University of Chicago, Denison University in Ohio, and the Harry S. Truman Library. He was also a lifetime trustee of the Cleveland Museum of Natural History.

Eaton died at Acadia Farms in Northfield, Ohio, leaving a personal fortune estimated at $200 million.

[Eaton's papers are held at the Western Reserve Historical Society in Cleveland, Ohio. See also Julius Griffin, "Commentary: Country Catches Up with Area Capitalist, Cyrus Eaton," in the Willoughby (Ohio) *News-Herald*, Sept. 16, 1991; and the entry on Eaton in the *Encyclopedia of Cleveland History* (1987). Obituaries are in the *New York Times* and the *Washington Post*, both May 11, 1979.]

KATHERINE A. S. SIEGEL

ECCLES, MARRINER STODDARD (Sept. 9, 1890–Dec. 18, 1977), banker, industrialist, and chairman of the Board of Governors of the Federal Reserve System, was born in Logan, Utah, the oldest of nine children of David Eccles and Ellen Stoddard. His father, a Scottish immigrant, made a fortune in the northwest lumber business and founded fifty-four banking and industrial enterprises in Oregon, Idaho, and Utah.

As a youth, Marriner worked in his father's railroads, lumber mills, and banks. He graduated from the high school level of Brigham Young College in Logan in 1909 and then served a proselytizing mission for the Mormon Church in Scotland. There he met May Campbell ("Maisie") Young, who married Marriner in July 1913. They had four children.

Upon the death of his father in 1912, Marriner assumed control of several of his father's business enterprises, formed the Eccles Investment Company, a family holding company, and managed Ogden First National Bank, Ogden Savings Bank, Utah Construction Company,

Amalgamated Sugar Company, Mountain States Implement Company, Sego Milk Products Company, the Eccles Hotel, and two lumber companies. In 1925 he joined with the Browning family of Ogden to form the Eccles-Browning Affiliated Banks and acquired several western country banks. On June 15, 1928, he and his brother George Eccles, Marriner Browning, and E. G. Bennett of Idaho Falls organized the First Security Corporation, the first multibank holding company in the United States.

During the early years of the Great Depression, faced with bank ruins and failing businesses, Eccles realized the need for a compensatory federal fiscal and monetary policy that would permit enhanced creation of credit (through lower interest rates and relaxed reserve requirements for banks) in depressed years and tighter controls in inflationary times. His talks to banking and business groups on this theme led to an invitation to testify before the Senate Finance Committee. He advocated federal deficit financing to take care of the destitute, to finance public works programs, and to refinance farm mortgages, and he suggested national economic planning.

Eccles helped write the Emergency Banking Act of 1933 and the Federal Deposit Insurance Corporation. Appointed assistant secretary of the Treasury in February 1934, he helped inaugurate the Federal Housing Act and revisions in the operation of the Federal Reserve banks. Eccles was nominated to the governorship of the Federal Reserve System and was approved by the Senate in February 1935. In 1936 he was appointed chairman of the Board of Governors of the revamped Federal Reserve System. He was reappointed to the board in 1944.

In 1935 the stock market started a year-long climb and Secretary of the Treasury Henry Morgenthau, Jr., responding to "sound money" advocates, advocated a return to a balanced budget. Eccles, however, saw no reason to retrench. Unemployment was still high, the nation's industrial capacity was still underutilized, and the carrying charges on the debt were less than 1 percent of the national income. During the recession of 1937–1938, a major economic downturn, Eccles persuaded President Franklin D. Roosevelt to embark on a deliberate policy of increased public spending. Programs of public construction, social welfare, cultural development, and military preparedness were expanded. A slow recovery followed.

During World War II, Eccles was a principal adviser to President Roosevelt on economic programs. He was an active participant in the Bretton Woods Conference that worked out the agreements creating the World Bank and the International Monetary Fund. He was also the leading spokesman in obtaining approval for the $3.5 billion loan to Great Britain in 1946. Similarly, he was a strong advocate of the Marshall Plan of 1948–1949, which helped to rebuild war-torn Europe.

After the war Eccles argued without much success for an anti-inflationary fiscal and monetary policy. When President Harry Truman failed to reappoint him as chairman of the Board of Governors in 1948, he remained on the board as vice-chairman and spoke out strongly against administration measures he regarded as fiscally harmful. Under his influence the Federal Reserve was able to free itself from domination by the Treasury in 1951. Eccles retired from the board the same year.

In 1950, Eccles was divorced from Maisie. He then married Sara (Sallie) Maddison Glassie, a socially prominent Washington, D.C., resident, on Dec. 29, 1951. Back in Utah and San Francisco, Eccles resumed active participation in the family's businesses, serving as chairman of the board of First Security Corporation, Amalgamated Sugar Company, and Utah Construction Company (then based in San Francisco). As the nation's monetary inflation continued and minerals became more valuable, Eccles directed Utah Construction into purchasing and working minerals. Operating worldwide, the company made substantial profits, as did other companies in which Eccles was involved. Utah Construction and Mining became Utah International in 1971 and merged with General Electric Corporation in 1976 in the largest corporate merger in United States history to that time.

In the 1960's, Eccles became active in speaking and writing about overpopulation, the Vietnam War (which he vigorously opposed), and the necessity of American recognition of the People's Republic of China. He served on the board of the American Assembly sponsored by Columbia University, founded the Marriner S. Eccles Library of Political Economy and the Marriner S. Eccles Graduate Fellowship in Political Economy at the University of Utah, and created the Marriner S. Eccles Foundation, which funded various cultural, scientific, and educational organizations, particularly in Utah.

In 1973 he established the Marriner S. Eccles Professorship of Public and Private Management at the Stanford University School of Business.

Eccles died in Salt Lake City. In 1982 the Federal Reserve Building in Washington, D.C., was named in his honor.

[The Marriner S. Eccles papers are in the Eccles Room at the Marriott Library, University of Utah, Salt Lake City. His memoirs are in Sidney Hyman, ed., *Beckoning Frontiers* (1951). Many speeches and articles are in Rudolph L. Weissman, ed., *Economic Balance and a Balanced Budget* (1940).

Biographies include Sidney Hyman, *Marriner S. Eccles* (1976); Jonathan Hughes, *The Vital Few* (1986); and Leonard J. Arrington, "Marriner S. Eccles," in Larry Schweikart, ed., *Encyclopedia of American Business History and Biography: Banking and Finance, 1913–1989* (1990). See also Arch O. Egbert, "Marriner S. Eccles and the Banking Act of 1935" (Ph.D. diss., Brigham Young Univ., 1967); Herbert Stein, *The Fiscal Revolution in America* (1969); "Sources of Marriner S. Eccles's Economic Thought," *Journal of Mormon History* 3 (1976), and *From New Deal to New Economics* (1981); and Sidney Hyman, *Challenge and Response* (1978). An obituary is in the *New York Times*, Dec. 20, 1977.]

LEONARD J. ARRINGTON

EGLEVSKY, ANDRÉ YEVGENYEVICH (Dec. 21, 1917–Dec. 4, 1977), ballet dancer, was born in Moscow, Russia, the son of Yevgeny Eglevsky, a colonel in the White Russian army, and Zoe Obranov. During the Russian Revolution, Mrs. Eglevsky and her two children fled to Constantinople, and then to Sofia, Bulgaria, where André developed a lung disease, necessitating the removal of a rib. Warned that her son would not survive the cold Balkan climate, Mrs. Eglevsky finally settled her family near Nice, France.

In order to strengthen the eight-year-old boy, André's mother had him take ballet lessons in Nice with Maria Nevelska, a graduate of the Imperial Ballet of the Bolshoi Theatre in Moscow, who claimed to have recognized her young pupil's promise after the first week. Nevelska later arranged for Eglevsky to audition with Michel Fokine, the choreographer for Diaghilev's Ballet Russe. Fokine was impressed with the boy, who was encouraged to study in Paris with other renowned dancers from the Imperial Ballet, including Lubov Egorova, Mathilde Kchessinska, and Alexandre Volinine. What academic schooling Eglevsky received was arranged around these lessons.

In 1931, while visiting Egorova's studio, Leonide Massine, a former member of the Diaghilev Ballet, saw the fourteen-year-old Eglevsky dance. Massine's choreographies dominated the repertoire of Colonel de Basil's Ballet Russe de Monte Carlo, and Massine was so impressed that he arranged for Eglevsky to make his professional dance debut as a member of its corps. In six months he was dancing lead roles for the company.

In 1933, Eglevsky went to London with the Ballet Russe, where he, Massine, and Alexandra Danilova, also a member of the troupe and his first famous partner, studied with Nicolas Legat, a former director of the Imperial Ballet. In *Heritage of a Ballet Master*, Eglevsky noted that his work had so improved under Legat's system that he left the Ballet Russe in 1935 to continue studying with the master.

Eglevsky performed with several dance companies in short engagements before joining Fokine, now directing the René Blum-Michel Fokine Ballet Russe de Monte Carlo in London, in 1936. He danced the lead parts in various Fokine ballets, such as *Les Sylphides*, *Prince Igor*, and *La Spectre de la Rose*, and created the roles of Leader of the Jesters and Leader of the Demons in his *Don Juan*.

In 1937, Eglevsky returned with Massine to the United States, where he had toured with the Ballet Russe in 1934. He became a permanent resident there and an American citizen in 1939. He soon left the Massine troupe to dance with the American Ballet, where he met his future wife, ballerina Leda Anchutina, whom he married in 1938 when he was appearing in *Great Lady*, a Radio City Music Hall musical comedy. The Eglevskys had three children, and their daughter, Marina, also became a dancer.

Eglevsky was in great demand as soloist and virtuoso, and he was especially famous for his pirouette turns, his beats, and his suspended leaps. He performed often for the Ballet Theatre, now the American Ballet Theatre, creating such roles as Paris in *Helen of Troy* by David Lichine, who shared Eglevsky's Ballet Russe training, and others in Massine's *Mademoiselle Argot* and John Taras's *Graziana*. For Ballet International he created the title role of Massine's *Mad Tristan* (*Tristan Fou*) and choreographed his own *Sentimental Colloquy* in 1944.

Eglevsky appeared in New York and Europe

in almost all the classic roles, often to considerable acclaim. Edwin Denby, a New York critic of the time, raved about his interpretation of Albrecht in *Giselle* in 1945, and Eglevsky also danced the prince in *Swan Lake*, the title role in *Apollo*, and other male leads in *The Nutcracker* and *Don Quixote*. During these years and throughout the 1950's he also partnered some of the outstanding prima ballerinas of the day, including Alicia Alonso, Melissa Hayden, Rosella Hightower, Nora Kaye, Tanaquil LeClercq, Alicia Markova, and Maria Tallchief.

In 1951, Eglevsky joined the New York City Ballet, under the direction of George Balanchine, and stayed there until his retirement in 1958. One source calls these years perhaps his most creative, a remarkable comment about a dancer at the end of his dancing career. He danced in many of Balanchine's new creations, including *Capricioso Brilliante*, *Caracole*, and *Western Symphony*, and he was especially noteworthy in *Scotch Symphony*. In 1952, while still associated with the New York City Ballet, he danced in *Death of Columbine* with Melissa Hayden in Charlie Chaplin's film *Limelight*, and in 1953 he performed with Maria Tallchief at the White House.

In 1944 the Eglevskys bought property in Massapequa, Long Island, N.Y., and settled there permanently in 1950. In 1955 they turned their garage into a dance studio, and began to teach ballet. The school prospered, thanks to his well-established reputation as a dancer, and soon the garage space proved too small. By 1957 he decided to build a studio in the area, financed by a series of dance engagements with Tallchief.

After his retirement from the New York City Ballet, Eglevsky commuted three days each week into the city to teach a men's class at Balanchine's School of American Ballet. His own last performance was on the Bell Telephone Hour on Sept. 30, 1960.

In 1961 he founded the André Eglevsky Ballet Company in Massapequa, which generally performed at local events and festivals. Eglevsky became increasingly involved with the dance company, creating his own staging for such full scale works as *Cinderella*, *Coppélia*, and *The Nutcracker*. During a tour of the company's annual performance of *The Nutcracker*, he died in Elmira, N.Y.

André Eglevsky was considered by many dance critics to be one of the greatest classical dancers of his generation. Undoubtedly the key words here are "classical" and "generation." Eglevsky was trained almost exclusively by émigrés from the Russian Imperial Ballet, and he was famous for his breathtaking, meticulous technique. The ballets in which he was most effective were ones that showed this effortless mastery to advantage, and the famous choreographers of his day—Fokine, Massine, Balanchine—also products of the Russian school, were able to combine his classical technique and their imaginations into very successful presentations.

It is therefore not surprising that at the end of Eglevsky's life he was still restaging the great classics of the nineteenth and early twentieth centuries for his own company. Nor is it surprising that in the last year of his life he collaborated in a "remembrance" of Nicolas Legat, who had created four personal dance classes for the young dancer in the mid-1930's that Eglevsky says later became his "bible."

It is the precise timing of Eglevsky's career as student, dancer, and teacher, however, that makes him a notable figure. Having been taught in the Russian manner by the very creators of the Ballet Russe companies, he then spent a long performing career dancing with people like Danilova and Tamara Toumanova, from this same background, and Kaye, Hayden, and Tallchief, who were not Russian-trained.

In the early 1950's, the young Jacques d'Amboise used Eglevsky as his style model. Later, when Eglevsky was a teacher at Balanchine's school, he began to work with an even newer generation of dancers, like Mikhail Baryshnikov, to whom he taught the role of Spectre in Fokine's *Spectre de la Rose*, as Fokine had taught him. Moreover, some remarkable American dancers, such as Fernando Bujones, Sean Lavery, and Patricia McBride were given early performing opportunities with Eglevsky's dance company. Thus, Eglevsky formed a kind of living link between the old Imperial Ballet School of prerevolutionary Russia and some of the most famous dancers in America in the late twentieth century.

[There are no full biographies of Eglevsky. His essay in *Heritage of a Ballet Master: Nicolas Legat* (1977) is useful, although it deals with only part of his career. There is some archival material on Eglevsky, mostly videotapes, at the New York Public Library, Performing Arts Research Center, Dance

Collection. An obituary is in the *New York Times*, Dec. 5, 1977.]

SANDRA SHAFFER VANDOREN

EICHELBERGER, CLARK MELL (July 29, 1896–Jan. 26, 1980), director of nongovernmental organizations, was born in Freeport, Ill., the son of Joseph Elmer Eichelberger and Olive Clark. His father was in the shoe business. At Union Elementary School, which he attended from 1902 to 1910, some of his teachers interested him in public affairs. He excelled at oratory and debating in high school. Eichelberger entered Northwestern University in 1914, intending to major in political science, but did not take a degree, leaving in 1917 to enlist in the army. He went to France with the American Expeditionary Force, working mostly as a stevedore. Inspired by President Woodrow Wilson's proposed League of Nations, he led discussions about it among soldiers. Eichelberger came out of this experience with a determination to do all that he could to end war once and for all.

Eichelberger studied at the University of Chicago from 1919 to 1920. Too restless to remain, he left and went to Washington, D.C., where he joined the Radcliffe Chautauqua System as a lecturer on international affairs. Often speaking about the League of Nations, he traveled to every state between 1922 and 1928. He made his first direct contact with the League of Nations at the close of his 1923 Chautauqua lecture tour; he arrived in Geneva in December of that year and was introduced to several statesmen and Secretariat members. He spent that winter in Europe studying the governments and conditions of nine different countries, becoming more eager than ever to work for the success of the League of Nations. In 1920 he met Rosa Kohler, an author and teller of children's stories, who was with the Chautauqua circuit. They were married on Oct. 6, 1924, and had no children.

In 1927, Eichelberger accepted the directorship of the Illinois chapter of the League of Nations Non-Partisan Association, founded in 1923 to educate the public about the League of Nations and to support American participation in it. He was appointed director of the Midwest office when the organization was enlarged in 1928.

In 1934, Eichelberger became national director of the League of Nations Association (LNA) in New York City. With Adolf Hitler in power in Germany and war fear growing, the LNA urged the American government to state the terms under which it would be willing to enter the League of Nations. Eichelberger harbored a second concern: to bring about American participation in the World Court. Supporting collective security against aggression, he broadcast from Prague and Geneva in 1938, weeks before the Munich Pact, that war could be avoided if the nations desiring peace were willing to fight to save Czechoslovakia.

In November 1939 the LNA helped organize the Commission to Study the Organization of Peace (CSOP), which was to develop plans for a new international arrangement to replace the League of Nations. Eichelberger was successively its director (1939–1964), chairman (1964–1968), and executive director (1968–1974). Soon thereafter, the LNA helped establish the Non-Partisan Committee for Peace Through Revision of the Neutrality Law, which sought to permit aid to countries victimized by aggression, an effort Eichelberger discussed with President Franklin D. Roosevelt on Sept. 7, 1939. In May 1940, the LNA assisted in the formation of the Committee to Defend America by Aiding the Allies (CDAAA). As national chairman of the CDAAA (1940–1941), Eichelberger called for victory over Nazi tyranny. He argued that American civilization could never survive otherwise.

Believing that winning the war and winning the peace could not be separated, Eichelberger, often called an unofficial secretary of state, conferred with President Roosevelt on Nov. 13, 1942, telling him it was imperative to establish peace machinery before the war ended. Roosevelt was aware how quickly postwar reaction against international cooperation could set in. From 1942 to 1943, Eichelberger served on a committee, chaired by Under Secretary of State Sumner Welles, that prepared the first draft of the United Nations Charter, and Eichelberger became the leader of the group of consultants from nongovernmental organizations that advised the American delegation to the San Francisco Conference (1945) at which the charter was completed.

In 1945 the name of the LNA was changed to the American Association for the United Nations (AAUN); Eichelberger was its executive director from 1947 to 1964. As editor of its monthly magazine, *Changing World*, he maintained that "public opinion is never static [and] it must be stimulated by constant discussion and information." He enlisted Eleanor Roosevelt as a volunteer to increase its membership nationwide. With the merger of the AAUN and the United States Committee for the United Nations to form the United Nations Association of the USA in 1964, Eichelberger devoted his energies to the CSOP.

Eichelberger initiated a weekly radio program, "The UN Is My Beat," on NBC, a series running from Apr. 8, 1949, to Oct. 25, 1953, on which he reviewed United Nations issues and activities. His philosophy that the work of the United Nations was all-encompassing was reflected in these broadcasts. Eichelberger wrote several books on the United Nations, revised at five-year intervals: *UN: The First Ten Years* (1955), *UN: The First Fifteen Years* (1960), *UN: The First Twenty Years* (1965), and *UN: The First Twenty-Five Years* (1970).

Eichelberger died in New York City.

[Eichelberger's papers, at the New York Public Library, include audiotapes of "The UN Is My Beat." Eichelberger's major work was *Organizing for Peace* (1977). An obituary is in the *New York Times*, Jan. 27, 1980.]

BERNARD HIRSCHHORN

EISELEY, LOREN COREY (Sept. 3, 1907–July 9, 1977), naturalist and educator, was born in Lincoln, Nebr., the son of Clyde Edwin Eiseley and Daisy Corey. Although both his parents had artistic ambitions—his father as an actor and his mother as a painter—the family household was, in Eiseley's memory, a bleak environment for a child. His father's job as a traveling hardware salesman often left the young boy alone with his mother, who had been stricken deaf as a child. The family was poor and moved often, with little in the way of a social life.

Thus began what Eiseley was to call his double life, comprising an outer life of school, brief friendships, and often difficult family interaction, and an inner life of imagination and adventure among the small creatures of the natural world he found in the fields and ponds around Lincoln. His inner life was fostered by an aunt and uncle who bought him books, took him to museums, and encouraged his thinking. To this uncle he would eventually partly dedicate his autobiography, with the inscription "without whose help my life would have been different beyond imagining."

After graduating in 1925 from high school in Lincoln, where he first determined that he would like to be a nature writer, Eiseley entered the University of Nebraska, where he focused his studies on zoology and English, writing poetry and joining the staff of the campus literary journal *Prairie Schooner*. His studies were interrupted by financial hardship, the death of his father in 1928, and his own deteriorating health. In 1929, diagnosed as having tuberculosis, he dropped out of college and began his wider explorations of the American West, sometimes working at odd jobs, sometimes hoboing on freight trains. Recovered from his tuberculosis, in the fall of 1930 he returned to the University of Nebraska, now as an anthropology major. His schoolwork continued sporadically, though he showed aptitude in both archaeology and paleontology, participating in summer field digs and working in the university's natural history museum. He graduated with a double major in English and anthropology in 1933.

Eiseley's fieldwork continued, first at the University of Pennsylvania, where he did graduate work in anthropology under the direction of Frank Speck, receiving the M.A. in 1935 and the Ph.D. in 1937, and then at the University of Kansas (1937–1944) and Oberlin College (1944–1947), where he held teaching positions. During this period his writing career also continued to develop. He participated in the New Deal Federal Writer's Project in 1936 and in 1942 published his first popular essay in *Scientific American*. In 1938 he married Mabel Langdon, who had been a curator at the University of Nebraska Fine Arts Collection and who continued her career in art administration throughout their marriage. They had no children, a decision Eiseley later attributed in part to his fear of passing on a madness he suspected in his mother's family.

In 1947, Eiseley received a grant for fieldwork in East Africa, which he declined in order to return to the anthropology department at the University of Pennsylvania, assuming the chairmanship formerly held by his mentor Frank Speck. This decision marked the end of Eiseley's significant fieldwork. His digs instead would now be in libraries and used book stores. His profuse reading—in poetry and philosophy as well as in natural history and the history of science—came to inform his writing as deeply as did his wanderings among ancient bones and living creatures.

Soon after his return to Philadelphia, where he would live the rest of his life, Eiseley began work simultaneously on two books on evolution, which would occupy his time throughout the better part of ten years. *The Immense Journey* (1957), his first and most popular book, brought together his scientific musings on evolution in a personal and accessible style. Critics hailed the clarity and eloquence of his writing. In *Darwin's Century: Evolution and the Men Who Discovered It* (1958), he presented the idea of evolution not as the discovery of one man but as the cumulative result of thoughts evolving through the minds of many men.

Other books followed. *The Firmament of Time* (1960) was concerned with the evolution of human thought, in particular the process by which natural explanations of the world, mankind, and life and death have replaced supernatural explanations in the Western mind, together with meditations on the meanings of the terms "human" and "natural." *Francis Bacon and the Modern Dilemma* (1962; corrected and expanded as *The Man Who Saw Through Time*, 1973) examined the life and times of the Elizabethan figure who, as a scientist, philosopher, and essayist, was a precursor to Eiseley. *The Unexpected Universe* (1969) offered Homer's Odysseus as a metaphor for science itself, a figure comparable to such later scientific voyagers as Captain James Cook exploring the Antarctic or Charles Darwin aboard the *Beagle*. (Elsewhere, though, the more doubting side of Eiseley wondered if Herman Melville's Captain Ahab, leading the *Pequod* and himself to destruction in his attempt to conquer nature, might not be a more accurate embodiment of Western science.) *The Invisible Pyramid* (1970) discussed the achievements of rocket science as an evolutionary development not unlike the evolution of molds and fungi. With *The Night Country* (1971) and the autobiographical *All the Strange Hours* (1975), Eiseley developed more fully the dichotomies of his childhood: loneliness and wonder, dark brooding and intellectual voyaging, fugitive existence and the search for a home in the world. In his final years he also returned to his earlier pursuit of poetry.

Although a scientist most of his life, Eiseley's writing is by no means a popularization of scientific ideas. Rather, his work registers the impact of modern scientific discoveries—the immensity of time, the loneliness of space, the mysterious wonders and the transient mutability of life—on a sensitive mind. Eiseley deeply valued the growth of knowledge and understanding, but his sensibility was essentially tragic, even when presenting the facts of the history of science. Loneliness suffuses his work, but so too do a sense of compassion and a fellowship with other creatures, both living and extinct. A naturalist, he lived the last thirty years of his life in a suburban apartment that did not allow him even a cat. As a teacher and administrator—he served two years as provost of the University of Pennsylvania (1959–1961) in addition to his duties as department chairman—he was deeply disturbed by the campus upheavals of the 1960's, yet he himself was a doubter troubled by orthodoxies. Such contradictions, far from detracting from his writing, give it much of its value. In 1971, as a professional scientist, he received the unusual honor of election to the National Institute of Arts and Letters. He died in Philadelphia.

[The chief repository of Eiseley manuscripts is the Loren Eiseley Seminar Room and University Archives, University of Pennsylvania, which also holds Jeanne DePalma Gallagher, *Bibliographic Card Catalog Index for the Writings of Loren Eiseley*. See also Kenneth Heuer, ed., *The Lost Notebooks of Loren Eiseley* (1987).

A fully researched biography is Gale Christianson, *Fox at the Wood's Edge* (1990). Other full-length studies include Andrew J. Angyl, *Loren Eiseley* (1983), which includes a useful annotated bibliography; Fred E. Carlisle, *Loren Eiseley: The Development of a Writer* (1983); and Leslie E. Gerber and Margaret McFadden, *Loren Eiseley* (1983). Hiram Haydn, Eiseley's long-term editor, includes anecdotes of Eiseley in his memoir *Words and Faces* (1974). Following Eiseley's death, Howard Nemerov presented a tribute, "Loren Eiseley: 1907–1977," *Proceedings of the American Academy of Arts and Letters* 2, no. 29 (1978). An obituary is in the *New York Times*, July 11, 1977.]

PAUL JOHNSTON

EISENHOWER, MAMIE GENEVA DOUD (Nov. 14, 1896–Nov. 1, 1979), wife of President Dwight D. Eisenhower, was born in Boone, Iowa, one of four daughters of John Sheldon Doud and Elivera Mathilda Carlson. John Doud had made a modest fortune in a meat-packing business begun by his father; he retired and moved the family to Denver when

Mamie was nine years old. She had a privileged childhood, reared in an elegant Victorian house that was built for Doud and his family. Mamie attended public schools in Denver and completed her education with a year at Miss Walcott's finishing school there. In her youth, she traveled with her family to Panama and the Great Lakes. Beginning in 1910, the Doud family spent the winter months in San Antonio, Tex.

In the winter of 1915, Mamie met Second Lieutenant Dwight D. ("Ike") Eisenhower, a recent West Point graduate stationed at Fort Sam Houston. They became engaged in February 1916. Mamie's father threatened to break off the engagement if Eisenhower followed through on his ambitions to become an army aviator. Doud said he would be irresponsible to allow his daughter to marry a man in such a dangerous profession. Mamie supported her father's ultimatum and Eisenhower declined a transfer to an aviation unit.

Dwight and Mamie were married on July 1, 1916, in the Doud family's Denver home. Mamie, who was accustomed to a rather settled existence, made the difficult transition to military living. During Eisenhower's military career, Dwight and Mamie moved twenty-five times, including seven moves in a single year. They lived at army base homes in Texas, the Panama Canal Zone, Colorado, Kansas, Georgia, and Maryland. From 1936 to 1939 the Eisenhowers lived in Manila, where Dwight was assigned in the Philippines as a military aide to General Douglas MacArthur. "I think I learned to be a good wife," Mamie wrote in a 1970 article for the *Reader's Digest*. "As Ike rose in rank and his responsibilities grew, I tried very hard to make our home a place of calmness and good cheer, where he could relax in the midst of his strenuous life."

After one of her husband's first transfers, Mamie Eisenhower sold her wedding presents and her household furniture, which would have been too much trouble to move, for $92 and could not afford to replace them for years. Because of this incident, she would never part with other family belongings. What was not in use went into storage, even when the Eisenhowers lived in the White House. She filled her closets and attics with old clothes.

Of her marriage, Mamie Eisenhower wrote in 1970: "We had our disappointments and our troubles, some of them devastating, yet between us there was a deep understanding, a feeling of contentment in each other's company."

There were difficult times in the Eisenhower marriage. Their first child died of scarlet fever at the age of three. Mamie Eisenhower could never speak of her first son without tears. "For a long time it was as if a shining light had gone out in Ike's life," she recalled. "Throughout all the years that followed, the memory of those bleak days was a deep inner pain that never seemed to diminish much." A second son, John Sheldon Doud Eisenhower, was born in 1922.

Mamie Eisenhower said that among the hardest times of their marriage "were the long periods when we were separated because there was no place for a wife where Ike was stationed." During World War II, when her husband was rising to prominence as supreme allied commander in Europe, she lived in an apartment in Washington, D.C. Dwight Eisenhower's wartime letters to his wife indicate that she was troubled by rumors about his alleged relationship with his military driver and aide Kay Summersby. Eisenhower assured his wife that the rumors were groundless and his letters affirm his deep affection for her.

During World War II, Mamie Eisenhower volunteered at service canteens and for the Red Cross. She also studied Spanish and played bridge with other military wives. After the war she said that she hoped to "unpack my furniture some place and stay forever." The Eisenhowers bought their first house in 1950 at Gettysburg, Pa., but did not live in it as a permanent residence for another eleven years. It is now a national historic site.

Though Mrs. Eisenhower was private and family-oriented, she was thrust into prominence in the 1940's as the wife of America's popular war hero. And for the next thirty-five years she was among the best known and most admired women in the world. For most of her life with Eisenhower, Mamie sought to remain in the background. "I was Ike's wife, John's mother, the children's grandmother," she told the *Philadelphia Inquirer* in a 1974 interview. "That was all I ever wanted to be."

The Eisenhowers lived at Ft. Myer, Va., from 1945 until 1948, when Dwight served as army chief of staff. They moved to New York City in June of 1948 when General Eisenhower was appointed president of Columbia University. Mrs. Eisenhower, who had talked her father out of enrolling her in college, had little

Eisenhower

enthusiasm for living in a university community. By arrangement with the trustees, Eisenhower relieved Mamie of the formal social schedule that had become a tradition during the long presidency of his predecessor, Nicholas Murray Butler. Socially, Dwight and Mamie preferred the company of army friends and their families to university officials and faculty. Mamie insisted that Dwight's Sundays be spent with her at their Morningside Drive residence and said that it was the only day that Eisenhower did not belong to Columbia. In 1950 when Eisenhower was named by President Truman as commander of NATO forces in Europe, Mrs. Eisenhower set up their residence in a fourteen-room villa outside of Paris, which had been redecorated by the French government for the Eisenhowers.

While in France, Mrs. Eisenhower received hundreds of letters urging her to use her influence to encourage General Eisenhower to become a presidential candidate in 1952. When Eisenhower decided to seek the presidency, Mamie was strongly supportive. With her warmth and vitality, she was viewed as one of her husband's assets in his successful race for the presidency. One of the reasons that Republican strategists encouraged Mrs. Eisenhower to make frequent public appearances with her husband in the 1952 campaign was that the Democratic presidential nominee, Adlai E. Stevenson, had been recently divorced.

As first lady in the 1950's, Mrs. Eisenhower took a more traditional role. She did not give speeches, never held formal White House press conferences, and said that she only went into the Oval Office four times, "and I was invited each time." At social gatherings, Mrs. Eisenhower was a gracious hostess, with a remarkable memory for faces and names. To the White House staff, there was never any question about her authority in running the executive mansion. She was a frugal housekeeper and frequently read food advertisements in local newspapers and clipped coupons to be used by the White House staff to hold down the food budget. Former chief usher J. B. West said of Mrs. Eisenhower: "Underneath that buoyant spirit, there was a spine of steel, forged by years of military discipline. . . . She understood the hierarchy of a large establishment, the division of responsibilities, and how to direct a staff. She knew exactly what she wanted, every moment, and exactly how it should be done."

Mrs. Eisenhower, who valued her privacy, trimmed down the White House social season, put staff members under a strict no-talking rule, and refused to put out a schedule of her visits outside the executive mansion. Disappointed by the lack of authentic presidential antiques, she worked to preserve the White House's history by launching efforts to recover antique furniture and china. President Eisenhower observed: "I personally think that Mamie's biggest contribution was to make the White House livable, comfortable, and meaningful for the people who came in. She was always helpful and ready to do anything. She exuded hospitality. She saw that as one of her functions and performed it, no matter how tired she was."

Though Mrs. Eisenhower kept a low public profile during her husband's presidency, she had considerable influence. Eisenhower acknowledged that he sought her advice about members of his administration and other political figures. "Mamie is a very shrewd observer," he once said. "She has an uncanny and accurate judgment of people with whom she was well acquainted. I got it into my head that I'd better listen when she talked about someone brought in close to me." It had done Secretary of the Treasury George Humphrey no harm that Mamie liked his wife; and Vice-President Richard M. Nixon, who was kept at a distance by the president, had a friend and defender in Mamie Eisenhower. On budget matters and economic problems, Eisenhower would seek his wife's opinions.

In 1952, Eisenhower was named one of the world's twelve best-dressed women by the New York Dress Institute, one of many best-dressed lists she appeared on. Women throughout the nation wore "Mamie pink," imitated her short bangs, and adopted her style of pastel-toned stockings. She was five feet, four inches tall and weighed 138 pounds. Her favorite vacation spot was Elizabeth Arden's Maine Chance health spa near Phoenix, Ariz.

Following President Eisenhower's heart attack in 1955, published reports maintained that Mrs. Eisenhower did not want him to seek another term in 1956. But she later divulged that she had privately encouraged her husband to run for another term. "I feared that for him to quit in the middle of things, to abandon what he deeply believed was his duty to his country, would do more violence to his health than to serve another four years."

Mrs. Eisenhower campaigned with her husband for reelection but made fewer public appearances in Eisenhower's second term. She further reduced the White House social schedule and, because she disliked flying, did not accompany Eisenhower on his 1959 and 1960 tours abroad. There were widely circulated rumors that she had a drinking problem. Mrs. Eisenhower said in a 1973 television interview that some people may have gotten that impression because she sometimes walked unsteadily as a result of a carotid sinus condition that affected her balance. In addition to her equilibrium problem, she also had claustrophobia. "I don't like being closed in," she told the *Philadelphia Inquirer*.

At the completion of Eisenhower's second term as president in January 1961, he and Mamie retired to their Gettysburg farm. Mrs. Eisenhower said that their years in Gettysburg were their best years as a family. They spent winters in Palm Springs, Calif., and also had a cottage in Augusta, Ga. Mrs. Eisenhower encouraged her grandson, David, to look up Julie Nixon, the daughter of the former vice-president, when he was attending Amherst and she was attending Smith College. The two were married in 1968. Mrs. Eisenhower also influenced her husband's endorsement of Nixon for the 1968 Republican presidential nomination. Following the death of her husband in 1969, Mamie Eisenhower continued to live in Gettysburg but was a frequent guest at the Nixon White House. Her public appearances were restricted to ceremonies honoring her late husband. She moved to the Sheraton Park Hotel in Washington, D.C., in 1978, but retained the use of her Gettysburg house. She died at Walter Reed Army Medical Center and was buried next to her husband in a small chapel at the Eisenhower Library in Abilene, Kans.

[Mrs. Eisenhower's papers are at the Eisenhower Library in Abilene, Kans. An interview is in the July 22, 1974, edition of the *Philadelphia Inquirer*. John S. D. Eisenhower edited *Letters to Mamie* (1978), Dwight D. Eisenhower's wartime letters to his wife. See "My Memories of Ike" in *Reader's Digest*, February 1970; Steve Neal, *The Eisenhowers* (1978); and the profile in Carl Sferrazza Anthony, *First Ladies* (1990). Obituaries are in the *New York Times* and *Philadelphia Inquirer*, both Nov. 2, 1979.]

STEVE NEAL

ELDER, RUTH (Sept. 12, 1904–Oct. 9, 1977), aviator, was born in Anniston, Ala., one of eight children of Mr. and Mrs. J. O. Elder. Elder retained her maiden name during her professional life and preferred to be called "Miss Elder" even when married. In her youth, she moved to Lakeland, Fla., where after one year in business school she became employed as a stenographer and then a dental assistant.

Inspired by Charles Lindbergh's and Richard Byrd's transatlantic flights in 1927, Elder took flying lessons from pilot George Haldeman, to whom she related her desire to be the first woman to fly across the Atlantic and who agreed to accompany her. She found financial backers who put up $35,000 for her plane, and later that year she arrived at Roosevelt Field on Long Island, N.Y., and became a public sensation when she announced her intention to fly across the Atlantic. Sporting knickers and her trend-setting "Ruth ribbons" trademark, a gypsy-like scarf wrapped around her head, the slender and vivacious beauty dazzled audiences with her pluck and charming smile.

Bold and unconventional, Elder embodied the last of the flapper generation. In press interviews, she reiterated her determination to make a crossing despite poor weather reports and the recent failed attempts of other flyers. On Oct. 11, 1927, shortly after receiving her pilot's license and five months after Lindbergh's landing in Paris, Elder and Haldeman departed from Roosevelt Field for Paris.

Elder and Haldeman flew in their single-engine Stinson plane, nicknamed the "American Girl," for thirty-six hours until a broken oil line forced both flyers to take periodic turns crawling down into the fuselage to bail out oil. Despite Haldeman's deliberate effort to avoid tumultuous weather just north of them, stormy winds fiercely jostled the overheated aircraft. Haldeman spotted an empty oil tanker below—the SS *Barendrecht*—and ditched the plane near the Dutch ship, 350 miles off the Azores. The *Barendrecht* immediately dispatched a small boat and rescue crew, who tossed ropes to the flyers. A concerned Elder, donning the only life jacket aboard the plane, cried out, "Take Haldeman first!" After both fliers safely boarded the *Barendrecht*, the plane exploded into flames and Elder, with lipstick in hand, remarked, "We will do it again."

Although Haldeman and Elder failed to reach Paris, they flew 2,623 miles, covering more miles over water than any previous aircraft. As Elder stepped ashore at the Azores, she was greeted by an enthusiastic crowd. In Paris, she was hailed by the Interallied Club, a French aeronautical society, as representing the "new spirit of American womanhood." King Alfonso XIII of Spain made Elder an honorary member of the Spanish air force. In New York City the National Women's Party congratulated her for "smashing the myth" that only "plain" and ordinary women can make a difference in the world.

Others were less enthusiastic. Winifred Stoner, founder of the League for Fostering Genius, stated that Elder could be of greater service to humanity as a typist. Similarly, Eleanor Roosevelt dubbed Elder's Atlantic flight "foolish," and renowned sociologist Katherine Davies maintained that Elder's accomplishment was unremarkable.

Movie, advertisement, and personal appearance contracts awaited Elder upon her return to the United States. She signed a contract with producer Florenz Ziegfeld to appear in one of his "Glorifying the American Girl" revues. In addition, Elder took to the vaudeville circuit, publicly recounting her dangerous transatlantic voyage. In June 1928, Elder appeared in the first of two silent pictures, *Moran of the Marines*, which included Richard Dix and future star Jean Harlow. The following year Elder demonstrated her flying skills opposite cowboy movie star Hoot Gibson in the *Winged Horseman*.

Elder also continued her flying career and in August 1929 entered the first Women's Air Derby. With Will Rogers officiating, Elder competed against other famous female aviators, such as Amelia Earhart, Pancho Barnes, and Ruth Nichols. The race ran from Santa Monica, Calif., to Cleveland, Ohio, with the pilots landing each night. Vying for cash prizes as well as advertisement and endorsement opportunities, Elder came in fifth place, just behind Blanche Noyes.

Elder was married and divorced six times; she married her first husband, schoolteacher C. E. Moody, at the age of eighteen. A few months before her Atlantic trip in 1927 she married Lyle Womack of Panama and a member of the Byrd South Pole Expedition in 1929. They divorced in 1928. Elder next married Walter Camp, Jr., president of Inspiration Pictures, Inc., a director of Madison Square Garden in New York City, and son of the renowned Yale football coach. They divorced in 1932. She next married George K. Thackery, then movie director Albert A. Gillespie, followed by Hollywood cameraman Ralph King, whom she married twice.

Elder's enormous popularity was understandable given the context of the 1920's. Aviation pioneers like Elder reaffirmed the importance of self-fulfillment while promoting the conquest of new frontiers. Elder resembled the alluring women adventurers common in the film and literature of the era. Unfortunately, Elder's celebrity status obscured her contribution to the advancement of women in aviation.

Elder had earned around $250,000 from motion pictures and public appearances, but later in life she told reporters that the money "slipped through her fingers" and disappeared. As the 1920's came to a close, so did Elder's place in the limelight. She attempted writing and briefly managed her own advertising agency. She then lived the remainder of her life in seclusion until her death in San Francisco.

[See "Ruth Elder's Ocean Flight," *Literary Digest*, Oct. 22, 1927; "The American Super-Girl and Her Critics," *Literary Digest*, Oct. 29, 1927; Russel Owen, "Ruth Elder's Revolt," *The Nation*, Nov. 23, 1927; Amelia Earhart, *The Fun of It* (1932); and Richard O'Connor, *Winged Legend* (1970). Obituaries are in the *New York Times* and the *Los Angeles Times*, both Oct. 11, 1977.]

KRISTINE WIRTS

ELLIOTT, WILLIAM YANDELL, III (May 13, 1896–Jan. 9, 1979), educator and government adviser, was born in Murfreesboro, Tenn., the son of William Yandell Elliott, Jr., a lawyer, and Annie Mary Bullock, a librarian. His father died when his son and namesake was three years old. As a result, William and his brother were reared principally by their mother in Murfreesboro and in Nashville, where she became librarian of the Vanderbilt University Law School. Elliott attended the Webb School, a private academy in Bell Buckle, Tenn., that emphasized the classics, and entered Vanderbilt in 1913. He concentrated on poetry and philosophy; edited the *Observer*, a literary magazine; served on the student council; and was a member of Phi Beta Kappa. Also at this time, Elliott joined an informal group of young poets that met regularly to read and discuss their poetry. Called the Fugitives, the group, which included future literary lions Donald Davidson, John Crowe Ransom, Allen Tate, and Robert Penn Warren, disdained the mythology of the Old South and possessed, according to Elliott, "the peculiar mixture of classic humanism, tragic irony, and a wry but courtly wit." Though poetry did not become his calling, Elliott continued to write verse, and his friendship with the other Fugitives lasted for the rest of his life.

After receiving his B.A. in 1917, Elliott enlisted in the United States Army and went off to war. When World War I ended, he was a first lieutenant with the 114th Field Artillery, Thirtieth ("Old Hickory") Division, of the American Expeditionary Force in France. Following the armistice, Elliott remained in France long enough to earn a certificate in French literature at the Sorbonne. Returning to Nashville in 1919, he enrolled in graduate school at Vanderbilt and resumed his association with the Fugitives. Elliott earned his M.A. in 1920 and was teaching English at his alma mater when he won a Rhodes Scholarship.

At Balliol College, Oxford, Elliott studied political philosophy under A. D. Lindsay, a highly respected tutor who had published a translation of Plato's *Republic* and works on the thought of Henri Bergson and Immanuel Kant. Elliott flourished in the unstructured environment of Oxford, absorbing, as he later wrote, "unhindered, the cream of a rich tradition of scholarship." He won the James Hall Foundation essay prize at Balliol in 1922 and was awarded his D.Phil. degree in 1923. He also indulged his poetic interest during his stay at Oxford as part of a circle that included Robert Graves, Anthony Eden, Oliver St. John Gogarty, and William Butler Yeats.

Elliott returned to the United States in the fall of 1923 to become an instructor in political science at the University of California at Berkeley. He was promoted to assistant professor in 1924, and a year later he moved to Harvard University as a lecturer and tutor in the department of government. After serving as an assistant professor from 1925 to 1929, he advanced to associate professor in 1929 and was made full professor in 1931. Elliott became Leroy B. Williams professor of history and political science in 1942. On June 28, 1923, Elliott married Barbara Pinkerton Foster; they had three children. His first marriage ended in divorce, and he wed Mary Louise Ward on Aug. 26, 1936; they had two children.

The 1920's and early 1930's were Elliott's most productive years as a scholar. He turned out a spate of journal articles based on his doctoral work at Oxford and ultimately published an expanded version of his dissertation, *The Pragmatic Revolt in Politics*, in 1928. The book was a spirited intellectual defense of rationalism and constitutionalism and a sharp critique of pragmatism, which Elliott believed undermined democracy and paved the way for fascism, syndicalism, and even Communism. He viewed pragmatism and social behaviorism as mechanistic dogmas little concerned with the vital question of moral personality. Although the controversial book vexed some of the followers of John Dewey and Harold Laski, it propelled Elliott to the front rank of young American political thinkers. His next two works, *The New British Empire* (1932) and *The Need for Constitutional Reform* (1935), were well received in academe.

The New British Empire, based on a series of lectures, was a sweeping economic, social, and political analysis of the transformation of a centralized colonial system into an association of cooperating nations. *The Need for Constitutional Reform* was a brief for a greater concentration of power in the American presidency and central government. One of Elliott's more provocative proposals advocated changing the states of the union into administrative units called "regional commonwealths."

In 1936, Elliott joined the academic recruits flocking to Washington, D.C., as a member of the research staff of the President's Committee on Administrative Management, chaired by Louis Brownlow. He contributed memoranda on presidential staffing to the Brownlow Committee's study of the federal government, which inspired the Reorganization Act of 1939 and the creation of the Executive Office of the President. In 1937, Elliott was appointed to the Business Advisory Council, a sounding board for economic policy assembled by Secretary of Commerce Daniel C. Roper and headed by investment banker W. Averell Harriman; he served on it for five years. Elliott must have found his employment in relatively minor New Deal posts fulfilling. For nearly thirty years thereafter, he set aside scholarship to commute between Harvard and the nation's capital, moonlighting as an all-purpose government expert.

Elliott had entered public service in the 1930's in the belief that the government of the United States had to be enlarged and strengthened as a bulwark against the "isms" infecting Europe. One of the earliest American critics of Mussolini's Italy and Hitler's Germany, he spoke out frequently on the need for war preparedness and other measures to deter German, Italian, and Japanese aggression. At one point, he suggested that the United States and Great Britain corner and put an embargo on the world's supply of nonferrous metals and other war matériel to prevent aggressor nations from obtaining the means with which to wage war. By 1940, his attacks on Charles A. Lindbergh and other American advocates of appeasement, and his support for President Franklin Roosevelt's efforts to aid the beleaguered Allies, had made Elliott an object of derision at heavily noninterventionist Harvard. Before Pearl Harbor changed the climate of opinion, he was regularly denounced by the student newspaper, the *Crimson*, and when Roosevelt sent fifty older destroyers to the British in exchange for the use of bases in the Western Hemisphere in the fall of 1940, Harvard protesters taunted Elliott with signs reading: "Send Fifty Over-Aged Professors to Britain."

Beginning in 1940, Elliott became a fixture in the labyrinth of government agencies created to ready the country for war. After serving on the National Defense Advisory Commission for a year, he went to work for its successor agency, the Office of Production Management (OPM). As an adviser on raw materials and international trade, Elliott argued strongly in favor of stockpiling tin and rubber in anticipation of Japanese actions cutting the United States off from its Asian sources. When the OPM was collapsed into yet another entity, the War Production Board (WPB), in 1942, Elliott was made director of its Stockpiling and Transportation Division. An able performance in that job resulted in his promotion to WPB vice-chairman of civilian requirements in May 1944. In this capacity, he was to oversee a new policy, propounded by WPB chairman Donald M. Nelson, allowing the unlimited manufacture of more civilian goods by small businesses. However, Nelson's replacement in August 1944 by Julius A. Krug, who was more amenable to the demands of the War Department and big business to slow the pace of industrial reconversion, limited Elliott's role in overall WPB policy. Thus, his protests against the "inroads being made on nonmilitary programs" to the detriment of the civilian economy went largely unheeded until his resignation in August 1945.

Later in 1945, Elliott became principal adviser to the House Special Committee on Postwar Economic Policy and Planning, chaired by Mississippi Democrat William M. Colmer. From this post he targeted Soviet Communism as the successor to fascism as the principal enemy of American democracy. After traveling with the committee to Europe for meetings with Joseph Stalin and other leaders, Elliott produced a hard-line report recommending that the Soviets be required to disclose their production figures, withdraw occupation forces from Eastern Europe, and open their society to Western journalists before they were granted American loans. Long skeptical of Stalin's intentions, he believed that the Soviet government was ignoring the needs of its people in the postwar period and using its vast resources to build up its armaments for confrontation with the West. At the same time, Elliott backed American economic assistance to war-ravaged Europe in order to prevent the continent's further deterioration in the face of the Communist threat. He had an opportunity to advance this view more forcefully during the Republican-dominated Eightieth Congress (1947–1949) as staff director of both the House Committee on Foreign Affairs and the House Select Committee on Foreign Aid, headed by Christian A. Herter of Massachusetts. The Herter Committee's detailed report of European conditions, the writing of which was supervised by Elliott, helped pave the way for congressional passage of the Marshall Plan in 1948.

The Truman administration availed itself of Elliott's wartime experience by making him assistant director of the Office of Defense Mobilization during the Korean crisis (1951–1953). He subsequently served the Eisenhower administration as a member of the Policy Planning Board of the National Security Council from 1953 to 1957 and advised Vice-President Richard M. Nixon and secretaries of state John Foster Dulles and Christian Herter. In the Kennedy administration, Secretary of State Dean Rusk retained Elliott as a consultant. Outside of government, Elliott chaired the foreign policy study group of the Woodrow Wilson Foundation and the Committee on American Education and

Communism, which advanced a program to teach the youth of the country the "cold, basic, hard facts about international Communism."

Although he was an established scholar with a long résumé in government, it was as a teacher, first and foremost, that Elliott made his mark. For thirty years he was in charge of the introductory course "Government 1" at Harvard and also taught political theory, comparative government, and international relations during his long career. A polished though somewhat undisciplined lecturer, Elliott preferred the tutorial as a pedagogical method. Even during his busiest government stints, he found time to meet with the most gifted of his students to discuss assigned readings and essays in weekly one-on-one sessions not unlike those he experienced at Oxford.

Tall, robust, with bushy eyebrows, outsized features, and booming voice, "Wild Bill" Elliott became a dominating figure in the department of government almost from his arrival at Harvard. His eclectic background, erudition, and charisma set him apart from most of his colleagues and generally attracted bright and ambitious undergraduates and graduate students. For his part, Elliott paid homage to another time-honored Oxford ideal by prepping his elite charges for careers in academe and important public service. Among his prize pupils were United Nations official Ralph Bunche, National Security Adviser McGeorge Bundy, President John F. Kennedy, Secretary of State Henry Kissinger, Canadian prime minister Pierre Elliott Trudeau, and noted political scientists Samuel H. Beer and Louis Hartz. Of these, Kissinger was Elliott's favorite.

The towering, flamboyant southerner and the short, austere, German-Jewish immigrant were an improbable but eminently successful match. Kissinger, who entered Harvard in 1947, regarded Elliott as a "man of great passion, great flashes of insight," more worldly and interesting than the rest of the faculty. Elliott, in turn, recognized in the younger man an "unusual and original mind" and soon came to view him as "more like a mature colleague than a student." He urged Kissinger to read widely and steered him toward political philosophy. Beyond fostering his intellectual development, Elliott encouraged Kissinger to attend graduate school, found him a job as a teaching assistant, and sent him to present papers at scholarly conferences as his mentor's stand-in. In 1951, as director of the Harvard Summer School (a post he held from 1950 to 1961), Elliott appointed Kissinger to head a pet project, the Harvard International Seminar, which brought young public officials and journalists from all parts of the world to spend the summer at Harvard, where they could learn that the United States was not the forbidding place portrayed by Communist propaganda. Through the seminar, which he made his own from 1952 to 1968, and his editorship of *Confluence*, a European-American foreign policy journal backed by Elliott and the Harvard Summer School, Kissinger was able to make important contacts that helped shape his later career. "Whatever I have achieved," Kissinger wrote in tribute to Elliott in 1963, "I owe importantly to his inspiration."

Elliott retired from Harvard in 1963. He then spent six years as university professor of philosophy, politics, and religion at American University in Washington, D.C. In the last twenty-five years of his life, Elliott also raised cattle, sheep, wild turkeys, and "fighting cocks" on his Hidden Valley Farm in Haywood, Va. He died there.

[The main collection of Elliott's papers is at the Hoover Institution for War, Revolution and Peace at Stanford University. There are also substantial manuscripts and a clipping file in the Harvard University Archives. The Vanderbilt University Archives has some Elliott material in its Fugitive-Agrarian Collection. In addition to the works mentioned in the text, Elliott was the author of *Industrial Mobilization and the National Security, 1950–1960* (1950) and the coauthor (with Neil A. McDonald) of *Western Political Heritage* (1949). Articles by Elliott include "Opportunities to Study for a Doctorate at Oxford," *School and Society*, Dec. 1928; "If America Goes Fascist," *American Mercury*, June 1938; "A Time for War," *Virginia Quarterly Review*, Autumn 1941; and "A Time for Peace?" *Virginia Quarterly Review*, Spring 1946.

Articles about Elliott are "Portraits of Harvard Figures: William Yandell Elliott," *Harvard Crimson*, Feb. 26, 1934; "New Boss, More Goods," *Time*, May 22, 1944; and "Ends and Means," *Newsweek*, Aug. 5, 1963. An appreciation of Elliott by Samuel H. Beer is in *Harvard Gazette*, Dec. 18, 1981. On Elliott and the Fugitives, see Louise Cowan, *The Fugitive Group* (1959). Bureau of Demobilization, *Industrial Mobilization for War* (1947), deals with Elliott's wartime government service. The Elliott-Kissinger relationship is explored in Stephen R. Graubard, *Kissinger: Portrait of a Mind* (1973); Ralph Blumenfeld and the Staff and Editors of the *New York Post*, *Henry Kissinger* (1974); Marvin Kalb and Bernard Kalb, *Kissinger* (1974); Peter Dickson,

Kissinger and the Meaning of History (1978); and Walter Isaacson, *Kissinger* (1992). Obituaries are in the *Boston Globe* and the *New York Times*, both Jan. 11, 1979; and the *Washington Post*, Jan. 12, 1979.]

RICHARD H. GENTILE

ELLIS, CLYDE TAYLOR (Dec. 21, 1908–Feb. 9, 1980), Congressman and rural electrification advocate, was born near Garfield, Ark., the son of Minerva Jane Taylor and Cecil Oscar Ellis, a farmer. Ellis was born in a farmhouse without electricity, and he remembered the trips to the local power company office with his father, who "pleaded with them to build lines into the hill country where we lived."

Ellis, the oldest of nine children, worked his way through high school in three years and began teaching in the rural schools near Garfield in 1927. For three summers he sold Bibles in the eastern states in order to earn tuition for college. In 1928 and 1929 he studied at the University of Arkansas in Fayetteville.

Ellis was superintendent of schools in Garfield from 1929 to 1934. He and members of the school board were unable to persuade the electric company to build power lines to the schools. He later attributed his lifelong devotion to the rural electrification program to this early struggle with an electric power monopoly.

He married Izella Baker on Dec. 20, 1931; they had two children. They were divorced in 1964.

Ellis studied law during the years he was a school superintendent. He was admitted to the Arkansas bar in 1933 and practiced law in Garfield and Bentonville, Ark. A Democrat, he was elected to the Arkansas General Assembly in 1932 at age twenty-three. He served in the state house of representatives in 1933–1934 and in the state senate from 1935 to 1938. Ellis introduced rural electrification legislation that was later used as a model by other states.

In 1938, Ellis defeated the incumbent Claud A. Fuller by 121 votes in the election for the United States House of Representatives. He said he was elected "solely on the power issue, the issue of the development of the White River." Ellis represented Arkansas's Third District in Congress for two terms, serving from 1939 to 1943. While in Congress, Ellis worked vigorously for rural electrification and water resources development. He unsuccessfully advocated the creation of an Arkansas Valley authority similar to the Tennessee Valley Authority. He criticized the United States Chamber of Commerce for opposing the Arkansas Valley plan, accusing the organization of supporting the "unscrupulously greedy interests of the American economic royalty." Ellis's career as an elected official ended in 1942 when he lost the Democratic primary race for the United States Senate.

Ellis became the general manager of the National Rural Electric Cooperative Association (NRECA) when it was founded in 1942. In 1943 he took a leave of absence to enter the United States Navy and served as a gunnery officer in an antisubmarine force in the North Atlantic during World War II. He resumed his post at NRECA in 1945. He frequently returned to the halls of Congress to lobby for the protection of rural cooperatives. He often battled private utility companies, accusing them of overcharging their customers and trying to "kill off" the cooperatives. He also criticized the administration of Dwight D. Eisenhower and in a speech delivered at NRECA's annual meeting in 1959 said, "This is a Wall Street-oriented big-business Administration through and through and I tell you it's the most powerful enemy any consumer-owned enterprise ever had."

While NRECA general manager, Ellis toured rural electrification projects in Russia with a Senate subcommittee and served as director of the Co-operative League of the United States of America. He also served on special advisory committees for the Department of Commerce and the Agency for International Development.

Because Ellis wanted to broaden his knowledge of management principles, he attended night classes at George Washington and American universities in Washington, D.C., and went back to the University of Arkansas for three six-week summer terms, where he completed a B.S. degree in business administration in 1958.

Ellis suffered a massive heart attack and stroke in the summer of 1965, from which his doctors initially feared he would not recover. He returned to his work at NRECA after his convalescence, however, and on Sept. 23, 1966, he married Camille Waldron Fitzhugh.

In 1966, Random House published Ellis's book, *A Giant Step*, which tells the story of NRECA and the development of the rural power system after the birth of the Rural Electrification Administration in 1935. One reviewer praised it for the force and clarity of its descriptions of "heartbreaking defeats along with spectacular victories." Ellis also wrote of his vision that rural electrification would "never be completed until the last person in the most remote area of the last country of the world who wants electric service has it." Ellis said he was not sure when he began to realize his obligation to help underdeveloped countries build their own cooperative rural electrification programs, but this endeavor, which took Ellis on journeys through Latin America, Africa, India, the Near East, and the Far East, was well under way by the time the book was published.

As a champion of rural electrification, Ellis won a reputation for his strong convictions and tireless energy. On his retirement from the NRECA in 1968, Vice-President Hubert H. Humphrey told Ellis, "Every time I see a light in rural America, it is a tribute to you." His opponents respected his effectiveness as a lobbyist, but criticized his tactics and his vision. In *Ellis in Wonderland: The Amazing Story of a Million-Dollar-a-Year Lobby and the Man Who Runs It* (1959), Glenn Martz wrote: "Mr. Ellis' social and economic blueprint for America is a veritable wonderland of Utopian dreams, brimming with such socialistic schemes as a giant public power grid which will eliminate private enterprise from the power field—harness America's falling waters for, in his words, 'the benefit of all the people.' "

Ellis served as a member of the National Water Commission from 1968 to 1970. He was also a special consultant to Secretary of Agriculture Orville L. Freeman during 1968. He was an assistant to Senator John L. McClellan (who had defeated Ellis for the senate nomination in 1942) from 1971 until 1977. In 1977 he returned to the Department of Agriculture and was employed there until his retirement in 1979. Ellis died in Chevy Chase, Md., and was buried in Arlington National Cemetery.

[Ellis's papers are in a special collection at the University of Arkansas Library in Fayetteville. An article by Ellis called "Power and Plenty" is in *Commonweal*, May 18, 1956. See also the book review of *A Giant Step* by Richard W. Gable in *Agricultural History*, Jan. 1969; and Orval E. Faubus, "Clyde T. Ellis: Lawmaker Led Movement to Electrify Rural America," *Arkansas Democrat*, July 23, 1989. Obituaries are in the *Arkansas Gazette*, Feb. 10, 1980; and the *New York Times*, Feb. 12, 1980.]

ROBYN BURNETT

ERNST, MAX (Apr. 2, 1891–Apr. 1, 1976), artist, was born in Brühl, Germany, the son of Philipp Ernst, a teacher of deaf mutes, and Luise Kopp. Ernst's father, a devout Roman Catholic and amateur painter of highly realistic images, was outraged by much of his son's art, which was, in part, a backlash against his father's structured realism. Ernst developed an early interest in the avant-garde. In high school he read the works of modern philosophers, including Max Stirner, Friedrich Nietzsche, and Sigmund Freud. He also studied abnormal psychology, making numerous visits to an insane asylum to study the art of the mentally ill.

Ernst entered the University of Bonn in the winter of 1909 as a philosophy student, but he directed much of his energy to refining his artistic ability. In college he became affiliated with Young Rhineland, a group of young German artists challenging traditional forms of poetry and painting. Ernst's first major showing took place at the German Autumn Salon in Berlin in 1913. Shortly thereafter he abandoned his studies in Bonn and moved to Paris.

Ernst's brief stay in Paris was interrupted by the outbreak of World War I in August 1914. Ernst's service in the German artillery in France and what is now Poland for the duration of the war affected his sense of self and the world, affirming in him a contempt for authority and tradition. Deeply moved by the war and the historical influences that gave rise to it, Ernst responded through his art. In 1918, shortly after his return to Cologne, Ernst married art historian Luise Strauss. They had one child, the American artist Jimmy Ernst, and they divorced in 1927. In Cologne, Ernst met artist-poet Jean Arp, founder of the dada movement. Ernst embraced the movement's aim to mock bourgeois sensibilities and, with Arp's help, organized the first dada exhibition in Cologne in 1919 and 1920. During this period Ernst developed his characteristic style of visually disturbing yet comically ingenious images, including *The Horse, He's Sick* (1920) and *The Elephant of Celebes* (1921). The dada exhibitions caused such uproars in Cologne that the occupying British army and local police closed them.

In 1922, Ernst settled in Paris, where his creative energies flourished, merging the illogical and the comical in works such as *Oedipus Rex* (1922) and *Revolution by Night* (1923). During this period Ernst formed some of his closest and most influential relationships with European artists and writers, including André Breton and Tristan Tzara. His closest and most enduring friend, however, remained poet Paul Eluard, whom Ernst first met in 1921.

By 1921, dadaism was succumbing to the growing ranks of surrealist artists and writers, who juxtaposed incongruent subject matter to convey their unconscious thoughts and emotions. Ernst fully embraced surrealism, employing its framework to combine philosophy and psychology with art. He experienced one of his most productive periods during the mid-1920's by revealing his latent childhood fears and open distaste for authority in such works as *Two Children Are Threatened by a Nightingale* (1924), *Ubu Imperator* (1924), and *The Blessed Virgin Chastises the Infant Jesus before Three Witnesses* (1926).

During this period Ernst engaged in a tremendous array of formal experiments, which continued through much of his productive career. He developed the technique of frottage—rubbings of wood, fabric, leaves, and other textured items—to inspire his unconscious mind in the creation of major works. A selection of Ernst's frottages was later collected in a book, *Histoire naturelle* (1926). The publication of three "collage-novels," *La Femme 100 têtes* (1929), *Réve d'une petite fille qui voulait entrer au Carmel* (1930), and *Une Semaine de bonté* (1934), marked yet another revolution in form. Cleverly recombining illustrations and phrases from popular nineteenth-century magazines and cheap novels, Ernst used his stories to critique popular culture. He also pioneered the process of decalcomania, the transfer of paint from one surface to another. Ernst even presaged American artist Jackson Pollock with the technique of oscillation, dripping and splashing paint over a canvas from a tin can full of holes.

Ernst's work became increasingly gloomy toward the onset of World War II, prompting many latter-day critics to suggest that the artist foresaw the destruction and decay that later beset Europe. The Third Reich placed Ernst's name on its blacklist in 1933. Ernst responded to the hostile Nazi regime with a series of penetrating images of catastrophe, including *The Petrified City* (1935), an eerily prophetic image of postwar Europe, and *The Angel of Hearth and Home* (1937), a remarkable portrait of advancing destruction. Ernst continued his reaction to the war after moving to the United States in such works as *Europe After the Rain II* (1940–1942).

In 1927, Ernst married Marie-Berthe Aurenche. He left her in 1936 to live with painter Leonora Carrington near Avignon, France. In 1939, Ernst was interned for a year in southern France as an enemy alien. When the Nazis defeated France and the French army surrendered, Ernst managed to escape prison and settle in the United States as a political refugee, receiving a warm welcome from New York City's artistic community. He married American art collector and gallery owner Peggy Guggenheim in December 1941.

Ernst's stormy personal life calmed when he left Guggenheim in 1943 to live with American painter Dorothea Tanning in Sedona, Ariz. They married three years later. The Arizona landscape inspired Ernst as much as his new wife's youthful exuberance, and in 1948 he became an American citizen. After moving to Arizona, Ernst began to experiment with sculpture, producing such notable works as *The King Playing with the Queen* (1944) and *Capricorn* (1948).

Ernst returned to France in 1953 and won the Grand Prize at the Venice Biennale the following year. He became a French citizen in 1958. The Guggenheim Museum in New York City hosted his last major exhibition in 1975. Although he never relented in his attack on modern civilization and culture, Ernst's later work became more lighthearted, striking a dramatic contrast to the earlier nightmarish visions and subversive fantasies that remain his most celebrated accomplishments. He died in Paris.

[See John Russell, *Max Ernst* (1967). Many of Ernst's writings are collected in *Beyond Painting* (1948). An obituary is in the *New York Times*, Apr. 2, 1976.]

FRANK MORROW

ERNST, MORRIS LEOPOLD (Aug. 23, 1888–May 21, 1976), lawyer, was born in Uniontown, Ala., the son of Carl Ernst, who ran a general store, and Sarah Bernheim. When Morris was two years old, his father took the family to New York City, where he prospered in the real estate business. Ernst was graduated from Williams College in 1909 and from New York Law School in 1912. In 1915 he married Susan Leerburger; they had one child before her death in 1922. The next year he married

Margaret Samuels, with whom he had two children. In 1915 he cofounded the firm of Greenbaum, Wolff and Ernst, with which he remained associated until his death. His specialty of censorship law and cases involving literary and artistic freedom gave the firm an unusual reputation.

Nettled by his defeat in a United States Customs Service book censorship case in 1927, Ernst determined to master the subject. "Very quickly I realized the inadequacy of my part-time preparation," he said in a rare introspective moment. "I started to make up for it by exhibitionism and have never recovered." He and William Seagle coauthored *To the Pure* the following year, the first of several jointly written volumes on freedom of expression in which Ernst argued the futility of attempting to define obscenity and focused on the irrational psychology of censorship. The book brought him a succession of celebrated censorship cases, all of which he won.

His most notable censorship case was the battle to have James Joyce's *Ulysses* admitted to the United States. Despite the book's reputation for literary excellence since its publication in Paris in 1922, its sexual frankness had kept it out of the United States legally, although blue paperbound copies had been smuggled in. In 1933, Bennett Cerf, head of the recently established publishing firm Random House, approached Ernst, who undertook to reverse the importation ban. Timing the proceedings to come up when the "liberal-minded" federal district Judge John M. Woolsey would be sitting, Ernst argued that the book should be considered in its entirety and as a work of literary merit. Woolsey agreed. His eloquent opinion was a landmark in the history of American censorship law. Random House, unable to afford Ernst's standard fee, agreed to pay him a 5 percent royalty on the hardbound edition of *Ulysses* and 2 percent on its Modern Library and paperback editions. While this arrangement provided a substantial lifelong income, Ernst was more pleased with the fame he had achieved.

Ernst opposed governmental censorship of any stripe, but drew the line at what he called "utter freedom" of expression. From 1929 to 1954, as co–general counsel of the American Civil Liberties Union, he pushed the ACLU into fighting literary censorship. He pressed his belief that because no workable definition of obscenity was possible, all prosecutions were inevitably arbitrary and speech about sex should be fully protected. Ernst represented Mary Ware Dennett in her successful battle to circulate *The Sex Side of Life* legally. "Sex wins in America," he proclaimed after prevailing on appeal in 1930. As general counsel for the Planned Parenthood Federation from 1929 to 1960, he led the first attacks on laws restricting the distribution and use of birth control information and devices. Ernst's greatest gift as a lawyer was his flamboyant ability to dramatize and publicize issues.

His involvement with the ACLU and Planned Parenthood was only part of his public activities. Ernst had been friendly with Franklin D. Roosevelt since Roosevelt, as governor of New York, named him to the state insurance commission. Later, at Roosevelt's direction, he spent considerable time in Washington, D.C., sometimes staying at the White House, talking to government officials, and reporting back to the president. One of these officials was his idol, Supreme Court Justice Louis D. Brandeis; another was Federal Bureau of Investigation director J. Edgar Hoover. During World War II, Ernst performed personal diplomatic chores for Roosevelt. This access became part of his essence.

By 1940, Ernst had become an obsessive anti-Communist. Battles with Communists in the National Lawyers Guild, which he had helped found, in the American Newspaper Guild, to which he was counsel, and the ACLU sharpened his attitude. He advocated a disclosure bill requiring all organizations to file information with the government concerning goals, finances, and membership. The ACLU, he thought, should abandon its doctrinaire approach, purge leftists, and compromise in the political arena. After the war he became more unyielding, and his professional relationship with Hoover blossomed.

It is easy and true to say this was the result of a pattern of behavior that began in the 1930's, but Ernst went further than most other informers. He protected the FBI whenever possible, calling himself "Hoover's lawyer," and he alerted the FBI to antibureau sentiments among ACLU members and to their plans to condemn it. While he may not have given specific names, he did pass confidential ACLU material to the FBI. His relationship with Hoover compromised his law practice: he would not sue *Red Channels* magazine for possibly libelous comments it made about one of his clients, journalist William L. Shirer.

Claiming that even unpopular causes were entitled to counsel, in 1957 Ernst undertook on behalf of the Dominican Republic government of General Rafael Trujillo an inquiry into the disappearance and death of Jésus de Galindez, a scholarly Basque exile and critic of Trujillo, who had vanished in New York City the year before. His 1958 report not only absolved Trujillo but found "no evidence of any nature . . . pointing toward [Galindez's] death or of any crime connected with his disappearance," evidence that only Trujillo could have had. The whole episode dismayed many of Ernst's friends and allies. He accepted the assignment to keep busy and his name prominent, just as he invented reasons to go to Washington to see a senator or Hoover.

His law practice was wide-ranging, with clients drawn from the worlds of literature, journalism, entertainment, and politics. Assistants did the spadework at his direction; he polished and controlled the final product. The best ideas were usually his (he had "one hundred solutions but only ninety-five problems," said a character lampooning him in a New York Bar Association sketch), and he never was bashful in taking the credit. In this manner Ernst wrote more than two dozen books, nearly half with several collaborators, about censorship and privacy, Communism in America, and sexual behavior. His own books considered the First Amendment, the leisure society, and large-scale business and government in addition to several volumes of diaries and memoirs. All were hastily drafted with a simplistic interpretation that allowed for quick reading.

Short, ever voluble, witty, informal, and nattily attired, Ernst rarely let a difference of opinion strain a friendship. "I only learn from people with whom I disagree," he said. His brisk, witty mind and breezy manner resembled a pogo stick in full flight. Ernst lived in a world of celebrities and let others know it. "He must know some unimportant people, but if so he never mentions them," noted Roger Baldwin, the longtime head of the ACLU. Ernst's clients and friends often overlapped. His shrewd sense of tactics and publicity was instrumental in his being the single most important civil liberties lawyer in the first half of the twentieth century. More than any other lawyer of his time, Ernst led the fight for literary, artistic, and reproductive freedom. He died in New York City.

[A large collection of Ernst's papers is at the Harry H. Ransom Humanities Research Center at the University of Texas. Hundreds of his letters to Roosevelt, bits of news and gossip he picked up that he thought might be useful, are at the Roosevelt Library in Hyde Park, N.Y. Ernst was author or coauthor of more than two dozen books and hundreds of articles in general and professional publications. See also Marquis James, "Morris L. Ernst," *Scribner's*, July 1938; Fred Rodell, "Morris Ernst," *Life*, Feb. 21, 1944; Edward Lindeman, "Multiple-Cause Crusader," *Saturday Review*, Nov. 13, 1948; Paul S. Boyer, *Purity in Print* (1968); William Shirer, *20th Century Journey* (1976); Bennett Cerf, *At Random* (1977); Harrison E. Salisbury, "The Strange Correspondence of Morris Ernst and John Edgar Hoover 1939–1964," *Nation*, Dec. 1, 1984; Jerold Simmons, "Morris Ernst and Disclosure," *Mid-America*, Jan. 1989; Samuel Walker, *In Defense of American Liberties: A History of the ACLU* (1990); and Edward DeGrazia, *Girls Lean Back Everywhere* (1992). An obituary is in the *New York Times*, May 23, 1976.]

ROGER K. NEWMAN

ETTING, RUTH (Nov. 23, 1896–Sept. 24, 1978), singer, was born in David City, Nebr., the daughter of Winifred and Alfred Etting; her father was a bank teller. Ruth's mother became ill and Ruth went to live with her paternal grandparents at age five. Her grandfather, George Etting, owned Etting Roller Mills and built the David City Opera House. Her father remarried after the death of his first wife, but Ruth remained with her grandparents.

As a young child, Etting showed no great interest in music and did not participate in any school musical activities. Growing up in David City, her only singing was as a member of the local Congregational church choir. She was not very interested in academics but enjoyed drawing and design. Etting completed high school at seventeen and soon after left for Chicago to attend the Academy of Fine Arts to study costume design. While attending school, she sketched costume designs for the wife of the manager of the Marigold Gardens nightclub. The manager and his wife liked Etting's work and invited her to the club to watch a show. Etting was enamored by the chorus, and soon after the manager offered her a job as a chorus member. For a time she attended school while working at the Marigold Gardens and another nightspot. But she was unable to keep up this pace and decided to quit school.

In 1919 a flu epidemic caused the Chicago government to close all nightclubs. Etting supported herself by painting Christmas cards. When the Marigold Gardens reopened, she rejoined the chorus. One evening the male singing star became ill. Etting knew his solo (she had been overheard quietly singing it along with the lead singer), and the manager asked her to dress in men's clothes and sing the solo, "Hats Off to the Polo Girl." Her performance went so well that Etting was asked to continue singing the solo for the duration of the show. Her voice was clear and sincere, and audiences loved her singing as well as her appearance.

Etting was young and inexperienced at negotiating business deals. She had no family in Chicago and was reluctant to tell her grandparents that she had quit design school and needed guidance. While singing at Marigold Gardens, she met the boisterous and outspoken Martin Moses ("Moe") Snyder, nicknamed "the Gimp." Before long, Snyder was her manager, and on July 12, 1922, they married. When elaborate floor shows began to disappear under Prohibition, Etting took a job at an Italian nightclub singing for tips. Later she moved to Chicago's College Inn at the Sherman Hotel. There she appeared with Abe Lyman and his orchestra on WLS radio programs. Columbia signed a recording contract with Etting around 1926. Her first recordings were "Let's Talk About My Sweetie" and "Nothing Else to Do." In 1927 she became a member of Florenz Ziegfeld's *Follies* in New York City. The 1930 *Follies* featured Ruth Etting singing "Ten Cents a Dance," a song that became associated with her throughout her singing career.

With the death of Ziegfeld in 1932 came a change in American entertainment. Etting left the *Follies* and appeared regularly on popular radio programs, such as "Chesterfield's Music That Satisfies." In 1933 she appeared in the movie *Roman Scandals* with Eddie Cantor. However, Etting's acting talents were never fully developed; most of her movie appearances featured her singing only.

As her manager, Moe Snyder oftentimes bullied agents, producers, and fans alike. He was temperamental and often alienated the very agents and producers he wished to impress. Although Etting was unhappy in her marriage, for many years she was too afraid of Snyder to leave him. In 1937, Etting made four recordings for Decca. After these recordings, she made no attempt to work. Sometime in August of that year, in front of guests, Snyder lost his temper and lashed Etting across the legs with his cane. Soon after, Etting sought a divorce, which was granted on Nov. 30, 1937.

Etting had worked for a brief time in 1935 with pianist and arranger Myrl Alderman. After her divorce she began seeing Alderman and they soon fell in love. When Snyder heard of this budding romance, he began harassing Etting by phone. In 1938, after she moved in with Alderman, Snyder came to their home and shot Alderman. Snyder was arrested and eventually served one year in prison for attempted murder. Alderman recovered, and he and Etting were married in December 1938 and soon settled in Colorado Springs, Colo. After World War II, the couple moved to Hollywood. In 1954, Metro-Goldwyn-Mayer obtained the rights to make a movie version of Ruth Etting's life. Doris Day played the role of Ruth Etting in the film, *Love Me or Leave Me*.

Although Ruth Etting had enjoyed a successful singing career and much popularity, her marriage to Snyder dampened her ambitions. In a later interview she said that she really did not enjoy her musical career because she associated it with her relationship with Snyder. She seemed quite content married to Alderman and not particularly bothered by her growing anonymity. She came out of retirement in 1946 to appear regularly on the "Rudy Vallee Hour." She also starred with Alderman on a radio show on WHN, a New York station.

Etting sang with a sincerity that touched American audiences, popularizing such songs as "It All Depends on You," "You Made Me Love You," "Ten Cents a Dance," "Mean to Me," and others that she recorded on the Columbia, Brunswick, and Decca labels. Etting's later recordings have a much richer and mature vocal sound and a more developed sense of rhythmic phrasing. She made recordings with early jazz musicians Rube Bloom, Joe Venuti, Eddie Lang, and the Dorsey brothers. She sang with Bing Crosby, Eddie Cantor, and other popular artists of the time. Etting continued to live in Colorado Springs until her death.

[Obituaries are in *Variety*, Sept. 27, 1978, and the *New York Times*, Nov. 6, 1978.]

JAN SHAPIRO

EVANS, BERGEN BALDWIN (Sept. 19, 1904–Feb. 4, 1978), college professor, author, and television host, was born in Franklin, Ohio, one of six children of Rice Evans and Louise Cass. His father, a country doctor, gave up his practice and entered the consular service. The family moved to Sheffield, England, when Bergen was four. He returned to Ohio during World War I, attending high school in Franklin and working in a paper mill. He entered Miami University at Oxford, Ohio, at the age of fifteen, where he worked on campus as a waiter and drew newspaper cartoons. Evans graduated with a B.A. in 1924 and was a member of Phi Beta Kappa; he went on to obtain an M.A. from Harvard University (1925), became a Rhodes Scholar at Oxford University (1928–1931), and then returned to Harvard to receive the Ph.D. in 1932. In 1932, Evans joined the faculty of Northwestern University as a lecturer, and he became a professor thirteen years later. He married Jean Whinery on Aug. 5, 1939. They had two children.

His writing career focused on the English language and its usage. He became best known for his tremendous wit. In his book *Comfortable Words* (1962), Evans investigated the meaning of words and how meanings change with time. He pulled his topics from everyday life, from experiences with people from all walks of life. Evans came to believe that most people were liars. He entered the lecture circuit with a piece entitled "Why Do People Tell Such Awful Lies?" Many were angered by his material but his popularity continued to grow. His book *The Natural History of Nonsense* (1946) reveals these feelings toward life and people.

One of the last successful network programs from Chicago was the low-key game show, Du Mont's "Down You Go" (1951–1956), which introduced the erudite Northwestern University professor, Bergen Evans. The show was created by Louis G. Cowan, who had a long history of successful game shows on radio and TV, including "Stop the Music." "Down You Go" was distinctively different from other network productions because of its Chicago base and its use of unknown talent. It emerged as one of the wittiest game shows on TV. "Down You Go" had a very simple format. Evans gave clues to the panel, which was supposed to guess a slogan, sentence, word, or phrase by adding a letter at a time. Members of the panel included Francis Coughlin, Toni Gilman, Robert Breen, and Carmelita Pope. Evans soon was making several times more money from broadcasting than from teaching. "I never cease to marvel," he commented, "that I am paid money for this at all."

In early 1955, Evans became the head of a staff of ten that prepared questions for "The $64,000 Question" and "The $64,000 Challenge." Contestants appeared over a period of several weeks in an effort to reach the $64,000 level. The television shows became known for their tough questions. A scandal erupted with charges that some contestants had been given answers in advance, but Evans's career and reputation remained untainted when he proved he knew nothing of the corruption on the shows. A later Evans show, "The Last Word" (1957–1959), which was also created by Cowan, dealt with etymologies. Evans conducted sophisticated panel discussions on the vagaries of the English language with Arthur Knight, June Havoc, and John Mason Brown.

Evans was master of ceremonies on other network TV and radio shows, including "Super Ghost" (1952–1953), "Of Many Things" (1953–1954), "English for Americans" (1961–1962), "Inquiry" (1961–1963), and "Words in the News" (1962–1963). His work on radio and TV earned him a George Foster Peabody Award in 1957 for excellence in broadcasting.

Throughout his television and radio career, Evans remained on the faculty at Northwestern, where for more than forty years he taught a course called "Introductions to Literature." He was so well liked and respected that his colleagues voted unanimously to let him continue to teach past retirement age as professor emeritus of English.

On campus, Evans had a reputation for being unconventional. He created a mild stir when he took the black American diplomat Ralph Bunche to the Northwestern Faculty Club long before the days of civil rights protests. Once, a minister called him to task for one of his ongoing attacks on the alleged infallibility of the Bible. Evans asked the minister to return for his next lecture. When the minister showed up with seventy fellow clergy, Evans changed his original prepared talk and spoke instead on the intimidation of the public by the clergy.

Evans died in Highland Park, Ill.

[Evans also wrote, with Cornelia Evans, *A Dictionary of Contemporary American Usage* (1957). An obituary is in the *New York Times*, Feb. 5, 1978.]

SARAH R. GARREN

EVANS, WILLIAM JOHN ("BILL") (Aug. 16, 1929–Sept. 15, 1980), jazz pianist and composer, was born in Plainfield, N.J., the son of Harry F. Evans and Mary Soroka. As a boy Evans played the flute, violin, and piano. He graduated from North Plainfield High School in 1946 and attended Southeastern Louisiana College, where he graduated in 1950 with a major in piano and a minor in flute.

Evans served in the United States Army from 1951 to 1954. He was stationed in Illinois, where he played the flute in an army band. During his off-duty hours he pursued his interest in jazz, performing as a pianist in nightclubs in Chicago. In 1955 he returned to the New York City area and did postgraduate work at the Mannes College of Music. He began in earnest his career as a jazz musician, playing piano with such noted jazz artists as Tony Scott and Charles Mingus. He studied the modal techniques of jazz composer George Russell, and began to incorporate them into his own improvisations and compositions. His piano solo on Russell's 1957 recording "All About Rosie," commissioned by the 1957 Brandeis University Festival of the Arts, brought Evans widespread recognition and praise.

The key factor in Evans's development as a musician was his replacement in 1959 of the pianist Red Garland in a sextet led by trumpeter Miles Davis. The ensemble included alto saxophonist "Cannonball" Adderley, tenor saxophonist John Coltrane, bassist Paul Chambers, and drummer Jimmy Cobb. Davis's influence on Evans was profound. During their brief association, Evans refined the distinctive improvisational and accompaniment style that would place his personal stamp on a whole generation of pianists. The sextet produced the Columbia Records album *Kind of Blue* (1959), which became the benchmark for modal improvising. Evans's piano playing combined his modal experience with Russell with the innovative modal style that Davis was exploring. The album represented a pathbreaking shift from improvising over a set of fixed harmonic progressions to the free use of church modes, which dated back to medieval sacred music.

After finishing his stint with the Davis group, Evans formed his own trio the same year. Before Evans, the trio was a setting that used the bass and drums as accompaniment to and reinforcement of the solo piano line. With Evans, drums and bass became central to the musical experience. By the early 1960's, he had forever changed the way trio playing will be evaluated. His classic ensemble included drummer Paul Motian and bassist Scott LaFaro. Much of what is generally considered the essence of Bill Evans's trio playing was produced during this collaboration, including the 1961 Riverside albums *Waltz for Debby* and *Live at Village Vanguard*. This creative outburst of the late 1950's through the early 1960's was cut short by the death of LaFaro in an automobile accident in 1961. It was not until Evans started to work with bassist Chuck Israels a year later that his concept of the unified trio continued to evolve. He recorded the highly acclaimed Verne album *Trio '65* with Israels and drummer Larry Bunker.

The trio remained Evans's preferred format and he continued to polish his signature style with various ensembles. He also made albums of duets with Jim Hall, Eddie Gomez, and Tony Bennett. A legendary solo performer, he recorded two albums with Verve, *Conversations with Myself* (1963) and *Further Conversations with Myself* (1967), where he improvised against a prerecorded track of his own playing. In 1973, Evans married Nenette Zazzara; they adopted one child.

Evans was a prolific composer. His compositions, however, were closely tied to his improvisational style and few became well-known standards performed by other artists. Despite health difficulties involving stomach ulcer and liver problems and a recurring struggle with drug addiction, Evans appeared in public and recorded regularly until just before his death in New York City. Davis paid homage to Evans with the ultimate accolade, remarking that "he played the piano the way it should be played."

Evans's influence on pianists extended beyond the trio setting into the realm of extended improvisations and reharmonization of popular melodies. One of the best ways to study Evans's approach is to look at transcriptions of his improvisatory performances, which are note-for-note renderings of his playing. His style encompassed long, flowing melodic lines with very sparse left-hand accompaniment and then beautiful full reharmonized chords with non-chord tone intervals of half and whole steps. Evans's compositions often utilized a few basic formulas or patterns combined into a complex structure over which he then improvised. His innovations have been incorporated into the vocabulary of a succeeding generation of jazz pianists, including Chick Corea, Herbie Hancock, and Keith Jarrett.

Evans received five Grammy awards and won the *Down Beat* critics poll five times, England's Melody Maker award (1968), and Japan's Swing Journal award (1969).

Evans died in New York City.

[A collection of materials relating to the life and work of Evans is located at Southeastern Louisiana University. See also Nat Hentoff, "Introducing Bill Evans," *The Jazz Review*, Oct. 1955; Mark C. Gridley, *Jazz Styles* (1978); Clifford J. Safane, "Bill Evans Conversations," *Jazz Forum*, Feb. 1979; and Gregory Eugene Smith, "Homer, Gregory, and Bill Evans? The Theory of Formulaic Composition in the Context of Jazz Piano Improvisation" (Ph.D. diss., Harvard University, 1983). An obituary is in the *New York Times*, Sept. 17, 1980.]

DENNIS THURMOND

EWING, OSCAR ROSS (Mar. 8, 1889–Jan. 8, 1980), corporation lawyer and political adviser, was born in Greensburg, Ind., one of two children of George McClellan Ewing and Jeanette ("Nettie") Moore. His father was a merchant of modest means. Influenced by an uncle who was a lawyer and circuit court judge, Ewing knew at an early age that he wanted to be a lawyer. After graduating from public high school in Greensburg in 1906, he worked his way through Indiana University. A philosophy major, Ewing (who hated the name Oscar and was known as "Jack"), was elected president of his class in both his junior and senior years.

After graduating from Indiana in 1910, Ewing entered Harvard Law School, where he was chosen editor of the *Harvard Law Review*. Again working to pay his tuition, Ewing ran out of money about halfway through the program. The dean of the law school, Ezra Ripley Thayer, thought so highly of Ewing that he personally loaned him the money to continue his education. Graduating in 1913, Ewing later not only repaid Thayer but established a revolving student loan fund in the dean's name.

Interested in politics from an early age, Ewing was elected secretary of the Decatur County (Indiana) Democratic Committee before he was old enough to vote. But he vowed he would never devote himself exclusively to politics until he was financially independent. Ewing married Helen Eliza Dennis on Nov. 4, 1915. They had two children.

In 1919, after one year of service in the United States Army stationed in Washington, D.C., Ewing joined the law firm of Hughes, Schurman and Dwight in New York City. (Charles Evans Hughes, a founding partner of the firm, was a former governor of New York and later chief justice of the Supreme Court.) When that firm was dissolved in 1937, Ewing became a cofounder of Hughes, Hubbard and Ewing, also in New York, remaining as a partner there until 1947, with Charles Evans Hughes, Jr. The practice, whose clients included the pharmaceutical giant Merck and Company and the Aluminum Company of America, was very successful.

Ewing entered the political arena in 1939, when he was named eastern states campaign manager for Paul McNutt, a former governor of Indiana who had been a fraternity brother of Ewing's at Indiana University, for the Democratic nomination for president in 1940. McNutt pulled out of the race when President Franklin D. Roosevelt announced he would run for a third term. In 1940, Ewing became assistant chairman of the Democratic National Committee after Judge Ferdinand Pecora, an important political figure in New York City, recommended him to President Roosevelt. As vice-chairman of the Democratic National Committee from 1942 to 1947, Ewing was largely responsible for running the 1944 convention in Chicago. He was instrumental in the nomination of Harry S. Truman over Henry Wallace to be Roosevelt's running mate.

After Truman's assumption of the presidency in 1945, Robert E. Hannegan, then chairman of the Democratic National Committee and a close friend of Truman's, urged the president to appoint Ewing administrator of the Federal Security Agency (now the Department of Health and Human Services). Ewing served in that post from Aug. 27, 1947, to Jan. 20, 1953. A social reformer who empathized with the downtrodden, he prized his new job because, as he said, "our agency, more than any other in the federal government, deals with human values. The degree to which we can give all citizens equal access to the basic human needs is the measure of practical democracy."

With the loss of Democratic control of both houses of Congress in the 1946 election, Ewing became convinced that Truman was paying too much attention to the conservative members of his administration, thereby alienating many of

Ewing

the liberal groups that had been essential to the winning coalition Roosevelt had forged. Ewing invited a small but influential group of liberal advisers to meet in his apartment in the Wardman Park Hotel in Washington, D.C., to discuss political strategy. This private informal body, which called itself the "Monday Night Group," met weekly from 1947 until the end of Truman's presidency in 1952. It included Clark Clifford, who was counsel to the president and the group's unofficial liaison with Truman.

The Monday Night Group changed the course of Truman's presidency. It laid out a liberal agenda, effecting Truman's upset election victory over Thomas E. Dewey in 1948 and forming the core of the Fair Deal, which guided the president for the rest of his term. Among the group's initial recommendations were such presidential actions as desegregating the armed forces and vetoing the Tart-Hartley bill.

In January of 1948, Truman requested a study of the possibilities for raising health levels in the interest of national welfare and security. Ewing advised Truman that only a prepaid system of government health insurance would meet the health and medical needs of all the people. In his report to the president entitled *The Nation's Health—A Ten Year Program* (1948), he pointed out the inadequacy of the voluntary system of health care, including voluntary insurance plans. The Ewing report was vigorously endorsed by Truman, who made it part of his political strategy in the 1948 campaign.

A peripheral but troubling question erupted right before the 1948 election on the matter of the partition of Palestine and the establishment of a Jewish state. Ewing investigated the legal claims of the Arabs and Jews to Palestine and found that under international law the Allies could dispose of Palestine—conquered from Turkey in World War I—as they wished. He told Truman that the Jews' title to a part of this conquered land became indisputable when the Allies transferred their title to it to them and advised him not to consent to any modification of boundaries as fixed by the United Nations except as it was agreeable to the Jews. Truman recognized de facto the state of Israel within several hours after it was proclaimed.

Ewing retired from government service and politics in January 1953 as the Truman presidency came to an end. His first wife died in June 1953, and he married Mary Whiting MacKay Thomas on Oct. 12, 1955. Wishing to live in a college town, he moved to Chapel Hill, N.C., in 1960. There he served the rest of his life as a director of the Research Triangle Foundation, a nonprofit organization that attracted corporations such as IBM to locate major research facilities in about 5,000 acres of land within the area bounded by the University of North Carolina, Duke University, and North Carolina State University. From 1963 to 1967, Ewing was also chairman of the Research Triangle Regional Planning Commission.

Ewing died at his home in Chapel Hill.

[Ewing's papers are at the Harry S. Truman Library in Independence, Mo. The Oral History Collection of Columbia University contains the transcript of a 1966 autobiographical interview with Ewing conducted by Peter A. Corning. The Harry S. Truman Library contains a transcript of an interview conducted by J. R. Fuchs in four sessions, April 29–30 and May 1–2, 1969. For Ewing's role in promoting national health insurance, see Monte M. Poen, *Harry S. Truman Versus the Medical Lobby* (1979). Ewing's Wardman Park Hotel group's activities are described in Cabell Phillips, *The Truman Presidency* (1966); and in Clark Clifford, *Counsel to the President* (1990). Obituaries are in the *New York Times*, Jan. 9, 1980 and the *Washington Post*, Jan. 9, 1980.]

BERNARD HIRSCHHORN

F

FAHY, CHARLES (Aug. 27, 1892–Sept. 17, 1979), jurist, was born in Rome, Ga., the son of Sarah Jonas and Thomas Fahy, a dry-goods merchant. One of eleven children, Fahy graduated from Rome High School in 1908 and took a preparatory course at the Darlington High School before entering the University of Notre Dame. After studying at Notre Dame for one year, he attended Georgetown University, where he received an LL.B. in 1914. He was admitted to the bar that same year and practiced law in Washington, D.C., until 1924.

Fahy served overseas from 1917 to 1919 in the United States Navy Reserve as a naval aviator with the British and American forces. He was awarded the Navy Cross for his heroism as a biplane pilot in World War I. Following military service, Fahy returned to law practice in Washington, D.C., then in 1924 moved to Santa Fe, N.Mex. because of his ailing health. After eight years of private practice, he became city attorney of Santa Fe in 1932. Fahy married Mary Agnes Lane of Washington, D.C., on June 26, 1929. They had four children.

His health improved, Fahy returned to Washington in 1933 at the request of a New Deal official who knew of his work in New Mexico. He was given two jobs in the Franklin D. Roosevelt administration, assistant solicitor in the Interior Department and chairman of the Petroleum Administrative board. In September 1935 he was named general counsel of the National Labor Relations Board, charged with directing the staff of the NLRB in the early years of the National Labor Relations Act (Wagner Act) of 1935.

Fahy successfully defended five of the crucial cases that upheld one of the landmark pieces of New Deal labor legislation, including *National Labor Relations Board* v. *Jones and Laughlin Steel Corporation* (1973), which is regarded as having established the constitutionality of the Wagner Act. The Supreme Court justices dubbed him "Whispering Charlie" for his soft-spoken voice and gentle demeanor. Fahy appeared in front of the United States Supreme Court on eighteen occasions regarding cases involving the Wagner Act. His arguments were wholly sustained sixteen times and partially sustained twice. His success attracted attention in administration circles, and Fahy later remarked that his work in defense of the Wagner Act was the most satisfying of his life.

President Roosevelt nominated Fahy for the post of assistant solicitor general in September 1940. In that capacity he helped negotiate the destroyers-for-bases deal with Great Britain, which received fifty American destroyers in exchange for American use of British bases. Fahy became solicitor general in November 1941, after his predecessor, Francis Biddle, became attorney general of the United States. One of Fahy's earliest cases as solicitor general involved the quarantining of Japanese Americans on the West Coast after the attack on Pearl Harbor. In a dramatic scene in front of the Supreme Court, Fahy declared that he could defend "with conviction" only portions of the government's program. The court sustained only those portions. In 1942, Fahy received an LL.D. from Georgetown University Law Center.

Fahy remained solicitor general until 1945, when he became the legal adviser and director of the legal division of the United States Military Government in Germany. He served as an adviser to the United States delegation to the San Francisco conference that led to the creation of the United Nations. The following year he served as a legal adviser to the State Department and was a member of the legal commission of the General Assembly of the United Nations. From 1947 to 1949 Fahy served as an alternate United States representative to the General Assembly.

While maintaining a private legal practice in Washington, D.C., Fahy served as the chairman of the President's Committee on Equality of Treatment and Opportunity in the Armed Services, which President Harry Truman created to examine segregation in the armed forces. Although Generals Dwight D. Eisenhower and Omar Bradley opposed integration, Fahy argued that all army school courses should be open to blacks. After two years of quiet meetings and exchanges of memorandums with the secretary of the army and the Joint Chiefs of Staff, Fahy and his committee prevailed. Army courses were opened to all enlisted men, regardless of race, and desegregation followed. President Truman named Fahy to the United States Court of Appeals in 1949; he assumed senior status in 1967.

Judge Fahy wrote frequently on the rights of criminals, insanity statutes, and racial desegregation. His 1955 opinion regarding the right of Americans to passports attracted national attention. The opinion expressed the unanimous decision of the Court of Appeals in forbidding the State Department to withhold passports from American citizens by "arbitrary" action. Fahy held that the right to travel was an inherent right under the Fifth Amendment. In the DeWitt Easter case in 1966, he wrote the principal opinion, which held that chronic alcoholism was a disease and not a crime.

A devout Roman Catholic and a lifelong Democrat, Fahy distinguished himself in the areas of individual liberties and the powers and limits of government. He continued to serve on the bench until his death in Washington, D.C.

[Obituaries and tributes are in the *Washington Post*, Sept. 18, 1979, and the *New York Times*, Sept. 19 and 20, 1979.]

RICHARD G. DEITSCH

FAITH, PERCY (Apr. 7, 1908–Feb. 9, 1976), musical composer, conductor, and arranger, was born in Toronto, Canada, one of eight children of Abraham Faith, a tailor, and Minnie Rotenberg. Percy's musical interests and ambitions began at an early age. He began playing the violin at age seven, but soon took up the piano. An uncle was a well-known violinist and encouraged his talents. At age eleven, Faith gave his first piano performance at the Iola Flicker, a local movie theater in Toronto. Thereafter, he performed regularly for silent movies, earning $3 per night. At age fifteen, he made his debut as a concert pianist at Massey Hall in Toronto.

Faith studied at the Canadian Academy and at age fourteen commenced a serious study of classical music with Frank Welsman at the Toronto Conservatory of Music. However, at age eighteen Faith severely burned his hands while putting out a fire on his five-year-old sister's clothing. Although he saved her life, he was unable to play the piano for some time. In spite of this, he took up arranging, studying harmony and composition. Financial difficulties prevented Faith from completing his studies at the conservatory. He was married in 1929 to a teenage sweetheart, Mary Palange, who remained his lifelong companion. They had two children.

A break came in 1934 when he was hired as an arranger and conductor by the Canadian Broadcasting Corporation. By 1937 he had his own program, "Music by Faith." The show was an enormous success and was eventually broadcast throughout North America and Hawaii. "Music by Faith" aired for seven years and was the most popular show on the network.

Advised by associates to go to the United States, in 1940 Faith auditioned for NBC's "The Carnation Contented Hour." He was hired as conductor for the popular radio show and moved to New York City. That year he became an American citizen. This was the start of an American career that would span three decades and three forms of American media: radio, television, and film. After the NBC engagement ended in 1947, he became musical director of "The Pause That Refreshes," a show on CBS sponsored by Coca-Cola, and later "The Woolworth Hour" (CBS, 1955–1957).

In 1951, Faith became musical director at Columbia Records. As head of the Artists and Repertoire Division, he helped develop such stars as Tony Bennett, Rosemary Clooney, Frankie Laine, Jerry Vale, Doris Day, Guy Mitchell, and Johnny Mathis. His own prolific recording career was under way as well. He recorded dozens of albums with Columbia, including both arrangements and original compositions. His most successful record was

"My Heart Cries for You"; "Brazilian Sleighbells" was also a big hit. Faith also arranged countless Broadway scores, including *Kismet*, *My Fair Lady*, *The Sound of Music*, and *Camelot*. These were great popular successes. He recorded arrangements of George Gershwin's music as well.

In 1960, Faith moved to Los Angeles, where he continued to work for Columbia Records. He turned his musical attention to the film industry he loved. His first film score, *Love Me or Leave Me* (1955), written with Georgie Stoll, received an Academy Award nomination. Other film scores were also successful, such as *The Third Day* (1963), *I'd Rather Be Rich* (1964), *The Love Goddesses* (1964), and *The Oscar* (1966). Later, he arranged Tara's theme from *Gone with the Wind* and the theme song from *A Summer Place*, both of which were originally composed by Max Steiner. In total, he wrote scores for eleven movies.

As determined as he was to succeed, Faith was equally determined to keep his private life out of the public eye. Unpretentious but also quite handsome, Faith, who loved Los Angeles, disdained the glitzy Hollywood social scene. He frequently visited Canada, but geography, time, and personal changes distanced him from his past. He found Canada too provincial and his old friends envious of his American success.

Perhaps Faith's greatest contribution to the musical world was to originate and develop the "easy listening" style, a distinctive blend of jazz, classical, and popular music that most closely resembled the semiclassical school of music associated with Andre Kostelanetz. He adored Kostelanetz but was also influenced by Tommy Dorsey and Frank Sinatra. Another Faith trademark was to turn a simple melody into a full-scale orchestration, loaded with violins and vivid tone color. At the peak of his popularity, Faith's own forty-five member orchestra performed his arrangements worldwide.

Some critics say he elevated "easy listening" to an art form. At the pinnacle of his career in the 1950's, he reflected an era, one that was to take its place in history as a quiet, unprovocative, and traditional time. His talents kept apace with the growth of radio, television, and film, and with great versatility he adapted to each. But his "background" music and "background" life-style may have kept him from reaching even greater heights of fame or critical acclaim. Faith died in Los Angeles after a four-year struggle with cancer.

[An obituary is in the *New York Times*, Feb. 10, 1976.]

LISA A. STAHL

FARAGO, LADISLAS (Sept. 21, 1906–Oct. 15, 1980), author and journalist, was born in Csurgo, Hungary, the son of Arthur Farago and Irma Lang. As a student at the Academy of Commerce and Consular Affairs in Budapest, from which he graduated in 1926, Farago developed a lifelong interest in war and international politics. He secured a position as a journalist in Budapest, and from 1928 to 1935 lived in Berlin as a foreign correspondent for the *New York Times*. As a correspondent for the Associated Press, Farago covered the Italian invasion of Ethiopia in 1935 and in that same year produced his first book, *Abyssinia on the Eve*. He also served as foreign editor of the London *Sunday Chronicle* in the mid-1930's.

He married Liesel Mroz on Mar. 22, 1934; they had one son. Farago became a naturalized United States citizen in the late 1930's, living in New York City.

Travel in Germany and the Middle East in the late 1930's and early 1940's inspired *Palestine at the Crossroads* and *The Riddle of Arabia* (both 1937) and *German Psychological Warfare* (1941). In 1942, Farago edited *The Axis Grand Strategy: Blueprints for the Total War*, a series of essays by leading German Nazis on their strategy and goals in World War II. The book was produced under the auspices of the Committee for National Morale, a voluntary organization of professionals in many fields dedicated to studying and promoting American morale during the war. Farago was research director for the committee from 1940 to 1942.

From 1942 to 1946 he served on the staff of the United States Office of Naval Intelligence as chief of research and planning. There followed a year as editor of *Corps Diplomatique* and three years (1947–1950) as senior editor of the magazine *United Nations World*. From 1950 to 1953 he was a consultant to Radio Free Europe.

By the early 1950's Farago had moved almost exclusively to full-time professional writing, and his output thereafter was voluminous. *Behind Closed Doors* (1950), coauthored with Rear Admiral Ellis M. Zacharias, was a study of the

Cold War. Much of Farago's writing focused on war, espionage, intelligence, and propaganda, including *War of Wits* (1954); *Burn After Reading: The Espionage History of World War II* (1961); *The Broken Seal: The Story of Operation Magic and the Pearl Harbor Disaster* (1967), on which the motion picture *Tora! Tora! Tora!* was partly based; and *The Game of the Foxes: The Untold Story of German Espionage in the United States and Great Britain During World War II* (1971). British historian Hugh Trevor-Roper stated that this last work revealed "more about the game of espionage, on a particular front, than anything so far published."

Other works included Farago's memoirs, *Strictly from Hungary* (1962), *The Tenth Fleet* (1962), about World War II American antisubmarine operations (growing out of his work with the Office of Naval Intelligence), and *It's Your Money: Waste and Mismanagement in Government Spending* (1964). *Patton: Ordeal and Triumph* (1964), a biography of General George S. Patton, Jr., was Farago's magnum opus and was adapted into the 1970 film *Patton.*

Farago created an international stir in 1972 with his assertion in a series of newspaper articles that Martin Bormann, a top aide to Adolf Hitler, was alive and living as a businessman in Argentina. It had been presumed until then that Bormann had died in Germany during the last days of World War II. Farago claimed that an Argentine intelligence officer, Juan José Velasco, had given him a photograph of the elderly Bormann and documents proving Bormann's presence in Argentina. But in December 1972, Velasco denied ever seeing Bormann and stated that the documents in Farago's possession were forgeries. In April 1973 the West German government announced that Bormann's remains had been unearthed in construction work in West Berlin. Farago stuck to his story, however, and published it in book form in *Aftermath: Martin Bormann and the Fourth Reich* (1974).

Farago died in New York City. Posthumous works included *The Secret American* (1981), a biography of J. Edgar Hoover, and *The Last Days of Patton* (1981).

As a scholarly yet lucid writer, Farago made recent history more accessible and popular to masses of readers, and the television programs and movies adapted from his works further widened his influence.

[An obituary is in the *New York Times*, Oct. 17, 1980.]

WILLIAM F. MUGLESTON

FARLEY, JAMES ALOYSIUS (May 30, 1888–June 9, 1976), politician and postmaster general, was born in Grassy Point, N.Y., the son of James Farley and Ellen Goldrick. His father was a brick manufacturer and member of the Democratic party in Republican-dominated Rockland County. At age eight, Farley campaigned for Democratic presidential candidate William Jennings Bryan. Two years later his father was killed by a horse, leaving a widow and five sons. His mother supported the family by operating a grocery store and saloon, where Farley worked in addition to his job as a machine boy at Morrissey's brickyard. He earned the nickname "Stretch" for his prowess as a first baseman on high school and semiprofessional baseball teams, and won a waltzing championship.

After graduating from Stony Point High School in 1905, he studied bookkeeping at the Packard Commercial School in New York City for nine months. He worked briefly as a bookkeeper in the Merlin, Keilholtz Paper Company in New York City and then joined Universal Gypsum Company, where he progressed from bookkeeper and company correspondent to salesman and sales manager by the time he left in 1926 to found James A. Farley and Company, which sold lime and cement to contractors. When the firm merged with five others in 1929 to form General Builders Supply Corporation, Farley served as president and director from 1929 to 1933 and again from 1949 to 1958.

A lifelong Democrat, Farley entered active politics in 1912, when he waged a successful postcard campaign for town clerk at Stony Point, becoming the first Democrat to hold that post since 1894. Farley then sent notes of thanks to every voter in the district, whether or not they had supported him. His unpaid activities included personal delivery of marriage licenses and door-to-door sales of hunting licenses on the Sunday before the opening of hunting season. He was reelected three times, leaving office in 1918 to become chairman of the Rockland County Democratic Committee. An early supporter of Alfred E. Smith's victorious campaign for governor, Farley was rewarded in 1919 with appointment as port warden of New York City at an annual salary of $5,000; he held that post for about a year until the Republican-controlled state legislature abolished it. On Apr. 28, 1920, he married Elizabeth A. ("Bess") Finnegan; they had three children before her death in 1955. In 1920 he was also elected supervisor at Stony Point.

In 1922, Farley helped Smith regain the Democratic nomination for governor over a challenge by William Randolph Hearst and was himself elected to the New York State Assembly. He was defeated for reelection in 1924, probably because of his opposition to the state law to enforce Prohibition. Nevertheless, he was a delegate to the 1924 Democratic National Convention in New York City, where he supported Smith and renewed his acquaintance with Franklin Delano Roosevelt. Governor Smith appointed Farley to the New York Athletic Commission; he became its chairman in 1925 and continued on the commission until 1933. Some of Farley's actions on the commission brought considerable criticism, particularly his rulings voiding fights between boxers of mixed weights and his practice of giving free fight tickets to friends.

Farley became secretary of the New York State Democratic Committee in 1928, while continuing as chairman of the Rockland County committee until the following year. In 1930 and again in 1932 he was elected chairman of the New York State Democratic Committee. In 1930 he was instrumental in Roosevelt's overwhelming reelection as governor. Farley immediately began to boom Roosevelt for the presidency. He toured eighteen states en route to the 1931 Elks convention in Seattle, establishing a vast network of political friendships, which he reinforced with personal letters, telephone calls, and a legendary memory for names and faces as well as details of the personal and family lives of his far-flung associates.

In 1932, with Senator Cordell Hull of Tennessee, he organized Democrats across the country in support of Roosevelt's presidential candidacy. As a delegate-at-large and Roosevelt floor leader at the 1932 Democratic National Convention, Farley helped Roosevelt supporter Senator Thomas J. Walsh of Montana win the permanent convention chairmanship over Jouett Shouse, chairman of the National Executive Committee and a Smith ally. Farley is credited with making the deal that gave the vice-presidential nomination to John Nance Garner in exchange for the backing of the Texas and California delegations, which secured the nomination for Roosevelt. Farley himself was elected national chairman on July 2, 1932, while continuing as chairman of the New York state committee. He campaigned vigorously for Roosevelt and came within 300,000 votes of predicting FDR's 7.5 million-vote plurality over Herbert Hoover.

President Roosevelt in 1933 appointed Farley as postmaster general, a position that traditionally entailed substantial patronage opportunities. Farley's criterion for dispensing jobs seems to have been party loyalty, particularly pre-1932 devotion to Roosevelt. Critics charged that he postponed making appointments until congressional sponsors of candidates demonstrated support for key pieces of administration legislation. Farley continued to reduce the United States Post Office debt and showed a $12 million surplus by the end of fiscal year 1934. Severe criticism followed the death of ten army fliers carrying airmail after the cancellation of contracts with commercial airlines in February 1934. Critics also castigated Farley for making gifts of special issue stamps to collectors. He did not have a major role in New Deal policy.

Farley managed the second Roosevelt presidential campaign in 1936 while on unpaid leave from the Post Office. Following his longstanding practice of personal contacts, 80,000 letters, signed "Jim" in his characteristic Irish green ink, went out to potential supporters. He again predicted a landslide over Alf Landon, accurately forecasting that Roosevelt would carry every state except Maine and Vermont. Farley published an autobiography in 1938 under the title *Behind the Ballots: The Personal History of a Politician*. But his enthusiasm for the Roosevelt administration began to cool. He resented the growing presence of such new advisers as Tommy Corcoran, particularly in light of his own waning influence, and disagreed with Roosevelt's attempted "purge" of anti–New Deal Democrats in 1938. Columnists spoke of a possible Farley run for governor of New York in 1938, perhaps in anticipation of a 1940 presidential bid. Widespread discussion of whether Roosevelt might seek a third term often included speculation about the presidential or vice-presidential nomination going to Farley, perhaps on a Hull-Farley ticket. Senator Carter Glass of Virginia nominated Farley for president at the 1940 Democratic National Convention, but when it was clear that Roosevelt would be renominated, Farley asked the convention to make the renomination by acclamation.

Soon afterward, Farley resigned as postmaster general and as chairman of the Democratic National Committee, allegedly to return to business. He became chairman of the board of the Coca-Cola Export Company. Although he publicly supported the Democratic ticket, he did not campaign vigorously as he had in 1932 and 1936. He remained chairman of the New York State Democratic Committee, supporting William O'Dwyer's unsuccessful 1941 campaign to become mayor of New York City and John J. Bennett's failed gubernatorial bid in 1942. Unanimously reelected as state chairman in 1944, Farley resigned the office in June of that year, claiming the press of his business obligations. At the 1944 Democratic National Convention, Farley denied that he had any personal ambitions. He supported Virginia Senator Harry F. Byrd for the presidential nomination and Kentucky Senator Alben Barkley for vice-president. After Roosevelt was nominated yet again, Farley publicly pledged his support for the Democratic ticket. But he took little part in the campaign beyond cosponsorship in September 1944 of a bipartisan appeal to keep religious and racial slurs out of the campaign.

Farley remained active in Democratic circles and attended the quadrennial conventions. He held various positions with Coca-Cola enterprises, traveling extensively as an international spokesman for the product, until a heart attack in 1972 led to his retirement the next year, when he was named honorary chairman. In 1948 he updated his autobiography, now entitled *Jim Farley's Story: The Roosevelt Years*. Farley was a member of the second Commission on Organization of the Executive Branch of the Government, chaired by former president Hoover from 1953 to 1955. In 1959 he joined James C. G. Conniff in writing *Governor Al Smith*. In 1968 he was again a member of the Electoral College, as he had been in 1932, 1936, and 1964.

Described as "a born joiner," Farley held lifelong membership in such clubs as the Elks, the Order of Red Men, and the Eagles; he served in many philanthropic, charitable, and civic organizations, including the Cordell Hull Foundation, the Alfred E. Smith Foundation, the Little League Foundation, the Boys Clubs of America, the Catholic Youth Organization, the Freedoms Foundation at Valley Forge, and the American Heritage Foundation. He was decorated by the governments of Venezuela and Panama, honored for his advocacy of foreign trade, and decorated by numerous Roman Catholic and Irish organizations such as the Knights of Columbus, the Friendly Sons of St. Patrick, and the Ancient Order of Hibernians. Farley received twenty-five honorary degrees and in 1974 Notre Dame University presented him with its Laetare medal.

In his later years, Farley made his home at the Waldorf-Astoria Hotel in New York City, where he died one month before he was to have attended his fourteenth Democratic National Convention, this time as its "chairman emeritus."

[Farley's papers are at the Library of Congress. The second of his two autobiographical volumes, mentioned above, was serialized in *Collier's*, June 21–July 19, 1947. An interview with Farley by Virginia V. Hamilton was published as "The True-blue Democrat," *American Heritage*, Aug. 1971. Doctoral dissertations include Earland I. Carlson, "Franklin D. Roosevelt's Fight for the Presidential Nomination, 1928–1932" (University of Illinois, 1956); and Gloria W. Newquist, "James A. Farley and the Politics of Victory: 1928–1936" (University of Southern California, 1966). Farley's association with Roosevelt is examined in James MacGregor Burns, *Roosevelt: The Lion and the Fox* (1956); Frank Freidel, *Franklin D. Roosevelt: The Triumph* (1956); Arthur M. Schlesinger, Jr., *The Age of Roosevelt*, 3 vols. (1957–1960); and William E. Leuchtenburg, *Franklin D. Roosevelt and the New Deal: 1932–1940* (1963). An obituary is in the *New York Times*, June 10, 1976.]

SUSAN ESTABROOK KENNEDY

FARRELL, JAMES THOMAS (Feb. 27, 1904–Aug. 22, 1979), novelist and critic, was born in Chicago, the son of James Francis Farrell, an express agency teamster and wagon dispatcher, and Mary Daly, a domestic servant. As the family increased, young James went to live with his maternal grandparents in 1907, growing up in fairly affluent but turbulent surroundings. He never lost touch with his own family.

From 1919 to 1923, Farrell attended Corpus Christi Grammar School, St. Anselm's Grammar School, and St. Cyril High School, where he earned letters in basketball, football, and baseball. Although he followed the classical curriculum and developed an interest in writing, he dreamed of becoming a big-league baseball player. Following graduation, Farrell worked as a telephone clerk at the Amalgamated Express Company; in September 1924 he enrolled in night school at DePaul University, where he studied history, sociology, and English composition. In March 1925 he went to work at a gas station; that June, he matriculated at the University of Chicago, planning to major in social science and prelaw.

Farrell, restless and intense, was an honor student and a voracious reader with a retentive memory. After studying English composition with Professor James Weber Linn, he decided that he wanted to write. In March 1927 he left the University of Chicago. That summer he hitchhiked to New York City, where he lived in cheap hotels, worked as a salesman, and read in the New York Public Library. By January 1928, Farrell had returned to Chicago; in the summer he reentered Linn's courses. For a while he was campus reporter for the *Chicago Herald Examiner.* Although Farrell's school compositions had appeared in the St. Cyril (High School) *Oriflamme* ("Danny's Uncle" in February 1921) and his essay "B & G Sandwich Shop" in Professor Linn's column in the *Chicago Herald Examiner*, his first published stories were "Slob," in *Blues* (June 1929) and "Studs," containing the germ of his Lonigan trilogy, in *This Quarter* (July–August–September 1930). Both stories employed the detailed realism that became his hallmark. After a second trip to New York City in the fall of 1929, Farrell returned to Chicago to write fiction. On Apr. 13, 1931, he married Dorothy Patricia Butler, a student at the University of Chicago; they left immediately for Paris, where, encouraged by Ezra Pound and Samuel Putnam, Farrell worked hard, writing ten hours a day, reading constantly, and living in poverty. Two personal events marred their stay: the death of their son five days after birth, and the death of Farrell's grandmother Daly. They returned to New York City in April 1932.

Settling in New York for the rest of his life, Farrell met many writers and social thinkers, and wrote steadily. In August 1933 he went for the first time to Yaddo, the artists' colony at Saratoga Springs, N.Y.; he returned for extended periods until August 1935. Here he completed the trilogy about Studs Lonigan that includes *Young Lonigan: A Boyhood in Chicago Streets* (1932), *The Young Manhood of Studs Lonigan* (1934), and *Judgment Day* (1935). *Studs Lonigan: A Trilogy* (1935) became an American classic. Using his own youthful experiences, Farrell created a character who showed how the mind and soul of a young Irish Catholic had been shaped by the modern urban and industrial world; Studs is victimized not by the environment but by a lack of will, and by the failure of family and society to help and guide him.

Although left-wing critics praised his novels for their realistic exposé of social problems, Farrell was never a member of the proletarian school of writers. Well-read in social theory, he offended editors of radical magazines with his essays and book reviews that did not follow the party line. His vision of the human need to grow through self-achievement had derived from such diverse sources as Ralph Waldo Emerson, Walter Pater, James Joyce, and Marcel Proust, as well as Karl Marx, John Dewey, and Theodore Dreiser. Sherwood Anderson, he wrote, inspired him "perhaps more profoundly than any other American writer."

Sympathetic with radical organizations and active in left-wing movements, Farrell spoke at the Communist-dominated American Writers' Congress in 1935; he defined the artist's role not as social and political propagandist but as truth teller in a world of endless process. "I have always believed," he said later, "that one must trust the unconscious and write out of it." In his Danny O'Neill pentology, begun in 1936, he reuses his Chicago experience from another point of view; the hero overcomes a background of social deprivation through hard work and education to become a writer.

Farrell's use of street language and his candid portrayal of racial and sexual scenes were attacked through litigation brought by censors; he won his first case in 1937, and again in 1944 and in 1948. In December 1936 he was one of the first to denounce Stalinist Communism and the Moscow trials. In 1937 he went to Mexico, as a member of the executive committee of the American Committee for the Defense of Leon Trotsky, to observe the John Dewey Commission of Inquiry as it took Trotsky's testimony regarding charges made against him at the Moscow trials. In 1941 he helped organize the Civil Rights Defense Committee; he served as its chairman from 1941 to 1945. In 1947 he joined the Workers' Defense Committee, and in 1948, the Executive Committee of the Workers Defense League. In 1950 he chaired the Committee against Jim Crow in Military Training, and he helped organize the International Congress for Cultural Freedom and the Fund for Intellectual Freedom. In 1955 and 1956 he was chairman of the American Committee for Cultural Freedom.

Farrell and his wife separated in August 1935 and were divorced in June 1940. On June 12, 1941, he married Hortense Aldren, an actress; they had one child. They separated in July 1951 and were divorced in 1955. He then remarried his first wife on Sept. 10, 1955; they separated again in 1958.

During the 1940's, Farrell became less angry and more stoical. He began his third series, the Bernard Carr (later changed to Clare) trilogy, which shows how a young writer in New York finally succeeds. He continued to travel: in 1949 he spoke at a peace conference in Paris, and in 1950, at the Berlin Congress for Cultural Freedom; in 1952 he was in Paris for the Festival of the Arts. He began his sixth European trip in 1954, and in 1956 a world lecture tour included Israel.

Meanwhile, Farrell had begun his fourth series, A Universe of Time, to run to perhaps thirty volumes. He completed only eight. Returning to his youthful experiences and using characters from earlier novels, he set about writing a "relativistic panorama of our times," showing "man's creativity and his courageous acceptance of impermanence." Farrell died in New York City.

[The Farrell papers are in the Charles Patterson Van Pelt Library, University of Pennsylvania. Neda M. Westlake describes the collection in *American Book Collector*, Summer 1961. See also Edgar M. Branch, *A Bibliography of James T. Farrell's Writings, 1921–1957* (1959), and his supplements in *American Book Collector*, Summer 1961, May 1967, Mar.–Apr. 1971, Jan.–Feb. 1976, and "Bibliography of James T. Farrell's Writings: Supplement Five, 1975–1981," *Bulletin of Bibliography*, Dec. 1982. A further bibliographical work is Jack Salzman, "James T. Farrell: An Essay in Bibliography," *Resources for American Literary Study*, Autumn 1976.

For biography and criticism see Edgar M. Branch, *James T. Farrell* (1971), with annotated bibliography; and Alan M. Wald, *James T. Farrell* (1978). An obituary is in the *New York Times*, Aug. 23, 1979.]

JOHN E. HART

FIEDLER, ARTHUR (Dec. 17, 1894–July 10, 1979), conductor and musician, was born in Boston, Mass., the son of Emanuel Fiedler and Johanna Bernfeld. His Austrian-born father was a violinist with the Boston Symphony Orchestra for twenty-five years. Although his grandfather and great-grandfather had also played the violin in Austria and young Arthur studied violin and piano, he had no immediate desire to become a musician. He attended neighborhood elementary schools and the Boston Latin High School, where he played the drum in a marching band called the Cadets. His mother was an accomplished amateur pianist and three sisters also studied music; two of them, Else and Rosa, went on to have professional careers.

Although his family was Jewish, his parents were not observant. Fiedler, who never entered a synagogue as a boy, later observed, "Music was the only religion in our family." As a boy, he studied with the distinguished pianist Carl Lamson even though he hated to practice. He would often look out Lamson's window at the patrol wagons pulling up to the police station next door. He would visit the neighborhood firehouse to play with the dalmatians and slide down the pole. These were the beginnings of Fiedler's lifelong fascination with police and fire departments. He eventually became an honorary fire chief in more than 250 cities. He tuned his car radio to police and fire frequencies and would often appear at large fires. He once said, "I've never left a concert for a fire, but I have left fires to go to a concert."

In 1910, after twenty-five years with the Boston Symphony, Emanuel Fiedler settled his family in Vienna. A year later, the family moved to Berlin, and about this time Arthur announced that he was not going on to a university. After a few menial jobs, he took his father's suggestion that he try music. He spent the summer of 1911 preparing for his audition at the Berlin Royal Academy of Music. It had thirteen openings; he placed thirteenth. He studied violin with Willy Hess, former concertmaster of the Boston Symphony; conducting with Arno Kleffel, formerly of the Cologne Opera House; and chamber music with pianist-composer Ernő Dohnányi. Many years later, with the composer in the audience, he conducted Dohnányi's *Variations on a Nursery Song* in honor of his old teacher.

At eighteen, Fiedler moved out of his father's house to assert his independence. To support himself, he played violin in cafés, toured with orchestras in the summer, and played in theater pit orchestras. It was his introduction to the kind of orchestral popular music he would later bring to the Boston Pops. The next year, he received an offer to serve as fourth assistant conductor of a small German opera house. Fiedler realized he would have to remain in Germany and work his way up if he was to have a successful career in conducting. The outbreak of World War I soon changed his plans.

Because he was a dual citizen of Austria and the United States, Fiedler was eligible for the Austrian draft. In 1915 he fled back to Boston, believing he was leaving his future behind him. He spent the summer playing violin for room and board on Nantucket Island until the Boston Symphony offered him a job playing second violin. He had learned how to support himself through lean times, and he had learned the hard work of professional preparation. It also helped that he was Emanuel Fiedler's son and Willy Hess's pupil.

In later life, Fiedler told an interviewer, "Something is driving me. . . . I just can't sit and twiddle my thumbs." Always restless and insistently independent, he switched from violin to viola because he thought it would be more interesting. In 1918 he was drafted into the United States Army, but after two weeks a doctor discharged him for flat feet. When he returned to the Boston Symphony, he played viola and doubled on violin, piano, organ, celesta, and percussion so often that he became known as the orchestra's "floating kidney." During the early 1920's he conducted an intense affair with Jeanne Eagels, a vivacious blonde actress best known for creating the role of Sadie Thompson in the stage adaptation of W. Somerset Maugham's short story, *Rain* (1922).

Fiedler found an outlet for his restlessness in 1924 when he formed a small orchestral group, the Boston Sinfonietta. Its first program on Oct. 30, 1925, combined light music with classical. For the next forty years, Fiedler used the Sinfonietta as his recording outlet for conducting "serious" music.

In 1926 he conducted the Boston Pops for the first time when conductor Agide Jacchia suddenly resigned his position just before the final concert of the season. Fiedler eventually became so closely associated with the Pops that many people believed he founded it, but it had actually been formed in 1885, four years after the founding of its parent orchestra, the Boston Symphony. Each spring, after completing its winter season, the orchestra, calling itself the Boston Pops, played a ten-week series of light classics modeled on England's famous Promenade Concerts. Although Fiedler applied to fill the vacant position immediately after conducting in Jacchia's place, the board of directors hired Alfredo Casella. The Italian conductor was unsympathetic to the Pops' repertoire and withdrew after three years.

In 1927, Fiedler had begun to think seriously about presenting great music to the public outdoors at no cost. Widely known and well liked by Boston society, he raised the necessary money for a series of Pops concerts in the Esplanade, a park along the Charles River. His program for the first concert, on July 4, 1929, included works by Antonin Dvořák, Giuseppe Verdi, and Richard Wagner, as well as Sigmund Romberg and Victor Herbert. Fiedler began the evening with John Philip Sousa's "Stars and Stripes Forever," the march that eventually became the Pops' signature piece. The first season of six outdoor concerts drew more than 208,000 people. In late January 1930 the directors finally offered the thirty-five-year-old Fiedler the directorship of the Pops Orchestra, which he held for the next half-century.

Although Casella had diminished the Pops' appeal, Fiedler soon demonstrated his gifts for programming and showmanship. He conducted palatable doses of classical music by such masters as Wagner, Mozart, and Beethoven, but he was also astutely aware of his audience's tastes. He began to introduce new works by such American composers as George Gershwin and Leroy Anderson, suites based on Broadway scores, and symphonic arrangements of songs associated with such popular performers as Frank Sinatra and the Beatles. Under his leadership, the Pops rose to greater popularity than ever.

White-haired and grandfatherly in appearance in his later years, he donned a Santa Claus hat for televised Christmas concerts. He also conducted the first evening of African-American composers, the first morning concerts for young people, and the first orchestral recording to sell one million copies—a then-unknown song by Jacob Gade called "Jalousie," which he had bought for fifteen cents in a Boston music store clearance. Eventually Fiedler and the Boston Pops would sell an estimated fifty million recordings.

Fiedler courted Ellen Bottomley for nearly ten years, beginning in 1932, when she was eighteen and he was thirty-seven. They often met in secret because of the opposition of her Catholic family. They married on Jan. 8, 1942, and had three children. During the Great Depression, Fiedler worked with the National Youth Administration Music Project to help form the national All-American Young People's Orchestra, and during World War II, he gave hundreds of concerts for USOs, veterans' hospitals, and army and navy bases. Although he had the first of five heart attacks in 1939, he enlisted in the United States Coast Guard as an apprentice seaman in 1943. After four months, he had a second and more serious coronary and left active duty to return to the Pops after his convalescence.

Over the ensuing years, Fiedler conducted the Boston Pops on national tours, on hundreds of recordings, and on radio and a television program called "Evening at Pops." Eventually, he formed a Boston Pops Touring Orchestra to augment the Boston Pops home orchestra, and he appeared with nearly every major and minor symphony orchestra in America. His celebrity grew even greater when he conducted the Boston Pops on the Esplanade for the Bicentennial celebration on July 4, 1976, before an estimated audience of 400,000. The televised program of Fiedler conducting "Stars and Stripes Forever" while young people clapped along and waved American flags is one of the more vivid images of the yearlong Bicentennial celebration.

Even though he became the nation's most famous conductor, it remained a bone of contention that he conducted the parent Boston Symphony only twice in his long career—in 1932, when a guest conductor was suddenly taken ill, and again in 1955. Even in 1956, during his twenty-fifth anniversary season, the Boston Symphony did not invite him to conduct. Serge Koussevitzky, musical director of the Boston Symphony from 1924 to 1949, had invited him to conduct in 1944 but suddenly withdrew the invitation in a fit of pique. It was a slight Fiedler remembered all his life.

Although he was genial and irreverent and usually well liked by his musicians, Fiedler could be acerbic and demanding. He would not be bound by anyone or anything that threatened to curtail his independence or authority. At the same time, despite his great success and his enormous popularity, Fiedler was often of two minds about his own career. He brought pleasure to millions of people and referred to those conductors who looked down on his music as "musical snobs" and "culture vultures." He also wondered from time to time, however, if he should have strived to become a major conductor of serious music. Many critics disapproved of his programs and his shenanigans on the podium, but one longtime associate observed, "Arthur can step up there and make an ordinary orchestra sound good, a good orchestra approach greatness, and a great orchestra—well, the regular conductor might be hesitant at inviting him back." In an appreciation accompanying Fiedler's obituary in the *New York Times*, John Rockwell called Fiedler "a genial, extroverted and vigorous exponent of populism in the realm of classical music" who provided "direct, efficient, no-nonsense conducting."

In 1977, President Gerald R. Ford awarded Fiedler the Medal of Freedom, the nation's highest civilian honor. In May 1979 he returned from treatment for an unspecified brain disorder to conduct the Pops in a triumphant concert in honor of his fifty years with the Boston Pops. He retired at the end of the season and died two months later of cardiac arrest at his home in Brookline, Mass.

[Of the three biographies published during Fiedler's lifetime, the most complete is Robin Moore, *Fiedler: The Colorful Mr. Pops* (1968). See also Carol Green Wilson, *Arthur Fiedler: Music for the Millions* (1968); James R. Holland, *Mr. Pops* (1972); and Harry Ellis Dickson, *Arthur Fiedler and the Boston Pops* (1981). See also interviews and sketches in *The Atlantic*, Feb. 1965; *TV Guide*, July 24, 1971; and the *Saturday Evening Post*, Sept. 1976. An obituary is in the *New York Times*, July 11, 1979.]

MICHAEL LASSER

FIELDING, JERRY (June 17, 1922–Feb. 17, 1980), film composer and bandleader, was born Joshua Itzhak Feldman in Pittsburgh, Pa., the son of Hiram Harris Feldman, a furniture salesman, and Esther Felman. Encouraged by his father's love of music, young Fielding took up the clarinet after a desire to be a trombonist proved impractical. He joined his school band and proved so adept that soon he was offered a scholarship to the Carnegie Institute for Instrumentalists in Pittsburgh. His tenure there was short-lived as his health suddenly deteriorated. Although his ailment was not diagnosed, the thirteen-year-old Fielding spent the better part of the next two years bedridden. He listened to the radio and became enamored of the big-band sound. He was also drawn to Bernard Herrmann's music for Orson Welles's groundbreaking radio dramas.

Sufficiently recuperated, Fielding saw no reason to prolong his education. Instead he went to work for Max Atkins at the Stanley Theater in Pittsburgh. Atkins was the orchestra's director, and he also taught arranging. Fielding, a fast study, was soon doing charts for the bands, and his natural aptitude was noticed by Alvino Rey. At seventeen he departed with Rey's band for New York City. Fielding's arrangements were often rejected by Rey because of their innovative quirkiness, but in 1940 his arrangement for "Picnic in Purgatory" was recorded and it sold well.

His stint with Alvino Rey ended when most of the band members were drafted. Fielding, however, was turned away from military service because of his frailty. He went to Los Angeles and was hired as vocal arranger for the Town Criers, led by Lucy Ann Polk. When the group joined Kay Kyser's band, Fielding went with them. By 1945 he had become Kyser's chief arranger and had begun a courtship with Ann Parks, a production assistant with the band. They married in December 1946 during a trip to Tijuana, Mexico. They adopted two children.

After arranging for Kyser's *Kollege of Musical Knowledge* on the radio, Fielding became bandleader on a succession of radio shows, including the "Jack Paar Show," "The Life of Riley," Mickey Rooney's "The Hardy Family," and "You Bet Your Life" with Groucho Marx. When Marx moved to television, Fielding stayed with him, and from 1949 to 1952 he had several weekly assignments including his own "Jerry Fielding Show." He joined a group called the Hollywood Writers Mobilization, which later became the Independent Progressive party. Under both guises the groups were considered by some to be fronts for the Communist party. When he was called to testify before the House Un-American Activities Committee in December 1953, Fielding refused to provide the committee with the names of his friends and political colleagues. Later he said, "I knew I'd be out of a job. By the time I got home the studio had called telling me not to report for work anymore."

Blacklisted in Hollywood, Fielding eventually found work in Las Vegas, where for several years he led the band in the Royal Las Vegas Hotel, which later became the Stardust. He recorded a number of albums for Decca Records and worked with many vocalists. In 1959, Betty Hutton was signed to do a television series, but she refused to work without Fielding. The network finally relented, and he was once more employable in Hollywood. Moving seriously into composition, Fielding's first film assignment was to write the score for *Advise and Consent* (1962). The director, Otto Preminger, was supportive of blacklist victims and, encouraged by writer Dalton Trumbo, gave Fielding the job. In the spring of 1963, Fielding's marriage ended. He had met Camille Williams, a dancer, in Las Vegas, and they were married on August 6 of that year; they had two children.

Fielding worked steadily in television, and he achieved fame with his theme for *Hogan's Heroes* (1965). In 1966 producer Daniel Melnick introduced Fielding to director Sam Peckinpah, and the two began a fruitful working relationship beginning with *Noon Wine* (1966) for the ABC series "Stage 67." *The Wild Bunch* (1969), a revisionist Western masterpiece, established the reputations of the director and his composer. Fielding's lengthy and diverse score for the movie was nominated for an Academy Award. Fielding received his second Academy Award nomination for his score to *Straw Dogs* (1971), which was also directed by Peckinpah. Fielding worked with other directors, including Michael Winner and Clint Eastwood. His score for Eastwood's *The Outlaw Josey Wales* (1976) was also nominated for an Academy Award. In 1971 he repaid a debt of faith to Dalton Trumbo by scoring Trumbo's directorial debut, *Johnny Got His Gun*, a harrowing antiwar story.

In 1977, Fielding suffered a heart attack. In the aftermath of his illness, he bemoaned the dearth of good directors and the lack of integrity in the work he was offered. He resented the fact that the studios retained ownership of the scores he and his colleagues were composing. He helped to initiate a lawsuit against the studios on behalf of the Composers and Lyricists Guild of America. The suit was only partially successful. He was a vocal member of the music branch of the Motion Picture Academy and was an avid campaigner for equal rights.

Fielding died of congestive heart failure in Toronto, Canada. He was awarded a posthumous Emmy for his score to *High Midnight* (1979).

Other notable credits include, for television, "The Chicago Teddy Bears" (1971), "McMillan and Wife" (1971–1977), "Bridget Loves Bernie" (1972–1973), and the television movie *A War of Children* (1972); and for motion pictures, *The Nightcomers* (1971), *Junior Bonner* (1972), *The Gambler* (1975), *The Killer Elite* (1975), *The Gauntlet* (1977), and *Escape from Alcatraz* (1979).

[See *Photoplay*, May 1973; *Film Music Notebook*, III (1977); Tony Thomas, ed. *Film Score: The Art and Craft of Movie Music* (1991), first published as *Film Score: The View from the Podium* (1979); and David Raksin, "A Conversation with Jerry Fielding," in *Soundtrack!* no. 23 (1980). Obituaries are in the *New York Times*, Feb. 19, 1980; and the *Los Angeles Times*, Feb. 20, 1980.]

NICK REDMAN

FIESER, LOUIS FREDERICK (Apr. 7, 1899–July 25, 1977), educator, chemist, and author, was born in Columbus, Ohio, the son of Louis Frederick Fieser and Martha Victoria Kershaw. Fieser served in the United States Army during World War I and then went on to receive his bachelor's degree in 1920 from Williams College, where he was a member of the football team. He received his Ph.D. in chemistry from Harvard University in 1924, studying under the brilliant scientist James Bryant Conant. Fieser did graduate work at Frankfurt am Main, Germany, from 1924 to 1925 and at Oxford University in 1925. He served for five years on the faculty of Bryn Mawr College before returning to Harvard, where he eventually became Sheldon Emery Professor of Organic Chemistry, a post that he held from 1939 to 1968. He was then named professor emeritus and remained in that position until his death.

On June 21, 1932, Fieser married Mary A. Peters, a fellow chemist who remained his scientific partner and writing collaborator throughout the rest of his career. They had no children. They coauthored numerous books, including *Organic Chemistry* (3d ed., 1956), *Steroids* (4th ed., 1959), *Introduction to Organic Chemistry* (1957), *Basic Organic Chemistry* (1959), *Style Guide for Chemists* (1960), *Advanced Organic Chemistry* (1961), *Topics in Organic Chemistry* (1963), and *Current Topics in Organic Chemistry* (1963). Their monumental five-volume work *Reagents for Organic Synthesis* remains a standard source. Siamese cats were an important part of their lives and were often referred to in sketches and in the introductions to their books. The Siamese cats would become a trademark of their joint efforts.

Fieser's career represented a paradox. His initial interest in naphthoquinones led in 1939 to an understanding of the structure and eventual synthesis of vitamin K, with important clinical medical implications. His parallel interest in cancer-causing hydrocarbons led to his book *Natural Products Related To Phenanthrene* (1936, 1937; rev. 3d ed., 1949), cowritten with his wife. His contributions to steroid chemistry also included the introduction of nomenclature to designate parts of the steroid structure that is universally employed by chemists throughout the world. His fascination with quinones and hydrocarbons continued throughout his career but was interrupted by World War II.

In 1940 Fieser was invited to join the National Defense Research Committee, which was responsible for the development of bombs, fuels, poison gases, and other potential chemical and explosive weapons. Fieser was assigned the task of developing the synthesis of new nitro compounds as possible explosives. With typical enthusiasm, he developed napalm, the gel explosive used in the Vietnam War. In addition, he participated in the development of an antitank grenade and several types of bombs and incendiary devices, which became important parts of the Allied arsenal during World War II.

After World War II, Fieser returned to his post at Harvard and the burgeoning field of steroid chemistry. He studied the potential carcinogenic effect of sterol compounds related to cholesterol and the antimalarial properties of lapachol derivatives. This latter research became important during the Vietnam War, when malaria was a problem among American troops.

In addition to his dozen books in organic chemistry, Fieser published nearly 350 research papers. He received numerous honors, including the Manufacturing Chemists' Association award for teaching (1959), the Norris Award for teaching (1959), and the American Chemical Society Award in Chemical Education (1967). He was elected to the National Academy of Sciences and was a recipient of the Katherine Berkan Judd prize for his work on cancer-producing hydrocarbons.

Following surgery to remove a lung tumor,

Fieser became an antismoking campaigner and was appointed to the Surgeon General's Advisory Committee on Smoking and Health in 1963. In addition to his skill as a research scientist, Fieser was well regarded at Harvard as a teacher. As Hans Heymann noted, "Who but Louis Fieser would delight in presenting himself to his undergraduate class wearing the 'Louie'—a bright orange sweatshirt bearing the lecturer's likeness and currently an article of trade at Harvard Square?" Fieser was instrumental in the development of low-cost plastic models of organic compounds that are now seen in nearly every organic chemistry laboratory and classroom in the world. His interest in the widest possible dissemination of information to students led to the production of one of the first instructional films on organic chemistry research techniques.

Fieser pursued his career with an elegance and perseverance best described by his mottoes, "Omnia possum" and "Labor omnia vincit." He died in Belmont, Mass.

[Fieser also wrote *The Scientific Method* (1964). See also Hans Heymann, "Louis Frederick Fieser," *Journal of Organic Chemistry*, May 1965. A review of Fieser's career by C. J. W. Brooks is in *Nature*, Dec. 22, 1977. An obituary is in the *New York Times*, July 27, 1977.]

PHILLIP THARP SWENDER

FINE, JOHN SYDNEY (Apr. 10, 1893–May 21, 1978), judge, politician, and governor, was born in Alden, Luzerne County, Pa., one of eleven children of Jacob W. Fine and Margaret Croop. His father was a mine worker with supervisory duties in the Glen Alden Company mine. The family moved to Nanticoke, Pa., where John completed high school in 1911. He received an LL.B. from Dickinson Law School in 1914 and established a law partnership in Wilkes-Barre in 1915. From 1917 to 1919, Fine served as a sergeant in an engineers unit of the American Expeditionary Force and then briefly attended the University of Dublin. He held offices in the legislative district and county Republican committees from 1919 to 1923.

A follower of Theodore Roosevelt's Progressive movement, Fine became attached to Governor Gifford Pinchot, who appointed him to fill a vacancy in the Luzerne County Common Pleas Court in January 1927. He was subsequently elected to regular ten-year terms in November 1927 and November 1939. Governor James H. Duff appointed him to the Superior Court in June 1947, and that November he was elected to a full ten-year term. On both courts he was often chosen to write opinions in cases dealing with labor law, compensation, real estate sales, divorce and domestic relations, evidence, and judicial powers. Characteristically concise, these legal statements were often innovative and reflected recognition of developments in society.

Fine continued to be a political leader in Luzerne County during his years on the bench, and he is reputed to have been its Republican boss except during the governorship of his fellow Luzerne County Republican Arthur H. James (1939–1943), who opposed Pinchotism and was allied to Philadelphia's old machine. Duff advanced Fine as the gubernatorial candidate to team with his own 1950 campaign for the United States Senate, and Fine won narrowly over the reform Democrat from Philadelphia, Richardson Dilworth. An increase in employment arising from the Korean War helped the Republican ticket, but Fine acknowledged the state's fiscal problems in his inaugural address. His administration inherited an obligation to increase teachers' salaries and to provide a veterans' bonus. Fine's struggles to obtain some form of broadly based tax shaped his four-year term and fragmented the Republican party. In 1951 a flat .5-percent income tax was defeated after a revolt by key Republican state senators. For his second biennial budget, Fine obtained a 1-percent sales tax, but only after months of criticism and ridicule. His pleas for a state constitutional convention to approve a graduated income tax were rebuffed by a public ballot in November 1953. In January 1954 he anticipated closing his administration with a \$17 million deficit, but it turned out to be over \$50 million.

Fine married Helene Pennebacker Morgan on Dec. 5, 1939. They had two children. She died on Apr. 23, 1951, as a result of an accidental fall during the gubernatorial campaign. The political atmosphere of open dialogue mixed with conviviality that had thus far characterized Fine's tenure ceased, and he vacated the governor's mansion in Harrisburg. At the 1952 Republican convention in Chicago he was rebuffed and vilified, a situation aggravated by television displays of his anger. The sales-tax controversy led to popular ridicule in the slogan "a penny for Fine." Favoring McCarthyism, Fine also made enemies by imposing a loyalty oath on state employees. He alienated others by authorizing state police raids to close down slot-machine gambling in social clubs.

The tax defeat of 1951 compelled him to ally with the Pennsylvania Manufacturers Association, causing an irreparable split with Senator Duff, and he softened his attitude toward the other old guard Pennsylvania Republican backers, the Pew brothers, the Mellon family, and the Philadelphia machine. To finance state Republican activities he collected money from state employees, insisting that these were voluntary contributions, but in 1954 a grand jury in Pittsburgh concluded that intimidation had taken place. Two of Fine's high administrators were indicted. More damaging, however, was his system of withholding funds from county and local Republican organizations. In the primaries of 1954 his political power evaporated permanently. Fine's lieutenant governor, Lloyd Wood, became the Republican gubernatorial nominee, but only because he appeared to be a congenial bridge between party factions. Fine was asked to play no part in the fall 1954 campaign.

Sometimes seen as an extension of Duff administration progressive public policies, many of Fine's programs attacked social problems he himself knew firsthand from his Luzerne County background. He oversaw a 25-percent increase in spending for education and the creation of vocational-technical area schools. He cracked down on gambling and liquor violations and reformed workmen's compensation and child adoption. The state took over local government welfare costs, and mental and physical health facilities were enlarged and subjected to licensing. His administration borrowed heavily through public authorities to circumvent legal limits on state indebtedness. He continued the highway and environmental protection policies of his predecessor. Fine assisted anthracite coal region representatives in seeking help from the federal government, and he created the Commission on Industrial Race Relations. He constituted expert commissions to study the tax problem and government reorganization. The latter, headed by Francis J. Chesterman, suggested eliminating the Department of Commerce, which was headed by Andrew John Sordoni, a self-made entrepreneur and Fine's link with the Pennsylvania Manufacturers Association. The idea was rebuffed, but Fine passed on the final Chesterman Committee report to his successor, George M. Leader. It included a major change Leader would adopt, the creation of the Governor's Office of Administration.

After his term, Fine settled in Loyalville, Pa. In the 1957 primaries he failed to be reelected to the Luzerne County Court of Common Pleas. In 1961 he was indicted for income tax evasion, but he was eventually acquitted. Vindicated by the state's failure to continue without the sales tax, which eventually reached 6 percent, Fine was chosen a delegate to the 1968 Republican convention, where he endorsed Richard M. Nixon.

An active Episcopal layman and a Freemason, Fine also belonged to many national fraternal, veterans, and social organizations. Making public appearances usually in a double-breasted suit and bow tie, he aged rapidly in appearance during the gubernatorial years. He died in Wilkes-Barre, Pa.

[Fine's gubernatorial papers are in the Pennsylvania State Archives, Harrisburg; a newspaper clipping file is in the Osterhout Library, Wilkes-Barre. The Government Documents Section, State Library of Pennsylvania, has copies of printed items from the Fine administration, including *A Record: Accomplishments of the Fine Administration*, revised as of Jan. 16, 1954. His governorship is discussed in Sylvester K. Stevens, "Duff and Fine," in Stevens, *Pennsylvania* (1968); and Paul B. Beers, "Tragic John Fine," in Beers, *Pennsylvania Politics Today and Yesterday* (1980). Judicial opinions can be found in *Luzerne Legal Register Reports*, vols. 24–39 (1927–1947); and *Pennsylvania Superior Court Reports*, vols. 161–166 (1947–1950). An obituary is in the *New York Times*, May 22, 1978.]

LOUIS M. WADDELL

FINLETTER, THOMAS KNIGHT (Nov. 11, 1893–Apr. 24, 1980), lawyer and government official, was born in Philadelphia, Pa., the son of Thomas Dickson Finletter and Helen Grill. Finletter's father and grandfather were judges of the Court of Common Pleas. Finletter attended the Episcopal Academy in Philadelphia from 1905 to 1910. After spending a year in France with his mother, he enrolled in the University of Pennsylvania, receiving a B.A. in 1915. He then entered the University of Pennsylvania Law School, but his studies were interrupted by service in World War I. Finletter served in France with the 312th Field Artillery, in which he attained the rank of captain by the war's end. He then returned to law school, receiving his LL.B. in 1920. On July 17, 1920, Finletter married Gretchen Blaine Damrosch, daughter of the conductor Walter Damrosch and granddaughter of the 1884 Republican presidential nominee, James G. Blaine. The couple had two children.

Thomas Finletter then made two breaks with his past. Dismayed by the Republican role in denying American entry into the League of Nations, he became a Democrat. He also decided to leave Philadelphia and practice law in New York City. From 1920 to 1926 he was a member of the Cravath and Henderson firm. He became a partner at Coudert Brothers in New York City, specializing in bankruptcy law. During the 1930's, in addition to his responsibilities at Coudert Brothers, Finletter committed to a part-time teaching post at the University of Pennsylvania Law School and published three law texts.

In March 1941, Finletter was named special assistant to the secretary of state. Two years later he became the executive director of the Office of Foreign Economic Coordination. His principal responsibilities consisted of acquiring strategic materials from abroad and diverting them from enemy use. He left the State Department in 1944 when Edward Stettinius, Jr., replaced Cordell Hull as secretary. Finletter returned to Coudert Brothers but served in May 1945 as a consultant to the American delegation to the United Nations Conference.

President Harry S. Truman named Finletter in July 1947 to chair an Air Policy Commission to examine all phases of military and civilian aviation. The commission heard 150 witnesses, including General Dwight D. Eisenhower and Admiral Chester W. Nimitz, and visited air facilities and aircraft factories. Its report, *Survival in the Air Age,* argued for a rapid expansion of the air force over the next five years to meet the impending threat of an air attack by the Soviet Union. The *New York Times* characterized it as "one of the most solemn reports on the defense of the United States ever prepared in time of peace," and it became a key Cold War document.

In May 1948, Finletter was appointed chief of the Economic Cooperation Administration in Great Britain. He served in this Marshall Plan post until June 1949. President Truman named Finletter secretary of the air force in April 1950. Finletter succeeded Stuart Symington, the first air force secretary, who had been an outspoken proponent of air force expansion beyond the president's budgetary constraints. Finletter was an equally ardent defender of expansion, but more politic in expressing the case. He particularly stressed strategic air capability as the cornerstone of the nation's defense. The outbreak of hostilities in Korea in June 1950 initiated tremendous expansion in defense outlays, and the air force gained disproportionately from that spending. When Finletter left his post at the end of the Truman presidency, the air force had grown well beyond the size he had called for in his report five years earlier.

Finletter returned to Coudert Brothers in 1953 but continued to engage in public affairs. He served as an adviser to Adlai Stevenson leading up to his 1956 and 1960 presidential campaigns. In 1954 he published *Power and Policy,* a reassertion of his beliefs that nuclear supremacy was the backbone of deterrence and that self-preservation came before economy. By the end of the decade he was arguing that a "missile gap" had emerged.

For all of Finletter's insistence on nuclear deterrence, he expressed a continuing hope of cultivating the rule of law rather than the use of force as the core of international policy. He was a founder of the United World Federalists, an antiwar organization, in the late 1940's, and he persistently explored arrangements to curb national aggression by the international application of the rule of law.

In 1958, Finletter sought the New York Democratic nomination for the United States Senate. Despite receiving endorsements from Eleanor Roosevelt and Herbert Lehman, he lost the nomination to Frank Hogan, Manhattan District Attorney.

President John Kennedy appointed Finletter United States ambassador to the North Atlantic Treaty Organization in 1961. He proved to be a key player in winning European support for American policy during the Cuban missile crisis. He continued in the position into the Johnson administration, resigning in July 1965.

Thus ended a quarter-century of significant, but largely anonymous government service. Finletter, then seventy-one, returned to New York City to practice law, write, and continue as a behind-the-scenes player in Democratic politics. His first wife died in 1969, and Finletter married Eileen Wechsler Geist on Jan. 13, 1973. He died in New York City.

[Finletter's papers from his tenure as secretary of the air force are at the Harry S. Truman Library, Independence, Mo. Finletter's range of policy interests can be found in his *Foreign Policy* (1958); and *Interim Report* (1968). An obituary is in the *New York Times*, Apr. 25, 1980. His oral history memoirs are on deposit at the Harry S. Truman Library and the Columbia University Oral History Collection.]

JOHN O'SULLIVAN

FISCHETTI, JOHN (Sept. 27, 1916–Nov. 18, 1980), political cartoonist, was born in Brooklyn, N.Y., the son of Italian immigrants Pietro Fischetti, a barber, and Emanuela Navarra. Giovanni, whose name was anglicized to John by friends, was the youngest of five children. Growing up in Brooklyn's Little Italy, Fischetti was surrounded by neighbors who were struggling to survive but who were protective of one another. "We were very much aware of being an island in this country, and so we clung together like Pilgrims," Fischetti said. When he was five years old, he was given a box of colored chalk at kindergarten and began drawing. He was soon showing artistic promise. By the age of thirteen, Fischetti had ambitions to become an editorial cartoonist. He greatly admired the political cartoons of Rollin Kirby of the *New York World*.

Fischetti, whose political views were shaped by the Great Depression, dropped out of Alexander Hamilton High School at the age of fifteen and, unable to find work, moved west on freight trains to Albany, Syracuse, Rochester, Buffalo, Erie, Cleveland, Chicago, and Kenosha, working at odd jobs, eating at soup kitchens and missions, and sleeping at shelters, transient camps, and in jail cells made available to the poor by police for a night. He returned to New York City and took a job as a cabin boy on the *Western World*, a Munson steamship. Fischetti spent a year at sea, sailing to Bermuda, South America, Barbados, and back to New York. On his return to Brooklyn, he worked as a free-lance artist and then enrolled at the Pratt Institute, where he studied commercial art for three years and graduated in 1940.

Until entering Pratt, Fischetti was inexperienced in any art medium other than pencil and paper. At Pratt, he learned to work with oils, watercolors, and pastels; he also studied sculpture. His passion and social consciousness began to emerge in his drawings. In choosing topics for his illustrations at Pratt, Fischetti later wrote: "I found that I naturally always chose something about the poor, the unfortunate, the put-upon. I saw the crummy places these people lived in and that not many people really cared about them. I grew to hate injustices and the people responsible for these injustices."

The writings of John Steinbeck illuminated Fischetti's vision of America. At Pratt, he produced a set of illustrations for Steinbeck's *The Grapes of Wrath*, which Steinbeck learned about after a public exhibition of Fischetti's work in Los Angeles. Steinbeck sought to have Fischetti's illustrations published in a special edition of the novel, but his publisher already had Thomas Hart Benton under contract.

Fischetti's first job out of Pratt was as an illustrator with the Walt Disney Studios in Burbank, Calif. He was among the animators for Mickey Mouse but grew to dislike the work, which he described as "an assembly line for artists." Fischetti later worked as a free-lance artist for the *Los Angeles Times*, then lived in San Francisco, moving in 1941 to Chicago, where he drew for *Coronet* and *Esquire* magazines. Later in 1941, he was hired as an associate political cartoonist for the *Chicago Sun*.

From 1942 to 1946, Fischetti served in the United States Army; he was assigned to the 999th Signal Corps as a radio operator and then to *Stars and Stripes*, the army newspaper, as a correspondent and cartoonist. Fischetti covered combat, the trial of Marshal Pétain, the fall of Nuremberg, and the liberation of the concentration camp at Dachau.

Returning to New York City in January of 1946, Fischetti worked as a free-lance illustrator for commercial clients, juvenile books, university magazines, advertising pamphlets, and for the *New York Times Magazine* and *Coronet*. On Oct. 25, 1948, Fischetti married Karen Mortenson, a flight attendant with the Scandinavian Airline System and a native of Denmark. They had two children. In 1950 the Fischettis moved from New York City to suburban Cos Cob, Conn. Fischetti became a cartoonist in 1951 with the Newspaper Enterprise Association and for ten years worked out of his home and an office in New York City for the NEA. Though he gained a national reputation during his decade with the news service, he grew frustrated with the requirement that he submit four or five cartoons to his editor for approval. Fischetti's cartoons appeared in more than 800 newspapers through the NEA syndicate, but he wanted more freedom in the selection of his cartoons.

One of his more powerful cartoons appeared in 1961 after the death of United Nations secretary-general Dag Hammarskjöld in a plane crash while on a peace mission in Africa. Fischetti drew a corner of the Secretariat Building at United Nations headquarters against a dark sky. In the lower right, he depicted a female peace figure, face in hands, head bent. The caption of the cartoon was: "My son, My son." Fischetti said that he got more reaction to the Hammarskjöld cartoon than to any other cartoon in his career. United Nations under secretary Ralph Bunche obtained the original Fischetti cartoon and placed it on display outside the secretary-general's office at the United Nations.

Fischetti joined the *New York Herald Tribune* in 1962 as an editorial cartoonist with an arrangement to work from his Connecticut home. Publisher John Hay Whitney, a multimillionaire who had served as American ambassador to Britain during the Eisenhower administration, told editors that Fischetti was to have complete editorial freedom. The *Herald Tribune* syndicated Fischetti's cartoons to seventy-five newspapers.

Fischetti's style influenced a generation of American editorial cartoonists. Before joining the *Herald Tribune*, he had begun working with brush and pen instead of the more traditional grease pencil, and began using dotted paper to achieve shades of gray in his cartoons. He introduced what he called "new look" cartoons that literally changed the shape of American cartooning. "John pioneered the modern-day horizontal-shape editorial cartoon in this country," Herbert Block of the *Washington Post* said. "It was popular in England and elsewhere, but for a long time the standard American editorial cartoon had been vertical. . . . John persevered against the herd instinct of editors who resisted the shape of his cartoons. And he probably would have been amused and outraged to find another generation of sheeplike editors feeling that a political cartoon was somehow unfashionable if it was not horizontal." Fischetti lamented the lack of creativity in political cartooning in the United States. He was disdainful of the cliché symbols used by some of his colleagues. "I haven't used Uncle Sam, a donkey or an elephant for years," he said in 1969.

After the *Herald Tribune* collapsed in 1967, Fischetti was hired by the *Chicago Daily News* and moved to Chicago. A memorable cartoon in 1968 showed an African-American man manacled with chains labeled "white racism" and the caption: "Why don't they lift themselves up by their own bootstraps like we did?" Fischetti was awarded the Pulitzer Prize for editorial cartooning in 1969. When the *Daily News* folded in March in 1978, Fischetti joined the *Chicago Sun-Times*, which was under the same ownership as the *Daily News* had been. Fischetti, who underwent triple heart bypass surgery in 1979 after suffering two heart attacks in the early 1970's, died of heart disease after collapsing at his Near North Side home.

"I've tried to use what talent I have to do my damnedest to make things just a little better, to alleviate some suffering and neaten up this spaceship we all live on for such a short time," Fischetti wrote in his autobiography. After his death, a national award for editorial cartooning was established in his memory and a Fischetti scholarship fund was organized for journalism students at Columbia College in Chicago.

[Fischetti's autobiography, *Zinga Zanga Za!* (1973), contains 150 of his political cartoons. A discussion of his influence is in Herbert Block, *Herblock: A Cartoonist's Life* (1993). Obituaries are in the *Chicago Sun-Times*, Nov. 19, 1980; and the *New York Times*, Nov. 20, 1980.]

STEVE NEAL

FLANNER, JANET (Mar. 13, 1892–Nov. 7, 1978), writer, was born in Indianapolis, Ind., one of three children of William Francis Flanner and Mary Ellen Hockett. Her father was co-owner of a mortuary. Her mother, a published poet and playwright, directed amateur performances at the YMCA and often toured the country, giving dramatic readings. Flanner attended Tudor Hall, a private academy that guaranteed its pupils automatic admission to the University of Chicago. In 1910, the family spent one year in Germany, an experience Flanner credited as the beginning of her love affair with Europe. Their stay in Germany was cut short by financial problems. After returning to Indianapolis, Frank Flanner committed suicide in February 1912.

Flanner

In the fall of 1912, Flanner enrolled at the University of Chicago, where she studied for two years and led an active social life. Although she respected the teacher Robert Morss Lovett and claimed he taught her how to write, for the most part she did not study or attend classes consistently. She withdrew from the university with failing marks in several courses and returned to Indianapolis in 1914. In 1917 she began to write brief reviews of vaudeville and burlesque shows for the *Indianapolis Star* and later had her own column, "Impressions in the Field of Art."

On Apr. 25, 1918, Flanner married a college friend, William Lane Rehm. The wedding was a surprise to friends and family. Many years later she confided to a cousin that she married to escape Indianapolis. In August 1918, shortly after beginning a new column for the *Star*, "Comments on the Screen," she moved to New York City, where she and Rehm rented an apartment in Greenwich Village. The marriage was short-lived, lasting until 1921, at which time Flanner left New York and traveled to Europe with the woman Solita Solano, a journalist whom Flanner's biographer calls "the first great love of Janet's life." Unlike the restrictive environment they experienced living in the United States near family and childhood friends, the atmosphere of Paris in the 1920's, each recalled, allowed them the freedom to live together openly. Their circle of acquaintances included Margaret Anderson, who started *The Little Review;* the novelist Djuna Barnes; Natalie Barney, whose famous salon was a gathering place for lesbian artists; Sylvia Beach, owner of the Shakespeare and Company bookstore; Ernest Hemingway; and Gertrude Stein. With Solano, Flanner first began her life as a writer in Paris.

Founded by the journalist Harold Ross, the *New Yorker* first appeared on Feb. 21, 1925. Jane Grant, the *New York Times* journalist married to Ross, wrote to Flanner in June 1925 and offered her the job as the *New Yorker*'s Paris correspondent. She accepted the offer, and her first column, "Letter from Paris," published under the pseudonym Genêt, appeared on Oct. 10, 1925. Flanner's Paris letter was to appear bimonthly at a length of 2,500 words.

Concurrently with writing for the *New Yorker*, Flanner wrote fiction. Her novel *The Cubical City* (1926) received good-to-lukewarm reviews. Especially in the early years, Flanner considered journalism merely a means of secure income and writing fiction her major occupation. Later, she tried translating, completing two of Colette's novels and Georgette Leblanc's memoir, *Souvenirs, 1895–1918: My Life with Maeterlinck*. She also wrote short stories, some of which were published in the *New Yorker*. Neither writing fiction nor translating matched the success of her "Letter from Paris," which she continued to write for fifty years.

Flanner's "Letter from Paris" reported on the art scene, the fashion scene, the publishing scene, and the street scenes of Paris. Genêt was an expert on music, theater, and food. Her mere mention of a subject, such as James Joyce's novel *Ulysses*, assured readers they, too, ought to know about it. The *New Yorker*, which also featured work by E. B. White and Dorothy Parker, promoted its image as sophisticated, but not pretentious; in this respect, Flanner's writing, shaped by Harold Ross's precise editorial style, did not explain, evaluate, or analyze, but was witty, incisive, intelligent, and distant. She refrained from using the word "I." Sometimes she recounted conversations or the exploits of literary friends. She often described art exhibits or films she had seen. She read ten newspapers each day and maintained a rich social life, attending art openings and film screenings, and conversing at the Deux Magots Café, as had been her habit since arriving in Paris. Her readership included Americans once familiar with Paris and who wished to remain so, albeit through the eyes of a talented insider, pointing out the names of indispensable head waiters in the same breath as new writers such as the young Samuel Beckett.

Flanner also wrote longer, factual profiles of individuals, such as the writer Edith Wharton, the dancer Isadora Duncan, and Pablo Picasso. These appeared in the *New Yorker*. On occasion, she wrote for *Arts and Decoration* and for *Vanity Fair*. By the mid-1930's, Flanner's writing began to incorporate French politics, and in 1936 she wrote a three-part profile of Adolf Hitler. Although she tried to keep this profile detached, in Germany, to her surprise, the profile was considered pro-Hitler.

In 1939, Flanner returned to America, distancing herself both geographically and emotionally from Parisian society. In 1944 she refused to write the text accompanying a book of photographs by Horst, repudiating what she called fashionable fascists and her early profession as their sometime chronicler. During her years in America, she continued to write profiles for the *New Yorker*, including a four-part study of Philippe Pétain, which was later published as the highly praised book *Pétain: The Old Man of France* (1944). In 1940, Flanner published *An American in Paris*, a collection of her profiles and of articles on crime in France. Also in 1940, Flanner met and fell in love with Natalia Danesi Murray, an Italian broadcaster, who remained her lover until Flanner's death. Around this time, Flanner and Solita Solano, who had lived together—albeit nonmonogamously—since their migration to Europe, gave up their residence together.

Upon her return to Europe in 1944, Flanner began to write and deliver news for French radio, a job she held until 1946. She also resumed writing "Letter from Paris," traveling throughout Europe to collect news from soldiers, statesmen, and prisoners of war. In Germany, she visited the concentration camp Buchenwald and attended the Nuremberg trials; later she produced several pieces on the Nazi regime. She also wrote letters from Capri, Trieste, Rome, Poland, and Vienna. In the spring of 1948, Flanner was made a knight of the Legion of Honor, in recognition of her years of scrupulous and passionate writing. Although she wore the ribbon on her lapel for the rest of her life, Flanner was depressed and saddened by the effects of the war and later remembered the postwar years as lonely and unhappy.

Flanner's articles became more political than they had ever been and, wary of this, her *New Yorker* editors, Harold Ross and William Shawn, often changed the tone of her letters significantly. With the rise of McCarthyism, Ross and Shawn warned her that the mood of the United States was changing, and they did not allow her to publish a profile of Léon Blum, France's first socialist and Jewish prime minister, after Blum died in 1950; they claimed not to want profiles of deceased figures, but Flanner felt their reasons were political. She opposed Senator Joseph McCarthy and his search for Communists, and without notifying the *New Yorker*, she traveled in 1952 to Bad Godesberg, Germany, to speak in defense of her friend and *New Yorker* colleague Kay Boyle, who was accused of being a Communist. During these years, Flanner also had to deal with the deaths of her mother in 1947 and of Harold Ross, whom she greatly esteemed, in 1951.

In 1954, Flanner published a profile of André Malraux. It was later included in her 1957 book, *Men and Monuments*, which was published to largely favorable reviews. In an article titled "French Ideas, American Dollars" (*Saturday Review*, May 11, 1957), reviewing both the book and Flanner's writing style, Francis Henry Taylor, director of the Worcester Art Museum, stated that Flanner, "a splendid, bright Medusa," had cast her gaze, and "[for] the first time in living memory artists and their works pass before the scrutiny of an informed foreign correspondent—a reporter equally at home in world politics and literature with none of the inevitable bias of the professor or the critic." Flanner felt this commendation best summed up the intentions of her writing.

During her later years, Flanner received many awards, including the National Book Award for her *Paris Journal: 1944–1965* (1965), a collection of her Paris letters. She acquired the nickname "America's Tocqueville." In 1971, Flanner published a second collection of her letters, *Paris Journal: 1965–1971*, and a collection of her prewar pieces, *Paris Was Yesterday, 1925–1939*, in 1972. The latter was a critical success. At the urging of Natalia Danesi Murray, she published *London Was Yesterday, 1934–1939* in 1975.

In late August 1975, Flanner, in ill health and surrounded by her oldest friends at Orgeval, France, wrote her final Paris letter. She died in New York City.

[The Library of Congress and the Harry Ranson Humanities Research Center at the University of Texas, Austin, have many of Flanner's papers. Flanner's biography, written by Brenda Wineapple, is entitled *Genêt: A Biography of Janet Flanner* (1989). See also *Janet Flanner's World* (1979) and *Darlinghissima: Letters to a Friend*, edited by Natalia Danesi Murray (1985). An obituary is in the *New York Times*, Nov. 8, 1978.]

MELISSA SOLOMON

FOGARTY, ANNE WHITNEY (Feb. 2, 1919–Jan. 15, 1980), fashion designer, was born in Pittsburgh, Pa., one of four children of Robert Whitney, an artist, and Marion Bosoranoff. Fogarty was early fascinated by clothes. At the age of five she shocked her mother by choosing a red hair ribbon to contrast with a pink organdy party dress. The color combination, unacceptable in the 1920's, later became one of Fogarty's favorite and most popular color schemes. When she was thirteen, she made what she later described as a "real, traditional garden-party dress . . . long, floating and elaborate." Because such dresses were not fashionable at the time, Fogarty wished to become a stage actress, so that she would wear her "dream dresses" in period plays.

While living at home, Fogarty wore many hand-me-down clothes from her three older sisters. She altered these dresses in various ways. Proud of a tiny waist—it was no larger than eighteen inches in adulthood—she cinched her sisters' clothes with boys' belts and otherwise completely redesigned them. She did not consider that what came so easily to her could someday develop into a career.

After graduating from high school in 1936, Fogarty attended Allegheny College in Meadville, Pa. In 1937 she transferred to the Carnegie Institute of Technology in Pittsburgh as a drama major. Two years later she enrolled in the East Hartman School of Design.

To pursue an interest in acting, Fogarty moved to New York City, where a sister (cookbook author Poppy Cannon) already resided. She worked as a model to support herself as she waited for acting parts. While modeling for designer Harvey Berin, she made incisive comments and suggestions about the clothes that revealed her natural talent in fashion. A year later she moved to Dorland International, which offered her a chance to help design. Evening art classes led to a meeting with Thomas E. Fogarty, Jr., a commercial artist, whom she married on Aug. 10, 1940. They had two children.

Not until 1947, after working as fashion publicist and stylist for Dorland, did Fogarty become assistant designer. That year Christian Dior introduced his "New Look," a radical change from the broad-shouldered, slim-hipped women's clothing of the war years. Cinched waists, tight bodices with rounded, natural shoulders, and full, calf-length skirts coincided perfectly with Fogarty's fantasy dresses. By 1948 she was designing for Youth Guild, a New York manufacturer of dresses for teens. Her cotton skirts with layers of bouffant petticoats were featured in *Harper's Bazaar*.

In 1950, Fogarty was hired by Margot Dresses, a producer of junior clothing. The combination of extreme femininity with simplicity of designs and fabrics made these moderately priced (well under $100 per dress) clothes in junior sizes 5–15 attractive to girls and women with "youthful figures." In 1951, *Mademoiselle* magazine gave Fogarty its Merit Award, and Bonwit Teller department store gave her its fashion award. Also in 1951, Fogarty was selected for the prestigious Coty American Fashion Critics Award, for her "paper-doll" silhouette.

On June 2, 1952, the *New York Times* offered two Anne Fogarty dress patterns for home sewers. Fogarty received the Neiman-Marcus fashion award in 1952 and the 20th Century World of Fashion Award from the Philadelphia Fashion Group in 1953. Two years later she was the recipient of the International Silk Association Award. At Margot Dresses, Fogarty also designed coats, suits, hats, costume jewelry, shoes, and lingerie. In 1957, her last year with Margot, she received the Cotton Fashion Award.

In 1958, Fogarty moved to Saks Fifth Avenue to design moderately priced misses' dresses. At Saks she produced new silhouettes, including an empire-waisted "camise" and a slim "relaxed sheath." Her designs for a round-the-clock wardrobe included lingerie, shoes, dresses, hats, and jewelry. Fogarty also found time to write. *Wife-Dressing*, advice for wives on how to dress to please husbands, was published in 1959.

Fogarty received the Sports Illustrated Magazine Designer of the Year Award in 1960. Pants, blouses, long evening dresses, and lounging jumpsuits, often in silk, cotton, or acetate, some trimmed in paillettes, were added to Fogarty's design repertoire. Her tenure with Saks Fifth Avenue ended in 1962, when she became president of Anne Fogarty, Inc., with Leonard Sunshine as her partner; also in that year she received the first American Express Annual Fashion Award.

Fogarty's company, located on Seventh Avenue in New York City, thrived, with reported annual sales of $7 million in 1968. Its divisions included Collector's Items (which was one of the first to use polyester double knits), Clothes Circuit, and A. F. Boutique. Fogarty was one of the first American companies to produce feminine, ruffled bikini bathing suits.

The Fogartys were divorced in the mid-1960's. On June 22, 1967, Fogarty married Richard Tompkins Kollmar, widower of newspaper columnist Dorothy Kilgallen. Kollmar died in 1971. By 1975, Fogarty had sold her company and was working from a studio in her townhouse at 45 East Sixty-eighth Street in Manhattan. Under the "Leisure-Pleasure" label she designed casual, functional clothes. Her 1977 marriage to Wade O'Hara ended in divorce. Fogarty continued to free-lance. For Shariella Fashions, she completed a spring-into-summer sportswear collection just before her death in New York City.

[A few garments designed by Fogarty are in the collection of the Fashion Institute of Technology's National Museum of Fashion in New York City. Early biographical material appears in the *New York World-Telegram*, July 2, 1947, and the *New York Times*, June 2, 1952. See also Imelda DeGraw, *25 Years/25 Couturiers* (1975), an exhibition catalog from the Denver Art Museum. Use of synthetic fabrics by Anne Fogarty, Inc., is described by Isadore Barmash in "Design and Technology Teamed," *New York Times*, Nov. 25, 1968. Caroline Rennolds Milbank traces Fogarty's career in *New York Fashion* (1989). For a feminist perspective of Fogarty's fashion philosophy, see Valerie Steele, *Women of Fashion* (1991). An obituary is in the *New York Times*, Jan. 16, 1980.]

THERESE DUZINKIEWICZ BAKER

FOLSOM, MARION BAYARD (Nov. 23, 1893–Sept. 28, 1976), businessman and public servant, was born in McRae, Ga., the son of William Bryant Folsom, a merchant, and Margaret Jane McRae. He was educated in the local schools and graduated from the University of Georgia at Athens with a B.A. in 1912; he then entered the Harvard Graduate School of Business Administration and was awarded an M.B.A. with distinction in 1914. He married Mary Davenport on Nov. 16, 1918; they had three children.

Folsom was hired by Eastman Kodak in Rochester, N.Y., in 1914; since he had taken a course in business statistics at Harvard, one of his first assignments at Eastman was in the statistical field. His employment was temporarily interrupted in World War I, when he served overseas in the United States Army as a captain in the Quartermaster Corps with the Twenty-sixth Division of the American Expeditionary Force. On his return from the war, he became a staff assistant to George Eastman and was asked to organize a statistical department to forecast sales and business conditions. He quickly rose from this position to be assistant to the president (Eastman) in 1921, assistant to the chairman of the board in 1925, assistant treasurer in 1930, treasurer from 1935 to 1953, and member of the board of directors from 1947 to 1952, and from 1958 to 1969.

Folsom's most enduring achievement at Kodak was in the area of pensions and retirement benefits. George Eastman, whom Folsom described as a rugged individualist who did not believe in pension plans, had devised a wage-dividend plan in 1912, paying bonuses based on profits. By 1927 these reached the equivalent of six to eight weeks' pay for employees with at least five years of service. Inefficient older workers lacking resources had to be kept on the company payroll, so Folsom took the lead in developing a pension plan for Kodak that enabled the firm to retire such workers without creating a burden for society. The company agreed upon Folsom's group annuity plan, the costs of which were paid from the bonus fund, which included life insurance and total disability as well. This work brought Folsom into contact with developments for a national social security program.

Folsom published his findings as "Old Age on the Balance Sheet" (*Atlantic Monthly*, September 1929): "Good management cannot keep employees . . . when they are no longer needed. . . . The solution lies in the inauguration of a sound and adequate pension plan." As more companies failed in the Great Depression, he came to feel that the federal government could not stand idly by. Following the 1929 stock market crash, Folsom began a study at Kodak (later expanded to include thirteen other firms) of the problem of stabilizing production and employment that became known as the Rochester Unemployment Benefit Plan, a precursor of unemployment insurance.

Because of Folsom's interest in old-age pension plans, President Franklin D. Roosevelt appointed him to the President's Advisory Board of the Committee on Economic Security (1934–1935) and as a United States employer delegate to the International Labor Conference at Geneva, Switzerland (1936). His role in the former was pivotal, and earned him the sobriquet "Chief architect of the Social Security Act of 1935." Edwin Witte, executive director of the United States Committee on Economic Security, which drafted the Social Security Act, remarked that Folsom's testimony to the Senate committee was particularly influential. In addition, as a member of the Federal Advisory Council on Social Security (1937–1938), Folsom had the major responsibility for convincing his business colleagues that government-sponsored old-age insurance would increase productivity and help to stabilize the economy.

Folsom was one of the original trustees of the Committee on Economic Development (CED), organized by Paul G. Hoffman (later administrator of the Marshall Plan) in 1942. A nonprofit, nonpartisan group of some of the nation's leading businessmen, the CED was formed to help business plan for quick reconversion and expanded production, distribution, and employment after the war, and to help determine through objective research economic policies that would encourage the attainment and maintenance of high production and employment. Folsom chaired the CED field development division from 1942 to 1944 and helped establish 2,900 local committees with 60,000 volunteer workers to maintain contacts with 2 million employers about jobs and opportunities in the postwar period.

Folsom resigned from this post in March 1944 to become staff director of the House of Representatives' Special Committee on Postwar Economic Policy and Planning (the Colmer Committee), designed to facilitate orderly demobilization and reconversion after the war. Just one year after the war's end, 90 percent of contract settlements and 95 percent of plant clearances had been completed. When the work of this body was finished in 1946, with eleven reports that would become the basis for legislation concerning postwar problems, Folsom returned to the CED. He was elected one of its six vice-chairmen and was chairman from 1950 to 1953.

Folsom was then under secretary of the Treasury from January 1953 to July 1955. During this period he represented the Treasury on a cabinet committee to determine how federal employee benefits compared with those of "progressive industrial concerns" in private industry, finding the lack of group life insurance and group health insurance as serious gaps in coverage. He therefore sponsored a group life insurance program for federal employees underwritten by private industry. Federal employees paid the rate generally contributed by workers in the private sector, with the federal government making up the difference.

As under secretary, Folsom also helped revise the federal income tax law (the Income Tax Revision Act of 1954) by recommending some twenty principle revisions of the tax code in order to encourage private capital investment and to remove some of the inequities. Folsom next worked with the Department of Health, Education, and Welfare on a study of old-age and survivors' insurance that resulted in extension of coverage and liberalization of benefits under the 1954 amendments to the Social Security Act.

President Dwight D. Eisenhower appointed Folsom secretary of health, education, and welfare on Aug. 1, 1955. He espoused an activist philosophy: under Folsom, medical research activities were expanded and important new health legislation was enacted, including programs for construction of research facilities, training more public-health personnel and nurses, and a continuing national survey of the extent and nature of illness among the population. He supported the Salk polio vaccine program instituted in 1955 and helped coordinate efforts to reduce the shortage of doses. He also broadened efforts to control air and water pollution. Although Folsom argued against lowering women's age of eligibility for Social Security benefits to age sixty-two (along with women's organizations, the United States Chamber of Commerce, and Catholic charities), the law was changed in 1956. Folsom was an advocate of Medicare. Along with other cabinet secretaries, he served on the cabinet committee that investigated narcotics traffic during 1956. The body recommended that the states develop treatment programs and increase penalties for drug pushers. A record number of persons were rehabilitated under the expanding vocational rehabilitation program.

The appearance of Sputnik in October 1957 gave great impetus to the movement to strengthen the teaching of science and mathematics, and bolstered education generally. Folsom, believing that the United States lagged behind other nations in the sciences and languages, lobbied from 1955 to 1957 for the passage of the National Defense Education Act (passed in 1958). When the bill passed, he deemed it "the most comprehensive federal-aid-to-education bill since the land-grant college act was passed in 1862." Funds for the services of the Office of Education were more than doubled during his tenure, educational research was expanded, and he streamlined the department's bureaucracy. In general, as he put it, "I had to avoid programs that would run counter to the

President's strong views that the federal government should not interfere with the functions of state and local governments."

After resigning the secretaryship on Aug. 1, 1958, Folsom, with the presidents of the Ford and Carnegie foundations, served on the New York State Committee on Higher Education, recommending in 1959 to Governor Nelson Rockefeller that the state increase funding for public undergraduate and graduate education, limit expenditures for private institutions, and discontinue tuition-free higher education. It proposed turning eleven state teachers' colleges into liberal arts colleges and establishing a revitalized university.

Throughout his business and federal careers, Folsom was active in local civic affairs, serving on school and college boards, bank boards, chambers of commerce, and entities in the Rochester, N.Y., area. He also published a number of articles on old age insurance, economic security, economic policy, higher education, and industrial relations.

In his writings, Folsom compared and contrasted the system of utilizing staff assistants in both business and government, noting that in the former the staff was personally selected and tended to remain in that company, whereas government staffers were short-term newcomers.

Folsom died in Rochester, N.Y., and was buried in Arlington National Cemetery.

[Folsom's papers are organized in the University of Rochester's rare books department. His writings include *Executive Decision Making* (1962). See also Edwin E. Witte, *The Development of the Social Security Act* (1962); Arthur Larson, *Eisenhower* (1968); and William Graebner, *A History of Retirement* (1980). An obituary is in the *New York Times*, Sept. 29, 1976. There is an oral memoir in the Columbia University Oral History Collection.]

JOSEPH N. HANKIN

FORD, MARY (July 7, 1924–Sept. 30, 1977), singer and guitarist, was born Iris Colleen Summers in Pasadena, Calif., the daughter of Jenny May ("Dorothy") White and Marshall Summers, a Nazarene minister. She attended high school in Pasadena and El Centro, Calif., but never earned a diploma.

Ford was taught to sing and play the guitar by her mother. She first performed with her parents and seven siblings as a religious music group on Pasadena's KPAS radio station. After two brief marriages in 1941 (to Dave Palmquist and Marvin Watson), she began performing on hillbilly radio shows in Los Angeles and making live appearances in the area. Show host Cliffie Stone commented that Ford had "an amazing ear. She sang quietly, succinctly, and always in tune. . . . She was a terrific rhythm [guitar] player, which was very hard to find."

In the summer of 1945, Ford auditioned for Les Paul, pioneer guitarist and audio technician, who gave her her stage name. Paul was married at the time, and he and Ford began an affair. They were involved in an automobile accident in 1948 that almost resulted in Paul's death. In 1949, Ford sang on a Les Paul recording for the first time. Seeing her prowess as a rhythm guitarist, Paul made her a permanent part of his stage act. After Paul was divorced from his wife, he and Ford were married in the midst of a busy touring schedule on Dec. 29, 1949.

During their first years together, Les Paul and Mary Ford made a number of experimental recordings utilizing Paul's pioneering overdubbing and multitrack techniques. On these recordings, Ford played guitar and stacked her voice in four- and five-part harmony. A transcription radio series, the "Les Paul Show with Mary Ford," was broadcast on NBC in 1950. Pursuing television work they eventually moved to New York City.

In their squalid home recording studio in Jackson Heights, Queens, Paul and Ford made the first of their most popular recordings, "How High the Moon," which featured an unprecedented twelve layers of guitar and vocal tracks. The song had already been heavily recorded by jazz artists, and Capitol Records, Paul and Ford's label, delayed releasing it. Capitol did release "Tennessee Waltz" (December 1950) and "Mockin' Bird Hill" (February 1951), recordings that demonstrated Paul and Ford's ease at moving between jazz, pop, and hillbilly styles. Their rendition of "Tennessee Waltz" successfully competed with Patti Page's, who had a hit with the song a month earlier. "Mockin' Bird Hill" became the second-largest selling disk in the country.

Their success persuaded Capitol to release "How High the Moon," which soon joined "Mockin' Bird Hill" at the top of the *Hit Parade* spots. It was the first single by a white act to reach the top of the rhythm and blues charts and influenced musicians in the United

States and Europe who would later become major rock stars, including Bill Wyman of the Rolling Stones, Jimmy Page of Led Zeppelin, and Paul McCartney of the Beatles. Within twenty-two weeks, Paul and Ford released several more hits, with record sales exceeding four million units.

They signed a new contract with Capitol in 1951, with the stipulation that Mary Ford would relinquish her stage name if the couple ever separated. Their live appearances were usually sold out. Offstage singers and instrumentalists were used to replicate the multitrack effects of their recordings. The live shows also featured cutthroat, virtuoso guitar battles between Paul and Ford. In a carefully rehearsed but seemingly spontaneous routine, Ford would match Paul's intricate guitar work lick for lick until, in exasperation, Paul would rip the plug out of her guitar amplifier.

In 1953, Les and Mary recorded their biggest hit, "Vaya con Dios," a Latin-flavored song released on June 1. It was uncharacteristically simple and tender, and won the hearts of the public, zooming to number one and remaining on the charts for nearly three months. In October 1953, the duo finally broke into television with the "Les Paul and Mary Ford Show," a five-minute-long segment that was essentially a Listerine commercial.

The relentless pace of recording and touring began to take its toll on Ford. She was borderline diabetic and developing an addiction to alcohol. On Nov. 26, 1954, she went into premature labor; the baby died four days later.

Rock and roll, emerging around 1955, proved to be the duo's downfall. The mellow and wholesome sound of Les, Mary, and other crooners of the day was lost on the modern audience. Record sales plummeted; their final release for Capitol was "Small Island" in 1958.

That same year, Paul and Ford adopted a baby girl, and in 1959 Ford gave birth to a son. Worn out with relentless touring and longing for a stable family life, Ford left Paul in 1963; they were divorced in 1964. Ford married Donald Hatfield, who had attended high school with her, in 1965 and abandoned show business for a quiet life in suburban Los Angeles. Her health, however, remained fragile. Overweight, alcoholic, and suffering from diabetes, she died after an eight-week diabetic coma at the age of fifty-three. She was buried in Forest Lawn cemetery in Covina Hills, Calif. Her grave marker bore the carving of a guitar and the title of her favorite song, "Vaya con Dios."

Most of Les Paul and Mary Ford's recorded output on Capital and Columbia was issued as 45 rpm singles. Their vinyl LP collections include, on Capitol, *Les and Mary* (1955), *The World Is Waiting for the Sunrise* (1974), *Very Best of Les Paul and Mary Ford* (1974), *Les Paul and Mary Ford: Their All-Time Greatest Hits* (1980); and, on Columbia, *The Fabulous Les Paul and Mary Ford* (1965).

[See Mary Alice Shaughnessy, *Les Paul: An American Original* (1993).]

DAVID L. JOYNER

FORMAN, CELIA ADLER (Dec. 7, 1889–Jan. 31, 1979), actress in the Yiddish theater, was born Tzirele Adler in New York, N.Y., the daughter of Jacob P. Adler and Dina Stettin, who were both actors. Her father, a tragedian, was a pillar of Yiddish theater and was also successful on Broadway. Her mother, one of Jacob Adler's several wives, earned renown for her acting in Britain and the United States and often worked with her husband. Forman later said of her birth: "I made my screaming appearance into our sinful world on the fourth floor of a tenement house on Clinton Street." Indeed, there was much to scream about. Her mother had arrived in New York from London only weeks before and soon would divorce Jacob Adler for his infidelity. She refused alimony out of pride and though the broken family continued to work together and enjoy success in the theater, Forman and her mother had to struggle to make ends meet.

Forman's mother married actor and playwright Sigmund Feinman, who treated Forman as if she were his own child. She used Feinman's last name until the age of eighteen, when she changed it to Adler for the stage. At the age of six months, Forman made her first appearance on stage. Terrified by the sight of her father in makeup, little Celia (as she became known soon after her birth) began to cry backstage during a play. Her mother quieted her until she had to perform (ironically, as a mother about to lose her infant child). Afraid to disturb Celia, her mother used her in place of a doll. Once on stage, Forman was in her element. She gave the audience such a curious, wide-eyed look that they broke out in laughter and applause.

Her second appearance, at the age of two-and-a-half, was also spontaneous, as were many of the Yiddish theater's finest moments. Forman's mother, angered by Adler's third wife's attempts to keep him from seeing her daughter, dressed Celia up in a fez and placed her on stage during a Turkish operetta in which Adler was starring. When Adler saw her, he picked her up and improvised lines of joy, to which Celia replied, "Quiet, there's a pway!"

Forman went on to play many child roles, but as a teenager she rebelled against the theater and left it. During this period, her stepfather died and Forman went to work as a piano teacher. Her mentor, Bertha Kalisch, brought Forman back to the theater by insisting that she costar with her in a production of Sudermann's *Die Heimat* (*Magda*). Forman received such a favorable review that she decided that her destiny was the theater.

Famous for her large, dark eyes and versatile facial expressions, Forman would earn a reputation as "the first lady of Yiddish theater." She starred in plays by Yiddish authors as well as in the translated dramas of Ibsen, Shakespeare, Shaw, Chekhov, Hauptmann, and others.

Her first formal success as a serious actress came in 1913 for her role in Ossip Dymou's *The Eternal Wanderer*. She is also remembered for her interpretations of Shakespeare's Desdemona and Ibsen's Nora. Her English-language performances include *Men in White*, *Success Story*, and *A Flag Is Born* in 1946 with Paul Muni. She made her last appearance on Broadway in 1961 in *Women in Horseradish*. But her greatest commitment was always to the Yiddish theater.

In 1918, Forman helped found the Yiddish Art Theater at the Irving Place Theater in Manhattan. There she met her first husband, actor Lazar Freed; they had one child. Married on Aug. 14, 1914, Forman and Freed divorced in 1919.

In 1930, Forman married her manager, Jack Cone, who died in 1955. In 1959 she married New York businessman Nathan Forman, whose death preceded hers by one month.

Forman eventually broke away from the Yiddish Art Theater to help found the Jewish Art Theater (*Naye Teatr*). She performed in nearly every European capital and in 1936 toured South America. During one performance in a village in Argentina, Forman was warned that a local dog always walked into the theater and howled in approval during performances. Annoyed, Forman nevertheless went on with the play. But when the dog failed to appear and not a howl was heard, she felt disappointed and wondered if she had acted well.

Though her formal education did not extend beyond high school, Forman regarded the theater as a realm of perpetual study and refinement of craft. To her advantage, she spoke a clear, beautiful Yiddish. She made great efforts to move Yiddish theater away from *shund* (literally "trash," or "low" theater) and toward *kunst* (literally "art," or "high" theater). Forman felt that the charming spontaneity of Yiddish theater's early years inhibited its evolution toward the more disciplined art form espoused by Jacob Gordin and other *kunst* playwrights.

Deeply proud of Yiddish culture, Forman worried over its demise. She blamed the decline of the Yiddish Art Theater on the star system, in which a star actor took the leading role in a play "whether or not the star fitted the role." The star would also automatically become manager, casting agent, director, and coach and would often succumb to self-promotion at the rest of the cast's expense. "This insidious poison," as Forman described the star system, set the actors in competition against each other for the limelight. Forman preferred repertory theater, in which actors played a variety of roles.

She also believed it was a mistake for Yiddish theater to imitate Broadway in order to attract an Americanized Jewish audience. "But just the opposite was the result," she wrote. "In aping Broadway, our theatre was shorn of the Jewish tone, the melody of Jewish charm. Why go to see Broadway imitated when one could go right to Broadway and see the real thing?"

In 1960, Forman's two-volume study, *The Yiddish Theater in America*, appeared in Yiddish. An English translation exists but remains unpublished.

Even after Forman entered a nursing home in 1975 well into her eighties, she continued to perform. A week before she died of a stroke at the Hebrew Home for the Aged in the Bronx in New York City, she performed several roles in a one-act monologue, and at the time of her death she was preparing for another performance.

[For Forman's memoirs of her family and theater life, see "Celia Adler Recalls," translated into English in Joseph C. Landise, ed., *Memoirs of the Yiddish Stage* (1984). See also David S. Lifson, *The*

Yiddish Theatre in America (1965); Nahma Sandrow, *Vagabond Stars* (1977); and Sandrow, "Yiddish Theater and American Theater," in Sarah Blacher Cohen, *From Hester Street to Hollywood* (1983). Extensive information on Forman's father can be found in Lulla Adler Rosenfeld, *Bright Star of Exile* (1977). An obituary is in the *New York Times*, Feb. 2, 1979.]

ALISON GARDY

FOX, VIRGIL KEEL (May 3, 1912–Oct. 25, 1980), organist, was born in Princeton, Ill., the son of Miles S. Fox, a real estate salesman and theater operator, and Birdie E. Nichols, an amateur singer. Virgil and his brother Warren grew up with a strong identification with local history and culture. Their maternal grandmother, Abigail Nichols, was one of the first woman doctors in the frontier days of Illinois settlement.

Virgil Fox began his musical study on the piano with Hugh Price, a local teacher. He switched to the organ reluctantly because at first he did not like its repertoire. However, he made such rapid progress that he was playing for church services at the First Presbyterian Church in Princeton by the age of ten and performing for large audiences outside his hometown by the time he was fourteen. In 1929, at the age of seventeen, he won the biennial contest of the National Federation of Music Clubs.

After graduating from high school in Princeton in 1930, Fox moved to Chicago to study with Wilhelm Middelschulte, an expert on the organ music of Johann Sebastian Bach. In 1931 he won a full scholarship to study with Louis Robert at the Peabody Conservatory in Baltimore, and in only one year he completed the artist's diploma, the first student to do so in such a short time. After a brief period of study with Marcel Dupré in Paris, Fox performed at Kingsway Hall in London. He gave his first New York City recital at Wanamaker's department store and performed to a standing-room crowd in 1933 at the Chicago World's Fair. In his career, Fox gave recitals at almost all of the 250 local chapters of the American Guild of Organists.

Throughout his career, Fox was a church organist. While a student at Peabody he played at St. Mark's Lutheran Church in Hanover, Pa. In 1938 he became the organist at the Brown Memorial Church in Baltimore. In that year he succeeded Louis Robert as head of the organ department at Peabody, a position he maintained until 1942, when he joined the United States Army Air Force. Stationed in Washington, D.C., Fox spent the war years performing to raise funds for the Air Force Aid Society. In 1946 he gave three major recitals sponsored by the Elizabeth Sprague Coolidge Foundation at the Library of Congress.

As a recitalist, Fox shared honors and critical acclaim with E. Power Biggs, but he earned an outstanding reputation with the public for his flamboyance as well as his musicianship. In order to make a piece more accessible to an audience, either in concert or on his numerous recordings, Fox occasionally changed the score. On tour he traveled with his own electronic organ, and late in his career he included a light show and flashy costumes in many of his concerts. He often spoke to his audiences, providing impromptu program notes, and occasionally he would ask his listeners to join him in singing a well-known hymn or patriotic song. While purists denigrated these departures from traditional concert decorum, audiences flocked to his concerts. At the height of his career, he was giving more than seventy concerts each year throughout the country. In addition, Fox recorded for the Capitol, RCA Victor, Columbia, and Command labels.

In 1946, Fox became the organist at Riverside Church in New York City. He declined the traditional responsibilities of choirmaster so that he could concentrate on his performing career, both inside and outside the church. Deeply religious, Fox sought to use music to inspire worship and nourish the spirit. He often spoke about the need to improve public taste in religious music, a process that he felt could only happen if the best of the organ repertoire was accessible to his congregations and audiences. His career at Riverside Church, which continued until 1965, included the dedication on Mar. 30, 1955, of the rebuilt five manual Aeolian-Skinner organ. On this occasion he was accompanied by the New York Philharmonic Orchestra, conducted by Dimitri Mitropoulos.

In 1936, Fox became the first American organist to give a major recital at Carnegie Hall for which audiences paid an admission. In addition to being the first American organist to play at the Cathedral of Notre Dame in Paris and on Johann Sebastian Bach's organ at St. Thomas Church in Leipzig, he performed at other major churches and cathedrals throughout Europe. On Dec. 15, 1962, he was joined by Catharine Crozier and E. Power Biggs in inaugurating the organ at Philharmonic (later Avery Fisher) Hall in Lincoln Center, and he performed a solo recital on this organ on Jan. 7, 1963. Fox continued to play with major symphony orchestras throughout the United States. His last symphonic appearance was with the Dallas Symphony Orchestra a month before his death in West Palm Beach, Fla.

[Clippings, programs, and reviews are in the Music Division of the New York Public Library for the Performing Arts at Lincoln Center. See also articles in *Etude*, Mar. 1952; *Musical America*, Dec. 1954; *High Fidelity*, Aug. 1963; P. J. Basch, "Virgil Fox," in *Music: The AGO and RCCO Magazine*, vols. 4 and 5 (1970–1971); A. Lawrence, "Virgil Fox, 1912–1980," in *The Diapason* (1980); and *The New Grove Dictionary of American Music* (1986). An obituary is in the *New York Times*, Oct. 6, 1980.]

BARBARA L. TISCHLER

FRANZBLAU, ROSE NADLER (Jan. 1, 1905–Sept. 2, 1979), psychologist and syndicated newspaper columnist, was born in Vienna, Austria, the daughter of Meyer Nadler, a manufacturer, and Rachael Breitfeld. The family came to the United States in the year of her birth. She married Abraham Norman Franzblau, a psychiatrist, in 1923. They had two children. She received a B.A. from Hunter College in 1926 and an M.A. and Ph.D. at Columbia University in 1931 and 1935, respectively. Her dissertation was published by Columbia University Press in 1935 as *Race Differences in Mental and Physical Traits, Studied in Different Environments*.

During Franzblau's nine years as a graduate student at Columbia, she continued a career as a teacher and principal in New York City high schools. In 1935 she began a five-year period of service as a personnel specialist for the National Youth Administration in Cincinnati, Ohio. In 1940 she was appointed director of personnel for the National Youth Administration in both Cincinnati and Columbus, Ohio. Three years later, Franzblau was named national director for the training of girls in the Washington, D.C., offices of the National Youth Administration, a post she held until 1944.

These positions led to several important public appointments. Between 1944 and 1946, Franzblau served as director of placement and overseas personnel training for the United Nations Relief and Rehabilitation Administration. She then assumed duties in 1946 at the New York City branch of the United States Office of Price Administration. In 1947 she was named associate director of the International Tensions Research Project for the United Nations Educational, Scientific, and Cultural Organization. Holding that post through 1951, she began in 1948 to work as a newspaper columnist as well.

Throughout this busy period as an administrator, Franzblau wrote a number of books. In 1944 she and Otto Klineberg wrote *National Youth Administration: Final Report* for the War Manpower Commission and in 1950 she collaborated with Klineberg on *Tensions Affecting International Understanding*. She authored or coauthored eight books, including such works as *The Menopause Myth*, published in 1976.

Franzblau also wrote articles for various popular magazines and professional journals. She authored a series entitled "Searchlight on Delinquency" in the *New York Post Magazine* from 1954 through 1955. A monthly feature initiated in 1967, "Your Family and You," appeared for two years in *Family Circle*. During that two-year period she was also a columnist for *Sales Management*, authoring a series entitled "How to Avoid the Tyranny of Executive Tensions." She also contributed articles to such popular magazines as *Seventeen* and *Cosmopolitan*.

Literary contributions were not Franzblau's only media activities. Between 1965 and 1970 she hosted a daily radio program, "Dr. Franzblau's World of Children," on WCBS in New York City. Like her popular writings, the program was an effort to present Freudian theory on various issues to the general public, including adolescence, juvenile delinquency, work-related stress, and self-image. Her question-and-answer column "Human Relations," which was syndicated in thirteen major newspapers between 1951 and 1976, was a sustained effort to translate for a general audience the intricacies of Freudian theory on issues ranging from sexuality and parenthood to social relations. Her surveys of guidance techniques for youths in Sweden, France, Denmark, and Great Britain, conducted in 1958, along with research in the juvenile-court procedures of Tel Aviv, Paris, Rome, and London in 1960, were also projects designed to apply Freudian precepts to contemporary issues.

Appearances on popular television talk shows—along with spots on radio programs such as "Girl Talk," "Noonday Line," and

"Contact"—were energetic attempts to popularize Freudian theory. By the time of her death in New York City, where she lived for the final thirty years of her life at 1 Gracie Terrace, she had established herself as an intellectual whose scholarly interests never set her apart from the community at large. Franzblau was committed to the spirit of Freud's original intent of constructing an analysis of the individual set squarely in the world producing that individual. Her conception of the ego had its theoretical roots in such classic works of Freud as *Civilization and Its Discontents*. Her work was as much a social commentary as it was a focus on the individual psyche.

[An obituary is in the *New York Times*, Sept. 3, 1979.]

MICHAEL J. EULA

FRICK, FORD CHRISTOPHER (Dec. 19, 1894–Apr. 8, 1978), baseball executive and journalist, was born on a farm outside Wawaka, Ind., the son of Jacob Frick and Emma Prickett. At the age of five his family moved to Brimfield, where Ford attended grade school.

Upon graduation from Consolidated High School in nearby Rome City in 1910, Ford worked on the Fort Wayne, Ind., *Gazette*. He entered DePauw University in 1911, where he combined his interest in sports, as a member of both baseball and track teams, with journalism, as a correspondent for several Terre Haute, Chicago, and Indianapolis newspapers.

Frick received his B.A. from DePauw in 1915 and briefly played semiprofessional baseball as a first baseman for the Walsenburg, Colo., team. Frick then taught English in the Walsenburg high school before becoming an assistant professor of English at Colorado College.

On Sept. 15, 1916, Frick married Eleanor Cowing. They had one child. The next year he left teaching to expand his part-time reporting for the *Colorado Springs Telegraph* into a full-time position.

In 1918, Frick joined the War Department's rehabilitation division as supervisor of training in Colorado, Utah, New Mexico, and Wyoming. In early 1919 he joined the staff of the *Rocky Mountain News* in Denver as a sports reporter. Later that year he returned to Colorado Springs to open an advertising agency and write an editorial column for the *Colorado Springs Telegraph*. Word of Frick's success as an editorial writer reached Arthur Brisbane, editor of the *New York Evening Journal*, and in 1922 Frick joined the sports staff of the *New York American* (both New York newspapers were part of the Hearst chain). In August 1923 he moved to the *Evening Journal*, where for eleven years he wrote a sports-page column covering the New York Yankees in the Grantland Rice tradition, often writing news in verse form. He became a ghost writer for Babe Ruth and Yankee manager Miller Huggins.

In May 1930, Frick was asked to fill in for the news editor of the *Evening Journal*, who had to miss his regular radio news broadcast due to illness. Frick's broadcast was so impressive that he was quickly signed to do a twice-daily sports broadcast on radio station WOR while still writing his newspaper column. In February 1934, Frick was named the first director of the National League Service Bureau, the publicity outlet for baseball's National League. On Nov. 8, 1934, Frick was elected president of the National League, replacing John A. Heydler, who had resigned because of poor health.

Among the immediate difficulties Frick faced was the poor financial state of three National League clubs, the Brooklyn Dodgers, the Boston Braves, and the Philadelphia Phillies. Frick was credited with putting all of the clubs back on firm financial footing by working out ways in which the clubs could pay their league obligations while avoiding bankruptcy. Frick also became a guiding force in the creation of the National Baseball Museum at Cooperstown, N.Y., which opened in July 1938, and he was instrumental in introducing night baseball into the major leagues.

Perhaps the most demanding and difficult moment of his presidency occurred with the racial integration of major league baseball in 1947. The St. Louis Cardinals threatened to strike rather than face the Brooklyn Dodgers, who had Jackie Robinson, the first black major league ballplayer, on their team roster. Frick's response was forthright: "If you do this you are through and I don't care if it wrecks the league for ten years—you cannot do this because this is America!" The players did not strike.

After serving for seventeen years as president of the National League, Frick was elected commissioner of baseball in September 1951. His election, however, did not come easily. The baseball owners had just removed A. B. ("Happy") Chandler as commissioner, and they were deadlocked between Frick and Warren Giles, the general manager of the Cincinnati Reds. Finally, Giles withdrew from the race "in the best interests of baseball" and was named National League president when Frick became commissioner.

As commissioner, Frick presided over baseball's greatest period of expansion, transition, and progress. The Boston Braves moved to Milwaukee, the St. Louis Browns moved to Baltimore, and the Philadelphia Athletics went to Kansas City. Perhaps the most memorable and controversial franchise shifts, however, were the movements of the Brooklyn Dodgers and New York Giants to Los Angeles and San Francisco, respectively. Frick also saw the creation of new clubs: the New York Mets, the Houston Colt .45's, the Washington Senators, and the California Angels. Under Frick's stewardship, baseball became big business with lucrative new television contracts that provided for World Series, All-Star Game, and game of the week coverage. New procedures under his tenure included the free-agent draft and the college-scholarship plan for students who signed professional baseball contracts while still in school.

While maintaining a quiet dignity as commissioner and as one known to eschew conflict and controversy wherever possible, Frick did have his moments in the spotlight of unwelcomed notoriety. Perhaps the most famous of these came during the controversy over the breaking of Babe Ruth's home run record by Roger Maris in 1961. During the season, when Maris appeared to bear down on Ruth's record, many media sources reported an alleged Frick remark that if Maris broke Ruth's season record of sixty home runs, it would have to be marked with an asterisk in the record book. Maris, he reasoned, played a 162-game schedule while Ruth's record was accomplished in just 154 games. There never was an asterisk placed in the record book when Maris, indeed, broke Ruth's home run mark, hitting sixty-one that season. Frick denied ever promoting the idea. As Frick related it, his ruling on the matter was quite simple and straightforward. If the record was broken in 154 games, the Maris mark would be recognized and the Ruth record dropped. If the Ruth mark still stood at the end of 154 games but was subsequently broken in the eight additional games of the season, then both records would be recognized as official and given equal billing in the record book. That is, in fact, the notation in the official record book.

Frick retired in November 1965 at the age of seventy-one after serving two seven-year terms as commissioner. In 1970 he was inducted into the Baseball Hall of Fame. He died in Bronxville, N.Y.

Frick's legacy to the game of baseball was summarized by the commissioner of baseball at the time of his death, Bowie Kuhn, who said that during Frick's tenure, when baseball experienced unprecedented expansion and transition, he brought to the game "integrity, dedication and a happy tranquility."

[Clippings and news releases pertinent to Frick's tenure as commissioner are available through Major League Baseball, Office of the Commissioner, New York City. Frick's memoirs are in *Games, Asterisks, and People* (1973). An obituary is in the *New York Times*, Apr. 10, 1978.]

GLENN N. SKLARIN

FROMAN, ELLEN JANE (Nov. 10, 1907–Apr. 22, 1980), singer, was born in St. Louis, Mo., the daughter of Elmer Ellsworth Froman and of Anna T. Barcafer, a teacher of piano and voice and a vocal soloist. After her parents were divorced in 1912, Froman and her mother returned to her mother's hometown, Clinton, Mo., where her mother supported them by teaching piano and voice in the local public schools. Although the family was not Catholic, Froman received her elementary education at a convent in Clinton. Froman's mother married W. J. Hetzler, the mayor of Columbia, Mo., in 1930.

As a child, Froman stuttered. A specialist in St. Louis recommended voice lessons, and the musical talent that she possessed was developed. Froman first studied voice and piano with her mother. She attended the high school division at Christian College (now Columbia College), in Columbia, where she appeared in musicals and plays. Interested in singing and writing, Froman continued to participate in musical theater during her two years at Christian College, from which she received an Associate of Arts degree with a major in French (1924). She then spent one year at the University of Missouri in Columbia, majoring in journalism.

Froman's first big break came when she sang the leading role in the journalism department's revue. A booker from St. Louis heard her and offered her a singing job in St. Louis. Froman decided to continue her musical studies and attended the Cincinnati Conservatory of Music. In 1930, after she sang "St. Louis Blues" at a party, Powel Crosley, Jr., asked her to sing on radio station WLW in Cincinnati. In 1932, Froman joined the Paul Whiteman band and made her first appearance at the Oriental Theater in Chicago. She also appeared on radio shows and performed in Chicago nightclubs. In March of that year, Froman moved to New York City, where she sang on local radio programs and in nightclubs and worked with such musicians as the Dorsey Brothers and Benny Goodman in the Lennie Hayton band. Froman married singer-entertainer Don Ross in September 1932; they had no children. By the time she appeared in *Ziegfeld Follies of 1934*, she had become a major singing star.

In 1940, Froman appeared in the Broadway show *Keep Off the Grass* with Ray Bolger and Jimmy Durante. President Franklin Roosevelt asked her to entertain American soldiers at Camp Dix, N.J., and thereafter she performed in USO shows at other bases. On Feb. 22, 1943, Froman was a member of a USO group on board the *Yankee Clipper*, a Pan American World Airways plane, when it crashed in the Tagus River, near Lisbon, Portugal. One of the few survivors, she was kept afloat in the icy river by the injured copilot of the plane, John Burn, until help came. Froman's right arm was broken in several places, two or three of her ribs were broken, her left leg was cut to the bone, and her right leg sustained a compound fracture so severe that it was nearly cut off. For weeks she was in critical condition. Burn and Froman were in the same Lisbon hospital for months, and a strong friendship developed. Over the next seven years, Froman strove to continue her career while undergoing twenty-five operations, spending a total of nearly three years in hospitals.

Froman progressed from singing in a wheelchair, to hobbling to the stage on crutches, to walking with a heavy brace on her right leg. She endured almost thirty bone grafts and operations before she was finally able to walk on her own. (In later years, she walked with a cane. She hid scars on her arms with long sleeves and her leg brace with long skirts.)

Froman traveled to Europe to entertain wounded American troops in hospitals and camps. She divorced Don Ross in 1948 and married John Burn; they were divorced in 1956. Froman appeared in the Broadway show *Laugh, Town, Laugh* (1942), and for the Broadway play *Artists and Models* (1943) she rehearsed in her hospital room. She weighed eighty-five pounds and was wearing a thirty-five-pound cast. Among the songs she recorded for Decca are "My Melancholy Baby," "I Only Have Eyes for You," and "Lost in a Fog." For Capitol she recorded "With a Song in My Heart," "That Old Feeling," "Blue Moon," "It's a Good Day," and others. In 1952, Froman's life was depicted in the movie *With a Song in My Heart*, starring Susan Hayward. Froman dubbed the vocals.

Struggling with enormous medical bills, Froman sued Pan American for $2.5 million in 1953. In 1957 the House of Representatives voted to pay her $138,000 as compensation for her wartime injuries.

In 1949, Froman became so depressed that she was admitted to the Menninger Clinic in Topeka, Kans. During her six-month stay, she became interested in helping emotionally disturbed children. In 1951, she established the Jane Froman Foundation for Emotionally Disturbed Children.

In spite of her injuries and constant pain, Froman starred in the television shows "USA Canteen" and "The Jane Froman Show." She also continued to sing in nightclubs, one of her last appearances being at the Flamingo, in Las Vegas. Froman retired in 1961 and moved back to Columbia, Mo., where she married a childhood friend, Rowland H. Smith, in 1962. She received a USO gold medal in 1968. In later years, Froman served as a trustee of Christian College (Columbia College), the Menninger Foundation, and the Missouri Society of Crippled Children and Adults.

The traditional training that Froman received was evident in her vocal delivery. (In the 1930's and 1940's, a musically educated popular vocalist was highly unusual.) Jane Froman was not a jazz or swing singer, but a vocalist of popular song, performing on the Broadway stage as well as in nightclubs. Her strongest appeal was in her heartfelt delivery of music and lyrics in a strong contralto voice. She died in Columbia, Mo.

[The Jane Froman collection is at Columbia College, Columbia, Mo. Articles concerning Froman include Arthur Mann, "Song in Her Heart," *Collier's*, Jan. 22, 1944; Rose Hyblut, "Comeback with Words and Music," *Etude*, Dec. 1948; and Jane Froman, "The Woman I Have Become," *Good Housekeeping*, Nov. 1952. An obituary is in the *New York Times*, Apr. 23, 1980.]

JAN SHAPIRO

FROMM, ERICH (Mar. 23, 1900–Mar. 18, 1980), psychoanalyst and social philosopher, was born in Frankfurt-am-Main, Germany, the son of Naphtali Fromm, a wine merchant, and Rosa Krause. The only child of a middle-class Orthodox Jewish family with a long rabbinical tradition on his father's side, he was particularly affected by his reading of the biblical prophets Isaiah, Amos, and Hosea, with their vision of universal peace and harmony and their confirmation of the ethical nature of history. His traditional religious upbringing rendered him in some ways closer in spirit to the late Middle Ages than to the twentieth century. The tension between the two worlds was a major creative force in his life.

Fromm considered his Talmudic teachers—J. Horowitz, Salman B. Rabinkov, Nehemiah Nobel, and his mother's uncle, Ludwig Krause—to be the most important influences in his life. All of them were strictly observant rabbis as well as tolerant humanists who constantly studied the Talmud and revealed no ambition to write and no desire for position or fame. Although Fromm gave up religious practices at the age of twenty-six because he "didn't want to participate in any division of the human race, whether religious or political," the principles and values of these teachers remained with him.

An early experience that cultivated Fromm's subsequent interest in psychoanalysis involved the death of an artist friend of the family who, when Fromm was twelve, committed suicide after the death of her father and had requested in her will to be buried with him. Fromm was fascinated by the preference of a beautiful young woman for death over life and art. The outbreak of World War I when he was fourteen convinced him that irrational behavior was not limited to the individual. The war came as a profound shock to Fromm, constituting what he felt was "the beginning of the process of brutalization that continues to this day."

After completing his secondary education in Frankfurt, Fromm attended the University of Heidelberg, where he studied psychology, philosophy, and sociology, earning a Ph.D. in 1922. His thesis was the social-psychological structure of three Jewish groups—the Karaim, the Hasidim, and the Reformists. In 1925 and 1926 he pursued additional studies in psychiatry and psychology at the University of Munich. He trained in psychoanalysis with Landauer and Wittenberg from 1926 to 1928 and completed his formal education at the Psychoanalytic Institute in Berlin. Upon graduating in 1931, he became a member of the Berlin Institute. Unlike many of his colleagues, who entered the psychoanalytical profession through the practice of medicine, Fromm never took a medical degree. He practiced psychoanalysis in Berlin, devoting part of his time to the application of psychoanalytical theories to social and cultural problems. During this period he and Frieda Reichmann, a physician and psychoanalyst he had married in June 1926, founded the Psychoanalytic Institute in Frankfurt; he lectured there during biweekly trips from Berlin. From 1929 to 1932 he taught at and was a member of the Institute for Social Research at the University of Frankfurt.

Fromm's reputation as a noted psychoanalyst grew with the appearance in 1930 of his essay "The Development of the Dogma of Christ" in *Imago*, a journal published by Sigmund Freud in Vienna, Austria. In the essay, published separately in 1931, he sought to interpret the doctrines and symbols of Christianity in light of the social and economic experiences of the early Christians.

Fromm was in Geneva, Switzerland, when Hitler came to power in Germany. Invited to lecture at the Chicago Psychoanalytic Institute, he traveled to the United States for the first time in 1933. He left Germany permanently the following year and became a naturalized American citizen in 1940. For a time he was associated with the child development theories of German-born psychoanalyst Karen Horney, but he eventually embarked on what Gregory Zilboorg, writing in the *Saturday Review*, called a search for the "essence of man, the meaning of human struggles, and the roots and growth and efflorescence of love in the deepest and universal, ethico-philosophical meaning of this word."

Fromm was a lecturer at the International Institute for Social Research of Columbia University in New York City from 1934 to 1939 and was a guest lecturer at Columbia in the 1940–1941 academic year. From 1941 to 1950 he served on the faculty at Bennington College in Vermont. He was also a lecturer at the American Institute for Psychoanalysis (1941–1942), at the New School for Social Research (1946–1956) in New York City, and at Yale University (1949–1950). Having divorced Frieda Fromm-Reichmann, he married Henny Gurland in July 1944; she died in 1952. He married Annis Freeman on Dec. 18, 1953.

In 1946, Fromm was one of the founders and trustees of the William Alanson White Institute of Psychiatry, Psychoanalysis, and Psychology in New York City, serving as chairman of its faculty from 1947 to 1950. In 1951 he accepted a professorship in the department of psychoanalysis at the medical school of the National Autonomous University of Mexico in Frontera and was head of the department from 1955 until he retired in 1965. Fromm also founded the Institute of Psychoanalysis and was its director from 1955 to 1965.

While a resident of Mexico, Fromm commuted regularly to the United States—for his teaching duties at the White Institute; at Michigan State University, where he was professor of psychology from 1957 to 1961; and at New York University, where he was adjutant professor of psychology from 1962 to 1980.

The ideas of Spinoza, Goethe, Marx, and Freud shaped Fromm's humanist philosophy. He saw in Marx's works the key to interpreting history and the manifestation, in secular terms, of the radical humanism expressed in the messianic vision of the Old Testament prophets. Fromm contended in *Marx's Concept of Man* (1961) that Marx developed his theory of socialism in response to the alienation of man from himself and from nature. Some years after his encounter with Marx's work he came under the influence of Freud. Originally a dogmatic and orthodox Freudian, Fromm gradually altered his views because he disagreed with Freud's concept of unconscious inner drives and his neglect of social and economic factors in his theories of the human mind. In *Beyond the Chains of Illusion* (1962), Fromm contrasted Freud's pessimistic view of humanity with Marx's "unbroken faith in man's perfectibility." He spent the years after 1928 attempting to work out a synthesis of Freudianism and Marxism.

Fromm described his introduction to Buddhism in 1926 as a kind of revelation, perceiving the Buddhist philosophy as a complete spiritual system, a way of life based on rationality devoid of mystification or appeal to revelation or authority. His initial experimentation with Buddhism was followed by an interest in Daisetz T. Suzuki's work on Zen Buddhism. The concepts, methods, and goals of Zen and psychoanalysis are compared in *Zen Buddhism and Psychoanalysis* (1960), which he edited with Suzuki and Richard DeMartino. A final contribution to Fromm's thought was J. J. Bachofen's study of matriarchal and patriarchal principles as applied not only to individual but to historical development. Through Bachofen's work Fromm grew to recognize the patriarchal bias of Freud's theories as well as the fundamental role of the mother figure in human life. His reading of the prophets, the Buddha, Marx, Freud, and Bachofen were fundamental influences on Fromm until the age of twenty-six; from that point his thinking can be perceived as an attempt to synthesize these ideas, none of which he abandoned, although he differed from the interpretations of their respective orthodox followers.

In more than twenty books, Fromm spoke of freedom in society, human destructiveness, and the concept of love. His system of personality acknowledges the individual's biological past but stresses his or her social nature; his pervasive thesis is that modern life has lost much of its meaning because people have sacrificed themselves to the machine and the superstate. Fromm was careful to base all of his theoretical conclusions about human psychic structure on observations of individual behavior made during forty years of practicing psychoanalysis. His most influential works are *Escape from Freedom* (1941), *Man for Himself* (1947), *The Sane Society* (1955), *The Art of Loving* (1956), and *To Have or to Be?* (1976).

Fromm's first book, *Escape from Freedom*, reprinted some twenty-five times by late 1965, is considered by many to be a landmark in psychology, intellectual history, and political philosophy—and his best work. In it he departed from standard Freudian theory by applying the techniques of psychoanalysis to the social process; the human instinct of destructiveness is not viewed as sexually derived behavior but as an attempt to overcome alienation and powerlessness. Tracing the development of human freedom and self-awareness from the Middle Ages to modern times, Fromm examined the tendency of emancipated beings to take refuge from the dehumanizing trends of contemporary civilization by turning to totalitarian movements such as Nazism. Instead of seeking "freedom from" the repressive character of technological society, people must join with others in the "freedom to" develop their creative powers.

Fromm examined these ideas further in *Man for Himself*, asserting that individuals must follow their own ethical standards rather than succumb blindly to authority. Based on the lectures he delivered at Yale, Fromm developed various character types that emerge as people react to socially imposed loneliness. The receptive character has insatiable demands and is willing to take but not to give. The hoarding character sees the outside world as a threat and avoids sharing what it has. The exploitative character satisfies its desires through force and cunning. The marketing character considers itself a commodity that can be bought or sold. The productive character alone is desirable, because it realizes its potential and, in so doing, devotes itself to the welfare and well-being of others.

Human beings in consumer-oriented society, Fromm argued in *The Sane Society*, have become estranged from their own behavior, becoming prisoners of the institutions they have created. To restore sanity, he urged that each individual develop high ethical standards in order to arrest the process of human robotization. The end product of the rebirth of enlightenment that would take place in all spheres of life would be a "humanistic communitarian socialism," within which human beings would be "restituted to [their] supreme place in society." *The Sane Society* served as inspiration for the naming of the National Committee for a Sane Nuclear Policy, which Fromm helped to organize in 1957. Always a socialist in spirit, he joined the Socialist party in the 1950's. His internationalism found expression in a symposium on socialist humanism, the proceedings of which he edited in 1965, and in his work with the peace movement of the 1960's.

In *The Art of Loving*, Fromm argued that the human need to destroy stems from an "unlived life," or the frustration of the life instinct. Love is the "only sane and satisfactory answer to the problem of human existence." Fromm described love in its various manifestations, contrasting immature love, based on superficialities, with mature love, "a mutually satisfying interpersonal union under the condition of preserving one's integrity."

Perceived as the culmination of Fromm's work at that time, *To Have or to Be?* maintains that two modes of existence are struggling for the spirit of humankind: the having mode, which concentrates on material possession and power and results in violence, and the being mode, which is based on love and results in productivity. Fromm views the having mode as bringing the world to the brink of psychological and ecological catastrophe and outlines a program for socioeconomic change.

The popularity of Fromm, especially among university professors and students of the 1960's, has led some observers to speak of a Fromm cult. Numerous social analysts, such as Christopher Lasch in the *Culture of Narcissism* (1979), have been inspired by Fromm's writings to continue his effort to psychoanalyze culture and society in a neo-Freudian and Marxist tradition.

Fromm died of a heart attack in Muralto, Switzerland.

[Fromm's other major publications include *Psychoanalysis and Religion* (1950); *The Forgotten Language* (1951); *Sigmund Freud's Mission* (1959); *Is World Peace Still Possible?* (1962); *War Within Man* (1963); *The Heart of Man* (1964); *May Man Prevail?* (1964); *You Shall Be as Gods* (1966); *The Revolution of Hope* (1968); *Social Character in a Mexican Village* (1970), with Michael Maccoby; *The Crisis of Psychoanalysis* (1970); *The Anatomy of Human Destructiveness* (1973); *Greatness and Limitations of Freud's Thought* (1980); *On Disobedience and Other Essays* (1981); and *For the Love of Life*, trans. Robert and Rita Kimber (1985). See also John H. Schaar, *Escape from Authority* (1961); Richard I. Evans, *Dialogue with Eric Fromm* (1966); J. S. Glen, *Erich Fromm* (1966); Bernard Landis and Edward S. Tauber, eds., *In the Name of Life* (1971); Don Hausdorff, *Erich Fromm* (1972); Jay Martin, *The Dialectical Imagination* (1973); and "Erich Fromm: Clinician and Social Philosopher," *Contemporary Psychoanalysis* (1979). Articles on Fromm appear in *Commonweal*, Mar. 14, 1969, and Mar. 15, 1974; *Nation*, Sept. 1, 1969; *New Republic*, Dec. 7, 1968; and *Saturday Review*, Apr. 11, 1959, and Dec. 14, 1968. Obituaries are in the *Chicago Tribune*, Mar. 19, 1980; *Los Angeles Times*, Mar. 19, 1980; *New York Times*, Mar. 19, 1980; and *Washington Post*, Mar. 19, 1980.]

SUSAN NEAL MAYBERRY

G

GABO, NAUM (Aug. 5, 1890–Aug. 23, 1977), painter, sculptor, and art theoretician, was born Naum Neemia Pevsner in Briansk, Russia. He was one of nine children of Boris Pevsner, a wealthy executive in the copper refining industry, and of Agrippine-Fanny Osersky, who came from a peasant background. As a student at the University of Munich (1910–1911), Gabo studied medicine and natural sciences. In 1912 he transferred to Polytechnic Engineering School in Munich, where he studied engineering; he also attended lectures on the history of art by Heinrich Wölfflin (1911–1912) and exhibitions by the avant-garde association of artists known as Der Blaue Reiter.

Renowned as a pioneer of the constructivist movement in sculpture, Gabo came under a number of artistic influences during his early years and throughout his artistic career. He traveled to Florence and Venice at the suggestion of Wölfflin in 1913 and visited his painter-sculptor brother Antoine in Paris the same year, thereby gaining exposure to the styles of cubism, Orphism, and futurism. In 1915 he changed his surname to Gabo in an effort to avoid confusion with his older brother Antoine.

From 1914 to 1917, Gabo and his brother Alexei lived in Copenhagen and in Oslo, where they were joined by Antoine in 1916. He returned to Russia with Antoine in 1917, lived in Berlin from 1922 to 1932, and then in Paris after Nazi storm troopers raided his studio in the latter year. In 1935 Gabo moved to London. He married Miriam Israels on Oct. 13, 1936; they had one child. Gabo lived in Cornwall, England, from 1939 to 1946, then immigrated to the United States, becoming an American citizen in 1952. His extensive travels developed his distinct political philosophy, which was integral to the evolution of his artistic and aesthetic theories.

Gabo's style incorporated twentieth-century materials, such as clear plastic and Plexiglas, in works that fused technology and science with art in the creation of transparent forms that were sometimes in motion and constructed (joined by glue, nails, strings, or welding). In his development of new spatial theories, Gabo combined two-dimensional lines with curved planes, creating a crisscross pattern as lines alternate direction on the various curved planes.

Gabo's early works, influenced by cubism, consist of figurative heads and busts constructed from metal disks and intersecting planes of cardboard, wood, and metal. Later he employed materials such as bronze and steel in seemingly weightless forms that curve in space. In 1920, Gabo created a motorized kinetic sculpture that may be regarded as the first mobile.

Gabo's later works are abstract, geometrical, and mathematically precise. He collaborated on architectural monuments and public buildings in Russia and Germany (1919–1931). These and later large-scale works in the United States express his philosophies concerning functions of space and determination of form. In 1955 he created an eighty-foot-high monumental sculpture constructed of steel and wire surrounding a transparent plastic core. Set in a plaza in the front of the Bijenkorf Department Store in Rotterdam, it is often regarded as the major constructivist monument.

Gabo communicated his aesthetic theories throughout his art, his teaching, and his publications. He believed that the order inherent in art and mathematics originates in nature and that the fourth dimension may be expressed in art. Further, he considered his works to be part of the whole of nature. A work should be constructed (not modeled or carved). An artist can develop a new philosophy of art through the implementation of new materials. Gabo stated that in a constructive sculpture, space, in and of itself, is a material and therefore is part of the object, which is capable of conveying volume.

After 1917 in Moscow, Gabo served as coeditor of the official art weekly *Izo* and taught at the state art school (1917–1920). From 1932 to 1935, he wrote articles for the publication sponsored by the Abstraction-Creation group in France. With Ben Nicholson and Leslie Martin, he published his theoretical writings on social and artistic qualities of constructivism in *Circle* magazine. Gabo also taught at the Bauhaus in 1928, was a visiting professor at the Harvard Graduate School of Architecture and Design (1953–1954), and gave the Mellon Lectures at the National Gallery of Art in Washington, D.C. (1959), which were published in 1962 under the title *Of Divers Arts*.

Gabo's greatest theoretical contribution was the publication of his aesthetic philosophy in the *Realist Manifesto* (also known as the *Constructivist Manifesto*) in conjunction with a joint exhibition with his brother Antoine. Through the oversight of an official, it was released in poster form as an official document that was displayed in locations reserved for governmental decrees. In this capacity, the manifesto exerted a strong influence on the artistic, social, and political climate of the day.

Gabo espoused controversial views in the manifesto, including statements against the use of art as a political instrument and assertions that art has an absolute and independent value, and may function as an expression of human experience and a means of communication. He affirmed the economic and political independence of the artist and rejected the imitation of nature in favor of the function of art in the discovery of basic natural forms. He deemphasized the function of color and emphasized the role of line in establishing direction. He favored the depiction of depth over the expression of volume, renouncing mass and static rhythms in favor of kinetic rhythms.

Those artists and trends inspired by Gabo's teaching, writing, and works include the De Stijl group in Holland, the avant-garde in Germany, British sculptors, kinetic art, op art, and minimal art. Gabo died in Waterbury, Conn.

[A substantial number of Gabo's sculptures, models, and drawings are at the Tate Gallery, London. His writings include "The Constructive Idea of Art," *Circle* (London) (1937); and "On Constructive Realism," in *The Tradition of Constructivism*, edited by Stephen Bann (1974). See also Ruth Olson and Abraham Chanin, *Naum Gabo and Antoine Pevsner* (1948); and Alexei Pevsner, *A Biographical Sketch of My Brothers Naum Gabo and Antoine Pevsner* (1964). An obituary is in the *New York Times*, Aug. 24, 1977.]

SUSAN EASTERLY

GABRIELSON, IRA NOEL (Sept. 27, 1889–Sept. 7, 1977), conservationist, was born in Sioux Rapids, Iowa, the son of Frank August Gabrielson and Ida Jansen. He attended the public schools of Sioux Rapids and graduated from its high school in 1906. He received the B.A. degree in biology from Morningside College in Sioux City in 1912. During the summers of 1911 and 1912 Gabrielson studied biology at the Lakeside Laboratory of Iowa State University at Lake Okoboji, and from 1912 to 1915 he taught biology at Marshalltown (Iowa) High School. On Aug. 7, 1912, he married Clara Speer. They had four daughters.

In 1915, Gabrielson moved to Washington, D.C., to work for the Bureau of Biological Survey of the United States Department of Agriculture. This agency was then engaged primarily in investigating relationships of birds and mammals to agriculture and the operation of predator- and rodent-control programs. From 1915 to 1918, Gabrielson studied economic ornithology and wildlife food habits. In 1918 he transferred from Washington to Portland, Oreg., as a member of the Bureau of Biological Survey's field force conducting experiments and demonstrations in the eradication of predatory animals injurious to livestock and of rodents hindering the cultivation and storage of grains. From 1918 to 1930 he headed the agency's rodent-control program in Oregon, North Dakota, South Dakota, and Iowa. Gabrielson was the Pacific Coast regional supervisor of rodent and predator control from 1930 to 1934. His work was credited with reducing the large number of animals harmful to agricultural production in the western states.

In 1935, Gabrielson returned to Washington to head the Division of Wildlife Research of the Bureau of Biological Survey under its dynamic new chief, Jay Norwood ("Ding") Darling, a famous newspaper cartoonist and conservationist. That same year he succeeded Darling as bureau chief and became largely instrumental in the development of the cooperative wildlife research unit program established by Darling. Under the program, research and demonstration projects were conducted in cooperation with land-grant colleges and conservation commissions in several states. The damage caused by birds, rodents, furbearing animals, predators, and other forms of wildlife to agricultural, grazing, or forested areas was studied, and selective methods of control were determined. The program gave important training to a large group of researchers who became a strong force in wildlife conservation.

Gabrielson was responsible for organizing the first North American Wildlife and Natural Resources Conference, which had been suggested by Darling and was called by President Franklin D. Roosevelt. Held in February 1936, the conference brought together biologists, administrators, and sportsmen to discuss new approaches to wildlife conservation. Gabrielson gave an address titled "A National Program for Wildlife Restoration," a subject that would receive his attention for years to come.

As chief of the Bureau of Biological Survey (1935–1940) and director of the Fish and Wildlife Service (1940–1946), Gabrielson was charged with administering a greatly expanding national wildlife refuge program. The program widened significantly under provisions of the Migratory Bird Hunting Stamp Act of 1934, which required receipts from hunting license stamps to be used to purchase and develop wetlands for the national refuge system. Between 1934 and 1941 the refuge system expanded from 1 million to more than 13 million acres. By 1941 there were 267 refuges in the system. Gabrielson visited nearly all of the refuges and inspected the living conditions of refuge personnel and their families, as well as the effectiveness of refuge operations.

Gabrielson's appointment as head of the Fish and Wildlife Service in 1940 gave him administrative responsibilities for fish culture and conservation in addition to those for wildlife conservation that he had performed as chief of the Bureau of Biological Survey. In the new area of responsibility he directed investigations of fishery resources and industries, operations of fish cultural stations, and surveillance of international fishery activities. In 1946 he was appointed by the Department of State as a delegate to the International Whaling Conference.

After thirty-one years of service, Gabrielson retired from the federal government in 1946 to become president of the Wildlife Management Institute. This organization, headquartered in Washington, D.C., had originated in New York City in 1911 as the American Game Protective and Propagation Association and was supported largely by wealthy sportsmen and gun companies. It had, however, promoted some traditional conservation ideas in an annual seminar, the North American Wildlife Conference, which brought conservationists together for discussion. Gabrielson's reputation as a scientific conservationist gave the institute new respect and prestige in the American conservation community.

As head of the Wildlife Management Institute, Gabrielson was in the forefront of many efforts for wildlife conservation and protection of parks and wilderness areas. During the 1950's he worked with David R. Brower, Howard C. Zahniser, and other leaders of conservation societies to prevent the construction of a dam at Echo Park in Colorado. In 1962, Secretary of the Interior Stewart Udall appointed him to a blue-ribbon advisory board on wildlife management in national parks, which recommended the maintenance or restoration of natural park environments to the greatest possible extent. From 1970 until his death, Gabrielson was chairman of the board of directors of the Wildlife Management Institute. Meanwhile, he had assisted in organizing the International Union for the Conservation of Nature and Natural Resources (1948) and the World Wildlife Fund (United States) (1961), and had directed studies of wildlife departments in thirty-one states and two Canadian provinces.

Although Gabrielson was popularly known as "Mr. Conservation," his principal scientific interest was probably ornithology. His collection of more than 8,000 bird skins, now preserved at the Patuxent (Maryland) Wildlife Research Center, is one of the best in the United States. He was coauthor of three ornithological books: *Birds of Oregon* (1940), *Birds: A Guide to the Most Familiar American Birds* (1949), and *Birds of Alaska* (1959). His general interest in wildlife was presented in three popular books: *Wildlife Conservation* (1941), *Wildlife Refuges* (1943), and *Wildlife Management* (1951). He also edited *Fisherman's Encyclopedia* (1951) and *New Fish Encyclopedia* (1964).

Gabrielson was a big, gregarious, affable man with a broad grasp of conservation issues. He filled leadership positions in numerous organizations with ease and grace, and received many professional awards for his contribution to conservation of natural resources. David R. Brower called him "the glue in the conservation movement" of the 1950's and 1960's. Gabrielson's home was near Oakton, Va., where he had maintained a wildlife sanctuary in cooperation with Fairfax County. He died in Washington, D.C.

[Records concerning Gabrielson's service in the Bureau of Biological Survey, U.S. Department of Agriculture, and Fish and Wildlife Service, U.S. Department of the Interior, are among records of these agencies in the National Archives, Washington, D.C. Some of his personal papers are in the conservation library of the Denver Public Library.

On Gabrielson's work during the 1930's, see Donald C. Swain, *Federal Conservation Policy, 1921–1933* (1963); and Theodore W. Cart, "New Deal for Wildlife: A Perspective on Federal Conservation Policy, 1933–40," *Pacific Northwest Quarterly*, July 1972. A general history of the wildlife conservation movement is James B. Trefethen, *An American Crusade for Wildlife* (1975). Obituaries are in the *Washington Post*, Sept. 9, 1977; *American Forests*, Nov. 1977; and *National Parks and Conservation*, Dec. 1977.]

HAROLD T. PINKETT

GALANTE, CARMINE (Feb. 21, 1910–July 12, 1979), gangster, was born in the East Harlem district of New York City, the son of immigrants from Castellamare del Golfo, a fishing village in Sicily. At age ten, he was sent to reform school, and at seventeen, he was serving time in Sing Sing for assault.

Upon his release from prison, Galante returned to New York City and was soon head of a gang on the Lower East Side. As "button man" for Vito Genovese, he carried out assassinations. Most notorious was the 1943 murder of Carlo Tresca, publisher and editor of *Il Martello* (The Hammer), an anarchist weekly. Genovese, who fled from the United States to Italy in 1937 to escape murder charges, was involved in the Italian narcotics trade and was a flunky for Benito Mussolini (one of whose official programs was to eradicate the Mafia). The murder of Tresca was a favor for Mussolini.

By 1952 Galante was a lieutenant in the Joe Bonanno crime family in New York City. Bonanno, like Galante's parents, was from Castellamare del Golfo. Bonanno's base of operations was a section of Williamsburg, Brooklyn, inhabited chiefly by immigrants from that village. His ambitions extended beyond the neighborhood: he was making inroads in Arizona, looking at Haiti and California, already running rackets in Canada. Galante (called Lillo or "The Cigar" in reference to his ever-present stogie), was Bonanno's main man in narcotics trafficking. He spoke several dialects of Italian and was fluent in Sicilian, Spanish, and French; thus he was the right man to travel abroad, arranging multimillion-dollar heroin deals. Having established the "French connection" from Italy through France and Montreal to New York, he became personal chauffeur to Bonanno, then an underboss.

In 1960, Galante was indicted for drug violations. The case ended in a mistrial after the jury foreman broke his back in a fall. Indicted again in 1962 on a narcotics charge, Galante was convicted and sent to the federal penitentiary in Lewisburg, Pa. He served twelve years of a twenty-year sentence before release on parole. Meanwhile, Bonanno, having failed to become *capo di tutti capi*, or boss of bosses, in the bloody Banana War, had been forced by the other capos to retire to Tucson, Ariz., after he suffered a heart attack in 1968. Genovese died in prison in 1969. His mentors gone, Galante, while still in Lewisburg, told associates he was going to be the next head of organized crime. He was openly critical of Carlo Gambino, the most powerful underworld boss in New York City by the end of the 1960's, for discouraging trafficking in drugs, opposing expansion of membership in families, and taking a disloyal attitude toward traditions of the Mafia.

Philip ("Rusty") Rastelli was head of the Bonanno family when Galante was paroled in 1974. He agreed to step down after his son-in-law was shot dead in a Brooklyn street. Galante next went after the drug trade Gambino had left untouched. In the next two years, more than twenty drug dealers in the Northeast were murdered, and the Bonanno family controlled almost all heroin passing through Canada to the United States. Its Canadian activities became so extensive that three lieutenants were settled in Canada under Steven Schwarz.

Besides narcotics, the Bonanno family's illegal activities under Galante consisted of gambling, labor racketeering, loan-sharking, truck hijacking, extortion, and bankruptcy fraud. Its legal businesses included cheese companies, trucking, refuse carting, and garment and jewelry companies. It dictated policy and rates for the American gambling syndicate in Canada.

In 1976, Gambino died a natural death. He had selected his brother-in-law Paul Castellano as his successor, but the real power in the family was Aniello ("Mr. Neil") Dellacroce. When Galante declared himself the next *capo di tutti capi*, a feud was inevitable. The Bonanno family had 200 soldiers; the Gambino family, 1,000. More than twenty died before the cease-fire of 1978, when Galante went to jail for violating parole by associating with known criminals.

The federal government placed Galante in solitary confinement in the penitentiary at Danbury, Conn., insisting they were protecting him because there was a contract on his life. Contending this assassination plot was a government invention, his lawyer, Roy Cohn, obtained his release. Galante immediately went to war, this time with the Genovese family, for control of drug operations in New York City. Mafia leaders had enough after eight Genovese soldiers were gunned down. At Boca Raton, Fla., Gerardo Catena, Santo Trafficante, Frank Tieri, Paul Castellano, Phil Rastelli (from prison), and Joe Bonanno (from retirement) agreed: Galante had to go.

On the afternoon of July 12, 1979, Galante was driven to the Joe and Mary Italian American Restaurant, in the Bushwick section of Brooklyn, to have lunch with the owner, Joe Turano, who was Galante's cousin. Galante, Turano, Leonard Coppolla (an associate), and two others were sitting at a table on the patio at the back of the restaurant when three masked gunmen entered. One of them stepped within six feet and fired both barrels of a shotgun. Galante, hit in the eye and chest, was hurled on his back, dead, his cigar still sticking straight out from the middle of his mouth. Coppolla also died instantly. Turano died en route to a hospital. The other two escaped unharmed, and disappeared.

The Bonanno family underboss at the time was Nicholas Marangella, who had run the organization during Galante's last stay in jail.

Galante and his wife Helen had three children. For the last twenty years of his life, however, he lived with Ann Acquavalla, who was married to his associate Steven Schwarz; they had two children. His official business was L&T Cleaners at 245 Elizabeth Street in the Little Italy district of New York City.

[See Gay Talese, *Honor Thy Father* (1971). An obituary is in the *New York Times*, July 13, 1979.]

CARMINE LUISI

GALLICO, PAUL WILLIAM (July 26, 1897–July 15, 1976), journalist and author, was born in New York City, the only child of Paolo Gallico and Hortense Erlich. His father, a concert pianist, composer, and music teacher, wanted Paul to become a musician and introduced him to many of the leading musicians of the early part of the century, but Gallico, a tall, muscular man who sensed that he had no musical talent, turned to sports. He attended public school in New York City, where he played football. In 1918 he served as a turret gunner in the United States Navy, then worked as a longshoreman, gym instructor, and translator to pay his way through Columbia University. He captained the college crew team and graduated with a B.S. degree in 1921. Also that year, Gallico married Alva Thoits Taylor, the daughter of a *Chicago Tribune* columnist. They had two children and divorced in 1934.

Following graduation, Gallico became a secretary for the National Board of Motion Picture Review. In 1922 he became a film reviewer for the *New York Daily News*, but complaints about the tone of his reviews led to his dismissal. In 1923 he began writing about sports. From 1924 to 1936 he was a columnist, sports editor, and assistant managing editor for the *Daily News*.

As a sportswriter during the 1920's, Gallico got firsthand experience and color for a story by challenging the athletic champions of the day. During a boxing match with Jack Dempsey, he was knocked out in one minute and thirty-seven seconds, but his story of the encounter, as well as his accounts of swimming against Johnny Weismuller, catching Dizzy Dean's fastball, skiing on an Olympic course, racing speedboats and automobiles, and golfing with Bobby Jones, made him nationally famous, and, perhaps, the highest-paid sportswriter in the country. In *Farewell to Sport* (1938) and *The Golden People* (1965), Gallico established a hagiography of sorts of those athletes, male and female, amateur and professional, whose feats had made the

1920's the "golden age." In 1927, Gallico founded the Golden Gloves amateur boxing competition. On Apr. 12, 1935, he married Elaine St. Johns, daughter of the writer Adela Rogers St. Johns; they divorced in 1936.

Gallico left the *Daily News* in 1936 and thereafter made his living as a free-lance writer, publishing more than one hundred short stories and articles. He was a contributing editor to the *Saturday Evening Post*, *Good Housekeeping*, and, after its founding in 1933, *Esquire*. In the 1930's and 1940's his stories were featured in the *Post*, *Cosmopolitan*, and other magazines with large circulations. He was a war correspondent for *Cosmopolitan* in 1943.

Gallico also wrote forty-one books, including *Confessions of a Story Writer* (1946), which includes a short autobiography, and eleven screenplays, including *The Clock* (1945), a World War II film starring Judy Garland, which he cowrote with Baroness Pauline Gariboldi, whom he had married in February 1939. They had no children and later divorced. *Lili* (1953), a musical film based on one of Gallico's novels was produced on Broadway in 1961 as *Carnival*. Gallico wrote the script for *The Pride of the Yankees* in 1942; the film starred Gary Cooper as baseball great Lou Gehrig and won an Academy Award nomination for best screenplay. *The Poseidon Adventure* (1969), a story about a luxury liner overturned by a tidal wave in the Atlantic, a three-star film in 1972, became the prototype for other disaster films. *The Adventures of Hiram Holliday* (1939, 1967) focused on a plump middle-aged copy editor and became a television series featuring Wally Cox.

Although Gallico's articles and books were popular successes, his only critical success was *The Snow Goose*, a 1941 O. Henry Memorial Award Prize Story, later published in book form and subsequently filmed in Canada. The tale, set in the Dunkirk evacuation in the early days of World War II, relates a hunchback's love for a beautiful girl and the way an injured goose brings the pair together. It became the model for many of his later children's novels, including several featuring Jeanne-Pierre, a guinea pig; *Manxmouse* (1968), relating the adventures of an animal with a mouse's body, a rabbit's ears, and a monkey's paws; and *Thomasina, the Cat Who Thought She Was God* (1958), in which a cat seems to return from the dead. Among his novels for adults were several about a charwoman, "Mrs. 'Arris," and her travels to several world cities, including one to Paris to buy a Dior gown.

Aside from *The Snow Goose*, Gallico's work received little attention from serious critics of literature. This was no cause for distress to him, however, for he once remarked, "In place of great literary fame, millions of people care about what I write and like me. What more do I want?" Elsewhere he said he was a "rotten novelist. I'm not even literary. I just like to tell stories and all my books tell stories." In 1973 he defended the sentimentality of his work against what he described as "the calamity howlers and the porn merchants. Sentiment remains far out in front among ordinary humans."

In 1950, Gallico began living abroad, in England, Liechtenstein, and Monaco, where he befriended Prince Rainier and Princess Grace. On July 19, 1963, he married Baroness Virginia von Falz-Fein. He died in Monaco of a heart attack.

[Best-selling novels by Gallico not mentioned in the text include *The Small Miracle* (1950) and *Love, Let Me Not Hunger* (1963). An obituary is in the *New York Times*, July 17, 1976.]

CLARENCE A. ANDREWS

GAMBINO, CARLO (Aug. 24, 1900–Oct. 15, 1976), racketeer, was born in Palermo, Sicily, and came to the United States as a stowaway, arriving in Norfolk, Va., in 1921 at the age of twenty-one. He settled in Brooklyn, N.Y., where several close relatives lived, and fell in with the borough's Mafia groups. During Prohibition Gambino took up bootlegging and kept at it after repeal. In 1937 he received a twenty-two-month sentence for conspiracy to defraud the government of liquor taxes in connection with an illegal still near Philadelphia. The conviction was thrown out eight months later because the evidence had been based on illegal wiretaps.

During World War II, Gambino specialized in stolen ration coupons. According to Joseph Valachi, the first Mafia member to testify publicly about the secret criminal society, Gambino "made over a million dollars from ration stamps during the war. The stamps came out of the [Office of Price Administration's] offices. First Carlo's boys would steal them. Then, when the government started hiding them in banks, Carlo made contact and the OPA men sold him the stamps."

Gambino became associated with the Mafia family headed by Vincent Mangano. When Albert Anastasia became boss of the family in 1951 upon Mangano's death, he made Gambino *sottocapo*, or underboss. Anastasia was shot to death on Oct. 25, 1957, while he was sitting in a barber's chair at the Park-Sheraton Hotel, his face covered with hot shaving towels. The murder's primary architect was Anastasia's Mafia rival, Vito Genovese. But most organized crime historians assign Gambino at least partial responsibility for the murder and suggest he arranged for Anastasia's bodyguards to leave the barbershop shortly before the shooting. Gambino, at any rate, became boss and consolidated his position by arranging to share power with Aniello Dellacroce, an Anastasia loyalist. Dellacroce became underboss and controlled the family rackets that relied on violence or the threat thereof, such as loan-sharking and extortion; Gambino focused on more subtle operations that ultimately proved more lucrative, including labor union corruption, construction bid-rigging, and monopolization of garbage collection. He also gained interests in a growing number of legitimate and quasi-legitimate enterprises that relied on Mafia muscle to scare competitors.

A few weeks after Anastasia's death, scores of mobsters from around the nation met at the Apalachin, N.Y., farm of Joseph Barbara. Police raided the "crime convention" and arrested about five dozen attendees, including Gambino. The meeting offered evidence of a national criminal conspiracy, which Federal Bureau of Investigation director J. Edgar Hoover had said did not exist. Gambino's crime family was one of the largest and most powerful, with hundreds of initiated members; each member, in turn, had his own group of criminal associates. Although its activities were largely limited to metropolitan New York, the network reached into New England, Pennsylvania, Florida, Nevada, and California.

Anastasia was merely the first of Gambino's rivals to fall. Genovese went to prison on a narcotics trafficking conviction; Joseph Bonanno, boss of another of New York's five Mafia families, was forced into retirement after a failed power play; Joseph Colombo, boss of the family bearing his name, was shot and critically wounded after he reportedly angered Gambino by staging public demonstrations to protest what he called persecution of Italian Americans by police and the FBI.

The newspapers called Gambino the "capo di tutti capi," the boss of bosses. But while he may have been the single most influential denizen of New York's underworld, the Mafia was not a corporation and Gambino was no chief executive officer. The Gambino family rackets were mostly autonomous operations run by various members or associates. Gambino provided a range of services, including contacts with corrupt police and politicians and protection from other criminals. He financed fledgling enterprises, criminal or legitimate. He was respected enough to arbitrate inter- and intra-family disputes, and powerful enough to make his decisions stick.

By the mid-1960's Gambino was constantly being subpoenaed to appear before grand juries. He would remain home as his lawyers filed medical documents certifying that he was too ill to appear, usually because of heart problems. Gambino's frail appearance belied his wealth and power. Small of frame and long of face, he dressed simply and was driven around in an inexpensive Buick or Chevrolet sedan by James ("Jimmy Brown") Failla. The boss and his family lived on the upper floor of a two-family brick house on Ocean Parkway in Brooklyn. Later they purchased a modest house in the Long Island community of Massapequa, where Gambino entertained mobsters and other associates at a large party each July 4. A government informer, Colombo family hanger-on Joseph Cantalupo, later described Gambino as "very even-tempered, very polite, very much the gentleman in the presence of others." Some even viewed Gambino as a bulwark against street crime. In 1973, when a jeweled crown was stolen from a statue of the Virgin Mary in a church in Brooklyn, newspapers reported that Gambino had ordered it returned. Eleven days after the theft, the FBI received an anonymous tip that the crown was in a locker at an airlines transfer terminal in Manhattan. It was.

Gambino's reputation undoubtedly was exaggerated, however. Peter Reuter, an economist who showed police claims of a Mafia monopoly on organized crime in New York City to be unfounded, once interviewed a police informer who insisted that Gambino received "25 percent of everything in the rackets." But the informer himself engaged in various fencing operations without making any payments to the Mafia.

Gambino and his wife, Kathryn Castellano, had four children. His son Thomas married a daughter of Thomas Lucchese, boss of another of the city's crime families. Gambino's sons ran trucking businesses in Manhattan's garment district and, according to prosecutors, used intimidation tactics to protect an illegal transportation cartel. Kathryn Gambino died in 1971, and her husband died five years later of a heart attack. His position was assumed by his cousin and brother-in-law, Paul Castellano.

[See also Thomas Plate et al., *Mafia at War* (1972); Paul Meskil, *Don Carlo: Boss of Bosses* (1973); the Gambino entry in Carl Sifakis, *The Mafia Encyclopedia* (1987); Howard Abadinsky, *Organized Crime* (1990); and Joseph F. O'Brien and Andris Kurins, *Boss of Bosses* (1991). An obituary is in the *New York Times*, Oct. 16, 1976.]

RICK HAMPSON

GARNER, ERROLL LOUIS (June 15, 1921–Jan. 2, 1977), jazz pianist and composer, was born in Pittsburgh, Pa., one of six children of Estella Darcus and Louis Ernest Garner, a factory worker who played guitar and mandolin. One brother, Linton Garner, became a noted pianist and arranger. Erroll Garner was largely self-taught in jazz piano. He began playing when he was very young and began performing professionally on Pittsburgh radio in 1928. Although he never learned to read or write music, Garner's technical skill and unique keyboard technique became legendary among both classical and jazz musicians. He had the uncanny ability, on hearing a piece of music, to play it immediately and with detailed accuracy.

Garner dropped out of Westinghouse House School in Pittsburgh to play with a local dance orchestra, and in 1939 went to New York City as a piano accompanist. He was inducted into the United States Army in 1942 but received a medical discharge less than a year later. He returned to New York City and worked in several nightclubs. He also substituted for pianist Art Tatum in Tatum's trio with guitarist Tiny Grimes and bass player Slam Stewart and played regularly with the ensemble when it became the Slam Stewart Trio in 1945. After the trio played an engagement at the Strand Theater in New York City in 1946, Garner got his first recording contract, with the Savoy Record Company. It led to his first hit, the ballad "Laura," which sold more than 500,000 copies.

Garner next played at nightclubs across the country and made several recordings with many record labels. He performed in Paris, France, in 1948, and on his return to the United States, he began playing at the Three Deuces club in New York City. By 1950 his reputation and audiences had grown, and he was the first modern jazz instrumentalist to perform solo in the United States, at the Cleveland Music Hall. In the same year he performed at Town Hall in New York City and signed an exclusive recording contract with Columbia Records. Garner is probably best known to the general public for his composition "Misty," which he wrote in the early 1950's. In 1957 he was chosen *Down Beat* magazine's best jazz pianist.

The most common style of left-hand piano accompaniment was then the stride technique, exemplified by the playing of Tatum, who initially based his left-hand accompaniment on the stride style perfected by Fats Waller and Earl ("Fatha") Hines. All of the early jazz pianists were influenced by this style, including Garner, but Garner soon abandoned this technique and developed a nonstride approach. He accomplished this by imitating the rhythm accompaniment used in big bands, such as that of guitarist Freddie Green of the Count Basie Orchestra. By the careful use of smooth left-hand keyboard voicing and a driving rhythmic feel, Garner was able to give the illusion in his piano solos that there was more than a single performer.

In 1958, Garner signed a contract with the impresario Sol Hurok and began a series of national and international tours. Although Garner had performed at all the major jazz venues, including the club Birdland in New York and the Blackhawk in San Francisco, he now concentrated on recitals and recordings. He recorded with the most influential jazz hornmen, including saxophonists Charlie Parker and Coleman Hawkins and trumpeter Dizzy Gillespie, and accompanied vocalist Sarah Vaughan. He performed frequently on television shows beginning in the 1950's, appearing on the "Tonight Show," "Today Show," and the "Ed Sullivan Show." Garner remained active until 1975, when he was diagnosed with emphysema; he died of a heart attack in Los Angeles.

[See Mimi Clar, "Erroll Garner," *Jazz Review*, Jan. 1959; James Doran, "Erroll Garner: A Discography Update," *Journal of Jazz Studies*, Fall/Winter 1979, and *Erroll Garner: The Most Happy Piano* (1985). An obituary is in *New York Times*, Jan. 3, 1977.]

DENNIS THURMOND

GARST, ROSWELL ("BOB") (June 17, 1898–Nov. 5, 1977), agriculturist and businessman, was born in Coon Rapids, Iowa, one of four children of Bertha Goodwin and Edward Garst, a general merchandiser and landowner. Garst graduated from Coon Rapids High School in 1916. He attended Iowa State College (now Iowa State University) for one semester and then transferred to the University of Wisconsin. Garst returned to Iowa State College in the fall of 1917 but dropped out the next spring to farm land owned by his father. He enrolled at Northwestern University in the spring of 1919 for only one quarter before dropping out again to join his brother Jonathan to farm in Canada. (In 1958, Grinnell College bestowed an honorary LL.D. on Garst.)

By 1921, Garst was engaged in dairy farming at Coon Rapids. On Jan. 30, 1922, he married Elizabeth Hanek, a schoolteacher from Cedar Falls, Iowa; the couple had five children.

Garst moved to Des Moines in 1926, where he founded the Garst Land Company, a real estate development firm. In Des Moines he became acquainted with agriculturist Henry A. Wallace, who interested Garst in hybrid seed corn. In 1930, Garst returned to farming at Coon Rapids, and in cooperation with Wallace planted fifteen acres of hybrid corn, which yielded 300 bushels of seed corn—10 percent of all the hybrid seed corn produced that year in the United States.

Convinced of the value of these high-yield seeds, Garst and fellow Coon Rapids farmer Charles W. ("Charlie") Thomas created the Garst and Thomas Hi-Bred Corn Company in 1931, and in 1932 Garst sold his dairy herd and mortgaged his farm to raise funds for the new company. By the late 1930's Garst and Thomas employed more than 850 representatives to sell their seed to farmers in Iowa, Nebraska, Kansas, Oklahoma, Arkansas, Missouri, and Colorado.

With the advent of the Great Depression and the election of Franklin D. Roosevelt as president, Garst was drawn into politics, not only as an outspoken agriculturist but also as a friend of Henry A. Wallace, the newly appointed secretary of agriculture. Sent to Washington, D.C., in 1933 by the Iowa Corn-Hog Committee, Garst played an important role in establishing the Department of Agriculture's corn-hog allotment program. He was so effective, in fact, that he was offered a post in the department, but he turned it down. Nonetheless, he had gained political stature, and in the late 1930's he was occasionally mentioned as a possible candidate for Iowa governor or congressman. Garst, however, had little interest in running for office. Although well connected with the Roosevelt administration, he remained a registered Republican, referring to himself as a "modern Republican" or an "independent Republican."

As World War II commenced, Garst was an internationalist. He supported supplying food to the Allies and endorsed the Lend-Lease Act. When the United States entered the war, he was often in contact with the Department of Agriculture, several times proving that he knew more about agriculture than the agency's experts, which led President Roosevelt to acclaim Garst as the "Henry Kaiser of American agriculture."

During the 1940's, Garst became a leading promoter of commercial fertilizer as a means to increase crop production. After the war, he continued his forays in innovation, undertaking experiments on his own farms to test measures that might improve crop and livestock productivity, such as using ground corn cobs as a feed or giving his stock urea, a synthetic protein, as a substitute for vegetable protein.

In 1955, Garst traveled to the Soviet Union and Eastern Europe. Despite the Cold War, he hoped to open markets for his hybrid seeds and to improve agricultural trade with Communist-bloc countries. Garst's efforts and expertise were well received by Communist agricultural leaders, and he succeeded in selling 5,000 tons of seed corn to the Soviet Union and Romania. Although his dealings with Communists elicited some harsh criticism, Garst continued to maintain and extend his ties with Eastern European customers. Indeed, when Soviet leader Nikita Khrushchev journeyed to the United States in 1959, he made a point of visiting Garst's farm at Coon Rapids, where Garst threw silage at the crowd of reporters as they obstructed Khrushchev's view. This incident gained wide coverage, making Garst nationally known as a "colorful" farmer.

Garst faced a serious health problem in 1962 when doctors removed his cancerous larynx. He learned to speak with a mechanical voice box, however, and the next year returned to the Soviet Union and Eastern Europe. At the same time, he also turned his attention to Latin America, where he sponsored a large-scale fertilizer demonstration program in El Salvador.

In 1970, Garst formally retired from Garst and Thomas. He had been very successful. In 1964, for example, Garst and Thomas produced 5 percent of all the hybrid seed corn produced in the United States. Additionally, Garst owned more than 2,500 acres, managed an additional 8,000 acres, and controlled large livestock operations, making him one of the most prosperous agribusinessmen in Iowa. (In 1979 Garst was posthumously installed in *Fortune* magazine's Business Hall of Fame.)

Garst had become famous for his agricultural knowledge and pragmatism, often expressed in a blunt and sometimes colorful manner. Though not a scholar, Garst authored several bulletins distributed by Garst and Thomas as well as a number of articles for farm magazines. In doing so he furthered his self-styled role as a "farm educator" or "farm innovator." While today's environmentalists would disagree with Garst's faith in the value of using fertilizers and other chemicals, grain cropping all land as much as possible, and putting additives into livestock feed, he nonetheless stayed true to his belief that the most important issue facing the world was the lack of food and that new agricultural technologies to increase production were a necessity as well as a boon to all farmers, especially American farmers. Garst died of a heart attack in Carroll, Iowa.

[Garst's papers are in the Special Collections at the Iowa State University Library. A selection of his letters appears in Richard Lowitt and Harold Lee, eds., *Letters from an American Farmer: The Eastern European and Russian Correspondence of Roswell Garst* (1987). Harold Lee, *Roswell Garst* (1984), is the only biography. Garst is also discussed in Hiram Drache, *Beyond the Furrow: Some Keys to Successful Farming in the Twentieth Century* (1976).

Obituaries are in the *Des Moines Register*, Nov, 6, 1977; and the *New York Times*, Nov. 7, 1977.]

THOMAS BURNELL COLBERT

GEER, WILLIAM AUGHE ("WILL") (Mar. 9, 1902–Apr. 22, 1978), actor, was born in Frankfort, Ind., the son of A. Roy Ghere, a farmer and later a railroad worker, and Katherine Aughe, a teacher. When Will was thirteen, his father left the family. Katherine moved her three children to Chicago in 1916. While attending Waller High School from 1916 to 1918, Will became involved in high school theater. The family returned to Frankfort in 1919, and Will graduated from Frankfort High School that same year. He entered the University of Chicago in 1919, graduating with a degree in botany in 1924. Later in 1924 he enrolled at Columbia University, but he soon left without completing a degree.

Geer made his professional acting debut in 1920 as a walk-on for the Sothern-Marlowe Shakespearean Repertory Company in Chicago. For the next few summers Geer appeared in stock company, tent show, and showboat productions on the Ohio and Mississippi rivers. In 1928, Geer joined Minnie Maddern Fiske's production of *The Merry Wives of Windsor* at the Knickerbocker Theater in New York City. From there, Geer continued with Fiske's touring company, which acted and sang at union halls and liberal political benefits. When Fiske died in 1931, Geer lost a major professional and political influence in his life and found himself unemployed in the midst of the Great Depression. He went to work as a steward on the Panama-Pacific Line, which operated ships between the east and west coasts of the United States. After an unsuccessful attempt to find steady work in films in Hollywood, Geer returned to theatrical work in Los Angeles. In 1934 and 1935 he helped to found the New Theatre Group, one of the numerous agitation and propaganda (or agit-prop) theater groups that grew out of the liberal and left-wing political activism of the New Deal years. Like many social activists of the 1930's, Geer looked favorably on the Soviet Union as a model workers' state, and he went to the Soviet Union for a few months in 1935 to work on a motion picture.

Geer returned to New York City in late 1935 to work in agit-prop theater, culminating in a tour of textile workers' union halls in New England in May 1936. In 1937, Geer appeared in New York City's Federal Theatre Project's production of *Unto Such Glory*. Sometime during the 1930's he started using the name "Geer" instead of "Ghere."

In 1938, Geer joined a summer tour with the John Lenthier Troupe, which raised funds for the Abraham Lincoln Brigade, a group of

Americans who were fighting alongside the Spanish Loyalists in the Spanish Civil War. The tour consisted of about thirty one-night stands at union halls and theaters in Pennsylvania, Virginia, Maryland, and Washington, D.C. On the tour, Geer worked with and fell in love with Herta Ware, a granddaughter of Ella Reeve ("Mother") Bloor, a suffragist and a founder of the American Communist Party. The wedding of Geer and Ware typified Geer's political activism. The wedding was advertised in left-wing newspapers, and admission was charged to raise funds for the New Theatre League. The public event was staged on Oct. 15, 1938, but the couple was not officially married until October 17. They had three children.

In 1939, Geer left for California to work on *Fight for Life*, a United States Film Service documentary. While in California he helped to organize migrant farm workers. In search of a ballad singer to accompany him, Geer met Woody Guthrie, a then-obscure folksinger and songwriter. They remained close friends until Guthrie's death in 1967.

Geer returned to New York City in late 1939 and took over the role of Jeeter Lester in the successful Broadway production of *Tobacco Road*. During the 1940's he appeared in various short-lived Broadway productions and also worked on radio. Starting in the late 1940's, Geer made a successful move to Hollywood films, when he often appeared as a character actor in Westerns, usually portraying a gruff but kindly old man.

In March 1951, Geer was called to testify before the United States House Un-American Activities Committee. Geer refused to give the committee any names of the people he had known as associates in the leftist causes he had supported since the 1930's. His refusal to supply names led to his being blacklisted in Hollywood and he could no longer find film roles. Geer and his wife separated in 1954. He found acting jobs off-Broadway and with touring companies. At his home in Topanga Canyon, outside of Los Angeles, Geer used his lifelong passion for gardening to develop the Theatricum Botanicum, a beautifully landscaped outdoor theater, where he staged weekend productions of Shakespeare.

By 1961 the McCarthy era was fading into history, and with it the blacklist. For the first time since 1953 Geer appeared in a film when the liberal director-producer Otto Preminger gave him a part in *Advise and Consent*. Other screen roles followed, including appearances in *In Cold Blood* (1967), *The Reivers* (1970), and *Jeremiah Johnson* (1973). He also appeared on television and continued his stage career, especially his longtime interest in Folksay Theatre. This art form used songs, skits, and tales to present American folklore to small audiences. During the 1940's and 1950's, Folksay evolved into hootennanies known for audience participation and topicality. During the 1960's and 1970's, Geer took shows, under the name "Will Geer's Americana" to theaters and college campuses across the country.

Geer reached the pinnacle of financial reward and public acclaim in the last six years of his life. From 1972 to 1978 he played Grandpa Walton on "The Waltons," a highly rated television series shown on CBS. In 1975 he won an Emmy award for best supporting actor in a dramatic series.

Geer's career spanned more than fifty years and included work on the stage, for radio, in films, and on television. His performing career mirrored the challenges and opportunities faced by actors during this era. Geer retained a deep commitment to social activism throughout his life, using his acting and ballad singing to entertain, increase social consciousness, and raise funds for political causes. Like other political activists sparked by the idealism of the New Deal era, Geer felt the backlash of McCarthyism. Unlike many of his fellows, however, he had the good fortune to live long enough to revive his career. Geer died in Los Angeles of a respiratory ailment.

[No book-length study of Geer has been written. See Sally Osborne Norton, "A Historical Study of Actor Will Geer: His Life and Work in the Context of Twentieth-Century American Social, Political, and Theatrical History" (Ph.D. diss., University of Southern California, 1980). An interview with Geer is Michael Ramirez, "I'm a Radical—and Proud of It!," *Coronet*, May 1977. An obituary is in the *New York Times*, Apr. 24, 1978; see also Joe Klein, "Will Geer: 1902–1978," *Rolling Stone*, June 1, 1978, for a tribute.]

PAUL A. FRISCH

GEISMAR, MAXWELL DAVID (Aug. 1, 1909–July 24, 1979), literary critic, was born in New York City, the son of Leon Geismar and Mary Feinberg. He was to spend most of his life in and around New York. In 1927 he graduated from Scarsdale High School in suburban Westchester County, where he was editor of the school magazine and was elected one of two captains of the baseball team, for which he played left field.

The summer after high school graduation Geismar went to work for the *Brooklyn Eagle*, where he reported on tennis for about three weeks, after which he was relieved of his duties for playing the sport better than he wrote about it. Sorry to leave the paper for which Walt Whitman had once served as editor, he moved on to the *Glen Cove Echo*, where he wrote assigned articles. In the fall of that year he took a job in an advertising agency and began to attend Columbia University. He soon left the advertising agency in favor of a more "manly" job—driving a furniture truck. He also worked in a garage and as a tutor. The next summer he was an assistant director of The Floating Hospital, a charitable organization for underprivileged children. The year after that he became its director. Meanwhile, at Columbia he took literature courses from Henry Ladd and Mark Van Doren and was elected to Phi Beta Kappa. In 1931, Geismar was awarded a B.A. degree; he was class valedictorian and received the Moncrief Proudfitt Fellowship in Letters.

He received his M.A. at Columbia in 1932, and on September 11 of that year he married Anne Rosenberg; the couple had three children. In 1933, Geismar received a teaching fellowship at Harvard, where he studied nineteenth-century literature.

After he left Harvard, Geismar's twelve-year academic career was centered exclusively at Sarah Lawrence College for Women (now called Sarah Lawrence College) in Bronxville, N.Y. At Sarah Lawrence, Geismar became a well-known figure, always wearing the same old brown hat pulled down over his eyes. He taught from 1933 until 1945 and spent summers on a farm in the Adirondack Mountains, where he played tennis and darts and built furniture. He left teaching in 1945 to become a full-time free-lance writer, historian, and critic. He maintained an office in his home on Winfield Avenue in Harrison, N.Y., from which he issued some twenty books and editions. His literary friends included Maxwell Perkins and Edmund Wilson.

He first established his reputation in 1942, with *Writers in Crisis: The American Novel 1925–1940*, a study of Lardner, Hemingway, Dos Passos, Faulkner, Wolfe, and Steinbeck. In it he showed that the Great Depression of the 1930's, considered by many to be destructive and the source of despair, was actually "a time of regeneration for the writer." His detailed chapter on Faulkner's career, written at a time when not one of Faulkner's books was in print, preceded Malcolm Cowley's heralded *The Portable Faulkner* by four years. While Cowley generally is credited with reestablishing Faulkner's reputation, Geismar should also be given his due.

Writers in Crisis was the first of a projected five-volume series of literary studies, with the overall title of *The Novel in America*, intended to cover a century of native prose. However, only three volumes in the series were published. Geismar's literary panorama continued with *The Last of the Provincials: The American Novel 1915–1925* (1947), and *Rebels and Ancestors: The American Novel 1890–1915* (1953). The former examined in detail Mencken, Lewis, Cather, Anderson, and Fitzgerald, while the latter treated Norris, Crane, London, Glasgow, and Dreiser. While he did not complete *The Novel in America* series, he did produce several arresting and controversial volumes during the last two decades of his life.

One of his most widely reviewed books was *Henry James and the Jacobites* (1963), which attempted to overturn the prevailing opinion that James was a great writer. Geismar saw James instead as a great entertainer. One critic called the book "one of the most furiously belligerent works of criticism written in modern times." Even more upsetting to some was Geismar's *Mark Twain: An American Prophet* (1970), in which he contended that Twain's best work was to be found in his later books, not in *The Adventures of Huckleberry Finn*. Geismar berated others for missing the significance of Twain's late social criticism.

Geismar's most accessible book is *American Moderns: From Rebellion to Conformity* (1958). Unlike those in *The Novel in America* series, it began as a collection of his articles and book reviews written for a broader audience. But, as in his other books, the central concern is with "the history of individual literary talents." These included Wouk, Cozzens, Marquand, Mailer, Salinger, Bellow, and Styron—as well as earlier figures such as Wolfe. The book's most heatedly discussed chapter was "By Cozzens Possessed," in which he asked of that author's best-selling novel, *By Love Possessed:* "Is love then merely a matter of glandular secretions, of aroused gristle, of muscular contractions, and dripping fluids? No, the point is that *By Love Possessed* has no love in it, nor does it understand, for all its rationalism, the meaning of the sexual love which it describes so anatomically."

When Geismar wasn't writing his own works of criticism and literary history, he was editing the works of others. He produced a *Whitman Reader* (1955), a *Ring Lardner Reader* (1963), a Mark Twain bestiary titled *The Higher Animals* (1976), and editions of works by Dreiser, Melville, London, and Anderson. Perhaps his most curious effort was a *Portable Thomas Wolfe* (1946). That volume with its oxymoronic title reduced all of Wolfe's sprawling, garrulous, and undisciplined output to 250,000 words. In 1966, Geismar became a senior editor at *Ramparts* magazine, and in 1970 he became a founding editor of *Scanlan's Monthly*.

During his seventy years Geismar acquired a number of awards, including a Guggenheim Fellowship (1943–1944), and a National Institute of Arts and Letters Grant in Literature for his criticism (1952). In 1970 he was a Boston University Libraries Fellow. He died of a heart attack in his hometown of Harrison.

[Geismar's manuscripts and correspondence are housed at the Mugar Library, Boston University. There is no biography. A profile is in the *Sarah Lawrence Alumnae Magazine*, Oct. 1940. Obituaries are in the *New York Times*, July 25, 1979; *Newsweek*, Aug. 6, 1979; *Publishers Weekly*, Aug. 6, 1979; and *A. B. Bookman's Weekly*, Aug. 20, 1979.]

ROBERT PHILLIPS

GETTY, JEAN PAUL (Dec. 15, 1892–June 6, 1976), oil producer and oil company executive, was born in Minneapolis, Minn., the only surviving child of George Franklin Getty and Sarah Catherine McPherson Risher. George Getty was an insurance lawyer in Minneapolis and might have remained one except that in 1903 he was sent to Bartlesville, Okla., by his firm to collect a debt. Bartlesville was then in the throes of an oil boom, and George Getty soon caught oil fever. His first well was a success and George thereafter moved his family to Oklahoma. Three years later he relocated his thriving oil business and his family to Los Angeles, eventually becoming a millionaire.

J. Paul Getty, as he always styled himself, was an indifferent student who scraped through a succession of preparatory schools and colleges until in 1914 he was awarded a bachelor's degree by Oxford University, which in those days made few demands upon students such as Getty.

The academic grind and much high living in Europe behind him, Getty returned to Oklahoma in 1914. Within two years he had made a small oil strike on his own and become a director of the family business, the Minnehoma Oil Company, returning to California in that capacity. Upon the death of his father in 1930, Getty became president of George F. Getty, Inc., as the firm was now called. His mother was now the principal shareholder. Until this time Getty had devoted himself chiefly to pleasure, marrying three times and pursuing with success a host of other women.

Although Getty was already rich thanks to his inheritance and to some extent his own efforts, during the Great Depression he set in motion a chain of deals that would eventually make him the richest man in America. Getty had many strengths as a businessman. His attention to detail was famous. He had exceptional negotiating skills and a sharp eye for a bargain. But what set Getty apart from his peers was the strategy he devised in the 1930's. At a time of business contraction, when most oil companies were retrenching, Getty determined to expand his holdings by buying at distressed prices companies with relatively low earnings but large oil reserves, betting that prosperity would return and multiply their value—as indeed it did.

The main impediment to his plans for expansion was his own mother, who owned 67 percent of the family business and was averse to taking risks. After years of wrangling, Getty developed an ingenious compromise. A Sarah Getty Trust was formed consisting of her shares in the business and some of J. Paul Getty's own assets. Getty was the sole trustee of this institution, which controlled most of the family wealth. He was not allowed to borrow against the trust's assets, but otherwise, except for a few trifling restrictions, he could do as he pleased. With his new freedom Getty battled the mighty Standard Oil Company of New Jersey for control of companies with proven oil reserves, including the Tidewater Associated Oil Company, doing so with such success that by the mid-1930's, when he himself was barely into middle age, Getty was worth about $50 million.

Before World War II broke out, Getty, who had traveled extensively in Europe and was fluent in French, German, and Italian, admired Hitler and the Nazi movement. After America's entry into the war, however, as if to atone for his sins, Getty threw himself into managing one of his holdings, the Spartan Aircraft Company, which produced airplane parts and trained pilots for the military. This was the only time during his long career when Getty behaved in what might be called a selfless manner.

After the war, with his fortune swollen by the increased value of oil, Getty took the final step that would result in his becoming a multibillionaire. Getty had failed earlier to gain an oil concession in the Persian Gulf area, but in 1948 he won the right from Saudi Arabia to drill in what was called the Neutral Zone, a disputed area claimed by both Saudi Arabia and Kuwait that the two countries had agreed to share. Getty won the Saudi concession by promising to make the usual payments and expenditures and offering to give King Ibn Saud record royalties for every barrel he pumped. Other companies were shocked by Getty's largess, but he anticipated that royalties would rise rapidly anyway, as they did, so his apparent generosity cost him little while giving him a jump on the competition. In 1953 Getty's first well came in and four years later *Fortune* magazine named him the richest man in America.

Getty controlled many companies, of which Tide Water Associated Oil Company, later Tidewater, was his chief vehicle overseas, while the Pacific Western Oil Company, which in 1956 he renamed the Getty Oil Company, contained the largest part of his American holdings. Getty developed Tidewater into one of the world's premier oil companies, making it the eighth "sister" to the seven that had dominated the world oil trade. In 1967 he folded it into Getty Oil, whose shares now made up most of the family wealth.

Not all the oil Getty touched turned to gold. In the 1950's he decided to build his own tanker fleet, doing so at a time when tankers were becoming a glut on the market. His decision, again made in the 1950's, to become a major oil refiner and distributor was also ill-judged, for this was a highly competitive market with small profit margins. But neither of these mistakes seriously impaired his fortune, which was solidly based on oil discovery and production. His investments in these areas, made with an eye toward long-term returns rather than speculative profits, were the solid foundation upon which his immense riches were based.

Unlike his public career, Getty's private life was a shambles. He married and divorced five times. When married, Getty paid little attention to his wives, preferring to maintain what was in effect a harem of concubines, while also pursuing numerous chance encounters. He neglected his five sons, two of whom predeceased him, and his grandchildren as well. Selfish and self-centered, he was also notoriously tightfisted, a trait that led to his best-known economy, the installation of a pay telephone in his great English country estate, Sutton Place.

Before purchasing Sutton Place, a stately home on sixty acres in Guildford, Surrey, twenty-three miles from London, Getty had lived for the most part in hotels. As was his custom, Getty acquired Sutton Place for a pittance, a sum equal to about $140,000 at the time, as its owner, the duke of Sutherland, was experiencing financial distress. Getty had been forced to abandon his footloose ways by the article in *Fortune* magazine in October 1957 that named him the richest man in America. Until then, although a legend in the oil business, Getty was little known to the general public. After 1957 his celebrity status made it impossible for him to live anonymously in hotel suites, and necessitated the move to Sutton Place.

Apart from his wealth and frugality Getty was most famous in his lifetime because of a bizarre incident that highlighted his shortcomings as a family man. One of his grandsons, Jean Paul III, was a well-known playboy and highly visible customer of Rome nightclubs. As the kidnapping of wealthy children was an Italian crime industry, with some 320 incidents taking place between 1960 and 1973, the prospect of seizing a grandson of America's, and possibly the world's, richest man was bound to occur to someone. In the event, on July 10, 1973, Jean Paul III was snatched off a Rome street and taken to what proved to be a series of hideouts in Calabria. Though ransom demands soon followed, Getty refused to pay, informing the press that he could not put his fourteen other grandchildren at risk by complying. Apparently he also suspected that the kidnapping was a hoax designed by family members to extort money from him.

In the months that followed more threatening notes were received, with the ransom demand ultimately reaching $3.2 million. On Nov. 10, 1973, a Rome newspaper received in the mail a human ear, said to be that of Jean Paul III. This was confirmed shortly afterward by two reporters from another paper who were supplied with snapshots of young Jean Paul III minus his right ear. The resulting publicity, reinforced by Jean Paul III's mother, whose unflattering remarks to the press about J. Paul Getty's parsimony must have hurt, forced the billionaire to cave in. He agreed to give $2.2 million himself, lending the balance to the boy's father, Jean Paul II, with repayment to be made from Paul II's income from the Sarah Getty Trust. Jean Paul III was discovered, alive, but not the ransom money, although the kidnappers were later arrested.

Getty will live on chiefly through the art museum in Southern California that bears his name. Getty was an avid art collector, starting what grew to be a substantial collection during the 1930's. Although it would provide the nucleus for his museum's holdings, his own collection was not a great one, primarily because in art, as in business, Getty always looked for bargains. This habit enabled him to make some shrewd purchases but also kept him from buying many great masters in the 1950's and 1960's when they were still relatively cheap. In addition, Getty bought with an eye toward avoiding taxes. At a time when the oil depletion allowance was the principal means of legally evading taxes for men in his business, Getty sheltered the largest part of his income by donating art objects to museums, especially his own.

Part of Getty's collection was stored in the main house of a sixty-four-acre citrus ranch in Malibu, Calif., which he had purchased after World War II. By the 1960's, though it was open to the public several days per week, the Internal Revenue Service was questioning whether such limited hours qualified the museum for tax-exempt status. These inquiries hastened Getty's decision to build a formal museum structure, which was opened on Jan. 16, 1974. The building cost $17 million to construct and housed a collection whose estimated worth at that time was $200 million. In addition to a large endowment, Getty made a promise, later fulfilled, to leave a major part of his holdings to the J. Paul Getty Museum.

When Getty died in 1976, he left a fortune of some $2 billion, divided between his personal holdings and those of the Sarah Getty Trust. Despite Getty's elaborate will, much litigation followed, initiated by disgruntled family members; unhappy female friends who, for the most part, received demeaningly small bequests; tax authorities; and complete strangers. In the course of resolving these disputes the Getty Oil Company was sold to Texaco for considerably more than its book value. The final yield was about $5 billion, of which the family received $3 billion and the museum $2 billion, making it the most lavishly endowed institution of its kind. Poetic justice had been served, with the museum becoming as famous for the high prices it would pay for works of art as Getty was for his bargain hunting.

Although Getty accumulated one of the great American fortunes, he made little mark on the country. He was not a pioneer or innovator like Henry Ford, simply better at business than most of his peers. Nor did he employ his wealth for noble purposes, as did Andrew Carnegie and John D. Rockefeller. Even his art patronage, for which he is most likely to be remembered, has been a mixed blessing: the huge endowment of the Getty Museum led it to inflate prices in what was already a booming art market. The full extent of the Getty legacy remained uncertain at the time of his death, in that his name was carried on by numerous very wealthy descendants.

[Getty was the author of *As I See It: The Autobiography of J. Paul Getty* (1976). Robert Lenzer, *The Great Getty: The Life and Loves of J. Paul Getty—The Richest Man in the World* (1986), as its title suggests, offers a celebrity approach to Getty's life. Obituaries are in the *New York Times*, June 7 and 11, 1976.]

WILLIAM L. O'NEILL

GILES, WARREN CRANDALL (May 28, 1896–Feb. 7, 1979), baseball executive, was born in Tiskilwa, Ill., the son of William Francis Giles, who owned a paint and contracting business, and Isabelle Slattery. After attending Moline High School and Jubilee College in Oak Hill, Ill., where he graduated in 1914, Giles entered Staunton (Va.) Military Academy, where he remained for two years. In the fall of 1916 he entered Washington and Lee University but left shortly thereafter to join the United States Army. He served on the western front as a lieutenant in the infantry and was wounded. He subsequently returned to Moline to work in his father's business.

While attending a meeting to discuss how to assure the financial stability of the local baseball team, Giles was so persuasive that he was selected by those present to become the club's new president in 1919. Under his direction the team's fortunes improved dramatically and in 1921 it won the Three I (Iowa, Indiana, Illinois) League pennant. Giles moved in 1922 to the front office of the St. Joseph club in the Western League. There, while making trades, he came to the attention of Branch Rickey, the owner of the St. Louis Cardinals in the National League, who was impressed by his honesty and reliability and selected him to head the Cardinal farm team in Syracuse (later in Rochester) in the International League. With Giles as general manager, this franchise won four pennants and two International League championships between 1928 and 1936.

Giles married Mabel Jane Foster Skinner in Chicago on Oct. 29, 1932. She died in 1943, and Giles never remarried. Their only child, William Yale Giles, was to follow in his father's footsteps as a baseball executive.

In 1937, Giles became general manager of the financially troubled Cincinnati Reds, then one of the worst teams in major league baseball. He served in this capacity until 1947, when he was elected president as a result of his successes, principal among them winning National League pennants in 1939 and 1940 and a World Series championship in 1940. During World War II, because of his own experience as a young man, he insisted that his draft-eligible players serve overseas. This policy no doubt weakened the franchise in Cincinnati, but it made him extremely popular as a patriotic citizen who put the interests of his country over the interests of his sport. It was the only time he would make baseball take a secondary role, although he always personally took a backseat to the interests of the game in his own career. In 1951 he was elected president of the National League after initially competing with Ford Frick for the position of commissioner of baseball in a seventeen-ballot marathon from which he withdrew, characteristically citing his commitment to the best interests of baseball as having a greater priority than his professional ambitions.

While president of the National League, Giles presided over rapid expansion. He insisted that teams that were not well supported in one city should go elsewhere. During his tenure the Braves moved from Boston to Milwaukee and then to Atlanta. More important, perhaps, he assured that the sport would remain truly the national pastime by helping baseball tap into the lucrative California market when the New York Giants moved to San Francisco and the Brooklyn Dodgers relocated to Los Angeles, although he denied saying "Who needs New York?" In addition, under his direction the National League expanded from eight to twelve teams, with an eastern and western divisional structure. He also oversaw the development of several new stadiums. Perhaps most significantly, under Giles's leadership the National League moved aggressively to hire both black and Latin American players, thereby getting a head start on the rival American League.

An affable yet strong-willed man, Giles developed numerous successful managers and players as well as baseball executives, most notably Gabe Paul, whose career began under Giles's auspices in the 1920's. Giles was known for his honesty and integrity and for his desire to modernize the National League yet with an eye toward its traditional past, once stating, "We are a game of tradition. The right kind of tradition has made baseball what it is, but blindly following tradition may lead into a rut. Baseball must always keep pace with the times." When he retired as president of the National League after the 1969 season, he was regarded by team owners as a consummate business manager. He became president emeritus of the National League in 1971, the same year he became chairman of the board of directors of the National Baseball Hall of Fame. Giles was elected to the Hall of Fame in 1979 and died of cancer that year in Cincinnati, where he had moved the National League headquarters during his presidency. Giles was buried in Moline, Ill.

[The National Baseball Hall of Fame Library, Cooperstown, N.Y., has a file on Giles. See also Gerald Holland, "Honest Warren Giles: He Always Strives to Please," *Sports Illustrated*, June 10, 1963. Obituaries are in the *New York Times*, Feb. 8, 1979; *Newsweek*, Feb. 19, 1979; and *Time*, Feb. 19, 1979.]

CHARLES R. MIDDLETON

GILLIAM, JAMES WILLIAM ("JUNIOR") (Oct. 17, 1928–Oct. 8, 1978), baseball player and coach, was born in Nashville, Tenn. Little is known about his early life. While he was an adolescent he hung around baseball parks in Nashville, where he was picked up by one of the traveling Negro League teams, the Baltimore Elite Giants, who placed him on their roster in 1945. He roomed with Roy Campanella while playing in Baltimore. A second baseman, Gilliam was tutored by Sammy Hughes, who taught him to be a switch-hitter.

After playing in the Negro League he was signed by the Brooklyn Dodgers as they vigorously set the pace for integrating major league baseball between 1947 and 1953. He was the eighth black player chosen by the Dodger organization and he was selected specifically because of his potential to replace the aging Jackie Robinson at second base. Gilliam, who was three times an all-star in the eastern circuit of the Negro National League, acquired while playing in Baltimore the sobriquet "Junior" because he was the youngest member of the team. His youth belied his seriousness about the sport, however; he had an avid interest in baseball and preferred to listen to the older players reminisce than carouse with the younger ones after games were completed. Early in his career he married Edwina A. Fields; the couple had four children.

Signed by the Dodgers in late 1950, Gilliam played two years in the International League; he led the league in runs scored in 1951 and 1952. In 1952 he also led in fielding. He was called up to the Dodgers in 1953, where he at first alternated with Jackie Robinson at second base, thereby enabling Robinson to play other less taxing positions and lengthen his career. Gilliam remained with the Dodgers from 1953 through 1966, moving with the team from Brooklyn to Los Angeles in 1958. From 1964 through 1966 while a player-coach, he insisted on hard play, hustles, and spirit, setting a tone around which younger athletes could rally and assuring Dodger victories in the late-season pennant races and in the World Series, which the Dodgers won in 1965.

Gilliam's career batting average was .265; in seven World Series he batted .211. His greatest strength lay in the fact that he was a versatile athlete who, in the course of his career, played six of the nine baseball positions (all but catcher, shortstop, and pitcher). A reliable and consistent player, Gilliam selflessly underpinned the more spectacular play of others who starred on the successful Dodger teams of the era.

Gilliam, whose salary was modest, especially by later standards, worked in the off-season as a salesman for Hiram Walker Breweries, promoting their beverages. He was also a member of the Screen Actors Guild by virtue of his appearance with Jerry Lewis in 1958 in the movie *The Geisha Boy*. Gilliam had ambitions to become a major league manager, but despite some experience as manager of the San Juan club in the Winter League, these remained unfulfilled at his death. He died in Englewood, Calif., after suffering a stroke. At the time of Gilliam's death only manager Walter Alston had served with the Dodgers for a longer time. The Dodgers dedicated both the playoff series and the 1978 World Series to his memory.

[For further information see John Halway, *Voices from the Great Black Baseball Leagues* (1975); Arthur R. Ashe, Jr., *A Hard Road to Glory* (1988); and "Off-Season Athletes on Off-Beat Jobs," *Ebony*, May 1962. Obituaries are in the *Pittsburgh Courier*, Oct. 21 and 28, 1978; *Newsweek*, Oct. 23, 1978; and the *New York Times*, Nov. 6, 1978. A tribute is in *Time*, Oct. 23, 1978.]

CHARLES R. MIDDLETON

GLUECK, SHELDON ("SOL") (Aug. 15, 1896–Mar. 10, 1980), professor of criminal law and criminology, was born in Warsaw, Poland, one of seven children of Charles Glueck and Anna Steinhardt. The Glueck family immigrated to the United States in 1903 and settled in Milwaukee, Wis. His father had owned a small steel shop in Poland, but after settling in Milwaukee he worked as a street peddler.

Sheldon Glueck worked in the solicitor's office of the United States Department of Agriculture from 1913 to 1917. During this time, he also took night courses in law at Georgetown University and night courses in the humanities at George Washington University. In 1917 he enlisted in the United States Army and for fifteen months served as sergeant with the "Rainbow Division" of the American Expeditionary Forces during World War I. Upon his return to the United States, he resumed his studies at George Washington University and received his B.A. degree in the humanities in 1920. Also in 1920, Glueck received an LL.B. and an LL.M. from the National University Law School, became a naturalized United States citizen, and passed the New York bar. He was employed by the United States Shipping Board from 1919 to 1922.

He was preparing to practice law in New York

when his older brother, Bernard Glueck, a forensic psychiatrist at Sing Sing prison, arranged for him to meet Eleanor Touroff, one of his graduate students from the New York School of Social Work. This marked the beginning of a remarkable intellectual partnership in social science research that would last fifty years. Glueck fell in love with Touroff and followed her to Boston, where she had taken a position as head of a settlement house. The couple were married on Apr. 16, 1922; they had one daughter, Joyce Glueck Rosberg, a poet, who died at age thirty-two.

In Boston, Glueck decided to continue his education. After being denied admission to Harvard Law School, Glueck was admitted to the Department of Social Ethics at Harvard University, an interdisciplinary precursor to the Sociology Department. In this department, Glueck received an M.A. in 1922 and a Ph.D. in 1924. His Ph.D. thesis focused on criminal responsibility, mental disorder, and criminal law and reflected his interests in sociology, law, and psychiatry. Meanwhile, his wife enrolled in the Graduate School of Education at Harvard. She received her M.Ed. degree in 1923 and her Ed.D. in 1925.

After serving as an instructor in the Department of Social Ethics at Harvard from 1925 to 1927, Glueck received an appointment at Harvard Law School as assistant professor of criminology. He was promoted to professor in 1932, and was named the first Roscoe Pound Professor of Law in 1950, a position he held until he became professor emeritus in 1963. Both Sheldon and Eleanor Glueck were given honorary doctorates by Harvard University in 1958, becoming the first husband-wife team to receive such a dual honor.

For more than forty years at Harvard Law School, Glueck and his wife studied the careers of juvenile delinquents and adult criminals, becoming internationally renowned for their research concerning the causes, treatment, and prevention of crime and delinquency. Seeking to merge theory and practice, the Gluecks' scholarly interests cut across the disciplines of law, sociology, psychology, biology, education, and social work.

The Gluecks conducted four major studies of delinquency and crime. Their first research project was a follow-up study of 510 male offenders who had been incarcerated at the Massachusetts Reformatory during the period 1911–1922. These offenders were studied over a fifteen-year span, resulting in three books, *Five Hundred Criminal Careers* (1930), *Later Criminal Careers* (1937), and *Criminal Careers in Retrospect* (1943). The second research project was a follow-up study of women who had been incarcerated at the Women's Reformatory in Framingham, Mass., which led to the publication of *Five Hundred Delinquent Women* (1934). A third major research effort focused on a sample of juveniles who had been referred by the Boston Juvenile Court to the Judge Baker Foundation (the existing court clinic at the time). These results were published in *One Thousand Juvenile Delinquents* (1934); a follow-up analysis produced *Juvenile Delinquents Grown Up* (1940). Each of these studies was characterized by meticulous documentation of the experiences of offenders *after* their involvement with the criminal justice system, and each study revealed high rates of continued criminal activity among these offenders.

In 1940 the Gluecks began work on their best-known study, *Unraveling Juvenile Delinquency* (1950). This ten-year project addressed the development of criminal careers and involved a detailed examination of 500 delinquents and 500 nondelinquents from disadvantaged neighborhoods in the Boston area. Then, for the next fifteen years, the Gluecks conducted an extensive follow-up of the original sample of delinquents and nondelinquents, resulting in the publication of *Delinquents and Non-Delinquents in Perspective* (1968).

Unraveling Juvenile Delinquency established the Gluecks as true pioneers in the study of crime and juvenile delinquency. Although they explored a wide range of factors related to crime, they were among the first researchers to focus special attention on the family and its role in generating juvenile delinquency. The *Unraveling* study demonstrated that the key factors in predicting juvenile delinquency were parental affection, supervision, and discipline. The Gluecks were the first researchers to collect and analyze data on both delinquents and nondelinquents, including careful tracking of their subjects into adulthood. Perhaps most important, they were also the first to promote the application of "prediction tables" for the early identification of potential juvenile delinquents, a methodology that prompted considerable criticism of their work.

Along with his extensive collaborative work

in criminology, Glueck focused attention on issues relating to criminal law and criminal procedure. He served as a member of the Supreme Court's Advisory Committee on Rules of Practice and Procedure. He also worked on the Model Penal Code of the American Law Institute. Glueck served as an adviser to Justice Robert H. Jackson during the Nuremberg Trials (see his works *War Criminals: Their Prosecution and Punishment* [1944] and *The Nuremberg Trial and Aggressive War* [1946]). He also had a longstanding interest in mental health, psychiatry, and the law, which was reflected in his books *Mental Disorder and the Criminal Law* (1925) and *Law and Psychiatry: Cold War or Entente Cordiale?* (1962). And, finally, throughout his career, he promoted reform of the administration of criminal justice (see *Crime and Justice* [1936], *Crime and Correction: Selected Papers* [1952], and *Roscoe Pound and Criminal Justice* [1965]).

During his career Glueck received many awards and honors. He was a fellow of the American Academy of Arts and Sciences, the American Psychiatric Association, and the American Association for the Advancement of Science. In addition, he was the recipient of the Isaac Ray Award of the American Psychiatric Association (1961); the August Vollmer Award of the American Society of Criminology (1961); the Gold Medal of the Institute of Criminal Anthropology at the University of Rome (1964); and the Beccaria Gold Medal from the German Society of Criminology (1964). Glueck's non-academic interests included writing plays, short stories, and children's stories and international travel. Although clearly successful in his profession, Glueck regretted not being able to have his plays produced on stage.

In 1980, eight years after his wife's death, Glueck died in Cambridge, Mass.

[The papers of Sheldon Glueck and the joint papers of Sheldon and Eleanor T. Glueck are located in the Harvard Law School Library. An interesting autobiography is *Lives of Labor, Lives of Love* (1977). See also Noah Gordon, "Five Signs on the Highroad," *Saturday Review*, Apr. 6, 1963, a profile.

An extensive bibliography of their work can be found in Sheldon and Eleanor T. Glueck, *Ventures in Criminology* (1964). See John H. Laub and Robert J. Sampson, "The Sutherland-Glueck Debate; On the Sociology of Criminological Knowledge," *American Journal of Sociology* 96 (1991), for an analysis of a debate between two of the leading criminologists of the twentieth century. See also John L. Laub and David de Lorenzo, *Pioneers in Criminology and Criminal Justice: Sheldon and Eleanor Touroff Glueck*, Harvard Law School Library (1992). Obituaries are in the *Washington Post*, Mar. 12, 1980; the *Boston Globe*, Mar. 12, 1980; the *New York Times*, Mar. 13, 1980; *Newsweek*, Mar. 24, 1980; and *Time*, Mar. 24, 1980.]

JOHN H. LAUB

GÖDEL, KURT FRIEDRICH (Apr. 28, 1906–Jan. 14, 1978), mathematician, logician, and educator, was born in Brünn, Moravia, a province of the Austro-Hungarian Empire (now Brno, the Czech Republic), the son of Rudolf Gödel and Marianne Handschuh. His father was a successful textile factory manager and owner. Kurt, the younger of two sons, attended a Lutheran elementary school in Brünn. At the age of ten he entered a German-language Gymnasium in the same city, where he was outstanding in mathematics, languages, and religion.

In 1924, Gödel entered the University of Vienna, intending to secure a degree in physics. However, his interests soon turned toward the logical foundations of mathematics, and he received his doctorate in mathematics in 1930. His dissertation and early research furnished the point of departure for an intellectually revolutionary paper published in January 1931, "Über formal unentscheidbare Sätze der *Principia Mathematica* und verwandter Systeme" ("On Formally Undecidable Propositions of the *Principia Mathematica* and Related Systems"). The paper appeared in the prestigious scientific journal *Monatshefte für Mathematik und Physik* and received immediate attention in the mathematical world. Its essential conclusions are now succinctly referred to as Gödel's Theorem.

The thrust of Gödel's Theorem may be summarized as follows. The two basic overall goals of any mathematical system, such as whole-number arithmetic, elementary algebra, and ordinary Euclidean geometry, had always been viewed as completeness and consistency. Gödel, using fundamental logic and working with the assumed "true" axioms of a system, proved that these objectives can never be fully realized. From a set of axioms in a *complete* mathematical system, it is possible to derive or prove the statement (or theorem) that so-and-so is true or alternatively that so-and-so is not true. In a *consistent* system, which simply means one free of contradiction, it is not possible to prove that so-and-so is true and concurrently not true.

The *Principia Mathematica*, referred to by Gödel in the title of his 1931 paper, is a three-volume work by Bertrand Russell (1872–1970) and Alfred North Whitehead (1861–1947), published between 1910 and 1913. In this text, an attempt was made to deduce all of mathematics from basic logical principles. What Gödel proved was that the Russell-Whitehead effort and ancillary endeavors by others, including David Hilbert (1862–1943), to reduce all of mathematics to an axiomatic, complete, and consistent system by means of logical principles was impossible. As a corollary to this, Gödel concluded that any consistent theory adequate even to encompass the arithmetic of whole numbers would be incomplete. This means that theorems must exist even in elementary arithmetic, let alone higher mathematics, that cannot be proved true or not true—or, in Gödel's words, are "formally undecidable."

The prominent mathematician Hermann Weyl (1885–1955) reacted to Gödel's discoveries—presumably tongue in cheek—with the observation "that God exists because mathematics is undoubtedly consistent and the devil exists because we cannot prove the consistency." Douglas Hofstadter phrases the reaction to Gödel's findings in this way: "It would be inaccurate to liken the publication of this result to a bombshell; thermonuclear explosion comes closer to the truth. . . . Mathematics will never be as it was before Gödel's theorem."

Gödel was a professor of mathematics at the University of Vienna from 1930 to 1938. He became a visiting member of the Institute for Advanced Study at Princeton University during the first year of its operation (1933) and returned for various periods in 1935, 1938, and 1939.

Having become a German citizen as a result of the *Anschluss* action against Austria in 1938, Gödel was declared "fit for garrison duty" in Hitler's armed forces in September 1939. On Sept. 20, 1938, he had married Adele Porkert Nimbursky, a nightclub dancer; they had no children. Since he was subject to military service, Gödel secured exit permits and American nonquota immigrant visas for himself and his wife. The couple arrived in Princeton early in 1940, and Gödel resumed his research activities at the Institute for Advanced Study, remaining there until his retirement in 1976. It was at Princeton that Gödel became a colleague and subsequently a close friend of Albert Einstein's; they were often seen walking together, engaged in conversation. In 1948, Einstein served as a witness during Gödel's naturalization proceedings. A 1959 analysis by Gödel of the theory of relativity was highly praised by Einstein.

Curiously, from 1941 to 1945 Gödel was listed as a member of the faculty of the Nazified University of Vienna, as Dozent für Grundlagen der Mathematik und Logik. He had, in fact, formally applied for a similar position in September 1939, his earlier professorship at the University of Vienna having been abrogated after the *Anschluss*. This application had been denied in a letter noting his association with Jewish-liberal circles, although he had not been identified as having taken a position for or against the Nazis. The nominal and obviously ineffective restoration of Gödel to the University of Vienna faculty during the war raises an interesting historical question. Whether it was done as a courageous act of defiance by members of the University of Vienna administration against their Nazi overlords, or was a crude effort to embarrass and humiliate Gödel, who had fled his homeland, cannot be determined.

Gödel, who had suffered bouts of physical and emotional ill health throughout his adult life, died in Princeton, N.J., of what his death certificate termed "malnutrition and inanition" caused by a "personality disturbance."

Variously characterized as the most important logician since Aristotle and the most brilliant intellect of the twentieth century, Gödel was the recipient in 1951 of the first Albert Einstein Award for achievement in the natural sciences. The famous mathematician John von Neumann, making the presentation address, summed up Gödel's lifework: "Kurt Gödel's achievement . . . is singular and monumental . . . it is a landmark . . . Gödel was the first . . . to demonstrate that certain mathematical theorems can neither be proved nor disproved with the accepted, rigorous methods of mathematics. . . . He proved, furthermore, that a very important specific proposition belonged to this class of undecidable problems—the question . . . whether mathematics is free of inner contradictions. The subject of logic will never again be the same."

[Gödel was the author of *Consistency of the Axiom of Choice* (1940) and "A Remark About the Relationship Between Relativity Theory and Idealistic Philosophy," in Paul A. Schilpp, ed., *Albert Einstein: Philosopher-Scientist*, vol. 2 (1959). See Solomon Feferman et al., ed., *Collected Works of Kurt Gödel*, 2 vols. (1986–1989). The best source on Gödel's life, with an extensive bibliography, is Gregory H. Moore's article in *Dictionary of Scientific Biography*, vol. 17 (1990).

On his work, see Ernest Nagel and James R. Newman, "Gödel's Proof," in James R. Newman, ed., *The World of Mathematics*, III (1956); Albert Einstein, "Remarks to the Essays Appearing in this Collective Volume," in Paul A. Schilpp, ed., *Albert Einstein: Philosopher-Scientist*, vol. 2 (1959); Edna E. Kramer, *The Nature and Growth of Modern Mathematics* (1970); Douglas R. Hofstadter, *Gödel, Escher, Bach* (1979); Morris Kline, *The Loss of Certainty* (1980); Philip J. Davis and Reuben Hersh, *The Mathematical Experience* (1981); Michael Guillen, "Gödel's Theorem, an Article of Faith," in his *Bridges to Infinity* (1983); Douglas R. Hofstadter, "Analogies and Metaphors to Explain Gödel's Theorem," in Douglas M. Campbell and John C. Higgins, eds., *Mathematics: People—Problems—Problems*, II (1984); Rudy Rucker, *Mind Tools* (1987); Raymond Smullyan, *Forever Undecided* (1987); Roger Penrose, *The Emperor's New Mind* (1989); and Raymond Smullyan, *Gödel's Incompleteness Theorems* (1992). An obituary is in the *New York Times*, Jan. 15, 1978.]

LEONARD R. SOLON

GOLDMARK, PETER CARL (Dec. 2, 1906–Dec. 7, 1977), inventor, was born in Budapest, Hungary, the son of Sandor (Alexander) Goldmark, a businessman, and Emma Steiner. His parents were divorced when he was eight; his mother remarried, and he moved with her to Vienna at the end of World War I. His early musical training in piano and cello had a profound effect on his career. He later attributed his intense attention to detail to the musical lesson that "a single note can ruin the beauty of an entire rendition."

As a youth, Goldmark was fascinated by everything electrical, in particular the nascent engineering fields of radio and television. He began his postsecondary studies at the University of Berlin, then transferred to the University of Vienna in 1925. While in Vienna, he developed his first patented invention, an auto horn that could be activated by the driver's knee. At this time he also sent away for a do-it-yourself television kit, assembled it with a friend, and watched on a postage stamp–size screen his first televised images—a flickering picture of a dancer broadcast from London. From the bathroom of his family home, Goldmark managed to enlarge the image size. His solution brought him yet another patent.

After receiving his Ph.D. in physics from the University of Vienna in 1931, Goldmark set up the television department for Pye Radio in Cambridge, England. Two years later he moved to New York City. After consulting for fledgling television and radio companies, Goldmark was hired by the Columbia Broadcasting System (CBS) in 1936 to explore the possibilities of television. He was chief television engineer until 1944. Also in 1936 he married Muriel Gainsborough Evans; they had no children and later divorced. In 1937 he became an American citizen.

In January 1940, Goldmark married Frances Charlotte Trainer; the couple would have four children. Three months after the wedding, at the end of their delayed honeymoon in Montreal, Goldmark saw a movie that profoundly affected his career. Because of his poor eyesight, he normally did not go to the movies, but this film, *Gone with the Wind*, was the first Technicolor movie he had seen, and he found it exhilarating. Throughout the film he was obsessed with the thought of applying color to television; he felt that black-and-white television, which was then under development, paled in comparison. A few months later he had created a prototype color television system; on Dec. 2, 1940, the first live color television broadcast took place on CBS's experimental channel. That same day, his son Peter, who would become president of the Rockefeller Foundation, was born.

World War II interrupted further development of Goldmark's color television system. In January 1942 he joined Harvard University's Radio Research Laboratory, where he turned his attention to the development of electronic countermeasures designed to confuse enemy radar, including the jammer, a shoe box–size device filled with electronic circuits that was carried by Allied aircraft in bombing raids over Germany and helped save the lives of thousands of Americans. In 1944 he became a member of the United States Navy's Office of Scientific Research and Development, where he helped develop an electronic decoy navy that was designed to deceive the Germans in advance of the Allied invasion of Normandy.

Back at CBS after the war, Goldmark, who had become director of engineering research and development in 1944, fought to open the UHF airwaves to color television, but was thwarted in his efforts by the Federal Communications Commission (FCC). Meanwhile, he perfected his mechanical, rotating-disk color television system, which the FCC approved in 1950. Shortly afterward, however, it was replaced by all-electronic systems that were compatible with the existing black-and-white transmissions.

Goldmark's work probably brought color television to the public a decade earlier than it might have otherwise, even though it was not in the form he had intended. Despite this setback, however, he did manage a few victories. The competition used a Goldmark innovation, the curved shadow mask, which produces better resolution at the edges of a television picture. Goldmark's color system did find wide application in closed-circuit television for industry, medical institutions, and schools because its camera was smaller, lighter, and easier to maintain than commercial television systems. His camera was later used by the National Aeronautics and Space Administration to beam back color pictures from the moon. The irony of the situation was not lost on the *New York Times*, which noted that "a color television system once deemed too crude for use on the ground has now been adopted as the sophisticated tool for the relaying of tinted images from space."

In the late 1940's, Goldmark and his development team revolutionized the music recording industry, which for half a century had relied on 78 rpm records. The genesis of his best-known invention, the LP, or long-playing record, occurred one evening in the fall of 1945, while the Goldmarks were visiting friends. After dinner their hosts played a new 78-rpm recording of Brahms's Second Piano Concerto. Goldmark was annoyed by its tinny sound, scratchiness, and clicks, but most of all by each record's short playing time: the concerto required six records.

Since Goldmark wanted to improve the quality as well as increase the playing time of recordings, he not only decreased the number of revolutions per minute to 33⅓ but also increased the number of grooves per inch, developed a sapphire stylus for the playing cartridge instead of the steel needle then in use, created a lightweight tone arm and new turntable drive, used vinyl instead of shellac to make records, and employed a new microphone to improve the quality of the recordings. But CBS's introduction of Goldmark's LP on June 21, 1948, was not an instant hit. Not until the musical *South Pacific* appeared on LP five years later did people start buying it—and other LPs—in droves. The LP's reign lasted about three decades, until it was made obsolete by the compact disc.

The 1950's brought two promotions for Goldmark, another divorce and marriage, and more inventions. In 1950 he became a vice-president of CBS and, four years later, president of CBS Laboratories, a post he held until his retirement. In 1954 he divorced his second wife and married his secretary, Diane Davis; they had two children. Meanwhile, Goldmark developed the rotating-drum line scanner, a system that allowed satellites to relay high-resolution images from space. This innovation would have tremendous military and scientific implications in the decades to come. On the other hand, the record player he developed for use in cars never caught on, but by showing the potential of owner-selected music for the automobile, it paved the way for the invention of the audio cartridge. By the late 1950's, Goldmark was talking about a tape cassette system for the home and automobile. In partnership with the 3M Company, his team developed a string of patents that laid the groundwork for the standard audiocassette.

In April 1958, Goldmark moved his CBS laboratory from New York City to Stamford, Conn., where he worked on his last invention, electronic video recording (EVR). This was the first device to play movies in the form of miniature film on one's own television set. Two decades later EVR led to the videocassette recorder. Goldmark never obtained full support of CBS for EVR because chairman William Paley saw the invention as a potential threat to his broadcasting enterprise. Once again, however, a Goldmark invention served to stimulate the industry and contributed to the videocassette boom of the 1980's.

Goldmark retired from CBS in December 1971 and formed his own company, Goldmark Communications Corporation, a subsidiary of Warner Communications. But in his last years Goldmark turned his attention away from the inventor's bench and toward, as his critics called it, "saving America." Inspired by his son Peter's "war on poverty" work, he became involved in establishing equal-opportunity and antipoverty programs in the Stamford area. On a broader scale, Goldmark believed that the congestion of the cities was the root of many social problems and promoted a solution he called the New Rural Society. He felt that the new communications technologies could relieve the urban burden by allowing a greater dispersion of the population into the countryside.

Goldmark died in an automobile crash on a highway in Westchester County, N.Y.

[The most complete account of Goldmark's life and inventions appears in his autobiography, *Maverick Inventor* (1973), written with Lee Edson. Information on the social innovations of his later years appears in Goldmark's *The New Rural Society* (1973). An obituary is in the *New York Times*, Dec. 8, 1977.]

PATRICK HUYGHE

GORDON, JOHN FRANKLIN (May 15, 1900–Jan. 6, 1978), engineer and business executive, was born in Akron, Ohio, the son of Frederick Farnum Gordon and Margaret Vance. His father was a commercial building contractor. When Gordon was seven, his family moved to Greeley, Colo., where he attended local schools. He entered the United States Naval Academy in 1918 and graduated in 1922. After the end of World War I, the navy needed fewer junior officers and encouraged midshipmen to resign at graduation. Gordon was among the nearly 150 in the class of 1922 who resigned. He then took advanced courses at the University of Michigan and was awarded an M.S. in mechanical engineering in 1923.

In September 1923, after being interviewed by some major automobile manufacturers, Gordon began work as a laboratory technician in the Cadillac Motor Car Division in Detroit. He was promoted in 1928 to assistant foreman of the experimental laboratory, to foreman in 1929, and to motor design engineer in 1933.

On Sept. 5, 1927, Gordon married Ruth Morrison; they had two children.

In 1940, Gordon was transferred to the Allison Aircraft Engine Division of General Motors in Indianapolis for work in forward engine design. At that time, the Allison Division was expanding to become the major producer of aircraft engines in the United States. Gordon's major project was to design and develop a powerful liquid-cooled aircraft engine, which demanded a very high degree of precision. His experience in producing precision automobile engines helped him design the high-horsepower aircraft engines for faster and bigger fighter planes. Meanwhile, he was also working with Cadillac on designing tanks and motorized artillery. Because of his efforts for the two divisions, Allison became the principal manufacturer of mass-produced, liquid-cooled aircraft engines for the Army Air Force during World War II, and Cadillac produced more than 170 precision parts for the Allison engines.

In June 1943, Gordon returned to Cadillac as chief engineer; later he was in charge of designing a motor and transmission for light tanks. Gordon became general manager of Cadillac and a vice-president of General Motors (GM) in 1946. With other engineers, he designed and developed Cadillac's high-compression, overhead valve V-8 engine. The 160-horsepower engine was less noisy, more efficient, more than 200 pounds lighter, and consumed 15 to 20 percent less fuel than the one it replaced. It later became an industry standard and dominated automotive production in the 1950's. Under Gordon's leadership, the Cadillac division broke all previous production and sales records for four consecutive years.

In July 1950, Gordon left Cadillac and became vice-president in charge of GM's engineering staff. The following January he was named group executive in charge of the body and assembly division. He was also elected to the GM board of directors and became a member of the Administration and Operations Policy committees. The general managers of three GM divisions, consisting of 38 plants with about 100,000 employees, reported to him. Gordon was in charge of decision making not only on automobiles but also on diesel engines, Frigidaire appliances, aircraft engines, and other consumer products. His major contributions included bringing out new models of all five General Motors cars in 1959—the first time in company history that had been accomplished. From 1950 to 1958, Gordon was chairman of the board of regents of the General Motors Institute in Flint, Mich.

In August 1958, Gordon was elected president and chief operating officer of General Motors, succeeding Harlow H. Curtice. He was also named chairman of the GM executive committee and a member of the finance committee. During his presidency of GM, Gordon supported the annual model change in automobiles with better design and quality—which, he believed, would advance technology and, at the same time, make used cars available to people who could not afford the new ones. He believed that the challenge of foreign competitors could be met only by maintaining leadership in quality, design, and innovation, and by increasing productivity, mechanization, and automation. Quality-minded, cost-conscious, and administratively capable, Gordon led GM through the recession and into the boom of the early and mid-1960's, when GM doubled its capital earnings and sales, and tripled its profits of 1958. The production of its North American operations and major overseas subsidiaries increased from 3,298,524 cars, trucks, and other kinds of vehicles in 1958 to 7,307,376 in 1965. In 1965, GM's market share was around 50 percent in North America and 30 percent worldwide. The profit ranking in *The Fortune Directory of the 500 Largest U.S. Industrial Corporations* showed that GM rose from 115th place in 1958 to twelfth in 1965. As the president of the world's largest manufacturing corporation, Gordon often made it known that the "people philosophy" was his philosophy, as well as General Motors', and that his achievements could not have been gained without the contribution of his colleagues and his employees.

Gordon was elected president of the Automobile Manufacturers Association in 1963. He retired as president of the General Motors Corporation in 1965. He was a member of GM's bonus and salary committee in 1966 and became its chairman in 1967.

Espousing the philosophy that "Without willingness to give and share, we cease to be human beings and we cease to be productive men and women," Gordon was very active in charity and civic work throughout his career, particularly with the United Foundation of Detroit. He served as a director of the Mayo Foundation in Rochester, Minn.; a trustee of the Citizen Council of Michigan; a member of the Oakland University Foundation; and a member of the board of governors of Providence Hospital in Detroit. He was named a member of the Academic Board of Advisers for the Naval Academy in 1966.

Gordon died in Royal Oak, Mich., after a brief illness. He was remembered as an outstanding top corporate executive with unusual ability in engineering, production, business, and leadership.

[Gordon's personal papers were given to the library of the General Motors Institute, Flint, Mich. Memorabilia and local newspaper clippings are in the National Automotive History Collection, Detroit Public Library. See also *Fortune*, Oct. 1950; "New President Made His Mark with Cadillac," *Detroit News*, Aug. 26, 1958; and "GM's John Gordon Looks to Leisure," *Detroit Free Press*, May 30, 1965. Obituaries are in the *New York Times*, Jan. 7, 1978; and the *Detroit Free Press*, Jan. 8, 1978.]

WEN-HUA REN

GORDON, KERMIT (July 3, 1916–June 22, 1976), economist, was born in Philadelphia, the son of H. B. Gordon and Ida Robinson. Gordon received his education in the Philadelphia public school system and graduated from Upper Darby High School. He attended Swarthmore College and worked as a police reporter for the *Philadelphia Evening Bulletin* to support himself. He graduated in 1938 with a B.A. degree in economics with highest honors. Gordon was a Rhodes Scholar and attended University College at Oxford University in the 1938–1939 academic year. During his stay in England he played on the lacrosse team and discussed important economic and world issues with his contemporaries Harlan Cleveland and Stephen K. Bailey.

Upon his return to the United States, Gordon served as a research candidate in economics at Swarthmore. After a one-year stint as an administration fellow at Harvard, Gordon served as an economist with the Office of Price Administration in Washington, D.C., from 1941 to 1943. He married Mary King Grinnell of Winnetka, Ill., on Dec. 25, 1941. The couple had three children.

Gordon served two years in the United States Army during World War II, assigned to the Office of Strategic Services as an economist. Discharged as a second lieutenant in 1945, he returned to Washington and became a special assistant in the Office of the Assistant Secretary of State for Economic Affairs. From 1943 until 1953 he served as a consultant to the Department of State and to the White House and helped in the preparation of the *Report of Foreign Economic Policies* in 1950. In 1951, Gordon also served as a consultant to the Office of Price Stabilization.

While maintaining his link with the State Department, Gordon became an assistant professor of economics at Williams College in Williamstown, Mass., in 1946. He was promoted to full professor in 1956 and was appointed to the William Bough Chair. Gordon served as associate to the administrator of the Merrill Foundation for Advancement of Financial Knowledge from 1947 until 1956.

Beginning in 1956, Gordon was an executive associate of the Ford Foundation. He was a director of economic development and administration at the foundation from 1960 until 1961 and also served on the foundation's board of trustees from 1967 to 1975. He resigned from Ford to prevent any conflict of interest between it and his work for the Brookings Institution, which began in 1965.

In 1961, Gordon became David A. Wells Professor of Political Economy at Williams College. He was also a visiting lecturer at Harvard University, the National War College, and the Massachusetts Institute of Technology and was a member of the board of editors for the *American Economic Review* from 1958 to 1960.

As a civil servant, Gordon was ever mindful of imprudent uses of taxpayer money. Instead of using a chauffeured limousine, he drove a government-confiscated jalopy. Gordon's wit and perception were highly regarded by his colleagues and superiors alike. Gordon was well known for beginning meetings by chatting about trivial matters and then progressing to more important issues. It was this combination of personal honesty, humor, and an ability to make penetrating assessments that attracted President John F. Kennedy to Gordon.

President Kennedy appointed Gordon to the three-man Council of Economic Advisers in 1961, serving with James Tobin and Chairman Walter W. Heller. The advisers submitted fiscal plans on how to stimulate economic growth in the country. Gordon advocated high employment, price stability, and rapid production growth. Pleased with Gordon's work on the council, Kennedy appointed him to succeed David E. Bell as budget director in 1962. Gordon held this position under both presidents Kennedy and Lyndon B. Johnson until 1965. Besides preparing the budget and developing sound fiscal policies, the Bureau of the Budget is also responsible for advising the president on the progress of work in other federal agencies. As director of the bureau, Gordon was noted for his positive use of fiscal policy, but he often favored free-market solutions to economic problems as well.

In 1965, Gordon became vice-president of the Brookings Institution, a private think tank financed primarily by endowments and grants from philanthropic foundations that conducts independent studies of economic, social, and political problems and sponsors conferences for government leaders and members of the private sector. The position of vice-president was newly created; Gordon was responsible for research and educational programs at Brookings.

Gordon also served as the first chairman of the Health Insurance Benefits Advisory Council, which advises the secretary of health, education, and welfare on the administration of the Medicare program. He assumed the presidency of the Brookings Institution in 1967. He then served on the Advisory Council on Social Security from 1969 until 1972. Gordon was a public member of the Pay Board in 1971 and 1972 and a member of the General Advisory Committee on Arms Control and Disarmament from 1969 to 1973. Gordon, a lifelong Democrat, held the last two positions under President Richard M. Nixon.

In 1974, Gordon published one of his last articles before his death in 1976. Entitled "Some Conjectures on Policy Problems in the 1970's," it predicted some of the major international economic problems that the United States would face in the coming decades. It also discussed inflation, the environment, and the performance of the public sector.

Gordon never received a Ph.D. and edited only one book, *Agenda for the Nation*, in 1968. He was respected as an economist from the oral tradition. According to his longtime friend and professional colleague Stephen Bailey, "Gordon had the capacity to see a complex intellectual landscape clearly and to anticipate its strategic and tactical possibilities." His legacy at the Brookings Institution included a growth in staff and an increase in scholarly publication, while stressing quality. When referring to books, he advocated "a shorter list, but a better one." He died of pancreatitis in Washington, D.C.

[Gordon's personal papers are in the Brookings Institution and Ford Foundation archives. The largest portion of his work is housed in the John F. Kennedy Library, National Archives and Records Administration. The Brookings Institution published a collection of memorial tributes to Gordon in 1977. An obituary is in the *New York Times*, June 23, 1976.]

DELIA CRUTCHFIELD COOK

GOUDSMIT, SAMUEL ABRAHAM (July 11, 1902–Dec. 4, 1978), physicist, was born in The Hague, Netherlands, the son of Isaac Goudsmit, a prosperous wholesaler, and Marianne Gompers, who operated a fashionable millinery shop. Although intrigued by the world of physics at age eleven, when he came across an article on solar spectra in a textbook belonging to his older sister, Goudsmit might have followed his mother into the millinery business had not her ill health forced her to close the shop in 1918, his last year in high school. Because he had done well in science and mathematics and lacked any interest in his father's business, Goudsmit entered the University of Leiden as a physics major in 1919.

His devotion to physics grew rapidly under the tutelage of Paul Ehrenfest, a distinguished physicist and teacher at Leiden. Goudsmit's instinctive gift for solving puzzles, nurtured during his childhood and fine-tuned by an eight-month course in detective work and a two-year course in deciphering hieroglyphics, was just the thing needed in the field of spectroscopy, to which he was immediately introduced at Leiden. Spectroscopy involves the analysis of the light given off by glowing gases. Each chemical element produces a unique pattern of spectral "lines" (each corresponding to a specific frequency of light given off by the atoms of the gas), and by decoding these patterns one can determine the detailed electron energy levels of the atom. At age eighteen Goudsmit published his first paper, in which he used relativity theory to explain the characteristic paired spectral lines of the alkali metals. His future collaborator, George Uhlenbeck, remarked later that this early paper foreshadowed the concept of electron spin, a discovery that was to make the two of them famous.

Goudsmit became thoroughly steeped in the data of spectroscopy during his years at Leiden, particularly in the multiplication or "splitting" of spectral lines that occurs when excited gases are subjected to the perturbing influence of magnetic fields. In 1924, Goudsmit worked half of each week with the acknowledged leader in the field of spectroscopy, Pieter Zeeman, in Amsterdam. Then, back in Leiden, Goudsmit tried to find the mathematical formulas that would make sense of the data. He published several papers on his findings.

Goudsmit's pursuit was at the forefront of physics research in 1925. The original quantum theory of the atom, proposed by Niels Bohr in 1913, had had many successes, but its limitations were becoming more and more apparent as time went on. To deal with the subtleties in complex spectra, Bohr had found that each energy state of each electron in an atom could be characterized by a distinct set of three "quantum numbers," all of them integers. But there were many empirical inconsistencies that could not be resolved.

Physicist Wolfgang Pauli proposed in early 1925 that a fourth quantum number be assigned to each atom; he stipulated that no two electrons in the atom could have the same set of four quantum numbers. Goudsmit quickly responded with the proposal, published in May 1925, that this fourth quantum number, which characterized values of the electron's angular momentum, had to have half-integer values (either plus one-half or minus one-half), but he was unable to offer any physical justification for the idea.

In the summer of 1925, Goudsmit tutored George Uhlenbeck, a student of Ehrenfest's who had just returned from Rome, on recent developments in physics, especially spectroscopy. During their discussions of spectra physics, Uhlenbeck asked conceptual questions that the empirically minded Goudsmit had never considered. Regarding Goudsmit's paper on Pauli's extra quantum number, the idea came to Uhlenbeck that "since each quantum number corresponds to a degree of freedom of the electron, the fourth quantum number must mean that the electron [has] an additional degree of freedom—in other words the electron must be rotating." Thus was born the concept of electron spin, the idea that the electron, instead of being static in its orbit, is an electrically charged body that spins like a top, either right side up or upside down, and therefore behaves like a magnet. The short note published by the two young physicists in 1925 describing this idea, with Ehrenfest's mixed blessing, met with considerable skepticism at first, partly because their explanation made the theoretical spectral line splittings be larger than the observed values by a factor of two. In 1926, Llewellyn H. Thomas showed that this troublesome factor could be accounted for as a relativistic effect, and soon the physics community came to accept the concept of spin as an inherent property of the electron. It received full theoretical justification with the publication of a paper on the theory of relativistic quantum mechanics by Paul A. M. Dirac in 1928. The idea of spin was also shown to apply to the nucleus of the atom when Goudsmit, collaborating with Ernst Back, published an analysis of the hyperfine structure of bismuth 209 in 1928.

In the summer of 1927, after having just returned from the University of Tübingen, where he had spent a year as a Rockefeller fellow, Goudsmit received his Ph.D. degree from the University of Leiden. He married Jaantje (Jeanne) Logher, a former designer in his mother's shop, on Jan. 19, 1927; they had one child and divorced in 1960.

In 1927, Goudsmit faced an unhappy prospect: unemployment. There were no European professorships in sight for the rising young physicist. So Goudsmit (along with George Uhlenbeck) accepted an instructorship at the University of Michigan, which was at that time attempting to build a world-class physics program. Advancing to the rank of professor in 1932, Goudsmit stayed on at Michigan until 1946, returning to Europe in 1938 on a Guggenheim Fellowship. During his stay at Michigan, Goudsmit published extensively in collaboration with his students, first on atomic spectra and later on neutron physics and electron scattering; he earned the reputation of being an excellent teacher.

In order to accept an assignment in the Radiation Laboratory of the Massachusetts Institute of Technology during World War II, Goudsmit took a leave of absence from the University of Michigan in 1941. He spent part of that time overseas; in England in 1943 he determined why British radar sets were failing the American Eighth Air Force, and later that year he was appointed scientific head of Project Alsos, an intelligence operation whose task was to determine the progress of war-related scientific research in Europe, especially German progress on an atomic bomb. From mid-1944 to mid-1945 the Alsos mission accompanied the Allied forces as they advanced through France, Belgium, the Netherlands, and Germany. Goudsmit concluded, much to the relief of the Allies, that the German uranium project was directed mainly toward constructing a uranium pile (reactor), with little prospect of producing a bomb. In 1947, Goudsmit published a book, *Alsos*, about his findings, and certain conclusions in it have been the subject of controversy ever since. Undoubtedly Goudsmit's feelings toward Germans and German science, making this book somewhat less than purely objective, were colored by the fact that his parents had been killed by the Nazis in the extermination camp at Auschwitz, and by the horror he felt when he saw firsthand how his boyhood home in The Hague had been destroyed. His suspicion of German scientists, most notably Werner Heisenberg, continued for many years thereafter.

In 1946, Goudsmit took a post at Northwestern University, where he remained until 1948. That year he became a senior scientist at Brookhaven National Laboratory, a prestigious research institution on Long Island in New York, where he remained until his retirement in 1970. Goudsmit's major research effort at Brookhaven was the development of a new type of mass spectrometer, used to make highly accurate measurements of the masses of nuclear isotopes, but his real contribution lay in his administrative accomplishments. From 1952 to 1960, Goudsmit was the chairman of the Physics Department at Brookhaven, and from 1952 to 1974 he was the editor of the *Physical Review*. He founded *Physical Review Letters* in 1958.

In addition, Goudsmit was a visiting professor at Rockefeller University from 1957 to 1974, and each year he taught a four-week course on nuclear physics at the Massachusetts Institute of Technology. In 1966 he coauthored a semipopular book on the nature of time. In 1960 he married for a second time, to Irene Bejach Rothschild.

After retiring from Brookhaven, Goudsmit became distinguished visiting professor of physics at the University of Nevada, Reno. Lamenting the pace, scale, cost, and influence that characterized physics after World War II, Goudsmit longed for the simpler times, when physics was done with "string and sealing wax," an era he knew was gone forever. To the end of his life, Goudsmit sought to help others appreciate the joy and beauty of physics. He died at the University of Nevada.

[Goudsmit's papers are in the archives of the American Institute of Physics, College Park, Md. The tapes and transcripts of three interview sessions, as well as microfilm copies of much correspondence and several manuscripts, are in the archives of the Sources for History of Quantum Physics, the American Philosophical Society, Philadelphia. A two-part biographical sketch is Daniel Lang, "A Farewell to String and Sealing Wax," the *New Yorker*, Nov. 7 and 14, 1953. Much information on Goudsmit,

Uhlenbeck, and the concept of electron spin is in Abraham Pais, *Inward Bound* (1986). A book dealing with the Alsos mission, and the exchange between Goudsmit and Heisenberg, is Mark Walker, *German Nationalism and the Quest for Nuclear Power* (1989). An obituary is in *Physics Today*, Apr. 1979.]

RICHARD K. GEHRENBECK

GRAUER, BENJAMIN FRANKLIN ("BEN") (June 2, 1908–May 31, 1977), radio and television announcer and commentator, was born in Staten Island, New York City, the son of Adolph Grauer, a surveyor and civil engineer, and Ida Kunstler Goldberg. At age seven, shortly after the family moved to Manhattan, he was plucked from a children's social dancing class by a motion-picture scout to begin a career at the Fort Lee (N.J.) movie studios, acting with such stars as Madge Evans, Theda Bara, and Pauline Frederick; in 1920 he starred in *The Town That Forgot God*. By then his career on Broadway had begun. He originated the role of Georgie Bassett in *Penrod* (1918), a play in which Helen Hayes was the ingenue, and eventually went on to the leading role of Tyltyl in Maurice Maeterlinck's *The Bluebird* (1923) and a part in the Theatre Guild production of *Processional* (1925). During World War I, dressed in an army officer's uniform, ten-year-old Grauer toured with a troupe entertaining at various army camps. He sold over $1 million in Liberty Bonds.

In 1925, Grauer's parents, having decided that he needed a more formal education than he was getting as a child actor, enrolled him in Townsend Harris High School in New York City. He went on to the City College of New York, graduating in 1930 with a bachelor's degree in English. He had been drama critic for the college's newspaper and editor-in-chief of its literary magazine. In his senior year he won the George Sandham Prize for Extemporaneous Speaking, although earlier in his college career he had almost failed a public-speaking course.

An ardent bibliophile, Grauer opened a small bookshop and mail-order book business after graduation, but was unsuccessful. For a short time he played juvenile roles on radio, and then, in October 1930, was hired by the National Broadcasting Company as a radio announcer. His first commercial sponsor chose him over ten others because he pronounced the sponsor's product "baloney," rather than the highfalutin "bologna."

Grauer's knack for extemporization enabled him to report many major news events over the next three decades, beginning in 1932 with the Los Angeles Olympic games and the Lindbergh baby kidnapping case. That same year he became the announcer for the long-running show of the gossip columnist Walter Winchell. Grauer, Winchell, and the comedian Milton Berle had all been in the cast of a Gus Edwards vaudeville revue as children.

In 1933, Grauer reported on the maiden flight of the dirigible *Akron*. That year his career and his life were nearly cut short. While he was describing a parade on Fifth Avenue in New York City, from a blimp hovering above, a trapdoor opened at his feet; he barely escaped plummeting to his death.

The first of his reportorial "scoops" occurred in 1934 when Grauer interviewed the first survivor ashore from the luxury liner *Morro Castle*, which burned off the New Jersey coast near Asbury Park. Later scoops included NBC-TV's first special event, the opening of the New York World's Fair in 1939, and the first on-the-scene news broadcast of Count Folke Bernadotte's assassination in Israel in 1948.

For many years, beginning in 1937, Ben Grauer (as he was known on radio and television) broadcast every presidential inauguration and, from 1944, covered every national Democratic and Republican convention, first on radio and then, in 1948, on television, sharing the microphone and camera with John Cameron Swayze. He remained on the air for sixteen consecutive hours, reporting the results of the 1948 Truman-Dewey-Wallace presidential contest.

During World War II, Grauer expanded on his World War I fund-raising activities, generating $15 million in defense and war savings bonds. In 1945, at war's end, he covered the United Nations Conference in San Francisco, following this with the Paris Conference of Allied Foreign Ministers in 1946. Other broadcasts from overseas included the 1947 solar eclipse in Brazil, the Berlin airlift and the Arab-Israeli war in 1948, Queen Elizabeth II's coronation in 1953, and the 1958 opening of the Brussels World's Fair. He broadcast from United Nations headquarters in New York on the Suez Canal crisis and Hungarian revolt in 1956, the Lebanese rebellion in 1958, and the

1960 meeting of the United Nations Security Council.

Grauer reveled in the spontaneity demanded by reporting special events, recognizing and accepting the fact that commentators cannot help being subjective, despite efforts to the contrary. This situation changed somewhat with the advent of television because, as he pointed out in an interview, the picture, not the announcer's choice of words, controlled the presentation. The spontaneity of his approach, however, as "one of the glibbest ad-libbers on the air" made him an ideal choice as host or moderator for quiz shows and panel discussions. With musical programs he ran the gamut from the folksiness of "Kay Kyser's Kollege of Musical Knowledge" to the urbane, understated announcing of the NBC Symphony Orchestra broadcasts conducted by Arturo Toscanini (1940–1954). Among his other programs on radio and early television were "Pot of Gold," "Mr. District Attorney," "Big Story," "Citizen's Searchlight," "Living," "Atlantic Spotlight" (NBC with the BBC), "Daily Business Trends," "Newslight," and "It's a Problem."

On Sept. 25, 1954, Grauer married interior designer Melanie Kahane; they had no children. Their shared interest in the decorative arts led to "Decorating Wavelengths," a five-minute, four-times-per-week talk show. Grauer's continued bibliophilia led to his amassing a library of well over 5,000 volumes of first and rare editions, housed in a separate apartment adjoining his Upper East Side residence. This love of books generated an interest in printing as an art strong enough for Grauer to become a recognized master of the hand printing press; for instance, he designed and printed his own Christmas cards. His abiding interest in the archaeology of Central America—an ambition, never fulfilled, was to excavate the site of a Mayan city he had seen while flying over the Guatemalan jungle—made him an ardent voice for the completion of the Pan-American Highway. His article "The Break in the Golden Brooch" (1951) describes the problem and offers his solution. He was also the author of *March on Pharaoh* (1932) and "How Bernal Diaz's 'True History' Was Reborn," in William Targ, ed., *Bouillabaisse for Bibliophiles* (1955) and was editor of *NBC News Picture Book of the Year* (1967–1969).

By the 1960's, Grauer had become Telstar's Spanish commentator and the producer-narrator of "Señor Ben and His Pan-American Highway of Melody," in addition to his English-language broadcasts. He retired from NBC in 1973 but continued broadcasting a weekly short-wave program, "New York, New York, with Ben Grauer," over the Voice of America. As noted in the *New York Times*, he also "continued the long tradition of delivering the countdown to midnight in Times Square for the Guy Lombardo telecasts on New Year's Eve."

Among Grauer's many honors were the George Foster Peabody Award for presidential convention-election coverage (1972), the establishment of a scholarship in his name at Columbia University's Graduate School of Journalism, and his decoration as a chevalier of the French Legion of Honor. He served as president of the National Music League, vice-president and trustee of the Overseas Press Club, and national secretary of the Academy of TV Arts and Sciences. He died, two days before his sixty-ninth birthday, in New York City.

[Grauer's articles include "Of Books and Words," *Publishers Weekly*, Nov. 23, 1946; and "The Break in the Golden Brooch," *United Nations World*, May 1951. See also "Handyman," *Time*, Mar. 15, 1948; "Ben Grauer Speaking," *Newsweek*, July 19, 1948; Bennett Cerf, "The Magic Grauer," *Saturday Review of Literature*, Feb. 17, 1951; and " 'Bluebird' on the Wing," *Theatre Arts*, July 1954. An obituary is in the *New York Times*, June 1, 1977.]

ALBERT TEPPER

GRIFFIN, JOHN HOWARD (June 16, 1920–Sept. 9, 1980), author, was born in Dallas, Tex., the son of Jack Walter Griffin, a wholesale grocery salesman, and Lena Mae Young, a musician; he was the second of four children. At the age of fifteen, Griffin responded to an advertisement for the Lycée Descartes, a boarding school in France, and requested admission. He stated that he had no money to pay fees but would do almost any type of work if he were admitted. The school accepted his offer. After graduating from the lycée, Griffin remained in France to study medicine and the humanities. When France was conquered by Germany in 1940, he abandoned his studies and took part in the French resistance movement. He returned to the United States, enlisted in the United States Army, and was sent to the South Pacific. There Griffin became involved in a United

States government project to prepare Pacific islanders for the possibility of American occupation; his job was to gain the trust of the natives.

During his stay in the South Pacific, Griffin's vision began to fail after an artillery attack during which he was knocked unconscious. His discharge papers indicated that his vision was 20/200, which meant that he was legally blind. Having abandoned his study of medicine, Griffin turned to musicology. In 1946 he spent several months in a Dominican monastery with a friend who was a monk. In later years he retreated to a monastery in difficult times.

By 1947, Griffin was totally blind and abandoned all hope of an academic career, deciding instead to raise hogs. A major turning point in his life came when he met the drama critic John Mason Brown, who suggested he become a writer. Griffin's subsequent novel, *The Devil Rides Outside* (1952), dealt with the struggle between faith and temptation. Although the book was banned in Detroit as being too sexually explicit, it received many positive critical reviews.

In June 1952, Griffin married one of his former piano students, Elizabeth ("Piedy") Holland; they had four children. In the fall of 1952 he was diagnosed with malaria and was soon confined to a wheelchair, paralyzed in all but his left arm. Griffin also was found to have diabetes. In spite of these devastating physical setbacks, his second novel, *Nuni*, was published in 1956. By the time of its publication he had fully recovered from the malaria.

In June 1957 Griffin's sight suddenly returned. Many people speculated that he had never really been blind; *Time* magazine suggested that his blindness had been hysterical. After regaining his sight Griffin became a staff reporter for *Sepia*, a black monthly magazine patterned on *Life* magazine. One of his undertakings for *Sepia* was a survey in November 1959, investigating the high suicide rate among southern blacks. In order to understand their plight, Griffin decided to "become" black. He flew to New Orleans and found a dermatologist who prescribed Oxsoralen, coupled with exposure to a sun lamp, to produce the desired change in complexion. Griffin reported that when he looked in the mirror, "the face and shoulders of a stranger—a fierce, bald, very dark Negro—glared at me from the glass. He in no way resembled me." He recorded his experiences first in *Sepia* and then in a book, *Black Like Me* (1961), that became a best-seller. Griffin was threatened and hanged in effigy by some of his white neighbors. In 1964 *Black Like Me* was made into a movie that was less successful than the book. His experiences led him to become an activist in the civil rights movement and his next book, *The Church and the Black Man* (1969), was a criticism of the way the Christian faith related to African Americans. After the death in 1968 of Thomas Merton (author of *The Seven Storey Mountain*), Griffin was asked by the Merton Legacy Trust to write Merton's biography. He worked for nine years on this project but was forced to give it up because of poor health.

Griffin died after suffering two years from kidney disease, lung congestion, heart attacks, and the amputation of a leg.

[See Jeff H. Campell, *John Howard Griffin* (1970); and Ernest Sharpe, Jr., "The Man Who Changed His Skin," *American Heritage*, Feb. 1989. An obituary is in the *New York Times*, Sept. 10, 1980.]

RENNIE SIMSON

GROPPER, WILLIAM (Dec. 3, 1897–Jan. 7, 1977), political cartoonist and painter, was born in New York City, the son of Harry Gropper, a scholarly man who could not hold a job, and Jennie Nidel, a seamstress who supported the family. The poverty Gropper knew as he grew up on the Lower East Side near the Williamsburg Bridge was the source of the social concerns that were central to his art. He left P.S. 171 at the age of fourteen to work at a menswear shop twelve hours a day, six days a week. Sometimes he brought clothes home to his mother, who always needed the work. He later commented that "the sweatshop gave us our livelihood but robbed us of our mother."

Gropper studied art at the Ferrer School in New York City from 1912 to 1915 and at the School of Fine and Applied Art beginning in 1915. The free-thinking Emma Goldman was something of an intellectual guide for the Ferrer School, where Gropper sketched from live models in the evenings with George Bellows, William Glackens, Robert Henri, Stuart Davis, and Man Ray. Henri took him to see the influential Armory Show in 1913.

In 1917 he joined the Sunday section of the *New York Tribune*; he was fired two years later for sympathizing too much with the victims he was assigned to cover. He contributed cartoons to many publications, some of them leftist in orientation, some of them mainstream. In 1919 he worked anonymously for *The Rebel Worker*, and in 1921 openly for *Revolutionary Age*, then for the *New Pioneer* and the *Labor Defender*. Through the years his satiric drawings, lambasting greedy, hoarding capitalists and cruel, irresponsible militarists, appeared in the *Nation*, *Dial*, *Smart Set*, and *New York Post*, the *New Republic*, *Vanity Fair*, *Esquire*, *Fortune*, *Holiday*, and others. His support for socialism and faith in the changes brought on by the Russian Revolution persisted.

In 1924, Gropper married Sophie Frankel, a bacteriologist; they had two children. Two years later, Gropper joined with other artists and writers in publishing *The New Masses*, for which he contributed many caricatures. The next year he visited the Soviet Union with Theodore Dreiser and Sinclair Lewis, and fifty-six of his drawings of the country were published in France in 1929. In 1930 he was a delegate to the Kharkov Conference in the Ukraine.

Among Gropper's political cartoons is one of a huge sheeted phantom brandishing a club in his right hand, a rope in his left, looming over a shouting mob itself and urging it forward like a kind of animus. In *Hunger in Germany* (1936) a cloaked skeleton—a personification of hunger—stands upon a charger ridden by Hitler, who looks back at it, as though to be encouraged. An international situation arose over a cartoon in the August 1935 issue of *Vanity Fair:* in a series of "unlikely historic situations," Hirohito was shown being awarded the Nobel Peace Prize. The Japanese government demanded an apology, which the American government, but not the artist, gave.

Gropper's work brought him awards and some acclaim. In 1936 the Museum of Modern Art in New York City purchased his oil painting *The Senate* (1935). Still one of his most famous pieces, it shows a pot-bellied legislator haranguing within a nearly empty section of the Senate chamber; only three of his colleagues are present, one of whom reads a newspaper while another rests with his hands folded upon his stomach, his feet stretched upon an adjacent chair. In 1937, Gropper traveled to the Dust Bowl in Oklahoma and the Texas Panhandle on a Guggenheim Fellowship. That same year the Metropolitan Museum of Art in New York City purchased *The Hunt* (1937), an oil painting featuring a frightening countryside scene of hunters and dogs.

His art also led to some confrontations. In 1943, after being selected by the War Department Art Advisory Committee to travel to Africa to make a pictorial record of the war, Gropper was denied a passport by the State Department. In 1953, because of his Communist sympathies, he was called before Senator Joseph McCarthy's congressional committee. After refusing to cooperate, he was given no shows in New York City until 1961. His series of fifty lithographs entitled *Caprichos* attacked the hypocrisy and vicious informing that McCarthyism brought on.

In 1947, with other invited artists, Gropper witnessed the unveiling of the Warsaw Ghetto monument. Declaring that "I'm not Jewish in a professional sense but in a human sense," he vowed to paint a picture every year in memory of the fallen instead of lighting a candle as prescribed by Jewish ritual. In the political cartoons there is no overt Jewish subject matter, but the concern for suffering may have been nurtured by the humanism he felt lay at the heart of Judaism. In 1965 he did make five stained-glass windows for Temple Har Zion of River Forest, Ill. The windows, showing stories from Genesis, contain chipped surfaces making for uneven reflections and a richness of surface treatment.

Gropper's figures are almost never reposeful or attractive in a classical sense. His older men are especially repulsive, both morally and physically. His younger men are full of violent rage. Women are shown less frequently; in the 1930's they are portrayed sympathetically—as seamstresses, for instance—while in his later work they become gaudy tourists and heavily made-up dates for old men. For Gropper, the world emerging after the horrors of World War II was not attractive, characterized by the rough capitalist system's victimizers and their victims, who do not fight back but simply go on with their suffering. In the end, it seems a world without hope.

Gropper could see little that was cheerful or uplifting. Such an all-encompassing view was skewed. But there was much accuracy in his revelations of the suffering endured by the afflicted and the dehumanizing qualities taken on by their tormentors. With Ben Shahn, Jacob Lawrence, Philip Evergood, and Jack Levine, he was a major social realist artist who used his art as an expression of outrage and as a weapon to change things for the better.

[See August L. Freundlich, *William Gropper: Retrospective* (1968); and Louis Lozowick, *William Gropper* (1983). An obituary is in the *New York Times*, Jan. 8, 1977.]

Abraham A. Davidson

GUGGENHEIM, MARGUERITE ("PEGGY") (Aug. 26, 1898–Dec. 23, 1979), patron and collector of modern art, was born into a prominent New York City family. Her mother, the former Florette Seligman, was the daughter of James Seligman, a powerful banker; her father, Benjamin Guggenheim, was the fifth son of Meyer Guggenheim, whose vast smelting and mining concern brought him one of the greatest fortunes in American history.

Guggenheim passed what she described as a miserable childhood. Educated mainly by governesses, she spent little time with her parents. Her father died in the sinking of the *Titanic* in 1912. He left less money than expected, so his widow and three daughters were forced to live less extravagantly, a change that gave Guggenheim a feeling of inferiority to her Guggenheim cousins that was to last all her life. After two years at the Jacoby School in New York City, her first real contact with girls her own age, Guggenheim graduated in 1915. She made her debut in 1916 and then took two short-lived jobs—helping new military officers buy uniforms, and as a receptionist and assistant for a dentist. More successful was her stint as clerk at the Sunwise Turn Bookshop, where she met a number of writers and intellectuals, including her future husband, Laurence Vail.

In 1920 she moved to Paris, where she was exposed to the ideas and people who would most shape her. She married the writer Laurence Vail—considered the "King of Bohemia"—in 1922; they had two children. The marriage proved tempestuous, however, and she left Vail for another writer, John Holms, in 1928 before divorcing Vail in 1930. Holms was perhaps her greatest love, but the affair was ended by his death in 1934. After an affair with a political radical named Douglas Garman, Guggenheim decided to open a gallery in London (she had moved to England in 1932). She knew little about art but was educated by Marcel Duchamp, who introduced her to the major surrealist artists. The gallery, which she named Guggenheim Jeune, opened with a Jean Cocteau show in 1938; shows of works by Wassily Kandinsky and of many other avant-garde artists followed. Although the gallery was successful in terms of publicity, it lost a great deal of money, so Guggenheim closed it to start a museum—still a money-losing venture but a more worthwhile one, she felt. These plans came to a halt with the advent of World War II.

Guggenheim, who had returned to France in the summer of 1939, decided to buy all the art she could, and with the guidance of a California dealer named Howard Putzel, set about purchasing "a picture a day." At a time when most people were thinking of little else than leaving Paris in the face of German danger, she bought two Constantin Brancusis, a René Magritte, an Alberto Giacommetti, a Georges Braque, and numerous other works, all at excellent prices because of the threatening political situation. Guggenheim finally had her collection shipped from Paris and then left on June 11, 1940, three days before the city's fall. After a year in Vichy France, Guggenheim and her family—including Vail, Vail's wife Kay Boyle, and their children—fled Europe for the safety of the United States, arriving on July 14, 1941. Max Ernst, with whom she had begun an affair, traveled with them and the couple married in December 1941. They were divorced in 1946, although their marriage had effectively disintegrated by 1942.

After she arrived in New York, Guggenheim began the hard work of establishing her gallery. She found a space, engaged the Viennese architect Frederick Kiesler to design the interior, and bought even more works of modern art so she could open with the widest possible selection. Her strengths were the pioneering moderns, like Pablo Picasso and Braque, and the surrealists, like Yves Tanguy and André Breton. The October 1942 opening proved a spectacular event, prompting one critic to remark, "My eyes have never bulged further from their sockets than at this show." Art of This Century, as the gallery was called, was indeed remarkably different from any other then in existence, and many of the innovations there, like unframed paintings, would later become standard. Through Art of This Century, Guggenheim established the careers of many young American artists, especially Jackson Pollock, Robert Motherwell, William Baziotes, Mark Rothko, Clyfford Still, and David Hare—the core of the New York school (abstract expressionism). Her role in this new movement was twofold: she and her gallery publicized surrealism, out of which abstract expressionism developed, and she supported its leading artists from the beginning.

Besides running her gallery and leading an exhausting social life, Guggenheim worked on her memoirs, *Out of This Century*, which appeared in 1946. The book was wildly controversial, detailing her affairs and flamboyant lifestyle, and bursting with cutting stories about most of the literati, thinly disguised by pseudonyms. Nevertheless, it was an entertaining and enlightening portrait.

In the summer of 1946, Guggenheim returned to Europe and decided to move permanently to Venice. After a closing exhibit at Art of This Century in May 1947, she did just that. She was invited to show her collection at the 1948 Venice Biennale, the first since the war, since it was obvious that hers was one of the most important collections of twentieth-century art. This invitation, the first official recognition of her achievement, was especially gratifying.

In 1949, Guggenheim bought an eighteenth-century palazzo on the Grand Canal in Venice that became her home and permanent exhibit-place. It opened to the public in 1951 and now houses her collection under the auspices of the Solomon R. Guggenheim Foundation in New York. (Solomon was her uncle.) Guggenheim lived happily there, watching her museum become one of Venice's top tourist attractions. She traveled, continued to collect, and wrote another book that picked up where *Out of This Century* left off. Published in 1960, *Confessions of an Art Addict* was less outrageous than her earlier memoir and did not stir up as much controversy. Guggenheim died in Padua, Italy. Her collection, which she had bought for $250,000, was worth over $40 million.

Guggenheim's contribution to modern art remains debatable. Some critics belittle her role, noting that she collected not solely on the basis of her own taste and instincts but on the advice of others. Many of her contemporaries disliked her on account of her miserliness and abrasiveness. Paradoxically, she could be generous—she supported many artists through stipends, for instance—and absolutely charming. What cannot be debated is the support she provided for young artists, and her ability to learn from others in developing her taste and thus amassing her formidable collection.

[Guggenheim's two books were published together as *Out of This Century: Confessions of an Art Addict* (1979). See also Angelica Zinder Rudenstine, *Peggy Guggenheim Collection, Venice: The Solomon R. Guggenheim Foundation* (1985); and Jacqueline Bograd Weld, *Peggy: The Wayward Guggenheim* (1986). An obituary is in the *New York Times*, Dec. 24, 1979.]

SARAH MCBRIDE

H

HAAGEN-SMIT, ARIE JAN (Dec. 22, 1900–Mar. 17, 1977), biochemist and educator, was born in Utrecht, the Netherlands, the son of Jan Willem Adrianus Haagen-Smit, a chemist, and Maria Geertruida van Maanen. He received his B.A. (1922), M.A. (1926), and Ph.D. (1929) from the University of Utrecht. Haagen-Smit married Petronella Francina Pennings in 1930; they had one child. His wife died in 1933, and on June 10, 1935, he married Maria Wilhelmina Bloemers; they had three children.

In 1929, Haagen-Smit began his career as chief assistant in organic chemistry at the University of Utrecht, serving there until 1936, when he came to the United States to lecture in biochemistry, at Harvard University. The next year he became associate professor of biochemistry at California Institute of Technology. He was promoted to professor of bio-organic chemistry in 1940, and in 1965 he became director of the plant environmental laboratory. He retired in 1971.

Haagen-Smit's early work extended his doctoral research on plant hormones, and while at Utrecht, he synthesized some naturally occurring plant hormones. He continued this work in California, and in 1944 he received a patent for a synthetic hormone that aided the body in healing wounds. Two years later he patented another hormone that helped in the healing of wounds in plants.

During the 1940's, Haagen-Smit became interested in the structure and usefulness of essential oils in plants. He analyzed the flavors of volatile oils contained in fruits and vegetables and established their chemical structures, work valuable to the food industry that brought him the 1949 Fritzsche Award of the American Chemical Society. Later research led to discoveries useful in industry and medicine. The development of paint products resulted from his study of oil of turpentine, for example.

Haagen-Smit's interest in the usefulness of plant compounds prompted a study of alkaloids found in cacti, some of which are effective in treating nervous disorders. During his career he expanded his research to include a variety of plants.

The work that brought Haagen-Smit to public prominence resulted from his residence in southern California. After World War II, Los Angeles began to experience serious air pollution. It was obvious to almost everyone that the smog hanging over the city was more than an aesthetic nuisance; it threatened the health of millions of persons.

While many accepted smog as an inevitable product of industry, the city adopted its first air pollution ordinance in 1946. This measure was ineffectual because it assumed that the easily identified sulfur compounds in the air were the major problem.

In 1949, as a member of the city's air pollution committee, Haagen-Smit accepted the task of determining the composition of the brown haze choking the city. His early studies showed that automobile exhaust was a major contributor, and cleanup measures quickly focused on reducing hydrocarbons. By 1955, Haagen-Smit argued that more efficient combustion in auto engines was insufficient because it would not reduce production of nitrogen oxides, formed when automobile engines heat nitrogen in the air.

By 1958, Haagen-Smit had begun to proclaim the fundamentals of a science of ecology. In *Science* he argued for sweeping conservation measures to control pollution. He warned that the "principal elements" of modern human society (air, water, space, and carbon-based energy) are limited and urged a broad-based response to air pollution including engineers, scientists, economists, and lawyers. He cautioned that the nationwide effort required would cost billions.

Any proposed solutions would need close scrutiny. Although atomic energy provided an alternative energy source, Haagen-Smit expressed serious concerns over the environmental dangers it posed. Pollution control devices on automobiles, touted by some as a panacea, would never be as effective for average drivers as in laboratory tests. To gauge the effects of air pollution on "the average person" was meaningless, he concluded, because the population affected was "so varied in reactions and responses" that the standard must be "the oversensitives—the sick, the young, and the very old."

On a 1959 television program, "The Next Hundred Years," Haagen-Smit explained that civic planning on the broadest scale was necessary. Efforts should be directed toward "creation of more and larger breathing spaces in the form of extensive parks and the complete revision of our thinking on public transportation. Even relocation of industry . . . may be necessary."

Haagen-Smit battled air pollution for the remainder of his career, always attempting to force recognition of its relationship to other problems. He decried the "rapid growth in population and industrial activity, marked by wastefulness of material resources, carelessness in regard to the future, indifference to many things of life, and a blind opposition toward anything that seems to threaten, in even a remote way, that which is termed prosperity."

Haagen-Smit remained optimistic, however. In regard to automobile air pollution, he declared in 1971, "We're so far over the hump I'm beginning to lose interest." While the average citizen did not see any improvement in air quality, Haagen-Smit noted scientific evidence to the contrary. He continued to call for pressure on government and industry to finish the battle, at the same time criticizing those making accusations without scientific evidence.

Widely recognized for his expertise, Haagen-Smit served on committees of the Atomic Energy Commission, the National Institutes of Health, and the National Academy of Sciences. He chaired the California Air Resources Board from 1968 to 1973 and the National Air Quality Criteria Advisory Committee for the Environmental Protection Agency. He was a member of the editorial boards of *Excerpts Medica*, *Atmospheric Environment*, and the Air Pollution Control Association of America.

Haagen-Smit received numerous awards, including the F. A. Chambers Award of the Air Pollution Control Association (1958); the Hodgkins Medal of the Smithsonian Institution; the Cottrell Award of the National Academy of Sciences (1972); the Monsanto Award of the American Chemical Society (1972); the Alice Tyler Ecology Prize (1973); the National Medal of Science (1973); and the Rheinland-Preis für Umweltschutz (1974). He died in Pasadena, Calif.

[Articles by Haagen-Smit include "Smell and Taste," *Scientific American*, Mar. 1952; "Essential Oils," ibid., Aug. 1953; "Air Conservation," *Science*, Oct. 17, 1958; "The Control of Air Pollution," *Scientific American*, Jan. 1964; and "Man and His Home," *Vital Speeches of the Day*, Apr. 28, 1970. Arnold Nicholson, "Los Angeles Battles the Murk," *Saturday Evening Post*, Dec. 19, 1959, recounts Haagen-Smit's first decade of involvement in air pollution control. An obituary is in the *New York Times*, Mar. 19, 1977.]

KEN LUEBBERING

HACKETT, ROBERT LEO ("BOBBY") (Jan. 31, 1915–June 7, 1976), jazz cornetist, was born in Providence, R.I., one of nine children of poor but hardworking parents; his father was a railroad blacksmith. At the age of eight Hackett started playing guitar, ukelele, and banjo, then violin at the age of ten, and finally a cornet purchased at a pawnshop; he was deeply inspired by phonograph records of the jazz trumpeter Louis Armstrong. At fourteen he quit high school after one year to play guitar in an orchestra at a Chinese restaurant in Providence; he later moved on to two large orchestras in the city's two ballrooms. During a one-night performance by Cab Calloway, Hackett sat in on cornet, his first gig on that instrument. After a 1934 summer engagement at a Syracuse, N.Y., hotel with Herbie Marsh's band, mostly on guitar, he went with Payson Ré to Cape Cod, Mass., improving his proficiency on cornet and scoring arrangements with clarinetist Pee Wee Russell. After playing both instruments in various Boston clubs, in 1936 Hackett took over leadership of Marsh's group at the

Theatrical Club, a prominent night spot in that city. He achieved local success, using arrangements by trombonist Brad Gowans.

In 1937, Hackett moved to New York City, where he was heralded by the music critic George Frazier as the successor to the legendary cornetist Bix Beiderbecke, who had died in 1931. By then, Hackett's command of the cornet had matured to a lyrical tone of exceptional clarity and inventiveness that rarely departed from the melody, whether he played "hot" Dixieland-style up-tempo numbers or delicately phrased intimate ballads. Alec Wilder described him as a poet, "never aggressive or noisy; rather . . . tender and witty."

A small man—five feet, four and a half inches and 125 pounds—who wore a thin mustache, he rarely had the power to hit high notes, but his warm style of playing reflected his personality. These musical attributes soon became apparent in performances with several society bands and in small jazz recording combos accompanying singers, notably Red McKenzie, Dick Robertson, and the Andrews Sisters—especially on their first hit recording, "Bei Mir Bist Du Schoen." In October 1937, Hackett joined Joe Marsala's hot jazz band as guitarist at the Hickory House but was already jamming on cornet with the Chicago-style jazzmen centered around impresario-guitarist Eddie Condon. The same year, he married his childhood sweetheart, named Edna; they had two children. Their son became a jazz drummer.

Bandleader Benny Goodman enlisted Hackett to play a delicate cornet rendition of Bix Beiderbecke's 1927 solo on "I'm Coming Virginia" at Goodman's epic Carnegie Hall concert on Jan. 16, 1938. After the concert, Hackett joined several Condon men to cut five tunes at the Brunswick studios. Released on the Commodore Record Shop label as the first independently made jazz records, they immediately introduced the listening public to freewheeling hot jazz in the Condon style; Hackett's solo on "Ja-da" brought him acclaim. These two performances established his reputation, and later that year he was hired to lead one of two jazz bands at Nick's night spot in Greenwich Village in New York City. He signed a recording contract for Vocalion with his own group but also was a prominent soloist on recordings of groups led by Condon, saxophonist Bud Freeman, and pianist Teddy Wilson. He backed vocalists Billie Holiday and Maxine Sullivan on records and became a fixture at Sunday afternoon jam sessions at Jimmy Ryan's on Fifty-second Street ("Swing Street").

Hackett formed a fourteen-piece swing band early in 1939, using arrangements by Buck Ram. It folded six months later, after having made only a few recordings. Deeply in debt, he joined Horace Heidt and His Musical Knights in September 1939, arranging, playing third trumpet, and providing cornet solos that gave the Heidt band a swinging quality it had previously lacked. In 1940 he provided the trumpet solos acted out by Fred Astaire in the film *Second Chorus* and resumed leading the band at Nick's. Dental surgery forced Hackett to curtail his horn blowing, whereupon Glenn Miller hired him as his big-band guitarist in July 1941. Though Miller had him purchase an electric guitar, he never plugged in the amplifier and was rarely audible. As his gums healed, however, Hackett played gorgeously lyrical cornet solos on several ballads of the Miller band, notably "Serenade in Blue" and "Rhapsody in Blue" but especially his famous twelve-bar solo on the medium-tempo "String of Pearls." During the orchestra's appearances, Hackett played soft jazz for dinner engagements and late-evening duets with trombonist Miller at dances; over the winter of 1941–1942 he rotated between guitar and the trumpet section. While too weak in the latter role, he nevertheless occupied the fourth trumpet chair during the last ten days of the Miller band's existence in September 1942.

Hackett joined NBC as a staff musician, toured with the dancer Katherine Dunham's revue in 1944, performed regularly at the Eddie Condon Town Hall concerts for the Armed Forces Radio Service in 1944 and 1945, and played lush obbligatos behind the singer Lee Wiley in several albums. During two years with Glen Gray and the Casa Loma Orchestra (1944–1946), he stopped his alcoholic drinking, and in 1946 he began a fifteen-year association with the ABC musical staff. Hackett, who had always idolized Louis Armstrong, provided background fills during Armstrong's band concerts and followed his advice to switch from cornet to trumpet. In 1951 he organized a studio orchestra of mostly strings, featuring himself on trumpet, for six romantic mood-music albums produced by Jackie Gleason. During the 1950's and 1960's he continued to record jazz under his own name; performed in concerts, on television, and at the Newport Jazz Festival; and toured with Jack Teagarden, Benny Goodman, and Tony Bennett. Ever versatile, he performed in a stunning session with bop trumpeter Dizzy Gillespie in 1971, the year he moved from the borough of Queens in New York City to West Chatham, Mass., on Cape Cod. There he played mostly locally, recording briefly under his own label, Hyannisport Records. He died in West Chatham.

A major force during the golden age of swinging and melodic jazz, Hackett has been characterized as the perfect blend of Armstrong and Beiderbecke, with his own unique technique. Ever a gentle man, he was reputed never to have said anything critical about anyone. Once pressed to comment on Adolf Hitler, he observed in typically subtle jazz humor that Hitler was at least "the best in his field."

[Published interviews with Hackett are in Whitney Balliett, *American Musicians* (1986); and John E. Heaney, "Jazz at the Overseas Press Club," *International Association of Jazz Record Collectors Journal*, Apr. 1989. His "hot" jazz life is illustrated in Eddie Condon and Hank O'Neal, *The Eddie Condon Scrapbook of Jazz* (1973). His work with the Miller band is covered in George T. Simon, *Glenn Miller and His Orchestra* (1974); and John Flower, *Moonlight Serenade* (1972). A sampling of the best Hackett LPs includes *The Hackett Horn* (Columbia JEE 22003); *The Commodore Years: Eddie Condon and Bud Freeman* (Atlantic SD2-309); *Glenn Miller: A Legendary Performer* (RCA CPM2-0693); *Night in Manhattan*, with Lee Wiley (Columbia JCL 656); *Jazz Session* (Columbia CL 6156); *Giants: Bobby Hackett, Dizzy Gillespie, Mary Lou Williams* (Perception PLP 19); and on several Eddie Condon Armed Forces Radio Service concert albums (Jazum). He may be seen on videotape leading a sextet on "Goodyear Jazz Concert" (1961). An obituary is in the *New York Times*, June 8, 1976.]

CLARK G. REYNOLDS

HALEY, JACK (Aug. 10, 1899–June 6, 1979), actor, was born John Haley in South Boston, Mass., to John Joseph Haley, a navigator, and Ellen F. Curley, a homemaker. Ellen Haley raised her two sons alone on a limited income after John Haley's death when the boys were young. Jack Haley was educated at Dwight Grammar School, where he gave the class address, and at Boston English High School. Rejecting his mother's wish that he become an electrician, he left home and a $15-per-week job as an apprentice electrician to pursue his dream of becoming an actor. "I ran away to New York," he later recalled, "to escape the jeers that everyone directed at my plans for a stage career."

Haley quickly moved on to Philadelphia, which offered more opportunities for an inexperienced actor than New York. There he found employment as a song plugger for the McCarthy Fisher Music Publishing Company. After Haley had worked for the company several months, the leader of an all-woman vaudeville act called at McCarthy Fisher in search of a light comic to front the act. Haley volunteered, and his show business career was on its way.

Haley quickly rose through the vaudeville hierarchy, moving from his first job with "The Lightner Girls and Alexander" to a song-and-dance comedy routine with a partner, Charley Crafts. In 1920, "Haley and Crafts" reached the pinnacle of vaudeville success, with a showcase performance at the famed Palace Theater in New York City, which ran for a record six months. After three years, Haley felt he was ready to move up to Broadway, and through his contacts on the vaudeville circuit was given a role in *Around the Town*, a revue put together by S. J. Perelman and Herman Mankiewicz. For the next ten years, Haley rarely had to go looking for work. Indeed, he was so busy that his marriage to Florence McFadden, a former Lightner dancer, took place on Feb. 25, 1921, between the matinee and the night show of *Gay Paree*, in which they both appeared. "No honeymoon," Haley later recalled. "After all, the show must go on . . . and on and on." The couple had two children in a marriage that lasted until Haley's death.

After *Gay Paree*, the Haleys worked with various traveling vaudeville troupes for several years. On their first trip to southern California, they fell in love with Los Angeles, and Jack Haley accepted a job as master of ceremonies at a theater in that city. He also appeared in a number of short films. In 1928, Haley gave up his steady work in Los Angeles for the lead in the traveling revue, *Good News*, in the hope that it would lead to bigger things.

Haley was soon offered the lead in the Broadway musical revue *Follow Thru* (1929), which provided him with his first big break. The show, which featured Haley mugging through a song-and-dance romp, "Button Up Your Overcoat," received ecstatic critical and popular acclaim. The *New York Times* asked why the heretofore unnoticed Haley, with "his capacities being what they evidently are, had not been fought for by Broadway musical comedy producers."

Broadway, however, still wasn't ready to sign on to the Haley admiration society. He had to stitch together a number of appearances in vaudeville, theater, and movie shorts before his next big success, the Broadway review *Take a Chance* (1932). Hollywood took some time to notice as well, even though he stole the film version of *Follow Thru* (1930) from matinee idol Charles Rogers. The *New York Times* noted, "Without [Haley] it would be just so many scenes of [Nancy] Carroll looking lovingly into the romantic eyes of Charles Rogers." After *Take a Chance*, however, Hollywood finally came calling, and Twentieth Century–Fox offered Haley a contract.

During the 1930's, Haley generally took the lead or second role in a series of lighthearted frolics that usually served as excuses for numerous song-and-dance routines. In *Sitting Pretty* (1933), *The Girl Friend* (1935), and *Pigskin Parade* (1936), Judy Garland's first feature film, Haley excelled at mixing hilarious slapstick, quick patter, and limber-limbed dance moves to drive the generally ridiculous plots. Even in truly inept films such as *Coronado* (1935), Haley received positive notices. His standout performance during this period was in *Wake Up and Live* (1937), a Darryl Zanuck–produced extravaganza costarring Patsy Kelly and Alice Faye, who often shared the screen with Haley.

These assignments would have made Haley a minor, if much beloved, Hollywood song-and-dance man if not for a peculiar twist of fate. Just as Metro-Goldwyn-Mayer was about to begin filming its mammoth movie version of Frank Baum's *The Wizard of Oz* (1939), Buddy Ebsen, picked to play the Tin Man, suffered an allergic reaction to the silver makeup the character required. Haley was given the part instead, and thus backed into a role that turned him into an American icon. At first, however, Haley was not sure it was worth it. "The costume was agony," he later recalled of the tin armor he was asked to clank around in. "When I wasn't working, I was on a reclining board. The only chance I had all day to get out of that costume was when Judy [Garland] was at school."

The addition of Haley was a happy one, for the three principals who played opposite Garland's Dorothy—Ray Bolger as the Scarecrow, Bert Lahr as the Cowardly Lion, and Haley—were all seasoned vaudevillians. Each contributed a bit of vaudeville to their performance, seemingly trying to outdo one another in each scene. Perhaps Haley's most memorable bit was his frantic waving back and forth as his cohorts loosened his rusted joints with the Tin Man's indispensable oil can. Although the film has been justifiably praised for its brilliant sound and visual effects and for its wonderful songs, it is Dorothy's relationship with her three escorts that bonds the audience with the story. The movie was a huge success at the box office, enjoying numerous releases. In 1976, CBS began showing the film on television, a yearly event that brought together many families in a ritualistic viewing experience. Once the film was released, Haley was no longer simply a song-and-dance man, he was the Tin Man.

Despite the acclaim, Haley did not receive a great upsurge in offers. After some respectable showings in *Moon Over Miami* (1941) with Don Ameche and Betty Grable, and *People Are Funny* (1945), among others, Haley realized that the era in which his talents could be appreciated on film had passed. He retired from acting in 1949, without regrets. "It's like being a washed-up fighter," he later explained. "He can go on kidding himself, taking one more fight getting hurt. Or he can move on." Rather than take on minor roles in inferior films, Haley focused his energy on real estate, in which he had been investing since the mid-1930's. Haley made a lot of money on these ventures, remarking, "A man had to be an idiot not to succeed in buying, selling and developing land in Southern California over the years." Jack Benny was more impressed, commenting, "Every time you drive down Wilshire Boulevard, you're trespassing on Jack Haley's property."

In addition to his real estate interests, Haley dedicated his time to charitable causes, most notably the American Guild of Variety Artists, of which he served as president. His biggest project with the guild was to set up a fund for old vaudevillians who "never had the breaks I've had." In 1969 he made a cameo appearance in *Norwood*, directed by his son Jack Haley, Jr., who became head of Twentieth Century–Fox. Just before his death of a heart attack in Beverly Hills, Haley reunited with Ray Bolger to present an Oscar at the 1979 Academy Awards ceremony, produced by his son.

[The Academy of Motion Pictures Library in Los Angeles maintains a substantial file on Haley. See Douglas McClelland, *Down the Yellow Brick Road: The Making of the Wizard of Oz* (1989). An obituary is in the *New York Times*, June 7, 1979.]

MICHAEL GOLDBERG

HALL, LEONARD WOOD (Oct. 2, 1900–June 2, 1979), politician, was born at Sagamore Hill in Oyster Bay, N.Y., to Franklyn Herbert Hall, a coachman at the estate of Theodore Roosevelt, and Mary Garvin. His father became chief messenger and eventually White House librarian after Roosevelt became president. Hall was named after General Leonard Wood, a friend of Roosevelt's; his godmother was Ethel Roosevelt Derby, one of Theodore Roosevelt's daughters.

After a public school education, Hall attended Georgetown University, earning an LL.B. degree from the law school in 1920. He was admitted to the New York bar in 1921, and he began an active law practice in New York City. His political career started in 1926, when he became a Republican campaign worker. The next year he was elected to the New York State Assembly, serving for two years, until he became Nassau County sheriff.

On May 10, 1934, Hall married Gladys Dowsey, who had two children from a previous marriage. That same year, he returned to the assembly and served until 1938, when the death of their candidate for the House of Representatives forced the Republicans to choose a new candidate only days before the election. Hall was selected and won the election, beginning a fourteen-year career in Congress.

Hall's congressional style was one of staying behind the scenes, getting things done in committee work. In 1941 he was elected chairman of the Republican Congressional Campaign Committee, a post he held for a decade. Other committee assignments included seats on the Select Committee to Investigate and Study Problems of Small Business; the Coinage, Weights, and Measures Committee; and the Rivers and Harbors Committee.

In April 1945, Hall traveled to Europe to inspect the Buchenwald concentration camp. This was one of many trips that he took to get firsthand information. The next month he spoke out to have Germans prosecuted for war crimes. In 1947, while acting as chairman of the House Interstate and Foreign Commerce Committee, Hall went to Europe with other congressmen to investigate problems with facilities that supported American air carriers. In 1951 he and Congressman Joseph Martin, Jr., of Massachusetts made a long tour of world trouble spots at their own expense. When they returned, they urged the American government to support the Nationalist Chinese government of Generalissimo Chiang Kai-shek to counter Chinese Communist expansion.

Hall did not run for reelection in 1952. At his wife's urging, he returned to Long Island to run for surrogate of Nassau County, a high judicial post. During this time, Hall was an insider in Dwight Eisenhower's campaign for the presidency. At one point, when there were questions about Richard Nixon's campaign finances, Hall acted as an intermediary to try to persuade Nixon to resign from the ticket; Nixon's famous "Checkers" speech in his defense was so effective, however, that this initiative was dropped.

Hall won his election but found almost immediately that he did not want to be a judge. Early in 1953 he found a way out when the position of chairman of the Republican National Committee became vacant. Hall, supported by President Eisenhower and Governor Thomas Dewey of New York, won the post easily. His judicial career had lasted less than four months.

Hall's four years as party chairman turned out to be the capstone of his political career. The six-foot, two-inch politician had a genial and gregarious political style, a vast memory for names, and an enormous repertoire of jokes. One of his hobbies was rewriting popular songs and adding humorous lyrics.

Hall's most important task as chairman was to organize Eisenhower's campaign for reelection in 1956. This was complicated in 1955, when the president suffered a major heart attack. There was widespread doubt that Eisenhower would be healthy enough to survive a second term. Hall organized speaking engagements for the president that helped dispel doubts. While he was active in convincing the country that Eisenhower should return to the White House, he also had to convince the president himself that a second term was a good idea. Once again, Hall was involved in an effort to remove Richard Nixon from the ticket, and once again the effort was quietly dropped.

In 1956, Hall bought a large house in Locust Valley, N.Y., six miles from the Roosevelt estate where he was born. After Eisenhower was reelected, Hall retired from his party position and became a permanent resident of Long Island.

Although he had a successful law practice in New York, Hall was not ready to leave politics. In 1958 he sought the nomination for governor of New York, and he seemed certain to win it. However, at the last minute, Nelson A. Rockefeller entered the race, and won. It was the first election that Hall ever lost. Late in 1958, Hall became campaign chairman of Richard Nixon's bid for the presidency. This aligned him against Rockefeller, who was also expected to run in 1960. In an interview made during the Nixon administration's final days, Hall said that of the seven presidents he had known, Nixon was the hardest working.

In 1965, Hall became chairman of the newly formed Nassau-Suffolk Regional Planning Board on Long Island. He served as chairman for ten years. After backing George Romney early in the 1968 Republican presidential race, Hall became a floor manager for Nelson Rockefeller at the national convention. That was the last convention in which he played a significant role. At the time of his death he was listed as a member of the steering committee for John Connally's 1980 presidential run.

Hall died in Glen Cove, N.Y., a few miles from his birthplace. His collection of hundreds of toy elephants was donated to the Nassau County Museum.

[A substantial file on Hall is at the Nassau County Museum Long Island Studies Institute at Hofstra University in Hempstead, N.Y. An obituary is in the *New York Times*, June 3, 1979.]

TERRY BALLARD

HALL, PAUL (Aug. 20, 1914–June 22, 1980), labor leader, was born in a small town near Birmingham, Ala., the son of Robert R. Hall, general chairman of the Brotherhood of Locomotive Engineers, and Minnie B. Discher. His father died when Paul was twelve years old. The impoverished family moved to Tampa, Fla., to live with relatives. Pride impelled Hall to leave school and seek work wherever he could find it. At the age of fifteen he became a professional prizefighter. As a middleweight he had seventy-five fights, with middling success, for small purses.

Still in his teens, Hall went to sea, sailing in the steward department before finding his permanent rating in the engineering department. As a professional seaman, he made numerous voyages before and during World War II, some of them in submarine-infested waters. He was active as a rank-and-file member of the Seafarers International Union (SIU) from its creation in 1938 as a successor to the ineffective and corrupt International Seamen's Union (ISU). In 1944, at the age of twenty-nine, he won his first union election as a dispatcher in Baltimore.

Within two years, Hall became the dominant figure of the SIU's autonomous Atlantic and Gulf Coast district, in effect leading his own national union. This was the result of his triumph in organizing the workforce of the Isthmian Fleet, a subsidiary of U.S. Steel, which was the largest shipping company in the world.

Hall married Margaret Rogers in February 1943 and divorced her in October 1948. He then married Rose Siegel Eldridge in 1950; they had two children.

With the death in 1957 of the legendary Harry Lundeberg, first president of the SIU and successor to Andrew Furuseth, who had assumed the ISU presidency in 1890, Hall became president of the SIU. Despite the smallness of its membership—the total number of AFL-organized seamen rarely exceeded 100,000 and after World War II was usually below 40,000—the head of the SIU played a major role within organized labor. Hall became the AFL-CIO's senior vice-president, chairman of its most important committees, and president of the AFL-CIO's Maritime Trades Department. The AFL-CIO, whose 8.5 million members made it the second-largest federation of unions in the world, provided unstinting and indispensable support for the maritime industry throughout Hall's lifetime.

Hall's life as a union leader was dominated by his conviction of the decline of American-flag shipping and the extreme importance of federal legislation to the maritime industry's survival. After taking control of his international union, Hall emerged as an Olympian figure in the industry, speaking not only for the seamen but also for shipowners and the shipbuilders. His major antagonists were the American oil companies with their foreign-flag tankers and farm groups with their focus on farm exports. In the face of higher manning costs and the desire to protect national interests, the Maritime Trades Department's foes came to include such unlikely allies as the State Department and the Defense Department, and Common Cause and Ralph Nader.

With exceptional deftness, Hall for nearly twenty years was able not only to hold off his formidable antagonists' efforts to modify or end favorable maritime legislation but also to achieve new beneficial laws, most notably the 1970 Merchant Marine Act. His greatest defeat was President Gerald Ford's veto in 1974 of the oil cargo preference bill, which would have preserved seamen's jobs and the nation's ability to meet its maritime needs for the foreseeable future. Because President Ford was a personal friend, a lifelong supporter of the SIU, and a beneficiary of the union's political funds, the veto was a crushing and unexpected blow.

Central to the SIU's political power was its Political Action Committee, which for years had collected and dispensed more money than any other American labor union. A left-handed compliment to the union's political effectiveness was a federal indictment of its entire executive board, including Hall, in 1970 for allegedly violating the Corrupt Practices Act. The gist of the charge was that seamen were coerced into making contributions for political action. The court two years later dismissed the indictment because of the delay in bringing the case to trial. Despite this outcome, the financial and human cost of the indictment was huge. Prior to its end, Hall suffered a serious heart attack; the union's secretary-treasurer and second in command died of heart attack.

The most colorful episodes of Hall's career involved his assistance to fellow unionists. Time and again unions in trouble turned to Hall for help, which always included his advice on tactics and strategy. A surprising number of unions, some of which were far larger than the SIU, were unable to plan an effective campaign or even to organize picket lines without his aid. The SIU freely gave substantial gifts and loans to hard-pressed organizations and, when needed, hundreds of seamen volunteered to participate in other unions' strike activities. A partial list of beneficiaries includes the Office Employees Union in its 1947 Wall Street strike, the International Ladies' Garment Workers' Union in its general strike of 1958, the American Federation of State, County and Municipal Employees Union in its organizational efforts in New York City and elsewhere in the mid-1960's, the Amalgamated Clothing Workers' difficulties in Canada, and César Chávez's organizational work in the 1970's.

As a close colleague of George Meany, Hall took on assignments that much larger unions shunned. When some Teamster locals disaffiliated from their International in the early 1960's and searched for an organizational home, Teamster leader Jimmy Hoffa succeeded in cowing nearly all of the labor movement into refusing them through a threat of retaliation. The SIU took Hoffa on, and battle was joined in half a dozen states and Puerto Rico between the 2 million Teamsters and the SIU, one-twentieth its size. The spectacular battle ended with the SIU's representing thousands of cab drivers in Chicago and former Teamsters in other places.

Hall was a closet intellectual, a voracious reader who had painfully educated himself during his early years of union office. Although a native southerner, he opposed Jim Crow laws and integrated his union in 1950. As he grew older, he took increasing pride in the SIU training school in Piney Point, Md. In a declining industry whose existence depended on his political skills, Hall preached that it was essential to have available an adequate number of trained new seamen and upgraded professional sailors. During the last ten years of his life, about one thousand recruits were trained each year for entry-level jobs, most of them dropouts from Appalachia or urban ghettoes.

One episode demonstrating Hall's influence is revealing. In the fall of 1975, during the New York City financial crisis, Governor Hugh Carey of New York State was unable to meet with President Ford. In Hall's Washington office, he vented his frustration at having a financial plan to save his state and being unable to do anything about it. Within minutes, Hall had the president on the telephone and arranged an appointment for the governor with Ford.

President Jimmy Carter, out of the country when Hall died in New York City, sent Vice-President Walter Mondale to speak at his funeral. Other eulogies were delivered by Governor Carey and Lane Kirkland, president of the AFL-CIO.

[No biography has been published, but some information is in Walter Sheridan, *The Fall and Rise of Jimmy Hoffa* (1972); Richard Billings and John Greenya, *Power to the Public Worker* (1974); Gerald R. Ford, *A Time to Heal* (1979); and Jewell and

Bernard Bellush, *Union Power and New York* (1984). An obituary is in the *New York Times*, June 24, 1980.]

PHILIP ROSS

HALSMAN, PHILIPPE (May 2, 1906–June 25, 1979), portrait photographer and writer, was born in Riga, Latvia, the son of Max Halsman, a dentist, and Ita Grintuch, a school principal. He became interested in photography at age fifteen, when he discovered an old view camera with glass plates in an attic, bought a book on how to use it, and began photographing anyone who would let him. After graduating from the Vidus Vacu Skola in Riga in 1924 with a B.A. degree, he continued his studies in Dresden, Germany, at the Technische Hochschule, majoring in electrical engineering. In 1928, his last year, realizing that he was not happy with engineering, he dropped out, although his grades were good. He then worked briefly for the publishing firm of Ullstein in Berlin.

While visiting Paris in 1930 to attend the wedding of his sister, Liouba, Halsman decided to remain; he took courses in art and philosophy at the Sorbonne. While photographing his fellow students and helping with photography assignments, he decided that this was his calling and set himself up as a professional photographer. Completely self-taught, and not caring for the diffused French style of photography, he developed his own, characterized by sharpness of image. For the next eight or nine years he worked in Paris as a fashion and portrait photographer, photographing such famous people as André Gide and Jean Giraudoux, and working for *Paris Vogue*, *Vu*, and *Voilà*. While photographing Gide, he invented the four-by-five-inch Halsman-Fairchild twin reflex camera (never commercially produced) because his own camera did not work fast enough to catch the subject's expression.

On Apr. 1, 1937, Halsman married Yvonne Moser, formerly his assistant; they had two children. In 1940, when Germany invaded France, he escaped to the United States with an emergency visa arranged by Albert Einstein. Unknown in the United States, he worked under contract with the Black Star photographic agency in New York City, barely earning enough to make ends meet. The turning point came when Halsman met Connie Ford, a model, and photographed her on a paper American flag. The photograph was bought by the cosmetics manufacturer Elizabeth Arden for an advertisement, and it won the Art Directors Club medal. Many assignments followed, and in 1942 he did the first of his 101 covers for *Life* magazine. In 1944 he was elected the first president of the American Society of Magazine Photographers, an honor repeated in 1954.

In 1949, the year he was naturalized as an American citizen, Halsman published his first book, *The Frenchman, a Photographic Interview*, with French comedian Fernandel; the photo captions, in the form of questions, were answered by the expression on the subject's face. This started a new trend in photography books and was widely copied. Other books followed: in 1953, *Piccoli*, a children's book written for his daughters; in 1954, *Dali's Mustache*, and in 1959, his famous *Jump Book*. This was a compilation of photographs of celebrities he had asked to jump during their sittings, to enable them to lose their inhibitions and drop their "masks." He called this his "science of jumpology."

Halsman worked in New York City as a free-lance photographer. Magazine assignments included commissions by *Life* in 1956 to find and photograph the world's most beautiful girls, by *Picture Post* of England in 1955 to photograph the world's foremost political and social figures, and by *Time* in 1962 to photograph "Reigning Beauties," the most beautiful queens and wives of presidents. His photographs also appeared regularly in *Saturday Evening Post* and *Look*. Among the subjects of his portraits were Winston Churchill, Dwight Eisenhower, Eleanor Roosevelt, Marilyn Monroe, and the Duke and Duchess of Windsor. His portraits of Albert Einstein, John Steinbeck, and Adlai Stevenson have appeared on American postage stamps; that of André Gide, on a French stamp.

Halsman's distinctive style is full of insight. He believed that a photographer must catch the essence of the subject; otherwise it is only an empty likeness. To reveal the interior person, one should talk to the subject and gain his or her confidence. Psychology and conversation are more important than technical expertise. Nevertheless, Halsman was a master of technique, innovative in lighting and composition, and possessed of impeccable timing. He often used props or manipulated photographs to achieve the desired effect. The most famous example of this is Salvador Dali suspended in midair, with furniture and cats.

Halsman was a member of the guiding faculty of the Famous Photographers School in Westport, Conn. (1963–1979); he taught a class on psychological portraiture at the New School for Social Research in New York City (1971–1979); and he was a professional lecturer (1967–1979).

Halsman was chosen one of the ten greatest photographers in a *Popular Photography* international poll taken in 1958. He received the Newhouse Citation of the Syracuse University school of journalism in 1963, the Golden Plate Award of Academic Achievement in 1967, and the American Society of Magazine Photographers Life Achievement award in 1975.

Halsman exhibited throughout the United States, and in Paris, London, and Tokyo. A major retrospective of his work was being held at the International Center of Photography in New York City at the time of his death. His photographs are held in the collections of the International Center of Photography, the *Life* Picture Collection, the Metropolitan Museum of Art, and the Museum of Modern Art in New York City; the Library of Congress and the Smithsonian Institution in Washington, D.C.; the New Orleans Museum of Art; and the Royal Photography Society in England.

Halsman, urbane and witty, was a superb raconteur. His playfulness and humor were evident in everything he did. His standards were high, yet he had inexhaustible patience and was noted for his kindness and generosity. He described himself as a happy pessimist. Halsman had brown eyes and black hair; was five feet, nine inches, tall; and weighed about 160 pounds. He died in New York City.

[Files in the International Center of Photography and the Museum of Modern Art contain magazine and newspaper clippings, transcripts of Halsman's lectures, exhibition notices, and examples of his greeting cards. Books not cited in the text are *Philippe Halsman on the Creation of Photographic Ideas* (1961); *Halsman on Sight and Insight* (1972); and Cornell Capa and Robert Walker, eds., *Halsman 1979* (1979), published to accompany the exhibition at the International Center of Photography. Halsman's articles include "People I've Shot," *American Magazine and Historical Chronicle* (1953); and "Philippe Halsman on Psychological Portraiture," *Popular Photography*, Dec. 1958. Two books by his wife, Yvonne Halsman, *Portraits* (1983) and *Halsman at Work* (1989), survey his work and contributions to photography. An interview with Ruth Spencer appears in the *British Journal of Photography*, Oct. 10, 1975. Obituaries are in the *New York Times*, June 26, 1979; and *Camera*, Oct. 1979.]

PAT BRAUCH

HAMER, FANNIE LOU (Oct. 6, 1917–Mar. 14, 1977), civil rights activist, was born in Montgomery County, Miss., the last of twenty children born to Lou Ella and Jim Townsend, who were sharecroppers. When she was two years old, the family moved to Sunflower County in hopes of economic improvement. Her father risked all he had to rent some land and purchase three mules, two cows, and some farm tools. The family made economic progress, but a neighboring white farmer poisoned their stock and forced them back to the dependency of sharecropping.

It was a hard life. The children, including Fannie Lou, had to drop out of school early to work in the fields. After completing their regular work, their mother would take the children from field to field "scrapping," taking what little cotton was left after the first picking. Eventually they would find enough to make a bale. Many times, the only food was cornmeal, an onion, or some flour gravy. Rags tied around their feet served as shoes, and clothes were repeatedly patched to make them serviceable. As a child, Fannie Lou wished she were white, but her mother repeatedly scolded her to be proud of who she was.

Hamer married Perry ("Pap") Hamer, a tractor driver, in 1944; they had two children. They worked on a white man's plantation, he a plower and she a field worker, a timekeeper (a recorder of workers' productivity), and the owner's house cleaner. They lived in a small house with cold running water but no working inside toilet. The owner refused to repair the broken fixture because he said the Hamers did not need one.

For eighteen years, Hamer lived this hard life, and would have died in it were it not for a protest meeting in nearby Ruleville in the summer of 1962. Angered at having been sterilized without her consent during a 1961 operation to remove a small uterine tumor, she decided to go to the meeting and there met James Bevel, James Forman, and other civil rights activists. Through their inspiration, she decided to join a group of black farmworkers determined to register to vote at the courthouse in Indianola. Until that meeting, she had never known she had the constitutional right to vote.

On Aug. 31, 1962, Hamer tried to register, but neither she nor any of the other eighteen aspirants could interpret the Mississippi constitution to the white registrar's satisfaction. On the way home, police stopped their bus, a black-owned vehicle used for transporting field hands, and arrested the driver for operating a bus of the "wrong color." When Hamer finally reached home, the plantation owner threw her off his land, insisting that her husband remain, however, until the crop was in. That night sixteen shots were fired into the house where she attempted to hide. She then became a fugitive.

Robert Moses of the Student Nonviolent Coordinating Committee (SNCC) saw Hamer's potential as a civil rights leader and invited her to a SNCC convention at Fisk University in Nashville in the fall of 1962. This meeting was the start of her total commitment to the cause. In January 1963 she tried to register again, feeling a sense of freedom because now there was nothing anyone could take from her. She had no job or house. This time she passed, but she could not vote until 1964 because she did not have the two required annual poll-tax receipts.

Hamer became increasingly active and outspoken in voter-registration drives and education. In June 1963 she attended a workshop in Charleston, S.C., with several other black women. They were arrested in Winona, Miss., on June 9, on the way home. Their crime was entering the whites-only bus station restaurant to eat. The women were roughly taken to the Montgomery County jail where they were beaten severely. Hamer was shoved on a bed facedown, and two black prisoners, supervised by a plainclothes policeman, were forced to beat her with a blackjack until they were exhausted. She tried to protect herself with her hands, which were beaten until they turned blue. The long-term results of the violence were a blood clot in one eye, kidney damage, and permanent injury to a leg. After three days with no medical care, she was finally released, through the efforts of James Bevel, Andrew Young, and a young law student named Eleanor Holmes Norton. She then learned that Medgar Evers, the field secretary of the National Association for the Advancement of Colored People, had just been assassinated in Jackson, the state capital.

None of this stopped Hamer. In the spring of 1964 she cofounded the Mississippi Freedom Democratic party, and her dramatic speech at the 1964 Democratic National Convention in Atlantic City helped galvanize the nation to right the wrongs of discrimination and forced the Democrats to mandate integrated state delegations in 1968.

In 1964, Hamer also attempted to run for the House of Representatives from Mississippi's Second Congressional District. She was not allowed on the regular ballot, so the Mississippi Freedom Democratic party established a "Freedom Ballot" that included all candidates, black and white. Hamer defeated incumbent Jamie L. Whitten on this unofficial ballot, in which those kept from the regular polls participated, 33,009 to 49. The following year she, Victoria Gray, and Annie Devine were the first black women to sit on the floor of the United States House of Representatives when they unsuccessfully protested the seating of the Mississippi delegation, including Whitten, that had been elected through a segregated ballot. In 1968 she was a member of the integrated Mississippi delegation to the Democratic National Convention in Chicago and was a committeewoman on the Democratic National Committee. Hamer was elected to the steering committee of the newly formed National Women's Political Caucus in 1971.

In 1965, Hamer helped organize a black cotton pickers strike, and in 1969 she established the 680-acre Freedom Farm Cooperative in Sunflower County. People began to call her "Pig Lady" because of her establishment, with the help of the National Council of Negro Women, of a "pig bank" that provided free pigs for blacks to breed, raise, and slaughter. Two piglets were to be returned to the "bank" from every newly born litter.

Hamer established Head Start in the Delta and acquired federal funding for housing projects. A large, dark-complected woman of some two hundred pounds with a strong voice, she never left Ruleville and Sunflower County, nor did she move from her simple three-room house into town until late in her life. Listeners frequently commented on the haunting eloquence of her words despite her bad grammar. "I've passed equal rights; I'm fighting for human rights," she said. "Ain't Gonna Let Nobody Turn Me 'Round," "I Woke Up This Morning with My Mind Set on Freedom," and "This Little Light of Mine" were three songs she loved to sing at rallies. Unlike other civil rights leaders of the 1960's, she was an uneducated older woman, not a well-educated male religious leader or student. She remained active despite a mastectomy for cancer in 1976. She died in Mound Bayou, Miss. The nation's civil rights elite gathered for her funeral.

[There are Fannie Lou Hamer papers in the Amistad Research Center, Tulane University (seventeen rolls of microfilm), and in the Moorland-Spingarn Research Center, Howard University, Washington, D.C. Interviews with and a vertical file on Hamer are in the Mississippi Department of Archives and History, Jackson. Consult also the Fannie Lou Hamer Collection in Special Collections, Coleman Library, Tougaloo College, Tougaloo, Miss.; and oral histories at Fisk University, Nashville, Tenn., and the University of Southern Mississippi, Hattiesburg.

A biography is Kay Mills, *This Little Light of Mine, The Life of Fannie Lou Hamer.* Among the numerous articles on Hamer are Jerry De Muth, " 'Tired of Being Sick and Tired,' " *The Nation*, June 1, 1964; Phyl Garland, "Builders of a New South," *Ebony*, Aug. 1966; Paule Marshall, "Fannie Lou Hamer, 'Hunger Has No Color Line,' " *Vogue*, June 1970; and Eleanor Holmes Norton, "Woman Who Changed the South: Memory of Fannie Lou Hamer," *MS*, July 1977. See also George Alexander Sewell and Margaret C. Dwight, *Mississippi Black History Makers* (1984). Obituaries are in the *New York Times*, Mar. 16, 1977, and the *Washington Post*, Mar. 17, 1977.]

JOHN F. MARSZALEK

HARRAH, WILLIAM FISK ("BILL") (Sept. 2, 1911–June 30, 1978), casino owner and car collector, was born in South Pasadena, Calif., the son of Amanda Fisk and John Garrett Harrah, an attorney, real estate speculator, and local politician. His mother's mental instability culminated in her suicide while Harrah was a student at Hollywood High School. A few years later, his father's investments suffered from the Great Depression, forcing Harrah to leave the University of California at Los Angeles. By 1932 the Harrahs were trying to make a living from a bingo parlor on the pier in Venice, Calif. Several times local magistrates hauled father and son into court and charged them with running a gambling establishment. His father sold the operation to Harrah for $500. By 1934 he had an annual income of between $25,000 and $50,000, but he disliked the questionable legal status of the business.

In May 1937, while traveling in Reno, Nev., Harrah found at last a city that encouraged gambling entrepreneurs. After an initial failure, Harrah opened a bingo parlor situated to take maximum advantage of pedestrian traffic. The place turned a modest profit and led Harrah to expand his business in the late 1930's and early 1940's. He formed partnerships with fellow businessmen, such as Virgil Smith, and courted the Raymond I. Smith family (no relation to Virgil), which owned Harolds Club, the largest casino in Nevada. When he learned that the owner of the Heart Tango Club was retiring, Harrah proved ruthless in the negotiations for the property. Shortly after Pearl Harbor, Harrah purchased the Japanese-owned Reno Club, largest of the city's bingo parlors; this was a key acquisition in Harrah's rise to prominence.

In 1946, Harrah opened his first large casino, and residents and tourists alike discovered a new approach to gambling that reflected the proprietor's emphasis on high quality and attention to detail. Harrah began to earn a reputation for sparing no expense to ensure a pleasant atmosphere. Unlike Benjamin ("Bugsy") Siegel, who was developing the Flamingo Hotel in Las Vegas into the state's first resort, Harrah remained content to reap profits from casino games rather than diversifying into entertainment and hotel accommodations.

Harrah's decade of achievement was amazing when one considers the turmoil in his personal life. According to his biographer, he led a "social life that would have exhausted Lothario, gagged Henry the Eighth, and left Casanova dehydrated and swearing lifelong celibacy." He also battled alcoholism. A compulsive gambler, Harrah lost heavily at the tables of neighboring casinos, but a near-fatal car accident in 1942 persuaded him to swear off high-stakes craps and to curtail his drinking.

A sober Harrah blossomed into a serious business leader who pioneered many aspects of the modern gambling industry. In 1946 he developed a daily profit and loss statement, and he started an internal surveillance system, nicknamed "Eye in the Sky," by which management kept track of both customers and employees. At Harrah's, managers handed new employees lengthy manuals that covered every aspect of their conduct. Pleasant, expensive surroundings were designed to appeal to women customers, who tended to be fanatical devotees of the slot machines, the major source of gaming revenues. Harrah also improved slot machine design, adding a candlestick top that lit up to show a player needed change or had won a jackpot. For keno, he developed a vacuum blower to select numbered balls and insisted that every ticket and drawing be photographed—all practices to ensure honesty. Finally, since the word "gambling" conjured up unsavory images, he pioneered the use of the euphemism "gaming."

By the early 1950's Harrah had become the trendsetter in gambling casinos, but he had not branched out into hotels. Eyeing Lake Tahoe's beautiful south shore, in 1955 he bought a small property next to Harvey's Wagon Wheel, the largest casino at Stateline, Nev. Harrah replicated his earlier strategic success as he gradually expanded. In December 1959, Harrah's South Shore Room opened with the largest dinner theater in northern Nevada, featuring the nation's best-known entertainers.

Meanwhile, Harrah solved the problem of the negative effect of Tahoe's harsh winters on profits. Making increased use of business experts, he commissioned from Stanford Research Institute (SRI) a study of the effect of low-cost bus service from the San Francisco area to the Tahoe casino. The SRI report showed that Harrah could profit even after paying for the transportation. Soon thousands of minorities and elderly from California's cities began to ride Harrah specials. As an unintended consequence Harrah brought casino gaming to the masses and achieved an extraordinary degree of social and racial integration.

Harrah believed that if he went into the hotel business, the accommodations would have to reflect the high reputation of his casino. In 1969 his Reno hotel was completed, and he made plans for a world-class hotel at Tahoe. In 1973, Harrah's Tahoe opened and gained instant recognition. Before its completion, Harrah achieved a major breakthrough for the gaming industry. In 1971 he sold part of his holdings to the public, and Harrah's became the first gaming company to be listed on the New York Stock Exchange (1973).

Yet as Harrah's financial life leaped from one success to another, his personal life was often tumultuous. He had six wives: Thelma Batchelor (1937–1948), Mayme Kandis Lucille ("Scherry") Teague Fagg (1949–1969), Bobbie Gentry (December 1969–April 1970), Mary Burger (August 1970–October 1971), Roxanna Darlene Carlson (October 1972–November 1973), and Verna Rae Frank (June 1974–June 1978). He and his second wife adopted two sons.

Harrah died in Rochester, Minn., from complications arising from heart surgery at the Mayo Clinic. At the time of his death, he controlled 83 percent of Harrah's stock, valued at $137 million, and had the largest private payroll in Nevada. Historians have called him the Henry Ford of casino gaming.

[Leon Mandel, *William Fisk Harrah* (1982), relies heavily on Harrah's two-volume "My Recollections of the Hotel-Casino Industry and as an Auto Collecting Enthusiast," Oral History Project, Special Collections, University of Nevada-Reno (UNR) (1980). See also oral histories from Harrah's associates in the Nevada gaming industry at UNR, and Harrah Miscellaneous Files at UNR and the Nevada Historical Society for numerous newspaper and magazine articles. Obituaries are in the *New York Times*, July 2, 1978, and the *Nevada State Journal*, July 1, 1978.]

GERALD THOMPSON

HARRIMAN, EDWARD ROLAND NOEL (Dec. 24, 1895–Feb. 16, 1978), financier and philanthropist, was born in New York City, the youngest of five surviving children of Edward Henry Harriman, a financier and executive of the Union Pacific and the Southern Pacific railroads, and Mary Williamson Averell. Among his siblings was William Averell Harriman, the financier and government official, four years his senior. Edward H. Harriman's estate was substantial, variously estimated between $70 million and $100 million upon his death in 1909.

When his family lived at 1 East Fifty-fifth Street in Manhattan, Roland played on the city streets and in Central Park. When he was ten years old, the family acquired a house at 1 East Sixty-ninth Street in New York City. His was no ordinary childhood, however; his summers were spent at the 20,000-acre family homestead in Orange and Rockland counties, N.Y. (Named Arden House, it was given to Averell by his mother in 1916; he, in turn, gave it to Columbia University in 1950, for use as a conference center.) There were also cruises on the family's yacht, *Sultana*, kept docked at Newburgh, on the Hudson River, and holidays at Island Park, the family ranch on the Snake River in Idaho.

Harriman's father took the family on most of his business trips; the boy had been in every state in the union but two (Alabama and North Dakota) by the time he was nine years old. When his father was ordered by his doctor to reduce his work load, the elder Harriman organized a scientific expedition to Alaska in 1899, which included among its scientists John Muir and John Burroughs. The group reached the Bering Sea. When the elder Harriman visited Japan in an attempt to link the steamship subsidiaries of his railroads with the Manchurian railroad in 1905, the family accompanied him. There were also many family trips to Europe.

Edward Harriman owned and raced trotting horses, so that it was not surprising that his youngest son became interested in the sport. Indeed, he was racing horses as an amateur by the time he was sixteen. Later this interest became a more serious avocation.

Harriman was educated at Groton, from which he graduated in 1913, and Yale (B.A., 1917). At Yale he majored in history and rowed on the varsity crew. Harriman married Gladys C. C. Fries on Apr. 12, 1917; they had two children. During World War I, Harriman served for ten months as an inspector with the rank of lieutenant in the United States Army Ordnance Department. Stricken with pneumonia and influenza, he was honorably discharged in January 1919. After regaining his health in California, he joined the Merchants Shipbuilding Corporation that November, a firm in which his brother Averell had an interest.

In 1922, Harriman joined W. A. Harriman Company, investment bankers in New York City, under the tutelage of his brother. The following year, he was made a vice-president; in 1927 the two brothers formed the banking firm Harriman Brothers and Company, and in 1931 the firm was merged with Brown Brothers and Company, with Roland as vice-president. Headquartered on Wall Street, Brown Brothers Harriman started with nine partners and about two hundred employees. In 1975, a few years prior to Harriman's death, there were twenty-nine partners and approximately one thousand employees. Nevertheless, its $360 million in assets in 1978 was a small fraction of such competitors as First National City Bank with its $18 billion in assets. As the firm grew, it husbanded its capital and maintained its partnership status while a competitor, J. P. Morgan and Company was forced to go public in 1940 upon the death of three of its partners. To forestall such a contingency, the Harriman brothers stipulated in their wills that their shares in the partnership should remain in the firm upon their deaths.

The firm performed specialized banking services for customers, mainly medium-sized corporations; it was not a member of the Federal Reserve System or the Federal Deposit Insurance Corporation. Its extensive overseas activities included a brisk stock brokerage business with English and Scottish investment firms. In 1968, Harriman and three other senior partners at Brown Brothers (Robert A. Lovett, secretary of defense under President Harry Truman; Prescott S. Bush, former senator from Connecticut; and Knight Woolley—all Yale men), moved "upstairs," literally and figuratively, to make way for the younger partners, one of whom was Robert Roosa, former undersecretary of the Treasury.

Harriman was president of the Bear Mountain Hudson River Bridge Company, which built the Bear Mountain Bridge (opened in 1924), making nearby state parkland more accessible from the east. Financing was arranged by W. A. Harriman and Company. His directorships at various times included the American Bank Note Company, the Delaware and Hudson Railroad, the Mutual Life Insurance of New York, the Oregon-Washington Railroad and Navigation Company, the Union Pacific Railroad (succeeding his brother Averell in 1946 as board chairman), the Anaconda Copper Mining Company, the Los Angeles and Salt Lake Railroad, the Oregon Short Line, the Royal Exchange Assurance Company, and Weekly Publications, publisher of *Newsweek*.

Politically, Harriman was a conservative Republican. An advocate of balanced budgets, he wrote articles on the subject for the *Saturday Evening Post* and the *Review of Reviews* in 1935; his speech on WEAF radio in August 1937 on the topic was reprinted in *Vital Speeches of the Day* (Sept. 15, 1937). His views were in sharp contrast with those of his brother Averell, who had left the Republicans in 1928 to vote for Governor Al Smith of New York for the presidency. As a Democrat, Averell became a New Deal administrator under Franklin D. Roosevelt, ambassador to the Soviet Union during World War II, and governor of New York. Of their political differences, Roland said, ". . . everything we have done in our business careers has been 50–50. I would say we are also 50–50 politically, because he is a Democrat and I am a Republican."

Harriman followed the philanthropic example of his mother and father. For example, he contributed to, and for a time was president of, the Boy's Club of New York, founded by his father. He and his wife established the Irving

Sherwood Wright professorship in geriatrics at New York Hospital–Cornell Medical Center and provided funds for cardiovascular research at the hospital. He joined the American Red Cross as a member of the board of governors in 1947, helped reorganize it after World War II, served as manager for the organization's North Atlantic area from 1944 to 1946, was its vice-president and national annual fund appeal chair in 1949, and was appointed its president by President Truman, to succeed General George Marshall in 1950. President Dwight Eisenhower reappointed him president in 1953. His other philanthropic board memberships included that of the American Museum of Natural History, for which he was also treasurer.

Harriman founded the Trotting Horse Club of America in 1924 and made it responsible for publishing the *Wallace's Register* and the *Yearbook* (which he purchased when they stopped publishing), to maintain breeding and racing records; assisted in the formation of the U.S. Trotting Association in 1938; and owned and operated the Historic Track in Goshen, N.Y. He was a steward of the Trotting Horse Club, president of the Orange County Driving Park Association, and president of the Hambletonian Society.

Harriman died in Arden, N.Y.

[Harriman's autobiography is *I Reminisce* (1975). Persia Campbell, *Mary Williamson Harriman* (1960), contains family vignettes. Articles are "Harriman of Goshen," *Sports Illustrated*, July 9, 1962; and "Brown Brothers, at Age 150, Grows with Care," the *New York Times*, Sept. 15, 1968. An obituary is in the *New York Times*, Feb. 17, 1978.]

HAROLD L. WATTEL

HARRIS, JED (Feb. 25, 1900–Nov. 15, 1979), theater producer and director, was born Jacob Hirsch Horowitz in Newark, N.J., one of five children of Meyer Wolf Horowitz, owner of a grocery store, and Esther Schurtz. Many sources report that he was born in Vienna, Austria, but that information was a bit of press-agent fakery. Harris was brought up in a traditional Jewish environment. He attended public schools in Newark and entered Yale University as a member of the class of 1921, but after excessive absences and unpaid fees, he left the university without completing his studies. After a girlfriend named Anita Greenbaum introduced him to the joys of the theater, he took a job in New York City as a junior reporter for *Billboard*, which crystallized his desire to become a prominent part of the Broadway scene.

In 1922, Harris borrowed $5,000 from the mother of a college friend and invested in his first venture, *The Romantic Age*, a play by A. A. Milne. The production was not successful enough to bear financial or professional fruits. He next worked briefly as a press agent in Chicago for a farce called *Applesauce*, then returned to New York, where he continued his career as a producer. By the time the 1927–1928 Broadway season hit full stride, Harris had four hits on the boards: *Broadway* (1926); *Coquette* (1927), with Helen Hayes; *The Royal Family* (1927); and *The Front Page* (1928). He gained much prestige from these shows plus a personal fortune. For example, he invested $11,000 in *Broadway* and earned some $1.3 million, and many playwrights hoped to have their plays produced by Harris. Because of his outstanding successes on Broadway, Harris's peers dubbed him "the Meteor." Noël Coward called him "destiny's tot."

During this same period, although he was married to Anita Green, Harris embarked on an affair with actress Ruth Gordon. Gordon became pregnant and journeyed to Paris, where she gave birth to their son, Jones Kelly. Although Harris's marriage to Green ended in divorce in 1928, Harris and Gordon never married. His marriage to actress Louise Platt, with whom he had one child, ended in divorce in 1944, and that to Beatrice ("Bebe") Allen in 1957 also ended in divorce in 1962.

Although few would deny his theatrical wizardry, Harris's personal relationships with directors, actors, and coproducers were notoriously stormy. The playwright and director George S. Kaufman once said that when he died he wanted to be cremated and have his ashes thrown in Harris's face. After Harris's death the *New York Times* noted that he was "a flamboyant man of intermittent charm." His own daughter Abigail once said, "I don't believe there is a person walking the face of the earth who would have a good word to say for my father."

Harris's fall from grace was almost as sudden and complete as his rise. He once had six flops in a row, particularly *The Lake* (1933), starring Katharine Hepburn. He recovered briefly, when he produced and directed Thornton Wilder's *Our Town* in 1938, but that production was clouded by the suicide of actress Rosamund Pinchot, who left behind a note quoting lines from the play, and by Wilder's insistence that Harris had ruined his prose in the play's graveyard scene.

Harris wrote in his autobiography, *A Dance on the High Wire* (1979), that from 1930 to 1947, a period during which he was actively engaged in the theater for ten seasons, he produced and directed only six productions that could be considered noteworthy—*Uncle Vanya* (1930), *The Green Bay Tree* (1933), *A Doll's House* (1937), *Our Town*, *Dark Eyes* (1943), and *The Heiress* (1947).

After the success of *The Heiress*, which had been adapted from Henry James's novel *Washington Square*, Harris made one other important contribution to the theater, when he directed Arthur Miller's *The Crucible* in 1953. His final work in the theater was in 1956, when he produced and directed *Child of Fortune*, to no great success. He spent his final years, far from wealthy, living in the Gorham and Royalton hotels in Manhattan. He died in New York City of congestive heart failure. Among the few mourners in attendance at his funeral were theater celebrities José Ferrer, Lillian Gish, Marc Connelly, and Jean Dalrymple.

[In addition to Harris's autobiography, see Martin Gottfried, *Jed Harris: The Curse of Genius* (1984). An obituary is in the *New York Times*, Nov. 16, 1979.]

LOUIS PHILLIPS

HARRIS, LEROY ELLSWORTH ("ROY") (Feb. 12, 1898–Oct. 1, 1979), composer, was born near Chandler, Lincoln County, Okla., on land claimed in a land rush by his father, Elmer Ellsworth Harris. Of his four siblings, one sister survived. His mother, Laura Broddle Harris, a former waitress, suffered from severe respiratory problems for about ten years, prompting the family to relocate to Covina, Calif., where the elder Harris farmed potatoes. His mother gave young Harris piano lessons, with emphasis on hymns and Mozart. At Covina Union High School he took up the clarinet, shortened his name to Roy, and played baseball and football. By his graduation in 1916, he was earning money farming, but his musical interests and piano skills remained strong. Harris served in a student division of the Army Training Corps in Berkeley from 1916 to 1918, ushering frequently at San Francisco Symphony Orchestra concerts in his spare time. He sporadically attended the University of California at Berkeley and of Los Angeles (UCLA) and studied music privately with numerous teachers. About 1922 he married Charlotte Schwartz, whom he called Davida; they had one child, with whom Harris lost touch, and were divorced in 1924. Not much is known about his second wife, Sylvia Feningston, whom he married in 1926.

In 1924, Harris began to study with Arthur Farwell, who encouraged him to compose, introduced him to the poetry of Walt Whitman, and helped Harris establish his unique concepts of harmony and voicings. In 1925 Harris completed his first orchestral composition, Andante, peformed by the Eastman School Orchestra. Aaron Copland urged him to study in Paris with Nadia Boulanger. He did so from 1926 to 1929, through the generosity of Alma Wertheim, a New York City arts patron, and two Guggenheim fellowships (1927, 1929). In 1929, Harris fell and injured his spine, forcing him to return to America for surgery and to compose away from the piano. In 1931 Harris received the Creative Fellowship for composing of the Pasadena Music and Arts Association. In 1932 he married his third wife, Hilda Hemingway; they were divorced in 1936. Also in 1932 he began teaching summer sessions at the Juilliard School of Music in New York City; among his students at Juilliard, where he continued teaching summer sessions until 1940, was composer William Schuman. The Concerto for Piano, Clarinet, and String Quartet (premiered in Paris, 1927) was his first work to be commercially recorded (1933). Harris wrote perhaps his most celebrated work, *Symphony 1933*, for Serge Koussevitzky and the Boston Symphony. (Recorded in 1934 by Columbia, it was probably the first commercial recording of an American symphony.) His friendship with Koussevitzky later resulted in commissions for the Third Symphony (1938), the Fifth Symphony (1942), and the Seventh Symphony (1952), although the conductor died before the Seventh Symphony's premiere.

With help from Elizabeth Sprague Coolidge, Harris promoted American chamber music, helping to found the Westminster Academy of Chamber Music at the Westminster Choir School in Princeton, N.J., where he taught from 1934 to 1938. (He received the Coolidge

Medal for "eminent service to chamber music" in 1942.) He also helped to organize the Composers Forum-Laboratory (1935) and participated in developing music festivals nationwide.

Harris researched folk music at the Library of Congress and became acquainted with such folk performer-scholars as Woody Guthrie and Burl Ives. Harris's work shows the profound influence of American folk melody and style, especially the Folksong Symphony (1940). The vocal parts of this work are within the abilities of a high school chorus. Harris strove to provide high-quality music accessible to amateur performers.

On Oct. 10, 1936, Harris married the accomplished Canadian pianist Beula Duffey, whom he renamed Johana (after Johann Sebastian Bach); they had five children. He wrote his Quintet for Piano and Strings as a wedding gift. In 1938 he developed a radio program for CBS called "Let's Make Music" and taught the summer session at Princeton. By 1939 he was acknowledged in the United States and in Europe as an outstanding composer. In 1943, Harris left his composer-in-residence position at Cornell University (where he had been since 1941) for Colorado, where he and Johana taught at Colorado College and enthusiastically collaborated on developing community musical activities.

In 1944, ABC commissioned the Sixth Symphony *(Gettysburg)*. Born in a log cabin on Abraham Lincoln's birthday, Harris felt kinship and admiration for the president, who was the subject of his tenth symphony, the *Abraham Lincoln* Symphony (1965, one hundred years after Lincoln's assassination), and his cantata *Abraham Lincoln Walks at Midnight* (1953). In 1945 Harris helped American forces abroad receive concerts, disks, and broadcasts as director of music for the Office of War Information.

Harris left Colorado to become composer in residence at Utah State Agricultural College in 1948. The following year, the family moved to Nashville, Tenn., where Harris served as composer in residence at George Peabody College for Teachers (now part of Vanderbilt University) and organized the Cumberland Forest Music Festival in Sewanee, Tenn. From 1951 to 1956 the Harrises taught at the Pennsylvania College for Women (now Chatham College) in Pittsburgh, where they organized the largest music festival for new music to date, the Pittsburgh International Festival of Contemporary Music. During this period, accusations that he was a Communist sympathizer (based on the dedication of his Fifth Symphony to the Soviet Union), although withdrawn, contributed to Harris's somewhat souring view of his homeland, which he said was revealed in the emotional Eleventh Symphony (1967).

Harris held positions at Southern Illinois University (1956–1957), Indiana University (1957–1960), and the Inter-American University in San German, Puerto Rico (1960–1961). He cofounded the International String Congress in 1959. Harris accepted a position at UCLA in 1961, and in 1964 the family moved to Pacific Palisades, Calif. He retired from UCLA in 1970 and became composer in residence at California State University, Los Angeles, until 1976. The Roy Harris Archive (now Collection) was founded at the university in 1973, and the Roy Harris Society was formed in 1979. Reawakened interest in his music cheered Harris before his death in Santa Monica, Calif.

Harris's early compositions have asymmetric rhythms and raw sonorities, sometimes criticized as technically underdeveloped. His later, more polished work is said by some to have less intensity. Harris summed up his own lifework thus: "My purpose has been to affirm tradition as our greatest resource, rather than to avoid it as our greatest threat."

[Harris's writings include "Problems of American Composers," in Henry Cowell, ed., *American Composers on American Music* (1933), repr. in Gilbert Chase, ed., *The American Composer Speaks* (1966); and "The Basis of Artistic Creation in Music," in Maxwell Anderson, Rhys Carpenter, and Roy Harris, *The Bases of Artistic Creation* (1942). See also Arthur Farwell, "Roy Harris," *Music Quarterly*, Jan. 1932; Nicolas Slonimsky, "Roy Harris," *Music Quarterly*, Jan. 1947; and Dan Stehman, *Roy Harris* (1984) and *Roy Harris: A Bio-bibliography* (1991)].

J. S. CAPPELLETTI

HARRIS, STANLEY RAYMOND ("BUCKY") (Nov. 8, 1896–Nov. 8, 1977), baseball player and manager, was born in Port Jervis, N.Y., the son of Thomas Harris, a coal miner, and Katherine Rupp. Harris moved with his family at age five to Pittston, Pa., and attended public school through the sixth grade. He began working in nearby coal mines in 1909 but aspired to become a professional baseball player like his older brother, Merle, who played in the minor leagues.

Harris participated in semiprofessional baseball as shortstop with Hamtown (Suburban League) in 1911 and in professional basketball with Pittston in 1916. Teammates nicknamed him Bucky because of his quick, jerky movements on the basketball court. The five-foot, nine-and-a-half-inch Harris, who batted and threw right-handed, started his professional baseball career as a light-hitting, poor-fielding 120-pound third baseman with Muskegon, Mich. (Central League), in 1916 and split the 1917 season with Norfolk, Va. (Virginia League), and Reading, Pa. (New York State League). His 1918–1919 campaigns were spent as second baseman and shortstop for Buffalo, N.Y. (International League), interrupted by a brief stint in the United States Army during World War I. The Detroit Tigers, New York Giants, and Philadelphia Athletics scouted Harris, but Washington Senators (American League) manager-owner Clark Griffith signed him for $4,500 in 1919. The day that Griffith saw him play, Harris was suffering from a broken finger yet made six hits and reached base all eight at-bats in a doubleheader for Buffalo.

Harris played regularly at second base for the Senators from 1920 to 1928, batting a career-high .300 in 1920. From 1921 to 1927 his batting average ranged between .267 and .289. A tough competitor, he played outstanding defense in the mold of his idol, Eddie Collins, and formed an effective double-play combination with shortstop Roger Peckinpaugh and first baseman Joe Judge. Harris in 1922 set a major league record for most putouts by a second baseman (479) and led his position in fielding (1927), putouts (1922–1923 and 1926–1927), errors (1923), and double plays (1923, 1925).

In 1924, at the age of twenty-seven, Harris was named player-manager, becoming the youngest manager in major league baseball history. The "Boy Wonder" promptly led Washington, a perennial second-division club, to its first pennant and World Series title. Washington upset the New York Giants in seven games, as Harris batted .333 with two home runs and handled fifty-four chances defensively. He established records for most putouts and assists by a second baseman in a Series game (eight each) and for a seven-game Series (twenty-six and twenty-eight). The Senators were league champions again in 1925 but lost a seven-game World Series to the Pittsburgh Pirates. Harris remained Washington manager through 1928, guiding the Senators to third- and fourth-place finishes. Washington traded Harris in October 1928 to the Detroit Tigers (American League) for infielder Jack Warner. Harris, who played briefly in 1929 and 1931, batted .274 lifetime with 1,297 hits, 506 runs batted in, and 166 stolen bases in 1,264 games.

Harris piloted five major league clubs in twenty-nine seasons spanning four decades. Only Connie Mack and John McGraw managed more major league seasons. Harris ranks as the third winningest (2,159 games) and second losingest (2,219) manager in major league history for a .483 career won-loss percentage. His clubs finished in the second division twenty times, but they always improved in Harris's first season at the helm. His managerial service included three separate stints with Washington and two with Detroit. Harris managed Detroit to five second-division finishes from 1929 to 1933. Owner Frank Navin wanted Harris to remain another campaign, but Harris resigned; he had, however, built the foundation for the Tigers' pennant-winning clubs of 1934 and 1935. He managed the Boston Red Sox to fourth place in 1934 and piloted Washington from 1935 to 1942. The Senators languished in the second division with poor talent, causing Harris to quit. Philadelphia Phillies owner Bill Cox hired Harris as manager for the 1943 season, but the pair clashed frequently. Cox fired Harris at mid-season when Harris accidentally learned about Cox's gambling activities. Harris dissuaded Philadelphia players from striking in protest against his departure. In 1944 and 1945 he returned to Buffalo (International League) as bench and general manager.

The New York Yankees in 1946 named Harris special assistant liaison between the players and management. In November 1946, Harris reluctantly assumed the Yankee managerial reins. Detroit offered Harris a $50,000-per-year contract to become the Tigers' general manager, but he already had accepted the Yankee position. Harris piloted the Yankees to the 1947 pennant and World Series title over the Brooklyn Dodgers in seven games, prompting *Sporting News* to name him major league manager of the year. In the 1948 All-Star game at St. Louis, Harris led the American League to a 5–2 triumph over the National League. Casey Stengel replaced Harris as manager after the Yankees finished a disappointing third in 1948. After managing the San Diego Padres (Pacific Coast

League) in 1949, Harris piloted the Washington Senators to five second-division finishes from 1950 to 1954. His managerial career ended successfully with the Detroit Tigers in 1955 and 1956. After being assistant general manager with the Boston Red Sox (1956–1960), he scouted for the American League Chicago White Sox (1962) and Washington Senators (1963–1971). He received the William J. Slocum Award in 1948 for service to baseball and was inducted into the National Baseball Hall of Fame in 1975.

Harris, a personable, smart, analytical, honest, outspoken, patient, and practical manager, had a gift for securing the best possible performance from even mediocre players. Besides staunchly defending his players, he employed sound, often daring baseball strategy. He rated pitcher Walter Johnson and outfielder Joe DiMaggio as his best performers.

Harris married Elizabeth Sutherland, the daughter of a United States senator from West Virginia, on Oct. 1, 1926. They resided in Washington, D.C., and had three children. Harris, who suffered from Parkinson's disease, died in a Bethesda, Md., retirement home on his eighty-first birthday.

[A Stanley ("Bucky") Harris file is in the National Baseball Library, Cooperstown, N.Y. The best early source remains Harris's autobiography, *Playing the Game: From Mine Boy to Manager* (1925). He outlined his managerial strategy in *Baseball: How to Play It* (1925). The most complete account of his career after 1925 is Edwin Pope, *Baseball's Greatest Managers* (1960). His managerial career is described in Shirley Povich, *The Washington Senators* (1954); Frederick G. Lieb, *The Detroit Tigers* (1946) and *The Boston Red Sox* (1947); and Frederick G. Lieb and Stan Baumgartner, *The Philadelphia Phillies* (1953). Obituaries are in the *Washington Post* and the *New York Times*, both Nov. 10, 1977.]

David L. Porter

HART, PHILIP ALOYSIUS (Dec. 10, 1912–Dec. 26, 1976), United States senator, was born in Bryn Mawr, Pa., the son of Philip Aloysius Hart and Ann Clyde. His paternal grandfather had emigrated from Ireland and worked as a landscape gardener and estate manager in the Bryn Mawr area. Hart's father was a banker who became president of the Bryn Mawr Trust Company. During his political career, Hart often referred to his father as the "only Democrat in Bryn Mawr."

Hart attended Waldron Academy and West Philadelphia Catholic High School before entering Georgetown University. At Georgetown he was elected president of the student body and graduated cum laude in 1934. After graduation he entered the University of Michigan Law School at Ann Arbor and received his degree in 1937. After being admitted to the bar the following year, he remained in Michigan, practicing law in Detroit until he entered the United States Army in 1943 as a captain.

Serving with the Fourth Infantry Division, Hart landed on Utah Beach at Normandy and was wounded seriously. He fought at the Battle of the Bulge and earned the Purple Heart, Bronze Star, and croix de guerre as well as other American and Allied decorations for valor. He was discharged as a lieutenant colonel in 1946. Hart's campaign literature and official biographies make only fleeting and incomplete references to his distinguished military record, a mark of the personal modesty that characterized his public life.

Returning to Detroit after his discharge, he attracted the attention of G. Mennen Williams, who had been elected governor of Michigan in 1948. Williams's election was the culmination of a remarkable rebuilding of the long-moribund Michigan Democratic party, and Hart was one of a number of young veterans and others drawn to the resurgent party because of liberal, activist ideas about government and public service. Williams appointed Hart Michigan's Corporation Securities Commissioner in 1949, beginning the career in public service that occupied the rest of his life. After an unsuccessful campaign for secretary of state in 1950, he served as director of the Michigan Office of Price Stabilization in Detroit in 1951 and 1952 and as United States attorney of the Eastern Michigan District in 1952 and 1953. In 1952 he was named "Outstanding Federal Administrator of the Year."

In 1953, following Dwight Eisenhower's election to the presidency, Hart resigned as United States attorney. After serving briefly as legal counsel to Governor Williams, he was elected lieutenant governor in 1954 and reelected in 1956. In 1958 he defeated incumbent Republican senator Charles E. Potter and began the first of three terms in the United States Senate.

In the Senate, Hart quickly established himself as a leader among the liberal Democrats rising to positions of power in the body. The generation of veterans who had entered politics after the war rapidly assumed leadership roles in national affairs in the mid-1950's, and Hart was one of the leaders on the Democratic side. He became a close ally of Senator Mike Mansfield of Montana, the majority leader, and served as a member of the Democratic Policy Committee.

While active in the area of labor legislation, Hart made his mark in the Senate primarily in the areas of civil rights and consumer legislation. He was a leading sponsor of the Drug Safety Act (1962), the Truth-in-Packaging Act (1965), the Truth-in-Lending Act (1966), and the Motor Vehicle Information and Cost Saving Act (1972), as well as major revisions of the antitrust laws. He served as floor leader for two landmark pieces of legislation, the Voting Rights Act (1965) and its extension in 1970, and the Fair Housing Act (1968). He played a leading role in the rejection of President Richard Nixon's nominations of Clement F. Haynsworth, Jr., and G. Harrold Carswell to the United States Supreme Court and was among the leaders of Senate opposition to the antiballistic missile defense system. His efforts to establish federal protection for Michigan's scenic Sleeping Bear Dunes led to the designation of that area as a national lakeshore. He was reelected to the Senate from Michigan twice, defeating Elly Peterson in 1964 and Lenore Romney in 1970.

Hart's support for consumer and civil rights legislation and organized labor, as well as his personal integrity, modesty, and simplicity, earned him the title "Conscience of the Senate" and the respect of his peers. While he frequently pointed out that his wife's inheritance had freed him from concern about providing for his large family so that he could pursue a career in public service, his reputation was as a senator of absolute integrity. A Senate office building was named in his honor in 1987.

Hart married Jane Cameron Briggs on June 19, 1943. She was the sister of his Georgetown roommate Walter ("Spike") Briggs and the daughter of Detroit industrialist and sportsman Walter O. Briggs, who owned both the Detroit Tigers and the Detroit Lions. Hart served as a director and officer of the Detroit Tigers and the Lions prior to his election to the Senate. He and his wife had nine children, one of whom died at an early age. Jane Hart was active and visible in the late 1960's and early 1970's as an opponent of the Vietnam War, frequently appearing at antiwar demonstrations while her husband was still publicly supporting the war. She also participated in the civil rights and world peace movements and was a proponent of major changes in the Catholic Church. Despite strong differences in their positions, especially on the Vietnam War, Hart was supportive of his wife's efforts, particularly when she was criticized for not conforming to the traditional role of a Senate wife.

In 1976, Hart chose not to stand for reelection to a fourth term in the Senate because he had been diagnosed with cancer. He died later that year in Washington, D.C., and was buried on Mackinac Island in Michigan, where he had a vacation home.

[Hart's papers are housed at the Archives of Labor History and Urban Affairs, Wayne State University, Detroit. See Nora Vreeland, *Philip A. Hart: Democratic Senator from Michigan* (1972), and the Library of Michigan, Biographical Vertical File. An obituary is in the *New York Times*, Dec. 27, 1976.]

WILLIAM H. MULLIGAN, JR.

HATHAWAY, DONNY (Oct. 1, 1945–Jan. 13, 1979), singer, composer, and arranger, was born in Chicago, the son of Hosea Hathaway and Druseller (later Huntley). He was brought up in St. Louis, in the Carr Square housing project, by his grandmother Martha Crumwell, also known as Martha Pitts, a gospel singer. Hathaway played the piano and sang gospel at an early age.

At three years old, he was performing in public. Billed as "Donny Pitts, the Nation's Youngest Gospel Singer," he accompanied himself on the ukulele. Hathaway was classically trained as a pianist, and could play the organ and drums. At age fourteen, he entered Vashon High School in St. Louis, where he was singled out as a musical prodigy. During his senior year, he played Grieg's Piano Concerto, as well as the accompaniment to Handel's *Messiah*. While in high school, he also took part in a music theory program at Washington University in St. Louis.

After graduating from high school in 1963, Hathaway attended Howard University in Washington, D.C., on a fine arts scholarship; he majored in musical theory. Professors at the school of music said he was too advanced to teach; they could only expose him to "new musical avenues." Hathaway was a straight-A student at Howard, where he met the singer Roberta Flack as well as his future wife Eulaulah; they had two children. To earn money to help pay for his education, Hathaway played the organ in churches and joined a jazz group, the Rick Powell Trio, composed of fellow classmates, which performed in a number of Washington clubs. He left Howard after three years because he couldn't keep up with his studies and the multiple offers for him to perform.

Hathaway worked in 1968 and 1969 as a producer with Curtis Mayfield's Curtom label in Chicago. There his duets with June Conquest resulted in his first hit in 1969, "I Thank You Baby." Work-related stress forced him to quit Curtom, and he signed with Chess Records as a staff musician-producer. He also worked free-lance with Uni, Kapp, and Stax Records with Woody Herman, Carla Thomas, and the Staple Singers. The following year he met tenor-saxophone great King Curtis at a music trade convention; Curtis introduced him to Atlantic Records, where Hathaway signed as a performer, writer, and producer in 1970. As a singer, he recorded "The Ghetto" (1970) and "Love, Love, Love" (1973). "The Ghetto" was a rhythm-and-blues hit and established his standing as an important figure in soul music.

As a composer, singer, and arranger, Hathaway made the charts in the popular as well as soul categories. Records he produced for Atlantic have been described as "authentic" soul, coming out of the gospel-blues tradition. Critics described the "remarkable intensity" of his music: "Using only the quality of his voice and the originality of his piano style; he didn't have to shout or grunt to convey passionate feelings."

From the beginning, his music was that of a preacher and storyteller. Each of his songs was a testimony, a sermon. In a 1973 interview, he said that preaching was his next "master plan." In fact, he was known for leaning out of the window of the seventeenth floor of the LaSalle Towers, where he lived in Chicago, and preaching to the winds.

From 1968 to 1973, Hathaway composed prolifically, including the score for the film *Come Back, Charleston Blue* (1972), which he also conducted. He sang the title song on the soundtrack with Valerie Simpson. Hathaway also wrote and sang the theme song for the television show *Maude*. Although he composed music for both films and television as well as songs recorded by Aretha Franklin and Jerry Butler, Hathaway is best known for his duets with former Howard classmate Roberta Flack. Their complementary voices, Hathaway's dramatic style offset by Flack's purity, brought "Where Is the Love" (1972) and "The Closer I Get to You" (1978) into the top five on the American music charts.

One of his best-known songs with Flack is the chart version of Carole King's "You've Got a Friend," which sold more than a million copies. According to Roberta Flack, "When we met in the studio to do 'You've Got a Friend,' he wrote the music at midnight, scored, did the whole job, and we were finished by 2 A.M."

Hathaway received numerous awards from the music industry, including a Grammy in 1972 for best popular vocal performance by a duo, group, or chorus for "Where Is the Love." He and Flack were also nominated for a Grammy for "The Closer I Get to You." Solo albums include *Everything Is Everything* (1970); *Donny Hathaway* (1971); *Donny Hathaway Live* (1972); *Extensions of a Man* (1973); and his posthumously released *In Performance* (1980), taken from live performances at New York's Bitter End and the Troubadour in Los Angeles. With Roberta Flack he recorded *Roberta Flack and Donny Hathaway* (1972), which sold more than 500,000 copies. At the time of his death he was working with Flack on *Roberta Flack Featuring Donny Hathaway* (1980).

Hathaway died at the age of thirty-three, as a result of a fall from the fifteenth floor of the Essex House Hotel in New York City. The death was ruled a suicide by the New York medical examiner, but many of Hathaway's friends questioned this finding. Although Hathaway had been hospitalized in the past for emotional problems, friends say he was in good spirits the evening of his death. After a dry spell, his career had appeared to be reviving; he was working again on an album, and "The Closer I Get to You" had just been nominated for a Grammy. According to the Reverend Jesse Jackson, who delivered the eulogy at his funeral, Hathaway's death seemed "to have been an accident. Donny died with his coat, scarf and cap on, and it's not likely that anyone would go through the preparation of putting on full attire just to jump out of a window." Hathaway was buried in Lake Charles Cemetery in St. Louis.

[See *The Illustrated Encyclopedia of Black Music* (1982); *Biographical Dictionary of Afro-American and African Musicians* (1982); *The Encyclopedia of Rock* (1968); and *The Guinness Encyclopedia of Popular Music* (1992). Reviews of albums may be found in *High Fidelity* for the year they were produced; *Stereo Review*, Jan. 1981, contains a review of *In Performance*. For a full discussion of his death see D. Michael Cheers, "The Mysterious Death of Donny Hathaway," *Ebony*, Apr. 1979. Obituaries are in the *New York Times* and the *St. Louis Post-Dispatch*, both Jan. 15, 1979. A tribute is in *Rolling Stone*, Mar. 8, 1979.]

MARCIA B. DINNEEN

HAWKS, HOWARD WINCHESTER (May 30, 1896–Dec. 26, 1977), motion-picture director, producer, and screenwriter, was born in Goshen, Ind., one of three children of Helen Howard and Frank Winchester Hawks, an executive in the paper mill industry. Because of his mother's poor health, the family moved to Pasadena, Calif., in 1906, where his father became vice-president of a hotel company. Hawks was educated at Pasadena High School (1908–1913); Throop College of Technology (now California Institute of Technology) where he studied woodworking and metalworking (1913–1914); Phillips Exeter Academy in New Hampshire (1914–1916); and Cornell University (1916–1917). He graduated from Cornell with a B.S. degree in mechanical engineering.

During his summer vacation from Cornell in 1916, Hawks worked at the Famous Players–Lasky Studio (then the production division of Paramount) in the property department. In 1917 he was working on the set of *The Little Princess*, starring Mary Pickford and ZaSu Pitts, when the director didn't come in to work. Hawks directed a few scenes so well that Pickford promoted him to assistant director.

Hawks left Hollywood later that summer to enter the Army Air Corps as a pilot in World War I. After his discharge in 1920, he worked in an aircraft factory, designing and flying planes. He also designed, built, and raced cars, a hobby he had begun in high school. When he later became a director, Hawks would often race cars and perform car stunts in his movies.

Hawks returned to Hollywood and to Paramount, working first as a film cutter, then assistant director, story editor, and casting director. In 1922 he wrote and directed two comedy shorts, which he financed himself. In 1923 he became producer of the feature film *Quicksands*, which he had also written. He left Paramount in 1924 and went to MGM, hoping to get a chance to direct. In 1925 he sold a story, "The Road to Glory," to Fox Studios on the condition that he be able to direct it. Thus began one of the longest and most versatile careers in American film.

Hawks worked under contract at Fox until 1929. Thereafter he worked as an independent producer and sold his projects to every major Hollywood studio. Altogether, he directed forty-three films in forty-four years. He also was an uncredited contributor to countless directing and scripting projects.

Hawks made films in almost every American genre, and each could well serve as one of the best examples of its type. He worked with equal ease in gangster movies (*Scarface*, 1932), action dramas (*The Crowd Roars*, 1932), screwball comedies (*Bringing Up Baby*, 1938), private-eye thrillers (*The Big Sleep*, 1946), military action (*Sergeant York*, 1941), musicals (*Gentlemen Prefer Blondes*, 1953), science fiction (*The Thing*, 1951), and Westerns (*Rio Bravo*, 1959).

Hawks's greatness was his ability to make characters come alive on the screen. To do this, he allowed his actors considerable latitude with the script, letting them develop the characters they portrayed. Male stars such as John Wayne, Humphrey Bogart, Cary Grant, and Gary Cooper gave some of the best performances of their careers in Howard Hawks films as did actresses such as Lauren Bacall, Carole Lombard, Rosalind Russell, and Angie Dickinson. Through their characters, these stars created American archetypes that persist today. He collaborated with a remarkable array of first-rate writers, including Ernest Hemingway, William Faulkner, and two of the best dialogue writers in Hollywood, Ben Hecht and Charles MacArthur.

Hawks maintained a high degree of control over production and the script, imparting all of Hawks's films with a distinctive signature. Common themes revolve around the camaraderie between adversaries in difficult situations. Whether they are gunfighters, aviators, hunters, detectives, newspapermen, or scientists, Hawks's characters attempt to uphold a rigorously defined code of conduct. A typical plot is the struggle of a flawed character to prove himself worthy of respect, by overcoming tendencies to disloyalty, cowardice, physical disability, or immaturity. Hawks's heroes respect their adversaries for upholding the same code of conduct while functioning under different circumstances. The heroes and adversaries are never threatened by each other but welcome the competition in order to surpass themselves.

Hawks received his only Academy Award nomination as best director in 1941 for *Sergeant York;* he lost to John Ford for *How Green Was My Valley*. His actor, actresses, and technical crews, however, took many nominations and awards. In 1975, he was presented with an honorary Oscar for his cumulative work. The Academy of Motion Picture Arts and Sciences cited him as "a giant of the American cinema whose pictures, taken as a whole, represent one of the most consistent, vivid, and varied bodies of work in world cinema."

Hawks appeared in four documentaries on his work: *The Great Professional—Howard Hawks,* a 1967 BBC-TV special with Peter Bogdanovich as interviewer; *Plimpton: Shootout at Rio Lobo,* a 1970 ABC-TV special produced and directed by William Kronick, featuring George Plimpton, John Wayne, and other cast members on the set of *Rio Lobo; The Men Who Made the Movies: Howard Hawks,* a 1973 PBS special produced, directed, and written by Richard Schickel as part of a series on veteran Hollywood directors for WNET, a New York station; and *Ein verdammt gutes Leben* (*A Hell of a Good Life*), a 1978 West German film written and directed by Hans Blumenberg.

Hawks married Athole Shearer on May 30, 1928; they had two children and Hawks adopted Shearer's child from a previous marriage. Hawks and Shearer divorced in 1940. On Dec. 10, 1941, Hawks married Nancy Raye Gross; they had one child before divorcing in 1948. His last marriage was to the former New York model Dee Hartford (born Donnan Higgins) on Feb. 20, 1953. They had one child and divorced in 1959. Hawks died at his Palm Springs, Calif., home from injuries sustained in a fall.

[A collection of Hawks's papers is in the Harold B. Lee Library, Brigham Young University. See Joseph McBride, *Focus on Howard Hawks* (1972), and *Hawks on Hawks* (1982); Donald C. Willis, *The Films of Howard Hawks* (1975); and Leland A. Poague, *Howard Hawks* (1982). Obituaries are in the *New York Times* and *Variety*, both Dec. 28, 1977.]

PATRICIA PALMER

HAWORTH, LELAND JOHN (July 11, 1904–Mar. 5, 1979), physicist, was born in Flint, Mich. At the time of his birth his parents, Paul Leland Haworth and Martha Ackerman, were living in New York City, where his father was a graduate student and lecturer in history at Columbia University. His mother, a former teacher, chose to return to her hometown for the birth of the first of their three children. In 1907 the family moved from New York City to Cleveland, Ohio, and in 1910, to West Newton, Ind., where Haworth spent the next eighteen years.

After graduating from West Newton High School in 1921, Haworth enrolled at Indiana University, where he earned a B.A. degree in physics in 1925 and an M.A. degree in physics in 1926. His first teaching position was as a physics instructor at the Arsenal Technical High School in Indianapolis (1926–1928). On July 2, 1927, Haworth married Barbara Mottier, a secretary; they had two children.

In 1928, Haworth was awarded a scholarship to the University of Wisconsin's Ph.D. program in physics. He received his doctorate in 1931 with the completion of his dissertation, "Secondary Electrons from Very Clean Metal Surfaces When Bombarded with Primary Electrons." During the last year of his graduate study, Haworth was a physics instructor at the University of Wisconsin. He continued to work there until 1937, when he received the Lalor Fellowship in physical chemistry from the Massachusetts Institute of Technology (MIT).

Haworth left MIT, after one year as a researcher in low-temperature physical chemistry, to become an associate professor of physics at the University of Illinois. His desire to be near his mother in Indiana, his father having died in 1938, was a major reason for his decision to leave MIT. Haworth soon found himself back at MIT, on leave from Illinois, to work at its radiation laboratory in support of the war effort. From 1941 to 1946 he worked with the microwave committee at the radiation laboratory on the development of microwave radar. From 1942 to 1943 he was group leader within the committee, and in 1943 he became division head. In 1944, Haworth, though absent from his duties for three years, was promoted to full professor at the University of Illinois.

In 1946, Haworth returned to his position as physics professor at the University of Illinois. On Apr. 15, 1947, he was contacted by the Brookhaven National Laboratory at Upton, N.Y., and invited in as a consultant. By July

1947, Haworth was assistant director in charge of special projects under Brookhaven's first director, Philip M. Morse. He supervised the expansion of Brookhaven's research facilities, including the building of the 30-megawatt graphite research reactor (BGRR) and the 3-giga-electron-volt proton accelerator (Cosmotron). On July 17, 1948, Morse resigned, returning to a professorship at MIT. Haworth was then named acting director of the laboratory, holding that position until October, when he officially became director of the Brookhaven National Laboratory. During his tenure as director, Haworth continued to oversee the construction of the BGRR and the Cosmotron, as well as a number of other projects, including the 30-GeV alternating gradient accelerator (AGS).

In addition to his work at Brookhaven, Haworth assisted the Department of Defense with projects that included the Vista project in 1951 and the East River project in 1952. He was also chairman of the Ad Hoc Committee on Combat Developments for the army in 1954, was a member of the Technological Capabilities Panel of the President's Science Advisory Committee from 1954 to 1955, and headed Project Atlantis for the navy in 1959.

In 1951, Haworth became vice-president of Associated Universities, Inc. (AUI), a nonprofit consortium of nine East Coast universities that was created to support major scientific research projects, including Brookhaven. Haworth served in that position until 1960 and was president from 1960 to 1961, after his predecessor, Lloyd V. Berkner, resigned. Haworth accepted the presidency reluctantly, placing a higher priority on his work at Brookhaven. As president, he was able to save AUI's 140-foot radio telescope in Green Bank, W.Va., after technical problems threatened to halt construction. He did this while recovering from surgery for colon cancer in the fall of 1959.

In February 1961, Haworth's wife died after a long illness. After fourteen years of service at Brookhaven, on Apr. 1, 1961, President John F. Kennedy asked Haworth to accept a position as a commissioner of the Atomic Energy Commission (AEC). As commissioner, Haworth was directly involved in the nuclear weapons program and in research and development of nuclear power and related technology.

In 1962, President Kennedy asked the AEC to write a report on the relationship between nuclear power and the United States economy. Haworth, assigned the role of principal author, completed the report, *Civilian Nuclear Power —A Report to the President—1962*, that same year. The report began the discussions in Congress on the need to support the research and development of all potential forms of energy in order to make the United States more energy independent. During his twenty-seven months with the AEC, Haworth supported the Limited Test Ban Treaty, ratified in 1963, which grew out of his concern for the environmental effects of nuclear testing.

As part of his work with the AEC, Haworth was a frequent visitor to the White House Office of Science and Technology. During his many visits, he met and fell in love with Irene Benik, who was secretary to the president's science adviser, J. B. Wiesner. Haworth and Benik were married on May 15, 1963. Around the same time, Haworth was being considered for the position of director of the National Science Foundation (NSF). On July 1, 1963, he succeeded Allen T. Waterman in that post. He remained there until 1969, when a reorganization of the NSF and the coming of a new presidential administration made his position uncertain.

After leaving the NSF in July 1969, Haworth became special assistant to the president of AUI and special consultant to the director of the Brookhaven National Laboratory. In addition to his work with the AUI and Brookhaven, he became a member of Oak Ridge Associated Universities (ORAU) in 1971. Haworth was named director emeritus of ORAU in 1978, the first person to be given that honor. Less than a year later, he died in Port Jefferson, N.Y.

Haworth was both a gifted scientist and a gifted administrator. Under his leadership the Brookhaven National Laboratory became a major center for high-energy physics research. Haworth also demonstrated his skills as director of the NSF by developing a number of major research projects and expanding the NSF's support of university-based scientific research.

[The archives of the Brookhaven National Laboratory, Upton, N.Y., 1946–1989, contain Haworth's papers covering his tenure as director. Papers of Philip Morse and Leland Haworth, 1946–1961 (20 microfilm reels), dealing primarily with Haworth's tenure at Brookhaven, are in the American Institute of Physics, Niels Bohr Library, New York City. References to Haworth's work at the MIT Radiation Laboratory are in the papers of Francis Wheeler Loomis,

1920–1976, in the archives of the University of Illinois at Urbana-Champaign.

An excellent biographical essay on Haworth by Maurice Goldhaber and Gerald F. Tape is in *Biographical Memoirs. National Academy of Sciences* 55 (1985). An obituary is in the *New York Times*, Mar. 6, 1979.]

TAMMY ANN SYREK

HAYDEN, ROBERT EARL (Aug. 4, 1913–Feb. 25, 1980), poet, was born in Detroit, Mich., to Gladys Finn, a former circus employee of Irish heritage, and Asa Sheffey, a black laborer. Because of societal proscriptions against interracial relationships, Gladys gave the infant up to a black couple, William and Sue Ellen Hayden, from whom young Robert derived his name and an early appreciation of African-American life and mores. In years to come, relations between the foster parents and natural parents—particularly his mother, who divorced Sheffey and married Albert Moore, a cabaret owner—were difficult.

Hayden never reproached his mother for giving him up; he later described her as a "beautiful woman, vivacious and fond of dancing." Grateful to her for introducing him to the theatrical and cultural life of Buffalo, N.Y., where he visited her on many occasions, Hayden found life with his foster parents trying because of their strict religious views. Hayden's sensitive nature and physical disability (extreme nearsightedness) were reproved by his natural father, resulting in strained relations between them throughout their lives. Because of his serious handicap, young Robert showed an early interest in things intellectual and bookish, rather than in sports or things considered more manly.

After elementary school in a poor area of Detroit, Hayden briefly attended the predominantly black Miller High School. Poor sight enabled him to transfer to the predominantly white Northern High School in another part of the city. Hayden referred to the school, with some sarcasm, as a "sight-saving school," in reference to his exposure to racial prejudice. While there, however, his first serious effort in fiction was made. He won a prize for a short story entitled "Gold."

In 1930, Hayden graduated from Northern High. During the harsh depression years that followed he did postgraduate study at Cass High School before entering Detroit City College (later Wayne State University) in 1932; he majored in Spanish. Unable to pass a required physics course Hayden did not receive his degree.

He left Wayne State in 1936 and began to pursue a literary career. Joining the Federal Writers Project of the Works Project Administration (WPA) to write poetry in 1936, Hayden developed his interest in African-American history and folklore. He came under the influence of both Richard Wright and Langston Hughes, key forces of the Harlem Renaissance. Wright's influence aroused in him an intense social consciousness and a fervor for protest.

During his years with the WPA, he showed an interest in Communism, but he never joined the Communist party and ultimately rejected its ideology as a means toward resolving black problems. At bottom, Hayden was, in his words, "a cultural assimilationist rather than a Marxist."

The 1930's and 1940's were apprenticeship years for Hayden. His experiences in the WPA found utterance in his first serious collection of poems, *Heart-Shape in the Dust* (1940). Hayden's reputation as a new and vital voice in American poetry was soon recognized. He was awarded the prestigious Jules and Avery Hopwood Prize for poetry by the University of Michigan in 1938 and in 1942. He was awarded a combined B.A./M.A. in 1944 from Wayne State University. In 1947 he received a Julius Rosenwald Fellowship in creative writing. Meanwhile, in June 1940 he married Erma Inez Morris, a concert pianist and music teacher.

While attending graduate school at the University of Michigan at Ann Arbor, Hayden became associated with the British-born poet W. H. Auden, who introduced him to new techniques of poetry associated with contemporary modernists such as William Butler Yeats.

This period of broadening poetic development and marriage contributed to his burgeoning religious faith. Indeed, his wife was responsible for his conversion to the Baha'i faith and its belief, he said, in "progressive revelation."

Despite his efforts to reflect the sensibilities of his race without consciously espousing black political causes, Hayden was seen less as a poet than as a *black* poet, which caused him consternation. He believed the problems between groups of people had more to do with class than with race, and he sought to express this view in his work.

In 1946, Hayden began teaching at Fisk University, in Nashville, Tenn., where he developed an intellectual independence and racial iconoclasm that was to create antagonism with black intellectuals throughout the 1950's and the 1960's. During the 1950's, for example, the overt racism felt but not directly experienced by Hayden himself was the inspiration for his series of poems about the pre–civil rights South, begun in his 1948 collection *The Lion and the Archer*.

During the 1950's, Hayden was awarded a Ford Foundation grant, which he used to travel in Mexico, where he learned firsthand about "the plight of the Mexican peon." This was the kind of class struggle that engaged his political consciousness. His experiences and observations during his Mexican travels found utterance in an acclaimed 1962 poetic collection, *A Ballad of Remembrance*.

The 1960's found Hayden confronted with his most turbulent times. Slipping into his fifties and never having been accepted as a voice for black leadership, he was labeled an Uncle Tom because of his assimilationist feelings.

Ironically, while ridiculed by militant students, his stature among his peers grew. A host of awards and acknowledgments followed him in his later years. In 1965 he won the Grand Prize for Poetry at the first World Festival of Negro Arts held in Dakar, Senegal. He was visiting poet-in-residence at Indiana State University in 1967. He left Fisk in 1969 to become full professor at the University of Michigan at Ann Arbor, a position he held until his death.

During the 1970's, Hayden continued to gain recognition for his poetry. His appointment in 1976 as poetry consultant to the Library of Congress was in addition to his being the recipient of honorary doctorates from four major universities. Honored also by the National Institute of Arts and Letters and the Michigan Foundation for the Arts, Hayden gained greater exposure through extensive public readings. He continued to publish until his death of heart failure at University Hospital in Ann Arbor, Mich.

[Hayden published nine collections of poetry. His *Collected Poems* (1985); and *Collected Prose* (1984) were edited by Frederick Glaysher. Numerous anthologies carry his poetry. See also John Hatcher, *From the Auroral Darkness: The Life and Poetry of Robert Hayden* (1984); Fred M. Fetrow, *Robert Hayden* (1984); and Pontheolla T. Williams, *Robert Hayden: A Critical Analysis of His Poetry* (1987). Critical discussions include Pontheolla T. Williams, "Robert Hayden: A Life upon These Shores," *World Order*, Fall 1981, a Baha'i publication. Obituaries are in the *New York Times*, Feb. 27, 1980, and *Jet*, Mar. 20, 1980.]

William F. Browne

HAYMES, RICHARD BENJAMIN ("DICK") (Sept. 13, 1918–Mar. 28, 1980), singer and actor, was born in Buenos Aires, Argentina. His father, an Englishman of Scottish descent, was a rancher, and his mother, Marguerite, was a concert singer and vocal coach. In 1919, after his ranch had suffered extensive locust damage, the elder Haymes moved his family to the United States. The family, including Dick's younger brother Bob (who had been a singer and lyricist), moved frequently before finally settling in California.

Thanks to voice training from his mother, Haymes developed a rich, warm baritone further distinguished by excellent phrasing and breath control. He worked first as a radio announcer and then successively as a singer with the Carl Hoff, Eddie Martin, and Orrin Tucker bands. Haymes got his first big career break in 1939 when Harry James hired him to replace Frank Sinatra, who had defected from James's band to become the featured vocalist with the Tommy Dorsey orchestra. Haymes had been writing songs and trying to sell them to various bandleaders. With the help of Larry Shayne, a music publisher, Haymes arranged a meeting with Harry James in the hopes of convincing him to add a Haymes song or two to his band's repertoire. James listened to the young songwriter's work and then, according to George Simon, author of *The Big Bands*, turned to Shayne and said, "I don't like the tunes too much, but I sure like the way the kid sings." Harry James's band was one of the most successful of the time. Performing as vocalist with the James band in concerts all over the United States and on the radio, Haymes soon became a household name. Songs associated with him from this period include "The Nearness of You," "Maybe," "Fools Rush In," and "How High the Moon."

But Haymes's loyalty to Harry James ran no deeper than that of his predecessor. He broke with James to join the Tommy Dorsey orchestra in 1943, then left Dorsey to sing briefly with Benny Goodman's band before becoming an independent single artist.

During the 1940's many people considered Haymes to be the equal of Bing Crosby and Frank Sinatra. He had two million-seller records, "You'll Never Know," in 1943, and "Little White Lies," in 1948. Other hits included "I'll Get By," "It Can't Be Wrong," " 'Til the End of Time," "Imagination," "The More I See You," "For You, for Me, for Evermore," and "Mam'selle." Although best remembered as a soloist, Haymes also recorded songs with the Andrews Sisters, Judy Garland, Ethel Merman, and other 1940's singing stars. Haymes's singing style was indebted to Bing Crosby and the crooning tradition. He projected a shyness and vulnerability when he sang, qualities well suited to the interpretation of love songs.

Because of his celebrity as a singer and his physical attractiveness, Haymes was much sought after by Hollywood. In 1944 he signed a contract with Twentieth Century–Fox, and thereafter acted and sang in a number of musicals: *Four Jills in a Jeep* (1944), *Irish Eyes Are Smiling* (1944), *Diamond Horseshoe* (1945), *State Fair* (1945), *Do You Love Me?* (1946), *The Shocking Miss Pilgrim* (1947), and *Carnival in Costa Rica* (1947). He made two pictures for Universal, *One Touch of Venus* (1948) and *Up in Central Park* (1948), and then worked on single-picture contracts for a variety of studios until his film career subsided in the early 1950's.

Haymes had a chaotic personal life. He married seven times. His first marriage, to Joanne Marshall, ended in divorce in the mid-1940's. He then married actress Joanne Dru; they had three children. He divorced Dru to marry Nora Eddington Flynn (the former wife of actor Errol Flynn) in 1949. He divorced Flynn to marry Fran Jeffries, a singer. He divorced Jeffries to marry actress Rita Hayworth in 1953; this marriage ended in 1955. Then, in 1958, Haymes married his seventh and last wife, Frances Ann Makris.

Haymes also had problems with the United States government. In 1944, when he was issued a draft notice, Haymes claimed that he was a citizen of Argentina and therefore exempt from the draft. Although he had a legal right to claim this exemption, and although his action produced no immediate negative consequences—indeed, it enabled Haymes to avoid military service just at the time when his careers as soloist and film star were taking off—his refusal to serve in the military came back to haunt him. When the Cold War spawned McCarthyism and many in the entertainment world were accused of being Communists or Communist sympathizers, the United States Immigration Service was tipped that Haymes was not an American citizen, and that despite having grown rich and famous in the United States, he had refused to serve in its army. Thus, during the years 1953–1954, Haymes lived under the threat of deportation, until the federal government dropped its case against him.

His problems with the federal government had a snowball effect. In 1953 the Actors Equity Association, presumably reacting to the negative publicity the Haymes affair generated, announced that Haymes had falsely listed Santa Barbara, Calif., as his place of birth when applying for membership in the association. Haymes's membership was suspended, which meant that he was effectively barred from performing in the United States. He only regained his union card when he became a United States citizen.

Meanwhile, Haymes was plagued by financial problems. Money had poured in when his career was on the rise, and he had not altered his life-style as his career began to go into decline. His many marriages and divorces led to burdensome alimony and child support payments. In 1953, teetering on the brink of bankruptcy, he was ordered to appear in court on alimony charges. Also in that year the Internal Revenue Service put a lien on his salary because of unpaid income taxes.

Haymes also suffered from alcoholism. But he gradually climbed out of the pit he had dug for himself. By the 1960's he was working regularly as a singer in Ireland, Great Britain, and Europe, and in the 1970's he had a modestly successful comeback in the United States. Haymes died of lung cancer in Los Angeles.

[An obituary is in the *New York Times*, Mar. 30, 1980.]

CAMILLE D'ARIENZO

HAYS, PAUL R. (Apr. 2, 1903–Feb. 13, 1980), judge, was born in Des Moines, Iowa, the son of S. Everett Hollingsworth Hays and Fae Susan Hatch. He graduated from Columbia University in 1924 and thereafter supported himself by teaching Greek and Latin while successively earning M.A. (1927) and LL.B. (1933) degrees from Columbia. On Feb. 1,

1924, Hays married Eleanor K. Williams; they had one child and divorced in 1943. After passing the New York bar, Hays joined the prestigious New York City law firm of Cravath, de Gersdorff, Swaine, and Wood in 1933.

In 1936, Hays left private practice to serve as counsel to the National Recovery Administration, and thereafter he held a variety of positions in other federal agencies, including the War Labor Board, the Office of Alien Property, the Resettlement Administration, and the Justice Department. He pursued a second career teaching law at Columbia University, as an assistant professor from 1936 to 1938, associate professor from 1938 to 1943, and professor from 1943 to 1971. From 1957 to 1961 he held the Nash lectureship at Columbia. From the mid-1940's on, Hays had a third career as a labor arbitrator. He served on the New York State Board of Mediation from 1940 to 1944 and on the New York City Board of Health from 1954 to 1960. On Nov. 19, 1949, he married Elinor Rice; they had no children. In 1952, Hays was appointed an arbitrator and helped to settle a particularly bitter New York longshoremen's dispute that had national implications.

In 1958, Hays became chairman of New York's Liberal party, a small but influential third party which, under Hays's leadership, played a key role in helping John F. Kennedy defeat Richard M. Nixon in the 1960 presidential election. Liberal party support helped Kennedy win a close contest in New York and thus its crucial electoral votes. After his election Kennedy rewarded Hays with an appointment to a judgeship on the prestigious Federal Court of Appeals for the Second Circuit, which sat in New York City and heard all appeals from the federal courts of New York, Vermont, and Connecticut. Hays's colleagues on the Second Circuit bench included such noted judges as Harold Medina, Irving Kaufman, and Thurgood Marshall.

As a jurist, Hays typically recoiled from using his court platform as a means to make law or to challenge other branches of the federal government. He regularly deferred to federal administrative agencies, which he saw as "not only experts on legislative procedures but specialists in problems [within their areas of concern, such as] education [and] mental health." In one of the most controversial and highly publicized cases of the Vietnam War era in 1971 Hays took the Nixon administration's side when it attempted to prevent the *New York Times* from publishing the so-called Pentagon Papers, a report of American involvement in Vietnam that documented the United States government's duplicity in the conduct of the war. The majority of the court, however, supported the *Times*.

In 1968, Hays voted to permit the importation of the erotic Swedish film *I Am Curious—Yellow*. Reviewing the film, which he described as depicting scenes of "sexual intercourse . . . some quite unusual," Hays nonetheless concluded that it met the Supreme Court's standard of acceptability, in that "it cannot be said that 'the dominant theme of the material taken as a whole appeals to a prurient interest in sex.' " The ruling enabled film distributors to import many more European movies that had "adult" content, and thereby pushed Hollywood producers to create films that offered more realistic portrayals of matters involving sex. The ruling was a key step in the process that has led to the almost total abolition of the government's power—whether at the local, state, or national level—to regulate and censor the sexual content of books, films, plays, and other materials.

Hays's most significant ruling was in the case of *Scenic Hudson Preservation Conference* v. *Federal Power Commission* in 1965. The Federal Power Commission intended to create a major nuclear-power-generating plant at Storm King, a particularly scenic point along the Hudson River. Its plan was challenged by Scenic Hudson, an environmental group. In writing the court's majority opinion, Hays ruled for the first time anywhere in the United States court system that such citizens' groups as Scenic Hudson could challenge the decision of a federal agency not only on economic grounds but on the basis of "aesthetic, conservational, and recreational aspects of power development." In doing so, Hays almost single-handedly opened up the field of environmental law.

In the course of his opinion, Hays noted that alternative sources of power had been proposed, and that four fishing groups "wished to show that the major spawning grounds for the distinct race of Hudson River striped bass was in the immediate vicinity of the Storm King project." Hays ruled that the whole fisheries question be taken into consideration again by the Federal Power Commission. Eventually the commission held to its prior decision, and Hays—speaking for the court—concurred. But Scenic

Hudson and other environmental groups had won the right to have their say in court. Hays had shown the way for the federal judiciary to consider environmental concerns, opening the door to passage of the federal National Environmental Policy Act a few years later.

Hays died in Tucson, Ariz., where he was vacationing.

[Hays's judicial opinions are in the *Federal Register*, second series. His comments in Monrad G. Paulsen, ed., *Legal Institutions Today and Tomorrow* (1959), the record of a symposium held at Columbia University, provide interesting insights into his legal beliefs. Hays's thoughts on labor negotiations and the proper role of the courts is detailed in his *Labor Arbitration: A Dissenting View* (1966). Other significant writings by Hays include "Formal Contracts and Considerations: A Legislative Program," *Columbia Law Review* 849 (1941); and "Federalism and Labor Relations in the United States," *University of Pennsylvania Law Review* 959 (1954). As regards the Pentagon Papers matter, see Sanford J. Ungar, *The Papers and the Papers* (1972). An official memorial tribute to Hays was published in 635 *Federal Reporter*, second series. An obituary is in the *New York Times*, Feb. 15, 1980.]

JOHN DAVID HEALY

HÉBERT, FELIX EDWARD ("EDDIE") (Oct. 12, 1901–Dec. 29, 1979), journalist and congressman, was born in New Orleans, La., the son of Felix Joseph Hébert, a streetcar motorman, and Lea Naquin, a teacher. A boyhood accident caused young Hébert to lose the sight of his left eye. He attended public and Catholic schools in New Orleans. At Jesuit High School he wrote for the school paper and managed athletic teams. He won awards for debate at Jesuit and at Tulane University, which he attended from 1920 to 1924 (he did not receive a degree).

Hébert's first profession was journalism. He was a sportswriter for the New Orleans *Times-Picayune* while still in high school. After working in public relations from 1926 to 1929, he became political editor of the *New Orleans States*. While in that position, he attacked Huey Long and members of his political machine daily in a front-page column. On Aug. 1, 1934, he married Gladys Bofill; they had one child.

In 1935, Huey Long was assassinated, but his organization remained. Four years later, Hébert became city editor and broke the story of corruption in state government, which resulted in criminal convictions of some members of the Long organization and came to be known as the "Louisiana Scandals."

In 1940, Hébert sought and won the Democratic nomination to the United States House of Representatives from the First Congressional District of Louisiana, defeating Joachim O. Fernandez, known as "Bathtub Joe." Hébert could hardly have failed in the political climate of reform he had helped to create. Since Louisiana was then a one-party state, the Democratic nomination was the equivalent of election to the office. It was an office which Hébert would hold for thirty-six years, until reformers of a later day rejected him and the principles for which he stood.

Typical of southern Democrats of the 1940's and 1950's, Hébert was a strong supporter of the military and an equally strong foe of Communism and racial equality. When he went to Congress in 1941, his first committee assignment was to the District Affairs Committee. From his position on that committee, he strove to promote good government but not self-government, for the District of Columbia, with its large African-American population. In later years, he opposed civil rights legislation and kept a junior Reserve Officers Training Corps program out of Louisiana because it would have been racially integrated.

In January of 1948, Hébert was appointed to fill a vacancy on the House Un-American Activities Committee. Richard Nixon joined the committee at the same time; the two got along well and remained friends over the years. Although he was on the committee for only one year, Hébert had a reputation as a hard worker who was concerned about treating witnesses fairly, although he himself might be unfair, if he genuinely believed that a witness was a Communist. He was committed to the work of the committee and did not leave it voluntarily. In the 1948 presidential election, Hébert supported the Dixiecrat candidate. After the election, the House Democratic Caucus, apparently with an eye to removing Hébert, adopted a rule requiring that all members of the Un-American Activities Committee be experienced lawyers. Since Hébert was not a lawyer, the rule permitted the party to replace him with a loyalist.

Hébert had his greatest impact on public policy in the area of national defense. In 1951 he chaired an Armed Services subcommittee that uncovered waste in military contracts, and in

1961 he publicized the number of retired military officers employed by defense contractors. However, the early 1960's was not a good time for the six foot, two inch, sturdily built congressman. The vision in his one functioning eye was deteriorating because of a cataract. In 1966, Hébert had successful surgery on the eye, which seemed to reenergize him. In 1970, after chairing a subcommittee investigation, he accused the military and the State Department of trying to cover up evidence related to the My Lai massacre in Vietnam, even though he had been a supporter of the Vietnam War.

By virtue of his seniority, Hébert assumed the chairmanship of the House Armed Services Committee in 1971, upon the death of Congressman L. Mendel Rivers of South Carolina. Following in the footsteps of previous Armed Services chairmen, he continued to give strong support to the military and to ensure continued appropriations of funds for defense installations in his district, as well as the New Orleans metropolitan area, part of which was outside his district. Hébert's predecessor as chairman had used the slogan "Rivers Delivers"; Hébert was less blatant and claimed to have instructed the Defense Department not to locate anything in his district on account of his chairmanship of the Armed Services Committee alone. A friend of the military, he said that he would take Pentagon officials to the woodshed and spank them when necessary.

Just as political scandals propelled Hébert to Washington, so scandals hastened his return home. In the 1974 elections, the American public reacted to the Watergate scandal by sending seventy-five new, liberal Democrats to Washington. They were instrumental in changing House Democratic procedures to require that committee chairmen be voted on by the party caucus—that is, all House Democrats—in a secret ballot. Hébert's promilitary stance and his general conservatism were unacceptable to them. He was one of three congressmen who were removed from their chairmanships. Hébert continued to serve on the Armed Services Committee until 1976 but did not seek reelection to the House. He died in New Orleans.

[Hébert's papers are at the Howard-Tilton Memorial Library of Tulane University. His autobiography is *"Last of the Titans": The Life and Times of Congressman F. Edward Hébert of Louisiana* (1976). A good summary of his career to 1971 is in Gay Cook and Pauline Jennings, "F. Edward Hébert: Democratic Representative from Louisiana," *Ralph Nader Congress Project: Citizens Look at Congress*, vol. 4 (1972). A description of his brief tenure on the Un-American Activities Committee is in Robert K. Carr, *The House Committee on Un-American Activities: 1945–1950* (1952). Information on the loss of his committee chairmanship is in *Congressional Quarterly Almanac* (1975) and *Congressional Quarterly Guide to Congress*, 2d ed. (1976). An obituary is in the *New York Times*, Dec. 30, 1979.]

PATRICIA A. BEHLAR

HEEZEN, BRUCE CHARLES (Apr. 11, 1924–June 21, 1977), oceanographer, was born in Vinton, Iowa. His father, Charles Christian Heezen, managed farm properties for an insurance company, then acquired his own farm near Muscatine, Iowa, on which he raised turkeys. His mother, Esther Christine Shirding, had taught dramatics in high school before their marriage and had considerable artistic talent. Bruce was their only child.

Heezen helped his father on the turkey farm (thereby acquiring a lifelong distaste for the product) and showed an early interest in science. In 1942 he enrolled at the University of Iowa; his studies were interrupted for two years during World War II, when he worked on his father's farm. In his third year of studies Heezen took a course in geology, and in the summer he collected conodont fossils in Nevada with a graduate assistant lecturer, Walter Youngquist. Fairly well on his way to a career in paleontology, in 1947 he attended a Sigma Xi lecture given by Professor Maurice Ewing of Columbia University.

Ewing invited Heezen to join him on an expedition at sea the following summer. At the last minute Heezen was put in charge of the work on the smaller of the two vessels, *Balanus*. He obtained two hundred photographs of the seafloor and many cores, which set him onto a career of studying the ocean floor. After receiving a B.A. from the University of Iowa in 1948 and spending more months at sea, he became a graduate student at Columbia University, where Ewing had just established Lamont Geological Observatory for his growing research group. Heezen received the M.A. in 1952 and the Ph.D. in 1957 from Columbia University. He was appointed research associate there in 1956, senior research scientist at Lamont Geological Observatory from 1956 to 1958, then assistant professor in the geology department at Columbia in 1960, where he advanced to associate professor in 1964. He never married.

Heezen's research began with a small number of sounding records in the North Atlantic. Early expeditions with an improved sounding device, the precision depth recorder, showed that vast areas of the seafloor were flat, and coring proved that the sediments were often coarse-grained sands. From the sequence of breaks in transatlantic cables caused by an earthquake in 1929, Heezen presented in 1952 the idea that turbidity currents can rapidly transport vast amounts of sediment far out to sea. These flows of sand and water created by submarine landslides had been first proposed by Reginald Daly and were demonstrated later by Philip Kuenen in tank experiments. After Ewing and Heezen determined that the Hudson Submarine Canyon was at least 15,000 feet deep, they proposed that turbidity currents can scour submarine canyons from the continental shelf. Later, with colleagues and students, Heezen found that deep currents caused by the Coriolis effect along the continental margins also transport and redeposit sediments in vast drifts on the seafloor.

The Mid-Atlantic Ridge was a feature that had been recognized but not surveyed. Using six profiles across the ridge obtained by Ewing and former colleagues at Woods Hole Oceanographic Institution, Heezen worked with research assistant Marie Tharp to create a map (1952). Tharp noted that on each profile, the crest of the ridge showed a deep valley. As more data came in from expeditions at sea, the great extent and continuity of the Mid-Atlantic Ridge became clear. Partly because of restrictions by the United States Navy on publication of contour charts, Heezen and Tharp instead produced in 1959 a three-dimensional physiographic diagram of the North Atlantic Ocean, after the style of Columbia geologist Armin K. Lobeck for terrestrial presentation. While plotting thousands of earthquakes to explain submarine cable breaks for Bell Laboratories, Heezen observed in 1952 that the earthquakes coincided with the rift valley that Tharp had noted, and concluded that the valley itself was a tension fault caused by earthquakes. In 1956, Ewing and Heezen proposed a world-girdling mid-ocean ridge system with an axial rift that was seismically active. Incorporated into the global system were the terrestrial rift valleys of eastern Africa, the San Andreas fault system in California, and the tension cracks near Iceland.

Over the next two decades, Heezen and Tharp in close collaboration produced physiographic diagrams of the South Atlantic, the Indian Ocean, the west-central Pacific, and finally the floors of all oceans. These panoramic views and globes, widely distributed chiefly by the National Geographic Society, clearly illustrate the 40,000-mile extent of the almost continuous seafloor mountain range and rift zone. A summary of the collaborative work, painted by Henrich Berann, was completed just before Heezen's departure on his final sea voyage in 1977.

Heezen at first proposed an expanding Earth to account for the new material being produced at the rift centers. It gradually became clear to oceanographers that the rifts represented plate boundaries, since the theory of global plate tectonics advocated that new material is thrust onto the seafloor at the rifts and older material descends at the deep trenches.

Heezen spent a great deal of time at sea, where he seemed to be indefatigable, ever fascinated by new information. He worked closely with his graduate students, who often accompanied him aboard ship. His interests extended to all aspects of seafloor sedimentation. He identified spiral patterns that appeared in deep-sea photographs as the tracks left by a bottom-dwelling acorn worm. He theorized that tektites dredged from the seafloor were evidence that a celestial object had exploded 700,000 years earlier. While analyzing cores from the Mediterranean with Dragoslav Ninkovich, he suggested that beds of ash there represented material from an explosive eruption of Santorini volcano in the Aegean Sea, which destroyed the Minoan civilization on Crete and was perhaps the origin of the legends of Atlantis.

Deep-sea photographs were a favorite tool of Heezen's, and hundreds of them appeared in the book he wrote with Charles D. Hollister, *Face of the Deep* (1971). In the late 1960's, Heezen began participating in United States Navy programs using submersibles and research submarines, so that he could see the undersea features directly and determine photo sites himself. He was aboard the navy research submarine *NR-1*, preparing for a dive near Iceland, when he died of a heart attack.

[Heezen's papers and underwater films are at the Smithsonian Institution Archives. His early work on turbidity currents was presented in "Turbidity Currents and Submarine Slumps, and the 1929 Grand Banks Earthquake," *American Journal of Science* (1952), with Maurice Ewing. Heezen's first physiographic diagram with Marie Tharp was presented in *The Floors of the Oceans, 1, The North Atlantic, Part 1, Physiographic Diagram of the North Atlantic*, Geological Society of America Special Paper no. 65 (1959), with Maurice Ewing and Marie Tharp. Later diagrams were published by the National Geographic Society (inserts in *National Geographic*, 1967–1970), with Marie Tharp. The final summary, *World Ocean Floor Panorama* (1977), with Marie Tharp, was sponsored by the Office of Naval Research. The study of ash from Santorini is "Santorini Tephra," in Walter F. Whittard and R. Bradshaw, eds., *Submarine Geology and Geophysics* (1965). Biographical accounts are A. S. Laughton, "Bruce C. Heezen," *Nature* 270 (1977); Marie Tharp, "Mapping the Ocean Floor—1947 to 1977," in R. A. Scrutton and M. Talwani, eds., *The Ocean Floor* (1982); Marie Tharp and Henry Frankel, "Mappers of the Deep," *Natural History*, Oct. 1986; and Paul J. Fox, "Bruce C. Heezen," *Oceanus*, Winter 1991/1992. An obituary is in the *New York Times*, June 23, 1977.]

ELIZABETH NOBLE SHOR

HELPERN, MILTON (Apr. 17, 1902–Apr. 22, 1977), forensic pathologist, was born in the East Harlem district of New York City, the son of Moses Helpern, a men's clothing cutter, and Bertha Toplon. He was educated entirely in the city, graduating from the College of the City of New York with a B.S. degree in 1922. He received his M.D. in 1926 from Cornell University Medical College and became an intern in the Cornell (Second) Medical Division of Bellevue Hospital, specializing in pathology.

For many years, the hospital's Department of Pathology and the Office of the Medical Examiner of New York City shared the same mortuary; as a result, students and doctors frequently assisted the examiner with routine autopsies. The medical examiner's office derived from the old coroner system, which was introduced early into the American colonies. However, by 1900 it was racked by corruption, since the coroners (one for each city borough) were elected political hacks with no medical training. In 1914 a commissioner appointed by the mayor to investigate the system recommended that it be replaced by a chief medical examiner for the city as a whole, with the examiner and his staff all to be doctors, pathologists, and microscopists, and subject to the Civil Service Law. In 1915 the state legislature passed the Medical Examiner Law, which became a prototype for many such laws.

In 1918 this law went into effect in the city, and Charles Norris was appointed the first chief medical examiner. When Helpern was doing his residency at Bellevue, he came into frequent contact with Norris, who regarded him as a personal protégé. Helpern said that although he enjoyed pathology as a resident, he was not particularly attracted to forensic medicine; he hoped to be named the head of a proposed hospital laboratory. The Great Depression ended the laboratory project, and it was only at the last hour of the last day for submitting applications that Helpern decided to take the civil service examination for assistant medical examiner. He passed and joined Norris's staff in April 1931.

Helpern married Ruth Vyner in July 1927; they had three children. She died in 1953, and Helpern married his secretary, Beatrice Liebowitz Nightingale, a widow with two children, in January 1955.

As a student at Cornell, Helpern had taught biology to help pay his tuition. He had been on the medical examiner's staff for perhaps six months when he was asked to replace another doctor who had been lecturing in legal medicine. Thus, about 1932, he began to teach with Thomas Gonzales, who became the second chief medical examiner, and Morgan Vance, also an assistant examiner, at Cornell, Columbia, New York University, and the New York Police Academy. The three doctors decided to combine their notes into a book, published in 1937 as *Legal Medicine and Toxicology*, which was long considered the definitive text in the field.

In 1943, Helpern was appointed deputy chief medical examiner, and became the third chief medical examiner of New York City in 1954. The medical examiner's office investigates a death in specific instances, which include death from criminal violence or in any "suspicious or unusual manner." The routine work of this office is to diagnose, for insurance purposes, the type of natural disease that killed someone. But much of the time the medical examiners assist law-enforcement agencies in the investigation or prosecution of a possible crime. As the chief medical examiner, Helpern testified at innumerable trials and was a key witness in several of the most sensational murder trials of his day. In the mid-1960's, he helped establish the guilt of Alice Crimmins in the murder of her children and was a chief witness in the bloody "career girl murders."

The extraordinary case of Dr. Carl Coppolino was his most memorable. Helpern said of this case: "Not only was the medico-legal aspect unique—it broke new ground in forensic toxicology—but the ballyhoo surrounding the trials was of an intensity that beat anything ever witnessed." In 1965, Dr. Carmela Coppolino was found dead in bed of an apparent heart attack and was certified as having died naturally. However, a number of inconsistencies and the agitated testimony of a former lover of her husband led to the decision that Helpern and his assistants should perform an autopsy, which concluded that she had been injected by her husband with a muscle relaxant that stopped her breathing. The difficulty was that the suspected drug breaks down quickly in the body into two substances normally found in tissues, and no one had ever searched for this particular compound in any body, living or dead. Nevertheless, Helpern's office proved conclusively that Coppolino had been murdered by lethal injection, and in 1967 her husband, over the vociferous protestations of his attorney, F. Lee Bailey, was given a life sentence.

From all accounts, Helpern made an excellent witness at such trials. Often called "avuncular," he had a sleepy-seeming manner and gave articulate responses in a warm voice. The *New York Times* called him a "prosecutor's dream," and a law-enforcement official who often dealt with him described him as "among the most remarkably convincing of experts." Because of these characteristics and because he and his associates did meticulous work, Helpern established a reputation as a "medical detective." During his years as chief medical examiner, he was involved in cases all over the world, either giving expert testimony or examining and interpreting evidence.

In 1960 the headquarters of the medical examiner's office was moved to 520 First Avenue. Helpern had the following inscription placed in the new lobby: "This is the place where death delights to help the living." In his memoirs, he insisted that one of the key functions of his office was to preserve the public's health, a field where death indeed "delights to help the living." For example, Helpern was instrumental in identifying carbon monoxide emissions as a cause of many otherwise mysterious deaths during the 1940's and subsequently helped to establish a citywide gas inspection program in 1951. In later decades he was effective in arranging organ transplants.

But it was probably in his lecturing, writing, and teaching that Helpern most fulfilled the precepts of his motto. His easy, articulate manner made him a sought-after speaker, and he loved to talk about his profession. "This job is not morbid," he once said. "You do these investigations in the interests of living people." Helpern wrote more than one hundred articles on his subject, as well as coauthoring an early classic. He became the head of the Department of Forensic Medicine at the New York University School of Medicine and served on the faculty of Cornell University Medical College. He also inspired the establishment of the Milton Helpern Library of Legal Medicine, which has developed one of the finest collections on forensic medicine in the country.

Helpern retired as chief medical examiner on Dec. 31, 1973. He was made a visiting professor at the Center for Biomedical Education at City College in 1974 and remained active as a speaker and in many professional organizations, some of which he had helped to found. He died in San Diego, Calif., while attending a convention of one such group.

Helpern's last year in office was plagued by instances of professional negligence and financial improprieties among his staff. Nevertheless, he is regarded as a pioneer in forensic medicine, responsible not only for deepening the understanding of that field in the medical world but also for making the activities of his office well known to the general public. In the latter sense, he was indeed a good servant of the forum, the public marketplace.

[The bulk of Helpern's manuscript materials are in the Milton Helpern papers at the National Museum of Health and Medicine in Washington, D.C.; there are also some materials in the New York University School of Medicine collections on individual doctors and in the Bernard Botein papers at the New-York Historical Society. Helpern's memoirs are *Autopsy* (1977), written with Bernard Knight. See also Marshall Houts, *Where Death Delights* (1967). Obituaries are in the *New York Times*, Apr. 23, 1977; and *Journal of Forensic Sciences*, Oct. 1977.]

SANDRA SHAFFER VANDOREN

HERBERG, WILL (June 30, 1901–Mar. 27, 1977), social philosopher and theologian, was born in Liachovitzi, Russia, the son of Hyman

Louis Herberg, a merchant, and Sarah Wolkov, a teacher. The family moved to Brooklyn in New York City in 1904. Hyman Herberg was unsuccessful in business and deserted his family around 1910; Will and his brother helped their mother with piecework at home. The family seems to have been mostly indifferent to their Jewish heritage.

Strongly encouraged by his mother, Will supplemented his work in elementary school and Boys' High School with a rigorous program of study at home in sciences and languages. He attended City College of New York from 1918 to 1920, when he was suspended, apparently for too many absences from the required courses in military science. To the end of his life he retained a great respect for formal, higher education, although most of his prodigious learning derived from a lifetime of voracious reading.

While at City College, Herberg joined the Communist party; subsequently, he directed the summer camps of the Young Workers' League and was elected to its "Politburo" with a special responsibility for agitprop. In the 1920's he wrote the first of the more than 300 articles he would publish in his lifetime. In 1929, Herberg remained loyal to Jay Lovestone when, on orders from Stalin, the Lovestonites were expelled from the American Communist party. For the next decade, Herberg helped edit *Revolutionary Age* (later, *Workers Age*). He also gave popular courses on Marxist theory at the Lovestonite New Workers School. From 1933 to 1954 he served as "educational director" of a local of the International Ladies Garment Workers Union —a position that gave him ample time to read and to write.

Herberg's range was remarkable. He undertook to clarify the "Negro question," to demonstrate the congruence of Marx and Einstein, and to rebut both Mike Gold and Edmund Wilson on the relation of literature to revolutionary action. He won recognition as a leading "theoretician" in the Lovestonite attempt to reclaim from the Stalinists the leadership of the Communist movement while eschewing the errors both of Trotskyites and of social democrats like Sidney Hook. He subscribed to Lovestone's belief that American culture had had an "exceptional" past and was therefore unlikely to have a future like that confidently charted by the Stalinists for all modern industrialized countries.

Throughout the 1930's, Herberg demonstrated the wide reading, the cocksureness, and the verbal extravagance of an effective polemicist. By 1940, however, Herberg—like most Lovestonites—had wearied of attempting to define a genuinely Marxist alternative to Stalinism. "Old-line social democracy, traditional Marxian orthodoxy, and Russian Bolshevism have all failed," he wrote, the victims of flawed philosophy and of an inveterate willingness to justify shabby, even criminal means by invoking illusory ends. The Lovestonites closed their school and discontinued their journal.

For a decade Herberg wrote comparatively little, but he read extensively in Judeo-Christian theology. He was especially impressed by the definition of the human predicament developed by Rienhold Niebuhr, whom Herberg was to declare "America's most searching contemporary theologian." He also found in Søren Kierkegaard, Nicholay Berdyayev, Karl Barth, Martin Buber, and Franz Rosenzweig justification for a "religious existentialism." At the same time, Solomon Schechter helped him explore the rabbinic tradition, which he had never carefully studied.

The dramatic reorientation of Herberg's thought was epitomized in his *Judaism and Modern Man*, which was published in 1951 as "a confession of faith"—an attempt to present "the truth of my existence as man and as Jew." He contrasted "Greco-Oriental" spirituality—otherworldly, impersonal, ahistorical—with the "biblical faith" common to Jews and Christians. Only a biblical faith would enable man to "transcend" the "tragic absurdity of existence"—"the self-defeating, self-destroying dynamic of human life conceived in its own terms." Only a "total and unreserved allegiance to the Living God" would save humanity from such pervasive modern "idolatries" as science, psychoanalysis, and Marxism.

The book was criticized by political radicals who deplored Herberg's "failure of nerve" and by some Jewish theologians who protested that Judaism was considerably less pessimistic about the moral and rational powers of men than was presented. But Herberg acquired a substantial audience for his book and for his lectures among college students and among a growing number of intellectuals like himself who could no longer commit themselves to Marxian socialism but hoped to find, in a modern interpretation of the theology of their forebears, a faith to live by.

Herberg felt obliged to distinguish genuinely

God-fearing affections from the flatulent self-satisfaction of the "religious revival" of the 1950's. His most influential book, *Protestant-Catholic-Jew* (1955; republished several times), maintained that a high percentage of the flood of Americans who joined churches and professed religious convictions in the post–World War II years did so in order to "belong." On the basis of a few specialized sociological studies, Herberg concluded that a large percentage of Americans were, in fact or in spirit, third-generation immigrants; alienated from the foreign ways of their grandparents, they were demonstrably unwilling to renounce their ethnicity as completely as had their parents. They refused to believe that to become Americans it was necessary for everyone to enter the same large "melting pot." The third generation, instead, celebrated the existence of a "triple melting pot" that encouraged Protestants, Catholics, and Jews to preserve their religious heritages even as they renounced their "foreign ways."

Implicit in this sociological explanation of the religious revival was the politically "good news" that most Americans now believed that all three religious communions were "legitimate." But, Herberg hastened to observe, there was a theological price to pay. Each communion had come to endorse, uncritically, the "American Way of Life"; each verged on becoming merely a "culture-religion"; each ignored or suppressed the prophetic element in authentic Judaism and Christianity.

Shortly after the publication of *Protestant-Catholic-Jew,* Herberg was appointed professor of Judaic studies and social philosophy (and later professor of philosophy and culture) in the graduate school of Drew University. He was a demanding but popular lecturer until his health forced him in 1976 to retire. He published anthologies on Maritain, Berdyayev, Buber, and Tillich (in *Four Existential Theologians*, 1958); on Buber (1956); and on Barth (1960). A representative sample of his many theological essays written in his years at Drew was published in 1976 as *Faith Enacted as History: Essays in Biblical Theology*.

Herberg also lectured and wrote extensively on social and political issues. He published angry polemics against modern "liberalism." He sharply censured the radical individualism of Martin Luther King, Jr., that led to the assertion of the right of civil disobedience. He criticized the "humanist" implications of Pope John XXIII's *aggiornamento.* He declared Senator Joseph McCarthy's "system of government by rabble-rousing" to be the "logical outcome" of Franklin D. Roosevelt's populist contempt for constitutional checks and balances. His wife, Anna Thompson, whom he married on July 6, 1925, died in 1959. They had no children. From 1961 until his death in Morristown, N.J., he was religion editor for William F. Buckley's *National Review*.

[Will Herberg's papers are in the library of Drew University, Madison, New Jersey. His hundreds of publications are listed in two books by Harry J. Ausmus, *Will Herberg: A Bio-Bibliography* (1986), and *Will Herberg: From Right to Right* (1987). John Patrick Diggins, *Up from Communism: Conservative Odysseys in American Intellectual History* (1975), compares Herberg's intellectual odyssey to those of Max Eastman, John Dos Passos, and James Burnham. A more recent interpretation is given in David G. Dalin, *From Marxism to Judaism: The Collected Essays of Will Herberg* (1989). The obituary notice in the *New York Times* (Mar. 28, 1977) and most other memorial notices are incorrect about the place and date of Herberg's birth and about the extent of his formal education.]

ROBERT D. CROSS

HERSHEY, LEWIS BLAINE (Sept. 12, 1893–May 20, 1977), director of the Selective Service System of the United States, was born in Angola, Steuben County, Ind. He came from a background of Mennonite farmers (who, historically, are pacifists). His father, Latta Freleigh Hershey, a farmer, was also sheriff of Steuben County, Ind.; his mother, Rosetta Richardson, died when Hershey was four years old. He was educated in the public schools of Steuben County and attended Tri-State College at Angola, Ind. As a student he alternated attendance at college with employment as a teacher, eventually earning the B.S. in 1912 and the B.A. and the Bachelor of Pedagogy in 1914. On Nov. 24, 1917, he married Ellen Dygert; they had four children.

Hershey joined the Indiana National Guard in 1911. He served on the Mexican border in 1916 during Pancho Villa's raids and was sent to France for active duty in the field artillery in 1918. This service convinced Hershey to make the military his career, so he entered the regular army with the rank of captain in 1920. Following a series of appointments to various staff and training schools, as well as duty posts, Hershey was made secretary of the Joint Army and Navy Selective Service Committee in 1936. This committee was charged with planning methods of raising necessary manpower in the event of a national emergency. When Congress established the first peacetime draft in American history on Sept. 16, 1940, Hershey's committee had the framework of a workable proposal in place. Hershey served as deputy director of Selective Service from 1940 to 1941 and as its director thereafter.

Throughout its history the Selective Service System operated through a network of local draft boards, a "group of neighbors who sit down together to decide whose boy goes and who stays," as Hershey described the process. At the height of World War II there were over 6,400 of these boards. The total manpower needs were established at the national level, where the general criteria for classification and induction were worked out. The local boards implemented the process with Hershey as general supervisor of the entire system.

Hershey was quick to admit the process was not a perfect one and that it contained elements that kept it from being a model of equality. The system was workable and was aided by a sense of obligation to serve during World War II. Hershey favored a universal military training program with very few deferments. He once commented, "If citizens don't see their responsibility to their nation or community, I don't know what's left."

When the 1940 draft law expired in 1947, Hershey was made custodian of draft records. With the passage of the Selective Service Act of 1948 he returned to his former position. When the Korean War began in 1950, the draft system under his direction quickly called up over 550,000 men.

During the initial period of the Vietnam War, there was not undue controversy over the draft. With escalation of the war, beginning in 1965, controversy arose. Because of various deferments, college students were not likely to be drafted, yet many campuses became centers of protest against the expanding war. Hershey felt that anyone who violated the Selective Service law should be reclassified and made eligible for induction at an early date. This was in keeping with his understanding of a 1956 executive order that interpreted the Selective Service Act of 1948. This interpretation caused a great deal of political controversy because many opponents of the war felt induction into the armed forces would be used as a punishment for protesting the war and the draft. In 1967, in a letter to local draft boards, Hershey suggested that action be taken against antiwar demonstrators by moving swiftly to induct them. President Lyndon B. Johnson urged Hershey to reconsider his stance and, as the result of a legal challenge, a United States Appeals Court ruled that such action constituted "a declaration of war against antiwar demonstrators" that had a "chilling effect on free speech."

President Richard M. Nixon wished to end the war and to lessen domestic controversy over his war-related policies. A lottery system for the draft was adopted by Congress on Dec. 1, 1969. In February 1970, Hershey was replaced as director of Selective Service and, simultaneously, was promoted to the rank of full general. In his thirty years in that post he had supervised the induction into the armed forces of more than 14.6 million draftees. In 1973 he retired from the army, the oldest person then on active service.

During his military career Hershey was awarded the Distinguished Service Medal and numerous awards from civic and patriotic organizations. Hershey died in Angola, Ind., where he was to attend graduation ceremonies at Tri-State University. He was buried in Arlington National Cemetery.

The almost universal support for World War II helped Hershey achieve his greatest accomplishments and affirmed his concept of the obligation for public service. That military service might be an onerous burden was foreign to him, and he seems never to have understood the opponents of the Vietnam War. This lack of understanding contributed to the controversy marking the last years of his service. Hershey did not feel an all-volunteer armed services would attract a sufficient number of recruits to meet national defense requirements; only the poor would volunteer, and then only during times of economic hardship. A man of strong will and energy, Hershey became a symbol of the military draft, but changing public attitudes toward the Vietnam War made his job, at the end, a thankless one.

[Tri-State University, Angola, Ind., has a memorial to Hershey and a collection of his memorabilia and papers. An obituary is in the *New York Times*, May 21, 1977.]

MICHAEL R. BRADLEY

HIGHET, GILBERT (June 22, 1906–Jan. 20, 1978), classicist, was born in Glasgow, Scotland, the son of Gilbert Highet, a postal telegraph superintendent, and Elizabeth Gertrude Boyle. In 1924 he graduated from Hillhead High School, where he edited the school magazine, already showing his disposition for writing. Later that year he entered the University of Glasgow, having received a full scholarship as the result of a competitive examination. Here he also edited the student magazine and was president of the Dialectic Society. He was awarded the M.A. degree in 1929, achieving first-class honors in the classics and receiving the Newlands Scholarship for study at Oxford University. Highet attended Balliol College at Oxford for the next three years and graduated with a B.A. in 1932, again with first-class honors, as well as with other university awards such as the Chancellor's Prize. On September 22 of the same year, he married Helen Clark McInnes, whom he had met during his first year at the University of Glasgow. His wife pursued a career in her own right as a novelist; they had one child.

Between 1932 and 1938, Highet became fellow and lecturer in classics at St. John's College, Oxford, serving first as a lecturer and then as a tutor. During these five years he served as editor of the *New Oxford Outlook*, a literary and political review, and cofounded the Oxford University Experimental Theatre Society. In 1936 he received the M.A. degree from Oxford, and in 1937 he came to the United States to teach at Columbia University at the invitation of its president, Nicholas Murray Butler. In the following year he was made full professor of Greek and Latin at Columbia, which was a notable achievement for a thirty-two-year-old man. Except for five years of leave during World War II, he remained at Columbia until his retirement. Between 1941 and 1946 he served first as a lieutenant in the British army, working as a liaison to the United States and Canada as a member of the British mission in Washington, D.C., and then, in the years 1945–1946 (after being promoted to lieutenant colonel), as part of the British military government in Germany, where he was concerned with acquiring Nazi party property and locating war booty taken by the Germans from occupied countries.

Highet returned to Columbia University in 1946, and in 1950 became Anthon Professor of Latin Language and Literature; both he and his wife became United States citizens in 1951. Highet achieved distinction and popularity as a teacher of the classics at Columbia. He was described by one former student as "unique, dominant, overwhelming in the best sense," and unmatched as a teacher. Large numbers of students attended his lectures because they were awed by his display of knowledge, stimulated by his enthusiasm for learning, and pleased by his theatrical approach, which included walking about the classroom and the ample use of gestures such as "waving his handkerchief." In his book *The Art of Teaching* (1950), Highet presented his ideas on teaching, which he considered more an "art" than a "science." Among the characteristics of a good teacher he included knowledge both of what is being taught and of the pupil, as well as love for the subject and fondness for the student. The work received national attention.

Highet's status as a classical scholar was enhanced by the publication of two books, *The Classical Tradition* (1949) and, especially, *Juvenal the Satirist* (1954), which he worked on for eighteen years and which was the first definitive work on the poet. The 1950's was a particularly busy period in Highet's career in teaching and writing (eight of his books were published in this decade). Between 1952 and 1954 he served as the principal book reviewer for *Harper's* magazine. In the latter year he became judge for the Book-of-the-Month Club, while for seven years, 1952 until 1959, he gave a weekly fifteen-minute radio talk, "People, Places and Books," which was initiated and sponsored by the Oxford University Press, first at WABF-FM and then at WQXR, both in New York City. The program was eventually carried by some three hundred radio stations, as well as by the British Broadcasting Corporation, the Voice of America, and a division of the United States Veterans Administration. The radio and television columnist of the *New York Herald Tribune*, John Crosby, wrote that each program was "extraordinarily well constructed, an essay in its particular field, and filled with exquisite satire." Highet published his radio talks in four books, beginning with *People, Places and Books* (1953). In 1958 he became chair of the editorial board of *Horizon* magazine. He was an inveterate reader both in fulfilling his professional duties and for his own gratification; he read while "putting on his socks" and even when shaving.

From 1965 until 1972, Highet was chair of the Greek and Latin department at Columbia. After the age of fifty he found some of the undergraduates too "arrogant" and teaching them to be too time-consuming; during the last twenty years of his career at Columbia he received the most pleasure instructing graduate students. In 1972 he retired, becoming professor emeritus, and in 1976 he discussed his "further reflections" and musings on teaching in *The Immortal Profession: The Joy of Teaching and Learning* (1976). Besides writing books, Highet also translated works, including Otto Kiefer's *Sexual Life in Ancient Rome* (with his wife, 1935), the three volumes of Werner Jaeger's *Paideia: The Ideals of Greek Culture* (1939, 1943, 1944), and poems for the *Oxford Book of Greek Verse in Translation* (1938). He was also a contributor to such periodicals as *Horizon*, *Virginia Quarterly Review*, *American Scholar*, *Classical Review*, and *Studies in Philology*. He died of cancer in New York City.

[The three other books containing Highet's radio talks are *A Clerk of Oxenford* (1954), *Talents and Geniuses* (1957), and *The Powers of Poetry* (1960). Three lectures he gave at Franklin and Marshall College are presented in *The Migration of Ideas* (1954), while the Spencer Trask Lectures presented at Princeton University in 1960 appear in *The Anatomy of Satire* (1962). Other books of his include *The Old Gentlemen* (1952), *Man's Unconquerable Mind* (1954), and *Poets in a Landscape* (1957), which is illustrated with photographs taken by Highet. See also the following articles: " 'Teaching Is an Art,' " *Newsweek*, Sept. 25, 1950; J. Harvey Breit, "Talk with the Highets," *New York Times Book Review*, Apr. 8, 1951; "Professor at Large," *Newsweek*, Nov. 15, 1954; "The Gilbert Highet Broadcasts," *Library Journal*, Feb. 15, 1958; Palmer Bovie, "Highet and the Classical Tradition," *Arion*, Spring 1967, which is a critical analysis of some of Highet's writings by a former student; and John F. Baker, "Gilbert Highet," *Publishers Weekly*, Apr. 12, 1976. An obituary is in the *New York Times*, Jan. 21, 1978.]

ALLAN NELSON

HILL, JOHN WILEY (Nov. 26, 1890–Mar. 17, 1977), public relations counsel, was born in Shelby County, Ind., the third of four sons of Theophilus Wiley Hill and Katherine Jameson. His father, whom Hill called a first-rate farmer but a poor business manager, lacked money for Hill's college education; thus, upon graduation from high school, Hill worked as a journalist for newspapers in Shelbyville, Ind., and Akron, Ohio, before studying English and journalism at Indiana University from 1910 to 1912. He left to work on the family farm. Hill claimed that on the farm he read from Everyman's Library up to fifteen hours a day. He briefly returned to Indiana University but did not receive a degree.

Hill worked as a journalist in the Midwest before moving in 1915 to Cleveland, where he married Hildegarde Beck, daughter of the first conductor of the city's symphony, on June 19, 1916. He was a reporter for the *Cleveland News* for two years, developed a newsletter aimed at local business executives for the Cleveland Trust Company, and in 1917 joined *Daily Metal Trade*, a steel publication, as financial editor. John Sherwin, Sr., head of the Union Trust Company, offered to retain Hill as a publicist. Having no other accounts, Hill insisted that Sherwin find him more clients. Sherwin secured Otis Steel, and Hill opened his corporate publicity firm in April 1927.

The Great Depression solidified Hill's career in public relations. He added a partner, Donald Snow Knowlton, in March 1933, and in November the new agency landed its flagship client, the American Iron and Steel Institute (AISI), the largest account in the nation. Like many business leaders, steel executives—and Hill—were horrified by the depression, but even more by what they considered the Roosevelt administration's intrusion into business decision making. Throughout his career Hill sought to educate Americans about the free-enterprise system, hoping they would reject government growth.

The first major crisis for the agency was the "Little Steel" strike of 1937, which resulted in the deaths of more than a dozen organizers. A subcommittee of the Senate Labor and Education Committee investigated the strike, including Hill and Knowlton's activities for the AISI and several steel firms. Senator Robert M. La Follette, Jr., suspected but could not prove agency involvement in antiunion "citizen's committees."

The agency grew rapidly during the 1930's and 1940's. Among its clients were the Petroleum Industrial Committee, Standard Oil of Ohio, Warner-Swasey, and the Cleveland Chamber of Commerce, along with several steel companies and the AISI. In 1938, Hill and

Knowlton opened a branch in New York City to attend to the steel account; Hill handled the New York business while Knowlton remained in Ohio. World War II brought increased business, and Hill's office soon outpaced Knowlton's. The two severed their partnership in 1947, with Hill running Hill and Knowlton, Inc., in New York, and Knowlton heading Hill and Knowlton of Cleveland; each held a minute portion of the other's company. Hill, who had separated from his wife by 1938, married Elena Karam on Dec. 2, 1949, and adopted two children.

Hill's connections with steel executives served the New York agency well. Republic Steel director Victor Emanuel retained Hill and Knowlton of New York during World War II for Aviation Corporation, and eventually for his entire conglomerate (Avco Manufacturing). Emanuel also set up Hill and Knowlton as counsel for the Aircraft Industries Association (AIA) to win military contracts after the war. Within fifteen years, Hill headed the largest public relations agency in the world.

Hill's relationship with his earliest clients established an important precedent for the agency. While many of his contemporaries favored flash and flamboyance, Hill modeled his career after Ivy Lee, who had worked directly with such magnates as the Rockefellers. Like Lee, Hill considered his role to be ensuring that the client's policies were sound and aligned with the public interest, and then publicizing them widely. A tall, long-faced man who dressed like a banker, Hill attended all board meetings of the AISI, Avco, and the AIA, all three of which remained clients for many years. Board participation by public relations counsel was not typical before Hill's career, and it symbolized the distinction between his agency and many others. Hill and Knowlton established its trade association clients as the definitive sources of statistical and other information on their industries for both the press and the government, in the process earning a reputation for honest, ethical representation.

Serving as the voice of big business, Hill accepted many controversial accounts. His agency counseled the steel industry through President Harry S. Truman's unpopular seizure of the mills to avert a strike in 1952 and President John F. Kennedy's attack on a price increase ten years later; the tobacco industry, beginning with the cigarettes-and-health scare of the mid-1950's, with a program that included formation of the Tobacco Institute in 1958; the Natural Gas and Oil Resources Committee (NGORC) from 1954 to 1956, when a lobbyist not affiliated with Hill and Knowlton attempted to bribe a United States senator, thereby killing the industry's hope for deregulation; and the pharmaceutical industry during the Kefauver hearings of the early 1960's. Although associations comprised the agency's biggest accounts, it also counseled corporations: Gillette, Procter and Gamble, Texaco, Studebaker, and Owens-Illinois.

Hill's was the first agency to open overseas offices, beginning in Europe in 1953; at his death there were eighteen offices overseas and thirty-six in the United States, together employing 560. The firm's education department, the only one in an agency of its size, prepared materials on business and industry for use in schools. Hill established stock purchase and profit-sharing programs, which effectively kept agency turnover to a minimum. Hill and Knowlton pioneered environmental public relations with a department that helped companies deal with new expectations growing out of the ecology movement. He also created a model for a firm that was bigger than its founder: beginning in 1960, he gradually withdrew from participation below the policy-making level and reduced his personal holdings in the agency. He retired as chairman and chief executive officer in 1962 but continued to occupy the corner office until his death in New York City.

[Hill's papers, including client files from 1947 to 1958, are in the Mass Communication History Center at the State Historical Society of Wisconsin, Madison. Hill wrote two books on his career: *Corporate Public Relations* (1958) and *The Making of a Public Relations Man* (1963). See George Felix Hamel, "John W. Hill, Pioneer of Public Relations" (M.S. thesis, University of Wisconsin-Madison, 1966); and Karen S. Miller, "Amplifying the Voice of Business: Hill and Knowlton's Influence on Political, Public and Media Discourse in Postwar America" (Ph.D. diss., University of Wisconsin-Madison, 1993), for lengthy scholarly treatments of Hill's career. An obituary is in the *New York Times*, Mar. 18, 1977.]

KAREN S. MILLER

HILTON, CONRAD NICHOLSON (Dec. 25, 1887–Jan. 3, 1979), hotelier, was born in San Antonio, N.Mex., one of eight children born to August Hilton, a Norwegian immigrant who arrived in the United States in the 1860's, and Mary Laufersweller, who was of German extraction. August Hilton was a trader, but at one time or another he engaged in a wide variety of other businesses. He ran a general store and the local post office, operated the New Mexico State Bank, dabbled in gold mining and refining, and sold farm equipment. Among his holdings was a $2.50-per-night boardinghouse, where his son had his first experience in the hotel business.

Hilton attended the New Mexico Military Institute in Roswell, for three years. In 1907 he entered the New Mexico School of Mines at Socorro, but dropped out in 1909 before being awarded a degree. During vacations he worked as a telegraph operator and day laborer. After leaving college he joined his father's bank and dabbled in politics, serving two sessions (1912–1913) in the state legislature. Hilton soon lost interest in government, and returned to work at the bank. He joined the United States Army in 1917 and served in France in the Quartermaster Corps. Hilton returned to New Mexico in January 1919, following his father's death in an automobile accident the preceding month. He then took over his father's several businesses.

In 1919, Hilton tried to purchase a bank in Cisco, Tex., a town then in the midst of an oil boom, for $5,000. He failed in this attempt and instead, with his partners, L. M. Drown and Jay C. Powers, purchased the fifty-room Mobley Hotel in the city for $10,000.

Finding the hotel business both to his liking and quite profitable, Hilton explored other properties in Texas. Later that year he purchased the Hotel Melba in Fort Worth, and the following year he acquired the 150-room Waldorf in Dallas. Others followed. By 1923, Hilton owned five hotels in Texas, with a total of 530 rooms and a value of around $250,000. At the end of the decade he was the largest hotel operator in the region.

Hilton came close to losing everything during the early years of the Great Depression. He closed down entire floors in his hotels, dismissed maids and other support staff, and removed telephones to save whatever he could. He even took a job at the rival Affiliated National Hotels to earn money. The turning point came in the second half of the 1930's, when the regional economy started to improve. Hilton changed his method of operation to suit the new situation. As he put it, "Up 'til then I had used two forms of operation. First, leasing my Texas dowagers and rejuvenating them, then building from the ground up on leased land, again in Texas." This was well enough during periods of prosperity, but in the depression scores of fine hotels had fallen into foreclosure and were acquired by speculators who knew next to nothing about hotel management. These properties now were being marketed aggressively and could be had at bargain prices. In 1935, Hilton purchased one such hotel, the Paso del Norte in El Paso. The second was the Gregg, in Longview, which he bought from a local doctor who discovered how difficult it was to run a hotel. Not only did Hilton obtain the property at far less than its value, but the doctor offered to lend the money for renovations. "This was as close as I ever came to being given a hotel," wrote Hilton.

While renovating existing properties, Hilton started buying distressed hotels on the West Coast, beginning in 1937 with San Francisco's Sir Francis Drake, a twenty-two story building with 450 rooms, which had cost $4.1 million to construct. Hilton and his group acquired the Drake for a cash outlay of $275,000. He then bought the Breakers, a bankrupt operation in Long Beach, Calif. Hilton settled the hotel's tax liabilities of $280,000 for $61,038, and then purchased its deeply discounted debt of $1 million for $110,000. He next turned inland, erecting a hotel in Albuquerque, N.Mex., the Albuquerque Hilton, which opened for business in 1939.

In 1943, Hilton bought the Hotel Roosevelt in New York City, and that October purchased the famed Plaza, at Fifth Avenue and Fifty-ninth Street, for $7.4 million. He also purchased the Town House in Los Angeles (1942) and the Mayflower in Washington, D.C. (1946), which ranked among the world's premier hostelries. His motto became "Across the Nation." These acquisitions marked a new phase in Hilton's career; now he was going after some of the nation's most prominent and largest hotels. The Stevens in Chicago was the largest hotel in the world, with 2,673 rooms. Like the other bargains Hilton acquired, it was in the midst of bankruptcy reorganization. In 1945 he began his campaign by buying up as many of the hotel's bonds as he could, at 25 cents on the dollar, accumulating $400,000 of them, then moved in to take over, for a total cost, including renovations, of $7.5 million. He renamed the Stevens the Conrad Hilton Hotel. The prize was Chicago's Palmer House, which in 1946 cost Hilton more than $19 million.

Hilton Hotels was incorporated in 1946, and the following year its common stock was listed on the New York Stock Exchange. This changed the structure of the Hilton holdings. Until then, each hotel operated as a stand-alone entity, controlled by Hilton but most of them with minority partners. Now the original securities holders were given Hilton stock in exchange for their interests. Hilton became the largest shareholder in the new entity, with stock worth over $9 million.

In the early 1940's, Hilton obtained his first foreign holdings, starting out in Mexico, and then on to Europe. As a result, he was well situated to capitalize on the tourism and business boom after World War II. In 1948, Hilton founded Hilton Hotels International, signaling his intention to concentrate more on foreign operations. His motto now became "World Peace through International Trade and Travel." The slogan "Across the Nation" was replaced by "Around the World." The first of the foreign hotels was the Castellana Hilton in Madrid (1953), which had been started by others and which Hilton bought out. In 1964, Hilton International shares were distributed to Hilton stockholders.

In 1949, Hilton capped his acquisitions spree with the $3 million purchase of controlling interest in the prestigious Waldorf-Astoria in New York City, which was acquired by Hilton Hotels in 1953. Now sixty-six years old, Hilton seemed content to rest on his laurels. "There's not much left to look around for, when you get the Waldorf-Astoria."

But there was more to come. In the early 1950's, Hilton became interested in the Statler chain of hotels, which had assets of over $110 million. Webb and Knapp, the real estate conglomerate directed by William Zeckendorf, made an offer for the decrepit chain, but Alice Statler, widow of the founder, did not want it to fall into the hands of nonhotel people. She was receptive to Hilton's willingness to make an offer of his own. So he did, it was accepted, and in 1954 Hilton acquired control of Statler for $100 million.

In 1958, Hilton organized Hilton Credit Company to operate Carte Blanche, a credit card company, to which Hilton Hotels transferred its credit-card lists, credit files, and other materials.

Hilton married three times. His first wife was Mary Barron; they had three sons. The eldest son, Conrad, Jr., better known as Nicky, became Elizabeth Taylor's first husband. Conrad and Mary Hilton divorced in 1934, a difficult move for the devout Catholic couple. In April 1942 he married the actress Zsa Zsa Gabor; they had one child. They separated in late 1944 and divorced soon after. In May 1977, Hilton married Mary Frances Kelly.

The marriage to Gabor signaled Hilton's emerging celebrity status. In the 1940's he was the subject of many magazine and newspaper articles that hailed him as the man who had revolutionized the hotel industry. This was an exaggeration. Rather, Hilton had the instincts of a showman. He knew how to capitalize on a hotel's reputation and had a feel for what the public wanted. These included telephones in elevators, in case guests wanted to keep in touch on the go, and hansom cabs at the Plaza. He also knew how to select managers; once they earned his trust, they received a free hand and better-than-average salaries.

In the 1950's, Hilton acted to standardize the newer hotels. He did so in the hope that businesspeople, then accounting for an increasingly large share of guests, would know what to expect from a Hilton. Although he sensed that a new age had arrived, Hilton's hotels remained in central cities, close to railroad terminals but far from airports.

The age of air travel and automobile throughways had dawned, but Hilton was unprepared to capitalize upon it. In his later years he missed opportunities and seemed to lose the decisiveness that made his empire possible. Not until later did he build hotels in suburbs and near highways. Hilton missed the motel boom; Kemmons Wilson recognized the opportunities of building a motel chain and created Holiday Inns, which might not have been so successful had Hilton moved more quickly. Carte Blanche was mismanaged and never amounted to much.

Bigger mistakes were to come. In 1964 (William) Barron Hilton, his second son, had visions of a resort-hotel network connected by air links. In order to accomplish this, the company would need an airline. After several feints, Barron urged his father to exchange Hilton International for a stake in Trans World Airways, which was done in 1967. In the years that followed, Hilton International thrived while TWA did poorly. The franchise business, initiated in

1966 under the name Statler Hilton (which later became Hilton) was managed timidly, and lost out to Holiday Inn, Marriott, Sheraton, and others.

By then Conrad Hilton had withdrawn from active management of the company. Barron Hilton, now president, took over from his father.

Hilton was a supreme opportunist, recognizing that during the last years of the Great Depression and the next two decades, values were out of line and business expansion would translate into large profits. Toward the end of his career, however, Hilton made several errors of omission and commission, and so his empire was not as strong or as large as it might have been had he exercised the same imagination he had shown earlier.

Until Hilton's activities in his growth period, most major hotels were individualistic, possessing characters of their own that were prized and preserved by on-site owners. Hilton saw value in this, and attempted to acquire existing hotels with such reputations. "I buy tradition and make the most of it," he once said. But Hilton also created and directed a chain of hotels, most of which were franchised, where travelers knew they could receive a degree of standardized treatment. At the time of his death in Santa Monica, Calif., his company owned or franchised 185 hotels and inns in the United States and 75 in foreign countries, ranging from Mexico City to Istanbul.

[Hilton's autobiography is *Be My Guest* (1957). See also Thomas E. Dabney, *The Man Who Bought the Waldorf* (1950). Articles on Hilton include Meyer Berger, "Conrad Hilton: Collector of Hotels," *New York Times Magazine*, Oct. 30, 1949; and "Connie Hilton: Hotel Empire," *Fortune*, June 1953. An obituary is in the *New York Times*, Jan. 5, 1979.]

ROBERT SOBEL

HIRES, CHARLES ELMER, JR. (Apr. 27, 1891–Mar. 19, 1980), businessman and philanthropist, was born in Philadelphia, one of five children of Charles Elmer Hires, Sr., and Clara Smith. The Hireses were a well-to-do Republican Quaker family. Charles E. Hires, Sr., had developed a popular carbonated beverage as a retail druggist in 1876; The Charles E. Hires Company was incorporated in 1890 and in 1900 the main production plant opened in Malvern, Pa., a suburb of Philadelphia. Hires Root Beer proved to be one of the most popular fountain soft drinks in the world and the company grew into a giant. It soon expanded into banking and the production of condensed milk. Charles Hires, Jr., graduated from Haverford Preparatory School in 1909 and then attended Haverford College near Philadelphia, graduating with honors in June 1913. During that summer, he went to work for his father's firm as a junior executive. On June 12, 1918, in Germantown, Philadelphia, he married Else M. Keppelmann. They had three children.

In 1920, Hires became president of the Charles E. Hires Company; his father became chairman of the board. When his father retired in 1924, Charles Junior took on the chairmanship as well. At his father's death in 1937, Hires became not only the undisputed corporate leader of the company but also the family patriarch. A cheerful, dynamic, and well-liked man, he led the business through its greatest period of growth and prosperity.

During the 1920's and 1930's, Hires switched the primary product of the company from a home-brewed fountain drink to a bottled (later canned) mass-produced national favorite rivaling such drinks as Coca-Cola, Pepsi, 7-UP, and Dr Pepper. In many respects, Hires became synonymous with root beer.

After World War II, under Hires's direction, the company opened plants in Boston, New Haven, Washington, Pittsburgh, Kansas City, Minneapolis, and Philadelphia. In 1950, Hires retired as president, remaining as chairman and later a member of the board of directors until 1960. The company expanded into the sugar industry, owning and operating the Hires Sugar Company's 25,000-acre plantation in Cardenas, Cuba, until it was sold in 1959, shortly after Fidel Castro's takeover of the Caribbean island nation.

In late 1960, Hires sold controlling interests in the parent company to Consolidated Foods, and retired. After retirement he became a full-time philanthropist. His generosity stemmed perhaps from a near-death experience after being kicked in the stomach while playing in a football game during his senior year at Haverford College. After eight hours in the operating room to repair a ruptured spleen, Hires was given little chance to survive. The *Philadelphia Ledger* even printed his obituary. Not only did he recover, but he was able to graduate on time and with honors. Afterwards, he became generous to a fault. As one friend later said, "he became a true Quaker."

During his last twenty years Hires gave much of his time and fortune to Haverford College. He frequently visited the campus to talk with students and faculty members. In the 1930's he had served on the board of directors of Lankenau Hospital in Philadelphia and was a director of the First National Bank of Philadelphia from 1941 to 1951. He was a charter member of the University of Pennsylvania Museum and an active member of the Arizona Sonoran Desert Museum in Tucson.

Hires maintained very close family ties throughout his life, and in his later years was a loving grandfather and great-grandfather. He died in Malvern, Pa.

Although none of his sons was active in the company, the Hires heritage continued. The rights to the famous Hires Root Beer, the oldest continuously marketed soft drink in the United States, were owned from 1980 to 1989 by Procter and Gamble, which sold them to Cadbury Beverages, Inc. of Stamford, Conn., in 1989.

[Obituaries are in the *Philadelphia Inquirer*, Mar. 21, 1980; and the *New York Times*, Mar. 22, 1980.]

WILLIAM HEAD

HITCHCOCK, ALFRED JOSEPH (Aug. 13, 1899–Apr. 28, 1980), was born in London, one of three children of Emma Whelan and William Hitchcock, a poultry dealer, greengrocer, and importer of fruit. His upbringing was strict. When Hitchcock was four or five years old, his father became annoyed by some of his carryings-on and sent him to the local police station with a note. The chief of police, following the note's instructions, locked the young boy in a cell for several minutes. "This is what we do to naughty boys," he somberly told Hitchcock. A number of biographers point to this early incident as a possible source of Hitchcock's ambivalent attitude toward the law. (Later in life, he told Marie Torre, a columnist for the *New York Herald Tribune*, about some of the things that frightened him: "Here's a list in order of adrenaline production: 1. Little children; 2. Policemen; 3. High places; 4. That my next picture won't be as good as the last one.")

Other aspects of Hitchcock's personality and artistry possibly can be traced to his enrollment as a young boy at St. Ignatius College, a Jesuit school in London. In an interview with fellow filmmaker François Truffaut, Hitchcock said of his early education, "It was probably during this period with the Jesuits that a strong sense of fear developed—moral fear—the fear of being involved in anything evil. I always tried to avoid it. Why? Perhaps out of physical fear. I was terrified of physical punishment."

As a teenager Hitchcock entertained ambitions to become an engineer, so his parents sent him to the School of Engineering and Navigation. While he studied mechanics, acoustics, and electricity, he developed and deepened his knowledge and love of films. Eventually he turned away from engineering and took up the study of art (and even navigation) in evening classes at the University of London. One of his first jobs was as an assistant layout artist in the advertising office of Henley's department store.

In 1920, Hitchcock became a title designer for silent films, and soon he was the head of the titling section of Famous Players, the London branch of a newly organized American film company. From Famous Players he moved to Gainsborough Pictures, where he wrote his first scenarios.

In 1923, when a director fell ill, Hitchcock volunteered to step in, and he directed his first film—*The Pleasure Garden*—in Munich. While making that film, he met Alma Reville, who served as his assistant director. Their marriage on Dec. 2, 1926, lasted until Hitchcock's death more than half a century later. They had one child, Patricia, who appeared in and worked on a number of her father's films.

After *The Pleasure Garden*, other silent films followed. Hitchcock's breakthrough came in 1929 with *Blackmail*, which is generally acknowledged to have been the first successful British talking movie. Other Hitchcock talkies preceded it, including *The Lodger* (1926), *Downhill* (1927), and *Easy Virtue* (1927), but the director's reputation greatly increased when he made *The Man Who Knew Too Much* (1934),*The 39 Steps* (1935), *The Secret Agent* (1936), *The Girl Was Young* (1937), and *The Lady Vanishes* (1938). New York film critics voted *The 39 Steps* the best-directed movie of 1935.

In 1938, Hitchcock visited the United States for the first time and signed a contract with Selznick-International. His first film for David Selznick, *Rebecca*, starring Laurence Olivier and Joan Fontaine, won an Academy Award as the best picture of 1940. From then until his final film, *Family Plot* (1976), Hitchcock was the preeminent director of suspense movies. His classic films included witty and imaginatively suspenseful scenes that have become part of the American collective memory, such as Robert Donat and Madeleine Carroll being handcuffed together on the bed in *The 39 Steps;* Cary Grant running from a very menacing crop-dusting plane in *North by Northwest;* Janet Leigh being stabbed in the shower in *Psycho* (we watch with horrified fascination the victim's dark blood circling the bathtub drain); hundreds of not-so-friendly birds attacking children running from a school playground in *The Birds;* and James Stewart's scuffle in a taxidermist shop in *The Man Who Knew Too Much,* where the hero is surrounded by stuffed leopards and bears. No doubt, every fan has his or her own list of favorite Hitchcockian moments (see, for example, Vincent Canby's article in the *New York Times,* Apr. 30, 1980). Such moments can provide the basis for a textbook on the meaning of film suspense.

Richard Mallett, reviewing *Stage Fright* for the June 7, 1950, issue of *Punch,* noted several aspects of the Hitchcock style: "alternation of tension with laughter, farce with melodrama, verisimilitude with cunning exaggeration." Hitchcock himself, remarking on his preoccupation with the macabre, once said that had he, and not Walt Disney, made the movie *Cinderella,* there would have been a dead body in the pumpkin. Mallet went on to describe Hitchcock's signature film endings, "The characteristic device that calls for the pursuit-climax to come with a final burst of speed through the innards of some large familiar building."

Another recurring element of Hitchcockian fun was a pursuit across or on some large, familiar national monument—for example, Cary Grant and Eva Marie Saint fighting villains on the presidential faces of Mount Rushmore in *North by Northwest* and Robert Cummings holding onto the sleeve of a Nazi spy who is dangling precariously from the crown of the Statue of Liberty in *Saboteur.* In addition, Hitchcock often focused on an innocent person tangled in a web of suspicion and forced to flee both the villian and the law. Frequently his films contained the message that only a thin line separated the innocent from the guilty.

From movies, Hitchcock branched into television. His half-hour show "Alfred Hitchcock Presents," which ran on CBS from 1955 until 1962 (then expanded to "The Alfred Hitchcock Hour," which ran for three years), was renowned not only for superb plots but for the wittily macabre introductions and closings made by Hitchcock himself. (Indeed, throughout his American period, one of Hitchcock's signatures was his brief appearance in each of his films.) Often his appearances were quite ingenious—in *Lifeboat* (1943), for example, there is a picture of Hitchcock in a newspaper advertisement for a weight-reduction product (appropriate, considering that Hitchcock was five feet, eight inches tall and sometimes weighed as much as 290 pounds).

As Hitchcock's professional stature grew, however, biographers and colleagues began to chronicle a darker side of his personal life. His practical jokes were frequently cruel, and he became noted for his obsession with his blond leading ladies (especially with Grace Kelly and Tippi Hedren), and for his cold and often indifferent treatment of actors.

MacDonald Carey, an actor who appeared in *Shadow of a Doubt* (1943), has provided a different view in his autobiography, *The Days of My Life:* "Of all the directors I ever worked with, Hitchcock . . . was the most human. Despite an enduring reputation for being cold to actors . . . he was the most approachable and consequently, the most memorable. I remember him, his wife Alma, and his daughter Pat as an oasis of warmth in the cold world of moviemaking."

Hitchcock received, among other honors, the Irving G. Thalberg Award of the Academy of Motion Picture Arts and Sciences in 1967. A United States citizen (he was naturalized on Apr. 20, 1955), he was knighted by Queen Elizabeth II of England in 1980.

During the final year of his life, afflicted with arthritis and kidney disease, Hitchcock worked on the script for a spy film, tentatively titled *The Short Night.* He died in Bel Air, Calif.

[See Eric Rohmer and Claude Chabrol, *Hitchcock: The First Forty-four Films,* translated by Stanley Hochman (1979); Donald Spoto, *The Art of Alfred Hitchcock* (1979), and *The Dark Side of Genius* (1983); Gene D. Phillips, *Alfred Hitchcock* (1984); and François Truffaut, *Hitchcock* (1984). An obituary is in the *New York Times,* Apr. 29, 1980.]

LOUIS PHILLIPS

HOBSON, JULIUS WILSON (May 29, 1919–Mar. 23, 1977), civil rights activist, was born in Birmingham, Ala. He typically gave his birth year as 1922, although government documents list it as 1919. His mother, Irma Gordon, a schoolteacher and principal, was apparently married only briefly to his father, Julius Hobson, about whom little is known. The father figure in young Hobson's life was Gordon's second husband, Theopolis Reynolds, who ran a dry cleaning plant and a drug store.

Hobson graduated from the Industrial (later Parker) High School in Birmingham and attended Tuskegee Institute from 1937 to 1940. He worked for a local paper company until April of 1942, when he joined the United States Army. Hobson was sent to Europe as a staff sergeant with the Ninety-second Division and served as an artillery spotter pilot. After a three-month stint at the university in Florence, Italy, he was honorably discharged in November 1945. He earned his B.S. degree in electrical engineering from Tuskegee in May 1946. While living briefly in Harlem, in New York City, Hobson attended classes at Columbia University; he then entered Howard University in Washington, D.C., for the fall 1946 semester. He did graduate work in economics at Howard under a number of prominent teachers, such as Otto Nathan and Eric Williams and the Marxist scholar Paul Sweezy.

In 1947, Hobson married Carol Jay Andrews; they had two children before divorcing in 1968. In 1948 he entered government service. His first post was as a desk attendant in the Library of Congress. He became a scientific and technical reference librarian in 1959. Hobson then moved to the Health, Education, and Welfare Department, where he was posted to the Division of Program Analysis and worked as a Social Security research analyst into the 1970's.

Hobson attributed the start of his civil rights activism to the days when he walked his young son past an all-white elementary school to an overcrowded and distant black school in Washington. His work in civic reform began in 1956, when he was elected president of his local civic association; he became vice-president of the Federation of Civic Associations that same year. He then was named to the executive committee of the National Association for the Advancement of Colored People, where his first major effort was to lead a suit against the city's police department, alleging racial discrimination in its promotion practices. In 1960, Hobson was elected chairman of the Washington, D.C., chapter of the Congress of Racial Equality (CORE). From then on, as he said, "I was locked into the whole business of protest."

During the next three years, he put up more than eighty picket lines at over 120 retail establishments. The result was the employment of more than 5,000 African-American workers. He later said, "My proudest achievement in this city is that I changed the complexion of employment downtown. When I started out with picket lines in 1960, a black clerk was as rare as a white crow." In response to a threatened boycott in 1962, the local bus company hired forty-four African-American drivers and clerks. Following Hobson's picketing of a major automobile dealership, black salesmen were hired. He used such unorthodox tactics as setting up banks of telephones in a local church, which were supposedly being used to communicate with demonstrators lining Route 40 in Maryland and Delaware. There were no such demonstrators. Through this ruse, Hobson was able to convince state officials to desegregate restaurants along Route 40. His work led to the integration of hospital services in Washington and to the desegregation of both patient wards and the physicians staff at the Washington Hospital Center. He achieved the latter by himself occupying a bed in an all-white ward.

In 1963, Hobson led 4,500 demonstrators to the steps of city hall, demanding that segregation in rental housing in Washington be outlawed. The campaign was successful. During the same year he rallied the community to participate in the March on Washington, which culminated in Martin Luther King, Jr.'s, "I Have a Dream" speech.

In mid-1963, Hobson was expelled from office by the national CORE leadership, allegedly for his militant stance; he did not endorse nonviolence. Hobson then joined a new black power organization called ACT. Among the more publicized events Hobson organized was the presentation to the press of long-range parabolic microphones designed to expose police brutality during arrests of blacks. Although the microphones were fakes, the police department allegedly upgraded its treatment of arrestees as a result.

Similarly, in 1964 Hobson held "rat rallies," driving into the affluent Georgetown section of Washington with numerous caged rodents. The goal was to publicize the need for a rat-suppression program in the black ghetto. Hobson threatened to "relocate" the rats to Georgetown. The city fathers capitulated and started an anti-rat program. It later developed that the rats were quietly drowned in the Potomac once the television crews had left the Georgetown venue.

Hobson began his campaign against inequality in the Washington schools in 1966 with *Hobson* v. *Hansen*. Armed with statistics, charts, and tables, he appeared before United States Circuit Court of Appeals judge J. Skelly Wright, maintaining that the public schools' "track system" was unfairly channeling black students into less academically rigorous ability groups. Thus, the schools, although officially desegregated, were actually discouraging black achievement, Hobson argued. On June 19, 1967, the court issued a sweeping ruling in Hobson's favor, dismantling the tracking system. On May 25, 1971, he won an order from the same court that the city equalize expenditures and teaching talent in all schools.

Following years of agitation by Hobson and others, the District of Columbia created an elective (as opposed to appointive) school board in 1968. Hobson ran for a seat on the board in the first local election in Washington since the 1870's. He was the only one of sixty-two candidates to win outright an at-large seat. Defeated a year later, he sought election to the United States House of Representatives in 1971 but lost to Walter Fauntroy. Hobson ran for election as vice-president of the United States in 1972 on the antiwar People's party ticket headed by Dr. Benjamin Spock. He became an enduring symbol for Washingtonians seeking increased self-government through statehood. When, in 1974, the city was allowed to vote for its first popularly elected city council in a century, he ran under the standard of the party he had helped to create, the D.C. Statehood party, and easily won a seat. He served in this post until his death. His last political effort, ultimately successful, was to institute a system of initiative, referendum, and recall for the District of Columbia.

In 1969, Hobson undertook a legal campaign to end federal job discrimination against blacks, women, and Mexican Americans. This ultimately contributed to the nondiscriminatory federal merit personnel system. As an active member of the Emergency Committee on the Transportation Crisis, he helped to prevent city planners from extending freeways through poor or black neighborhoods and successfully fought fare increases on the buses.

Hobson wrote several books. With coauthor Janet Harris, he wrote *Black Pride: A People's Struggle* (1969), aimed at young people. He also published *Damned Children* (1970) and *Damned Information* (1971).

In December 1969, Hobson married Justine (Tina) Lower Clapp, a divorced government official and peace activist with two children. Publicly criticized for marrying a white woman, he never waivered in either his public or his private devotion to her. During the 1970's, Hobson taught courses, often titled "Social Problems and the Law" at American University and Trinity College, both in Washington, D.C. He was also on the staff of the innovative Antioch School of Law, where he was named Charles Huston Professor of Law in 1973.

Hobson, who was diagnosed as having cancer in 1971, wrote in a letter to his son Julius Hobson, Jr., just days before his death in Washington, D.C., that "perhaps the greatest destructive force in life is hate—because of sex, race, religion or ethnic origin. We have seen what this has done to us, as well as to others. I look forward to the day when my people can be as easy beyond their neighborhoods as Tina and I have been within our family."

Much about Hobson's life was shrouded in mystery and fraught with contradictions. His second wife told the press, following revelations four years after his death that he had become a "confidential source" for the Federal Bureau of Investigation until June 1966, that he had "manipulative skills and [a] penchant for trickery," often disguising what he did for strategic goals.

Although a classic agitator who made "a studied effort to stay to the left of practically everybody," he was also a career government worker. A man whose public persona was built on outrage ("I sleep mad," he once said), he was in his private life a devoted son, husband, and father. A militant, he never owned a gun and even dismissed the Secret Service guards assigned to him as a candidate for national office because he felt the detail was a waste of taxpayers' money. A vocal advocate of black power, he insisted on taking his white wife to public meetings and was one of the earliest civil rights leaders to denounce incipient black racism.

[The Julius W. Hobson Collection is located in the Martin Luther King Memorial Library, Washington, D.C. Obituaries are in the *Washington Post*, Mar. 24, 1977; the *New York Times*, Mar. 25, 1977; and *Newsweek*, Apr. 4, 1977. Tributes appeared in the *Washington Post*, *Washington Star*, and *Washington Afro-American* at the time of his death.]

JOSEPH DREW

HODGE, ALBERT ELMER ("AL") (Apr. 18, 1912–Mar. 19, 1979), radio and television actor, was born in Ravenna, Ohio, the only child of Albert Elmarian Hodge, a tailor-clothier, and Jessie Jeannette Eldridge. He graduated from Ravenna High School in 1930 and then attended Miami University in Oxford, Ohio; he graduated in 1934 with a B.A. degree, having majored in speech. While at Miami, Hodge was a member of the track team, cheerleading squad, boosters' club, glee club, student-faculty council, dramatic honorary society, and Delta Tau Delta fraternity. He acted in many theatrical productions, produced or directed others, and often served as master of ceremonies for university functions.

After graduating, Hodge toured for one year with the Casford Players theatrical troupe. He then was an announcer and classical music program copy writer for the Cleveland, Ohio, wired radio experiment, an early version of Muzak. In late 1935 he was hired at $35 per week as an announcer and copy writer at radio station WXYZ in Detroit. The station's driving force was Detroit businessman George W. Trendle, who, together with free-lance scriptwriter Fran Striker, developed the concept for a Western serial adventure program that debuted on Jan. 30, 1933, as "The Lone Ranger." Aired thrice weekly, the program soon became a national favorite, and in an attempt to capitalize on its popularity, Trendle and Striker created a modern, urban version of the genre, "The Green Hornet," which premiered on Jan. 31, 1936.

Hodge was personally selected by Trendle for the lead role of Britt Reid on "The Green Hornet." He played the character from 1936 to 1943 while continuing to work for the station in other capacities: writing copy, announcing, producing, directing, and doing color commentary for college football games. In the fall of 1937, Hodge was instrumental in forming the Detroit local of the American Federation of Radio Artists and was elected its first president in January 1938.

On Nov. 30, 1936, Hodge married his first wife. Al and Elizabeth Hodge had one child and were divorced in 1946. Hodge served as a lieutenant junior grade in the United States Navy from 1943 to 1945. He briefly returned to WXYZ and then left for New York, where he worked regularly in radio and television dramas and soap operas. In the late 1940's he married his second wife, Doris. They and her two children lived in Manhasset, N.Y.

On June 27, 1949, the fledgling Dumont Television Network inaugurated the first televised children's science-fiction adventure serial, "Captain Video and His Video Rangers." The program featured the exploits of a futuristic superhero and self-proclaimed "Guardian of the Universe, dedicated to the destruction of all forces of evil." Operating from a secret mountain headquarters and assisted by a faithful young companion (the Video Ranger), a corps of secret agents, and myriad pseudoscientific devices, he waged an ongoing struggle against a variety of earthly and interplanetary villains.

Despite meager production budgets, a grueling five-nights-per-week schedule, and the vagaries of live television in its formative era, "Captain Video" became enormously popular and spawned a series of imitators that helped propel its initially earthbound plot lines into space. When the first Captain Video was replaced, Hodge assumed the role in the winter of 1950. Standing six feet, two inches, and weighing 190 pounds, with a commanding presence and an authoritative voice, he was perfect for the role and became firmly identified with it, even after the final episode was aired on Apr. 1, 1955. From Sept. 5, 1953, to May 29, 1954, a half-hour variant, "The Secret Files of Captain Video," aired every other Saturday morning, featuring complete science-fiction adventures and often starring Hodge. On Oct. 19, 1954, Hodge appeared before a subcommittee of the Senate Judiciary Committee investigating links between juvenile delinquency and violence in children's television programming; he defended his program for minimizing violence while emphasizing cooperation, fair play, and good taste.

At its height, "Captain Video" was shown on Dumont's flagship New York station, WABD, and more than 150 affiliates. However, the network incurred major financial losses in an unsuccessful effort to compete with CBS, NBC, and ABC, and in 1955 the Dumont Television Network operation was terminated and the program was canceled. For a time, Hodge continued to appear in his Captain Video persona on "Captain Video's Cartoons," hosting juvenile cartoon and adventure programs until his Dumont contract expired in August 1957. At the height of his popularity he had made $600 per week playing Captain Video, and even more making personal appearances; he now found it difficult to get television work in New York City, being typecast in his former role. He therefore went to California, where from 1958 to 1960 he made commercials, was a radio disc jockey, and had a few minor television roles. For a time after returning to New York, Hodge had a continuing role on the radio soap opera "Ma Perkins." His final television work involved hosting a short-lived local New York program, "Space Explorers," in the fall of 1961.

Hodge and his second wife were divorced in 1961, and within a year he married Jane Virginia Osborne. He held a succession of jobs, including real estate salesman, lecturer, proofreader, clothing salesman, and security guard. In July 1975 he left his wife and moved into a Manhattan hotel, subsisting mainly on a $312 monthly Social Security check. Hodge's final years were spent forgotten and in declining health from emphysema and chronic bronchitis, compounded by a drinking problem. His body, surrounded by memorabilia and fan letters from his radio and television heyday, was found in his room by the hotel manager and a policeman.

Hodge portrayed heroic figures who generated wide audience appeal and considerable fan following. As Captain Video, he captured national attention as the first television science-fiction hero and extolled positive virtues to a viewing audience that avidly followed the new medium and its stars. The program provided an opportunity for hundreds of actors to gain television experience while instilling mass interest in space exploration that would long outlast the show itself.

[Material on Hodge's early years and university life is available at the Miami University and Kent State University libraries and archives. The Billy Rose Theatre Collection of the New York Public Library for the Performing Arts at Lincoln Center contains clipping files on Hodge, WXYZ, the Dumont Television Network, and "The Green Hornet" and "Captain Video" programs. Information on Hodge's career at WXYZ is in Dick Osgood, *WYXIE Wonderland* (1981). The "Captain Video" program is detailed in Donald M. Glut and Jim Harmon, *The Great Television Heroes* (1975). An obituary is in the *New York Times*, Mar. 22, 1979.]

EDWARD J. TASSINARI

HOOD, CLIFFORD FIROVED (Feb. 8, 1894–Nov. 9, 1978), steel industry executive, was born on a farm near Monmouth, Ill., the only child of Edward Everett Hood and Ida Florence Firoved. His family soon moved to another farm, near Cameron, Ill., where he first went to school, walking three miles each way, then attended high school in Galesburg. His first paying job came at age ten, working as a water boy for a threshing crew and earning fifty cents per day. Hood probably would have become a farmer if a young electrical engineer who was working on the new interurban line between Monmouth and Galesburg had not come to room with his family. They became friends and often went squirrel hunting together. That friendship influenced Hood to go to college and study engineering.

In 1915, Hood graduated from the University of Illinois with a B.S. degree in electrical engineering. While a student he had managed the annual show of electrical equipment, which gave him the opportunity to meet manufacturers. After graduation he went to work for the Packard Electric Company of Warren, Ohio, as a sales engineer and assistant manager of cable sales. In 1917 he married Emilie R. Tener; they adopted two children. In the same year he took a job as an operating clerk with a leading producer of electrical cable, American Steel and Wire, at its Worcester, Mass., facility. A subsidiary of United States Steel Corporation, American Steel and Wire Company also produced wire rope and steel cable. Hood was there only six weeks before being inducted into the army; he spent two years with a coast artillery unit and was discharged with the rank of lieutenant. He returned to American Steel and Wire in 1919 as a foreman in the electrical cable department. In 1925 he was promoted to assistant superintendent of the South Works in Worcester and became superintendent in 1928.

In 1932, Hood moved again, to assistant manager of Worcester district operations and then to manager in 1933. He displayed his skills in managing production, piling up an exemplary record, and in 1935 he was brought to American Steel and Wire headquarters in

Cleveland, Ohio, as vice-president in charge of operations. In 1937, Hood became executive vice-president and on Jan. 1, 1938, he was elected president, with day-to-day responsibility for a company with 70,000 products—from watch springs and piano wire to Erector-set girders and cyclone fence. During World War II, he managed major plant expansions at Worcester; Gary, Ind.; and Pittsburg, Calif. In 1943 he married his second wife, Mary Ellen Tolerton, his first wife having died a few years earlier. After the war he developed an incentive plan for management that in 1953 was extended to all of U.S. Steel.

Hood might have gone no further than this because U.S. Steel was a holding company with dozens of semiautonomous subsidiaries, each with its own board of directors, and with comparatively little movement of operating personnel between the units. After World War II, however, senior management believed that it was critical to the long-term health of the corporation that it acquire significant new raw material sources, modernize its physical plant, expand into new product lines, and tighten managerial control. Hood's demonstrated abilities in production management made him an obvious choice to implement these changes. Thus, in 1950 he became president of Carnegie-Illinois Steel Corporation, the largest subsidiary of U.S. Steel, which was undertaking major expansion, and simultaneously joined the board of directors and the executive committee of United States Steel Corporation of Delaware, the operating subsidiary of the holding company. In 1951, Carnegie-Illinois and two other major subsidiaries were merged with the Delaware company to form the United States Steel Company; Hood took the top production position of executive vice-president for operations.

In March 1951, U.S. Steel began construction of the largest single expansion in steel industry history, the $450 million Fairless Works in Morrisville, Pa., a few miles north of Philadelphia and across the Delaware River from Trenton, N.J. This was U.S. Steel's first major facility in the eastern United States, where it would position the company to compete more effectively with Bethelem Steel in the region. A site on the Delaware River was also critical because it permitted U.S. Steel to receive high-quality ores directly from major deposits it had discovered in Venezuela and Labrador. Hood, who was named a director of U.S. Steel in November 1952, managed 4,000 contractors employing 10,000 workers on the 4,000-acre Fairless site. He later told a journalist that what he liked best was "dealing directly with men and materials, organizing them together." He brought the new works on line in just over twenty-one months, an industry record for building a facility.

On Jan. 1, 1953, Hood became president of a reorganized U.S. Steel Corporation; the operating subsidiary, the U.S. Steel Company, had been dissolved. For the first time since the creation of the U.S. Steel Corporation in 1902 the company had a centralized management, with Hood, a knowledgeable steel man, as president. He was responsible for operations and sales, which were based in Pittsburgh, Pa., and spent nearly half his time visiting company facilities; Benjamin F. Fairless, the former president of the holding company, who now served as chairman, had responsibility primarily for public relations and worked from New York City, while Enders Voorhees chaired the Finance Committee, also in New York.

In 1954, Roger Blough replaced Fairless as chairman, and in 1955 Blough announced a multibillion dollar program to rebuild and expand U.S. Steel over the next twenty-five years, the beginning of which was overseen by Hood. At the same time, Hood was reelected president and appointed to the newly created position of chief administrative officer. In 1956, Hood was elected chairman of the board's Executive Committee and opened a new corporate research center in Monroeville, Pa. At this time the American steel industry was investing less in research and development than any other industrial sector; U.S. Steel and other major American steel firms were largely ignoring important technological developments, including the basic oxygen process, which cut the open-hearth's eight-to-ten hour heat time to just forty-five minutes. The vaunted expansion plans of U.S. Steel focused exclusively on rounding out existing facilities. This approach looked cost-effective but actually reduced efficiency in American plants (largely because of crowding and poor layouts that increased materials handling). At the same time, foreign competitors were building new plants, using the superior basic oxygen process, and locating them at deep-water sites (like the Fairless Works) to take advantage of the rich ores available from new mines in the developing world.

U.S. Steel also aggressively raised prices throughout the 1950's, even in the recession year 1958, when the industry was operating at only 60 percent of capacity. The aggressive pricing followed by the oligopolistic American steel industry, coupled with a devastating steelworkers strike in 1959, led steel consumers both to a serious search for substitutes, particularly aluminum and plastics, and to their first significant purchases of foreign-made steel. From 1959 the American steel industry began a dramatic, long-term decline, which did not end until the early 1990's. Thus, Hood's retirement as president on May 5, 1959, coincided with a major turning point in the history of the American steel industry.

Hood remained on the board of directors and the executive committee until 1967 but focused his energies on humanitarian and civic concerns. He was a member of the National Council on Alcoholism where he chaired an industrial advisory committee in 1960 that encouraged the creation of hundreds of corporate rehabilitation programs. An active Baptist, he also supported such organizations as the American Enterprise Institute, American Cause, and the Freedoms Foundation. In 1976 he helped found the Christian Businessmen's Fellowship. In 1969 he moved to Palm Beach, Fla., where he died.

[See portraits of Hood and discussions of changes at U.S. Steel in *Fortune*, Apr. 1951, Feb. 1953, and Jan. 1956; and *Business Week* May 7, 1955. See also William T. Hogan, *Economic History of the Iron and Steel Industry in the United States* (1971); Robert W. Crandall, *The U.S.* Steel *Industry in Recurrent Crisis* (1981); Bruce E. Seely, ed., *Encyclopedia of American Business History and Biography: Iron and Steel in the Twentieth Century* (1988); and Paul A. Tiffany, *The Decline of American Steel* (1988). An obituary is in the *New York Times*, Nov. 15, 1978.]

FRED CARSTENSEN
ELDON BERNSTEIN

HOWARD, ELSTON GENE ("ELLIE") (Feb. 23, 1929–Dec. 14, 1980), baseball player, was born in St. Louis, Mo., the only child of Wayman Hill Howard, a high school principal and graduate of Tuskegee Institute, and Emmaline Webb, a professional dietitian. After starring in baseball, football, and basketball in high school and declining several college athletic scholarships, Howard began his professional baseball career with the Kansas City (Mo.) Monarchs of the Negro League in 1949; he batted .375 for the Monarchs in 1950. While with the Monarchs, he roomed with Ernie Banks, later a Hall of Fame infielder with the Chicago Cubs. After two years in the army (1951–1953), Howard played with Muskegon (Mich.) in the Class A Central League, the Kansas City Blues in the American Association, and Toronto in the International League, where in 1954 he batted .330 (22 home runs and 109 runs batted in) and was named the most valuable player in the International League. On Dec. 14, 1954, he married Arlene Henley; they had three children.

In 1955, Howard became the first African American to play for the New York Yankees. First signed as an outfielder, he had been converted to catcher in the minor leagues, a move widely criticized at the time for seeming to delay the racial integration of the Yankees. Howard's career marks were no doubt lower because, even after his promotion to the parent club, he was a second-string catcher behind Yogi Berra for six seasons. During these years, however, he was a valued utility man who proved his versatility within manager Casey Stengel's platoon system. "Thank God, I was able to play more than one position," Howard recalled. "That's what kept me going, the ability to fill in at first base and the outfield." He batted .314 for the Yankees in 1958, and he received the Babe Ruth Award as the outstanding player in the World Series with the Milwaukee Braves that year.

As the regular catcher for the 1961 Yankees, arguably the greatest baseball team ever assembled, Howard batted .348, hit 21 home runs, and batted in 77 runs. In 1963 he batted .287, had 28 home runs and 85 runs batted in, and was named the most valuable player in the American League, the first African American to receive this honor. The following season, his salary was raised to $55,000, and in 1965 to $70,000. An agile athlete who was six feet, two inches tall and weighed about 200 pounds, Howard received the Gold Glove Award as the outstanding defensive catcher in the American League in 1963, when he had a fielding average of .994, and again in 1964, when he set a major league record for putouts in a season at his position. Late in 1967 he was traded to the Boston Red Sox, the team that subsequently won the pennant. He appeared with the Red Sox in all seven games of the World Series against the Cardinals that year.

Howard retired as an active player at the end of the 1968 season and returned to the Yankees as an on-field coach and later a front-office assistant. The first African-American coach in the American League, he coached the Yankees for ten seasons. He declined an offer to manage in the Yankees' minor league system, though he aspired to become a major league manager. Although he was denied the opportunity, his name was often mentioned among major league managerial candidates in the mid-1970's.

The Yankees won pennants in nine of the first ten years Howard was a member of the team. He played on nine American League All-Star and four world championship teams; had a career batting average of .274 in 1,605 games over 14 major league seasons; and had a total of 167 home runs. In 54 World Series games, he batted .246 and hit five home runs. Never a flamboyant player, he was a leader by example on the field and, both as a player and coach, a peacemaker in the clubhouse.

Early in his career, Howard suffered the indignities of segregation during spring training in St. Petersburg, Fla., where he lived with a family. "The camp would break at the end of the day," he remembered, "and you had to go back across the tracks to the black section to dress while the white boys would go back to the hotel to dress." Even after receiving the MVP award in 1963, he was unable to rent an apartment for spring training in 1964. Still, he was soft-spoken on racial issues. His teammate Jim Bouton recalled that once he was "involved in an argument about civil rights" with Howard, Howard's wife, and an elderly sportswriter: "Arlene and I were the militants." Bill White, a black baseball player, a Yankee broadcaster, and later president of the National League, eulogized him at his funeral as "a fighter in his own quiet way."

After joining the Yankees, Howard lived with his family in Teaneck, N.J., where he was active in charity work and community affairs. Baseball "has given me all the things I never had, and it has granted me the opportunity to give my children a nice home and send them to college," he told a reporter in 1964. His teammate and fellow coach Dick Howser believed that Howard "epitomized the Yankee tradition." Before his death, Howard invested in a minority-owned printing business in Manhattan. He died in New York City of myocardinitis.

[See "The New 'Mr. Yankee,' " *Ebony*, Oct. 1964; and Peter Golenbock, *Dynasty* (1975). Obituaries appear in the *New York Times*, the *Washington Post*, and the *Chicago Tribune*, all Dec. 15, 1980.]

GARY SCHARNHORST

HOWE, JAMES WONG (Aug. 28, 1899–July 12, 1976), cinematographer, was born Wong Tung Jim in Kwangtung, China. In 1904 his parents immigrated to the United States, where they settled in Pasco, Wash. His first schoolteacher, presumably trying to hasten the assimilation process, combined his name with that of his father, Wong Howe, to produce the more "American" name James Howe. Many years later, when he had already established a professional identity in Hollywood, Howe readopted the middle name Wong for the very reason he had first given it up: its hint of the exotic.

Howe's parents were the first Chinese merchants in Pasco, owning successively a general store and a restaurant. "Jimmy," as he came to be known in this period and thereafter, was the only Chinese in his class at school and was frequently the object of racial taunts. Often called upon to defend himself, he became a skillful boxer, and in his teens he fought professionally, earning fees of $10 to $100 per bout.

After his father's death in 1914, Howe began to drift south along the coast of California, working as a boxer, a farm laborer, and a delivery boy for a commercial photographer. In Los Angeles he worked as a bellhop in a Beverly Hills hotel and was fired after two weeks for what he recalled as "smacking a Korean whose looks didn't appear quite right."

Out of work in Los Angeles, Howe had a chance meeting that changed the course of his life. After watching a film crew work on a Mack Sennett comedy that was being shot on location in Chinatown, he asked a cameraman about work. He was advised to apply at Jesse Lasky's Famous Players studio. When he did, he was judged to be too small to handle the daunting bulk of a movie camera, but he was offered a job sweeping up scraps of film in the editing room.

By 1917 he was working as a slate boy for Cecil B. DeMille, who was keenly aware of Howe's interest in cameras and assigned him to assist studio photographer and cameraman Alvin Wyckoff. This work allowed Howe to refine his own ideas about photographing still close-ups, and he was occasionally permitted behind the movie camera to shoot retakes. The convergence of these related skills occurred in 1922, when DeMille assigned Howe the job of taking portrait shots of actress Mary Miles Minter. Howe constructed a black velvet frame to modify the bleaching effect of studio lighting on Minter's pale blue eyes. The enormous success of this solution established Howe as a technician who could make a camera deliver a credible illusion of reality on command and led Minter to request him as cameraman on her next film, *Drums of Fate* (1923). By 1925, Howe had become director of photography at Paramount.

In the half century between *Drums of Fate* and *Funny Lady* (1975), Howe's last film, the credit "Photographed by James Wong Howe" came to stand for exceptionally high photographic production values. One reason for Howe's technical and artistic success was that he always subordinated virtuoso cinematography, which would call attention to itself, to visual strategies that seemed integral to particular scripts and characterizations. Howe's credo was "Keep it simple and true."

The inventiveness of this approach first became apparent in *The King on Main Street* (1925) when he rode backward in the front seat of a roller coaster while cranking a camera at Adolphe Menjou and Bessie Love. In *Transatlantic* (1931), Howe used deep focus, lighting a shot so that all elements, whether in the shallow or deep spaces of the frame, were equally in focus. It should be pointed out that he employed this technique a decade before Gregg Toland, who is frequently credited with inventing it for *Citizen Kane* (1941). In *Adventures of Tom Sawyer* (1937) Howe worked in Technicolor and produced realistic color quality. Perhaps the most famous of his technical solutions was for *Body and Soul* (1947) when he roller-skated around a prizefighting ring with a hand-held camera in order to represent the subjectivity of John Garfield's point of view as a fighter. Similarly, he used subjective point-of-view shots for both matador and bull in *The Brave Bulls* (1951).

For his notable contributions to filmmaking, Howe became much sought after, highly paid, and famous. He photographed such leading ladies as Marlene Dietrich, Norma Shearer, Myrna Loy, Gloria Swanson, Merle Oberon, and Joan Crawford. He worked with such great directors as Howard Hawks, Erich von Stroheim, Victor Seastrom, Fritz Lang, Michael Curtiz, Raoul Walsh, Joshua Logan, and Martin Ritt, among others. Nominated for sixteen Academy Awards, he received two, for *The Rose Tattoo* (1955) and *Hud* (1963).

The magnitude of Howe's achievement becomes clear when one considers the range of projects with which he was associated in his long career. Some of these include *The Thin Man* (1934), *The Prisoner of Zenda* (1937), *Yankee Doodle Dandy* (1942), *Come Back, Little Sheba* (1953), *Picnic* (1955), *The Sweet Smell of Success* (1957), and *The Heart Is a Lonely Hunter* (1968).

Howe married the former Sonora Babb on Sept. 16, 1949; the couple had no children. Howe died in Los Angeles.

[For more information about Howe's career, see Charles Higham, *Hollywood Cameramen* (1970); Win Sharples, "A Discussion with James Wong Howe," *The Filmmakers Newsletter* (1973); and "Last Seminar with a Hollywood Legend" in *American Cinematographer* (1976). Obituaries are in the *New York Times*, July 13, 1976; and the *New York Post*, July 16, 1976.]

DAVID COREY

HOWE, QUINCY (Aug. 17, 1900–Feb. 17, 1977), journalist and historian, was born in Boston, the son of Mark Antony De Wolfe Howe, an editor and biographer, and Fanny Huntington Quincy. Through his mother, Howe was a descendant of Josiah Quincy, a president of Harvard University and mayor of Boston. After attending St. George's School in Newport, R.I., Howe studied at Harvard and graduated with honors in 1921. While living in England for a year, he studied at Christ's College, Cambridge. He returned to Boston in 1922.

Following in his family's literary tradition, Howe joined the Atlantic Monthly Company in 1922 as an editor for *Living Age*, a scholarly magazine of reprints and translations from foreign journals. When the magazine was sold in 1928, Howe stayed with the *Atlantic Monthly* as an assistant to Ellery Sedgwick, the magazine's editor. Archibald Watson, who had acquired *Living Age*, moved the journal to New York City and hired Howe in 1929 as editor in chief.

As editor of *Living Age*, Howe put his own distinctive imprint on the magazine. In addition to selecting and translating articles of significance from the international press, Howe wrote a monthly analysis of world politics and culture. His first book, *World Diary: 1929–1934*, published in the fall of 1934, was a provocative, iconoclastic study of the years before World War II and of the forces that caused the Great Depression.

An advocacy journalist, Howe was a reformer in the tradition of New England liberalism. In 1932 he took part in a motorcade that brought food to striking miners in Harlan County, Ky.; opposed legislation to restrict immigration; and was active in prison reform. A director of the American Civil Liberties Union from 1932 to 1940, he was a fighter against censorship. But it was in foreign policy that Howe drew attention in the 1930's. A critic of dictatorships of the left and the right, he was sympathetic to the emerging nationalist movements in the colonial empires of the Old World. He was a member of the left-wing American League Against War and Fascism. In his writings of the 1930's, Howe stressed the dangers of American intervention in another world war.

From 1935 to 1942, Howe was among the more influential figures in book publishing as the editor in chief of Simon and Schuster. He was hired by Max Lincoln Schuster, with whom he worked closely in the selection of manuscripts. During his tenure as editor, Howe improved the quality of the firm's nonfiction catalog, producing books that were topical and commercially successful. While Howe was the senior editor, Simon and Schuster published the first two volumes of Will and Ariel Durant's *The Story of Civilization*. Howe personally edited and wrote the introduction for the British editorial cartoonist David Low's *Cartoon History of Our Times* (1939) and edited Ambassador Joseph E. Davies's *Mission to Moscow* (1941).

As a writer, he became one of Simon and Schuster's more controversial authors. In *England Expects Every American to Do His Duty* (1937), Howe challenged the pro-British policy of the American establishment and made the argument that the United States should not be led into a war to preserve Britain's colonial empire. "It is not Britain's strength but Britain's weakness that America has to fear," wrote Howe. "America's destiny hinges upon the destiny of the British Empire not because that Empire is strong but because it is weak. And the stronger America becomes, the more England needs that strength during the first century of its decline." Howe asserted that "ever since the unpleasantness of 1776 the American Dominion has been making the world safe for the British Empire." The book provoked controversy in the United States and England, including a debate in the House of Commons, and a satirical verse about Howe by H. G. Wells.

In 1939, Howe published *Blood Is Cheaper Than Water*, an analysis of the battle between isolationists and interventionists for American public opinion. Norman Cousins, reviewing the book for *Current History*, wrote, "even if the side you choose is not Howe's, you will have to acknowledge the brilliance with which he states and presents the issue." His fourth book, *The News and How to Understand It* (1940), was an engaging portrait of American journalism with profiles of prominent columnists and radio commentators. By the time of the book's publication, Howe had become a well-known radio personality. He was among the first journalists to move from print to electronic journalism.

With his Yankee twang, Howe brought the war home to millions of Americans as a radio commentator. He was among a group of broadcast journalists, including Edward R. Murrow, William L. Shirer, Elmer Davis, H. von Kaltenborn, and Eric Sevareid, who were thrust into prominence by World War II. Ironically, Howe, who had been an outspoken noninterventionist, said that his life began when his broadcasting career was launched in 1938 during the Czechoslovakian crisis. He analyzed the Munich Agreement for the Mutual Broadcasting System in 1938 and from 1939 to 1942 aired three commentaries per week for WQXR, a New York City radio station. Upon joining CBS in 1942, he was a pioneer in establishing news analysis as an important ingredient of broadcast journalism. Howe, who modified his isolationist views after the fall of France in 1940, was widely acclaimed for his insightful reporting, his encyclopedic knowledge of world affairs, and his fairness. Viewed by his contemporaries as the most authoritative and perceptive of news analysts, he elevated the standard for broadcast journalism. Instead of reading the news, Howe told his listeners what national and world events would mean to them.

Making the transition to television after the war, Howe was a commentator on the CBS evening news until he was dropped in 1947, at the urging of a sponsor. His removal as a nightly commentator was criticized by the *New York Times* and may have ultimately strengthened the independence of the CBS news division. Writing in the November 1943 *Atlantic Monthly*, Howe had warned about threats to the integrity of broadcast journalism: "Give government its head, and radio becomes a Federal monopoly. Give the radio industry its head and you get more and more power concentrated into fewer and fewer hands. Give the sponsors who support radio their heads and radio becomes the voice of private American industry."

After losing his commentary slot, Howe continued reporting for CBS and earned critical praise, along with Murrow and Douglas Edwards, for coverage of the 1948 Republican and Democratic national conventions in Philadelphia. He left CBS in 1949 and taught journalism at the University of Illinois from 1950 to 1954. Howe returned to network television in 1954, resuming his commentary for ABC News, where he made broadcasts for the next fourteen years. He received a George Foster Peabody Award in 1956 and an Overseas Press Club Award in 1959 for his coverage of world affairs. From 1961 to 1965, Howe edited *Atlas* magazine, which published reprints from the world press.

In the mid-twentieth century, Howe became one of the nation's more admired historians. Inspired by the journalist-historians Mark Sullivan and Frederick Lewis Allen, he spent twenty-five years writing a three-volume history of the twentieth century, *A World History of Our Times*. The first volume, which covered the period from 1900 to the World War I armistice, was published to popular and critical acclaim in 1949. The second volume, which covered the period between the two world wars, appeared in 1953. The concluding volume, *Ashes of Victory: World War II and Its Aftermath*, was published in the fall of 1972. Panoramic in scope and richly detailed, Howe's trilogy was an impressive achievement. "Mr. Howe's manner of putting all the pieces together, of reappraising the war in the light of its consequences, and of making sense out of chaos is indeed unique," John Toland wrote in reviewing *Ashes of Victory* for the *New York Times*. "He leads the reader through the maze of politics and war with the endearing arrogance of a school teacher who cares."

Howe married Mary L. Post on May 14, 1932; they had two children. Howe died in New York City. In a letter to Edward R. Murrow's wife, Janet, after Murrow's death, Howe had written: "Ed was a perfectionist, in other words an artist, and his genius lay in the way he organized, channeled and eventually exhausted and expended all that was in him. Nobody can say where this spark comes from. Whenever and wherever it appears, it is a kind of miracle." Howe had a similar spark.

[Some of Howe's correspondence is in the Houghton Library, Harvard University. His career as a publishing executive is discussed in John Tebbel, *Between Covers* (1987). For background on Howe's broadcasting career, see Irving E. Fang, *Those Radio Commentators!* (1977); David Halberstam, *The Powers That Be* (1979); Ann M. Sperber, *Murrow: His Life and Times* (1986); and William L. Shirer, *A Native's Return*, vol. 3 of his *Twentieth Century Journey* (1990). An obituary is in the *New York Times*, Feb. 18, 1977.]

STEVE NEAL

HUBBARD, ROBERT C. ("CAL") (Oct. 31, 1900–Oct. 17, 1977), athlete, was born in Keytesville, Mo., to Robert P. Hubbard and Sally Ford who were farmers. He graduated from Glasgow High School, where he played football and ran track, and worked at odd jobs until 1922, by which time he stood six feet, four inches tall and weighed 250 muscular pounds.

Cal Hubbard chose to attend Centenary College in Shreveport, La., in order to play football under coach "Bo" McMillin, a sportsman he had admired since youth. Hubbard quickly proved his prowess in the line at both guard and tackle, playing both offense and defense (teams did not then platoon). He transferred to Geneva College in Beaver Falls, Pa., when McMillin moved there in 1925. He had to sit out the 1925 football season because of the school's eligibility rules, but returned to the playing field with a vengeance in 1926, leading the Geneva team to an upset victory over Harvard. It was the first opening-game defeat in Harvard football history. McMillin later concluded that Hubbard was simply "the greatest football player of all time," a sentiment that other less partisan observers would substantiate.

Hubbard graduated from Geneva College with a B.A. in 1927, after an impressive college career there. He married Ruth Fishkorn that November; the couple had two children before her death in 1962. Also in 1927, Hubbard accepted an offer to play linebacker for the New York Giants in the National Football League. The sporting press called him "the Perfect Tackle" in admiration of his abilities. Extremely agile despite his size, he could run one hundred yards in eleven seconds to the end of his career and had coordinated lateral movement—he frequently tackled ball carriers from behind after they had passed him.

In 1928 the Giants' schedule included a trip to Green Bay. Hubbard, who hated big cities, fell in love with Wisconsin. He forced the Giants' management to trade him to the Green Bay Packers under threat of his imminent retirement. He played for the Packers until 1934, when he left to coach college football at Texas A&M.

He returned to the Packers to play the 1935 season. In 1936, after announcing his retirement from professional football, Hubbard resigned with the Giants as a substitute for "just one game." He played six, including what may have been his finest performance in a victory over the Detroit Lions that year. In the second half Detroit ran every play away from his side of the line—a remarkable silent tribute to the thirty-six-year-old linebacker.

Even while still playing professional football, in 1928 Hubbard began a career as a baseball umpire. He worked in the minor leagues until 1936, when he was brought up to the American League. His mobility, speed, and gentle sense of humor served to make him an outstanding official. He used to tell batters coming to the plate that they should swing at close pitches because he might call a ball a strike "accidentally." In reply to batters' complaints about his strike zone, he would remind them not to get too close, lest he step on them. In 1941 and 1942, Hubbard served as head coach at Geneva College while continuing to work as a major league umpire.

In 1951, Hubbard was injured in a hunting accident, when a stray shotgun pellet cost him the sight in one eye. He retired immediately, only to have the American League bring him back the next year as assistant supervisor of league umpires. In 1954 he was appointed supervisor, a post he held until he retired from baseball in 1969. His most controversial proposal as supervisor of league umpires was an initiative to legalize the spitball; his fellow umpires rejected his recommendation by a narrow margin.

In 1963, Hubbard was elected as a charter member of the Professional Football Hall of Fame. Also that year he married Mildred Sykes; they settled in Milan, Mo., and later in St. Petersburg, Fla. In 1976 he was elected to the Baseball Hall of Fame, thus giving him the unprecedented status of winning the highest honor in two professional sports.

Cal Hubbard was a big bear of a man, but those who knew him say he was a gentle giant. He was down to earth, roughhewn, and rather plain. He enjoyed the company of bird dogs, hunting quail, and playing chess. His enviable skill at duplicate bridge earned him ranking as a life master. Yet despite a lifetime of athletic success, awards, and accolades, he remained unpretentious. He liked to sit drinking coffee by the pot at the local café in Keytesville, or later in Milan, and when prevailed upon by his friends and neighbors, regale them with tales from the big leagues. He died in St. Petersburg.

[See Martin Appel and Burt Goldblatt, *Baseball's Best* (1977); and George Sullivan, *All Time Greats* (1969). An obituary is in the *New York Times*, Oct. 18, 1977].

WILLIAM E. ESPOSITO

HUBLEY, JOHN (May 21, 1914–Feb. 21, 1977), animated filmmaker, art director, and painter, was born in Marinette, Wis., the only child of John Raymond Hubley, a small businessman, and Verena Kirkham. He graduated from Iron Mountain High School, Iron Mountain, Mich., in 1932. Then, having always wanted to be an artist, he attended Los Angeles City College and the Art Center of Los Angeles.

In 1936, Hubley went to work at Disney Studios. Disney artists were encouraged to attend classes at night; and it was in these classes, especially in those taught by John Graham, that Hubley sharpened his skills in composition, drawing, painting, and art history. He apprenticed on the studio's first feature, *Snow White and the Seven Dwarfs* (1937), beginning as a background painter and moving to art direction, which involved designing both the background and the composition of the shot. For *Pinocchio* (1940) and *Bambi* (1942), he was associate art director, and for *Fantasia* (1941), he designed the "Rite of Spring" sequence, an imaginative vision of the creation of the world.

While Disney training was invaluable to the artists who worked there, the younger members of Disney's creative staff were not always content with the studio's rigid assembly-line production methods or the restrictions on their creative freedom. Hubley and his colleagues pressed for both artistic and economic reform. A strike at Disney Studios in 1941 ended the family atmosphere that had long been a hallmark of Disney's growing empire.

Not welcomed back after their participation in the strike, many of the former Disney artists joined army production units. Hubley served in the First Motion Picture Unit, directing United States Navy training films. In 1941 he married Claudia Ross Sewell; they had three children and were divorced in 1955.

In 1945, Hubley, along with several other ex-Disney artists, founded United Productions of America (UPA), a studio formed as a direct artistic challenge to Disney realism. As Hubley put it, UPA style "re-examined animation and its function. . . . It was greatly influenced by the modern French painting school: Klee, Picasso, Matisse, Miro—in terms of creating forms and shapes other than the literal one."

Hubley supervised the studio's *Ragtime Bear* (1949), its first theatrical release using the UPA style. The story concerned a nearsighted businessman who vacations with his nephew in the mountains. The uncle, an amalgam based on a stubborn old Hubley relative, the W. C. Fields persona, and actor Jim Backus's vocal characterization, became the irascible Mr. Magoo, UPA's most celebrated character. More interested in working on new ideas than in repeating prior successes, Hubley moved on to other projects, among them *Rooty Toot Toot* (1952), on which he was supervising director, and the Academy Award–nominated *Gerald McBoing Boing* (1951), a more collective studio effort based on a character created by Dr. Seuss.

During the period of the House Un-American Activities Committee and McCarthyism, the pressure from Columbia, UPA's parent studio, to purge UPA of people suspected of Communist affiliation or activity resulted in Hubley's eviction from the studio. Refusing to be a "friendly witness" or to participate in bribery that would maintain his political neutrality, Hubley opened Storyboard Productions. Storyboard specialized in television commercials, a venture that allowed him to continue working, since the use of a "front man" maintained his anonymity. Throughout its existence, Storyboard produced many award-winning spots, including the Maypo series, starring "Marky Maypo," whose "I want my Maypo!" became a popular and highly successful campaign.

In 1955, Hubley married Faith Elliott, a former film editor, script supervisor, and music editor; they had four children. Although they made commercials in order to "buy the groceries," as Hubley put it, they had promised in their marriage vows to make at least one personal film each year, stressing artistic values over those of mass production. In 1956, they produced their first joint film, *The Adventures of an* *, commissioned by the Guggenheim Museum. *Adventures* was a breakthrough, not only in its goal—to introduce modern, nonobjective art to a wider audience—but also in its technique—eliminating the "inking and painting" process in animation, which resulted in rigid and awkward drawings, and replacing it with the use of wax crayons and watercolors, creating a "resistant" texture that was optically superimposed onto painted backgrounds.

Their films continued to experiment with visual stylization, using multiple exposures and drawing directly on paper to produce a freer style. In addition to their remarkably innovative graphics, the Hubleys approached sound in a unique way, creating their musical tracks first and prerecording dialogue. In three of their films—*Moonbird* (1959), *Windy Day* (1967), and *Cockaboody* (1973)—they recorded the voices of their children, then created visuals to complement the children's worlds of imagination, reality, and play. They also utilized the talents of jazz composers and musicians, among them Benny Carter, Dizzy Gillespie, Ella Fitzgerald, Oscar Peterson, and Quincy Jones, always experimenting with the delicate relationship between sound and image. Throughout this period and after they had stopped making television commercials, the Hubleys worked on many of the animated segments produced by Children's Television Workshop ("Sesame Street" and "The Electric Company"), a commercial effort that allowed them to continue their commitment to more personal filmmaking.

The Hubleys produced about one personal film a year, some dealing with political and social issues, such as hunger (*Children of the Sun*, 1960), war (*The Hole*, 1963, and *The Hat*, 1964), the runaway growth of cities (*Urbanissimo*, 1966), environmental problems (*Of Men and Demons*, 1970), and the population explosion (*Eggs*, 1970); others dealt with more intimate concerns, such as young love (*The Tender Game*, 1958) and childhood (*Moonbird, Windy Day*, and *Cockaboody*). In 1962, the Hubleys produced *Of Stars and Men*, a fifty-three-minute film based on the works of Harlow Shapley, whose abstract concepts about the universe, time, space, matter, and energy seemed perfectly suited to animation's ability to visualize them. In 1963 the Hubleys conceived an idea for a film using the improvised dialogue of Dizzy Gillespie and George Matthews. *The Hole*, produced at the time of the Cuban missile crisis, deals with issues that range from insurance to nuclear war, and stands as a quintessential Hubley work, combining improvised dialogue with stylized graphics and sound. It won the Academy Award for best animated short subject in 1963, an honor the Hubleys had previously received for *Moonbird* in 1959, and were to repeat with the *Tijuana Brass Double Feature* in 1966. Their films continued to win scores of international prizes, including four more Academy Award nominations. In 1976 they produced a feature film for CBS, entitled *Everybody Rides the Carousel*. Based on the work of psychologist Erik Erikson, the film takes the audience on rides that suggest various stages in the life cycle and comments poignantly on questions of human development. In an effort to share their unique approach to art and life with young artists, the Hubleys taught a course on the visualization of abstract concepts at Yale University School of Art.

At the time of Hubley's death in New Haven, Conn., during coronary bypass surgery, the Hubleys were involved in a collaboration with cartoonist Garry Trudeau, based on the latter's comic strip, "Doonesbury." "A Doonesbury Special," a half-hour television program produced for NBC, looks at the way in which 1960's activists attempt to adjust to the realities of the 1970's. The film, completed by Faith, won both an Academy Award nomination and a Special Jury Prize at the Cannes Film Festival. Hubley films continued to receive global recognition, and in 1985 the Hubley Studio was honored by the Academy of Motion Picture Arts and Sciences with a retrospective of their films. In the early 1960's, Hubley was elected president of ASIFA (the international association of animated filmmakers), a post he held until his death.

John Hubley summarized his artistic goals by stating, "These aims seem realizable: to increase awareness, to warn, to humanize, to elevate vision, to suggest goals, to deepen our understanding of ourselves and our relationships with each other." Hubley's work, both on his own and in collaboration with his wife, represents the fulfillment of those goals.

[Many Hubley works are available on film and videotape from Pyramid Film and Video, Santa Monica, Calif., and from Light Year Entertainment, New York City. Hubley's contributions to the art of animation are described in Charles Solomon, *Enchanted Drawings: the History of Animation* (1989). An obituary is in the *New York Times*, Feb. 23, 1977.]

SYBIL DEL GAUDIO

HUGHES, ALBERT WILLIAM (Jan. 21, 1891–Mar. 22, 1979), retailing executive, was born in Skaneateles, N.Y., to Lillian Foote and Charles John Hughes, a hardware retailer. In 1903 the family relocated to Hamilton, N.Y., where Hughes received his high school education at Colgate Academy and then attended Colgate University, from which he graduated Phi Beta Kappa in 1911. He also took his first job in Hamilton, working in a variety store, doing various chores—cutting cheese, filling kerosene cans, sorting stock—for twenty-four cents per day "and all the candy [he] could eat."

After graduation from Colgate, Hughes took a position at the Hill School, in Pottstown, Pa., teaching Latin. Students gave him the nickname "Caesar," but he did not want to make teaching his career; he wanted to go into business. Among the students at Hill School were two sons and two nephews of James Cash Penney, founder of the J. C. Penney stores, whom he met when Penney visited the school. Penney had opened the Golden Rule store in Kemmerer, Wyo., in 1902, with the slogan "Live better for less." The Golden Rule sold only on a cash-and-carry basis and carried only soft goods with low margins but high turnover. To open new stores, Penney used a unique partnership system in which each store manager was a one-third owner of the store he managed and paid for his share through his work; thus there was no initial capital requirement to become a manager and part owner. Managers also had absolute autonomy in running their stores, deciding everything from the selection of goods and pricing to advertising. Supposedly Penney tried to dissuade Hughes from leaving teaching, telling him he could make only $75 per month, but Hughes insisted on pursuing retailing. In 1919, after eight years of teaching, Hughes moved to Moberly, Mo., to work for Penney; his salary was more than promised, a full $100 per month; the Moberly store would be, in Penney's opinion, a true test of Hughes's ability: "For any man that can sell merchandise in Missouri can sell it anywhere." On July 6, 1920, Hughes married Gertrude Whitaker; they had three children.

In Moberly, Hughes worked for one of Penney's best store managers, John F. Weber, and like his first job in a variety store, Hughes did everything—swept floors, sold shoes, washed windows, and unpacked merchandise. He also learned to sell. When he finished his apprenticeship with Weber, Hughes moved to Eureka, Utah, as first man in the Penney store there, which had been opened in 1909 by Earl Corder Sams, Penney's first partner in 1907, who had become company president in 1914 (serving in that office until 1946). Hughes became manager in 1923 and quickly made his mark, generating the best sales and highest profits achieved at the Eureka store. Ironically, Sams reprimanded Hughes for his profits—they were excessive, revealing that Hughes was taking too large a margin on each sale. Penney intended to make its profits from high volume, not high margins, but Hughes had demonstrated that he both understood and could implement Penney's single-minded focus on high-quality customer service.

Late in 1924, Hughes moved to Athens, Ga., to open and manage a new store. In 1926, because of his unbroken success as a retail store manager, Sams brought him to Penney headquarters in New York City to work in the personnel department. By then the company had 750 stores in forty-five states and sales of $116 million. In 1930, Sams appointed Hughes assistant to the president; in 1933 he was elected to the board of directors and in 1937 became a vice-president and head of personnel. In 1939 Hughes designed and implemented a retirement plan covering all Penney employees. In 1940 he was promoted to executive vice-president, becoming the designated successor to Sams. In 1942 Penney surpassed Woolworth's and became the nation's third largest nonfood merchandiser in the United States, behind only Sears, Roebuck and Montgomery Ward. In 1946, with total sales approaching $700 million, Penney retired from his position as chairman of the board, taking the title of honorary chairman; Sams moved up to chairman and Hughes became the company's third president.

Hughes faced a variety of challenges to maintaining Penney's growth. The company had a substantial majority of its stores west of the Mississippi River; expansion would have to come in the East, against well-established competitors. Penney stores still sold low-margin goods that had made the Golden Rule stores a success—soft goods such as work clothes, yard goods, men's shirts, women's hosiery, blankets, sheets, and house dresses; it still did not sell hardware, home appliances, cosmetics, or jewelry and did not offer credit sales or a catalog.

Hughes, known for his bright bow ties, pursued an aggressive expansion, emphasizing moving stores into larger facilities, typically rented to give the company maximum flexibility in choosing locations. By the middle 1950's the company was opening nearly three dozen new stores annually, and Penney soon had stores in every state except Alaska and Hawaii. Because each store manager was wholly responsible for operation of that store, Hughes kept the central office focused first on developing capable managers and service-oriented staff, declaring in 1956, "Our chief interest is in people. It is all a matter of having the right man in the right place with a sense of responsibility and the authority that goes with it." His second objective was assuring that the central buying organization offered managers quality merchandise at competitive prices; nearly 90 percent of goods sold in the chain carried the Penney label. To ensure uniform quality in its goods, Hughes opened a company laboratory in New York. He maintained supervision of the nearly 1,700 stores through an eight-man operating committee with thirty-five district managers organized into five zones. The emphasis on people and service gave Penney a fine reputation among customers, while its lean structure gave it the industry's lowest expense ratio.

In 1958, Hughes became chairman of the board. Sales had surpassed $1.4 billion, more than twice the level of 1946; profits were nearly $47 million. The company had no debt, having financed its highly successful expansion entirely out of retained earnings. That same year, the company began to offer sales on credit and opened its first discount store and its first full-line department store, which carried white goods (home appliances), hardware, cosmetics, and jewelry. In 1962 the company decided to open a catalog division, publishing its first catalog in 1963.

Hughes continued as chairman until 1964 and served on the board until 1969. Under his leadership, the J. C. Penney Company had grown into a full-line dry-goods competitor and moved into second place among American merchandisers, behind only Sears. Hughes retired to his home in suburban Larchmont, N.Y., and pursued his favorite hobby of gardening. He died in New Rochelle, N.Y.

[Copies of speeches by Hughes and other material are located in the J. C. Penney archives in Dallas, Tex. See articles in *Time*, June 20, 1949; *Fortune*, Sept. 1950; the *New York Times*, June 24, 1956; and *Investor's Reader*, Jan. 6, 1960. An obituary is in the *New York Times*, Mar. 23, 1979.]

FRED CARSTENSEN
ELDON BERNSTEIN

HUGHES, HOWARD ROBARD, JR. (Sept. 24, 1905–Apr. 5, 1976), industrialist, aviation pioneer, and filmmaker, was born in Humble, Tex., the son of Howard Robard Hughes, a mining engineer who had made a modest fortune as an oil wildcatter, and Allene Gano, a Dallas heiress. Hughes spent much of his early years in Houston, then attended the Fessenden School in West Newton, Mass. (1920–1921) and the Thacher School (1921–1922) in Ojai, Calif. He later took courses at the California Institute of Technology.

Hughes's education ended after his father's death in 1924, when he took over the management of the Hughes Tool Company. The company had been formed to manufacture an invention of his father's, the first successful rotary bit for drilling oil wells through rock. The cone-shaped drill came to be used throughout the world; its success provided the basis for the enormous fortune accumulated by Hughes.

On June 1, 1925, Hughes married Ella Rice, a Houston socialite; they had no children. The marriage ended in divorce in 1929, and a half year later Hughes began making motion pictures in California. His first film, *Hell's Angels* (1930), cost $4 million to produce, at the time the most expensive film ever made; it grossed $8 million and made actress Jean Harlow a star. Of the dozen films made by Hughes, the most memorable included *Scarface*, with Paul Muni and George Raft (1932), and *The Front Page* (1931), with Pat O'Brien. *Scarface*, a thinly disguised biography of Al Capone, was a box office success, and received critical acclaim. The *New York Times* described it as "a stunning picture, efficiently directed and capably acted." Hughes soon came to be regarded as a filmmaker of great ability and daring. His most sensational and publicized production, *The Outlaw*, starred his discovery, Jane Russell. Russell's audacious portrayal of the half-breed girl Rio, who falls in love with Billy the Kid, caused such a furor of protest that Hughes delayed the general release of the film, completed in 1942, until 1946.

From 1930 through 1945, Hughes gained a reputation in aviation as a daring, even reckless, pilot. He established a number of speed records in a plane of his own design, particularly a record of 352 miles per hour on Sept. 13, 1935. He twice won the Harmon International Trophy, previously awarded to Charles A. Lindbergh and Wiley Post, as the best aviator of the year. In July 1938, Hughes flew around the world in record time, ninety-one hours and fourteen minutes. He also crashed on several occasions. In July 1946, in Beverly Hills, Calif., Hughes suffered critical injuries testing the XF-11, a high-speed, long-range reconnaissance plane. He spent five weeks in the hospital and did not fully recover for months.

In January 1939, Hughes purchased 12 percent of Trans World Airlines (TWA); eventually he owned over 75 percent of the company's stock. For the next twenty years, although he never held any type of management position, he monitored nearly every aspect of corporate activity. He particularly maintained a veto over any major financing proposals and required that his personal approval be obtained for any fleet procurement.

Hughes took a direct, comprehensive, and intelligent interest in aircraft design. During World War II, Hughes and the industrialist Henry J. Kaiser received a government commission to build the world's largest cargo plane. The War Production Board envisioned a "flying boat" made entirely of nonstrategic material. Kaiser eventually withdrew from the project and the venture took several years to complete. Hughes invested over $40 million in federal funds and his own money in what proved to be a nationally publicized fiasco. On Nov. 2,

1947, Hughes piloted the gigantic craft, three stories high with a wingspread of 320 feet and derisively labeled the "Spruce Goose," one mile across the harbor at Long Beach, Calif. Despite its size, the plane had the appearance of aerodynamic efficiency. It never flew again, however, and eventually became a tourist attraction at Long Beach.

During the 1930's and 1940's, Hughes participated to the fullest in the glamour life-style of Hollywood. He was romantically involved with film actresses including Bette Davis, Jane Russell, Katharine Hepburn, Ginger Rogers, and Olivia de Havilland. Several of his biographers allege that he also had relationships with a number of Hollywood's leading men, including Cary Grant and Tyrone Power. The popular novelist Harold Robbins allegedly based much of his novel *The Carpetbaggers* on Hughes and his coterie. Hughes remained single from his divorce in 1929 until his marriage to actress Jean Peters in 1957; they had no children and were divorced in 1971.

Hughes's exploits as a pilot brought him a ticker tape parade in New York City, a medal from the United States Congress, and a visit with President Franklin D. Roosevelt at the White House. Yet even in his early years, Hughes gave evidence of the need for privacy and secrecy that became obsessive later in his life. He conducted business in odd places, at unusual hours, and often in rumpled clothes and tennis shoes; he seemed constantly suspicious of those around him. From his mother, Hughes had acquired a dread of germs and disease, an affliction that grew worse as years passed.

The debacle of the Spruce Goose did not mark the end of cooperation between Hughes and federal agencies. For more than a quarter of a century, Hughes worked with the Central Intelligence Agency and other government entities on a number of projects, including the development of ship-to-shore lasers for use against military installations in Cuba. In a strange and exceedingly costly scheme known as Operation Jennifer, Hughes cooperated with the CIA in a venture that resembled a science fiction story. In 1970, the Hughes publicity machine revealed that Hughes would construct a ship to explore the floor of the Pacific Ocean, hundreds of miles southwest of Hawaii, for precious metals. The real object of the *Glomar Explorer* was to recover a sunken Soviet submarine in order to salvage nuclear warheads and cipher machines believed to be on the vessel. The CIA proposed to build a $350 million ship longer than three football fields and equipped with a derrick that would lower a giant claw to the bottom of the ocean and snatch the submarine to the surface. Despite the expenditure of $500 million over the next several years in the planning and construction of the *Glomar Explorer*, the project's 1974 recovery effort was only partially successful. In 1975, the *Philadelphia Inquirer* analyzed the long history of the relationship between Hughes and the government and concluded that he had obtained federal contracts worth $6 billion between 1965 and 1974.

After World War II, Hughes again turned his attention to the film industry. In 1948, he acquired a controlling interest in the Radio-Keith-Orpheum (RKO) Corporation for $8,825,000. His management of the corporation often coincided with his conservative political views; he sought to purge RKO of "left-wing influences" and made several anti-Communist films, such as *The Woman on Pier 13* (1949), originally titled *I Married a Communist*, and *Jet Pilot* (1957), which starred Janet Leigh as a Soviet spy posing as a defector. These films proved to be financial disasters and, combined with complaints about his erratic management style, led to stockholder suits that charged Hughes with running the studio with "caprice, pique and whim." In 1954 he responded to the suit by writing a personal check for over $23 million for all the outstanding stock, thus becoming the first person to be sole owner of a major motion picture studio. But Hughes soon lost interest in making movies and sold most of RKO to the General Tire and Rubber Company for $25 million. He merged a small part of RKO into the Atlas Corporation in exchange for 11 percent of the stock of that company.

Not surprisingly, given the amount of his company's government funding, Hughes engaged in much political wheeling and dealing. These operations were normally handled by his chief aides, of whom the most important were Noah Dietrich and Robert Maheu. Dietrich began working for Hughes in 1925, and his successful management of the Hughes Tool Company and Hughes Aircraft provided the financing for Hughes's film career as well as for his eccentric and extravagant life-style. Dietrich produced annual profits as high as $55 million.

After his dismissal over a trivial incident in 1957, Hughes relied upon Robert Maheu, a former agent for the Federal Bureau of Investigation.

Maheu had many dealings with the administration of President Richard M. Nixon, and during the Watergate investigations, it was revealed that Hughes had contributed $100,000 to Nixon. This was not the first financial connection between Hughes and the Nixon family. During the 1960 presidential campaign, the Hughes Tool Company made an unrecorded loan of $205,000 to Donald Nixon, younger brother of Richard Nixon. Publication of the circumstances of the loan materially assisted John F. Kennedy's campaign against Nixon. Some of Hughes's biographers have advanced the theory that since Maheu was known to be friendly with the chairman of the Democratic National Committee, Lawrence O'Brien, the Watergate burglary may have been an attempt to discover what O'Brien knew about Nixon's dealings with Hughes, particularly about the legality of the $100,000 contribution. Specific allegations centered upon $50,000 that Charles G. Rebozo spent on behalf of Nixon. In December 1970, Hughes dismissed Maheu as abruptly as he had fired Dietrich.

Beginning in 1961, Hughes engaged in a fierce battle for control of TWA, a struggle often seen as a forerunner of corporate takeover struggles in the 1980's. A group of Wall Street banks, which had made loans to Hughes for purchase of aircraft, gained operating control of the corporation and sued Hughes for violation of the antitrust laws and mismanagement. Hughes, who at least nominally still controlled a majority interest in TWA, at first indicated a willingness to settle the suit, but eventually filed a countersuit charging that the banks and insurance companies had conspired against him. He asked for a judgment in excess of $500 million. Court hearings on the case continued for several years as Hughes's position became weaker because of his refusal to respond to subpoenas to appear personally before the courts. Abruptly, in April 1966, Hughes ended his role in the case by putting his 78 percent interest on the market. He received $566 million, at the time the largest check ever to be received by one person at one time. *Fortune* magazine, which described Hughes as "the spook of capitalism," declared him the richest man in America.

By the early 1960's, Hughes's fear of personal contact had become pathological. Once, when his wife asked to talk to him, he directed her to stand at the door and shout to him while he remained in bed. When she asked the reason, he replied, "Germs." Hughes absolutely refused to shake hands with anyone in his later years. His aides wrapped their hands in paper tissues when serving him food or drinks. In November 1966, Hughes moved into the penthouse of the Desert Inn, in Las Vegas, Nev., for an indefinite stay. When, after some weeks, the hotel management asked that he leave, Hughes purchased the hotel; he did not leave his suite for four years.

The purchase of the Desert Inn marked the beginning of Hughes's Nevada gambling empire. In part he acquired casinos for tax purposes. He had been paying considerable taxes on the interest from the proceeds of the TWA sales, money that the Internal Revenue Service classified as "passive" income. Hughes discovered that gross casino revenue, classified as "active" income, could be used to offset the passive interest so long as the active income was at least four times greater than the interest. Casino income legally saved Hughes millions of dollars in taxes. He presented himself as a savior of the gambling industry in Nevada by rescuing it from control by organized crime.

By 1969, Hughes had invested $50 million in hotels and casinos in Las Vegas and had become the largest single employer in Nevada. His casino operations, which in Las Vegas included the Desert Inn, the Sands, the Frontier, and the Castaways, and additional casinos in Reno, accounted for 17 percent of all gambling revenue in Nevada. He owned over 15,000 acres of land in Nevada and had purchased Air West. The governor of Nevada, Paul D. Laxalt, assisted Hughes in obtaining the necessary gambling licenses despite his refusal to appear personally before the state gambling commission. Anxious to rid Nevada of underworld influences, Laxalt believed Hughes's ownership of the casinos would improve their reputation. For his part, Hughes promised to finance a medical school for the University of Nevada, pledging donations of $200,000 to $300,000 per year over a twenty-year period. Doubts remain as to whether Hughes ever fulfilled his pledge. Hughes also envisioned Las Vegas as the site of a gigantic regional airport, declaring he planned a whole new concept of air travel in which an SST and jumbo jet airport would serve Nevada, California, and Arizona. Not surprisingly, this visionary prediction made Hughes extremely popular in southern Nevada; the *Las Vegas Sun* compared him to Sir Isaac Newton.

In December 1971, Hughes became a central figure in one of the most publicized and bizarre literary hoaxes in American history. This strange affair began when McGraw-Hill announced its intent to publish an "autobiography" of Howard Hughes. Clifford Irving, an obscure American novelist living on the Spanish island of Ibiza, had received $750,000—a $100,000 advance and a check for $650,000 made out to H. R. Hughes, for a 230,000-word manuscript. Irving purportedly based his "autobiography" on more than one hundred interviews he claimed to have taped with Hughes. The $650,000, allegedly a payment to Hughes for his cooperation, had been deposited in a Swiss bank account under the name Helga R. Hughes, a pseudonym for Irving's wife, Edith. The publisher also released statements attributed to Hughes, including one that read, "I believe that more lies have been printed and told about me than any living man; therefore it was my purpose to write a book which would set the record straight."

The Hughes Tool Company immediately labeled the book a hoax. As the affair gained worldwide attention, Hughes granted his first newspaper interview in fourteen years. Speaking from Nassau in the Bahamas to seven journalists gathered in California, he talked for almost three hours, easily proving his identity to the reporters, denying that he had ever met or ever heard of Irving, and promising he would file a lawsuit to halt publication. Responding to a query as to why he had fired Robert Maheu the previous year, Hughes described his former chief aide as dishonest—"he stole me blind." Maheu sued for slander and libel and in 1974 received over $2.8 million, one of the largest compensatory damage awards in American judicial history. McGraw-Hill and Time-Life Corporation, which had serial rights to the "autobiography," continued to defend Irving's book. The matter became a media circus for the next two months, as investigators, handwriting experts, and former Hughes employees endeavored to prove or disprove Irving's claims. Gradually, it became clear that Irving had borrowed details in the "autobiography" from published accounts and that his wife had made the Swiss bank deposit. Finally, McGraw-Hill conceded in February 1972 that the book was a hoax. Irving and his wife eventually served jail sentences for their fraud, which had cost McGraw-Hill over $1 million.

In his declining years, Hughes became ever more suspicious and obsessed with privacy, and surrounded himself with a group of men—mostly of the Mormon Church, selected because they did not drink or smoke—who served him as bodyguards, clerks, messengers, nurses, cooks, and valets. His requirements for privacy led him to travel only by night, and he continually moved his residence—Boston; Los Angeles; Nassau, the Bahamas; Managua, Nicaragua; London; and Acapulco, Mexico. Wherever he went, Hughes arranged to obtain a penthouse or the entire upper floor of a luxury hotel. For days he would sit or lie on his bed, eating haphazardly and watching films for more than twenty-four hours before being able to sleep. Hughes's lifelong passion for movies contrasted with his distaste for television. He came to believe that television emitted radiation causing constipation and sterility. Near the end of his life, Hughes often ate only one meal a day; his exercise consisted solely of walking between his bed, his chair, and the bathroom.

During his interview with reporters over the Irving hoax, Hughes dismissed as lies and distortions stories of his bizarre behavior, but witnesses later corroborated the stories. His hair had grown halfway down his back, his fingernails were of inordinate length, and he weighed ninety-four pounds.

Hughes continued to generate publicity even after his death from acute kidney failure while flying from Acapulco to Houston, where he was buried. A large number of claimants appeared to press for a share of his personal estate, estimated to be in excess of $650 million. Executors of his will spent a great amount of time and money attempting to find a valid will, even going so far as to hire a psychic. Detectives searched buildings where Hughes had lived and worked. Hundreds of spurious wills appeared, offered by people from all over the world. One of these, left on the desk of the president of the Mormon Church in Salt Lake City, appeared for a time to have some validity but ultimately proved to be false. Finally, in May 1977, the executors divided the estate among twenty-three surviving relatives of Hughes.

[Records relating to the Hughes estate are held in courts in Los Angeles County, Calif.; Clark County, Nev.; and Harris County, Tex. See also Stephen Fay, *Hoax* (1972); Donald L. Bartlett and James B. Steele, *Empire: The Life, Legend, and Madness of Howard Hughes* (1979); Suzanne Finstad, *Heir Not Apparent* (1984); Robert Maheu and Richard Mack, *Howard Hughes* (1985); Robert W. Rummel, *Howard Hughes and TWA* (1991); Robert Maheu and Richard Mack, *Next to Hughes* (1992); and Charles Higham, *Howard Hughes* (1993). An obituary is in the *New York Times*, Apr. 6, 1976.]

JOHN B. DUFF

HUMPHREY, HUBERT HORATIO, JR. (May 27, 1911–Jan. 13, 1978), United States senator and vice-president of the United States, was born in Wallace, S.Dak., one of four children of Hubert Horatio Humphrey, a druggist, and Christine Sannes, a former teacher born in Norway. Humphrey was raised in Doland, S.Dak., where his father, one of the town's few Democrats, had established a drugstore. After education in the local school system, Humphrey enrolled in 1929 at the University of Minnesota in Minneapolis. Little more than a year later, hard times overtook the family business. Humphrey left the university to help his father start a new drugstore in Huron, S.Dak., a larger city sixty miles to the south of Doland. To qualify as a pharmacist, he took a six-month course at the Capitol College of Pharmacy in Denver, and for the next five years worked side by side with his father. On Sept. 2, 1936, Humphrey married Muriel Buck, a student at Huron College; they had four children. The following year, he told his father that he did not wish to become a pharmacist and, at age twenty-six, he returned to the University of Minnesota.

Humphrey said that in addition to his father, the formative influences in his life were the Dakota dust bowl and the University of Minnesota. In his political science classes, he was an outspoken defender of populist causes, often continuing his orations on the steps outside class, amid a circle of undergraduates. Warm, funny, outgoing, and high spirited, he formed lifelong friendships with professors and students alike.

In June 1939, having received his B.A. with high honors, Humphrey was awarded a graduate fellowship at Louisiana State University, where the following year he received his M.A. with a thesis titled "The Political Philosophy of the New Deal." Some of his professors encouraged him to enter politics. Back in Minneapolis, he took a teaching assistantship. But Muriel was pregnant and Humphrey needed higher-paying work. He found it as director of a worker-education program for the Works Progress Administration. The position brought him into contact with trade-union officials, and he began addressing labor groups. With faculty friends he discussed running for Congress, but the radical Farmer-Labor party and the New Deal Democrats split the liberal vote in his district; there seemed no chance to take the seat from the Republicans. Then another venue opened, in that city races in Minnesota were nonpartisan. Humphrey's speeches had come to the attention of Farmer-Labor elders who were looking for new blood in Minneapolis's city hall. Endorsed for the 1943 mayor's race by the city's Central Labor Union, Humphrey, "dashing out of nowhere," as the press reported, made such a strong showing that, even though he lost the election, the Republican incumbent's backers tagged him as a prospect for high office.

Humphrey was a Democrat though, and he went to Washington to advise the Democratic National Committee that the only way for their party to get ahead in Minnesota was to merge with the Farmer-Laborites. His timing was right; the national ticket needed Minnesota's votes in 1944. On the Farmer-Labor side the real impetus for coalition building came from the worldwide drive of Communists and their sympathizers, who were forming popular fronts everywhere against the fascists attacking the Soviet Union. Humphrey emerged from the founding convention as 1944 state campaign chairman of a united party.

In 1945, Humphrey ran again for mayor of Minneapolis, this time with the backing of both labor and business. Denouncing "the leeches of crime, vice and corruption," he won election by the biggest majority in the city's history to that time. In office he was a reformist. He installed a police chief trained by the Federal Bureau of Investigation, who closed down the gambling rackets. But Humphrey kept the police out of labor disputes even when strikers broke the law against mass picketing. Mindful that a 1946 national magazine article had labeled Minneapolis "the capital of anti-Semitism in America," Humphrey organized a "self-study" in which 600 volunteers, Christian and Jew, black and white, walked side by side, taking note of discriminatory practices in shops, offices, factories, churches, and schools. As a result, the city council passed Humphrey's pioneering Fair Employment Practices Law. When he stood for reelection in 1947, he won by a record 102,696 votes to 52,358.

Up to this time, Humphrey enjoyed solid support from the Left, and in 1944, after President Franklin Roosevelt named former vice-president Henry Wallace secretary of commerce, Humphrey wrote to Wallace that Minnesota was expecting him to be the presidential candidate in 1948. But in 1946, Wallace made a speech urging that the United States accept the Soviet Union's communizing of Eastern Europe. This was too much for Humphrey, who broke with Wallace. And at the same time that the Cold War began in earnest, left-wingers in the Democratic-Farmer-Labor (DFL) party staged a coup in which pro-Communist forces won control of statewide caucuses and the party convention.

Battle was joined, both in the state and in the nation. On the wider front, in 1947, Humphrey joined in forming the Americans for Democratic Action (ADA), whose aim was to establish a non-Communist political and labor force on the Left. He declared, "We're not going to let the political philosophy of the DFL be dictated from the Kremlin." Led by future governor Orville Freeman, loyalists organized in every Minnesota county and precinct, won back control at the 1948 state convention, and nominated Humphrey to run against the Republican incumbent, Joseph Ball, for the Senate.

At the Democratic National Convention that year, ADA leaders were looking for a way to blunt the third-party candidacy of Wallace, who had Communist support. Their strategy was to commit the convention to the strong civil rights program put forward by the President's Commission on Civil Rights but deemed too divisive by party chiefs. This was Humphrey's opportunity. A comer, a proven vote getter, and a midwesterner for civil rights, he was picked to speak for the minority resolution. His eight-minute address summoning the Democratic party to "get out of the shadow of states' rights and walk forthrightly into the sunshine of human rights" ultimately proved persuasive. With the preamble "We highly commend President Truman for his courageous stand on the issue of civil rights," the Humphrey-Biemiller plank carried the day, 651.5 votes to 582.5. Delegates from four southern states stomped out to nominate Strom Thurmond as the Dixiecrat candidate for president.

In Minnesota, Humphrey's civil rights leadership took the momentum away from the Wallace camp. And against his senatorial opponent Ball, Humphrey had every advantage except money. Ball had introduced the most punitive of the union curbs in the Taft-Hartley Act. He had alienated former governor Harold Stassen by voting against the Marshall Plan, and was no match for Humphrey as a campaigner. "In his speeches [Humphrey] lets the corn grow high," the *New Republic* commented. "But Humphrey is not shallow. He has a well-knit liberal philosophy and a powerful urge to right wrongs." On election day, Humphrey led Ball by 243,000 votes, to become the first Democrat elected to the Senate from Minnesota.

Some have seen in Humphrey a resemblance to the protagonist of the 1939 movie *Mr. Smith Goes to Washington*. He was young and intent on reform. He thought he could win repeal of the union-curbing Taft-Hartley Act, but ran up against the redoubtable Senator Robert Taft and lost. He thought he could put through a civil rights bill, but was routed by the usual southern filibuster. He introduced fifty-seven bills—for a safe and healthy workplace, for school construction, for extending Social Security, and for aid to farmers and small businesses—but not one brought action. One senior southerner, Harry Byrd of Virginia, remarked that Humphrey's bills, if enacted, would cost a ruinous $30 billion. In reply, Humphrey attacked the huge tax bill being put through unchallenged by the Dixiecrat-Republican alliance. After studying oil-depletion allowances, family partnerships, and capital-gains preferences, all the loopholes by which he saw the rich escaping from paying their share of taxes—Humphrey held the floor for two days. All of his twenty-seven amendments but one were voted down.

In 1954, disgusted with Republican scheming to pin the "soft on Communism" label on Democrats, Humphrey introduced an outrageously opportunistic bill to ban the Communist party. It outdid the Republicans and, only slightly modified, was swiftly adopted as the Communist Control Act of 1954. Though it undermined his reputation as a staunch defender of civil rights and ignored Oliver Wendell Holmes's doctrine that ideas, however odious, should be dealt with only in the competition of the marketplace, Humphrey's maneuver assured his reelection and helped the Democrats win back control of both houses of Congress in 1954. When Lyndon Johnson of Texas took over as Senate majority leader, he assigned Humphrey to the powerful Foreign Relations Committee and began using him as go-between with the small group of unruly Senate liberals that Johnson liked to call "bomb-throwers." On the Foreign Relations Committee, Humphrey was outspoken for NATO, for Israel, and for Nehru's India. He was also in a position to champion the idea that government-owned surplus crops could be bought by needy countries with their own currencies. Authorized by the Agricultural Trade Development and Assistance Act of 1954, the program became a major component of postwar foreign-trade policy.

People had begun to talk about Humphrey as a future president even when he was mayor, but opportunity did not come his way until 1956. On the strength of a talk with Adlai Stevenson, he did what nobody had done before by openly declaring his candidacy for vice-president. Stevenson decided to let the delegates pick the nominee, and Humphrey, running far behind Estes Kefauver and John F. Kennedy, suffered bitter defeat.

But Humphrey was resilient. He used his membership on a minor subcommittee to advocate nuclear disarmament and, here as elsewhere, he was prescient. The success of the Soviet Sputnik satellite brought the issue of ballistic missile technology to the forefront, and Humphrey proposed a ban on nuclear testing. Humphrey's hearings and speeches were noted in Moscow, where Soviet premier Nikita Khrushchev was looking for "peaceful co-existence" with the West. In 1958, when Humphrey visited Moscow, the two statesmen held an eight-hour conference that made world headlines and lifted Humphrey into serious contention for the Democratic presidential nomination. His strategy as a candidate in 1960 called for capturing a few early primaries where his farm and labor backing would be strongest. This same course was also chosen by Senator John F. Kennedy, however. Outgeneraled and above all outspent, Humphrey was flattened in the primaries, first in Wisconsin and then in West Virginia.

When Kennedy picked Johnson as his running mate, Mike Mansfield of Montana was elected Senate majority leader, and Humphrey accepted the post of majority whip. His conciliatory style and affable demeanor helped line up the votes. Moreover, Kennedy's New Frontier agenda consisted in good part of legislation Humphrey had pioneered: the Peace Corps, the Job Corps, Food for Peace. He won Kennedy's agreement to create the Arms Control and Disarmament Agency, which Humphrey had endorsed since 1955. Further, when Kennedy signed the Limited Nuclear Test Ban Treaty in 1963, he turned to Humphrey and said, "Hubert, this is yours."

When Kennedy was assassinated in Dallas in 1963, Lyndon Johnson proclaimed that his mission as the new president was to carry out what Kennedy had begun. Top priority was to go to the civil rights bill, the most comprehensive in a hundred years, with Senate whip Humphrey in charge. He led his liberals with firmness. Against Johnson's counsel, he accepted amendments. He outmaneuvered Georgia's formidable Richard Russell's filibustering efforts. He praised Minority Leader Everett Dirksen of Illinois for abandoning the Republican alliance with the southern Democrats. But, in the end, it was Humphrey, cajoling Republican votes that even Dirksen could not deliver, who amassed the necessary two-thirds majority to break the hitherto unbeatable filibustering of the southern Democrats.

In his memoirs Humphrey called passage of the Civil Rights Act of 1964 his greatest achievement. He had every right to make the claim. The early 1960's saw enactment of other major legislation that Humphrey had introduced years before—in health (Medicare), in education (vocational training), and in welfare (Social Security entitlements). Food stamps also sprang from an early Humphrey initiative. All this commended him to Johnson. Humphrey's hopes for high office had been nearly extinguished by his harsh defeat at the hands of Kennedy in 1960, but Johnson offered him the vacant vice-presidency. And when Johnson, determined to win the election of 1964 on his own merits, passed over Attorney General Robert Kennedy for the number-two spot, Humphrey got the nod. Humphrey felt obligated to Johnson for the rest of his life.

The Johnson-Humphrey team carried 61 percent of the vote. From his vice-president, Johnson demanded absolute loyalty. Accordingly, Humphrey marched in step with the president's Great Society program of sweeping domestic reforms and worked avidly for the passage of the Voting Rights Act of 1965. But Humphrey's unswerving devotion to Johnson could not last, for the administration had inherited a major involvement in Southeast Asia. President Kennedy had shored up a shaky South Vietnamese regime against a spreading Communist-led insurrection. Johnson sent American combat forces into the jungle war. The crucial first step was to unleash American air power against the Communists. To Johnson's astonishment, Humphrey spoke out against the chosen course at a National Security Council meeting: "Political opposition would mount steadily" he said, accurately foreseeing the public's response to the war.

Infuriated, Johnson banished his vice-president from all consultations. The freeze-out lasted until nearly a year later, when Humphrey began to speak up publicly for the war. When Johnson ordered 200,000 ground troops to Vietnam in 1965, the vice-president called the decision "tremendous," and soon he was the administration's loudest proponent of the war in Vietnam. While protesters at home burned draft cards, Humphrey toured Southeast Asia and proclaimed, "The tide of battle has turned in our favor." Humphrey's old ADA friends were shocked. A writers' group said, "The vice president has betrayed the liberal movement."

Then came the 1968 Tet offensive, which persuaded many Americans that the United States was not winning the war, as its leaders had claimed. There followed the New Hampshire presidential primary, in which Senator Eugene McCarthy of Minnesota almost outpolled Johnson. Thereupon, Robert Kennedy entered the race for the Democratic nomination. Johnson announced that he would not seek reelection, calling for a partial halt to the bombing in Vietnam, which led to the opening of peace talks in Paris.

Humphrey decided to run for the presidency. His strategy was to leave the primaries to McCarthy and Kennedy, and to go after delegates from the more numerous nonprimary states. With his strong ties to Democratic regulars, Humphrey was able to corral entire delegations from big states like Pennsylvania. After Robert Kennedy was assassinated as he celebrated victory in the California primary, Humphrey won the Democratic nomination. But he had trouble distancing himself from the president, especially on the Vietnam War. For though Johnson was now seeking peace, he was adamant against "concessions," a position that Nixon, the Republican nominee, assured the president he shared. The Paris talks remained deadlocked.

The 1968 Democratic National Convention in Chicago was a disaster for Humphrey. Pressed from all sides to show that he was his own man, he offered a Vietnam resolution proposing new terms to end the fighting. Thereupon, President Johnson blocked Humphrey's move and dictated a stand-pat resolution on Vietnam that Humphrey accepted. Students who had flocked to Chicago to demonstrate for peace rose in anger and frustration. Mayor Richard Daley and his police were ready for them, and the protesters were clubbed and kicked, and dragged to patrol wagons in full view of cameras televising the melee nationwide during coverage of the convention. Humphrey's acceptance speech was grimly received.

After the catastrophic Chicago convention, Humphrey's opinion-poll rating sank. He trailed Nixon by twenty-six points and, at 27 percent was only seven points ahead of the third-party candidate, George Wallace of Alabama. His funds dried up. His only chance was to stake out his own position on Vietnam. At Salt Lake City, on September 30, he finally declared that if the North Vietnamese restored the demilitarized zone between North and South Vietnam, he as president would call off all bombing of North Vietnam, in the cause of peace. Johnson did not like it, but the speech gave Humphrey maneuvering room.

After Salt Lake City, Humphrey's campaign surged. The antiwar demonstrators who had dogged him everywhere had been appeased. Organized labor, fearing George Wallace's blue-collar appeal in the North, threw its power behind the Humphrey candidacy. In mid-October the president's emissaries in Paris reported a breakthrough. If the United States stopped its bombing, they reported, the North Vietnamese were ready to start substantive talks to end the war. Aware of the developments in Paris, Anna Chan Chennault, the China-born vice-chairman of the Republican Finance Committee, set out to avert a development whose success could swing the November election to Humphrey. Using her personal contacts with Saigon, she informed South Vietnamese president Nguyen Van Thieu that he would get a better deal from a Republican president and, to this end, urged that South Vietnam hold off taking part in the Paris talks. Late in October, President Johnson satisfied himself that he had a commitment from the North Vietnamese and prepared to announce the cessation of bombing. At this point, President Thieu, who had thus far gone along with the American efforts, suddenly withdrew his cooperation. Johnson, aware through radio intercepts of Chennault's intervention, went ahead and on October 31 announced that the United States was halting the bombing of North Vietnam and would meet the North Vietnamese on November 6 to start peace talks.

When Saigon's decision to hold back from the Paris talks became known, Humphrey's hopes were dashed. Nixon won 301 electoral votes, to 191 for Humphrey (Wallace took 46, all in the South). The popular vote was so close (31,785,480 to 31,270,533) that a single vote change in each of the nation's 250,000 precincts would have put Humphrey ahead. His own later assessment was that in four years as Johnson's vice-president he had "lost some of my identity and personal forcefulness. . . . I ought not to have let a man who was going to be a former president dictate my future."

Humphrey tried again four years later. The retirement of Eugene McCarthy in 1970 had given him the opportunity to return to Washington as Minnesota's junior senator. But in 1972 the Vietnam War still dragged on, and at that year's Democratic National Convention, Humphrey's Vietnam record doomed his bid to defeat the antiwar candidacy of his onetime protégé, Senator George McGovern of South Dakota. In 1976 party regulars beseeched him to enter the New Jersey primary in hopes of stopping Jimmy Carter. At the last minute Humphrey drew back, saying that a fourth try for the top was "ridiculous—and the one thing I don't need at this stage of my life is to be ridiculous."

In fact, he had a health problem. A bladder infection had required radiation treatment in 1973, and in 1976 he had emergency surgery to remove the bladder. He recovered and won his fourth Senate term that fall. But he was terminally ill with cancer. In 1977 the Senate made him its deputy president pro tem; President Carter invited him to the Camp David talks on Israel-Egypt peace; and in October he addressed the House and Senate. On December 22, Vice-President Walter Mondale took him home to Minnesota. He died less than a month later, in Waverly, Minn. His wife, Muriel Humphrey, succeeded him in the Senate.

Considered the most accomplished public speaker of his generation, Humphrey may also have been the best-qualified presidential candidate in the period after World War II. But he lacked the necessary ruthlessness to achieve that office. Men were not afraid of him. When, through the vicissitudes of politics, he, and not Lyndon Johnson, stood for the White House in 1968, he could not bring himself to break with his unpopular and overbearing chief. Defeated, he passed into history as one of those eminent lawmakers who shaped the nation but never governed it.

[Humphrey's papers are at the Minnesota Historical Society. His writings include *The Cause Is Mankind* (1964); *The War on Poverty* (1964); *Beyond Civil Rights* (1968); and his memoirs, *The Education of a Public Man* (1976). Biographies are Winthrop Griffith, *Humphrey* (1965); Robert Sherrill and Harry Ernst, *The Drugstore Liberal* (1968); Albert Eisele, *Almost to the Presidency* (1971); Edgar Berman, *Hubert* (1979); and Carl Solberg, *Hubert Humphrey, a Biography* (1984). An obituary is in the *New York Times*, Jan. 14, 1978.]

CARL SOLBERG

HUTCHINS, ROBERT MAYNARD (Jan. 17, 1899–May 15, 1977), educator, was born in Brooklyn, N.Y., the son of William James Hutchins and Anna Laura Murch. Both his father and paternal grandfather were Presbyterian ministers. In 1907 the family moved to Oberlin, Ohio, where his father became a professor at Oberlin Theological Seminary. Brilliant, popular, and trained by his upbringing to self-discipline, Hutchins moved easily through the Woodland Avenue public school (skipping seventh grade) and Oberlin Academy. He entered Oberlin College at age sixteen. Although Hutchins would later refer to Oberlin as a "Puritan island," its idealism and cultivation of intellectual independence almost certainly shaped the views on higher education he later brought to the presidency of the University of Chicago.

After two years at Oberlin, Hutchins entered the United States Army in September 1917, serving in the Ambulance Corps in Italy. He was awarded the Italian croce di guerra. Although a pacifist, he had a powerful sense of duty and felt a strong moral obligation to support his country, a position he again adopted when marshaling the resources of the University of Chicago in World War II, in spite of having vigorously opposed America's entry into the war. (Wartime research at Chicago produced the earliest controlled nuclear chain reaction, a seminal step in the development of the atomic bomb.)

Hutchins entered Yale College as a junior in 1919, distinguishing himself in spite of having to work part-time. He became president of the debating team and won the DeForest Oratory Medal, as had his father. He was elected to Phi Beta Kappa and Wolf's Head honor society. Still, Yale disappointed him; he acidly characterized the experience as not truly intellectual, but a social rite of passage for the privileged. As an antidote, at the end of his junior year he enrolled in the Yale Law School, where he later claimed he began his "formal education." Voted most likely to succeed, he graduated summa cum laude from Yale College in 1921 with a B.A. degree.

On Sept. 21, 1921, shortly after his graduation from Yale, Hutchins married Maude Phelps McVeigh, an artist of strong temperament, style, and some talent; they had three children. The marriage became exceedingly strained in the latter years of Hutchins's presidency of the University of Chicago and ended in divorce in 1948.

After teaching briefly at a preparatory school in Lake Placid, N.Y., Hutchins became secretary to the Yale Corporation in January 1923, the first of several senior-level positions offered him at a very young age. As secretary, he was responsible for relations with the Yale trustees and for fund-raising and public relations. By all accounts, Hutchins was stunningly attractive, gracious, magnetic, irreverent, witty, and urbane. He was also brilliant, a gifted orator, hardworking, and highly principled. These qualities seem to have led others, and Hutchins himself, to believe he could handle positions of enormous responsibility normally thought to require far more experience than he had.

Hutchins received his LL.B. from Yale in 1925, magna cum laude. Continuing the pattern of meteoric ascension in his chosen careers, he was made associate professor, full professor, then acting dean, and then in 1927 was named dean of the Yale Law School. Hutchins sought to infuse the law school with scholarly research and with academics from other disciplines, particularly the social sciences. He was not himself a scholar, and he seemed to underestimate the complexity and difficulty of the connections between the empirical social sciences and the law. At the same time, he brought new intellectual energy to the law school.

In July 1929, at age thirty (and now dubbed by the press "the boy wonder"), Hutchins was named president of the University of Chicago. Chicago was one of America's two or three premier research universities, but its undergraduate college had little distinction, either socially or academically. In his ensuing twenty-two-year tenure, Hutchins chose to pour his intellect, prestige, and energy into a remaking of Chicago's undergraduate education that assaulted both the conventional curriculum and pedagogy and the power structure of the faculty. He precipitated a debate over the meaning and manner of undergraduate education that made him and the university subjects of national attention.

Hutchins disdained all that was vocational or preprofessional in undergraduate education. He believed American education was misguided in seeking to mold education to society's needs. Rather, he believed, with a passion and single-mindedness some saw as arrogant and simplistic, that undergraduate education should seek the truth and cultivate the ability to reason, specifically through moral philosophy and metaphysics.

The undergraduate experience Hutchins sought to impose on the University of Chicago—in the main, successfully—was interdisciplinary and deeply intellectual. Wholly prescribed and built around a content of great Western classics and a pedagogy of discussion and inductive Socratic reasoning, it permitted the admission of students after their sophomore year of high school and encouraged students to move at their own pace, their progress measured through comprehensive examinations.

A core element, never fully implemented, was the "great books" curriculum, built around 250 works by 50 writers. (Of these writers, only two lived in the twentieth century.) Hutchins's emphasis on the great books, moral philosophy, and Socratic pedagogy originated, or at least came to be associated, with the philosopher Mortimer J. Adler, whom Hutchins brought to Chicago from Columbia University, where he had taught a "great books" curriculum. Brilliant, abrasive, and a consummate promoter, Adler recommended the readings to Hutchins, who had expressed a desire to become better educated. By 1930, Hutchins and Adler were teaching their "great books" seminar, a practice they continued throughout Hutchins's tenure. It came to exemplify the Chicago undergraduate experience.

The University of Chicago during the Hutchins years was a place of extraordinary excitement for those faculty who believed fervently in the mission of undergraduate teaching and for many brilliant young minds, largely of unconventional bent, who were stimulated by Chicago as they could have been by no other place. The intellectuality and academic integrity Hutchins championed remain characteristic of the university, as does some of the iconoclasm so vividly symbolized by Hutchins's celebrated abolition of big-time football.

The Chicago undergraduate curriculum did not survive Hutchins's departure from the university in 1951. It ran too counter to the interests of students, particularly of veterans returning from World War II, who wanted an undergraduate education that had more bearing on careers. The curriculum also ran counter to the desire of most young persons to follow their own intellectual interests, to experiment with various kinds of studies, and to make their own choices—wishes incompatible with Hutchins's concept of a proper undergraduate education.

The curriculum also was never really accepted by the regular Chicago faculty, who remained committed to their disciplines and their scholarship. Graduates of the college were treated as underprepared by many graduate schools, including those of the University of Chicago, and were required to complete additional coursework before admission to serious graduate work.

The Hutchins curriculum, while stimulating and challenging, was in some ways simplistic and narrowing, antiempirical, and even antiscientific. It rewarded those who were articulate and verbally aggressive, but it could be discouraging or frustrating to those who were not. Although the Chicago idea survived only at St. John's College, Annapolis, Md., Hutchins's concepts of curriculum and pedagogy, set forth vividly in his 1936 polemic, *The Higher Learning in America*, remain staples of American higher educational philosophy.

In 1939, President Franklin D. Roosevelt declined to nominate Hutchins for a post on the United States Supreme Court, an appointment for which Hutchins had discreetly lobbied. He was probably damaged politically by his opposition to American involvement in World War II, then confined to Europe. He was offered instead the chairmanship of either the Securities and Exchange Commission or the Federal Communications Commission, but declined, thus effectively closing the door on the prospect of a career in governmental service.

In 1945, Hutchins was made chancellor of the University of Chicago, following a protracted controversy with the faculty. While the new title strengthened his power to set educational policy and freed him from administrative routine, it also signaled his failure to remake the university according to his own ideal. Although he remained active as chancellor and as editorial chairman of the *Encyclopaedia Britannica* (for which the university had assumed editorial responsibility in 1943 under a profitable royalty agreement), Hutchins increasingly busied himself with projects outside the university. These included the Commission on the Freedom of the Press, which in 1947 published a number of reports highly critical of the press, and the Committee to Frame a World Constitution, active from 1945 to 1947.

In May 1949, Hutchins married Vesta Sutton Orlick, his secretary and editorial assistant at *Encyclopaedia Britannica*. She had a daughter who took the Hutchins name.

In 1951, Hutchins left Chicago to become associate director of the Ford Foundation, where by 1953 his creation and control of independent or semi-independent "funds" to support educational projects put him seriously at odds with the foundation's board of directors. In a compromise move, in 1954 he became president of the Fund for the Republic, which the Ford Foundation had earlier established as, in Hutchins's words, "a wholly disowned subsidiary" that worked to protect civil liberties.

The Fund for the Republic supported many farsighted projects—on Hollywood blacklisting, government loyalty-security programs, housing practices contributing to segregation, and the effects of McCarthyism on education—that soon made it the center of sustained attack by right-wing groups and the House Un-American Activities Committee. Its policy of providing grants to southern organizations actively promoting integration increased the controversy. While the independent and idealistic Hutchins remained largely undaunted by right-wing opposition, his high-handed management style created problems with his board and almost cost him his presidency.

In 1959, the Fund for the Republic established the Center for the Study of Democratic Institutions at Santa Barbara, Calif., with Hutchins as chairman. The center embodied Hutchins's conception of the ideal intellectual community, with resident fellows meeting daily to define and discuss questions critical to democratic ideas and institutions. At the center, Hutchins broadened his thinking on education. In *The Learning Society*, published in 1968, he argued for lifelong learning as the new educational modality. Later, he addressed ethical and legal issues regarding provision of equal public education for all sectors of society.

Perhaps best remembered for its four Pacem in Terris convocations of the 1960's and 1970's, the center sponsored numerous public forums and produced some published works. Hutchins later told the *New York Times*, "The Center is not a very good center, but it is the only one there is. It has significance as representing something that ought to be done." The center remained dependent on Hutchins, unable to grow and change because of his dominant presence, yet unable to flourish either after his resignation as chairman in 1974 and as president in 1975. Hutchins died in Santa Barbara. The center, already in financial distress, was moved to the University of California at Santa Barbara, where it continued a modified program until 1987.

[Hutchins's papers are housed in the Joseph Regenstein Library, Special Collections, at the University of Chicago. Pertinent material is also at Yale University Library, Manuscripts and Archives; Princeton University, Mudd Library (Fund for the Republic Papers); the University of California at Santa Barbara Library, Special Collections (Center for the Study of Democratic Institutions, papers, audiotapes and videotapes); and Berea College Archives (family correspondence).

Hutchins's major published writings include *No Friendly Voice* (1936); *Education for Freedom* (1943); *Saint Thomas and the World State* (1949); *Morals, Religion, and Higher Education* (1950); *The Democratic Dilemma* (1952); *The Great Conversation* (1952); *The Conflict in Education in a Democratic Society* (1953); *The University of Utopia* (1953); *Some Observations on American Education* (1956); *Freedom, Education and the Fund* (1956); and *Zuckerland!* (1968).

Biographies include Harry S. Ashmore, *Unseasonable Truths* (1989); and Mary Ann Dzuback, *Robert M. Hutchins* (1991). See also Dwight MacDonald, *The Ford Foundation* (1956); and Frank K. Kelly, *Court of Reason* (1981). Articles include Joseph Epstein, "The Sad Story of the Boy Wonder," *Commentary*, Mar. 1990; Edward Shils, "Robert Maynard Hutchins," *American Scholar*, Spring 1990; Benjamin McArthur, "A Gamble on Youth: Robert M. Hutchins, the University of Chicago and the Politics of Presidential Selection," *History of Education Quarterly*, Summer 1990; and Mary Ann Dzuback, "Hutchins, Adler, and the University of Chicago," *American Journal of Education*, Nov. 1990. An obituary is in the *New York Times*, May 16, 1977.

Oral history interviews are available in the Ford Foundation Archives.]

D. BRUCE JOHNSTONE

HUTTON, BARBARA WOOLWORTH (Nov. 14, 1912–May 11, 1979), heiress, was born in New York City, the only child of Edna Woolworth and Franklyn Laws Hutton. Barbara's father, a stockbroker, was a founding partner of the E. F. Hutton brokerage firm. Her mother was the daughter of Frank Woolworth, who amassed millions with his chain of five-and-ten-cent stores. In his youth a poor store clerk, Woolworth was driven to success by the Protestant work ethic and Darwinian social philosophy. Despite his wealth, he was never accepted by New York society. Stung by this, he had social aspirations for his offspring but remained suspicious of foreign men who, he believed, were titled fortune hunters. Ironically, his granddaughter's life exemplified both his aspirations and his fears.

Hutton's early life was lonely and tragic. Her father, an alcoholic womanizer, was distant and abusive; her mother, shy and insecure. When she was just four, her mother was found dead in their New York apartment. While the cause of death was reported as chronic illness, no attempt was made to investigate, and medical records mysteriously disappeared. Most likely, Edna Hutton committed suicide after humiliating reports of her husband's infidelities were made public. After her mother's death, Hutton lived with relatives in California and rarely saw her father.

Hutton was a plump, blond, pretty child but unsure of herself and painfully aware of her wealth. Her doubts about her appearance escalated despite the fact that she blossomed physically. She wrote as a teenager: "I shall be an old maid. Nobody can ever love me. For my money, but not for me." Some of these feelings probably derived from her father, who was distant, rejecting, and cruel. Moreover, when Hutton was nine, a family butler remarked that she was fat and not very pretty, and that nobody would ever want to marry her except for her money. An imaginative, intensely lonely girl, she was the object of jealousy and had virtually no friends. She did, however, have Ticki Tocquet, her governess and surrogate mother, who traveled with her all over the world.

Hutton attended the Santa Barbara (Calif.) School for Girls (1924–1926), Miss Hewitt's School in New York City (1926–1928), and graduated from Miss Porter's School for Girls in Farmington, Conn., in 1930. When her grandfather died in 1919, he had left $78 million to his mentally infirm wife, Jennie. Jennie died five years later, and Hutton inherited $28 million. Since Hutton was only twelve, her father became guardian of her wealth. He shrewdly invested it, and when she came of age, she was worth in excess of $50 million.

Hutton's adult years were dominated by childhood experiences. She went from husband to husband in search of the acceptance and love she never had. As self-destructive as her father and as insecure as her mother, she tried to buy affection. Fascinated by Europe and in search of the social standing she had never had, she mistook title for class. Her succession of titled European husbands made her the object of hatred and scorn in America. Seeking the attention so lacking in childhood, she became one of the most publicized women of her time for her many marriages and extravagant life-style.

In June 1933, Hutton wed Prince Alexis Mdivani, against her father's wishes. Some have contended that Mdivani wanted $2 million to marry her, but a prenuptial agreement afforded him half that sum. The Mdivanis divided their time between Paris and New York and made frequent trips to the Orient and Tangier. After meeting the Danish aristocrat Count Heinrich Haugwitz-Hardenberg-Reventlow, Hutton divorced Mdivani in May 1935 and married Reventlow within twenty-four hours. They had one son.

The Reventlows' stormy marriage lasted six years. During that time, on her attorney's advice, Hutton renounced her American citizenship in 1937. The move, designed to save her taxes and safeguard her son's inheritance, was poorly received. The American press, which had sensationalized her extravagant life-style and foreign husbands, now said she was depriving America of its rightful share of the profits from her grandfather's stores. Although Hutton had little to do with managing Woolworth's, she was accused of exploiting the employees. Her visits home were attended by demonstrations and abuse. To add to her troubles, her divorce from Reventlow in 1941 resulted in an international custody battle over her son.

The American press, unfortunately, was not so diligent in reporting Hutton's generosity. She gave generously to the Musician's Emergency Fund, New York Foundling Hospital, the Metropolitan Museum of Art, the Whitney Museum, the Juilliard School of Music, San Francisco Opera Company, and the New York Philharmonic. During the war, she made generous gifts to the American Red Cross as well as the British Red Cross. While living in Tangier, she established a scholarship fund to support the education of needy children. She was, additionally, very generous to friends and staff.

Hutton settled in Los Angeles and married Cary Grant on July 8, 1942 (the exact date of her marriage is disputed). Grant, a successful actor, was the only husband who earned his keep, but his devotion to his career undermined the marriage, which was legally terminated in 1945.

Hutton's later years were marked by a succession of wrong marriages. She drank heavily and consumed massive amounts of barbiturates. A heavy smoker, she also suffered from anorexia. As her marriages failed, so did her physical and emotional health. She nearly died of an ovarian tumor that rendered her infertile, of an intestinal blockage, and later in life, after a suicide attempt. The death of her thirty-six-year-old son, Lance Reventlow, in an airplane crash in 1972 was the final blow. Hutton spent the last five years of her life driven nearly mad by grief, drugs, and alcohol, bedridden, and physically and financially dissipated.

But first there were four marriages and three divorces, beginning with Prince Igor Troubetzkoy, whom she wed on Mar. 1, 1947, and divorced in July 1951, in Mexico; a second divorce was granted in October 1951, in France. Her next husband was Porfirio Rubirosa, whose sexual conquests included Jayne Mansfield and Zsa Zsa Gabor. Married on Dec. 30, 1953, they actually lived together for only fifty-three days, during which time Rubirosa collected $1 million in gifts and $2.5 million in cash. They divorced in 1955. On Nov. 8, 1955, Barbara married Baron Gottfried von Cramm, a world-renowned tennis player and a homosexual. Although they were married for five years, the relationship was never consummated. After their divorce in 1960, Barbara turned to younger men and married Prince Raymond Doan Champaçak on April 8, 1964. Champaçak, an artist, was believed to be a fortune hunter.

Tragedy pursued Hutton. Three former husbands died in automobile accidents and her son in a plane crash, her mother and a cousin committed suicide, and her father succumbed to liver cirrhosis. Most of her marriages were loveless; some were sexless. She lived for many years in Tangier but spent her last years in Los Angeles, where she died. The years preceding were blurred by drugs, suicide attempts, and psychosis. Her fabulous wealth was just as dissipated, chiefly by her husbands, her extravagance, her generosity, and her attorney, who allegedly pocketed the proceeds from the sale of her art and jewelry collections. When she died, only $3,500 was left of her $50 million fortune.

The legacy of Frank Woolworth met an ironic end with his granddaughter, a tragic victim of his Horatio Alger success.

[Hutton published two books: *The Enchanted* (1934) and *The Wayfarer* (1957). On Hutton, see Dean Jennings, *Barbara Hutton* (1968); Philip Van Rensselaer, *Million Dollar Baby* (1979); and C. David Heymann, *Poor Little Rich Girl* (1984). An obituary is in the *New York Times*, May 13, 1979.]

LISA A. STAHL

I

INGELFINGER, FRANZ JOSEPH (Aug. 20, 1910–Mar. 26, 1980), gastroenterologist and medical editor, was born in Dresden, Germany, the only child of Joseph Ingelfinger, an assistant professor of bacteriology at the University of Göttingen, and Eleanor Holden, an American teacher. His parents had met during one of his mother's trips to Europe; the family immigrated to Boston in 1922. Ingelfinger attended Phillips Andover Academy, then received his B.A. in English in 1932 from Yale, where he played on the football team.

Ingelfinger became an American citizen in 1931. The country was in the midst of the Great Depression, and jobs in the financial world were scarce, so his senior year Ingelfinger decided to take the science courses he needed to enter medical school. He graduated with an M.D. from the Harvard School of Medicine in 1936.

"Don't do what everybody else is doing" was Ingelfinger's motto. Unsurprisingly, then, he decided to specialize in gastroenterology, an uncommon field in the 1930's. In Philadelphia he worked with T. Grier Miller and William Osler Abbot, who designed the intestinal tube, and became interested in studying the properties of the intestine's motility (motions and contractions) and absorption.

Only four years after receiving his M.D., Ingelfinger was appointed chief of gastroenterology at Boston University Medical School's Evans Memorial Hospital, where he began a twenty-seven year career as a researcher and teacher. He was among the first to transform gastroenterology from a descriptive discipline into a quantifiable science. He often experimented on himself and would put tubes through his nose and mouth in order to study the physiology of the esophagus, stomach, and intestines. Ingelfinger trained fifty-seven researchers, or "Fingerlings," as they were called; most became leaders in academic medicine around the world.

Ingelfinger's laboratory made fundamental contributions to the understanding of the human digestive system. Ingelfinger and his team used intraluminal manometry (the study of the pressures of gases) to observe intestinal motility. They devised the mecholyl test and perfusion techniques to investigate intestinal absorption. They also examined blood flow through the liver to determine its role in various diseases. Ingelfinger felt his most important contribution was the documentation of the megaloblastic anemia that can follow a complete gastrectomy.

In 1961, Ingelfinger became chief of the Boston University Medical Services at Boston City Hospital. Over the next six years, he transformed it into a leading center of teaching. Ingelfinger liked to teach by the Socratic method, in which he asked questions in a way that induced students to find the answers for themselves. Known as "the Boss" among his trainees, he inspired both fear and respect. Tall, thin, bald, with rounded shoulders and an authoritarian manner, he arrived at work at 7:15 in the morning and left at 6 in the evening. "We work Saturdays," he told trainees, but they ended up working Sundays and holidays as well. "Demanding, humbling, but always stimulating" was the way one trainee described his experience under Ingelfinger. Devoid of pomp or egotism, Ingelfinger spoke his mind, and when he did not know something, he simply said, "I don't know." When aggravated, however, he had the curious habit of chewing on his tie or shirtsleeve to vent his frustration.

Ingelfinger was fiercely competitive, and

hated to come in second. At the annual picnic at his summer home in Ipswich, Mass., he would organize a football game among the trainees, select the most athletic ones for his team and, according to one trainee, leave "a pathetic aggregation of obese, lame, near-sighted residents to serve as the loyal, but impotent, opposition." Ingelfinger would play two positions at once, quarterback and running back, so that he almost always had the ball.

He began a third career in 1967 as editor of the *New England Journal of Medicine*. Over a ten-year period, he boosted the journal's circulation from about 100,000 to 170,000, and the number of articles submitted for publication increased 140 percent. Ingelfinger's editorship encouraged innovation and provoked controversy. He loved debate and lively correspondences in the letters-to-the-editor section. He insisted on strict scientific review and evaluation of articles submitted. Using his background as a college English major, he expected articles to be written in lucid, readable, and, if possible, entertaining prose. He focused on issues of medical ethics, and did not hesitate to publish anti-establishment views of medicine.

While Ingelfinger was editor of the *New England Journal of Medicine*, Lewis Thomas wrote a regular column for it, "Notes of a Biology Watcher," which eventually became the National Book Award winner *The Lives of a Cell* (1974). Ingelfinger also published Norman Cousins's controversial account of how he overcame a collagen disease by taking high doses of vitamin C, laughing a lot, and avoiding doctors and hospitals. Cousins later expanded the article into the best-selling book *Anatomy of an Illness* (1979).

Ingelfinger had some unconventional views regarding medicine and the doctor-patient relationship. He felt patients expected too much of physicians and needed to realize that doctors could not cure everything. He advocated two forms of preventive medicine: old-fashioned self-discipline and keeping oneself informed. On the other hand, he said, "Doctors fail to appreciate how patients feel. They take too much for granted, don't realize how little the patient understands, how much the patient needs to be talked to." He was against patients' "shopping" around or switching from doctor to doctor. But he also felt a doctor should "take time to explain his impressions and recommendations to the patient . . . [in] terms that the patient can understand . . . [and] language that is distinctly non-authoritarian."

During his editorship, Ingelfinger devised the hotly debated "Ingelfinger Rule," which requires that any material published in the *Journal* not have been published previously. The rule became a standard practice for other medical journals and, as a result, researchers have become less willing to talk to reporters or show them work.

"The Finger," as he was known among colleagues, stepped down from his editorship in 1977. Two years earlier, he had, ironically, diagnosed himself as having cancer of the esophagus. An operation in 1975 removed part of his digestive tract. He continued to lead an active life despite subsequent radiation and chemotherapy treatments, but eventually his deteriorating physical condition forced him to retire.

Ingelfinger said he had "few regrets" about his life. He had married Sarah Shurcliff on Aug. 23, 1941; they had two children. He continued his hobbies of gardening, watercolor painting, and music after he retired. He died in Boston.

[Biographical articles include "Franz Ingelfinger, M.D.: A Redoubtable Character," *Journal of the American Medical Association*, Feb. 1, 1980; Edward Huth, "Franz Ingelfinger, 1910–1980," *Annals of Internal Medicine*, June 1980; Joseph A. Ingelfinger, "Franz Ingelfinger in the Summer—Memorial Remarks for My Father," *Gastroenterology*, Sept. 1980; Arnold S. Relman, "Franz J. Ingelfinger, 1910–1980," *New England Journal of Medicine*, Apr. 10, 1980; R. M. Donaldson, "Franz J. Ingelfinger: His Accomplishments," *Gastroenterology*, May 1981; and Michael D. Levitt, "Franz J. Ingelfinger: The Man," *Gastroenterology*, May 1981. Obituaries are in the *New York Times*, Mar. 27, 1980; and *Lancet*, Apr. 5, 19, and 26, 1980.]

ALISON GARDY

INGERSOLL, ROYAL EASON (June 20, 1883–May 20, 1976), naval officer, was born in Washington, D.C., the son of Royal Rodney Ingersoll, a naval officer, and Cynthia Eason. He grew up in Annapolis, Md., and in his mother's hometown of LaPorte, Ind., during his father's long absences at sea, and attended school in both communities. Appointed to the United States Naval Academy from Indiana, he graduated in 1905. Ingersoll's first assignment as a passed midshipman was on the battleship *Missouri* in the "Great White Fleet"; he then had duty aboard the battleship *Connecticut* and at the Portsmouth Peace Conference. After a course of study in ordnance, his father's specialty, he served on the *Connecticut* during the world cruise of the White Fleet (1907–1909). His father, who was then a captain, was the fleet's chief of staff at the beginning of the cruise. On June 29, 1910, Ingersoll married Louise Van Harlingen; they had two children. Their son died in combat while serving on the aircraft carrier *Hornet* at the Battle of Midway in 1942.

Promoted to ensign in 1907 and to lieutenant in 1910, Ingersoll taught at the United States Naval Academy for two years, beginning in 1911. He then served two years on the staff of the commander in chief, Asiatic Fleet, after which he remained in the Far East as executive officer of the cruiser *Cincinnati*. In 1916, as a lieutenant commander, Ingersoll was assigned to the communications office in the Office of Naval Operations. The communications office supervised telephone and telegraph communications, radio dispatches, and all of the navy's code work. A small office in peacetime, it expanded significantly once the United States entered World War I. By the end of the war Ingersoll was in charge of more than two hundred persons who handled thousands of messages daily. A frequent visitor to his office was Assistant Secretary of the Navy Franklin D. Roosevelt. After the armistice, Ingersoll was detached for duty in Paris to handle communications between the American delegation to the peace conference and Washington.

Ingersoll returned to sea in 1919, serving briefly on the *Connecticut* and then as executive officer of the powerful new battleship *Arizona*. During the 1920's, Ingersoll, who had been promoted to commander in 1921, was rotated through several more shore billets, including a stint as head of counterespionage at the Office of Naval Intelligence (ONI), a year of study at the Naval War College (1926–1927), and a year on the faculty of that institution. Although it was another officer who made the most direct contribution, it was during Ingersoll's tenure at ONI that the United States Navy began to decipher Japanese codes. In 1928, Ingersoll became assistant chief of staff to Admiral William Veazie Pratt, commander of the battle fleet. As a captain, Ingersoll returned to Washington, D.C., in 1930 for three years of duty in the Division of Fleet Training in the Office of the Chief of Naval Operations, where he wrote the manuals on tactics and war instructions.

In 1933, Ingersoll began a two-year tour at sea, commanding in turn the cruisers *Augusta* (Chester Nimitz succeeded him in that command) and the *San Francisco*, which he brought into commission. Ingersoll's next billet was in the War Plans Division of the Office of the Chief of Naval Operations. During this time he was temporarily detached to serve as a technical expert at the London Naval Conference of 1936; he returned to London at the start of 1938 to confer with British representative Capt. T. S. V. ("Tom") Phillips on parallel action between the Royal Navy and the United States Navy in the event of war in the Far East. Later in 1938, Ingersoll was promoted to rear admiral and assigned to command a division of heavy cruisers in the Pacific. When war broke out in December 1941, he was assistant chief of naval operations. He received command of the Atlantic Fleet on Jan. 1, 1942.

Ingersoll's new command covered an area from Brazil to Iceland with naval bases in Trinidad, Bermuda, and Newfoundland, as well as along the east coast of the United States. Ingersoll had vast responsibilities but relatively little public recognition because naval warfare in the Atlantic did not involve battles between great task forces and fleets, as did naval war in the Pacific. Rather, Atlantic operations involved escorting convoys, antisubmarine warfare, and several large amphibious operations in North African and European waters. Ingersoll had no command authority over the routing of convoys or over the amphibious operations of 1943 and 1944 in the Mediterranean and in the English Channel. Throughout the war, however, he was charged with assigning ships to convoy escort and made the important decision, once sufficient numbers of escort carriers became available in 1943, to send those carriers on aggressive antisubmarine patrols rather than restricting them to close support of convoys.

Ingersoll's command supervised the training of crews of newly commissioned ships for all types of naval warfare. The Atlantic Fleet, for example, operated what historian Samuel Eliot Morison called the United States Antisubmarine University, consisting of fifteen antisubmarine training centers as well as separate sonar schools. In addition, the fleet's Training Command maintained training facilities for surface warfare and amphibious operations. Ships slated for Pacific operations also took their training under Ingersoll if they had been built in shipyards along the Atlantic coast.

Promoted to admiral July 1, 1942, Ingersoll had little to do beyond the routine by November 1944, for the sea-lanes in the Atlantic were under Allied control. His superiors believed he could be of much use in the Pacific, however, so he was assigned to San Francisco as commander, Western Sea Frontier, to take charge of all naval activity, including shore establishments, in eleven western states. To facilitate Ingersoll's tasks he was also given the titles of deputy commander, United States Fleet, and deputy chief of naval operations. If he could not issue the requisite orders under one title, he almost certainly could under the other.

The pressing problem Ingersoll faced was to straighten out what was becoming a supply nightmare. With operations in the western Pacific becoming larger and more distant from West Coast bases, and with an invasion of Japan looming, a logistics logjam had developed. No one in authority seemed to have an accurate idea of what supplies were available or where they were: at a forward base, at sea en route to a base, in a warehouse in California or Oregon, or at a naval depot in some interior state. Too many ships were being dispatched to forward bases where there was no warehouse space for their cargoes, necessitating the wasteful use of ships as floating warehouses. Ingersoll's task was to bring order to this chaos. Assisted by logistics expert Paul Pihl and reserve officer Clark Clifford, he implemented a more efficient use of ships destined for the war zone and established an IBM system to keep track of cargoes and the availability and location of supplies.

A superb leader of men and a masterful planner throughout his career, Ingersoll was always low-key and self-effacing. Reflecting on the war, he said that he had earned the "croix de chair" for commanding an LMD, a "Large Mahogany Desk." He retired on July 1, 1946. At the time of his death in Bethesda, Md., Ingersoll was the senior officer on the retired list of the navy.

[By far the best source on Ingersoll is his oral history, "Reminiscences of Admiral Royal E. Ingersoll," Oral History Research Project, Columbia University (1965). Also of use are Samuel Eliot Morison, *History of United States Naval Operations in World War II*, 15 vols. (1947–1962), particularly vols. 1 and 10; James R. Leutze, *Bargaining for Supremacy* (1977); Duncan S. Ballantine, *U.S. Naval Logistics in the Second World War* (1949); and Clark G. Reynolds, *Famous American Admirals* (1978). An obituary is in the *New York Times*, May 22, 1976.]

LLOYD J. GRAYBAR

ITURBI, JOSÉ (Nov. 28, 1895–June 28, 1980), concert pianist and conductor, was born in Valencia, Spain, one of four children of Ricardo Iturbi, a bill collector for a local gas company and piano tuner in his spare time, and Teresa Baguena, an opera singer who performed in *Carmen* only hours before Iturbi was born. As a child, Iturbi accompanied his father when he tuned pianos, and he developed a love for the instrument. He began taking lessons at the age of four, and a year later was enrolled in the Escuela de Música de María Jordan. At the age of seven, Iturbi began studies at the Conservatorio de Música in Valencia and first began to make a living from his music: at a silent movie house, he played a twelve-hour shift until after midnight, and then for a little extra money, he would play dance music until two in the morning, stopping only to eat the sandwiches his mother made for him.

When Iturbi was thirteen, a local journalist inspired the citizens of Valencia to raise enough money to send him to the Conservatoire de Musique in Paris. He supported himself there by performing all night in cafés and graduated at the age of seventeen with top honors. He then went to Zurich, where the director of the Geneva Conservatory heard him play at a fashionable café and offered him a teaching position. Iturbi spent the years 1919–1923 at Geneva as the head of the piano faculty at the conservatory, a position once held by Franz Liszt.

On June 8, 1916, Iturbi married Maria Giner, one of his pupils; she played the piano in cafés while Iturbi taught at the Geneva Conservatory. They had one daughter. Iturbi's wife died in 1928 and his daughter took her own life in 1946.

Iturbi's fame as a pianist quickly spread through Europe. He made his London debut in 1928 and toured with the composer Igor Stravinsky. In October 1929 he debuted in the United States with the Philadelphia Orchestra, playing Beethoven's G Major Concerto. He proceeded to give more concerts in the next four years than any other pianist before him except Ignace Jan Paderewski. In 1930 he gave seventy-seven concerts on one American tour, and by

1950 Iturbi had surpassed Paderewski in the number of concerts.

In 1933, Iturbi went to Mexico intending to play four concerts, but popular demand induced him to play nineteen. He was then given the opportunity to form his own orchestra and become a conductor. Iturbi became known for conducting while simultaneously playing the piano and keeping the beat with his head. Some critics said he tried to do too much on stage. Orchestras in the United States began seeking Iturbi as a conductor. After serving as a guest conductor with most of the country's major orchestras, he became the regular conductor and musical director of the Rochester Philharmonic in 1936.

Iturbi did not limit his interests to music. He once said, "Life is like a meal and music is the roast beef. But what good is the roast beef by itself? I must have my coffee and dessert and cigar." Iturbi's other interests included amateur boxing, flying, and motorcycle riding. He often flew to his concert engagements in his own plane and liked to spar with former New England featherweight champion Don Perone.

Iturbi became an American citizen in 1943. During World War II, he wrote to President Roosevelt, stating that he wanted to fly for the Army Air Forces. His age prevented him from doing so, but he enrolled in the Civilian Air Patrol (1942) and performed for war bond drives.

In 1944, Iturbi resigned as conductor of the Rochester Philharmonic in order to pursue a career in Hollywood. He became known for his appearances in *A Song to Remember* (1945), in which his hands were photographed as those of Frederic Chopin playing the piano, as well as in films such as *Anchors Aweigh* (1945), *Thousands Cheer* (1943), *That Midnight Kiss* (1949), *Music for Millions* (1944), and *Holiday in Mexico* (1946).

Some critics accused Iturbi of "going Hollywood." He lived flamboyantly in Beverly Hills, supported by his earnings from movies, concerts, and record sales. In 1946, Iturbi received a check for $118,029 in royalties from RCA Victor—at the time the largest amount paid to an artist as six months' royalties. Most of the royalties came from *A Song to Remember*, for which Iturbi received no screen credit because he was under contract to another studio, and from his record of Chopin's Polonaise in A-flat, which sold over 800,000 copies. Some believed Iturbi's luxurious life-style was a compensation for the childhood he never had. "When I walk onto the stage of a concert hall today," he once said, "I have to prove that I can still play the piano."

Iturbi was also criticized for playing with little emotional depth, though he displayed dazzling technical ability. Despite his detractors, most of whom were classical musicians, Iturbi succeeded in popularizing classical music for the American public. People who had never been to a concert became familiar with classical music through the movies, then flocked to see Iturbi perform on stage.

Iturbi had a colorful personality, given to extreme expressions of generosity and devotion, on the one hand, and anger and disgust, on the other. He offended a number of people on several occasions, such as the time he withdrew from a concert in which jazz clarinetist Benny Goodman was the soloist, because he did not believe in mixing classical and jazz music, even though he played and enjoyed boogie-woogie. Also, while conducting a concert in Cleveland, he scolded members of the audience who were eating hot dogs during the performance. Iturbi insulted women musicians by suggesting they would never attain the musical competence that men had. Nevertheless, he once said of his sister Amparo, who played the piano and often toured with him, that he was "her worst enemy," because he overshadowed her though he believed her to be the better pianist.

Iturbi died in Hollywood.

[Further information on Iturbi can be found in "Piano Playboy," *Time*, June 17, 1946; Pete Martin, "The Prodigious Señor," *Saturday Evening Post*, Oct. 25, 1947; Charles O'Connell, *The Other Side of the Record* (1947); Pete Martin, *Hollywood Without Makeup* (1948); Arthur Bronson, "Fantastic José Iturbi," *American Mercury*, Jan. 1950; "What Happened to Jose?," *Time*, May 21, 1951; and Richard Lamparski, *What Ever Became of . . . ?*, 5th ser. (1974). An obituary is in the *New York Times*, June 29, 1980.]

ALISON GARDY

J

JACOBS, PAUL (Aug. 24, 1918–Jan. 3, 1978), journalist, author, labor leader, and social activist, was born in New York City, the son of Julius Jacobs, a businessman, and Tecla Schmidt. A graduate of Townsend Harris High School, he attended City College of New York and the University of Minnesota.

Jacobs's formal education gave way to an intense interest in social and labor problems of the 1930's and 1940's. Calling himself a "professional revolutionist," he was an organizer for the International Ladies' Garment Workers Union (1941–1943). For another two years (1946–1948) he served as race relations specialist for the American Jewish Committee. This was the first professional application of his inherited affiliation with the Jewish faith of his parents. From 1948 to 1951 he was international representative of the Oil Workers International Union.

A major portion of Jacobs's varied career opened in 1956 as staff member at the Center for the Study of Democratic Institutions in Santa Barbara, Calif. That connection continued until 1969, and he was an associate of the research staff of the Center for the Study of Law and Society, at the University of California Berkeley, from 1964 to 1972. Overlapping that was his growing interest in national events. In 1970 he accepted an associate fellowship at the Institute for Foreign Policy Studies in Washington, D.C.

While these assignments were in force, Jacobs contributed many articles to newspapers and magazines. Among them were the *Atlantic Monthly*, *Harper's*, the *Reporter*, *Commentary*, *Commonweal*, *New Politics*, *Economist*, *Dissent*, *New America*, and even *Playboy*. Publications he particularly liked were *Mother Jones* (1974–1976) and *Newsday* (from 1977).

Jacobs produced one book after another on socially inflammatory issues. These began with *Old Age and Political Behavior* (1959), in which friends Frank Pinner and Philip Selznick joined. His next partner was Michael Harrington, and in 1961 they brought out *Labor in a Free Society*. There followed *Dead Horse and the Featherbird* (1962); *State of the Unions* (1963); *Is Curly Jewish?* (1965), describing his boyhood; with Saul Landau, *The New Radicals: A Report With Documents* (1966); *Dialogue on Poverty* (1967); *Prelude to a Riot: A View of Urban America From the Bottom* (1968), an investigation of African-American civil rights; *Between the Rock and the Hard Place* (1970), a description of Jewish-Arabic relations; with Saul Landau and Eve Pell, *To Serve the Devil* (1971), a history of American minority groups; and *The Red, Black and Brown Experience in America* (1971).

One of Jacobs's characteristics was to move into new means as well as new subjects. Thus he became a producer of public television programs, for which he frequently served as commentator. A notable program he helped develop was a 1972 documentary, *The Jail*, which was filmed in the San Francisco County Jail. Describing it as "candidly exploring most aspects of jail life," John J. O'Connor of the *New York Times* rated it as "valuable television."

The 1958 Sigma Delta Chi award for distinguished public service in magazine journalism honored Jacobs, for exposing the Atomic Energy Commission's activities in Nevada. In the May 16, 1957, issue of the *Reporter*, Jacobs set out his views under the title "Clouds from Nevada." The Sigma Delta Chi magazine, *Quill*, summarized this as follows:

"Paul Jacobs' report on the AEC's weapons-testing program was outstanding. Official secrecy hampered his investigation; the climate of opinion insured that the questions raised by his disclosures would be unpopular. Yet he dug out a comprehensive set of facts—and presented them compellingly—so that Americans were alerted to a real danger and provoked to discussion of policies that have deep significance for people everywhere." This award recognized Jacobs's exploration of the nuclear test site which he subsequently believed was the source of the cancer of which he died.

Jacobs spent the years 1943–1946 in the United States Army Air Forces, from which he was discharged with the rank of sergeant. He married Ruth Rosenfield on Jan. 1, 1939; they had no children. Jacobs died in San Francisco.

[Jacobs's papers and files are at the University of California at Santa Barbara and at the Center for the Study of Democratic Institutions, also in Santa Barbara. See *Quill*, May 1958. Obituaries are in the *New York Times* and the *Washington Post*, both Jan. 5, 1978.]

IRVING DILLIARD

JACOBY, NEIL HERMAN (Sept. 19, 1909–May 31, 1979), economist, was born in Dundurn, Saskatchewan. After being educated in local schools and receiving a bachelor's degree from the University of Saskatchewan in 1930, he enrolled at the University of Chicago, where he received his Ph.D. in economics in 1938. He also worked as a supervisor in the legal and research department of the Saskatchewan Taxation Commission, and before then had been a supervisor in the legal and research division of the province's Department of Finance. He married Claire Gruhn; they had two children.

Jacoby became an assistant professor of finance at Chicago in 1938. Two years later he was promoted to associate professor, and in 1942 he became a full professor. In 1948 he transferred to the University of California at Los Angeles, where he was named the first dean of the Graduate School of Business Administration.

Jacoby, who did not write a book until late in his career, had a reputation as a competent but rather colorless political economist who considered tax policy the preferred method of regulating the economy. Jacoby favored cutting taxes in times of recession as a stimulus, and raising them in periods of boom to dampen inflationary forces. If administered properly by government, such a program would balance out over the economic cycle. Because of his views Jacoby was considered by some to be a moderate Keynesian, which was not the case in that he believed government spending increases during recessions, a mainstay of Keynesian thought, have only a small initial effect and take hold only after the recessions end, thus possibly proving inflationary. Furthermore, he generally favored corporate over individual tax cuts, since the former would stimulate investment while the latter might have inflationary consequences. At the time, these stances placed him squarely in the moderate Republican camp.

In the summer of 1953, President Dwight Eisenhower named Jacoby to the three-person Council of Economic Advisers (CEA). He served from Sept. 15, 1953, until Feb. 9, 1955. During Jacoby's tenure Arthur Burns was chairman of the CEA and one of Eisenhower's closest advisers on economic policy. The president saw no reason for the CEA to continue, and permitted its funding only to please Burns. He did not meet with Jacoby and Walter Stewart, the other CEA member; their views were transmitted to Eisenhower through Burns.

Eisenhower entered office at a time when the economy was in recession. At the CEA, Jacoby generally supported Burns in calling for lower taxes and decreased government spending, a policy criticized by liberals and conservatives alike. The former thought lower spending would only exacerbate the recession, while conservatives like Secretary of the Treasury George Humphrey opposed tax cuts at a time when the federal budget was unbalanced.

Burns and Jacoby argued that through corporate tax cuts, the government could produce the greatest impact with the least intervention in the economy. They won the day when Eisenhower became convinced that without tax cuts, the recession would deepen and Eisenhower, the first Republican president since Herbert Hoover, would further identify the party with hard times.

Jacoby later argued that taxes on the wealthy and the poor should be cut, while those on the middle class should be increased. He reasoned that a tax cut for the upper brackets would encourage investment and savings (at the time, marginal tax rates exceeded 90 percent for the very rich), while that for the lower ones would enhance economic equity and stimulate consumption. Since most Americans were in the middle brackets, small tax increases there would be needed to balance the cuts elsewhere but could be absorbed without undue pain. He also supported ending the tax-exempt status for municipal bonds, arguing that it led to social inequities and diverted investment capital from the private sector.

After leaving government service in 1955, Jacoby returned to UCLA as dean of the Graduate School of Business. In 1957, Eisenhower named him United States representative to the United Nations Economic and Social Council, and in 1965 he was named to the Agency for International Development, to report on the role of American investment and aid in Taiwan's economic growth.

Jacoby's subsequent publications reflected his new interests. *Can Prosperity Be Sustained?* (1956) reiterated his stance in favor of tax-based direction of the economy. This was followed by *European Economics—East and West* (1967) and *The Progress of People* (1969). Other Jacoby publications included *The Polluters* (1972), *Corporate Power and Social Responsibility* (1973), *Multinational Oil* (1974), and *Bribery and Extortion in World Business* (1977).

The wide range of topics covered in these books indicates a broadening of Jacoby's interests. But a reading of them demonstrates the failures of his kind of analysis during the 1970's. Jacoby's experiences and analysis fit well into the world in which deflation and inflation, recession and expansion, were alternatives to be diagnosed and for which prescriptions might be offered. In the wake of the oil shock of 1973, the American economy experienced stagflation, the combination of stagnation of growth and inflation, a phenomenon for which macroeconomists were unprepared. In such an atmosphere tax cuts often brought more inflation, and tax increases often depressed even further an economy on the brink of double-digit unemployment. Nor did Jacoby realize that America's economic hegemony of the post–World War II period had drawn to a close, calling for a new set of policies. He now advocated the establishment of planning commissions to help guide the nation's industries. He welcomed the expansion of multinational corporations as assisting the development of Third World countries and stimulating trade.

Jacoby retired as dean in 1968 and became Armand Hammer professor of business economics and policy. He served as chairman of President Nixon's Task Force on Economic Growth and as a member of the Pay Board from 1971 to 1973. He died in Los Angeles.

[There is no full-scale biography of Jacoby. James Collins contributed an essay on his life and scholarship to Robert Sobel and Bernard Katz, eds., *Biographical Directory of the Council of Economic Advisors* (1988). An obituary is in the *New York Times*, June 1, 1979.]

ROBERT SOBEL

JAMES, DANIEL, JR. ("CHAPPIE") (Feb. 11, 1920–Feb. 25, 1978), United States Air Force general, was born in Pensacola, Fla., the son of Daniel James, a lamplighter and coal-dolly operator at the local gas plant, and Lillie Anna Brown, a schoolteacher. The youngest of seventeen children (ten had died before his birth), James grew up on Alcaniz Street, in a black area of Pensacola. The early experience of facing the strict color line of the South, as well as admiring the frequent overflights from the nearby Pensacola Naval Air Station, shaped his commitment to integration and his pride in the military as he rose through the ranks of the air force officer corps to become America's first black four-star general.

James completed his education through the seventh grade under his mother's instruction. She considered Pensacola's black schools unsuitable, and taught her own and the neighborhood children through the junior high school level in her Lillie A. James Private School, which the children called "Miz Lillie's" school. James credited his parents, especially his mother, with imbuing him with a dedication to academic excellence and a loathing for racial prejudice. His mother taught him to stress leadership qualities, spiritual strength, love of country, and what James referred to later in life as the Eleventh Commandment: "Thou shall not quit."

After graduating from Washington High School in 1937, James enrolled at Tuskegee Institute in Alabama. In those dark days of the Great Depression, it took contributions from the entire family to pay for his education. James quickly became involved in campus academics and social activities, using his six-foot, four-inch height and 200-plus pounds to play tackle on the football team and his affable personality to make friends. One of those friends, Dorothy Agusta Watkins, married James on Nov. 3,

1942, after a prolonged and sometimes stormy courtship; they had three children.

After being expelled from Tuskegee in 1942, James pursued his dream of becoming a combat pilot. He became a licensed pilot and flight instructor in the segregated Army Air Corps Aviation Cadet Program at Tuskegee. Later he entered the program himself (the alumni became known as the Tuskegee Airmen) and earned a commission as a second lieutenant in the Army Air Force in July 1943. During World War II, James underwent fighter training at Selfridge Field, Mich., and trained pilots for the all-black Ninety-ninth Pursuit Squadron, which flew combat missions in Europe. By 1945, James had adopted the Black Panther insignia, a sign that he said characterized him as a "different breed of cat. This Black Panther fights for his country." In subsequent years, James took pride in claiming he was the original black panther, although he strongly disavowed the separatist tactics of the militant Black Panther party in the late 1960's.

While on temporary duty at Freeman Field, Ind., in April 1945, James and one hundred other black officers challenged the Army Air Corps policy of segregation by demanding service at the whites-only officers club. All the blacks were arrested and sent to Godman Field, Ky., for disciplining, but only three (not including James) were selected for trial. The noted NAACP lawyer Thurgood Marshall agreed to represent the black flyers, all three of whom were acquitted in this early "test case" of military segregation. James later took pride in recalling this event as the first civil rights sit-in and in his friendship with Thurgood Marshall, who in 1967 became the first African-American member of the Supreme Court.

For the next three decades James served in a wide variety of stations and combat roles in the air force. From 1946 to 1949, James served at Lockbourne Air Force Base (AFB) in Ohio, after which he transferred as a fighter pilot and flight leader to Clark Field in the Philippines. At Clark, James experienced an especially tense situation at the white officers club when he first requested service. All the whites ignored him with the exception of a Texan named Claude ("Spud") Taylor. A strong bond existed between the two officers until Taylor died during the Korean War. The Jameses honored the memory of Taylor by naming their second son Claude (and nicknaming him "Spud").

In July 1950, James left for duty in the Korean conflict. While in Korea, he flew 101 combat missions in P-51 and F-80 aircraft. In May 1951, James was transferred to Griffiss AFB, N.Y., and later to Otis AFB, Mass., where he served as commander of various fighter-interceptor squadrons. In 1954, while at Otis, James won the Young Man of the Year Award from the Massachusetts Junior Chamber of Commerce for his community involvement and frequent speeches on Americanism.

In 1957, James completed the Air Command and Staff School program at Maxwell AFB, Ala. His next duty took him to the Office of Deputy Chief of Staff for Operations, Air Defense Headquarters, in Washington, D.C. Upon completion of that duty in 1960, James became assistant director, and later director, of operations, Eighty-first Tactical Fighter Wing and then commander of the Ninety-second Tactical Fighter Squadron, Royal Air Force Station, in Bentwaters, England. From 1964 to 1966, James was director of operations, and training and deputy commander for operations, at Davis-Monthan AFB, Ariz.

In December 1966, James began his service in the war in Southeast Asia as a combat pilot, deputy commander for operations, and vice-commander of the Eighth Tactical Fighter Wing, commanded by his close friend Robin Olds (later commandant of the United States Air Force Academy). James flew seventy-eight combat missions over North Vietnam, many in F-4 Phantom jets in the dangerous airspace above the Hanoi/Haiphong Harbor area. On Jan. 2, 1967, he led a squadron that destroyed seven enemy MIG jets in the famous "Bolo MIG Sweep" action, which accounted for the highest number of kills for a single mission during the war. James added to his reputation as a fierce combat pilot by recording one kill and several probable kills during his service in Southeast Asia.

James's next duty was as vice-commander of a tactical fighter wing at Eglin AFB, Fla., for two years beginning in 1967. In August 1969, James took command of Wheelus AB, Libya, the largest such facility outside the United States. He presided over the sensitive evacuation of that air base, ordered by the new military strongman Muammar al-Gadhafi. Also in 1969, Tuskegee Institute awarded a belated degree to its now-famous student.

In March 1970, James became the first military officer to serve as Deputy Assistant Secretary of Defense for Public Affairs. This high-visibility position, coupled with his recent success in Libya, positioned him for promotion to the elite corps of generals. On July 1, 1970, James was appointed brigadier general, but not without controversy. Many in the media speculated that his promotion was timed to fill the slot of the recently retired Benjamin O. Davis, Jr., the first black general in the air force. The suggestion that his promotion was based on race rather than on talent and achievement rankled James. He further took umbrage at criticism from militant blacks who referred to him as a "Tom" and "puppet of the establishment." James declared publicly to his detractors: "I didn't just walk in here; I fought every step of the way. I got here because I'm damned good." At that time, he had logged over 10,000 air hours, flown 179 combat missions, and commanded units and bases around the world.

By Aug. 1, 1972, James had added another star to his shoulder board as a major general, and on June 1, 1973, he had tacked on the third star, as a lieutenant general. In the following year, James became vice-commander of the Military Airlift Command, Scott AFB, Ill. He was named the armed forces' first black four-star general on Sept. 1, 1975 (one of only thirty-six four-star generals in the entire military), and assumed dual command of the North American Air Defense Command (NORAD) and the United States Air Force Aerospace Defense Command (ADCOM) at Peterson AFB, Colo. The new commander of NORAD/ADCOM held extensive power, including responsibility for the surveillance and defense of North American airspace, and direction of 63,000 service personnel around the world and the nuclear-resistant NORAD facility 4,675 feet into Cheyenne Mountain in the Colorado Rockies. The most awesome power he held, however, was authorization, as the only person other than the president, to "push the button" (to launch a nuclear attack).

James retired on Feb. 1, 1978. His military record noted twenty-four major citations, including the Distinguished Service Medal, the Distinguished Flying Cross with two oak leaf clusters, the World War II Victory Medal, the Korean Service Medal with four service stars, and the Vietnam Service Medal with two bronze service stars. He also received numerous civilian awards, including the George Washington Freedom Foundation Medal in 1967 and 1968; the Arnold Air Society's Eugene M. Zuckert Award in 1970; the Capital Press Club, Washington, D.C., Salute to Black Pioneers Award (1975); the Blackbook Minority Business and Reference Guidance Par Excellence Award (1976); and the United Negro College Fund's Distinguished Service Award (1976). In 1970, James was listed in *Ebony* magazine as one of its "100 Most Influential Black Americans."

While in Colorado Springs to give a speech on Americanism and self-help, James died of a heart attack. A number of distinguished figures—including Vice-President Walter Mondale, Secretary of Defense Harold Brown, senators Edward W. Brooke and Barry Goldwater, and Mayor Walter Washington of Washington, D.C.—attended the funeral. James was buried in Arlington National Cemetery.

[Some of James's speeches are on tape at the Tuskegee Institute Archives. The Secretary of the Air Force, Office of Information, has useful information on his military career and professional life, and the Albert F. Simpson Historical Research Center, Maxwell AFB, Ala., has information on his unit histories and his air force career. An official air force biography of James is available from the Secretary of the Air Force, Office of Information, Command Service Unit, Bolling AFB, D.C. The wing historian on any air force base will obtain information on James and provide it to interested parties.

For biographies, see James R. McGovern, *Black Eagle* (1985); and J. Alfred Phelps, *Chappie* (1991). Useful background articles are "General-to-Be Is a Black Panther," *Washington Post*, Feb. 1, 1970; "Black Colonel Getting General's Rank," *New York Times*, Jan. 26, 1970; Carolyn DuBose, "Chappie James: A New Role for an Old Warrior," *Ebony*, Oct. 1970; and Alex Poinsett, "Gen. Daniel (Chappie) James, Jr.: New Boss of the Nation's Air Defense," *Ebony*, Dec. 1975. An obituary is in the *New York Times*, Feb. 26, 1978.]

IRVIN D. SOLOMON

JANSSEN, DAVID (Mar. 27, 1930–Feb. 13, 1980), actor, was born David Harold Meyer in Naponee, Nebr. His father, Harold Meyer, was a banker, and his mother, Berneice Dalton, was a showgirl who appeared in the *Ziegfeld Follies*. When Janssen was an infant, his parents were divorced, and he toured with his mother in Ziegfeld's production of *Rio Rita*. They subsequently moved to Hollywood, where his mother married Eugene Janssen. David assumed his stepfather's surname.

While still in his teens, Janssen played small roles in several minor films, making his debut in *It's a Pleasure* (1945), a musical with Sonja Henie. Janssen attended Fairfax High School in Los Angeles, where he was a leading athlete. After leaving school, he continued his acting career. In 1951, at age twenty-one, he signed a long-term contract with Universal-International Studios, but he appeared in only two movies, *Yankee Buccaneer* (1952) and *Bonzo Goes to College* (1952), before being drafted into the army.

Resuming his acting career after discharge, Janssen had featured roles in a number of films where his good looks and raspy voice could be seen and heard to advantage. Among his movies in the 1950's were *To Hell and Back* (1955), *Toy Tiger* (1956), and *The Girl He Left Behind* (1956). In 1957 he won his first major television assignment in "Richard Diamond, Private Detective." In the role that Dick Powell had originated on radio, Janssen played a former policeman who becomes a private detective and uses his old contacts on the police force to help him solve crimes. The series had resourceful Diamond using his car phone to check in with his answering service, represented by a sexy-voiced woman known only as "Sam." "Sam," played by budding actress Mary Tyler Moore, was seen in silhouette; only her shapely legs were visible. During this time, Janssen also appeared in many other television plays.

By the early 1960's, no longer under contract to Universal-International, Janssen graduated to leading roles in such second-level movies as *Ring of Fire* (1961), *King of the Roaring Twenties* (1961), and *My Six Loves* (1963). He seemed fated, however, to remain on a lower rung of the ladder to stardom until he was signed to play the title role in the enormously successful television series "The Fugitive." Premiering on Sept. 17, 1963, the series cast Janssen as Dr. Richard Kimble, a physician falsely accused of murdering his wife. Pursued by an implacable police lieutenant named Gerard (Barry Morse), Kimble spent each episode playing a significant role in the lives of people he met during his flight and narrowly escaping capture by Gerard. He also continued his relentless search for the elusive one-armed man he saw fleeing from his house on the night of his wife's murder. The final episode, aired on Aug. 29, 1967, drew one of the largest audiences in television history. Over a quarter-century later, in 1993, "The Fugitive" was turned into a well-received motion picture starring Harrison Ford as Dr. Kimble.

Although Janssen could now command larger parts, his popularity on television did not translate into full-fledged stardom in films. He continued to play substantial roles in such movies as *The Green Berets* (1968), *The Shoes of the Fisherman* (1968), and *Marooned* (1969). He also starred in two other television series that drew on his laconic, understated personality: in "O'Hara, United States Treasury" (1971–1972) he was an investigative agent for the government, and in "Harry O" (1974–1976), he played Harry Orwell, a world-weary former policeman, injured in the line of duty, who becomes a part-time private detective. Neither series achieved the enormous popularity of "The Fugitive." There were other television shows in the 1970's, most notably "A Sensitive, Passionate Man" (1977), in which the actor played a self-destructive alcoholic.

Janssen died of a massive heart attack in Malibu, Calif. At the time he was filming a television play about Father Damien, known as the Leper Priest. Two months after his death, a heated dispute over his will arose between his mother and his widow, Dani Greco, whom he had married in 1972. (An earlier marriage to Ellie Graham had ended in divorce in 1969, after ten years.) Janssen's mother claimed that her son's will, which left a reported $2 million to his widow, was either forged or signed under duress. Dani asserted that there had been strife between mother and son for many years, going back to her allegedly having left him in an orphanage from age eight to age twelve. Janssen's mother denied this claim.

Although he never achieved top-ranking stardom on the big screen, David Janssen displayed a low-key style and brooding, enigmatic personality that came across effectively on television.

[See Alvin H. Marill, "The Television Scene," *Films in Review*, Dec. 1980; and Ed Robertson, *The Fugitive Recaptured* (1993). An obituary is in the *New York Times*, Feb. 14, 1980.]

TED SENNETT

JARMAN, WALTON MAXEY (May 10, 1904–Sept. 9, 1980), corporate executive, was born in Nashville, Tenn., the son of James Franklin Jarman and Eugenia Maxey. His father, a devout Southern Baptist, was a partner in the J. W. Carter Shoe Company until he founded the Jarman Shoe Company in 1924. The elder Jarman left the Carter Company because he was disturbed by the "un-Christian" behavior of his business associates and wished to operate his own company along different lines. The strong religious convictions that motivated the father were also characteristic of the son throughout his life.

After attending public schools in Nashville, Jarman spent three years studying engineering at the Massachusetts Institute of Technology. Although he had a good record there, he left in 1924, at the end of his junior year, to join his father's newly organized Jarman Shoe Company. On Oct. 10, 1928, he married Sarah McFerrin Anderson; they had three children.

The Jarman Shoe company began with a capitalization of $130,000. Highly successful in producing low-priced, high-quality shoes, the firm had $1 million in sales in 1925. Jarman was named secretary-treasurer of the firm that year, a post he held until he became president of the company in 1932. Also in 1932, the company was reorganized and renamed General Shoe Company. Jarman's father remained as chairman of the board and chief executive officer, but because of failing health he turned over increasing responsibilities to his son. By the time of his father's death in 1938, Jarman had assumed full control of the affairs of the company. General Shoe was listed on the New York Stock Exchange the following year, and Jarman began an expansion program that would make the company a leader in the manufacturing and retailing of shoes and apparel. He acquired a number of shoe companies and expanded operations into Mexico (1942), Peru (1946), and Israel (1950). By the mid-1950's, General Shoe had become a major importer and exporter of shoes and related products, with direct investments in six countries and licensing arrangements in seventeen others. Jarman also led the company into acquiring retail outlets for shoes and apparel.

Jarman's ambitious growth plan for the company attracted the attention of the Justice Department. Between 1950 and 1955 General Shoe had acquired nineteen shoe companies and was faced with antitrust violation charges. In 1956, Jarman was obliged to sign a consent decree that effectively prohibited further expansion in the shoe business until 1961. His response was to continue the expansion thrust in another direction. In 1956, General Shoe made a major move into the high end of merchandising with the acquisition of Bonwit Teller, a department store, and Tiffany's, a prestigious jewelry firm, both in New York City. Jarman had been introduced to the New York scene in 1953, when his company had acquired I. Miller & Sons, a high-priced women's shoe concern, and Whitehouse & Hardy, a high-end retailer of men's shoes and clothing. With these acquisitions, Jarman began spending a great deal of time in New York, usually flying back and forth from Nashville on a weekly basis. In many respects, the acquisition of Bonwit Teller and Tiffany's marked a high point for Jarman and General Shoe. The company continued to grow, acquiring additional retail and manufacturing companies, and was renamed Genesco in 1959 to reflect its new status. By 1961, Genesco comprised sixty-five companies making and retailing men's, women's, and children's shoes and apparel.

Jarman was widely known and respected, and his company was growing larger, if not more profitable. He was noted regularly in the business pages of the *New York Times*, was featured in *Fortune* magazine, and spoke frequently on business and political affairs. By the time Jarman retired from active management in 1969, Genesco had peaked in terms of growth and profitability. The price of its stock in 1968 had exceeded $58 per share; it had plunged to less than $3 per share by 1974. Jarman's son, Franklin Maxey Jarman, who had also studied engineering at MIT, succeeded him as chairman of the board and attempted to reorganize the company in the face of declining sales and profits. The economic climate of the 1970's, coupled with the debt load of Genesco, left little margin for error, and Franklin Jarman failed in his efforts. He was ousted by the Genesco board in a bitter confrontation in 1977.

These were difficult years for the elder Jarman. He was not in agreement with his son's direction of Genesco and often opposed him publicly. After leaving the board of Genesco in 1974, he was no longer actively involved in the affairs of the company he had worked so diligently to create and was obliged to observe its decline from the sidelines. Jarman's strong religious convictions seem to have sustained him in these trying years. Beginning as a teenager, when he helped his father in a program to distribute free Bibles by mail, and despite a consuming business career, he had actively practiced his faith. He read the Bible regularly, taught Sunday School classes, supported the Moody Bible Institute and the American Bible Society, and published two books on the Bible: *O Taste and See* (1957), a compilation of Scriptures, and *A Businessman Looks at the Bible* (1965). In his last years he became increasingly involved in the Southern Baptist Convention and served a term as vice-president of the organization. He also helped to establish the Christian Bible Society in Nashville, to promote Bible reading. He died in Nashville.

[Jarman's speeches include "Turmoil in the Market Place," *Vital Speeches of the Day*, Dec. 1, 1961; and "The Genesco Formula for Growth," in Newcomen Society in North America, *Newcomen Addresses* (1968). See also Richard Hammer, "The Cold-blooded Dreamer of Nashville and Seventh Avenue," *Fortune*, Feb. 1961; and Eleanor Carruth, "Genesco Comes to Judgment," *Fortune*, July 1975. An obituary is in the *New York Times*, Sept. 10, 1980.]

GEORGE P. ANTONE

JOHNSON, HARRY GORDON (May 26, 1923–May 8, 1977), economist, was born in Toronto, Canada, to middle-class intellectuals. He received a B.A. from the University of Toronto in 1943, in the field of political economy. At that time, Toronto was noted for its strength in economic history under Professor Harold Innis. After a year of teaching at St. Francis Xavier University at Antigonish, Nova Scotia, Johnson went overseas with the Canadian infantry in World War II. At the end of hostilities, he attended Cambridge University while still in the army, receiving a second bachelor's degree in 1946. His college professor at this time was the noted Marxist economist Maurice Dobb.

Johnson pursued graduate studies back in Toronto in 1947, obtained an M.A. from Harvard in 1948, and returned to Cambridge in 1951. After his second stint at Cambridge, Johnson capped off his educational career by acquiring a Ph.D. at Harvard in 1958. The latter degrees were attained en passant, as it were, because over the same years, Johnson was a lecturer at Cambridge (1949–1956) and a professor in economic theory at the University of Manchester, England (1956–1959). As a student, Johnson never failed to impress his professors, and fellow students found him unfailingly helpful and accommodating. In 1948 he married Elizabeth Scott Serson, an editor and writer who served for many years as the chief editor at the University of Chicago Press. The couple had two children.

In 1959, Johnson took a professorship at the University of Chicago, which remained his academic home until his death. After 1966, Johnson served each year for one term at the London School of Economics and Political Science and two quarters at the University of Chicago.

Johnson's main contribution to the field of economic theory was in the analysis of the effects of relative changes in a country's domestic money supply on its international balance of payments. He is perhaps best known, however, for his astringent attacks on the "Keynesians," whose advocacy of interventionist governmental fiscal policies were in ascendancy on college campuses in the 1950's and 1960's. Johnson's attacks helped dampen the influence on economics of the more radical wing of the Keynesians (largely the Cambridge University group dominated by Joan Robinson). Despite his anti-Keynesian stance, Johnson never completely adopted the Chicago school, which holds that the level of the nominal national income is largely determined by the supply of money and that discretionary monetary and fiscal policies cause instability in the functioning of the economy. Nor did Johnson take a purely noninterventionist approach to the societal problems of affluent economies.

Johnson's approach to economics was eclectic, but an abiding influence on him was Professor Dennis H. Robertson of the London School of Economics and Cambridge University. Robertson's period model of macroeconomics was distinguished from the Keynesian national income model because Robertson clearly implied a necessary change in the money aggregate as the economy moved from one level to another. As is made clear in the book Johnson cowrote with his wife, *The Shadow of Keynes* (1978), Johnson was upset by the shabby treatment of Robertson by the dominant Keynesian clique at Cambridge in the 1950's.

Johnson's study of monetary effects on international trade and the balance of payments led him to the insight that under a regime of fixed exchange rates, inflation was an international phenomenon. He believed, in other words, that an excess supply of money in one major economy would spill over to its trading partners and the price level would rise in both countries.

Thus, in agreement with Milton Friedman of the Chicago School, Johnson became a strong advocate of freely floating exchange rates as the one method of adjusting trade and the balance of payments among a group of trading countries operating under different monetary and fiscal regimes.

Johnson was an advocate of an international division of labor and of open economies operating in free markets. Early on, he exposed the fallacies and the structural imbalances resulting from the forced industrialization policies for development advocated by Raúl Prebisch and his followers. Nevertheless, Johnson was sympathetic to programs of the welfare state designed to ease the hardships suffered by individuals bearing the brunt of the transition costs of structural shifts in the economy, and he advocated some fail-safe assistance for those whose social or physical handicaps prevented them from fully participating in the economy. Johnson was also concerned about the uneven investment in "human capital" in a private economy, which means that educational resources were not distributed optimally between the rich and poor.

Johnson was a visiting professor at many universities, and he delivered papers at innumerable conferences. He never severed his ties to Canada, and he appeared often at the conventions of Canadian social scientists. He served on various Canadian commissions on the Canadian economy, and he was the mainstay on the research staff of the (Porter) Royal Canadian Committee on Banking and Finance in 1962.

In his last years, Johnson divided his time teaching at the University of Chicago and the Graduate School of International Relations at Geneva. Noted as a rather heavy drinker, he suffered a mild stroke in 1975 and died two years later in Geneva.

Johnson was the author of some 500 articles and 19 books and was the editor of 24 additional texts. He served at various times as editor of *Economica*, the *Review of Economic Studies*, the *Journal of International Economics*, and the *Journal of Political Economy*. Among his noteworthy publications were the books *International Trade and Economic Growth* (1958), *Aspects of the Theory of Tariffs* (1971), and *On Economics and Society* (1975), as well as the articles "Optimum Tariffs and Retaliation," *Review of Economic Studies* (1954) and "Monetary Theory and Policy," *American Economic Review* (June 1962).

He was president of the Canadian Political Science Association and chairman of the Association of University Teachers of Economics. He was president of the Eastern Economic Association at the time of his death. Johnson was awarded the Prix Mondial Nessim Habif of the University of Geneva and the Bernhard Harms Prize of the University of Kiel.

[See Grant L. Reuber and Anthony Dalton Scott, "Harry G. Johnson," *Canadian Journal of Economics*, Nov. 1977. Memorial articles by William Max Corden, David Laidler, Arnold C. Harberger, David Wall, and Richard E. Caves are in the *Journal of Political Economy*, Aug. 1984. An obituary is in the *New York Times*, May 10, 1977.]

ELI SCHWARTZ

JOHNSON, MALCOLM MALONE (Sept. 27, 1904–June 17, 1976), journalist, was born in Clermont, Ga., the eldest of seven children of William M. Johnson, a lawyer, and Willie Estelle Bolding, a teacher and school principal before her marriage. He grew up in nearby Gainesville. His father died in the influenza epidemic of 1918, shortly after Johnson turned fourteen. His mother took in boarders to help make ends meet and later invested profitably in real estate. Johnson graduated from Gainesville High School in 1922.

Johnson attended Mercer University in Macon, Ga., from 1922 to 1926 but did not graduate. He was a controversy-stirring editor of the school newspaper, and in 1924 he began to work for the *Macon Telegraph* under Mark Ethridge, later the publisher of the *Louisville Courier-Journal*. In 1926, Johnson wrote a series of articles exposing the criminal activities of the Ku Klux Klan in Tombs County, Ga., that gained national attention and, along with a recommendation from Ethridge, led to a job offer from the *New York Sun*. Johnson began working for the *Sun* on Sept. 24, 1928, initially planning to return to the *Macon Telegraph* in a few years. Once in New York City, however, he fell in love with both the city and his new job.

On Dec. 4, 1928, Johnson married Emmie Ludie Adams; they had four children. Johnson's early *Sun* assignments included the failure of the Bank of the United States, the burning of the cruise ship *Morro Castle*, and the Lindbergh kidnapping.

In 1933, Johnson attended the meeting in Heywood Broun's apartment at which the

Newspaper Guild was founded. He was an active early member and tried unsuccessfully to establish a Guild chapter at the *Sun*. By the late 1930's, however, Johnson had ceased to be active in the Guild, and the *Sun* formed its own editorial union.

For nine years, Johnson was the *Sun*'s Broadway columnist, and he frequently served as a critic. After the United States entered World War II, however, he moved back to general news. From February 1945, he was a Pacific correspondent, covering the invasions of Iwo Jima and Okinawa, and the Japanese surrender. He was also with the first group of correspondents to tour Hiroshima after the atomic bomb was dropped.

Johnson was both an industrious legman and a polished writer. To him, being a reporter meant doing everything, and he took pride in getting the most out of any story—small or large. In fact, what started out as a routine crime story—the murder of Thomas Collentine, a hiring boss on the docks, in April 1948—turned into the biggest story of Johnson's career. While covering the murder, he became convinced that there was a major story in what was wrong on the waterfront. He dug for about six weeks, with little to show for his efforts. "Then I had some lucky breaks," Johnson later wrote. "One was meeting and gaining the confidence of an informant, an ex-convict, who had worked with the racketeers. His story set the pattern, and he steered me to other sources." Johnson's editors gave him the time he needed, and he worked on the story, single-handed, for five months.

The *Sun* received a spectacular payoff: a twenty-four-part, front-page series that ran from Nov. 8 to Dec. 10, 1948, under the title "Crime on the Waterfront." It exposed an interlocking system of shakedowns, kickbacks, loan-sharking and terrorism, as well as union officials who exploited their members in order to maintain a hold on lucrative waterfront rackets and a shipping industry without the inclination or the will to challenge the racketeers. Johnson and his family were the target of numerous threats, but he continued to write on the subject, doing some 300 follow-up articles in 1949. His articles led to three official investigations of waterfront crime and the formation of the Waterfront Commission in 1953.

On May 2, 1949, it was announced that Johnson had won the 1948 Pulitzer Prize for local reporting. "Look, I worked hard on the stories—sure," he modestly said after hearing the news. "But I had luck, too. I've worked hard on other stories and fallen flat on my face."

On Jan. 3, 1950, after more than twenty years at the *Sun*, Johnson lost the job he loved when the paper was sold to the *New York World-Telegram*. Johnson wrote the article about the sale for the paper's final issue on January 4—in effect, the 117-year-old paper's obituary. Newspaper people consider that article one of Johnson's best, but it always held bitter associations for him. "No *Sun* man would want a by-line on that story," he said, and it ran without one.

Johnson, who had been the *Sun*'s star reporter, received job offers from several other New York City papers, but the demise of the *Sun* had left him bitter about newspaper publishers in general. He took the most lucrative offer, which was from King Features Syndicates, which distributed his articles through International News Service. He was a special-assignment reporter for that wire service from 1950 to 1954, covering the Kefauver hearings on organized crime, among other things, but he was never happy there.

Meanwhile, Johnson's "Crime on the Waterfront" articles continued to generate attention. In June 1949 he sold the movie rights to the Monticello Film Company. In 1950 he published a book, *Crime on the Labor Front*, based largely on material from those articles. Between 1951 and 1953, Budd Schulberg wrote eight scripts for a film to be titled *Crime on the Waterfront*, which evolved from a documentary into a fictional piece. By 1953, the movie rights had reverted back to Johnson, and he sold them directly to Schulberg. In July 1954 the movie *On the Waterfront* opened; it won eight Academy Awards in 1955, including that for best picture.

The same month that *On the Waterfront* opened, Johnson left reporting for good, taking a job with the public relations firm of Robinson-Hannigan and Associates. The firm was sold to Hill and Knowlton two years later, and Johnson continued there, working on a variety of accounts and eventually becoming a vice-president.

In 1966, Johnson's eldest son, Haynes, won a Pulitzer Prize. To date, they are the only father and son to have won reporting Pulitzers. In 1968, Johnson was one of three editors of the book *Current Thoughts on Public Relations: A*

Collection of Speeches and Articles by Members of Hill and Knowlton, Inc. In 1969 he wrote movingly about the *Sun's* final days in an article for the *Silurian News*; "To the *New York Sun*—In Fond Remembrance" was reprinted in the 1974 book *Shoeleather and Printer's Ink*, edited by George Britt. Johnson retired from Hill and Knowlton in 1973. He made his home in Killingworth, Conn., after his retirement and died in nearby Middleton.

[Useful articles are Don Anderson, "Johnson Prize Story Began as Routine Task," *New York Sun*, May 3, 1949; Murray Kempton, "Interlude," *New York Post*, July 30, 1954; and Haynes Johnson, "He Was My Best Friend as well as My Father," *Washington Post*, June 18, 1978. Obituaries are in the *Washington Post*, June 18, 1976; and the *New York Times*, June 19, 1976.]

LYNN HOOGENBOOM

JOHNSON, MORDECAI WYATT (Jan. 12, 1890–Sept. 10, 1976), university president and clergyman, was born in Paris, Tenn., the son of the Reverend Wyatt Johnson, a former slave who was a stationary engine operator in a mill, and Caroline Freeman, a homemaker. After his grammar school education in Paris, he entered the Academy of Roger Williams University in Nashville (1903). When the school was destroyed by fire in 1905, he completed the term at Howe Institute in Memphis. In the fall of 1905 he entered the Preparatory Department of Atlanta Baptist College (Morehouse after 1913), where he completed his high school studies. During his college years, also at Atlanta Baptist College (1907–1911), he was strongly influenced by President John Hope, Dean Samuel Howard Archer, and Professor Benjamin Brawley, from whom he learned a mastery of language and a deep respect for learning placed in the service of others. A leading student at the college, Johnson played varsity football and tennis, was on the debating team, and sang in the glee club and chorus. As a result of his outstanding academic record, he was appointed to the faculty and taught history, economics, and English for two years. He also served as acting dean of the college from 1911 to 1912. During the summers of 1912 and 1913, he studied at the University of Chicago and received a second B.A. degree in 1913. From 1913 to 1916 he was enrolled at the Rochester Theological Seminary, graduating with the degree of Bachelor of Divinity in 1916. The most important intellectual influence on him was Walter Rauschenbusch, whose doctrine of the Social Gospel aimed to place Christianity in the service of social and economic reform. During his studies at Rochester he was the pastor of the Second Baptist Church in Mumford, N.Y.

On Dec. 25, 1916, Johnson married Anna Ethelyn Gardner; they had five children. From 1916 to 1917, Johnson was a secretary of the International Committee of the YMCA, working in the Southwest. In 1917 he became pastor of the First Baptist Church of Charleston, W.Va., and established a reputation as a brilliant orator and community organizer. In Charleston he organized the Rochdale Cooperative Cash Grocery and the Charleston branch of the NAACP. From 1921 to 1922 he was on leave from his church to study at Harvard University, where he received the Master of Sacred Theology degree in 1922. A year later he was awarded an honorary Doctor of Divinity degree by Howard University in recognition of his application of religion to social problems.

In June 1926, Johnson was selected the first Negro president of Howard University. His place in history is secured by the record of his transformation of Howard during his thirty-four-year tenure. His appointment as president was regarded as a test of whether, in the context of a segregated society, a Negro president could lead a high-quality university, since all of the leading black colleges and universities at the time—Fisk, Hampton, Spelman, Shaw, Morgan, Talladega, and Lincoln—had white presidents. Equally significant was the impact of segregation on educational opportunities for blacks, who were barred by statute from attending the white universities of the South (where the majority of the black population lived), and there was no provision for professional or graduate education in the racially separate institutions that those states maintained for black students. During most of Johnson's administration, Howard trained 48 percent of the nation's black physicians, 49 percent of the black dentists, and 96 percent of the black lawyers. The academic quality of Howard was therefore of national significance.

In the 1920's Howard's instructional facilities were inadequate, its library and laboratory development substandard, and its faculty poorly paid. The most serious problem was the uncertainty of continuing federal support because

Johnson

there was no statutory authority for the annual appropriations to Howard that had been granted by Congress since 1879. Only two of the university's schools and colleges were accredited, liberal arts and dentistry. The academic problems in the professional schools, notably law and medicine, were particularly severe. On Dec. 13, 1928, Congress enacted legislation amending the charter that Howard had received in 1867 to provide for annual appropriations. In recognition of this landmark change, Johnson was awarded the NAACP's Spingarn Medal "for the highest achievement of an American Negro" on July 2, 1929.

In the early years of his administration, Johnson succeeded in winning government approval of a twenty-year development plan and in attracting the financial support of the Rockefeller Foundation, the General Education Board, and the Rosenwald Fund. During his tenure, Howard's annual budget rose from $700,000 to $8 million, and twenty major buildings were added to the physical plant, increasing its value from $3 million to $34 million. In the first decade of his presidency the faculty doubled, library resources doubled, and the scientific equipment of laboratories tripled. During his administration each school and college of the university was accredited, and each was conducting instruction and research in new facilities. Most significant was the transformation of the professional schools. The school of law became a full-time day school, was admitted to membership in the Association of American Law Schools, and developed a program in civil rights litigation that led to the Supreme Court's landmark decision, *Brown* v. *Board of Education* in 1954. In the College of Medicine, there was a complete rebuilding of the faculty that paralleled the improvement in physical facilities, substantially enhancing the quality of instruction and research. The college of liberal arts faculty in the 1930's and 1940's included the largest number of blacks with Ph.D.'s in the nation, and many of its departments were headed by scholars of international reputation, such as Alain L. Locke, Ernest E. Just, E. Franklin Frazier, Charles H. Wesley, Rayford W. Logan, Ralph J. Bunche, and Abram L. Harris. The award of the university's first Ph.D., in chemistry, in 1958 was perhaps the clearest indication of a new level of maturity as an institution committed to graduate instruction and research.

Despite a reputation for strong, even authoritarian, leadership, Johnson was a champion of academic freedom. During the McCarthy era, he publicly fought all efforts by the Federal Bureau of Investigation and congressional committees to interfere with outspoken Howard faculty. Among the nation's university presidents, Johnson was also the outstanding spokesman for countries then under the colonial domination of Britain, France, Belgium, and the Netherlands. He was one of the early American supporters of Indian independence from Britain, and lectured widely on the life and work of Mohandas Gandhi. It was one of these lectures, at Crozer Theological Seminary in Philadelphia, that introduced Gandhi's philosophy of nonviolent social action to Martin Luther King, Jr., when he was a seminarian, thus eventually changing the center of gravity of the civil rights movement in the United States.

During Johnson's tenure, Howard attracted students from more than ninety countries. He articulated the view that Howard was providing progressive leadership not only for black Americans but also for Africa, Asia, and the Caribbean, at the time when there was a contest between the Soviet Union and the United States for the allegiance of nonaligned countries. He insisted that Howard, continuing the tradition of its abolitionist founders, was a "world university" open to all races and religions, a microcosm of a future in which democratic values would shape higher education in all countries. The central figure in the development of Howard into a major American university, Johnson retired in 1960. In 1962 he was appointed to the District of Columbia Board of Education, where for the next three years he was a prominent critic of the inequitable funding of schools in poor neighborhoods and the persistence of racial discrimination in schools even after the elimination of mandated racial segregation.

Johnson was honored by Liberia and Ethiopia for his leadership in education. His wife died in 1969, and he married Alice Clinton Taylor King on Apr. 12, 1970. In 1973 the Howard University administration building was named in his honor. He died in Washington, D.C.

[The most complete collection of material on Johnson's administration at Howard is in the Mooreland-Spingarn Research Center at Howard University. There is no biography of Johnson, but see Benjamin G. Brawley, "Mordecai W. Johnson" in his *Negro Builders and Heroes* (1937); Edwin R. Embree, "Lord High Chancellor," in his *13 Against the Odds* (1944); Michael R. Winston, ed., *Education for Freedom* (1976); Broadus N. Butler, "Mordecai Wyatt Johnson: A Model of Leadership in Higher Education," *Howard University Magazine*, Jan. 1977; and Benjamin E. Mays, "The Relevance of Mordecai Wyatt Johnson for Our Times," inaugural address in the Mordecai Wyatt Johnson Lecture Series (1978). A comprehensive bibliography is James P. Johnson, Janet L. Sims, and Gail A. Kostinko, *Mordecai Wyatt Johnson* (1976). An obituary is in the *New York Times*, Sept. 11, 1976.]

MICHAEL R. WINSTON

JOHNSON, NUNNALLY HUNTER (Dec. 5, 1897–Mar. 25, 1977), film writer, producer, and director, was born in Columbus, Ga., the son of James Nunnally Johnson, a mechanic who later headed the Columbus pipe and sheet metal department of the Central of Georgia Railroad, and Johnnie Pearl Patrick. Johnson did not use his middle name in his professional life.

After serving as a second lieutenant in the cavalry in World War I, Johnson worked for the *Enquirer Sun* in Columbus. Late in 1919 he moved to New York City, where he wrote for the *Brooklyn Daily Eagle*, the *New York Evening Post*, and the *New York Herald Tribune*. At the same time he was publishing short stories, most notably in the *American Mercury*, the *Smart Set*, and the *Saturday Evening Post*; one of them was adapted for the silent screen as *Rough House Rosie* (1927). In 1930 he published a collection of his short stories, *There Ought to Be a Law*.

Johnson was married in 1919 to Alice Love Mason, an editor at the *Brooklyn Daily Eagle*; they had one child. In March 1927, he married Marion Byrnes, also of the *Eagle* staff; they had one child. These in-house marriages, both of which ended in divorce, were a source of considerable amusement among Johnson's coworkers.

Although the adaptation of his *Saturday Evening Post* story gave Johnson a screen credit before he ever saw Hollywood, his official film career began in 1932, when he went to Hollywood as a writer. His first film was an adaptation called *A Bedtime Story* (1933), for which he did not receive a screen credit. The unusual pattern of his later career was established within the next two years, when he began to serve first as associate producer and then as producer on projects that he had written. For the next forty years, he produced nearly all of his films, wrote seventy-seven of them, and occasionally directed them as well.

Johnson was known for a relentless professionalism that became a bankable asset for the movie studios and moguls with whom he was associated. John Houseman described him as "both a successful film writer and one of the handful of educated WASPs on whom Darryl Zanuck counted to write, produce, and, occasionally, direct the more sophisticated items in his vast annual output of motion pictures."

The record bears out this claim. After writing both *The House of Rothschild* and *Kid Millions* in 1934, Johnson wrote *Thanks a Million* (1935), which was Twentieth Century–Fox's second film and a box office smash that made the studio financially solvent. Johnson worked for Fox from then on. This association provided his initial and later collaborations with director John Ford, but Johnson's range extended well beyond John Ford Westerns to include costume dramas, comedy, war films, and suspense thrillers. Johnson's 1930's output concluded with *Prisoner of Shark Island* (1936), *Rose of Washington Square* (1939), and *Jesse James* (1939), all of which he wrote and produced.

On Feb. 4, 1940, Johnson married Dorris Bowdon, an actress; they had three children. At the start of the 1940's there was a quantum leap in the already high quality of Johnson's productions with *The Grapes of Wrath* (1940) and *Tobacco Road* (1941), both directed by John Ford. During that decade he also produced such film noir classics as *The Woman in the Window* (1944) and *The Dark Mirror* (1946), as well as *Life Begins at Eight-thirty* (1942), *The Keys of the Kingdom* (1944), *Along Came Jones* (1945), and *The Senator Was Indiscreet* (1947).

In the 1950's and 1960's, Johnson's films displayed maturity, confidence, and consolidation. After producing the memorable films *The Gunfighter* (1950) and *How to Marry a Millionaire* (1953), Johnson wrote and directed *The Man in the Gray Flannel Suit* (1956), a film that epitomized the zeitgeist of the decade. A year later he wrote, directed, and produced one of his greatest films, *The Three Faces of Eve*. In the 1960's, Johnson returned solely to writing with *Mr. Hobbs Takes a Vacation* (1962), *Take Her, She's Mine* (1963), *The World of Henry Orient* (1964), and *The Dirty Dozen* (1967).

Although none of these projects brought Johnson his own Academy Award, he may fairly be said to have provided the armature for the academy's recognition of others: John Ford and Jane Darwell for *The Grapes of Wrath* and Joanne Woodward for *The Three Faces of Eve.* He died in Los Angeles.

[An accurate and inclusive biography is Tom Stempel, *Screenwriter: The Times of Nunnally Johnson* (1980). The Hollywood years are covered in *The Letters of Nunnally Johnson*, edited by Dorris Johnson and Ellen Leventhal (1981). An obituary is in the *New York Times*, Mar. 26, 1977.]

DAVID COREY

JONES, HOWARD MUMFORD (Apr. 16, 1892–May 11, 1980), author and historian, was born in Saginaw, Mich., the only child of Frank Alexander Jones, a salesman and small businessman, and Josephine Whitman Miles, a hairdresser; both parents were descended from New England emigrants to the West. The family moved to Milwaukee, and, a few years before his father's death in 1906, to La Crosse, Wis. In his autobiography Jones later recalled his schooling and his newspaper route, his German and Norwegian neighbors, and his mother's working days. He finished high school in 1910, then took a two-year normal-school preteaching course, held summer jobs as a typist for the novelist Hamlin Garland and on the railroad, and wrote regional prose and poetry. His first publication was *A Little Book of Local Verse* in 1915.

Meanwhile, he entered the University of Wisconsin, where he studied with O. J. Campbell and William Ellery Leonard; he was awarded the B.A. in 1914. He then went to the University of Chicago, where he found broader intellectual horizons. He received the M.A. in 1915 and the following year published his thesis, a translation of Heine's *North Sea* cycle, with commentary on Heine's and Swinburne's North Sea poetry. In 1916 he became adjunct professor of English and general literature at the University of Texas. Thus began his connection with the South.

His first stay at the University of Texas ended in the wake of conflict between the university and Governor Jim Ferguson; discontented with the precarious financial situation at Texas, he accepted an offer from State University of Montana at Missoula. There he continued writing poetry, saw something of labor struggles in Butte, and on July 18, 1918, married Clara McLure. They had one child and were divorced in 1925.

In these years he began to develop his new concept of the relation of American culture to Europe, emphasizing the manifold influence, especially of Latin cultures, on the Americans. He was called back to the University of Texas in 1919 as associate professor of comparative literature and remained there until 1925. This period was one of scholarly achievement, much activity in university dramatic productions, frequent public speaking, and varied writings. It ended with a leave of absence in 1924 and 1925, spent in Chicago on research in Franco-American cultural relations. There he met Bessie Judith Zaban, a brilliant student, whom he married in 1927 (she would later be his coeditor on *The Many Voices of Boston* [1976]). There too he received a letter from the new University of Texas administration dismissing him without cause, but soon thereafter he accepted an offer from the up-and-coming University of North Carolina.

Jones described his five years at the University of North Carolina as some of "the more blessed" years of his life, characterized by congenial colleagues, rewarding activities (founding a college bookstore and continuing to produce dramas and to write for magazines) and the publication in 1927 of his first major academic study, *America and French Culture (1750–1848)*, for which he later received the American Historical Association's Jusserand Medal. His extraordinary poetic talent came into full bloom in a volume of translations of Romanesque lyric that was published, with P. S. Allen, in 1928.

From that time on he moved rapidly forward in the academic world. He became professor of English at the University of Michigan in 1930, published a biography of the early Americanist Moses C. Tyler (1933), and was awarded a Guggenheim Fellowship for the period 1932–1933, which he devoted to research for his biography of poet Thomas Moore, *The Harp That Once* (1937).

In 1936 he received an honorary doctorate at the Harvard Tercentenary and was almost simultaneously offered a professorship, at a time when the Harvard Department of English was losing some of its most significant faculty. Jones was different from the traditional Harvard English professors, and graduate students were amused to hear how he sat on his desk singing cowboy songs to his class. But he was a popular lecturer, offering large courses in English and American literature and successful seminars on American writers.

It would be difficult to list more than a small sampling of his scholarly production, which included numerous monographs and collections of essays and addresses (including *The Theory of American Literature* in 1948 and *American Humanism* in 1957); anthologies (*Major American Writers*, with E. E. Leisy, in 1935); editions (Edgar Allan Poe in 1929 and *Letters of Sherwood Anderson*, with Walter B. Rideout, in 1953); commentaries (*One Great Society*, for the American Council of Learned Societies in 1959); and many articles on literature, education, and American traditions. He remained productive even after retirement, writing his "magisterial trilogy" on American civilization, *O Strange New World* (1964), which was awarded a Pulitzer prize for general nonfiction, *The Age of Energy* (1971), and *Revolution and Romanticism* (1974)—massive studies of the intricate evolution of culture in the Americas. These studies were successful even though they were sometimes overloaded with material and not always clear in definition. He also wrote innumerable reviews and articles in learned journals and "quality" magazines—*Atlantic*, *Scribner's*, the *Saturday Review of Literature*—and some of the finest reviews ever printed in a newspaper, during his tenure as literary editor of the *Boston Transcript* (1938–1940).

Jones was president of the American Academy of Arts and Sciences (1944–1951); chairman of the American Council of Learned Societies (1955–1959), chairman of the Weil Institute (1959–1960) (see his study *Belief and Disbelief in American Literature*, based on lectures he delivered for the institute), recipient of the Phi Beta Kappa medal (1973), and president of the Modern Language Association (1965). His array of honorary degrees is stupendous.

Jones's career at Harvard was happy, with one exception: his term as dean of the Graduate School of the Arts and Sciences (1943–1944), during which his plans for reform were not adopted. He resigned suddenly from that position, the "gaudy title" of which, he noted, concealed the fact that "I had responsibilities but no authority."

Jones later served with the Provost Marshal General's Office in reeducation of German prisoners at Fort Kearny, writing texts for them on American history and conditions. In 1950 the Joneses went to Munich to work in the newly founded Amerika-Institut. They made two journeys to Israel, where in 1964 Jones lectured on America at the Hebrew University of Jerusalem. He held several visiting lectureships at American universities, both before and after his retirement from Harvard as Abbott Lawrence Lowell Professor of Humanities in 1962.

Jones remained productive as ever—eleven of his books were published after 1962. His phenomenal capacity for reading and writing was undiminished nearly to the end, as were his firm public views—he refused to accept posts at institutions that insisted on special oaths for teachers, and he presented forcefully his stands on academic freedom, civic concerns, the role of the humanities, the traditional principles of the Enlightenment, and the significance of American contributions to world civilization, especially in literature and philosophy. He died in Cambridge, Mass., still at work at age eighty-eight, urging deeper American explorations of distant world civilizations and preparing a study of the American West.

His faith, he had written, was that of a Stoic. His great guides were Goethe and Jefferson. As he was recalled by the Harvard faculty of arts and sciences, Jones was indeed "the least parochial of American scholars."

[Jones's papers are in the Harvard University Archives; the collection contains most of his publications, including early newspaper articles, contributions in prose and poetry to many periodicals, and notes for courses, but does not include much personal correspondence. Harvard University official files contain many materials written by Jones, as do the *Harvard Library Bulletin*, which he revived and edited in 1966, and the *Harvard Alumni Bulletin* (later *Harvard Magazine*). Pertinent material appears in publications of the many organizations of which he was a member or officer. Richard M. Ludwig's *Aspects of American Poetry* (1962), a Festschrift to mark Jones's retirement, contains a complete bibliography for the years 1913–1961. See also Jones's autobiography, *Howard Mumford Jones* (1979).

Obituaries are in the *Boston Globe*, May 12, 1980, and the *New York Times*, May 13, 1980; see also the memorial minute presented to the faculty by a committee headed by Jerome Buckley, in the *University Gazette* (May 22, 1981), reprinted in W. J. Bate, Michael Shinagel, and James Engell, eds., *Harvard Scholars in English (1890–1990)* (1992).]

REGINALD H. PHELPS

JONES, JAMES RAMON (Nov. 6, 1921–May 9, 1977), novelist, was born in Robinson, Ill., the son of Ramon Jones, a dentist, and Ada Blessing. Discovery of oil on his grandfather's farm had brought an affluence to the Joneses that dwindled during the early 1930's with the Insull stock scandal. Like his older brother and younger sister, Jones attended the local schools. He was interested in literature and sports but never became a school athlete. When he graduated from high school in 1939, money for college was no longer available. His father advised him to join the army.

After a summer construction job in Findlay, Ohio, Jones tried to enlist in the Canadian army but was refused. On Nov. 10, 1939, he joined the United States Army Air Corps and was sent to Fort Slocum, N.Y. On December 18 he was shipped by way of the Panama Canal to Hickham Field, Hawaii. Unable to qualify as a pilot because of poor eyesight, he requested a transfer to the infantry. In September 1940 he was assigned to Schofield Barracks near Honolulu. At the post library he discovered the novels of Thomas Wolfe and realized, he said, that "I had been a writer all my life without knowing it." He began submitting poems and stories for publication without success.

Sensitive and impressionable, Jones was deeply moved by the changes and losses in his family and in the people around him. In March 1941 he learned of the death of his mother, on December 7 of that year he witnessed the Japanese attack on Pearl Harbor, and in March 1942, he received word that his father had committed suicide. Later that year he attended writing classes at the University of Hawaii; on December 6, the Twenty-fifth Infantry Division, of which he was a member, was sent to Guadalcanal; they landed on December 30.

Jones's outfit saw action immediately. On Jan. 12, 1943, he received a head wound from enemy shrapnel but returned to duty after a week. Later, killing a Japanese soldier in hand-to-hand combat left him emotionally distraught. He reinjured a chronically weak ankle and was hospitalized. In May, Jones was shipped back to the United States, to Kennedy General Hospital in Memphis, Tenn. In November, rather than be discharged, Jones elected to remain in the army, but on "limited service" only. Nonetheless, he was assigned to a combat outfit at Camp Campbell, Ky., that was preparing for duty overseas. Denied a furlough, he went AWOL, returning home to Robinson, Ill. Here he met Lowney and Harry Handy; she loved to help young writers. Jones stayed with them, but after two weeks, reported to Camp Campbell. Still angry with his assignment, he again went AWOL. Back in Robinson, he drank too much, was arrested, and jailed. Returned to Camp Campbell, he was reduced in rank and reassigned to a supply unit composed of wounded veterans. Although later promoted to sergeant, he still found conditions so intolerable that he could not work on his novel. Again he went AWOL. When he returned, he was sent to a hospital for psychiatric observation. Partly through the intercession of the Handys, he was given a medical discharge on July 6, 1944, and granted a small disability pension. After visiting Thomas Wolfe's home in Asheville, N.C., he returned to Robinson and settled in with the Handys to write. Lowney Handy had already become both his mentor and his lover.

In 1945, Jones enrolled in a writing class at New York University. He showed the manuscript of his novel to Maxwell Perkins at Scribner's. Perkins rejected it, but on learning that Jones, who had returned to Illinois, was planning to write about life in the peacetime army, urged him to do so and offered an unprecedented option of $500.

Encouraged by the Handys and, after Perkins's death in 1947, by editors Burroughs Mitchell and John Hall Wheelock, Jones set to work, writing slowly and painfully from 5:30 in the morning to midafternoon. The result, *From Here to Eternity* (1951), with its amazing intensity and shocking realism, has been called the finest novel on soldiering ever written. Jones had, Wheelock said, extracted an "exalted kind of poetry" from a "plethora of realistic detail." The movie rights brought $82,500. With millions of copies sold, the novel was both an artistic and a financial success.

After working for a while in Hollywood, Jones returned to Robinson to help Lowney Handy establish the Handy Artist Group at nearby Marshall, Ill., a place where young writers came to live and write. Jones invested heavily in the project and built his own quarters, where he worked and housed his collection of books, jazz records, guns, knives, Meissen porcelain, and chessboards. In 1952, Jones received the National Book Award and met other writers, including Norman Mailer and William Styron.

Always, whether at the Handy Group or traveling, often by jeep and trailer with Lowney and other members of the group, Jones maintained his daily writing schedule. *Some Came Running* (1958), the story of a writer returning to his hometown in search of real values, was not well received by critics. In late 1956, having finished his novel, Jones went to New York City to see his publishers. There he met Gloria Patricia Mosolino, an actress and writer. They were married on Feb. 27, 1957, in Haiti, and lived for a while at the Handy Group. When Lowney Handy attacked Gloria with a knife, they left, never to return. After a short stay in New York, where Jones wrote *The Pistol* (1959), they sailed for Europe on Apr. 12, 1958. After four months in London, they settled in Paris.

In Paris the Joneses' apartment on the Ile St. Louis became a center for expatriates during the 1960's. With boundless energy, Jones maintained a large correspondence, worked on movie scripts, met artists and editors, helped aspiring young writers, and finished the second volume of his projected war trilogy, *The Thin Red Line* (1962), which some critics called "the best combat novel" of the generation. He traveled to New York, Jamaica, and Greece and Spain, usually with his wife and two children. In February 1973, he went on assignment to Vietnam for the *New York Times Magazine*, stopping in Hawaii on his way back. He recorded his findings in *Viet Journal* (1974).

Longing to return to America, Jones accepted a teaching position for the 1974–1975 academic year at Florida International University in Miami. In 1975 the family rented, then bought, a house in Sagaponack, N.Y., where he all but finished his war trilogy. He died of congestive heart failure in Southhampton, N.Y.

[Major collections of Jones's manuscripts and letters are in the Beinecke Rare Book and Manuscript Library, Yale University; the James Jones Archives of the Humanities Research Center of the University of Texas at Austin; and the rare book room of the Firestone Library, Princeton University. Additional materials are in the Mugar Memorial Library, Boston University; the Houghton Library, Harvard University; the Kenneth Spencer Research Library, University of Kansas; the Fales Library, New York University; the special collections, University of Oregon Library; and in the estate of James Jones. Materials about the Handy Group are in the Brookens Library Archives, Sangamon State University, Springfield, Ill.

Additional titles by Jones are *Go to the Widow-Maker* (1967); *The Ice-Cream Headache and Other Stories* (1968), *The Merry Month of May* (1971), *A Touch of Danger* (1973), and *WWII* (1975). *Whistle* (1978), the third volume of the war trilogy, was completed by Willie Morris in the author's own words. Correspondence is in George Hendrick, ed., *To Reach Eternity, The Letters of James Jones* (1989). A collection is James R. Giles and J. Michael Lennon, eds., *The James Jones Reader: Outstanding Selections from His War Writings* (1991).

See also John R. Hopkins, *James Jones: A Checklist* (1974); Willie Morris, *James Jones, a Friendship* (1978); James R. Giles, *James Jones* (1981); George Garrett, *James Jones* (1984); and Frank McShane, *Into Eternity* (1985). An obituary is in the *New York Times*, May 10, 1977.]

JOHN E. HART

JONES, JIM (May 13, 1931–Nov. 18, 1978), cult leader, was born James Warren Jones in Crete, Ind. The only child of James Thurman Jones, a disabled veteran, and Lynetta Putnam, a waitress and factory worker, he grew up in a shack without plumbing in nearby Lynn. His abusive father backed the Ku Klux Klan, while his doting mother embraced progressive politics. Neither parent attended church.

The parents separated in 1945, and Jones moved with his mother to Richmond, Ind. There he worked as an orderly in a hospital where he boarded while attending high school. After completing high school in January 1949, Jones entered Indiana University. On June 12, 1949, he married Marceline Baldwin, a nurse he had met at the hospital. They had one son and adopted seven children of various races.

In 1950 the Joneses moved to Indianapolis, where Jones sporadically attended Butler University, receiving a B.Ed. in 1961. A Marxist, he decided to promote socialism through the ministry. In 1952 he tried Methodism before becoming a faith healer by "removing cancers" through fakery with chicken livers.

In 1954, Jones opened Indianapolis's first biracial church, renamed Peoples Temple in 1955. The church set up a soup kitchen, operated nursing homes, and practiced racial equality. In 1960 the Temple joined the Disciples of Christ, which ordained Jones in 1964. To make blacks feel welcome, Jones, who had high cheekbones, dark eyes, and black hair, falsely claimed to be part Indian. In 1961, Jones became director of the Indianapolis Human Relations Commission, and he spent the following two years on a mission to Brazil.

Jones predicted nuclear war and in 1965 settled with fifty or more followers in Redwood Valley, Calif., about 100 miles north of San Francisco. Blacks became a majority in the Temple when branches opened in San Francisco and Los Angeles. In 1972 the headquarters moved to San Francisco, where Jones cultivated radical celebrities like Angela Davis and Huey Newton, and liberals like Mayor George Moscone, who in 1976 appointed Jones to the San Francisco Housing Authority.

Life inside the Peoples Temple grew strange. At closed services Jones stomped on the Bible, denounced the "Sky God," and claimed to be Buddha, Christ, and Lenin reincarnated. "I come as God Socialist!" he boasted. Declaring that the ends justified the means, he insisted that members call him Father, that they live communally, and that they give all property to the church, which became authoritarian. On top of the ruling hierarchy was Jones, next a dozen "angels," then about 100 mostly white members of the Planning Commission, and finally the 2,000 or so predominantly black members.

Jones punished wrongdoers in "catharsis" sessions, either with paddlings of up to a hundred or more blows or by forcing them to box against larger, stronger opponents. The Planning Commission held nightlong confrontations about sex. Claiming to be the world's only true heterosexual, Jones had sex with both female and male members but always assumed the dominant position. In 1973 he faced a lewd conduct charge, which was dropped.

In 1974 the Temple leased 3,842 acres of South American jungle from Guyana's Marxist government, and members began clearing the "Promised Land" for agriculture. During 1977, amid bad publicity, lawsuits, and relatives' complaints, Jones and nearly 1,000 followers—three-quarters black, two-thirds female, almost one-third under eighteen—moved to Jonestown. Social Security and welfare checks followed.

Charges that overwork, poor food, harsh punishments, tranquilizers, armed guards, censored mail and phone calls, and Jones's nightly harangues over loudspeakers made Jonestown tantamount to a concentration camp led Congressman Leo J. Ryan to visit in late 1978. The canny, flamboyant California Democrat's entourage included Charles Garry and Mark Lane (Jones's attorneys), eight reporters, and four relatives of Jonestown residents. On November 17 they flew from Georgetown, Guyana, to Port Kaituma and proceeded overland to Jonestown. After being treated to an impressive barbecued pork dinner and a rock concert, Ryan and a reporter learned that a few residents wanted to leave. Ryan decided to process defectors the next day.

On November 18, Ryan interviewed persons whose relatives had expressed concern. All decided to stay. However, as word spread that several people planned to leave with Ryan, tension grew, and one resident attacked the congressman with a knife. Lane and Garry saved Ryan's life.

Ryan's party, including sixteen defectors, boarded a truck for the airstrip. Two aircraft arrived, but with insufficient seats, so defectors boarded first. As a small Cessna, loaded with defectors, roared down the runway, a tractor pulling a flatbed trailer, presumably sent by Jones, blocked the plane's way. Most defectors had boarded the larger Otter, while Ryan and the reporters stood aside.

Suddenly, Larry Layton, a false defector aboard the Cessna, began shooting, and men on the flatbed trailer fired at those standing outside the Otter. Layton was overpowered and removed from the small plane, along with two injured defectors, and the pilot took off. By then the gunmen had started back to Jonestown. Ryan, one defector, and three reporters lay dead. Others had fled into the jungle. Nearby Guyanese soldiers did nothing.

Meanwhile, Jones, a pill-popping hypochondriac in declining health, demanded that his followers commit mass "revolutionary suicide." Temple members had rehearsed "white nights" many times. Adults used syringes to squirt cyanide-laced, grape-flavored punch down children's throats before drinking the poison themselves. Although armed guards ringed the gathering, few resisted.

Mark Lane, Charles Garry, and two residents escaped into the jungle. Two elderly people survived. Jones ordered three high-ranking leaders to leave with half a million dollars in cash. These were Jonestown's only survivors. Authorities found 914 bodies. All had been poisoned, including Jones's wife, except three who were shot—Jones, one of Jones's mistresses, and an unidentified male. Jones left his estate to the Communist party.

In Georgetown a Temple loyalist, with assistance, killed her three children and herself.

Jones's birth son and other members of the touring Jonestown basketball team survived, as did more than $10 million in Temple assets. Layton was charged in San Francisco with conspiring to kill Ryan and, after a mistrial in 1981, was convicted in 1986.

[Peoples Temple Archives are at the California Historical Society, San Francisco. The best books are Shiva Naipaul, *Journey to Nowhere* (1981); Tim Reiterman with John Jacobs, *Raven* (1982); and David Chidester, *Salvation and Suicide* (1988). Important articles are in the *New York Times*, Sept. 2, 1977; Nov. 19–27, 29, 1978; and Mar. 15, 1979; the *New York Times Magazine*, Feb. 25, 1979; and Nov. 18, 1979; the *San Francisco Sunday Examiner-Chronicle*, Sept. 17, 24, 1972; Aug. 7, 14, 1977; Nov. 19, 26, 1978; and Dec. 10, 1978; and the *San Francisco Chronicle*, Aug. 20, 1977; June 15, 1978; and Nov. 20–25, 1978. Obituaries are in the *Los Angeles Times*, Nov. 24, 1978; and the *New York Times*, Nov. 26, 1978.]

W. J. Rorabaugh

JONES, JOHN MARVIN (Feb. 26, 1882–Mar. 4, 1976), congressman, wartime administrator, and judge, was born near Valley View, Tex., the fourth of eleven children of Horace K. Jones, a farmer, and Theodocia ("Docia") Gaston Hawkins. After finishing the curriculum of the local public school, he farmed briefly in partnership with his brother Delbert and then taught school for a year. Dissatisfied with both farming and teaching, Jones sought additional education and graduated in 1905 from Southwestern University, a small Methodist school at Georgetown, Tex., where he was a member of the debate and baseball teams. He declined a scholarship from Vanderbilt University for graduate study in English and registered at the University of Texas School of Law. Excelling in oratory, he graduated in 1908 and was admitted to the Texas bar.

Jones established his law practice in Amarillo, a relatively new town of fewer than 10,000 in the center of the rapidly developing Panhandle section of northwestern Texas. He soon secured a retainer from one of the largest ranches in the area and eventually specialized in representing farmers and ranchers in damage suits against railroads. His practice was lucrative, but Jones wanted a political career and used his travels to regional county courthouses to solicit political support. In his first campaign he defeated ten-term incumbent John Hall Stephens and two other rivals in the 1916 Democratic primary for the Thirteenth Congressional District. Given the lack of significant Republican opposition, the primary victory was tantamount to election. During the campaign, for reasons never fully explained, he stopped using his first name; henceforth he was Marvin Jones.

In the House of Representatives, Jones quickly became a protégé of John Nance Garner and established a close friendship with Sam Rayburn, a law school acquaintance. His first vote was cast in support of President Woodrow Wilson's war resolution in April 1917; later he joined the United States Army and served briefly as an enlisted man at Fort Polk, N.C. Jones supported the Prohibition and women's suffrage amendments and was generally a loyal Wilsonian Democrat.

Increasingly his attention turned to agriculture. Because his sprawling West Texas district was so agriculturally diverse, ranging from cattle and wheat in the northwest to cotton in the southeast, Jones became an expert on a variety of farm commodities. During the 1920's, he sought lower transportation rates, expanded rural credit, and the development of export markets for surplus production, but he displayed little enthusiasm for the McNary-Haugen Farm Bill because he feared it would lower the price of cotton. When the Democrats organized the House in 1931, he succeeded to the chairmanship of the powerful House Agricultural Committee. Although by nature not a highly partisan individual, Jones came to detest what he believed was President Herbert Hoover's unwillingness to support government aid for depression-stricken farmers.

Following the victory of fellow Democrat Franklin D. Roosevelt in the 1932 presidential election, Jones anticipated legislative actions aimed at improving agricultural conditions. He was not disappointed. Even before taking office, Roosevelt asked Jones and Professor William I. Myers of Cornell University to begin drafting an executive order (no. 6084, Mar. 27, 1933) that would consolidate all farm credit agencies into one new organization, the Farm Credit Administration. During the next five years, Jones sponsored and helped guide through Congress an imposing number of farm bills, including the Agricultural Adjustment Acts of 1933 and 1938, the Jones-Connally Cattle Act, the National Soil Conservation and Domestic Allotment Act, and the Jones-Costigan Sugar Act.

At times Jones clashed with Secretary of Agriculture Henry A. Wallace and those he referred to as the "bright boys" of the New Deal, but generally his policy was to support "the man on the other end of the avenue." Although clearly one of the most powerful members of Congress during the 1930's, Jones attracted little public attention. Soft-spoken and mild-mannered, Jones, who was unmarried, largely ignored the social aspects of Washington life, preferring to read a book or to take a quiet walk or an occasional fishing trip.

On Apr. 9, 1940, Roosevelt appointed Jones a judge of the United States Court of Claims with the proviso that he remain in the House and continue to shepherd agricultural matters until after the fall elections. Consequently, Jones did not join the court until January 1941. He remained on it until early 1943 when, again at Roosevelt's request, he took a leave of absence to become agricultural adviser to James F. Byrnes, director of the newly created Office of Economic Stabilization. One of Jones's initial assignments was to serve as president of the first International Conference on Food and Agriculture held at Hot Springs, Va., May 18–June 3, 1943. Representatives from forty-four countries attended. One result of the conference was a resolution calling for the establishment of a permanent world food organization. This goal was reached in 1945 when the United Nations Food and Agricultural Organization (FAO) was formed.

When Jones returned from the Hot Springs Conference in 1943, he received a call from Roosevelt asking that he become war food administrator, a position left vacant by the resignation of Chester Davis. Fearing the job was political suicide, Jones consented only after receiving assurances that his judicial leave of absence would be continued. He was sworn in on June 29, 1943. Jones had little enthusiasm for administrative details and instead devoted much of his efforts to public relations campaigns to stimulate the production and conservation of food. He sought to resign after a year, but Roosevelt insisted that he remain for the duration of the war. On May 22, 1945, shortly after Roosevelt's death and the end of the war in Europe, Jones sent his resignation to President Harry S. Truman and returned to the court on July 1. Two years later President Truman named him chief justice of the Court of Claims, a position he held from July 10, 1947, until his retirement on July 14, 1964. Even then, though well into his eighties, Jones remained remarkably active, filling temporary vacancies on various courts of appeal across the nation and working on his memoirs. He died in Amarillo shortly after his ninety-fourth birthday.

[Jones's papers are in the Southwest Collection, Texas Tech University, Lubbock. His publications include *How War Food Saved American Lives* (1947); *Should Uncle Sam Pay—When and Why?* (rev. ed. 1963); and Joseph M. Ray, ed., *Marvin Jones Memoirs* (1973). A biography is Irvin M. May, Jr., *Marvin Jones* (1980). Obituaries are in the *Amarillo Daily News*, Mar. 5, 1976, and the *New York Times*, Mar. 6, 1976. The Columbia Oral History Project has a lengthy interview with Jones by Dean Albertson (1952); there are shorter reminiscences at the Lyndon B. Johnson Library (1969) and the Harry S. Truman Library (1970).]

PETER L. PETERSEN

JOSEPHSON, MATTHEW (Feb. 15, 1899–Mar. 13, 1978), author, was born in Brooklyn, N.Y., the son of Julius Josephson, a banker, and Sarah Kasendorf. Josephson's family was well off; his father, interested in politics, encouraged political discussion. Young Josephson showed an early and wide-ranging interest in literature. He graduated from Old Boy's High School in Brooklyn.

At Columbia University, from which he received a B.A. degree in 1920, he concentrated his studies in French literature. He lived for a while in Greenwich Village and then departed for France with his wife, Hannah Geffen, whom he had married on May 6, 1920. They had two children. In Montparnasse, Josephson was a member of the expatriate community of artists and writers that became known as the "Lost Generation." His experience with the avant-garde led eventually to his *Life Among the Surrealists: A Memoir* (1962), considered an outstanding chronicle of Parisian cultural life in the interwar years. While in Paris he befriended E. E. Cummings, William Carlos Williams, and Malcolm Cowley.

For a time Josephson concentrated on poetry, but his forte was prose writing, and he became an eminent biographer and journalist. He served as editor of various experimental literary magazines: *Secession* (1922–1924), which he cofounded with Gorham Munson, *Broom* (1922–1924), and *Transition* (1928–1929). He also served as book editor for the Macaulay

Company (1929) and assistant editor at the *New Republic* (1931–1932).

Josephson offered early encouragement to the poet Hart Crane, whom he met in 1919. He became prominently involved with the left-wing literary movement of the 1930's. While never a Communist, Josephson sympathized with Communists and cowrote a manifesto for the Communist party in the 1932 election. His memoir of these times, *Infidel in the Temple, A Memoir of the Nineteen-Thirties*, is a valuable document.

Josephson's experience in France and his associations in the 1930's help to explain his two chief areas of literary output: French literature and American capitalism. The Great Depression had a particular effect on Josephson. For the *New Republic*, he wrote articles dealing with social problems arising from the depression. This experience generated his most famous book, *The Robber Barons: The Great American Capitalists, 1861–1901* (1934). This well-received work traces the careers of John D. Rockefeller, Andrew Carnegie, J. P. Morgan, E. H. Harriman, and Henry Clay Frick. Even those, such as historian Allan Nevins, who rejected Josephson's critical view of these industrialists, felt the book was vivid and compelling. A similar critical history was *The Politicos, 1865–1896* (1938).

Josephson's writing style was accessible and dramatic without sacrificing historical accuracy. For *Robber Barons*, *Politicos*, and others, he was elected in 1947 to the National Institute of Arts and Letters, and for *Edison: A Biography* (1959) he received the Francis Parkman Prize in 1960. His final biography, *Al Smith: Hero of the Cities* (1969), was cowritten with his wife and received the Van Wyck Brooks Prize for biography and history.

It has been said that Josephson brought an understanding of the French people to his biographies of Zola (1942) and Stendhal (1946). Critics praised his French biographies, with the exception of *Victor Hugo: A Realistic Biography of the Great Romantic* (1942), which was treated as below the standards set by his other biographies.

Josephson was a visiting professor at the University of California at Santa Cruz at his death.

[Josephson's papers are in the Beinecke Rare Book and Manuscript Library, Yale University. Other works of significance by Josephson include *The President Makers: The Culture of Politics and Leadership in an Age of Enlightenment, 1896–1919* (1940); *Sidney Hillman: Statesman of American Labor* (1952); and *The Money Lords: The Great Finance Capitalists, 1925–1950* (1972). An obituary is in the *New York Times*, Mar. 14, 1978.]

RONALD H. RIDGLEY

K

KANAGA, CONSUELO DELESSEPS (May 25, 1894–Feb. 28, 1978), photographer, was born in Astoria, Oreg. Her father, Amos Ream Kanaga, was a lawyer and, for a time, district attorney of Astoria, but gave up his practice intermittently to pursue a lifelong interest in agrarian affairs and publish several magazines on farming. Her mother, Mathilda ("Tillie") Carolina Hartwig, compiled and wrote a history of Napa Valley, Calif., published in 1901 and still in use. She had three siblings, two of whom survived.

Kanaga had no formal education beyond high school but apparently was encouraged to be a journalist by her father. After the family moved to San Francisco sometime in the early 1900's, Kanaga landed a job as a reporter and feature writer on the *San Francisco Chronicle* in 1915. Increasingly, her interest turned to photography and she stayed on in this rare career for a woman in that era, until 1919.

Kanaga's first job was to write an article; a photographer was sent along to take pictures. Kanaga would, in her own words, "sort of arrange the pictures." Her editor, delighted with the results, urged her to try her hand in the darkroom. Soon she was taking a camera on her assignments and spending the rest of her time printing, developing, and enlarging her own photographs as well as those of the rest of the staff photographers. At first, her work was simple, everything sharp and etched with no nuances. She worked with a large view camera, which, according to Kanaga, developed discipline because the photographer was forced to organize the subject carefully, using the whole frame. Early on, she mastered the use of a small amount of flash powder and continued to use it throughout her career for more dramatic effects, finding the results "preferable, softer and more pleasing compared with contemporary flash effects." She always mixed her own developer. She maintained, "That's what the art of photography means. A photograph that's been carefully printed, it's as different as day to night." Her assignments included everything from society events to covering farm workers' strikes. An idealist from earliest childhood, Kanaga refused job offers from the conservative William Randolph Hearst publication the *San Francisco Examiner* and worked only for the *San Francisco Chronicle* and then for a short time moved to the *San Francisco Daily News*.

About 1918, Kanaga joined the California Camera Club. While there she discovered Alfred Stieglitz's publication *Camera Work*. Through it, she first became aware of the early work of such photographers as Paul Strand, Julia Margaret Cameron, Clarence White, Gertrude Käsebier, and, of course, Stieglitz. In 1919 she began to lose interest in journalism and longed to try her hand at "pictorial photography." In the same year she married a young mining engineer, Evans Davidson. However, she had great difficulty reconciling her marriage and her career as a news photographer with her desire to experiment with pictorialism. Her love of city life began to separate her from her husband's interests, which resulted in an informal separation. In 1922, Kanaga departed for New York City, a journey that took her many months to complete as she free-lanced her way across the United States as a journeyman photographer by car, rail, and boat, finally arriving in New York City in September. In order to support herself, she went to work for a William Randolph Hearst publication, the *New York American*. She had hesitated to take the job, but she justified it by vowing to take pictures for Mrs. Hearst's "Hundred Neediest," a photogravure feature popular during the Christmas season. Her work brought her to the attention of Stieglitz, who became so impressed with her images of poor people that he offered her the use of his developer formulas. Kanaga's sincerity as a photographer was borne out by her philosophy: "The great alchemy is your attitude, who you are, what you are. When you make a photograph, it is very much a picture of your own self. That is the important thing. Most people try to be striking to catch the eye. I think the thing is not to catch the eye but the spirit." Kanaga was convinced that a medium like photography could change the world. She said Stieglitz asked only one question of photographers: "What have you got to say?" It was in answer to this question that she measured her own work and that of others.

Kanaga's contact with poverty and with African Americans inspired the two main themes that appear in many of her finest pictures. She was, in fact, one of the earliest photographers to take a serious interest in photographing African Americans. Although she was also very interested in still life, nature, abstraction, and architecture, her personal concern was always with the human condition. At the urging of the California philanthropist and art collector Albert Bender, she spent a year (1927) in Europe and several months in Kairouan, Tunisia, where she met and married her second husband, a charismatic Irishman and writer, James Barry McCarthy. While there, she took more than one hundred negatives, hoping to publish a book. After returning to New York City in 1928, Kanaga accepted a job in the studio of the noted photographer Nickolas Muray, where she learned to refine her skills at developing, printing, and retouching, thus making it possible to open her own studio. In December 1930, Kanaga returned to San Francisco, where she established her own studio and renewed her relationship with West Coast photographers. She was invited to participate in the landmark Group f.64 exhibition of California photographers who had rebelled against pictorialism in favor of sharply focused "super realism."

Despite the fact that Kanaga's four contributions to the exhibition were singled out for their excellence, she refused to join the f.64 movement and kept her status as an independent artist throughout her career. Although she joined the Film and Photo League and did some assignments for the Works Progress Administration (WPA) during the Great Depression, Kanaga never formally associated herself with any one movement, either politically or socially. She was always fiercely independent in thought and action. When her second marriage ended badly, she pulled her life together and began to plan a portfolio of studies of African Americans, even moving into Harlem with two young black women for several months. In 1936, while on assignment for the WPA project the Index of American Design, she met and married (on May 28) her third and last husband, the artist Wallace Bradstreet Putnam, who worked for the *Sun* newspaper. She was forty-two years old, five years older than Putnam. He was supportive of Kanaga's career and shared her radical views. Her most productive work was done in the late 1940's and early 1950's, when she and her husband visited Maitland, Fla., and Tennessee. Her work was also beginning to appear in exhibitions.

In 1955 two of Kanaga's photographs were part of Edward Steichen's landmark exhibition The Family of Man, presented at the Museum of Modern Art in New York City. After the *Sun* folded, she was the main support of the family, having taken a job as a free-lance photographer for *Woman's Day* magazine. Kanaga and Putnam moved to rural Yorktown Heights, N.Y., a much less inspiring atmosphere for her work as a photographer. In her lifetime, her photographs appeared in sixteen exhibitions, six of which were devoted exclusively to her work. In 1974 she had a one-person exhibition at the Blue Moon and the Lerner-Heller Gallery, jointly, in New York City, and, by 1976, a small but important exhibition at The Brooklyn Museum. In 1977 her work was shown at the Wave Hill Center for Environmental Studies, the Bronx, N.Y., followed by participation in the now historic re-creation of the original f.64 exhibition at the University of Missouri, St. Louis, in 1978. She died at her home in Yorktown Heights, still virtually unknown except by her peers and a few fiercely loyal friends. Her death was attributed to emphysema caused by incessant smoking and the harsh and dangerous chemicals she chose to use to produce her prints. Only a few of those exceptional prints are known to have entered the art market. Her productivity was comparatively limited, but that was a choice she made. In 1982, Wallace Putnam gave Kanaga's 2,500 negatives and the 373 prints she owned to The Brooklyn Museum. At her death, her entire estate was valued at only $1,345. Her talent was finally acknowledged in 1993, when her first major retrospective was presented at The Brooklyn Museum.

[See Barbara Head Millstein and Sarah M. Lowe, *Consuelo Kanaga* (1992). An obituary is in the *New York Times*, Mar. 2, 1978.]

BARBARA HEAD MILLSTEIN

KANTOR, MACKINLAY (Feb. 4, 1904–Oct. 11, 1977), novelist, was born in Webster City, Iowa, the son of John Marvin Kantor, a confidence man who deserted the family, and Effie Rachel MacKinlay, a writer and newspaper editor. Kantor and his sister were raised by their mother, who edited the *Webster City Freeman-Tribune*. At the age of ten, he became an avid student of the Civil War after a salesman left sample pages from a Civil War encyclopedia at his home. Kantor, the great-grandson of a Union Army officer, grew up in a family that had vivid memories of the war. Eleven of his ancestors and relatives had fought for the North. A favorite aunt, who lived in Galena, Ill., had known Ulysses S. Grant and regaled him with stories. Kantor marched with the Grand Army of the Republic in Memorial Day parades, became an accomplished fifer, and was a member of the Association of Civil War Musicians. "There is no reason in fife music," he once said, "but there is all the emotion of the ages."

Moving with his family, Kantor attended high schools in Chicago and Des Moines before returning to Webster City in 1921. His mother was then the editor of the *Webster City Daily News*, and Kantor worked as a reporter for the newspaper. Encouraged by his mother, he began writing poetry and short stories. At the age of eighteen, he won a statewide short story contest sponsored by the *Des Moines Register*. "Suddenly, I knew that I could write, and some people knew it too," Kantor said.

Following his graduation from Webster City High School in 1923, Kantor was seriously injured in an automobile accident. His left thigh was shattered. The tall, slender Kantor walked with a limp for the rest of his life. During his long recovery from the accident, Kantor decided to pursue a literary career.

Kantor moved to Chicago in 1925 and attempted without success to get a reporting job on a major daily newspaper. In the process, he made valuable contacts and became a frequent contributor to the *Chicago Tribune*'s "Line O Type" column and the feature supplements of other newspapers. He subsidized his writing career by working as a clerk in the Cook County treasurer's office, for the Mandel Brothers department store, and as the assistant advertising manager for the American Flyer Company, a manufacturer of toy trains. On Sept. 2, 1926, he married Florence Irene Layne; they had two children.

Kantor's first novel, *Diversey* (1928), was among the earliest fictional treatments of the Chicago organized-crime syndicate. Senator Coleman Blease of South Carolina denounced the novel as "the dirtiest thing I have ever read." But Fanny Butcher, the *Chicago Tribune*'s literary critic, wrote that Kantor had shown "a real gift for storytelling, and he makes a thriller out of his tale."

Kantor, who was still struggling to support his family on his writing income, returned to Iowa and worked briefly as a reporter for the *Cedar Rapids Republican* (1927) and as a columnist for the *Des Moines Tribune* (1930–1931). A second Chicago novel, *El Goes South* (1930), attracted less attention than his first book. His third novel, *The Jaybird* (1932), focuses on a Civil War veteran and fife player who has become the town drunk. The Civil War was a recurring theme in Kantor's fiction, and he wrote about it with power and narrative force. In April 1932, he and his family moved to Westfield, N.J., where he started writing his most ambitious work.

In preparation for his novel about the battle of Gettysburg, Kantor had spent years working with primary source materials and attending encampments of the United Confederate Veterans; studied journals, letters, and diaries written by soldiers on both sides of the conflict; and made extensive use of the archives of the United States and Confederate States war departments. Kantor also gained firsthand knowledge of the battlefield and town in visits to Gettysburg.

Long Remember (1934) is a superb fictional account of the Battle of Gettysburg, written from the perspective of the soldiers and residents of the town. Allen Tate, who reviewed Kantor's novel for the *Nation*, wrote: "There is no book ever written which creates, so well as this, the look and smell of battle. As a spectacle of war, this book has no equal."

Kantor's Gettysburg novel established his literary reputation, not just as a novelist but as one of the nation's respected authorities on the Civil War. *Long Remember*, which was a selection of the Literary Guild, was a commercial success. National magazines, which had previously rejected his short stories, competed for his byline in the wake of *Long Remember*.

The Voice of Bugle Ann (1935), Kantor's most enduringly popular novel, set in the wooded hills of Missouri, is about a man who risks hanging to avenge his foxhound. The novel was adapted into a Metro-Goldwyn-Mayer motion picture in 1936.

Kantor's second Civil War novel, *Arouse and Beware* (1936), is about two Union soldiers escaping from a Confederate prison camp. *The Romance of Rosy Ridge* (1937) is a novel about the relationship between a Yankee veteran and the daughter of a former Southern officer. From 1936 until 1939, Kantor had an affair with Margaret Leech Pulitzer, a novelist and historian who influenced his development as a writer. Kantor aided Leech in her research for *Reveille in Washington* (1941), a history of the nation's capital during the Civil War. Kantor reviewed Leech's book favorably for the *New York Times*. "Peggy's greatest influence was on his prose, which became leaner, cleaner, during those years," Tim Kantor wrote of his father's relationship with Leech. Kantor made no reference to his affair with Leech in *I Love You, Irene* (1972), a memoir of his marriage. The Kantors built a home in Sarasota, Fla., in 1936 and traveled widely.

During World War II, Kantor served as a war correspondent for the *Saturday Evening Post* and flew with the British Royal Air Force. He attended gunnery school in England and flew eleven combat missions with the 305th Bomb Group of the United States Army's Eighth Air Force. He became a close friend and confidant of General Curtis LeMay, and was the coauthor of LeMay's autobiography, *Mission With LeMay* (1965). Kantor flew six more missions during the Korean conflict. He said that his wartime experience brought a new dimension to his writings.

Kantor's 1945 novel, *Glory for Me*, written in verse, focused on the resettlement of three World War II veterans in a small midwestern town. His story was rewritten into a screenplay by Robert E. Sherwood and adapted into the 1946 motion picture *The Best Years of Our Lives*, which received nine Academy Awards.

An autobiography of his formative years, *But Look, the Morn* (1947), was written with warmth and affection and dedicated to the residents of his Iowa hometown. Kantor, who was a tireless researcher, spent nearly two years patrolling New York City's Twenty-third Precinct with police officers in gathering background for *Signal Thirty-two* (1950), a novel about New York policemen.

But the Civil War remained Kantor's passion. He published *Lee and Grant at Appomattox* (1950) and *Gettysburg* (1952) for Random House's Landmark Books, a popular juvenile series. His 1955 Civil War novel, *Andersonville*, which won the Pulitzer Prize, was an authoritative history of the notorious Confederate prison camp where 50,000 Union soldiers were held. "Andersonville reduced them to a single pattern: they were stamped out of that pattern by the enormous heavy die of confinement, like a row of toy tin wretches holding hands," wrote Kantor, who had spent more than a quarter century gathering his research for the novel. Henry Steele Commager, who reviewed *Andersonville* for the *New York Times Book Review*, called it "the greatest of our Civil War novels." Kantor later wrote *Silent Grow the Guns and Other Tales of the American Civil War* (1958) and *If the South Had Won the Civil War* (1961).

Spirit Lake (1961), an epic historical novel about an 1857 Indian massacre of Iowa settlers, received mixed reviews and was a commercial disappointment. Although the book was long on historical detail, it was overwritten and disjointed. Kantor blamed the literary establishment, not the decline of his writing skills, for the disappointing reception of his later books. *Beauty Beast* (1968), a novel about a nineteenth-century slave owned by a sexually frustrated Southern woman, was an embarrassment. Kantor struck back at his critics in *Missouri Bittersweet* (1969), writing with bitterness and scorn in his second book of memoirs.

His final historical novel, *Valley Forge* (1975), was well researched but plodding and contrived. Though the reviews were negative, Kantor still had a following. The novel, written for the United States Bicentennial, went into five printings and was an alternate selection of the Book-of-the-Month Club. Kantor died of congestive heart failure in Sarasota, Fla.

Kantor had few peers at bringing the American past vividly to life. He wrote with sentiment about the small town values of the heartland. More than any American novelist since Stephen Crane, Kantor wrote with realism and clarity about the Civil War. "You've got to write about what you believe in, and nothing else," he said of his writing.

[Kantor's papers are at the Library of Congress. The University of Iowa has papers relating to *Andersonville*. Tim Kantor, *My Father's Voice* (1988), is a biography by Kantor's son. *Author's Choice* (1944), a collection of MacKinlay Kantor's short stories, includes reminiscences by the author of his early career. Commager's review is in the *New York Times Book Review*, Oct. 30, 1955. An interview with Kantor is in the *Philadelphia Inquirer*, Nov. 25, 1975. An obituary is in the *New York Times*, Oct. 12, 1977.]

STEVE NEAL

KAUFMANN, WALTER ARNOLD (July 1, 1921–Sept. 4, 1980), scholar, teacher, and translator of German literature and philosophy, was born in Freiburg im Breisgau, Germany, the son of Bruno Kaufmann, a lawyer, and Edith Seligsohn. The family lived in Berlin until late 1938, when Kaufmann fled the Nazis alone and settled in the United States. He became an American citizen in 1944.

Williams College admitted Kaufmann as a sophomore in the spring 1939 semester. There he was influenced by two prominent philosophers: John William Miller, whose metaphysics of history was grounded in the human "free act proposing systematic consequences," and James Bissett Pratt, who offered physiological interpretations of religious phenomena. Both of these strains of thought were later manifested in Kaufmann's own thought, such that the habitual disagreements between Miller and Pratt seemed to be resolved in the work of their student. Kaufmann claimed that the Williams course that influenced him most was Pratt's on comparative religion.

Kaufmann married Hazel Dennis on July 12, 1941; they had two children. After receiving his B.A. from Williams in 1941, he enrolled at Harvard University, convinced by both Miller and Pratt that it was the only worthwhile place in America for graduate work in philosophy. He earned his M.A. in 1942, but interrupted his doctoral studies in 1944 to enlist in the United States Army, serving first in the Army Air Forces and then in military intelligence, including fifteen months in Germany. Upon his honorable discharge in 1946, he returned to Harvard and received his Ph.D. in 1947 with a dissertation titled "Nietzsche's Theory of Values." He was immediately hired to teach at Princeton University, where he spent the rest of his career except for visiting professorships at Cornell (1952), Columbia (1955), Heidelberg (1955–1956), the University of Washington (1958), the University of Michigan (1959), Hebrew University in Jerusalem (1962–1963, 1975), Purdue (1966), and Australian National University in Canberra (1974).

In 1950, Kaufmann published his first and most influential book, *Nietzsche: Philosopher, Psychologist, Antichrist*, a revolutionary interpretation that single-handedly destroyed the hitherto dominant myth, promulgated by Crane Brinton, George Santayana, and others, that Nietzsche was a proto-Nazi. In place of this myth, Kaufmann provided his own: that Nietzsche was an existentialist. This question has been quite controversial.

Kaufmann's contributions in this book, in the next twenty years of his philosophical books, and in his best-selling translations or retranslations of most of the corpus of Nietzsche, were important not only to scholarship but also to the development of the 1960's and 1970's counterculture. It was Kaufmann's version of Nietzsche that, for better or worse, impressed many young minds in that era, from college students to Bob Dylan. *From Shakespeare to Existentialism* (1959), published in England as *The Owl and the Nightingale* (1960), was particularly significant among Kaufmann's other books in establishing existentialism as the leading Anglo-American intellectual tendency of the mid-twentieth century, both in the ivied halls and in the streets. Thus, Kaufmann remained a major American cultural force for the latter half of the twentieth century. Evidence of his stature as fountainhead of the existentialism that pervaded the student movements of the 1960's is that in 1962 the Princeton undergraduates named him a Witherspoon Lecturer, the highest honor that they could formally give to a faculty member.

Other major works of this period were *Critique of Religion and Philosophy* (1958), *The Faith of a Heretic* (1961), *Cain, and Other Poems* (1962), and *Tragedy and Philosophy* (1968); and (as editor) the anthologies *Existentialism from Dostoevsky to Sartre* (1956) and *Religion from Tolstoy to Camus* (1961).

Kaufmann was a tireless translator, not only

of Nietzsche but also of a great variety of German authors and poets, notably Goethe, *Faust: Part One and Sections from Part Two* (1961). He edited several anthologies of his translations of German poetry. His translations are readable and accurate, yet occasionally cater more to popular culture than to high scholarly standards of adherence to the text. For example, he allowed a comic book hero and Bernard Shaw's play to affect his decision to render Nietzsche's key term *Übermensch* by the false cognate "overman" instead of the more descriptive "superman." As a translator, anthologist, and editor, he has been accused of manipulating authors to serve his own existentialist interpretation rather than letting either them or the issues speak for themselves.

In 1965, Kaufmann published his other truly revolutionary work, *Hegel: A Reinterpretation*, which, along with his often reprinted article, "The Hegel Myth and Its Method" (1951), and his anthology, *Hegel's Political Philosophy* (1970), are benchmarks of the Anglo-American Hegel renaissance that began in the 1950's. With Hegel as with Nietzsche, Kaufmann's forte was in dispelling prevalent myths about the thinker—for example, the allegations that Hegel regarded Napoleon as "the world-soul on a horse" and history as the inexorable "march of God" through time. His fundamental method in this book, as in the Nietzsche book, was to discover the private consciousness of the thinker. This kind of analysis appeals more to the "intelligent laity" than to specialists in the field. His scholarly detractors claim that Kaufmann's conclusions about Hegel's and Nietzsche's psyches are too speculative—for example, his idea that Hegel's fathering of an illegitimate child materially affected the content of the *Phenomenology of Spirit*. These detractors have dubbed the posthumous psychoanalysis of philosophers "Kaufmannization."

Kaufmann's most effective writing was done in the first two decades of his thirty-year public career. Yet his last decade was no less prolific, and includes *Without Guilt and Justice: From Decidophobia to Autonomy* (1973), *Traveling Mind* (1976), *Existentialism, Religion and Death* (1976), *Religions in Four Dimensions: Existential and Aesthetic, Historical and Comparative* (1976), and *The Future of the Humanities* (1977). Toward the end of his life he became absorbed with the relationship of the arts, especially photography, to philosophy, religion, and particularly ethics. He began to illustrate his philosophical books with his own photographs, had several one-person shows, and in 1978 published *Man's Lot*, a trilogy of photographs and commentary comprising *Life at the Limits*, *Time Is an Artist*, and *What Is Man?* His last major work was a self-illustrated trilogy, a massive philosophical exegesis called *Discovering the Mind:* vol. 1, *Goethe, Kant, and Hegel*; vol. 2, *Nietzsche, Heidegger and Buber*; vol. 3, *Freud Versus Adler and Jung* (1980).

The consensus among his contemporaries at Princeton was that Kaufmann was extremely self-contained, even for an academic. His world consisted of nineteenth- and twentieth-century German thought and literature—and very little else. He was not liked by either graduate students or his colleagues. If he was a favorite of undergraduates, it was only because of the reputation and influence of his books. Indeed, the reading lists for his usually well-attended courses were filled with his own titles.

Kaufmann died in Princeton, N.J.

[Autobiographical and other source materials are in the alumni archives of the Williams College Library and the faculty archives of the Seeley G. Mudd Library at Princeton University.]

Eric v. d. Luft

KEENEY, BARNABY CONRAD (Oct. 17, 1914–June 18, 1980), historian, educator, and first chair of the National Endowment for the Humanities (NEH), was born in Halfway, Oreg., the son of Maud Barnaby Conrad and Robert Mayro Keeney, a metallurgical engineer. The family moved frequently, finally settling in Hartford, Conn. After his graduation in 1936 from the University of North Carolina, Keeney attended Harvard University, where he received his master's degree in 1937 and his doctorate in 1939, both in medieval history. He immediately began teaching at Harvard. On June 27, 1941, Keeney married Mary Elizabeth Critchfield; they had three children.

War interrupted Keeney's Harvard career. Enlisting in 1942, he served in Europe as an army intelligence officer. While engaged in combat, he risked his life to gather information. After receiving the Purple Heart, Bronze Star, and Silver Star, he left active duty as a captain in 1945.

He returned to Harvard's history department,

only to be wooed away to Providence, R.I., as assistant professor of history at Brown University in 1946. Keeney's dissertation, *Judgment by Peers*, published in 1949, concerned the institutional and ideological origins of democratic constitutionalism. He continued to publish articles in medieval history during his early career. A full professor by 1951, he became dean of Brown's graduate school in 1952 and, a year later, dean of the college. War again interrupted Keeney's academic career: he went to Washington in 1951 amid the Korean conflict to work for the Central Intelligence Agency (CIA) and returned to Brown the following year.

Keeney became president of Brown University in 1955. An admitted elitist, he believed in "superior opportunities for superior students" at every educational level. He set high standards for Brown students and faculty but worried about gifted young people who could not develop their potential because of inferior schools. Identifying undereducated teachers as part of the problem, Keeney decided to improve their opportunities. In 1957, Brown instituted a Master of Arts in Teaching program. Aspiring and present teachers took regular liberal arts courses, concentrating on their specialty, while taking methodological courses in education.

Keeney also recognized, years before affirmative action became a maxim, that elite colleges were not properly serving minorities. He instituted an informal but aggressive policy of encouraging black students to apply to Brown and Pembroke (Brown's women's college), and almost tripled the graduate school enrollment in part to increase opportunities for minorities and women denied admission to other prestigious universities. He also established a relationship between Brown and predominantly African-American Tougaloo College in Mississippi. During his tenure, Keeney enforced fair housing regulations for off-campus students and ordered fraternities to eliminate discriminatory clauses from their charters or leave their national organizations.

His more tangible accomplishments at Brown included raising more than $85 million, more than doubling its physical plant, almost doubling its land area, and doubling its faculty. In addition, he initiated Brown's medical education program. After a decade on the job, Keeney remarked, a university president "gets pleased with his work . . . . That is a dangerous state of affairs." Having achieved all his goals, he resigned July 1, 1966, to face new challenges as the first chair of the National Endowment for the Humanities (NEH).

Keeney played a crucial role in the development of the NEH. In 1963, the American Council of Learned Societies, the Council of Graduate Schools of the United States, and the United Chapters of Phi Beta Kappa created the Commission for the Humanities, naming Keeney as its chair. Its 1964 *Report for the Humanities* received wide and favorable attention in the media and Congress. The bill establishing the National Foundation for the Arts and Humanities easily passed Congress, and President Lyndon B. Johnson signed it in September 1965.

Keeney's term (1966–1970) was decisive for the NEH. Its organization into divisions, its development of a permanent professional staff, its establishment of grant procedures, and its selection of a prestigious and active oversight council occurred in those years. Keeney's effective lobbying also ensured the NEH's permanence and steady growth.

However, Keeney—the only chair appointed without regard to political affiliation—found himself engaged in a philosophical argument over the mission of the NEH. Academics considered the NEH an organization for financing scholarly research. With an eye on Congress, Keeney promoted programs that would serve a more general public. In his last two years, when "relevance" became the byword on college campuses, the NEH extended its definition of humanities to encompass subjects like peace, urbanization, and ethnicity. Keeney suggested that his most significant general achievement as NEH chair was to reduce "the breach between those who deal directly with human problems, and those who seek insight into them through professional study."

When President Richard M. Nixon limited him to one term, Keeney elected to remain in Washington as the chief executive officer of the Washington Consortium of Universities. The six-year-old consortium of Georgetown, George Washington, Catholic, American, and Howard universities wanted to create a strong, prestigious entity that would provide a first-class education at less cost. As CEO, Keeney was expected to have sufficient clout to achieve a consensus among university presidents and academic deans. Within months, however, he realized that maintaining the status quo was more important to individualistic deans and department heads than elevating the reputations of their schools. Keeney tendered his resignation effective July 1971, the first anniversary of his appointment. His only legacy was an impressionistic report suggesting several options for creating a viable graduate-level consortium. None was effectively implemented.

The Claremont Graduate School (CGS) next sought Keeney's expertise. Part of the Claremont (California) Colleges, CGS appointed Keeney its first president, effective in 1971 upon his resignation from the consortium. It selected him because he retained his reputation as a "fixer" and a fund-raiser. Besides making CGS financially sound, Keeney was able to carry out his philosophy of graduate education: preparing tomorrow's college teachers. He retired from CGS in 1976.

The quiet of Keeney's retirement was broken briefly in 1978 when *New Times* revealed that he secretly worked for the CIA while Brown's president. He made no apologies for this relationship; he was serving his country.

Keeney's post-Brown career had been devoted to promoting his philosophy of a liberal arts education in a changing world: "It has been abundantly demonstrated that education of itself does not solve social problems, but it is equally clear that a population with general education properly used enlarges the talent of society to solve them." During these years he wrote and lectured on the humanities and on education for both academic and public audiences. In a typical "Keeneyism," he noted, "It must be clearly understood that the scholar does not lose dignity by being intelligible."

Keeney succeeded in making academia more intelligible to the public and vice versa. He died in Providence, R.I.

[Keeney's papers are in the University Archives, Brown University, Providence, R.I. The only lengthy treatment of Keeney is Michael Edward Diffily, "Barnaby Conrad Keeney" (Ph.D. diss., Boston College, 1988). See also *Brown Alumni Monthly*, Oct. 1955 and June–July 1980. An obituary is in the *New York Times*, June 19, 1980.]

SUSAN ROSENFELD

KELLER, JAMES GREGORY (June 27, 1900–Feb. 7, 1977), Catholic priest, was born in Oakland, Calif., the son of James Keller and Margaret Selby. His father owned and operated a haberdashery shop. In 1910, at one of the religious instruction classes that Keller attended in preparation for his first communion, he was greatly influenced by the remark of a parish curate that of the boys present, one of them "may become a priest someday and do some good for the world." By the time he was twelve, he had decided to become a priest, and he was accepted at St. Patrick's Minor Seminary (high school) in Menlo Park, Calif., in 1914. During the spring of 1918, his senior year, Keller's vocation was temporarily suspended when he left school to work in an uncle's candy store. However, by the summer he had decided to return to the seminary, and after catching up on his school work, he entered St. Patrick's Major Seminary in the fall.

As a seminarian, Keller was impressed by talks delivered by members of the Maryknoll Missionary Society, which had been founded in 1911, and by the spring of 1921 he had decided to become a Maryknoll missioner. His bishop gave permission for the change, and the Maryknoll Society accepted his application; in 1921, Keller began his studies at the Maryknoll Seminary in Ossining, N.Y. In 1924 his Maryknoll superiors sent him to Catholic University to study for a master's degree in medieval history; he received his S.T.B. from this institution in 1924 and his M.A. degree in 1925. On Aug. 15, 1925, he was ordained a priest at his parish church in Oakland by Archbishop Edward J. Hanna of San Francisco.

During the next five years, Keller was stationed at Maryknoll House in San Francisco, where he publicized Maryknoll activities, recruited candidates, and solicited funds: he was also managing editor of the society's magazine, *The Field Afar*. Although he never served in the foreign mission fields, he did visit some of these areas, such as China and Korea, in 1928 in the entourage of Auxiliary Bishop John J. Dunn, director of the Society for the Propagation of the Faith of the archdiocese of New York. In January 1931 he was transferred to New York City to open and direct a Maryknoll center; his activities included numerous speaking engagements promoting Maryknoll's work as well as fund-raising. In 1933, while organizing a benefit concert for the society at the Metropolitan Opera House, Keller beheld the light of a single match in the dark auditorium and was reminded of the ancient Chinese saying that was to become the motto of the future Christopher movement: "It is better to light one candle than to curse the darkness."

In 1943, Keller, with the assistance of *New York Times* reporter Meyer Berger, wrote his first book, *Men of Maryknoll*, in which he presented the heroic accomplishments of his colleagues in the foreign missions. Two years later Keller founded the ecumenical Christopher movement and devoted the next quarter-century, until his retirement in 1969, to its development. The term Christopher is derived from the Greek meaning "Christ-bearer," which indicates the missionary orientation of the organization. Keller wanted "to make every person a missioner"; he advocated individual initiative and responsibility to upgrade human values in all fields of human activity, especially those areas that have maximum influence on the public: government, literature, education, labor-management relations, and entertainment. He argued that only 1 percent of human beings promoted evil in the world; he called for "another 1 percent" to promote good and positive activities.

The structure of the Christopher movement was simple. There were no membership lists, meetings, or dues because individual responsibility and action were the basic themes. In 1946 the publication of the four-page *Christopher News Notes* began. By the end of the year the circulation amounted to 45,000 copies and kept increasing, reaching about 1 million in the early 1960's. In 1947, Keller launched a writing contest with a prize of $15,000 for fiction and nonfiction works that were not antagonistic to "Christian principles."

In 1948 the first of Keller's some twenty-five books on Christopher topics, *You Can Change the World*, which embraced many of the themes and concepts in the *News Notes*, was published. A year later, *Three Minutes a Day* appeared; it contained daily meditations directed toward motivating people to be active rather than passive in dealing with modern world problems. The publisher of this book sent a copy to the Bell Syndicate, recommending it become the basis for a daily column; eventually three hundred dailies published such a column under the above title. In 1954, Keller offered a one-minute program titled "Christopher Thoughts for the Day," free to radio stations across the country, and in just under a decade 1,900 stations were broadcasting it. Earlier, Keller had begun using motion pictures to circulate the Christopher message; the first film, *You Can Change the World*, was directed by Leo McCarey and featured such stars as Jack Benny, Eddie ("Rochester") Anderson, and Bing Crosby. By 1952 television programs were being developed, and by the beginning of the next decade some five hundred Christopher programs had been made and shown weekly on almost three hundred stations, reaching an estimated audience of approximately 3 million. Keller also initiated the Christopher Awards, presented each year for books, motion pictures, and television productions.

Although a Maryknoll missioner, Keller never worked in the foreign mission field. Instead he spent many of the years since his ordination raising funds for and speaking in behalf of the Maryknoll society, first in California and then in New York City. During the last thirty years of his life he turned his attention via the Christopher movement to motivating and stimulating "the individual" from all walks of life to use his or her talents to do good and thus combat evil. In a sense his mission field became all the people of the United States, and he was very successful reaching people and delivering his message of individual initiative and responsibility in promoting Christian principles and the "highest human good." He did this in a world torn by the effects of World War II and the spread of Communism. He produced many books to spread this Christopher message and in doing so served as a Christopher role model for all individuals in all fields of endeavor. The movement he founded survived him and is still significant today.

Keller died in New York City.

[Keller's papers relating to the Christophers are housed at the Christopher Headquarters, New York City. The best source for the life of Keller is his autobiography, *To Light a Candle* (1963). Besides those listed above, his books include *The Priest and a World Vision* (1946); *One Moment Please* (1950); *Careers That Change Your World* (1950); *Government Is Your Business* (1951); *Just for Today* (1952); *All God's Children* (1953); *Stop, Look and Live* (1954); *Give Us This Day* (1956); *It's Your Day* (1957); and *A Day at a Time* (1958).

A biography on Keller is Richard Armstrong, *Out to Change the World* (1984). See also "Calling All Christophers," *Time*, Apr. 14, 1947; Harvey Breit, "Talk with Father Keller," *New York Times Book Review*, Sept. 25, 1949; and "Christopher Number One," *Good Housekeeping*, Oct. 1956. An obituary is in the *New York Times*, Feb. 9, 1977.]

ALLAN NELSON

KELLY, EMMETT LEO (Dec. 9, 1898–Mar. 28, 1979), circus clown, was born in Sedan, Kans., the son of Thomas Kelly, a railroad section foreman, and Mollie Schimick. By the time Emmett began school his father had retired from the railroad and purchased a small farm near Cabool, Mo. There he attended a one-room schoolhouse for eight years.

A fair student with definite artistic abilities, Kelly failed to graduate from the eighth grade because he was needed on the farm before the school year ended. Following the end of his formal education his mother enrolled him in a correspondence art course at the Landon School of Cartooning. Kelly quickly proved to be an able cartoonist, and in 1917, following the completion of this course, he embarked upon a career as a cartoonist and entertainer. His first job consisted of presenting chalk-talks in which he used his cartooning skills to convert words into illustrations. Throughout the remainder of his life Kelly continued to perfect this form of art and used it whenever he performed in nightclubs.

In 1920, Kelly secured a position as a cartoonist with the Adagram Film Company of Kansas City, a firm that created animated advertisements for use in the local movie theaters. While working there Kelly created the cartoon character that eventually evolved into his alter ego, the clown Weary Willie. Throughout his life Kelly maintained that his first ambition as a boy, as a young man, and as an adult was to be an artist. Along the way, however, he attended a circus, worked for a short time as the manager of the carnival sideshow "Spidora," learned to work on the single trapeze, and fell in love with "trouping," the term used by circus performers for living on the road and working under the canvas big top.

Kelly received his first real circus contract from Howe's Great London Circus in 1921 when he signed on to perform principally as a trapeze aerialist and double as a clown. On opening day, however, his incorrectly rigged trapeze resulted in a poor performance and the cancellation of the aerialist portion of his contract. Kelly, who still considered himself a trapeze artist, spent his first season performing as a whitefaced clown while studying the various aerialist acts and honing his own skills. The following year he returned to the single trapeze with the John Robinson's Circus and remained there for three seasons. There he met a young aerialist named Eva Moore, and they were married between shows on July 21, 1923, over the objections of her father and the circus manager. The couple had two children. They became known as the Aerial Kellys and worked together on a double trapeze. Over the years, Kelly continued to double as a clown in order to fulfill his growing family and financial responsibilities. In 1935 the Kellys divorced.

During his early years as a clown, Kelly performed in whiteface, using a zinc oxide and lard makeup with black or red greasepaint outlining the eyes, nose, mouth, and eyebrows. In the back of his mind, the cartoon tramp he had created slowly began to take form and finally emerged as his true clown identity. Prior to the Great Depression, Kelly's ragged tramp clown was considered dirty-looking and unacceptable. By 1933, however, the American public was ready to embrace the forlorn, melancholy little hobo who, according to Kelly, "always got the short end of the stick and never had any good luck at all, but who never lost hope and just kept trying."

Dressed in a tattered and torn suit with numerous mismatched patches, oversized shoes, a green shirt, and a derby, Kelly's alter ego, Weary Willie, performed a number of routines that became his trademarks. The most famous of these relied on two props, a broom and a spotlight, and Willie's relentless determination to sweep up every last circle of light in the darkened arena before the show began. In 1942 he took this routine to Madison Square Garden, where he opened with the Ringling Brothers and Barnum and Bailey Circus.

During the 1944 season Mildred Ritchie, a young aerialist performer, joined the Ringling Brothers tour. She and Kelly married on Apr. 27, 1944, while the show played in New York City. Before the circus moved on to its next engagement the couple had agreed to end the marriage.

In 1954, Kelly published his autobiography, *Clown*. The same year a young German acrobat named Elvira ("Evie") Gebhardt arrived at Ringling and soon caught Kelly's attention. They were married on Apr. 21, 1955. The Kellys left Ringling Brothers and circus life in the spring of 1956 and moved to Sarasota, Fla., where they raised their two daughters.

Kelly's career as a clown extended far beyond the circus arena. At the end of his first circus season he began performing as a clown in night clubs and small theaters. In 1940 he debuted on Broadway in a production of *Keep Off the Grass*, receiving favorable reviews. A decade later he portrayed a murderous clown in the David O. Selznick film *The Fat Man* (1950) and then appeared as Weary Willie in Cecil B. DeMille's *The Greatest Show on Earth* (1952). Following his retirement from Ringling Brothers, Kelly opened at the Roxy in an ice show, spent a season as the Brooklyn Dodgers' mascot, performed in Sarah Caldwell's production of the opera *The Bartered Bride*, appeared in European movies and on European and American television, and served as the technical director of a *General Electric Hour* television feature based on his life. For sixteen years he played long summer engagements at clubs in Lake Tahoe and Reno.

During his "trouping" years Kelly performed with the greatest traveling circuses of his day including Sells-Floto, Cole Brothers and Clyde Beatty Combined, Bertram Mills in England, and thirteen seasons with Ringling Brothers and Barnum and Bailey. Emmett Kelly's work as Weary Willie elevated the art of clowning and the status of the clown and earned him a place in the Clown Hall of Fame in Delavan, Wis. He was posthumously inducted on Apr. 23, 1989.

[Kelly's autobiography, *Clown* (1954), was written with F. Beverly Kelley. See also John H. Towsen, *Clowns* (1976); and John Culhane, *The American Circus: An Illustrated History* (1990). An obituary is in the *New York Times*, Mar. 29, 1979.]

DIANE E. COOPER

KENNEDY, GEORGE CLAYTON (Sept. 22, 1919–Mar. 18, 1980), experimental geophysicist, educator, and researcher, was born in Dillon, Mont., the son of Clayton Tierny Kennedy and Maude Coley. He claimed to have been educated by itinerant teachers, but at the age of sixteen he won a scholarship to Harvard University. There he received his B.A. degree in geochemistry in 1940, his M.A. degree in geochemistry in 1941, and his Ph.D. in geology in 1946. Kennedy was a geologist at the Alaska branch of the United States Geological Survey from 1942 to 1945 and a physicist at the United States Naval Research Laboratory in Washington, D.C., in 1945. He was a junior research fellow at Harvard from 1946 to 1949 and an assistant professor from 1949 to 1953. Kennedy married Sally Slocum on Oct. 1, 1951; they had three children and were later divorced. On May 11, 1968, he married Ruth Porter; they had no children.

From 1953 to 1969, Kennedy was a professor of geology, and from 1969 to 1980 professor of geology and geochemical science, at the Institute of Geophysics and Planetary Sciences at the University of California at Los Angeles. He published on such topics as the hydrothermal solubility of silica, volcanology, contact metamorphism, solubility in the gas phase, problems in geochemistry, the effects of volatiles, thermal expansion at high pressure and the synthesis of large diamonds, and the physics of high pressures.

Kennedy and his coworkers developed a popular and much-copied version of the opposed-anvils high-pressure apparatus, which he later abandoned in favor of a piston-cylinder apparatus capable of pressures up to 80 kilobars. He measured the pressure-volume-temperature relations of water–carbon dioxide mixtures and solutions, thereby providing petrologists and geochemists with data necessary for thermodynamic calculations for many equilibrium reactions. Along with his research associates Kennedy determined phase relationships in sodium chloride–water and silicon dioxide–water systems that became models for salt and silicate systems at high pressures. The Kennedy law of melting resulted from the establishment and subsequent experimental verification of the relationship between volume change and temperature of melting.

Kennedy applied his law of melting to the determination of the temperature of the Earth's outer core. He concluded that the core must have a partly subadiabatic temperature gradient and, therefore, that corewide convection was impossible. Based on contemporary models of convection in the core, the consequence of his conclusion was that the Earth could have no magnetic field. For a number of years attempts were made to solve the "Kennedy paradox"; models of convection in the core that began to emerge in the 1990's were consistent with Kennedy's thermal model.

Kennedy's calibration of the high-pressure scale provided standards used in laboratories worldwide and established targets for theoreticians concerned with extrapolation to pressures higher than those possible in Kennedy's laboratory. Until the final month of his life, Kennedy continued to carry out experiments that required the combined genius and skill of a physicist and a surgeon, yet were elegant in conceptual simplicity. He was capable of doing delicate measurements of utmost sensitivity within the confines of apparatus that sustained high pressures and temperatures.

In the late 1950's, Kennedy became a fellow of the American Mineralogical Society and the American Academy of Arts and Sciences and was a member of the Geological Society of America and the Society of Economic Geology. He received a special award from the American Mineralogical Society in 1956 for his contributions to geological research. He was an associate editor of *Orchid Digest* and vice-chairman of the Explorers Club (1967–1968). Kennedy was known internationally for his collections and knowledge of primitive art and orchids.

[A brief biography of Kennedy is in the dedication of the special issue honoring him of *Journal of Geophysical Research*, Dec. 10, 1980.]

RAGHU N. SINGH

KENTON, STANLEY NEWCOMB (Dec. 15, 1911–Aug. 25, 1979), composer, bandleader, educator, and pianist, was born in Wichita, Kans., the eldest child of Floyd Kenton and Stella Newcomb. During Kenton's youth, his father was variously a tombstone salesman, mechanic, carpenter, roofer, and operator of several unsuccessful businesses. When Kenton was six weeks old, the family moved from Wichita to La Jara, Colo., and then, in 1917 to Los Angeles, Calif. Kenton, his two sisters, and their mother grew very close because of Floyd's instability and frequent absences from home. To augment the family's income, his mother acquired a piano and began to give lessons in the home.

By 1922 the family had moved to Huntington Park, Calif., where Kenton spent a large amount of time by himself. His mother initially offered piano instruction to his sisters, but neither of them was interested. Kenton, however, was eager to learn the piano, but his mother's teaching technique frustrated his need to play songs by ear and approach the piano on his own terms. In the summer of 1923 the Kentons were visited by Billy and Arthur Kenton, cousins from Portland, Oreg., and Kenton was excited by the music they played, which was influenced by the new "hot" jazz. His mother had abandoned attempts to teach him, and he moved from teacher to teacher.

In 1924 the family moved to Bell, Calif., where Kenton began taking lessons from Frank Hurst, an organist at a Los Angeles theater. By the end of six months, Kenton had begun to make significant progress because of his all-consuming interest in music. After he heard a jazz band perform at one of the beaches near Los Angeles, he began to practice five to ten hours per day. Kenton himself recalled that "from the time I was fourteen years old, I was all music. Nothing else even entered my mind."

Kenton's abilities as a musician led to his election as president of his high school student body in 1928; he also organized groups to play at school and outside functions. Kenton continued his studies with Hurst and by the time he was fifteen had begun to write jazz arrangements. In 1928 he sold his first arrangement (of Drigo's *Serenade*) to a Long Beach group. Hurst had encouraged Stan to listen to the important jazz performers of the day—Benny Carter, Louis Armstrong, and Earl ("Fatha") Hines—and Kenton's writing style was especially influenced by Carter. As Kenton improved as a player and writer, Hurst encouraged him to seek a new teacher, whom Kenton found in Tony Arreta, an important Hollywood and vaudeville music writer. Kenton's studies with Arreta made him aware of the possibilities of arranging and the use of orchestral color and gave him a better understanding of the use of instruments and their timbre.

After graduating from high school, Kenton received an offer from Al Sandstrom to work with Art and Jack Flack's six-piece combo in a San Diego café (actually a speakeasy). The band also played for vaudeville acts and various other entertainers. Kenton returned home within six weeks and found work with area musicians that led to an engagement in Las Vegas, Nev., a stepping-stone for more important professional engagements. He joined the American Jazz Band, a six-piece band led by Frank Gilbert, doubling on piano and banjo and as one of the featured vocalists. He left the Gilbert band after a year and a half and performed with bands throughout the West.

Kenton's first professional break came in 1933, as pianist and arranger for Everett Hoagland's ensemble, which was idolized by many young Californians for its new, advanced form of jazz performances. He next worked as an assistant music director for Earl Carroll's Theater Restaurant and as an arranger for Russ Plummer (1935–1936), Gus Arnheim (1936–1937), and for various movies and radio stations. While working for Plummer, Kenton met Violet Peters; they were married in July 1935. They had one child and were divorced.

In 1937, Kenton decided to give up performing and arranging to devote himself to serious study of composition, theory, harmony, solfège, and conducting. As his teacher he chose Charles Dalmores, a prominent composer, conductor, and classical musician in Los Angeles. After a year of study, Kenton returned to theater work, composing, and working with bands in the area but dissatisfied with these playing experiences. In 1939 and 1940 he planned the formation of his own group. He continued to write "experimental" arrangements but did not record during this period. He felt that his arrangements were musically sound but lacked a unique style. He had considerable experience as a player and as an arranger, but his knowledge of conducting was academic. He then tried to build a repertoire of original compositions and arrangements as a basis for a rehearsal band (an experimental orchestra). The Kentons rented a cabin in the mountains near Idyllwild, Calif., where Kenton worked on his music.

The Kentons then moved back to Los Angeles, where he organized a thirteen-piece rehearsal band. He was able to arrange a performance at the Pavilion, a ballroom in Huntington Beach, in January 1941, which was followed by performances at ballrooms in Los Angeles. The group's enthusiastic reception led to a booking in the Rendezvous Ballroom in Balboa Beach, Calif., for the summer of 1941. The group, first known as the Stan Kenton Orchestra, developed a steady and dedicated following and its big-band sound began to receive wide acclaim throughout the area. Maurice Cohen, owner of the Hollywood Palladium, which had opened in the fall of 1940 and where only the top name bands appeared, hired the band, and it opened on Nov. 25, 1941. Thanks largely to the loyal fans from the Rendezvous, the band drew record-breaking crowds.

The Artistry in Rhythm Orchestra, as the group was called beginning in 1943, was innovative in a number of ways. Kenton had absorbed the teachings of Dalmores and had studied the writings and the playing of the traditional jazz masters (Hines, Carter, Armstrong, and Duke Ellington), as well as the music of George Gershwin. He combined these influences to create a modern big band sound. The orchestra began its first nationwide tour in January 1942 and concluded with a weeklong performance at the Roseland Ballroom in New York City. In 1943, Kenton was hired for Bob Hope's coast-to-coast radio show. After completing thirty-nine weeks with Hope, he left to undertake a second nationwide tour. By 1946 the enlarged Artistry in Rhythm Orchestra (eighteen pieces) had become the country's most popular big band. It was chosen Band of the Year by *Look* magazine, and its members won more than 60 percent of the votes in polls taken by *Down Beat*, *Metronome*, and *Variety*. By 1947 the band had grown to twenty pieces and was known as the Stan Kenton Progressive Jazz Orchestra. In the spring of that year, tickets for its concert schedule in New York City sold out within twenty-four hours. The group was again voted the number-one band in the *Down Beat* poll. In June 1948 more than 15,000 fans attended a Progressive Jazz Orchestra concert at the Hollywood Bowl.

Although the 1950's was a period of decline for most big bands, Kenton and his band continued to attract large audiences, primarily because of the popularity of its recordings. Kenton had begun his recording career with Decca Records in 1941 and switched to Capitol Records in 1943. His continued search for the appropriate combination of jazz and classical music resulted in the forty-three piece Innovations in Modern Music Orchestra, with strings, woodwinds, brass, and percussion. This orchestra made two nationwide tours in 1950 and 1951 and was hailed by the *New York Times* as "the first successful attempt to bridge the gap between classical and jazz music." Even though the response to this group was positive, it was difficult to keep such a large ensemble on the road. Kenton was approached by Capitol to produce a series of recordings introducing new artists and for the band to serve as the backup orchestra, which kept them in the public eye.

While his career had prospered during the 1950's and 1960's, Kenton's personal life was a shambles. After his divorce from Violet, he married Ann Richards, who had sung with the band, on Oct. 18, 1955; they had two children. Because of his daughter's inability to accept Richards, this marriage also ended in divorce. In July 1967, Kenton married Jo Ann Hill; they had no children and were divorced. He spent his last years in the company of his longtime companion and manager, Audree Coke, who indicated that the two were married in Mexico a few years before Kenton's death.

In the 1950's and 1960's, Kenton turned his attention to jazz education. He established the first of his jazz clinics for teenage musicians at Indiana and Michigan State universities in 1959, followed by another at Redlands University in California in 1966. He also founded the Los Angeles Neophonic Orchestra in 1965 and the highly successful Modern Music Tour in 1966, of which *Time* said, "Kenton's orchestra has created the most original sound in music." In the 1960's and 1970's, Kenton's initial experiment with Afro-Cuban music, as seen in his *Cuban Fire* and *Viva Kenton* albums of 1958, was furthered with the addition of a Latin percussionist to his orchestra. He also enlarged the orchestra by experimenting with strings and an expanded brass section. Influences of jazz fusion, as well as the more traditional swing and bop, appeared in his music and his musicians of this period.

Kenton occupies an ambiguous position in the history of jazz and American music. His public success was offset by condemnation by the jazz establishment, and his considerable talents as an arranger and pianist were overshadowed by those of superior sidemen and staff arrangers whom he attracted to his organization. Works by Pete Rugolo, Shorty Rogers, Gerry Mulligan, Neal Hefti, Bill Russo, Johnny Richards, and others enhanced Kenton's reputation as a jazz arranger. The exciting jazz soloists and vocalists who performed with Kenton's groups included Anita O'Day, June Christy, Lee Konitz, Art Pepper, Stan Getz, Zoot Sims, Pepper Adams, Maynard Ferguson, Kai Winding, Laurindo Almeida, and Shelly Manne. Kenton's commitment to perpetuating jazz performance through education was instrumental in the founding of the National (now International) Association of Jazz Educators. He was partly responsible for the appearance of big bands in public school education and a revival of interest in music written in that tradition. He died in Hollywood following a stroke.

[Biographies of Kenton include Hans Joachim Dietzel and Horst H. Lange, *Stan Kenton* (1959); Pete Venudor and Michael Sparke, comps. and eds., *The Standard Stan Kenton Directory* (1968); Christopher A. Pirie and Siegfried Mueller, *Artistry in Kenton* (1969); William F. Lee, *Stan Kenton* (1980); Charles Garrod, *Stan Kenton and His Orchestra*, 3 vols. (1984–1991); and Anthony J. Agostinelli, *Stan Kenton* (1986). An obituary is in the *New York Times*, Aug. 26, 1979.]

WARRICK L. CARTER

KERNER, OTTO, JR. (Aug. 15, 1908–May 9, 1976), governor and federal judge, was born in Chicago, the son of Rose Barbara Chmelik and Otto Kerner, an attorney and federal appellate judge. Raised in the wealthy Chicago suburb of River Forest, he graduated from the prestigious Chicago Latin School in 1926 and went on to earn his B.A. at Brown University in 1930. After spending the 1930–1931 academic year at Trinity College, Cambridge University, Kerner earned his J.D. at Northwestern University Law School in 1934.

On Oct. 20, 1934, Kerner married Helena Cermak Kenlay, daughter of former Chicago mayor Anton Cermak, who had been killed in Miami in March 1933 by an assassin's bullet intended for President Franklin D. Roosevelt. His marriage further cemented his political future in Chicago's sizable Czech community, of which both his father and Mayor Cermak had been longtime leaders. Kerner and his wife had no children, but her daughter from a previous marriage, Mary, had a son and a daughter. When Mary was killed in an automobile accident in 1954, the Kerners adopted her two young children as their own.

After his admission to the Illinois bar in 1934, Kerner joined the law firm of Cooke, Sullivan, and Ricks, where he served for one year as an associate. In 1935 he became a partner in his father's firm, Kerner, Jaros, and Tittle, where he worked chiefly with major corporate clients. His association with the firm lasted until 1947 but was interrupted for five years by military service during World War II.

Having joined the elite Black Horse Troop of the Illinois National Guard in 1934, Kerner was called to active duty as a captain with the Thirty-third Infantry Division of the United States Army in March 1941. A year later he was transferred as a major to the Ninth Infantry Division; in 1942 and 1943 he served with distinction in the North African and Sicilian campaigns. After a brief stint at Fort Sill, Okla., Kerner was promoted to lieutenant colonel and reassigned to the Thirty-second Infantry Division, with which he served in the Philippines and Japan from July to December 1945. He was discharged from active duty in March 1946, but he remained in the National Guard until 1951, when he retired as a major general. For his battlefield service he received the Soldier's Medal and the Bronze Star.

In 1947, Kerner, already a rising star in the Cook County Democratic party, was appointed United States attorney for the Northern District of Illinois. After seven years in that position, in 1954 he was tapped by the Democratic political machine to run for Cook County judge. His election put him in charge of the largest administrative court in the nation. Reelected in 1958, Kerner resigned from his county judgeship in 1960 to run for governor. As the candidate endorsed by the Democratic state convention, he defeated two rivals in the party primary and went on to swamp incumbent Republican governor William G. Stratton in November. His half-million vote victory (2,594,731 to 2,070,479) far exceeded the statewide victory margins of both Democratic presidential candidate John F. Kennedy and popular Democratic senator Paul H. Douglas, establishing him instantly as a major figure in the national party. In 1964 he was reelected by a smaller, but still substantial margin (2,418,394 to 2,239,095 for businessman—and later senator—Charles Percy).

As governor, Kerner faced Republican majorities in both houses of the legislature but nevertheless managed to win approval of his program to improve Illinois state finances, including increases in both the state sales tax and the corporate tax rate. Aided by the general economic prosperity of the early 1960's, the state's financial position improved, benefiting Kerner politically. He also established credentials as a champion of black civil rights, winning passage of a statewide fair employment practices law though failing to obtain open housing legislation. Throughout his two terms, Kerner maintained good relations with the Cook County machine, especially its powerful leader, Chicago mayor Richard J. Daley. But the educated and urbane governor never seemed to fit comfortably with the machine that had launched his career; indeed, his aloof, almost aristocratic, bearing and his reputation for personal integrity were useful to Daley and his colleagues in countering popular stereotypes of them and their work.

Kerner's second term as governor coincided with Lyndon Johnson's presidency and was dominated by the same forces. In 1965, 1966, and 1967, he was forced to mobilize the National Guard in order to quell race-related urban violence (in Chicago in 1965 and 1966, and Cairo in 1967). Kerner's decisive actions in these instances and his long association with the National Guard, coupled with his record as a sincere supporter of civil rights, made him an ideal choice for Johnson, in the wake of rioting in July 1967, to head the President's National Advisory Commission on Civil Disorders. This eleven-member commission included leading figures from both houses of Congress, Roy Wilkins of the National Association for the Advancement of Colored People (NAACP), and other private-sector representatives. In March 1968, in the Kerner Report, the commission captured headlines by pronouncing that the United States was "moving toward two societies, one black and one white—separate and unequal." The report, which called for an ambitious agenda of reforms in housing, law enforcement, employment, and welfare, was greeted enthusiastically by civil rights leaders but lukewarmly by President Johnson, who stated that the billions of dollars needed for such a program would not likely be forthcoming. No major legislation resulted from the commission's report.

Two months before the Kerner Report was released, Kerner had shocked the leaders of both parties in Illinois by announcing that, for personal reasons (widely thought to include the poor state of his wife's health) he would not run for a third term as governor. Whether by prearrangement or not, within a week of the report's issuance, President Johnson nominated him to the United States Court of Appeals for the Seventh Circuit (the same court on which his father had served). Despite the public opposition of South Carolina Republican senator Strom Thurmond, who announced that he was protesting the spirit of the Kerner Report rather than Kerner's specific qualifications as a jurist, he was confirmed by the Senate on a voice vote. In May 1968 he resigned as governor to assume his seat on the bench.

To all outward appearances, Kerner continued to be a model public servant as a circuit court judge. His name had never been linked with corruption, even by his political enemies, and he seemed to have reached the position to which he had always aspired. ("It is my life," he later said of the judgeship.) In mid-December 1971, however, a federal grand jury dropped the bombshell that he was among several former Illinois public officials implicated in illicit stock deals that had been uncovered by a two-and-a-half-year federal investigation into the activities of Illinois horse racing interests. Indicted on nineteen counts of conspiracy, income tax evasion, mail fraud, and lying to a grand jury, Kerner asserted his innocence but asked to be relieved of his duties as judge pending final resolution of the charges; he continued to receive his $42,500 annual salary.

The indictment charged that Kerner (along with his friend, one-time state revenue director Theodore Isaacs) had, as a result of an agreement reached in 1962, purchased $356,000 worth of racing stock in 1966 for only $70,158 (the 1962 price of the stock), then had immediately sold the stock at its face value, reaping a large profit. At the time the initial stock agreement had been made, it was alleged, Kerner had used his influence as governor to benefit the racing officials from whom he purchased the stock; then, after selling the bargain stock, he had falsified his income tax records by dating the date of purchase so that he could record the profits as long-term capital gains and thereby pay a much lower tax rate than he would have had to pay if listing them as regular income. It was further charged that during investigations of the issue by the Internal Revenue Service, Kerner had lied about one of the entries on his 1967 tax return.

On Feb. 19, 1973, following a dramatic thirty-five day trial, Kerner was convicted on seventeen counts—the first sitting federal appeals court judge to be found guilty of a felony. Remaining dignified and civil in this time of crisis, and believing himself the victim of a political vendetta by Republicans (his prosecutor was a future Republican governor of Illinois, James Thompson), Kerner announced immediately after his conviction that he would never give up the battle for vindication. The matter, he contended, was "more important than life itself, because it involves my reputation and honor, which are dearer than life itself." In April 1973, Judge Robert Taylor sentenced him to three years in prison and a fine of $50,000 (terms much lighter than the maximum sentence of eighty-three years in prison and $93,000 in fines). Kerner's appeal was turned down by a Special Court of Appeals in October 1973, and eight months later his last hope for exoneration expired, when the Supreme Court refused to hear the case. On July 29, 1974, with impeachment the only other option, he finally resigned from the bench and began his prison term at the minimum-security Federal Correctional Facility in Lexington, Ky.

The final years of Kerner's life were extremely difficult. In addition to his conviction, the year 1973 saw the death of his wife. In May of the following year, as he was waiting to hear the fate of his appeal to the Supreme Court, he suffered a heart attack. Then, just seven months after his incarceration, he was diagnosed as having advanced lung cancer. On Mar. 6, 1975, he was released from prison to undergo surgery. With a brief respite from illness, Kerner plunged energetically into the cause of prison reform, speaking widely and serving as a consultant to Lewis University's Special Services Center, which was involved in motivational work with prison inmates. Of particular concern to him was the callous handling of prisoners by federal prison administrators. Kerner's financial troubles continued to pile up during 1975, as the tax court denied his earlier claim of a $21,658 deduction for donating his personal papers to the Illinois State Historical Library. In the spring of 1976, his health failed again—this time permanently. After a brief period of hospitalization during which Illinois's two United States senators tried hard, but without success, to persuade President Gerald Ford to grant him a presidential pardon, Kerner died in Chicago.

For all the pain of his felony conviction and removal from the federal bench he so loved, Kerner enjoyed the compensation of substantial public support and goodwill until the end of his life. After his release from prison he was formally honored for his good works by both the Chicago branch of the NAACP and the Illinois Academy of Criminology. Though he never succeeded in disproving the charges on which he was convicted, his many years of effective public service, his unwavering dignity and composure, and especially his humanitarian contributions as an advocate of prison reform in the last year of his life combined to make him seem respectable despite what he referred to as his "indiscretion" while governor.

[There are two collections of Kerner's papers: his official gubernatorial papers are in the Illinois State

Archives, and the Illinois State Historical Library houses his personal and family papers, as well as the bulk of his official papers while serving as governor and federal judge—including many relating to his work as head of the National Advisory Commission and to his appeals of his conviction. No biographical studies of Kerner have been produced. See Hank Messick, *The Politics of Prosecution* (1978), concerning Kerner's trial. Obituaries are in the *Chicago Tribune*, the *New York Times*, and the *Washington Post*, all May 10, 1976.]

GARY W. REICHARD

KIEWIT, PETER (Sept. 12, 1900–Nov. 2, 1979), construction magnate, was born in Omaha, Nebr., the fifth of six children of Anna Schleicker and Peter Kiewit. Although father and son bore the same name, the son never styled himself "Junior."

In 1884, Kiewit's father founded a small masonry contracting firm. Upon his death in 1914, two older sons took over the business, renaming it Peter Kiewit Sons in his honor.

Until his graduation from Omaha's Central High School in 1918, Kiewit worked for his brothers as water boy, timekeeper, carpenter's helper, and finally apprentice bricklayer before entering Dartmouth College, which he left after a year. (In 1960, Dartmouth recognized his brief stay by awarding him an honorary doctor of law degree, a gesture amply reciprocated in 1964 when Kiewit donated $500,000 to Dartmouth for construction of a computer center.)

After returning to Omaha in 1919, Kiewit again worked for his brothers, first as bricklayer, next as foreman, and finally as estimator and construction supervisor. On Jan. 22, 1922, he married Mary Drake, the daughter of a well-known bridge builder. They had two children.

The construction business prospered during the 1920's as it acquired contracts for buildings in and around Omaha. Kiewit's older brothers left the firm, which he reorganized in July 1931 as Peter Kiewit Sons' Company (hereafter PKS) with assets of $125,000 and himself as president and chief stockholder.

Shortly before, Kiewit had undergone what proved to be one of the formative experiences of his life. In 1930 he was stricken with phlebitis, a chronic inflammation of the veins, and after nine months in various hospitals was told by doctors he could never again lead an active life. Kiewit ignored these warnings and resumed work, although for the next fifteen years he was often hospitalized by recurrences of the disease. Because he never knew when illness might incapacitate him, Kiewit developed a management style that would become his trademark—he sought out talented young men, gave them on-the-job training, promoted them to ever more responsible positions if they proved able, and finally allowed them to purchase (nonvoting) shares in the company so that they might prosper with it, with the proviso that they sell back their shares if they left the company. In this way Kiewit built a loyal and highly motivated management team capable of supervising jobs in his absence. However, he retained ultimate control of PKS by keeping all voting stock in his own hands.

PKS grew during the 1930's, for Kiewit felt that the government would attempt to stimulate the depressed economy by means of public works projects, and he borrowed money to buy heavy earth-moving equipment. Thus PKS was in a position to bid successfully for the dam and irrigation projects that soon began under the New Deal.

This intuition was an example of what many construction men saw as Kiewit's uncanny ability to divine the future direction of their industry, for PKS always seemed poised to take advantage of the next boom in building. For instance, Kiewit's expansion of his company's scope of operations despite the depression of the 1930's gave PKS the capacity to undertake over half a billion dollars in defense contracts during World War II.

Meanwhile, in 1941, Kiewit created a holding company, Peter Kiewit Sons Inc. (hereafter PKS Inc.) to control the various companies he had established or acquired. Although PKS, Kiewit's original construction company, remained the most important of the new parent company's subsidiaries, the Kiewit empire consisted of some thirty others by the time of his death.

Where other contractors downsized after the end of the wartime boom, Kiewit diversified into strip mining and quarrying to provide employment for his earth-moving equipment during lean times. Thus PKS was able to take advantage of the highway building boom of the 1950's and in 1952 won a $1.2 billion contract (the second largest ever awarded to that time) to build a plant for the Atomic Energy Commission at Portsmouth, Ohio.

Kiewit was frequently away from home during the years in which he built his business empire, and he and his wife grew apart; they separated in 1943 and divorced in 1951. On July 2, 1952, Kiewit married Evelyn Stotts Newton, the widow of an early business associate. Many who knew the couple credited her with changing her husband's outlook on life. Although he never neglected his various business enterprises, Kiewit became more involved in social, civic, and philanthropic endeavors after his second marriage, serving on the boards of trustees of a number of colleges, universities, museums, and hospitals, and giving over $20 million to such institutions before his death.

In 1962, Samuel Newhouse, who owned a string of newspapers throughout the United States, secretly negotiated to buy the *Omaha World-Herald* from its local owners for $40.1 million. Omaha business and civic leaders were outraged when news of the impending deal leaked out. Kiewit, who normally shunned publicity, dramatically stepped forward at the eleventh hour to save the paper from "foreign" ownership by topping Newhouse's offer, financing the deal himself with surplus cash and securities from the coffers of PKS Inc.

During the 1960's, PKS won contracts for numerous urban transportation projects, and with the onset of an energy crisis in the 1970's, PKS Inc. soon became one of the nation's ten largest coal producers and its profits from mining would rival those of PKS from construction.

In January 1977, Kiewit's second wife died. On Feb. 18, 1978, he married Marjorie Harkins Buchanan, a widow with four grown children and a fellow member of the United Presbyterian Church's national board.

Perhaps because of his early brush with invalidism, Kiewit took a keen interest in medical affairs and physical fitness. In 1976 he received the University of Nebraska's Distinguished Service to Medicine Award and in the same year gave $4 million for the construction of the Kiewit Physical Fitness Center at Creighton University. As his seventy-ninth birthday approached, Kiewit appeared to be in excellent health. However, in August 1979, he was thrown from a horse and hospitalized with broken ribs at Clarkson Hospital in Omaha—already the recipient of over $1 million in Kiewit gifts. In September, he was readmitted to Clarkson, where doctors removed his left lung after discovering a tumor. He left the hospital on October 19, only to be readmitted four days later with a bleeding ulcer. He underwent surgery to correct the problem but died a week later.

Kiewit's will provided for the transfer of PKS Inc. to its employees, for upon his death his voting stock was canceled and henceforth control of the company was based on ownership of common stock—60 percent of which was held by employees. The common stock still owned by Kiewit was transferred to the Peter Kiewit Foundation, which was gradually to sell it to employees and use the proceeds to continue the philanthropic work begun by its founder. Similar arrangements were made for employee ownership and control of the *Omaha World-Herald.*

Nonetheless, an obituary in the *New York Times* introduced a measure of controversy concerning Kiewit's career by suggesting that PKS public works projects had often "dragged far behind schedule at exorbitant costs to taxpayers." The charge did not go unanswered, for the president of Kiewit's *Omaha World-Herald* replied with an able defense of Kiewit's reputation. However, a posthumous taint of scandal arose in 1981 when PKS pleaded "no contest" to charges it had rigged bids for Army Corps of Engineer projects between 1970 and 1976.

[See Harold B. Meyers, "The Biggest Invisible Builder in the World," *Fortune*, Apr. 1966; Hollis J. Limprecht, *The Kiewit Story* (1981); and Jill Bettner, "The Ultimate Meritocracy," *Forbes*, Aug. 1, 1983. Obituaries are in the *Omaha World-Herald*, Nov. 3, 1979; and the *New York Times*, Nov. 4, 1979, with a reply on Dec. 18, 1979.]

ROMAN ROME

KINTNER, ROBERT EDMONDS (Sept. 12, 1909–Dec. 20, 1980), journalist and broadcast company executive, was born in Stroudsburg, Pa., the son of Albert H. Kintner, superintendent of schools in Stroudsburg, and Lillian M. Stofflet. After graduating from Swarthmore College in 1931, he became a reporter with the *Stroudsburg Record* for two years, then joined the staff of the *New York Herald Tribune*, earning $17.50 per week. Initially assigned to Wall Street, he was soon sent to the *Tribune*'s Washington bureau. In 1937, Kintner began a four-year partnership with fellow *Tribune* reporter Joseph Alsop, Jr., producing a syndicated political column titled "Capital Parade," which appeared in ninety-five newspapers nationwide. The collaboration also produced two popular books, *Men Around the President* (1939) profiling President Franklin D. Roosevelt's New Deal political advisers, and *American White Paper: American Diplomacy and the Second World War* (1940) anticipating Roosevelt's response to war in Europe. Kintner and Alsop also wrote political commentary for popular magazines, including the *Saturday Evening Post* and *Life*. On Mar. 9, 1940, Kintner married Jean Rodney, a theatrical producer; they had three children.

In 1941 the war effort ended the "Capital Parade" partnership; both reporters joined the armed services, with Kintner serving in the War Department Bureau of Public Relations of the Army Air Force. He received a medical discharge in 1944, as a lieutenant colonel, after suffering the lifetime loss of hearing in the right ear following a precipitous drop in altitude during a flight over North Africa. Kintner began his broadcasting industry career in 1944, as director of public relations for the American Broadcasting Company (ABC), originally the Blue Network of the National Broadcasting Company (NBC). It had been purchased from NBC by Edward J. Noble, who had made his fortune inventing Life Saver candies. By war's end Kintner headed the radio system's fledgling news operation. In 1948, ABC inaugurated television service in competition with the Dumont Network, NBC, and the Columbia Broadcasting System. On Jan. 1, 1950, Noble named Kintner ABC president with a seven-year contract at $75,000 per year.

Kintner's personality and drive suited the needs of the struggling network. Kintner kept his own counsel in a brusque, often moody, manner. Tough, confident, and inexhaustible, the five-foot, nine-inch, 180-pound executive badgered subordinates and was often intolerant of the mistakes of others. A heavy drinker and chain smoker, the hard-driving Kintner slept little, often arriving at his office at 6 A.M., monitoring the company's smallest details and harassing secretaries to tears. At times, a softer side would emerge, characterized by thoughtful gestures, gracious notes, and gifts. Kintner was given to bow ties and expensive suits; his trademark was his cuff links, of which he reportedly owned two hundred pairs. Cataracts troubled him throughout his adult life; he had operations on both eyes and wore thick-lensed glasses.

Kintner's personal drive brought significant results despite his shoestring budgets. During his seven-year ABC tenure he directed the third-place network toward profitability and respect by combining police and Western action series with a viable and extensive news operation. Kintner added sixty television stations to the ABC affiliate network while reducing a 1949 debt of $519,000 to $142,000 in 1952, and finally turning a profit of $5.2 million in 1955. In 1951 he accepted a special Peabody Award presented to ABC for refusing to cooperate with *Red Channels'* anti-Communist blacklist. In 1954, Kintner was praised for his decision to televise the Army-McCarthy hearings.

Despite his success Kintner was forced to resign as ABC president in October 1956, three years after the ABC-United Paramount Theaters merger created a new corporate management team under Leonard Goldenson. Kintner resented his new executive subordinates. Personality clashes arose, references to Kintner's excessive drinking increased, and Goldenson noted that ABC's financial success had not matched that of network rivals. Within three months of his departure from ABC, Kintner was hired by NBC as executive vice-president in charge of the color television development program. In July 1958, Kintner succeeded Robert Sarnoff as president of NBC, becoming the first person to be chief executive officer of two broadcast networks.

Mirroring his ABC experience, Kintner made NBC a solid second network behind CBS, promoting action dramatic series and an aggressive, expansive news department. He established NBC News as a separate network division and the biggest in the industry, keying on the success of news anchormen Chet Huntley and David Brinkley to surpass CBS in news-viewer popularity. News programming provided a solid viewer base leading into the nighttime entertainment lineup.

When network quiz show scandals rocked the industry, an embarrassed Kintner appeared before a congressional investigating committee in November 1959, publicly apologizing for his network's involvement and blaming the show's producers for the deception. He initiated the "NBC White Paper" series, telling his corporate colleagues that the way to regain viewer confidence was with an energized news department that represented a higher level of programming.

NBC grossed $500 million in billings in 1965, which reportedly accounted for 25 percent of the earnings of the parent company, Radio Corporation of America. As a reward for his success, Kintner in September was designated chairman of the board and president of NBC, with a salary of $200,000 per year and a seat on the RCA board of directors. However, within three months, he was fired. Apparently his alcoholism, generally controlled since his arrival at NBC, had flared up again, convincing RCA president Robert Sarnoff that Kintner was unable to assume his new responsibilities.

As part of a ten-year, $583,000 severance settlement, Kintner remained with NBC until Apr. 1, 1966, when he became a special assistant to President Lyndon B. Johnson, a friend since the 1930's, in Washington, D.C. Kintner's responsibilities, at $30,000 per year, included directing the White House research and speech writing office, presiding over White House staff meetings, setting the agenda for cabinet meetings, recruiting business executives for government service, and advising the president on "image" matters. As a result of failing eyesight and the prospect of surgery, Kintner was forced to resign his White House duties in June 1967. He died in Washington, D.C.

[Short personal profiles of Kintner are in *Time*, Nov. 16, 1959; *Newsweek*, Dec. 20, 1965; and the *New York Times*, Oct. 24, 1965, and June 14, 1967. His tenure at ABC is discussed in Sterling Quinlan, *Inside ABC* (1979); and at NBC in Reuven Frank, *Out of Thin Air* (1991). An obituary is in the *New York Times*, Dec. 23, 1980.]

DAVID BERNSTEIN

KIRCHWEY, FREDA (Sept. 26, 1893–Jan. 3 1976), journalist, editor, and publisher, was born Mary Frederika Kirchwey in Lake Placid, N.Y., one of four children of George Washington Kirchwey, a law professor and criminologist, and Dora Child Wendell, a high school English teacher. Her early years were influenced by an extended family that at various times included her paternal grandparents, paternal aunts, and her maternal grandmother.

Kirchwey received an excellent formal education at the Horace Mann schools in New York City and at Barnard College, from which she graduated in 1915 with a major in history. She credited much of her education to dinner table conversations with her highly educated family and to participation in the progressive reforms of her day. She joined the picket line of a shirtwaist factory workers' strike; she worked for woman suffrage. She learned best by firsthand experiences, and she made sense of her world by writing about it as early as high school and college. At Barnard she wrote editorials to get sororities (then called fraternities) abolished because of their discriminatory nature; she prevailed. Upon graduation from Barnard College she started her first job; she also married Evans Clark in a civil ceremony on Nov. 9, 1915, keeping her maiden name. The Kirchwey-Clarks had three sons, two of whom died in childhood.

Kirchwey's first paid position in journalism was writing for a sporting newspaper, *The Morning Telegraph* (1915–1916), where she continued using words to advocate her causes. In this case, she manipulated her assignments to cover news for the society page into clever stories advocating woman suffrage. For several months in 1918 she was an editorial assistant on *Every Week*, a literary magazine, until its demise in June, and then she spent two months with the *New York Tribune*. In August of that year, Kirchwey applied for an opening on the *Nation*, asking managing editor, Henry R. Mussey, her former economics professor, to recommend her. She wrote, "If you think I'm the man for the job, will you put in a word for me?" She jointed the staff of the newly reorganized crusading journal under the editorship of Oswald Garrison Villard. In 1918 she began her lifelong career on the *Nation*, one of the oldest American political journals. She was hired to read, clip, and file articles for the journal's International Relations Section (IRS). Soon she wrote pieces for this section, and in June 1919 she was promoted to editor of the IRS. Kirchwey read all that she could to understand the changing world, and she talked to people whom she respected to expand her knowledge. During those formative years of building an expertise in international affairs, Kirchwey came to know and respect Chaim Weizmann and his support of Zionism. This early and continuing friendship profoundly influenced her positions later in her life. During World War II she would advocate a homeland for the Jews.

Kirchwey influenced the journal's policies as she advanced into increasing positions of authority on the *Nation*, becoming the managing editor in 1922, literary editor in 1928, and executive editor of a board of four in 1933. By 1937, she owned, edited, and published the journal. In 1943, to offset difficult financial times, Kirchwey transferred ownership of the

Nation into a nonprofit organization called Nation Associates. She remained president of Nation Associates, and editor and publisher of the *Nation*, until her retirement in 1955.

Kirchwey's writings touched on many important themes in social and political history. In the 1920's she was particularly interested in changing mores and relationships between men and women. She used her journal to explore these issues, soliciting articles for a series titled "New Morals for Old." Such diverse writers as Charlotte Perkins Gilman, Joseph Wood Krutch, H. L. Mencken, and Beatrice Hinkle contributed to the series, which Kirchwey later edited into the book *Our Changing Morality* (1924). In another series, "These Modern Women," (1926–1927) in the *Nation*, she asked a number of prominent women (whose identities were not disclosed) to share their points of view on men, marriage, children, and jobs. She showed her reliance on psychology, the science of the 1920's, by having the life stories of these women analyzed in the *Nation* by a neurologist, a behaviorist psychologist, and a Jungian psychoanalyst.

Kirchwey may have been searching for answers from these women, since she and Evans were experiencing marital difficulties at the time. Early in 1930, when their son Jeffrey became very ill, they called a marital truce. Kirchwey took a leave of absence to try to nurse Jeffrey back to health, but to no avail. After his death she took almost three years off before coming back to work full-time. When she did return, she merged her life with that of the *Nation* to an inordinate degree. Kirchwey also changed her focus from domestic issues and those having to do with women to international affairs. In part this was due to the rise of international fascism.

During the 1930's, 1940's, and 1950's, Kirchwey focused the *Nation*'s coverage on problems arising from the Great Depression and the spread of fascism. She filled the *Nation* with details of the horrors in Nazi Germany and fascist Spain. She began to call herself a "militant liberal" and insisted that the *Nation*, which had been a pacifist journal, begin to advocate collective security, and, eventually, war. She pressed for homes for refugees from fascism, and specifically a national homeland for the Jews. When the United States declared war, Kirchwey gave a voice to those leaders ousted from power by fascists in their countries by publishing their views in a new "Political War" section of the *Nation*.

During World War II and thereafter, Kirchwey fought against censorship and for civil liberties. She wrote about the devastating effects of the atomic bomb in Hiroshima and Nagasaki and held a public forum to contemplate the terrible results of this new technology and the need for public control and peaceful uses of atomic power. She published the results of that forum in the book *The Atomic Era: Can It Bring Peace and Abundance?* (1950).

After she retired from the *Nation* in 1955, Kirchwey continued to write about and work for issues that mattered to her. She wrote articles for the *Gazette and Daily* of York, Pa., and was the Women's International League for Peace and Freedom's delegate to the United Nations. She continued her long-term commitment to restoring democratic rule to Spain by work on the Committee for a Democratic Spain. Her husband died in 1970. Kirchwey died in St. Petersburg, Fla.

[The Freda Kirchwey Papers at Schlesinger Library, Radcliffe College, contain extensive correspondence, speeches, and writings. While information about Kirchwey appears in many archives of figures of her day, the Dorothy Kirchwey Brown Papers, Schlesinger Library and the Oswald Garrison Villard Papers, Houghton Library, Harvard, are most helpful.

Kirchwey's many unsigned editorials are in the annotated copies of the *Nation* in the New York Public Library (although they may not be available owing to their extremely fragile state).

Secondary literature includes Warner Oliver, "Oh, Stop That, Freda," *Saturday Evening Post*, Feb. 9, 1946; and Sara Alpern, *Freda Kirchwey: A Woman of the Nation* (1987), and "In Search of Freda Kirchwey," in Sara Alpern, J. Antler, E. I. Perry, and I. W. Scobie, eds., *The Challenge of Feminist Biography* (1992). Obituaries are in the *New York Times*, Jan. 4, 1976; the *Washington Post*, Jan. 10, 1976; Carey McWilliams, "The Freda Kirchwey I Knew," the *Nation*, Jan. 17, 1976; and *Barnard Bulletin*, Jan. 26, 1976.]

SARA ALPERN

KIRKUS, VIRGINIA (Dec. 7, 1893–Sept. 10, 1980), literary critic and author, was born in Meadville, Pa., the daughter of Frederick Maurice Kirkus, an Episcopal clergyman, and Isabella Clark. Kirkus spent her early childhood in Wilmington, Del., where her father was for twenty-five years rector of Trinity Church. She attended the Missus Hebbs School in Wilmington and the Hannah More Academy in Reisterstown, Md. In 1916 she graduated from Vassar College, where she majored in English, and in 1917 she took education courses at Teachers College of Columbia University.

Kirkus's first employment was teaching English and history for three years at the Greenhill School in Wilmington. In 1920 she returned to New York City to become assistant fashion editor for *Pictorial Review*, then edited the "back of the book" section of *McCall's* magazine and wrote her first book, *Everywoman's Guide to Health and Personal Beauty* (1922). In 1923 she edited *Robert Bacon, Life and Letters*.

Around 1925, Kirkus became head of the children's books department of Harper and Brothers, where she continued until 1932, when the Great Depression forced Harper's to discontinue publishing children's books. The firm gave Kirkus six months to look for another position; she spent two months visiting her family in Europe, where her father was temporarily assigned to the American Church in Munich.

During her homeward voyage, Kirkus decided that instead of taking another editorial job she would start a new service for booksellers, providing them with prepublication reviews of books, as guides to their ordering and promotion. By January 1933, Kirkus had persuaded twenty publishers to let her review advance proofs of their new books, and the Virginia Kirkus Bookshop Service began sending review bulletins to her first ten bookseller subscribers, who paid $10 per month for the service. After three months she established a sliding scale for subscriptions, ranging from $2.50 per month for small shops to $15 for the largest. During the first year she reviewed almost a thousand books, and established a reputation that rapidly increased the size of her clientele and encouraged publishers to provide her with galley proofs. In 1935, Kirkus was persuaded by Joseph Wheeler, director of the Enoch Pratt Library in Baltimore, to offer her service to libraries. By the mid-1950's her rates for library subscriptions ranged from $19 to $32, depending on the size of their book budgets. Kirkus also added book clubs, literary agents, radio and television stations, and even publishers to her list of clients. By 1950 she had over 1,500 subscribers and four assistants, and she was reviewing more than 4,000 books per year.

In 1935, with Frank Scully, Kirkus wrote two children's books of games, *Fun in Bed for Children* and *Junior Fun in Bed*. On June 4, 1936, Kirkus married Frank Glick, personnel director of a New York City department store; they had no children. The ceremony was performed by her father and Rabbi Samuel H. Goldman. In 1943 the Virginia Kirkus Bookshop Service was located at 38 Bank Street, in Greenwich Village, where they had an apartment above the ground-floor office space of her business.

The Glicks had a country house in Redding Ridge, Conn. It was the subject of Kirkus's book *A House for the Weekends* (1940), in which she described the joys of restful rural weekends and gave advice on acquiring, restoring, and maintaining a weekend cottage in the country. Another book derived from the house in Redding Ridge was *The First Book of Gardening* (1956). Kirkus was also a frequent contributor to the *Saturday Review*.

Kirkus retired in 1962 and moved her permanent residence from New York City to Redding Ridge. In 1971 she sold her business, which then had 4,600 subscribers, to the *New York Review of Books*. At that time she judged that her evaluations of the 16,000 books she had reviewed during the past thirty years had been right about 85 percent of the time. She admitted, for example, underestimating Hervey Allen's *Anthony Adverse*, which she thought was too long, and Thomas Wolfe's *Of Time and the River*, which she thought "would have only snob appeal." On the other hand, she anticipated the success of such books as John Steinbeck's *Tortilla Flat*, Alan Paton's *Cry, the Beloved Country*, Ernestine Gilbreth Carey's *Cheaper By the Dozen*, Herman Wouk's *The Caine Mutiny*, and many more.

Kirkus was a member of the Cosmopolitan Club of New York, P.E.N., the American Library Association, and the League of Women Voters. In one of her biographical summaries she said that her principal recreational interests were horseback riding and dancing. During World War II she served on the selection board for Armed Services Editions and on the Booksellers Authority, in Washington, D.C. She was president of the Mark Twain Library in 1953 and 1954 and was a member of the Governor's Commission on Rural Libraries in Connecticut from 1961 to 1964.

Kirkus died in Danbury, Conn.

[A story on the tenth anniversary of the Bookshop Service is in *Publishers' Weekly*, Mar. 27, 1943.

Obituaries are in the *New York Times*, Sept. 11, 1980; and *A.L.A. Yearbook*, 1981.]

DAVID W. HERON

KNOWLES, JOHN HILTON (May 23, 1926–Mar. 6, 1979), physician, physiologist, and foundation administrator, was born in Chicago, the son of James Knowles, a business executive, and Jean Laurence Turnbull, an artist. His father had been a World War I flying ace and eventually retired as vice-president of the Rexall Drug Company. Many of the Knowles's ancestors were physicians, including his grandfather, Frederick M. Turnbull, a psychiatrist at Massachusetts General Hospital (MGH); but it was the influence of Dr. George Klinkerfuess, a general practitioner in Normandy, Mo., that settled the eight-year-old on a career in medicine. The family had moved to Normandy when Knowles was an infant; when he was about twelve, they moved to suburban Belmont, Mass.

Knowles was a star athlete in several sports at Belmont Hill School, as well as a fine pianist, but was not distinguished for his academic achievements. The same was true at Harvard, from which he received his B.A. in 1947. Knowles won letters as a baseball pitcher, a hockey goalie, and a squash player. With his classmate Jack Lemmon, the future Academy Award winner, he played jazz piano, composed show music, and acted in a Hasty Pudding revue.

Ten of the eleven medical schools to which Knowles applied, including Harvard, rejected him. Although his academic record at Harvard was poor, he did very well as a medical student at Washington University in St. Louis (1947–1951), receiving his M.D. cum laude and winning awards in both internal medicine and pathology. This change in his academic success can be ascribed to his newly serious attitude; he applied himself diligently to the scholarly pursuits that his many extracurricular activities had previously enticed him to neglect.

Knowles served his internship at MGH from 1951 to 1952. One day in the emergency room he met a new cytology technician, Edith Morris LaCroix, whose assignment was to help him pump the stomach of a person who had taken an overdose of pills. Knowles and LaCroix were married on June 13, 1953, and had six children.

Except for service from 1953 to 1955 as a lieutenant in the Naval Reserve Medical Corps, administering the cardiopulmonary laboratory at the Portsmouth (Va.) Naval Hospital and from 1956 to 1957 as a postdoctoral fellow in physiology at the universities of Rochester and Buffalo, Knowles was at MGH for twenty years, working his way up through the ranks. He was assistant resident in medicine from 1952 to 1953, resident in medicine from 1955 to 1956, chief resident in medicine from 1958 to 1959, chief of the Pulmonary Disease Unit from 1959 to 1961, director of medical affairs from 1961 to 1962, and general director from 1962 to 1972 the youngest in MGH's history. All the while he taught intermittently at Harvard Medical School, becoming professor of medicine in 1969.

In the late 1950's, Knowles's primary interest shifted from clinical medicine to the social, political, and economic aspects of medicine. He soon became an outspoken and controversial critic of the health-care establishment in speeches, press interviews, articles (both popular and scholarly), and books. He was especially critical of the private sector and was an early supporter of Medicare to alleviate the callousness of the health-care delivery system. He also advocated that hospitals and other health-care institutions emphasize preventive rather than curative medicine, which was potentially more beneficial to patients, but more difficult to administer and less profitable for individual physicians. Such attitudes did not endear Knowles to the American Medical Association (AMA), although the American Hospital Association strongly endorsed him.

The notorious "fight" between Knowles and the AMA was in reality a dispute between Secretary of Health, Education, and Welfare Robert H. Finch and the AMA, with Knowles caught in the middle. Just before President Richard Nixon's first inauguration in 1969, secretary-designate Finch told both Nixon and Knowles that Knowles was his first choice to be assistant secretary for health and scientific affairs. Nixon promised Finch that he would appoint Knowles to this post if Finch could garner sufficient support for Knowles within the health-care community. Nearly every important professional medical association supported Knowles except the most important one, the AMA, a very conservative group and traditionally a heavy contributor to Republican coffers.

The AMA never disclosed publicly its specific objection to Knowles. It merely presented a list of its own recommendations for the position, conspicuously omitting Knowles's name. Depending upon which source one consults, the AMA opposed him either because of his views as such, however he presented them, or because he was flamboyant and a gadfly, whatever his views. Nixon finally succumbed to pressure, both from the AMA and from members of Congress who were beholden to the AMA, and in June 1969 selected Roger O. Egeberg instead of Knowles. Apparently Egeberg was more acceptable to the AMA because he was more subdued. The irony was that Egeberg and Knowles held similar ideas about the role of medicine in society.

From 1972 until the end of his life, concurrent with being professor of medicine at New York University, Knowles was president of the Rockefeller Foundation. He loved this work best of all. In retrospect, even though he would have accepted the federal appointment if it had been offered, Knowles doubted he could have survived long as a Washington, D.C., insider, and after government service the trustees of the Rockefeller Foundation probably would not have been interested in him.

As a philanthropic administrator, Knowles's main goal was to increase the leadership and participation of the private sector in socioeconomic change. He believed in the people leading themselves, not in the government leading the people, but also that if the people did not lead themselves, then the government would have to step in and take them by the nose. In order to prevent this kind of intervention, Knowles looked for ways to encourage private citizens to help make health care more equitably delivered and of better quality. Under his guidance, the Rockefeller Foundation also undertook projects in international agricultural development, energy conservation, and peacemaking. His focus was always on what the individual could do if given the right tools and the right motivation, not on what the group could do for the individual.

Knowles died at MGH in Boston after a brief struggle with pancreatic cancer.

[Knowles was the author of *Respiratory Physiology and Its Clinical Applications* (1959) and the editor of *Hospitals, Doctors, and the Public Interest* (1965); *The Teaching Hospital* (1966); *Views of Medical Education and Medical Care* (1968); and *Doing Better and Feeling Worse: Health in the United States* (1977). Obituaries are in the *New York Times*, Mar. 7, 1979; and *Forum on Medicine*, Aug. 1979.]

ERIC V. D. LUFT

KOHLER, WALTER JODOK, JR. (Apr. 4, 1904–Mar. 21, 1976), industrialist, politician, and governor, was born in Sheboygan, Wis., the son of Walter J. Kohler, Sr., and Charlotte Henrietta Shroeder. His father was president of the Kohler Company, a manufacturer of bathroom fixtures and, from 1929 to 1931, was the Republican governor of Wisconsin.

After completing grade school in Sheboygan, Kohler graduated from Phillips Academy in Andover, Mass., in 1921 and graduated from Yale with a Ph.B. in 1924. He then joined the Kohler Company, where he was active in engineering and ceramic research. In 1929 he moved into marketing and sales. He became a director in 1936 and corporate secretary a year later.

Kohler became a lieutenant in the Naval Reserve in 1942 and went on active duty in 1943 as an air combat intelligence officer in the Pacific. He participated in the Solomon Islands campaign that year and served on the aircraft carrier *Hancock* in 1944 and 1945. Kohler returned to the Kohler Company when the war ended and in 1947 became president of the Vollrath Company, founded by a maternal great-grandfather.

In 1948, Kohler entered politics as a delegate at large in the Republican National Convention in Philadelphia. Two years later, when Governor Oscar Rennebohm of Wisconsin announced he would not seek a third term, Kohler obtained the Republican nomination and defeated Democrat Carl Thompson for the governorship. In 1952 he defeated William Proxmire to win a second term, receiving 400,000 more votes than his Democratic opponent. These same candidates were in opposition again in 1954, with Kohler winning a bare 51 percent of the vote. During these six years the Republicans held a decisive majority in both houses of the Wisconsin legislature (never fewer than 25 seats in the 33-seat state senate, nor fewer than 88 of the 100-seat state assembly), all executive offices, both United States Senate seats, and at least eight of ten seats in the House of Representatives.

During his three terms, Kohler took advantage of a supportive legislature to cut income taxes and raise salaries of government employees. There was continuation from the Rennebohm governorship of an extensive building program for the University of Wisconsin, the state college system, and needed state buildings. In agriculture there was an extensive program of disease control among farm animals, particularly cattle.

Kohler declined to run for a fourth term in 1956. However, when the controversial Senator Joseph McCarthy died in 1957, he ran for the remainder of his Senate term. Kohler won the Republican primary against six other candidates and opposed Democrat William Proxmire, who had failed to unseat Kohler when they sought election in 1952 and 1954. This time Proxmire defeated Kohler by more than 120,000 votes. Kohler returned to Sheboygan to become chairman of the board of the Vollrath Company.

Kohler's position on Senator McCarthy in the election of 1952 has a peculiar relevance to his own political stance. In 1951, McCarthy had been critical of the loyalty of General George C. Marshall in connection with his search for traitors in the federal government. When Dwight Eisenhower was campaigning for the presidency in 1952, he was openly critical of McCarthy's attack on General Marshall in a speech in Denver, and it was anticipated that Eisenhower would defend Marshall's loyalty in a forthcoming speech in Milwaukee. However, Kohler and others boarded Eisenhower's train on the way to Milwaukee and persuaded Eisenhower not to discuss the Marshall matter further in Wisconsin, in order not to jeopardize McCarthy's chances for reelection.

Kohler married Celeste McVoy Holden on Nov. 14, 1932. They had two children, and were divorced in 1946. On Nov. 8, 1948, Kohler married Charlotte McAleer; they had no children.

During his later years Kohler was active in various civic causes, particularly the American Cancer Society. He also was a member of the American Legion, Veterans of Foreign Wars, and several other military and fraternal organizations. He died in Sheboygan, Wis.

[There is a vast collection of Kohler's speeches and documents about his political activities in the Archives of the State Historical Society of Wisconsin. Obituaries are in the *Capital Times* (Madison), Mar. 22 and 27, 1976; *Wisconsin State Journal*, Mar. 23, 1976; and the *New York Times*, Mar. 23, 1976.]

AARON J. IHDE

KOSTELANETZ, ANDRE (Dec. 22, 1901–Jan. 13, 1980), orchestra conductor, was born in St. Petersburg, Russia, the son of Nachman Kostelanetz and Rosalie Dimscha. Both of his parents were amateur musicians and encouraged their son's musical interests. It is said that one day, when he was five, he was enjoying a band concert in a park while on a vacation in Germany with his parents. Inspired by the music, young Andre started to conduct, and when the bandleader paused to observe the child's efforts, the musicians responded to the direction of the small conductor. He attended St. Peter's School from 1911 to 1918, and was a student of conducting at the St. Petersburg Conservatory from 1920 until 1922. He supported himself by working as an accompanist and coach at the Mariinsky Opera until it closed in February 1922. Although emigration from Russia was illegal, he then left the country and rejoined his family, who had previously gone to New York. He was hired as a rehearsal accompanist at the Metropolitan Opera in New York City. Kostelanetz met George Gershwin at the latter's New York apartment in 1926, and over the years Gershwin's music constituted one focus for his conducting talents. He became a naturalized American citizen in 1928.

In 1930, Kostelanetz was named conductor of the CBS Broadcasting System's symphony orchestra. His musicianship contributed to the success of a number of radio programs, particularly the "Chesterfield Hour." During his early years on the radio, Kostelanetz developed his own instrumentation and microphone technique, which others emulated. A number of big band leaders who later achieved fame, including Jimmy and Tommy Dorsey, Glenn Miller, and Mitch Miller, played for Kostelanetz during the early 1930's. Major opera and instrumental soloists, notably Rosa Ponselle, Lawrence Tibbett, Lucrezia Bori, Kirsten Flagstad, and Jascha Heifetz, were featured on the "Chesterfield Hour." While some early critics regarded Kostelanetz as a mere popularizer, a majority came to recognize his intelligence, efficiency, and musicianship. He was well known in the industry for the excellent results he got from his musicians despite a minimum number of rehearsals. Many of his recorded interpretations of the music of popular composers of the day were well received, although purists objected to his medleys of classical selections and popular music.

Kostelanetz enjoyed an enormous success as a recording artist, producing more than two hundred recordings for Columbia Records that earned $52 million in sales. He also conducted the musical scores for several Hollywood films. In 1936 he directed his future wife, the soprano Lily Pons, in the film *That Girl From Paris.* They were married on June 2, 1938, and were divorced in 1958; the couple had no children. Kostelanetz's 1960 marriage to Sara Gene Orcutt, a medical technologist, ended in divorce in 1969.

During World War II, Kostelanetz led a number of orchestras consisting of uniformed personnel in Europe, Southeast Asia, and North Africa. In the early 1940's he identified and purchased a device that made it possible for his musicians to determine whether they were using the proper pitch without having to rely entirely on the ear. Word of this innovation soon reached the United States Navy, which made use of it in conjunction with its sonar system. The machine played a vital role in helping the Allies locate enemy submarines.

In the late 1930's, Kostelanetz first conducted summer concerts for the New York Philharmonic, and in 1953, as guest conductor, began a series of recordings with that orchestra. In May 1963 he originated and directed a series of Promenade concerts in Philharmonic Hall, New York City, during the months of May and June, normally considered an unpropitious time of year for such an initiative. These events became increasingly popular and helped expand the Philharmonic's audience. Kostelanetz remained their artistic director for sixteen years. The repertoire for these concerts often featured seldom-heard compositions by well-known composers, mixed with premieres of new compositions, standard "pops" selections, and encores rarely if ever heard at regular Philharmonic concerts. The series was finally ended in 1978 because of its prohibitively high cost of production. From 1974 to 1979, Kostelanetz also led a series of summer concerts in New York's Central Park. One such occasion in the summer of 1979 drew an audience of between 200,000 and 250,000 persons, believed to be a record for a concert of serious music. Total attendance during that six-year period was estimated at approximately 1 million persons. Kostelanetz served as a guest conductor of the Philharmonic for twenty-seven consecutive seasons (1952–1979), longer than any other person in its history. He also led many of the major orchestras of the United States, Europe, Japan, and Israel.

As a conductor, Kostelanetz gave a good deal of attention to the music of the nineteenth-century European romantics, but he also put considerable emphasis on the work of twentieth-century American composers. He commissioned a number of works by prominent American composers, including Virgil Thomson, Alan Hovhaness, Ferde Grofé, Aaron Copland, Jerome Kern, William Schuman, Paul Creston, and others. A good many of these have remained in the standard concert repertoire. Kostelanetz once commented, "If I can leave an inheritance of a growing audience for the concert hall, I have accomplished everything. All the rest are second-class accomplishments." A mild-mannered individual who achieved considerable success and became wealthy, he was able to indulge his love for valuable works of European and Oriental art. He died of a heart attack while vacationing in Port-au-Prince, Haiti.

[Kostelanetz's memoirs, *Echoes* (1981), were written with Gloria Hammond; there is no published biography. See Howard Shanet, *Philharmonic* (1975). Obituaries are in the *New York Times* and the *Washington Post*, both Jan. 15, 1980.]

KEIR B. STERLING

KOUSSEVITZKY, OLGA NAUMOFF (July 15, 1901–Jan. 5, 1978), patroness of the arts and wife of conductor Serge Koussevitzky, was born in Samara (now Kuibyshev), Russia, the daughter of Alexander Naumoff and Anna Ouchkoff. Her father was a minister in the imperial government. Her mother was a member of the wealthy Ouchkoff family, tea importers and patrons of the arts. Olga Naumoff was educated privately. In 1917 the Russian Revolution forced her family to flee to the West, where they settled in Nice, France.

In 1929, Naumoff accompanied her aunt Natalia and Natalia's husband, the orchestra conductor Serge Koussevitzky, to the United States as companion and secretary. Natalia Ouchkoff had married Serge Koussevitzky in 1905. She used her wealth to promote her husband's talent and vision. In 1909 the Koussevitzkys had acquired a music publishing company and in 1910, a symphony orchestra. He published the work of young Russian composers, such as Sergei Prokofiev, Sergei Rachmaninoff, Aleksander Scriabin, and Igor Stravinsky, and subsequently introduced the new music in his concerts. In 1920 he and his wife fled Russia. He continued to publish and perform the music of young European composers, such as Arthur Honegger, Maurice Ravel, and Albert Roussel. In 1924 he was hired to conduct the Boston Symphony and during his twenty-five years there he premiered 110 new works, the majority of them by American composers, such as Samuel Barber, Aaron Copland, Roy Harris, Walter Piston, and William Schuman, in effect establishing their careers. In this environment, Olga Naumoff became acquainted with many of the important musical personalities of her time.

Koussevitzky desired to bring music to ever-larger audiences. In the summer of 1936 he began to perform at the Berkshire Music Festival at Tanglewood in Lenox, Mass., which has grown into one of the world's most famous and ambitious summer music festivals. In 1940 he established the Berkshire Music Center, a summer school for talented young musicians, where he taught conducting; young Leonard Bernstein was a student in his first class. Staff and students maintained ties throughout their lives, forming a network of America's musical elite. By 1969 the festival and school were staffed by alumni, as Koussevitzky had envisioned.

In 1941, Naumoff became an American citizen. The following year her aunt Natalia died. On Aug. 15, 1947, Naumoff and Serge Koussevitzky were married at Seranak, his home at Tanglewood.

In 1949, Koussevitzky retired from the Boston Symphony Orchestra. Leonard Bernstein and the Koussevitzkys traveled to Israel, where the two men were to conduct the Israel Philharmonic. Koussevitzky observed the close bond between her husband and Bernstein. "He came to regard him almost as a son," she said. Koussevitzky died on June 4, 1951. That year his wife served as president of the Koussevitzky Music Foundation, which he had established to commission new music, and to give awards, scholarships, and prizes at the Berkshire Music Center. In this capacity, Koussevitzky continued her husband's mission: "I saw the path he lighted for those of us who were close to him—his associates and pupils." In 1956 she served as president of the American International Music Fund. She also served on the scholarship fund of the International Federation of Music Clubs.

In addition, Koussevitzky supported the Harlem School of the Arts, the Benjamin Britten Club, the Nadia Boulanger Memorial Fund, and the MacDowell Colony. In 1961 she was president of the Musicians Club of New York, which awards cash prizes and performance opportunities to young musicians. Among Koussevitzky's awards for service were the Spirit of Achievement Award, given by the Albert Einstein College of Medicine, and the Medal of Honor of the National Arts Club.

Koussevitzky's talent for caricature was evident from her teens, when she drew family members and acquaintances as a hobby. Gradually she amassed a sizable collection of these pictures. She illustrated critic Samuel Chotzinoff's book of interviews, *A Little Night Music* (1964). In 1971, the Hammond Museum in northern Westchester County, N.Y., mounted an exhibition of her caricatures, "Captured Moments," that included such musical figures as Vladimir Horowitz, Igor Stravinsky, and Arturo Toscanini. Koussevitzky recalled, "I would meet these great personalities, see them perform, and later in the evening or the next morning I would do a caricature from memory. The stronger the musical impression, the easier it was to do the caricature."

Koussevitzky remained active in the music world to the end of her life. She was a familiar figure at concerts in New York City in winter and at the Berkshire Music Festival in summer, where she opened the festival. On the Sunday closest to July 26, the anniversary of her husband's birthday, she held a memorial service and served slices of birthday cake at Koussevitzky's graveside.

At her death in New York City, Leonard Bernstein commented, "How I shall miss our dear Olga—that fragile Rock of Gibraltar on whom so many of us depended for significant links with a past of love and beauty."

[The scores of the compositions commissioned by the Serge Koussevitzky Musical Foundation are in the Library of Congress. In 1967 a collection of documents, scores, and memorabilia was given to the Music Department of the Boston Public Library. Drawings, photographs, and other material are in the archive of the Boston Symphony Orchestra. Some of Koussevitzky's caricatures are in the Library of Congress. Koussevitzky left an unfinished autobiography. Her writings include "I Beseech You to Look," in *This I Believe*, vol. 1, edited by Edward P. Morgan (1952), and "Virtuoso of the Double Bass," *Saturday*

Review of Literature, July 31, 1954. See also "Serge Koussevitzky, Mentor of Young Composers," *New York Times*, July 23, 1944; Nicolas Slonimsky, "The Koussevitzky Mission," *Saturday Review of Literature*, June 30, 1951; "The Composer Is the Key," *New York Times*, June 23, 1968; Albert Kupferberg, *Tanglewood* (1976); Joan Peyser, *Bernstein* (1987); Aaron Copland, *Copland, Since 1943* (1989); and Andrew Pincus, *Scenes from Tanglewood* (1989). An obituary is in the *New York Times*, Jan. 7, 1978.]

JOHN C. REINERS

KRONENBERGER, LOUIS, JR. (Dec. 9, 1904–Apr. 30, 1980), drama critic, writer, and editor, was born in Cincinnati, Ohio, the son of Louis Kronenberger, a merchant, and Mabel Newwitter. He attended Hughes High School, then the University of Cincinnati from 1921 to 1924 but left to begin a writing career in New York City before obtaining a degree. In 1926 he obtained his first full-time position, as an editor for the publishing house Boni and Liveright, which published his first novel, *The Grand Manner*, in 1929. He joined the editorial staff of Alfred A. Knopf in 1933 and edited *An Anthology of Light Verse* (1935). Kronenberger began his association with publisher Henry R. Luce's periodicals in 1936, first with *Fortune* magazine as a feature writer, then on that magazine's board of editors from 1936 to 1938. He became drama critic for *Time* magazine in 1938, where his reviews made him known nationally. He married Emily L. Plaut on Jan. 29, 1940, and they had two children. In the same year he became drama critic for *PM* magazine, a position he held until 1948, although he resumed writing for *Time* and continued to do so until 1961.

Kronenberger also had an extensive academic career: at Columbia University in New York City as lecturer on English Restoration drama 1950–1951; as a visiting professor at City College of New York, 1953–1954; at Stanford University in California in 1954 and 1963; at New York University in 1958; at Harvard in Massachusetts and Oxford in England in 1959; a return to Columbia University in 1961, a year in which he was also a Christian Gauss Seminar lecturer in criticism at Princeton University in New Jersey; and at the University of California at Berkeley in 1968. His lengthiest teaching stint was as professor of theater arts at Brandeis University in Waltham, Mass., from 1952 to 1980. He also held the position of full-time librarian at Brandeis from 1963 to 1967.

Among his other noteworthy positions were director of the Writing Colony, Yaddo Corporation, in Saratoga Springs, N.Y.; a consultant to the New York Public Library for the Performing Arts in New York City; a member of the National Institute of Arts and Letters, serving as secretary from 1953 to 1956; and a fellow of the American Academy of Arts and Sciences and Guggenheim Foundation, 1969–1970.

Kronenberger edited or compiled several literary collections, including *The Portable Johnson and Boswell* (1947), *George Bernard Shaw* (1953), *Cavalcade of Comedy* (1953), *The Cutting Edge* (1970), *Atlantic Brief Lives* (1971), and *The Last Word* (1972). He was particularly fond of the eighteenth century and its authors. He edited *An Eighteenth Century Miscellany* (1936) and wrote *Kings and Desperate Men* (1942) and *Marlborough's Duchess* (1958). *The Thread of Laughter* (1952), on English stage comedy, was applauded by literary critic Edmund Wilson as "the very best thing on the subject." Wilson went on to ascribe genuine sophistication and polish to the work and wrote most aptly of Kronenberger's civilized attitude toward life and letters. His *A Month of Sundays* (1961) was valued as a richly imagined and sophisticated divertissement with an element of the fantastic.

His memoirs, *No Whippings, No Gold Watches* (1970), best revealed Kronenberger's literary nature. Its modest subtitle is *The Saga of a Writer and His Jobs*. A quintessential man of letters, Kronenberger claimed only the title of writer. He rejected the placement of his memoirs in the category of autobiography, however, writing that he had merely produced a subjective memoir of places and people he worked at and with.

Kronenberger also wrote for the stage, and in all his writing and teaching guises he managed to be at the center of culture, observing the American scene, particularly from the 1930's to the 1950's, but his scholarly pursuits of the seventeenth and eighteenth centuries also shaped his personality as well as his journalistic endeavors. He was especially fond of the urbane conversation of literary and cultural figures and enamored of intellectual salons and literary parties. His relations with some of the most contentious contemporary figures, such as the authoritarian Luce and elegant Knopf, were genial. Kronenberger came closest to political associations while working at *PM*, where the staff adhered to a liberal-left position and some followed a hard-line Stalinist Communism. He was ill at ease with his colleagues at *PM*, his liberalness having more to do with literary culture than with political polemics.

It is of interest that Kronenberger spent much of his life in publishing and with the theater as a critic, playwright, and friend of actors, producers, directors, but in his autobiography he wrote of the academic world and the literary world, not giving the dignity of the category "world" to either the theater or publishing. It would seem that he preferred the roles of tangential observer, commentator, and analyst to the rough competitive market arenas of theater and publishing.

Kronenberger's last book, a biography of Oscar Wilde, was published in 1976. He had moved in 1963 to Brookline, Mass., where he died after suffering from Alzheimer's disease for several years.

His remarks about academia were unusually cogent. University life, he wrote, is as enclosed and anomalous as court life and in other ways is like the world of corporations despite the efforts of academics to disassociate themselves from the corporate style. While there are differences in enlightened views, cultural values, and disinterested goals, there are similarities in structures and hierarchy where titles and consciousness of them are important in both worlds. Such insights add to Kronenberger's achievements as a man of letters.

[In addition to *No Whippings, No Gold Watches* (1970), see portraits in *Saturday Review*, May 14, 1955, and *Theatre Arts*, Oct. 1955. Kronenberger is also discussed in W. A. Swanberg, *Luce: A Man and His Empire* (1972). An obituary is in the *New York Times*, May 2, 1980.]

HENRY WASSER

KUHLMAN, KATHRYN (May 9, 1907–Feb. 20, 1976), preacher and faith healer, was born near Concordia, Mo., the daughter of Joseph Kuhlman and Myrtle Walkenhorst. Her mother was a Methodist; her father, the mayor of Concordia, was a nominal Baptist who had a deep aversion to preachers. At age fourteen, she was converted under the ministry of a traveling evangelist, describing the experience as "my first contact with the power of God . . . . the beginning of everything."

At the age of sixteen, Kuhlman left school and went to Oregon to work with her sister, Myrtle, whose husband, Everett Parrott, was a Methodist evangelist. Kuhlman sang and played the piano for the Parrotts' small-town services. When her sister's stormy marriage came to an abrupt end, the two destitute women rented a hall in Boise, Idaho, and Kuhlman began a preaching ministry that would last until her death.

For the next ten years she held services throughout Idaho, Utah, and Colorado. Kuhlman finally settled in Denver, Colo., in 1933 and built the Kuhlman Revival Tabernacle shortly thereafter. Aided by her first radio broadcasts, her storefront congregation grew to 2,000 within three years.

In 1938, Kuhlman married Burroughs A. Waltrip, whom she had met when he had appeared as a guest preacher at the Tabernacle. Their courtship was clandestine, for Waltrip was married; after he had divorced his wife (they had four children), he and Kuhlman were married surreptitiously by a local justice of the peace, over the protests of her close friends and advisers; they had no children. Kuhlman and the man she always called "Mister" probably separated sometime in 1944; Waltrip served her with divorce papers four years later. Kuhlman spent the rest of her life fending off the disapproval of her constituents, attempting to keep the entire affair as secret as possible.

After she left Waltrip, Kuhlman moved east, leaving Denver and the adverse publicity generated by her divorce. She covered a wide area of the middle Atlantic and southern states, but gradually spent more and more time in western Pennsylvania. The town of Franklin, where she began preaching in 1946, emerged as a base.

At about the same time, the emphasis of Kuhlman's ministry shifted dramatically; some of her listeners claimed that they had been healed of various maladies during her sermons. Such claims led to increased demands for her preaching, and in 1948 Kuhlman held her first services in Pittsburgh's Carnegie Hall. By the early 1950's the healings had brought her national prominence.

Kuhlman's meetings were centered on herself. A tall, slender woman with auburn hair worn in a Shirley Temple style of long curls parted in the middle, she possessed a radiant smile. She conducted her services with enormous energy and spoke in a dramatic yet folksy style. As Kuhlman's ministry grew, so did the trappings: impeccably dressed ushers, large choirs, and theatrical buildups to her appearance on stage. Critics questioned her extensive art collection, the vast array of gaudy dresses that she wore, and, toward the end of her career, her private jet. A deeply insecure woman, Kuhlman was an inflexible administrator. She was close to only a few trusted aides, two of whom remained with her for over thirty years.

Kuhlman's theology defied traditional categories. Though she eventually joined the American Baptist Convention, she disclaimed any specific doctrine, declaring that "God doesn't have preferences in theology." Her greatest emphasis was on the Holy Spirit as the agent of God's salvation and healing; this gave her the appearance of being a Pentecostal. Conservative evangelicals and fundamentalists, distrusting such doctrines as well as her claims of supernatural healings, held her at arm's length. Kuhlman's only relationship with a mainstream congregation was after 1968, when Pittsburgh's First Presbyterian Church allowed her to use its building for her meetings. However, she was never fully accepted by Pentecostals either: her failure to preach the necessity of a second "work of grace" accompanied by the supernatural phenomenon of speaking in tongues, and her description of Pentecostals as "fanatics," made her an outcast in their eyes as well. She walked in a theological shadow world.

Kuhlman never took credit for the healings that occurred during her services, nor did she claim to know any formulas to effect them. Insisting that her primary goal was to "save souls," she had an extremely strong view of the sovereignty of God in healing. "I cannot heal a single person," she maintained. "God does the healing. Whom He heals and whom He chooses not to heal is His business." Kuhlman's supporters produced medical evidence of the authenticity of the healings; her detractors cited the lack of medical evidence, maintaining that the ailments were self-diagnosed.

In 1965, Kuhlman went to Pasadena, Calif., at the invitation of some local pastors. Pasadena became a second base of her ministry, and she soon moved into the Shrine Auditorium, from which she conducted services during the final decade of her life. Radio broadcasts had long since become a normal part of her services, and in the late 1960's she began to produce television broadcasts as well. Her book *I Believe in Miracles* sold more than one million copies; this and the CBS shows brought her worldwide fame and made her the best-known female evangelist since Aimee Semple McPherson. However, the expensive productions also placed enormous financial demands on the ministry. The number of services that she conducted increased dramatically, as did the geographical range with several trips overseas. Close associates of Kuhlman maintained that the resulting pressures caused a severe decline in her health. She died in Tulsa, Okla., surrounded by questions concerning lawsuits by a former aide, disputes over her will, and allegations of a grown son from her marriage.

[Kuhlman's papers and a number of tapes of her television shows are in the Billy Graham Center at Wheaton College, Ill. Eight books were published under her name, including *I Believe in Miracles* (1962) and *God Can Do It Again* (1976). Biographies include Alan Spraggett, *Kathryn Kuhlman* (1970); and Jamie Buckingham, *Daughter of Destiny* (1976). Obituaries are in the *New York Times*, Feb. 22, 1976; and in *Christianity Today*, Mar. 12, 1976.]

FREDERICK W. JORDAN

KUNITZ, MOSES (Dec. 19, 1887–Apr. 20, 1978), biochemist, was born in Slonim, Russia, a center of Talmudic studies before its occupation by the German army early in World War II. Kunitz was educated in Slonim before his immigration to the United States; further information about his upbringing has been lost.

Kunitz settled in New York City in 1909 and obtained work in a hat factory, pursuing his education on a part-time basis at the Cooper Union Evening School of Chemistry, which he entered in 1910. His brother and his fiancée, Sonia Bloom, joined him later. Kunitz and Bloom were married in 1912 and had two children; he became an American citizen in 1915.

In 1913, Kunitz became a laboratory assistant to Jacques Loeb, an eminent cell physiologist, at the Rockefeller Institute in New York City; he remained there for the rest of his scientific career, a period spanning almost sixty years. Loeb, head of the department of physiology at Rockefeller, valued Kunitz's adept and meticulous lab work and encouraged him to pursue a research career.

Kunitz graduated from Cooper Union in 1916 with a B.S. and then spent two years at Cooper Union's Electrical Engineering School, transferring in 1919 to the Columbia University

School of Mines, Engineering, and Chemistry. In 1922, Kunitz became a graduate student at Columbia. He received a Ph.D. in biological chemistry in 1924 and was appointed to the staff of the Rockefeller Institute with the title of assistant.

Kunitz published his first papers on protein behavior with Loeb in 1923. After Loeb's death in 1924, John Howard Northrop became head of the department of general physiology. Kunitz's collaboration with Northrop in determining the chemical nature of enzymes, which had mystified scientists for a century, constitutes his major contribution to science. Kunitz was made an associate at the Rockefeller Institute in 1926, the year the physiology department moved to Princeton, N.J. After the death of his wife in 1938, he married Rebecca Shamaskin, an émigré from Slonim, in 1939.

Kunitz's knowledge of the chemistry and physical properties of proteins had been gained through his experiments with gelatin under Loeb; Northrop, who had devised a thesis regarding the protein nature of enzymes in the mid-1920's, called upon Kunitz to put that knowledge to the test. Northrop and Kunitz collaborated on the isolation of the two major digestive enzymes, pepsin and trypsin, in crystalline form in 1930 and 1931, and in the decades that followed Kunitz isolated some eighteen additional enzymes and precursors in crystalline form, confirming Northrop's thesis that enzymes are proteins and further elucidating their high specificity in biological reactions.

In addition to studying the chemistry of enzymes, Kunitz made major advances in determining the physical properties and activities of proteins in general. In 1935 he was one of the first researchers to demonstrate that certain inhibiting proteins of the stomach and pancreas prevent digestive enzymes from breaking down the living tissues in which they are formed. One of his papers, "The Kinetics and Thermodynamics of Reversible Denaturation of Crystalline Soybean Trypsin Inhibitor" (1948), demonstrated the process whereby denatured proteins are restored to their original or normal condition.

Called by Roger Herriott the "crystallizer of last resort for many younger enzyme chemists," Kunitz demonstrated a remarkable ability to isolate compounds in the laboratory and pioneered the methodology for enzyme purification. In 1940 he crystallized ribonuclease, the enzyme responsible for the scission of ribonucleic acid (RNA) in living cells; in 1948 he did the same with deoxyribonuclease. This work became particularly important in later biomedical studies of the chemistry of the nucleic acids. Kunitz's work on the purification of proteins opened the door to other medical breakthroughs, including the purification of bacteriophage and the crystallization of diphtheria antitoxin by Northrop, and the crystallization of tobacco mosaic virus by another colleague, Wendell M. Stanley.

Responding to a request by the Office of Scientific Research and Development during World War II, Kunitz isolated hexokinase in crystalline form; this enzyme was thought to be involved in the action of mustard gas upon living tissue. Kunitz, who had been made a full member of the Rockefeller Institute in 1949, returned to New York in 1950 when the Princeton branch of the institute was closed. In 1953, with the conversion of the Rockefeller Institute to university status, he became professor emeritus, a title he held until his retirement in 1972. He spent numerous summers working at the Marine Biological Laboratory in Woods Hole, Mass., to which he commuted from his summer home in Falmouth Heights, Mass.

Kunitz received the Carl Neuberg Medal of the American Society of European Chemists and Pharmacists in 1957, on the occasion of which Northrop praised him as "a research worker of the first rank in his chosen field," who brought to his laboratory research the qualities of "imagination, ingenuity, persistence, great technical skill, mathematical facility, and a thorough theoretical knowledge."

Kunitz died in Philadelphia. Described by his colleagues as a self-effacing man who was uncomfortable in the spotlight, Kunitz "did not write reviews that integrated his studies into the developing thought of the time," but concentrated his energy and scientific resourcefulness on the task at hand. His researches, laid out in papers described as models of scientific reporting, contributed in the short term to scientific breakthroughs that enabled his colleagues Northrop and Stanley to share the Nobel Prize for chemistry in 1946, and in the long term to important advances in enzymology that bioscientists continue to build upon.

[Kunitz's papers are in the Rockefeller Archive Center in Pocantico Hills, N.Y. His most significant publication is *Crystalline Enzymes* (1948), with John H. Northrop and Roger M. Herriott. See also the profile by Roger M. Herriott in *Biographical Memoirs. National Academy of Sciences* 58 (1989); and George W. Corner, *A History of the Rockefeller Institute* (1964). An obituary by Roger M. Herriott is in *Nature*, Sept. 28, 1978.]

MELISSA A. DOBSON

L

LABAREE, LEONARD WOODS (Aug. 26, 1897–May 5, 1980), historian and educator, was born near the Persian (now Iranian) village of Urumia, one of two children of Benjamin Woods Labaree and Mary Alice Schauffler, American missionary teachers at a Presbyterian college for Persia's Nestorian Christians. In 1904 his father was killed by Kurdish tribesmen, who mistook him for another missionary. Soon thereafter his mother returned to the United States with her children. Taking up residence in Connecticut, she became superintendent of New Britain City Mission and also taught part-time in Hartford Seminary's missionary program. Labaree attended Hotchkiss School in Lakeville, Conn., before enrolling at Williams College in 1915. When the United States entered World War I in 1917, he volunteered for service as a balloon pilot, received his commission as second lieutenant, and served in the Twenty-eighth Balloon Company of the Army Air Service from 1917 to 1919. After the war he resumed his college education and graduated with honors from Williams College in 1920. On June 26, 1920, just weeks after his graduation, he married Elizabeth Mary Calkins of New London; they had two children.

In the fall of the same year Labaree entered graduate school at Yale University, where he was a student of the noted colonial historian Charles M. Andrews. In 1923 he completed his M.A. degree, and the following year he began his forty-five-year career on the Yale faculty, starting at the rank of instructor. Three years later, after he had received the Ph.D., he was promoted to assistant professor. From 1929 to 1930 he served as Carnegie Visiting Professor at Armstrong College of Durham University in England. Because of the Great Depression, promotions at Yale, as elsewhere, were virtually frozen. Labaree's appointment as assistant professor was renewed periodically, but it was not until 1938, by which time he had succeeded Andrews as Yale's colonial historian, that he was made associate professor and granted tenure. He was elevated in 1942 to professor and became Durfee Professor and then Farnam Professor of History in 1946, the chair his mentor had held.

Labaree authored a number of important scholarly monographs on various aspects of colonial American history. Included among them are *Royal Government in America: A Study of the British Colonial System Before 1783* (1930), which won the American Historical Association's Justin Winsor Prize; *Milford, Connecticut: The Early Development of the Town as Shown in Its Land Records* (1933), his M.A. thesis, which was issued in the Connecticut Tercentenary series; *Royal Instructions to British Colonial Governors, 1670–1776* (1935), which he collated and edited as an outgrowth of his monograph from 1930; and *Conservatism in Early American History* (1948), which was based on his Anson P. Stokes Lectures at New York University in 1947. In addition, he edited five volumes of *The Records of the State of Connecticut* (*1782–1796*) during the decade from 1941 to 1950, when he served as official historian for the state of Connecticut.

Labaree's greatest contributions to his profession were made as editor of historical texts. His editorial skills became evident early in his professional career. In 1933 he embarked upon a fourteen-year term as editor of the Yale Historical Publications series, sponsored by the Yale Department of History. In this capacity Labaree helped shape and steer through the press some forty volumes of diverse historical texts, most of which originated as doctoral dissertations. However, it was as editor-in-chief of *The Papers of Benjamin Franklin* (1959) that Labaree achieved preeminence.

Labaree's reputation for exhaustive research, meticulous attention to detail, and sound judgment made him an obvious candidate to lead what was, at the time, one of the most ambitious editorial enterprises in the history of American book publishing. When Yale University, in partnership with the American Philosophical Society, decided to publish a new and definitive edition of the papers of Benjamin Franklin, they chose Labaree to head the project. In 1954, Labaree took charge of a small group of scholars who began the painstaking job of locating and copying all the surviving Franklin papers. In a tour-de-force of editorial enterprise, they assembled copies of 27,800 widely scattered manuscript documents, then transcribed and edited the first fourteen volumes of a collection that is expected to run to forty-five volumes when completed (about the year 2006).

Five years of intensive searching, sorting, collating, and transcribing preceded publication of the first volume, although in 1957, on the 250th anniversary of Franklin's birth, the editors offered a preview of things to come by bringing out a small volume of letters under the title *Mr. Franklin*. Two years later the first volume of the *Papers* appeared. The academic community praised it and subsequent volumes and credited Labaree with setting editorial standards for thoroughness, accuracy, and clarity that made the project the model of its kind. Those standards have not been surpassed by the editors of the papers of other founding fathers. In 1969 Labaree retired from Yale. At that time, fourteen volumes of the *Papers* and a new scholarly edition of the *Autobiography of Benjamin Franklin* (1964) had been published.

In retirement at Northford, where he and his wife had restored an old Connecticut farmhouse, Labaree remained active. His historical knowledge, together with his reputation for common sense and impartiality, earned him positions as town moderator and chairman of the local planning board. He continued to conduct historical research and edited, for the New Haven Colony Historical Society, a three-volume history of the socially and politically important Shepard family. He died at his Northford home.

[Labaree's professional papers, including his correspondence relating to the *Franklin Papers*, are at Sterling Library, Yale University. He edited and contributed to *Essays in Colonial History* (1931) and wrote "The Nature of American Loyalism," *American Antiquarian Society Proceedings*, Apr.–Oct. 1944, and "In Search of 'B. Franklin,' " *William and Mary Quarterly*, Apr. 1959. Obituaries are in the *New York Times*, May 8, 1980; *American Antiquarian Society Proceedings*, Oct. 1980; and the *New England Quarterly*, Dec. 1980.]

CHARLES D. LOWERY

LANG, FRITZ (Dec. 5, 1890–Aug. 2, 1976), film director, was born in Vienna, Austria, the son of Anton Lang, an architect, and Paula Schlesinger. As a youth, Lang studied architecture at the Technische Hochschule (Technical High School) in Vienna. At age twenty he left home and traveled to North Africa, Asia Minor, Russia, China, Japan, and the Pacific, supporting himself by selling drawings, painted postcards, and cartoons. In 1913 he settled in Paris in order to paint, and he had an exhibition there in 1914. At the outbreak of World War I, Lang returned to Vienna and was conscripted into the Austro-Hungarian army. Wounded four times, he was discharged as a lieutenant and began writing screenplays in 1916 while convalescing for a year in a Vienna hospital.

After the war, Lang worked in Berlin with the producer Erich Pommer, as a script reader, writer, and eventually director of films for the Decla Bioscop Company, before forming his own film production concern. His directorial debut was *Halbblut* (The Half-breed) in 1919, the first of many Lang films in which a man is destroyed by his love for a woman. In 1920, Lang married popular writer Thea von Harbou, who collaborated on his German screenplays; they had no children.

While in Berlin, and later in Hollywood, Lang used cinema to explore a personal fascination with, in his words, "cruelty, fear, horror and death." His filmmaking style is characterized by grandeur of scale, striking visual compositions and sound effects, suspense, and narrative economy—including the minimalist techniques for enlisting the audience's imagination to evoke horror. A progenitor of the film noir movement, Lang was preoccupied throughout his career with the dark side of human nature: vengeance, violence, and the criminal mind. The heroes of his films are brought down by injustice, bad women, or the iron laws of fate.

Lang's first successful effort was *Der müde Tod* (The Tired Death, 1921, released in the United States as *Between Two Worlds*), which inspired Douglas Fairbanks's 1924 feature, *The Thief of Bagdad*. It was followed by *Dr. Mabuse, der Spieler* (1922), a two-part portrait of a master criminal, and *Die Niebelungen* (1924), released in the United States in two parts, *Siegfried* and *Kriemhild's Revenge*. Based on the thirteenth-century Siegfried epic, it was intended to restore pride in Germany's cultural heritage.

Metropolis (1927), a powerful expressionistic drama about a futuristic slave society, was a stunning technical achievement; despite its simplistic message it remains a classic. The production nearly bankrupted the UFA studio, and Lang formed his own production company for his next film, *Spione* (Spies, 1928). It was followed by *Woman in the Moon* (1929); and *M* (1931), starring Peter Lorre as a compulsive child-murderer. *M*, the first German sound film, remains the acknowledged masterpiece of Lang's German period, and was his personal favorite.

"If Adolf Hitler had never existed," wrote the critic Andrew Sarris, "Fritz Lang would have had to invent him on the screen." Lang, who was not Jewish, used a madman in an asylum to espouse Nazi doctrines in the 1932 film *Das Testament des Dr. Mabuse* (The Last Will of Dr. Mabuse). After it opened, in 1933 he was summoned by Joseph Goebbels, Hitler's propaganda minister, and invited to supervise Nazi film production. Instead, Lang fled Germany for Paris the same day, leaving behind a personal fortune and a vast collection of primitive art. In 1933, Thea von Harbou divorced him and joined the Nazi movement. After making one film in France in 1934 (*Liliom*, starring Charles Boyer), Lang signed a one-picture contract with David O. Selznick of Metro-Goldwyn-Mayer and moved to Hollywood, where for the next twenty years he worked in such various genres as thrillers, war and crime dramas, and Westerns.

Although he became an American citizen in 1935, Lang retained his monocle and a Continental formality of bearing for some years. He developed a strong penchant for the American West—living for weeks at a time on Indian reservations—and for American slang. His Hollywood debut, *Fury* (1936), a study of mob violence starring Spencer Tracy and Sylvia Sidney, was a huge commercial and critical success. It was followed by *You Only Live Once* (1937); *You and Me* (1938); two Westerns for Twentieth Century–Fox, *The Return of Frank James* (1940) and *Western Union* (1941); and a series of war films, thrillers, and melodramas, including *Hangmen Also Die* (1943), which Lang wrote in collaboration with Bertolt Brecht; *Ministry of Fear* (1944); and *The Woman in the Window* (1944) and *Scarlet Street* (1945), both starring Edward G. Robinson. The later films, mostly crime dramas, included Clifford Odets's *Clash by Night* and *Rancho Notorious*, a Western starring Marlene Dietrich (1952); *The Big Heat* (1953); *The Blue Gardenia* (1953); *Human Desire* (1954); *Moonfleet* (1955), a costume drama; *Beyond a Reasonable Doubt* (1956); and *While the City Sleeps* (1956).

The distinctiveness of Lang's European and American periods reflects an extraordinary adaptation: to a new country, language, and studio environment, as well as to cinematic sound and color. Critics have never been able to reconcile the two phases. The early German films, which gained a wide international following, were brilliantly innovative but self-conscious to the point of didacticism, relying heavily on interior sets, monumental architecture, and expressionistic devices such as painted backdrops and stylized action. The American movies, on the other hand, reflected a more mature style, and the resources (as well as the commercial influences) of Hollywood. Forced to make shorter, tighter films for a mass audience, Lang earned further recognition for his visual and thematic craftsmanship, but he chafed at the limitations of the studio system, favoring lower-budget films over which he could exercise artistic control.

A tall, physically imposing figure, and a perfectionist by nature, Lang could be a temperamental and dictatorial presence on the set. His differences with producers ultimately prompted his departure from Hollywood in 1956. He directed two low-budget films in India, and in 1959 returned to Germany, where he directed his final film, *The Thousand Eyes of Dr. Mabuse*, in 1960. In 1963 he portrayed himself in the film *Mépris* by Jean-Luc Godard, released in the United Sates as *Contempt*. Lang was awarded the French Officier d'Art et des Lettres. He died in Los Angeles.

[See Peter Bogdanovich, *Fritz Lang in America* (1968); Paul M. Jensen, *The Cinema of Fritz Lang* (1969); Andrew Sarris, "Fritz Lang, the Prophet of Our Paranoia," the *Village Voice*, Aug. 16, 1976; Herman G. Weinberg, *Fritz Lang* (1979); E. Ann Kaplan, *Fritz Lang: A Guide to References and Resources* (1981); Lotte H. Eisner, *Fritz Lang* (1986); and Reynold Humphries, *Fritz Lang: Genre and Representation in His American Films* (1988). An obituary is in the *New York Times*, Aug. 3, 1976.]

JEFFREY SCHEUER

LANGER, WILLIAM LEONARD (Mar. 16, 1896–Dec. 26, 1977), historian, was born in Boston, Mass., the son of Karl Rudolf Langer, a florist, and Johanna Rockenbach. He attended Harvard University, from which he received the B.A. in 1915, the M.A. in 1920, and the Ph.D. in history in 1923. He married Susanne Katherine Knauth, a philosopher, on Sept. 3, 1921; they had two children. They were divorced in 1942, and he married Rowena Morse Nelson on Apr. 9, 1943.

Langer began his teaching career at Worcester Academy (1915–1917) and continued it at Clark University as assistant professor of history (1923–1925) and associate professor (1925–1927). He moved to Harvard University as assistant professor (1927–1931), associate professor (1931–1936), Coolidge Professor of History (1936–1964), and emeritus in 1964. During his association with Harvard and as an early advocate of regional studies, he served as founder and director of the Harvard Russian Research Center (1954–1959) and the Harvard Center for Middle Eastern Studies (1954–1956); he was also a friend of and guide for the Harvard-Yenching Institute for Chinese and Far Eastern Studies and the National Association for Armenian Studies and Research. Langer was visiting professor and lecturer at the University of Chicago (1926), Columbia University (1931), Yale University (1933), and the Fletcher School of Law and Diplomacy at Tufts University (1933–1934, 1936–1941).

As a soldier in World War I, in the St.-Mihiel and Argonne engagements, Langer rose from private to sergeant. In addition to his distinguished academic career, Langer was a key figure in the American intelligence community. A member of the Board of Analysts, Office of Coordinator of Information (1941–1942), he became chief of the Research and Analysis Branch, Office of Strategic Services (1942–1945), special assistant for intelligence analysis to the secretary of state (1946), and assistant director of the Central Intelligence Agency (1950–1952). After 1952, Langer served as a consultant to the CIA. In all, he spent thirty years dealing with the problems and organization of foreign intelligence including nine years on the President's Foreign Intelligence Advisory Board (1961–1969).

Langer's first significant book was *The Diplomacy of Imperialism* (1935). His view was that Hitler's *Mein Kampf* was an extraordinary medley of amateur politics and amazing insights into international problems and possibilities, and that Hitler "showed reckless courage in realizing German dreams, nightmarish as some of them were." He also asserted that Britain and France knew that the 1919 peace settlements reflected not justice but a passion for revenge. Langer later believed Hitler to be a menace to the entire world.

Our Vichy Gamble (1947), written with S. Everett Gleason, vigorously defended American Vichy policy that veered toward Marshal Philippe Pétain and away from General Charles de Gaulle. Langer believed Pétain and Pierre Laval had acted as they thought best for France. The French government, contemplating a libel suit against Langer and Gleason, turned for advice to Allen Dulles and Henry Hyde, former intelligence comrades of Langer's. On their counsel, the libel suit was dropped. Langer also justified American Vichy policy as providing a listening post on the Continent and an opportunity to maintain contact with a traditional ally.

A dispute also arose between Langer and Charles Beard and Harry Elmer Barnes, both isolationists, with respect to World War II. The bones of the argument were in *The Challenge to Isolation* (1952) and *The Undeclared War* (1953), both written with S. Everett Gleason. Barnes labeled Langer a "court historian." Langer and Gleason, however, won the prestigious Bancroft Prize for the 1953 work.

As president of the American Historical Association (1957), Langer broke new ground in his presidential address, emphasizing the need for deeper study and more extensive reference by historians to the teachings of modern psychology.

In 1959, Langer was a member of President Eisenhower's Commission on National Goals, on which his responsibility as analyst was the role of the United States in world affairs.

Turning to yet another approach to history, Langer published *Political and Social Upheaval 1832–1852* (1960), in which he interpreted the extraordinary change and uncertainty of those two decades in demographic terms.

In and Out of the Ivory Tower (1977), Langer's autobiography was offered as a corrective to the student unrest of the 1960's. In it, he sought to remind ahistorical skeptics that the United States was the freest and most rewarding land in history.

Langer took pride in his memberships in the American Philosophical Society, the Council on Foreign Relations, and the American Academy of Arts and Sciences, and his fellowship at the Center for Advanced Study in Behavioral Sciences (Stanford) in its early days. A lifelong enthusiastic golfer, he took delight in his memberships in the Essex and Oakley country clubs. Langer died in Boston.

[Langer's papers are in the Harvard University Archives. An obituary is in the *New York Times*, Dec. 27, 1977.]

HENRY WASSER

LASSWELL, HAROLD DWIGHT (Feb. 13, 1902–Dec. 18, 1978), political scientist, was born in Donnellson, Ill., to Anna Prather, a schoolteacher, and Linden Downey Lasswell, a Presbyterian minister. Upon graduation from Decatur High School as class valedictorian at age sixteen, Lasswell enrolled on a scholarship at the University of Chicago, where he received a B.A. in philosophy and joined the political science department as a teaching assistant (1922–1924) and instructor (1924–1927). He undertook extensive postgraduate training at the universities of London, Geneva, Paris, and Berlin while working on his doctoral dissertation from 1923 to 1925. Lasswell completed his Ph.D. in 1926 under the direction of Charles Merriam, a pioneer in the behavioral approach to the study of politics at the University of Chicago. While he was in Europe, he focused on the still relatively novel works of Sigmund Freud and underwent psychoanalysis as a patient of Theodore Reik's, one of Freud's foremost disciples. Lasswell's doctoral dissertation was published in 1927 as *Propaganda Technique in the World War* and is still recognized as a seminal study on the psychological foundations of communication theory.

Lasswell spent the bulk of his professional career as a professor of political science at the University of Chicago from 1922 to 1938 and as a professor of law and political science at Yale University from 1946 to 1971. During the period 1939–1945, he served as the director of the War Communication Research Division at the Library of Congress. During his stay in Washington, Lasswell began to attract national attention for his bold theories on the use of psychoanalysis for the study and practice of politics. In particular, his application of orthodox Freudian methods to the study of world leaders led to his successful predictions of the rise of totalitarian dictatorships throughout the world.

Lasswell established himself as a pioneering scholar in the field of political science with the publication of two seminal works: *Psychopathology and Politics* (1930) and *World Politics and Personal Insecurity* (1935). In both studies, he relied upon classical Freudian precepts to contend that world political leaders' actions and belief systems were most clearly understood and predictable in the context of a psychoanalysis of each leader and that psychoanalytical methods would revolutionize not only the study of politics but also the nature of politics itself in the twentieth century.

According to Lasswell, psychoanalysis provided the first truly "scientific" basis for politics and would result in its transformation throughout the globe by using therapeutic methods of "preventive politics" to eliminate rather than perpetuate the causes of political conflict. For many, his propositions as a whole led to the "undemocratic" conclusion that political life and behavior were predictable and controllable through a supposedly infallible Freudian methodology.

Overlooked by many of his critics was Lasswell's revisionary breakthrough that political behavior was heavily influenced by the drives of the unconscious and that politics and individual personality were inseparably bound together. Lasswell boldly contended that the political quest for power by many world leaders emerged from their attempts to overcome low self-esteem. He extended his approach to the analysis of entire political systems and established a continuum in which contrasting governmental systems were aligned with a matching personality type for citizens of each distinct regime (in this context Nazism bespoke psychological disorder, and western democracy represented well-adjusted personalities).

Despite the appearance of these two monumental works, Lasswell's unique approach to the study of politics largely was ignored by his professional peers. Indeed, from 1937 to 1950 he did not write one article in a journal of political science. Instead, Lasswell's prolific output of scholarly research found an audience among psychiatrists. He continued to advance the psychoanalytical study of politics in psychology journals. In part, his rejection by his peers in political science was attributable to his laborious prose style, a self-contained language of complex nuances and meanings. Beginning in the 1950's, however, Lasswell began to receive the belated recognition of political scientists. As a younger generation of scholars entered the field after World War II, Lasswell's work gained a broader professional acceptance, especially his theories on the psychological impact of political symbolism upon a citizenry. His full acceptance by his profession was formally acknowledged by his election as president of the American Political Science Association in 1955.

Throughout the 1960's, Lasswell continued to teach at Yale University and write an impressive body of studies on political value systems. In 1971 he retired from Yale to accept an appointment as a distinguished professor at the John Jay College of Criminal Justice. From 1972 to 1976, Lasswell was the recipient of many academic awards and distinguished professorships, including one at Temple University and another at Columbia University. In 1975 he retired from active teaching to work as the cochairman and later president of the Policy Sciences Center in New York City to complete his research on the topic of human rights. Four studies on this theme were published posthumously. He died at Roosevelt Hospital in New York City.

[An anthology of Lasswell's writings is *The Political Writings of Harold D. Lasswell* (rev. ed. 1979). A detailed bibliography of his work is in Michael Lerner, "A Bibliographical Note," in Fred Greenstein, *Personality and Politics* (rev. ed. 1975). There exists a broad range of scholarly assessments of Lasswell's writings, among them, Fred Greenstein, "Harold D. Lasswell's Concept of Democratic Character," *Journal of Politics*, Aug. 1968; Arnold Rogow, ed., *Politics, Personality, and Social Science in the Twentieth Century: Essays in Honor of Harold Lasswell* (1969); Martin Deutsch, "What Is Political Psychology?" *International Social Studies Journal* 35 (1983); and Robert Horwitz, "Scientific Propaganda," in Herbert J. Storing, ed., *Essays on the Scientific Study of Politics* (1962). An obituary is in the *New York Times*, Dec. 20, 1978.]

RONALD LETTIERI

LAURENCE, WILLIAM LEONARD (Mar. 7, 1888–Mar. 19, 1977), science reporter, was born Leid Siew in the village of Salantai, Lithuania, the son of Lipman Siew and Sarah Preuss. His father, a devout orthodox Jew, devoted most of his time to religious studies, so it generally fell to his mother to run the family's small shop, which dealt mostly in medicines.

Laurence's early education consisted mainly of instruction in Hebrew, German, and Russian from a local tutor. Following his bar mitzvah at age thirteen, he enrolled in a school of Talmudic study. By then, however, he had begun to read avidly in science, literature, and philosophy; the intellectual perspectives derived from that reading placed him sharply at odds with the school's religious teachings. As a result, his teachers soon viewed him as a troublemaker, and he was dismissed from the school.

His dismissal thoroughly alienated him from his father, and rather than live in the shadow of parental disapproval, Laurence moved to the city of Libau (Liepaja), Latvia, where he earned his living as a Hebrew tutor. Here his sympathy for radical political ideas drew him to local dissidents, and in 1905 he participated in a revolt against Latvia's Russian rulers.

The rebellion was ultimately crushed, and Laurence found himself faced with the threat of arrest. After escaping to Germany concealed in a barrel, he immigrated to the United States. He first worked briefly at a textile factory in Brooklyn, N.Y., then in 1906 moved to Boston, where he took a job delivering flowers and enrolled in high school. Two years later, having saved enough money for tuition, he entered Harvard.

Lack of funds forced Laurence to leave Harvard after his third year. In 1913 he became an American citizen, and a year later he reentered Harvard to complete his last year of undergraduate study. But the school refused him a degree because he had failed to complete certain course requirements, and although he received a cum laude in philosophy, he left Harvard in 1915 without officially graduating.

During his final undergraduate days, Laurence did special tutoring in Greek philosophy and, in the process, showed himself to be a master in remedial instruction. Soon thereafter, as an employee of the Roxbury School, he began tutoring Harvard students on a regular basis. Following service in the United States Army during World War I and a period of study at the University of Besançon in France, he returned to Boston in 1919 and opened his own tutoring establishment, the Mt. Auburn Tutoring School.

Laurence closed his school in 1921 to study law, first at Harvard and later at Boston University, from which he received a law degree in 1925. He never practiced law, however, and in 1926, after trying his hand at writing plays, he took a job as a general reporter for the *New York World*. There, Laurence found his true calling. When assigned to cover a lecture by James MacKaye challenging Einstein's theory of relativity, he produced a story that demonstrated his rare gift for reducing modern scientific theory to easily comprehended terms that led him eventually to be dubbed the "Boswell" of modern American science. Largely on the strength of that story the *New York Times* hired him as its full-time science reporter in 1930. He married Florence Davidow on Dec. 19, 1931; they had no children.

Laurence soon emerged as a leader in his new journalistic specialty. In 1934 he helped to found the National Association of Science Writers, and two years later he shared a Pulitzer Prize with four other science reporters for his coverage of Harvard's Tercentenary Conference of Arts and Sciences. In 1940 the American Institute of New York City awarded him a fellowship, citing his "pre-eminent record of reporting brilliantly . . . the achievements of science and technology."

Laurence was more than just a good chronicler of modern scientific progress. Thanks to his remarkable ability to envision the practical applications of a given development, he was also one of its catalysts, and on a number of occasions his reportage led to noteworthy advances in science. It was an article of his, for example, that prompted the Squibb Company to investigate further the medicinal uses of sulfadiazine. In another piece, he reported Vladimir Zworykin's thoughts on a supermicroscope for use in television. In so doing, he hastened the development of television by making Zworykin's superiors at Radio Corporation of America finally realize the value of a concept that they had ignored when Zworykin first raised it. Perhaps Laurence's most noteworthy contribution to science came in 1949, when in the course of reporting on the pain-relieving potentials of manufactured cortisone, he tracked down a little-known African plant whose seed could be used as a base for that drug.

No journalist had a quicker or deeper grasp of modern physics than Laurence. In 1940, taking his cue from a brief note in a science journal on efforts to isolate an isotope of uranium known as U-235, he produced the first lengthy discussion in the popular press about atomic energy and its enormous energy-generating powers. In the final months of World War II, this prescient piece of reporting led to Laurence's recruitment into the United States Army's top-secret Manhattan Project, charged with developing the atomic bomb. There he was assigned to draft the press releases that were to go out when the weapon finally became an actuality. In the process he observed most phases of the enterprise, including the detonation of an atomic bomb over Nagasaki, Japan, on Aug. 9, 1945, while he flew on an instrument plane. On returning to the *Times* shortly thereafter, he produced a series of articles on the history of this weapon and its wartime uses that earned him a second Pulitzer Prize.

Known afterward as "Atomic Bill," Laurence later wrote several books on atomic energy, among them *Dawn Over Zero* (1946) and *Men and Atoms* (1959). In 1956 he became science editor for the *Times*, a position that he held until his retirement in 1964. In his final years he served as a science consultant to the New York World's Fair and to the National Foundation–March of Dimes. He died in Majorca, Spain.

[A small collection of manuscripts and clippings on Laurence is in the archives of the *New York Times*, New York City. Laurence's writings include *The Hell Bomb* (1951) and *New Frontiers of Science* (1964). For Laurence's coverage of the Manhattan Project, see Meyer Berger, *The Story of the New York Times* (1951). The best published biographical source is Robert Simpson, "The Infinitesimal and the Infinite," *New Yorker*, Aug. 18, 1945. An obituary is in the *New York Times*, Mar. 19, 1977. Transcripts of lengthy interviews with Laurence are in the Biographical and Oral History Collection, Columbia University Libraries, New York City.]

FREDERICK S. VOSS

LAWSON, JOHN HOWARD (Sept. 25, 1894–Aug. 11, 1977), screenwriter, was born in New York City, the third child of Simeon Levy (later S. Levy Lawson) and Belle Hart. His father was the general manager in the United States and Canada for Reuters, the British news agency. In addition to tours of Europe, America, and Canada with a private governess, Lawson was educated at the Halstead School in Yonkers, N.Y., the Cutler School in New York City, and Williams College, where he determined to become a professional playwright. At Williams he was not permitted to join the staffs of either the school paper or the literary magazine because he was a Jew, even though he was one of the latter's most prolific contributors. He graduated in 1914 and went overseas as an ambulance driver during World War I, where he met Kay Drain, an American YMCA worker, who became his first wife.

Lawson began writing his first produced play, *Roger Bloomer*, while in France in 1918; some have speculated that the work was influenced by his brother's suicide. It was performed on Broadway in 1923 and is recognized as the first American expressionist play. His next play, *Processional*, about a coal miner oppressed by a capitalist figure called "The Man in the Silk Hat," was produced by the Theatre Guild in 1925. The following year he joined the New Playwrights Theatre, a group of avant-garde writers including John Dos Passos and Mike Gold, which produced *Nirvana* (1926), a failure after four performances, and *The International* (1928), an expressionistic musical about a rebellious young man who is a metaphor for world revolution. While acclaimed by those with Marxist sympathies, it ran for only twenty-seven performances.

In 1928, Lawson accepted an offer to write dialogue for Metro-Goldwyn-Mayer (MGM), which had just converted from silent films to talkies. After writing the talking sequence for *Flesh and the Devil* (originally released in 1926), and titles for *The Pagan* (1928), he wrote screenplays for *Dynamite* (1929), *The Ship from Shanghai* (1930), *Our Blushing Brides* (1930), and *The Sea Bat* (1930). He then returned to New York City to mount *Success Story* (1932), a play about Jewish middle-class workers struggling between capitalism and radicalism, for the Theatre Guild. Though it had mixed reviews, *Success Story* was Lawson's longest-running play, with 121 performances.

Lawson married his second wife, Susan, in 1930; they had two children. He accepted a contract from RKO Radio Pictures to write *Bachelor Apartment* (1931) in order to support his family. He then returned to MGM where, in 1933, studio head Louis B. Mayer announced a 50-percent cut in pay for all nonunion personnel. Lawson joined with Dudley Nichols, Oliver H. P. Garrett, and Ralph Bloch to revive the old Screen Writers Guild, originally founded in 1921, with the purpose of defending "the economic interests of authors in the film industry." He was the first to sign the Guild's "Code of Working Rules" and was elected its first president.

Both the chilly reception he received at MGM for his activism and the nonrenewal of his contract may have prompted Lawson's more radical involvement with the Communist party of the United States as he worked full-time at organizing the Guild. After a series of artistic failures in 1934—an unsuccessful film adaptation of *Success Story* for RKO called *Success at Any Price* and the simultaneous Broadway openings and closings of *The Pure in Heart* and *The Gentlewoman*—Lawson engaged in a public exchange of criticism and insult with the New York critics Percy Hammond, Brooks Atkinson, and Richard Garland, who referred to Lawson as "America's professional promising playwright." Feeling rejected by the New York establishment and ineffectual as a revolutionary, Lawson volunteered to write for the *Daily Worker* while in Alabama to research a play on the Tennessee Coal and Iron strike. When his articles about the strike appeared in the *New York Post*, he was arrested and run out of Alabama with orders not to return. After he wrote *Party Wire* (1935) for Columbia Pictures, and a treatise on Marxist dramatic theory, *Theory and Technique of Playwriting* (1936), his strike play *Marching Song* (1937) was produced by the Theatre Union. While praised in the *Daily Worker*, it was panned by the Broadway critics and ran for only sixty-one performances.

Lawson returned to Hollywood to write *Blockade* (1938) for the independent producer Walter Wanger and to organize for the Communist party. Additional screenwriting projects during this period were *Personal History* (later *Foreign Correspondent*, 1940), *They Shall Have Music* (1939), *Earthbound* (1939), *Four Sons* (1940), and *Action in the North Atlantic* (1942), which starred Raymond Massey and Humphrey Bogart. In 1943, Bogart starred in another Lawson-scripted film, *Sahara*, for Co-

Lazarsfeld

lumbia. Lawson's final Hollywood films were also for Columbia, including *Women at War* (1943), *Counter-Attack* (1945), and *The Jolson Story* (1946), from which Lawson had his name removed because of his dissatisfaction with the racist interpretation added to his script. *Smash-Up: The Story of a Woman* (1947), starring Susan Hayward, was the last film Lawson wrote before being blacklisted from Hollywood.

Lawson was called before the House Un-American Activities Committee as an unfriendly witness on Oct. 27, 1947. After being refused the opportunity to read a prepared statement, he was cited for contempt of Congress for refusing to confirm or deny his membership in the Communist party. Convicted in April 1948 and sentenced to one year in prison, Lawson entered the Ashland, Ky., Federal Reformatory on June 9, 1950. He shared a cell with Dalton Trumbo, another member of the "Hollywood Ten," which also included Adrian Scott, Samuel Ornitz, Albert Maltz, Ring Lardner, Jr., Edward Dmytryk, Lester Cole, Herbert Biberman, and Alvah Bessie. After his release, Lawson continued to write under a pseudonym and published several critical works, including *Theory and Technique of Playwriting and Screenwriting* (1949), *The Hidden Heritage* (1950), *Film in the Battle of Ideas* (1953), and *Film: The Creative Process* (1964). He spent the balance of his life working on a massive autobiography, which failed to find a publisher. Lawson died of complications from Parkinson's disease in San Francisco, Calif.

[Lawson's papers are in the Morris Library, Southern Illinois University of Carbondale, Ill., which has published *Lawson Biography and Inventory of John Howard Lawson Papers* (1971), indexing more than one hundred boxes of manuscripts and published materials. The New York Public Library for the Performing Arts at Lincoln Center contains an extensive clipping file on Lawson as well as his published works. A major biography is Gary Carr, *The Left Side of Paradise: The Screenwriting of John Howard Lawson* (1984). Obituaries are in the *New York Times*, Aug. 14, 1977; the *New York Post*, Aug. 15, 1977; and *Variety*, Aug. 17, 1977.]

SHARON CUMBERLAND

LAZARSFELD, PAUL FELIX (Feb. 13, 1901–Aug. 30, 1976), sociologist and a self-professed "managerial scholar," was born in Vienna, Austria, the son of Robert Lazarsfeld and Sofie Munk. His father was a lawyer with a penchant for defending impecunious political activists; as a result, the family's circumstances were modest. His middle-class Jewish family, though of limited means, expected its offspring to be educated, and Lazarsfeld ultimately enrolled at the University of Vienna. He first planned on a career in law but his interest changed to mathematics, and his doctorate, awarded in 1925, was in applied mathematics.

No sooner had Lazarsfeld begun teaching mathematics and physics in a Gymnasium in Vienna than his attention was diverted to social and psychological issues. Alfred Adler had trained Lazarsfeld's mother as a psychologist, and the young mathematician developed an intellectual attraction to Adler, whose opposition to Freud had a strong sociological tinge. Adler had been instrumental in educational reform in Vienna, and Lazarsfeld became, in his words, an "amateur 'educator,' " working as a counselor in socialist children's camps and as a tutor in high schools for working-class youths. That involvement reinforced his interest both in Marxism—he had earlier been active in the Socialist Student Movement—and in social science.

As a graduate student, Lazarsfeld had been exposed to writers prominent in science and the philosophy of science, particularly Ernst Mach, Henri Poincaré, and Albert Einstein. In his doctoral dissertation he had applied Einstein's theory of gravitation to the movement of the planet Mercury. If he had studied social science instead of mathematics, it is unlikely that he would have been exposed to these intellectual influences, for the social sciences were then dominated by philosophical and speculative approaches. Instead, he came to realize that in the social sciences, as in all science, the research procedures by which truths are uncovered are central to the successful development of a field. That focus on methodology became the hallmark of Lazarsfeld's work and, through him, helped to shape American sociology.

A turning point in Lazarsfeld's thinking came with the arrival at the University of Vienna, in 1923, of two distinguished German psychologists, Charlotte and Karl Bühler. Lazarsfeld attended their seminars and was asked by them to teach statistics. He established and directed an independent research center, the Division of Applied Psychology. He conducted consumer research for European and American firms as well as research in basic social psychology—which he was teaching at the university—and he encouraged graduate students to do their dissertations on data collected by the center. His own study of youth and occupational choice (published in *Jugend und Beruf*, 1931) demonstrated the limited opportunities for advancement available to working-class youngsters.

The criticism of a draft of that study by Charlotte Bühler and Lazarsfeld's response to it had a permanent effect on his later work. Lazarsfeld later wrote that she had "objected strenuously" to the compassionate tone of the section on proletarian youth, in which he had disparaged the bourgeoisie because of its exploitative practices. He rewrote the section, and the discussion became descriptive and detached. This episode contributed to the later controversy over the value-free stance of American sociology that was led by C. Wright Mills. In his voluminous subsequent publications, there is no hint that Lazarsfeld had ever been a Marxist.

Noteworthy in *Jugend und Beruf* was the demonstration of the importance of social-class position in determining life chances. Although class position was a central focus among both Marxist and non-Marxist sociologists, little empirical work had been done in Europe or in America using it as an explanatory variable. Lazarsfeld was one of the first to use that pivotal concept in an empirical study.

In 1933, Lazarsfeld won a Rockefeller Foundation traveling fellowship that brought him to the United States. Political unrest in Austria led to his request for an extension of the award, and by the fall of 1935, he decided to remain. Capitalizing on a position he had secured with the New Jersey Relief Administration, Lazarsfeld established a research center at the University of Newark in 1936, with himself as the director. The following year, he was appointed the director of the Office of Radio Research (ORR) at Princeton University, which had been established to study the effect of radio on American society.

Lazarsfeld's being in so prestigious a position was partly a result of his reputation as an innovator among a group of young "empiricists" to whom he had demonstrated the spurious effect certain variables such as age could have on correlations in statistical studies. He also had impressed Robert Lynd, the Columbia University sociologist whose study *Middletown* had, in some respects, paralleled that of Marienthal, a village that Lazarsfeld had investigated in Austria. Lynd set out to find Lazarsfeld a job in an academic world that was inhospitable to both foreigners and Jews. Lynd wrote one prospective employer that the Austrian did not look very Jewish, only to receive the reply that "Lazarsfeld shows clearly the marks of his race." Lynd finally convinced Hadley Cantril, a Princeton psychologist, that Lazarsfeld was the person for ORR. Not until much later was Lazarsfeld able to overcome his feelings of marginality that resulted from his foreignness, his Jewishness, and his marked accent.

At ORR, Lazarsfeld worked with Frank Stanton, the director of research of the Columbia Broadcasting System (later the president of that network), who was an associate director of ORR; together they became pioneers in the new field of mass communications. In 1939, ORR was transferred to Columbia University, where Lazarsfeld soon joined the department of sociology. ORR became the Bureau of Applied Social Research (BASR) and in 1945 was incorporated into the Columbia University structure. Lazarsfeld molded the bureau along the lines that he had developed in Vienna, and graduate training in sociology at Columbia came almost to require an apprenticeship in the research center. The graduate students who passed through it included some of the most distinguished sociologists in the United States and abroad. Lazarsfeld credited Charlotte Bühler with giving him an example of how a research institute should be organized. Yet he was aware that some members of the Vienna center had felt exploited by her, a charge later made against him as director of BASR.

In its early stages, ORR and then BASR were given only token financial support by their universities. Lazarsfeld conceived of a funding system whereby the research would be backed by grants from foundations, businesses, and government bureaus so that he would be free of the fiscal constraints imposed by inadequate university support. Doing research on contract for outside interests was a major innovation that spread throughout the academic world and represented a turning point in the history of American universities.

Lazarsfeld's aim was to use BASR and the classroom to develop methods for the study of individual and mass behavior using the rigor of mathematics. His own specialty was mathematical sociology. As might be expected, given the diverse sources of BASR's funding, the studies produced varied from simple market research surveys—such as—"Should Bloomingdale's Maintain Its Restaurant?"—to more basic inquiries, such as studies of voter preferences in the presidential elections of 1940 and 1948. The latter research made voting behavior an essential part of a new specialty, political sociology, another of Lazarsfeld's substantive interests.

BASR became a dominant influence in sociology at Columbia and, through its graduate students, in American sociology and beyond. Although Lazarsfeld gave up the directorship to become the chairman of the sociology department in 1951, his influence at BASR never waned. Columbia displaced the University of Chicago as the preeminent sociology department in the country. In retrospect, Lazarsfeld used BASR to institutionalize empirical research in the social sciences. That is, research was organized within the bureau, it was funded from outside the university, and it became collaborative—the single scholar doing an empirical study became outmoded; Lazarsfeld almost always had collaborators. His major methodological approach was the social survey. That method, which exemplified Lazarsfeld's mission to "quantify complex experiences," involved a number of components, including a sample of the population to be studied, an interview or a questionnaire whose questions or "items" reflected the objective of the research, and a statistical analysis of the responses that related them to the age, race, ethnicity, gender, social class, education, occupation, and religion of the respondents. Survey research dominated not only American sociology but also public opinion and mass communications, fields in which Lazarsfeld also achieved prominence.

Many distinguished Columbia faculty members—including C. Wright Mills—did survey research under the auspices of BASR. What could be called the "Columbia school of sociology" shaped the field in postwar America.

Lazarsfeld had his detractors. Some argued that the most important aspects of human experiences were so elusive that they were not subject to quantification or that sociology was a humanity as well as a social science, thereby requiring something analogous to artistic insight. Mills argued that Columbia's sociology was dehumanizing in its insistence on value detachment, and he refused to teach graduate students. Others charged that too often BASR's products were "little studies" of obscure fragments of social life. Some objected to the idea of the sociologist-for-hire enabling capitalists to manipulate consumers. Interestingly, sometimes the captains of industry suffered from the far-from-perfect state of market research. BASR's study of the social psychology of automobile buying produced several reports for the Ford Motor Company that it used to plan what became the Edsel.

Much of the criticism was unwarranted. Lazarsfeld had always believed that good sociology required a combination of insight, quantification, and a variety of methods. His study of Marienthal had used not only quantitative methods, including interviews and what came to be known as "unobtrusive measures" (such as the circulation of books from workers' libraries), but also qualitative methods, such as participant observation and life-history analysis. Lazarsfeld's name was equated with quantitative methods, but he always gave qualitative approaches their full measure.

Lazarsfeld had two collaborators in the Marienthal study, Hans Zeisel and Marie Jahoda. He married Jahoda, who had been his student; they had one child and were divorced by 1933. Lazarsfeld married twice more, each time to a former student and collaborator: Herta Herzog and Patricia Kendall, who at the time of his death was distinguished professor of sociology at Queens College of the City University of New York. He and his third wife had one child.

Lazarsfeld conducted many market research studies of limited sociological interest and importance—he used the alias Elias Smith to hide their authorship—but his substantive work was marked by a search for explanation and for theory. He worked closely with Robert K. Merton, the equally brilliant Columbia theoretician, and together they demonstrated the interdependence of theory and empirical research. When critics argued that survey research, by focusing on live respondents, neglected historical influences, Lazarsfeld added a historian to the sociology faculty, an unprecedented appointment.

During the convulsions in the American university attendant on the war in Vietnam, the sociology department at Columbia came under attack. Ironically, the Marxist approach, which Lazarsfeld had left behind him in Austria, was one of the intellectual spearheads in this. To some extent, quantification, attention to methodological detail, and value neutrality were sacrificed to new approaches, which frequently were ideologically motivated. BASR lost its predominant position in 1977 and was merged with other research centers at Columbia and became the Center for Social Science. Lazarsfeld died in New York City.

During his lifetime, Lazarsfeld received many honors. He was appointed Quetelet professor of social sciences at Columbia in 1962, the title reflecting both his perduring interest in mathematics and his ambivalence about calling himself a sociologist. After retiring from Columbia he became distinguished professor of sociology at the University of Pittsburgh (1969–1976). His legacy includes a focus in social science on empirical studies, a self-consciousness with the procedures used to conduct survey research, sophisticated statistical analysis, and the creation of institutional conditions that promoted research and the training of graduate students.

[Lazarsfeld's papers are in the Rare Books Division of the Columbia University Library. Papers, reports, and files of the BASR are in the Lehman Library at Columbia University, and the Lazarsfeld Archives at the University of Vienna contain a collection of his books and papers. The Clearwater Publishing Company, New York City, also has materials from BASR. Lazarsfeld's many publications include *Six Papers on Statistical and Educational Psychology* (1930); *Die Arbeitslosen von Marienthal* (1933), with Marie Jahoda and Hans Zeisel; *The People's Choice* (1944), with Bernard Berelson and Hazel Gaudet; *Voting* (1954), with Bernard Berelson and William N. McPhee; *The Language of Social Research* (1955), with Morris Rosenberg; *Personal Influence* (1955), with Elihu Katz; and *The Academic Mind* (1958), with Wagner Thielens, Jr.

On Lazarsfeld and his work, see Paul Lazarsfeld, "An Episode in the History of Social Research: A Memoir," *Perspectives in American History* (1968); James S. Coleman, "Paul F. Lazarsfeld: The Substance and Style of His Work," in Robert K. Merton and Matilda White Riley, eds., *Sociological Traditions from Generation to Generation* (1980); and David Sills, "Paul Lazarsfeld: 1901–1976," *Biographical Memoirs. National Academy of Sciences* (1987). An obituary is in the *New York Times*, Sept. 1, 1976.]

SIDNEY H. ARONSON

LEAF, WILBUR MUNRO (Dec. 4, 1905–Dec. 21, 1976), writer and illustrator of children's books, was born in Hamilton, Md., the son of Charles Wilbur Leaf, a printer, and Emma India Gillespie. Leaf, a third-generation descendant on both maternal and paternal sides of Maryland families, was educated at public schools in the Washington, D.C., area. He received a B.A. from the University of Maryland in 1927 and an M.A. in English literature from Harvard in 1931. During summer vacations from college, he worked on such jobs as road construction in Virginia, ranching in Montana, and as a deckhand on a British tramp steamer carrying coal from Baltimore to Dublin, Ireland. He also went to Army Reserve officers camp.

For approximately ten years before Leaf began writing and illustrating children's books, he taught in preparatory schools and worked in publishing. From 1929 to 1931 he taught English and coached football in Belmont, Mass., and Wynnewood, Pa. He worked briefly for Bobbs-Merrill as a manuscript reader before being employed by Frederick A. Stokes, Publishers, as an editor and director from 1932 to 1939. Leaf married Margaret Butler Pope of Washington, D.C., on Dec. 29, 1926; the couple had two children.

Leaf's first children's book, *Grammar Can Be Fun* (1934), was inspired when he overheard a mother in the New York City subway struggling to explain to her child why "ain't" was ungrammatical. The book illustrated other frequent mistakes in grammar with prankish personified stick figures. *Grammar Can Be Fun* became the first in a series of ten semididactic titles, all in a similar format, on a variety of important childhood subjects covering manners, safety, health, history, geography, patriotism, reading, and science. The last book in this series was *Metric Can Be Fun!* (1976).

Over a period of forty-two years, Leaf wrote, illustrated, or collaborated with other artists on more than forty books, mostly for readers aged three to nine. Although he had no formal art training, Leaf's unique style and simple pen-and-ink drawings succeeded in large part due to their sincerity, refreshing humor, common sense, and broad range of interest. His writing was clear and easily understood; his ideas appealed directly to a wide range of readers.

His best-known book, *The Story of Ferdinand* (1936), was written in "forty minutes one rainy Sunday afternoon" and illustrated by his friend Robert Lawson. The story of a gentle young bull who would rather sniff at flowers than fight in a bullring, *Ferdinand*

Leaf

immediately captured the imagination of young and old alike and became both a perennial best-seller and a modern American classic. The seemingly simple story struck a deep emotional chord with the public.

Leaf maintained that his whimsical tale, a mere eight hundred words long, had no inherent message. But many readers including critics, established a canon of symbolic interpretation and controversial analysis around peace-loving Ferdinand. Discussion ranged from psychoanalytic theory to various political ideologies, including antiwar support during the Vietnam War. Speaking on behalf of her late husband during a fiftieth-anniversary celebration for the book held in 1986, Margaret Leaf stated what she believed to be the book's message, "that Ferdinand has the courage to refuse to do what he knows is wrong for him." However, Leaf himself always maintained that the message was not his but rather Ferdinand's and that readers should get the message from Ferdinand according to their own need. Leaf also explained that he chose a passive bull named for the Spanish king so that it would stand out among the countless juvenile books on dogs, cats, and other common animals already in print.

In 1938, Walt Disney Studios bought the movie rights to *Ferdinand* for $800, which Leaf divided among himself, Robert Lawson, and the book's publisher, Viking Press. The Oscar-winning animated film version was remarkably true to the book and remained popular even after its re-release on videotape. Ferdinand also inspired original music scores as well as numerous popular recordings; various merchandise items including diamond pins, toys, board games, and cereal favors were successfully sold to Ferdinand's fans. During the late 1930's and 1940's, Ferdinand was one of the most popular characters in children's literature and was translated into sixty languages. At the time of Leaf's death it had already sold 2.5 million copies in the United States.

Leaf collaborated with Robert Lawson on two additional books. *Wee Gillis* (1938), a fable set in Scotland about a small boy who resolves a family clan conflict as well as a personal problem, earned a Caldecott honor award in 1939. Their third and last book together was a version of *Aesop's Fables* (1941). *Noodle* (1937), the story of a dachsund, was illustrated by Ludwig Bemelmans. *Turnabout* (1967) was a departure from Leaf's usual style, using full-color artwork to educate as well as entertain children about the proper treatment of animals.

From 1938 to 1960, Leaf wrote and edited a "Watchbirds" column for the *Ladies' Home Journal* using his trademark stick characters to teach children rules of etiquette based on kindness and helpfulness. These monthly columns, which gave Leaf his widest adult readership, were published in a series of four books as well as in an omnibus, *Flock of Watchbirds* (1946).

In 1942, Leaf enlisted in the United States Army, serving in the Pentagon and Europe during World War II and earning the rank of major before he left in 1946. During his service he collaborated with Dr. Seuss (Theodore Geisel) to produce an army field manual on malaria entitled *The Story of Ann*, short for anopheles mosquito. While unorthodox in presentation, their pamphlet was widely circulated to Allied forces in the Pacific and went into nearly seven million copies.

The war years began a long and productive relationship with the government. Leaf's publications included a series of political pamphlets supporting the postwar Marshall Plan and a goodwill handbook on the United Nations. He also helped write some of President Franklin D. Roosevelt's fireside chats and later worked with President Lyndon B. Johnson's War on Poverty program.

From 1961 to 1964 he served the State Department as an emissary for American democratic ideals and the promotion of literacy and good books for children. Accompanied by his wife, Leaf made three tours of duty to over twenty countries in Europe, Asia, and the Middle East as part of a cultural and educational exchange program. Together the Leafs lectured and shared their commitment with cultural attachés, writers and publishers, educators, librarians, students, and children, with Leaf using his particular style to illustrate his talks. A direct result of these cultural exchanges was the booklet *I Hate You! I Hate You!* (1968), which Leaf wrote and illustrated. He later considered it his most satisfying work. In keeping with Leaf's philosophy of international unity and concern for children all over the world, its message was one of tolerance and understanding between races, nationalities, and religions.

Leaf, who loved and respected children, did not sentimentalize or speak down to them. He remained steadfast in his belief that basic education was the "hottest commodity" in the world and books the backbone of education. An early book for children on ecology and the environment, *Who Cares? I Do*, was published in 1971.

Leaf's concern with adult attitudes and behavior was evident in his collaboration with William C. Menninger, the noted psychiatrist, on *You and Psychiatry* (1948). Other adult works included *Listen, Little Girl, Before You Come to New York* (1938) and the book and lyrics for a musical comedy, *You Can Take It, Columbus* (1949), produced by the Connecticut Playmakers of Old Greenwich, Conn. Leaf also wrote under two pseudonyms, Mun (*Lo, the Poor Indian*, 1934) and John Calvert (*Gwendolyn the Goose*, 1946).

Leaf was a small, dynamic man possessing high energy, good humor, a keen intellect, and deep convictions. Although semiretired, Leaf continued to accept speaking engagements, using his famous chalk talks, until shortly before his death. He died of cancer at his home in suburban Garret Park, Md.

[No biography of Leaf exists. See Lee Bennett Hopkins, *Books Are by People* (1969); Margaret Leaf, "Happy Birthday, Ferdinand!" *Publishers Weekly*, Oct. 31, 1986; and Michael P. Hearn, "Ferdinand the Bull's 50th Anniversary," *Washington Post Book World*, Nov. 8, 1986. A curriculum guide to *The Story of Ferdinand*, by Sonia Landes and Molly Flender, was published in 1987. Obituaries are in the *New York Times*, Dec. 22, 1976; and the *Washington Post*, Dec. 23, 1976.]

MARY SUE D. SCHUSKY

LEAR, WILLIAM POWELL (June 26, 1902–May 14, 1978), aeronautical engineer, entrepreneur, and inventor, was born in Hannibal, Mo., the son of Reuben Lear, a carpenter, and Gertrude Elizabeth Powell. Lear was raised in an abusive, broken home; in 1913 his mother moved with him to Chicago, where she married Otto Kirmse. Lear was fascinated by electronics and airplanes and dropped out of Englewood High School in 1919 to work at an airplane hangar in Grant Park. The following year he left Chicago for the West Coast, taking odd jobs on the way.

Regular work proved hard to find, so in September 1920, Lear joined the United States Navy and was sent to the Great Lakes Training Station north of Chicago to study radio. Discharged six months later because of manpower cutbacks, Lear began working for Western Union as a teletype operator. His first business venture was Quincy Radio Laboratories, which in 1922 began manufacturing and servicing single-tube radios. The same year he married Ethel Peterson; they had two children, one of whom died in infancy.

Lear continued his interest in aviation; having relocated to Oklahoma, in 1925 he built his first aircraft from a kit, a one-seater Lincoln Sport. On Oct. 4, 1926, after obtaining a divorce, he married Madeline Murphy; they had two children and were divorced in 1931. After returning to Chicago, center of the American radio industry, Lear became a consultant to several radio manufacturers, helping them overcome technical problems. By 1928 he was again manufacturing radios, with his nine-tube design incorporating many of his theories.

Lear also began to develop a design for an inexpensive car radio, which resulted in his first patent. The radio was marketed by Galvin Manufacturing Company in 1930 under the name Motorola and was an immediate success. Lear now formed his second company, Lear-Wuerfel, with another engineer, Bob Wuerfel. By 1931 he was a sought-after radio engineer. He indulged his interest in aircraft, and as a result of his flying experience became intrigued with the problems of aerial radio receiving and navigation. He dissolved Lear-Wuerfel and opened Lear Developments in July 1931 at the Curtiss-Reynolds Airport in Glenview, Ill., to manufacture airplane receivers for navigation.

Short of capital to fund his interest in radio navigation, Lear in 1934 adapted turret-type tuners for use in radios. He sold the idea to RCA for $50,000 cash and $40,000 per year for five years, money that was used to underwrite Lear Developments. In January 1935, Lear Developments unveiled the radio direction finder, the Learoscope. Since domestic sales were sluggish, Lear attempted to sell his devices to foreign governments, including Japan, but was blocked by the State Department. Fighting off takeover offers from Bendix Corporation, he moved to Roosevelt Field in Mineola, N.Y., in 1938, broke with his partners, and set up Lear Radio, where a work force of forty assembled receivers, transmitters, and direction finders.

In 1939, Lear patented fifteen new inventions, among them automatic trailing antennas and an automatic direction finder, ADF-6, a device so sophisticated that it could be used for blind landings.

Lear now expanded his company with new

investors, changed its name to Lear Avia, and moved his base of operations to the Vandalia airport, ten miles north of Dayton, Ohio. His factory soon employed 300 workers working in four continuous shifts.

While his business life was on a sound footing, Lear's personal life remained turbulent. In 1936 he married Margaret Radell, who divorced him within eighteen months. He set up trust funds for three of his children but made no provisions for his daughter Mary Louise, from whom he was estranged.

By 1940, Lear Avia was flourishing, with annual sales of $912,000. The war in Europe would help Lear further expand his business; research and development offices were opened in New York City and Hollywood. The following year Lear Avia submitted fourteen patent applications to the government; among them were a number of designs for airplane electromechanical devices that incorporated the "fastop" clutch for controlling wing and aileron surfaces, replacing the hydraulic systems then in use. Sales of Lear Avia products went up 60 percent in 1941, to $1.6 million; and by 1945 the company employed 4,000 people.

Lear's personal life began to stabilize; on Jan. 5, 1942, he married Moya Marie Olsen; they had four children. At the end of the war, Lear bought out his partners, moved the company to Grand Rapids, Mich., and renamed it Lear Incorporated. At the same time he took it public with an initial share offering of 450,000 priced at $5 each. The deal made Lear a multimillionaire.

Lear's biggest interest in the postwar era was designing a true autopilot. The United States Air Force awarded Lear Incorporated a $128,000 development grant; Lear delivered the C-2 prototype in early 1947. A second design for the F-80 jet, the F-5, was developed the same year. The contract subsequently awarded to Lear Incorporated for a modified F-5 was worth nearly $1 billion over the next twelve years, as the mechanism was installed in all American combat aircraft. Another Lear success was the VGI (Vertical Gyro Indicator), installed in all American military aircraft. Lear sales by 1954 climbed to $54 million.

Lear now entered aircraft production; his Learstar was a modified Lockheed Lodestar design, which flew at 300 miles per hour and had a cruising range of 3,800 miles. On a personal level, in 1956 he became the first private pilot from the West to fly into Moscow.

Lear's interest in aircraft production induced him to begin thinking about building an aircraft of his own design, the SAAC-23, which would eventually emerge as the Lear Jet. In order to invest in the aircraft's design and production, Lear in 1962 sold his shares and interests in Lear Incorporated for approximately $12.5 million; the agreement also allowed him to keep the Lear Jet name, which would be developed under the aegis of his new company, Lear Jet Corporation.

Lear now moved his base of operations to Wichita, Kans., having negotiated a generous development package with the city. He budgeted $12 million for the development of the first Lear Jet prototype. The production line was to move directly into production tooling, rather than waiting for modifications to the prototype before beginning production. Lear's contributions to the project were especially marked in the electronics and avionics designs. On Oct. 7, 1963, Lear Jet 801-L made its maiden flight, and performed flawlessly. On July 31, 1964, the Lear Jet received its FAA certification. The aircraft was an immediate success as the first commercially produced business jet; by June 1965 the company had orders for more than 100 aircraft at $600,000 apiece. Other jet designs were quickly developed.

Lear did not rest on his laurels; the same year, he invented the eight-track car stereo player, which was immediately franchised by Ford and RCA Victor.

By 1967, cash flow problems forced Lear to sell his company. His next interest was an environmentally advanced steam-powered automobile engine. Lear now formed Lear Motors to research the project. Despite innumerable setbacks, Lear in June 1970 signed a contract with California to develop a steam-powered bus. Two years later, the California Steam Bus Project declared the prototype a success. It predicted that with adequate funding a general-use steam engine would be ready for use within a decade. The funding was not forthcoming from either the government or the private sector, however, and Lear was forced to abandon the project by 1975.

Lear turned again to aircraft design; his proposed Learstar 600 was a turbofan jet aircraft with a projected speed of 600 miles per hour, a range of 4,000 miles, and a passenger capacity of fourteen. The plane's revolutionary design incorporated extensive use of epoxy resin composites, greatly reducing the aircraft's weight. While the design was never built, Lear used the experience to design a composites-based twin-propeller aircraft, the Lear Fan.

Lear never saw the Lear Fan fly, however; his health began to fail. In early 1978 he was diagnosed with acute leukemia. He died in Reno, Nev. His family scattered his ashes over the Pacific.

[See L. E. Leipold, *William P. Lear* (1967); Victor Boesen, *They Said It Couldn't Be Done* (1971); and Richard Rashke, *Stormy Genius* (1985). A documentary film is *By the Seat of His Pants*, narrated by Lloyd Bridges (1975). An obituary is in the *New York Times*, May 15, 1978.]

JOHN C. K. DALY

LEEMANS, ALPHONSE E. ("TUFFY") (Nov. 12, 1912–Jan. 19, 1979), professional football player, was born in Eloise, Wis., one of four children of Joseph and Hortense Leemans, immigrant Belgian miners. Leemans spent most of his childhood in Superior, Wis., where he earned the nickname "Tuffy" by playing with, and sometimes physically dominating, older boys in pickup football games. After playing football in high school and graduating in 1931, Leemans enrolled in the University of Oregon, but he later transferred to George Washington University in the District of Columbia.

During the 1930's, George Washington was a major collegiate football power, and Leemans was its star. Between 1933 and 1935, Leemans gained 2,382 yards on 490 rushing attempts. He was also among the team's leaders in passing and receiving, and he played defense as well. Following his senior season Leemans was chosen to appear in the 1936 College All-Star Game against the National Football League (NFL) champion Detroit Lions. Leemans's selection owed a great deal to a local Washington sportswriter who mailed in ballots for Leemans wrapped around bits of straw, suggesting he had more votes than he really did. In addition to playing, Leemans was also supposed to report on the College All-Star Game as a correspondent for the *Washington Herald*. His modesty, expressed as an inability to write about himself even though he was the star of the pregame scrimmages, brought a quick end to his journalistic career. Leemans was selected as the collegians' most valuable player after their 7–7 tie with Detroit.

After the College All-Star Game, Leemans reported to the New York Giants, who had chosen him as the second overall pick of the inaugural NFL draft. As a rookie Leemans became the first Giant to lead the league in rushing, gaining 830 yards on 206 carries. Leemans was the only first-year player named to the official all-league team.

Leemans played the right halfback position in Giants coach Steve Owens's unique A-formation offense. The right halfback's responsibilities were similar to those of the tailback in the more conventional single-wing offense. Only six feet tall and weighing 180 pounds, Leemans called the plays and was used variously as a runner, receiver, or passer. Coach Owens ran the A formation as a two-platoon system. Leemans and the other starters would begin the game and play both offense and defense. Then, at some point, the second platoon would replace them and also play offense and defense. This lack of specialization prevented Leemans and other players of his era from accumulating statistics equal to those of today's football players. In his time, however, Leemans was considered to be a workhorse.

Leemans played for the New York Giants from 1936 until 1943, spending his last season as a player-coach. During that time the Giants had a combined regular season record of 53 wins, 27 losses, and 8 ties. They played in the NFL championship game in 1938, 1939, and 1941. In the 1938 championship game Leemans scored on a six-yard touchdown run to help the Giants beat the Green Bay Packers 23–17. In 1941 his thirty-one-yard pass to George Franck accounted for the Giants' only touchdown in a 37–9 loss to the Chicago Bears.

Leemans married Theodora Rinaldi in 1938. The couple had two children.

Throughout his career Leemans was known less as a player blessed with speed and physical talent than as one who achieved success through determination and competitive desire. *New York Times* sportswriter Arthur Daley said Leemans had "an uncanny knack of squirting out of the grasps of tacklers for extra yardage." He played his best when the game was on the line.

Unlike other players, Leemans's career was not disrupted by military service during World War II. A head injury suffered in a 1942 game against the Chicago Bears left him deaf in one ear. Leemans ended his NFL career with 3,142 yards and 17 touchdowns rushing, 2,324 yards and 25 touchdowns passing, and 422 yards and 3 touchdowns on 28 pass receptions. He was an all-pro selection in 1936 and 1939, and the Giants retired his jersey.

Following his football retirement, Leemans moved to Silver Spring, Md., where he became a successful businessman. He owned a mini-bowling lane and had a number of other investments; he also coached at Bishop Carroll High School in Washington, D.C. Leemans was elected into the National Football League Pro Football Hall of Fame in Canton, Ohio, in July 1978. In addition he was chosen by the Pro Football Hall of Fame Selection Committee as a back on the official All-Time Team of the 1930's.

Leemans remained interested in football up until the time of his death in Hillsboro Beach, Fla. He had gone to Florida with his wife and another couple to see the Super Bowl.

[Memorabilia and newspaper clippings are in the National Football League Pro Football Hall of Fame in Canton, Ohio. An interview with Leemans appears in Myron Cope, *The Game That Was: The Early Days of Pro Football* (1970). See also Tom Bennett et al., *The NFL's Official Encyclopedic History of Professional Football* (1977); and Don R. Smith, *Pro Football Hall of Fame All Time Greats* (1988). An obituary is in the *New York Times*, Jan. 20, 1979.]

HAROLD W. AURAND, JR.

LEHMANN, LOTTE (Feb. 27, 1888–Aug. 26, 1976), operatic and concert soprano, was born in Perleberg, Germany, the daughter of Carl Lehmann, a minor official of a benevolent society, and Marie Schuster. Her full christened name was Charlotte Sophie Pauline Lehmann. After elementary education in Perleberg and studies at the Ulrich Lyceum in Berlin, she enrolled for private vocal training at the Royal High School of Music in Berlin. She and the distinguished teacher Etelka Gerster were incompatible, and it was not until she began to study with Mathilde Mallinger, a star of Bayreuth and Berlin who had created Eva in *Die Meistersinger*, that her voice was properly placed. Lehmann was offered an engagement with the Hamburg Opera, where she made her professional debut as the Second Boy in Mozart's *Die Zauberflöte* on Sept. 2, 1910. Stage experience in a multitude of small parts, and singing under such eminent conductors as Arthur Nikisch and Otto Klemperer, developed her as an artist. A real breakthrough came in 1912 with her success in her first major role, Elsa, in *Lohengrin*. After this came other leading parts: Sieglinde in *Die Walküre*, Eva in *Die Meistersinger*, Micaela in *Carmen*, Elisabeth in *Tannhäuser*, and many others.

In 1916, Lehmann moved to the Court Opera in Vienna. After a successful debut in August as Agathe in *Der Freischütz*, in October she became a star when she created the role of the Composer in the premiere of the revised version of Richard Strauss's *Ariadne auf Naxos*. This began her long association with Strauss, who had requested her for the role and whose guidance and coaching became a major influence on her career. In addition to *Ariadne*, she sang in the Vienna premieres of *Die Frau ohne Schatten* (1919), *Intermezzo* (1924), and *Arabella* (1933). In 1914, Lehmann had begun her international career by singing Sophie in Strauss's then-new *Der Rosenkavalier* in London under Thomas Beecham; that fall in Hamburg she added the trouser role of Octavian, and in 1924 in London she sang what became her greatest part, the Marschallin. It was her role in this opera for the rest of her career, and the role in which she sang her farewell to opera in 1946.

Lehmann's years in Vienna saw a succession of triumphs. She sang an immense number of roles—the variety and range of which her later American career gave little indication: Puccini and Massenet, Mozart and Tchaikovsky, as well as Beethoven, Wagner, and Strauss. She and the Moravian soprano Maria Jeritza divided the loyalties of the knowledgeable Viennese public.

Lehmann had an appeal that went beyond the glowing beauty of her voice. She even managed to convert her vocal defects—and she was the first to admit that there *were* defects—into strengths. For example, her breathing was flawed, but she managed to turn the necessity of snatching a breath into a dramatic asset, creating an illumination of character from a moment of physical frailty. And she was able to do this on the recital platform as well as on the operatic stage, touching her audiences with the sense that they were hearing an aspiring, though imperfect, human being, like themselves.

Lehmann moved beyond central Europe in the 1920's with a season in South America (Buenos Aires, Montevideo, Rio, São Paulo) in 1922, London in 1924 and annually thereafter through the 1930's, Paris in 1928, and Brussels and Stockholm in 1929. In 1926 she began the series of appearances at the Salzburg Festival that continued until the Nazis took over Austria in 1938. Throughout her career she sang with the greatest conductors: Nikisch, Klemperer, Thomas Beecham, Franz Schalk, Richard Strauss, Bruno Walter, and Arturo Toscanini.

On Apr. 28, 1926, Lehmann married Otto Krause; they had no children. In October 1930 she made her American debut, not at the Metropolitan Opera in New York City, where her rival Maria Jeritza reigned, but at the Chicago Civic Opera, whose company was then the equal, in artistry and opulence, of the Metropolitan. As Sieglinde, Elsa, and Elisabeth she convinced the American critics that she was a first-rank German lyric soprano, and it was in these seasons (1930–1932) that she began the song recitals in which she continued to enchant audiences after her operatic days were over.

With the rise of Hitler, Lehmann's German career effectively ended, for while she was not Jewish, and indeed had been invited by Hermann Göring to sing in Berlin, she preferred not to perform where Nazis ruled. After 1938, Austria heard her no more. She became an American citizen in 1945, eleven years after she made her Metropolitan debut following the departure of Jeritza from the company. She sang there for twelve seasons, until a final *Rosenkavalier* in February 1945. Her last operatic appearances were in the same work with the San Francisco Opera in 1945 and 1946. A reduced operatic schedule was balanced by an increased number of lieder recitals, where the purely vocal demands were not as great, and where her deepening interpretative insights increasingly illuminated the rich world of song for an ever more affectionate public. No singer did more than Lehmann to bring a knowledge of German song to American audiences.

On Feb. 16, 1951, just a few days before her sixty-third birthday, Lehmann sang her farewell concert at Town Hall in New York City. Though there were later a few recitals elsewhere, it was in effect the end of her singing career.

After Lehmann retired to Santa Barbara, Calif., she became a distinguished teacher of such renowned pupils as Marilyn Horne, Grace Bumbry, Carol Neblett, Jeannine Altmeyer, Maralin Niska, and Janet Baker. When she returned to Austria in 1955 for the reopening of the State Opera, where she had sung so brilliantly for so many years, the outpouring of affection of the Viennese public proved that their most beloved singer had not been forgotten. In 1962 Lehmann helped stage the Metropolitan revival of *Der Rosenkavalier* with Régine Crespin in the role of the Marschallin. She painted, sculpted, wrote, and recorded recitals of poetry, exhibiting tireless creative energy. With advancing years, declining strength necessarily limited her activities. Lehmann died in Santa Barbara.

[Lehmann's papers are in the Lotte Lehmann Archives of the Library of the University of California, Santa Barbara. See her autobiography, *Midway in My Song*, translated by Margaret Ludwig (1938). She also wrote books on her operatic roles, *My Many Lives*, translated by Frances Holden (1948), and *Five Operas and Richard Strauss*, translated by Ernst Pawel (1964); and on her song interpretations, *More Than Singing*, translated by Frances Holden (1945), and *Eighteen Song Cycles* (1971). The standard biography is Beaumont Glass, *Lotte Lehmann* (1988), which includes a complete discography compiled by Gary Hickling; the usefulness of hearing Lehmann's recordings listed therein cannot be overstated. Also valuable are P. L. Miller, "Lotte Lehmann," *Record News* (1960); and Harold C. Schonberg's appreciation in the *New York Times*, Nov. 4, 1962. An obituary is in the *New York Times*, Aug. 27, 1976.]

THOMAS FURCRON

LEIBOWITZ, SAMUEL SIMON (Aug. 14, 1893–Jan. 11, 1978), criminal defense lawyer and judge, was born Samuel Simon Lebeau in Jassy, Romania, the only child of Bina and Isaac Lebeau, who were Orthodox Jews. His father was a moderately successful merchant who owned a dry-goods store. In 1897, uncomfortable with government-sanctioned anti-Semitism, the family migrated to the United States. They arrived in New York City on March 17 and settled on the Lower East Side in the borough of Manhattan.

Soon after their arrival, a friend who had been in America slightly longer advised Isaac that he would be more successful if he "Americanized" his name. Isaac took the advice and immediately hired a lawyer to change the family name to Leibowitz, the name the friend suggested as "more American."

By 1906 the family had purchased a home in the East New York–Cypress Hills section of Brooklyn, and Isaac Leibowitz had opened a dry-goods store on Fulton Street in the downtown area of Brooklyn. Samuel was educated in the city's public schools and attended Jamaica High School in Queens.

In 1912, at the age of eighteen, Leibowitz entered the Colleges of Agriculture and Law at Cornell University. Although he had been a mediocre student, he became intrigued by the law and started to excel academically. He also plunged into campus life. The five-foot, eleven-inch, slim young man participated in various sports, made the debating team, and served as president of the Cornell Congress (a public issues forum). He also pursued his interest in theater and became the first Jewish member of the Cornell Dramatic Club. After graduation in 1915, Leibowitz returned to Brooklyn, where he worked for several law firms, including that of Michael F. McGoldrick, then Brooklyn's most prominent attorney.

In 1919, unhappy with a civil practice and the lack of opportunity to litigate, Leibowitz opened his own firm on Court Street in Brooklyn and began to specialize in criminal law. The decision to become part of the criminal bar was actually made earlier. His interest began during the summer before he graduated, when he spent much of the time watching criminal cases tried in the Brooklyn courts. The life-and-death drama of those trials fascinated him. He also recognized that opportunities in other, more lucrative areas of law would be limited. He calculated that as a successful criminal lawyer he would be able to attract clients by building a reputation for winning. His first case, which he handled pro bono, was clearly a losing one against a perpetual drunk who had admitted to stealing $7 and a bottle of whiskey from a saloon. To the surprise and outrage of both the judge and the assistant district attorney, Leibowitz pleaded his client not guilty, and won. The self-confidence he displayed in the courtroom, and the techniques that he employed—diligent preparation that included anticipation of the prosecutor's case, a dramatic courtroom presentation, the skilled use of expert witnesses, and, especially, careful attention to the jury—became the hallmark of the Leibowitz style.

On Dec. 25, 1919, after an arduous courtship, Leibowitz married Belle Munves, a graduate of the Manhattan Institute of Music (now Juilliard), who gave up the idea of pursuing a career as a concert pianist. They had three children.

As his reputation grew, Leibowitz began to attract many widely publicized cases. Ultimately he won 139 of 140 capital cases, including the defense of Al Capone and other mob figures of the 1920's and 1930's. In 1931, after he had won acquittals for two police officers on charges of corruption brought by the Seabury Committee, which had been investigating corruption in the police department and the lower courts, a grand jury indicted Leibowitz and his associate on one count of suborning perjury and one count of conspiring to have four witnesses give perjured testimony. The indictments were dismissed on appeal, on the grounds of legal insufficiency. The Appellate Division later reinstated one charge, which was dismissed by the Brooklyn district attorney.

In his most celebrated case, Leibowitz in 1933 undertook the defense of the Scottsboro Boys, nine young black men accused of raping two white vagabonds in Alabama. Robert Leibowitz, his son and biographer, suggests that his father was "motivated by an amalgam of genuine outrage and a compelling desire to increase the realm of his renown." Working pro bono, Leibowitz seized on the absence of blacks on jury rolls to argue, through successive appeals to the Supreme Court (*Norris* v. *Alabama*, 1935), that the defendants' due-process rights were violated. Leibowitz's arguments prevailed, forcing Alabama to include African Americans on its jury rolls. The decision prevented Alabama from executing the men. However, Leibowitz did not win their freedom, and all nine served long prison terms. On his retirement from the bench in 1969, Leibowitz told a reporter from the *New York Times* that his proudest accomplishment was "that I got the first black man on a jury in the South in the history of the United States."

In 1941, Leibowitz was sworn in as a judge of the Kings County Court; he became a justice of the New York State Supreme Court of Kings County in 1962, when the courts were merged. On the bench he remained a controversial figure, a strong supporter of capital punishment who was known for meting out harsh sentences. In one of his most widely publicized actions as a judge, Leibowitz, between 1949 and 1951, led a grand-jury investigation that uncovered a connection between high-ranking police officials and Harry Gross, who ran a multimillion-dollar bookmaking operation for organized crime. Several high-ranking police officials were convicted and jailed.

Leibowitz defended the severity of his sentences and merciless treatment of criminals by citing his experience at the criminal bar: "For 22 years I lived with them all—Scarface, Capone, all of them. I know what you do with a dangerous snake. [If] you can't take the fangs out, at least you put him away where he can't bite anybody."

In 1953, without leaving the bench, Leibowitz sought the Democratic nomination for mayor of New York City; when it did not look as if he would be successful, he accepted nomination on a fusion ticket. His acceptance speech emphasized law and order. In August, saying that he was unable to raise the $1 million he considered the necessary minimum for waging a credible campaign, Leibowitz withdrew from the ticket.

In September 1963, when Leibowitz reached the age of seventy, the mandatory retirement age for judges, the Association of the Bar of New York objected to granting him an extension. Citing his lack of judicial temperament, "his habitual arrogance and discourtesy to lawyers and litigants, his frequent embroilment in distasteful and grossly unjudicial incidents," the association argued that continuation of Leibowitz on the bench was "contrary to the public interest and not in the best interest of the administration of justice." Nevertheless, the Board of the New York State Judicial Conference extended Leibowitz's tenure for three two-year terms, the maximum allowed under the law.

After he retired from the bench, Leibowitz remained active in private practice, teaching, and lecturing until his death in Brooklyn, N.Y.

[The Samuel Simon Leibowitz papers (and audiotapes) are in the Department of Manuscripts and University Archives, Cornell University Libraries. See Alva Johnson, "Let Freedom Ring," *New Yorker*, June 4 and 11, 1932; Quentin Reynolds, *Courtroom* (1950); and Robert Leibowitz, *The Defender* (1981). An obituary is in the *New York Times*, Jan. 12, 1978.]

NEDDA C. ALLBRAY

LENNON, JOHN WINSTON ONO (Oct. 9, 1940–Dec. 8, 1980), singer, guitarist, and songwriter, was born in Liverpool, England, the son of Alfred ("Freddie") Lennon, a merchant seaman, and Julia Stanley. Lennon's father was absent during his early childhood and later estranged from Julia Lennon. It was decided that Lennon's best chance for a stable upbringing was with his mother's married but childless older sister, Mary Elizabeth ("Mimi") Smith, in the Liverpool suburb of Woolton. Lennon's mother taught him his first guitar chords and indulged him by letting him skip school to rehearse with his early bands. The abandonment by his father and his mother's death on July 15, 1958, after being struck by an automobile had a profound effect on him.

Lennon's inventiveness, particularly the ability to twist the language, was evident in his earliest years. Beginning as a seven-year-old student at Dovedale Primary School, then at Quarry Bank Grammar School (1952–1957) and the Liverpool College of Art (1957–1960), he entertained his friends by writing booklets of parodies and nonsense verse, illustrating them with cartoons and caricatures. His penchant for quirkily illustrated and linguistically fractured poetry and prose found full flower in his books *In His Own Write* (1964) and *A Spaniard in the Works* (1965). A third collection, *Skywriting by Word of Mouth*, was published posthumously (1986).

When the rock-and-roll revolution came to England in 1955, Lennon and his friends were attracted primarily to its antiauthoritarian postures. Around the same time, skiffle—a folk blues form from the American South, often played on makeshift instruments—took root in England. Under these influences, Lennon formed his first band, the Black Jacks—renamed the Quarry Men after a week—in March 1957. In true skiffle fashion, the group's instrumentation included guitars, banjos, and drums augmented by tea chest basses and washboards.

At a performance at the annual summer garden fete at St. Peter's Church in Woolton on July 6, 1957, Lennon met Paul McCartney, a budding musician two years younger than he but more accomplished on the guitar. Lennon invited McCartney to join his group. This was the start of one of the most famous and productive songwriting partnerships in the history of popular music. Lennon and McCartney became prolific writers, both individually and together, but agreed early on that all their music would be published under both their names. In their earliest songs—"Love Me Do," "Hello Little Girl," "Love of the Loved," and "There's a Place"—one hears an amalgam of Everly Brothers harmonies, plaintive blues-inspired melodies, a hint of theater music (an influence to which McCartney was particularly susceptible), and, somewhat more submerged, the modal quality of English folk song.

George Harrison joined the group in 1958, completing the nucleus of the Beatles, the name they adopted in mid-1960. By then they had abandoned acoustic guitars and washboards in favor of electric guitars. Stuart Sutcliffe, an art college friend of Lennon's, was briefly enlisted to play electric bass (which McCartney took over when Sutcliffe left at the end of 1960), and Pete Best joined the Beatles as drummer.

The group's sound was formed in the nightclub scene in Hamburg, Germany, which the Beatles first visited in 1960. In Hamburg they played six or seven hours a night, not only expanding their repertoire but also evolving from an unpolished ensemble into a cohesive, if somewhat wild, band. When Brian Epstein, the manager of a Liverpool record store, offered to manage the group on Dec. 3, 1961, Lennon not only accepted but also capitulated to Epstein's direction that the group abandon its leather jackets and its anarchic stage show in favor of suits, ties, and professional demeanor. In June 1962, Epstein secured the group a contract with Parlophone, a subsidiary of EMI Records. On August 16, Pete Best was replaced on drums by Ringo Starr. A week later, Lennon married Cynthia Powell, a girlfriend from art school.

On Sept. 4, 1962, the Beatles went to EMI's Abbey Road Studios in London to record their first 45-rpm single. Their producer, George Martin, had wanted their debut to be "How Do You Do It?," a catchy tune by Mitch Murray, a professional songwriter, and they did tape the song at the session. Lennon and McCartney argued for their own material, however, and persuaded Martin to release "Love Me Do" instead. The record placed respectably on the British charts.

At a time when the standard pop group configuration was a featured singer and a backup band, the Beatles were a cohesive ensemble, and each member sang. At a time when record producers selected songs for groups, the Beatles maintained creative control. Lennon and McCartney became a virtual hit factory, and in 1963 the Beatles had four number one singles: "Please Please Me," "From Me to You," "She Loves You," and "I Want to Hold Your Hand."

Beatlemania exploded in England in 1963, when the group became fixtures on radio and television programs and were seized upon by the press. They toured constantly, and when Lennon's son Julian was born on April 8, 1963, he had little time to visit his wife and child between jaunts. When "I Want to Hold Your Hand" topped the American pop charts early in 1964, the group arranged a brief but triumphant trip to the United States that included performances at the Washington Coliseum in the nation's capital and Carnegie Hall in New York City. There were also three consecutive appearances on the "Ed Sullivan Show," performances that reached more than 70 million people each and launched Beatlemania in the United States.

The rise of Beatlemania, however, doomed the group's stage shows, which could hardly be heard over the din of screaming fans. The recording studio became the band's creative venue. The first two albums, *Please Please Me* and *With the Beatles* (both 1963) mixed original material and versions of American rhythm-and-blues hits. The standouts, however, were the Lennon-McCartney songs, but even in those early days their work was distinguishable: Lennon's songs tended to be dark or introspective, McCartney's sunny and outgoing.

That dichotomy grew clearer with the Beatles' third album, *A Hard Day's Night* (1964), part of which was the soundtrack from the group's first feature film. Lennon's love songs—"I Should Have Known Better," "You Can't Do That," and "I'll Cry Instead," for instance—were peculiar in that they tended to focus largely on anger, jealousy, and disappointment. The film *A Hard Day's Night* established all four Beatles as comic actors with good instincts, possibly because the script, written by Alun Owen, focused on and magnified each of the Beatles' distinct personas.

On the album *Beatles for Sale* (1963) Lennon's dark and sometimes self-critical songs, such as "I'm a Loser" and "I Don't Want to Spoil the Party," again counterbalanced McCartney's brighter ones. During this period the strains of touring and the Beatles' necessarily cloistered life-style began to tell in Lennon's work. *Help!*, the title song for the group's fifth album and second film (1965), had the veneer of an up-tempo pop song, but as Lennon explained, it was actually a lament for lost independence and a confession of insecurity.

Lennon

Lennon's songs in this period continued to paint pictures somewhat more complex than typical for pop songs. "You've Got to Hide Your Love Away," "Ticket to Ride," "It's Only Love," and "You're Going to Lose That Girl" on the *Help!* album focused on the complications of love rather than its unalloyed joys. On the *Rubber Soul* album (1965), "Norwegian Wood" cryptically described an extramarital affair and "Nowhere Man," for all its gorgeous choral harmonies, is an expression of complete detachment.

By 1966 Lennon and Harrison had become increasingly unhappy about touring. The *Revolver* album (1966), with its expanded instrumentation and electronic effects, took their music well beyond what could be reproduced on stage. By the end of the summer 1966 tour, the Beatles resolved not to tour again.

Before they reconvened in the recording studio in November, Lennon went to Almería, Spain, to make a solo appearance in Richard Lester's antiwar film *How I Won the War.* In Almería, Lennon wrote "Strawberry Fields Forever," a song in which his lyrics veer toward the impressionistic rather than the plainly descriptive. Yet its lithe, floating melody and the subtleties of Martin's production gave the impression of complete lucidity.

In early 1967 the Beatles recorded *Sgt. Pepper's Lonely Hearts Club Band*, a defining work of late-1960's psychedelia in which Lennon's outstanding contributions include "Lucy in the Sky with Diamonds" and "Being for the Benefit of Mr. Kite!" Only a few weeks after *Pepper* was released, the group appeared on the global television broadcast "Our World," singing the Lennon song "All You Need Is Love," which helped transform Lennon into a spokesman for the idealism of the younger generation. His impressionistic "I Am the Walrus" was the centerpiece of *Magical Mystery Tour*, a television film and album the group produced at the end of 1967.

In early 1968 the Beatles were in Rishikesh, India, to pursue one of Harrison's fascinations, transcendental meditation, with the Maharishi Mahesh Yogi. When they returned to England, they had enough material for the thirty-song double album *The Beatles* (1968), also known as *The White Album.* Lennon's contributions were fantasy pieces, such as "Cry Baby Cry"; the bluesy screamers like "Yer Blues"; and a few gentle ballads, such as "Julia."

Perhaps the most puzzling track was Lennon's "Revolution 9." Just as his fascination with nonsense imagery made its way into his music in 1966, his interest in avant-garde sound painting erupted in this astonishingly evocative piece of musique concrète.

Around this time, Lennon had become involved with Yoko Ono, a Japanese avant-garde conceptual artist. Their relationship brought Lennon's marriage to an end. In July 1968 Lennon presented his own conceptual art show in London, "You Are Here." On Nov. 8, 1968, Cynthia Lennon was granted a divorce, and about a week later Lennon and Ono released their first avant-garde recording, *Unfinished Music No. 1: Two Virgins*, for which they appeared nude on the album cover. By the end of the year, Lennon and Ono were inseparable, a situation that caused considerable friction during the Beatles' recording sessions for the album and documentary film *Let It Be* (recorded in 1969, released in 1970). Lennon and Ono were married on Mar. 20, 1969, in Gibraltar, and for their honeymoon they staged what they called a "Bed-In for Peace"—a week-long run of interviews. On April 22, Lennon officially changed his middle name from Winston to Ono.

During another bed-in, in Montreal, from May 26 to June 3, Lennon and Ono wrote and recorded "Give Peace a Chance," a song that was quickly taken up by the peace movement and chanted at anti-war marches around the world. They next embarked on a stream of avant-garde productions. *Unfinished Music No. 2: Life with the Lions* and *The Wedding Album* continued the series of experimental albums. The couple took time out from their activities to accommodate sessions for the final Beatles album, *Abbey Road*, during the summer.

For Lennon the Beatles were over. For a while he recorded with a changing group of musicians under the name Plastic Ono Band. On Sept. 13, 1969, a version of that group (which included the guitarist Eric Clapton) played at a concert in Toronto; the recording of the performance was released two months later. Lennon's early solo songs could be chillingly autobiographical. "Cold Turkey" (1969) was a musically and lyrically harrowing evocation of his intermittent heroin problem.

In April 1970, Lennon and Ono checked into the Los Angeles clinic of Dr. Arthur Janov, who specialized in primal scream therapy. Lennon became disenchanted with Janov but emerged from the therapy with a painful yet astonishing album, *Plastic Ono Band* (1970). Childhood and adolescent traumas are recurring themes. Lennon took a softer stance in parts of the album *Imagine* (1971). The title track offers the kind of naively utopian view for which he had become famous.

Late in 1971 the Lennons moved to New York City because Lennon's problems with the United States Immigration and Naturalization Service, which wanted to deport him because of a 1968 drug conviction, prevented his leaving, lest he not be allowed to return. His battle with the government continued until 1976, when he was given a green card. Soon after arriving in New York, Lennon befriended the leaders of the radical and antiwar Yippies, Abbie Hoffman and Jerry Rubin. He adopted an "artist-as-journalist" persona and wrote a stream of topical (but not very good) songs for the album *Some Time in New York City* (1972).

Lennon's marriage was tenuous in the early 1970's, and he and Ono separated between October 1973 and February 1975. Signs of the strain could be heard on his *Mind Games* (1973) and *Walls and Bridges* (1974) albums. After his reconciliation with Ono, Lennon stepped out of the public eye for five years, mainly to raise their son Sean, who was born on Oct. 9, 1975.

In 1980 Lennon decided to return to public life and began writing songs, as did Ono. The songs turned into a dialogue about relationships and during the summer Lennon and Ono recorded the *Double Fantasy* album (1980). Lennon was in top form, both as a songwriter and as a singer.

On Dec. 8, 1980, just a few weeks after the album was released, Lennon was shot to death by Mark David Chapman, a demented fan, outside his home, the Dakota Apartments, in New York City. In 1984, Ono released *Milk and Honey*, the sequel to *Double Fantasy* that she and Lennon had been working on, as well as several posthumous albums of interviews, concert recordings, and studio outtakes.

[Lennon's personal papers are in the possession of Yoko Ono. On his work with the Beatles, see Hunter Davies, *The Beatles* (1968); Philip Norman, *Shout!* (1981); Mark Lewisohn, *The Beatles Recording Sessions* (1988), and *The Complete Beatles Chronicles* (1992). Biographies include Ray Coleman, *Lennon* (1984); Jon Wiener, *Come Together* (1984); and Kevin Howlett and Mark Lewisohn, *In My Life* (1990). Personal memoirs include Cynthia Lennon, *A Twist of Lennon* (1978); May Pang and Henry Edwards, *Loving John* (1983); Pete Shotton and Nicholas Schaffner, *John Lennon in My Life* (1983); and Julia Baird and Geoffrey Giuliano, *John Lennon My Brother* (1988). Published interviews are in Jann Wenner, ed., *Lennon Remembers* (1971); David Scheff, ed., *The Playboy Interviews with John Lennon and Yoko Ono* (1981); and Andy Peebles, ed., *The Lennon Tapes* (1981). On Lennon's writings, art, and films, see James Sauceda, *The Literary Lennon* (1983); and John Robertson, *The Art and Music of John Lennon* (1990). A collection of essays, articles, and interviews is Elizabeth Thomson and David Gutman, eds., *The Lennon Companion* (1988). An obituary is in the *New York Times*, Dec. 9, 1980.]

ALLAN KOZINN

LEVENSON, SAMUEL ("SAM") (Dec. 28, 1911–Aug. 27, 1980), folk humorist, was born in New York City, the son of Hyman Levenson, a tailor, and Rebecca Fishelman. The family moved from East Harlem to the Lower East Side and then, in 1924, to the borough of Brooklyn, where Levenson attended Franklin K. Lane High School. His mother's death when he was thirteen strengthened Levenson's ties to the rest of his family. Years later, when he was a contestant on the television show "I've Got a Secret," a picture was shown of a group of men and Levenson playing various musical instruments. What was his secret? The other men were his brothers.

Levenson's earliest interest was music. He studied the violin, practicing six or seven hours daily rather than playing with his friends. When he entered Brooklyn College in 1930, the need for financial security led him to prepare for teaching. After graduating in 1934 with a B.A. in Romance languages, Levenson began to teach. He simultaneously attended Columbia University, from which he received a master's degree in Romance languages in 1938. He taught successively at Erasmus Hall, Abraham Lincoln, and Samuel J. Tilden high schools, all in Brooklyn.

Levenson loved working with students and teachers. In light of his talents, he was appointed to a counseling position, in which he helped students (and parents) with their problems. Many were counseled at his apartment, the numbers increasing to such a degree that the Levensons moved to a house, where there would be more room and privacy.

On Dec. 27, 1937, Levenson married Esther

Levine, whom he had known since high school. They had two children. The Levensons spent summers in the Catskill Mountains, where Esther's aunt had a farm. In 1940 friends recommended Levenson for the job of master of ceremonies at a nearby resort, where he perfected his humorous routines. The favorable response led to work at more prestigious resorts. From being paid with free room and board, Levenson went on to earning $25 for an evening's performance at the Nevele Hotel. Other leading hotels vied for the services of "Sam Levenson, Folk Humorist," as he billed himself. His success meant hard work for Levenson, who could not perform extemporaneously. His seemingly effortless performances required extensive preparation.

Levenson was also making public appearances in New York City, after school and on weekends, at fund-raisers, social gatherings, and organizational functions. At first his pay was in the $5 range, but soon it rose to $15 and more. A good number of performances, however, were done at no charge.

Realizing that he could no longer combine teaching and counseling with his increasingly numerous performances, Levenson took a leave of absence in 1945. He performed at more and more functions and in nightclubs and was frequently a guest on the television shows of Jack Benny, Milton Berle, Ed Sullivan, and Rudy Vallee. When Arthur Godfrey took a leave from his show in 1959, for medical reasons, Levenson took over. He was such a hit that CBS signed him to a five-year contract. The programs on which he appeared included "The Arthur Godfrey Show," "The Jack Paar Show," "Password," "Two for the Money," and, of course, "The Sam Levenson Show." Even at the height of his success, Levenson devoted more than two-thirds of his personal appearances to charitable, religious, educational, and similar causes.

Although no longer a teacher in the formal sense, Levenson remained one in a broader perspective. His humor emphasized values, and he was tireless in the pursuit of social justice. His humor was intertwined with instructive, philosophical, and thought-provoking concepts. These traits were displayed in Levenson's books. The first portion of his *Everything but Money* (1966) is in good measure autobiographical, covering his early years. Among his other books are *Meet the Folks* (1948), *Sex and the Single Child* (1969), *In One Era and out the Other* (1973), and *You Can Say That Again, Sam!* (1975).

Levenson was unpretentious, warm, and gentle. The illustrations that he used in his routines were drawn from his own and his family's experiences. "Family" can be interpreted broadly here, since his stories of Jewish family life evoked a positive response from other ethnic groups as well. After a performance by Levenson at the White House, President Dwight D. Eisenhower said, "You know, Sam, when you talked about the tribulations of the Levensons, I thought you were talking about the Eisenhowers."

On receiving an honorary doctorate from Brooklyn College in 1976, Levenson said, "I have never uttered a word of humor at the expense of any human being, at the expense of any group. I have tried to use the words of kindness and generosity, trying to build peace and affection between people." Upon Levenson's death of a heart attack, Bishop Francis Mugavero of the Roman Catholic diocese of Brooklyn said, "Sam Levenson was a saint."

[The Sam Levenson archive at Brooklyn College includes manuscripts, recordings, television tapes, and photographs. A taped interview with Esther Levenson by Murray M. Horowitz is also in the archive. See Earl Wilson, "Unforgettable Sam Levenson," *Reader's Digest*, Jan. 1982. An obituary is in the *New York Times*, Aug. 29, 1980.]

MURRAY M. HOROWITZ

LEVITT, ARTHUR (June 28, 1900–May 6, 1980), public official, was born in Brooklyn, N.Y., the son of Israel Levitt and Rose Daniels. In 1917 he joined the United States Army as an infantry private. After the war, he attended Columbia University, from which he received his bachelor's degree in 1921 and his law degree in 1924. Immediately after graduation, he was admitted to the New York bar and opened his own law practice. On June 30, 1929, he married Dorothy Wolff, a schoolteacher; they had one child, Arthur Levitt, Jr., who would grow up to be a leading Wall Street businessman and president of the American Stock Exchange.

In 1941, Levitt reentered the army, this time as a captain in the Judge Advocate General's Corps. By the end of World War II, he had been promoted to colonel and was in charge of the Corps' training center in the borough of

Queens in New York City. He maintained his connections to the military for many years thereafter, serving in the reserves and doing regular two-week tours of duty every summer. He was decorated with the medal of the Legion of Merit.

Levitt was also active in community affairs: he was a member of the American Legion; a Mason (thirty-third degree); a member, and later president, of the Union Temple of Brooklyn; and a member of the board of directors, starting in 1950, and vice-chairman of the Brooklyn chapter of the American Red Cross.

Levitt entered politics soon after the war ended. In 1946, he served as campaign manager for the reelection bid of the scandal-scarred Democratic minority leader of the New York State Assembly, Irwin Steingut. In 1952 he was appointed to the New York City Board of Education by Mayor Vincent R. Impellitteri and was elected its president in 1954.

In September of that year, Levitt was asked by gubernatorial candidate W. Averell Harriman to join the Democratic-Liberal ticket as the candidate for comptroller of New York State. The previous candidate had been forced to withdraw from the race because of a damaging scandal. It was just a few weeks before the election, but on Nov. 2, 1954, with help from Harriman's coattails, Levitt was elected comptroller. He remained in Albany long after Harriman was gone, for a record six consecutive four-year terms.

Levitt redefined the office of comptroller by pursuing an aggressive nonpartisan program of audits. Year after year, his staff turned out investigative reports that probed the management and disbursal of public funds statewide. Levitt, who liked to be called "Colonel," acquired a reputation as steady, conservative, and serious. His audits, which included evaluations of procedures and management performance, in addition to the more customary balance-sheet data and budgetary accountings, were known for both their thoroughness and their fairness.

In 1961, at the urging of a group of disenchanted Democratic leaders, Levitt decided to seek the Democratic nomination for mayor of New York City. The ensuing primary campaign against incumbent Mayor Robert F. Wagner proved to be the only time Levitt ever lost an election. He was regarded as unbeatable in his reelection campaigns for state comptroller and survived the Republican ascendancy in Albany when Nelson A. Rockefeller dominated New York State politics. When the Democrats regained control of the state house in 1974, after Rockefeller had been appointed vice-president by Gerald Ford, Levitt won election to his sixth and final term with a victory margin of over 2 million votes.

Meanwhile, Levitt gained power within the New York Democratic organization. In 1965, he was chairman of the party's state convention. He also served as a delegate to the Democratic national conventions in 1968, when Hubert Humphrey was nominated, and in 1976, when Jimmy Carter was nominated.

When Levitt declined to stand for reelection in 1978, he did not support the Democratic nominee to succeed him as state comptroller, New York City comptroller Harrison J. Goldin. Levitt, who had always tried to take a nonpartisan approach to the fiduciary duties of the comptroller, was concerned by Goldin's partisan reputation. He also was worried that Goldin would be inclined to make aggressive use of state pension funds to relieve New York City's fiscal crisis, an action that Levitt considered a violation of the comptroller's fiduciary responsibilities. Instead, despite his long career as a leader of the Democratic party in New York State, Levitt informally supported the more conservative Republican nominee Edward V. Regan as his successor. Regan won the election.

After he retired from public office, Levitt took a job in New York City, as an investment officer at the Lincoln Savings Bank. He was at his desk when he died.

[Levitt's papers from his time as New York State comptroller (1955–1978), including correspondence, speeches, reports, subject files, and appointment schedules, are in the New York State Archives. Over 400 pages of transcribed interviews with his family, colleagues, and associates are available at the Oral History Office at Columbia University as part of the Arthur Levitt Project. An obituary is in the *New York Times*, May 7, 1980.]

OWEN D. GUTFREUND

LEVY, GUSTAVE LEHMANN (May 23, 1910–Nov. 3, 1976), investment banker, was born in New Orleans, La., the son of Sigmund Levy, a container manufacturer, and Bella Lehmann. After his father's death in 1923, his mother took him and his two sisters to live in

France. In 1927, after attending the American School in Paris, he returned to New Orleans to enter Tulane University. However, his mother could not afford the tuition, so he left New Orleans again in 1928 and moved to New York City, where he lived for the rest of his life. He procured a job as a runner at Newborg and Company, a small Wall Street brokerage, and worked his way up within the firm, eventually becoming a stock trader. From 1928 until 1932, Levy attended night classes at New York University, but he never completed enough credits to obtain his degree. Newborg and Company went out of business in 1932, in the aftermath of the stock market crash, and Levy joined the millions of Americans who were unemployed during the Great Depression. Fortunately, he got another job in 1933, working on the foreign bond desk of Goldman Sachs and Company at a starting salary of $27 per week. On Mar. 7, 1934, Levy married Janet Wolf; they had two children.

With the exception of a brief hiatus during World War II (1942–1945), when he served as a lieutenant colonel in the Air Corps, Levy spent the rest of his life working for Goldman Sachs. Soon after he started at the firm, he was transferred to the stock trading desk, where he began to take positions for the firm's account instead of just executing orders for customers and making money on the commissions. He soon established himself as a hardworking, profit-making trader and a skilled arbitrageur with a talent for taking advantage of market inefficiencies. When he returned from the war in 1945, he was made a partner.

During the 1950's, Levy expanded Goldman's trading operations to include block trading and risk arbitrage. His aggressive trading style helped Goldman Sachs to emerge as one of the handful of firms that would dominate these markets for decades. This dominance helped the firm to expand its activities in related activities, including underwriting, corporate finance, mergers and acquisitions, and commercial paper. Levy's reputation as an ambitious and zealous trader with good instincts continued to grow. In 1969 he was named senior partner and chairman of the Managing Committee of Goldman Sachs, taking over for Sidney J. Weinberg, who had run the investment bank for many years.

Colleagues and competitors alike regarded Levy as a tough and occasionally difficult man, but he was generally well respected. He was known as a relentless businessman who thrived in the competitive world of Wall Street. Under his leadership, Goldman Sachs continued to grow and expand, all the while remaining a highly profitable partnership. Unfortunately, his tenure at the firm was marred by a major securities scandal. In 1970, the firm had marketed commercial paper for the failing Penn Central Transportation Company, even as the railroad giant was on the verge of bankruptcy. The partnership was dragged into litigation, and in 1974 it was forced to pay settlements amounting to millions of dollars to investors who had bought the worthless Penn Central commercial paper.

In connection with his career as an investment banker, Levy served on numerous corporate boards, including New York Telephone, May Department Stores, Foster Grant, Keebler, Samsonite, Studebaker-Worthington, Norton Simon, Patagonia, the Bowery Savings Bank, and Braniff Airways. He was a director of the New York Chamber of Commerce and Industry, as well as of the Economic Development Council of New York City. From 1967 to 1969 he was chairman of the board of governors of the New York Stock Exchange.

Levy was a vigorous fund-raiser and supporter of philanthropic causes, and he was active in civic affairs. He was a supporter of the Federation of Jewish Philanthropies, and served that organization as president from 1957 to 1959. In 1962, Levy was appointed chairman of the Mount Sinai Hospital and Medical Center, as well as of the Mount Sinai Medical School. From 1970 to 1976, he was a commissioner of the Port of New York Authority. He served, on a pro bono basis, as a distinguished adjunct professor of finance at New York University (1971–1976). Levy was treasurer of the Lincoln Center for the Performing Arts and a trustee of the Museum of Modern Art, both in New York City, and a trustee of the John F. Kennedy Center for the Performing Arts in Washington, D.C. His skill as a fund-raiser was often called upon to aid Republican politicians. In particular, he was active in the presidential campaigns of Richard M. Nixon and Gerald R. Ford, the gubernatorial campaigns of Nelson A. Rockefeller, and the mayoral campaigns of John V. Lindsay.

Levy died in New York City.

[There are very few published sources about Levy's life. A number of oral history interviews mention Levy in *The Way It Was*, compiled by the editors of *Institutional Investor* (1988). An obituary is in the *New York Times*, Nov. 4, 1976.]

OWEN D. GUTFREUND

LHÉVINNE, ROSINA (Mar. 29, 1880–Nov. 9, 1976), pianist and teacher, was born Rosina Bessie in Kiev, Ukraine, the younger of two children of Jacques Bessie, a Dutch diamond merchant, and Maria Katch. There were violent anti-Semitic riots in Kiev during Rosina's first year, and the Jewish Bessie family was fortunate to be permitted to move to Moscow in 1881 or 1882. Rosina was seriously stricken with diphtheria in 1884, and were it not for her mother's insistence that the doctors perform a risky tracheotomy (a new and untested procedure at that time), she would not have survived. An outcome of the "miracle" of her survival was that her mother was fiercely overprotective of Rosina throughout her early years. She was educated at home by private tutors and was not allowed outside during the long Moscow winters.

The Bessies lived a cultured and relatively comfortable life. Both parents were amateur pianists, and their apartment housed two grand pianos. Rosina began to study piano privately at the age of six with Antonin Galli, a Moscow Conservatory graduate. At the age of nine she was accepted into the lower school of the Moscow Conservatory, which had been established by Anton Rubinstein in 1862. Admission to the Conservatory was extremely competitive, especially for Jews, as Tsar Alexander III had established a quota limiting the number of Jews to no more than 3 percent of the student body. Rosina studied with S. M. Remesov in the lower school during her first year; when he suddenly took ill her temporary substitute teacher was fourteen-year-old Josef Lhévinne, who at that time was one of the Conservatory's top piano students. Among their other classmates at the Moscow Conservatory were Sergey Rachmaninoff and Aleksandr Scriabin.

Rosina entered the upper school of the Conservatory at the age of twelve. Her primary teacher was Vasily Safonov. She made her public orchestral debut at the age of fifteen, playing Chopin's Piano Concerto no. 1 in E Minor with the Conservatory Orchestra conducted by Safonov. Josef Lhévinne attended this concert and later claimed that it was then that he fell in love with her. She graduated from the Moscow Conservatory in 1898 with a gold medal, the youngest woman ever to receive the school's highest honor. She and Josef were married a week after her graduation.

During the first year of their marriage the Lhévinnes made their two-piano debut in Moscow, playing Anton Arensky's Second Suite for Two Pianos at a benefit concert. At this time Rosina made the decision to abandon her solo career and devote her energies to her husband's. In the fall of 1899 they relocated to Tiflis (Tbilisi), where he had been offered a position as professor at the local conservatory. They stayed there for two years. Although life in Tiflis was relatively comfortable, Rosina knew that Josef's career was stagnating in the remote Georgian city, and at her suggestion they relocated to Berlin. Her instincts about the best environment for her husband's career proved correct, and after a successful year in Berlin he was appointed to the faculty of the Moscow Conservatory.

Josef Lhévinne's first American tour was in 1906. It proved to be successful, and in the summer of 1906 Rosina prepared to join him for his second American tour. They planned an extended stopover in Paris, where the first of their two children was born.

The Lhévinnes made their American two-piano debut in Chicago on Feb. 17, 1907. Their two-piano recitals consisted primarily of solo works played by Josef, with one or two works for two pianos played by both of them. Rosina would not play solo works at this time, again deferring to the primacy of her husband's career. Their two-piano performances were well received, and Madame Lhévinne was praised by critics and audiences for her technical proficiency and fine musicianship.

Josef Lhévinne continued to tour Europe and the United States from 1907 to 1914. The family made their permanent home in Wannsee, a suburb of Berlin. By this time he had amassed a large following of students, and she filled in for him as their primary teacher while he was away on tour. Because they were Russian citizens, when World War I broke out they were subjected to internment in Wannsee; this lasted from 1914 until 1919.

As soon as the war was over the Lhévinnes immigrated to the United States and made their home in Kew Gardens, Queens, a neighborhood in New York City. Josef began touring again, and although Rosina joined him for occasional two-piano recitals, she spent most of her time teaching in Queens.

In 1924 the Lhévinnes joined the original faculty of the Juilliard Graduate School, which was established by the Juilliard Musical Foundation to provide advanced musical training for talented performers. They shared the same studio, and she was considered to be the better teacher by many of their students.

Rosina was devastated by her husband's death of a heart attack in 1944, and worried that Juilliard would not renew her teaching contract without her husband. Instead, her teaching and performing careers were to blossom after her husband's death. She moved from Queens to Manhattan to be closer to Juilliard, then located at 122d Street and Broadway, and expanded her roster of students. Her students, among them Van Cliburn, John Browning, Tong Il Han, Adele Marcus, Mischa Dichter, Ralph Votapek, Martin Canin, David Bar-Illan, and Jeffrey Siegel, won many of the national and international piano competitions. Beginning in 1956 she also taught at the Aspen Music School in Colorado during the summer months. Lhévinne also taught summer master classes at the Los Angeles Conservatory of Music from 1946 to 1955, at the University of California at Berkeley in 1961, and at the University of Southern California from 1971 to 1974.

Lhévinne embarked upon a solo performing career in 1956, at the age of seventy-six, playing Mozart's Concerto in C Major, K. 467 with the Aspen Festival Orchestra. During the next seasons she played solo works with orchestras across the country. In January 1963, a few months before her eighty-third birthday, Lhévinne performed Chopin's Piano Concerto no. 1 in E Minor with the New York Philharmonic under the direction of Leonard Bernstein for four performances. The performances (one of which was broadcast nationwide over CBS radio) met with great critical acclaim, and were the highlights of her solo career.

Rosina Lhévinne taught at Juilliard until a few months before her death at the age of ninety-six at the home of her daughter in Glendale, Calif. As a teacher and performer, Lhévinne was one of the last carriers of the art of late-nineteenth-century Russian pianism. Known for her warmth and devotion to her students, she frequently became as concerned with their personal lives as with their musical training. Her dedication to her art and to the people with whom she shared it was unwavering.

[Memorabilia (including newspaper clippings and photographs) from the Lhévinnes' career at Juilliard is in the Juilliard School Library, New York City; other clippings are held by the Music Division of the New York Public Library at Lincoln Center. See also Rosina Lhévinne's foreword to the 1972 edition of Josef Lhévinne's book *Basic Principles in Pianoforte Playing* (originally published in 1924). The most extensive source on the Lhévinnes is Robert K. Wallace, *A Century of Music-Making* (1976), which includes a bibliography, discography, and filmography. Obituaries are in the *New York Times*, Nov. 11, 1976, and the *Juilliard News Bulletin*, Feb. 1977. An extensive tribute by Harold C. Schonberg is in the *New York Times*, Nov. 21, 1976.]

JANE GOTTLIEB

LIBBY, WILLARD FRANK (Dec. 17, 1908–Sept. 8, 1980), chemist, was born in Grand Valley, Colo., the son of Ora Edward Libby and Eva May Rivers, who were farmers. When he was five years old, the family, which included four other children, moved to an apple ranch near Sebastopol, Calif. Libby entered the University of California, Berkeley, in 1927, originally intending to become a mining engineer. He found chemistry more interesting, however, and received the B.S. in that discipline in 1931. He received the Ph.D. from Berkeley two years later, after studying low-energy radioactive nuclei with the noted physical chemists Gilbert N. Lewis and Wendell M. Latimer.

Upon completing his doctorate, Libby was appointed instructor in chemistry at Berkeley. On Aug. 9, 1940, he married Leonor Lucinda Hickey, a teacher; they had two children. The following year, Libby (now an associate professor) took a sabbatical year at Princeton University on the first of three Guggenheim fellowships. His research was interrupted, however, by the entry of the United States into World War II. Libby joined Nobel laureate Harold C. Urey at Columbia University as part of the Manhattan Project, for which he developed gaseous-diffusion techniques for separating uranium isotopes. This work allowed the isolation of fissionable uranium-235 from the more abundant uranium-238, a necessary step in the construction of the atomic bomb dropped on Hiroshima.

In 1945, Libby moved to the University of Chicago as professor of chemistry and began conducting research at its Institute of Nuclear Studies. Recent discoveries had revealed that cosmic rays hitting atoms in the upper atmosphere produced neutrons that were readily absorbed by nitrogen atoms. This absorption created an unstable isotope that decayed to radioactive carbon-14, found to possess a half-life (the time required for half the atoms in a sample to decay to stable isotopes) of 5,730 years. Libby theorized that the amount of carbon-14 in the biosphere was constant because the creation of new atoms would be balanced by the decay of old ones. More important, he believed that radiocarbon was rapidly oxidized to carbon dioxide and absorbed by plants through photosynthesis. Organisms consuming these plants would absorb carbon-14, which would remain at a constant level until the organism died.

Libby's ideas provided a method to determine the ages of organic material based on the known decay rate of radiocarbon atoms. Measuring the amount of carbon-14 in a sample would reveal the time since the organism died. The accuracy of this proposed technique was quickly tested by measuring the radioactivity present in redwood and fir samples whose ages were precisely known through tree-ring dating techniques. Libby also tested historical artifacts of known age to confirm his hypothesis. After his announcement of his findings in 1949, the radiocarbon method emerged as the basic technique for dating events of the last 70,000 years. For his work in developing radiocarbon dating, Libby won the Nobel Prize for chemistry for 1960. Although more sophisticated tree-ring analysis during the 1960's disclosed systematic fluctuations in the carbon-14 concentration in the atmosphere and led to recalibration of the radiocarbon time scale, the method has remained a fundamental tool for archaeology and geology.

Libby's reputation as one of the nation's leading nuclear scientists led to significant government service. In 1954, President Dwight D. Eisenhower appointed Libby to the Atomic Energy Commission (AEC), the first chemist to serve on the body. Libby's chief interest was the study of fallout from nuclear weapons testing. A political conservative, Libby argued that fallout was less of a danger than an inadequate American nuclear arsenal, and that Americans would have to learn to live with it. He was also involved in the development of international efforts for peaceful uses of atomic energy, including Eisenhower's "Atoms for Peace" program. He served as vice-chairman of the American delegation to the First International Conference on Peaceful Uses of Atomic Energy, which met in Geneva in 1955.

Libby resigned from the AEC in 1959 to become professor of chemistry at the University of California, Los Angeles (UCLA). Three years later he was appointed director of the university's Institute of Geophysics and Planetary Physics, a position he held concurrently with his professorship. Libby's research interests became increasingly diverse over the next two decades and included geochemistry, lunar and space research, environmental concerns, earthquake protection, and civil defense. In 1966, Libby divorced his wife and soon thereafter married Leona Woods Marshall, a professor of environmental engineering at UCLA; they had no children.

Libby's environmental interests led to his membership on the Presidential Task Force on Air Pollution (1969–1970), the second position in the Nixon administration for which he had been considered. In late 1968, rumors began to circulate that Libby was President-elect Nixon's choice as science adviser. Libby's well-known ultraconservative political views alarmed many of his scientific colleagues, who protested that he would be a questionable choice for this position. Libby received no further consideration. During his Los Angeles years, Libby served as an adviser to several state governments on topics related to environmental and radiation questions. He retired from UCLA in 1976. He died in Los Angeles.

Tall and powerfully built, Libby presented an imposing figure. Fellow Nobel laureate Glenn T. Seaborg described him as a "painstaking, patient, and effective teacher" who also had a "wide-ranging curiosity." Libby gained significant recognition during his career, including the Charles Frederick Chandler Medal of Columbia University (1954), the Elliott Cresson Medal of Franklin Institute (1957), and the Willard Gibbs Medal of the American Chemical Society (1958). Libby was a member of the National Academy of Sciences, the American Academy of Arts and Sciences, and the American Philosophical Society.

[The Willard Frank Libby Papers, including two hundred linear feet of manuscript material, are housed in the Department of Special Collections, UCLA Library. See also his *Collected Papers*, edited by Rainer Berger and Leona Marshall Libby, 7 vols. in 5 (1981). Libby's major published works, in addition to numerous journal articles, include *Radiocarbon Dating* (1952); *Isotopes in Industry and Medicine* (1957); *Science and Administration* (1961); and a posthumous volume edited by Leona Marshall Libby, *Solar System Physics and Chemistry* (1981). An obituary is in the *New York Times*, Sept. 10, 1980.]

GEORGE E. WEBB

LILLY, ELI (Apr. 1, 1885–Jan. 24, 1977), businessman and philanthropist, was born in Indianapolis, Ind., the eldest son of Josiah K. Lilly and Lilly Ridgely. His paternal grandfather, Eli Lilly, founded the pharmaceutical company that bore his name. The family lived in an affluent section of town, the "new north side." Their cottage at remote Lake Wawasee, in Kosciusko County, provided an idyllic setting and respite from urban life. From his grandfather, young Lilly learned Indian legends and folklore of the region. Excursions on the lake stimulated his interest in native American archaeology.

Lilly's childhood was not always pleasant. His father's strong influence left a lasting impression, and Lilly's accomplishments in life were attempts to please the father he idolized and adored. His mother's relationship with her eldest son was less than affectionate. He felt unloved and shifted his affection to an aunt.

At the age of ten, Lilly began washing bottles during summer vacations at his grandfather's plant. After graduating from Shortridge High School in 1904, he entered the Philadelphia College of Pharmacy, from which he received a degree in 1907. On Aug. 29, 1907, Lilly married Evelyn Fortune, a childhood sweetheart; they had three children, two of whom died in infancy.

At the family firm, Lilly was first appointed the head of the newly created Economic Department, established to save money and improve efficiency, in 1907. His first important contribution was a plan to produce multiple copies of manufacturing formulas through a blueprinting process, thus facilitating an increase in production. In 1909, Lilly became superintendent of the manufacturing division. By the beginning of World War I, he was familiar with the views of Frederick W. Taylor, whose book *The Principles of Scientific Management*, he later declared, had the most profound influence on the company. A bonus system, a guaranteed wage, an improved method for filling gelatin capsules, and the hiring of efficiency experts all represented Lilly's conversion to Taylor's scientific management philosophy.

Following the war, Lilly was promoted to vice-president and was in charge of the manufacturing and scientific divisions. He began straight-line production, utilizing automated conveyor systems. This technological innovation, which improved productivity and efficiency, transformed the company into a major force in the pharmaceutical industry. Yet Lilly himself could hardly have anticipated the impact scientific research would have on the company balance sheet and the whole of humanity.

Pharmaceutical research had started in Europe at the beginning of the twentieth century. American dependence on European sources of chemicals left many American companies scrambling to find substitutes after June 1914. Sensing their vulnerability, Josiah Lilly organized the Scientific Department to conduct experimental research. He and Eli Lilly hired George Henry Alexander Clowes, a British chemist, as director of biochemical research.

They soon made inroads against diabetes. Clowes surmised it was possible to use insulin, a fluid extracted from the pancreas of sheep and cattle, hypodermically to help sufferers of the metabolic disorder digest essential nutrients in food to prevent starvation. Insulin became available for public use in October 1923. The American Diabetes Association belatedly presented George Clowes the Banting Medal in 1947 for his contributions. As for Lilly, he could boast of an increase in company profits well into the 1920's and basked in his father's praise.

Under Lilly's leadership the company developed liver extract for the treatment of pernicious anemia in 1930. The effects of Lilly's self-imposed work load in the 1920's and the failure of the Lillys to have another child led to their divorce in 1926. On Nov. 27, 1927, Lilly married Ruth Helen Allison, who had been his secretary. They had no children.

In 1932, Lilly became president of the family firm, a position he held until 1948. The business showed strong sales and hefty profits during the Great Depression. Paradoxically, Lilly's disdain for President Franklin D. Roosevelt's New Deal was not evident in the manner in which he managed his labor force. He created jobs for workers in order to avoid layoffs and refused to slash the payroll in light of massive unemployment. His management philosophy paid off handsomely. In sharp contrast to the auto, steel, and coal industries, the company did not experience the labor unrest so prevalent during the period. The economic crises had a minimal impact on the firm's plans for plant expansion. Convinced that the company's future hinged upon scientific research, Lilly planned the construction of facilities adequate to accommodate such an undertaking. The Lilly Research Laboratories was dedicated in 1934.

Following the Japanese attack upon Pearl Harbor in 1941, Lilly directed his energies toward the war effort. Production of blood plasma was a major undertaking, and by the end of the war, the company accounted for 20 percent of the nation's total output. In addition, its typhus vaccine and the antiseptic Merthiolate helped to combat disease and infection. Lilly also cooperated with Oxford University scientist Howard Florey to produce penicillin in 1941. Lilly's accomplishments as president from 1932 through 1948 were reflected in the increase in aggregate sales from $13 million to $117 million. The company payroll expanded from 1,700 to 6,900 during the same period.

On Feb. 8, 1948, Josiah Lilly died; Eli served as chairman and, beginning in 1953, as honorary chairman. As chairman, Lilly's greatest accomplishment was working with Jonas Salk in producing the polio vaccine. He reassumed the chairmanship for three years after his brother Josiah's death in 1966. He became honorary chairman once again in 1969 and never retired officially.

Lilly's interest in archaeology brought him great recognition. In 1930 he began collecting native American artifacts indigenous to Indiana, and he played an important role in the Indiana Historical Society. Lilly's curiosity about Indiana's prehistoric past served as inspiration for his first book, *Prehistoric Antiquities of Indiana* (1937). The work was, according to his biographer James H. Madison, a significant attempt to develop "a chronological synthesis and taxonomy of prehistoric cultures in Indiana." His most ambitious writing project, however, was as contributor to and sole financier of the book *Walam Olum or Red Score: The Migration Legend of the Lenni Lenape or Delaware Indians* (1954), an ethnological study of an indigenous Indiana tribe. His appreciation of history led to the 1934 purchase and restoration of the William Conner property, an early-nineteenth-century homestead in Noblesville, Ind., north of Indianapolis. Lilly's project emulated Henry Ford's Greenfield Village and John D. Rockefeller, Jr.'s, Williamsburg. Such restorations, he believed, could somehow replace something missing in the modern American character.

As he grew older, Lilly became less involved in company business. He and his wife traveled extensively. Stays at Lake Wawasee replenished his spirit and provided a source of solitude from which he renewed his strength. Woodworking and collecting valuable Chinese art also occupied his time, as did community service. Lilly, a progressive Republican, remained active in state and national party politics.

Ruth Lilly died in 1973. Lilly then began planning for his own death. His will bequeathed his Indianapolis home to Indiana University for a presidential residence. Lilly's vast wealth, including company stock, bonds, real estate, and cash, was valued in excess of $165 million. Lilly willed his estate to his favorite institutions and charitable causes. Those receiving special consideration included the Indianapolis Museum of Art, Butler University, Wabash College, the Indiana Historical Society, the Children's Museum of Indianapolis, and the Lilly Endowment.

Lilly believed strongly that human beings have the capacity for self-improvement, provided they employ self-analysis. His monetary worth did not exceed his faith in humanity and his conviction that "the improvement of character in the world is the most important thing to accomplish." Lilly died in Indianapolis.

[Lilly's personal papers are in the Lilly Archives, Lilly Center, Eli Lilly and Company, Indianapolis, Ind. James H. Madison's unauthorized biography, *Eli Lilly* (1989), is the definitive study to date. An obituary is in the *New York Times*, Jan. 25, 1977.]

JEAN W. GRIFFITH, JR.

LIPPINCOTT, JOSEPH WHARTON (Feb. 28, 1887–Oct. 22, 1976), author, publisher, and sportsman, was born in Philadelphia, Pa., the son of Joshua Bertram Lippincott and Joanna Wharton. Lippincott's maternal grandfather was Joseph Wharton, an industrialist who was a founder of Swarthmore College and helped to establish the Wharton School of Finance and Commerce at the University of Pennsylvania. Wharton and his family retained interest in the Wharton Tract, in southeastern New Jersey, that covered 148,000 acres. This land was until the 1950's the largest privately owned acreage east of the Mississippi. His paternal grandfather, Joshua B. Lippincott, began his publishing career in 1827, bought out his employer in 1836, and founded the J. B. Lippincott Company. He acquired Grigg, Elliot, and Company in 1850 and incorporated J. B. Lippincott Company in 1885.

At a young age, Lippincott met many important writers at his parents' home who contributed to *Lippincott's Monthly Magazine* (1868–1914). The humorist Bill Nye and the cartoonist Frederick Opper, according to Lippincott, were his greatest influences. "J. W.," as he was called, spent almost a year in Wyoming on the same ranch where Owen Wister had researched material for *The Virginian*. While in Wyoming, he developed a love of horses and outdoor life.

Lippincott graduated from the Episcopal Academy of Philadelphia, where he was an editor of the school magazine. In 1904 he enrolled at the Wharton School. Graduating with a B.S. degree in 1908, Lippincott was awarded the Terry Prize for the highest class average. That summer he served as a companion and courier for his grandfather Wharton and Andrew Carnegie while they traveled in Europe. He met Kaiser Wilhelm II on his yacht in Kiel, along with many of Germany's warlords. Carnegie's stories helped young Lippincott develop an interest in libraries.

Lippincott began his publishing career as an office boy in 1908, then moved to dusting books in the shipping department. He claimed that this gave him an appreciation of clean literature. Lippincott married Elizabeth Schuyler Mills in October 1913; they had three children. His wife died in 1943, and Lippincott married Virginia Jones Mathieson on Sept. 20, 1945.

Lippincott, who was promoted to vice-president in 1915, served in the United States Naval Reserve during World War I. He became the fourth president of the family firm in 1926 and president of the National Association of Book Publishers in 1929. When he retired from the latter presidency in 1933, Lippincott gave a speech titled "Are the Classics Dying Out?" His controversial remarks on the increase of book production in the midst of the Great Depression captured headlines across the country.

In 1940 the company merged with Carrick and Evans of New York City, a general publisher, and with Frederick A. Stokes of Philadelphia, which had an extensive list of juvenile books. His many trips abroad for the company sealed friendships with English and other European authors, such as Hilaire Belloc, E. V. Lucas, Sir Hall Caine, and Sir Gilbert Parker, all of whom had published extensively with the family firm. In addition, Lippincott added the Lonsdale Library of Sports, Games, and Pastimes to the company. Published jointly with Seeley, Service and Company of London, the books were on boxing, big-game hunting in Africa, fox hunting, and cricket.

Under his leadership, the J. B. Lippincott Company opened an editorial branch in New York City in 1941 and its staff more than tripled. Furthermore, in 1944 the company established an employees' profit sharing trust (one of the first in the country). Lippincott became chairman of the board in 1949, holding this position until his retirement in 1959.

Besides heading the family's publishing house, Lippincott was an accomplished writer and sportsman. All of his seventeen books for juveniles were technically correct yet pleasing to read. Many are still in print. His first book, *Bun, a Wild Rabbit* was published in 1918. It was followed by *Red Ben, the Fox of Oak Ridge* (1919). *Wilderness Champion* (1944) sold more than 25,000 copies. *The Wahoo Bobcat* (1950) and *Wilderness Champion* were both selections of the Junior Literary Guild.

At six feet tall and weighing 165 pounds, Lippincott was an expert sportsman, and many of his expeditions were the basis of his novels. He enjoyed pigeon shooting with Ernest Hemingway and deer hunting with F. Van Wyck Mason. In 1933 he spent a month in the Yukon Territory. This trip was also the focus of his book *The Wolf King* (1933). Lippincott participated in big-game hunts in Alaska, Canada, Mexico, Germany, and Austria. Three of his trophy heads are among the largest on record. Lippincott served as master of the hounds of the Huntingdon Valley hunt, played polo, raced yachts, and showed dogs and horses. His passion for nature was also evident in his membership in the National Geographical Society, the

Pennsylvania Audubon Society, and the Zoological Society of Philadelphia.

Lippincott's love of books was also visible in his philanthropic activities. He served as a director of the Free Library of Philadelphia, the Athenaeum Library, and the Council of Books in Wartime. He was a member of the boards of the Philadelphia City Institute, Abingdon Hospital, the Mercantile Library, and the Franklin Institute. With the support of the American Library Association, Lippincott established the Joseph W. Lippincott Award in 1937. The award includes a certificate and a monetary prize for outstanding achievement in librarianship. The award presentation was suspended during World War II and resumed in 1950.

Lippincott was chairman of the board of libraries for the University of Pennsylvania and secretary and a member of the board of trustees for the Moore Institute of Art, Science, and Industry. He was also a supporter of the Academy of Natural Sciences.

Lippincott died in Huntingdon Valley, Pa.

[Other books by Lippincott include *Gray Squirrel* (1921); *Persimmon Jim the 'Possum* (1924); *Long Horn, Leader of the Deer* (1928); *The Red Roan Pony* (1934); *Chisel-Tooth the Beaver* (1936); *Animal Neighbors of the Countryside* (1938); *Black Wings, the Unbeatable Crow* (1947); *The Phantom Deer* (1954); *Old Bill, the Whooping Crane* (1958); and *Coyote, the Wonder Wolf* (1964). See also "Joseph Wharton Lippincott," *Publishers Weekly*, Nov. 25, 1933; "Take a Bow: Joseph Wharton Lippincott," *ibid.*, May 19, 1945; and Stewart Freeman, *Toward a Third Century of Excellence* (1992). An obituary is in the *New York Times*, Sept. 23, 1976.]

DELIA CRUTCHFIELD COOK

LISAGOR, PETER IRVIN (Aug. 5, 1915–Dec. 10, 1976), journalist, was born in Keystone, W.Va., one of four children of Paris Lisagor, who ran a small general store, and Fanny Simpkins. Growing up in the coalfield region of McDowell County, Lisagor moved to Chicago in 1930 and graduated from Marshall High School on the city's West Side. A star high school athlete, Lisagor first had an ambition to play professional baseball. He attended Northwestern University in 1933, then transferred after a year to the University of Michigan at Ann Arbor, earning a B.A. degree in political science in 1939. At Michigan, Lisagor excelled as a second baseman on the Wolverine baseball team and as a writer and editor for the *Michigan Daily*. Playing under the name of "Pete Lyons," he had a brief minor league baseball career in Iowa. Lisagor recalled that his baseball salary amounted to "$65 a month and hamburgers."

After graduation from Michigan, Lisagor joined the sports department of the *Chicago Daily News* and was named the newspaper's American League baseball writer, covering the Chicago White Sox. After three years on the sports beat, he left the *Daily News* to become a general reporter in the Chicago bureau of the United Press. He married Myra K. Murphy in 1942; they had two children.

During World War II, Lisagor served in the United States Army's Eleventh Armored Division. For two of his three years in the Army he was assigned to *Stars and Stripes*, serving as managing editor of the London edition in 1944 and 1945 and as editor of *Stars and Stripes* magazine in Paris in 1945. Following his discharge in 1945, he worked briefly as news editor of the *Paris Post*, then returned to Chicago late in the year and rejoined the *Daily News* as a general news reporter.

As a member of the *Daily News* staff, Lisagor covered Chicago's city hall and Illinois government. In February 1947 he wrote a series of articles exposing the substandard conditions of Illinois mental hospitals. In reaction to Lisagor's articles, the Illinois General Assembly launched an investigation of mental institutions and adopted reforms, including a new personnel code to raise professional standards in mental hospitals. Largely because of the mental health series, Lisagor was awarded a Nieman Fellowship at Harvard University for the 1948–1949 academic year and studied international affairs. On returning to the *Daily News* he was assigned to the foreign desk and spent a year in New York as United Nations correspondent.

Beginning in 1950, Lisagor reported on national politics and the presidency as a Washington, D.C., correspondent and special writer for the *Daily News*, and from 1959, as chief of the Washington bureau. From the Korean War through the era of détente, Lisagor also covered international affairs. In more than a quarter century of Washington reporting, Lisagor gained a reputation as one of the nation's most incisive political analysts. Bringing the tough style of Chicago front-page journalism to the nation's capital, he was renowned for asking hard questions of senior officials with wit and irreverence. In 1969, when White House press secretary Ronald Ziegler attempted to explain to a press briefing that General Lewis Hershey had not been fired as Selective Service System director but had been "promoted" to an advisory position, Lisagor cut Ziegler short by asking: "How did he take the good news, Ron?" In a political town, Lisagor set a standard for fairness. "An old editor once told me to walk down the middle of the street and shoot windows out on both sides," Lisagor said of his nonideological approach to political writing. In a 1970 *Time* magazine profile, Lisagor was described as "the newspaper correspondent conceded by his colleagues to be Washington's all-around best."

Lisagor's writing style was distinctive. While covering Soviet premier Nikita Khrushchev's 1959 visit to the United States, Lisagor wrote: "Traveling with Khrushchev is like holding a stick of dynamite with a sputtering fuse. This man has an endless repertoire of moods. He can flit from a touching recital of his life as a soiled coal miner dreaming of a Communist paradise to a fist-clenching menace." In the wake of the violence that erupted at the 1968 Democratic National Convention in Chicago, overshadowing Hubert H. Humphrey's nomination for the presidency, Lisagor wrote: "Humphrey could have gotten a better deal in bankruptcy court."

Lisagor was adept at scooping his competitors on major news developments. Using excellent sources, he gave his readers the inside story of the Korean War. John F. Kennedy shared with Lisagor his strategy for debating Richard M. Nixon in 1960 and, later, for dealing with Khrushchev. In December 1966, Lisagor reported the first authentic account of the dispute between the family of the late President Kennedy and author William Manchester over the publication of Manchester's *The Death of a President* in 1967. Lisagor disclosed the family's efforts to delete from the book Jacqueline Kennedy's personal recollections about the aftermath of her husband's assassination. In his final interview as president, Lyndon B. Johnson acknowledged to Lisagor that he should have involved the public more in decision-making about the Vietnam War. Johnson also told Lisagor that he had failed to build trust among younger Americans.

Tall and athletic in build, Lisagor had a good-natured demeanor and a wry sense of humor. A master storyteller with a hearty laugh, Lisagor was well liked by his colleagues and the people he covered. "His personal authority was so immense, he was so smart and funny and tough of mind, so unconnable, that he was taken very seriously by his peers," journalist David Halberstam wrote of Lisagor in 1979. "It was Lisagor, smart, quick, verbal, who always seemed to be able to define an event in a few words."

For all of his accomplishments as a print journalist, it was as a television personality that Lisagor developed a national following. He was the most frequent guest interviewer on NBC's "Meet the Press" and a regular on CBS's "Face the Nation." In February 1967, Lisagor became a panelist on "Washington Week in Review," a political commentary show aired by the Public Broadcasting Service. Two years later he joined "Agronsky & Co.," a nationally syndicated public affairs program. Lisagor won a George Foster Peabody Award in 1974 for his contributions to broadcasting news.

Lisagor was a major influence in the development of the Watergate scandal as a serious news story at a time when the journalistic and political establishments were reluctant to pursue it. Lisagor, who had known Richard M. Nixon for more than two decades, believed that President Nixon had known about the 1972 break-in of the Democratic National Committee offices and that he had directed the cover-up. He was convinced that Nixon's obsession with secrecy and his personal control of political operations had led to the scandal. What Lisagor wrote for the *Daily News* and said on television about Watergate had enormous impact. "He had ultimate peer power," Halberstam wrote of Lisagor's influence in shaping the nation's perception of Watergate. Although he was a leading member of the journalistic establishment and shaper of conventional wisdom, Lisagor was sometimes off the mark in assessing the mood of voters beyond Washington. He seriously underestimated, for example, the strength of Ronald Reagan's challenge to Gerald R. Ford for the 1976 Republican presidential nomination.

Early in 1976, Lisagor was diagnosed with lung cancer and began receiving radiation and chemotherapy. He directed *Daily News* coverage of both political conventions that summer and continued writing his column, but reduced his television appearances. He died at Northern Virginia Doctors Hospital. By order of President Ford, Lisagor was buried in Arlington National Cemetery. "He was a journalist in every sense of the term, fair and thorough," said Ford. Secretary of State Henry A. Kissinger remembered Lisagor as "the Renaissance man of the Washington Press." The Chicago Society of Professional Journalists presents annual awards for distinguished journalism in Lisagor's name. His headstone at Arlington is inscribed with a tribute from President Johnson: "Americans will always respect the responsibility with which you have carried forward the strategic freedom of the press."

[A profile "Horizontal in Washington," is in *Time*, Aug. 17, 1970. Lisagor discussed his philosophy of journalism with Timothy Crouse in *The Boys on the Bus* (1973). David Halberstam noted Lisagor's influence in *The Powers That Be* (1979). Obituaries are in the *Chicago Daily News* and the *New York Times*, both Dec. 11, 1976.]

STEVE NEAL

LOMBARDO, GAETANO ALBERT ("GUY") (June 19, 1902–Nov. 5, 1977), bandleader and violinist, was born in London, Ontario, Canada, the oldest son of Gaetano Lombardo, a tailor, and Angelina Paladino. Both parents were musically inclined. At the age of twelve Gaetano, who had become known as "Guy," began taking violin lessons. His brothers also received training on musical intruments: Carmen on the flute and saxophone, Lebert on the drums (later shifting to trumpet), and Victor on the saxophone. His brother Joseph was the one nonmusical family member. Two sisters, Rose Marie and Elaine, were later affiliated with their brother's band, the former as a vocalist and the latter as the wife of singer Kenny Gardner.

In 1919, Guy, Carmen, and Lebert left school to become professional musicians, and by the early 1920's, their band was playing regularly in London. The youths, calling themselves "the Royal Canadians," moved to Cleveland, Ohio, in 1924 for an engagement at the Claremont Café. It was there that the group's style, including playing a melody legato and using the musical medley, began to evolve. One of the café's patrons was Jules Stein, an agent who later represented the Lombardos and founded the Music Corporation of America.

A personable individual, Lombardo catered to the dancers in his audience and made use of the then-new technology of radio to gain a following by broadcasting on a Cleveland station. He became a naturalized citizen in 1926 and married Lilliebell Glenn the following year. They had no children.

In 1927 the band moved to the Grenada Hotel in Chicago. A critic praised the musicians as the "sweetest jazzmen on any stage this side of heaven." Slightly modified, this phrase was used to describe the band's music throughout its career.

The Royal Canadians moved to New York City in 1929 at the behest of Jules Stein and opened at the Roosevelt Grill, thus beginning a thirty-three-year association that lasted until the grill closed and the band moved to the Waldorf-Astoria. After arriving in New York, brother Victor joined the group and they established the tradition of playing on New Year's Eve, performing their theme song, "Auld Lang Syne," at midnight. The band gave its forty-eighth and last New Year's performance on Dec. 31, 1976.

The Royal Canadians were featured on several radio programs, including "The Robert Burns Cigar Show" and "Lady Esther Serenade," and was one of the three groups hired on a permanent basis for "Spotlight Bands." Although they appeared in motion pictures beginning in 1934, their activity on television was mainly limited to specials and the New Year's Eve show.

The band made its first recordings for Gennett in 1924. In 1934, Lombardo signed a contract with Decca Records, beginning an affiliation lasting for more than twenty years. During that time, the musicians regularly produced best-sellers, including at least four records that sold more than 1 million copies each.

Also in 1934, Lombardo and bandleaders Rudy Vallee, Richard Himber, and Abe Lyman joined Paul Whiteman to form a Committee of Five for the Betterment of Radio. Hoping to avoid any outside censorship of radio similar to the "clean film" movement against sexually suggestive material in the movies, this review board met each Friday to examine songs published during the week. If any were found to be objectionable, the publisher was asked to revise the lyrics. If this was not done, the song was cited on a list that was sent to orchestra leaders who broadcast nationwide.

Throughout his career, Lombardo was an astute businessman. His investments included a music publishing company, the Port-O-Call

Restaurant in Tierra Verde, Fla., and the East Point House at Freeport, N.Y. Lombardo also was deeply involved in motorboat racing. He was national speedboat champion from 1946 to 1952. He was nearly killed in 1948 when he hit some floating debris during competition, and his wife prevailed on him to halt this activity in 1957, although he continued boating for pleasure and was in the forefront of attempts to promote safe boating.

In 1954, Lombardo began producing extravaganzas at the Jones Beach Theater in Wantagh, N.Y. Robert Moses, the state parks commissioner, induced the bandleader to enter this very successful activity, which lasted for twenty-three years.

In addition to their other performances, the Royal Canadians were noted for their appearances at each presidential inaugural ball, beginning with that for Franklin D. Roosevelt in 1933 and continuing through that for Jimmy Carter in 1977.

Though derided by jazz lovers as "the King of Corn" or "Guy Lumbago," Lombardo and his band were so well known for playing "the sweetest music this side of heaven" that he became one of the most popular leaders in the history of American dance music. A major factor contributing to the Royal Canadians' success was that in the numbers they played, the melody was always recognizable and singable, and the tempo danceable. Moreover, the group had a distinctive, easily identified sound. The Lombardo band also introduced more than four hundred songs, some of which—"Boo Hoo," "Sweethearts on Parade," "Seems Like Old Times," and "Little Coquette"—became enduring popular hits. Many of these tunes were composed by Lombardo's brother Carmen.

Lombardo died in Houston, Tex., from complications following open-heart surgery. At his funeral, he was eulogized by Robert Moses and by bandleader-singer Phil Harris, who said that his friend was "one of a kind who would continue to live on through his music." A bridge over the Thames River in London, Ontario, and an avenue in Freeport, N.Y., bear his name.

[Band and family memorabilia are in the Guy Lombardo Music Centre in London, Ontario. Book-length coverage of Lombardo is Saul Richman, *Guy* (1978). See also B. Herndon, *The Sweetest Music This Side of Heaven* (1964); Guy Lombardo and J. Altschul, *Auld Acquaintance* (1975); B. F. Cline, *The Lombardo Story* (1979); and Thomas A. DeLong, *Pops: Paul Whiteman, King of Jazz* (1983).

Probably the most complete collection of recordings is the six-LP set *The Best of Guy Lombardo and His Royal Canadians* (Reader's Digest, RD4-161), which contains extensive program notes. Two compact disc collections are *Guy Lombardo: 16 Most Requested Songs* (Columbia CD, CK 44407) and *Best of Guy Lombardo and His Royal Canadians* (Curb CD, D2-77390). Brian Rust, *The American Dance Band Discography: 1917–1942* (1975), holds much detailed material on the earlier portion of the Royal Canadians' recording endeavors. An obituary is in the *New York Times*, Nov. 7, 1977.]

BARRETT G. POTTER

LONGWORTH, ALICE LEE ROOSEVELT (Feb. 12, 1884–Feb. 21, 1980), socialite, was born in New York City, the only child of Theodore Roosevelt and Alice Hathaway Lee. Two days after she was born, her mother died, and care of the infant Alice passed to her paternal aunt, Anna Roosevelt Cowles, while Theodore Roosevelt grieved in Dakota Territory. Alice lived in New York City and Sagamore Hill, Long Island, receiving periodic visits from her father until Dec. 2, 1886, when Theodore married Edith Kermit Carow; thereafter, the three made their home at Sagamore Hill. Eventually Alice had four stepbrothers and one stepsister.

Alice received an irregular education. Intelligent, curious, and precocious, she studied broadly on her own and was often tested by her father, who administered oral examinations. Although bright and pretty, Alice thought of herself as lethargic and shy. Until she was thirteen she had to wear heavy leg braces to offset the effects of childhood polio. Alice matured in Albany, N.Y., New York City, and Washington, D.C., as Theodore's burgeoning political career necessitated the family's moves to those locations. Alice desired a reassuring closeness with her busy father, and suffered emotionally from his distance from her and his preoccupation with his career. Meanwhile, illness and childbearing distracted Edith from nurturing Alice. Alice rebelled against their disinterest by refusing to be confirmed in the church, playing poker for money, and choosing friends of whom her parents disapproved.

Theodore Roosevelt assumed the presidency in September 1901, and Alice became "First Daughter." In January 1902 she made her formal debut at a party given at the White

House. Slender, graceful, and attractive, Alice soon thereafter christened Kaiser Wilhelm's American-made yacht and simultaneously launched herself into the international spotlight. The press nicknamed her "Princess Alice," an undemocratic but affectionate title that recalled Alice's high spirits and intuitive understanding of her semiofficial position as First Daughter. Theodore sent Alice to Cuba and Puerto Rico as his emissary. She made a highly publicized goodwill tour of four countries during the 1905 Russo-Japanese War settlement. The mikado, the dowager empress of China, and Korean and Filipino leaders treated Alice as visiting royalty.

At home, Alice engaged in entertainments calculated to capture her father's attention. She mimicked his friends. She drove unchaperoned and too fast. She smoked in public. She carried her pet snake to parties, ate broccoli with gloved fingers, and befriended the nouveau riche, a group her father abhorred. Thousands of fans attended her public appearances while the press recorded it all. To her parents' relief, on Feb. 17, 1906, Alice wed Congressman Nicholas Longworth of Ohio in a celebrated White House ceremony. The Longworths honeymooned in Cuba and then traveled to Europe, where the royalty of England, France, and Germany entertained them. Then the Longworths returned to Washington, where Nick launched a successful campaign for a third term in the House of Representatives.

In the 1908 Republican sweep Nick won reelection. Alice appeared at her husband's political rallies, but generally decreased her public appearances. She refused to conform to Washington's byzantine social codes. Alice gained fame as a hostess who could encourage friendly and enlightening dissent between political enemies. Their famed parties often ended with Nick's violin performances (he was talented enough to be a professional musician) or all-night games of high-stakes poker.

After her marriage, Theodore used Alice as a political sounding board. She enthusiastically supported her father's 1912 third party attempt, despite Nick's awkward position of being son-in-law of the Progressive party leader, and one of Ohio's Republican party heirs-apparent. That year, Theodore Roosevelt failed to win the presidency, Nick suffered his only congressional defeat, and the Longworths retreated to the family mansion in Cincinnati.

Nick won reelection in 1914 without his wife's assistance. Alice instead joined her father to campaign for America's rapid entry into World War I. She did no war work, but instead acted in her now customary role of congressional watchdog and bipartisan lampooner. After the war ended, Alice joined with the Irreconcilables to oppose American involvement in the League of Nations. In 1920, Alice joined the Ohio Republican Committee and stumped for Warren G. Harding, whom she called "not a bad man, just a slob." In 1925, Nicholas Longworth was elected Speaker of the House, a position he retained until his death in 1931. On Feb. 14, 1925, at age forty-one, Alice gave birth to her only child, Paulina. Contemporary gossip attributed Paulina's paternity to Senator William E. Borah, but Nick Longworth adored his daughter.

Alice's political savvy, her Oyster Bay family loyalty, and her infamous wit made her an outspoken critic of her distant cousin, President Franklin Delano Roosevelt (FDR), and his New Deal. Though prompted to run for Nick's vacant seat in 1932, she declined; that year she supported Herbert Hoover for president. After FDR's victory, Alice wrote her autobiography, *Crowded Hours* (1933). She attended the 1936 Republican convention as a delegate and redoubled her attacks on New Deal Democrats in her short-lived, syndicated newspaper column, a conservative counterpoint to her first cousin Eleanor Roosevelt's "My Day."

During World War II Alice campaigned for isolationist presidential candidate Robert Taft. She served as an officer of the American First Committee, an organization committed to keeping the United States out of World War II. Alice considered the gyrations of the House Un-American Activities Committee in the 1950's a great spectator sport. In later life, as "Washington's other monument," she devoted herself to dishing up political polemics at her notorious dinner parties. Presidents Kennedy, Johnson, Nixon, and Ford courted Alice. She attended Washington's most prestigious political and social gatherings even after she turned ninety, wearing her trademark broad-brimmed hat.

Famed for controversial actions in early life, her later celebrity rested upon such witticisms as comparing Thomas E. Dewey to "the groom on a wedding cake," and calling FDR "two-thirds mush and one-third Eleanor." Of President Lyndon B. Johnson's televised display of his gall-bladder operation scars, she opined, "I suppose we should be grateful it wasn't a prostate operation." Mrs. Longworth asserted that "Wendell Willkie sprang from the grass roots—of the country clubs of America," and that Calvin Coolidge looked "as though he had been weaned on a pickle." Perhaps her most famous witticism was the slogan embroidered on her favorite pillow, "If you haven't got anything nice to say, come and sit by me." Critics accused Alice of mean-spiritedness, but Washingtonians knew it was better to be jibed at than ignored by "Mrs. L."

Alice's breadth of acquaintances, her political insights, her celebrity status, and her penchant for "comforting the afflicted and afflicting the comfortable" made her one of the capital's most influential women, a combination power broker and political goad.

Longworth died in Washington just after her ninety-sixth birthday.

[The Library of Congress houses Alice Roosevelt Longworth's correspondence, diaries, scrapbooks, and a clipping and photograph file. Nicholas Longworth's papers are also deposited at the Library of Congress, while the Longworth family papers are located in the Cincinnati Historical Society. The Roosevelt family papers are divided between the Library of Congress and the Theodore Roosevelt Collection, Harvard University. Alice Roosevelt Longworth's autobiography is *Crowded Hours* (1933).

Michael Teague's *Mrs. L: Conversations with Alice Roosevelt Longworth* (1981) is a biography based on oral interviews. Other biographies are James Brough, *Princess Alice* (1975); Howard Teichmann, *Alice: The Life and Times of Alice Roosevelt Longworth* (1979); and Carol Felsenthal, *Alice Roosevelt Longworth* (1988). For other aspects of her life, see Stacy A. Rozek, " 'The First Daughter of the Land': Alice Roosevelt as Presidential Celebrity, 1902–1906," *Presidential Studies Quarterly*, Winter 1989; and Stacy Rozek Cordery, "Theodore Roosevelt's Private Diplomat: Alice Roosevelt and the 1905 Far Eastern Junket," in Natalie A. Naylor, Douglas Brinkley, and John Allen Gable, eds., *Theodore Roosevelt: Many-Sided American* (1992). Also of value is Sylvia Jukes Morris, *Edith Kermit Roosevelt: Portrait of a First Lady* (1980). Obituaries are in the *New York Times*, and the *Washington Post*, both Feb. 21, 1980. The Columbia University Oral History Collection contains transcripts of an interview with Alice Roosevelt Longworth.]

STACY A. CORDERY

LOWELL, RALPH (July 23, 1890–May 15, 1978), banker, was born in the Chestnut Hill section of Boston, the son of John Lowell, an attorney, and Mary Emlen Hale. A descendant of one of the oldest and most prominent families in Massachusetts, he numbered among his ancestors poets, shipping and textile magnates, scholars, and clergymen. There is even a town named for the family: Lowell, Mass. Lowell received his early education at the Volkmann School in Boston and at El Rancho Bonito in Mesa, Ariz. He then became a member of the sixth generation of Lowells to attend Harvard when he entered in 1908. He graduated in 1912 with a B.A. degree in anthropology magna cum laude and with membership in Phi Beta Kappa. Following graduation, he traveled around the world with a friend and Harvard classmate, Richard Wigglesworth. They arrived in Baroda, India, in time to be present at the wedding of Harvard classmate, Prince Jaisinhrao.

When Lowell returned to Boston, he became a salesman with the brokerage firm of Curtis and Sanger, where he remained until 1916, when he left to become secretary to the president of the First National Bank of Boston. He left the bank in 1917 to serve in the United States Army. On Sept. 1, 1917, he married Charlotte Loring, the daughter of Lindsley Loring, a businessman in the Boston suburb of Westwood; they had seven children. He served in the army until 1919, advancing to the rank of lieutenant colonel. He was stationed in Plattsburgh, N.Y., and later at Camp Lee, Va., where he served as the senior instructor in the Officers Training School. Following his discharge, he remained in the army reserves and from 1919 to 1923 served as a civilian aide in Massachusetts to the secretary of war.

When Lowell returned to Boston, he became head of the stock department of Lee, Higginson and Company, and in 1937 he was made a partner and manager of the Boston office of Clark, Dodge and Company. Five years later, he left the brokerage business when he became chairman of the board of the Boston Safe Deposit and Trust Company, of which he was elected president in 1946. He remained in this position until 1959, acting also as the chief executive officer of the bank. In 1963 he "retired" in order to travel, to devote more time to charitable and civic activities and to spend more time with his family.

Lowell was the perfect example of a proper

Bostonian. His family were both "movers and shakers" and humanitarians, and he followed their example. At one time he served on twenty-six boards of directors of corporations and businesses, and he gave his financial expertise in the area of fund-raising to hospitals, charities, and cultural endeavors.

One of his outstanding efforts came as a result of a Lowell family bequest. In 1836, under the will of his ancestor John Lowell, Jr., a family trust was established that created the Lowell Institute. In 1943, Ralph Lowell inherited the trusteeship of the Lowell Institute from its president, A. Lawrence Lowell. Two years later, acting upon the advice of a friend, Harvard president James B. Conant, he organized the Lowell Institute Cooperative Broadcasting Council. The council consisted of thirteen universities and cultural institutions in the Boston area that joined together to prepare programming for adult educational programs for broadcast by a number of area commercial stations. An outgrowth of this early effort was the creation and licensing in 1951 of the radio station WGBH-FM, which was devoted entirely to cultural, educational, and noncommercial programming. In 1955, WGBH-TV began regular broadcasting as one of the first educational television stations in the nation. In 1965 it honored Lowell by naming its studios for him.

Harvard was another of Lowell's primary interests. He was a member of its policy-making Board of Overseers and served as its president in the years 1957–1958. He was class treasurer and class agent of the class of 1912. Lowell also was a trustee for a number of schools in the Boston area.

As Lowell's hair grew white, he reminded one of former president William Howard Taft. When those who knew of his various charitable, civic, and cultural contributions attempted to publicize them, he turned the attention away from himself, remarking how blessed he had been to have been given so much, and that he had the responsibility to give back, in order to help his fellow man.

Lowell died in Boston.

[Lowell's papers, memorabilia, and family records may be found at the Massachusetts Historical Society. See also Edward Weeks, *The Lowells and Their Institute* (1966). An obituary is in the *New York Times*, May 16, 1978.]

BETTY B. VINSON

LOWELL, ROBERT TRAILL SPENCE, JR. (Mar. 1, 1917–Sept. 12, 1977), writer and teacher, was born in Boston, Mass., the son of Robert Traill Spence Lowell, a naval officer, and Charlotte Winslow. Descended on both sides from prominent New England families, he numbered among his relatives the writer and diplomat James Russell Lowell (1819–1891), the poet Amy Lowell (1874–1925), an early governor of Plymouth Colony, Edward Winslow (1595–1655), and the Revolutionary War general John Stark (1728–1822). Except for brief periods when his father was stationed in Washington and Philadelphia, Lowell grew up in Boston. He attended the Brimmer and the Rivers schools in Boston and St. Mark's in Southboro, Mass., where he played football and began writing. He was encouraged in his writing by the poet Richard Eberhart, who was a teacher at St. Mark's. In 1935, Lowell entered Harvard University, where a cousin, Abbott Lawrence Lowell, had recently retired as president. On the advice of the novelist Ford Madox Ford, Lowell transferred from Harvard to Kenyon College in Gambier, Ohio, in 1937 to study with the poet John Crowe Ransom. At Kenyon, where he majored in classics, he was awarded a B.A. summa cum laude in 1940.

On Apr. 2, 1940, Lowell married Jean Stafford, whom he had met at a summer writing seminar—and who would precede him in becoming a successful writer. Their courtship had been interrupted a few days before Christmas 1938 by an automobile accident that forced the reconstruction of Stafford's face. Lowell was at the wheel. He had been drinking and illegally left the scene. Although he had proposed to her before the accident and considered themselves engaged, the incident started a rumor that he married her to prevent a costly injury suit. The couple had no children and moved to Baton Rouge, La., where Lowell continued his studies at Louisiana State University with Robert Penn Warren, and Stafford worked in the offices of *The Southern Review*. In March 1941, Lowell converted to Roman Catholicism, and in September of that year, the couple moved to New York City, where for the next nine months Lowell worked as an editorial assistant for the Catholic publishing firm of Sheed and Ward and came under the influence of the British historian Christopher Dawson. In 1942, at the invitation of Allen Tate and his wife, Caroline Gordon, the Lowells joined the Tates in Monteagle, Tenn., where during the winter all four writers worked on separate literary projects.

In 1942, Lowell tried unsuccessfully to enlist in the armed services. Bad eyesight was given as the reason for his rejection. Called for induction in August 1943, he refused to report. In a letter to President Franklin D. Roosevelt, dated September 7, he stated his opposition not to the war but to the Allied aims of unconditional surrender and saturation bombing, and to an ignored, imminent threat of world Communism. In October 1943 he was found guilty of draft evasion and sentenced to prison for a year and a day. Five months later, he was paroled to Bridgeport. He and his wife lived in nearby Black Rock, Conn.

Lowell's first collection of poems, *Land of Unlikeness*, was published in 1944. Critical of the nation's loss of spiritual direction and its embrace of materialism, the volume presented Lowell as a formalist and "consciously a Catholic poet." Its poems recalled the harsh religious and satirical lyrics of seventeenth-century British poets as well as the recent work of Tate and the highly allusive techniques of Ezra Pound and T. S. Eliot. Using heroic language, Lowell evoked the heroic energies of a personal and national past that, if revived, might redirect the people and nation toward likeness to God and Saint Augustine's City of God. Many of the poems were rewritten and incorporated with dramatic monologues and new, more compassionate and elegiac works into Lowell's second collection, *Lord Weary's Castle* (1946). The volume's formalism, heroic language, ironies, cautions, and calls for individual and social change seemed ideally suited to the postwar temper. It brought Lowell the 1947 Pulitzer Prize in poetry, a grant from the American Academy and National Institute of Arts and Letters, a Guggenheim Fellowship, and an appointment as consultant in poetry to the Library of Congress for the period 1947–1948.

By the autumn of 1946, Lowell's marriage to Stafford was over, although they were not legally divorced until June 1948. Before their marriage, perhaps as early as 1935, Lowell had exhibited manic behavior and shown signs of mental instability. In the spring of 1949, following his participation in the controversial awarding of the Bollingen Prize for poetry to Pound and his efforts to unseat Agnes Smedley as director of the writer's colony at Yaddo, in upstate New York, he experienced the first in a series of breakdowns that occurred periodically for the rest of his life. Recovered from the breakdown, on July 28, 1949, he married the writer Elizabeth Hardwick, whom he had met at Yaddo. They had one child. In 1950, after teaching at the Kenyon School of Letters and a semester of teaching at the University of Iowa, the Lowells went to Europe for an extended stay. While they were abroad, his third volume, *The Mills of the Kavanaughs* (1951), appeared. It contains two of his most enduring works, "Falling Asleep over the Aeneid" and "Mother Marie Therese."

In Europe, Lowell suffered another brief breakdown. After recovering, he was able in 1952 to teach in Austria at the Salzburg Seminar on American Studies and, in 1953, to return to teaching posts at the Kenyon School of Letters and the State University of Iowa. The following year, while lecturing at the University of Cincinnati, he received word of his mother's dying in Italy. He arrived too late to see her alive. After returning with her body, he suffered the most severe of his early breakdowns. Following treatment, he and his wife moved to Boston, eventually settling in a house on Marlborough Street a short distance from the house his parents had occupied. In 1956, Lowell taught at Boston University. In 1958, while awaiting the publication of his next volume of poems, *Life Studies* (1959), he taught summer school at Harvard University.

In contrast to *Lord Weary's Castle*, which had embodied the values of the New Critics and an "escape from personality" advocated by Eliot, *Life Studies* moved to looser verse techniques and an "expression of personality." In it Lowell used the mental problems that had surfaced during the previous decade to weigh the social lives and psychologically damaging influences of his parents and his own efforts to achieve a stable, middle-class life. Its "confessional" tone and personal investments of ordinary objects with symbolic values helped set the style for subsequent British and American poetry. In existential fashion, what one chose for oneself, one chose for others. The volume's final poem, "Skunk Hour," with its admission that "My mind's not right," was awarded the Guinness Poetry Prize in 1959, and in 1960, the volume received the National Book Award for poetry. Its success prompted the Boston Arts Festival to commission a new poem, "For the Union Dead," and assisted in Lowell's receiving a Longview Foundation Award and a Ford Foundation grant to study opera (1960).

In September 1960, the Lowells moved to New York City, and during the next decade the political views that had long been a part of Lowell's poetry were put into political action. The change coincided with the efforts of politicians to include cultural figures in their attempts to revitalize the nation. Lowell was invited to the inauguration of John F. Kennedy and later to the White House by President Kennedy in May 1962 and became a spokesman abroad for American policies. In 1962, on completion of a year of teaching at the New School for Social Research in New York City, Lowell traveled to South America, where he experienced still another breakdown. The next year, after being treated, he accepted a position at Harvard University, commuting from New York City to teach there two days per week. The position continued until 1970, when he left the United States for England. In 1965, invited by President Lyndon B. Johnson to the White House Festival of the Arts, Lowell used his international stature and the occasion to protest the country's recent involvements in Vietnam and the Dominican Republic. The attacks on Johnson's policies continued in "Waking Early Sunday Morning" (1965) and in his adaptation of Aeschylus' *Prometheus Bound* (1967), as well as in public remarks. In September 1967, Lowell was one of a number of prominent cultural figures who took part in the Pentagon March against the war in Vietnam, and in 1968 he worked to gain Senator Eugene McCarthy the Democratic nomination for president.

During this period, Lowell published *Imitations* (1961), *For the Union Dead* (1964), *Near the Ocean* (1967), and *Notebook 1967–68* (1969), as well as his version of Jean Racine's *Phèdre* (1961) and a dramatic transformation of works by Nathaniel Hawthorne and Herman Melville into *The Old Glory* (1965). He received a number of awards for these works, including, in 1962, the Bollingen Prize for translation for *Imitations* and, in 1965, an Obie Award for the "Benito Cereno" segment of *The Old Glory*. In 1966, Lowell was the first American writer in serious contention for the poetry professorship at Oxford University; the person finally selected was the British poet Edmund Blunden.

Much like *Life Studies*, *Notebook 1967–68* struck out in a new direction with its autobiographical, free verse, fourteen-line sonnetlike segments. In a verse line that strove for novelty and distinction, it recorded the banalities and excitements of daily events. Lowell revised, expanded, and republished the volume as *Notebook* (1970), then augmented, divided, and reorganized it into *History* (1973) and *For Lizzie and Harriet* (1973), issuing it with a new volume of poems, *The Dolphin* (1973), written after his move to England. Prompted in part by the results of the 1968 presidential election and an offer of a visiting professorship at All Souls College at Oxford University, Lowell moved to England in early 1970. Almost immediately on his arrival in England, a teaching offer at the University of Essex was extended. Abroad alone, Lowell soon became involved with the writer Lady Caroline Blackwood. Since his breakdowns were often preceded by blatant extramarital involvements, his wife thought this involvement presaged another breakdown—and, indeed, one did occur.

Upon his recovery, Lowell continued his relationship with Blackwood; in September 1971, their son was born. In October 1972 he divorced Hardwick and married Blackwood in Santo Domingo. Details of their involvement and marriage are recorded in *The Dolphin*, which in 1974 brought Lowell his second Pulitzer Prize in poetry. In February 1975, Lowell resumed his teaching at Harvard. *Selected Poems* appeared in 1976, and a new volume, *Day by Day*, was issued the following year. It broke with the sonnetlike structure that had marked the last three volumes and in 1978 brought Lowell a posthumous National Book Critics Circle Award for poetry. On the way to take up his teaching duties at Harvard, Lowell died in New York City. His unfinished translation of Aeschylus' *Oresteia* (1978) was published posthumously, and in 1987 his *Collected Prose*, edited by Robert Giroux, appeared.

[The New York Public Library and the Houghton Library at Harvard University have extensive holdings of Lowell's manuscripts and letters. A major biography is Ian Hamilton, *Robert Lowell* (1982). On the Lowell family background, see Ferris Greenslet, *The Lowells and Their Seven Worlds* (1946); Edward Weeks, *The Lowells and Their Institute* (1966); and Clemens David Heymann, *American Aristocracy* (1980). On his poetry, see Hugh B. Staples, *Robert Lowell* (1962); Jerome Mazzaro, *The Poetic Themes of Robert Lowell* (1965); and Steven Gould Axelrod, *Robert Lowell* (1978). Anthologies of criticism include Thomas Francis Parkinson, ed., *Robert Lowell* (1968); Jerome Mazzaro, ed., *A Profile of Robert Lowell* (1971); Jonathan Price, ed., *Critics on Robert Lowell* (1972); Steven Axelrod and Helen Deese, eds., *Robert Lowell* (1986); and Jeffrey Meyers, ed., *Robert Lowell* (1988). On Lowell's political involvements, see Norman Mailer, *The Armies of the Night* (1968); and Alan Williamson, *Pity the Monsters* (1974). Steven Axelrod and Helen Deese have also compiled a bibliography, *Robert Lowell: A Reference Guide* (1982). Obituaries are in the *New York Times*, Sept. 13, 1977; and the *Times* (London), Sept. 14, 1977.]

JEROME MAZZARO

LOWENSTEIN, ALLARD KENNETH (Jan. 16, 1929–Mar. 14, 1980), political activist, was born in Newark, N.J., and grew up in Westchester County, N.Y. His father, Gabriel Abraham Lowenstein, a doctor, taught at the Columbia College of Physicians and Surgeons and then gave up medicine to run a successful restaurant business. His mother was Augusta Goldberg. Lowenstein graduated from the Horace Mann School in New York City in 1945. After graduating with a B.A. in 1949 from the University of North Carolina at Chapel Hill, where he had been active in the nascent civil rights movement, Lowenstein went to work in Washington, D.C., as a legislative assistant to liberal Senator Frank P. Graham of North Carolina. In the early 1950's he presided over the National Student Association, and in the 1952 presidential campaign Lowenstein chaired the national organization of Students for [Adlai] Stevenson. Later that year he began working for Eleanor Roosevelt at the United Nations. He received a law degree from Yale University in 1954, and as a young lawyer he actively championed the cause of Namibian independence.

After failing to win a congressional seat from Manhattan in 1960, Lowenstein taught law and politics at Stanford University from 1961 to 1962, where he also served as an assistant dean of men, and at the University of North Carolina from 1963 to 1964. In 1963 he mobilized students from Yale and Stanford to work with the Student Nonviolent Coordinating Committee (SNCC) in its efforts to register African Americans to vote and to hold a "freedom election" in Mississippi. He then recruited college students for the Mississippi Freedom Summer of 1964 and sought to play a leading role in the voter-registration campaign. Lowenstein's attempts to move the Freedom Summer headquarters from Mississippi to New York, however, and to prevent SNCC from receiving legal assistance from the leftist National Lawyers Guild alienated SNCC militants. When Lowenstein supported President Lyndon B. Johnson's compromise proposal in 1964 on the seating of the Mississippi delegation at the Democratic National Convention which the Mississippi Freedom Democratic party opposed as a sell-out, the rift between SNCC and Lowenstein and other white liberals became an unbridgeable gulf. On Nov. 25, 1966, he married Jennifer Lyman; they had three children and were later divorced.

In the fall of 1967, as vice-chairman of the Americans for Democratic Action, Lowenstein planned a revolt against Johnson's renomination. Recruiting converts on college campuses, in the peace movement, and among dissident Democrats, he built a movement to "dump Johnson." After senators Robert Kennedy of New York and George McGovern of South Dakota rejected his plans to run against the president in the Democratic primaries, Lowenstein found his candidate in Senator Eugene McCarthy of Minnesota and engineered the challenger's impressive showing in the 1968 New Hampshire primary election. Lowenstein attracted large numbers of liberals to the "peace" candidacy of McCarthy, and Johnson ultimately withdrew from the race.

In November 1968, after moving to Long Beach on Long Island, Lowenstein was elected to Congress from New York's Fifth District in Nassau County. He served one term before being defeated for reelection and then failed to win in four subsequent attempts. In 1977 he was appointed by President Jimmy Carter to be the American representative to the United Nations Commission on Human Rights; later that year he became the United States alternative representative for United Nations Special Political Affairs.

Returning to private law practice with Layton and Sherman in New York in 1978, Lowenstein continued to travel widely on behalf of peace and justice, particularly to Africa, where he helped mediate a settlement in Rhodesia. Dennis Sweeny, formerly a close friend of Lowenstein's at Stanford and his protégé in the civil rights movement, shot him to death in his Rockefeller Center law office. In a tribute to a "life devoted to reason and justice," President Carter stated: "From the sit-ins to the campuses to the halls of Congress, Al Lowenstein was a passionate fighter for a more humane, more democratic world."

[Lowenstein's papers are in the University of North Carolina, Chapel Hill. See William H. Chafe, *Never Stop Running: Allard Lowenstein and the Struggle to Save American Liberalism* (1993). His account of apartheid in South Africa and his own campaign against it is *Brutal Mandate* (1962). A collection of his speeches and writings is Gregory Stone and Douglas Lowenstein, eds., *Lowenstein* (1983). An obituary is in the *New York Times*, Mar. 15, 1980.]

HARVARD SITKOFF

LUBIN, ISADOR (June 9, 1896–July 6, 1978), economist, government official, and educator, was born in Worcester, Mass., one of three children of Harris Lubin, a Lithuanian immigrant who owned a chain of clothing stores, and Hinda Francke. Lubin worked in his father's clothing stores before entering Clark College in 1912. He received a B.A. in economics from Clark in 1916. After spending several weeks at an ROTC training camp in Plattsburgh, N.Y., in the summer of 1916, Lubin enrolled in the University of Missouri graduate program, where he studied under economist Thorstein Veblen. He was an undergraduate instructor at Missouri in 1917.

World War I interrupted Lubin's academic career. Between January and July of 1918 he worked under Veblen as a statistician for the United States Food Administration, assisting him in several studies of midwestern food production. From July 1918 to September 1919, Lubin was a special expert for the War Industries Board.

In 1919, Lubin resumed his graduate studies at the University of Michigan, and in 1920 he joined the faculty as an assistant professor of economics. He worked at Michigan until 1922, when he joined the staff of the Robert Brookings School of Economics and Government. He became a member of the Brookings faculty in 1923 and also taught at the University of Missouri as an assistant professor of economics in 1924. In 1926 he received a Ph.D. from the Brookings School.

During the 1920s, Lubin concentrated on the economic problems of the coal industry, visiting coal mines in England and Germany in 1925. His research during this period resulted in the publication of two books: *Miners' Wages and the Cost of Coal* (1924) and *The British Coal Dilemma* (1927), the latter written with Helen Everett. Lubin argued that lower prices and declining wages in the coal industry were caused by overproduction, and he advocated the nationalization of coal mines to reduce excess capacity.

Lubin married Alice E. Berliner, the daughter of gramophone inventor Emile Berliner, on Sept. 15, 1923. They had a daughter before their divorce in 1928. In that year Lubin became an adviser to the Senate Committee on Education and Labor, which was investigating unemployment. He spent eight months during 1929 in Europe researching a book on government regulation of the radio industry. The project was never completed, however, because upon his return to America, Lubin was assigned to help a Senate subcommittee draft legislation for a public works program. In 1930, Lubin was an economic adviser for the Senate Committee on Manufacturers, which was conducting a study of business organizations.

President Franklin D. Roosevelt appointed Lubin commissioner of labor statistics in May 1933. Lubin and his staff collected statistics on unemployment, wages, productivity, industrial accidents, and the cost of living. Under Lubin's supervision, the Bureau of Labor Statistics modernized the methods of collecting and disseminating economic data and introduced a new cost-of-living index to provide the federal government with a better picture of the nation's economic health. On Feb. 29, 1932, Lubin married Ann Shumaker, the editor of *Progressive Education*. She died in 1935, shortly after giving birth to Lubin's second daughter.

Lubin took a leave of absence from the Bureau of Labor Statistics in July 1940 to work in the labor section of the National Defense Advisory Board. He was also deputy director of the labor division of the Board's successor, the Office of Production Management. In these positions Lubin helped settle labor disputes that threatened production in defense-related industries.

In May 1941, Roosevelt asked Lubin to establish an office in the White House to monitor defense production statistics and to serve as special statistical assistant to the Lend-Lease program. In 1942 he became director of the Statistical Analysis Branch, Munitions Assignment Board of the Combined Chiefs of Staff, which involved preparing the statistical charts for the War Room in the White House. Lubin went to London in December 1942 to confer with British officials on the standardization of statistical classifications.

In January 1945, Lubin visited occupied Germany to prepare a report on economic conditions for the American military. Following this tour, he became the American representative to the Allied Reparations Commission meeting in Moscow in March 1945, where he worked closely with United States ambassador W. Averell Harriman. For health reasons, Lubin turned down President Harry S. Truman's request to serve on the Japanese reparations commission, but he continued to serve on the German commission until he resigned all of his government positions in January 1946.

Afterward, Lubin became president and chairman of the board of Confidential Reports, Inc., a theatrical accounting firm owned by several large motion-picture studios, including United Artists, Columbia Pictures, and Warner Brothers. He headed Confidential Reports until 1951. He also joined the board of directors of Decca Records. Lubin also became chairman of the executive committee of the Franklin D. Roosevelt Foundation in 1950, a position he held until his death.

During the postwar period Lubin became interested in foreign economic development and technical aid. From 1947 to 1949 he was the American representative to the Economic and Employment Commission of the United Nations Economic and Social Council (ECOSCO). In 1950, President Truman appointed Lubin the American representative to ECOSCO itself, and from then until 1952 he was also a member of the United States delegation to the United Nations General Assembly. In both positions he stressed the need to provide technical and financial assistance to developing countries and especially the need to transfer industrial technologies. At the conclusion of the 1951–1952 General Assembly session he married Carol Riegelman (then a member of the International Labor Organization staff) in Geneva, Switzerland, on Jan. 30, 1952. The couple had no children.

In addition to Lubin's participation in United Nations affairs, he was always deeply involved in the development of Israel. He first visited Palestine in 1929, and maintained a strong interest in the region from that time. He became an active board member of various organizations, such as the Palestine Economic Corporation, the American Joint Distribution Committee and the Weizmann Institute of Science. In 1960 he became the representative of the United Israel Appeal to oversee the use of contributions in the immigration of settlers to Israel. He continued as a consultant until his death.

In January 1955, Governor W. Averell Harriman of New York named Lubin head of the state industrial commission. Lubin's appointment was blocked by conservative legislators who were suspicious of his New Deal background. Harriman refused to withdraw the appointment and, after several weeks, the Senate Labor Committee approved the nomination.

As industrial commissioner, Lubin advised Harriman on labor policies and advocated an antipoverty program based on a study he had commissioned as head of the Franklin D. Roosevelt Foundation. The study criticized the federal government's failure to deal with the chronically poor and called for industrial training measures to eliminate the causes of poverty. Although a few welfare reforms and test projects were implemented, Lubin lacked the funding for a comprehensive poverty program.

At the end of Harriman's term in 1959, Lubin was named Arthur T. Vanderbilt Professor of Public Affairs at Rutgers University, from which he retired in 1961. During the 1960's and 1970's he continued to work as a consultant for a number of governmental and private agencies, including the Bureau of the Budget, the Twentieth Century Fund, and the American Jewish Committee. Lubin died of heart failure at his home in Annapolis, Md.

[Lubin's papers are in the Franklin D. Roosevelt Library, Hyde Park, N.Y. Lubin published several books and numerous articles, including *Government Control of Prices During the War* (1919), written with Stella Stewart and Paul Garrett; *The Absorption of the Unemployed by American Industry* (1929); and *The British Attack on Unemployment* (1934), written with Arthur Cheney Clifton Hill, Jr. Lubin's work is discussed in Joseph Dorfman, *Thorstein Veblen and His America* (1934); Donald T. Critchlow, *The Brookings Institution, 1916–1952* (1985); and Rudy Abramson, *Spanning the Century: The Life of W. Averell Harriman, 1891–1986* (1992). An obituary is in the *New York Times*, July 8, 1978.]

LEONARD DEGRAAF

LUNT, ALFRED DAVID, JR. (Aug. 12, 1892–Aug. 3, 1977), actor and director, was born in Milwaukee, Wis., the son of Alfred David Lunt, a lumberman and land agent, and Harriet Washburn Briggs. The senior Lunt died in 1894. As a child, Lunt produced his own plays in a toy theater. In 1899 his mother married Carl Sederholm, a Swedish-born doctor.

Lunt attended public school in Milwaukee through the second grade and then entered the private Milwaukee Academy. In 1906 he entered Carroll College Academy, affiliated with Carroll College, in Waukesha, Wis. He enrolled at Carroll College in 1910.

Lunt was active in school theatricals produced by the Carroll Players, a group run by a progressive teacher named May Rankin. Tall (six feet, three inches) and handsome, he played many leads and was appreciated throughout Wisconsin and even beyond the state's borders because of bus tours he made with Carroll College's glee club, on whose programs he gave recitations. One of his unconventional devices—playing with his back to the audience—began to emerge during his Carroll days. Lunt was also an able painter but decided against becoming a set designer or architect in favor of acting. Among his other talents was cooking; he became a gourmet chef.

In 1912, Lunt transferred to Emerson College of Oratory in Boston. He left after landing a job with the Castle Square Theater, a noted stock company, and making his professional debut in *The Aviator*. He remained until 1915, performing mainly in potboilers and playing mostly men much older than himself.

After becoming the beneficiary of a trust fund, Lunt bought real estate in the Wisconsin village of Genesee Depot in 1914. Over the years, he developed the property into a beautiful estate that provided an outlet for his love of farming and gardening and became his refuge from the rigors of his profession.

In 1916 and 1917, Lunt was primarily the leading man to a series of touring female stars. Most influential on his development was Margaret Anglin, an artist of the highest standards, with whom he toured in several unimportant plays. He also acted in outdoor stagings of three Greek tragedies and *As You Like It*.

Lunt made his Broadway debut in *Romance and Arabella* (1917), a flop in which he managed to gain considerable attention. It led to a job in a touring production of *The Country Cousin*, by Booth Tarkington and Julian Street. Its producer, George C. Tyler, hired Lunt for his summer-stock company in Washington, D.C., in 1919. During the rehearsals, Lunt met and fell in love with English-born actress Lynn Fontanne, five years his senior; they were married on May 26, 1922. As the Lunts, they became a practically inseparable acting team, recognized by many as America's finest. They had no children.

They acted together for the first time in the company's production of *Made of Money*. While Fontanne toured in *Made of Money*, Lunt found his breakthrough role on Broadway as the title character in Booth Tarkington's *Clarence* (1919). It was typical of his dedication that, to guarantee an authentic effect when Clarence played the piano and saxophone, he learned to play the instruments well enough so that offstage musicians were not needed. After its run in New York, Lunt toured nationally with the play. In later years he continued to tour with his productions, playing in even the most out-of-the-way venues. He kept the idea of the "road" alive when most other stars had abandoned it.

Following his 1921 appearance in another Tarkington play, *The Intimate Strangers*, Lunt displayed his versatility by shifting from the light comic roles he had been playing to that of a rakish gambler in Alfred Savoir's *Banco* (1922). He also appeared in several mediocre silent films. Back on Broadway in 1923, he appeared with Fontanne in *Sweet Nell of Old Drury* and without her in John Drinkwater's *Robert E. Lee* and Sutton Vane's *Outward Bound*.

Lunt and Fontanne were not considered an acting team until they costarred in the Theatre Guild's extremely popular production of Ferenc Molnár's romantic comedy *The Guardsman* (1924). The Guild, devoted to producing artistically respectable plays of doubtful commercial value (although hits were welcome), had a no-star policy, which was fine with the Lunts, who accepted lesser billing because they believed that the play came first. The Lunts also earned far less than they could have under commercial managements because they respected the plays the Guild produced. They often quarreled with the Guild's management but kept returning to it, even after they and two other partners had formed Transatlantic Productions in 1934.

During the rest of the 1920's, the Guild presented Lunt in New York and on tour in one new play or revival after the other. Lunt appeared alone in four plays, including Eugene O'Neill's *Marco Millions* (1928). The Lunts appeared together in eight plays, including three by George Bernard Shaw and two by S. N. Behrman. Lunt's parts represented an exhausting list of strikingly varied characterizations.

In the 1930's the Lunts appeared in seven important plays and one failure. Memorable were Maxwell Anderson's *Elizabeth the Queen* (1930), Robert E. Sherwood's *Reunion in Vienna* (1931) and *Idiot's Delight* (1936), Noël Coward's *Design for Living* (1933), Shakespeare's *The Taming of the Shrew* (1935; revived 1940), Jean Giraudoux's *Amphitryon* 38 (1937), and Anton Chekhov's *The Seagull* (1938). They also made their only significant sound film, *The Guardsman* (1931), based on their 1924 hit. Lack of creative control made movie acting unattractive to them.

During the 1940's the Lunts were first seen in Robert Sherwood's *There Shall Be No Night* (1940), highly controversial because of its antipacifism, and S. N. Behrman's *The Pirate* (1942), developed as a play with which to tour army camps (the tour had to be canceled owing to Fontanne's ill health). In 1943 the Lunts moved to London, where they remained throughout the war, often performing during rocket raids. Their production of Terence Rattigan's *Love in Idleness* (1944), which they took to soldiers in Europe, came to America as *O Mistress Mine* (1946). It was their biggest commercial hit (452 performances) and ended only because of Lunt's illness. It and their next three plays (by S. N. Behrman, Noël Coward, and Howard Lindsay and Russel Crouse) were commercial fluff redeemed only by the Lunts' matchless artistry. Finding the right plays to suit each of them proved increasingly difficult, and their choices made them seem old-fashioned. The Lunts regained critical respect with their seventeenth team effort, Friedrich Dürrenmatt's black comedy *The Visit* (1958) (unsuccessfully premiered in England as *Time and Again*), directed by Peter Brook. It opened the Lunt-Fontanne, a Broadway theater renamed in their honor. Age and illness took their toll (Lunt went blind), and following *The Visit*, Lunt did not act again on stage.

Although they ignored Hollywood's blandishments, the Lunts occasionally did radio plays and, late in life, acted in several television productions, including their final shared performance, *The Magnificent Yankee* (1965). In the mid-1930's Lunt began to direct most of his productions, even when another was credited; he displayed outstanding directorial ability. Later, he free-lanced as a director, staging plays (notably Jean Giraudoux's *Ondine* [1954], with Audrey Hepburn and Mel Ferrer, for which he won a directing Tony) and operas for other performers. The Lunts, who undertook to develop many young actors, created a Lunt-Fontanne repertory company when they toured in the late 1930's. High costs prevented them from establishing the troupe in New York.

The Lunts preferred to preserve their energy by living quietly. They became wealthy and often contributed to favorite charities. Although generally apolitical, during World War II they were active in causes to raise funds for the Allies. Completely devoted to one another, no hint of scandal marred their lives.

Lunt, a professional for fifty-two years, was a master technician who brought deep emotional reserves to any role he played, seeking only to find the truth in it. Both comedy and drama were grist for his eclectic mill, although he is best remembered for his acting in high comedy. He worked from the outside in, seeking some physical attribute or prop (his "green umbrella") to help him get a handle on a character. Lunt was a perfectionist who rarely grew bored with a part, even in a long run, and would be experimenting even at the last performance. For all his brilliant talent, he remained shy and modest, and experienced doubts about his work throughout his career. Although hard put to articulate his acting methods, he insisted that there were no inviolable rules. He was an unselfish actor who thought it his responsibility to serve the playwright, not himself. His partnership with Fontanne was exceptionally close, and the two never ceased to amaze by the diligence with which they prepared. They possessed a thorough understanding of every element of their roles and were renowned for their unusual professional commitment and symbiotic acting style. They developed a unique method of overlapping each other's lines in such a way that both could be heard.

Although he possessed a temper, Lunt was normally in control emotionally. Still, he needed Fontanne (who died in 1983) to calm him when he was under stress. His many awards included an acting Tony for *Quadrille* (1954) and the Presidential Medal of Freedom (1964). Lunt died in Chicago.

[Important papers are in the Wisconsin State Historical Society, Madison, and the New York Public Library for the Performing Arts at Lincoln Center. The best biography is Jared Brown, *The Fabulous Lunts* (1986). Also helpful are George Freedley, *The Lunts* (1958); and Maurice Zolotow, *Stagestruck* (1964). A obituary is in the *New York Times*, Aug. 4, 1977.]

SAMUEL L. LEITER

LYONS, LEONARD (Sept. 10, 1906–Oct. 7, 1976), gossip columnist, was born Leonard Sucher in New York City, one of four children of Bronna Harnick and Moses Leib Sucher, a worker in the garment industry. His father had immigrated to New York from Romania in 1896 after the death of his wife, and by 1897 he had saved enough money to send for his three children and his sister-in-law, Bronna Harnick, whom he married on her arrival in the United States.

By the time Lyons was eight years old, his father had died, and financial need necessitated that the older children leave school and go to work in the sweatshops. His mother opened a candy stand on the Lower East Side in Manhattan. An excellent student, Lyons attended P.S. 160 at Rivington and Suffolk streets, where he won an award for his drawing ability. He also sang in the synagogue choir. He went on to the High School of Commerce, night school at the City College of New York, and St. John's University Law School.

In 1928, Lyons passed the New York bar examination while working for the firm of Armstrong, Keith, and Kern. Two years later he set up his own law practice. Also in 1930 he began work at the *Jewish Daily Forward*, where the editor of the English-language section of the paper renamed the young reporter Leonard Lyons (Lyons being an anglicization of Leonard's father's middle name, Leib). Lyons eventually assumed the new name in his personal as well as his professional life. He was hired in 1934 by the *New York Post* to write a daily column about Manhattan night life. "The Lyons Den," as the daily piece came to be known, was an enormous success. Chatty and lightweight, the column quoted celebrities more often than it talked about them. In effect, Lyons became the mouthpiece of Broadway characters, and he was soon the most famous gossip columnist in the nation's largest city. A *New Yorker* profile published in 1945 characterized him as a table-hopping journalist who avoided cruel gossip in favor of anecdotes about celebrities desirous of being in the limelight. Lyons later related that he became a columnist because he wrote detailed letters to a girl named Sylvia Schonberger, who told him that he ought to be with a newspaper. They met when he was twenty-two. They were married in November 1934 and had four children.

A slight, dark-haired man, Lyons had an unusual daily routine: On a typical day Lyons had breakfast with his family at about 6 A.M., before going to sleep until noon. Then he began his daily rounds of the trendy restaurants. By 1 P.M. he might be at Sardi's in the theater district, then move on to other restaurants frequented by celebrities, usually stopping by the Algonquin Hotel on Forty-fourth Street to visit with the literary notables at its famed round table. By 3 P.M. he was heading toward his office at the *New York Post* on South Street, where he began work on his column. He allegedly maintained an extensive filing system with obscure details about the people who appeared in his column. At about 6 P.M. Lyons returned to his apartment on Central Park West for a nap before heading out for the evening. By 7:30 P.M. he was off again, often to a Broadway opening and then to such elegant spots as La Côte Basque, "21," and the Russian Tea Room. Lyons did not like alcohol and tended to drink coffee when he sat down at people's tables.

"The Lyons Den" was syndicated to more than one hundred newspapers with a total circulation of 15 million, appearing every day but Sunday for forty years. It appeared for the last time on May 20, 1974. Lyons died in New York City and was buried at Beth Moses Cemetery in Pinelawn, Long Island, N.Y.

[See Russell Maloney, "These Things Are Fated," *New Yorker*, Apr. 7, 1945; and "Gentle Gossip," *Time*, June 3, 1974. An obituary is in the *New York Times*, Oct. 8, 1976.]

NANCY V. FLOOD

M

MacARTHUR, JOHN DONALD (Mar. 6, 1897–Jan. 6, 1978), insurance and real estate magnate, was born in Pittston, Pa., one of seven children of William Telfer MacArthur, a coal miner who became a Baptist evangelist, and Georgiana Welstead. Shortly after the turn of the century, the family relocated to Illinois, then moved again to Nyack, N.Y., in 1910. By this time the Reverend MacArthur's ministry had gained national prominence, and he often preached to audiences of 5,000 to 6,000 persons. At age thirteen, John, a bright but headstrong student, entered the Wilson Academy in Nyack. Having earned failing marks and a reputation as a prankster, he dropped out of school after the eighth grade.

When his mother died in 1915, MacArthur left Nyack to rejoin his three elder brothers in Illinois. He went to work as a salesman for his oldest brother Alfred's Central Standard Life Insurance Company. Three months later, he became the firm's top producer. In 1917 he sold a million dollars' worth of policies. Eager to enter World War I, MacArthur joined the United States Navy and then the Royal Canadian Flying Corps, but left both because he could not get the combat orders he sought. He later failed in an attempt to stow away on board a troopship.

Inspired by two newspapermen brothers of his—Telfer, who owned Pioneer Press, a chain of suburban newspapers, and Charles, an award-winning journalist—MacArthur worked briefly as a copyboy and then a cub reporter for the *Chicago Herald and Examiner*, but soon returned to a career in insurance. He married Louise Ingalls in 1919; they had two children.

By 1927, he had become sales vice-president of State Life Insurance of Illinois, at an annual salary of $10,000. Ambitious, driven, and prescient enough to see a salary as a limitation to someone gifted with his sales ability, MacArthur, again with help from Alfred, struck out on his own. In 1928 he purchased Marquette Life of Jerseyville, Ill., a small and ailing company, for $7,500. At the time Marquette listed liquid assets of less than $16. He moved its office to Chicago and rebuilt the company by selling insurance policies door-to-door during the Great Depression.

The collapse of the New York Stock Exchange on Black Friday, Oct. 25, 1929, and the ensuing financial chaos nearly bankrupted the life insurance industry. Later in life, MacArthur recalled his cocky stance during the depression: "I had shot my mouth off to my brothers about making a big success," he remembered, "so I couldn't throw in the sponge when things got tough." His late entry into the business actually proved his salvation. MacArthur recalled, "I didn't have any assets, but I didn't have any liabilities, either, and the liabilities were destroying the big firms," which could not economically collect premiums of less than $5. MacArthur not only sold policies with $1 monthly premiums but also accosted people on Chicago's streets and sold them insurance for anything they could afford—including their lunch money.

In 1935, seven years after acquiring his first company, MacArthur borrowed the money to purchase Banker's Life and Casualty for $2,500, a move that almost put him out of business when four of the firm's policyholders filed claims during the first month of his ownership. His assets shrank to a bare $100, yet he survived and took advantage of the depression by selling policies to clients left stranded by failed firms.

In 1938, MacArthur launched an innovative system—selling life insurance through the mail. He placed ads and mailed out thousands of flyers. The phenomenal response to this novel gambit underwrote his nationwide expansion.

MacArthur divorced his wife early in 1937 and married Catherine Hyland, his secretary and bookkeeper, in 1938.

In the 1940's MacArthur sold hundreds of thousands of low-cost policies. After World War II, his security-conscious customers bought more expensive coverage. By the 1950's, Bankers Life was a virtual insurance empire. MacArthur was its sole owner. *Fortune* magazine anointed him one of the nation's richest business tycoons. His corporate philosophy of privately held assets allowed him total freedom of operation. "Go public?" he once exclaimed to an interviewer. "What for? This way I've got nobody to quarrel with. My life is a million times easier." He repeated his formula of buying small, bankrupt insurance firms a dozen times or more. As of July 1958, his companies employed a sales staff of more than 5,000, servicing 3 million clients with $5.5 billion in policies.

MacArthur drove an old Cadillac, wore drip-dry shirts, and always flew economy class; never failing to point out to more free-spending colleagues, "My tail fits nicely in a tourist seat." The MacArthurs moved to Palm Beach County, Fla., in 1958, and he began to invest in land, eventually purchasing over 100,000 acres, about 25,000 of them in Palm Beach County alone. In addition to his insurance holdings and Florida land, MacArthur owned several development companies and shopping centers, hotels, banks, paper and pulp companies, 19 office buildings and 6,000 apartments in New York City, publishing firms, and radio and television stations.

Although MacArthur never gained the fame of his brother Charles (the husband of the actress Helen Hayes, and collaborator with Ben Hecht on the Pulitzer Prize–winning play *The Front Page*) or of his cousin General Douglas MacArthur, by the 1970's, he was one of the country's two surviving billionaires and certainly the more accessible (shipping magnate Daniel K. Ludwig was the other; Howard R. Hughes, J. Paul Getty, and H. L. Hunt predeceased them). In his sixties, MacArthur owned and worked from a small hotel, the Colonnades, in the minuscule community of Palm Beach Shores on Singer Island, on the north side of Palm Beach Inlet. A plain-living person who eschewed maids, butlers, chauffeurs, public relations men, and bodyguards, he held court each morning in the hotel's coffee shop with a band of cronies, running his financial empire from his breakfast table. One profile of him put it thus: "With a rumpled shirt and baggy wash-and-wear slacks, MacArthur looks less like a billionaire than a retired postal clerk." Whenever the Colonnades' staff was shorthanded, MacArthur pitched in wherever needed—from the front door to the reception desk.

Diagnosed with stomach cancer in 1970, MacArthur continued his workaday life. During the recession of the mid-1970's there was a strip of bankrupt or near-bankrupt high-rise condominiums on the oceanfront in North Palm Beach. MacArthur purchased one of these buildings for a few cents on the dollar, slashed each unit's asking price, and gave every purchaser a Cadillac Sedan de Ville. At a time when condominium sales stood moribund in that community, he sold out his property in weeks.

John D. MacArthur, "arguably the most successful salesman in history," died in West Palm Beach, Fla. Although he was known as a pragmatic and closefisted billionaire, his will directed the establishment of two philanthropic organizations: the John D. and Catherine T. MacArthur Foundation, to which he bequested $700 million, and the Retirement Research Foundation, both "for charitable and public service purposes." He divided the balance of his estate, worth $70–$80 million, between his wife (half) and his children (one-quarter each).

[See Lewis Beman, "The Last Billionaires," *Fortune*, Nov. 1976; A. J. Mayer and A. Bentley, "The Richest Men in America," *Newsweek*, Aug. 2, 1976; and The John D. and Catherine T. MacArthur Foundation, *John D. MacArthur* (1978–1988). An obituary is in the *New York Times*, Jan. 7, 1978.]

W. M. P. Dunne

McBRIDE, MARY MARGARET (Nov. 16, 1899–Apr. 7, 1976), journalist, author, and radio personality, was born in Paris, Mo., the daughter of Thomas Walker McBride and Elizabeth Craig. Her father was a farmer who liked to keep moving; he acquired farms, improved them, and then traded them. Her maternal grandfather was a Baptist preacher, and from him, as well as from her mother, she acquired a strong sense of morality. At the age of eight she took the temperance pledge and was faithful to it for the rest of her life. Mary Margaret (she was never called Mary) was educated in a one-room schoolhouse and then in the Paris grade school. At the age of eleven she was sent to the William Woods School in Fulton, Mo., through the beneficence of her Great-Aunt Albina, who had an interest in the institution and wanted her grandniece to become a teacher (and eventually principal of the Woods School). After her graduation in 1916, her great-aunt also financed McBride's studies at the University of Missouri. However, from her youth McBride had wanted to be a writer; and true to her ethical code, after one year she told her great-aunt, who terminated her financial support. McBride then supported herself by minding faculty children and working on the *Columbia* (Mo.) *Times* as copyboy, reporter, and society editor for $10 per week. She graduated in 1919 with a Bachelor of Journalism degree.

Through a friend McBride obtained a position on the *Cleveland Press* in 1920. Later that year she took a job in the publicity department of the Interchurch World Movement in New York City. After a few months, through a former associate in that organization, she became a reporter and feature writer on the *Evening Mail*. When the paper was sold in 1924, McBride became a free-lance writer, and for the next ten years she produced articles for such periodicals as *Cosmopolitan, Good Housekeeping, Harper's, Scribner's, McCall's*, and *Collier's*. A four-part article about jazz written in collaboration with Paul Whiteman was one of her first pieces and was published in the *Saturday Evening Post*. In 1926 the article appeared as a book titled *Jazz*. She also wrote other books in this period, including *Charm*, with Alexander Williams (1927); four travel books with Helen Josephy, beginning with *Paris Is a Woman's Town* (1929); and *The Story of Dwight Morrow* (1930).

McBride received sizable fees for her articles and was able to travel to Europe, to invest in the stock market, and, by the end of the 1920's, to live on Park Avenue. However, the stock market crash of 1929 hurt her financially, and because of the subsequent depression, by the end of 1931 there was no longer a demand for her articles.

During the next three years McBride had difficulty in obtaining writing assignments. Thus, in 1934 she auditioned for a position as woman commentator for an afternoon radio program on radio station WOR. She was hired, and paid $25 per week to broadcast for half an hour each day, posing as a grandmotherly individual, Martha Deane, who talked about her "grandchildren" and dispensed advice on taking care of children and managing the household. McBride soon found this pretense uncomfortable, and one day told her audience that she was not a grandmother, nor was she married; she stated that she would just be herself and talk about her current and past experiences. The listener response was positive; after a while she eliminated the household hints and just talked and did interviews. In her style and approach McBride was a pioneer of later radio and television talk shows. She ad-libbed and had the ability to make her guests feel comfortable, thus enabling them to talk freely. During her radio career she interviewed people from Eleanor Roosevelt and Harry Truman to plumbers, businessmen, fencing champions, small boys, and housewives. She spoke with a Midwestern accent, in a voice described as "homey" and "folksy."

McBride broadcast for WOR as Martha Deane until 1940, doing a forty-five-minute program from 1936. In 1937 she undertook a fifteen-minute daily program under her own name for CBS; in 1940 it was broadcast nationally. McBride found the fifteen-minute format constraining, and in 1941 she went to work for NBC, which gave her forty-five minutes each day. In 1950 she moved to ABC, where she remained until 1954. During her twenty years in radio McBride's large and very loyal audience was composed largely of housewives who enjoyed listening as a respite from their daily routine. In 1939, 1944, and 1949 she observed the anniversaries of her radio program with gala celebrations; the last two, held in Madison Square Garden and Yankee Stadium, respectively, were attended by huge crowds. The loyalty of her fans extended to the products of her sponsors. At first McBride hesitated to accept sponsors, but then she laid down some ground rules: she would not accept a product without first using it herself; alcohol and tobacco were never accepted. She became a "super salesman" and had a long waiting list of would-be sponsors.

McBride never married. Food was one of her abiding interests and was often a topic of discussion on her programs; she often nibbled while broadcasting. In 1954 she moved to West Shokun, N.Y. Although retired, she continued to broadcast and, until 1956, to write a syndicated newspaper column for the Associated Press. Between 1954 and 1960 she did programs for NBC, and from 1960 until 1976 she broadcast a syndicated program for *New York Herald Tribune* Radio. She also broadcast a local program over WGHO in Kingston, N.Y., until a few months before her death. She died in West Shokun.

[The three travel books McBride wrote with Helen Josephy that are not mentioned in the text are *London Is a Man's Town* (1930); *New York Is Everybody's Town* (1931); and *Beer and Skittles* (1932). Autobiographical works include *Here's Martha Deane* (1936); *How Dear to My Heart* (1940), which presents some of her early childhood experiences; *A Long Way from Missouri* (1959), which covers the years 1919–1934; and *Out of the Air* (1960), which deals with her radio years. See also Barbara Heggie, "Profiles: The Forty-Five-Minute Tempo," *The New Yorker*, Dec. 19, 1942; Philip Hamburger, "Mary Margaret McBride: A Super Saleswoman Shares Adventures of Mind and Stomach with a Host of Radio Listeners," *Life*, Dec. 4, 1944; and Allen Churchill, "Mary Margaret McBride," *American Mercury*, Jan. 1949. Also of value is Isabella Taves, *Successful Women and How They Obtained Success* (1943). An obituary is in the *New York Times*, Apr. 8, 1976.]

ALLAN NELSON

McCARTHY, JOSEPH VINCENT ("JOE") (Apr. 21, 1887–Jan. 13, 1978), baseball manager, was born in the Germantown area of Philadelphia and attended high school in that city; information on his parents is scanty. While still a student, he suffered a broken kneecap while playing a sandlot game of baseball. From 1905 to 1907, McCarthy attended Niagara University, but he left without a degree when offered a chance to play baseball for the minor-league Wilmington, Del., team. McCarthy then played for a succession of seven minor league teams, playing both infield and outfield positions and maintaining a batting average of .300 to .325. His earlier knee injury hampered his speed and kept him from having a real chance at a major league career. In 1919, McCarthy became player-manager for the American Association team in Louisville, Ky. In 1921 he stopped playing to serve as manager only. On February 14 of that year he married Elizabeth ("Babe") McCave.

In his association with the Louisville ball club, McCarthy established a reputation for producing winning teams and, equally important for his later career, as an excellent teacher who sent on to the major leagues players who had received sound, all-around training.

The Chicago Cubs of the National League hired McCarthy as manager in 1926 despite the fact that he had never played a single inning in the major leagues. In this position McCarthy began to show the hard-bitten style of leadership that would mark his managerial career. (He was often called "Marse Joe" because his management was likened to that of a plantation overseer.) When he found Grover Cleveland Alexander, the Cubs' best pitcher, to have a negative and uncooperative attitude, McCarthy quickly traded him to another team. By 1929, McCarthy had led the Cubs from a last-place finish to the league pennant. However, the Cubs lost the 1929 World Series to the Philadelphia Athletics of the American League. Public opinion in Chicago and disappointment by the Cub's owner led to McCarthy's resignation in the face of certain dismissal. He was hired immediately by the New York Yankees, where he spent the greater part of his career. In 1932, his second year with the Yankees, McCarthy's team played the Chicago Cubs in the World Series and defeated them soundly.

From 1933 to 1935 the Yankees finished consistently in second place, but McCarthy was increasingly putting his personal stamp on the team. With the departure of Babe Ruth to the Boston Braves in 1935, McCarthy completely dominated the team. In 1936 the Yankees clinched the American League title by September 9, the earliest date at which the title had ever been won. In the second game of the World Series for that year, the Yankees broke or tied eleven records for a single World Series game. A sequence of World Series victories from 1936 to 1939 gave rise to the phrase "Yankee dynasty," a team dominance of major league baseball marked by a cold, efficient, machinelike style of play that was all business. This dynasty was fueled by a steady stream of well-trained players moving up from an extensive farm club system in the minor leagues. During this period, the Yankees achieved a winning percentage of .702.

McCarthy was a firm believer in discipline. He maintained strict control over his team even in the locker room after a winning series. He discouraged rowdiness, practical jokes, and individualistic behavior. His favorite player was Lou Gehrig because, said McCarthy, "he always showed up, he didn't cause any trouble, and he hit."

McCarthy was also a fine teacher, even when dealing with talented athletes. Joe DiMaggio, who McCarthy said had more natural talent than any player he ever managed, said of McCarthy, "Never a day went by when you didn't learn something from [him]." McCarthy demonstrated this teaching ability by showing stars like Tommy Byrne how to play new positions. Byrne came to the Yankees as a pitcher who had just received the largest bonus for signing ever paid to a rookie player. McCarthy turned him into an effective first baseman.

McCarthy was often selected as the American League all-star manager, a post he filled seven times between 1936 and 1946. On at least one occasion in 1940, McCarthy was passed over for this honor merely because league officials thought somebody else deserved a chance to manage. In the 1937 all-star game, McCarthy received the unprecedented opportunity to name all members of the roster without the involvement of league officials or fans.

World War II had a major impact on the 1942 baseball season, as many experienced players were drafted into the armed forces. McCarthy proved his skill as a manager by whipping inexperienced players into league pennant winners in 1942 and 1943. He was also named manager of the year in a major league sportswriters poll for a third time in 1943, earlier awards having been given in 1936 and 1938.

The stress of managing the wartime and postwar Yankees began to tell on McCarthy's health. His blood pressure was quite high, aggravated by a quick temper and occasional heavy drinking. He retired in 1946 but returned to the game in 1948 to manage the Boston Red Sox for two years, retiring permanently in 1950. McCarthy was named to the Baseball Hall of Fame in 1957. Unique in sports annals in that he won a pennant in both the National and American leagues, McCarthy also had the distinction of winning seven World Series, four of them in succession, all while managing the New York Yankees.

McCarthy spent the last years of his life with his wife on their farm near Buffalo, N.Y. He enjoyed hunting, fishing, and the theater. He died from pneumonia in Buffalo and was buried there.

[A collection of Joe McCarthy memorabilia is at the Baseball Hall of Fame in Cooperstown, N.Y. An obituary is in the *New York Times*, Jan. 14, 1978.]

MICHAEL R. BRADLEY

McCLELLAN, JOHN LITTLE (Feb. 25, 1896–Nov. 27, 1977), United States senator, was born in Sheridan, Ark, the only son of Isaac Scott McClellan, a farmer who became a lawyer, and Belle Suddeth, who died during her son's infancy. Young McClellan attended local schools but gained his most valuable education for his future career by simultaneously studying law in his father's office, beginning in 1908. Although only seventeen years old, he was admitted to the bar in 1913 by a special act of the Arkansas legislature. That same year he married Eula Hicks; they had two children and were divorced in 1919. McClellan practiced law until the summer of 1917, when he joined the United States Army; he had attained the rank of first lieutenant in the Signal Corps by the time he was mustered out in early 1919.

Returning to civilian life, McClellan moved to Malvern, Ark., not far from Sheridan. Throughout the 1920's his legal career blossomed. For the first six years of the decade he served as city attorney; for the remaining four years he functioned as a state prosecuting attorney. In 1922 he married Lucille Smith; they had three children.

A brief hiatus in his public career during the early years of the Great Depression notwithstanding, the 1930's were the first of McClellan's many years in national politics. (Interestingly, his father had given him his middle name in honor of their congressman, John Little.) McClellan was elected to the House of Representatives in 1934 and in 1936. General support for President Franklin Roosevelt's New Deal policies characterized his voting record during these two terms, but he did oppose an antilynching measure, the president's plan to pack the Supreme Court, and a government reorganization bill. In 1938, McClellan unsuccessfully challenged Arkansas senator Hattie Caraway for her seat, losing a close Democratic primary (winning that primary was then tantamount to election). McClellan, who after the death of his second wife had married Norma Myers Cheatham in 1937 (they had one child), believed that his opposition to the reorganization bill had cost him victory; a third contender in the primary, J. R. Venable, believed that McClellan had been cheated through fraudulent vote counting. McClellan returned to private law practice but four years later handily won Arkansas's other Senate seat. It was the first of six successive elections to the upper house.

During his first two terms as senator, McClellan served on a wide variety of committees but sponsored no major bill. His voting record during these dozen years was that of a typical conservative southern Democrat of that era. Staunchly anti-Communist and internationalist in foreign policy, he was concerned with what he deemed excessive appropriations for waging the Cold War. Hoping to draw industry and commerce southward, he supported the Taft-Hartley Act of 1947, lower minimum wages, and various other measures that were anathema to organized labor. A confirmed segregationist, he opposed his party's civil rights platform plank in 1948 and legislative measures that threatened the racial status quo in the South. Somewhat surprisingly, in 1950 he backed a resolution calling for a constitutional amendment that would grant equal rights to women.

McClellan gained national notice after his election for a third term in the Senate. As the ranking minority member of the Permanent Investigations Subcommittee of the Senate Committee on Government Operations, he clashed with the group's chairman, Senator Joseph R. McCarthy, during the explosive hearings on Communism that began in 1953. At one point McClellan, furious with McCarthy's methods, briefly boycotted the hearings. Asserting that he was as anxious as anyone to uncover Communists in America, he persistently sought to blunt the bullying tactics of the Wisconsin junior senator. One historian characterized McClellan as "the real terror of the Subcommittee, cadaverous and saturnine and pursuing everyone with a rasping logic." Along with every other Democratic senator, he voted for the censure of McCarthy on Dec. 2, 1954.

Once the Democrats regained control of the Senate as a result of the 1954 elections, McClellan became chairman of the Committee on Government Operations as well as of its Permanent Investigations Subcommittee. He continued in this capacity throughout his last three full terms in office. During these eighteen years, as the ranking member of the Senate watchdog committee, he presided over some of the most spectacular investigations in modern American history.

Congressional investigation of corruption and racketeering in organized labor dated back to the turn of the century but had remained generally dormant until the 1950's, when increased publicity evoked demands for reform. Efforts by the AFL-CIO to purge its offending locals of malfeasance proved ineffective, and on Jan. 30, 1957, the Senate established the Select Committee on Improper Activities in the Labor and Management Field. Better, and more simply, known as the McClellan Committee, the group, led by McClellan and its tenacious chief counsel, Robert F. Kennedy, offered a series of dramatic investigations and disclosures before issuing its final report in 1960. Witnesses during nationally televised committee hearings gave startling details of widespread embezzlement, violence, dishonest elections, and assorted wrongdoings on the part of certain unions. The committee's investigation of the International Brotherhood of Teamsters and its president, David Beck, provided the most vivid examples. Beck was forced to resign the presidency and was later convicted of income tax evasion and grand larceny. (Ironically, the defiant teamsters replaced Beck with the even more notorious James R. Hoffa.)

Much of the success of the committee was due to the relentless pursuit of witnesses by McClellan, whom Kennedy called "the most devastating cross-examiner I have ever heard." McClellan, in turn, strongly supported the confirmation of his youthful chief counsel as attorney general. Largely as a result of the committee's disclosures, Congress passed the Landrum-Griffin Act (1959), which more effectively empowered the government to fight corruption in organized labor but at the same time added provisions that pleased anti-union forces.

During these years McClellan and his committee probed other criminal activities. Operating during the early 1950's, the Senate's Kefauver Committee had publicized the activities of the Mafia, but national attention became focused only with the arrest of fifty-eight mobsters at a meeting in Apalachin, N.Y., in November 1957. In the fall of 1963 the committee heard electrifying testimony from Joseph Valachi, a convicted murderer and member of the powerful criminal organization, concerning the leadership, structure, and activities of "La Cosa Nostra." Concluded McClellan, "There exists in America today what appears to be a close-knit, clandestine, criminal syndicate."

The 1960's also witnessed the revelation of scandals and dubious ethical behavior within the government itself. The McClellan Committee, voting along strict party lines, exonerated the Department of Agriculture, and implicitly the Kennedy administration, from any legal wrongdoing with regard to their dealings with Billie Sol Estes, a well-connected Texas businessman who had been arrested and charged with various offenses. More sensational was the committee's investigation in 1963 of the Department of Defense's award of a lucrative contract for the production of the TFX aircraft for the military. General Dynamics received the contract despite studies by the Pentagon, Air Force, and Navy that indicated that a rival firm (Boeing) could produce a better and less expensive plane. The committee pointed an accusing finger at Secretary of Defense Robert S. McNamara and two of his subordinates, the latter having previously been connected with General Dynamics. The investigation and bitter controversy that began in February ended only with the assassination of President Kennedy in November.

Issues of law and order also received the attention of McClellan and his committee during the turbulent 1960's. Distressed by what he deemed the folly of the Supreme Court in its far-ranging decisions that gave new rights to the accused, especially in *Miranda* v. *United States* (1966), and also by the rioting and violence that were sweeping the nation's college campuses and cities, McClellan called for sterner measures to safeguard the fabric of society. The Omnibus Crime Control and Safe Streets Act of 1968, among other enactments, extended legal provisions for wiretapping. Two years later McClellan introduced the even more sweeping Organized Crime Control Act. He chaired a committee that investigated campus disorders and applauded the action of national guardsmen that resulted in the deaths of four student protesters at Kent State University in 1970.

By this time, however, McClellan had begun to sour on American military involvement in Vietnam. In 1969 he voted to prohibit the introduction of American troops into Laos and Cambodia, and two years later he supported the Mansfield Amendment that called for the withdrawal of American troops from Vietnam within nine months after the release of American prisoners of war.

McClellan resigned the chairmanship of the Government Operations Committee in 1973 to head the Appropriations Committee. He remained on the Judiciary Committee, where he helped to draft a revision of the United States Criminal Code. Suffering from a heart condition, he announced that he would not seek reelection in 1978. He died in Little Rock, Ark. At the time he was the second most senior member of the Senate and one of its most powerful members. His deeply rooted conservative views were controversial, but few questioned his personal probity or legal and political skills.

[To date there is no collection of McClellan's papers. Individual items appear sporadically in various manuscript holdings. Similarly, no book-length biography exists. An obituary is in the *New York Times*, Nov. 29, 1977.]

ROBERT MUCCIGROSSO

McCORMACK, JOHN WILLIAM (Dec. 21, 1891–Nov. 22, 1980), Speaker of the House of Representatives, was born in Boston, Mass., the son of Joseph H. McCormack, a stonemason, and Mary Ellen O'Brien. He grew up in the poor but proud Irish-American neighborhood of South Boston. After his father's death, he left school and, at age thirteen, went to work to support his mother and two younger brothers. He was employed as a Western Union messenger and an errand boy for a small brokerage firm in Boston's financial district before being hired to work in the law office of William T. Way for $4 per week. Impressed with his conscientiousness, Way befriended the young man, lent him books from his law library, and encouraged him to seek a legal career. Approaching his twentieth birthday, McCormack took a second job as a part-time bookkeeper for a tailoring firm to earn money for classes conducted by prominent Boston attorney Charles H. Innes for young men unable to attend law school. Armed with knowledge gained from Way, Innes, and law student friends, he passed the state bar examination in 1913, the last year the examination could be taken by candidates without a high school education.

In the next few years, McCormack developed a respectable law practice by taking on and winning the mostly civil cases of his neighbors.

Meanwhile, McCormack involved himself in the political campaigns that were the lifeblood of his community. After helping to organize the election efforts of other candidates for public office and speaking in their behalf at street corner rallies, he was elected as a delegate to the Massachusetts Constitutional Convention in the spring of 1917. Although a relatively minor figure at the conclave, McCormack had an opportunity to observe the state's most prominent lawyer-legislators in action. The experience further whetted his appetite for a political career.

During the Constitutional Convention, which opened two months after American entry into World War I, McCormack was drafted into the United States Army. He spent the war at Camp Devens, Mass., and Fort Lee, Va., and left the service with the rank of sergeant major. In 1919, McCormack entered and won another political contest, ousting a sitting member of the Massachusetts House of Representatives in the Democratic primary, which, in the Irish sections of Boston, was tantamount to election. On June 9, 1920, he married M. Harriet Joyce, a concert singer who had been under contract to the Metropolitan Opera; they had no children.

After two terms in the House, McCormack advanced to the state senate in 1922. Reelected in 1924, he was chosen minority floor leader. In the latter role, McCormack demonstrated considerable leadership ability, battling to preserve Progressive Era labor and social welfare reforms in an increasingly conservative, Republican-dominated legislature. In the spring of 1926 he scored a rare Democratic triumph when he persuaded a majority of his colleagues to support bills to create and fund the first state-run hospital for cancer patients in the United States.

Later that year, McCormack sought national office by mounting a primary challenge to James A. Gallivan, a six-term congressman. Though he was defeated soundly by the popular incumbent, his issue-oriented, gentlemanly campaign was viewed favorably by district voters. Thus, when Gallivan died in April 1928, McCormack, whose campaign literature trumpeted him as the "logical" Democrat, swept to an easy victory over a crowded field of contenders in a special election. He went on to win a full term in the fall and was returned to Congress routinely for the next forty years.

Early in his congressional career, McCormack's diligent committee work and adherence to party discipline gained the attention of the House Democratic leader, John Nance Garner of Texas, who saw in the younger man the makings of a good lieutenant. Consequently, after Garner became Speaker in 1931, McCormack was given a seat on the prestigious Ways and Means panel, a rare promotion for a congressman with less than two terms of seniority. He also was made a member of the "Board of Education," an informal, after-hours group of House members convened regularly by Garner and his fellow Texan and protégé Sam Rayburn for serious political discussion and poker playing.

As one who strongly favored government intervention in the economy for the benefit of the needy, McCormack proved an effective spokesman for and defender of President Franklin D. Roosevelt's meliorative antidepression program and became a congressional favorite of the White House. Legislatively, he played a role in the drafting of the Social Security Act of 1935 and, as a member of the Ways and Means Committee, helped to fashion such major New Deal revenue proposals as the "soak the rich" tax of 1935 and the undistributed profits tax of 1936. He even championed Roosevelt's proposal to reorganize the Supreme Court in 1937.

In 1934, the reliable McCormack was the choice of party leaders to chair the Special Committee on Un-American Activities rather than Samuel Dickstein of New York, a flamboyant figure who introduced the resolution creating the body; Dickstein became vice-chairman. The McCormack-Dickstein Committee, as it came to be known, was charged with investigating Nazism, fascism, organized anti-Semitism, and Communism, which McCormack, a devout Catholic, regarded as the principal enemy of religion and American family life. The panel probed Nazi ties to American public relations firms and the activities of the Friends of the New Germany, the Silver Shirts, and other subversive groups; heard frank testimony in executive session from a variety of witnesses, including a Nazi propagandist and leading members of the American Communist Party; and issued a report proposing, among other things, a law to require registration of all agents of foreign governments that was enacted by Congress in 1938. The overall inquiry was conducted quietly and efficiently by trained professionals hired by McCormack, and when he presided over committee hearings, witnesses were examined in an orderly courtroom fashion with legal counsel present. McCormack's low-key, thoughtful stewardship of the special committee contrasted sharply with the lurid performances of many of the congressional inquisitors who came later.

In 1937, McCormack supported Sam Rayburn's candidacy for House majority leader against John J. O'Connor of New York, the anti–New Deal chairman of the Rules Committee. In so doing, he convinced ten of eleven New England colleagues to back Rayburn, ensuring the Texan's victory. In 1940, Rayburn, who had ascended to the Speakership, returned the favor by helping McCormack defeat Clifton Woodrum of Virginia for majority leader. McCormack, who had eschewed races for mayor of Boston and United States senator to remain on the congressional leadership track, thus became the first New Englander to enter the Democratic hierarchy.

The short, stocky, mild-mannered Rayburn and the tall, thin, sometimes volatile McCormack maintained their amicable partnership for the next twenty-two years. As Rayburn's deputy, McCormack was noted for his sharp, highly partisan debating style. According to one observer, he had the "ability to confound his opponents when he held the best of the argument and to confuse them when he did not." Within party ranks, he also gained a reputation as a compromiser, mediating successfully between the interests of the urban northerners and rural southerners who made up the New Deal coalition.

When the European crisis intruded on the American domestic scene in the latter part of the 1930's, McCormack was at first ambivalent about it. His record on foreign affairs up to 1939 closely resembled that of another Irish-American from Massachusetts, isolationist United States senator David I. Walsh. Like Walsh, he opposed the League of Nations and the World Court, and favored military preparedness and strict neutrality. Moreover, McCormack's view of the Spanish Civil War as a life-and-death struggle between Communism and Christianity led him to support General Francisco Franco's Nationalist cause and the arms embargo that aided Franco's ultimate victory. At the same time, he was a harsh critic of Nazi Germany and the Soviet Union for their persecution of Jews and Catholics.

The outbreak of war in Europe in September 1939 and the steady advance of Hitler's armies in 1940 alarmed McCormack, causing him to break with isolationism and embrace President Roosevelt's cautious course toward interventionism. He backed Roosevelt's cash-and-carry proposal, repeal of the embargo on the sale of arms and munitions to belligerents, and the destroyers-for-bases deal. Following his elevation to the post of majority leader in the fall of 1940, he played an even more important role in advancing the administration's foreign policy and war preparations in Congress.

Accordingly, Roosevelt designated McCormack to introduce his lend-lease bill early in 1941, and the House clerk was instructed to number the "aid to Britain" legislation H.R. 1776, to give it a patriotic veneer and make it more palatable to the majority leader's anti-British Boston Irish constituents. McCormack helped lead the successful fight for lend-lease in the spring of 1941 and was instrumental in winning passage of the extension of the military draft later that year. He convinced Roosevelt to have the latter measure brought forward first in the Senate, where it had substantial support and triumphed easily, and then rounded up enough wavering Democrats to eke out a one-vote victory on the House floor. After Pearl Harbor, McCormack completed his conversion to internationalism by embracing legislation sponsored by J. William Fulbright of Arkansas and others calling for American participation in "international machinery" to maintain world peace in the postwar period.

Finding the domestic policies of President Harry Truman as congenial as those of Roosevelt, McCormack lined up votes for the Employment Act of 1946, Truman's veto of the Taft-Hartley Act of 1947, and the extension of rent control in 1948. He was even more enthusiastic about Truman's Cold War foreign policy, vigorously supporting economic and military aid for Greece and Turkey (1947) and for Korea and Formosa (1950). As he often did, McCormack went further than the administration's hard line in 1951 by introducing a resolution calling upon the United Nations to declare Communist China the aggressor in the Korean War. With Republican Dwight D. Eisenhower as president, McCormack assumed the role of partisan scold, attacking especially the "New Look" policy, which cut the military budget and force levels and relied upon massive retaliatory power to deter potential aggressors.

Sounding a theme that would be echoed by Senator John F. Kennedy of Massachusetts and other Democratic presidential contenders in 1960, the majority leader accused Eisenhower of weakening America's defenses at a time when they faced serious Communist threats in Eastern Europe and Asia.

Though he chaired the pro-Kennedy Massachusetts delegation to the 1960 Democratic National Convention and assisted the senator's campaign, McCormack's relationship with his home state's favorite son was awkward at best. Besides the wide gulf that separated the two Irish Catholics in age and social background, Kennedy and McCormack often found themselves on opposite sides in the Democratic party turf battles of the 1940's and 1950's. In 1947, Kennedy had been the only member of the Massachusetts congressional delegation to spurn McCormack's petition urging President Truman to pardon seventy-three-year-old Boston mayor James Michael Curley, who was serving a prison sentence for mail fraud. Nine years later, Senator Kennedy supported the ouster of a longtime McCormack ally, William ("Onions") Burke, as Massachusetts Democratic party chairman. For his part, McCormack allowed his name to be used in a write-in campaign that overwhelmingly defeated Adlai E. Stevenson in the 1956 Massachusetts presidential primary and embarrassed Kennedy, who had endorsed Stevenson and hoped to be his running mate.

The uneasy relations extended into the Kennedy presidency, with McCormack assisting the American Catholic hierarchy in its successful effort to scuttle the president's aid to education bill in 1961 because it did not include funds for parochial schools. And the Massachusetts rivalry continued by proxy, as the president's brother, Edward, and McCormack's favorite nephew, Edward J. McCormack, Jr., engaged in a bitter primary battle for a Senate seat that was finally won by Kennedy in 1962.

Sam Rayburn's illness and death brought John McCormack's election successively as Speaker pro tempore in August 1961 and as the first Catholic Speaker of the House in January 1962. As Speaker, McCormack labored dutifully for Kennedy's ambitious agenda, which included an income tax cut, civil rights legislation, and a program of medical care for the elderly. However, he proved unable to get it through the conservative coalition of Republicans and southern Democrats, many of whom chaired the relevant committees.

Kennedy's assassination in November 1963 placed Speaker McCormack first in line to succeed the new president, Lyndon B. Johnson, under the provisions of the Presidential Succession Act of 1947 until the new vice-president, Hubert H. Humphrey, took the oath of office in January 1965. The positioning of the elderly McCormack a "heartbeat away" from the presidency caused many in Congress to reexamine the succession issue. Consequently, a constitutional amendment, providing for the naming of a new vice-president in the event of a vacancy, was passed by Congress later in 1965 with the approval of McCormack, who had been uncomfortable with his new status. The Twenty-fifth Amendment was ratified by the states in 1967.

The Speaker worked easily and effectively with Johnson, another protégé of Rayburn's who had voted for McCormack for House majority leader in 1940. Still, because of Johnson's own virtuosity as a legislative horse trader, the aging Speaker and his Senate counterpart, Majority Leader Mike Mansfield, got little credit for the passage of the Kennedy program and the stream of social legislation that became the new president's Great Society. In fact, McCormack's leadership was under almost constant attack throughout the 1960's by a new generation of liberal Democrats led principally by Richard Bolling of Missouri. They regarded McCormack as an ineffectual leader committed to the defense of a rigid and anachronistic committee system and the southern oligarchy that controlled it. The younger Democrats were further alienated by McCormack's unwavering support for the expanding intervention in Vietnam and his endorsement of legislation to curb the activities of antiwar demonstrators. As a result, Morris Udall of Arizona mounted a challenge to McCormack's reelection as Speaker in the Democratic caucus in January 1969 but lost by a 178–58 vote.

Though he survived the liberal uprising, McCormack's Speakership was damaged beyond repair by a major scandal that broke in October 1969. *Life* magazine reported that his chief aide, Martin Sweig, and lawyer Nathan Voloshen, a McCormack friend of twenty years, had accepted money to influence a number of criminal cases and government contracts and had conducted their illicit business from McCormack's office. McCormack denied any involvement in their wrongdoing, professing complete ignorance of their activities. Though his long career seemed to have reached its end, the beleaguered seventy-eight-year-old Speaker sought to save face by declaring his candidacy for reelection in 1970.

Early in 1970, McCormack weathered a no-confidence vote initiated by antiwar congressman Jerome Waldie of California in the Democratic Caucus and, in May, he was cleared by the courts of complicity in the schemes of Sweig and Voloshen. With his office and honor intact, McCormack dropped his plans for reelection and announced his retirement. Before leaving the House, he oversaw the passage of legislation granting the vote to eighteen-year-olds and the Equal Rights Amendment.

After the death of his wife, who had been ailing through much of his 1970 ordeal, McCormack returned to Boston in 1971. In his remaining years, he spent much of his time in an office maintained for him in the McCormack Post Office Building, one of the many city monuments bearing his name. There he reminisced with old friends and granted occasional interviews with journalists and scholars. McCormack died in Dedham, Mass.

[McCormack's papers, largely consisting of constituent letters, are in Mugar Memorial Library at Boston University. Some McCormack correspondence is at the presidential libraries of Lyndon B. Johnson, John F. Kennedy, Franklin D. Roosevelt, and Harry S. Truman, and at the Sam Rayburn Library in Bonham, Tex. A biographical study of McCormack is Lester I. Gordon, "John McCormack and the Roosevelt Era" (Ph.D. diss., Boston University, 1976). "The New Speaker," *Newsweek*, Jan. 15, 1962; "Mr. Speaker," *Time*, Jan. 19, 1962; "McCormack: A Symbol Retires," *Time*, June 1, 1970; "Mr. Speaker Yields the Gavel," *Newsweek*, June 1, 1970; and Richard W. O'Donnell, "From Andrew Square to the Speaker's Chair," *Yankee*, Apr. 1976, are brief surveys of his life and career. *Political Profiles* for the Truman years (1978), the Eisenhower years (1976), the Kennedy years (1976), the Johnson years (1976), and the Nixon-Ford years (1979) also contain articles on McCormack.

See also Neil MacNeil, *Forge of Democracy* (1963); William V. Shannon, *The American Irish* (1963); Richard Bolling, *House Out of Order* (1964) and *Power in the House* (1968); Walter Goodman, *The Committee* (1968); Warren F. Kimball, *The Most Unsordid Act* (1969); Robert W. Winter-Berger, *The Washington Pay-Off* (1972); Herbert S. Parmet, *Jack* (1980); and Ronald M. Peters, Jr., *The American Speakership* (1990). Obituaries are in the *Boston Globe*, the *New York Times*, and the *Washington Post*, all Nov. 23, 1980. Oral history interviews with McCormack are on deposit at Boston University and the Kennedy and Johnson presidential libraries.]

RICHARD H. GENTILE

McCOY, GEORGE BRAIDWOOD (Jan. 14, 1904–Dec. 22, 1976), radio talk-show host and character actor, was born in Florida, the son of George McCoy and Nellie Braidwood. He grew up in the Washington Heights neighborhood of Manhattan in New York City. McCoy attended P.S. 132 elementary school but never graduated; he had no other formal education.

McCoy's first job was escorting subway passengers home on rainy nights from the stop at 181st Street in Manhattan, using an umbrella he borrowed from a friend. McCoy held various other odd jobs, such as office worker, swimming instructor, publicist, and salesman, hawking everything from Easter egg dye to automobiles. He also did a short stint as a reporter for the New York City News Association. In 1928 he was a publicist and bodyguard for Governor Alfred E. Smith during his presidential campaign.

During the Great Depression, McCoy mastered the art of the "freebie." He was known to frequent the Waldorf-Astoria at happy hour for the free snacks and cigarettes. Famous as New York City's number-one gate-crasher, McCoy began sneaking into Broadway plays after intermission, having discovered that most theaters did not use door checks. He was also known to attend—uninvited—conventions and other public dinners, for the food, brandy, and cigars that could be obtained without charge.

But it was at the 1939 World's Fair in New York City that McCoy's freeloading reached its apogee. He actually lived at the fair for several months, sleeping in the Royal Scot train car that was on loan from Britain and feasting on free samples of food, wine, and beer. While residing at the fair, McCoy found that he could procure a shave, haircut, or massage for free at promotional demonstrations. Eventually, he sold the story of his stay at the World's Fair to *Life* magazine.

It was also at the World's Fair that McCoy's radio career began. While working for a publicity firm, Voices Inc., McCoy was assigned to help with the broadcast of a "Man in the Street" interview show from the fair, which Voices had agreed to produce. When the scheduled announcer was late for the first show, McCoy filled in for him until he arrived. Within a week, the announcer had quit and McCoy had become the regular host, referring to himself as "The Real McCoy."

McCoy's show aired irregularly at first because of difficulty in finding and keeping a sponsor. But by the summer of 1940, it was running six nights per week, on such NBC-network stations as WHOM in Jersey City and WEAF in New York City. The show was usually broadcast from the street. The initial location was the midway at the World's Fair, but eventually the show moved on to other spots such as Ripley's Odditorium on Broadway and the outside steps of the Astor Hotel. Most of McCoy's interviewees were passersby he flagged down and asked about their occupation, their love life, and anything else that came to his mind. His guests tended to speak candidly about themselves and their opinions, but on those occasions when they became nervous, McCoy would simply reassure them that "nobody was listening but my relatives." Occasionally, McCoy had scheduled guests appear on the show, such as a female glass-eater who munched razor blades during the interview.

McCoy's radio career was interrupted when he enlisted in the United States Army shortly after the Japanese attack on Pearl Harbor in 1941. Initially, he was assigned to an antiaircraft unit, but his inability to learn anything about guns resulted in a permanent assignment to kitchen police duty. In Algiers, McCoy met Andre Baruch, who was in charge of the army's radio station there, and who helped him get into Special Services.

At Special Services, McCoy worked in circulation for the military newspaper *Stars and Stripes* and hosted a radio show for GI's in Algiers and, later, Rome. The show in Algiers, called "The Sidewalks of North Africa," was modeled after McCoy's show in Manhattan, and had him interviewing GI's on the streets of Algiers. McCoy rarely interviewed officers, preferring instead to give the enlisted men something to write home about. In Rome, the format was slightly different, with McCoy broadcasting from the balcony of the Piazza Venezia, the same place where Mussolini had delivered his speeches. McCoy would open his Rome broadcasts by jokingly asking the soldiers gathered below if there was "anyone here from out of town?" Both of McCoy's overseas shows differed from his show back home in that they were not broadcast live, since they had to be inspected by the censors from the Office of War Information.

McCoy resumed his civilian broadcasting career after the war ended, but according to contemporary reviewers, the show had grown stale. With the advent of television, McCoy forsook radio and began a new career as a character actor, appearing in such programs as "Studio One" and "Philco Television Presents." His "neutral" face allowed him to play a variety of roles: priests, inmates, detectives, and black marketeers. In his characteristic self-deprecating style, McCoy acknowledged that he was the world's worst actor.

McCoy supplemented his income from acting and broadcasting by driving a cab. He often spent his nights cruising the streets of Manhattan for fares and then entertaining them with jokes he carried with him, written on index cards.

McCoy married Esther Goetz, an artist, in 1951; they had no children. In the years prior to his marriage, McCoy had often claimed that "marriage was a luxury I can't afford."

McCoy continued to act on television until the 1970's, appearing mostly on daytime soap operas. He also continued to drive a taxicab in New York City, where he died.

[See "Broadway Voices: Wisecracker and Mimic Cash in on Bedlam," *Newsweek*, Aug. 26, 1940; Milton Bracker, "From Grover's Corners to Algiers," *New York Times*, Nov. 21, 1943; and Philip Minoff, "The Fabulous McCoy," *Cue*, May 19, 1951. An obituary is in the *New York Times*, Dec. 23, 1976.]

JOHN GILLOOLY

McCOY, TIM (Apr. 10, 1891–Jan. 29, 1978), actor, cavalry officer, and cowboy, was born Timothy John Fitzgerald McCoy in Saginaw, Mich., the son of Timothy Henry McCoy and Cathrin Fitzpatrick. His father was the police chief of Saginaw. McCoy graduated from the local high school and, in 1908, entered St. Ignatius College in Chicago. Although he studied hard, he became increasingly immersed in such tales of cowboy life as Owen Wister's *The Virginian*. Some years before, McCoy had met with "Buffalo Bill" Cody, and he had learned to ride the wild horses imported by a railroad freight agent into Saginaw. When the Miller Brothers Wild West Show came to Chicago, McCoy's mind was made up. He left college in the late spring of 1909 to become a cowboy.

McCoy ended up in Wyoming, where he worked the range, went on cattle drives, encountered bank robbers and bounty hunters, and met Indians. In his autobiography dedicated in part to "the buffalo-hunting warriors of the Great Plains," it is apparent that his contact with the Arapaho, particularly his "brother" Goes In Lodge, had a profound influence on his life. He was given the name Black Eagle by the Blackfeet and High Eagle by the Arapaho. He named his Wyoming ranch the Eagle's Nest.

In 1917, McCoy read an article in the *Denver Post* concerning former president Theodore Roosevelt's proposal to mount cavalry to fight "the Hun" in Europe, previous to American involvement in World War I. McCoy decided he would recruit a full squadron of 400 cowboys from Montana and Wyoming and wrote to Roosevelt of his plan. Roosevelt telegraphed, "Bully for you! Do proceed." President Woodrow Wilson quashed Roosevelt's proposal, but when America became involved in the war, McCoy enlisted. He served as a cavalry officer and was mustered out with the rank of lieutenant colonel, having never seen combat. In 1919 he was appointed adjutant general of the state of Wyoming. The job carried with it the rank of brigadier general, making him a one-star general at the age of twenty-eight. McCoy retired from the army with the permanent rank of full colonel-cavalry.

At this time McCoy resumed his friendship with the Indians and with General Hugh Scott, a former Indian fighter. They together explored Custer's battlefield at the Little Big Horn. Later McCoy would discover previously unknown facts about the battle through conversation with Indians who had been there.

Through his knowledge of Indian customs and sign language, McCoy became an expert on Indians, and it was this expertise which first involved him in Hollywood in 1923. Hollywood needed 500 long-haired Indians for the Western epic *The Covered Wagon*, and someone who could communicate with the Indians. McCoy, bored with his job and life on his ranch, jumped at the opportunity to be a technical adviser. When the film was released in Los Angeles, at Grauman's Egyptian Theater, McCoy and fifty Indians performed a live prologue on stage. Both film and prologue were a success and ran for eight months before relocating to London, where McCoy and another group of Indians were booked into the Pavilion Theatre in Piccadilly Circus.

When McCoy returned to Hollywood in 1926, it was as MGM's only Western star. In his career McCoy acted in more than eighty films for several different companies, including Paramount, Columbia, Puritan, and Monogram. He successfully adjusted from the silent to the sound era. As a cowboy actor, he developed a unique style and look. Articulate and well-spoken, with a distinctive military bearing, he stood out among his more roughneck contemporaries. Although he was probably the fastest on the draw of all the screen cowboys, he chose a more austere image. He dressed all in black and wore first a white hat, then the black hat; for the hero to dress in black was unusual.

But it was the attitude toward the Indians in several of his films that is truly distinctive. In the silent films, particularly, authenticity was stressed in depicting Indians and Indian life. McCoy included many of his Indian friends in the films. One of his most extraordinary series Westerns was *End of the Trail* (1932). With a bigger budget than normal and with McCoy, for once, almost completely in control of the project from start to finish, the film is unique in its sympathetic portrait of the Indian.

McCoy also starred in *The Indians Are Coming* (1930), which was released in both silent and sound versions; *The One Way Trail* (1931); *War Paint* (1926); and *Winners of the Wilderness* (1927); the latter two, in critic Jon Tuska's opinion, are "rare incidences of compassion amid hundreds of Westerns picturing Indians as mindless savages." His best series was made in the 1940's at Monogram, known under the collective title of *The Rough Riders*. Buck Jones, Raymond Hatton, and McCoy starred as three veteran United States marshals. Although produced in the space of a week or so, the films were well made. The series came to an abrupt end because McCoy was recalled to active duty with the army. Buck Jones died in Boston's Cocoanut Grove nightclub fire in 1942.

In addition to his acting career, McCoy starred in Ringling Brothers and Barnum and Bailey Circus from 1935 to 1938 and in other Wild West Shows. His Colonel Tim McCoy's Real Wild West and Rough Riders of the World had only a month's run in 1938 and was a financial disaster.

McCoy's career was interrupted by World War II. He had asked for active duty after losing the Wyoming Republican primary for a United States Senate seat in 1942, and served in France and Germany as a liaison officer between ground and air tactical units. He received the Bronze Star for bravery under fire.

After the war, there were few big-screen opportunities for him in Hollywood, so McCoy turned to television, hosting his own show, the "Tim McCoy Show" (1950–1955), which won an Emmy in 1952. The show varied in time from fifteen to ninety minutes and consisted of McCoy speaking about Indian lore, demonstrations by "all that bunch of Indians I had used in pictures for years," and film clips.

McCoy's final films were cameo appearances in *Around the World in Eighty Days* (1956), as the officer commanding the United States Cavalry unit that rescues Phineas Fogg; in *Run of the Arrow* (1957), as the army officer who signs the peace treaty with the Sioux; and in *Requiem for a Gunfighter* (1965).

In his lifetime McCoy received thirteen campaign medals and decorations for heroism, including the Bronze Star and the Legion of Honor. He was inducted into the National Cowboy Hall of Fame in 1974.

McCoy married Agnes Miller in 1917; they had three children. The marriage ended in divorce in 1931. On Feb. 14, 1946, he married Inga Arvad; they had two children.

At the age of seventy-one, McCoy joined the Tommy Scott and His Country Caravan show, demonstrating his skill with a gun and a bullwhip. He toured 300 days per year with the show until he was in his eighties. When he retired, he kept busy writing his autobiography. McCoy died in Nogales, Ariz., where he had lived for twenty years.

In an interview, McCoy stated: "I am one of the few men that I know of who has done everything he ever wanted to in life. . . . Any time an idea ever came to me, I made it come true."

[See Tim McCoy, *Tim McCoy Remembers the West, an Autobiography* (1977), written with Ronald McCoy; Darryl Ponicsan, "High Eagle: The Many Lives of Colonel Tim McCoy," *American Heritage*, June 1977; and Leo Miller, *The Great Cowboy Stars of Movies and Television* (1979). An obituary is in the *New York Times*, Jan. 31, 1978.]

MARCIA B. DINNEEN

McCREARY, CONN (June 17, 1921–June 28, 1979), thoroughbred jockey and trainer, was born in St. Louis, Mo., the son of John McCreary. After graduating from high school in St. Louis, McCreary traveled to Lexington, Ky., hoping to make his fortune at the racetrack. His mother had bought him a bus ticket, and had pinned inside his jacket a note declaring that her son had permission to travel.

Once in Lexington, he set out on foot for Dixiana Farms, a bluegrass training ground he had heard about. He was given a ride that day by Steve Judge, a noted trainer for the Woodvale Farm of Royce G. Martin, who hired him immediately as a stable boy. McCreary soon became a jockey and never left racing.

McCreary rode in 8,802 races and produced 1,251 winners during a twenty-one-year career from 1939 to 1959. His mounts earned a total of $7,822,624. Although he won his first race in 1939 at Chicago's Arlington Park, his first big win came in 1941 in the Blue Grass Stakes, where he rode Our Boots to victory over Whirlaway, the horse that would set a Kentucky Derby record ten days later and go on to win the Triple Crown.

Aboard Pensive in 1944, McCreary won the Kentucky Derby and the Preakness, but fell short of the Triple Crown when he was beaten in a photo finish with Bounding Home in the Belmont Stakes. In the Derby, he came from thirteenth place to win the contest.

McCreary's life as a jockey was marked by both hot and cold streaks. His career seemed to end in 1950, when a succession of losses caused him to hang up his tack. A comeback attempt in 1951 seemed equally futile until Broadway restaurateur Jack Amiel entered the picture. His three-year-old colt, Count Turf, a none-too-promising son of 1943 Triple Crown winner Count Fleet, had won only sprint races and was a "field horse" in the Derby. Even Count Turf's trainer had given up, refusing to travel to Kentucky for the race. McCreary rode Count Turf to a Kentucky Derby win, taking the lead in the stretch and winning by four lengths going away. Returning to New York City by train, McCreary and Amiel admired the gold cup. "I wish they had a little one for the jockey," Conn said. "I'd rather have it than the money." The next year, Churchill Downs began the custom of presenting the winning jockey with a replica of the Kentucky Derby winner's cup.

McCreary's second Derby win ended the long

slump for the jockey, who returned to form as one of the top thoroughbred riders of the day. Among his later triumphs were the Flamingo and Preakness on Blue Man in 1952, and the Palm Beach and Widener handicaps at Hialeah, in Florida, in 1953 on Oil Capital. He was also successful riding Stymie, a noted stretch-run horse whose abilities matched McCreary's talents. His second and final retirement from riding came in 1959.

Throughout his career, McCreary was among the most popular jockeys in the country. Known as the "Mighty Mite" and "Convertible Conn," he stood four feet, two inches tall and weighed just ninety pounds at the beginning of his racing career. He was noted for his ability to save a horse until late in a race, gaining a reputation as a come-from-behind rider. Although he earned fame for his dramatic stretch runs, which required perfect timing, he was equally adept at taking a lead early and holding it for an entire race.

He took several bad falls as a rider, including one at Aqueduct racetrack in New York in 1944, in which he landed on his head. He continued riding for the next month before headaches forced him to a doctor in Miami, where X rays revealed he had a fractured skull.

After his retirement from riding, McCreary remained active in horse racing as a trainer from 1960 until 1968, when poor health forced him to retire. Horses trained by McCreary included the champion Irish Rebellion, and the stakes winners Mara Lark and Selari's Miss.

In 1974, McCreary became the forty-eighth jockey elected to the Hall of Fame of the National Museum of Racing in Saratoga Springs, N.Y., joining America's top jockeys and horses. At the time of his induction, he was working in the press box of Calder Park in Miami, Fla.

He remained in Florida, working in the publicity departments of various Miami racetracks over the years, and was in the process of moving to Ocala when he died of a heart attack.

McCreary was married twice. He had four children with his first wife, Norma, and two with his second wife, Dorothy.

[Obituaries are in the *New York Times* and the *Daily Racing Form*, both June 30, 1979.]

RICHARD CONIGLIONE

McCULLOCH, ROBERT PAXTON (May 9, 1911–Feb. 25, 1977), inventor, industrialist, and land speculator and developer, was born in St. Louis, Mo., the son of Mary Grace Beggs and Richard McCulloch; the McCullochs pioneered industrial development in the area. Even before attending Stanford University, where he received an M.E. degree in 1931, he had already developed the reputation for being a thinker and a tinkerer. McCulloch married Barbara A. Briggs on Sept. 8, 1934; the couple had four children.

In 1936 he founded McCulloch Engineering, the first of many companies that would bear his name. McCulloch Engineering developed and refined small and medium motors and was especially successful in developing a centrifugal supercharger for its motors. In 1943, McCulloch sold the company to Borg Warner Corporation. Six months later, using the $1 million proceeds from the sale of his first company, he formed McCulloch Aviation, which specialized in manufacturing lightweight engines, especially those designed for the aviation industry. He later expanded the corporation to make gyroplanes, a cross between a helicopter and a small plane. Unfortunately, the company was never able to find a market for this product.

Despite his success to this point in his life, it was the purchase of a tract of land near what was to become the Los Angeles International Airport, and the innovative products provided by a third McCulloch concern, the McCulloch Corporation, founded in 1945, that would make him a truly wealthy man and provide the riches for his future endeavors. Utilizing technology developed by his aviation company and adapting it to the two-cycle engine, in 1948 McCulloch produced the first portable chainsaw light enough to be used by an ordinary man. His company quickly branched out to produce gas heaters, post-hole diggers, golf carts, outboard motors, snowmobile engines, and even helicopters. In 1973 he sold McCulloch Corporation to the Black and Decker Manufacturing Company in a transaction that netted him stock valued at over $66 million.

Meanwhile, in 1958, McCulloch founded the McCulloch Oil Corporation. In 1960 he merged this closely held enterprise with the Cuban American Oil Company, which was listed on the American Stock Exchange. Clearly, one of the purposes of this $22 million transaction was to obtain the Cuban American Oil Company's listing, for barely a month after the merger, the new entity wrote off all its Cuban investments as worthless. In the following decade, the company acquired, by purchase or merger, a number of oil and gas concerns, interests in coal and silver mining, and two air transportation businesses. At its height, McCulloch Oil Corporation had oil, gas, and mining interests stretching from the North Slope of Alaska south to Colombia.

McCulloch came up with a variety of creative means to finance the development of his properties. One of the first to sell limited partnerships to members of the general public, thereby enabling them to take advantage of tax incentives previously available only to the rich, he leveraged the oil company's resources by minimizing its risks and costs while at the same time enjoying a large percent of its profits. He also entered into an innovative agreement with Investors Diversified Services, a huge mutual fund organization, to sell shares in several joint oil and gas exploration programs.

One of the first to see the synergies possible between the mining industry and other endeavors, in the early 1960's McCulloch began to develop mining land he owned. In December 1963 he initiated land sales at a site he called "Lake Havasu City" in the Arizona desert. Located on the shores of the Colorado River, this "instant" city had a population of tens of thousands scarcely a decade later. McCulloch hired C. V. Wood, Jr., the creator of Disneyland, to build the city and spared no expense to ensure its success. He built schools and hospitals, created an artificial lake, and imported and planted 11,000 palm trees. His promotional instincts were uncanny: he brought professional motorboat racing to the area and sponsored lucrative fishing tourneys on his man-made lake. He utilized a McCulloch-owned airline to fly prospective homeowners to Lake Havasu City from all corners of the country. What would make Lake Havasu City different from all the other land-development schemes of the time (including other McCulloch projects in Colorado, Arizona, and Nevada) was the purchase of London Bridge from the City of London in April 1968. McCulloch spent $2,460,000 for the property itself and $7,500,000 to disassemble it, transport it halfway around the world, and then reassemble it over his man-made lake. The landmark proved to be an unbelievable coup, for it garnered publicity from the media and provided an identity and an attraction that was lacking in all other similar projects.

At the height of its prosperity, McCulloch Oil had over a dozen affiliates involved in all aspects of mining; oil and gas discovery, recovery, and transmission; and land development. In consideration of the firm's impressive record of profit growth, investors accorded it a high price-earnings ratio, enabling the company to issue stock for other acquisitions on most favorable terms. All, however, was not well. As did most other land-development companies, McCulloch Oil accounted for real estate sales in full in the year in which they were made, even if they had been made on an installment basis—as most were. This accounting convention resulted in the immediate reporting of huge profits, thus supporting a bloated price-earnings ratio. At roughly the same time the desert states' land boom cooled, the Accounting Principles Board forced McCulloch Oil Company to restate its earnings figures to reflect *only* actual payments. As a result, corporate earnings fell precipitously, the gloss on the stock tarnished, and its price fell by nearly 80 percent.

In an effort to stimulate sales, the company increased its sales force and began to engage in practices of dubious legality. Even this did not turn the company around. In 1976 the McCulloch Oil Company was forced to take a $60 million write-off when it abandoned the land-development business and sold its real estate operations. By the time of McCulloch's death, many lawsuits had been filed against his company and investigations were under way by the Securities and Exchange Commission, the Federal Trade Commission, and the Department of Housing and Urban Development. Originally his death was thought to have been caused by a heart attack, but an autopsy revealed that it was the result of a fatal mixture of barbiturates and alcohol.

There was one final act to the tragedy of the McCulloch Oil Company: shortly after McCulloch's death, Black and Decker sold its shares in the company to a group that used this block of shares to gain control of the company and then effectively liquidate it.

[There is little available information in print on McCulloch; material can be found in the financial press, including the articles "How to Build a River in the Arizona Desert to Flow Under the London Bridge," *Esquire*, Feb. 1969; "McCulloch Oil Hits a Gusher with Big Arizona Land Holdings," *Barron's*, Mar. 31, 1969; and "McCulloch's Empire Shrinks Once Again," *Business Week*, July 28, 1973. Mc-

Culloch's London Bridge scheme led *Newsweek*, *Esquire*, and the *Saturday Review of Literature* to cover his endeavors. His companies' annual reports, various filings with the Securities and Exchange Commission such as the 10-K and 10-Q, and company prospectuses all provide some background on McCulloch. Obituaries are in the *New York Times* and the *Los Angeles Times*, both Feb. 26, 1977.]

THEODORE P. KOVALEFF

McDONALD, DAVID JOHN (Nov. 22, 1902–Aug. 8, 1979), labor organizer and union leader, was born in Pittsburgh, Pa., the son of Welsh-born David McDonald, a steelworker and union activist, and Mary Agnes Kelley. He grew up in a working-class and pro-union atmosphere. He attended both public and parochial schools in the Pittsburgh area, receiving a high school diploma in 1918. He originally aspired to work in the theater and took classes at the Drama School of the Carnegie Institute of Technology, from which he earned a certificate of graduation in 1932.

McDonald was employed by several steel companies in the Pittsburgh area beginning at age fifteen. He worked successively as a stock boy, steelworker, and machinist's helper. The pivotal moment of his life occurred in 1923, when he applied for and was offered the post of private secretary to Philip Murray, then vice-president of United Mine Workers of America. First as Murray's aide and then as his protégé, McDonald traveled around the United States and served as a union organizer and coordinator in the coalfields of the Appalachian South. While traveling in this capacity he met his first wife, Emma Lou Price, another union employee. They were married on Aug. 4, 1937; the couple had one child. This marriage ended in divorce in 1947.

By the time the Council of Industrial Organizations (CIO) was formed in 1935, McDonald was one of labor's best-known union organizers. He was made secretary-treasurer of the Steel Workers Organizing Committee, a group that intended to organize steelworkers throughout the United States and Canada. This organizing drive culminated in the formation of the United Steelworkers of America in 1942, with Murray as president and McDonald as its international secretary-treasurer. McDonald was very detail-oriented and he was scrupulously honest in his management of union money. These characteristics earned him a well-deserved reputation for efficiency and honesty in his own union, in the world of unionism, and in the world at large. Indeed, his influence within the union movement and his reputation for probity led to many calls to serve in federal agencies during World War II, and with such charitable and civil organizations as the American Red Cross, the Community Chest, the American Cancer Society, the American Heart Association, and the National Conference of Christians and Jews.

In order to deal with the necessary correspondence and business arrangements in these assignments, McDonald hired a private secretary, Rosemary McHugh. They were married on Jan. 3, 1950, and had no children. Just prior to their marriage, McDonald had served as a delegate to the World Federation of Trade Unions Conference in London. At that meeting he had taken a leading role in breaking up the federation by arguing that some of its Communist-dominated member unions had made the organization unworkable. McDonald also participated in the creation of its successor, the International Confederation of Trade Unions.

When Murray died in 1952, McDonald was the natural choice to succeed him as head of the steelworkers. McDonald advocated what he called "democratic capitalism." This idea, partially borrowed from CIO president John L. Lewis, with whom he had worked closely in the 1930's, sees the relationship between management and labor as a partnership between equals who depend on each other for the partnership to work. McDonald argued that all partnerships involve occasional disagreements, but that once the disagreement is mediated, the partnership must begin to work again. An industry had to be successful if its workers were to earn a living, but to make the industry successful its workers must provide an honest day's work for an honest day's pay. His emphasis on the idea of partnership prompted many business leaders to view McDonald as a union "conservative" and to establish close personal ties with him. These ties led to his union's success in the 1950's but would eventually damage McDonald's standing with members in 1964.

As head of the United Steelworkers, McDonald was also an important official in the CIO. He played a key role in guiding organized labor to a time of growth and increasing political power, accomplishments that must be viewed as almost extraordinary when viewed against a background of McCarthyism and probusiness conservatism.

McDonald had a good working relationship with the administration of Dwight D. Eisenhower and with many business leaders in the steel industry, and in 1953 he successfully negotiated an agreement that recognized the needs of both workers and the steel industry by using his concept of democratic capitalism. He toured the United States with Ben Fairless, president of U.S. Steel, to advocate union-management agreements to solve problems without strikes. He was asked to serve on a special national security committee by President Eisenhower and thereafter communicated with Eisenhower frequently about economic issues. In 1956, McDonald successfully negotiated another contract beneficial to steel workers by using his personal contacts.

John F. Kennedy attracted McDonald's attention in 1956 when Kennedy made an unsuccessful attempt to win the Democratic vice-presidential nomination. McDonald invited Kennedy to address the United Steelworkers convention that year. A bitter steel strike in 1959 that lasted 116 days convinced McDonald that an even stronger partner was needed in government at the national level, and he intensified his support for Kennedy.

Economic growth was slow during the 1960's, and United Steelworkers contracts did not show the big gains registered in the 1950's. Many union members objected to the support McDonald gave to Lyndon Johnson when he was vice-president because they viewed Johnson as a reactionary. Despite a successful contract negotiation in 1962, many union members came to feel that McDonald was too closely allied with industry leaders and political figures to understand the needs and aspirations of working people. In a close and somewhat questionable election, I. W. Abel was elected head of the United Steelworkers in 1964. McDonald retired to Palm Springs, Calif., in 1965, where he remained isolated from union activities until his death.

Because of his skill at negotiation, his ability to win members for the union during times of both economic expansion and contraction, and his skill at public relations, McDonald was a giant among union leaders whose stature was enhanced by his style of leadership. He associated as a peer with the labor leaders of his era.

[With Edward A. Lynch, McDonald coauthored *Coal and Unionism* (1939). He also wrote an autobiography, *Union Man* (1969). An obituary is in the *New York Times*, Aug. 9, 1979.]

MICHAEL R. BRADLEY

McDONNELL, JAMES SMITH, JR. (Apr. 9, 1899–Aug. 22, 1980), aeronautical engineer and business executive, was born in Denver, Colo., the third son of James Smith McDonnell and Susie Belle Hunter. After living several years in Colorado, the McDonnell family returned to their home near Little Rock, Ark., where McDonnell's father was a successful storekeeper and cotton merchant. Young McDonnell attended local schools, delivered newspapers on horseback, and built a ham radio station in his parents' attic before leaving for Princeton University in 1917. McDonnell graduated from Princeton with a bachelor's degree in physics in 1921. Determined to design, build, and fly airplanes, McDonnell continued his education at the Massachusetts Institute of Technology, where he earned a master's degree in aeronautical engineering in 1925. While at MIT, McDonnell received an appointment as a cadet at the Army Air Corps Flying School at Brooks Field, San Antonio, Tex. In 1924, McDonnell earned his pilot's license and was commissioned a second lieutenant in the reserves.

After spending much of 1924 working as a gypsy pilot, McDonnell took a series of jobs at small aircraft factories. The first was at Huff, Daland Airplane Company in Ogdensburg, N.Y., where he worked as a test pilot and engineer. In 1925, McDonnell became assistant chief engineer with Stout Metal Airplane Company in Dearborn, Mich., and served as a member of the team that developed the Ford Trimotor, the "Tin Goose," one of the most widely recognized and durable airplanes ever built. Beginning in 1925, McDonnell worked for Consolidated Aircraft Company as a stress analyst; in the years 1926–1927 he worked for Hamilton Aero Manufacturing Company as chief engineer.

Responding to the country's enthusiasm for Charles Lindbergh's successful flight across the Atlantic, in 1928 McDonnell founded his first airplane company, McDonnell and Associates, in partnership with James C. Cowling and a classmate from MIT, Constantine L. Zakhartchenko. The trio planned to produce an affordable two-seat, low-wing monoplane, propelled by a Warner Scarab engine, designed to compete in the Guggenheim safe airplane competition that carried a prize of $100,000. With McDonnell at the controls, the experimental "Doodlebug" crashed during a demonstration flight. McDonnell continued trying to refine and market the plane, but the Great Depression forced him to give up his business. He sold the "Doodlebug" to the National Advisory Committee for Aeronautics (NACA) where it was used for wind-tunnel stress experiments.

In 1931, McDonnell joined Great Lakes Aircraft as a test pilot and engineer. Two years later he moved to Glenn L. Martin Company in Baltimore, where he was chief project director for landplanes. He worked on several projects developing twin-engine bombers, including the Martin B-10 and the B-12. Anticipating the need for defense aircraft generated by the growing conflicts in Europe and Asia, McDonnell resigned from Martin to raise the $165,000 he needed to found McDonnell Aircraft Corporation.

McDonnell opened his business on July 6, 1939, in St. Louis. McDonnell chose St. Louis because it was the home of American Airlines and Curtiss-Wright; the site of Lambert Air Field, a major military base; and an area rich in skilled labor. Moreover, McDonnell believed that aircraft industries located near either coast were potential targets for foreign aggression. After a profitless first year, McDonnell Aircraft began to thrive when war production efforts provided McDonnell with contracts for parts from other airline companies. In 1941 McDonnell Aircraft won a United States Navy contract to design and build its first plane, a prototype for a bomber-destroyer. This experimental work was supplemented by contracts directing McDonnell to begin research and development in the application of jet propulsion engines to aircraft. In 1943 McDonnell Aircraft received a navy contract to design, develop, and build a jet-engine, carrier-based, fighter plane, the FH-1 Phantom I, the first jet to exceed 500 miles per hour. The Phantom was the first in a series of jet fighter planes successfully produced through the 1950's that created a secure economic base for McDonnell's company. "Mr. Mac," as McDonnell was known, believed that the planes he and his teammates built absorbed a vital spirit from the efforts of the people who made them. By naming the jets "Phantom," "Banshee," and the like, McDonnell made the connection between his planes and the spirit world explicit.

McDonnell's success in building military aircraft and selling them to the United States and its allies fit with his belief "that only from a foundation of strength can peace be successfully waged." Throughout the Cold War years, McDonnell supported the United Nations, serving as a member and eventually as national chairman of the United States Committee for the United Nations.

Although McDonnell was known as an exacting and demanding employer, his primary emphasis as head of McDonnell Aircraft was on the importance of teamwork. Curious by nature and taking an interest in all aspects of his company's work, he stressed the importance of "management by participation" to create machines as complex and as critical to the national defense as he believed his aircraft to be.

McDonnell's interest in missiles and spacecraft began with a navy contract in 1944 to build the Gargoyle, a radio-controlled, glide bomb. McDonnell's teams had begun research and experimentation on manned spacecraft before the Russian Sputnik launch in 1957. In 1959, McDonnell accepted a National Aeronautics and Space Administration (NASA) project to develop and produce America's first spacecraft, the Mercury Friendship. Mercury space capsules carried the first six American astronauts to orbits in outer space. For the Gemini project, McDonnell supervised the development and manufacture of space capsules carrying two astronauts. The space capsules Gemini 7 and Gemini 6 made the first manned rendezvous in outer space in December 1965. McDonnell believed that "space science and exploration [is] . . . a creative and psychological substitute for war."

In 1966, Douglas Aircraft Company, a manufacturer of both military and commercial aircraft, reported serious financial problems and solicited merger invitations. McDonnell negotiated the merger that resulted in creation of the McDonnell-Douglas Corporation in 1967. The merger provided the Douglas divisions with McDonnell's financial stability and added commercial airlines—the highly profitable DC series of passenger planes—to McDonnell's primarily military business. McDonnell continued as chief executive officer of McDonnell-Douglas until 1972, when he became chairman of the board. Until his death he was actively involved in the decisions that made McDonnell-Douglas one of the largest and most profitable airplane and spacecraft manufacturers in the world.

McDonnell married his first wife, Mary Elizabeth Finney, on June 30, 1934. On Apr. 1, 1956, seven years after Mary's death from cancer in 1949, McDonnell married Priscilla Brush Forney. McDonnell had two children from his first marriage and he adopted Mrs. Forney's three children. McDonnell suffered a stroke in mid-July 1980 and died at his home in Ladue, a suburb of St. Louis.

[See Douglas J. Ingells, *The McDonnell-Douglas Story* (1979); and Bill Yenne, *McDonnell-Douglas: A Tale of Two Giants* (1985). *Scotsmen Caught Young* (1981) and *Much May Be Made of a Scotsman: The Story of McDonnell-Douglas* (1990) are house publications available from McDonnell-Douglas Corporation, St. Louis. Obituaries are in the *St. Louis Post-Dispatch*, Aug. 22, 1980; the *St. Louis Globe-Democrat*, Aug. 23–24, 1980; the *New York Times*, Aug. 23, 1980; and the *Washington Post*, Aug. 23, 1980.]

WENDY HALL MALONEY

McGINLEY, PHYLLIS (Mar. 21, 1905–Feb. 22, 1978), poet and author, was born in Ontario, Oreg., the daughter of Daniel McGinley, a rancher, and Julia Kiesel. In 1908 the family moved to Colorado, where she and her brother attended a rural school. After her father's death, her mother took the children to Ogden, Utah, where Phyllis attended Ogden High School and the Sacred Heart Academy. She went on to the University of Southern California, then completed her studies at the University of Utah in Salt Lake City, graduating in 1927. She then taught school, first in Ogden for a year and then at a New Rochelle, N.Y., high school from 1929 to 1934, writing poetry and prose pieces at the same time.

After writing the children's operetta *The Toy-Shop* (1928) and after several of her poems were published in national magazines, such as the *New Yorker*, McGinley gave up teaching and moved to New York City, holding various jobs, including copywriter at an advertising agency and poetry editor for *Town and Country* briefly in 1937. In that year she married Charles L. Hayden, a telephone company executive. They moved to Larchmont, N.Y., and had two children. Until her husband's death in 1972, she often drew on their suburban family life and domestic issues as a source for her ironic, affectionate, and often witty light verse. Katherine White, fiction and poetry editor at the *New Yorker*, is credited with advising McGinley when she began submitting her work to the magazine in the 1920's to switch from "the same sad song all our lady poets sing" to a more playful style.

McGinley's first collection of verse, *On the Contrary*, was published in 1934, and was followed by *One More Manhattan* (1937) and *A Pocketful of Wry* (1940), all of which were well received. Three more collections followed. By the time *The Love Letters of Phyllis McGinley* was published in 1954 her popularity was firmly established. The book, about the joys of suburbia, sold 40,000 copies and critics took notice. E. H. Smith wrote in the *New York Herald Tribune Book Review*, "An honest review is in much danger of sounding like a love letter to Phyllis McGinley." Charles Jackson of the *New York Times* claimed she had restored delight to poetry, as well as "a magical sense of communication and intimacy between herself and the reader."

McGinley's first honors included several awards from Catholic groups, such as the Christopher Medal (1955), and much of her work reflected her strong religious beliefs. She wrote a devotional book for children, *A Wreath of Christmas Legends* (1967), and essays about Catholic saints, collected in *Saint-Watching* (1969), the last of her eighteen books. She had begun writing children's books in 1944 (*The Horse Who Lived Upstairs*), and *Wonderful Time* (1966) was named one of the best of the year by the *New York Times*. She won the Pulitzer Prize in 1961 for her collection *Times Three: Selected Verse from Three Decades with Seventy New Poems* (1960), for which poet W. H. Auden, himself a masterful writer of light verse, wrote the foreword. *Times Three* included new poems and verse from seven volumes published from 1934 to 1954. She was the first writer to win the Pulitzer for light verse.

McGinley also wrote the lyrics for *Small Wonder* (1948), a musical revue, and the narration for the film *The Emperor's Nightingale* (1951). In 1955 she was elected to the National Academy of Arts and Letters. Her two other volumes of essays are *Province of the Heart* (1959), in which she praised her suburban village, and *Sixpence in Her Shoe* (1964), about being a wife and mother. She wrote more prose than poetry in her later years, contributing articles to national women's magazines. Near the end of her career she said of the light-verse writer, "in times of unrest and fear it is perhaps his duty to celebrate, to single out some of the values we can cherish, to talk about some of the few warm things we know in a cold world." McGinley died in New York City, where she had returned after the death of her husband.

Like an Erma Bombeck who rhymed, McGinley became an important source of suburban wit during the 1950's and 1960's. Although McGinley and her eighteen books and numerous short publications were in the limelight for nearly four decades and critics claimed she was sure to enjoy lasting prominence, she is now largely forgotten. Most of her work, except for a few of her children's books, is either out of print or gathering dust on library shelves.

[See Auden's foreword in *Times Three*; Linda Wagner-Martin, *Phyllis McGinley* (1971); and portraits in *Catholic World*, Sept. 1957, and *Saturday Review*, Dec. 10, 1960. An obituary is in the *New York Times*, Feb. 23, 1978.]

CAROL BURDICK

McINTYRE, JAMES FRANCIS ALOYSIUS (June 25, 1886–July 16, 1979), Roman Catholic prelate, was born in New York City, the only child of James F. McIntyre and Mary Pelley. The family lived on East Twenty-eighth Street in Manhattan and was supported by James McIntyre's construction job. After Mary McIntyre's death in 1896, Frank was raised by a cousin, Mary Conley. He served as an altar boy at his parish churches, St. Stephen's and St. Ignatius Loyola, and was interested in studying to be a priest, but he left school at age thirteen to support his father, who had become an invalid. He took a job as a messenger in the financial district and worked nights toward his high school degree.

McIntyre rose quickly on Wall Street. He became office manager for the investment firm of H. L. Horton and Company and had been offered a partnership at another firm when his father died in 1915. McIntyre then resigned and began preparing for the priesthood. He graduated from St. Joseph's Seminary in the Dunwoodie neighborhood of Yonkers, N.Y., and was ordained a priest in 1921 by Patrick Hayes, archbishop of New York. After several years as a parish priest at St. Gabriel's Church in Manhattan, McIntyre was named vice-chancellor of the archdiocese. In 1934 he became chancellor, with broad administrative authority over the church's richest diocese and its 2,000 priests. He was a member of Cardinal Hayes's inner circle and lived in the cardinal's residence on Madison Avenue behind St. Patrick's Cathedral.

In 1940, Pope Pius XII appointed McIntyre an auxiliary bishop, and five years later Hayes's successor, Cardinal Francis Spellman, appointed him vicar general of the archdiocese. The following year the pope appointed McIntyre coadjutor (assistant) archbishop of New York, without right of succession to Spellman. Spellman traveled frequently and focused on international and national affairs, leaving the day-to-day operation of the vast archdiocese to McIntyre. Although many priests found McIntyre intolerant and stern, it was generally agreed that his business talents—which ranged from a command of shorthand to expertise in mortgage restructuring—made him perfect for the job.

In 1948, McIntyre was named archbishop of Los Angeles and San Diego, becoming one of many Spellman aides appointed to sees around the United States. A close friend of Pius XII's and easily the most influential American cardinal, Spellman was effusive on the subject of his departing aide: "In the nine precious years that we have lived and worked and prayed together, he has been to me all things that one man can be to another. Like Joseph, he has fostered close to his holy heart the little people of the archdiocese."

The booming Los Angeles archdiocese was a daunting administrative challenge, but over the next two decades McIntyre presided over one of the most dramatic building and development campaigns in the history of the Catholic Church in America. He began by establishing secretariats and commissions for vocations, communications, archives, cemeteries, and liturgy, founded a new charitable fund, built a new administrative building, and refurbished St. Vibiana's Cathedral.

In McIntyre's first fifteen years in Los Angeles, the archdiocese's Catholic population doubled, and the number of Catholic schools rose from 141 to 347. He opened parochial schools at the rate of one a month and in the process became known as "the brick-and-mortar bishop." He also lobbied vigorously and successfully for legislation in 1951 that exempted church schools from property taxes and later in the 1950's led the fight against two attempts to repeal the law.

In 1952 the pope named McIntyre to the College of Cardinals, making him the first cardinal from the western United States and one of four Americans in the college. On Jan. 12, 1953, he was elevated at St. Peter's Basilica in Vatican City. McIntyre said the appointment reflected the pope's affection for "the City of the Angels," and his new title was a source of pride among many Angelinos. The *Los Angeles Daily News* reported that McIntyre "has in this comparatively short period won the esteem and affection of the entire community for his effective leadership in many civic and social welfare projects."

The election of Pope John XXIII in 1958 and the convocation of the Second Vatican Council marked the beginning of an era of liberal change, in which McIntyre's conservatism seemed increasingly dated. When the council considered allowing the Mass, the most important Catholic worship ceremony, to be said in vernacular languages, McIntyre vehemently urged retention of Latin, adding that "active participation is frequently a distraction." In 1963, McIntyre told reporters that "there is no such thing as separation of church and state to any man who believes in God. It's a shibboleth. . . . There can't be any separation of church and state unless you want to be a Communist or a materialist—and if you want to, that's your privilege."

Once known mostly as an administrator, McIntyre in his later years became a prominent clerical hard-liner; John Cogley, then religion editor of the *New York Times*, wrote in 1964 that "he has been described by more than one Vatican observer as the most reactionary prelate in the church, bar none—not even those of the Curia," the Vatican's administrative body.

McIntyre's attitudes toward race and the civil rights movement also angered many Catholics. Particularly controversial was his refusal to join other church leaders in supporting California open-housing legislation. He said he did not want to involve the church in politics, but critics noted that he strongly opposed a bill in the state legislature that would have liberalized the abortion law. McIntyre called abortion "legalized murder." Despite his conservative reputation, *America* magazine concluded that the archdiocese of Los Angeles was far ahead of other American jurisdictions in heeding the suggestions and spirit of the council.

McIntyre retired as archbishop in 1970 and was succeeded by Timothy Manning. He spent several years as a parish priest at St. Basil's Church in Los Angeles before failing health confined him to St. Vincent Medical Center.

[See James Hennesey, S.J., *American Catholics* (1981); and Francis J. Weber, *Called as Disciples, Sent as Apostles* (1985). For a critical view, see John Cooney, *The American Pope* (1984). Obituaries are in the *New York Times* and the *Los Angeles Times*, both July 17, 1979.]

RICK HAMPSON

McLEAN, ROBERT (Oct. 1, 1891–Dec. 5, 1980), newspaper publisher, was born in Philadelphia, the second of four children of William Lippard McLean, a newspaper publisher, and Sarah Burd Warden. When McLean was four years old, his father bought the Philadelphia *Evening and Sunday Bulletin* at an executor's sale and subsequently transformed it into the city's largest newspaper.

After graduating from the Hill School, in Pottstown, Pa., McLean entered Princeton University, where he served as managing editor of the *Daily Princetonian*. He majored in political history and received a Litt.B. degree in 1913. McLean then went to work for his father's newspaper, first as a truck driver in the Circulation Department, and eventually in every other department of the newspaper.

McLean joined the prestigious First Troop of Philadelphia City Cavalry in 1915, and served with them under General Pershing on the Mexican border in the years 1916–1917. After American entry into World War I in 1917, McLean received a commission as lieutenant in the cavalry of the United States Army Reserve Corps. He soon transferred to the field artillery and was assigned to training duty at Camp Meade, Md., and Fort Sill, Okla. He was discharged with the rank of major in 1919, and was thereafter referred to as "the Major."

After returning to Philadelphia, McLean married Clare Randolph Goode on Apr. 28, 1919. They had no issue, but they later adopted two children.

Continuing his rise through the ranks at the *Bulletin*, McLean was elected its vice-president in 1922. In 1924 the elder McLean retired from the board of directors of the Associated Press (AP), a joint news-gathering organization, and his son Robert was elected to take his seat.

McLean became first vice-president of the AP in 1936, and its president in 1938. In 1941, McLean expanded the AP's operations to include services to radio stations.

McLean's father started turning over control of the *Bulletin* to his son in 1928. When William McLean died in 1931, the newspaper company elected Robert McLean the new president of the Bulletin Company, the newspaper's parent corporation. McLean helped the newspaper survive—and even expand—during the lean years of the Great Depression. He was one of the nation's first newspaper publishers to establish a pension and health insurance program for his employees. As a nominally Republican newspaper, the *Bulletin* opposed President Franklin D. Roosevelt's domestic New Deal policies, though not so vehemently as other partisan publications.

Like many other East Coast Republicans, McLean supported Roosevelt's efforts to increase American involvement in international affairs. After the nation's entry into World War II, the Roosevelt administration invited McLean to become a member of a fact-finding mission to England to study war conditions. McLean also accepted a Truman administration invitation in 1946 to travel to east Asia, where he and two other newspaper publishers met with Emperor Hirohito of Japan and Chinese Nationalist leader Chiang Kai-shek.

McLean and the AP ran afoul of federal antitrust law in the early 1940's, as the result of the organization's policy of excluding any new member that was opposed by an existing member. The Department of Justice began an antitrust lawsuit in 1942, after the exclusion of the Chicago *Sun*, and the ruling against the AP was upheld by the Supreme Court in a 1944 decision, which forced the AP to change its restrictive membership policies.

McLean and the *Bulletin* prospered in the immediate postwar years, when favorable economic conditions helped newspapers to prosper everywhere. In 1947, McLean's company acquired the Philadelphia *Record*, which had been financially crippled by a Newspaper Guild strike. The Bulletin Company also acquired radio station WCAU and subsequently started an affiliated television station. That same year, McLean received honorary doctorates from Princeton and Columbia universities.

The advent of television, as well as the growing number of automobiles, hampering delivery of afternoon newspapers, eventually began to take its toll on afternoon newspapers in the 1950's. With a circulation of 761,000 in 1947, the *Bulletin* ranked as one of the largest afternoon newspapers in the nation, but circulation declined to 725,000 by the 1960's.

McLean was a strong proponent of freedom of the press, and criticized the Truman administration in 1951, after the president complained about newspapers and magazines publishing "secret" information. A more local conflict arose in 1963, when the *Bulletin* initiated a lawsuit to allow its reporters to gain access to patrons' records of books borrowed from the Philadelphia Public Library.

In 1957, McLean decided to cut back on his activities. He resigned from the presidency of the AP, although he continued as a director and member of the executive committee until 1968. In 1959, McLean relinquished the presidency of the *Bulletin* to his nephew and ascended to the honorary position of chairman of the board.

In 1964, McLean completely severed his ties with the *Bulletin* and moved to Montecito, Calif., where he had bought the *Santa Barbara News-Press* and an affiliated radio station. He served as the newspaper's chairman until his death in 1980. Shortly after Robert McLean's death, the McLean family sold their interests in the *Bulletin* to the Charter Media Company. The newspaper's circulation had declined to 400,000, and it had become increasingly unprofitable. The newspaper ceased circulation in 1982.

McLean was an able newspaperman who built up a newspaper with a reputation for accuracy and avoidance of sensationalism. His newspapers benefited from the prosperity of the immediate postwar years but eventually succumbed to the growing power of television and rush-hour traffic congestion that decimated the ranks of afternoon newspapers throughout the nation.

[The newspaper "morgue" of the *Bulletin*, located in the Urban Archives of Temple University, Philadelphia, contains several files on Robert McLean and his family. There is no biography, but information about the McLean family and the *Bulletin* can be found in E. Digby Baltzell, *Philadelphia Gentlemen* (1958); Nathaniel Burt, *The Perennial Philadelphians* (1963); and Donald Paneth, *The Encyclopedia of American Journalism* (1983). The *Bulletin* published a detailed company history in its June 1, 1955, issue. Freedom-of-the-press issues are addressed in Robert

E. L. Taylor, *Robert McLean's "Bulletin" and a Look at Our Free Press in 1987* (1988). An obituary is in the *New York Times*, Dec. 7, 1980.]

STEPHEN G. MARSHALL

McQUEEN, TERENCE STEPHEN ("STEVE") (Mar. 24, 1930–Nov. 7, 1980), actor, was born in Indianapolis, Ind. (his birthplace is often incorrectly given as Slater, Mo.). He was reputedly named after a bookmaker by his father, whose own name was probably Terrence William McQueen. Nothing certain is known about McQueen's father, who was possibly a pilot, except that he left home when McQueen was six months old. He may not have been married to McQueen's mother. With his father gone, McQueen and his mother, Julia Crawford, moved in with her uncle, Claude Thompson, in Slater, Mo. When McQueen was nine, his mother tried to raise him alone in Indianapolis briefly, only to return him to her uncle while she went to California alone.

The next few years of McQueen's life were almost idyllic—he lived on a well-ordered farm with a great-uncle who treated him as if he were a son. When he was twelve, his mother reappeared and took him to Beech Grove, Ind., and then to Los Angeles. There McQueen did badly in schooling, got into trouble for stealing, and was violently at odds with his new stepfather, a man named Berri. In the autumn of 1944 he was sent by his parents to California Junior Boys' Republic in Chino, Calif. After initially resisting the reform school's program, McQueen fell under the influence of a superintendent who restored his sense of self-worth. He left Chino in April 1946, ending his formal education at the ninth-grade level. Years later, he established a scholarship fund for the school and revisited it regularly.

While McQueen was at Chino his stepfather died, and his mother moved to New York City, where he rejoined her. He quickly had a falling out with her and left. (McQueen and his mother were never again close, but he was with her when she died in 1965.) He signed on as a deckhand on a tanker bound for the West Indies, only to jump ship in the Dominican Republic and work his way back to the United States. After a period of drifting, he joined the United States Marine Corps in April 1947. While serving in Georgia, he was repeatedly promoted and busted and spent six weeks in the brig for being absent without leave. In the Marine Corps he learned auto mechanics, a skill he cultivated through the rest of his life. After he was discharged in April 1950, he returned to New York and made a meager living with odd jobs.

At a friend's suggestion, McQueen began studying acting at the Neighborhood Playhouse in 1951, using his GI Bill benefits. In 1952 he debuted onstage with one line in a Yiddish-language play and soon earned a scholarship to the Uta Hagen–Herbert Berghof School. During this period he began competing in motorcycle races on Long Island, cultivating another lifelong avocation.

The summer of 1952 brought McQueen minor roles in little theater productions with Margaret O'Brien, Ethel Waters, and Melvyn Douglas. In the next few years he occasionally did television work, and in 1955 he won one of five scholarships awarded to 2,000 applicants to Lee Strasberg's Actors Studio. Through these years he supported himself with full-time nonacting jobs.

In mid-1956, McQueen replaced Ben Gazzara in *A Hatful of Rain* on Broadway, winning critical praise that bolstered his confidence as an actor. During this time he met Neile Adams, a dancer and actress, whom he married in California on Nov. 2, 1956; they had two children. While in California he played a walk-on part in *Somebody Up There Likes Me*, starring Paul Newman. The next year McQueen got his first featured film role in *Never Love a Stranger* (1958). In 1958 he made *The Great St. Louis Bank Robbery* (1959) and starred in a now-classic science fiction movie, *The Blob* (1958).

McQueen's ability to project strength and vulnerability simultaneously helped win him the lead in a new television series, "Wanted—Dead or Alive," which premiered on Sept. 6, 1958. As professional bounty hunter Josh Randall, McQueen made an inherently unappealing character likable and firmly established his screen persona as a rugged laconic loner. Three years in this series transformed him into a nationally known figure.

Meanwhile, McQueen made *Never So Few* with Frank Sinatra in 1959 and costarred with Yul Brynner in *The Magnificent Seven* (1960), a Western that certified his big-screen appeal. After "Wanted—Dead or Alive" left the air in 1961, McQueen turned his back on television to concentrate on films and formed his own production company.

After an unsatisfactory attempt at comedy in *The Honeymoon Machine* in 1961, McQueen reestablished his image in *Hell Is for Heroes* and *The War Lover* in 1962. He then made the film that elevated him to the first rank of box office stars: *The Great Escape* (1963), a big-budget production about a famous Allied prisoner-of-war breakout during World War II. McQueen quietly stole the picture playing Hilts, the "Cooler King"—an indomitable loner. The film also allowed him to showcase his motorcycle skills in a chase scene and won him a best-acting award at the Moscow Film Festival.

Over the next several years McQueen played shiftless losers in *Love with the Proper Stranger* (1963), *Baby, the Rain Must Fall* (1965), and *The Cincinnati Kid* (1965). His career reached a new level in 1966, when he starred in *The Sand Pebbles* as an alienated American sailor stationed in China in a performance that earned him his only Oscar nomination. The same year he also starred in *Nevada Smith*, an undistinguished spinoff from *The Carpetbaggers*.

McQueen's career reached a different kind of plateau in 1968 when he starred in *Bullitt*, a taut action film that certified his growing box office status; his stunt driving in a high-speed car-chase episode reinforced the public's identification of him with the characters that he played. That same year he also made *The Thomas Crown Affair*, the only film in which he played a rich and powerful character. By the late 1960's, McQueen was making a million dollars a movie, a figure that would more than triple over the next decade.

In 1971, McQueen starred in two racing films, *Le Mans* and *On Any Sunday*. He played a fading rodeo contestant in *Junior Bonner* (1972), a bank robber in *The Getaway* (1972), a French prisoner on Devil's Island in *Papillon* (1973), and a fire chief in *The Towering Inferno* (1974), his last "superstar" role. In September 1971, McQueen and his wife were divorced. He married Ali MacGraw, his costar in *The Getaway*, on July 13, 1973, in Cheyenne, Wyo.; they had no children.

McQueen's screen persona underwent a change in the late 1970's. In 1978 he played against type in an adaptation of Henrik Ibsen's *An Enemy of the People*. Warner Brothers thought the film so noncommercial that it blocked distribution. In 1980 McQueen appeared in his last two films: *Tom Horn* presented him as a frontiersman overtaken by civilization, and in *The Hunter* he played a modern-day bounty hunter.

McQueen's marriage to MacGraw ended in 1978. In January 1980 he married Barbara Minty, a model. He died in Juárez, Mexico, of lung cancer.

[The Academy of Motion Picture Arts and Sciences Margaret Herrick Library in Beverly Hills, Calif., has both the Steve McQueen/Neile Adams Collection, which includes personal scrapbooks and photographs from McQueen's family life and early film career, and the Steve McQueen Collection, which mostly comprises McQueen's professional and business papers. Cataloging the latter collection began in 1992.

Biographies include Malachy McCoy, *Steve McQueen* (1974); Tim Satchell, *Steve McQueen* (1981); William F. Nolan, *McQueen* (1984); Neile McQueen Toffel, *My Husband, My Friend* (1986), a memoir by his first wife; and Marshall Terrill, *Steve McQueen* (1993). Casey St. Charnez, *The Films of Steve McQueen* (1984), has biographical information and numerous photographs. There are obituaries in the *New York Times* and the *Los Angeles Times*, both Nov. 8, 1980.]

R. Kent Rasmussen

McWILLIAMS, CAREY (Dec. 13, 1905–June 27, 1980), writer and social critic, was born in Steamboat Springs, Colo., the son of Jeremiah Newby McWilliams and Hattie Casley. His father, who served in the Colorado state senate, prospered as a cattle rancher and land dealer during World War I but lost heavily in the aftermath of the wartime boom.

In 1922, McWilliams was expelled from the University of Denver for his involvement in a St. Patrick's Day celebration that got out of hand; he then enrolled at the University of Southern California (USC), earning money for his education with a full-time job in the business office of the *Los Angeles Times*. He delighted in shunning the school's institutions, including fraternities and its prized football team, and gravitated to other students who shared his unconventional attitudes. Especially interested in literary criticism, he participated in several student literary endeavors despite the demands of his job. He continued at USC for both his undergraduate and law degrees, which he received in 1927.

McWilliams then joined the prestigious Los Angeles law firm Black, Hammack and Black but was still able to enjoy a bohemian life-style. He practiced law for a decade while developing the literary interests he had shown as a student. He contributed to such publications as *L. A. Saturday Night*, the *San Franciscan*, and the *Overland Monthly*. Encouraged by H. L. Mencken, McWilliams undertook a biography of the satirist Ambrose Bierce. The product of careful research, *Ambrose Bierce: A Biography* (1929), was widely and favorably reviewed. McWilliams married Dorothy Hedrick in 1930; they had one child and were separated in 1935. They were divorced thereafter. In 1941, McWilliams married novelist Iris Dornfeld; they had one child.

The onset of the Great Depression led to a period of social protest in California that increasingly engaged McWilliams's attention. A longtime friend of social critic Louis Adamic, he took a special interest in strikes by agricultural workers and studied the farm labor question. McWilliams gathered enough material to write *Factories in the Field*, published in 1939, the same year as John Steinbeck's *The Grapes of Wrath*. Inevitably the two books were compared, the *New York Times* reviewer calling *Factories* "equally masterful."

Earlier in 1939 McWilliams had given up his law career to accept appointment as head of the California Division of Immigration and Housing. Newly elected Democratic governor Culbert Olson gave McWilliams a mandate to revive the agency that had become moribund under Republican governors. He had authority to investigate migrant labor, immigrants, and some forms of rural housing. After the attack on Pearl Harbor, McWilliams arranged for the House Committee on Inter-State Migration (the Tolan Committee) to hold hearings in California on the situation of the Japanese Americans residing on the West Coast. He hoped this would buy time and that the animosity then so evident against the Japanese-American community would diminish. McWilliams underestimated the depth of feelings, and when the hearings were held (too late to head off the clamor for relocation), even liberals such as Governor Olson spoke against the Japanese.

During his four-year tenure, McWilliams became involved in disputes over wages and working conditions and made important political enemies. The election of Republican Earl Warren as governor in 1942 ended any chance McWilliams had of remaining in office. He turned to writing, completing seven major studies within the decade. *Ill Fares the Land* (1942) reflected McWilliams's interest in migrant labor. *Southern California Country: An Island on the Land* (1946) and *California: The Great Exception* (1949) undertook a wide-ranging and provocative analysis of the Golden State. The remaining four dealt with the social problems of minority groups. One of them, *Brothers Under the Skin* (1943), became a best-seller, in part because its publication coincided with the zoot-suit riots in Los Angeles. *Prejudice* (1944) looked in some depth at the long-term resentments behind the relocation of Japanese Americans, as well as the prospects for resettlement; *A Mask for Privilege* (1948) was an investigation of anti-Semitism; and *North from Mexico* (1949) discussed Mexican Americans in the United States. McWilliams's recognition as an authority on the sociology of prejudice brought him many speaking engagements and radio appearances.

In 1945, McWilliams accepted a position as West Coast contributing editor to the *Nation*, an important journal of opinion. The post was not demanding and offered only a token stipend, but as the years passed it brought him more in touch with the magazine's staff, then headed by Freda Kirchwey, and with eastern liberalism. The *Nation* was in the thick of the controversies that raged between liberals and the Right in postwar America and that also created fractures within American liberalism. McWilliams moved to New York City in early 1951 to become associate editor, which gave him an ideal forum for addressing the domestic and international questions that engaged American intellectuals.

In 1948, McWilliams supported Henry Wallace's Progressive candidacy for president, believing that Wallace, far more than President Harry Truman, identified the issues that mattered. McWilliams was appalled by the persecution of suspected Communists that began under Truman and grew even more outrageous after the issue of anti-Communism was co-opted by Senator Joseph McCarthy of Wisconsin. Although McWilliams believed that McCarthyism posed the greatest threat to civil liberties, he also jousted with the American Civil Liberties Union, which he felt was tepid in its defense of civil liberties, and with what he considered the "chic" anti-Communism of organizations like the American Committee for Cultural Freedom (which had been receiving

Central Intelligence Agency subsidies, he later discovered). The *Nation* escaped direct attack by McCarthy, but its position was always financially precarious and McWilliams devoted much time to assisting Kirchwey in fending off threats to the magazine.

McWilliams succeeded Kirchwey as editor in 1955 and endeavored to solidify the magazine's finances and to freshen its list of contributors. Hunter Thompson, James Baldwin, Willie Morris, and Ralph Nader were among the young writers he introduced to readers of the *Nation*. Financial constraints kept McWilliams from practicing investigative journalism on a consistently large scale, but he was able to increase the use of special issues to give more substantial coverage to topics such as civil rights, FBI abuses, the Central Intelligence Agency, corruption in New York City, and the emergence of the radical Right. The periodical was a consistent critic of the death penalty, inhuman prison conditions (Patrick Buchanan, later a prominent conservative, wrote an article in this series), America's Vietnam policies, and the military-industrial complex. McWilliams sympathized with the goals of the 1960's protest movement but did not like its violence and disagreed with its rhetorical style.

In 1975, McWilliams retired, having spent four decades identifying many of the questions that engaged American liberalism. On many occasions, McWilliams was called a socialist, a Communist, and a soft-headed liberal. He was not any of these, he insisted in his memoirs, but rather a Western radical, a radical who was concerned with issues rather than with the theoretical precision of his own arguments. He died in New York City.

[The papers of Carey McWilliams are at the University of California, Los Angeles. An oral history transcript is also there. Other materials are at the Bancroft Library, University of California, Berkeley. In addition to the titles mentioned in the text, McWilliams's major works include *The New Regionalism in American Literature* (1930), edited by Glen Hughes; *Louis Adamic and Shadow America* (1935); *Witch Hunt* (1950); and the compilation *The California Revolution* (1968). Most informative are Carey McWilliams, *The Education of Carey McWilliams* (1979); and Greg Critser, "The Making of a Cultural Rebel, Carey McWilliams, 1924–1930," *Pacific Historical Review*, May 1986. See also Robert E. Burke, *Olson's New Deal for California* (1953); Leonard Downie, Jr., *The New Muckrakers* (1976); Richard H. Pells, *The Liberal Mind in a Conservative Age* (1985); Sara Alpern, *Freda Kirchwey* (1987); and Kevin Starr, *Material Dreams* (1990). An obituary is in the *New York Times*, June 28, 1980.]

LLOYD J. GRAYBAR

MAN RAY (Aug. 27, 1890–Nov. 18, 1976), artist, was born Emmanuel Radnitsky in Philadelphia, the first of four children of Melach Radnitsky, a tailor, and Manya Louria (or Lourie), both Russian-Jewish immigrants. He assumed the single combined first and last name of Man Ray when his entire family adopted the surname Ray in 1911. The family moved to Brooklyn, N.Y., in 1897, where Man Ray, with family encouragement, early manifested his enduring fascination with gadgets, objects, and inventions as well as with art.

While attending Boys' High School from 1904 to 1908, Man Ray's passion for art grew, initially in visits to the New York museums and later when he saw the first modern works shown in the city, in 1908. Graduating from high school in 1908 with a determination to become an artist, he daringly refused a scholarship to study architecture. After two brief and unsatisfactory stints at more established art schools, with Alfred Stieglitz's encouragement and then with the mentorship of Robert Henri at the life drawing sessions at the anarchist Ferrer School, Man Ray became a largely self-taught artist. Establishing a lifelong pattern, he improvised, sometimes copied, more often invented, and constantly learned from his friends.

Man Ray, particularly inspired by the cubist works at the Armory Show of 1913, absorbed the iconoclasm of the young poets, radicals, and artists then giving a new flavor to New York life. That year he moved out of the family home first to Manhattan and then to a little cottage in an artists' colony in Ridgefield, N.J. In these years he painted a series of cubist canvases, coedited an avant-garde journal (its one issue included poetry by Ezra Pound and William Carlos Williams), wrote and self-published poetry, and drew antiwar political cartoons for Emma Goldman's *Mother Earth News*. In May 1914 he married Adon Lacroix, a Belgian-born, French-speaking poet; they had no children. In 1915, at his first one-person show at the Daniel Gallery in Manhattan, an important collector bought six of his cubist paintings, providing both the money and the incentive for him to rent a studio in New York City. Man Ray also bought a camera, chiefly to document his own art works. At this time he met Marcel Duchamp, who became his closest friend and strongest artistic influence.

In the next five years, Man Ray largely moved away from conventional painting to other media—collage, photography, the assemblages from found materials, and aerographs—creating a rich variety of works that demonstrate, despite the marks of Duchamp's influence, a formed artistic style. *The Rope Dancer Accompanies Herself with Her Shadows* (1916), influenced by Duchamp's then unfinished assemblage *The Bride Stripped Bare by Her Bachelors, Even* (1915–1923) and painted from a collage, illustrates the multiple media and influences that became a fixed part of his style. *The Revolving Doors* (1916–1917), a series of ten collages accompanied by a text, rendered mysterious Man Ray's developing theories of art by creating deliberate confusion between abstraction and representation.

Self-Portrait (1916) was his first publicly exhibited proto-dada object, a canvas with two doorbells and buzzer that frustrated viewers by not ringing when pressed. He painted *Suicide* (1917) with a commercial airbrush—a "pure cerebral activity," he asserted, since the artist never touched the work's surface. And he created his first photographic images. Portraits and reproductions of works of art brought him a living without trudging to an office. He experimented with puns, whimsies, shadows, and symbols, such as the eggbeater and its shadow that became the photograph titled *Man* (1918) and the flashbulb reflectors, six clothespins, and shadow that became *Woman* (or *Shadow*) (1918), both suggestive of Duchamp's "readymades."

The New York art world provided Man Ray with stimulating companions, but efforts to create a climate for modernism and dada in the city failed, and he found no buyers for his newer, less inhibited work. In about 1918 he and his wife separated, although they did not divorce until 1937. His marriage having collapsed, Man Ray burned a number of his older works, borrowed $500, and set off to Paris in July 1921.

Paris both rewarded and disappointed him. Welcomed by the dadaists as a precursor, he fell immediately into their social scene. His first show, under dada auspices, however, proved that Paris also offered no market for his paintings. But commissions for portrait and fashion photography soon assured him a livelihood and allowed him to create images that established his reputation as a master photographer. While Man Ray never quite overcame his prejudice that photography rated below painting as an art form, he, in fact, maintained his avant-garde reputation in large part through the invention, or more strictly the reinvention (since Fox Talbot had done them in the 1830's) of the photogram, the cameraless photograph created by placing objects on photosensitive paper and exposing them to light.

With his rayographs, as Man Ray called them, he had, said writer Jean Cocteau, unlearned painting by making "paintings with light." To Tristan Tzara, a leader in the dada movement, he had transformed a machine-age art from mechanical to mysterious: common objects were "set, softened, and filtered like a head of hair through a comb of light." He further removed photography from any suspicion that it offered an objective rendering of the world by perfecting solarization, which created demarcating lines around images by controlled introduction of light during the developing process. Man Ray's reputation among French artists as well as in the fashion industry grew even as American critics, dubious about photography as art, viewed him as an illusionist, a trickster, and an entrepreneur.

Man Ray's success, however, was undeniable. The subjects of his portraits included Georges Braque, Pablo Picasso, Henri Matisse, Gertrude Stein, Francis Poulenc, and Ernest Hemingway in the arts as well as such social notables as Nancy Cunard and the Marquise Casati, whose double-exposed face with two pairs of eyes both pleased its subject and became a surrealist icon. His several experimental films commanded enthusiastic audiences among the Paris literati and remain a subject for scholars of the film. His images of women—nudes, faces, complex distortions, punning surreal compositions, such as the famous *Le Violon d'Ingres* (1924) with its violin F-shaped sound holes on his model's naked back—remain among his most influential works. His art appeared frequently both in exhibitions and in various magazines, ranging from avant-garde publications to *Vogue* and *Harper's Bazaar*.

Man Ray earned a good living and generally enjoyed his expatriate life in the Paris art community. His liaison with beautiful women, particularly Kiki, a nightclub singer and painters' model known as "Queen of Montparnasse," and Lee Miller, the famous model and photographer, inspired major works. His best-known painting of the Paris years, *Observatory Time—The Lovers* (1932–1934) (also known as *The Lips*), began with a photograph of Kiki's lips and emerged years later as a giant vision of Miller's lips floating in the sky over Paris. By the time World War II forced Man Ray to return to the United States in 1940, he had become a major figure in international art: a leading modernist photographer with a vast body of work, an occasional painter of notable surrealist images, an indefatigable creator of surrealist objects, and a pioneer in making fashion photography adventuresome.

The return to the United States, where Man Ray had never gained acceptance as an artist, was difficult. He stayed only briefly in New York City, largely avoiding the art world, and soon migrated to Los Angeles. There, in the "beautiful prison" of California, as he described it, he found respect as a pioneer of modernism, opportunities to paint and to exhibit his work, and a few admirers who bought enough of his work to keep him going. He also met Juliet Browner, a dancer; they were married on Oct. 24, 1946. They had no children. Man Ray was never fully comfortable in Hollywood, never felt the respect for his calling as a dedicated iconoclastic artist that had always consoled him in Paris, and was never financially secure. In March 1951 the Man Rays sailed for France.

During the next quarter century Man Ray continued to paint, to make objects, to commission replicas of his objects ("To create is divine," he wrote. "To reproduce is human."), to write—including an autobiography, *Self Portrait*, in 1963, and to cooperate in the monumental exhibitions of his work mounted with increasing frequency as his reputation as a creator of the modern style continued to grow. His place in art history was secured in the 1960's as dadaesque objects again flourished and photographic images gained acceptance as works of art. Major exhibitions in Paris in 1962, in Los Angeles in 1966, in Rotterdam in 1971, in Paris in 1972, and in New York in 1974 demonstrated renewed appreciation of his lengthy career. He died in his studio in Paris.

Man Ray never achieved the reputation as a painter to which he aspired, could never accept with grace his seminal role in the history of photography, and always longed for an acceptance by American art critics that he never quite achieved in his lifetime. Nonetheless, his place in twentieth-century art continued to grow after his death. The National Museum of American Art mounted *Perpetual Motif: The Art of Man Ray* in 1988, a retrospective exhibition that traveled to Los Angeles, Houston, and Philadelphia during the next two years. The French government in the early 1990's constructed a replica of his studio in the Pompidou Center as a monument to the American whom France has adopted as one of its national treasures.

William Copley, one of his patrons, termed him "the Dada of us all." He brought together an astonishing number of the characteristics that have been labeled "postmodern" in the art made in the years since his death. He created objects only to photograph them; he dissolved the line between unique and reproducible objects; he pioneered manipulated and cameraless photography; he veered from medium to medium; he incorporated machine-made and artist-crafted objects into hybrids; he rejected craft and technique for concept and idea; he combined words and images in startling and humorous juxtapositions; he was a cheerful surrealist, a nonideological dadaist, a tinker and inventor, an American and a European, a conjurer of dreams but usually not of nightmares. He sought to "amuse, bewilder, annoy, and inspire" rather than to shock—or to confront the full terrors of the twentieth-century world. Some critics cannot forgive his insouciance and his lack of development over his long career, but many see in his transformations of the material world what critic Andy Grundberg has described as "new ways of envisioning what art can be." As the always articulate Man Ray noted, "All opinion is transient, and all work is permanent."

[Merry A. Foresta et al., *Perpetual Motif* (1988), is the best introduction to Man Ray's work. Neil Baldwin, *Man Ray* (1988), is a reliable and detailed biography. Both volumes have useful bibliographies; the Foresta volume lists manuscript collections. Man Ray's autobiography, *Self Portrait* (1988), is unreliable but essential. See also Rosalind Krauss and Jane Livingston, *L'amour fou* (1985). Brief critical evaluations of Man Ray's work include Chuck Nicholson, "To Amuse, Bewilder, Annoy and Inspire," *Artweek*, Feb. 8, 1986; Andy Grundberg, "A Revival of Interest in a World Gone Awry," *New York Times*, Dec. 4, 1988; and Deborah Solomon, "The Resurrection of Man Ray," *New Criterion*, Mar. 1989. An obituary is in the *New York Times*, Nov. 19, 1976.]

ROBERT D. MARCUS

MARCUSE, HERBERT (July 19, 1898–July 29, 1979), philosopher, social theorist, and political activist, was born in Berlin, Germany, the son of Carl Marcuse and Gertrud Kreslawsky, upperclass German Jews. After serving with the German army in World War I, he went to Freiburg to pursue his studies. He received his Ph.D. in literature in 1922 and, following a short career as a bookseller in Berlin, returned to Freiburg in 1928 to study philosophy with Martin Heidegger. Marcuse's first published article (1928) attempted a synthesis of the philosophical perspectives of phenomenology, existentialism, and Marxism, a synthesis that decades later would be carried out by Jean-Paul Sartre and Maurice Merleau-Ponty.

Marcuse argued that Marxist thought had degenerated into a rigid orthodoxy and thus needed "phenomenological," or concrete, experience to revivify the theory; at the same time, Marcuse believed that Marxism neglected the problem of the individual, and throughout his life he was concerned with individual liberation and well-being in addition to social transformation and the possibilities of a transition from capitalism to socialism.

In 1933, Marcuse published a major review of Marx's just-published *Economic and Philosophical Manuscripts of 1844*; the review anticipated the tendency to revise interpretations of Marxism from the standpoint of the works of the early Marx. His study *Hegel's Ontology and Theory of Historicity* (1932) contributed to the Hegel renaissance that was taking place in Europe. These works revealed Marcuse to be an astute student of German philosophy, and he was emerging as one of the most promising theorists of his generation.

Also in 1933, Marcuse joined the Institut für Sozialforschung (Institute for Social Research) in Frankfurt and soon became deeply involved in interdisciplinary projects that included working out a model for radical social theory, developing a theory of the new stage of state and monopoly capitalism, and providing a systematic analysis and critique of German fascism. Marcuse identified with the Critical Theory of the institute and throughout his life was close to Max Horkheimer, Theodor W. Adorno, and others in the institute's inner circle. Critical Theory attempted to develop a theory of the contemporary era, and Marcus was deeply involved in its studies of contemporary culture, society, and politics.

Later in 1933, Marcuse—a Jew and a radical—fled from Nazism and moved to Geneva. The following year he immigrated to the United States.

The Institute for Social Research was granted offices and an academic affiliation with Columbia University in New York City, where Marcuse worked until 1940. His first major work in English, *Reason and Revolution* (1941), traced the genesis of the ideas of Hegel, Marx, and modern social theory. It demonstrated the similarities between Hegel and Marx and introduced many English-speaking readers to the Hegelian-Marxist tradition of dialectical thinking.

Marcuse became an American citizen in 1940. In 1941 he joined the Office of Strategic Services and then worked in the State Department in Washington, D.C., becoming the head of the Central European Section of the Office of Intelligence Research by the end of World War II and remaining there until 1951. Marcuse saw his government service as a way to participate in the struggle against fascism. He published *Eros and Civilization* in 1955, a work that attempted an audacious synthesis of Marx and Freud and sketched the outlines of a non-repressive society. While Freud argued in *Civilization and Its Discontents* that civilization inevitably involved repression and suffering, Marcuse argued that other elements in Freud's theory suggested that the unconscious contained evidence of an instinctual drive toward happiness and freedom. This evidence is articulated, Marcuse suggested, in daydreams, works of art, philosophy, and other cultural products. Based on this reading of Freud and study of an emancipatory tradition of philosophy and culture, Marcuse sketched the outlines of a non-repressive civilization that would involve libidinal and nonalienated labor, play, free and open sexuality, and production of a society and culture that would further freedom and happiness. His vision of liberation anticipated many of the values of the 1960's counterculture and helped Marcuse to become a major intellectual and political influence during that decade.

Marcuse argued that contemporary society produced "surplus repression" by instituting socially unnecessary labor, unnecessary restrictions on sexuality, and a social system organized around profit and exploitation. In light of the technological advancements and society's prospects for increased abundance, Marcuse called for the end of repression and for the creation of a new society. His radical critique of society and its values, together with his call for a nonrepressive civilization, elicited a dispute with his former colleague Erich Fromm, who accused him of endorsing nihilism and hedonism. Marcuse had earlier attacked Fromm for excessive conformity and idealism, and repeated these charges in the polemical debates following the publication of *Eros and Civilization*.

In 1958, Marcuse became a professor of politics and philosophy at Brandeis University; during his tenure he was one of the most popular and influential members of its faculty. He published a critical study of the Soviet Union in 1958 (*Soviet Marxism*) that broke the taboo in his circle of cultural theorists against speaking critically of the Soviet Union and Soviet Communism. While attempting to develop a many-sided analysis of the Soviet Union, Marcuse focused his critique on Soviet bureaucracy, culture, values, and the differences between the Marxist theory and the Soviet version of Marxism-Leninism. Distancing himself from those who interpreted Soviet Communism as a bureaucratic system incapable of reform and democratization, however, Marcuse pointed to potential "liberalizing trends" countering the Stalinist bureaucracy, which eventually materialized in the 1980's under Mikhail Gorbachev.

Next, Marcuse published a wide-ranging critique of both advanced capitalist and Communist societies in *One-Dimensional Man* (1964). This book theorized the decline of revolutionary potential in capitalist societies and the development of new forms of social control. Marcuse argued that "advanced industrial society" created false needs that integrated individuals into the existing system of production and consumption. Mass media and culture, advertising, industrial management, and contemporary modes of thought all reproduced the existing system and attempted to eliminate negativity, critique, and opposition. The result was a "one-dimensional" universe of thought and behavior in which the aptitude and ability for critical thinking and oppositional behavior was withering away.

Not only had capitalism integrated the working class, the source of potential revolutionary opposition, but the ruling elite had developed new techniques of stabilization through state policies and the development of new forms of social control. Thus Marcuse questioned two of the fundamental postulates of orthodox Marxism: the revolutionary proletariat and the inevitability of capitalist crisis. In contrast with the more extravagant demands of orthodox Marxism, Marcuse championed nonintegrated forces of minorities, outsiders, and radical intelligentsia, and attempted to nourish oppositional thought and behavior through promoting radical thinking and opposition.

One-Dimensional Man was severely criticized by orthodox Marxists and theorists of various political and theoretical commitments. Despite its pessimism, it influenced many in the New Left as it articulated their growing dissatisfaction with both capitalist and Soviet Communist societies. Moreover, Marcuse continued to defend demands for revolutionary change and the new, emerging forces of radical opposition, thus winning him the derision of establishment forces and the respect of the new radicals.

One-Dimensional Man was followed by books and articles that articulated New Left politics and critiques of capitalist societies: "Repressive Tolerance" (1965), *An Essay on Liberation* (1969), and *Counterrevolution and Revolt* (1972). "Repressive Tolerance" attacked liberalism and those who refused to take a stand during the controversies of the 1960's. It won Marcuse the reputation of being an intransigent radical and ideologue for the Left. *An Essay on Liberation* celebrated all of the existing liberation movements, from the Viet Cong to the hippies, and exhilarated many radicals while further alienating establishment academics and those who opposed the movements of the 1960's. *Counterrevolution and Revolt*, by contrast, articulated the new realism that was setting in during the early 1970's, when it was becoming clear that the most extravagant hopes of the decade were being dashed by a turn to the right and "counterrevolution."

In 1965, Brandeis refused to renew his teaching contract, and Marcuse soon thereafter received a position at the University of California at San Diego (in La Jolla), where he remained until his retirement in 1970. During this period, Marcuse published many articles and gave lectures and advice to student radicals all over the world. His work was often discussed in the mass media. Never surrendering his revolutionary vision and commitments, Marcuse continued to defend Marxist theory and libertarian socialism until his death. His students began to gain influential academic positions and to promote his ideas, making him a major force in American intellectual life.

Marcuse dedicated much of his work to aesthetics, and his final book, *The Aesthetic Dimension* (1978), briefly summarizes his defense of the emancipatory potential of aesthetic form in so-called high culture. Marcuse thought that the best of the bourgeois tradition of art contained powerful indictments of bourgeois society and emancipatory visions of a better society. Thus he attempted to defend the importance of great art for the projection of emancipation and argued that cultural revolution was an indispensable part of revolutionary politics.

Marcuse's work in philosophy and social theory generated fierce controversy, and most studies of his work are highly tendentious and frequently sectarian. In retrospect, Marcuse's vision of liberation—of the full development of the individual in a nonrepressive society—distinguished his work, along with his sharp critique of existing forms of domination and oppression. Marcuse's work lacked the sustained empirical analysis that characterized some versions of Marxist theory as well as the detailed conceptual analysis found in many versions of political theory. Yet he constantly showed how science, technology, and theory itself had a political dimension and produced a solid body of ideological and political analysis of many of the dominant forms of society, culture, and thought during the turbulent era in which he lived.

Marcuse was married three times. He and his first wife, Sophie, had one child before her death in 1951. He next married Inge Werner on Feb. 19, 1955; she died in 1974. His third wife was Erica Sherover, whom he married on June 21, 1976.

Marcuse died in Starnberg, Germany.

[Marcuse's unpublished papers are in the Stadtsbibliothek, Frankfurt, Germany. Works by Marcuse not mentioned in the text include *Negations* (1968) and *Studies in Critical Philosophy* (1972). See also Douglas Kellner, *Herbert Marcuse and the Crisis of Marxism* (1984); Robert Pippin, Andrew Feenberg, and Charles Webel, eds., *Marcuse: Critical Theory and the Promise of Utopia* (1988); and John Bokina and Timothy J. Lukes, *Marcuse: New Perspectives* (1994). An obituary is in the *New York Times*, July 31, 1979.]

DOUGLAS KELLNER

MARQUARD, RICHARD WILLIAM ("RUBE") (Oct. 9, 1889–June 1, 1980), baseball player, was born in Cleveland, Ohio, one of five children raised in a middle-class household. Drawn to baseball at an early age, Marquard was a batboy for the American League Cleveland team (then the Broncos, later the Indians). Growing to six foot three by his midteens, Marquard became an accomplished left-handed pitcher. In all likelihood, he graduated from high school in Cleveland, but there is no evidence of any participation in interscholastic sports. As he related in an interview with Lawrence Ritter in the 1960's, his father, Frederick Marquard, was against his determination to be a major league pitcher and even, in the face of Rube's defiance, refused to speak to his son until late in Marquard's baseball career.

At age seventeen, Marquard tried to hook up with Waterloo of the Iowa State league. Given no advance contract, he rode freight trains to Iowa, where he won one game but, still given no contract, left the team and returned home. He was signed by Indianapolis of the American Association in 1907 and won twenty-three games with Canton (Ohio) that year and twenty-eight with Indianapolis in 1908, striking out 250 batters. A perfect game against Columbus late that year so impressed scouts that the eighteen-year-old phenom was offered an $11,000 signing bonus by the New York Giants, the largest ever paid up to that date. The "$11,000 Beauty" (as he was labeled) so disappointed the Giants and manager John McGraw in the next two full seasons, however, that sportswriters started to dub him the "$11,000 Lemon."

The origins of Marquard's nickname are not entirely clear. While still in the minors, he (or his fastball) was likened in appearance to Rube Waddell, then a star left-handed pitcher for the Philadelphia Athletics. Despite accounts stressing Marquard's urbane demeanor, dependability, and sobriety (he claimed to have never smoked or drunk alcohol), the nickname stuck.

Over the next three years, Marquard became the best left-handed pitcher in the National League, winning seventy-three games between 1911 and 1913. This turnaround is credited to Wilbert Robinson, then a Giants coach, who helped him control his curveball and mix his pitches. In 1912 he won his first nineteen decisions, an achievement never since equaled. His only two World Series victories came in the 1912 series with Boston. He and Christy Mathewson (his longtime roommate), the league's premier right-handed pitcher, teamed up in three consecutive World Series from 1911 to 1913.

By the end of 1912, Marquard was a New York celebrity. He began a vaudeville career and in 1913 teamed with the actress Blossom Seeley in a popular dance act. At the time, she was married to Joseph Kane, who won a $4,000 settlement from Marquard in an alienation of affection case. Marquard and Seeley were married in 1913; this marriage ended in divorce in 1920.

Marquard's baseball career began to falter as early as 1914, when he lost twelve consecutive games en route to a 12–22 season. Nevertheless, that year he did win a twenty-one-inning complete game against Pittsburgh. He dickered with the Brooklyn team of the short-lived Federal League prior to the 1915 season, but McGraw prevented his jumping to that league. In April 1915 he pitched his only major league no-hitter, against Brooklyn, but soon fell into greater disfavor with McGraw. In an unusual maneuver, McGraw permitted Marquard to trade himself to Brooklyn, a team managed by Wilbert Robinson, for $7,500 later in the season. After 1915, Marquard was inconsistent, winning only ninety-six games in ten more seasons (five with Brooklyn, one with Cincinnati, and the last four with the Boston Braves). He pitched in two World Series with Brooklyn, but lost his only three decisions. A broken leg and appendicitis, respectively, afflicted his 1919 and 1924 seasons. Only twice did he win more than thirteen games in a season.

Marquard finished his career with a record of 201 wins and 177 losses (some record books show 204–179) and an estimated earned run average of 3.08. He turned to minor league managing from 1926 until the early 1930's, even umpiring in the Eastern League in 1931. He then left baseball and worked several years as a betting-window clerk at various racetracks in Florida and in the Baltimore area, where he settled in 1930.

Marquard married Naomi Wrigley in 1921; upon her death in 1954, he married Jane Ottenheimer. Marquard died of cancer at his home in Baltimore.

Forty years after retiring as an active player, Marquard was featured along with several other early ballplayers in the book *The Glory of Their Times*, in which he recounted his adventures in baseball, stating that he "loved every minute of [it]." It must be acknowledged that some of his assertions of fact are not documented elsewhere. For example, his claim that his father was the city engineer of Cleveland during his youth is not verified in official sources. Some believe that his profile in the Ritter book was responsible for his selection in 1971 by the Veterans Committee (for the pre-1925 era) for election into the Hall of Fame, while others point out that in 1971 this committee expanded the number of its selections to four per year. A. W. Laird ranked him as thirty-seventh among all major league pitchers playing between 1893 and 1987 in *Ranking Baseball's Elite*, and among the top ten left-handed pitchers in the history of the game. While others (such as Bill James) may not list Marquard among the very best southpaw pitchers of all time, his credentials are clearly on a par or exceed many of his fellow baseball Hall of Famers.

[Pitching statistics for Marquard appear in *Total Baseball*, 2d ed., edited by John Thorn and Pete Palmer with David Reuther (1991). The major source on his life is Lawrence Ritter, *The Glory of Their Times* (1966). An obituary is in the *New York Times*, June 3, 1980.]

MARVIN D. LEAVY

MARSHALL, SAMUEL LYMAN ATWOOD ("SLAM") (July 18, 1900–Dec. 17, 1977), journalist, military historian, and soldier, was born in Catskill, N.Y., the son of Caleb Carey Marshall, a British-born brickmaker, and Alice Medora Beeman. After a series of moves, his family settled in Niles, Calif., in 1912, and for the next two years Marshall was a juvenile actor with the Western Essanay Company. Following yet another move in 1915, he attended high school in El Paso, Tex. In 1917 he enlisted in the United States Army, where he advanced rapidly from the rank of private in the engineering corps to first lieutenant of infantry. He was the youngest army officer in World War I, seeing action in the Soissons, St. Mihiel, Meuse-Argonne, and Ypres-Lys campaigns.

Marshall's formal education was limited to a

year at the Texas College of Mines after his release from the army in 1919. By 1923 he was established as a sports editor and then city editor of the *El Paso Herald.* He left that paper in 1927 for the *Detroit News,* where for the next thirty-five years (interrupted by military service) he worked variously as chief editorial writer, military critic, and foreign correspondent. Inevitably known as "Slam" because of his initials, Marshall traveled the world in search of stories for his paper, for the North American Newspaper Alliance, and for magazines. He reported from Latin America in the 1930's, from both Europe and the Pacific during World War II, from Korea in the 1950's, from the Congo and Southeast Asia in the 1960's. By his own count, he covered twenty-one wars. He wrote hundreds of articles, many of them technical papers for the military, in which he analyzed a broad range of subjects, from Jimmy Doolittle's historic raid on Tokyo in May 1942, to the psychological stress suffered by combat infantrymen.

Marshall produced thirty books, most of which were based on firsthand observation. Their popularity was in large measure a result of his crisp, clear, often vivid prose style, his eye for the telling detail, and his keen sense of what it was like to be a soldier on the battlefield, which he once described as "the lonesomest place which men may share together." He developed that theme in *Men Against Fire* (1947), an unsparing and controversial study of World War II troop training and battlefield performance. In it, Marshall argued that only 25 to 30 percent of American soldiers carrying hand weapons in combat had fired them—the result, he wrote, of inadequate preparation and the military command's widespread misunderstanding of the fear and uncertainty that all troops must feel in combat. The army responded to the book by redesigning its training procedures over the next two years, incorporating a number of Marshall's suggestions. His critics were not persuaded by either his evidence or his conclusions.

With the onset of World War II, Marshall renewed what became a lifelong association with the United States Army. Commissioned as a major in 1942, he initially worked in the office of Secretary of War Henry L. Stimson, where he developed procedures for indoctrinating enemy prisoners of war. He wrote or edited dozens of training manuals and organized the Army News Service. He was one of the key figures in shaping the army's wartime research operations in the development of tactical weapons.

In 1943, Marshall became chief combat historian in the Central Pacific, where he took part in the Twenty-seventh Division's invasion of the Gilbert Islands and the Seventh Division's invasion of the Marshall Islands. There he pioneered interviewing techniques that became standard for combat historians in every theater. Convinced that headquarters reports were often misleading, Marshall insisted on interrogating combat soldiers in company units as soon after a battle as possible, relying on the group memory of the particular moment, when joined to other such reports, to provide an all-encompassing picture of the larger battle that no one person was in a position to describe. Through this attention to detail his books had their impact on both civilian and professional military readers.

Marshall was transferred to Europe in time for D day, as the chief historian for the European Theater, participating in the Normandy and Brittany invasions, the siege of Brest, the airborne invasions of Holland, and the major campaigns in Germany. In a memorable moment, he and Ernest Hemingway "liberated" Paris on Aug. 25, 1944. In the company of seven other Americans, they inadvertently entered the city some minutes before the arrival of the French forces, and well in advance of the American troops waiting in the suburbs, while rear-guard German units were still present. Amid sniper fire and occasional explosions, Marshall and Hemingway drove triumphantly down the Avenue Foch to the Hotel Claridge and that night had dinner at the Ritz.

For his service in both world wars and later in Korea, the army awarded Marshall the Distinguished Service Medal, the Legion of Merit, the Bronze Star with oak leaf cluster, and the Combat Infantry Badge. He received the Legion of Honor and the croix de guerre with palm from France, and the Ardennes Medal from Belgium. He was subsequently decorated by the governments of Italy, Ethiopia, and Israel.

Marshall left the army in 1946 but was recalled to active duty two years later, as the Cold War intensified. Assigned to the Pentagon, he assisted in staff planning for the North Atlantic Treaty Organization. In 1951, while serving as chief combat historian in Korea, he was promoted to brigadier general, the rank he held at his death.

Although he returned to civilian life in 1952, Marshall continued to cover the Korean War and later reported on the Sinai War between Israel and Egypt in 1956, the war in Lebanon in 1958, and the Vietnam War between 1960 and 1967. He periodically consulted with the Defense Department and various military commands until 1977. Among his many books are *Island Victory* (1944), *Bastogne* (1946), *The River and the Gauntlet* (1953), *Pork Chop Hill* (1956), *Night Drop* (1961), *The American Heritage History of World War I* (1964), and *Battles in the Monsoon* (1967).

Marshall married Ruth Elstner in 1920; they had one child and were divorced. His second wife, Ives Westervelt, developed multiple sclerosis shortly after their marriage in 1932. She died of the disease in 1952. Marshall married Catherine ("Cate") Finnerty on Mar. 10, 1954; they had four children.

[Marshall's papers are at the University of Texas, El Paso. His memoirs, *Bringing Up the Rear*, were edited by Cate Marshall (1979). Marshall described his entry into Paris in "How Papa Liberated Paris," *American Heritage*, Apr. 1962. See also *The Infantry News*, 1951. An obituary is in the *New York Times*, Dec. 18, 1977.]

ALLAN L. DAMON

MARTINEZ, MARIA (1887?–July 20, 1980), American Indian potter, was born to Reyes Peña and Tomas Montoya. Her father eked out a living for the family of six working variously as a farmer, a carpenter, and a cowboy. There is no record of Martinez's birth and her biographers have chosen dates ranging from 1881 to 1887. She lived her entire life in the pueblo of San Ildefonso, N.Mex., a small group of adobe houses clinging to the eastern bank of the Rio Grande about twenty miles northwest of Santa Fe. As a child, Martinez, whose name in the Pueblo language Tewa was Po-Ve-Ka, liked nothing more than to watch her aunt, the accomplished potter Nicolasa Peña, at work. Using ancient techniques, Peña would roll coils of clay between her moistened hands to form a tall cylinder that she would then push out into a graceful contour, smoothing the finished product with a round stone. Finally, the dried pot would be painted in a variety of clay slips and baked in a wood fire. As they had been for centuries, these perfectly round, polychrome pots, created without the benefit of a potter's wheel or kiln, would be used in the households of the pueblo. Martinez absorbed this tradition from her aunt and at the age of seven or eight began to mold crude plates and bowls.

Martinez attended the government grammar school in her pueblo until 1896, when the tribal council chose her and her sister Desideria as two of the children to be sent to St. Catherine's Indian School in Santa Fe. After two years, Martinez returned to San Ildefonso. Unsure of her next step, she spent some time doing odd jobs for the teacher in the government school. In 1904 she married Julian Martinez, also from San Ildefonso, in a traditional early morning service at the pueblo. That afternoon, the newlyweds were on a train headed for the World's Fair in St. Louis, Mo., where they spent four and one-half months with a group of pueblo Indians demonstrating traditional dancing and pottery making. This was Martinez's first public recognition as a potter.

The couple went home to San Ildefonso where Martinez gave birth to four sons and a daughter who died at birth. In 1907, Julian Martinez was hired by Edgar L. Hewett, director of the School of American Research, to excavate prehistoric pueblo sites. Hewett, who had heard that Martinez was an accomplished potter, asked her to clarify some technical issues by reproducing pots based on shards found on the Pajarito Plateau. Though some reports claim that these shards had an unusual black finish, the artifacts were not black and Martinez reproduced them using the methods still common in San Ildefonso, though she did so with distinguished artistry. Hewett eagerly purchased all these pots and assured her that he would find a market outside the pueblo for any more she would produce.

Sometime during this period, Julian Martinez, who painted the patterns on the pots that his wife molded, began to experiment with the firing process. By smothering the fire with horse manure, he generated smoke that carbonized the pots, leaving a rich black finish. Though many credited him with discovering this process, he actually built upon a living tradition practiced in the pueblos around San Ildefonso. However, he did succeed in refining the technique to create a uniquely lustrous black surface which resembled metal more than clay. The Martinezes' real innovation came around

1918, when Julian drew a pattern on unpolished clay that Maria then rubbed smooth with a round stone; after firing, this produced a glossy black design on a matte black background. Because polishing a fine pattern was difficult and time-consuming, Julian began instead to paint his patterns with a watery clay slip onto an evenly smoothed surface. This method produced the stunningly beautiful contrast of matte black patterning on a mirror-like ground for which the Martinezes became known. The first recorded purchase of a piece of decorated black-on-black ware was by the Museum of New Mexico in 1920.

Over the next few decades, as increasing interest in Indian cultures generated an Anglo market for pueblo pottery and newly constructed government highways brought communities like San Ildefonso within easy reach of tourists, Martinez's flawless and unusual pots became highly sought after. The small pieces of black ware which she would have sold at the pueblo for three to six dollars in 1924 brought up to $1,500 in galleries at the time of her death in 1980. The Smithsonian Institution in Washington, D.C., and the Wheelwright Museum in Santa Fe both mounted retrospectives of her work. She received countless awards and honorary degrees, was chosen to lay the cornerstone of Rockefeller Center, and was invited to the White House by four presidents: Hoover, Franklin Roosevelt, Eisenhower, and Johnson.

Yet even as her fame spread throughout the world, Martinez passionately clung to the traditional pueblo conception of pottery making as a communal endeavor. Indeed, her greatest impact was as a teacher. As early as 1920, she became self-conscious about the financial rewards her pottery brought and asked her husband if she could teach others to make black ware. She always encouraged the sale of other women's pots, often hiding her own on a back shelf. Placing no particular value on her signature and not wanting to disappoint tourists, she would gladly take up a ballpoint pen or pencil and sign any pot that might possibly have been made by her. In the 1920's, she signed "Marie," a change in spelling that Chester Faris, the director of the Indian School in Santa Fe, thought would appeal to Anglos; in the 1950's, she began signing "Maria." With the exception of a few experimental pieces, she never decorated her own pots. After her husband's death in 1943, her daughter-in-law Santana worked with her until 1956 and then her son Popovi Da, a collaboration that lasted until her virtual retirement in 1971. In 1974 the Martinez family began holding summer workshops at the Idyllwild campus of the University of Southern California, which spread the craft of pueblo pottery to non-Indian artists.

When Martinez died in 1980, pottery making was the single most important source of income for the pueblos of the Rio Grande. Largely through her sharing of skills and knowledge, San Ildefonso had been transformed from a poor, remote village to a craft center. Martinez became painfully aware of the dilution of Indian traditions resulting from these changes and, during the last years of her life, she urged the young of San Ildefonso to maintain the culture she had done so much to revive.

[See Carl E. Guthe's *Pueblo Pottery Making* (1925); Alice Marriott, *Maria: The Potter of San Ildefonso* (1948); Susan Peterson, *The Living Tradition of Maria Martinez* (1977); Susan Brown McGreevy, *Maria: The Legend, The Legacy* (1982); and Richard L. Spivey, *Maria*, 2d ed (1989). Films of Martinez working include *Hands of Maria* (1967); *Maria the Potter of San Ildefonso* (1967); and *Maria of the Pueblos* (1971). Obituaries are in the *New York Times* and the *Albuquerque Journal*, both July 22, 1980.]

CORINNE T. FIELD

MARX, HERBERT ("ZEPPO") (Feb. 26, 1901–Nov. 30, 1979), vaudeville performer, stage and movie actor, and theatrical agent, was born in New York City, the fifth of five sons of Samuel Marx, a tailor, and Minnie Schoenberg.

Zeppo was not an original member of the Four Marx Brothers, a vaudeville act organized in 1912 and composed of his older brothers, Groucho, Gummo, Harpo, and Chico. Various explanations of his nickname have been offered, but Chico suggested it was a variation on the rural nickname Zeb, which Zeppo acquired while the family lived on a farm near Chicago during World War I.

Only after America's entry into that war, when Gummo was inducted into the United States Army, was Zeppo drafted into the Four Marx Brothers by their mother to preserve the logic of the group's name and to replace Gummo as the team's straight man. Thus, Zeppo, who joined the act just before it made the transition from vaudeville to the Broadway stage, was never a part of the zany antics of his brothers; instead, he played the romantic lead in their stage and screen comedies. He appeared in the Marx Brothers' first Broadway show, *I'll Say She Is!* (1924), as well as the later plays *The Cocoanuts* (1925) and *Animal Crackers* (1928) and in their first five movies: *The Cocoanuts* (1929), *Animal Crackers* (1930), *Monkey Business* (1931), *Horse Feathers* (1932), and *Duck Soup* (1933).

In reviews of these films, Mordaunt Hall, a critic for the *New York Times*, sketched the film persona of Zeppo in a few deft strokes. In one review, Hall referred to him as "the sober Zeppo" and "the staid member of the family." In another, Hall contrasted what he called Groucho's "corkscrew humor," Chico's "distortions of English," and Harpo's pantomime, which aroused "riotous laughter," with Zeppo's "sedate" manner.

Zeppo, acknowledged by Groucho to be the funniest of the brothers in real life, was an underrated talent. For example, when Groucho was hospitalized in 1930, Zeppo appeared on stage as Groucho and the audience was unaware of the switch. Only later, when Zeppo failed to appear in his own role, was the ruse discovered. As Groucho admitted, Zeppo's "roles were thankless, and . . . all he was required to do was show up. It's not that he didn't have talent; he simply had three older brothers ahead of him." Dissatisfaction with the role of straight man, inherited from brother Gummo, led Zeppo to leave the Four Marx Brothers in 1934.

In 1927, Zeppo married Marion Benda, an actress. They had one child and were divorced in 1954.

The first two Marx Brothers movies were filmed in Astoria (in the borough of Queens, New York City) while the brothers continued to appear on Broadway, but in 1931 they moved to California to make their third movie at Paramount Studios in Hollywood. Zeppo left the comedy team in March 1934 to become a theatrical agent with Orsatti and Brene. His letter of resignation, made public by Groucho, read, "I'm sick and tired of being a stooge. . . . I have only stayed in the act until now because I knew that you [Groucho], Chico and Harpo wanted me to."

Zeppo soon established a successful agency of his own, but he represented his brothers only once, during negotiations with RKO in 1937. Groucho was dissatisfied with Zeppo's efforts because, as Zeppo later explained when asked why he was not his brothers' agent, "I arranged one deal—$250,000 for them to do *Room Service*. Groucho said it should have been $350,000." Zeppo gave up the account, and the brothers thereafter maintained a close personal relationship.

Zeppo left show business altogether when he sold his theatrical agency in 1948. He had already become a manufacturer of airplane parts, and his company had produced the clamping devices used to carry the atomic bombs dropped on Japan at the close of World War II.

In September 1959, Zeppo married Barbara Blakely, a divorcée who was a dancer at the Riviera in Las Vegas. He later adopted her son from her first marriage. The couple divorced in May 1973, and three years later, Barbara Marx became the fourth wife of the singer Frank Sinatra.

In 1969, Zeppo and a partner, Albert D. Herman, patented a "dual watch" worn on the wrist to monitor the heartbeat. The invention consisted of a conventional watch and a "control" watch set to operate according to a patient's heartbeat. If the pulse rate increased or decreased, the two watches fell out of synchronization and an alarm sounded.

Although he was remembered only as the team's former straight man, Zeppo was included when the Four Marx Brothers were inducted into the Hollywood Hall of Fame in January 1977. Although too ill to attend the ceremony, he had the satisfaction of knowing his somewhat reluctant contribution to American film comedy was recognized.

Despite poor health, Zeppo attempted to intervene in a bitter fight between Erin Fleming, Groucho's longtime companion and business manager, and Groucho's son, Arthur, over who would be named Groucho's conservator and thus control the failing comedian's wealth. Zeppo's offer to serve as conservator was acceptable to Fleming, but his statement that Groucho loved her and that she brought him happiness made him unacceptable to the other side, and he was not appointed. When Groucho died on Aug. 19, 1977, Zeppo was not invited to the funeral. He held a news conference at which he angrily charged that he was being ostracized because of his defense of Erin Fleming.

Two years later, Zeppo, the last survivor of the Marx Brothers' act, died in Palm Springs, Calif.

[The Zeppo Marx file and the Marx Brothers files, in the Billy Rose Theatre Collection in the New York Public Library for the Performing Arts, contain materials on Zeppo's career. Marx Brothers biographies with information on Zeppo include Joe Adamson, *Groucho, Harpo, Chico, and Sometimes Zeppo* (1973); Groucho Marx and Richard J. Anobile, *The Marx Bros. Scrapbook* (1973); and Wes D. Gehring, *The Marx Brothers* (1987). "Zeppo's Last Interview," given to Barry Norman in 1979, is in the *Freedonia Gazette*, Nov. 1981 and Summer 1982. Obituaries are in the *Los Angeles Times*, Nov. 30, 1979; and the *New York Times*, Dec. 1, 1979.]

ROMAN ROME

MARX, JULIUS HENRY ("GROUCHO") (Oct. 2, 1890–Aug. 19, 1977), vaudeville performer and star of stage, screen, radio, and television, was born in New York City, the third of five sons of Samuel Marx, a tailor, and Minnie Schoenberg.

It is sometimes difficult to separate fact from fantasy in dealing with Groucho's life. For instance, *Who's Who in America* long listed his date of birth as Oct. 2, 1895, although he was actually born five years earlier—a discrepancy apparently resulting from a Hollywood studio's desire to make Groucho and his brothers appear younger than they were to create an "image of zany boys rather than insane middle-aged men."

Groucho himself was never one to let facts stand in the way of a good story. For example, Groucho insisted he was named Julius after an uncle who, despite ample evidence to the contrary, convinced Groucho's mother he was wealthy. Uncle Julius took advantage of Minnie's hope that he would leave his "fortune" to his namesake to sponge off the Marx family. However, when he died his entire estate consisted of "a nine ball that he had stolen from the poolroom, a box of liver pills, and a celluloid dickey."

Groucho's stage name, derived from his grumpy disposition, was bestowed in 1916 by Art Fisher, a monologist known for giving nicknames to fellow vaudeville performers.

Groucho was the first of the brothers to embark on a career in show business, as a boy soprano. One by one, three of his brothers—first Gummo, then Harpo, and finally Chico—joined him. The Four Marx Brothers soon emerged as a singing act that played small-town vaudeville circuits until, according to Groucho, a mule launched the brothers on their career in comedy. During a performance in Nacogdoches, Tex., word spread inside the theater that a mule had run away, and the bored audience went outside to watch the fun. Furious over this snub, the brothers hurled ad-libbed insults at the Texans when they returned to the theater after the mule's recapture and, much to their surprise, the audience roared with laughter.

America's entry into World War I temporarily separated the Four Marx Brothers. When the act was reconstituted, brother Zeppo replaced Gummo as the team's straight man. Already one of the hottest acts in vaudeville, they made the transition to musical comedy with the Broadway hits *I'll Say She Is!* (1924), *The Cocoanuts* (1925), and *Animal Crackers* (1928).

During this long apprenticeship in vaudeville and on the Broadway stage, Groucho developed the persona familiar to moviegoers everywhere. For instance, in the play *Fun in Hi Skule* (1912), Groucho played a professor and for the first time wore the frock coat that became his standard costume. Another trademark—the ever-present long, fat cigar used to punctuate his comic thrusts—was originally a useful stage prop: "If you forget a line all you have to do is stick the cigar in your mouth and puff on it until you think of what you've forgotten." Groucho's admission provides evidence that, contrary to legend, Marx Brothers sketches were usually carefully plotted; however, Groucho and company frequently ad-libbed, and successful lines were written into the script for subsequent performances.

One of Groucho's most distinctive features—a black greasepaint mustache—was first used when he arrived for a performance too late to paste on the false mustache he wore in the act and instead applied a smear of greasepaint beneath his nose.

His speech was deliberately uncultured—even uncouth—and his language was often illogical and usually insulting as he poured forth streams of non sequiturs. The wisecrack and pun were his stock-in-trade, and his most vicious satire was reserved for those who held themselves in too high regard. Nonetheless, many critics have suggested that few people were actually offended by Groucho's verbal assaults, for, as Albin Krebs put it, Groucho's insults were "never really unkind," as his humor was intended "to deflate rather than annihilate." As Groucho explained to an interviewer, he sought to make people laugh at themselves rather than "to evoke malicious laughter at the other fellow."

Other stage characteristics associated with Groucho were his strange, crouching walk, often described as a "lope," and his dark, leering eyes behind steel-rimmed glasses beneath bushy eyebrows that went up and down like elevators whenever an attractive woman came into view.

On stage—and some would argue in his private life as well—Groucho's attitude toward women was marked by a strange blend of misogyny and lechery, and he always treated them with a rough equality devoid of any false sense of chivalry. Thus Margaret Dumont, who played the quintessential grande dame in numerous Marx Brothers productions, was more the butt of Groucho's roughhouse humor than an object of his lust.

On Feb. 4, 1920, in Chicago, Groucho married Ruth Johnson, Zeppo's dance partner in the vaudeville show *Home Again*. The couple's children—Arthur and Miriam—have published books about their famous father. In July 1942, Ruth, who had developed a serious drinking problem, obtained a divorce on the grounds of cruelty. Some critics have charged that life with Groucho drove Ruth—as well as two later wives and both his daughters—to alcoholism.

Between 1929 and 1933, the Four Marx Brothers made five movies for Paramount Pictures: *The Cocoanuts* (1929), *Animal Crackers* (1930), *Monkey Business* (1931), *Horse Feathers* (1932), and *Duck Soup* (1933). At the outset of this extremely productive period, however, Groucho nearly suffered a nervous breakdown when the stock market crash of October 1929 wiped out his entire savings ($240,000). The experience left him with an acute case of insomnia that plagued him the rest of his life and a profound sense of financial insecurity that often led to obsessive behavior about money. Despite his fears, Groucho never faced poverty; in 1929 he was earning $2,000 per week appearing on Broadway in *Animal Crackers* at night while filming *The Cocoanuts* by day at Paramount's Astoria, N.Y., studios, and he would soon be collecting royalties on his first literary endeavor, *Beds* (1930).

In 1934, Zeppo left the team, and the three remaining Marx Brothers were lured to Metro-Goldwyn-Mayer (MGM) by that studio's head of production, Irving Thalberg, with the offer of a three-film contract. Thalberg died during the making of the second movie, but the fruit of this brief collaboration was *A Night at the Opera* (1935) and *A Day at the Races* (1937).

In 1938, Zeppo, now a prominent theatrical agent, negotiated a lucrative contract for his brothers with RKO Pictures to star in a film adaptation of the Broadway play *Room Service*. Most critics panned the film, which was the only one made from material and characters the brothers had not helped to develop. They returned to MGM to make three more films—*At the Circus* (1939), *Go West* (1940), and *The Big Store* (1941)—but none was on a par with their earlier work, and the brothers announced their "retirement" from the movies.

Groucho attempted to launch a new career for himself apart from his brothers, and indeed he would be the only one to succeed as a "solo act." In 1934, Groucho and Chico had starred in a radio comedy, "Flywheel, Shyster, and Flywheel," and Groucho became convinced that radio was a "softer racket" than slapstick comedy, for there were no lines to learn, no falls to take, no makeup to apply, and few rehearsals to attend. During the early 1940's he made numerous guest appearances on radio before finally landing a weekly show of his own ("Blue Ribbon Town") in 1943; however, he was dropped by the sponsor, Pabst Blue Ribbon Beer, the next year and replaced by Danny Kaye.

On July 21, 1945, Groucho, now fifty-four, married again, to Catherine ("Kay") Mavis Gorcey, a twenty-four-year-old actress and the former wife of Leo Gorcey of the "Dead End Kids." The couple, who had one daughter, were divorced in May 1950.

In 1946 the Marx Brothers returned to film and made *A Night in Casablanca*, after which Groucho, Harpo, and Chico again went their separate ways. Groucho appeared alone in the film *Copacabana* (1947), and in October 1947 he became the host of a new radio show, "You Bet Your Life." The show's quiz format, devised by producer John Guedel, enabled Groucho to bounce wisecracks off announcer George Fenneman and to needle contestants before asking them questions for prize money. The popular show won Groucho a Peabody, radio's equivalent to the Oscar, in 1948. In 1950 the show was brought to television, and Groucho also appeared for the last time with his brothers, in the movie *Love Happy*. In 1951, Groucho won an Emmy Award and also made the film *A Girl in Every Port* with Marie Wilson and William Bendix.

In August 1932 the Four Marx Brothers had appeared together on the cover of *Time*. In December 1951, Groucho appeared alone on its cover. He had achieved fame apart from his brothers.

On July 17, 1954, Groucho, now sixty-three, married for a third time, to Eden Hartford, a twenty-four-year-old photographer's model. The couple had no children and were divorced in December 1969.

Groucho, a public-school dropout, was proud of his literary achievements. He collaborated with Norman Krasna on a play, *Time for Elizabeth*, about a businessman who retires to avoid paying income taxes—a particular bugbear of Groucho's, who wrote a lampoon on the subject, *Many Happy Returns* (1942), and who frequently complained about the amount taken from his income by the government. The play, written with Groucho in mind, opened on Broadway in 1948 with Otto Kruger in the lead role and closed after only eight days.

In 1959, he published the autobiographical *Groucho and Me* and boasted that he had written every word without the help of a "ghost." He next discussed love, sex, and sundry other topics in *Memoirs of a Mangy Lover* (1963). Groucho was elated when, in 1965, the Library of Congress asked him to donate his letters—some of which would be published as *The Groucho Letters* (1967).

During these years of literary activity, Groucho withdrew somewhat from public view, for in 1961, after fourteen years on radio and television, "You Bet Your Life" was finally canceled. A new show, "Tell It to Groucho," had only a brief run.

By 1971, Groucho, who was again divorced and living alone, had become something of a recluse. At this point, however, Groucho hired Erin Fleming, an attractive Canadian-born actress, as his secretary—although she would soon be referred to in the press as his "companion and business manager"—and she brought him back in the public eye.

On May 6, 1972, Groucho performed at Carnegie Hall to a sold-out house before journeying to France, where he was honored by the Cannes Film Festival and made a Commandeur des Arts et Lettres by the French government.

In April 1974, he received a special Academy Award, and in his acceptance speech he thanked Fleming, "who makes my life worth living and who understands all my jokes." Two years later, he published *The Secret Word Is Groucho*, a book about his radio and television career.

In January 1977, the Four Marx Brothers were inducted into the Hollywood Hall of Fame. Harpo and Chico were dead and Zeppo was too ill to participate; Groucho was the only brother able to attend the ceremony. Shortly after this moment of triumph, however, Groucho again made headlines in a different way. Despite these recent successes, Groucho's faculties had been failing, and in 1974 Fleming had been named his temporary conservator. In April 1977, she petitioned the courts to name her permanent conservator. However, Groucho's son Arthur contested her request and asked instead that he be appointed. Groucho became the object of a sensational court battle of which he was probably only dimly aware. It might be said that Groucho, sometimes called the "King of Leer" because of his lecherous ogling of women, was transformed into "King Lear" as his companion and his son battled for control of his fortune, estimated at $2.5 million.

Despite ill health, Zeppo testified in support of Fleming because, he said, Groucho was in love with her and she brought him happiness. In the end, Groucho's grandson, Andrew Marx, was named conservator.

After Groucho's death at Cedars-Sinai Medical Center in Los Angeles, Bank of America, the executor of his estate, sued Fleming, charging that she had exploited her relationship with Groucho to obtain a 50 percent share of Groucho Marx Productions, two houses, and other gifts totaling $400,000. In April 1983, a California jury (by a 9–3 vote) found against her in a verdict that trial lawyer Melvin Belli said defied logic and could only have been written by Groucho. "If anyone would make sense out of it they'd have to get Groucho, Zeppo, Harpo, and Chico" to explain it.

[Groucho's papers are in the Library of Congress. The Groucho Marx file and the Marx Brothers files in the Billy Rose Theatre Collection at the New York Public Library for the Performing Arts contain materials on Groucho's career. Works on Groucho by his children include Arthur Marx, *Life with Groucho* (1954) and *Son of Groucho* (1972); and Miriam Marx Allen, *Love Groucho: Letters from Groucho Marx to His Daughter Miriam* (1992). Useful biographies include Charlotte Chandler, *Hello, I Must Be Going: Groucho and His Friends* (1978); and Hector Arce,

Groucho (1979). Obituaries are in the *New York Times*, Aug. 20, 1977; and *Variety*, Aug. 24, 1977.]

ROMAN ROME

MARX, MILTON ("GUMMO") (May 21, 1893–Apr. 21, 1977), vaudeville performer and theatrical agent, was born in New York City, the fourth of five sons of Samuel Marx, a Jewish tailor who immigrated to the United States from the former French province of Alsace in the early 1880's, and Minnie Schoenberg, the daughter of show people. Before coming to America from Germany, her father had been a traveling magician and her mother a harpist. Her brother, whose stage name was Al Shean, became part of the Gallagher and Shean vaudeville act. Minnie Marx is often credited with launching her sons' careers in show business, and her early efforts on their behalf was the subject of *Minnie's Boys*, a musical comedy that had a brief run on Broadway in 1970.

Although his name appears as "Moses Marks" on his birth certificate (in the New York City Municipal Archives), Gummo was originally known as Milton. He once said he acquired his nickname as a youngster because he always had holes in his shoes and wore gumshoes (rubbers) over them even when it was not raining. But his brother Groucho claimed a monologist named Art Fisher pinned the name on Gummo during a vaudeville tour because of his fondness for wearing gum-soled shoes.

Gummo told Richard J. Anobile that he first appeared on stage inside a ventriloquist's dummy held by his uncle, Harry Shean, while Gummo spoke and operated the mechanical parts from within the dummy. The act was not a success. Soon after, in 1907, Gummo, a boy tenor, teamed up with brother Groucho and a girl named Mabel O'Donnell to form the Three Nightingales. The next year, brother Harpo joined the group, which became the Four Nightingales and played small towns in the Midwest and South. In 1910 the boys' mother, who would assume the name Minnie Palmer and advertise herself as "Chicago's only lady producer," moved her family to that city because most booking agents for the small-town vaudeville circuit were located there.

The act expanded to become the Six Mascots, composed of Groucho, Gummo, Harpo, a bass singer, and two female singers. When the women quit, Minnie and her sister Hannah replaced them until the act was reorganized as the Three Marx Brothers and Company (it became the Four Marx Brothers in 1912, when brother Chico joined the act). They toured the small-town circuit in a show called *Fun in Hi Skule*, in which, for the first time, comedy, rather than music, was emphasized. Gummo was cast as straight man—a role he found unrewarding—and this later played a part in his decision to leave the stage.

In 1914, Al Shean wrote a new act for the Four Marx Brothers entitled *Home Again*, with Gummo again playing the handsome straight man. After several months on the road, the show opened in New York City, where in February 1915, it played the Palace, the pinnacle of the vaudeville circuit.

After the United States declared war on Germany in 1917, Gummo entered the United States Army as a private. Although he spent the war in Illinois, military service proved to be a pivotal event in his life, for he left the act and never returned. Gummo was replaced by Zeppo, the youngest Marx brother, who became straight man to Groucho, Chico, and Harpo. Thus Gummo was not a member of the Four Marx Brothers when the team opened on Broadway in *I'll Say She Is!* (May 19, 1924). He has been called the most obscure of the Marx brothers because he did not appear in any films. Nonetheless, he played a prominent role in the various musical acts involving the Marx brothers during their early days in vaudeville and was a member of the group when it made the transition from a musical act to the comedy team that became famous. Gummo later attributed his brothers' success entirely to himself—"I quit the act."

Even before entering the army, Gummo thought of leaving the stage, for he believed himself "a pretty lousy actor." As early as 1916, he had begun selling paper boxes used by grocers and butchers to hold merchandise. By day he called on potential customers in whatever town the team happened to be playing; at night he appeared on stage with his brothers. After leaving the army in 1918, Gummo found employment as a salesman in the garment industry in New York City. On May 2, 1929, he married Helen Theaman von Tilzer, a young widow who was pregnant when her husband died in February 1928. Gummo adopted the girl; the couple also had a son.

On Aug. 17, 1932, the *New York World-Telegram* announced two Marx Brothers openings on Broadway: Harpo, Groucho, Chico, and Zeppo in *Horse Feathers* at the Rialto Theatre, and Gummo Marx, Inc., at 1375 Broadway. Gummo's venture into dress manufacturing during the Great Depression proved unsuccessful. However, failure in the garment industry brought Gummo back into show business, for he launched a new and highly successful career as a theatrical agent.

When Zeppo, who left the Marx Brothers act in 1934, opened a theatrical agency, Gummo ran the New York office. In 1937 he moved to California, where his brothers had taken up residence in 1931, and soon became a partner in the agency, which was known as Marx, Miller, and Marx until it was sold in 1948. When Groucho, the only brother to succeed as a solo performer after the team retired from films, began a new career in television, Gummo served as his personal business manager and also established an agency of his own in Beverly Hills.

Gummo died in Palm Springs, Calif.

[The Gummo Marx file and the Marx Brothers files in the Billy Rose Theatre Collection at the New York Public Library for the Performing Arts contain materials on Gummo's career. Marx Brothers biographies with information on Gummo include Kyle Crichton, *The Marx Brothers* (1950); Groucho Marx and Richard Anobile, *The Marx Bros. Scrapbook* (1973); Hector Arce, *Groucho* (1979); and Wes D. Gehring, *The Marx Brothers* (1987). An obituary is in the *New York Times*, Apr. 22, 1977.]

ROMAN ROME

MASON, FRANCIS VAN WYCK (Nov. 11, 1901–Aug. 28, 1978), author, was born in Chicago, the son of Francis Payne Mason and Ermagarde Coffin. As a boy he lived in Paris and Berlin with his grandfather, Frank H. Mason, American consul general in those cities. The outbreak of World War I stranded him in Europe. Before the United States entered the conflict, sixteen-year-old Mason enlisted as an ambulance driver and saw frontline service at the battle of Verdun. A proficiency in French, German, and Spanish later led to his employment as a military interpreter. He received the croix de guerre with two palms, and the Medaille de Sauvetage, and was elected to the Legion of Honor. In 1918 he was commissioned a second lieutenant in the United States Army Expeditionary Forces.

Mason returned home in 1919 to resume his education, first at the Berkshire School in Sheffield, Mass. (1919–1920), and then at Harvard. He graduated in 1924 with a B.S. in literature and intended to enter the foreign service. Instead, he started a business importing embroidery, rugs, and rare books. Acting as his own purchasing agent, Mason traveled frequently to the Caribbean, Europe, and North Africa. He kept his military affiliation with Squadron A of the New York National Guard's Seventh Cavalry (1924–1929).

Mason married Dorothy Louise Macready on Nov. 26, 1927; they had two children. Early in 1928 he gave up his business, moved from New York City to Riderwood, Md., and began writing full time. To maintain his army association, he transferred to the Maryland field artillery as a sergeant, and eventually received promotion to lieutenant (1930–1933).

Mason's first book, *Seeds of Murder* (1930), introduced his protagonist Captain Hugh North, an army intelligence officer "of incisive thought as well as action," according to a *New York Times* reviewer. North, whom Mason eventually promoted to major and colonel, starred in twenty-three novels. The plots took him to Africa, the Balkans, Cuba, Europe, the Middle East, and the Orient. The colorful and exciting backgrounds of these stories originated from Mason's own wanderings, and their complicated plots enthralled and captured a loyal coterie of fans. Another *New York Times* review summed up the author and his hero: "Van Wyck Mason and . . . North never let one down when it comes to mystery thrillers."

Even before the first North book reached the bookstores, Mason, who often worked on as many as four books at once, produced the historical novel *Captain Nemesis* (1931). During his career he gradually shifted from mystery to history, occasionally interspersing contemporary war stories.

Mason's most successful historical fiction effort was the Revolutionary War novel *Three Harbours* (1938), which he wrote while living in Bermuda (1936–1939). *Three Harbours* sold more than 120,000 hardcover copies and lingered on best-seller lists for nearly a year. It was the first of a tetralogy that included *Stars on the Sea* (1940), *Rivers of Glory* (1942), and *Eagle in the Sky* (1948).

With twenty-one books in print after his first decade of writing, Mason, under the pseudonym Ward Weaver, began the 1940's with *Hang My Wreath* (1941). When the Japanese attacked Pearl Harbor, he requested active duty and the army called him up in early 1942. The following year, he received orders to Europe for duty with the General Staff Corps of the Supreme Allied Headquarters civil and military government section, as chief historian. Mason wrote some of the first official dispatches concerning the D-day invasion. By the time of his release from active duty in 1945, he had been promoted to full colonel. Despite the demands of wartime military service, Mason wrote another Ward Weaver book, *End of Track* (1943), and followed it with three war novels written under the pseudonym Frank W. Mason: *Q-Boat* (1943), *Pilots, Man Your Planes!* (1944), and *Flight into Danger* (1946). After returning to civilian life, as Van Wyck Mason he composed the thrillers *Saigon Singer* (1946) and *Dardanelles Derelict* (1949), and the historical novel *Cutlass Empire* (1949).

His wife's illness, which began with a stroke in 1950 and led to her death in 1958, reduced Mason's output in the 1950's. He began with the award-winning *Valley Forge* (1950). In rapid succession he published *Proud New Flags* (1951), *Golden Admiral* (1953), *Blue Hurricane* (1954), *Silver Leopard* (1955), *Captain Judas* (1955), *Our Valiant Few* (1956), *Lysander* (1956), *The Young Titan* (1959), and *Return of the Eagles* (1959), the majority of them historical novels.

Mason married his longtime secretary, Jeanne-Louise Hand, on Oct. 3, 1958. They purchased a home in Bermuda and took up residence there in 1963. Long a member of the American Society of Bermuda, Mason served as its president from 1960 until 1978, when he suffered a heart attack and drowned while swimming near his home at Southampton, Bermuda.

Mason wrote or edited sixty-five books during a literary career that spanned five decades. Late in life he succinctly commented, "Started writing in 1928. Still at it!" Matching actions to words, at the time of his death, Mason had a major work, *Armored Giants*, based on the 1862 battle between the world's first iron-clad warships, *Monitor* and *Merrimack*, completed in draft form. (It was published in 1980.) All told, Mason wrote twenty-one books in the 1930's, fourteen in the 1940's, and fifteen each in the 1950's and 1960's. A *New York Times Book Review* article, commenting on his prolific writing style, stated: "That is all, for the moment, Mr. Mason plans, but this is only Sunday and there is a whole week ahead."

[See relevant articles in the *New Yorker*, Nov. 5, 1938, and Nov. 30, 1946; *Saturday Review of Literature*, Nov. 12, 1938; *New York Times*, Nov. 13, 1938, Nov. 24, 1946, and Oct. 20, 1957; *Boston Transcript*, Nov. 19, 1938; *New York Times Book Review*, Feb. 15, 1948, June 21, 1959, Jan. 31, 1960, Feb. 26, 1961, May 19, 1968, and Sept. 30, 1973; *New York Herald Tribune Book Review*, May 27, 1951, and Sept. 27, 1959; *Chicago Sunday Tribune*, June 14, 1959; *New York Herald Tribune Lively Arts*, Mar. 19, 1961; *Best Sellers*, Sept. 1, 1969; and *Los Angeles Times*, Oct. 28, 1980.

Obituaries are in the *Washington Post*, Aug. 30, 1978; the *New York Times*, Nov. 6, 1978; and *AB Bookman's Weekly*, Nov. 6, 1978.]

W. M. P. Dunne

MAUCHLY, JOHN WILLIAM (Aug. 30, 1907–Jan. 8, 1980), computer scientist, was born in Cincinnati, Ohio, one of two children of research physicist Sebastian Jacob Mauchly and Rachel Scheidemantel, both of German ancestry. Mauchly attended high school in Chevy Chase, Md., while his father was a department head at the Carnegie Institution in Washington, D.C. He entered Johns Hopkins University in 1925 to study engineering and was permitted to begin graduate study in physics in 1927 without receiving an undergraduate degree. He received his doctorate in 1932, writing a dissertation on the molecular spectroscopy of carbon monoxide.

Mauchly taught physics at Ursinus College in Collegeville, Pa., from 1933 to 1941. He became interested in statistical analysis and weather prediction, which led him to study the existing electromechanical devices for making large numerical calculations. In 1941, Mauchly joined the Moore School of Electrical Engineering at the University of Pennsylvania. He took a defense training course in electrical engineering, where he met John Presper Eckert, a twenty-two-year-old graduate instructor who had a similar interest in electronic calculations.

The Moore School had contracts with the United States Army Ballistics Research Laboratory to construct electromechanical machines to calculate artillery firing tables. Mauchly wrote a seminal proposal in 1942, "The Use of High-Speed Vacuum Tube Devices for Calculating," which proposed a new type of completely electronic computational device. In

April 1943, the army contracted with Mauchly and Eckert to implement the proposal.

Mauchly and Eckert led a fifty-person team that constructed the Electronic Numerical Integrator and Computer (ENIAC), the first digital computer. Mauchly developed the mathematical theory and specifications for the new machine; Eckert supplied the engineering expertise, constructing ENIAC out of parts of existing IBM punch-card tabulators, vacuum tubes, and switches. "Get a machine out fast with off-the-shelf parts, that was the name of the game for ENIAC," was how Eckert described their work.

Construction of ENIAC was completed in December 1945. It weighed thirty tons, used nearly 18,000 vacuum tubes, and cost $486,000, but it performed numerical calculations one thousand times faster than previous electromechanical calculators. The army moved it to Aberdeen (Md.) Proving Ground in 1947 and used it for nearly ten years to design wind tunnels, study cosmic rays, and make other calculations before retiring it in 1955.

While completing work on ENIAC, Eckert and Mauchly also began work on another computer for the army, the Electronic Discrete Variable Automatic Calculator (EDVAC). After completion by others at the Moore School in 1952, EDVAC used only 2,000 vacuum tubes but was several times faster than ENIAC.

Mauchly and Eckert had filed patent applications for their computer technology in 1944. In early 1946 the University of Pennsylvania adopted a patent policy that required faculty to relinquish all patent rights or leave the university. Mauchly and Eckert resigned from the faculty on Mar. 22, 1946.

The pair founded the world's first commercial computer-manufacturing firm, the Electronic Control Company, setting up business in an office over a clothing store in Philadelphia. Eckert's family of Philadelphia real estate developers provided the initial funding, and other relatives and friends invested several hundred thousand dollars. The pair changed the company's name to the Eckert Mauchly Corporation in 1947.

Eckert and Mauchly marketed a proposed Universal Automatic Computer (UNIVAC), which would contain fully stored programs with software subroutines and use magnetic-tape input and output. They obtained contracts with the Bureau of the Census, Prudential Insurance Company, and the A. C. Nielsen Company. Designing and constructing the new computer took much longer than expected, however, and the two underestimated the amount of money necessary to finance their company's initial years of operation.

The company also contracted with the Northrop Corporation in 1947 to construct a small experimental computer for the guided missile program, the Binary Automatic Computer (BINAC). This was really two computers working in tandem, each one checking on the other, which created a "fail-safe" system using internal stored programs.

During this period, Mauchly also influenced the field of computer software by developing one of the first high-level computer languages, short code. This allowed computer programs to be written in mnemonic symbols of alphanumeric text rather than in the binary code of machine language.

In 1948, Mauchly married his second wife, Kathleen McNulty, a mathematician who had been a programmer on the ENIAC project. His first wife, Mary Walzl, whom he had married on Dec. 30, 1930, had died in a drowning accident in Atlantic City, N.J., in 1946.

Cost overruns, delays in payments, and other development problems caused difficulties for the new company. These came to a head when the company's major investor died in a plane crash in 1949. The following year Mauchly and Eckert sold their company to the Remington Rand Corporation, receiving a payment for their patent rights and salaried positions of $18,000 for the next eight years. Their company, now a division of Remington Rand, completed work on UNIVAC I in March 1951 and delivered the first UNIVAC to the Bureau of the Census in June 1951. The computer had only 5,000 vacuum tubes, but it was twenty-five times faster than ENIAC. It gained nationwide prominence when the Columbia Broadcasting System used it for a televised prediction of the winner of the 1952 presidential election. A total of forty-six UNIVACs were built by Remington Rand, which became Sperry Rand in 1955 and then UNISYS Corporation in 1986.

Mauchly was Sperry Rand's director of UNIVAC applications research until the late 1950's, when he lost his security clearance because of attendance at left-wing meetings while in college. Sperry Rand offered him a position in sales, but he resigned in 1959 to form his own consulting firm, Mauchly Associates. He continued to develop computers and created the critical path method (CPM) for computer scheduling. He founded Dynatrend in 1967, which offered consulting services in weather forecasting and stock market trends. Mauchly rejoined Sperry Rand as a consultant in 1973. He died undergoing heart surgery, in Abington, Pa.

Although unsuccessful as entrepreneurs, Mauchly and Eckert achieved fame as the inventors of the world's first electronic digital computer. Mauchly's later years were marred by litigation concerning the patent rights to ENIAC. In 1973 a federal judge ruled that patent rights held by Mauchly and Eckert were invalid because their innovations appeared to be based on earlier work by Iowa State University professor John Vincent Atanasoff. Many members of the computer science community criticized the judge's conclusions and continued to regard Eckert and Mauchly as the fathers of the electronic computer. In 1979 the Association of Computing Machinery chose to name its prestigious Eckert-Mauchly Award in their honor.

[Mauchly's correspondence and personal papers are housed at the University of Pennsylvania's Van Pelt Memorial Library in Philadelphia. There is no full-length biography, but useful portraits are in Robert Slater, *Portraits in Silicon* (1987); and James Cortada, *Historical Dictionary of Data Processing: Biographies* (1987). Articles by Mauchly in *IEEE Spectrum*, Apr. 1975; *Datamation*, Nov. 1979; and *Annals of the History of Computing*, July 1982; and by J. Presper Eckert in *Computerworld*, June 22, 1992, provide firsthand accounts of their work. Nancy Stern, *From ENIAC to UNIVAC: An Appraisal of the Eckert-Mauchly Computers* (1981), covers the business as well as the technological aspects of Mauchly's work, which are also described in the first two episodes of *The Machine That Changed the World*, a five-part series produced for the Public Broadcasting Service in 1992. Portions of ENIAC are displayed at the Smithsonian Institution, while others are at the Moore School. An obituary is in the *New York Times*, Jan. 9, 1980.]

STEPHEN G. MARSHALL

MEAD, MARGARET (Dec. 16, 1901–Nov. 15, 1978), anthropologist, was born in Philadelphia, Pa., one of five children of Edward Sherwood Mead, an economics professor at the Wharton School of the University of Pennsylvania, and Emily Fogg, a feminist and sociologist. Her parents raised their children in various towns in New Jersey and Bucks County, Pa., from which her father commuted to his work in Philadelphia. Margaret Mead graduated from the New Hope School for Girls in Pennsylvania and enrolled at DePauw University in Greencastle, Ind., in 1919. After an unhappy year, she transferred to Barnard College in New York City. There, in her senior year, she discovered her life's work, under the influence of anthropology professor Franz Boas and his assistant, Ruth Benedict, for whom Mead's affection was intense, reciprocal, and unending. At the same time she carried on a placid courtship with her fellow Pennsylvanian, Luther Sheeleigh Cressman, a theology student who had secretly been her fiancé since her teens. They were married on Sept. 3, 1923, a few months after Mead received her B.A. degree from Barnard. She received both her M.A. degree (1924) and Ph.D. (1929) from Columbia University.

Partly at Mead's urging, Cressman left the clergy for sociology, then anthropology, and eventually became a distinguished archaeologist. For Mead marriage was less compelling than her work, which in 1925 took her across the world to American Samoa. Boas sent her there on her first field trip, to undertake "a study in heredity and environment based on an investigation of the phenomenon of adolescence among primitive and civilized peoples." Her task, as she described it, would "involve working almost entirely with women, and should therefore add appreciably to our ethnological information on the subject of the culture of primitive women."

En route home after five and a half months of fieldwork, Mead fell into a shipboard romance. Reo Franklin Fortune was a brilliant young New Zealander, bound for graduate studies in psychology at Cambridge University in England (and destined to switch professions and become an anthropologist). He and Mead corresponded when Mead was back in New York, joylessly reunited with Cressman. In 1926, Mead became an assistant curator at the American Museum of Natural History, an association that lasted until her death. She completed her doctorate and finished the manuscript for *Coming of Age in Samoa* (1928), the first and best known of her thirty-two books, which asserted that there were ways and ways not only of getting through puberty but of doing almost anything.

If Samoans could get through adolescence without pain and clumsiness, then so might Americans and Europeans.

Mead and Cressman were divorced in the summer of 1928. She proceeded with plans to return to the South Seas to do more fieldwork, in partnership with Fortune, whom she married in Auckland, New Zealand, on Oct. 8, 1928. Together they headed for the Admiralty Islands, where they began work that led to his *Manus Religion* and her *Growing Up in New Guinea* (1930). In 1930 they returned to New York, then went to Nebraska on an assignment from the American Museum of Natural History to do a summer of fieldwork with a tribe of native Americans, the result of which was *The Changing Culture of an Indian Tribe* (1932). Mead and Fortune received grants in 1930 that allowed them to begin work in the Pacific the following fall.

Studying the different ways sex roles were stylized in three Melanesian tribes—the Arapesh, Mundugumor, and Tchambuli—Mead took decreasing pleasure in her teamwork with Fortune. The strain between the two had grown acute by Christmas of 1932, when they encountered British ethnographer Gregory Bateson, who was doing fieldwork of his own in the Pacific. Fortune was the odd man out in the ensuing romantic triangle. The three returned to their native countries, and Mead and Fortune divorced in 1935. Mead wrote *Sex and Temperament in Three Primitive Societies* (1935), a report of her studies of the New Guinea cultures; taught her first course at Columbia University; and kept in close touch with Bateson, whom she married in Singapore on Mar. 13, 1936.

For two years their collaboration was idyllic. First they worked in Bali (1936–1938), where they devised new research methodologies using film and photography, and then with a New Guinea tribe called the Iatmul in 1938. As World War II loomed, the couple returned to New York, where Mead gave birth to her only child, Mary Catherine Bateson. Motherhood, she was determined, would not conflict with her and Bateson's writing or with their work on the applications of social science to international crises.

Mead somehow managed to balance her domestic life with an ever-expanding array of outside commitments. In 1940 she began a two-year teaching stint at Vassar College in Poughkeepsie, N.Y. During World War II she commuted to Washington, D.C., to work on the National Research Council's Committee on Food Habits and went to England for the Office of War Information to study the relationships between British citizens, especially young women, and American troops. She and Benedict launched an ambitious postwar project sponsored by the United States Navy called Research on Contemporary Cultures at Columbia. All this was hard on her marriage, and she and Bateson were divorced in October 1950.

Setting up housekeeping in Greenwich Village with Rhoda Métraux, a widowed fellow anthropologist who also had a child, Mead did her best to keep up with old and new friends, her own large family, and all her former in-laws. Once a protégé, she became more and more a mentor to her students and her assistants at the Institute for Intercultural Studies, which she had established in 1944 at the American Museum of Natural History. In 1953, around the time she coined the term "post-menopausal zest," she returned with two young fieldworkers to Peri village in Manus. In *New Lives for Old* (1956), she described how World War II had affected the people she and Fortune had studied twenty-five years earlier.

Mead continued to write books and articles, give speeches, and agree to more responsibilities. She continued the teaching she had been doing since 1934 at Columbia University (and would do all her life) and was a visiting lecturer at the University of Cincinnati School of Medicine's Department of Psychiatry (1957–1978) and at the Menninger Foundation in Topeka, Kans. (1959). She also taught at Fordham University in New York City (1968–1970). A devout Episcopalian, always ecumenical and interdisciplinary, she took on roles with the World Council of Churches, Planned Parenthood, the United Nations, the World Federation of Mental Health (president, 1956–1957), the National Academy of Sciences, the American Anthropological Association (president, 1960), and the American Association for the Advancement of Science (president, 1975, and chairman, 1976). She spoke out for various environmental causes, made appearances on late-night television talk shows, and wrote a monthly column, one of many collaborations with Métraux, for *Redbook* magazine. As the 1970's waned she was physically thin and quite irritable, which turned out to be symptoms of pancreatic cancer, of which Mead died in New York City.

Five years after her death Mead's reputation was subjected to a severe attack from Derek Freeman, a New Zealand–born professor at the Research School of Pacific Studies at the Australian National University. Freeman based his charges on fieldwork he had conducted over six years, beginning in 1940, in Western Samoa. He asserted in *Margaret Mead and Samoa: The Making and Unmaking of an Anthropological Myth* (1983) that Mead had seriously misrepresented her first subjects' culture and character. Mead's research, Freeman contended, had been conceived as part of Boas's philosophical struggle against biological determinism and was conducted in unscholarly haste. Mead's young natives, said Freeman, had duped her. Her champions rose to Mead's defense, in print and in a series of spirited colloquia, but Freeman still challenged her reputation. Other posthumous critics, particularly indigenous scholars in the islands Mead had studied, regarded her as a coconspirator in neocolonialism. By portraying South Pacific natives in terms of savagery, cannibalism, and wanton sexuality, they asserted, she reinforced belief in Western colonialist supremacy and in a distortedly romanticized view of the Pacific Islands.

Mead's early fieldwork may have been hurried and imperfect, but in the mid-1920's, when she went off to Samoa, little formal training in field methods existed anywhere. Several years later, when Columbia University offered its first course in the subject, she was one of its first teachers. If in her early travels she was guilty of some wrong answers, she kept on asking what many strongly felt were the right and most urgent questions. The question one colleague said Mead took to Samoa was one she kept asking all her life: "How can we understand ourselves?," not "How can we understand others?"

[Mead's papers are in the Library of Congress in Washington, D.C. Her publications *Coming of Age in Samoa*, *Growing Up in New Guinea*, and *Sex and Temperament in Three Primitive Societies* were published in one volume, *From the South Seas* (1939). Other major works are *New Lives for Old* (1960); *Balinese Character*, with Gregory Bateson (1962); *Culture and Commitment* (1970); and the autobiographical *Blackberry Winter* (1972). Biographies include Jane Howard, *Margaret Mead* (1984); and Mary Catherine Bateson, *With A Daughter's Eye* (1984). See also Luther S. Cressman, *The Golden Journey* (1988); Derek Freeman, *Margaret Mead and Samoa* (1983); and Lenora Foerstel and Angela Gilliam, *Confronting the Margaret Mead Legacy* (1992).]

JANE HOWARD

MEANY, WILLIAM GEORGE (Aug. 16, 1894–Jan. 10, 1980), labor leader, was born in Harlem in New York City, the second of eight surviving children of Michael Joseph Meany, a plumber and union official, and Anne Cullen. At age five, George Meany (his given first name was never used) moved with his family to the Bronx. He attended Public School 29 there from 1899 to 1908, and Morris High School the following year. Although a good student, Meany dropped out of school at the age of fourteen. The most important influences upon the young Meany were trade unionism, partisan politics, Irish nationalism, and Roman Catholicism.

In keeping with the values of the insular community in which he grew up, Meany followed in his father's footsteps by signing on in the fall of 1910 as an unskilled helper to a local plumber. At his father's insistence, Meany enrolled in a nearby trade school, where he studied plumbing at night for an academic year. Meany worked for another three years as a plumber's apprentice and then took the journeyman plumber's exam, which he passed on his second try in 1915. After a brief probationary period, Meany on Jan. 10, 1917, became a full-fledged member of the Manhattan-Bronx local of the United Association of Journeymen and Apprentices of the Plumbing and Pipe Fitting Industry of the United States and Canada. At first he showed relatively little interest in the union's affairs, preoccupied as he was with family responsibilities. His father died suddenly in 1916, and when the United States entered World War I in April 1917, Meany's older brother John immediately enlisted in the army, leaving George Meany, at the age of twenty-two, as the sole provider for his mother and six younger siblings. As a journeyman plumber, Meany could command an hourly wage that was high enough to shoulder his considerable burden, but only if the work proved steady, which it seldom did. As a result, he had to supplement his income with money earned from playing semiprofessional baseball. By then a big, burly man, Meany earned something of a reputation as a nimble catcher. He also found time during this period to conduct a four-year courtship of Eugenie Augustina McMahon, a clothing worker and member of the International Ladies' Garment Workers' Union; they were married on Nov. 26, 1919, and had three children.

Soon after marrying, George Meany became active in the plumbers' union local 463. A practical man, Meany may have been attracted by the higher pay and greater security of a union official's life. At least as important, however, appears to have been a growing awareness that he had the brains and ability to go farther. His wife, whose own union was then in a militant, organizing phase, also seems to have encouraged him. Of course, he also had the example of his own father to guide him, and so Meany in 1919 ran for and won a seat on local 463's executive board. In September 1922, when a business agent's position opened in the local, Meany pursued it and again won, at which point he became a full-time union official.

Meany proved unusually adept at his new job, which consisted of monitoring contract compliance at job sites. Much of the work was essentially legalistic, and Meany soon developed what proved to be a lifelong interest in legal concepts and terminology. He first came to the attention of the plumbers' union leadership in 1927, when he took the then-heretical step, among older union officials at least, of seeking and winning a court injunction to defeat a lockout. He soon became secretary of the New York Building Trades Council, a job that provided only a nominal salary but enabled him to meet influential politicians and labor leaders, who were impressed by this well-dressed and well-spoken union official.

In the late 1920's and early 1930's, Meany parlayed those attributes into a major advance within New York's trade-union hierarchy. First came his election in 1932 as one of the thirteen vice-presidents of the New York State Federation of Labor. Only two years later Meany was elected its president, a fortuitous time for labor leadership, since the state legislature was then considering a whole host of bills labor wanted. By testifying before committees, making speeches, and dueling with reporters, Meany contributed significantly to the passage of groundbreaking workers' compensation, unemployment insurance, and health and safety laws. Meany also won praise for the way he handled the other parts of his job, most notably his dogged and clever bargaining with city and federal officials over wage rates for public employees, and his ability to hold together New York's endlessly feuding building trades' unions.

His record brought Meany to the attention of the American Federation of Labor, which by 1939 was looking to replace the aging and increasingly ineffective AFL secretary-treasurer, Frank Morrison. Meany's independence from the AFL's various power blocs and experience as lobbyist and spokesman struck AFL officials as the right credentials for the New Deal era. His steadiness also made him attractive. A moderate during a radical period in American labor history, Meany had contributed to the AFL's resurgence during the late 1930's in the face of a continuing challenge from the new Congress of Industrial Organizations (CIO), led by AFL renegade John L. Lewis. And so on Oct. 12, 1939, the AFL's national convention ratified his appointment, and Meany was on his way to Washington and the national stage. During World War II, Meany served as a permanent AFL representative on the National War Labor Board (NWLB), where he emerged as a blunt, tough spokesman for unions seeking wage increases. Meany at that time also became deeply concerned with foreign policy issues. Always hostile to Communists, he became ever more so during the war. In keeping with that view, Meany led the AFL boycott of the World Federation of Trade Unions (WFTU), formed in 1945, for its decision to admit Soviet trade unions. Attacking them as creatures of the Soviet state, Meany helped establish a rival federation, the International Confederation of Free Trade Unions (ICFTU), which eventually won the allegiance of all labor federations save those of the Soviet Union and its allies. Meany hailed the Truman administration's Cold War policies and strongly supported American military intervention in the Korean conflict. He blasted John L. Lewis in a memorable speech at the 1947 AFL convention for Lewis's willingness to work with American Communists.

Meany's one other major achievement as AFL secretary-treasurer lay in the realm of political action. The AFL had traditionally pursued a policy of independence from all political parties, preferring instead an opportunistic neutrality. But with the Republican-controlled Eightieth Congress's passage of the Taft-Hartley Act in 1947, opposed by all labor leaders, support within the AFL for political neutrality suffered a mortal blow. Meany, determined to oust the GOP majorities in Congress, worked to establish Labor's League for Political Education (LLPE), which the AFL formally created in December 1947. Collaboration during 1948 between the CIO's Political Action Committee (PAC) and the LLPE proved instrumental in electing Truman to a full term in his own right, and in returning control of Congress to the Democrats. In recognition of Meany's record, the AFL elected him its president when incumbent William Green died in 1952.

As AFL president Meany continued along the course he had charted in his lesser trade-union roles. A strong opponent of labor corruption, he persuaded the AFL chieftains to expel the racketeer-influenced International Longshoremen's Association (ILA) in 1953, and several other corrupt affiliates, most notably the Teamsters union, several years later. He played a major part in the quest for labor unity, working out with CIO general counsel Arthur J. Goldberg the terms of the AFL merger with the CIO in 1955. With that development, Meany became president of the AFL-CIO and the undisputed spokesman for the American labor movement. Meany also expanded upon his earlier commitment to labor's participation in partisan politics following the AFL-CIO merger by persuading the federation to pursue an electoral alliance with the Democrats, and by establishing the Committee on Political Education (COPE), a permanent AFL-CIO vehicle for influencing the election of public officials. He played a similarly important part in winning federation support for civil rights legislation and court decisions aimed at dismantling legalized segregation.

Although intimately involved in the crafting and passage of much so-called Great Society legislation in the mid-1960's, Meany by then had become a highly controversial figure within liberal circles. His early and vociferous support for American military intervention in Vietnam, which he saw as entirely consistent with the containment policy adopted in the late 1940's, alienated liberals and left-wing laborites. So, too, did his criticism of affirmative action programs aimed at compelling labor unions to set aside a certain number of jobs for nonwhites. Meany's inability to reverse the decline in the fraction of the workforce organized into unions that had begun in the late 1950's, and seeming lack of interest even in trying to do so, also alienated labor militants, most notably United Auto Workers Union (UAW) president Walter Reuther. A product of the New Deal liberal era, Meany struck 1960's liberals and new leftists as increasingly dated and "conservative." His resistance to wage-control policies and reservations about feminism as well as environmental legislation that cost jobs also hurt him among middle-class liberals. Meany's stodgy, rigid, and often dismissive manner contributed to his loss of prestige, as did his indifference to matters of image. He often appeared in public puffing on cigars, playing golf with influential politicians, and sunning himself during AFL-CIO conclaves at luxurious hotels in Bal Harbour, Fla., images that undercut his credibility as a spokesman for the American working class.

Meany's isolation from reform elements grew during his final decade as AFL-CIO president. Although labor strongly supported Jimmy Carter's election as president in 1976, Meany never enjoyed a real rapport with the Georgian, who showed little warmth to Meany the man, and failed to deliver the labor reform legislation that the AFL-CIO had wanted from the Carter administration. Increasingly feeble from severe arthritis in the late 1970's, Meany finally resigned his office and installed a handpicked successor in November 1979. Two months later he died of a heart attack in Washington, D.C.

A controversial figure for most of his career and never more so than toward its end, Meany nonetheless proved to be one of the most influential labor leaders in American history. If formally only the chief clerk of a federation whose member unions had most of the real power, Meany proved adept at guiding them more like the head of a centralized western European labor movement than any other American labor leader, before or since. In many ways Meany was the prototype of the modern American labor leader: strongly supportive of a market system and firmly believing in the need for unions both to humanize and sustain it, militantly hostile to Communism as a betrayal of workers' highest aspirations, practical when dealing with employers and government officials but zealous in protecting unions' autonomy from both, and temperamentally committed to gradualist reform. The quintessential organization man, Meany was, as he himself sometimes reminded listeners, a labor leader who had never walked a picket line, organized a local, or led a strike. It was precisely those qualities that made him so novel, successful, and controversial a figure throughout his long career.

[Meany's papers are in the George Meany Memorial Archives, Silver Spring, Md. See Joseph C. Goulden, *Meany* (1972) and Archie Robinson, *George Meany and His Times* (1981). Three important articles are John Corry, "The Many-Sided Mr. Meany," *Harper's*, Mar. 1970; Byron E. Calame, "Labor's Durable King of the Hill," *Wall Street Journal*, Oct. 23, 1973; and Robert H. Zieger, "George Meany: Labor's Organization Man," in Melvyn Dubofsky and Warren Van Tine, eds., *Labor Leaders in America* (1987). An obituary is in the *New York Times*, Jan. 11, 1980.]

DAVID L. STEBENNE

MERCER, JOHN HERNDON ("JOHNNY") (Nov. 18, 1909–June 25, 1976), lyricist, composer, and singer, was born into a fairly well-to-do family in Savannah, Ga., the son of George A. Mercer, a lawyer and real estate salesman whose ancestors had emigrated to the colonies from Scotland in 1747, and Lillian Ciucevich, the daughter of an Austrian merchant who settled in Savannah in the 1850's. Johnny had three older half-brothers from his father's first marriage, and one sister. The Mercer boys were sent to Woodberry Forest School near Orange, Va., where Mercer seemed more interested in poetry and music than academics, writing his first song at age fifteen (a jazz number entitled "Sister Suzie, Strut Your Stuff"). Upon graduation in 1927, Mercer worked briefly and unsuccessfully in his father's business, which by then was sinking as a result of an overall decline in real estate prices. George Mercer finally had to liquidate his assets and borrow $15,000 to "stay off the charity rolls." When he died in 1940 at age seventy-three he owed his creditors $300,000 (a debt that Mercer repaid years later to clear his father's name).

Mercer's mother wanted him to be an actor, and he joined the Savannah Little Theater in 1927 at her urging. Later that year, the group went to New York City to participate in the Belasco Cup, a one-act play competition, from which the group emerged with first prize. Mercer subsequently decided to remain in New York, making his Broadway debut in 1928 in Ben Jonson's *Volpone*, followed by other minor roles. He failed the audition for a singing part in the *Garrick Gaieties of 1930*, but succeeded in placing one of his songs in the show. He also succeeded in captivating one of the dancers from the *Gaieties*, Ginger Meehan, whom he married on June 8, 1931. They had two children. The newlyweds moved to Brooklyn and Mercer divided his time between trying to make it as a songwriter and struggling to earn a living as a runner on Wall Street.

Mercer was familiar with the work of other songwriters and poets. In the early 1930's he was fortunate to make the acquaintance of such noteworthy contemporaries as Yip Harburg, Vernon Duke, and Hoagy Carmichael. At first, Harburg served as a mentor (they collaborated on one song, "Satan's Li'l Lamb," which appeared in the Broadway revue *Americana* in 1932), teaching him how to work a song to perfection, even if it required using *Roget's Thesaurus* and a rhyming dictionary. It was, however, Mercer's southern background, his ear for dialect, and his familiarity with such African-American forms as jazz and blues that gave his lyrics both charm and poignancy. In 1933 he released his first hit, "Lazybones," for which Carmichael had provided the music. Shot through with authentic southern regionalism, it was quite a contrast to the mock-folksiness offered by New York songwriters.

It was also in 1933 that Mercer began a two-year association with the Paul Whiteman Orchestra, as a vocalist, emcee, and songwriter for Whiteman's radio program. His growing success as a lyricist and recording artist (particularly his duets with Jack Teagarden) led to a songwriting and acting contract with RKO Studios, taking Mercer to Hollywood in 1935 to write songs for and appear in two pictures, *Old Man Rhythm* and *To Beat the Band*. Although Mercer never acted in another picture, he got a foothold in Hollywood as a songwriter with the 1936 hit "I'm an Old Cowhand" (sung by Bing Crosby in the movie *Rhythm on the Range*). His songwriting work for the movie *Hollywood Hotel* (1937), which featured Benny Goodman's orchestra, led to his joining Goodman's "Camel Caravan" radio program as a vocalist. Other hit songs in the 1930's included "Goody, Goody" (1936) and "And the Angels Sing" (1939), both Goodman vehicles, as well as "Jeepers Creepers" (1938), inspired by actor Henry Fonda's midwestern twang, and "Day In, Day Out" (1939), another big-band favorite. During this period his collaborators included Richard Whiting, Harry Warren, Rube Bloom, and Jimmy Van Heusen, among others.

Mercer

Mercer said he preferred to work from an already composed melody, and the quality of his lyrics depended often on the quality of the material he was given. As he described it (in an oft-repeated story), he would sit at the typewriter and type dozens of alternative lines, then weed out the poor ones until he had what he wanted. His feeling for the rhythmic subtleties of jazz is unparalleled among Tin Pan Alley songwriters, and a large number of Mercer songs (such as "Skylark" and "Satin Doll") went on to become essential jazz vocal repertoire. Although capable of the urbane wordplay that flavored many Broadway hits of the era, Mercer was at his best when he reflected on images of small-town America (trains, back roads, front porches), and he was able to do so without being trite. His collaborations with Harold Arlen were particularly successful because Arlen was able to provide the requisite mixture of jazz and blues Mercer needed as a framework for his stories. Their first hit, "Blues in the Night" (1941), was so impressive that the producers of a movie it was to be featured in changed the title of the film (originally *Hot Nocturne*) to fit the song. Later collaborations with Arlen included "That Old Black Magic" (1942) and "One for My Baby (and One More for the Road)" (1943), a torch song that became inextricably associated with Frank Sinatra (much as Mercer's "Come Rain or Come Shine" became identified with Judy Garland and "Satin Doll" with Ella Fitzgerald).

In 1942, Mercer (along with Glenn Wallichs and Buddy DeSylva) founded Capitol Records, where as president and talent scout he helped develop the careers of such major stars as Nat King Cole, Peggy Lee, Stan Kenton, and Jo Stafford. While Mercer had no great interest in the record business as such, and later sold his interest in the company, the Capitol catalog remains a significant part of his legacy.

Although Mercer wrote the music for seven Broadway shows, none of them was a big hit. Most of his 1,500 songs were written for the movies. The last of the great Tin Pan Alley songwriters, his career unfortunately was maturing just as the Broadway musical theater was changing its emphasis from "the song" to "the show," a transition Mercer found difficult. In 1946 he and Arlen collaborated on *St. Louis Woman*, a black folk drama in the tradition of *Porgy and Bess*, but it closed after only 113 performances. Later efforts, even good shows such as *Li'l Abner*, were also relative flops, unable to compete with such new, plot-based musicals as *South Pacific* and *Guys and Dolls*. Hollywood also was in transition. As the studios gradually gave up producing original musicals in favor of remakes of successful Broadway shows, Mercer was relegated to writing "movie themes," beginning with "Laura" in 1945 (although as late as 1954 he was writing material for an original musical film, *Seven Brides for Seven Brothers*). He shared Academy Awards for best song for his lyrics to "On the Atchison, Topeka, and the Sante Fe," written with Harry Warren for *The Harvey Girls* (1946), and "In the Cool, Cool, Cool of the Evening," written with Carmichael for *Here Comes the Groom* (1951). But Tin Pan Alley was rapidly fading; record sales had replaced sheet music as the major revenue source in popular music, and the market had moved toward rock and roll (and its antecedents, rhythm and blues and country) and the teenage consumer.

As the market shifted, and the thirty-two-bar "A-A-B-A" format became less viable, songwriters like Mercer had an uphill climb. By the 1950's, Mercer was working without a collaborator, setting words to instrumentals such as "Autumn Leaves" (1950) and "Midnight Sun" (1954). He continued to achieve pronounced success with these efforts, as well as with movie themes, such as "Moon River" (1961) and "Days of Wine and Roses" (1962), both of which, with music composed by Henry Mancini, won Academy Awards. As late as 1965 a Mercer song, "Summer Wind," could be seen at the top of the charts. His songs from this period exhibited a recurrent theme of wistful recollection of time past.

Mercer was a reluctant melody-writer, perhaps because he lacked musical training, but he wrote words and music for a couple of musicals (*Daddy Long Legs*, *Top Banana*), as well as for a few hits ("Dream," "I'm an Old Cowhand," "Something's Gotta Give"). A dedicated craftsman, he traced his musical heritage back to the Englishman William S. Gilbert (of Gilbert and Sullivan), but he will be remembered as the most American of songwriters, whose songs served as themes for such classic jazz and ballad singers as Billie Holiday, Sinatra, and Tony Bennett.

By all accounts a convivial fellow (who could become quite temperamental after a few drinks), Mercer liked to swim and paint watercolors, as well as play tennis and golf. He maintained a home in Savannah, Ga., and an apartment in New York, but his main residence was in Los Angeles. Mercer died at his home in Bel-Air, eight months after undergoing brain surgery, from which he never recovered. In 1982 his widow donated a collection of memorabilia to Georgia State University in Atlanta, including all his published songs, photographs, letters, and awards.

[Essays on Mercer appear in Gene Lees, *Singers and the Song* (1987); and Philip Furia, *The Poets of Tin Pan Alley* (1990). Bob Bach and Ginger Mercer put out an annotated edition of Mercer's lyrics entitled *Our Huckleberry Friend* (1982). There is a compilation of Mercer songs by Capitol artists, *Too Marvelous for Words* (CDP 7 96791 2). Also of interest is a recording of Mercer singing his material, entitled simply *Johnny Mercer* (also on Capitol, C2 792125 2). An obituary is in the *New York Times*, June 26, 1976.]

JOSEPH BLUM

MERCHANT, LIVINGSTON TALLMADGE (Nov. 23, 1903–May 15, 1976), government official and diplomat, was born in New York City, one of two children of Huntington Wolcott Merchant and Mary Floyd Tallmadge. His ancestors on his father's side included Oliver Wolcott, George Washington's secretary of the Treasury; and, on his mother's side, William Floyd, a signer of the Declaration of Independence. "Livy," as his friends usually called him, was educated at the Hotchkiss School in Lakeville, Conn., and at Princeton University; he graduated in 1922 and 1926, respectively. Following graduation from Princeton, Merchant pursued a successful career as an investment counselor with the prominent Boston firm of Scudder, Stevens, and Clark, becoming a partner in 1930. On Dec. 10, 1927, he married Elizabeth Stiles of Washington, D.C.; the couple had three children.

After the United States entered World War II, Merchant began what would be a twenty-year career with the State Department. His first position, as assistant chief of the division of defense materials from 1942 to 1945, proved an especially demanding one in view of the critical importance and sensitivity of procurement issues during wartime. In 1945 he was appointed chief of the war areas division, another post in which Merchant's expertise in economic matters served him in good stead. Later that year, he accepted his first overseas assignment, becoming the counselor for economic affairs at the American Embassy in Paris. In 1947, in the middle of a two-year stint back in Washington as chief of the State Department's aviation division, he formally joined the foreign service.

In 1948, Merchant was posted to China as the counselor of the American Embassy in Nanking. In that position he witnessed the final stages of the Chinese civil war. The Nationalist government of Chiang Kai-shek, to which he was accredited, disintegrated in front of Merchant's eyes, its remnants fleeing to Taiwan with the establishment of the Communist regime in October 1949. Like many of his colleagues serving with the United States diplomatic corps in China at that time, Merchant had grown disillusioned with the corruption and isolation of Chiang's government and believed that some form of rapprochement should be pursued between the United States and the People's Republic of China. Consequently, he joined the State Department's "China hands" in advocating formal recognition of the government of Mao Tse-tung.

Merchant continued to advocate that position upon his return to Washington late in 1949 to assume his new job as the deputy assistant secretary of state for Far Eastern affairs. But, like the man he served under for much of that time, Assistant Secretary Dean Rusk, Merchant never forcefully advanced his personal views. Indeed, Merchant's trademark throughout his career was the low-key, team-player approach favored by most career foreign service officers. During his two years as deputy assistant secretary of state, he participated regularly in the often rancorous policy debates concerning China, Korea, Japan, and Indochina without ever becoming strongly associated with a particular policy orientation.

In November 1951, Merchant was named special assistant to the secretary of state on mutual security affairs. The next year, he was again posted to Paris, this time as deputy for political affairs to the United States special representative in Europe. He served simultaneously as the alternate United States special representative to the North Atlantic Treaty Organization Council. Merchant remained in that position until early 1953, having attained the rank of ambassador in 1952. Among his other responsibilities, Merchant played an important role in the development and supervision of the European Recovery Program.

At the time of Dwight D. Eisenhower's accession to the presidency in January 1953, Merchant ranked as one of the foreign service's most respected diplomats. That reputation solidified during the Eisenhower years, as Merchant was increasingly tapped for the most important and difficult diplomatic assignments. He served as assistant secretary of state for European affairs from 1953 to 1956, and again from 1958 to 1959; in 1959, he was named under secretary of state for political affairs, the third-highest-ranking position within the State Department and a post he maintained until the early days of the John F. Kennedy presidency.

During his first tour of duty as head of the European bureau, Merchant helped Eisenhower and Secretary of State John Foster Dulles respond to the changes in Soviet policy that occurred after Joseph Stalin's death in 1953, played a leading role in the "Big Four" (comprising Soviet, American, British, and French heads of state) summit meeting at Geneva in 1955, and served as a senior adviser to Eisenhower at the Berlin conference of 1954 and the London, Geneva, and Paris conferences of 1955. Those conferences dealt primarily with East-West issues, European security, and the German question. In addition to those duties, both Eisenhower and Kennedy dispatched Merchant on a number of delicate negotiating missions. Among other matters, he helped promote an improvement in United States–Panamanian relations following a dispute in 1959 over the canal zone, and he worked to achieve a temporary rapprochement between Pakistan and Afghanistan following a flare-up in tensions between those rival nations in 1961.

Merchant also served two separate stints as United States ambassador to Canada, from 1956 to 1958 and again from 1961 to 1962. Although relations between the United States and Canada have historically been placid, during his tenure in Ottawa, Merchant needed to respond with unusual sensitivity to a burgeoning anti-Americanism that had become a potent force in Canadian political life. The pervasive American economic presence and cultural influence within the country fueled Canadian resentment toward the United States, helping propel conservative nationalist John G. Diefenbaker into the prime ministership in the general elections of June 1957. Merchant did his best to ease the ensuing strain in relations between the two NATO allies. Utilizing the calm personal demeanor, command of details, and diplomatic professionalism that formed his stock-in-trade, he helped soothe angry voices on both sides of the border.

Following his retirement from the foreign service in 1962, Merchant served as the United States executive director of the World Bank from 1965 to 1968. He died at his home in Washington, D.C., after suffering a heart attack.

[Merchant's papers are in the Rare Books and Special Collections Department, Firestone Library, Princeton University. Merchant has not yet been the subject of a biography, nor has he received more than cursory treatment in the general literature on American foreign relations. A useful, but brief, treatment of his early diplomatic career, by Edward C. Keefer, can be found in *Historical Dictionary of the Korean War*, edited by James I. Matray (1991). Obituaries are in the *New York Times* and the *Washington Post*, both May 17, 1976.]

ROBERT J. MCMAHON

METCALF, LEE WARREN (Jan. 28, 1911–Jan. 12, 1978), lawyer and United States senator, was born and grew up on a 300-acre farm near Stevensville, Mont., the son of Harold Everett Metcalf, a bank cashier, and Rhoda Ann Smith. After graduating from the local public high school, he attended the University of Montana for one year, then transferred to Stanford University in California, where he studied history and economics. He returned to Montana to study law. In 1936 he received both the B.A. from Stanford and the LL.B. from the University of Montana School of Law.

In November 1936, Metcalf was elected to represent Ravalli County in the Montana State House of Representatives. The following year he was appointed an assistant attorney general for the state. He rose to the position of first assistant attorney general and served in that position until 1941, when he resigned to enter private law practice in Hamilton, Mont. On Aug. 20, 1938, he married Donna Albertine Hoover of Wallace, Idaho. They had one foster son.

After the United States entered World War II, Metcalf enlisted in the army and was selected for officer candidate school. He was commissioned in 1943 and served as a staff officer with the Fifth Corps during the Normandy invasion. In subsequent campaigns he served with the Sixtieth Infantry Regiment, Ninth Infantry Division, First Army. As Allied troops entered Germany, he helped to organize the occupational police and civilian court systems. After the German surrender, he supervised housing and repatriation of displaced persons, helped to draft the ordinance for the first free local elections in Germany, and supervised elections in Bavaria. He was discharged in April 1946 with the rank of first lieutenant.

After returning to Montana, Metcalf won a nonpartisan election in 1946 to a six-year term as an associate justice of the Montana Supreme Court. In 1952 he was elected as a Democrat to the United States House of Representatives from Montana's First District, composed of the mountainous western third of the state. He served in the House for eight years, holding membership in the Education and Labor Committee and the Interior and Insular Affairs Committee during most of that period. In his last term he won a seat on the powerful tax-writing Ways and Means Committee. A bold and energetic congressman, Metcalf established a record during his four terms in the House as a vociferous opponent of private power companies, a supporter of federal aid to education, and an ardent conservationist. He vigorously crusaded for the protection of public lands from private exploitation and the preservation of wildlife habitats.

During the 1950's the congressional seniority system placed conservative southern Democrats in many of the key leadership positions in the House. As a liberal Democrat, Metcalf frequently opposed the leadership of his own party as well as the Republican Eisenhower administration. In 1957 he joined with other liberals to found the Democratic Study Group, which advocated policy positions rejected by the party leadership, and participated in an unsuccessful attempt to reduce the power of the conservative chairman of the House Education and Labor Committee. Two years later he participated in another unsuccessful reform movement—this time to make it more difficult for the conservative Rules Committee to block liberal legislation.

In 1960, Metcalf ran for the Senate and won the seat by a narrow margin despite a Republican victory in the Montana presidential race. He was reelected in 1966 and 1972.

Metcalf brought his interests in conservation of natural resources, education, and consumer protection to the Senate. His committee assignments included Interior and Insular Affairs, Public Works, Government Operations, and Energy and Natural Resources. In 1962 he introduced a bill that he termed "Save Our Streams" to protect recreational resources from damage caused by interstate highways. He withdrew the bill after the Federal Highway Administration incorporated its principles into its regulations. He also sponsored the Senate version of the Wilderness Act to protect natural areas from exploitation. In 1965 he achieved a major goal of his political career with the passage of the Elementary and Secondary Education Act, providing federal financial aid to education.

As a consumer advocate, Metcalf continued to focus public attention on the privileges accorded to privately owned utilities. In his 1967 book *Overcharge*, coauthored by Vic Reinemer, he compared the electric rates of investor-owned utilities with those charged by publicly owned ones and concluded that customers of the private companies paid an average of $60 per year in excess charges. His proposals for tighter supervision failed to pass, however.

Perhaps as a result of his service in the House, where he had participated in two major revolts against the established ways of the institution, Metcalf was convinced that organizational reform was the only way to make Congress more responsive to the public interest. In 1965 he was appointed to the newly established Joint Committee on the Organization of Congress, which made a number of recommendations for reform and laid the groundwork for the Legislative Reorganization Act of 1970, the first serious reform of congressional organization and procedures since 1946. The 1970 law established the Joint Committee on Congressional Operations, which Metcalf cochaired for the remainder of his Senate career.

A legislative supporter of Democratic presidents John F. Kennedy and Lyndon B. Johnson, Metcalf was elected acting president pro tempore of the Senate in 1963. As one of the most consistently liberal members of the Senate, he frequently opposed the legislative proposals of Republican president Richard M. Nixon. In 1970 he cast the only Senate vote against Nixon's omnibus crime bill, asserting that it would take away the basic rights of individuals. Washington radio commentator Joseph McCaffrey likened Metcalf to a bulldog: "Once he digs his teeth into an issue he stays with it. . . . The tougher it is, the more tenacious he becomes."

Metcalf died in Helena, Mont., where he had made his home.

[Metcalf's papers are at the Montana Historical Society in Helena. See Richard D. Warden, *Metcalf of Montana* (1965); and D. A. Burke et al., "The Legacy of Lee Metcalf," *Living Wilderness*, June 1979. Obituaries are in the *New York Times* and the *Washington Post*, both Jan. 13, 1978.]

VAGN HANSEN

METCALFE, RALPH HAROLD (May 30, 1910–Oct. 10, 1978), congressman and athlete, was born in Atlanta, Ga., the son of Clarence Metcalfe and Maria Attaway. The family moved to Chicago in 1917. He attended Tilden Technical High School there, and he showed early promise as a track star. In 1930, running as a member of the Chase Athletic Club, he won the AAU junior 100-yard dash in 9.7 seconds. On June 11, 1932, Metcalfe broke the world record in the 220-yard dash and tied the record for the 100-yard dash. His principal opponent at this time was Thomas ("Eddie") Tolan, Jr., of Detroit. These two men are said to have marked the beginning of black domination of the short races.

In the 1932 Olympics, held in Los Angeles, Metcalfe won the silver medal in the 100-meter dash and the bronze in the 200-meter dash, finishing behind Tolan. At the 1936 Olympics in Berlin, he finished second in the 100-meter race, just behind Jesse Owens. Metcalfe received a gold medal as a member of the American 100-meter relay team. Although Germany won more gold medals than any other nation at the 1936 Olympics, Hitler was angered by the black domination of these track and field events.

In 1936, Metcalfe earned a Ph.B. degree from Marquette University in Milwaukee, and in 1939 the M.A. degree from the University of Southern California. He taught physical education and political science and was track coach at Xavier University in New Orleans from 1936 to 1942 and served in the United States Army from 1942 to 1945, rising to the rank of first lieutenant. While in the army he organized and directed the physical education program for troop training, a service for which he received the Legion of Merit. On July 20, 1947, Metcalfe married Madelynne Fay Young; they had one child.

Back in Chicago after the war, Metcalfe held a number of high-profile positions. He was a member of the Chicago Commission on Human Relations from 1945 to 1949 and headed the Illinois Athletic Commission from 1949 to 1952. He was elected committeeman for the Third Ward in the Democratic organization and served on the Chicago City Council from 1955 to 1970.

Metcalfe was elected to the United States House of Representatives in 1970, representing the First District of Illinois. The district had been in the hands of a black congressman since 1928 when Oscar De Priest, a Republican, had been elected. Metcalfe was reelected to Congress in 1972, 1974, and 1976; he won the 1978 primary election as well but died before the general election. He was opposed by black militants until he spoke out against police brutality in 1972.

Metcalfe was a member of the House Committee on Interstate and Foreign Commerce and the subcommittee on Transportation and Commerce as well as the subcommittee on Consumer Protection and Commerce. He also served on the House Committee on Merchant Marine and Fisheries and was chairman of its subcommittee on the Panama Canal. Metcalfe was secretary of the Democratic Study Group and vice-chairman of its task force on crime and drug abuse. He was member of the Democratic Steering and Policy Committee in 1975.

Metcalfe was a director of the National Council to Control Handguns. He served in several groups aimed at fostering the well-being of African-American people: the NAACP, the Urban League, the Joint Negro Appeal, the Mahalia Jackson Scholarship Fund, and the Dr. Martin Luther King Urban Progress Center; he established the Ralph H. Metcalfe Youth Foundation. He was also involved with groups promoting athletic excellence: the Athletic Advisory Commission and the Midwest chapter of United States Olympians. He was elected to the Helms Athletic Foundation, the United States Track and Field Hall of Fame, the National Track and Field Hall of Fame, and the Black Athletes Hall of Fame.

Metcalfe died in Chicago of an apparent heart attack.

[The most complete account of Metcalfe's athletic career is in Arthur R. Ashe, Jr., *A Hard Road to Glory* (1981). An obituary is in the *New York Times*, Oct. 11, 1978.]

DONALD F. TINGLEY

MEUSEL, ROBERT WILLIAM (July 19, 1896–Nov. 28, 1977), baseball player, was born in San Jose, Calif., the son of Charles F. Meusel, a teamster, and Mary Smith. The youngest of six children, Robert was raised in Los Angeles and followed his three older brothers into athletics. His brother Emil ("Irish") Meusel starred for the Philadelphia Phillies and New York Giants. After graduating from Los Angeles High School in 1916, Robert started his baseball career on a semiprofessional team in Arizona. The following year he played on a minor-league ball team in Vernon, a Los Angeles suburb, in the Pacific Coast League. After batting .311 as a part-timer in 1917, Meusel served in the United States Navy, where he sharpened his baseball skills by playing for navy squads against major league teams. He returned to Vernon for the 1919 season and his .337 batting average earned him a contract with the New York Yankees in 1920.

Tall and rangy at six feet, three inches and 190 pounds (hence his nickname "Long Bob"), Meusel played briefly at third base before shifting to the outfield midway through his rookie season. With eleven home runs, his slugging prowess and powerful throwing arm garnered praise, yet his performance was overshadowed by Babe Ruth's initial season in Yankee pinstripes. Ruth's fifty-four home runs surpassed the output by each of the major league's other fifteen franchises except for the Philadelphia Phillies.

In 1921, Meusel emerged as a star, batting .318, tying for second in the American League in home runs (24), and finishing third in runs batted in (135). He also placed third in total bases (334) and first in outfield assists (28) as the Yankees won their first pennant in team history. That October, he played against his brother Emil, then a star outfielder for the New York Giants, in the 1921 World Series. Following the Yankees' defeat, Meusel joined his friend Babe Ruth on an unsanctioned barnstorming tour. As a result, Baseball Commissioner Judge Kenesaw Mountain Landis suspended both men for the first thirty-eight days of the 1922 season. On Dec. 14, 1921, Meusel married Edith Cowan; they had one child.

Meusel undermined his tremendous physical skills with a surly attitude that exasperated fans, Yankees management, and the press. Longtime Yankees manager Miller Huggins criticized Meusel's attitude as "one of just plain indifference." Although few players of his generation matched his batting power, strong throwing arm, and running speed, Meusel never satisfied those who felt his talents should have produced greater results. Despite a lifetime batting average of .309 that included five years with more than 100 RBIs, Meusel's languid style left fans questioning his desire and hustle.

Meusel's throwing arm has been regarded as the strongest in major league history by national magazines and baseball experts like Casey Stengel. Indeed, after Meusel led the American League in outfield assists in his first two complete seasons in the outfield, opposing runners rarely tested his arm. Yet his throwing talents did not appease critics who felt he did not hustle after balls hit to his post in left field.

A quiet man both on and off the diamond, Meusel did not enjoy a good working relationship with the New York press until late in his career. Famed sportswriter Frank Graham described Meusel's character when he said, "He's learning to say hello when it's time to say goodbye."

During a game against Detroit in 1924, Meusel precipitated one of the worst brawls in the annals of the game. In the top of the ninth inning, the Yanks were comfortably ahead of the Tigers 10–6 when the Detroit hurler Bert Cole threw several pitches that nearly beaned batter Babe Ruth. When Meusel, following Ruth in the lineup, was struck in the back by a Cole fastball he charged the pitcher and swung wildly at him. The confrontation escalated when Tigers manager Ty Cobb ran in from his center-field position and Babe Ruth ran toward him. Soon, players from both teams and most of the 18,000 fans in attendance had rushed the field and were embroiled in fights. Policemen came onto the field, but they proved no match for the fighters. The umpires could only declare the game forfeited to the Yankees. Meusel and Cole were suspended for ten days and fined for their roles in the riot; Ruth was also fined $50.

Ironically, Meusel enjoyed his greatest individual success on the 1925 Yankees squad that finished an ignominious seventh out of eight teams in the American League. Babe Ruth missed much of the season as a result of his infamous "bellyache," and Meusel led all American League batters with 33 home runs and 138 RBIs. A key member of the Yankees' "Murderers' Row" that terrorized pitchers throughout the 1920's, Meusel hit for the cycle three times in his career (an American League record), belted more than 40 doubles in five different seasons, and knocked in 1,005 runs during his ten-year Yankee career. His .311 overall batting average with New York ranked sixth in team history and he stood in the top ten in team doubles, triples, and RBIs. A smart base runner, Meusel led the Yanks in stolen bases five times and finished second in the American League with 26 stolen bases in 1924 and 24 in 1927. He stole home twice during World Series games, once in 1921 and again in 1928.

Yet Meusel did not excel in World Series play for the Yankees, who were pennant winners six times between 1921 and 1928. Although he led Yankee batters with a .300 average in the 1922 World Series, he batted only .225 with one home run over his thirty-four World Series games. His muff of a fly ball in the decisive seventh game of the 1926 World Series propelled the St. Louis Cardinals to a 3–2 triumph and the championship.

Following a mediocre .261 average in the 1929 season, the Yankees sold Meusel's contract to the Cincinnati Reds in the National League, where he closed out his major league career in 1930. He played the following two years in the minor leagues at Minneapolis and Hollywood. After retiring from the game, Meusel worked for fifteen years as a security guard at the United States Navy base at Terminal Island, Calif., and lived in nearby Redondo Beach. He died in Downey, Calif., where he lived with his wife and daughter.

[The Baseball Hall of Fame Library in Cooperstown, N.Y., contains clippings on Meusel's baseball career. See also John J. Ward, "Bob Meusel, the Rookie Who Slugs Like Babe Ruth," *Baseball Magazine*, Sept. 1920; and Frank Graham, *The New York Yankees: An Informal History* (1943). An obituary is in the *New York Times*, Nov. 30, 1977.]

STEPHEN WEINSTEIN

MEYER, ANDRÉ BENOIT MATHIEU (Sept. 3, 1898–Sept. 9, 1979), financier, was born in Paris, France, the son of Jules Meyer, a small businessman, and Lucie Cerf. After what would be considered a secondary school education in the United States, André Meyer obtained a post as messenger for a financial house that was a member of the French Bourse (stock market). From there he became a trader at the Bourse, where he caught the attention of David David-Weill, who headed the small but prestigious banking firm of Lazard Frères and who provided him with a job in which he learned the rudiments of investment banking.

In 1922, Meyer married Bella Lehman, with whom he had a son (Philippe) and a daughter (Francine). Among his grandchildren at the time of his death were Patrick Gerschel, Laurent Gerschel, and Marianne Gerschel Merrick, all of whom became partners at Lazard, and who were his daughter Francine's children. There were also five great-grandchildren.

In 1927, Meyer was named a partner at Lazard, where for the next fourteen years he was involved in a series of spectacular underwritings and organizations, the most famous of which was the creation of Sovac, a pioneering finance company.

Meyer recognized the dangers posed by Adolf Hitler and the National Socialist party in Germany, and he later claimed to have helped fund a plot to assassinate the Nazi leader. When France surrendered to Germany in 1940, Meyer took his family to the United States, where he found a place at the American branch of Lazard, working with the firm's chief executive officer, Frank Altschul. When Altschul retired in 1943, Meyer became its senior partner. Five years later he became an American citizen.

There were three kinds of investment banks in the period immediately after World War II. The best known were those concentrating on brokerage, especially the larger ones, known as "wire houses." Merrill Lynch, Pierce, Fenner and Beane, and E. F. Hutton were the best known of these. They concentrated on serving small as well as some larger customers by buying and selling stocks and bonds for their accounts. The second type of investment banks were those that concentrated on raising capital for clients by selling their new issues of stock and bonds to individual and institutional accounts. Kuhn Loeb and Morgan Stanley were among the leaders in this category. Both types of firms had ambitions to expand into other areas; Merrill would enter underwriting, while some investment banks purchased brokerages or started their own, in attempts to become what later would be called "financial supermarkets."

Meyer had no such ambitions for Lazard. Rather, under his leadership Lazard concentrated on offering advice to corporations and individuals regarding their investments and occasionally purchasing properties so as to sell them later at a substantial profit. Typically, Lazard would structure a deal for a client and then, when it was necessary to raise funds by marketing securities, would put together a syndicate, including wire houses and investment banks, and direct its efforts. Meyer described the practice as "financial engineering." No one was more adept at the practice. David Rockefeller, one of his clients and associates, called him "in many ways, the most creative financial genius of our time in the investment banking field."

Meyer was at the height of his power and influence during the conglomerate era of the 1970's, when Lazard advised many companies seeking to grow through acquisitions. One of these was International Telephone and Telegraph (ITT), which was headed by Harold Geneen, the most famous conglomerator of his time. Meyer engineered Lazard's purchase of Avis Rent a Car System for around $7 million; a few years later it was sold to ITT for $52 million in stock.

Meyer preferred to operate behind the scenes, leaving the spotlight to younger partners, such as Felix Rohatyn, who was ITT's banker and who had a seat on ITT's board of directors. Rohatyn engineered the Avis purchase and many others of the Geneen era. He also served such Lazard clients as Schenley, Radio Corporation of America, United Aircraft, Lone Star Cement, and Transamerica. If most readers of business pages concluded that Rohatyn was the star on Wall Street, industry insiders realized that Meyer was the real power at Lazard and that Rohatyn's successes were in great measure due to Meyer's patronage.

Meyer's other activities included philanthropies and art. He was a major benefactor of New York University, the Louvre in Paris, and the Museum of Modern Art in New York. He was active in politics, making donations to both the Republican and Democratic parties to ensure influence and access no matter who was in power. He was an adviser to Jacqueline Kennedy and helped draft her prenuptial contract when she married Aristotle Onassis.

Despite his successes, Meyer was never truly secure after fleeing Europe. He had no confidants or close friends. "Did I ever trust anyone?" he responded to his granddaughter. "No, but I wished I could have." He lived in the Carlyle Hotel, because, said Rohatyn, "he wanted to be able to go downstairs on any day and check out and leave—to just shut the door, turn in the key, pick up his airplane ticket, and go."

At the time of his death, Meyer's worth was estimated at around $250 million, although some thought it was closer to $500 million. His successor as Lazard chairman was Michel David-Weill, who once headed the firm's Paris branch but who had worked with Meyer in New York for several years. This came as a surprise to those outside the firm who had expected Rohatyn to succeed Meyer. By then, however, Rohatyn had gained celebrity status as the banker who had engineered New York City's recovery from its 1975 financial crisis and was more valuable to the firm as a deal maker than as an executive.

[Cary Reich, *Financier: The Biography of Andre Meyer* (1983), is a critical biography of André Meyer. For a view of Lazard in this period, see Karen W. Arenson, "Lazard Prospers on Plan Bequeathed by Meyer," in the *New York Times*, Sept. 11, 1979. Obituaries are in the *New York Times* and the *Washington Post*, both Sept. 11, 1979.]

ROBERT SOBEL

MIELZINER, JO (Mar. 19, 1901–Mar. 15, 1976), stage designer, was born in Paris, France, the second son of Leo Mielziner, a portrait painter, and Ella MacKenna Friend, a fashion and arts journalist. After the family's return to America in 1909, his parents encouraged his talent for painting. At age fifteen, Mielziner left the Ethical Culture School in New York City, having received a scholarship to the Pennsylvania Academy of Fine Arts. In September 1918 he enlisted in the United States Marine Corps and served briefly in World War I.

In 1919 he received the Pennsylvania Academy's Cresson traveling scholarship for two successive years. Touring Europe, Mielziner observed revolutionary changes in staging and theatrical design, worked under Viennese designer Oscar Strand, and visited designer-visionary Gordon Craig in Rapallo, Italy.

Having decided on a theater career, Mielziner worked in June 1921 as actor, stage manager, and assistant designer for Jessie Bonstelle's famous stock company in Detroit. Mielziner then apprenticed himself to three men who had introduced modernist design ("the New Stagecraft") to Broadway: he painted scenery in the

New York studio of Joseph Urban, and when the Theatre Guild hired him in 1923 as a bit-actor and assistant stage manager, Mielziner worked under Robert Edmond Jones and Guild designer Lee Simonson.

By 1924, Mielziner was working with the "frenetic haste" he would later decry. The Theatre Guild first hired him to design Ferenc Molnár's *The Guardsman*, starring Alfred Lunt and Lynn Fontanne (1924). He did four plays that first season, and eight the next; commissions kept piling up. Mielziner later complained that staff costs forced designers "to accept more commissions than any man would wish to take on during a season." Though he preferred to "brood" on a design project, he rarely found the time during his hundred-hour workweeks. By 1976, he had designed the sets, lighting, and often the costumes for more than three hundred (some count four hundred) productions. Given the pressure, the high overall quality of his designs is astonishing.

Beginning his profession when few theater professionals understood the full potential of scene design, Mielziner had to learn for himself and then teach others the often subtle ways to enhance the script and the actors' work. Some early collaborators were hard to convince: in 1935, Maxwell Anderson wanted literal, realistic sets for the slum dwellers and gangsters in his verse tragedy *Winterset;* it took long arguments and a foggy-night walk near the Brooklyn Bridge to win his consent to Mielziner's poetically moody under-bridge view, a widely praised and reproduced stage design invariably pictured in theater histories and stage-design texts.

Mielziner regarded lighting as an essential part of his work. Using miniature stage lights in his studio, he previewed their effects on the colors of his designs and then planned the production's lighting, saving grateful producers costly hours of lighting installation and rehearsal.

Mielziner's concepts often reshaped new plays, as was strikingly demonstrated when his innovative solutions to the problems of staging and lighting Arthur Miller's radically innovative *Death of a Salesman* (1949) helped crystallize its emotionally stunning final form. Mielziner's design broke through the proscenium arch by extending a forestage platform into the audience, liberating Broadway stage design from its traditional "picture frame."

Mielziner worked with Broadway's finest producers and creative talents for most of his fifty-year career, his design credits covering many of the period's best plays and musicals. Among them were Eugene O'Neill's *Strange Interlude* (1928); *Street Scene* (1929) and three more plays by Elmer Rice; six plays by S. N. Behrman, including *Biography* (1932) and *No Time for Comedy* (1939); nine by Maxwell Anderson, ending with *Anne of the Thousand Days* (1948); Sidney Howard's *Dodsworth* and *Yellow Jack* (both 1934); actress Katharine Cornell's productions of *The Barretts of Wimpole Street* (1931), *Romeo and Juliet* (1934), and *Saint Joan* (1936); John Gielgud's 1936 New York appearance in *Hamlet; The Women* (1936); *Susan and God* (1937); *On Borrowed Time* (1938); Robert E. Sherwood's *Abe Lincoln in Illinois* (1938); *Watch On the Rhine* (1941); *The Glass Menagerie* (1945); *A Streetcar Named Desire* (1947), and five others by Tennessee Williams; *Mr. Roberts* (1948); *Tea and Sympathy* (1953); *Picnic* (1953); and *After the Fall* (1964). Some of the musicals were George and Ira Gershwin's political satire *Of Thee I Sing* (1931); seven by Richard Rodgers and Lorenz Hart, including *On Your Toes* (1936), *The Boys from Syracuse* (1938), and *Pal Joey* (1940); *Annie Get Your Gun* (1946); *Finian's Rainbow* (1947); five by Richard Rodgers and Oscar Hammerstein, Jr., including *Carousel* (1945), *South Pacific* (1949), and *The King and I* (1951); Frank Loesser's *Guys and Dolls* (1950) and *The Most Happy Fella* (1956); *Gypsy* (1959); and *1776* (1969).

In World War II, as a major in the Army Air Forces (1943–1945), Mielziner wrote the technical manual on camouflage. In 1945 he was asked by the State Department to design the setting and lighting for the first meeting of the United Nations in San Francisco. In 1965 he designed a portable stage for the East Room of the White House. He consulted on a number of major American theaters built in the 1960's, among them the Vivian Beaumont at Lincoln Center in New York City and the Mark Taper Forum at the Los Angeles Music Center.

The first of Mielziner's five Antoinette Perry ("Tony") awards was unusual in honoring an entire ten-production season (1948–1949), one that included designs for *Mr. Roberts, Summer and Smoke, Anne of the Thousand Days, Death of a Salesman, South Pacific,* and *A Streetcar Named Desire*. In 1955 he received an Academy Award for his color art direction of the film *Picnic*.

Mielziner married actress Jean MacIntyre in 1938; they had three children. At the time of his death in New York City, they had been separated for many years.

[Mielziner's files, papers, and drawings are at the New York Public Library for the Performing Arts at Lincoln Center; his scrapbooks are at Boston University's Special Collections Division. Major repositories of his scene paintings are at the New York Public Library, the McNay Museum of San Antonio, the Museum of the City of New York, and the University of Texas Theatre Collection.

Mielziner wrote two books: *Designing for the Theatre* (1965) and *The Shapes of Our Theatre* (1970).

An early appreciation is in John Mason Brown, "Youngsters in Stage Designing," *Boston Transcript* June 6, 1925, summarized in *Literary Digest*, July 18, 1925. An obituary by Albin Krebs and an appraisal by Clive Barnes are in the *New York Times*, Mar. 16, 1976.]

DANIEL S. KREMPEL

MILK, HARVEY BERNARD (May 22, 1930–Nov. 27, 1978), politician and gay rights activist, was born in New York City, the second of two children of Minerva Karns and William Milk, a retail clothing businessman. He grew up in suburban Woodmere, Long Island, where he graduated from high school in 1947.

Milk entered the United States Navy in 1951 after graduating from the Albany (N.Y.) State College for Teachers, where he belonged to the Kappa Beta fraternity. He served during the Korean conflict as a chief petty officer on a submarine rescue ship. Upon his return to New York in 1955, Milk taught high school briefly before becoming an actuarial statistician at Great American Insurance Company. In 1963 he was hired as a financial researcher with Bache and Company. Milk received numerous promotions during his five years with Bache, but his abrasive honesty and the split between his personal and professional life ensured that he never fully committed himself to his business career.

While still with Bache, Milk began the personal transformation from staid financial analyst to gay political activist. Before the 1960's, Milk carefully shielded his homosexuality from high school, college, naval, and business friends. At the same time, he was gradually coming to terms with his sexual orientation. His change began with his love of the opera. Through his lover Jack Galen McKinley, Milk became involved in the experimental theater work of Tom O'Horgan. O'Horgan, director of *Hair*, *Jesus Christ Superstar*, and *Lenny*, hired McKinley as stage manager for *Hair*. When McKinley became stage director of the production in San Francisco in 1968, Milk quit Bache, moved west, and went to work as a financial analyst. After his relationship with McKinley ended, Milk left finance altogether to serve as aide to O'Horgan on a failed attempt to film *Lenny*, and later as associate producer of O'Horgan's short-lived Broadway production *Inner City*. In 1972 the long-haired and bearded Milk and his current partner, Scott Smith, moved permanently to San Francisco, where they opened a photography store.

The tall, gangly Milk first ran for city supervisor in 1973, cultivating support from the generation of liberated gays descending upon San Francisco. He campaigned as a gay populist against the politically conventional gay Democratic establishment, symbolized by the powerful Alice B. Toklas Memorial Democratic Club, which was closely allied with the city's liberal political establishment. He combined his commitment to gay liberation with a broader interest in building a progressive coalition among San Francisco's ethnically, racially, and sexually diverse neighborhoods. He joined traditional techniques of neighborhood politics with his ribald humor to produce a unique campaign style. Although he lost, Milk garnered over 17,000 votes, mainly from the gay neighborhood around Castro Street, and became the self-proclaimed "Mayor of Castro."

In 1975, George Moscone, a liberal state senator with a pro-gay legislative record, was elected mayor of San Francisco. Moscone appointed Milk to the Board of Permit Appeals, Milk's first public office after a second failed campaign for supervisor in 1975. Milk soon announced his intention to run for the state assembly. Even though he wore suits and had cut his hair, Milk failed again. The Milk-controlled San Francisco Gay Democratic Club (later renamed in memory of Harvey Milk) developed out of this defeat.

In 1978, Milk finally won election as city supervisor. He rode the crest of the changing population of the city, which provided the atmosphere for the rise of the progressive movement he came to symbolize. In 1977, these new voters had mandated district elections for city supervisors, changing the political landscape of the city. The district system immediately produced new faces on the board, not only Milk, but also the first Chinese American, the first black woman, and Dan White, a conservative supervisor from a white ethnic neighborhood.

During 1978, under Supervisor Milk's strong leadership, the city passed a gay-rights ordinance, which prohibited discrimination in employment and housing on the basis of sexual orientation, and allocated funds for Gay Freedom Day activities. Also, the city's police chief announced a drive to recruit gays and lesbians to the force.

Milk's progressive coalition also pushed issues critical to the elderly, the working class, Asian Americans, and African Americans. Working with Moscone, Milk advocated renter rebates and limits on real estate development. He received national attention for his campaign against dog litter, which illustrated Milk's interest in practical neighborhood issues, his sense of humor, and his genius for public relations.

National notoriety also resulted from Milk's 1978 campaign against the Briggs state initiative, one in a series of conservative attempts to repeal or halt gay and lesbian political and legislative advances. The proposal, by John Briggs, a conservative state senator from southern California, would have prohibited gays and lesbians from teaching in the public schools. Additionally, the initiative would have mandated the firing of any employee failing to report knowledge of a gay colleague.

The anti-Briggs campaign was mounted by an array of homosexual and heterosexual organizations. Milk opposed Briggs in a series of impassioned debates, during which he reinforced his messages of hope and gay liberation. The antibias campaign turned what appeared at first to be a certain victory for the initiative into a landslide defeat. Milk emerged from the victory with increased stature on the board of supervisors, and state and national recognition as a gay leader.

Less than three weeks later, Milk and Moscone were murdered by Dan White. After surreptitiously entering San Francisco City Hall to avoid the building's metal detectors, White entered the office of Mayor Moscone and shot him four times, twice directly to the head after he had fallen to the floor. White then reloaded his Smith & Wesson with dum-dum bullets, especially powerful cartridges, before heading to Supervisor Milk's office. He shot Milk five times, again shooting his victim twice to the head after he had fallen, presumably to ensure that he was dead. Milk was cremated and his ashes were scattered in the Pacific Ocean just outside the Golden Gate Bridge.

The murders appeared to be a premeditated action by a troubled political rival. White had supported the Briggs initiative, opposed Milk's progressive coalition on virtually every issue, was the only supervisor to vote against the gay-rights ordinance, and blamed the two men for his own political troubles, which had culminated in his resignation weeks earlier. However, after a prosecution many deemed ineffectual and the notorious "Twinkie defense," in which his lawyers claimed White's judgment was impaired because he consumed too much junk food, White was found guilty only of voluntary manslaughter, and given the lightest possible sentence for an admission of murder.

The "White Night Riots" that followed Dan White's sentencing signaled the refusal of gays, lesbians, and their supporters to stop the progress that Harvey Milk had committed himself to achieving. Several thousand people surged from the Castro District to City Hall demanding justice. Barred from City Hall, they attacked the building, burned police cars, and taunted police lines. After three hours, the police made a foray into the crowd, which led to considerable fighting. After the riot had faded at City Hall, police moved into the Castro itself, attacking people randomly and rampaging through several gay bars. The night ended with at least sixty-one police officers and one hundred gays injured, a dozen police cars burned, and total property damage of roughly $250,000.

The next evening, the gay community held a birthday party for Harvey Milk, who would have been forty-nine. Approximately twenty thousand people danced along Castro Street in honor of the man who became a symbol of the gay rights movement with his own liberation, his unorthodox politics, his courage, his martyrdom, and his ardent commitment to the liberation of gays and lesbians. He is memorialized not only by the Harvey Milk Democratic Club, but by the Harvey Milk High School in New York City and the annual Harvey Milk Memorial Parade in San Francisco.

[The Harvey Milk Archive is currently supervised by Scott Smith, who plans eventually to donate the archive to the San Francisco Public Library. The most extensive biography is Randy Shilts, *The Mayor of Castro Street* (1982). John D'Emilio, "Gay Politics, Gay Community," *Socialist Review*, Jan.–Feb. 1981 (more accessible through D'Emilio's 1992 collection of essays *Making Trouble*), discusses the creation of the Castro gay and lesbian community. The assassinations are covered in Mike Weiss, *Double Play* (1984). Obituaries and tributes are in all the San Francisco newspapers and in the *New York Times*, Nov. 28, 1978. *The Times of Harvey Milk* (1984), an Academy Award–winning documentary, focuses on Milk's political career in San Francisco.]

DAVID C. SLOANE

MILLER, HENRY VALENTINE (Dec. 26, 1891–June 7, 1980), novelist and essayist, was born in the Yorkville sector of Manhattan in New York City, the son of Heinrich Miller, a gentleman's tailor, and Louise Marie Nieting, both of the first generation born to German immigrants. He grew up in an unquiet home, echoing with the babbling of his retarded sister Lauretta and the frequent disputes between his easygoing father and his domineering mother. The hatred Miller felt for his frigidly critical mother may well have motivated his unceasing search for an ideal relationship with a woman.

When Miller was a few months old, his parents moved to Williamsburg, in Brooklyn, where he attended Public School No. 85 and the Eastern District High School. Despite being considered a "wild Indian," he graduated second in his class in 1909. Beginning with the standard children's books and moving on to a set of Harvard Classics given him as a birthday present, Miller read widely and eclectically. He attended the City College of New York for a few months before quitting over difficulties with *The Faerie Queene*. He showed promise as a pianist and in 1915 decided to study toward a concert career but instead married his teacher, Beatrice Sylvas Wickens, on June 15, 1917. They had one child before the marriage ended in divorce in December 1923.

Miller wanted early on to write but did not commit himself to a career as an author until age thirty-two. Before that he worked at countless jobs, including waiting on customers in his father's tailor shop and clerking for the Atlas Portland Cement Company; he was a ranch hand in California, where he claimed to have met the anarchist Emma Goldman; and he sorted mail in the War Department in Washington, D.C. In 1920 he applied for a job as a messenger for Western Union but was hired instead as employment manager, a position he held until his resignation in November 1924. During a three-week vacation in 1922, he produced a book-length typescript, *Clipped Wings*, a series of vignettes of Western Union messengers, which has never been published.

The major, catalytic event of Miller's writing career was his meeting with June Mansfield Smith, a taxi dancer born Juliet Edith Smerth in the Bucovina region of Romania, then part of Austria-Hungary; they were married on June 1, 1924. She encouraged him to leave Western Union and write 350-word prose sketches. June peddled these vignettes, signed "Mansfield," to customers in the restaurants where she worked as a waitress. Through 1927 Miller wrote mainly under her name, publishing a few articles in such magazines as *Young's* and *Snappy Stories*. The couple's real income came from June's casual jobs and, more important, from a succession of her male admirers. In 1928, Miller wrote *Moloch* (published in 1992), using his wife's name to convince one of her patrons, known to him only as "Pop," to finance a trip to Europe for the talented young "authoress." In April he and June departed for nine months in London, Paris, Vienna, Budapest, Cracow, Prague, and Marseilles. On their return to New York, Miller drafted *Crazy Cock* (published in 1992), a novel about his life with June. None of the longer works that he had written thus far showed much promise or succeeded in attracting a publisher. In mid-February 1930, June packed Henry off alone to France.

The true beginning of Miller's creative life came during his first year in Paris, when he began to evolve a quasi-fictional persona whom he called Henry Miller. This picaresque character, improvident, resourceful, generous, ruthless, petty, grandly iconoclastic, sycophantic, and determined to write, would appear henceforth in a loosely connected series of autobiographical fictions in which the details and associations in Miller's actual life merged with his fantasies. Thus, Miller proclaimed his Brooklyn voice, his raffish tone, and a theme: the rebel liberating himself from the life-denying canons of society. The eponymous narrator in *Tropic of Cancer* (1934), surviving in Paris through borrowing, begging, and moving in with friends, follows the general outlines of Miller's life from autumn 1931 through 1932. His most constant companion, benefactor, and parasite—the roles alternated—through 1939

Miller

was Viennese-born writer Alfred Perlès, who would appear as Carl in *Tropic of Cancer*. Anaïs Nin, obsessive diarist and wife of an American banker, was the most important of Miller's lovers and muses during the same period. Inspired by Nin's 1932 book on D. H. Lawrence, Miller began a study of Lawrence.

Tropic of Cancer was published by Obelisk Press in 1934 in Paris and was immediately banned in Britain and the United States on grounds of obscenity, initiating a pattern that would dog Miller into the 1960's. However, his novel was praised by Cyril Connolly, T. S. Eliot, George Orwell, Ezra Pound, and, a few years later, Edmund Wilson: Miller soon became, arguably, America's best-known unread author. Others were strong in their disapproval: George Bernard Shaw admitted that Miller could write well but said that he had "totally failed to give any artistic value to his verbatim reports of bad language." *Tropic of Cancer* attracted the attention of the young British writer Lawrence Durrell, who would become Miller's most important literary friend. Their correspondence, begun in 1935, would continue until Miller's death.

Black Spring (1936) and *Max and the White Phagocytes* (1938), both collections of essays and word portraits, and *Tropic of Capricorn* (1939), written partly in the naturalistic style of the earlier *Tropic of Cancer*, were also published in Paris. "Jabberwhorl Cronstadt," a sketch of the writer Walter Lowenfels, and "Into the Night Life," both collected in *Black Spring*, are dadaist melanges of dream sequences, canny judgments, and lunatic flights, and they establish Miller as perhaps the most successful American practitioner of surrealism. With *Tropic of Capricorn* Miller began to work his way back in time through his life in New York. Sometimes raw and savage, Miller's early books are marked by a ribald, life-celebrating humor. In 1939 Miller's first book to appear in America, *The Cosmological Eye*, consisting of selections from *Black Spring* and *Max and the White Phagocytes*, was published by James Laughlin of New Directions. These publications added to Miller's acclaim in critical circles but not much to his income, since his more sensational titles could not be imported into the United States or Britain.

With the approach of World War II, Miller left Paris for Greece, where he spent five months visiting Durrell. Miller left Greece on Dec. 28, 1939, to return to New York. *The Colossus of Maroussi* (1941) is his memoir of his Greek experience and an exuberant portrait of George Katsimbalis, the Colossus of the title. Neglected by earlier commentators, many now consider *The Colossus of Maroussi* Miller's best book, with its integrated descriptions of culture, scene, and character.

While the United States mobilized for war, Miller, guided by a pacifism based on his ego-driven independence, spent a year touring the country by car. He did not like what he saw in the people—"the bleak absence of anything vital or meaningful"—and wrote *The Air-Conditioned Nightmare*, withholding its publication until 1945 because he did not wish to criticize his fellow citizens in the middle of a world conflict.

Beginning in June 1942, Miller boarded with friends in Hollywood, where he avoided writing for the film industry by announcing that he would not work for less than $1,000 per week. On a trip back east in September 1944, he met a twenty-year-old Bryn Mawr graduate, Janina M. Lepska, whom he married on December 18. They settled in a cottage on Partington Ridge, Big Sur, in California, a wild stretch of the coast forty miles south of Monterey. Miller and Lepska—she preferred to be called by her last name—had a daughter and a son before her divorce from Miller in November 1952. Miller estimated that his income from writing had run approximately $500 per year, but with the Allied victory the Paris sales of the *Tropic of Cancer*, *Tropic of Capricorn*, and *Black Spring* to GI's made him a millionaire in francs. Before he could arrange the transfer of currency, however, the franc was devalued and his wealth shrank considerably.

From 1942 through 1960, Miller's major project was the writing of *The Rosy Crucifixion* trilogy, the concluding volumes of his autobiographical fictions, which first appeared abroad and later in English as *Sexus* (1949), *Plexus* (1953), and *Nexus* (1960). The publication history of Miller's works is complicated: Obelisk Press in Paris brought out the first edition of *Sexus*, but the novel went through sixteen editions, including at least five piracies, before the first American authorized edition, by Grove Press, appeared in 1965. Many of his other titles encountered similar fates. *The Rosy Crucifixion* was not well received by either critics or Miller's oldest literary allies. Durrell cabled him to withdraw and revise *Sexus*, saying that it was vulgar and poorly written. To his chagrin Miller became sought after in the 1960's as a guru of the counterculture, and strangers would walk unannounced into his home to proclaim him.

Miller's confessional bent led him to write *The Books in My Life* (1952), which lists the one hundred authors and individual books that most influenced him. The same sort of self-revelation is implied by the title of *The Complete Book of Friends* (1988), which is far from complete and in which Miller maintains that his best friend was his "racing wheel," his bicycle.

Although he was never to be rich, Miller was finally able to travel almost at will, and in 1953 he spent seven months in France with Eve McClure, whom he had married the preceding December after they shared an idyllic nine months at Big Sur. Then the marriage turned sour as Eve drank and Henry scolded, and in 1960 he returned to France without Eve, whom he would divorce in 1962. During this trip he met and fell in love with Renate Gerhardt, English-language editor for his German publisher. He searched western Europe in vain for an ideal home, and Renate rejected him.

Tropic of Cancer was finally published in America in 1961 by Barney Rosset of Grove Press, and the ordeal that Miller had dreaded began with a string of prosecutions for obscenity. Well over a million copies were sold in the first year, and during the same period there were more than sixty court cases. By 1964, when the Supreme Court lifted the ban on *Tropic of Cancer* and thus effectively ended all censorship on grounds of obscenity, Miller was "the most litigated author of all time." In 1963 he bought a house in Pacific Palisades, a quiet upper-middle-class suburb of Los Angeles, and never again seriously considered moving to Europe.

Miller's fascination with the Far East lasted throughout his life; he produced a study of Yukio Mishima in 1972 and often courted Asian women. It is ironic that he, after writing about sexuality in the first person for much of his life, would in his final years, endure a sexless union with Hiroko Tokuda (a Japanese nightclub singer and pianist whom he married Sept. 10, 1967, lived with for two years, and divorced in 1977) and apparently unconsummated love affairs (with Lisa Lu, a Chinese actress, and Brenda Venus, sometime model and starlet who claimed to be Amerindian). Miller died quietly of cardiovascular failure at his home in Pacific Palisades.

Miller kept writing to the end of his life, and even after his death the flood of publications did not stop. (A descriptive bibliography of primary writings, including foreign editions, runs more than 1,000 pages.) *The World of D. H. Lawrence*, edited from material produced by Miller in the 1930's, appeared the month after his death, followed by two early novels and by various collections of letters. A posthumous work attributed to him, *Opus Pistorum* (1984), was not in fact written by Miller but consists of pornographic episodes sold under his name in 1941.

Miller was influenced by an international set of writers that included James Fenimore Cooper, Marie Corelli, Knut Hamsun, Theodore Dreiser, Jean Giono, François Rabelais, D. H. Lawrence, James Joyce, Blaise Cendrars, Fyodor Dostoyevsky, and Walt Whitman. Miller in turn influenced Durrell, Lawrence Ferlinghetti, Jack Kerouac, Norman Mailer, and many others, and his reputation in France earned him the Legion of Honor in 1975.

An internationalist despite his boast—also true—of being plain "Henry Miller from Brooklyn," Miller was a compulsive and prodigious correspondent, and his lifetime production probably exceeded 200,000 letters. Published selections of his letters to Durrell, Nin, Emil Schnellock, a friend from his boyhood, and French writer Joseph Delteil show rare spontaneity and freshness. His letters to Hiroko Tokuda and to Brenda Venus, published posthumously, are qualitatively weaker.

Miller may well be the most controversial of all modern authors: he has been both extolled as the greatest figure in twentieth-century American literature and written off as a pornographer and self-propagandist—"*Leaves of Grass* gone to seed" in Harry Levin's phrase. At various times he was attacked, on tenuous grounds, for being pro-fascist, anti-Semitic, and misogynistic. He was elected to membership in the National Institute of Arts and Letters in 1957. Miller often said that he hated pornography and that his explicit descriptions of human sexuality stemmed from his need to portray human nature in all its aspects. The literary character Henry Miller notwithstanding, Miller in the flesh was a profoundly gentle man, able to captivate his hearers on almost any subject, speaking English, French, or German with the

Brooklyn accent that he never lost. The most reasoned evaluations credit him with writing both very well and very badly, sometimes in the same book. His best work appeared in the 1930's and early 1940's. Miller himself confidently, and vainly, expected to win the Nobel Prize in literature.

Miller's accomplishments are considerable. He asserted the right of the writer to create without heeding censorship statutes or the tacit restraints of social propriety, and the *Tropic of Cancer* case transformed the freedom that Miller had claimed for himself into the law of the land. His best essays are models of inspired insight—studies of Arthur Rimbaud, Nin, the painter Hans Reichel—and of vivid writing. The English critic Herbert Read noted his "ability to combine the aesthetic and prophetic functions." Miller was consistently a reformer and a romantic who proclaimed, in a robust and unself-pitying voice, the eventual triumph of humankind, even as he issued jeremiads against materialism and money, war, barbarism, crass stupidity, and a host of other perceived evils. He can with considerable justice be called the Whitman of American prose.

[The major archive of Miller's manuscripts, correspondence, and other documents is stored in some 127 boxes at the University of California, Los Angeles. Important collections of 600 or more pages of material are at the University of Texas at Austin, the University of Virginia, Indiana University, Southern Illinois University at Carbondale, and Dartmouth College. Files on the litigation over *Tropic of Cancer* are at the Library of Congress and the University of Minnesota. Nine other libraries in the United States list significant holdings. Among Miller's other publications are *Aller Retour, New York* (1935), *What Are You Going to Do About Alf?* (1935), *Money and How It Gets That Way* (1938), *Hamlet* (with Michael Fraenkel, 1939), *The World of Sex* (1940), *The Wisdom of the Heart* (1941), *Sunday After the War* (1944), *Maurizius Forever* (1946), *Remember to Remember* (1947), *The Smile at the Foot of the Ladder* (1948), *Quiet Days in Clichy* (1956), *A Devil in Paradise* (1956), *Big Sur and the Oranges of Hieronymus Bosch* (1957), *To Paint Is to Love Again* (1960), *Stand Still Like the Hummingbird* (1962), *Insomnia; or, The Devil at Large* (1971), *My Life and Times* (1971), *Gliding into the Everglades* (1977), and *Mother, China, and the World Beyond* (1977).

The best biography is Robert Ferguson, *Henry Miller: A Life* (1991), but Jay Martin, *Always Merry and Bright* (1978), remains the most detailed. There are two essential bibliographies: Lawrence J. Shifreen, *Henry Miller: A Bibliography of Secondary Sources* (1979), includes useful annotations; and Lawrence J. Shifreen and Roger Jackson, *Henry Miller: A Bibliography of Primary Sources* (1993), describes Miller's publications in all languages. The best general commentaries are Annette Kar Baxter, *Henry Miller, Expatriate* (1961), George Wickes, *Henry Miller* (1966); Kenneth C. Dick, *Henry Miller: Colossus of One* (1967); William A. Gordon, *The Mind and Art of Henry Miller* (1967); Ihab Hassan, *The Literature of Silence: Henry Miller and Samuel Beckett* (1967); and Leon Lewis, *Henry Miller: The Major Writings* (1986). Valuable focused studies include Thomas H. Moore, ed., *Henry Miller on Writing* (1964); E. R. Hutchinson, *Tropic of Cancer on Trial* (1968); Bertrand Mathieu, *Orpheus in Brooklyn* (1976); and Erica Jong, *The Devil at Large* (1993). *The Henry Miller Odyssey* (1969), a film by Robert Snyder, captures Miller's manner and conversation. An obituary is in the *New York Times*, June 9, 1980.]

IAN S. MACNIVEN

MILLETT, FRED BENJAMIN (Feb. 19, 1890–Jan. 1, 1976), educator and scholar, was born in Brockton, Mass., one of two sons of Daniel Edwin Millett and Mary Avalina Churchill Porter. He grew up in nearby Whitman, a small town where his grandfather owned a dairy farm. His father, widely read though largely self-taught, worked in a nearby shoe factory. A fragile child, Millett developed an early interest in books and libraries. In 1908 he graduated from Whitman Public High School as valedictorian and entered Amherst College.

The Amherst years were sometimes difficult socially for the shy youngster, orphaned before his second college year. Nonetheless, he majored in English, participated in literary and theatrical events, made Phi Beta Kappa, and received his B.A. in 1912, magna cum laude.

A position as lecturer in English took him to Queen's University at Kingston, Ontario, where he remained until 1916. Summer graduate study at the University of Chicago led to a fellowship, but in 1918 the draft intervened. Following six months as a private stationed in Florida in the Medical Corps, Millett earned the rank of second lieutenant at Officers Training School.

In 1919, Millett went to the Carnegie Institute of Technology as assistant professor of English. Although promoted to associate professor in 1926, he left the following year to accept a second assistant professorship at the University of Chicago. He completed his Ph.D. at Chicago in 1931 and in 1932 he regained the rank of associate professor.

These were tumultuous times at Chicago, where President Robert Maynard Hutchins was fighting hard for educational reform. Though Hutchins's emphasis on liberal undergraduate education appealed to Millett, there was also conflict with the dynamic president. Thus, in 1937, he accepted an appointment as visiting professor at Wesleyan University in Middletown, Conn., escaping from what he called "the tensions precipitated at Chicago by Robert Maynard Hutchins and his gang of intellectual camp-followers." However tense, Millett's time at Chicago was productive. By 1937 he had edited and significantly revised a respected work of the 1920's, *Contemporary British Literature* (1935), coedited *The Art of the Drama* (1935) with Gerald E. Bentley, and coedited an anthology, *The Play's the Thing* (1936).

Millett's appointment at Wesleyan, to him a "less contentious academy," became permanent in 1939. His passion for educational reform, especially in the humanities, discomfited some of his colleagues, but others were enthusiastic. Among the latter were Wesleyan president Victor Butterfield and Professor Nathan Pusey, later president of Harvard University. As the years passed, Millett's intellectual breadth and gifted teaching were increasingly acknowledged by his peers. From 1943 to 1958 he directed Wesleyan's Honors College. Under his aegis, this center for independent and often interdisciplinary research evolved as a cherished campus institution.

Millett's impact on Wesleyan was most evident in his work on the design and implementation of a new freshman humanities program. Firmly convinced of the unique contributions of the humanistic disciplines to civilization, he was equally certain of the need for greater curricular and instructional creativity to engage student interest. As consultant in 1942 and 1943 to the humanities division at the Rockefeller Foundation for a study on the rebirth of liberal education, he had additional opportunity to consider strategies. On campus, he became a central figure in Wesleyan's exploration of new ways to present literature, religion, philosophy, and the fine arts to students. He directed Wesleyan's Honors College from 1943 until his retirement in 1958. The new Humanities Program, initiated in 1943, became the foundation of undergraduate education at the college for many years. Its aim was a creative, interdisciplinary exploration of the Western intellectual tradition. Small discussion groups were led by professors from different disciplines to function as "experienced learners," not experts. A required "arts laboratory" to give first-year students "some personal experiences of the materials and methods of the . . . arts" provided hands-on experience to balance analysis and criticism. For fifteen years Millett, a beloved teacher, served as the program's director. Though Wesleyan was not alone in introducing such changes, the university moved early in directions that became increasingly fashionable over succeeding decades.

During these years Millett also continued to write and publish. Alone and with others, he produced books praised for their impeccable scholarship and widely used as texts and works of reference. Although not on the front lines of research, he was far more than a codifier. His wide knowledge of English literature, a passion for bibliography, a commitment to be useful to students and teachers, a delight in pedagogic innovation, and a blessedly clear style characterized publication after publication.

Especially useful were his revisions and updatings of earlier works. *Contemporary American Authors* (1940) presented brief analyses, biographies, and bibliographies of more than two hundred writers. *A History of English Literature* (1943) was the sixth edition of a very well known work by William V. Moody and Robert M. Lovett, first published before World War I. Here, as in several subsequent editions, and indeed in much of Millett's work, the challenge was to connect solid but outdated scholarship to the present. *The Rebirth of Liberal Education* (1945), more controversial than Millett's other work, argued for the primacy of the humanities in liberal education. It was attacked by some critics as disparaging and misunderstanding the natural and social sciences. His 1950 books *Reading Fiction*, *Reading Drama*, and *Reading Poetry* offered students and teachers instruction in rigorous, yet personal, methods of analysis to support close reading.

Millett was named Olin Professor of English in 1952. From 1952 to 1954 he served as president of the American Association of University Professors, using the office to attack Senator Joseph McCarthy and the members of the House Un-American Activities Committee as vigilantes intent on destroying the academy's traditional freedoms. After his retirement in 1958, Millett served briefly as Distinguished Professor of English at the State University of New York at Albany. Otherwise he divided his time between his Whitman home and Cape Cod, working on his journals and maintaining his interest in all the arts, as well as some scholarly activity. He edited the eighth edition of *A History of English Literature* in 1964, alert as ever to new literary developments.

A lifelong bachelor and something of a loner, Millett was on excellent terms with his family, especially one nephew. His great passion was the theater, and he was also devoted to book collecting. Millett died in Brockton.

[Millett's unprocessed papers, including the journals written in retirement, are housed in the Wesleyan University Archives, as are documents he submitted during his lifetime. His published works include "And Gladly Wolde He Lerne," *Wesleyan University Alumnus*, Feb. 1958; and *Professor* (1961). He was also the coauthor of *Minor British Novelists* (1967) and *Minor American Novelists* (1970). See also Edward H. Hastings, "For F.B.M.: A Last Assignment," *Wesleyan University Alumnus*, Spring 1976. An obituary is in the *New York Times*, Jan. 2, 1976.]

URSULA S. COLBY

MINGUS, CHARLES, JR. (Apr. 22, 1922–Jan. 5, 1979), jazz musician and composer, was born in Nogales, Ariz., the son of Charles Mingus, a retired sergeant in the United States Army, and Harriett Sophia Philips. His mother died five months after he was born. Mingus was raised in the Watts district of Los Angeles by his father and stepmother. His first major musical influence was the black gospel music of the Holiness Church.

By the age of eight, Mingus played the trombone, and in junior high he began to play the cello. At Jordan High School he switched to the string bass and began private studies with bassist Red Callender. Next, he took classes in piano, theory, and composition with Lloyd Reese. In 1943 he began five years of lessons with Herman Rheinschagen, former bass player with the New York Philharmonic.

Mingus's formal education was not successful. As a light-skinned black man he was the brunt of racial prejudice from whites and darker blacks alike. His sensitive nature was already in a state of rebellion. Only his high IQ saved him from going to Boyle Heights, a school for problem children.

In 1942, Mingus worked in a band led by Barney Bigard. This led to a job with Louis Armstrong, but in 1943 he was fired just before a tour of the southern United States. Mingus was so vehement in his refusal to stand for racial prejudice that Armstrong was afraid he would be murdered. He joined the Lee Young Sextet (1943) and then helped form the Strings and Keys trio (1944). In 1945 he played informal jam sessions with the genius of bebop, Charlie Parker (interestingly, Mingus at first was not impressed). Mingus toured with Lionel Hampton (1947–1948) and then with the Red Norvo trio (1950–1951), which he left when a white bassist took his place just before a television broadcast.

In 1951, Mingus moved to New York City, where he played with Miles Davis and then Charlie Parker. In 1952 he helped form one of the first musician-owned record companies, Debut Records. In January 1953 he joined one of his most admired musical and compositional influences, Duke Ellington. But on February 3 he was fired. During an intermission at a concert at the Apollo Theatre in Harlem, trombonist Juan Tizol made racial slurs about Mingus's musicianship. A fight broke out and Tizol, holding a bolo knife, chased Mingus across the stage; Mingus grabbed a fire ax, chased Tizol, and chopped his chair into splinters.

In 1953, Mingus booked perhaps the best bebop band of all time (with Charlie Parker, Dizzy Gillespie, Bud Powell, Max Roach, and himself) for a concert at Massey Hall in Toronto on May 15. This was recorded and issued on Debut Records. By this point, he had played with the leading figures of jazz and was recognized as a major performer and innovator on string bass. Still playing, Mingus moved more toward composition. In 1954 he helped to form the earliest cooperative group of the modern jazz era, the Jazz Composer's Workshop. By 1955 he was the leader of the Charles Mingus Jazz Workshop, which essentially played only his music.

Beginning with the recording of *Pithecanthropus Erectus* in January 1956, Mingus extended the frontiers of jazz composition by the use of varying tempos, extended form, pedal points, and collective improvisation. The music, with its intense passions, had an unmistakable Mingus sound. One of the reasons was that

Mingus preferred to sing or play—not write down—parts for his players.

Mingus reached new artistic heights in 1959 with the LPs *Blues and Roots* (Atlantic) and *Mingus Ah Um* (Columbia). The latter contained two of his most popular pieces, "Goodbye Pork Pie Hat" and "Better Git It in Your Soul."

A musical debacle occurred on Oct. 12, 1962, at an improperly prepared concert at Town Hall in New York City. Longtime associate trombonist Jimmy Knepper refused a music-writing assignment, and Mingus punched him in the mouth. Knepper instituted legal charges. Inept recording engineers added to problems the night of the concert. Undaunted, on Jan. 20, 1963, Mingus recorded what many believe to be his finest album, *Black Saint and the Sinner Lady* (Impulse).

In the spring of 1966, Mingus was evicted from his apartment on the Lower East Side in New York City. This low point in his life was captured in the documentary film *Mingus* (1968), by Thomas Reichman. Soon afterward, he suffered a nervous breakdown and was sent to Bellevue Hospital. For most of the period 1967–1968 he was professionally inactive. He began a slow return to the world of performance in 1969. But Mingus was not himself: he took no solos, he did not talk to the audience, he let musicians read music, and his bass playing was not assertive.

In 1971, Mingus was awarded a Guggenheim Fellowship for composition. His imaginative and at times semipornographic autobiography, *Beneath the Underdog*, edited by Nel King, was published in 1971. He played at the Newport Jazz Festival in 1972. At a recording session, arranger-collaborator Sy Johnson said, "He's his old self. He just yelled at the band." At the end of the year, he was elected to the *Down Beat* Hall of Fame.

During his remaining years Mingus traveled extensively with his band and continued to compose music for large ensembles; especially important is "The Shoes of the Fisherman's Wife Are Jive Ass Slippers," recorded on *Let My Children Hear Music* (Columbia). In 1979 he collaborated with pop singer Joni Mitchell on her album *Mingus* (Asylum).

Mingus was married five times. He was first married when he was only sixteen, but the union was quickly annulled. He married Canilla Jeanne Gross on Jan. 3, 1944; they had two children and were divorced in 1947. He married Celia Nielson on Apr. 2, 1951; they had one child. She left him on their anniversary in 1958. He married Judy Starkey in the early 1960's; they had two children. By 1966 he was living alone. In 1975 he married his manager, Susan Graham Ungaro.

In November 1977, medical tests revealed that Mingus had amyotrophic lateral sclerosis, better known as Lou Gehrig's disease. On June 18, 1978, he was a guest of honor at a jazz party at the White House. In pursuit of a spiritual healer he and Susan then went to Cuernavaca, Mexico, where he died. In accordance with his wishes, his widow flew to India with his cremated remains and scattered his ashes in the Ganges River.

[Hundreds of Mingus's musical scores are in the collection Let My Children Hear Music at the Library of Congress, Music Division. The most valuable biography is Brian Priestley, *Mingus* (1982). See also H. Lukas Lindenmaier and Horst J. Salewski, *The Man Who Never Sleeps* (1983); and Tom Moon, Stephen Davis, and Charles Mingus, "In the Mingus Archives," *Musician*, June 1989. An excellent collection of his compositions is Sue Mingus, ed., *Charles Mingus* (1991). An obituary is in the *New York Times*, Jan. 9, 1979.]

JOHN VOIGT

MITCHELL, MARTHA ELIZABETH BEALL (Sept. 2, 1918–May 31, 1976), political wife and national celebrity, was born in Pine Bluff, Ark., the only child of George Virgil Beall, a cotton broker, and Arie Ferguson, a teacher of elocution. She had a half brother from her mother's first marriage, which had ended in divorce. She attended a private school for six years before transferring to the local public school; a move that was caused by her father's financial losses in the market crash of 1929. After graduating from Pine Bluff High School in 1937, she attended Stephens College in Columbia, Mo., for one year, the University of Arkansas for a year, and the University of Miami for two-and-a-half years before earning a B.A. in history in 1942.

After one unhappy year of teaching in Mobile, Ala., she returned to Pine Bluff, trained as a certified Red Cross volunteer-aide, and then worked at the local hospital for a year. In May 1945, she was employed as receptionist to the commanding officer at the Pine Bluff Arsenal. When the commander was transferred to Washington, D.C., in July 1945, she requested reassignment with him. She was employed for the next year at the Office of the Chief Chemical Warfare Service, where she became a research analyst. While at Chemical Warfare, she met an army captain from Virginia, Clyde W. Jennings, Jr., and they were married on Oct. 5, 1946. The couple moved to Forest Hills in Queens, N.Y., where Jennings was a partner in a handbag manufacturing firm. After the birth of their only son, the Jenningses moved into Manhattan, and around 1954 Martha Jennings went to work for the Plymouth Shops, first as a sales clerk and later as an assistant buyer. After eleven years of marriage, the Jenningses were divorced on Aug. 1, 1957. On December 30 of that year, Martha Jennings married John Newton Mitchell of New York, an attorney whom she had met through friends several years earlier. The Mitchells had one daughter. For eleven years the couple lived in New York City and the suburban communities of Greenwich and West Norwalk, Conn., and Rye, N.Y.

In 1968, President Richard M. Nixon appointed John Mitchell, his former law partner and campaign manager, United States attorney general. The Mitchells moved to Washington, D.C., where Martha Mitchell immediately set her own style as a political wife. She did not observe the traditional reserve and decorum expected of most cabinet spouses, saying she saw no reason why a wife should not speak for herself. As one biographer has noted, Mitchell was "an outspoken, willful Southern conservative. . . . She had strong, often vituperative opinions about many of the politically charged issues of the day, and she was not afraid to express them publicly."

In her early days in Washington, Mitchell's outspoken criticisms were directed at antiwar protestors, whom she described as "liberal Communists" (even though she, too, argued that "the Vietnam war stinks"), and "liberal academics," whom she blamed for "all the troubles in this country." She also was critical of labor and civil rights officials as well as the Supreme Court and fashion designers.

Mitchell became most famous for her middle-of-the-night phone calls to the press. One call to the *Arkansas Gazette* demanded that they "crucify" Senator J. William Fulbright for his opposition to a Nixon Supreme Court nominee. Although her public statements sometimes were politically embarrassing to the administration, during the first Nixon term both the president and John Mitchell seemed tolerant of and even amused by her outspokenness. President Nixon encouraged the "spunky" Martha to "give 'em hell," and John Mitchell called her his "unguided missile" who made him laugh.

A Gallup poll in November 1970 found that Mitchell was better known than many public figures, with an unusually high recognition factor of 76 percent, 43 percent positive and 33 percent negative. She was second only to the president in the number of requests received for public appearances and speeches, and for several years she was said to have received as many as a thousand letters per month. She was the only cabinet wife ever voted one of the ten most-admired women in the world. Many citizens regarded her as a folk heroine and felt she was one of the few honest political figures in Washington. Others, however, were outraged by what they believed were her narrow, conservative opinions and her outlandish behavior.

Mitchell's publicity for her opinions obscured recognition of her public service. While in Washington she assisted the Salvation Army, worked on antidrug, antipornography, and antipollution campaigns, and organized information seminars for the new cabinet spouses. According to the Washington *Star*, she never ignored a charity appeal and would willingly "pose, sip tea, taste preview menus, dance, speak Swahili, or simply make an appearance" if asked.

Mitchell's distinctive and flamboyant physical appearance added to her notoriety. She had bleached blonde hair that was teased, sleekly coiffed, and sprayed. As one source described her: "She was cute, a feisty little thing in stiletto heels and frowsy dresses and a Southern drawl with matching dimples."

In March 1972, John Mitchell resigned as attorney general to head Nixon's reelection campaign. Martha Mitchell, as a prominent speaker, had been a member of the Committee to Reelect the President (CREEP) for over a year. Members of Nixon's staff complained that they found working with Martha Mitchell difficult. One Nixon aide described her as "a southern charmer one moment, and absolutely impossible the next." As long as she remained ardently pro-Nixon, however, her peccadilloes and difficult behavior were tolerated. After the Watergate break-in in June 1972, she was suddenly viewed as an embarrassment and a threat. She learned of the break-in while on a trip to California where she was attending Nixon reelection functions. Mitchell later recounted a harrowing story of being forcibly restrained in a California hotel room by a CREEP security agent who pulled her telephone out of the wall after she called a member of the press. She also reported that she had been injected with a sedative against her will. After being detained for several days in California, she flew to Westchester County, N.Y., where she related her ordeal to a reporter before again being given a security guard. After the California incident was publicized, one segment of the press circulated stories from so-called inside sources that she was mentally ill and an alcoholic. Others, especially women reporters who had gotten to know Martha Mitchell, argued that she was being victimized by Nixon loyalists.

Shortly afterward, John Mitchell resigned as Nixon's campaign manager, citing concern for his wife's happiness and welfare. The couple returned to Manhattan. In early 1973, as the Watergate investigation began to implicate her husband, Mitchell publicly accused "Mr. President" of being deeply involved in the Watergate affair. She condemned Nixon for letting her husband and others take the blame and demanded that the president resign, predicting that if he did not, he would be impeached. By this time her nocturnal phone calls, unbridled public comments, and rumored drinking problem had caused many to doubt her seriousness and credibility, and her early warnings implicating Nixon in Watergate were ignored. Mitchell objected publicly when the Senate Watergate Investigation Committee concluded that she did not have enough evidence to testify before them, though later observers would note that many of her "dial-a-headline prophecies had an uncanny way of panning out."

Through the summer and fall of 1973, the strains of public life and Watergate took their toll on the Mitchell marriage. On Sept. 10, 1973, Mitchell awakened to learn that her husband had left her without warning or arrangements for financial support. He never afterward saw or spoke to her. In spite of her estrangement from her husband and their only daughter, who remained with John, Martha Mitchell continued to declare publicly that her husband was a scapegoat for the president. She also said Nixon was responsible for the destruction of her marriage.

In July 1974, Mitchell filed for a legal separation and support payments from her husband. Because of John Mitchell's failure to pay temporary support prior to that time, and because of the court's delay in rendering a judgment on her suit until his involvement in the Watergate case had been resolved, she became increasingly indebted. She worked on her autobiography and various magazine articles, and made public appearances, but her declining health and periods of depression interfered with her productivity and her ability to earn any significant income. In the fall of 1975, she learned she had multiple myeloma, a rare form of bone cancer. Most of her last few months were spent in hospitals. Shortly before her death in May 1976, the court ordered John Mitchell to pay the outstanding support that had been granted months earlier in their separation agreement. Martha Mitchell, still the legal wife of John Mitchell, died in debt in New York City. She was buried in Bellwood Cemetery in her hometown of Pine Bluff, Ark.

Martha Mitchell became a celebrity because she not only engaged the national public's attention but also had a populist appeal to a large group of Americans who were frustrated by the feeling that their politicians were deceptive and dishonest. While detractors viewed her as destructive and a publicity seeker, admirers saw her as patriotic and forthright. Observers of Martha Mitchell created a popular slogan, "Martha Was Right," a description that applies to her whether she is remembered as the Cassandra or "heroine of Watergate," or its victim.

[See Charles Ashman and Sheldon Engelmayer, *Martha, the Mouth that Roared* (1973); "Martha Mitchell," Madeleine Edmondson and Alden Duer Cohen, *The Women of Watergate* (1975); "Martha Mitchell," Eleanora W. Schoenebaum, ed., *Political Profiles: The Nixon/Ford Years* (1979), and Winzola McLendon, *Martha: The Life of Martha Mitchell* (1979). Examples of supportive articles by women reporters are Shana Alexander, "Love Song to Martha Mitchell," *Newsweek*, Apr. 30, 1973; Vivian Cadden, "Martha Mitchell Goes It Alone," *McCall's*, Jan. 1974; and Ellen Goodman, "Here's to the Crazy Ladies," *Ms.*, May 1977. Also of value are "Martha Mitchell's View from the Top," *Time*, Nov. 30, 1970; and Vivian Cadden, "Martha Mitchell: The Day the Laughing Stopped," *McCall's*, July 1973. Obituaries are in the *New York Times*, June 1,

1976; the *Washington Post*, June 1, 1976; and *Time*, June 14, 1976.]

MARILYNN WOOD HILL

MONRONEY, ALMER STILLWELL ("MIKE") (Mar. 2, 1902–Feb. 13, 1980), congressman and senator, was born in Oklahoma City, Okla., the son of Almer Ellis Stillwell Monroney and Mary Wood. He attended public schools there and was graduated Phi Beta Kappa from the University of Oklahoma with a B.A. degree in 1924. He then spent five years as a reporter and political writer for the *Oklahoma News*. In 1929, Monroney became president of his father's furniture store, the oldest in Oklahoma. He successfully administered it until 1938, when he was elected as a Democrat to the United States House of Representatives, the first of six consecutive terms.

A member of the House Banking and Currency Committee, Monroney gained distinction while serving as vice-chairman of the Joint Committee on the Organization of Congress. With Senator Robert M. La Follette, Jr., he wrote the Legislative Reorganization Act of 1946, which reduced the number of Senate committees from thirty-three to fifteen and House committees from forty-five to nineteen. It also improved the quality of the committee professional staffs, promoting a growth in technical expertise. In 1945, Monroney received the first Collier's Award for Distinguished Congressional Service for his efforts on legislative reorganization, international cooperation, and domestic stabilization. His reputation was that of a "moderate liberal" who supported most New Deal and Fair Deal measures.

In 1950, Monroney was elected to the United States Senate; he was reelected in 1956 and in 1962. As a senator, he served on the Appropriations, Commerce, Banking and Currency, and Post Office and Civil Service committees. On each of these he chaired important subcommittees. He also chaired the Special Committee on the Organization of Congress and cochaired the Joint Committee on the Organization of Congress during the Eighty-Ninth and Ninetieth Congresses (1965–1969). He wrote the Federal Aviation Act of 1958; the Federal Aid to Airports acts of 1958, 1959, 1961; and the Permanent Certification of Feeder Airline acts of 1957 and 1961. He sponsored measures to modernize and increase civil and military air-cargo equipment and capacity. He also wrote legislation defining rules for supplemental carriers, the small-business segment of aviation, in 1960 and 1961. For these and other endeavors on behalf of the industry, Monroney became known as "Mr. Aviation," and in 1961 he was awarded the Wright Brothers Memorial Trophy for public service in aviation.

Further significant pieces of legislation written by Monroney alone or with others include the Automobile Labeling Act of 1958; the Monroney-Clark Federal Aid to Education amendment, providing matching funds to states in the National Defense Act of 1961; the Small Producers Lead and Zinc Stabilization Bill of 1961; and Senate Resolution 264 (1958), proposing an International Development Association as an affiliate of the World Bank.

In addition to being noted for his efforts to assist small business, Monroney was recognized as one of the leading advocates of upstream flood control. The Upper Washita Flood Control District in Oklahoma was the first such district in the nation. It gained Monroney the distinction of being the "Big Daddy of Little Dams." Moreover, he was a leading supporter in the Senate of the oil industry and of natural-gas producers seeking assistance in development and exemption from federal regulation. (In Oklahoma oil or gas was found in seventy of seventy-seven counties, and by 1960, 47 percent of the total land area was either in production or under lease.) Monroney was a leader in the fight to turn back assaults on the 27.5 percent depletion allowance permitted oil and gas producers for income-tax purposes. In Oklahoma he was also known as a strong friend of the rural electric cooperatives and helped build the telephone cooperatives, which by 1960 reached 78 percent of the state's farms.

As a United States senator, Monroney was widely recognized for his work in behalf of international assistance, aviation, rural development, and protection of the oil and natural-gas producers. In the 1950's he was a staunch opponent of Senator Joseph McCarthy, and in 1960 he led the unsuccessful drive for Adlai Stevenson's third nomination as the Democratic presidential candidate. After the Democratic National Convention he sponsored legislation calling for free time on television for the "great debate" by presidential candidates John F. Kennedy and Richard M. Nixon. While he had a broad international and national outlook, Monroney viewed issues through the prism of their possible effect on Oklahoma's economic growth. And it was economic strength, not military might, that he believed would ultimately determine the "battle between collective state communism and free enterprise democracy."

Monroney was an unsuccessful candidate for reelection in 1968. He maintained his Washington residence, served as an aviation consultant, was a member of several boards of directors, and held membership in a wide range of organizations. Described by *Time* as "friendly as an Airedale pup," Monroney was six feet tall and lean with "straight attractive features." He married Mary Ellen Mellon on July 3, 1932; their son, Michael, stumped for his father during his senatorial campaigns. Monroney died in Rockville, Md. His body was cremated, and some of the ashes were deposited in a niche in the Washington Cathedral; the rest were scattered on the grounds of the Mike Monroney Aeronautical Center in Oklahoma City.

[The Carl Albert Center, University of Oklahoma, is the repository for Monroney's papers. Unfortunately, more than 90 percent of his congressional papers were destroyed by the National Archives, at the authorization of his office, in 1973, leaving the collection with only the Senate years and some congressional reorganization files from his service in the House. A register of material destroyed by the National Archives is in the accession folder of the collection. Obituaries are in the *Washington Post*, the *Daily Oklahoman*, and the *New York Times*, all Feb. 14, 1980.]

RICHARD LOWITT

MONTOYA, JOSEPH MANUEL (Sept. 24, 1915–June 5, 1978), congressman and senator, was born José Manuel Montoya in Peña Blanca, N.Mex., the son of Thomas O. Montoya and Frances de La. His father, after mining gold in Arizona, returned to New Mexico to become sheriff of Sandoval County. On Nov. 9, 1940, Joseph Montoya married Della Romero. They had three children.

Although his family was not wealthy, it was influential. Both parents traced their ancestry to seventeenth-century Hispanic roots. This was significant in New Mexico, where Hispanics in the northern part of the state proudly claimed unbroken descent from Spanish settlers, in contrast to those who came across the Mexican border as late as the twentieth century and who generally had a mixed Spanish-Indian genealogy.

Montoya attended Bernalillo (N.Mex.) High School before entering Regis College in 1931. He transferred to Georgetown University in 1934, where he received the LL.B. in 1938. The following year he was admitted to the New Mexico bar and began practicing law in Santa Fe. Later he was admitted to practice before both the state supreme court and the United States Supreme Court.

If one can be politically precocious, that term fit Montoya. While still a student at Georgetown, he was elected in 1936 to the New Mexico House of Representatives representing Sandoval County. At the conclusion of the 1937 legislative session, he was named its outstanding legislator by his colleagues. Reelected in 1938, he was selected majority floor leader by his fellow Democrats for the 1939 and 1940 sessions. In 1940, at the required minimum age of twenty-five, Montoya was elected to the New Mexico state senate. In that chamber he was elected Democratic whip and chaired the judiciary committee. Montoya served in the state senate through 1946 and was elected to that body again in 1952. He also served in the state's executive branch when he was elected lieutenant governor in 1946, 1948, 1954, and 1956.

Losing the 1950 Democratic primary for the state's only congressional seat to Antonio M. Fernandez, Montoya returned to his law practice and managed the Western Freight Lines, which he had purchased in 1945 and whose principal activity was hauling materials for the Los Alamos nuclear program. Later he would acquire substantial commercial real estate in New Mexico, becoming a millionaire by the 1970's.

Before Montoya took office for his fourth term as lieutenant governor, Congressman Fernandez died in November 1956. The next February, Montoya was selected by a caucus of Democratic leaders to be the party's candidate for the vacant House seat. He won the Apr. 9, 1957, special election over Republican Tom Bolack. Both later said this was the most difficult campaign of their careers.

Montoya was reelected to the House in 1958, 1960, and 1962, but his modest plurality in that last contest made him vulnerable to a future challenge. As a member of Congress, where he served on the judiciary committee, Montoya did not make a national reputation but diligently pursued the interests of his constituents. Representing one of the nation's poorest states, he supported programs to aid the economically disadvantaged, as well as subsidies for wheat and cotton, key commodities in his state.

In late 1962, Dennis Chavez, who represented New Mexico for nearly three decades in the United States Senate, died. The state's Republican governor, Edwin L. Mechem, resigned in order to be appointed to the vacant Senate seat by his lieutenant governor, Tom Bolack. Through the state's unusual preprimary endorsing system, Montoya and Mechem were nominated in 1964 to contest the Senate seat. The Mechem-Montoya struggle was a contrast of stature and ideology, pitting "Big Ed," a Goldwater Republican, against "Little Joe," a lifelong liberal Democrat. For a dozen years, Mechem had been the only Republican victor for statewide office. Handicapped in this contest by the opprobrium of his virtual self-appointment to the Senate in 1962, Mechem lost to Montoya in 1964 by an unexpectedly large margin.

In 1970, Montoya retained office by defeating Goldwaterite Anderson Carter. During his second term, Montoya served on the Senate committee that investigated the Watergate break-in. The televised hearings did not benefit him to the extent that national television exposure often can. As the last senator in rotation, his questions mainly reiterated inquiries made by other senators, and his comments seemed closely dependent on his notes. Soon afterward Montoya was the target of unsupported allegations that he had pressured the Internal Revenue Service to grant him favorable treatment because he was chairman of the Senate committee that oversaw the agency's budget. He was also harmed by reports of improprieties related to a shopping center he owned in Santa Fe.

Seeking a third term in 1976, Montoya lost by a huge margin to former astronaut Harrison Schmitt. Thus ended the political career of the "barefoot boy from Peña Blanca." Montoya had held elective office for thirty-eight years, losing only twice.

Although his family name could be considered an asset, at least twice it was a liability. He lost the 1950 congressional primary to Antonio Fernandez by 2,000 votes because another Joe Montoya on the ballot collected 10,000 votes. In the 1962 election, he was faced with an opponent who claimed he was the actual Joe Montoya. Only after the congressman presented papers in court confirming that he had surrendered his birth name of José did he prevail.

Montoya's final loss signaled a major change in New Mexico's political profile. The influx of people from other parts of the nation diluted the strength of the Hispanic voters in the state. By the 1950's, the "Little Texas" voters in the eastern and southern counties were giving their support to candidates who reflected their conservative origins in the American South. At the same time, Republican strength grew in Albuquerque, which had nearly one-third of the state's voters, as newcomers with college educations and other middle-class attributes rejected the patronage system that was a prominent feature of the state's Democratic politics.

Stricken with an incurable kidney ailment, Montoya died after a brief hospitalization in Washington, D.C.

[Montoya's papers are at the University of New Mexico Library; these are primarily from his files as a United States Senator. See also John Littlewood and Frederick Allen, *Joseph M. Montoya: Democratic Senator from New Mexico* (1972). Obituaries are in the *Albuquerque Tribune*, June 5, 1978; and the *Albuquerque Journal*, the *New York Times*, and the *Santa Fe New Mexican*, all June 6, 1978.]

THOMAS P. WOLF

MOREELL, BEN (Sept. 4, 1892–July 30, 1978), engineer and chief of the United States Navy Bureau of Yards and Docks, was born in Salt Lake City, Utah, the son of Samuel Moreell and Sophia Sossnitz. After living in New York City he was raised in St. Louis, Mo. He graduated from Washington University in 1913 with a B.S. degree in civil engineering and from 1913 to 1917 worked for St. Louis's public works department. In 1917 he was appointed a lieutenant (j.g.) in the navy's Civil Engineer Corps (CEC). After serving during World War I in the public works office of the naval base at Ponta Delgada, Azores Islands, he was the plant engineer at the destroyer and submarine base at Squantum, Mass. (1919–1920). He served as a public works officer in Haiti (1920–1924) and at the Norfolk Navy Yard in Portsmouth, Va. (1924–1926). He was then assistant design manager in the Bureau of Yards and Docks (BuY&D) (1926–1930) and a public works officer at Bremerton and the Thirteenth Naval District (1930–1932). He planned and constructed the ship model basin of the Admiral David W. Taylor Model Basin, Carderock, Md. (1930–1932). In 1929 he published the widely acclaimed *Standards of Design for Concrete.* On Oct. 23, 1923, he married Clara Julia Klinksick; they had two children.

After studying in France in 1932 and 1933, Moreell served as project manager of shipbuilding and repair facilities in the storage and submarine base section of BuY&D from 1935 to 1937, and as the public works officer of the Naval Base and Fourteenth Naval District at Pearl Harbor in late 1937.

That December, President Franklin D. Roosevelt nominated Moreell to a four-year term as chief of BuY&D with the grade of rear admiral, making him the first non–Naval Academy man and one of the youngest to fill the post. In addition to inspecting facilities in the Atlantic and Pacific, he had two large graving docks built at Pearl Harbor and devised the sectional dry dock, sections of which could be connected to form docks of any desired size. He also obtained permission to form skilled craftsmen into Naval Construction Battalions (CBs or Seabees), who could be sent overseas.

Moreell helped the navy's expansion after 1940 by building bases at Samoa and the Aleutian Islands and by providing training and housing facilities for enlisted naval personnel, whose numbers were augmented from 125,000 in 1941 to 3 million in 1945. After the Lend-Lease bill became law in March 1941, he had bases built on sites from Newfoundland to British Guiana that the British rented or gave to the United States in exchange for fifty destroyers. On Nov. 3, 1941, President Roosevelt nominated him for a second term.

During World War II, Moreell found substitutes for scarce materials and increased his CEC force from 125 men in December 1941 to 10,860 by the end of the war. These men supervised construction at naval and Marine Corps facilities as well as any required by the other naval bureaus. For example, the nineteen naval air bases of 1941 grew to eighty with many satellite fields. Most of Moreell's construction work was done by Contractors, Pacific Naval Air Bases, a separate organization that involved naval personnel and eight large construction companies. He saved money by using cost-plus-fixed-fee contracts rather than cost-plus-percentage-profits contracts.

Most of the $9.25 billion in spending that Moreell supervised was for the naval bases and facilities in the Pacific theater, but he used Seabees worldwide. Early in the war, the Seabees were unarmed civilians who could not legally defend themselves if attacked. But with building sites often in war zones, Moreell in January 1942 showed that advanced base construction could proceed only with military personnel under military command. Volunteers were given military ranks and training, and he had to promise organized union labor that they would either work overseas or build only while training; the rest of the domestic work would be done by private contractors and civilian labor.

The first Seabee Battalion was composed of 3,000 men representing some sixty skills. They disregarded organized trade lines and did whatever work was assigned to them. After being trained at major camps such as those near Little Creek, Va., at Davisville, R.I., and at Port Hueneme, Calif., they went overseas. Special groups were formed to build and maintain air bases and fire director bases. Also trained were thirty stevedore battalions.

Seabees involved in amphibious landings, often as integral parts of Marine combat divisions, built naval bases and airfields from which the next operation could be launched. To use as building blocks for barges, piers, and even floating dry docks, they built sheet steel into five-by-seven foot cubes. At their peak, the CBs included 360,000 officers and men, 83 percent of whom worked overseas.

On Feb. 2, 1944, President Roosevelt nominated Moreell a vice-admiral, and he subsequently became the youngest vice-admiral in the navy and also the first CEC officer to hold that rank.

The postwar demobilization of Moreell's personnel was swift. They were reduced to 400 officers and 20,000 men by June 30, 1946. In his last naval billet (1945–1946), he served as director of procurement and materials, and at President Truman's order he controlled the petroleum and coal industries when their workers struck. He was able to bring owners and workers into agreement. He was retired on Oct. 1, 1946. He headed the Turner Construction Company for a short time, was board chairman and chief executive of the Jones and Laughlin Steel Corporation (1947–1958), and in the 1960's was board chairman of the conservative Americans for Constitutional Action, a group devoted to anti-Communism and inculcating patriotism. Six years after the death of his second wife, he married Cecilia Anderson, who died in 1971. He married Jesse Grimm later that year. He received many American and foreign service medals, honorary degrees, and engineering society awards. He died at Oakland, Pa.

[See Ben Moreell, "The Seabees in World War II," United States Naval Institute *Proceedings* (Mar. 1962). Brief summaries of Moreell's work appear in the annual reports of the secretary of the navy for the period 1936–1946 and in Admiral Ernest J. King's official reports for the period 1942–1946. Basic documentation of his career lies in the records of the BuY&D in the National Archives, Washington, D.C. See also United States Bureau of Yards and Docks, *Building the Navy's Bases in World War II* (1946); Paolo E. Coletta and K. Jack Bauer, eds., *United States Navy and Marine Corps Bases*, 2 vols. (1985); and Paolo E. Coletta, "Vice Admiral Ben Moreell," in Stephen Howarth, ed., *Men of War: Great Leaders of World War II* (1992). Obituaries are in the *New York Times*, July 31, 1978; and the *Washington Post*, Aug. 1, 1978.]

PAOLO E. COLETTA

MORGENTHAU, HANS JOACHIM (Feb. 17, 1904–July 19, 1980), political scientist, was born in Coburg, Germany, the son of Ludwig Morgenthau, a physician, and Frieda Bachmann. An only child, he suffered from the attentions of a neurotic and authoritarian father, and, as a Jew, from the rampant anti-Semitism that existed in Germany even before Hitler's rise to power. When his father forbade him to major in literature, Morgenthau pursued a law degree from the University of Munich and was admitted to the German bar in 1927.

Morgenthau earned his doctorate in law at the University of Frankfurt in 1929; his thesis was entitled "The International Judicial Function and the Concept of Politics." His research for this project had persuaded Morgenthau that not law but politics was the determining force in international relations. This insight led him to change careers, and in 1932 he became an instructor in political science at the University of Geneva, Switzerland, just in time to escape Hitler's seizure of power in Germany. Morgenthau remained in Geneva until 1935; he married Irma Thormann on June 3 of that year. They had two children. The couple moved to Madrid, Spain, where Morgenthau taught in the 1935–1936 academic year. They immigrated to the United States in 1937, and Morgenthau became a naturalized citizen in 1943.

Morgenthau held many academic positions, but his association with the University of Chicago, which began with a visiting appointment from 1943 to 1945 and concluded with his retirement in 1968, was the longest and most important. During his tenure at Chicago, Morgenthau was a visiting professor at a variety of institutions, including the University of California at Berkeley in 1949 and Harvard University in 1951, 1959, 1960, and 1961. He served also as a consultant to the State Department from 1949 to 1951, and again from 1961 until his death. He similarly assisted the Department of Defense from 1961 to 1965. From 1950 to 1968 he directed the Center for the Study of American Foreign Policy at the University of Chicago. After retiring from Chicago he was on the faculty of the City College of New York for six years, and from 1974 until his death, that of the New School for Social Research in New York City.

Morgenthau became well known in academic circles for his writings in the 1940's and 1950's, which did much to establish the study of international relations as a distinct and respected field. But his name became known to the general public only in the 1960's, when he joined with other opponents of the Vietnam War to build a powerful case against it. Though in time their thesis, that fighting in Southeast Asia threatened rather than strengthened American security, would be widely accepted, the initial result was a campaign of slander, encouraged by the administration of President Lyndon B. Johnson, which represented Morgenthau as a dangerous leftist.

The irony of such attacks was that Morgenthau was generally regarded as a conservative critic of the American diplomatic tradition, his name frequently joined with those of Walter Lippmann, the columnist and political philosopher, and George F. Kennan, the diplomat and historian. The approach of this school of thought was usually called "realist," as against the presumed "idealist" tradition of American foreign policy.

Although Morgenthau was a prolific author, his influence resulted chiefly from his major work, *Politics Among Nations: The Struggle for Power and Peace*, which first appeared in 1948. His aim in this book was twofold: to explore the principles governing international politics and to suggest how those principles could be employed by the United States to keep the peace and defend the nation's national interests. His first goal was particularly difficult, because in the United States, foreign relations had been viewed for the most part in three ways: as a branch of recent history; as a series of legal issues; or as a moral problem, the solution to which entailed creating a more perfect world order.

The tendency to view international relations in terms of ethics had long been an Anglo-American trait and was heightened by American belief in the United States' unique status and mission. Morgenthau wished to point the field away from ethics and to focus instead on how nations actually behaved toward one another, thereby basing the study of foreign relations on empirical principles. To this end, he sought to leaven the reformist impulses of American diplomacy with aspects of the harder-edged continental perspective. Thus, he boldly began the first chapter of *Politics Among Nations* with this statement: "International politics, like all politics, is a struggle for power."

Critics often charged that to Morgenthau, the "pope" of realism, as some called him, power politics comprised the whole of international relations. They were wrong. Morgenthau believed Americans had been able to cultivate false notions about the world owing to their political and geographical isolation in the nineteenth century. Being safe had enabled them to develop a political ideology stressing what he called "humanitarian pacifism and anti-imperialism." However, as the dangers to the United States increased, such thinking had become harmful to the conduct of foreign relations.

On the other hand, Morgenthau admired many aspects of the American political heritage, did not believe that the ends of the state justified any and all means, and recognized that statesmen and diplomats were not motivated solely by material considerations. But he wanted Americans to understand that righteousness is an insufficient basis for the achievement of national goals. In an amoral world, moral force has its limits. This remains hard for Americans to grasp, and was harder still in the 1940's, when many still hoped to return to some form of isolation from world politics.

In stressing that power politics was the basis of international relations, Morgenthau was at pains to dispel an American misconception that, as he put it, "men have a choice between power politics and its necessary outgrowth, the balance of power, on the one hand, and a different, better kind of international relations on the other." The truth was, as he would explain in detail, "that the balance of power and policies aimed at its preservation are not only inevitable, but an essential stabilizing factor in a society of sovereign nations."

Balance-of-power politics was not desirable for its own sake, Morgenthau argued, but in the absence of world peace a stable balance of power was the most to be hoped for. World peace was the goal toward which international politics should be directed, but to achieve it required a world state, he believed, an obvious impossibility under present circumstances. Morgenthau did, however, think it was realistic for the United States to break out of the superpower deadlock of the Cold War and to restore diplomacy as the link between hostile nations. He concluded his argument with this passage: "Diplomacy can make peace more secure than it is today, and the world state can make peace more secure than it would be if nations were to abide by the rules of diplomacy."

These were, it should be evident, not the words of one who believed that might makes right, as some critics seemed to feel, but those of a humane thinker who saw the world as it was, not as it should be, and yet who never abandoned the hope that through enlightened statecraft it might still become a fit place to live in. They also point up the irrelevance of another criticism sometimes made of Morgenthau, that he did not change with the times. By 1948, Morgenthau had arrived at the principles on which he believed international relations should be conducted. The only reason for changing them would have been if events had proven Morgenthau to be mistaken, which they did not. The sixth and final edition of his *Politics Among Nations*, which appeared posthumously in 1985, was in substance the same as the first, and equally as reliable a guide to understanding international relations.

It is true that Morgenthau did not adapt to changing fashions in political science, which may have disturbed those who did. Few outsiders will take such a charge very seriously. Indeed, to a layman, the most impressive aspect of Morgenthau's work was that it did not rely on arcane formulas or esoteric methods but on logic. He did not hide behind a professional mask, rather he expressed his ideas clearly, relying on his reasoning powers to carry the day.

Morgenthau died in New York City. Henry

Kissinger, the former secretary of state, paid tribute to him both as a scholar and as a man. Professionally, Morgenthau had made contemporary international relations a major academic discipline. Personally, Kissinger remembered Morgenthau as a "gentle, loving man," a great teacher, with a "slightly sardonic sense of humor which never stooped to the malicious."

[Morgenthau's papers are on deposit at the Alderman Library of the University of Virginia. A brief memoir by Morgenthau is "An Intellectual Autobiography," *Society*, Jan./Feb. 1978. It appears in Kenneth Thompson and Robert J. Myers, eds., *A Tribute to Hans Morgenthau* (1977), a collection of his essays and addresses. See also Greg Russell, *Hans J. Morgenthau and the Ethics of American Statecraft* (1990), a positive interpretation, and Martin Griffiths, *Realism, Idealism and International Politics* (1992), which is more critical. An obituary is in the *New York Times*, July 21, 1980. A tribute by Henry Kissinger is in the *The New Republic*, Aug. 2 and 9, 1980.]

WILLIAM L. O'NEILL

MORISON, SAMUEL ELIOT (July 9, 1887–May 15, 1976), historian and educator, was born in Boston, the son of John Holmes Morison, a lawyer, and Emily Marshall Eliot. He was inspired to become a historian by his grandparents, historian Samuel Eliot and Emily Marshall Otis. Summers on Maine's Mt. Desert Island led to an affection for the Down East coast and made him into an inveterate sailor; he also acquired a fondness for horseback riding. Educated at two preparatory schools, Noble's School in Boston and St. Paul's School in Concord, N.H., he entered Harvard in 1904, graduating cum laude with a B.A. in history in 1908. After studying at three universities in France for a year, he took his M.A. at Harvard in 1909 and his Ph.D. in 1912. On May 28, 1910, he married Elizabeth Amory Shaw ("Bessie") Greene, a painter of Boston. They had four children before she died in 1945. After teaching history at Radcliffe College and the University of California at Berkeley, he joined the history faculty at Harvard in 1915, an appointment he retained for the rest of his teaching career. In 1941 he became Jonathan Trumbull Professor of American History and retired in 1955.

Morison's powerful narrative style of writing forged him into an articulate champion of his country's liberal past and a deft purveyor of these traditions to scholars and general readers alike. An abiding kinship with seafarers in general and with the New England founders of America in particular led him to focus on the political successes of these individuals, beginning with the two-volume revised doctoral dissertation celebrating his own great-great-grandfather: *The Life and Letters of Harrison Gray Otis, Federalist, 1765–1848* (1913; revised edition 1969). He admired the religious leaders of Puritan Massachusetts, Jeffersonian idealists, Andrew Jackson as common man, and Alexander Hamilton for the orderliness and discipline without which Morison believed freedom cannot flourish.

In his admiration of Woodrow Wilson's idea for the League of Nations, the young historian enlisted in the army in 1918 and worked as a peace commission staff member for the Baltic region until June 1919, when he resigned in opposition to Wilson's compromises to Allied diplomatic demands at the Versailles conference and returned to Harvard to teach. Disillusioned over the role of historians as social and political activists, Morison equally turned away from the prevailing school of American progressive relativist historical writing (that which was influenced by contemporary issues) and, without distorting objective facts or rigorous research, followed the advice of former senator Albert Beveridge to write personalized, subjective history, as in *The Maritime History of Massachusetts, 1783–1860* (1921). He was inspired mostly by the style of American historian Francis Parkman.

In 1922 he welcomed the invitation of Oxford University to be the first Harold Vyvyan Harmsworth Professor of American History, a position he held for three years (1922–1925). In 1925 he returned to his post at Harvard. The American dream and national unity were the theme of his two-volume *Oxford History of the United States, 1783–1917* (1927), expanded and revised as *The Oxford History of the American People* (1965), which formed the basis for *The Growth of the American Republic* (1930), coauthored with Henry Steele Commager. In this volume, he countered "debunkers" of American idealism and the traditional New England past, including such historical relativists as Carl L. Becker, midwestern regionalists epitomized by Frederick Jackson Turner, and especially economic determinist Charles A. Beard. Morison's refutation of Beard's contention that economic motives lay behind the writing of the

Constitution and the entry of the United States into both world wars appeared in a devastating review essay, "History Through a Beard," in the *Atlantic Monthly* in 1948.

Yet his own regionalism provided the foundations for his articles in the pages of the *New England Quarterly*, which he founded in 1928 and edited for a time, and in several books that revived scholarly interest in the Puritans: *Builders of the Bay Colony* (1930), *The Puritan Pronaos* (1936, reissued in 1956 as *The Intellectual Life of Colonial New England*), and the three-volume *Tercentennial History of Harvard College and University, 1636–1936* (1935–1936).

From 1925 until 1974, Morison increasingly devoted his time to retracing the voyages and reliving the experiences at sea of early European and American seafarers, celebrating their heroism as explorers but not their subsequent heavy-handed activities as empire makers. His first achievement in this venue was his greatest—the two-volume biography of Christopher Columbus, *Admiral of the Ocean Sea* (1942), the research for which was conducted on several voyages (1937–1940) of the Harvard Columbus Expedition under his command undertaken to prove Columbus's navigational genius. The book won the Pulitzer Prize, as did *John Paul Jones: A Sailor's Biography* (1959). His crowning dual seafaring epics were the two volumes of *The European Discovery of America: The Northern Voyages* (1971) and *The Southern Voyages* (1974), the latter published when Morison was eighty-seven years old.

Rare among American historians, Morison advocated American intervention in World War II. Early in 1942 he persuaded President Franklin D. Roosevelt to give him a commission as a lieutenant commander in the United States Naval Reserve and to permit him to write the semiofficial history of the navy's wartime operations and to observe combat operations on vessels of his own choosing. He thereupon served aboard eight warships in both oceans but, oddly, never aboard an aircraft carrier or submarine, the two ship types that proved most decisive. Leaning heavily on a small staff of historians, he applied his organizational skills and adept turn of phrase to produce the epic fifteen-volume *History of United States Naval Operations in World War II* (1947–1962). As with most of his multivolume works, a popular condensation followed: *The Two-Ocean War* (1963), a one-volume work. He attained the rank of captain late in 1945 and retired as rear admiral in 1951.

Although elected president of the American Historical Association in 1950 and an outspoken conservative, anti-Communist historian, the already very private Morison rapidly turned away from institutional affiliations. In 1949 he married his cousin Priscilla Barton Schackelford of Baltimore; she died in 1973. They had no children. In his later years, Morison—ever tall, sea-wizened, and with awesome countenance—enjoyed eminence as the dean of American historians, famed for his independence from "schools" of historical interpretation, his narrative style, and his gift for storytelling. He died in Boston.

[Morison's papers are housed at the Harvard University Archives and formed the basis for the biography by Gregory M. Pfitzer, *Samuel Eliot Morison's Historical World* (1991), which, however, suffers from inaccuracies concerning his naval service. Autobiographical books are *One Boy's Boston, 1887–1901* (1962) and *Spring Tides* (1965). *Sailor Historian* (1977), edited by his daughter Emily Morison Beck, is a collection of essays. Other anthologies of essays include *By Land and by Sea* (1953) and *Vistas of History* (1964).

Biographical essays are William Bentinck-Smith, "Samuel Eliot Morison," *Proceedings of the Massachusetts Historical Society*, vol. 88 (1976); and Wilcomb E. Washburn, "Samuel Eliot Morison, Historian," *William and Mary Quarterly*, July 1979. See also Bernard Bailyn et al., "Memorial Minute: Samuel Eliot Morison," *Harvard Gazette*, June 10, 1977; Parker Bishop Albee, Jr., "Portrait of a Friendship," *The New England Quarterly*, June and September 1983; and K. Jack Bauer, "Bibliography of Writings of Samuel Eliot Morison," *North American Society for Oceanic History Newsletter* (1977). An obituary is in the *New York Times*, May 16, 1976.]

CLARK G. REYNOLDS

MORTIMER, CHARLES GREENOUGH (July 26, 1900–Dec. 25, 1978), food industry executive, was born in Brooklyn, N.Y., the son of Charles Greenough Mortimer, an inventor, and Cecilia Clara Dessoir. The family soon moved to suburban East Orange, N.J., where Mortimer attended public high school. At graduation he enlisted in the United States Naval Reserve, which assigned him to a submarine engineering training program at nearby Stevens Institute of Technology in Hoboken, N.J. At the same time, he got a job as an export department clerk with National Aniline and Chemical Company and soon realized that his interest lay in sales, not engineering. In 1921 he left Stevens to take a full-time sales job with R. B. Davis Baking Powder Company. He quickly climbed the organizational ladder, successively working as district manager, a division manager, then general sales manager.

In 1923, Mortimer married Marion Mather Lewis, who died in childbirth three years later. In 1927, Mortimer married again, to Elizabeth Kempley Atterbury; they had three children.

In 1924, Mortimer accepted a position with the Madison Avenue advertising agency George Batten Company. As an account executive, he was given several grocery accounts, including Sanka coffee. A German named Ludwig Roselius had developed Sanka as a replacement for his decaffeinated Kaffee Hag, which the American government had seized during World War I; Roselius hired the Batten agency to handle the advertising. When Mortimer took over the account, he visited Roselius's plant, learning the intricacies of coffee blending and production; he then introduced a campaign based on the slogan "Now a Coffee Even for Substitute Drinkers." The campaign was successful enough to persuade executives of the Postum Cereal Company (makers of Postum, the leading coffee substitute, developed by Charles W. Post in 1895) that Sanka was a strong competitor; Postum bought the marketing rights to Sanka in 1928 and promptly transferred the advertising account to Young and Rubicam. Within weeks, Mortimer learned of an opening for an advertising assistant at Postum and was hired. He had responsibility for advertising and merchandising of two products: Calumet baking powder and Sanka. In 1930, Mortimer was named merchandising manager for a group of products including Calumet baking powder, Sanka, Log Cabin syrup, Certo, and Sure Jell.

In 1929, Postum, in partnership with the Goldman Sachs investment firm, paid about $22 million for Birds Eye Frosted Foods, a marginally successful company that produced only frozen haddock, thereby acquiring Clarence Birdseye's 168 patents, including those controlling his quick-freezing process, the Birds Eye brand name in frozen foods, and rights to the name General Foods; it adopted that name for itself. Thus Postum became General Foods, where Mortimer would spend the rest of his business career.

Mortimer was a highly effective marketing executive. In 1928 Sanka had been sold only in the New York City area. By 1935, in the face of the Great Depression and a pricing strategy that made Sanka expensive, Mortimer had made Sanka into a national brand and had doubled sales. To do this, he shifted the advertising away from its emphasis (which he himself had developed) on Sanka as a substitute for coffee to a campaign making two points: Sanka was a coffee that let people sleep; Sanka was itself an excellent brand of coffee. He initially focused on print media, relying principally on humorous commentaries. In the summer of 1935, Mortimer added radio advertising. At that time, this meant sponsoring a program. Sanka was soon sponsoring a dramatic half-hour program featuring Helen Hayes; it was a striking success, perhaps drawing the largest audience of any dramatic program then on radio.

In 1938, Mortimer moved up to vice-president for advertising and in 1943 became vice-president for marketing and operations. Here he continued General Foods' creative leadership in using radio as a primary marketing medium, most prominently through the "Maxwell House Coffee Hour" radio variety show, Jack Benny's half-hour show sponsored by Jell-O, and Kate Smith's program sponsored by Swans Down flour and Calumet baking powder. These shows featured such leading entertainment figures as Abbott and Costello, Frank Morgan, Lanny Ross, and Meredith Willson. In 1950, Mortimer was elected to the board of General Foods and promoted to operating vice-president for Birds Eye. Again his flair for marketing made its mark: Birds Eye froze thousands of snowballs, then sold them in July as part of a promotional campaign. In 1952 he moved up to executive vice-president, and on Apr. 1, 1954, became president, in part because of the recognition by the board of directors that marketing was central to General Foods' future success. Though General Foods was one of America's largest food companies, it was earning anemic profits, well below the average for American business and for its competitors in the food business; faced a host of aggressive competitors in virtually every market; had to cope with a rapidly evolving American food market, as consumers switched to convenience foods and became much more willing to try new foods; and was surprisingly far behind smaller competitors in seeking foreign markets.

Mortimer soon restructured management to

improve information available to top management and to delegate more responsibility to divisional vice-presidents. He also completed an important rationalization of the sales organization; until 1953 a single salesman handled a startling array of products from several different groups, which made it difficult both for the salesman to handle the individual products effectively and for the managers responsible for production to be accountable for marketing. Under the new structure, General Foods products were grouped into five divisions, each of which had full responsibility for production and marketing. Mortimer supported this strengthened marketing organization with huge expenditures on advertising—General Foods became the largest food advertiser in the country and ranked fifth in expenditures among all advertisers, behind only General Motors, Procter and Gamble, Colgate-Palmolive, and Ford. He also began a strong foreign expansion. General Foods had long ignored foreign markets; in 1953, when it finally created a separate international division, it had a single foreign subsidiary, in the United Kingdom. By the time Mortimer retired as chairman in 1965 (he had been promoted in 1959), General Foods was operating in seventeen and marketing in ninety-three foreign countries. Between 1958 and 1962 he vastly strengthened General Foods' ability to serve its customers through a system of regional warehouses. Finally, he led General Foods much more deeply into research. By 1959 it had the largest private food research laboratory in the United States, and had raised research expenditures from barely 0.5 percent of sales to 1.3 percent.

Mortimer was a restless and demanding corporate leader. His nickname was "How Soon Mortimer" because he always wanted to know when a job would be done. He declared that "knowing more about the total company than any other person around" was the first requirement of his job. So he typically met daily with senior managers and asked fifty executives to send him weekly confidential reports discussing "whatever they damned well please." He sharpened his sense of what the company was doing by dropping in on executives, checking the shelves of grocery stores to see how his products were doing, and talking with customers. He also took new products home to test them himself. His family so liked Spanish Minute Rice that he canceled the test marketing and put it directly on the market; it was an immediate success. Probably General Foods' biggest failure under Mortimer's leadership was a line of gourmet frozen foods introduced in 1956. Bypassing usual distribution channels, General Foods tried to sell the line through upscale department stores and advertised the line only in high-brow magazines. By the time Mortimer canceled the line in 1960, it had cost the company $30 million.

During Mortimer's time as president (1954–1959) and chairman (1959–1965), General Foods' annual sales grew from $825 million to $1.5 billion and the number of employees from 18,000 to 30,000. More important, it moved from making only a small profit to earning one of the best in the food industry and one well above the average for American industry. Mortimer's ability as a business executive was recognized through appointments to the boards of directors of major corporations that included Ford, Bell and Howell, First National City Bank, and Mobil Oil, on which he remained active until mandatory retirement in 1975. Until his death he served on the boards of the Federal Street Fund (now the State Street Fund) in Boston. Mortimer was a trustee of Smith College and the Stevens Institute of Technology and was national chairman for the Emancipation Centennial United Negro College Fund Development Campaign (1963–1964).

When he was away from General Foods, Mortimer's passion was his Westfall Farm in New Jersey, where he managed a world-class breeding program for Holstein-Frisian dairy cattle for fourteen years and developed a stable of Morgan horses, considered the best in New Jersey; in 1968 he donated the herd to the state.

Mortimer died in Orleans, Mass.

[Further information on Mortimer can be found at the Kraft General Food Archives, Morton Grove, Ill.; his business papers are housed at the University of Wyoming. See also Lawrence M. Hughes, "General Foods Organizes Management and Markets for the Next 10 Years," *Sales Management*, July 15, 1955; and *Time*, Dec. 7, 1959. An obituary is in the *New York Times*, Dec. 29, 1978.]

FRED CARSTENSEN
ELDON BERNSTEIN

MORTON, ROGERS CLARK BALLARD (Sept. 19, 1914–Apr. 19, 1979), congressman and cabinet member, was born in Louisville,

Ky., the son of David Cummins Morton, a physician and milling business executive, and Mary Harris Ballard, a homemaker. An older brother, Thruston B. Morton, served three terms as a congressman and from 1957 to 1969 was a United States senator from Kentucky. Morton attended public schools in Jefferson County, Ky., before transferring to Woodberry Forest School, near Orange, Va. He graduated from Woodberry Forest in 1933 and entered Yale University, pursuing studies toward a degree in business and political science. While at Yale, he played on the basketball team. After graduation in 1937, he entered the College of Physicians and Surgeons at Columbia University. He left within a year, having found that a medical career was not to his liking. Morton returned to Louisville, where he joined the family milling business, Ballard and Ballard. On May 27, 1939, he married Ann Prather Jones; they had two children.

In 1941, Morton enlisted in the United States Army as a private in the field artillery. After being sent to Officers' Candidate School, he served in the European Theater and rose to the rank of captain by the time of his discharge in 1945. After World War II, he returned to Louisville and became president of Ballard and Ballard in 1946. While in Louisville, Morton helped manage the successful congressional campaigns of his older brother, Thruston. In 1951, the family firm merged with the Pillsbury Company, and Morton became a corporate vice-president and director.

In the early 1950's, Morton moved to Talbot County, Md., where he purchased a thousand-acre farm to raise beef cattle and operate a cattle-feeding business. In Maryland, he revived his interest and involvement in Republican party politics. Residing in the then predominantly Democratic First Congressional District of Maryland, he managed the 1960 campaign of Republican candidate Edward T. Miller. Two years later, Morton himself ran as the Republican candidate for the First District, and won. Following that victory, he was reelected to the next three Congresses. During his first three terms, Morton served on the committees on the Interior and Insular Affairs, the Merchant Marine and Fisheries, and the Select Committee on Small Business. In 1969 he was assigned to the powerful Ways and Means Committee.

Morton's voting record in Congress mirrored the conservative views of his district and indicated a general adherence to party positions. On environmental issues he drafted legislation establishing the Assateague Island National Seashore, developed laws preserving estuarine areas, and sponsored an oil-pollution control bill. He was the sponsor of President Richard M. Nixon's major environmental package, a belated supporter of the 1964 Civil Rights Act, and an opponent of a 1968 open-housing bill favored by President Nixon.

In the Republican maneuvering for the 1968 presidential nomination, Morton supported Richard Nixon. At the Republican party convention in August, he served as floor manager for Nixon's nomination. In April 1969, two months after the resignation of Ray C. Bliss, Morton was chosen chairman of the Republican National Committee, a post in which he acted as the chief spokesperson for administration policies. Earlier, his older brother had held the post. For nearly the next twenty-one months Morton was both National Committee chairman and a congressman. Mounting friction between the White House staff and the National Committee led to Morton's resignation of the chairmanship in late 1970.

In January 1971, President Nixon named Morton secretary of the interior. While serving in the post, one of the major issues he faced was the construction of the controversial Alaska pipeline. In May 1972, Morton approved the pipeline, although legal maneuvers by environmentalists blocked the start of construction until April 1974. Other issues impacting agencies under his administration included the November 1972 Native American takeover of the Bureau of Indian Affairs Building in Washington, D.C., and the winter 1973 siege at Wounded Knee, S.Dak., where several hundred Oglala Sioux and their supporters returned to take a stand on Native American lands and Native American rights. Their return led to armed conflict with federal officials for several months in early 1973 (Wounded Knee was the site of an 1890 massacre of 300 Native Americans by the United States Army). In the 1972 presidential campaign, Morton served as spokesperson for the Nixon campaign. Following Nixon's reelection, Morton continued as secretary of the interior.

In August 1974, following Nixon's resignation, President Gerald R. Ford appointed Morton to a committee overseeing the transition of administration. Under the Ford presidency, Morton became secretary of commerce in March 1975, a post he held until February 1976, when he became a counselor to the president for economic and domestic policy matters. The Commerce post was not without controversy; Morton came into conflict with the House Commerce Committee for initially refusing to supply the names of American firms participating in the Arab boycott of Israel. In April 1976, he became chairman of President Ford's campaign committee. Following Ford's defeat at the polls, Morton resigned from politics and returned to his farm and custom boatbuilding business. He died in Easton, Md.

[Morton's papers are in the Modern Political Collections of the Special Collections Department, University of Kentucky Library, Lexington. An obituary is in the *New York Times*, Apr. 20, 1979.]

FRANK R. LEVSTIK

MOSCONE, GEORGE RICHARD (Nov. 24, 1929–Nov. 27, 1978), mayor of San Francisco, was born in San Francisco, the son of George J. Moscone, a prison guard, and Lena ("Lee") Monge. Growing up in the city's Cow Hollow district, he attended St. Ignatius High School and won all-city basketball honors in 1947 and 1948. He served in the naval reserve, was president of his college fraternity, and received the B.A. from the University of the Pacific in 1952. Moscone married Eugenia ("Gina") Bondanza on June 19, 1954; they had four children. In 1956 he earned the J.D. from the University of California's Hastings Law School in San Francisco, and he was admitted to the California bar in 1957.

Moscone became a partner in the law firm of a childhood friend, Charles O. Morgan. He was a member of the San Francisco County Democratic Committee from 1960 to 1969, taught law at Lincoln University in San Francisco from 1960 to 1964, and was a member of the San Francisco Board of Supervisors from 1963 to 1966.

A liberal, Moscone won election to the California State Senate in 1966, the year Ronald Reagan won the governorship, and fought Reagan's attacks on welfare and mental health funding. His proudest legislative achievement was securing state funding for school lunches for 750,000 California children in 1970. Moscone was elected senate majority leader and often marched with César Chávez and the United Farm Workers in their quest for better working conditions. The capitol press corps in Sacramento voted him "Most Effective Democratic Senator" in 1969, the year he became a member of the law firm of Hansen, Bridgett, Marcus and Jenkins. During this busy time, Moscone also wrote for legal journals.

In 1974, Moscone entered the California gubernatorial primary but dropped out in favor of Edmund G. ("Jerry") Brown, Jr. The annual stays in Sacramento left him little time for his family, so he directed his career closer to home. In 1975, he decided to run for election as successor to the colorful Joseph Alioto as mayor of San Francisco.

Then, as now, San Francisco had a cosmopolitan culture but suffered from perceived ills: "hippies" in the Haight-Ashbury district, homosexuals in Castro Valley, and rampant political crime. Nearly 100 political bombings and 14 political murders occurred in the decade before 1975 as Black Muslim "Zebra" killers, the Symbionese Liberation Army, and the New World Liberation Front tried to disrupt the political process.

New high-rise buildings, decaying neighborhoods, and unrepresentative city government plagued the city. Its supervisors were elected "at large" rather than from specific districts. Power blocs, such as the Civic League, froze the poor, blacks, Asians, and homosexuals out of city offices. Moscone tried to change that cliquishness and to help the city create supervisorial districts and to require supervisors to live in their districts. He faced a childhood friend, conservative supervisor John Barbagelata, in the December runoff election, which he won with the help of Jim Jones and volunteers from his People's Temple. With Moscone as mayor, new people came into office, including Harvey Milk, an acknowledged homosexual as supervisor for the Haight-Ashbury and Upper Market Street.

After his January 1976 inauguration, Moscone acted on his reforming principles and broadened participation in city government by appointing homosexuals to city boards and Jones to the city's housing authority. Moscone faced three immediate challenges after his election: a virtual war with radical groups, a strike by municipal workers, and the sale of the San Francisco Giants baseball team to a Canadian group.

The problems with the radicals were beyond

his control. The thirty-eight-day strike was settled with concessions from the Board of Supervisors, and Moscone threatened a lawsuit against the Giants while working to keep the team in the city. His efforts paid off when the Giants decided to stay in San Francisco. Moscone served as a delegate to the Democratic National Convention in 1976.

More challenges arose in 1977 when Barbagelata organized a move to overturn the political reforms of the year before and to cut the terms of Moscone and other elected officials from four to two years. The challenge failed at the polls.

When Miami, Fla., repealed its laws protecting homosexuals, San Francisco's large gay community became alarmed. In June 1977, homosexuals Jerry Taylor and Roger Hillsborough, a city gardener, were attacked and Hillsborough was killed. The gay community reacted in protest, and Moscone moved to help them and to calm their fears. The city hall flag flew at half-staff for Hillsborough. Violent crime came to the fore when three gunmen killed five and wounded eleven in Chinatown's Golden Dragon Restaurant. Moscone offered a $100,000 reward for their apprehension.

In January 1978 a two-year drought and water rationing ended. In April, the city celebrated the centennial of its famous cable car lines. Then, on Nov. 18, 1978, came tragedy: the suicides of Jim Jones and 911 of his followers who had left San Francisco and reestablished their temple in Jonestown, Guyana. The news of the suicides compounded the malaise many San Franciscans felt for their city and its new inhabitants.

One segment of the population saw Moscone and Milk as "symbols of a once glorious city that had become dirty and dangerous." One of those was Dan White, a former policeman, a conservative, and a gay-basher. White had resigned as a San Francisco supervisor on November 10 because of the position's low salary but came to Moscone's office on November 27 to ask to be reinstated. Moscone had already selected another individual to fill the post. White shot and killed Moscone in the mayor's office and then killed Milk in his City Hall office. He surrendered at the police station where he had once been an officer. At the memorial service for Moscone and Milk on the steps of City Hall, Joan Baez sang "Kumbaya," "Amazing Grace," and "Oh, Freedom." Leo T. McCarthy, speaker of the California Assembly, spoke a fitting epitaph, calling Moscone "a power broker for the poor."

[Moscone left no publicly accessible papers. See *The Harvey Milk Gay Democratic Club Presents Harvey Milk's Birthday, 1982* (1982); Randy Shilts, *The Mayor of Castro Street: The Life and Times of Harvey Milk* (1982); and Mike Weiss, *Double Play: The San Francisco City Hall Killings* (1984). Oral history interviews conducted by Ann Lage with Arlen F. Gregorio and John V. Jervis, and by Arlene Lazarowitz with Omer L. Rains, can be found at the University of California, Berkeley. Obituaries are in the *Los Angeles Times*, Nov. 28, 1978; the *New York Times*, Nov. 28 and 29, 1978; and the *Washington Post*, Nov. 29, 1978.]

LAWRENCE CARROLL ALLIN

MOSTEL, SAMUEL JOEL ("ZERO") (Feb. 28, 1915–Sept. 8, 1977), actor, comedian, and painter, was born in the Brownsville section of Brooklyn, N.Y., the son of Israel Mostel and Cina Druchs. Israel Mostel, who had emigrated from eastern Europe to New York in 1898, managed vineyards and a slaughterhouse and acted as lay rabbi in his Orthodox Jewish community. Druchs, born in Poland and reared and educated in Vienna, immigrated to America in 1908. She became Mrs. Celia Mostel, housewife and mother to eight children, including four from Israel's first marriage. In 1917 the family moved to the Lower East Side of Manhattan.

Young Samuel was strongly influenced by Jewish tradition and humor and also became multilingual through his parents. He attended P.S. 188 on Houston Street from 1921 to 1926, advanced rapidly through junior high school, and entered Seward Park High School in 1928. Mostel showed promise in painting, visiting New York City museums regularly to study works of art. He participated in art classes given by the Educational Alliance, a program organized to acculturate Jewish immigrants. Painting soon became the focus of his life.

After he graduated from high school in 1931, Mostel studied fine arts and literature at the City College of New York (CCNY). In 1935 he earned a B.A. from CCNY and began graduate work at New York University (NYU); though he intended to earn an M.A. and then to teach, Mostel soon dropped out of NYU, working at various blue-collar jobs and traveling to Louisiana and Mexico.

In 1937 he was hired through the Federal Art Project of the Works Progress Administration (WPA). Only twenty-two, he was the youngest painter in the program. Mostel painted murals and taught art classes to Jewish youth in New York City. His employer described him as "a very satisfactory teacher, highly intelligent" but also remarked negatively about his "clowning all the time." Mostel lectured for the WPA in numerous museums, where he developed a reputation as a comedian, and began to entertain at parties and fund-raisers to earn extra money. He was a large man, fitting Irving Howe's description of Yiddish actors as "men of vitality and heft, accustomed to filling the spaces of the stage." His waistline increased and his brown hairline receded as the years advanced. Often he wore a thick mustache, and sometimes a beard, especially in his later years.

In February 1942, Mostel obtained a part-time job doing stand-up routines at the progressive Café Society Downtown. He was christened "Zero" by press agent Ivan Black, who thereby implied a similarity between Mostel and the Marx Brothers: Groucho, Harpo, and Chico; the name also suggested that Mostel was "starting from nothing." Mostel's zany pantomime and biting social satire quickly won him a following and a degree of fame.

Mostel rose meteorically in 1942, performing on national radio, on Broadway, at New York's Paramount Theatre, and in a Metro-Goldwyn-Mayer film, *DuBarry Was a Lady*. He soon appeared at top nightclubs and on radio shows nationwide, earning as much as $5,000 per week. America's radio columnists named him the "Number One New Star of 1943." However, Mostel's career was put on hold in March 1943, when he was drafted into the United States Army. He served only a few months before being honorably discharged, ostensibly for a physical disability. But Mostel's biographer Jared Brown notes that Mostel "was under suspicion as a radical," which may have prompted his early dismissal. Mostel then performed overseas for the American troops.

On July 2, 1944, Mostel married his second wife (the first, Clara Sverd, left him in 1941 after two years of marriage), Kathryn ("Kate") Harkin, a Rockette from an Irish-Catholic family; the couple had two children.

From 1946 to 1949, Mostel studied drama with Donald Richardson. He debuted as Mr. Peachum in a Duke Ellington remake of *The Beggar's Opera* entitled *Beggar's Holiday*. In 1948 he appeared on a television series, "Off the Record," and in a television movie, *The Man Who Came to Dinner*.

Mostel developed a dual personality that shifted rapidly from serious intellectual to zany comic, depending on his environment. His political characterizations onstage, along with his background and milieu, brought him under suspicion by zealous anti-Communists; he was denounced as a Communist in *Counterattack* and *Red Channels*, and thereafter blacklisted and denied employment as an actor. The family subsisted for nearly a decade on money Kate earned from jobs and money Zero earned from occasional sales of his paintings.

Mostel was called to testify before the House Un-American Activities Committee (HUAC) on Oct. 14, 1955. He invoked the Fifth Amendment, refusing to cooperate with the committee by naming any of his friends or acquaintances as Communists or Communist sympathizers. His loyalties and personal convictions regarding censorship and blacklisting, together with his pride, precluded any possibility of Mostel's acting as a "friendly witness" for the HUAC; though he experienced deep depression during the blacklist, he was well satisfied with his performance in court.

In 1957, Mostel appeared in the unsuccessful Broadway comedy *Good as Gold*. In May 1958 he played Leopold Bloom in *Ulysses in Nighttown*, an off-Broadway production of a segment of the James Joyce novel, directed by Burgess Meredith. Mostel's phenomenal performance earned him universal acclaim from theater critics and the Obie Award for the best off-Broadway performance of the 1958–1959 season. His agent, Toby Cole, arranged an equally successful European tour of the play; Mostel was elected best actor by the International Critics Circle at the Théâtre des Nations festival in Paris.

On Jan. 13, 1960, a careening bus struck Mostel as he exited a taxi, crushing his left leg. Complicated surgery restored use of the leg, but it was never the same again. After much physical therapy, Mostel was cast as John in Eugene Ionesco's *Rhinoceros*, which opened on Jan. 9, 1961, at Broadway's Longacre Theatre. Mostel's innovative transformation from human to rhinoceros using mime instead of makeup was "side-splitting and terrifying," said Howard Taubman of the *New York Times*. Mostel's was the outstanding Broadway performance of 1960–1961, for which he received his first Antoinette Perry ("Tony") Award.

Mostel considered offers for the role of Falstaff in Shakespeare's *Henry IV* but was instead persuaded to play the lucrative role of Pseudolus in Stephen Sondheim's slapstick musical comedy *A Funny Thing Happened on the Way to the Forum*. The production opened at the Alvin Theatre on May 8, 1962, and was heralded as a great success by the New York City critics. Despite its "low comedy" format, the play was a box office smash.

For a time, the billboard above the Alvin Theatre simply stated "Zero," sufficing to attract scores of theatergoers. *Forum* won six Tony awards, one of which went to Mostel for the best performance by an actor in a musical. *Cue* magazine named him "Entertainer of the Year." But Mostel's large ego was often a burden to his colleagues; librettist Larry Gelbart described Mostel as "a giant talent . . . and a giant pain in the ass."

Mostel's reputation soared. He was invited to give the Theodore Spencer Memorial Lecture at Harvard University. The lecture, entitled "Mostel on the Art of Comedy," was given on May 20, 1962. Mostel's delivery was unique, interspersed with outrageous jokes, noises, and facial expressions. The theoretical basis was derived from nineteenth-century drama critic George Meredith, who argued that comedy is engendered by "a climate of free intellectual activity." Mostel cited the censure of both Nazis and Puritans as inhibition of this "activity." He advised the audience to "throw your hair shirt into the flame" to revitalize American comedy. Mostel's words met with thunderous applause.

His next major character was the dairyman Tevye in *Fiddler on the Roof*. The musical underwent much revision before arriving at the Imperial Theatre on Broadway. Mostel influenced the score, script, direction, and performance; his knowledge of Jewish tradition vastly improved the final production. When the musical opened on Sept. 22, 1964, Harold Taubman said Mostel and Tevye "were ordained to be one." *Newsweek* claimed that "Broadway has a new king and divinity, and there are no rivals in sight." *Fiddler* won nine Tony awards, with Mostel winning best actor in a musical for the 1964–1965 season. Moreover, he also was given the Sholem Aleichem Award, the New York Drama Critics Award, and the Outer Circle Award, and he was named the "Year's Outstanding Actor" by the Yiddish Theatrical Alliance. In June 1966, Zero and Kate were honored with a reception at the White House.

A variety of projects followed, beginning with the film version of *A Funny Thing Happened on the Way to the Forum* in 1966. Also in 1966 he collaborated with Paddy Chayefsky and Burgess Meredith on a repertory theater company, but the enterprise was soon aborted. In 1968, Mostel performed in an unappealing film, *Great Catherine*, and then costarred with Gene Wilder in what many critics believe to be his best film, the zany Mel Brooks comedy *The Producers*. Further film work followed, including *The Great Bank Robbery* (1969), *The Angel Levine* (1970), *The Hot Rock* (1972), *Marco* (1973), *Once upon a Scoundrel* (1973), and *Foreplay* (1975).

Mostel had his first solo painting exhibition at the ACA Galleries in New York in 1973. Critics approved his intense, sophisticated style, though sales were unimpressive.

Mostel starred in an acclaimed BBC/CBS production of the opera *Gianni Schicci* in 1975. In 1976, *Fiddler* was successfully revived on Broadway, with Mostel again appearing as Tevye. In 1976 he starred as a blacklisted comedian in the film *The Front*, a poignant tribute to performers who had suffered under McCarthyism.

In 1977, Mostel took the role of Shylock in Arnold Wesker's *The Merchant*, a play based on Shakespeare's *The Merchant of Venice* in which a slim Shylock opposes the law requiring Antonio's death and fights in court to save his life. Resorting to a liquid diet, Mostel shed a hundred pounds in four months. Just before the opening performance, he collapsed and was hospitalized. On September 8, in Thomas Jefferson University Hospital, Philadelphia, Mostel suffered a fatal aortic aneurysm. He was remembered with memorial art exhibits at the New York Public Library and in a television program, *Adding Up to Zero*.

[See Jared Brown, *Zero Mostel: A Biography* (1989). Also of key interest are Max Waldman, *Zero by Mostel* (1965); and Kate Mostel and Madeleine Gilford, *One Hundred Seventy Years of Show Business: With Jack Gilford and Zero Mostel* (1978). See also Craig Zadan, *Sondheim & Co.* (1986); and Marian Seldes, *The Bright Lights: A Theatre Life* (1984). An obituary is in the *New York Times*, Sept. 9, 1977.]

STUART W. STROTHMAN

MOWRER, EDGAR ANSEL (Mar. 8, 1892–Mar. 2, 1977), journalist and author, was born in Bloomington, Ill., the son of Rufus Mowrer, a businessman, and Nell Scott. The most influential person in Mowrer's life as a child, he wrote, was his older brother Paul Scott Mowrer. The family moved in 1898 to the South Side of Chicago, where Mowrer grew up and graduated in 1909 from Hyde Park High School. He enrolled that fall at the University of Michigan but transferred the next year to the University of Chicago.

In January 1911, he left school in Chicago bound for Paris to visit his brother, a foreign correspondent for the Chicago *Daily News*. Mowrer spent a year attending lectures at the Sorbonne, writing, and immersing himself in the student life of the Latin Quarter. On a train from London to Liverpool, England, on his way home to Chicago, he encountered a young Englishwoman, Lilian May Thomson, who also had studied in Paris and became a noted writer. Later, Mowrer wrote to his brother that he had met the woman he intended to marry. He returned to the United States and the University of Michigan, where he received a B.A. in 1913. After graduation he returned to Paris, intending to become a writer of essays and literary criticism.

That pursuit was short-circuited by the outbreak of World War I. When Paul Mowrer left Paris in 1914 to cover the fighting in Belgium, he recruited his brother to take over the Paris office of the Chicago *Daily News*. Paul wrote that his brother "took to journalism like a squirrel to a tree. He had judgment, facility, and initiative. . . . With his insatiable curiosity [he] combined a determined courage."

As a correspondent, Edgar Mowrer covered the German offensive against Belgium, coming under fire and at one point observing the action from a church belfry, where he shared champagne with a Belgian artillery observer. His eyewitness dispatches were among the first battlefront descriptions of the war by an American journalist. In the spring of 1915, Mowrer was assigned to the Chicago *Daily News*'s Rome bureau. He and Lilian Thomson were married in London on Feb. 10, 1916, and she joined him in Rome. They had one child, a daughter.

In Italy, Mowrer met Benito Mussolini and covered the Italian army's retreat at Caporetto. Mussolini, then a newspaper editor, favored Italy's joining the Allies. After recovering from a near-fatal case of influenza, Mowrer was named Rome bureau chief and reported on the rise of fascism in Italy until he accepted the post of Berlin bureau chief in 1923.

In Germany, Mowrer chronicled the rise of the Nazis in dispatches that won him the Pulitzer Prize for foreign correspondence in 1933. He was among the first journalists to recognize the threat Adolf Hitler represented to European peace. His book *Germany Puts the Clock Back* (1933; revised edition, 1939), describing the decline of the Weimar Republic and the rise of the Nazis, was banned in Germany. Because of Hitler's displeasure with the book, Nazi officials ordered Mowrer to resign as chairman of the Foreign Press Association. Backed by his colleagues, he refused to resign until the Nazis released an elderly Austrian Jewish newspaper correspondent whom they had arrested. After being expelled from Germany, Mowrer returned to Paris in 1934, replacing his brother, who had been named editor of the *Daily News*. From this post he covered the early days of the Spanish civil war, Hitler's escalating demands, and France and Britain's appeasement policies. Mowrer's reporting so outraged the Nazis that Propaganda Minister Joseph Goebbels once said that he would give a division of troops to capture him. Mowrer also reported from the Soviet Union and China. By 1937, both Mussolini and Stalin had expelled him from their countries.

In 1940, Mowrer left France just ahead of the advancing German army, writing dispatches along the way from cafe tables and park chairs and, once, typing a report on the hood of a car. Using an old visa that he had altered to obscure the date, he slipped across the border into Spain. Mowrer returned to the United States and was assigned to the *Daily News* Washington bureau. After the United States entered World War II, he became deputy director of the United States Office of Facts and Figures under Archibald MacLeish, an operation that later merged with the Office of War Information (OWI). Mowrer, an outspoken critic of Vichy France, resigned the post in 1943 after his trip to North Africa for the OWI was held up by the State Department because of his anti-Vichy views.

The *Daily News* did not rehire Mowrer as a correspondent, but he became a commentator on world affairs for the *New York Post*. In that position he traveled back to Europe as a war correspondent in 1944. The *Post* dropped Mowrer's column in 1948, but another syndicate picked it up. After the war he concentrated on calling attention to the peril of Soviet expansionism. He was an ardent anti-Communist who urged a hard line against the Soviet Union. Peaceful coexistence, he wrote, "was the opium of the West." He wrote three books analyzing postwar American foreign policy: *The Nightmare of American Foreign Policy* (1948), *Challenge and Decision* (1950), and *An End to Make-Believe* (1961). In them he made an "appeal to free men to make victory in the Cold War their immediate purpose. . . ."

In 1957, Mowrer became North American editor of a new magazine, *Western World*. Published in English and French, it was described as "offering a truly intercontinental forum, a continual two-way conversation" between North Atlantic nations. The magazine folded in 1960 owing to lack of funds. Mowrer continued writing his syndicated column and other articles until his retirement in 1969. He lived his remaining years in Tamworth, N.H. Mowrer died while visiting the island of Madeira, off Portugal.

[Mowrer's papers are in the Library of Congress, Manuscript Division. A collection of letters received by Mowrer from readers of his column (1952–1969) is in the State Historical Society of Wisconsin, Madison. Books by Mowrer include *Immortal Italy* (1922), *This American World* (1928), *Sinon; or, The Future of Politics* (1930), *The Dragon Wakes* (1939), *Global War* (1942, with Marthe Rajchman), *A Good Time to Be Alive* (1959), *Triumph and Turmoil* (1968), and *Umano and the Price of Lasting Peace* (1973, with Lilian Thomson Mowrer). Mowrer also authored scores of articles throughout his career. His series of articles written with William Donovan, "Fifth Column Lessons for America" (1940), was distributed to all newspapers in the United States and was reprinted by the American Council on Public Affairs. See also Lilian T. Mowrer, *Journalist's Wife* (1937). An obituary is in the *New York Times*, Mar. 4, 1977.]

MARY ANN WESTON

MULLIN, WILLARD HARLAN (Sept. 14, 1902–Dec. 21, 1978), sports cartoonist, was born in Warren County, Ohio, just north of Cincinnati, the second son of Milo Mullin, a dairy farmer, and Marie Ballard. He was named for his mother's sister, Willa Ballard. In 1906 the family moved to Los Angeles, where Milo Mullin became appraiser of the port of Los Angeles. Mullin recalled the source of his ambitions as a cartoonist: "I'm not an artist, I'm a cartoonist. I got the notion from my mother's first cousin, Claire Victor Dwiggins, who did one of the first Sunday cartoons in New York in 1906 and who had the rights to draw Tom Sawyer and Huckleberry Finn. When I was 10 years old, I knew it would be my career forever."

After Mullin graduated from Los Angeles High School in 1920, he went to work lettering signs for Bullock's, a local department store. In 1923 he joined the staff of the *Los Angeles Herald*, first as a spot illustrator and retoucher and later as an assistant sports cartoonist. On July 20, 1929, he married Helen Tousley; they had two children.

Dissatisfied with his subordinate position on the *Herald* staff (his sports cartoons were usually drawn at night, after a full day of retouching), in 1934 Mullin moved to New York to work for the *World-Telegram*; the next year he took over as regular sports cartoonist. From 1935 until the *World-Telegram* ceased publication in 1966, six days a week the first page of the paper's sports section featured a four- or five-column cartoon Mullin. He also worked extensively as a free-lance illustrator; his work was published in national magazines, including *Life*, *Look*, *Newsweek*, and the *Saturday Evening Post*, and in books, most notably a number of editions of *Henke's Encyclopedia of Sports*. A Mullin cartoon graced the front cover of *Time* when the New York Mets won the National League pennant in 1969.

For most of his career, Mullin lived in Plandome, N.Y., where he often worked, delivering his daily drawings to the newspaper office by a series of relay messengers. He traveled extensively as well, covering sporting events all over the United States; he watched Joe Louis fight twenty-five times. After the demise of the *World-Telegram*, Mullin continued his work as free-lance illustrator; his lifework amounted to some 10,000 cartoons.

On his retirement in 1971, Mullin was honored by the National Cartoonists Society as "Sports Cartoonist of the Century," a tribute both to the achievements of his long career and to the influence of his approach on American sports cartooning. Previously sports cartoonists had been gag men; very few achieved a national reputation. Mullin kept the humor ("Under his touch, a foot in a spiked shoe became hilarious," wrote sports columnist Red Smith), but most of his daily pieces had the analytical focus and bite of a political cartoon. A Mullin cartoon often was organized around a central portrait of a current sports figure rendered in realistic detail, with smaller caricatured scenes in a loose, spontaneous line on the periphery making the editorial point.

Mullin was a lover of word games, and his verbal invention included inspired Brooklyn patois, humorous verse, and Latin aphorisms as tag lines; his pieces incorporated allusions to Sir Walter Scott, Walt Whitman, the Bible, Oliver Wendell Holmes, and Shakespeare. The tone of Mullin's work ranged from rough slapstick to heartfelt eulogies for departed sports heroes.

Admired and imitated by cartoonists as an exemplary craftsman, Mullin was best known to the general public as the creator of symbols for baseball teams, including the doltish New York Giant, the breechclouted Boston (later Milwaukee) Brave, and the riverboat gambler St. Louis Swifty for the Cardinals; his most famous creation was the Brooklyn Bum, the seedy symbol of the Brooklyn Dodgers who sported a beret and sunglasses on moving to Los Angeles in 1958, yet remained as bedraggled and disreputable as ever.

In his youth a championship-level squash player, Mullin remained an affectionate devotee of sports even as he became a sharp observer of human folly and hypocrisy on and off the field. His detailed and knowledgeable treatments of football, baseball, boxing, horse racing, and yachting demonstrate his intense interest in competition of all sorts. He admitted that assignments on rowing gave him trouble, mostly because the repetitive drawings required gave him little scope for humorous invention: "Eight guys in a shell doing the same thing—I'd be so bored by the time I got to the stroke that I'd be sick to my stomach." Mullin's scornful pieces on professional wrestling are among his funniest of the 1950's; one shows a crowd of spectators at a wrestling match, each with a hole in his head.

As Mullin's lack of interest in women's athletics indicates, the world of sports journalism in which he moved was an intensely masculine one. He was a convivial man who took pleasure in the company of other journalists and sportsmen; according to Red Smith, Mullin called Joe Louis "a newspaperman's champion because he always finished in time for the first edition. The guys could get their work done and make it to the bar at Shor's or Leone's with hours to go before closing time." Mullin was a founding member of the Village Green Reading Society, a social club whose members included the sportswriters Stanley Woodward, Frank Graham, Red Smith, and Grantland Rice, and football coach Herman Hickman; the organization had "more to do with eating, drinking and reciting than reading," said his obituarist.

Mullin was honored many times by organizations of journalists and cartoonists. In 1971 a retrospective exhibition of his work was held at the Artium Gallery in Port Washington, N.Y. Mullin died in Corpus Christi, Tex.

[The largest single holding of Mullin's work, around 300 drawings, is at the Syracuse University Library; other examples are at the Baseball Hall of Fame in Cooperstown, N.Y., and the Football Hall of Fame in Canton, Ohio. His memoirs are *A Hand in Sport* (1958), written with Dave Camerer. See also Joseph Durso's feature in the *New York Times*, Jan. 10, 1971; Red Smith, "Looking Back with Willard Mullin," *New York Times*, July 1, 1978; and *Cartoonist Profile*, Sept. 1978 (an interview). An obituary is in the *New York Times*, Dec. 22, 1978.]

JOSEPH WITEK

MUÑOZ MARÍN, LUIS (Feb. 18, 1898–Apr. 30, 1980), Puerto Rico's first elected governor, was born in San Juan, P.R., the only son of Luis Muñoz Rivera and Amalia Marín. His father, known as "the George Washington of Puerto Rico," had won for the island a degree of autonomy from Spain before Puerto Rican independence. Following the Spanish-American War of 1898, Muñoz's father became resident commissioner for the island in Washington, D.C., and worked to convince Congress to grant Puerto Ricans American citizenship and their own elected legislature.

Muñoz grew up in the United States and Puerto Rico, though he spent most of his early years in New York City and Washington, D.C. He attended the Georgetown Preparatory School and then Georgetown University from 1912 to 1916. As a student, he began free-lance writing for the *Baltimore Sun* and national magazines.

Muñoz attended Georgetown Law School, but following his father's death in 1918, he left for New York, where he lived as a free-lance writer. There he met Muna Lee, a poet from Mississippi; they were married on July 1, 1919, and had two children. Muñoz was a poet in addition to being a political commentator with a socialist perspective. Among the publications Muñoz contributed to during these years were the *Nation*, *New Republic*, *Smart Set*, and *American Mercury*. He was the editor of *La revista de Indias*, a magazine about Latin American culture, and translated poems by Walt Whitman and Carl Sandburg, among others, into Spanish. In 1917, Muñoz published two books, *Borrones* and *Madre Haraposa*.

From 1916 to 1918, Muñoz was a secretary to the Puerto Rican representative to the United States Congress and continued to advocate socialism. By the time he entered Puerto Rican politics in 1926, he had switched his allegiance to the new Liberal party. During this period, Muñoz became editor and publisher of the newspaper *La Democracia*, through which he urged Puerto Rico's total independence from the United States, a stand that he would later reverse. Muñoz criticized his father for being too conservative and unaware of the needs of the *jíbaros* (peasants). He expressed these ideas in "Puerto Rico, the American Colony," an essay published in *These United States* (1925).

In 1932, Muñoz was elected to the senate of the island's legislature. Through his connections to President Franklin D. Roosevelt, he was able to ensure that millions of dollars flowed to Puerto Rico through the Puerto Rican Reconstruction Administration at the height of the Great Depression. This achievement made him popular on the island. As a Liberal party senator in Puerto Rico, he led a drive to have the widely disliked governor Robert Gore removed from office, and he pushed through the legislature a bill that would divide and distribute large sugar company landholdings among the *jíbaros*. Believing that Puerto Rico's problems were more economic than political or cultural, Muñoz felt this land distribution was critical to Puerto Rico's shift to greater economic self-sufficiency. He battled against the Nationalists, who sought immediate independence for the island. Muñoz thought independence would be a disaster because Puerto Rico was dependent on continued aid from the United States. Therefore, political independence would mean misery for the majority of Puerto Ricans.

Muñoz clashed with the sugar barons and the leaders of the Liberal party over his stand on independence and land reform. He broke with the party in 1937 and went on to form the Popular Democratic party in 1938, organizing landless *jíbaros* in the countryside under the motto "Bread, Land and Liberty." In preparation for the elections in 1940, Muñoz personally visited almost two-thirds of all the legislative districts and sent recordings of his speeches to be broadcast over loudspeakers in places he could not reach.

Muñoz spoke out against the longtime practice of selling one's vote for two dollars, saying the voter could have "justice or two dollars. But you can't have both." He promised to break up large landholdings, to set a minimum wage, to regulate the sugar industry, to encourage new business, and to improve rural electrification. He told voters that if his party failed to do these things, they should be voted out of office. "Distrust all politicians—even me," he said. After his victory, he added, "If we turn out to be crooks, we've at least taught the Puerto Rican people how to kick us out."

Muñoz received the greatest number of votes of any candidate in 1940, and was elected president of the senate. The opposition, however, was strong in the legislature. Nevertheless, Muñoz managed to push a number of bills through, including a tax exemption for all property assessed at $1,000 or less, an elimination of the salt tax and sales tax, a dramatic increase in the income tax, and the establishment of a minimum-wage commission.

With the support of Governor Rexford G. Tugwell, appointed in 1941, Muñoz developed agriculture and industry and set up the Land Authority to redistribute land to the *jíbaros*. Over the next decade, tens of thousands of acres were redistributed in the form of one-acre plots that were coordinated into farms and worked on a profit-sharing basis. Electricity, water, and transportation cooperatives were formed in order to provide these services at a low cost. About 28,000 public and private housing units were constructed by 1949.

Tugwell came under attack by some congressmen for supporting "socialist experiments" in Puerto Rico, but Muñoz's popularity boomed on the island and impressed even the congressional critics. In 1944 the Popular Democratic party obtained twice as many votes as all the other parties combined and filled the majority of legislature seats. Muñoz began to push for industrialization in order to raise the average annual income for Puerto Ricans, which he felt would encourage families to have fewer children and, in this way, would slow a population explosion that threatened to undermine the island's capacity to support itself by agriculture.

Industrialization, however, required that Puerto Rico have more control over its own resources. Puerto Rico was, at the time, almost entirely dependent on sugar, tobacco, and coffee exports to the United States. Mainland obstacles to the island's economic development included a quota on Puerto Rican sugar, high freight rates on Puerto Rican exports (at one time making it three times less expensive to ship goods from Belgium to New York than from Puerto Rico to New York), and competitive mainland manufacturers who undersold the Puerto Ricans whenever they tried to diversify their industries. Muñoz urged the United States to grant Puerto Rico greater political autonomy, saying the island needed "more vitamins and less aspirin."

During World War II, Puerto Ricans suffered as the United States rechanneled its resources toward the war in Europe and the Pacific. Because factories on the island had to shut down or reduce production, almost half of Puerto Rico's families had no income at all. Muñoz launched Operation Bootstrap, an economic recovery program that became one of his landmark achievements. The program attracted American investment by offering new industries a twelve-year tax exemption, assistance with labor problems, and plant construction. By 1953, more than 200 plants employed over 15,000 workers on the island, the greatest number ever employed outside the sugar industry. Puerto Rico began producing rayon, nylon, shoes, and electronic components. From 1940 to 1950, the island's income almost tripled and unemployment dropped 9 percent, despite enormous population growth.

In 1947, Muñoz's wish for greater Puerto Rican autonomy came true. Congress granted Puerto Rico the right to elect its own governor, and Muñoz was the first to be elected, in 1948. Nationalists, who insisted on immediate independence, tried to seize the Puerto Rican government and assassinate President Harry S. Truman. They also targeted Muñoz.

In 1950, the island was granted the right to create its own constitution and have it approved by popular vote. Congress approved the constitution, and Puerto Rico became a commonwealth on July 25, 1952. Its new political status gave the island its own flag and the right to make domestic laws and elect its own officials without congress's approval. Muñoz favored commonwealth status over independence because he felt the commonwealth ensured the island's fiscal and cultural autonomy while giving Puerto Ricans the benefits of American citizenship, federal aid, and access to mainland markets.

Muñoz was reelected in 1952. He put provisions into the constitution that limited the governor's power and ensured minority parties at least one-third of the legislative votes. He also embarked on Operation Serenity, an ambitious education program that upgraded instruction while preserving Puerto Rican culture and rural traditions. Muñoz was governor of Puerto Rico until 1964, when he refused to run for a fifth term. He entered the island's senate, and in 1968, at the age of seventy, began reducing his activity in politics.

A large, bearlike man with sad, dark eyes, Muñoz had a capacity to work eleven hours straight while chain-smoking cigarettes. His marriage to Muna Lee, which had been strained over many years, ended in 1940. He married his longtime companion, a literature professor named Inés María Mendoza, in 1947; they had two children. Muñoz died in San Juan.

[Muñoz Marín's autobiography is *Memorias* (1982). See also Enrique Lugo-Silva, *The Tugwell Administration in Puerto Rico* (1955); Ruth Gruber, *Puerto Rico* (1960); Thomas Matthews, *Luís Muñoz Marín* (1967); and Enrique Bird Piñero, *Don Luís Muñoz Marín* (1991). An obituary is in the *New York Times*, May 1, 1980.]

ALISON GARDY

MUNSON, THURMAN LEE (June 7, 1947–Aug. 2, 1979), baseball player, was born in Akron, Ohio, one of four children of Ruth and Darrel Munson; his father was a farmhand. At age eight he moved with his family to Canton, Ohio, where his father drove long-distance trucks. At Canton-Lehman High School, Munson made All-State in baseball, football, and basketball. He graduated in 1965 and entered Kent State University in Kent, Ohio, with an athletic scholarship. There he starred as a football linebacker and made the 1968 All-American team as a baseball catcher. The New York Yankees picked Munson first in the 1968 free-agent draft. After dropping out of college, Munson played some 100 minor league games with Binghamton, N.Y. (Eastern League), in 1968 and Syracuse, N.Y. (International League), in 1969 and then joined the Yankees that September. On Sept. 21, 1968, he married Diane Lynn Dominick; they had three children.

The Yankees rebuilt their team around Munson and star outfielder Bobby Murcer. In 1970, the five-foot, eleven-inch, 190-pound right-handed Munson helped lift New York from fifth to second place in the American League East with a .302 batting average. The Baseball Writers' Association of America voted him American League Rookie of the Year. In 1971 he tied the club record for best fielding average by a catcher (.998). A sensational 1973 season saw him bat .301 with twenty home runs and win the first of three consecutive Gold Glove defensive awards. A classic field general, Munson handled pitchers in a masterly fashion and threw out base stealers with perhaps the league's quickest release.

Catchers Carlton Fisk of the Boston Red Sox and Johnny Bench of the Cincinnati Reds received more publicity and acclaim, though. Munson led Fisk in every offensive department except home runs, but fans voted Fisk to start the 1973 All-Star Game. Munson, however, started at catcher for the American League in the 1974 through 1976 All-Star games. His best major league season came in 1975, when he compiled the third-best batting average (.318) in the American League and the most runs batted in (102) by a Yankee since 1964.

In 1976, Yankee manager Billy Martin named Munson the first club captain since Lou Gehrig had been given the title in 1939. Munson led the Yankees to their first American League pennant since 1964, batting .302 with seventeen home runs, 105 runs batted in, and fourteen stolen bases. He hit .435 in the Championship Series against the Kansas City Royals and his eight singles set a five-game Championship Series record. He batted .529 with nine hits in the World Series against the Cincinnati Reds, setting four-game World Series records for most singles (8), assists by a catcher (7), and players caught stealing (5). The Reds, however, went on to sweep the Series. The Baseball Writers' Association of America selected Munson the American League's Most Valuable Player.

In 1977, Munson batted .308 with eighteen home runs and 100 runs batted in. The Yankees defeated Kansas City in the Championship Series and the Los Angeles Dodgers in the World Series, their first world title since 1962. Munson batted .320 in the World Series with eight hits, one home run, and three runs batted in. A financial dispute with Yankees owner George Steinbrenner ended in March 1978, when he signed a four-year contract averaging $420,000 annually. Munson batted .297 in 1978, but arm troubles, tendinitis, and creaky knees limited his home run production. The Yankees vanquished the Boston Red Sox in a dramatic Eastern Division playoff game, Kansas City in the Championship Series, and Los Angeles in the World Series, as Munson again batted .320 with eight hits and seven runs batted in.

Munson had become a licensed pilot in 1977 and often flew his plane between New York and his home in Canton, near Cleveland. He died in the crash of his Cessna Citation, a twin-engine jet, while attempting to land at Akron-Canton Airport. The Yankees, who had denied Munson's requests to be traded to the Cleveland Indians to be nearer his family, retired his uniform number 15.

Statistically, Munson rivaled Fisk as the best American League catcher of the 1970's. In 1,423 career games, he batted .292 with 113 home runs and 701 runs batted in. In addition to making the American League All-Star Team seven times (1971, 1973–1978), Munson surpassed a .300 batting average in five seasons and drove in 100 or more runs three times. No other Yankee has garnered both American League Rookie of the Year and Most Valuable Player honors. Despite these accomplishments, Munson never enjoyed popularity. He frequently feuded with fans, the press, and management. Many players, however, respected him for his line-drive clutch hitting, competitive spirit, and willingness to play even when he was injured and in pain. Munson held the team together with his hard work and courage.

[The National Baseball Library, Cooperstown, N.Y., holds files on Munson's career. Thurman Munson and Martin Appel, *Thurman Munson* (1978), contains Munson's personal reflections on his baseball career. See also Bill Libby, *Thurman Munson* (1978); Larry Keith, "He's a Dish Only Behind the Plate," *Sports Illustrated*, Sept. 13, 1976; and Don Lauck, "What Makes Thurman Run," *Sport*, June 1978. An obituary appears in the *New York Times*, Aug. 3, 1979.]

DAVID L. PORTER

MURCHISON, JOHN DABNEY (Sept. 5, 1921–June 14, 1979), financier, was born in Tyler, Tex., the elder of two sons of Clinton Williams Murchison, an oilman, and Anne Morris. During the 1920's and 1930's his father accumulated an estate of more than $100 million, largely through the trading of oil leases acquired on credit, and then diversified his investments into banking, insurance, and numerous other areas.

John Murchison graduated from the Hotchkiss School in Connecticut and entered Yale University in 1940 but joined the Army Air Corps after the bombing of Pearl Harbor. He was commissioned a first lieutenant, flew more than fifty combat missions as a fighter pilot in the Mediterranean and South China theaters of war, and was awarded the Distinguished Flying Cross and the Air Medal. He returned to Yale after demobilization in 1945 and graduated with a degree in political science in 1947. Meanwhile he had met Lucille ("Lupe") Gannon, and he married her on Mar. 9, 1947. The couple had four children.

Murchison's first job was with a bank in Santa Fe, N.Mex., where he had moved to alleviate his asthmatic condition. In 1948 his father persuaded him to return to Dallas and oversee the family business operations. In 1942 his father had set up a partnership, Murchison Brothers, in the names of John and his younger brother, Clint Murchison, Jr. The privately held firm oversaw investments made by their father in more than one hundred companies.

One of the early Murchison Brothers investments involved the purchase of 13 percent of the stock of the New York publishing house Henry Holt, Inc. Both brothers obtained seats on the board of directors and prompted the firm's expansion into the lucrative textbook market during the postwar baby-boom period.

John and Clint used the investments placed by Murchison Brothers as the means to take active roles in numerous firms engaged in banking, life insurance, housing, road construction, mining, and other activities. John eventually began to specialize in investments involving insurance and banking, while Clint concentrated on construction and real estate. A business associate recalled that "Clint Jr. loved everything that had to do with construction and John liked everything that did not have to do with construction."

The Murchison Brothers investments were kept low-key until the early 1960's, when the brothers made a well-publicized takeover attempt of the Alleghany Corporation, a diversified holding company whose assets included the New York Central Railroad. After a bitter proxy battle with Woolworth heir Allan P. Kirby, the brothers won formal control of the company. Their victory turned out to be illusory, however, since Kirby remained a major shareholder and was able to veto all of the Murchisons' financial proposals. The brothers sold their Alleghany holdings a few years later.

During the early 1960's John was also instrumental in developing the small mountain town of Vail, Colo., into a major ski resort. His investments in the region and regular visits (he and Lupe were avid skiers and the epitome of jet-setters) focused attention on the area's magnificent ski trails. By 1964 Vail was listed in the same league as Cortina, St. Moritz, and other world-class ski resorts.

John and Lupe admired modern art. They collected the works of Frankenthaler, Rauschenberg, and other contemporary artists during John's frequent business trips to New York. (John and Clint maintained a suite at the Carlyle Hotel as their New York residence.) Texas society initially held modern artists in contempt; the Dallas Museum of Fine Arts had refused to exhibit the works of Picasso because he was a Communist. John and Lupe were instrumental in organizing the Dallas Museum of Contemporary Art, which became a leading avant-garde art museum in the West, but they also acquired holdings of Renoir, Courbet, Matisse, and other traditional artists. The Dallas Museum of Contemporary Art eventually merged with the Dallas Museum of Fine Arts, and John became a member of the latter's board of directors.

Murchison Brothers obtained more publicity after its purchase of a National Football League (NFL) franchise in 1959 and development of the Dallas Cowboys. Within ten years of its creation the Cowboys became a contender for the NFL title when the team reached the 1970 Super Bowl. Although both brothers had equal co-ownership, Clint took the active role in developing the public image of the team, paying particular attention to the Dallas Cowboys cheerleaders, while John limited his involvement to attending football games.

Shortly before his death in 1969, Clint Murchison, Sr., had obtained tax-free transfers of his large personal fortune into a number of trusts established for his children and grandchildren. Murchison Brothers, however, soon began treating the assets held in trusts as the firm's own property and used them as pledges for loans to finance Murchison Brothers' business ventures during the 1970's.

The estimated wealth of Murchison Brothers grew during the early 1970's as the prices of oil and Texas real estate boomed after the Arab oil embargo and the creation of the Organization of Petroleum Exporting Countries. By the middle of the decade, the brothers' assets totaled several hundred million dollars, but their debts may have been of equal magnitude. Since Murchison Brothers was a private partnership, financial reports were not available for public inspection. The two brothers gave personal guarantees of money loaned to them, so bankers and other creditors never demanded any outside audit of the firm's finances.

John eventually began to have doubts about the wisdom of combining all his business operations with those of Clint. The younger brother was becoming increasingly dependent on drugs and alcohol, making less reliable business deals, and relying more on the advice of sycophants and procurers than the recommendations of the firm's experienced business experts.

During the late 1970's, John began initiating many of his business deals outside the Murchison Brothers' organization, in order not to endanger them with debt from previous bad deals approved by Clint. This divergence of the brothers' operations and the increasingly unsteady condition of Murchison Brothers' finances went largely unnoticed until after the time of John's death from a heart attack on June 14, 1979.

John's son, John Dabney Murchison, Jr., was eventually forced to initiate litigation against Clint (who by then had declared himself to be a born-again Christian) to obtain the trust funds that were being withheld from him by Murchison Brothers. The publicity generated by the lawsuit made bankers aware of the extent to which the Murchison Brothers' operations depended on unsecured credit. The once-unthinkable fall in prices of both oil and Texas real estate during the 1980's doomed the Murchison Brothers' overleveraged operations. Clint Murchison, Jr., and the firm were forced into bankruptcy; the hollow shells of the Murchison Brothers operations were sold, and the firm's skimpy actual assets were distributed to creditors.

[There is no biography of John Murchison, but the Murchison family has been the subject of numerous books and articles. The best of these is Jane Wolfe, *The Murchisons: The Rise and Fall of a Texas Dynasty* (1989), which includes numerous interviews with members of the Murchison family and supersedes two earlier works: John Bainbridge, *The Super Americans* (1972); and James Presley, *A Sage of Wealth* (1978). Journalistic treatments of Murchison Brothers' business operations are Robert Lubar, "Henry Holt and the Man from Koon Kreek," *Fortune*, Dec. 1959; and "High Finance: Texas on Wall Street," *Time*, June 16, 1961. An obituary is in the *New York Times*, June 16, 1979.]

STEPHEN G. MARSHALL

MURPHY, GARDNER (July 8, 1895–Mar. 18, 1979), psychologist, was born in Chillicothe, Ohio. His father, Edgar Gardner Murphy, an Episcopal priest, had moved his family there from Laredo, Tex., earlier in 1895. In 1899 the family moved to Montgomery, Ala., where the father continued his career as a churchman until 1901. Gardner's mother, Maud King Murphy, was from Concord, Mass. In 1902, Gardner and his older brother, DuBose, moved with their mother to Concord, from there to Branford, Conn. (around 1904), and then to New Haven. His father, who remained in the South until 1908, had left the ministry to become executive secretary of the Southern Education Board. In this capacity he became involved in child-labor issues. In 1908 he retired because of ill health and rejoined his family in New Haven.

Murphy's literary interests and activities may well have been strengthened by his New England experience. His liberalism was nurtured and developed by his father's interest in the civil and educational rights of blacks and whites, both children and adults, and by his efforts after leaving the ministry to improve the human condition.

In 1908, Murphy entered high school in New Haven, and in 1910 he received a scholarship to attend the Hotchkiss School in Lakeville, Conn. He graduated with honors in June 1912 and entered Yale College that fall. After the death of his father in 1913, and possibly because of this event, Murphy developed an interest in psychic research and chose to major in psychology. He was also influenced by the writings of William James.

Murphy received his B.A. degree from Yale in 1916 and went on to Harvard for graduate work in psychology, receiving his M.A. degree in 1917. The United States had entered the European war that spring, and Murphy enlisted in the Yale Mobile Hospital Unit, with which he served in France. Eventually he was commissioned a second lieutenant in the United States Army Corps of Interpreters; he received his honorable discharge on July 7, 1919.

Still wearing his uniform, Murphy visited the psychology department at Columbia University, where he met Robert S. Woodworth, chairman of the department. He began his doctoral studies there that fall. In 1920, following Murphy's presentation of a research project without notes, Woodworth recommended him for a teaching position in the Columbia Extension Division. He received his Ph.D. from Columbia in 1923 and that fall introduced a course in the history of psychology that began with Democritus, Plato, and Aristotle. In 1925 he was promoted from lecturer to instructor.

On Nov. 27, 1926, Murphy married Lois Barclay, a graduate of Vassar College. At the time she was studying at the Union Theological Seminary, adjacent to the Columbia campus. They had two children. In 1928, Lois began teaching psychology courses at Sarah Lawrence College in Bronxville, N.Y., where she remained until 1952. In 1931 she and Murphy published their landmark book, *Experimental Society Psychology*.

In 1929, Murphy was promoted to assistant professor, having completed his classic study, *An Historical Introduction to Modern Psychology*, the previous year. This work and his published articles in the field of social psychology and personality theory, as well as his introductory psychology textbooks, established his scholarly reputation nationwide.

In 1932, Murphy was awarded the prestigious Nicholas Murray Butler Medal by Columbia University for his achievements as a teacher and scholar. From 1921 to 1940 he was one of the most respected and admired teachers at Columbia College. He was chosen president of the Eastern Psychology Association in 1941, and in 1943 he was elected president of the American Psychological Association—the highest accolade in his field.

In 1939, Murphy was offered a full professorship at the City College of New York, where the department of psychology had at last been given its independence from the department of philosophy. The members of the department voted unanimously to elect Murphy as chairman if he would accept the professorship. He accepted and arrived there in the fall of 1940.

Murphy had conditioned his acceptance on a considerable expansion of laboratory and office space and the appropriation of $10,000 for laboratory equipment. These conditions were met, and the offerings of the department were considerably expanded to include a two-semester course in experimental psychology and courses in social psychology and personality, the latter being taught by Murphy himself. As at Columbia, Murphy soon became known as an outstanding teacher and research mentor. Many of his students pursued experimental research in social psychology, perception, and personality under his guidance. Several became well-known psychologists in their own right, including Harold Proshansky, who later became president of the Graduate Center of the City University of New York. Among Murphy's many publications during his City College years was his influential book *Personality: A Biosocial Approach to Origins and Structure* (1947).

By 1946, Murphy had assembled a brilliant staff of psychologists from the New York City area and established an M.A. program in clinical psychology. Its remarkable popularity and success led Murphy and his colleagues to propose a doctoral program in psychology as well; but by 1952 it had become clear that such approval could not be given to a single department in only one of the several city colleges. Consequently, Murphy accepted an offer to become director of research at the Menninger Foundation in Topeka, Kans., in 1952, and he and his family moved there that fall. He stayed with the foundation until 1968. A glimpse into the nature of his research can be seen from the titles of some of the books he published during his Topeka years: *In the Minds of Men* (1953), *Human Potentialities* (1958), *Development of the Perceptual World* (1960, with Charles M. Solley), and *Encounter with Reality* (1968, with Herbert Spohn).

During his years at City College and with the Menninger Foundation, Murphy continued his interest in psychic research (begun in the 1920's while at Columbia) at the American Society for Psychical Research in New York City. He introduced rigorous scientific methodology to the research work done there and served as the society's president from 1962 to 1971. During the summer of 1942 he also taught a course on psychic research at Harvard, and in 1945 he lectured on parapsychology at the New School for Social Research in New York City. In 1961 he published *The Challenge of Psychical Research* (with Laura A. Dale) and *Freeing Intelligence Through Teaching*. His last book on his research at Menninger, *Outgrowing Self-Deception* (1975), was the first of two that he wrote with Morton Leeds. The second, *The Paranormal and the Normal*, was his final book and was published posthumously in 1980.

In 1968, Murphy and his family moved from Topeka to Washington, D.C., where he remained until his death. For five years he was a guest professor at George Washington University there, lecturing on personality theory.

In 1972 the American Psychological Foundation of the American Psychological Association awarded Murphy the gold medal for lifetime achievement: "To a senior American psychologist in recognition of a distinguished and long-continued record of scientific and scholarly accomplishment." Murphy closed his response to the lengthy citation with these words: "You have given me a gold medal, lovely symbol of our dedication to science. I can give you in return only the hope that the present rigid barriers between the sciences and the humanities may, in your generation, yield to a more generous perspective."

[Virtually all of Murphy's papers were lost during a family move, according to Lois Murphy. Additional publications by Murphy include *An Outline of Abnormal Psychology* (1929), as editor; *Approaches to Personality* (1932) with Friedrich Jensen; *General Psychology* (1933), *Public Opinion and the Individual* (1938), with Rensis Likert; *William James on Psychical Research* (1960), edited with R. O. Ballou; *Psychological Thought from Pythagoras to Freud* (1968); *Asian Psychology* (1968), edited with Lois Murphy; and *Western Psychology* (1969), edited with Lois Murphy.

The most comprehensive review of his life and works remains Lois B. Murphy, *Gardner Murphy* (1990). Other sources of information on Murphy include Edwin G. Boring and Gardner Lindzey, *History of Psychology in Autobiography* (1967); and Lawrence Nyman, "Recollections: An Oral History of the Psychology Department of the City College of the City University of New York" (1976), which is available from the psychology department of CUNY. An obituary is in the *New York Times*, Mar. 21, 1979.]

JOHN G. PEATMAN

MURPHY, ROBERT DANIEL (Oct. 28, 1894–Jan. 9, 1978), diplomat and business executive, was born in Milwaukee, the son of Francis Patrick Murphy, a saloon owner and railroad worker, and Catherine Louise Schmitz. "It was assumed in our family that I could scarcely expect formal education beyond grade school," Murphy reflected in his memoirs, "and it was not easy to get even that far." He proved an excellent student, however, and after graduating from Gesu Parochial School in 1909, he attended Marquette Academy, a parochial high school, on a four-year scholarship. After graduation, he attended Marquette University briefly before accepting a clerical position in Washington, D.C., with the United States Post Office in 1916. His job enabled him to attend George Washington University Law School in the evenings, from which he received a law degree in 1920.

In 1917, Murphy joined the State Department, beginning what would be a remarkable forty-two year diplomatic career. He was assigned first to the American legation in Bern, Switzerland, as a code clerk. Admitted to the foreign service in 1921, following his marriage on March 3 of that year to Mildred Claire Taylor, with whom he had two children, Murphy served briefly as a vice-consul at Zurich and, from 1921 to 1925, at Munich. At the latter post, he witnessed firsthand Adolf Hitler's failed beer hall putsch. His German experience impressed upon Murphy the devastating human consequences brought by extreme economic and political instability. Yet, as he later lamented, "I saw nothing to indicate that the American Government or people were even mildly interested in the political developments which seemed so ominous and significant to us on the spot." The young diplomat also became an expert on France during the interwar years, serving continuously in Paris from 1930 to 1940, first as consul and then as counselor of the embassy. With the German victory over France in June 1940, the State Department appointed Murphy to the politically sensitive position of chargé d'affaires to the newly established Vichy government.

Shortly thereafter, President Franklin D. Roosevelt tapped Murphy for a diplomatic assignment of even greater sensitivity. Hopeful that the French might eventually be brought back to the war against Germany, the president dispatched the veteran Foreign Service officer to French North Africa in order to establish contacts with the French military leadership there. Murphy determined quickly that that leadership remained staunchly anti-German. With Roosevelt's blessing, in early 1941 he negotiated a preliminary, and highly secret, economic agreement with General Maxime Weygand, commander of the 150,000 French troops stationed in Africa. It promised American aid to the French colony in Algeria and the French protectorates in Tunisia and Morocco in the hope that American support might help drive a wedge between the North African French and the Vichy regime.

Following American entry into the war, Murphy's surreptitious organization of potential "fifth-column" activity in North Africa assumed even greater salience to Roosevelt. In mid-1942, the president selected North Africa as the site for the first American amphibious landing of the war and ordered Murphy to help secure the support, or at least the neutrality, of French forces. Murphy ultimately struck a deal with Weygand's successor, Admiral Jean Darlan, which was concluded just as United States troops landed on North African beaches on Nov. 7–8, 1942. Darlan agreed to sever his ties to the Vichy regime and to cooperate with the Allied invaders in return for American backing. The so-called Darlan deal sparked much criticism in the United States since the admiral's anti-Semitic and anti-British prejudices were well known, turning Murphy almost overnight into a controversial public figure. Yet his superiors unstintingly praised Murphy's role in the North African campaign. Commanding General Dwight D. Eisenhower wrote that Murphy had done "a grand job"; President Roosevelt was so pleased with his emissary's work that he named Murphy his "personal representative in North Africa with the rank of Minister."

Murphy remained attached to Eisenhower's command for most of the rest of the war. He served as the general's political attaché throughout the North African fighting and the invasion of Italy, helping, among other matters, to negotiate the Italian armistice. Following the cross-channel landings of June 1944, Roosevelt appointed Murphy to serve as Eisenhower's political adviser on German affairs. In that capacity, Murphy attended the Potsdam Conference in July 1945. He stayed in Germany during the early postwar years as the chief diplomatic adviser to the United States High Commission. During that period, which included the Berlin crisis of 1948, Murphy became intensely suspicious of the Soviet Union.

After a short stint back in Washington as director of the State Department's Office of German and Austrian Affairs, President Harry S. Truman selected Murphy in 1949 to be the United States ambassador to Belgium. Three years later Truman transferred Murphy to Tokyo, where he became the first postwar United States ambassador to Japan.

Before Eisenhower's election as president in 1952, Ambassador Murphy already ranked as one of the foreign service's most experienced and most respected diplomats. His calm and affable demeanor together with his trademark prudence and evenhandedness endeared him to peers and superiors alike. The accession of his friend and former associate to the presidency, however, vaulted Murphy to even greater prominence. In 1953, Eisenhower appointed Murphy assistant secretary of state for United Nations affairs; then, later in the year, promoted him to deputy under secretary of state, the third-highest-ranking position in the State Department. Even more important than his rank was Murphy's personal relationship with Eisenhower; the president regularly tapped his former political attaché to perform the most delicate diplomatic assignments.

Two of the most important of those concerned the Middle East. In 1956, following the Egyptian seizure of the Suez Canal, Eisenhower dispatched Murphy to London and to Paris in order to help avert an immediate military confrontation. Although that confrontation ultimately occurred, Eisenhower later remarked that Murphy had played an extremely valuable role by making clear the staunch American opposition to the Anglo-French use of force. Then, in 1958, Eisenhower sent Murphy to Lebanon to help prepare the way for the dispatch of 14,000 American troops to that politically volatile nation.

In 1959, Murphy retired from the foreign service. His proved an unusually active retirement. Until being incapacitated by a stroke in November 1977, he served as chairman of Corning Glass International and as a director of the Corning Glass Works. Murphy also accepted an occasional call for further public service, helping President Richard M. Nixon make his major diplomatic appointments in 1969 and serving on the Foreign Intelligence Advisory

Board under President Gerald R. Ford in 1976. Murphy died at his home in New York City.

[Murphy's papers are at the Hoover Institution, Stanford University. His memoir of his diplomatic career, *Diplomat Among Warriors* (1964), is invaluable. See also the oral histories at Princeton University, Princeton, N.J., and at the Eisenhower Library, Abilene, Kans. Murphy has not yet been the subject of a biography, but aspects of his career are covered in numerous works about World War II and Cold War diplomacy, including William L. Langer, *Our Vichy Gamble* (1947); and H. W. Brands, *Cold Warriors: Eisenhower's Generation and American Foreign Policy* (1988). An obituary is in the *New York Times*, Jan. 10, 1978.]

ROBERT J. MCMAHON

MURTAUGH, DANIEL EDWARD ("DANNY") (Oct. 8, 1917–Dec. 2, 1976), baseball player and manager, was born in Chester, Pa., the son of Daniel Joseph Murtaugh, a shipyard worker, and Nellie McCarey. Murtaugh grew up in the Seventh Ward, a poor Irish-American neighborhood in Chester, a shipbuilding city south of Philadelphia on the Delaware River. Small and wiry as a youth, he played sandlot baseball and was known for his grit and hustle. Murtaugh also became a skilled fielder under the tutelage of George Noblitt, an elderly former minor leaguer. By the time he graduated from Chester High School in 1935 he was a capable all-around ballplayer.

After receiving no professional baseball offers, Murtaugh went to work in the Chester shipyards. He took a number of low-skilled and hazardous jobs between 1935 and 1937, including that of passer boy on a rivet gang; for thirty-four cents per hour he caught hot rivets in a cup. He also worked for a time as a wheat puffer in a cereal factory, shooting kernels out of a cannonlike machine.

Murtaugh got his first baseball break in 1937 at a tryout camp held in Chester by Fritz Lucas, a scout for the St. Louis Cardinals. He impressed Lucas sufficiently to win a contract with the Cardinals Class D farm team in Cambridge, Md., for $200 per month. He played second base, his preferred position, as well as shortstop and hit .297 and .312 in two seasons. He moved up in the Cardinals farm chain to Rochester, N.Y., Columbus, Ohio, and Houston, Tex., over the next three years, splitting his time between second base, third base, and shortstop. Although at five feet, nine inches, and 160 pounds he possessed little power, Murtaugh developed into a dependable singles hitter.

In search of infield help, the last-place Philadelphia Phillies purchased Murtaugh from the Cardinals during the 1941 season. Playing mostly at second base, Murtaugh hit an unimpressive .219 in eighty-five games but led the National League with eighteen stolen bases. He hit .241 in 1942 and .273 in 1943 for the team, which finished eighth (last) and seventh, respectively, in those years. In 1944 he joined the United States Army and saw action as an infantryman in Europe. Shortly after his return to the Phillies in 1946, he was sent back to the Cardinals and assigned once again to their Rochester farm team, where he had his best offensive year ever—batting .322, with 174 hits and sixty-two runs batted in—and was acquired by the Boston Braves in the off-season. When he was unable to break into the Braves starting infield in 1947, Murtaugh was sent to the club's farm team in Milwaukee, where he went forty-two consecutive games without an error, set an American Association record with a fielding average of .988, batted .302, and hit a career-high seven home runs. Subsequently, the Braves traded him to the Pittsburgh Pirates.

Murtaugh became the Pirates regular second baseman, collecting 149 hits, hitting .290, and driving in 71 runs in 1948. He also led National League second basemen in putouts, assists, and double plays, surpassing the totals of such stellar rivals as Jackie Robinson of the Brooklyn Dodgers and Red Schoendienst of the Cardinals. Murtaugh's solid performance helped the Pirates, who had tied for seventh place in 1947, move up to fourth. He slumped badly in 1949, however, batting only .203 and losing his regular second base job. Murtaugh rebounded in 1950 by hitting .294, his highest average as a major leaguer, and regained his place in the starting lineup. After the season, Pittsburgh general manager Branch Rickey gave him a blank contract and asked Murtaugh to fill in the salary amount he thought he deserved. He is said to have written in $15,000, more than he had earned up to that time.

Murtaugh struggled at the plate again in 1951, ending the season with a woeful .199 batting average for a weak Pirates club, which finished in the National League cellar. Realizing that his steady infield play was probably not enough to keep him in the big leagues, he asked Rickey for the opportunity to manage a team in the Pittsburgh farm system. In his nine erratic seasons in the major leagues, Murtaugh had appeared in 767 games, collected 661 hits, and compiled an overall batting average of .254.

In 1952, Murtaugh was installed as player-manager for the New Orleans Pelicans of the Southern Association. While he played regularly the Pelicans were contenders for the league pennant, but when a severe leg injury sidelined him, the team lost momentum and finished in fifth place. Restricted to pinch-hitting duties, Murtaugh gained more experience managing from the bench in 1953 but New Orleans again finished fifth. When he retired as a player in 1954 and devoted all of his energies to managing, the Pelicans were able to move up to a tie for second place. Murtaugh left New Orleans after three years to escape the constant verbal abuse of Pelicans fans. Murtaugh's next managerial post, in Charleston, W.Va., proved even less fulfilling. Insolvent and in last place, the team released him in mid-season.

In 1956 the new general manager of the Pirates, Joe L. Brown, who had been Murtaugh's boss in New Orleans, hired him to manage Pittsburgh's Williamsport, Pa., farm club. Before he got to Williamsport, however, Murtaugh was tapped by Brown to fill a vacancy on the Pirates coaching staff. He served as first-base coach under manager Bobby Bragan, a former Phillies teammate. The Pirates' poor showing in 1956 and 1957 and the flamboyant Bragan's public comments denigrating the abilities of some of his players brought about his dismissal in August 1957. After veteran coach Clyde Sukeforth declined the job, Brown made Murtaugh interim manager.

Although the Pirates ended the 1957 season at the bottom of the National League, they had played better than .500 ball in fifty-one games under Murtaugh and he was given a chance to lead the club again. By 1958 young players recruited under the Rickey regime (1950–1955) were maturing and Brown had added to the team's depth with deft acquisitions. Pitchers Bob Friend, Vernon Law, and Elroy Face, along with such everyday players as Roberto Clemente, Dick Groat, Bill Mazeroski, Bob Skinner, and Frank Thomas, came into their own in 1958 and propelled the Pirates to an unexpected second-place finish, eight games behind the Milwaukee Braves. As a result, Murtaugh, after his first full season at the helm of the Pirates, won manager of the year honors in the National League.

In contrast to the brash Bragan, Murtaugh had a low-key style and great empathy with the players. A nondrinker who preferred chewing tobacco and cigars, he kept his men relaxed and focused and was careful not to pry into their activities off the field. Although he was never considered much of a strategist among managers, Murtaugh occasionally resorted to a little innovation. In 1958 he had Pirates scout Ray Welsh, a former track coach, devise an intensive running program for the team during spring training. This conditioning probably helped the Pirates avoid serious injuries and advance six places in the standings.

Despite high expectations, Pittsburgh finished a disappointing fourth in 1959. In 1960, however, everything came together for "Danny and the Pirates." During the off-season Murtaugh intervened with Brown to prevent the trade of shortstop Groat to Kansas City for slugger Roger Maris. Groat went on to hit .325 that year and was the National League's Most Valuable Player. In addition, Clemente batted .314 and established himself as one of baseball's premier outfielders, and Law won twenty games and the Cy Young Award. The 1960 Pirates captured the National League pennant by eight full games over Milwaukee and went on to win the World Series. Despite being decisively outhit (91–60) and outscored (55–27) by the powerful New York Yankees, the Pirates eked out victories in four games to become the first baseball champions from Pittsburgh since 1925. Mazeroski's dramatic ninth-inning home run in the seventh game of the series was the telling blow.

In the next four years the Pirates finished above .500 only once (1962) and no higher than fourth place, while Groat was traded away, Law was hampered by a sore arm, and relations between Murtaugh and Clemente soured. Although Clemente won two batting titles under Murtaugh (1961 and 1964), the manager came to view his superstar as a prima donna who took himself out of ball games for dubious illnesses. The two had a number of angry confrontations and by 1964 were hardly communicating. Later that year Murtaugh discovered he had a serious heart ailment and left managing to become a Pirates scout and front-office troubleshooter.

During the 1967 season, Harry Walker was dropped as the Pirates manager and Brown brought Murtaugh out of retirement. Under Murtaugh's direction, Pittsburgh won thirty-nine games and lost thirty-nine, ending up in sixth place. More important, Murtaugh, who prided himself in his handling of players, made peace with Clemente, who won his fourth league batting championship in 1967. Nevertheless, Murtaugh refused Brown's entreaties to stay on as manager and in 1968 returned to the front office as director of player acquisition and development.

When the Pirates floundered under Larry Shepard in 1969, Brown again called upon Murtaugh, who had been cleared to return to the dugout by his doctor. He soon met the challenge of molding a new crop of promising young Pirates into a winning ballclub. His 1970 team was led by Clemente and included slugger Willie Stargell, catcher Manny Sanguillen, and problematic pitcher Dock Ellis. The successful handling of Ellis, who later claimed to have pitched a no-hitter while on LSD, may have been one of the great psychological triumphs of Murtaugh's career. After taking the National League Eastern Division crown and losing the league playoffs to the Cincinnati Reds in 1970, the Pirates won a second World Series for Murtaugh in 1971, beating the Baltimore Orioles in seven games.

The heart problem that had plagued Murtaugh intermittently since 1964 and made him miss more than a month of the 1971 regular season caused him to quit managing once more and go back to scouting.

Murtaugh returned briefly to manage the National League team in the 1972 All-Star Game and then was rehired by the Pirates in late 1973 after the firing of Bill Virdon. Murtaugh's 1974 and 1975 teams, led by Stargell, Dave Parker, and pitcher Jerry Reuss, won the Eastern Division titles but lost in the playoffs to the Los Angeles Dodgers and Cincinnati Reds. In his last season, 1976, the Pirates ended up second in the National League East, nine games behind the Philadelphia Phillies. When he retired for the last time, in October 1976, Murtaugh had compiled a record of 1,115 victories and 950 losses (a winning percentage of .540) in fifteen years of managing. His teams won two world championships and he was named National League manager of the year three times (1958, 1960, and 1970). The Pirates retired his number 40 in 1977.

Murtaugh had married Kathleen Patricia Clark, another Chester native, on Nov. 29, 1941, and had three children. He died in Chester two days after suffering a stroke.

[The National Baseball Library in Cooperstown, N.Y., has a clipping file on Murtaugh. Biographical material is in Myron Cope, "Baseball's Mr. Mischief," *Saturday Evening Post*, May 9, 1959, and Harold Rosenthal, *Baseball's Best Managers* (1961). Murtaugh's records can be found in the 1951 *Baseball Register* and Joseph L. Reichler, ed., *Baseball Encyclopedia* (1988). A good short history of the Pirates for the Murtaugh years is in Donald Dewey and Nicholas Acocella, *Encyclopedia of Major League Baseball Teams* (1993). See also Roger Birtwell, "Cards Pulled a Murtaugh," *Baseball Digest*, June 1949; Dick Groat and Bill Surface, *The World Champion Pittsburgh Pirates* (1961); Furman Bisher, "Murtaugh the Persistent," *Baseball Digest*, Feb. 1961; Jay H. Smith, *The Managers* (1976); and Bob Addie, "Danny Murtaugh: The Gentle 'Buccaneer,' " *Baseball Digest*, Mar. 1977. Obituaries are in the *New York Times*, Dec. 3, 1976; and the *Sporting News*, Dec. 18, 1976.]

RICHARD H. GENTILE

MUSE, CLARENCE (Oct. 7, 1889–Oct. 13, 1979), singer, actor, and director, was born in Baltimore, Md., the son of Alexander Muse, a shoe-shine man, and Mary Kellams, a homemaker who raised her son to appreciate the benefits of a strong educational background. He was educated in the Maryland school system.

After completing his secondary education, Muse enrolled at Dickinson School of Law in Carlisle, Pa. In 1911, with a major in international law, Muse became the first African American to graduate from Dickinson. It was there that he met Dean William A. Tricket, a man whose personal credo would become Muse's own: "I have never met a man or woman with enough intelligence to insult me." Upon graduating, Muse moved to Washington, D.C., where he tried to establish a law practice but found that few African-American attorneys were able to practice or to appear in court.

Undaunted and determined to make a living, in 1912 Muse began his show-business career as a singer on the Hudson River showboats in New York and at Palm Beach, Fla., cafés and resorts. As a young man who had sung while in law school in order to pay the tuition, Muse was no stranger to the stage. After the season's end in Palm Beach, he traveled to Jacksonville, Fla., where he met Tim Moore, who had his own

Muse

touring stock company. Muse traveled with this group of actors for about seven years before he eventually settled in New York City in 1912 with his first wife, Ophelia ("Billie") Muse, and young son. There he joined the Lincoln Players, with whom he performed for about three years.

Muse left the Lincoln Players in 1916 to become one of the founding members of the Lafayette Players. Not long after joining its ranks, he became one of the troupe's most prominent actors. Starring in several critically acclaimed productions from 1916 to 1923—including *Dr. Jekyll and Mr. Hyde, The Master Mind*, and *Fine Feathers*—Muse was a pioneer in the creation of black theater that challenged the stereotypically degrading parody of African-American life that was popular at the time—the minstrel show. In a 1915 *New York Times* review, Lester Walton remarked, "When visiting the Lafayette Theatre one can expect to see great and meritorious effort being made . . . and an endeavor to prove that the Negro can do more than sing and dance." Of Muse's 1915 performance in *The Master Mind*, a critic commented that he gave "splendid delineation of his character, playing with well contained restraint that added force and power to his presentation." Following his years as an actor on the New York stage, Muse lived from 1923 to 1929 in Chicago, where he was the founder and manager of the Chicago School of Dramatic Art. He also organized shows for the Royal Gardens Theatre. At the end of Muse's stage career, he had appeared in more than 200 plays.

In 1929, Muse was hired by William Fox of Hollywood's Fox Studios to play the leading role of Uncle Napus in *Hearts in Dixie*, the second talking film and the first all-black musical. Following this performance, Muse went on to star in a total of 219 Hollywood productions, including *Huckleberry Finn* (1931); *The Count of Monte Cristo* (1934); *Broadway Bill* (1934); *So Red the Rose* (1935); *Way Down South* (1939); *Broken Strings* (1940); *Heaven Can Wait* (1943); and *Porgy and Bess* (1959).

Hollywood's dearth of roles for black actors during the 1930's, 1940's, and 1950's was reflected in Muse's frequently recurring role as the subservient, docile "Uncle Tom" character. Nevertheless, he was a man whose intelligence and dignity could not be stifled by the confines of stereotypes. In his 1989 study of African Americans in film, Donald Bogle observed: "What was most intriguing was that Muse seemed miscast because his slave was too excruciatingly intelligent. His dialect was obviously faked and forced. . . . No other black performer of the period ever had quite such an effect. . . . Muse always seemed to be standing at a great distance, looking on with his large questioning eyes and sadly shaking his head."

In 1934, Muse moved to Perris, Calif., where he became involved in community affairs. With the Perris Valley Chamber of Commerce, he founded the Perris Valley Activities Committee, which sponsored local charitable functions. Muse was also an early member of the Screen Actors' Guild, and was active in the Negro Actors' Guild.

In 1939, Muse collaborated with Langston Hughes and cowrote the screenplay for *Way Down South*. He composed the film's theme song, "When It's Sleepy Time Down South," which became a hit after Louis Armstrong recorded it two years later. Muse also wrote eleven spirituals for the film, which were recorded by the Hall Johnson Choir; Muse was the first African American to star with the choir. One year later Muse independently produced, wrote, and starred in *Broken Strings* (1940), the story of a black classical violinist who loses the use of his left hand, then regains it by enthusiastically applauding his son's performance at a "swing" music recital.

At the peak of his film career in the 1940's, Muse became involved in the international movement against fascism by articulating the connection between racism at home and totalitarianism abroad. In an Apr. 22, 1942, interview with Jack Young from the *New York Times*, he declared: "Discrimination is part of the evil of fascism which we are fighting on a worldwide scale. The day of master and slave is over. We win the war and it's out—there'll be no more lynching anywhere."

In 1943, Muse returned to the stage and became the first African American to direct a Broadway show, his production of *Run, Little Chillun*. This folk play was one of the most popular artistic undertakings commissioned by President Franklin D. Roosevelt's Federal Theatre Project. In June 1949, Muse was divorced from his second wife, Willabella Marchbanks, with whom he had one child. In August 1954 he married Irene ("Ena") Claire Kellman.

During the 1950's, Muse starred in the films *County Fair* (1950); *My Forbidden Past* (1951), and *So Bright the Flame* (1952). He also hosted a radio show in Los Angeles called "Night Owl Roost." After taking a hiatus from acting in the 1960's, he appeared in films of the 1970's that included *Buck and the Preacher*, with Sidney Poitier (1972); and *Car Wash* (1976). Muse's final film appearance was in 1979, in Francis Ford Coppola's *The Black Stallion*.

Muse died in Perris, Calif. On Oct. 7, 1993, the 104th anniversary of his birth, Muse had his star placed on the Hollywood Walk of Fame.

[Muse published a pamphlet titled *The Dilemma of the Negro Actor* (1932). See Henry T. Sampson, *Blacks in Black and White* (1977); and Donald Bogle, *Toms, Coons, Nannies, and Bucks* (1989). Articles are in *Chicago Defender*, Feb. 26, 1949; *Amsterdam News*, Dec. 10, 1949, Dec. 20, 1979, and Dec. 27, 1979; *Ebony*, Sept. 1972; *Sepia*, Oct. 1976; *Essence*, Apr. 1977; *Encore*, Apr. 18, 1977; and *Jet*, Nov. 4, 1976, and Mar. 23, 1978. Obituaries are in the *New York Times*, Oct. 17, 1979; and *Jet*, Oct. 20, 1979. A taped interview is in the Hatch-Billops Collection of the Schomburg Center for Research in Black Culture, New York City.]

LaRose Parris

N

NABOKOV, NICOLAS (Apr. 17, 1903–Apr. 6, 1978), composer, educator, and writer, was born Nikolai Dmitrievich Nabokov to Dmitri Dmitrievich Nabokov and Lydia von Falz-Fein in Novogrudok, near Lyubcha, in the Minsk region of Russia. His influential family included an uncle who had served as a liberal member of the Russian Duma and the novelist Vladimir Nabokov, who was a first cousin.

Nabokov received his early education at the Imperial Lyceum in St. Petersburg (1911). After studying under Vladimir Ivanovich Rebikov in St. Petersburg and Yalta (1913–1920), he attended the Stuttgart Conservatory (1920–1922) and the Berlin Hochschule für Musik (1922–1923), where he studied under Paul Juon and Ferruccio Busoni. He earned the degree of license ès letters in 1926 from the Sorbonne in Paris, and lived in France until 1933.

That year, Nabokov traveled to the United States, where on invitation from the Barnes Foundation, he delivered a series of lectures on European music. Remaining in the United States, Nabokov became professor of music history, music theory, and composition, and chair of the department of music at Wells College in Aurora, N.Y., a position he held from 1936 to 1941. He taught at St. John's College in Annapolis, Md., from 1941 to 1944 and was professor of composition at the Peabody Conservatory of Music in Baltimore from 1943 to 1945 and from 1947 to 1951. He had become an American citizen in 1939.

Nabokov was adviser for cultural affairs for the United States military government in Germany from 1945 to 1947, serving as deputy chief of film, theatre, and music control for Germany. He was coordinator of interallied negotiations for information media and special adviser to Ambassador Robert D. Murphy on Cultural and Russian Matters. In 1947 he was editor in chief of the Russian Broadcast Unit of the Voice of America. He later served as secretary-general of the Congress for Cultural Freedom from 1951 to 1963 and adviser for internal cultural affairs to the mayor of West Berlin and the Berlin Senate from 1963 to 1978.

Nabokov served as composer-in-residence and adviser on arts at the Aspen Institute for Humanistic Studies in Colorado from 1969 to 1978. He lectured on aesthetics at the State University of New York in Buffalo from 1970 to 1971 and at New York University from 1972 to 1973. He also taught at the American Academy in Rome and at the City University of New York. On Mar. 23, 1970, he married Dominique Cibiel; they had no children.

Nabokov contributed to modern cultural consciousness through his many efforts as an organizer and supervisor of music festivals throughout the world. He is best known for his work on behalf of the internationalization of world music. He organized "Masterpieces of the Twentieth Century" (Paris, 1952), "Music in Our Time" (Rome, 1954), and "East-West Music Encounter" (Tokyo, 1961). He was artistic director of the Berlin Music Festival from 1963 to 1968 and served as adviser to the Festival of Israel. Later he was appointed to establish a regular festival in Iran called the Teheran Biennale.

Nabokov's compositional style incorporated Russian folk melodies and rhythms that were blended with compositional procedures of a generally universal character. He communicated many of his views on music in such publications as *Old Friends and New Music* (1951), a book of essays and memoirs; *Igor Stravinsky*

(1964); and *Bagázh: Memoirs of a Russian Cosmopolitan* (1975).

Fluent in four languages and decorated with the Grand Cross Order of Merit of West Germany and the Chevalier Legion of Honor of France, Nabokov created works with an international flavor. His output included two operas; three symphonies; flute and piano concertos; vocal, choral, and orchestral concert pieces; and five ballets. His compositions include his first major work for chorus, an oratorio entitled *Job* (1933), which comprises fifteenth- and sixteenth-century monophonies of a dramatic character.

Nabokov's ballets include *Ode; or, Meditation at Night on the Majesty of God, as Revealed by Aurora Borealis*, which was produced by Serge Diaghilev's Ballets Russes in 1928, and *Union Pacific*, produced in Philadelphia in 1934. *Ode*, based on a poem by the eighteenth-century Russian poet and scientist Lomonosov, is eclectic in style, containing arias, duets, choruses, and instrumental interludes and focusing on both the poetry and the deism of eighteenth-century Russia. To accentuate such themes, he highlighted simple elements, using an economy of music materials in a manner similar to that of Mikhail Glinka. *Union Pacific* emphasizes folk elements through the combination of American popular and folk tunes and takes as its subject the history of the transcontinental railroad. Perhaps his best-known ballet score was *Don Quixote*, which he composed for George Balanchine and the New York City Ballet in 1965.

In his later years Nabokov divided his time between New York and Paris; he died in New York City.

[See David Ewen, ed., *Composers Since 1900—A Biographical and Critical Guide* (1969); Oscar Thompson, *International Cyclopedia of Music and Musicians* (11th ed., 1985); and Nicolas Slonimsky, *Baker's Biographical Dictionary of Musicians* (8th ed., 1991). An obituary is in the *New York Times*, Apr. 7, 1978.]

SUSAN EASTERLY

NABOKOV, VLADIMIR VLADIMIROVICH (Apr. 23, 1899–July 2, 1977), writer, was born in St. Petersburg, Russia, the eldest of five children of Vladimir Dmitrievich Nabokov, a criminologist, politician, and editor, and Elena Ivanovna Rukavishnikov. The family belonged to tsarist Russia's aristocracy, and Nabokov enjoyed a privileged upbringing, divided between his parents' country estate fifty miles south of St. Petersburg, and a house on the capital's most fashionable street. Nabokov's father was a prominent liberal politician, a founding member of the Constitutional Democratic party, and the party's leader on the floor of the First Duma, the Russian parliament, in 1906. For protesting the disbanding of the Duma, he was imprisoned and barred from political office; after his release he became publisher and editor of the daily *Rech'*, St. Petersburg's leading liberal newspaper.

Nabokov had an English governess from the age of two, and his mother read English fairy tales to him at bedtime. Like her husband, she had a deep and broad love of the arts, especially literature, and she fostered in her favorite child his imaginative sensibility and exceptional memory.

At age six, Nabokov began to be taught by a French governess. It was not until 1906 that he learned to read and write in Russian, with the help of a village schoolteacher. That year he also discovered butterflies, which became a lifelong passion, and within two years he had mastered the known butterfly species of the earth. From 1907, Nabokov had a succession of Russian tutors. His family thought he might become a painter, and provided him with lessons under artists of the caliber of Mstislav Dobuzhinsky.

In January 1911, at age eleven, he began formal schooling at the liberal Tenishev school in St. Petersburg. Here the fiercely individualistic Nabokov objected to the enforced communality and civic-mindedness the teachers tried to instill in the students, but he was popular, a zealous goalkeeper at soccer, a good boxer, and, in the words of one teacher, produced "a most favorable impression with his moral decency." At school he studied German, and he read voraciously in French, Russian, and English.

In 1914, Nabokov began to write poetry and was soon composing prolifically. In the summer of 1915, at his family's country estate, he met his first love, Valentina Shulgin, the "Tamara" of his autobiography, the "Mary" of his first novel. When in 1916 his maternal uncle died, leaving him an estate worth several million dollars, he drew on his inheritance to publish his first book of poems, ardent but conventional love lyrics for Valentina.

After the February Revolution of 1917,

Nabokov's father once more entered political life as chancellor of Russia's first provisional government, and his son continued to resist the increasing pressure at school to participate in debates and write essays on Russia's political turmoil. Nabokov's last term at Tenishev School would have ended in December 1917, but when the October Revolution came, his father, fearing his eldest sons might be conscripted into the army, had Nabokov take his final exams early and go with his younger brother to the Crimea.

The rest of the family soon joined them there, leaving virtually all of their material wealth behind. During 1918 the Nabokovs stayed first at Gaspra, then on the outskirts of Yalta, while the Crimea changed hands several times. After the Germans retreated, a Crimean provisional government was established, with V. D. Nabokov as its minister of justice. In April 1919, the Crimea fell to Bolshevik troops, and the Nabokov family escaped from Sevastopol harbor on a Greek merchant ship as machine-gun fire strafed the waters.

In May 1919 the Nabokovs reached London. Vladimir entered Trinity College, Cambridge, in October 1919, reading modern and medieval languages (Russian and French) and zoology. He soon dropped zoology to leave himself more time for soccer, women, and the nostalgic Russian verse he had been composing on a daily basis since his severance from his homeland. In 1920 his father moved to Berlin—which was rapidly becoming the center of the Russian émigré community—to establish the liberal Russian daily *Rul'*. Nabokov had already published widely—poems in Russian and English, even a scientific article on butterflies—but now, adopting the pen name Vladimir Sirin to distinguish his byline from his father's, began to ply *Rul'* with his verse.

On Mar. 28, 1922, Nabokov was on vacation with his family in Berlin when his father was assassinated by two Russian monarchists. Nabokov revered his father and never forgot the horror of that night. In May he completed his B.A. exams, earning second-class honors. Throughout his years at Cambridge he had not been particularly attentive to his studies, preoccupied instead with his poems, prose, translations, and scientific articles. After graduation he took up residence in Berlin. In 1923, Nabokov began composing Pushkinian verse dramas, stories, and a five-act, quasi-Shakespearean verse play before settling firmly into prose fiction in 1924.

Though Paris supplanted Berlin as the center of Russian émigré life after 1924, Nabokov chose to remain in Germany, partly in the hope that his difficulties with the language would act as a vacuum seal to isolate and preserve his Russian, partly because of Véra Evseevna Slonim, whom he had met in 1923. Nabokov and Slonim were married on Apr. 25, 1925. She had been interested in his work for years and had typed his manuscripts for the last year and a half. As his wife, she would be his muse, editor, typist and secretary, cook, chauffeur, research and teaching assistant, business manager, legal adviser, and bibliographer. They had one child, Dmitri.

In 1925, Nabokov published his first novel, *Mary*. He was supporting himself and Véra primarily as a private tutor of English and French, and even gave lessons in tennis and boxing. He continued to write numerous stories, published mostly in *Rul'*, and in 1927 began his second novel, *King, Queen, and Knave*. Early in 1929 he and his wife traveled to the eastern Pyrenees for his first butterfly expedition since the Crimea. On this trip he conceived the idea for his third novel, *The Defense*, which he completed by the end of the summer.

The Defense was published in serial form in the Paris-based *Sovremennye zapiski*, the most important literary journal of the emigration; it published all his remaining Russian novels. Although Nabokov had won praise from discerning readers since the early 1920's, his publishing mostly in Berlin had limited the growth of his reputation; *Rul'* was far too costly in Paris to have a readership among émigrés there. *The Defense*, one of the finest novels Nabokov would ever write, astonished its émigré audience. Nina Berberova, after Nabokov the most important new novelist to emerge in the emigration, wrote of her reaction to the first installment of *The Defense:* "A tremendous, mature, sophisticated modern writer was before me, a great Russian writer, like a Phoenix, was born from the fire and ashes of revolution and exile. Our existence from now on acquired a new meaning. All my generation were justified. We were saved." Ivan Bunin, the elder statesman of émigré letters and soon to become the first Russian Nobel laureate for literature (1933), commented: "This kid has snatched a gun and done away with the whole older generation, myself included."

Nabokov continued to write prolifically, publishing the novella *The Eye* (written 1929–1930), the novels *Glory* (1930), *Camera obscura* (1931), and *Despair* (1932). In November 1932 he traveled to Paris for a first, triumphant, literary tour. Returning to Berlin, he began what would be by far his most ambitious project, the novel *The Gift*, which necessitated research into the life of the writer Nikolai Chernyshevsky that took up most of 1933 and much of 1934. As Hitler consolidated his power in Germany, Nabokov broke off work on *The Gift* to write the highly poetic but dystopian antitotalitarian fable, *Invitation to a Beheading* (1935).

In 1935 came the first translation of one of his novels into English. Dissatisfied with the result, he decided to translate the next, *Despair*, himself. His success made him eager to obtain a job anywhere in the English-speaking world. Nothing was forthcoming. But the fact that his wife was a Russian Jew, and the fact that Hitler in late 1936 had appointed one of his father's killers head of Russian émigré affairs, made it imperative that Nabokov find a way out of Germany.

Nabokov tested the Paris literary scene in early 1937, writing some pieces in French, then with Véra and their three-year-old son, settled on the Côte d'Azur, completing *The Gift* in early 1938 and writing two plays for the new Russian Theater in Paris. Unable to obtain a work permit, he was destitute, despite a small advance for his first American novel, *Laughter in the Dark*, his own retranslation and rewriting of *Camera obscura*.

In Paris at the end of 1938, sensing that the coming war would obliterate the Russian emigration in Europe, Nabokov wrote his first novel directly in English, *The Real Life of Sebastian Knight* (completed in January 1939). But although he was still trying to find an escape from the Continent, he had not yet switched definitively to English. He wrote a Russian novella, *The Enchanter*—the original of *Lolita*—and began a last, never-to-be-completed, Russian novel. A friend, the novelist Mark Aldanov, had been offered a summer post at Stanford that he was unable to accept; he passed the job on to Nabokov.

At last Nabokov could take his family to the United States. Just in time, they obtained the *visas de sortie*, borrowed the money for the fare, and left Paris in mid-May 1940, after German tanks had already crossed into France.

Nabokov

They arrived in New York City on May 28. Excited by America's intellectual freedom, Nabokov immediately felt at home in a way he never had in émigré Europe. But he lived a hand-to-mouth existence, writing reviews for the *New York Sun* and—thanks to a meeting with Edmund Wilson, who thought him the most brilliant man he had ever met—the *New Republic*. In June 1941, en route to Stanford, where he would teach summer courses in creative writing and in Russian literature, Nabokov discovered his first new species of butterfly, an event that confirmed his enchantment with America.

In the 1941–1942 academic year Nabokov was a visiting lecturer at Wellesley College, a post designed to allow him time to write. *The Real Life of Sebastian Knight* was published in December 1941, and his stories began to appear in the *Atlantic*. While living at Wellesley, Nabokov also began to sort out the lepidoptera collection at Harvard's Museum of Comparative Zoology, and until 1948 remained there as a research fellow, producing many articles and a monograph on North American butterflies.

Unable to find a permanent academic post, Nabokov divided his time in 1942 and 1943 between poorly paid lecture tours, his work at the museum, and writing. From 1943, settled in Cambridge, Mass., he taught Russian language at Wellesley College, studied butterflies, and wrote stories for the *Atlantic*, poems for the *New Yorker*, and his first novel in America, *Bend Sinister*, for which he had been awarded a Guggenheim Fellowship.

On July 12, 1945, Nabokov became an American citizen. That summer, serious heart palpitations forced him to quit his heavy smoking, and his physique thereafter changed from its early gauntness to the comfortable cushioning of later years.

At Wellesley, Nabokov introduced intermediate Russian language classes in 1945 and Russian literature in 1946, but despite being able to handle Russian better than anyone else in the United States and English better than almost any American, he could not find a permanent job until Morris Bishop, a fellow *New Yorker* writer, invited him to teach at Cornell University. He began there in 1948, at first teaching only Russian literature. Meanwhile he was writing his autobiography, *Speak, Memory*, which he published serially, mostly in the *New Yorker*. In 1950 he began to teach "Masterpieces of European Fiction"—soon to become one of Cornell's most celebrated courses—while composing *Lolita* and preparing an annotated translation of Pushkin's *Eugene Onegin*.

Nabokov completed *Lolita* by late 1953, working mostly in the summers, which he typically spent with his wife in search of new butterflies in the Rocky Mountains. In need of further income while he was completing *Lolita*, he wrote another novel, *Pnin*, which was published in several installments in the *New Yorker*.

Since no American publisher dared touch *Lolita* because of its intense, intimate treatment of child abuse, the novel was first published in Paris in 1955. Graham Greene commended it as one of the best books of the year. A British newspaper editor and morals crusader, John Gordon, read the novel on Greene's recommendation and promptly launched a campaign against it. The book rapidly became a cause célèbre, and was at last published in America in August 1958. All the advance publicity ensured excellent sales—100,000 copies in three weeks, the best since *Gone with the Wind*—and allowed Nabokov to retire from Cornell in 1959.

Nabokov had meanwhile been spending his time completing *Pnin*, and his translation and commentary of *Eugene Onegin*, now swollen to four volumes. In the wake of *Lolita*'s success, his son Dmitri began to translate his father's Russian novels, starting with *Invitation to a Beheading* (1959).

In late 1959, Nabokov visited Europe. While there, he received a cable from Stanley Kubrick, inviting him to Hollywood to write the screenplay for *Lolita*. He agreed, and spent the period February–October 1960 in California. Dmitri, meanwhile, had won an opera contest in Italy, and late in 1960 his parents returned to Europe to be near him. There, in Nice, Nabokov began *Pale Fire*, completing it in December 1961 at the Montreux Palace Hotel, Montreux, Switzerland, where he would spend the rest of his life.

Throughout the 1960's Nabokov's oeuvre expanded at both ends, in new fiction and translations of the old. Between late 1965 and late 1968, he wrote his longest and most complex novel, *Ada*. Its publication in 1969—with its ecstatic front-page review in the *New York Times Book Review*, *Time* cover story, *Playboy*-serialization, Literary Guild selection, and Book-of-the-Month-Club selection—probably marked the high point of his career.

In the early 1970's Nabokov wrote two more novels, *Transparent Things* (1970) and *Look at the Harlequins!* (1973); completed the translations of his early Russian novels and his stories into English; and closely supervised the translations of old and new novels and stories into French and even (with his wife's help) German. The work load proved too much for a man in his late seventies. While chasing butterflies on a slope in the Alps in 1975, he had a serious fall, and a series of infections kept him in the hospital for much of the next two years, too weak to write out more than a fraction of the new novel, *The Original of Laura*, that was already complete in his head. He died in Lausanne.

Nabokov's works were banned in the Soviet Union until 1986, but among Russian émigrés since the beginning of the 1930's and among the Russian readers who discovered his works decades later, he has been widely regarded as the best Russian novelist of the century. And to many in the United States he has produced the finest body of work of any American novelist since World War II.

In an age that favored discreet egalitarianism, Nabokov celebrated his sense of his own difference and wrote with elegance and an unabashed desire for distinctiveness and distinction. His style was sinuous, sensuous and cerebral, playful, deceptive and allusive, and above all, artful.

His novels foreground art, and to some have seemed simply artificial. To others, he used artifice to celebrate the power and test the limits of human consciousness. A gifted storyteller and an inventive rethinker of narrative form, he devised in his best novels unprecedented structures and styles that both expressed and arose from unique combinations of fictional character and circumstance. In works like *The Gift*, *Lolita*, *Pale Fire*, and *Ada*, he showed how the novel could move beyond stolid realism without lapsing into arid experiment.

[Most of Nabokov's manuscripts are in two major collections, both restricted: the Library of Congress (Russian and English novels and stories to 1962) and the Berg Collection, New York Public Library (correspondence, diaries, early notebooks, late manuscripts). Other collections, mostly of correspondence, include the Bakhmeteff Archive, Columbia University Library, and the Edmund Wilson Collection, Beinecke Library, Yale University.

Apart from the works mentioned in the text, published Nabokoviana includes four collections of stories, *Nabokov's Dozen* (1958), *A Russian Beauty*

 Nevers

(1973), *Tyrants Destroyed* (1975), and *Details of a Sunset* (1976); *Poems and Problems* (1971) and his collected Russian poems, *Stikhi* (1979); the play *The Waltz Invention* (1966); the posthumously collected *The Man from the USSR and Other Plays* (1984); translations of *Alice in Wonderland* into Russian (1923) and of *Three Russian Poets* (1945) and *The Song of Igor's Campaign* (1960) into English; a critical book, *Nikolay Gogol* (1944); the posthumously edited *Lectures on Literature* (1980), *Lectures on Russian Literature* (1981), and *Lectures on Don Quixote* (1983); *Strong Opinions* (1973), a collection of interviews and other public prose; and three posthumous collections of letters: *The Nabokov-Wilson Letters* (1979), *Perepiska s sestroy* (1985), and *Selected Letters, 1940–1977* (1989).

Brian Boyd's *Vladimir Nabokov: The Russian Years* (1990) and *Vladimir Nabokov: The American Years* (1991) supplant Andrew Field's conjectural and error-ridden *Nabokov: His Life in Part* (1977) and *VN: The Life and Art of Vladimir Nabokov* (1986). Alfred Appel, Jr., and Charles Newman, eds., *Nabokov: Criticism, Reminiscences, Translations, and Tributes* (1970); Alfred Appel, Jr., *Nabokov's Dark Cinema* (1974); and Peter Quennell, ed., *Vladimir Nabokov: A Tribute* (1979), contain biographical material. The standard bibliography is Michael Juliar, *Vladimir Nabokov: A Descriptive Bibliography* (1986). The journal of *The Nabokovian* (formerly *Vladimir Nabokov Research Newsletter*) has listed current scholarship since 1978. Among the most fruitful of sixty or so critical books are Alfred Appel, Jr., ed., *The Annotated Lolita* (1970); Ellen Pifer, *Nabokov and the Novel* (1980); Brian Boyd, *Nabokov's Ada: The Place of Consciousness* (1985); Donald Barton Johnson, *Worlds in Regression: Some Novels of Vladimir Nabokov* (1985); Julian Connolly, *Nabokov's Early Fiction: Patterns of Self and Other* (1992); and Michael Wood, *The Magician's Doubts: Nabokov and the Risks of Fiction* (1994). Among essays, Robert Alter's in Appel and Newman, in Quennell, and in his own *Partial Magic* (1975) stand out.

Nabokov was interviewed often on television. Among the best interviews are those by Patrick Wilson and Lionel Trilling for the Canadian Broadcasting Corporation, Nov. 1958; by Peter Duval Smith, for the BBC, Nov. 1962; by Robert Hughes, for National Educational Television, Jan. 1966; by James Mossman, for BBC-2, Oct. 1969; and by Bernard Pivot, for French television's "Apostrophes," May 1975. Harvard University has tapes of Nabokov readings; Cornell University and Wellesley College libraries have tapes or transcripts of reminiscences by Nabokov's colleagues and students. An obituary is in the *New York Times*, July 5, 1977.]

BRIAN BOYD

NEVERS, ERNEST ALONZO ("ERNIE") (June 11, 1903–May 3, 1976), athlete, was born in Willow River, Minn., the son of George and Mary Nevers. His parents, who had immigrated to the United States from Nova Scotia, Canada, were innkeepers in several small towns in northeastern Minnesota during Nevers's childhood. He attended high school in nearby Superior, Wis., where his brother worked. At Superior Central High School, Nevers developed into an outstanding basketball player and played American-style football for the first time. In 1918 the family's home was destroyed by fire, and the beginning of wartime Prohibition diminished George Nevers's income in the hotel business. He moved the family to California the same year and settled in Santa Rosa, where Ernie joined his parents after completing the school year in Wisconsin.

Nevers attended high school in Santa Rosa in 1919 and helped organize the school's first football team. The following year he returned to Superior, where he was a star athlete in four sports, and completed his high school education before returning to California. After spending a year at Santa Rosa Junior College to remedy a foreign language deficiency, he entered Stanford University in 1922.

At Stanford, Nevers became a star athlete in basketball, football, and baseball. He was best known as the six-foot, 205-pound smashing fullback who helped lead the Stanford team, coached by Glenn ("Pop") Warner, to the Rose Bowl. Having broken both ankles during the course of the season, Nevers was not expected to play in the game on Jan. 1, 1925, against the Notre Dame team, coached by Knute Rockne and featuring the famed "Four Horsemen" in the backfield. Despite heavily taped ankles and a noticeable limp, he was the outstanding player on the field in a 27–10 Stanford defeat, gaining 114 yards in 34 carries. His courage and stamina won him national recognition. The following season Nevers was an All-America selection despite playing for a subpar Stanford team. In three seasons, he led Stanford to an overall won-lost-tied record of 22–5–1. In comparing Nevers to Jim Thorpe (whom he had also coached in college), Coach Warner remarked: "Nevers could do everything Thorpe could do. And Ernie always tried harder. Ernie gave 60 minutes of himself in every game." Nevers's jersey number 1 was retired upon his graduation.

After his final season at Stanford, Nevers turned professional and organized the Jacksonville (Florida) All-Stars in order to capitalize on a pro football boom triggered by Harold ("Red") Grange's signing with the Chicago Bears. As one of the most publicized football players ever, Grange drew 40,000–50,000 fans to Bears games. Previously, a crowd of 10,000 was considered excellent in the NFL. He was paid $25,000 to play in two last games, one of which was against Grange and the Bears in Jacksonville in January 1926. Nevers outperformed Grange despite a 19–6 Chicago victory. The Jacksonville team disbanded shortly thereafter.

In the fall of 1926, Nevers signed with the Duluth Eskimos of the National Football League (NFL) and became the centerpiece of a legendary barnstorming tour. Owner Ole Haugsrud, a high school classmate, agreed to pay him $15,000 and a percentage of the larger gate proceeds. The team began its tour on September 20 and played twenty-nine league and exhibition games before it disbanded on the West Coast in early February with a record of 19–7–3. Nevers played in all but twenty-seven minutes of the games and outshone Red Grange, who played in the rival American Football League that year. He was unanimously selected as all-NFL fullback in a poll conducted by a Green Bay, Wis., newspaper. The following season he served as player-coach for Duluth, but despite his superb play the Eskimos had a 1–8–0 record on the road.

Beginning with the 1926 season, Nevers played three years of major league baseball with the St. Louis Browns, who gave him a $10,000 signing bonus and $7,000 per season. A journeyman pitcher, he ended his career with a record of six wins and twelve losses and a 4.64 earned run average. He is best known for giving up two of Babe Ruth's record-setting sixty home runs in 1927. Nevers also played one season of pro basketball for a Chicago team in 1926.

After sitting out the 1928 football season because of a back injury, Nevers returned to the NFL in 1929 with the Chicago Cardinals and led the league in scoring with eighty-five points. He also registered one of the best single-game performances in NFL history. On November 28, against the rival Chicago Bears, he made a record six touchdowns and kicked four extra points in a 40–7 victory. In that game he scored all of his team's points. Nevers had outstanding seasons with the Cardinals in 1930 and 1931, serving as player-coach in 1930. He was selected to the all-NFL team as a fullback in each of his seasons with Chicago. A wrist injury forced him to retire after the 1931 campaign. In five NFL seasons, he scored 301 points.

Nevers was assistant coach at Stanford from 1932 to 1935 and served in the same capacity at Iowa in 1937 and 1938. He was head coach at Lafayette College in Pennsylvania in 1936. Returning to the NFL in 1939 as head coach of the Chicago Cardinals, he finished with a disappointing 1–10 record. During World War II, he served in the South Pacific as a captain in the United States Marine Corps. After the war, Nevers was briefly involved in setting up the Chicago Rocket franchise in the All-America Football Conference. He soon returned to California and settled in Tiburon near San Francisco, where he worked in public relations for a wholesale liquor company and hosted a radio sports program. In 1926, Nevers had married Mary Elizabeth Haegerty, who died in 1943. He married Margery Luxem in 1947; they had one child. Nevers was elected to both the National Football Foundation's College Football Hall of Fame and the Pro Football Hall of Fame. *Sports Illustrated* selected Nevers as the best college player of all time, and he was a Football Writers of America choice for All-Time All-America team. He died in San Rafael, Calif.

[A file and newspaper clippings are in the Pro Football Hall of Fame in Canton, Ohio. A biography of Nevers is Jim Scott, *Ernie Nevers* (1969). See also David S. Neft and Richard M. Cohen, *Pro Football* (1987); Richard Whittingham, *Saturday Afternoon* (1985); and Dan Daly and Bob O'Donnell, *Pro Football Chronicle* (1990). An obituary is in the *New York Times*, May 4, 1976.]

JOHN M. CARROLL

NEWHOUSE, SAMUEL IRVING (May 24, 1895–Aug. 29, 1979), communications executive, was born Solomon Neuhaus in New York City, the eldest of eight children of Meier Neuhaus and Rose Arenfeldt, Jewish immigrants from eastern Europe. When he was two, the family moved to New Jersey. He grew up in Bayonne and surrounding communities. His sickly father fared badly in the garment industry. In 1902 the family name was changed to Newhouse, and Solomon became Samuel.

In 1908, Newhouse finished the eighth grade at Bayonne's P.S. 7. He spent the summer commuting to the Gaffney School in New York City, where he studied bookkeeping, stenography, and typing. That fall he was hired as an office boy for the Bayonne magistrate Hyman Lazarus, who became his mentor. Excellent with numbers, ambitious, determined, hard-working, and very short, Newhouse soon had increasing responsibilities. By 1912 these included overseeing the *Bayonne Times*, in which the judge had gained a controlling interest. Instructed to "look after the paper" until it could be sold, the teenaged Newhouse (self-described as "a brash kid") transformed a chronic money-loser into a profitable operation.

In June 1916, after four years of night classes at the New Jersey College of Law, Newhouse passed the state bar examinations. After losing his first case because of a rigged jury, he concentrated on business—overseeing the *Times* and managing the judge's law firm (the largest practice in the country). In 1922, for $98,000 Newhouse and Lazarus acquired control of the *Staten Island* (N.Y.) *Advance*, a property in dire straits. Newhouse made it profitable within a year. In 1923 his name went on the masthead as publisher, the first time it so appeared. In May 1924, Newhouse acquired control of the *Advance* with the aid of two partners (bought out in 1927 for $198,000). On May 24, 1924, he married Mitzi Epstein, a student at the Parsons School of Design; they had two sons.

The death of Lazarus in November 1924 led Newhouse to end his ties in Bayonne and concentrate on the *Advance*, which under his direction was increasingly profitable. Retained earnings provided him enough capital to take over the *Long Island Daily Press* (1932), which he soon made profitable by cutting costs, stimulating circulation, and promoting advertising. Following this pattern, Newhouse bought other financially straitened newspapers and took them out of the red. In 1940 *Editor and Publisher* recognized Newhouse's increasing importance by adding him to its list of American chain publishers because he controlled dailies in major population areas: the *Advance*, the *Long Island Daily Press*, the *Newark Star-Ledger* (he bought the *Ledger* in 1935, subsequently merging it with the *Star-Eagle*), the *Long Island Star-Journal* (the result of the 1938 acquisition and merger of the *Long Island City Star* and the *North Shore Journal*), and the *Syracuse Herald-Journal* (a 1939 acquisition and merger).

Despite a continuing increase in his holdings, Newhouse remained little known outside the newspaper industry. He eschewed publicity or editorial control, unlike William Randolph Hearst and other press lords. Newhouse did not concern himself with an individual newspaper's editorial content, only with its business matters. The takeover of the *Jersey* (City) *Journal* in 1945 resulted in litigation that forced him onto the witness stand, but in the main Newhouse continued to act secretively. His 1940's acquisitions of the *Syracuse Post-Standard* (1942) and the Harrisburg (Pa.) *Patriot* and *Evening News* (1947) were undertaken by agents; his involvement remained unknown for some time.

Newhouse's choice of acquisitions caused press critic A. J. Liebling to describe him as "a journalist chiffonnier" (ragpicker). But in 1950 he acquired his first property with stature that was not losing money, buying the Portland *Oregonian* for $5.5 million. Subsequently Newhouse paid $6.25 million for the *St. Louis Globe-Democrat* (1955). Later that year, borrowing bank money for the first time to finance a purchase, he paid, in what *Editor and Publisher* described as "the biggest transaction to date in American newspaper history"—$18.6 million for the *Birmingham* (Ala.) *News*, the *Huntsville* (Ala.) *Times*, and their three radio and one television stations. Newhouse already owned broadcast properties and would acquire more. In 1959 he took over Condé Nast (whose magazines included *Vogue* and *Glamour*) as well as Street and Smith (the oldest United States magazine firm). Merging it into Condé Nast restored the latter's profitability.

An obdurate manager given to nepotism, Newhouse endured well-publicized labor problems over the years. His style of paternalism, coupled with an aggressive cost-consciousness, especially rankled newsroom employees. Their union, the American Newspaper Guild, called its first strike, in 1934, against the *Long Island Daily Press*. Newhouse remained a bête noire to the Guild ("The Union Busting Duke of Staten Island" is how it characterized him in the 1930's). He also had his problems with the craft unions; the dispute they initiated at the *Oregonian* in 1959 led to an unsuccessful strike that officially lasted five years, four months, and twenty-five days. The publisher's successful handling of the unions from the 1930's on presaged the newspaper industry's ultimate triumph over organized labor in the 1980's.

Newhouse continued making deals into the 1970's, including the purchase of the *Bayonne Times* (1971), which he immediately merged into the *Jersey* (City) *Journal.* In 1962, Newhouse set a record for the highest price paid for newspapers in one city: $42 million for the *New Orleans Times-Picayune* and *States-Item;* in 1967 he broke that record with $54.2 million for the *Cleveland Plain Dealer.* In his quest for acquisitions he drove the price of newspaper properties up. His last transaction, in 1976, is likely to remain among the biggest American newspaper deals: in a bidding contest he paid more than $300 million for the Booth chain's eight Michigan dailies and the Sunday supplement *Parade.* Newhouse died in New York City from the effects of a stroke.

Newhouse's life is a genuine Horatio Alger story: poor immigrant boy builds a media empire worth a fortune. At his death that empire controlled thirty-one newspapers in twenty-two American cities, a string of magazines, radio and television stations, cable-television systems in a score of areas, and diverse assets such as an airport in Massachusetts. Newhouse never could articulate his urge to own newspapers. His brother Theodore once asserted that "he might as well have collected shoe factories." Because of Newhouse's emphasis on business management rather than editorial control, the empire had flaws: in the mid-1970's a journalism review list of the nation's "ten worst" big-circulation dailies included three Newhouse papers. Yet the *New York Times* rightly commended him for giving "the voices" of his newspapers freedom in an age of increasing consolidation.

[The only copy available to the public of Newhouse's privately printed *A Memo for My Children as Related to and Written by David Jacobs* (1980) is in the Library of Congress. Detailed biographies are John A. Lent, *Newhouse, Newspapers, Nuisances* (1966); and Richard H. Meeker, *Newspaperman* (1983). For Newhouse's relations with the American Newspaper Guild in the 1930's, see Daniel J. Leab, *A Union of Individuals* (1970). An obituary is in the *New York Times,* Aug. 30, 1979.]

DANIEL J. LEAB

NIELSEN, ARTHUR CHARLES (Sept. 5, 1897–June 1, 1980), market research engineer and business executive, was born in Chicago, Ill., the son of Rasmus Nielsen and Harriet Burr Gunn, both of whom were accountants. Nielsen attended grammar school in Berwyn, Ill., and Morton High School in Cicero, Ill. He graduated as class valedictorian from the University of Wisconsin in 1918, with a B.S. in engineering, earning the highest grades of any engineering student in the school's history. He spent the next year in the United States Naval Reserve, serving on the USS *Manchuria* as an ensign. On June 15, 1918, he married Gertrude B. Smith; they had five children.

Upon returning to the United States, Nielsen worked as an engineer for several Chicago companies until he decided to set out on his own in 1923. With $45,000 in investments from former fraternity brothers, he founded the A. C. Nielsen Company to make surveys of the performance and production techniques of industrial equipment. Although the company came close to failing on two occasions, it survived into the 1930's, when the Great Depression severely undermined the equipment manufacturing businesses that were Nielsen's biggest clients. In order to stave off bankruptcy, in 1933 Nielsen developed a new service that measured the retail flow of grocery and drugstore products. Product manufacturers, eager to use this information to help direct their advertising and production strategies, immediately supported the venture, and the A. C. Nielsen Company's fortunes were assured. The Nielsen Food and Drug Index, the first of its kind, made the Nielsen Company the leading marketing research company in the nation.

In 1938, Nielsen responded to the suggestions of radio station owners and developed a means for electronically measuring the size of a radio program's audience. He first obtained the patent on a device that measured which station a radio was tuned to; he then instituted a system that used numerous incentives to convince 1,000 radio listeners in the Midwest to install the Nielsen Audimeter and to send in the film that recorded the machine's results every two weeks. From these findings, Nielsen compiled the Nielsen Radio Index, then sold the results to radio networks, advertisers, and ad agencies.

Unlike food and drug research, the radio ratings field was not wide open. Nielsen had several competitors, including the network-supported Cooperative Analysis of Broadcasting (CAB), and C. E. Hooper. Hooper was the leader in the field, utilizing the relatively inexpensive system of telephone interviews to determine program ratings. When the Nielsen Company went national, however, the radio industry dropped its support of the CAB, leaving the field to Nielsen and Hooper. Nielsen, having learned the advantages of industry domination, bought out Hooper's national operation in 1950. Those in the radio business began greeting each other with, "How's your Nielsen?" instead of "How's your Hooper?" as they had previously.

A. C. Nielsen Company was thus well positioned to take advantage of the interconnected explosion in television audience and consumer spending of the post–World War II era. In 1950, Nielsen adapted the Audimeter for television and quickly assumed 90 percent control of the television rating industry. Families that installed an Audimeter were asked to keep a diary of the shows they watched, and were compensated a dollar or two per week plus free television repair services. All went well for the Nielsen Company until 1958, when the quiz show scandals that had rocked Americans' confidence in the medium led to a Commerce Department investigation into possible tampering with television ratings figures. Although no action was taken at the time, congressional committees began their own investigations into the accuracy and influence of the ratings services.

In 1961 the Nielsen Company began Nielsen Media Service, a ratings service for magazine advertisers, in part because to Nielsen it seemed much less likely to incur congressional scrutiny. Nielsen pulled out of the radio ratings business in 1963, largely because the Audimeter could no longer distinguish between the ever-growing number of stations on the dial. Although Nielsen's media ratings services had received the most public attention, food and drug research brought in 80 percent of the company's revenues.

Congress reopened the television ratings controversy in 1963, when Democratic congressman Oren Harris of Arkansas, who had gained fame exposing the extent of the game show scandals, launched a full-scale investigation of Nielsen and seven competitors. The investigation revealed some dramatic inconsistencies in the Nielsen Company's techniques, and the national media soon picked up the story. Magazines ranging from the *Saturday Evening Post* to the left-leaning *Nation* reiterated the charges of congressional critics that television ratings were widely unreliable, on the one hand, and responsible for television being a "vast cultural wasteland," on the other. Many critics, from congressmen to the *Saturday Review*'s Goodman Ace, blamed the ratings services—personified as "Mr. Nielsen"—for encouraging television executives to produce such top-rated shows as "The Beverly Hillbillies" instead of "quality productions." Nielsen, however, disavowed playing the role of tastemaker, arguing, "We're like baseball umpires. No one likes them, but they're essential to the game." Indeed, as one television executive explained, "Ratings are used by all the advertising agencies with which we deal. Since our sole financial support comes from payments by advertisers," he explained, networks needed the ratings to justify advertising costs. The only alternative to depending on ratings in a market-driven economy would have been for the government to provide monetary support for network programming, which no congressman was willing to suggest.

The charge about the accuracy of the ratings had more merit. Nielsen claimed that "Nielsen families" were demographically representative of a cross section of Americans, referring to his critics as "ignoramus[es] in the ABC's of statistical mathematics." But congressional investigators found Nielsen families to be skewed toward lower-middle-income groups—those who had enough money to buy a television set, yet appreciated the small remunerations the Nielsen Company paid for the bothersome task of keeping Audiolog diaries. The Nielsen Company's researchers were often unwilling to take the additional time needed to hunt down those who fit a specific demographic group and often substituted anyone who was willing to participate. The Audiologs provided the most graphic evidence of the unreliability of ratings. One woman wrote in her log that she kept her radio on for her dog to listen to, and "my dog enjoys it as much as a dog can." Another wrote that she opposed Jack Paar's views on integration, so she deliberately turned to another show when he came on. Nielsen countered that these were aberrations the committee had chosen for shock value, but the weight of evidence gathered by the committee seemed to point to real flaws in the Nielsen Company's methods.

Although the media and industry experts predicted the imminent death or reconstruction of the ratings business, the Nielsen Company weathered the storm and went on largely as before. In the 1970's the Nielsen Company instituted information services for petroleum companies and replaced the Audimeter with the Storage Instantaneous Audimeter, which gave the company ratings results every fifteen minutes. Nielsen retired as chairman of the board in 1976 and was succeeded by his son, Arthur C. Nielsen, Jr., who had been president of the company since 1957. The A. C. Nielsen Company by that time had subsidiaries in twenty-three countries, with almost $400 million in yearly revenues. Nielsen died in Chicago; he designated $2.4 million of his $47 million estate to charity.

[Articles on the A. C. Nielsen Company include "How's Your Nielsen," *Newsweek*, Mar. 13, 1950; *Time*, Jan. 14, 1957; "TV Ratings—The Men Behind Them," *Newsweek*, May 18, 1959; "Nielsen's Romance with Magazines," *Business Week*, July 15, 1961; *Time*, Apr. 12, 1963; "Broadcast Ratings Lose Spell," *Business Week*, Apr. 13, 1963; Kenneth Woodward, "Ambush at Omaha Pass," *The Nation*, May 4, 1963; Bard Lindeman and Alan Patureau, "Television Ratings on Trial," *Saturday Evening Post*, Feb. 8, 1964; *Saturday Review*, Jan. 2, 1965; "TV Ratings Stay Clear," *Business Week*, Sept. 10, 1966; and *Saturday Review*, May 12, 1970. An obituary is in the *New York Times*, June 4, 1980.]

MICHAEL GOLDBERG

NILES, JOHN JACOB (Apr. 28, 1892–Mar. 1, 1980), folksinger, music collector, and composer, was born in Louisville, Ky., the son of John Thomas Niles, a farmer who was a singer and square dance caller, and Lula Sarah Reisch, a church organist. Niles attended public school in Louisville. At home, he learned to play the piano from his mother and to play stringed instruments from his father. While still in elementary school, Niles received a store-bought three-stringed dulcimer from his father with the admonition that in the future he would need to make his own instrument. At the age of twelve, the gift dulcimer was replaced by one of Niles's own construction. During his high school years, he began collecting folk music from his region. In 1907, Niles gave his first paid performance as part of a Chautauqua group. In 1909 he graduated from DuPont Manual High School in Louisville.

Following graduation, Niles became a surveyor, an occupation that took him throughout Kentucky and expanded his interest and involvement in folk music collection. While traveling, Niles would give performances for local churches and other interested groups. In 1917 he enlisted as a private in the Aviation Section of the Army Signal Corps. While serving in France in 1918, he nearly lost his life in a plane crash that left him partially paralyzed. Not until the mid-1920's was he again able to walk normally. After his discharge, Niles remained in France, attending the University of Lyons and the Schola Cantorum in Paris, expanding his background in classical music. In late 1919, he returned to the United States, where he studied at the Cincinnati Conservatory of Music and continued to give folk song concerts.

In the early 1920's, Niles moved to New York City. While there, he met contralto Marion Kerby, and they created a folk song program with which they toured in the United States and Europe. Niles supplemented his musical earnings with a variety of positions, including nightclub emcee, horse groom, and rose gardener. In addition, he contributed stories to *Scribner's Magazine*. Starting in 1928, he was a driver for famed photographer Doris Ulmann. Together, they traveled the southwestern United States, where she photographed and he collected more folk material. By the 1920's, Niles's earliest folk song collections were published and available to the public. Chief among them were *Impressions of a Negro Camp Meeting* (1925); *Singing Soldiers* (1927); *Seven Kentucky Mountain Tunes* (1929); and *The Songs My Mother Never Taught Me* (1929, with Douglas S. Moore).

During the 1930's, Niles's concert performances expanded to nearly fifty per year, he collected songs in the states of southern Appalachia, and he engaged in an outpouring of folk song publication, collection, and arranging. The publications focused on Appalachia and included *Songs of the Hill-Folk* (1934), *Ten Christmas Carols from the Southern Appalachian Mountains* (1935), and *Ballads, Carols and Tragic Legends from the Southern Appalachian Mountains* (1937). On Mar. 21, 1936, Niles married Rena Lipetz, a free-lance writer; they had two children. The popularity of his concerts and compositions led to a recording contract with RCA Victor. In 1939 he recorded his first album, *Early American Ballads*.

Early in the 1940's, Niles began work on an oratorio titled *Lamentations*, prompted by Hitler's actions in Europe. Meanwhile, he released two more albums, *Early American Carols and Folk Songs* (1940) and *American Folk Lore* (1941). Folk song collections continued to be released as *The Singing Campus* (1941), *The Anglo-American Ballad Study Book* (1945), and *The Anglo-American Carol*

Study Book (1948). Niles even found time to write a book for children, *Mr. Poof's Discovery* (1947). Concert performances in the United States continued to draw audiences who appreciated his dulcimer playing and high-pitched falsetto song styling.

Writing, recording, performing, and collecting continued throughout the 1950's. Musical experts estimate Niles collected more than 1,000 folk tunes during his career, a feat earning him the title "Dean of American Balladeers." Further song collections were published and released in the decade: *The Shape-Note Study Book* (1950) and the *John Jacob Niles Suite* (1952). In 1950, Niles completed *Lamentations*, started a decade earlier, an expression of opposition to authoritarian rule, be it fascist or Communist. Late in the decade, RCA Camden issued *John Jacob Niles: Fiftieth Anniversary Album* (1957) and Tradition Records released *I Wonder as I Wander* (1958). While he collected vast numbers of folk songs Niles is probably best remembered for three songs of his own composition: "I Wonder as I Wander," "Go 'way from My Window," and "Black Is the Color of My True Love's Hair."

The early 1960's brought forth an outpouring of publications from Niles: *The Ballad Book of John Jacob Niles* (1961), *Folk Carols for Young Actors* (1962), *Folk Ballads for Young Actors* (1962), and *John Jacob Niles Song Book for Guitar* (1963). In the last half of the decade, albums titled *John Jacob Niles: Folk Balladeer* (1965) and *The Best of John Jacob Niles* (1967) were released. With advancing age, Niles began to limit concert performances to the eastern United States.

During the last decade of his life, Niles remained close to his Boot Hill Farm near Lexington, Ky. While there, he undertook the last major project of his career, setting to music twenty-two poems of Thomas Merton, a Trappist monk and author who lived at Gethsemani Abbey near Bardstown, Ky. In 1972, he published the *Niles-Merton Song Cycles*. Four years later, *The John Jacob Niles Bicentennial Song-Book* was released. Niles died at Boot Hill Farm.

[Niles's papers are in the Special Collections Department of the University of Kentucky Library, Lexington. See also David F. Burg, "John Jacob Niles," *Kentucky Review* 2 (1980). An obituary is in the *New York Times*, Mar. 3, 1980.]

FRANK R. LEVSTIK

NIN, ANAÏS (Feb. 21, 1903–Jan. 14, 1977), diarist and novelist, was born in Neuilly, France, the oldest child (and only daughter) of Joaquín Nin y Castellanos and Rosa Culmell de Nin, both musicians born in Cuba. Nin's father, who was studying music in Paris at the time of his daughter's birth, later became well known as a composer and concert pianist. The family lived in Germany, Cuba, and Belgium before Joaquín Nin abandoned his family in the south of France in 1913. Rosa took her three children to Barcelona before settling in New York City in 1914. Nin's schooling, both parochial and public, included only a few months of high school; she dropped out of Wadleigh High School in April 1919. Briefly she modeled for artists and devoted her time to reading and writing.

Nin married Hugh Parker Guiler on Mar. 3, 1923, during a visit to Cuba. Guiler, a 1919 graduate of Columbia University, was a banker with National City Bank in New York, then in Paris and London, before returning to New York City during World War II. When he left his job with the bank more than a decade later, he changed his name to Ian Hugo and worked as a copper engraver and art-film maker, but continued to earn money as a financial adviser. Guiler and Nin were married for fifty-five years.

The diary that Nin began when she was eleven years old, just before her arrival in New York City, grew over the next fifty years to some 35,000 pages. She had what she called an "obsession with preserving, portraying, recording." While living with her husband in Paris from 1925 to 1939, she filled a new diary volume at least every three months. She turned their home in Louveciennes, a forty-five-minute train ride from Paris, into a center of social and literary activity. She wrote short stories and a brief study of D. H. Lawrence, whom she credited with her sexual awakening. *D. H. Lawrence: An Unprofessional Study* (1932) caught the attention of Henry Miller.

Nin had sexually awakening affairs with both Miller and (briefly) his wife, June, and she began acting out the Don Juan behavior of her father, culminating in a brief incestuous sexual liaison with him in 1933. During her eight-year affair with Miller, they shared a literary passion that would have a profound effect on both their lives and their work. Nin grew as an artist, publishing *The House of Incest* (1936), a prose poem; and *The Winter of Artifice* (1939), three novellas; as well as the introduction to Miller's *Tropic of Cancer* (1934). All three books were published for Miller and Nin under the imprint of their Siana editions or Seurat series. This publishing venture, run by Jack Kahane's Obelisk Press, operated out of Miller's apartment in rue Villa Seurat and was financed by Nin. She also rented a houseboat on the Seine River in Paris, where she carried on an affair with (among others) Gonzalo More, a Peruvian Marxist. During the 1930's she also had close friendships with Antonin Artaud, Lawrence Durrell, René Allendy, and Otto Rank. The latter two men were her analysts and lovers. Long disillusioned with Catholicism, Nin took psychoanalysis as her religion. She spent two periods of several months each in the years 1934–1935 working in New York City at Rank's analytical practice, experiences she used in "Hotel Chaotica" (published as "The Voice").

After fleeing the war in Europe at the end of 1939, Nin and Guiler settled in New York City. When the literary establishment shunned her poetic, abstract, introspective fiction, she bought her own printing press (Gemor Press). With the assistance of Gonzalo More (who gave his name to the press), she began reprinting her first two volumes of fiction and new short stories entitled *Under a Glass Bell* (1944) and *This Hunger* (1945)—all illustrated by her husband ("Ian Hugo"). She also wrote erotica for a dollar a page, drawing on her own experiences and those of her friends—including More, Miller (who soon drifted to California), Eduardo Sanchez (a cousin), actress Luise Rainer, poet Robert Duncan, Caresse Crosby, and Gore Vidal. Both Vidal and a good review of her short stories by Edmund Wilson helped to secure her first trade publisher for a full-length novel. *Children of the Albatross* (1947), based on her circle of young gay artists in Greenwich Village, would become the first of five works in her "Proustian novel," eventually titled *Cities of the Interior.*

By 1950, Nin had begun dividing her life between New York City, where she lived with her husband, and Los Angeles, where she lived with her second "husband," Rupert William Pole, whom she had met in 1947. Pole, about fifteen years her junior, worked for the Forest Service before becoming a junior high school teacher. He often gave readings with Nin, who continued to publish novels: *The Four-Chambered Heart* (1950) concerns a love affair with a Marxist revolutionary on a houseboat in the Seine; *A Spy in the House of Love* (1954) follows numerous adulterous affairs of "Sabina" in New York City; and *Seduction of the Minotaur* (1961) is set in Acapulco, which had become Nin's favorite vacation spot.

As the diary volumes grew, Nin was torn between her desire to publish them and her fear of hurting her husband and family. Occasionally an edited version of a portion of her diary was rejected by various publishers. In addition to writing her diary and fiction, Nin wrote nonfiction essays, collected in *The Novel of the Future* (1968) and *In Favor of the Sensitive Man* (1976). She also acted in films, appearing in several of Ian Hugo's art films, including the first two, *Ai-Ye* (1950, twenty-two minutes) and *Bells of Atlantis* (1952, nine minutes). She also acted in Maya Deren's *Ritual in Transfigured Time* (1946) and Kenneth Anger's *Inauguration of the Pleasure Dome* (1950).

After her final volume of fiction, *Collages* (1964), Nin began publishing *The Diary of Anaïs Nin* (seven volumes, 1966–1980). The first volume, which was rewritten and severely expurgated (no husband or sexual activities were included), began with her meeting Miller in the late fall of 1931. The appearance of her diaries, beginning in her sixty-third year, coincided with the rise of the women's movement and the Age of Aquarius, concerned with inner exploration and freedom. Nin articulated the Lawrentian world for women, an "obedience to the urge that arises in the soul" (as Lawrence called it).

Nin's literary style was occasionally satirized in the national press, and her appearance was emulated by many. She dressed dramatically in black, wore heavy makeup, and piled her hair above or behind her head. Lawrence Durrell called her a "diva." She spoke to university students across the country. More important than her fame, however, was her contribution to the genre of autobiography. No woman has left such an extensive portrait of her inner life: her diary is the "first real portrait of the artist as a woman," said the feminist Kate Millett. Miller had predicted decades earlier that Nin's complete diary would take its place beside those of St. Augustine and Proust. And Maxwell Geismar, though he charged her with mendacity, claimed she was the "best known diarist since Samuel Pepys."

After her death in Los Angeles, admirers held large public memorial services in that city, San

Francisco, New York City, and Washington, D.C. An even greater fame came posthumously with the publication of her erotica, *Delta of Venus* (1977) and *Little Birds* (1979). Her exotic looks and her name have become legendary. The French house of Cacharel named a perfume for her (Anaïs, Anaïs), Gore Vidal wrote her into five of his novels, more than a dozen students have written doctoral dissertations on her work, and five books of criticism have appeared.

[Nin's original and rewritten diaries are with her papers at UCLA; fiction manuscripts are at Northwestern University, Evanston, Ill.; and erotica manuscripts are at UCLA and at the Kinsey Institute, Indiana University. Additional published works by Nin are *Waste of Timelessness and Other Early Stories* (1977); *The Early Diary of Anaïs Nin*, 4 vols. (1978–1985); *Henry and June* (1986); and *Incest* (1992). Her letters are collected in *A Literate Passion*, edited by Gunther Stuhlmann (1987). The first full biography is Noël Riley Fitch, *Anaïs* (1993). Critical studies include Evelyn Hinz, *The Mirror and the Garden* (1973); Benjamin Franklin V and Duane Schneider, *Anaïs Nin* (1979); Sharon Spencer, *Collage of Dreams* (1981); Nancy Scholar, *Anaïs Nin* (1984); and Linde Salber, *Anaïs Nin* (1992). Bibliographies include Benjamin Franklin V, *Anaïs Nin* (1973); and Philip K. Jason, *Anaïs Nin and Her Critics* (1993). Of three journals devoted to her life and work—*Anaïs, Seahorse*, and *Under the Sign of Pisces*—only the first is still being published. Robert Snyder's *Anaïs Nin Observed* is a sixty-minute documentary film. An obituary is in the *New York Times*, Jan. 16, 1977.]

NOËL RILEY FITCH

NOLAN, BOB (Apr. 1, 1908–June 15, 1980), composer and singer, was born Robert Clarence Nobles in the timberlands of New Brunswick, Canada, the son of Harry Byron Nobles, a tailor, and Florence Nobles. Raised by aunts in Boston, where he could receive an education, he developed a keen interest in American folk music. His father, after receiving a medical discharge from the United States Army Air Service, moved to the dry climate of Tucson, Ariz., to recuperate from lung damage and changed the family name to Nolan (as more American- and Irish-sounding). Young Clarence joined him there at age fourteen and soon acquired a deep appreciation for the awesome beauties of the western desert. Inspired also by such nineteenth-century romantic poets as Byron and Shelley, he applied their styles to his own poems about the natural wonders of the desert; these poems, which did not yet include the cowboy, provided themes for songs he later composed. Another source of musical inspiration was trains with their whistles, to which he was exposed when wanderlust took him traveling around the country after high school. His first song, "Way Out There," followed this theme of the rails; he wrote it while singing with a Los Angeles Chautauqua troupe in 1929.

As Bob Nolan he joined the Rocky Mountaineers, a western musical group of instrumentalists and two other singers in Los Angeles in 1931 to provide the baritone voice and yodeling; the lead was sung by Leonard Slye (later named Roy Rogers). But he left the group after a few months in favor of steady work as a golf caddie at an exclusive country club. In September 1933, Slye and Tim Spencer prevailed upon Nolan to join them in forming a western vocal ensemble, the Pioneer Trio. Determined to outclass the few other popular western singing groups, the three men developed an original style of clear, precise harmonizing in unison, both singing and yodeling, an unprecedented feat. Slye also played lead guitar; Nolan, the bass fiddle. The trio gained a local following on Los Angeles radio programs. In order to provide breaks in their singing and to enrich their sound, the vocalists in early 1934 added an accomplished Texas cowboy fiddler, Hugh Farr, who eventually also sang occasional bass parts. That March they changed their name to Sons of the Pioneers and then added Farr's brother Karl on guitar. The Farr brothers blended perfectly with the vocal trio to round out its unique sound.

The popularity of the Sons of the Pioneers stemmed from their close, seemingly effortless harmonies, their string accompaniment, and especially the original song compositions of Nolan and Spencer. Nolan set the pace by breaking with the customary cowboy sentimentalism to paint romantic images of nature embodied in the western plains and the men who tamed that land and its herds of cattle. He first wrote the poetic words, then set them to music. His first hit, "Tumbling Tumbleweeds," recorded by the Sons of the Pioneers for Decca in 1934, captured this flavor, became the group's theme song, and was sung by Gene Autry in the 1935 Western film that had the same title as the song. The deep feeling and vocal coloring with which the Sons of the Pioneers sang these melodies were marked by Nolan's unusual baritone voice, as on his 1935 gospel song "When I Leave This World Behind"; the ethereal "Blue Prairie," which he helped Spencer compose; his added yodeling on "Echoes from the Hills"; and the rollicking "Roving Cowboy," which later became Hank Williams's theme song as "Happy Cowboy." Nolan wrote over 1,200 songs, his second most famous one being "Cool Water" (1936, a hit in 1941); Spencer wrote several hundred, usually hits for the Sons of the Pioneers, notably "The Everlasting Hills of Oklahoma" and "Cigareets, Whusky and Wild, Wild Women" in 1947 and "Room Full of Roses" in 1949.

In 1936 the Sons of the Pioneers appeared with Bing Crosby in the motion picture *Rhythm on the Range* and made their first road tour, to perform at the Texas Centennial in Dallas with Will Rogers. The same year Spencer left the group and was replaced by an exceptionally powerful and clear tenor, Lloyd Perryman, who remained with the Pioneers after Spencer returned late in 1937 to sing lead when Slye moved on to a cowboy movie career under the name Roy Rogers. Slye, however, rejoined the Sons of the Pioneers in December 1937 for a recording session of outstanding Nolan tunes for Columbia, including another gospel-railroad song, "When the Golden Train Comes Down," and Nolan singing lead on "Song of the Bandit." By the end of that year Spencer's brother Glenn had joined to write songs and act as business manager, and Pat Brady was added to relieve Nolan on the bass fiddle, provide comedy in public performances, and occasionally sing tenor.

The Sons of the Pioneers appeared in many western cowboy films, including twenty-nine with Charles Starrett and forty-one with Roy Rogers, sometimes with speaking parts. Their movie roles were usually incongruous, however, for although their smooth, gentle harmonies complemented the cowboy singers, with whom they evoked the mythology and mystique of the legendary cowboy, the lyrics remained almost spiritual in contrast to the rambunctious six-gun plots of these films. Eventually billed as Bob Nolan and the Sons of the Pioneers, because his voice was usually featured, the group created a poetic western sound that captured popular imagination in America and Europe during the 1930's and 1940's. The music was not western swing, which aimed primarily at energetic dancing, nor was it the hillbilly folk music of the rural Midwest, whose practitioners, however, imitated or borrowed heavily from the Sons of the Pioneers' western flavor to help fashion "country" music.

Nolan remained the foundation of the Sons of the Pioneers as World War II brought personnel replacements: stuttering Shug Fisher filled in for Brady, and tenor Ken Carson for Perryman. The Sons of the Pioneers had their own radio show, "Sunshine Ranch," appeared as guests on other programs, toured constantly, and recorded again for Decca until 1945, when they switched to RCA Victor, adding orchestral accompaniment for a fuller sound. The group also produced hundreds of radio transcriptions. In 1947 the Sons of the Pioneers were honored by trade journals as the most popular western vocal group in the world.

Nolan married his fiancée Clara in 1941; they had one child. A private and deeply religious man who admired the philosophical writings of Spinoza, he elected to follow Tim Spencer into retirement from the Sons of the Pioneers in 1949, in order to devote his time to song writing; he did not leave until a replacement had been found whose voice closely matched his own, Tommy Doss. In the 1950's, Nolan made guest appearances on a new Sons of the Pioneers radio program and replaced Doss on Sons of the Pioneers records with Perryman and Ken Curtis (later the scruffy Festus on television's "Gunsmoke") during the period 1955–1957. By then, however, the unique western musical creations of Nolan and the Sons of the Pioneers had gone the way of the singing movie cowboy, always to remain the epitome of the golden age of pure western popular music. Nolan's contribution had been immense. Said music historian Hugh Cherry, "Bob Nolan is to western music what Zane Grey was to the western story." Nolan died in Los Angeles.

[The fullest treatment of Nolan's life is in Ken Griffis, *Hear My Song* (1974). A remembrance by Griffis is "Reflections on Bob Nolan," *JEMF* [John Edwards Memorial Foundation] *Quarterly*, Summer 1980. The founding of the Sons of the Pioneers is treated in Elise Miller Davis, *The Answer Is God* (1955), a biography of Roy Rogers and Dale Evans. The place of Nolan and the Sons of the Pioneers in the history of western music is treated in Douglas B. Green, *Country* (1988). Representative record album collections are *The Best of the Sons of the Pioneers*, RCA ANL1-3468 (1966); *Sons of the Pioneers*, Columbia 37439 (1982), featuring the late 1937 recordings of mostly Nolan compositions; and *Sons of the Pioneers: Empty Saddles*, MCA-1563 (1983), with liner notes by Laurence J. Zwisohn.]

CLARK G. REYNOLDS

NOYES, WILLIAM ALBERT, JR. (Apr. 18, 1898–Nov. 25, 1980), chemist and teacher, was born in Terre Haute, Ind., the son of William Albert Noyes, a noted chemist, and Flora Elizabeth Collier. He graduated from Urbana High School in Illinois in 1914, then attended Grinnell College in Iowa for two years. He next enrolled at the University of Illinois, but left to enlist in the United States Army in April 1917 and served as an officer in the 308th Signal Corps Battalion while stationed in France from June 1918 until February 1919. He was granted a B.A. degree from Grinnell while he was in France and received an American Field Service fellowship, which allowed him to continue his studies at the University of Paris, from which he received the Docteur ès Science degree in 1920, and at the University of Geneva.

Noyes's wartime experience in France was part of a lifelong association with that country. He was first introduced to the French language and culture at the age of ten, when his father arranged for him to live for several months with a French teacher in a small village near Paris, and he married Sabine Onnillon of Paris on June 10, 1921. They had one child. In recognition of his contributions to the study of chemistry, the French government awarded him the rosette d'Officier de la Honneur in 1956.

Noyes returned to the United States in 1920 to take up a teaching fellowship at the University of California at Berkeley. He went on to teach chemistry at the University of Chicago (1922–1929), Brown University (1929–1938) in Providence, R.I., and the University of Rochester (1938–1963) in New York. He became chairman of the department of chemistry at Rochester in 1939 and later served as dean of the graduate school and the College of Arts and Sciences. He was also director of the University of Rochester's chemistry research laboratory.

Noyes was a productive and prolific scientist throughout his long career. He did research in electrochemistry, photochemistry, vapor pressures, reaction kinetics, fluorescence, and spectroscopy. His major accomplishments were in the photochemistry of ketones and chemical kinetics and he published extensively in this and related areas. He also published several books, including *Photochemistry of Gases* with P. A. Leighton in 1941. He actively promoted the scholarship of other chemists through his work as editor of the various publications of the American Chemical Society. From 1939 to 1949 he edited *Chemical Reviews*, a journal his father edited from its inception in 1924 to 1926. From 1950 to 1962 he edited the *Journal of the American Chemical Society*, as did his father from 1902 to 1917, and from 1952 to 1964 the *Journal of Physical Chemistry*. Noyes also served on numerous governance committees for the society. In 1947 he was elected president of the society, an office his father held in 1920. He also played a significant role in the affairs of the International Union of Chemistry. He participated regularly in the meetings of the union, was vice-president of the organization from 1947 to 1951, and in 1959 was elected to a three-year term (1960–1963) as president, the first American to be so honored since before World War II.

Noyes's distinguished career in the academic world was matched by an equally distinguished career as a spokesman, consultant, and adviser on scientific and technical matters to national and international agencies. From 1940 to 1946 he was employed by the federal government, first as section chairman (1941–1942), then as a staff member (1942–1946), of the National Defense Research Committee. He also joined the staff of the Technical Division of the army's Chemical Warfare Service (1942–1947). In this capacity he was primarily concerned with the development of protective measures in the event of gas warfare. Following the war, Noyes served as chairman of the Chemical Warfare Committee of the Research and Development Board (1948–1950). In 1951 he was appointed the chief scientific adviser to the head of the United States Chemical Corps. During this same time period he served as a consultant to the Atomic Energy Commission.

On the international level, Noyes was a delegate to the 1946 London conference that drafted the initial plans for the United Nations Educational, Scientific, and Cultural Organization (UNESCO). He was an alternate delegate to a 1948 conference and participated in the educational and technical needs surveys of a number of underdeveloped countries. In September 1951 he was named to the United States

National Commission for UNESCO, a commission composed of one hundred prominent leaders in education, science, and the arts that advised the federal government on UNESCO affairs.

Noyes was the recipient of many honors during his long and notable career. In 1948 he received the Medal for Merit from the United States and the King's Medal for Service in the Cause of Freedom from Great Britain. In 1954 he was awarded the Priestley Medal by the American Chemical Society. In 1957 he received the Willard Gibbs Award in recognition of his contributions to chemistry as a teacher, researcher, and government adviser. He was given the Charles Lathrop Parsons Award in 1970 by the American Chemical Society for outstanding public service. He was a member of the American Association for the Advancement of Science, the National Academy of Sciences, and the American Academy of Arts and Sciences, and he was active in the lobbying effort that encouraged Congress to establish the National Science Foundation in 1950.

After Noyes retired from the University of Rochester in 1963, he joined the faculty of the University of Texas at Austin on a part-time basis. At the time of his death in Austin he was Ashbel Smith Professor Emeritus of Chemistry.

[See "Dedicatory Number in Honor of William Albert Noyes, Jr.," *Journal of the American Chemical Society*, Nov. 1962.]

GEORGE P. ANTONE

O

OAKIE, JACK (Nov. 12, 1903–Jan. 23, 1978), actor, was born Lewis Delaney Offield in Sedalia, Mo., the son of James Madison Offield and Mary Evelyn ("Ev") Jump. His mother was an educator who founded schools in Sedalia and in Muskogee, Okla., where the family moved when Offield was five years old.

When he was nine, his father died. His mother opened an all-girl school in Muskogee and sent Offield to live with his maternal grandmother in Kansas City, Mo., where he finished his public schooling in 1917. He then joined his mother in New York City, where she had taken a teaching position, and attended a Roman Catholic military school for boys.

In 1919, Offield began working in a Wall Street brokerage house as a telephone clerk. His office clowning and impersonations led to his participation in a charity production of *Babes in Toyland* in 1922. Since he was playing the Jack of Hearts, the musical director dubbed him "Jack." New York acquaintances had already given him the nickname "Okie" because of the accent he had picked up in Oklahoma. Offield combined the two nicknames and had his name listed in the show's program as "Jack Oakie." He used this name professionally for the rest of his life but never changed his legal name.

Oakie's success in *Toyland* and two other charity shows encouraged him to abandon Wall Street for show business. He soon joined the chorus of George M. Cohan's *Little Nellie Kelly* (1922). Over the next five years he was in *Peggy-Ann*, John Cort's *Sharlee*, and the Shuberts' *Innocent Eyes* and *Artists and Models*. During intervals he teamed with Lulu McConnell to tour the vaudeville circuit with *At Home*. By 1927, Oakie had achieved headliner status on Broadway, but Charles Lindbergh's trans-Atlantic flight inspired him to risk everything by going to Hollywood to get into films.

Almost immediately after he arrived in Los Angeles in June 1927, Oakie landed parts in *Finders Keepers* and two other films. His flair for visual comedy, characterized by his famous "double takes," got him a contract with Paramount in 1928. While finishing *Someone to Love*, his last silent film that year, Oakie and other Paramount contract actors were ordered to report for voice tests. He escaped the test when a director friend invited him to begin work immediately on a new sound film, *The Dummy*. His performance in that "talking" film assured his continued success as an actor; over the next decade he appeared in more than fifty films.

In 1929 alone Oakie made ten films, including *Fast Company*, an adaptation of *Elmer the Great*, a Broadway hit about a baseball player that remained Oakie's favorite film role. Between 1930 and 1932 he made nearly twenty films. At age twenty-eight he played a college freshman in *Touchdown*, the first of the collegiate comedies with which he became identified. He also had featured parts in two W. C. Fields classics, *If I Had a Million* and *Million Dollar Legs*, both from 1932.

The half-dozen films Oakie made in 1933 include *College Humor* and *Alice in Wonderland*, in which he violated his personal policy of never wearing makeup by appearing in an enormous mask as Tweedledum. His mother made a rare screen appearance in *Too Much Money*. In 1934, Oakie made three more Paramount films as well as *Looking for Trouble* for United Artists. The following year he worked with Clark Gable in Twentieth Century–Fox's *Call of the Wild*. In 1935 he made *The Big Broadcast of 1936,* and in 1936 he appeared in *Collegiate* for Paramount and two films for Fox. Oakie made five films in 1936, including *That Girl from Paris,* his first for RKO. The same year he married Venita Varden. The couple separated two years later; their divorce was finalized on Feb. 16, 1945. They had no children.

By the mid-1930's Oakie was established as a film star. His strong identification with college themes led to his having a radio show, "Jack Oakie College" (also known as "Jack Oakie's College"), which ran on CBS from Dec. 29, 1936, through Mar. 22, 1938. The format had Oakie as president of a school bearing his name and incorporated such collegiate trappings as an opening yell; otherwise, it was a typical variety show. Benny Goodman's orchestra provided the music through 1937, and Judy Garland was a regular performer.

After making five films in 1937, Oakie made four in 1938, including *The Affairs of Annabel* and *Annabel Takes a Tour* with Lucille Ball, and then spent half the year in Europe. When he returned home, he felt that Hollywood had written him off for his absence. It happened, however, that he had sailed back from Europe on the same ship as Charles Chaplin's brother Syd, on whose recommendation Chaplin soon invited Oakie to act in *The Great Dictator* (1940). Oakie's flamboyant portrayal of "Napolini, *Il Duce* of Bacteria," earned him an Oscar nomination for best supporting actor, and he afterward called working with Chaplin the highlight of his career.

Oakie's work with Chaplin reestablished a demand for him as an actor. Nevertheless, the frequency of his screen appearances slackened; over the next decade he made half as many films as he had made during the 1930's. After making two films in 1950 he was off the screen until he had a cameo in *Around the World in Eighty Days* in 1956.

During the early 1950's, Oakie married actress Victoria Horne; they had no children. It was at this time that he began appearing on television. In 1950 he performed in Ken Murray's and Jack Carter's variety shows. He was on "The Shower of Stars" twice in 1955, and in 1958 he made his dramatic television debut on "The Kraft Television Theatre" and "Studio One in Hollywood." The good notices that his "Kraft" performance earned brought him new film roles. His last feature film appearances were in *The Wonderful Country* in 1959, *The Rat Race* in 1960, and the Rock Hudson–Doris Day film *Lover Come Back* in 1962.

The same year in which he made his last feature film, Oakie had his first guest role on a television series, "Target!: The Corruptors," about a crime-fighting journalist. In 1963 he was in three episodes of the hillbilly sitcom "The Real McCoys." A year later he was in an episode of "The Breaking Point," a medical drama. In 1964 he also played an ex-vaudevillian in a Disney television special, "Kilroy." According to rumor, he turned down a generous offer to play the same kind of role in a regular television series. His last television appearance was in 1972, on Johnny Carson's special, "Sun City Scandals."

Largely retired from show business during the last decade of his life, Oakie lived quietly with his wife on his San Fernando Valley ranch in Los Angeles. He died in Northridge, Calif.

[The University of Southern California's Cinema-Television Library has materials that Oakie donated during his lifetime, as well as items later donated by his widow. The collection includes radio and television scripts, a scrapbook from the "Jack Oakie College" radio series, photographs, and audiotapes. The film archive of the Academy of Motion Picture Arts and Sciences in Beverly Hills, Calif., has a restricted collection of Oakie's home movies. The Western History Research Center of the University of Wyoming in Laramie has a large collection of Oakie memorabilia. *Jack Oakie's Double Takes* (1980) is an illustrated collection of autobiographical vignettes written for magazines during the 1970's. Obituaries are in the *New York Times* and the *Los Angeles Times,* both Jan. 24, 1978.]

R. KENT RASMUSSEN

OBERON, MERLE (Feb. 19, 1911–Nov. 23, 1979), movie and television actress, was born Estelle Merle O'Brien Thompson in Port Arthur, Tasmania, Australia, to John Thompson, a major in the British army, and Charlotte Constance Selby, a homemaker. Major Thompson, who had taken his pregnant wife to visit his sister in Tasmania, died just before Oberon was born. Charlotte Thompson found it necessary to remain in Tasmania with her husband's family. When Oberon was seven, her mother moved them to India, first to Bombay and then to Calcutta, where they lived with Thompson's brother, a British government official.

In Calcutta, Oberon attended elite private

schools, then took classes at La Martinere College, learning French and Hindustani. She also appeared in dance productions by the Calcutta Amateur Theatrical Society. Numerous acquaintances and strangers praised her beauty and urged her to consider a career as a movie actress. Oberon took these suggestions to heart, and when she was sixteen she accompanied her uncle to England. Once in London, she enrolled in a dance course and convinced her uncle to return to India without her, promising she would follow when the course was completed. As soon as her uncle's ship left port, she cashed her return ticket to finance her prospective acting career.

After Oberon failed to support herself as an actress, she took a job as dance hostess at the Café de Paris in London, a position she felt was beneath her. She had to eat, however, and the pay covered her expenses and provided free dinners. While working as a dancer, she took the name Queenie O'Brien.

Her first screen test turned into a comedy of errors. Just as the test began, she was suddenly kissed and hugged by an actor, who received a sharp slap for his effort. Although the director had failed to explain that the actor's advances were included in the scene, Oberon was not given a second chance. Soon afterward, however, she began getting small parts in local film productions and was able to quit her job at the café. In 1932, she caught the eye of producer Alexander Korda, who offered her a five-year contract with the newly established London Film Productions. Korda, however, insisted that she take the name Oberon, rather than O'Brien, explaining to her, "Everybody in New York is named O'Brien."

Between 1932 and 1933, Oberon appeared in feature roles in a number of unremarkable British films, none of which received much notice in the United States. At the time, American critics generally relegated English productions to B-movie status and treated these films—when they noticed them at all—with condescension. However, the fortunes of both British films and Merle Oberon were to change dramatically with Korda's production of *The Private Life of Henry VIII* (1933). The movie's boisterous, irreverent approach had little in common with the pious tone found in most British historical films. Distributed by United Artists, it garnered widespread praise by critics, gained an Academy Award nomination for Best Picture, and scored at the box office; Charles Laughton, playing the rather debauched Henry, received an Academy Award. Although Oberon, playing Henry's second wife, Anne Boleyn, was on screen but a short time, she received glowing notices. Most commented upon her "stunning" looks and "statuesque" manner and predicted great things to come.

Oberon did not fulfill her promise immediately, thanks in part to Korda's strategy of casting her as an Oriental siren. Oberon, of course, had as much Asian ancestry as Anne Boleyn, but reality was of limited concern to Korda. Instead, publicists were able to weave strands of mystery around her persona, liberally sprinkling a girlhood in Tasmania and Calcutta, and fluency in Hindustani, into their press accounts about the new sensation. All that British and American audiences required on film was the diligent use of eyeliner to accent Oberon's almond eyes and a secretive, alluring screen presence—their imagination did the rest. While such films as *Thunder in the East* (1933) gained Oberon some positive notices and a growing American audience, they were far from the star vehicles she desired.

Although Korda's follow-up attempt at historical revisionism, *The Private Life of Don Juan* (1934), failed to sell many tickets or give Oberon much exposure, his subsequent effort, *The Scarlet Pimpernel* (1935), was a triumph for all concerned. In a tale of political intrigue set in Revolutionary France and anti-Revolutionary England, Oberon played the wife of the dashing double-agent, Sir Percy Blakeney, alias the Scarlet Pimpernel, played by Leslie Howard. Raymond Massey contributed a brilliant performance as a sinister French agent intent on exposing the ever-elusive Pimpernel. Although Oberon's part was not demanding, the press continued to heap accolades on her screen allure, and the film's critical and popular success raised her stock considerably.

Fortunately for Oberon, producer Samuel Goldwyn had arranged a cooperative agreement with London Film Studios, and decided to develop Oberon further as a star. Much to Oberon's satisfaction, Goldwyn thought her better suited playing "a straightforward English girl" than assuming the ideal of an Englishman's Oriental. Playing the lead in prestige pictures like *The Dark Angel* (1935) and *These Three* (1936), Oberon at last reached star status. Her career was temporarily derailed when she was involved in a serious auto accident that scarred her face. After several months of reconstructive surgery, however, Oberon's most marketable characteristic was restored to its near-perfect state. In her return to the screen, *The Divorce of Lady X* (1938), she showed a fine comic touch in the Korda-produced comedy of manners.

Oberon reached the pinnacle of her career with her role as Cathy in Goldwyn's production of *Wuthering Heights* (1939). She was cast opposite an extraordinarily intense Laurence Olivier as Heathcliff, and the two mesmerized audiences with their passionate performances. The film, directed by William Wyler, seems a bit overwrought today, but both the filmmaker and the players received lavish praise from reviewers. Olivier received an Academy Award nomination; for Oberon, the performance was perhaps her best.

Although Oberon managed to keep her star status (at least measured by her appearances on the covers of the glossies), nothing she did after 1940 equaled her triumph in *Wuthering Heights*. She married Korda in the summer of 1939, but the war kept him in Britain a great deal of the time, and Oberon settled in Hollywood. *Lydia* (1941), their sole collaboration, displayed Korda's standard sumptuous production values, but also revealed Oberon's limitations as an actress. For the remainder of the war, she appeared mostly in World War II–related movies, which were often benefits for war relief. In 1944, Oberon announced her separation from Korda, and she formally divorced him in 1946. Soon after, she married cinematographer Lucien Ballard. The marriage lasted until 1949, during which time Oberon appeared in numerous forgettable films, including *Temptation* (1946) and *Berlin Express* (1948).

During the 1950's, Oberon made occasional appearances in films, and more frequent appearances on television, including *Cavalcade* (1955) and *The Man Who Came to Dinner* (1954). In 1957 she married the wealthy Italian-born Mexican industrialist Bruno Pagliai, adopted two children, and, except for a few film and television appearances, retired from acting, becoming renowned as a hostess to the Hollywood set. In 1972 she donated a building to the Actors' Studio West, which was named the Merle Oberon Playhouse. The following year, Oberon attempted a comeback, producing and starring in *Interval*, the story of an aging beauty who falls for a younger man. While the film disappeared quickly, the story did not—Oberon left Pagliai for her young lead, Robert Wolders, and married him in 1978. She died in Los Angeles.

[Much useful information is in the clippings file at the Academy of Motion Pictures Arts and Sciences library in Los Angeles. See James Robert Parish and Don E. Stanke, *The Glamour Girls* (1975); Charles Higham, *Merle* (1983); and Charles Higham and Roy Moseley, *Princess Merle* (1983). A obituary is in the *New York Times*, Nov. 24, 1979.]

MICHAEL GOLDBERG

O'BRIEN, ROBERT DAVID ("DAVEY") (Dec. 11, 1917–Nov. 18, 1977), athlete, was born in Dallas, Tex., to David E. O'Brien, a cashier, and Ella Mae Keith, a schoolteacher. After his parents divorced in 1920, Davey and his older brother were raised by his mother with the help of her brother, Boyd Keith. Davey was a troubled child who may have spent time at the Juliette-Fowler Home, an orphanage, in Dallas. His life began to turn around, however, after he won a medal for being the best camper at a summer camp in Missouri—the family still has this medal. Despite his small size—he was five feet, seven inches tall, and weighed just 150 pounds—O'Brien became the star quarterback of Woodrow Wilson High School's football team in Dallas, leading it to the state playoffs in 1935, his senior year. He also played baseball and threw the javelin for Wilson.

Actively recruited by many colleges, O'Brien chose Texas Christian University (TCU). There in his sophomore year he played understudy to quarterback "Slingin' Sammy" Baugh on famed coach Dutch Meyer's "Horned Frogs." O'Brien took over as quarterback when Baugh decided to become a professional. He took part in every offensive play his team made, including kicking TCU field goals and punting. As was then the custom, he also played defense, pulling down sixteen interceptions during his TCU career. In 1937, O'Brien threw for over 1,000 yards and missed only fourteen minutes of TCU's entire schedule. He demonstrated amazing endurance on the field: after being tackled by much bigger opponents, he would bounce up and help them get to their feet. Sportswriter Grantland Rice, after watching the diminutive Texan, observed, "The lad must be stuffed with scrap iron." Local papers called him "The Mighty Mite," and the nickname stuck.

In 1938, O'Brien surpassed his performance of the year before, throwing passes for 1,733 yards and nineteen touchdowns with only four interceptions. In addition, he rushed for almost 500 yards that season. His team won all ten of its regular-season games, and O'Brien stunned the sporting world by winning the coveted Heisman Trophy over numerous rivals from more prestigious eastern teams. In addition, he is still the smallest player ever to win the Heisman. Arriving in New York City by train to accept his award, O'Brien was met by mounted police, including pseudo–Texas Rangers in full regalia, waiting outside Penn Station to escort him on horseback to be greeted by New York City mayor Fiorello La Guardia at City Hall. After receiving the Heisman, O'Brien still had the Sugar Bowl and the possibility of his team's national championship ahead of him. Despite the glare of national publicity, he led his team to victory over Carnegie Tech by a score of 15 to 7, in the process throwing a touchdown and kicking a field goal.

In 1939, O'Brien graduated from TCU with a B.A. in geology. The Philadelphia Eagles of the National Football League (NFL) signed him to a two-year contract by offering him a $12,000 bonus. In his first season he passed for 1,324 yards, thereby breaking the NFL record set by his college teammate, Baugh. O'Brien was named to the league's all-star team, even though his own team only managed to win one game that year. As he told a friend later, "I always knew I was small, but I never knew how small I was" until the first time he saw the Chicago Bears defensive line. Despite O'Brien's determination and his impressive passing yardage, his team lost all but one game in 1940, too. In two years as a pro, he threw for 2,600 yards and eleven touchdowns—but he also was responsible for thirty-four interceptions.

O'Brien decided to leave professional football when his contract expired at the end of the 1940 season. The Eagles management wanted to win, not just to set records. O'Brien joined the Federal Bureau of Investigation (FBI) in December and remained with the agency for more than ten years. There he made $3,200 per year, rather less than the $10,000 per year the Eagles had been paying him. He served in field offices in Kansas City, Mo., Washington, D.C., and Springfield, Ill., before returning to the FBI academy in Quantico, Va., as an instructor. O'Brien taught recruits self-defense skills and firearms use. He achieved the unprecedented (and still unmatched) feat of shooting ten consecutive perfect scores on the pistol target range over a period of two days. His name is still listed, along with those agents who have shot a single perfect score at the pistol range, on a large plaque in the hallway at the FBI Academy. He was remembered by fellow agents for his patience in teaching recruits the shooting art. While a pistol instructor at Quantico, he met and befriended fellow firearms instructor Clarence Kelley, a future FBI director. They remained close friends until O'Brien's death in 1977.

O'Brien resigned from the FBI in 1951 and moved to Texas to enter the oil business. Initially he worked in public relations for Hunt Oil, but in 1962 he went into business for himself.

He married Frances Buster in 1939; the couple had three children and were divorced in 1957. He married Janie Russell in 1963; they had no children.

O'Brien was elected to the Professional Football Hall of Fame in 1955. He spent the last years of his life working for Dresser-Atlas Oil Tools as a marketing representative. He was Tarrant County Democratic party chairman in the 1950's. Among the many honors and awards he received was *Sports Illustrated*'s Silver Anniversary Award in 1960. He was particularly gratified because it was only given to twenty-five former collegiate athletes twenty-five years after lettering who had distinguished careers in business, politics, and philanthropy—the world outside sports. He died of cancer in his home city of Dallas.

[See Allison Danzig, *The History of American Football* (1956). An obituary is in the *New York Times*, Nov. 19, 1977.]

WILLIAM E. ESPOSITO

OCHS, PHIL (Dec. 19, 1940–Apr. 9, 1976), singer and songwriter, was born Philip David Ochs in El Paso, Tex., the son of Jacob Ochs, an army physician, and Gertrude Phin. After Jacob was sent overseas during World War II, the family moved to New York City to stay with his parents. Returning home in 1945, Jacob was hospitalized for manic-depression. Released in 1947, he tried to establish a private practice, but recurring mental illness reduced him to work as a physician in tuberculosis hospitals.

Given the effects of his father's military experience, it is little wonder that Ochs developed the antiwar attitudes that inspired protest songs like "I Ain't Marching Any More" and "Draft Dodger Rag."

Ochs attended public school first in Far Rockaway, in the borough of Queens, then in Perrysburg, N.Y., where he displayed a talent for the clarinet. After the family moved to Columbus, Ohio, he attended the Marion Franklin School. At the age of fifteen, he successfully auditioned for the Capitol University Conservatory of Music in Columbus, Ohio. After one year there, Ochs entered Staunton Military Academy in Virginia; Barry Goldwater's son Michael and future Watergate conspirator John Dean were among his classmates. In 1958, Ochs enrolled at Ohio State University, where he majored in journalism and wrote for the student newspaper, the *Lantern*. He and his roommate, Jim Glover, formed a group called the Sundowners. They performed songs by Pete Seeger and the Kingston Trio, as well as original material by Ochs. After being passed over for the editorship of the *Lantern*, one semester short of graduation, Ochs followed Glover to New York City, where he hoped to launch his career as a folksinger.

Arriving in Greenwich Village, Ochs found Glover living with Jean Ray on Thompson Street. Glover and Ray later formed a duo ("Jim and Jean") and recorded a number of Ochs's songs on their album *Changes*. Through them, Ochs met Alice Skinner, whom he married on May 16, 1963; they had one child. By January 1965 the couple had separated, although they did not divorce until 1973.

In 1962, Greenwich Village was the center of a folk music revival. Like Bob Dylan, Tom Paxton, and Dave Van Ronk, Ochs began playing the clubs and cafés, including the Gaslight and Gerde's Folk City. He continued to write topical songs like "Ballad of the Cuban Invasion," "Fifty Mile Hike," and "The Ballad of Billy Sol," many of which were published in *Broadside*. Ochs was earning a reputation as one of the leading protest singers of the day, second, perhaps, only to Bob Dylan, with whom he would perform at the Newport Folk Festival in 1963.

By February 1964, Ochs's star was on the rise. After signing a contract with Elektra, he recorded his first album, *All the News That's Fit to Sing* (1964). The title reflected Ochs's belief that every newspaper headline contained a potential song. Songs like "One More Parade," "The Ballad of William Worthy," "Lou Marsh," and "Too Many Martyrs" introduced some of his recurrent themes: pacifism, politics, public apathy, and civil rights. Ochs performed at colleges and in concert halls across the country, promoting his album. He performed again in Newport, then traveled south to the Mississippi Caravan of Music. There, when officials discovered the bodies of three murdered young civil rights workers—James Chaney, Michael Schwerner, and Andrew Goodman—Ochs wrote and performed "Here's to the State of Mississippi," a savage indictment of southern racism that appeared on his second album, *I Ain't Marching Anymore* (1965). On Jan. 6, 1966, he realized a dream—a solo concert at Carnegie Hall in New York City. It was to become the basis for his last album with Elektra, *Phil Ochs in Concert* (1966).

After signing with A&M records, Ochs spent the summer of 1966 in Los Angeles, recording *Pleasures of the Harbor* (1967). While some critics applauded it as his most beautiful work, others saw it as an overproduced monstrosity. It was, however, Ochs's best-selling album to date and contained two of his most popular songs: "Crucifixion," a song commemorating John F. Kennedy's assassination, and "Outside of a Small Circle of Friends," a condemnation of the apathetic mind-set that allowed a Queens neighborhood to ignore the murder of Kitty Genovese.

Ochs was one of the foremost critics of the Vietnam War. Unlike many of the protesters, however, he had a strong patriotic streak evident in early songs like "The Power and the Glory" and "The Hills of West Virginia." Even the antiwar "Draft Dodger Rag" poked fun at those whose refusal to serve was based on expediency rather than conscience. "The War Is Over," which appeared on the album *Tape from California* (1968), became a peace-movement anthem. Ochs performed at numerous antiwar concerts and organized peace rallies in Los Angeles and New York in 1967. His experience in Chicago at the 1968 National Democratic Convention, however, would dramatically change his life.

Ochs joined Jerry Rubin and the Youth International Party at their Festival of Life in Chicago in August 1968, where he played for the protesters who were being beaten in the streets.

Ochs saw the violence as the last gasp of democracy in America, with the Chicago police representing a fascist military machine that threatened to destroy the nation. Something inside of him died in Chicago, and he knew it: the cover of his next album, *Rehearsals for Retirement* (1969), bore a picture of his tombstone. After Chicago, Ochs began to doubt the antiwar movement's ability to promote change. He also questioned his own effectiveness as a singer-songwriter in raising the political consciousness of his audience.

For Ochs, after 1970, America's only hope lay in revolution, and the only hope for revolution was to have Elvis Presley become Che Guevara: he therefore donned Presley's gold lamé suit and went on tour. In a concert at Carnegie Hall on Mar. 27, 1970, Ochs performed songs by Elvis and Buddy Holly. Some of these were included on his album *Phil Ochs' Greatest Hits* (1970), which, ironically, contained only new material. Ochs was booed, and the first show was shortened because of a bomb scare. During the intermission, Ochs put his hand through the box office window in a fit of rage prompted by a disagreement with Carnegie Hall management; he played the second show with a bandaged hand, lecturing the audience between songs. By the end of the concert, he seemed to have won some fans over. The evening was captured in a live album, *Gunfight at Carnegie Hall* (1974).

Between 1967 and 1969, under his brother Michael's management, Ochs grossed over half a million dollars. In the 1970's, however, finding it increasingly difficult to write, he drank heavily and was arrested several times for fighting and drunk driving. He traveled and performed in South America, Australia, and Africa. In Tanzania, three men attacked him and damaged his vocal cords. After learning of Salvador Allende's murder in Chile (September 1973) upon his return home, Ochs organized a concert to aid Chilean refugees. The concert, at the Felt Forum in New York City on May 9, 1974, was a stunning success thanks to the surprise appearance of Bob Dylan. On May 11, 1975, Ochs sang "The War Is Over" at a Central Park rally in New York City celebrating the end of the Vietnam War. It was a fitting swan song.

Ochs's drinking continued. He adopted a new identity, John Butler Train; carried weapons to protect himself from enemies real and imaginary; and lost most of his money attempting to open a bar called Che's in New York City. Finally he stopped drinking and went to stay with his sister, Sonny Tanzman, in Far Rockaway, where he lived quietly until Apr. 9, 1976, when he hanged himself. His body was cremated and his ashes scattered in Scotland.

[Ochs's diaries and notebooks are in the hands of his daughter, Meegan, in Los Angeles. His scores are in three collections: *Songs of Phil Ochs* (1964); *The War Is Over* (1968); and *The Complete Phil Ochs: Chords of Fame* (1978). Posthumous releases include *A Toast to Those Who Are Gone* (1986); *The War Is Over: The Best of Phil Ochs* (1988); *The Broadside Tapes I* (1989); *There but for Fortune* (1989); and *There and Now: Live in Vancouver* (1990). Marc Eliot, *Death of a Rebel* (1979), the only full-length biography to date, includes a discography through 1976. See also Tom Nolan, "The Last Days of Phil Ochs: God Help the Troubadour Who Tried to Be a Star," *New West*, June 21, 1976; and John Berendt, "Phil Ochs Ain't Marchin' Anymore," *Esquire*, Oct. 1976. Obituaries are in the *New York Times*, Apr. 10, 1976; the *Washington Post*, Apr. 11, 1976; the *Village Voice* (New York), Apr. 19, 1976; and *Rolling Stone*, May 20, 1976. *Chords of Fame* (1983), directed by Michael Korolenko, is an eighty-eight-minute docudrama of Ochs's life.]

WILLIAM M. GARGAN

O'DONNELL, KENNETH PATRICK (Mar. 4, 1924–Sept. 9, 1977), presidential adviser, was born Patrick Kenneth O'Donnell in Worcester, Mass., the son of Cleo O'Donnell, the football coach of the College of the Holy Cross and St. Anselm's College, and Alice Guerin. (Known as Kenneth his entire life, he had the order of his names legally reversed in the 1960's.) Following graduation from Worcester Classical High School in 1942, the Irish Catholic O'Donnell joined the United States Army Air Corps, flying thirty missions as a B-17 bombardier over Europe during World War II. Afterward, he attended Harvard University, from which he graduated with a B.A. in government in 1949. While at Harvard he was quarterback and captain of the football team and the roommate of Robert F. Kennedy, an end on the varsity football team and brother of the future president of the United States. On Sept. 19, 1948, O'Donnell married Helen Sullivan; the couple had five children.

O'Donnell began his longtime association with the Kennedys in 1946, when Robert enlisted him to work for John Kennedy's inaugural congressional campaign in the North End area in Boston. Despite disliking Joseph P. Kennedy, the candidate's conservative father, O'Donnell admired John Kennedy for his war record. O'Donnell played a key role in Kennedy's election to the Senate over Henry Cabot Lodge, Jr., in 1952. It was O'Donnell who persuaded Robert Kennedy to assume control of the campaign, which O'Donnell felt was heading toward "absolute catastrophic disaster." After Kennedy's victory, O'Donnell continued as a paper salesman while holding the position of the senator's unpaid state representative in Massachusetts. In 1957 he assisted Robert Kennedy, now counsel to the Senate Rackets Committee, as an administrative assistant, and he remained in Washington, D.C., the next year as a member of Senator John Kennedy's staff. During Kennedy's 1960 presidential campaign, he emerged as a principal organizer.

As one of Kennedy's most trusted friends and a member of the advisory group dubbed the Irish Mafia, O'Donnell officially served the new administration as appointments secretary. Unlike the stereotypical Irish politician, the wiry, dour, and abrasive O'Donnell was a man of few words, most of them "no." His thin, small mouth and unsmiling eyes and defiant face seemed to punctuate his expletives. So protective was the "iceman" of the president that he refused many visitors entry to the Oval Office. Consequently, with the president's concurrence, the genial Evelyn Lincoln, Kennedy's personal secretary, permitted staffers and select outsiders passage through her office. In this way, the president had the best of both worlds, for he could tell those he really did not want to see to contact O'Donnell; those who were more familiar with procedures merely went through Lincoln's office. O'Donnell also made travel arrangements for Kennedy; he himself traveled so anonymously that outsiders mistook him for a Secret Service agent. He also controlled the use of White House limousines and helicopters and White House office space. Moreover, he acted as liaison with the Federal Bureau of Investigation and the Secret Service. Jacqueline Kennedy once called O'Donnell the "wolfhound," because whenever he entered the room, she knew that her husband had to return to work.

O'Donnell so earned Kennedy's trust that he became one of the few people with whom the president was completely open. Along with David Powers, another longtime friend of Kennedy's, he amused the president with shared reminiscences. Because of his fierce loyalty, O'Donnell also felt free to speak bluntly to Kennedy. Suspicious of most people, he was particularly sensitive to those who might seek to use the president.

During the 1960's, O'Donnell remained a New Deal Democrat who believed that government should help the dispossessed; he was also one of the few Irish Catholics in Massachusetts who thought that red-baiter Joseph McCarthy was a discredit to his country. How much influence O'Donnell had on Kennedy's ideology and policy is disputable. Press Secretary Pierre Salinger once claimed that O'Donnell had more impact on Kennedy's key decisions than any other adviser. Arthur Schlesinger, Jr., labeled O'Donnell an important liberal influence. Other Kennedy aides played down O'Donnell's importance on policy, arguing that "Ken was oriented toward people, not issues." One thing is certain: Kennedy did not always take O'Donnell's advice. He went against O'Donnell in speaking frankly on the issue of his religion during the 1960 campaign, in selecting Lyndon Johnson as his vice-presidential candidate, and in deciding to push civil rights legislation in 1963 in the face of O'Donnell's contention that it would wreck other proposed programs.

Ironically, it was O'Donnell who not only planned the arrangements for Kennedy's last trip to Texas in November 1963, but he also sold Kennedy on the political importance of visiting Dallas, despite the advice of others. Following Kennedy's assassination on November 22, O'Donnell saw to it that Kennedy's remains left Dallas that same day, even though local officials insisted that an autopsy first be performed.

Of all Kennedy's personal advisers, O'Donnell remained in the new administration the longest, regardless of past differences with Johnson. His new position as a special assistant to the president was a symbiotic one—the new president needed a Kennedy intimate to win the support of northern political leaders for the approaching 1964 presidential campaign. The president also used O'Donnell as a liaison with Attorney General Robert Kennedy, who was Johnson's chief antagonist and who had vice-presidential aspirations in 1964. For O'Donnell's part, he wanted to prevent the presidential election of Republican Barry Goldwater. He consequently sought to prevent a rift in the Democratic party for which the Kennedyites would be blamed. Most important, he believed that, as Johnson's adviser, he could best protect Robert Kennedy's interests. While Kennedy had virtually no chance for the vice-presidency, O'Donnell was in a good position to assist Robert Kennedy's successful efforts to win the Democratic Senate election in New York. During 1964, O'Donnell served as a special assistant to the president and as executive director of the Democratic National Committee.

Resigning in January 1965, O'Donnell returned to Massachusetts, where he lost the gubernatorial primary race against state attorney general Edward J. McCormack the next year. In 1968, disgusted by the Vietnam War, he advised Robert Kennedy to seek the presidency. Following Kennedy's assassination in June, O'Donnell helped to shape the peace plank for the party platform, which was defeated at the Democratic National Convention in August. Afterward, O'Donnell returned to his public-relations firm in Boston and assisted his brother in a printing business. In 1970, in collaboration with David Powers, he published a ghostwritten memoir, *"Johnny, We Hardly Knew Ye,"* detailing their association with John Kennedy. That same year, O'Donnell lost another bid for the Democratic gubernatorial nomination in Massachusetts, this time placing a disappointing fourth in the primary. In his two races, O'Donnell lacked the money, statewide recognition, and flair needed to be a successful candidate.

An intensely private person, O'Donnell managed to keep his family out of the spotlight. His wife died in January 1977; later that year he married Asta Hanna Helga Steinfatt. O'Donnell died in Boston from undisclosed illnesses apparently induced by alcoholism.

[There is manuscript material on O'Donnell in the John Fitzgerald Kennedy Library in Boston. An O'Donnell oral history exists at the Lyndon Baines Johnson Library in Austin, Tex. Information on O'Donnell's association with John Kennedy can be found in Kenneth P. O'Donnell and David F. Powers with Joe McCarthy, *"Johnny, We Hardly Knew Ye": Memories of John Fitzgerald Kennedy* (1970). See also Lewis Chester, Godfrey Hodgson, and Bruce Page, *An American Melodrama: The Presidential Campaign of 1968* (1969); Donald Smith, "Where Are They Now? The Camelotians," *New York Times Magazine*, Nov, 4, 1973; Herbert S. Parmet, *Jack: The Struggles of John F. Kennedy* (1980); and James N. Giglio, *The Presidency of John F. Kennedy* (1991). An obituary is in the *New York Times*, Sept. 10, 1977.]

JAMES N. GIGLIO

O'MALLEY, WALTER FRANCIS (Oct. 9, 1903–Aug. 9, 1979), major league baseball club owner, was born in the Bronx in New York City, the son of Edwin J. O'Malley and Alma Feltner. The only child of a successful dry goods merchant and onetime commissioner of public markets of New York City, O'Malley received his secondary education at the Culver Military Academy in Indiana. A gifted student, he graduated from the University of Pennsylvania with an engineering degree in 1926. He was attending Fordham University Law School when his father went bankrupt in 1929, but by working three part-time jobs, O'Malley earned his law degree in 1930. On Sept. 15, 1931, he married Kay Hanson; they had two children.

During the Great Depression, O'Malley built a lucrative legal practice by specializing in bankruptcies. That work and his investments made him a multimillionaire. He owned the New York Subways Advertising Company, was co-owner of a building supply company and a building block company, and invested in a railroad, a utility, and a brewery. He later served on the boards of several banks and corporations.

O'Malley's involvement with major league baseball began in 1941 when the Brooklyn Trust Company, a major creditor of the Brooklyn Dodgers baseball club, chose him to succeed Wendell Willkie as attorney for the club. As his fascination with baseball increased, O'Malley acquired one-quarter of the team's stock shares by 1944 and soon devoted his full energy to its fortunes.

By 1950, having become the team's principal owner, O'Malley forced his rival, Branch Rickey, to sell his quarter-interest in the club for $1.05 million and resign as club president. Over the next seven years, O'Malley presided over the National League's most victorious and prosperous franchise, a team that accounted for 44 percent of the league's gross profits and annually attracted over a million fans to the club's aging Ebbets Field. In a large measure O'Malley's business acumen and personal involvement in the club's operations accounted for this success. A demanding owner, O'Malley assembled a corps of loyal subordinates, including vice-presidents Fresco Thompson and Emil J. ("Buzzy") Bavasi, who served for many years. So did Walter Alston, whom O'Malley chose to be the team's field manager in 1954. Although Alston never enjoyed the security of a multiyear contract, O'Malley annually renewed Alston's contract for the next twenty-two seasons, during which time the Dodgers won seven National League pennants and four World Series championships.

While profiting from his Dodger operations, O'Malley also became a powerful figure in the major league baseball establishment. By serving on key committees, including a twenty-eight-year stint with the owners' powerful Executive Council, he became the game's leading policymaker. More powerful than any baseball commissioner of his time, O'Malley contributed to the ouster of Commissioner A. B. ("Happy") Chandler in 1950 and to the appointment of three successor commissioners, each of whom deferred to O'Malley's advice on such important matters as the expansion of the major leagues, the establishment of divisional playoff series, the negotiating of national television contracts, and collective bargaining with the Major League Players Association.

As a baseball innovator O'Malley was the catalyst behind the expansion of the major leagues when he decided to move the Dodgers from their long-established Brooklyn location to Los Angeles. In the mid-1950's he fretted over the limited financial prospects of his Dodgers' Ebbets Field location. Inspired by the examples of three owners who had profited by relocating their teams, he sought to transfer his team to a larger stadium with more abundant parking facilities. To this end he pressured New York City officials to provide him with an acceptable site where he could build a modern park. He underscored his determination to move in 1953 when he sold Ebbets Field to a realtor, then took a five-year lease on the old park. In 1957, when this threatening decision failed to persuade city officials to provide a suitable location, O'Malley struck a tentative deal with a Los Angeles official for a promising site and acquired the territorial rights to the Los Angeles area by purchasing the minor league Los Angeles Angels franchise from the Chicago Cubs. The Los Angeles City Council ceded 300 acres of land for O'Malley's proposed stadium project and agreed to spend almost $4.75 million for improvements. In return O'Malley deeded the Angels' stadium to the city and agreed to pay an annual property tax of $350,000 when his privately financed park was completed. A complex settlement, the matter was not fully resolved until 1958, when a public referendum approved the deal by a narrow margin.

O'Malley's scheme to relocate the Dodgers to Los Angeles included the transfer of the New York Giants to San Francisco. In obtaining the National League's permission for these relocations, the owners' influence in league councils was decisive. O'Malley successfully defended the westward movements before a congressional subcommittee in 1957.

The public announcement of the impending departures of the Dodgers and Giants evoked a storm of angry criticism. But O'Malley's West Coast movement transformed major league baseball from a regional to a truly national presence and hastened the expansion of the major leagues to twenty-eight teams, including six West Coast clubs, by 1993.

Once removed to Los Angeles in 1958, the Dodgers played their next four seasons at the Memorial Coliseum, a converted football field, while awaiting the construction of Dodger Stadium. Despite the Coliseum's inadequacies as a baseball park, the Dodgers drew 1.8 million fans in 1958, and the following year a record total of 270,000 fans jammed the Coliseum to watch the Dodgers win three World Series games.

In 1962, O'Malley opened his new $20 million Dodger Stadium, a structure he designed and financed. That year the Dodgers set a major league attendance record by hosting 2.7 million spectators. Over the next seventeen seasons, during which time the team won six National League championships and two World Series titles, annual attendance averaged better than 2 million and included a seasonal record of more than 3.3 million. For this enviable achievement, some critics credited merely the team's location in the nation's second most populous urban region, but O'Malley's promotional skills enhanced this advantage. O'Malley offered the lowest ticket prices, sold the most season tickets, set the highest standards for park maintenance, and profited more from concession sales than ticket sales. But his zeal for profits was sometimes excessive. Thus critics forced him to provide drinking fountains at the park and faulted him for negotiating a lucrative local television contract that allowed the fewest games to be televised of any club. And when the major leagues expanded to twenty teams by 1962, O'Malley permitted the new American League California Angels to enter his Los Angeles territory, but his penurious policies as that team's landlord soon persuaded the Angels to relocate in Anaheim.

When O'Malley turned over the presidency of the Dodgers to his son Peter in 1970, his franchise was valued at $50 million. In 1975 he received the first Busch Award for "meritorious service to baseball." Until his death from heart disease in Rochester, Minn., O'Malley continued to serve as the Dodgers' board chairman and remained an influential force in baseball.

[The National Baseball Library at Cooperstown, N.Y., has a large file of articles, clippings, and photographs of O'Malley. The Los Angeles Dodgers baseball club is another excellent source of materials. Critical sketches of O'Malley are in Roger Kahn, *The Boys of Summer* (1972); Harold Parrott, *The Lords of Baseball* (1976); and Don Kowet, *The Rich Who Own Sports* (1977). O'Malley's career with the Dodgers can be followed in Donald Honig, *The Los Angeles Dodgers* (1983); Neil J. Sullivan, *The Dodgers Move West* (1987); and Stanley Cohen, *Dodgers!* (1990). O'Malley's place in the history of major league baseball is covered in David Q. Voigt, *American Baseball*, vol. 3 (1983). Useful articles include Melvin Durslag, "A Visit with Walter O'Malley," *Saturday Evening Post*, May 14, 1960; Bill Veeck, Jr., "The Baseball Establishment," *Esquire*, Aug. 1964; Ray Kennedy, "Who Are These Guys?" *Sports Illustrated*, Jan. 31, 1977; and David Q. Voigt, "They Shaped the Game," *Baseball History*, Spring 1986. Obituaries are in the *Los Angeles Times* and the *New York Times*, both Aug. 10, 1979.]

DAVID QUENTIN VOIGT

O'NEILL, C. WILLIAM ("BILL") (Feb. 14, 1916–Aug. 20, 1978), judge and governor, was born in Marietta, Ohio, the second son of Charles T. O'Neill, a lawyer, and Jessie Arnold.

One of the top ten high school debaters in the country, O'Neill began his political career when he was elected to the Ohio state legislature at the age of twenty-two, while he was a Phi Beta Kappa economics and sociology student at Marietta College, from which he graduated in 1938. O'Neill was reelected in 1940 while at Ohio State University Law School, from which he earned an LL.B. in 1942, and again while serving in Europe with General George Patton's Third Army. He married Betty Hewson on July 29, 1945; they had two children.

After serving as Republican state convention chairman in 1948, O'Neill was elected Ohio's youngest attorney general in 1950. Reelected twice, he initiated federal-state cooperation in drug treatment services and refused to finance segregated public school districts. He started one of the first efforts to end pollution of Ohio's rivers, prosecuting some cities for municipal environmental waste.

When he was elected governor of Ohio by a landslide victory in 1956 over Democrat Michael V. DiSalle, O'Neill already had eighteen years of state government experience. Described by the *New York Times* as "a short, stocky man with sharp blue eyes and a friendly smile . . . a sort of boy-wonder in Republican politics," he enjoyed a legislative majority and, initially, a friendly press.

Governor O'Neill got his entire legislative package passed: expansion of public education, reorganization of courts, and increases in public employees' salaries based on efficiency. Of his other initiatives, the emergency interstate highway construction program (insisted on by him after so many years of commuting from Marietta to Columbus) was the most successful. His administration introduced the safety painting of white lines on the sides as well as the center of highways. Upon taking office, he had to deal with a six-month-old telephone strike rife with sabotage. He called in the National Guard to restore service and threatened to expand its deployment if an agreement was not soon reached. It was.

To attract top talent, O'Neill increased state salaries (but not fringe benefits) for key cabinet posts; when he realized that the state would nevertheless be uncompetitive, he persuaded the legislature to nullify the increases. Public opinion polls rated him "indecisive." In 1958 he lost his reelection bid to his 1956 opponent, DiSalle, who ran on a right-to-work platform.

O'Neill resumed teaching law and political science at Bethany College in West Virginia and practicing law with his brother in Marietta, Ohio, as he had done while a state legislator. Out of political office only two years of his adult life, he was elected to the Ohio Supreme Court in 1960. Governor James A. Rhodes appointed him chief justice in 1970, calling him "a man of trust."

O'Neill firmly believed in the separation of

powers and dissented when the court modified drug sentences as a "usurpation of the executive pardoning power." His decisions were balanced. He voted to overturn the conviction of a homicide defendant who was forced into a police lineup despite his request for his lawyer.

But it was in the free press–free trial arena that O'Neill most eloquently drew on his political experiences. He had long been a friend of the press; twice the Ohio Newspaper Correspondents Association voted him "Outstanding State Legislator." However, when press-trial conflicts emerged, his approach most often was first to require exhaustion of all procedures designed to ensure fair play, including careful jury selection and sequestration, adjournments, and change of venue. He unequivocally adjudged that all pretrial hearings were to be open to the press to benefit both the crime victim and defendant: "The issues in such hearings are often the competence, efficiency, judgment, courage and behavior of the police, the prosecutor, the defense counsel, the court employees and the judge. Because of corruption or malice, a secret judicial proceeding may be and has been used to railroad accused persons charged with crimes. . . . The . . . victims of crime are entitled to know what is going on" (*State ex rel. Dayton Newspapers, Inc.* v. *Phillips*, 1978).

In 1972, O'Neill wrote rules of "superintendency" for the Ohio lower courts that reduced the caseload of 5,885 personal injury cases to 2,223 and 1,897 criminal cases to 142 by year's end. In 1974, he was voted the outstanding appellate court judge by the Association of Trial Lawyers of America. In 1975 the American Judicature Society honored him for "being a prime mover in reforming Ohio's judicial system; and . . . a catalyst to bring about improvements." As chairman of the National Conference of Chief Justices in 1978, he lobbied for press coverage of court proceedings and the extensive use of audiotapes and videotapes. Through all his elective and legislative victories, his opinions as attorney general, and judicial decisions, O'Neill remained primarily a modest person of few pretensions.

O'Neill had a history of heart attacks, one while governor, in 1958, and another, in 1970, at a judicial conference in Tennessee. Finally, in 1978, after complaining of chest pains, he was admitted to a hospital in Columbus, Ohio, where he died.

[O'Neill's personal papers are in his family's possession; some memorabilia of his public life are in the collection of the Law Library of the Supreme Court of Ohio. Obituaries are in the *Marietta Times*, Aug. 21, 1978; the *New York Times*, Aug. 21, 1978; and the *Washington Post*, Aug. 22, 1978.]

MARY ELLEN SWEENEY PERRI

ONSAGER, LARS (Nov. 27, 1903–Oct. 5, 1976), theoretical physical chemist, was born in Oslo, Norway, the son of Erling Onsager and Ingrid Kirkeby. His father was a barrister. After completing secondary school in Oslo, he pursued chemical engineering in Trondheim at the Norges Tekniske Hogskole, receiving the Ch.E. degree in 1925.

By then Onsager had read widely in the chemical literature and found a flaw in the recently published Debye-Hückel theory of electrolytes. He visited Peter Debye in Zurich and brashly told him the theory was flawed with respect to the treatment of conductivity and diffusion. Following a discussion of the matter, Debye offered Onsager an assistantship at the Eidgenössische Technische Hochschule, a position he held until 1928.

Onsager then came to Baltimore as an instructor at Johns Hopkins University, where he was to lecture to freshman chemistry students. The term was a disaster, for the lectures were above the abilities of the students and Onsager was not about to come down to their level. Removed from the assignment after one term, he used the free time to study the statistical theory of irreversible processes and continued the development of his concepts of reciprocal relations.

Brown University offered him an appointment the next fall but kept him out of the undergraduate classrooms. He taught statistical mechanics to graduate students and guided the research of Raymond Fuoss, the only student who could understand his lectures on electrolyte systems. It had been known for some time that temperature gradients in a liquid or a gas cause ions or molecules to diffuse. During this period, Onsager turned his attention to the study of this effect, thermal diffusion. This work provided ideas on his concepts of reciprocal relations and later proved valuable to the Manhattan Project when separation of uranium isotopes became a critical objective.

During his five years at Brown, Onsager devoted much time to the study of statistical theories of systems at thermal equilibrium, the statistical study of transport processes, and particularly the mobility of dissolved ions in the presence of electrical fields.

Since the Great Depression was at its low point in 1933, the university decided it could no longer afford a theoretician who taught only a few specialized students and whose research was beyond the understanding of more than a handful of physical scientists. Onsager then went to Europe to give lectures and visit theoreticians who understood his research.

Onsager was wanted at Yale, however, by Herbert Harned, a leading electrochemist; Onsager was happy to accept the Sterling Fellowship in 1933. Yale officials were embarrassed to learn that Onsager had no Ph.D. He had published two papers on reciprocal relations, but the summary sent to the Norges Tekniske Hogskole had not been accepted as being of thesis quality. His supporters at Yale suggested that any of his published papers might serve as a dissertation, but Onsager insisted on writing one on new work. The Ph.D. was granted by Yale in 1935 for "Solutions of the Mathieu Equation of Period 4π and Certain Related Functions." Onsager was now clearly entitled to a professional position, and even before the dissertation was finished, he was appointed assistant professor of chemistry in 1934; he was later promoted to associate professor in 1940.

In 1945, Onsager became a naturalized American citizen and was honored by Yale when he became the J. Willard Gibbs professor of theoretical chemistry. The honor was particularly appropriate since Willard Gibbs had pioneered in clarifying subtle relationships in physics, chemistry, and mathematics half a century earlier. Onsager was essentially continuing in the same realm of scholarship.

Onsager's career at Yale was a fruitful one, although his classroom presentations were never memorable and most students referred to his two graduate courses as Advanced Norwegian I and II. Even his ability to direct the research of others was clearly limited. His influence was largely restricted to those highly gifted in mathematics and the behavior of solutions of electrolytes.

Onsager early developed an interest in the details of what was taking place in solutions of electrolytes. These solutions had been studied for the previous half-century with respect to the presence of positive and negative ions in them. The basic concepts of their behavior were well established by the end of World War I. However, a number of chemists and physicists were becoming aware of secondary problems that the general theories had not really addressed. Onsager did much to clarify a number of these questions.

Onsager's study of the statistical theories of transport processes in general, and particularly his studies of thermal diffusion and the mobility of ions in electrolytic solutions—that is, the influence of electric fields on the ions—led to very general results concerning the rates of irreversible processes. These results, known as Onsager's reciprocal relations, have to do with the rates of reciprocal effects. As an example of reciprocal effects, consider thermal diffusion, the effect of a temperature gradient in a liquid or a gas on the diffusion of ions or molecules. The effects reciprocal to these, that concentration gradients cause an energy flow in such systems, were also known. Another example is the effect of a concentration gradient of one species of ion in a solution on the diffusion of a second species and the effect of a concentration gradient of the second species on the diffusion of the first. Onsager proved from very general arguments that the coefficients associated with any such pair of reciprocals are simply related.

These reciprocal relations permit the prediction of the magnitude of one effect from a measurement of the reciprocal effect. It is perhaps of even more fundamental theoretical interest that these relations follow from the symmetry of the laws of mechanics with respect to time, that is, time-reversal symmetry, but these ideas did not really catch on before the last part of World War II. In 1968, Onsager received the Nobel Prize in chemistry.

In 1933, when he visited electrochemist Hans Falkenhagen in Austria, Onsager met Falkenhagen's sister-in-law, Margarethe ("Gretl") Arledter. A rapid romance led to their marriage on Sept. 7, 1933, immediately before his return to the new position at Yale. They had four children. In addition to their home in New Haven, Conn., the Onsagers bought a 100-acre farm near Tilton, N.H., where they grew fruits and vegetables and enjoyed cross-country skiing and swimming.

When Onsager reached age seventy, Yale made him, against his wishes, emeritus professor. He then arranged for an appointment as distinguished university professor at the University of Miami and spent most of his remaining time there. He died in Coral Gables, Fla.

[Microfilms of Onsager's letters, research notes, and papers are in Sterling Memorial Library, Yale University. Onsager's first journal articles dealing with reciprocal relations are "Reciprocal Relations in Irreversible Processes I" and ". . . II," *Physical Review* 37 (1931), and 38 (1931). His Nobel Prize address, "The Motion of Ions: Principles and Concepts," is in *Nobel Lectures—Chemistry (1963–1970)* (1972). The best biography of Onsager is H. Christopher Longuet-Higgins and Michael E. Fisher, in *Biographical Memoirs of Fellows of the Royal Society*, vol. 24 (1978); see also Stefan Machlup's entry in *Dictionary of Scientific Biography*, vol. 18 (1990). Joseph O. Hirschfelder, Charles F. Curtiss, and R. Byron Bird, *Molecular Theory of Gases and Liquids* (1954), gives an extensive application of the Onsager reciprocal relations. An obituary is in the *New York Times*, Oct. 6, 1976.]

AARON J. IHDE

OWENS, JAMES CLEVELAND ("JESSE") (Sept. 12, 1913–Mar. 31, 1980), track athlete and Olympic gold medalist, was born in Oakville, Ala., the tenth surviving child of sharecroppers Henry Owens and Emma Fitzgerald. In the early 1920's the family moved to Cleveland, Ohio, where Henry and his older sons found work in steel mills. The youngest Owens underwent a name change when an elementary schoolteacher mistook his drawled "J. C." for "Jesse."

At Cleveland's Fairmount Junior High School, Owens's athletic talent and ambitions were nourished by a dynamic physical education teacher, Charles Riley, who continued to coach Owens in high school. Owens set several interscholastic track records at East Technical High School, and at age nineteen attempted to win a place on the 1932 United States Olympic team. He failed in that endeavor, but in 1933, after a spectacular senior year of high school competition, he accepted a work-study "scholarship" to attend Ohio State University. Guided by coach Larry Snyder, Owens immediately began setting Big Ten and national track records. As a sophomore, on May 25, 1935, at the Big Ten championships in Ann Arbor, Mich., he set new world records in the 220-yard dash (20.3 seconds), the 220-yard low hurdles (22.6 seconds), and the broad jump (26 feet, 8¼ inches) and tied the world record in the 100-yard dash (9.4 seconds).

As the first member of his family to finish high school or attend college, Owens was poorly prepared for the academic requirements of his physical education major. Coming from a home bereft of books and a technically oriented high school lacking in academic aspirations, he could scarcely read. In order to keep him athletically eligible, advisers steered him away from basic courses in math and science. After the first term, he remained on academic probation and was allowed to compete athletically only because the rules of eligibility were loosely enforced.

Personal as well as academic problems hounded Owens. In the wake of a highly publicized California romance during a western track tour, he came under legal pressure from the city of Cleveland to marry his high school sweetheart, Minnie Ruth Solomon, with whom he had fathered a daughter three years earlier. They were married in July 1935 and had two more daughters.

In intercollegiate track meets prior to the 1936 Olympic Games in Berlin, Germany, Owens's constant nemesis was Eulace Peacock, a strong sprinter and long jumper from Temple University. Before he suffered a hamstring injury at the Penn Relays in the spring of 1936, Peacock beat Owens five of six times in direct competition. Had it not been for the bad hamstring (which became aggravated during the Olympic trials), Peacock might well have seized some or all of the gold medals won by Owens. In the summer of 1936, however, Owens stood beside heavyweight boxer Joe Louis as the most visible of all African-American athletes in the racially segregated nation. Just six weeks before the Berlin games, Louis succumbed to the blows of German Maximilian Schmeling. At the Berlin Olympics in early August, Owens dominated the track and field competitions by winning gold medals and breaking world records in the 100- and 200-meter dashes and the 400-meter relay, in addition to winning the gold medal in the broad jump.

Against an international backdrop of tension and fear, Adolf Hitler ceremoniously attended the games and cheered for German athletes. The emotionally charged scene gave birth to one of the most dramatic of sports myths. Hitler supposedly snubbed Owens, refusing to shake his hand after his victories, and allegedly stormed out of the stadium enraged that Owens's athleticism refuted the Nazi dogma of Aryan superiority. Endearingly simple and morally satisfying, this yarn is untrue; it was largely concocted by American sportswriters. Moreover, German athletes won more medals overall than the American athletes.

At the end of the track and field portion of the Berlin Olympics, the American track team departed for exhibitions in several major European cities. Arranged by the Amateur Athletic Union (AAU) as a means of paying Olympic travel expenses, the tour quickly turned sour for the athletes. Owens not only felt fatigued and homesick, he also had several stage and screen offers to capitalize on because of his Olympic success. He refused to go on from London with the coaches and athletes to Stockholm, Sweden, and took a steamer back to the United States. The AAU immediately banned him from any further amateur athletic competition in the United States.

Although most of the business and entertainment offers turned out to be bogus, agent Marty Forkins arranged several endorsements in the black press and numerous fee-paying appearances on radio shows and at banquets and ball games. Republican presidential candidate Alf Landon paid Owens to stump for black votes in the autumn of 1936. Shortly after that ill-fated effort, Owens received word of his selection as Associated Press Athlete of the Year. He then left for Havana, Cuba, to run a well-paid race against a horse, creating another facet of the Jesse Owens myth. Years later he would be depicted as a poor boy who achieved Olympic fame only to be unable to find a job back home in racist America; supposedly he had to chase horses in order to survive financially. In truth, Owens made about $20,000 in the autumn of 1936. He bought himself a new Buick sedan, a complete wardrobe of clothes and jewelry for his wife, and a large, modern, and fully furnished house in Cleveland for his parents.

From 1937 to the onset of World War II, Owens bounced around from one project to another—barnstorming with various musical and athletic groups, supervising recreational activities on Cleveland's playgrounds, and running exhibition races at both major league and Negro League baseball games. One of his projects, a dry-cleaning business in Cleveland, went bankrupt in 1939. Undeterred, he moved his family to Columbus, hoping to finish his undergraduate degree. He assisted Snyder in the coaching of track at Ohio State and opened another dry-cleaning shop. He continued to fail academically, and just a few days after the Japanese attack on Pearl Harbor, he gave up hopes for a baccalaureate degree. During World War II, several brief government jobs led to an assignment as director of black personnel at Ford Motor Company in Detroit, under Ford's powerful head of labor relations, Harry Bennett.

Shortly after the war, Owens moved to Chicago, where in 1950 he joined the board of directors of the South Side Boys Club and later served on the Illinois State Athletic Commission and the Illinois Youth Commission. In 1950 he was selected by Associated Press sportswriters as the greatest track athlete of the past half century. In the early 1950's he emerged as a Cold War patriot, hailing the United States as a land of unsurpassed opportunity. He frequently linked athleticism and patriotism in speeches to schools, youth groups, and civic clubs. In 1955 he went to India, Malaya, and the Philippines under the auspices of the Department of State, to make speeches, conduct athletic clinics, and grant interviews lauding the virtues of the American way of life and government. In 1956 he attended the Olympic Games in Melbourne, Australia, as one of President Dwight D. Eisenhower's three handpicked goodwill ambassadors, then served for a time with the president's People-to-People Program on behalf of Americanism.

In 1960, Owens joined with Ted West, a former advertising adviser for the *Chicago Defender*, to create Owens-West and Associates, a sales and promotional agency. While West attended to the business details, Owens brought in clients. The door to mainstream commercial endorsements opened in the 1960's and college youths began rejecting the traditional work ethic and patriotism represented by Owens. Owens spent much of his time on the road, addressing business and athletic groups.

He carelessly neglected to file income tax returns for the years 1954 to 1962 and in 1965 was indicted for tax evasion. Liable to a prison sentence and large fine, Owens pleaded no contest. He was found guilty as charged, but federal judge J. Sam Perry leniently required only payment of the back taxes and a small fine because he deemed Owens to be a "good citizen." Owens, insisted Judge Perry, was tirelessly "supporting our country and our way of life and our democracy," while others were "running over this country offering their blood and going out to other countries and aiding and abetting the enemy openly."

Not only did Owens's type of patriotism stand in sharp contrast to the antiwar movement during the Vietnam era, he could not even think kindly of the civil rights movement of the 1960's. Wed to the pragmatic and moderate remedies associated with his childhood hero, Booker T. Washington, Owens thought the Reverend Martin Luther King, Jr., too fiery in his speeches and too confrontational in his tactics. Owens could not understand the revolt of black athletes in the 1960's and certainly not the anger expressed by Olympic athletes Tommie Smith and John Carlos in their black-power salutes on the awards podium at Mexico City in 1968. Appalled, Owens urged Smith and Carlos to apologize, but they dismissed him as an "Uncle Tom."

In *Blackthink: My Life as Black Man and White Man* (1970), Owens assaulted "fire-fanning blackthinkers" as "pro-Negro bigots" and "professional haters" who did not represent the "silent black majority" working for respectability rather than revolution in the United States. Cooperating with ghostwriter Paul G. Neimark, Owens insisted that laziness, more than racial prejudice, condemned American blacks to failure. "If the Negro doesn't succeed in today's America, it is because he has chosen to fail." Such unguarded statements brought howls of protest from black readers and reviewers, prompting Owens to tone down his message with another book, *I Have Changed* (1972), also written with Neimark. In truth, he changed little; he merely translated his moderate middle-class prescription into more diplomatic terms. At the Munich Olympics in 1972, two angry black athletes also demonstrated on the victory podium, provoking Owens to engage in another futile effort of mediation.

During the 1970's, Owens fully identified himself with big business. At business conventions and in media advertisements, he regularly represented such corporations as Sears, United Fruit, United States Rubber, Johnson and Johnson, Schieffelin, Ford Motor Company, and American Express. The most lucrative deal was a long-term contract with Atlantic Richfield Company (ARCO) for the exclusive commercial use of his name and for financial support of the annual ARCO Jesse Owens Games for boys and girls.

In addition to athletic and business groups, Owens appealed to conservative religious gatherings in the 1970's. He claimed to be a "born again believer" and in *Jesse: A Spiritual Autobiography* (1978), again written with Neimark, he charted numerous personal crises through which prayer and the presence of God had sustained him. In print and speeches he "emphasized God, mother, country, hard work, and clean living," recalled an old track teammate, "and he got it across very well." He became a "professional good example," as journalist William O. Johnson, Jr., put it, and "a kind of all-round super combination of nineteenth-century spellbinder and twentieth-century p. r. man, . . . glad-hander, evangelistic small-talker."

In 1972 he received an honorary doctor of athletic arts degree from Ohio State University, some compensation for the bachelor's degree he never obtained. In 1974 the National Collegiate Athletic Association gave him the Theodore Roosevelt Award for distinguished achievement since retirement from athletic competition, and in that same year he was elected to the Track and Field Hall of Fame. In 1976, President Gerald Ford honored him with the highest civilian recognition, the Medal of Freedom, for being "a source of inspiration" for all Americans. In 1979, President Jimmy Carter presented him with the Living Legends Award for his "dedicated but modest" endeavors "to inspire others to reach for greatness."

Owens and his wife left Chicago in the early 1970's for the sunnier climate of Scottsdale, Ariz. In December 1979 he was diagnosed with lung cancer, probably the result of many years of heavy smoking. After his death in Tucson, Ariz., four months later, memorial statues, plaques, track meets, streets, and paths proliferated from Berlin to Los Angeles and from the Ohio State campus to the roadside of Oakville, Ala. As Owens himself said, "In America, anyone can become somebody." He was buried in Chicago.

[Owens wrote a fourth autobiographical work with Paul Neimark, *The Jesse Owens Story* (1970), but while those works are essential for Owens's views they are filled with factual inaccuracies. Barbara Moro's 1961 interviews with Jesse and Ruth Owens are in the Illinois State Historical Library at Springfield. See also Richard D. Mandell, *The Nazi Olympics* (1971); William O. Johnson, Jr., *All That Glitters Is Not Gold: The Olympic Game* (1972); and William J. Baker, *Jesse Owens: An American Life* (1986). An obituary is in the *New York Times*, Apr. 1, 1980.]

WILLIAM J. BAKER

P

PAGE, JOSEPH FRANCIS ("JOE") (Oct. 28, 1917–Apr. 21, 1980), baseball player, was born in Cherry Valley, Pa., the son of Joseph Page, a coal miner, and Lurena Couch. The oldest of seven children, Page was encouraged to pursue a baseball career by his father, a coal miner and sometime semiprofessional baseball pitcher.

When he was ten, Page's family moved to Cheswick, Pa., where he played sandlot and semiprofessional baseball, graduating from Springdale High School in 1935. For a time he worked as a coal miner. In 1936, Page was struck by a car and spent eleven months in a hospital, his left leg severely injured. Eventually a bone graft was performed, saving his leg from amputation.

After a lengthy recovery period, Page returned to baseball. In 1938 he attended a Pittsburgh Pirate tryout and was signed as a pitcher for their McKeesport farm team in the Class D Pennsylvania State Association in 1939, but he was released before the season began. In 1940, Page tried out for the Butler Yankees of the same league and made the team.

From 1940 to 1943, Page moved up through the New York Yankees farm system, despite various physical problems. He was hospitalized for ten days in 1942 when he collapsed from stomach ulcers while en route home from spring training. On Feb. 25, 1941, he married Catherine Aquina Carrigan; they had no children.

After a 14–5 record and a 3.05 earned run average with Newark in the International League in 1943, Page made the Yankees in 1944, winning five of his first six starts and being named by manager Joe McCarthy to the American League All-Star team. In June, Page injured his left shoulder in a base-running fall, then lost six games in a row and was sent back to Newark. He returned to New York in 1945, but over the next two years he developed a reputation as a talented pitcher who never realized his potential owing to a fondness for late nights and drink. In May 1946, McCarthy berated Page aboard a team flight for breaking training and squandering his ability.

In 1947, Page signed a special contract whereby he received an extra $500 every two weeks if he behaved himself and forfeited $500 if he violated curfew. During spring training, Yankees president and part-owner Larry MacPhail suggested to new manager Bucky Harris that Page be converted to a relief pitcher. For a time, Page roomed with Yankees star centerfielder Joe DiMaggio on the road, in the hope that DiMaggio's discipline and professionalism would provide an example for the fun-loving but insecure Page.

Page faced being released because of his poor showing in the young season, when on May 26 he was brought in to pitch relief against the Boston Red Sox before a record crowd at Yankee Stadium as New York trailed early in the game. The first batter Page faced reached base on an error, filling the bases with none out. Page fell behind three balls and no strikes on the next two hitters but struck out both, then retired the third on a fly out. New York rallied to win the game and went on to win the pennant easily. With performances such as this, Page emerged as a relief pitching specialist, appearing in 56 games, winning 14, and saving 17 with an earned run average of 2.48. In the World Series against the Brooklyn Dodgers, Page pitched in four games, saving the first and receiving credit for a victory in the deciding seventh.

Page had an off year in 1948 but recorded his

finest season in 1949 with a 13–8 mark in 60 appearances, a 2.59 earned run average and 27 saves. He pitched in three games during the 1949 World Series, winning the third and saving the fifth as the Yankees defeated the Dodgers in five games.

In January 1950, Page was the first winner of the Babe Ruth Memorial Award as the outstanding player in the 1949 World Series. Plagued by hip problems and a loss of velocity on his fastball, Page struggled to a 3–7 record and a 5.04 earned run average in 37 games, ending the season with the Kansas City farm club. The next year, Page suffered from physical problems during spring training and was sent down to Kansas City in May, pitching there briefly, then to San Francisco later that year and to Syracuse in 1952. In 1954, Page entered the Pittsburgh Pirate training camp in Fort Pierce, Fla., and requested a tryout. He pitched well enough to sign a contract but after seven relief appearances he was released in June.

After retiring from baseball, Page operated taverns in Irwin and Laughlintown, Pa., until the mid-1970's. In 1955 he was divorced from his first wife, and soon thereafter he married Mildred Brown. They had three children.

Page suffered a heart attack in 1970 and within a twelve-month period underwent heart surgery and throat cancer surgery. For a time in the early 1970's, Page was victimized by an imposter in the New Jersey area who exploited his name. This led to a highly unflattering article about Page in *Sport* magazine in March 1973 that was based primarily on sensationalized information provided by the imposter. In May 1973, Page sued the magazine for libel. A settlement was approved by the Federal District Court in Pittsburgh in February 1976, with Page receiving $25,000.

Page was in failing health in his final years. After being hospitalized with heart problems for several weeks, he died of heart failure in Latrobe, Pa.

With his flamboyant demeanor, good looks, and flair for the dramatic, Page brought a heightened appreciation to the craft of relief pitching. Standing six feet, three inches tall and weighing 215 pounds, he possessed a live fastball and, as he revealed after his career had ended, a supply of graphite oil concealed on the inside of his belt to discolor the baseball when necessary. He was the first relief pitcher after World War II to be used consistently in game-saving situations. Pitching in an era when baseball's popularity reached new peaks, Page created excitement whenever he made an appearance on the mound.

[A clippings file on Page is at the National Baseball Hall of Fame in Cooperstown, N.Y. See also Joe Page, "I Was Baseball's Bad Boy," *Saturday Evening Post*, May 22, 1948, written with Joe Trimble; and Milton Gross, *Yankee Doodles* (1948). A poignant portrayal of Page's final years can be found in W. C. Heinz, *Once They Heard the Cheers* (1979). Obituaries are in the *New York Times*, Apr. 23, 1980, and the *Sporting News*, May 10, 1980.]

EDWARD J. TASSINARI

PAL, GEORGE (Feb. 1, 1908–May 2, 1980), film producer and director, was born in Cegléd, Hungary, the son of George Pal, Sr., a noted Hungarian actor. His mother, Maria Pal, was also an actor. He received his formal education in architecture at the Budapest Academy of Arts but subsequently turned to illustration at age twenty-two and eventually became head of the cartoon department at the Berlin UFA film studio. He established his own small studio in 1932, the first of several studios he would create in Europe before his move to America in 1939. Pal married Zsoka Grandjean in 1930; they had two children. She encouraged their initial move from Budapest to Berlin because of a lack of financial opportunity there. They left Germany in 1933, when the Nazis assumed political control, to go to Prague, where he opened a studio, only to move once again. He set up studios in Paris in 1934, and later in Holland in 1935.

Supported in his work by commercial advertisers in Holland, Pal developed some of his early special-effects animation techniques that would eventually make him internationally famous. Initially using tobacco products such as cigarettes and tobacco leaves to provide unusual photographic images in making commercials that were shown in movie theaters, Pal began experimenting with animating puppets for film. He employed a stop-motion animation process with wooden puppets and quickly discovered a new commercial potential outlet for his creative impulses: eight-minute movies featuring animated puppets, which he termed "Puppetoons." Pal's film studio in Einhover, Holland, was devoted to producing these animated movies, and it became the largest animation production facility in Europe prior to World War

II. Pal created more than two hundred Puppetoon films in Europe; later Puppetoons produced in America were designed for children and frequently espoused a moral or a lesson. In fact, several of the forty-two Puppetoons that Pal produced for Paramount Pictures in America were heavily propagandistic, attacking the Nazi militarism of that time.

In part because of this growing Nazi threat in Europe, the Pals decided to move to America. George Pal had produced a special-effects-laden commercial in the 1930's entitled *The Ship of the Ether*, which caught the favorable attention of an American audience. He delivered a lecture at Columbia University in 1938, and when Columbia invited him back for another lecture in 1939, after Germany had just invaded Poland, the Pals decided that it was an appropriate time to make a permanent move to the United States. Approximately a decade later, George Pal became a naturalized American citizen.

In America, Paramount hired Pal to head his own animation studio, where he was encouraged to continue making his Puppetoons. Unlike his earlier films in Europe, which were merely animated commercials, the Puppetoons he made in America during the 1940's were strictly for entertainment. Pal received both critical and popular acclaim for his early efforts in Hollywood. He won an Academy Award in 1943 for his Puppetoon animation, and a comic book of his entitled *George Pal's Puppetoons* made its appearance. However, because of the increased costs involved in producing the Puppetoons, as well as the growing popularity of television, Pal turned his attention away from short film subjects around 1948 in order to work on feature-length movies.

Paramount backed George Pal's production of *Destination Moon* in 1949, and despite his difficulty in getting firm support from the studio, the film was released to critical acclaim in 1950. Subsequently, *Destination Moon* has been cited by numerous film critics as a seminal movie in the development of the science-fiction film. Satisfied with his work, Paramount backed Pal in another science-fiction feature, *When Worlds Collide* (1951). Pal went on to produce a number of other important films, including *The Great Rupert* (1949), *War of the Worlds* (1953), *Houdini* (1953), *The Naked Jungle* (1954), *The Conquest of Space* (1955), *The Power* (1968), and his last movie, *Doc Savage, the Man of Bronze* (1975). Pal's forte in the motion pictures that he produced was designing special effects, and the film industry recognized his important contributions by giving him Academy Awards for special effects for *Destination Moon, When Worlds Collide*, and *War of the Worlds*.

The first film that Pal directed was *Tom Thumb* in 1958, which he also produced. He directed and produced several more feature films, including *The Time Machine* (1960); *Atlantis, the Lost Continent* (1961); *The Wonderful World of the Brothers Grimm*, which he codirected with Henry Levin (1962); and *The 7 Faces of Dr. Lao* (1964). Two of his films, *Tom Thumb* and *The Time Machine*, subsequently won Academy Awards for special effects. Projects that he had hoped to film, but could never find the appropriate financial support for, included sequels to both *The Time Machine* and *When Worlds Collide*, the latter entitled *After Worlds Collide*, which, like its predecessor, was based on the novels of science-fiction author Phillip Wylie.

George Pal was known by his associates as a man of great vision who was often kind to others. He was sometimes called the "Gentle Producer," and people who worked for him frequently described him as always smiling, considerate, and laid-back—rare traits for a high-profile Hollywood personality. Pal is frequently cited by motion-picture scholars and historians as being the father of the modern science-fiction film. His great strength as both producer and director was his ability to have superior special effects in his movies despite being hindered by relatively low production budgets. Pal helped to transform science fiction, a cinematic genre that was typically regarded as second-rate, into something worthy of being taken seriously. His science-fiction films ranged from the highly realistic, documentary type, to slap-dash adventure, to folklore-inspired fantasy, to classic interpretations of H. G. Wells. Pal's important contributions to early special-effects moviemaking during the 1950's and 1960's helped to pave the way for later producer-directors such as George Lucas and Steven Spielberg.

Pal died at his home in Beverly Hills.

[See Gail Morgan Hickland, *The Films of George Pal* (1977). Articles written about Pal include Sondra Gorney, "The Puppet and the Moppet," *Hollywood Quarterly*, July 1946; D. S. Johnson, "The Five

Faces of George Pal," *Cinefantastique*, Fall 1971; Ed Naha, "The Worlds of George Pal," *Starlog*, Dec. 1977; James Burns, "Pal's Puppetoons," *Fantastic Films*, Oct. 1979; and Samuel Maronie, "George Pal, 1908–1980: From 'Puppetoons' to 'The Power,' " *Starlog*, Sept. 1980. Obituaries are in the *New York Times*, May 4, 1980; and *Variety*, May 7, 1980.]

GARY HOPPENSTAND

PALEY, BARBARA CUSHING ("BABE") (July 5, 1915–July 6, 1978), socialite, was born in Boston, Mass., to Katharine Stone Crowell and the well-known brain surgeon Harvey Williams Cushing. A popular socialite of the 1930's and 1940's, she was best known for her fashion style and her marriage to William S. Paley, founder of the Columbia Broadcasting System (CBS).

There appears to be a family dispute as to how the nickname "Babe" originated. One source attributed it to Barbara Cushing's oldest sister Minnie, who named Babe after a favorite doll. Another claims it was because Babe was the youngest of five children.

Bred by her mother to marry wealth, Babe graduated from the exclusive Westover School in 1933 and made her debut into society the following year, at the Ritz-Carlton in Boston, despite the fact that her father had lost his money in the stock market crash of 1929. Babe then left Boston for New York City where she secured an entry-level job at *Glamour* magazine. During the 1930's, while living in New York City, Babe and her two older sisters, Betsey and Minnie, made a sensation in New York high society and were known as the "Fabulous Cushing Sisters." Fashion doyenne Diana Vreeland described the Cushing girls as very American. "They had a basic sense of taste, a basic look about the bones in their faces. . . . There was a moment when they were extraordinary."

Babe was the most beautiful and glamorous of the trio. In 1939, Babe moved to *Vogue*, where she became a fashion editor and was frequently photographed by such legendary photographers as Horst P. Horst and Edward Steichen.

On Sept. 21, 1940, Babe Paley married Stanley Grafton Mortimer, Jr. Mortimer was from an aristocratic American family that included John Jay, first chief justice of the Supreme Court, as well as one of the founders of Standard Oil of California. The Mortimers frequently entertained at home, and soon after the marriage Babe retired from *Vogue* and had two children. In 1943, Stanley Mortimer joined the United States Navy. When he returned from the Pacific, he was drinking and having severe mood swings. On May 29, 1946, Babe divorced Mortimer in Florida on the grounds that he was "habitually intemperate from the voluntary use of alcoholic liquors."

Before her divorce became final, Babe began seeing the recently separated William S. Paley, who was also seeing socialite Janet Stewart. Commenting on the two romances became a favorite parlor game among New York society. Then Babe had a severe attack of phlebitis and was hospitalized for a month. Paley visited her at the hospital every evening, bringing in dinners from the city's most elegant restaurants. In the hospital their relationship flourished.

Babe married William Paley on July 28, 1947, and became the stepmother of his two adopted children. The wedding was followed by a grand honeymoon in Europe. They settled into a life in and around New York City, commuting between an apartment in the St. Regis Hotel and their estate on Long Island known as Kiluna Farm. The couple had two children.

Babe, whom her husband described as a perfectionist, transformed their Kiluna Farm estate into a place of rare beauty. Gardening was her passion and every winter she would have her plans for the gardens drawn. In the spring and summer the vegetables and flowers would grow in a variety of landscape designs. Babe's attention to detail also manifested itself in her extraordinary appearance. Her attention to clothes made her a regular on America's Ten Best Dressed List. In fact, she made the list so many times that in 1959, according to her husband, she asked that her name be dropped in order to "spare [the] children the joshing of their schoolmates." In 1958 she was named to Fashion's Hall of Fame, which William Paley called "a perpetual honor."

Paley pretended to be indifferent to her fashion reputation, and she told *Women's Wear Daily* that "Lots of women go overboard on clothes. . . . Once you get where you're going, you forget what you have on, so why fuss?" Yet author Truman Capote and radio personality Tex McCrary felt Paley's stylish position meant more to her than she let on. "She didn't want to be fashionable," said McCrary. "She wanted to be *fashion*."

Babe Paley devoted her life to her demanding and successful husband, who once confided to *New York Times* society columnist Charlotte Curtis that Babe taught him how to handle himself in dealing with their high-society friends.

Babe Paley died at home of cancer the day after her sixty-third birthday. The Reverend Frank N. Johnston read the eulogy, calling Babe Paley "a beacon of perfection in this era of casual convenience."

[See William S. Paley, *As It Happened; a Memoir* (1979); Lewis J. Paper, *William S. Paley and the Making of CBS* (1987); Sally Bedell Smith, *In All His Glory* (1990); and David Grafton, *The Sisters: The Lives and Times of the Fabulous Cushing Sisters* (1992). An obituary is in the *New York Times*, July 7, 1978.]

JOANNA WOLPER

PARSONS, TALCOTT (Dec. 13, 1902–May 8, 1979), sociological theorist, was born in Colorado Springs, Colo., the son of Edward Smith Parsons and Mary Augusta Ingersoll. His father, an ordained Congregational minister, was a professor of English and later president of Marietta College in Ohio.

Parsons received his early education in the public schools of Colorado Springs and graduated from the Horace Mann School for Boys in New York City in 1920. He then entered Amherst College, where he majored in biology and philosophy and was elected to Phi Beta Kappa. While at Amherst he became interested in economics and decided to pursue graduate education in the social sciences.

After graduating from Amherst, Parsons attended the London School of Economics (1924–1925), where he was strongly influenced by the prominent anthropologist Bronisław Malinowski. In 1925 he received a fellowship to attend Heidelberg University, where in 1927 he earned the Ph.D. in sociology and economics. At Heidelberg he became familiar with the writings of the German intellectual Max Weber and other European scholars whose works were largely unknown in the English-speaking world. In the period 1926–1927, while completing his thesis on the concept of capitalism of Werner Sombart and Max Weber, Parsons returned to Amherst, where he taught economics.

On Apr. 30, 1927, Parsons married Helen Bancroft Walker; they had three children. In the fall of 1927 he joined the faculty at Harvard, where he taught economics and began an academic affiliation that spanned forty-six years. In 1931 he became an instructor in sociology. He served as assistant professor (1936–1939), associate professor (1939–1944), and full professor (1944–1973). From 1946 to 1956 he chaired the new department of social relations, which he had founded and which promoted interdisciplinary links within the behavioral sciences. In addition, from 1943 to 1946, Parsons was a member of the staff of the Harvard University School for Overseas Administration. He also was a consultant to the Foreign Economic Administration from 1944 to 1946.

Parsons was a visiting summer professor of sociology at Columbia University (1933 and 1935), the University of Chicago (1937), visiting professor of social theory at Cambridge University (1953–1954), and a fellow of the Center for Advanced Study in the Behavioral Sciences at Stanford University (1957–1958). He was a member of the Eastern Sociological Society and the American Sociological Association, serving as president of the former in 1941 and the latter in 1949. He was a member of the American Philosophical Society and a fellow of the American Academy of Arts and Sciences, of which he was president in 1967.

Parsons's first book translated Max Weber's *The Protestant Ethic and the Spirit of Capitalism* (1930). In 1947 he completed a translation of Weber's *The Theory of Social and Economic Organization*. With these translations and with the publication of a series of scholarly works in which he developed his own theories and analytical abstractions, Parsons came to be recognized as the most significant figure in American sociology from the 1930's through the 1960's.

Parsons's original works began with the publication of the *Structure of Social Action* (1937), which introduced the ideas of European scholars Vilfredo Pareto, Emile Durkheim, and Weber while setting forth his own theory of society. Some of his subsequent books were *The Social System* (1951); *Structure and Process in Modern Societies* (1960); *Social Structure and Personality* (1964); *Sociological Theory and Modern Society* (1967); and *Action Theory and the Human Condition* (1978). In these works he attempted to construct a systematic general theory of human social activity that he deemed necessary for sociology to develop as a mature academic discipline.

Within sociology, Parsons was recognized as

one of the founders of the "structural functional" school. However, according to sociologist Daniel Bell, "Such an amorphous phrase offers little clue to his intentions and achievements. What Parsons sought to do was to reformulate the ideas of Max Weber and Emile Durkheim . . . into a comprehensive theory of human action . . . that would serve as a framework for understanding the entire range of social relationships."

In Parsons's construct, every society contains four major systems, each based on the simpler systems beneath it and shaped by the more sophisticated system above it. In his hierarchy, at the base is the behavioral system (biology), then the personality system (psychology), the social system (sociology), and the cultural system (anthropology). According to Parsons, each society must satisfy certain functional tasks through social institutions such as the polity, the economy, the family, and religion. This perspective sees society as a system of functionally interrelated parts that remain generally stable over time and change in an orderly fashion.

Parsons was highly controversial. His abstract constructions were criticized as irrelevant since they lacked empirical application. Because the functionalist model stresses stability and order and plays down social change and conflict, his critics claim that it tolerates inequality. He has been scorned by many for his abstruse writing style, his cumbersome use of terminology, his tenacity, and his dogmatism.

Parsons died in Munich, Germany, where he was to give a lecture. His obituary in the *New York Times* noted that when he retired from Harvard in 1973, a large number of colleagues and past and present students gathered to honor him, and that he was responsible for the education of three generations of students, including many prominent sociologists. It described him thus: "Professor Parsons . . . propounded abstract theories about human social systems that were highly controversial. Despite this he achieved something like immortal status as a man of thought."

[Parsons's extensive papers are in the Harvard University Archives, Pusey Library. Parsons is difficult to read; a good summary of his work is found in John Macionis, *Sociology* (1987). Two short paperbacks by Parsons are recommended as a starting place: *Societies* (1966) and *The System of Modern Societies* (1971). An article by sociologist Daniel Bell in the *New York Times*, May 13, 1979, gives an excellent account of Parsons's contributions to sociology. Two books that discuss Parsons's theories in the context of history are Alvin Gouldner, *The Coming Crisis of Western Sociology* (1970); and Lewis Coser, *Masters of Sociological Thought* (1971). An obituary is in the *New York Times*, May 9, 1979.]

WILLIAM L. VINCENT

PATMAN, JOHN WILLIAM WRIGHT (Aug. 6, 1893–Mar. 7, 1976), congressman, was born in a log cabin in Patman's Switch, Tex., a town that no longer exists, to Emma Spurlin and John Newton Patman, a poor tenant farmer, part-time blacksmith, and devout fundamentalist Baptist. A good student, Patman graduated from high school in Hughes Springs, Tex., in 1912. He then worked and saved his money in order to attend law school at Cumberland University in Lebanon, Tenn. He received an LL.B. in 1916 and had a brief law practice in Hughes Springs before joining the United States Army in 1917. In February 1919 he married Merle Connor. They had four children. She died in 1967 and he married Pauline Tucker the following year.

Patman settled in Linden, Tex., and in 1920 he won a seat in the Texas House, where he made the acquaintance of Sam Ealy Johnson and his tall young son, Lyndon Baines Johnson. He admired the elder Johnson as an honest legislator who worked hard for his agrarian constituents. Likewise, Johnson admired Patman as a man who "always votes for the people." In the Texas House, Patman assailed the Ku Klux Klan as "un-American" and sponsored a resolution to condemn it. The resolution was tabled by a vote of sixty-nine to fifty-four. Although the Klan opposed Patman's reelection, he won in 1922 and waged a campaign in the next session against agricultural corporations. At the request of the governor, Patman accepted appointment as district attorney for Texarkana, a town notorious for graft, gambling, and prostitution. He won election in his own right in 1924 while carrying a pistol to protect himself against threats by gangsters.

In 1928, Patman ran for the United States House of Representatives, vowing to fight for farmers and against big corporate influences in the Treasury Department, the Federal Reserve, and the Federal Trade Commission, which remained political targets for the rest of his life. He accused the incumbent, Eugene Black, of voting for the Railroad Act of 1920 to benefit the principal holders of railroad securities, Wall

Patman

Street bankers. Also, Patman asserted, fourteen years in the House was enough for any man. "Give a Young Man a Chance," was his slogan. The young man won by 3,000 votes and would serve forty-seven years in the House of Representatives.

Patman's district then included eleven counties with a population of about a quarter of a million. It was so poor that in 1935 it was estimated that less than two-thirds of 1 percent of the population had ever filed an income tax return. Beginning his tenure in the special session of 1929, Patman vowed that he would not "regard the House as a morgue where new members must lie on a marble slab for several sessions" awaiting the right to speak. A few months into his career he introduced a bill to give war veterans an immediate cash payment of the paid-up life insurance promised them in 1924. As the veterans' bonus would cost the government the astronomical sum of $2 billion, Patman proposed issuing new currency to pay for it, a proposition that revealed him as an inflationist. The veterans' bonus bill failed then and again in 1932, when it provoked a massive veterans' march on Washington and a riot that President Hoover put down with military force. In 1935, Congress finally passed the veterans' bonus over President Roosevelt's veto. Known as a "funny money man," Patman ignored House Speaker John Nance Garner's orders to desist in seeking a bonus payment. He paid the penalty for it by being denied a seat on the House Banking and Currency Committee for eight years, which, he calculated, delayed his ascendancy to its chair by sixteen years.

Patman depicted the monopoly of capital as the country's greatest sin and the farmer its principal victim. Monopolies in banking, he insisted, bred additional monopolies in manufacturing, distribution, and even retailing, which went to the heart of woes endured by small-town merchants such as his constituents. A defender of "independent business," he endeared himself to fellow Democrats by attacking Republicans for "making the rich richer and the poor poorer." Patman assailed Secretary of the Treasury Andrew Mellon in 1932, demanding his impeachment on the grounds that his banking, shipping, aluminum, and oil interests directly benefited from decisions he made in the name of fiscal policy. He accused Mellon of having illegally acquired more property than anybody was entitled to possess. When President Herbert Hoover ended the impeachment process by appointing Mellon to be ambassador to Great Britain, Patman called it a "presidential pardon."

During the Great Depression, Patman crusaded against chain stores at a time when several southern states enacted laws taxing chains by the store; the more stores it had in a state, the larger the tax paid by a retail corporation. But the Supreme Court struck down a Florida law that endeavored to foster "equality of opportunity" by taxing big chains, and Patman made himself the House's champion of small business by proposing a national "fair trade" law to protect independent grocers and wholesalers. This resulted in the Patman-Robinson Act. However, when Patman proposed other "fair trade" laws, he aroused consumer interest groups who pointed out that Patman advocated limiting the number of competitors while opposing price competition. He proposed, in effect, a retailers' cartel.

A tall, heavy-set, pink-cheeked man with glasses and curly hair, Patman's smallish facial features gave him a somewhat cherubic look, an impression he reinforced with sincerity in fighting for the underdogs of the marketplace. Yet he had a streak of vanity and thrived on publicity, relishing the adulation of small-town grocers, druggists, and hardware dealers who endorsed his message assailing a conspiracy of big capital in New York City. World War II brought political and economic changes to Texas, and Patman adjusted. East Texas hungered for economic development, which mobilization offered. Patman endorsed a campaign to build a steel plant in Longview that would fabricate pipelines for the booming oil industry. When Dallas and New York bankers ignored Patman and other East Texans' petitions for loans to build a pilot plant, the Reconstruction Finance Corporation subsidiary, the Defense Plant Corporation, helped organize the Lone Star Steel Company. Defense industries sprouted all over Texas during the war thanks to $1.6 billion of government money, far and away the highest figure invested in any southern state.

Still, Patman fought big banks, foundations, and the Federal Reserve and enjoyed a reputation as the House's last "populist." He played a major role in creating the Small Business Administration during World War II, and he was the coauthor of the Employment Act of 1946, which created the Council of Economic Advisers. Patman was the principal author of legislation creating a national system of credit unions for the savings of ordinary workers, and he wrote the bills that gave the president stand-by authority to impose the price controls President Richard Nixon used in 1972. He tried to investigate the Watergate break-in in 1972 to no avail. In the early 1960's, Patman highlighted abuses by tax-exempt foundations and promoted legislation that corrected them. However, his fight against the Federal Reserve Board and its alleged connections with big banks and their interlocking directors failed to win passage of legislation. He also sought to make credit more available to ordinary citizens through savings and loans associations that duplicated banking functions. In later years the House Banking Committee rebelled against what was said to be his high-handed rule of the committee, and shortly before his death it ousted him as its chairman. He died at the Bethesda Naval Medical Center in Maryland.

[The Patman Papers are in the Lyndon Baines Johnson Library in Austin, Tex. Biographical material is in Fred J. Cook, "Foundations as a Tax Dodge," *Nation*, Apr. 20, 1963; Paul Duke, "The Oddball Crusade of Congressman Patman," *Saturday Evening Post*, Mar. 7, 1964; Hubert Kay, "The Warrior from Patman's Switch," *Fortune*, Apr. 1965; "Wright Patman: A Lonely 'Populist,'" *Business Week*, July 23, 1966; Robert Sherrill, " 'The Last of the Great Populists' Takes On the Foundations, the Banks, the Federal Reserve, the Treasury," *New York Times Magazine*, Mar. 16, 1969; Robert Sherrill, "A Minor National Monument," *Nation*, Feb. 1, 1971; Walter Shapiro, "The Profit Motive and the Public Interest," *Ramparts*, May 1971; Janet Louise Schmelzer, "The Early Life and Early Congressional Career of Wright Patman: 1894–1941" (Ph.D. diss., Texas Christian University, 1978); and Jordan A. Schwarz, *The New Dealers* (1993).

Patman also figures in New Deal histories such as Ellis W. Hawley, *The New Deal and the Problem of Monopoly* (1966); in Lionel V. Patenaude, *Texans, Politics and the New Deal* (1983); and in two books about Lyndon Johnson: Robert A. Caro, *The Years of Lyndon Johnson* (1982); and Robert Dallek, *Lone Star Rising* (1991). An obituary is in the *New York Times*, Mar. 8, 1976.]

JORDAN A. SCHWARZ

PATTERSON, WILLIAM ALLAN ("PAT") (Oct. 1, 1899–June 13, 1980), airline executive, was born in Honolulu, territory of Hawaii, the son of William Patterson, overseer of a large sugar plantation, and Mary Castro. Patterson had an unsettled childhood. Following a bitter strike at the Waipahu sugar plantation, Patterson's father was transferred to Puerto Rico, where he contracted malaria. In 1906, Patterson and his mother, who had remained in Hawaii, were reunited with his father in San Francisco. The older Patterson, however, died before the end of the year, and mother and son returned to Hawaii.

In 1912, Mary Patterson traveled to San Francisco to attend business school, leaving her son in a local military academy. An unhappy Patterson promptly ran away from school and sailed for San Francisco as a cabin boy on a four-masted sugar transport. Realizing that Patterson would not remain in Hawaii while she was in San Francisco his mother enrolled him in John Swett Grammar School. Graduating in 1914, Patterson found employment as an office boy at the Wells Fargo Nevada Bank in San Francisco (later, Wells Fargo Bank and Union). He remained with the bank for the next fifteen years, continuing his education by taking night courses at Humbolt High School and, later, the American Institute of Banking. On June 20, 1924, he married Vera Anita Witt. They had two children.

The turning point in Patterson's career came in March 1927, when he approved a loan for $5,000 to Vern C. Gorst, owner of Pacific Air Transport (PAT). Holding a contract to fly the mail between Seattle and Los Angeles, Gorst desperately needed funds to keep his struggling enterprise alive. Having given Wells Fargo a stake in the success of the airline, Patterson soon found himself closely monitoring, then actively participating in, Gorst's company. Patterson ended up reorganizing the airline's bookkeeping, revamping its purchasing procedures, and serving as the company's financial adviser.

Drawn ever deeper into the developing airline industry on the West Coast, Patterson resigned his position at the bank on Apr. 15, 1929, shortly after PAT was acquired by the Boeing Airplane Company, and became assistant to Philip Johnson, Boeing's president. Patterson took charge of Boeing's airline division, which included Boeing Air Transport, the airmail contractor on the western half (Chicago–San Francisco) of the prized transcontinental route.

At a time of industry consolidation, Boeing's airline network grew over the next two years to include Stout Air Services, a midwestern company; Varney Air Lines, which operated routes in the Pacific Northwest; and National Air Transport, which operated the eastern half (New York–Chicago) of the transcontinental airmail route. On July 31, 1931, Patterson became vice-president of United Air Lines, a new management company intended to oversee the component parts of Boeing's burgeoning airline complex. He also served as president of the individual airlines, which retained their separate identities.

In 1934 a senatorial investigation into alleged improprieties in the awarding of airmail contracts led to a restructuring of the airline industry. Because the Air Mail (Black-McKellar) Act of 1934 prohibited mail contractors from holding interests in other aviation enterprises, United had to sever its connection with Boeing. Patterson, promoted to president of United Air Lines (now an operating company), directed the merger of the individual airlines into a single entity. The process was officially completed on May 1, 1934, resulting in the formation of the largest airline in the United States.

United became a pacesetter during the 1930's. Concerned with passenger amenities, Patterson in 1930 introduced stewardesses on airliners. In 1937 he approved the industry's first flight kitchens. United also led the way in promoting safety, applying radio technology to communications and navigation. A paternalistic manager, Patterson placed great store in the "human touch" in dealing with the airline's employees. During United's early years, he took pains to maintain a personal relationship with the company's workers. Later, as the airline grew, he sought to institutionalize this managerial approach through a system of benefits and training, administered by one of the industry's first personnel departments. The absence of major labor difficulties during a time of union unrest testifies to the success of his efforts.

Patterson's major problem during the 1930's was United's continued reliance on the outmoded Boeing 247. In March 1933, United became the sponsor and exclusive operator of the first modern all-metal airliner. The speedy Boeing transport could take passengers from New York to San Francisco (with refueling stops) in the then impressive time of twenty hours. The next year, however, the much superior Douglas DC-2 appeared. As United's competitors reequipped their fleets with DC-2s, and larger DC-3s, Patterson continued to operate the now inferior Boeings. Not until 1937 did United acquire DC-3s and again become competitive with its transcontinental rivals.

The post–World War II years saw United expand slowly, mirroring Patterson's conservative approach. While other airlines eagerly sought new routes from the Civil Aeronautics Board, Patterson was content with securing authority to compete with Pan American Airways on the San Francisco–Honolulu route. During this same period, the Douglas DC-6B—a sturdy, economical, and profitable transport that could fly coast-to-coast in ten hours—became United's premier airliner.

Patterson's innate caution led him to reject both turboprop and first-generation jet equipment during the 1950's. He preferred to await the development of more economical pure-jet airliners. This decision proved wise, as United continued to prosper while operating its piston-engine equipment. At the end of the decade, when increased competition forced him to act, Patterson selected the Douglas DC-8 for United. Although this placed his company nearly a year behind rival operators who acquired Boeing 707s, Patterson believed that United had secured superior equipment.

In 1960, Patterson demonstrated that he was capable of taking a bold gamble when he decided to acquire Capital Airlines. On June 1, 1961, following lengthy negotiations, United absorbed Capital, with its 7,000 employees and far-flung route structure. This made United the largest airline in the Western world, with 267 aircraft serving 116 cities.

In 1963, Patterson became chief operating officer and chairman of the airline's board of directors. Two years later, in his last major decision, the conservative Patterson again surprised the industry by placing the largest order in history for commercial aircraft: $375 million for 112 Boeing 727s, 737s, and Douglas DC-8s.

Patterson retired on Apr. 28, 1966. Acknowledged as one of the five giants of the early airline industry (the others being C. R. Smith of American, Edward V. Rickenbacker of Eastern, Juan Trippe of Pan American, and Howard Hughes of TWA), he lived comfortably in retirement until succumbing to pneumonia in Glenview, Ill.

[Frank J. Taylor, *"Pat" Patterson* (1967), is an admiring, anecdotal biography; Robert van der Linden, "William Allan Patterson," in William M.

Leary, ed., *Encyclopedia of American Business History and Biography: The Airline Industry* (1992), offers a brief, reliable account of his life. Information on United Air Lines can be found in Frank J. Taylor, *High Horizons* (1951); and R. E. G. Davies, *Airlines of the United States Since 1914* (1982). An obituary is in the *New York Times*, June 14, 1980.]

WILLIAM M. LEARY

PAUL, ALICE (Jan. 11, 1885–July 9, 1977), women's rights activist, organizer, and lawyer, was born in Moorestown, N.J., the eldest of four children of William Mickle Paul and Tacy Parry. Her father was the founder and president of Burlington County Trust Company, a real estate investor, and the owner of a working farm. Paul's mother attended Swarthmore College. Accompanying her mother to a suffrage meeting was one of Paul's earliest recollections.

Paul attended Quaker schools in Moorestown and matriculated to Swarthmore, where she earned a B.S. in biology in 1905. During her last year at Swarthmore, Paul developed what was to become a lifelong interest in political science and economics. She was elected to Phi Beta Kappa and Pi Gamma Mu in recognition of her academic excellence. In 1906, Paul completed a College Settlement Association Fellowship at the New York School of Philanthropy. She earned an M.A. degree in sociology in 1907 from the University of Pennsylvania and began research on the legal status of women. In the fall of 1907 she continued her studies in social work on a Quaker Fellowship at Woodbridge, England.

While working as a London caseworker, Paul became involved in the British suffrage movement as a protégé of the militant Pankhursts—Christabel, Emmeline, and Sylvia. With American suffragist Lucy Burns, Paul learned the more defiant tactics of the Women's Social and Political Union that the two later employed to secure passage of the Nineteenth Amendment.

Paul returned to the United States in 1910 and resumed her graduate studies at the University of Pennsylvania. In 1912 she completed a Ph.D. in sociology with her dissertation, "The Legal Position of Women in Pennsylvania." Paul continued suffrage work within the ranks of the National American Woman Suffrage Association (NAWSA). After a disagreement on strategy with Carrie Chapman Catt and other NAWSA leaders, Paul and Burns founded the Congressional Union of the NAWSA in 1913, which became an independent organization the following year. The "New Suffragists" decided to employ the more strident tactics of British feminists, but, because of Paul's Quaker beliefs, without the violence. The focus to obtain woman suffrage shifted from a states' rights, state-by-state battle to one that utilized the vote of women in western states and declared war on President Woodrow Wilson and the Democratic party. Paul founded the National Woman's Party (NWP) in 1916, serving as chairperson until 1921, and was instrumental in gaining women's voting rights in 1920. Actively involved in protests, Paul served time in jail for her participation in demonstrations. Like many suffragists, Paul was charged with disturbing the peace and unlawful assembly.

After the Nineteenth Amendment was ratified in 1920, Paul, with characteristic single-mindedness, decided to press on for equal rights for women in all areas of life. Beginning in 1921 she served the NWP on the executive committee and as chair of the international relations committee. From 1927 to 1937 she chaired the Woman's Research Foundation. In the midst of harsh criticism from those who favored protective legislation for women, Paul wrote the Equal Rights Amendment (ERA) in 1923 and saw it introduced in Congress for the first time that December. Meanwhile, Paul continued her education. She earned three law degrees: an LL.B. from Washington College of Law (1922) and an LL.M. (1927) and D.C.L. (1928) from American University. A small income from her father's estate allowed Paul to devote all of her time and legal expertise to women's rights.

In the 1930's, Paul chaired the nationality committee of the Inter-American Commission of Women, representing the Women's Consultative Committee on Nationality of the League of Nations. She also served on the executive committee of Equal Rights International. Her goal was to obtain an international equal rights treaty. By the late 1930's, Paul had garnered enough support to found the World Party for Equal Rights for Women, or the World Women's Party. After serving for two years as chair of the WWP in Geneva, Paul returned to the United States in 1941.

Paul was elected national chair of the NWP in 1942. The remainder of her career with the NWP was marked by disagreement among its members, some brought on by normal personality conflicts and internal politics, some by a perception that Paul sought the limelight for personal gratification. She was a perfectionist and demanded dedication and loyalty from those around her, but no more than she was willing to give. Because of her resolve, Paul was instrumental in the placement of a passage on gender equality in the preamble of the United Nations Charter.

Paul's work for equality allowed little time for intimate, long-term relationships. There is no evidence that Paul ever considered marriage. After returning to the United States in 1941, she resided with her sister Helen. When Helen passed away, Paul and her closest friend, feminist Elsie Hill, shared a home until Elsie's death in the late 1960's.

Paul's intensity and the ranks of the NWP would not allow the ERA to die; it was repeatedly introduced in Congress until it passed in 1972 and was sent to the states for ratification. As late as 1969, Paul still protested on the front lines, both for women's equality and against the Vietnam War. Historian Amelia Frye believes Paul's primary contribution, other than securing passage of the Nineteenth Amendment and fighting for equal rights, was in establishing nonviolent civil disobedience as a model form of protest across the nation. Paul continued to lobby for the ERA until a stroke disabled her in 1974. She died in Moorestown, erroneously believing that, with only three additional states needed for ratification, the Equal Rights Amendment would soon become a reality.

[The National Women's Party, Washington, D.C., holds all of Paul's papers in connection with her work there. Microfilm Corporation of America has duplicated most of the NWP documentation. The Library of Congress has a collection of papers on her involvement with the Equal Rights Amendment. The Schlesinger Library, Radcliffe College, Harvard University, has a small collection of personal papers. Her home in Moorestown has been restored by the Alice Paul Foundation and contains a collection of memorabilia, as does the Moorestown Friends High School. "Conversations with Alice Paul: Woman Suffrage and the Equal Rights Amendment," an interview conducted by Amelia Frye in 1973, can be found at the Suffragists Oral History Project, University of California at Berkeley. See also William L. O'Neill, *Everyone Was Brave* (1969); Christine A. Lunardini, *From Equal Suffrage to Equal Rights* (1986); and "Alice Paul," in G. J. Barker-Benfield and Catherine Clinton, eds., *Portraits of American Women* (1991). An obituary is in the *New York Times*, July 10, 1977.]

TERESA L. LAYTON

PAUL, WILLIAM DARWIN ("SHORTY") (Jan. 31, 1900–Dec. 13, 1977), the inventor of buffered aspirin and a pioneer in the fields of sports medicine and rehabilitation medicine, was born in Brooklyn, N.Y., the second of four children of immigrants Max Paul and Sarah Siegfried. His father, who immigrated to the United States from his birthplace in Warsaw, was descended from a family of Polish Jewish book dealers. Max Paul was intellectually inquisitive and aggressive, and conversant in several languages in which he read aloud to his wife each evening after a day of factory work. Paul's mother, born in Galicia, absorbed the content of her husband's reading, although she remained functionally illiterate. The Pauls conversed in Polish, Yiddish, and German; their children cultivated English.

When Max Paul was killed in a streetcar accident in 1912, family leadership devolved upon the older son, Maurice, who encouraged "Willie" to follow up his high school diploma from Eastern District High School in Brooklyn with study in New York City's Polytechnic School. A professor there recognized the young man's gifts and arranged for a scholarship for him to study medicine at the University of Cincinnati, where Paul took both his undergraduate and medical degrees, supporting his education as a chemical laboratory technician.

After meeting and marrying Louise Ebeling in 1930, Paul moved to Iowa City, Iowa, for a residency at the University of Iowa Hospital. That initial one-year commitment became instead a lifetime career at the university, where he became assistant professor of medicine in 1941, associate professor in 1946, and professor in 1954. The university granted him emeritus honors in 1965.

William D. Paul's research and clinical medical practice improved the quality of medical care for people worldwide, especially in light of the buffered aspirin he developed. Paul had been stymied whenever a rheumatic patient could not deal with the unpleasant side effects of pain-suppressing (and acidic) aspirin. In 1944, Dr. John Krantz of the University of Maryland developed an antacid by reacting aluminum propoxide with glycine, forming a compound he dubbed "alglyn." Krantz sent five pounds of the new alglyn to Paul at about the same time that one of Paul's Iowa colleagues, Dr. Kate Daum, complained that aspirin offered her no relief from her recurring severe headaches because of uncomfortable aspirin-related reactions. Paul mixed powdered aspirin and the new alglyn into capsules and gave them to Dr. Daum, telling her it was a new headache medication. She took the compound and reported timely and effective pain relief without the usual side effects. Buffered aspirin was born. A similar opportunity to combine alglyn with penicillin made Paul the first physician to administer that drug orally.

When the Bristol-Myers Company expressed interest in marketing Dr. Paul's buffered aspirin, he teamed up with Joseph I. Routh and R. L. Dryer to conduct the necessary laboratory research. Clinical studies with 238 subjects, 37 of whom submitted to blood analyses, documented not only that the buffer provided increased comfort for aspirin users, but that the aspirin-with-buffer promoted pain relief in half the time that aspirin alone required. Bristol-Myers used this fact in its marketing slogan for Bufferin, "Twice as Fast." Doctors Paul and Routh promoted a similar application of a buffering compound to antacid tablets which resulted in another marketing coup, the development of Rolaids by the American Chicle Company and the Chattanooga Chemical Company.

Paul's contributions to medicine were the result of pioneering vision. From 1931 to the end of his career he published on internal medicine, handling issues as diverse as mechanism of pain in peptic ulcer; oxygen consumption and nitrogen metabolism; the relationships between bronchial asthma and heart disease; and complications that arose with the administration of the new drug penicillin. Paul introduced the administration of penicillin by mouth, on which he reported in 1945. From 1943 on, medical journals published his articles on rheumatology dealing with the effects of aspirin, fever therapy, palindromic rheumatism, and the efficacy of vitamin D treatments. He published in these specialties before they were officially recognized and given board certification. His genius was in applying laboratory research to clinical practice. When he learned about endoscopy, the technique of viewing the interiors of hollow organs, he adopted it and thus through his publications (beginning in July 1941) introduced a tool and a technique that is now routine for internists. He was similarly among the pioneers in using electrocardiography and in treating diabetes with insulin (on which he began publishing in 1932). In the field of physical therapy, he published on post-polio rehabilitation techniques as early as 1943 and pioneered in the combination of exercise and curare in 1949. During the polio epidemics of the 1950's he was head of the Polio Department of the University Hospital, where he further developed rehabilitation protocols.

In spite of a distinguished scientific career that included dozens of articles in scientific journals, offices in numerous professional societies, development of new medicines, and pioneering work in surgery, gastroenterology, and diabetes therapy, the first sentence in Paul's obituary in the *Iowa City Press-Citizen* identified him as the popularly recognized "University of Iowa football and basketball team physician from 1932 to 1971." During his long association with university athletes the four foot, eleven inch tall doctor gained the sobriquet "Shorty," a nickname in which he apparently delighted. He told with glee of an occasion when hulking football players picked him up by each arm and carried him along with his own feet high off the ground.

Working among comparative physical giants, Shorty Paul practically invented the specialty of sports medicine and was one of the few physicians who worked consistently with university athletic teams at that time. He was without peer, as most coaches were content to rely on mere trainers to tape joints and give rubdowns. Paul was a team physician whom the athletes trusted. His considerable self-confidence and feisty personality protected students from any coach who might want to send a badly injured player back into the game. He served the interest of the coaches, too, by capably diagnosing athletic injuries. He elevated sports medicine to a respectable level by conducting responsible research and publishing his results in the field. Paul's published research into the effects of deep tissue heat on blood circulation, on protective taping, and on the effects of diet on athletes have been applied in locker rooms throughout the world.

Colleagues remembered Paul for his innate intelligence, his propensity for hard work, his mercurial temper, his unfeigned "Napoleon complex," his "crusty" demeanor, and his interests in music, history, languages, and art. University of Iowa policy at the time forbade any personal or even institutional financial profit from the results of university research. However, by way of appreciation and compensation, Bristol-Myers commissioned quality-control research through the University of Iowa laboratories. Paul felt that whatever funding came to the university that way offset the time he spent with the football and basketball teams, as opposed to seeing patients. Paul died in Iowa City after a brief illness.

[No biography of Paul exists. Two examples of his published work are W. D. Paul, R. L. Dryer, and J. I. Routh, "Effect of Buffering Agents on Absorption of Acetylsalicylic Acid," *Journal of the American Pharmaceutical Association*, Scientific Edition, Jan. 1950, and W. D. Paul, "Crash Diets and Wrestling," *Journal of the Iowa Medical Society*, Aug. 1966. Interviews with family members and colleagues provided much of the above information. Obituaries are in the *Iowa City Press-Citizen*, Dec. 13, 1977; and the *New York Times*, Dec. 21, 1977.]

THEODORE N. THOMAS

PAYNE-GAPOSCHKIN, CECILIA HELENA (May 10, 1900–Dec. 7, 1979), astronomer, was born in Wendover, England, the eldest of three children of Edward John Payne and Emma Leonora Helena Pertz. Her father, a lawyer, musician, and Oxford scholar, died when Payne was four years old. After seeing her first meteor at the age of five, she declared both her intention to become an astronomer and her haste, in case there should be no research left when she grew up. In 1923, Payne received her B.A. degree from Newnham College, Cambridge University, where she studied astronomy under Edward A. Milne. There she was also introduced to the Bohr atom by the Danish physicist himself, and in accordance with the university regulations for women, she was seated in his advanced course, by herself, in the front row. Awarded a National Research Fellowship to do graduate work, she came to the United States, having been told by Leslie J. Comrie, who was going to teach at Swarthmore College, that a woman would have a better chance to win a research post in astronomy in America than in Britain.

Studying at Radcliffe College, Payne joined the Harvard College Observatory, which, under the directorship of Edward C. Pickering, was known for having encouraged the research of such famous women astronomers as Annie Jump Cannon, Williamina Paton Fleming, Antonia Maury, and Henrietta Leavitt. In 1925, Payne received the first astronomy Ph.D. from Radcliffe. Her dissertation on stellar atmospheres, described by Edward A. Milne as an "attractive story and a work of reference," sold out as a book. In the early 1900's, Henrietta S. Leavitt had made the important discovery of the relation between a star's magnitude and its period of luminosity. It was a critical astronomical yardstick, and Payne sought to explain the variations. In their history *Astronomy in the 20th Century* (1962), Otto Struve and Velta Zebergs termed Payne's dissertation "undoubtedly the most brilliant Ph.D. thesis in astronomy." Payne was the first astrophysicist to determine the high dominance of hydrogen and helium in the cosmos, a theory that Henry Norris Russell at first discouraged but later supported. In 1926 she became the youngest astronomer ever "starred" in Jacques Cattell's *American Men of Science* (1947).

After obtaining American citizenship in 1931, Payne married Dr. Sergei I. Gaposchkin on Mar. 6, 1934, and took the name Cecilia Payne-Gaposchkin. They had three children. Before her marriage, Payne had developed new ways of determining stellar magnitudes from photographic plates. With her husband, a Russian astronomer whom she had met in Germany in the early 1930's, she focused on the study of variable stars and contributed significantly to the understanding of novae, variable stars that suddenly increase in brilliance by thousands of times over the original and then decrease in brightness over a period of months, and their relationships to the life histories of stars. Together they examined 1,500 specimens in several million observations and published their conclusions in *Variable Stars* (1938), which became a standard source for researchers.

In 1938, Payne-Gaposchkin received her first Harvard rank under the presidency of James Bryant Conant when she was named Phillips astronomer and a lecturer at the Harvard College Observatory; she had been a permanent member of the staff since 1927. The appointment, however, was not a faculty position except in its duties; the courses Payne-Gaposchkin taught were not listed in the Harvard catalog until after World War II, in keeping with President Abbott Lawrence Lowell's long-standing policy that no female could receive an appointment from the Harvard Corporation. Indeed, she had even experienced difficulties observing on Harvard-owned telescopes, for male directors of astronomical observation stations, usually located in isolated areas, believed it was too dangerous to have women observe alone, and improper for them to spend the night in the company of men. Regardless of her formal university status, Payne-Gaposchkin participated in numerous research projects conducted by the observatory's staff, and she worked independently. In addition to her study of variable stars and stellar atmospheres, she discovered the exploded nova of Hercules and photographed the fragments, and she worked on spectroscopy and the structure of the galactic system. For her outstanding scientific achievements, she was honored in 1952 by Radcliffe College with an Award of Merit. Her books include *Stars in the Making* (1952), *Introduction to Astronomy* (1954), *Variable Stars and Galactic Structure* (1954), and *Galactic Novae* (1957).

The first woman to achieve the rank of full professor at Harvard through regular faculty promotions, Payne-Gaposchkin was named a professor of astronomy in 1956, and from 1956 to 1966 she served as chair of the university's astronomy department. The American Association of University Women honored her in 1957 for her significant contributions to "the broadening of our understanding of the ages and lifetimes of stars and stellar systems." She was appointed astronomer at the Smithsonian Astrophysical Observatory in 1965, and in 1976 she received the Henry Norris Russell Prize, the most distinguished honor of the American Astronomical Society, which in 1934 had awarded her the Annie Jump Cannon Medal. Smith College, Western College for Women, Wilson College, and Cambridge University conferred honorary degrees on her. She died of lung cancer in Cambridge, Mass.

Throughout her life, Payne-Gaposchkin advocated a balanced life of career and homemaking for women. In *Cecilia Payne-Gaposchkin: An Autobiography and Other Recollections* (1984), she reflected on the past discrimination she had experienced as a female scientist, "a tale of low salary, lack of status, slow advancement," but she also exulted in her achievement of having, through dogged persistence, reached professional heights that were beyond her wildest dreams. In these same recollections, her daughter, Katherine Haramundanis, described Payne-Gaposchkin as a "Renaissance woman": at once scholar, linguist, generous neighbor, cultivated traveler, playgoer, musician, clever wit, political independent, keen scientist, and warm mother.

[An obituary is in the *New York Times*, Dec. 8, 1979.]

BARBARA B. JACKSON

PEI, MARIO ANDREW (Feb. 16, 1901–Mar. 2, 1978), educator and philologist-linguist, was born in Rome, Italy, the son of Francesco Pei and Luisa Ferri. His father owned and managed a pharmacy, the failure of which led to the family's immigration to the United States to settle in New York City in 1908.

Having completed his first two years of schooling in Italy, Mario Pei entered parochial school in New York at the age of seven. Quickly becoming bilingual in English and the native Italian spoken at home, he proved himself an exemplary student at the Saint John Evangelist Elementary School. At age thirteen he won a scholarship to Saint Francis Xavier High School, where he excelled in Greek, Latin, and French. Upon graduation in 1918 Pei became a sixth-grade teacher at the Saint Francis Xavier Grammar School (1918–1920) and enrolled for evening courses in mathematics and sciences at the College of the City of New York.

Pei spent most of the following year in Havana, Cuba, as private tutor to the nephews of President Mario García Menocal, primarily for English and French, during which time Pei became fluent in Spanish. He then revisited Italy on a grant from the Italian government. Upon his return to the United States in 1921, he resumed his studies at City College, shifting to a liberal arts major in French, and taught foreign languages at Regis High School (1921–1922), Fordham Preparatory School (1921), and the Franklin School (1922–1923). In 1923 he was invited to teach Latin and Romance languages at City College and at its prestigious preparatory school, Townsend Harris High School, a position he continued to hold until 1937. On June 25, 1924, Pei married Pearl Glover of Oklahoma, a pianist who remained his lifelong companion. They had no children.

While holding simultaneous full-time high school and part-time college teaching positions, Pei pursued his undergraduate degree as a part-

Pei

time evening student for seven years. He distinguished himself at City College, being elected to Phi Beta Kappa and receiving his B.A. degree magna cum laude in 1925. In the same year he was naturalized an American citizen. By this time Pei was dedicated to teaching and was thoroughly imbued with his passion for languages and philology. He embarked upon an ambitious study of world classics in the original Greek, Latin, French, Italian, and Spanish and began to work through German, Russian, and Hebrew texts and grammars. In 1928, Pei began his formal graduate studies at Columbia University in ancient and medieval languages and literature, including Sanskrit, Old Church Slavonic, Gothic, Old French, and Medieval Romance dialects. He wrote and published his dissertation, *The Language of the Eighth-Century Texts in Northern France*, and was awarded the Ph.D. degree in Romance philology and comparative linguistics in 1932.

The following year, Pei joined the faculty at Columbia University as a nontenured lecturer in French and was promoted in 1937 to assistant professor of Romance languages. In 1946 he was promoted to associate professor of Romance philology, with tenure, and in 1953 he became a full professor, a position he held until his retirement in 1969 as professor emeritus. Pei also held special posts as a NATO lecturer at the universities of Lisbon and Coimbra in Portugal (1961); as a visiting professor at the University of Pittsburgh (1962–1963), Rutgers University (1963–1964), and Seton Hall University (1970–1972); and as a visiting lecturer at Brigham Young University (1970, 1972).

Pei's writing career began in the mid-1920's with articles, editorials, and some translations for such popular periodicals as *Il Progresso Italo-Americano*, *United America*, and *Atlantica*. Beginning in the 1950's he contributed hundreds of articles to popular periodicals, including *Town and Country*, *Holiday*, the *New York Times Magazine*, *Reader's Digest*, *Saturday Review*, *Saturday Evening Post*, and a host of others in the United States and abroad.

At the invitation of a respected London publisher, Pei translated from Italian Vittorio Ermete de Fiori's biography of Benito Mussolini, *Mussolini: The Man of Destiny* (1928), which established Pei's reputation as a translator. He wrote, coauthored, translated, compiled, or edited more than fifty books. His dissertation, *The Language of the Eighth-Century Texts in Northern France*, published by Columbia in 1932, drew praise in Romance language circles worldwide. His intimate knowledge of Romance philology and early fascination with the medieval era led to *French Precursors of the "Chanson de Roland"* (1948) and the scholarly historical novel *Swords of Anjou* (1953), which was acclaimed both for its authentic recreation of Moorish Spain and medieval France as well as its readability and appeal to a modern audience. *The Italian Language* (1941) proved valuable for scholars and laymen alike as a reference work and textbook both in the Italian language and in comparative historical linguistics; it was revised and reprinted in 1954.

He served also as associate editor of *Romanic Review*, *Modern Language Journal*, and *Symposium* and was on the editorial board of *Romance Philology*.

The advent of World War II dramatically elevated once-isolationist America's interest in the languages and customs of foreign countries, which marked a turning point in Pei's writing career. He was called upon by the federal government to serve as a consultant and lecturer at the United States Army Language School in Monterey, Calif.; to broadcast in French, Italian, German, Dutch, Czech, and Romanian for Radio Free Europe and Voice of America; to prepare English lessons for Spanish-speakers for broadcast in Latin America; and to work with the Office of War Information and the Office of Strategic Services on a number of war-related language projects. Using his knowledge of several well-known and lesser-known languages, Pei created a utilitarian thirty-seven-language course called "War Linguistics," out of which grew *Languages for War and Peace* (1943). The book, revised as *The World's Chief Languages* in 1947, served many years as a textbook and reference work of descriptive outlines of each of the languages included. It was further revised and reprinted in 1960.

This seminal work led to Pei's pioneering efforts on behalf of a new branch of linguistics, geolinguistics, a term coined by one of his graduate students, Joseph Costanzo. In 1965, Pei founded the American Society of Geolinguistics in New York City, with the stated aim of gathering and disseminating up-to-date knowledge concerning the distribution and relative importance of the world's present-day languages in terms of their economic, political, and cultural value; their genetic, historical, and geographic relationships; and their current usage in spoken and written form. The growth of geolinguistic centers since 1965 has been significant in the United States and abroad.

Pei's concept of language as a cohesive force in the world and his vision of a linguistically, politically, and economically united global society of nations is evident in his books *English: A World-Wide Tongue* (1944); *The American Road to Peace: A Constitution of the World* (1945); and *One Language for the World and How to Achieve It* (1958); which Pei sent to heads of state throughout the world. *The Story of Language* (1949, rev. ed. 1965), by far the most widely read of his writings, reflects most strongly his belief that language is the unifying thread of civilization and that language the story of humanity. Pei's love for and comparative studies of English resulted in *The Story of English* (1952), which was revised and retitled *The Story of the English Language* in 1967.

Trained in historical and comparative philology and linguistics, Pei never espoused any school of modern linguistics. He did, however, remain abreast of the changes taking place in the field of linguistics and used his gift for simplification and clarification to narrow the gulf between the terminological creativity of linguists and intellectuals and newcomers to linguistics. *A Dictionary of Linguistics* (1954), revised as *Glossary of Linguistic Terminology* (1966), was written to bridge the gap between ongoing terminological coinages and the three previous works generally available to the American student of linguistics. His *Invitation to Linguistics: A Basic Introduction to the Science of Languages* (1965) is an attempt to cut a broad, clear, central path through the developing jungle of intertwining terms and conflicting theories; to explain and clarify the two well-known branches of linguistics, historical (diachronic) and descriptive (synchronic); and to program the future of the newly founded branch of geolinguistics. Similarly, *Language of the Specialists: A Communications Guide to Twenty Different Fields*, written in collaboration with a team of specialists (1966); *Language Today: A Survey of Current Linguistic Thought* (1967), with Katherine Le Mée, Don L. F. Nilsen, and others; *Words in Sheep's Clothing* (1969); *Double-Speak in America* (1973); and *Weasel Words: The Art of Saying What You Don't Mean* (1978), which targets the proliferation of ambiguous euphemisms, are all attempts to build a bridge of reference resources to keep language comprehensible, useful, and functional as a tool of communication between the specialist and the nonspecialist.

Pei's ongoing concern with sociopolitical issues was voiced in *The American Road to Peace: A Constitution for the World* (1945), a blueprint for ending all war and maintaining world peace; *The Consumer's Manifesto* (1960); *Our National Heritage* (1965); and *The America We Lost: The Concerns of a Conservative* (1968), to which William F. Buckley, Jr., wrote the introduction.

Pei's talent and merit as a teacher, mentor, and writer who had perfected to a fine art the transmission of his knowledge and his vision to posterity are amply documented in his considerable legacy of scholarly and popular publications, students who have served on the faculties of distinguished universities around the world, and a grateful and better-educated audience at large for whom he transformed the study of language from a formidable task into an engrossing pursuit.

Pei died in Glen Ridge, N.J., where he was in active retirement.

[Manuscript collections with material on Pei are in the libraries at Boston University and Columbia University. John Fisher and Paul A. Gaeng, ed., *Studies in Honor of Mario Pei* (1972), includes a lengthy listing of Pei's published writings before 1971. An obituary is in the *New York Times*, Mar. 5, 1978.]

MARGARET A. HOWARD

PERDUE, ARTHUR WILLIAM (Aug. 8, 1885–June 27, 1977), businessman, was born in Whitesburg, Md., the second son of Levin W. Perdue and Martha Ellen Adkins. Perdue's father was a lumberman, a millman, and then a farmer at the age of fifty-eight.

As a boy, Perdue worked in his father's sawmill, feeding logs and shoveling sawdust into the furnace. Once a tract of lumber was used up, the family moved to another small town near a new tract. Their first move was to Libertytown, Md., when Perdue was twelve years old. The following year he left the mill and tried his hand at farming, but failed. He went back to the sawmill and soon could do the tasks of a grown man, such as firing boilers and working as the lever-man behind the sawyer, who set the pace for the mill. When the family moved to Friendship, Md., Perdue became a sawyer,

Perdue

and ran the mill until he was twenty-one years old. His father paid Perdue $1.50 for a ten-hour day, 50 percent more than he paid his other employees.

Perdue's father stopped operating the sawmill in 1909, when he decided to become a full-time farmer. By then, Perdue, who had also been going to school since the age of five, had saved enough money to attend business school. He moved to Salisbury, Md., at the age of twenty-three to enroll in the business program at Eastern Shore College. He received his diploma on June 18, 1908.

While at business school, Perdue worked in a men's clothing store in Salisbury. One of his clients, a Dr. C. C. Ward, who owned a drugstore in nearby Crisfield, offered Perdue free room and board if he would work for him. Perdue agreed, and the two became good friends. Though Perdue learned about medicine in his job at the drugstore, it was only a matter of time before he grew restless. He wanted to meet more people and earn more money. Ward promised him a Maxwell car if he would stay on, but Perdue refused and headed back to Salisbury when he was twenty-five.

In Salisbury, Perdue got work as a messenger for the Adams Express Company, which later became Railway Express. Within a year, he began working for the Baltimore, Chesapeake and Atlantic Railroad as well. His job took him to a number of cities linked to Baltimore. The next year, he transferred to the Norfolk–New York City line, where he worked for four years. He was then promoted to cashier in the Salisbury office. Two years later, he was placed in charge of the office.

Perdue's earliest contact with the chicken business occurred when he bought fifty leghorn chickens around 1907. But he turned them over to his mother because he was too busy with his other jobs to care for them. Perdue got his first inkling of the larger possibilities poultry could offer when he noticed increasing numbers of chickens and eggs being loaded on the Norfolk–New York railroad line. He talked with poultry men in the Salisbury area and noticed they were all financially prosperous. In 1917, Perdue decided to enter the poultry business.

But he stayed with the express company for a few more years, in part because he wanted to earn enough money to purchase a house for his wife, Pearl Parsons, whom he had married on May 23, 1917. Once they had a house, Perdue bought twenty-three laying hens, and he and his wife began the business. Their only child, Franklin, was born in 1920. By then Perdue was able to buy their first car, a Model T, to replace the motorcycle he and his wife had used for three years. Pearl ran their chicken house while Perdue continued to work on the railroad. In 1925, they built their first hatchery, with a 5,400-egg capacity. Later that year they hired their first part-time employee, a nephew.

Because his father had been in debt until two years before his death, Perdue decided to begin his business slowly, on a cash basis, and never to borrow money. His conservative approach paid off during the Great Depression. With no debts, and his house, hatcheries, chickens, and feed all paid for in cash, Perdue did not suffer as much as many others. In 1933 he was able to add two incubators and hire his first full-time employee.

Perdue was a strict Methodist. No one in the business worked on Sundays. No eggs were packed, and no chickens were fed on that day for many years. Perdue described himself as having a "deep faith in God." "I know," he once said, "that a greater Power than mortal man has been at work throughout my life." His deep sense of certainty was matched by his unassuming, humble manner and what one friend described as "gentlemanliness."

Perdue's self-discipline, constant attention to detail, and frugality set the tone of his business. He worked from dawn to dusk with a one-hour lunch and a twenty-minute nap every day. After dinner he might read a poultry magazine or listen to the radio, but he would check the chickens before bed. When a friend asked him why he didn't "take it slower," Perdue replied, "I'm afraid I might get to like it."

Perdue's technique of raising chickens received acclaim. He paid extra for excellent mating breeds. The hatcheries were tidy. Dropping boards were cleaned daily and fountains were washed. There was sufficient water, ventilation, and light. His chickens were on a strict feed schedule. They were brooded in complete confinement and never touched the ground, which reduced their exposure to disease. Nor were they overcrowded.

When Franklin was ten years old, Perdue gave him fifty chickens of his own and a piggy bank. Franklin was expected to care for the chickens and keep records on them. His son officially joined the company in 1939, and though Franklin was more ambitious and fast-paced than his father, there was said to be no rivalry between the two. In 1940, they ventured into the broiler business, and in 1944, when Franklin became a full partner, the company name was changed to A. W. Perdue and Son. That same year, they built their first large hatchery, which held up to 198,000 eggs and produced 50,000 broiler chicks per week.

Pearl Parsons Perdue died of tuberculosis in 1942. Perdue married his brother Lawrence's widow, Edith Dennis Perdue, on Dec. 3, 1945.

Franklin officially took over guidance of the company in 1948 and built it into an integrated broiler operation, that is, one that hatches eggs, raises chickens, prepares feed, and processes and markets the broilers in house. In 1960, in order to keep expanding, Perdue, or "Mr. Arthur," as he was affectionately known, took out the first loan of his lifetime.

The parent-to-child transition is one of the greatest obstacles any family-owned business faces. About 75 percent of such businesses do not survive the transition. Of the 25 percent that do, 65 percent are liquidated or sold within the first two years of transition. The fate of the Perdue business is an exception. Perdue and his son were known for their unusually close relationship. Perdue let Franklin make his own mistakes, even though he worried about rapid and costly expansion.

When he was not working, Perdue was often in the garden, tending his rose bushes, or collecting and writing poetry. In his late eighties, he spent part of each day visiting friends in nursing homes. He died in Salisbury, Md.

[See Gordon Sawyer, *The Agribusiness Poultry Industry* (1971); Frank Gordy, *A Solid Foundation . . . The Life and Times of Arthur W. Perdue* (1976); Lawrence Freeny, "Arthur and Frank Perdue: Chicken Kings," *New York Times*, Sept. 12, 1976; and Edward M. Perdue, *Our Family Heritage: The Perdues of the Eastern Shore of Maryland* (1988). An obituary is in the *New York Times*, June 28, 1977.]

ALISON GARDY

PERELMAN, SIDNEY JOSEPH (Feb. 1, 1904–Oct. 16, 1979), humorist and author, was born in Brooklyn, N.Y., the only child of Russian Jewish immigrants Joseph Perelman and Sophia Charra. He grew up in Providence, R.I., where his father embarked on a series of unsuccessful occupations including running a dry goods store and raising chickens. Perelman later wrote, "to this day I cringe at the sight of a gizzard." His early ambition was to be a cartoonist and as a young boy he remembered drawing cartoons in his father's store on the long cardboard strips around the bolts of gingham.

In his youth Perelman read a wide variety of books popular at that time, including *Graustark*, *Girl of the Limberlost*, *Scaramouche*, the Horatio Alger success stories, and the novels of Charles Dickens. His habit of voracious reading continued throughout his lifetime and was the springboard for his writing. In 1917 he received a writing prize in a nationwide essay contest but his primary interest was still cartooning.

While attending Classical High School, his attention turned to movies and vaudeville. He held down a number of after-school jobs, including electroplating automobile radiators, a hazardous job that exposed him to acid fumes. At the insistence of his parents, he quit but quickly found work in a department store. In 1921 he entered Brown University in Providence as a premedical student. He later became an English major and joined the staff of the college humor magazine, the *Brown Jug*, as a cartoonist. In his senior year Perelman became editor of the magazine. It was at Brown that he met the novelist Nathanael West, who became his closest friend and his brother-in-law, when Perelman married Laura West on July 4, 1929. Perelman left Brown in 1924, one course short of graduation because he had failed the math requirement. Years later Brown University awarded the humorist an honorary degree.

Perelman then moved to Greenwich Village in New York City, where he was a cartoonist at *Judge*, a weekly humor magazine, from 1924 until 1929. He produced cartoons weekly, with such captions as "I've got Bright's disease and he's got mine." He also wrote short humorous pieces and his characteristic writing style began to emerge. Al Hirschfeld, the caricaturist and Perelman's good friend remembered: "He used to do these one-line jokes and then they became two lines and then they became six lines and finally the editors said to him, 'Listen, Sid. Why are you bothering with the drawing? Why don't you just extend the caption?' Which is what he did and that's how he started writing."

In 1929 he moved from *Judge* to *College Humor*, where his unique style of prose became evident. In 1929 a collection of his magazine pieces, *Dawn Ginsbergh's Revenge*, was published by Horace Liveright. It garnered attention from Groucho Marx who was looking for a writer for an upcoming movie. The subsequent collaboration between Perelman and the Marx Brothers resulted in *Monkey Business* (1931) and *Horse Feathers* (1932). Later Perelman recalled, "I did two films with them, which in its way is perhaps my greatest distinction in life, because anybody who ever worked on any picture for the Marx Brothers said he would rather be chained to a galley oar and lashed at ten-minute intervals until the blood spurted from his frame than ever work for those sons of bitches again."

Over the next decade Perelman worked periodically in Hollywood. He and Laura and their two young children divided their time between their farm in Bucks County, Pa., and their home in Greenwich Village. Between 1932 and 1956, Perelman contributed to eleven screenplays, some individually, some collaboratively with his wife. Perelman detested Hollywood and quickly left after each lucrative project. Back East, they wrote Broadway plays. Two comedies, *All Good Americans* (1933) and *The Night Before Christmas* (1941), had brief Broadway runs and were later made into films. Tragedy befell the Perelmans in 1940, when Nathanael West and his wife were killed in a car accident.

Perelman had begun to write pieces for the *New Yorker* in 1931 and continued for almost half a century. His early magazine pieces were published in the collection *Strictly From Hunger* (1937) and *Look Who's Talking!* (1940). Random House continued to publish his collections, which included *The Dream Department* (1943), *Crazy Like a Fox* (1944), and *Keep It Crisp* (1946). He circled the globe with Hirschfeld and together they wrote and illustrated *Westward Ha!, or, Around the World in Eighty Clichés* (1948). From 1940 to 1960, Perelman published no fewer than 171 short comic essays, which were published in *The Road to Miltown or, Under the Spreading Atrophy* (1957) and *The Rising Gorge* (1961).

Perelman teamed up with Ogden Nash in 1943 to write a successful musical, *One Touch of Venus* (music by Kurt Weill). This Broadway hit freed him financially from Hollywood. He would not return until 1955, when he wrote the script for Mike Todd's production of *Around the World in Eighty Days* (1956). Despite Perelman's feelings of contempt and disdain for Todd and film writing in general, he produced a script that won the Academy Award. Perelman was later to say "misery loves copy." His acclaim as an Oscar winner led to writing assignments for television, including "Malice in Wonderland," three sketches about Hollywood that aired on the cultural series "Omnibus" in 1959. In 1962 he wrote a theatrical comedy, *The Beauty Part*, which starred Bert Lahr. The play opened Dec. 26, 1962, to good reviews at the Music Box Theater on Broadway, but it closed on Mar. 9, 1963, because of a publicity blackout resulting from a New York City newspaper strike.

The Perelmans returned from a long stay in England toward the end of 1969, and Laura died the following April. A few months later, Perelman, unable to work, sold his farm and Laura's belongings and moved to London. He told a reporter, "I've had all the rural splendor I can use, and each time I get to New York it seems more pestilential than before." Once in London, he immediately embarked on an eighty-day trip around the world in imitation of the Jules Verne character Phineas Fogg. He returned to New York in May 1972, and for the next seven years he continued to write and travel. In 1975 *Vinegar Puss*, his twentieth book, was published; *Eastward Ha!* appeared in 1977 and recounted his sixth trip around the world.

Perelman died in his sleep of natural causes in his Gramercy Park apartment in New York City. Although he had described himself as a crank, those who knew him thought otherwise. The writer Paul Theroux observed: "Perelman's friends liked him very much. He was generous, he was funny, he was enormously social, he didn't boast. . . . When he talked in his croaky drawl he did so in the elaborate way he wrote, with unlikely locutions and slang and precise descriptions diverted into strings of subordinate clauses."

Perelman was a uniquely American writer who was credited by one critic as having a "profound gift for derangement." His style is easily recognized by his acerbic wit and skilled wordplay. His writing is exuberant yet filled with puns and deadpan humor. He once described his style as "mélange, a mixture of all the sludge I read as a child, all the clichés, liberal doses of Yiddish, criminal slang, and some of what I was taught in a Providence, Rhode Island, school by impatient teachers." Perelman used his mastery of the English language and ingenious syntax to parody everyday subjects—books, travel, advertisements, films. His hallmark was magnifying the ordinary situations that plague humans.

[For examples of Perelman's writings see his books *The Best of S. J. Perelman* (1947); *The Road to Miltown; or, Under the Spreading Atrophy* (1957); *The Most of S. J. Perelman* (1958); and Richard Marschall, ed., *That Old Gang o' Mine: The Early and Essential S. J. Perelman* (1984). An obituary is in the *New York Times*, Oct. 18, 1979.]

VIRGINIA WYLY

PIATIGORSKY, GREGOR (Apr. 17, 1903–Aug. 6, 1976), violoncellist, was born in Ekaterinoslav (now Dnepropetrovsk), Ukraine, to Paul I. Piatigorsky and Maria Amchislavsky. Gregor Piatigorsky received his first instruction on the cello from his father, a violinist, and from local instructors. On his seventh birthday his father gave him a full-size cello. "Even before I could pluck the strings, it was next to me at all meals and next to my bedside at night," he recalled in *Cellist*, his 1965 autobiography.

When Gregor was eight years old, his father left the family behind and traveled to St. Petersburg to study violin with Leopold Auer. Young Gregor was forced to find work in order to support his mother and siblings. He played cello in nightclubs and in a silent movie theater. Eventually his father gave up his aspirations for a career as concert violinist and moved the family to Moscow. There in 1911 Piatigorsky auditioned successfully at the Imperial Conservatory and won a scholarship. He studied with Alfred von Glehn.

Having demonstrated his independence at such an early age, young Piatigorsky found it difficult to submit to his father's authority. When the family returned to Ukraine, Gregor remained in Moscow, maintaining a rigorous schedule of early morning practice, daily conservatory study, and nightly performances in restaurants.

In 1917, at age fourteen, Piatigorsky joined the Zeitlin Quartet and auditioned for and won the first cello chair with the Imperial Opera orchestra, which afforded him invaluable experience in the performance of the music of opera, ballet, and symphony. He gave recitals and participated in various chamber music performances.

The Russian Revolution imposed great hardships upon Piatigorsky. Musicians were conscripted into the service of the Communist party. The Zeitlin Quartet was renamed the Lenin String Quartet and was assigned to play in factories and workers' clubs. When Piatigorsky's application for a permit to study abroad was denied, he decided to leave Russia surreptitiously. In 1921 he and fellow musicians on tour near the Polish border crossed the Sbruch River and arrived safely in Lvov, Poland.

Piatigorsky briefly found work with the Warsaw Philharmonic before moving on to Leipzig, where he studied with Julius Klengel. "He never lectured or antagonized his students," Piatigorsky later said. "He worked from each student's best strength." Most of Klengel's students lived together in a rooming house and the cello was their principal preoccupation. To Piatigorsky it was "a cello paradise, a beehive on the verge of drowning in its own honey."

In 1923 he completed his studies with Klengel and moved to Berlin, where he came to the notice of pianist Artur Schnabel, who engaged him to perform in the premiere of Arnold Schoenberg's *Pierrot Lunaire*. Wilhelm Furtwängler, conductor of the Berlin Symphony, invited him to audition for the first cello position in the orchestra. He played with the Berlin Symphony from 1924 to 1928 and also gave solo concerts in Berlin and toured the Baltic countries. In 1926 he taught cello at the Scharwenka Conservatory in Berlin. He commented, "I taught between the rehearsals and I often practiced after concerts at night." He joined a sonata partnership with Artur Schnabel and Karl Flesch. They concertized vigorously, commissioned new works, and enjoyed their fame, their high fees, and "the joyous traveling and playing together."

In Berlin, Piatigorsky married Lydia Antik. He referred to his marriage briefly in his autobiography: "Very musical and alert, she was ambitious and had great charm. My bachelorhood turned into a stormy life that, after nine childless years, ended in peaceful divorce. Faithful to cello, she later married the eminent French cellist Pierre Fournier."

In 1928 he resigned from the Berlin Philharmonic to devote his energies to a career as a cello virtuoso. That year impresario Alexander Merovitch arrived from Russia with two young protégés, pianist Vladimir Horowitz and violinist Nathan Milstein, with plans to promote their careers in the West. He offered Piatigorsky similar career management. The three musicians

Piatigorsky

were about the same age and eager to become world famous. Merovitch called them "the Three Musketeers," and they immediately became lifelong friends. Merovitch encouraged each to develop a repertoire appropriate to the virtuoso, avoiding "ungrateful" works, composing transcriptions, and perfecting showpieces. He arranged ambitious American concert tours for them, and Piatigorsky's first tour began in Oberlin, Ohio, on Nov. 5, 1929, with pianist Valentin Pavlovsky. On Dec. 29, 1929, he appeared with the New York Philharmonic at Carnegie Hall under conductor Willem Mengelberg, playing the Dvořák Cello Concerto. "In his hands, the instrument shed its reputed limitations. . . . He is one of the most poetic and sensitive performers now before the public," said *New York World* critic Samuel Chotzinoff. He was dubbed "the cellist sensation of the season" and "the American Casals."

For the next twenty years he lived the busy life of the traveling virtuoso, appearing throughout the United States, Canada, Europe, South America, and Asia with every major symphony orchestra and conductor in the world.

In 1933, to commemorate Brahms's centenary, Piatigorsky performed all of the composer's works for piano and strings with Paul Hindemith and Bronislaw Huberman.

On Jan. 31, 1935, he joined conductor Arturo Toscanini in the world premiere of the cello concerto composed for him by Mario Castelnuovo-Tedesco. On Feb. 22, 1935, he played the premiere of *Concerto Lirico* for cello by Nicolai Berezowski, with conductor Serge Koussevitzky. In that year he performed the cello version of the "Italian Suite" from *Pulcinella*, a collaboration between himself and Igor Stravinsky. In subsequent years he introduced cello concertos by Sergey Prokofiev (1940), Paul Hindemith (1941), and Sir William Walton (1957).

Piatigorsky also composed for the cello: *Pliaska, Scherzo, Variations on a Theme by Paganini for Cello and Piano or Orchestra*, and various transcriptions which he included in his concerts.

On Jan. 26, 1937, Piatigorsky married Jacqueline de Rothschild, a talented amateur musician and daughter of Baron Édouard de Rothschild. The couple had two children. In 1939 the family moved to the United States, and Piatigorsky became an American citizen on Aug. 29, 1942.

Piatigorsky stood six feet, three inches tall, and was able to establish an easy rapport with his audiences. The press often noted the priceless Stradivarius cello he took with him on tours. He owned the "Baudiot," made in 1725, and the "Batta," made in 1714, which rank among the world's finest instruments. He succeeded in winning acceptance of the cello as a serious musical instrument. A 1939 article in *Newsweek* noted: "He has spurred wide public interest in an instrument which, long extolled for its virtue in ensemble work, has been rather grudgingly acknowledged as a first-rank solo vehicle." A growing number of cello virtuosos began to appear on the concert scene.

In 1949 he curtailed his touring schedule. In twenty years of concertizing he had given more than 1,000 recitals and had made nearly 250 appearances with orchestras. Now he wished to devote more time to his family, his teaching, and his recording. That year he formed with violinist Jascha Heifetz and pianist Artur Rubenstein what *Life* magazine called "the Million Dollar Trio." They performed a series of trio concerts.

From 1961 to 1976 the Heifetz-Piatigorsky concerts performed chamber music throughout the United States. On occasion they were joined by violinist William Primrose and pianist Leonard Pennario. Recordings of some of these performances with RCA Victor won Grammys from the National Academy of Recording Arts and Sciences in 1961, 1962, and 1963.

Piatigorsky was also a committed teacher. In 1940 he became director of chamber music in the Berkshire Music Center's summer program. From 1942 to 1949 he taught at the Curtis Institute in Philadelphia. In 1957 he presented a master class at Boston University. From 1962 until his death he was cello professor at the University of Southern California in Los Angeles.

In 1970, Leonard Bernstein honored Piatigorsky's debut in the United States forty years earlier, leading the New York Philharmonic and Piatigorsky in Strauss's *Don Quixote*. Two years later, Piatigorsky joined conductor Pierre Boulez and the New York Philharmonic in Dvořák's Cello Concerto, which he had played at his first appearance with that orchestra in 1929. On May 20, 1973, the Chamber Music Society of Lincoln Center presented a gala concert to honor Piatigorsky's seventieth birthday.

Piatigorsky was awarded honorary Doctorate of Music degrees from Temple University, Columbia University, University of California at Los Angeles, and other institutions. He received the Brandeis Gold Medal in 1954 and was inducted into the French Legion of Honor in 1955. He died in Los Angeles, Calif.

[The Gregor Piatigorsky collection, including manuscripts and printed music, and correspondence can be found in the Library of Congress, Washington, D.C. See also Jacqueline Piatigorsky, *Jump in the Waves* (1988), his wife's memoir. Articles include " 'Cello's Renaissance: Great Soloists Effect Revival of a Neglected Institution," *Newsweek*, Mar. 6, 1939; "Big Cello," *Time*, Feb. 19, 1951; "Master Class," *Time*, May 13, 1966; Hubert Saal, "Gregor the Great," *Newsweek*, Nov. 9, 1970; and "For Piatigorsky," *New York Times*, May 22, 1973. There are two performances on videocassette: *Artur Rubenstein*, Kultur V1102 (1977), and *Heifetz and Piatigorsky*, Kultur V1101 (1977). An obituary is in the *New York Times*, Aug. 7, 1976.]

JOHN C. REINERS

PICKFORD, MARY (Apr. 8, 1892–May 29, 1979), actress and film producer, was born Gladys Louise Smith in Toronto, Ontario, Canada, the eldest of three children of John Charles Smith and Charlotte Hennessey. Her father was a printer when she was born and a bartender in 1898, when he died. His wife took in sewing to support the family. Gladys received only about six months of formal education, at the McCaul Street School, eventually teaching herself to read.

Charlotte Smith, half a year after her husband's death, allowed six-year-old Gladys to debut with the Valentine Stock Company in *The Silver King*. Gladys soon worked for other stock companies, mainly in popular melodramas, and received a helpful boost when she was hired to tour Canadian and American towns in *The Little Red Schoolhouse* (1901). By the time "Baby Gladys Smith," as she was billed, toured in *The Fatal Wedding* (1903), her younger sister and brother as well as her mother were also given parts. Through the efforts of Charlotte—with whom Gladys maintained an extremely close personal and professional relationship until her mother's death in 1928—the family appeared together as much as possible, including several New York City productions, such as *Edmund Burke* (1905). Most of their time was spent touring, often for grueling one-night stands.

Fifteen-year-old Gladys became Mary Pickford when she landed a starring role in *The Warrens of Virginia* (1907), produced and directed by David Belasco. She performed in the hit show on Broadway and on tour for two years. Her siblings, who continued acting, took the Pickford name as well.

Although the nascent silent film industry was then frowned upon by many stage actors, Pickford began making movies in 1909 for American Mutoscope and Biograph Company. Its chief director was the redoubtable D. W. Griffith, who had a potent influence on her acting, which favored emotional inspiration over technical preparation. Her early films were short features churned out on an average of one per week, beginning with *Her First Biscuits* (1909). By 1911, when she married fellow actor Owen Moore, who frequently costarred with her, she had made eighty-one films, in both New York and Hollywood, where the movie industry was putting down roots. Pickford played a surprisingly wide variety of characters, including prostitutes and Indians, but with her sunny good looks, inner radiance, and trademark golden curls, the diminutive (five feet, one inch) actress captured fans' hearts with her portrayals of preteens and adolescents. When she bobbed her hair in the 1920's, many fans were indignant.

Pickford took a deep and intelligent interest in everything about the filmmaking business, even selling her own scenarios to Biograph. Her income ($10 per day at the start) grew astronomically as did critical approval, and she was quickly elevated to star status. Because of Biograph's policy of not publicizing its players, however, it was some time before the public knew her name.

Carl Laemmle's Independent Motion Picture Company lured Pickford away for a much higher salary in 1911, but she was unhappy with the quality of their work, broke her one-year contract after thirty-four films, and signed on with the Majestic Company in Chicago only to leave them in 1912 after five movies so that she could return to Griffith at Biograph. By now, thanks to Laemmle's publicity, Pickford's name spelled major stardom. She was known by various sobriquets, such as "Little Mary" and "The Girl with the Curls."

She made another twenty-four Biograph films, such as *The Schoolteacher and the Waif* (1912), *Friends* (1912), and *The New York Hat* (1913), all of them exploiting her youthful appeal. She returned to Broadway to play a blind girl in the Belasco hit *A Good Little Devil* (1913), and her film reputation drew droves of customers to the play. Producer Adolph Zukor starred Pickford in a Famous Players Company movie version. Her $500-per-week salary (soon doubled, then quadrupled, then boosted to $10,000 per week) was inducement enough to abandon theater for the movies, and she proceeded to make thirty-four Zukor-financed films, among her first five being *Hearts Adrift* (1914) and *Tess of the Storm Country* (1914). Publicity for the latter touted her as "America's foremost film actress." Pickford was quickly becoming the most popular superstar of her day.

Although admired by her coworkers for her professionalism, bonhomie, and work ethic, Pickford was also a shrewd, even ruthless, businesswoman whose clout grew so great that Zukor gave her the unprecedented authority to serve as her own producer. After *Tess*, she made eighteen features by 1917 for Famous Players Film Company and Famous Players–Lasky Corporation (a 1916 merger) under such directors as James Kirkwood, Allan Dwan, Sidney Olcott, and John B. O'Brien. With the exception of *The Eagle's Mate* (1914), these films were mostly mediocrities that exploited her archetypal Victorian image as a pure-hearted optimistic, virginal, and patriotic but feisty and even hoydenish youngster, one who—even when burdened by poverty—is often responsible for the moral and physical well-being of others. Her sentimental films then and later often idealized the working classes and knocked the socially superior. By 1917, Pickford was earning well over $1 million annually.

Despite her actual years and the fact that she occasionally played age-appropriate roles, the public liked to imagine her as no more than sixteen. By no means a superlative actress, she was outstanding within the range of her specialty and had precisely those magnetic qualities that supersede artistic talent in the composition of a movie star. Still, most of her films dated quickly.

From 1917 to 1919, Pickford made four features for Artcraft Pictures, several of them counted among the era's classics, including *The Poor Little Rich Girl* (1917), directed by Maurice Tourneur, with Pickford as the neglected child of wealthy parents; *Rebecca of Sunnybrook Farm* (1917), filmed by Pickford's favorite director, Marshall Neilan, and concerning a poor girl residing with mean-spirited relatives; and *Stella Maris* (1918), directed by Neilan, with Pickford revealing memorable versatility in the sharply contrasted roles of a mistreated cockney maid and a wealthy invalid child.

In 1918, Pickford founded the Mary Pickford Company, its films to be financed and distributed by First National. This arrangement earned her more than $250,000 per film, but more important, gave her complete artistic control. Three films resulted, one of them the artistically and commercially outstanding *Daddy Long Legs* (1919), directed by Neilan, with Pickford playing an orphan looked after by a secret benefactor. During the same year, she cofounded the film distribution organization United Artists, with Griffith and stars Douglas Fairbanks, Charlie Chaplin, and William S. Hart. (The board's composition eventually changed.)

Pickford and Fairbanks, two of America's greatest movie stars, were married in 1920, creating the most idealized marriage in Hollywood history (she had divorced Moore earlier that year). They reigned over Hollywood from their Beverly Hills Tudor mansion, Pickfair. The marriage crumbled, however, and the world's most popular couple were divorced in 1936. In 1937, Pickford wed sometime movie actor and orchestra leader Charles ("Buddy") Rogers, twelve years her junior, with whom she lived out her days. She had no natural children by any of her spouses, having become sterile during a 1912 abortion, but she and Rogers adopted two children.

Pickford made sixteen films for United Artists, including the tremendously profitable *Pollyanna* (1920), with Pickford playing the orphaned "glad girl" of the title, and *Suds* (1920), about another cockney servant. Films in which she starred and also produced were *Little Lord Fauntleroy* (1921), with Pickford playing both the role of the eponymous, overdressed rich boy and that of his mother; a remake and improved version of *Tess of the Storm Country* (1922); *Rosita* (1923), about a Spanish street singer, one of her rare nonadolescent roles; *Little Annie Rooney* (1925), with the thirty-three-year-old star playing a twelve-year-old; *Sparrows* (1926), with Pickford as the loving guardian of a group of captive juveniles; and *My Best Girl* (1927), Pickford's final silent, in which she was a poor shop girl.

Her four sound features were *Coquette*

(1929), for which her portrayal of a southern belle won an Academy Award, although her voice was unremarkable; *The Taming of the Shrew* (1929), her sole costarring vehicle with Fairbanks, which revealed her inexperience in Shakespeare and was a box office letdown; *Kiki* (1931), which, to the dismay of her fans, allowed her to flaunt some sex appeal; and *Secrets* (1933), a period romantic comedy. Her directors included Ernst Lubitsch, Neilan, William Beaudine, Sam Taylor, and Frank Borzage. Following the failure of her final three efforts, and realizing that she was trapped in a role type from which commercial considerations would not allow her to escape and that talkies were not as amenable to her abilities as silent movies, Pickford retired from acting after *Secrets*.

Pickford, who amassed a fortune by her investments, produced nine mostly forgettable movies from 1936 to 1949. Until she sold her share of United Artists in 1951 for $3 million, she remained a contentious member of the board. She toured in vaudeville in 1933 and a one-act play in 1934 but her plans for a screen comeback (she was considered for the lead in *Sunset Boulevard*) came to naught. From the 1930's through the 1950's she occasionally hosted radio programs. An archconservative, she applauded fascism in the 1930's and toyed with the idea of running for Congress. Several religiously oriented (Christian Science) books bore Pickford's byline, as did the 1935 novel *The Demi-Widow* and her 1955 memoirs, *Sunshine and Shadow*. An alcoholic recluse in her later years, she made her final public appearance (televised from Pickfair) in 1976 to receive a special Academy Award. "America's Sweetheart," still a Canadian citizen, died in Santa Monica, Calif.

[Pickford's career is discussed in many books about the history of American films, such as Kevin Brownlow's *The Parade's Gone By* (1968). Scott Eyman has authored the definitive biography, *Mary Pickford: America's Sweetheart* (1990). Also worth examining are Kemp Niver, *Mary Pickford, Comedienne* (1969); Robert Windeler, *Sweetheart: The Story of Mary Pickford* (1974); and Booton Herndon, *Mary Pickford and Douglas Fairbanks* (1977). Major collections of Pickford's films are at the Library of Congress, Washington, D.C., and the Museum of Modern Art, New York City. An obituary is in the *New York Times*, May 30, 1979.]

SAMUEL L. LEITER

PIERCE, ROBERT WILLARD (Oct. 8, 1914–Sept. 6, 1978), evangelist and humanitarian, was born in Fort Dodge, Iowa, the son of Fred Asa Pierce, a carpenter, and Flora Belle Harlow Evison. The youngest of seven children, he moved with his family to Greeley, Colo., and then, at age twelve, to Los Angeles. Shortly thereafter the family joined the Grace Church of the Nazarene, and Pierce experienced Christian conversion. When his father died unexpectedly, Pastor Earle Mack became a major force in his life. In his early teenage years, Pierce served as a street-corner preacher. He attended high school in Los Angeles and then entered nearby Pasadena Nazarene College. Although he considered himself of inferior talent and was best known for his pranks, Pierce was elected student body president during his junior year. He did not return to Pasadena for his senior year, and on Nov. 24, 1936, he married Ruth Lorraine Johnson. They had three children.

In his twenties, Pierce served as an itinerant evangelist for the Church of the Nazarene on the West Coast, as a young evangelist for the World Christian Fundamentals Association, as a general manager of the Eureka Jubilee Singers, as a fledgling filmmaker, and as an assistant minister with his father-in-law, Floyd B. Johnson, at the Los Angeles Evangelistic Center. He was ordained by the First Baptist Church of Wilmington, Calif., in 1940.

Pierce had found his work with young people especially fulfilling, and when he learned that the many local Youth for Christ (YFC) rallies that had developed since the late 1930's were becoming a national organization, he eagerly joined Torrey Johnson, Billy Graham, Merv Rosell, and others in the new movement. In 1944 he accepted an invitation from the Seattle organization to lead its rally. A year later he was named a YFC vice-president at-large, which required him to return to itinerant evangelism but on a more extensive scale. When Madame Chiang Kai-shek invited Youth for Christ to conduct a series of youth rallies in China, YFC president Torrey Johnson asked Pierce to lead the effort. Although his wife was suffering from a major illness and he lacked adequate travel funds, he departed for the one-month trip in the fall of 1947. His trip resulted in nearly 18,000 Christian conversions and proved to be a life-changing experience for Pierce. He was deeply moved by missionaries who, despite meager resources, were performing heroic works of compassion with lepers, blind outcasts, and poor schoolchildren. Pierce pledged to commit funds regularly from his own limited income to help one specific needy child. Thus was born the model for what later became the expressed purpose of his World Vision organization, "To meet emergency needs in crisis areas through existing evangelical agencies and individuals."

Soon thereafter, in the midst of the Chinese Communist Revolution, Western missionaries were forced to leave China. However, with the havoc created by the Korean War, Pierce found a new mission field. He visited South Korea on the eve of the war and strongly empathized with the suffering of people who through most of the twentieth century had experienced foreign occupation. When the Korean War began in June 1950, he gained recognition as a war correspondent for the *Christian Digest*, thus assuring his continued presence in South Korea. Pierce combined a willingness to share in the suffering of those to whom he ministered with an ability to persuade American Evangelicals to fund his humanitarian efforts. During the war he wrote in his Bible, "Let my heart be broken with the things that break the heart of God." Pierce's passion and natural speaking skills created a powerful effect when he addressed American audiences during his periodic trips home. Evangelist Billy Graham described him as "the greatest raiser of money for missions I ever knew." Through documentary films, radio broadcasts, and personal appearances, Pierce helped support orphanages, child-care homes, and hospitals. To help organize his fund-raising efforts he created World Vision, Inc. in September 1950.

Especially noted for its orphan sponsorship program, World Vision grew to become a large, multifaceted worldwide relief and mission organization. After Pierce's death it became the largest voluntary relief organization in the world, the largest independent Protestant mission organization in North America, and one of the most important centers for strategic planning for Christian mission. The number of sponsored children grew from 8,000 in Korea and Taiwan in 1956 to 23,000 in 1967 (Pierce's last year as World Vision president) to more than 1 million in the 1990's.

Pierce often was unable to control his emotions and time. When Ted Engstrom and other World Vision leaders in the 1960's brought discipline to the organization's accounting procedures and transformed it into a model of financial accountability, Pierce was resentful and he resigned in 1967. Years of constant travel and inadequate attention to diet and sleep took their toll on Pierce's mental and physical health and his relationships with his family, from whom he separated for a period. He spent his last years seeking to recover from a major neurological and psychological breakdown. He died of leukemia in Los Angeles, Calif., leaving as his legacy an organization that continued to grow.

[The Robert Pierce Papers (1947–1978) are located at Samaritan's Purse, Boone, N.C. Books authored by Pierce include *The Untold Korean Story* (1951); *The Korean Orphan Choir* (1965); and *Big Day at Da Me* (1968). Norman B. Rohrer, *Open Arms* (1987), is an able history of the World Vision organization. Pierce's daughter, Marilee P. Dunker, movingly describes the effect on his family of Pierce's constant traveling in the biographical *Days of Glory, Seasons of Night* (1984). See also Richard Gehman, *Let My Heart Be Broken* (1960); Franklin Graham with Jeanette Lockerbie, *Bob Pierce* (1983); and John Robert Hamilton, "An Historical Study of Bob Pierce and World Vision's Development of the Evangelical Social Action Film" (Ph.D. diss., University of Southern California, 1980). An obituary is in *Christianity Today*, Oct. 6, 1978.]

WILLIAM C. RINGENBERG

PISTON, WALTER HAMOR (Jan. 20, 1894–Nov. 12, 1976), composer and teacher, was born in Rockland, Maine, the son of Walter Hamor Piston, a bookkeeper, and Leona Stover. All of his ancestors were of Yankee origin except for his paternal grandfather, Antonio Pistone, who left Italy to resettle in New England. Neither of Piston's parents was particularly musical, nor did he express an interest in music until his early teens.

In 1905 the Piston family moved to Boston, and three years later Walter entered the Mechanic Arts High School, where he studied mechanical drafting and woodworking, all the while hoping to become a painter. He also developed an interest in music, taking piano and violin lessons and playing in the school orchestra. Upon graduating in 1912 at the age of eighteen, Piston worked briefly as a draftsman for the Boston Elevated Railway. Later that year, torn between a career in music and art, he decided to study at the Normal Art School instead of the New England Conservatory of Music since the tuition was free. There he majored in painting and took courses in architectural design and the humanities. He continued his studies in violin and piano and supported himself (as he would for the next ten years) playing both instruments in bands at dance halls, restaurants, and hotels, and at social events.

Piston graduated from the Normal Art School in 1916, enlisted in the United States Navy in 1917, and played saxophone in the Aeronautics Division Band for the next two years. (He learned enough of the instrument in three days to pass the audition.) Stationed at the Massachusetts Institute of Technology, he also found time to study piano at the Boston Musical Association and to play violin in its orchestra. In 1919, after deciding not to pursue a career as an orchestral violinist, Piston enrolled at Harvard University as a special student and a year later, at the age of twenty-six, as a regular student. There he majored in music (taking courses in theory, counterpoint, composition, harmony, and orchestration) and conducted the student orchestra. (He also took courses in English, French, Italian, Greek, European history, and aesthetics.) On Sept. 14, 1920, he married Kathryn Nason, a talented artist and classmate at the Normal Art School. Childless by choice, they remained married for fifty-six years.

Upon graduating from Harvard summa cum laude with Phi Beta Kappa honors in 1924, Piston received a John Knowles Paine Traveling Fellowship from the university and spent the next two years with his wife in Paris, studying composition at the École Normale de Musique with Paul Dukas and privately with Nadia Boulanger, a noted teacher who inspired a generation of composers. He also met a number of prominent musicians and artists who had flocked to Paris.

After returning to the United States in 1926, Piston settled in Belmont, Mass., and accepted a teaching position at Harvard, where he remained until 1960, becoming a full professor in 1944 and Walter Naumburg Professor of Music (a newly endowed chair) seven years later. A popular teacher of music theory and composition, noted for his wide-ranging intellect, wit, and pragmatism, Piston supervised the education of many important scholars and composers, including Leonard Bernstein, Elliott Carter, Jr., and Irving Fine. He wrote four textbooks: *Principles of Harmonic Analysis* (1933), *Harmony* (1941), *Counterpoint* (1947), and *Orchestration* (1955). (The detailed drawings of instruments in the last book are all his own except for one.) All of the texts are noted for their stress on students' deducing basic principles as opposed to learning theoretical rules, and several are still popular at colleges.

Despite his reputation as a teacher, Piston is primarily remembered for his compositions. His seventy-six works, composed over forty years, have established him as one of America's outstanding composers. Averaging three major works every two years, Piston produced a diverse body of masterfully structured compositions (primarily in large classical instrumental forms), including eight symphonies, a ballet titled *The Incredible Flutist* (the suite from which is his most popular work), two violin concertos, five string quartets, and many other chamber pieces for various combinations. Most of his music was commissioned; the Boston Symphony Orchestra premiered eleven of his works between 1927 and 1971. (Serge Koussevitzky, conductor of the orchestra from 1924 to 1949, was an important proponent of Piston's music.)

Piston, who has been called a neoclassicist, developed a modern harmonic and rhythmic vocabulary within classical structures. This is especially true of his early works (1926–1938), which have been described as Gallic, cultivating objectivity, clarity, elegance, and wit. Moreover, they have a distinct international flavor, uniting musical elements of West and East—classical, folk, popular, and jazz. One music historian wrote, "Having assimilated the most important trends in the musical art of our time, he has combined them into a style that bears the imprint of his own personality."

In his later works, especially after 1965, Piston became increasingly personal, lyrical, and complex (especially harmonically). A wide emotional range and great melodic breadth are hallmarks of this style. Classical and romantic elements vie for the forefront, clashing in violent opposition. One historian described his music as "poised and refined on the outside and brooding and passionate on the inside." Another commented on the sense of struggle in Piston's music—"the conflict between clarity and confusion, restraint and sensuality, wit and gloom, and humanity and loneliness." This struggle was in part a reflection of the physical difficulties that plagued Piston during his last years, including diabetes, failing sight and hearing, and a broken hip.

Piston remained a central figure on the American musical scene throughout his career. His numerous honors and prizes include a Guggenheim Fellowship, Coolidge Medal, Naumburg Award, two Pulitzer Prizes (one for his Third Symphony in 1948 and one for his Seventh Symphony in 1961), and three New York Music Critics Circle Awards. He was elected to the National Institute of Arts and Letters in 1938, the American Academy of Arts and Sciences in 1940, and the American Academy of Arts and Letters in 1955. In 1969 the French government decorated him with the Officier dans l'Ordre des Arts et des Lettres, and two years later the governor of Vermont presented him with an award for excellence in the arts. Piston died in Belmont, Mass.

[Piston's papers are in the Boston Public Library and the Library of Congress. See David Ewen, ed., "The Composer Speaks," in *Book of Modern Composers* (1961); and Peter Westergaard, "Conversation with Walter Piston," *Perspectives on New Music*, vol. 7 (1968). For a full-length biography, see Howard Pollack, *Walter Piston* (1982). Also see Howard Pollack, *Harvard Composers: Walter Piston and His Students, From Elliott Carter to Frederic Rzewski* (1992). A shorter source is Oliver Daniel, ed., *Walter Piston* (1964), a booklet celebrating Piston's seventieth birthday. Obituaries are in the *New York Times* and the *Boston Herald*, both Nov. 13, 1976.]

PETER S. GARDNER

PONS, LILY (Apr. 12, 1898–Feb. 13, 1976), coloratura soprano, was born Alice Josephine Pons in Draguignan, France, near Cannes, the daughter of Maria Naso, an Italian, and Auguste Pons, a French engineer and automobile enthusiast. Lily first studied piano as a young child. At age thirteen, she enrolled at the Paris Conservatory, aspiring to become a concert pianist.

Near the end of World War I, Pons became very ill and was forced to discontinue her piano studies for approximately two years. After she recovered from her illness she played piano at French hospitals for wounded soldiers. It was said that one soldier asked her to sing and when the audience stopped applauding, Pons realized that her voice was something out of the ordinary. Soon after Lily convinced the manager of the Théâtre des Variétés, Max Dearly, to hire her as an actress and singer. She was selected to perform a small role in one of the productions. Her talents were immediately acknowledged and many believed Pons was destined for the highest goal of French actors—the Comédie Française—but in 1923 she decided to quit the stage and married August Mesritz, a wealthy retired Dutch lawyer and publisher who was considerably older than Pons. Mesritz recognized Pons's rare talent and encouraged her to concentrate on developing her voice. He arranged for her to study with the renowned Spanish voice teacher Alberti di Gorostiaga, and Pons diligently studied one hour every day for three years with Gorostiaga. It has been said that Pons and her husband even followed Gorostiaga on his vacations in order to avoid missing a lesson.

In 1928, Pons made her operatic debut in the title role of *Lakmé* at the opera house of Mulhouse in Alsace, France. During the next two years she performed in various French provinces. On one such occasion, retired opera singers and artist agents Maria Gay and Giovanni Zenatello heard Pons and encouraged her to audition for the Metropolitan Opera in New York City. At this time, Pons was not well versed in opera repertoire, as were other vocalists aspiring for the Met, but one of the Met's leading coloraturas, Amelita Galli-Curci, was forced to withdraw because of illness and a replacement coloratura was needed. Even though Pons had unimpressive credentials and a limited repertoire of only five opera roles, Zenatello and Gay persuaded Giulio Gatti-Casazza, manager of the Metropolitan Opera, to audition her. Another version of the story has it that Gay and Zenatello heard Pons in Gorostiaga's studio (arranged by the teacher) and were so impressed that they signed a management contract with her, and sent her to the United States to be heard by Gatti-Casazza.

Her audition at the Met led to a five-year contract, and she made her debut in January 1931 at a matinee performance in the title role of *Lucia di Lammermoor*. There were no press releases about the new singer, but when the Met audience heard Pons sing they were quickly enamored of her voice and stage presence. Soon people stood in line at the box office to attend Pons's performances. By March 1931 the relationship with Gay and Zenatello had soured, with Pons claiming that after agent fees she received very little salary. Gay countered that Pons's voice was still undeveloped when they met and that her vocal imperfections were corrected through her influence. Gay took Pons to court, stating that her intervention and expertise made Pons into "a sensation," but both parties decided on an out-of-court settlement.

Pons's voice may not have been as big as those of her coloratura colleagues but in her favor was the ease and clarity with which she sang above high C. She reached high F (more than two octaves above middle C) in the "Bell Song" of *Lakmé*. Her petite stature and good looks were unlike the usual full-figured opera singers. Pons stood five feet tall, weighed ninety-five pounds, and had dark hair and eyes. She sang for twenty-eight seasons with the Met, appearing 198 times in ten roles, most notably the roles of Lucia, Lakmé, Gilda (*Rigoletto*), Rosina (*The Barber of Seville*), Olympia (*The Tales of Hoffman*), Philine (*Mignon*), Amina (*La Sonnambula*), the title role in *Linda di Chamounix*, the Queen of Shemakhan (*Le Coq d'or*), and Marie (*La Fille du Régiment*). Although she was asked to sing in other operas, Lily Pons wisely refused, stating in 1972, "My voice is like a flute. It has projection. No matter how loud the conductor, I never force my voice. . . . I will stay in my repertory—Lucia, Rosina, Gilda—and that's all."

Throughout her singing career, Pons suffered from a nervous stomach before every performance, but her public presence was always professional and regal. In a 1941 *New York Times* interview, conducted in the same year she became an American citizen, Pons said that she changed her opera costumes every year for the public and that she was also superstitious, her lucky number being thirteen. In the public eye, even during her retirement, Pons maintained an air of sophistication and a well-dressed appearance. At one point, she was on the list of America's best-dressed women.

Pons separated from Mesritz in 1931 and two years later they divorced. In 1938 she married musician and conductor André Kostelanetz; they divorced in 1958. Pons also was one of the Metropolitan Opera stars who appeared in major films—*I Dream too Much*, a Jerome Kern musical score with actor Henry Fonda (1935); *That Girl from Paris* (1936); and *Hitting a New High* (1937). In addition to the Met, she performed with opera companies in San Francisco, Chicago, Buenos Aires, Rome, Monte Carlo, Paris, and London. She also made recordings for Columbia Records, appeared on radio and television, and made yearly national and international concert tours. She sang repertoire from opera scenes and popular light classics. For a brief period, Pons also sang regularly on radio with Kostelanetz's orchestra. They also performed together overseas, entertaining American troops during World War II. When she toured the India-Burma war theater, she received the Asiatic-Pacific service ribbon.

Pons celebrated her twenty-fifth anniversary with the Met on Jan. 3, 1956, after which she began singing less frequently. During her Met tenure, Pons maintained homes in New York City and Connecticut. On Apr. 12, 1958, she made her farewell appearance at the Met as Lucia but returned once more for a concert performance in 1960.

During retirement, she moved from New York and bought a home in Palm Springs, Calif., an apartment in Dallas, Tex., where she had several close friends; and a home in Cannes. She was president of the Opera Guild of Palm Springs, which staged familiar opera scenes for elementary schoolchildren in the area.

Even though Pons's singing career had officially ended, she never stopped singing for herself and friends. She became friends with pianist Earl Wild and made an informal tape, with Wild on piano. Still on good terms with his former wife, Kostelanetz invited Pons to appear again with his orchestra, and when he received the informal tape of herself and Wild, Kostelanetz again asked her to perform in concert with him. Pons finally consented in 1972 and appeared with her former husband's orchestra at Philharmonic Hall in New York. She astonished old friends, colleagues, and critics with her vocal performance. Her voice demonstrated remarkable resilience for her age. After a brief illness, Pons died of pancreatic cancer in Dallas.

Pons was not a dramatic singer—she had intonation problems and at times her upper-middle range was inconsistent with the clarity and beauty of her high tones—but no one can deny her feat of singing Lucia's mad scene an octave up from the written part. Among the honors bestowed upon her was chevalier of the French Legion of Honor. A Maryland town was renamed Lilypons in her honor.

[See Lanfranco Rasponi, *The Last Prima Donna* (1982). Obituaries are in the *New York Times*, Feb. 14, 1976; *Variety*, Feb. 18, 1976; and *Opera News*, Apr. 3, 1976.]

JAN SHAPIRO

PORTER, KATHERINE ANNE (May 15, 1890–Sept. 18, 1980), short story writer, novelist, and essayist, was born Callie Russell Porter in Indian Creek, Tex., the daughter of Harrison Boone Porter, a farmer, and Mary Alice Jones. Her mother died shortly before Porter's second birthday. Harrison Porter never recovered from her death. He sold the farm and moved to Kyle, Tex., where his mother, Catherine Anne Porter, raised his children in a strict Methodist household. Despite the severity of her upbringing, Porter loved her grandmother for providing the only love and stability she had ever known. She used Catherine as a model for the leading character in one of her most moving stories, "The Jilting of Granny Weatherall."

After her grandmother's death in 1901, her father moved the family to San Antonio, where Porter studied at the Thomas School for Girls, a private institution that offered training in the dramatic arts. Harrison Porter could not afford to keep her there for more than two years. The family then moved to Victoria, Tex., where Porter and her sister supported the household by giving singing and drama lessons. On June 20, 1906, Porter, aged sixteen, married John Henry Koontz, a twenty-year-old railroad worker on the Southern Pacific. Koontz was a Catholic, and Porter, attracted to the Roman ritual, converted to her husband's faith in 1910. Nevertheless, their marriage did not last. Porter left Koontz in 1914 and traveled to Chicago, where she worked as an extra in movies. After her divorce became final in June 1915, she adopted her grandmother's name, with a slight variation in spelling.

That year, Porter moved to Dallas, where she contracted tuberculosis. While staying at the Carlsbad Sanatorium in Texas, she met Kitty Barry Crawford, who, along with her husband, ran a weekly newspaper, the *Fort Worth Critic*. After Porter recovered, the Crawfords hired her as a reporter and columnist, marking a turning point in her career. She gave up her dreams of the stage and turned her attention to writing. In 1918, Porter accepted a position with the *Rocky Mountain News* in Denver, where she became the drama critic. Her career was interrupted once again, however, when she contracted influenza and almost died during the 1918 epidemic. Porter later used this experience as the basis of her story "Pale Horse, Pale Rider."

In 1919, Porter left Denver for New York City, where she supported herself by doing publicity work and ghostwriting. Living in Greenwich Village, she met several Mexican artists, including Adolpho Best-Maugard. She developed a keen interest in Mexican life and culture, and her enthusiasm led to her writing the story for a ballet by Best-Maugard for Anna Pavlova, which was performed in Mexico in 1923. In the fall of 1920, Porter traveled to Mexico as a correspondent for the *Magazine of Mexico*. Through her friendships with Mexican artists and revolutionaries, she became involved in the country's political struggles and was forced to flee Mexico briefly before being invited to return by President Álvaro Obregón to organize a traveling exhibition of popular Mexican folk art.

Based on her trips to Mexico, Porter wrote "María Concepción" and "The Martyr," both published in *Century Magazine* shortly before her return to New York City. These experiences continued to provide her with material for several more stories over the next ten years, including "Virgin Violeta," "Flowering Judas," "Hacienda," and "That Tree."

In 1925, Porter married Ernest Stock, an Englishman studying at the Art Students League in New York. They lived together briefly in a Connecticut farmhouse, but the marriage failed. The couple later divorced. In August 1927, Porter went to Boston to protest on behalf of Italian political activists Nicola Sacco and Bartolomeo Vanzetti, who had been convicted of murder. She was present at Charlestown prison to witness their executions. The *Never-Ending Wrong*, not published until 1977, is a testament to her involvement with the anarchists' cause. Throughout 1927, Porter did research for a biography of Cotton Mather in Salem, Mass., an effort that was never completed. She also worked on several short stories, including "Magic" and an early version of "The Fig Tree." Returning to New York in 1929, Porter found a job as copy editor at Macaulay and Company. Physically and emotionally ill as the result of an unhappy love affair, Porter spent five months recuperating in Bermuda while writing her biography of Mather.

Her career continued to flourish. "The Jilting of Granny Weatherall" appeared in 1929 in *transition*, one of the leading avant-garde journals of the day; that same year "Theft" was accepted by *Gyroscope*, and the next year *Hound and Horn* published "Flowering Judas," the story that firmly established Porter as a short story writer of the first rank. In April 1930, Porter returned to Mexico. There she met Eugene Dove Pressly, an American working as a secretary at the Crane Foundation. After she was awarded a Guggenheim Fellowship in February 1931, Porter and Pressly sailed for Europe on the SS *Werra*. The trip from Veracruz to Bremen, Germany, provided the inspiration for Porter's best-selling novel *Ship of Fools* (1962).

After their arrival in Germany, Pressly left for Spain in search of a diplomatic position; Porter remained behind in Berlin and worked on "The Leaning Tower" and "The Cracked Looking-Glass." At a party she met Hermann Göring, who accompanied her to a nightclub. Years later, Porter would insist that she had tried to warn the United States of the rising danger of Nazism. In fact, however, there is no evidence to support her claim.

She spent the next two years traveling in Europe, living briefly near Pressly in Basel, Switzerland, where he had been posted. She and Pressly finally settled in Paris, where they were married on Mar. 11, 1933. Although the marriage was beset with problems, Porter's years with Pressly were among her most productive. She published limited editions of *Katherine Anne Porter's French Song-Book* (1933) and *Hacienda* (1934) as well as a commercial edition of *Flowering Judas and Other Stories* (1935). She also published "The Circus" and "The Grave," two of four stories that featured the character Miranda, a young girl who represented in some ways Porter's alter ego.

Porter and Pressly returned to the United States in 1936. Unhappy in her marriage, she left Pressly and stayed at an inn in Doylestown, Pa., where she finished "Noon Wine" and "Old Mortality." Despite an attempted reconciliation in New York, the couple separated in 1937 and divorced on Apr. 9, 1938. Ten days later, Porter married Albert Russel Erskine, a graduate student and business manager of the *Southern Review* whom she had met on a visit to Tennessee. This marriage, too, ended in divorce, on June 19, 1942. Porter, who had no children, never married again.

The publication in 1939 of *Pale Horse, Pale Rider* to highly favorable reviews did much to solidify Porter's reputation. She was invited to writers conferences, appeared on the lecture circuit, and was offered teaching assignments at Stanford, the University of Michigan, and the University of Virginia. She was elected to the American Institute of Arts and Letters in 1941 and appointed a Fellow of the Library of Congress in 1944, the same year Harcourt, Brace published *The Leaning Tower, and Other Stories*.

It was the publication of the best-selling *Ship of Fools*, however, that brought Porter fame as well as fortune. For it, Porter was awarded the Emerson-Thoreau Medal for prose fiction by the American Academy of Arts and Sciences. She also sold the movie rights for more than $400,000. In 1966 *The Collected Stories of Katherine Anne Porter* (1965), generally considered to be Porter's crowning achievement, garnered her both the Pulitzer Prize and the National Book Award. In her last years Porter lived in College Park, Md.; she died in Silver Spring. Her remains were taken back to Indian Creek and placed beside her mother's grave in the small cemetery there.

[Porter's personal papers and manuscripts along with 2,000 volumes of her private library are in the Katherine Anne Porter Room at the McKeldin Library of the University of Maryland, College Park. The Beinecke Rare Book and Manuscript Library at Yale University, the Harry Ransom Center of the University of Texas at Austin, and the Allen Tate and Caroline Gordon collections at Princeton University also contain significant material. See Kathryn Hilt and Ruth M. Alvarez, *Katherine Anne Porter* (1990), for primary and secondary bibliographies.

Joan Givner, *Katherine Anne Porter*, rev. ed. (1991), is the most detailed and accurate biography of Porter. Specialized biographies include Clinton Machann and William Bedford Clark, *Katherine Anne Porter and Texas* (1990); James T. F. Tanner, *The Texas Legacy of Katherine Anne Porter* (1990); and Thomas Walsh, *Katherine Anne Porter and Mexico* (1992). Interviews with Porter are collected in Joan Givner, ed., *Katherine Anne Porter: Conversations* (1987), and in Enrique Hank Lopez, *Conversations with Katherine Anne Porter* (1981). *Katherine Anne Porter* (1988), a documentary, was produced by Films for the Humanities. An obituary is in the *New York Times*, Sept. 19, 1980.]

WILLIAM M. GARGAN

POTOFSKY, JACOB SAMUEL (Nov. 16, 1894–Aug. 5, 1979), labor leader, was born in Radomyshl, Ukraine, Russia, the son of Simon and Rebecca Potofsky. His father managed a glass factory in Kiev before the family immigrated to the United States in 1905. Potofsky continued his elementary education in Chicago, where the family settled. At age fourteen he left school to join his father at work in the garment industry, becoming a floor boy performing odd tasks for the firm of Hart, Schaffner and Marx. Laboring by day, he attended the Chicago Hebrew Institute at night, seeking the knowledge to become what one historian has characterized as a "half-intellectual."

Like many of his Russian-Jewish immigrant peers, Potofsky developed an interest in trade unionism, joining Pantsmakers' Local 144 of the United Garment Workers of America (UGW). In 1910 he participated in a dramatic strike against Hart, Schaffner and Marx, an industrial conflict that reshaped unionism in the garment trades and spawned a new immigrant generation of labor leaders.

Potofsky and his immigrant cohort exemplified a type of unionism that sought to organize all workers, regardless of skill, nationality, or gender, and that merged political and economic action. Partly as a result of the 1910 strike and the socialist unionism represented by Chicago's immigrant clothing workers and garment union members in other cities, the UGW split. Dissatisfied with the policies and practices of the UGW and unable to make their influence felt effectively, the immigrant workers formed their own union in 1914, the Amalgamated Clothing Workers of America (ACW), with Sidney Hillman as president.

Although barely into his twenties, Potofsky had experience as a shop secretary and treasurer of his pantsmakers' local. In 1916, Hillman invited Potofsky to New York to assist in establishing the ACW's national headquarters and to serve as the union's assistant general secretary-treasurer, a position he held for eighteen years.

Potofsky helped to create what rapidly became known as the "new unionism." The ACW practiced a form of unionism unlike that of other American labor organizations. Potofsky and his union endorsed socialism and independent labor politics; stood almost alone in defending the Soviet Union; and built its own small welfare state for members based on union-operated banks, cooperative housing developments, health plans, and educational and recreational programs. Potofsky remarked later in life, that what lies at the core of unionism is "its heart and soul, not its money." By the 1920's, he had a commanding presence: he was nearly six feet tall, with aquiline features and a small Van Dyke beard that made him appear an intellectual, no disgrace within the ACW, which numbered quite a few intellectuals and "half-intellectuals" among its leaders. For three decades (1916–1946) Potofsky served as Hillman's lieutenant, doing "whatever needed to be done in the union."

In 1934, Potofsky married Callie Taylor, a former clothing worker; they had three children. That same year he became assistant president of the ACW, a position he held until 1940. The New Deal years saw Potofsky's role in the labor movement grow, and his politics and philosophy shift. As President Franklin D. Roosevelt's labor policies brightened the prospects for unionism, Potofsky organized the nonunion shirtmakers in New Jersey and eastern Pennsylvania and the textile workers in southern Appalachia. When Hillman and the ACW in 1935 joined John L. Lewis in forming the Committee for Industrial Organization within the American Federation of Labor, Potofsky became a key leader in the new organization, serving as a member of the first executive board of the CIO when it became the independent Congress of Industrial Organizations in 1938.

Politically, Potofsky moved away from his socialist roots, first deserting the Socialist party in 1936 for the New York–based American Labor party and then drifting into the Liberal party (1948) and finally the Democratic party. By the end of the 1930's, Potofsky had committed himself to the New Deal Democratic welfare state, and he worked closely with Hillman to link the CIO's Political Action Committee to the Democratic national party. Also like Hillman and other Jewish-American labor leaders who had once thought of themselves as secular internationalists, Potofsky during the 1930's, in response to the rising threat of Nazism, grew increasingly involved in Jewish community affairs and in the cause of labor Zionism. In 1940, Hillman chose Potofsky to serve as general secretary-treasurer of the ACW, a position of great importance because Hillman devoted himself to serving Roosevelt as a wartime labor adviser.

When Hillman died in 1946, the ACW members turned to Potofsky as his successor. Also in 1946, Potofsky's wife died. In 1951 he married Blanche Lydia Zetland, the widow of a Brazilian exporter.

As president of the ACW from 1946 until his retirement in 1972, Potofsky led the union during a period of hard times for the labor movement. Through aggressive organizing campaigns, the ACW added more than 100,000 new members to the union (reaching a peak of almost 385,000 in 1972), including many southern textile workers and many African-American, Hispanic-American, and Asian-American garment workers. Under Potofsky's leadership, the ACW remained dedicated to social unionism, funding health centers and cooperative housing for members as well as supporting the movement for civil rights.

Potofsky was one of the CIO leaders firmly committed to the reunification of the labor movement through a merger with the AFL consummated in 1955, at which time he became a vice-president and executive council member of the united AFL-CIO. Within the merged labor movement, Potofsky represented a social unionism that endorsed welfare benefits for all citizens, and he urged the labor movement to unite behind John F. Kennedy's New Frontier and Lyndon Johnson's Great Society domestic programs. Potofsky broke with the majority of his colleagues on the AFL-CIO executive council over the war in Vietnam, linking himself and his union to the antiwar movement between 1970 and his retirement in 1972.

At the time of his retirement, Potofsky was one of the last survivors of the generation of labor leaders whose families had left eastern and southern Europe to build a new life in the United States and who turned to trade unionism and the CIO to realize their dreams of a freer and more equal society. Potofsky exemplified the amalgamation of Yiddish culture, secular socialist unionism, labor Zionism, and labor Americanism into what became an American version of social democracy. Potofsky died in New York City.

[The Potofsky Papers are part of the records of the Amalgamated Clothing Workers of America, housed at the Labor-Management Documentation Center, Catherwood Library, New York State School of Industrial and Labor Relations, Cornell University. Part of the collection is available on microfilm through University Publications of America. Steve Fraser, *Labor Will Rule, Sidney Hillman and the Rise of American Labor* (1991), surpasses all previous histories of the ACW and offers the fullest account of the union and reform circles in which Potofsky moved. An obituary is in the *New York Times*, Aug. 6, 1979.]

MELVYN DUBOFSKY

POTTER, CHARLES EDWARD (Oct. 30, 1916–Nov. 23, 1979), United States senator, was born in Lapeer, Mich., one of three children of farmers Fred Potter and Sarah Elizabeth Converse. Potter attended public schools in Lapeer, where he was active in football and track. He entered Michigan State Normal College (now Eastern Michigan University) at Ypsilanti in 1934, where he studied social science and supported himself by working in a sawmill, a cannery, and an automobile plant. During senior year he also worked part-time as a social worker in Ypsilanti, and he received his B.A. degree in 1938.

Potter was administrator of the Cheboygan County Bureau of Social Aid from 1938 to 1942. He married Lorraine Esther Eddy on Nov. 25, 1939. The couple had no children.

Potter enlisted in the United States Army in May 1942, completed the officers training course, and was commissioned a second lieutenant the following December. He served with the Twenty-eighth Infantry Division in France, Luxembourg, and Germany, and was wounded three times. A land mine in Colmar, France, damaged both of Potter's legs during the Battle of the Bulge in 1945; and one was amputated at the knee and the other at the hip. He recuperated at the Walter Reed Hospital and received an honorable discharge as a major in July 1946. He was awarded the Silver Star, Bronze Star, the French croix de guerre, and three Purple Hearts.

Potter began work in 1946 as a vocational rehabilitation adviser for the United States Department of Labor Retraining and Reemployment Administration in Washington, D.C. He resigned that position in June 1947 to return to Michigan and to campaign as the Republican candidate for the House of Representatives seat of the late Frederick V. Bradley in the Eleventh District. He won the Aug. 26, 1947, special election by a two-to-one vote, and was reelected in 1948 and 1950.

While a member of the House of Representatives, Potter took a conservative stand on domestic issues but a liberal internationalist position on foreign policy. His voting record mirrored that of the senior Michigan senator, Arthur H. Vandenberg, who was Potter's political mentor. Potter became a member of the Education and Labor Committee and the House Committee on Un-American Activities. In the latter post he was instrumental in reopening a congressional investigation of Communist influence in the Hollywood film industry.

Vandenberg's death in 1952 resulted in a four-way Republican primary contest for his vacated Senate seat. Potter won the nomination and faced the Democratic candidate, Blair Moody, in the general election. Potter accused Moody of being a "captive of the little band of overlords who rule the CIO" (Congress of Industrial Organizations) and a minion of "Moscow-trained" CIO president Walter Reuther. Senator Joseph R. McCarthy of Wisconsin went to Michigan to campaign for Potter, who won the election by a wide majority.

Potter entered the United States Senate along with the first Republican majority in two decades. He became a member of the Interstate and Foreign Commerce Committee, where he regularly supported the Eisenhower administration's foreign policy programs, including its proposed development of the St. Lawrence Seaway. Potter was also a member of the committees on appropriations, government operations, and rules and administration.

Potter was also appointed a member of the Senate Subcommittee on Permanent Investigations, which held hearings during spring 1954 on charges brought by the United States Army against Senator McCarthy. During the course of the hearings Potter became convinced that Senator McCarthy's aide, Roy Cohn, had attempted to exercise improper influence on army officials. Potter signed the majority committee report, which criticized McCarthy and his aides but also issued his own independent report, which also criticized army officials. In the later Senate vote to censure McCarthy, Potter voted in favor of censure. Because Potter had an indisputably anti-Communist record his opposition to McCarthy marked the end of the latter's influence.

Potter had no primary challengers in 1958, but he faced a popular Democratic candidate, Philip Hart in the general election. Hart was a former United States attorney who had made a name for himself by prosecuting Communists in the early 1950's and was then elected Michigan lieutenant governor by a five-to-one margin. Hart had the strong support of the automobile industry's labor unions, and Republican candidates were hampered by the 1958 recession, which was attributed to the fiscal policies of the Eisenhower administration. Hart defeated Potter by a wide margin in the 1958 general election.

Because Potter had been a strong supporter of the Eisenhower administration while in the Senate, the president offered him the post of under secretary of commerce after his electoral defeat. Potter declined the offer and retired to a farm in suburban Queenstown, Md. He later became active in real estate ventures and lobbying. Potter registered as a lobbyist for the Committee of American Tanker Owners, Inc. On May 11, 1960, Potter married his second wife, Mary Elizabeth Bryant Wismer, a widow with two children.

In 1965 he founded the real estate and securities brokerage firm Charles E. Potter Company. That same year he published *Days of Shame*, which discussed his role in the Army-McCarthy Hearings. Potter described the time as "a period of strange and hysterical nonsense, brought on by a haunted man who had an overpowering need to be the center of attraction but whose ambitions had no substance."

During his post-Senate years Potter also acted as a fund-raiser for the Republican party. In 1972, during President Richard M. Nixon's administration, he joined the Finance Committee of the Committee to Re-Elect the President (CREEP), which later attained notoriety during the unfolding of the Watergate scandal. Although John Mitchell, Maurice Stans, and many CREEP members were indicted, tried, and received prison terms, Potter was not touched by the scandal. In possible deference to his Senate experience and physical condition, Potter was not even called to testify at any of the numerous congressional hearings.

Before the full scandal came to light, Potter accepted an appointment as one of three trustees in charge of President Nixon's leftover campaign funds, the Campaign Liquidation Trust, which totaled approximately $3.5 million. Potter disagreed with fellow trustee Stans over the use of the campaign funds for payment of the rapidly mounting legal bills of indicted Watergate defendants. Potter refused to use the trust funds to pay the legal expenses of anyone who did not hold an official position in the campaign organization, such as White House Chief of Staff H. R. Haldeman, presidential counselor John Ehrlichman, and Nixon himself. Potter also insisted that the trust fund provide reimbursement for legal fees of campaign officials indicted on felony charges only if they were found innocent.

In 1972 he also founded Potter International, Inc., a consulting and public relations firm.

Potter was also a director of the National Capitol Life Insurance Company and associated with several other business firms involved in business consulting and sales of securities and real estate, including Swesnick, Blum and Potter Securities Corporation, the International Development and Engineering Company, and Potter and Kornmeier International.

Potter died in Washington, D.C., and was buried in Arlington National Cemetery in Virginia.

[Potter's papers are at the Michigan Historical Collection of the University of Michigan, Ann Arbor. Relevant papers are also located in the Homer Ferguson Papers at the same location and in the Arthur Vandenberg Collection at Clarke Historical Library at Central Michigan University in Mount Pleasant. Potter's role in the McCarthy hearings is mentioned in Roy Cohn, *McCarthy* (1968); Robert Griffith, *The Politics of Fear* (1970); Lately Thomas, *When Even Angels Wept* (1973); and Richard M. Fried, *Men Against McCarthy* (1976). Potter's involvement with the Campaign Fund Liquidation Trust is described in the *Washington Post*, Mar. 30 and Aug. 14, 1974. An obituary is in the *Washington Post*, Nov. 25, 1979.]

STEPHEN G. MARSHALL

POWERS, FRANCIS GARY (Aug. 17, 1929–Aug. 1, 1977), pilot and espionage agent, was born in Burdine, Ky., one of six children of Ida Ford and Oliver Powers. His father, a coal miner, encouraged young Gary to seek a career that would pay more money than coal mining. Powers, ever since his first flight at the age of fourteen, dreamed of nothing but flying.

Oliver Powers moved his family to Detroit, Mich., so that he could work in a defense plant during the last year of World War II. When the war ended, he moved his family to Virginia, where Gary completed his high school education at Grundy High School in Pound, Va. After high school he entered Milligan College in Johnson City, Tenn., intending to pursue premedical studies. In his junior year, he dropped out of the premedical program but continued to study biology and chemistry. In his senior year, he applied for the Air Force cadets, and upon graduation from college in 1950 he joined the Air Force as an airman. After finishing basic training, he entered flying school as a second lieutenant and in 1952 achieved the rank of first lieutenant. He met and married Barbara Gay Moore, a secretary at Turner Air Force Base near Albany, Ga., where he was stationed. They were married in April 1954.

In late 1955, Powers and several other pilots were recruited by Major William Collins to work for the Central Intelligence Agency (CIA). By joining the agency, he officially had to resign his commission in the Air Force, purportedly becoming Francis G. Palmer, a pilot for the Lockheed Aircraft Corporation. In reality, he and the other military pilots began training to fly the U-2 reconnaissance aircraft. (The CIA had worked with Lockheed to develop the U-2 aircraft, specifically designed for high-altitude photoreconnaissance flights in order to observe Soviet military installations.) Powers and the other pilots signed an agreement stating they would fly espionage missions over the Soviet Union for the CIA for three years then return to the military with ranks equal to those airmen who stayed in the Air Force. As cover for their flights, he and the other pilots were stationed with a Second Weather Observation Squadron informally known as Detachment 10-10 based at Incirlik Air Force Base near Adana, Turkey. From there, they flew to Pakistan, the starting point of their reconnaissance flights.

On May 1, 1960, following a period of reduced flights during temporary warming of relations between the United States and the Soviet Union, Powers undertook what was termed to be a normal surveillance flight from Peshwar, Pakistan to Bodo, Norway. Powers piloted United States Air Force U-2 reconnaissance plane #360 across the Soviet Union. As the plane approached the Russian city of Sverdlovsk, a Soviet missile battery spotted the plane and hit it with a surface-to-air missile. Powers tried desperately to keep the craft in the air, but it had been severely damaged and he had to bail out over Soviet territory.

When Powers ejected, the stunned Sverdlovsk townspeople rushed to his aid thinking he was a Soviet air force pilot. They detained Powers but did not treat him harshly even when they learned that they were holding a United States Air Force pilot. Had the plane been destroyed by the explosive charges on board or by the impact of the crash, Powers might have been able to convince the Soviets he was not an American pilot. However, the explosives failed to detonate, and the crash did not destroy all the physical evidence. Soviet authorities took the remains of the airplane to Moscow for further examination.

When CIA officials lost contact with Powers, the National Aeronautics and Space Administration which was in charge of the cover mission, immediately issued a statement that it had lost contact with a weather observation airplane near the Soviet border. Soviet premier Nikita Khrushchev released evidence to show this was not the case, and as he brought forth more and more material obtained from Powers and the plane's wreckage, it became clear that Powers was the pilot of a military photoreconnaissance plane and had conducted espionage against the Soviet Union.

The Soviets, especially Khrushchev, were enraged to learn that the United States was spying on them during a supposed thaw in Soviet-American relations. The premier ended a summit conference designed to lessen Cold War tensions and open more formal relations between the two superpowers. At first the United States tried to deny the incident, saying it was not true. Eventually, in the face of overwhelming evidence, President Eisenhower admitted the espionage flights.

Powers's own damning testimony before a Soviet court revealed that he had knowingly violated Soviet airspace under orders of the Central Intelligence Agency. He provided a comprehensive account of the events leading up to the crash of the U-2. Powers pleaded guilty to the charges against him and the Soviet court sentenced him to ten years in prison. He had only served two years when a spy swap was arranged. On Feb. 10, 1962, Powers was taken to Glienicker Bridge, which spanned the Havel River and connected East and West Germany. He was told to walk to the other end of the bridge; simultaneously, American intelligence officials released the celebrated Soviet agent Rudolf Abel at the other end.

Powers returned home to confront many people who were ashamed that he had not committed suicide or at least remained silent. His wife considered him to be a "coward, not a hero." Their marriage, which had been strained before the incident, collapsed under the turmoil surrounding his actions. They were divorced in February 1963.

For a short time after he returned to the United States, Powers worked for the Air Force, but he soon resigned and rejoined the CIA full-time at its headquarters in Virginia, instructing U-2 pilots on what to do if they were ever downed over enemy territory. During his brief employment in Virginia he met and later married Claudia Edwards Downey, a psychometrist (a statistical measurer of variables for psychological tests) employed by the CIA. They were married on Oct. 24, 1963, and had one child.

In the late 1960's, Powers moved to southern California, where he worked on the U-2 project at a Lockheed plant in suburban Van Nuys. While working there he wrote a book about his experiences entitled *Operation Overflight* (1970). Shortly after the book was published, Powers was fired from his job at Lockheed. Longing to return to flying, he went to work for Los Angeles radio station KGIL as a traffic reporter. During the early 1970's he left KGIL and went to work for an aircraft communications firm, then returned to KGIL.

In November 1976, Powers was hired as a helicopter traffic reporter for KNBC in Los Angeles. On Aug. 1, 1977, he was flying over Encino, Calif., when his helicopter ran out of fuel. Unable to return to Van Nuys Airport, Powers crashed near a Little League baseball field. He and George Spears, a cameraman who had been covering brushfires near Santa Barbara, Calif., were killed in the crash. Some believed Powers's death was part of a conspiracy, since they could not believe that such an experienced pilot would have let his aircraft run out of fuel. President Jimmy Carter granted permission for him to be buried in Arlington National Cemetery.

Even in death, Powers was able to shed more light on the shadowy U-2 program. After the funeral, his uncle introduced the press to a longtime friend of his nephew's, Sammy Snipes. Snipes had been one of Powers's fellow U-2 pilots and the press conference was the first time he had acknowledged this to anyone, even his family.

[David Wise and Thomas B. Ross, *The U-2 Affair* (1963), is a complete account of the incident. Barbara Powers, *Spy Wife* (1965), provides unique insights from the perspective of a spy's wife. Francis Gary Powers and Kurt Gentry, *Operation Overflight* (1970), is a firsthand account of the incident. Michael R. Beschloss, *MAYDAY* (1986), is a comprehensive account. Francis Gary Powers and Harold S. Burman, trans., *The Trial of the U-2* (1960), is a compilation of Powers's testimony and translation of eyewitness accounts and testimony given in the Soviet Supreme Court about the incident. Fred J. Cook, *The U-2 Incident* (1973), written for children, provides a wealth of valuable information not detailed in other sources. An obituary is in the *New York Times*, Aug, 2, 1977.]

BRIAN B. CARPENTER

PRESLEY, ELVIS ARON (Jan. 8, 1935–Aug. 16, 1977), singer and actor, was born in Tupelo, Miss., the surviving twin of a stillborn brother, Jessie Garon. His father, Vernon Elvis Presley, was a sharecropper, laborer, and truck driver who spent two and a half years in Parchman Penitentiary for check forgery when Elvis was a young boy; his mother, Gladys Love Smith, was a housewife and part-time nurse's aide. As a boy in Tupelo, Presley soaked up music by attending the First Assembly of God Church and by listening to popular music on the radio. In 1945 his mother bought him a guitar and instruction book and he taught himself to play. That year, at the age of ten, he won second prize at the Children's Day of the Mississippi-Alabama Fair and Dairy Show, singing "Old Shep."

The Presley family moved to Memphis, Tenn., in September 1948 and found an apartment in a public housing project. Presley majored in shopwork at the L. C. Humes High School, where he won the senior talent show with another rendition of "Old Shep." He graduated in 1953 and worked first on a munitions assembly line and then as a truck driver, while studying to become an electrician. He was still listening to popular music—country music, white and black gospel music, and black rhythm and blues—on the radio, on records, and in Memphis music halls and nightclubs. He dreamed of becoming a movie star (he patterned his hair after motion-picture actor Tony Curtis) and of becoming a singer (he patterned his crooning style after Dean Martin). He began singing during musicians' breaks at a nightclub on the outskirts of Memphis.

In the summer of 1953, soon after high school graduation, he visited the Memphis Recording Service, home of Sam Phillips's Sun Records. Presley wanted to record something for his mother, and he left with an acetate disk of "My Happiness" and "That's When Your Heartaches Begin." At the time, Sun Records was a struggling label for black rhythm and blues artists, and Phillips was looking for a white singer who could "sing black." A year later, Phillips was still trying to break black rhythm and blues into the white market. He remembered Presley and called him back to the studio. The session that took place on July 5, 1954, was one of the great events in popular musical history. Backed up by two local musicians, Bill Black on bass and Scotty Moore on guitar, Presley began running through the songs he knew by Arthur Crudup, a popular black writer and blues singer. The session did not go well until Presley began improvising on the Crudup song "That's All Right, Mama." Phillips suddenly heard something startling. Presley's ringing, bell-like voice and his tightly controlled, wild energy had transformed Crudup's growl of resentment into a joyous, barbarous yawp of liberation. It was a definitive moment, arguably the birth of rock and roll.

"That's All Right" was released on July 19, 1954, with a cut of "Blue Moon of Kentucky" on the flip side. First aired on Dewey Phillips's Memphis radio program, the song was an immediate and enormous hit. Presley quickly followed it with "Good Rocking Tonight," a hard-driving rock song, and signed with impresario Colonel Thomas A. Parker. He continued to record hit after hit while touring large and small towns across the South as the Hillbilly Cat. He appeared on the "Grand Ole Opry" radio program and became a regular on the weekly "Louisana Hayride" radio broadcast. His records began moving from the regional charts onto the national hit lists. His first nationwide hit was "Baby, Let's Play House" in July 1955, and Phillips sold Presley's contract and five master disks to RCA Victor for $35,000. In April 1956, "Heartbreak Hotel," Presley's first recording for RCA, was an unprecedented number one on all three charts: country, pops, and rhythm and blues.

During 1956, while his records dominated the market, Presley appeared on all the major network television variety shows, first on the Jan. 18, 1956, "Stage Show," produced by Jackie Gleason and hosted by the Dorsey brothers, then on the "Milton Berle Show" (twice) and the "Steve Allen Show." The most notable was his third appearance on the "Ed Sullivan Show" on Jan. 6, 1957, when cameras showed him only from the waist up to hide his gyrations during his performance. His string of hits in 1957 and 1958 included "I Want You, I Need You, I Love You," "Blue Suede Shoes," "Hound Dog," "Don't Be Cruel," "Love Me

Tender," "Too Much," "All Shook Up," "That's When Your Heartaches Begin," "(Let Me Be Your) Teddy Bear," "Loving You," "Jailhouse Rock," "Don't," "Blue Christmas," "Trouble," "Wear My Ring Around Your Neck," "Hard Headed Woman," "One Night," "A Fool Such As I," and "A Big Hunk of Love."

Presley's film career began in 1956, with *Love Me Tender*, followed by *Loving You* and *Jailhouse Rock* in 1957 and *King Creole* in 1958.

Presley's spectacular success had as much to do with changes in American culture as with his own talents, formidable though they were. In retrospect, it is clear that a youth culture was developing that would make young whites receptive to Elvis's mimicry of the hip, sexually liberated, irreverent stances of the black male subculture. A tidal wave of black musical creativity was ready to sweep over the mainstream white audience. Presley was the catalyst, but he was more: his voice, face, and body communicated a sense of freedom that American youth craved in the 1950's, and he artfully learned how to give teenagers just what they needed to drive them out of their minds. And, as it happened, American youth culture's desire for this liberation was an international phenomenon, and so Elvis became the agent for making American rock and roll the first truly global popular culture.

Presley's career was interrupted when he was inducted into the United States Army on Mar. 4, 1958. He served for two years, mostly in the Third Armored Division in Friedberg, Germany. When he returned to the United States in 1960, his mother was dead, and he gave himself over completely to the schemes of Colonel Parker, who encapsulated him in a deadening series of twenty-seven formula films between 1960 and 1969. In films such as *G.I. Blues* (1960), *Blue Hawaii* (1961) *Girls! Girls! Girls!* (1962), *Fun in Acapulco* (1963), *Paradise Hawaiian Style* (1966), *Clambake* (1967), *Speedway* (1968), and *The Trouble with Girls* (1969), Presley was reduced to an embarrassing self-caricature, with only the occasional electrifying musical number to remind audiences why he was a star. Contractually limited to recording only songs from the movie sound tracks, his musical career declined.

On Dec. 3, 1968, Presley made his first television performance in eight years—the legendary 1968 comeback special, sponsored by the Singer Company. It featured a lean, dynamic Presley costumed in black leather, pounding through twenty-seven numbers, including "If I Can Dream," which became his first hit in years. A hit album followed, *From Elvis in Memphis*, and then more hits, such as "In the Ghetto," "Kentucky Rain," and "Suspicious Minds." Presley capped his success by signing a long-term contract to headline at the International Hotel (now the Hilton) in Las Vegas, Nev., performing a pair of month-long shows a year, from July 1970 until his death in 1977. Including road shows, Presley gave a total of 1,126 live performances during this period. Heavily into the martial arts, he choreographed his performances with karate kicks and thrusts; his lavishly arranged numbers were backed by an enormous orchestra with triumphal effects; and his chief influence became Tom Jones, a master of the Las Vegas musical art.

No matter how much he and his entourage misunderstood and misused it, Presley still had a monumental talent, which he displayed in one more notable television special, *Aloha from Hawaii*, on Jan. 12, 1973, which featured Presley's hit version of "My Way" and was beamed by satellite for worldwide viewing. *Aloha* attracted the largest television audience in history up to that time.

On Oct. 9, 1973, Presley divorced his wife, Priscilla Ann Beaulieu Presley, whom he had met in Germany when she was fourteen. They had been married on May 1, 1967, and had one daughter. After his divorce, Presley embarked on a period of self-indulgence. A binge eater who never lost his taste for the fat-laden southern cooking of his boyhood, he had to be stuffed into his lavish Las Vegas costumes. His lifestyle of women, drugs, and a potentate-like entourage was coupled with a fog of theosophy and martial arts. His obesity and consumption of prescription drugs made his stage shows grotesque, although even in his last concerts his magnificent voice could make a song such as "Unchained Melody," in which he accompanied himself on the piano, an unforgettable and awe-inspiring experience. He died of heart-failure, brought on by cumulative drug abuse, at Graceland, his mansion in Memphis. The funeral was on a scale befitting a king. More than 100,000 attended the wake. The governor of Mississippi declared a day of mourning. In Tennessee, the governor had the state's flags lowered to half mast. President Jimmy Carter issued a tribute from the White House. The casket rode to the cemetery in a white Cadillac limousine, preceded by a silver Cadillac, trailed by sixteen more white Cadillacs, the "Mystery Train" of Elvis's classic recording, which was "sixteen coaches long." His tomb, now relocated to Graceland, is the most visited grave in America.

Presley—a legend in life—was no less so in death. The Elvis myth centers on Graceland and on a staggering production of Elvis kitsch and collectibles. His fans' posthumous veneration of Elvis is part self-parodistic, part sincere. There is accurate insight in the attention American popular culture pays to Presley: his career was significant. By ushering in the age of rock, he redefined American popular music and produced music that will be loved as long as rock and roll endures. Presley helped shift the criterion of American popular music from European to black American standards of musical excellence. He also helped redefine the American idea of success. Before Presley, social status meant conforming to the American pseudoaristocracy's pretension for the sophisticated and selective European tradition. After him, the dreams of the masses ruled. In Presley there was something like the apotheosis of the democratic idea, both its apogee and its nadir; for better or worse, his was greatness in the democratic mode.

As befits a mythic hero, alleged sightings of Presley after his death have received attention in the popular press. Scores of professional Elvis impersonators have held their own conventions. Rock singers such as Alannah Myles ("Black Velvet") and Laurie Anderson ("Hiawatha") have sung about him, and rock groups have continued to pay him tribute by recording his songs. His legendary status gained official recognition on Jan. 8, 1993, when a portrait of Presley graced the first commemorative postage stamp dedicated to a rock and roll singer. It had the largest printing (500 million) of any commemorative in history, yet it sold out almost immediately.

[There are extensive collections of Presley memorabilia at Graceland and at the Elvis Hall of Fame in Gatlinburg, Tenn. A guide to such material and more is Jane and Michael Stern, *Elvis World* (1987). CD boxed-set reissues of his songs include *Elvis, The King of Rock 'n' Roll: The Complete Fifties Masters* (1992) and *From Nashville to Memphis: The Essential '60s Masters* (1993). His films are all available on video, as are his 1968 Singer television special and *Aloha from Hawaii*. Biographical works include Jerry Hopkins, *Elvis* (1971); Albert Goldman, *Elvis* (1981); Dave Marsh, *Elvis* (1982); Elaine Dundy, *Elvis and Gladys* (1985); Priscilla Beaulieu Presley, *Elvis and Me* (1985); and Peter Guralnick, *Last Train to Memphis: The Rise of Elvis Presley* (1993). For detailed chronologies of his life, see Wendy Sauers, *Elvis Presley: a Complete Reference* (1984); Lee Cotton, *All Shook Up: Elvis Day-by-Day, 1954–1977* (1985); and Patricia Pierce, *The Ultimate Elvis: Elvis Presley Day by Day* (1994). For analysis of his music and the legend, see Greil Marcus, *Mystery Train* (1975), and *Dead Elvis* (1991); Robert Matthew-Walker, *Elvis Presley: A Study in Music* (1979); and Joseph A. Tunzi, *Elvis Sessions: The Complete Recorded Music of Elvis Presley, 1953–1977* (1993). See also the documentary *Elvis, The Great Performances* (1990); among the better docudramas are *Elvis* (1990) and *Elvis and the Colonel* (1993). An obituary is in the *New York Times*, Aug. 17, 1977.]

RICHARD GID POWERS

PRIMA, LUIGI ("LOUIS") (Dec. 7, 1911–Aug. 24, 1978), jazz trumpeter, singer, and composer, was born in New Orleans, La. His older brother, Leon, was a professional trumpeter, and a sister, Mary Ann, performed on the piano. Initially, Prima studied the violin. He began his study on the trumpet at age nine and progressed so rapidly that at age eleven he formed a highly successful band that featured Irving Fazola.

Upon graduation from Jesuit High School in New Orleans, Prima performed with his own band at local nightclubs. He later toured and performed in Chicago, New York City, and Los Angeles. In 1932 and 1934 he performed with Red Nichols and His Five Pennies in Cleveland. He also appeared regularly in the orchestras of the Saenger Theater and Loew's State in New Orleans.

Prima's musical style was both unique and entertaining. Known more for being an entertainer than a jazz trumpet virtuoso, he patterned himself after Louis Armstrong. At best, Prima was a clowning entertainer who used obnoxious language even when performing duets with the band's female singers, Lily Ann Carol and Keely Smith. His typical performance included some acrobatics and comedy supported by a high-energy show.

From the 1930's through 1973, Prima recorded extensively and appeared in many commercial films. From 1939 to 1942 he invested in and operated a small recording company.

Prima had residences during this period in New York City and New Orleans.

High-energy performances brought him the opportunity to accompany well-known musicians in films. His film appearances include *Swing It*, with Pee Wee Russell (1936); *After the Thin Man* (1936); *Manhattan Merry-Go-Round*, with "Cab" Calloway (1936); *Swing Cats Jamboree* (1938); *Rose of Washington Square* (1939); *New Orleans Blues* (1943); *Rhythm Masters* (1948); *Shack out on 101* (1955); *The Benny Goodman Story* (1956); *Jazz Ball* (1956); *The Wildest* (1957); *Senior Prom*, with Bob Crosby (1958); *Hey Boy! Hey Girl!* (1959); *Twist All Night* (1961); *Playgirls International* (1963); *The Man Called Flintstone* (1966); *The Jungle Book* (1967); *A Summer Without Boys* (1973); and *Rafferty and the Gold Dust Twins* (1975).

Coupled with his appearance in many films was Prima's recording of such popular hits as "Sing, Sing, Sing," "Little Boy Blew His Top," "Robin Hood," "It's the Rhythm in Me," "A Sunday Kind of Love," and "That Old Black Magic."

Throughout the 1950's and 1960's, Prima toured with his own big band. In 1953, he married his vocalist, Keely Smith; they were divorced in 1961. He married Gia Maione in 1963; they had two children.

Prima died in New Orleans, of pneumonia, having been in a coma for three years following brain surgery.

[See Al Rose, *I Remember Jazz* (1987); Richard S. Sears, *V-Discs: A History and Discography* (1980); Arnold Shaw, *Black Popular Music in America* (1986); and Garry Boulard, *Just a Gigolo: The Life and Times of Louis Prima* (1989).]

LEMUEL BERRY, JR.

PRINZE, FREDDIE (June 22, 1954–Jan. 29, 1977), comedian and actor, was born in New York City, the only child of Karl Prinze, a tool-and-die maker, and Mary Prinze, a factory worker. Prinze, who jokingly called himself a "Hungarican," developed much of his humor from his mixed ethnicity. His mother, a Puerto Rican Roman Catholic who spoke little English, urged her son to attend mass every Sunday; his father, a Hungarian Jew who spoke three languages, sent his son to a Lutheran elementary school. Prinze grew up on West 157th Street in the predominantly Puerto Rican neighborhood of Washington Heights on Manhattan's Upper West Side. His childhood friends described him as an overweight child who joined local street gangs for his own protection. Prinze, however, never engaged in physical fights; he used his quick wit to cut down his adversaries.

Prinze enrolled in the High School for the Performing Arts with strong interests in ballet and drama but soon realized that his grandest talent lay in his unique street humor. Drawing on his ethnic background to develop his trademark characterization of Puerto Rican street life, he performed in Manhattan nightclubs, including the Improv and Catch a Rising Star. He left high school in 1973, lacking enough credits to graduate, and dedicated himself to a career in entertainment. He continued to work the New York club circuit, often without pay.

Prinze's rise to national success was meteoric. In 1973, just months after he left high school, he was invited to make his television debut on the "Jack Paar Show." It was his appearance on the "Tonight Show Starring Johnny Carson" in December 1973, however, that launched his career. Television producer James Komack saw Prinze's performance on the "Tonight Show" and, shortly thereafter, cast him in a costarring role in a new television series. Set in the East Los Angeles barrio, "Chico and the Man" pitted an ill-tempered Anglo automobile mechanic (Jack Albertson) against his wisecracking Chicano employee (Prinze), focusing on the ethnic and generational differences between the two characters. The show premiered on NBC in September 1974 and was an immediate hit.

Following the success of "Chico and the Man," Prinze was catapulted from the street life of Washington Heights to the glamorous, high-profile life of a Hollywood celebrity. He made numerous appearances on television specials, completed his only television movie, *The Million Dollar Ripoff* (1976), and performed his stand-up routine in Las Vegas. In October 1975, Prinze married Katherine Elaine Cochran; they had one child.

Prinze did not cope well with his sudden and enormous success. His initial love affair with Hollywood quickly faded, and he made offhand remarks to friends about taking his own life. He developed an alarming dependency on drugs, often taking an excess of tranquilizers, especially quaaludes, to calm himself. His problems eventually devastated his marriage, and in December 1976 his wife filed for divorce. Ironically, Prinze's personal problems did not detract from his professional success. "Chico and the Man" continued to be one of the most-watched television shows. Prinze appeared as a guest host on the "Tonight Show," and more appearances were scheduled. In January 1977 he performed at President Jimmy Carter's pre-inaugural celebration in Washington, D.C. Despite his professional success, however, Prinze was rapidly succumbing to the pressures of public life.

During the early morning hours of Jan. 28, 1977, Prinze's depression overcame him. Facing a charge of driving under the influence of drugs, a legal challenge from a former business associate, and his impending divorce, Prinze made numerous telephone calls to his family and friends. Business manager and close friend Marvin Snyder arrived at Prinze's hotel room in West Los Angeles just as Prinze ended a telephone conversation with his estranged wife, drew a loaded gun, and shot himself in the head. Prinze died the next day in a Los Angeles hospital. In response to a legal action brought by Prinze's mother to recover claims on several life insurance policies, a jury determined that his death was not suicide because he was under the influence of drugs when he shot himself.

[An account of Prinze's shooting and an obituary are in the *New York Times*, Jan. 29 and 30, 1977, respectively.]

FRANK MORROW

PURTELL, WILLIAM ARTHUR (May 6, 1897–May 31, 1978), United States senator and manufacturer, was born in Hartford, Conn., the son of Thomas M. Purtell and Nora O'Connor, tobacco workers in the Connecticut River Valley. He became a newsboy at age eight, a grocery errand boy at age ten, and at age thirteen he added the job of janitor of an apartment house. He left school at age fifteen to work full-time as a water boy on a construction site. He was also a file clerk in an insurance office and a car checker in the New Haven Railroad freight yards. Purtell was never ashamed that he had to leave high school to support his family, but he became defensive when anyone pointed out his lack of education.

Purtell enlisted in the United States Army during World War I, served overseas in the radio section of the Signal Corps (1918–1919), and was discharged as a corporal. During the war, he became engaged to Katherine Cassidy, a nurse serving with the Allied Expeditionary Forces. They were married Dec. 30, 1919, and had two children.

After his marriage, Purtell joined a Hartford manufacturing concern as a salesman. In 1929, on the proverbial shoestring, he and a few friends organized the Holo-Krome Screw Corporation, using several of Purtell's inventions to produce high-quality screws. It was one of the first nonunion Connecticut firms to have an employee profit-sharing program and to pay wages comparable with those of similar, unionized industries in the area.

Just before World War II, Purtell was named president, treasurer, and general manager of Billings and Spencer, an almost bankrupt Hartford firm that manufactured forging machinery and tools; he was chairman of the board from 1944 to 1947. After reorganizing it, assuring employees that their jobs were secure, and making the company an important contributor to the war effort, he left in 1947. He remained president of Holo-Krome until 1952. During these years, Purtell was also involved with Sparmal Engineering Corporation (1938–1952), Colts Manufacturing Company, Hartford Connecticut Trust Company, Veeder-Root, Hartford Gas Company, and National Fire Insurance Company.

In 1950 the politically inexperienced Purtell was an unsuccessful candidate for the Republican gubernatorial nomination against John Davis Lodge. Nevertheless, on May 27, 1952, at the Republican state convention, he was nominated to oppose Senator William Benton. Warned that a manufacturer was considered "poison" as a candidate for elective office, Purtell determined to learn the reasons for this attitude. In an article for the *Saturday Evening Post* (Apr. 5, 1952), he listed them as the failure of manufacturers to communicate well with workers, the inability of manufacturers to abandon a naturally conservative role, and the willingness of manufacturers to let politicians be the leaders.

On Aug. 29, 1952, Purtell was appointed by Governor Lodge to fill the vacant Senate seat of the recently deceased Brien McMahon, a Democrat, until a successor could be elected in November. Purtell was in the unusual position of filling one Senate seat while running for the other, but because his Senate service could not be continuous, he gained no seniority by the appointment. Purtell accepted the appointment in order to change the things he was always complaining about.

Purtell conducted his campaign on the issues of the Korean War, Communism, and corruption, and he changed his mind about having Senator Joseph R. McCarthy of Wisconsin, a foe of Benton, campaign for him. When first nominated, Purtell announced that he would beat Benton without help but later appeared with McCarthy in the state. His campaign sights were set on "ruinous taxation, ruinous extravagance, and ruinous debt." Purtell achieved a surprising triumph and supported McCarthy a few years later by opposing a resolution censuring the Wisconsin Republican for "failure to cooperate" with a Senate subcommittee. Purtell was one of the first Connecticut Republicans to support Dwight D. Eisenhower's run for the presidency.

After Eisenhower's nomination, Purtell's Senate campaign was pitched to the theme "Give Ike a Republican Senate," and he remained a supporter of Eisenhower's policies. Purtell felt that the government, under Franklin Roosevelt and Harry Truman, took over basic powers that belonged to the people; the Democratic Fair Deal domestic agenda was a philosophy of favoritism, influence, and easy money. Benton remarked that Purtell's philosophy made Senator Robert Taft of Ohio look like "a left-wing New Dealer." After Purtell defeated Benton by 90,000 votes, he resigned all business positions and directorships.

In his one Senate term, Purtell was a member of the Interstate and Foreign Commerce, Labor and Public Welfare, and Post Office and Civil Service committees, and several subcommittees concerned with juvenile delinquency, welfare and pension plan legislation, surface transportation, and health. One of his most important assignments was an appointment by Vice-President Richard Nixon to an eight-member bipartisan Senate select committee to investigate lobbying, campaign contributions, and corrupt political practices (1956). He was a delegate to the Interparliamentary Union meetings in Austria (1954) and in Finland (1955), and a member of the American delegation to the International Conference on the Peaceful Uses of Atomic Energy in Geneva (1955).

One of Purtell's first acts after taking his elected seat in the Eighty-third Congress (1953–1955) was to request congressional approval of a flood-control compact among the Connecticut River Valley states. He later asked for presidential authorization (1955) of income-tax refunds for flood victims. Purtell was also identified with many issues in the health field, especially with an amendment to the Social Security law, which President Eisenhower signed, that prevented preemption by federal or state agencies of child welfare services in urban areas already adequately covered by voluntary agencies. His other interest was labor issues. He cosponsored amendments (1953, 1955) to the National Labor Relations Act making any kind of discrimination by employers or labor organizations an unfair labor practice and advanced an administration proposal (1954) to amend the Taft-Hartley Act by requiring a government-conducted vote before a union could strike. He was also chairman of a Senate Office Building commission that approved funds to build what is now the Dirksen Senate Office Building.

In foreign policy, Purtell opposed pressing France to give full self-government in its former colony of Indochina, the Bricker amendment (limiting presidential treaty-making powers), and giving authority to Congress to veto presidential trade agreements. He favored permitting members of the armed forces serving abroad to be tried for off-duty offenses in foreign civil courts, penalizing foreign aid recipients trading with Communist China, passage of the "defend Formosa" resolution, and a three-year extension of the reciprocal trade program. Purtell cosponsored a resolution asking the State Department to urge Great Britain to "consult" the people of Cyprus concerning their future.

Purtell was unsuccessful in his bid for reelection in 1958 because of his neglect of Connecticut interests and voter apathy for the Republican party. He retired to West Hartford and resumed his manufacturing interests. With his ready wit, remarkable memory, and forceful delivery, he was in demand as an after-dinner or featured speaker on special occasions, such as Memorial Day observances. He died in West Hartford.

In Washington, Purtell had lived quietly, shunning the limelight as much as possible. Before his Senate service, however, he had been active in civic affairs. After World War I he was prominent in the American Legion. He was director of the Hartford Red Cross during World

War II, a former governor of Hillyer College (now the University of Hartford), a member of the state interracial commission, and director of the Connecticut State Prison, and a member of the Board of Parole.

Purtell was also a life member of the American Society of Tool and Manufacturing Engineers and the American Supply and Machinery Manufacturers Association, president of both the Manufacturers Association of Hartford County and the Manufacturers Association of Connecticut, and a director of the United States Chamber of Commerce.

[Purtell's papers are not available to the public. The White House Central Files, Dwight D. Eisenhower Library, Abilene, Kans., have correspondence from Purtell's Senate office. The National Archives has the records of the Senate committees on which Purtell served. The Senate Historical Office has a small file on Purtell; some of the biographical material was edited by Purtell or by his widow after his death. The Connecticut State Library, Hartford, has information on Purtell's 1952 Senate appointment in the governors' papers of John Davis Lodge. The Holo-Krome Screw Corporation, West Hartford, now a subsidiary of the Danaher Corporation, has material on Purtell in its archives. The Washingtonia Division, District of Columbia Public Library, has a clipping file on Purtell covering his years in Washington. See also his autobiographical article, "I'm a Boss, and What's Wrong with That?," *Saturday Evening Post*, Apr. 5, 1952. Obituaries are in the *New York Times* and the *Hartford Courant*, both June 1, 1978.]

MARTIN J. MANNING

R

RAFT, GEORGE (Sept. 26, 1895–Nov. 24, 1980), actor, was born in New York City, the son of Conrad Ranft and Eva Glockner. He changed his name to Raft in 1917. Raised in poverty in a rough neighborhood on the west side of the city known as Hell's Kitchen, Raft had only a limited education. At an early age he frequented pool parlors and dance halls, worked for bootleggers, and associated with local gangsters such as his childhood friend Owney Madden. He was also a semiprofessional baseball player and an unsuccessful bantamweight boxer.

Raft's talent for dancing led to a professional career in dance halls that included the Audubon Ballroom and Churchill's Sunken Gardens. While working as a dancer he is said to have frequently served as a gigolo. His life in the nightclub field began as a dancer in Texas Guinan's troupe. He also appeared in a vaudeville touring company billed as "The Fastest Dancer in the World." Fred Astaire said that Raft was an extraordinary dancer who did "the fastest, most exciting Charleston I ever saw." Hardworking and anxious to succeed, Raft prospered as a nightclub performer. His acquaintance with gangsters who owned many of the clubs undoubtedly contributed to his steady employment.

In 1923, Raft married Grace Mulrooney. They lived together for less than a year and then separated. His wife, a Roman Catholic, objected to divorce for religious reasons, but Raft continued to support her during their long estrangement, which continued until her death in 1970. They had no children.

Raft's handsome, well-defined features as well as his dancing ability and ambition helped him find work as an extra in Warner Brothers crime films and a small part in *Queen of the Night Clubs* (1929). This was followed by appearances in such mediocre motion pictures as *Quick Millions* (1931) and *Dancers in the Dark* (1932). He also appeared with Loretta Young in *Taxi* (1932), but it was in *Scarface: Shame of a Nation* (1932), with Paul Muni, Ann Dvorak, and Karen Morley, that he gained widespread recognition on the screen. The movie, directed by Howard Hawks, was an adaptation by Ben Hecht of a book about Chicago crime by Armitage Trail. Paul Muni starred as Scarface Tony Camonte, a role roughly comparable to the real-life gangster Al Capone. Raft capably played the part of a henchman, Gino Rinaldi, who flipped a coin almost incessantly throughout the picture. The inane trait firmly established the character, who was eventually murdered by Camonte (Muni). Raft immediately became a highly recognized actor and Hollywood personality and was assured of future roles, especially in crime pictures. The film also resulted in typecasting him as a gangster, crooked cop, or other disreputable figure with sleek hair and flashy clothes. Raft said, "My celluloid hoodlums were always well-dressed, soft-voiced, and underplayed." He claimed that was the manner of most gangsters he knew in real life. He also said his tough image on the screen was "my gimmick, it was the way, the only way, the public would accept me."

Following his breakthrough in *Scarface*, Raft appeared with Mae West and Constance Cummings in *Night After Night* (1932). One critic wrote that his well-groomed hair and his eyes were reminiscent of Rudolph Valentino's. In *The Bowery* (1933) he was cast with the highly popular Wallace Beery and Fay Wray. In *Bolero* (1934), with Carole Lombard, Raft made a favorable impression as a graceful dancer. The character he played, however, was another low-down type who worked his way out of honky-tonks by using women as stepping-stones to build a career. Although Raft's popularity increased with the public, he seldom received rave reviews. At best, critics usually considered his performances workmanlike, albeit wooden. On some occasions he received extremely harsh criticism. When he played the title role in *Johnny Allegro* (1949), a character on the right side of the law, a critic commented, "Nothing with any vague resemblance to vivid acting is contributed by Mr. Raft, who has become one of the most indifferent and comatose actors extant."

From 1931 to 1967, Raft appeared in about sixty motion pictures, and he performed with many of Hollywood's leading stars. Among his movies were *Souls at Sea* (1937), with Gary Cooper; *They Drive by Night* (1940), with Humphrey Bogart and Ann Sheridan; and *Manpower* (1941), with Edward G. Robinson and Marlene Dietrich. Many of his films were low-budget productions, but he gained acceptance with moviegoers and in 1946 earned $450,000, which made him one of Hollywood's highest-paid performers. His career might have been enhanced further if he had not rejected the roles played by Humphrey Bogart in *The Maltese Falcon* and *Casablanca*. Raft was careless with money and lost large sums at the racetrack and other sporting events. In 1965 the Internal Revenue Service prosecuted him for tax evasion, claiming that he owed the government $75,000 in back taxes.

As his fortunes declined and opportunities for roles faded, Raft returned to nightclubs. Prior to Fidel Castro's rise to power, he worked as an entertainment director at the Capri Hotel in Havana. He was also host at the Colony Club, a London gambling casino, until the British government banned his entrance into the country because of his association with underworld figures. In the late 1960's he worked in public relations at the Beverly Hills office of the Las Vegas Riviera hotel.

The impact that Raft's personality made on the public is reflected in three films that were produced based on his life. He appeared in two of them, *Broadway* (1942) and *Some Like It Hot* (1959). In the latter, the character Spats Colombo was actually a self-parody. In *The George Raft Story* (1961), Ray Danton played the part of George Raft. If Raft did not achieve rank as an outstanding actor, he nevertheless succeeded in establishing his style and individuality on the screen and appealed to a worldwide audience. He died in Hollywood.

[Material on Raft is in the New York Public Library for the Performing Arts at Lincoln Center. See also John Baxter, *The Gangster Film* (1970); and Lewis Yablonsky, *George Raft* (1974). An obituary is in the *New York Times*, Nov. 25, 1980.]

ERNEST A. MCKAY

RAND, SALLY (Feb. 2, 1904–Aug. 31, 1979), dancer and actress, was born Helen Gould Beck in Elkton, Mo., the daughter of Mary Annette Kisling and William Beck. Her mother was a schoolteacher and correspondent for several Kansas and Missouri newspapers; her father was a career military man who separated from his wife before World War I and remarried in France.

Rand, raised in the Quaker faith, stated that her desire to be an actress was stimulated in high school and college (both apparently in Columbia, Mo., though there is no evidence that she completed either level of education). In the 1950's and 1960's she took college classes in the sciences in California. In 1976, on the occasion of her fiftieth reunion at Christian College in Columbia, Mo., she said that to get rid of her Missouri accent cost her $10,000 and took twice as many hours as it did to earn a college degree. She also claimed to have put six younger brothers through college.

Rand left home at age thirteen to help support her mother. She spent her teenage years in Chicago and Kansas City, studying ballet in Chicago and working as a model in life classes at the Chicago Art Institute and as a cigarette girl in Chicago speakeasies. Her first show-business exposure, as a chorus girl in Kansas City, led *Kansas City Journal* critic Goodman Ace to recommend Rand for Gus Edwards's juvenile vaudeville company, School Days. In 1920 she appeared in a *Ziegfeld Follies*–type revue at the Marigold Gardens in Chicago. Later in the 1920's she worked as an acrobatic dancer, including one season with Ringling Bros. Circus, substituting as a flyer for a brief time.

In 1924, stranded in California with the Billy Seabury Troupe, Rand appeared in the first of twenty-five silent films, playing bit parts. Her first film was *The Dressmaker from Paris* (1924) and the last, after a six-year absence from Hollywood, *Bolero* with George Raft (1934). In 1927, as Billy Beck, she was under contract to Cecil B. DeMille and appeared as Mary Magdalene's slave girl in his *The King of Kings*. DeMille is credited with selecting the name Rand, from a Rand-McNally atlas on his desk; Rand chose Sally as a good name for theater marquees. Although she returned to dancing and touring with the introduction of talkies, in 1929 she settled in Glendora, Calif.

In 1930, while appearing in New York with a brother as The Rands, her name first appeared in the newspapers following her brother's altercation with a director. Subsequently, she was constantly covered by the press, often as a result of arrests for indecent behavior in her invention, the fan dance. Rand's fame began in 1932 when, following a tour in *The World Between* that closed in Chicago, she obtained a $75-per-week job as dancer in a speakeasy. Broke, she decided to adapt her classical ballet training to the taste of the club's patrons. A pile of moth-eaten ostrich plumes at a costume maker's reminded her of Pavlova's *Dying Swan* and of "the white herons that used to float through the moonlight on nights of the harvest moon." Fans were cheaper than an expensive wardrobe, and a pair of white, twenty-one-inch-stem, double-willowed ostrich fans, ordered from Henry Sittenberg in New York at $125 each, arrived the day her job was to begin. A late rehearsal prevented her from obtaining a chiffon nightgown she intended to wear, however, and so that night her famous fan costume debuted through chance.

In the spring of 1933, Rand's application for a dancing job at Chicago's Century of Progress World's Fair was rejected. At a benefit the night before the fair's opening, she appeared as Lady Godiva, "wearing only my long blonde hair." The next day, she was hired for $125 per week; by the end of the second year, she was making $3,000 per week. It was claimed that she "practically single-fanned" saved the fair from slow death. In August 1933, Rand was arrested four times in one day on a charge that her fans failed to constitute a decent costume.

Rand's legitimate acting career never progressed beyond infrequent appearances in summer stock, first in 1935 in Skowhegan, Maine, as Sadie Thompson in *Rain* (with a young Humphrey Bogart in a small role). Other appearances included *They Knew What They Wanted* and *Susan and God* (both in 1938), and *Mary of Scotland* and *The Little Foxes* in the 1960's. More successful was a stint in 1963 as Ann Corio's replacement in *This Was Burlesque* in New York City. In April 1964 she narrated an NBC television special on carnivals.

Rand continued her fan-dance appearances at fairs, nightclubs, carnivals, and theaters, touring up to forty weeks of the year, until May 1979, when she gave her final performances in Albuquerque and Santa Fe, N.Mex. By 1950 she reportedly had worn out five hundred sets of fans. Initially, her performances were considered outrageously immoral, but by the end of her career her act was considered camp nostalgia, devoid of prurience. Physically, Rand and her act changed little over forty years. At five feet tall and 113 pounds, she claimed in her sixties that her figure still measured the same (36–24–37) as it had at her peak. Rand's act was consistently six minutes long, performed under blue light to the music of Chopin's Waltz in C-Sharp Minor and Debussy's "Clair de Lune." Its success was not so much in what she revealed as in what she projected onto the fantasies of onlookers. She believed in mystery and illusion, often stating, "The Rand is quicker than the eye" when asked about her adroit fan manipulation. In 1934 she added a bubble dance to her act. To Rand, the fan dance, which she compared to a frieze of nymphs, was less abstract and more successful, while the bubble dance was more like the classic acanthus-leaf pattern.

A master of publicity, Rand called herself a ballet dancer or a "terpsichorean artiste," claimed never to have appeared in a burlesque show, and rejected the names stripper, exotic dancer, and even fan dancer. She was variously billed the Babson of the Bubble-Dance, the Fan-Waving Financier, the Nabob of Nudity, the Tycoon of Terpsichore, the Queen of the Bubble-Bounders, and her own favorite, Her Sexellency. She always insisted on the "pristine purity of her dance and the classicalness of its line." Wanting to be considered an intellectual, she spoke often to civic clubs, dressed in a tailored suit, cocky little hat, and an "air of genuine gentility." She often took time from her professional performances to dance for free at local benefit shows for schools, charities, and churches (with her clothes on).

Rand was wed three times. Her marriage in 1942 to Thurkel ("Turk") Greenough, a rodeo cowboy, ended three years later in divorce. Her second marriage, to Harry Finklestine, failed because, she said, he was "a young girl casualty"; they adopted a son in 1948. Her final marriage in 1954, to Fred Lalla, a Los Angeles plaster contractor, ended in divorce in the 1960's. Rand died in Glendora, Calif., her home of fifty years.

[Michigan State University, East Lansing, owns a 35-minute taped oral history of Rand made in 1968 by Studs Terkel and broadcast Jan. 9, 1973. A sizable clipping file on Rand is in the New York Public Library for the Performing Arts at Lincoln Center. There is extant film footage of Rand's fan and bubble dances. Obituaries are in the *New York Times* and *Los Angeles Times*, both Sept. 1, 1979, and in *Variety*, Sept. 5, 1979.]

DON B. WILMETH

RANDOLPH, ASA PHILIP (April 15, 1889–May 16, 1979), labor and civil rights leader, was born in Crescent City, Fla., the second of two sons of Elizabeth Robinson and James William Randolph, a minister of the African Methodist Episcopal Church. Philip Randolph spent his childhood in Jacksonville, Fla., and completed high school in 1907 at the Cookman Institute, a missionary school. In 1911, because it was impossible for a young black man to find meaningful work or to develop a career in Jacksonville, Randolph left for New York City. Although he dutifully promised his mother that he would return at the end of the summer, he had left Jacksonville for good to find a job and become a Shakespearean actor. Randolph never received a major acting role in New York, but through acting he began to develop the deep, resonant voice and superb oratory that came to characterize his persona. In addition to studying acting, Randolph attended classes at City College and the Rand School of Social Science, where he steeped himself in social economics and Marxian socialism, but because of the eclectic curriculum he chose he never attained a degree.

Randolph's move to New York, and especially to the Harlem section of Manhattan where he settled, coincided with the first major wave of African-American migration into the city. There were 65,000 blacks in the city in 1910; by 1920 the number had risen to 152,000. Harlem became the center for cultural, political, and economic activity among African Americans, and Randolph was at home in this cauldron of intellectual and cultural activity. While he attended college classes, Randolph spent a large part of his early years in New York as a magazine editor and street-corner orator. The soapbox orators of the time, including Marcus Garvey of the Universal Negro Improvement Association (the back-to-Africa movement), provided much competition and intellectual stimulus for Randolph, but he more than held his own. Indeed, he claimed great pleasure in having presented Garvey to his first audience in Harlem.

It was also during this early period that Randolph began a relationship with two individuals who would be lifelong companions and associates. In 1914, Randolph met Chandler Owen, a writer, and Lucille Green, a widow and cosmetologist. Randolph and Green were married in November of that year and were separated only by her death in 1963. In 1917, after several efforts with Owen to organize black workers in Harlem had failed, Randolph joined him in founding the *Messenger*, a magazine that took a radical stance against racial discrimination and on economic issues.

Randolph was committed to the idea that the "rights of men are more sacred than the rights of property" and saw the solution to the racial problem in America wholly in economic terms. Accordingly, both employers and unions that discriminated against black workers and denied them access to jobs felt his wrath. During World War I, Randolph saw little hope for the advancement of black workers through the organized labor movement, especially as long as it was led by Samuel Gompers, whom Randolph termed "the chief strike breaker in America."

The *Messenger* was especially outspoken in its opposition to the participation of the United States in World War I and was particularly opposed to the involvement of blacks in the war because of the country's racist military and domestic policies. Randolph's loud opposition to the war led to his arrest as a war protester. While Attorney General A. Mitchell Palmer described the *Messenger* as the ablest African-American publication, he also called Randolph "the most dangerous Negro in America." Palmer tried to influence the Post Office Department to deny the *Messenger* third-class mailing privileges and thus silence the magazine, but the postmaster general, acknowledging that the *Messenger* was protected by the First Amendment to the Constitution, refused to grant the attorney general's request. The arrest charges were also dropped.

In 1925 began the job that was to occupy first claim on his time throughout the remainder of his long life. In that year, already thirty-six years old and, in the view of one observer, "a man whose time had passed him by," Randolph accepted the invitation of a group of New York–based Pullman Company porters to lead the efforts to organize the Brotherhood of Sleeping Car Porters (BSCP). Though he was not a porter, the porters' selection of Randolph as president of the organization made sense. Despite his reservations about the efficacy of the general labor movement for blacks, Randolph had previously tried to organize black workers, including elevator operators and waiters on passenger ships. He also was the editor of a magazine that could serve as the new union's journal, and because he was not a porter the Pullman Company could not fire him. As general organizer of the BSCP, Randolph immersed himself in his work and with the able assistance of trusted lieutenants, especially Milton P. Webster of Chicago, organized BSCP locals in the major railway centers throughout the nation. With what became characteristic bravado, Randolph vowed to "bring the Pullman Company to its knees."

Like most nascent and financially weak organizations, the BSCP struggled during most of its early history. The Pullman Company publicly ignored it and abstemiously refused to bargain with the union. The BSCP received almost the same reception from general organized labor, especially the American Federation of Labor (AFL), some of whose member unions still had constitutional bars against the membership of black workers, and whose organizing philosophy centered on crafts rather than on industry-wide groups.

It was during this difficult period that Randolph exhibited remarkable leadership skills and brought together disparate elements of both blacks and whites to aid the porters' cause. Randolph believed that "public opinion [was] the most powerful weapon in America," and he used every available venue to keep the BSCP's message before the public. Moreover, through the union's troubled early years, Randolph carried himself with such dignity and personal incorruptibility that he came to personify the porters' cause.

The public opinion campaign he waged, combined with his personal stature, enabled Randolph to maintain support for the union among a solid core of porters, numerous community leaders and public officials, and large numbers of average citizens, even as the nation endured the severe deprivation of the Great Depression. It was not until 1935, after the National Labor Relations Act improved overall the bargaining power of unions, that the Pullman Company entered into negotiations with BSCP over the wages and working conditions of porters. That same year, during the bitter split between the AFL and the unions that became the Congress of Industrial Organizations (CIO), the BSCP received an international charter from the AFL.

Through a decade of struggle Randolph had kept faith with his pledge to make the BSCP the sole bargaining agent for Pullman porters. In 1937 the union and the company signed their first agreement, which gave the porters pay increases, shorter hours, and overtime pay; Randolph became a larger-than-life personality. Through his personal charisma he had succeeded in making the BSCP a major civil rights organization for African Americans, not just a union of sleeping car porters.

By 1937, Randolph was a major spokesman on behalf of blacks, especially the working class, and was participating in a wide range of labor and civil rights activities. In 1935 he was elected president of the National Negro Congress, a broad-based organization of black rights organizations, a position he held until he resigned in 1940 with a warning to black leaders to eschew the involvement of whites, and especially Communists, in black organizations. Indeed, Randolph became—and remained—deeply anti-Communist because of Communist efforts to take over the BSCP and because of Communists' success in exercising wide influence over the National Negro Congress.

Randolph launched the most important period of his career at the outset of World War II, when he used his union to lead an assault on the nation's racist domestic policy. As the war spread in Europe and the administration of President Franklin D. Roosevelt edged closer to supporting the Allied forces, Randolph noted that while the Great Depression was ending for white Americans little had changed for blacks. Unlike his opposition to World War I, Randolph was not opposed to American efforts to rid the world of Adolf Hitler, but he was convinced that if the nation went to war, Americans could not suffer the misery of war, either on the battlefield or at the home front, and return to the same kind of domestic racial policy that existed in 1940. The clearest evidence of change, he believed, would lie in improved employment and working conditions for blacks.

Accordingly, in 1941 Randolph called on the federal government to outlaw racial discrimination in employment and hiring and to end segregation in the nation's armed forces, and he promised to organize a massive march on Washington, D.C., by blacks to demand compliance. When he announced his call for a march on July 1 and organized the March on Washington Movement (MOWM)—largely an arm of the BSCP—Randolph for the first time took a purely racial stance on an economic issue. Unlike his efforts to gain multiracial support for the union, this time he argued that MOWM leadership and membership should be all black. The time had come, he said, for "Negroes to fight their own battles." He called for what became known as the "Double V" Campaign—African Americans would be willing to fight against Nazism and later Japanese aggression abroad but they would also fight at home to rid the nation of the tyranny of racism.

In his initial call for a march, Randolph claimed that 10,000 blacks would demonstrate in the capital, but within weeks black newspapers picked up his cause, and as the spring of 1941 wore on the number was escalated to 50,000. The MOWM became the largest mass movement of blacks since Garvey's Universal Negro Improvement Association of the 1920's. As the summer approached Randolph raised his claim of the number of protesters to 100,000 and national leaders began to worry.

Randolph had directed the march threat at President Roosevelt, through his insistence that the president issue an executive order meeting the MOWM's demands. In an effort to defuse the issue the president sent his wife, Eleanor, who had a good reputation as a friend of African Americans, and Mayor Fiorello La Guardia of New York City, a friend and confidant of Randolph's, to talk the BSCP leader into calling off the march. The president thought that the nation could ill afford the spectacle of thousands of black citizens demonstrating in the streets of the capital, especially when the German propagandists looked for any excuse to highlight disharmony within the United States. His disquiet was heightened by the fact that Washington was a southern city which in 1941 had a white police force wholly willing to use harsh action to clear the streets of the black protesters.

All of their entreaties went to naught. Randolph, with the steadfast support of Walter White, executive secretary of the National Association for the Advancement of Colored People (NAACP), informed the president's emissaries that nothing short of a presidential executive order would halt the march.

The impasse led to direct conversations in June between MOWM leaders and the White House, including the president, but failed to end or delay the threat of the march. Thus, on June 25, in order to stave off domestic disruption, President Roosevelt signed Executive Order 8802, which mandated an end to discrimination in hiring and union membership for companies and unions that did business with the government and established the Fair Employment Practice Committee (FEPC) to oversee compliance.

Executive Order 8802 was in many ways a significant victory, but Randolph suffered much abuse in the black press and among some of the younger members of the MOWM leadership for having accepted a compromise. Bayard Rustin, who became one of Randolph's most devoted and trusted aides, was prominent among the detractors. Though they recognized that for the first time since the Civil War blacks had forced the government to admit its complicity with racial discrimination and to accept its responsibility to end that policy, they faulted Randolph for not holding out for the whole package. The executive order did not mention segregation in the military, for example, and the FEPC was at best a weak entity. But Randolph knew something that others did not; the MOWM had been a march in name only, and it was highly improbable that 10,000 marchers, certainly not 100,000 people, would have appeared in Washington at the appointed time. He knew that his was a big bluff that had succeeded, and that large numbers of people had continued to maintain that they would march because of their personal commitment to him. He had gotten the best deal he could at the time and would use his new influence to work for improvements in the future.

During the years following World War II,

Randolph carried on his work with organized labor and continued to stress the relationship between economic improvement and civil rights for African Americans. In 1955, after the AFL/CIO merger reunited the organized labor movement, Randolph accepted a seat on the executive council of the new organization and used his position to press for an end to union discrimination. Moreover, he insisted that black workers be given leadership positions within the organized union movement. In 1959, after having made little progress on that front, Randolph took the leadership in forming the Negro American Labor Council (NALC), which was to be all black, fight for employment for African-American workers, and press for black "participation in the executive, administrative, and staff areas of unions."

Early in 1963 he again called for a march on Washington during the late summer. Using the NALC's organizational structure and the organizing genius of Rustin, Randolph cobbled together the national leadership to make the march come off. On August 28, millions across the nation and around the world heard on radio and television the memorable words of Dr. Martin Luther King, Jr., president of the Southern Christian Leadership Conference, as he stood before the throng of more than 200,000 that stretched from the Lincoln Memorial to the Washington Monument and spoke of his dream for America. Many thought that King was the organizer of the march, but the fact is that it was Randolph's march and in his speech that day Randolph reminded America that "the sanctity of private property takes second place to the sanctity of the human personality."

The March on Washington for Jobs and Freedom, which federal officials tried to stall as they had the proposed march in 1941, led almost directly to the passage of the Civil Rights Act of 1964 and the Voting Rights Act of 1965. After the march Randolph continued as president of the BSCP until he retired in 1968 and saw his union disappear after its merger into the Brotherhood of Railway and Airline Clerks. In retirement, Randolph spent most of his time as an elder statesman for both the civil rights and organized labor movements, operating mainly from his home in New York City, where he died.

[The papers of the Brotherhood of Sleeping Car Porters are at the Chicago Historical Society. The papers of the National Association for the Advancement of Colored People at the Library of Congress, Washington, D.C., also contain considerable information on Randolph, as does the collection of interviews on Randolph in the Columbia University Oral History Collection in New York City. Jervis Anderson, *A. Philip Randolph: A Biographical Portrait* (1972), is the only study of his full life. Edwin R. Embree, *Thirteen Against the Odds* (1944); and Julius Adams, *The Challenge: A Study in Negro Leadership* (1949) each devotes a chapter to Randolph. Essays on Randolph are included in John Hope Franklin and August Meier, eds., *Black Leaders of the Twentieth Century* (1982); and Melvyn Dubofsky and Warren Van Tine, eds., *Labor Leaders in America* (1987). See also Brailsford R. Brazeal, *The Brotherhood of Sleeping Car Porters* (1946); Theodore Kornweible, *No Crystal Stair: Black Life and the Messenger, 1927–1938* (1975); William H. Harris, *Keeping the Faith* (1977), "A. Philip Randolph: A Study in Charismatic Leadership," *Journal of Negro History*, Summer 1980, and *The Harder We Run* (1982); and Paula F. Pfeffer, *A. Philip Randolph* (1990). An obituary is in the *New York Times*, May 17, 1979.]

WILLIAM H. HARRIS

RANDOLPH, LILLIAN (Dec. 6, 1914–Sept. 12, 1980), entertainer, was born in Knoxville, Tenn., the younger daughter of Jesse and Jane Randolph. The family moved to Cleveland, Ohio, where Lillian attended public school. Her older sister Amanda, an established performer in New York City nightclubs, inspired her to enter the entertainment field. Her career in the entertainment industry spanned five decades and included nightclub, radio, television, motion picture, and personal appearances. Lillian began as a singer on radio station WJR in Detroit, Mich., where she also performed in nightclubs. She remained in Detroit for another two years, acting in the drama "Lulu and Leander" on WXYZ Radio.

In 1936 she moved to Los Angeles, Calif. She spent the first seven years there as a popular singer in nightclubs. She had a strong voice and enthusiastic delivery that propelled her to a productive career in radio. Her first network radio role was as Mammy on the "Al Jolson Show." Randolph next performed on Edward G. Robinson's "Big Town" series and worked regularly in radio until the 1950's.

Until the 1960's, African-American performers were limited to roles that white management deemed appropriate, such as maids, butlers, or singers. These characters were based on white minstrel show interpretations of black figures with exaggerated facial expressions and a "negroid" dialect. Randolph spent three months studying with a white vocal coach to master that dialect. She soon portrayed the stereotypical black maid on several radio comedies during the 1940's and 1950's: "Beulah," "The Billie Burke Show," "My Mother's Husband," and "The Remarkable Miss Tuttle." Her most famous maid character was Birdie Lee Coggins on "The Great Gildersleeve." She also played Madam Queen on the "Amos 'n' Andy" show.

Randolph's portrayals of a black maid in a white household represented a typical stereotyped role. While displaying warmth, understanding, and common sense, she was a confidante of the white family members. The black housekeeper, emitting self-confidence and an implacable personality, could deflate the central character, such as Gildersleeve, with a verbal jab, delivered with courtesy and deference. Randolph's dynamic persona and perfectionism made her the master of these roles.

Because the stereotypical black maid was also a popular movie character, Randolph soon found work in films while continuing to perform on radio and in nightclubs, encouraged by Edward Stevenson, a designer with RKO Studios who had seen her nightclub act. Initially, she acted in several "race" movies such as *Life Goes On* (1938). She performed in more than thirty films, many of them comedies, and often in the role of the maid. Her most noteworthy films included *Little Men* (1940); *West Point Widow* (1941); four Great Gildersleeve movies, in which she reenacted the role of Birdie Lee Coggins (1942–1944); *The Adventures of Mark Twain* (1944); *It's a Wonderful Life* (1946), playing her favorite and memorable role as Annie the maid; *The Bachelor and the Bobby-Soxer* (1947); *Once More My Darling* (1949); *That's My Boy* (1951); *Bend of the River* (1952); *Hush, Hush, Sweet Charlotte* (1964); *Once Is Not Enough* (1975); *Magic* (1978); and *The Onion Field* (1979), in her last and most dramatic role, as a foster mother pleading for the life of her accused son.

During the 1940's and 1950's, the National Association for the Advancement of Colored People protested the small number of blacks working in the entertainment field and the stereotypical roles, speech, and mannerisms that limited African-American performers. The Great Gildersleeve and Randolph's character Birdie were especially criticized for "malicious maligning of minorities" in the minstrel tradition. Several regularly employed African-American entertainers, such as Randolph and Eddie ("Rochester") Anderson, spoke out publicly against the protests. Randolph stated that she had no problems in radio "except the criticism from Negro groups." Moreover, she said, these portrayals "do not affect the Negroes' past, present, and future."

In 1952 the American Federation of Television and Radio Artists (AFTRA) considered a resolution "to prohibit the usual stereotype portrayal of Negroes on radio." Randolph, the only black delegate to this and other AFTRA conventions, argued successfully that the resolution would put blacks out of work by giving those roles to white actors.

In the 1950's several popular radio programs were adapted for television, and Randolph continued her roles as Madam Queen on "Amos 'n' Andy," Birdie on "The Great Gildersleeve," and Beulah. During the 1960's and 1970's, she showed a broader range of talent on the first "Bill Cosby Show" (1969–1970), "Mannix" (1970), "Room 222" (1970), and "That's My Mama" (1974); as the voice of the aged Miss Pittman on "The Autobiography of Miss Jane Pittman" (1974); on "Sanford and Son" (1975) and "The Jeffersons" (1976); and as Sister Sara in "Roots" (1977).

Randolph married boxer Jack Chase, who died, and then Garcia McKee in 1954. She had at least two children. Randolph loved the entertainment field and continued to work professionally until her death. In 1956, after CBS dropped the "Amos 'n' Andy" show, Randolph and other cast members created a touring company called the "TV Stars of Amos 'n' Andy." The effort was short-lived because CBS threatened legal action. For ten years she provided the voice of the cook in the "Tom and Jerry" cartoons. During the 1960's, Randolph, McKee, and daughter Barbara toured the Far East, entertaining at American military bases and nightclubs. She also made television commercials for Wesson Oil, Pacific Telephone, and American Airlines.

Randolph was a music and drama coach for many years and created her own singing group, the Lillian Randolph Singers, which toured the country and gave professional advice to aspiring singers and actors. She also was involved in church and charity work, such as the Benevolent Variety Artists, which she sponsored. A private person whose greatest enjoyment was her family, she died in Arcadia, Calif.

Although Randolph is mainly remembered for stereotypical roles, she is important as one of the few talented African-American entertainers who was regularly employed in the early days of radio and television and helped to open the door for others. She was inducted into the Black Filmmakers Hall of Fame in Oakland, Calif., in 1980.

[A biographical file is at the Black Filmmakers Hall of Fame. An interview with Randolph and discussion of her AFTRA activities are in Estelle Edmerson, "A Descriptive Study of the American Negro in United States Professional Radio, 1922–1953" (M.A. thesis, University of California at Los Angeles, 1954). See also Donald Bogle, *Blacks in American Films and Television* (1988). An obituary is in the *New York Times*, Sept. 17, 1980.]

FRANCES T. GIGLIO

RATHBONE, MONROE JACKSON ("JACK") (Mar. 1, 1900–Aug. 2, 1976), oil company executive, was born in Parkersburg, W.Va., the son of Monroe Jackson Rathbone, manager of an oil refinery, and Ida Virginia Welch. In the period 1918–1919, during World War I, he served as a second lieutenant in the United States Army. He returned to studies at Lehigh University after the war and graduated in 1921 with a degree in chemical engineering. On Apr. 22, 1923, he married Eleanor Groves. They had two children.

In 1921 Rathbone joined Standard Oil Company of Louisiana at the firm's Baton Rouge refinery and began a rapid advance through that company's management, rising from assistant to the general superintendent in 1926 to company president in 1936. He instituted changes in the Louisiana company, most notably introducing the fluid catalytic oil-cracking process. He gathered together a talented group of engineers and scientists and pushed for research on better quality fuel with less energy waste, artificial rubber, and other products. These developments positioned the company well for World War II production demands and expansion.

In 1944, Standard Oil Company (New Jersey), among the world's largest corporations, appointed Rathbone president and director of another affiliate, Esso Standard Oil Company, and he moved to New Jersey. Five years later he became a director of the parent company, with responsibility for employee and public relations, and the contact director for the Esso affiliate. Rathbone's 1951 report on the prospect for petroleum chemicals provided a base for Standard Oil (New Jersey) and its affiliates to move rapidly into that business. In 1954 he became president of the company and from 1960 to 1965 he served as chief executive officer and was chairman of the board from 1963 until his retirement.

In 1960, Rathbone pushed to completion the decentralization begun in 1927 of Standard Oil from a producing to holding company, which required restructuring the role of management as well as that of the affiliate companies. The parent company controlled funds and research and sought to develop leaders with a worldview while the affiliates handled operations. With modifications this reorganization endured for more than twenty years. Also in 1960, under a Department of Justice decree, Standard Oil (New Jersey) and Socony Mobil Oil Corporation began to dissolve their jointly owned affiliate, Standard-Vacuum Oil Company, which had operated principally east of Suez, Egypt. This dissolution enabled Jersey to develop one of its most profitable affiliates, Esso Standard Eastern, in 1962.

Rathbone became interested in the Greening the Earth Program of the United States and the United Nations to provide cheap fertilizer from petrochemicals. Under his leadership Standard Oil (New Jersey) moved rapidly in that area, thereby creating an exciting period at the company, which poured millions into fertilizer plants around the globe. No corresponding infrastructure existed to deliver and market the fertilizer produced, however, and not every farmer knew how to use the product. After investing almost $500 million Standard Oil (New Jersey) sold the plants and absorbed the loss.

During the 1960 reorganization Rathbone pushed the consolidation of all domestic affiliates into the Humble Oil and Refining Company (now Exxon Corporation), a move that increased profits as well as the competitive position of Standard Oil (New Jersey) within the United States. A glutted market in the same year led to long debates over the posted price for oil from the Middle East and Venezuela. Rathbone then decided to reduce the posted price closer to actual market price. Within a month five oil-producing nations created the Organization of Petroleum Exporting Countries. While Venezuela's Dr. Juan Pablo Perez Alfonso more than any other individual deserved the title "Father of OPEC," some United States oil company executives credited Rathbone with that questionable title.

Rathbone constantly sought more petroleum to increase the reserve supplies of Standard Oil (New Jersey) by purchasing companies with such supplies and by pressing the company's exploration units to search for oil and natural gas in likely regions. The oil strike in Libya in 1959, after competing companies had ended their search, proved sensational. Of greater importance, however, Rathbone pushed the company into the acquisition of vast acreages in the Gulf of Mexico, where in 1962 it began offshore production. The company later found oil off the California coast.

Rathbone proved to be an outstanding leader and executive. His reorganization of company operations increased efficiency and profits, and his constant search for oil for production and reserves left Standard Oil (New Jersey) in a strong position for later operations.

He retired in 1965, but his interest in the company continued until his death in Baton Rouge. He vigorously fought the company's name change to Exxon Corporation in 1973 but later graciously admitted that the new name was needed. He became active in many organizations, including the Exxon Education Foundation, and devoted much time to young people. He received ten national and international awards for executive leadership and innovation as well as numerous honorary degrees.

[Two of the best of numerous sketches of Rathbone are "Rathbone of Jersey Standard," *Fortune*, May 1954; and Walter Guzzardi, Jr., "How Rathbone Runs Jersey Standard," *Fortune*, Jan. 1963. The best account of his career with Standard Oil is Bennett H. Wall, C. Gerald Carpenter, and Gene S. Yeager, *Growth in a Changing Environment: A History of Standard Oil Company (New Jersey), 1950–1972, and Exxon Corporation, 1972–1975* (1988). See also George S. Gibb and Evelyn Knowlton, *The Resurgent Years, 1911–1927: The History of Standard Oil Company (New Jersey)* (1956); and Henrietta Larson, Evelyn Knowlton, and Charles S. Popple, *New Horizons, 1927–1950: The History of Standard Oil Company (New Jersey)* (1971). An obituary is in the *New York Times*, Aug. 3, 1976.]

BENNETT H. WALL

RAY, MAN. See MAN RAY.

REED, STANLEY FORMAN (Dec. 31, 1884–Apr. 2, 1980), justice of the United States Supreme Court, was born in Minerva, Ky. (near Maysville), the only child of John A. Reed and Frances Forman. His father was a medical doctor and his mother served for a time as registrar general of the Daughters of the American Revolution. He received B.A. degrees from Kentucky Wesleyan College (1902) and Yale College (1906), then attended the University of Virginia Law School and Columbia Law School. He married Winifred Elgin of Minerva on May 11, 1908; they had two children. After attending the Sorbonne in Paris, Reed returned from France and was admitted to the Kentucky bar in 1910. He began practicing law in Maysville and served in the state general assembly from 1912 to 1916. During World War I he served in the Army Intelligence Division.

Reed's principal client was the Chesapeake and Ohio Railroad—Maysville was on the main line. Another client was the Burley Tobacco Growers' Association, which led to his appointment as general counsel for the Federal Farm Board (1929–1932) and then the Reconstruction Finance Corporation (1932–1935). While with the RFC, Reed supported a gold repurchase plan, and he was given the task of arguing the gold clause cases (1935) before the United States Supreme Court. He successfully argued that the federal government held the power to abrogate the gold clauses in private contracts requiring payment in gold specie. President Franklin D. Roosevelt then appointed Reed solicitor general, making Reed the administration's spokesman in arguments before a usually hostile Supreme Court. Reed's biggest loss was in *Schechter Poultry Corporation* v. *United States* (1935), in which the Court held that the National Industrial Recovery Act (1933), with its program of industry codes, was unconstitutional. When the Court also attacked the Agricultural Adjustment Act of 1933 on similar grounds (*United States* v. *Butler*, 1936), the props of the early New Deal recovery program were taken away. In 1937, Roosevelt thereupon announced a plan to "pack" the Supreme Court with additional new justices. While this plan failed, the Court took note of its plight and in 1937 upheld the pro-union National Labor Relations Act of 1935.

Justice Willis Van Devanter retired from the Court in May 1937 and Senator Hugo L. Black was chosen as Roosevelt's first appointment to the high court. When George Sutherland announced his retirement, Roosevelt named Reed to the Court and the new justice was sworn in on Jan. 31, 1938.

Reed's judicial position on the Supreme Court is difficult to categorize. In nearly twenty years as a justice, he never authored a truly landmark decision among his more than 200 opinions. As would be expected from the man who argued the *Schecter* case, he was favorable to administrative agencies and the executive branch, as well as to labor, although he did vote against President Harry Truman's seizure of the steel mills in 1952 during the Korean War. His most outstanding opinions concerned equality for African Americans. He wrote the Court's 1944 opinion in *Smith* v. *Allwright*, abolishing whites-only Democratic primary elections in Texas and the majority opinion in *Morgan* v. *Virginia* (1946), upholding the Interstate Commerce Commission's ban on racially based seating on interstate bus lines. On the other hand, he rejected relief in certain cases involving Japanese Americans during World War II.

In 1949, Reed was subpoenaed to appear as a character witness in the trial of Alger Hiss on a perjury charge relating to Hiss's testimony before the House Un-American Activities Committee, in which he had resolutely denied admitted Communist Whittaker Chambers's allegation that he was a spy. Reed, who had appointed Hiss his assistant while he was solicitor general, testified on Hiss's behalf, as did fellow justice Felix Frankfurter. Reed was never accused of complicity with Hiss; in fact, Reed voted in 1951 to uphold the convictions of eleven Communist leaders of violating the Smith Act, which prohibited the advocacy of the violent overthrow of any government in the United States (*Dennis et al.* v. *United States*).

Reed had a unique view in the areas of religious freedom and church-state relations. For example, in 1948 in *McCollum* v. *Board of Education* he dissented when the Court struck down an in-school program of voluntary religious education by teachers of religion (without pay). He was against censorship but was no friend of criminal defendants. In *United States* v. *Kahringer* (1953), he wrote the Court's opinion holding that a taxpayer could be required to disclose illegal gambling wages to the Internal Revenue Service, and in 1947 he wrote the opinion (since modified) in *Adamson* v. *California*, allowing a district attorney to comment on the failure of a murder suspect to take the witness stand. Reed believed that this issue of criminal administration was properly left to the states. In short, Reed was often viewed as the swing vote in matters before the Court. He retired from the Court in 1957; his seat on the bench was taken by Charles E. Whittaker.

Reed was chairman of two federal commissions—Roosevelt's Commission on Civil Service Improvement and President Dwight D. Eisenhower's Civil Rights Commission. Although he held the latter post after retiring, because he held emeritus status as a federal judge, he soon resigned. He continued to sit on cases before the Court of Claims and the Court of Appeals for the District of Columbia circuit for a number of years. He moved to Long Island, N.Y., shortly before he died in Huntington. At the time of his death, he was the longest-living Supreme Court justice.

[Reed's papers are at the University of Kentucky in Lexington. A valuable study of Reed's career by C. Herman Pritchett is in Leon Friedman and Fred Israel, eds., *Justices of the United States Supreme Court, 1789–1978* (1980). See also C. Herman Pritchett, *The Roosevelt Court: A Study in Judicial Politics and Values, 1937–1947* (1948); and F. William O'Brien, *Justice Reed and the First Amendment* (1958). One view of the Hiss affair is provided in Whittaker Chambers, *Witness* (1952). An obituary is in the *New York Times*, Apr. 4, 1980. An official tribute from his fellow justices is in 100 *Supreme Court Reporter* (1979).]

JOHN DAVID HEALY

REESE, HELOISE BOWLES (May 4, 1919–Dec. 28, 1977), columnist and author, was born in Fort Worth, Tex., one of twin daughters of Charles Louis Bowles and Amelia Harrison. Educated in Forth Worth public schools, Heloise attended the Texas School of Fine Arts in 1938 and earned diplomas from both Felt and Tarrent Business College and Draughn's Business College in 1939. She married Army Air Forces pilot Adolph Risky on Jan. 5, 1941. After two miscarriages, they adopted one child. Risky was shot down and killed in 1943 and he was buried in Cambridge, England.

In 1946, Heloise married another Army Air Forces captain, Marshall ("Mike") Cruse, after a three-week courtship. In 1948 they were stationed in China, where she wrote much of the material for her later book, *Heloise in China* (1972); the couple returned to Texas in early

1950. Still plagued by miscarriages (five more in five years), Heloise finally gave birth to a girl on Apr. 15, 1951. Captain Cruse's Air Force assignments took the family from Waco, Tex., to Arlington Va., in 1953 and then Hawaii in 1958. There Heloise amassed a record 12,000 hours of volunteer nurse's-aide service. But the woman who once claimed to have been the only girl to take shop class at her high school needed another outlet for her incredible energy and curiosity about how things work.

From a chance remark at a navy officers' cocktail party, Heloise approached the editor of the *Honolulu Advertiser* and offered to write a column free for six weeks to prove that she could do it. The column, begun in 1959 as "Readers' Exchange," encouraged people to write in both questions and responses to other readers' questions about common household problems. It proved to be so popular that the paper's circulation rose 40 percent in less than three years. By the time it was syndicated by King Features in 1961, the column had been retitled "Hints from Heloise," and she was receiving thousands of letters weekly, including one avalanche of more than 200,000 requests for a small booklet she wrote on laundry tips and offered free to readers. It was the largest delivery of mail to an individual in the postal history of Hawaii.

Concentrating on easily available materials, Heloise's hints featured often bizarre uses for such things as peanut butter, mayonnaise, vegetable dyes, and nylon netting—which was advocated for everything from scrubbing to haute couture. For example, she advised using rubber fruit jar rings to prevent ice trays from sticking to the bottom of the freezer compartment, sprinkling baking soda to deodorize carpets before vacuuming, and using mayonnaise to remove furniture scratches. The zeal with which Heloise offered time and money-saving suggestions to help the overworked housewife perhaps explains the fervor of her readers, who sent their favorite tips to Heloise. She then tested them, often improved them, and passed them on in both the daily columns and the six books she compiled: *Heloise's Housekeeping Hints* (1962); *Heloise's Kitchen Hints* (1963); *Heloise All Around the House* (1965); *Heloise's Work and Money Savers* (1967); *Heloise's Hints for the Working Woman* (1970); and the book written nearly two decades before, *Heloise in China* (1972).

Active in the American Red Cross, Heloise was the recipient of the Silver Lady Banshee Award for outstanding columnist from the Actors and Writers Professional Organization (1964); the Writer's Award from the Headliners clubs in Austin, Tex. (1964), and in San Antonio (1968); the Howe Press award for work with the blind (1971); the International Trophy from the Perkins School for the Blind, Boston, Mass. (1972); and the International Ecology Award, Paris, France (1973). She was also named Woman of Achievement by Theta Sigma Phi (now Women in Communications) (1962) and Ecology Woman of the Year (1972–1973).

In her lifetime, Heloise battled a number of health problems, which included not only the seven miscarriages, but a stomach tumor, trigeminal neuralgia, arteriosclerosis and heart disease (aggravated by constant smoking), and a cracked vertebra suffered in an accident with a drunk driver. In fact, her health was so precarious that she had her own funeral planned for several years before her death and her tombstone carved and installed by 1975, with the epitaph, "Heloise, Every Housewife's Friend."

Frequent radio and television appearances gave her fans the opportunity to see and identify their champion, and Heloise always gave them something to remember. One of her favorite devices was to spray paint her hair—purple, green, blue, or red—to match the outfit she was wearing. Around her home office, she often wore her own designs of Hawaiian muumuus, fashioned from anything from curtains to bedsheets. Her concern for being her own unique fashion statement extended even to her choice of burial attire—a red silk Japanese wedding robe she habitually wore on New Year's Eve.

In 1966 the Cruses moved to San Antonio, Tex., a popular military retirement post chosen for its similarity to her beloved Hawaii climate with its tropical foliage, availability of good military hospitals, low cost of living, and most important for Heloise's work, speedy mail service. The Cruses, however, divorced soon thereafter. In 1970, Heloise married and divorced Houston businessman A. L. Reese, taking back her maiden name.

Heloise died of pneumonia in San Antonio while hospitalized for a heart attack. Mourners at her funeral were given red carnations and heard her one copyrighted song, "There Are No Phones in Heaven." Considered by Heloise to be her philosophy of life, the song calls for people to share their feelings of love and appreciation before it is too late.

The columns remained in syndication to more than 600 American and foreign papers even after her death, as daughter Poncé Cruse continued the household hints, first as "Heloise II," and then as simply "Heloise."

[See Maxine Cheshire, "Dishrags to Riches: The Saga of Heloise," *Saturday Evening Post*, Mar. 2, 1963; Jane Howard, "Heloise, the Most-Needed Housewife," *Life*, Apr. 21, 1967; and Ian Frazier, "Nobody Better, Better Than Nobody," *New Yorker*, Feb. 21, 1983. Obituaries are in the *New York Times* and the *San Antonio Express*, both Dec. 30, 1977.]

DOROTHY S. ("DOREY") SCHMIDT

REID, ROSE MARIE (Sept. 12, 1906–Dec. 18, 1978), bathing suit designer, was born in Cardston, Alberta, Canada, one of seven children of William Elvie Yancey, a storekeeper and farmer, and Marie Hyde, a seamstress. When Reid was young, the family moved to a Mormon community in Wieser, Idaho, where she graduated as valedictorian of her high school class at the age of sixteen. Her family was poor and she did not pursue further education. As a child she worked on farms and in stores and learned to sew from her mother. A sixth-generation Mormon, she felt that women should remain at home with their children. An early first marriage, which soon ended in divorce, took her out of Idaho in 1933 to Vancouver, British Columbia. She married Jack C. Reid, a professional swimming instructor, on Nov. 20, 1935. She did not begin designing swimwear until after the birth of the first of her three children.

Until the 1930's, bathing suits were made of heavy wool, which made it difficult to swim. Reid designed a suit for her husband made of duck cloth, which he tried to market. An avid swimmer herself, Reid in 1938 made a woman's bathing suit of heavy cotton with shoelaces going up the sides for comfortable swimming. She wore the suit to a swim meet and caught the eye of an executive from the Hudson's Bay Company, a Canadian department store, and he ordered a dozen of the suits.

Reid did not want to go into business but her husband did, and the orders for bathing suits began coming in. Reid gathered together sixteen women with sewing machines to complete her first orders. The first year of business brought a gross income of $10,000, with which the Reids invested in sixteen sewing machines and established Reid's Holiday Togs, Ltd. The following year, her bathing suits were used by the participants in the 1937 British Empire games in Australia.

Reid tried to balance raising children and running her nascent business. Despite her husband's criticism that she neglected the business for her children, Reid often took them on business trips to New York's fabric retailers. Her six-week-old daughter, Sharon, became the youngest baby to fly across the country before 1938.

Reid was divorced on Apr. 10, 1946. She purchased her former husband's half of the company. By this time, she had captured 50 percent of the swimsuit market in Canada. Jack Kessler, an acquaintance and a clothing salesman in Seattle, convinced her to move to California. He became her partner and invested $50,000 in her swimsuit business. They established a plant thirty miles from the Los Angeles airport.

Reid began experimenting with weaving silver and gold metallic yarn into the fabric of bathing suits, and, on Dec. 20, 1946, the company debuted a new line of swimwear, including a gold metallic bathing suit that sold for an unprecedented $90. She was the first to transform the bathing suit from a dull uniform into a fashion item. She also quadruped its price. Reid felt that women should "feel as dressed in a bathing suit as in an evening gown." She wanted to make bathing suits that would flatter all types of female figures and developed models to complement six body types: the heavy-busted, the large-hipped, the pudgy or mature, the petite, the tall, and the "perfect" body. She developed an innovative line of swimwear that included such features as inside brassieres, tummy-tuck panels, stay-down legs, spiral stays in strapless suits, and laces up the sides. She was the first to introduce dress sizes in swimwear and the first to use stretchable fabrics and colors in bathing suits.

Beginning in 1946, Reid's sales increased by more than $1 million each year. In 1960, the company's sales came to $18.4 million, amounting to almost 10 percent of total sales of women's bathing suits in the nation.

Between 1950 and 1956, Reid built a line of bathing suits around the idea of "imagineering," the concept that a woman needed different bathing suits for different situations, such as sunning, swimming, and lounging. Another marketing technique involved breaking with the tradition of selling only one line of suits each year. Reid created a late-summer line and a winter line for cruises, Florida vacations, and Christmas presents. She created at least one hundred designs each season.

It soon became necessary to build another factory. Located in the San Fernando Valley, the factory cost $2 million and employed 1,100 workers, bringing the total number employed in the two factories to 1,900. The new factory, which began operations in October 1960, featured a fifty-foot swimming pool that was used as a test basin for fabrics as well as a recreation facility for employees on the weekends. Concerned about strengthening employer-employee relations in an increasingly high-skilled enterprise, the Reid Company staged two upscale fashion shows for its employees so that assembly line workers could have the satisfaction of seeing the finished products.

In the 1950's Reid was one of the Big Four bathing suit designers in California, the heart of the swimwear industry, even though she designed only for women. Her bathing suits were sold all over the country and to forty-six other nations. She was noted for elegant, understated swimsuits that preserved an element of modesty despite fashion trends toward increasingly more bare skin. She refused to design bikinis, calling them "hideous, vulgar, and immoral," and broke with her company over the bikini issue. Reid's work was recognized by her winning the American Designer Sportswear Award and the Academy Award of Design, both in 1958. Two years after she left the company in 1961, the factory folded. Reid sold the right to use her name in 1964 to the Jonathan Logan Company, which still puts out bathing suits under her name.

After she left the company, Reid began designing a synthetic-fiber wig for women under the name Reid-Meredith. She also moved to Provo, Utah, to live near her grandchildren and continue her missionary work for the Mormon Church. She died in Provo. There was some confusion as to her age in obituaries, because throughout her career Reid preferred to say she was six years younger than she was really was. She felt that appearing younger was necessary to retain her credibility in a fashion industry that appealed to young people.

[See the biography, *Rose Marie Reid*, written by her daughter Carole Burr and Roger Peterson (1994). See also Gloria Ricci Lothrop, "A Trio of Mermaids—Their Impact upon the Southern California Sportswear Industry," *Journal of the West*, Jan. 1986; "Introducing Workers to Product," *Business Week*, Nov. 20, 1954; "Well Suited by the West," *Sports Illustrated*, Nov. 28, 1955; "Swimsuits Around the Calendar," *Fortune*, Feb. 1956; "Styling Buoys Swim Suit Maker," *New York Times*, Oct. 8, 1960; and Lena Lencek and Gideon Bosker, *Making Waves* (1989). Obituaries are in the *New York Times* and the *Los Angeles Times*, both Dec. 22, 1978.]

ALISON GARDY

RENALDO, DUNCAN (Apr. 23, 1904–Sept. 3, 1980), actor, was born Casile Dumitree Cughienas in Romania. Almost nothing is known about his early years because of his own apparent unwillingness to supply such information. What does seem likely is that he arrived in Baltimore in the early 1920's aboard a coal ship, changed his name several times, married his first wife, Suzette, fathered a son, and worked his way into the motion-picture business in New York. His first starring role in a feature film was *Fifty-Fifty* in 1925.

Renaldo was signed by Metro-Goldwyn-Mayer in 1928. His first role in a major film was that of Esteban, a tragic romantic figure in *The Bridge of San Luis Rey* (1929), based on the novel by Thornton Wilder. The film was a combination silent movie and talkie, with spoken sequences at the beginning and end of the film. It was a critical, but not a financial, success. Reviewers liked the film but thought it too intellectual for the average moviegoer.

In March 1929, Renaldo went to Africa for nine months of location shooting for the film *Trader Horn*. He played a romantic lead opposite Edwina Booth in this early talkie that became known for its big budget look. The film cost $2 million, which made it one of the most expensive movies of its time. Critics praised the film for its documentary accuracy of the African landscape and predicted correctly that it would be a hit.

With his wavy hair and Latin good looks, Renaldo seemed destined for a long and successful career as a leading man. When he got home from Africa in 1930, however, he was sued for divorce by his wife, who also sued his costar Booth, for alienation of affection. Booth won her case, but after Renaldo's divorce was finalized in 1930, Suzette notified federal authorities that the information on the passport that he used to travel to Africa was incorrect—it claimed that he had been born in Camden, N.J. When *Trader Horn* premiered in Hollywood in 1931, Renaldo was facing perjury charges and deportation as an illegal alien. He was convicted and served eighteen months at the McNeill Island Federal Prison in Washington State. He was to have been deported upon his release, but President Franklin D. Roosevelt gave him a full pardon that allowed him to resume his film career.

The scandal had stalled his career as a romantic lead, but he found work at Republic Studios starting in 1937, making low-budget Western feature films and serials with such newcomers as Gene Autry and Roy Rogers. In the 1941 film *Outlaws of the Desert*, which starred William Boyd as Hopalong Cassidy, Renaldo played an Arab sheik. In 1939 he married Lea Rosenblatt and the marriage ended in divorce seven years later. The couple had three children.

Renaldo got the part of Lieutenant Berrendo in *For Whom the Bell Tolls*, which was released in 1943 and starred Gary Cooper and Ingrid Bergman. The years of prerelease publicity for this epic rivaled that of *Gone with the Wind* and the film was a major success. Renaldo's part was small, however, and little of the excitement about the film translated to him. It was his last major feature film.

From 1945 to 1950, Renaldo also starred in eight films as the Cisco Kid, a character that had been brought to the screen in the silent film era; Warner Baxter won the Academy Award for best actor in 1929 for his portrayal of the Cisco Kid in *In Old Arizona*. The character was based on the short story "Robin Hood of the Old West" by O. Henry. In 1949, Renaldo was asked to go back to the role for a syndicated television series. He accepted the part and convinced longtime vaudeville actor Leo Carrillo to join him as a comic sidekick. Renaldo argued that for the television series there should be less violence than in the movie versions, and he portrayed a sort of Don Quixote of the Old West. Renaldo was proud of the fact that the Cisco Kid never killed anybody. The series, which aired from 1951 to 1956, was a major success and for the first time in his career the actor was a household name. Renaldo, who did his own stunts, broke his neck in 1954 when a dropped boulder that was supposed to miss him made a direct hit. A total of 156 episodes were produced. By the time the last show was filmed in 1955, Renaldo had so many injuries from doing his own stunts that he was no longer able to mount a horse. Also in that year, he married his third wife, Audrey.

The actor retired to a ranch in Santa Barbara, Calif. He impressed interviewers as a thoughtful and soft-spoken man who was filled with endless enthusiasm for the acting profession and for the role that made him famous. Because the shows had been filmed in color, they had a long life in reruns in the 1960's and 1970's. He was often called upon to make public appearances as the Cisco Kid, which he did with great enthusiasm, often accompanied by the horse Diablo that he rode in the television series. Until his death in 1961, costar Carrillo was a frequent visitor to the ranch.

Renaldo was active in the Old Spanish Days of Santa Barbara, a festival that he once chaired. In 1973 the rock group War recorded a song called "Cisco Kid," which Renaldo promoted with a television appearance. He died in Santa Barbara.

[There is a substantial file on Renaldo at the New York Public Library for the Performing Arts at Lincoln Center. See also Evelyn M. Truitt, *Who Was Who on Screen* (1983). An obituary is in the *New York Times*, Sept. 4, 1980.]

TERRY BALLARD

REYNOLDS, MILTON (1892–Jan. 23, 1976), industrialist, was born in Albert Lea, Minn., where his father was a threshing-machine salesman. After dropping out of high school, he became an automobile salesman, and at the age of twenty was an independent tire dealer. By 1918 he was a millionaire, only to become bankrupt within four years. During the next eight years Reynolds rode a financial roller coaster, which resulted in three bankruptcies. Sometime in the early 1920's, Reynolds married Edna Loeb, who died in 1952. They had two children.

Reynolds moved to Chicago in the early 1920's and became a stock market speculator. He was nearly wiped out in the 1929 stock market crash. After two days of searching for new business ideas he purchased a printing shop that sold commercial signs with the intention of manufacturing the equipment used in sign making. The company, Print-A-Sign, proved another of Reynolds's successes.

During World War II, Reynolds engaged in several businesses, the most successful being the importation of silver cigarette lighters from Mexico, which earned him at least $500,000. While on a business trip to Buenos Aires in 1945, Reynolds came upon an early ballpoint pen invented by László Biro, a Hungarian journalist. While ballpoint pens were new on the market, they dated to 1888, when John Loud patented a version of them that never went into production. A type of ballpoint pen was invented in Czechoslovakia by Frank Klimes in the early 1930's and manufactured by him and Paul V. Eisner. The first of these instruments, called the Rolpen, was produced and marketed in Prague, in 1935, but this patent expired during World War II, when Klimes was in a concentration camp.

Biro, who had fled to Paris when Germany invaded Hungary, went to Argentina and sold the rights to Henry George Martin, a British promoter, who then organized a company to manufacture the pen, called the Eterpen. Some pens were produced and given away the United States government for distribution to servicemen.

The pen was a novelty. Not only could it write on almost any surface (as well as underwater) but it was leakproof, which made it a favorite with airmen. The Biro interests licensed its patents for American production to Eversharp Inc. and Eberhard Faber in May 1945. Stories of the new pen were featured in the press, but Eversharp and Eberhard Faber did not move swiftly into production.

Without revealing his motives to Biro or Martin, Reynolds returned to the United States, where he obtained a patent on a pen that delivered ink by gravity flow rather than the capillary action method featured in the Biro patent. Reynolds began production on Oct. 6, 1945, before the Biro interests could enter the American market.

Reynolds marketed the pens through the Gimbel Brothers department store in Manhattan, where they went on sale on Oct. 29, 1945, for $12.50. The pens were an instant success; Gimbels sold $100,000 worth of them the first day, and then notified Reynolds it would take all he could deliver. In the first three months Reynolds was able to sell 2 million pens through 60,000 retail outlets in the United States and thirty-seven foreign countries. Reynolds's company, Reynolds International Pens, had been capitalized at $26,000; after this three-month period, it had earned total revenues of $5.7 million, with a net income of $1.6 million. Gimbels accounted for the sale of 100,000 pens itself. It was one of the most successful new-product introductions in American history.

Stung by Reynolds's success, Eversharp and Eberhard Faber moved into production in December, which prompted Reynolds to seek a preliminary injunction against them for harming his sales. The injunction was denied, with Judge Paul Leahy concluding there were too many conflicting questions to act without a jury trial. Eversharp and Eberhard Faber introduced the Repeater pen in May 1946. But Eterpen was able to ship ballpoint pens manufactured in Argentina to the United States in March, where they were sold as Biromes at R. H. Macy and Company for $19.95. Reynolds responded that he soon would introduce a second pen with an improved ink chamber that would permit the pen to write for four years without refilling.

Other companies also entered the field, which was saturated by autumn of 1946. In February 1947, Macy's was able to advertise the sale of a Reynolds pen, the Rocket, for 98 cents; the next day Gimbels advertised the Rocket for 94 cents. The great ballpoint pen bonanza had ended. By 1948, the pens were selling at 39 cents.

As legal threats faded and pen production slowed, Reynolds turned to other interests. In mid-1947 he announced that he intended to break Howard Hughes's record of a round-the-world flight of ninety-one hours and fourteen minutes. Reynolds claimed the flight was also scientific in nature, since he intended to investigate rumors of mountains higher than Mt. Everest.

Reynolds refitted a surplus Air Force light attack bomber and teamed up in 1947 with veteran flyer William P. Odom to make the flight in less than seventy-nine hours. At refueling stops Reynolds mingled with well-wishers and distributed more than 1,000 ballpoint pens.

Soon after his return Reynolds sold his pen business and returned to manufacturing machinery and signs, but his business was more a hobby than anything else. In 1953, after the death of his first wife, he married Manuela Selas and relocated to Mexico. Reynolds died in Chicago, and his body was returned to Mexico for burial.

Rhine

[There is no biography of Milton Reynolds or, for that matter, a history of the ballpoint pen. Researchers in the field have to make do with articles in business magazines, of which there were many in the mid-1940's. See, for example, "Writes Anywhere," *Business Week*, May 26, 1945; "At Pens' Points," *Business Week*, Dec. 8, 1945; "Furor Over Pens," *Business Week*, Mar. 2, 1946; "Reynolds Offers Model 2," *Business Week*, Apr. 20, 1946; "Battle of the Pens," *Business Week*, May 4, 1946; "Fountain-Pen Scramble," *Fortune*, July 1946; and "Ball Point Bonanza," *Business Week*, Feb. 22, 1947. An obituary is in the *New York Times*, Jan. 25, 1976.]

ROBERT SOBEL

RHINE, JOSEPH BANKS (Sept. 29, 1895–Feb. 20, 1980), psychologist, was born in Waterloo, Pa., the son of Samuel Ellis Rhine and Elizabeth Ellen Vaughan. Rhine, the second of five children, spent his childhood in a fairly isolated mountain region of southern Pennsylvania, where people, including his mother, believed in omens, prophetic warnings, and other supernatural occurrences. His father, a farmer, merchant, and occasional public school teacher, scoffed at these psychic stories and discouraged any belief in them.

At the age of four, Rhine began accompanying his father when he taught school during the winter months between farming seasons. He learned to read by the age of five. His father encouraged him to study hard, and his mother wanted him to be a minister. Rhine did develop a strong interest in religion because of the influence of some devout relatives, the books to which he was exposed, and a seemingly natural philosophical disposition from which he developed a questioning mind. Rhine was eager for answers to perplexing questions about the nature of man, the meaning of existence, man's place in the universe, and other issues of an epistemological and metaphysical nature. Rhine's family moved eleven times from one small farming community to another during his elementary school years. Being rather shy and a bookworm, he was often teased and attacked by other students and frequently had to "fight his way to social acceptance," which helped him develop a tenacity and ability to stand up for his beliefs.

In 1910 the Rhine family moved to Marshallville, Ohio, where his father rented a farm from their neighbor, whose daughter, Louisa Ella Weckesser, taught in the local elementary school. Weckesser was four years older than Rhine but had much the same philosophical temperament. She was impressed with his maturity and integrity. He was thoughtful, quiet and self-confident, and had a passion for learning. They spent hours discussing religion and philosophy and soon developed a close relationship. In 1916 they both enrolled in the College of Wooster, Rhine as a student in the Department of Religion with the intention of becoming a minister, but he was soon frustrated by what he perceived to be the overly restrictive nature of religion. The next year he joined the United States Marine Corps and won the gold medal in the President's Rifle Match of 1919. After his discharge that year with the rank of sergeant, he enrolled at the University of Chicago, where Weckesser was also a student. They were married on Apr. 8, 1920, and had four children. Two years later, Rhine received his B.S. degree and his wife an M.S. degree. In 1923, Rhine received his M.S. degree in biology and Louisa a Ph.D.

From 1923 to 1924 the Rhines worked as assistant plant physiologists at the Boyce Thompson Institute for Plant Research in Yonkers, N.Y. From 1924 to 1926, Rhine was an instructor in botany at West Virginia University in Morgantown. He received a Ph.D. in 1925 from the University of Chicago, where his interest in psychic research germinated.

Disillusioned with orthodox religion but intrigued by questions concerning the nature of man posed by philosophy and religion, Rhine saw psychic research as an area in which to use science to address such questions. This possibility was suggested in a lecture on spirit survival by Sir Arthur Conan Doyle and by such books as Henri Bergson's *Creative Evolution* and William McDougall's *Body and Mind* and *Psychical Research as a University Study*. McDougall, a widely respected psychologist and advocate of psychic research, was chairperson of the Department of Psychology at Harvard University. Rhine moved to Cambridge to work with him in the summer of 1926, and to take advanced courses in psychology and philosophy. McDougall, however, was beginning a year's sabbatical, but the Rhines remained at Harvard until McDougall accepted the chairmanship of the newly formed Psychology Department at Duke University in Durham, N.C., and offered Rhine a research fellowship.

Beginning in 1927 as an evaluator of the mediumistic material of Dr. John F. Thomas,

Rhine

Rhine adopted an experimental approach to psychic research that he and McDougall called parapsychology. In 1930, Rhine, McDougall, and two of McDougall's former students, Karl Zener and Helge Lundholm, created the Parapsychology Laboratory at Duke University, which marked the beginning of the first sustained, systematic, and scientific study of psychic phenomena under controlled laboratory conditions in a university setting. Rhine was concerned with understanding the human mind and how it acquired knowledge, because, in his view, this determined one's "approach to life, living, and problem solving. For it is by what we are mentally even more than by what we are bodily that we identify and regulate ourselves." One fundamental question addressed by Rhine was whether the acquisition of knowledge is limited to the parameters of time and space as governed by the physical laws of the universe or whether the human mind can transcend scientific law and come to know things through means other than the known senses.

From 1930 to 1934, Rhine and his associates conducted 90,000 experiments with a wide variety of subjects to demonstrate the existence and functioning of psychic phenomena, which he termed extrasensory perception, or ESP, meaning perception without the mediation of sensation, including such phenomena as clairvoyance, telepathy, and precognition. Clairvoyance, the ESP of objects, is the ability to know objects and objective events without the use of the senses. A standard test of clairvoyance was to ask subjects to identify the order of cards with distinctive symbols in a shuffled deck hidden from their view. Telepathy, the ESP of another's mental activity or mind reading, is direct thought transference from one person to another without the intervention of any physical form of energy transmission. Rhine tested for telepathy by asking a subject, or "sender," to think of symbols on each card in a special deck while another subject, or "receiver," was locked in another room and simultaneously tried to state which card the sender had in mind. In these experiments, the score or number of successes is compared to the chance rate of scoring by appropriate mathematical and statistical principles of probability. Rhine obtained some impressive results and was convinced of the existence of ESP. He also discovered that these paranormal phenomena obeyed certain laws or were affected by certain conditions and subject characteristics.

In 1934, Rhine published his work in *Extra-Sensory Perception*, and although some scientists confirmed many of his findings, the book was roundly criticized by many scholars, some of whom questioned Rhine's methods and objectivity. Others pointed to the failure of many researchers to replicate Rhine's results, and still others maintained that Rhine's findings could be explained by factors other than ESP, such as natural laws, coincidence, fraud, and trickery. Nevertheless, Rhine doggedly pursued his work and remained devoted to the scientific method in exploring the dynamics of ESP. In 1937 he published much of the same material in a less technical volume, *New Frontiers of the Mind*. This book became a nonfiction best-seller and made ESP cards a commercial commodity.

In March 1937, Rhine founded the *Journal of Parapsychology*. In 1940 he became director of the Parapsychology Laboratory and with four of his assistants published *Extra-Sensory Perception After Sixty Years*. This volume surveyed and critically examined all the research evidence for and against ESP up to that time. It temporarily silenced many of Rhine's critics. During the 1940's Rhine broadened his research interests to include a related paranormal phenomenon, known as psychokinesis (PK), the ability of the mind to directly influence material objects, for example, to move objects without touching them or to influence the fall of dice on a dice toss. On July 30, 1962, the Foundation for Research on the Nature of Man was founded in Durham with the Institute for Parapsychology as its research unit. This organization allowed Rhine to continue his work after his retirement from Duke in 1965. He died at his home in Hillsborough, N.C.

J. B. Rhine is one of the most controversial figures in the history of psychology. He initiated a new branch of psychology, parapsychology, and for almost half a century he was the dominant force in that field throughout the world. Some have stated that his name is synonymous with parapsychology. He defined the concepts of parapsychology, developed its methods, and provided instruments for evaluating its basic principles.

[Rhine's authorized biography is Denis Brian, *The Enchanted Voyager: The Life of J. B. Rhine* (1982). Rhine's other books include *The Reach of Mind* (1947); *New World of the Mind* (1953); *Parapsychology: Frontier Science of the Mind* (1957), coauthored with J. G. Pratt; *Parapsychology Today* (1968), coedited with R. Brier; and "Telepathy and Other Untestable Hypotheses," *Journal of Parapsychology*, June 1974. Insights into Rhine's character can be found in Sally Rhine Feather, "Joseph Banks Rhine from a Daughter's Perspective," a paper delivered at the 100th annual convention of the American Psychological Association, Washington, D.C., 1992. An obituary is in the *New York Times*, Feb. 21, 1980.]

PETER J. WESTON

RITCHARD, CYRIL (Dec. 1, 1898–Dec. 18, 1977), actor, director, and producer, was born in Sydney, New South Wales, Australia, to Herbert Trimmnel-Ritchard and Margaret Collins. His father was a successful businessman and hotel owner and his mother was a homemaker. He studied at Jesuit primary and secondary schools and attended St. Aloysius College and the University of Sydney. His father hoped he would become a doctor, but he opted for the theater. In 1917 the gangling nineteen-year-old made his theatrical debut as a chorus boy. Over the next seven years he became a respected actor, singer, and director in his native country. Years later he declared, "I always think the way I developed comedy acting was as I was taken to my room to be spanked by my father, I had to think of something to make him laugh. If I could, it was a pretty weak spanking."

When his career began he not only cut short his medical studies but also his family name. As he explained, "It couldn't fit on the marquee, so I gave the first part to my dog." In 1925 he made his debut on the London stage with Madge Elliott, whom he married in 1935. The couple so charmed London and Australian audiences over the next several years that Noël Coward dubbed them "the musical Lunts."

During World War II, Ritchard performed in several serious plays in London. His most notable success was in 1942 as Algernon Moncrieff with Sir John Gielgud in Oscar Wilde's *The Importance of Being Earnest*. Between 1943 and 1945 he spent most of his time touring Egypt and Europe to entertain Allied troops. In 1946 he moved to New York, where in 1947 he made his Broadway debut with Gielgud in the Theatre Guild's well-received production of William Congreve's comedy *Love for Love*.

The tall, elegant man—he stood six feet, two inches tall and weighed 194 pounds—with the "lordly presence" soon followed that triumph with another in 1948, when he starred in John Van Druten's comedy *Make Way for Lucia*. In 1949 he returned to London to star in *Ann Veronica*. The next year he starred in the London production of *The Schoolmistress*. His transatlantic life reached its pinnacle in 1952 when he starred with Katharine Hepburn in George Bernard Shaw's *The Millionairess* in both London and New York productions. In addition, in 1958 he performed with Cornelia Otis Skinner on Broadway in a musical version of Samuel Taylor's *The Pleasure of His Company*.

His greatest role was his triumph in 1954 as Captain Hook opposite Mary Martin's Peter Pan on Broadway in a musical version of J. M. Barrie's classic play. The *Christian Science Monitor* review noted, "In the course of a marvelously inventive performance, he runs the acting gamut from Restoration comedy to British review. He not only runs it, he dances it in versatile exhibitions of the tango, tarantella, and waltz." For his efforts he won the 1954 Tony Award for best supporting actor. He repeated the performance in a live color production on NBC-TV on Mar. 7, 1955, and again on Jan. 3, 1956. He and the entire cast received rave reviews. In November 1955 the production received the Sylvania Award for being the "television show of the year."

Sadly, at the height of his professional acclaim his wife died on Aug. 8, 1955. He had been devoted to her for twenty years. Even long after her death he always referred to her as "my dearest darling." To help deal with his grief he immersed himself in his work. In late 1955 he appeared on the "Milton Berle Show" and on "Mr. Peepers." In February 1956 he costarred with Julie Harris in NBC-TV's production of Ferenc Molnár's *The Good Fairy*. In July he returned to NBC in their adaptation of *Die Fledermaus*, entitled *Rosalinda*. That fall he appeared with Celeste Holm in NBC's *Jack and the Beanstalk*. He capped this great run with his starring role in Gore Vidal's 1957 stage comedy *Visit to a Small Planet*.

In addition to acting on television, he directed numerous plays in London and New York. Among his most critically acclaimed Broadway successes were *The Reluctant Debutante* (1956) and *The Jockey Club Stakes* (1973). Ritchard's movie appearances were few: *Piccadilly* (1929), *Half-a-Sixpence* (1967), and Peter Ustinov's 1975 ABC-TV comic movie *Swordplay*.

Although his career peaked in the 1950's, Ritchard continued to direct and perform all over the world until the end of his life. In 1965 he starred in the musical stage play *The Roar of the Greasepaint, the Smell of the Crowd* in New York City. In 1972 he returned to Broadway in the musical *Sugar.* Two years later he directed and performed in the *The Gypsy Baron.*

Throughout his life Ritchard was something of a bon vivant. He once remarked, "I live far beyond my means, which is about the only way to live in a Central Park West apartment." He also had a country house in Ridgefield, Conn., and was a member of the Fifth Avenue Club, also called the Knickerbocker Club.

On Nov. 25, 1977, during a matinee performance of *Side by Side by Sondheim* in Chicago Ritchard suffered a massive heart attack on stage. He was taken to Northwestern Memorial Hospital where he eventually lapsed into a coma and died three weeks later. He was buried in Ridgefield, Conn.

Cyril Ritchard will no doubt be remembered for his square and smiling pale face and for his half century as one of the most elegant and stylish actors in the history of the English-speaking theater. Yet as he himself noted in 1970, he will always be remembered as Captain Hook. He wryly said, "I feel when I die that's all people will feel I have done." Probably not! Besides, most people still probably see Captain Hook as Cyril Ritchard, not Cyril Ritchard as Captain Hook.

[A profile of Ritchard appears in Marjorie Dent Candee, ed., *Current Biography Yearbook* 1957. Obituaries are in the *New York Times*, Dec. 19, 1977; the *Washington Post*, Dec. 19, 1977; and *Variety*, Dec. 21, 1977.]

William Head

ROBB, INEZ EARLY CALLAWAY (Nov. 29, 1900–Apr. 4, 1979), journalist, was born in Middletown, Calif., the daughter of Abner Kenton Callaway and Adah M. Asbill. Her parents lived in Caldwell, Idaho, but were staying with her maternal grandparents during her mother's difficult pregnancy. The Callaways lived in California for four or five years, and her father worked for the state highway department. When the family returned to Caldwell, he had fruit-packing and seed and grain businesses. As a young girl, Robb lived on the edge of Caldwell on a two-acre farm that was part of the land homesteaded by her paternal grandfather.

Robb attended school in Caldwell from September 1910 to December 1913. Later she wrote about her years growing up there, a small town near Boise where fire hydrants were nonexistent and the horse-drawn water wagon "circumnavigated Caldwell twice a day . . . [and] kids followed the white barrel-shaped wagon as if it were a latter-day Pied Piper." In 1914 she moved to Boise to live with an aunt, Nell Callaway, and attended Boise High School from January 1914 until her graduation in June 1918. She was class president in 1915 and 1916 and was on the staff of the school newspaper, *Courier*, every year from 1914 to 1917.

Robb took her first newspaper job at age fifteen, when she was a high school reporter on the *Evening Capital News.* Her first byline story was an account of an airplane ride with a barnstorming aviator at the Idaho State Fair in Boise. No other reporter at the *News* wanted the assignment, so she volunteered.

Robb won a $200 College Women's Club scholarship to the University of Idaho, which she attended from October 1918 to June 1920. She then worked for a year at the *Daily Statesman* in Boise. In August 1921 she transferred to the University of Missouri School of Journalism, from which she graduated in 1924 with a B.A.

Following her graduation, Robb went to work as a daily assignment reporter for the *Tulsa Daily World*, earning $40 per week. She spent twenty-seven months there. In September 1926 Robb traveled to Chicago with a scrapbook filled with her clippings. Joseph M. Patterson, the publisher of the *Chicago Tribune*, offered her $75 per week to work on the Sunday edition of the *New York Daily News.* She moved to New York City and worked for eighteen months as an assistant editor. In May 1928, Robb became society editor of the *Daily News.* She took over the column with the byline Nancy Randolph. She said she could not understand how she could be a society reporter because "I don't like champagne and I buy my hats in bargain basements." She married J. Addison Robb, an advertising executive and author, on Sept. 16, 1929; they had no children.

As a society reporter and editor of the *Daily News* from 1928 to 1938, Robb covered the coronation of King George VI of England (1936), the marriage of the Duke and Duchess of Windsor (1937), the America's Cup races of 1937, polo matches, prize fights, horse shows, the resorts and watering holes of the rich and famous, nightclubs, yacht races, the opera, weddings, and countless parties. Her emphasis on eyewitness reporting of society and society events set a standard and became a model for subsequent reporting. It was said that she treated society affairs as "real news," and that "she rolls up her sleeves and gets to work like a police reporter when the occasion seems to demand tenacity." Once, to get a story from close up, she crashed a society wedding disguised as a widow in deep mourning.

Robb left the *Daily News* in 1938 to work for the International News Service (INS). For fifteen years she wrote a five-days-a-week general news column, "Assignment: America," that appeared in the Hearst newspapers (including the *New York Journal-American*). In 1939 she was one of the reporters who traveled on the train with the king and queen of England during their six-week tour of Canada and the United States. In the summer of that year she flew across the Atlantic when Pan American inaugurated its European service. She stayed in England to write a series of reports on that nation at war, and she went to Ireland to do a story on the first American contingent to arrive there.

Robb returned from England in the spring of 1942 and less than a year later was off to cover World War II. In January 1943 she and Ruth Cowan of the Associated Press were the first women to be accredited as war correspondents during the North African invasion. They traveled on a ship carrying the first two companies of Women's Auxiliary Army Corps (WAACs) to North Africa—the first contingent of WAACs sent overseas. In Algiers she and Cowan got a cold reception from the chief of the Associated Press bureau, who did not approve of women correspondents. While at the front, Robb watched the retreat of the American forces and the advance of the Germans commanded by Field Marshal Erwin Rommel. When the correspondents' plane left the front without Robb, she rode back to Algiers in a truck.

In 1945, Robb covered the inaugural sessions of the United Nations in San Francisco. She also made a trip around the world by plane in fewer than six days, breaking a record. She traveled to Germany in the spring of 1946 and to South America that summer. In Argentina she interviewed Juan Perón and Argentine cabinet officials. In Chile, Robb had the unusual experience of interviewing two presidents on successive days—the first president resigned the day he gave the interview. She visited Uruguay and Brazil on this trip as well.

In the fall of 1947, Robb flew to Texas City, Tex., to cover a series of explosions that had leveled the harbor area. She arrived shortly after the first series of explosions, and just as another blast showered bricks and pieces of metal all around her. She was blown to the ground by the blast, which reportedly flattened the taxi she had left moments before and killed several people standing nearby.

Robb was one of the few reporters allowed inside Westminster Abbey to cover the wedding of Philip Mountbatten and Princess Elizabeth of England in 1947. For her coverage of that event she received the George R. Holmes Memorial Award for distinguished reporting, the first woman to be so honored. In 1953 she covered the coronation of Queen Elizabeth II.

On May 7, 1948, Robb received the Missouri Honor Award for Distinguished Service in Journalism from the University of Missouri School of Journalism. The citation noted that the award was "in recognition of her long series of stories of great events and interviews with famous leaders at home and abroad; the spirit of adventure, sense of humor, and understanding of newsworthy situations which have made her one of the greater reporters of her times; and her never-failing zest for journalism as a great profession." In accepting the award, Robb said, "I have tried for many years to be a credit to the profession I have loved passionately since we embraced each other when I was not quite fifteen. When I was in grammar school, I was told that one could not love an inanimate thing. But the newspaper profession is an exception: No one can deny that it is animate!"

In 1953, Robb left the INS to write a daily opinion column for the Scripps-Howard newspapers and United Features Syndicate. Until her retirement in 1969, this column was carried in close to 140 newspapers in the United States and Canada. Her columns dealt with women and fashion, her family life, life in the American West, manners and morals in American life and politics, contemporary church architecture, Hungarian freedom fighters, civil liberties and citizenship, and the importance of education and the teaching profession in America. She also wrote a front-page series investigating the story in Paris behind the Algerian crisis. Her style was described as "a lively use of the vernacular with a sense of humor, and underneath is a solid foundation, a knowledge of the classics and a deep regard for them."

In 1957, Robb received the New York Newspaper Women's Club Award for the best column in any field. At that time her column appeared five nights weekly in the *New York World Telegram and Sun*. Her work also was published in the *Saturday Evening Post*, the *Saturday Review of Literature*, the *New Republic*, and *Vogue*. In 1962, Robb published her only book, *Don't Just Stand There*, a collection; many of the pieces had first appeared in her column.

Robb died in Tucson, Ariz.

[See *Mademoiselle*, May 1940; and "Scripps-Howard Gets Inez Robb's Column," *Editor and Publisher*, Oct. 24, 1953. Obituaries are in the *New York Times* and the *Washington Post*, both Apr. 6, 1979; and in the *Chicago Tribune*, Apr. 8, 1979.]

AMY SCHEWEL

ROBESON, PAUL LEROY (Apr. 9, 1898–Jan. 23, 1976), singer, actor, linguist, and political activist, was born in Princeton, N.J., the fifth and last child of Maria Louisa Bustill and William Drew Robeson. His mother, a teacher at the Robert Vaux School in Philadelphia, was of mixed black, Delaware Indian, and white origin, and the daughter of one of Philadelphia's most advantaged and distinguished black families. His father, a former slave, graduated from Lincoln College in 1878 and was an ordained minister at the Witherspoon Street Presbyterian Church in Princeton.

The Robeson family suffered a reversal of fortune, beginning in 1900, when William lost his Princeton pastorate and culminating in 1904 with the death of Maria Louisa in a household fire. In 1907 the family moved to Westfield, N.J., and in 1910 to Somerville. One of the few blacks attending Somerville High School, Robeson excelled academically, competed with distinction in oratorical and debating contests, and showed considerable athletic promise. During his senior year he placed first in a competitive scholarship exam for Rutgers College. Unlike his brothers, who attended all-black colleges, Robeson decided to enroll at Rutgers.

Ambitious and eager to prove himself in a white setting, Robeson began his studies at Rutgers in 1915. Academics came first: he worked hard and earned the scholastic distinction he sought. There he also experienced his first taste of fame. In 1917, Walter Camp named Robeson to his roster of college football stars (because of the war, no official All-American team was picked) and in 1918 selected him for the All-American team. With his name splashed on sports pages throughout the country, Robeson put Rutgers on the map and learned that success could do much to break down racial barriers. He graduated from Rutgers in 1919, a member of Phi Beta Kappa, winner of numerous oratorical awards, an All-American in football, and the recipient of twelve varsity letters in sports.

After graduation Robeson moved to Harlem in New York City and began law classes at New York University. Leaving Rutgers and settling into city life proved a difficult transition. Robeson disliked New York University, and in February 1920 he transferred to Columbia University. He worked to pay rent and tuition and tried to keep his hand in athletics, coaching football at Lincoln University and playing basketball with Harlem's St. Christopher team.

In Harlem, Robeson met his future wife, Eslanda ("Essie") Cardozo Goode, a descendant of the prominent Sephardic Jewish Cardozo family and a graduate of Columbia University. She was a histological chemist at Presbyterian Hospital in New York City, the first black staff member of the hospital. They were married on Aug. 17, 1921, and had one child.

With his wife's encouragement, Robeson began to consider career possibilities other than law. Professional football offered good money, and Robeson played with the Akron Pros (1920–1921) and the Milwaukee Badgers (1921–1922) but soon tired of the game. During his college years he had occasionally earned money singing, and in Harlem he had taken advantage of performing opportunities, among them his acting debut in June 1920, playing the title role in the Harlem YWCA's revival of Ridgely Torrence's *Simon the Cyrenian*.

In late February 1923, Robeson graduated from Columbia Law School and began seeking work. The racist hostility he met while working for a firm specializing in estates discouraged him, so in 1923, when he was offered the lead in a new Eugene O'Neill play, *All God's Chillun Got Wings*, Robeson jumped at the opportunity. Although the play's subject matter—interracial marriage—sparked a storm of controversy in New York City and throughout the country, Robeson earned both timely exposure and fine reviews for his performance in *Chillun* as well as in a revival of *The Emperor Jones* staged by the Provincetown Players that same year.

Accompanied by musician, composer, and singer Lawrence Brown, Robeson made his formal concert debut in April 1925 at the Provincetown Playhouse (MacDougal Street Theatre). Performing a program composed entirely of black spirituals and folk songs, Robeson and Brown scored a huge personal and professional success. Proof came when the Victor Talking Machine Company offered Robeson and Brown a recording contract. That summer Robeson traveled to London to perform in a revival of O'Neill's *The Emperor Jones.* In England, he sang on the radio, thus formally introducing himself to the British public: it was the beginning of a long and intense friendship that would last for decades.

In 1926, Robeson and Brown undertook their first American concert tour under the management of James B. Pond. Although they received good reviews, audiences were often small and the traveling difficult, and for all their effort, they made little money. Discouraged, Robeson hoped to put his name back in the limelight with his performance in Frank Dazey and Jim Tully's play *Black Boy*, but reviewers almost universally panned the play, and it closed after only three weeks.

Hurriedly Mrs. Robeson began booking dates for another tour to begin in February 1927. This tour proved even more disastrous than the first. In the spring she told Robeson that she was pregnant. Essie and Paul had discussed having a child earlier and Paul had made it clear that he was not ready. Essie's news left him stunned and angry. When their son was born in November 1927, Robeson was in Paris, on tour with Lawrence Brown.

The years 1928–1932 were a time of great professional achievement for Robeson. Late in 1927, when work prospects had looked particularly bleak, he signed a contract with a white producer, Caroline Dudley Reagan, agreeing to appear in an American revue in the fall of 1928. Shortly after signing the contract, he was offered the role of Joe in a London production of *Show Boat*, by Jerome Kern and Oscar Hammerstein II, based on a novel by Edna Ferber. Much to everyone's surprise, the London *Show Boat* was a smash hit, with Robeson's singing of "Ol' Man River" the production's chief drawing card. Soon Robeson was giving concerts at the Drury Lane Theatre as well as performing in the musical. Robeson's presence and physical appearance—he was arrestingly handsome—combined with his deep, sonorous voice and shy, boyish manner, had an almost magical effect on British audiences. They lionized him, and within a short time he found himself courted by British socialites. It was an exhilarating experience, and when the time came to return to the United States to fulfill his contract obligations, Robeson refused.

The Robesons took up permanent residence in England, and Robeson and Brown earned a name for themselves touring Europe and the British provinces. In May 1930, Robeson played the role of Othello opposite Peggy Ashcroft in Maurice Browne's London production of the play. It was the first time since Ira Aldridge, the great black actor whose portrayal of the Moor in the 1860's won plaudits throughout Britain and the Continent, that a major theatrical production had cast a black man in the role. Initially reviewers hailed Robeson's performance, but later assessments were more critical. Robeson was chided, in particular, for his failure to affect the bearing of a military man.

Coincidental with the *Othello* opening, Eslanda Goode Robeson's *Paul Robeson, Negro* was published. The book, which received mediocre reviews, exacerbated problems within the Robeson marriage. By the end of 1930 the couple had separated, and their relationship continued to deteriorate over the next two years. In 1932, Essie announced publicly that she was suing for divorce. Robeson had planned to marry a white Englishwoman, but she rejected him. Her refusal devastated Robeson. By the end of 1932, Essie had canceled divorce proceedings, and the couple proceeded to work out a marital arrangement satisfactory to them both.

Robeson threw himself into his work. It was a settled and focused Robeson who in the spring of 1933 performed in *All God's Chillun Got Wings*. Directed by André Van Gyseghem and produced by Roland Adam, the production proved a huge critical success and perhaps the most brilliant acting performance of Robeson's career. In May, Robeson sailed for New York to star in a film version of *The Emperor Jones.* America's racial business-as-usual hit Robeson like a slap across the face, and he was irritated and annoyed throughout the filming. The racist underpinnings of the American film industry coupled with the black community's criticism of his willingness to play the role of the corrupt emperor disheartened him, and he returned to England determined to pursue future movie opportunities in the British film industry.

Robeson made five films set in Africa and produced by British film studios between 1934 and 1937: *Sanders of the River* (1935), *My Song Goes Forth* (1937), *Song of Freedom* (1937), *King Solomon's Mines* (1937), and *Jericho* (1937). For the British film industry these "Empire films" offered a viable means of competing with the gigantic American film industry. For Robeson they provided an alternative to America's stereotypical portrayal of blacks. With each film he was initially enthusiastic, confident it would broaden the public's understanding of Africa, but each proved a disappointment. It took Robeson five years to comprehend the futility of trying to alter stereotypical views of Africa through the medium of British films.

During the filming of *Sanders of the River*, Robeson viewed footage shot in central Africa by filmmaker Zoltan Korda. The 160,000 feet of film recorded details of African life, including music, speech, dancing, and rituals never before seen in the West. The footage fascinated, moved, and inspired Robeson. He had discovered an important piece of his identity, and for the next several years he feverishly studied African languages and cultures.

At the end of 1934, Robeson made his first trip to the Soviet Union, accepting an invitation by the Russian film director Sergei Eisenstein to visit and discuss a film based on the life of Toussaint L'Ouverture. During the summer of 1936 he returned to the Soviet Union for a concert tour and extended vacation. Russia filled the gap left by Robeson's growing disenchantment with England. Robeson was particularly impressed by the Soviet Union's seemingly complete absence of racial prejudice, its policy toward minorities, and its national arts program. Concerning his own treatment there, he later commented that for the first time he walked the earth with complete dignity. In 1936, Robeson and Eslanda announced they would send their son to the Soviet Union to complete his schooling, primarily as a way of sparing him the experience of American and British racism.

In the summer of 1936, while Essie and their son took a three-month tour of Africa and Robeson finished work on two films set in Africa, civil war broke out in Spain. For the next three years Robeson devoted his full energy to working for the Popular Front Republican government's efforts to resist General Franco's rise to power. He spoke, sang, visited Madrid and Barcelona, and attended numerous fund-raisers. Spain focused his sense of mission, forcing him into the political arena. Once he was there, Robeson never left.

Although the Republicans would lose the fight in Spain, among popular front groups the fervor to combat fascism remained strong. For Robeson, this translated to rallies to aid Spanish refugees and a renewed commitment to using his artistic talents and charismatic personality to fight for the rights of the oppressed. After a brief summer trip in 1939 to the United States, Robeson returned to England for his last British film, *Proud Valley*. Written and directed by his close friend and Communist party member, Herbert Marshall, *Proud Valley* was the film of which Robeson was most proud.

On Sept. 3, 1939, as the Robesons finished preparations for a permanent return to the United States, England and France declared war on Germany. On Nov. 5, 1939, CBS Radio premiered Robeson singing John LaTouche and Earl Robinson's "Ballad for Americans." Public response to this rousing, patriotic piece was overwhelming. For the next two years, as Robeson crisscrossed the country on tour, "Ballad for Americans" preceded him. To American audiences Robeson was the ballad's nameless hero, a symbol of national unity and spirit.

In October 1943, after trial runs in Cambridge, Mass., and Princeton, N.J., Robeson played the role of Othello in Margaret Webster's Broadway production of the Shakespeare play. His portrayal was a historic event, the first time in American history that a black man had played the role on Broadway. Commercially the production set a precedent also: 296 Broadway performances, the longest run on record for any American Shakespeare production. *Othello* on the road likewise proved a rousing success. For nearly a year and a half (1944–1945) the production toured the United States and Canada, methodically excluding, as stipulated by Robeson, any city (including Washington, D.C.) that enforced segregated seating.

The *Othello* years were pivotal in Robeson's career as an artist and political activist. Although he had attained great success prior to 1942, his popularity now reached its apex. Robeson was awarded the NAACP's coveted

Robeson

Spingarn Medal in 1945 and concluded the year with a spectacular winter-spring (1945–1946) American concert tour. Throughout, he drew record crowds, and by June 1946 had more than seventy dates booked for the following year. As his career skyrocketed, Robeson increasingly assumed the role of spokesman for a variety of issues: the rights of oppressed minorities and of the working class, the fight to defeat fascism, an American policy of friendship with the Soviet Union, the struggle to attain lasting peace. American audiences loved Robeson and therefore tolerated his increasingly frequent political commentary as part of the price they paid to hear his magnificent voice.

Personally, however, Robeson found it difficult to restrain his onstage politicking. He resented audiences who listened to his "pretty" songs but ignored his political message. With the wave of lynchings that followed the war, Robeson's political commitments took on more serious tones. By the summer of 1946 he was virtually obsessed with the causes he espoused, in particular the fight to gain passage of a federal antilynching bill and the Council on African Affairs–sponsored drive to raise money for famine-stricken Africa. In 1946, Robeson met with President Harry Truman to discuss the passage of antilynching legislation. Robeson had already publicly criticized the new administration and denounced England and Churchill as well, all the while vigorously defending the Soviet Union. In contrast to NAACP secretary Walter White's conciliatory meeting with the president a few weeks earlier, the meeting between Truman and Robeson was brief and stormy. The chief executive treated the Robeson delegation with near contempt, and Robeson reacted in kind.

The tide turned quickly for Robeson. In the spring of 1947 the city council of Peoria, Ill., voted not to allow Robeson use of any public gathering place for an upcoming concert appearance. The reason: Robeson's "un-American" beliefs. Peoria was just the first in a long line of towns, cities, and organizations that would ban Robeson from their stages and concert halls.

In 1947, Robeson announced he would temporarily give up professional concertizing in order to devote himself full-time to politics, and throughout 1948 he campaigned aggressively for the Progressive party candidate, Henry Wallace. Despite Wallace's dismal showing in the 1948 elections, Robeson continued politicking. On tour in Europe during the early months of 1949, he again condemned the Truman administration and British imperialism. The State Department by this time had Robeson under constant surveillance.

In April 1949, Robeson attended the Congress of the World Partisans of Peace in Paris. Reports from the press quoted him as saying that no American black would go to war on behalf of the United States against the Soviet Union. The report was widely circulated in the American press and elicited heated reaction. The vast majority of Americans—blacks and whites alike—viewed it as next to treason.

Robeson returned to the United States early in the summer of 1949, in time for the Smith Act trials, which resulted in the incarceration of several of his closest Communist friends. The June 1949 marriage of his son to a white Columbia student, Marilyn Paula Greenberg, drew additional adverse reaction. By the end of the summer it was clear that Robeson had lost the support of establishment black leadership. In June 1949, Columbia Artists Management canceled eighty-five scheduled concerts. As longtime friends and allies fell by the wayside and his professional horizons shrank before his eyes, Robeson redoubled his attack, determined that his views would be heard.

On Aug. 27, 1949, Robeson was scheduled to appear at an outdoor concert in Peekskill, N.Y. The concert never took place, however. Instead, a protest demonstration, organized by local veterans' organizations, degenerated into a riot that left several concertgoers seriously injured. Robeson never got near the concert grounds, for friends who had received word of the violence whisked him back to safety in New York City. Most eyewitnesses claimed that local police had allowed rioters free rein, and public opinion throughout the country condemned the Peekskill violence. Robeson was infuriated, and when supporters asked him to perform in Peekskill the following week, he agreed. For the second concert, state and local police were on hand in large numbers, as well as an army of 3,000 volunteers gathered by Leon Strauss of the International Fur and Leather Workers Union (CIO). No violence occurred until concertgoers began to leave, at which point protesters stoned and overturned cars. The second riot lasted well into the night and left 150 people injured seriously enough to require medical attention. After Peekskill, organizations were more reluctant than ever to sponsor Robeson concerts, and supporters, frightened of reprisals, left the Robeson ranks.

Under heavy criticism in the United States, Robeson made preparations for a European tour. But, in July 1950, he was refused a passport. For eight years Robeson would fight to regain his right to travel abroad. In the interim he remained a prisoner in his own country. Between 1950 and 1955 virtually all of the organizations with which he was associated were declared subversive by the attorney general. Denied access to the concert stage, radio, television, and recording studios, Robeson was closely watched by the FBI and other federal, state, and local agencies. During these years his only backers were the remnants of the radical left wing—the Communist party, Council on African Affairs, the Civil Rights Congress, and the National Negro Labor Council. His only forum was the short-lived journal *Freedom* (1950–1955).

Robeson turned to black churches for support, but they feared reprisal, and many turned him away. Worse still, the black establishment, most notably the NAACP (led by Roy Wilkins) openly attacked him. Likewise, Robeson was rebuffed by the white liberal "vital center": Eleanor Roosevelt reportedly refused to let him appear on her television program, and other whites followed suit. Stripped of his livelihood, Robeson's income fell precipitously from the 1944 high of $200,000 to $16,000 in 1956. In 1956 the Robesons were forced to sell their home in Connecticut. For the first time in his life, Robeson had time on his hands.

In the meantime, American blacks made tremendous gains in the area of civil rights, exemplified by *Brown* v. *Board of Education* in 1954, the young Martin Luther King's 1955–1956 bus boycott in Montgomery, Ala., the 1957 Civil Rights Act, and the beginning of school integration in Little Rock, Ark. Ironically, Robeson had no part in any of this. As far as the burgeoning civil rights movement was concerned, he was a forgotten man.

In 1956, at the age of fifty-eight, Robeson had prostate surgery and, for the first time in his life, worried about his physical well-being. There was still no end in sight as far as the passport denial was concerned, and continued litigation was proving costly. Nikita Khrushchev's 1956 revelations concerning the extent of Stalin's crimes, and the divisions that resulted, almost totally destroyed what was left of the Communist party in America. Finally, in the first months of 1958, cracks began to appear in the anti-Communist wall. Robeson was granted permission to give concerts in several American cities as well as to travel within the Western Hemisphere. Then, in June, came the news Robeson had been waiting for: he had been granted a passport. He left America for England almost immediately. He did not return until December 1963.

Robeson was sixty years old when he returned to England. Devastated by World War II, Great Britain was dependent on the United States for financial and military aid, and while the British treated Robeson regally on stage, they made it quite clear that they preferred he keep his politics to himself. Disappointed with England, Robeson began a five-year sojourn in the eastern bloc nations. There he was showered with awards and honorary degrees, and acclaim for his concert performances. It was the closest Robeson had come in years to the glory days of the past.

Still, Robeson felt like a man without a country. To compound matters, both he and Essie were ill, Essie with breast cancer and Robeson with both physical and emotional ailments. They were hospitalized for a time in Moscow. In 1960 the Robesons began a long and grueling tour of New Zealand and Australia, with plans to move on to India and China. The undertaking proved too much, however. They returned to England, where in 1961 Paul was placed in a sanatorium outside London to undergo treatment for physical and emotional problems. In September 1963 they entered a sanatorium in East Berlin. After three months, doctors decided Robeson was fit to travel, and the couple returned to the United States. Essie died in 1965, and Robeson went to live with his sister in Philadelphia, where he remained in seclusion for the rest of his life. Both Paul and Eslanda Robeson were buried in Ferncliff Cemetery in Hartsdale, N.Y.

[The Robeson Family Archives, a vast collection of over 50,000 items located at the Moorland-Spingarn Research Center at Howard University in Washington, D.C., includes newspaper clippings, correspondence, letters, and diaries. The biggest drawback of this collection is that it represents Eslanda Robeson far better than Paul Robeson. See his autobiography, *Here I Stand* (1958). Biographies include Eslanda Robeson, *Paul Robeson, Negro* (1930);

Shirley Graham, *Paul Robeson, Citizen of the World* (1946); Marie Seton, *Paul Robeson* (1958); and Martin B. Duberman, *Paul Robeson* (1989). See also Philip S. Foner's collection of Robeson's writing and speeches, *Paul Robeson Speaks* (1978). An obituary and follow-up articles are in the *New York Times*, Jan. 24, 25, 27, and 28, 1976.]

SHEILA TULLY BOYLE
ANDREW BUNI

ROCHE, JOSEPHINE ASPINWALL (Dec. 2, 1886–July 29, 1976), coal operator, government official, and labor leader, was born in Neligh, Nebr., the only child of John J. Roche, a conservative coal mine operator, and Ella Aspinwall. She received her B.A. from Vassar College in 1908, returned to her family in Denver, Colo., and worked as a probation officer of the Denver Juvenile Court for one year. She then enrolled at Columbia University, from which she graduated with an M.A. in sociology in 1910.

For the next two years Roche did settlement work for the New York Probation Society. In 1912 she returned to Denver and became Denver's first policewoman. After leaving the police force, she served as executive secretary of the Colorado Progressive Society and as director of the Girls Department of Denver's Juvenile Court; her work with Denver's poor and delinquent children in this latter post reinforced liberal and radical ideas she had been developing since college.

Her national service began in 1915 with her appointment as special agent for the Commission for Relief in Belgium. Shortly after the United States entered World War I, President Woodrow Wilson called her to Washington, D.C., to appoint her director of the Foreign Language Education Service and make her a member of the Committee on Public Information. In the two posts she worked with editors of foreign-language newspapers to provide information about the government's goals and actions to America's non-English-speaking population. In 1923 she was named director of the editorial division of the United States Children's Bureau, an agency that provided immigrants with information on health, education, immigration laws, and other matters.

While serving in Washington, Roche attempted to combine marriage with her career but found the two incompatible. She married Edward Hale Bierstadt on July 2, 1920; they had no children and their marriage ended two years later.

In 1925, Roche returned to Denver, where she served as referee of the Juvenile Court until her father's death in 1927. Roche inherited his minority holdings in the Rocky Mountain Fuel Company, Colorado's second-largest coal company. She angered fellow shareholders when she defended striking miners to the Colorado Industrial Commission. She angered them even more by proposing that the United Mineworkers of America (UMW) be asked to unionize the company's employees. When irate stockholders sold their shares, Roche bought them, thus acquiring a majority interest in Rocky Mountain Fuel.

She quickly appointed friends of the UMW as company managers and she assumed the post of vice-president. After allowing the UMW time to organize the workers, she signed a contract with the union that was described as a Magna Carta of industrial democracy and that gave her workers the highest wages in Colorado's mines. During an ensuing price war, many miners loaned one-half their pay for several months to the company to keep it in business. The company operated until inherited debt forced it into bankruptcy in 1944. During the early days of the National Recovery Administration, Roche helped develop the National Bituminous Coal Code and worked tirelessly as a member of the Bituminous Coal Authority.

In 1934 she became the first woman to run for governor in Colorado: she won the city vote, but lost the more conservative rural vote. Although unsuccessful in her bid for elective office, she attracted the attention of President Franklin D. Roosevelt, who appointed her assistant secretary to the Treasury that same year, putting her in charge of the United States Health Service. She also became the Treasury's representative on the Committee on Economic Security, which formulated the recommendations on which the Social Security Act was based. In 1935, Roosevelt named Roche chair of the executive committee of the National Youth Administration. In 1937, after the Social Security Act had been passed, Roosevelt established the Interdepartmental Committee to Coordinate Health and Welfare Activities with Roche as its chair.

In the same year she resigned her Treasury position to return to Colorado to manage her coal company after the death of its president.

Roosevelt was so reluctant to let her go that he announced that the position would be held open indefinitely to await her return. Secretary of the Treasury Henry Morgenthau, Jr., called her the "ablest and most sincere advocate of public health."

She returned to Washington in 1939. As chair of the Interdepartmental Committee to Coordinate Health and Welfare Activities, she took on the forces controlling health care, most notably the American Medical Association (AMA). In an effort to provide universal access to basic health care services, Roche used a wealth of evidence amassed by the United States Public Health Service, the Committee on Social Security, and earlier committees. She supported the Social Security committee's declaration that voluntary insurance held no promise of success. The AMA fought her efforts, labeling them "socialized medicine." The *New York Times* supported Roche, claiming that the AMA opposed "any encroachment on the traditional social and economic prerogatives of the private practitioner."

Roche's committee called for an extension of public health services, maternal and child health care, care for recipients of public assistance and low income persons, disability insurance, and a comprehensive health care program to be developed in cooperation with the states. Her recommendations were included in the Wagner Bill presented to Congress in 1939.

Roche served as president of the National Consumers' League from 1939 until 1944. After World War II, she worked in Europe for two years, writing about the European coal industry for the *New York Herald Tribune*.

She became the first director of the UMW's welfare and retirement fund in 1947, remaining active with the fund until 1971. She left under a dark cloud, however, after being convicted of mismanagement of funds for depositing large amounts of pension funds in non-interest-bearing accounts in a bank largely owned by the UMW. Roche conceded poor judgment in her court testimony, saying, "There's no excuse, perhaps for it all. I know how terrible it looks to have so much money sitting there." She and John L. Lewis had feared a shortage of ready cash in an emergency, she explained, a fear bred of the costly labor battles of the depression era. In retrospect she agreed that more money should have been invested.

Roche's reputation as a tough but caring public servant resulted in several colorful stories about her. As a child she reportedly asked to go to her father's mine and, upon being told that it was too dangerous, replied, "If it is too dangerous for me, why is it not too dangerous for the men?" Another story concerns a meeting held to work out details of the coal code. When Roche was asked to leave the audience and join the male speakers on the platform to add some beauty to the proceedings, she replied, "What this meeting needs is not beauty but guts."

Whatever the authenticity of those stories, Josephine Roche certainly made her own path as an independent woman in a society not used to one. She championed causes important to the lives of those who had few powerful friends, and accomplished a number of significant "firsts" for women.

Roche died in Bethesda, Md.

[Roche's papers are located in various collections in the National Archives, the Franklin D. Roosevelt Library, and the Hoover Institution. There is also a collection of her papers in the Western Historical Collections, University of Colorado. Her only publication is *Wage Earning Women and Girls in Baltimore; A Study of the Cost of Living in 1918*. The *Proceedings of the National Health Conference, July 18, 19, 20, 1938* covers a substantial part of the debate on that issue. For other aspects of her career, see "Woman Unravels an Industrial Knot," *New York Times Magazine*, Feb. 7, 1932; "Miss Roche Resigns Her Post in Treasury," *New York Times*, Oct. 28, 1937; "A Union Angel," *Business Week*, June 17, 1944; "Battler for Miners," *Business Week*, Apr. 8, 1967; George Lardner, "UMW Fund Chief Criticizes Hoarding," *Washington Post*, Dec. 9, 1971; and "U.M.W. Must Pay Fund $11.5 Million," *New York Times*, Jan. 8, 1972. An obituary is in the *New York Times*, July 31, 1976.]

KEN LUEBBERING

ROCKEFELLER, JOHN DAVISON, 3D (Mar. 21, 1906–July 10, 1978), philanthropist, was born in New York City, the son of John Davison Rockefeller, Jr., a philanthropist and heir to the Standard Oil fortune, and Abby Greene Aldrich. As the eldest of five sons (he also had an older sister), he was reared to assume his father's role as the steward of the family's commitment to social service through investment in worthy causes. The Rockefeller Baptist faith was reflected in his devotion to duty and serious purpose; his mother's warmth and good humor were expressed in his capacity for friendship.

The Rockefellers maintained homes in New York City; Pocantico Hills in West Tarrytown, N.Y.; and Seal Harbor, Maine. The children enjoyed the rich opportunities for recreation available in these environments. Rockefeller was enrolled in four different private schools from the age of six, but he was a weak student, suffered from bad health, and was painfully shy. At age fifteen he was judged ready for a college preparatory regimen and entered the Loomis School at Windsor, Conn. A mediocre student at Loomis, Rockefeller struggled with a phobia about his appearance—he was tall, thin, and sharp featured—but by his senior year he was involved in boxing and debating, was on the tennis team, and was elected to the student council. He also made his father proud by saving half of his allowance and donating it to charity.

In choosing to attend Princeton instead of Brown, his father's college, Rockefeller made one of many efforts to temper the stifling paternal influence that he faced at home and later in such organizations as the Rockefeller Foundation, where he was surrounded by mature executives of formidable accomplishment who were reluctant to grant initiative to a younger and greatly privileged man without professional expertise. At Princeton, he began to display the intellectual and social skills necessary to succeed as a social leader. He lettered in tennis as a freshman, joined the Cap and Gown Society, taught English to immigrants for three years, and graduated in 1929 with high honors in economics, eighty-fifth in a class of 437. His senior thesis was on industrial relations, a subject of intense interest to his family since the 1914 Ludlow Massacre during a strike at the family-owned Ludlow Fuel and Iron Company in Colorado.

While attending college, Rockefeller developed interests that would inform his career as a philanthropist. Some influential professors were eugenicists, and he took an independent reading course on Malthus. In 1928 his father had him appointed to the board of directors of the Bureau of Social Hygiene, the means through which the elder Rockefeller invested money in social science research and action programs in criminology, sex education, and birth control. Rockefeller became especially interested in birth control and population issues. When the Bureau was terminated in 1934, he wrote to his father that he intended to maintain a strong interest in birth control. The elder Rockefeller also drew his son into his work with the League of Nations. The younger Rockefeller spent the summer of 1928 as an intern in the Information Section of the League's office in Geneva, Switzerland, thus beginning a lifelong engagement with international relations. He urged his father to allow him to make a world tour after graduation, overcame objections that it would appear to be a rich boy's frivolous grand tour, and traveled through Russia, China, and Japan, concluding his trip with work for an Institute for Pacific Relations conference in Japan. He returned home to begin apprenticeship in his father's New York office in December 1929, shortly after the start of the Great Depression, with an abiding interest in Japanese culture and in improving American relations with Asian people.

Rockefeller married Blanchette Ferry Hooker on Nov. 11, 1932. A Vassar woman and president of her class, Blanchette traced her lineage to the Puritan founders of Connecticut. Her father was a leading manufacturer and a Republican party activist. Possessed of a zest for life and socially at ease, she proved an ideal mate for a sometimes inhibited spouse. Of their four children, their only son, John Davison Rockefeller, IV, known as Jay, carried on the family tradition of public service as governor of West Virginia (1976–1985) and United States Senator from West Virginia (beginning in 1985).

Despite the support of a strong family, independent wealth provided by trusts that his father established for all of his children, and many significant and demanding appointments to the managing boards of such organizations as the Rockefeller Foundation, Colonial Williamsburg (Va.), and the American Museum of Natural History in New York City, Rockefeller was unable to find a sense of individual accomplishment in his work. He suffered from agoraphobia, the fear of public places, and the resulting involuntary reclusion and his characteristic modesty reinforced the impression that his younger brother Nelson was the man to watch among their generation.

While Rockefeller's father, an only son, had been the principal heir to a growing fortune that offered many exciting opportunities for pioneering work in philanthropy, Rockefeller joined his father's work in a period of radical economic retrenchment. His father's aggressive giving, new tax laws, and the decision to divide resources relatively equally among five sons meant that Rockefeller would have much less financial leverage as a philanthropist than his father enjoyed.

Rockefeller made two major efforts to reorient both the Rockefeller Foundation and Colonial Williamsburg to reflect his vision of a new international order. He felt that future events increasingly would be shaped in the non-Western world, was especially concerned by the economic and demographic problems of Asia, and wanted to correct the American lack of appreciation for non-Western cultures. Rockefeller hoped to move the focus of the Rockefeller Foundation from university research in the West to the application of knowledge for social transformation in the less developed world. He also hoped that the emphasis of Colonial Williamsburg would gradually be shifted from historical preservation to educational programs that would explain the virtues of democracy and a free economy. He was disappointed in both of these efforts.

Rockefeller served in the United States Navy during World War II with the rank of lieutenant commander. Work on an interagency task force devoted to planning postwar policy for Japan proved good preparation for a 1952 invitation from John Foster Dulles to join the Japanese peace treaty negotiations, with special responsibility for improving cultural relations. Also in 1952 Rockefeller revived the Japan Society, which promoted a series of cultural exchanges that helped to normalize relations between the United States and Japan. The following year he created the Population Council to promote research on population control. In the same year, Rockefeller, seeking to improve food supplies in the Far East, organized the Council on Economic and Cultural Affairs to provide assistance for Asian farmers (it was renamed the Agricultural Development Council in 1963). In 1956 he organized the Asia Society in an effort to heal the Cold War atmosphere of suspicion that followed the Communist takeover of China. Rockefeller became the American leader with whom prominent Asians most often sought counsel, and a persistent voice for cooperation and moderation in foreign affairs.

In 1955, Rockefeller assumed the chairmanship of a committee of civic leaders who were working to create Lincoln Center, a new home for the performing arts on New York City's Upper West Side. This project was a source of frequent anguish for fourteen years as the scale and scope of the plan grew. Rockefeller was the key figure in raising the more than $184 million needed to complete the project and in forging consensus among the diverse group of impresarios, government officials, and social leaders whose cooperation was essential to the center's success. When he resigned from the Lincoln Center board of directors in 1969, a section of New York City had been revived and an international center of excellence in the performing arts had been firmly established.

Rockefeller's lobbying was responsible for President Lyndon Johnson's statement in his 1965 state of the union address that he would seek new ways to deal with the explosion in world population and the growing scarcity of world resources. Working through the Population Council, Rockefeller was an important influence during the 1960's in organizing scientific and public opinion that questioned the wisdom of population growth. In 1970, President Richard Nixon appointed Rockefeller chairman of the Commission on Population Growth and the American Future. The commission's 1972 report made a strong case for an aggressive national policy to promote family planning, but Nixon disappointed Rockefeller by disassociating himself from the report's recommendations on sex education and abortion and by ignoring the rest of the work.

Rockefeller also made a major effort to influence public policy on corporate philanthropy. Much concerned by the hostility directed toward the Rockefeller Foundation during the 1950's by populist and anti-Communist congressional zealots, Rockefeller argued that private foundations played a vital role in promoting constructive social change. He was the key figure in the creation of the Commission on Private Philanthropy and Public Needs in 1972 and lobbied Congress for regulatory and tax laws under which private giving could flourish. Rockefeller also saw great potential in the civil rights and youth movements. He described his vision of the United States as a pluralistic democracy that emphasized cooperation between public and private institutions in *The Second American Revolution* (1973).

When Rockefeller was killed in an automobile accident involving a teenage driver in the town of Mount Pleasant, N.Y. (near the family estate at Pocantico Hills), he was still involved in promoting his interests in population, international relations, and the arts. Following a memorial service at Riverside Church in New York City and national editorial recognition of his immense contributions to the arts, Asian-American relations, and research in population and agriculture, he was buried in the Rockefeller Cemetery near the Pocantico estate, close to the graves of his parents. His major collections of Oriental and American art were donated to the Asia Society in New York and the Fine Arts Museum of San Francisco, respectively. He lived up to the family credo that much is expected from those to whom much is given. The Protestant ethic and the missionary impulse were still present in his makeup, but they were overlaid with a secular and cosmopolitan humanism.

[Rockefeller's papers are in the Rockefeller Archive Center, North Tarrytown, N.Y. See John E. Harr and Peter J. Johnson, *The Rockefeller Century* (1988) and *The Rockefeller Conscience* (1991). Peter Dobkin Hall's review essay on these books, "What You See Depends On Where You Stand," *Philanthropy Monthly*, Nov. 1991 and Jan./Feb. 1992, analyzes Rockefeller's role as leader of the philanthropic establishment. An obituary is in the *New York Times*, July 11, 1978.]

JAMES W. REED

ROCKEFELLER, NELSON ALDRICH (July 8, 1908–Jan. 26, 1979), businessman, philanthropist, and public official, was born in Bar Harbor, Maine, the third of six children of John Davison Rockefeller, Jr., and Abby Greene Aldrich, both of whom were from wealthy and socially prominent families. His father, also a businessman and philanthropist, was the son and namesake of John D. Rockefeller, Sr., founder of the Standard Oil Company and of one of the great American family fortunes. His mother was the daughter of Nelson W. Aldrich, a longtime Republican senator from Rhode Island and a major figure within his party.

Raised in New York City and at the family's summer home in Seal Harbor, Maine, Rockefeller knew a life of extraordinary, if unostentatious, privilege. Educated by private tutors; at the Lincoln School in Harlem, which he attended from 1917 through 1926; and at Dartmouth College, from 1926 to 1930, he eventually overcame a reading problem later diagnosed as dyslexia to become a good and exceptionally energetic student. Although a member of a family known for its sober, even severe, bearing and social awkwardness, Rockefeller was from an early age both gregarious and charming. And while he had acquired moderate political views from his father, which the progressive Lincoln School reinforced, unlike many of his relatives, he seems never to have exhibited any insecurity over the predatory business practices his grandfather had used to amass the family fortune, and for which he had become notorious. Hard work at Dartmouth led to Rockefeller's election to Phi Beta Kappa and to a B.A. in economics cum laude. He married Mary Todhunter Clark, the offspring of a rich and long-established Philadelphia family, on June 23, 1930; they had five children.

Although younger than his brother John D. Rockefeller 3d, Rockefeller soon emerged as the leader of his generation of Rockefellers by virtue of his energy, charm, ambition, and a talent for skillful infighting. He demonstrated all of those qualities in his first real job, as the rental agent of Rockefeller Center during the depths of the Great Depression. Responsible for finding tenants for the complex of office buildings in New York City during some very lean years, Rockefeller did so with great success, thanks to effective public relations and below-cost pricing practices that reminded some of his rivals of his grandfather. Although his aggressive tactics sparked a $10 million lawsuit from a rival developer, Rockefeller's overall performance proved so successful that by the 1940's the complex was earning a profit. Inclined toward compromise with organized labor, he negotiated a comprehensive agreement with the construction unions responsible for building Rockefeller Center that allowed the work to go forward without strikes. And when a mural commissioned from Diego Rivera by Rockefeller for the center briefly threatened to arouse public controversy, he managed to have it removed without great incident. In recognition of those achievements, his father named him president of Rockefeller Center in 1938.

By the late 1930's, Rockefeller's interests were shifting to the international scene, and in particular to Latin America, where his family had numerous investments. By that point a militant anti-Communist, he had become concerned during a tour of the area in 1937 about the possibility of upheaval there unless the quality of life of the region's masses was improved. Most concerned about Venezuela, where the Rockefeller family had large oil company interests, he made a long visit there in 1938, began learning Spanish, and pushed Standard Oil executives in the country to improve its general welfare. With the coming of World War II, Rockefeller's interests in the area broadened, and he became increasingly preoccupied with combating Axis influence there. Impressed with his work and eager to develop bipartisan support for his administration during an election year, President Franklin Roosevelt in August 1940 appointed Rockefeller coordinator of inter-American affairs. He spent the next four years ferreting out some 2,000 South American firms that were doing business with the Axis countries, pressuring them to cease and desist such commercial activity.

His blacklist efforts proved so successful that in November 1944 Roosevelt appointed him assistant secretary of state for Latin American affairs. He served in that post during an important nine-month period in which the shape of postwar collective security arrangements were being decided. Although a supporter of the emerging United Nations (UN), Rockefeller believed strongly that its charter should not bar the United States from entering into regional security arrangements, which he believed necessary to counter Soviet influence. Over the outraged protests of his superiors at the State Department, Rockefeller managed to persuade Michigan senator Arthur Vandenberg, the ranking Republican on the Senate Foreign Relations Committee, that the UN charter should allow such alliances. With Vandenberg's backing, Rockefeller's position prevailed, thereby laying the legal foundation for such future organizations as the North Atlantic Treaty Organization (NATO) and the Southeast Asian Treaty Organization (SEATO). So seriously had Rockefeller offended his superiors at the State Department, however, that they persuaded President Harry Truman to fire him on Aug. 23, 1945.

Over the next four years, Rockefeller remained active in international affairs. He took the lead in finding a site for the United Nations headquarters in New York City and persuading his father to donate the $8.5 million needed to acquire it. Rockefeller continued his Latin American development efforts by establishing two private organizations to promote them. He also served briefly in the Truman administration again during the period 1950–1951 as an adviser to its assistance programs for the Third World. Finding his recommendations for more ambitious efforts consistently ignored, Rockefeller quit and returned to New York, where he played a leading role in the Rockefeller Brothers Fund, a nonprofit foundation that by 1951 was the country's fourth largest.

Rockefeller supported Dwight D. Eisenhower's successful presidential campaign the following year, and soon after taking office, the new president named him chairman of the Advisory Committee on Government Organization. With Milton Eisenhower and Arthur S. Flemming, he fashioned several proposals for reorganizing executive branch agencies, the most important of which led to the creation of a new cabinet-level Department of Health, Education, and Welfare (HEW). During its early period of operation (1953–1954), Rockefeller served as its under secretary. Still interested more in international affairs, Rockefeller sought and won appointment as a foreign policy aide to the president. Formally the special assistant for Cold War strategy, he was responsible for seeing that the leading foreign policy arms of the government placed greater emphasis on economic and cultural, as opposed to purely military, competition with the Soviet Union and its allies. Although he put forward several initiatives that won wide attention in the press, such as Atoms-for-Peace and Open Skies, the Eisenhower administration never implemented them. Out of step with the more cautious and fiscally conservative Eisenhower and his chief advisers, Rockefeller opted to resign his post at the end of 1955 and return to New York.

Soon he began planning to run for public office. Rockefeller quickly secured the backing of New York Republican state chairman L. Judson Morhouse, who engineered Rockefeller's appointment to a state commission on a constitutional convention. Using the post to develop support across the state for a gubernatorial candidacy in 1958, Rockefeller managed to deter other Republicans from running and in August 1958 was nominated by the party's state convention. Although a weak public speaker at first, Rockefeller's energetic and informal electioneering and, more important, his enthusiastic embrace of most New Deal liberal ideas and his extraordinary financial resources soon won him support even in traditionally Democratic areas. Although his views differed little from those of his opponent, Democratic incumbent W. Averell Harriman, Rockefeller made headway by faulting Harriman's lack of independence from Democratic party "bosses" when making appointments and his failure to balance the state's budget. Aided by a recession that made 1958 a bad year for many incumbents, Rockefeller surprised political professionals by easily defeating Harriman that November by a margin of almost 600,000 votes.

Rockefeller's election to the highest office in what was then the nation's most populous state instantly made him a leading figure on the national political stage, a prominence magnified by the generally poor Republican showing in the 1958 elections. As governor in 1959, Rockefeller attracted attention by pushing successfully for greater state spending on housing, education, and the mentally ill, and for tax increases on fuel, cigarettes, and personal incomes to pay for those initiatives. He also raised eyebrows by pushing an abortive program to subsidize the construction of home bomb shelters, which he claimed were needed to protect New Yorkers from the risk of nuclear war. A hawk and a spender, to use the political terminology of his day, Rockefeller soon began thinking about a presidential race to promote those views. Rebuffed by more moderate and conservative party leaders in the Midwest and the West, who supported Vice-President Richard Nixon's candidacy for president in 1960, Rockefeller declined both becoming a candidate and Nixon's offer of the vice-presidential nomination. Even so, the public policy prescriptions he had developed by drawing upon research commissioned by the Rockefeller Brothers Fund influenced the Republican platform that year and, even more heavily, the campaign of Nixon's successful opponent, John F. Kennedy.

As governor of New York in the early 1960's, Rockefeller continued along the lines he had earlier laid out, adding an environmental program aimed at cleaning up his state's air and waterways, and assistance to mass transit serving New York City. Although he was a strong advocate of nuclear power, the legislature blocked most of his efforts in that field, as it did his proposal for revising the state's health insurance system. In most respects Rockefeller had begun to emerge by the end of his first term as a leading liberal of the 1960's variety, concerned with improving education, the environment, and addressing the growing problems of the poor, and willing to tax, spend, and eventually borrow more to do so. His substantial record and a rising level of state income propelled him to an easy reelection in November 1962, despite his divorce in March that year.

The early favorite for the 1964 Republican presidential nomination, Rockefeller grievously wounded his chance by choosing to marry Margaretta ("Happy") Fitler Murphy, a divorcee, on May 4, 1963; they had two children. His remarriage to a much younger woman so soon after his divorce enraged moral traditionalists within his own party, who retaliated during the 1964 Republican presidential primaries. Hampered, too, in seeking the presidential nomination by a reputation as a liberal that he tried unconvincingly to run away from, Rockefeller lost to conservative Arizona senator Barry Goldwater. In a memorable address to the Republican National Convention that year, Rockefeller denounced right-wing extremists within his own party, winning praise from liberal Republicans and Democrats alike, but forever alienating conservatives.

In 1966, weakened by his unsuccessful presidential campaign and personal problems related to it, Rockefeller faced a serious challenge to his reelection to a third term. Increasing crime and even higher taxes had bred considerable public dissatisfaction with his record, especially among middle-income voters. Marshaling the enormous financial resources at his disposal, Rockefeller managed to eke out a narrow victory in a four-way contest thanks to strong support from black and Jewish voters. Deeply disturbed by that result, Rockefeller increasingly inclined away from controversial liberal stands, most notably in the area of criminal justice.

Still hoping for another chance at the presidency, Rockefeller wavered as the 1968 election approached. Although privately supportive of American entry into the Vietnam War, he had never taken a clear public stand on what by early 1968 had become the leading issue. Deciding in the spring of that year to make a last-minute effort to win the Republican nomination, he offered himself quite opportunistically as an antiwar candidate, only to back away from that position once he lost again to Richard Nixon. With Nixon's election to the presidency in November 1968 came the end to any real prospect of a Rockefeller presidency.

By the late 1960's, Rockefeller had lost much of his earlier appeal, both with liberals, who disliked his growing conservatism, and the broad middle class, concerned with the rising cost of living. Even so, he managed to win yet another term as governor of New York in 1970 by running his most lavishly financed campaign ever, which emphasized his determination to fight drug abuse and crime more generally, preserve traditional values of home and family, and keep taxes from going up any further. During his fourth and final term as governor, Rockefeller presided over the construction of a massive set of public buildings in the state capital, which were used to house the state bureaucracy his administration had greatly enlarged, and further expansion of the state's system of higher education. Rockefeller lost more of his remaining luster with liberals, however, when he opted to quash a riot at Attica state prison in September 1971 by force, which led to the deaths of twenty-nine inmates and ten hostages. Still in command of the New York political scene in the early 1970's, shrinking state budgets were by then undermining his ability to finance existing programs. That situation encouraged Rockefeller to accept when President Gerald Ford asked him in August 1974 to take the vice-presidency Ford had earlier vacated. Sworn in on Dec. 19, 1974, Rockefeller served in the post for a little over two years. He spent the remainder of his life in New York City, pursuing a lifelong interest in collecting modern art, and died there.

Although something of a prophet without honor in his own party, Nelson Rockefeller nonetheless made a lasting impression on public affairs in both New York State and the nation. Like John F. Kennedy, whose views he essentially shared, Rockefeller was a transitional figure who began as a supporter of the reforms associated with the New Deal, and by the late 1950's had begun to embrace the newer liberal agenda as more appropriate to the changed conditions facing the nation. Animated by the same basic worldview as the Democrats' Great Society program, Rockefeller's policies on the state level proved, if anything, even bolder than Kennedy's and Lyndon Johnson's did in Washington. Like them, he believed strongly in an activist state that used the fruits of social scientific research to address contemporary problems, what some later called "technocratic liberalism." And to an entire generation of Americans, Rockefeller stood as the foremost example of liberal Republicanism in a party ever more dominated by its most conservative elements. He symbolized, too, a more glamorous, cosmopolitan and "European" kind of politician than the American system had typically produced. And yet, for all of his achievements, Rockefeller's career left a thoroughly ambiguous legacy, one that raised the possibility of a more urbane, generous, and paternalistic brand of Republicanism, and doubts that it could ever prevail.

[Rockefeller's papers are in the Rockefeller Archive Center, Pocantico Hills, N.Y. There is no good scholarly study of Rockefeller, although there are authorized campaign biographies and books about him written by former aides. See the biography by Joseph E. Persico entitled *The Imperial Rockefeller* (1982). The most penetrating analyses are in the following articles: Richard Austin Smith, "The Rockefeller Brothers," *Fortune*, Feb. and Mar. 1955; William Manchester, "Nelson Rockefeller's Moral Heritage," *Harper's*, May 1959; Duncan Norton-Taylor, "Nelson Rockefeller, A Record to Fit the Times," *Fortune*, June 1, 1967; Jack Newfield, "The Case Against Nelson Rockefeller," *New York*, Mar. 9, 1970; and William Kennedy, "Rocky Is 64, Going on 35," *New York Times Magazine*, Apr. 29, 1973. Also helpful are two books by John E. Harr and Peter J. Johnson: *The Rockefeller Century* (1988) and *The Rockefeller Conscience* (1991). An obituary is in the *New York Times*, Jan. 27, 1979.]

DAVID L. STEBENNE

ROCKWELL, NORMAN PERCEVAL (Feb. 3, 1894–Nov. 8, 1978), illustrator, was born in New York City, the younger son of Jarvis Waring Rockwell, an office manager for a textile firm, and Nancy Hill.

Young Rockwell, who was thin and poorly coordinated, wore glasses and corrective shoes. He also showed an early aptitude for art. "All I had was the ability to draw," he related in his autobiography. "I began to make it my whole life. . . . Gradually, my narrow shoulders, long neck, and pigeon toes became less important to me. . . . I drew and drew and drew."

Rockwell left Mamaroneck (N.Y.) High School in his sophomore year (1909) to study art full-time. Eventually he enrolled at the Art Students League in New York City, where he studied anatomy under George Bridgeman and illustration under Thomas Fogarty.

With Fogarty's help, Rockwell obtained his first professional assignment, illustrating Carl H. Claudy's children's book *"Tell Me Why" Stories* (1912). This led in 1913 to work at *Boys' Life*, a magazine issued by the Boy Scouts of America. Rockwell soon was named art director.

Rockwell worked steadily illustrating children's books and magazines, but the subject matter and the editorial restrictions dissatisfied him. In 1916 he decided to restart his career by painting a cover for the *Saturday Evening Post*, the best-selling magazine of the day (the first American weekly to sell one million copies) and the most prestigious for an illustrator. As part of the Curtis Publishing Company empire, the *Post* commanded the respect of readers and of advertisers. The greatest illustrators—J. C. Leyendecker, Howard Chandler Christy, Coles Phillips, and James Montgomery Flagg—painted *Post* covers. Rockwell considered imitating the stylized brilliance of these illustrators, but a friend, the cartoonist Clyde Forsythe, dissuaded him, telling him to draw what he did best—children.

In March 1916, Rockwell carried two paintings to the Philadelphia offices of the *Saturday Evening Post*. The art editor, Walter Dower, and the editor in chief, George Horace Lorimer, were persuaded to look at the unsolicited work, and they were impressed. Lorimer bought the pictures and requested more.

Rockwell's first of 323 *Post* covers was published on May 20, 1916. Other magazines soon became interested in his work; his drawings would eventually appear on covers for *Literary Digest*, *Life*, *Judge*, *Leslie's*, *American*, *Country Gentleman*, *Look*, *McCall's*, *Family Circle*, and *TV Guide*.

In general, a Rockwell illustration was a meticulously researched, carefully planned, and often impishly humorous scene of everyday American life. The scene was rendered with a photograph-like realism in oils on canvas, in a style that some critics admired and others frankly deplored. The painstaking authenticity with which Rockwell invested his illustrations makes them an invaluable record of American culture.

As his illustrations appeared regularly in national magazines, advertisers took note and began to solicit his services. Technical advances in photo-offset lithography after 1910 and the rise of mass-market magazines such as the *Post* made pictorial advertising technically and economically feasible for more and more companies. With photography still little used in advertising, companies or their advertising agencies sought illustrators like Rockwell. After Lorimer advised Rockwell to charge twice as much for an advertisement as he received for a cover, Rockwell's pledge never to do advertisements was forsaken, and during his career he drew for ads selling products as diverse as socks and steel.

Reasonably confident of his future, Rockwell married Irene O'Connor in the fall of 1916. They had no children. Although he failed his Selective Service physical, Rockwell did enlist, with the connivance of a recruiter, in the United States Navy during World War I. He illustrated a camp newspaper in Charleston, S.C., and continued to paint magazine covers while in uniform.

During the 1920's, financial success and public acclaim followed Rockwell's prodigious output of magazine covers and advertisements. In 1921 alone, thirty-one magazine covers and six advertisements were published. Since painting with live models in a studio proved to be a major obstacle to this torrid pace, Rockwell experimented with photographing models.

In 1925, Rockwell began painting an annual picture for the Boy Scouts of America, at no fee. These were published as *Boys' Life* covers and other Scout materials regularly until 1976. The Silver Buffalo, scouting's highest award, was presented to Rockwell in 1939 in recognition of this work.

Lorimer honored Rockwell by selecting him to paint the *Post*'s first four-color cover, which appeared on Feb. 6, 1926. Rockwell remained free to sell his work wherever he chose, but few of his covers appeared on any magazine except the *Post* after this time. By 1929 he had become the magazine's premier illustrator.

"The Doctor and The Doll," perhaps the most representative of all Rockwell illustrations, appeared as a *Post* cover on Mar. 9, 1929. The picture shows a kindly doctor listening with his stethoscope to the "heartbeat" of a young girl's doll. This combination of a whimsical story painted with exquisite detail was the hallmark of Rockwell's work.

Norman and Irene Rockwell were divorced on Jan. 14, 1930. He married Mary Rhoads Barstow on Apr. 17, 1930; they had three children. A difficult professional period followed these personal changes, for Rockwell lost confidence and delight in painting the events of everyday American life. He produced costume pictures based on the writings of Charles Dickens or similar to the illustrations of N. C. Wyeth and Howard Pyle. The quality of the work remained high, but Rockwell found little inspiration in the America of the 1930's.

The Rockwells moved to Paris in 1932 for seven months. Rockwell took courses in modern art and contemplated abandoning illustration. He accepted liquor and cigarette advertising to maintain his income as he sorted out his future.

Illustrating a 1936 edition of Mark Twain's *The Adventures of Tom Sawyer* was the turning point. The success of the project vindicated both the subjects and the techniques of Rockwell's earlier work. In an *American* magazine guest editorial (May 1936), Rockwell rededicated himself to painting the "commonplace" events of American life.

Lorimer's death in 1937 troubled Rockwell because he revered the editor's advice. He merely tolerated Lorimer's successor, Wesley Stout, although he did accede to Stout's nagging that he use photography to liven up his illustrations with fresh perspective. Rockwell did many story illustrations for *American* magazine, a *Post* rival, during Stout's tenure as *Post* editor.

In May 1939, the Rockwells moved to Arlington, Vt., where they had had a summer home since 1937. Rockwell hired Gene Pelham, a local artist, to take black-and-white photographs of local residents in their everyday clothes and surroundings to serve as references for his paintings. Rockwell's illustrations became more detailed and more vivid records of American life.

Ben Hibbs succeeded Stout as *Post* editor in 1942. Rockwell described Hibbs as having "iron in his soul" for the dramatic changes he made in the *Post*'s appearance and editorial direction. In 1943, the *Post* published Rockwell's "The Four Freedoms," a series of paintings entitled "Freedom of Speech," "Freedom of Worship," "Freedom from Want," and "Freedom from Fear," which were inspired by a 1941 speech by President Franklin D. Roosevelt. An enormously successful government War Bond drive was developed around "The Four Freedoms" after their publication in the *Post* on Feb. 21 and 27 and Mar. 6 and 13, 1943. The pictures, in which extremely abstract concepts were given pictorial meaning through judicious use of detail, are regarded as Rockwell's masterpieces.

A disastrous studio fire on May 15, 1943, destroyed many paintings, props, and records. Rockwell turned the event into a cartoon for the *Post*, published July 17, 1943, and had a new studio built in West Arlington, Vt.

The *Post* of Nov. 24, 1951, carried a Rockwell cover showing a grandmother and her grandson bowing their heads to say grace over a restaurant meal. Their thankfulness in the midst of the materialism surrounding them drew an emotional response from many *Post* readers. "Saying Grace," as the picture came to be titled, was later voted by *Post* readers the most popular of Rockwell's covers. On Oct. 11, 1952, Rockwell's portrait of Dwight Eisenhower appeared as a *Post* cover. Rockwell's first formal portrait of a public figure gave him new credentials as an artist.

In November 1953, the Rockwells moved to Stockbridge, Mass. There his career reached its zenith. Major advertising campaigns for Pan American World Airways and for Crest Toothpaste were begun, and one for Massachusetts Mutual Life Insurance Company continued. Rockwell covers had become the single biggest feature of the *Saturday Evening Post*. An extra 250,000 copies were printed and sold every time a Rockwell cover appeared. In 1960, Curtis Publishing brought out Rockwell's autobiography, *My Adventures as an Illustrator*, which Rockwell wrote in collaboration with his son Thomas.

Mary Rockwell died in August 1959. Rockwell then married Mary ("Molly") Pundersen, a retired schoolteacher, on Oct. 25, 1961, in Stockbridge. That same year, the *Post*'s severe financial problems surfaced. Changes made to save the magazine frustrated Rockwell. He found his cover ideas no longer welcomed by new editors intent on making the *Post* into a "sophisticated, muckraking magazine." A small portrait of Jacqueline Kennedy inside the Oct. 26, 1963, issue was Rockwell's last illustration for the *Saturday Evening Post*.

Rockwell soon accepted an assignment from *Look* magazine. Inside the Jan. 14, 1964, issue was "The Problem We All Live With," depicting an African-American child being escorted to school by four U.S. marshals. This was a powerful and unexpected picture from Rockwell, but he got few opportunities to do similar work. He remained active and well paid for his illustrating—he reported his 1971 income as $1.4 million—but he did not work regularly for any magazine or advertiser.

In 1971, the *Saturday Evening Post*, which had gone bankrupt in 1969, was revived by new owners. Rockwell posed for a cover photograph on the first issue, but he did not contribute any new art to the magazine. He painted a number of portraits at this time. Among them were actors Walter Brennan (1973) and John Wayne (1974) for the National Cowboy Hall of Fame in Oklahoma City.

In 1972, Bernard Dannenberg Galleries of New York City, organized a sixty-year retrospective to showcase Rockwell's achievements. A trust to preserve his personal collection of paintings was established in 1973 under the stewardship of the Old Corner House in Stockbridge. President Gerald Ford awarded Rockwell the Medal of Freedom in 1977.

Rockwell's last published work was the cover of *American Artist* in July 1976. Rockwell painted himself draping a "Happy Birthday" banner across the Liberty Bell, with his paintbrushes at his feet. He died in Stockbridge, where he was also buried.

Rockwell described himself as an illustrator. "I'm no fine arts man," he said in a *Forbes* interview (June 1, 1972). "I've done ads, books, you name it." Rockwell's art was designed to sell something. Editors purchased his illustrations to make their magazines attractive or to reflect editorial opinion. Advertisers commissioned Rockwell pictures to promote and to create goodwill for their products and services. Unlike "fine art," Rockwell's art had to please his clients, their public, and, finally, himself. It had to have broad appeal and to conform to the limits of space, of deadlines, and of editorial policy imposed by the printed page.

More than 2,000 Rockwell paintings were published between 1911 and 1976. Besides magazine covers, advertisements, short stories, and novels, Rockwell illustrations appeared in virtually every commercial art market: posters for movies, charities, and War Bond drives; calendars; Christmas cards; United States postage stamps (1959 and 1963); and a record album cover (1968).

Many Rockwell illustrations are licensed for reproduction today by their copyright owners as posters, porcelain plates and figurines, and collectibles.

[A significant collection of Rockwell's paintings, papers, and related materials is housed at the Norman Rockwell Museum in Stockbridge, Mass. Fifty canvases and Boy Scout–related materials are at the National Scouting Museum in Murray, Ky. Comprehensive collections of the published works are at the Norman Rockwell museums in Philadelphia and in Rutland, Vt. Rockwell's autobiography, written with his son Thomas, is *My Adventures as an Illustrator* (1960); he also wrote *How I Make a Picture* (1979). See also Arthur Guptill, *Norman Rockwell, Illustrator* (1946); Thomas Buechner, *Norman Rockwell, Illustrator and Artist* (1970); Donald Stoltz and Marshall Stoltz, *Norman Rockwell and the Saturday Evening Post* (1976); William Hillcourt, *Norman Rockwell's World of Scouting* (1978); Donald Walton, *A Rockwell Portrait* (1978); Susan Meyer, *Norman Rockwell's People* (1981); and Laurie Norton Moffatt, *Norman Rockwell: A Definitive Catalogue*, 2 vols. (1986). An obituary is in the *New York Times*, Nov. 10, 1978.]

FRED BRINCKERHOFF

ROCKWELL, WILLARD FREDERICK (Mar. 31, 1888–Oct. 16, 1978), industrialist engineer, and inventor, was born in Dorchester, Mass., a suburb of Boston. He was the eldest of five sons of Frederick Joshua Rockwell, a contractor, and Catherine Herr. Rockwell graduated from the Mechanical Arts High School in Boston and attended Massachusetts Institute of Technology from 1905 to 1909, receiving a B.S. degree in mechanical arts. On June 4, 1908, he married Clara Whitcomb Thayer; they had five children.

After graduation Rockwell was an efficiency engineer with Scovell and Company, an industry-survey firm. In 1915 he was hired as factory manager of the Torbensen Axle Company (later Eaton Manufacturing) of Cleveland, Ohio. In 1918, Rockwell served as a civilian specialist in the Motor Transport Division of the Quartermaster Corps and advocated the use of heavy trucks for the armed forces. (He was made lieutenant colonel in 1930, thus gaining the abiding nickname "The Colonel.") At war's end he became vice-president for marketing and engineering at Torbensen. In 1919 a dispute over a proposal for an improved axle caused him to leave the firm and buy a small axle company, Wisconsin Parts, in Oshkosh, Wis.

Rockwell designed and patented a double reduction gear for axles that he induced Ruggles Truck Company to try. At that time Eaton Manufacturing began to manufacture a similar gear. Rockwell successfully sued for infringement of his patent. Rockwell had arrived in the industry because he had a product that truck manufacturers could not do without. In 1933, Timken-Detroit Axle Company, the largest producer of heavy-duty axles, made Rockwell president of its subsidiary Wisconsin Parts.

In 1925, while his axle company was developing and prospering, Rockwell was asked by the Mellon family of Pittsburgh to take over Equitable Meter and Manufacturing Company as president. The Mellons also asked him to take over Standard Steel Spring Company in 1936. In 1933, Rockwell was simultaneously president of Timken-Detroit, chairman of Standard Steel Spring, and chairman and president of Pittsburgh Equitable Meter.

Rockwell strung together chains of companies specializing in automobile parts, thereby making possible the 1953 merger of Standard Steel Spring (which made springs and bumpers for passenger cars, and truck and farm implement parts) with Timken-Detroit (which made axles for truck and tractor manufacturers) into the Rockwell Spring and Axle Company, with Rockwell as chairman. It was one of the largest suppliers of parts to the automotive industry. "If it moves, we probably make something on it" became a Rockwell boast.

Pittsburgh Equitable had acquired several affinity companies and became Rockwell Manufacturing in 1945. Rockwell was president until 1947, when he became chairman of the board. This arm of his empire had been acquired for the sake of diversification because in the recession after World War I, Rockwell had been caught with a glut of truck axles. He was looking for products that were in the same broad manufacturing category but not subject to the same economic pressures. Rockwell Manufacturing became the leading manufacturer of valves and measurement and control equipment for gas, oil, chemical, water, and other fluid products.

Rockwell saw the benefits of mergers and acquisitions years before most American industrialists. Through sound judgment and incredible energy, he began buying companies in related fields during the 1920's and 1930's. Expansion went from heavy-duty axles to all types of automobile springs, coils, and universal joints. Rockwell made his acquisitions through the exchange of stock and often left the management of purchased companies intact. He bought management, plants, patents, and facilities. Acquired companies usually became divisions. Standard business reference sources such as *Moody's Industrials* detail the scores of companies acquired by Rockwell over the years.

Rockwell maintained the associations with the military he had begun during World War I and worked on experimental truck and tank design. Thus, he was poised to benefit from the rearmament of the country for World War II. It is estimated that Timken-Detroit filled 80 percent of the United States Army's axle requirements, and that Standard Steel and Spring produced about 75 percent of the heat-treated tank armor plate. During the war Rockwell was director of production for the Maritime Commission and served on the executive committee of the Army and Navy Munitions Board and on the Requirements Committee of the War Production Board.

Rockwell's son, Willard Frederick Rockwell, Jr., who had worked in every department of the company since the mid-1930's, spearheaded the development of the company beyond the 1960's. In 1958 Rockwell Spring and Axle was renamed Rockwell Standard. At the time it was doing $250 million in annual sales. Rockwell served as chairman of the board of Rockwell Standard until 1967, when he became honorary chairman.

In 1967, Rockwell Standard merged with North American Aviation to form North American–Rockwell, thereby merging precision engineering with the high technology of aerospace. Six years later, Rockwell Manufacturing was merged into North American–Rockwell and became Rockwell International.

Rockwell received scores of industrial awards and served on numerous civic, business, and public affairs boards. He was a lifelong Republican, an outspoken critic of big government, and a promoter of free enterprise. In 1964 a collection of his papers, speeches, and sayings entitled *The Rebellious Colonel Speaks* was published by McGraw-Hill. He died in Pittsburgh, Pa.

[There is no biography of Rockwell, but his son Willard and the Rockwell Foundation published *A History and Genealogy of the Rockwell and Thayer Families* in 1984. See Robert Sheehan, "Cool Col. Rockwell, and the Companies He Keeps," *Fortune*, Mar. 1954; and John Leland Atwood, *North American Rockwell* (1970).]

SUSAN VAUGHN

RODGERS, RICHARD CHARLES (June 28, 1902–Dec. 30, 1979), composer, was born in Hammels Station, Long Island, N.Y., the second son of William Abraham Rodgers, a successful New York physician, and Mamie Levy. Rodgers grew up in a large brownstone on the Upper West Side of Manhattan in New York City; his maternal grandparents lived with the family, and his father's medical office was on the first floor. Rodgers described his childhood as filled with unpleasant altercations between various members of his extended family, and early on he found music to be an escape from the household tensions.

Both of his parents were regular theatergoers, and his mother was an accomplished pianist. She frequently accompanied his father's singing of songs from their favorite Broadway musicals and operettas. Rodgers began to play the piano by ear when he was about four years old; although he was given some formal piano lessons when he was six, he remained largely self-taught. His parents supported and encouraged their son's obviously prodigious musical talents, especially because he was strongly attracted to the theater music they both loved.

Rodgers attended New York City public schools. He showed relatively little interest in his academic studies, but took advantage of every opportunity to attend theater performances with his parents or grandparents. He was especially impressed with the musicals of Jerome Kern.

Rodgers wrote his first complete song while at summer camp in 1916. His first copyrighted song, "Auto Show Girl," with lyrics by David Dyrenforth, was registered on June 30, 1917. He wrote his first complete musical comedy, *One Minute, Please,* that same year. The work, with book by Ralph G. Engelsman and lyrics by Engelsman and Rodgers, was presented by the Akron Club as a benefit for the *New York Sun*'s tobacco fund, which sent cigarettes to American troops overseas. A second amateur production, *Up Stage and Down,* with book by Myron D. Rosenthal and lyrics by Rodgers, was presented by the Infants Relief Society at the Waldorf-Astoria Hotel in March 1919. Several of the songs from this show ("Twinkling Eyes," "Asiatic Angles," "Butterfly Love," "Love Is Not in Vain," and "Love Me by Parcel Post") were his first to be published.

Rodgers was introduced to his longtime partner and lyricist Lorenz ("Larry") Hart in 1918. Both men were interested in achieving new and higher artistic standards for the American musical stage. Their first collaboration was the amateur production *You'd Be Surprised,* which was presented at the Plaza Hotel in New York City on Mar. 6, 1920.

Rodgers left high school in 1919 to enroll in extension courses at Columbia University. He and Hart wrote the Columbia Varsity Show of 1920, *Fly with Me.* The show impressed the Broadway producer Lew Fields, who hired them to write the music and lyrics for their first professional production, *Poor Little Ritz Girl,* which ran for 119 performances on Broadway from July to October 1920. This production proved to be somewhat of a disappointment for Rodgers and Hart, as some of their original songs for the show were replaced without their consent with songs by Sigmund Romberg.

In 1921, Rodgers left Columbia University to pursue more focused musical studies at the Institute of Musical Art, the predecessor institution to the Juilliard School. He studied there until 1923, taking harmony classes with Percy Goetschius and ear-training with George Wedge. The next Rodgers and Hart professional production was *The Melody Man,* which ran for only fifty-six performances on Broadway during May and June 1924. Rodgers became very depressed with his prospects for success in the musical theater at this time, and considered taking a job in the babies' underwear business. This decision was abandoned, however, after he and Hart received an invitation to collaborate on a music revue presented by New York's prestigious Theatre Guild Junior Players. *The Garrick Gaieties* of 1925, whose cast included Peggy Conway, Lee Strasberg, and Sanford Meisner, was their first success. It was followed by *Dearest Enemy* (1925), *The Girl Friend* (1926), *Lido Lady* (1926; their first London production), *Peggy-Ann* (1926), *Betsy* (1926), *One Dam Thing After Another* (1927), *A Connecticut Yankee* (1927), *She's My Baby* (1928), *Present Arms* (1928), *Chee-Chee* (1928), *Spring Is Here* (1929), and *Heads Up!* (1929).

The 1930's began with *Simple Simon* (1930), which included the song "Ten Cents a Dance." Throughout this time Rodgers and Hart experimented with possibilities of varying the standard musical comedy formula of "set pieces," working to integrate music, text, and dance to create a unified dramatic whole. This integration was apparent in *On Your Toes* (1936), which included choreography by George Balanchine. In *Babes in Arms* (1937), each song functioned as a "plot" song. *The Boys from Syr-*

acuse (1938), which was based on *The Comedy of Errors,* was the first musical comedy to be based on a play by Shakespeare.

During the 1930's, Rodgers and Hart were hired by Hollywood film studios to produce songs for several films. Among them were *The Hot Heiress* (1931); *Love Me Tonight,* which starred Maurice Chevalier (1932); *The Phantom President,* with George M. Cohan (1932); *Hallelujah, I'm a Bum!,* with Al Jolson (1933); *Dancing Lady* (1933); *Manhattan Melodrama* (1934), *Hollywood Party,* with Jimmy Durante (1934); *Mississippi,* with Bing Crosby and W. C. Fields (1935); *Dancing Pirate* (1936); and *Fools for Scandal* (1938). The work in Hollywood was not artistically satisfying for Rodgers, however, and he was anxious to return to the New York stage.

Rodgers also composed some nontheatrical works in the 1930's. In 1936 he and Hart were invited by Paul Whiteman to compose a concert piece for vocal soloist and symphony orchestra. *All Points West* was premiered by Whiteman and the Philadelphia Orchestra with baritone Ray Middleton as soloist on Nov. 27, 1936. His *Nursery Ballet* (1938) for piano and orchestra was also premiered by Paul Whiteman.

In 1939, Rodgers was commissioned by the Ballet Russe de Monte Carlo to compose the music for a ballet. *Ghost Town* was presented at the Metropolitan Opera House in November 1939; Rodgers conducted all five performances.

Like many musical theater composers of his time, Rodgers relied on others to prepare the orchestrations of his works. Among his principal orchestrators were Hans Spialek and Robert Russell Bennett.

The 1940 musical *Pal Joey* was, to Rodgers, "the most satisfying and mature work I was associated with during all my years with Larry Hart." Based on short stories by John O'Hara, it achieved the team's goal of complete integration of music and text.

Hart was an alcoholic, and during the early 1940's his working habits became increasingly erratic as his health deteriorated. Rodgers realized that he would have to find a new lyricist, and he began working with Oscar Hammerstein II in 1942. Hart died on Nov. 22, 1943. A film on his collaboration with Hart, *Words and Music,* was released in 1948.

Rodgers's collaboration with Hammerstein was marked by the enormous success of their first musical, *Oklahoma!* (1943). The show, which featured choreography by Agnes de Mille, had 2,212 performances during its initial five-year run on Broadway. Two million copies of the sheet music and more than 500,000 copies of the original cast album (one of the first "original cast albums" to be produced) were sold during this time. The show received a special drama award from the Pulitzer Prize committee in 1944.

During the run of *Oklahoma!,* Rodgers and Hammerstein created the successful musicals *Carousel* (1945) and *Allegro* (1947). In 1945 they were invited by Twentieth Century–Fox to write the music and lyrics for the film *State Fair,* which included the song "It Might As Well Be Spring."

In 1943 the team established a publishing house, Williamson Music, which was named for both of their fathers. They also took on the role of producers at this time, presenting the Irving Berlin musical *Annie Get Your Gun* (1946) as well as several shows by other composers and lyricists.

They also produced, in association with Leland Hayward and Joshua Logan, their own musical *South Pacific* (1949), which is considered to be one of their greatest successes. The show ran for 1,925 performances and received the Pulitzer Prize for drama in 1950. Among the original cast members were Mary Martin and Ezio Pinza.

The King and I, which was also produced by the team, ran for 1,246 performances on Broadway from 1951 to 1954. It was followed by *Me and Juliet* (1953), *Pipe Dream* (1955), and *Flower Drum Song* (1958). The final Rodgers and Hammerstein musical was *The Sound of Music* (1959), which ran for 1,443 performances from 1959 to 1963 and received the 1959 Tony Award for best musical. Hammerstein died on Aug. 23, 1960.

Film versions of many of the Rodgers and Hammerstein musicals were made during the 1950's and 1960's. Rodgers was invited to compose the music for several television productions: the United States Department of Navy show *Victory at Sea* (1952), *Cinderella* (1957), and *Winston Churchill—the Valiant Years* (1960).

After Hammerstein's death Rodgers searched for new collaborators, sometimes choosing to write the song lyrics himself. This was the case in his 1962 musical *No Strings,* which ran for

580 performances. In *Do I Hear a Waltz?* (1965) he collaborated with Stephen Sondheim. His last musicals, *Two by Two* (1970), *Rex* (1976), and *I Remember Mama* (1979), did not achieve the notable success of his earlier shows. (The last show, which had lyrics by Martin Charnin, was originally produced by Rodgers and Hammerstein as a nonmusical play in 1944.)

In 1962, Rodgers was invited by Lincoln Center president William Schuman to serve as president and producing director of the Music Theater of Lincoln Center. The project, designed to produce musical theater works in Lincoln Center's New York State Theater during the summer months, lasted for only six seasons.

Rodgers married Dorothy Feiner on Mar. 5, 1930; they had two children. Their daughter Mary has composed several musicals, including *Once upon a Mattress* (1967), *The Mad Show* (1973), and *Working* (1978).

Rodgers received many honors and awards during his lifetime. He was elected to membership in the National Institute of Arts and Letters in 1955 and received the Kennedy Center Honors award from President Jimmy Carter in 1978. He served on the boards of the American Theatre Wing, Barnard College, the Juilliard School, the John F. Kennedy Center for the Performing Arts, the National Council on the Arts, and the Dramatists Guild.

Rodgers contributed generously to artistic and civic projects. In 1965 the Rodgers and Hammerstein Foundation established the Rodgers and Hammerstein Archive of Recorded Sound at the New York Public Library at Lincoln Center, which is one of the world's largest recorded sound collections. In 1970 he supported the creation of a $1 million recreation center and 1,932-seat theater in Mount Morris (now Marcus Garvey) Park in Harlem, where he had played as a child. He established generous scholarship funds at the Juilliard School, the American Theatre Wing, and the American Academy of Dramatic Art. In 1978 he donated $1 million to a special endowment fund to support the creation of new musical theater projects in New York.

Rodgers died in New York City. He had composed about 1,500 songs, had 42 musicals on Broadway, and seen numerous revivals of these works throughout the world.

Rodgers was admired by many of his colleagues for his apparent ease in composing. He could compose at any time or place, with or without a piano. In his collaborations with Hart he often wrote the music before the lyrics, while with Hammerstein he worked the other way around.

Rodgers's life was devoted to the musical stage. He was a careful businessman and systematic in his work habits. Dapper in dress, he resembled a successful businessman rather than a harried theater artist. With his collaborators Larry Hart and Oscar Hammerstein II, Richard Rodgers achieved his goal of bringing the American musical theater to new artistic heights.

[Rodgers's papers are housed in the Library of Congress. His autobiography is *Musical Stages* (1975). Book-length biographical sources include Deems Taylor, *Some Enchanted Evenings* (1953); David Ewen, *Richard Rodgers* (1957), rev. as *With a Song in His Heart* (1963); Samuel Marx and Jan Clayton, *Rodgers and Hart* (1976); Ethan Mordden, *Rodgers & Hammerstein* (1992); and Bert Fink, *Rodgers and Hammerstein Birthday Book* (1993).

Complete lists of Rodgers's songs and shows are found in the *Richard Rodgers Fact Book* (1965; supp. 1968); the *Rodgers and Hammerstein Fact Book*, edited by Stanley Green (1980); and *Richard Rodgers*, compiled by Steven Suskin (1984). Analytical discussion of his music is found in Milton Kaye "Richard Rodgers" (Ph.D. diss., New York University, 1969). Standard song anthologies are *The Rodgers and Hart Song Book* (1951); and *The Rodgers and Hammerstein Song Book* (1958).

An obituary is in the *New York Times*, Dec. 31, 1979.]

JANE GOTTLIEB

ROLF, IDA PAULINE (May 19, 1896–Mar. 19, 1979), biochemist and physiologist, was born in New York City, the daughter of an electrical engineer, and grew up in the Bronx, N.Y. She graduated from Barnard College in 1916 and received a Ph.D. in biological chemistry and physiology in 1920 from the College of Physicians and Surgeons of Columbia University.

While studying at Columbia, Rolf also began working as a biochemistry assistant at the Rockefeller Institute (now Rockefeller University) in Manhattan, winning her position in part because of the large number of young men who were overseas fighting in World War I. Rolf worked in the institute's Department of Chemotherapy and Department of Organic Chemistry and eventually became an associate at the institute, where she remained until the late

1920's. In 1920, Rolf married Walter Demmerle, a building contractor; the couple had two children.

Over the next twenty years, Rolf worked in the areas of chemotherapy and organic chemistry while studying homeopathy, osteopathy, and yoga. In 1940 her interest in yoga led her to use a series of yoga exercises to help a friend, a piano teacher, regain the use of her hand and arm that had been disabled in an accident. Rolf later referred to this incident as the beginning of Rolfing, a short-term method of physical therapy. She began refining the therapy over the next decade, integrating exercises she learned from osteopath Amy Cochran. Rolf then traveled extensively in the United States, Canada, and Europe, teaching and lecturing on the method, which she called structural integration.

The primary purpose of Rolfing is to realign the body, thus restoring its natural balance, through the physical manipulation of the connective tissue that surrounds the body's bones and muscles, "moving the soft tissue toward the place where it really belongs," as Rolf described the method. She also stressed that Rolfing was not strictly a medical practice and was intended to enhance a person's overall health rather than simply treat specific symptoms. After a successful series of Rolfing sessions, a person would not only experience the relief of painful physical conditions but also an improvement in the body's general functioning and psychological well-being. Rolf eventually developed a treatment program consisting of ten hour-long Rolfing sessions. "This is the gospel of Rolfing," she wrote in *Ida Rolf Talks About Rolfing and Physical Reality* (1978). "When the body gets working appropriately, the force of gravity can flow through. Then, spontaneously, the body heals itself."

Rolfing became more widely known around the world after she began holding workshops on structural integration at California's Esalen Institute in the mid-1960's, at the invitation of Gestalt therapist Fritz Perls. The therapy was given the name of "Rolfing" by her students. In the summer of 1970 a group of Rolfers met at Esalen with the intention of establishing a headquarters for the growing number of Rolfers. The initial meeting led to the creation of the Guild for Structural Integration, which eventually became the Rolf Institute, founded in 1973 in Boulder, Colo. Rosemary Feitis, who had been trained at Esalen, assisted Rolf in the writing of her two books, the first of which was *Rolfing: The Integration of Human Structures* (1977), which focused on the principles of Rolfing. *Ida Rolf Talks About Rolfing,* which features an introduction by Feitis, was written to provide the public with a less formal look at the subject.

By 1978 Rolf was quite ill and was rarely able to travel. She died the following year in a nursing home in Bryn Mawr, Pa.

[See Rolf's article "Gravity: An Unexplored Factor in a More Human Use of Human Beings," *Systematics,* June 1963; and Don Johnson, *The Protean Body: A Rolfer's View of Human Flexibility* (1977). An obituary is in the *New York Times,* Mar. 21, 1979.]

GILLIAN G. GAAR

ROSE, ALEX (Oct. 15, 1898–Dec. 28, 1976), labor union official and political leader, was born Olesh Royz in Warsaw, Russian Poland, the son of Hyman Royz and Faiga Halpern. Rose's father, a well-off tanner and trader in raw hides, provided a comfortable life. Discrimination against Jews prevented Rose from continuing his education after graduating from high school, and he immigrated to the United States in 1913.

In 1914, with the outbreak of World War I, his parents no longer were able to send money, so Rose abandoned his plan to become a doctor and sought employment. Using his anglicized name, he worked as a millinery operator for $6 per week and joined the Cloth Hat, Cap and Millinery Workers' International Union (CHCMW), becoming recording secretary of its Local 24 in 1916.

Active in the Labor Zionist organization, Rose enlisted in 1918 in the British army's "Jewish Legion," serving as a private in Palestine, Egypt, and Syria. Returning to the United States in 1920, he married Elsie Shapiro, a Russian immigrant also active in Zionist politics, on July 7, 1920; they had two children. That year, Rose resumed his union involvements, becoming Local 24's secretary-treasurer in 1923 after a three-year campaign he led to oust the local's Communist party–affiliated leadership. In 1927, Rose was elected vice-president of the CHCMW, remaining in that post when his union merged with the United Hatters of North America to form the United Hatters, Cap and Millinery Workers International Union in

1934. The union represented about 40,000 workers when Rose was elected president of the United Hatters in 1950, succeeding Max Zaritsky. At the time of Rose's death, the union represented about 16,000, a decline from a peak of nearly 100,000 members that was due in large part to foreign competition and Americans' decreasing inclination to wear hats.

During the 1930's, Rose encountered organized crime in the garment industry, sustaining personal attacks that led him to carry a gun for protection. He called at the 1953 American Federation of Labor and 1956 AFL-CIO conventions for the expulsion of unions controlled by organized crime. AFL-CIO president George Meany appointed Rose head of the Appeals Committee at the 1957 AFL-CIO convention; it considered a recommendation that the International Brotherhood of Teamsters be ousted from the federation if it did not reform itself. When Rose's attempt to negotiate a compromise reform plan failed, his committee's recommendation of ouster was approved by a convention vote.

Rose believed that it was the role of the union to help stabilize industry. Even though Rose led a strike in 1953 and 1954 against the Hat Corporation of America, he wrote in a column in the *New York World-Telegram* of Aug. 25, 1949, that "the class struggle is a thing of the past in my union and in many others." Throughout the 1950's, the United Hatters invested union funds in corporations employing its members to keep the businesses afloat.

Rose's renown reached considerably farther than the presidency of a relatively small union might suggest because of his significant role in politics. In 1936, Rose, along with David Dubinsky, leader of the International Ladies Garment Workers Union (ILGWU), and others, organized the American Labor Party (ALP), originally formed as the New York chapter of John L. Lewis's Labor's Non-Partisan League. Established specifically to give socialists and others a way to vote for the pro-labor Franklin D. Roosevelt without voting Democratic, the ALP tallied almost 300,000 votes for Roosevelt and also drew votes for the victorious Democratic gubernatorial candidate, Herbert Lehman. After the 1936 election, Dubinsky and Rose agreed that the ALP should be permanent, and Rose served as its state secretary and director from 1936 to 1944. According to Dubinsky, Rose was a born political strategist. In the 1937 New York City mayoral race, the ALP backed the victorious Republican-Fusion candidate Fiorello La Guardia, garnering almost half a million votes on its line for him. When ALP legislators turned to Rose for direction on state labor legislation, George Meany, then president of the New York State Federation of Labor, was angered and broke politically with Rose and the ALP.

Rose and Dubinsky, both leaders of moderate AFL unions, broke with the ALP in 1944 when their faction was defeated in party primaries by the Left-CIO contingent. They formed the Liberal party, which was confined to New York State, with Rose as vice-chairman. It became a major force by championing Harry Truman's underdog presidential bid in 1948. In 1954, using the threat of a Liberal party endorsement of an Independent or Republican candidate for governor, Rose helped secure the Democratic nomination for W. Averell Harriman, who won in November. Similarly, rebuffing President Lyndon Johnson, the Liberal party refused to back the 1966 Democratic gubernatorial nominee Frank O'Connor, running on its own line Franklin D. Roosevelt, Jr., who drew more than 500,000 votes, throwing the election to Nelson A. Rockefeller.

Rose was a prime mover in getting Dubinsky and the ILGWU, then the backbone of the Liberal party, to support John F. Kennedy early for the presidency. He also promoted Lyndon Johnson for the 1960 vice-presidential slot and brought Johnson into closer contact with labor and liberals. Arriving at a November 1963 AFL-CIO convention, a hatless President Kennedy, aware of Rose's practice of sending hats to presidents, said to Dubinsky, "Tell Alex I left the hat in the car."

In New York City mayoral politics, under Rose's leadership the Liberal party in the 1960's asserted its power and disapproval of the Democratic party machine by backing for a third term Democratic mayor Robert F. Wagner, who ran as a reform candidate after being spurned by the Democratic organization. Rose viewed Wagner's 1961 victory as one of his major successes. In 1965, the Liberal party supported the successful Republican mayoral candidate, John V. Lindsay. Such was the vote-getting power of the Liberal party that Lindsay ran successfully for a second term on the Liberal party line alone in 1969, after losing the Republican primary.

Rose was a close confidant of New York governor Hugh Carey, being one of the few notable political leaders to endorse Carey in the 1974 Democratic gubernatorial primary. The Liberal party enjoyed the benefits of patronage from the administrations of Wagner, Lindsay, and Carey. Rose's backing of Republicans like Lindsay and Jacob Javits and moderate Democrat Daniel Patrick Moynihan against liberal Bella S. Abzug in the 1976 Democratic senatorial primary was not without controversy. The party's lateness in coming out against the war in Vietnam grew out of Rose's closeness to Johnson.

Building on a party enrollment of only 108,000 and his union and labor movement base, Rose demonstrated a political astuteness that led to his being elected a presidential elector five times. Speaking with an accent and combining the mien of a tall and courtly Victorian gentleman with the savvy adeptness of a political tactician, Rose remained active in politics until his death in New York City. He was succeeded in the Liberal party leadership post by Raymond B. Harding, a key lieutenant during Rose's later years.

[Papers of the United Hatters and a file on the Liberal party are available at the Taminent Institute–Robert F. Wagner Labor Archives at the Bobst Library, New York University. See J. M. Budish, *History of the Cloth Hat, Cap and Millinery Workers* (1926); Donald Robinson, *Spotlight on a Union* (1948); and David Dubinsky and A. H. Raskin, *David Dubinsky: A Life with Labor* (1977). An obituary is in the *New York Times*, Dec. 29, 1976.]

MARJORIE FREEMAN HARRISON

ROSEBURY, THEODOR (Aug. 10, 1904–Nov. 25, 1976), bacteriologist, was born in London, England, the son of Aaron Rosebury and Emily Dimesets. His father was a union organizer and writer who wrote a history of the British labor movement. Aaron Rosebury moved his family to New York in 1910, where he continued his involvement in union organizing and writing. Emily Rosebury ran two boardinghouses in New York, which provided most of the family income. Theodor Rosebury was registered as an American citizen when his father was naturalized in 1916.

Rosebury attended City College in New York City from 1921 to 1923 and graduated from New York University in 1924. He received his D.D.S. from the University of Pennsylvania School of Dental Medicine in 1928. Dissatisfied with dentistry as a profession, Rosebury joined the Department of Bacteriology at the College of Physicians and Surgeons at Columbia University in 1930 as an instructor. Rosebury was promoted to assistant professor in 1935 and to associate professor in 1944. He remained at Columbia until 1951 when he was appointed a full professor in the bacteriology department of Washington University School of Dentistry in St. Louis. He retired as professor emeritus in 1967.

Rosebury married Lilly Aaronson in 1925. The couple had two children and were divorced in 1948. On Nov. 21, 1949, Rosebury married his second wife, Amy Pearl Loeb, a psychotherapist. The couple had no children.

Rosebury, an active researcher, published four books and some 150 learned articles. His scholarship and wide range of research interests allowed him to establish a reputation in three fields of study: causation of dental diseases, bacterial microorganisms hosted by mankind, and biological warfare.

In his book *Peace or Pestilence*, Rosebury wrote that he became interested in biological warfare as a consequence of Hitler's rise to power. He had heard news reports suggesting that the Germans might use germs as weapons if they went to war again. After the United States entered World War II, Rosebury joined the Biological Warfare Center at Camp Detrick in Maryland, where he served as civilian head of the Airborne Infection Project from 1943 to 1945. The scientists involved in this investigation used a cloud chamber to test the effect of inhaling various infective agents. In 1945, Rosebury received a decoration from the War Department for exceptional civilian service. Though some of this biological research was classified, in 1947 Rosebury published a monograph, *Experimental Air-Borne Infection*, that described the test chamber, the problems involved in its use, and the infectious agents tested, including their dose and lethality.

By 1949, however, Rosebury had become uneasy with the prospect of germ warfare. In that year, in his book *Peace or Pestilence*, he explained the motivation behind the biological warfare investigation at Camp Detrick, but he also warned the American public about the potential danger of the experiments at Camp Detrick. Rosebury's expertise in the area of biological warfare led the United Nations

Atomic Energy Commission to hire him in 1950 to compile an international bibliography on biological warfare.

Microorganisms Indigenous to Man was published in 1962. This book, a comprehensive compilation of the literature on the normal flora, or microbiota, associated with mankind, served as a useful reference for medical research. In *Life on Man*, published in 1969, Rosebury attacked "the myth that dirt and germs are always our enemies." This discussion of harmless microbes occurring naturally in man was written for readers without a scientific background. It won a special commendation in the 1971 National Book Awards science category. The last book Rosebury completed before his death, *Microbes and Morals—The Strange Story of Venereal Disease*, was published in 1971. Rosebury attempted to educate his readers and to dispel many of the misconceptions that surrounded venereal diseases, including the notion that Columbus and his crew introduced venereal disease to Europe upon their return from Hispaniola.

Rosebury called attention to himself and his progressive political views in 1965 when he invited Herbert Aptheker, a historian of African-American affairs and the director of the American Institute for Marxist Studies, to be his house guest. Aptheker arrived in St. Louis on February 13 to speak at the local chapter of the W. E. B. Dubois Club. Rosebury met Aptheker at the airport and put him up overnight. This incident was covered by the city papers and offended the Dental School faculty at Washington University, many of whom demanded that Rosebury be dismissed. Since there was no evidence that Rosebury had openly advocated his political philosophy in the classroom or on campus, and since Rosebury was in a tenurial position, the university administration had no grounds to fire him outright. But Rosebury, who had a history of coronary heart disease, was eased out: first, he was given a medical leave of absence in 1966, and then he was offered early retirement from the faculty with full benefits at the end of his year's sick leave. Despite the tension created by this incident, university officials did not lose sight of Rosebury's contributions to science and to the school. When announcing Rosebury's leave of absence, Washington University provost George E. Pake acknowledged that "he is nationally and internationally known as an outstanding scientist in his field and in his years here has brought a new research dimension to the School of Dentistry."

Rosebury moved to Chicago in 1966 and then to Massachusetts, where in 1974 he settled in the small country town of Conway. He continued to write during his retirement and was working on two books at the time of his death.

[Rosebury's research papers are held by Morehouse College in Atlanta, Ga. Articles on developments arising from the Aptheker speech are in the *St. Louis Globe-Democrat*, Oct. 15, 1965; and the *St. Louis Post-Dispatch*, Nov. 18, 1965. An obituary is in the *New York Times*, Nov. 28, 1976.]

LYNNE E. OHMAN

ROSENSTEIN, NETTIE ROSENCRANS (Sept. 26, 1893–Mar. 13, 1980), fashion designer, was born in Vienna, Austria, to Sarah Hoffman and Joseph Rosencrans, a dry goods merchant. In 1899 the Rosencrans family moved to America, settling in New York City. Her parents soon opened a dry-goods shop on Lenox Avenue at 118th Street, where Nettie learned about and developed a passion for fabrics. She was soon making doll's clothes and by age eleven had begun to make clothes for herself. She worked standing up at her mother's sewing machine because she was too short to reach the foot pedal while sitting. In 1913 she was still sewing only for herself and perhaps a few family friends. On October 12 of that year she married Saul Rosenstein; the couple had two children.

Rosenstein's sister Pauline had a millinery shop and sent her clients to Nettie for dresses, and by 1917 Nettie had begun a dressmaking business in her own home. Supposedly this business generated such a flow of traffic in and out of her Harlem brownstone that a local policeman came to the house to investigate what could generate such traffic. By 1921 she was employing fifty seamstresses and moved her business out of the brownstone, opening Nettie Rosenstein, Inc., in a shop on East Fifty-sixth Street. She had ceased to make dresses to order and began making ready-to-wear garments, thus creating one of the first prototypes of the modern high-fashion retail specialty store.

Rosenstein never had any formal design training; in fact, she never even learned to sketch. While working in her parents' store she designed her clothing by simply draping fabric on herself, then proceeded to cut and sew the fabric.

She continued this unorthodox approach after she opened her own business, hiring models on which she would drape bolts of fine fabrics, developing each pattern directly on the model. After opening the Fifty-sixth Street shop, one of her customers brought in a buyer from I. Magnin, who immediately recognized the quality of the designs and fabrics and the potential market for ready-to-wear high fashion dresses. Soon other leading stores—Neiman-Marcus, Bonwit Teller, Nan Duskin—were carrying Nettie Rosenstein dresses. Priced as high as $500, they were among the most expensive off-the-rack clothes in America.

Despite her success, Rosenstein retired from business in 1927, but she went back to work in 1930, first as a designer for Corbeau et Cie. In 1931 she opened her own wholesale business on Forty-seventh Street, focusing almost exclusively on evening dresses. She had two partners in this venture, her sister-in-law Eva Rosencrans and Charles Gumprecht, a capable businessman who played a major role in making fashionable ready-made women's clothing a major industry. It was his responsibility to organize the comparatively large volume manufacture of Rosenstein designs. The business reached an unprecedented volume, surpassing $1 million in sales in 1937.

Rosenstein regularly visited Europe, seeking inspiration for new evening dress designs. By the 1930's, Vionnet and Chanel were both designing simple black dresses, to highlight the gold jewelry favored by their wealthy clients. Rosenstein pared down the style, later stating that "It's what you leave off a dress that makes it smart." According to designer Bill Blass, Rosenstein "practically invented the little black dress for Americans." She created endless variations on the same basic theme and established the "little black dress" as the dominant evening fashion for more than two decades and well into the 1950's. In 1938 she received the Lord and Taylor Achievement Award and the Neiman-Marcus Achievement Award.

In 1942, Rosenstein moved her business to 550 Seventh Avenue, in the heart of New York City's garment district, and expanded her line of clothing, adding daytime dresses. In 1946 this line won the Fashion Trades Award for Best Design. Rosenstein also decided to expand into new product lines, creating the Nettie Rosenstein Accessories Company to make costume jewelry and handbags. In the same year she created Nettie Rosenstein Perfumes, Inc. Each of these businesses succeeded and brought her added recognition, including a prestigious Coty Award in 1947 for consistent good design and a second Coty in 1960 for accessories. Indeed, Rosenstein was one of the few designers—Anne Klein was another—to earn two Cotys. Rosenstein attracted high-visibility clients, such as Dinah Shore, Hildegarde, and Norma Shearer, and Mamie Eisenhower asked Rosenstein to design her gowns for the presidential inaugural balls in 1953 and 1957. Rosenstein was considered the "great classicist" of American fashion design, and one example of her "little black dress," as well as both inaugural gowns, is in the permanent costume collection of the Smithsonian Institution in Washington, D.C.

In 1961, Rosenstein retired from active management of her dress business but continued for several more years to oversee the accessories and perfume business. She died in New York City.

[See Josephine Ellis Watkins, *Fairchild's Who's Who in Fashion* (1975); and Eleanor Lambert, *World of Fashion: People, Places, Resources* (1976). An obituary is in the *New York Times*, Mar. 15, 1980.]

FRED CARSTENSEN
ELDON BERNSTEIN

ROSENSTIEL, LEWIS SOLON (July 21, 1891–Jan. 21, 1976), industrialist and philanthropist, was born in Cincinnati, Ohio, the only child of Elizabeth Johnson and Solon M. Rosenstiel, a commercial broker. He attended Cincinnati's University School and Franklin Prep and hoped to become an All-America football player and a doctor. Both of these goals were thwarted when he suffered an eye injury playing football at the age of sixteen. While hospitalized in Milton, Ky., he accepted a job offer from his uncle, David L. Johnson, owner of the Susquemac Distilling Company in that city. During his eleven years of employment at the distillery, Rosenstiel worked his way up from meal-room helper to superintendent. He never returned to school nor did he obtain a college education.

When Prohibition became the law of the land in the United States in 1920, the Susquemac distillery closed, and Rosenstiel turned to a variety of jobs, including selling shoes and bonds. Winston Churchill, whom Rosenstiel met fortuitously during a vacation on the French Riviera in the 1920's, advised him to prepare for the repeal of Prohibition. Accordingly, Rosenstiel began to buy and sell medicinal alcohol and warehouse receipts to accumulate a supply of aged whiskey. In 1923 he bought Schenley Products Company of Schenley, Pa., which had an inventory of four thousand barrels of whiskey.

Over a five-year period, Rosenstiel also purchased the Joseph S. Finch distillery in Pittsburgh from Sol Rosenbloom; it held 500,000 gallons of Golden Wedding brand whiskey and a concentration permit—a federal license to store whiskey—something Rosenstiel had been unable to obtain when he purchased Schenley. Short of cash, he had to borrow $75,000 from Rosenbloom to consummate the purchase. To round out his line of products Rosenstiel acquired distribution rights for a number of high-quality European brands of wines, liquors, and cordials in 1932.

On July 11, 1933, the Schenley Distillers Company (in 1949 it became Schenley Industries) was chartered in Delaware with the aid of a $2,990,000 stock issue arranged by Lehman Brothers. The new corporation was confronted with a tax bill of $12 million in 1933 when Pennsylvania enacted a floor tax on all liquor in the state. Rosenstiel's law firm fought the tax as unconstitutional and won. When Prohibition was repealed on Dec. 5, 1933, Rosenstiel already owned four distilleries, a large inventory of aged whiskeys, and a varied product line. Schenley Industries grew under Rosenstiel and at one point owned plants in seven states, Puerto Rico and the Virgin Islands, and eight foreign countries.

In the industry Rosenstiel was known as an innovator and a "battler" and was fondly nicknamed the "Chairman." He held the reins of the firm closely, even to the point of approving every advertisement for every Schenley product—no mean feat when in 1957 the company employed twelve advertising agencies with an ad budget of close to $14 million. As an employer, he provided workers with liberal health and welfare benefits and ensured equal opportunities. A gold medal from the George Washington Carver Institute was bestowed on him in 1950 for his fair employment practices. In 1964 he promoted Charles T. Williams to a vice-presidency at Schenley, the first black to win such a high-level position in any American industry.

In the post–World War II period, the big four of the industry were Seagram's, with about 25 percent of the market; Schenley and National Distillers, with 14 percent each; and Hiram Walker, with 10 percent. Ever since Prohibition's repeal, the industry had been subject to extensive federal and state government oversight, so that the firms were in continual battle with authorities over taxes, antitrust matters, product definitions, and distillery and withdrawal processes. In addition, after the war the industry had to deal with a declining market for distilled spirits and changing liquor tastes. In particular, the move from whiskey to vodka hurt Schenley badly since it had built its reputation on bourbon. In March 1968, Rosenstiel sold his interest in Schenley to Meshulam Riklis of Glen Alden and Rapid-American Corporations and, in October, retired as chairman and chief executive officer of the company.

Rosenstiel was married five times. His marriage to Dorothy Heller on Oct. 3, 1917, ended with her death in 1944. They had three children. To memorialize the happy union, he established the Lewis S. and Dorothy H. Rosenstiel Foundation. Subsequent marriages were shorter and less successful than the first. On June 19, 1946, he married Leonore Cohen Kattleman; they had one child and were divorced in September 1951. On Dec. 14, 1951, he married a cousin, Louise Rosenstiel, but the marriage lasted less than a year. Susan Lissman Kaufman became his fourth wife on Nov. 30, 1956; they divorced in 1966, five years after they separated. On June 7, 1967, Blanka Wdowiak, a Polish national, became his fifth wife. Rosenstiel died in Mount Sinai Hospital in Miami Beach, and he was buried in Cincinnati.

Rosenstiel's business triumphs were many: the development of the Schenley Packed Column to facilitate conversion from beverage alcohol to industrial alcohol during World War II; the design of a mass-production process for penicillin during the war; the founding of the Bourbon Institute; and the successful passage of the Forand bill, which lengthened from eight to twenty years the period distillers could hold whiskey before paying withdrawal taxes (1959). He wrote about the liquor industry and always interested himself in the economic problems of the country. His "Plan for Sustained Prosperity" appeared as a monograph in the July 29, 1949, issue of *U.S. News and World Report.*

At the time of his retirement from Schenley,

Rosenstiel's stock holdings were worth an estimated $30 million, and his real estate (in New York, Connecticut, and Miami Beach) was valued at more than $2 million. During his lifetime Rosenstiel donated more than $100 million to educational institutions and philanthropies, including Brandeis and Notre Dame universities and Mount Sinai hospitals in New York and Miami Beach.

[No biography of Rosenstiel has been published. Articles about his work in the liquor industry can be found in the *New York Times*, May 22, 1955, Aug. 14, 1966, and Oct. 4, 1968; *Printers Ink*, May 30, 1958; and the *New York Journal American*, July 29, 1961. An obituary is in the *New York Times*, Jan. 22, 1976.]

HAROLD L. WATTEL

ROSENWALD, LESSING JULIUS (Feb. 10, 1891–June 25, 1979), business executive, philanthropist, and art collector, was born in Chicago, Ill., the eldest of five children of Julius Rosenwald and Augusta R. Nusbaum. In 1895, his father, Julius, a merchant, purchased a 25 percent financial interest in Sears, Roebuck and Company, then a Chicago-based mail-order house, for $37,500 and became vice-president. Six years later, Julius Rosenwald increased his stake in Sears through investing an additional $1 million, and in 1908 he became president of the firm. As Sears grew into one of the largest companies in the United States, Rosenwald became extremely wealthy. He was a civic-minded individual who inculcated his philosophy of philanthropy into his children.

Lessing was named after Lessing Rosenthal, his father's best friend, a Chicago attorney and a community activist. As a youngster Rosenwald attended the University of Chicago's elementary and secondary schools, then studied chemistry at Cornell University (1909–1911).

In September 1911, at age twenty, he began his career at Sears as a shipping clerk. His father believed that his son should not be given any preferential job opportunities within the company. On Nov. 6, 1913, Lessing married Edith Goodkind; they had five children.

Rosenwald spent his entire working career at Sears. By doing many different jobs, he gained a comprehensive view of the company's operations. After serving in the United States Navy during World War I, he returned to Sears in 1920, as general manager of its Philadelphia plant. In 1930, after several promotions, he was named executive vice-president. Rosenwald also held several administrative posts, such as vice-chairman of the board (January 1931–June 1932), and chairman of the executive committee. When his father died in 1932, he became chairman of the board. While chairman of Sears, Rosenwald also was an industrial representative on the Regional Labor Board (1934). In January 1939, after seven years at the helm of Sears, he resigned (at age forty-eight) in order to devote his life to philanthropy, collecting rare books and prints, and community activities.

Although retired from corporate America, Rosenwald remained active in local and national affairs. For example, in 1939 he served as a member of the Philadelphia Labor Mediation Tribunal and arbitrated labor disputes. In the early 1940's he held a number of local and federal government posts: member of the local board of appeals of the Selective Service System (October 1940), head of the Office of Production and Management's silk commodity section in Washington, D.C. (August 1941), chief of the Bureau of Industrial Conservation (September 1941), and its director when the bureau became a division. In January 1943, after several major conservation efforts and accomplishments, he resigned when a number of federal agencies were reorganized to form the War Production Board.

Upon his return to Philadelphia, Rosenwald devoted his attention to collecting, philanthropy, and civic activities. In early 1943, as president of the American Council for Judaism, he opposed the establishment of a Jewish state in Palestine. Rosenwald believed that such a state would not solve the problems of Jews but, rather, would endanger Jews throughout the world and would create additional tension in the Middle East. Instead, he sought to increase migration of Jews to the United States and to other countries, in order to disseminate Jewish intellectuals throughout the world.

Also in 1943, Rosenwald began donating valuable art and rare books to the United States government. His largess included gifts to the National Gallery of Art—some 6,500 prints and drawings—and to the Library of Congress—rare books and reference materials. During the 1950's, Rosenwald continued his lifelong passion of collecting rare prints and books. He amassed the largest collection of any twentieth-century living collector and purchased many major pieces of art and rare books as he traveled throughout the world. For example, while vacationing in Buenos Aires, Argentina, he had bought a collection of German Expressionist prints and drawings. His philosophy as a collector was to make purchases for the love of art rather than for investment.

In 1960, Rosenwald donated approximately 130 acres of his 159-acre estate (built in 1939) to Abington Township, Pa. He retained about thirty acres for his personal use by converting an old greenhouse into a home where he resided with his wife and maintained his collection. Over the next few years, the township developed the land and dedicated it as Alverthorpe Park.

In 1961, Rosenwald served as a honorary consultant on rare books to the Library of Congress, to which he contributed more than 700 rare volumes. In addition to his gifts, and other philanthropic and community activities, Rosenwald spent much of his time in the 1960's and the 1970's with his collection of rare books and prints, served on a number of boards, and met with scholars and other collectors to discuss his collection. During his lifetime, he donated some 25,000 prints and drawings and nearly 8,000 rare books worth $35 million to the United States government. Rosenwald, one of the greatest collectors of art in modern times, died at his estate, Alverthorpe, in Jenkintown, Pa.

[An article by Rosenwald, "Reminiscences of a Print Collector," is in *American Scholar*, Autumn 1973. See also *New Yorker*, Mar. 10, 1973; Fred Ferretti, "The Treasure of Jenkintown, Pa.: Lessing Rosenwald's 25,000 Prints," *Art News*, Mar. 1973; Library of Congress, *Catalog of Gifts, Lessing J. Rosenwald to the Library of Congress, 1943–1975* (1977); James C. Worthy, *Shaping an American Institution* (1984); and Michael Patrick Allen, *The Founding Fortunes* (1987). An obituary is in the *New York Times*, June 26, 1979.]

JOSEPH C. SANTORA

ROSS, NELLIE TAYLOE (Nov. 29, 1876–Dec. 20, 1977), governor of Wyoming and director of the United States Mint, was born near St. Joseph, Mo., one of four children of James Wynns Tayloe, a merchant and farmer, and Elizabeth Blair. Because of poor health and the early death of her mother, Nellie Tayloe attended public schools intermittently and received private tutoring. She took additional courses to become a kindergarten teacher, but her health ruled out a classroom career. Later she said that "early in my teens I was vain as a peacock, loved pretty clothes." She grew to a woman of medium height, with brown hair, "and very large, expressive blue eyes." Stylish hats would become a characteristic feature of her public appearances later in life.

She married William Bradford Ross, a lawyer, in Omaha, Nebr., on Sept. 11, 1902. The couple had four sons, one of whom died in an accident in February 1906. Over the next fifteen years, William Ross became an important figure in the Wyoming Democratic party. His wife raised their children and was active in the Episcopal Church, the Boy Scouts, and the Cheyenne Woman's Club, where she developed the qualities that would one day help her meet the demands of public office. In 1922, William Ross was elected governor of Wyoming. He became ill during the autumn of 1924 and died on October 2 with more than two years of his term remaining.

Since it occurred more than thirty days before the next general election, Ross's death left the state's politicians with the problem of picking a successor to serve the unexpired term. Both Republicans and Democrats held conventions to select candidates, and the Democrats chose Nellie Tayloe Ross. "I was overwhelmed," she said later, "and the first thing I knew I was committed."

Ross did not campaign in the short time that remained before the election. In two public letters, she pledged to carry out her husband's program and to do nothing that would justify the charge that "women should not be entrusted with high executive office." She received 43,323 votes to 35,527 for her Republican opponent, Eugene Sullivan, and was the only Democrat in Wyoming to win a statewide race. Sworn into office on Jan. 5, 1925, she became America's first woman governor. Miriam A. Ferguson of Texas had also been elected governor in 1924, but she was inaugurated two weeks after Ross, who became a national celebrity overnight. "My opinion was asked on absurdly irrelevant subjects," she later said; for example, people wrote to inquire if she intended to replace all male state employees with women.

During the two years of her governorship, Ross faced a Republican legislature and a state government dominated by her political enemies. She insisted that certain banking legislation not restrict the powers of the governor and used the threat of the veto to have such language removed from the bill. She enforced Prohibition and once removed a county sheriff for misconduct involving the liquor laws. The episode for would cost her votes in the next election.

One of Ross's close advisers was Joseph C. O'Mahoney, a Catholic who had ambitions for the United States Senate. This association brought forth charges that there was an invisible government in the Ross administration at a time when the Ku Klux Klan had influence in Wyoming politics. She vetoed a bill providing for a special election in the event that one of Wyoming's senators could not serve. Republicans alleged that "A vote for the woman Governor is a vote for a Democratic Senator" since one of the incumbent senators, the elderly Francis E. Warren, seemed likely to die before his term ended in 1930, which would enable Ross to appoint O'Mahoney.

To run against Ross in 1926, the Republicans nominated Frank C. Emerson, an engineer, arguing that the governorship was not for women. After an intense battle, Ross was defeated by a little more than 1,300 votes.

Despite her defeat, Ross became vice-chairman of the Democratic National Committee in 1928 after having seconded Alfred E. Smith's nomination at the national convention that same year. In a pamphlet that she wrote in support of Smith, she argued that his election would produce a president "who thinks of government in terms of the men, women, and children it should help." Over the next four years, she directed Democratic activities aimed at female voters. The party, she wrote in 1930, believed that "women are not voters merely, but co-workers with men." She campaigned for the Democratic ticket vigorously in 1932 and became close to Eleanor Roosevelt. Early in 1933, she urged the First Lady and other women in the party to consider the numerous applications women sent in for federal appointments.

Ross was appointed director of the United States Mint and took office on May 3, 1933. The operations of the Mint were curtailed because of the Great Depression, leaving Ross with only a skeleton force of employees. During the two decades that followed, she dealt with the inflow of gold into the United States as the economy improved. She also directed the management of coinage during World War II, including the unpopular zinc-coated penny. When she left office in 1953, she had been responsible for approximately two-thirds of the domestic coinage that the Mint had produced since its founding in 1792. In retirement, Ross was still in demand as a speaker. After celebrating her one-hundredth birthday in 1976, she died the following year. Her funeral was held in Cheyenne, where she was buried.

The accident of her husband's death had brought Nellie Ross into politics and national prominence. As governor and as a federal official, she became a leader among the political women who exercised influence during the New Deal years. A newspaper reporter said of Ross that she was a woman who "when called on, can meet any and every situation with distinction, yet always remain feminine."

[There is a collection of Ross papers at the University of Wyoming in Laramie and additional official records at the Wyoming State Archives in Cheyenne. The Franklin D. Roosevelt Library and the Harry S. Truman Library have information on her public career, as do the Joseph C. O'Mahoney papers at the University of Wyoming. Among her published writings are "The Governor Lady: Nellie Tayloe Ross," *Good Housekeeping*, Aug., Sept., and Oct. 1927; "Progress, Prohibition and the Democratic Party," *Scribner's Magazine*, May 1928; *Twelve Reasons Why Women Should Vote for Smith* (1928); and "Should Women Support the Administration's Policies?" *Congressional Digest*, Oct. 1930. See also Cecelia Hennel Hendricks, "When a Woman Governor Campaigns," *Scribner's*, July 1928; and Mabel Brown, ed., *First Ladies of Wyoming, 1869–1990* (1990). An obituary is in the *New York Times*, Dec. 21, 1977.]

LEWIS L. GOULD

ROTH, LILLIAN (Dec. 13, 1910–May 12, 1980), actress and singer, was born in Boston, Mass., the elder child of Arthur Roth (formerly Rutstein), a salesman, and Katie Silverman. Her stagestruck parents named her after the famed singer Lillian Russell and put her on the stage shortly after their move to New York City when she was six. She had her first theatrical role in *The Inner Man* in 1917, but her breakthrough play was *Shavings* in 1920. "Just turned eight," she later wrote with little regard for arithmetic, "I was billed as 'Broadway's Youngest Star.' "

Sometimes alone and sometimes with her younger sister, Ann, Roth toured the vaudeville circuit. The sisters were billed first as "Lillian Roth and Co.," and then later as "The Roth Kids." In between Broadway and touring engagements, Roth went to New York's Professional Children's School, from which she graduated in 1923. She also attended the Clark School of Concentration in 1924.

In her autobiography, Roth recalled an unhappy childhood. Her alcoholic father never made a substantial living, and the family depended on the children's earnings. Despite Roth's avowed devotion to her mother, Katie Roth comes across in her daughter's memoir as a hard taskmistress overly ambitious for her daughter's theatrical success.

Lillian Roth made the transition to adult roles at the age of fifteen, when the Shubert organization booked her to star in the Chicago run of its revue *Artists and Models*. She continued to appear in revues throughout the late 1920's, starring in such productions as Florenz Ziegfeld's *Midnight Follies* and Earl Carroll's *Vanities of 1928*.

In 1929, Paramount Pictures offered Roth a contract with the studio. Roth played a comic supporting role in the Ernst Lubitsch musical *The Love Parade* (1929) and leading roles in films including *The Vagabond King* (1930), *Honey* (1930), *Animal Crackers* (1930), and *Madam Satan* (1930). Her vivacious on-screen personality brought her increasing fame and, she later claimed, $1 million in income in the early 1930's.

Shortly after her arrival in Hollywood in 1929, Roth became engaged to David Lyons, an assistant director. When Lyons died in 1930, she fell into a depression and began to drink heavily. She married airman William Scott later that year, but the marriage dissolved within a few months. She had no children by him or by any other husband.

Roth continued to act in films, but she also continued to drink. In 1933 she married New York City judge Ben Shalleck and temporarily retired from show business. As Mrs. Shalleck she was socially active and engaged in frequent charity work. According to her 1954 autobiography, she consolidated her alcoholism during this marriage. The Shallecks were divorced in 1939, and Roth plunged into a relationship with Mark Harris, a playboy with underworld connections. Despite his physical abuse of her and a dependence on alcohol that exceeded even her own, she married Harris in 1940. During their stormy marriage, he spent most of her remaining money and continued to abuse her. She had the marriage annulled before the end of the year.

In 1941, Roth was briefly married to salesman Edward Leeds, with whom she moved back to Los Angeles. Unable to work and often sick because of her alcohol dependence, she subsisted on checks from her family for several years. In 1945 she returned to New York and checked into a mental hospital in Westchester County for six months of therapy and drying out.

Upon her release from the hospital in mid-1946, Roth secured work from her old friend Milton Berle, but she quickly began drinking again and could not fulfill her professional commitments. Her despair during this period of her life finally prompted her to join Alcoholics Anonymous (AA), an organization she would later publicize heavily. With help from fellow AA members, Roth stopped drinking. Her recovery enabled her to find singing engagements in nightclubs.

In 1947 she married Burt McGuire, a friend from AA who had been an advertising executive before alcoholism had overwhelmed him. McGuire became Roth's manager. Together the pair went on an extended concert tour of Australia and New Zealand in 1947 and 1948. There they helped organize AA groups in their spare time. Born of Jewish parents, Roth converted to Roman Catholicism shortly after her marriage to McGuire, who had been raised a Catholic.

Roth found increasing work in nightclubs around the country. Her comeback was given a boost in 1953, when she was honored on Ralph Edwards's popular television program, "This Is Your Life." During her appearance on the program, she sang for a national viewing audience. She also discussed her triumph over alcoholism.

In 1954 that triumph was further highlighted in Roth's autobiography, *I'll Cry Tomorrow*, coauthored by Mike Connolly and Gerold Frank. Critical response to the book was mixed. Nevertheless, the combination of Roth's tale of her lurid descent into alcoholism and her recovery, and her final message of hope attracted readers, and the book sold well. In 1955, Metro-Goldwyn-Mayer bought the film rights to the book, which it made into a motion picture that same year; Susan Hayward played Roth on the screen and won an Oscar nomination for her performance.

Between nightclub engagements in the mid-1950's, Roth continued to write. In 1958 she produced *Beyond My Worth*, a group of essays chronicling her life since the publication of *I'll Cry Tomorrow*. More lighthearted than her first book, it rejoiced in her successful comeback as an entertainer and described her newfound role as inspiration to alcoholics and other sufferers. Despite its verbal and photographic images of a happier Lillian Roth, the book suggested that the singer-actress still experienced spells of profound depression.

Roth's comeback was crowned in 1962 by her portrayal of the hero's mother in the musical comedy *I Can Get It for You Wholesale* on Broadway. She would not play on Broadway again until 1971, when she appeared in the musical *70 Girls, 70*. She spent most of the 1960's and 1970's in semiretirement, doing occasional nightclub work and regional theater. In 1963 she and McGuire were divorced. Her final film appearance was a brief role in the 1979 film *Boardwalk*. Lillian Roth died in New York City.

[The Billy Rose Theatre Collection of the New York Public Library for the Performing Arts maintains several clipping files on Roth. In addition to her two autobiographical works, the best source on Roth's life and career is her entry in *Notable Names in the American Theatre* (1976). An obituary is in the *New York Times*, May 13, 1980.]

TINKY ("DAKOTA") WEISBLAT

ROVERE, RICHARD HALWORTH (May 5, 1915–Nov. 23, 1979), political journalist, was born in Jersey City, N.J., the son of Lewis (formerly Louis) Halworth Rovere, an electrical engineer born in France, and Ethel Josephine Roberts, a native of Jamaica. Although Rovere envied colleagues whose ethnic identity was clear, his mixed and mysterious heritage—British and Swedish, French or Italian, presumably black, and possibly Jewish—left him "deprived . . . of self-knowledge" but gave him a detachment useful in his profession. His father's insistence that Rovere's boyish assertions be backed up with evidence and his mother's love of poetry inculcated in him a passion for accuracy and words. Apart from frequent visits to Washington, D.C., and travels to other points on the globe, Rovere lived his entire life in New York City and its environs. With his parents moving about once a year, he grew up primarily in the Prospect Heights section of Brooklyn. He attended the public schools (reluctantly), the Unitarian church (infrequently), the Boy Scouts (regularly), the movies (weekly), and Ebbets Field (as often as he could). "I was a Brooklynite," he recalled, "not a New Yorker, and I was less a Brooklynite than a proud defender of whatever part of the borough I happened to live in."

Viewing school as a "rude intrusion" on his life, Rovere was so indolent a scholar that his despairing parents sent him at age fourteen to the Stony Brook School in Stony Brook, N.Y., in hopes of rescuing him for college. He continued his academic slump, "had a brief seizure of fundamentalist Presbyterianism," and went out for the football team. Neck surgery following an injury during football practice confined Rovere to a hospital bed for several weeks in his junior year and changed his life. He did some serious reading, devoured periodicals, honed his writing style, and became an editor of the school's newspaper. After an unhappy semester at Storrs Agricultural College (now the University of Connecticut), Rovere in January 1934 transferred to Bard College at Annandale-on-Hudson, N.Y., where he drifted until radicalized by the Great Depression. In his third year he became editor of the *Bardian*, transforming it into "an Annandale *Pravda*." In 1936 he joined the Communist party as Dick Halworth and met and admired its leading literary light, Granville Hicks, but loathed its insufferably dull catechistic cell meetings.

An unemployed college graduate in 1937, Rovere did household chores for room and board at the Hickses' primitive home in Grafton, N.Y. In the spring of 1938, on Hicks's recommendation, Rovere commenced an editorial job with *New Masses*, a weekly that slavishly followed the Communist line. Disenchanted in the late summer of 1939 by the Nazi-Soviet pact and chagrined that he had tolerated the totalitarianism of the American Communist Party, Rovere quit the *New Masses* and broke with the party. Over the next two years he supported himself as a free-lance. Lack of steady employment did not deter him and Eleanor Alice Burgess from marrying on Dec. 20, 1941; they had three children. For a brief period in 1942 Rovere was an editor with the *Nation* and in 1943 for *Common Sense*, but by early 1944 he was again free-lancing.

In May 1944, after he had portrayed Thomas E. Dewey as the "Man in the Blue Serge Suit" for *Harper's,* Rovere realized his ambition to join the staff of the *New Yorker.* Over the next four years he profiled political and nonpolitical subjects, including two shyster lawyers whose bizarre story was reprinted as *Howe & Hummel* (1947). While covering the 1948 presidential campaign, Rovere was asked by William Shawn, managing editor of the *New Yorker,* to write a "Letter from Washington" every three or four weeks, "not to chronicle the action . . . but to find . . . meaning . . . in it, and to find out what the best-informed and most reflective people *thought* about it." Rovere welcomed the security that came with having his own department. As a transient from exurban Dutchess County, N.Y. (where he and his family had moved in 1946), observing Washington through the monocle of the *New Yorker,* Rovere enhanced his detachment and relied not on personal contacts with public figures, but on "material that is fixed in the record and cannot be repudiated." For thirty-one years Rovere's columns were models of penetrating analysis, objectivity, clarity, wit, and style.

The "Letter from Washington"—concentrating on politics, economics in a broad sense, and foreign policy—was critical from a liberal perspective, but not partisan. Rovere's more pointed political commentary appeared as separate articles or as books. His *General and the President* (1951), written with Arthur M. Schlesinger, Jr., harshly criticized Gen. Douglas MacArthur and warmly supported Harry S. Truman's Korean policy. Rovere's *Affairs of State* (1956) pictured a pious and duplicitous John Foster Dulles and an irresponsible Republican party held in check by Dwight D. Eisenhower, whose chief virtue was his inaction; his influential *Senator Joe McCarthy* (1959) portrayed a con artist whose considerable talent made him a dangerous demagogue; *Goldwater Caper* (1965) had sympathy for Barry Goldwater the man but contempt for his ideas and supporters and suggested that the huge Democratic majority in 1964 was more a tribute to the fallen John Kennedy than a compliment to Lyndon Johnson; and *Waist Deep in the Big Muddy* (1968) was "an outburst of anger and torment, a prolonged cry of pain over Vietnam" and a rejection of his earlier support for intervention in Korea.

Rovere was also a literary critic. His introduction to the 1950 Modern Library edition of *Light in August* contributed to the William Faulkner revival, his perceptive introduction to the *Orwell Reader* (1956) acknowledged his debt to George Orwell, and his *Esquire* article "The Question of Ezra Pound" (September 1957) helped gain that poet's release from a mental hospital.

Rovere was never more amusing, perceptive, and influential than in his *Esquire* essay, which was reprinted in the collection *American Establishment and Other Reports, Opinions, and Speculations* (1962), a book that identified the "American Establishment" as Ivy League clubmen in three-piece suits. A spoof with phony footnotes, it ridiculed C. Wright Mills's *Power Elite.* Ironically, many readers missed its satire. With repetition the "American Establishment," to Rovere's amusement, achieved the status of received truth. The article was taken seriously by the extreme left (who rushed it to Fidel Castro), the political center (with the Library of Congress searching for the article's fictitious sources), and the extreme right (with the article confirming the conspiracy notions of the John Birch Society). With tongue in cheek, Rovere uttered a phrase, imagined a type, and invented a hypothesis that in the 1960's intruded into every discussion about who governed.

In the 1970's Rovere's earlier neck injury again caused problems. After a surgeon botched the removal of a malignancy from his neck, Rovere spent the remaining five years of his life "in unceasing, racking, accelerating pain." During his last three and a half months, in the Vassar Brothers Hospital in Poughkeepsie, N.Y., Rovere twice underwent surgery to achieve cervical fusion (to repair a "broken" or technically "dislocated" neck). He died in Poughkeepsie.

[Rovere's papers are in the State Historical Society of Wisconsin at Madison. He wrote two autobiographies, *Arrivals and Departures* (1976) and *Final Reports* (1984), the foreword to which by Arthur M. Schlesinger, Jr., is particularly valuable. Obituaries are in the *New York Times,* Nov. 24, 1979; and in the *New Yorker,* Dec. 10, 1979.]

ARI HOOGENBOOM

RUBICAM, RAYMOND (June 16, 1892–May 8, 1978), advertising agency executive, was born in Brooklyn, N.Y., the youngest of eight children of Joseph Rubicam and Sarah Maria

Bodine. His father, a failed businessman, became a trade journalist. His mother contributed poetry to *Godey's Lady's Book*.

After his father's death, when Rubicam was five, the children were dispersed. Rubicam's schooling stretched across the country as he stayed with relatives in New Jersey, Pennsylvania, Ohio, Texas and, finally, Denver, Colo., where he lived with his brother Harry. A troubled youth, he ran away twice. At age fifteen, he left school and went to work full-time as a shipping clerk's helper for $5 per week. Rubicam originally wanted to be a lawyer but, lacking funds for college, became interested in writing.

At age eighteen, Rubicam decided to make his way to the ancestral home of his family, Germantown, Pa. It took him a year, during which he worked as a bellhop, usher, movie projectionist, door-to-door salesman, and general hand on cattle cars. At times he lived as a hobo. In 1912, Rubicam settled with relatives in Philadelphia and submitted free-lance feature stories to newspapers there. As a result of these stories, he was able to secure a cub reporting job at a Philadelphia newspaper that paid him $12 per week. Next he sold automobiles, but found the commissions provided too erratic an income for a young man interested in marriage. In 1916, looking for a better-paying job, he chose the field of advertising, which combined his experience as writer and salesman.

Rubicam wrote two ads for Philadelphia companies, a maker of plug tobacco and a truck firm, and tried selling them to the advertisers. The tobacco company referred him to its agency, F. Wallis Armstrong. He visited that agency, sent his ads in with a secretary, and was told to wait. After nine days of waiting, he sent Armstrong an angrily worded note and went home. The next day Armstrong interviewed him, telling him, "Those ads you wrote didn't amount to much, but this letter has some stuff in it."

Armstrong, who hired Rubicam as a copywriter for $20 per week, treated his employees poorly, ridiculing and threatening them. Despite this, Rubicam lasted three years at the agency before taking a job with N. W. Ayer, also in Philadelphia. At Ayer he wrote "The Instrument of the Immortals" ads for Steinway pianos, a slogan that was used by the company for decades. For the E. R. Squibb Company he developed the slogan "The Priceless Ingredient of every product is the honesty and integrity of its maker." He also worked on campaigns for Rolls-Royce and International Correspondence Schools.

In 1923, Rubicam and John Orr Young formed Young & Rubicam (Y&R). Young was an account executive and new business solicitor who had shared an office with Rubicam at Armstrong and later moved to Ayer with him. In 1924, Young convinced General Foods to give Y&R its toughest product: Postum, a poor-selling, noncaffeinated hot beverage. Postum became the agency's first major account, and Rubicam's ads stressed its soothing qualities. These ads won a Harvard-Bok Award, and the success of this campaign earned Y&R numerous other General Foods accounts, including, Jell-O, Sanka coffee, and Calumet baking powder. Other well-known clients were Arrow shirts, the Borden Company, Four Roses whiskey, General Electric radios, Gulf Oil, International Silver, Johnson baby powder, Packard automobiles, Parke Davis drugs, and Travelers Insurance.

Y&R immediately gained a reputation as a creative agency and followed what was to become known as the image school of advertising. The agency developed personalities for its products and eschewed the claim and reason-why ads popular since the time of John E. Kennedy and Claude Hopkins, who wrote for Lord & Thomas during the first decade of the twentieth century.

In 1926, Y&R moved to New York City, and in 1927 Rubicam became its president. He was made chairman in 1944 and retired later that year. He was the agency's chief executive officer and principal stockholder from 1927 to 1944. In the 1970's, Y&R grew to be the country's largest agency, billing more than $1 billion in 1977, the year before Rubicam's death, and $2.3 billion by 1980.

Rubicam's background was in print, but his agency became a noted producer of radio shows, developing new talent and sponsoring some of the most popular radio programming of the 1930's and 1940's. Among the talent brought to the airwaves by Y&R was Jack Benny. Y&R clients also sponsored Kate Smith, Fred Allen, and Arthur Godfrey.

Although Y&R advertising was known for its creativity, Rubicam also introduced intensive, scientific marketing to the business. In 1932, he hired Dr. George H. Gallup away from his professorship at Northwestern University. In the sixteen years Gallup worked for Y&R, he performed numerous surveys and studies of consumer media use and advertising responses for the agency.

Rubicam published an advertising trade publication, *Tide,* which he bought from Time, Inc., in 1930. He remained a majority owner of the magazine until 1948. He was chairman of the board of the Audience Research Institute, a public opinion and attitude research company of which George Gallup was president. At age forty, he purchased a farm at Danboro, in Bucks County, Pa., and bred Aberdeen Angus cattle and Berkshire hogs. He was chairman of the American Association of Advertising Agencies in 1935 and was named to the American Advertising Federation's Hall of Fame in 1974 and to the Copywriters Hall of Fame in 1975. Rubicam served as special assistant to the chairman of the War Manpower Commission in 1942. He was also a trustee of Colgate University's American Graduate School of International Management from 1947 to 1952.

Rubicam married Regina McCloskey on Nov. 30, 1916; they had three children and were divorced in 1939. On Sept. 16, 1940, he married Bettina Hall; they had two children. He died in Scottsdale, Ariz.

Rubicam is among the advertising industry's most respected figures. Among his admirers were David Ogilvy, who said that Rubicam was "the strongest influence in my life as an advertising man," and William Bernbach, who praised his writing.

[Articles on Rubicam are in *Outlook,* Jan. 1935; and *Advertising & Selling,* award no. (1938). An excellent discussion of his life and work is in Stephen Fox, *The Mirror Makers* (1984). An obituary is in the *New York Times,* May 9, 1978.]

RICHARD L. TINO

RUKEYSER, MURIEL (Dec. 15, 1913–Feb. 12, 1980), poet, author, and social activist, was born in New York City, the daughter of Lawrence Rukeyser and Myra Lyons. She graduated from the Fieldston School in 1930 and then attended Vassar College in Poughkeepsie, N.Y., from 1930 to 1932; she also was a student at Columbia University in New York City during the summers of 1931 and 1932. While a student at Vassar, Rukeyser was the literary editor for the leftist undergraduate journal *Student Review.* In 1931 she drove south with two friends to cover the controversial trial in Scottsboro, Ala., of nine black youths accused of raping two white girls. During her brief stay in Scottsboro, she and her friends were detained by police and charged with contempt of court after they were seen speaking with black reporters and they were connected to a black student conference. This experience is evident in her poem "The Trial" and may have established her interest and commitment to social causes and those wrongly accused of crimes.

Most of her poetry written during her undergraduate days centered more on personal than social or political issues, and after leaving Vassar to pursue a writing career, she began publishing poems in such periodicals as *Poetry.* In 1935 she became an associate editor for *New Theater* magazine and took a flying course in order to learn the mechanics of aviation for her collection of poems *Theory of Flight* (1935). These poems contained descriptions of the structure of a plane in addition to aspects of her own adolescence and reflections of social concerns. She received critical attention for this first collection, and although it won the Yale Series of Younger Poets competition, it was labeled overburdensome with obscure details by some reviewers.

In 1936, Rukeyser traveled to London and then to Spain, where she reported on the People's Olympiad, which had been organized by workers sports clubs in protest against the official Olympic Games being held in Nazi Germany. Upon her return to the United States she became active in the cause of Spanish loyalists. Her second volume of poems, *U.S. 1,* was published in 1938, and one of the most striking poems in the collection, "The Book of the Dead," details the story of a West Virginia mining town dying of silicosis. One reviewer, however, commented that "while having come into her own," she had yet to "fuse the personal and social."

Rukeyser followed this collection with *A Turning Wind* (1939), *The Soul and Body of John Brown* (1940), *Wake Island* (1942), *Beast in View* (1944), *The Children's Orchard* (1947), and *The Green Wave* (1948). Three collections were published in 1949, *Orpheus, Elegies,* and *The Life of Poetry,* and her later works are *Selected Poems* (1951), *One Life* (1957), *Body of Waking* (1958), *Waterlily Fire* (1962), *The Orgy* (1965), *The Outer Banks* (1967), *The*

Speed of Darkness (1968), *Twenty-nine Poems* (1970), *The Traces of Thomas Hariot* (1971) *Breaking Open* (1973), and *The Gates* (1976). In 1979 a comprehensive volume of her poetry was published and critics raved about the vast nature of her work, which reflected American history from the Great Depression to the Vietnam War. Thomas Lask, in a *New York Times* review, commented: "Poetry was never an artifice to Muriel Rukeyser, never a decoration on life. The woman and the poet were one. She was always committed. What that commitment meant to her is the substance of her richly rewarding book." A posthumous collection, *More Nights*, was published in 1981.

Rukeyser also translated the work of other poets, including Octavio Paz, Gunnar Ekelöf, and Bertolt Brecht. Her books for children were *Come Back Paul* (1955), *I Go Out* (1961), *Bubbles* (1967), and *Mazes* (1970). She had one child but there is no information on whether or not she ever married. She also wrote a play, a biography (*Willard Gibbs*, 1942), and for motion pictures and television. Her academic career included serving on the faculty of Sarah Lawrence from 1956 to 1967 and on the board of directors for the Teachers-Writers Collaborative in New York from 1967 to 1980.

Rukeyser was recognized throughout her life with numerous fellowships, awards, and prizes. She was twice poet-in-residence at Yaddo in Saratoga Springs, N.Y., and received the National Institute of Arts and Letters Award in 1942 and the Copernicus Award and Shelley Award in 1977. In addition she won a Guggenheim Fellowship in 1943 and an American Council of Learned Societies Fellowship in 1963. She was a member of the National Institute of Arts and Letters and the Society of American Historians. She also served as president of PEN (Poets, Playwrights, Essayists, Editors, and Novelists) from 1975 to 1976.

In a January 1979 interview for *Ms.* magazine, Rukeyser commented to Louise Bernikow: "The heart of the reimagining is rebellion, breaking through old thought." She also spoke of women poets: "I wish we were better. I wish the cute and coy elements were purged. I know it's attractive, but it isn't what I need in poems. I think a lot of June Jordan, Alice Walker, and Audre Lorde. Black women know how to rebel. I try to hold in my mind somebody who sees it all—some future unborn black woman poet." Walker was one of the up-and-coming black women writers who had studied under Rukeyser at Sarah Lawrence.

A long time resident of Greenwich Village in New York City, she died there of a heart attack after suffering from two strokes.

[See J. M. Brinnin, "Social Poet and the Problem of Communication," *Poetry*, Jan. 1943; R. Eberhart, "Art and Zeitgeist," *Poetry*, Dec. 1948; John Ciardi, ed., *Mid-Century American Poets* (1950); J. R. Caldwell, "Invigoration and a Brilliant Hope," *Saturday Review of Literature*, Mar. 11, 1950; Randall Jarrell, *Poetry and the Age* (1953); Louise Bogan, *Selected Criticism* (1955); D. Nyren, ed., *A Library of Literary Criticism* (1960); E. Carruth, "Closest Permissible Approximation," *Poetry*, Feb. 1963; L. Lieberman, "Critic of the Month," *Poetry*, Apr. 1969; "Craft Interview with Muriel Rukeyser," *New York Quarterly*, Summer 1972; L. Bernkow, "Breaking Open: New Poems by Muriel Rukeyser," *Ms.*, Apr. 1974; Edmund Wilson, ed., *Collected Essays of John Peale Bishop* (1975); "Back Tooth: Dream-Drumming, Islands, Poems," *Ms.*, Oct. 1976; Robert Coles, "Muriel Rukeyser's 'The Gates,'" *American Poetry Review*, May–June 1978; and Louise Kertesz, *The Poetic Vision of Muriel Rukeyser* (1980). An obituary is in the *New York Times*, Feb. 13, 1980.]

WENDEE JACOBSON

RUPP, ADOLPH FREDERICK (Sept. 2, 1901–Dec. 10, 1977), college basketball coach, was born in Halstead, Kans., one of six children of Henry Rupp and Anna Lichti, farmers who were immigrants from Austria and Germany, respectively. After playing high school baseball, Rupp entered the University of Kansas in 1919. While an undergraduate he played guard on the basketball team coached by Forrest ("Phog") Allen, whose record of most collegiate games won was to be surpassed by Rupp himself in 1968. While at Kansas, Rupp studied the sport with James Naismith, who had invented the game of basketball and was on the faculty, and who had been the university's first head coach in the sport.

After graduating with a B.A. degree in 1923, Rupp taught high school at Burr Oak, Kans. (1923); at Marshalltown, Iowa (1923–1926), where his first wrestling team won a state championship; and at Freeport, Ill. (1926–1930), where his basketball teams were consistent winners. In the summers he worked on his masters degree in educational administration at Columbia University in New York City. He received his masters in 1930, and that year he was hired by the University of Kentucky as its head basketball coach. He remained in this position for forty-two years until the university's mandatory retirement regulations forced him, despite his public resistance, to retire in 1972 at the age of seventy. On Aug. 29, 1931, he married Esther Schmidt. The couple had one son.

Rupp brought the University of Kentucky into prominence in collegiate basketball. He won his first game in 1930 by a wide margin and never looked back. In the course of his career his teams were known for the up-tempo, fast-break playing style that Rupp popularized. He recruited principally in the hills of Kentucky and surrounding states, and he benefited by the then-unusual adoption of athletic scholarships by the Southeastern Conference (SEC) early in his career. This enabled him to attract youths from small towns who otherwise would have been unable to attend the university. He taught them on the court, and because of his faculty appointment he helped keep many of them in school. He unabashedly gave all A's to his players when they enrolled in his classes, saying that to do otherwise was to admit that he had taught them nothing.

Rupp became a legend well before he retired. Over his career he won 879 games. His teams won twenty-seven SEC championships and one National Invitational Tournament title. In compiling a winning percentage of .825, Rupp went to the NCAA tournament on eighteen different occasions and won the championship four times (1948, 1949, 1951, and 1958). He produced seven Olympic gold-medal winners, twenty-four All-Americans, and twenty-eight professional players. He also co-coached the American Olympic gold medal team in 1948. Although his career victories record was broken in the junior college ranks in 1987 by Dick Baldwin, coach at Broome Community College in Binghamton, N.Y., it is likely to stand in major college basketball.

In the late 1940's, during the basketball point-shaving scandals, Rupp professed that such activities were impossible in his program. Subsequent investigations revealed that some of his players not only shaved points but purposely lost games, that the university had given illegal cash payments to basketball players, and that Rupp had used ineligible players in games. These revelations caused the NCAA to penalize Kentucky for rules violations and the SEC to suspend his program for the 1952 season, which the university subsequently canceled. That he survived these scandals was a measure of his popularity.

Like other coaches in both the SEC and the Atlantic Coast Conference, Rupp consistently resisted the recruitment of black basketball players until the late 1960's. The consequences of this decision were most apparent when an all-white Kentucky team, ranked number one in the country, lost to Texas Western University with five black starters in the 1966 NCAA championship game. The contrast between the two teams changed the game, and within five years both conferences were fully integrated.

Throughout Rupp's career, his teams were known for their intense play and their close man-to-man defense. He achieved results by rigorous preparation that included practices during which no one talked except the coach and players were expected to give their best effort at all times. Rupp ran a disciplined organization dominated by his own egotism and an iron fist. In later years, however, as his health began to deteriorate due to a heart attack and chronic diabetes, he began to project a more caring image, at least in the press. On his death, John Wooden called him "an amazing man" and Bear Bryant said that he was "a legend." Lou Carnesecca, the coach at St. John's University, summed it up best: "Hey, down in Kentucky, he's as famous as the Derby."

After his retirement in 1972, Rupp, who authored *Championship Basketball* (1948–1956), became President of the Memphis Tams and subsequently vice-chairman of the board of the Kentucky Colonels in the American Basketball Association. His career accomplishments, which included SEC Coach of the Year (1963–1966, 1968–1972), and UP/API National Coach of the Year in 1951, 1959, and 1966, were recognized by his election to the Kansas Hall of Fame, the Helms Athletic Foundation Hall of Fame, and the Basketball Hall of Fame. He died in Lexington, Ky., about a year after the dedication there of the Rupp Arena, which stands as a lasting monument to his accomplishments.

[See "Bluegrass Sage," *Newsweek*, Jan. 6, 1947; Collie Small, "The Crafty Wizard of Lexington," *Saturday Evening Post*, Feb. 15, 1947; "The Baron," *Time*, Jan. 12, 1959; Ray Cave, "The Old Master Has a New Kind of Winner," *Sports Illustrated*, Feb. 19, 1962; John Lake, "The Baron Scores," *Newsweek*, Feb. 12, 1968; and Barry McDermott,

"The Cain-Tuck-Eee Jubilee," *Sports Illustrated*, Dec. 20, 1976. An obituary is in the *New York Times*, Dec. 12, 1977.]

CHARLES R. MIDDLETON

RUSSELL, ROSALIND (June 4, 1912–Nov. 28, 1976), actress, was born in Waterbury, Conn., to James Edward Russell, a trial lawyer and bank director, and Clara McKnight; both parents were of Irish descent. The fourth of seven siblings (she quipped that she was "the ham in the middle"), she enjoyed a comfortable upbringing. After graduating from a Waterbury convent school, she attended Marymount College at Tarrytown-on-the-Hudson, N.Y., from 1926 to 1928, leaving in her sophomore year to study at the American Academy of Dramatic Arts, from which she graduated in 1929. For her first professional engagement, in 1929, she appeared in twenty-six different plays in thirteen weeks of summer stock at Saranac Lake, N.Y.

This experience led to a winter stock company job (1929–1930) for E. E. Clive in Boston. Her New York City career began with a part in a popular revue, *The Garrick Gaieties* (1930). After working in stock companies in New Jersey, New York, and Massachusetts, she landed a role in a Broadway flop, *Company's Coming* (1931). For the next three years she struggled, taking what few jobs there were, but making no impact. In 1934, while touring in *The Second Man* on the so-called subway circuit, she was seen by a talent scout and sent to Hollywood. She was so annoyed by the way she was treated during her screen test by Universal Studios that she wangled a test at Metro-Goldwyn-Mayer. Because Universal held an option on her, she fooled its head, Carl Laemmle, into thinking her so ridiculous-looking that he was happy to get rid of her. Metro signed her to a seven-year contract. During those seven years she appeared in twenty-seven films.

She made her film debut in a minor role in *Evelyn Prentice* (1934), with William Powell and Myrna Loy. She was cast quickly in a series of forgettable vehicles, such as *West Point of the Air* (1935) and *Reckless* (1935). Many of her parts were second leads or "other women" roles, in which she competed for the hero's affections with the likes of Jean Harlow or Joan Crawford. After appearing in *Casino Murder Case* (1935), however, she was promoted to female leads, although she was still often cast as a love rival.

She had her first really good part in *Craig's Wife* (1936), based on George Kelly's play about a compulsively fastidious housewife. Then came such efforts as *Under Two Flags* (1936), *Night Must Fall* (1937), *The Citadel* (1938), *The Women* (1939), *His Girl Friday* (1940), *Hired Wife* (1940), *No Time for Comedy* (1940), *The Feminine Touch* (1941), and *Design for Scandal* (1941).

On Oct. 25, 1941, Russell married Danish-born agent and producer Frederick Brisson. The couple had one child.

Also in 1941, she left Metro to accept a five-year contract with Columbia that allowed her to free-lance. Ultimately, she did another twenty-four movies, three of them produced by Independent Artists, a company she set up with her husband. Too many, though, were undistinguished artistically and commercially. Among them were *Take a Letter, Darling* (1942), *My Sister Eileen* (1942), *Sister Kenny* (1946), *The Guilt of Janet Ames* (1947), *Mourning Becomes Electra* (1947), *The Velvet Touch* (1948), *Picnic* (1955), *Auntie Mame* (1958), *A Majority of One* (1961), *Five Finger Exercise* (1962), *Gypsy* (1962), *The Trouble with Angels* (1966), *Oh Dad, Poor Dad, Mamma's Hung You in the Closet and I'm Feeling So Sad* (1967), and *Mrs. Pollifax—Spy* (1971).

These roles displayed Russell's versatility as a character actress capable in both drama and comedy, although she is best remembered for her comedies, in which she displayed a range that extended from slapstick to witty repartee. Her one-line description of acting goes, "Acting is standing up naked and turning around very slowly." Respected for her unflinching professionalism, she was an untemperamental and disciplined artist who researched each role diligently and gave her directors complete respect. "I do it his way, no matter how much I may disagree with him," she wrote.

A tall, rangy, and dynamic brunette, with a husky voice likened to the Ambrose Lightship calling to its mate, she was not comfortable in the sex-symbol, glamour-girl category; she was better cast as the not-quite-beautiful type who won men by her smartness in words and clothes. (Russell herself was known for her fashion sense.) Beginning in the early 1940's, in such films as *Take a Letter, Darling*, she exploited her brittle but fundamentally warm personality in career-woman roles (she once said they totaled twenty-three) that included doctors, lawyers, and executives. These business-suited women matched wisecracks with or bossed around such leading men as Fred MacMurray, Brian Aherne, Melvyn Douglas, Clark Gable, and Walter Pidgeon. The best example is *His Girl Friday*, an outstanding screwball comedy remake of *The Front Page*, in which Russell (as pinstriped reporter Hildy Johnson—originally a part written for a male) and Cary Grant (as her hardbitten editor) engaged in a memorable clash of comic temperaments, their rapid-fire dialogue overlapping under Howard Hawks's skillful direction. She hated to be typed, though, and constantly fought for roles that provided variety and depth. One of her finest roles was as the Kansas spinster schoolteacher in *Picnic*. It was one of several important roles she played in films based on Broadway plays.

A woman of integrity who preferred her family and friends to superstardom, she refused to play by many of Hollywood's rules, but when the stakes were high enough could use her wiles to advance her career. To get the role of the bitchy Sylvia in *The Women*, a film she practically stole from Norma Shearer and Joan Crawford, she showed director George Cukor how she could play the part in six different ways. Then, to get the star billing she wanted, she called in sick during the filming until her goal was accomplished.

Apart from USO appearances and a role in a Noël Coward one-act as part of a Hollywood benefit during World War II, Russell did not return to the stage until 1951. After a series of film flops that left her wondering whether she still could act, she was a smash in a touring production of *Bell, Book, and Candle*. Her sagging career was greatly boosted when, despite limited dancing and singing ability (she declared, "I don't sing, I gargle"), she added musical comedy to her repertoire, playing Ruth in the hit *Wonderful Town* (1953), with a score by Leonard Bernstein and a book by Adolph Green and Betty Comden. Russell introduced such tunes as "Ohio" and "One Hundred Easy Ways to Lose a Man," and did a hilariously vigorous conga with a crew of Brazilian naval cadets. *Time* said she "represents the triumph of personality over technique." The part, later reprised for a television production, brought her many awards, including a Tony, and led to her garnering movie musical roles.

She hit Broadway paydirt again in *Auntie Mame* (1956), her greatest success, in which she played the outrageously campy title role for a year and a half before leaving to make the profitable movie version. Her interpretation of the role was based on her sister, who she said was remarkably like Mame. She later declared that she and director Morton Da Costa made considerable contributions to Jerome Lawrence and Robert E. Lee's script. Mame's line, "Life is a banquet, and most poor sons-of-bitches ["suckers" in the film] are starving to death!," inspired the title of Russell's autobiography.

Russell's career also involved several television shows, including her last acting performance, *The Crooked Hearts* (1972). In addition, she displayed some writing talent, making uncredited improvements in many of her scripts, crafting magazine articles, and coauthoring the screenplay for *The Unguarded Moment* (1956) and (using her mother's name), *Mrs. Pollifax—Spy*.

In the 1970's her career slowed down because she suffered from rheumatoid arthritis, an illness about which she undertook to educate the public. She had always been a tireless fundraiser for worthwhile causes. A favorite cause was the Sister Kenny therapy for polio victims; indeed, she overcame Hollywood's reluctance to make a movie about the Australian nurse. For her multiple charitable activities, Russell received the Gene Hersholt Humanitarian Award in 1973, presented during the Academy Awards ceremony. She received four nominations for the Oscar itself but never won. Her many other honors included having a theater in Waterbury named after her in 1955. In 1974, there was a revival of interest in her and she began to appear in sold-out one-woman shows featuring clips from her films. The same year she was awarded the prestigious National Artist Award by the American National Theatre and Academy. She died in Beverly Hills, Calif.

[Russell's autobiography (written with Chris Chase) is *Life Is a Banquet* (1977). There are good accounts of her film career in David Shipman, *The Great Movie Stars: The Golden Years* (1970) and Ethan Mordden, *Movie Star: A Look at the Women Who Made Hollywood* (1983). Other helpful accounts include Joe Hyams, "Rosalind Russell," *Theatre Arts*, June 1961; and "The Comic Spirit," *Time*, Mar. 30, 1963. An obituary is in the *New York Times*, Nov. 29, 1976.]

SAMUEL L. LEITER

S

SALTONSTALL, LEVERETT (Sept. 1, 1892–June 17, 1979), United States senator, was born in the Boston suburb of Chestnut Hill, Mass., the son of Richard M. Saltonstall, an attorney, and Margaret Brooks. Saltonstall, whose forebears had resided in Massachusetts since 1630, had many ancestors who had been in public service. Among them was a great-grandfather (also named Leverett Saltonstall), who had been in the United States House of Representatives from 1838 to 1843. Saltonstall completed his secondary education at the Noble and Greenough School in Boston in 1910. He received his B.A. degree in 1914 and a law degree in 1917, both from Harvard. On June 27, 1916, Saltonstall married Alice Wesselhoeft, daughter of a distinguished Boston surgeon. The couple had six children. Following graduation he volunteered for service with the United States Army during World War I. Upon his commissioning as a lieutenant, he was assigned to the 301st Field Artillery in France.

After the war, Saltonstall returned to Boston. He was admitted to the bar and began the practice of law in the office of his uncle, Endicott P. Saltonstall, in 1919. The next year he joined his father's firm and entered politics with election to the board of aldermen in the Boston suburb of Newton. In 1922, Saltonstall ran as a Republican for a seat in the Massachusetts legislature, the General Court. In what he described as his "shoe leather" campaign Saltonstall, who had helped found the Newton American Legion post in 1919, made the rounds of his district in Newton on foot, stopping at groceries, soda fountains, clubs, and anywhere else he could meet people. Despite spending only $17, he won and entered the Massachusetts house in January 1923 for his first of seven terms. Saltonstall won respect for his integrity and for his mastery of the issues and soon became identified with various reforms. Among them was a compulsory automobile insurance bill he introduced. Its enactment made Massachusetts the first state to have such a law. From 1929 through 1936 he served as speaker and consistently fought the still common shakedown measures, bills intended to cause various businesses sufficient inconvenience so that the targeted businessmen would bribe the sponsoring legislators to drop their support of the shakedown schemes.

In 1936, Saltonstall was defeated in a race for the lieutenant governorship, the last time he would lose an election. Two years later he opposed the legendary James Michael Curley, former mayor of Boston, for governor. Curley made a monumental error when he picked up on a Boston newspaper's recent reference to Saltonstall, who was conspicuous for his long face and protruding chin, as a man with a Back Bay name and a South Boston face and said that Saltonstall "may have a South Boston face, but he doesn't dare show it in South Boston." Saltonstall, whose face would in time be called an American "antique," had long worked assiduously to court Boston's large ethnic vote. He of course proceeded to South Boston, a neighborhood where many blue-collar voters of Irish ancestry lived, to shake hands and exchange greetings and to turn Curley's quip to his advantage at every rally he held by retorting that he might indeed have a South Boston face, that he was proud of it, and that it would still be the same face after the election. Saltonstall won. Soon after his inauguration in early 1939 he placed his stamp on the governor's office by going in person to a truck drivers' union local to promise fair arbitration if the drivers would end a strike that was paralyzing the delivery of milk and other perishable foods in the Boston area. After additional negotiations at the State House, the drivers resumed work and found the settlement to their liking.

Taking advantage of an expanding economy and his own skill at trimming waste in government, Saltonstall was able to lower taxes while securing social reforms such as unemployment insurance and old-age assistance that he had advocated in his inaugural address. On international matters he broke with Republican tradition in his state by endorsing President Franklin D. Roosevelt's efforts to support Great Britain during the early years of World War II. By the time he had completed three terms as governor Saltonstall had helped reshape the Republican party in Massachusetts from one of parochialism and conservatism to one of liberalism.

In 1944, Saltonstall won the United States Senate seat vacated by Henry Cabot Lodge, Jr., who had resigned to enter military service, by a record margin of nearly 500,000 votes. During his first term he gained appointment to the Naval Affairs Committee and the Committee for the District of Columbia. He became expert on military matters, continuing on the Naval Affairs Committee and then serving on the Armed Services Committee after the National Security Act of 1947 provided for unification of the armed forces. Saltonstall worked hard to shape the details and then secure passage of the act, which also established the Central Intelligence Agency as an independent body. He consistently backed the Roosevelt-Truman policy of internationalism by voting for such measures as the Bretton Woods agreement, the United Nations charter, aid to Greece and Turkey, and the Marshall Plan. In domestic matters he voted for the amendment limiting future presidents to two terms in office and for the Taft-Hartley labor relations bill.

Saltonstall won reelection in 1948 and again served on the Armed Services Committee; he also earned a place on the Appropriations Committee. Always an advocate of Massachusetts interests, Saltonstall opposed construction of the St. Lawrence Seaway, which would draw business away from the state, and gained the nickname of "Mr. Fish" for his backing of measures to help the declining New England fishing industry. Saltonstall established a good working relationship with John F. Kennedy, who entered the Senate in 1953. It was understood that in a year Saltonstall was campaigning he could refer to a popular measure as the Saltonstall-Kennedy bill; if Kennedy were running, the junior senator from Massachusetts would have the privilege of speaking of the Kennedy-Saltonstall bill. He and Kennedy collaborated to secure establishment of the Cape Cod National Seashore Park and to gain federal insurance for communities devastated by floods, a matter of special interest to New England in the late 1950's.

In 1952, Saltonstall strongly backed Dwight D. Eisenhower for president. When Saltonstall was unexpectedly nominated for vice-president from the floor of the Republican National Convention, he hastened to assure a concerned Richard Nixon that since Eisenhower was registered in New York, a second eastern candidate should not be on the ticket. Nixon went on to gain the vice-presidential nomination on the Republican ticket that swept to victory in the fall election.

The laconic Saltonstall did not speak much from the floor of the Senate; he did his homework carefully and exerted his influence in committee deliberations and in give-and-take discussions. On three occasions he was bypassed for his party's top Senate leadership position but did become Republican whip and was one of the party's eight top congressional leaders to meet weekly with President Eisenhower.

Saltonstall was against McCarthyism but was hesitant to speak out against the demagogic Wisconsin senator when Senator Ralph Flanders of Vermont introduced a measure to censure McCarthy in 1954. Saltonstall, who was waging a successful campaign for reelection, immediately began receiving a large volume of mail on both sides of the matter. Flanders's resolution was referred to committee. When the vote was taken on the Senate floor after the elections, Saltonstall became the only member of the Republican leadership (party senators divided evenly on the measure) to join in censuring McCarthy. That same year Saltonstall voted against a bill to make membership in the Communist party illegal. Saltonstall took other stands that were unpopular with the Republican right in the 1950's. He backed the confirmation of General George Marshall as secretary of defense in 1950 and endorsed President Truman's recall of General Douglas MacArthur from command in Korea the following year.

In addition to his identification with defense appropriations and foreign aid, Saltonstall supported many civil rights measures and voted to amend the Senate rules to limit filibuster when it was being used to thwart the enactment of civil rights bills. He was a spokesman for education and worked diligently to shape the details of the bill that established the National Science Foundation. He was later named to the National Historical Publications Committee and also served as a regent of the Smithsonian Institution. Saltonstall did not seek reelection in 1966. He died at his farm in Dover, Mass., where he had long resided.

[Saltonstall's papers are at the Massachusetts Historical Society in Boston. Saltonstall's memoirs, *Salty: Recollections of a Yankee in Politics*, as told to Edward Weeks, were published in 1976. An earlier perspective on his career is in Leverett Saltonstall, "Notes of a Novice Senator," *American Mercury*, Aug. 1946. See also Joseph F. Dinneen, "Brahmin from Boston," *New Republic*, Feb. 24, 1947; and Edgar Litt, *The Political Cultures of Massachusetts* (1965). An obituary is in the *New York Times*, June 18, 1979.

Saltonstall was interviewed for several oral history projects relating to political contemporaries. The most substantial of these interviews are at the Eisenhower Administration Project, Columbia University, the John F. Kennedy Library, and the Lyndon Baines Johnson Library.]

LLOYD J. GRAYBAR

SANDERS, HARLAND DAVID ("COLONEL") (Sept. 9, 1890–Dec. 16, 1980), restaurateur and entrepreneur, was born near Henryville, Ind., the eldest son of Wilbert Sanders, a butcher, and Margaret Ann Dunleavy, a homemaker. When Harland was five years old, his father died, leaving a widow and three children. In 1897, in an effort to support the family, Sanders's mother found employment in a canning factory in Henryville, Ind. Harland was left to care for his younger brother and sister and had his first opportunity to prepare meals. Because of his family's poverty, Sanders's education was limited to the sixth grade. In November 1906, after his mother remarried, Sanders enlisted in the United States Army and served a short hitch in Cuba.

In 1908 he married Josephine King in Jasper, Ala., where he had moved after leaving the service. The couple had three children. Sanders's first marriage ended in divorce in 1947.

While working for the Illinois Central Railroad, Sanders took correspondence courses for a law degree from Southern University. He had access to a local judge's law library and used his off-hours to visit local lawyers who explained legal terminology to him. Dismissed from the railroad during this period, Sanders switched to law and represented his clients with some success from the mid-1910's to the early 1920's. Unfortunately, Sanders got into a brawl with a client in open court. Although he was found innocent of an assault and battery charge, the altercation destroyed his practice. For most of the next two decades, Sanders worked at a variety of jobs throughout the southeastern United States as a railroad fireman, a plowman, a buggy painter, a filling station operator, and an insurance salesman.

In the summer of 1929, Sanders and his family moved to Corbin, Ky., where he opened a filling station. Tourists and traveling salespeople stopping at his station often asked where they could find a tasty meal. Sensing a good business opportunity, Sanders opened a small restaurant adjacent to his filling station, which soon became locally famous for its fried chicken. The famed restaurant critic Duncan Hines stopped at Sanders's restaurant during the mid-1930's and listed it in his popular *Adventures in Good Eating*. Shortly thereafter, Sanders added a motel to his restaurant and filling station complex.

In 1937, Sanders attempted to start a chain of restaurants within Kentucky, but his efforts proved unsuccessful and he was forced to sell them. Two years later, he opened a second motel and restaurant complex in Asheville, N.C., but it failed after two years. During the 1940's, Sanders put aside dreams of expansion and contented himself with running his Corbin motel, restaurant, and filling station complex. In the mid-1930's, Sanders had been given an honorary colonel's commission by Governor Ruby Lafoon. In 1949 he was similarly honored, this time by Kentucky's lieutenant governor, Lawrence Weatherby. Soon thereafter, Sanders began to refer to himself as "Colonel" Harland Sanders and to use the title as part of his signature. To complete his transformation from southern redneck to southern gentleman, he grew a mustache and goatee and began to wear a white suit and black tie all the time. Also in 1949, he married Claudia Ledington, an employee whom he had known since the early Corbin years. They had no children.

Meanwhile, Sanders continued to tinker with his recipe for frying chicken. By 1952 he had perfected his "secret recipe of eleven herbs and spices." His secret recipe and his use of a pressure cooker as part of the chicken frying process made his chicken unique in terms of external crispness, internal tenderness, and all-around flavor.

In 1954, Sanders made his first attempt to franchise "Colonel Sanders Kentucky Fried Chicken," but signed up only five restaurants in two years. When plans were announced for a new interstate highway in Kentucky that would bypass Corbin and Sanders's restaurant, he sold his Corbin business for $75,000. Following this sale in 1956, Sanders and his wife moved to Shelbyville, Ky., near Louisville, and he began a new franchising effort. He traveled the nation, personally meeting with thousands of restaurant owners to promote his chicken and to sell franchises to retail it. Initial sales were slow, but by 1960 he had franchised more than two hundred outlets. Three years later, thanks to his remarkably effective salesmanship and promotion, Sanders's "finger lickin' good" chicken was available in more than six hundred outlets. Colonel Sanders Kentucky Fried Chicken had become the largest fast-food chain in the United States.

In 1964, overwhelmed by his rapid success and his advancing age, Sanders sold his firm for $2 million to Kentucky businessman John Y. Brown, Jr., and Tennessee businessman Jack Massey. He remained a director of the company, with an annual salary of $40,000, and acted as its goodwill ambassador. Sanders had retained the rights to sales in Canada and there established a nonprofit charitable foundation that turned over his profits to charitable and educational organizations. In 1974, Sanders estimated that his foundation contributed nearly $250,000 to charitable causes annually. Throughout the 1960's, Sanders made personal appearances and television commercials to promote his fried chicken. His likeness in advertisements and on signs above every Kentucky Fried Chicken store soon made him one of the most widely recognized men in the world.

In 1971, Brown sold Kentucky Fried Chicken to Heublein Incorporated, a manufacturer of packaged foods and premixed drinks. Sanders retained his public relations post, but he was outraged by changes Heublein made in the food offered at his namesake restaurants and brought suit against the corporation in 1974. Later that year the suit was settled out of court in Sanders's favor for more than $1 million. Also in 1974, Sanders published his autobiography, *Life as I Have Known It Has Been Finger Lickin' Good.* In subsequent years failing health reduced his public appearances to a minimum.

[Sanders's autobiography and John Ed Pearce's *The Colonel: The Captivating Biography of the Dynamic Founder of a Fast-Food Empire* (1982) are the two main sources for information about Sanders's career. Obituaries are in the *New York Times* and the *Louisville Courier-Journal*, both Dec. 17, 1980; and in *Time*, Dec. 29, 1980.]

FRANK R. LEVSTIK

SAYPOL, IRVING HOWARD (Sept. 3, 1905–June 30, 1977), lawyer and judge, was born on the Lower East Side of Manhattan in New York City, the son of Louis Saypol, a building contractor, and Minnie Michakin. He attended city public schools and St. Lawrence University in Canton, N.Y. While taking night courses at Brooklyn Law School, he met Adele D. Kaplan, whom he married on Sept. 29, 1925. They ran a court-reporting and messenger service until he was admitted to the bar in 1928. From 1929 to 1934 he was an attorney for New York City. He then went into private practice in the city. In 1945, Saypol was appointed an assistant United States attorney for the Southern District of New York. Four years later he became United States attorney, making him the chief prosecutor for the federal government in the Manhattan area.

Saypol's tenure as a United States attorney, one of the most crucial in the history of the office, coincided with the rapidly intensifying Cold War between the United States and the Soviet Union. He emerged as a central figure in a series of highly controversial federal trials involving national security issues. These cases, which drew international attention, both reflected and contributed to a growing alarm in the United States over the threat of Soviet Communist subversion and espionage. In 1949, Saypol successfully prosecuted Eugene Dennis and ten other American Communist leaders for conspiring to advocate the violent overthrow of the federal government. Their convictions, initially upheld by the Supreme Court, greatly limited the activities of the American Communist Party during the early Eisenhower era.

The same year, Saypol guided the federal prosecution of alleged Communist spy Alger Hiss. In hearings before the House Un-American Activities Committee into possible Communist infiltration of the federal government, former Communist Whittaker Chambers had identified Hiss as a fellow member of a Communist underground organization in Washington in the 1930's that had engaged in espionage for the Soviet Union. Hiss, a former high-ranking State Department official, vehemently denied the accusations. Committee member Richard M. Nixon, who gained national prominence through his role in the case, relentlessly pressed the investigation of Hiss. The federal government was unable to prosecute Hiss for espionage because the statute of limitations had expired. Instead, he was indicted by a federal grand jury in New York on perjury charges for having lied to investigators about his former Communist involvement. After a lengthy court battle, Saypol secured Hiss's conviction for perjury in January 1950. Hiss steadfastly maintained his innocence during and after the trial. His defenders decried a miscarriage of justice and labeled the government's handling of the case an anti-Communist witch hunt. Hiss's conviction was upheld on appeal.

In 1950, Saypol named New York lawyer Roy M. Cohn his confidential assistant to aid in the prosecution of national security cases. Cohn later acted as counsel to Senator Joseph McCarthy during his hearings into Communist infiltration of the government. Saypol's most renowned case was the Rosenberg spy trial. He personally directed the prosecution of Julius and Ethel Rosenberg following their arrest in June 1950 for having passed atomic secrets to the Soviet Union. The government, through Saypol, alleged that the husband and wife duo had recruited Ethel's brother David Greenglass into their espionage network. In 1944 and 1945, during World War II, Greenglass had relayed to the Rosenbergs information concerning America's secret atomic bomb project at Los Alamos, N.Mex., where, as an army enlisted man, he had worked as a machinist. The Rosenbergs had conveyed the information to their Soviet contact, a consular official who had departed the United States in 1946 and thus escaped apprehension. Also arrested in connection with the espionage ring were scientists Harry Gold and Morton Sobell. Greenglass and Gold confessed to authorities and testified for the government. The Rosenbergs and Sobell emphatically denied any involvement with Soviet espionage and insisted on their innocence. In one of the most discussed criminal trials ever, the Rosenbergs were found guilty in April 1951. As the purported leaders of the espionage network, they were sentenced to death. Their conviction and sentence sparked widespread protest. The other members of the ring received long prison terms. After a final appeal was denied by the Supreme Court, the Rosenbergs were executed in 1953.

Critics accused Saypol of manipulating the jury into convicting the Rosenbergs because they were Communists. He was also castigated as one of the first users of managed television news, for he publicly claimed he had an additional witness whom he later withdrew, accusing him of lying. While the weight of contemporary scholarship is that the Rosenbergs did pass atomic secrets, the same evidence suggests that what they conveyed was not particularly valuable to the Soviets. The evidence also indicated that they were not dedicated Soviet agents but rather peripheral participants in an espionage operation. In retrospect it is clear that the Rosenbergs were treated harshly for acting as the go-betweens for Greenglass and other real spies—all of whom escaped with their lives. The most sinister accusation against Saypol is that he conspired with trial judge Irving Kaufman to persuade the Justice Department to ask for the death sentence not only for Julius, but also for Ethel, against whom the government had a weaker case.

In 1952, Saypol began serving the first of two fourteen-year elected terms as a trial-level justice of the New York Supreme Court. His most famous case while on the bench involved a dispute in 1966 with Congressman Adam Clayton Powell, Jr., who represented Harlem. Powell refused at first to pay a libel judgment for having referred to a certain Esther James, in the course of allegations concerning corruption in the New York City Police Department, as "a bag woman," meaning a go-between for gamblers and corrupt police. Saypol threatened to hold Powell in contempt but forbore issuing an actual order. Powell was eventually censured by Congress and lost his seat. In 1975, Saypol ruled that Grand Central Terminal in New York City, the largest and most famous railroad station in the United States, was not subject to landmark-preservation laws, a decision that was later overturned on appeal.

In 1976, Saypol was indicted on charges that he gave choice assignments to lawyers who appeared before him in exchange for their steering $20,000 worth of business to one of his three children, who was a professional appraiser and auctioneer. Although cleared of the accusations, Saypol was deeply affected by the experience. His close friend Cohn, quoted in the *New York Times*, characterized his mood: "He was in a state of disbelief that something like that could have happened." Saypol, who was ill with cancer, died a year later at his Upper East Side residence. He had been working reduced hours and was scheduled to retire from the bench at the end of the year.

[For further information on Saypol and the Hiss and Rosenberg trials see Allen Weinstein, *Perjury: The Hiss-Chambers Case* (1978), and Ronald Radosh and Joyce Milton, *The Rosenberg File: A Search for the Truth* (1983), respectively. The Powell episode is addressed in Kent M. Weeks, *Adam Clayton Powell and the Supreme Court* (1971). An obituary is in the *New York Times*, July 1, 1977.]

JOHN DAVID HEALY

SCHARY, DORE (Aug. 31, 1905–July 7, 1980), producer and writer, was born Isidore Schary in Newark, N.J., the son of Herman Hugo Schary and Belle Drachler. His immigrant parents ran a kosher catering business, Schary Manor. Schary attended public school and received a traditional Jewish education but dropped out of Central High School at age fourteen. He worked at various jobs, including china buyer, haberdashery salesman, and printer's devil for the *Newark Call*. Six years later, frustrated by his lack of education, he returned to Central High School and, inspired by an English teacher to become a writer, finished high school in ten months. Schary returned to the *Call* as reporter and feature writer. He also wrote publicity for a lecture tour by Rear Admiral Richard E. Byrd.

But Schary's passion was the theater. He joined an amateur theater group at the Newark YMHA, working as assistant drama coach under Moss Hart, and shortened his given name for the stage. In 1927, Schary joined Hart at a Catskills resort, where he honed his producing, directing, writing, and acting skills. Though he landed bit parts on Broadway, playing opposite Paul Muni in 1927 and Spencer Tracy in 1928, he continued to work at playwriting. In 1932 a play attracted the attention of film producer Walter Wanger, who wired New York: "Hire Dore Schary. She writes with a lot of vigor—for a woman." Schary eagerly accepted Columbia's offer of $100 per week to write. He moved to Hollywood with his wife Miriam Svet, an artist, whom he had married on Mar. 5, 1932. They had three children.

Schary arrived in Hollywood "with thirty-six dollars, two clean shirts, and my wife." Though Columbia Pictures dropped his option after three months, he hung on as a free-lance writer, turning out eleven scripts in one year. Soon he established a reputation as a reliable and speedy craftsman with a steady flow of ideas. In 1938, Metro-Goldwyn-Mayer hired him as a scriptwriter. His script for *Boys' Town* (1938), starring Spencer Tracy and Mickey Rooney, won an Oscar with its appealing portrayal of small-town America, a message pervading other Schary MGM scripts like *Young Tom Edison* (1940), starring Mickey Rooney. These credits led MGM to make Schary head of its low-budget or "B" production unit. The B films established Schary's reputation as an executive producer with a talent for choosing good scripts, matching them with directors and actors, and meeting a production schedule and budget without sacrificing quality.

A brief stint at David O. Selznick's Vanguard Productions in 1943 and 1944 led to work at RKO, where Schary made four very profitable movies, including *The Farmer's Daughter* (1947), featuring Loretta Young, and *The Spiral Staircase* (1946), starring Dorothy McGuire as a mute. In 1947, RKO promoted him to executive vice-president in charge of production. Schary then supervised a groundbreaking, controversial movie on anti-Semitism, *Crossfire* (1947), directed by Edward Dmytryk, with Robert Ryan. Schary defended his decision to expose anti-Semitism, citing childhood experiences of prejudice and what he learned while lecturing to GIs during the war. The movie won Schary several awards, including the Golden Slipper Club Award for Humanitarianism (1947), the Thomas Jefferson Award of the Council Against Intolerance in America (1947), and the One World Motion Picture Award (1948).

An outspoken liberal, Schary came under attack for his testimony before the House Un-American Activities Committee in October

1947. He stated that he "would hire Communists and non-Communists alike on the basis of ability," believing that the Constitution protected the expression of unpopular political opinions and that it was illegal to fire a person for political views. However, when producers instituted a blacklist in November 1947, Schary accepted the onerous responsibility of announcing the new industry policy, leading to his criticism by left-wing groups. In 1948, RKO's new owner, billionaire Howard Hughes, halted Schary's "message" movies, and Schary returned to MGM as head of production, the chosen successor to Louis B. Mayer.

At MGM Schary produced more than 250 movies, trying "to maintain a balance between being a picture maker, a citizen, and a creative artist." His movies at MGM included such money-makers as *Battleground* (1949), *Show Boat* (1951), and *Quo Vadis* (1951), as well as such classic musicals as *On the Town* (1949), *An American in Paris* (1951), *Singin' in the Rain* (1952), and *Seven Brides for Seven Brothers* (1954). He balanced these entertainment movies with such serious films as *Bad Day at Black Rock* (1954) and *The Blackboard Jungle* (1955). Schary clashed repeatedly with Mayer, arguing that "movies must reflect what is going on in the world." Schary also pursued personal and political commitments that included not only support for liberal Democrats but also a growing dedication to creative Judaism. He wrote innovative services for youth at the Brandeis Camp Institute and developed new rituals to celebrate Hanukkah. He also started to study Hebrew again, helped found the University of Judaism in Los Angeles, and became a champion of the new state of Israel. In 1956 he produced a film on the history of the Democratic party that was shown at the party's national convention. Just what led to his being fired later that year is debated: Mayer's scheming, MGM's declining profits, failure to convert to widescreen technology, Schary's increasing involvement in Democratic politics, and his visible Jewish commitments are all cited.

Schary left Hollywood and returned to New York City, writing a play on his hero, Franklin Delano Roosevelt. *Sunrise at Campobello* opened on Broadway during the 1957–1958 season, running for 556 performances. The play about Roosevelt's struggle to overcome polio won five Tony awards and was named Best Play of 1958. Schary produced a movie version two years later. *Sunrise at Campobello* embodied Schary's talents and many of his political commitments. Such a combination subsequently eluded him, though he tried writing and producing several other plays that were commercial failures. His final play, about the founder of Zionism, *Herzl*, written with Amos Elon in 1976, closed after one performance.

In the 1960's, Schary devoted increasing time to community service, especially liberal projects for social change. He served as national chairman of the Anti-Defamation League of B'nai B'rith from 1963 to 1969. In 1970, Schary became New York City's first commissioner of cultural affairs under Mayor John V. Lindsay. Near the end of his life, he wrote an autobiography, *Heyday* (1979). He died in New York City.

[Besides his autobiography, Schary wrote *For Special Occasions* (1962), an account of his childhood and his parents' catering business. His plays are *Sunrise at Campobello* (1958); *One by One* (1964); and *Brightower* (1970). His screenplays are *Young and Beautiful* (1934); *Outcast* (1937); *Boys' Town* (1938); *Young Tom Edison* (1940); *Edison the Man* (1940); *Behind the News* (1941); *It's a Big Country* (1952); *Battle of Gettysburg* (1956); *Sunrise at Campobello* (1960); and *Act One* (1963). An obituary is in the *New York Times*, July 8, 1980.]

DEBORAH DASH MOORE

SCHIPPERS, THOMAS (Mar. 9, 1930–Dec. 16, 1977), conductor, was born in Kalamazoo, Mich., the son of Peter Schippers, a distributor of Westinghouse products, and Anna Nanninga. Schippers was a keyboard prodigy. He began piano studies at four, performed in public at six, and by the age of eight he performed regularly on a local radio station. He also sang in the choir of a local church, where he often practiced the organ so late into the evening that he spent the night there.

An academic prodigy as well, he graduated from high school at thirteen. At fifteen he entered the Curtis Institute of Music in Philadelphia to study organ and graduated in 1947, completing the four-year course in two. After one semester at Yale University, where he took philosophy courses and studied composition with Paul Hindemith, he returned to Philadelphia to study piano and composition with Olga Samaroff. At her suggestion, he audited a conducting class at the Tanglewood Music Center at Lenox, Mass., and at eighteen, he took second prize in a conducting competition held by the Philadelphia Orchestra.

Although his father tried to dissuade him from pursuing a musical career, he took a job as organist at a church in Greenwich Village in New York City. A neophyte opera group, the Lemonade Opera, rehearsed at the church, and he became their coach and conductor. This led to a major career break. When one of his singers auditioned for Gian Carlo Menotti's opera, *The Consul*, Schippers's piano accompaniment so impressed Menotti that the composer hired him as musical supervisor of his company. *The Consul* opened in Philadelphia on Mar. 1, 1950. Two weeks later fate again intervened when the conductor fell ill and Schippers conducted the New York premiere. He then went to Italy to conduct Menotti's film score for *The Medium* (1951). On Dec. 24, 1951, he directed the NBC-TV world premiere of Menotti's *Amahl and the Night Visitors*.

After a brief tour of duty with the United States Army in Germany, he served as resident conductor of the New York City Opera from 1952 to 1955 and also appeared as guest conductor with the Boston Symphony, the Philadelphia Orchestra, and the NBC Symphony. When Schippers conducted the New York City Opera in the world premiere of Aaron Copland's *The Tender Land* (1954), a critic for the *New Yorker* said he combined "taste and energy with the rare faculty of conveying musical ideas by means of gestures that is the indispensable talent of the born conductor." He led the New York premiere of Menotti's *The Saint of Bleecker Street* (1954) and in 1955 made his debut at La Scala Opera in Milan with the same opera.

The year 1955 marked the beginning of his lengthy associations with the New York Philharmonic and the Metropolitan Opera. After his Philharmonic debut on March 26, *New York Times* critic Olin Downes called him "a conductor of very exceptional gifts." Of his Metropolitan debut on December 23, Howard Taubman of the *New York Times* wrote, "Schippers knows how to keep his forces together. . . . He keeps things moving but is wise enough to give the singers a certain flexibility."

Schippers was an imposing presence on the podium: six foot three and handsome, with dark brown eyes, curly dark-gold hair, and a resonant voice. He memorized all his scores, including more than one hundred operatic works, and maintained an arduous daily work schedule. In 1958, he and Menotti cofounded the Festival of Two Worlds in Spoleto, Italy, a summer showcase of international talent. Schippers remained artistic director of the festival until 1976, led most of its orchestral and operatic performances, and developed many new artists.

In the summer of 1959 he shared the podium with Leonard Bernstein when the New York Philharmonic toured the Soviet Union, and in 1960 he became the first American conductor to open a Metropolitan Opera season. Between 1961 and 1963, he guest conducted the New York Philharmonic, the San Francisco Symphony, the La Scala Opera, where he led the world premiere of Manuel de Falla's *Atlantida* (1962), and made his debut at the Bayreuth (Germany) Festival (1963), conducting Wieland Wagner's production of *Die Meistersinger*. In 1964 he led the American premiere of Menotti's *The Last Savage* at the Metropolitan Opera.

On Apr. 17, 1965, Schippers married Elaine ("Nonie") Phipps, the daughter of Michael Grace Phipps, director of the W. R. Grace steamship line. Immediately after the ceremony, which took place in Manhattan, the couple flew to Berlin, where he conducted the Berlin Philharmonic. Following the 1965–1966 season, he traveled with the Metropolitan Opera Company on its first European tour in fifty-six years. Schippers was chosen to open the 1966 season, and the new auditorium, at the Lincoln Center for the Performing Arts with the world premiere of Samuel Barber's *Antony and Cleopatra*.

When Leonard Bernstein stepped down as conductor of the New York Philharmonic in 1969, Schippers was considered his likely successor. The post went instead to Pierre Boulez, but in 1970 Schippers was named music director of the Cincinnati Symphony, replacing Max Rudolf. In 1972 he was appointed Distinguished Professor of Music at the College-Conservatory of Music of the University of Cincinnati, where he taught conducting. He and his wife divided their time between residences in Cincinnati and Manhattan, but in January 1973 Nonie Schippers died after a prolonged bout with cancer. They had no children.

In 1974, Schippers had perhaps the greatest success of his career by leading the Metropolitan Opera production of Mussorgsky's *Boris Go-*

dunov (a combination of the 1869 version and the 1872 revisions), regarded as the most complete performance ever heard in America, possibly in the world. In 1975 he led the American premiere of Rossini's *The Siege of Corinth*, in which Beverly Sills made her Metropolitan Opera debut. From 1975 to 1976 he toured Europe and the Soviet Union, served as director of Special Projects for the RAI, Italy's radio and television network, and was affiliated with the Archigiana, an international music school in Siena.

In 1976 his artistic partnership with Menotti ended. Menotti said Schippers had become too expensive for the Spoleto Festival; Schippers replied that Menotti had turned against performers who enjoyed more attention than he did. In 1977, Schippers was diagnosed with lung cancer and gave up his post as music director of the Cincinnati Symphony to become its conductor laureate. He was appointed music director of the Santa Cecilia Academy Orchestra in Rome, but had to cancel his initial concerts there in October owing to his illness. He died in New York City that December and left the bulk of his $5 million estate to the Cincinnati Symphony.

[Schippers's personal papers, scores, and book collection are held in the Archives and Rare Books Department at the University of Cincinnati Library. Profiles appear in *Opera News*, Sept. 17, 1966; *Newsweek*, Oct. 19, 1970; and *Saturday Review*, May 20, 1972. See David Ewen, comp. and ed., *Musicians Since 1900* (1978). An obituary is in the *New York Times*, Dec. 17, 1977.]

SUSAN FLEET

SCHORER, MARK (May 17, 1908–Aug. 11, 1977), writer, was born Marcus Robert Schorer in Sauk City, Wis., the second of four children of William Carl Schorer, a manufacturer, and Anna Walser. In grammar school, Marcus and a younger friend and rival, August Derleth (who would become a prolific regional writer), haunted the village library. In high school, the literary pair read Oscar Wilde and J. K. Huysmans. Although Marcus did not fancy himself a decadent, he found in the name "Mark" (bestowed on him by a sympathetic teacher who penned Emerson's words "God speed the mark!" in a gift book) a new identity, and he preferred tippling bootleg whiskey and practicing the oboe to playing ball and slaying rabbits.

Deciding to teach and write after receiving his B.A. from the University of Wisconsin (on a Zona Gale Fellowship) in 1929, Schorer recalled the onerous nickel chores that he had performed for his grandfather and persuaded the roughhewn old German immigrant to send him to Harvard for a year. In Cambridge, Mass., the tall, midwestern youth, in quest of maturity, earned a master's degree under the highly civilized professor and poet Robert Hillyer. After graduation he returned to the University of Wisconsin for doctoral studies.

While preparing for a career in academe, Schorer began to write fiction. During the summer of 1931, he entered into a joint literary venture with the more disciplined Derleth, renting a cottage on the Wisconsin River and churning out Gothic yarns for *Weird Tales*. In 1933 he turned to the writing of short stories for magazines such as *Harper's* and *Scribner's*. Two years later he brought out his first novel, *A House Too Old*, based on the historical Sauk City and on the splendid dwelling that his grandparents had built there twenty-two years earlier for his parents. Unfortunately, Schorer's tedious nostalgia undermined this generational psychic saga of the American Dream killed by greed.

A Mary L. Adams Fellowship in the period 1935–1936 enabled Schorer to plan an ambitious book on the mind and poetry of William Blake. He received his Ph.D. in 1936, and on August 15 of that year he married Ruth Tozier Page of Madison, Wis., and New York City. They had two children. The young scholar taught at Dartmouth College his first year out of Wisconsin and then left to teach at Harvard. In 1940 the affable, sensitive, witty Schorer was appointed a Biggs-Copeland instructor. The following year he published his second novel, *The Hermit Place*, a tense psychological tale of two married sisters haunted by their separate and secret memories of the same dead lover.

Assisted by Guggenheim Fellowships in 1941 and 1943, Schorer worked on his study of Blake, which he began writing in Laguna Beach, Calif., continued on a sheep ranch near Roswell, N.Mex., and finally completed in Cambridge. During this time, he also wrote stories, literary essays, and newspaper reviews. With his Blake book in press and with the expansion of American universities after World War II, Schorer left Cambridge in 1945 to become an associate professor at the University of California, Berkeley. His erudite *William*

Blake: The Politics of Vision (1946) depicts the poet less as an enraptured mystic than as a man of the world, a visionary rationalist, who "demanded too much of art because he hoped for so much from life."

At Berkeley, Schorer taught courses in contemporary literature, critical theory, and story writing. In 1947 he gathered thirty-two of his stories under the title *The State of Mind*. Gracefully restrained but biting, they dramatize memorable conflicts between nationalities, classes, parents, and children. That same year Schorer was made a full professor at Berkeley and a fellow of the Kenyon College School of English (later the School of Letters, Indiana University).

Fascinated by critical theory and the problem of the novel, Schorer continued to read widely. In 1948 he received another Guggenheim fellowship, this time to write, to study novel theory, and to edit an anthology of criticism. In 1949 he became director of the Christian Gauss Seminar at Princeton University, lecturing there on his theoretical and critical interests. In 1950 he published *The Story: A Critical Anthology*, a brilliant guide to understanding through close reading and concrete illustrations the limits and possibilities of a complex art form, as well as its relation to the novel.

After a stint as visiting professor at Harvard in 1952, Schorer, recognized as a leading New Critic, traveled to Italy as a Fulbright fellow. There he lectured at the University of Pisa, completed his third novel in a Florentine *pensione*, worked on a biography of D. H. Lawrence, and began researching backward his authorized biography of Minnesotan Sinclair Lewis, who had died in Rome the year before. Like the writer from Sauk Centre's Main Street, the writer from Sauk City's Water Street had also dreamed of escape, of elegant romance and spirited bonhomie, of literary fame and good fortune.

Schorer published his third, and last, novel in 1954. With a symmetry and a delicacy reminiscent of Henry James, the two-part *The Wars of Love* discloses how four childhood friends destroy one another as adults. While still working on his Lewis biography, which he then imagined would take about two years to write, Schorer continued to edit texts and to write on other literary and critical subjects. He was a visiting professor at the University of Tokyo in 1956 and a fellow at the Center for Advanced Study in the Behavioral Sciences in Stanford, Calif., from 1958 to 1959. In 1960 he became chairman of Berkeley's department of English and a Bollingen fellow.

Finally, in 1961, after more than nine years of what became an obsessive involvement in the project, Schorer completed his massive *Sinclair Lewis: An American Life*. Marvelously controlled and eminently readable, the 867-page Book-of-the-Month Club selection was praised by most reviewers; a few, however, found the linkage between Lewis's inner life and public expression inadequate, attributing the biographer's caustic gratuities to perhaps the exorcism of private demons. At any rate, Schorer's superb effort and the by-products of his great enterprise—sundry articles, a pamphlet, a collection of criticism on Lewis, and introductions to paperback editions of Lewis's best novels—stimulated a Sinclair Lewis revival in the 1960's.

Following his year as a Fulbright professor at the University of Rome, Schorer stepped down as department chairman at Berkeley in 1965, but he remained active in scholarly and literary associations. In 1966 appeared *Colonel Markesan and Less Pleasant People*, a collection of the horror and science fiction collaborations that he and Derleth had dreamed up years before on the banks of the Wisconsin River. In 1968, Schorer published more recent selections, *The World We Imagine*, nineteen of his finest essays, prefaces, and lectures on books, writers, and ideas, among them the eloquent "Technique as Discovery" and "The Burdens of Biography." His biography, *D. H. Lawrence*, also appeared that year; written sporadically over two decades, it was far less comprehensive than the Lewis life, but was packed with illuminating insights about Lawrence's development.

At the time of his death in Oakland, Calif., Schorer's *Pieces of Life* (1977), a collection of ten short stories interlaced with eleven dark autobiographical sketches, was in press. He left unfinished a biography of choreographer George Balanchine, in whose New York school Schorer's daughter taught dance.

[Schorer's papers are at the Bancroft Library, University of California, Berkeley. Other books written or edited in whole or part by Schorer include *Direct Communication, Written and Spoken* (1943), *Criticism: The Foundations of Modern Literary Judgment* (1948, rev. 1958), *Society and Self in the Novel* (1956), *The Novelist in the Modern World* (1957), Lawrence's *Lady Chatterley's Lover* (1959), *Modern*

British Fiction (1961), Lewis's *I'm a Stranger Here Myself and Other Stories* (1962), *American Literature* (1965), *Galaxy: Literary Modes and Genres* (1967), *The Literature of America: Twentieth Century* (1970), and Lawrence's *Sons and Lovers: A Facsimile of the Manuscript* (1977). An obituary is in the *New York Times*, Aug. 18, 1977.]

MARTIN BUCCO

SEBERG, JEAN DOROTHY (Nov. 13, 1938–ca. Aug. 31, 1979), actress, was born in Marshalltown, Iowa, the daughter of Ed Seberg, Jr., a pharmacist, and Dorothy Arline Benson, a schoolteacher. (The family name became Seberg when her paternal grandfather changed his name from Carlson after emigrating from Sweden.)

Seberg grew up in an archetypal midwestern American setting. She attended public schools, played in the school band, taught Sunday School, worked at her father's drugstore, and was a bit of a tomboy. She won an American Legion oratory contest, was teen chairman of the Iowa March of Dimes, and was elected lieutenant governor of Iowa Girls State.

Seberg's mother wanted her to be a writer, and her father wanted her to be a doctor, but she wanted to act from the time she was twelve and was later active in school dramatics. Prophetically, she appeared in a school film production of *Sabrina Fair* as a middle-class American girl who goes to Paris.

In order to please her parents, Seberg enrolled at the University of Iowa. While she was still a freshman, her high school drama coach entered her name in a worldwide competition that film director Otto Preminger was conducting to find a lead for a big-budget film production of George Bernard Shaw's *Saint Joan*. The competition, which eighteen thousand girls had entered, climaxed in the fall of 1956 when Seberg was named the winner; she was instantly transformed into a national celebrity.

Seberg worked on *Saint Joan* in the glare of unprecedented publicity, only to see it open in 1957 to uniformly unfavorable reviews. Critics generally blamed her flat performance for the film's failure. Devastated by hostile reactions to the film, she went into seclusion in Nice, France, beginning an almost permanent exile from the United States.

Late in the summer of 1957 Seberg made a second film with Preminger: *Bonjour Tristesse* (1958), about a sophisticated adolescent obsessed with her father. Critical reaction was kinder, but Seberg's application to the Actors Studio in New York City was ignored, and Preminger turned her contract over to Columbia Pictures. She then had small supporting roles in *The Mouse That Roared* (1959) and *Let No Man Write My Epitaph* (1960).

On Sept. 6, 1958, Seberg married François Moreuil, an American-educated French lawyer who helped her make contacts in the French film industry. The marriage lasted almost exactly two years. Meanwhile, Jean-Luc Godard cast Seberg as the American mistress of a French criminal played by Jean-Paul Belmondo in *À Bout de Souffle*. The expressionless face and flat, hesitant voice that had been limitations in her first films became strengths in this film, helping her establish a new screen image ambiguously mixing wholesomeness and amorality.

Godard's film was a success in France and played to good reviews as *Breathless* in the United States (1961). Although Seberg had squandered the instant stardom that Preminger had handed her with *Saint Joan*, she now became a star of the French New Wave and later gained reacceptance in Hollywood as an international film personality.

Throughout the early 1960's, Seberg continued to work in France, playing morally ambiguous roles in such films *La Récréation (Playtime*; 1963), *Les Grandes Personnes* (*Time out for Love*; 1963), and *L'Amant de cinq jours* (*The Five Day Lover*; 1963), which were also released in the United States. Her fluency in French was improving rapidly, but she almost always played American characters. In 1963, Seberg made *In the French Style*, her first purely English-language film since 1958; however, this film was essentially an adaptation of her New Wave work. Critical reaction to this film was so favorable that Columbia offered her a greatly improved contract.

Seberg married another Frenchman, author Romain Gary, who was twenty-five years her senior, on Oct. 16, 1963. They had two children and divorced in 1970.

Seberg's strongest performance in an American film was probably *Lilith*, a 1964 adaptation of a J. P. Salamanca novel directed by Robert Rossen. In a break from her American-in-Paris roles, she played a schizophrenic having an affair with a sanatorium attendant. Seberg received good notices, but the film itself was panned. The next year Universal cast her in a big-budget production, Mervyn LeRoy's *Moment to Moment* (1966). Through the remainder of the decade she continued to work on both sides of the Atlantic. Her best-known American films during this period were *Paint Your Wagon* in 1969 and the 1970 disaster film *Airport*.

What was probably Seberg's last significant role came in *Ondata di calore* (*The Dead of Summer*) in 1970. She gave a powerful performance as a schizophrenic American stranded in Morocco. Just as she was maturing as an actress, however, she was approaching an emotional breakdown from which she would never recover.

Seberg was known as an active supporter of black nationalist causes in the United States throughout the 1960's. In May 1970, Joyce Haber, a Hollywood gossip columnist, published an item about an unnamed actress said to be carrying the baby of a Black Panther leader; the item could only have been about Seberg, who was then pregnant. When *Newsweek* ran the story in its Aug. 24, 1970, issue, it named Seberg as the actress in question. It was later revealed that the FBI had fabricated and planted the story in order to discredit Seberg because of her black nationalist sympathies.

When Seberg saw the *Newsweek* story, she was seven months into a problematic pregnancy, and she and Gary had recently agreed to separate. Reading the story put her over the edge. Convinced that there was a bizarre conspiracy to destroy her, she immediately went into labor. In Geneva, on Aug. 23, 1970, she delivered a daughter who survived just two days. Seberg never recovered emotionally. Gary later claimed that every year thereafter she attempted to kill herself on the anniversary of her daughter's death.

Seberg's film career stalled in 1972. She had become too old to be an ingenue, but was still too young for interesting character roles. None of the eleven films that she made during her last decade is of outstanding interest. While searching for a new direction in her career, she met Dennis Berry, a young American actor and would-be filmmaker who had grown up in France. They capped a brief affair by flying to Las Vegas, Nev., where they were married on Mar. 12, 1972.

During her last year Seberg lived with a young Algerian actor, Ahmed Hasni, with whom she went through a wedding ceremony in May 1979, although she remained legally married to Dennis Berry. On the night of Aug. 30, 1979, she disappeared after leaving her Paris apartment. Nine days later she was found dead in a parked car; she had apparently used barbiturates to take her life the night she had disappeared. Several days later Romain Gary accused the FBI of causing her death with its 1970 actions. On Sept. 14, 1979, the FBI publicly admitted that it had indeed fabricated the pregnancy story to discredit Seberg.

On Dec. 2, 1979, Gary shot himself to death, leaving a note disavowing any connection between his suicide and that of Seberg.

[The fullest biography is David Richards, *Played Out* (1981). See also Charles Champlin, "The Death of an Actress," *Los Angeles Times*, Sept. 12, 1979; Lee Grant, "Jean Seberg: Did Gossip Kill Her?" *Los Angeles Times*, Sept. 23, 1979; and John McCormick, "What Have They Done to Ed and Dorothy Seberg's Girl?" *Los Angeles Times*, Sept. 23, 1993. Obituaries are in the *New York Times* and the *Los Angeles Times*, both Sept. 9, 1979.]

R. Kent Rasmussen

SHAW, LAWRENCE TIMOTHY ("BUCK") (Mar. 28, 1899–Mar. 19, 1977), football coach, was born on a farm near Mitchelville, Iowa, the son of Timothy Shaw and Margaret Kelly. After playing football at Stuart High School and for a year at Creighton University, in Omaha, Nebr., Shaw transferred to Notre Dame University, where he became one of Knute Rockne's greatest linemen (1919–1921). An all-around athlete, he was also a shot-putter for Notre Dame's track team. A six-foot, 175-pound tackle, he played on Notre Dame football teams that lost one game in three seasons. During the 1920 season, Shaw blocked five punts and helped lead Notre Dame to its first national championship, and as a senior in 1921, he was also the team's kicker and converted thirty-eight points after touchdown. Shaw was selected an All-American in 1921. Soon afterward he married Majorie Bowerman; they had two children.

Influenced by Rockne, Shaw passed up a professional football career to become a coach. On Rockne's recommendation, he was hired by the University of Nevada in 1922 as an assistant coach. Shaw moved to North Carolina State in 1924 as head football coach, then returned to Nevada in 1925 in a similar capacity. It was at the University of Santa Clara, a small Jesuit institution fifty miles south of San Francisco, that Shaw stepped out of Rockne's shadow. Working as a line coach from 1929 to 1935, and after 1936 as Santa Clara's head coach, he turned a losing football team into a national power. At the end of his first Santa Clara season, the Broncos played in the 1937 Sugar Bowl.

Soft-spoken, calm, and thoughtful, the prematurely silver-haired Shaw (known as the Silver Fox) developed a reputation as one of football's innovators. Leonard J. Casanova, Shaw's assistant and successor at Santa Clara, said that what set Shaw apart from other coaches of his era was an ability to change. With one of the nation's most explosive offensive teams and the home-field advantage, Louisiana State University (LSU) was heavily favored over Santa Clara in the 1937 Sugar Bowl. "At a time when multiple defenses were unheard of, Buck designed and used six different defenses against LSU," recalled Casanova. By shifting his defense throughout the game, the Santa Clara team kept LSU off balance and won a 21–14 victory. It was the critical game of Shaw's career.

In Shaw's tenure at Santa Clara, he compiled a 47–10–2 record and national ranking in five of his seven years. He took on formidable teams from large universities and defeated Oklahoma, Arkansas, Texas A&M, Michigan State, Purdue, Stanford, California State, and UCLA. His unbeaten, untied 1937 team returned to the Sugar Bowl in 1938 and held LSU scoreless for the first time in fifty games, and Shaw became the first coach to win back-to-back Sugar Bowl championships. The football stadium at Santa Clara was later named Buck Shaw Stadium.

In 1941, Shaw was offered the head coaching job at Notre Dame, but Shaw, who avoided personal involvement in recruiting and disliked public speaking, declined the position, which went to Frank Leahy of Boston College. Shaw never regretted his decision. "You're a teacher without tenure," he said of the pressures of college coaching. "The history teacher doesn't have to send his class out before 64,000 people on Saturday to compete against classes from other schools, classes which may have much better material than he has. But you send your class out and your status keeps changing, according to what happens to it out there."

Shaw resigned as the Bronco coach in 1943, when Santa Clara suspended football for the duration of World War II, and served in a United States Army ROTC athletic program. After the war San Francisco businessman Tony Morabito, a Santa Clara graduate, signed Shaw to coach a new professional football team, the San Francisco 49ers, in a new league, the All-American Football Conference (AAFC). Because the AAFC would not begin play until the 1946 season, Morabito allowed Shaw to coach at the University of California at Berkeley in the 1945 season.

Moving into the professional ranks in 1946 as the first coach of the San Francisco 49ers, Shaw controlled every aspect of the franchise. In his nine years as coach of the 49ers, Shaw shaped his team into a football powerhouse, compiling a .614 winning percentage. While he had been renowned for his defensive genius at Santa Clara, as a professional coach, he developed a razzle-dazzle offensive attack that made professional football more exciting. He built the team around quarterback Frankie Albert, whose favorite receiver was Alyn Beals, who had played for Shaw at Santa Clara. Shaw was among the first professional football coaches to sign and play African Americans, including Joe ("The Jet") Perry in 1948. Although Perry had only junior college and United States Navy football experience, Shaw recognized Perry's potential to become a professional star. Perry went on to become the league's all-time rushing leader in sixteen seasons and a member of the Professional Football Hall of Fame.

From 1946 through 1949, the 49ers played in the All-American Football Conference and were runners-up for four seasons in the Western Conference to the Cleveland Browns. Shaw's 49ers defeated the Browns in their first meeting in 1946 and broke Cleveland's twenty-nine-game undefeated streak in 1949. The Browns, however, defeated the 49ers in the 1949 AAFC championship game by 21–7.

Shaw's 1948 team won twelve of fourteen games, finishing second to the Browns. With speed, power, and durability, the 49ers of 1948 ran for more yardage than any team in professional football history. Led by halfback Johnny Strzykalski and Perry, the 49ers rushed for 3,663 yards, averaged 6.1 yards per carry and 262 yards per game, and ran into the end zone for 495 points.

When the AAFC merged into the National Football League (NFL) in 1950, the 49ers faced tougher competition. Shaw had his only losing season with the 49ers in his first year in the NFL. He responded to the challenge by rebuilding with new talent. Within four years, Shaw had signed five future members of the Professional Football Hall of Fame: quarterback Y. A. Tittle, running backs Hugh McElhenny and John Henry Johnson, and tackles Leo Nomellini and Bob St. Clair.

Although Shaw's 49er teams were winners and crowd pleasers, they never won a championship. Twice the 49ers were unbeaten at midseason, then were hobbled by injuries and lost crucial games. Under Shaw the 49ers were at their best against top teams, winning five consecutive games against the Detroit Lions, a team that won the NFL championship in 1952 and 1953. Frustrated that Shaw couldn't deliver a title, Morabito fired him after the 1954 season despite Shaw's winning teams in eight of his nine 49er seasons. When he left, the team faltered. The 49ers in the post-Shaw era had three coaches in the next four years and one winning season.

In the spring of 1955, Shaw became the Air Force Academy's first football coach. He built another winning program before resigning in January 1958. Shaw had planned to retire but was lured back into the NFL by the Philadelphia Eagles. He took the job on the condition that the Eagles sign a veteran quarterback. Norm Van Brocklin of the Los Angeles Rams was acquired in a trade. The Eagles, who won two of twelve games in 1958, finished tied for last in the Eastern Conference.

Numerous personnel changes were made over the next year, and the Eagles improved their record in 1959 to 7–5 and a tie for second in the Eastern Conference. Van Brocklin led the Eagles to a 49–21 upset over the New York Giants in a game that was a turning point in Shaw's rebuilding program.

In 1960, Shaw was voted NFL Coach of the Year after the Eagles won the league championship. After losing the season opener to Cleveland, they won nine games in a row and finished with an 11–2 record. When his regular linebackers were injured early in the season, Shaw persuaded center Chuck Bednarik to become the last of the sixty-minute men, playing every down on offense and defense. The Eagles defeated Vince Lombardi's Green Bay Packers, 17–13, in the NFL championship game. Shaw was the only coach to beat the legendary Lombardi in a playoff game. "I can't think of a better time to bow out," Shaw said in announcing his retirement after the game. "I can't soar any higher than being the head coach of a world championship professional football team."

Shaw became vice-president of the Royal Container Corporation of San Francisco. In retirement, Shaw served as a university regent for Santa Clara. He was inducted into the Helms Foundation Football Hall of Fame in 1960 and the National College Football Hall of Fame in 1972. He died of cancer in Menlo Park, Calif.

[Shaw's Santa Clara Teams are featured in Marty Mulé, *Sugar Bowl* (1983). A chapter on Shaw is in Y. A. Tittle, *I Pass!* (1964). Obituaries are in the *New York Times* and the *Philadelphia Inquirer*, both Mar. 20, 1977.]

STEVE NEAL

SHEEN, FULTON JOHN (May 8, 1895–Dec. 9, 1979), clergyman, author, and radio and television preacher, was born in El Paso, Ill., the oldest of four children of Delia Fulton and Newton Morris Sheen, variously a farmer and storekeeper. Sheen's original first name Peter was dropped at a young age; he later added John, his confirmation name. In 1901 the family moved to Peoria, Ill., where he attended St. Mary's School and the Spalding Institute, a Roman Catholic high school, from which he graduated in 1913. The same year Sheen entered the College and Seminary of St. Viator at Bourbonnais, Ill., where he earned B.A. (1917) and M.A. (1919) degrees. He completed his seminary studies at the Seminary of St. Paul in St. Paul, Minn., and, on Sept. 20, 1919, was ordained a Catholic priest for the Peoria diocese. Following ordination, Sheen pursued graduate studies at the Catholic University of America (S.T.B. and J.C.B., 1920), the University of Louvain, Belgium (Ph.D., 1923), the Sorbonne in Paris, and the Pontifical Athenaeum Angelico in Rome (S.T.D., 1924). In 1925, while teaching dogmatic theology at St. Edmund's College in Ware, England, he was awarded an agrégé en philosophie by the University of Louvain.

Sheen seemed destined for an academic career. Concerned that he might have become too "high-hat" in Europe, however, his bishop summoned him back in 1925 for assignment as assistant pastor at St. Patrick's, one of Peoria's poorest parishes. Sheen proved himself a dedicated priest, unaffected by his experiences in Europe, and the following year was sent to teach at the Catholic University in Washington, D.C. After one year on the theology faculty, academic and ecclesiastical infighting, never Sheen's forte, forced his reassignment to the department of philosophy, where he swiftly attained professorial rank and served until 1950.

Starting with the publication in 1925 of his neo-Thomist dissertation, *God and Intelligence in Modern Philosophy* (with an introduction by his friend G. K. Chesterton), Sheen produced, nonstop until his death, more than sixty books (every one dedicated to Mary, mother of Christ) as well as countless articles in journals and magazines. Academic colleagues criticized this brilliant and learned man's decision to settle for derivative scholarship and to become a popularizer and spiritual author. Yet it cannot be denied that, over the decades, millions of readers, including the well-educated and many non-Catholics, found his writings intellectually engaging as well as inspiring.

It was as a preacher and public speaker that Sheen rose to fame and achieved his greatest influence. As a young priest, he was much sought after for his extraordinary speaking abilities. Eventually he received such prestigious invitations as to deliver the Lenten sermons at St. Patrick's Cathedral in New York City, something he did, to packed congregations, for many years. Sheen proved an equally compelling evangelist whether in a pulpit, before a radio microphone, or on a television stage. In 1930 he was chosen by the National Council of Catholic Men to be the regular speaker on a new radio program it was sponsoring. The "Catholic Hour," broadcast on NBC, quickly became an enormous success and made Sheen an international figure. From 1930 to 1952 he drew a worldwide audience of millions to the Sunday evening program. Sheen sometimes received on a single day as many as 10,000 letters from his listeners, one-third of them non-Catholics. In 1940 he conducted the first religious service ever televised, appearing on forty sets on Long Island. Sheen also gave instruction courses on Catholicism for large groups of inquirers and privately introduced into the Catholic faith such prominent individuals as Clare Boothe Luce, Henry Ford II, and Heywood Broun.

As both a writer and a public speaker, Sheen was a relentless, but nonthreatening, apologist for and communicator of Catholic teachings and viewpoints. His favorite target, to the point of obsession, was atheistic Communism; but he always insisted that his anti-Marxism was aimed at the philosophy, not at the people subjected to it. He also railed at Freudian psychoanalysis to the consternation and embarrassment of Catholics in the profession (and also Catholic patients), an error he publicly acknowledged in later years. Utterly orthodox theologically, Sheen was capable of speaking out on controversial social justice and other political issues. For example, from the time of the atomic bombing at Hiroshima, he attacked nuclear war as immoral.

In 1950, Pope Pius XII sent Sheen to New York City as national director of the Society for the Propagation of the Faith, and in 1951 the Pope also appointed him auxiliary to the archbishop of the New York diocese, Francis Cardinal Spellman. With this appointment came his consecration as a bishop. Sheen's fame and popularity helped to make him effective as the chief fund-raiser and spokesperson for Catholic missionaries around the world. John Tracy Ellis, the historian, reported that Sheen told him personally that in 1955 fund-raising had reached "$24,600,000 of which one million was my personal contribution."

Sheen had acquired so much disposable income through royalties and honoraria, and in 1952 he had become one of the early stars of network television. His "Life Is Worth Living" series ran first on the Dumont network (1952–1955) and later on ABC (1955–1957) for half an hour on Tuesdays at 8 P.M. Eventually reaching more than 20 million viewers, he competed successfully against the shows of popular entertainers such as Milton Berle and Frank Sinatra. Thousands of Catholic families would stop everything to turn on their new black-and-white television sets to watch brilliant, handsome Bishop Sheen, their champion, who represented to them all that was best in the Church and in America. Thousands of non-Catholics tuned in as well. From a broadly Christian, not specifically Roman Catholic, perspective, Sheen taught and preached on such topics as freedom, pleasure, war and peace, love, and, of course, Communism. *Time* magazine described his television style in its Apr. 14, 1952, cover story: "Sheen's voice (with a wisp of a brogue) ranges from tremulous whispers to Old Testament rage. His hands finger the chain of his pectoral cross, or spread outward in supplication, or hammer down a point in the air, or thrust skyward." And all who watched the show could expect without fail Sheen's colorful episcopal garb, including beanie, cross, and cape; the office background with library and statue of Mary; the blackboard, used as a teaching aid, with "JMJ" (Jesus, Mary, Joseph) scribbled devotionally on top; the running gag about his "angel," the stagehand who, off camera, would clean the board; and the dramatic "God loves you," always perfectly timed, to conclude the show. Many commented on Sheen's eyes which *Time* characterized as "one of the most remarkable pairs of eyes in America, looking out from deep sockets, pupil and iris almost merged in one luminous disk which creates the optical illusion that he not only looks at people but through them and at everything around them." A second series, "The Bishop Sheen Program" ran from 1961 to 1968 but never enjoyed the same popularity.

In 1966, Pope Paul VI appointed Sheen, then seventy-one years old and inexperienced as a diocesan administrator, bishop of Rochester, N.Y. Sheen, who had participated in Vatican Council II and was generally comfortable with its reforms, struggled valiantly, but too often with a pre–Vatican II administrative style, to lead the diocese according to the new spirit in the Church. After three years of much fighting and frustration, he received permission to resign. Sheen returned to live in New York City where he continued, quietly but by no means entirely out of the public eye, to preach and write to the extent his declining health allowed until his death.

Many who knew Sheen have accused him of vanity; theatrical style and obvious enjoyment in his own success contributed to this impression. Otherwise he is remembered as a good and admirable man of great personal charm whether with the mighty or the lowly. He prayed for an hour every day, led a fairly simple life, and gave most of his money to charity. That he was a source of spiritual awakening and renewal for many people over many years is well-documented. In the pre–Vatican II years of the 1940's and 1950's, no Roman Catholic was better known within or without the Church. Sheen both symbolized and contributed significantly to the movement of Roman Catholics, many of them recent arrivals from the countries of Europe, into mainstream American life.

[The Archbishop Fulton John Sheen Archives are kept at St. Bernard's Institute on the campus of the Colgate-Rochester Divinity School in Rochester, N.Y. Sheen's autobiography is *Treasure in Clay* (1980). His two most popular books were *Peace of Soul* (1949) and *Life of Christ* (1958). See also John Tracy Ellis, *Catholic Bishops: A Memoir* (1984); Kathleen Riley Fields, "Bishop Fulton J. Sheen: An American Catholic Response to the Twentieth Century" (Ph.D. diss., University of Notre Dame, 1988); and Peter W. Williams, "Fulton J. Sheen," in Charles H. Lippy, ed., *Twentieth-Century Shapers of American Popular Religion* (1989). Obituaries are in the *New York Times*, Dec. 10, 1979; and the *National Catholic Reporter*, Dec. 21, 1979.]

JAMES N. LOUGHRAN, S.J.

SHELDON, WILLIAM HERBERT (Nov. 19, 1898–Sept. 16, 1977), psychologist, was born in Warwick, R.I., the son of William Herbert Sheldon and Mary Abby Greene. His father, a naturalist, as well as a judge of hunting dogs and a hunting guide, was a friend of William James, Harvard's famous philosopher who had also become a pioneer in American psychology. James was the child's godfather, although any far-reaching influence is questionable since James died in 1910. Sheldon was close to his father during his childhood and absorbed his father's interest in nature.

During his college years at Brown University he spent his summers as an assistant ornithologist to his father in Rhode Island and Massachusetts. After completing his B.A. degree in 1918 Sheldon served with the United States Army as a second lieutenant during World War I. He went to the Southwest in 1919 as an oil field scout and became a wolf hunter on a sheep ranch in New Mexico the following year. In 1921 he took a high school teaching position in Roswell, N.Mex., while also completing an M.A. thesis in psychology at the University of Colorado in 1923.

At this point Sheldon became an instructor in psychology and sociology at the University of Texas in Austin. A year later he became an instructor at the University of Chicago while completing his Ph.D. in psychology there in 1926. He remained at Chicago another year as an assistant professor before moving to a similar position at the University of Wisconsin. At Madison, Sheldon began interviewing students with the object of classifying them into human types.

In 1930 he returned to the University of Chicago to pursue an M.D., which he finished in 1933. Following completion of his internship in Chicago in 1934, Sheldon spent two years in Europe as a traveling fellow in psychiatry and religion. During this period he also worked with Carl Jung and Ernst Kretschmer. While in England he met Bill Wilson, the founder of Alcoholics Anonymous, and had a philosophical influence in developing the foundations of that organization.

Sheldon returned to Chicago in 1936 as professor of psychology at the Chicago Theological Seminary. However, his real interest lay not in classroom teaching but in research. He had been exploring, for more than a decade, the relation of physical characteristics of men to their temperaments. He was able, in 1938, to move into full-time research at Harvard University.

American involvement in World War II found him back in Europe as a lieutenant colonel in the United States Army Air Forces. After the war ended Sheldon became director of the constitution clinic at the Columbia University College of Physicians and Surgeons in 1946. He relinquished this appointment in 1958 as he had become absorbed in other responsibilities. In 1951 he had assumed two new positions, becoming director of research at the Biological Humanics Foundation in Cambridge, Mass., and clinical professor of medicine and director of the constitution clinic at the University of Oregon Medical School. He joined the Institute of Human Development at the University of California, Berkeley, as a research associate in 1955. In 1961 he added the position of chief of the research facility at the Rockland State Hospital in Orangeburg, N.Y.

Since childhood, Sheldon had a passion for classification. At age twelve he began collecting coins. Almost immediately he created a system of classification that later resulted in two numismatic books: *Early American Cents* (1948) and *Penny Whimsey* (1958). His professional research and work focused on developing a classification system that correlated constitutional types and personality characteristics. The basic classifications he evolved were endomorph, mesomorph, and ectomorph. The endomorph had a bulky body, an extroverted personality, was highly emotional, and apt to weep under stress. The mesomorph was sturdily built with a muscular body, had an extroverted personality, and was prone to express his views by physical action. The ectomorph, tall and thin, was introverted, inhibited, thoughtful, and inclined to seek privacy when under pressure.

In 1940, Sheldon published *The Varieties of Human Physique*, which discussed the three types with the aid of nude photographs showing front, side, and back views of college males with discussion of the characteristics of each person. He later added a numerical classification that permitted numerical treatment of deviation from a basic class. Using a system of rankings for each class, ranging from 1 to 7, he broadened the clarity of class treatment. A person of purely endomorphic class might be placed in the 711 class, the pure mesomorph as 171, and the pure ectomorph as 117. A 354 classification would represent a fairly typical mesomorph.

Sheldon's personal life was one of a search for position. His restless nature was evident in his frequent change of academic affiliation. He enjoyed recognition, but on his own terms. His great ambitions were constantly frustrated by seeming lack of academic support for his far-reaching plans and led to his accepting new projects without abandoning earlier ones. He had difficulty in finding financial support for his studies. His strongest source of financial assistance in the last quarter of his life was Eugene McDermott, the founder of Texas Instruments, who provided research funds after 1948.

Sheldon was married twice, the first time to Louise Steiger, whom he wed in 1925, followed by a divorce three years later. In 1943 he married Milancie Hill. They had two children. His final years were lived in Pawtucket, R.I. He frequently commuted to his Cambridge office at the Biological Humanics Foundation. It was in that office that he died of a heart attack.

[See the short biographies of Sheldon in *International Encyclopedia of the Social Sciences*, vol. 18 (1979), which lists the titles of eleven books published between 1936 and 1974; and Raymond J. Corisini, ed., *Encyclopedia of Psychology*, vol. 3 (1984). An obituary is in the *New York Times*, Sept. 18, 1977.]

AARON J. IHDE

SHOR, BERNARD ("TOOTS") (May 6, 1903–Jan. 23, 1977), saloonkeeper, was born in Philadelphia, Pa., the third child of Abraham Shorr, a German immigrant of Austrian descent, and Fanny Kaufman, who was born in Russia. They lived over their candy store, "a

Jewish family in a Catholic neighborhood." Although some have suggested the nickname "Toots" was a corruption of "Tootsie," Shor denied any knowledge of its derivation. Young Toots learned to play baseball on the sandlots, to shoot pool in church recreation centers, and to fight in the streets. Recalling his detour through a church to escape from a pursuing gang, he explained, "Those bums would have to genuflect when they passed the altar. I didn't have to break stride." He went to South Philadelphia High School, often cutting classes to hustle pool. Although he would have preferred a boxing career, he attended Drexel Institute part-time and the Wharton School at the University of Pennsylvania for a year. He said he never brought it up because "I wouldn't want people to think I was educated."

Shor worked for a cousin's shirt company and for a time represented BVD underwear as a traveling salesman, but he preferred city life. In Atlantic City, N.J., he was hired as a lifeguard despite the fact that he could not swim. He quit as cashier at a cousin's nightclub and was told, "You'll always be a bum." Shor returned to Philadelphia to hustle pool and shoot dice, but confided to a friend, "This town's not big enough for me."

Broke but optimistic, Toots moved to New York City in 1930, living rent-free in the Central Park South apartment of a cousin. Unemployed, he philosophized, "I don't want to be a millionaire; I just want to live like one." Street tough and confident, he worked at a succession of speakeasies as a greeter, bouncer, and occasional bookmaker. In November 1934, Shor married a former showgirl, Marion ("Baby") Volk; they had four children. Columnist Mark Hellinger introduced Toots as the "classiest bum in town" at Billy La Hiff's Tavern, a speakeasy frequented by former mayor Jimmy Walker and newspapermen Ring Lardner, Ed Sullivan, and Walter Winchell. Toots was hired as manager. In 1936 he bought the tavern with borrowed money. That same year he won $50,000 betting on his beloved New York Giants, then lost it all on the World Series. Those were exciting days for Shor. "I was learning how to live," he reminisced. "I learned how important it was to be a spender."

His world was his saloon, a haven for politicians, mobsters, and Ziegfeld showgirls, but in 1939 Shor was forced to sell the tavern to pay a gambling debt. Out of action, he waited for another opportunity. It arrived with a tip from Horace Stoneham, owner of the New York Giants, that the Sixth Avenue el tracks would be razed. Shor borrowed $50,000 to buy a property at nearby 51 West Fifty-first Street, and bandleader Eddy Duchin gave Shor a blank check to establish the restaurant's credit. News of Duchin's check spread like "wild flowers," as Samuel Goldwyn put it; Shor never had to cash the check.

Proud to be called "saloonkeeper," he opened Toots Shor's in 1940. During World War II he patriotically chastised those who complained about the midnight curfew: "Any bum that can't get drunk by midnight ain't tryin'." Shor, who weighed as much as 275 pounds, was "an oversized cherub" to friends, an uncouth loudmouth to critics. In 1943 the Office of Price Administration determined that Toots Shor's had exceeded its red meat quota by more than 100,000 points. For a time, all he could serve from the animal kingdom was chicken and eggs. After the war, the restaurant operation expanded and Toots added sports murals—"hand-painted pictures," he called them.

Toots Shor's "the saloon with a soul," was a showcase for entertainers, athletes, and sportswriters, and a hangout for Shor's friends like Joe DiMaggio and Frank Sinatra. Shor earned, and enjoyed, his reputation for hard drinking and his notoriety for verbally abusing customers. While friends cherished his references to them as "crumb bums" and "creeps," some visiting celebrities, like Charlie Chaplin and Joe Namath, resented his blunt insults. Occasionally Shor fired off a classic, as when a patron, complaining of bad service, threatened to tell all of his friends to stay away: "Tell him," Toots suggested. Shor was extremely sentimental and a serious mourner, organizing the funerals of departed friends and honoring their memories with prodigious drinking bouts. In 1955, Shor sued Sherman Billingsley for more than $1 million after the Stork Club owner said on television, "I wish I had as much money as he owes." They settled for $48,500. Shor was featured on "This Is Your Life," a program that his pal comedian Jackie Gleason called the "worst TV show he ever saw." In 1959, Shor sold the lease of his restaurant for $1.5 million. He reopened the next year at 33 West Fifty-second Street, lost money, and was closed for failure to pay taxes. Before looking for a new location, Shor vacationed in Europe and guessed, "I'm probably the only bum who went to Europe and came back as ignorant as when I left."

The ground breaking in October 1960 for the new Toots Shor's at 5 East Fifty-fourth Street was attended by numerous luminaries, including Chief Justice Earl Warren and former heavyweight champion Jack Dempsey. When the restaurant opened, with a mortgage secured through the intervention of Jimmy Hoffa, it looked like the old place: oak floors, wood paneling, and a circular bar. Again the menu featured roast beef hash, but no dishes that contained garlic or that Shor could not pronounce. Friends and celebrities returned, but not as frequently. Business fell off gradually. The restaurant was bankrupt in 1971. Subsequently, four new Toots Shor's opened, all of them owned by National Restaurant Management. Shor died in New York City.

[See John Bainbridge, "Toots's World," *New Yorker*, Nov. 11, 18, and 25, 1950, reprinted as Bainbridge's *The Wonderful World of Toots Shor* (1951); and Bob Considine, *Toots* (1969). Obituaries are in the *New York Times*, Jan. 25 and 26, 1977.]

ARNOLD MARKOE

SHUMLIN, HERMAN ELLIOTT (Dec. 6, 1898–June 14, 1979), theatrical producer and director, was born to George Shumlin and Rebecca Slavin in Atwood, Colo., where his parents were attempting to raise sheep. That venture failing, they moved successively to Illinois and Indiana before settling in 1906 in Newark, N.J., where Shumlin grew up. Financial need forced Shumlin to quit school at age fifteen; he held jobs at a hardware factory and a railroad yard.

In 1924, after working for a New Jersey office promoting Metro films, he wrote for two show-business papers, the *New York Clipper* (1921–1924) and *Billboard* (1924–1925). A job in 1925 as a press agent for musical librettists Laurence Schwab and Frank Mandel preceded employment as general manager for producer-director Jed Harris. Shumlin turned to producing in 1927; his first four productions were box office flops, with *Celebrity* (1927), *The Command Performance* (1928), *Tonight at 12* (1928), and *Button, Button* (1929) between them running for a total of 118 performances. In 1930 he had his first success with John Wexley's 285-performance anti–capital punishment melodrama about men on death row, *The Last Mile* (1930), which made Spencer Tracy a star. Shumlin followed with one of Broadway's most memorable productions, Vicki Baum's *Grand Hotel* (1930), a 444-performance hit that also marked his directorial debut (he directed most of his later productions). The smooth movement of the large-cast, episodic play's panoramic action, set in various parts of a big hotel, was facilitated by Shumlin's use of a jackknife stage, wheeled platforms that folded into the wings at either side as required. When the production opened, Shumlin owned only a single suit and a pair of shoes, but within a week he splurged $675 on clothes.

Shumlin, who spent 1931 in Hollywood as an assistant producer to Samuel Goldwyn, had two more Broadway successes during the decade. *The Children's Hour* (1934), a first drama by Lillian Hellman (Shumlin's play reader at the time), managed 691 showings. This impressive work, about juvenile mendacity and suspected lesbianism in a girls' school, created a storm of debate and was the first of several Shumlin productions dealing with sensitive issues. Because the play was banned in Boston, Shumlin took on the Massachusetts state legislature and managed to get that body to alter its censorship procedures. Until business policies separated them, Shumlin was closely associated with Hellman, staging five of her plays. Their next blockbuster was her stinging blow at turn-of-the-century southern capitalism, *The Little Foxes* (1939), starring Tallulah Bankhead.

Shumlin's failures during the 1930's included *Clear the Wires!* (1932); *The Bride of Torozko* (1934); *Sweet Mystery of Life* (1935); Hellman's *Days to Come* (1936); and Thornton Wilder's *The Merchant of Yonkers* (1938), directed by Max Reinhardt and later revised as the still-popular *The Matchmaker* (the source of *Hello, Dolly!*). As a free-lance director, he staged *Ten Minute Alibi* (1933) and S. N. Behrman's *Wine of Choice* (1938).

Shumlin followed *The Little Foxes* with a string of theatrical successes in the early 1940's: James Thurber's and Elliot Nugent's seriocomic defense of academic freedom, *The Male Animal* (1940); *The Corn Is Green* (1941), Emlyn Williams's semiautobiographical account of a compassionate schoolteacher and an intellectually gifted boy in a Welsh mining town, which revived Ethel Barrymore's career; and Hellman's drama about invidious fascism, *Watch on the Rhine* (1941). Shumlin also directed the movie version (1943), starring Bette Davis and Paul

Lukas. His only other film was *Confidential Agent* (1945), with Charles Boyer and Lauren Bacall. He worked as a director on two flops handled by other producers: *A Passenger to Bali* (1940), on which he assisted John Huston without credit, and Behrman's *The Talley Method* (1941). After *Watch on the Rhine*, Shumlin only rarely had something to show for his labors, either as a director or producer. Lesser offerings he both produced and staged included *The Great Big Doorstep* (1942); his final Hellman play, *The Searching Wind* (1944); *Only in America* (1959); his only off-Broadway show, *Transfers* (1970); and *Flowers* (1974). Works he directed for others included *Kiss Them for Me* (1945), in which Judy Holliday debuted; *Jeb* (1946); *The Biggest Thief in Town* (1949); *Candida* (1952), his only classic revival, starring Olivia de Havilland; *Regina* (1953), a revival of the opera version of *The Little Foxes*; *Tall Story* (1959); *Little Moon of Alban* (1960); *Dear Me, the Sky Is Falling* (1963); and *Spofford* (1967), notable because it was his only effort as a playwright (he adapted it from a Peter De Vries novel).

Amid this succession of less-acclaimed productions, Shumlin retained the ability to mount important works. His three significant stagings from later in his career were the impressive, long-running (808 performances) Jerome Lawrence and Robert E. Lee play about the Scopes "monkey" trial, *Inherit the Wind* (1955), starring Paul Muni; and two controversial dramas by German playwright Rolf Hochhuth, *The Deputy* (1964) and *Soldiers* (1968). *The Deputy*, which suggested that the pope allowed Roman Jews to die at the hands of the Nazis during World War II, stirred up a storm of protest and was picketed nightly.

Shumlin, who presented a professorial appearance, was a tall, mustached, bespectacled, tastefully dressed, bullet-headed man who took to shaving his head. Although capable of seeming imperious, the intense, chain-smoking producer and director had a warm side as well and, with actors, was considered an understanding, patient, and encouraging figure. A man of many (usually short-lived) enthusiasms, he often supported liberal causes and was even branded a Communist for his social and political views. His outspoken opinions ranged from world politics to theatrical policies, including his frustration at the limited time permitted for rehearsals; his distaste for the hit-and-miss nature of commercial theater (he wanted to run a profit-sharing permanent company); and his anger with the United States Department of Labor and Actors Equity over their restrictions on the importation of nonstar English actors for English roles. Noted for his sponsorship of socially committed drama, he told an interviewer that any play he did had to contain "people who are recognizable as human beings, written by an author who understands human beings. And reflecting the times in which we are living."

A meticulous director with a scholarly bent, Shumlin was concerned not only about the communication of ideas and feelings but with the precise way of visualizing the action, down to whether a phone was lifted with the left or right hand. Still, his direction was typically of the self-effacing sort that allowed the play priority over directorial flourishes. His willingness to go out on a limb for a play whose ideas he favored helped him both make and lose fortunes in theatrical production; at one time he owned a Manhattan townhouse on the Upper East Side hung with modern masterpieces (he favored nudes). Much of his livelihood derived from the film sales of plays he produced. His first two marriages, to actresses Rose Keane and Carmen Englander, ended in divorce. His third wife was producer Diana Green Krasny; Shumlin had no children. He died in New York City.

[Archival materials are located in the Herman Shumlin Collection, State Historical Society of Wisconsin. See also the Herman Shumlin clippings file at the Billy Rose Theatre Collection at the New York Public Library for the Performing Arts. The most complete account of his career is Gary Blake, "Herman Shumlin: The Development of a Director" (Ph.D. diss., City University of New York, 1973); it contains a useful bibliography. Obituaries are in the *New York Times*, June 15, 1979; and *Variety*, June 27, 1979.]

SAMUEL L. LEITER

SHUSTER, GEORGE NAUMAN (Aug. 27, 1894–Jan. 25, 1977), author and college president, was born in Lancaster, Wis., the son of Anthony Shuster, a contractor and bridge builder, and Elizabeth Nauman. He attended Catholic parochial and boarding schools and graduated from the University of Notre Dame in 1915. American entrance into World War I ended his work as a journalist in Chicago. Perhaps because of his German heritage, he was unenthusiastic about the war; but, unwilling not to participate in a defining American experience, he enlisted and served in France as a sergeant in Army Intelligence. Before returning to the United States, he was in the army of occupation in Germany and studied at the University of Poitiers in France; European institutions and culture would fascinate him for the rest of his life.

From 1920 to 1924, Shuster was chairman of the Department of English at Notre Dame. His first book, *The Catholic Spirit in Modern English Literature* (1922), was aimed at the public rather than the scholar. Nevertheless, he passionately believed that Notre Dame had an obligation to produce scholars and scholarship, and he was disappointed at the unwillingness of a new group of college administrators to commit themselves to that goal. He resigned in 1924 and, the next year, published an angry article, "Have We Any Scholars?" (*America*, Aug. 15, 1925), in which he concluded that in Catholic colleges there were too many students and too few teachers for scholarship to flourish. And he observed, in passing, that lay teachers were treated as "necessary evils or cheap benefits." For many years thereafter Shuster did not feel welcome at Notre Dame. On June 25, 1924, he married Doris Parks Cunningham; they had one child.

For the next thirty-five years Shuster lived in the New York area. He taught English at St. Joseph's College for Women (1925–1935). In 1925 he became an editor of *Commonweal*, a journal founded the year before by a group of laymen to review, from a Catholic perspective, literature, the arts, and public affairs. Shuster's early contributions were epitomized in *The Catholic Spirit in America* (1927), in which he attempted to show that the "Catholic intellect" is different from the "American intellect," and argued that the republic would benefit from more extended commerce between the two. He was particularly indignant at the anti-Catholicism engendered by Al Smith's presidential campaign in 1928.

Shuster admired German culture and sympathized with Germany's economic problems after World War I. In *The Germans* (1932), he glibly dismissed the "ideas" of Adolf Hitler as "no more commendable for wisdom or practicableness than are the notions of the average United States Senator." But in his *Strong Man Rules* (1934), he apologized for his lack of prescience; thereafter he eloquently denounced the Nazis' assaults on individual and religious freedom. In 1936, *Commonweal* urged that America boycott the Olympic Games in Berlin; for this, Shuster was criticized by some American bishops.

Shuster was forced to resign from *Commonweal* in 1937. Most American Catholics wholeheartedly supported General Francisco Franco's rebellion in Spain. Shuster, in an article titled "Some Reflections on Spain" (Apr. 2, 1937), found it "shocking" that "Catholics are ready to ignore the manifest brutality, reactionary political method and intellectual simplicity of the Francoites." The ensuing uproar convinced Shuster, he later reported, "that for Catholic New York the world outside the United States was either Communist or Fascist, and that therefore they had opted for Fascism." Unable to persuade his colleagues that fascism was as inimical to Catholicism as Communism, Shuster felt obliged to resign.

He returned to the graduate work in English that he had begun at Columbia in 1924. In 1940 he published his dissertation, *The English Ode from Milton to Keats*, which late in life he declared the most enduring of his many books, because the most scholarly. But instead of becoming a professor, in 1939 he became acting president (in 1940 president) of Hunter College in New York City, at that time the largest public women's college in the world. He served with distinction for twenty years.

Very early in his tenure he became convinced that "you ought not to educate a woman as if she were a man, or to educate her as if she were not"—a paradox he sought to resolve by urging that Hunter's traditional liberal arts curriculum be complemented with a "vocational inlay" of domestic science and office skills. More important, perhaps, by his ready availability to students and his enthusiastic participation in student activities, he helped convey his confidence in them as young adults and as women. He encouraged and went out of his way to reward distinguished faculty scholarship. And, though he was obliged to battle both Communist party members on the faculty and McCarthyites in the community, in 1952 he publicly commended junior faculty members who, as advisers to student clubs, shared in student enthusiasms and risked sharing in student mistakes.

Shuster was especially delighted to claim that Hunter, partly because of its location on Park

Avenue, had become "the greatest community center to be found anywhere in the world." He strengthened its adult education program. He believed that its concert series and its many visiting lecturers, including friends like Heinrich Brüning, Jacques Maritain, Georges Bidault, Stefan Zweig, and Sigrid Undset, could effectively educate the whole city.

During his presidency Shuster found time for many civic duties. He served on the Enemy Alien Board during World War II. He attended the conferences that established UNESCO, and served as the American representative on UNESCO's executive board until 1962. For eighteen months in the years 1950–1951, he was deputy for Bavaria to the high commissioner for Germany, responsible for promoting American policies in politics, economics, education, and law. From 1954 to 1964 he was a director of the Carnegie Endowment for International Peace. He also wrote *Religion Behind the Iron Curtain* (1954) and *In Silence I Speak*, a biography of József Cardinal Mindszenty (1956).

Shuster retired from Hunter in 1960 and the following year returned to Notre Dame, where he founded the Center for the Study of Man in Contemporary Society. The center sponsored a series of conferences titled "Family and Fertility," in the hope of developing in the church respect for the "complexity" of the role of sexuality in human life. Naturally, Shuster was disappointed with the blunt proscriptions of the papal encyclical *Humanae vitae* (1968).

Shuster's center also sponsored a study of Catholic elementary and secondary schools, which concluded with the recommendation that Catholics concentrate their limited resources on the secondary schools. It also recommended that more laymen be given leadership positions in the parochial schools.

Shuster resigned as director of the center in 1969. He had been a trustee of Notre Dame since 1967; he resigned in 1971. He died in South Bend, Ind.

[The largest collection of Shuster's papers is in the archives of the University of Notre Dame; there are also papers in the archives of Hunter College, City University of New York. Thomas E. Blantz, *George N. Shuster: On the Side of Truth* (1993), is a full-length biography. Shuster's brief "Autobiography" and "Spiritual Autobiography" are reprinted in *On the Side of Truth*, edited by Vincent P. Lannie (1974). On Shuster's years as a journalist, see Rodger Van Allen, *The Commonweal and American Catholicism* (1974). Shuster's *The Ground I Walked On* (1961) is an instructive interpretation of those aspects of his Hunter College presidency that he found most memorable. An obituary is in the *New York Times*, Jan. 27, 1977.]

ROBERT D. CROSS

SILVERHEELS, JAY (May 26, 1919–March 5, 1980), actor, was born Harold Jay ("Harry") Smith on the Six Nations Indian Reserve near Brantford, Ontario, Canada. A Mohawk Indian, he was the son of Captain A. G. E. Smith, the most decorated Canadian Indian soldier during World War I; little is known about his mother. Along with his nine brothers and sisters, he was raised on his family's farm on the reserve.

Silverheels left the Brantford Collegiate Institute at the age of seventeen to play professional lacrosse in Toronto. Because of his athleticism, he became one of the greatest professional lacrosse players in Canada by the mid-1930's. Since he always ran on the balls of his feet with his heels up and had blinding speed, he became known to family members, to Mohawk Indians, and to lacrosse devotees as "Silverheels," the stage name he used throughout his acting career. Nine years before his death, he legally changed his surname to Silverheels. Besides his legendary skills in lacrosse, he was a semiprofessional hockey player; a football, track, and wrestling star; and winner of the Eastern States Middleweight Golden Gloves Boxing Championship in the United States in 1937. He was also an established horseman, a skill that later proved beneficial in his acting career.

In 1938, Silverheels was "discovered" by the comedian Joe E. Brown during a lacrosse match. Brown served as his mentor, promoting Silverheels's slow rise to fame by introducing him to the Hollywood film industry. Silverheels became a member of the Screen Actors Guild and, soon after, found himself working as an extra, making $16.50 per day falling off horses in battle scenes in Hollywood Westerns. For nearly ten years, he struggled to make a living as an extra in B Westerns and in memorable motion pictures such as *Drums Along the Mohawk* (1939).

Silverheels's first major screen role was as an Aztec prince in *Captain from Castile* in 1947. The following year, he had a bit part in the film classic *Key Largo* (1948). In all, Silverheels performed in 32 Westerns and all 221 television episodes of "The Lone Ranger." Besides *Captain from Castile*, his major film credits included playing Geronimo in *Broken Arrow* (1950); costarring in *The Lone Ranger* (1956) and *The Lone Ranger and the Lost City of Gold* (1958); and appearing in *Brave Warrior* (1952), *Saskatchewan* (1954), *True Grit* (1970), and *The Man Who Loved Cat Dancing* (1973). He also appeared in numerous television episodes, including "Cade County" and "Love American Style," as well as in television commercials.

Although he was by no means the first Native American to succeed in Hollywood, Silverheels was the leading actor playing Native American roles from 1940 to 1970. Much of his fame as an actor stemmed from his role as Tonto in the "Lone Ranger" television series, which he re-created in two full-length motion pictures. As a result of his earlier film credits and his horsemanship skills, Silverheels was selected to costar as Tonto opposite John Hart and, later, Clayton Moore. This highly successful ABC network program, a television version of the famous radio program created by Fran Striker in 1933, ran from 1949 to 1957 and has been widely syndicated in reruns around the world since its final episode.

Unlike the forceful, articulate Lone Ranger, Tonto had no mask, no silver bullets, rode a pinto horse named Scout, and spoke in butchered English. As the friendly and loyal Indian companion of "Kemo-sabe," Tonto was presented as a decent man of innate wisdom who could track down "bad hombres" with the best of them. Despite being criticized by many politically active Indians for playing this clearly subservient role, Silverheels's character was the first major Indian film hero and paved the way for other Native American actors, such as Chief Dan George, Graham Greene, and Will Sampson. Until Silverheels, Indian actors—with the exception of Will Rogers, who played cowboys—had largely been relegated to the roles of foils or villains in Western epics.

In 1960, Silverheels protested the way Native Americans were portrayed in films, sending letters to President Dwight Eisenhower, Vice-President Richard Nixon, and the executives of the three major television networks. He also assisted aspiring actors and in 1963 founded the Indian Actors Workshop in Hollywood, working later with Jonathan Winters and Buffy Sainte-Marie in this endeavor. As a result of his reputation in the film industry, Silverheels became the first Native American to have his star set in Hollywood's Walk of Fame along Hollywood Boulevard.

In 1974, Silverheels obtained a license to work as a harness racing driver and raced competitively with his horse Tribal Dance. His racing days ended when he suffered a stroke that left him paralyzed. After being treated for a heart condition, he died in the Motion Picture and Television Country House at Woodland Hills, Calif. He was survived by his wife, Mary Di Roma, and their four children.

[Biographical materials on Silverheels's life are found at the library of the Woodland Cultural Centre, Six Nations Indian Reserve, Brantford, Ontario. On Native Americans in Hollywood, see Gretchen M. Bataille and Charles L. P. Silet, eds., *The Pretend Indians* (1980). An obituary is in the *New York Times*, Mar. 6, 1980.]

LAURENCE M. HAUPTMAN

SKAGGS, MARION BARTON (Apr. 5, 1888–May 8, 1976), grocer, was born in Aurora, Mo., the son of Samuel M. Skaggs, a Baptist minister and grocer, and Nance E. Long. Samuel moved his large family, numbering twelve children, to nearby Kato, Mo., when Marion, the fourth child, was very young. At Kato, in the Ozarks region of southwestern Missouri, Samuel opened a grocery store. In a 1926 interview in *American Magazine*, Marion explained that he "got his first smell of groceries" in that store, and "loved it." After a short stay in Kato, the elder Skaggs was ordained as a Baptist minister, and then relocated his family to Newtonia, Mo., where he took up his first position as a Baptist minister for an annual salary of $600. The Skaggs family supplemented this ministerial salary with subsistence farming on twenty acres. Marion helped on the farm, and he also trapped and sold rabbits. Looking back at his childhood, Marion claimed that his single-mindedness contributed to his later success as a grocer: "But whether I studied, or hoed, or trapped, I thought of groceries. Father wanted me to be a minister, but I had other plans."

Skaggs gained his first practical grocery experience at age fourteen, when he spent his summer vacation working in a store at Granby, Mo., about five miles from Newtonia. Here Skaggs learned about the precarious financial plight small grocers faced when they extended credit to their customers. "Right there, I decided that my store, if I ever got one, would do a cash business only." Marion ended his formal education with graduation from high school and entered into his first business venture at the age of nineteen, when he became partners with Oscar Skaggs, his eldest brother, in a restaurant, confectionery, and meat market in Diamond, Mo. On Oct. 28, 1907, Marion married Estella Iona Roselle; they had at least three children. About this time, Samuel moved his family to Anadarko, Okla., where he took another position as a Baptist minister. Marion and Oscar Skaggs sold their business in Diamond to join the family in Oklahoma, where they became partners with their father in another grocery store. Later, Marion recollected his six years in Oklahoma as the only stagnant period in his career: "I'm sorry to say, not a single important, progressive idea about selling groceries or increasing trade percolated through my mind. I was in a rut."

When Samuel Skaggs's health began to decline, he moved his family to the high desert country around American Falls, Idaho, where he took up a homestead and founded another grocery store. Marion soon sold his business in Oklahoma, moved to Idaho, and himself became a homesteader. To make ends meet, he started a well-drilling business with a brother-in-law. Marion's singlemindedness still prevailed: "My only object in drilling wells was to get enough money ahead to buy a grocery store. As I worked, I could look out across the sagebrush and the dust and desolation, and see my model store." On Aug. 15, 1915, Marion bought his father's tiny (eighteen by thirty-two feet) grocery store for $1,088.

By 1926, Marion Skaggs owned 428 stores in ten western states. The Skaggs credo was: "He who serves best, profits most." The key to Marion's success was building volume sales by taking only a small profit. In 1926 he got together with the New York investment house Merrill Lynch to broker a merger with Safeway, a southern California grocery chain with 322 stores. Originally known as Sam Seelig stores, the chain had adopted the "Safeway" name in 1925. By 1927, the revitalized Safeway chain run by Skaggs operated 915 stores, which earned $1.9 million in profits on sales of $69 million. In 1931, Safeway Stores, Inc., owned 3,527 stores, the largest number of stores in its history. Though the number of stores in the chain declined steadily during the depression era—a situation common to chain grocery stores of this period—both store size and chainwide sales increased. In 1937, Safeway Stores had sales of over $380 million and profits of more than $3 million. Among American grocery store chains, only the Great Atlantic and Pacific Tea Company (A&P) had greater sales and profits.

Skaggs led an intensely private life following an interview he gave to *American Magazine* in 1926. The interview resulted in a flood of 8,000 letters, one of which threatened to murder Skaggs and his family and bomb Safeway Stores unless a ransom of $10 thousand was paid. The extortionists were apprehended, and no harm came to Skaggs and his family, but thereafter he kept his personal life out of the public eye. While Skaggs encouraged his executives to join civic organizations, he did not join these organizations himself, and he avoided public speaking and public appearances. On June 6, 1941, Skaggs resigned as the chairman of Safeway Stores, Inc., in order to give his full time to personal and philanthropic affairs. Skaggs donated more than $300,000 to construct the Skaggs Community Hospital in Branson, Mo., a twenty-five-bed facility that was dedicated on Jan. 8, 1950. In addition, Skaggs owned a game preserve in the Ozarks. Wild deer, elk, and buffalo roamed within twenty-nine miles of fence. He worked with the Missouri Conservation Commission to release into the wild 100 deer annually. Skaggs spent his retirement in Piedmont, an exclusive community in the San Francisco Bay area.

As one of the pioneers of retail grocery chains, Skaggs dramatically changed the ritual of grocery shopping. The volume buying and large grocery outlets pioneered by Skaggs gave American consumers cheaper prices and more convenient shopping.

[Skaggs's desire for privacy undoubtedly led him to leave no known manuscripts and few public accounts of his life. Two articles in popular magazines provide some insight, though few hard facts: Magner White, "This 'Sagebrush Hick from Idaho' Heads 357 Big Stores," *American Magazine*, Aug. 1926; and an untitled piece in *Newsweek*, Aug. 24, 1935. For a brief description of Skaggs's role in the history of Safeway Stores, Inc., see Safeway Stores, Inc., *Our Fiftieth Year* (1975); and *Everybody's Business: An Almanac* (1980). Obituaries are in the *San Francisco*

Chronicle, May 9, 1976; and the *New York Times*, May 10, 1976.]

PAUL A. FRISCH

SKINNER, CORNELIA OTIS (May 30, 1901–July 9, 1979), actress, playwright, and author, was born in Chicago, the daughter of Otis Skinner and Maud Durbin, actors who were on tour at the time. Otis Skinner had learned his craft in supporting roles to the leading Shakespearean actor, Edwin Booth. His wife retired from the stage when their daughter was born. The Skinners maintained a home in Bryn Mawr, Pa., where Skinner was brought up.

Skinner grew tall and lanky in her adolescence, features she was to convert to a dignified, commanding presence onstage and off. She spent two years as a student at Bryn Mawr College but found she could not grasp anything as abstract or as rote-taught as mathematics. In the company of her mother, a woman of considerable cultivation, Skinner continued her education in Paris at the Sorbonne, where she gained a deep appreciation of European civilization, especially Parisian, and received classical training in theater from Jacques Copeau and Emile Debelly, the latter of the Comédie Française. Upon returning to America, Skinner made the rounds of casting calls; the prominent producer Winthrop Ames gave her several small roles. She made her Broadway debut in Clemence Dane's *Will Shakespeare* at the National Theater in January 1923, having first appeared professionally in a small role in *Blood and Sand* with her father's company (1921). For him she wrote an adaptation of a novel, *Captain Fury*, which opened in 1925. Roles came regularly thereafter, and Skinner appeared in the light, forgettable comedies and dramas that filled the large number of theaters on Broadway. Among the plays were *Tweedles, In the Next Room, The Wild Westcotts, In His Arms*, and *White Collars*.

Skinner married Alden S. Blodgett, a wealthy banker and sportsman, on Oct. 2, 1928; they had one child. Combining the careers of wife, mother, and professional actress, Skinner was soon as busy as ever, with increasing emphasis on writing. She thought in terms of a produced play or monologue as she wrote, because for her, speech, movement, and ideas were inseparable. As a monologist, she took the parts of several characters, a technique that English audiences accepted readily. She had appeared there in a well-received monologue version of *The Wives of Henry VIII*; other multicharacter productions were *The Empress Eugenie* and *The Loves of Charles II*.

In 1938, Skinner brought the dramatization of Margaret Ayer Barnes's novel *Edna, His Wife*, which treated three women, to New York City. Taking all of the roles, she sharply etched the position of women in American society and its slow evolution. She toured widely in *Edna*, which was enthusiastically received by the public, although the New York critics were more restrained in their reviews. American audiences preferred her in fully produced and cast plays, and she was highly successful in the title role of George Bernard Shaw's *Candida* (1935) and as Lady Britomart in Shaw's *Major Barbara* (1946), as well as Mrs. Erlynne in Oscar Wilde's *Lady Windermere's Fan* (1946). In 1944 she played Emily Hazen, wife of an American diplomat, in Lillian Hellman's *The Searching Wind*, which had a long run at the Fulton Theater and an extensive national tour.

The 1930's marked the heyday of a new medium, network radio, which could make good use of the monologue technique. Skinner was heard frequently on the networks, and her name and style became known even in remote places, like the small Arkansas town where a fifteen-year-old boy never forgot her portrayal of a middle-aged midwestern wife who, as she is being poled down Venice's Grand Canal in a gondola with her husband, comments on the vastly different world they are briefly glimpsing. Skinner was a frequent guest on the sophisticated yet extremely popular radio show "Information Please" in the late 1930's and early 1940's, matching wits with such diverse characters as the saturnine columnist Franklin P. Adams and the Russian-born actor-director Gregory Ratoff. Her scripts for the prime-time radio serial "William and Mary" raised the show above the average for the genre.

During the years when her son was growing up, Skinner was a dutiful, loving mother and wife. The family lived in a mansion on Long Island's fashionable North Shore, where she wrote many pieces in the easy, conversational style that was her trademark. Among her subjects were her experiences as a neophyte wife and mother of one son and stepmother to two more. Many of her sketches appeared in the *New Yorker, Harper's Bazaar, Ladies' Home Journal*, and other magazines. Her greatest success was a best-selling book, written with a close friend, Emily Kimbrough, about an unescorted trip to Paris the two young girls took in the 1920's. Published in 1942 as *Our Hearts Were Young and Gay*, the book charmed millions with such anecdotes as the night they spent locked out on one of the towers of the Cathedral of Notre Dame, and another in a brothel, which they had mistaken for a tourist hotel. Condensed in *Reader's Digest*, made into a motion picture in 1944, and dramatized by Jean Kerr in 1948, the story reached millions more.

Skinner obviously enjoyed putting her thoughts and experiences down on paper, but she never thought of giving up the stage. "Acting," she said, "is less painful than writing—and faster." Her one foray into scholarship was *Madame Sarah* (1967), a biography of Sarah Bernhardt. It was praised by most critics for its verve rather than its scholarship, but the influential French writer André Maurois, praised the book highly. In a more relaxed vein, Skinner wrote the story of one of the most successful collaborations in the theater, that of two close friends, *Life with Lindsay and Crouse* (1976). Over the years her essays were collected in three volumes, *Tiny Garments* (1932), *That's Me All Over* (1948), and *Bottoms Up* (1955). Her reminiscences of the Skinner and Blodgett families are in *Family Circle* (1948), which, while in no sense an autobiography or even a memoir, contains much about the lives of her and her relatives.

During the early postwar years the theater saw relatively little of Skinner. Long the enemy of ethnic discrimination, especially anti-Semitism, she became active in the National Conference of Christians and Jews. In 1951 she was elected its secretary and in 1960 was national chairman of the observance of Brotherhood Week, for which she received a silver plaque in 1961.

There was at least one theatrical project, however, that had been close to Skinner's heart for a long time: a monodrama in which she would portray a number of characters reflecting the types upon which Parisian life rested at the turn of the century. In 1951 she undertook a research trip to Paris, where she accumulated facts of Parisian life in the 1890's and read many memoirs, scandalous and otherwise, of this era. The result was a monodrama that is widely considered her greatest success in that form, a revue called *Paris '90*. Opening on Broadway in the spring of 1952, it was praised by a majority of critics. Walter Kerr, of the *New York Herald Tribune*, was especially enthusiastic.

In *Paris '90* Skinner portrayed fourteen characters, and audiences for years after delighted in relating the dialogue of their favorites to friends. One member of Skinner's audience recalled two with particular admiration: the younger of a pair of spinster Boston schoolteachers in Paris for the summer, and the mistress of an aged cabinet minister as she rides in her own carriage in his funeral cortege. In the first, the younger spinster, looking forward eagerly to a day in the Bois de Boulogne, exclaims to her rather dour companion, "Why, the grass must be simply spahkling," and, yes, she has remembered to place the book of irregular verbs in their picnic basket. At the other end of the social scale, the worldly-wise courtesan, smiling sweetly at the wife who rides by, ignoring her, muses, "So, he has finally died. And in his *own* bed. And when I think of the times I was sure he was going to die in *mine*!" Both characters, true to life as they were, were yet pure Skinner. Ten years later Skinner published much of the results of her researches into fin-de-siècle Paris in *Elegant Wits and Grand Horizontals* (1962).

One last Broadway triumph remained for Skinner after *Paris '90*, and it was a notable one, a fully produced play entitled *The Pleasure of His Company*, which she wrote with Samuel Albert Taylor. She shared the leading roles with Cyril Ritchard and Dolores Hart, and the dialogue sparkled with repartee. The play opened at the Longacre Theatre in 1958 and toured nationally in 1960. The dean of New York critics, Brooks Atkinson of the *New York Times*, was delighted with the show, applauding every element of good acting: "taste, distinction . . . wit," combined with voice, eyes, and movement.

The rest of Skinner's life was devoted largely to writing. After her husband died in 1964, she left the mansion on Long Island, where they had lived for nearly forty years, for an equally baronial apartment in New York City. Tall, dark, and stately, well-spoken yet informal, Skinner was the ideal club woman, but her social life consisted of much more than tea at the Colony or the Cosmopolitan (she was a member of both). Theatrical people, especially playwrights, producers, and directors, were among her closest friends. She died in New York City of a cerebral hemorrhage.

[There are no accessible papers bearing on Cornelia Otis Skinner. There is no biography. An obituary is in the *New York Times*, July 15, 1979.]

ALBRO MARTIN

SLATER, JOHN CLARKE (Dec. 22, 1900–July 25, 1976), physicist, was born in Oak Park, Ill., the son of John Rothwell Slater, a professor, and Katharine Southland Chapin. When Slater was four years old, the family moved to Rochester, N.Y., where his Harvard-educated father became head of the English department at the University of Rochester. Slater attended public school, excelling in math and science, and from an early age exhibiting a fascination with mechanical and electrical devices. Through his father's personal library, he was exposed to such classics of scientific literature as Albert A. Michelson's *Light Waves and Their Uses*.

Slater entered the University of Rochester in 1917 with a major in science. His research in atomic and molecular physics began in his senior year while a laboratory assistant; he conducted research for a special honors thesis on the effect of change of pressure on the intensities of the Balmer spectral lines of hydrogen, for which he used Niels Bohr's 1913 paper on atomic structure. Slater completed his undergraduate work in three years and received a B.A. from Rochester in 1920.

In the fall of that year, Slater entered Harvard graduate school on an assistantship under Percy W. Bridgman. For three years, during which Slater pursued his M.A. and then his Ph.D., he collected laboratory data for Bridgman, who was pioneering the study of phenomena at high pressure. Bridgman supervised Slater's doctoral dissertation on the compressibility of alkali halide crystals and influenced his philosophical orientation, instilling in him the virtues of scientific pragmatism. Slater's focus was thereafter on the development of theories that explain observable phenomena, specifically the development of quantum theory and its application to molecular and solid-state problems.

While completing his dissertation, Slater was intrigued by laboratory results that could not be explained by current scientific thinking. "I was convinced," he later wrote, "that the quantum theory of 1923 was not adequate to describe the nature of molecules and solids, and resolved to do my best to help in the development of more adequate theories."

Awarded a Ph.D. in physics in 1923, Slater spent the following year traveling in Europe, then the center of advances in theoretical physics, on a Sheldon Fellowship from Harvard. "Seldom in the history of science has there been a more exciting decade than that from 1923 to 1932," he later wrote, referring to the scientific breakthroughs in quantum theory and wave mechanics that signaled a final break with classical physics. Slater conducted research on the emission and absorption of energy in atoms at the Cavendish Laboratory in Cambridge, and then in Copenhagen, where he met many of the physicists at the forefront of the quantum revolution, including Niels Bohr, Werner Heisenberg, and Wolfgang Pauli. In 1924, Slater collaborated with Bohr and Hans Kramers on a paper titled "The Quantum Theory of Radiation," which followed from Slater's idea that a radiation field guided the light quanta, and that a set of "virtual oscillators," whose frequencies were determined by the Bohr frequency condition instead of those of classical orbital motions, were associated with the atom. This idea was described by a colleague as "a sort of forerunner of the duality principle," or particle-wave theory of light, and served as a foundation for Heisenberg's matrix mechanics. It propelled Slater to international recognition in the scientific community.

Returning to the United States in June 1924, Slater became an instructor of physics at Harvard. He advanced to associate professor in 1929, a position he retained until 1930. In 1926, Slater married Helen Frankenfeld; they had three children and were divorced in 1952.

Slater's first paper using quantum mechanics, "Radiation and Absorption on Schroedinger's Theory" (1927), focused on the binding energy of helium. In 1929 he published what is regarded as his most important paper, "The Theory of Complex Spectra," in which he introduced determinantal wave functions for a system of many electrons, now referred to as the Slater determinants. In June 1929 he traveled to Europe on a Guggenheim Fellowship, spending much of his time in Leipzig. He applied his determinantal method to the study of solids while focusing on cohesion in metals and on ferromagnetism.

When he returned to Harvard in February 1930, Slater was asked by Karl Compton, president of the Massachusetts Institute of Technology, to join MIT as head of the physics department. Slater accepted, and remained at MIT through 1951, presiding over a veritable shift in the center of quantum physics and wave mechanics, and the emerging technologies thereof, from Europe to the United States. Slater overhauled the physics curriculum at MIT and introduced the textbooks that brought him additional renown, including *Introduction to Theoretical Physics* (with N. H. Frank, 1933), *Microwave Transmission* (1942), and *Quantum Theory of Molecules and Solids* (4 vols., 1963–1974). His *Modern Physics*, published in 1955, is still considered an excellent introduction to quantum theory at the undergraduate level. Elected to the National Academy of Sciences at the age of thirty, Slater influenced scores of physicists at MIT and thus helped bring the United States into an age of unprecedented industrial and technological growth following World War II. In 1951, Slater became institute professor at MIT, a position he held until 1966, when he retired.

Throughout the 1930's and into the 1940's, Slater shifted his focus from atomic structure to the structure of molecules and solids. He worked on energy bands in metals, the structure of alloys and insulating crystals, and superconductivity. His attempt to find better methods of calculating the binding energy of molecules led to his invention in 1937 of the "augmented-plane-wave method," application of which gradually increased with the introduction of high-capacity digital computers in the 1950's.

During World War II, Slater worked, both in the MIT radiation lab (1940–1945) and on the technical staff of Bell Telephone Labs (1941–1945), on the development of microwave radar, developing a theory of magnetrons that made possible advances in magnetron design. In 1945 he concentrated on converting MIT's wartime laboratory into a research facility having broad civilian implications, specifically in the areas of electronics and nuclear science. He spent the 1951–1952 academic year at the Brookhaven National Laboratory on Long Island, N.Y., studying the phenomenon of neutron diffraction with the aim of applying that to the magnetic properties of solids. In 1954 he married Rose Mooney, a fellow physicist.

Anticipating his mandatory retirement from MIT in 1966, Slater in 1964 accepted the position of research professor of physics and chemistry at the University of Florida in Gainesville. Though he regretted leaving MIT, he noted that by the 1960's the physics department there "had been literally captured by the nuclear theorists." In Gainesville he joined the Quantum Theory Project founded by physicist Per-Olov Löwdin. He retired from this position in June 1976, one month before his death of a heart attack at his home on Sanibel Island, Fla.

Slater received the Irving Langmuir Prize of the American Physical Society in 1967. In 1971, President Richard M. Nixon awarded him the Medal of Science for "wide-ranging contributions to the basic theory of atoms, molecules, and matter in the solid form." As a participant in the quantum revolution in physics, Slater conducted research that helped open the door to postwar technologies such as solid-state electronics, microwave and satellite communications, computers, and the laser.

[Slater's papers are in the American Philosophical Society Library, Philadelphia. A taped interview and its transcript are at the American Institute of Physics, Center for History of Physics, in New York City; also there are taped interviews with Thomas Kuhn, John Van Vleck, and Charles Wiener that include material on Slater. Selected correspondence is in the Edwin M. Hall collection at Houghton Library, Harvard University. Slater's scientific autobiography is *Solid-State and Molecular Theory* (1975). A profile is Philip M. Morse, in *Biographical Memoirs. National Academy of Sciences* 53 (1982). See also *Wave Mechanics*, edited by William C. Price, Seymour S. Chissick, and Tom Ravensdale (1973). Obituaries are in the *New York Times*, July 27, 1976; and *Physics Today*, Oct. 1976.]

MELISSA A. DOBSON

SLICHTER, LOUIS BYRNE (May 19, 1896–Mar. 25, 1978), geophysicist, was born in Madison, Wis., the son of Mary Louise Byrne, an elementary school teacher, and Charles Sumner Slichter, a professor of applied mathematics at the University of Wisconsin. Slichter had three brothers, who all attained prominence: Sumner Huber became professor of economics at Harvard University; Donald Charles became president of the Northwestern Mutual Life Insurance Company; and Allen McKinnon founded the Pelton Steel Casting Corporation.

Slichter attended local schools and graduated from the University of Wisconsin with a B.A. in mechanical engineering in 1917. He then worked briefly for the General Electric Corporation in Schenectady, N.Y., on steam turbines. Later in 1917 he enlisted in the United

States Naval Reserve as an ensign. His first assignment was to a research team in the National Research Committee's submarine committee, headed by Max Mason. Mason had been trained in mathematics by Slichter's father and joined the University of Wisconsin graduate school faculty. Slichter worked with Mason on submarine detection devices at the Navy Experimental Laboratory in New London, Conn., then transferred to the Royal Navy's Subchaser Base at Plymouth, England, in 1918. He was discharged in 1919.

After the war ended, Slichter resumed his studies at the University of Wisconsin and obtained a Ph.D. in physics in 1922. From 1922 to 1924 he was employed by the Submarine Signal Corporation, a Boston firm specializing in detection of undersea mineral deposits.

In 1924 he joined with Mason again to create a consulting firm, Mason, Slichter and Hay, in Madison, Wis., which provided geophysical prospecting advice to mining companies. On Oct. 20, 1926, Slichter married Martha Merry Buell; the couple had two children.

Mason was largely occupied with the presidency of the University of Chicago during the years 1925–1928, so most of the practical work was left to Slichter and Hay. In 1927 the latter left, so the firm was reorganized as Mason, Slichter and Gauld, with Brownlee B. Gauld. That same year Slichter published his first paper, "Geophysical Prospecting Methods," a chapter in Robert Peele's *Mining Engineering Handbook*. Meanwhile, Mason had joined the staff of the Rockefeller Foundation; he became its president in 1929. As business conditions worsened after the onset of the Great Depression, the partners decided to dissolve the firm in 1930, and Slichter returned to the academic community.

Slichter taught briefly at the California Institute of Technology (1930–1931). He then went to the Massachusetts Institute of Technology (MIT) to organize its geophysics program. He was an associate professor of geophysics in 1931, then a full professor (1932–1945). During this time Slichter did research involving the detection of subsurface structures, building upon his commercial experience. In 1932 he published a groundbreaking paper with mathematician Rudolph E. Langer, titled "The Theory of the Interpretation of Seismic Travel-Time Curves in Horizontal Structures." He also did experimental work with his graduate students, including analysis of data, employing electrical currents generated by underground telephone circuits borrowed from the local telephone company during the early morning hours, to measure the electrical conductivity of the earth's crust. Using portable seismographs that he had helped design and construct, Slichter performed experiments based on explosions at local quarries. He also published a seminal paper on radioactivity and slow-speed heat conduction through the earth's mantle, "Cooling of the Earth," in *Bulletin of the Geological Society of America* (1941).

After the outbreak of World War II, Slichter joined the antisubmarine committee created by the National Academy of Sciences, at the request of the Department of the Navy, to evaluate antisubmarine techniques. The committee's recommendations for more basic and applied research led to the creation of a section of the National Defense Research Committee dealing with antisubmarine research; Slichter traveled on its behalf to England in 1941 to ascertain the status of British antisubmarine research and warfare. After the creation of the Office of Scientific Research and Development (OSRD), Slichter joined the OSRD Division 6, concerning antisubmarine warfare, in 1942. He worked on electromagnetic submarine detection devices and was later involved in torpedo design. He was awarded a Presidential Certificate of Merit in 1948.

Slichter taught briefly at the University of Wisconsin (1946–1947), then went to the University of California at Los Angeles (UCLA) to organize its Institute of Geophysics, the first such institute in the nation devoted to research. While at UCLA, Slichter became interested in earth tides and began publishing a series of papers on the subject. He still retained an interest in the practical side of his subject, and published "The Need of a New Philosophy of Prospecting" as the 1960 Jackling Lecture, when he received the Daniel C. Jackling Award from the American Institute of Mining and Metallurgical Engineers.

In 1961, in response to a growing space program, the name of the institute at UCLA was changed to Institute of Geophysics and Planetary Physics. Slichter resigned as its head in 1962 and became an emeritus professor in 1963. His retirement was followed by the publication of a festschrift, *Papers in Geophysics in Honor of Louis Byrne Slichter* (1963).

After his retirement Slichter retained an office at the university and continued his research, primarily in the UCLA gravity program, and in projects measuring earth tides and other geophysical data in Antarctica. He died in Los Angeles.

Slichter was one of the first and foremost American geophysicists, combining practical business consulting experience, theoretical studies, experimental work, and administrative duties. His research covered analysis of subsurface structures through electroconductive and seismographic studies, as well as earth tides, seismology, and electromagnetic prospecting methods. Slichter Hall at UCLA and Slichter Foreland in Antarctica were named in his honor.

[Though there are no papers or archival collections of Slichter's available, his correspondence is recorded in the papers of Max Mason, at the American Institute of Physics, Neils Bohr Library, New York City. There is no book-length biography of Slichter, but biographical information is available in John Burchard, *QED: MIT in World War II* (1948); Clarence E. Palmer, "Louis Byrne Slichter: Builder of the Institute of Geophysics and Planetary Physics," *Journal of Geophysical Research* 68 (1963); Mark H. Ingraham, *Charles Sumner Slichter* (1972); and Robert Rakes Shrock, *Geology at M.I.T. 1865–1965*, vol. 1 (1977). Obituaries are in the *New York Times*, Mar. 26, 1978; and *Geological Society of America. Memorials*, by C. F. Kennel (1980).]

TAMMY ANN SYREK

SMITH, GERALD L. K. (Feb. 27, 1898–Apr. 15, 1976), minister, political organizer, and publisher, was born in Pardeeville, Wis., the only son and second child of Lyman Z. Smith, a traveling salesman and farmer, and Sarah Henthorn, a teacher. Smith began his education in a one-room, rural school on his father's property, attended elementary school at Viola, Wis., and graduated from high school at Viroqua, Wis., where he participated in debate and track. He enrolled at Valparaiso University in 1915, where he worked at part-time jobs, including preaching, and earned as many as forty credits in a single semester, enabling him to graduate in 1918 with a B.A. in biblical studies.

Smith decided to follow his father and grandfather, unpaid lay preachers for small Disciples of Christ churches, into the ministry and returned to Wisconsin after graduating from college, preaching at Soldiers Grove, Footville, and Beloit, Wis., then in Kansas, Illinois, and Indianapolis, Ind. On June 22, 1922, he married Elna M. Sorenson, whom he met while preaching at Footville. They had one adopted son, Gerald L. K. Smith, Jr., who was estranged as an adult from his parents.

In the spring of 1929, Elna Smith contracted tuberculosis and the Smiths moved to the South for her health. Gerald Smith accepted the position as pastor of the large Kings Highway Christian Church in Shreveport, La. Despite arriving shortly before the stock market crash, he improved the church's finances and membership and became prominent in the community as a charity fund-raiser. He became acquainted with Senator Huey Long when Long intervened to save the homes of some of Smith's congregants threatened with foreclosure. Smith attached himself to Long's political machine, an unpopular move with his wealthy congregation, many of whom disliked Long's program of taxation of the rich.

In the summer of 1933, Smith resigned to avoid being fired and briefly joined the Silver Shirt Legion of William Dudley Pelley, a demagogue headquartered in North Carolina, who modeled his movement on the German Nazi party. Smith, however, saw no future with Pelley and became a paid organizer for Long. Beginning in early 1934 he toured the United States organizing clubs for Long's Share Our Wealth Society and promoting Long's plan to confiscate and redistribute the incomes of millionaires. Arrogant and boastful among weaker individuals, Smith was servile among stronger men such as Long, and his charismatic oratory recruited millions of members to Long's movement. When Long was assassinated in September 1935, on the verge of declaring his candidacy for president, Smith delivered a moving eulogy to more than 150,000 mourners at his funeral on the grounds of the state capitol. "He was the Stradivarius whose notes rose in competition with jealous drums, envious tomtoms," Smith said.

Smith campaigned for Long's successor, Richard W. Leche, in the Democratic primary of January 1936, dipping his hands in red dye to proclaim that the opposing ticket had the blood of Huey Long on its hands, calling down Long's voice from heaven—and achieving a response from a loudspeaker in a tree. With the election won, Smith was no longer useful to the Long machine and lost out in a power struggle with

Long's lieutenants Seymour Weiss and Robert Maestri, who wanted to discontinue the Share Our Wealth Society and support President Franklin D. Roosevelt's reelection campaign in return for New Deal patronage. Smith left Louisiana, seeking another politician whom he could serve. On Jan. 27, 1936, he spoke in Macon, Ga., at a mass gathering of supporters of Governor Eugene Talmadge, an enemy of Roosevelt, who was testing his potential as a presidential candidate. "We're going to get that cripple out of the White House," Smith said of Roosevelt.

After Talmadge failed to emerge as a credible presidential candidate, Smith joined the crusade of Francis E. Townsend, a California physician whose solution to the Great Depression was to provide $200 monthly stipends to everyone older than sixty who retired, thus priming recovery by an infusion of spending and opening jobs to younger workers. Smith spoke at Townsend's annual convention of the Townsend Recovery Plan supporters as well as the convention of the National Union for Social Justice of Father Charles E. Coughlin, the radio priest, a bitter foe of Roosevelt. In the fall Townsend, Smith, and Coughlin created the Union party, whose candidate for president was North Dakota congressman William Lemke. Despite the oratorical prowess of Smith and Coughlin, Lemke polled only 891,858 votes and failed to carry a single state.

For the next three years Smith delivered speeches and raised money to fight Communism. In 1936 he founded the Committee of One Million as the vehicle for his political activities. The next year he befriended Henry Ford, who financed his radio speeches and used him as an antiunion speaker in his plants. Smith claimed that Ford introduced him to the issue of anti-Semitism. In 1939, Smith settled in Detroit, and three years later he campaigned for the Republican nomination for the United States Senate, polling more than a hundred thousand votes but finishing second.

After his loss in 1942, Smith moved to the far-right fringes of politics. During the campaign he founded a political-religious journal, *The Cross and the Flag*, which became his mouthpiece for the rest of his life. In 1943 he founded the America First party as the successor to the Committee of One Million; it was succeeded in turn by the Christian Nationalist party in 1946 and by the Christian Nationalist Crusade in 1948. Smith remained active in politics, supporting candidates in every presidential election and running for president himself in 1944, 1948, and 1956 but never polling more than a few thousand votes.

The issues in Smith's crusades changed as he grew older: preaching in the 1920's, politics in the 1930's, anti-Semitism in the 1940's, anti-Communism in the 1950's, and religious fundamentalism in the 1960's. Smith was most notorious for his hostility to Jews in his speeches and in the pages of *The Cross and the Flag* and numerous tracts. He claimed Jews were responsible for the crucifixion of Jesus and also blamed them for causing the Great Depression and for inspiring World War II. He praised Hitler, who he said had done much good for Germany, and he denied the reality of the Holocaust. Smith claimed presidents Woodrow Wilson, Harry S. Truman, and Franklin D. Roosevelt were Jews or, at the very least, were dominated by Jews. He sold the notorious forgery *The Protocols of the Elders of Zion*, which claimed Jews plotted to destroy Christianity and enslave Gentiles. In his later years Smith encouraged younger anti-Semites and provided them with articles and information for their publications.

One of the more famous orators in the United States, Smith claimed to have spoken to more people, in audiences, than had any of his contemporaries. Journalist H. L. Mencken considered Smith the best rabble-rouser he had ever heard. As Smith grew older, and as television replaced radio, he turned increasingly to the written word to reach audiences. Effective in direct-mail solicitations for money, he became a millionaire, purchased Victorian homes, jewelry, antiques, and expensive cars, and indulged his hobbies of raising miniature horses and goats.

During the 1950's, Smith's career was in temporary eclipse, but he emerged in the 1960's as an entrepreneur of religious shrines. In 1966 he dedicated the Christ of the Ozarks at Eureka Springs, Ark., a statue twice the size of the better-known Christ of the Andes and half that of the Statue of Liberty. In 1968 he began staging a passion play in an amphitheater at Eureka Springs, and it became the largest outdoor production in the United States. He also built a religious-art gallery and a Bible museum in the languishing Ozark resort and revived its tourist trade. At his death in 1976 he was buried at the foot of the Christ of the Ozarks. He will best be remembered as an anti-Semitic hate monger who preached bigotry in the guise of Christianity and Americanism.

[Smith's papers are in the Bentley Historical Library of the University of Michigan. He self-published an autobiography, *Besieged Patriot* (1978). Glen Jeansonne, *Gerald L. K. Smith: Minister of Hate* (1978), is the only biography. See also David H. Bennett, *Demagogues in the Depression, American Radicals in the Union Party, 1932–1936* (1969); and the chapters on Smith in Leo P. Ribuffo, *The Old Christian Right: The Protestant Far Right from the Great Depression to the Cold War* (1983). An obituary is in the *Arkansas Gazette*, Apr. 24, 1976.]

GLEN JEANSONNE

SMITH, HARRY ALLEN (Dec. 19, 1907–Feb. 24, 1976), journalist, humorist, and author was born in McLeansboro, Ill., one of the nine children of Henry Smith and Adeline ("Addie") Allen. The family left McLeansboro before H. Allen's ninth birthday. His only memories of the town were of falling headfirst down a well and later out of a hay loft, experiences he felt constituted "an adequate preparation for a career in journalism—the equivalent of four years in college." The family moved to Decatur, Ill., and then to Defiance, Ohio, before settling in 1919 in Huntington, Ind., where his father obtained a job in a poultry house.

Here Smith attended St. Mary's Parochial School through the eighth grade, when he abandoned his formal education. He worked as a farm laborer, a chicken plucker, and a shoeshine boy. When he was fifteen, he got his first newspaper job as a proofreader with the *Huntington Press* and quickly rose to the position of reporter. His stay in Huntington ended two years later when he wrote a ribald story that a friend copied and circulated in the local high school. After a copy of "Stranded on a Davenport" made its way to the principal's office, Smith was arrested. He had to pay a $22.50 fine for writing and circulating "lewd, licentious, obscene, and lascivious literature" and, effectively a social outcast, immediately left town. He later called the story "the bawdy screed that was to send me forth into the world, a disgrace to heaven, home and mother."

Smith, who shortened his name to H. Allen, spent the next twenty years as an itinerant newspaperman, moving from town to town and paper to paper. Along the way he developed and refined his talent for perceiving and exposing the underlying absurdity in the situations he encountered. He worked first as a reporter in Jeffersonville, Ind., and then in Louisville, Ky., for the *Evening Post* and the *Times*. At the age of nineteen he became editor of the daily *Sebring American* in Florida, where he met Nelle Mae Simpson, a graduate of the University of Missouri School of Journalism and society editor for the paper. They were married Apr. 14, 1927.

When the *American* folded in 1927, Smith worked briefly for the *Tribune* in Tulsa, Okla., before moving on to the *Denver Post*. It was in Denver that the Smith's two children were born. In 1929 he left the *Post* and went to New York City where he was employed as a feature writer for United Press until 1934. He then worked for several radio and film companies before joining the *New York World-Telegram* in 1936 as a rewrite man and later a feature interviewer and composer of humorous articles.

Smith said of his years as a wandering reporter, "among other things, I saw a good part of the United States, I became editor of a small daily newspaper, part owner of a weekly, . . . learned to dance and gave it up as a ridiculous striving for something that can best be attained in a boudoir, read the works of O. Henry, caught a fish, hit a preacher, got married, [and] begat two first-rate children." He also completed his education by reading voraciously. The influence of authors such as Anatole France, Mark Twain, and H. L. Mencken can be seen in his work. It was, however, his own knack for finding the ignoble hidden in the noble or the pathetic in the pompous that made him one of the nation's most popular interviewers. If he tired of doing typical interviews, and he often did, he livened things up by introducing a new and unexpected element. For instance, once when scheduled to interview the actress Olivia de Havilland, he instead asked her to interview an ardent fan about the fine points of autograph collecting. She not only agreed, but conducted a funny and informative interview.

Smith's first full-length book, *Robert Gair*, was published in 1939 and garnered favorable reviews, but his second, *Mr. Klein's Kampf*, (1940) received little notice. His long years of apprenticeship as a writer finally paid off with publication in 1941 of the best-selling *Low Man on a Totem Pole*. In this collection of interviews, autobiographical sketches, and trivia,

Smith returned to what he did best, observing the world around him and reflecting it back filtered through his own slightly skewed perspective. He would, with few exceptions, follow this recipe throughout his writing career which spanned forty years, thirty-seven books, and an almost continual stream of magazine articles.

The popularity of *Low Man on a Totem Pole* led the United Feature Syndicate to offer Smith a job writing a daily syndicated column called "The Totem Pole." He accepted and left the *World-Telegram* in 1941. The column was a success, but Smith believed the onset of World War II would cause newspapers to tighten their budgets by discarding newer features. Since he already had numerous magazine assignments as well as a contract to write another book, in April 1942, he canceled the contract on his last newspaper job.

Smith's books reportedly sold 1.4 million copies between 1941 and 1946. Throughout the 1940's he was rarely off the best-seller lists with books such as *Lost in the Horse Latitudes* (1944), in which he took a humorous look at Hollywood. He noted, for example, that Hollywood geniuses come in three sizes, "those who are geniuses and speak about it frequently; those who are actually not geniuses but somebody told them they were so they do everything but wear badges proclaiming it; and genuine geniuses who keep their mouths shut about their affliction and do their work."

In the mid-1940's, Smith moved his family to suburban Mt. Kisco in Westchester County, N.Y. *Larks in the Popcorn* (1948) recounts his trials as a gentleman farmer and introduces the collection of expatriate New York theater and literary personalities who were his country neighbors. Although the majority of his writing was based on actual people and events, he did write an occasional piece of sheer fiction. One of these, *Rhubarb* (1946), about a cat who inherits a million dollars and a baseball team, was made into a successful motion picture in 1951.

Through the 1950's and 1960's, Smith continued to turn out almost one book per year. Two of his best from the period are *The Rebel Yell* (1954), a satire on people's tendency to lament the passing of the "good old days", and *The Pig in the Barber Shop* (1958), a humorous travel book about Mexico. In 1967 he moved to Alpine, Tex., a small town he first visited in 1947 while collecting material for *We Went Thataway* (1949). Smith continued to write prolifically until his death while on a visit to San Francisco. His last book, *The Life and Legend of Gene Fowler*, was published posthumously in 1977.

Bergen Evans, in his introduction to *The World, the Flesh and H. Allen Smith*, calls him an American humorist in the tradition of Mark Twain and James Thurber. He adds that future historians will be indebted to Smith for his insight and for his honesty in depicting American culture. Smith himself never forgot his roots in journalism. When asked to characterize his work he answered, "I am generally referred to as a humorist but I don't particularly care for the designation. I prefer to think of myself as a reporter, a reporter with a humorous slant. I am funny in the sense that the world is funny." At another time, he defined a humorist as "a fellow who realizes, first, that he is no better than anybody else, and second, that nobody else is either." Taken together these two statements perhaps best describe Smith's philosophy and his work.

[Smith's papers are at Southern Illinois University. His autobiography is *To Hell in a Handbasket* (1962). His other major published works include *Smith's London Journal* (1952); *Let the Crabgrass Grow* (1960); *How to Write Without Knowing Nothing* (1961); and *The Great Chili Confrontation* (1969). A biographical sketch is in Bergen Evans, *The World, the Flesh and H. Allen Smith* (1954). An obituary is in the *New York Times*, Feb. 25, 1976.]

ANNA B. PERRY

SMITH, HOWARD WORTH ("JUDGE") (Feb. 2, 1883–Oct. 3, 1976), United States congressman, was born in Broad Run, Va., in rural Fauquier County, the third child of William Worth Smith, a farmer, and Lucinda Lewis, a homemaker. Smith's parents, though only children at the time, remembered seeing Confederate and Union troops in Virginia during the Civil War. Their memories of the Civil War and Reconstruction were passed on to Howard, their first son.

Smith was educated successively in a one-room school, Bethel Military Academy, and the University of Virginia, where he enrolled in 1901 and received a law degree in 1903. Following admission to the bar, he practiced law in Alexandria. This was a time when some candidates for public office in Virginia were Confederate veterans. In later years, Smith would tell an interviewer that if a candidate "had an empty sleeve, he could be elected to anything."

On Nov. 4, 1913, Smith married Lillian Violett Proctor; they had two children. Lillian Smith died in 1919, and Smith's parents took the two small children to Cedar Hill, the family farm. In 1922, Smith became judge of the Corporation Court in Alexandria. On June 27, 1923, he married Ann Corcoran, the twenty-two year old woman who took care of his children. They had no children. In 1928, Smith was appointed judge of the Sixteenth Circuit of Virginia. Even after becoming a congressman, he continued to be known as Judge Smith.

In 1930, Smith, a Democrat, was elected to the United States House of Representatives from Virginia's Eighth Congressional District, which had once been represented by James Madison. The tall, slim, dark-haired Democrat, with his old-fashioned wing collar and pince-nez, took a giant step toward political power when he became a member of the House Rules Committee in 1933, the same year that Franklin D. Roosevelt became president. Smith at first supported Roosevelt's New Deal but later opposed the National Industrial Recovery Act, Roosevelt's "court-packing" plan, and the Fair Labor Standards Act. Roosevelt responded by unsuccessfully attempting to purge him by supporting his opponent, W. E. Dodd, in the 1938 Democratic primary.

Smith considered himself a defender of the Constitution against those, such as New Dealers, who would transform it; however, a major law bearing his name did injury to the First Amendment. The Smith Act of 1940, among other things, criminalized speech that advised or urged insubordination or disloyalty in the military. It also prohibited teaching, advocating, or advising "the necessity, desirability, or propriety" of overthrowing government by force or violence. If Smith had had his way, his bill would also have resulted in the deportation of aliens who suggested changing the American form of government, even by peaceful, legal means. Such wording, however, did not appear in the final version, which Congress enacted over little opposition. Smith would later complain of the Supreme Court's interpretation of his law, whereby convictions under the act were made difficult.

In 1955, Smith became chairman of the House Rules Committee, which controls the flow of bills to the floor and determines whether floor amendments will be permitted. His chairmanship, together with his role as leader of the conservative coalition of southern Democrats and Republicans, made Smith a powerful figure in the House of Representatives. He frequently exercised his power by refusing to schedule hearings on bills he opposed. He did this in 1958 in regard to Alaskan statehood, but the chairman of the Interior and Insular Affairs Committee called the bill to the floor as privileged legislation, which did not need a rule. The House passed the bill.

Smith's Rules Committee was notorious for its obstruction of civil rights legislation. By the 1960's, however, Smith and the conservative coalition were out of step with the dominant political forces in the nation. In 1961 the House enlarged the Rules Committee to strengthen the hand of liberals. Smith recognized that he could not keep the Civil Rights Act of 1964 bottled up in committee, but he still hoped to defeat it on the floor. When Title VII, banning discrimination in employment based on race, color, religion, or national origin was before the House, he proposed an amendment to add "sex" after "religion." The ensuing debate was largely facetious, but the bill was passed with the amendment. Smith's motivation in offering his amendment has been debated. Some have said that he did it in jest. Others believe that he was quite serious. Clearly, he opposed the legislation and would have been pleased if his amendment had caused its defeat. But, if the bill became law, in all likelihood he wanted to ensure that white women would have no less protection than black women. Smith had been a sponsor of an equal rights amendment as far back as 1945.

Although Smith ceased to be the powerful figure he had once been, he did not decide to leave Congress. That decision was taken by others. Reapportionment brought more liberals into his district, and his conservative constituents were unhappy with him for not leaving the increasingly liberal Democratic party. Smith was defeated in the Democratic primary by a liberal candidate, who in turn was defeated by a conservative Republican in the 1966 general election. At age eighty-three, Smith did not easily adjust to retirement. He died in Alexandria, Va.

[Smith's papers are at the Alderman Library of the University of Virginia. Smith's own writings include

"NLRA—Abuses in Administrative Procedure," *Virginia Law Review*, Mar. 1941; and "In Defense of the House Rules Committee," *Congressional Reform: Problems and Prospects*, edited by Joseph S. Clark (1965). For an interview after his defeat, see "An Elder Statesman Looks at U.S. Today," *U.S. News and World Report*, Oct. 31, 1966. The only full-length biography is Bruce J. Dierenfield, *Keeper of the Rules* (1987). Shorter biographical pieces are numerous. A good one is "No. 2 Man in House," *New York Times*, Aug. 23, 1960. For extensive discussion of the Smith Act, see Zechariah Chafee, Jr., *Free Speech in the United States* (1941). Smith's views on Alaskan statehood can be found in Claus-M. Naske, *An Intrepretative History of Alaskan Statehood* (1973). On his role in the passage of the Civil Rights Act of 1964, see Carl M. Brauer, "Women Activists, Southern Conservatives, and the Prohibition of Sex Discrimination in Title VII of the 1964 Civil Rights Act," *Journal of Southern History*, Feb. 1983. An obituary is in the *New York Times*, Oct. 4, 1976.]

PATRICIA A. BEHLAR

SMITH, WILLIAM EUGENE (Dec. 30, 1918–Oct. 15, 1978), photographer, was born and grew up in Wichita, Kans., where his father, William Henry Smith, was a prosperous executive and part owner of a grain company who later served as president of the Wichita Board of Trade. His mother, Nettie Lee Caplinger, had a controlling personality and, for both good and ill, played an important part in her son's career practically until her death in 1955. An enthusiastic amateur photographer, she was largely responsible for Smith's interest in picture-taking, which by his early teens amounted to a passion.

Smith began his formal education at Wichita's Roman Catholic Cathedral Grammar School. In 1932 he enrolled in Cathedral High School, which he attended for three years, but completed his secondary education at North High School in 1936.

Smith's interest in photography began in his eleventh year, when he took his first picture and began to develop his prints in an improvised darkroom. Within another few years he was rarely without a camera close at hand, and he had a reputation in high school for taking pictures of fellow students in sometimes embarrassing circumstances. In 1934 he sold his first news photograph to the *Wichita Eagle* and began hanging around its editorial offices, where the chief photographer and future Pulitzer Prize winner, Frank Noel, gave him encouragement and advice. By his final year of high school, Smith was supplying photographs on a regular basis to both the *Eagle* and the *Wichita Beacon*.

Mounting business difficulties, spawned in part by the Great Depression, led to the senior Smith's suicide in the spring of 1936. While this tragedy did not leave his widow and two sons destitute, there was not enough money to pay for Smith's college education. As a result, he entered the University of Notre Dame the following fall on a scholarship that required him to work as the school's photographer. College did not suit Smith, who much preferred his photographic pursuits to academic study. Dropping out of Notre Dame after one semester, he set out for New York City, to study at the New York Institute of Photography.

Eventually joined by his mother, Smith was soon trying to make his way as a news photographer, and after working briefly for *Newsweek* in 1937, he began working as a free-lancer. By the fall of 1939 he had a contract with *Life* magazine to work for that publication two weeks out of every month and was also supplying pictures to *Collier's* and a number of other periodicals.

During this early phase of his career, Smith started to develop some strong convictions about photography. For him, it was not enough simply to record what he saw. To be worthwhile, he thought, a picture must express the thoughts and emotions of its maker. As time went on, that belief deepened still further, and he pursued its realization with a sometimes maniacal intensity.

On Dec. 9, 1940, Smith married Carmen Martinez; they had four children. The early years of his marriage coincided with growing unhappiness over *Life*'s treatment of his work, and shortly after America's entry into World War II, Smith severed his affiliation with that publication to work primarily for *Parade*. In the year following, he became a war correspondent for *Flying* magazine and, by late 1943, was on a United States aircraft carrier covering the air war in the Pacific. Accompanying planes on air missions did not satisfy Smith's increasing desire to record the war close-up, and in May 1944, hoping for better chances to see the ground war, he returned to *Life*. His wish was granted; over the next year, he covered several major military operations in the Pacific.

Smith's wartime work includes some of the finest pictorial journalism of World War II, and many of his pictures had a crisp and sometimes raw immediacy that set new standards in front-line photography. The high quality of his reporting was largely the result of an unusual willingness to take risks under fire, and on May 22, 1945, that willingness brought his war correspondent's career to an end in the battle for Okinawa. Standing up to turn his camera on soldiers diving for cover against an enemy mortar attack, he suffered severe wounds, the recovery from which was long and painful.

Although remaining on *Life*'s payroll, Smith did not use a camera for a year after being wounded. When he finally did, he produced a picture that became a classic in modern photography. Entitled "The Walk to Paradise Garden," the picture showed two of his children ambling in a forest. Its success marked the beginning of Smith's most productive years. His stories for *Life* dating from 1947 through 1954, among them "Country Doctor" and "Spanish Village," raised the picture essay to new levels of excellence and earned for their creator a reputation as one of the country's foremost photojournalists.

These triumphs coincided with a deterioration in Smith's stability that manifested itself in financial difficulties, reliance on drugs and alcohol, and increasing alienation from his wife and children. The distancing from his family led to extramarital affairs—one of which produced a child out of wedlock—and in 1968, Smith divorced his wife. On Aug. 28, 1971, he married Aileen Mioko Sprague; they were divorced in 1978.

In spite of his personal problems, Smith continued to be productive. After leaving *Life* in 1955, primarily over disputes about editorial control of his work, he agreed to do the photographs for Stefan Lorant's projected book on Pittsburgh (finally published in 1964). Work on that project spurred Smith to do his own pictorial portrait of the city, which took the form of an extensive photo essay in *Modern Photography Annual* (1959). Following a large retrospective exhibition of his work in 1971 at the Jewish Museum in New York City, he launched a project to document the often tragic effects of industrial pollution (specifically, mercury poisoning) on the inhabitants of Minamata, Japan. The resulting pictures, some of the most impressive of his later career, appeared in many publications around the world and eventually became the basis for a widely acclaimed book, *Minamata* (1975), which Smith wrote with his second wife.

In 1977, Smith moved to Tucson to teach at the University of Arizona and to oversee the arrangement of the massive archive of his lifework at the school's newly established Center for Creative Photography. By now the many years of abusing drugs and alcohol had taken their toll, and he died in Tucson.

[The main repository for Smith's work, as well as his personal papers, is the Center for Creative Photography, University of Arizona, Tucson; a compilation of the papers, by Charles Lamb and Amy Stark, was published in 1983. In addition to issues of *Life*, important published sources containing Smith's work include W. Eugene Smith and Carole Thomas, *Japan . . . A Chapter of Image* (1963); W. Eugene Smith, *His Photographs and Notes* (1969); William S. Johnson, ed., *W. Eugene Smith* (1981); and Glenn G. Willumson, *W. Eugene Smith and the Photographic Essay* (1992). Chief among the biographical writings on Smith is Jim Hughes, *W. Eugene Smith* (1989). Obituaries are in the *New York Times*, Oct. 16, 1978, and, by Jim Hughes, in *Popular Photography*, Dec. 1978.]

FREDERICK S. VOSS

SPORN, PHILIP (Nov. 25, 1896–Jan. 23, 1978), electric company executive, was born in Folotwiner, Austria, one of four children of Isak Sporn, a teacher, and Rachel Kolker. His parents later immigrated to the United States, and Sporn became a naturalized citizen in 1907. He was first involved with utilities while a student at Stuyvesant High School in New York City, working as a lamplighter for the New York Edison Company. Sporn graduated from Columbia University in 1917, with a degree in electrical engineering.

Sporn worked for the Crocker-Wheeler Manufacturing Company from 1917 to 1919, then became a utility engineer with the Consumers Power Company. In 1920 he joined the American Gas and Electric Company (AGE) as a protection engineer. On Sept. 23, 1923, Sporn married Sadie Posner; they had three children.

AGE promoted Sporn through a variety of posts: communication engineer, transmission and distribution engineer, and chief electrical engineer. He became the chief engineer of AGE and its subsidiaries in 1933, and testified on their behalf at the congressional hearings that resulted in the Public Utilities Holding Companies Act of 1935. The company was then the largest investor-owned electric utility system in the nation and owned twenty subsidiaries providing electricity in Ohio, Indiana, Kentucky, Tennessee, Virginia, West Virginia, Michigan, Pennsylvania, and New Jersey. The 1935 law required the divestiture of all noncontiguous subsidiaries and caused a drastic reorganization or dissolution of most utility holding companies. AGE, however, already had a compact and interrelated system, so it had only to spin off two utilities in Pennsylvania and New Jersey. Sporn supervised AGE's reorganization and became its executive vice-president in 1945. When his mentor, AGE president George Tidd, retired in 1947, the board of directors named Sporn as his successor.

AGE grew rapidly during the following decades, as Sporn introduced important innovations in the generation, transmission, and distribution of electricity. AGE received the Charles A. Coffin Award for "distinguished pioneering of advanced engineering concepts" in 1954, for its construction of high-voltage transmission lines and high-pressure generators. In 1958, Sporn changed the company's name to American Electric Power (AEP), to reflect the company's spin-off of gas subsidiaries in the previous decades. He disapproved of gas and electric companies' being owned by the same holding company, believing that such dual ownership destroyed any initiative for either subsidiary to compete or introduce innovations to improve customers' services.

Under Sporn, AEP constantly increased generating plant capacity well beyond predicted future needs, then used its sales force to create larger demands for electric power. AEP persuaded large industrial firms like Kaiser Aluminum to relocate plants in its service area by offering special discounts for high-volume users of electricity. It also encouraged sales of electric appliances in order to increase the consumption of electricity by residential customers and promoted the concept of the all-electric house, in which electricity would power the heating and air-conditioning, as well as lighting and all appliances.

Sporn supported the development of nuclear power as an alternative means of fueling generating plants. He initiated a multi-utility consortium that constructed one of the nation's first nuclear power plants, operated by the Commonwealth Edison Company at Dresden, Ill. Sporn also served on a number of committees advising the United States Atomic Energy Commission and on other government-industry committees, and frequently testified before Congress about nuclear power. He predicted that by the year 2000, nuclear power plants would be generating 50 percent of the electricity used by Americans.

Sporn never accepted the industry's overly optimistic predictions about nuclear technology's economic benefits (some proponents predicted that nuclear power would eventually make electricity "too cheap to meter"). Instead, he advocated more research into traditional sources of electric power—coal, oil, and gas. Sporn had only criticism for the period's nascent environmental movement, however, which he saw as the source of unnecessary regulations that would drive up the cost of electricity.

Sporn retired from the AEP presidency on Dec. 1, 1961, but remained active on the AEP board of directors and as a member of its executive committee. Simultaneously with Sporn's retirement, the board of directors created the AEP System Development Committee to oversee the firm's engineering and technological activities, and to focus on research into new forms of energy generation. Sporn was appointed the committee's full-time chairman. He continued to serve on numerous governmental and international advisory committees regarding nuclear energy, including Israel's Sea Water Conversion Commission.

Prior to his retirement, Sporn had written *Heat Pumps* (1947) and *The Integrated Power System* (1950). After retiring he became a prolific writer, publishing *Energy: Its Production, Conversion and Uses in the Service of Man* (1963); *Foundations of Engineering* (1964); *Research in Electric Power* (1966); *Technology, Engineering and Economics* (1969); *The Social Organization of Electric Power Supply in Modern Societies* (1971); and *Energy in an Age of Limited Availability and Delimited Applicability* (1976). In all, Sporn, published a total of 200 books and articles. He was a member of Columbia University's council for the School of Engineering and its Graduate School of Business. Sporn died in New York City, while walking to his AEP System Development Committee office, where he worked as consultant.

During his lifetime he was known as "Mr. Public Utility," and was considered the nation's top expert in the areas of electric utility engineering, economics, and marketing. His leadership at AEP inspired many of the industry's policies through the 1960's, particularly the rapid growth of generating facilities to feed a constantly increasing, utility-inspired demand for electric power. Although Sporn was one of the first utility executives to question nuclear power, he did so solely on economic grounds. Like virtually everyone else in the industry, he was blind to the environmental costs of electricity production in general, and of nuclear power in particular. The accidents at Three Mile Island in 1979 and at Chernobyl in 1986, and subsequent highlighting of the dangers of nuclear power and radioactive waste, have tarnished Sporn's reputation as a prophet.

[The Sporn collection is part of the American Electric Power company archives, located at the corporate library of the American Electric Power Service Corporation, Columbus, Ohio. Many of his speeches and articles were published in the three-volume *Vistas in Electric Power* (1968). There is no biography of Sporn, but he was interviewed in *Business Week*, Apr. 23, 1949, and profiled in *Business Week*, June 16, 1956. His role as the utility industry pace-setter is described in Richard Hirsch, *Technology and Transformation in the American Electric Utility Industry* (1989). His role in the debate over nuclear power is described in Irvin C. Bupp and Jean-Claude Derian, *The Failed Promise of Nuclear Power* (1981). The Newcomen Society of North America has published a short company history: W. S. White, Jr., *American Electric Power* (1982); also see William W. Corbitt, *And There Was Light: The Story of American Electric Power* (1992). An obituary is in the *New York Times*, Jan. 24, 1978.]

STEPHEN G. MARSHALL

SPROUL, ALLAN (Mar. 9, 1896–Apr. 9, 1978), banker, was born in San Francisco, Calif., the second son of Robert Sproul, a Scottish immigrant employed as a freight auditor by the Southern Pacific Railroad, and Sarah Elizabeth Moore. After attending schools in San Francisco and Berkeley, Calif., Sproul entered the University of California at Berkeley (UCB) in 1914. He left in 1918 and joined the Army Air Corps. He trained as a fighter pilot and was sent to England, but the war ended before he flew any combat missions. After being discharged with the rank of second lieutenant, Sproul returned to UCB. He graduated from the College of Agriculture in 1919 with a B.S. degree in agricultural economics, specializing in pomology.

Sproul worked briefly for a farm produce distributor, the California Packing Company, and then served as an agricultural adviser for two Southern California banks. A friend working at the Federal Reserve Bank of San Francisco suggested that he apply there for a job, and Sproul became head of the bank's Division of Analysis and Research in 1920. On Apr. 2, 1921, Sproul married Marion Meredith Bogle, who had been a UCB classmate; they had three children.

Sproul soon became assistant to the bank's chairman, John Perrin, and was appointed secretary of the bank in 1924. His job required frequent trips to Washington, D.C., to assist Perrin in monetary policy conferences with officials from other Federal Reserve banks. Sproul's abilities impressed Benjamin Strong, the head of the Federal Reserve Bank of New York, as well as Strong's deputy and eventual successor, George L. Harrison, who offered Sproul a post at their bank.

Sproul joined the New York bank as assistant deputy governor and secretary to Harrison on Mar. 1, 1930. He was also assigned to its foreign department, where he became involved in international monetary affairs. Sproul assisted Harrison at several international monetary conferences, at which he became acquainted with such foreign bankers as Montagu Norman, head of the Bank of England.

Sproul became Harrison's assistant in 1934 and was promoted to vice-president in 1936. In September 1938, Sproul became manager of the bank's Open Market Account, which conducted open market operations (sales and purchases of Treasury bills and securities) for the entire Federal Reserve System. After Harrison resigned from the bank's presidency in 1940, Sproul became the third president of the bank on Jan. 1, 1941. He also became vice-chairman of the Open Market Committee, the policy-making group that guided the open market operations.

Sproul's initial years as bank president were occupied with the demands of wartime finance. In 1942, the Department of the Treasury and the Federal Reserve Board announced a fixed pattern of prices for government securities for the duration of the war. Sproul disagreed with this policy, which he believed subordinated the Federal Reserve System's monetary powers to the Department of the Treasury.

Sproul also assisted the government in developing plans for the postwar international economic order. He disagreed with some of the tenets of the Employment Act of 1946, fearing its inflationary consequences. He also disagreed with the major provisions of the proposed International Monetary Fund, but strongly supported the International Bank for Reconstruction and Development (the World Bank). He was offered the latter's presidency in 1946 but decided to remain with the New York bank.

After the outbreak of the Korean War, Sproul was involved in negotiations between the Federal Reserve System and the Treasury Department concerning appropriate government monetary policy. He participated in the 1951 accord that allowed the Federal Reserve Board to exercise a larger degree of independence in setting monetary policy than during World War II.

Sproul considered inflation one of the worst dangers facing the nation, and he deplored the tendency to focus monetary policy solely on preventing the recurrence of a depression. He also criticized the growing influence of "monetarists" such as Milton Friedman and others at the University of Chicago, whom Sproul believed were offering an oversimplified view of monetary policy. His frequent debates on the Open Market Committee concerning these issues aggravated his ulcers, and required him to follow a diet of milk and bland foods for a week after each committee meeting.

In February 1956, the bank's board of directors reappointed Sproul to another five-year term. He resigned from his position several months later, citing a desire to spend more time with his family. Some observers speculated that his unexpected retirement (five years before the mandatory retirement age of sixty-five) was the culmination of a long-running dispute with the Department of the Treasury over the administration's "bills-only" policy, which restricted the Federal Reserve Board's debt-management powers.

After leaving the presidency of the New York Federal Reserve Bank on Apr. 30, 1956, Sproul and his wife settled in the San Francisco suburb of Kentfield, in Marin County. Sproul became a director of the American Trust Company, which later merged with the Wells Fargo Bank. In 1969 he became a director of the holding company, Wells Fargo and Company. He gave a monthly talk to the board of directors concerning monetary policy, credit conditions, and other economic issues. He also served as a director of the Kaiser Aluminum and Chemical Corporation (1957–1968).

Sproul also served in various nongovernmental organizations, such as the Committee for Economic Development and the Twentieth Century Fund, during the 1960's. In 1960 he was a member of a committee appointed by the president of the World Bank to examine the role of foreign aid in the economic development of India and Pakistan. He found the existing program acceptable, the main bottleneck being the lack of responsible officials and administrators.

In 1961, President John F. Kennedy appointed Sproul chairman of a special task force that studied America's balance-of-payments problem and various domestic economic issues. During the later 1960's, Sproul disapproved of American involvement in Vietnam. He became upset by the inflation resulting from the increased military spending and apparent lack of coherent fiscal and monetary policies.

After his wife died in 1973, Sproul cut back on his activities and gave only an occasional speech at the Wells Fargo Bank. He resigned from his directorship in 1975 but remained a special consultant. Sproul died at his home in Kentfield, Calif., and was buried at Sunset View Cemetery, El-Cerrito, Calif.

Sproul, who termed himself a Republican "with independent leanings," played a conservative role in the operation of the nation's central banking system. He was very protective of the role of the Federal Reserve System, particularly that of the New York Federal Reserve Bank, in formulation of national monetary policy, and he fought against encroachments into this role by the Department of the Treasury.

[Sproul's official papers are at the Records Management and Archives Division of the Federal Reserve Bank of New York; his personal papers are at the Bancroft Library, University of California, Berkeley. Lawrence S. Ritter, ed., *Selected Papers of Allan Sproul* (1950), is a useful selection of Sproul's speeches and writings. He is mentioned in Marriner Eccles, *Beckoning Frontiers* (1951). Sproul's role in the 1951 accord is analyzed in Joseph L. Lucia, "Allan Sproul and the Treasury-Federal Reserve Accord, 1951," *History of Political Economy*, Spring 1983. The "bills only" dispute is mentioned in Edward H. Collins, "A Change at the Top of the New York 'Fed,' " *Banking*, July 1956; and Milton Friedman and Anna Jacobson Schwartz, *A Monetary History of the United States 1867–1960* (1963). An obituary is in the *New York Times*, Apr. 11, 1978.]

STEPHEN G. MARSHALL

STAFFORD, JEAN (July 1, 1915–Mar. 26, 1979), novelist and short story writer, was born in Covina, Calif., the youngest of four children of John Richard Stafford and Mary Ethel McKillop. At age six, Stafford moved with her family from California to Colorado, where her eccentric father wrote Western stories for pulp magazines under the names Jack Wonder and Ben Delight, and her mother ran a boardinghouse near the University of Colorado campus in Boulder. Stafford's writing weaves together the various strands of her upbringing: the natural grandeur of the West, isolation and loneliness in youth and adolescence, and her struggle against what she regarded, with a strong sense of shame, as the cramped, spiritually impoverished world of her parents. Late in her life, she wrote to her sister Marjorie Pinkham, "For all practical purposes I left home when I was 7."

A series of traumas scarred Stafford's early life. While attending the University of Colorado, where she earned concurrent bachelor's and master's degrees in 1936, she witnessed the suicide by shooting of her friend Lucy McKee. After a year studying philology in Heidelberg, Germany, she returned to Boulder, where she met the poet Robert Lowell at a writers' conference. In 1938 she was severely injured in an automobile accident in which Lowell was driving and had to undergo reconstructive facial surgery. Her other brother died in World War II. Stafford taught briefly at Stephens College in Columbia, Mo., but disliked teaching. She also worked at the *Southern Review* in Baton Rouge, La., and lived with Lowell in New York City and Tennessee before moving to Boston, where (despite suing him in connection with the accident) she married him on Feb. 4, 1940.

Stafford gained overnight celebrity with the publication of her first novel, *Boston Adventure*, in 1944. The book is a coldly satirical account of initiation into Boston society, as seen by the daughter of a modest immigrant family. Reviews in Boston were mixed, but Howard Mumford Jones in the *Saturday Review of Literature* called it "memorable and haunting," adding, "Miss Stafford is a commanding talent, who writes in the great tradition of the English novel." The *New Yorker* compared *Boston Adventure* to the work of Proust for its "ceaseless vivisection of individual experience." According to Thomas Lask in the *New York Times*, the novel was "mandarin and embroidered, yet it conveyed with claustrophobic exactness the ingrown, hothouse atmosphere" of its Brahmin setting. The book brought Stafford the Merit Award from *Mademoiselle* magazine in 1944. In 1945, she won a Guggenheim Fellowship and a $1,000 award from the American Academy and National Institute of Arts and Letters.

Although she spent most of her adult life in the East, Stafford never escaped the psychic tolls of her Western youth; literary success brought her little happiness, and her physical and emotional health remained frail. The marriage to Lowell was disastrous and ended in divorce in 1948. She spent most of 1947 at the Payne Whitney Clinic in New York City, being treated for alcoholism and depression that would continue to plague her throughout her life. An autobiographical story in the *New Yorker* titled "Children Are Bored on Sunday" marked her return to writing and the beginning of a long association with that magazine, including twenty-one stories and several articles over a decade and a close, thirty-year relationship with its fiction editor, Katharine White.

Stafford's second novel, *The Mountain Lion* (1947), was a striking departure from, and to some critics an improvement on, her first. Written in a sparer style, it treats the coming of age of a brother and sister in high-country Colorado, and the interplay of gender and nature. Orville Prescott in the *New York Times* called it "a sad, poignant, satiric story, definitely not an enjoyable one." Stafford married Oliver Jensen, a staff photographer for *Life* magazine, on Jan. 28, 1950; they were divorced in 1953. Her third and final published novel, *The Catherine Wheel* (1952), set in Maine, was written while she was living with Jensen in New York City and at her house in Damariscotta Mills, Maine. An autobiographical novel, *The Parliament of Women*, was never completed, but two chapters appeared as stories: "An Influx of Poets," in the *New Yorker* (1978), and "Woden's Day," in *Shenandoah* (1979).

During the 1950's, Stafford wrote for the *New Yorker*, *Harper's Bazaar*, the *Sewanee Review*, and other magazines. Her story "In the Zoo" won the O. Henry Prize in 1955. That same year, she developed writer's block. In the summer of 1956, while on a nonfiction assignment in London for the *New Yorker*, Stafford was introduced to the journalist A. J. Liebling; they were married on Apr. 3, 1959. It was the third marriage for each, and the four and a half years they shared in New York were the happiest of Stafford's life. After Liebling's death in 1963, she moved to his house in East Hampton, N.Y. Although she virtually ceased to write short stories after marrying Liebling, Stafford turned out numerous nonfiction articles, several children's books, and *A Mother in History* (1966), a nonfiction account of a three-day interview with Marguerite C. Oswald, the mother of Lee Harvey Oswald. Her *Collected Stories* (1969), which originally appeared in the *New Yorker* and other magazines, earned her the Pulitzer Prize for fiction in 1970. The Pulitzer jury cited the "range in subject, scene and mood" in these bleak but elegantly crafted tales, which are often autobiographical. Their central characters, mainly women and adolescents, inhabit a harsh, unromantic America: a place of loneliness and loss where innocence dies hard, social convention weighs on the individual, and experience is a cruel teacher. After that, she won several grants and fellowships but wrote little. In 1976, she suffered a stroke that resulted in aphasia, impairing her speech and vision. She died in White Plains, N.Y.

[Works by Stafford not cited in the text include *Children Are Bored on Sunday* (1953); *The Interior Castle* (1953), which contains "Boston Adventure," "The Mountain Lion," and "Children Are Bored on Sunday"; *Elephi, the Cat with the High IQ* (1962); *The Lion and the Carpenter and Other Tales from the Arabian Nights Retold* (1962); and *Bad Characters* (1964). See also William Leary, "Jean Stafford, Katharine White, and the *New Yorker*," *Sewanee Review*, Fall 1985; Mary Ellen Walsh, *Jean Stafford* (1985); David Roberts, *Jean Stafford* (1988) and "Jean and Joe," *American Scholar*, Summer 1988; Charlotte M. Goodman, *Jean Stafford* (1990); William Leary, "Jean Stafford," *Sewanee Review*, Summer 1990; and Ann Hulbert, *The Interior Castle* (1992). An obituary is in the *New York Times*, Mar. 28, 1979.]

JEFFREY SCHEUER

STEWART, DONALD OGDEN (Nov. 30, 1894–Aug. 2, 1980), humorist, playwright, and screenwriter, was born in Columbus, Ohio, the third (and last) child of Clara Ogden and Gilbert Holland Stewart, a lawyer and Ohio circuit court judge. Self-conscious about his family's modest wealth and his own physical appearance (he wore glasses and had buck teeth that required braces), Stewart grew up longing for wealth and social acceptance. When fellow students teased him unmercifully during his freshman year of high school (calling him Duck Lip and Four Eyes), he convinced his parents to send him to Phillips Exeter Academy in Exeter, N.H., in 1909. He warmed to Exeter's rigorous academic program and its more tolerant and success-oriented student body.

Stewart graduated from Exeter in 1912 and returned to Columbus, only to suffer a series of disillusionments. He learned that his mother was an alcoholic and that his father had been indicted for stealing money from the Columbus Law Library. The case never came to trial (Gilbert Stewart died that fall), but Stewart was humiliated by the adverse publicity. In addition, his adored older brother Bert died just prior to his father's death. Although Stewart had an older married sister, he assumed the primary care of his mother.

Despite these family tragedies, Stewart entered Yale in 1912 with a scholarship and loans from family friends. He majored in English, having discovered a latent passion for the arts (particularly music and literature), and was appointed assignments editor of the *Yale Daily News*. He was especially proud of being tapped for membership in the elite Skull and Bones Society. He graduated in 1916 and took a job with American Telephone and Telegraph (AT&T) serving in Birmingham, Ala., Pittsburgh, and Chicago before he was drafted in 1918.

Stewart enrolled in the Naval Officers Training School in Chicago, where he served as an instructor for the duration of World War I (his poor eyesight kept him from overseas duty). After the war he went to work for AT&T in Minneapolis, where he met and established an immediate rapport with F. Scott Fitzgerald and began to reorient himself toward a literary rather than a business career.

Stewart left AT&T in the spring of 1920, worked briefly and lucratively for a private manufacturing company in Dayton, Ohio, and then moved in late 1920 to Greenwich Village in New York City, where writers such as Fitzgerald were beginning to define their careers through the New York magazines. Fitzgerald introduced Stewart to Edmund Wilson, then an assistant editor for *Vanity Fair*, which published Stewart's parody of James Branch Cabell, followed by similar parodies of contemporary writers as they "reimagined," in their distinct styles, famous events of American history. After these sketches were collected and published as *A Parody Outline of History* (1921), they captured the attention of a wider audience. Stewart followed up with *Perfect Behavior* (1922), a series of essays that lightheartedly mocked the etiquette books of the day. By the time Stewart traveled in Europe (1922–1923), he had established himself as a popular American satirist.

Stewart's career as a satirist shifted somewhat after he experienced the "shock" of modernist art in Paris, where he met Ernest Hemingway and other expatriate artists who were finding Paris artistically congenial and energizing. Stewart's reading of T. S. Eliot's "The Waste Land" shortly after its publication in 1922 influenced his decision to attempt more serious satire, which resulted in *Aunt Polly's Story of Mankind* (1923). This dark parody of middle-class greed and social hypocrisy caught Stewart's readers off guard, and the book was a critical and financial failure. Although Stewart had hoped to attack the "many sacred cows which Mark Twain had somehow overlooked," he realized later that he was "singularly unfitted both by nature and education" for the role of "Chief American Gadfly," and he returned to his more whimsical style. *Mr. and Mrs. Haddock Abroad* (1924) details the naive and nonsensical behavior of Mr. and Mrs. Haddock and their smug daughter, Mildred, on board an ocean liner for Europe, and its deadpan speech and non sequiturs make for the slapstick humor characteristic of what Stewart called his "crazy humor" mode.

Stewart completed *Mr. and Mrs. Haddock Abroad* during his second trip to Europe in 1924, at which time he went with Ernest Hemingway to the July festival in Pamplona, Spain, and then returned to America for a cross-country lecture tour (characterized by witty after-dinner speeches). Stewart arranged for the first American publication of Hemingway's *In Our Time* by Boni and Liveright (1925), and he contracted with the firm as well for his own next book, *The Crazy Fool* (1925). During the summer of 1925, Stewart returned to Europe and once again traveled with Hemingway to the Pamplona festival. This second trip inspired Hemingway's *The Sun Also Rises* (1926), in which Stewart is the prototype for Jake Barnes's friend Bill Gorton. "A few of the quips" were his, Stewart said later, and overall the book struck him "as little more than a very clever reportorial tour de force."

The Crazy Fool, which utilized Stewart's favorite Horatio Alger success formula as the basis for its humor, attracted attention in Hollywood. Stewart went to work as a screenwriter for Metro-Goldwyn-Mayer (MGM) in late 1925, although he initially found screenwriting uncongenial. He completed *Mr. and Mrs. Haddock in Paris, France* (1926) while on MGM's payroll. He also courted Beatrice Ames, whom he had met in Paris the previous summer. They were married on July 24, 1926, and had two children. The Stewarts honeymooned in France, where Stewart showed off his bride at Gerald and Sara Murphy's Villa America in Antibes. Here were gathered many of Stewart's artist friends, including Robert Benchley, Dorothy Parker, Scott and Zelda Fitzgerald, Archibald and Ada MacLeish, and Ernest and Hadley Hemingway. Stewart was saddened that fall in Paris to witness Hemingway's vindictive streak. Hemingway had written a poetic parody of Dorothy Parker that he read aloud at the MacLeishes. Stewart found the poem—and Hemingway's public reading of it—in poor taste, and told Hemingway so. It was the end of their friendship.

When the Stewarts returned to America in late 1926, they stayed briefly in Hollywood before moving to New York City. During 1927 and 1928, Stewart wrote a weekly column for the *Chicago Tribune*, published short humorous pieces in the *New Yorker*, and tried his hand at play writing. He hoped to make "the transition from the satirical world of *Aunt Polly* and *The Crazy Fool* into the depths of living characters and current human problems." His first attempt, a collaboration with Max Mercin called *Los Angelos*, lasted two weeks on Broadway. Stewart believed that producer George M. Cohan had seriously compromised the play into a "tasteless melodrama" about Hollywood, and he was dismayed that he himself "cared more about money" than about "artistic standards"—he had left his name associated with the work.

Stewart continued to experiment with play writing, hoping to end his career as a "professional 'humorist.' " He debuted as an actor in Philip Barry's play *Holiday* in 1928. Stewart had no intention of being an actor, but he hoped to learn more, at first hand, about dialogue by acting in a play. The play enjoyed a successful run, and in 1929 Stewart wrote his own successful play, *Rebound*, a humorous love story that was voted one of the ten best plays of 1929–1930.

Although Stewart continued play writing, he had little success and returned to screenwriting after the publication of his final book of humor. *Father William* (1929) was a satire of a successful businessman, Austin Seabury, who decides (not unlike Stewart) that laughter and enjoyment are life's chief rewards. By the time the Stewarts moved to Hollywood, Stewart had begun to recognize screenwriting as a craft worthy of respect. The Stewarts remained in Hollywood until shortly before their divorce in 1938. Stewart married Ella Winter Steffens, the widow of muckracker journalist Lincoln Steffens, on Mar. 4, 1939. He continued to sustain the reputation he had earned during the 1930's as one of the best and most highly paid screenwriters. He defined the good screenwriter as an adapter, one who knows when to leave someone else's material alone and when to change it. He disliked being one of many collaborators on a script, and he resisted being "the man to write the first draft." Someone would eventually change it so as to gain the screen credits. Stewart's easygoing manner and humor made him a popular scriptwriter. He said of his film work that he always tried to give "a laugh at the end." Stewart's best-known films include *The Prisoner of Zenda* (1937), *The Philadelphia Story* (Stewart's adaptation of Philip Barry's play that won Stewart an Academy Award, 1940), and *Keeper of the Flame* (1942).

During the late 1930's and 1940's, Stewart was increasingly involved in political activities. He was president of the Hollywood Anti-Nazi League and of the League of American Writers (he helped to organize the 1937 Writers Congress in New York City), and he was a board member of the Screen Writers' Guild. Stewart became known for his nagging of President Franklin D. Roosevelt on various liberal issues to such an extent that Roosevelt was said to order "orange juice, coffee and his first 10 telegrams of protest from Donald Stewart" upon awaking.

Increasingly, Stewart's leftist sympathies made him vulnerable to the attack of the House Committee on Un-American Activities, and in 1950 he joined the ranks of artists who found themselves blacklisted. By 1951 he and Ella had moved to London, where they remained until his death. Although Stewart did some film work in England (essentially dubbing English dialogue for European films) and some work for Hollywood by way of correspondence, his last years were relatively unproductive.

Although Stewart's work as a humorist and screenwriter gained recognition in his lifetime, he is probably best remembered today for his associations with those, such as Fitzgerald and Hemingway, who achieved more permanent literary fame. Stewart's contemporaries, such as John Dos Passos, noted his rangy gait and charm, and they appreciated his self-effacing humor and easy wit, which allowed Stewart to see himself, and the society of his day, with a refreshing candor.

[See Stewart's autobiography, *By a Stroke of Luck!* (1975). He also appears in the various biographies, memoirs, and letters of his literary contemporaries. See in particular John Dos Passos, *The Best Times* (1966); Carlos Baker, *Ernest Hemingway* (1969); and Linda Patterson Miller, ed., *Letters from the Lost Generation* (1991). An obituary is in the *New York Times*, Aug. 3, 1980.]

LINDA PATTERSON MILLER

STILL, CLYFFORD (Nov. 30, 1904–June 23, 1980), painter, was born in Grandin, N.Dak., the son of an accountant who moved his family in 1905 to Spokane, Wash. Five years later the family moved to southern Alberta, Canada, near Bow Island, to homestead. Throughout Still's school years, the family traveled between Canada and the home that they retained in Spokane. He began drawing and painting at an early age, collected art books and prints, and developed an intense interest in the old masters and such late-nineteenth-century American painters as Albert Pinkham Ryder, whose canvases share a sensuous paint surface with those of Still. He also studied and memorized many works of the composers Chopin, Beethoven, and Schubert, which he played on the family piano.

Still traveled to New York City in 1925 for the first time and enrolled in the Art Students League, where, upon completing forty-five minutes of class time, he departed; he later remarked on this experience that "the exercises and results I observed I had already explored for myself some years before and had rejected most of them as a waste of time." He spent the rest of the year in New York City looking at paintings in galleries and museums, but he was often disappointed by the discrepancies between his imagination and the reality of some works of the old masters that he had seen reproduced in prints and books.

In the fall of 1926, Still enrolled at Spokane University. He left after the spring semester in 1927 to return to Canada to continue his self-directed studies in philosophy and literature. In the fall of 1931 he reenrolled at Spokane University after receiving a teaching fellowship in art. He received a B.A. degree in 1933 and became a teaching fellow at Washington State College (now University) in Pullman. He received his M.A. degree from Washington State in 1935 and was an instructor in fine arts there from 1935 to 1940 and an assistant professor from 1940 to 1941. Still left the university because he found the demands on both his time and his independence too taxing to pursue his painting. He did, however, continue to represent the Fine Arts Department at oral examinations and tutored Rhodes scholar nominees informally in the fine arts.

During the late 1930's and the 1940's, Still's paintings were dark and cryptic, some with forms that were autoerotic in nature, as in a pair of works from the period 1936–1937 in the permanent collection of the San Francisco Museum of Art. (Still never gave his paintings titles. He merely designated the year in which they were painted, and in early exhibits a letter was added for identification. At his first one-man show in New York City, the gallery assistants invented and attached titles for their own amusement.) Still held onto the Romanticist ideal of an artist's work transcending his culture. His longing for a solitary vision echoed that of Paul Cézanne, for example, a painter he admired for his pursuit of themes, forms, and a singular way of seeing the world. In the summers of 1934 and 1935, Still painted realistic landscapes at Trask Foundation (today known as Yaddo) in Saratoga Springs, N.Y.

At the end of the 1940–1941 academic year, Still resigned from Washington State College and moved to California, a state that would play a large part in Still's professional life. From December 1941 until the summer of 1943, he worked in the industries of war—shipbuilding in Oakland, as a steel checker for the United States Navy in the building of the submarine *Coucal*, and in San Francisco as a material-release engineer for Hammond Aircraft, which made assemblies for the Douglas A-20 airplane. He continued to paint during this period and many canvases were included in his first one-man exhibit, which opened at the San Francisco Museum of Art (now the San Francisco Museum of Modern Art) on Mar. 1, 1943.

In 1943, Still met the painter Mark Rothko in Berkeley, Calif., who brought Still to the attention of Peggy Guggenheim, an early supporter of the New York School of painters. Rothko offered Still encouragement and was the only one of the abstract expressionists with whom Still established a long-standing relationship. (Still was later to accuse Rothko of borrowing his painterly style from one of Still's pieces.) In the same year Still accepted a professorship at the Richmond Professional Institute (now Virginia Commonwealth University), a division of the College of William and Mary. Although he had a teaching schedule of thirty-two hours per week, Still produced a large body of work, as well as the only lithographs he ever was to produce, a series of twenty-one with which Still experimented with a variety of techniques and applications in the medium.

The size and nature of some of Still's works in this period challenged the status quo of art professionals. He often invoked an attitude of secrecy and self-importance that sometimes did not endear him to his peers. He was never comfortable in the cultural ranks of New York City and saw his struggle as one of a lonely artist having no allegiances to any of his contemporaries, such as William Baziotes, Franz Joseph Kline, Jackson Pollock, and Barnett Newman. In 1944, while in Richmond, he wrote in his notes: "Ultimately, there will be no explanation, logically [of my work] whatever the psychologists or psychoanalysts may pretend. Their tools are too clumsy and utterly meaningless." In 1946, before the opening of his one-man exhibit at Peggy Guggenheim's Art of This Century Gallery in New York City (he had previously hung his black painting of 1945, or PH-314, in the Autumn Salon show there), his first major New York show, he wrote: "It is frequently remarked that all the successful artists look like business-men. The fact is, they are shrewd, political, sensitive, and tough business-men who dabble in painting. Of good intelligence and fair insight, a spark of creative revolt can scarcely be found in the entire lot."

Still accepted a teaching post in 1946 at the California School of Fine Arts in San Francisco, where he initiated a successful graduate program in painting that became known throughout the world. Still also advised students to open their own private gallery, which they did at 527 Bush Street and was then known as the Metart Gallery. In 1947 and 1948, Still briefly played a role in the formation of a major new art school to be located on Eighth Street in Manhattan, New York City, and to be called Subjects of the Artist—a joint effort of West Coast and East Coast painters. Only practicing artists would be invited to teach there. Unfortunately, Still backed out after disagreements over curriculum and staff. He later commented on this experience: "It is probably the most foolish hope I ever had."

Meanwhile, Still's large, partially paint-covered canvas "1947-H No. 2" was hung in the Third Exhibition of Painting at the California Palace of the Legion of Honor (1948–1949). The piece, as were many of his works, was violently attacked in the San Francisco press. In a letter to the editor the *San Francisco News* printed a perennial complaint about abstract art: "This is nothing but an insult to the taxpayers of San Francisco. . . . This type of 'art' is certainly not art at all but some sort of chicanery being foisted upon the art-loving public, and if my small voice can be heard I demand the removal of this horrible monstrosity from this fine arts museum." Such a reaction was common to the compositions of color and nonrepresentational form in the works of such painters in the 1950's as Baziotes, Kline, Adolph Gottlieb, Robert Motherwell, and the "action painter" Pollock, who literally dripped paint onto a canvas that lay on the floor. It was not until a few critics, such as Harold Rosenberg and Clement Greenberg, championed such work that those artists became well known around the world. Although Still clearly produced his most praised body of work in the 1950's, his work was not well known to the public at large in that decade, and his works were not shown in Europe until 1992, twelve years after his death. He began to distance himself from his dealer Betty Parsons, at whose New York gallery he had one-man shows in 1947, 1950, and 1951, and from his contemporaries. He described New York in the early 1950's as a place "where the showdown fight really goes on—it's bloody red. . . . New York offers a slash in the belly. You know your friend has a knife and will use it on you."

Although Still often remembered the expansive and bleak landscapes of Canada and Washington that he had known as a youth, he declared that his canvases of flamelike color denied any sense of landscape or representational form. A new kind of pictorial space opened up for him and he broke with the spatial methods of Renaissance perspective, as well as with cubism and the Paris School. Three-dimensional picture space was being replaced in his work by a two-dimensional realm of paint and the canvas surface. Some scholars saw this as revolutionary, while others, such as Robert Rosenblum, saw its relationship to the sublime in nature in examples of German Romanticist landscapes.

In 1950, after his one-man exhibition at the Metart Gallery (the last before its closing), Still resigned from the California School of Fine Arts and moved to New York City, although he would often travel back to California. In 1951 he began teaching at the City University of New York, first at Hunter College and then at the Teacher Education Program at Brooklyn College, where he taught graphic techniques. In 1952 the Museum of Modern Art in New York put together "Fifteen Americans," an exhibition of new works, and Still contributed seven works to the show. This was Still's last public exhibition until November 1959, when he showed seventy-two paintings, all selected by the artist himself, at the Albright (now Albright-Knox) Art Gallery in Buffalo, N.Y. Still enforced his complete control of how the works were displayed and handled—for example, he required that certain works had to remain together if they were to be shown at all. He did let the blue-chip Marlborough-Gerson Gallery of New York City represent him and first showed there in November 1970. In May 1975 he donated a permanent installation of thirty-three canvases to the San Francisco Museum of Modern Art. In 1978, Still was elected to the American Academy and Institute of Arts and Letters, and the largest one-man show ever devoted to a living artist, seventy-nine paintings by Still, was on display at the Metropolitan Museum of Art in New York City from November 1979 to February 1980. Still's allegiances to Buffalo's Albright-Knox Gallery and the San Francisco Museum of Modern Art prompted him to leave thirty-one and seventy-eight works, respectively, to each of these institutions.

Clyfford Still moved to a small farm in Maryland in 1961 and died of cancer at Sinai Hospital in Baltimore. He was survived by his wife, Patricia, and their two children.

[Further information on Still can be found in Dorothy Miller, ed., *Fifteen Americans* (1952); Ti-Grace Sharpless, *Clyfford Still* (1963); Irving Sandler, *The Triumph of American Painting* (1970); John P. O'Neill, ed., *Clyfford Still* (1979); and Thomas Kellein, ed., *Clyfford Still, 1904–1980: The Buffalo and San Francisco Collections* (1992). Profiles are in *Time*, Nov. 29, 1963; and *Newsweek*, Dec. 22, 1969. An obituary is in the *New York Times*, June 25, 1980.]

RICHARD FUMOSA

STILL, WILLIAM GRANT, JR. (May 11, 1895–Dec. 3, 1978), composer, was born in Woodville, Miss., the son of William Grant Still, Sr., who died while his son was an infant, and Carrie Lena Fambro. Shortly after his father's death, his mother moved to Little Rock, Ark., to live with her mother. His mother's marriage to Charles B. Shepperson, a railroad postal clerk, was a turning point in Still's young life. Shepperson, a cultured black man, introduced the phonograph to their home, which enabled Still to listen to European classical music. His first venture into music began with the study of the violin.

Upon graduation from high school in 1911, Still enrolled in Wilberforce University in Ohio, where his quick mind and innate talent enabled him to learn several instruments in a short time. He also learned to appreciate orchestral music while serving as a leader of the student band. Still left college before obtaining a degree after he was accused of compromising a female student's virtue. He set out for Columbus, Ohio, where he naively hoped to earn enough money playing the popular music of the day to return to college eventually. A byproduct of his experience in Columbus was his exposure to jazz, folk music, and other forms of popular music, all of which were to interact with his formal musical training in the years ahead.

In 1915 he married Grave Bundy, the young woman whose accusations forced him to leave Wilberforce. The marriage was a failure almost immediately. Although they had four children, Still and his wife lived apart for most of their married lives, each pursuing separate interests, and they finally divorced in 1932.

Still corresponded with W. C. Handy, the great blues innovator, whom he had met briefly in Columbus. Handy invited Still to come to Memphis, where he became part of Handy's band and played cello and oboe. Traveling the back roads and byways of the Deep South, he met people far different from any he had previously known, an experience that would influence his composition the remainder of his life.

In 1917, Still returned to Oberlin College, but he was bored with the school routine after his adventures on the road with Handy, and he left after a few months to join the United States Navy in 1918. After his discharge that same year, and unable to find work as a musician, he returned to Oberlin to continue his studies in composition. He soon dropped out again, this time traveling to New York City, where he once more found employment with Handy, as both band member and arranger. While he was working for Handy and for his publishing company, an opportunity arose for Still to become the recording director of the noted Black Swan Phonograph Company in New York City, a position that enabled him to meet well-known musicians, such as the modernist Edgar Varèse. He began studies with Varèse and learned how to develop his individuality as an experimentalist. Later, Still studied music composition with the noted composer George W. Chadwick of the New England Conservatory of Music.

Still began composing full-time in the mid-1920's, writing such chamber music pieces as *From the Land of Dreams* (1924) and *From the Black Belt* (1926); full-orchestra pieces, including *Darker America* (1924) and *From the Journal of a Wanderer* (1925); and the ballet *La Guiablesse* (1927). These early works led to his winning the Harmon Award in 1928 for the "most significant contribution to American Negro culture."

The 1930's were also very productive years. In 1931, Still rewrote one of his early successes, *Africa*, to create the *Afro-American Symphony*, probably his most famous work. European critics considered this work "a bridge between the old world and the new." In 1934 he won a Guggenheim Fellowship and received several commissions, writing *Kaintuck* (1935) for the League of Composers, *Lenox Avenue* (1937) for the Columbia Broadcasting System, and the theme song for the New York World's Fair of 1939–1940. In 1936 he became the first black to conduct a major United States orchestra—the Los Angeles Philharmonic. Still's creative involvement with radio began in 1935, and his position as arranger-conductor for the popular radio show "Willard Robison and His Deep River Orchestra" made Still the first black to lead a white radio orchestra in New York City. While in Hollywood in the late 1930's, where he wrote several songs for motion pictures, Still met Verna Arvey, a concert pianist and part-time writer, whom he married on Feb. 8, 1939. They had two children. Arvey wrote the librettos for most of Still's operas.

During World War II, Still wrote several works of a patriotic nature, including *In Memoriam: The Colored Soldiers Who Died for Democracy* (1944), and continued to write and receive awards throughout the 1940's, 1950's, and 1960's. In 1944 he won the prize for the best overture in a competition administered by the Cincinnati Symphony Orchestra. His ballet *Troubled Island* (1938), with a libretto by Langston Hughes, was produced by the New York City Opera in 1949. In 1953 alone, he received the Freedom Foundation Award for *To You, America* (1952) and the George Washington Carver Achievement Award. In 1961 he won a contest for a work dedicated to the United Nations (*The Peaceful Land*). He also received honorary degrees from Wilberforce (1936), Howard University (1941), Oberlin (1947), the New England Conservatory of Music (1973), and the Peabody Conservatory of Music (1974), among several other universities.

Never able to rid himself of the label of black composer, which he detested, Still had the support of major classical musicians and composers of his day. He was championed by Leopold Stokowski, who wrote that Still's "musical nature [gave] him the power to fuse into one unified expression our American music of today with the ancestral memories laying deep within him of African music." In the introduction to the only in-depth study of the composer's life, his wife's *In One Lifetime* (1983), B. A. Nugent said that Still believed "racial barriers should be dissolved through exemplary acts and gentle persuasion rather than demolished through the militant explosions of marches and uncivil riots."

For Still, the black music movement of the 1960's ("soul music") strayed from the expansive musical development initiated by such originals as Handy and Duke Ellington. The militants claimed that Still wrote Euro-American, not Afro-American, music, but several black composers, including Ulysses Kay, Arthur Cunningham, and Olly Wilson, recognized Still as a pioneer.

Still died in Los Angeles after a series of strokes.

[Verna Arvey, *In One Lifetime* (1984), contains a complete listing of Still's compositions. Mariam Williams, "Profile," *Phylon*, Spring 1951, offers a short portrait of Still. Robert Bartlett Haas, ed., *William Grant Still and the Fusion of Cultures in American Music* (1972), offers the most extensive examination of Still's place in American musical history. Obituaries are in the *New York Times*, Dec. 6, 1978; and the *New York Amsterdam News*, Dec. 9, 1978.]

WILLIAM F. BROWNE

STOKOWSKI, LEOPOLD ANTHONY (Apr. 18, 1882–Sept. 13, 1977), conductor and composer, was born in London, England, the son of Annie Moore and Kopernik Stokowski, said by some to be a Polish diplomat and, by others, a cabinetmaker. As a young child, he studied violin, piano, and organ. In 1895, at age thirteen, he was admitted to the Royal College of Music (at the time the youngest student in the school's history), where he studied organ with Stevenson Hoyte and theory and composition with Walford Davies and Sir Charles Stanford. Stokowski was awarded a diploma in organ performance in 1900. In 1902 he was engaged as organist and choirmaster at the Church of St. James, Piccadilly, and in 1903 received his B.M. degree from Queen's College, Oxford. In 1905 he accepted the position of organist of St. Bartholomew's Church in New York City (until 1908) while continuing to study during the summers in Paris, Berlin, and Munich. His first appearances as a conductor were in Paris in 1908 and in London in 1909.

Herman Thumann, music critic of the *Cincinnati Enquirer*, recommended Stokowski for the position of music director of the Cincinnati Symphony Orchestra. Stokowski conducted the orchestra from 1909 to 1912, revitalizing the musical life of the city. Admired by many as a gifted yet idiosyncratic conductor, he was rejected by others as too much the showman. He married Olga Samaroff, a pianist and critic, in 1911 (they were divorced in 1923) and became an American citizen in 1915.

Stokowski's successes in Cincinnati prepared him for his next position, as conductor and, later, music director of the Philadelphia Orchestra. Their twenty-six-year relationship brought international renown to both director and orchestra; the Philadelphia Orchestra eventually rivaled the great orchestras of New York City, Boston, and Chicago. Stokowski led the orchestra from 1912 to 1936 and shared the position of music director with his successor, Eugene Ormandy, from 1936 to 1938. In 1922 he received the Edward Bok Award of $10,000 as "the person who has done the most for Philadelphia."

Stokowski was a strong advocate of modern music. He conducted the premieres of Rachmaninoff's Symphony no. 3, Piano Concerto no. 4, and Rhapsody on a Theme of Paganini; Ives's Fourth Symphony; Copland's Dance Symphony; and Antheil's Fourth Symphony; and the American premieres of Stravinsky's *The Rite of Spring*, Mahler's Eighth Symphony, Berg's *Wozzeck*, and Schoenberg's *Gurrelieder*, to name only a few. In 1971 it was estimated that Stokowski had presented more than 2,000 premieres in at least 7,000 concerts. Stokowski's own compositions include a symphony, concertos for piano and for violin, choral works, and organ pieces.

The Philadelphia audiences in the 1920's and 1930's were not always receptive to these new works. When listeners began to grumble during a performance of Webern's Symphony, Stokowski walked off the stage; after the audience quieted down, he returned and began the piece again. During his tenure with the Philadelphia Orchestra, he took it upon himself to reprimand audiences for making too much noise, for not being receptive enough to new music, and for knitting during concerts. These reprimands were given in Stokowski's vague (clearly non-British) accent that no one could quite place. (His use of this accent, however, was not consistent, and some people questioned whether Stokowski contrived his accent to add an international flair to his public image.)

In addition to championing new works, Stokowski was well known for his orchestral transcriptions, particularly of the works of Johann Sebastian Bach. Harold Schonberg stated, "His Bach transcriptions were considered monstrosities by most musicians, who in addition were outraged over his free hand with the orchestration of sacred masterpieces. Intellectuals simply laughed at him." These transcriptions renewed a phrase coined during Stokowski's Cincinnati days: "to Stokowski-ize." The Bach transcriptions were very popular with many; Donald Brook stated that Stokowski, "by making the many excellent [Bach] transcriptions . . . has probably done more than any other musician in the United States to promote the understanding and appreciation of Bach's immortal works by the masses of American music-lovers."

These disparate critical opinions concerning Stokowski's Bach transcriptions illustrate the great divide regarding the merits of the whole of his work. Virgil Thomson, for example, cited Stokowski's ambition and vanity as well as his "lack of a sound musical culture" and "lapses of musical taste." Thomson was surprised that, given Stokowski's "violation of musical tradition," he was held in such high regard. Indeed, Stokowski always had the support of respected musicians. Rachmaninoff considered the Philadelphia Orchestra, under both Stokowski and Ormandy, the greatest with which he had performed. Rather than try to arrive at the ultimate judgment of Stokowski, it would be wiser to consider that his art was expansive, encompassing both vision and vanity. David Ewen put it succinctly when he said, in 1943, "Stokowski is Stokowski, which is to say he is a genius and a charlatan in one, a great artist and a circus performer."

In 1926, Stokowski married Evangeline Brewster Johnson, heiress to the Johnson and Johnson fortune; they had two children and were divorced in 1937.

When Stokowski felt he could "improve" the orchestration of even the greatest composers, he did not hesitate, stating, "You must realize that Beethoven and Brahms did not understand instruments." Although he has been criticized for having added percussion where none was called for by the composer, doubled passages with instruments of his choice, and made extensive cuts in the music, it is forgotten that most conductors of the period did the same, even the "purist" Toscanini. Even Brook allows that his interpretations were not always consistent and that he allowed himself "to be 'carried away' by the music and, as a result, strongly emotional passages are sometimes exaggerated."

The overall effect was of the utmost importance to Stokowski; while he at times went painstakingly over the smallest details of a score, he would, on other occasions, concentrate almost exclusively on the "larger meaning" of the work at hand, often talking to his musicians about philosophical or literary topics that, at first, seemed unrelated to the purpose of the music. Sibelius is reported to have said of Stokowski, "He is a very fine man, I am sure, a very interesting man, and interested in many things—but not, I think, in music." Reputedly, Stokowski sometimes rehearsed only particular passages of a work, even new works; this led some to criticize passages that were not technically perfect. His supporters argued that it was Stokowski's spontaneity and freedom from rigid approaches to the music that led to the great sonority and lyricism of the orchestra and to the profound interpretation of the composition.

Stokowski conducted most of the repertoire without a score. In 1929 he went one step further and abandoned the use of a baton; this flamboyant approach, criticized by some as yet another example of his histrionics and vanity, was seen by many as the perfect medium by which Stokowski shaped the "Philadelphia sound." (Some musicians did, however, consider him an extremely difficult conductor to follow.) Stokowski encouraged free bowing and experimented with seating in an effort to improve the sonority of his orchestra; he placed the violins to the left and the cellos to the right and variously rotated or eliminated the position of concertmaster.

Experimenting with lighting effects, Stokowski had spotlights focused on his head and hands, casting huge shadows on the walls and ceilings. Although he was called vain for some of these effects, he argued that the purpose was to allow the musicians to see his expressive gestures.

For all the debate about Stokowski's contributions to orchestral music, the consensus today is that Stokowski created one of the world's major orchestras, an ensemble of great power and subtlety. Harold Schonberg stated, "More than any conductor in the history of music, Stokowski was governed by sound, pure sound. Sound meant more to him than construction, shape, or logic. . . . Stokowski got more *sound* out of the music than others did. The other great conductors could get more *music* out of the music."

Stokowski's personality attracted the attention of newspaper columnists and society writers, and he did little to avoid publicity. He was tall, elegant, and always meticulously dressed, and had a halo of blond hair. He achieved the fame normally reserved for movie stars, receiving large salaries and exciting the public with his romantic adventures, such as his 1938 trip to Europe with Greta Garbo.

Stokowski, an early advocate of orchestral recordings, made his first recording with the Philadelphia Orchestra in 1917. He continued throughout his career to research methods of improving the quality of orchestral recording and became an expert in acoustics and recording techniques (at times in conjunction with record companies). Stokowski was featured in several films: Disney's *Fantasia* (1941), for which he was music director, is his most famous appearance; he had important roles in *100 Men and a Girl* (1937), *The Great Broadcast of 1937* (1936), and *Carnegie Hall* (1947).

In 1938, Stokowski left Philadelphia to begin an independent career that included not only guest conducting but founding new orchestras. In 1940 he founded the All-American Youth Orchestra, with which he made a well-publicized tour of South America in the summer of 1940; the orchestra also toured the United States and Canada in 1941. In the 1940's, Stokowski occasionally conducted the NBC Symphony Orchestra, founded and conducted the New York City Symphony Orchestra (1944) and the Hollywood Bowl Symphony Orchestra (1945), and was a frequent guest conductor of the New York Philharmonic from 1946 to 1950.

In 1945, Stokowski married the millionairess Gloria Vanderbilt; he was sixty-three, and she was twenty-one. They had two children and were divorced in 1955.

From 1955 to 1960, Stokowski was the principal conductor of the Houston Symphony Orchestra, and in 1962 he was cofounder of the American Symphony Orchestra. In 1972 he resigned as its conductor and returned to London, where, in celebration of his ninetieth birthday, he led the London Symphony Orchestra in the identical program he had conducted with this orchestra sixty years earlier.

Shortly before his ninety-fourth birthday, Stokowski recorded an album of well-known overtures with the National Philharmonic. For Mozart's *Don Giovanni* Overture, he supplied a concert finale, as had Otto Klemperer and Ferruccio Busoni, to its inconclusive ending. Drawing on the music that underscores Don Giovanni's descent into hell—the point at which Mozart introduces trombones—he utilized this passage to give the overture power and personality.

Stokowski continued to conduct until July 1975, at the Vence Festival in France, and recorded until 1977. He died in Nether Wallop, Hampshire, England.

In 1965, Stokowski had presented the world premiere of Charles Ives's Fourth Symphony. What he said about Ives's work and about composers in general can be applied to his own career: "His music is full of contradictions. . . . Some composers have no contradictions. Everything is according to their system. . . . We must give our education of music, of philosophy and of everything connected with human life, subtlety. We must give it elasticity, so we can bring into our conception of culture all the possibilities of life which are often very contradictory."

[Stokowski published *Music for All of Us* (1943). See David Ewen, *Dictators of the Baton* (1943); Donald Brook, *International Gallery of Conductors* (1951); Harold C. Schonberg, *The Great Conductors* (1967); Edward Johnson, ed., *Stokowski* (1973), with discography and lists of compositions and transcriptions; Robert Chesterman, ed., *Conversations with Conductors* (1976), for a 1969 "interview" by Glenn Gould; A. Hodgson, "The Stokowski Sound," *Records and Recording* 20 (1977); Abram Chasins, *Leopold Stokowski* (1979); Oliver Daniel, *Stokowski* (1982); Preben Opperby, *Leopold Stokowski* (1982), with discography; and W. A. Smith, "Leopold Stokowski: A Re-Evaluation," *American Music* 1 (1983). An obituary is in the *New York Times*, Sept. 14, 1977.]

JOSEPH CORONITI

STONE, EDWARD DURELL (Mar. 9, 1902–Aug. 6, 1978), architect, was born in Fayetteville, Ark., the son of Benjamin Hicks Stone and Ruth Johnson. After studying art at the University of Arkansas from 1920 to 1923, Stone joined his older brother, a practicing architect, in Boston. There he took courses at night through the Boston Architectural Club while pursuing an apprenticeship with the firm of Coolidge, Shepley, Bulfinch, and Abbott. In 1926, Stone won a competition entitling him to study architecture, first at Harvard (1926) and then at the Massachusetts Institute of Technology (1927). At MIT, under the sponsorship of Professor Jacques Carlu, Stone won the Rotch Scholarship, which allowed him two years' study and travel in Europe (1927–1929).

Stone's early career was marked by rapid growth in ability and reputation. When Stone returned to America in 1929, he found employment with Schultze and Weaver and helped design the interior of the Waldorf-Astoria Hotel in New York City; he then joined a consortium of architects working on Rockefeller Center and created the interior of Radio City Music Hall. Further designs followed, such as the Mandel House in Mount Kisco, N.Y. (1933), and plantation buildings for Henry R. Luce at Moncks Corner, S.C. (1936). In 1936, Stone opened his own firm, Edward Durell Stone and Associates, in New York City and, with Philip Goodwin, completed his first major building, the Museum of Modern Art (1937). It was hailed upon its completion as an embodiment in glass and concrete of the art it was meant to extol. At the same time, Stone built a house for the museum's president, A. Conger Goodyear, in Old Westbury, N.Y.; it was the first design in which Stone used the overhanging roof that would become a trademark.

Over the next decade Stone's commitment to the International Style was affected by two major influences. During a trip across America in 1940, he met Frank Lloyd Wright and visited Taliesin West; his observations and conversations there converted him to acceptance of indigenous materials, a change reflected in the redwood exterior of a "House of Ideas" he built for *Collier's* magazine later that year. He was also affected by his military experience; as a major in the United States Army Air Corps (1942–1945), Stone for the first time designed buildings for structure, not beauty. His first commission after the war, for the El Panama Hotel in Panama City (1946), reflected these developments; his design incorporated cantilevered balconies derived from control towers, and used local decorations. Two more resort hotels, in San Salvador and Montego Bay, Jamaica, followed.

Stone's growing reputation was underscored by several major commissions: a 900-bed hospital in Lima, Peru (1950); a medical center in Palo Alto, Calif. (1955), and a new Fine Arts Center for the University of Arkansas (1951), which awarded him a belated college degree (*honoris causa*) in return. Stone had married Orlean Vandiver on Dec. 5, 1931; they had two children. They were divorced in 1951, and on June 24, 1953, Stone married Maria Elena Torchio, who converted him to what Stone called "romanticism." They were divorced, and in 1972 he married Violet Campbell Moffat. The final stage in Stone's career brought him his greatest fame and greatest controversy.

The first fruit of this change was the American Embassy in New Delhi, India (1954). The embassy building, placed at the edge of a reflecting pool, was protected from direct sun by a concrete grillwork across the entire facade, and by an overhanging roof such as in the

Goodyear house. The building was set on a platform, so that it seemed to float above the sheltered parking area. This prizewinning design was followed by the Graf house in Dallas, Tex. (1956), which employed a similar screen across the second floor, and by Stone's own townhouse in Manhattan, which he renovated in 1956 with a four-story screen covering the entire facade. Stone repeated these motifs in a number of major projects over the next decade, such as the National Geographic Society's headquarters in Washington, D.C. (1964), which floats on a two-story base with overhang. Its roof is marked by a second overhang, and the window mullions are made into false columns.

This last motif brought Stone criticism, because it masked the true form of the building; however, Stone wanted to reduce the visible weight of his structures, making them appear to float just above their environment. Perhaps the best-known example of this effort is the building he designed in 1959 for the art collector Huntington Hartford. The pierced-concrete facade of the New York Cultural Center (as it is now known), at Columbus Circle in New York City, appears to hover on structural piers that are split at the second-story level by large circular voids. The effect is, for many viewers, unsettling, though for others it is liberating.

This is not to say that Stone repeated himself; indeed, few architects ever faced the number of design challenges Stone faced. For the American Pavilion at the Brussels World's Fair in 1958, for example, Stone was asked to encase multiple display areas within a single structure, at the same time preserving eleven willow trees that had been planted on the site at the end of World War I. His solution was to make the pavilion a 340-foot-diameter cylinder, and he suspended a translucent roof inside to transmit natural light to the trees.

With his reputation at its peak, Stone was asked to design buildings whose demands exceeded any architect's ability to succeed. He built two efficient, but hardly beautiful, skyscrapers: the fifty-story General Motors Building in New York City (1964–1968) and the eighty-story Standard Oil Building (later the Amoco Building) in Chicago (1974). Neither building was a total success; the General Motors Building was attacked for its plaza design, and the Standard Oil Building's marble facade did not withstand Chicago winters. Stone's most controversial commission was for the John F. Kennedy Center for the Performing Arts in Washington, D.C. (1971). No roof overhangs or false columns could disguise the fact that Stone had been asked to design a warehouse, some 630 feet long and 300 feet wide; the lobbies that separate the three performance spaces are nearly 100 feet high. Although the building was a functional success, Stone was condemned for "architectural populism."

Throughout his forty-five year career, Stone fulfilled the architect's prime directive: he gave his clients what they wanted. And occasionally, as at the Pepsico World Headquarters in Purchase, N.Y. (1971–1973), Stone could give his clients something more: an image of themselves and their ideals in stone, metal, and glass, set before the world for admiration. Although he did not challenge the limits of twentieth-century American architecture, Edward Durell Stone certainly helped define them.

Stone died in New York City.

[Stone wrote about his early years in *The Evolution of an Architect* (1962); his transformation to "romanticism" is recorded in *Recent and Future Architecture* (1967). See also obituaries in the *New York Times*, Aug. 8, 1978; and the *AIA Journal*, Sept. 1978.]

HARTLEY SPATT

STRAND, PAUL (Oct. 16, 1890–March 31, 1976), photographer and filmmaker, was born in New York City, the only child of Jacob Strand, a salesman, and Matilda Arnstein, both of Bohemian-Jewish descent. Raised in a middle-class home, Strand went to public schools until age fourteen, when his parents transferred him to the Ethical Culture School, a private, progressive school that stressed humanism and social reform. At age seventeen Strand took a photography course with Lewis W. Hine, a science teacher at the school who was to become a major photographic force in the social reform movement.

Hine took the class to the Photo-Secession Gallery owned by Alfred Stieglitz, one of the most important photographers of the day and an important force in the rapidly evolving art world of the United States. Strand, seeing works of the contemporary masters of photography at the gallery, resolved to make photography his life's work.

Strand worked as an office boy in his father's firm from 1909 to 1911. When the firm was bought out, he took a job for a few months in an

Strand

insurance company, then quit to become a professional photographer. Strand supported himself with his photography until 1918, doing portrait work and traveling around the country taking pictures of college campuses. Around 1913 he became a regular visitor to Stieglitz's Photo-Secessionist Gallery and was gradually welcomed into the group of avant-garde artists who gravitated there. During that time he developed a close protégé-mentor relationship with the older Stieglitz that lasted into the 1930's.

While still in his twenties, Strand created many of his best-known photographs. Strongly influenced by the abstract paintings of Picasso and Braque, Strand employed extreme close-ups, odd camera angles, and unusual croppings to create photographic abstractions in which the objects photographed become secondary to the interplay of light, shadow, line, and form. Among the best known of this group of photographs are "Abstraction, Bowls" and "Abstraction, Porch Shadows." Although Strand soon abandoned his abstract work, dismissing it as "experimental," he continued to employ the compositional principles explored in those images throughout his photographic career. During the same period, Strand created an innovative series of candid street portraits taken mainly in the poor sections of Manhattan. Catching subjects unawares was difficult, since the bulky cameras and heavy tripods of the time were quite conspicuous. Strand succeeded in capturing the images he wanted by mounting a false lens on one side of his camera while taking photos through another lens that he kept partially hidden under his arm. The candor with which the subjects are revealed in the resulting close-ups is often both startling and confrontational. Photos from this period were exhibited in a one-person show at Stieglitz's gallery in 1916.

Strand was drafted into the United States Army in 1918 and served eighteen months as a hospital X-ray technician, after which he spent a few years doing advertising photography. In 1922 he began a ten-year career as a free-lance cinematographer. He spent a $2,500 inheritance to purchase a state-of-the-art, highly maneuverable motion-picture camera that was ideally suited to filming action scenes, and took whatever jobs came along, filming sporting events, college graduations, newsreel footage, and action sequences for Hollywood films.

In 1922, Strand married Rebecca Salsbury, an artist. When their modest income allowed, the couple traveled in the Northeast and in the Southwest, where Strand pursued his still photography.

In 1932, with more-versatile movie cameras drastically cutting the demand for Strand's specialty work and his marriage nearing an end, Strand was looking for new directions. He traveled to Mexico, where he pursued his personal photography with renewed vigor, creating a series of photographs published in 1940 as *Photographs of Mexico*, a limited-edition portfolio of twenty exquisitely handprinted photogravures. He also embarked on a filmmaking project for the Mexican government; the result was a sixty-five minute movie titled *Redes*, released in the United States in 1936 as *The Wave*. Strand cowrote and filmed this part documentary, part fictional work celebrating a strike by poor Mexican fishermen who were fighting against their economic exploitation.

Soon after Strand's return to the United States in 1934, he and a group of friends traveled to the Soviet Union to observe Russian film and theater. During his two-month stay, he met with the filmmaker Sergei Eisenstein as well as other Russian artists. When he returned to the United States, Strand worked for Pare Lorentz on a documentary film about the Dust Bowl titled *The Plow That Broke the Plains*. In 1937 he formed a cooperative documentary filmmaking company, Frontier Films, with Ralph Steiner and Leo Hurwitz. Strand's leftist political leanings are abundantly clear in the seven documentaries produced by the company, most of which emphasized the need to fight for social equality and civil liberties. He was most intimately involved with the two-hour *Native Land* (1942), which dealt with the subject of union busting and the violation of the civil liberties of labor-union activists in the 1930's.

Strand married his second wife, Virginia Stevens, in 1936; this marriage ended in 1949. After World War II Strand grew disenchanted with what he saw as an increasingly repressive political and social climate in the United States. In 1950, after completing a photography book, *Time in New England*, he left the United States for France, where he lived until his death. About his self-imposed exile, Strand commented, "It was not in any way a rejection of America; it was a rejection of what was happening in America just then." In February 1951 he married Hazel Kingsbury, a professional photographer. During his last twenty-five years Strand created five photography books, each linked to a specific geographic location and each created in collaboration with a different writer: *La France de profil* (1952), *Un Paese* (1955), *Tir a'Mhurain* (1962), *Living Egypt* (1969), and *Ghana: An African Portrait* (1976). Strand died at his home in Orgeval, France.

Strand considered himself an artist whose chosen medium was photography, and he tended to associate mainly with painters, sculptors, and writers rather than with other photographers. He was a quiet, intense person whose still photography generally avoids high drama and instead emphasizes a vibrant yet subtle unity of elements that invites the viewer to peruse the entire image and linger over its details. A demanding craftsman and an artistic perfectionist, he was legendary for laboring over a negative for hours or even days, producing one or two prints, and then never printing the negative again. His work is not easily categorized, as his best photographs run the gamut from portraiture to landscape to cityscape to close-up. Though he has not received great popular recognition, his reputation among photographers and art critics places him as one of the major photographers of the twentieth century. His work has been exhibited widely in the United States as well as in Mexico and Europe, including a major retrospective at the Museum of Modern Art in New York in 1945, the first such exhibit of a photographer's work in the museum's history.

[Strand's papers are at the Center for Creative Photography in Tucson, Ariz. His negatives and prints are at the Aperture Foundation, Millerton, N.Y. Materials relating to his career in filmmaking are in the Library of Congress. Biographical and critical material as well as collections of Strand's photographs can be found in *Paul Strand: Sixty Years of Photographs* (1976); Sarah Greenough, *Paul Strand: An American Vision* (1990); and Maren Strange, ed., *Paul Strand: Essays on His Life and Work* (1990). An obituary is in the *New York Times*, Apr. 2, 1976.]

DAVID SAFIER

STRONG, ELMER KENNETH, JR. ("KEN") (Aug. 6, 1906–Oct. 5, 1979), baseball and football player, and professional football coach, was born in West Haven, Conn., the son of Elmer Kenneth Strong. Strong began his athletic career at West Haven High School, but he first achieved national renown at New York University. There he was an outfielder on the baseball team. It was in football, however, that Strong gained his greatest fame. After spending 1925 on the freshman team and 1926 as a blocking back, Strong became the star of Coach Chick Meehan's two greatest New York University teams.

Strong was a triple-threat football player, equally skilled at running, passing, and kicking. During his senior year the six-foot, 200-pound back and placekicker led the East in scoring with 162 points. In New York University's most important game that season, a victory over Wally Steffens's as-yet undefeated Carnegie Tech team, Steffens declared Strong to be "the greatest football player I ever saw." Strong finished his collegiate career as an All-American, with what was then a collegiate record total of 2,100 yards gained.

Strong began his professional sports career in 1929 after graduating from New York University. That season he signed with the New Haven, Conn., farm team of the New York Yankees, batting .285 with twenty-one home runs. Strong played in 1930 with Hazelton in the New York–Penn League, where he had a .373 batting average with a league record of forty-one home runs. On June 8, 1930, he hit four successive home runs against Wilkes-Barre, also a league record. The next season, while playing for Detroit's top farm team in Toronto, Strong's promising professional baseball career came to an end. A severe wrist injury made it impossible for him to throw from the outfield.

Strong's second career, as a professional football player, also began in 1929, as an off-season adjunct to his more promising baseball career. Although offered a contract with the New York Giants, he signed instead with the Staten Island Stapletons, becoming that team's dominant player. When the Staten Island franchise folded following the 1932 season, Strong joined the Giants in 1933 and tied for the National Football League's lead in scoring sixty-four points. That season Strong also began a string of outstanding performances in championship play. After winning the Eastern Division, the Giants met the Chicago Bears at Chicago's Wrigley Field for the 1933 National Football League championship. Strong kicked three extra points and scored a touchdown in the fourth quarter on an eight-yard pass from Harry Newman. The

Bears came back to win the game in the closing minutes, however.

Strong secretly married Amelia Hunneman, a showgirl known professionally as Rella Harrison, in 1929. The couple lived apart as soon as the honeymoon was over. In 1931, divorced from Hunneman, Strong married Mabel Anderson. They had one child.

In 1934 the Giants, led by Strong and Ed Danowski, again topped the National Football League's Eastern Division and met the Bears in the championship game, this time at the Polo Grounds in New York City. Freezing weather had turned the field into a sheet of ice, and at the beginning of the fourth quarter, the Giants trailed 13 to 3. In a desperate attempt to gain better traction, they switched from cleats to sneakers. Strong scored on touchdown runs of forty-two and eleven yards, and kicked two extra points as the Giants came back to win 30 to 13.

In the 1935 championship game Strong scored all seven of the Giants' points in a 26–7 loss to the Detroit Lions. He left the Giants in 1936 after a salary dispute and signed with the New York Yankees of the short-lived American Football League. When the Yankees collapsed after one season, Strong attempted to rejoin the Giants, but found he had been banned by the National Football League for having left his team. Strong's suspension only lasted one year, and he returned to the Giants for the 1939 season. Bleeding ulcers forced him to retire in 1940. At that point he had scored 322 career points, more than anyone else in National Football League history. When World War II caused a shortage of players, Strong was asked to return to the Giants. He did, serving as a placekicking specialist from 1944 until 1947. Strong tied for the league lead in field goals his first year back, with six, and he kicked extra points in the 1944 and 1946 National Football League championship games. During this last phase of his career Strong had little contact with the violent side of football. He rarely wore shoulder pads while kicking and was one of the few players to take the field with a wristwatch.

Following his playing career Strong worked in public relations and as a liquor salesman. In 1950 he coauthored the book *Football Kicking Techniques* with Emil Brodbeck. It was the first book to use motion-picture studies to demonstrate the proper methods of kicking. Strong returned to the Giants as a kicking coach from 1962 through 1965.

Strong's official career statistics of 1,321 yards gained on 363 rushing attempts, and his 479 points scored on 33 touchdowns, 167 extra points, and 38 field goals pale beside modern records. They reflect, though, the slower pace and less accurate record keeping of the pre–World War II game. Strong was elected to the National Hall of Fame and National Football Foundation College Football Hall of Fame for his play with New York University. In 1967 he was elected to the Pro Football Hall of Fame in Canton, Ohio. The National Football League's Hall of Fame Selection Committee named Strong to the All-Time Team of the 1930's as a running back.

Strong died in New York City.

[Memorabilia and newspaper clippings are in the National Football League Pro Football Hall of Fame in Canton, Ohio. See Robert Leckie, *The Story of Football* (1968); and the oral histories in Richard Whittingham, *What a Game They Played* (1984). An obituary is in the *New York Times*, Oct. 6, 1979.]

HAROLD W. AURAND, JR.

SUGIURA, KANEMATSU (June 5, 1892–Oct. 21, 1979), biochemist and cancer research pioneer, was born in Tsushima-shi, just west of Nagoya, Japan, the youngest of seven children of Seisuke Sugiura and Miyono Aoki. His father, a dyemaker, kendo master, and former samurai, died of cancer when the boy was only eight, plunging the family into financial difficulties. Thus, even though he was a top student, at the age of thirteen he was an apprentice in the hardware trade.

While Sugiura's older brother Kamasaburo was serving as the official interpreter for the American railroad tycoon Edward H. Harriman in negotiations with the Japanese government in 1905, Harriman became entranced by demonstrations of the ancient Japanese martial arts of jujitsu and kenjitsu. He decided to bring five Japanese boys, including Kanematsu, to the United States to entertain President Theodore Roosevelt and other prominent Americans with displays of judo and kendo. After six months, Harriman offered full financial support to any of the five who chose to stay in America. Only Sugiura accepted the offer, and he did so despite his homesickness, because he knew it was his only chance for a college education. He lived in New York City with the Harriman family physician, William G. Lyle, attended P.S.

69 and, from 1908 to 1911, Townsend Harris Hall High School. After school he worked in the laboratories of Roosevelt Hospital.

When Harriman died of cancer in 1909, leaving $1 million to found the Harriman Research Laboratory (HRL) at Roosevelt Hospital, Sugiura decided to dedicate his life to cancer research. He started working under Lyle at HRL as an assistant chemist in 1911, and in 1912 began studying the chemotherapy of cancer. At the same time he was attending evening classes as an undergraduate at the Polytechnic Institute of Brooklyn, from which he received his B.S. in chemistry in 1915. Two years of summer classes at Columbia University earned him the M.A. in chemistry in 1917.

In the early twentieth century the medical community in general considered the hypothesis odd that since cancer was probably caused by certain chemical insults, it could be cured or managed by chemicals. Nevertheless, Sugiura and his colleages at HRL remained steadfast in their early commitment to developing drug therapies for cancer.

HRL promoted Sugiura to associate chemist in 1917. However, that same year the Harriman family withdrew its support and the facility was forced to close. Sugiura was immediately hired by Dr. James Ewing as an assistant chemist at the Memorial Hospital for Cancer and Allied Diseases, formerly the New York Cancer Hospital. He continued to hold his old HRL title until 1928, and from 1923 to 1931 he was the Harriman Research Fund fellow at New York University and Bellevue Hospital College of Medicine. Memorial promoted him to research chemist in 1925. The same year Kyoto Imperial University awarded him an Sc.D. that, although only honorary, was regularly treated as if earned—and on that basis alone, he was always thereafter known as "doctor."

On Oct. 20, 1923, Sugiura married Zoë Marie Claeys; they had one daughter.

Sugiura's early research sought to identify specific carcinogens, first among inorganic salts, and then among the diets of various lands and peoples, and eventually among hormones and enzymes. At Memorial he also investigated possible uses of X rays and other radiation in treating cancer and, under Ewing's direction, originated some tumor transplantation techniques, such as the trocar method, that were still in use half a century later. By 1940 he had published eighty-two scientific papers.

Thanks to the intercession of several prominent American physicians and scientists, including Dr. Cornelius P. Rhoads, then director of Memorial Hospital and chief of the Medical Division of the U.S. Chemical Warfare Service, Sugiura was not interned during World War II, although he was still a Japanese citizen. His movements were severely restricted, however, and he lived out the war under virtual house arrest, cut off from the main focus of his research but still able to continue his work. The government permitted him to travel between his home on the Grand Concourse in the Bronx and the old Memorial Hospital at 106th Street and Central Park West, Manhattan, but refused to let him go to his usual workplace, the new Memorial Hospital at 444 East Sixty-eighth Street, Manhattan, where research with radioactive isotopes was being conducted. He weathered this political storm well, and kept his high spirits intact. He became an American citizen in 1953.

After the war Sugiura resumed the full scope of his search for effective chemotherapies for malignancies. In 1947 he was made an associate member of the recently founded Memorial Sloan-Kettering Institute for Cancer Research, serving as head of the Solid Tumor Section of the Division of Experimental Chemotherapy. In 1959 he became a member of the institute, and in 1962 an emeritus member.

During this later period of his career, Sugiura concentrated on the chemotherapeutic properties of compounds whose palliative effects had been discovered either during or just after the war, including nitrogen mustards, purines, pyrimidines, steroids, antimetabolites such as methotrexate, and antibiotics such as mitomycin C. At Sloan-Kettering he analyzed literally thousands of imaginable carcinostats and suspected carcinogens for more than one hundred transplantable tumors. This research enjoyed marked success and resulted in many practical advances in patient care.

Even long after his retirement, Sugiura kept active in his field, commuting nearly every day from his home in Harrison, N.Y., to the Sloan-Kettering Institute's Walker Laboratory in Rye, N.Y. At the time of his death in White Plains, N.Y., he was involved in research with laetrile and believed in its limited efficacy.

[Sugiura's papers are archived in the Aichi Cancer Center, Nagoya, Japan. A brief autobiography is "Reminiscence and Experience in Experimental

Chemotherapy of Cancer," *Medical Clinics of North America*, May 1971. Obituaries are in the *New York Times*, Oct. 23, 1979; and *Cancer Research*, July 1980. The entry written and proofed by Sugiura himself for *Who's Who in the East, 1942–1943* settles the question of whether he was born in 1890 or 1892.]

ERIC V. D. LUFT

SUTTON, WILLIAM FRANCIS, JR. ("WILLIE") (June 30, 1901–Nov. 2, 1980), notorious bank robber, was born in Brooklyn, N.Y., the son of William Francis Sutton, a blacksmith, and Mary Ellen Bowles, a native of Ireland. He attended both public and parochial schools. An intelligent boy with a retentive memory, he earned excellent grades and learned to dress well, though not ostentatiously. He later credited his aunt Alice, a half sister of actress Billie Burke, with teaching him social graces.

But Sutton also acquired antisocial habits early, breaking into a department store at age ten, then entertaining his friends with his stolen money. Interestingly, his early ambition was to become a criminal lawyer; in later years he thought he would have been a good one.

At age fifteen, after being caught stealing quarters from his teacher's purse, he left school to work as an errand boy for a Brooklyn bank. Then he became a mail clerk for an insurance company but lost his job when he was caught stealing rolls of postage stamps. A romance at age seventeen led Sutton into big-time thievery. In 1919 the pair wanted to marry, and when her father objected, she helped Sutton steal $16,000 from her father's safe, and then fled with him to Albany, N.Y. There the father and the police caught up with them. Sutton was placed on probation and ordered never to see the girl again.

In July 1921, Sutton was charged with murdering a man with whom he had quarreled. He fled, changing his identity. Then he was falsely accused of robbing a safe, so he changed his identity again. In 1923, he was arrested on charges of robbery and murder. He spent nine months in jail before a jury found him not guilty.

Sutton began planning a career as a bank robber. One day, watching an armed guard letting employees into a bank before business hours, he saw the guard admit a Western Union messenger. Soon, in one uniform or another, Sutton was persuading guards at the banks and jewelry stores to admit him before business hours. When the manager walked in, Willie was waiting with a gun. He earlier had learned how to circumvent burglar alarms and to use tools to break locks and open safes. He also had become an amateur metallurgist.

In 1926, Sutton was arrested for breaking into a bank and sentenced to five to ten years in Sing Sing Prison at Ossining, N.Y. Three months later he was transferred to Dannemora Prison in northeastern New York. He was there in August 1929 when inmates rioted, burning and destroying everything they could. A few days later he was paroled.

Sutton married Louise Leudemann on Oct. 21, 1929. They had one child and were divorced in 1947 soon after he was again sentenced to prison. Their daughter, Jeane, was to grow up hardly knowing her father—she saw him only two or three times until he was an old man. In *Look* magazine (May 20, 1952), a Jeanne Courtney claimed to be Sutton's second wife.

In prison he studied psychology and other subjects, either by reading books from prison libraries or by correspondence courses. He supplemented his studies with carefully plotted plans and schemes for escaping. At Sing Sing in 1932, he and another inmate used prison ladders to climb over the wall on a dark night. In 1945 he crawled through a sewer under the walls of Eastern State Penitentiary, but he was caught immediately. On Feb. 3, 1947, he and four other convicts, disguised as guards, used ladders to climb over the walls of "escapeproof" Holmesburg Prison during a snowstorm.

Out of prison, Sutton used makeup and a varied wardrobe to conceal his identity, and he avoided areas where police would look for him. As a consequence the William F. Sutton who had escaped from Holmesburg in 1947 attracted widespread public attention as "Willie the Actor" in 1950's magazine feature stories.

Despite his makeup and precautions, on Feb. 10, 1952, Sutton was recognized by twenty-four-year-old Arnold Schuster, a presser in a tailor shop. After Sutton's subsequent arrest despite some police bungling, Schuster was interviewed on television. On Mar. 8, 1952, Schuster was found shot to death. Sutton denied having anything to do with the murder, and he was not charged. He was found guilty, however, of a 1950 bank robbery and was sentenced to a minimum of thirty years in prison, where he began working with writer Quentin Reynolds on an "autobiography," dedicating it to his daughter.

Despite his lengthy sentence, Sutton was released from prison for the last time on Dec. 24, 1969, because he was suffering from emphysema. From 1923 until his release, Sutton had spent a total of thirty-three years in prison.

He spent his remaining years with his sister, Helen Mottola, in Spring Hill, Fla., north of Tampa. There he and writer Edward Linn composed a second "autobiography," *Where the Money Was*. The book both repeats and updates the 1953 book, again using fictitious names for some people. Despite the book's title, Sutton denied ever saying that he robbed banks "because that's where the money was." He said that he robbed banks "because I loved it. . . . I was more alive when I was inside a bank, robbing it, than at any other time in my life." Late in life Sutton estimated that he had stolen almost $2 million from banks and merchants—and he had little to show for it.

Sutton died in Spring Hill, Fla., and was buried in an unmarked grave in the family burial plot in the Flatbush section of Brooklyn. Because he wanted no publicity, it was more than two weeks before the news media, which had given him so much publicity, learned Sutton was dead.

[Further biographical information can be found in Willie Sutton, *Where the Money Was* (1976), with Edward Linn; Erle Stanley Gardner, "The Case of Willie Sutton," *Look*, May 6 and 20, 1952; and Quentin Reynolds, *I, Willie Sutton* (1953). An obituary is in the *New York Times*, Nov. 19, 1980.]

CLARENCE A. ANDREWS

SYMES, JAMES MILLER (July 8, 1897–Aug. 3, 1976), railroad executive, was born in Glen Osborne, Pa., near Pittsburgh, the son of Frank H. Symes and Clara Heckert. His father was a lifelong employee of the Pennsylvania Railroad (retiring as a baggage master), and the younger Symes resolved to make the railroad his career as well. After completing Sewickley High School in 1914, he enrolled in a secretarial course at the Carnegie Institute of Technology to prepare for a clerical position. In 1916 the Pennsylvania Railroad (PRR) offered him a job in Pittsburgh as clerk and car tracer if he would play on the semiprofessional baseball team it sponsored. He accepted. On Sept. 27, 1919, he married Fern Elizabeth Dick, also a PRR clerk. They had one child.

In 1920, Symes became chief statistician for the PRR's Cleveland-based Lake Division. Two years later, he entered the operating department—the traditional route to executive management—when he was named division freight movement director. His abilities impressed the superintendent, Martin W. Clement—a future PRR president—and the two men began a friendship that boosted Symes's career. In 1923, when Clement became general manager of the Central Region (which included the Lake Division), he promoted Symes to regional train movement director. In 1926, Clement went to the railroad's Philadelphia headquarters as assistant vice-president in charge of operations. Symes soon moved up to become general manager of passenger transportation for the Western Region in Chicago. In 1929, Symes was transferred in the same capacity to the Eastern Region, based in Philadelphia.

When Clement was appointed acting president in 1934, he promoted Symes to chief of freight transportation for the entire railroad. In this capacity Symes became interested in national issues affecting the railroad industry. He served as a member of President Roosevelt's Eastman committee—created to encourage voluntary reduction of the nation's overbuilt rail network—and in 1935 took a leave of absence from the PRR to serve as the Association of American Railroads' vice-president for operations and maintenance. Living in Washington, D.C., for the next four years, Symes had a front-row seat as railroad executives, academics, and politicians discussed various strategies—including consolidations and mergers—to enable railroads to compete more effectively with other modes of transportation.

In 1939, Symes returned to the Western Region, first as general manager and then as vice-president. In 1947, Symes became vice-president of operations, historically one of the final stepping-stones to the railroad's presidency. But he drew fire from his colleagues when he proposed to replace the railroad's 4,100 steam locomotives with diesels. Clement himself finally embraced the $400 million program, eventually recognizing the economies inherent in the plan. It was a huge undertaking, and the PRR did not fully retire steam until 1957.

Meanwhile, the PRR's financial health deteriorated. It recorded its first net operating deficit in 1946, and its postwar operating ratio (the portion of gross revenues used for operations) rarely fell below 85 percent. Obsolete rolling stock, a physical plant exhausted by wartime demands, competition from highway and air transportation, too many money-losing passenger trains, and the economic decline of the industrial Northeast were but a few of the railroad's difficulties.

In 1949, Clement created the post of board chairman as a way to give up running the railroad but remain a national spokesman for the PRR and the railroad industry. The presidency went to Walter S. Franklin, and Symes became vice-president (executive vice-president in 1952). In 1954, Symes finally became president. It was once again the railroad's highest office, the chairmanship having been abolished with Clement's retirement in 1951.

Symes pressed forward on three fronts. First, he implemented a modernization program on as large a scale as the railroad's finances would permit. Projects included construction of two facilities in the "world's largest" category: an automated classification yard at Conway, near Pittsburgh, and the Samuel Rea car building and repair shop at Hollidaysburg, Pa. The PRR also led the industry in adopting intermodal truck trailer-on-flatcar shipments—Truc-Train, in PRR parlance.

Second, Symes preached the gospel of regulatory reform. He warned that if railroads were not given more flexibility in setting rates, and if government subsidies remained lopsided in favor of highway users and airlines, bankruptcy and government ownership were inevitable. His forecasts went largely unheeded.

Finally, Symes returned to an idea that he first studied in the 1930's—consolidation. Mergers, he argued, would allow railroads to eliminate redundant services and facilities and would reduce labor costs. For the PRR, he proposed in 1957 a merger with archrival New York Central. The two lines had many similarities. They served the same type of industrial customers in the Northeast and Midwest, were heavily burdened by passenger services, operated numerous parallel lines, and were experiencing serious financial problems. His suggestion initially met with skepticism among New York Central executives. But by 1960, fearing that it might be shut out by other Northeastern roads studying consolidation, the Central opened talks with the PRR. Within two years, the stockholders of both companies had approved the merger, and hearings began before the Interstate Commerce Commission.

Symes retired from the PRR on Sept. 30, 1963, shortly before the Interstate Commerce Commission (ICC) approved the merger with the New York Central. (Since 1959, he had been the company's chairman of the board, a title revived from the Clement era.) He continued to serve as a PRR director through five years of litigation that followed the ICC's decision. On Feb. 1, 1968, the Pennsylvania and New York Central joined to form the Penn Central. Symes stayed on an additional year as director.

The merger failed to produce the results that Symes had promised. The Penn Central continued the downward spiral of its predecessors and in 1971 became the largest American company to that date to enter bankruptcy. When reorganization plans failed, the federal government—ironically, as Symes had prophesied—stepped in to form the Consolidated Rail Corp. (Conrail) from the Penn Central and other bankrupt Northeastern lines. The Penn Central fiasco finally convinced Congress of the need for regulatory reform. Bolstered by government deregulation of the railroad industry, Conrail eventually began posting impressive profits—as Symes had predicted railroads would do if given freedom of the marketplace.

Symes's thinking about mergers was theoretically sound, but he chose the wrong partner for the PRR. The Pennsylvania and New York Central were too similar. Their merger magnified their problems while diluting their strengths. Nor, surprisingly, did Symes sufficiently appreciate the depth of the century-old rivalry between the two roads. "Red team" versus "Green team" clashes undermined management through the Penn Central era. However, the Penn Central set a precedent for numerous subsequent mergers that strengthened the railroad industry and reaped many of the benefits he had envisioned.

Symes died in Feasterville, Pa.

[Papers relating to Symes's presidency are in the PRR collection at the Hagley Museum and Library, Greenville, Del. See "The Future . . . What Jim Symes Is Doing About It," *Railway Age*, Sept. 14, 1954; Herrymon Maurer, "New Signals for the Pennsy," *Fortune*, Nov. 1955; Joseph R. Daughen and Peter Binzen, *The Wreck of the Penn Central* (1971); and Stephen Salsbury, *No Way to Run a Railroad* (1982). Obituaries are in the *Philadelphia Inquirer*, Aug. 4, 1976; and the *New York Times*, Aug. 5, 1976.]

MICHAEL BEZILLA

T

TANDY, CHARLES DAVID (May 15, 1918–Nov. 4, 1978), entrepreneur and manufacturer, was born in Brownsville, Tex., one of two children of David Lewis Tandy and Carmen McLain. Tandy's father was a partner in a wholesale leather goods business servicing shoe manufacturers. The company was headquartered in Fort Worth, where Charles was educated. He entered Rice University in 1935 but dropped out to work for his father. He later returned to school, graduating from Texas Christian University in 1940. He attended Harvard Graduate School of Business before entering the United States Navy in 1941.

Stationed in Hawaii during World War II, Tandy was assigned the task of selling war bonds, which occasionally took him to hospitals, where he saw many injured veterans working at crafts projects as a means of rehabilitation. Tandy wrote to his father, recommending that the elder Tandy produce leatherworking kits for such purposes. Discharged in 1947, Charles became a vice-president of his father's firm and expanded the leathercraft line from hospitals to prisons, schools, and summer camps. He and his father bought out the partners of his father's company in 1950 and renamed it the Tandy Leather Company.

On Oct. 25, 1945, Tandy married Gwendolyn Purdy Johnston. She had two children from a previous marriage; they remained married until her death in 1967. A man of few interests outside of business, Tandy was considered affable and loquacious by outsiders, but his professional standards were almost impossibly high; employees that did not meet those standards were seldom fired, however, but reassigned to positions that maximized their abilities. Tandy's requirement for his executives included working Saturday mornings and answering their own telephones, as he himself did.

Having made a success of what was largely a mail-order business, Tandy in 1951 embarked on an ambitious plan to open retail outlets. Realizing that crafts customers, used to "doing it themselves," were comfortable in a "nuts and bolts" workshop atmosphere, Tandy positioned the stores in low-rent locations. He paid managers small salaries but offered them a healthy percentage of the profits and equity in the store. Thirty-one stores were opened in the first three years, and by 1962, 140 were in operation. The strong incentives for manager effort helped ensure that Tandy's work ethic—"If you can't get your job done in five days, do it in seven"—was followed to the same extent at the retail level as it was at the corporate level.

Tandy purchased his first company, American Handicrafts, in the early 1950's and acquired additional retail stores and an expanded line of crafts kits. He overreached in 1955, however, when as president he sold Tandy Leather to American Hide and Leather Company, which had been in financial distress, but whose executives assured Tandy that the firm was on the upward swing. When Tandy realized that the only way he could save Tandy Leather (a matter of family pride) was to buy the parent company, he did just that, even though it plunged the firm into losses of more than $250,000.

To recover financially, Tandy began looking for other acquisitions and product lines. Another financially troubled company, Radio Shack, a small Boston-based chain of nine consumer electronics stores, approached Tandy, and after some hesitations, he bought the business in 1963 that would become a household name. Once again, however, he was faced with a financial crisis, including almost $1 million in unpaid bills; much of the accounts receivable was uncollectable. Following the pattern he had established with Tandy Leather stores, Tandy brought the total number of Radio Shack outlets to 530 by 1969 and more than 2,800 by the end of 1973.

In the 1970's, Tandy began approaching American manufacturers about producing privately labeled goods for his stores; he found them unwilling to do so at his price. Tandy Corporation thus began to manufacture many of its own electronics kits, and by the late 1970's, the firm had sixteen factories in North America, one in Japan, and one in Korea.

The key to Tandy's phenomenal success in building a billion-dollar company with more than 7,000 stores worldwide was not only his ability to spot profitable new products, like CB radios and personal microcomputers, but also his ability to turn around losing products, situations, and companies. By the time of his death, he was the undisputed merchant prince of Fort Worth. The twin seventeen-story towers of the eight-block-square Tandy Center formed "one whole side" of the city's new skyline, "the name in lights carrying for miles through the darkness," according to one *Forbes* writer.

As Fort Worth's leading businessman, Tandy served on various civic boards and associations including the Fort Worth Art Association, Fort Worth Community Theater, Trinity Improvement Association, Texas Christian University (trustee), Rockefeller University, and Fort Worth Chamber of Commerce, and on the boards of directors of First United Bancorp, Pier 1 Imports, Stafford-Lowdon, Kimbell's, Alcon Labs, and Dillard's. He was honored as a distinguished alumnus by Texas Christian University in 1967 and was given the silver award from *Financial World* in 1976 and the Distinguished Business Leadership Award from the University of Texas at Arlington in 1976, and was named business executive of the year by Texas Wesleyan University in 1976.

Tandy married Anne Burnett Windfor on June 12, 1969. She was described by *Fortune* magazine as "a wealthy woman in her own right from a socially prominent, pioneer Texas family . . . [with] one of the most extensive collections of modern art in the country." Their showcase home was designed by I. M. Pei and could accommodate both large numbers of guests and the formidable art collection. Despite his wealth, Tandy consistently worked twelve- and fourteen-hour days, six days a week. This schedule, combined with his chain-smoking of cigars, probably contributed to his first heart attack in 1968, to gall bladder surgery in 1972, and to a heart attack in 1978 that resulted in his death. The Charles D. and Anne Burnett Tandy Foundation was established after his death to fund civic, community, charitable, and arts projects.

[See relevant articles in *Business Week*, Sep. 8, 1962, Apr. 17, 1978, Aug. 31, 1987, and Mar. 14, 1988; *Forbes*, Nov. 15, 1969, Sep. 1, 1975, Mar. 5, 1979, Nov. 24, 1980, Apr. 11, 1983, and Nov. 5, 1984; *Financial World*, Mar. 15, 1976, and Mar. 15, 1978; and *Fortune*, Nov. 12, 1979, and Apr. 29, 1985; see also James L. West, *Tandy Corporation: "Start on a Shoestring"* (1968). An obituary is in the *New York Times*, Nov. 6, 1978.]

DOROTHY S. ("DOREY") SCHMIDT

TANNER, EDWARD EVERETT, III ("PATRICK DENNIS") (May 18, 1921–Nov. 6, 1976), writer, was born in Evanston, Ill., the son of Edward Everett Tanner, Jr., a stockbroker, and Florence Thacker. Tanner attended Evanston High School as well as several private schools in Evanston and Chicago and then entered the Art Institute of Chicago. At this time he adopted the pseudonyms Patrick Dennis and Patrick Tanner, names he would use the rest of his life to protect his privacy.

Before joining the American Field Service in 1942, Tanner worked in Chicago for the Stebbins Hardware Company and Columbia Educational Books, Inc. As an ambulance driver during World War II, Tanner saw service on the Arabian Peninsula and in North Africa, France, and Italy. Wounded twice, he was awarded two Purple Hearts posthumously.

In 1945, Tanner moved to New York City, where he worked as an account executive for the advertising agency of Franklin Spier, Inc., then as an advertising manager for Creative Age Press, and finally as the promotion manager for *Foreign Affairs*. He remained at the magazine from 1951 until Jan. 1, 1956. From 1957 to 1971 he served as the drama critic at the *New Republic*. On Dec. 30, 1948, Tanner married Louise Stickney, a writer; they had two children.

Tanner was the ghostwriter for four books

before he started writing his own novels. His first published novel was *Oh, What a Wonderful Wedding* (1953), written under the name Virginia Rowans. A *New York Times* book review on June 28, 1953, stated: "Miss Rowans writes with a fine feminine realism and few of the foibles of our competitive society escape her." In 1954, *House Party* was published, again with the author listed as Virginia Rowans.

Tanner's best-known book, *Auntie Mame*, his first under the pseudonym Patrick Dennis, appeared in 1955. It had been submitted to fifteen publishers over a period of five years, before Vanguard Press brought it out. Although he had spent more than a year working out the plot, the story of an eccentric, middle-aged woman from Beekman Place in New York City, as told by her nephew, had been written in only ninety days. As Tanner later told a reporter for *Life* magazine: "I write fast or not at all. I write in the first person, but it is all fictional. The public assumes that what seems fictional is fact; so the way for me to be inventive is to seem factual but be fictional."

Auntie Mame received favorable notices. "The humor, broad at times," wrote Robert W. Henderson in his review, "is coupled with satire on phony *avant-garde* intellectuals, racial prejudices as evident in suburban communities, and snobbism in general." The acclaim received by *Auntie Mame* altered Tanner's life, bringing the author both wealth and fame. It remained on the best-seller list for two years, selling more than two million copies in hard cover, paperback, and translations. *Auntie Mame* has also enjoyed a long life on the stage and screen. Featuring Rosalind Russell, the stage adaptation of the novel ran on Broadway from Oct. 3, 1956, to June 28, 1958. Russell also played the lead in the movie of *Auntie Mame*, released on Dec. 4, 1958. The novel was adapted once more, this time into the musical *Mame*, which was produced both on Broadway and as a movie.

Tanner published his next two books in 1956, *Guestward Ho!* and *The Loving Couple* by Virginia Rowans. For a period of eight weeks in 1956, Tanner had three novels on the *New York Times* best-seller list—a record that has never been broken. (Tanner, however, discovered the downside of this experience: "You're competing with yourself in the bookstores.") In 1957, Tanner published his next book, *The Pink Hotel*, written by Patrick Dennis and Dorothy Erskine. In 1958, *Around the World with Auntie Mame* appeared. Within a few months, it sold 130,000 copies. In 1961, he published *Love and Mrs. Sargent*, his last work under the pen name of Virginia Rowans.

The rest of Tanner's work was published under the name of Patrick Dennis: *Little Me* (1961), *Genius* (1962), *First Lady* (1964), *Joyous Season* (1965), *Tony* (1966), *How Firm a Foundation* (1968), *Paradise* (1971), and *Three-D* (1972). In all, Tanner wrote twelve novels under the pseudonym of Patrick Dennis and four novels under the pen name of Virginia Rowans.

There have also been four adaptations of his work for other media. In addition to the different reworkings of *Auntie Mame*, *Little Me* (the fictitious memoirs of an actress) was adapted by Neil Simon and produced on Broadway in 1962, starring Sid Caesar. Two television series were based on Tanner's work: "Guestward Ho!" (1960–1961) and "The Pruitts of Southhampton" (1966–1967).

In 1965, Tanner moved temporarily to Mexico City but returned to New York in 1970, where he died at his home on Park Avenue.

[Some of Tanner's manuscripts are at Yale University and at Boston University. See L. Berquist, "The Man Behind Auntie Mame," *Look*, Jan. 20, 1959; John G. Fuller, "Trade Winds," *Saturday Review*, Feb. 25, 1961; and Haskel Frankel, "What's in a Name or Two?" *Saturday Review*, Aug. 1, 1964. An obituary is in the *New York Times*, Nov. 7, 1976].

BURNHAM HOLMES

TATE, JOHN ORLEY ALLEN (Nov. 19, 1899–Feb. 9, 1979), poet, essayist, and literary critic, was born in Winchester, Ky., the youngest of the three sons of John Orley Tate, a lumberman, and Eleanor Custis Varnell. Tate's maternal ancestry stemmed from Fairfax County, Va., the land Tate portrayed in his novel *The Fathers* (1938). As he grew up, Tate was surrounded by a multitude of books, among them an 1800 edition of *Lyrical Ballads*, annotated in his great-grandfather's hand, along with popular novels and histories, the choices of his mother, who was a compulsive and indiscriminate reader.

Tate's formal schooling was haphazard: he attended the Tarbox School in Nashville, Tenn.; the Cross School, a private classical academy in Louisville, Ky.; and, for a year, the

Tate

Georgetown University Preparatory School before entering Vanderbilt University in the fall of 1918. Illness caused him to receive his B.A. degree there in 1923, a year late. In his junior year he was invited to a meeting of a literary group made up largely of Vanderbilt professors—among them John Crowe Ransom, Donald Davidson, and Walter Clyde Curry. Its members met every two weeks for critical deliberations on poetry, though Tate recalled their dialogue as more philosophic and aesthetic than literary. With his espousal of Baudelaire and the symbolists, Tate introduced into the discussions a sometimes jarring but always stimulating note of modernism.

The group published a magazine, *The Fugitive* (April 1922–December 1925), which, by the time of its demise, had launched the careers of four distinguished literary figures: Ransom, Tate, Davidson, and Robert Penn Warren. Warren, an undergraduate from Guthrie, Ky., had joined the group in 1924 and formed a lasting friendship with Tate. These four, joined by the novelist Andrew Lytle, went on to form the core of Agrarianism, a serious attack in the 1930's on the cultural ills of industrialism. The *Fugitive* gave rise as well to a view of poetry as a radically distinct mode of knowledge, engendering a school of literary theory—the New Criticism—which, augmented by the work of fellow Vanderbilt graduate Cleanth Brooks, dominated the academic world for some three decades. For Tate, *The Fugitive* afforded contact with the larger world of letters; his correspondence with Hart Crane introduced him to the writings of T. S. Eliot, Jules Laforgue, and Ezra Pound and led to his allegiance with the avant-garde in poetry and criticism.

Tate married the writer Caroline Gordon on Nov. 2, 1924, and the two moved to New York City. There they became a part of the lively literary scene, along with Malcolm Cowley, Edmund Wilson, Mark Van Doren, Gorham Munson, Slater and Susan Brown, Kenneth Burke, and other notables. During most of the 1920's, Tate made a bare living as a free-lance writer, subsisting mostly on commissions for reviews in the *New York Herald Tribune*, the *Nation*, and the *New Republic*. Gordon worked as secretary for Ford Madox Ford and began her own career as a novelist. In 1925 the Tates rented half of an old house in Patterson, N.Y., where Hart Crane joined them for a brief and stormy interval. This period in Tate's life, though spent in poverty and discomfort, provided the leisure to examine his basic convictions; he had already begun to qualify his reservations about the South and during the next few years would carry on a thoughtful and productive correspondence with his Agrarian friends.

Now, however, Tate worked with increasing intensity at his poetry and perfected the prose style that would characterize his best writing: sharp, formal, imperious. He began work on his biographies of Stonewall Jackson (1928) and Jefferson Davis (1929) and wrote a good many of his most brilliant poems—"Ode to the Confederate Dead," "Mr. Pope," "Death of Little Boys," "Causerie"—included in *Mr. Pope and Other Poems* (1928). These promising achievements earned him a Guggenheim Fellowship, which, with Gordon's reception of a similar grant in 1929, allowed the couple to spend the next two years abroad.

In Europe, the Tates stayed in London and Paris, spent some time with Warren at Oxford, and renewed friendships with Ford Madox Ford, John Peale Bishop, and Léonie Adams; they came to know Eliot, Herbert Read, Ernest Hemingway, Gertrude Stein, and other American expatriates who frequented Sylvia Beach's bookstore. They then moved back to Tennessee, to live for a while in Benfolly, an antebellum house on the Cumberland River bought for them by Allen's brother Ben. Benfolly became a haven for numerous fellow writers, including Katherine Anne Porter, Malcolm Cowley, and the poet Robert Lowell, who pitched a tent on the front lawn to have the benefit of Tate's tutelage. The Fugitive-Agrarian writers came over frequently from Nashville, continuing the discussions that would soon issue in their controversial manifesto *I'll Take My Stand* (1930).

In this milieu Tate's thought was increasingly occupied with the distinctions between traditional culture and its modern secular counterpart. During these years he produced some of his most celebrated poems: "Sonnets of the Blood" (1931), "Last Days of Alice" (1931), "The Mediterranean" (1932), "Sonnets at Christmas" (1934), and "The Meaning of Life" (1935). Two of his poems, "Winter Mask" (1943) and "Seasons of the Soul" (1944), indicated a new and deeper spiritual orientation. He also published a number of articles in periodicals, later collected in several volumes. *Re-*

actionary Essays on Poetry and Ideas (1936) and *Reason in Madness* (1941) contained such major critical pieces as "Tension in Poetry," "Miss Emily and the Bibliographers," "Narcissus as Narcissus," and "What Is a Traditional Society?" Tate occupied the chair of poetry at the Library of Congress (1934–1944), held the position of poet in residence at Princeton (1939–1942), and was editor of the *Sewanee Review* (1944–1946).

Tate converted to Roman Catholicism in 1950, as Caroline had done in 1947; their friend the French philosopher Jacques Maritain was his sponsor. Together the Tates edited a noted anthology of short stories, *The House of Fiction* (1950). Shortly afterward they went to live in Minneapolis, where Tate held a professorship at the University of Minnesota from 1951 until his retirement in 1968. In 1955, after thirty-one years of a turbulent marriage and a close intellectual and literary collaboration, the Tates separated; they were divorced in 1959. They had one child. Tate and Isabella Stewart Gardner were married Aug. 27, 1959, and divorced in 1966. On July 30, 1966, he married Helen Heinz; they had three children, one of whom died in infancy.

In the 1950's and 1960's, Tate was at the height of his power and his acclaim. Two essays written in 1951, "The Angelic Imagination" and "The Symbolic Imagination," made clear the overtly theological nature of his criticism. In poetry, he embarked upon an ambitious undertaking, more in the mode of Dante than anything he had before written; he was to complete, however, only three parts of the projected nine-part series: "The Maimed Man," "The Swimmers," and "The Buried Lake" (1952–1953). He was awarded the Bollingen Prize for Poetry (1956), the Brandeis University Medal Award for Poetry (1961), and the Dante Society Gold Medal (1962), and was elected to the American Academy of Arts and Letters (1964) and the American Academy of Arts and Sciences (1965); he served as president of the National Institute of Arts and Letters in 1968. Tate died in Sewanee, Tenn.

[Tate's papers are in the Princeton University Library. He published a memoir, *Memoirs and Opinions* (1975). Collections of his letters include *The Literary Correspondence of Donald Davidson and Allen Tate*, edited by John Tyree Fain and Thomas Daniel Young (1974); *The Republic of Letters in America*, edited by Thomas Daniel Young and John J. Hindle (1981); *The Lytle-Tate Letters*, edited by Thomas Daniel Young and Elizabeth Sarcone (1987); and *Exiles and Fugitives*, edited by John M. Dunaway (1992). Accounts of his early work with the Fugitives are Louise Cowan, *The Fugitive Group* (1959); and John Lincoln Stewart, *The Burden of Time: The Fugitives and Agrarians* (1965). Interpretations of his work include *Sewanee Review*, Autumn 1959, a tribute to Tate; Roger K. Meiners, *Last Alternatives* (1963); George Hemphill, *Allen Tate* (1964); M. E. Bradford, *Rumors of Mortality* (1969); Louise Cowan, *The Southern Critics* (1971); Radcliffe Squires, *Allen Tate* (1971) and, as editor, *Allen Tate and His Work* (1972); James Larry Allums, "Allen Tate and the Poetic Way" (Ph.D. diss., University of Dallas, 1978); Robert S. Dupree, *Allen Tate and the Augustinian Imagination* (1983); Lewis Simpson, "The Critics Who Made Us: Allen Tate," *Sewanee Review*, Summer 1986; and Gale Carrithers, *Mumford, Tate, Eiseley* (1992). An obituary is in the *New York Times*, Feb. 10, 1979.]

LOUISE COWAN

TAUBER, MAURICE FALCOLM (Feb. 14, 1908–Sept. 21, 1980), librarian and consultant, was born in Norfolk, Va., the son of Abraham Albert Tauber, a tailor, and Leona Miller, a seamstress. Both parents were immigrants from eastern Europe. When Tauber was six, his father died. Starting at age fourteen he helped support his mother and siblings by working part-time as a newsboy. This set the pattern for his lifelong belief in the mutually enriching nature of hard work and study.

In 1925, Tauber's family moved to West Philadelphia, where he graduated from high school second in his class (1926), then enrolled at Temple University. His sophomore year proved propitious in two ways. First, he started part-time evening work in the university library. Second, he met his future wife, Rose Anne Begner; they were married on May 15, 1932, and had two children.

Upon graduation in 1930 with a B.S. in English and sociology, Tauber enrolled in the University of Pennsylvania Law School on a scholarship. After three months, the onset of pleurisy with incipient tuberculosis required half a year's rest. This illness finished his savings and his legal studies, and in the fall of 1931 Tauber was working full-time at Temple's library in the acquisitions and cataloging departments. He became his generation's preeminent authority in these specialties, which he combined with related library book-processing activities and called "technical services."

Tauber worked in Temple's library until 1938, progressing to the head of the Catalog Department in 1935, after completing a B.S. in library service at Columbia University in 1934. He then enrolled in the Master's in Education program at Temple (awarded in 1939); his thesis, was titled "Moving Picture Censorship in the State of Pennsylvania." Tauber took a characteristically objective approach while pointing out the potential dangers to democracy that censorship entails. He affirmed "the liberal ideal of Americans to see all sides of a question, whether one believed in it or not."

In 1938, Tauber began his studies for the Ph.D. at the University of Chicago's Graduate Library School. In 1939 he became research assistant to Dean Louis Round Wilson, organizing his papers, doing biographical research, and, most important, surveying many academic libraries around the country in preparation for their joint definitive text, *The University Library* (1945). The survey techniques that Wilson taught him formed the basis for Tauber's many years of consulting at hundreds of libraries. In gratitude Tauber wrote *Louis Round Wilson* (1967).

In 1939, Tauber published his first major scholarly article in the prestigious *Library Quarterly*. He wrote of his efforts at library cooperation in Philadelphia through building a "union catalog" of all holdings in the region. He focused on many of the technical problems but highlighted the importance of this cooperative effort "to aid scholars." He early championed centralization of technical services and coordination of multiple types of libraries.

Tauber completed his Ph.D. in 1941. His dissertation, "Reclassification and Recataloging in College and University Libraries," derived from experience at Temple plus extensive historical and survey work. He argued that large academic and research libraries should shift from the Dewey classification system to the one used at the Library of Congress. One national standard could minimize duplication and variation of effort. He used these arguments in many subsequent publications and proposals, persuading the bulk of large academic and research libraries in the United States (and some abroad) to adopt the Library of Congress classification. He saw technical standards as a means for clarification, cooperation, and centralized efficiencies of scale.

Soon after graduation Tauber obtained the dual assignment of instructor at Chicago's Graduate Library School, and chief of cataloging in the library. In addition he continued to survey and consult for other libraries, including the libraries at Columbia University. This led to his appointment there in 1944 with another dual assignment: assistant professor at the School of Library Service and assistant director of technical services for the library. By 1949 he had become a full professor, and from 1954 to 1976 was the Melvil Dewey professor of library service. He taught an entire generation of librarians, showing particular solicitude for foreign Ph.D. students. He collaborated with seven student "associates" to write his magnum opus, the encyclopedic textbook *Technical Services in Libraries* (1954).

From 1948 to 1962, Tauber edited one of the principal journals of librarianship, *College and Research Libraries*. He promoted many studies and articles designed to broaden the scope of the profession while applying principles of scientific research and management to its operations.

In keeping with his "work-study" beliefs, Tauber continued to survey individual libraries. Several of these studies were monumental in scope, particularly the ones at Cornell (1948) and Columbia (1958), and especially his exhaustive review of over 150 libraries in Australia while on a Fulbright Fellowship in 1961. This survey alone, comprising three large volumes along with extensive popular press coverage in Australia, contributed significantly to the development of improved library service for a whole continent. When Australian prime minister Robert Menzies visited the White House in 1964, President Lyndon Johnson invited Tauber to be present. One important feature of Tauber's surveys and consulting was that they frequently led to increased funding and new building designs for libraries, as well as improvements in technical processes. After twenty-five years of such experience, he solidified this approach at a conference he organized in 1965 on library surveys (published 1967).

In 1959, Tauber's wife's health began to fail. Her five-year illness, combined with his own health problems, had a progressively dampening effect on his energies. Nevertheless, he continued his enthusiasm for the technical improvements of libraries. In 1963 he showed an interest in the beginnings of computerization by coediting *Book Catalogs*, describing a computer-produced alternative to the traditional card catalog based on machine-readable records. His last monograph was *Library Binding Manual* (1972), a highly technical review of the binding industry and its standards for libraries.

Tauber's interests were extensive, and so were his contacts in the library field. He wrote many biographical sketches, ever recognizing the achievements of others. Starting in 1966, he began to review his own accomplishments and had his archival management students begin to sort and index parts of his voluminous correspondence, amounting to some 75,000 items. This collection documents his thorough research and helpfulness in all areas of librarianship.

In the midst of many ongoing publication projects and library surveys, Tauber died in New York City. The tributes of his colleagues included the endowment in 1981 of the Maurice Tauber Foundation to sponsor lectures in librarianship and information science. Though the bulk of his career preceded the computer age, his thoroughness of detail and specification of technical standards did much to lay the foundation for the coming age of library automation.

[Tauber's papers are in the Rare Book and Manuscript Library of the Columbia University Libraries. Other major publications include *Cataloging and Classification* (1960) and *Classification Systems* (1961), as well as hundreds of articles, book reviews, and technical survey reports in the library press. For an exhaustive bibliography of Tauber's writings, along with several biographical appreciations, see Marion C. Szigethy, *Maurice Falcolm Tauber* (1974). For further biographical material, see Kurt S. Maier, "Maury," *American Libraries*, Dec. 1976, and "Maurice F. Tauber," *Leaders in American Academic Librarianship, 1925–1975* (1983). An obituary is in the *New York Times*, Sept. 26, 1980. In 1974, Tauber recorded his reminiscences for the Columbia University Oral History Project. Other tapes and pictures are included among the papers.]

CHARLES C. STEWART

TEUBER, HANS-LUKAS ("LUKE") (Aug. 7, 1916–Jan. 4, 1977), neuropsychologist and educator, was born in Berlin, Germany, one of two sons of Eugen Teuber and Rose Knopf. Teuber's interest in psychology was sparked at an early age by his parents, behavioral scientists who, under the auspices of the Prussian Academy of Sciences, founded a field station for the observation of chimpanzees in Tenerife, the Canary Islands; this colony was later made famous by the German gestalt psychologist Wolfgang Köhler, whose studies in Tenerife were documented in *The Mentality of Apes* (1924).

Teuber received a classical education at a private German preparatory school and at the Collège Français in Berlin, where he studied from 1926 to 1934 and received a baccalaureate degree. His intellectual interests were diverse: he enjoyed Greek and Roman literature, poetry, the natural sciences, and semantics. From 1935 to 1939 he studied at the University of Basel in Switzerland, where he pursued an interdisciplinary course of study and was a member of a discussion group that centered on the philosophy of science, specifically the dynamics between the natural and social sciences. It was at Basel that Teuber first became exposed to the workings of the central nervous system. Other courses included biology and zoology, embryology, and comparative anatomy.

Teuber was granted a fellowship for study at Harvard in 1939, but the outbreak of war in Europe postponed his arrival in the United States until 1941. On August 1 of that year, having settled in Cambridge, Mass., Teuber married Marianne Liepe, a student at Vassar; they had two children. He became an American citizen in 1944.

Teuber interrupted his graduate studies in psychology at Harvard between 1944 and 1946 to serve in the United States Naval Reserve. He was stationed in California, where he worked closely with Dr. Morris B. Bender, head of neurology at the San Diego Naval Hospital. The experience, Teuber later wrote, provided "the final and decisive push in the direction of my chosen field." Teuber and Bender published numerous joint papers on brain injury, specifically on visual and perceptual problems suffered by brain-damaged war veterans. It was Teuber's first encounter with the paradoxical notion that casualties of war can provide insight into normal functioning. As he later put it, "Certain kinds of blindness can illuminate sight, and certain forms of paralysis can tell us something about the normal bases of voluntary movement . . . [and] the acquired amnesias of the injured brain can point us in the direction in which answers to the riddle of memory can be sought."

After receiving his Ph.D. in experimental psychology from Harvard in 1947, Teuber became a research associate at the New York University (NYU) College of Medicine, where he continued his research in brain injury; he later became a professor in the department of psychiatry and neurology and in the NYU psychology department. From 1947 to 1961 he was also head of the psychophysiological laboratory at the NYU-Bellevue Medical Center, which, under his administration, became an internationally renowned research center.

It was at the NYU laboratory that Teuber's research methodology, now considered standard procedure in neurological testing and diagnosis, was developed. Studying a group that ultimately comprised more than 500 brain-injured veterans from World War II and the Korea and Vietnam conflicts, augmented by children and adults who had suffered non-war-related brain injury, Teuber developed a battery of tests designed to evaluate tactile, auditory, and visual functioning. The purpose of these tests was to reveal the neurological impairment or deficit responsible for various behavioral manifestations. The reliability of the tests was ensured by Teuber's strict use of control groups and by the principle of the "double dissociation of symptoms," which sought to ascribe definitively a particular deficit to a particular lesion. He also delineated the distinction between external sensory stimulation and internal, self-initiated movement, which causes in individuals what he called a "corollary discharge." Teuber's work with the brain-injured was most significant in understanding how the brain functions with regard to visual, particularly spatial, perception.

Teuber and his wife lived in Dobbs Ferry, N.Y., a suburb of New York City, until their move to Arlington, Mass., in 1961, when Teuber joined the staff of the Massachusetts Institute of Technology (MIT) as a professor and head of the psychology department. At that time, psychology was subsumed in the department of economics and social science at MIT. Teuber restructured staffing and curriculum, and by 1964, MIT conferred full departmental status on psychology and Teuber was named chairman. According to one colleague, under Teuber's direction "the MIT department became an almost compulsory stopping-off point in the U.S.A. for scientists from throughout the world with interests in brain function and psychology."

Throughout his career Teuber published more than 200 papers and monographs on neuropsychology. He was noted for his interdisciplinary approach; as he said, "The converging evolutions of experimental psychology, physiology, and microanatomy, together with comparative and developmental studies, are bound to take us ever closer toward our common goal: that of gaining a rational understanding of ourselves." He could read fluently in Latin, ancient Greek, English, French, and German, and was a gifted speaker in the latter three languages; his lectures at MIT drew standing-room-only crowds. In later life, he traveled with increasing frequency to Europe to promote the interchange of scientific information and personnel. He held several visiting lectureships, including that of Eastman professor at Oxford University in the 1971–1972 academic year.

Among the awards Teuber received were the Karl Spencer Lashley Award for Research in Neurobiology of the American Philosophical Society (1966), the Apollo Achievement Award of the National Aeronautics and Space Administration (1969), the Kenneth Craik Award in Experimental Psychology from St. Johns College, Cambridge, England (1971), and the James R. Killian Faculty Achievement Award from MIT (1976–1977). He sat on the editorial boards of several scientific journals, including *Journal of Comparative and Physiological Psychology* (1956–1968) and the *Journal of Psychiatric Research* (1961–1964).

Teuber disappeared while swimming off Virgin Gorda in the British Virgin Islands, where he was vacationing with his wife; he was presumed to have suffered a heart attack and drowned.

[*Perception* (1978), vol. 8 of *Handbook of Sensory Physiology* (1978), was coedited by Teuber and contains the text of an address he delivered at the 21st International Psychological Congress in Paris, "The Brain and Human Behavior." A profile by Leo M. Hurvich, Dorothea Jameson, and Walter A. Rosenblith is in *Biographical Memoirs. National Academy of Sciences* 57 (1987). Obituaries are in the *New York Times*, Jan. 7, 1977; and *Nature*, Mar. 31, 1977.]

MELISSA A. DOBSON

THOMPSON, STITH (Mar. 7, 1885–Jan. 10, 1976), folklorist, was born in Bloomfield, Ky., the son of John Warden Thompson and Eliza McClaskey, who were farmers. He grew up mostly in Indianapolis, Ind., where he completed his secondary education at Manual

Training High School. Throughout his career, his strong interest in his midwestern roots influenced both his choice of folklore as a field of study and his determination to locate his research in Indiana. He was distantly related to Abraham Lincoln, and his appearance—tall and loose-jointed—was reminiscent of that famous relative.

Thompson began his university schooling at Butler University in Indianapolis, which he attended for two years; simultaneously, he worked as an office boy at the Bobbs-Merrill Publishing Company, where he came into contact with established authors including James Whitcomb Riley.

Following two years of high school teaching in Springfield, Ill., Thompson moved to the University of Wisconsin to complete his undergraduate education, receiving his B.A. in 1909; at Wisconsin he became interested in folklore and in the oral literature of the North American Indians. He then spent two years teaching high school English in Portland, Oreg., where he worked during summers as a lumberjack; there he learned Norwegian and more folklore. He continued his formal education as a university fellow at the University of California, where he received his M.A. in 1912, and then as a research fellow at Harvard University, where he received a Ph.D. in 1914; his dissertation, "A Study of the European Tales Among the North American Indians," was done under the direction of George Lyman Kittredge.

After teaching English at the University of Texas (1914–1918), Colorado College (1918–1920), and the University of Maine (1920), Thompson became associate professor of English at Indiana University, where he remained for the rest of his academic career (1921–1955); there he organized folklore studies and directed the composition program. On June 14, 1918, he married Louise Faust, a student at the University of Texas; they had two children.

Thompson's steadily increasing reputation brought international renown to the folklore program at Indiana, which became a world center for folklore studies. During his years at Indiana, among other significant projects, he produced his massive publication, a standard reference work on folklore to the present, the six-volume *Motif-Index of Folk-Literature* (1935; rev. 1953–1958). He also revised and enlarged Antti Aarne's *Verzeichnis der Märchentypen*, which ultimately appeared as the Aarne-Thompson publication *The Types of the Folktale* (1971).

Thompson was president of the American Folklore Society (1937–1940) and member and officer of other folklore societies, American and international. In 1947 he set up the folklore program at the University of Venezuela, working as a consultant with the Ministry of Education there. In the 1951–1952 academic year he was a Fulbright professor in Norway, and in the 1956–1957 academic year he held a Guggenheim Fellowship. Thompson retired in June 1955 but maintained his interests in writing and fieldwork, and accepted visiting professorships at the universities of Texas, Kansas, and Hawaii.

Thompson's major and lasting achievement as a folklore scholar lay in the codification of accumulated folktales, to enable their study through their history and geography. His methodology was empirical, intended as a counterweight to earlier, less scholarly, treatments of folktales that were often vaguely general and symbolically oriented. He pursued careful documentation not only of the materials themselves—often previously unrecorded if they came originally from oral tradition—but also of their social history and geographical dispersion. An extensive work force of colleagues, both students and other faculty, over time developed the process of motif hunting under Thompson's supervision; many of the resulting finds became part of the *Motif-Index*.

Thompson also devoted time and energy to ensuring that folklore studies would receive the respect he was determined to prove they deserved. At Indiana, he served as dean of the Graduate School (1947–1950). He also worked to strengthen the institution's doctoral program in folklore, its professorship of folklore, and its summer institutes in the field. His abilities as an academic organizer were closely connected to his international network of scholarly contacts and his ongoing concern with international relations, which he worked to further and to support.

Thompson died in Columbus, Ind. A bust of him is in Ballantine Hall at Indiana University, in recognition of his contributions to the institution and the field of folklore studies. Known as "the Dean of American Folklore," he legitimized the study of folklore as a university discipline in the United States, with his scholarly writings and with his organization of the Folklore Institute at Indiana University.

[See *Western Folklore*, Oct. 1976; and *Journal of American Folklore*, Jan. 1977. An obituary is in the *New York Times*, Jan. 12, 1976.]

MARGIE BURNS

THORNTON, DANIEL I. J. (Jan. 31, 1911–Jan. 18, 1976), rancher and politician, was born in Hall County, Tex., the son of sharecroppers Clay C. Thornton and Ida Fife. He worked in the cotton fields while attending Posley Community School at Slaton, Tex. At the age of twelve he became involved with livestock work through the local 4-H Club, and four years later he was elected president of the Texas State 4-H Club.

After graduating from Lubbock High School in 1930, Thornton attended Texas Technological College (now Texas Technological University) in 1930 and 1931, and the University of California at Los Angeles (UCLA) in 1932. He supported himself by working as a movie extra at the Warner Brothers studios, as a gas station operator, and as a derrick rig hand in the oilfields at Wilmington, Calif.

On Apr. 7, 1934, Thornton married Jessie Willock, who had been a fellow student at UCLA. Thornton's father-in-law lent him $37,000 in 1937 to begin ranching operations in Springerville, Ariz. Thornton established a highly profitable herd of Hereford cattle and soon repaid the loan. In 1941 he shifted his ranching operations to Colorado's "Western slope" and established the 2,000-acre Thornton Hereford Ranch in Gunnison, Colo. He selectively bred his herd's strains to produce the Thornton Triumphant cattle. The new strain was very profitable: two bulls sold for $50,000 each in 1945; and in 1947 he sold a herd of 250 head for almost $900,000, which was the industry's largest single cattle sale up to that time.

Thornton first ran for public office in 1948, as the successful Republican candidate for Colorado's eleventh senatorial district. In 1950 the incumbent Republican governor Ralph Carr died five weeks before the election, and the Republican leaders selected Thornton as Carr's replacement. Most political observers believed Thornton to be merely a sacrificial candidate, but he waged an unexpectedly active campaign and won an upset victory over the Democratic candidate, Walter Johnson. When Thornton was inaugurated on Jan. 9, 1950, he became the youngest governor in the nation at the age of thirty-nine.

Thornton generally promoted conservative fiscal policies, although he increased state advertising expenditures to promote tourism and lobbied for a long-range highway construction plan. He also sponsored the appropriation of $1 million to purchase land in Colorado Springs, which was donated to the United States Air Force in exchange for its selection of Colorado Springs as the site of the United States Air Force Academy.

Thornton strongly supported Dwight D. Eisenhower's effort to obtain the Republican nomination for the presidency in 1952, and clashed with Senator Eugene Millikin, a supporter of conservative contender Robert Taft. Although Millikin led the Colorado delegation at the 1952 Republican convention, Thornton succeeded in persuading fifteen of the state's eighteen delegates to support Eisenhower, who won the presidential nomination on the first ballot. Thornton was mentioned as a possible vice-presidential candidate in 1952 (and again in 1956), but the position went to Senator Richard M. Nixon.

Thornton chose not to run again for governor in 1954 and also declined the Republican nomination for the United States Senate election in that same year. After leaving office he served on a fact-finding commission appointed by President Eisenhower to evaluate South Korea's economic and military strength.

After two years of ranching, Thornton decided to return to political life. He became director of the farm campaign division of the Republican National Committee and ran for the Senate seat vacated by Millikin. His opponent was John A. Carroll, a "liberal–New Deal" Democrat who had the backing of the state's most important Democratic leader, Governor "Big Ed" Johnson. Thornton's supporters accused Carroll of being a "pinko" during the campaign, but he won nevertheless. Although President Eisenhower carried Colorado by more than 131,000 votes, Thornton, who was a well-publicized friend of the president's, lost by a margin of nearly 2,770 votes. The Democratic party took control of both houses of the Colorado legislature.

In 1958, Thornton made an unsuccessful attempt in the primary election to win the Republican nomination for Colorado's Second District congressional seat, but lost the primary election to State Representative John G. Mackie. President Eisenhower subsequently appointed Thornton special ambassador to Paraguay.

In 1959, Thornton was the subject of an investigation by the Securities and Exchange Commission (SEC) into misreporting of financial conditions by the Hamilton Oil and Gas Corporation, which he served as an officer and director. The SEC eventually filed criminal charges against Hamilton's president, former Notre Dame football coach Frank Leahy, but no charges were filed against Thornton.

Thornton eventually phased out his livestock operations and closed down his Gunnison ranch in 1961. He thereafter concentrated on various financial undertakings and served as a director of Financial Industrial Fund, Inc., Cycle Manufacturing Company, and the National Western Stock Show. Thornton helped establish the Colorado 4-H Foundation, and in 1976 the Colorado 4-H Foundation established a memorial fund in his name.

Thornton's wife died in 1972; he married Geraldine M. McCabe on July 7, 1973. He had no children. After retiring from his business operations and directorships in 1974, Thornton moved to Carmel Valley, Calif., where he died of a heart attack.

Thornton represented the combination of conservative businessman and politician who usually became a supporter of the isolationist wing of the Republican party, yet he backed Dwight Eisenhower's presidential campaign and established a personal friendship with the new president. Thornton's relationship with the president, however, was insufficient to win in Colorado after the resurgence of the Democratic party in the late 1950's.

[Thornton's gubernatorial papers are at the Colorado State Archives, Denver; Texas Technological University, Lubbock, has extensive clippings on his business and political career, with a microfilm copy at the Colorado Historical Society, Denver. Various correspondence is in the Agnes Wright Spring Collection at the University of Colorado's Western Historical Collection, Boulder, and in the Ralph Carr Collection at the Colorado Historical Society. Curtis Martin, "The 1956 Election in Colorado," *Western Political Quarterly*, Mar. 1957, and "Political Behavior in Colorado," *Colorado Quarterly*, Summer 1957, contain useful information. Obituaries are in the *New York Times*, and the *Washington Post*, both Jan. 20, 1976.]

STEPHEN G. MARSHALL

TIOMKIN, DIMITRI (May 10, 1894–Nov. 11, 1979), composer and pianist, was born in the Ukraine (of partly Jewish extraction, according to Nicolas Slonimsky); he was the son of Zinovie Tiomkin, a noted pathologist, and Maria Tartakovsky. He remembered little of his early childhood in Poltava, nor did he respond well to introductory music schooling in Saint Petersburg. At thirteen, however, he was enrolled in the Saint Petersburg Conservatory. There Tiomkin studied piano under Felix Blumenfeld, the teacher of Vladimir Horowitz, and composition under Alexander Glazunov. After hours, he frequented the café world of Petersburg artists and intellectuals. He also played the piano to accompany silent movie and vaudeville shows, including an appearance by the famous German comedian Max Linder.

Like many musicians in an aristocratic society, Tiomkin supported himself by giving piano lessons to the children of the rich. After his second term at the conservatory he was sent to the country estate of Ivanoskoye Selo as the household musician for the Princess Bariatinsky, daughter of the assassinated tsar Alexander II. He also served in the household of Count Sheremetiev, where he tutored Miss Ruby, the count's black mistress, and gained from this New Orleans native his first exposure to ragtime and jazz.

During the Russian Revolution, Tiomkin entertained soldiers in the Arctic port of Murmansk, served in an anti-cholera squad, and was briefly imprisoned while in the service of a suspect general. He finally escaped Russia in 1920, when his estranged father managed to bring the young man to Berlin. Tiomkin's relations with his father did not improve, but he did continue his musical studies with Ferruccio Busoni, whose rigorously classical training complemented the florid romanticism of Glazunov. Tiomkin was by this time a pianist of some accomplishment. He played the Liszt A Major Concerto with the Berlin Philharmonic before moving to Paris in 1924 with the virtuoso Mickel Kariton. It was there that the famous bass Fyodor Chaliapin advised Tiomkin of the opportunities for musicians in the United States. Chaliapin suggested that the classically trained Tiomkin adopt a more popular and flexible style suitable for entertaining the American masses.

Tiomkin and Kariton embarked on a vaudeville tour in 1925. Their two-piano act was the finale for a show featuring the Albertina Rasch Dancers. Its New York debut was greatly benefited when a former patron, Prince Serge Obolensky (by that time married to Alice Astor), turned it into a major society event. Tiomkin married Albertina Rasch in 1927 and always credited the Austrian ballerina for enhancing his show business sense.

Tiomkin's United States recital debut, which took place in Carnegie Hall in November 1927, included a brief "Quasi Jazz" of his own devising. Apart from some light marches and dances published in Paris, this work was Tiomkin's first significant musical composition. Further concertizing followed in New York and Paris. Tiomkin's greatest success came with the famous 1928 concerts in which he introduced the music of George Gershwin to Paris.

When Albertina Rasch was invited to choreograph dance sequences in some early Hollywood musicals, Tiomkin went along and provided original accompaniment in such films as *Devil May Care* and *Lord Byron of Broadway* (both 1930). The couple also established a presence in New York, where Tiomkin produced an unsuccessful show (*Aha!*) in 1930 and where Rasch established a short-lived tea room near Carnegie Hall.

Back in Hollywood, Tiomkin committed himself to the movies. (His pianistic career ended decisively in 1937 when a broken bone failed to heal properly.) Although he had little formal compositional training, the erstwhile classicist had become a formidable showman. His first dramatic film assignments were the 1931 version of Tolstoy's *Resurrection* and *Alice in Wonderland* (1933). A friendship with the director Frank Capra led to Tiomkin's scoring *Lost Horizon* (1937), his first major success. Tiomkin's musical exoticism was perfectly suited to this adventure in the mythical Shangri-La, and the success of the film made Tiomkin a recognized Hollywood figure. That same year he became an American citizen, and in 1938 he made his conducting debut at the Hollywood Bowl, leading a suite of music from *Lost Horizon* together with a program of the Albertina Rasch Ballet. Tiomkin scored many other films for Capra, including *You Can't Take It with You* (1938), *Mr. Smith Goes to Washington* (1939), *Meet John Doe* (1941), *It's a Wonderful Life* (1947), and several wartime documentaries in the "Why We Fight" series.

Surprisingly, this very Russian musician became the leading composer for Hollywood Westerns, including *Duel in the Sun* (1946), *Red River* (1948), *The Big Sky* (1952), *Gunfight at the O.K. Corral* (1957), *Rio Bravo* (1959), and *The Alamo*, with the song "The Green Leaves of Summer" (1960). "A steppe is a steppe is a steppe" was Tiomkin's explanation when queried about his unlikely success at scoring American subject matter. The most famous Western of all was *High Noon* (1952), for which Tiomkin devised the novel idea of a ballad ("Do Not Forsake Me, Oh, My Darlin' ") to be sung over the action. The song and the music were a considerable factor in the film's success and earned Tiomkin his first two Academy Awards. They also inspired a trend toward "title songs," since producers were quick to sense the opportunities for publicity and subsidiary income. Tiomkin, a shrewd businessman, was not shy in this department, having secured the rights to his song before the picture's release.

Tiomkin's acceptance speech for his third Oscar (for *The High and the Mighty*, 1954) evoked considerable laughter when he thanked not the usual cinema colleagues but Brahms, Strauss, Wagner, and other composers of the past. Through such wisecracks (delivered with mingled innocence and irony in a thick Russian accent) and through a love of press agentry and high living, Tiomkin became a celebrity. The most famous composer in Hollywood, he was thought by some to epitomize the shallowness often attributed to film music. One critic described *The Fall of the Roman Empire* (1964) as "a stereophonic score that not only drowns out most of the dialogue but also effectively obliterates the sound of Gibbon revolving in his grave." Nevertheless, Tiomkin's extravagant orchestrations in the Russian style, lavishly embroidered with percussion and flutter-tongued brasses, provided colorful and exotic backgrounds for some of Hollywood's best-remembered movies. Other famous Tiomkin scores include *Portrait of Jennie* (1949), *Cyrano de Bergerac* (1950), *The Thing* and *Strangers on a Train* (1951), *Land of the Pharaohs* (1955), *Giant* and *Friendly Persuasion* (1956), and *The Guns of Navarone* (1961). He won a total of four Oscars and twenty nominations for his music and songs, which accompanied more than 120 films.

Albertina Rasch died in 1967. Tiomkin then moved to London and, in 1972, married Olivia Patch, who survived him. He had no children.

His last venture was a return to producing in the first Soviet-American coproduction, the musical biography *Tchaikovsky* (1971). He died in London.

[Tiomkin's papers are collected at the Cinema-Television Library and Archive of the University of Southern California. His memoir, *Please Don't Hate Me* (1959), written with Prosper Buranelli, is anecdotal and occasionally inaccurate. The most vivid account of Tiomkin's personality is Gary Stevens, "Shave Phone, Put on My Bill," in *Variety*, Feb. 9, 1980, p. 34. For critical appreciations see Christopher Palmer, *Dimitri Tiomkin* (1984) and *The Composer in Hollywood* (1990). There are surveys of the life and music in Tony Thomas, *Music for the Movies* (1973); and in William Darby and Jack Du Bois, *American Film Music* (1990). An obituary is in the *New York Times*, Nov. 14, 1979.]

JOHN FITZPATRICK

TISHMAN, DAVID (Apr. 22, 1889–June 18, 1980), real estate developer and businessman, was born in New York City, the son of Julius Tishman, a Russian-Jewish immigrant, and Hilda Karmel. The upwardly mobile Julius Tishman rose from selling dry goods, to owning a department store, to constructing, in 1898, his first tenement at 519 East Thirteenth Street in Manhattan, thereby founding the family real estate dynasty.

David Tishman became the leader of the dynasty's second generation. He was the oldest son and the first of five brothers to join his father in the business, in 1909, after graduating from New York University Law School. He married Ann Valentine in 1914; the couple had three children.

Tall, with an aristocratic bearing, David was the leader of Julius Tishman and Sons while it developed into the most successful of New York City's speculative owner-builders during the 1920s. Following the construction of a successful luxury apartment building at 125 East Seventy-second Street, the Tishmans built seventeen more luxury apartment buildings along Park Avenue and its side streets running from the East Seventies to the Nineties, creating a line of elegant "prewar" buildings that remains prime real estate today.

By the mid-1920's the Tishmans were constructing buildings, as well as buying and selling buildings and building sites, all over New York City. As the family became richer, its members also became involved in philanthropy. During the 1920's, David Tishman participated in the organization and construction of the Sydenham Hospital, which his father had been instrumental in founding.

After serving as vice-president of Julius Tishman and Sons under his father from 1912 to 1928, David Tishman took over as president in 1928 as the company went public and renamed itself Tishman Realty and Construction, Inc. During the Great Depression, Metropolitan Life and various banks took ownership of many residential buildings away from Tishman Realty and Construction, but the Tishman Company continued to run the properties for them.

As president of the family company until 1948, David Tishman's main achievements took place in the post–World War II period, when Tishman Realty and Construction pioneered the modernization of its residential holdings and led the renaissance of real estate development. Tishman was the first major New York City landlord to replace ice boxes with electric refrigerators. He then led his company from building residences to building more-lucrative office towers.

Tishman's construction of an office tower at 445 Park Avenue at Fifty-seventh Street marked three firsts: it was the first new office building in New York City after World War II, the first office building located north of Grand Central Terminal, and the first office building in the world to feature central air-conditioning. This building spurred the development boom in office buildings on the East Side of Manhattan between Forty-seventh and Fifty-seventh Streets.

David Tishman's creativity in financing also showed itself during this period. He persuaded Metropolitan Life to sell back to the family those Park Avenue residential buildings that it had taken over during the Great Depression. He then re-sold the buildings as cooperatives, in the process making a handsome profit.

David's concept of the Tishman Company was family-oriented. Of his three brothers who had joined the firm, Louis had died in 1931, but younger brothers Paul and Norman were active rivals for the succession to the presidency. After the war, David brought his sons Robert and Alan into the company from the United States Navy, where they had both served, and later brought in his nephews John, Edward, William, and Peter. In 1948, David made the decision to move up to chairman and chose his brother Norman, whose specialties were leasing and finance, as president, passing over his brother Paul, who had been construction chief.

A major achievement for the company under David Tishman's chairmanship was the construction, in 1956, of its new headquarters at 666 Fifth Avenue, a well-located building featuring clean vertical lines, an open lobby, a waterfall, and a penthouse restaurant. In the tight market for real estate loans in 1956, Tishman initiated a creative financing arrangement for the building, a "sale/leaseback" with Prudential Life Insurance Company.

As David Tishman became less active in the day-to-day management of the company in the late 1950's, he started a second career devoted to charitable activities, especially at New York University (NYU). His help in initiating its building drive following World War II and his work as a trustee of the university's Law Center had already earned him NYU's Meritorious Service Award in 1955. In 1958 he became a member of the university's medical board, in 1960 he was given an honorary LL.D. degree, and in 1961, he was made a trustee of the university. He became a life trustee in 1974.

In 1962, when his wife died, David stepped aside from the family business for a while; Norman took over as chairman, and David's son Robert became president. In 1966, David married Beatrice Levinson Rosenthal. When Norman died in 1967, David resumed the chairmanship. During the 1960's, the management of the construction arm of the company had passed on to David Tishman's nephew, John, who ran it as a service company, building for others. Its biggest job in the 1960's was the management of the construction for New York's World Trade Center.

The completion of the World Trade Center created a glut of office space, contributing in the 1970's, to Tishman Realty and Construction's biggest loss ever: the forty-four-story office building at 1166 Sixth Avenue. When General Telephone and Electric backed out of an arrangement to lease it and decided to move to Connecticut instead, Tishman was left with an empty building, causing his company to lose $70 million to $80 million before the New York State Employees Retirement System acquired the $100 million building for $37 million through foreclosure.

After this loss, in the troubled real estate market of 1976, Tishman Realty and Construction decided to liquidate and sell one of its three divisions, Construction and Research, along with its name and T-shaped girder logo, to the Rockefeller Center Corporation. David Tishman's official retirement as chairman coincided with this sale. The other two divisions of the company continued under the leadership of his sons, with Alan Tishman heading Tishman Management and Leasing Corporation, and Robert Tishman and his son-in-law Jerry I. Speyer heading Tishman Speyer Properties.

John Tishman continued to run Tishman Realty and Construction during the period of ownership by the Rockefeller Center Corporation. After David Tishman's death in New York at the age of ninety-one, John Tishman was able, with sixteen partners, to buy the company back from Rockefeller Center Corporation in 1981.

[See Tom Shachtman, *Skyscraper Dreams*, (1991), a record of New York City real estate developers. See also William G. Blair, "Tishman Company Back on Its Own Once More," *New York Times*, Feb. 10, 1980. An obituary is in the *New York Times*, June 19, 1980.]

ROSALYN SHAOUL

TOBEY, MARK (Dec. 11, 1890–Apr. 24, 1976), artist, was born in Centerville, Wis., one of four children of George Baker Tobey, a carpenter and farmer, and Emma Jane Cleveland. When Tobey was four, his family moved to Trempealeau, Wis., where he attended the local public schools. Although he had no formal exposure to art in school, he taught himself to draw by copying magazine covers, and learned about form by carving animal figurines out of the soft red stone found near his home. When Tobey was sixteen, the family moved to Hammond, Ind., near Chicago. Because of financial difficulties at home, Tobey dropped out of school in order to contribute to the family income.

While working at a series of low-paying jobs in Chicago, including blueprint boy for the Northern Steel Works and shipping clerk for a printing company, Tobey took Saturday classes at the Art Institute of Chicago, where he studied watercolor and was first exposed to art history and the works of the old masters.

After working for a time illustrating a mail-order catalog of women's clothing, Tobey moved to New York City in 1911 and settled in Greenwich Village, then the home of a thriving community of artists and writers. To support himself, he took a job as a fashion illustrator with *McCall's* magazine, earning forty dollars per week. His skill as a caricaturist and charcoal portraitist soon enabled him to leave the world of commercial art behind. His first one-man show, featuring portrait drawings, was held at the Knoedler Gallery in 1917. Tobey later noted that portraiture paid well, but that it involved "too many dinner parties."

Around 1918, Tobey became an adherent of the Baha'i faith, which teaches that all religions, despite their apparent diversity, really aim at finding an identical truth. Baha'i thereafter had a profound influence on both his life and work, providing him with aesthetic principles that emphasized unity in the visual sphere.

In 1922, Tobey moved to Seattle, Wash., which despite many comings and goings over the decades thereafter became his home base. He taught art in a progressive school run by Nellie Cornish. At about this time, he discovered what he called "multiple space," a personal version of cubism. He concluded that "all life is six-sided. . . . Even a piece of paper has six sides; my finger does; my hand does. Everything is six-sided." Also during this period, he was introduced to Chinese calligraphy by a Chinese artist studying at the University of Washington.

Tobey traveled to Europe in 1925 and settled for a time in Paris. He subsequently traveled to Greece, Turkey, and the Near East, where he studied Arabic and Persian calligraphy. In 1927 he returned to the United States and for the next four years divided his time between Seattle, Chicago, and New York City. He had one-man shows in both Chicago and New York City in 1928. Major works from this period include *Odalisque, Man Scratching Himself*, and *Middle West*.

From 1930 to 1938, Tobey lived and taught as artist in residence at Dartington Hall, a progressive school and cultural center in Devonshire, England. There he met such artists and intellectuals as Aldous Huxley, Pearl Buck, Arthur Waley, and Rabindranath Tagore, who like himself were interested in merging Western and Eastern viewpoints. In 1934 he traveled to the Far East, visiting China and Japan, where he lived for a month in a Zen monastery and studied painting, calligraphy, and meditation techniques. Back at Dartington Hall in 1935, influenced by his experiences in the Orient, Tobey began to develop his distinctive nonobjective painting style, "white writing." The white writing technique consists of a mazelike interlace of delicate white lines. In such paintings of this period as *Broadway Norm* and *Welcome Hero*, one is reminded of works by Jackson Pollock, but Tobey's paintings are much smaller, are usually done in tempera, and have an exquisite delicacy.

Tobey returned to the United States in 1938. He still had one foot in the representational Western tradition of art and was not yet ready to embrace the abstract, white writing style he had invented. By 1940 he was painting landscapes characterized by undulating hill forms, typified by his *White Night* (1942). Then for two years he painted shoppers and workers congregating in and about Seattle's markets; *E Pluribus Unum* (1942), which shows a crowd of a hundred or more small figures assembled before the stalls of vendors, typifies his best work from this period. Even when he employed white writing in this period, as in his 1943 painting of a great cathedral, *Gothic*, his lacelike, intermeshing white lines sometimes combined to suggest recognizable forms. But gradually Tobey turned more and more to his white writing style and used it to convey spiritual/intellectual concepts rather than impressions of physical objects. He covered his canvases from corner to corner with a myriad of small dots and lines, creating a network of densely integrated brushstrokes owing much to Eastern calligraphic traditions. White writing paintings such as *Tundra*, from 1944, and *Written Over the Plains*, from 1950, offer the viewer an impression of groundlessness and expansiveness. Tobey remarked, "I like best to see in nature what I want in my painting. When we can find the abstract in nature we find the deepest in art." Although his white writing anticipated the wiry all-over nonobjective paintings of Pollock and shared with abstract expressionists the search for a sense of the cosmic in art, he stands apart from them in that he ignored the Jungian-surrealist or forceful automatism that often underpinned abstract expressionist works.

By the 1950's, Tobey was recognized as one of America's most important, imaginative, and original painters. During the last twenty-five years of his life his works were exhibited at major museums and galleries throughout the

United States and Europe. He was elected to the National Institute of Arts and Letters in 1956. In 1960 he moved to Basel, Switzerland, where with his friend Pehr Hallsten, a Swedish-American scholar, he lived in a house formerly occupied by Paul Klee. He died in Basel.

The major collections of Tobey's works are in New York City, at the Museum of Modern Art and the Metropolitan Museum; in London, at the Tate Gallery; and in Paris, at the Musée National d'Art Moderne.

[William C. Seitz, *Mark Tobey* (1962), is a carefully documented and informative study of the artist's life and work up until 1962. The Seattle Art Museum, *Tobey's Eighty: A Retrospective* (1970), includes many plates of the artist's works and photographs of him and his friends and associates. The Galerie Bayeler's catalog, *Exhibition, December 70–February 71* (Basel, Switzerland, 1970), includes very good color illustrations and some interesting statements by the artist. Eliza E. Rathbone, *Mark Tobey, City Paintings* (1984), covers the artist's city and town subjects of the 1940's and 1950's. An obituary is in the *New York Times*, Apr. 25, 1976.]

ABRAHAM A. DAVIDSON

TOBIN, AUSTIN JOSEPH (May 25, 1903–Feb. 8, 1978), career government official, was born in Brooklyn, N.Y., the son of Katharine A. Moran and Clarence J. Tobin. His father was active in Democratic politics as secretary to John McCooey in the Municipal Civil Service Commission and was a career court reporter in Brooklyn. Tobin attended local Catholic schools and graduated from St. John's Preparatory School in 1921 and as salutatorian from Holy Cross College in 1925 with a B.A. On Dec. 9, 1925, he married Geraldine Thomasina Farley; they had two children.

In the period 1925–1927, Tobin worked in a Manhattan law firm while attending night law school at Fordham University. He had already developed an interest in the economic development of the New York region, and in 1927 he joined the Port of New York Authority (created by compact between New Jersey and New York State in 1921), as a law clerk. After earning his LL.B. degree in 1928, Tobin was appointed assistant attorney; in 1930 he was named real estate attorney and given responsibility for land condemnation work connected with the Port Authority's early projects—the George Washington Bridge, the Manhattan rail terminal, and the Lincoln Tunnel; in 1934 he began work on tax disputes involving the bistate agency and in 1935 he was appointed an assistant general counsel.

During his college years, Tobin had shown a talent for organizing people to carry out complex projects. By the mid-1930's he was displaying these traits in his legal work defending the Port Authority against private suits and against the Internal Revenue Service's efforts to tax Port Authority salaries and its bonds. From 1938 to 1942 he led a nationwide campaign to block the Roosevelt administration's attempts to strip all governmental bonds of tax-exempt status. The effort, which was successful, showed Tobin's ability to bring together a coalition of disparate groups and highlighted his tactical skills. In 1942, despite opposition from those who doubted that Tobin had real administrative talents, the Port Authority's commissioners reached down into the ranks and named him executive director.

When Tobin assumed office in July 1942, the Port Authority's operating facilities were limited to two tunnels under the Hudson and four bridges (three to Staten Island). Within a year, Tobin and his aides had identified several new projects that the agency might undertake—regional truck terminals, a large Manhattan bus station, marine terminals in Brooklyn and Manhattan and along the New Jersey shore, and the modernization and expansion of the region's three airports. Tobin then marshaled a staff of experts—in transportation planning, engineering, law, political analysis, finance, and public relations—that would allow the agency to evaluate the feasibility of action in each of these areas and to devise political strategies that could win support from the two states for the agency's plans.

Between 1945 and 1965, all of the planned projects were added to the Port Authority's domain: airports at Newark, La Guardia, and Idlewild (now Kennedy); truck terminals in New York City and Newark; the Manhattan bus terminal; and marine terminals at Newark, Elizabeth, Hoboken, and Brooklyn (although New York City rejected Tobin's offer to modernize city-owned piers). In addition, the agency built a second and then a third tube for the Lincoln Tunnel, which brought more cars and buses into Manhattan; it joined with Robert Moses and the Triborough Bridge and Tunnel Authority to expand the regional highway system; it resisted undertaking commuter rail projects but finally agreed to operate the old Hudson and Manhattan Railroad (now Port Authority Trans Hudson); it urged that a gigantic new airport be constructed in New Jersey; and it built the largest office center in the world, the World Trade Center.

Throughout these decades Tobin was the central figure in setting priorities, in guiding staff analysis, and in challenging skeptics and opponents at legislative hearings and in public meetings. He successfully resisted demands for patronage appointments and favoritism in contracts, emphasizing the importance of "avoiding politics" as a crucial ingredient in his agency's work. Because the Port Authority did not have taxing power but instead relied on income from tolls and rents, Tobin emphasized the need for each project to be self-supporting; this standard permitted him to use the rallying cry of "businesslike efficiency" in attracting support from the press and civic leaders, in fending off demands that the agency take on deficit-producing projects, and in persuading his own executives to operate airports, marine terminals, and other enterprises at high levels of effectiveness. Tobin's concept of public responsibility extended beyond narrow cost-benefit analysis, however; he encouraged his staff to devise innovative programs for tenant relocation and for affirmative action.

Tobin's first wife died in 1966. On June 29, 1967, he married Rosaleen C. Skehan, a lawyer for the Port Authority; they had no children. Tobin remained as the agency's executive director until 1972, but his final years were filled more with conflict than with achievements. He continued to urge that a new airport be built in New Jersey, but that project was blocked. He faced increasing demands that Port Authority revenues be used to meet growing deficits on the region's commuter railroads, and his firm resistance cost him political support in both state capitals. The immense size and cost of the World Trade Center turned some supporters of the agency's vision into doubters. In December 1971, Tobin decided that the strain of the job overwhelmed the sense of challenge that he had enjoyed for nearly thirty years in office, and he resigned. In the next several years, Tobin served as an unpaid adviser with the Executive Service Corps, providing managerial advice to government agencies in the Far East, Israel, and other areas. He died of cancer in Manhattan.

[Tobin's papers, including his weekly reports to the board of commissioners, together with related newspaper articles, are available at the library of the agency (since 1972 titled the Port Authority of New York and New Jersey). For analyses of Tobin and his work, see Annmarie H. Walsh, *The Public's Business* (1978); Jameson W. Doig, "To Claim the Seas and the Skies," in Jameson W. Doig and E. C. Hargrove, eds., *Leadership and Innovation* (1987); and Terry L. Cooper and Jameson W. Doig, "Austin Tobin and Robert Moses," in T. L. Cooper and N. D. Wright, eds., *Exemplary Public Administrators* (1992). An obituary is in the *New York Times*, Feb. 9, 1978.]

JAMESON W. DOIG

TODMAN, WILLIAM SELDEN ("BILL") (July 31, 1916–July 29, 1979), television producer, was born in New York City, the son of Frederick Simpson Todman and Helena Diana Orlowitz. His father was an accountant and author of books on finance. Todman completed his high school education at the Ethical Culture School in New York City. He received a B.S. from Johns Hopkins University in 1938 and a B.A. from New York University in 1941.

Between 1938 and 1941, Todman worked as a free-lance radio writer and producer in New York City, joining WABC radio as a writer and producer from 1941 through 1943. In 1943 he became agency supervisor of the Biow Company, an advertising agency in New York City, and writer and director of the "Connie Boswell Show," a radio program broadcast over the Blue Network (later part of the American Broadcasting Company). The next year Todman joined the "Anita Ellis Sings" radio show as director and writer. In 1945 and 1946 he was a writer for the "Treasury Salute" radio dramas.

In 1946, Todman teamed up with Mark Goodson to form Goodson-Todman Productions. They had met in 1941, while Todman was a writer for "Battle of the Boroughs," a local radio quiz show in New York City. Goodson was the show's emcee. Their careers were intertwined for the remainder of Todman's life. Goodson and Todman were package producers, a broader role than producer. They came up with the ideas for their shows, developed the ideas, hired all of the shows' employees, and oversaw a research department that located their guests or contestants. In short, they delivered completely packaged programs to the purchasing networks or advertisers. Although Goodson and Todman collaborated in the fullest sense, bouncing ideas off each other, the major responsibilities of their production company were divided. Goodson took charge of the programs' contents, while Todman, with his advertising background, handled the business aspects. In the broadcasting industry, these highly successful producers were known as The Boys; they were also referred to as the Gold Dust Twins, the Quiz Kids, and Flotsam and Jetsam.

Their first collaboration was "Winner Take All," a radio quiz program. Goodson came up with the idea, and Todman pitched it to Columbia Broadcasting Company (CBS) in 1942, but it was rejected by the network. CBS viewed the show as "a glorification of gambling with a disproportionate emphasis upon raising the ante. We might as well dramatize a poker game!" In 1946, CBS approached Todman for ideas for new radio programs. Todman presented the network with a revised script of the "Winner Take All." This time CBS bought the proposed show, which pioneered what became standard game show techniques, such as two or more contestants trying to answer a question at the same time, and allowing the winning contestant to return on subsequent shows until the person was defeated. Its success encouraged the pair to produce other game shows, including "Stop the Music" and "Hit the Jackpot." These radio shows and the later television programs that Goodson and Todman produced broke new ground in broadcasting. They were spontaneous programs that appealed to the competitive and acquisitive instincts of the American listening and viewing audience.

In February 1950, Todman and Goodson joined the newly emerging television broadcasting industry with the airing of "What's My Line?" on CBS. The show was hosted by John Daly with permanent panelists Dorothy Kilgallen, Arlene Francis, and Bennett Cerf, and a different celebrity panelist each week. Contestants worked in unusual occupations, and it was the task of the panelists to guess the occupations. The panelists had a limited number of questions, and the contestants could only give "yes" or "no" answers. The closing segment of each show featured a celebrity guest who intentionally disguised his or her voice. The blindfolded panel tried to determine the celebrity's identity. In its first year, "What's My Line?" won the Michael Award of the Academy of Radio and Television Arts and Sciences for the best panel show. In this era of live programming, "What's My Line?" was watched by millions of Americans every Sunday evening. One television critic claimed the program was "destined to become part of television history, American culture, the Sunday-night-after-the-Sunday-morning ritual." The show ran for seventeen years, leaving the air in 1967. The only program to run longer up to that time was the "Ed Sullivan Show."

Other successful quiz and game shows packaged for television by Goodson and Todman included "I've Got a Secret," "Password," "The Name's the Same," "Two for the Money," "Judge for Yourself," "By Popular Demand," "Play Your Hunch," and "Get the Message." At the time of Todman's death, Goodson-Todman had four shows on television: "The Price Is Right," "Match Game," "Tattle Tales," and "Family Feud."

In the 1960's, Goodson-Todman produced and filmed television dramatic series. These included "The Web," "Philip Marlowe," "The Legend of Ethan Allen," "Jefferson Drum," "The Rebel," "Branded," and the critically acclaimed "The Richard Boone Show." The duo produced one feature motion picture, *Ride Beyond Vengeance*, and coauthored the *Winner Take All Home Quiz Book* in 1949.

Todman and Goodson also had other communications interests. Todman served as vice-president of Capitol City Publishing Company, a holding company that controlled seventeen newspapers and radio station KOL in Seattle.

Todman married Frances Holmes Burson on Dec. 17, 1950; they had two children.

Todman and Goodson packaged the quiz and game shows that drew large audiences and helped to shape the first three decades of American television. Two generations of television viewers knew the phrase "A Mark Goodson–Bill Todman Production," the credit seen and heard at the close of each of their programs. Todman died in New York City.

[See James Poling, "Programs Packaged to Go," *Collier's*, May 24, 1952; John Daly, Mark Goodson, Bill Todman, Arlene Francis, and Bennett Cerf, "This Is Our Line," *Theatre Arts*, May 1954; and Gilbert Rogin, "Lords of Fun and Games," *Sports Illustrated*, June 24, 1963. An obituary is in the *New York Times*, July 31, 1979.]

PAUL A. FRISCH

TRISTANO, LEONARD JOSEPH ("LENNIE") (Mar. 19, 1919–Nov. 18, 1978), jazz pianist and composer, was born in Chicago, the second of four sons of Michael Tristano, a pharmacist, and Rosemary Milano. He began playing the piano by age four, but he did not receive formal instruction until later in childhood. Around 1923, he started losing his sight. Although his blindness has been attributed to his birth during an influenza epidemic or to a severe case of measles, the cause is unknown. Tristano did not do well in school, and he was relegated to a class for children with physical and mental handicaps. By age nine he was completely without sight, and his parents sent him to a state residential school for the blind. Tristano's interest in music was encouraged there. He received lessons on piano, drums, and a number of wind instruments. One night while listening to the radio, he heard jazz trumpeter Roy Eldridge, which profoundly influenced his musical development. By age twelve, he was performing on piano, clarinet, and tenor saxophone.

In 1938, Tristano entered the American Conservatory of Music in Chicago. He finished his work for a Bachelor of Music degree in three years and was just one exam shy of a master's degree when he left the school in 1943. While at the conservatory he composed classical works, including a string quartet. During this time he played clarinet in Dixieland bands and tenor saxophone and piano in rhumba bands. After leaving the conservatory, he taught advanced students at the Christiansen School of Popular Music. He later said that "students who wanted to learn taught me how to teach." For example, alto saxophonist Lee Konitz, then fifteen, came to study with Tristano, starting an association that lasted for more than two decades. Tristano attracted other important students, including composer William Russo. Among his students was the singer Judy Moore, whom he married in July 1945. They had one child and were divorced in 1953.

Tristano insisted, despite conventional wisdom, that jazz could be taught. He also maintained that the heart of jazz was improvisation, not orchestration. He asked his students to listen to and be able to sing the recorded improvisations of jazz masters such as Eldridge and Lester Young. He defined the true jazz improvisers as "pure, uncontrived players who were bursting with energy and ideas, but who released all that energy slowly." His coterie of associates grew, and the writer Phil Featheringill called him the "father-confessor" of young Chicago beboppers. (Bebop was the complex style of jazz then in the avant-garde.) Some critics, especially Barry Ulanov of *Metronome*, a magazine for which Tristano occasionally wrote, began promoting his work. Also at this time he made his first recordings, four solo piano recordings and a session with trombonist Earl Swope, both released posthumously.

Tristano moved to New York City in 1946. Already he was stretching the harmonic limits of jazz, pushing it toward functional, if not formal, atonality. His early engagements in the New York City area proved unsuccessful, but he soon was recording with a trio of guitar and bass. One side, "I Can't Get Started," has been cited by jazz historian Gunther Schuller as "one of the most prophetic recordings in all jazz history." Tristano was active on the New York scene, playing with many major musicians, including alto saxophonist Charlie Parker, percussionist Max Roach, and bassist-composer Charles Mingus. Tristano's work had a marked influence on Mingus's music. He also resumed teaching, attracting as students tenor saxophonist Warne Marsh and guitarist Billy Bauer.

When Konitz arrived in New York in 1948 and resumed his studies, Tristano created the Lennie Tristano Sextet, which proved his most notable ensemble. The group sounded very different from other jazz ensembles of the time. Its sound was characterized by long, intricate, precisely played ensemble figures, the use of counterpoint, and the light, flutelike sound of the saxophones. The sextet recorded for Capitol in 1949. At one session the group, without the drummer, performed four numbers that were freely improvised, with no predetermined meter or tonality. Two performances were erased, and Capitol refused to release the other two. They were released only after New York disc jockey "Symphony Sid" Torin repeatedly broadcast copies he had obtained. These sides presaged the free improvisation of the 1960's.

What some saw as willfulness gave rise to criticisms of Tristano's work. Critics charged his music was overly intellectual and lacked rhythmic vitality. Tristano maintained that "feeling" rather than raw emotion was central to true improvisation. He contrasted what he saw as egotistical technical displays with improvisation that revealed a player's inner self. On a technical level, he emphasized the creation of melody that flowed freely over the bar lines, creating the effect of polymeter. Despite the critical brickbats, Tristano's recordings influenced the growing "cool" jazz movement popular in the 1950's.

In 1951, Tristano opened the Lennie Tristano School of Music in New York City, where he and his advanced students gave private lessons. The loyalty of his students, some of whom refused lucrative jobs to continue their studies, was cause for suspicion. Al Haig, a prominent pianist, referred to him as "the witch doctor." But many of his students found in him a practical philosopher who could guide their musical development and help them deal with life. "He once said that you would play better after you had read *War and Peace*," according to Russo. "He encouraged us to read, to learn about the world, to enlarge ourselves." At one point, he even considered abandoning music and studying psychology. He discouraged students from looking on jazz as a way to make a living, instead encouraging them to practice it as an art that would lead them to a better understanding of themselves. Many of his students became teachers.

Also in 1951, Tristano formed Jazz Records, but the label released only one two-sided single recorded during his lifetime. His use of multitrack recording and tape manipulation, an early use of that now-common technology, on two tracks of *Lennie Tristano*, an album he recorded for Atlantic in 1955 caused further controversy. In 1956 he closed his school after most of the other teachers left to pursue their own careers. He moved to Long Island and continued a rigorous—ten hours per day, six days per week—teaching schedule in his home. Though he had a contract with Atlantic, he chose to record infrequently, with only two albums being issued before his death twenty-two years later. The most significant, *The New Tristano*, was released in 1962. This solo piano album, which he recorded himself in 1962, represents the pinnacle of Tristano's art. From 1958 to 1965, he led groups with Marsh and sometimes Konitz at the Half Note in New York City. The performances led to Tristano's only appearance on national television, on the religious program "Look Up and Live."

During this period Tristano attracted some of his important later students, notably pianist Connie Crothers and tenor saxophonist Lenny Popkin. Crothers and pianist Liz Gorrill were among his noted female pupils. Crothers has said that unlike other teachers, she felt Tristano took her as seriously as his male students. Tristano maintained that women had more potential as improvisers because they tended to be more intuitive and were less concerned with instrumental prowess for its own sake.

In the last years of his life, Tristano increasingly withdrew from the jazz scene. He married Carol Miller in 1961; they had two daughters, one of whom, with encouragement from her father, became a drummer. For a few years Tristano enjoyed a degree of domestic peace. His piano was in the kitchen, and he often played with his children around his legs. His marriage, however, broke up bitterly in 1964. About this time, he suffered the first in a series of chronic health problems that plagued him until his death.

Tristano traveled to Europe in the fall of 1965 to take part in a historic piano summit in Berlin. The program included two pianists, Earl Hines and Teddy Wilson, who had influenced him early in his career, and the popular modernist Bill Evans, who, though not a Tristano student, reflected the Tristano influence and helped spread it to the next generation of pianists. In 1968, at the invitation of former pupils, Tristano traveled to England to perform. But he concentrated his energies on teaching and produced concerts featuring three of his prized students—Sal Mosca, his student since 1947, Gorrill, and Crothers. Tristano died at his home in Jamaica, Queens, in New York City. Since his death, a number of recordings of his performances have been released on the revitalized Jazz Records.

[Tristano's articles "What's Wrong with the Beboppers" and "What's Right with the Beboppers" are in *Metronome*, June and July 1947 (respectively). He also wrote "Why Don't They Leave Me Alone?," *Down Beat*, Dec. 3, 1952. A chapter is devoted to Tristano and Konitz in Ira Gitler, *Jazz Masters of the Forties* (1966); Gunther Schuller's analysis of "I Can't Get Started" is in his *The Swing Era* (1988). See also Barry Ulanov, "Master in the Making," *Metronome*, Aug. 1949, and "The Means of Mastery," *Metronome*, Sept. 1949; Nat Hentoff, "Multitaping Isn't Phony: Tristano," *Down Beat*, May 16, 1956; Dick Hadlock, "Lennie Tristano," *Down Beat*, Oct. 30, 1958; Bill Coss, "Lennie Tristano Speaks Out," *Down Beat*, Dec. 6, 1962; Bob Dawbarn, "Tristano: Never Mind History, All I Want to Do Is Play Music," *Melody Maker*, Nov. 13, 1965; Gundrun Endress, "Lennie Tristano Talks . . . ," *Jazz Monthly*,

Feb. 1966; Alan Surpin, "Lennie Tristano: Feeling Is Basic . . . ," *Down Beat*, Oct. 16, 1969; and John Francis McKinney, "The Pedagogy of Lennie Tristano" (Ph.D. diss., Fairleigh Dickinson University, 1978). An obituary is in the *New York Times*, Nov. 20, 1978. C. Sheridan, "Lennie Tristano," *Jazz Podium*, Feb. 1979, a long obituary in German, includes a good, concise discography. Discussions of Tristano's work published after his death include Robert Palmer, "The Teachings of Lennie Tristano," *Rolling Stone*, Apr. 5, 1979; and Francis Davis, "Tristanoitis: The Legacy of Lennie Tristano," the *Village Voice*, June 4, 1991.]

DAVID DUPONT

TRUMBO, JAMES DALTON (Dec. 9, 1905–Sept. 10, 1976), screenwriter and novelist, was born in Montrose, Colo., the son of Orus Bonham Trumbo, a sometimes shoe salesman and beekeeper, and Maud Tillery. Although he attended the University of Colorado (1924–1925), the University of California, Los Angeles (1926), and the University of Southern California (1928–1930), Trumbo had to leave college without a degree because he ran out of money. He spent his early years as a writer fulfilling the classic stereotype of the struggling artist in a variety of blue-collar jobs: car washer, railroad section hand, and for nine years first a bread-wrapper and later an estimator on the night shift of a Los Angeles bakery. Between 1925 and 1933 he wrote eighty-eight short stories and six novels, all of which were rejected by the book and magazine editors to whom he offered his work. After a brief stint as a reader at Warner Brothers, he sold his first screenplay, *Jealousy*, to Columbia Pictures in 1934, and his first novel, *Eclipse*, to a London publisher in 1935. Over the next five years he wrote two more novels, *Washington Jitters* for Knopf in 1936, and *Johnny Got His Gun* for Lippincott in 1939. The latter, a powerful, antiwar novel centered on the thoughts of a hospitalized World War I soldier who has lost his arms, legs, sight, and hearing, won the American Booksellers Award for 1939. *Johnny Got His Gun* was finally made into a film in 1971, using Trumbo's script, and received the International Critics Award and a Special Grand Prize at the Cannes Film Festival. In 1940 he published his fourth novel, *The Remarkable Andrew*, which he turned into a film script in 1942.

Between 1935 and 1945, Trumbo alone or in collaboration with other screenwriters worked on the scripts of twenty-one films for RKO, Columbia, Paramount, Twentieth Century–Fox, and MGM. His first important screenwriter's credit was for RKO's *A Man to Remember*, which was named one of the ten best films of 1938. His screen adaptation of Christopher Morley's novel, *Kitty Foyle*, helped Ginger Rogers to win an Oscar as Best Actress in 1940. Three of his scripts for MGM were given awards by *Boxoffice Magazine*: *A Guy Named Joe*, in 1943; *Thirty Seconds over Tokyo*, also named one of the ten best films of 1944; and *Our Vines Have Tender Grapes* in 1945. In addition to his screenwriting, Trumbo wrote stories for a variety of national magazines, including *Vanity Fair*, *McCall's*, the *Saturday Evening Post*, and two left-wing publications, *The New Masses* and *Masses and Mainstream*. He also served briefly as a war correspondent with the United States Army Air Force. Trumbo married Cleo Beth Fincher on March 13, 1938; the couple had three children.

As the post–World War II period began, Trumbo was one of the highest-paid writers in Hollywood, commanding as much as $3,000 per week for his services or $75,000 a script under his five-year contract with MGM. But by 1949 he was in prison, anathema to the film industry, and nearly penniless. The coming of the Cold War had led the United States House of Representatives Un-American Activities Committee (HUAC), under the chairmanship of J. Parnell Thomas of New Jersey, to investigate allegations of subversion and propagandizing in Hollywood by Communists and fellow travelers. Named as a subversive by members of a conservative group calling themselves the Motion Picture Alliance for the Preservation of American Ideals, Trumbo was summoned to the HUAC hearings in Washington in October 1947 to explain his membership in the Communist party in 1943 and his editorship of the *Screen Writer*, the official organ of the Screen Writers' Guild. Refusing to give the committee any information about his politics, he was tried, found guilty of contempt of Congress (as were nine other witnesses who, with Trumbo, comprised the "Hollywood Ten"), and sentenced to pay a $1,000 fine and to serve a year in prison. After the Supreme Court refused to review the case, Trumbo entered the federal prison at Ashland, Ky., in June 1950. "It was a place of quality," he said later, "as evidenced by the fact that the head librarian was a Congressman."

Assigned to work in a storeroom, Trumbo

had access to a typewriter and used it to write a screenplay. Released ten months later, in April 1951, and unable to sell the script under his own name, Trumbo sold it on the black market. He had been placed on the Hollywood blacklist, which had been compiled four years earlier, in the aftermath of HUAC's investigations, by top-level movie executives from both coasts meeting secretly in New York at the Waldorf-Astoria.

The blacklist, which has never been fully disclosed and the existence of which was denied for years, reportedly contained as many as three hundred names of writers, directors, actors, and others who were suspected of Communist party affiliation or Communist sympathies. For Trumbo the blacklist meant both personal and financial hardship. Unable to work in Hollywood, he was forced to sell his beloved mile-high ranch eighty miles from Hollywood. He moved to Mexico where he churned out some eighteen low-budget scripts, which he marketed under a pseudonym for a fraction of the fees he had once been able to command. Trumbo later wrote in the *Nation* that the worst part of his ordeal was not the loss of income or property: "The more terrible wound," he said, was "the loss of a profession." For a decade, Trumbo toiled in anonymity. Then his screenplay for *The Brave Bulls*, which was credited to "Robert Rich," won the Academy Award in 1957. Finally free to write under his own name again, Trumbo created the screenplays for two overtly liberal pictures, the big-budget spectaculars *Spartacus* and *Exodus*, both released in 1960. Before his death in Los Angeles, Trumbo wrote scripts for many other films, including MGM's *Hawaii* in 1966, *The Fixer* in 1968, and *Papillon* in 1973.

[Trumbo's papers are at the University of Wisconsin, Madison. His letters, edited by Helen Manfull, are collected in *Additional Dialogue: Letters of Dalton Trumbo, 1942–1962* (1970). His account of his experience with HUAC is found in *The Time of the Toad: A Study of Inquisition in America* (1972). An obituary is the *New York Times*, Sept. 11, 1976.]

ALLAN L. DAMON

TUGWELL, REXFORD GUY (July 10, 1891–July 21, 1979), economist, political adviser, and governor of Puerto Rico, was born in Sinclairville, N.Y., south of Buffalo. His father, Charles Henry Tugwell, was a cattle dealer and entrepreneur; his mother, Dessie Rexford, was a former schoolteacher.

Tugwell attended primary school near home but later transferred to Masten Park High School in Buffalo, from which he graduated in 1911. His early work in his father's canning factory aroused his sympathies for the overworked and underpaid employees. Although generally vigorous, he suffered from asthma all his life.

With an eye toward finance and commerce, Tugwell entered the University of Pennsylvania's Wharton School in Philadelphia, from which he received the B.S. in 1915 and a master's degree in 1916. He was an instructor in economics at the Wharton School (1915–1917) and assistant professor of marketing at the University of Washington (1917–1918). His Ph.D. dissertation, "The Economic Basis of Public Interest," was published in 1922.

After managing the American University Union in Paris for a year, he paused at home for a year to consider where next to go. In 1920 he began his service in the department of economics at Columbia University. He became a popular teacher, particularly in Columbia's innovative course on contemporary civilization. He rose to full professor in 1931.

Tugwell married Florence E. Arnold in 1914; they had two children and were divorced in 1938. In the same year he married Grace Falke; they had two children.

Although the Wharton School had a broadly conservative economics program, as did Columbia University, Tugwell acquired a generous view of what federal policy in the field ought to be. He was helped by the dynamic outlook of his Wharton School associate Simon Patten. He was also impressed by Thorstein Veblen's institutional approach to economics, as well as Frederick W. Taylor's time-and-motion-study production controls then being made famous in Henry Ford's automobile plants. Tugwell's out-of-academe influences included H. G. Wells's fictional and nonfictional musings on progress and the means for obtaining it. John Dewey, a fellow professor at Columbia, taught him the need for experiment in planning.

In a larger sense, Tugwell was responsive to the Populist and Progressive movements of his time, which introduced ideas and actions by government sponsors and the cooperative worker-capitalist programs of such innovators as Bolton Hall, Upton Sinclair, and Edward A. Filene.

The greatest impression made on Tugwell during his Wharton School years was the persecution endured by Scott Nearing, of somewhat similar background to Tugwell's. Nearing's efforts to plead the cause of workers in his writings and university classes caused him to be dropped in 1915 from Wharton's staff, beginning Nearing's long career of disaffection with American traditions.

At Columbia, Tugwell became known for his views on government, social planning, and experiment. His articles in both academic journals and such general-interest publications as the *New Republic* further increased his visibility. In 1927 he visited Soviet Russia, and the following year he published a positive view of Communist accomplishments in his *Soviet Russia in the Second Decade*. That same year he contributed advice on farm policy to Governor Alfred E. Smith of New York, the Democratic presidential candidate, and turned from the Republican to the Democratic party.

Tugwell was critical of the Hoover administration's reaction to the Great Depression and published his thoughts in *Mr. Hoover's Economic Policy* (1932). During the presidential elections of that year, Tugwell advised the Democratic nominee, Franklin D. Roosevelt, on campaign issues.

After Roosevelt's 1932 victory, Tugwell was called to Washington, D.C., to plan ways to fight the continuing depression. He became Secretary of Agriculture Henry A. Wallace's assistant secretary and later rose to under secretary of agriculture (1934–1937). In the Department of Agriculture, Tugwell developed a program not only to end the Great Depression but also to put the nation on a road to better and more satisfying living. He described his purposes in *The Battle for Democracy* (1935).

The heart of Tugwell's program was deficit spending. Economically, he argued that the money could be readily replenished once production was revived. Constitutionally, he pointed out that the nation's basic document said nothing about business and such related matters as health, the role of cities, and world relations. They were thus areas subject to change and amendments.

Hence, in the economic crisis Tugwell felt free to ask for higher taxes on those with large incomes and inheritances. He requested $5 billion for relief and for getting purchasing power back into the hands of the needy and unemployed. As head of the Resettlement Administration, Tugwell sought funds to move farmers from worn-out soil to better land, where they would profit from expert government advice and from soil conservation. Public enterprises and regulatory agencies would control large-scale operations.

Over the next several years there was government action in all these areas, but all were underfunded, and relatively little was accomplished. There was some movement by farmers, but more because of drought and flood than as a result of subsidies. The problem inspired John Steinbeck's *The Grapes of Wrath* (1939), but not enough took place to do more than institutionalize government subsidies, mainly to large farmers.

There were plans for greenbelts, model areas to which farmers and others of urban background but loyal to New Deal purposes could be moved in an organized way and which would be kept beautiful as well as practical under planning regulations. Three such programs materialized, and they were credited with influencing the form and substance of post–World War II suburbs, created to satisfy housing needs rather than to set standards for model towns.

Tugwell resigned from the Department of Agriculture in 1936—he left Columbia officially the next year—and accepted his friend Charles Taussig's offer of a vice-presidency of the American Molasses Company, a sinecure he left early in 1938, when Mayor Fiorello H. La Guardia of New York City appointed him chairman of the city's Planning Commission. Tugwell broke new ground with a city budget intended to balance its duties to citizens with broadening their rights to include human privileges such as minority opportunities in jobs and civil service.

In 1940, Secretary of the Interior Harold L. Ickes asked Tugwell to visit Puerto Rico and report on large corporations that illegally monopolized land. Tugwell became friendly with the progressive politician Luis Muñoz Marín who was instrumental in having him appointed chancellor of the University of Puerto Rico in 1941. Shortly afterward, the United States Senate confirmed Tugwell as governor of Puerto Rico.

Tugwell took office at a difficult time, with German submarines isolating Puerto Rico from its sources of supply and customers. During the next five years he became an authority on the island's social and cultural needs. He fought for laws favoring the poor and set up planning and budget bureaus, but he was frustrated by traditional attitudes favoring the island's elite. Tugwell recounted his adventures in *The Stricken Land* (1947). The government later published his official papers as governor.

In 1946, Tugwell accepted the invitation of President Robert M. Hutchins to direct the University of Chicago's Institute of Planning (through 1950), as well as to serve as professor of political science (through 1957). His hopes of turning planning into legislation, however, were limited. The Great Depression had been cured by war needs, and the new priority was control of nuclear weapons. Although Tugwell disagreed, his *A Chronology of Jeopardy, 1945–1955* (1955) did not meet the anxieties of the Cold War. Public opinion was less willing to credit Soviet dictator Stalin with benign intentions than was Tugwell. Holding that only superior power would control Stalin, President Harry Truman and the Congress preferred that funds be allotted to Cold War expenses rather than to civic or social needs. Disappointed, Tugwell worked for Henry A. Wallace's Progressive party in the 1948 presidential campaign.

In 1959, when Hutchins established the Center for the Study of Democratic Institutions in Santa Barbara, Calif., Tugwell joined him as a senior fellow and retired from the University of Chicago. More important, he became recognized as the outstanding memorialist of the New Deal and an advocate for President Roosevelt's policies, for such works as *The Democratic Roosevelt* (1957), *The Enlargement of the Presidency* (1960), *The Brains Trust* (1968), and *Roosevelt's Revolution* (1977), the last a personal memoir of his first year in Washington. *Off Course, from Truman to Nixon* (1971) was a critical review of the presidency as practiced by Roosevelt's successors, with conjectures as to how Roosevelt would have handled the crises that followed his death. Although none of Tugwell's works in this vein sold well, they constituted a unique appraisal of the New Deal era for those examining its premises and results.

Tugwell died in Santa Barbara, Calif.

[Tugwell's papers are in the Franklin D. Roosevelt Library, Hyde Park, N.Y. *The Light of Other Days* (1962) is his autobiography. See also *The Diary of Rexford G. Tugwell: The New Deal, 1932–1935*, edited by Michael V. Namorato (1992). Also of value is Bernard Sternsher, *Rexford Tugwell and the New Deal* (1964). An obituary is in the *New York Times*, July 22, 1979.]

LOUIS FILLER

TUNNEY, JAMES JOSEPH ("GENE") (May 25, 1897–Nov. 7, 1978), heavyweight boxing champion, was born in a flat above a grocery store to Irish Catholic parents who lived at 414 West Fifty-second Street in New York City. When Gene was three months old his father, John Joseph Tunney, a longshoreman, moved the family to Perry Street in Greenwich Village. There Gene attended St. Veronica's Parochial School, demonstrating an early interest in the arts. Classmates considered him a bit of a prig because of his interest in Greek and Roman history and his fastidiousness with language and deportment. At thirteen, he appeared on the school stage as the prince in *Romeo and Juliet*, and he liked reciting speeches by Portia, Antonio, and Shylock.

Gene's mother, Mary Lydon, born at Castle Bar in County Mayo, was a devout woman and hoped that one of her three sons would become a priest. Gene's father was a fight fan who idolized Jim Corbett, Bob Fitzsimmons, and John L. Sullivan. John Tunney frequented Owney Geaghan's boxing club on the Bowery, where the great John L. Sullivan had fought, and there was defeated in a boxing match against the house pro. He gave his son boxing gloves for his tenth birthday, hoping the skinny lad would learn to protect himself from neighborhood toughs. Gene boxed all day with his brothers and companions, going home with a swollen nose, bloody lips, and "a terrific headache." He based his boxing style on the columns of *New York Evening World* sportswriter Bob Edgren, repeatedly practicing a straight left and a right swing, once on an inflated turkey crop that he tied to a transom after the family's Thanksgiving meal. None of the Tunney boys entered the priesthood, but a sister did become a nun.

Initially, Tunney fought as a means of physical conditioning. He sparred with volunteers at the local firehouse, played center in local basketball, and handball with parish priests. He ran marathon at La Salle Academy, from which he graduated in 1915, and organized sprints around Central Park with neighborhood friends. On warm summer nights Tunney could be seen jogging up Fifth Avenue behind big green double-decker buses. He liked to swim off the pier at West Tenth Street and frequently dove from barges and transatlantic steamers into the Hudson River. He suffered a concussion after diving with arms to his sides from the top deck of the SS *Majestic*.

Boxing was as much a part of Tunney's teen years as breathing, he later recalled. Scuffling with rivals in the Gophers and Hudson Dusters, two youth gangs who fought for West Side bragging rights, taught Tunney a valuable lesson "in the manly art of self-protection." A healthy respect for "the other fellow's fists" cautioned him to size up his opponents before challenging them. Tunney's defensive instincts characterized his boxing and business careers. He emulated "Handsome" Jack Goodman, a light heavyweight who also lived on Perry Street. Tunney followed him through the streets of the city's West Side, imitating his short, snappy stride. At school and at smokers held by Catholic clubs, the Christian Brothers encouraged Tunney's interest in boxing, hoping to channel his surplus energy. But a bout with Leonard Ross failed to impress onlookers. The promoter of a competing smoker thought Tunney "too awkward and wild" to have a future in prizefighting.

In his middle teens, Tunney fought nightly in West Side smokers for ginger ale and a stale ham sandwich. By day he worked at the Ocean Steamship Company, earning five dollars weekly as a fifteen-year-old office boy and eleven dollars weekly later as a mail clerk. Promotion to freight classifier when he was seventeen brought seventeen dollars per week and correspondence courses in business, mathematics, and English in the hope he would one day rise to the rank of dock superintendent. But the work proved monotonous; Tunney was "itching for excitement." During breaks, he would spar with junior clerks, pushing desks and file cabinets out of the way to provide ring space. Fight club evenings were "rough and tumble" and proved a good training ground "where nearly anything went."

Tunney's first encounter with a professional boxer came when he was sixteen. He sparred three rounds with twenty-six-year-old Willie Green, a veteran of 168 fights, and was beaten up so badly he decided the next morning he would never go up against a professional again. Three weeks later, however, he battled Green a second time and held his own, following that with two savvy showings against the veteran, which made the 133-pound challenger the talk of the West Side. Tunney's first fight as a professional came when he was a 140-pound eighteen-year-old. He received eighteen dollars from the Sharkey Athletic Club for his seventh-round knockout of Bobby Dawson. Four fights quickly followed, a draw and three wins, two by knockout. Tunney became a 150-pound fighter of "careful" habits. He had learned to counterpunch, feint, and side step, and to time his attacks.

In early 1917, Tunney clung to his daytime job at the steamship company, poised between two careers and unsure if there was a future for him in fighting. American entrance into World War I complicated matters further. Tunney failed a physical with the United States Marine Corps in May of that year because of an elbow injury. He took a summer job as a lifeguard in Keansburg, N.J., hoping the sun and exercise would expedite the healing process, and in June 1918 he was aboard a troop ship bound for France. He boxed as a member of the American Expeditionary Force to avoid guard duty. Despite breaking a knuckle in a preliminary bout in Tours, he went on to defeat southpaw K. O. Sullivan and American amateur light heavyweight champion Ted Jamison to win the AEF's light heavyweight championship in Paris in 1918. He returned to the United States the following year.

Late in 1919, while on a boxing exhibition in the Rhineland, Tunney confessed to a newspaper man his ambition of one day defeating Jack Dempsey, the "Manassa Mauler," who earlier that year had become world heavyweight champion. The boast seemed absurd. Even after Tunney won the United States light heavyweight title in 1922 with a twelve-round decision over Battling Levinsky, critics charged the six-foot, one-and-a-half-inch, 175-pound Tunney was a "synthetic fighter" with small, brittle hands and little punching power. That critique seemed substantiated when Tunney lost his title later that year to Harry Greb. Tunney, blind and out on his feet at the end of the fight, collapsed at his dressing room door. It would be the only loss of Tunney's career. He fought the "Pittsburgh Windmill" four more times in four years and, following the final fight in St. Paul, Greb predicted that Tunney would beat Dempsey.

Despite victories over the leading contenders of his era, including Georges Carpentier, Tommy Gibbons, and Bartley Madden, Tunney was a nine-to-five underdog when he fought Jack Dempsey at Philadelphia's Sesquicentennial Stadium on Sept. 23, 1926. Dempsey, slowed by three years of inactivity, was no match for the now 187-pound "fighting marine." Tunney dominated the ten-round title fight, fought in a driving rain before 144,468 spectators, the largest crowd yet to see a sporting event in North America. Tunney's superior speed and careful study of Dempsey's ring style led to a first-round right that landed flush on the champion's jaw. Dempsey, badly battered, never recovered.

A rematch fought Sept. 22, 1927, at Soldier Field in Chicago created the most famous moment in the history of boxing. The first six rounds were a replay of the first Tunney-Dempsey fight, with Tunney's counterpunching keeping him in command. Then, fifty seconds into the seventh round, Dempsey caught Tunney against the ropes with a left-hand lead and floored the sagging Tunney with six more blows, only two of which Tunney later remembered. For the first time in his career Tunney was on the canvas. Dempsey, however, refused to go immediately to the furthest neutral corner, and this led to a six-second delay in referee Dave Barry's count, the so-called long count. Tunney rose on nine, fifteen seconds after his knockdown, escaped Dempsey's charge, and won the final three rounds of the fight, retaining his championship.

Tunney defended his title only one additional time, knocking out a longshot, New Zealander Tom Heeney, in the eleventh round on July 26, 1928, in New York. Tunney retired from the ring following his marriage to Mary Josephine ("Polly") Lauder, heir to the Carnegie estate, on Oct. 3, 1928. They had four children, one of whom, John Varick Tunney, became a United States senator from California. Gene Tunney had become a millionaire through boxing and made a second fortune as a corporate executive. He served as chairman of the board of American Distilling Company and of the McCandless Corporation and served on boards for Schick, Technicolor, Inc., the Industrial Bank of Commerce, and many other companies. He became national chairman for the National Foundation for American Youth and directed athletics and physical fitness programs for the United States Navy in World War II. He traveled extensively, made friends with George Bernard Shaw, Thornton Wilder, and other members of the literary community, and even lectured on Shakespeare at Yale. He died in Greenwich, Conn.

Tunney's place in boxing history seems secure. He lost only one of sixty-three recorded bouts, defeated Dempsey twice, and was the first heavyweight champion to retire undefeated. An untraditional pugilist, Tunney, with his emphasis on speed, footwork, and defense in boxing, transformed the sport from a bare-knuckled bloodbath into something approaching a science. Tunney's status as a cultural icon has not gone unchallenged, however. Though his ascendancy was briefly interpreted as a Horatio Alger success story, critics later charged that his "unspectacular efficiency" in the ring and "bookish social climbing" outside it "failed to touch the heart of America."

The prize ring, with its million-dollar gates, became in Tunney's day a forum for competing social values and notions of manhood. Dempsey's offensive ring style made him the "noble savage," while Tunney's studied ring strategy made him the first of the truly modern boxers. His career, he claimed, was guided by the simple principle that "thinking, practicing and doing" made champions in all walks of life.

[Tunney's two autobiographies are *A Man Must Fight* (1932) and *Arms for Living* (1941). He also wrote "My Fights with Jack Dempsey," in *The Aspirin Age* (1949), edited by Isabel Leighton; the foreword to Alexander Johnston, *Ten and Out* (1927); and "The Blow That Hurts," *Atlantic Monthly*, June 1939. See also Edward Van Every, *The Life of Gene Tunney, the Fighting Marine* (1927); and Nat Fleischer, *Gene Tunney* (1931). Biographic sketches are found in Paul Gallico, *Farewell to Sport* (1940), and *The Golden People* (1965); Grantland Rice, *The Tumult and the Shouting* (1954); Mel Heimer, *The Long Count* (1969); and Benny Green, *Shaw's Champions* (1978).

For the cultural context of the Tunney-Dempsey fights see Heywood Broun, "It Seems to Heywood Broun," *Nation*, Aug. 8, 1928; William E. Leuchtenburg, *The Perils of Prosperity, 1914–1932* (1958); John William Ward, *Red, White, and Blue* (1969); Roderick Nash, *The Nervous Generation* (1970); Lawrence W. Levine, "Progress and Nostalgia: The Self-Image of the 1920's," in Lawrence W. Levine and Robert Middlekauff, *The National Temper* (1972); Randy Roberts, *Jack Dempsey* (1979); Frank Winer, "The Elderly Jock and How He Got That Way," in Jeffrey H. Goldstein, ed., *Sports, Games and Play* (1979); Benjamin G. Rader, "Compensatory Sports Heroes: Ruth, Grange and Dempsey," *Journal of Popular Culture* 16 (Spring 1983); and Elliott J. Gorn, "The Manassa Mauler and the Fighting Marine: An Interpretation of the Dempsey-Tunney Fights," *Journal of American Studies* 19 (1985). An obituary is in the *New York Times*, Nov. 8, 1978.]

BRUCE J. EVENSEN

U–V

UNTERMEYER, LOUIS (Oct. 1, 1885–Dec. 17, 1977), anthologist, editor, and poet, was born in New York City, the son of Emanuel Untermeyer, a jewelry manufacturer, and Julia Michael. His parents were prosperous and cultured, and his mother read often to him from the classics. As a child he loved Gustave Doré's illustrations of Dante's *Inferno*, and fifty years later, he would publish several volumes of French fairy tales illustrated by the French artist. Though he aspired to be a composer, at the age of seventeen he dropped out of DeWitt Clinton High School after failing geometry and entered the family jewelry business. Later he became vice-president of the company and manager of the firm's Newark factory. He resigned in 1923 to study and write. Untermeyer married Jeannette Starr, a poet, in 1907; they had three children, two of whom were adopted. The couple divorced in 1926, and were married again from 1927 to 1933. From 1926 to their divorce in 1927 he was married to Virginia Moore; they had one child. In 1933, Untermeyer married Esther Antin, a lawyer. They divorced in 1948. That same year he married Bryna Ivens, an editor of children's books. This marriage lasted until his death.

As early as 1912, Untermeyer sponsored young poets such as Robert Frost, Ezra Pound, Vachel Lindsay, Wallace Stevens, and T. S. Eliot by helping them get their poetry published. He began his own writing career as a music and poetry critic, becoming a contributing editor of *The Masses* and the *Liberator*. Together with Robert Frost, Van Wyck Brooks, and others, he founded *Seven Arts* magazine. From 1934 to 1937 he was poetry editor of the *American Mercury*. He was also an occasional lecturer at colleges and universities. For a while he worked as a radio commentator, and late in life he was a panelist on the television program "What's My Line?" During this period he was accused of being a Communist and resigned from the show. By the late 1940's he had begun to write critical biographies.

Untermeyer delivered the Henry Ward Beecher lectures at Amherst College (1937), was poet-in-residence at the University of Michigan (1939–1940); cultural editor at Decca Records (1943–1956), consultant in poetry at the Library of Congress (1961–1963), and for a quarter of a century chair of the Pulitzer Prize poetry jury. In 1960 he was appointed consultant to the Britannica Library in American and British poetry. He was the United States representative to an international cultural conference in India (1961) and conducted seminars in American poetry in Japan (1962). Throughout his life he was also involved in Jewish scholarship.

Untermeyer was an anthologist of eclectic taste, the subjects of his collections included limericks, parodies, food and drink, candy, humor, erotica, biblical flora, short stories, juvenile literature, and adventure fiction. His poetry anthologies, such as *A Treasury of Great Poems* (1955), *The Golden Treasury of Poetry* (1959), and *The World's Great Stories* (1964), are still used in high schools throughout the United States. The most famous of his anthologies, *The Golden Treasury of Poetry*, became a household volume.

Untermeyer claimed that most people liked poetry, and he did much to disprove the myth that poetry is a highbrow art. He credited "the non-conformers and innovators in art, science, technology and human relations, who, misunderstood and ridiculed in their times, have shaped our world." Untermeyer himself liked to think that he was "a bone collector with a mind of a magpie."

During World War II, Untermeyer worked for the Office of War Information, where he was editor of the Armed Forces Editions—classic works as well as contemporary writing published for the military. He had traveled widely and lived in Vienna for two years, where he had joined the intellectual life of the city, associating with Sigmund Freud, Arthur Schnitzler, Max Reinhardt, and the Zweig brothers. On his many trips he befriended Dorothy Thompson, art historian Bernard Berenson, Siegfried Sassoon, Ezra Pound, William Butler Yeats, and Robert Frost, who became his close friend and whose letters to Untermeyer were published in 1963.

Besides anthologies, Untermeyer published a few volumes of his own prose and verse as well as an appraisal of E. A. Robinson and a collection of letters from Ezra Pound. He wrote introductions to works of such varied writers as Horace, Emily Dickinson, Omar Khayyam, Heinrich Heine, Emerson, Edmond Rostand, and Robert Frost. He also edited the Grimm brothers' *Fairy Tales*, and, in 1965, he wrote *Bygones, An Autobiography*, which dealt mainly with his four marriages. Like his friend Robert Frost, he had a deep love for country life and in his latter years lived on a farm he rehabilitated in Newtown, Conn. In all he produced more than ninety books.

Untermeyer died in Newtown, Conn.

[Autobiographical works by Louis Untermeyer include his *From Another World* (1939). An obituary is in the *New York Times*, Dec. 20, 1977.]

DANIEL SPICEHANDLER

UTLEY, FREDA (Jan. 23, 1898–Jan. 21, 1978), author, lecturer, and journalist, was born in London, England, one of two children born to Emily Williamson and William Herbert Utley, an editor and journalist. She attended Prior's Field, Surrey (1911–1915); King's College of London University (1920–1923), from which she received a B.A. (with first-class honors); Westfield College of London University (1924–1926), from which she received an M.A. (with distinction); and the London School of Economics (1926–1928), where she was a research fellow.

A promising academic career was aborted by her decisions to join the British Communist party in 1927, to visit the Soviet Union that same year, and to marry a Soviet citizen, Arcadi Jacovlevitch Berdichevsky, in 1928; they had one child. During the next two years Utley lived with her husband in Japan, returned briefly to England, and in 1930 finally settled down, she thought, in Moscow, where she was a senior scientific worker at the Institute of World Economy and Politics. In 1936, Berdichevsky fell victim to the massive purges then sweeping Russia; he disappeared into the Gulag Archipelago, where he died on Mar. 30, 1938. Having retained her British passport, Utley was able to escape with her son to England.

Her year in that country enabled Utley to write *Japan's Feet of Clay* (1937), a best-selling critique that established her reputation. In 1938 she traveled to China as a war correspondent for the *London News Chronicle*; her experiences led her to write *China at War* (1939). The following year she immigrated to the United States with her son and her mother. In 1940, certain that her husband was dead, she published her scathing autobiographical indictment *The Dream We Lost: Soviet Russia Then and Now* (reprinted as *Lost Illusion*, 1948). In it she revealed her disillusionment with the Soviet system, which, though aggravated by her husband's arrest on the usual trumped-up charges, was mainly a function of innumerable discrepancies she discovered between her earlier idealization of Stalin's regime and the savage realities of his rule by terror.

Although her attack on Soviet Communism appeared after the Stalin-Hitler pact had been signed, and was therefore politically more acceptable than it would have been a year earlier, Utley could not fully capitalize on it because of her unpopular argument that Nazi Germany should be encouraged to attack the Soviets. She hurt herself in other ways as well.

Utley made the mistake of admitting to immigration authorities in 1940 that she had been a member of the British Communist party. This enabled the Justice Department to seek her expulsion the following year, nominally because of her Communist past, but really, she believed, in retaliation against her article "Must the World Destroy Itself?," published in *Reader's Digest*, which urged Britain to make peace with Hitler. Though friends saved her from deportation, Utley's obsessive anti-Communism, a natural outcome of her experiences in the Soviet Union, limited her opportunities as a lecturer and journalist during the war years, when the Soviet Union and the United States were allies.

The coming of the Cold War made Utley's message more attractive, thus benefiting her career. In 1944, Congress passed and President Roosevelt signed a private bill introduced by Jerry Voorhis, a liberal congressman from California who would subsequently lose his seat to Richard Nixon, allowing Utley to reenter the United States from Canada on an immigrant visa. She settled in New York City and promptly applied for citizenship, becoming naturalized five years later. Utley's *The China Story* (1951), an attack on American supporters of Communist China, made the best-seller lists. It was her last successful book. In later years her career sagged because, except on the issue of Communism, she was never comfortable with conservatives, and her association with Senator Joseph McCarthy of Wisconsin alienated liberals. Her last book was *Odyssey of a Liberal: Memoirs* (1970), which describes, in a sketchy and fragmented way, her life up to 1941. It includes scattered references to her later years.

Fiercely polemical, uncompromising, and utterly lacking in political judgment, Utley was at the same time remarkable for her honesty. Indeed, it might be said of her that she was honest to a fault, as when she refused to lie to the immigration authorities in 1940. This was strikingly demonstrated by her 1950 testimony before the subcommittee of Senator Millard Tydings, which was investigating Senator McCarthy's charge that Owen Lattimore of Johns Hopkins University was the Soviet Union's chief secret agent in the United States. Although Utley hated Lattimore, whom she had known in Moscow during the 1930's and could never forgive for whitewashing the purges that had taken her husband's life, she refused to characterize him as a spy: "To suggest that his great talents have been utilized in espionage seems . . . as absurd as to suggest that Mr. Gromyko or Mr. Molotov employ their [*sic*] leisure hours . . . in snatching documents." The senators were not impressed by this comparison, and her testimony, since she made no sensational charges, did Lattimore little harm—although she had hoped it would.

Utley was the reverse of an opportunist, her success in the 1950's resulting from longstanding convictions that had only recently become fashionable. During her career she met numerous other writers and intellectuals, a large number of whom she broke with, or was dropped by, because of her ruthless integrity and single-mindedness. These included Bertrand Russell, George Bernard Shaw, Pearl Buck, John Paton Davies (who was dismissed from the foreign service during the McCarthy era), and others. Her recollections of them were usually uncharitable. An exception is her portrait of Agnes Smedley, a journalist Utley met in China, who supported Chinese Communism to the end of her life. Utley described her as "one of the few spiritually great people I have ever met."

In calling herself a liberal, Utley did not identify with twentieth-century liberalism but, rather, with the nineteenth-century tradition of free thought and rationalism in which she had been raised. She never subscribed to most conservative principles, and claimed never to have liked conservatives as a group, although she was fond of certain individuals. She was a crusading anti-Communist for principled as well as personal reasons but had no interest in capitalism, either intellectually or financially. She was most comfortable with writers like Max Eastman and Sidney Hook, ex-Marxists like herself who had not become true believers in some other religious or economic system.

Utley is likely to be remembered more as a witness than as a writer. Her experience of being seduced by Communism in her youth, and later growing out of it, was shared by many other Western intellectuals. But she was one of the few who suffered directly as a result of Stalin's crimes. She held all Communists accountable for this, and would fight them, their friends, their sympathizers, and whoever got in her way, for the rest of her life. If she carried it too far and was sometimes unjust, there remains something splendid about her one-woman war against tyranny.

Utley died in Washington, D.C.

[Obituaries are in the *New York Times*, Jan. 23, 1978; and the *Washington Post*, Jan. 25, 1978.]

WILLIAM L. O'NEILL

VAN, BOBBY (Dec. 6, 1930–July 30, 1980), actor and dancer, was born Robert Stein in New York City, the son of Harry Stein and Mina Anapolsky, vaudeville performers who used the stage names Harry King and Minna Ann. Van made his first appearance at the age of four, when his parents introduced him into their act in Atlantic City, N.J.

Van attended public schools in New York City and took music classes at the Metropolitan Vocational High School (now the High School of Performing Arts). He had no formal classes in dance, but his father (who had been a choreographer for the Ziegfeld Follies) coached him in dancing. Van played the trumpet and started his own band at the age of fifteen, later adding some dancing and ad-libbed comedy routines. He initially billed himself Bobby King but changed his stage name because "there were too many Kings in the business." The idea for his new stage name came from his sister, who had a crush on the actor Van Johnson.

Van first performed at resorts in the Catskill Mountains northwest of New York City and entertained troops for the United Service Organizations (USO). After World War II ended, he appeared at hotels and supper clubs, as well as on radio and television. He made his Broadway debut with Gwen Verdon in the revue *Alive and Kicking*, which had an eight-week run at the Winter Garden Theater on Broadway (1950), and then appeared in *Red, White and Blue* at the Paramount Theater in Los Angeles and on a subsequent tour (1950).

Van's California theater appearances caught the attention of motion-picture producer Joe Pasternak, who brought Van under contract to Metro-Goldwyn-Mayer (MGM). His first movie role was a minor part in the Mario Lanza star vehicle *Because You're Mine* (1952). He was then paired with Debbie Reynolds in his next two movies. In *Skirts Ahoy* (1952), Van and Reynolds played themselves as performers in a "show within a show," and in *The Affairs of Dobie Gillis* (1953), he played the title role.

Van's best movie roles came in 1953. In *Small Town Girl* he astounded audiences with his talent and energy in the "Take Me to Broadway" reprise (the "Hippity-Hop" dance, choreographed by Busby Berkeley), during which he bounced in rhythm for five minutes around the motion picture's set. The number was later shown in *That's Entertainment, Part 2* (1976). Later in 1953, Van appeared in *Kiss Me Kate*, playing Gremio, a suitor of Ann Miller's Bianca. Their show-stopping number "Tom, Dick and Harry" was also shown in *That's Dancing* (1985). During this period Van married actress Diane Garrett, who appeared in minor roles in MGM films.

Despite favorable reviews, Van's motion-picture career never took off. Audience tastes were changing and movie musicals were declining in popularity. MGM focused its efforts on projects produced by Pasternack's rival, Arthur Freed, who chose to give the number of choice roles to better-known dancers like Fred Astaire and Gene Kelly. "I spent three years in Hollywood, starting at nineteen," Van recalled. "I was washed up when I was twenty-one and came back to New York. The day of the lavish musical was over."

Van returned to Broadway for the 1954 revival of Richard Rodgers and Lorenz Hart's 1936 musical *On Your Toes* at the 46th Street Theater, performing Ray Bolger's original role. He later went to London for an appearance in a variety show at the Palladium in 1958. He played Will Parker in the Los Angeles Civic Light Opera's performance of *Oklahoma!* (1960), and Joey in San Diego's Circle Arts Theater's *Pal Joey* (1961). During this time he also made numerous television appearances on the "Ed Sullivan Show," the "Jackie Gleason Show," the "Ford Star Jubilee," "Kraft Music Hall," and other variety shows.

Van returned to Hollywood in the early 1960's as the choreographer for two Jerry Lewis films, *The Ladies' Man* (1961), and *It's Only Money* (1962). He appeared with Mamie Van Doren in *The Navy vs. the Night Monsters* (1966), choreographed dances for the Miss America pageant, directed television commercials, and appeared in a made-for television movie, *The Lost Flight* (1969). In 1968, Van married Elaine Joyce; they had one child.

Van's theatrical career rebounded with his critically acclaimed performance as the lawyer Billy Early in the popular 1971 revival of *No, No, Nanette* at the 46th Street Theatre on Broadway. Van played 861 performances with costars Ruby Keeler, Patsy Kelly, and Helen Gallagher. He considered this role as one of his two favorites (the other being Will Parker in the 1960 Los Angeles performance of *Oklahoma!*), and it earned him a 1971 Tony nomination. Van and Gallagher repeated their show-stopping number, "You Can Dance with Any Girl You Can" at the televised 1972 Tony Awards program.

Van's success on Broadway led to several movie offers, but these did not revive his motion-picture career. He appeared in what critics termed a "stultifyingly boring melodrama," *The Doomsday Machine* (1972), and he played the role of a USO entertainer in an unpopular musical remake of *Lost Horizon* (1973). He produced and cohosted a televised musical, "The Bobby Van and Elaine Joyce Special" (CBS, 1973), and hosted the game show "Show-offs" (ABC, 1975). Van returned to Broadway in 1975, playing the title role in *Doctor Jazz* at the Winter Garden Theater. Although critics praised Van's performance, they panned the show, which closed after five performances.

Van returned to television and hosted more game shows: "The Fun Factory" (NBC, 1976), and "Make Me Laugh" (syndicated, 1979). He appeared in another made-for television movie, *Bunco* (1976), was choreographer and assistant producer of several Miss America pageants, and hosted four Mrs. America pageants.

His last public appearance was as host of the 1980 Mrs. America pageant. He died of cancer several months later, in Los Angeles.

Bobby Van was a multitalented entertainer—singer, dancer, comedian and musician—whose career spanned twenty-five years of performances in resorts, nightclubs, theater, motion pictures, radio, and television. He was noted for his energy, breezy manner, and ever-present smile, and his dance routines covered the gamut from softshoe to energetic tap numbers. Reviewer Brooks Atkinson considered him "an extraordinarily able dancer and a thoroughly agreeable performer," but Van came to the movies at a time when Hollywood (and the genre of big-budget musicals) was in the process of being supplanted by television. Critics, producers, and the public considered him a likable and dependable talent, and he remained popular until his death.

[The Billy Rose Theatre Collection of the New York Public Library for the Performing Arts at Lincoln Center has a file of newspaper articles and reviews about Van, as well as a videotape of his performance with Helen Gallagher at the 1972 Tony Awards. There is no biography of Van. Obituaries are in the *New York Times*, Aug. 1, 1980; and *Dance Magazine*, Oct. 1980.]

STEPHEN G. MARSHALL

VANCE, VIVIAN (July 26, 1912–Aug. 17, 1979), actress, was born Vivian Roberta Jones in Cherryvale, Kans., one of six children of Robert Jones and Mae Ragan. Soon after her birth, the family moved to Independence, Kans., where she later studied drama with William Inge. The family subsequently settled in Albuquerque, N.Mex., where Vance's talents flowered at the Albuquerque Little Theatre. Her dramatics teacher, Vance Randolph, helped her not only with technique but also with her stage name. The directors of the theater group were so impressed with Vance's acting that they took up a collection to send her to New York City to study with Eva Le Gallienne.

Upon her arrival in Manhattan in 1932, Vance was disappointed to learn that the school was overenrolled, so she lost thirty-four pounds and started auditioning on her own. "New York was a lot tougher to crack than Albuquerque," she later recalled, "but of course I couldn't go back." Despite her misgivings, Vance was hired her first time out, for the Broadway show *Music in the Air*. In her spare time, she sang at the Biltmore Roof, the Club Simplon, and other nightclubs, developing an impressive following.

Two years later, when *Music in the Air* closed, Vance became the understudy for Ethel Merman, the star of *Anything Goes*. Vance's Broadway break came in 1937 with *Hooray for What!* when the star left before opening night. During the summer of 1941, Vance met and married actor Philip Ober; they had no children. Later that year she starred in *Let's Face It* on Broadway, with Danny Kaye and Eve Arden, for an eighty-five-week run. Vance and her troupe were among the first entertainers sent to the European Theater during World War II, traveling from North Africa to Italy. In 1945, after the war, she went to Chicago to take the leading role in *The Voice of the Turtle*.

During this run Vance suffered a nervous breakdown. "One day I was up and about," she recalled, "the next I was lying in bed in my hotel room, my hands shaking helplessly . . . weeping hysterically from causes I didn't know." The breakdown left her incapacitated for two years, and she retired to her ranch in Cubero, N.Mex. In 1951, Mel Ferrer called Vance to reprise her role as the "other woman" in *The Voice of the Turtle* at the La Jolla Playhouse in La Jolla, Calif. At first she refused the offer, associating the play with her breakdown. But Ferrer was insistent, and Vance finally agreed.

On July 28, 1951, Desi Arnaz, writer Jess Oppenheimer, and Vance's friend director Marc Daniels drove to the La Jolla Playhouse to audition Vance for the role of Ethel Mertz, Lucy's neighbor on the new television show "I Love Lucy." Many actresses had already read for the part and been rejected. Hiring was difficult because William Frawley had been cast as Fred Mertz. The actress had to look as if she could be married to Frawley (who was sixty-four years old), yet not be so old that she could not realistically be involved in Lucy's shenanigans. Of her performance in *The Voice of the Turtle*, a *Los Angeles Times* critic wrote: "Miss Vance is excellent as the thick-skinned but essentially tenderhearted actress."

Apparently Arnaz reached the same conclusion about Vance's abilities, because after the first act he leaned over to his companions and said, "I think we found our Ethel Mertz." They agreed. Arnaz went backstage during the intermission and told Vance they wanted her to try out for the show. She replied, "What do I want to get mixed up in that for? It's only a television show. I'm up for a picture at Universal." Nonetheless, she read for the part the following week, then left with her husband for their ranch in Cubero, N.Mex. The rest of the negotiations were conducted by telephone, and rehearsals began in three weeks. Vance was only thirty-nine years old when she landed the plum role of Ethel Mertz.

When "I Love Lucy" became a hit, Vance was not initially happy with the public's identification of her with Ethel Mertz. After all, "Ethel is a frump. She's frowsy, blowsy, and talks like a man." She also disliked being considered Frawley's wife because of the twenty-five-year age difference. "He should be playing my father," she complained. As the years passed, however, Vance no longer minded when people called her "Ethel." In 1954 she won an Emmy as the best supporting actress in a series for her work on "I Love Lucy."

In March 1959, Ober sued for divorce. That same summer, Vance met John Dodds, a literary agent seven years her junior. They were married on Jan. 16, 1961, and moved into a 125-year-old white colonial in suburban Stamford, Conn. Vance became active in the Connecticut Association for Mental Health.

Early in 1962, Lucille Ball came east for a visit and handed Vance a script for a new series, to be called "The Lucy Show." "Lucy, don't take it out," Vance said, "I won't read it." Six months later, Vance was in Hollywood taping the show. "I don't believe I'd have started the show without Vivian," Ball said. Vance left the cast after three years, citing difficulties commuting from one coast to another, but every year she returned to California to guest-star in Lucy's shows.

In 1974 the Doddses moved to Belvedere, Calif., near San Francisco. Vance died there five years later.

[See Bart Andrews, *The "I Love Lucy" Book* (1985). An obituary is in the *New York Times*, Aug. 18, 1979.]

LAURIE ROZAKIS

VAN VLECK, JOHN HASBROUCK (Mar. 13, 1899–Oct. 27, 1980), Nobel laureate physicist, was born in Middletown, Conn., the only child of Hester Laurence Raymond and Edward Burr Van Vleck, a mathematician. Raised in Madison, Wis., where his father taught at the University of Wisconsin beginning in 1906, he attended public schools and the University of Wisconsin. His father was heir to a comfortable fortune, and the family often summered in Europe. With his parents, and later his wife, Van Vleck traveled over much of the world. He was unathletic, but from his father he learned to enjoy hiking, and he followed college football throughout his life. Van Vleck was a precocious child; memorizing railway timetables was his hobby. In adulthood he was able to travel without referring to a printed schedule.

An outstanding undergraduate, Van Vleck majored in physics at the University of Wisconsin, but he did not settle on a career in mathematical physics until he began graduate study at Harvard in the spring of 1920. He completed his doctorate in 1922 and by 1927 was a full professor at the University of Minnesota. On June 10, 1927, he married Abigail June Pearson; they had no children. He spent most of his career at Harvard (1922–1923, 1934–1969), with shorter terms at the University of Minnesota (1923–1928) and the University of Wisconsin (1928–1934). He was often invited to lecture at other universities in America and in Europe.

Van Vleck is known as the father of modern magnetism, for he established much of the foundation of the quantum theory of paramagnetism. He also made pioneering contributions to spectroscopy and chemical physics. He belonged to the first generation of theorists in American physics, entering the discipline just as it was "coming of age," to use his phrase. The success that he enjoyed in the 1920's also owed a good deal to the University of Minnesota. His first professorship there carried light teaching duties, and it allowed him time to develop his research.

Magnetism was what Van Vleck called his first love. His entry into that field was marked by his discovery of the general theory of magnetic (and electric) susceptibilities in gases, in 1927, soon after the advent of quantum mechanics. This general theory, along with experimental substantiation and extensions to related topics, made up his masterpiece, the 1932 text *The Theory of Electric and Magnetic Susceptibilities*. The book also contained the germ of the crystal field theory, which Van Vleck and his students William Penney and Robert Schlapp developed in 1932 to describe paramagnetic salts (particularly salts containing rare-earth ions).

In paramagnetic materials, magnetic moments of electrons in various quantum states align themselves with an external field; the object of any theory is to discover which of those quantum states are occupied. The crystal field theory considers only energy perturbations of the quantum states of a paramagnetic ion that arise from electrostatic effects, but by 1935 Van Vleck was able to suggest how to account for perturbations from molecular bonding of the ion to the rest of the crystal. Physical chemists have since expanded this suggestion into ligand field theory.

The exchange of energy between paramagnetic ions and vibrations in the salt crystal lattice (the phenomenon of paramagnetic relaxation) first attracted Van Vleck's attention in 1939. He continued to study relaxation and paramagnetic materials, particularly crystals containing rare earths, through 1975.

Ferromagnetics were a recurring concern of Van Vleck's from 1931. Ferromagnetic materials (such as iron) have intrinsic magnetic moments, in contrast with the induced moments of paramagnetics. They are, however, far more complex than paramagnetics, and neither Van Vleck nor anyone else achieved a fundamental understanding of them.

Magnetism was not Van Vleck's sole concern. Beginning in 1927, he (and his students) delved into molecular spectroscopy. His most notable discovery in that area (stemming from wartime research on radar, and published in 1947) was a spectral absorption line for the water molecule near 1.3 cm wavelength. This absorption line made impractical a proposed radar system that would have operated at about that wavelength.

Between 1932 and 1935, Van Vleck and his students investigated chemical physics, in particular the methane molecule. They were able to reconcile the seemingly disparate theories of atomic orbitals and molecular orbitals. Such reconciliations appeared in Van Vleck's work in several areas.

Van Vleck's familiarity with magnetic theory, spectroscopy, and radio frequency techniques (radar and magnetic relaxation) put him in a central position in the development of magnetic resonance techniques in the late 1940's and early 1950's. Although he published comparatively little on resonance topics, his close contact with experimentalists, such as Edward Purcell's nuclear magnetic resonance group at Harvard, frequently expedited their research.

In the middle of his career Van Vleck established himself as a capable administrator. He directed the theory group at the Radio Research Laboratory (the radar countermeasures laboratory) at Harvard from 1943 to 1945. Also at Harvard, Van Vleck was chairman of the physics department from 1945 to 1949, and from 1951 to 1957 he shaped the interdisciplinary Division of Engineering and Applied Physics, as its first dean.

In 1951, Van Vleck became Hollis Professor of Mathematics and Natural Philosophy at Harvard, and in 1952 and 1953 he was president of the American Physical Society. He was elected to the United States National Academy of Sciences, as well as several foreign academies. The greatest of his many honors was the Nobel Prize, which he shared with his student Philip Anderson, and with N. F. Mott, in 1977.

Van Vleck an open and generous man, was known to most acquaintances as Van. He took care that his collaborators received their share of credit for work done with him, if not more. He died at his home in Cambridge, Mass.

[Van Vleck's papers are divided between the Harvard University Archives and the Center for History of Physics, American Institute of Physics. A selection of his early correspondence was microfilmed as part of the Archive for History of Quantum Physics. Van Vleck published two books, *Quantum Principles and Line Spectra*, Bulletin of the National Research Council, no. 54 (1926), and *The Theory of Electric and Magnetic Susceptibilities* (1932), as well as more than 180 articles. Bibliographies are included in obituary notices by Brebis Bleaney, "John Hasbrouck Van Vleck," *Biographical Memoirs of Fellows of the Royal Society*, 1982; and by Philip W. Anderson,

"John Hasbrouck Van Vleck," *Biographical Memoirs. National Academy of Sciences*, 1987. Also relevant is Frederick Fellows, "Van Vleck, John Hasbrouck," in *Dictionary of Scientific Biography*, suppl. II (1990). An obituary is in the *New York Times*, Oct. 28, 1980.]

FREDERICK FELLOWS

VENUTI, GIUSEPPE ("JOE") (Sept. 16, 1903–Aug. 14, 1978), jazz violinist and bandleader, was born in Philadelphia, the son of Giacomo Venuti and Rosa LaMacchia, Italian immigrants to the United States (some sources give conflicting data regarding his birth). Venuti's parents' occupations are unknown, though Venuti once stated that all the men in his family were sculptors. He attended public school in South Philadelphia, where one of his classmates was guitarist Salvatore Massaro (later known as Eddie Lang); both played in the school orchestra. Venuti reportedly studied with Michel Sciapiro before beginning his professional career as a musician at the age of fifteen. Venuti was married at least once, to a woman named Sally. It is certain that this marriage occurred prior to 1936. Close friends indicate that he had no children and was divorced from Sally in the late 1940's or early 1950's.

It may be that the facts of Venuti's personal life are unclear because he wanted it that way. He believed that his private life was his concern and no one else's. He once said, "Music is my whole life, see, and that's it." Moreover, he was noted as a consummate practical joker; indeed, one former colleague said that Venuti was "the greatest joker who ever lived and was inclined to exaggerate." Perhaps this aspect of his personality led him to suppress the truth, rearrange the details, and provide contradictory stories about the life he led before he became a notable personage.

Early in his career Venuti joined with Eddie Lang to form a duo that performed in Atlantic City, N.J. Lang, the first guitarist to make an international reputation as a jazz soloist, was noted both for his chord patterns and his single string performances. Lang's very successful partnership with Venuti would result in more than seventy sides of recorded music. Soon recognized for his own virtuosity, Venuti was awarded the nickname "Four-string Joe" because of his ability to play with the back of the bow underneath the violin, with the loosened hairs of the bow sounding all four strings at once.

From 1924 to 1927, Venuti, often working with Lang, performed with the Jean Goldkette Orchestra, as well as with other top jazz men of the time. In September 1926 the violinist began his recording career with a group named "Venuti's Blue Four." This group has been described as having a unique style and "a tonal finesse and jazz-chamber-music quality hitherto unknown."

During the years 1927–1928, Venuti played with groups led by Roger Wolfe Kahn and Don Voorhees. He and Lang also jointly led their own band in New York City until they joined the famous Paul Whiteman Orchestra in mid-1929. Venuti was so seriously injured in an auto accident in mid-1929 that it was thought he might never play again. But he did recover. Following his recovery, he free-lanced for recording studios, and with theater bands. In 1934 he took a small group to England. In 1936, he was picked for *Down Beat* magazine's "All-Star Swing Band."

From the mid-1930's until 1943, Venuti led his own big band. One of his vocalists was Kay Starr, later a very big star. His band included as sidemen most of the great white performers from the Goldkette and Whiteman era. (Without doubt Venuti had informal contacts with black jazz greats of his time, though musicians were generally color-segregated in the 1920's and 1930's. Integrated performances were the exception even in the 1930's.) When not fronting his own band, Venuti appeared with groups led by cornetist Red Nichols, composer Hoagy Carmichael, and Tommy and Jimmy Dorsey.

During the 1940's, Venuti did both movie and recording studio work for Metro-Goldwyn-Mayer in Hollywood. For a time he was musical director of the popular "Duffy's Tavern" radio show. A close friend of Bing Crosby's, the violinist appeared on the singer's radio shows during the late 1940's and early 1950's. He often had a small speaking part as well as an opportunity to perform.

In 1953, Venuti toured in Europe. At mid-decade he was working for radio station bands in Los Angeles. In December 1956 he appeared on Jackie Gleason's CBS-TV memorial tribute to trombonist Tommy Dorsey. The following year he composed a jazz violin concerto, which he performed with the Seattle Symphony. Apart from these highlights, the violinist lived and worked in relative obscurity as a consequence of changing musical tastes, namely the demise of the big bands in favor of rock music, and the growth of television together with the declining popularity of radio shows featuring live music. During the 1960's he was active mainly in the Los Angeles, Las Vegas, and Seattle areas, eventually settling in the last-named city.

After nearly twenty years of obscurity Venuti returned to prominence with an appearance at Dick Gibson's Colorado Jazz Party in 1967, the first of many appearances at this annual event through 1976. His comeback was enhanced by participation at the 1968 Newport Jazz Festival, where his performance showed that age had not diminished his technical skill or his ability to "swing" musically.

In 1969 the violinist was chosen the "most impressive soloist" at London's Jazz Exposition. He was afflicted with a serious illness in April 1970. Fortunately, he was able to resume playing and in 1975 performed an important role in the New York Jazz Repertory Company's tribute to cornetist and former associate Bix Beiderbecke at the Newport Jazz Festival in New York City. At the same time he was honored by the Newport Jazz Hall-of-Fame.

Venuti became a legend in the music business both for his performances and his reputation as a practical jokester. His success as a bandleader was limited, however, perhaps because he did not take the business aspects of music seriously, preferring, instead, to front a small group that allowed him more flexibility and the opportunity to play his instrument. Moreover, he was adept at putting both critics and his fellow musicians in their places when they did or said something of which he disapproved.

Venuti's wonderful tone, unerring intonation, and superb technique, combined with his rhythmic sense, earned him a justified reputation as a great jazz violinist who influenced others, such as Stephane Grappelli and Jean-Luc Ponty. He recorded and performed until shortly before his death in Seattle, from lung cancer.

[There is no full-length biography of Venuti. Anecdotes and illustrations may be found in Walker, *The Wonderful Era of the Great Dance Bands* (1964); Herb Sanford, *Tommy and Jimmy: The Dorsey Years* (1972); Richard M. Sudhalter and Philip R. Evans, *Bix: Man and Legend* (1974); and Thomas A. DeLong, *Pops: Paul Whiteman, King of Jazz* (1983).

Extensive discographical data are contained in Brian Rust, *The American Dance Band Discography: 1917–1942* (1975), and *Jazz Records: 1897–1942* (1978). Venuti's work in films is covered in David Meeker's *Jazz in the Movies* (1981).

Representative recordings include a two-LP set *Stringing the Blues* with Joe Venuti and Eddie Lang (Columbia CoC2L24); *Nightwings: Bucky Pizzarelli with Joe Venuti* (Flying Dutchman LP, BDLI-1120); *Joe Venuti and Dave McKenna: Alone at the Palace* (Chiaroscuro CR-D-160), and *Joe Venuti and Zoot Sims* (Chiaroscuro CR-D-142). The last two noted are compact discs and include extensive liner notes.

An obituary is in the *New York Times*, Aug. 16, 1978. A longer tribute is in the *International Musician*, Sept. 1978. "Viva Venuti!," a eulogy by Norman P. Gentieu, including several photographs, is in the International Association of Jazz Record Collectors *Journal*, Apr. 1979.]

BARRETT G. POTTER

VIDOR, FLORENCE (July 23, 1895–Nov. 3, 1977), actress, was born Florence Cobb in Houston, Tex., and then acquired the surname of her mother, Ida's, second husband, John F. Arto. Florence was "discovered" by King Vidor, a native of Texas who was soon to be a Hollywood director, and who was searching for a beautiful woman to star in the film that would launch his career. He saw Florence in the back of an open touring car on Houston's Main Street and, according to his autobiography, learned her identity by tracing the ownership of the car. John Arto refused to let Florence appear in Vidor's films; it was not until after her marriage to King Vidor in 1915 that she moved to Hollywood and made her first appearance in his work.

Called at one point in her career "the first lady of the screen," Florence Vidor is not usually considered among the top stars of Hollywood's silent era, although the olive-skinned, five-foot-four-inch beauty appeared in numerous starring and supporting roles for various studios, including Vitagraph, Paramount, Morosco, Fox, and Famous Players–Lasky. Her first role was an uncredited bit part in *A Tale of Two Cities* (1917) as the young woman who walked to the guillotine with William Farnum. As Mimi, her last words to him were, "Won't you hold my hand?" The scene was so powerful, audiences left the film asking, "Who was the girl in the guillotine cart with Farnum?" Vidor herself was greatly surprised at the acclaim, which brought her a string of film offers.

Known for poise and elegance, Vidor worked with Cecil B. DeMille in *Old Wives for New* (1918), with Thomas H. Ince in *Lying Lips*

(1921), and with Ernst Lubitsch in *The Patriot* (1928). Her versatility can be demonstrated by the range of her roles: from a Russian princess in *The Grand Duchess and the Waiter* (1926) opposite Adolphe Menjou, to a frazzled mother in *Are Parents People?* (1925). Her regal bearing was perfectly suited to period costumes and brought her many roles in historical romances. Described by the *New York Times* as having "large brown eyes, a small and peculiarly attractive mouth and a well-sheared Eton bob," she was considered "fascinating" and "refreshing" by critics. She was praised most especially for her work with Sessue Hayakawa, from whom she said she learned everything she knew about acting. Typical of her critical reception was the *Chicago Daily Tribune* review of *The White Man's Law* (1918) with Hayakawa: " 'Some girl!' You're due to exclaim when you behold Florence Vidor. . . . She has a most attractive personality, a ready smile, and frank uplifting eyes that are very winning."

Vidor was memorable as the female lead in the story of pirate Jean Lafitte in Frank Lloyd's *The Eagle of the Sea* (1926). Perhaps her most striking portrayal was in the title role of *Barbara Frietchie* in Thomas H. Ince's 1924 version of the Clyde Fitch stage play about the Civil War heroine. Ince asserted that Vidor's "innate charm and beauty" typified "the best of American womanhood."

Despite these forays into historical epics, light comedy became Vidor's forte with the popularization of the marital farce by screenwriter Elinor Glyn, DeMille, and Lubitsch. Combining aristocratic and humorous themes, these films gave Vidor the opportunity to widen her artistic range. Although the parts capitalized on the aloof beauty for which she had become known, they also put Vidor in comic settings that afforded her a down-to-earth quality. Her dark complexion, which allowed her to play many half-caste roles, also served to humanize her characterizations.

She separated from King Vidor in 1923. In a *Daily Mirror* interview in 1924, she said she believed that an actress could do better work for a director to whom she was not married. She went on to say that they had no intention of divorcing and that they were still good friends. In 1925, however, she was granted a divorce from King Vidor on the grounds of desertion. She did not ask for alimony, asserting that she could support herself. She retained custody of their only child.

Florence Vidor's career came to an abrupt end in 1929 when she appeared in her first talkie, the melodrama *Chinatown Nights*. Her Texas accent was incompatible with the image the film-going public had of her. The *New York Times* review stated that "it is astonishing that Florence Vidor . . . should have been asked to act the part she has in *Chinatown Nights*."

Vidor gave up her film career after marrying the violinist Jascha Heifetz in 1928. They had two children before divorcing in 1945. At the time of her death she was living a solitary existence in Pacific Palisades, Calif.

[The New York Public Library for the Performing Arts at Lincoln Center contains clippings and scrapbooks of reviews and publicity material. For filmographies see *Films in Review*, Jan. 1970; John Stewart, comp., *Filmarama*, vols. 1 and 2 (1975, 1977); and Leslie Halliwell, *Halliwell's Filmgoer's Companion*, 9th ed. (1990). See also Kalton C. Lahue, *Ladies in Distress* (1971), and King Vidor's autobiography, *A Tree Is a Tree* (1953). An obituary is in the *New York Times*, Nov. 6, 1977.]

CAROL R. BERKIN

VON BRAUN, WERNHER. See BRAUN, WERNHER VON.

W

WALLENDA, KARL (Jan. 21, 1905–Mar. 22, 1978), high wire walker, or funambulist, was born near Magdeburg, Germany, the son of Englebert Wallenda, a trapeze artist and animal trainer, and Kunigunde Jameson, a dancer and slack wire artiste. A fourth-generation performer, Karl spent his childhood traveling with the Wallenda Circus, his father's arena show, and after his parents divorced, the Grotefent Circus, his mother and stepfather's arena show. During those years he learned the basic skills of an acrobat and became a master balancer. By the time he was ten, Wallenda had developed his own handstand and balancing act, which he performed in the beer halls of Magdeburg throughout World War I to help support his mother and younger stepsiblings. Wallenda obtained his formal education by attending what he estimated to be 160 different schools between 1911 and 1920, as his family's arena show rarely stayed in the same town for more than two weeks.

Following World War I, Wallenda was employed as a coal miner, the only noncircus job he ever held. In 1921, he answered an ad placed by funambulist Louis Weitzmann for a young handstander. From Weitzmann, Wallenda learned to walk the high wire. During the eight months they worked together, their trademark trick consisted of Weitzmann's performing a headstand on the wire while Wallenda did a handstand on Weitzmann's feet. They also performed a number of publicity skywalks above natural and man-made spans.

By 1925, Wallenda had formed the nucleus of his own high wire troupe, the Great Wallendas, and had added the high pole to the list of aerial acts he could perform. Under Karl's direction, the original four-member troupe made high wire pyramids their trademark. By 1947, the year they premiered the three-tiered, seven-man pyramid, the Great Wallendas had expanded to twenty-three members capable of performing seven different aerial acts.

Wallenda married Martha Schepp, a ballerina who did not perform in his troupe, in 1927, shortly before the birth of their daughter and the troupe's first foreign tour. After his divorce in 1934, Wallenda married Helen Kreis, the troupe's top-mounter, on July 18, 1935. They had a daughter and adopted a son. All three of Karl's children, and later his grandchildren, followed him on to the high wire. In about 1940, Wallenda became a naturalized American citizen.

Wallenda performed with a number of German circuses including the Circus Malve, Circus Strassburger, Circus Gleich, and his own Wallenda Circus, prior to receiving a contract with the Cuban Circo Santos y Artegas in 1927. While working in Havana that year, the Great Wallendas' performance was seen by the American John Ringling, who offered them a one-year contract with Ringling Brothers and Barnum and Bailey Circus. Wallenda planned on returning to Europe at the end of that first season. Instead, his troupe remained with Ringling Brothers for sixteen out of the next eighteen seasons, increasing in size as Wallenda persuaded family members to come to the United States and work with him. More than thirty men and women walked the high wire with Wallenda during his career, and at least two-thirds of them were members of his family.

Wallenda, who believed the true circus artiste always created his own routines, took his stunts one step beyond what was considered the ordinary realm of possibility. He conceived his famous seven-man, three-tiered pyramid during the winter of 1938 and spent the next eight years assembling a crew willing to attempt the dangerous trick. In 1946, Wallenda presented the idea to John Ringling North, who felt it was too dangerous and refused to support him. At the end of that season, Karl and his troupe left Ringling Brothers and Barnum and Bailey Circus and began work on what he referred to as "the world's greatest high wire achievement," the seven-man pyramid.

Once the trick was perfected, circuses clamored to book the Great Wallendas. In order to support his twenty-three member troupe, Karl created six additional aerial acts for them to perform. With so many acts at his disposal, Karl decided to open Circus Wallenda, a one-ring, European-style spectacle with aerial and ground acrobatics, clowning, big cats, and a baby elephant, to tour the United States. Circus Wallenda worked winter dates in Florida before opening its touring season in January 1947. Twelve months later it closed in debt.

During the next dozen years, Wallenda managed to book the seven-man pyramid in a number of circuses, performing it without mishap until Jan. 30, 1962. During that afternoon's performance at a Shrine Circus in Detroit, Karl's nephew Dieter Schepp lost control of his balance pole and fell to the arena floor, pulling two other troupe members off the wire with him and leaving the rest of the troupe clinging to the wire. The accident resulted in the deaths of Schepp and Richard Faughan, Wallenda's son-in-law, and in the paralysis of Wallenda's adopted son, Mario. The Great Wallendas performed the pyramid only three more times, at Ft. Worth in 1963, for the DuPont Show, and in 1977 for the NBC movie *The Great Wallendas*. Each time film crews recorded the feat.

In 1966, Karl attempted to retire from the high wire but, convinced that "the rest of life is just time to fill in between doing the act," he kept getting lured back for "one final walk." During the 1970's he performed a number of skywalks across a variety of natural and man-made spans, including Tallulah Gorge in Georgia, the Houston Astrodome, Philadelphia Stadium, Maryland's Capital Center, and London's Clapham Commons. In 1974 he set the world high wire distance record by walking a wire 1,800 feet long across King's Island, Ohio. In 1978, while walking between two hotels in San Juan, P.R., Wallenda fell 120 feet to his death.

[See Ron Morris, *Wallenda* (1976); and Delilah Wallenda and Nan DeVincentis-Hayes, *The Last of the Wallendas* (1993). See also David Lewis Hammarstrom, *Behind the Big Top* (1980); and John Culhane, *The American Circus* (1990). An obituary is in the *New York Times*, Mar. 23, 1978.]

DIANE E. COOPER

WALSH, RAOUL (Mar. 11, 1887–Dec. 30, 1980), motion-picture actor and director, was born in New York City, the son of Thomas Walsh and Elizabeth Brough. His father, an Irish immigrant, became a clothes cutter for such firms as Brooks Brothers and grew prosperous in the wholesale garment business. Young Raoul met many celebrities visiting the Walsh home, including the actor Edwin Booth, the boxer John L. Sullivan, and the author Mark Twain.

Walsh attended New York public schools. Despondent after his mother's death from cancer in 1903, he dropped out of high school and joined an uncle, Matthew Walsh, on a schooner bound for Cuba. (Though obituaries indicate a matriculation at Seton Hall University, Walsh never alluded to college in his autobiography or interviews.)

Walsh soon abandoned ship and became a trail hand, driving longhorns across the Rio Grande from Mexico. In 1905 he worked on a ranch in Montana and then wandered to San Antonio, Tex., where he got his first acting role, as a Ku Klux Klan member on horseback in a theatrical production of *The Clansman*. Upon his return to New York City, Walsh found that his cowboy skills facilitated a movie career. He played on-horseback leads in *A Mother's Love* and *Paul Revere's Ride*, both shot in New Jersey for the Pathé Brothers. Next, Walsh acted in Biograph one- and two-reelers opposite future silent stars Lillian and Dorothy Gish and Mary Pickford, and he met D. W. Griffith, whom he later declared his directorial mentor.

In 1910, Walsh was part of a historic company—Griffith, cameraman Billy Bitzer, the Gish sisters, and actor Donald Crisp—who assembled at Grand Central Terminal in New York City for a cross-country train trip. They would make their films for the Biograph Company in Hollywood. "Most of the personnel, including myself," Walsh would remember, "regarded our job as a meal ticket and good fun." In California, Walsh acted in, and directed uncredited, one- and two-reelers, mostly

Westerns; bought a Stutz Bearcat in 1911; and became, he said, "the first Hollywood actor-director to own an automobile."

Walsh's first major directing assignment, for Griffith, was *Life of General Villa* (1914). He traveled into Mexico and befriended Pancho Villa, filming the revolutionary's army as it battled from Juárez to Mexico City. Walsh also delivered a legendary acting cameo for Griffith in *The Birth of a Nation* (1915), playing John Wilkes Booth in the dramatic reenactment of the assassination of Abraham Lincoln.

After that, Walsh went home to New York and a behind-the-camera contract with an up-and-coming studio, Fox. He directed the first gangster feature ever, *The Regeneration* (1915), and *Carmen* (1915) and *The Serpent* (1916), starring Theda Bara. Then Walsh returned to California, assigned to Fox's new studio, where he remained as principal director until 1935.

Walsh's most popular silent film was a Fox loan-out to United Artists, the acrobatic spectacle *The Thief of Bagdad* (1924), with Douglas Fairbanks. Walsh called it "the first picture to cost a million dollars." Among his important Fox films in a two-decade residence were *What Price Glory?* (1926), a free-spirited, fist-flying rendition of the Maxwell Anderson–Lawrence Stallings antiwar comedy; *Sadie Thompson* (1928), in which he returned to acting opposite Gloria Swanson's charismatic femme fatale; and *The Big Trail* (1930), the Western that introduced John Wayne.

Walsh retired from acting in 1929, having lost an eye in a freak auto accident the year before. Thereafter, he wore his signature eye patch and a cowboy hat, cultivating his image as a rugged "he-man" director, although, his actors concurred, he was actually kindly and gentle. "A dear, dear man," actress Jane Russell described him. "He acted gruff, but he was a marshmallow inside."

At first Walsh free-lanced after his Fox contract expired. Then he signed up with Warner Brothers in 1939 for what, most critics agree, would be his most significant years of filmmaking. He directed gangster film classics such as *The Roaring Twenties* (1939), *High Sierra* (1941), and *White Heat* (1949); fine period pictures such as *The Strawberry Blonde* (1941); *They Died with Their Boots On* (1941); and *Gentleman Jim* (1942); and unusual film-noir syntheses with traditionally non-"noir" genre subjects, such as the truckers' saga *They Drive by Night* (1940) and two Westerns, *Pursued* (1947) and *Colorado Territory* (1949). By every indicator, Walsh felt comfortable at Warners, where he worked with such contract actors as Humphrey Bogart, James Cagney, and Errol Flynn.

Still, there are some who prefer Walsh's leisurely 1950's films, with their emphasis on female characters, such as Jane Russell's *The Tall Men* (1955) and *The Revolt of Mamie Stover* (1956). As one critic pointed out about Walsh's 1955 film set in World War II: "Most of *Battle Cry*'s 149 minutes' running time is devoted to the likes of Mona Freeman, Nancy Olson, Dorothy Malone . . ."

Walsh's last film was a Western, *A Distant Trumpet* (1964). Then he retired to his ranch in Simi Valley, Calif., where he lived with his third wife, Mary Edna Simpson, whom he had married in 1941. (His first marriage, from 1916 to 1927, was to Miriam Cooper, a major silent film star.)

In 1973, Walsh was a featured director on the acclaimed PBS series produced by Richard Schickel, "The Men Who Made the Movies," and in 1974 he was honored with a retrospective of sixty-seven films at New York's Museum of Modern Art. Still, his fame on these occasions was fleeting. Few Americans are aware of his prolific directorial career, which spans the history of the Hollywood studio system and is filled with expertly told genre stories—Westerns, gangster films, comedies, period pieces—in which moviedom's greatest stars appear.

"His best films are genuinely exciting—though neither profound nor pretentious," wrote critic Andrew Sarris. But others have noted a dark, Freudian underside to many of Walsh's genre films—*High Sierra*, *Pursued*, and *White Heat*, for example—that have made them disturbing and psychologically potent.

[Walsh's autobiography, *Each Man in His Time* (1974), is more anecdotal than factual. See also Kingsley Canham, *The Hollywood Professionals*, vol. 1, *Michael Curtiz, Raoul Walsh, Henry Hathaway* (1973); Phil Hardy, ed., *Raoul Walsh* (1974); and an interview in Richard Schickel, *The Men Who Made the Movies* (1975). An obituary is in the *New York Times*, Jan. 3, 1981.]

GERALD PEARY

WARNER, JACK LEONARD (Aug. 2, 1892–Sept. 9, 1978), motion-picture executive, was born Jack Eichelbaum in London, Ontario, Canada, one of twelve children born to Polish-born Benjamin Eichelbaum, a peddler, and Pearl Eichelbaum. In 1894 the family settled in Youngstown, Ohio. Jack never attended high school. He began his career in show business by singing and dancing at neighborhood film projection showings run by his brothers Samuel (1888–1927), Harry (1881–1958), and Albert (1884–1967).

The Warner brothers ("Warner" became the family name by 1907) were fascinated with film acquisition and distribution. They opened their first "permanent" theater in 1905 in an empty Newcastle, Pa., store. They formed the Duquesne Amusement Supply Company in Pittsburgh and eventually opened arcades in Norfolk, Va.; Baltimore, Md.; Atlanta, Ga.; and San Francisco. After selling the company in 1912, they returned to Youngstown. After the opening showing in Hartford, Conn., of *Dante's Inferno*, Jack followed Sam on the road to exhibit this popular film. Jack and Sam began producing their own films in 1917, while Harry and Albert established themselves in New York City to arrange the exhibition of those films as well as the production of other "Warner Features." Jack focused on San Francisco, where he bought a small film theater; he rejoined Sam in Los Angeles in 1917 and continued absorbing all aspects of film production.

Both Sam and Jack enlisted in the Army Signal Corps during World War I and arranged the production of *Open Your Eyes*, a documentary assigned by the military, with Jack acting his only film "lead." The four brothers' first big success followed from their decision to buy rights to Ambassador James W. Gerard's best-selling 1917 book *My Four Years in Germany*; their film version grossed about $1.5 million in 1919. Returning that same year to Los Angeles, Sam and Jack filmed several serials, including *The Tiger's Claw* and A *Dangerous Adventure* (1922), and won production contracts with Mack Sennett for a series of Monte Banks comedies.

The four brothers incorporated themselves as Warner Brothers Pictures, Inc., in 1923, and in 1925 concluded a contract with Western Electric to form Vitaphone, a company dedicated to developing sound pictures. Jack enlisted Babe Ruth for a film, but *Babe Comes Home* (1926) was not popular. Rin-Tin-Tin, a dog found in the trenches of World War I, starred in a series of highly successful Warner pictures until his death in 1932.

On Aug. 6, 1926, Warner Brothers opened *Don Juan*, starring John Barrymore, in New York City. Although the voices of its actors were not recorded, the picture was the first ever to contain a fully synchronized musical score designed to complement the action. Warner Brothers topped this technological feat on Oct. 6, 1927, when New York audiences heard the first words on film, spoken by Al Jolson in *The Jazz Singer*. Tragically, just as the era of sound motion pictures began, Sam Warner, overworked, died in California.

On July 7, 1928, the Warners offered *Lights of New York*, the first full-length all-talking film. They also bought in that year the Stanley Company of America and extensive interests in First National Pictures, which they would eventually own outright. They thus inherited a large Burbank lot and an ever-growing roster of illustrious stars and directors. Always on the lookout for new talent, Jack and his brothers issued contracts to three young stars of the Broadway show *Penny Arcade*; James Cagney, Pat O'Brien, and Joan Blondell eventually became Hollywood stars.

As vice-president and production chief at Warner Brothers, Jack supervised many of the artistic and financial details, from the selection of stories and directors to the use of actors, set costs, and scheduling. He also invested in hotel, restaurant, and racetrack enterprises. Although a Republican, Jack joined the Hollywood group backing Franklin D. Roosevelt's presidential candidacy.

Critics often complained about Jack's penny-pinching, resulting in low-budget production costs and sets, but a listing of some of the Warner Brothers films calls to mind some of the greatest visual scenes, memorable scripts, and acting performances of the American screen. Classic films in a variety of genres were authorized and supervised by Jack. Such impressive films as *Little Caesar* (1930), *The Public Enemy* (1931), and *The Life of Emile Zola* (1937) brought fame to the studio. Max Reinhardt's A *Midsummer Night's Dream* (1935) was the first successful sound film based on a Shakespeare play. Some films effected legal changes, such as Paul Muni's performances in *I Am a Fugitive from a Chain Gang* (1932) and *Black Fury* (1935). *Green Pastures* (1936) presented an all-black cast. Warner Brothers produced a string of memorable Busby Berkeley musicals during the 1930's, including six in the yearly Golddiggers series (1933–1938). Warner felt that Berkeley's *42nd Street* (1933) helped lift the national spirit during the darkest days of the Great Depression. Michael Curtiz worked numerous wonders for the Warners, including his direction of a series of popular films pairing Errol Flynn with Olivia de Havilland, such as *Captain Blood* (1935) and *The Adventures of Robin Hood* (1938). As World War II was fermenting in Europe, the studio produced the first major American antifascist film, the fact-based *Confessions of a Nazi Spy* (released May 1939).

Effective for one year from Apr. 17, 1942, Jack Warner served as a lieutenant colonel in a motion-picture unit of the Army Air Forces and produced several films for the military—*Winning Your Wings* was his first. He and his brothers donated more than $7 million of the proceeds from Irving Berlin's *This Is the Army* (1943) to the Army War Relief Fund and much of the profits from *Hollywood Canteen* (1944) went to that canteen operation. During the war Warner Brothers produced such movie classics as *Casablanca* (1942), *Watch on the Rhine* (1943), and *Destination Tokyo* (1943). Warner gave several eloquent speeches about his studio's wartime obligations to the American public and the film industry's subsequent urgent peacetime duties—educative as well as entertaining. Commitment to education included the Warner American History series. There also was comic cartoon relief, in the form of Bugs Bunny and other classic Warner cartoon characters. Warner was particularly proud of what he designated as the "happy" and patriotic film, *Yankee Doodle Dandy*, which opened in New York City in 1942. In 1944, Canada recognized his production of *The Shining Future* with an award on behalf of its sixth war loan drive, and California's Richmond Shipyard honored his father, the immigrant who had labored as cobbler, peddler, and butcher, by naming its last Liberty ship the *Benjamin Warner*. After Germany's defeat, Warner accepted the Hollywood Foreign Correspondents First World Peace Award for *Hitler Lives?* On the occasion he remarked, "The politically free screen must fight evil with truth. It must combat intolerance by revealing how decent people behave." Despite awards, honors, profits, and artistic achievements during the 1940's, Warner had to deal with some tense wartime union problems, such as an eight-month Screen Actors Guild strike, which was settled in 1945.

In the late 1940's the studio continued to produce its variety of film types and in the 1950's Jack led Warner Brothers into the 3-D fad, represented by the popular *House of Wax*. Although Warner had responded positively to Roosevelt's request to film Ambassador Joseph E. Davies's book, *Mission to Moscow*, with its sympathetic view of Russia and Russians, during the war, he had to defend that film before a McCarthy-era congressional committee. There he explained that the studio had always terminated employment of any anti-American director. To avoid antitrust action, Warner Brothers separated their production and theater-ownership functions in 1955 and thereafter started focusing on television production. In 1956 the brothers sold most of their stock in Warner Brothers, although Jack became the largest company stockholder by repurchasing one-third of the stock.

On Aug. 5, 1958, only weeks after his brother Harry's death, Warner suffered a near-fatal accident on the Riviera, from which he amazingly recovered. At the end of that year he dismissed his son from the studio. Jack Warner headed production until Seven Arts took over the company in 1965, whereupon he became president of Warner–Seven Arts Studio; in 1967, he sold his shares and resigned as production chief, but remained on the board as vice-chairman. After his retirement from the studio (1969), when it merged with Kinney National Service, and his disastrous attempt at Broadway production (*Jimmy*, 1969), he became president of Jack Warner Productions. His productions of the 1960's and 1970's included *My Fair Lady* (1964), *Who's Afraid of Virginia Woolf?* (1966), *Camelot* (1967), *Bonnie and Clyde* (1967), *Dirty Little Billy* (1972), and *1776* (1972). He also financed the distribution of *Whatever Happened to Baby Jane?* (1962).

Key honors Jack Warner received include the President's Medal of Merit and the Irving G. Thalberg Memorial Award (1958) for consistent high-quality film production work. He married his first wife, Irma Claire Salomon, on Oct. 14, 1914; they had one son, Jack Warner, Jr. After Jack and Irma divorced in the 1930's, he married Ann Paige Boyar Alvarado in 1936. He died in Los Angeles.

Jack Warner's early life had demonstrated how familial cooperation, immigrant determination, and intuitive ingenuity combined to make the Warner name outstanding in twentieth-century America's cultural life. He and his brothers moved as a unit and, after mastering their standards for financial and entertainment success, they continued—especially Jack as semiofficial studio spokesman—to sustain a commitment to the American public, which they sought to entertain and inform. Jack claimed to have supervised more than 5,000 Warner Brothers films; he would classify himself as a rare, true "producer," who knew everything about every aspect of filmmaking.

[Jack Warner's autobiography, coauthored with Dean Jennings, is *My First Hundred Years in Hollywood* (1964). On the Warner family and studios, see Ted Sennett, *Warner Brothers Presents* (1971); Charles Higham, *Warner Brothers* (1975); James R. Silke, *Here's Looking at You, Kid* (1976); William R. Meyer, *Warner Brothers Directors* (1978); Clive Hirschhorn, *The Warner Bros. Story* (1979); Rudy Behlmer, ed., *Inside Warner Bros., 1935–1951* (1985); and Cass Warner Sperling and Cork Millner, with Jack Warner, Jr., *Hollywood Be Thy Name: The Warner Brothers Story* (1994). Obituaries are in the *Washington Post*, Sept. 11, 1978; and *Variety*, Sept. 13, 1978.]

MADELINE SAPIENZA

WARREN, LINDSAY CARTER (Dec. 16, 1889–Dec. 28, 1976), United States congressman and comptroller general, was born in Washington, N.C., the son of Charles Frederic Warren, a lawyer, and Elizabeth Mutter Blount. After graduating from the Bingham School in Asheville in 1906, Warren studied at the University of North Carolina at Chapel Hill from 1906 to 1908, continuing on at the law school there in 1911 and 1912. Warren was admitted to the bar in 1912 and practiced law in Washington. He married Emily Harris on Jan. 28, 1916. They had three children.

Warren served as attorney of Beaufort County from 1912 to 1925, during which he also chaired the county's Democratic executive committee. In 1917 and 1919 he was a member of the North Carolina state senate, acting as president pro tem his second term. He participated in 1919 on the state code commission for compiling the consolidated statutes and in 1920 chaired the special legislative committee on workmen's compensation acts. From 1923 to 1925, Warren represented Beaufort County for one term in the state general assembly.

First elected in 1924, Warren, a Democrat, represented North Carolina in the United States House of Representatives from March 1925 through October 1940. An expert on farm legislation and government reorganization, Warren quickly earned the respect of his colleagues. By early 1939, Washington correspondents ranked him among the ten most effective United States representatives. Reporters praised Warren as a dynamic, eloquent, able, and influential leader, strategist, and legislator.

Warren generally supported the New Deal and the internationalist policies of President Franklin D. Roosevelt. He backed the Economy Act of 1933, the Gold Reserve Act of 1934, and the Work Relief and Social Security acts of 1935. He came out against the fair labor standards bill of 1938 and organized the water bloc resisting the Transportation Act of 1940, which placed inland waterways under Interstate Commerce Commission regulation. On international issues, Warren favored providing economic assistance to the Allies and building up American defense. He supported the Reciprocal Trade Agreements Act of 1934, the naval expansion bill of 1938, the Neutrality Act of 1939, and the Selective Service Act of 1940.

Warren chaired the House Accounts Committee from 1931 to 1940 and served on the Joint Committee on Government Reorganization. He adamantly favored the reorganization bill of 1938, which would have empowered President Roosevelt to transfer, consolidate, or abolish federal government departments and agencies, select six new administrative assistants, and curtail budgets of commissions. The House, however, rejected the legislation because it would have consolidated many independent agencies into cabinet-level departments and authorized the president to revamp the civil-service system and create new government departments. Warren cosponsored the Reorganization Act of 1939, which removed these controversial features. Leading the floor debate, Warren argued that the executive branch had ballooned to 150 agencies encompassing 500 bureaus, resulting in enormous cost to the taxpayers and providing wasteful duplication of effort. Congress approved Warren's measure, which was more acceptable to conservative Democrats than the 1938 bill.

While serving in the Congress, Warren remained active in both state and Democratic party affairs. The governor appointed him in 1931 to the North Carolina Constitutional

Commission. Warren chaired the North Carolina Democratic State Convention in 1930 and 1934, was temporary chairman and keynote speaker at the North Carolina State Democratic Convention in 1938, and served as a delegate at large to the Democratic National Convention in 1932 and 1940.

In August 1940, President Roosevelt appointed Warren to a fifteen-year term as comptroller general of the United States. He did not begin his assignment until Nov. 1, 1940, because he was still serving as acting House majority leader. As comptroller general, Warren supervised the 15,000-member General Accounting Office, an agency established by Congress to check on government financial transactions, overseeing the making of its rules and regulations, the establishment of procedures for appropriations and accounting of various government departments, the settlement of government claims and accounts, the auditing of government corporations, and the investigation of and reporting on the use of public funds. Under Warren, the General Accounting Office set up efficient operating procedures and reduced its employees to 5,904 by 1954.

Warren hoped to eliminate duplication, waste, and inconsistency in governmental departments and agencies by creating uniform, cost-efficient accounting systems. The War Department, army, navy, and other federal departments and agencies had committed numerous contract abuses during World War II. Congress cooperated with Warren's office after the war, placing 101 government corporations under its budgetary and auditing controls. Warren's office conducted audits of the Tennessee Valley Authority, the Reconstruction Finance Corporation, the Atomic Energy Commission, the War Shipping Administration, the Maritime Commission, the air force, and other federal agencies and departments. In 1947, Warren, Secretary of the Treasury John Snyder, and Director of the Budget Fred Lawton inaugurated a joint accounting program to ensure better government accounting of all federal departments and agencies. Congress in 1950 authorized Warren's office to implement joint accounting. Most government departments and agencies cooperated with the joint accounting program, but it took time to make the system fully operative within the vast Department of Defense.

Warren frequently appeared before Congress to endorse or condemn various reorganization plans. He backed President Harry Truman's request for broad authority to reorganize the government's executive agencies, but criticized the establishment of the Hoover Commission as a waste of public funds. Warren denounced the commission's recommendation to reduce the staff and functions of the General Accounting Office as an invasion of congressional rights.

Warren retired for health reasons as comptroller general on May 1, 1954, eighteen months before his term expired. The General Accounting Office's exacting scrutiny of government expenditures under Warren's leadership ultimately saved the government about $915 million. Warren returned to Washington, N.C., where he joined the Beaufort County Red Cross as general chairman in November 1954. He served in the North Carolina state senate from 1959 to 1962. Warren died in Washington, N.C.

[Warren's papers are located in the Southern Historical Collection at the University of North Carolina, Chapel Hill. Richard Polenberg, *Reorganizing Roosevelt's Government* (1966); and David L. Porter, *Congress and the Waning of the New Deal* (1980), recount Warren's congressional role on reorganization legislation. David L. Porter, "Representative Lindsay Warren, the Water Bloc, and the Transportation Act of 1940," *North Carolina Historical Review* 50 (July 1973), details his role in opposing federal regulation of inland waterways. "More Scandals to Come Out," *U.S. News and World Report*, Feb. 15, 1952; and relevant articles in the *New York Times*, Apr. 1, 1954, and May 1–3, 1954, recount Warren's activities as comptroller general.]

DAVID L. PORTER

WARREN, SHIELDS (Feb. 26, 1898–July 1, 1980), experimental pathologist, was born in Cambridge, Mass., the son of William Marshall Warren, dean of Boston University's College of Liberal Arts, and Sara Bainbridge. His paternal grandfather had been the first president of Boston University. He attended Boston University, where he graduated with a B.A. in biology in 1918. He received an M.D. degree from Harvard University Medical School in 1923. On Aug. 11, 1923, he married Alice Springfield; they had two children.

Warren was the first assistant in pathology in the laboratory at Boston City Hospital, where he worked from 1923 to 1925. His initial research was in diabetes, which became the subject of the first of the nine medical textbooks he would write. But he soon shifted his focus to the study of cancer and the way in which it spreads.

In 1925, Warren began teaching at Harvard Medical School as an instructor in pathology. In 1936, he became an assistant professor, and, in 1948, a full professor. Warren was known for having a calm, dry manner. One colleague described him as a riveting speaker who had "no pretension whatsoever." In 1927, he began a fifty-year career as a pathologist at New England Deaconess Hospital, where he became chief pathologist in 1946. He also served other hospitals in the Boston area.

Warren's research in the 1930's supported his theory that the lymphatic system might play a role in transmitting cancer cells from one part of the body to another. His observations led to the modern surgical practice of removing the lymph nodes close to cancerous tissue. Warren also proposed the idea that some people might be more predisposed than others to cancer and multiple cases of cancer.

By the time the world knew of atomic energy, Warren and a small number of other scientists had already shown in many experiments that radiation overdoses caused injury and death. His knowledge and experience came into play during World War II, which ended with the atomic bombing of two Japanese cities, Hiroshima and Nagasaki. Warren entered the Naval Reserve as a captain in 1943, and served on the scientific advisory board of the Army Institute of Pathology as an expert consultant to the surgeon general. But Warren's most important duty came after the war.

In 1945, he led the medical team of the United States Navy's technical mission to Japan. Warren concluded that the majority of deaths in Hiroshima and Nagasaki were caused by the explosion's radiation and not by the bomb blast itself. The second greatest cause of death, he said, was "flash burns" from the explosion's blinding light. He was given credit for conducting the first systematic study of radioactive fallout. With "ground zero" marking the location where the bomb was dropped, Warren's study noted that flesh burns were observed within a 2.5-mile radius of ground zero. The study concluded that lethal radiation effects were uncommon beyond a mile radius of ground zero, though some beyond that limit were still exposed to ionizing radiation. Such exposure caused a delayed reaction in human blood cells, similar to damage done by overexposure to X rays. A typical delayed reaction would occur two weeks after exposure and might appear as leukemia or forms of anemia.

Warren examined survivors of the atomic blast and found specific symptoms associated with acute radiation. In the short term, damage was done to the bone marrow as well as the lymphoid and gastrointestinal tissue. In the long run, sterility, genetic damage, and cancer could appear. His conclusions helped set safety standards for people who work with atomic energy and radiation.

In 1946, Warren was an officer of the Naval Medical Section during the atomic tests on Bikini atoll. He outlined the first program in biology and medicine for the Atomic Energy Commission (now the Department of Energy), and in 1947 was appointed the first director of its Division of Biology and Medicine. That same year, Congress funded the division with $5 million for cancer research. Eventually, the division discovered positive uses of radiation, such as the treatment of diseases with radioisotopes. Warren was director of the division until 1952.

His interest in the beneficial uses of radiation prevented Warren from joining scientists who called for an end to nuclear bomb tests after World War II. He felt not only that nuclear energy had peaceful purposes but also that mankind must learn to control its dangers. The Division of Biology and Medicine developed a radiation meter that could be commercially produced at a cost between $10 and $15, compared with a $200 Geiger counter, which was then being used to detect radiation.

In a public hearing on Mar. 17, 1950, Warren told the Joint Congressional Committee on Atomic Energy that "there was no ground for fears that an atomic blast would cause widespread sterility or other debilities." As evidence, he pointed to the stable birth rate in Nagasaki and Hiroshima, and claimed that there was "no unusual rate of abnormality among children born since then." He said that penicillin and streptomycin, among other antibiotics, would serve to "eliminate so far as possible secondary effects produced by overwhelming infections."

In the same year as the public hearing, Warren claimed that radioactive tracers had allowed pathologists to revolutionize their techniques in locating diseased tissue and thus provided solutions to previously unsolved problems. For years he studied the positive effects radiation could have on cancerous tissue. In the mid-1940's, with Olive Gates, Warren developed the "cervical smear," which is used to diagnose cancer of the cervix.

From 1955 to 1963, Warren was the United States representative to the United Nations Scientific Committee on the Effects of Atomic Radiation. He was elected to the National Academy of Sciences in 1962 and, in that same year, was given the Albert Einstein Medal and Award for the study of the pathological effects of ionizing radiation on human beings. Warren's other contributions include the development of techniques that enabled pathologists to improve their cell sections for analysis under the electron microscope.

In the last five years of his life, Warren began researching the connection between cancer and the endocrine system. He died in his family's summer home in Mashpee, Mass.

[Warren's published works include *The Pathology of Diabetes Mellitus* (1930), with P. M. LeCompte; *A Handbook for the Diagnosis of Cancer of the Uterus* (1947), with Olive Gates; *Introduction to Neuropathology* (1950), with Samuel P. Hicks; *The Medical Effects of the Atomic Bomb in Japan* (1956), edited with Ashley W. Oughterson; and *The Pathology of Ionizing Radiation* (1961). An obituary is in the *New York Times*, July 8, 1980.]

ALISON GARDY

WATERS, ETHEL (Oct. 31, 1896–Sept. 1, 1977), singer, actress, and Christian evangelist, was born in Chester, Pa., the daughter of Louise Anderson, who was raped at knifepoint at the age of twelve by John Waters. Her father, whom she never knew, was murdered by poison when Waters was three. She had a half sister, born to her mother in a later marriage, and perhaps as many as three half brothers from her father, by Waters's own account. Raised by her maternal grandmother, Sally Anderson, and living sometimes with two aunts whom she described as sometimes abusive alcoholics, Waters had an early childhood marked by constant moving that fostered toughness and street smartness. Sally Anderson found occasional employment as a live-in housekeeper and cleaning woman but was often unable to feed and house herself and Waters properly. Nevertheless, her faith and personal strength influenced Waters, and she remembered her grandmother's example throughout her life.

Growing up in the slums and red-light districts of Philadelphia and its outlying areas, Waters was no stranger to desperation. She learned to fend for herself early on, occasionally stealing food to keep from going hungry. Her friends and acquaintances included the neighborhood prostitutes and petty thieves. Her grandmother, a devout Catholic, enrolled Waters, at age nine, in a multiracial Catholic school in Philadelphia. The nuns inspired awe, respect, and a lifelong love of God that sometimes stood in stark contrast to her daily existence.

In April 1910, at the age of thirteen, Waters married Merritt ("Buddy") Purnsley, ten years her senior; they had no children. The marriage, approved by her mother, with whom she had had little contact, was characterized by physical abuse and lasted less than a year. A number of years later she married and divorced Edward Mallory; they had no children.

Waters began working in hotels and apartment houses as a chambermaid and waitress. In her autobiography, *His Eye Is on the Sparrow*, she recalled that her dream was to become the personal maid and companion of a wealthy woman who would take her around the world; she also fantasized about being a star of the stage. On Oct. 31, 1917, Waters sang at a local Philadelphia nightclub, Jack's Rathskeller. She was soon hired, billed as Sweet Mama Stringbean—"They called me that," she said, "because of my lissome and willowy form." Urged on by Braxton and Nugent, a successful vaudeville team, she began singing and dancing at the Lincoln Theatre in Baltimore with Maggie and Jo Hill, as the third member of the Hill Sisters. At this time she obtained permission from W. C. Handy to perform his "St. Louis Blues," a much-requested song and one of many that she made famous. Later successes included "Dinah," "Takin' a Chance on Love," and "Stormy Weather."

During World I, the Hill Sisters and Sweet Mama Stringbean played vaudeville clubs and carnivals in Detroit, Cincinnati, Atlanta, Savannah, and small towns in the South and Midwest. They encountered the viciousness of Jim Crow laws in both the North and the South, as well as the resentment of southern blacks. While playing in Birmingham, Ala., Waters met the great black performers of the day—Ma Rainey, Legge McGinty, Alice Ramsey, and others, many of whom she had seen years before at the Standard Theater in Philadelphia.

When Waters returned to Philadelphia after the breakup of the Hill Sisters and a year on the road, she had a two-week engagement at the Standard Theater, the city's premier showcase for black performers; only a few years before, she had "watched shows from the peanut gallery" there. In those early years, her blues singing was her trademark.

Waters moved to New York City and found work singing at Edmond's Cellar and other small clubs in Harlem, and at Rafe's Paradise in Atlantic City, N.J. She recorded "Down Home Blues" and "Oh, Daddy" on the Black Swan label, a record followed by a number of other popular blues hits that led to a tour with Fletcher Henderson's Black Swan Jazz Masters. Waters later recorded with Benny Goodman, Tommy and Jimmy Dorsey, and other white musicians on the Columbia label. In the summer of 1924 she filled in for the black singing star Florence Mills at Sam Salvin's Plantation Club on Broadway, alongside Josephine Baker and Bessie Allison.

Although Waters won praise for her renditions of classic blues songs, she declined the opportunity to play Paris, an offer that Josephine Baker accepted. Waters's first Broadway appearance was in the all-black revue *Africana* (1927), which then toured the Midwest. She next appeared in Lew Leslie's 1930 production *Blackbirds* and, following an eight-month tour of Europe that included performances in Paris and at the Palladium in London, she starred in the 1931 revue *Rhapsody in Black*. Her first movie, *On with the Show*, was released in 1929.

In the early 1930's the Cotton Club in Harlem featured such well-known black performers as Cab Calloway and Duke Ellington. Waters's rendition there of "Stormy Weather" caught the attention of Irving Berlin, who cast her in his musical *As Thousands Cheer*, a highly successful hit in which she became the first black performer in an otherwise all-white cast and the highest-paid woman on Broadway. In 1935 she costarred with Beatrice Lillie in the Shubert show *At Home Abroad*, which ran at the Winter Garden and (in 1936) at the Majestic. This success was followed by *Mamba's Daughters*, which opened to critical acclaim in January 1939 at the Empire Theatre. In it, Waters was the first black actress to star on Broadway in a dramatic role. As Petunia Jackson in *Cabin in the Sky* (1940), Waters sang "Takin' a Chance on Love." The play subsequently went on the road and in 1943 was made into a movie starring Waters, Lena Horne, and Louis Armstrong. Waters also appeared in the film *Cairo* (1942).

Despite a string of successful plays, films, and recordings, by the late 1940's Waters found little work, was plagued by financial troubles, and fought to keep from losing her home in California by accepting minor bookings. But by 1948 she was back in Hollywood, filming the Twentieth Century–Fox production of *Pinky* (1949), directed by Elia Kazan. For her portrayal of Granny in this story of the troubles of a black girl who passes for white, Waters won an Oscar nomination for best supporting actress.

Before the release of *Pinky*, Waters was approached to star in the Carson McCullers play *The Member of the Wedding*. At first she objected to the story because "there was no God in this play." When the producers allowed her to give the role of Berenice Sadie Brown her own interpretation, she signed a contract. Julie Harris was cast to play Frankie, the thirteen-year-old heroine. The play opened on Broadway at the Empire Theatre, to universal acclaim, on Jan. 5, 1950, and had a long run before being made into a movie in 1952. Waters received the New York Drama Critics Award for her stage appearance in *Member*. She sang her signature song, "His Eye Is on the Sparrow," a hymn taught to her by her grandmother, and the title of her first autobiography, in the play.

During the 1950's and 1960's, Waters appeared frequently in the one-woman show *An Evening with Ethel Waters*, despite her great size (at one point she weighed almost 350 pounds and moved with difficulty). She was in the film *The Sound and the Fury* (1959) and had a number of small roles on television shows.

A turning point in Waters's life came in 1957 when, while on tour, she was invited to the Billy Graham Crusade at Madison Square Garden in New York City. She soon took an active role in Graham's crusades, marking a transformation in her spiritual and professional life by singing in the Crusade choir.

In a long career as a singer and an actress that began in the honky-tonk clubs of black America and ended in Christian evangelist crusades with mainly white audiences, Waters had a large and devoted following. She is remembered as much for the obstacles she overcame as for her contributions to twentieth-century American culture. She died in Chatsworth, Calif., at the home of friends.

[Waters wrote two autobiographies: *His Eye Is on the Sparrow* (1951) and *To Me It's Wonderful* (1972), the latter of which corrects the erroneous birthdate given in the former. A biography is Juliann DeKorte, *Finally Home* (1978). An obituary is in the *New York Times*, Sept. 2, 1977.]

JONATHAN G. ARETAKIS

WATT, DONALD BEATES (May 3, 1893–Nov. 27, 1977), educator and organization head, was born in Lancaster, Pa., one of five children of Peter T. Watt and Laura L. Geiger. His father, a Scottish immigrant, was cofounder of the Watt and Shand Department Store in Lancaster. His mother raised Watt with religious zeal, and the Presbyterian Church and the YMCA were important influences on his developing value system. Watt took an early liking to outdoor activities; he started camping at the age of eight and hiking at twelve. After attending public schools in Lancaster, Watt went to the Lawrenceville School (1908–1912) in New Jersey. While there, he directed the school summer camp for underprivileged boys.

At Princeton University majoring in psychology from 1912 to 1916, Watt underwent a change in his religious mindset, from a strictly literal belief in the Bible to a greater understanding of it as history and poetry. During his college years he traveled to Europe for the first time. Upon his graduation, he served in the British-Indian army in Mesopotamia (Iraq) as a YMCA secretary. From 1916 to 1919, as a lone American among British and Indian troops, Watt learned to adjust to European and Asiatic customs. During World War I, his job was to make the troops as comfortable as possible. To that end, Watt organized social and religious activities for the soldiers. After the war, he traveled across the deserts of Persia. He felt at home in unusual and distant places.

Upon returning to the United States, Watt went to work as treasurer for a family enterprise, a cement factory near Catskill, N.Y. In Catskill, he met and married Leslie Somers, the sister of the local Presbyterian minister's wife, on Mar. 25, 1922. They had three children. With the sale of the cement company, Watt began graduate study in psychology at the University of Pennsylvania in 1924.

Watt then spent three years at the University of Pennsylvania and at Yale University. Despite failed preliminary examinations for the Ph.D., he went to Germany in 1926 to study German. During this summer vacation, he spent one month in a German home and a second month hiking in the mountains. This experience foreshadowed the pattern he would adopt for his bold educational experiment.

When Watt returned to the United States, he accepted a post to organize and head a student personnel department at Syracuse University. He led a group of college students on a hiking tour of France, Germany, and Switzerland. When the Great Depression struck in 1931, Watt was asked to take a leave of absence from his post at Syracuse. He went to New York City, where he took a volunteer job with the Inquiry, a group of sociologists in the YMCA and YWCA movements who studied group dynamics and the discussion method.

This group refined and developed communication based on consensus. Using personal experience, small groups worked together with a skilled leader on solving a specific problem, in a setting conducive to fruitful discussion. In 1931, Watt and two colleagues from the Inquiry went to Geneva to study the methods used in the summer schools conducted by the League of Nations Societies. They were unsuccessful in their attempts to persuade the League societies to use the discussion method. However, out of this failure emerged the plan for the Experiment in International Living.

The first experiment, designed to create sympathetic understanding across national lines, sought to bring fourteen teenage American boys together for one month with an equal number of European boys. The experiment was designed to give American youth an opportunity to live in European homes and to share the outdoor life of Europeans. Watt's first prospectus outlined the purposes: To learn, by living and thinking with them, how French and German boys live and think; to make friends among them by being a friend to them; to make a real beginning of speaking one of their languages; to visit places of cultural and historical importance. Despite the depression, a group of twenty-three boys participated in the first experiment in 1932 in Switzerland.

After this, Watt felt committed to make mountain climbing an important feature of the experiment summer. Other changes were made in succeeding years. The group camp was eliminated and the home stay instituted. Visitors were to speak the language of their hosts. Visitors and hosts were to live together for two months; the first month in a home, the second traveling in the host country. Females were included in the second year. Watt listened to experimenters. His seriousness of purpose was reflected in constant reexamination and changes in the program.

To find young experimenters for the second-year program, Watt embarked on a three-month trip to visit independent schools. During the early years of the experiment, he and his wife were the salespeople and the office staff. The second experiment (1933) in Germany proved controversial because of the rise of Nazi power.

From the third experiment on, groups went to France. There were strong objections to overcome. For example, Watt was told by one authority, "The French do not take strangers into their homes." Watt, undeterred, prevailed in his search for French homes. Similar obstacles were overcome in southern Italy, Latin America, Mexico, and Nigeria. In each instance, Watt was challenged to find people willing to join the experiment.

Each year, the numbers of people the experiment served and the geographical area it covered grew. In 1937, Watt moved from Syracuse to Putney, Vt. The experiment program was incorporated in 1942 and became codified in a series of publications, including, among others, leaders' and experimenters' handbooks. As the experiment grew, Watt found natives to represent the different countries involved. These nationals became the experiment directors and attended general international meetings.

By the time Watt retired, the experiment had grown considerably to include the School for International Training, established in 1961. Today, the school offers degrees in international studies and has trained more Peace Corps volunteers than any university. Still at its core is the central idea that people learn to live together by living together. Learning by experience in the home of another national is basic to effective education for international understanding, Watt believed. For his efforts, Watt received recognition from the governments of Germany, France, Chile, and Japan. He died in Lancaster.

[Watt's papers are located at the headquarters of the Experiment in International Living's successor organization, World Learning, Inc., in Brattleboro, Vt. He wrote three books, *Investment Banking as a Career* (1929), a vocational monograph, and *Intelligence Is Not Enough* (1967) and *Letters to the Founder* (1977), about his experience with the experiment. A videotape, "Back to the Future" (1989), is available from the experiment. Obituaries are in the *New York Times*; the *Lancaster Intelligencer Journal*; and the *Lancaster New Era*, all Nov. 28, 1977.]

JACOB L. SUSSKIND

WATTS, FRANKLIN MOWRY (June 11, 1904–May 21, 1978), publisher and author, was born in Sioux City, Iowa, the son of John Franklin Watts, a Baptist minister, and Amanda Mowry. Watts was raised primarily in Northampton, Mass. His father was well-read in history, economics, and sociology, and the family had a substantial library, which cultivated in Watts a strong interest in literature. He attended Boston University and received a B.A. in business administration in 1925.

Watts owned a bookstore, the Book Nook, in Lawrence, Kans., and was a book buyer for the George Innes Company of Wichita, Kans., and L. S. Ayers and Company in Indianapolis from 1925 to 1932. He worked as the sales manager for several publishing firms in New York City, including Vanguard Press from 1932 to 1934, Julian Messner from 1934 to 1950, and Heritage Press from 1936 to 1950.

In September 1942, Watts started his own publishing company, Franklin Watts, Inc., at 285 Madison Avenue in New York City, and was its president until 1969 and vice-chairman from 1970 to 1978. Franklin Watts, Inc., published its first book, *Voices of History: Great Speeches and Papers of the Year*, edited by Watts himself, in October 1942. Although the book did not sell well, it received favorable reviews. The second book published by the company was *How to Write Better Letters* by Marcel M. Swartz. It was a great success, with more than 100,000 copies sold in the company's first ten years. It was the first of the company's line of eight-and-a-half-by-eleven-inch paperback home reference books, preceding such successful titles as *Houses for Homemakers* (1945) by Royal Barry Wills, which sold more than 400,000 copies in one year.

Watts's experience as a salesman enabled him to recognize the growing demand for children's books. He decided to publish a volume on trains for children, many of whom had never seen a steam engine. *Little Choo Choo*, written by

Helen Hoke, was published in 1943, and by 1952 had sold more than 140,000 copies. Watts married Hoke on May 25, 1945. In addition to writing for children, she was a distinguished children's book editor for publishers, including Holt, Messner, Reynal and Hitchcock, and McKay. She joined Franklin Watts, Inc., as its vice president in 1948 and served as editor in chief from 1948 to 1956.

Watts's famous First Books series began with *An Airplane Rebus* by Jeanne Bendick, which had disappointing sales when first published. Watts changed the title into *The First Flying Book* (later retitled *The First Book of Airplanes*) after he had carefully checked in the New York Public Library and found that the word "first" had been used in about forty-two bibliographic entries, but none for a children's series. Thus was initiated a successful children's series that ran continuously up to some 300 titles during Watts's presidency. Many of the volumes were written by well-known authors. The series covered a variety of subjects, such as nature, geography, history, and sports, and included *The First Book of Stones, The First Book of World War II*, and *The First Book of Japan*. All the First Books were uniform in size and price, but varied in length, type styles, illustrations, and reading level.

Watts started to seek a merger in 1956 because he felt the company was not making enough of a profit to finance internal expansion. On Mar. 26, 1957, Franklin Watts, Inc., was sold to Grolier Enterprises, Inc., with Franklin and Helen Watts retaining 20 percent of the stock. After the merger, the company expanded its publishing business (about 100 new titles a year) and personnel, increased its sales over the industry averages every year, and became one of the leading publishers of juvenile books.

The acknowledged aim of Franklin Watts, Inc., was "never to underestimate the intelligence or overestimate the knowledge of the reader." Its goal was "to enrich the minds and hearts of children for generations to come." Watts continuously solicited ideas from librarians, teachers, writers, and colleagues for children's publications. The juvenile series Terrific Triple Titles began with the anthology *Horses, Horses, Horses* by Phyllis Fenner, which sold more than 22,000 copies in its first six months. It was followed by about twenty others, including *Elephants, Elephants, Elephants; Ghosts, Ghosts, Ghosts; Jokes, Jokes, Jokes;* and *Doctors, Doctors, Doctors*. In 1966 Watts initiated another successful children's series, Let's Find Out, which was geared toward first- and second-grade readers. Watts's books, with their fine design and low price, sold very well to libraries and schools as well as to the general public. Watts was also involved with Keith Jennison in publishing large-type books for the visually handicapped. The first such title was *Profiles in Courage*.

Being a distinguished publisher of children's books, Watts also wrote for children. Among his publications were *The Complete Christmas Book* (1958), which he edited, and *Let's Find Out About Christmas* (1967), *Let's Find Out About Easter* (1969), *Corn* (1977), *Rice* (1977), *Wheat* (1977), *Oranges* (1978), *Peanuts* (1978), and *Tomatoes* (1978).

In addition to working for his own companies, Watts developed a series of more than fifty nonfiction juvenile titles for Doubleday, the Real Books. He also created a series of adult titles for Pocket Books, and was the editor of *Pocket Book Magazine* from 1954 to 1956. He frequently wrote articles advising would-be authors and sharing with other publishers his experience in the publishing business.

In 1969 Watts retired from the presidency of Franklin Watts, Inc., to establish Franklin Watts, Ltd., a joint venture with Grolier International, in London, England. He was the managing director there from 1970 to 1976. There was no direct business relationship between the London and American companies. It published both original books and anglicized versions of some Franklin Watts, Inc., books.

In 1976, Watts retired to return to New York City to found the Franklin Book Corporation, an independent book company. Watts was a member of the American Book Publishers Council and the Government Book Program advisory committee. He was also a member of a United States Department of State advisory committee on international book projects. Watts died at Doctors Hospital in New York City.

[Articles by Watts include "Juveniles in the Post-war World," *The Retail Bookseller* 48 (Nov. 1945); "A Publisher Looks at Series," *Library Journal* 87 (Jan. 15, 1962); "Getting a Children's Book Published," *The Writer* 78 (Oct. 1965); "Meeting 'A Crisis in Prosperity,' " *Publishers Weekly*, Jan. 2, 1967; and "Franklin Watts Starts London Publishing Company," *Publishers Weekly*, Nov. 17, 1969. See also "Watts Marks Tenth Anniversary," *Publishers Weekly*, Oct. 25, 1952; and "Watts Celebrates Publication of 100th First Book," *Publishers Weekly*, June 8, 1959. Obituaries are in the *New York Times*, May 23, 1978; and *Publishers Weekly*, June 5, 1978.]

WEN-HUA REN

WAYNE, JOHN (May 26, 1907–June 11, 1979), actor, was born Marion Michael Morrison in Winterset, Iowa, one of two children of Clyde L. Morrison, a pharmacist, and Mary Margaret Brown. He was close to his father but estranged from his mother, who favored his brother, Robert. Clyde Morrison needed dry air because he suffered from tuberculosis, so the family moved to Palmdale, Calif., on the edge of the Mojave Desert. In 1916, after Clyde's attempt at farming had failed, the family moved to Glendale, Calif. Having grown into a tall, rangy, athletic teenager, Marion won a football scholarship to the University of Southern California in 1925. The same year he began to work as a scenery mover in the prop department at Fox Film Studio. Because of his imposing size—he was six feet, four inches tall and weighed over 200 pounds—he began to appear as an extra in movies about college athletes and in Westerns.

In 1926, Marion met John Ford, the director who was to have a decisive impact on his career. Ford sensed a raw potential in the strapping though callow young man and recommended him to Raoul Walsh, who was looking for an actor to play the starring role of a wagon-train leader in an epic Western, *The Big Trail* (1930). Walsh, who felt that despite his inexperience, Marion had the presence to become an action movie hero, cast him in the role and gave him a new, rugged-sounding name, John Wayne. The film, which was shot in Fox's new widescreen process and had an unusually high budget for the period, was not a success. In his first major part Wayne was often physically awkward and delivered his lines in a drawling monotone, but he had the he-man swagger that in time made him a Hollywood icon.

The film's failure put Wayne's career on hold, and for the next nine years—one of the longest apprenticeships in movies—Wayne toiled unrewardingly in a series of B pictures for Columbia, Universal, and Warner Brothers, as well as for "Poverty Row" factories like Mascot, Monogram–Lone Star, and Republic. During this prolonged B period, Wayne made almost seventy features, mostly Westerns and contemporary action stories that recycled the same narrative formulas over and over: typically, the films were shot in three to six days, on extremely tight budgets, and ran no more than an hour. Shooting them back to back, Wayne later recalled, he often could not remember which movie he was in.

Not until 1939, when John Ford cast him as the Ringo Kid in *Stagecoach*, did Wayne get another chance to crawl out of his B-movie rut. This time both the actor and the film achieved a notable success. In a star-making entrance, Wayne seemed to materialize out of the desert as the camera lunged forward to greet him. As a generic stereotype, a Man of the West who did what he had to do, Wayne was vocally and facially inexpressive but moved well, walking with the slow, sure stride that became part of his signature. He looked entirely at home on the range.

But *Stagecoach* did not lift Wayne out of B films. He was billed below Claire Trevor, his *Stagecoach* costar, in two routine Westerns, and looked uncomfortable partnering Marlene Dietrich in three movies designed to showcase her newly Americanized persona. Wayne was under contract to Republic Pictures, a minor studio, and throughout the 1940's he appeared in the formula action fare that was the studio's specialty.

Wayne's career went into high gear only when Howard Hawks cast him in *Red River* (1948). As a dictatorial cattle baron, Wayne played a role that questioned the tall-in-the-saddle heroism that had become his stock-in-trade; his reactionary, emotionally wounded character was challenged and corrected by his stepson, an enlightened pioneer (played by Montgomery Clift, a high-strung "Method" actor from New York, and Wayne's iconographic and temperamental opposite). Now in his early forties, Wayne had acquired a grizzled, weather-beaten quality that deepened his acting and, breaking up his lines with naturalistic pauses, he had learned to use his voice effectively.

Entering the most ambitious phase of his career, Wayne appeared in John Ford's famed cavalry trilogy in which he played soldiers driven by patriotism and respect for tradition. In *Fort Apache* (1948) he was a company man who enshrined the memory of his commanding officer, a tyrant and a fool, in order to keep up troop morale. In *She Wore a Yellow Ribbon* (1949) he was an about-to-retire career officer who led one final, heroic attack against marauding Indians. And in *Rio Grande* (1950) he played what was to become a standard John Wayne part, that of a disciplinarian who whips a group of callow young men into fighting shape—in *The Sands of Iwo Jima* (1949) he had played exactly the same role in a different genre and earned his first Oscar nomination. *Rio Grande* was the first of five films Wayne made with Maureen O'Hara. Opposite O'Hara in *The Quiet Man* (1952), directed by John Ford, Wayne gave his one convincing performance as a romantic lead.

In 1944, Wayne was a founding member of the Motion Picture Alliance for the Preservation of American Ideals, an organization dedicated to expelling Communists from the film industry. He became obsessed by his anti-Communist activities, and for the rest of his life he remained devoted to Senator Joseph McCarthy and proud of his part in compiling the Hollywood blacklist. By the late 1940's, the actor and his roles had merged, and a "John Wayne" part became a virtual synonym for a particular kind of manly code of conduct and a superheated Americanism. The actor's ideological convictions were an implicit factor in most of his films, but on a few occasions Wayne made the mistake of using his work as a platform for his political fundamentalism. In 1952, for instance, he produced and starred in *Big Jim McLain*, an overwrought, simpleminded anti-Communist diatribe.

In 1956, Wayne starred for Ford in *The Searchers*, a career high point. As Ethan Edwards, a loner who lives in and understands the great outdoors, and is driven by his hatred of Indians, Wayne portrayed a character representing the dark side of the American West. The role required Wayne to be more brooding and to create more of an inner life than he had ever done before; the steepest acting challenge in his career occurred in the film's climactic scene, in which his character is torn between killing or accepting the niece who was abducted by Indians and who now says she feels more Indian than white.

In the late 1950's and 1960's, as he became a Hollywood elder statesman, Wayne played a series of stalwart veterans who gave strength to others. He helped drunkards, played by Dean Martin in *Rio Bravo* (1959) and by Robert Mitchum in *El Dorado* (1967), to reclaim their self-respect, and he turned an easterner (James Stewart) into a western hero in *The Man Who Shot Liberty Valance* (1962).

As a vocal proponent of American involvement in the Vietnam War in the 1960's, Wayne again became as famous for his opinions as for his acting. To support his position that America needed to defend South Vietnam from the Communist hordes sweeping down from the north, he produced, directed, and starred in *The Green Berets* (1968), the first pro-war major studio feature about Vietnam, and excruciating both politically and cinematically. (Wayne's first directorial effort, *The Alamo* [1960], was another labor of love on a patriotic theme, and only marginally better.) Despite poisonous reviews *The Green Berets* made money, a fact Wayne was proud of; the film did well, he said, because it made statements Americans both wanted and needed to hear.

When he appeared as Rooster Cogburn in *True Grit* (1969), Wayne was "forgiven" for *The Green Berets*. He won an Oscar for his performance as a gruff, expansive, seldom-sober bounty hunter who softens as he helps a young woman track the man who killed her father. Sending up his image in broad, deft strokes, Wayne had never been as loose or amusing before, and like many big stars near the ends of their careers, he depended on and played to the affectionate memories of his fans.

Wayne never stopped working, and he retained his popular rating longer than any other star; but for the rest of his career he was mired, for the most part, in a series of routine Westerns. On the few occasions when he tried to bend his image, he stumbled. Late in the day he tried to climb onto the police-movie bandwagon popular in the 1970's, but in *McQ* (1974) and *Brannigan* (1975) he was too old and too slow-moving for the genre. *The Shootist* (1976), in which he played a celebrated gunslinger dying of cancer, was a fitting valedictory.

Wayne was respected by coworkers for his professionalism and dedication. His need to keep working, however, helped to undermine his three marriages. His first marriage, to Josephine Saenz, a pious Panamanian uninterested in her husband's career, lasted from 1933 to 1945; they had four children. His second marriage, to Esperanza ("Chata") Baur Diaz, a Mexican, was volatile and short-lived; they were married in 1946 and divorced, noisily, in 1953. They had no children. Wayne's third marriage, to Pilar Palette Weldy, a Peruvian actress, was his longest and happiest—they were married in 1954 and separated in 1973. They had three children.

Wayne was private about his private life, but when a cancerous lung was removed in 1964, he spoke out, announcing that he had just fought and won his greatest battle. He was equally public in 1979 about his second and fatal battle with cancer. Wayne died in Los Angeles.

On his deathbed Wayne was awarded a congressional medal that honored "John Wayne, American." The debate over Wayne's ability as an actor continues. He had no versatility whatever—he was ludicrous as Genghis Khan in *The Conqueror* (1956) and as a Roman centurion in *The Greatest Story Ever Told* (1965); the only time he did not sound like "John Wayne" was when he spoke with a reasonably convincing Swedish accent in *The Long Voyage Home* (1940). If he lacked the transformative skills of Laurence Olivier (whom he respected), he did have the ability to "play himself," or what audiences accepted as an authentic self-projection. At his best, out on the American desert and prairie, he was a natural, unassuming performer who never let the viewer catch him acting.

Wayne probably appeared in more unwatchable films than any other star of his stature. From first to last, his career was littered with formula Westerns and war pictures but, working with Ford and Hawks, he also starred in some of the most enduring Westerns ever made. If, finally, Wayne is more icon than actor, firmly implanted in American culture as the embodiment of a stolid, patriotic, honor-bound American masculinity, he is an indelible part of the way American films have depicted how the West was won.

[See Allen Eyles, *John Wayne* (1979), for the most complete account of Wayne's films. Pilar Wayne, with Alex Thorleifson, *John Wayne, My Life with the Duke* (1987), is the most vivid account to date of the star's off-screen life. See also Mark Ricci, Boris Zmijewsky, and Steve Zmijewsky, *The Films of John Wayne* (1970); Maurice Zolotow, *John Wayne* (1974); and Judith M. Riggin, *John Wayne, a Bio-Bibliography* (1992). An obituary is in the *New York Times*, June 12, 1979.]

FOSTER HIRSCH

WEAVER, WARREN (July 17, 1894–Nov. 24, 1978), mathematician, was born in Reedsburg, Wis., the second of two sons of Isaiah Weaver, a pharmacist, and Kittie Belle Stupfell. After a somewhat lonely childhood in the then small town of Reedsburg, the family moved to Madison, where Warren graduated from high school in 1912. He attended the University of Wisconsin from 1912 to 1917, receiving a B.S. in mathematics in 1916 and a C.E. (Civil Engineer) degree in 1917.

Weaver's teaching career began at Throop College (later the California Institute of Technology) in Pasadena, Calif., as an assistant professor of mathematics. After less than a year of teaching he was drafted into the United States Army and served in the newly formed National Research Council Unit. He worked mainly at the National Bureau of Standards, developing aviation equipment. In 1919, upon completion of his service in World War I as a second lieutenant, he returned to his teaching career in Pasadena and on Sept. 4, 1919, married his college classmate Mary Hemenway. They had two children.

In the fall of 1920, Weaver joined the faculty of the University of Wisconsin. The next twelve years at Madison comprised the rest of his academic career. His Ph.D. in 1921 was in mathematical physics, and his collaboration with Max Mason, a mathematical physicist who had been Weaver's most admired undergraduate professor, led to the publication of *The Electromagnetic Field* in 1929, for many years a widely used text for graduate students in physics. By 1928, Weaver was a full professor and chairman of the mathematics department.

When Max Mason became president of the Rockefeller Foundation in New York City in 1930, he invited Weaver to join his staff. The newly reorganized foundation was shifting its focus of support into the area of natural sciences. Weaver's vision of research in biological fields, which included undertaking a long-range program to fund research in experimental and quantitative biology, met with approval, and he was invited to become director of the newly defined Division of Natural Sciences (renamed the Division of Natural Sciences and Agriculture in 1951 to reflect the expansion of interest in funding agricultural research) of the Rockefeller Foundation. The decision to leave Madison was not an easy one for the Weavers. In his 1970 autobiography *Scene of Change: A Life-*

time in American Science, Weaver wrote that although he loved to teach, he "lacked that strange and wonderful creative spark that makes a good researcher." He accepted the opportunity in New York City, and in January of 1932 began a new career in science administration and philanthropy. The *President's Review and Annual Report* of the Rockefeller Foundation during Weaver's tenure there, as well as *The Story of the Rockefeller Foundation* (1952) by Raymond B. Fosdick, delineate the changes and refocusing of the Rockefeller Foundation under the leadership, enthusiasm, and vision of Warren Weaver. Weaver saw research in molecular biology as the dependable way to gain an understanding of life processes and to seek solutions to various health problems. Again in his 1970 book *Scene of Change,* he expressed the conviction that "the most important thing I have ever been able to do was to reorient the Rockefeller Foundation science programs. . . . between 1932 and my retirement in 1959 the total of the grants made in the experimental biology program which I directed was roughly ninety million dollars." Following his retirement from the Rockefeller Foundation in 1959, Weaver served as vice-president of the Alfred P. Sloan Foundation, where he was praised upon his retirement in 1964 for uncommon imagination and integrity. The building at New York University that houses the Courant Institute of Mathematical Sciences is named Warren Weaver Hall.

During World War II, Weaver served as chairman of the Fire Control Division (D-2) of the National Defense Research Committee of the Office of Scientific Research and Development, working on sighting systems and designing and developing a successful electrical antiaircraft gun director. In addition, remembering the devastation of such European libraries as those at Heidelberg, Louvain, and the Sorbonne, during World War I, Weaver, with the support of the Rockefeller Foundation and the American Library Association, set up a program to give subscriptions of professional journals to these libraries. At the end of the war these journal collections were distributed. From 1943 to 1946 he served as chief of the Applied Mathematics Panel of the National Defense Research Committee, where his skills as an administrator and facilitator between the military and the Washington bureaucracy allowed him to coordinate effectively a group of research mathematicians at ten universities across the country. For his contributions during the war years he received the Medal for Merit of the United States and the British King's Medal for Service in the Cause of Freedom, both in 1948.

One of Warren Weaver's strongest continuing commitments was to the promotion of a broad public understanding of science. Toward the end of World War II he prepared a series of intermission programs sponsored by U.S. Rubber, each a talk given during breaks in the New York Philharmonic Symphony Society radio broadcasts by a research scientist who discussed his own work. These talks were assembled in a 1947 book entitled *The Scientists Speak,* edited and introduced by Weaver. Several years later Weaver put together a similar program for television, the Bell Telephone Science Series, eight programs that each focused on a particular field of science. After these programs were shown on national television, copies were distributed free of charge to schools, colleges, and churches. This commitment continued in his service to the American Association for the Advancement of Science (AAAS), where he not only served as president in 1955, but became the first chairman of the AAAS Committee on the Public Understanding of Science and helped organize the Council for the Advancement of Science Writing.

In 1963, Weaver combined a special interest in the theory of probability and a penchant for presenting scientific information to the layperson in the writing of *Lady Luck: The Theory of Probability.* This popular book was reprinted in a slightly revised version in 1982. In 1965, for his many contributions to the public understanding of science, Weaver was awarded both UNESCO's Kalinga Prize for literary excellence in scientific writing, and the Arches of Science Award of the Pacific Science Center.

Although his professional life was very demanding, Weaver's hobby of collecting materials about *Alice in Wonderland* and the Reverend Charles Dodgson (Lewis Carroll) must not be overlooked. His collection, with special emphasis on foreign-language translations, includes over seven hundred items. In 1964, Weaver's book *Alice in Many Tongues* was published by the University of Wisconsin Press. Weaver died after a fall in New Milford, Conn.

[The Warren Weaver collection is now housed at the University of Texas in Austin. See the profile by

Mina Rees in *Biographical Memoirs. National Academy of Sciences* 57 (1987). A Warren Weaver interview is included in the Oral History Project at Columbia University, Spring 1961. Weaver files are in the Rockefeller Archive Center in Pocantico Hills, N.Y. An obituary is in the *New York Times*, Nov. 25, 1978.]

NANCY J. HERRINGTON

WEICKER, LOWELL PALMER (Oct. 14, 1903–Nov. 25, 1978), business executive, was born in Stamford, Conn., the second child of Theodore Weicker, a German-born chemist who in 1904 acquired a substantial interest in E. R. Squibb and Sons and built it into a major American pharmaceutical firm, and Florence Edith Palmer, a daughter of his father's partner, Lowell M. Palmer.

After attending grade school in Connecticut and the Culver Military Academy (1919–1921), Weicker graduated from the Lawrenceville School (1922) and earned a B.S. from Yale (1926). On Oct. 22, 1927, he married Mary Hastings Bickford; they had four children (including Lowell P. Weicker, Jr., who later became a United States senator and the governor of Connecticut). They were divorced in 1951, and on June 6, 1953, he married Beverly Kraft Topping. They were divorced in 1965, and he married Antoinette Francois Littell.

In 1927, Weicker joined E. R. Squibb and Sons. In 1928 the company sent him to France to manage and expand its European interests. Weicker contributed substantially to the company's diversification overseas. In 1930, while in Paris, he acquired Lenthéric, a French perfume and toiletries company, significantly expanding that aspect of Squibb's business in America and Europe. Weicker became a director of Squibb in 1932. On returning to the United States in 1936, he became vice-president in charge of sales and advertising. In 1941 he became Squibb's president, a post he held (with the exception of service in the armed forces during World War II) until 1953, when Squibb merged with the Mathiesen Chemical Corporation.

Weicker served in the Army Air Forces from 1942 to 1945, most notably overseas as deputy director of intelligence on the staff of General Carl Spaatz. Weicker's extensive knowledge of Europe and his fluency in French, German, and Italian were of assistance in the development of a strategic bombing policy during the war's latter months in Europe. Weicker, who attained the rank of colonel, was awarded the Bronze Star and the croix de guerre with palms, as well as an Order of the British Empire.

At war's end Weicker returned to Squibb and helped lead it to increasing prosperity. The company's net earnings nearly doubled between 1946 and 1951. Although the company faced increased competition (especially in antibiotics), its sales of antibiotics, vitamins, cosmetics, anesthetics, and diverse pharmaceutical supplies soared. By 1951 its annual sales, which in 1946 had been about $59 million, were over $100 million.

The Mathiesen Chemical Corporation, which had expanded dramatically in the late 1940's, aggressively recruited Squibb's officers. After World War II, the Palmer and Weicker families reduced their holdings in Squibb; between 1949 and 1951 alone, these holdings decreased by 15 percent. But the Palmers, the Weickers, and various family trusts still held nearly half of Squibb's stock, and thus once they agreed to a merger, it took place quickly. To the tune of $100 million, five shares of Mathiesen common stock were exchanged for every three shares of Squibb. The Palmer and Weicker families' and the family trust shares were placed in a voting trust; Weicker was not one of the trustees.

In 1953, Weicker—on the recommendation of President Dwight D. Eisenhower—became an assistant secretary-general of the North Atlantic Treaty Organization (NATO), in charge of production and logistics. Moving once again to Europe, he served NATO efficiently and had some success in reducing unnecessary bureaucratic procedures before resigning in 1956.

That same year, on returning to the United States, Weicker became president of Bigelow-Sanford, then one of the leading domestic producers of rugs and carpets. Weicker worked diligently, intelligently, and ruthlessly to revive a once-profitable company that sustained losses during the early 1950's and that in 1954 earned a little more than $107,000 on sales of over $68 million. Weicker dropped traditional product lines, sold off money-losing operations, fired many executives, and transferred 80 percent of Bigelow-Sanford's manufacturing from New York State and Connecticut to South Carolina, where labor was cheaper.

Putting Bigelow-Sanford's house in order (to use Weicker's words) initially resulted in further losses. But ultimately he succeeded in transforming an old manufacturing firm and placing it on a profitable footing. In 1958 the company lost $1.7 million, but by 1964 there had been five consecutive profitable years, earnings had risen to $3 million annually, and sales had increased to over $82 million.

Weicker continued as Bigelow-Sanford's president until 1968, when he became chairman. In 1970, Sperry and Hutchinson, as part of diversification, bought the firm. Weicker became chairman of the board's executive committee, retiring to honorary status in 1976. During these years he continued to serve as a director of various companies. He died in New York City.

Born into well-to-do circumstances that gave him a confidence, allowed him to follow his own inclinations, and eased his way into the business world, Weicker did well, heading two very different types of companies. In essence he was a journeyman executive who believed that "basically all business is the same. . . . You deal with costs and inefficiencies . . . you deal with people." A demanding man, whose personal relationships were not always easy, Weicker (notwithstanding his personal wealth) is representative of many of the American business executives of his time.

[An obituary is in the *New York Times*, Nov. 27, 1978.]

DANIEL J. LEAB

WELCH, LEO DEWEY (Apr. 22, 1898–Oct. 21, 1978), banker and business executive, was born in Rochester, N.Y., the son of William Frederick Dewey, a mason, and Mary Elizabeth Compton. He attended public schools in his native city and worked his way through the University of Rochester, graduating with a B.A. degree in 1919. He served in the United States Navy Reserve during World War I.

In 1919, Welch joined the National City Bank of New York (NCB), having entered the college training class three years before. His first foreign post was in Buenos Aires, Argentina. In Montevideo, Uruguay, during this assignment he met Veronica Purviance, a prominent socialite from Kansas City, Mo. They were married on Jan. 27, 1926, in the cathedral in Montevideo; they had one child before her death in 1970. In 1929 he was transferred to Santiago, Chile, where he was successively manager and supervisor of the NCB branch office there. While in Chile he also served as a director of the Banco Central de Chile. He was decorated with the Order of Chile in October 1933.

In 1934, Welch returned to Buenos Aires as supervisor of NCB's River Plate branches in Argentina and Uruguay. Welch also served as a director of the Banco Central de la República de Argentina between 1936 and 1940. As director of the United States Chamber of Commerce in Argentina in 1936 and 1937, he spoke out about the way the Argentine government allegedly discriminated against American business interests when allocating foreign exchange to importers. He also served as president of the Corporación para la Promoción del Intercambio (Argentine Trade Promotion Corporation) from 1941 to 1943. In 1943 he returned to New York City as vice-president in charge of NCB's Caribbean operations. Under the new regime of General Juan Peron, he was no longer welcome in Argentina.

In October 1944, Welch left the NCB to become treasurer of the Standard Oil Company of New Jersey (Jersey Standard), later to become the Exxon Corporation. Welch's appointment marked a change in the role of Jersey Standard's treasurer's department. In order to prepare itself for the postwar financial environment and for new international business opportunities, the company needed a new type of treasurer, who could oversee this new area of strategic concern in addition to performing traditional responsibilities. Welch's experience placed him in a position to assess the implications for the company of the planned international economic recovery. In the fall of 1945, Welch was a member of a party of senior Jersey Standard executives sent to determine what remained of its affiliated companies' organizations in western Europe. In 1952 he served as chairman of the Committee on Latin America of the Business Council of the departments of State and Commerce. The following year Welch was elected a director of Jersey Standard, a vice-president in 1956, and executive vice-president and a member of the executive committee in 1958. He became the eighth chairman of Jersey Standard in 1960. In addition, in 1956 Welch revived his association with NCB, which had been renamed First National City Bank of New York, serving as director until 1968.

Although Welch was a Republican, in early

1963 he was appointed by President John F. Kennedy as board chairman and chief executive officer of the new Communications Satellite Corporation (COMSAT), which was created to set up a worldwide communications satellite system. COMSAT was the first modern United States government–sponsored, private-sector, profit-making corporation. It had been established by the United States Congress the previous year. Welch was chosen for his extensive international business experience, which would be valuable in promoting COMSAT to America's allies and in complex negotiations with government agencies in Washington, D.C., and with foreign nations. He also oversaw financial affairs of COMSAT, including its initial stock offering in June 1964, which was a great success. Nearly 200,000 Americans invested $500 each in half of the $200 million stock issue. The other half of the stock was sold to "common carrier" corporations, including the American Telephone and Telegraph.

In July 1964, Welch brought together COMSAT and eighteen telecommunications companies from other Western countries in the International Telecommunications Satellite Consortium (INTELSAT) as co-owners of a prospective global communications space network; the American corporation held 61 percent of the ownership. By the spring of 1965, another twenty-six countries had joined the consortium. In April, Welch oversaw the successful launch of INTELSAT I (*Early Bird*), an experimental satellite with some operational capacity. COMSAT was to achieve its objective as a result of a technological breakthrough, the high-altitude, stationary INTELSAT satellite. This satellite cost only a fraction of previous satellites and allowed COMSAT to be financially independent of the government. Using an INTELSAT III satellite, global commercial satellite communications involving sixty-four countries were first established in 1968.

Welch underwent surgery for a kidney ailment in May 1965 and retired from active direction of the company at the end of November, having completed the establishment phase of the corporation. He remained on the corporation's board of directors until 1977. He also continued to be a gentleman farmer on his 900-acre cattle farm near Berryville, Va., which he had purchased in 1963. In 1971, Welch was named chairman of the National Arbitration Panel, a position he held until 1976. Welch died in an automobile accident while vacationing near Cuernavaca, Mexico.

[See Henrietta M. Larson, Evelyn H. Knowlton, and Charles S. Popple, *History of Standard Oil Company (New Jersey)* (1971). An obituary is in the *Washington Post*, Oct. 25, 1978.]

RICHARD A. HAWKINS

WEST, MAE (Aug. 17, 1893–Nov. 22, 1980), actress and playwright, was born in Brooklyn, N.Y., the first of three children of John P. West and Matilda Delker-Dolger. Her father, an occasional prizefighter, ran a livery stable and later was a private detective and real estate salesman. Her mother was a model and dressmaker. West's formal education was limited, consisting mainly of sporadic tutoring and dancing lessons. At around the age of seven she began appearing in amateur performances. The first was at the Royal Theater on Fulton Street in Brooklyn, where she sang and danced, wearing a satin dress with spangles; she won first prize. Her professional career started in Hal Clarendon's stock company in New York as Little Nell. By 1911 she was in vaudeville with Frank Wallace, a song-and-dance man. She married Wallace on Apr. 11, 1911, in Milwaukee, but within a few months they went their own ways without a legal separation or divorce.

By September 1911, West had created a favorable impression in a revue called *À la Broadway and Hello Paris* in the Folies Bergère cabaret. During that same year, she was in another revue, *Vera Violetta*, which starred Al Jolson at the Winter Garden in New York City. Her vivacity attracted attention and in 1912 she appeared at the Moulin Rouge in *A Winsome Widow*, produced by Florenz Ziegfeld, Jr. Ambitious and energetic, she developed a vaudeville act that same year featuring ragtime tunes and garish costumes. A critic writing in *Variety* noted that she lacked "that touch of class that is becoming requisite in the first class houses." Nonetheless, to another critic she had "a style and willowy abandon that is intoxicating." She was one of the few women in vaudeville to perform without a partner. She continued to refine her material and later in 1912 was well received at Hammerstein's, a theater where she sang "Isn't She the Crazy Thing?" and "Everybody's Ragtime Crazy." Four years later, however, a critic claimed that she "may only be admired for her persistency in believing she is a big-time act." West achieved stardom with Ed Wynn in the musical comedy *Sometime* (1918) at the Shubert Theatre. She introduced a dance that combined the cooch and the shimmy called "the Shining Shawabble." Her songs included "All I Want Is Just a Little Lovin'." Within the next year and into the early 1920's, she returned to vaudeville, where she became well established as a lively entertainer whose trademarks were a suggestive manner and an easygoing way of saying her lines.

West entitled the first play she wrote *Sex*; it opened on Broadway in 1926. It was crude and vulgar and became the target of the Society for the Suppression of Vice. After forty-one weeks, the police arrested the cast and West received a $500 fine, one day at the Jefferson Market Prison, and nine days at the workhouse on Welfare Island. When she completed her sentence she announced that she had collected material for a dozen plays.

West's most successful play, *Diamond Lil* (1928), capitalized on the stage personality she had assiduously created over the years. West appeared as a singer friend of a Bowery saloon keeper and an acquaintance of underworld figures in the 1890's. In the play, she offered her most memorable line, "Why don't you come up sometime and see me?" When the play opened in Brooklyn, Robert Garland, critic for the *New York Evening Telegram*, wrote, "It's worth swimming to Brooklyn to see her descend those dance hall stairs and be present while she lolls in a golden bed reading 'The Police Gazette.' " At that same time, West's *Pleasure Man* (1928), a poorly crafted, tasteless play, was produced at the Biltmore Theater. At the end of the first performance the police arrested the cast for violating the penal code for obscenity. The court dropped the case after a mistrial, but the play did not reopen.

The Constant Sinner (1931), another play written by West, opened at the Royale Theatre in New York. It closed in Washington, D.C., after two performances when the district attorney threatened to take action because the "theme, language, and postures" were "lewd and lascivious."

West went to Hollywood in 1931 to make her first motion picture, *Night After Night* (1932), adapted from a Louis Bromfield story. She rewrote many of her own lines for the role of Maudie Triplett, the girlfriend of gangster Joe Anton (played by George Raft). In this film, West received the support of such polished performers as Constance Cummings, Alison Skipworth, Roscoe Karns, and Louis Calhern. In one scene, a hatcheck girl remarks, "Goodness, what beautiful diamonds," and West replies with another of her famous lines, "Goodness had nothing to do with it, dearie." In the midst of the Great Depression, the mass appeal of this picture bolstered the shaky financial position of Paramount Pictures and established West as a film star.

In *She Done Him Wrong* (1933), based on her play *Diamond Lil*, West played Lady Lou, a sentimental saloon keeper who protests her innocence. Her rendition of the risqué song "Frankie and Johnnie" was a high point of the movie. Swinging and swaying, speaking slowly with a nasal intonation, she was the floozy with the heart of gold.

West had successfully carried her stage persona over to film. Neither her lines nor her actions varied from one picture to another. Although her range may have been limited, she realized that she had struck a chord with the public. When she could not think of a new line, she rewrote an old one. She once said, "It isn't what I do, but how I do it. It isn't what I say, but how I say it, and how I look when I do it and say it."

She Done Him Wrong was notable for featuring an unknown young actor, Cary Grant, whom West had selected to appear with her in the picture. Grant also appeared with her in *I'm No Angel* (1933). The two films broke box office records for the year. In the latter comedy West played Tira, a circus queen who put her head in a lion's mouth twice a day. *Belle of the Nineties* (1934), adapted from a story by Mae West, with Roger Pryor and music by Duke Ellington's band, was another financial success. By 1935, she received a salary of almost half a million dollars, which made her one of the highest paid stars in Hollywood, along with such performers as Charlie Chaplin, Marlene Dietrich, and Gary Cooper.

Despite the popularity of West's pictures, the daring implications of her material roused many objections concerning indecency. Some audiences found such songs as "I Like a Guy What Takes His Time" offensive rather than amusing. Adverse reactions to her work contributed to the establishment of the Catholic League of Decency. The league objected to *Klondike Annie* (1936), a film that led to stricter supervision of the Motion Picture Production Code instituted in 1930 by the Association of Motion Picture Producers.

Although the sexual aspect of West's films lessened, she remained a major attraction at the box office in *Go West, Young Man* (1936) with Warren William and Randolph Scott, which lampooned a Hollywood glamour girl named Mavis Arden. In *Every Day's a Holiday* (1938) she played Peaches O'Dea, who sold the Brooklyn Bridge. Ironically, one of her best-known films, *My Little Chickadee* (1940), came out after the enforcement of stricter censorship. Its success undoubtedly owed much to the brilliance of W. C. Fields; he and West made a memorable pair.

Her style, however, was wearing thin and by the early 1940's West's film career was essentially over. Late in life, she made unfortunate appearances in *Myra Breckinridge* (1970) and *Sextette* (1978), which did not enhance her reputation as an entertainer. Long past her prime, she was merely a relic of her past. In all, West made twelve motion pictures and the persona she had created made an enduring impact on American society. During World War II, servicemen affectionately named inflatable life-jackets "Mae Wests" in honor of her buxom figure.

As her film career wound down in the 1940's, West returned to Broadway in a play she had written entitled *Catherine Was Great* (1944). She was hailed by one reviewer as having given one of the "really batty performances of the year." West's role seemed to combine Diamond Lil and a parody of Queen Victoria. It ran six months and then toured the country.

At the age of sixty-one, West built a nightclub act in Las Vegas that continued to portray her as an alluring and spicy character. The act included nine tall young musclemen. She also appeared on radio and television.

In private life, West lived quietly and reportedly neither drank nor smoked. Although she frequently denied that she had ever married, Frank Wallace sued her for divorce in 1942. Alleging that she associated with criminals, he sought alimony. The marriage ended with a secret financial arrangement. She never married again, but Paul Novak, a former member of her nightclub act, was her companion for the last twenty-six years of her life. Three months after suffering a stroke, West died at her Los Angeles home. She was buried in Green-Wood Cemetery in Brooklyn.

[Material on West is in the New York Public Library for the Performing Arts at Lincoln Center. Her autobiography is *Goodness Had Nothing to Do with It* (1959). Carol Marie Ward, *Mae West: A Bio-Bibliography* (1989), includes a discography and a filmography. See also June Sochen, *Mae West: She Who Laughs, Lasts* (1992). An obituary is in the *New York Times*, Nov. 23, 1980.]

ERNEST A. MCKAY

WHEELOCK, JOHN HALL (Sept. 9, 1886–Mar. 22, 1978), poet, critic, and editor, was born in Far Rockaway, Queens, N.Y., the son of William Efner Wheelock and Emily Charlotte Hall. Among his ancestors was Eleazar Wheelock, founder of Dartmouth College. Wheelock's father was a prosperous physician, a botanist, a lawyer, and a substitute French horn player for the New York Philharmonic. Wheelock was to write one of his finest poems, "The Gardener," about his father and his plantings, which Wheelock took to be artistic creations of strict order. It was his mother who introduced the boy to poetry, urging him to memorize a poem a week. All his life he could quote substantial blocks of poetry. He knew all his own poems by heart, and at his public readings he rarely consulted a book.

Wheelock, who had one of the longest careers in American letters (his first book was published in 1905 and his last in 1978), had early brushes with literary greatness. In an interview in *The Paris Review* he stated he had seen Walt Whitman, whom his father had pointed out as the great poet stood in the bow of a New York ferry boat. But since Wheelock was a baby at the time, he carried no memory of the occasion. Wheelock also touched the sleeve of Algernon Swinburne, an occasion he would not forget, since as a college student in 1906 he had made the pilgrimage to "The Pines" in London for a glimpse of his poetic hero.

Wheelock loved the ocean. He was born near the Atlantic Ocean, and his father's medical practice enabled the family to afford both a residence in Manhattan and a home in East Hampton, on the South Fork of Long Island. As an adult Wheelock retreated there, to the house to which he returned for over eight decades, spending part of each summer. He walked the beaches, mentally composing poems that he later wrote down. The Atlantic Ocean appears in many of them, as does eastern Long Island, to which he referred by its Native American name, "Bonac."

Wheelock's first published poem—a translation from Ovid—appeared in the paper of the Morristown School (N.J.) in 1900. He enrolled at Harvard in 1904 and became a friend of Van Wyck Brooks, also a student. In 1905 they anonymously published *Verses by Two Undergraduates*, which sold about half a dozen copies at twenty-five cents each. It later became a valuable collectors' item. Another Harvard friend was Maxwell Perkins. Wheelock edited the *Harvard Monthly*, was named class poet, and graduated Phi Beta Kappa in 1908.

His father urged him to continue studies toward a Ph.D in literature, with an academic career in mind. Wheelock studied at the University of Göttingen in 1909 and the University of Berlin in 1910. He earned no degree but acquired a few fashionable dueling scars. The only doctorate he received was an honorary Doctor of Humane Letters from Otterbein College, decades later.

Wheelock's first job was as a clerk in Scribner's Book Store on Fifth Avenue in New York City, a position he held from 1911 until 1926. In 1911 he published his second book, *The Human Fantasy*. It brought him recognition as a considerable poet at the age of twenty-five. His Harvard friend Maxwell Perkins had become an editor at Charles Scribner's Sons, the publisher whose offices were located above the bookstore. Perkins urged Wheelock to leave the store for an editorial opening upstairs. In 1932, Wheelock became a director, and later that year he was elected secretary of the corporation. Eventually he replaced Perkins as editor in chief. In all he remained with Scribners from 1911 until 1957, when he retired. Wheelock once described editorial work as the "dullest, hardest, most exciting, exasperating and rewarding of perhaps any job in the world."

Among the authors Wheelock edited were Thomas Wolfe, Marjorie Kinnan Rawlings, Allan Nevins, Charles A. Lindbergh, and James Truslow Adams. He also edited the poet Louise Bogan until she imagined a quarrel between them and took her work elsewhere. When he was in his late sixties, Wheelock created a publishing innovation by establishing the Scribner Poets of Today series. Rather than publishing individual volumes of verse, he packaged three poets per volume. He published eight such collections, including twenty-four new poets, between 1954 and 1961. Among his discoveries were May Swenson, James Dickey, Louis Simpson, and Joseph Langland. He said of the series, "All my choices turned out well."

The Human Fantasy brought Wheelock more than critical attention. It brought the personal attentions of Sara Teasdale, famous poet of countless love lyrics. She wrote Wheelock letters, began to visit Scribners daily, and declared her love. Apparently Wheelock, who was gangling and had protruding ears, was involved with another woman. He also was timid. In a letter to Harriet Monroe, Teasdale described him as "the shyest person I ever knew." Wheelock did not marry until Aug. 25, 1940—when he was fifty-four. He and his wife, Phyllis de Kay, had no children.

Influenced by Percy Shelley and Algernon Swinburne, Wheelock was a lyric poet of feeling. He recognized that his work was considered unfashionable. "Feeling has been rather played down by modern poets, partly as a result of what the world has been through with its depressions and wars. The nerve of feeling has been exhausted," he said in an interview. Nevertheless, he was highly honored during his lifetime. He received the Ridgely Torrence Memorial Award (1956), the Borestone Mountain Award (1957), the Gold Medal of the Poetry Society of America (1972), and the Bollingen Prize (1962), which he shared with Richard Eberhart. He was a member of the National Institute of Arts and Letters, and a chancellor of the Academy of American Poets. Allen Tate called him "one of the best poets in English." He died in New York City.

Wheelock published fourteen books of poetry, an insightful study of the genre titled *What Is Poetry?* (1963), and several editions and translations, the most important being *Editor to Author: The Letters of Maxwell Perkins* (1950).

[Most of Wheelock's papers are at the Library of Congress. The E. S. Bird Library at Syracuse University has some of his correspondence. His other major publications include *The Beloved Adventure* (1912); *Dust and Light* (1919); *The Black Panther* (1922); *The Bright Doom* (1927); *Poems, 1911–1936* (1936); *Poems Old and New* (1956); *The Gardener and Other Poems* (1961); *Dear Men and Women* (1966); *By Daylight and in Dream* (1970); *In Love and Song* (1971); *Afternoon: Amagansett Beach* (1978); and *This Blessed Earth* (1978).

No biography has been written. For biographical insights, see Louis Untermeyer, *The New Era in American Poetry* (1919); John Nelson, ed., *Wisdom: Conversations with the Elder Wise Men of Our Day* (1958); William Cahill and Molly McKaughan, "The Art of Poetry, XXI," *Paris Review*, Fall 1976, an interview with Wheelock; A. Scott Berg, *Max Perkins* (1978); and William Drake, *Sara Teasdale, Woman and Poet* (1979).

Obituaries are in the *New York Times*, Mar. 23, 1978; and the *Washington Post*, Mar. 24, 1978.]

ROBERT PHILLIPS

WHITE, CHARLES WILBERT (Apr. 2, 1918–Oct. 3, 1979), artist, was born in Chicago, Ill., the son of Charles White and Ethel Gary. He won a scholarship to the Chicago Art Institute and attended Saturday classes, then studied at the New York Art Students League. He later attended the Taller de Gráfica Popular and the Esmeralda School of Painting and Sculpture, both in Mexico City. Childhood sketches and high school newspaper cartoons were early evidence of White's artistic ability. His mother gave him a paint set for his seventeenth birthday, and he began his artistic career in earnest. His earliest extant works are three portraits of women done between 1935 and 1937. During this time he was a member of the Art Craft Guild, directed by African-American cultural leader George E. Neal, and White came into contact with other black artists such as Margaret Taylor Goss, Bernard Goss, William Carter, and Eldzier Cortor. The guild and similar organizations in other creative arts formed a community of black intellectuals who were inspired by the Harlem Renaissance in New York City and were influenced by socialist zeal, the result of the Great Depression in the United States and fascism abroad. These influences are reflected in White's early paintings, which for the most part depict the black working class. A number of his early works, for example, *Laborers* (1936–1937), were done in charcoal, a medium in which many critics considered he displayed his finest talent.

Mural painting, an art form promoted by the Works Progress Administration in public buildings, was utilized by White in *Five Great American Negroes*, completed in 1940 for the Chicago Public Library. This work is a depiction of African-American history and includes portraits of Booker T. Washington, Frederick Douglass, Sojourner Truth, Marian Anderson, and George Washington Carver. In the center of the mural is a tree, representing a historical symbol for lynching. The presence of the tree and the seriousness of all five figures would indicate that in White's estimation the brutality suffered by blacks during slavery was not at an end at the time the mural was painted. In 1943 he completed another mural, *Contribution of the Negro to American Democracy*, for the Hampton Institute in Virginia. It included such figures as Crispus Attucks, Nat Turner, Denmark Vesey, Booker T. Washington, and George Washington Carver.

His work during World War II showed the influence of modern artistic tendencies, particularly cubism. While living in New Orleans from 1940 to 1941 he attended a Pablo Picasso retrospective exhibit, and Picasso's cubistic style is clearly evident in some of White's work, for example, *The Soldier* and *Head of a Man*. During the war he received two Rosenwald fellowships, and in 1945 he was artist in residence at Howard University in Washington, D.C. In 1946 he divorced his first wife, black sculptor Elizabeth Catlett.

He went to Mexico in 1947 to study at the Taller de Gráfica Popular. He later wrote that he attended this institute because "they deal with issues that spring from the problems of the people in their fight to overcome oppression."

After his study in Mexico he worked as a cartoonist for the *Daily Worker* and *Congress Vue* in New York City. His cartoons were bitter and satirical comments on the injustices suffered by blacks. In the late 1940's he focused his efforts on creating a link between painting and music with such works as *Blues Singer, Songs*, and *The Flutist*. His friend and fellow artist Ernest Crichlow referred to these paintings as softer and less polemical than many of White's earlier works. At this time he also became interested in his African heritage, which is evident in his work during the 1950's.

The beginning of the decade marked a number of significant events in his life. In 1950 he married Frances Barrett; they had two children. His two-year bout with tuberculosis followed by a long hospitalization had a profound influence on his work, both philosophically and technically. When his doctors advised him that paint was harmful to his health, he turned to graphics and drawings as a means of expression. Many of his drawings focused on women, whom he portrayed with much compassion as strong and loving matriarchs. Among the best known of these works are *The Mother* (1952), *Ye Shall Inherit the Earth* (1953), and *Solid as a Rock* (1954). From 1950 to 1953 he was an instructor at the Workshop School of Art in New York City.

In 1956 he left New York for Los Angeles, Calif., because his doctors felt the move was necessary to restore his failing health. A number of critics have suggested that White's work during this period showed a spiritual presence of ancestors, an African kinship. The characters seem intense and mythic rather than realistic. This effect can be seen in the drawings *Dawn* and *Nocturne* (both 1960). Each portrays the head of a woman free from any social reference. The images, as Peter Clothier stated, "have the quality of spirit and speak to us out of the language of myth." This emphasis on the language of myth is seen in the works produced by White for the remaining decades of his life.

The works of the 1960's and 1970's also reflected an emphasis on his heritage, which is evident in such works as *Mayibuye Afrika* (a tall barefoot figure reminiscent of an African tribesman), *Go Tell It on the Mountain*, *Move On Up a Little Higher*, *Mother Courage*, and *I've Known Rivers* (after the poem by Langston Hughes). As Clothier said, these later works combined "the experience of the American street with the awesome heritage of Africa." One of the most impressive works reflecting this emphasis was *Birmingham Totem*, a tribute to the four children killed in the bombing of an Alabama church in 1964. From the mid-1960's on, his works reflected the anger felt by many blacks during the civil rights movement. White's anger is visible in such works as *The Wall* and *Dream Deferred* (again after a Hughes poem). He was the illustrator of Philip Sterling's well-known children's book *Four Took Freedom* (1967). In 1968 he executed a series of drawings entitled *I Have a Dream*, in memory of the recently assassinated Reverend Martin Luther King, Jr. White's remaining years were devoted to honoring individual African Americans, both known (such as civil rights leader Mary McLeod Bethune) and unknown.

Harry Belafonte, a close personal friend, summed up White's contribution as "his artistic interpretation of Negro Americans—the poetic beauty of Negro idiom." Throughout his artistic career, White portrayed only black people and their "struggle to survive in this racist country." At the time of his death in Los Angeles, White was teaching at the Otis Art Institute. White's works are part of the collections of forty-nine museums, including the Metropolitan Museum of Art in New York City and the Museum of Fine Arts in Boston. He has had fifty-three one-man shows and his works have been exhibited in 123 institutional exhibitions.

[White illustrated numerous books including *Songs Belafonte Sings* (1962) and Lerone Bennett, *The Shaping of Black America* (1975). Commentaries on his works appear in the catalogs of numerous exhibits of his art. See also *Images of Dignity: The Drawings of Charles White* (1967). A documentary film by Moro Carlton, *Scenes of the Life of Charles White*, was produced by Pyramid Films. An obituary is in the *New York Times*, Oct. 6, 1979.]

RENNIE SIMSON

WHITE, MINOR MARTIN (July 9, 1908–June 24, 1976), photographer, was born in Minneapolis, Minn., the only child of Charles Henry White, a bookkeeper, and Florence Martin, a dressmaker. White's introduction to photography was through his maternal grandfather, an amateur photographer and avid collector of lantern slides. White was given his first camera (a box Brownie) when he was ten years old and inherited all of his grandfather's equipment when he was twelve, including a carbon arc projector and several hundred slides. He graduated from West High School in Lake Calhoun, Minn., in 1927. During his adolescence he confided his growing awareness of his homosexuality in his diary, which was discovered and read by his family. He never married or had children.

White attended the University of Minnesota, where he studied botany and poetry and learned the rudiments of photography. He dropped out in 1931 but returned and completed his B.A. degree in 1933. For five years he devoted himself to poetry while working twelve hours per day as a houseboy and waiter. After completing a sonnet sequence of one hundred poems, he took up photography again in 1937 when he moved to Portland, Oreg., where he took a job as a night clerk. In 1938 he was hired by the Works Progress Administration (WPA) to take a series of photographs of local architecture. He spent an additional two years teaching for the WPA in Portland and eastern Oregon.

In 1941 he participated in his first national photography show, the *Image of Freedom* exhibition at the Museum of Modern Art in New

York City. The museum bought some of his photographs for its permanent collection. In 1942 he had his first one-man show, at the Portland Museum of Art, and his photographs were first published in *Fair Is Our Land*, edited by Samuel Chamberlain.

White served with the Army Intelligence Corps in the Pacific from 1942 to 1945 and was awarded the Bronze Star. After his discharge he moved to New York City, where he met some of the most notable American photographers, including Alfred Stieglitz, Edward Steichen, and Nancy and Beamount Newhall, who codirected the Museum of Modern Art's photography department. He was greatly influenced by Stieglitz and his theory of equivalence, or the metaphoric power of photographic images. Encouraged by his colleagues, White took graduate courses in art history and aesthetics at Columbia University.

After turning down an offer to work with Steichen at the Museum of Modern Art, White left New York for San Francisco in 1946 to teach at the California School of Fine Arts, where he taught until 1952 and began a lifelong friendship with photographer Ansel Adams, who taught him to trust and use the beauty of natural light in his photography. At the same time White met another important photographer, Edward Weston, whose starkly powerful black-and-white photographs were a major influence on his work.

In 1947, White completed *Second Sequence/ Amputations*, his first nonnarrative photographic series. At this time he began to concentrate on large format, straightforward photography that had a psychoanalytic approach in its content. In 1952, White and other important photographers—including Dorothea Lange, Adams, and the Newhalls—cofounded the influential photography journal *Aperture*, which he helped edit until his death.

In 1952, White moved to Rochester, N.Y., where for three years he arranged exhibits at George Eastman House, including *The Pictorial Image* in 1955. During his tenure in Rochester he organized *How to Read a Photograph*, an exhibition of his photographs at the San Francisco Museum of Art in 1953. He also created his first group of photographs of the landscape of the eastern United States, *Sequence 10/Rural Cathedrals*. After several unhappy years in Rochester, White quit his job at Eastman House in 1955. He taught part-time at the Rochester Institute of Technology from 1955 to 1964 and held workshops throughout the country.

A deeply spiritual man, White was interested in mysticism and comparative religions, especially those of the Far East. In the late 1950's he came under the influence of the Russian mystic G. I. Gurdjieff, Zen Buddhism, and Gestalt psychology. His studies in philosophy and religion profoundly influenced his thinking about photography as well as his teaching methods.

In 1959, White exhibited his largest group of photographs, *Sequence 13/Return to the Bud*, at George Eastman House. An invitation to teach a workshop in Portland inspired the first of many cross-country trips during which he avidly photographed the landscape of the American West. Returning to Rochester, White initiated full-time resident workshops in his home, where students received formal instruction and were expected to help out with daily housekeeping. In the spring 1959 issue of *Aperture*, entitled "The Way Through Camera Work," he published his philosophy on the art of photography.

In 1965, White went to the Massachusetts Institute of Technology to start a photography program in the school's department of architecture to introduce students to the creative possibilities of the visual arts. In 1969 he published *Mirrors, Messages, Manifestations*, the first book-length compilation of his photographs and including 243 photographs and excerpts from White's journals and theoretical writings.

In 1970, White had a major one-man exhibition at the Philadelphia Museum of Art and received a Guggenheim Foundation Fellowship. In 1975, a year after his first European trip, he had his first important European exhibit in Paris. In 1976 he received an honorary doctorate from the San Francisco Art Institute. He died of a heart attack in Boston.

In the practice of his art and his devoted nurturing of new photographers White became one of the most influential figures in post–World War II American photography. His elegantly observed compositions are celebrations of the intimate textures of wood, stone, earth, and organic forms. White strove to endow his work with a sense of the sacred, which he believed to be the root of all creativity.

[White's photographic archives and personal papers are at Princeton University in New Jersey. Illustrated volumes that include generous selections from White's writings include Michael E. Hoffman, ed., *Minor White: Rites and Passages* (1978); and Minor White, *Mirrors, Messages, Manifestations* (1969). Catalogs that include biographical material are Abe Frajndlich, *Lives I've Never Lived* (1983); Ansel Adams et al., compilers, *Minor White: A Living Remembrance* (1984); and Peter C. Bunnell, *Minor White: The Eye That Shapes* (1989). An obituary is in the *New York Times*, June 26, 1976.]

CHRISTINE STENSTROM

WHITEHEAD, WALTER EDWARD (May 20, 1908–Apr. 16, 1978), businessman, was born in Aldershot, England, the son of Walter and Amy Whitehead. He attended local schools and graduated from Aldershot County High School. In 1925 he went to work in London for the advertising department of General Accident Assurance Company and subsequently rose through its ranks. On Sept. 14, 1940, Whitehead married Adinah ("Tommy") Thomas; they had one child.

Whitehead's interest in sailing led him to join the Royal Navy Volunteer Reserve (RNVR) in 1937; he was called up for active duty after the outbreak of World War II. At the time he had a mustache, which was forbidden by naval regulations, so he grew a beard, which was permitted. Whitehead was inducted as a sublieutenant in 1939 and initially served on HMS *Impregnable*, stationed in Plymouth, where he was responsible for training signalmen. He eventually reached the rank of commander and traveled around the world with assignments related to selection and training of officers and the maintenance of morale.

Whitehead remained in the RNVR in London after the end of the war, running an organization he had persuaded the Admiralty to create for helping discharged naval officers adjust to civilian life. After his discharge from the Royal Navy in 1946, Whitehead became general secretary of the British Association for Commercial and Industrial Education, an organization that sought to improve the morale and training of British workers. From 1947 to 1950 he was head of the Industrial Section of the Economic Information Unit of the Treasury, where he acted as an industrial troubleshooter for Chancellor of the Exchequer Sir Stafford Cripps.

During his postwar work Whitehead became acquainted with industrialist Frederic Hooper, who had served briefly in the Ministry of Labour. After Hooper became managing director of Schweppes in 1948, he invited Whitehead to work with him. Whitehead joined the beverage company as its advertising manager in 1950. After a subsequent stint as Schweppes's London sales manager, he was offered the job of general manager of all of the company's overseas operations. In 1952 he was named to the board of directors of Schweppes (Overseas) and was assigned to expand its international sales. Whitehead changed the company policy of shipping beverages bottled in England, arranging for local bottlers in other nations to use local water with the concentrated flavoring sent from England, thereby greatly lowering shipping costs and decreasing prices.

Whitehead came to America in 1953 as president of Schweppes (USA) and established a relationship with the Pepsi-Cola Company that would involve Schweppes's reciprocal dilution and bottling of Pepsi-Cola in England. At that time Pepsi-Cola was far behind Coca-Cola in international sales, and sought to expand its overseas operations.

Schweppes retained the prominent advertising firm of Ogilvy, Benson and Mather to handle American advertising, with the dual aim of popularizing gin and tonic (made with Schweppes tonic water) as a year-round drink and ensuring that the decline in the beverage's price was not perceived as the result of a drop in quality. Ogilvy set up a campaign centered on Commander Whitehead as a personality who embodied not only Schweppes, but also the British Empire. Ogilvy's distinctive advertisements soon made Commander Whitehead a popular celebrity. Whitehead recalled, "It wasn't long before I saw caricatures of myself in cartoons. Stand-up comedians, disc jockeys and radio announcers mimicked my British accent."

Schweppes originally planned to assign Whitehead to America for only two years, but he stayed longer because of the phenomenal rise in sales. Schweppes (USA) soon became a separate subsidiary of the parent company. He oversaw the diversification of Schweppes beverages other than tonic and successfully introduced Schweppes bitter lemon and Schweppes ginger ale into the United States.

From 1959 to 1961, Whitehead hosted a half-hour program on WQXR (a New York City radio station devoted to classical music) called "This Is Britain." He enjoyed the opportunity to interview entertainers and public figures, "not only beguiling myself but helping my listeners to focus on some highlights of British humor, character and culture." The program was sponsored by such firms as Jaguar cars and British Railways; Whitehead did not allow Schweppes to buy commercial time on the show.

Business success brought Whitehead governmental honors. He was made a member of the Order of the British Empire in 1961. He worked with the British government to improve exports and international sales during the mid-1960's, and in 1965 he helped organize and was named chairman of the British Exports Marketing Advisory Committee (BEMAC). He wrote the first pamphlet issued by BEMAC, which urged British businessmen to copy American marketing techniques. Whitehead deplored the fact that the British public and elite looked down on business operations as merely "trade," considering military service, civil service, and the professions as the only types of honorable work. After his work with BEMAC, Whitehead was named a commander of the British Empire in 1967.

Whitehead's American success brought him further promotions within the company. He became chairman of Schweppes (USA) and president of another Schweppes subsidiary, L. Rose and Company (America). When Schweppes merged with Cadbury, a candy company, to become Cadbury Schweppes in 1969, Whitehead became a director of the new firm. He also served as outside director of Cunard and of the General Cigar Company.

Retiring from Cadbury Schweppes in 1971, Whitehead divided his time during his retirement years between homes in Stamford, Conn., and Nassau, the Bahamas, enabling him to enjoy his hobbies of sailing, skiing, swimming, running beagles, and fox hunting. He died in Petersfield, England.

Whitehead's steady rise from relatively humble origins to wealth, business success, and government honors was due to intelligence, charm, and hard work, as well as to the brilliant Schweppes advertising campaign that personified him in Americans' minds as the embodiment of British aristocracy. Ironically, Whitehead was not the product of Oxford or Cambridge; he obtained his formal education at a state-supported high school. He openly stated that his success resulted from his adoption of American marketing methods and an American attitude toward business, and he repeatedly urged his countrymen to follow his example.

[There is no book-length biography of Whitehead. Whitehead published *How to Live the Good Life* (1977). His wife's memoirs are Tommy Whitehead, *The Beard and I* (1965), published in Great Britain as *Schwepped Off My Feet* (1966). David Ogilvy described some of his relationship with Whitehead in *Confessions of an Advertising Man* (1964). Schweppes's relationship with the Pepsi-Cola Company is discussed in J. C. Louis and Harvey Z. Yazijian, *The Cola Wars* (1980). See also Douglas A. Simmons, *Schweppes: The First Two Hundred Years* (1983). Obituaries are in the *New York Times*, Apr. 18, 1978; and the *Times* (London), Apr. 19, 1978.]

STEPHEN G. MARSHALL

WIENER, ALEXANDER SOLOMON (Mar. 16, 1907–Nov. 6, 1976), physician and educator, was born in Brooklyn, N.Y., the son of George Wiener, an attorney, and Mollie Zuckerman; his parents had emigrated from Russia in 1903. In 1922, Wiener graduated from Boys High School in Brooklyn, where he was a member of the mathematics team and president of the mathematics club. He was recognized early for his academic brilliance and received a scholarship and cash stipend to attend Cornell University in Ithaca, N.Y. He majored in biology, took advanced mathematics courses, wrote poetry under a pseudonym that was published in the Cornell daily paper, devised original math problems that were published in the *American Mathematics Monthly*, and was elected to Phi Beta Kappa.

After graduating in 1926 with a B.A. in biology, Wiener entered the Long Island College of Medicine (now SUNY Downstate Medical Center), where he graduated in 1930 with an M.D. While in medical school, he did research at the Jewish Hospital of Brooklyn in collaboration with doctors Max Lederer and Silik H. Polayes on human blood groups and their transmission by heredity; the resulting work was published in the *Journal of Immunology* in June 1929. He continued to focus on blood group research during his two-year internship at the hospital. In 1930 he received the Jerome Lewine Prize for his work at the hospital. In 1932 he devised a method for measuring linkages in human genetics, which he published in the journal *Genetics*. He remained at Jewish Hospital after his internship as the head of the

Division of Genetics and Biometrics and entered into private practice. He married Gertrude Rhoda Rodman on June 15, 1932; they had two children. Three years after his marriage he established Wiener Laboratories, which he directed for many years. Also that year he was instrumental in the passage of a New York State law upholding the validity of blood tests in paternity suits. In 1938 he was appointed serologist in the Office of the Chief Medical Examiner of New York City, a post he held until his death.

Working with Karl Landsteiner (who received the Nobel Prize in Medicine in 1930 for the discovery of the four main blood types), Wiener codiscovered in 1937 the Rh factor (its name derived from the Rhesus monkey, in which the factor was first identified), a finding first published in January 1940 in the *Proceedings of the Society for Experimental Biology and Medicine*. The Rh factor is a protein, found on the red blood cell surface, that functions as an antigen. Wiener and Landsteiner found by way of serological testing that approximately 85 percent of the Caucasian population had such a factor on their red blood cells. At the time of their discovery, they did not connect the Rh factor with any medical pathology; the connection came later when Wiener was working at the Jewish Hospital and noted a transfusion failure that he expected to be routinely successful. His investigation found that the failure resulted from an Rh incompatibility between Rh-positive and Rh-negative individuals. He also showed that the sensitization of Rh-negative people to Rh-positive blood was the chief cause of intragroup hemolytic transfusion reactions. In collaboration with H. Raymond Peters, he demonstrated that this sensitization might not appear on the first transfusion of Rh-positive blood to an Rh-negative individual and could show up only after a second transfusion of Rh-positive blood and lead to a life-threatening reaction. Rh-negative females can become sensitized as a result of a pregnancy with an Rh-positive child, because the Rh antigen can cross the placental barrier and thereby stimulate the mother to produce antibodies against the Rh factor; in turn, these antibodies cross back into the fetus and clump its red blood cells. As a result of Wiener's work, Rh testing of patients and donors before transfusions became routine. This knowledge was applied prophylactically during World War II in the treatment of battlefield casualties. Further research by Philip Levine (who also worked with Landsteiner at Rockefeller University and was in communication with Wiener at the time), led to the discovery that the Rh incompatibility was the cause of erythroblastosis fetalis, a blood disease in newborns. Levine's theory had the shortcoming of not explaining the varied manifestations of the disorder or why sensitized mothers had no discernible antibodies in their sera. Wiener succeeded in demonstrating that there must be two major forms of Rh antibodies, one he termed bivalent antibody, which was demonstrable by saline agglutination, and the other univalent, or blocking, antibody, which was capable of coating but not clumping red cells. In 1944 he developed the blocking test for univalent antibodies and, in 1945, the conglutination test. These tests perfected the diagnosis of erythroblastosis fetalis and led to the adoption of routine prenatal testing of Rh and Rh-antibody titration to detect before birth the possibility of the occurrence of the disorder.

Wiener became increasingly absorbed in the problem of how to save the lives of babies who would otherwise die from erythroblastosis fetalis. He spent much of his time, including even his leisure hours at the piano, thinking about how to solve this problem. He realized that the only solution possible would require Rh factor–compatible blood transfused at birth, a procedure he began at the Jewish Hospital. Infants having cases of the disorder so severe that additional compatible blood did not help spurred Wiener to develop a technique to transfuse them successfully. Working from 1944 to 1946, he developed a process of exsanguination to replace the damaged blood of the infants, a delicate transfusion method by which compatible blood is slowly substituted for the baby's own blood until all the incompatible blood is removed. When this procedure came into wide use the lives of thousands of potential victims were saved.

In 1939, Wiener joined the Department of Forensic Medicine at New York University, becoming an associate professor in 1967 and a full professor in 1968. In 1952 he was instrumental in compelling the use of blood tests in cases of assault and homicide and was called upon to serve as an expert witness in criminal cases for many years.

Wiener's analysis that Rh antibodies, and indeed all antibodies, defined serological specificities that are extrinsic attributes of antigenic substances demonstrated that there is no one-to-one relationship between antigen and antibody, implying that there is an unlimited number of possible antibodies and that the limitations to the number of serological specificities characterizing an agglutinogen were left to the imaginations and talents of researchers in developing new antisera.

Wiener and his coworkers established the existence of twenty-five different serological specificities. Discoveries of such specificities, in addition to their significance in prevention of hemolytic transfusion reactions, is also important in forensic medicine, for example, in cases of disputed parentage, criminal cases, tracing racial relationships in physical anthropology, and animal husbandry.

Wiener published more than 500 articles on blood grouping and blood transfusions. His books include *Blood Groups and Transfusions* (1935; 3d ed., 1943), a standard textbook on the subject; *The Rh-Hr Blood Types* (1954); *Heredity of the Blood Groups* (1958); and *Advances in Blood Grouping*, vol. 1 (1961), vol. 2 (1965), vol. 3 (1970).

In the 1960's, Wiener continued research work in the coding and nomenclature of blood groups. His numerous scientific awards included the Silver Medal from the American Society of Clinical Pathologists for his exhibit on the Rh factor (1942); the Alvarenga Prize for discovery of eight Rh blood types and their heredity (1945); the Lasker Award (1947); and the Passano Foundation Award (1951). Dr. Wiener's students at the Jewish Hospital remembered him as a serious person with a gentle voice, quiet demeanor, and a graying mustache. He died of leukemia in New York City.

[See Irmengarde Eberle, *Modern Medical Discoveries* (1948). An obituary is in the *New York Times*, Nov. 7, 1976.]

LESLIE S. JACOBSON

WILDER, ALEXANDER LAFAYETTE CHEW ("ALEC") (Feb. 16, 1907–Dec. 24, 1980), songwriter and composer, was born in Rochester, N.Y., one of four children of George Wilder, a bank president, and Lilian Chew. His father died when he was three years old, and his twin brother died in childhood. He described himself as "an odd boy who was always reading books who never fought or even played with other children but who made people laugh." He went to private schools in Rochester. When his family moved to Garden City, N.Y., on Long Island, he attended the St. Paul School. Eventually, the Wilders moved to Park Avenue in New York City, where he graduated from the prestigious Collegiate School. After failing his Regents examination he abandoned his plan to attend Princeton University. Instead, he returned to Rochester and enrolled at the Eastman School of Music, where he studied composition with Edward Royce and counterpoint with Herbert Inch. At Eastman he made many lifelong professional friends, including Mitchell Miller (later famous as "Mitch" Miller, who had a popular sing-along show on television in the 1960's), an oboist; John Barrows, a french horn player; and Jimmy Carroll, a clarinetist.

In the early 1930's, Wilder began a career of arranging and composing popular songs in New York City. Most of his music was written with specific performers, including Mildred Bailey, Cab Calloway, Bing Crosby, and Ethel Waters, in mind. In 1939 he formed the Alec Wilder Octet, in which he played the harpsichord and Mitch Miller played the oboe; the other six instrumentalists played clarinet, flute, bass clarinet, bassoon, string bass, and drums. For this group, Wilder composed a series of experimental compositions that blended popular song, jazz, and classical elements. Wilder's innovations were not well received. He later noted, "They were gunned down by the jazz boys because they had a classical flavor and they were gunned down by the classical boys because they had a jazz flavor."

In the 1940's Wilder wrote arrangements for big bands and individual performers, such as Frank Sinatra and Mabel Mercer. His best-known works from this period include "I'll Be Around," "It's So Peaceful in the Country," and "While We're Young." Despite a string of hit songs and fame within the popular music world as a skilled arranger, Wilder was restless and hungered for challenges. He later commented, "I was hip-deep in the pop music world, and I hated it."

The challenge Wilder sought came in the early 1950's, when John Barrows moved to New York City and encouraged Wilder to try writing chamber music. At Barrows's prompting, Wilder began to compose serious works that combined elements of big band swing and popular song with classical genres. Eventually, he wrote more than 300 "serious" compositions, including pieces for orchestra, wind ensemble, and chorus. He was a prolific composer who wrote quickly at the piano and rarely edited his first ideas. Volumes of concert music were written while he continued to write popular songs. Much of his concert music was composed for friends; characteristically, he never asked them for any remuneration.

In the 1960's, Wilder began work on his celebrated book, *American Popular Song: Great Innovators, 1900–1950* (written with the editorial assistance of James T. Maher). The book, finally published in 1972, examines 800 songs submitted for copyright in the first half of the century. Wilder stated what his principles were for examining these songs: "I should make clear that my criteria are limited to the singing (melodic) line and include the elements of intensity, unexpectedness, originality, sinuosity of phrase, clarity, naturalness, control, unclutteredness, sophistication, and honest sentiment. Melodrama, cleverness, contrivance, imitativeness, pretentiousness, aggressiveness, calculatedness, and shallowness may be elements which result in a hit song but never in a great song." The modest Wilder totally ignored his own contribution to the American song tradition, omitting any mention of his songs. His book led to a weekly series on National Public Radio, in which Wilder hosted a gallery of America's greatest songwriters.

Wilder was something of an eccentric. He favored "seedy" surroundings when he composed because it forced him "to create a little loveliness." Wilder could work anywhere, including on trains and in airport terminals. Maine was the only place where Wilder put aside his pen: he would go there to relax.

Wilder never had a permanent home. He lived out of three suitcases at the Algonquin Hotel on West Forty-fourth Street in Manhattan and the Sheraton Hotel in Rochester, N.Y. He spent much of his time riding on trains, which he loved. Wilder never married. Throughout his life he maintained the curiosity and vitality of a child and was noted for his loyalty to his friends. He was a delicately constructed, tall man. His long, handsome face featured deep-set eyes, heavy eyebrows, and a small thin mustache. He said that fear and terrible teeth controlled his life. He found out that he had very little calcium in his bones and was in constant fear of breaking an arm or a leg. In the 1930's, he broke his leg jumping off a Fifth Avenue bus on his way to meet his mother. He spent six months on his back in a polio splint.

It is difficult to determine how much music Wilder wrote because many of his songs were written on small pieces of manuscript paper and tossed aside or left behind in piano benches and desk drawers in the homes of friends. His concert music was written primarily for friends who played wind instruments. As the reporter Whitney Balliett of the *New Yorker* wrote, "He occupies his own space in the world of formal music and that's it." Although he composed music for more than fifty years, very few recordings of his music are available. Wilder died of lung cancer in Gainesville, Fla.

[Wilder's *Letters I Never Mailed* (1975) is a kind of autobiography that reveals Wilder's unique personality by presenting a series of letters he wrote, never mailed, and saved; the intended recipients of these letters include relatives, friends, and people in the musical and literary worlds. Whitney Balliett, "The President of the Derriere-Garde," *New Yorker*, July 9, 1973, is an incisive and appreciative profile. An obituary is in the *New York Times*, Dec. 25, 1980.]

MATTHEW MARVUGLIO

WILDT, RUPERT (June 25, 1905–Jan. 9, 1976), astrophysicist and educator, was born in Munich, Germany, the son of Gero and Hertha Wildt. A combination of a love of astronomy, especially the planets, cultivated as a boy and a Ph.D. in chemistry, received in 1927 from the University of Berlin, led to his desire to found a new discipline, which he would call cosmochemistry. Toward this goal, Wildt worked as a research assistant at the observatory of Bonn University (1928–1929) and at the University of Göttingen (1930–1934).

Wildt's first great discovery occurred at Göttingen. He theorized that certain absorption bands in the red spectra of Jupiter and the other outer planets, first observed by the astronomer Vesto Slipher, were due to the presence of methane and ammonia. Prior to Wildt's theory, astronomers had believed that Jupiter's spectrum was similar to the sun's. Wildt's theory was later confirmed by the Pioneer and Voyager space probes. Whereas hydrogen and helium make up most of the atmospheres of Jupiter and the outer planets, ammonia and methane were indeed found and are important minor components.

Wildt's progress was interrupted by the rise of Hitler in Germany. Although not Jewish, Wildt was deeply involved with, and became engaged to, a young Jewish woman. When Hitler became chancellor in 1933, Wildt wrote to his mother that he was determined to leave Germany. Academic concerns may also have stimulated his desire to leave. The nazification of higher learning in Germany after 1933 did not elate academics. Professors were either forced to accept the inevitable, and thus keep their jobs, or emigrate, if they could, or die at the hands of the Nazis, which some did. Wildt had a difficult time when he decided to emigrate in 1934, for foreigners were more interested in helping Jews to escape. Finally, with the help of an American colleague, Henry Norris Russell, Wildt was named a Rockefeller fellow in 1935 at the Mt. Wilson Observatory in California, which facilitated his departure. His Jewish fiancée, who had previously become the paramour of a high-ranking SS officer, did not leave with Wildt.

In 1936, Wildt entered the Institute for Advanced Study at Princeton University, eventually becoming a research associate, a post he kept until 1942. At Princeton, Wildt continued his studies of the Jovian planets. In this area he was rather an innovator, for these planets provided few easy clues to their constitutions and origins; therefore, many astronomers neglected them. Wildt was an exception. In 1938 he hypothesized that the masses of Jupiter and Saturn were composed mainly of compressed hydrogen, which would cause them to have low densities. Thus the Jovian planets would be similar to the sun in their interior structures. The following year Wildt provided the answer to a puzzle that had confused astronomers for a long time. Solar gases are at least 5,000 times more opaque than gases on earth, but until Wildt, nobody had discovered why. He showed that negative ions of hydrogen were absorbing the flow of radiation from the inside of the sun, thus causing the opacity. This theory, later verified through laboratory experimentation and reproduction, was expounded in Wildt's paper "Electron Affinity in Astrophysics," published in *Astrophysical Journal* in March 1939. For these two theories Wildt received the Eddington Gold Medal of the Royal Astronomical Society of England in 1966.

Wildt became an American citizen in 1942. Prior to his naturalization, while still at Princeton, the German government, uneasy about the "brain drain" of the 1930's, had sent Wildt's former fiancée to the United States to entice him back to Germany. Wildt rebuffed her, and she returned to Germany, where she later died in a concentration camp.

During World War II, Wildt assisted in work organized under the Office of Scientific Research and Development, through the Office of Field Service and the National Defense Research Committee. He continued his government employment intermittently throughout his career, becoming, for example, a consultant to the Goddard Institute for Space Studies of the National Aeronautics and Space Administration.

In 1942, Wildt became associate professor of astronomy at the University of Virginia, where he remained until 1946. During his four years in Charlottesville, he advanced a major theory of the composition of the Jovian planets. He claimed that the interiors of the outer planets consist of large, metallic, rocky cores encircled by ice and compressed hydrogen, above which are deep and dense layers of atmosphere. Data from the Pioneer and Voyager space flights have not confirmed this theory, however, hinting instead that the interiors have much smaller cores and contain hydrogen not just compressed but also in various forms.

In 1946, Wildt left the University of Virginia for a professorship at Yale University. He remained at Yale until he retired in 1973; from 1966 to 1968 he was chairman of the department of astronomy. His later career was devoted to the administration and direction of various astronomical societies. Wildt's particular interest was the Association of Universities for Research in Astronomy (AURA), which operates two centers: Kitt Peak National Observatory in Arizona and the Inter-American Observatory in Chile. Wildt was either president, chairman of the board, or director of AURA from 1958 to 1976. During his tenure at Yale he accepted visiting professorships at the University of Basel (1947), the University of California at Berkeley (1958), and the National University of Mexico (1963).

Upon his retirement from Yale, Wildt moved to Orleans, Mass., the hometown of his wife, Katherine Eldredge, whom he had married on Oct. 26, 1962. He died of cancer and was buried there.

[A complete list of Wildt's numerous publications can be found in S. K. Runcorn, ed., *High Pressure Physics and Planetary Interiors* (1972), a book dedicated to Wildt on the occasion of his retirement. An excellent eulogy by Wendell C. DeMarcus, his first Ph.D. student, is in *Icarus* (1977). An obituary is in the *New York Times*, Jan. 11, 1976.]

DANA L. SAMPLE

WILEY, BELL IRVIN (Jan. 5, 1906–Apr. 4, 1980), historian, was born in Halls, Tenn., the sixth of thirteen children of Ewing Baxter Wiley, a minister, teacher, and farmer, and Anna Bass, a teacher. His grandmother, Fredonia Abernathy Bass, was a Confederate widow whose stories intrigued him. Two Civil War veterans, Union soldier George Washington Bunker and Confederate Will Martin, were often in his home and helped implant a deep interest in the Civil War into the young child's mind.

Wiley graduated from Halls High School and then Asbury College in Wilmore, Ky., with a B.A. in 1928. Wiley would always be indebted to his debate teacher, Zachary T. Johnson, for his career. While teaching at Asbury and coaching the debating team, Wiley did graduate work at the University of Kentucky, receiving an M.A. in English in 1929. At Yale, Wiley received a Ph.D. in history in 1933; his dissertation, done under Ulrich B. Phillips, was published in 1938 as *Southern Negroes, 1861–1865*. C. Vann Woodward said in 1964, "His book still stands as the best general treatment of this important subject in existence." Wiley was among the first to write about blacks, women, and common soldiers.

In 1934, Wiley became professor and head of the history department at Mississippi State College for Women at Hattiesburg. During the summers, he taught at Peabody College in Nashville. On Dec. 19, 1937, Wiley married Mary Frances Harrison; they had two children. In 1938, Wiley went to the University of Mississippi as professor of history and head of the department.

Wiley's most influential book, *The Life of Johnny Reb, the Common Soldier of the Confederacy* (1943), dealt with a largely neglected subject of the Civil War. "They had such very, very rich humor," observed Wiley of the Confederates, and he quoted letters and diaries to let Johnny Reb speak for himself. Throughout his career, he was ready to challenge accepted views, as he did by questioning the need for the war itself in this book: "This inescapable urge of blue and gray to intermingle and to exchange niceties suggests that—grim war though it was—the internecine struggle of the sixties was not only in some aspect a chivalric war but that it was in many respects a crazy and a needless war as well."

Joining the army in 1943, Wiley became lieutenant colonel in three years, serving as a staff historian with the Second Army and as assistant historical officer at headquarters, Army Ground Forces, during World War II. In 1946 he became head of the history department at Louisiana State University, and in 1949 he settled in Atlanta as professor of history at Emory University. In 1952 he completed *The Life of Billy Yank, the Common Soldier of the Union*, which David Donald called "a major contribution to American social history." David M. Potter said, "Out of an immense depth of knowledge Professor Wiley pictures the Union soldier with a fullness that leaves no aspect of his life and few areas of his thought unrevealed."

Wiley became president of the Southern Historical Association in 1955 and fought to end its policy of racial segregation. At the SHA annual meeting on Nov. 10, 1955, papers in support of integration were read by William Faulkner, Dr. Benjamin E. Mays, president of Morehouse College, and Cecil Sims, which were published as *The Segregation Decisions* (1956), with a foreword by Wiley. He examined the reasons for Confederate defeat, in *The Road to Appomattox* (1956), saying, "The South had reason to believe that it could achieve independence. That it did not was due as much, if not more, to its own failings as to the superior strength of the foe."

One of his students, Henry T. Malone, recalled, "Wiley's greatest enjoyment when lecturing comes in quoting from the letters and diaries of semiliterate Civil War soldiers." Wiley contributed to the increasing popularity of his field by supporting Civil War Round Tables, and from 1959 to 1960 he was president of the Atlanta Round Table. In the 1940's and 1950's, Civil War Round Tables were formed, with members from a wide variety of occupations, to encourage public interest in the war through meetings, where leading historians lectured, and battlefield trips. In 1981 the New York Round Table established the Bell I. Wiley

Award, often presented to a hero of battlefield preservation.

In the 1965–1966 academic year, Wiley was Harmsworth Professor of American History at Oxford University, and he published *Lincoln and Lee* in 1966. He was chairman of the executive committee of the National Civil War Centennial Commission; with two of its officials, Allan Nevins and James I. Robertson, Jr. (his former student), Wiley compiled the two-volume *Civil War Books: A Critical Bibliography* (1967–1969).

A debate raged in 1970 at Emory University over whether black students should be admitted under separate admissions standards. Wiley believed in a single standard and said so in the newspaper debate. Earlier, he had lost friends because he supported integration. Now he was being criticized again because of his conviction that equality could not be compromised.

After giving the summer commencement address in 1974, Wiley retired from Emory. He continued to teach as visiting professor at the University of South Carolina (1974), Tulane University (1975), Agnes Scott College, where he was historian in residence (1975–1977), and the University of Kentucky (1977). Saying "women have always held more fascination for me than men," in 1975 Wiley published *Confederate Women*, a study of Mary Chesnut, Varina Davis, and Virginia Clay. Mary Boykin Chesnut was the most famous Confederate diarist: *A Dairy from Dixie* (1905) was revised as *Mary Chesnut's Civil War* (C. Vann Woodward, ed., 1981); Varina Howell Davis was the wife of the Confederate president and the author of *Jefferson Davis, Ex-President of the Confederate States of America. A Memoir by His Wife* (1890); Virginia Clay was the author of *A Belle of the Fifties* (1904).

In 1978, Wiley wrote a new introduction to *The Life of Johnny Reb* in which he reflected on the history of the South and the Civil War: "The 'lowly' people gave a better account of themselves than did the more privileged members of Southern society. They quarreled less than those who were rated their superiors. . . . They bore their hardship . . . with less complaint than the bigwigs. . . . Generally speaking they were not the drab, improvident, depraved, ignoramuses depicted in *Tobacco Road* and other fictional works. Many of them were deeply religious." His last project was *Slaves No More: Letters from Liberia, 1833–1869* (1980), which he edited.

Bruce Catton has given an appraisal of Wiley's contribution to the study of the Civil War: "Of all the books that have been written . . . the ones that will truly live are Bell Wiley's." Wiley died in Atlanta.

[Wiley's papers are in Woodruff Library at Emory University, Atlanta. See also Gene Moore, "Focus: Bell I. Wiley," *Georgia Magazine*, Mar. 1973; John Duncan, "A Historian in His Armchair: An Interview with Bell Wiley," *Civil War Times Illustrated*, Apr. 1973; Henry T. Malone, "Bell Irvin Wiley: Uncommon Soldier" and John Porter Bloom, "Bibliography of Bell Irvin Wiley," in James I. Robertson, Jr., and Richard M. McMurry, eds., *Rank and File, Civil War Essays in Honor of Bell Irvin Wiley* (1976); and John Barnwell, "Bell Irvin Wiley," in Clyde N. Wilson, ed., *Twentieth-Century American Historians* (1983). Obituaries are in the *Atlanta Constitution*, Apr. 6, 1980; the *Washington Post*, Apr. 7, 1980; the *New York Times*, Apr. 7, 1980; and the *Journal of Southern History*, Aug. 1980.]

RALPH KIRSHNER

WILHELMINA (May 11, 1939–Mar. 1, 1980), fashion model and author, was born Wilhelmina Behmenburg in Cullemborg, the Netherlands, the daughter of Willy Robert Behmenburg and Klasina von Straten. At age four, she briefly toyed with the idea of apprenticing in her father's butcher shop.

After attending Blumenhof Grammar School in Oldenburg, Germany, Wilhelmina immigrated to the United States in 1954, settling in Chicago with her parents. "Soon I dreamed a new dream . . . stimulated by my first exposure to American fashion magazines," she said, even the old issues she purchased from secondhand stores for the English and the fantasy. She attended Waller High School, from which she graduated in 1958. While still a student, she enrolled in a local modeling school and took the professional name Winnie Hart, which she used just two years, eventually switching to her first name alone.

In 1960, Wilhelmina launched a seven-year modeling career in Paris that ultimately flourished in both Europe and America. She appeared on nearly 300 magazine covers, including 28 covers of *Vogue*. Standing five feet, eleven inches, and looking even taller with a mane of dark hair piled high over doelike eyes and delicate cheekbones, she boasted that she was "one of the few high-fashion models built like a woman." Along with Suzy Parker, Capucine, and Veruschka, Wilhelmina epitomized the classical aristocratic look that was the style standard of the 1950's and 1960's. Famous for her hollow-cheeked, haut monde look, she never approved of the natural, earthy image that arrived in the 1970's with Lauren Hutton, Cheryl Tiegs, and Margaux Hemingway: "If I had to start all over again, I would never make it. Not in this day of girl-next-door, California-blond, outdoor types."

On Feb. 15, 1965, Wilhelmina married V. Bruce Cooper; they had two children. In 1967, at the height of her modeling career, she formed Wilhelmina Models with Cooper, later expanding the agency to represent writers, directors, and performers as well. As president of Wilhelmina Models, located in New York City, she headed an agency that, at the time of her death, was second in size only to Eileen Ford's.

Graceful and elegant in her modeling, Wilhelmina was equally respected as a professional by her peers as a model manager. She was an impressive figure, usually clothed in black against the white backdrop of her office, never slouching while regally seated behind her desk as she would greet clients at eye level. Wilhelmina's agency represented some of the most important young models of the period: Naomi Sims, Iman, Barbara Carrera, Jessica Lange, and Connie Sellecca. Wilhelmina was a member of the International Model Managers Association, the Screen Actors Guild, the American Federation of Television and Radio Actors, and the Fashion Group. She died of lung cancer in Greenwich, Conn., near her residence in Cos Cob.

[Wilhelmina wrote *The New You* (1978). An obituary is in the *New York Times*, Mar. 3, 1980.]

STEVEN D. JONES

WILLIAMS, THOMAS HARRY (May 19, 1909–July 6, 1979), historian, was born in Vinegar Hill, Ill., the only child of William Dwight Williams, a schoolteacher and lead miner, and Emeline Louisa Collins. His mother died in 1911, and he moved with his father to a farm near Hazel Green, Wis. Williams graduated from high school in 1927 and entered Platteville State Teachers College, Wis., where he earned a B.Ed. in 1931.

At the University of Wisconsin in Madison, Williams received a Ph.M. in 1932 for a thesis on Benjamin Wade that was directed by Carl Russell Fish. He received a Ph.D. in 1937 with a dissertation on "The Committee on the Conduct of the War: A Study of Civil War Politics." His mentor was William Best Hesseltine, and Richard Nelson Current was a fellow graduate student.

On Sept. 2, 1937, Williams married Helen Margaret Jenson; the couple had no children and were divorced in 1947. Williams married Estelle Skolfield on Dec. 27, 1952; they had one child. She was an instructor in the English department at Louisiana State University, and she would help her husband research his books.

Williams was an instructor at the University of Wisconsin's extension division from 1936 to 1938, before going to the University of Omaha (1938–1941), where he became assistant professor. In 1941, he joined the history department of Louisiana State University in Baton Rouge, where he would remain until his retirement in 1979, save for the 1966–1967 academic year, when he was Harmsworth Professor of American History at Oxford University. His first book, *Lincoln and the Radicals* (1941), was a revision of his dissertation, sparking a debate on Lincoln as politician and party leader. Leadership, both military and civilian, would remain Williams's interest for the rest of his career.

Lincoln and His Generals was a 1952 Book-of-the-Month Club selection in which Williams studied Lincoln as commander in chief. Williams stressed the "modern" aspects of the Civil War, particularly the command system that the Union developed. Williams focused on Lincoln as a war director from the perspective of modern war, which made the book valuable to professional soldiers and specialists alike. He called Lincoln "a great natural strategist, a better one than any of his generals." In his review of the book, Allan Nevins said, "The reader will gain as clear and shrewd an overall comprehension of the Northern effort from this volume as from any other in print." It was also stylistically outstanding. Williams had the ability to write vivid vignettes of his characters, such as those of zoologist Colonel Theodore Lyman. What Bell I. Wiley said of Williams's *P. G. T. Beauregard: Napoleon in Gray* (1955) explains why Williams's books could also appeal to the public: "It presents a clear view of campaigns and the problems of high command. . . . It is absorbingly interesting."

Williams gained recognition as an eminent historian of the South, serving as editor from 1947 to 1978 of the Southern Biography Series, published by Louisiana State University Press. In 1959, Williams became president of the Southern Historical Association. He served on the Louisiana Civil War Centennial Commission and often spoke to Civil War Round Tables. In addition, Williams wrote the chapter on "The American Civil War" in *The New Cambridge Modern History*, vol. 10 (1960).

Americans at War: The Development of the American Military System (1960) begins in the eighteenth century and ends with World War II. Williams observed that war is almost never purely military, particularly in a democracy, and said Ulysses S. Grant and William Tecumseh Sherman "understood the political nature of the war." With his interest in political biography, Williams was in an excellent position to write about high command. He contrasted Lincoln and Jefferson Davis as war leaders and administrators, demonstrating again that a familiarity with the military is not the most important qualification for a director of war. Williams's portrait of a president as a soldier, *Hayes of the Twenty-third: The Civil War Volunteer Officer*, was published in 1965.

A showman in the classroom, Professor Williams occasionally appeared in a Civil War uniform. Not surprisingly, his large, popular classes filled up immediately at registration. Students could learn as much from him informally as in class, since he was generous with his time. Williams also served as vice-president of the Ulysses S. Grant Association, and the first volume of Grant's papers was published in 1967.

Huey Long: A Biography appeared in 1969 and won the Pulitzer Prize plus the National Book Award for history and biography. Reviewers praised Williams's extensive use of oral history interviews. Some critics were surprised at the unusually sympathetic treatment of Long, who, Williams said, "created in Louisiana a domination not seen before or since in an American state, one-man rule of all three branches of government." Estelle Williams said her husband "had first become interested in him while a student at the University of Wisconsin in the early 1930's. Harry and his fellow graduate students would gather in the Wisconsin Union building and listen when Huey made his famous national broadcasts." She quoted Williams as saying, "He seized our imagination. He seemed to hold out hope."

Williams was president of the Organization of American Historians (1972–1973). In 1977, Williams noted, "The men I have been drawn to in history are, notably, Abraham Lincoln, Huey Long, Lyndon Johnson—great power artists." He also said, "I subscribe to a version of the great man theory of history." Especially interested in American populism, he was as bold and original in political biography as in military history. He did not share the prevailing low opinion of President Lyndon B. Johnson, and at the time of his death in Baton Rouge, La., he was writing a life of Johnson.

The History of American Wars from 1745 to 1918 was published posthumously in 1981. After noting how *Lincoln and His Generals* changed the course of Civil War writing from tactical to strategic, Frank E. Vandiver said that Williams's "constant searching for new interpretations, his constant goading of others to originality, make his life in Civil War history one of the most important in the last half century."

[Williams's papers are in the Troy H. Middleton Library, Louisiana State University, Baton Rouge, La. Further information can be found in Joseph G. Dawson III, "T. Harry Williams," in Clyde N. Wilson, ed., *Twentieth-Century American Historians* (1983); and Frank E. Vandiver, "Williams and His Generals," in Roman J. Heleniak and Lawrence L. Hewitt, eds., *The Confederate High Command and Related Topics: The 1988 Deep Delta Civil War Symposium: Themes in Honor of T. Harry Williams* (1990). *Selected Essays of T. Harry Williams* (1983) includes a biographical introduction by Estelle Williams. Obituaries are in the *New Orleans Times-Picayune*, the *New York Times*, the *Washington Post*, all July 7, 1979; and in the *Journal of Southern History*, Nov. 1979.]

RALPH KIRSHNER

WILLS, CHILL (July 18, 1902–Dec. 15, 1978), actor, was born in Seagoville, Tex., to entertainers Robert B. Wills and Fanny Rublee. Chill was his real name, a fact he attributed to being the seventh child born in his family. ("they ran out of common names time they got to me") or the hot weather that year in rural Texas ("they wanted to cool me off"). Other times he claimed he was delivered by a Doctor Chillins and named in his honor. He was "educated" in medicine shows, honky tonks, and burlesque halls. He learned to sing in the Dallas First Baptist Church and later joined a professional singing group in Burkeburnett, Tex. He added humorous monologues to his singing performances and moved to Chicago at fifteen to play a hick straight man in burlesque for $60 per week.

Wills said he "graduated from Minsky's to vaudeville" in the 1920's. In one memorable New Year's Eve performance, Wills portrayed the old year, and the new year was played by two-year-old Mickey Rooney. In 1936, Wills made his last vaudeville appearance on stage in San Francisco beside ventriloquist Edgar Bergen. Wills said he turned to nightclubs because vaudeville houses were closing so quickly, "I got afraid I'd get locked in one." He formed a country and western singing group, Chill Wills and the Avalon Boys. They appeared in films and played themselves in *Way Out West* (1937), which starred comedians Stan Laurel and Oliver Hardy. The group also played themselves and sang in a Hopalong Cassidy film, *The Bar 20 Rides Again* (1936). The group split up in 1938.

In that year Wills was discovered by a movie executive while performing his routine at the Trocadero, a nightclub in Hollywood, Calif. His craggy features, raspy voice, rural Texas twang, twice broken nose, wry humor, and uncomplicated sincerity made him a natural to play supporting roles in Westerns. He made six pictures in a series for RKO studios that starred George O'Brien. Wills played a garrulous prevaricator appropriately called Whopper Hatch. He performed in an average of three or four movies, mostly Westerns, each year for the next forty years. He portrayed a number of character roles, usually as some hero's sidekick and almost never played a villain. Although he performed opposite some of the biggest stars in Hollywood, including Walter Pidgeon, Gary Cooper, Robert Taylor, and John Wayne, Wills was known for stealing scenes. For example, he stood out as the rangy, laconic deputy sheriff in *Boom Town* (1940), which starred Clark Gable, Spencer Tracy, Claudette Colbert, and Hedy Lamarr. Wills performed in several musicals, including *Meet Me in St. Louis* (1944) and *The Harvey Girls* (1946). Perhaps his greatest stretch was playing a monsignor in *The Cardinal* (1963).

In 1939, Wills married Betty Chappele and settled in North Hollywood. They had two children. Betty died in 1957. Wills married Novadeen Googe in Las Vegas, Nev., in 1973. They were the first couple married at the new MGM Grand Hotel and Casino.

Despite his many acting roles, Wills is perhaps best remembered as the voice of Francis the Talking Mule in a series of six popular and successful comedy films between 1950 and 1955. Regarding his role as Francis, Wills quipped, "I'm kind of proud to be speaking for a jackass. These days so many people are speaking for themselves." Wills also wrote or ad-libbed nearly a third of the mule's lines. In addition, Francis memorabilia, from record albums to wind-up toys, sold briskly. For selling hundreds of thousands of dollars of United States defense bonds during the Korean War, Wills and Francis received public acclaim from Generals George C. Marshall and Dwight D. Eisenhower and Vice-President Alben Barkley.

In 1960, Wills played Beekeeper, a lovable, whiskey-guzzling, humorous sidekick to John Wayne's Davy Crockett in *The Alamo*. Wayne, who also directed the picture, hired a publicist and paid him an unprecedented $125,000 to promote the film, which secured seven Oscar nominations, including one for Wills as best supporting actor. Wills, believing that this opportunity would not pass his way again, hired his own press agent and flooded the Hollywood press with garish, self-promoting ads such as: "We of the *Alamo* cast are praying—harder than the real Texans prayed for their lives in the Alamo—for Chill Wills to win the Oscar . . . Your Alamo Cousins." Comedian Groucho Marx placed his own ad in reply: "Dear Mr. Chill Wills, I am delighted to be your cousin, but I voted for Sal Mineo." Wayne chastised Wills in an open letter to *Daily Variety*, saying that he was sure Wills's "intentions were not as bad as his taste." Wayne's criticism brought a stinging reply from *Los Angeles Times* columnist Joe Hyams, who quipped: "For John Wayne to impugn Chill Wills's taste is tantamount to Jayne Mansfield criticizing a stripper for too much exposure." Neither *The Alamo* nor Wills won an Academy Award.

Wills invested his money in a series of business ventures, including a restaurant chain and his own brand of chili, splitting his time between his acting career and business management. He became active in politics toward the end of his life and expressed an interest in running for governor of Texas. The closest he got to elective office, however, was warming up audiences at fund-raising rallies for Alabama governor George Wallace in 1971.

As the nation's taste for Westerns began to diminish in the 1960's, so did opportunities for the aging character actor. He starred in the television series "Frontier Circus" (1961–1962) and "The Rounders" (1966–1967). One of his most memorable film performances was in Sam Peckinpah's *Pat Garrett and Billy the Kid* (1973). His last role was in the television movie *Stubby Pringle's Christmas* (1978). He died of cancer at his home in Encino, Calif.

[See Emanuel Levy, *And the Winner Is . . .* (1987), and Mason Wiley and Damien Bono, *Inside Oscar* (1993). Obituaries are in the *Los Angeles Times*, Dec. 16, 1978; and the *New York Times*, Dec. 17, 1978.]

DAVID M. ESPOSITO

WINSLOW, OLA ELIZABETH (Jan. 5, 1885–Sept. 27, 1977), biographer, was born in Grant City, Mo., one of three children of William Delos Winslow, a local banker, and Hattie Elizabeth Colby.

Winslow matriculated at Stanford University in 1903 and received her B.A. degree in 1906. She taught English in private preparatory schools in San Francisco from 1907 to 1911, when William W. Guth, president of the College (now the University) of the Pacific, hired her as an English instructor. The following year Winslow became assistant professor of English; she continued in that capacity until 1914, when she earned her M.A. at Stanford.

In September 1913, Guth assumed the presidency of Goucher College in Baltimore and a year later hired his protégée to chair the small English department at the all-female school, a post Winslow would hold for thirty years. Winslow was elevated to assistant professor in 1917. In 1919, after controversy erupted over the appointment of a man to replace retiring dean Eleanor Lord, President Guth compromised with angry faculty and students by naming Winslow assistant dean, a position she held until 1921. In 1920, Winslow was promoted to associate professor of English.

While in Baltimore, Winslow began doctoral studies at Johns Hopkins University and spent her summers between 1916 and 1922 at the University of Chicago, where she worked under noted English literature scholar John Matthews Manly. Winslow produced a dissertation entitled "Low Comedy as a Structural Element in English Drama from the Beginnings to 1642," and earned her Ph.D. from Chicago magna cum laude in August 1922. Meanwhile, Winslow continued to teach both English and American literature at Goucher, and between 1941 and 1943 she even developed and taught a course in cryptography for the United States Navy.

Many years of research at Yale University libraries led to Winslow's publication of *Jonathan Edwards, 1703–1758* (1940), one of three books she produced while at Goucher. Odell Shepard of the *New York Times Sunday Book Review* praised the effort for its wide appeal, its scholarly contribution, and its vivid prose. A committee chaired by noted journalist Burton J. Hendrick agreed and unanimously awarded Winslow's work the Pulitzer Prize for biography for 1941.

Winslow left Goucher in 1944 to take a one-year visiting professorship in English at Wellesley College. She was to assume the teaching duties of two professors who had gone on leave, one an Americanist and the other an English literature specialist; Winslow was chosen because of her expertise in both areas. Within the year Wellesley accepted Winslow as a permanent part of the faculty, assigning her primarily to American literature classes. At the same time Winslow served on an English department committee responsible for faculty evaluation, promotion, and tenure. Though by all accounts an excellent teacher, Winslow soon tired of her role as educator. She asked for and received an appointment as research professor for the 1949–1950 academic year, retiring from Wellesley in the spring of 1950 with the rank of professor of English emeritus.

Winslow's years in retirement were her most productive. Between 1950 and 1962 she spent her winters on the English faculty of the Radcliffe College Seminars. She lived most of the year in her house near Sheepscot, Maine, where she continued to write. Winslow also kept a humble, sparsely furnished Boston apartment during these years and devoted her winter days to research in various area libraries. Her later researches produced no fewer than ten books, all of which were historical or biographical, including *Meetinghouse Hill, 1630–1783* (1952), *Master Roger Williams* (1957), *Samuel*

Sewall of Boston (1964), *Portsmouth, the Life of a Town* (1966), *John Eliot: Apostle to the Indians* (1968), *Old South Church* (1970), and *A Destroying Angel: The Conquest of Smallpox* (1974). Winslow also lived and worked in England at various times; one four-month research period in particular resulted in yet another biography, *John Bunyan* (1961).

Winslow never married and had no children. Rather, she was the perfect picture of the solitary, serious, prodigious, and careful scholar. Her interests in later life shifted from teaching to research, from literature to biography and history. She remained productive well into her eighties and had contracts with three publishers at the time of her death at Miles Memorial Hospital in Damariscotta, Maine, at the age of ninety-two.

[Winslow also wrote *Low Comedy as a Structural Element in English Drama* (1926) and edited *American Broadside Verse* (1930). See also *The Stanford Alumni Directory* (1911); College of the Pacific *Bulletin* (1914); Anna Heubeck Knipp, *The History of Goucher College* (1938); "Pulitzer Prizes of 1941," *The Saturday Review of Literature*, May 10, 1941; "Pulitzer Prizes Awarded for 1940," *Publishers Weekly*, May 10, 1941; "Goodbye Messrs. Chips," *Time*, July 3, 1950; and Frederic O. Musser, *The History of Goucher College, 1930–1985* (1990). An obituary is in the *New York Times*, Oct. 3, 1977.]

RAYMOND D. IRWIN

WINSTON, HARRY (Mar. 1, 1896–Dec. 8, 1978), gem merchant and jeweler, was born in New York City, one of four children of Jeanette Harivmen and Jacob Winston, owner of a small jewelry store. At the age of eight, one year after his mother's death, Winston and his sister accompanied his asthmatic father to Los Angeles. His two brothers remained in New York, where they worked for antiques dealers. Winston attended public school until the age of fifteen, when he left high school in order to work full-time for his father in the jewelry business.

Winston demonstrated his acumen for identifying gems at the age of twelve, when he spotted an emerald priced at 25 cents in a tray of junk jewelry in a pawnshop window. It turned out to be a two-carat stone, which he resold two days later for $800. His salesmanship was developed while working for his father, selling jewelry to oil prospectors in saloons. In 1920, with almost $2,000, he set up his first business, the Premier Diamond Company, at 535 Fifth Avenue, in New York City. Two years later, by buying shrewdly at auctions and wholesale markets, he accumulated $10,000 in cash and jewelry worth $20,000. Unfortunately, an employee absconded with all his assets. Winston persisted in his efforts to remain self-employed, however, securing a loan from a branch of the New Netherlands Bank. Taking advantage of changes in jewelry fashion in the 1920's, when many of the Victorian and Edwardian items such as stomachers, corsage ornaments, and tiaras were no longer desirable, Winston sent mailings to people listed in the *Social Register* and obtained the names of attorneys and judges who would know about estates to be probated, then wrote to ask if the jewelry was for sale. He removed the gems, recut the stones to achieve greater brilliance, and gave them a modern setting.

Winston's first major estate purchase was that of Rebecca Darlington Stoddard of New Haven, Conn., in 1925, obtained through the president of a branch of the New Netherlands Bank, who gave him a letter of introduction to her husband. Allowed to appraise the collection, Winston made an offer of $1.2 million, knowing he would outbid everyone else, if he could have six months to sell it. Stoddard agreed; Winston found buyers, received $1.25 million for the jewels, and earned a $125,000 commission.

In 1926, Winston acquired the estate jewels of Arabella Huntington for $1.2 million, financed by the New Netherlands Bank, which gave him publicity when it was reported in the society columns of the major newspapers of the day. In December 1930 Winston's successful bid on a thirty-nine-carat emerald-cut diamond—the largest diamond sold at a public auction in the United States—initiated his reputation as a purchaser of large stones. Although Winston is identified mainly with diamonds, his purchase of the "Lucky" Baldwin estate in 1930 included a twenty-six-carat ruby that was ranked as one of the six top rubies in the world.

In 1932, Winston closed Premier Diamond Company and opened Harry Winston, Inc., which manufactured its own line of jewelry. On Feb. 10, 1933, he married Edna Fleishman; they had two children. His son Ronald later headed the firm.

In 1935, when Winston bought the 726-carat Jonker diamond for $700,000 from De Beers Company, which had earlier purchased it for

$350,000, the *New York Times* reported the purchase as establishing Winston's name worldwide. Winston had Lazare Kaplan cut the stone into eleven individual stones, together valued at $2 million. The Jonker 1 was sold for $1 million to King Farouk of Egypt.

Ironically, King Farouk turned out to be, according to Winston, his only problem client. In 1951 he ordered the Catherine the Great emerald and the Star of the East diamond, neither of which he paid for on delivery. When he was deposed in 1952, he returned the emerald but claimed to have left the diamond in Egypt and to be unable to pay for it. This proved to be untrue, and it took Winston ten years of litigation to retrieve the diamond from a Swiss vault.

Winston's love of big stones continued to bring him fame and success. His showmanship was vividly demonstrated by the exhibit called the *Court of Jewels*, which toured the country from 1949 to 1953. This display included the 46-carat Hope diamond, which carried a legend of bringing misfortune to its owners; the 95-carat Star of the East; the 94-carat pair of diamonds known as the Indore pear shapes, the 126-carat Jonker 1 emerald-cut diamond, the 31-carat McLean diamond, the 46-carat Mabel Boll diamond, and the 337-carat Catherine the Great sapphire. Winston was fascinated by the history of ownership as well as the intrinsic value of the gems, and used these histories to enhance interest in the stones. He was known to call some of his gems his babies, as he did the 62.5-carat diamond that carried his name.

Winston was one of a select group of jewelers (sightholders) who could buy uncut stones from De Beers Consolidated, which controlled 85 percent of the diamond market. His biggest purchase occurred in 1974, when he paid $24.5 million for uncut diamonds. In 1978 he made the largest emerald purchase in history from the government of India.

Winston wanted to have his own mine so that he would not have to pay commissions to De Beers. He tried to accomplish this in Angola, Sierra Leone, the Ivory Coast, and Venezuela. He was not successful, and in the case of Sierra Leone, almost was excluded from De Beers. He negotiated a compromise and received a reduced commission rate.

In 1958, Winston donated the Hope diamond to the Smithsonian Institution in Washington, D.C., after owning it for ten years. This was one of several important gems he presented to the Smithsonian's Hall of Gems and Minerals. Others were an uncut diamond in memory of Sir Ernest Oppenheimer, chairman of the board of De Beers, and the 127-carat Portuguese diamond.

Winston, short (five feet, four inches) and dapper, was called "a little Napoleon." The only full-face photo of him appears in the *New York Times* obituary. He contended that Lloyd's of London, his insurer, did not want his face photographed, as a security precaution, which only added to his mystique. The deliberate advertisement of his diamonds, however, in ads for Maximilian furs, Lucky Strike cigarettes, and Revlon cosmetics, kept his name, if not his face, highly visible.

Winston amassed a gem collection that ranked second only to that of the British Crown. Of some 300 major diamonds ranked by the Gemological Institute, Winston at one time had owned 60. When he died in New York City, he was the premier diamond merchant of Fifth Avenue, with salons in France and Germany and diamond-cutting factories in Israel, France, Germany, Portugal, Puerto Rico, and Arizona.

[See Harmon and Elsie Tupper, "King of Diamonds," *Cosmopolitan*, Apr. 1947; Lillian Ross, "Profiles: The Big Stone," *New Yorker*, May 8 and 15, 1954; James Stewart-Gordon, "Harry Winston, Ace of Diamonds," *Reader's Digest*, Jan. 1978; Christopher P. Anderson, "Interview with Harry Winston," *People*, May 15, 1978; David Koskoff, *The Diamond World* (1981); and Laurence Krashes, *Harry Winston* (1984; 2d ed., 1986). An obituary is in the *New York Times*, Dec. 9, 1978 (correction on Dec. 10).]

BARBARA L. GERBER

WOLFE, BERTRAM DAVID (Jan. 19, 1896–Feb. 21, 1977), political activist and author, was born in Brooklyn, N.Y., the son of William D. Wolfe and Rachel Samter. His father had run away from home at thirteen, leaving the town of Kempen in what is now Poland and making his way to New York City, where he worked in a variety of odd jobs. Wolfe was a good student and received a B.A. cum laude from the City College of New York in 1916. Following graduation he joined the English faculty at Boys High School in Brooklyn. On Apr. 18, 1917, Wolfe married Ella Goldberg, a Spanish teacher; they had no children.

Revolutionary developments in Russia in 1917 inspired in Wolfe a deepening interest in

Communist ideology and radical political activity. After the United States entered World War I the same year, he joined the Socialist party. Wolfe, who harbored pacifist sentiments, was drawn to the party because of its initial opposition to American involvement in the war. Influenced by the emergence of a Bolshevik government in Russia, he became affiliated with the party's more radical leftist wing. By February 1919 he had authored, along with journalist John Reed, the "Manifesto of the National Council of the Left Wing of the Socialist Party," a proclamation calling for strikes and direct revolutionary action by unemployed veterans and jobless defense workers. The same year Wolfe participated in the formation of the American Communist Party. He devoted himself to working on behalf of the party over the next decade.

Indicted in 1919 under New York's criminal anarchy law, Wolfe fled with his wife to California. Under the name of Arthur Albright he engaged in a variety of radical activities, including service as a California delegate to the Communist party convention in Michigan in 1920. Indicted again, he and his wife went to Mexico. Wolfe worked in Mexico City as an English teacher from 1922 through 1925. In 1925 he received an M.A. degree in romance languages from the University of Mexico. Expelled by the Mexican government for spreading Communist ideas among railroad workers, he returned to New York City and in 1926 became the director of the Workers School, a post he held through 1928. The Communist-affiliated school provided instruction in Marxist economics, Communist ideology, and the radical organization of workers.

In 1929, Wolfe attended the third meeting of the Communist International (Comintern) in Moscow as an American delegate and member of the executive committee. He became disillusioned over the direction Communism was taking under new Soviet leader Joseph Stalin. On his return home he joined in the ideological debate splitting the American Communist Party. Wolfe allied himself with the anti-Stalinist wing of the party led by Jay Lovestone. When Lovestone, Wolfe, and others refused to support the Comintern's official Stalinist line, they were expelled from the party. As a member of the Lovestoneite faction Wolfe began a systematic criticism of Stalinism, which eventually evolved into a repudiation of Communism itself. Nonetheless, this period of Wolfe's life was characterized by a tireless attempt to invoke Marxist-Leninist tenets in the face of Stalinist realities in the Soviet Union. His political activism combined with an energetic teaching and writing schedule. At the Workers School he offered such courses as "The Economics of Present Day Capitalism," "The Nature of the Capitalist Crisis," and "Marxist Economics." He also taught mathematics and English at the Eron Preparatory School through 1934, while authoring numerous pamphlets, essays, articles, and book reviews. Wolfe earned a second M.A. in Romance languages from Columbia University in 1932. In 1934 he collaborated with Diego Rivera on the book *Portrait of America*, featuring his commentary and the Mexican artist's work.

Also in 1934, Wolfe was a visiting lecturer in Spanish literature at Stanford University. He published another collaboration with Rivera, *Portrait of Mexico*, in 1937. In 1939, Wolfe completed *Diego Rivera: His Life and Times* and *Keep America Out of War: A Program*, written with the socialist Norman Thomas. By then he had made an open break with Stalin, calling Nikolai Bukharin's trial an "infamous and murderous farce." Bukharin's execution in 1938 was a turning point for Wolfe. He began to wonder whether Leninism itself spawned the excesses of Stalin. The signing of a nonaggression pact between Stalin and Adolf Hitler in 1939 prompted Wolfe to begin work on a critical study of the Russian Revolution and its meaning. Nine years in the writing, his book *Three Who Made a Revolution: Lenin, Trotsky, Stalin* appeared in 1948. Highly acclaimed, it was eventually translated into twenty-eight languages.

During World War II, Wolfe continued to speak out against Stalin. He lectured on the dangers of new subjugations in a postwar Europe dominated by the Soviet dictator. Wolfe and his supporters were attacked by the Communist Political Association as "Trotskyites" and "fascists" whose opposition to Stalin lent support to Hitler.

In 1951, Wolfe created an Ideological Advisory Unit for the State Department's Voice of America International Broadcasting Division. Its purpose was to fight Soviet propaganda, and to undermine its effects in the West and in such Soviet-controlled areas as North Korea. The unit's radio broadcasts sought to unmask the totalitarian nature of the Soviet system, attacking the alleged morality of Communism itself. Wolfe remained with the State Department through 1954. During this period he also worked as a fellow in the Russian Institute of Columbia University.

After leaving government Wolfe resumed his career as a free-lance author, while holding a variety of academic and research posts. In 1956 and 1957 he served as a research fellow in the Russian History Project and from 1961 to 1962 he was a distinguished visiting professor of Russian History at the University of California, Berkeley. He continued writing at a feverish pace, publishing such books as *Six Keys to the Soviet System* (1956), *Khruschchev and Stalin's Ghost* (1957), and *Communist Totalitarianism: Keys to the Soviet System* (1961). In 1966, Wolfe was named a research associate at the Hoover Institution on War, Revolution, and Peace. Through the late 1960's he continued to produce books, such as *Marxism: 100 Years in the Life of a Doctrine* (1965), *The Bridge and the Abyss: The Troubled Friendship of Maxim Gorky and V. I. Lenin* (1967), and *An Ideology in Power: Reflections on the Russian Revolution* (1969).

A historian who himself was a primary historical source, Wolfe had known many Soviet leaders and was a central figure in the first decades of the American Communist movement. He shared with scholars and political leaders his impressions of such ex-Communists as V. F. Calverton and Whittaker Chambers. He communicated with a variety of American political and corporate heads, such as Richard Nixon, Gerald Ford, Ronald Reagan, and Joseph Coors. Wolfe suffered severe burns when his bathrobe caught fire at his home in Menlo Park, Calif. He was transported to the Santa Clara Valley Medical Center in San Jose, but his injuries proved fatal.

[Wolfe's papers are at the Hoover Institution, Stanford University. His autobiography, *A Life in Two Centuries*, was published posthumously in 1978. See also Robert Hessen, ed., *Breaking with Communism: The Intellectual Odyssey of Bertram D. Wolfe* (1990), which includes a bibliography of Wolfe's writings. An obituary is in the *New York Times*, Feb. 22, 1977.]

MICHAEL J. EULA

WOOD, PEGGY (Feb. 9, 1892–Mar. 18, 1978), actress and writer, was born in Brooklyn, N.Y., the daughter of Eugene Wood, a feature writer for the *New York World*, and Mary Gardner. Her parents named her Margaret. As a girl, Wood studied piano and singing in preparation for a career in grand opera. Upon graduation in 1909 from Manual Training High School in Brooklyn, she determined that her singing was not of operatic quality; but possessed of a lovely trained voice, a tall, slim figure, blue eyes, blond hair, and comely features, she decided to seek a role in musical comedy. She managed to obtain an introduction to Arthur Hammerstein and in 1910 landed in the chorus of Victor Herbert's *Naughty Marietta* on Broadway. Since there were eight Margarets among the cast, she adopted Peggy as her stage name.

In 1911 she won the role of Vera Steinway in *The Three Romeos*. Other roles in musical comedies in the years 1913–1915 culminated in her second appearance in *Naughty Marietta* in 1916 as the lead. Thus, Wood had progressed from chorus girl to star in just over five years. She scored a big hit in 1917 as Ottilie in Sigmund Romberg's *Maytime* and remained with the show for two years. The *New York Times* theater critic observed that she was "not only her own amiable, spirited and comely self, but portrayed the unhappily married woman of thirty and the faded woman of sixty with a skill in technique, a subtlety and finesse of feeling, which were truly memorable." Zelda Sears, who wrote the script and lyrics for *The Clinging Vine*, in which Wood starred, spoke of "the rapture of working with a singer who is 100 per cent. actress and an actress who is 100 per cent. singer."

After further successes Wood felt ready to "step out of comic opera into drama." In 1925 she asked for and got Katharine Cornell's part in the original Broadway production of *Candida* when Cornell left the cast. Wood's interpretation of George Bernard Shaw's heroine encouraged her ambitions as a serious actress. Roles in Shakespeare soon followed. Her 1926 characterization of Lady Percy in *Henry the Fourth, Part One* was described as having warmth as well as beauty." In 1928 she played Portia in the George Arliss production of *The Merchant of Venice*, both in New York and on tour.

In 1926 and 1927, Wood toured with John Drew in the road company of *Trelawny of the Wells*. Her account of this adventure, which turned out to be Drew's last performance, is lovingly detailed by Wood in a *Saturday Evening Post* article entitled "Splendid Gypsy" (Sept. 3, 1927), published in book form the following year. In years following, she wrote numerous articles for the *Post* as well as for the *Ladies Home Journal*, *Woman's Home Companion*, *Theater Arts Monthly*, *Arts and Decoration*, *Harper's*, and *Collier's*, and for many newspapers. She also published several books.

Wood made her London debut in Noël Coward's *Bitter Sweet*, which opened at His Majesty's Theatre on July 18, 1929, to rave notices. The London *Daily News* critic wrote that "Mr. Coward has been lucky in his leading lady, Peggy Wood. She has charm, naturalness and personal distinction and sings remarkably well. If only American film stars in the talkies had such beautiful speaking voices—one seldom hears English as well spoken—we should be very happy." More Broadway performances preceded her third Shakespearean role, as Katherine in *The Taming of the Shrew*, in Berkeley, Calif., in 1934.

On Apr. 7, 1937, Wood opened in the title part of a play she cowrote with Ward Morehouse entitled *Miss Quis*. This story of an eccentric housekeeper turned heiress received lukewarm reviews. In the spring of 1938, Wood returned to the London stage in another Coward production, *Operette*, and remained there to do *Theatre Royal* the following spring. In John Van Druten's *Old Acquaintance*, presented in December of 1940, Wood was praised as having given "the best performance of her career—honest, aware and lucidly projected" for her memorable portrayal of Mildred Drake. Once again, Coward supplied a vehicle for Wood's considerable talents; his *Blithe Spirit*, in which Wood played Ruth, the perplexed and beleaguered second wife, opened in November 1941.

Until her memorable performance as the Mother Superior in the 1965 film version of *The Sound of Music*, for which she received an Academy Award nomination for best supporting actress, Wood's film credits were few and far between. She was, however, a pioneer in the industry, appearing as early as 1919 in the silent film *Almost a Husband*. Her highly successful portrayal of a lovable Norwegian-American matriarch, in the eight-year run of the weekly television series *Mama*, began in 1949. For this characterization, she was honored in 1951 by King Haakon of Norway, receiving the Order of St. Olaf.

On Feb. 14, 1924, Wood married John Van Alstyn Weaver, a poet, novelist, and playwright. They had one child. Their happy marriage came to an end in 1938 when John Weaver died of tuberculosis. On Oct. 1, 1946, she married William A. Walling, an executive in the printing business, who died in 1973.

Wood had a lifelong dedication to Actors Equity, of which she was a founder and subsequently a vice-president. She also served on its council from 1919 to 1940. The actress was a participant in the 1919 actors strike that protested low wages and unfair working conditions for chorus personnel. In 1959, Wood assumed the presidency of the American National Theatre and Academy (ANTA), a position she held until 1966. Active in the Episcopal Actors Guild, she served as its vice-president from 1950 to 1964. As a member of the American Theatre Wing she acted in *Blithe Spirit* in various bases of the Eighth Air Force in Britain during World War II.

Throughout her career, Wood appeared in more than seventy Broadway plays. Her last performance was with Ethel Barrymore Colt in *A Madrigal of Shakespeare* in Westport, Conn., in 1967, but she continued to be active in theater organizations until her death in Stamford, Conn.

[Among Wood's books containing biographical information are *Actors and People* (1930); *How Young You Look* (1941); and *Arts and Flowers* (1963). Other books by her are *The Flying Prince* (1927, written with her father); *The Splendid Gypsy: John Drew* (1928); *The Star Wagon* (1936); and her play, coauthored with Ward Morehouse, *Miss Quis* (1937). See also Mary B. Mullet, "Peggy Wood Seems Like Such a Nice Girl," *American Magazine*, Aug. 1926. For information on Wood's involvement with theatrical organizations see Barbara Ann Simon, "Twentieth Century American Performing Arts as Viewed Through the Career of Peggy Wood" (Ph.D. diss., New York University, 1981). An obituary is in the *New York Times*, Mar. 19, 1978.]

JAMES A. RAWLEY

WOODWARD, ROBERT BURNS (Apr. 10, 1917–July 8, 1979), chemist and Nobel laureate, was born in Boston, Mass., the only child of Arthur Chester Woodward and Margaret Burns. His father died in October 1918, during the great influenza epidemic. Woodward's mother, an accountant and realtor, was of Scottish ancestry; on the basis of the name, Woodward claimed a relationship to Scotland's national poet, Robert Burns. Margaret Woodward soon remarried, but she and her young son were abandoned by her second husband.

By the time he was two, Woodward knew the alphabet and could count to one hundred. He received a chemistry set when he was eight years old and gradually went beyond the set's basic contents and procedures. Woodward later claimed that by the age of twelve he had performed essentially all the experiments in Ludwig Gattermann's *Practical Methods of Organic Chemistry*, a then widely used college textbook. Woodward received his elementary and high school education in the public schools of Quincy, the Boston suburb where he lived. He graduated from high school in 1933 and that fall, at the age of sixteen, enrolled at the Massachusetts Institute of Technology to study chemistry. In 1937, James Flack Norris, professor of chemistry and director of the organic chemistry research laboratory at MIT, said of Woodward, "When he entered the Institute as a freshman he already had as much knowledge of organic chemistry as a man normally acquires during four years of enrollment in undergraduate classes."

Woodward was dropped from MIT at the close of the fall 1934 semester. Routine and certain kinds of discipline were never his forte. Woodward quickly let it be known that he had no plans to attend formal classes; he would spend all his time in the library and chemical laboratory and show up only for his final examinations. Woodward also forgot about the requirement for physical education, which became his undoing. After a semester working for the MIT department of biology, Woodward, with the assistance of Norris, enrolled once again for the fall 1935 semester. The faculty recognized Woodward's abilities, and a special curriculum was designed for him. Woodward experimented in his own laboratory, he could spend as little time as he desired in formal classes, he had to take final examinations, and he had to satisfy the physical education requirement. Woodward received the B.S. degree in June 1936 and the Ph.D. degree, at age twenty, in June 1937. The *Boston Globe* of June 8, 1937, reported the following remarks from an interview with Norris upon Woodward's graduation: "We did for Woodward what we have done for no other student in our department, for we had no student like him in the department. Woodward is brilliant but, unlike some scholars, he will not burn out suddenly. We are convinced that he will make a distinguished name for himself in the scientific world."

Upon receiving his Ph.D. degree, Woodward became an instructor in chemistry at the University of Illinois for the summer of 1937. This brief affiliation ended in a mutual parting of the ways owing to his brash personality. Woodward then went to Harvard as research assistant to Elmer P. Kohler, head of the division of organic chemistry there. In September 1938, Woodward became a junior fellow of the Society of Fellows at Harvard. This appointment allowed him total freedom for study and research in chemistry and his other interest, mathematics. While a member of the society, Woodward planned the syntheses of many complex natural products. To accomplish these he needed graduate and postdoctoral students; a fellow of the society was on his own.

Consequently, Woodward resigned this fellowship in January 1941 to become an instructor in the department of chemistry at Harvard. He was promoted to assistant professor in 1944, associate professor in 1946, and full professor in 1950. Woodward became the Morris Loeb professor in 1953 and the Donner professor of science in 1960. He occupied this position, which freed him from all formal teaching responsibilities, until he died.

During his years as a fellow, Woodward collected and correlated isolated and muddled data from the chemical literature that appeared as a series of publications in 1941 and 1942 that came to be known as Woodward's rules. These rules related ultraviolet absorbance bands to the structure of certain unsaturated ketones. On the heels of Woodward's rules came the synthesis of quinotoxine in collaboration with William von Eggers Doering in 1944. The goal was quinine, and it was generally agreed that the synthesis of this compound would require the production of quinotoxine, which, the German chemist Paul Rabe reported in 1918, could be turned into quinine. Woodward had turned twenty-six just one day prior to the completion of this synthesis.

In 1944, Woodward joined the joint British-American war effort on the structure and synthesis of penicillin. He correctly postulated the structure for this antibiotic in that same year. Woodward solved or contributed to the elucidation of the structures of many complex chemical compounds. One of note resulted from work performed in collaboration with Geoffrey

Wilkinson and reported in 1952 on an iron "sandwich" compound of unique structure, ferrocene.

Woodward formulated the Octant Rule in 1961. He utilized the instrumental technique of optical rotatory dispersion to describe the molecular geometry of certain ketones. And in 1965, as a consequence of work involved in the synthesis of vitamin B_{12}, the Woodward-Hoffman Rules were announced. This concept used the theory of wave mechanics to understand the pathways for chemical reactions and to predict the spatial arrangement of atoms in organic molecules involved in cyclization reactions.

In 1964, Woodward received a National Medal of Science, and in 1965 he was the sole recipient of the Nobel Prize in chemistry. It was awarded to him for "meritorious contributions to the art of chemical synthesis." The Woodward-Hoffman Rules earned the Nobel Prize in chemistry for Roald Hoffman in 1981. Had Woodward not died in 1979, it is probable that he would also have shared in this award.

After 1944, Woodward accomplished total syntheses of patulin (1950), cholesterol (1951), cortisone (1951), lanosterol (1954), lysergic acid (1954), strychnine (1954), reserpine (1956), chlorophyll (1960), the tetracyclines (1962), colchicine (1963), cephalosporin C (1965), prostaglandin $F_{2\alpha}$ (1973), and the most complex synthesis of all, vitamin B_{12} (1976). This last, begun in 1960, was an international collaboration between Woodward and his students at Harvard and Albert Eschenmoser and his students at the Eidgenössische technische Hochschule in Zurich. The synthesis of the antibiotic erythromycin A in 1980 was Woodward's last. It was a ten-year effort and completed after his death by his Harvard group under the direction of Yoshito Kishi, a once visiting professor at Harvard.

In 1963, CIBA-Geigy created the Woodward Research Institute at the company's headquarters in Basel, Switzerland. Here Woodward could choose his own research, with the proviso that it be connected in some fashion with living organisms. The first project was the total synthesis of the natural antibiotic cephalosporin C, which became the topic of Woodward's Nobel lecture. The institute was closed after Woodward's death.

Noted for lecturing flawlessly without text or notes, Woodward spent many hours preparing his "theatrical performance." His public lectures always had the same title, "Recent Advances in the Chemistry of Natural Products." His blue suit and light blue tie were constant and legendary. He claimed never to have slept for more than three or four hours per night. He had little time for family life or holidays. Woodward smoked three and a half packs of unfiltered cigarettes per day, and he was a heavy consumer of alcohol. He was addicted to puzzles and games, read widely, and loved a party. He abhorred physical exercise.

Woodward married Irja Pullman on July 30, 1938; they had two children and were divorced in 1946. On Sept. 14, 1946, Woodward married Eudoxia Muller; they had two children and were divorced in 1972. Woodward died of a heart attack at his home in Cambridge, Mass.

[Woodward's personal papers, correspondence, and photographs are in the Harvard University Archives. For excellent biographies, see Alexander Todd and John Cornforth, "Robert Burns Woodward," *Biographical Memoirs of Fellows of the Royal Society* 27 (1981); and Mary Ellen Bowden and Theodor Benfey, *Robert Burns Woodward and the Art of Organic Synthesis* (1992), for which the Beckman Center for the History of Chemistry provides a traveling exhibit as a complement. An obituary is in the *New York Times*, July 10, 1979.]

GERALD I. SPIELHOLTZ

WRIGHT, JAMES ARLINGTON (Dec. 13, 1927–Mar. 25, 1980), poet, was born in Martins Ferry, Ohio, a small steel-mill town, the son of Douglas Wright, a steelworker, and Jessie Arlington. Neither of his parents attended school beyond the eighth grade, which might in part account for the unpretentiousness of his poetry, its compassion for the unfortunate, and its anger against society's injustices. He spent much of his childhood on a small farm on the outskirts of the town. His experience in both the industrial and rural landscape helped to shape his vision and poetic range, for Wright wrote poems of both pastoral beauty and industrial plunder, and his antipastorals, depicting the collisions between the two worlds, stand as some of the finest "ecological" poems composed in the second half of the twentieth century.

Wright was enrolled in a vocational training program at Martins Ferry High School when two teachers took note of his ability and urged him to study literature. Wright served in the army during World War II in the Pacific and Japan. He graduated from Kenyon College in

Gambier, Ohio, in 1952, where he received the Robert Frost Poetry Prize and was also influenced by the traditionalist stylistics of poet John Crowe Ransom. After a year as a Fulbright Scholar at the University of Vienna, Wright earned his M.A. (1954) and Ph.D. (1959) degrees from the University of Washington, where he came under the tutelage of one of America's preeminent lyric poets, Theodore Roethke. During the 1950's he also struck up friendships with other notable American poets, such as Robert Mezey, Anne Sexton, Donald Hall, Robert Bly, W. S. Merwin, William Duffy, and John Logan. Wright taught English at Macalester College in St. Paul, the University of Minnesota, and then at Hunter College in New York City from 1966 until his death.

Wright married Liberty Kardules in 1952; they had two children and were later divorced. He married Anne Runk, a sculptor, in 1967. Many of his later poems and volumes are dedicated to her. She seems to have had a stabilizing influence on the poet's life, and her companionship was deeply important to Wright.

Wright's poetry came to national attention with the publication in 1957 of his first volume, *The Green Wall*. The poems—lyrics and narratives—employ carefully crafted traditional forms, often rhymed in iambic meter and logically developed. As Wright himself acknowledged, the poems in this collection were greatly influenced by the works of Robert Frost and Edward Arlington Robinson. *The Green Wall* was widely praised by critics who preferred traditional and formalistic styles. Although many of Wright's poems are about grief, the outcasts and downtrodden of society, and the demands of love, his poems convey an elusive and mystical quality, a mysterious beauty that enthralls his admirers.

Not all critics praised Wright's early work. Some believed his talent was too strictly guided by traditional forms and that the lyric power and contemporary relevance of his poems were buried in technical skill. The conflict between those critics who stress innovative technique and significant statement on the human experience and those who praise foremost the use of traditional forms in the art of poetry arose with each of Wright's books.

The publication in 1963 of *The Branch Will Not Break*, the poet's third collection of poems, marked a significant break with traditional techniques. The style used in these poems and the works composed throughout the remainder of Wright's career is called deep image poetry, or poems of emotive imagination. They are highly visionary and subjective works in which leaps in imaginative association are made. Wright's friendship with Robert Bly may have influenced his change in style. His translations of such German and Spanish surrealist poets as Georg Trakl, Hermann Hesse, César Vallejo, Juan Ramón Jiménez, and Pablo Neruda also may have influenced him. Like many of his contemporaries, Wright may have become bored with the limitations of traditional forms and found them inadequate in conveying the imaginative experience of humanity in the second half of the twentieth century.

Wright was broad-shouldered and short, bearded, and unassuming. He generally wrote in the early morning hours and carried a small brown notebook wherever he went, handwriting his poems in a slightly cramped style before crafting them on a typewriter. A prolific artist, he received the Brandeis University Creative Arts Award, an Academy of American Poets Fellowship, the Melville Cane Award from the Poetry Society of America, and the Pulitzer Prize in 1972 for his *Collected Poems* (1971).

Summarizing his own work, Wright once wrote: "I have written about the things I am deeply concerned with—crickets outside my window, cold and hungry old men, ghosts in the twilight, horses in a field, a red-haired child in her mother's arms, a feeling of desolation in the fall, some cities I've known." An article in the *New York Times Book Review* in 1972 stated: "Our age desperately needs his vision of brotherly love, his transcendent sense of nature, the clarity of his courageous voice. . . . His *Collected Poems* proves James Wright to be a truly rare and beautiful poet . . . it forces on us the recognition that James Wright is among the masters of our day."

Wright continued composing through the 1970's and completed his final volume of poems just before his death, from cancer, in New York City. His wife enlisted many of Wright's friends to edit the book and *This Journey* was published posthumously in 1982.

Wright's poetry has deeply influenced many younger poets. He left a legacy of dedication to the art, of compassion for human beings, and of dogged attention to the mysteriousness of life, the details of its strangeness, its brutality, and its beauty.

[Additional books of poems by Wright are *Saint Judas* (1959); *Shall We Gather at the River?* (1968); *Salt Mines and Such* (1971); *Two Citizens* (1973); and *To a Blossoming Pear Tree* (1977). See also William Heyen and Jerome Mazzaro, "Something to Be Said for the Light: A Conversation with James Wright," *Southern Humanities Review* 6 (1972); and Dave Smith, ed., *The Pure Clear Word: Essays on the Poetry of James Wright* (1986). Obituaries are in the *New York Times* and *Newsweek*, both Mar. 27, 1980.]

STUART BARTOW

WRIGHT, JOHN JOSEPH (July 18, 1909–Aug. 10, 1979), Roman Catholic cardinal and philosopher, was born in the Dorchester section of Boston, the oldest of six children of John Joseph Wright, a clerk in a paper factory, and Harriet L. Cokely. After graduation from Boston Latin School, the city's public high school for its most gifted students, he enrolled in Boston College, a Catholic, Jesuit-run institution, from which he graduated with a B.A. in 1931. He began his academic career as a journalism major but decided against journalism as a profession when he found himself incapable of interviewing the mother of a girl who had recently committed suicide. He entered St. John's Seminary in Brighton, Mass., to study to become a Catholic priest. After receiving an S.T.L. degree in 1932, he was admitted to the Pontifical Gregorian University in Rome, Italy, where he received an S.T.D. degree in 1939. Cardinal Wright would eventually receive more than twenty honorary degrees from colleges and universities in Canada and the United States.

Meanwhile, on Dec. 8, 1935, he was ordained a priest. After finishing his studies in Rome, he was appointed a professor of philosophy at St. John's Seminary in Boston, where he remained on the faculty until 1944. In 1942 his doctoral thesis was published as *National Patriotism in Papal Teaching*, which emphasized the war as paradox for the Christian. Nonetheless, Wright's acknowledgment of moral dilemma does not mean the negation of patriotism in Catholic doctrine. By this juncture it was apparent that he had already been deeply influenced by French philosophy. Throughout his career the writings of Henri deLubac, Jacques Maritain, Cardinal Emmanuel Suhard, and Étienne Gilson all loomed as a crucial influence upon his thinking. Indeed, his interest in French life in general had begun while he was still a child, when he listened to veterans of the United States Expeditionary Force in World War I talk about their experiences in France. As a young man he began a collection of books about Joan of Arc that eventually numbered 6,000 volumes. His love of France and things French was further stimulated by doing parish work in Périgueux, France, during vacations from his Roman theology studies. His interest in France extended to rural folk songs, poetry, and the music of Claude Debussy. When elevated to a bishopric, he had his crosier designed in France and had the fleurs-de-lis embroidered on his bishop's miter.

In 1943 he was named secretary to the archbishop of Boston, William Cardinal O'Connell; he retained this position when O'Connell was succeeded by Archbishop (eventually Cardinal) Richard J. Cushing. Wright became a monsignor and a papal chamberlain in 1944 and was named a domestic prelate in 1946. A year later, on June 30, 1947, he was named an auxiliary bishop of Boston. Between 1950 and 1959 he served as the first bishop of the newly created see of Worcester, Mass., supervising some quarter million Catholics. In 1959 he was named the bishop of Pittsburgh, shepherd to some 850,000 Catholics, a position he retained until 1969. During this period he published *Words in Pain* (1961) and *The Christian and the Law* (1962). He also contributed to *Dialogue for Reunion* (1962). These writings reveal Wright's struggle to unite God and human needs. For Wright, the objective of modern Catholicism is to avoid anarchism, without slipping into philosophical dogmatism. In 1960, the *Catholic Mind* devoted an entire issue to consideration of Cardinal Wright's thought.

Elevated to cardinal in 1969, Cardinal Wright entered office at a moment of spreading ecclesiastical skepticism. This was especially true among European priests. Expanding his intellectual horizons to include the study of liberal Dutch theologians, Cardinal Wright argued for renewed dedication by priests to the principles of faith that had prompted them to join the priesthood in the first place. He called for the reassignment of skeptical priests to hardship posts in the third world as a means of renewing their Christian commitment. Taking an increasingly strong stand regarding priests who questioned their vows, he pointed out that "there is nothing that cures subjectivism like the impact of other people's problems." He added that skepticism and doubt were "not so severe that hard work won't cure" them.

In keeping with these ideas, he called upon priests to renew their vows of celibacy and ecclesiastical obedience once per year. Considering the spirit of the age, his positions did not come at an opportune moment. Expressed only a few years after the Vatican II Council had instituted many liberal reforms, they did not find a friendly audience in Europe. Dissenting priests reacted strongly against Cardinal Wright's call for a yearly renewal of vows, likening the idea to the loyalty oaths of the McCarthy era in the United States.

Indeed, Cardinal Wright's positions were not received particularly well in the United States either. His call to 1,200 priests to attend a mass at St. Patrick's Cathedral in New York City in 1970 in order to renew their promises of celibacy and obedience drew only thirty-five responses. The episode was a clear embarrassment to the Vatican. As the Reverend Charles Curran, a liberal theologian at Catholic University in Washington, D.C., suggested, "Why is it that when they want to test us, it's always on celibacy or obedience—and never on anything basic like faith, hope or charity?"

Nonetheless, Cardinal Wright persisted with his conservative campaign. In an interview in *U.S. News and World Report* in 1970, he argued that modernism was akin to being morally adrift. In the midst of the forces of modernism, he argued, Christianity was under siege. Accordingly, he suggested that Christian ethics must stand out with a clarity and a moral vision not characteristic of modern society.

Seen from this vantage point, the cardinal's curious mixture of conservatism and liberalism becomes comprehensible. While opposing liberalism within his church, he remained committed to it outside the church. This self-styled "theological conservative" always remained the "social liberal." He forged strong ecumenical bonds among Catholic, Jewish, and Protestant leaders while serving as bishop of Pittsburgh. He championed civil rights. At the height of the Vietnam War he called for a cessation of bombing and for peace negotiations with the National Liberation Front. But meanwhile he remained conservative in matters of church doctrine, for example, by strongly supporting Pope Paul VI's call for a ban on artificial means of birth control.

Suffering from cataracts and polymyositis, a neuromuscular disorder affecting his legs, he was confined to a wheelchair by 1978. He died at the Youville Rehabilitation and Chronic Disease Hospital in Cambridge, Mass. He was buried in a family plot in Brookline, Mass.

[For more information on Wright, see articles in *Jubilee*, Feb. 1956; *Look*, Oct. 23, 1962; and *Sign*, Nov. 1962. An obituary is in the *New York Times*, Aug. 12, 1979.]

MICHAEL J. EULA

WRIGLEY, PHILIP KNIGHT (Dec. 5, 1894–Apr. 12, 1977), businessman and baseball executive, was born in Chicago, one of two children of William Wrigley, Jr., founder of the chewing gum company that bears his name, and Ada Elizabeth Foote. Beginning in 1907, William Wrigley had invested heavily in advertising, particularly of a new gum called Spearmint, and by 1911 sales of the William Wrigley, Jr., Company were measured in millions.

The family lived first in an apartment on North Dearborn Street near Lincoln Park, then moved to a house in the suburbs. Wrigley attended a boys' school, the Chicago Latin School, although he was often absent when the family was out of town. In midsummer and the coldest months of winter they frequently visited Lake Geneva, Wis., then acquired a summer house at Harbor Point, Mich., where Philip learned to sail. He recalled winter visits to Thomasville, Ga., where his father bought him his first horse.

In the fall of 1911 he entered Phillips Academy in Andover, Mass., where he was an average student and a good athlete, excelling in lacrosse. He left before graduating. After being tutored by Paul Harper, a law student and son of the president of the University of Chicago, Philip was admitted to Yale University, then to Stanford. He persuaded his father, however, to let him go instead (at the age of twenty) to Australia to establish a gum factory in Melbourne. The plant was functioning successfully when Philip returned in 1916 to Chicago, where he enrolled as a special student in chemistry at the University of Chicago.

In 1917, when the United States entered World War I, Philip Wrigley applied unsuccessfully for cavalry training, then enlisted as a fireman third class in the Naval Reserve, and was assigned to a new aviation unit at the Great Lakes Naval Training Station. He was commissioned an ensign on Dec. 6, 1917, and put in charge of an aviation mechanics' school, where he remained until his discharge as a lieutenant in February 1919.

On Mar. 26, 1918, he married Helen Blanche Atwater of Garden City, N.Y., the daughter of a Wrigley Company vice-president. They had three children.

In 1920 he became a vice-president of the Wrigley Company, while his father began construction of the Wrigley Building in Chicago, bought an interest in the Chicago National League Baseball Club, organized the Boulevard Bridge Bank (which in 1933 became the National Boulevard Bank), and in 1921 bought the Los Angeles Angels. On Feb. 10, 1925, Philip Wrigley was elected president of the company, and his father assumed the chairmanship of the board, which he held until his death in January 1932.

The Wrigley Company survived the Great Depression, paid regular dividends, gave a general pay increase in 1933, started an unemployment compensation plan in 1934, and a pension plan in 1935. Philip Wrigley later confessed to voting once for Franklin D. Roosevelt.

The company fared less well in 1936, but Wrigley maintained and increased its advertising, which included radio sponsorship of Guy Lombardo and His Royal Canadians and full-page ads in *Simplicity* and *Woman's Day*. His active interest in the company's advertising continued even after his son William succeeded him as president in 1961 and he became chairman of the board.

Wrigley was an enthusiastic horseman and yachtsman. He had several small boats during his early childhood at Harbor Point; he recalled that his father bought him a thirty-foot sloop named the *Wasp* when he was eleven years old. His largest boat was a ninety-eight-foot cruiser named *Speejacks*, which he bought in 1925, renamed *Fame*, and kept on the Great Lakes until 1941, when he gave it to the United States Navy. In 1930, Wrigley established an Arabian horse ranch named el Rancho Escondido on Catalina Island.

Catalina was also for several years the training camp of the Chicago Cubs, which were a source of occasional pleasure and frequent anxiety to Philip Wrigley from the time when he became sole owner and president of the Chicago National League Ball Club (as the Cubs were formally known) in 1934. The Cubs won the National League pennant three times between 1934 and 1945. Thereafter, in spite of frequently changes of managers, coaches, and pitchers, they were a consistent source of expense and disappointment. Although these tribulations continued for thirty years, during which Wrigley received several serious offers to buy the Cubs (whose home stadium on the North Side is Wrigley Field), he refused to sell the team.

Wrigley died in Elkhorn, Wis., of a gastrointestinal hemorrhage that occurred as he was watching the Cubs on television.

[Wrigley's principal biography is Paul M. Angle, *Philip K. Wrigley* (1975). See also Robert Boyle, "A Shy Man at a Picnic," *Sports Illustrated*, Apr. 14, 1958; "The Island Kingdom of P. K. Wrigley," *Forbes*, Nov. 1, 1970; and Seth King, "Wrigley: a 7-Cent Bonanza," *New York Times*, May 9, 1971. An obituary is in the *New York Times*, Apr. 13, 1977.]

DAVID W. HERON

Y–Z

YAWKEY, THOMAS AUSTIN ("TOM") (Feb. 21, 1903–July 9, 1976), baseball club owner, was born Thomas Yawkey Austin in Detroit, Mich., the son of Thomas J. Austin, a businessman, and Augusta Lydia Yawkey. The elder Austin, who was associated with his father-in-law, William Clyman Yawkey, in lucrative timber and mining ventures in the midwestern United States and Canada, died of pneumonia when his only son was seven months old. Subsequently, young Tom Austin lived with his maternal uncle, William Hoover Yawkey, and his wife, Margaret Alice Williams Draper. William Hoover Yawkey had taken over the vast Yawkey family holdings in November 1903 after the death of his father. He was also the owner of the Detroit Tigers baseball team from 1904 through the 1907 season, after which he sold half his interest and remained a silent partner until his death in 1919. Tom grew up across the lake from Detroit in Sandwich, Ontario, and in New York City, where his uncle moved his offices after 1910. In Sandwich, the boy came into contact with many of the Tiger players who were dinner guests of his uncle. The great outfielder Ty Cobb became a particular friend. Following his mother's death in 1918, Tom was adopted by his uncle and aunt and soon thereafter changed his name to Thomas Austin Yawkey.

At the Irving School in Tarrytown, N.Y., Yawkey played baseball, basketball, and football and competed for the coveted Edward T. Collins Trophy, awarded to the school's preeminent student-athlete and named for Irving alumnus Eddie Collins, who achieved great fame as a major league second baseman. Though he never won the trophy, Yawkey was runner-up in both his junior and senior years. He studied chemistry, mining, and metallurgy at the Sheffield Scientific School, a division of Yale University, and received his B.S. in 1925. On June 18, 1925, he married Dora Elise Sparrow, an artist's model and beauty-contest winner from Birmingham, Ala.; they adopted one child.

After college Yawkey settled in New York City and assumed control of his family's far-flung investments, which included lead and silver mines, oil fields, paper mills, and much timber land. By the age of thirty, Yawkey's personal fortune was estimated to be more than $20 million and he was well known in sporting circles as an accomplished hunter and fisherman. At this time, Ty Cobb and Eddie Collins, to whom Yawkey had become particularly close, convinced their young friend to emulate his uncle and such other millionaire sportsmen as Jacob Ruppert, who owned the New York Yankees, and William Wrigley, owner of the Chicago Cubs, by purchasing a major league baseball franchise. He bid unsuccessfully for the New York Giants and spurned a half interest in the Brooklyn Dodgers before buying the most troubled franchise of the depression era, the Boston Red Sox of the American League. As of 1932, Boston had languished in last place for eight of the previous ten years. In 1932 the team had a record of 43 wins and 111 losses, ended up 64 games behind the first-place New York Yankees, and drew a total attendance of only 182,000. Yawkey paid $1 million for the Red Sox in February 1933 and hired Collins as his general manager. Although he continued to manage and expand his already considerable business portfolio, Yawkey devoted most of the remainder of his life to baseball.

After settling the many debts incurred by the

previous owners, Yawkey plowed $750,000 into a major renovation of Fenway Park, the team's home in the Back Bay section of Boston. In 1934 more than 15,000 new seats were added to the park, the fire-plagued wooden center-field stands were replaced with concrete bleachers, and a thirty-seven-foot-high wall made of sheet metal and steel was erected in left field. The latter, dubbed the "Green Monster," became one of the most famous features of America's major league ballparks. Yawkey and Collins also sought to refurbish their team's personnel by purchasing baseball talent from such cash-poor teams as the St. Louis Browns, the Philadelphia Athletics, and the Washington Senators. Yawkey thus spent over $1 million between 1933 and 1937 to acquire a host of new players, including such standouts as catcher Rick Ferrell, pitcher Lefty Grove, shortstop-manager Joe Cronin, and first baseman Jimmie Foxx. As a result of some of these acquisitions, the "Gold Sox" or "Yawkeybilts," as they were called, were able to move up four notches to fourth place in the standings in both 1934 and 1935, and to bring crowds back to Fenway Park.

When the team slipped back to sixth place in 1936, Yawkey and Collins adopted a new strategy to make their club a major force in the American League. Instead of relying on retreads, they decided to recruit and develop their own players in a minor league farm system modeled after the successful operations of Branch Rickey of the St. Louis Cardinals and George Weiss of the Yankees. Yawkey hired Billy Evans, a shrewd former major league umpire, to direct the farm effort. In relatively short order, Evans saw to it that such stars as Ted Williams, Dom DiMaggio, Bobby Doerr, Tex Hughson, and Johnny Pesky were advanced through the minor league system to the Red Sox. The gambit paid off as Red Sox teams, composed mainly of former farmhands, finished second to the Yankees in four of the next six years (1937–1942), and Williams established himself as one of baseball's greats by hitting for a prodigious .406 average in 1941. Yawkey was so committed to his steadily improving team that he turned down the opportunity to buy the dominant Yankees in 1944.

After nearly three years of separation, Yawkey and Dora Elise Sparrow divorced in November 1944. On December 22 of the same year he married Jean Remington Hollander Hiller, a once-married model for a fashionable New York women's clothing store; the couple had no children.

The Red Sox seemed to begin to fulfill Yawkey's dream by winning the first postwar pennant in 1946. Though they lost the World Series that year to the St. Louis Cardinals, it was expected that the talent-laden Red Sox would often represent the American League in the fall classic. However, after narrowly losing out in 1948, 1949, and 1950, the team did not contend seriously for another pennant for seventeen years. During this lean period, when the rival Yankees captured fifteen American League flags and ten World Series championships, critics focused on owner Yawkey's easygoing paternalism as the root cause of the Red Sox malaise. Like his uncle, who gave Detroit pitchers $100 bills for beating Cleveland and took the Tigers out on drinking sprees after victories, Yawkey idolized and spoiled his players. He paid them generously and they seldom, if ever, suffered pay cuts or even fines for poor performance or misbehavior. In the early years of his ownership Yawkey worked out with the team and took favored players on hunting and fishing trips to his expansive game preserve in Georgetown County, S.C. Later, he doted on tempestuous superstar Ted Williams, defending him from hostile Boston sportswriters and making sure that his salary was always higher than that of the Yankees' Joe DiMaggio. Despite consistent strong performances from Williams and his successor as Yawkey's favorite, Carl Yastrzemski, the Red Sox usually finished a distant third or worse in the American League from 1951 to 1967 and were viewed by the team's critics as the self-satisfied country club of baseball.

In these years Yawkey spent lavishly to sign high-priced "bonus babies," most of whom failed to become stars or even dependable regulars. General managers and field managers hired by the owner, including such experienced baseball hands as Joe Cronin, Lou Boudreau, Bucky Harris, and Pinky Higgins, turned out largely one-dimensional teams, stressing right-handed power hitting suited to the contours of Fenway Park over speed and defense. Moreover, the Red Sox front office eschewed signing black players in the postwar era, including two who ultimately gained immortality as vital cogs on championship Dodgers and Giants teams. Both Jackie Robinson, who had been given a tryout at Fenway Park, and Willie Mays, who played for a Birmingham, Ala., Negro League team that used the same park as Boston's farm team in that city, were passed over by Yawkey's men in the 1940's. When the Red Sox finally made utility infielder Elijah ("Pumpsie") Green their first black player in 1959, they were the last major league team to integrate, twelve years after Robinson had taken the field for Brooklyn.

In an effort to make the Red Sox operation more businesslike, Yawkey appointed Dick O'Connell, who had handled the team's finances and advised the owner on tax matters, as general manager in 1965. Though he lacked the professional baseball credentials of his predecessors, O'Connell used his employer's resources wisely to revive an atrophied organization and assemble teams that won pennants in 1967 and 1975. Yawkey was especially proud of the 1967 Red Sox, who came from ninth place in 1966 to win the next American League title on the last day of the season. Built around Carl Yastrzemski, whom the owner regarded as his finest all-around player, this "Impossible Dream" team had a tough, no-nonsense manager, Dick Williams, and included Tony Conigliaro, Jim Lonborg, Rico Petrocelli, George Scott, and Reggie Smith. In 1975, two hard-hitting rookie outfielders, Fred Lynn and Jim Rice, led a well-rounded Boston club that captured the Eastern Division title and swept the defending champion Oakland A's in the league playoffs. The World Series that followed, which the Red Sox lost to the powerful National League champion Cincinnati Reds in seven games, was among the most exciting in modern baseball history. The sixth game of the series, played at Fenway Park, televised to millions and won by Boston on a dramatic twelfth-inning home run by catcher Carlton Fisk, is considered by many knowledgeable fans to be the greatest game ever played.

Even as the Red Sox teams in 1967 and 1975 failed to win the world championship Yawkey had sought for so long, they popularized baseball in Boston and New England and made their owner's investment profitable in the last decade of his life. Records show that Yawkey's Boston American League Baseball Company lost money for eighteen of the twenty-seven years it existed as a corporation (1933–1960). A proprietorship after 1960, the Red Sox continued to be unprofitable through 1966. Between 1967 and 1975, however, the franchise became a reliable moneymaker. Season attendance averaged 1.7 million, best in the American League, and the team's games were broadcast on seven television stations and fifty radio outlets.

Though a shy, very private man, Yawkey had influence in the inner circle of owners who ran major league baseball. As vice-president of the American League from 1956 to 1973, he was instrumental in the selection of his longtime friend and associate Joe Cronin as league president in 1959. Yawkey was also noted for his philanthropic activities in Boston and South Carolina, where he owned two plantations and spent his winters. He was a member of the executive committee of the Jimmy Fund of Boston, which raised money for the children's cancer research of Dr. Sidney Farber. Under the patronage of Yawkey and the Red Sox after 1952, the Jimmy Fund became one of the best-known charities in New England. In Mt. Pleasant, S.C., Yawkey donated generously to local hospitals and churches and was the principal benefactor of Tara Hall, a Catholic-run school for troubled boys. An ardent conservationist, he left 15,000 acres of his coastal property, as well as $10 million in a trust to finance its care, to the state of South Carolina in his will. The land was to be preserved in its natural state and its wildlife protected.

One of the last of baseball's sportsman-owners, Yawkey accepted his failure to win a championship with equanimity. He told one journalist, "In baseball, just like in hunting, you have to take the good with the bad. There's a lot of luck involved. After all, it's only a game." After Yawkey's death in Boston, the city named a street adjacent to Fenway Park in his honor. He was inducted into the Baseball Hall of Fame posthumously in 1980.

[The National Baseball Library in Cooperstown, N.Y., has an extensive clipping file on Yawkey. Biographical material is in the *New York Times*, Feb. 26, 1933; Bill Cunningham, "Starch for the Red Sox," *Collier's*, Aug. 5, 1933; American Historical Company, *Yawkey, Richardson, and Allied Families* (1939); Arthur Daley, "Superfan," *American Magazine*, June 1951; and James Simon Kunen, "The Man with the Greatest Job in Boston," *Boston Magazine*, Sept. 1975. Frederick G. Lieb, *The Boston Red Sox* (1947); Dan Shaughnessy, *The Curse of the Bambino* (1990); and Peter Golenbock, *Fenway* (1992) are popular histories of the Red Sox containing much about Yawkey and his ownership of the team. See also Jack Mann, "The Great Wall of Boston," *Sports Illustrated*, June 28, 1965; Al Hirshberg, *What's the Matter with the Red Sox?* (1973); Jules Tygiel, *Baseball's Great Experiment* (1983);

and Ed Linn, *The Great Rivalry* (1991). Obituaries are in the *Boston Globe* and the *New York Times*, both July 10, 1976; and the *Sporting News*, July 24, 1976.]

RICHARD H. GENTILE

YOUNGDAHL, LUTHER WALLACE (May 29, 1896–June 21, 1978), lawyer, judge, and governor, was born in Minneapolis, Minn., the son of John Carl Youngdahl, a grocer, and Elizabeth Johnson. Both his parents were devout Swedish Lutherans. They did a remarkable job of instilling in all of their children their belief in the values of Christian faith, education, and hard work. One of Luther Youngdahl's brothers became a college dean, one became a minister, and one became a member of the United States Congress.

Youngdahl graduated from South High School in Minneapolis in 1915. After attending the University of Minnesota from 1915 to 1916, he transferred to Gustavus Adolphus College, a small, Lutheran college located in St. Peter, Minn., from which he graduated with a B.A. degree in 1919. A strongly built and athletic person, Youngdahl played football in high school and college and was a lifelong advocate of the value of exercise and physical fitness.

Like many young men of his generation, Youngdahl interrupted his college studies to serve in the United States Army during World War I. He entered as a private and was demobilized as a second lieutenant after his brief period of service.

Youngdahl entered the Minnesota College of Law in 1919, and received his LL.B. in 1921. After passing a civil service exam for the post—an experience that fortified his belief in the value of a merit system rather than patronage as the means to fill government offices—Youngdahl became the assistant city attorney for Minneapolis in 1921 and served until 1924. For the next six years he practiced law as a partner in a Minneapolis law firm. From 1930 to 1936 he served as a judge on the Minneapolis Municipal Court; here he became convinced that many of the "criminals" who appeared before his bench were emotionally troubled and would benefit more from psychiatric care than from incarceration. He was elected district judge of the Hennepin County (Minneapolis) Court in 1936 and served on this court until 1942, when he won election as an associate justice of the Minnesota Supreme Court.

In 1946, Youngdahl resigned from the court to run for governor of Minnesota on the Republican ticket. He was elected in that year, and again in 1948 and 1950. On Sept. 27, 1951, he resigned the governorship to accept an appointment as a federal judge for the United States District Court for the District of Columbia from President Harry S. Truman. After retiring from the federal bench in 1966, Youngdahl continued to serve as a senior judge, trying cases part-time until his death.

Youngdahl spent much of his life demonstrating that there was no conflict between being a good Christian and becoming a successful politician. He spoke often on the relationship between Christianity and politics, maintaining that Christians should take political affairs seriously because "government is the machinery by which society makes its moral decisions." Viewing politics as a calling and proud of his record as a vote-getter, Youngdahl applied his Christian ethics to his decisions and actions as a governor, always placing the people's welfare above the concerns of special-interest groups.

Believing that volunteerism was insufficient to help the weakest members of society, and that these people therefore needed the help of a caring government, he used the power of his office to have laws passed to protect the weak, and he mobilized public opinion to achieve social reform. In his first term as governor he launched a moral crusade to enforce the state's laws against gambling and those that regulated the sale of liquor; this action was prompted by his strong conviction that lack of respect for the law induced by laxity in law enforcement had a particularly injurious effect upon children. In 1947 the state legislature passed his bill to outlaw slot machines and also passed his bill to increase state aid to the public schools significantly.

This self-styled "liberal Republican" was particularly proud of his Youth Conservation Act; this act implemented a series of programs to prevent juvenile delinquency and to rehabilitate young people in prison. Unafraid to step into political thickets, Youngdahl waged a two-year campaign to improve the treatment and care of the mentally ill in the state's hospitals, institutions that had been characterized as "snakepits." He took on the conservatives in his own party and eventually won his fight to pass the Mental Health Policy Act, the greatest achievement of his second administration. On Oct. 31, 1949, Youngdahl lit a bonfire on the grounds of the Anoka State (Mental) Hospital to destroy a heap of discarded straitjackets and shackles to dramatize a new program that would emphasize rehabilitation rather than restraints.

As a federal judge, Youngdahl is best remembered for his May 2, 1953, ruling in the case of *United States* v. *Lattimore*. In the midst of McCarthyism and anti-Communist fever, the federal government charged that Owen J. Lattimore, a professor at Johns Hopkins University, had committed perjury in 1952 when he denied before the Senate Internal Security Subcommittee (the McCarran committee) that he was a sympathizer with or promoter of Communism or Communist interests. Youngdahl dismissed the indictment because it was so nebulous and indefinite that it violated the Sixth Amendment and the accused's right to be informed of the nature and cause of the accusation against him. He also noted that the government's allegation was in conflict with the First Amendment because it restricted freedom of belief and expression. "When public sentiment runs high," he wrote, "we must be particularly alert not to impair the ancient landmarks set up in the Bill of Rights."

Youngdahl married Irene Annet Engdahl, daughter of a Lutheran minister and a high school English teacher, on June 23, 1923. The couple remained married and shared a rich partnership for fifty-five years; they had three children. Youngdahl loved to spend time with his family, engaging in such indoor pursuits as discussions about religion and politics and family sings at the piano, and in such outdoor pursuits as ice-skating parties, hikes, picnics, and fishing trips. Youngdahl died in Washington, D.C., and was buried in Arlington National Cemetery.

[Youngdahl's papers are held by the Minnesota Historical Society in St. Paul; other source material is at the Gustavus Adolphus College archives. Youngdahl's book, *The Ramparts We Watch* (1962), offers a summation of his ideas about democracy and includes his three inaugural addresses as governor. Robert Esbjornson, *A Christian in Politics: Luther W. Youngdahl* (1955), is the only biography; it includes Youngdahl's opinion in the Lattimore case. Obituaries are in the *Washington Star*, June 22, 1978; the *Washington Post*, June 22, 1978; and the *New York Times*, June 23, 1978.]

BERNARD HIRSCHHORN

ZANUCK, DARRYL FRANCIS (Sept. 5, 1902–Dec. 22, 1979), motion-picture producer and screenwriter, was born in Wahoo, Nebr., to Frank Zanuck, a hotel operator, and Louise Torpin. In 1910, Zanuck moved with his tubercular mother to Los Angeles, where he attended the Page Military Academy. Shortly after his mother was married in Los Angeles to a man he never respected, young Zanuck began to take off several days from school to look around movie sets or view films at the theater with his father, who had moved to the West Coast. At age eight, he reportedly appeared in his first Western, as an Indian extra at Edendale, near Glendale. His mother and stepfather decided to entrust him to the care of his maternal grandparents in Oakdale, Nebr. He remained in school until the eighth grade, with later studies at the Manual Training High School. At age fourteen he lied about his age and enlisted in the United States Army. He went to New Mexico with the Sixth Nebraska Infantry; in France in World War I, he served as a private with the Thirty-fourth Division, until that unit's dissolution, whereupon he transferred to the Thirty-seventh Division; he served as a runner, or messenger, and also boxed as a bantamweight in regimental matches. When Zanuck's grandfather, who had always nurtured his creativity, gave several of Zanuck's frontline letters to Nebraska newspapers for publication, he resolved to become a writer.

After his discharge from the army in 1920, Zanuck found varied employment in California as a boxer, shirt salesman, longshoreman, newspaper subscription handler, hair tonic salesman, and founder of an advertising venture, Darryl Poster Service: in short, about eighteen different occupations in one year. After selling a story he had written, "Mad Desire," for $500 to *Physical Culture* magazine, which published it in 1923, he aspired to become a Hollywood screenwriter. Also in 1923, he sold *Habit: A Thrilling Yarn That Starts Where Fiction Ends and Life Begins* (containing "Habit," "The Scarlet Ladder," "Say It with Dreams," and "The Forgotten City") to film studios for $11,000 and soon found short-term gag-writing positions with Mack Sennett, Carter DeHaven, Harold Lloyd, Charlie Chaplin, and especially Sydney Chaplin. Zanuck worked with Joseph P. Kennedy's FBO (Federal Booking Office, RKO's predecessor) at $150 per week, writing twenty-four episodes each of the two-reelers *The*

Telephone Girl and *The Leatherpusher*. After a brief period with Fox Film Company, he was hired by Warner Brothers in 1924 as a scriptwriter for the Rin-Tin-Tin series. Within four years, Zanuck's weekly salary had increased from $250 to $5,000. Then and throughout his career, he sometimes wrote screenplays under the pen names Gregory Rogers, Melville Crossman, and Mark Canfield.

By 1927, Zanuck, who had acquired extensive knowledge about the mechanics of filmmaking, was promoted to executive producer at Warner Brothers. He produced "the first talkie," *The Jazz Singer* (1927), then worked to create spectacular sound effects for the biblical–World War I epic, *Noah's Ark* (1929), starring Dolores Costello and directed by Michael Curtiz. He featured Fanny Brice in her first film appearance, *My Man* (1928), scripted by Zanuck, writing as Mark Canfield. Zanuck rose to general production chief at Warner Brothers in 1929, then chief executive in charge of all production in 1931. Despite successes with such films as *Little Caesar* (1930), *Doorway to Hell* (1930), *Public Enemy* (1931), *I Am a Fugitive from a Chain Gang* (1932), and the biography films *Disraeli* (1929), *Alexander Hamilton* (1931), and *Voltaire* (1933) starring George Arliss, Zanuck suddenly left the Warners on Apr. 15, 1933. Though Metro-Goldwyn-Mayer (MGM) had expressed interest in hiring Zanuck, on April 18 he joined Joseph M. Schenck, president of United Artists, in cofounding Twentieth Century Pictures, of which Zanuck became vice-president. Producing eighteen films during the company's first eighteen months, Zanuck enjoyed immediate successes as a producer, starting with *The Bowery* (1933).

When Twentieth Century merged with Fox Films in 1935, Zanuck became vice-president and chief of all production. With Twentieth Century–Fox, Zanuck earned the name of "liquidator" as he laid off studio employees, a cost-cutting tactic he would repeat in 1962. His first production, *Metropolitan* (1935), starring Lawrence Tibbett, opened at Radio City Music Hall to critical though not popular acclaim; but his second, *Thanks a Million* (1935), starring Dick Powell, "made" Twentieth Century–Fox, Zanuck would proudly state. MGM's William Goetz, a son-in-law of Louis B. Mayer, became a Twentieth Century Pictures stockholder at its creation, which Mayer helped Schenck and Zanuck finance; Goetz brought more stars and directors to strengthen the roster brought in by Fox; in addition, Zanuck would eventually recruit Tyrone Power, Don Ameche, and Alice Faye. In the 1930's Twentieth Century–Fox amply demonstrated its strength, producing almost a dozen films with the child star from Fox, Shirley Temple; musical favorites such as *Alexander's Ragtime Band* (1938); Westerns and comedies; Jack London stories such as *The Call of the Wild* (1935) and *White Fang* (1936); children's classics such as *Kidnapped* (1938); and film biographies such as *The Story of Alexander Graham Bell* (1939), *Young Mr. Lincoln* (1939), and *Stanley and Livingstone* (1939). Zanuck hired the petite Norwegian Olympic ice-skating champion Sonja Henie, whose first film in her contract series was *One in a Million* (1936). The early 1940's saw John Ford's direction of the award-winning version of John Steinbeck's depression classic *The Grapes of Wrath* (1940) starring Henry Fonda, and of Richard Llewellyn's best-seller, *How Green Was My Valley* (1941).

In 1937, Zanuck became the first recipient of the Irving G. Thalberg Memorial Award, which recognized consistently creative film producers; after his accepting this award two subsequent times (1944 and 1950), the Academy made it a once-in-a-lifetime honor.

Before Pearl Harbor, Zanuck publicly urged the United States to join Great Britain in the war; he served on the Advisory Council to the Chief Signal Officer and, in October 1940, had already begun coordinating efforts between Hollywood (through the Research Council of the Academy of Motion Picture Arts and Sciences) and the federal government in regard to a fair, competitive manner of awarding contracts among Hollywood studios to produce government films, especially training series for the Signal Corps and the marines. Still serving as producer, coproducer, or executive producer of several "entertainment" films (often expressing or motivated by wartime events), Zanuck oversaw production of various films released during the war years. Most were popular, except for his personal favorite, *Wilson* (1944). He was also instrumental in the Academy's establishment of the Academy Foundation (1944), a restoration project that enlarged the Library of Congress Paper Prints Collection.

Commissioned in January 1941, Zanuck served as a reserve lieutenant colonel in the Signal Corps, with a promotion to colonel in

January 1942. His overseas duty included the preparation of training films (such as *Winged Victory*, 1944). As an observer, he traveled with Lord Mountbatten's commandos; next, he prepared a film on American military operations in the Aleutian Islands; finally, he devoted two months to documenting the North African campaign (*At the Front*, produced for public release in 1943) and wrote *Tunis Expedition*, which was published by Random House in 1943.

At least on two occasions during the war years, Zanuck and Twentieth Century–Fox came under the close scrutiny of Senator Harry S. Truman's Special Committee to Investigate the National Defense Program, established in April 1941. Though the efforts of the highly respected Truman Committee focused on such matters as the construction and maintenance of military camps and the overall condition of defense production, it also looked into the military's supposed favoritism in awarding four studios (Twentieth Century–Fox, Paramount, MGM, and RKO) the above-mentioned filming contracts. In 1943 the Truman Committee summoned Zanuck, Frank Capra, and other producers and directors associated with being "Hollywood colonels," since the committee was questioning the rapidity of assigning high military rank to Hollywood personalities involved directly with the war effort. Zanuck heeded General George C. Marshall's recommendation to place himself on the inactive list (effective May 31). In 1944, Zanuck received the Legion of Merit for "exceptional bravery under fire."

Postwar filmmaking saw a return to the wide variety of subject matter that had brought success to Twentieth Century–Fox in the 1930's, ranging from traditional Westerns to historical romance such as *Anna and the King of Siam* (1946), featuring Gertrude Lawrence; from the suspenseful *The Razor's Edge* (1946) to the delights of the Christmas classic *Miracle on 34th Street* (1947); from Elia Kazan's social commentary films, *Gentleman's Agreement* (1947) and *Pinky* (1949) to the psychological dramas of *The Snake Pit* (1948) and *Twelve O'Clock High* (1950); from the melodrama of *A Letter to Three Wives* (1949) to the adaptations of Ernest Hemingway's popular works *The Snows of Kilimanjaro* (1952) and *The Sun Also Rises* (1957). There were such biblical epics as *David and Bathsheba* (1951) and *The Robe* (1953); the latter's premiere on Sept. 17, 1953, in New York inaugurated Hollywood's utilization of CinemaScope, a filming process that utilizes a special wide-angle lens that makes the images appear clear and distinctly larger and deeper. Zanuck applied the CinemaScope process to Michael Curtiz's *The Egyptian* (1954) and the on-location romance *Three Coins in the Fountain* (1954).

During the Korean War, Zanuck was placed on active duty in Washington by Secretary of Defense Louis Johnson and was asked to prepare a film under $1 million about the war. Zanuck disliked the official script of the film, however, and produced his own version for free by utilizing stock Fox newsreel footage. The film was released within two weeks, and Zanuck resigned his reserve commission. A 1969 request by Zanuck for the Department of Defense to review his military record resulted in his restoration to full colonel, retired, in the United States Army.

In 1956, Zanuck resigned as production head at Twentieth Century–Fox to establish, in conjunction with a Fox contract, DFZ Productions, the eventual headquarters of which was in Paris. During the 1960's and 1970's he emphasized on-location filming and often contributed several scripts under the Canfield name, such as *The Crack in the Mirror* (1960) and *Hello—Goodbye* (1970). Some of Hollywood's last epic-sized films were produced under Zanuck's auspices, such as the comedy *Those Magnificent Men in Their Flying Machines* (1965) and *Hello, Dolly!* (1969). DFZ Productions was also noted for several war movies based on historical reenactments, including *The Longest Day* (1962), Hollywood's definitive black-and-white tribute to D day as based on Cornelius Ryan's book, and *Tora! Tora! Tora!* (1970), the color epic recreating the diplomatic treachery, military tactics, and human errors leading to Pearl Harbor.

Zanuck returned to the company with which he had created so many artistic and financial successes to be Twentieth Century–Fox's president from 1962 to 1969 during one of its bleakest financial periods, and then its chairman and chief executive officer from 1969 to 1971. Despite presiding over the release of the costly *Cleopatra* (1963), he was able to reinvigorate the studio's financial status with the successes of *The Sound of Music* (1965), *Patton* (1970), and *M*A*S*H* (1970). Working mainly in New York City, he named his son as vice-president in charge of production in 1963. But internal rivalries within the studio pressured Zanuck, as chairman of the board, to dismiss his son Richard from the company and so fracture the Zanuck dynasty. In 1971 the elder Zanuck himself was compelled to resign and assume the meaningless title of chairman emeritus.

Hardworking and energetic, full of ideas and sensitive to details, Zanuck was once called a "jumping jack executive." "Napoleonic" was an epithet commonly applied to him, owing to his small size, athletic stature, and the magnitude and forcefulness of his ideas. His fierce attention to all aspects of film production was rewarded during his lifetime as demonstrated by the best-film Academy Awards for *How Green Was My Valley* (1941), *Gentleman's Agreement* (1947), and *All about Eve* (1950).

His marriage to Virginia Fox (a former actress who had starred with Buster Keaton), lasted from January 1924 until his death. Most of their life was spent in Santa Monica, Calif., until Zanuck moved to Europe and New York City in 1956. Ill, he returned on Apr. 7, 1973, to her and to their Palm Springs house, Ric-Su-Dar, named after their three children. Zanuck died in Palm Springs.

[An authorized biography of Zanuck is Mel Gussow, *Don't Say Yes Until I Finish Talking* (1971), which includes a filmography. See also Leonard Mosley, *Zanuck* (1984); Stephen M. Silverman, *The Fox That Got Away* (1988); and Marlys J. Harris, *The Zanucks of Hollywood* (1989). Discussion about Zanuck's resignation from Warner Brothers, his three-time winning of the Thalberg Memorial Award, his wartime leadership of the Research Council, and his incorporating the Academy Foundation appear in *Academy Awards: An Ungar Reference Index* (1982), compiled by Richard Shale. Zanuck's resignation from Warner Brothers is also discussed in Bob Thomas, *Thalberg* (1969); and James Robert Parish and Don E. Stanke, *The Debonairs* (1975). Obituaries are in the *New York Times*, Dec. 24, 1979; and *Variety*, Dec. 26, 1979.]

MADELINE SAPIENZA

ZECKENDORF, WILLIAM (June 30, 1905–Sept. 30, 1976), real estate developer, was born in Paris, Ill., the son of Arthur Zeckendorf, a merchant, and Byrd Rosenfield. In 1908 the family moved to Cedarhurst, Long Island, where Arthur went into the shoe business. In 1917 they moved into Manhattan, and William entered the New York City public school system. When he was sixteen years old, he passed the regents exam and was allowed to graduate early from high school. He attended New York University from 1922 to 1925 before dropping out during his junior year, when he went to work for his uncle, Samuel Borchard, a real estate agent.

This job marked the beginning of Zeckendorf's long career in real estate. In his first year in the business, he established himself as a hardworking property manager. He attracted the attention of Leonard S. Gans, who ran a real estate brokerage firm, and in 1926 Gans hired him to run the firm's new property management division. By 1928, Zeckendorf had worked his way up to become a full-fledged broker and had closed his first deal. On Sept. 20, 1928, he married Irma Levy. They had two children before getting divorced in 1934.

In 1930, after he successfully brokered the sale of a $3 million site on the West Side, he was made a partner of Leonard S. Gans. Eight years later, he left the firm to become vice-president of Webb and Knapp, a real estate concern that owned and managed a portfolio of properties. On Dec. 10, 1940, he married for a second time, to Marion Griffin.

Under Zeckendorf's influence, Webb and Knapp began to expand dramatically. For example, in 1942 he was able to persuade Vincent Astor to retain Webb and Knapp to manage his huge portfolio of properties. Then, in 1945, Zeckendorf began his best-known real estate deal. Starting with the purchase of a large plot from the Swift meat packing company, he assembled control of a huge stretch of land along the East River north of Forty-second Street. Almost immediately thereafter, he learned that the city was desperately seeking a site suitable for the headquarters of the United Nations (UN). He sold the riverfront tract, realizing a handsome profit for Webb and Knapp. In 1947, Zeckendorf was named president of Webb and Knapp.

Zeckendorf became widely known as a shrewd and perceptive real estate trader, and also as an ambitious and creative developer. While the UN deal was perhaps his most famous deal, it was by no means his only major one. Under his leadership, Webb and Knapp took on numerous high-profile clients, including Gimbels, Montgomery Ward, Time, Inc., the Guaranty Trust Company, and Macy's. The firm was involved in several large-scale developments, including many Title 1 urban redevelopment projects. It took part in the development of Century City in Los Angeles, Mile High City in Denver, L'Enfant Plaza in Washington, D.C., Kips Bay Plaza in New York City, and Place Ville-Marie in Montreal. Many of New York City's most famous office buildings and hotels were owned or managed by Webb and Knapp at one time or another, including the Chrysler Building.

Some of Zeckendorf's most ambitious projects for New York City never came to fruition. One of these was the original plan for the UN site, where he had planned to build office space, apartment buildings, an opera house, a hotel, a convention hall, a marina, and a helicopter pad. He had also proposed a huge mixed-use development on the West Side with a rooftop airport, and at one time he announced plans to build an office tower atop Grand Central Terminal.

In 1949, Zeckendorf hired I. M. Pei, who was then an assistant professor of architecture at Harvard, as Webb and Knapp's in-house architect. Then, in 1952, he created a new unit of the company that would act as general contractor for all of the company's projects. Now, with divisions that handled real estate brokerage, architectural design, construction contracting, and building management, Webb and Knapp had become a full-service, integrated real estate services firm. The firm's net worth reportedly grew to $75 million by 1957 from a prewar level of under $1 million. Zeckendorf bought a house in Greenwich, Conn., built up his wine cellar to 20,000 bottles, and provided financial backing for dozens of Broadway shows. He donated more than $1 million to Long Island University, where he served as chairman of the Board of Trustees for many years. This era of prosperity would prove to be Webb and Knapp's zenith, and Zeckendorf's as well.

In 1962, when Webb and Knapp was dangerously overextended, construction delays and cost overruns caused a serious deterioration of the firm's financial position. Despite a series of contractions and spin-offs, the company was unable to satisfy its creditors and was forced into bankruptcy in 1965, with assets of only $21 million and debts of $80 million. The bankruptcy trustee filed suit against Zeckendorf to recover some of the assets he had withdrawn from the company as it floundered. Earlier, Zeckendorf had cosigned some of the Webb and Knapp notes, so he was forced to file for personal bankruptcy protection in 1968. This marked the end of Zeckendorf's career as a high-flying real estate developer and turn-around specialist. Over the preceding two decades he had profoundly affected the urban landscape, building new neighborhoods and reshaping old ones.

After emerging from bankruptcy, Zeckendorf continued to be active in the real estate world, serving as a consultant and adviser to General Property Corporation, a new real estate firm started by his son, William Zeckendorf, Jr. On Mar. 5, 1968, his wife, Marion, died in a plane crash. He married Alice Bache on Dec. 21, 1972, but this union was short-lived, and by 1975 he had gotten a divorce and married a fourth time, to Louise Malcolm; they had no children. Zeckendorf died of a stroke in New York City.

[Zeckendorf wrote an autobiography, *Zeckendorf* (1970), with Edward McCreary. The Columbia University Oral History Office has an interview with I. M. Pei, which includes discussion of Zeckendorf. Relevant information on Zeckendorf appears in articles in the *New Yorker*, Dec. 8, 1951; *Newsweek*, Aug. 16, 1954; *Life*, Feb. 12, 1965; and *Forbes*, Mar. 1, 1969. An obituary is in the *New York Times*, Oct. 2, 1976.]

OWEN D. GUTFREUND

ZELLERBACH, HAROLD LIONEL (Mar. 25, 1894–Jan. 29, 1978), businessman, music and art patron, and philanthropist, was born in San Francisco, the second son of Isadore Zellerbach and Jennie Baruh. He was the grandson of Anthony Zellerbach, founder of the firm that later became the Crown Zellerbach Corporation. Harold Zellerbach and his family were major figures in the economic and cultural development of the city of San Francisco.

Anthony Zellerbach immigrated to the United States from Bavaria with his brother, Mark, and settled in San Francisco in 1868. Beginning as a small trader in general merchandise, he established a paper jobbing firm in 1870. The firm prospered in tandem with the expanding California economy and by the turn of the century A. Zellerbach and Sons had eighteen locations in and around San Francisco and a sales office in Los Angeles. Within the first decade of the century the firm was reorganized as the Zellerbach Paper Company with Isadore Zellerbach as president. Thanks in large part to

Isadore's business acumen, the firm quickly expanded and opened new offices in Portland, Seattle, San Diego, and Salt Lake City.

Harold Zellerbach attended the University of California at Berkeley for two years (1913–1915) and then transferred to the University of Pennsylvania, from which he received a B.S. in economics in 1917. That same year, on April 19, Zellerbach married Doris Joseph; the couple had three children and their marriage continued for sixty-one years.

Zellerbach followed his older brother, James David, into the family firm and was immediately appointed personnel manager. His brother had joined the company four years earlier, in 1913, upon completing his B.S. degree at the University of California. This would establish the pattern of leadership at Zellerbach Paper—James David followed by Harold Lionel—until the elder brother's death of a brain tumor in 1963.

Over the next ten years Isadore Zellerbach and his two sons led the firm into a major period of expansion. By the mid-1920's Zellerbach Paper was the major distributor of paper products in the West and had moved into manufacturing. In 1924 the Zellerbach Corporation was formed as a holding company to operate the paper company and other subsidiaries. In 1928 the company merged with the Crown Willamette Paper Company, at that time the second largest paper manufacturing firm in the country. Louis Bloch of Crown Willamette became chairman of the board of the merged companies, whose name became the Crown Zellerbach Corporation. Isadore Zellerbach was named president of the new corporation, with James David Zellerbach as executive vice-president. Harold Zellerbach was appointed vice-president of the parent corporation and president of Zellerbach Paper Company, thus assuming direct responsibility for the management of the original firm. In 1938, James David Zellerbach moved up to the presidency of Crown Zellerbach and Harold Lionel Zellerbach was named executive vice-president to succeed him. He held this position for almost twenty years, until 1956. From 1928 to 1959 he served as a director of Crown Zellerbach, and in 1957 followed his brother as chairman of the board. In 1959, upon reaching mandatory retirement age, he relinquished an active role in the management of the company. He thereafter held the honorary post of consulting director and continued to take a vigorous interest in the affairs of Crown Zellerbach until his death. His son, William Joseph Zellerbach, succeeded him as president of the Zellerbach Paper Company in 1961. By the time Harold Zellerbach retired from active management in 1959, Crown Zellerbach had become one of the world's largest producers of forest-related products, including pulp and paper products, lumber, plywood, and chemicals. The company was an acknowledged leader in forest management and had long been recognized for enlightened personnel policies and practices. The growth and continuing success of this company are directly attributable to the talent and energy of Harold Zellerbach, working in tandem with his brother.

Harold Zellerbach's career in business was matched by his lifelong interest in the arts and public service. He worked continuously to promote the development of the arts in all forms in San Francisco. He served as a board member for the San Francisco Associated Council of Arts, the San Francisco Symphony, the Art Institute, the Ballet Guild, the Opera Association, and the San Francisco Performing Arts Center. He was also a trustee of the Fine Arts Museum of San Francisco. His active participation in promoting the arts in his home city was backed up by a major financial commitment. Harold Zellerbach and his family contributed heavily to support and develop the arts community. He headed the Zellerbach Family Fund and was instrumental in arranging a $1 million gift to the University of California at Berkeley to support the construction of a campus theater. The Harold and Doris Zellerbach Fund provided $1 million to underwrite the construction of a performing arts building in San Francisco, and the same fund provided $500,000 for a similar purpose at his alma mater, the University of Pennsylvania. In 1973 he was a founding member of the Foundation for the Arts and Humanities, a private foundation to promote the arts and humanities on a national level.

Zellerbach was politically active and regularly supported candidates on the national level. Though he maintained ties with both political parties, he himself was a liberal. He supported such politicians as Jacob Javits, the liberal Republican senator from New York, and Adlai Stevenson, the Democratic candidate for president in 1952 and 1956. In 1956, Stevenson appointed Zellerbach to the fifty-member National Business Council, made up of business and financial leaders who supported Stevenson in the campaign of that year.

During World War II, Zellerbach served on the War Production Board, and in the 1950's he was chairman of the Zellerbach Commission on European Refugees. This commission, established in 1957 and supported by private funds, was organized to address the "hard-core" refugee problem that remained from World War II. A commission report in 1959 estimated that approximately 40,000 refugees remained in camps in Europe, with an additional 100,000 refugees from behind the "Iron Curtain." The Zellerbach report recommended that the United States take in 50,000 of these refugees within the next two years.

Harold Lionel Zellerbach was a man of broad concerns and activities. A successful businessman, an avid supporter of the arts, and a man of wide-ranging public interests, Zellerbach was energetic and active to the very end. He died while aboard a cruise ship in Honolulu harbor.

[A brief history of Crown Zellerbach, with comment on the role of Harold Zellerbach, may be found in R. O. Hunt, *Pulp, Paper and Pioneers: The Story of Crown Zellerbach Corporation* (1961). An obituary is in the *New York Times*, Jan. 31, 1978.]

GEORGE P. ANTONE

ZUKOFSKY, LOUIS (Jan. 23, 1904–May 12, 1978), poet and critic, was born and raised on Christie Street in New York City's Lower East Side, one of five children of Pinchos Zukofsky, a night watchman and a pants presser in a men's clothing factory, and Chana Pruss. His parents were immigrants from the town of Most in the province of Kovna in what later became Lithuania. A precocious child, Zukofsky learned Longfellow's "Hiawatha" by heart at age five. He attended public elementary school and Stuyvesant High School, making excellent marks. When he was ten or eleven, his family moved to 111th Street in East Harlem. In 1919, Zukofsky entered Columbia University, where he began to write poetry.

Zukofsky absorbed the lessons of the European modernists quickly, reading Hilda Doolittle (H. D.) and the Imagists in 1920. After sending him several rejections, Harriet Monroe's prestigious *Poetry* magazine published his sonnet "Of Dying Beauty" in its January 1924 issue. In 1926 he wrote "Poem Beginning 'The,' " his first major work. He sent the piece to Ezra Pound, who published it in the spring 1928 issue of his journal *Exile*. At Pound's insistence, Zukofsky traveled to Rutherford, N.J., to meet William Carlos Williams, with whom he developed a lifelong friendship. With Pound's encouragement, Monroe published more of Zukofsky's poetry. In 1928 he finished the first four "movements," as he called them, of a long work that would contain twenty-four movements in all and engage his attention for many decades. Titled "A," the work was very much in the experimentalist, high modernist mode prevalent in the 1920's and showed the influence of Pound's *Cantos*. In 1929 Zukofsky wrote a perceptive essay, "Ezra Pound: His Cantos," which was published in the short-lived French literary journal *Echanges*.

Zukofsky had difficulty finding a suitable job after graduation from Columbia in 1923. With Pound's assistance he was given a teaching assistantship in English and comparative literature at the University of Wisconsin for the 1930–1931 academic year. He continued his work on "A," finishing the next three movements in 1930. In Madison he received an extraordinary invitation from Monroe, instigated by Pound, to edit a special issue of *Poetry* devoted to those poets of his generation whom he respected and read. With contributions from Robert McAlmon, S. Theodore Hecht, George Oppen, Williams, and Carl Rakosi, the February 1931 "Objectivists" issue of *Poetry* gave birth to a new movement. Zukofsky's assistantship at the University of Wisconsin was renewed, but despite new friends in Madison, such as poet Lorine Niedecker, he turned it down and moved back to New York City in June 1931.

At the height of the Great Depression, Zukofsky subsisted through various writing and editorial jobs, among them working for George Oppen and To Press, which published *An "Objectivists" Anthology* in 1932. Pound and Tibor Serly, a violinist and composer, provided him with money for a European trip. He sailed for France in the summer of 1933, to spend time in Paris, Budapest, and in Rapallo, Italy, where he visited Pound.

In 1934 he wrote his brilliant poems "Mantis" and " 'Mantis,' An Interpretation" about the helplessness of the poor. Like many artists of this time, Zukofsky escaped poverty himself by working for the Works Progress Administration (WPA) of President Franklin D. Roosevelt's New Deal. While supervising one WPA project in 1934, Zukofsky met a young musician and composer, Celia Thaew, whom he began to date. They were married on Aug. 20, 1939, and had one child. In 1937 he completed the eighth movement of "A," and in 1938 he began the first half of the ninth movement, which he finished the following year. He finished the tenth movement of "A" the following year and was encouraged when a collection of his work, *55 Poems*, was published in 1941.

Zukofsky wrote little poetry during the 1940's. He quit the WPA in April 1942 and spent that summer and early fall with his wife in Diamond Point, N.Y. He worked at various jobs until he found a position in February 1947 as instructor of English at the Polytechnic Institute of Brooklyn, from which he retired nearly twenty years later as associate professor. In 1947 he began his long critical and philosophical piece, *Bottom: On Shakespeare*, and in 1948 he published his anthology *A Test of Poetry*. He returned to "A," finishing the second half of the ninth movement and the eleventh movement in 1950. After his father's death in 1950 he started the twelfth movement of "A," a moving portrayal of his father and family that, when finished the following year, had become longer than the previous eleven movements. His son Paul began to demonstrate remarkable gifts as a violinist, and his parents spent time and money encouraging him. Paul made his debut at Carnegie Hall when he was only thirteen.

The family traveled to England and France in the summer of 1957; Zukofsky taught a course in poetry at San Francisco State College the following summer. While the local poetry community celebrated his visit, he was becoming disappointed at his failure to reach a wider audience. In the summer of 1959 the Zukofskys traveled to Mexico with Oppen, resuming their acquaintance after almost thirty years. Another friendship grew through correspondence with Cid Gorman, who published the first half of "A" (movements one through twelve) in 1959. The following year Zukofsky finished *Bottom: On Shakespeare*. One section of it, *Pericles*, was set to music by Celia Zukofsky.

During the 1960's Zukofsky continued work on "A" and on a translation of the Latin poet Catullus. Recognition was slow in coming. His book of recent short poetry, *After I's*, was published in 1964. In 1965 he published the first volume of *ALL, The Collected Shorter Poems, 1923–1958*. *Poetry* devoted its entire October issue that year to "A"-14 and to appreciative reviews of *ALL*, *After I's*, and *Bottom*. Zukofsky retired in 1965. He and Celia moved from Brooklyn to Manhattan, and eventually to suburban Port Jefferson on Long Island, N.Y. *ALL, The Collected Short Poems 1956–1964* appeared in 1966, and *Prepositions: The Collected Critical Essays of Louis Zukofsky* was published in 1967. Two of his important works of fiction, *Ferdinand* and *It Was*, were published together in 1968. In his final years in Port Jefferson, Zukofsky worked on his experimental collection *80 Flowers*, which was published posthumously. He died unexpectedly while the complete "A" was being prepared for publication.

An unrelenting experimenter, Zukofsky was always appreciated by other poets but received no widespread public recognition during his lifetime. The contemporary "Language" poets name him, along with Guillaume Apollinaire and Gertrude Stein, as the most important influence on their work. His "Objectivists" movement of the 1930's has received renewed critical attention, but he himself has yet to receive the attention worthy of his subtle art. Zukofsky's sheer bravura technical ability is without equal in twentieth-century American poetry, but his lack of lyricism will probably forever consign him to a reputation as a poet's poet.

[The Zukofsky Archive is at the Humanities Research Center at the University of Texas at Austin. His *Collected Fiction* was published in 1990, and his *Complete Short Poetry* in 1991. Major critical works include Carroll F. Terrell, ed., *Louis Zukofsky: Man and Poet* (1979); Barry Ahearn, *"A": An Introduction* (1983); and Michele J. Leggott, *Reading Zukofsky's 80 Flowers* (1989). An obituary is in the *New York Times*, May 14, 1978.]

TIM REDMAN

ZUKOR, ADOLPH (Jan. 7, 1873–June 10, 1976), motion-picture executive, was born in Ricse, Hungary, the son of Jacob Zukor, a merchant, and Hannah Liebermann. His parents both died when Zukor was a child, and he was raised by his maternal uncle, a rabbi. At age twelve Zukor was apprenticed to a storekeeper in Szanto. When he completed his apprenticeship in 1888, he immigrated to the United States where he became a furrier's assistant in New York City; his first job was sweeping the floor for two dollars per week. After four years of learning the fur business, Zukor moved to Chicago, started his own business, and prospered as a manufacturer of fur scarves. On Jan. 10,

1897, he married Lottie Kaufman; they had two children. Their daughter Mildred would marry the son of Marcus Loew, the founder of Metro-Goldwyn-Mayer.

In 1900, Zukor, a soft-spoken man of small stature, returned to New York City to continue in the fur business. He also invested in a penny arcade that needed funds for equipment including kinetoscopes, devices through which an individual could watch a loop of film. The profitability of the arcade prompted Zukor and his associates to open other arcades on the East Coast. Zukor soon gave up the fur business to concentrate on the management of these arcades. Above his busy Fourteenth Street Arcade in New York City, Zukor opened the Crystal Hall Theater where customers could watch a fifteen-minute show of three motion pictures for a nickel. Zukor, who liked to sit in the audience and study viewer reaction, became convinced that there was a future in screening motion pictures in a theater setting rather than in arcades. He sold his interest in the arcades, and with William A. Brady, a theatrical manager and aspiring producer, as his new partner he began showing novelty films in the theaters they owned. This venture had some success, but it began to decline within a year and Zukor turned to showing films with a plot in the theaters he still controlled.

After experiencing another financial setback, Zukor hedged his bets in 1910 by merging most of his theaters into a vaudeville circuit headed by Marcus Loew, also a one-time furrier. It was the second time he and Loew had been business associates. As a cost-cutting measure vaudeville was then substituting movies for some of its traditional variety acts. Zukor, however, retained his independent ownership of several other theaters in New York, Newark, and Boston and became interested in showing feature-length films rather than the one-reel films of twelve to fifteen minutes then standard.

Zukor, who had already screened an imported three-reel film, *The Passion Play*, at his own theaters in 1910, grew interested in emulating the new European practice of filming popular plays and having dramatic stars repeat their roles on film. His aim was to attract middle-class patrons, or as an early biographer put it, to "kill the slum tradition" in the movies. Zukor was only one of several ambitious producers moving in this direction, but he was well versed in many areas of the growing industry and plunged in with unsurpassed success. After breaking with Loew, he spent $35,000 for the rights to the four-reel French production of *Queen Elizabeth* starring the renowned Sarah Bernhardt. Although the best theaters in New York were owned by theatrical producers who took a dim view of motion pictures, Zukor succeeded in engaging Daniel Frohman's Lyceum for what proved to be a notably successful premiere of *Queen Elizabeth* on July 12, 1912. Zukor's agents had already begun to line up rentals in other cities. The film's success helped Zukor advance in the rapidly growing film industry.

To produce films himself, Zukor established the Famous Players Film Company. Using the slogan "Famous Players in Famous Plays," his new company prospered despite initial resistance by many of the performers and producers whose cooperation he needed. Among his studio's early, successful productions were *The Prisoner of Zenda*, starring James Hackett; *Tess of the D'Urbervilles*, with Minnie Maddern Fiske; and *The Count of Monte Cristo*, with James O'Neill. An agreement with Broadway producer David Belasco allowed Zukor to film *A Good Little Devil*, in which Mary Pickford was then appearing. Already experienced in motion pictures, she achieved unprecedented stardom after appearing in Zukor's 1914 hit *Tess of the Storm Country*. To direct many of these early projects Zukor secured the veteran Edwin Porter who also had a financial interest in the company. D. W. Griffith, whom Zukor had sought as a director, believed that Zukor's stage-bound formula would be too restrictive for his own talents and film ideas and so he declined the Famous Players offer. Griffith, of course, was right about the future course of the film industry: before long, Zukor's studio would have to follow the lead of some of its more prescient competitors and seek original screenplays and develop its own stars. But these changes in the industry came because the public's demand for films had soared after Famous Players had taken the major step of making high-quality films of an hour or more in length.

To meet the needs of exhibitors, Zukor increased production from five films in 1912 to thirty in 1913 as Famous Players became the major producer of the day. In 1914, Zukor contracted with William Hodkinson's newly established distributing organization, Paramount Pictures Corporation, to provide half the 104 films Paramount would require for its annual operations. Paramount, which would advance the costs of production, made similar arrangements with other studios including the Los Angeles–based Feature Pictures Company run by Jesse Lasky, until then Zukor's major competitor. Zukor, whose own interest increasingly centered on financial matters, soon had to replace his Manhattan studio with a superior facility at Long Island City. He also worked with Mack Sennett in financing and distributing the "Keystone Kops" and other Sennett comedies.

Zukor has been described by historian Kevin Starr as "Hollywood's preeminent business intelligence" during the years 1914–1924. His operations were characterized by relentless expansion and by ruthlessness in discarding associates who no longer suited Zukor's requirements. In 1916, Zukor engineered a merger with the Feature Pictures Company to form a new film-production company, Famous Players–Lasky. Zukor was president, Lasky became vice-president and head of West Coast operations, and Cecil B. DeMille was named director-general. Lasky and DeMille had been with Feature Pictures. Samuel Goldfish (later known as Samuel Goldwyn) was also an executive in the company. Then in 1917, Zukor gained control of Paramount Pictures Corporation, ending the arrangement that had allowed Hodkinson's Paramount to use its cash advances to influence the type of films Zukor could make. Finally, in 1919, he turned to Kuhn, Loeb, a major New York investment bank, to underwrite a stock issue of $10 million he needed to expand aggressively into the ownership of theaters, the third—and at the time, the most profitable—element in the motion-picture industry. He began by purchasing major theaters in New York City and Los Angeles. Within a decade Paramount (the name under which Famous Players–Lasky began releasing its films in the mid-1920's) controlled more than 1,000 theaters.

Until 1924, when the Loew's theater chain countered Zukor's expansion by organizing the Metro-Goldwyn-Mayer studios as its production arm, Paramount was the most successful company in the film industry which by then was becoming dominated by vertically integrated companies that, like Paramount, combined production, distribution, and exhibition. As early as 1921 the Federal Trade Commission began to investigate the business practices of Paramount and eventually those of its major competitors. But the investigations were noted more for producing thousands of pages of testimony than in ending allegedly unfair trade practices such as block booking that required independent exhibitors to accept dozens of a studio's routine films (usually a year's output) in order to secure rights to show potential hits featuring major stars such as Mary Pickford. At one time or another Rudolph Valentino, Wallace Reid, Gloria Swanson, Pola Negri, Clara Bow, and Western stalwart William S. Hart appeared in Zukor's films.

Maintaining the arrangement that allowed Lasky to control production, Zukor preferred to reside in the East (the source of the capital he required) and lived on an estate in Rockland County near New York City. With films booming during the 1920's the corporation built a thirty-nine-floor Times Square office building that also housed the landmark Paramount Theater. Paramount adjusted slowly but successfully to the sound revolution in motion pictures of the late 1920's and by 1930 was compiling record profits. With more new stars under contract, including Gary Cooper, Claudette Colbert, Maurice Chevalier, and Marlene Dietrich, the studio seemed destined for an even brighter future. However, troubles enveloped Zukor and other members of management once the Great Depression hit the film industry and precipitated the exposure of the reckless manner in which Paramount's expansion had been financed. Lawsuits initiated by creditors and major stockholders who resented the profligate use of company funds forced Paramount into receivership in 1933.

Zukor, whose power in the organization was sharply curtailed, was willing to sacrifice Lasky and other long-term associates and apparently was in danger of being entirely ousted from Paramount's management himself. The proceedings cost him dearly financially, but he managed to regain considerable influence in the beleaguered company thanks to squabbles among various factions and the court's decision to appoint him a trustee in order to utilize his intimate knowledge of the film industry and of Paramount itself which had five hundred subsidiary companies. High-profile names such as attorney Elihu Root, Jr., and financier Joseph P. Kennedy (who was brought in as a consultant) were involved in the byzantine legal proceedings and their aftermath. Zukor temporarily moved to Hollywood to help guide the company, which soon rebounded at the box office with films starring such radio and stage personalities as Mae West, Bing Crosby, and Bob Hope. Critically acclaimed directors such as Ernst Lubitsch and later Billy Wilder and Preston Sturges were also identified with the studio.

When the company emerged from bankruptcy in 1935, Zukor accepted the chairmanship of the board. The appointment afforded Zukor a measure of status while allowing investors to believe that new president John E. Otterson would avoid the excesses of Zukor's long regime. Otterson quickly became the victim of still another struggle for power that allowed Zukor to regain some say in policy matters. As chairman, Zukor remained interested in the entertainment industry and predicted a bright future for television when others thought of it as a fad. Paramount, in fact, became the first major studio to go into television production. A generation earlier Zukor had shown a similar interest in radio, and for a while Paramount had held a half interest in the Columbia Broadcasting System until forced to sell during the Great Depression. In 1949, Zukor received a special Academy Award for lifetime contributions to the motion-picture industry. Into his nineties Zukor, something of an icon of the old Hollywood, held the title of chairman emeritus and still attended board meetings. To recognize his hundredth birthday Paramount (acquired by the conglomerate Gulf and Western following a stockholders' revolt in 1965) established film scholarships in Zukor's name at fifteen universities. He had long since sold his estate to a group that developed a golf course on it but maintained apartments in both New York City and Los Angeles. He died in Los Angeles.

[A collection of stills and scripts comprising the Paramount Studio Archives is at the Margaret Herrick Library of the Academy of Motion Pictures Arts and Sciences, Beverly Hills, Calif. No personal papers of Zukor are in this collection. The place to begin a study of Zukor is with his memoir (considerably understated), *The Public Is Never Wrong: The Autobiography of Adolph Zukor* (1953), written with Dale Kramer; and Will Irwin, *The House That Shadows Built* (1928). Herbert G. Luft, "Remembering Adolph Zukor," *Films in Review*, Dec. 1976, is useful as are these works on the film industry: Robert Sklar, *Movie-Made America: How the Movies Changed American Life* (1975); Tino Balio, ed., *The American Film Industry* (rev. ed. 1985); and Kevin Brownlow with John Kobal, *Hollywood: The Pioneers* (1979). See also James Robert Parish, *The Paramount Pretties* (1972); I. G. Edmond and Reiko Mimura, *Paramount Pictures and the People Who Made Them* (1980); Kevin Starr, *Inventing the Dream: California Through the Progressive Era* (1985); Eileen Bowser, *The Transformation of Cinema, 1907–1915* (1990); and Richard Koszarski, *An Evening's Entertainment: The Age of the Silent Feature Picture, 1915–1928* (1990). "Paramount," *Fortune*, Mar. 1937, should be consulted for its corrosive examination of Zukor's financial maneuverings. An obituary is in the *New York Times*, June 11, 1976.]

LLOYD J. GRAYBAR

INDEX GUIDE

TO THE SUPPLEMENTS

INDEX GUIDE

INDEX GUIDE

INDEX GUIDE

INDEX GUIDE

INDEX GUIDE

INDEX GUIDE

INDEX GUIDE

INDEX GUIDE

INDEX GUIDE

INDEX GUIDE

INDEX GUIDE

INDEX GUIDE

INDEX GUIDE

INDEX GUIDE

INDEX GUIDE

INDEX GUIDE

INDEX GUIDE

INDEX GUIDE

INDEX GUIDE

INDEX GUIDE

INDEX GUIDE

INDEX GUIDE

INDEX GUIDE

INDEX GUIDE

INDEX GUIDE

INDEX GUIDE

INDEX GUIDE

INDEX GUIDE

INDEX GUIDE

INDEX GUIDE

INDEX GUIDE

INDEX GUIDE

INDEX GUIDE

INDEX GUIDE

INDEX GUIDE

INDEX GUIDE

INDEX GUIDE

INDEX GUIDE

INDEX GUIDE

INDEX GUIDE

INDEX GUIDE

INDEX GUIDE

INDEX GUIDE

INDEX GUIDE

INDEX GUIDE

INDEX GUIDE

INDEX GUIDE

INDEX GUIDE

INDEX GUIDE

ARAPAHOE COMMUNITY COLLEGE
3 1717 00067 6561
FOR REFERENCE
DICTIONARY OF AMERICAN BIOGRAPHY
CSS